PRISMA'S

Swedish-English Dictionary

THIRD EDITION

University of Minnesota Press
Minneapolis

Published in the United States in 1997 by the University of Minnesota Press
111 Third Avenue South, Suite 290
Minneapolis, MN 55401-2520
http://www.upress.umn.edu

Printed in the United States of America on acid-free paper.

A catalog record for this book is available from the Library of Congress

ISBN 0-8166-3163-8

The University of Minnesota is an equal-opportunity educator and employer.

06 05 04 03 02 01 00 99 98   10 9 8 7 6 5 4 3 2 1

Foreword

This dictionary has been compiled by Bokförlaget Rabén Prisma's Dictionary Editorial Office by Eva Gomer and Mona Morris-Nygren in collaboration with Erik Durrant, Michael Knight, Hans Nygren, Michael Phillips, Sture Sundell, and Gösta Åberg. The lexicographic advisor was Bertil Molde. It contains approximately 59,000 headwords and 15,000 phrases, expressions, and other language constructions. The third edition contains approximately 500 new headwords.

The selection of headwords reflects modern language usage. Technical terms within different fields, everyday usage, and slang expressions are abundantly represented. Even certain registered trademarks have been included.

For the benefit of non-Swedish readers in particular, the book includes pronunciation and stress for the Swedish headwords as well as information about inflections of nouns, verbs, and adjectives. The principles employed are explained in "Notes on the Use of the Dictionary."

The grammatical apparatus is the simplest possible. Self-explanatory expressions rather than grammatical terminology have been used whenever possible.

All important available dictionaries and reference works have been consulted in the compiling of this dictionary. Those extensively consulted include *Collins Dictionary of the English Language, Collins Cobuild English Language Dictionary, The Concise Oxford Dictionary, The Advanced Learner's Dictionary of Current English, The American Heritage Dictionary, Svartvik-Sager Engelsk universitetsgrammatik, Illustrerad svensk ordbok, Svensk ordbok, Svensk Handordbok,* and *Nyord i svenskan från 40-tal till 80-tal.*

ANVISNINGAR

Allmänt

De svenska uppslagsorden återges i sträng bokstavsordning, alltså t.ex. **bildäck, bildöverföring, bilersättning.** Facktermer anges med *tekn., mil., sport. etc.* (se förkortningslistan på s. 16). I översättningarna har amerikanska alternativ markerats med *AE.*

Använda tecken

Om ett uppslagsord har flera betydelser anges olika ordklasser med hjälp av romerska siffror. Klart åtskilda betydelser inom varje ordklass anges med arabiska siffror, mindre betydelseskillnader med semikolon.

| står efter den del av ett uppslagsord som återkommer i ett eller flera följande uppslagsord. Dessutom används det någon gång av tydlighetsskäl för att visa hur ett ord är sammansatt, t.ex. **bil|drulle**

- betecknar, när | är utsatt, avskild del av uppslagsord. I sammansättningar och avledningar betecknar det hela det föregående uppslagsordet, t.ex. **berör|a, -ing** (= **beröra, beröring**), **fasad, -klättrare** (= **fasad, fasadklättrare**).

-- anger att den följande orddelen skall avskiljas med bindestreck. Observera alltså skillnaden i artikeln **svensk|amerikan** med sammansättningar mellan **-amerikansk** (= **svenskamerikansk**) och **--engelsk** (= **svensk-engelsk**).

~ inuti artiklarna betecknar hela uppslagsordet, t.ex. **arm** *gå ~ i ~, med ~arna i kors.*

( ) används dels för kompletterande förklaringar, t.ex. **hösäck** *(tom)* haysack; *(full)* sack of hay, dels för alternativa ord och fraser, t.ex. *ta ett hinder (sport.)* jump (take, clear) a hurdle (fence).

[ ] används dels kring uttalsbeteckningarna, dels för att ange ord eller del av ord som kan utelämnas, t.ex. **fönsterlucka** [window]shutter.

Stavning

Bortsett från rena undantagsfall har brittisk stavning iakttagits i hela ordboken. De viktigaste skillnaderna mellan brittisk och amerikansk praxis framgår av nedanstående uppställning:

Brittisk engelska	*Amerikansk engelska*	
travelling, waggon	traveling, wagon	I amerikansk engelska bibehålls enkelt l och p efter obetonad vokal.
colour, neighbour	color, neighbor	Ändelsen -our motsvaras i amerikansk engelska av -or.
metre, theatre	meter, theater	-re i ordslut motsvaras i amerikansk engelska oftast av -er.
cheque, plough, catalogue, programme	check, plow, catalog, program	Bokstavsföljder som betecknar ett enda ljud förenklas i amerikansk engelska.
defence	defense	-ce i ordslut motsvaras i amerikansk engelska ibland av -se.

Förkortningar *se s. 16.*

Oregelbundna verb

Imperfekt- och supinumformer av oregelbundna svenska verb står upptagna som uppslagsord med hänvisning till infinitivformen.

De svenska ordens uttal

Till tjänst för utländska läsare anges där så behövs de svenska ordens accent och uttal. Accenten anges med tecknet ' före den betonade stavelsen, såväl i uppslagsorden som i uttalsparenteserna (i vissa fall före betonad vokal). *I ord vilkas uttal följer den grundregel som säger att två- och flerstaviga ord har betoningen på första stavelsen och grav accent ges dock ingen anvisning om accenten.* I övrigt används en förenklad ljudskrift som i huvudsak ansluter sig till det internationella fonetiska alfabetet. Den intresserade hänvisas till de engelskspråkiga anvisningarna (Notes on the use of the dictionary, s. 10).

Böjningsformer

Substantivs, adjektivs och verbs böjning anges med hjälp av en kod som återfinns i de engelska anvisningarna (Notes on the use of the dictionary, s. 13).

NOTES ON THE USE OF THE DICTIONARY

General

The Swedish headwords are arranged in strict alphabetical order, e.g. **bildäck, bildöverföring, bilersättning**. Field labels appear in italics before the English translation, e.g. *tekn., mil., sport.* (see list of abbreviations, p. 16). American alternatives of the English translations are marked *AE*.

Symbols

If a headword has more than one meaning, each different part of speech is indicated by means of a roman numeral. Entirely different meanings within each part of speech are indicated by arabic numerals, smaller differences in meaning are indicated by a semi-colon.

| stands after the part of a headword that reappears in one or more successive entries. It is also sometimes used for the sake of clarity to show how a word is made up, e.g. **bil|drulle**

- indicates the part of the entry, separated by |, or (in compounds and derivatives) the entire preceding entry, e.g. **berör|a, -ing** (= beröra, beröring), **fasad, -klättrare** (= fasad, fasadklättrare).

-- indicates that the following word element is preceded by a hyphen. Note the difference, in the article on **svensk|amerikan** and its compounds, between **-amerikansk** (= **svenskamerikansk**) and **--engelsk** (= **svensk-engelsk**).

~ within the article indicates the entire headword, e.g. **arm** *gå ~ i ~, med ~arna i kors.*

( ) is used for complementary explanations, e.g. **hösäck** (*tom*) hay-sack; (*full*) sack of hay, and for alternative words and phrases, e.g. *ta ett hinder* (*sport.*) jump (take, clear) a hurdle (fence).

[ ] is used round the phonetic transcription and round a word or part of a word that can be omitted, e.g. **fönsterlucka** [window]shutter.

Spelling

With a very few exceptions British spelling has been used throughout the dictionary. The most important differences in spelling between British and American English are listed below.

British usage	American usage	
travelling, waggon	traveling, wagon	A double consonant is sometimes written as a single consonant.
colour, neighbour	color, neighbor	The ending -our is written as -or.
metre, theatre	meter, theater	-re at the end of a word is usually written as -er.
cheque, plough, catalogue, programme	check, plow, catalog, program	Letter combination denoting a single sound are sometimes simplified.
defence	defense	-ce at the end of a word is sometimes written as -se.

Abbreviations *see p. 16.*

Irregular verbs

The past participle and the supine of irregular Swedish verbs are given as headwords with a reference to the infinitive.

PRONUNCIATION OF THE SWEDISH WORDS

Tone and stress

There are two kinds of tone in Swedish: the acute accent, or singletone, and the grave accent, or double-tone. The acute accent is a falling tone, as in English beggar, calendar. It occurs in words of one syllable and in a few words of two or more syllables. In this dictionary the acute accent in words of two or more syllables with the stress on the first syllable is always indicated in the phonetic transcription. The grave accent, which is characteristic of the Swedish language, occurs in words of two or more syllables. It is also a falling tone, but the second syllable begins on a higher pitch than the first. The main stress usually lies on the first syllable and there is a strong secondary stress on the second syllable.

Most Swedish words of two or more syllables have the stress on the first syllable and the grave accent.

Words with the following endings have the stress on the last syllable:

-age [-'aːʃ]	-gogi [-gå'giː]	-ment
-ang [-'aŋ]	-graf	-nom [-'nåːm]
-ans	-grafi [-gra'fiː]	-nomi [-nå'miː]
-ant	-ik	-skop [-'skåːp]
-at	-ion	-tet
-ens	-ism	-tris
-ent	-ist	-ur
-eri [-e'riː]	-log [-'låːg]	-ör
-ess	-logi [-lå'giː]	-ös
-gog [-'gåːg]		

Words with the following endings have the stress on the penultimate syllable:

-abel [-'aːbel]	-ering [-'eːriŋ]	-istisk [-'istisk]
-ator [-ˣaːtår]	-inna [-ˣinna]	-logisk [-'låːgisk]
-era [-'eːra]	-issa [-ˣissa]	-nomisk [-'nåːmisk]

In words that are not pronounced in accordance with these rules, the stress is rnarked. When only the stress is indicated, this is done by means of an accent before the stressed syllable in the headword. The stress may also be indicated in the phonetic transcription, where one is given (see below).

Pronunciation

The first column contains the Swedish letters and the second column the phonetic symbols used in this dictionary.

Vowels

a	[aː]	as in father. E.g. *far* [faːr].
	[a]	similar to the first element in the English diphthong in time, the French a in la, the German a in kann. E.g. *hatt* [hatt].
e	[eː]	has no exact English equivalent, is pronounced as in French les, German mehr. E.g. *leta* [ˣleːta], *se* [seː].
	[e]	as in let. E.g. *detta* [ˣdetta].
i	[iː]	as in three. E.g. *lida* [ˣliːda].
	[i]	similar to the i in fit. E.g. *sitta* [ˣsitta].
o	[oː]	similar to the vowel in too. E.g. *ropa* [ˣrɷːpa].
	[o]	similar to the vowel in put. E.g. *hon* [hɷnn].
u	[uː]	has no English equivalent. Tongue position as for [eː] above, but lips rounded. E.g. *luta* [ˣluːta], *hus* [huːs].
	[u]	similar to English [ə] in letter, but lips rounded. E.g. *kulle* [ˣkulle].
y	[yː]	similar to the French u in rue, the German u in früh, but lips more protruded and rounded. E.g. *gryta* [ˣgryːta], *sy* [syː].
	[y]	short [yː], compare French lune, German müssen. E.g. *syster* [ˣsyster], *hylla* [ˣhylla].
å	[åː]	similar to the vowel in saw. E.g. *båt* [båːt].
	[å]	as in long. E.g. *lång* [låŋ].
ä	[äː]	before r similar to the first element in the diphthong in bear. E.g. *bära* [ˣbäːra]. In other cases less open as in French chaise.

E.g. *träd* [trä:d], *läsa* [ˣlä:sa], *säl* [sä:l].

[ä] before r as in carry. E.g. *värre* [ˣvärre], *ärta* [ˣärta]. In other cases similar to e in set. E.g. *mätt* [mätt].

ö [ö:] before r similar to the vowel in bird. E.g. *höra* [ˣhö:ra]. In other cases the sound is similar to the vowel in French deux, German Öl.

[ö] before r similar to the vowel in English cup, but lips rounded. E.g. *dörr* [dörr]. In other cases similar to the final vowel in English better. E.g. *höst* [höst].

Consonants

b	[b]	as English b.
c	[s]	as in sea. E.g. *cykel* ['sykel].
ch	[ʃ]	as in shall. E.g. choklad [ʃɷk'la:d]
ck	[k]	as English k.
d	[d]	as English d, but pronounced with the tongue against the back of the upper teeth.
f	[f]	as English f.
g	[g]	as English g in great, good, before a, o, u, å or unstressed -e. E.g. *god* [gɷ:d], *gul* [gu:l], *fågel* ['få:gel].
	[j]	as English y in yes, before e, i, y, ä, ö and after l and r. E.g. *ge* [je:], *gynna* [ˣjynna], *göra* [ˣjö:ra], *arg* [arj].
	[k]	as English k, before t. E.g. *sagt* [sakt].
gj	[j]	as English y in yes. E.g. *gjort* [jɷ:rt].
gn	[ŋn]	E.g. *regn* [reŋn].
h	[h]	as English h.
j	[j]	as English y in yes. E.g. *ja* [ja:].
k	[k]	as English k, before a, o, u, å. E.g. *kall* [kall], *kål* [kå:l].
	[ç]	similar to the initial sound in child, but without the beginning t-sound, compare German ich. Comes before e, i, y, ä, ö. E.g. *kela* [ˣçe:la], *kyla* [ˣçy:la], *kött* [çött].
l	[l]	as English l.
m	[m]	as English m.
n	[n]	as English n.
ng	[ŋ]	as in song. E.g. *mangel* ['maŋel]. Note no g-sound should be heard after the ŋ-sound as it is in English.
p	[p]	as English p.
q	[k]	as English k.
r	[r]	similar to English r but rolled.
rd	[rd]	similar to rd, rt in ford, cart in British pronunciation. In the pho-
rt	[rt]	netic transcription written rd, rt. E.g. *bord* [bɷ:rd], *sort* [sårt].
rs	[rs]	pronounced as sh in shall. In the phonetic transcription written rs. E.g. *brorson* [ˣbrɷ:rså:n].
s	[s]	as English s in see (voiceless).
sch	[ʃ]	similar to sh in she. E.g. *marsch* [marʃ], *dimension* [dimen'ʃɷ:n],
si(on)		*själv*[ʃälv], *skjuta* [ˣʃu:ta], *stjärna* [ˣʃä:rna]. (Most Swedes use a dif-
sj		ferent sound, which is, however, difficult for foreigners to produce.)
skj		
stj		
t	[t]	as English t, but pronounced with the tongue against the back of the upper teeth.
ti(on)	[ʃ]	see sch etc. above.
tj	[ç]	similar to the initial sound in child but without the initial t-sound, compare German ich. E.g. *tjänst* [çänst], *tjuv* [çu:v].
v, w	[v]	as English v.
x	[ks]	never pronounced gs, as in example.
z	[s]	pronounced as English s in see (voiceless).

Other phonetic symbols

In addition to the phonetic symbols given after the Swedish letters above, the following symbols are used:

'   indicates acute accent. E.g. *allting* ['alltiŋ].
ˣ   indicates grave accent. E.g. *arton* [ˣaːrtån].
:   indicates long vowel. E.g. *adjö* [a'jöː].
-   is used when only part of the word is transcribed. E.g. *piano* [-'aːnɷ].

A consonant following a short, stressed vowel is written twice. E.g. *banjo* ['bann-].

It has not been considered necessary to give the pronunciation of ch, sch, stj where they are pronounced [ʃ], of -sion, -tion where they are pronounced [-ʃɷːn], of ng where it is pronounced [ŋ] or of c where it is pronounced [s].

No pronunciation is given for compounds. The reader is referred to the separate words which make up the compound. Within an article containing several headwords the first word normally gives the stress and pronunciation of the following words, but not the accent. For practical reasons only one pronunciation has often been given for words which have two or more possible pronunciations.

INFLECTION OF NOUNS, ADJECTIVES, AND VERBS

The following codes are used:

Nouns

The forms given are: sg indefinite – sg definite – pl indefinite.

s1   flicka – flickan – flickor
      toffel – toffeln – tofflor
      ros – rosen – rosor

s2   pojke – pojken – pojkar
      dag – dagen – dagar
      dager – dagern – dagrar
      dagg – daggen – no pl
      sky – skyn – skyar
      mun – munnen – munnar
      lämmel – lämmeln – lämlar
      kam – kammen – kammar

s3   rad – raden – rader
      doktor – doktorn – doktorer [-'tɷː-]
      filosofi – filosofin – filosofier
      djungel – djungeln – djungler
      kollega – kollegan – kolleger
      pilgrim – pilgrimen – pilgrimer
      konsul – konsuln – konsuler [-'suː-]
      parallellogram – parallellogrammen – parallellogrammer

s4   bryggeri – bryggeri*et* – bryggeri*er*
        fängelse – fängels*et* – fängels*er*
        studium – studi*et* – studi*er*
        drama – drama*t* – dram*er*

s5   sko – sko*n* – sko*r*
        hustru – hustru*n* – hustru*r*

s6   äpple – äpple*t* – äpple*n*
        schema – schema*t* – schema*n*

s7   träd – träd*et* – träd
        damm – damm*et* – no pl
        garage – garag*et* – garage
        fönster – fönstr*et* – fönster
        kummel – kuml*et* – kummel
        kapitel – kapitl*et* – kapitel
        gram – gramm*et* – gram

s8   faktum – faktum[et] – fakta or faktum
        centrum – centret or centrum[et] – centra or centrum
        natrium – natrium[et] or natriet – no pl

s9   studerande – studerande*n* – studerande
        hänsyn – hänsyn*en* – hänsyn

The same codes are used for nouns which have no plural form. For nouns with the following cornmon endings no code is given in the entry.

-ang [-'aŋ]	*-en -er*	**-ion**	*-en -er*
-ant [-'ant]	*-en -er*	**-ism**	*-en no pl*
-are	*-n =*	**-iss|a** [-ˣissa]	*-an -or*
-at [-'at]	*-en -er*	**-ist** [-'ist]	*-en -er*
-else	*-n -r*	**-log** [-'lå:g]	*-en -er*
-ent [-'ent]	*-en -er*	**-ning**	*-en -ar*
-er	*-n =*	**-nom** [-'nå:m]	*-en -er*
-eri [-e'ri]	*-[e]t -er*	**-sk|a**	*-an -or*
-ersk|a	*-an -or*	**-tet** [-'te:t]	*-en no pl*
-ess [-'ess]	*-en -er*	**-tris** [-'tri:s]	*-en -er*
-het	*-en -er*	**-ur** [-'u:r]	*-en -er*
-ing	*-en -ar*	**-ör** [-'ö:r]	*-en -er*
-inn|a [-ˣinna]	*-an -or*	**-ös** [-'ö:s]	*-en -er*

Indeclinable nouns are marked *n* or *r* (common gender). For irregular nouns which do not fit the above paradigms the inflected forms are given in full, together with the gender if this is not evident from the forms.

Adjectives

The forms given are: positive – neuter positive – comparative – superlative.

a1   stark – stark*t* – stark*are* – stark*ast*
        stilig – stilig*t* – stilig*are* – stilig*ast*
        lätt – lätt – lätt*are* – lätt*ast*
        röd – rött – röd*are* – röd*ast*

fri – fri*tt* – fri*are* – fri*ast*
vit – vi*tt* – vit*are* – vit*ast*
blond – blon*t* – blond*are* – blond*ast*
tunn – tun*t* – tunn*are* – tunn*ast*
följsam – följsam*t* – följsamm*are* – följsamm*ast*
allmän – allmän*t* – allmänn*are* – allmänn*ast*

a2   ädel – ädel*t* – ädl*are* – ädl*ast*
vacker – vacker*t*– vackr*are* – vackr*ast*

a3   rutten – rutte*t* – ruttn*are* – ruttn*ast*
trogen – troge*t* – trogn*are* – trogn*ast*
försigkommen – försigkomme*t* – försigkomn*are* – försigkomn*ast*

a4   gängse – gängse – *mera* gängse – *mest* gängse
defekt – defekt – *mera* defekt – *mest* defekt

a5   begåvad – begåva*t* – *mera* begåvad – *mest* begåvad
komisk – komisk*t* – *mera* komisk – *mest* komisk
prydd – prytt – *mera* prydd – *mest* prydd
svulten – svulte*t* – *mera* svulten – *mest* svulten

The comparison of adjectives which do not fit these paradigms is indicated in full in the entry.

Verbs

Conjugations (infinitive, present tense, past tense, supine, past participle):

v1   kalla – kallar – kallade – kallat – kallad
dagas – dagas – dagades – dagats

v2   böja – böjer – böjde – böjt – böjd
breda – breder – bredde – brett – bredd
skilja – skiljer – skilde – skilt – skild
blygas – blyg[e]s – blygdes – blygts
brännas – bränn[e]s – brändes – bränts
klämma – klämmer – klämde – klämt – klämd
tända – tänder – tände – tänt – tänd

v3   köpa – köper – köpte – köpt – köpt
mista – mister – miste – mist – mist
lyfta – lyfter – lyfte – lyft – lyft
skvätta – skvätter – skvätte – skvätt – skvätt
begynna – begynner – begynte – begynt – begynt
hjälpas – hjälp[e]s – hjälptes – hjälpts

v4   tro – tror – trodde – trott – trodd

As a rule verbs belonging to *v1* are not marked. The past tense and the supine of *irregular verbs* are written out.

Förkortningar   Abbreviations

a adjektiv   adjective
absol. absolut   absolute[ly]
abstr. abstrakt   abstract
adj. adjektiv[isk]   adjective, adjectival
adv adverb   adverb
AE. amerikansk engelska   American English; [in] U.S.
akad. akademi   academy
allm. allmän[t]   general[ly]
anat. anatomi   anatomy
a p. a person
arkeol. arkeologi   archaeology
arkit. arkitektur   architecture
astr. astronomi   astronomy

bank. bankväsen   banking
bergv. bergväsen   mining
best. bestämd   definite
beton. betonad [-at]   stressed
bibl. bibliskt   biblical
bildl. bildlig[t]   figurative[ly]
biol. biologi   biology
bokb. bokbinderi   bookbinding
bokför. bokföring   book–keeping
boktr. boktryckeri   printing
bot. botanik   botany
byggn. byggnadskonst   building

data. databehandling   data processing
demonstr. demonstrativ[t]   demonstrative
dep deponens   deponent
determ. determinativ[t]   determinative
dial. dialektal[t]   dialectal[ly]
dipl. diplomatterm   diplomacy

eg. egentlig[en]   literal[ly]
ekon. ekonomi   economy
elektr. elektrisk, elektroteknisk   electrical, electrotechnical
elektron. elektronisk, elektronik   electronic, electronics

fack. fackspråk   technicalterm
fem. femininum   feminine
film. filmterm   cinema
filos. filosofi   philosophy
fisk. fiskeriterm   fishing
flyg. flygväsen   aviation
fonet. fonetik   phonetics
foto. fotografikonst   photography
fys. fysik   physics
fysiol. fysiologi   physiology
fäkt. fäktterm   fencing
fören. förenad (–t)   adjectival form
förh. förhållande   relation[ship]

förk. förkortning   abbreviation
försäkr. försäkringsväsen   insurance

gen. genitiv   genitive
geogr. geografi   geography
graf. grafisk term   printing
gruv. gruvterm   mining term
gymn. gymnastik   gymnastics

hand. handelsterm   commercial term
her. heraldik   heraldry
hist. historisk[t]   historical[ly]
hopskr. hopskrivs, hopskrivet   written as one word
högt. högtidlig[t]   formal[ly]

ibl. ibland   sometimes
imperf. imperfektum   past tense
indef. indefinit   indefinite
inf. infinitiv   infinitive
interj interjektion   interjection
interr. interrogativ(t)   interrogative
iron. ironisk[t]   ironic[ally]
i sht i synnerhet   particularly

jakt. jaktterm   hunting
jfr jämför   compare
jordbr. jordbruk   agriculture
jur. juridik   law
järnv. järnvägsväsen   railway term

kat. katolsk   Catholic
kem. kemi   chemistry
kir. kirurgisk term   surgery
kokk. kokkonst   cookery
koll. kollektiv   collective[ly]
komp. komparativ   comparative
konj konjunktion   conjunction
konkr. konkret   concrete
konst. konstterm   art
konstr. konstruktion   construction
kortsp. kortspel   card game
kyrkl. kyrklig term   ecclesiastical
lantbr. lantbruk   agriculture
lantm. lantmäteri   land-surveying
litt. litterär[t], litteratur   literary, literature
log. logik   logic

mat. matematik   mathematics
med. medicin   medicine
meteor. meteorologi   meteorology
mil. militärterm   military term
miner. mineralogi   mineralogy
mots. motsats   opposite
mus. musik   music

17

myt. mytologi mythology
mål. målarterm painting

n neutrum neuter
neds. nedsättande derogatory
neg. negation negative
ngn någon somebody
ngt något something

opers. opersonlig impersonal
opt. optik optics
ordspr. ordspråk proverb
o.s. oneself

parl. parlamentarisk term parliamentary term
pass. passiv, passivum passive
perf. part. perfekt particip, past principle
pers. person[lig] person[al]
pl pluralis plural
poet. poetisk[t] poetical[ly]
polit. politik politics
poss. possessiv[t] possessive
post. postterm postal term
predik. predikat, predikativ[t] predicate, pre-dicative[ly]
prep preposition preposition
pres. presens present [tense]
pron pronomen pronoun
psykol. psykologi psychology

r reale common gender
radar. radarteknik radar
radio. radioteknik radio engineering
rel. relativ[t] relative
relig. religion religion
ret. retorisk[t] rhetoric[ally]
rfl reflexiv[t] reflexive
ridk. ridkonst equestrian term
rumsbet. rumsbetydelse spatial sense
räkn räkneord numeral

s substantiv substantive
s.b. somebody
schack. schackterm chess
sg singularis singular
självst. självständig[t] pronoun
sjö. sjöterm nautical term
skeppsb. skeppsbyggeri shipbuilding
skol. skolväsen education

skämts. skämtsam[t] jocular[ly]
sl. slang slang
slaktar. slaktarterm butchering term
sms. sammansättning[ar] compound[s]
snick. snickarterm joinery
s.o. someone
spel. spelterm game
sport. sportterm sporting term
spr. språk language
språkv. språkvetenskap linguistics
ss. såsom as
stat. statistik statistics
s.th. something
subj. subjekt subject
sup. supinum supine
superl. superlativ superlative
särskr. särskrivs, särskrivet written as two words
sömn. sömnad sewing

t. till to
tandläk. tandläkarterm dentistry
teat. teaterterm theatre
tekn. teknologi, teknisk technology, technical
tel. telefon telephone
teol. teologi theology
text. textilterm textiles
tidsbet. tidsbetydelse temporal sense
trädg. trädgårdsskötsel gardening
tullv. tullväsen customs
TV. television television

ung. ungefär approximately
univ. universitetsterm university
uttr. uttryck(ande) expression expressing

v verb verb
vanl. vanlig[en] usual[ly]
vard. vardagligt colloquial[ly]
versl. verslära prosody, metrics term
vetensk. vetenskaplig scientific
veter. veterinärväsen veterinary term
väv. vävnadsteknisk term weaving

zool. zoologi zoology

åld. ålderdomlig[t], föråldrad (–t) acchaic

äv. även also

A

A

1 a [a:] *s6* a; ~ *och o* alpha and omega; *har man sagt ~ får man säga b* in for a penny, in for a pound
2 a *prep, se a conto, a dato, a priori*
à 1 of, containing; *5 påsar ~ 20 gram* 5 bags of 20 grammes [each] **2** *2 biljetter ~ 1 pund* 2 tickets at £1 each **3** or; *3 ~ 4 dagar* 3 or 4 days; *det tar 2 ~ 3 veckor* it takes from 2 to 3 weeks
AB (*förk. för aktiebolag*) Ltd.; *AE.* Inc.
abakus ['abba-] *s2* (*räkneram, arkit.*) abacus
abandon [abaŋ'dåŋ] *s3* abandon
abbé *s3* abbé **abbedissa** abbess
abborr|e [-å-] *s2* perch **-grund** *s7, ung.* perch angling shallow **-pinne** small perch
abbot [-åt] *s2* abbot
abbots|döme *s6*, **-värdighet** abbacy
abc [abe'se:] *s6* ABC **-bok** ABC-book, primer
ABC-stridsmedel ABC weapons
abderitisk [-'ri:-] *a5* Gothamite
abdik|ation abdication **-era** abdicate
abdom|en [-'då:-] *n el. r, best. form -en, pl -en, äv. -ina* abdomen **-i'nal** *a5* abdominal
aber ['a:-] *n* but, drawback, catch; snag
aberration aberration; *kromatisk ~* chromatic aberration; *sfärisk ~* spherical aberration
Abessinien [-'si:-] *n* Abyssinia **abessin|ier** [-'si:-] *s9*, **-[i]sk** [-'si:-] *a5* Abyssinian
abiturient matriculation candidate; *numera ung.* General Certificate of Education [A-level] candidate
ablation *fack.* ablation
ablativ *s3* ablative
ablution *kyrkl.* ablution
abnorm [-'nårm] *a1* abnormal **-itet** abnormity, abnormality; malformation, deformity
abolition abolition **-ism** abolitionism **-ist** abolitionist
abonne'mang *s7* subscription (*på* to, for)
abonnemangs|avgift subscription [rate (fee, price)]; *tel.* telephone rental **-biljett** season ticket (*på* for) **-föreställning** performance for season-ticket holders
abonn|ent subscriber; (*konsert-, teater- etc.*) season-ticket (seat, box) holder **-era** subscribe (*på* to, for), contract (*på* for); *~d buss* hired (private) bus; *~d föreställning* closed (private) performance
a'bort [-å-] *s3* abortion; *spontan ~* miscarriage; *göra ~* terminate pregnancy **-era** abort, miscarry
abor'tiv abortive **-medel** abortifacient
abort|lag law on abortion **-sökande** applicant for abortion **-ör** abortionist
abradera *geol.* abrade
abrakadabra [-'da:bra] *s7* abracadabra
abrasion *geol.* abrasion
ab'rupt *a1* abrupt, sudden
abscess [-'sess] *s3* abscess

ab'sid *s3* apse, apsis
ab'sint *s3* absinth[e]
abskissa [-'skissa] *s1* abscissa
abso'lut I *a1* absolute; *en ~ omöjlighet* an utter impossibility **II** *adv* absolutely, utterly, certainly, definitely; *~ inte* definitely not, by no means, not at all; *den ~ bästa* by far the best; *han vill ~ gå* he insists on going **-belopp** absolute value
absolution absolution
absolut|ism 1 absolutism **2** (*helnykterhet*) teetotalism, total abstinence **-ist 1** absolutist **2** (*helnykterist*) teetotaller, total abstainer
absolvera [-å-] **1** absolve (*från* from) **2** finish, complete; *~ en examen* pass an examination
absorb|ator [-år-] *s3* (*i solfångare*) absorber **-era** absorb; *~d dos* absorbed dose
absorption [-p'ʃɷ:n] absorption
absorptions|förmåga power of absorption **-kylskåp** absorption[-type] refrigerator **-kärl** absorption drum **-medel** absorbent, absorber
abstinens abstinence **-besvär, -symtom** withdrawal symptom
abstrahera abstract; *~ från* disregard
ab'strak|t I *a1* abstract **II** *adv* abstractly, in the abstract **-tion** [-k'ʃɷ:n] abstraction
abstraktionsförmåga ability to think in abstract terms
ab'strus *a1* abstruse
absurd [-'urd *el.* -'u:rd] *a1* absurd, preposterous **-itet** *s3* absurdity, absurdness
a cappella [ka'pella] *mus.* a cappella
accelerando [aksele'randå] *adv o. s6* accelerando
acceleration [aks-] acceleration; *~ vid fritt fall* acceleration of free fall, acceleration due to (of) gravity
accelerations|fil [aks-] acceleration lane **-förmåga** acceleration capacity
acceler|ator [akse-] *s3* accelerator **-era** accelerate, speed up **-ometer** [-'me:-] *s2* accelerometer
accent [aks-] accent; (*tonvikt*) stress **-tecken** accent
accentuer|a [aks-] accentuate, stress **-ing** accentuation
ac'cept [aks-] *s3* **1** (*växel*) acceptance, accepted bill; *dokument mot ~* documents against acceptance **2** (*-ering*) acceptance **-abel** *a2* acceptable; passable **-ans** [-'tans] *s3* acceptance **-ant** acceptor **-era** accept; *vard.* buy **-vägran** nonacceptance
accession [akse'ʃɷ:n] acquisition; acquest **accessionskatalog** acquisition catalogue
accessoarer [aksesɷ'a:rer] accessories
accesstid [ak*ˣ*sess-] *data.* access time
acci'denstryck [aks-] job-printing, job[bing] work **-eri** jobbing printer
accis [ak'si:s] *s3* excise [tax, duty], inland duty **-fri** exempt from excise [duty] **-pliktig** liable to excise [duty]
ace'tat [-s-] *s7, s4* acetate **-silke** acetate [rayon]
aceton [asse'tå:n] *s4* acetone
acety'len [-s-] *s3, s4* acetylene, ethyne **-gas** acetylene [gas] **-lampa** acetylene lamp **-svetsning** oxyacetylene welding
ace'tylsalicylsyra [-s-] acetylsalicylic acid

aciditet [-s-] acidity **acidos** [-'då:s] *s3, med.*
acidosis
ack oh [dear]!; *högt.* alas!; ~, *om han vore här!*
oh, if only he were here!
ackja *s1* Lapp sledge
acklamation acclamation; unanimous vote; *väljas med* ~ be voted by (with) acclamation
acklimatiser|a acclimatize; ~ *sig* become acclimatized, begin to feel at home **-ing** acclimatization, acclimation
ackommodation accommodation
ackommodations|förmåga accommodation **-växel** *hand.* accommodation bill
ackommodera accommodate
ackompanja|tris, -tör [-å-] accompanist
ackompanj|e'mang [-å-] *s7* accompaniment; *till* ~ *av* to the accompaniment of **-era** accompany
ackord [a'kå:rd] *s7* **1** *mus.* chord **2** (*arbete*) piecework [contract], piece rate; *arbeta på* ~ work at piece rates (by contract), do piecework **3** *jur.* agreement, composition [with one's creditors] **-era** (*köpslå*) negotiate (*om* about, for), bargain (*om* for)
ackords|arbete piecework **-lön** piece rate **-pris** piece price, piecework price **-sättning** rate fixing
ackrediter|a **1** *dipl.* accredit (*hos, vid* to), furnish with credentials **2** *hand.* open a credit for [a certain amount] (*hos en bank* at a bank); *bank. äv.* authorize **3** *väl ~d hos ngn* in a p.'s good books **-ing** accreditation
ackumul|ation accumulation **-a'tiv** *a5* accumulative **-ator** *s3* accumulator, [storage] battery **-era** accumulate; *~d ränta* accrued (accumulated) interest
acku'rat *a1* accurate **-ess** accuracy, exactitude, precision; *med all* ~ adroitly, expertly
ackusativ [ˣacku-]*s3* accusative; *i* ~ in the accusative **-objekt** direct object
ackuschörska [-ˣʃö:r-] *s1* midwife
ackvirera procure
ackvisi|tion **1** (*förvärv*) acquisition **2** *hand.* canvassing **-tör** canvasser; *försäkr.* insurance agent
acne *se akne*
a conto [a 'kåntå] on account **--betalning** payment on account
actionfilm [*ung.* äkʃn-] action film (*AE.* movie)
acyklisk [a'syk-] *a5* acyclic
adagio [a'da:dʒå] *s6 o. adv* adagio
Adam och Eva *bot.* elder-flowered orchid
adams|dräkt *i* ~ in one's birthday suit **-äpple** Adam's apple
adap|tation adaptation, adjustment **-ter** *s2* adapter, adaptor **-tera** adapt, adjust **-tion** [-p'ʃɔ:n] *se adaptation*
a dato [a ˣda:tɔ] from date **--växel** time (term) bill, time draft (note)
ADB (*förk. för automatisk databehandling*) A.D.P. (automatic data processing)
ad'd|end *s3* addend **-era** add up (together), cast [up]; *absol. äv.* do sums **-ering, -ition** addition
additionsmaskin adding machine
addi'tiv *s7 o. a1* additive
ade'kvat *a1* adequate, equivalent; apt

adel ['a:-] *s2* **1** (*härkomst*) noble birth **12** (*samhällsklass*) nobility; *i Storbritannien äv.* peerage **3** (*ädelhet*) nobility
adels|brev patent of nobility **-dam** noblewoman, titled lady **-kalender** peerage [book]
adelskap *s7* knighthood; baronetcy; peerage
adels|man nobleman, titled gentleman **-märke** mark of nobility **-privilegium** privilege of the nobility **-stånd** nobility **-titel** title **-välde** aristocracy
adenoid [-ɷ'i:d] *a5, n sg obest. form undviks* adenoid; *~a vegetationer* adenoids
a'dept *s3* pupil, beginner, novice
aderton [ˣa:rtån] eighteen **-de** eighteenth **-[de]del** eighteenth [part]
adertonhundra eighteen hundred **-femtio** eighteen [hundred and] fifty **-nittiotalet** *på* ~ in the [eighteen] nineties **-talet** *på* ~ in the nineteenth century
aderton|tiden *vid* ~ about 6 p.m., about six o'clock in the evening **-årig** *a1* eighteen- -year-old; ~ *vänskap* a friendship of eighteen years' standing; *en* ~ *pojke* a boy of eighteen **-åring** a boy (girl *etc.*) of eighteen, an eight--year-old boy (*etc.*) **-årsåldern** *i* ~ about eighteen [years of age]
adhe|sion [ade-] adhesion **-sionskraft** adhesive power **-'siv** *a5 o.* *s7* adhesive
ad hoc|-grupp, -utskott ad hoc committee
adiantum [-ˣann-] *s3, bot.* maidenhair [fern]
adjektiv *s7* adjective **-isk** *a5* adjectival
adjungera [-jung-] call in; co-opt; *~d ledamot* co-opted member; *~d professor* visiting professor
adjunkt [-'juŋkt] *s3* assistant master [at a secondary school]; *jfr kyrko-, pastorats-*
adjutant aide[-de-camp] (*hos* to)
adjö [a'jö:] **I** *interj* goodbye; *högt.* farewell; *äv.* good day (morning *etc.*); ~ *så länge* goodbye for now, so long **II** *n* farewell, adieu; *säga* ~ *till ngn* say goodbye to s.b., bid s.b. goodbye
adla [ˣa:d-] **1** (*i Storbritannien*) raise to the peerage; (*om eng. lågadel*) knight, make a baronet, confer a knighthood (*etc.*) on **2** *i sht bildl.* ennoble **adlig** *a1* noble, aristocratic, of noble family; ~ *krona* nobleman's coronet; *upphöja i ~t stånd* raise to the nobility
administration administration, management
administrations|apparat administrative machinery **-kostnader** management (administrative, general) costs
administr|a'tiv *a1* administrative; *på* ~ *väg* by administrative means, departmentally **-atör** administrator **-era** administrate, manage
admittans [-'ans *el.* -'aŋs] *s3, elektr.* admittance
admonition admonition
ad notam [ad ˣnɷ:tam] *ta* ~ pay attention to, obey, heed
adolescens [-'ʃens *el.* -'sens] *s3* adolescence
adonis [-'dɷ:-] *s2* Adonis
adop|tera [-å-] adopt **-tion** [-p'ʃɔ:n] adoption
adoptiv|barn [-ˣti:v-] adopted child **-föräldrar** adoptive parents **-hem** adoptive home, home of adoption
adrena'lin *s4* adrenaline **-avsöndring** adrenaline secretion
a'dress **1** (*bostadsuppgift*) address; *utan* ~ (*om*

brev etc.) unaddressed, undirected; *ändra* ~ change one's address; *han sade det med* ~ *till mig* his remark was meant for me; *paketet har inte kommit fram till sin* ~ the parcel has not reached its destination 2 *(lyckönskningsskrivelse o.d.)* [illuminated] address
adress|at addressee; *(på postanvisning e.d.)* payee; *(på paket e.d.)* consignee **-debatt** *parl.* debate on the address
adresser|a address, send, direct; *(om varor)* consign **-ing 1** *(-erande)* addressing **2** *(adress)* address
adresseringsmaskin addressing machine
adress|förändring change of address **-kalender** [street] directory **-kort** dispatch note, address form **-land** [country of] destination **-lapp** [address] label (tag) **-ort** [place of] destination **-plåt** address plate **-postanstalt** post office of destination, receiving post office **-register** register of addresses **-ändring** *se adressförändring*
Adriatiska havet [-i'a:tis-] the Adriatic [Sea]
adsor|bera [-å-] adsorb **-ption** [-p'ʃɔ:n] adsorption
adstringerande [-ŋ'ge:-] *a4* astringent *(äv.* ~ *medel)*
aducera anneal
aducerings|järn malleable [cast] iron **-verk** malleable iron foundry
A-dur A major
advent *s7* Advent; *första [söndagen i]* ~ Advent Sunday **-ist** Adventist
advents|kalender Advent calendar **-tid** [the season of] Advent
ad'verb *s7* adverb **-i'al** *s7* adverbial [modifier] **-i'ell** *a5* adverbial
adversativ [ˣadd- *el.* -ati:v] *a5* adversative
advocera plead *(för* for; *mot* against); quibble
advokat lawyer, *(juridiskt ombud)* solicitor, *(sakförare vid domstol)* barrister[-at-law], *(pläderande)* counsel; *(i Skottland)* advocate; *AE.* attorney[-at-law], counselor[-at-law] **-arvode** attorney's (solicitor's) fee (charge) **-byrå** law-service office *(firm of* solicitors, solicitor's firm, law office **-fiskal** *ung.* prosecuting counsel, prosecutor **-knep** legal quibble **-kontor** *se* -byrå
advokat|orisk [-'tɔ:-] *a5* quibbling, pettifogging **-päron** *se* avokado **-samfund** bar association; *utesluta ur* ~*et* disbar; *Sveriges A*~ [the] Swedish Bar Association
advoka't|yr *s3* quibbling, casuistry **-yrke** legal profession; *avstänga från utövande av* ~*t* disbench; *slå sig på* ~*t* enter the legal profession
aerob [aä'rå:b] **I** *s3* aerobe, aerobium *(pl* aerobia) **II** *a5* aerobic
aerobiologi [ˣaärå-, ˣaärɔ-] aerobiology
aerobisk [aä'rå:b-] *a5* aerobic; ~ *träning* aerobics *(behandlas som sg el. pl)*, aerobic exercises *(pl)*
aero|drom [aärå-, aärɔ'drå:m] *s3* aerodrome **-dyna'mik** [*äv.* ˣaä-] aerodynamics *(pl, behandlas som sg)* **-dynamisk** [-'na:-, *äv.* ˣaä-] aerodynamic **-gram** [-'gramm] *s7* aerogram, aerogramme, air letter **-lo'gi** *s3* aerology **-logisk** *a5* aerologic[al] **-'naut** *s3* aeronaut **-nau-'tik** *s2* aeronautics *(pl, behandlas som sg)*

-'**plan** aeroplane, aircraft; *AE. äv.* airplane **-sol** [-'såll] *s3* aerosol -'**stat** *s3* aerostat **-sta'tik** aerostatics *(pl, behandlas som sg)*
afa|'si *s3, med.* aphasia **-sisk** [-'fa:-] *a5,* **-tiker** [-'fa:-] *s9,* **-tisk** [-'fa:-] *a5* aphasic
af'fekt *s3* [state of] emotion **-betonad** *a5* emotional, agitated **-erad** [-'te:-] *a5* affected; mannered, theatrical; *vard.* la-di-da **-fri** unemotional, dispassionate, impassive
affektionsvärde [-kˣʃɔ:ns-] sentimental value
affinitet affinity
affisch [a'fiʃ] *s3* poster, bill, placard; *sätta upp en* ~ post (stick) a bill
affischer|a post (stick) bills, post **-ing** billposting; ~ *förbjuden* stick no bills, billposting prohibited
affisch|klistrare *se affischör* **-pelare** poster (advertising) pillar **-tavla** hoarding; *AE.* billboard
affischör bill|poster, -sticker
af'fär *s3* **1** *(firma)* business, [business] firm, concern, establishment, enterprise **2** *(transaktion)* transaction, deal, operation; ~*er* business; *en dålig* ~ a bad bargain; *en fin* ~ a good stroke of business, a bargain; *bortrest i* ~*er* away on business; *göra* ~*er i* do business in; *göra stora* ~*er på Sydamerika* do a lot of business with South America; *ha* ~*er med* do business with; *inlåta sig på en* ~ enter into a business transaction; *prata* ~*er* talk business; *slutföra en* ~ close a deal; *hur går* ~*erna?* how is business? **3** *(butik)* shop; *särsk. AE.* store; *inneha en* ~ keep (own) a shop; *stå i* ~ be a shop assistant; *öppna en* ~ start a business, open a shop (store) **4** *(angelägenhet)* affair, matter, concern; *göra stor* ~ *av ngt* make a great fuss about s.th.; *ordna sina* ~*er* settle one's affairs; *sköt dina egna* ~*er* mind your own business **5** *(rättsfall)* case **6** *(spekulation)* venture
affärs|angelägenhet business matter; *i* ~*er* on business **-anställd** shop employee (assistant, worker); *AE. äv.* store clerk **-bana** *gå* ~*n* go into business **-bank** commercial bank **-begåvning** gift for business **-besök** business call **-biträde** shop assistant; salesman, *fem.* saleswoman; *AE.* [sales]clerk **-bokföring** financial accounting **-brev** business letter **-byggnad** shop building **-centrum** shopping centre (precinct) **-drivande** *a5, statens* ~ *verk* government-owned enterprises and public utilities **-folk** businessmen, business people **-förbindelse** business connection; *stå i* ~ *med* have business relations with **-föreståndare** shopkeeper, storekeeper **-företag** business firm (enterprise), company; *AE. äv.* corporation **-gata** shopping street **-handling** business document; ~*ar (post.)* printed matter *(sg)*, commercial papers **-hemlighet** trade secret **-hus 1** *(byggnad)* business (commercial) property **2** *(företag)* business firm (company, house) **-händelse** *bokför.* business transaction **-idkare** businessman, *fem.* businesswoman, tradesman, *fem.* tradeswoman **-innehavare** shopkeeper, storekeeper **-inredning** shop fittings *(pl)* **-jurist** solicitor; company lawyer, legal adviser (advisor) [of a company]; *AE. äv.* attorney **-knep** business trick **-korrespon-**

dens commercial correspondence **-kretsar** business circles **-kutym** se -sed **-kvarter** shopping (business) area **-kvinna** businesswoman **-liv** business [life], trade; *inom ~et* in business **-lokal** business premises (*pl*), shop **-läge 1** (*lokalitet*) business site, store location **2** (*konjunktur*) business conditions (*pl*), state of business (the market) **-man** businessman **-meddelande** business communication **-medhjälpare** se -biträde **-metoder** business methods **-moral** business ethics (*pl*) **-mässig** *al* businesslike **-resa** business trip **-rörelse** business **-sed** commercial (business, trade) practice (custom) **-sinne** business sense, nose (flair) for business **-ställning** business position (standing) **-tid** business hours (*pl*) **-transaktion** business deal (transaction) **-uppgörelse** business transaction, closing of a deal **-vana** business experience **-verk** se *under affärsdrivande* **-verksamhet** business [activity] **-vän** business friend **-värde** good will **-världen** the business (commercial) world, business life

afghan [af'ga:n] *s3*, **-[i]sk** *a5* Afghan[i] **Afghani'stan** *n* Afghanistan

aflatoxin aflatoxin

aforis|m aphorism **-tisk** *a5* aphoristic

Afrika ['a:-] *n* Africa

afrikaans [-'ka:ns] *r* Afrikaans

afri'k|an *s3* African **-and** *s3* Afrikaner **-ansk** [-'ka:nsk] *a5* African

afro|-amerikansk Afro-American **--asiatisk** Afro-Asian

afrodisiakum [-'si:a-] *s8* aphrodisiac

afrofrisyr Afro

afton [-ån] *-en aftnar* evening; *i ~* this evening; *i går ~* yesterday evening; *i fredags ~* last Friday evening; *om ~en* in the evening; *sent på ~en* late in the evening; *det lider mot ~* the day is drawing to a close **-andakt** evening prayers (*pl*) **-bön** evening prayers (*pl*); *läsa ~* (*äv.*) say one's prayers [at bedtime] **-dräkt** evening dress **-gudstjänst** evening service **-klänning** evening gown **-kurs** evening classes (*pl*) **-kvist** *på ~en* in the early evening **-måltid** evening meal, supper **-psalm** evening hymn **-rodnad** sunset glow; afterglow **-skola** evening (night) school **-sol** evening sun **-stjärna** evening star **-stund** *ung.* twilight hour **-sång** evensong; vespers (*pl*) **-tidning** evening paper **-underhållning** evening entertainment **-vind** evening breeze

1 aga *s1* (*turkisk titel*) ag[h]a

2 aga I *s2* flogging, caning **II** *v1* flog, cane; *den man älskar den ~r man* (*ung.*) the ones we love, we chasten

agar[-agar] *s3* agar[-agar]

agat agate

agave [a'ga:ve] *s5* agave; (*hundraårsväxt*) century plant, American aloe

agenda [a*xˣ*genda] *s1* **1** (*föredragningslista*) agenda **2** *parl.* order paper

agens ['a:-] *s3*, *kem.* agent

agent agent (*äv. språkv.*), representative; (*handelsresande*) travelling salesman, [commercial] traveller; *hemlig ~* secret agent **-provision** [agent's] commission

agentur agency; representation **-affär** agency [business] **-avtal** agency agreement **-firma** agency [firm]

agera act; *de ~nde* the performers, the actors, *koll.* the cast (*sg*)

agg *s7* grudge, rancour; *bära* (*hysa*) *~ mot ngn* have a grudge against s.b.

agglome'ra|t *s7* agglomerate **-tion** agglomeration

agglomerer|a agglomerate **-ing** agglomeration, sintering

agglutin|ation agglutination **-era** agglutinate; *~nde språk* agglutinative language

aggre'gat *s7* unit (set) [of machinery], plant, installation

aggregationstillstånd [-*ˣ*ʃɷ:ns-] state of aggregation

aggression [-e'ʃɷ:n] aggression

aggres'siv *a1* aggressive **-itet** aggressiveness

agio ['a:giɷ] *s6* agio

agitation agitation, campaign **agitationsmöte** propaganda meeting

agit|ator *s3* agitator, propagandist **-a'torisk** *a5* agitatorial, agitational **-era** agitate (*för* for); (*vid val*) canvass, do canvassing; *~ upp en opinion* stir up [an] opinion

1 agn [aŋn] *s1* (*blomfjäll*) palea (*pl* paleae) **2** (*på säd*) husk; *~ar* husks, chaff (*sg*); *skilja ~arna från vetet* separate the wheat from the chaff; *som ~ar för vinden* as chaff before the wind

2 agn [aŋn] *s7* (*vid fiske*) bait, gudgeon

agna [*ˣ*aŋna] bait

agnat [ag'na:t] agnate **-isk** *a5* agnatic; *~ tronföljd* agnatic succession

agnost|icism [agnås-] agnosticism **-iker** [ag-'nås-] *s9*, **-isk** [ag'nås-] *a5* agnostic

ago'ni *s3* agony

agorafo'bi *s3* agoraphobia

a'graff *s3* agraffe, clasp, buckle

a'grar *s3* agrarian **-förbund** agrarian league **-parti** agrarian party

agremang [-'maŋ] *s7* agrément, approbation **-er** [-'maŋ-] *pl* **1** (*nöjen, behag*) amenities **2** (*bekvämligheter*) material comforts **3** (*prydnader*) ornaments

agrikul'tur agriculture **-'ell** agricultural

agro|nom agronomist **-no'mi** *s3* agronomy **-nomisk** *a5* agronomic[al]

ah oh **a'ha** aha, oho

aids *r, med.* AIDS (*förk. för acquired immune deficiency syndrom*)

air [*ung.* ä:r] *s3* air **-bag** [-bägg] *s2* (*krockkudde*) airbag

Aisopos ['aisåpås] Aesop

aiss [ajs] *s7* A sharp

aj [ajj] oh, ow; (*starkare*) ouch

à jour [a'ʃɷ:r] *a4, föra ~* keep up to date; *hålla ngn ~ med* keep s.b. informed on (as to), keep s.b. posted on

ajourner|a [aʃɷr-] adjourn; *parl.* prorogue, recess; *~ på obestämd tid* recess **-ing** adjournment, prorogation

ak'acia *s1* acacia

akade'mi *s3* **1** (*konst- etc.*) academy **2** *univ.* university, institution **3** (*vetenskaplig*) society, association **-elev** academy student

akademiker [-'de:-] **1** (*med akademisk examen*) university graduate **2** (*medlem av akademi*) academician
akademi|ledamot, -medlem member (fellow) of an academy (a society), academician
akadem|isk [-'de:-] *a5* academic; ~ *avhandling* doctoral dissertation, thesis; ~ *kvart* (*ung.*) quarter of an hour's allowance; *avlägga* ~ *examen* take a university degree, graduate **-iskt** *adv* academically; ~ *bildad* with a university education
a'kantus *s2*, *bot.*, *arkit.* acanthus
akilles|häl [a*kill-] Achilles heel **-sena** Achilles tendon
akleja [-*leja] *s1* columbine, aquilegia
akne *s5* acne
akri'bi *s3* accuracy
akro'bat acrobat **-'ik** *s3* acrobatics (*sg o. pl*) **-isk** [-'ba:-] *a5* acrobatic
akrofo'bi *s3* acrophobia
akromat achromat, achromatic lens **-isk** [-'ma:-] *a5* achromatic
akro'nym *s3* acronym
akropol [-'på:l] *s3* acropolis
akrostik|on [a'kråstikån] *-onet, pl -on el. -er* acrostic
a'kryl *s3* acrylic fabric **-at** *s7, s3* acrylate **-fiber** acrylic fibre **-harts** acrylic resin **-syra** acrylic acid
1 akt *s3* **1** (*handling*) act **2** (*ceremoni*) ceremony, act **3** (*avdelning av skådespel*) act **4** (*handling, dokument m.m.*) document, deed, record, file **5** *konst.* nude
2 akt *oböjligt s, förklara i* ~ proscribe, outlaw
3 akt *oböjligt s* (*uppmärksamhet, avsikt*) attention; *i* ~ *och mening* with intent, on purpose (*att* to); *ge* ~ *på* pay attention to; *giv* ~*!* attention!; *stå i giv* ~ stand at attention; *ta sig i* ~ be on one's guard (*för* against); *ta tillfället i* ~ seize the opportunity
akta 1 (*vara aktsam om, vårda*) be careful with, take care of; (*skydda*) guard, protect (*för* from); (*vara aktsam med*) be careful with; (*se upp för*) mind, look out for; ~ *huvudet* mind your head; ~*s för stötar* fragile, handle with care; ~*s för väta* keep dry, to be kept dry **2** *rfl* take care (*för att göra* not to do), be on one's guard (*för* against), look out (*för* for); ~ *er!* look out!, take care!; *han* ~*de sig noga för att komma i närheten av mig* he gave me a wide berth **3** (*ge akt på, lägga märke till*) take notice of **4** (*värdera, skatta*) esteem, respect **5** *han* ~*r inte för rov att stjäla* he thinks nothing of stealing **aktad** *a5* respected, esteemed
akter ['akt-] **I** *s2* stern; *från för till* ~ from stem to stern **II** *adv* aft; ~ *ifrån* from the stern; ~ *om* abaft; ~ *ut* (*över*) astern, aft **-däck** quarterdeck, afterdeck **-kant** aft side **-kastell** stern castle **-lanterna** stern light **-lastad** [down] by the stern, stern-heavy
akterlig *a1* abaft
akter|salong aftersaloon **-segel** aftersail **-seglad** *a5* left behind **-skepp** stern **-snurra** [boat with] outboard motor **-spegel** stern
akterst ['akt-] *adv* furthest astern **aktersta** ['akt-] *a i superl.* the sternmost (aft[er]most)
akter|städerska saloon stewardess **-stäv** stern-

post
aktie ['aktsie] *s5* share; ~*r* (*koll.*) stock (*sg*); *en* ~ *på nominellt 100 kronor* a share of a par value of 100 kronor; *bunden* ~ restricted share; *ha* ~*r i ett bolag* hold shares in a company; *teckna* ~*r* subscribe to (for) shares
aktie|bolag joint-stock (limited) company; *AE.* stock (incorporated) company **-bolagslag** *BE.* Companies Act; *AE.* General Corporation Act **-brev** share (*AE.* stock) certificate **-börs** stock exchange (market) **-delning** stock split **-emission** share (*AE.* stock) issue **-fond** unit trust; *AE.* mutual fond **-innehav** holding of shares (*AE.* stock), shareholding, *AE.* stockholding **-kapital** joint stock, share capital; *AE.* capital stock **-kupong** [share] coupon **-kurs** price of shares **-majoritet** share majority; (*friare*) controlling interest **-mantel** share (*AE.* stock) certificate **-marknad** share (*AE.* stock) market **-portfölj** shares held, share portfolio **-post** block of shares; shareholding **-sparare** small investor **-sparklubb** investors' club **-stock** share capital **-teckning** subscription for shares; *AE.* capital stock subscription **-utdelning** dividend **-ägare** shareholder; *AE.* stockholder
akti'n|id *s3, kem.* actinide series **~er** actinide series **-isk** [-'ti:-] *a5* actinic **-ium** [-'ti:-] *s8* actinium
aktion [ak'ʃɔ:n] action
aktions|basis basis of action **-grupp** action group **-radie** range (radius) of action; cruising range
aktiv ['akt-] *a1* active, brisk, lively, busy; ~*t avfall* hot waste; ~*t kol* activated carbon (charcoal), active carbon
aktiva ['akt-] *pl* assets; ~ *och passiva* assets and liabilities
aktivator *s3* sensitizer; activator
aktiver|a activate, make [more] active **-ing** stimulation, activation, boost; *elektron.* sensitization; activation
aktiv|isera *se aktivera* **-ism** activism **-ist** activist **-itet** activity, activeness
aktivum ['akt-] *s4, språkv.* active [voice]
aktning 1 (*respekt*) respect (*för* for) **2** (*uppskattning*) esteem **3** (*hänsyn*) regard (*för* for), deference (*för* to); *av* ~ *för* out of consideration for, in deference to; *med all* ~ *för* with all deference to; *hysa* ~ *för* have respect for; *stiga i ngns* ~ rise in a p.'s esteem; *vinna allmän* ~ make o.s. generally respected
aktnings|bevis token of esteem **-bjudande** *a4* **1** commanding respect, imposing **2** (*ansenlig*) considerable **-full** respectful **-värd** *a1* entitled to (worthy of) respect; ~*a försök* creditable attempts
aktra, aktre *a4* after
aktris actress
aktsam *a1* careful (*med, om* with, of); prudent **-het** care[fulness], prudence
akt|samling file, dossier **-studie** nude **-stycke** [official] document
aktuali|sera 1 (*föra på tal*) bring to the fore; *frågan har* ~*ts* the question has arisen **2** (*modernisera*) bring up to date **-tet** topicality, topic of interest, news [value]
aktualitetsvärde topicality value

aktuarie [-'a:-] *s5* **1** (*vid ämbetsverk, ung.*) registrar, recording clerk **2** *försäkr.* actuary
aktu'ell *a1* [of] current [interest], topical, timely; ~ *fråga* burning (topical) question; *de ~a varorna* the goods in question; *det är mycket ~t just nu* it's very much in the news these days; *jag har inte siffran ~ just nu* I can't remember the exact figure just now
aktör actor
akupunktur acupuncture
akust|ik acoustics (*pl, behandlas som sg*) **-iker** [a'kus-] acoustician
akustikplatta sound-insulating board
akustisk [a'kus-] *a5* acoustic; (*utan förstärkare äv.*) unplugged; ~ *gitarr* acoustic guitar
a'kut *a1* acute; urgent; ~ *accent* acute accent; ~ *smärta* (*äv.*) sharp pain **-mottagning** casualty department **-sjukvård** emergency treatment
akvama'rin *s3* aquamarine
akva'rell *s3*, **-färg** watercolour **-ist** watercolourist
akvarie|fisk [-'va:-] aquarium fish **-växt** aquarium (aquatic) plant
akvarium [-'va:-] *s4* aquarium
akva'tint *s3*, **-gravyr** aquatint
akvatisk [-'va:-] *a5*, ~ *energi* aquatic energy
akvavit *s3* aquavit; schnap[p]s (*pl* schnap[p]s)
akve'dukt *s3* aqueduct
al *s2* alder
alabaster [-'bast-] *s2* alabaster
à la carte [alla'kart] à la carte
ala'dåb *s3* aspic (*på* of)
A-lag first team (string); *bildl.* topnotchers (*pl*)
a'larm *s7* alarm; *falskt ~* false alarm; *slå ~* sound (beat) the alarm **-anordning** alarm device **-beredskap** state of emergency
alarmer|a alarm, sound the alarm **-ing** raising the alarm
alarm|klocka alarm bell **-signal** alarm signal; *flyg.* air-raid warning **-system** alarm system
Alaska [a'laska] *n* Alaska
alba *s1* alb
al'ban *s3* Albanian **Albanien** [-'ba:-] *n* Albania **albansk** [-'ba:nsk] *a5* Albanian **albanska 1** (*språk*) Albanian **2** (*kvinna*) Albanian woman
albatross [-'tråss, *äv.* -'alba-] *s3, zool., golf.* albatross
albi'gens *s3* Albigensian; ~*er* (*äv.*) Albigenses
albinism albinism **albino** [-'bi:-] *-n, pl albiner* albino
Albion ['albiån] *n* Albion
album ['all-] *s7* album
albu'min *s4, s3* albumin, albumen **-u'ri** *s3* albuminuria
alde'hyd *s3* aldehyde
aldrig 1 never; ~ *i livet!* not for the life of me!, *vard.* not on your life!; ~ *mera* never again, nevermore; ~ *någonsin* never once; *nästan ~* hardly ever; *bättre sent än ~* better late than never; *du kan ~ tro hur roligt vi har haft* you'll never guess what fun we had; *du är väl ~ sjuk?* you're not ill, are you?; *man skall ~ säga ~* never say never **2** (*i koncessiva förbindelser*) *som ~ det* like anything; ~ *så litet* the least little bit; *du kan göra ~ så många invändningar* no matter how much you object; *om*

man också är ~ så försiktig however careful you are
alert [a'lärt] **I** *a1* alert, watchful; lively **II** *s2*, *på ~en* on the alert
Aleuterna [-'levt-] *pl* the Aleutian Islands
alexan'drin *s3* Alexandrine [verse]
alf *s3* elf
alfa *s6* alpha **-aktivitet** alpha rhythm (wave)
alfabet ['ʹalfa- el. -'e:t] *s7* alphabet
alfabetiser|a teach how to read **-ingskampanj** literacy campaign
alfabetisk [-'be:- el. ʹalfa-] *a5* alphabetic[al]; ~ *ordning* alphabetical order
alfa|numerisk [-'me:-] alphanumeric, alphameric **-partikel** alpha particle **-strålar** alpha rays **-strålning** alpha ray
alfresko [-'fresko̊] *adv*, **-målning** fresco
al|fågel old squaw, oldwife **-förrädare** Steller's eider
alg [-j] *s3* alga (*pl* algae)
algebra ['alje-] *s1* algebra **-isk** [-'bra:-] *a5* algebraic[al]
Alger [-'ʃe:r] *n* Algiers **algerier** [-'ʃe:-] Algerian, Algerine **Algeriet** [-ʃe'ri:-] Algeria **algerisk** [-'ʃe:-] *a5* Algerian, Algerine
algo|log algology **-logi** *s3* algological
algo'ritm *s3* algorithm, algorism
alhi'dad *s3* alidad[e]
alias ['a:-] alias
alibi ['a:li- el. ʹa:li-] *s6* alibi; *bevisa sitt ~* prove an alibi; *han hade vattentätt ~* he had a cast-iron alibi
alien|ation alienation **-era** alienate
alifatisk [-'fa:-] *a5* aliphatic
alika ['ali- el. ʹali-] *s1* jackdaw; *full som en ~* drunk as a fish, dead drunk
alisa'rin *s4, s3* alizarin
alka *s1* auk
alkali ['all- el. -'ka:-] *s4* alkali **-beständig** alkali-proof **-metall** alkali metal
alkal|isera alkalize **-isk** [-'ka:-] *a5* alkaline; ~ *jordartsmetall* alkaline earth [metal]; ~ *reaktion* alkaline reaction **-iskt** [-'ka:-] *adv*, *reagera ~* have an alkaline reaction
alkaloid [-o̊'i:d] *s3* alkaloid
al'kan *s3* alkane, paraffin
alkekung little auk, dovekie
alke'm|i [-çe-] *s3* alchemy **-ist** alchemist
al'ken [-k-] *s3* alkene, olefine
alkis ['alkis] *s2* dipso
alkohol [ʹall- el. -'hå:l] *s3* alcohol; spirit **-begär** craving for drink **-fri** nonalcoholic; ~ *dryck* soft drink **-förgiftning** alcoholic poisoning **-halt** alcoholic strength **-haltig** *a1* alcoholic; ~*a drycker* alcoholic beverages, *AE.* alcoholic (hard) liquors
alkohol|iserad [-'se:-] alcoholized **-isk** [-'hå:-] *a5* alcoholic **-ism** alcoholism, dipsomania
alkoholist alcoholic, dipsomaniac, habitual drunkard **-anstalt** alcoholism treatment unit **-vård** treatment of alcoholics
alkohol|missbruk abuse of alcohol **-prov** sobriety test **-påverkad** *a5* under the influence of drink **-sjukdom** alcoholic disease **-skadad** *a5* alcoholic **-stark** strong, high-proof **-svag** low-proof **-test** alcohol test; (*vid trafikkontroll*) breath test, breathalyser test

alkotest *se alkoholtest*
alkov [-'kå:v] *s3* alcove; recess [in a wall]
alkyd|harts [-ˣky:d-] alkyd resin **-lack** alkyd varnish
alkyl [-'ky:l] *s3* alkyl
all I *pron* **1** *fören.* all; (*varje*) every; *~e man på däck* all hands on deck; *~a tiders* (*vard.*) great, super, swell, smashing; *av ~a krafter* with all one's energy, with might and main; *av ~t hjärta* with all one's heart; *för ~ del!* not at all!, don't mention it!, you're welcome!; *för ~ framtid* permanently; *en gång för ~a* once and for all; *i ~ enkelhet* in all simplicity, quite informally; *i ~ evighet* for ever and ever, ad infinitum; *i ~a fall* nevertheless, all the same; *i ~ hast* hurriedly, (*i brev*) in haste; *i ~ tysthet* very quietly, in strict secrecy; *med ~ aktning för* with due respect to; *mot ~t förnuft* absurd, absolutely senseless; *på ~a fyra* on all fours; *på ~t sätt* in every way; *till ~ lycka* fortunately enough; *under ~ kritik* beneath [all] criticism, miserable; *utan ~ anledning* for no reason at all, without any reason [whatever]; *utom ~ fara* out of danger, completely safe, past the crisis; *utom ~t tvivel* without any (beyond all) doubt; *gå ~ världens väg* go the way of all flesh; *ha ~ anledning till missnöje* have every reason to be dissatisfied; *~a barn i början* you must learn to creep before you run; *~a goda ting är tre* all good things are three in number; *~ vår början bliver svår* all things are difficult before they are easy; *han har ~a utsikter att lyckas* he has every chance of succeeding; *vad i ~ sin dar* (*i ~ världen*) *säger du?* what on earth are you saying? **2** *självst.* all; *~a* all, (*varenda en*) everybody, everyone; *~as krig mot ~a* (*skämts.*) free for all; *~as vår vän* our mutual friend; *~t eller intet* all or nothing; *~t som ~t* all told, all in all; *trots ~t* after all; *ngns ~t i ~o* a p.'s factotum; *500 kronor i ett för ~t* a lump sum of 500 kronor; *en för ~a och ~a för en* one for all and all for one; *av ~t att döma* as far as can be judged; *sätta ~t på ett kort* stake everything on one card, put all one's eggs in one basket; *det är ej ~om givet* it is not given to everybody; *det är inte guld ~t som glimmar* all is not gold that glitters; *fartyget förliste med man och ~t* the ship went down with all hands; *han var ~t annat än glad* he was anything but happy; *när ~t kommer omkring* after all is said and done; *plikten framför ~t* duty first **II** *a* (*slut*) over; *hennes saga var ~* that was the end of her
alla *se all*
allaktivitetshus multi-activity centre
allaredan [-ˣre:-] already
all|bekant wellknown **-daglig** everyday; commonplace, ordinary
alldeles quite; altogether; absolutely, entirely, completely, all; exactly; *~ häpen* completely taken aback; *~ mörkt* pitch-dark, pitch-black; *~ nyss* just now; *~ omöjligt* utterly impossible; *~ rätt* perfectly right; *~ säkert* absolutely certain; *~ för tidigt* far too early, all too soon; *det gör mig ~ detsamma* it is all the same (all one) to me; *det är ~ i sin ordning* it is quite in order (quite all right); *kjolen är ~ för lång* the

skirt is much too long
allden'stund inasmuch as; because, since; *jur.* whereas
allé *s3* avenue; walk
alle'gat *s7* voucher
allego'r|i *s3* allegory **-isera** allegorize **-isk** [-'gɔ:-] *a5* allegoric[al]
allegretto [-'grettå] *s6 o. adv* allegretto
allegro [-'le:grå] *s6 o. adv* allegro
allehanda I *oböjligt a* all sorts of, of all sorts, miscellaneous **II** *oböjligt s* all sorts of things, sundries
allemansrätt *ung.* right of common
allena [-ˣle:- *el.* -'le:-] *oböjligt a o. adv* alone **-rådande** *a4* in sole control; universally prevailing
allenast [-ˣle:- *el.* -'le:-] only; *endast och ~* [only and] solely, exclusively
aller'gen [-j-] *s7*, *s4* allergen
aller'g|i *s3* allergy **-iker** [-'lärr-] allergic person **-isk** [-'lärr-] *a5* allergic (*mot* to)
allergitest allergy (scratch) test **allergolog** allergist
allernådigst [-ˣnå:-] Most Gracious
alle|sammans all of them (*etc.*); *adjö ~!* goodbye everybody! **-städes** everywhere; *~ närvarande* omnipresent, ubiquitous
all|farväg highroad; *vid sidan av ~en* off the beaten track **-god** all-bountiful **-helgonadag[en]** [-ˣhell-] All Saints' Day
allians [-'aŋs] *s3* alliance **-fri** nonaligned; *~ politik* policy of non-alignment **-fördrag** treaty of alliance **-ring** eternity ring
alliera *rfl* ally o.s. (*med* to) **allierad** *a5* allied (*med* to); (*friare*) connected (*med* with); *de ~e* the allies
alligator *s3* alligator
allihop all [of us *etc.*]
allitter|ation alliteration **-era** alliterate
allmakt omnipotence
allmoge *s2* peasantry, country people (folk) **-dräkt** peasant costume **-konst** folk art **-stil** rustic style
allmos|a *s1* alms (*pl*); *-or* alms; *leva av -or* live on charity
allmoseutdel|are almsgiver; (*katolsk präst*) almoner **-ning** almsgiving
allmän *a1* (*vanlig*) common, ordinary; (*gemensam el. tillgänglig för alla*) general; (*som gäller för alla*) universal; (*som står i samband med stat, kommun el. regering*) public; (*gängse*) current, prevalent; *~t bifall* universal approval; *~t bruk* (*sedvänja*) prevalent custom, (*användning*) general use; *~ idrott* athletics (*pl*); *~ landsväg* public highway; *~na meningen* public opinion; *~ rösträtt* universal suffrage; *det ~na* the community, the [general] public; *det ~na bästa* the public (common, general) good (weal); *i ~t bruk* in general use; *i ~na handeln* in general commerce, on the market; *i ~na ordalag* in general terms, (*fritt*) vaguely; *på ~ bekostnad* at public expense; *tallen är ~ i dessa trakter* the pine is common in these parts
allmän|belysning general lighting **-bildad** *ung.* well-informed, well-read **-bildande** *ung.* generally instructive **-bildning** all-round educa-

tion; general knowledge **-farlig** ~ *brottsling* dangerous criminal **-giltig** generally applicable, of universal application **-giltighet** universal applicability **-gods** commonplace things **allmänhet 1** ~*en* the public; *den stora* ~*en* the general public, the man in the street; *i* ~*ens intresse* in the interest[s] of the public; ~*en äger tillträde* open to the public **2** *i* ~ in general, as a rule; *i största* ~ very generally, in very broad terms

allmän|medicinare *se allmänpraktiker* **-mänsklig** human; universal; broadly humane **allmännelig** [ˣall- *el.* -'männe-] *a5* catholic; universal; *en helig* ~ *kyrka* the Holy Catholic Church

allmänning common [land]
allmän|nytta public good (utility) **-nyttig** for the public good (weal), for the commonweal; ~*t företag* public utility company; *för* ~*t ändamål* for the use of the public, for purposes of public utility **-orientering** *en* ~ *i ämnet* a general introduction to the subject **-politisk** ~ *debatt* general political debate **-praktik** general practice **-praktiker** general practitioner **-praktiserande** ~ *läkare* general practitioner **-preventiv** ~*a åtgärder* public-preventive measures

allmänt *adv* commonly, generally, universally; ~ *bekant* generally known; *en* ~ *hållen redogörelse* a general account; *det talas* ~ *om henne* she is the talk of the town; *det är* ~ *känt* it is common knowledge

allmäntillstånd *med.* general condition
allo *se all I 2*
alloker|a allocate **-ing** allocation
allom [-å-] *se all I 2*
allomfattande all-embracing, comprehensive, general
allonge [a'låŋʃ] *s5 (på växel)* allonge, rider **-peruk** full-bottomed wig
allo|pat allopath[ist] **-pa'ti** *s3* allopathy
allra of all; very; ~ *först (sist)* first (last) of all; ~ *helst* most of all, above all; ~ *högst* at the very most; ~ *överst* topmost; *de* ~ *flesta* the vast majority; *det* ~ *heligaste* the holy of holies, *(friare)* the sanctuary; *av* ~ *bästa kvalitet* of the very best quality; *i* ~ *högsta grad* in (to) the highest possible degree; *med* ~ *största nöje* with the greatest pleasure; *göra sitt* ~ *bästa (äv.)* do one's level best; *den kostar* ~ *minst 20 kronor* it costs 20 kronor at the very least; *han är* ~ *högst 40 år* he is 40 at the very most; *jag kommer med det* ~ *första* I shall come at the earliest possible opportunity **allra|högst** *den* ~*e* the Most High **-käraste** [-ˣçä:-], **-käresta** [-ˣçä:-] *s9* most beloved, dearest of all

all|rengöringsmedel all-purpose cleaner **-riskförsäkring** comprehensive insurance
all round, allround *oböjligt a, se allsidig*
allrum multipurpose room
alls at all; *ingenting* ~ nothing whatever (at all); *inget besvär* ~ no trouble whatever (at all); *inte* ~ *trött* not at all (a bit) tired
all|seende *a4* all-seeing **-sidig** *a1* all-round, comprehensive; *skänka en fråga* ~ *belysning* shed light on all aspects of a question **-sköns**

[-ʃ-] *oböjligt a, i* ~ *ro* completely undisturbed, at peace with the world
allsmäktig [ˣalls- *el.* -'mäktig] almighty, omnipotent; *Gud* ~ Almighty God
allström universal current
allströms|motor universal motor **-mottagare** universal receiver
allsång community singing, sing-along, singsong
allt I *pron, se all* **II** *s7, se världsalltet* **III** *adv,* ~ *framgent* from now on, from this time forward, henceforth, henceforward[s]; ~ *som oftast* fairly often; *i* ~ *större utsträckning* to an ever increasing extent; *du hade* ~ *rätt ändå* you were right after all; *hon blir* ~ *bättre* she is gradually improving, she is getting better and better

allt|efter according to **-eftersom** as **-emellanåt** from time to time, every now and then **-fort** still **-för** too, quite (altogether, all, only, far) too; ~ *liten* far too small; ~ *mycket av det goda* too much of a good thing; *det är* ~ *vänligt av er* it is too kind of you; *det gör jag blott* ~ *gärna* I shall be only too happy to do it

alltiallo [-ˣallω] *n el. r* right-hand man; maid-of-all-work; factotum
alltid always, ever; *för* ~ for ever (good), forever; *det blir väl* ~ *någon råd* something is sure to turn up; *du kan ju* ~ *fråga honom* you can always ask him, why don't you ask him?
allt|ifrån ever since **-igenom** through and through, throughout; thoroughly; *en* ~ *lyckad fest* a very successful party; *han är* ~ *ärlig* he is thoroughly honest **-ihop[a]** all [of it], the whole lot
allting ['all-] everything
alltinget [ˣall-] *(på Island)* the Althing
allt|jämt still **-mer[a]** increasingly, more and more **-nog** in short, anyhow **-omfattande** all-embracing **-samman[s]** all [of it (them *etc.*)], the whole lot [of it *etc.*] **-sedan** ~ *dess* ever since then **-så** so then; *(följaktligen)* accordingly, consequently, thus **-uppslukande** *bildl.* all-absorbing

allu|dera allude *(på* to) **-sion** allusion
alluv|i'al *a5* alluvial **-ium** [-'lu:-] *s8* alluvium
allvar *s7* earnestness, seriousness; gravity; *på fullt* ~ seriously, in real earnest; *på fullaste* ~ in all seriousness; *göra* ~ *av ett löfte* fulfill a promise; *ta ngn på* ~ take s.b. seriously; *är det ditt* ~? are you serious?, do you really mean that?; *detta är mitt fulla* ~ I am quite serious; *jag menar* ~ I am serious, I really mean it, *vard.* I mean business; *stundens* ~ *kräver* the gravity of the situation demands, in this hour of crisis we must; *vintern har kommit på* ~ winter has come to stay
allvarlig *a1* serious, grave; earnest; ~*a avsikter* serious intentions; ~ *fara* grave danger; ~*a förmaningar* serious admonitions; *se* ~ *ut* look serious (grave); *ta en* ~ *vändning* take a turn for the worse **allvarligt** *adv* seriously; ~ *sinnad* serious-minded; ~ *talat (äv.)* joking apart
allvarsam *a1* serious, grave; *en* ~ *min* a serious (grave) expression; *hålla sig* ~ keep serious, *(för skratt)* keep a straight face

allvars|diger fraught with gravity **-ord** serious word

all|vetande *a4* all-knowing, omniscient **-vetare** person with a vast fund of general knowledge; *iron.* oracle, know-all **-vis** all-wise **-ätare** omnivore

alm *s2* wych-elm, witch-elm

almanacka *s1* almanac, calendar; (*fick-*) diary

aln [a:-] *s2, ung.* ell (= *45 eng. tum*)

aloe *s5* aloe **-hampa** aloe fibre

alp *s3* alp

alpacka [-ˣpacka] *s1* **1** (*lama*) alpaca **2** (*tyg*) alpaca **3** *miner.* nickel (German) silver

alpbestig|are alpine climber **-ning** alpine climbing

Alperna ['alp-] *pl* the Alps

alp|flora alpine flora **-glöd** alpenglow **-hydda** [alpine] chalet

al'pin *a5* alpine **-ism** alpinism **-ist** alpinist

alp|jägare *mil.* alpine rifleman **-landskap** alpine landscape **-ros** rhododendron **-stav** alpenstock **-viol** cyclamen

alruna [ˣa:l-] *s1* mandrake, mandragora

alsikeklöver alsike [clover]

alster ['als-] *s7* product, production; *koll. äv.* produce, (*böcker*) works (*pl*)

alstr|a produce, manufacture; *elektr.* generate; *bildl.* engender **-ing** production, manufacture; generation; procreation

alstrings|drift generative instinct **-duglig** *biol.* reproductive **-förmåga, -kraft** generative power; productivity **-linje** *se generatris*

alt *s2, mus.* (*manlig*) alto (*pl* altos), counter–tenor; (*kvinnlig*) alto, contralto

al'tan *s3* [roof] balcony; terrace

altar|bord communion table, altar **-duk** altar cloth

altare *s6* altar; *~ts sakrament* the Eucharist

altar|kläde antependium **-kärl** sacred vessel **-ljus** altar candle **-ring** altar rails (*pl*) **-skrud** vestment **-skåp** triptych, reredos **-tavla** altarpiece **-tjänst** altar service, liturgy **-uppsats** retable

alteration agitation, anxiety

alter ego ['alter 'e:gɷ] alter ego

altererad [-'re:-] *a5* flurried, excited

altern|a'tiv I *s7* alternative **II** [*äv.* 'alt-] *a5* alternative **-era** alternate

alt|fiol viola **-horn** althorn

alti'tud *s3* altitude

alt|klarinett alto clarinet **-klav** alto (viola) clef

alto|cumulus [-'ku:-] *meteor.* altocumulus **-stratus** [-'stra:-] *meteor.* altostratus

altru|ism altruism **-ist** altruist **-istisk** *a5* altruistic

alt|röst [contr]alto [voice] **-saxofon** alto saxophone **-stämma** [contr]alto voice; [contr]alto part **-violin** viola

aluminera aluminize

aluminium [-'mi:-] *s8* aluminium; *AE.* aluminum **-brons** aluminium bronze **-folie** aluminium foil **-kastrull** aluminium saucepan **-legering** aluminium alloy **-oxid** aluminium oxide, alumina **-plåt** sheet aluminium

a'lumn *s3* alumnus (*pl* alumni), *fem.* alumna (*pl* alumnae)

alun *s7* [potash] alum **-skiffer** alum shale **-stift**

stick of alum; styptic pencil

alv *s2, geol.* subsoil, undersoil

alveol [-'å:l] *s3* alveolus (*pl* alveoli)

amal'gam *s7, s4* amalgam **-era** amalgamate **-fyllning** amalgam stopping (filling)

amanuens *s3* assistant university teacher (librarian, archivist *etc.*), assistant, amanuensis; (*vid ämbetsverk*) chief (principal) clerk; (*vid kansli*) third secretary

amaryllis [-'ryll-] *-en amaryller* amaryllis

amason [-'så:n] *s3* Amazon **-drottning** Amazon queen

Amasonfloden the Amazon

amatör amateur (*på* of, at) **-bestämmelser** amateur rules (regulations) **-boxning** amateur boxing **-brottning** amateur wrestling **-foto** amateur snapshot **-fotograf** amateur photographer **-idrott** amateur athletics (*pl*) (sport) **-mässig** *a1* amateurish **-regler** amateur rules **-skap** *s7, hans ~* his amateur status **-skådespelare** amateur actor **-spelare** amateur player **-sändare** amateur transmitter **-teater** amateur theatricals (*pl*) **-tävling** (*fri idrott*) amateur meeting

ambas'sad *s3* embassy **ambassa'dris** *s3* ambassadress

ambassad|råd [embassy] counsellor **-sekreterare** *förste* (*andre, tredje*) ~ first (second, third) secretary [of (to, at) an embassy] **-ör** ambassador

ambi|tion ambition **-tiös** [-'ʃö:s] *a1* zealous, aspiring, pushing; (*plikttrogen*) conscientious

ambiva'l|ens *s3* ambivalence **-ent** *a4* ambivalent

ambra *s2* ambergris

ambros|ia [-'brɷ:-] *s1* ambrosia **-isk** *a5* ambrosial, ambrosian

ambulans [-'ans *el.* -'aŋs] *s3* ambulance **-flygplan** ambulance (hospital) plane, air ambulance **-förare** ambulance driver **-personal** paramedics (*pl*)

ambulatorisk [-'tɷ:-] *a5* ambulatory

ambuler|a *ung.* move (travel) [from place to place] **-ande** *a4* itinerant, travelling

amen [ˣamm- *el.* 'amm-] amen; *säga ja och ~ till allt* (*ung.*) agree to anything; *så säkert som ~ i kyrkan* as sure as fate

americium [-'ri:-] *s8* americium

Amerika [a'me:-] *n* America; *~s förenta stater* the United States of America

amerika|arv *ung.* dollar inheritance **-brev** letter from America **-feber** America fever

ameri'kan *s3, -are* [-ˣka:-] *s9* American **-isera** Americanize **-isering** Americanization **-ism** *s3* Americanism **-ist** Americanist

amerikan|sk [-'ka:nsk] *a5* American **-ska 1** (*språk*) American **2** (*kvinna*) American woman

amerika|resa trip (journey) to America **-svensk** Swedish-American

ametist amethyst

amfeta'min *s3, s4* amphetamine

amfibie [-'fi:-] *s5* amphibian **-artad** [-a:r-] *a5* amphibious **-båt** amphibious craft **-fordon** tracked landing craft **-plan** amphibian [plane] **-stridsvagn** amphibious tank

amfibisk [-'fi:-] *a5* amphibious

amfiteat|er [ˣamfi- *el.* -ˣfi:-] amphitheatre **-ra-**

lisk [-'ra:-] amphitheatric[al]
amfora ['amfåra] *s1* amphora
a'mi *s3* muffler; comforter
amidplast [aˣmi:d-] polyamide
a'min *s3, s4* amine **-harts** aminoplastic [resin]
aminosyra [-ˣmi:-] amino acid
ami'ral *s3* **1** *mil.* admiral **2** *zool.* red admiral
-itet *s7* admiralty; ~*et* (*Storbritannien*) the Admiralty Board, *AE*. Navy Department
amirals|flagg admiral's flag **-person** flag officer, admiral **-skepp** flagship, admiral's ship
amma I *s1* wet nurse **II** *v1* nurse, suckle, breast-feed; *hon ~r barnet själv* she feeds the baby herself, she breast-feeds the baby
ammoniak [-'mɷ:-] *s2* ammonia
ammo'nit *s3* ammonite
ammonium [-'mɷ:-] *s8* ammonium **-karbonat** ammonium carbonate
ammunition *s3* ammunition; munitions (*pl*); *lös* ~ practice ammunition; blank cartridge *skarp* ~ live ammunition
ammunitions|depå ammunition dump **-fabrik** munitions factory **-fartyg** ammunition ship **-förråd** ammunition supply (stores) **-gördel** cartridge belt; bandoleer **-väska** ammunition pocket
amne'si *s3* amnesia
amnes'ti *s3* amnesty; *få* ~ obtain [an] amnesty; *bevilja ngn* ~ grant s.b. an amnesty **-kungörelse** act of indemnity
amning breast-feeding, nursing, suckling
amok [a'måck] *oböjligt s* amuck, amok; *löpa* ~ run amuck
a-moll A minor
amoral|isk [-'ra:-] *a5* amoral **-itet** amorality
amorbåge Cupid's bow
a'morf [-å-] *a1* amorphous
amo'rin *s3* cupid
amorter|a [-å-] amortize, pay off by instalments; ~ *ett lån* pay off a loan **-ing** repayment by instalments, amortization
amorterings|belopp amortization [amount (payment)] **-fri** ~*tt lån* straight loan, loan payable in full at maturity **-lån** instalment credit (loan); sinking-fund loan **-plan** amortization schedule **-tid** period of amortization **-villkor** terms of amortization (repayment)
amo'rös *a5* amorous
1 ampel [ˣamp-] *s2* (*för växter*) hanging flowerpot; (*hänglampa*) hanging lamp
2 ampel ['amp-] *a2, ampla lovord* unstinted praise (*sg*)
amper ['amp-] *a2* pungent, sharp; biting, stinging
ampere [-'pä:r] *s9, s5* ampere **-meter** *s2,* **-mätare** ammeter **-timme** ampere-hour
amper'sand *s3* ampersand
amplifiera amplify
ampli'tud *s3* amplitude **-modulering** amplitude modulation
am'pull *s3* ampoule, ampul[e]; *Storbritannien äv.* ampulla
amput|ation amputation **-era** amputate
amsaga [ˣamm-] tall story, old wives' tale
amt *s7, ung.* shire, county
amu'lett *s3* amulet
amygda'lin *s3, s4* amygdalin

amylacetat [-ˣmy:l-] amyl acetate
amöba [-ˣmö:-] *s1* amoeba
1 an [ann] *hand.* to
2 an [ann] *av och* ~ up and down, to and fro; *gå av och* ~ *i rummet* (*äv.*) pace the room
ana have a feeling (presentiment); ~ *oråd* suspect mischief; *intet ont ~nde* unsuspecting; ~ *sig till ngns tankar* divine a p.'s thoughts; *det lät* ~ it hinted at (gave an inkling of); *du kan inte* ~ *hur glad jag blev* you have no idea how glad (happy) I was; *vem kunde* ~ *det* who would have suspected that; *det ante mig* I suspected as much
anabapt|ism Anabaptism **-ist** Anabaptist
anabol [-'bå:l] *a1* anabolic; ~ *asteroider* anabolic steroids **-ism** anabolism
anacka [aˣnacka] *se anagga*
anaerob [anaä'rå:b] **I** *s3* anaerobe, anaerobium (*pl* anaerobia) **II** *a5* anaerobic
anagga [a'nagga] dash it!, dang it!
anagram [-'gramm] *s7* anagram
anako'lut *s3* anacoluthon (*pl* anacolutha)
anakonda [-ˣkånda] *s1* anaconda
anako'ret *s3* anchorite
anakronis|m anachronism **-tisk** *a5* anachronistic
analfa'bet *s3,* **-isk** *a5* illiterate **-ism** illiteracy
analfena anal fin
analgetikum [-'ge:-] *s8* analgesic
analog *a1* analogous (*med* to); ~ *klocka* analog[ue] watch
analogi *s3* analogy; *i* ~ *med* on the analogy of **-bevis** analogical evidence **-bildning** analogical formation, analogy **-maskin** analog computer
analogisk *a5* analogic[al]
analogislut analogism
ana'lys *s3* analysis (*pl* analyses) **-era** analyse
analyt|iker [-'ly:-] analyst **-isk** *a5* analytic[al]
analöppning anus
anamm|a [a'namma] **1** receive, accept; ~ *nattvarden* partake of the Holy Communion **2** (*tillägna sig*) appropriate, seize **3** *fan ~!* damn [it]!, damn and blast!, hell! **-ande** *s6* acceptance
anam'nes *s3* anamnesis (*pl* anamneses)
ananas [ˣa:- *el.* ˣann-] *s9* pineapple
ana'pest *s3* anap[a]est
anar'k|i *s3* anarchy **-isk** [a'narr-] *a5* anarchic[al] **-ism** anarchism **-ist** anarchist **-istisk** *a5* anarchistic
anarkosyndikalism anarchosyndicalism
anastigmat anastigmat
anatema [-ˣte:- *el.* -'te:-] *s6* anathema
ana|tom [-'tå:m] *s3* anatomist **-to'mi** *s3* anatomy **-tomisal** dissecting-room **-tomisk** [-'tå:-] *a5* anatomical
anbefall|a 1 (*ålägga, påbjuda*) enjoin, charge; ~ *ngn tystnad* enjoin silence upon a p.; *läkaren -de honom vila* the doctor ordered him to rest **2** (*förorda, rekommendera*) recommend, advocate; ~ *på det varmaste* sincerely recommend, commend; ~ *sin själ i Guds hand* commend one's soul to God
anbelanga *vad mig ~r* as far as I am concerned
anblick sight; appearance, aspect; *en ståtlig* ~

an imposing appearance; *vid ~en av* at the sight of; *vid första ~en* at first sight
anbring|a (*sätta, ställa*) place, put; (*sätta på etc.*) mount, affix, fit, apply **-ande** *s6* placing, mounting *etc.*
anbud (*köp-*) bid; (*sälj-*) offer; (*pris*) quotation; *lämna ~ på* send in a tender for; *~ infordras härmed på* tenders are invited for
anbuds|formulär tender form **-givare** tenderer, bidder **-givning** [-'ji:v-] tendering, bidding **-kartell** tendering cartel
anciennitet seniority; *efter ~* by seniority
and *-en änder* wild duck; *jfr gräs-*
anda *s2* **1** (*andedräkt, andhämtning*) breath; *med ~n i halsen* out of breath, (*med spänning*) with bated breath; *ge upp ~n* give up the ghost, expire; *hålla ~n* hold one's breath; *hämta ~n* catch one's breath; *kippa efter ~n* gasp for breath; *tappa ~n* lose one's breath; *allt som liv och ~ har* everything that lives and breathes **2** (*stämning*) spirit; *i en ~ av samförstånd* in a spirit of understanding; *i samma ~* in the same spirit; *samma ~s barn* kindred spirits; *tidens ~* the spirit of the age; *när ~n faller på* when the spirit moves him (*etc.*), *vard.* when he (*etc.*) is in the mood **3** (*mod, disciplin*) morale
andakt *s3* devotion; *med ~* in a devotional spirit; *förrätta sin ~* perform one's devotions
andakts|bok devotional manual **-full** devotional; devout **-stund** devotional hour **-övningar** devotions, devotional exercises
Andalusien [-'lu:-] *n* Andalusia
andanom [-å-] *se ande 1*
andante [-ˣdann-] *s6 o. adv* andante
andas *dep* breathe, respire; *~ in* breathe in, inhale; *~ ut* breathe out, exhale, *bildl.* breathe freely; *~ djupt* take a deep breath, breathe deeply
ande *s2* **1** (*själ*) spirit; (*intelligens*) mind, intellect; *i ~ns rike* in the spiritual (intellectual) world; *i andanom* in the spirit, in one's mind's eye; *~n är villig, men köttet är svagt* the spirit is willing, but the flesh is weak; *de i ~n fattiga* the poor in spirit **2** (*övernaturligt väsen*) spirit, ghost; *Den helige ~* the Holy Ghost (Spirit); *ngns onda ~* a p.'s evil spirit; *tjänande ~* ministering spirit; *de avlidnas andar* the spirits of the dead **3** (*personlighet, natur*) spirit, mind; *en stor ~* a spiritual giant; *besläktade andar* kindred spirits **-besvärjare** raiser of spirits, exorcist **-besvärjelse** raising of spirits, exorcism **-drag** *se andetag* **-dräkt** breath; *dålig ~* bad breath **-fattig** (*om pers.*) dull, vacuous, inane; (*om sak*) uninspired
andel share (*i* of); *ha ~ i ett företag* have an interest in a business
andels|bevis scrip [certificate] **-förening** co-op[erative] [society], co-op **-företag** coop[erative] undertaking **-lägenhet** time-share apartment (flat); *AE.* condominium **-mejeri** coop[erative] dairy **-slakteri** coop[erative] slaughterhouse
andemening spirit, inward sense
Anderna ['and-] *pl* the Andes
ande|skådare seer [of visions], visionary **-skådning** [-å-] preternatural insight, second

sight **-tag** breath; *i ett ~* [all] in one breath; *till sista ~et* to one's last breath; *ta ett djupt ~* take a deep breath **-viskning** ghostly whisper **-värld** spirit[ual] world **-väsen** spirit[ual] being]
and|fådd *a1* out of breath, breathless; *vard.* winded, puffed **-fåddhet** breathlessness, shortness of breath **-hämtning** breathing, respiration **-hämtningspaus** breathing space
andjakt duck shooting
andlig *a1* **1** (*själslig*) spiritual; (*psykisk, förstånds-*) intellectual, mental; *~t liv* intellectual life; *~ odling* cultural life; *~a värden* spiritual values; *barnets ~a utveckling* the child's mental development **2** (*gudfruktig*) spiritual, sacred, religious; (*kyrklig*) ecclesiastical; (*prästerlig*) clerical; *~ makt* spiritual power; *~ orden* religious order; *~t stånd* clerical order; *~a sånger* sacred songs; *~t ämbete* ecclesiastical appointment; *inträda i det ~a ståndet* take [holy] orders **andligen** mentally, intellectually, spiritually
andlös breathless; *~ tystnad* dead silence
andmat *bot.* duckweed
andning breathing, respiration; *konstgjord ~* artificial respiration; *andra ~en* second wind
andnings|apparat breathing apparatus; respirator **-organ** respiratory organ **-paus** breathing space (spell) **-svårigheter** *se andnöd* **-vägar** respiratory system (*sg*)
andnöd difficulty in breathing, respiratory distress
1 andra [ˣandra:] *se andraga*
2 andr|a ['andra] *-e* **I** *pron, se annan* **II** *räkn* second; *A~ Mosebok* Exodus; *~ våningen* (*i bet. 1 trappa upp*) first (*AE.* second) floor; *ett ~ klassens hotell* (*neds.*) a second-rate hotel; *för det ~* in the second place, secondly; *-e opponent, se andreopponent; -e styrman* second mate; *den ~ maj* the second of May, (*i brev*) 2nd May (May 2); *göra ett ~ försök* make a second attempt, *vard.* have another go; *ha en uppgift ur ~ hand* have information second-hand; *köpa i ~ hand* buy second-hand; *det får komma i ~ hand* it will have to come second (later)
andrag|a state; advance, put forward, mention, set forth; *~ till sitt försvar* plead in one's defence **-ande** *s6* statement; advancing *etc.*
andragradsekvation equation of the second degree
andrahands|- second-hand **-lägenhet** sublet apartment **-pris** resale price **-uppgift** second-hand information **-värde** trade-in value
andrakammarval elections to the Second Chamber [of the Swedish Riksdag]
andraklass|are second-form boy (girl) **-biljett** second-class ticket **-kupé** second-class compartment **-vagn** second-class carriage (coach; *AE.* car)
andra|placering *han fick en ~* he came second **-plansfigur** insignificant person
andre *se 2 andra*
andreaskors [-ˣdre:as-] *konst.* St. Andrew's cross, saltire
andre|maskinist second engineer **-opponent** opponent appointed by candidate for a doctor-

ate **-pilot** copilot, second pilot **-styrman** second mate
androgen [-'je:n] I *a5* androgenic II *s7, s4* androgen
andrum room to breathe; *bildl.* breathing space **and|truten** *a3* out of breath, breathless; winded **-täppa** *s1* shortness of breath **-täppt** *a4* short of breath; *vard.* short-winded
andäktig *a1* devout; attentive **-het** devoutness; attentiveness
andäktigt *adv* devoutly; attentively; *lyssna ~ på ngn* hang on a p.'s words
anekdot [-'då:t] *s3* [humorous] anecdote, amusing story **-isk** *a5* anecdotal, anecdotic
ane'm|i *s3* anaemia **-isk** [-'ne:-] *a5* anaemic
anemometer [-'me:-] *s2* anemometer; (*vindmätare äv.*) wind gauge
anemon [-'å:n *el.* -'ω:n] *s3* anemone
aneroidbarometer [-ω*'i:d-] aneroid barometer
aneste'si *s3* anaesthesia
anestesio|log anaesthetist; *AE.* anesthesiologist **-logi** *s3* anaesthetics (*pl, behandlas som sg*); *AE.* anesthesiology
anestet|ikum [-'te:-] *s8,* **-isk** [-'te:-] *a5* anaesthetic
anfader [*a:n-] ancestor
anfall attack; *i sht mil.* assault, charge; (*sjukdoms-* etc.) fit; *ett hysteriskt* ~ a fit of hysteria; *i ett* ~ *av vrede* in a fit of anger; *gå till* ~ attack, charge; *rikta ett* ~ *mot* direct an attack against
anfalla attack; assail, assault
anfalls|krig aggressive war **-mål** objective **-plan** plan of attack **-robot** offensive missile **-spelare** attacker, forward **-vapen** offensive weapon **-vinkel** angle of attack
anfang [-'faŋ, *äv.* *an-] *s3, boktr.* initial [letter]
an|flygning [*ann-] approach [path]; homing **-fordran** demand; *att betalas vid* ~ payable on demand **-frätning** corrosion; pitting **-frätt** *a4* corroded; ~*a tänder* decayed teeth; ~ *av rost* rusty
anfäkt|a harass; haunt; assail; ~*s av tvivel* be haunted by doubts **-else** tribulation [of spirit], vexation; obsession
anför|a 1 (*leda*) lead, command, be in command of; ~ *en orkester* conduct an orchestra **2** (*andraga, framhålla*) state, say; ~ *besvär* complain (*över* of); ~ *besvär mot ett beslut* appeal against a decision; ~ *som bevis* bring (enter) as evidence; ~ *som skäl* give as reason; ~ *till sitt försvar* plead in one's defence **3** (*citera*) quote, cite; *på det -da stället* in the passage cited **-ande** *s6* **1** lead[ership], command[ing]; *mus.* conductorship **2** (*yttrande*) statement; speech, address; *hålla ett* ~ give an address, make a speech **-are** commander, leader; *mus.* conductor **-ing** *direkt* ~ direct speech; *indirekt* ~ indirect (reported) speech, *AE.* indirect discourse
anförings|sats inserted clause **-tecken** quotation mark, inverted (turned) comma **-verb** leading verb
anförtro ~ *ngn ngt* entrust s.th. to s.b., entrust s.b. with s.th.; ~ *ngn en hemlighet* confide a secret to s.b.; *hon* ~*dde mig att* she confided

to me the fact that; ~ *sig åt* entrust o.s. to, (*ge sitt förtroende*) confide in
anförvant relation, relative, [family] connection
ange 1 (*upplysa om, uppge*) inform, state, mention; ~ *noga* specify, detail; ~ *skälet till* state the reason for; *det angivna skälet* the reason given; *det på fakturan angivna priset* the invoice[d] price **2** (*anmäla för myndighet*) report, inform against, denounce; ~ *ngn för polisen* inform against s.b., report s.b. [to the police]; ~ *sig själv* give o.s. up (in charge) **3** ~ *takten* (*mus.*) indicate tempo, *bildl.* set the pace; ~ *tonen* set the tone
angelsaxare [aŋel*saks-] *se anglosaxare*
angelägen [*anje-] *a3* (*om sak*) urgent, pressing, important; (*om pers.*) anxious (*om* for); ~ *om att göra* anxious to do, desirous of doing (to do); ~ *om att vara till lags* anxious to please; *visa sig mycket* ~ (*äv.*) be overanxious **-het 1** (*sak, ärende*) matter, affair, concern; *inre ~er* internal affairs; *sköta sina egna ~er* mind one's own business **2** (*betydelse, vikt*) urgency
angelägenhetsgrad degree of priority (urgency)
angenäm [*anje-] *a1* pleasant, agreeable; *det var ~t att träffas* it was a pleasure to meet you
angina [aŋ*gi:-] *s1* angina; ~ *pectoris* angina pectoris
angiv|a [*anji:-] *se ange* **-are** informer **-else** information, denunciation, accusation; (*tull-* etc.) declaration **-eri** informing
angler ['aŋ(g)-] *s9* Angle
angli|cism [aŋ(g)li-] *s3* Anglicism **-kansk** [-'ka:nsk] *a5* Anglican; ~*a kyrkan* Anglican Church, (*statskyrkan i England*) Church of England **-sera** anglicize
anglo|-amerikansk ['aŋ(g)lω-] Anglo-American **-'fil** *s3* Anglophil[e]
anglosax|are [aŋ(g)lω*saks-] *s9,* **-isk** [-'saks-] *a5,* **-iska** [-'saks-] (*språk*) Anglo-Saxon
Angola [aŋ*gå:la] *n* Angola
ango'l|an [aŋg-] *s3,* **-ansk** [-'a:nsk] *a5* Angolan
angora|garn [aŋ*gå:ra-] angora [wool] **-get** Angora goat **-kanin** Angora rabbit **-katt** Angora cat **-ull** (*från -get*) mohair; (*från -kanin*) angora [wool]
angostura [aŋgå*stu:ra] *s2* angostura; (*smakessens vanl.*) angostura bitters (*pl*)
angrepp attack (*mot, på* on)
angrepps|punkt point of attack (application) **-vapen** offensive weapon
angripa attack, assault, assail; (*inverka skadligt på*) affect; (*skada*) injure; (*fräta på*) attack, corrode, rust; ~ *ett problem* tackle (approach) a problem
angrip|are assailant, aggressor **-en** *a5,* ~ *av röta* damaged by rot; ~ *av sjukdom* diseased, struck down by illness; *metallen är* ~ *av rost* the metal has gone rusty
angränsande *a4* adjacent, adjoining, next
angå concern; (*avse, beträffa*) have reference to; *saken* ~ *r dig inte* it is no concern of yours, *vard.* it's none of your business; *vad mig ~r* as far as I am concerned **-ende** regarding, concerning, as regards, as to, as for

angöra 1 ~ *hamn* make port; ~ *land* make land **2** (*fastgöra*) make fast
angörings|hamn [-j-] port of call **-plats** lay-by
anhalt *s3* halt; *AE.* way station
anhang *s7* following; (*patrask*) rabble; (*hejdukar*) tools (*pl*), hirelings (*pl*); *vard.* crew, gang; *hans* ~ his likes (*pl*)
anhop|a heap (pile) up, amass; ~ *sig* accumulate **-ning** piling up; accumulation; ~ *av trupper* troop concentration
anhyd'rid *s3* anhydride
anhåll|a 1 (*fängsla, arrestera*) apprehend, arrest, take into custody **2** (*begära*) ask (*om* for), apply (*om* for), request, demand; ~ *hos ngn om ngt* apply to s.b. for s.th.; ~ *om en flickas hand* ask for a girl's hand [in marriage]; ~ *om snar betalning* request [an] early settlement; *om svar -es* (*o.s.a.*) an answer will oblige (R.S.V.P.) **-an** *r, pl saknas* request, demand (*om* for); *enträgen* ~ entreaty, solicitation; *ödmjuk* ~ supplication **-ande** *s6* (*arrestering*) arrest; (*häktning*) apprehension
anhängare follower, adherent (*av, till* of); (*av idé*) supporter, advocate
anhängiggöra [ˣanhäŋigjö:ra] ~ *vid domstol* bring into court; ~ *ett mål vid domstol* bring an action before a court of law; ~ *rättegång mot* take legal proceedings against
anhörig *subst. a* relative; *mina ~a* my family; *närmaste ~[a]* next of kin
ani'lin *s2, s7* aniline **-färg** aniline dye **-förgiftning** aniline poisoning **-penna** indelible pencil, copying pencil
ani'mal *a5*, **-isk** *a5* animal
animer|a animate; *stämningen var mycket ~d* there was a gay atmosphere **-ad** *a5* animate; ~ *film* animated cartoon
animis|m animism **-tisk** *a5* animistic
animositet animosity
aning *s2* **1** (*förkänsla*) presentiment (*om* of; *om att* that); foreboding; hunch; *ond* ~ misgiving **2** (*föreställning*) notion, idea, feeling; *jag hade ingen* ~ *om* (*äv.*) I never suspected **3** (*smula, något litet*) *en* ~ a little, a trace, *vard.* a touch, a tiny (wee) bit, *kokk.* a dash, a sprinkle
anings|full apprehensive; expectant **-lös** unsuspecting
anis *s2* (*växt*) anise; (*krydda*) aniseed **-'ett** *s3* anisette
anjon [ˣann-] *s3* anion
anka *s1* **1** [tame] duck **2** (*tidnings-*) hoax, canard
1 ankare *s6, s9* (*laggkärl*) *ung.* anker, firkin
2 ankare *s6* **1** *sjö. o. bildl.* anchor; *kasta ankar* cast (come to, drop) anchor; *lätta ankar* weigh anchor; *ligga för ankar* ride at anchor **2** *elektr.* armature **3** *byggn.* brace, cramp [iron] **4** (*i ur*) lever escapement
ankar|fly *s6* fluke, flue **-fäste** hold[ing-ground] **-klys** hawse[pipe] **-kätting** anchor chain **-plats** anchorage **-spel** anchor gear, capstan **-spole** armature coil **-stock** anchor stock **-tross** mooring (anchor) cable **-ur** lever watch
ank|bonde drake **-damm** duck pond
ankel ['ank-] *s2* ankle[bone] **-led** ankle joint **-lång** ankle-length **-socka** ankle sock; *AE.* anklet

anklaga ~ *ngn för ngt* accuse s.b. of s.th., charge s.b. with s.th.; *den ~de* the accused; *med ~nde miner* accusingly; *sitta på de ~des bänk* stand in the dock, *bildl.* stand accused, be under fire
anklagelse accusation, charge (*för* of); *rikta en* ~ *mot ngn* make an accusation against s.b.; *ömsesidiga ~r* cross accusations **-akt** bill of indictment **-punkt** count **-skrift** [written] indictment
anklang approval; *vinna* ~ meet with (win) approval; *väcka* ~ *hos ngn* appeal to s.b.
anknyt|a attach, join, unite (*till* to); connect, join (link) up (*till* with); *bibanan -er till stambanan vid C.* the branch line connects up with the main line at C.; *berättelsen -er till verkliga händelser* the story is based on real events **-ning** connection, attachment, link; *tel.* extension
anknytningsapparat extension telephone
ankomm|a 1 (*anlända*) arrive (*till* at, in); *~nde post* incoming (inward) mail; *~nde tåg* (*i tidtabell o.d.*) [train] arrivals **2** (*bero*) depend (*på* on); *vad på mig -er* as far as I am concerned; *det -er på henne att se till det* it is up to her to see to that **-en** *a5* **1** (*anländ*) arrived **2** (*ngt skämd*) *-et kött* tainted meat; ~ *fisk* (*frukt*) fish (fruit) going bad **3** (*ngt berusad*) tipsy, merry
ankomst [-å-] *s3* arrival; *vid ~en till stationen* on my (*etc.*) arrival at the station **-datum** date of arrival **-hall** arrival hall **-tid** time of arrival
ankr|a anchor **-ing** anchoring, anchorage
ankrings|förbud anchoring prohibition **-plats** anchorage
anlag *s7* **1** *biol.* rudiment, germ, embryo (*till* of) **2** (*medfött*) talent, gift, aptitude (*för* for); *med.* tendency (*för* to), disposition (*för* towards); ~ *för fetma* tendency to put on weight; *musikaliska* ~ a gift for music; *ärftliga* ~ hereditary disposition (*sg*); *ha goda* ~ have a gift, be gifted, have good mental powers
anlagd *a5* **1** *se anlägga* **2** *praktiskt* ~ of a practical turn; ~ *på förtjänst* planned (set up) on a profit basis
anlags|bärare *med.* carrier **-prov** aptitude test **-prövning** aptitude testing **-test** aptitude test
anledning (*skäl*) reason (*till* for, of); (*orsak*) cause, occasion (*till* for, of); *av vilken* ~ ? for what reason?, on what account?; *med* (*i*) ~ *av* on account of, owing to, in view of, because of; *med* ~ *härav* in view of this fact, for this reason, such being the case; *utan all* ~ without any (for no) reason; *vid minsta* ~ on the slightest provocation; *ge* ~ *till* give occasion to, cause; *ha* ~ *till missnöje* have cause for dissatisfaction; *det fanns ingen* ~ *till oro* there was no cause for alarm; *han hade all* ~ *att resa* he had every reason to leave; *på förekommen* ~ *får vi meddela* we find it necessary to point out
anlete *s6* visage, countenance, face; *i sitt ~s svett* by the sweat of one's brow **anletsdrag** feature, lineament
anligg|a ~ *mot* bear on **-ningsyta** contact surface
anlit|a 1 (*vända sig t.*) apply (turn) to (*ngn för* a p. for); ~ *advokat* engage (go to) a lawyer; ~ *läkare* call in a doctor; *vara mycket ~d* be

in great demand, be successful (popular) **2** (*tillgripa*) have recourse to, resort to; ~ *lexikon* use (make use of) a dictionary; ~ *telefonen* use the telephone; ~ *vapenmakt* resort to arms; *en ofta ~d utväg* an expedient often resorted to **-ande** *s6, med ~ av* use being made of, with the aid of

anlopp 1 (*ansats*) run-up **2** (*rusning*) rush **3** (*anfall*) assault, attack (*mot* upon)

anlupen *a3* tarnished, discoloured; ~ *av fukt* tarnished by damp

anlägg|a 1 (*bygga*) build, construct, erect; (*grunda*) found, set up; ~ *en park* lay out a park **2** (*planera*) plan, design; ~ *mordbrand* commit arson **3** (*börja bära, lägga sig t. med*) take to, begin to wear, put on; ~ *skägg* grow a beard, let one's beard grow; ~ *sorg* put on mourning; ~ *kritiska synpunkter på* adopt a critical attitude towards **4** (*anbringa*) ~ *förband på ett sår* dress a wound, apply a bandage to a wound; *se äv. anlagd* **-are** builder, constructor; founder; designer **-ning 1** *abstr.* foundation; erection, construction **2** *konkr.* establishment; (*fabrik*) works (*pl*), plant, factory premises (*pl*); (*byggnad*) building, structure

anläggnings|arbetare construction worker **-kapital** fixed capital **-tillgångar** fixed (capital) assets

anlända arrive (*till* at, in); ~ *till* (*äv.*) reach

an|löpa 1 *sjö.*, ~ *en hamn* call at (touch) a port, put into a port **2** *tekn.* temper, anneal **-löpning** *tekn.* tempering, annealing **-löpningshamn** port of call

anman|a demand, request, urge (*ngn att s.b. to*); ~ *ngn att betala* demand payment from s.b. **-ing** request; *utan ~* without reminder; ~ *vid ~* on demand

anmarsch advance

anmod|a request, call upon; (*enträget*) urge; instruct; demand **-an** *r* request; *på ~ av mig* at my request

anmäl|a *v2* **1** (*tillkännage, meddela*) announce, report; ~ *en besökande* announce a visitor; ~ *flyttning* give notice of changed address (residence); ~ *förhinder* send word to say one is prevented from coming; ~ *ngt för polisen* report s.th. to the police; ~ *sig för tjänstgöring* report for duty; ~ *sig som sökande till* put in an application for, apply for; ~ *sig till en examen* enter for an examination; ~ *sitt utträde ur en förening* withdraw one's membership from a club, resign from a club **2** (*recensera*) review **-an** *r* **1** announcement, notification (*om* of); report **2** (*recension*) review **3** (*tull-*) declaration **-are 1** (*angivare*) informer **2** (*recensent*) reviewer

anmälnings|avgift [-ä:-] registration fee; (*t. tävling etc.*) entry fee (money) **-blankett** registration (application) form **-lista** list of applicants (entrants) **-plikt** obligation to report [regularly] to police *etc.* **-tid** period of notification; (*idrott*) entry time

anmärk|a 1 (*påpeka, yttra*) remark, observe **2** (*klandra, ogilla*) find fault (*på with*); ~ *på* criticize; *han hade ingenting att ~ på* he found no fault with **-ning 1** (*yttrande, påpekande*) comment, remark, observation **2** (*förklaring*)

remark, comment, observation, annotation; (*i bok*) note, footnote **3** (*klander*) objection, criticism, complaint **4** *skol.* bad [conduct] mark; *få ~* be given a bad mark

anmärknings|bok conduct book; report card **-värd** *a1* **1** (*märklig*) remarkable **2** (*beaktansvärd*) notable, noteworthy; (*märkbar*) noticeable

ann *se annan 1*

annaler [-'na:-] *pl* annals, records

annalkande I *s6* approach[ing]; *vara i ~* be approaching **II** *a4* approaching; ~ *fara* imminent danger; *ett ~ oväder* a gathering storm

anna|n *-t andra* **1** other; (*efter självst. pron*) else; *en ~* another, (*självvst. äv.*) somebody (someone, anybody, anyone) else; *ingen ~* nobody else; *ingen ~ än* no other than; *ingen ~ än du* no one [else] but you; *någon ~* somebody (anybody) else; *en och ~ gång* occasionally, once in a while; *gång efter ~* time and again, time after time; *tid efter ~* from time to time; *av en eller ~ anledning* for some reason or other; *jag är av ~ mening* I am of another opinion, I don't agree; *en ~ gång är en skälm* tomorrow never comes; *bland annat, se under bland*; *på ett eller -t sätt* somehow or other; *ha -t att göra* (*vard.*) have other fish to fry; *lova är ett och hålla ett -t* it is one thing to make a promise and another thing to keep it; *säga ett och mena ett -t* speak with [one's] tongue in [one's] cheek; *hon är allt -t än vacker* she is anything but beautiful; *vi talade om ett och -t* we talked about one thing and another, we chatted; *inte -t än jag vet* as far as I know; *hon gör inte -t än gråter* she does nothing but cry; *hon kunde inte -t än skratta* she could not help laughing, she could not but laugh; *alla andra* all the others, (*om pers. ofta*) everybody else; *alla de andra* all the others (the rest); *en ann är så god som en ann* one man is as good as another **2** (*ej lik*) different; *det är en ~ historia* that's a different (another) story; *något helt -t än* something quite different from (to)

annan|dag ~ *jul* the day after Christmas Day, (*i Storbritannien*) Boxing Day; ~ *pingst* Whit Monday; ~ *påsk* Easter Monday **-stans** elsewhere; *ingen ~* nowhere else

annars 1 (*i annat fall*) otherwise, or [else], else **2** (*för övrigt*) otherwise, else; *var det ~ något?* was there anything else? **3** (*i vanliga fall*) usually; *mera trött än ~* more tired than usual

annat *se annan*

annekter|a annex **-ing** annexation

an'nex *s7* annex[e] **-byggnad** annex[e], wing

annexion [-k'ʃɔ:n] annexation

annexsjukhus branch hospital

annihil|ationsstrålning annihilation radiation **-era** annihilate

anno [ˣannɔ *el.* 'annɔ] in [the year]; *från ~ dazumal* (*ung.*) ancient, *skämts.* antediluvian, as old as the hills

annons [-'åns *el.* -'åŋs] *s3* advertisement, *vard.* ad[vert] (*om* about); (*födelse- etc.*) announcement; *enligt ~* according to your advertisement, as advertised; *sätta in en ~ i en tidning* put an advertisement in a paper, advertise in a

paper **-ackvisitör** advertising agent **-bilaga** advertisement supplement (section) **-byrå** advertising agency
annonser|a 1 (*tillkännage, söka etc.* genom annons) advertise (*efter* for; *om ngt s.th.*) **2** (*tillkännage*) announce **-ing** advertising
annons|kampanj advertising campaign **-organ** advertising medium **-pelare** advertising pillar; *AE.* billboard **-plats** advertisement space **-pris** advertising charge **-sida** advertisement page **-spalt** advertisement column **-tavla** advertisement board; *AE.* billboard **-taxa** advertisement rate **-text** copy
annonsör advertiser, space buyer
annor|ledes, -lunda otherwise, differently; *såvida ej ~ föreskrivs* unless otherwise prescribed; *han har blivit helt -lunda* he has changed completely, he is quite a different man **-städes** elsewhere, somewhere else
annotation note **annotationsblock** [scribbling] pad; *AE.* memo pad **annotera** note (take) down, make a note of
annu'ell *a1* annual **annuitet** *s3* **1** (*på lån*) annual instalment **2** (*livränta*) annuity, life interest **annuitetslån** instalment credit; annuity loan
annullation *försäkr.* cancellation
annuller|a cancel, withdraw, annul; (*kontrakt, äv.*) nullify; vitiate **-ing** cancellation, withdrawal, annulment, revocation, nullification
annulleringsklausul cancellation clause
a'nod *s3* anode **-batteri** anode battery **-spänning** anode voltage
ano'ma|l *a1* anomalous **-'li** *s3* anomaly **-listisk** *a5* anomalistic
ano'mi *s3* anomie, anomy
ano'nym *a1* anonymous **-itet** anonymity
anor *pl* ancestry (*sg*), ancestors; lineage (*sg*); *bildl.* progenitors, traditions; *ha gamla ~* be of ancient lineage, *bildl.* have a long history, be a time-honoured tradition (custom); *det har ~ från antiken* it dates back to classical times
anorak ['ano- *el.* -'rack] *s3* anorak; windcheater
anord|na arrange, put in (bring into) order, set up, organize; *~ lekar* get up games **-ning** arrangement, preparation, setup; (*apparat*) apparatus, device; (*utrustning*) outfit; *~ar* (*hjälpmedel o.d.*) facilities
anore'xi *s3* anorexia
anpart [ˣann-] share, portion
anpass|a adapt, suit, adjust (*efter* to), bring in line with **-bar** *a5* adaptable **-ling** turncoat, yes man; (*medlöpare*) fellow traveller, camp follower **-ning** adap[ta]tion, adjustment, accommodation
anpassnings|förmåga adaptability **-svårigheter** adjustment problems; *han har ~* he finds it difficult to adapt himself (fit in)
anrik [ˣa:n-] of ancient lineage
anrik|a [ˣann-] concentrate, enrich, dress; *~t kärnbränsle* enriched nuclear fuel **-ning** concentration, enrichment
anrikningsverk dressing plant; (*för stenkol*) washing plant
anrop call; *mil.* challenge; *sjö.* hail **anropa** call [out to]; *mil.* challenge; *sjö.* hail; *~ Gud om hjälp* invoke God's help

anropssignal call sign (signal)
anryck|a *v2*, **-ning** *s* advance
anrätt|a prepare, cook, dress **-ning 1** (*anrättande*) preparation, cooking **2** (*rätt*) dish; (*måltid*) meal; *göra heder åt ~arna* do justice to the meal, *vard.* tuck in[to], eat with gusto
ans *s2* care, tending; (*av jord*) dressing; (*av häst*) grooming **ansa** tend, see to; cultivate
ansaml|a collect, gather; *~ sig* (*om t.ex. damm*) settle **-ing** collection; (*av vatten*) pool [of water]; (*av skräp*) heap [of rubbish]
ansats 1 (*sats*) run-up; *mil.* bound, rush; *höjdhopp utan ~* standing high jump; *framryckning i ~er* advance by rushes **2** (*början*) start; (*försök*) attempt; (*impuls*) impulse (*till* to); (*tecken*) sign (*till* of); *visa ~er till förbättring* show signs of improvement **3** *mus.* striking of a note **4** *tekn.* shoulder, projection
ansatt *a4* afflicted (*av* with); *hårt ~* hard pressed, in a tight corner
an|se 1 (*mena*) think, consider, be of the opinion; *man ~r allmänt* it is generally considered; *han ~r sig orättvist behandlad* he considers himself unjustly treated **2** (*betrakta*) consider, regard, look upon; *jag ~r det som min plikt* I consider it my duty; *det ~s sannolikt* it is considered likely; *han ~s som vår största expert* he is regarded as our leading expert **-sedd** *a5* (*aktad*) respected, esteemed, distinguished; (*om firma etc.*) reputable; *väl ~* of good repute **-seende** *s6* **1** (*gott rykte*) reputation, standing, prestige **2** (*aktning*) esteem, respect **3** *utan ~ till person* without respect of persons; *i ~ till* considering **-senlig** [-e:-] *a1* considerable, large
ansikte *s6* face, countenance; *ett slag i ~t* (*bildl., vard.*) a smack in the eye; *det är ett slag i ~t på alla musikälskare* it is an insult to all music lovers; *han blev lång i ~t* his face fell; *kasta en anklagelse i ~t på ngn* throw an accusation in a p.'s face; *skratta ngn rätt upp i ~t* laugh in a p.'s face; *stå ~ mot ~ med* stand face to face with; *säga ngn ngt rakt i ~t* tell s.b. s.th. [straight] to his face; *tvätta sig i ~t* wash one's face; *vara lång i ~t* have a face as long as a fiddle
ansikts|behandling facial [treatment] **-drag** features (*pl*) **-form** shape of a p.'s face **-färg** colouring, complexion **-kräm** face cream **-lyftning** face-lift (*äv. bildl.*) **-mask** face pack, mask **-servett** face tissue **-skydd** face protection; (*andnings-*) mask **-uttryck** [facial] expression **-vatten** skin tonic (lotion)
ansjovis [-'ʃɔ:-] *s2* anchovy **-burk** tin of anchovies
anskaff|a procure, obtain, buy, acquire; provide **-ning** procurement, acquisition, purchase; provision
anskaffnings|kostnad acquisition (initial) cost; *sälja till ~* sell at cost price **-pris** initial (purchase) price **-provision** new business commission **-värde** purchase (initial) value
anskri outcry, scream
anskriven *a5, väl* (*illa*) *~ hos ngn* in (out of) favour with s.b., in a p.'s good (bad) books
anskrämlig [-ä:-] *a1* hideous, ugly, forbidding
anslag 1 (*kungörelse*) notice, placard, bill; *sätta*

upp ett ~ stick up a bill **2** (*penningmedel*) provision; grant; subsidy; (*stats-*) appropriation; *bevilja ett* ~ make a grant **3** (*komplott*) design, plot **4** *mus.* touch **5** *filmens* ~ *är glatt* (*ung.*) the film strikes a happy note **6** (*projektils etc.*) impact

anslags|beviljande *a4*, ~ *myndighet* [appropriation] granting authority **-bevillning** voting of supplies **-kraft** force of impact **-tavla** notice (*AE.* bulletin) board **-äskande** budget estimate

ansluta connect (*till* with); ~ *sig till ett avtal* accede to (enter into) an agreement; ~ *sig till ett parti* join a party; ~ *sig till ngns åsikt* agree with a p.['s opinion]; *nära* ~ *sig till* be on much the same lines as

anslut|en *a5* connected (*till* with); associated (*till* with), affiliated (*till* to) **-ning 1** (*förbindelse*) connection (*till* with); *tel.* extension **2** (*stöd*) support; (*uppmuntran*) support, patronage; *i* ~ *till* in connection with; with (in) reference to; *i* ~ *till vårt brev* further to our letter; *vinna allmän* ~ gain general support

anslutnings|avgift connection charge **-flyg** connecting airline; air connection **-linje** *järnv.* branch line **-trafik** connecting traffic

anslå 1 (*kungöra*) ~ *en kungörelse* put up a notice; ~ *en tjänst ledig* advertise a post as vacant **2** (*anvisa*) assign, set aside, earmark (*till* for); (*pengar*) grant, allocate, allow **3** (*uppskatta*) estimate, rate, value **4** *mus.* strike; *jfr äv. slå an* **-ende** *a4* pleasing, attractive; *en* ~ *predikan* an impressive sermon

anspann *s7* team

anspel|a allude (*på* to), hint (*på* at) **-ning** allusion (*på* to)

anspråk claim, demand; pretention; *avstå från* ~ *på* waive a claim; *göra* ~ *på* lay claim to; *göra* ~ *på ersättning* claim compensation; *motsvara ngns* ~ satisfy (meet) a p.'s demands; *ta i* ~ claim, demand, make use of; *ta ngns tid i* ~ take up a p.'s time

anspråks|full pretentious, assuming; (*fordrande*) exacting **-fullhet** pretentiousness; exactingness **-lös** unpretentious, unassuming, modest, quiet, moderate **-löshet** unpretentiousness, modesty; *i all* ~ in all modesty, in a very modest way

anspänn|a 1 (*häst*) harness **2** *bildl.* strain, brace **-ing** *bildl.* exertion, strain, tension

anstalt *s3* **1** (*institution*) institution, establishment, home **2** (*anordning*) arrangement, preparation; step; *vidtaga ~er för* take steps to, make arrangements for

anstalts|behandling institutional treatment **-vård** institutional care

anstift|a cause, provoke; ~ *en sammansvärjning* hatch a plot; ~ *mordbrand* commit arson **-an** *r, på* ~ *av* at the instigation of **-are** instigator (*av* of), inciter (*av* to)

anstolt [ˣaːn-] proud of one's descent (pedigree)

anstorm|a, -ning assault

anstryk|a (*grundmåla*) prime; paint **-ning 1** (*målning*) coating, priming **2** (*skiftning*) tinge, shade, colour **3** (*tycke, prägel*) touch, trace, suggestion; *utan minsta* ~ *av förakt* without the slightest trace of contempt

ansträng|a *v2* strain; (*vara påkostande för*) try, tax; ~ *sig* exert o.s., endeavour; ~ *sig till det yttersta* do one's very utmost, make every possible effort; *läsning -er ögonen* reading is a strain on one's eyes; *-d* strained, (*om skratt e.d.*) forced **-ande** *a4* strenuous, trying, taxing; ~ *arbete* hard work **-ning** effort, exertion, strain, endeavour; *med gemensamma ~ar* by united efforts; *utan minsta* ~ without the slightest effort

ansträngt *adv* in a forced manner; *han log* ~ he gave a forced smile

anstucken *a5* infected, tainted (*av* with)

anstå 1 (*passa, vara värdig*) become, befit; be becoming (befitting) for; *det -r inte mig att* it is not for me to **2** (*uppskjutas*) wait, be deferred (put off, postponed); *låta ngt* ~ let s.th. wait, postpone s.th. **anstånd** *s7* delay, respite, grace; *begära en veckas* ~ *med betalning* request a week's respite for payment

anställ|a 1 (*i tjänst*) employ, engage, hire, appoint; *fast -d* [permanently] employed; on the [permanent] staff; *vara -d* be employed (*hos ngn* by s.b., *vid* at, in) **2** (*anordna*) bring about, cause; ~ *blodbad* start a massacre; ~ *ett gästabud* give a banquet; ~ *skada* cause damage **3** (*företaga*) make; ~ *betraktelser över* contemplate; ~ *efterforskningar* institute inquiries; ~ *examen* hold an examination; ~ *förhör* subject [s.b.] to interrogation

anställ|d *subst. a* employee **-ning** employment, situation, job, position, post; (*tillfällig*) [temporary] engagement

anställnings|betyg testimonial, reference; *mil.* service record **-förmån** fringe benefit; perquisite, *vard.* perk **-intervju** interview **-kontrakt** contract of employment, service contract **-skydd** job security **-tid** period of employment, length of service **-trygghet** job security **-villkor** terms of employment

anständig *a1* respectable, decent, decorous; (*passande*) proper; (*hygglig*) decent **-het** respectability; propriety; decency

anständighetskänsla sense of propriety **anständigtvis** in common decency, for decency's sake

anstöt *s2* offence; *ta* ~ *av* take offence at, be offended at; *väcka* ~ give offence, offend **-lig** *a1* offensive (*för* to); objectionable

ansvar *s7* responsibility; (*ansvarsskyldighet*) liability; *på eget* ~ on one's own responsibility, at one's own risk; *vid laga* ~ under penalty of law; *bära ~et för* be responsible for; *ikläda sig ~et för* take the responsibility for; *ställa ngn till* ~ *för* hold s.b. responsible for; *yrka* ~ *på ngn* prefer a charge (accusation) against s.b., demand a p.'s conviction

ansvara be responsible (*för* for), answer (*för* for); ~ *för en förlust* be liable for a loss; *jag ~r inte för hur det går* I assume no responsibility for the consequences

ansvarig *a5* responsible, answerable, liable; *göras* ~ be made (held) responsible; ~ *utgivare* [legally responsible] publisher **-het** responsibility, liability; *begränsad* ~ limited liability; *bolag med begränsad* ~ limited [liability] company

ansvarighetsförsäkring [third party] liability insurance

ansvars|befrielse discharge [from liability] **-fri** free of responsibility **-frihet** freedom from responsibility; *bevilja* ~ grant discharge; *bevilja styrelse* ~ adopt the report [and accounts] **-full** responsible **-förbindelse** contingent liability **-försäkring** *se ansvarighetsförsäkring* **-kännande** *se -medveten* **-känsla** sense of responsibility **-lös** irresponsible **-löshet** irresponsibility **-medveten** responsible, conscious of one's responsibility **-påföljd** legal penalty **-yrkande** ~ *mot ngn* demand for a p.'s conviction

ansvällning swelling; enlargement

ansätta press, attack, beset, harass; *jfr ansatt*

ansök|a ~ *om* apply for **-an** *r, som pl används pl av ansökning* application (*om* for); *avslå en* ~ refuse (reject, deny) an application; *inlämna en* ~ make an application **-ning** application; petition; *inkomna ~ar* lodged applications

ansöknings|blankett application form **-förfarande** application procedure **-handling** application [paper, document] **-skrivelse** letter of application **-tid** period of application; *~en utgår den* applications must be sent in by the

anta *se antaga*

antabus ['anta-] *r* Antabuse **-kur** Antabuse treatment

antag|a 1 (*mottaga*) take, accept; ~ *en plats* take (accept) a post; ~ *en utmaning* accept a challenge; ~ *som elev* admit as a pupil **2** (*godkänna*) accept, consent to, approve; ~ *en lag* pass a law **3** (*göra t. sin, övergå t.*) adopt, assume, embrace; ~ *fast form* (*bildl.*) take definite shape, *fys.* solidify; ~ *kristendomen* adopt Christianity; ~ *namnet* take the name of; *under -et namn* under an assumed name **4** (*anlägga*) put on, assume; ~ *en dyster min* put on a gloomy expression, *vard.* look miserable **5** (*anställa*) engage, appoint **6** (*förmoda*) assume, suppose, presume; *AE. äv.* guess; *antag att* suppose (supposing) that; *jag antar att vi skall vänta här* I take it [that] we are to wait here

antag|ande *s6* **1** (*jfr antaga 1–5*) acceptance; adoption, assumption; engagement, appointment **2** (*förmodan*) assumption, supposition, presumption, guess **-bar** *a5* acceptable; reasonable **-lig** *a1* **1** (*rimlig*) reasonable, plausible; (*sannolik*) probable, likely **2** (*antagbar*) acceptable; admissible; eligible **-ligen** probably, very likely, presumably **-ning** admission

antagnings|byrå *Centrala ~n* Central Student Admissions Office; (*i Storbritannien*) Universities Central Council on Admissions **-nämnd** admissions board

antagon|ism antagonism **-ist** antagonist, adversary **-istisk** *a5* antagonistic

antal *s7* number, amount, quantity; *ett stort ~ böcker* a great number of books; *minsta ~ besökare* the fewest visitors; *i stort ~* in great numbers; *sex till ~et* six in number; *höra till de levandes ~* be numbered among the living

Antarktis [-'ark-] *n* the Antarctic [Zone]

antarktisk [-'ark-] *a5* Antarctic

antast|a 1 (*ofreda*) molest; ~ *kvinnor på gatan*

accost women in the street **2** (*klandra*) ~ *ngns heder* throw doubt on a p.'s honour, discredit s.b. **-lig** *a1* assailable; challengeable

antavla [*ˣa:n-] genealogical table; (*friare*) family tree

anteceden|tia, -tier [-'dentsia, -er] antecedents

antecip|ation anticipation, forestalling **-a'tiv** *a5, jur.* anticipatory **-era** anticipate, forestall

anteckn|a note, make a note of, write down; (*uppteckna*) record; ~ *till protokollet* enter in the minutes, record; ~ *sig* put one's name down (*för* for, *som* as) **-ing** note, annotation, memorandum

antecknings|block notepad, writing pad **-bok** notebook, memo book

ante|datera antedate **-diluviansk** [-'a:-] *a5* antediluvian

an'tenn *s3* **1** *radio.* aerial, antenna; *radar.* scanner **2** *zool.* antenna (*pl* antennae); feeler

ante|pendium [-'pend-] *s4* antependium **-penultima** [-'ulti-] *s1* antepenult

anti|biotikum [-'å:-] *s8*, **-biotisk** [-'å:-] *a5* antibiotic **-chambrera** [-ʃam-] *ung.* wait for an audience **-cyklon** anticyclone, high **-fo'ni** *s3* antiphony **-frysvätska** antifreeze [fluid] **-gen** [-'je:n] I *s7*, *s4* antigen II *a5* antigenic **-hista'min** *s4* antihistamine **-hjälte** antihero

an'tik I *a1* antique, old[-fashioned] **II** *r*, *~en* classical antiquity; *~ens historia* ancient history **-behandling** antique finish, antiquing **-handel** *se antikvitetshandel* **-isera** classicize; imitate classic style

anti|kleri'kal anticlerical **-'klimax** anticlimax **-konceptio'nell** *a5* contraceptive **-'krist** *s3* Antichrist **-kropp** *med.* antibody

antikva [-*ˣti:k-] *s1, boktr.* roman [type]

antikv|ari'at *s7* second-hand bookshop **-arie** [-'a:rie] *s5* antiquary **-arisk** [-'a:risk] *a5* antiquarian; ~ *böcker* second-hand books **-erad** [-'e:rad] *a5* antiquated, outmoded **-itet** antique

antikvitets|handel antique shop; curio shop **-handlare** antique dealer **-samlare** collector of antiques **-värde** antique value

Antillerna [-'till-] *pl* the Antilles

antilogaritm antilogarithm

anti|'lop *s3* antelope **-ma'kass** *s3* antimacassar **-materia** [*ˣanti-*] antimatter

antimilitar|ism antimilitarism **-ist** antimilitarist **-istisk** *a5* antimilitaristic

antimon [-'å:n, *äv.* -'o:n] *s7, s3* antimony

antingen [-ŋ-] **1** (*ettdera*) either; ~ *skall han lämna rummet eller också gör jag det* either he leaves the room or I do **2** (*vare sig*) whether; ~ *du vill eller inte* whether you like it or not

antipartikel antiparticle

anti|pa'ti *s3* antipathy (*mot* to) **-patisk** [-'pa:-] *a5* antipathetic[al] **-pod** [-'po:d *el.* -'på:d] *s3* **1** (*rak motsats*) antipode **2** *~er* (*folk, plats*) antipodes **-podisk** [-'pɔ:-] *a5* antipodal **-robot** antimissile **-robotvapen** antimissile weapon

antise'mit *s3* anti-Semite **-isk** *a5* anti-Semitic **-ism** anti-Semitism

antisep't|ik *s3* antisepsis **-ikum** [-'sept-] *s8*, **-isk** [-'sept-] *a5* antiseptic

antision|ism anti-Zionism **-ist** *s3*, **-istisk** *a5* anti-Zionist

anti|statisk [-'sta:-] *a5* antistatic **-statmedel** [-ˣsta:t-] antistatic agent **-'tes** *s3* antithesis (*pl* antitheses) **-tetisk** [-'te:-] *a5* antithetic[al] **-to'xin** antitoxin **-ubåtsvapen** antisubmarine weapon

antivivisektion|ism antivivisectionism **-ist** antivivisectionist

antologi *s3* anthology

anto'nym *s3* antonym

antra'cit *s3* anthracite, hard coal

antrakos [-'kå:s] *s3, med.* anthracosis

antropo|log anthropologist **-logi** *s3* anthropology **-logisk** *a5* anthropological **-morf** [-'mårf] *a5* anthropomorphic **-morfism** [-å-] anthropomorphism **-morfistisk** [-'fiss-] *a5* anthropomorphic **-sof** [-'så:f] *s3* anthroposophist **-so-'fi** *s3* anthroposophy

anträda set out (set off, embark) [up]on; begin

anträff|a find, meet with **-bar** *a1* in; at home; available

Antwerpen *n* Antwerp

antyd|a 1 (*flyktigt omnämna*) suggest, hint at **2** (*låta förstå*) intimate (*för* to), imply, give [s.b.] to understand; (*ge en vink om*) hint [to s.b.] **3** (*tyda på*) indicate; *av -d art* of the kind indicated; *som titeln -er* as the title implies

antyd|an *r, som pl används pl av antydning* **1** (*vink*) intimation (*om* of), hint **2** (*ansats, första början*) suggestion (*till* of) **-ning** (*i förtäckta ordalag*) insinuation; (*vink*) hint; (*spår*) trace **-ningsvis** roughly, in rough outline

antågande *s6* advancing, advance, approach, approach[ing]; *vara i ~* be approaching, be on the way

antänd|a set fire to, set ... fire, ignite, light **-lig** *a1* inflammable **-ning** ignition

anus ['a:-] *s2* anus

anvis|a 1 (*visa, utpeka*) show, indicate, point out; *~ ngn en plats* show s.b. to a seat **2** (*tilldela*) allot, assign; *han ~des ett rum på baksidan* [*av huset*] he was given a room at the back **3** (*utanordna*) allot, assign **-ning 1** (*upplysning, instruktion*) direction, instruction; *få ~ på* be directed (referred) to; *ge ngn ~ på* direct (refer) s.b. to **2** (*utanordning*) assignment, remittance

anvisningsprovision arranger's fee

använd|a 1 (*begagna, bruka*) use (*till* for), make use of; *~ tid* (*pengar*) *på* spend time (money) on (in); *~ glasögon* wear glasses; *~ käpp* carry (use) a stick; *~ socker* take sugar; *~ väl* make good use of; *färdig att ~s* ready for use **2** (*ägna, nedlägga*) devote; *~ mycken energi på att* (*äv.*) put a great deal of effort into; *väl -a pengar* well-spent money **3** (*tillämpa*) apply (*om regel*), adopt (*om metod*)

användarvänlig user friendly

använd|bar *a1* fit for use; (*nyttig*) useful (*till* for); serviceable (*om kläder*), practicable (*om metod*); *föga ~* of little use **-ning** use; (*av regel*) application; (*av pers.*) employment; *jag har ingen ~ för den* it is of no use to me; *komma till ~* be used, prove useful

användnings|område [field of] application, area of use **-sätt** mode of application; (*tryckt*

---

instruktion) directions for use

aorta [aˣårta] *s1* aorta

apa I *s1* monkey; (*svanslös*) ape; simian; *neds.* cat, cow, bitch **II** *v1*, *~ efter* ape, mimic

apache [a'paʃ] *s5* apache

apanage *s7* ap[p]anage

apart [-'a:rt, *äv.* -'art] *a4* striking, remarkable, distinctive

apartheidpolitik [a'pa:rt-] apartheid [policy]

apa't|i *s3* apathy **-isk** [-'pa:-] *a5* apathetic

apa'tit *s3* apatite

apbrödsträd baobab, monkey bread tree

apekatt (*upptågsmakare*) monkey, clown; (*efterhärmare*) mimic, parrot

apel ['a:-] *s2* apple [tree] **-kastad** *a5* dapple-grey

apel'sin *s3* orange **-juice** orange juice **-marmelad** [orange] marmalade **-saft** (*pressad o.d.*) orange juice; (*koncentrerad*) orange squash **-skal** orange peel **-träd** [sweet] orange [tree]

Apenninerna [-'ni:-] *pl* the Apennines

aperitif [-'tif] *s3* apéritif

apertur aperture

apex ['a:-] *s3, astr.* [solar] apex

AP-fonden *se pensionsfond*

aphelium [ap'he:-] *s4* aphelion (*pl* aphelia)

aphus monkey house

aplanat aplanatic lens

aplik simian, simious

a'plomb *s3* (*säkerhet*) equanimity, self-confidence, self-possession; (*eftertryck*) emphasis, stress

apmänniska apeman

apné *s3* apnoea

apogeum [-ˣge:-] *s4* apogee

apo|ka'lyps *s3* apocalypse **-kalyptisk** [-'lypt-] *a5* apocalyptic **-kromat** apochromat, apochromatic lens **-kryfisk** [-'kry:-] *a5* apocryphal; *de ~a böckerna* the Apocrypha

apollofjäril [aˣpållⱭ-] apollo

apolo'get [-g-] *s3* apologist **-ik** ['-tik] *s3* apologetics (*pl, behandlas som sg*) **-isk** *a5* apologetic

apologi *s3* apologia, apology

apople|ktisk [-'plekt-] *a5* apoplectic **-'xi** *s3* apoplexy

apostel [-'påst-] *s2* apostle

a posteriori [-ˣⱭ:ri *el.* -ˣå:ri] a posteriori; empirical

Apostlagärningarna the Acts [of the Apostles]

apost|lahästar *använda ~na* use shanks's pony (*AE.* shanks's mare) **-olisk** [-'Ⱐ:-] *a5* apostolic[al]; *den ~a trosbekännelsen* the Apostles' Creed

apostrof [-'strå:f] *s3* apostrophe **-era** apostrophize

apo'tek *s7* pharmacy; dispensary; chemist's [shop]; *särsk. AE.* drugstore **-are** [-ˣte:-] pharmacist, *i Storbritannien* [dispensing] chemist; *AE.* druggist

apoteks|biträde dispenser **-vara** pharmaceutical preparation

apoteos [-'å:s] *s3* apotheosis (*pl* apotheoses)

apparat apparatus; *vard.* gadget, contrivance; (*anordning*) device, appliance; *sätta igång en stor ~* (*bildl.*) make extensive preparations

apparatur equipment; apparatus
apparition appearance
ap'pell *s3* call; *mil.* roll call, muster; *jur.* appeal **appellation** *jur.* appeal **appellationsdomstol** court of appeal
appellativ *s7, s4* appellative, common noun
appellera appeal
append|i'cit *s3* appendicitis **-ix** [-'pend-] *s7* appendix; *anat.* [vermiform] appendix
applicer|a apply (*på* to) **-ing** application
applikation *sömn.* appliqué
app'låd *s3* applause; *kraftiga ~er* enthusiastic (loud) applause (*sg*), *AE. o. vard.* a big hand; *hon hälsades med en ~* she was greeted with applause **-era** applaud; cheer, clap **-åska** storm of applause
apport [-'årt] *interj* retrieve; fetch it **-era** fetch; *jakt.* retrieve
apposition apposition
apprecier|a appreciate, revalue **-ing** appreciation, revaluation
appr|etera finish, dress **-e'tur, -e'tyr** *s3* finishing, dressing
approxim|ation [-rå-] approximation **-a'tiv** *a5,* **-era** approximate
apri'kos *s3* apricot [tree]
april [-'ill, *äv.* -'i:l] *r* April; *narra ngn ~* make an April fool of s.b.; *~ ~! April fool!* **-skämt** April fools' joke **-väder** April weather
a priori [-ˣω:- *el.* -ˣå:-] a priori
à-pris price per unit, unit price
apro'på I *adv* by the bye (way); *helt ~* incidentally; casually; quite unexpectedly **II** *prep* apropos of, with regard to **III** *s6, s4, som ett ~ till detta* in this connection, as an illustration of this
apter|a adapt (*till* to; *för* for); (*anpassa*) adjust **-ing** adaptation; adjustment
ap'tit *s3* appetite; *ha ~ på livet* have an appetite for life; *ha god ~* have a hearty appetite; *~en kommer medan man äter* appetite comes with eating
aptit|lig [-'ti:t-] *a1* appetizing; savoury (*ej om söta rätter*); (*lockande*) inviting; (*smaklig*) tasty; (*läcker*) delicious; (*för ögat*) dainty **-lös** *vard.* off one's feed **-retande** *a4* appetizing, tempting; *vard. äv.* mouthwatering **-retare** apéritif, appetizer
ar *s9, s7* are; *1 ~ (ung.)* 119.6 square yards
ara *s1, zool.* macaw
a'rab *s3* Arab, Arabian **-e'sk** [-'besk] *s3* arabesque
Arabien [a'ra:-] *n* Arabia
arab|isk [a'ra:-] *a5* Arabian, Arabic; Arab **-iska** *s1* **1** (*språk*) Arabic **2** Arab[ian] woman **-stat** Arab state **-världen** the Arab world
Aragonien [-'gω:-] *n* Aragon
aragon|ier [-'gω:-] *s9,* **-isk** [-'gω:-] *a5* Aragonese
aralia [a'ra:-] *s1, bot.* aralia
arame|isk [-'me:-] *a5* Aramaic; Aram[a]ean **-iska** *s1* Aramaic
arbeta work, be at work (*med* with); (*tungt*) labour; (*mödosamt*) toil; (*fungera*) operate, work; *~ bort* get rid of, eliminate; *~ ihjäl sig* work o.s. to death; *~ på att* strive to; *~ på ngt* work at s.th.; *~ upp en affär* work up a busi-

ness; *~ upp sig* improve [in one's work]; *~ ut sig* wear o.s. out; *~ över* be on (work) overtime; *~ sig trött* tire o.s. out with work; *~ sig upp* work one's way up, make one's way [in the world]; *tiden ~r för oss* time is on our side; *det ~s för att få honom fri* forces are at work to release him (get him aquitted)
arbetad *a5* manufactured, worked; (*om yta*) finished; (*om metall*) wrought
arbetarbostäder workmen's dwellings
arbetar|e worker; labourer; *vard.* workfolk, *AE.* workfolks (*pl*); (*i motsats t. arbetsgivare*) employee; *se äv.* diverse-, fabriks-, kropps-, verkstadsarbetare **-klass** working class **-kommun** labour union **-parti** Labour Party **-regering** Labour Government **-rörelse** labour movement **-skydd** industrial welfare
arbetarskydds|fond *~en* [the Swedish] work environment fund **-lag** labour welfare act; (*i Storbritannien*) Factory Acts (*pl*) **-nämnd** labour welfare council **-styrelse** *~n* [the Swedish] national board of occupational safety and health
arbete *s6* work; *abstr. äv.* labour; (*sysselsättning*) employment, job; (*möda*) toil; *~n i äkta silver* real silver handicraft products; *ett ansträngande ~* hard work; *ett fint ~* fine workmanship; *offentliga ~n* public works; *med sina händers ~* by the labour of one's hands; *ha ~ hos* be employed by; *mista sitt ~* lose one's job; *nedlägga ~t* stop work, go on strike, strike, down tools; *sätta i ~* put to work; *vara under ~* be in preparation, be under construction; *vara utan ~* be out of work (unemployed)
arbeterska working woman, woman worker
arbetsam *a1* industrious, hard-working; (*mödosam*) laborious
arbets|analys work analysis **-avtal** labour contract (agreement) **-bas** *s2* foreman, *fem.* forewoman; *vard.* boss **-beskrivning** working instructions; operational directions **-besparande** *a4* labour-saving **-besparing** saving of labour **-bi** worker [bee] **-bord** worktable; desk **-bänk** [work]bench **-börda** workload, amount of work to be done **-dag** working day, *i sht AE.* workday **-domstol** labour (industrial) court, (*i Storbritannien*) Central Arbitration Committee; *~en* [the Swedish] labour court **-duglig** able to work, fit for work; able-bodied **-fred** industrial peace **-fri** *~ inkomst* unearned income **-fysiologi** industrial physiology **-fält** sphere (field) of activity **-för** *a5* fit for work, able-bodied; *~ ålder* working age; *partiellt ~* physically handicapped **-fördelning** *ekon.* division of labour; *~en* the distribution of the work **-förhållanden** working conditions **-förmedling** employment office, jobcentre; *~en (i Storbritannien)* the Employment Service Agency **-förmåga** capacity for work **-förtjänst** earnings (*pl*), pay
arbetsgivaravgift general payroll tax
arbetsgivar|e employer; master **-förening** employers' association; *Svenska A~en* [the] Swedish Employers' Confederation **-parten** the employers **-uppgift** particulars supplied by employer [regarding salaries *etc.*] **-verk** *A~et*

[the Swedish] national agency for government employers

arbets|glädje pleasure in one's work **-grupp** [working] team **-handskar** protective gloves **-hygien** industrial (occupational) hygiene **-hypotes** working hypothesis (theory) **-häst** carthorse **-inkomst** wage earnings (*pl*), income from work **-inrättning** workhouse institution **-insats** work done; work effort, performance **-inställelse** stoppage of work, strike; lockout **-intensitet** rate of working **-intensiv** labour-intensive **-kamrat** workmate **-kapacitet** working capacity **-karl** workman **-kläder** working clothes; dungarees (*pl*) **-konflikt** labour dispute (conflict) **-kraft** labour, manpower; *en bra ~ a* good worker **-kraftsreserv** manpower reserve **-lag** gang [of workmen], team **-lagstiftning** protective labour legislation, protective legislation for the workers **-ledare** foreman (*fem.* forewoman), supervisor **-ledning** [labour] management **-liv** working life **-livscentrum** centre for working life **-livserfarenhet** [professional] experience **-lokal** workroom; factory premises (*pl*) **-lust** zeal, zest **-läger** work camp **-lön** wages (*pl*), pay

arbetslös unemployed, out of work; *en ~* an unemployed person; *de ~a* the unemployed **-het** unemployment

arbetslöshets|försäkring unemployment insurance **-kassa** unemployment fund **-understöd** unemployment benefit (*AE.* compensation); *vard.* dole

arbetsmarknad labour market

arbetsmarknads|departement ministry of labour; *AE.* department of labor **-konflikt** *se arbetskonflikt* **-minister** minister of labour; *AE.* secretary of labor **-nämnd** *Statens a~* [the Swedish] national board for government employees **-politik** labour market policy **-styrelse** *~n* [the Swedish] national labour market board; (*i Storbritannien*) the Manpower Services Commission **-utbildning** vocational advancement **-utskott** *~et* [the Swedish parliamentary] standing committee on the labour market

arbets|material working material **-medicin** industrial (occupational) medicine **-metod** method of work[ing] **-miljö** work environment **-moment** suboperation, work operation **-myra** working-ant: *bildl.* busy bee **-människa** hard worker **-namn** [tentative] working title **-narkoman** workaholic **-nedläggelse** [work] stoppage, strike **-oduglig** unfit for work **-oförmåga** incapacity for work; disablement **-oförmögen** unable to work, incapacitated; (*varaktigt*) disabled, invalid **-ordning** work[ing] plan; programme **-ovillig** *se -skygg* **-pass** shift, working period **-plats** place of work; *byggn. äv.* [working] site; (*lokal*) [factory] premises (*pl*), office **-plikt** obligation to work **-prestation** output of work, performance **-program** working programme **-projektor** overhead projector **-psykologi** occupational psychology **-ritning** workshop drawing **-ro** quiet (peace of mind) essential for work; good working atmosphere **-rock** work-coat; smock **-rum**

workroom, study **-rätt** *jur.* labour law **-skygg** workshy **-studieingenjör** work-study engineer **-studieman** time and motion study man **-studier** time and motion study (*sg*) **-stycke** workpiece, piece to be machined **-styrka** labour force, number of hands **-sökande** job-seeker **-tag** *vara i ~en* be hard at work **-tagare** employee; (*arbetare*) wage earner (*AE. worker*); (*tjänsteman*) salaried employee **-takt** working pace; (*i motor*) power stroke; *han har en hög ~* he works quickly **-tempo** *se -takt* **-terapeut** occupational therapist **-terapi** occupational therapy **-tid** working hours, hours of work (*pl*); *efter ~ens slut* after hours **-tidsförkortning** reduction in working hours **-tillfälle** vacant job, job opportunity **-tillstånd** work permit **-uppgift** task, assignment **-utskott** working committee (party) **-vecka** working week, *i sht AE.* work week **-villkor** working conditions **-värdering** job evaluation **-växling** job rotation

arbitrage *s7* **1** *hand.* arbitrage, foreign exhange dealings (*pl*) **2** *jur.* arbitration, arbitral award **-affärer** *pl, se arbitrage 1*

arbi'trär *a5* arbitrary

ardennerhäst [-ˣdenner-] Ardennes carthorse

Ardennerna [-'denn-] *pl* the Ardennes

area ['a:-] *s1* area **are'al** *s3* area, space; (*jordegendoms*) acreage

arekapalm [aˣre:-] betel palm, areca

arena [aˣre:na] *s1* arena; *bildl.* scene of action **-teater** theatre-in-the-round, arena theatre

areometer [-'me:-] *s2* hydrometer

arg [-j] *a1* (*vred*) angry (*på ngn* with s.b.; *på ngt* at s.th.); *AE. o. vard.* mad; (*illvillig*) malicious, ill-natured; (*ilsken*) savage; *~ fiende* bitter enemy; *en ~ hund* a savage (vicious) dog; *~a konkurrenter* keen competitors, (*starkare*) ruthless rivals; *ana ~an list* suspect mischief, *vard.* smell a rat; *bli ~* get angry (*på ngn* with s.b.); *~a katter får rivet skinn* quarrelsome dogs get dirty coats (come limping home) **-bigga** *s1* shrew, vixen

Argentina [-ˣti:-] *n* Argentina, the Argentine **argent|inare** [-ˣti:-] *s9*, **-insk** [-'ti:-] *a5* Argentine, Argentinean

argon [-'å:n *el.* 'arg-] *s4* argon

argsint [ˣarj-] *a1* ill-tempered, irascible

argument *s7* argument **argumentation** argumentation, arguing **argumentationsanalys** argument analysis

argumenter|a argue **-ing** *se argumentation*

argusögon *med* ~ Argus-eyed, vigilant

aria ['a:-] *s1* aria

arier ['a:-] *s9*, **arisk** ['a:-] *a5* Aryan, Arian

aristo|krat aristocrat **-kra'ti** *s3* aristocracy **-kratisk** [-'kra:-] *a5* aristocratic

aritmet|ik *s3* arithmetic **-isk** [-'me:-] *a5* arithmetic[al]; *~t medium* arithmetic mean; *~ serie* arithmetic progression, (*summa*) arithmetic series

1 ark *s2* ark; *förbundets ~* the Ark of Covenant; *Noas ~* Noah's Ark

2 ark *s7* sheet [of paper]; (*del av bok*) sheet, section; *falsade ~* folded sheets

ar'kad *s3* arcade

Arkadien [-'ka:-] *n* Arcady, Arcadia

arkadisk [-'ka:-] *a5* Arcadian
arka|iserande [-'se:-] *a4* archaizing **-isk** [-'ka:-] *a5* archaic **-ism** *s3* archaism
Arkangelsk [-'kaŋ-] *n* Archangel
arkebuser|a [-k-] shoot **-ing** execution by a firing squad
arkeo|log arch[a]eologist **-lo'gi** *s3* arch[a]eology **-logisk** [-'lå:-] *a5* arch[a]elogical
arkipe'lag [-k-] *s3* archipelago
arki'tekt [-ki- *el.* -çi-] *s3* architect **-kontor** architect's office
arkitektonisk [-ki-, -çi-, -'tω:-] *a5* architectural, architectonic **arkitektur** architecture
ar'kiv [-k-] *s7* archives (*pl*); (*dokumentsamling* *äv.*) records (*pl*); (*bild- o.d.*) library; (*ämbetsverk*) record office **-alier** [-'va:-] *pl* records; rolls **-arie** [-'va:-] *s5* archivist; keeper of public records; *förste ~* senior archivist
arkiver|a file **-ing** filing
arkiv|exemplar (*lagstadgat*) statutory copy; (*hand.*) voucher copy; (*kontorsterm*) file copy **-forskning** archival research work **-skåp** filing cabinet
Arktis ['ark-] *n* the Arctic [zone]
arktisk ['ark-] *a5* Arctic
arla [ˣa:r-] early [in the morning]
1 arm *a1* (*stackars, fattig*) poor; (*utblottad*) destitute; (*usel*) wretched, miserable
2 arm *s2* arm; (*av flod, ljusstake etc.*) branch; *lagens ~* the arm of the law; *med ~arna i kors* with folded arms; *med öppna ~ar* with open arms; *på rak ~* (*bildl.*) offhand, straight; *bjuda ngn ~en* offer a p. one's arm; *gå ~ i ~* walk arm in arm; *hålla ngn under ~arna* (*bildl.*) back up (support) s.b.; *slå ~arna om halsen på ngn* fling one's arms [a]round a p.'s neck
armada [-ˣma:-] *s1* armada
armatur 1 *elektr.* [electric] fittings (*pl*); (*ljus-*) lighting fitting **2** *tekn.* (*tillbehör*) accessories (*pl*); (*ankare*) armature
arm|band bracelet **-bandsur** wristwatch **-bindel** armlet, armband; *med.* sling **-borst** crossbow **-brott** fractured (broken) arm
arm|båga *~ sig fram* elbow o.s. along **-båge** elbow
armbågs|led elbow joint **-rum** elbowroom **-veck** crook of the arm
armé *s3* army **-attaché** army attaché **-chef** commander in chief of the army **-förband** army troops (*pl*), army unit **-fördelning** [army] division **-förvaltning** army administration **-gevär** service (army) rifle **-kår** army corps **-ledning** army headquarters (*pl*) **-lotta** member of the Women's Royal Army Corps (W.R.A.C.); *AE.* member of the Women's Army Corps (WAC); *vard.* Wrac, *AE.* Wac **-museum** army museum
Armenien [-'me:-] *n* Armenia **armen|ier** [-'me:-] *s9*, **-isk** *a5* Armenian **-iska 1** (*språk*) Armenian **2** (*kvinna*) Armenian woman
armer|a (*beväpna*) arm; (*förstärka*) reinforce; *~d betong* reinforced concrete **-ing** (*beväpning*) armament; (*förstärkning*) reinforcement
armeringsjärn reinforcing bar (iron)
arméstab army staff
arm|foting *zool.* brachiopod, lamp shell **-gång** travelling along the [horizontal] bar **-håla** arm-

pit **-krok** arm in arm; *gå ~* walk arm in arm
armod *s7* poverty, destitution
armring bangle, bracelet
armslängd *på ~s avstånd* at arm's lenght
arm|styrka strenght of [one's] arm **-stöd** elbow rest; (*på stol*) arm [of a chair] **-svett** underarm perspiration, body odour (*förk.* B.O.)
arom [a'rå:m] *s3* aroma, flavour **-atisk** [-'ma:-] *a5* aromatic; *~ förening* aromatic compound; *~t kolväte* aromatic hydrocarbon **-glas** brandy (balloon) glass
arrak ['arrack] *s2* arrack, arak
arrang|emang [-ŋʃe- *el.* -nʃe-] *s7, s4* arrangement; organization **-era** arrange; organize; (*iscensätta*) stage
arrangör [-ŋ'ʃö:r *el.* -n'ʃö:r] arranger; organizer
arrendator *s3* tenant [farmer], leaseholder; lessee
arrende [aˣrende *el.* a'rende] *s6* (*-förhållande*) lease, tenancy; (*-tid*) lease; (*-avgift*) rent[al]; *betala* (*få*) *1 000 pund i ~* pay (get, receive) a rent of 1,000 pounds **-avgift** rent[al] **-gård** leasehold [property], tenant holding **-kontrakt** lease, tenancy agreement **-nämnd** regional tenancies tribunal
arrende|ra lease, rent, take on lease; *~ ut* let out on lease, lease out **-tid** lease
ar'rest *s3* custody, detention; *mil.* arrest; (*lokal*) jail, gaol, *mil.* guardroom; *AE.* brig (*särsk. i fartyg*); *mörk ~* confinement in a dark cell; *sträng ~* close arrest; *sitta i ~* be [kept] in custody; *sätta i ~* place under arrest
arrester|a arrest, take into custody **-ing** arrest[ing] **-ingsorder** warrant [of arrest]
arriärgarde [-ˣä:r-] rearguard
arrog|ans [-'ans *el.* -'aŋs] *s3* arrogance, haughtiness **-ant** [-'ant *el.* -'aŋt] *a1* arrogant, haughty; *vard.* high and mighty
arrowrot ['arråo-] arrowroot
arsel *s7* arse, bum, backside; *AE.* ass
arse'nal *s3* arsenal (*äv. bildl.*), armoury
arse'nik *s3* arsenic **-förgiftning** arsenic poisoning **-haltig** *a1* arsenical
ar'sin *s3* arsine
art [a:rt] *s3* **1** (*sort*) kind, sort **2** (*natur*) nature, character **3** *biol.* species
arta [ˣa:rta] *rfl* shape; *~ sig väl* shape well; *vädret tycks ~ sig* the weather is looking up
arte'fakt *s3* artefact; *AE.* artifact
arteri'ell *a1* arterial
arterioskleros [-'å:s] *s3* arteriosclerosis
artesisk [-'te:-] *a5*, *~ brunn* artesian well
artfrämmande foreign to the species; extraneous
artifici'ell *a1* artificial; (*konstlad*) sham; *~ insemination* artificial insemination; *~ intelligens* artificial intelligence
artig [ˣa:r-] *a1* polite, courteous (*mot* to); (*svagare*) civil (*mot* to); (*uppmärksam*) attentive (*mot* to) **-het** politeness, courtesy; attention; *av ~* out of politeness; *säga ngn en ~* pay s.b. a compliment, flatter s.b.
artighets|betygelse mark of courtesy **-fras** polite phrase **-visit** courtesy call
artikel [-'tick-] *s2* article **-serie** series of articles

artikul|ation articulation **-era** articulate
artilleri artillery, ordnance **-eld** artillery fire, gunfire **-förband** artillery unit **-kår** artillery corps **-pjäs** gun, piece of ordnance **-regemente** artillery regiment; *AE.* artillery group
artillerist artilleryman, gunner
artist (*målare etc.*) artist; (*om skådespelare, musiker e.d.*) artiste **-eri** artistry **-isk** *a5* artistic **-namn** (*skådespelares*) stage name
artnamn specific name
arton [ˣaːr-] *se aderton*
artrik rich in species
ar'trit *s3* arthritis
ar'tros [-å-] *s3* arthrosis
art|skild specifically distinct **-skillnad** specific difference, differentia
ar'tär *s3* artery
arv *s7* inheritance, (*testamenterad egendom*) legacy; *biol.* inheritance; (*andligt*) heritage; *få ett stort* ~ come into a fortune; *få i* ~ inherit; *gå i* ~ be handed down; *lämna ngt i* ~ *åt ngn* leave s.th. [as a legacy] to s.b.; *skifta* ~ divide an inheritance, distribute an estate (the estate of a deceased person); *den är ett* ~ *efter min mor* my mother left it to me; *rött hår är ett* ~ *i släkten* red hair runs in the family
arve|del share of an inheritance **-gods** hereditary (family) estate; inheritance
arv|fiende hereditary foe **-furste** hereditary prince **-följd** succession **-gods** *se arvegods*
arving|e *s2* heir, *fem.* heiress; *utan -ar* without issue, heirless
arvlös disinherited; *göra* ~ disinherit, cut out of a will
arvod|e *s6* remuneration; (*t. läkare etc.*) fee **-era** pay by fee
arv|prins hereditary prince **-rike** hereditary kingdom
arvs|anlag gene **-anspråk** claim to an inheritance (the succession) **-berättigad** entitled to an inheritance
arvskifte distribution of an estate; division of an inheritance
arvs|lott share (portion, part) of an inheritance **-massa** germ plasm; hereditary factors (*pl*) **-rätt** *jur.* law of succession (inheritance) **-skatt** death (succession) duty, inheritance tax **-tvist** dispute about an inheritance
arv|synd original sin **-tagare** *se arvinge* **-tant** wealthy aunt [who may leave me (*etc.*) money]
1 as *s7* (*djurlik*) carcass, carrion
2 as *s2, myt.* As (*pl* Æsir)
asalära Æsir cult
asbest ['ass-] *s2* asbestos **-os** [-'åːs] *s3* asbestosis **-platta** asbestos mat (plate)
asch [aʃ] pooh!
asept|ik *s3* asepsis **-isk** [a'sept-] *a5* aseptic
asfalt [ˣass-] *s3* asphalt, bitumen **-beläggning** asphalt surface; tarmac; (*i motsats t. grusväg ofta*) road metal **-era** asphalt, coat with asphalt
asfalt|kokare tar boiler **-läggare** asphalter **-papp** asphalt roofing felt **-tjära** mineral tar
asfull *vard.* tight, canned, smashed, dead drunk
asiat *s3* Asian **-isk** *a5* Asian **Asien** ['aː-] *n* Asia; *Främre* ~ the Middle East; *Mindre* ~ Asia Minor

asi'mut [*äv.* 'aː-] *s3* azimuth
1 ask *s2, bot.* ash [tree]; *av* ~ (*äv.*) ash[en]
2 ask *s2* box; (*bleck-*) tin [box]; *en* ~ *cigaretter* a packet of cigarettes
aska I *s2* ashes (*pl*); (*av visst slag*) ash; *ur ~n i elden* out of the frying pan into the fire **II** *v*, ~ [*av*] knock the ash off
A-skatt *ung.* pay-as-you-earn (P.A.Y.E.)
askblond ash blond
as'k|es *s3* asceticism **-et** *s3* ascetic **-etisk** [-'keː-] *a5* ascetic[al] **-etism** asceticism
ask|fat ashtray **-grå** ashen, ashgrey **-kopp** *se askfat* **-onsdag** Ash Wednesday
askorbinsyra [-ˣbiːn-] ascorbic acid
askregn shower of ashes
Askungen Cinderella
askurna cinerary urn
asoci'al *a1* antisocial, asocial **-itet** social maladjustment
1 asp *s2, zool.* rapacious carp
2 asp *s2, bot.* aspen; *av* ~ (*äv.*) aspen
as'pekt *s3* aspect
aspir|ant applicant, candidate (*till* for); trainee; *bildl.* aspirant (*på, till* to); *mil.* cadet **-ation** aspiration **-era 1** *språkv.* aspirate **2** ~ *på* aspire to, aim at
aspi'rin *s4* aspirin
asp|löv aspen leaf **-virke** aspen [wood]
1 ass *s7, se assurera*
2 ass *s7, mus.* A flat
Ass-dur A flat major
asse'gaj *s3* assegai, assagai
assembler|are [-ˣbleː-] *data.* assembler **-ingspråk** assembly (assembler) language
assessor [aˣsessår] *s3* assessor; deputy judge
assiett [a'ʃett] *s3* (*tallrik*) small plate; (*maträtt*) hors d'œuvre dish
assimil|ation assimilation **-era** assimilate
assist|ans [-'ans *el.* -'aŋs] *s3* assistance **-ent** assistant; (*tjänstetitel*) clerical officer **-era I** (*hjälpa till*) assist; act as assistant **II** (*hjälpa*) assist, help
associa|tion association **-tionsförmåga** ability to form associations **-'tiv** *a5* associative
associer|a associate; ~ *sig med* associate with **-ing** association
assonans [-'aŋs *el.* -'ans] *s3* assonance
assuradör *m* insurer; (*sjöförsäkr. äv.*) underwriter; (*livförsäkr. äv.*) assurer
assurans [-'ans *el.* -'aŋs] *s3* insurance **-belopp** insured value
assurer|a insure; ~*t brev* insured letter **-ing** insurance
Assyrien [a'syː-] *n* Assyria **assyr|ier** *s9*, **-isk** *a5* Assyrian **-iska 1** (*språk*) Assyrian **2** (*kvinna*) Assyrian woman
astat astatine
aste'n|i *s3* asthenia, astheny **-iker** [-'teː-] *s9*, **-isk** [-'teː-] *a5* asthenic
aster ['ast-] *s2, bot.* aster
aste'risk *s3* asterisk
asteroid [-ɵ'iːd] *s3* asteroid, minor planet
astigmat|iker [-'maː-] *s9*, **-isk** [-'maː-] *a5* astigmatic -ism astigmatism, astigmia
astma *s1* asthma **-anfall** attack of asthma
astmat|iker [-'maː-] *s9*, **-isk** [-'maː-] *a5* asthmatic

astra'kan *s3* (*skinn*) astrakhan
ast'ral *a1* astral **-kropp** astral body
astro|biologi astrobiology **-fy'sik** astrophysics (*pl, behandlas som sg*) **-geologi** astrogeology **-kemi** astrochemistry **-log** astrologer, astrologist **-lo'gi** *s3* astrology **-logisk** [-'lå:-] *a5* astrological **-me'tri** *s3* astrometry **-'naut** *s3* astronaut **-nau'tik** astronautics (*pl, behandlas som sg*) **-nom** astronomer **-nomi** *s3* astronomy **-nomisk** *a5* astronomic[al]; ~ *enhet* astronomical unit; ~ *navigation* celestial navigation, astronavigation
asur *se azur*
a'syl *s3* asylum, [place of] refuge; (*fristad*) sanctuary **-rätt** right of asylum **-sökande** *s* person seeking asylum
asymme'tr|i *s3* asymmetry **-isk** [-'me:-] *a5* asymmetric[al]
asymptot [-'tå:t] *s3* asymptote
asynkron [-'å:n] asynchronous
atavis|m *s3* atavism **-tisk** *a5* atavistic, atavic
ate|ism atheism **-ist** atheist **-istisk** *a5* atheistic[al]
ateljé *s3* studio; (*sy- etc.*) workroom
A'ten *n* Athens
atenare [-ˣte:-] *s9*, **atensk** [-'te:nsk] *a5* Athenian
ater'man *a5* athermanous
atlantdeklarationen [-ˣlant-] the Atlantic Charter
Atlanten [-'lant-] *n* the Atlantic [Ocean]
atlant|fartyg [-ˣlant-] transatlantic liner **-pakten** the North Atlantic Treaty **-paktsorganisationen** the North Atlantic Treaty Organization (NATO) **-ångare** *se atlantfartyg*
1 atlas ['att-] *s3* (*tyg*) satin
2 atlas ['att-] *s3* (*kartbok*) atlas (*över* of); (*kota*) atlas
Atlasbergen [ˣatt-] *pl* the Atlas Mountains
at'let *s3* athlete; (*stark man*) strong man, Hercules **-isk** *a5* athletic
atmo'sfär *s3* atmosphere **-isk** atmospheric[al]; ~*a störningar* atmospherics; *radio. äv.* [radio] interference **-tryck** atmospheric pressure
a'toll [-å-] *s3* atoll
atom [a'tå:m] *s3* atom **-bomb** atom[ic] bomb, A-bomb, fission bomb **-drift** atomic propulsion (operation) **-driven** nuclear-powered, atomic-powered **-energi** *se kärnenergi* **-forskare** nuclear scientist **-forskning** nuclear research **-fysik** nuclear physics **-klocka** atomic clock **-kraft** *se kärnkraft* **-kärna** [atomic] nucleus **-massa** atomic mass; *relativ* ~ relative atomic mass **-masseenhet** [unified] atomic mass unit, dalton **-mila** nuclear reactor; (*äldre namn*) atomic pile **-nummer** atomic (proton) number **-reaktor** nuclear reactor **-sopor** nuclear waste (*sg*) **-sprängning** nuclear fission **-teori** atomic theory **-ubåt** nuclear[-powered] submarine **-ur** *se -klocka* **-vapen** nuclear (atomic) weapon **-vikt** atomic weight **-värde** valency, *särsk. AE.* valence **-åldern** the atomic age
ato'mär *a5* atomic
ato'nal *a5* atonal
ATP [ate'pe:] *r* (*förk. för allmän tilläggspensionering*) *se tilläggspensionering*

atrium ['a:-] *s4* atrium **-hus** atrium house; courtyard house
atro'f|i *s3*, **-iera[s]** *v1* atrophy **-isk** [-'trå:-] *a5* atrophic
atro'pin *s7, s3* atropin[e]
att I *infinitivmärke* to; ~ *vara eller inte vara* to be or not to be; ~ *åka skidor är roligt* skiing is fun; *genom* ~ *arbeta* by working; *av utseendet* ~ *döma* judging (to judge) by appearances; *envisas med* ~ *göra ngt* persist in doing s.th.; *efter* ~ *ha misslyckats* having failed; *vanan* ~ *röka* the habit of smoking; *skicklig i* ~ *sy* good at sewing; *sanningen* ~ *säga* to tell the truth; *han lämnade landet för* ~ *aldrig återvända* he left the country never to return; *han var rädd* ~ *störa henne* he was afraid of disturbing her; *han är inte* ~ *leka med* he is not [a man] to be trifled with, he is not one to stand any nonsense; *jag kunde inte låta bli* ~ *skratta* I could not help laughing; *vad hindrar honom från* ~ *resa* what prevents him from going **II** *konj* that; *på det* ~, *så* ~ [in order] that, so that; *under det* ~ while; whereas; *vänta på* ~ *ngn skall komma* wait for s.b. to come; *förlåt* ~ *jag stör* excuse my (me) disturbing you; ~ *du inte skäms!* you ought to be ashamed of yourself!; ~ *jag inte tänkte på det!* why didn't I think of that!; *utan* ~ *ngn såg honom* without anyone seeing him; *frånsett* ~ *han inte tycker om musik* apart from the fact that he does not like music; *jag litar på* ~ *du gör det* I rely on your doing it, I am relying on you to do it; *jag trodde* ~ *han skulle komma* I thought [that] he would come; *jag är glad* ~ *det är över* I am glad [that] it is over; *så dumt* ~ *jag inte kom ihåg det* how stupid of me not to remember it; *säg till honom* ~ *han gör det* tell him to do it
attaché [-'ʃe:] *s3* attaché **-väska** attaché case
at'tack *s3* attack (*mot, på* on); (*sjukdoms-*) attack, fit **-era** attack **-plan** fighter [aircraft] **-robot** air-to-surface missile
attent|at *s7* attempt (*mot ngn* on a p.'s life), attempted assassination; (*friare*) outrage (*mot* on) **-ator** *s3* would-be assassin; perpetrator of an (the) outrage
at'test *s3* attestation (*på* to); certificate, testimonial **-era** attest, certify
atti'ralj *s3* apparatus; paraphernalia (*pl*)
attisk ['att-] *a5* Attic; ~*t salt* Attic salt (wit)
atti'tyd *s3* attitude; posture, pose
atto- atto-
attrahera attract
attrak|tion [-k'ʃɵ:n] attraction, appeal **-tionsförmåga** [power of] attraction **-'tiv** *a1* attractive, appealing **-tivitet** attractiveness, attractivity, attraction
at'trapp *s3* dummy
attri|buera *v1*, **-'but** *s7* attribute **-bu'tiv** *a1* attributive
att-sats that-clause
aubergine [åbær'ʃinn] *s5* aubergine; *AE.* eggplant
audi'ens [au-] *s3* audience; *få* ~ *hos* obtain an audience of (with); *mottaga ngn i* ~ receive s.b. [in audience]; *söka* ~ *hos* seek an audience with

audio|gram [audiɷ'gramm] s7 audiogram **-logi** s3 audiology **-meter** [-'me:-] s2 audiometer **-me'tri** s3 audiometry **-visuell** se audivisuell

audi|'tiv [au-] a5 auditory **-torium** [-'tɷ:-] s4 (sal) auditorium; (åhörare) audience **-tör** judicial adviser (advisor) [to a regiment]; (vid krigsrätt) judge advocate

audivisu'ell [au-] a1 audiovisual; ~a hjälpmedel audiovisual aids

augiasstall [ˣaugias-, äv. -ˣgi:as-] Augean stables (pl)

augur [au-] augur; soothsayer **-leende** ung. conspiratorial smile

augusti [au'gusti] r August

augustiner [augus'ti:-] s9 Augustine friar

augustin[er]|munk Augustine friar **-orden** Order of St. Augustine

Augustinus [augus'ti:-] St. Augustine

auktion [auk'ʃɷ:n] [sale by] auction, [public] sale (på of); exekutiv ~ compulsory auction; köpa på ~ buy at an auction; sälja på ~ sell by auction **-era** ~ bort auction [off], auctioneer, sell by auction **-ist** se auktions|förrättare, -utropare

auktions|bridge auction bridge **-bud** bid at an auction **-förrättare** auctioneer **-kammare** auction rooms (pl) **-utropare** auctioneer, auctioneer's assistant

auktor ['auktår] s3 author; (sagesman) authority, informant

auktoris|ation [au-] authorization **-era** authorize; ~d revisor chartered accountant **-ering** se auktorisation

auktori|ta'tiv [au-] a1 authoritative; på ~t håll in authoritative circles **-tet** authority **-tetstro** belief in authority **-'tär** a5 authoritarian

auktorskap s7 authorship

auktorsrätt copyright

aula ['au-] s1 assembly hall, lecture hall; AE. auditorium

aura ['au-] s1 aura

aureomy'cin [au-] s7 aureomycin

aurikel [au'rickel] s3, s2, bot. auricula

auskult|ant [au-] **1** skol., ung. student teacher observing classroom methods **2** med. auscultator **-ation 1** skol. attending classes as an observer **2** med. auscultation, stethoscopy **-era 1** skol. attend classes as an observer **2** med. auscultate

auspicier [au'spi:-] pl auspices; under ngns ~ under the auspices of s.b.

Australien [au'stra:-] n Australia

austral|iensare [-ˣensa-] s9, **-ier** [-'stra:-] s9, **-isk** [-'stra:-] a5 Australian **-neger** Australian aborigene, native Australian

autar'ki [au-] s3 autarchy; (självförsörjning) autarky, anarchy

autent|icitet [au-] authenticity, genuineness **-isk** [-'tenn-] a5 authentic

aut|ism [au-] autism **-ist** autistic person **-istisk** a5 autistic

autodafé [au-] s3 auto-da-fé

autodi'dakt [au-] s3 autodidact, self-taught person **-isk** a5 autodidactic, self-taught

auto|gen [autɷ'je:n] a5 autogenous **-giro** [-'ji:-] s5 autogiro, gyroplane

autograf [au-] s3 autograph **-isk** a5 autographic[al] **-jägare** autograph hunter

auto|'klav [au-] s3 autoclave; sterilizer **-krat** autocrat **-kra'ti** s3 autocracy **-kratisk** [-'kra:-] a5 autocratic

automat [au-] automatic machine, automaton; (varu-) slot machine; vending machine, automat; (person) automaton **-gevär** automatic [rifle]

automa|'tik [au-] s3 automatism **-tion** automation

automatiser|a [au-] introduce automatic operation; automate; tel. automatize **-ing** automation, automatization

automat|isk [autɷ'ma:-] a5 automatic; ~ databehandling automatic data processing **-kanon** automatic gun **-låda** (i bil) se -växel **-pistol** automatic [pistol] **-svarv** automatic lathe **-telefon** dial (automatic) telephone **-vapen** automatic weapon **-växel** tel. automatic switchboard; (i bil) (-växellåda) automatic gearbox (transmission), (-växling) automatic gear-change

automo'bil [au-] s3 [motor]car, automobile

auto|nom [au-] a5 autonomous; ~a nervsystemet autonomic nervous system **-nomi** s3 autonomy **-pilot** automatic pilot, autopilot

auto'psi [au-] s3 autopsy, postmortem examination

auto|strada [autɷˣstra:da] s1, se motorväg **-ty'pi** s3 halftone [plate]

av I prep **1** vanl. of; ~ god familj of good family; född ~ fattiga föräldrar born of poor parents; en man ~ folket a man of the people; en man ~ heder a man of honour; drottningen ~ England the queen of England; ett tal ~ Churchill a speech of Churchill's (jfr 2); turkarnas erövring ~ Wien the conquest of Vienna by the Turks; ingen ~ dem none of them; ägaren ~ huset the owner of the house; hälften ~ boken half [of] the book; en klänning ~ siden a dress of silk, a silk dress; byggd ~ trä built of wood; till ett pris ~ at a (the) price of; en del ~ tiden part of the time; i två fall ~ tre in two cases out of three; ett avstånd ~ fem kilometer a distance of five kilometres; det var snällt ~ dig it was kind of you; vad har det blivit ~ henne? what has become of her? **2** (betecknande den handlande, medlet) by; ~ en händelse by chance; ~ misstag by mistake; ~ naturen by nature; ett tal ~ Churchill a speech made by Churchill (jfr 1); författad ~ Byron written by Byron; hatad ~ många hated by many; leva ~ sitt arbete live by one's work **3** (betecknande orsak) a) (t. ofrivillig handling el. tillstånd) with, ibl. for, b) (t. frivillig handling) out of, c) (i en del stående uttryck) for, on; ~ allt mitt hjärta with all my heart; ~ brist på for want of; ~ den anledningen for that reason; ~ fruktan för for fear of; ~ nyfikenhet out of curiosity; ~ olika orsaker for various reasons; ~ princip on principle; darra ~ köld (rädsla) shiver with cold (fear); gråta ~ glädje weep for joy; leva ~ fisk live on fish; skrika ~ förtjusning scream with delight; utom sig ~ raseri beside o.s. with rage **4** göra ngt ~ sig själv do s.th. by o.s. (of one's own accord); det faller ~ sig själv[t] it is a matter of course; det *går* ~ *sig själv*[*t*] it runs by (of) itself **5** *(från)* from; *(bort från)* off; ~ *egen erfarenhet* from [my own] experience; ~ *gammalt* from of old; ~ *gammal vana* from force of habit; *svart* ~ *sot* black from soot; *en present* ~ *min mor* a present from my mother; *få (köpa, låna, veta) ngt* ~ *ngn* get (buy, borrow, learn) s.th. from s.b.; *gnaga köttet* ~ *benen* gnaw the meat off the bones; *hoppa* ~ *cykeln* jump off one's bicycle; *stiga* ~ *tåget* get off the train; *ta* ~ [*sig*] *skorna* take one's shoes off; ~ *jord är du kommen* from dust art thou come; *det kommer sig* ~ *att jag har* it comes from my having; *vi ser* ~ *Ert brev* we see from your letter **6** *(oöversatt el. annan konstruktion)* ~ *bara tusan* like hell; *med utelämnande* ~ excluding; *rädd* ~ *sig* timid, timorous; *bryta nacken* ~ *sig* break one's neck; *njuta* ~ enjoy; *vara* ~ *samma färg* be the same colour **II** *adv* **1** ~ *och an* to and fro, up and down; ~ *och till* now and then, occasionally **2** *(bort*[*a*]*, ner, i väg)* off; *ge sig* ~ start off; *ramla* ~ fall off *(hästen* the horse); *stiga* ~ *tåget* get off the train; *ta* ~ *till höger* turn [off to the] right; *torka* ~ *dammet* wipe off the dust **3** *borsta* ~ *en kappa* brush a coat, give a coat a brush; *diska* ~ *tallrikarna* wash up the plates; *klä* ~ *ngn* undress s.b.; *lasta* ~ unload; *rita (skriva)* ~ copy; *svimma* ~ faint away **4** *(itu)* in two; *(bruten)* broken; *benet är* ~ the leg is broken; *åran gick* ~ the oar snapped in two

a'val *s3* bank guarantee for a bill

avancemang [-aŋse-] *s7* promotion **avancemangsmöjlighet** promotion prospect[s *pl*], opportunity for promotion **avancera** advance; be promoted, rise; ~*d* advanced, progressive, *(djärv)* bold, daring

avannonsera *(t.ex. radioprogram)* sign off

avans [-'aŋs] *s3* profit, gains *(pl)*

avant|garde [a^xvaŋt- *el.* a'vant-] van[guard]; *konst. o.d.* avant-garde **-gardism** avant-gardism **-gardist** avant-gardist **-scenloge** stage box

avart variety; *(oart)* degenerate species

avbalk|a partition off **-ning** partitioning off; *konkr.* partition

avbasning [-ba:s-] beating; *(upptuktelse)* scolding

avbeställ|a cancel **-ning** cancellation **-nings-avgift** cancellation fee

avbeta graze; crop

avbetal|a pay off, pay by instalments **-ning** *(belopp)* instalment; *(system)* hire-purchase plan, *AE.* installment buying; *köpa på* ~ buy on the hire-purchase plan

avbetalnings|kontrakt hire-purchase contract **-köp** *(entaka)* hire-purchase transaction; *koll.* hire-purchase **-villkor** hire-purchase terms

avbetning [-e:-] grazing; cropping

av|bild representation; copy; *han är sin fars* ~ he is the very image of his father **-bilda** reproduce; draw, paint **-bildning** reproduction

avbitartång nippers *(pl)*; *en* ~ a pair of nippers

avblås|a bring to an end; *(strid)* call off; *se äv. blåsa av* **-ning** sport. stoppage of game

avbländ|a shade; *foto.* stop down; *se äv. blända av* **-ning** shading *etc.*

avboka cancel

avbrott 1 *(uppehåll)* interruption, break; *(upphörande)* cessation, stop[page], intermission; *(i radioutsändning)* breakdown [in transmission]; *ett* ~ *i fientligheterna* a cessation of hostilities; *ett angenämt* ~ a pleasant break; *ett kort* ~ *i regnandet* a short break in the rain; *utan* ~ without stopping, continuously, without a break **2** *(motsats)* contrast, change; *utgöra ett* ~ *mot* make a change in, break the monotony of

avbrottsförsäkring loss of profits insurance

avbruten broken

avbryta break off, interrupt; cut off; ~ *ngn (vard.)* break (butt) in on s.b.; ~ *en resa* break a journey; ~ *ett samtal* cut short a conversation; ~ *förhandlingar* break off negotiations; ~ *sitt arbete* stop work, leave off working; ~ *sig* check o.s., stop speaking; *se äv. bryta av*

av|bräck *s7 (skada)* damage, injury; *(men)* disadvantage; *lida* ~ suffer a setback **-bränning** *hand.* deduction [from profits], incidental expenses **-bröstning** *mil.* unlimbering **-bytare** replacement, relief, substitute; *(för chaufför)* driver's mate; *(vid motortävling)* co-driver **-böja** decline, refuse; ~ *ett erbjudande* decline an offer; ~*nde svar* refusal, answer in the negative **-böjning** *radar.* deflection **-bön** apology; *göra* ~ apologize **-börda 1** *(samvete)* unburden **2** *rfl* free o.s. of; ~ *sig en skuld* discharge a debt

av|dagataga [-^xda:-] put to death **-damning** *ge ngt en* ~ give s.th. a dust **-dankad** *a5* discharged, discarded

avdel|a *(uppdela)* divide [up] *(i* into), partition [off]; divide off; *mil.* detail, tell off **-ning** *(del)* part; *(avsnitt)* section; *(av skola, domstol)* division; *(av företag)* department, division; *(sjukhus-, fängelse-)* ward; *(i skåp)* compartment; *mil.* detachment, unit; *(av flotta, flyg)* division, squadron

avdelnings|chef *(i departement)* *ung.* undersecretary; *(i ämbetsverk)* head of a department; *(i affär)* departmental manager **-direktör** principal administrative officer **-kontor** branch [office] **-sköterska** ward sister, head-nurse

avdik|a *(mark)* drain; *(vatten)* drain off **-ning** [-i:-] draining, drainage

avdomna *se domna*

avdrag 1 deduction; *(beviljat)* allowance; *(rabatt äv.)* reduction; *(på skatt)* abatement, relief; ~ *för inkomstens förvärvande* professional outlay (expenses *pl*); *efter* ~ *av omkostnaderna* expenses deducted; *med* ~ *för* after a deduction of; *göra* ~ *för* deduct; *yrka* ~ *med 1000 pund* claim a deduction of 1,000 pounds **2** *boktr.* proof [sheet], pull, impression

avdraga 1 *(draga ifrån)* deduct, take **2** *boktr.* pull

avdragsgill deductible; ~*t belopp* allowable deduction

av|dramatisera play down **-drift** *sjö.* drift; leeway; *(projektils)* deviation

avdunst|a evaporate; *(försvinna)* clear off (out) **-ning** evaporation

av|döda ~*t vaccin* killed-virus vaccine **-döma** decide, judge

avel ['a:-] *s2* breeding, rearing
avels|djur breeder; *koll.* breeding-stock **-hingst** stallion, studhorse **-reaktor** breeder [reactor] **-sto** brood mare **-sugga** *ung.* prize sow **-tjur** breeding bull
avenbok [ˣa:-] *s2* hornbeam, ironwood
ave'ny *s3* avenue
aversion [-r'ʃɷ:n] aversion (*mot* to)
av|fall 1 (*avskräde*) waste, refuse; (*köks-*) garbage, rubbish; (*vid slakt*) offal; *radioaktivt ~* radioactive waste[s *pl*] **2** *bildl.* falling away, backsliding; (*från parti*) desertion, defection; (*från religion*) apostasy **-falla** fall away (*från* from); desert (*från* from), turn deserter (apostate), defect **-fallen 1** (*om frukt etc.*) fallen **2** (*mager*) thin, worn; *-fallna kinder* pinched cheeks
avfalls|kvarn [garbage] disposer **-kärl** dustbin; *AE.* garbage (trash) can **-produkt** waste product; *kem.* residual product
av|fart[sväg] slip road, turn-off; exit [road] **-fasa** bevel, slope, cant **-fasning** bevel **-fatta** word, indite; (*avtal*) draw up; (*lagförslag*) draft **-fattning** version; wording, draft **-fetta** defat, degrease **-flytta** move [away] **-flyttning** removal; *de är uppsagda till ~* they have been given notice to quit **-flöde** outflow, effluent
avfolk|a [-å-] depopulate, unpeople **-ning** depopulation **-ningsbygd** depopulated region, depressed area
av|fordra *~ ngn ngt* demand s.th. from (of) s.b., call upon s.b. for s.th.; *~ ngn räkenskap* call s.b. to account (*över* for) **-frosta** [-å-] defrost **-frostning** [-å-] defrosting **-fuktning** dehumidification
avfyr|a fire [off], discharge **-[n]ing** firing [off], discharge **-[n]ingsramp** launch[ing] pad
av|fälling apostate, renegade, backslider **-färd** departure, going away, start **-färda** [-ä:-] **1** (*skicka*) dispatch, send off **2** (*bli färdig med*) dismiss (finish with) (*ngn* s.b.); finish (*ngt* s.th.); *jag låter inte ~ mig så lätt* I am not going to be put off that easily **-färga 1** (*beröva färgen*) decolour, bleach, decolorize **2** *se färga* **-färgning** bleaching, discolouration **-föda** offspring, progeny, brood; *I huggormars ~* (*bibl.*) O, generation of vipers
avför|a 1 (*bortföra*) remove, carry off **2** (*utstryka*) cancel, cross out (*från from*); *~ från dagordningen* remove from the agenda; *~ ur ett register* strike off a register **-ing 1** removal, cancelling **2** *med.* evacuation [of the bowels], motion; *konkr.* motions (*pl*), faeces (*pl*) **-ings-medel** laxative; purgative
avgas exhaust [gas] **-renare** exhaust purifier [device] **-rening** exhaust emission control **-rör** exhaust pipe **-ventil** exhaust valve
avge 1 (*ge ifrån sig, avsöndra*) emit, give off; yield **2** (*lämna, avlägga*) give; *~ ett omdöme om* give (deliver) an opinion on; *~ protest* make (lodge) a protest; *~ sin röst* cast one's vote; *~ vittnesmål* give evidence, testify
avgift [-j-] *s3* charge; (*medlems- etc.*) fee, dues (*pl*); (*tull-*) duty; (*hamn-*) dues (*pl*); (*för färd*) fare; *extra ~* surcharge, additional charge; *för halv ~* at half price (fare, fee); *mot ~* at a fee; *utan ~* free of charge

avgifta [-j-] detoxify; detoxicate
avgifts|belagd *a5* subject to a charge **-belägga** put a charge on **-fri** free [of charge]
av|giva *se avge* **-gjord** decided; (*påtaglig*) distinct; definite; *-gjort!* done!, it's a bargain!; *en ~ förbättring* a marked improvement; *en ~ sak* a settled thing; *en på förhand ~ sak* a foregone conclusion
av|gjuta take a cast of **-gjutning** casting; *konkr.* cast **-gnaga** gnaw off; *~ ett ben* pick a bone **-grena** *rfl* branch off **-grening** branch; (*rör*) branch pipe
avgrund *s3* abyss, precipice; (*klyfta*) chasm; (*svalg*) gulf; *bildl.* pit; (*helvete*) hell
avgrunds|ande infernal spirit, fiend **-djup I** *a5* abysmal, unfathomable **II** *s7* [abysmal] depths (*pl*), abyss **-kval** *pl* pains of hell **-lik** *a5* abysmal, hellish
avgräns|a demarcate, delimit; *klart ~d* clearly defined **-ning** demarcation, delimitation
av|gud idol, god **-guda** idolize, adore (*äv. bildl.*)
avguda|bild idol; image of a god **-dyrkan** idol worship, idolatry **-dyrkare** idol worshipper, idolater (*fem.* idolatress)
avguderi idolatry
avgå 1 leave, start, depart; (*om fartyg äv.*) sail (*till* for); *~ende tåg* (*i tidtabell o.d.*) outgoing trains, departures [of trains] **2** (*avsändas*) be sent off (dispatched) (*till* to); *~ende brev* outgoing letters; *~ende gods* outward goods **3** *bildl.* retire, resign; *~ med döden* decease; *~ med seger* come off (emerge, be) victorious **4** (*vid räkning*) be deducted; *78 kr ~r för omkostnader* less 78 kronor for expenses **5** (*förflyktigas*) evaporate, vanish
avgång 1 departure, (*fartyg äv.*) sailing (*från* from; *till* to, for) **2** (*persons*) retirement, resignation; *naturlig ~* natural wastage
avgångs|betyg leaving certificate **-examen** final (leaving) examination **-hall** departure hall **-hamn** port of departure **-signal** starting signal **-station** departure station **-tid** time of departure **-vederlag** severance pay; *vard.* golden handshake
avgäld rent [in kind]
avgäng|a thread off **-ning** threading off
avgör|a decide; (*bedöma*) determine (*huruvida* whether); (*slutgiltigt bestämma*) settle, conclude **-ande I** *a4, ~ beslut* final decision; *~ betydelse* vital importance; *~ faktor* determining factor; *~ prov* crucial test; *~ seger* (*steg*) decisive victory (step); *~ skäl* conclusive argument; *~ stöt* decisive blow; *~ ögonblick* critical (crucial) moment **II** *s6* (*jfr avgöra*); deciding, decision; determination; settlement; conclusion; *i ~ts stund* in the hour of decision; *träffa ett ~* make a decision
av|handla (*förhandla om*) discuss; (*behandla*) deal with, treat [of] **-handling** (*skrift*) treatise; (*akademisk*) thesis, dissertation; (*friare*) essay, paper (*över* on) **-hjälpa** (*fel*) remedy; (*missförhållande*) redress; (*nöd*) relieve; (*brist*) supply; (*skada*) repair; *skadan är lätt att ~* the damage is easily repaired (put right) **-hopp** *polit.* defection **-hoppare** *polit.* person seeking political asylum, defector **-hugga** hew (lop) off; chop (cut) off; (*knut o.d.*) sever **-hysa**

evict **-hysning** [-y:-] eviction **-hyvla** plane smooth; (*borttaga med hyvel*) plane off (away) **-hyvling** [-y:-] planing down (off, away); *bildl.* dressing down

avhåll|a 1 (*hindra*) keep, restrain, deter, prevent (*från* from) **2** (*möte o.d.*) hold **3** ~ *sig från a*) keep away from, *b*) (*nöjen o.d.*) abstain from, *c*) (*att uttala sin mening*) refrain from, *d*) (*undvika sällskap med*) shun, avoid; ~ *sig från att röka* abstain from smoking **-en** *a5* beloved, dear[ly loved], cherished; (*svagare*) popular **-sam** *al* temperate, abstemious **-samhet** temperance, abstemiousness; *fullständig* ~ total abstinence

av|hämta fetch, call for, collect **-hämtning** collection; *till* ~ (*om paket*) to be called for **-hända** deprive [s.b.] of; ~ *sig* part with **-hängig** [-häŋig] dependent (*av* on) **-hängighet** [-häŋig-] dependence **-härda** soften, wet **-härdning** softening, wetting **-härdningsmedel** [water] softener **-höra** listen to; (*obemärkt*) overhear; (*förhöra*) examine

a'vi *s3* advice, notice; ~ *om försändelse* dispatch note

aviat|ik *s3* aviation **-iker** [-'a:ti-] aviator

avig *al* **1** wrong; inside out; (*i stickning*) purl **2** (*om person*) awkward

avig|a *sl,* **-sida** *sl* wrong side, back, reverse; *det har sina -sidor* it has its drawbacks **-vänd** *a5* turned inside (wrong side) out

1 avisa [a*vi:-] *sl* newspaper

2 avisa [*a:v-] *vl* de-ice

aviser|a advise, notify, inform **-ing** (*aviserande*) advising; (*avi*) advice

avisoväxel [a*vi:-] bill payable at a fixed date after sight, after-sight bill

avista [a*vista] at sight, on demand **-växel** sight draft (bill)

av|jonisering deionization **-jämna** level, make even; (*kant*) trim; *bildl. se avrunda* **-kall** *n,* ge (*göra*) ~ *på* renounce, waive, resign **-kapa** cut off

avkast|a 1 throw off; ~ *oket* shake off the yoke **2** *ekon.* yield, bring in; (*om jord äv.*) produce, bear **-ning** proceeds (*pl*), return[s *pl*], yield; (*behållning*) takings (*pl*); (*vinst*) profit; (*gröda etc.*) produce; *årlig* ~ annual yield (returns *pl*); *ge god* ~ yield well

avkastnings|förmåga earning capacity **-grad** rate of return

av|klara clear, clarify; *se äv. klara av* **-klinga** wear off; *fys.* decay, disintegrate **-klingning** [radioactive] decay, disintegration **-klingningsbassäng** decay tank **-kläda** undress; divest (strip) of; *se äv. klä av* **-klädning** [-ä:-] undressing *etc.* **-klädningshytt** dressing cubicle; (*på badstrand*) bathing hut **-kok** decoction (*på* of) **-komling** [-å-] descendant; child **-komma** [-å-] *sl* offspring, progeny; *jur.* issue **-koppla** uncouple; disconnect; *se äv. koppla av* **-koppling** *tekn.* uncoupling, disconnection; (*avspänning*) relaxation **-korta** shorten, curtail; (*text*) abridge, abbreviate; (*minska*) reduce, diminish **-kortning** [-å-] shortening; abbreviation; reduction, diminution **-kriminalisera** decriminalize **-kristna** dechristianize **-kristning** dechristianization

-krok out-of-the-way spot (corner); *han bor i en* ~ he lives at the back of beyond (*AE. vard.* the sticks) **-kräva** ~ *ngn ngt* demand s.th. from s.b. **-kunna** *vl* pronounce, deliver, pass; (*lysning*) publish; ~ *ett utslag* record a verdict **-kvista** trim [a felled tree] **-kyla** cool, refrigerate; *bildl.* cool down, dampen **-kylning** cooling, refrigeration, chilling **-köna** [-ç-] *en helt ~d varelse* a completely sexless creature

avla [*a:v-] beget, conceive; (*om djur o. bildl.*) breed, engender; ~ *av sig* multiply

av|lagd *a5,* ~*a kläder* discarded (cast-off) clothes (clothing); *jfr avlägga* **-lagra** deposit in layers; ~ *sig* be deposited in layers **-lagring** deposit, stratum (*pl* strata), layer

avlast|a (*befria från last*) unload; (*varor*) discharge; unship; *bildl.* relieve **-are** shipper, consignor, sender **-ning** unloading; discharge; *fys.* stress-relieving, load-relieving; *bildl.* relief

avlat [*a:v-] *s3* indulgence

avlats|brev letter of indulgence **-krämare** seller of indulgences

avled|a carry off; (*vatten*) drain, draw off; (*friare*) turn away (off), divert; (*blixt*) conduct; *språkv.* derive; ~ *misstankarna från* turn away suspicion from; ~ *ngns uppmärksamhet* divert a p.'s attention **-are** conductor; *bildl.* diversion **-ning** conduction; diversion; *språkv.* derivative

avledningsändelse derivative ending (suffix)

avlelse [*a:v-] conception; *den obefläckade* ~*n* the Immaculate Conception

avleverera deliver [up]

av|lida die, expire, pass away (on, over) **-liden** *a5* deceased, dead; *den -lidne* the deceased, *AE.* the decedent; *den -lidne president R.* the late President R.

avling [*a:vliŋ] propagation, breeding **avlingsduglig** procreative, reproductive

av|liva put to death, kill; (*sjuka djur*) destroy; *bildl.* confute, scotch **-livning** [-i:v-] putting to death, killing *etc.* **-ljud** ablaut [vowel], gradation **-locka** ~ *ngn en bekännelse* draw a confession from s.b.; ~ *ngn en hemlighet* worm (lure) a secret out of s.b.; ~ *ngn ett löfte* extract a promise from s.b.; ~ *ngn ett skratt* make s.b. laugh; ~ *ngn upplysningar* elicit information from s.b.

avlopp [out]flow, outlet; sewer, drain; (*i badkar o.d.*) drain, plug-hole

avlopps|brunn cesspool, sink, sump; gully **-dike** drainage ditch **-ledning** drainpipe; sewer **-rör** discharge (waste) pipe, drainpipe, sewer; (*för ånga*) exhaust pipe **-trumma** drain, sewer **-vatten** waste water; sewage

av|lossa fire [off], discharge **-lossning** discharge **-lusa** delouse **-lusning** [-u:-] delousing **-lutning** alkali removing **-lyftning** lifting off, removal; relief **-lysa** suspend, cancel, call off **-lysning** suspending *etc.* **-lyssna** listen to; (*ofrivilligt*) overhear; ~ *telefonsamtal* tap [the wires] **-lyssning** (*av telefon*) wire-tapping **-lyssningsapparat** listening (bugging) device **-lång** oblong, oval, elliptical **-låta** (*utfärda*) issue; (*avsända*) dispatch, send off **-lägga 1** (*kläder*) leave off; lay aside (by) (*äv. bildl.*) **2** ~ *en bekännelse* make a confession; ~ *besök* *hos* pay a visit to, call upon; ~ *ed* take an oath, swear; ~ *examen* pass an examination; ~ *rapport om* report on; ~ *räkenskap för* render an account of, account for **-läggare** *bot.* shoot, layer; *bildl.* offshoot, branch

avlägs|en *a3* distant; remote; *-na släktingar* distant relatives; *i en* ~ *framtid* in the remote future; *inte ha den -naste aning om* not have the remotest (faintest) idea about **-et** *adv* remotely, distantly; ~ *liggande* (*äv.*) remote, out--of-the-way, far-off

avlägsna remove; (*avskeda*) dismiss; (*göra främmande*) estrange, alienate; ~ *sig* [*från*] go away, leave, retire, withdraw, (*för ögat*) recede

avlämn|a (*varor*) deliver; (*t. förvaring*) leave, give up; (*inlämna*) hand in; (*resande*) drop, set down **-ande** *s6* delivering *etc.*; *mot* ~ *av* against [the] delivery of **-ing** delivery

avlänka deflect, deviate

avläs|a read [off]; ~ *ngt i ngns ansikte* read s.th. on a p.'s face **-are** meter inspector **-bar** readable **-ning** reading

avlön|a pay, remunerate **-ing** pay, remuneration; (*arbetares*) wages (*pl*); (*tjänstemans*) salary; (*prästs*) stipend

avlönings|dag payday **-kuvert** pay packet **-lista** payroll

av|löpa (*sluta*) end; (*utfalla*) turn out; ~ *lyckligt* turn out well, end happily

avlös|a (*vakt*) relieve; (*följa efter*) succeed; (*ersätta*) replace, displace; *teol.* absolve **-are** relief (*äv. mil.*); successor **-ning** relieving *etc.*; *mil.* relief; *teol.* absolution

avlöva strip of [its] leaves, defoliate; *~d* leafless; *~s* (*äv.*) shed its leaves

avmagnetiser|a demagnetize; (*fartyg mot minor*) degauss **-ing** demagnetization; (*av fartyg*) degaussing

avmagring [-a:-] growing thin; loss of weight

avmagrings|kur reducing (slimming) cure **-medel** slimming (reducing) preparation

avmarsch march[ing] off, departure

1 avmaska (*vid stickning*) cast off

2 avmask|a (*befria från mask*) deworm

avmaskning deworming

avmasta dismast

avmatt|a weaken, enfeeble; (*utmatta*) exhaust **-as** grow weak, languish, flag, lose strength **-ning** flagging, weakening, languor, relaxed vigour

avmattningstendens weakening trend

avmobiliser|a demobilize **-ing** demobilization

av|montera dismantle, dismount **-måla** paint; (*beskriva*) depict; *glädjen -de sig i hans ansikte* joy was depicted in (on) his face **-mäta** measure; (*i lantmäteri*) trace out, measure up; (*straff o.d.*) mete out **-mätning** measuring *etc.*; measurement **-mätt** *a4* measured, deliberate; (*reserverad*) reserved, guarded

avmönstr|a 1 (*avlöna*) pay off, discharge **2** (*avgå från tjänstgöring*) sign off **-ing** paying-off *etc.*

av|navla [-na:v-] cut the umbilical cord **-njuta** enjoy **-nämare** buyer, purchaser, consumer, customer

avnöt|a wear off **-ning** wearing off; *geol.* abrasion, detrition

avog *a1* unkind **avoghet** averseness, aversion (*mot* to) **avogt** *adv* unkindly; ~ *stämd mot ngn* unfavourably disposed towards s.b.

avokado [-'ka:-] *s5* **1** (*träd*) avocado **2** (*frukt*) avocado [pear], alligator pear

avpass|a fit (*efter* to); *bildl. äv.* adapt, adjust (*efter* to); ~ *tiden för* time, choose the right time for **-ning** fitting, adaption, adjustment

avpatruller|a patrol **-ing** patrolling

avplock|a (*frukt*) pick, gather; (*buske o. friare*) strip **-ning** picking *etc.*

avpolitisera make nonpolitical, unpoliticize

avpolletter|a *bildl.* dispose (get rid) of **-ing** dismissal

avporträtter|a portray **-ing** portrayal

avpressa ~ *ngn ngt* extort (extract) s.th. from s.b.

avprick|a tick [off] **-ning** checking

avprickningslista check list

avprov|a test, try, give a trial; (*avsmaka*) taste, sample **-ning** testing *etc.*

avprägla stamp; ~ *sig* stamp (imprint) itself (*i, på* on)

avputs|a clean, finish, polish **-ning** cleaning *etc.*

av|raka shave [off] **-reagera** abreact; ~ *sig* work off one's annoyance, *vard.* let off steam **-reda** thicken **-redning** thickening

avregistrer|a strike off a register; (*fordon*) deregister **-ing** deregistration

av|resa I *v3* depart, leave, set out, start (*till* for) **II** *s1* departure, leaving, setting out (*till* for) **-resedag** day of departure

avrevider|a *boktr.* revise **-ing** *boktr.* revising

av|rigga unrig, untackle **-ringning** ring[ing]-off **-rinna** flow (drain) away (off); *låta* ~ drain, stand to strain **-rinning** runoff, outflow **-riva** tear off **-rivning** tearing off; *kall* ~ cold rubdown **-romantisera** deglamorize **-rop** suborder **-ropa** suborder

avrund|a round [off]; *~d summa* round sum **-ning** rounding [off]

avrust|a demobilize, disarm; *sjö.* lay up **-ning** disarmament; *sjö.* laying up

av|rustningskonferens disarmament conference **-råda** ~ *ngn från ngt* advise (warn) s.b. against s.th., dissuade s.b. from s.th.; ~ *ngn från att komma* advise s.b. against coming (s.b. not to come), dissuade s.b. from coming **-rådan** *r* dissuasion, discouragement **-räkna** deduct, discount; ~ *mot* apply against; *detta ~t* making allowance for that **-räkning** deduction, discount; *hand.* settlement [of accounts]; *i* ~ *mot* in settlement of, to be deducted from; *betala i* ~ pay on account **-rätta** execute, put to death (*genom* by); ~ *genom hängning* hang; ~ *med elektricitet* electrocute **-rättning** execution, putting to death; electrocution **-rättningsplats** place of execution **-röja** clear away **-röjning** clearing away, removal **-rösa** demarcate, set landmarks **-rösning** [-ö:-] of demarcation **-rösningsjord** uncultivated land

av|sadla unsaddle **-sadling** [-a:-] unsaddling **-saknad** *r* want; *vara i* ~ *av* lack, be without **-salta** desalinate, desalt **-salu** *oböjligt s, till* ~ for sale **-sats** *s3* ledge, shelf; (*trapp-*) landing

avse 1 (*hänsyfta på*) concern, bear upon, have

reference to, refer to **2** (*ha i sikte*) have in view, aim at **3** (*ha för avsikt*) mean, intend; *~dd för* intended (designed, meant) for; *~ende* concerning, bearing upon, referring to

avseende *s6* (*syftning*) reference; (*beaktande*) consideration; (*hänseende*) respect, regard; *i alla ~n* in all respects, in every way; *i rättsligt ~* from a judicial point of view; *i varje* (*intet, detta*) *~* in every (no, this) respect; *med* (*i*) *~ på* with regard (reference, respect) to, regarding, concerning; *utan ~ på person* without respect of persons; *fästa ~ vid* take notice of, pay attention (heed, regard) to; *förtjäna ~* deserve consideration; *ha ~ på* have reference to, refer to; *lämna utan ~* pay no regard to, take no notice of, disregard

av|segla sail, leave (*till* for) **-segling** sailing, departure **-sela** unharness

avsevärd *al* considerable, appreciable; *~ rabatt* substantial discount

avsides aside; *~ belägen* remote, out-of-the-way; *ligga ~* lie apart **-replik** aside

avsigkommen [-å-] *a3* broken-down; *se ~ ut* look shabby (seedy)

avsikt *s3* (*syfte*) intention; purpose; object, end; (*uppsåt*) design, motive; *jur.* intent; *i ~ att* for the purpose of; *i bästa ~* with the best of intentions; *med ~* on purpose; *med ~ att* with the intention of (+ *ing-form*), *jur.* with intent to; *utan ~* unintentionally; *utan ~ att såra* without intending to hurt; *utan ond ~* without [an] evil intent; *ha för ~ att* have the intention to, intend to; *vad har hon för ~ med det?* what is her purpose in doing that?

avsikt|lig *al* intentional; (*överlagd*) deliberate **-ligt** intentionally, on purpose

av|sjunga sing **-skaffa** abolish, get rid of, do away with; put an end to; (*upphäva*) repeal **-skaffande** *s6* abolishing *etc.*; abolition; repeal

avsked [-ʃ-] **1** (*entledigande*) dismissal, discharge; (*tillbakaträdande*) retirement, resignation; *begära ~* hand in one's resignation; *få ~* be dismissed; *få ~ med pension* retire on a pension; *få ~ på grått papper* be dismissed forthwith, *vard.* be turned off, be sacked; *ta ~ från* resign, leave **2** (*farväl*) parting, leave-taking, leave; farewell; *i ~ets stund* at the moment of parting; *ta ~ av* say farewell to, take leave of **avskeda** dismiss, discharge, give notice to; *vard.* fire, sack

avskeds|ansökan resignation; *inlämna sin ~* hand in one's resignation **-besök** farewell visit **-föreställning** farewell performance **-hälsning** parting greeting **-kyss** parting kiss **-ord** parting word **-tagande** *se avsked* 2 **-tal** valedictory (farewell) speech

avskepp|a ship [off] **-ning** shipping [off]; *klar till ~* ready for shipment **-ningshamn** port of shipment

avskild secluded; isolated; *leva ~ från* live apart from **-het** retirement, seclusion; isolation

avskilj|a separate, detach; (*avhugga*) sever, cut off; (*avdela, t.ex. med skiljevägg*) partition [off] **-are** separator

avskjut|a fire, discharge; (*raket*) launch **-ning** firing, discharge; launching; (*av vilt*) shooting

off **-ningsbas** launching base **-ningsramp** launch[ing] pad

av|skrap *s7* scrapings (*pl*), refuse; *bildl.* dregs **-skrapa** scrape [off]

avskrift copy, transcript[ion]; *bevittnad ~* attested copy; *~ens riktighet bekräftas* I (we) certify this to be a true copy; *i ~* in copy

avskriv|a 1 (*kopiera*) copy, transcribe; *rätt -et intygas* true copy certified by **2** *hand.* write off; depreciate **3** *jur.* remove from the cause list **-ning 1** *hand.* writing off; (*summa*) item written off; *vara på ~* (*bildl.*) fall (go, pass) out of use **2** copying

avskräck|a *v3* frighten (*från att* from + *ing-form*); (*förhindra*) deter; (*svagare*) discourage; *han låter mig ~ sig* he is not to be intimidated **-ande** *a4* (*om exempel*) warning; (*om straff*) exemplary; (*om verkan*) deterrent; *verka ~* act as a deterrent

av|skräde *s6* refuse; (*efter slakt o.d.*) offal; (*friare*) rubbish **-skrädeshög** refuse (rubbish) heap

av|skum scum; skimmings (*pl*); *bildl. äv.* scum, dregs (*pl*) **-skuren** *a5* cut [off], severed; isolated

avsky [-ʃy] **I** *v4* detest, abhor, loathe **II** *s2* disgust (*för, över* at); abhorrence (*för* of); loathing (*för* for); *känna ~ för* feel a loathing for; *vända sig bort i ~* turn away in disgust **-värd** *al* abominable, detestable; *-värt brott* heinous crime

av|skära 1 *se skära av* **2** *~ återtåget* intercept the retreat **-skärma** screen off; *radio.* shield **-skärmning** screening; *radio.* shielding **-skärning** cutting off; (*genomskärning*) section

avslag *s7* refusal, declining; (*på förslag*) rejection; *få ~ på* have turned down; *yrka ~* move the rejection of the proposal **avslagen** *a5* rejected *etc.*, *se avslå*; (*om dryck*) stale, flat; dead **avslagsyrkande** motion for the rejection [of a proposal (bill)]

av|slappnad relaxed **-slappning** slackening, relaxation **-slipa** grind, polish [off]; (*om vatten*) wear away (down); (*juvel*) cut; *bildl.* rub off, polish **-slipning** grinding *etc.* **-slockna** die away; go out

avslut *hand.* contract, bargain, deal; (*bokslut*) balancing [of one's books]

avslut|a 1 (*göra färdig*) finish [off], complete; (*ge en avslutning*) conclude, bring to an end; (*göra slut på*) end, close; *~s* be finished off; come to an end; *sammanträdet ~des* the meeting was closed **2** (*göra upp köp o.d.*) conclude; (*räkenskaper*) balance **-ning 1** (*avslutande*) finishing off, completion; conclusion, concluding **2** (*avslutande del*) conclusion, finish; (*slut*) end, termination; *skol.* break-up [ceremony]; speech day; *AE.* commencement

avslutningsvis by way of conclusion, in conclusion

av|slå 1 *se slå av* **2** (*vägra*) refuse, decline, reject **3** (*avvärja*) repulse **-slöja** unveil; *bildl.* expose, unmask, disclose **-slöjande** *s6* unveiling; *bildl.* disclosure, revelation

avsmak dislike, distaste; (*starkare*) aversion (*för* to), disgust (*för* with); *få ~ för* take a dislike to; *känna ~* feel disgusted; *väcka ~* arouse

disgust
avsmak|a taste; (*prova*) sample **-ning** tasting
avsmaln|a narrow [off]; (*långsamt*) taper **-ande** *a4* narrowing; tapering
av|sminka remove make-up **-smälta** (*om snö etc.*) melt away; (*om säkring*) fuse
av|snitt sector; (*av bok*) section, part; (*av följetong etc.*) instalment **-snöra** cut off **-snörning** cutting off **-somna** pass away; *de saligen ~de* the [dear] departed **-spark** *sport.* kickoff **-spegla** reflect, mirror; *~ sig* be reflected **-spegling** reflection **-spela** play back **-spelning** playback; (*spelande*) playing back **-spisa** put off; *vard.* fob off **-spänd** relaxed **-spändhet** relaxation **-spänning** relaxation (slackening) [of tension], easing off **-spärra** bar, block; shut (cordon) off (*från* from); *mil.* blockade; (*med rep o.d.*) rope (rail, fence) off; (*avstänga*) close (*för* for) **-spärrning** barring *etc.*; (*område*) rope-off area; (*polis-*) cordon
avstalinisering de-Stalinization
av|stamp take-off **-stanna** stop, come to a standstill, cease; (*om samtal o.d.*) die down **-stava** divide [into syllables] **-stavning** division into syllables, syllabi[fi]cation **-stavningsregel** syllabi[fi]cation rule **-steg** departure, deviation; *~ från den rätta vägen* lapse from the right path **-stickare** (*utflykt*) detour, deviation; (*från ämnet*) digression **-stigning** alighting **-stjälpa** tip, dump **-stjälpning** tipping, dumping **-stjälpningsplats** tip, dumping-ground **-stressad** relaxed **-stressande** relaxing **-stycka** parcel out, divide **-styckning** parcelling out, division **-styra** prevent; avert, ward off **-styrka** discountenance, oppose; recommend the rejection of **-styrkande** *s6* disapproval; rejection
avstå give up, relinquish, cede (*till* to); *~ från* give up, relinquish; (*avsäga sig*) renounce, waive; (*låta bli*) refrain from, pass up; (*undvara*) do without, dispense with; *jur.* remise **-ende** *s6* giving up *etc.* (*från* of)
avstånd *s7* distance; (*till målet*) range; *på ~ at* a distance, (*i fjärran*) in the distance; *på vederbörligt ~ at* a discreet distance; *på 6 m ~* (*äv.*) six metres away; *hålla ngn på ~* keep s.b. at a distance (at arm's length); *ta ~ från* dissociate o.s. from, (*avvisa*) repudiate, (*ogilla*) deprecate, take exception to; disclaim
avstånds|bedömning determination of distance[s *pl*] **-bestämning** range-finding **-inställning** *foto.* (*abstr.*) focusing; (*konkr.*) focusing lever **-mätare** rangefinder; *tekn.* telemeter **-tagande** *s6* dissociation, repudiation (*från* of); deprecation (*från* of); disclaiming (*från* of)
avstäm|ma *bokför.* tick (*AE.* check) [off]; *radio.* tune [in] **-ning** *bokför.* tick; *AE.* check; *radio.* tuning **-ningsindikator** tuning indicator, magic eye **-ningskrets** tuning circuit
avstämpl|a stamp; *~ en aktie* have a share stamped **-ing** stamping **-ingsdag** *järnv. o.d.* day of issue; *post.* date of postmark
av|stänga shut off; (*inhägna*) fence in (off), enclose; close; (*avspärra*) bar, block; (*vatten o.d.*) turn off; (*elektrisk ström*) cut off; *bildl. äv.* exclude; *gatan avstängd* no thoroughfare

-stängning shutting off *etc.*; (*område*) enclosure **-stängningsventil** stop valve **-stöta** reject **-stötning** rejection **-stötningsprocess** rejection process **-svalna** cool [down, off], grow cool; *bildl.* wane **-svalning** cooling **-svavla** [-a:v-] desulphurize **-svavling** sulphur removal, desulphurization **-svimmad** *a5* in a faint (swoon); *falla ~ till marken* fall fainting to the ground **-svärja** ~ [*sig*] abjure; forswear **-svärjning** abjuration; foreswearing **-syna** inspect and certify **-synare** inspector **-syning** official inspection **-syningsförrättning** inspection **-såga** saw [off]; *~d* (*vard.*) finished, washed up **-säga** *rfl* resign, give up; (*avböja*) decline; (*frisäga sig från*) disclaim; renounce; *~ sig kronan* abdicate; *~ sig allt ansvar* renounce all responsibility **-sägelse** resignation; renunciation; abdication
avsänd|a send [off], dispatch; ship; post **-are** sender; (*av gods*) consignor, consigner, shipper; (*av postanvisning*) remitter, remittor **-ning** dispatch; shipment **-ningsavi** dispatch note; shipping bill
avsätt|a 1 (*ämbetsman*) remove, dismiss; (*regent*) depose, dethrone **2** (*varor*) sell, find a market for, dispose of **3** (*lägga undan*) set (put) aside, reserve **4** (*bottensats*) deposit **5** (*upprita*) set off; *~ märken* leave marks (traces) **-bar** *a5* dismissable, removable; (*om vara*) marketable **-ning 1** (*ämbetsmans*) dismissal, removal; (*regents*) deposition, dethronement **2** (*varors*) sale, market; *finna god ~* meet with a ready market, sell well **3** *bokför.* appropriation
avsättnings|möjligheter *pl* market potential (*sg*) **-område** market [area] **-svårigheter** *pl* marketing problems; *~ för stål* a poor market for steel
avsök|a scan **-ning** scanning
avsöndr|a (*avskilja*) separate [off], sever, detach; (*utsöndra*) secrete; *~ sig* isolate o.s.; *~s* separate off, be secreted **-ing** separation, severance; secretion; isolation **-ingsorgan** secretory organ
avta *se ta av*
av|tacka thank s.b. for his (her) services **-tacklad** *a5* thin and worn, haggard
avtag|a 1 *se ta av* **2** (*försvagas, minska*) decrease, diminish; (*om månen*) wane; (*om storm o.d.*) abate, subside; (*om hälsa, anseende*) decline, fail, fall off **-ande** *s6* decrease, diminution; waning; abatement; decline; *vara i ~* be on the decrease, grow less, (*om månen*) be on the wane **-bar** *a5* removable, detachable
avtagsväg turn[ing]
avtal *s7* agreement; contract; (*mellan stater*) treaty, agreement, convention; *enligt ~* as agreed upon; *träffa ~ om* come to (make) an agreement about (concerning, for); **avtala 1** (*träffa avtal*) agree (*med* with; *om* about) **2** (*överenskomma om*) agree upon; (*tid*) fix, appoint; *ett ~t tecken* a prearranged sign; *på ~d plats* at the appointed place; *som ~t var* as arranged
avtals|brott breach of [an] agreement ([a] contract) **-brytare** violator of an agreement **-enlig** [-e:n-] *a5* as agreed [upon], as stipulated **-förhandlingar** *pl* wage negotiations, pay

talks **-mässig** a5 contractual **-rätt** law of contract **-rörelse** collective bargaining, wage negotiations (pl) **-stridig** contrary to agreement (contract)

av|tappa (låta rinna ut) draw [off], tap (ur from, out of); (tömma) draw **-tappning** drawing etc.; (av valuta) drain **-teckna** draw, sketch (efter from); ~ sig stand out, be outlined (mot against) **-tjäna** work off; ~ fängelsestraff serve a prison sentence **-tona** konst. shade off **-torka** wipe [off], wipe down, clean; (tårar) dry, wipe away **-torkning** wiping [off] etc. **-trappa** de-escalate **-trappning** de-escalation **-trubba** blunt, dull; tekn. bevel [down] **-trubbning** blunting

avtryck 1 imprint, impression; (kopia) print **2** boktr. proof [impression], print; (omtryck) reprint; konst. reproduction

avtryck|a impress, imprint; boktr. print [off], copy [off]; (omtrycka) reprint **-are** (på gevär) trigger; foto. shutter lever

avträd|a give up, leave, surrender; (landområde) cede; (avgå från) retire, withdraw **-ande** s6 giving up etc.; cession, retirement, withdrawal

avträde s6 **1** jur. compensation **2** (hemlighus) privy

av|tvagning [-a:g-] washing [away] **-tvinga** ~ ngn ngt extort s.th. from s.b., wring (force) s.th. out of s.b. **-två** wash [off]; bildl. wash away; (beskyllning) clear o.s. of **-tyna** languish; (om pers. äv.) pine away, decline **-tynande I** s6 [gradual] decline **II** a4 languishing **-tåg** s7 departure, marching off; (friare) decampment; fritt ~ liberty to march off **-tåga** march off, decamp **-täcka** uncover; (staty) unveil **-täckning** uncovering etc. **-täcknings-ceremoni** unveiling ceremony **-tärd** worn, emaciated, gaunt

avund s2 envy; blek av ~ pale with envy; känna ~ mot (över) feel envious of; väcka ~ arouse envy

avund|as dep envy **-sam** a1 envious **-samhet** enviousness **-sjuk** envious, jealous (på, över of) **-sjuka** enviousness, envy

avunds|man ung. antagonist, enemy; han har många -män there are many who bear him a grudge **-värd** a1 enviable

avvakta (svar, ankomst) await; (händelsernas utveckling) wait and see; (lura på, invänta) wait (watch) for; ~ lägligt tillfälle wait for an opportunity, mark time; ~ tiden bide one's time; förhålla sig ~nde play a waiting game; intaga en ~nde hållning adopt a wait-and-see policy

avvaktan r, i ~ på while waiting for, pending, hand. awaiting, looking forward to

av|vand [-a:n-] a5 (om dibarn) weaned **-vara** endast i inf. spare **-vattna** drain [off], dewater **-vattning** dewatering, drainage **-veckla** (affär o.d.) wind up; (friare) liquidate, settle **-veckling** winding up; liquidation; settlement **-verka** (hugga) fell; AE. cut, log; (slutföra) accomplish, finish **-verkning** (huggning) felling, disforestation

avvik|a 1 (från regel) diverge; (från ämne) digress; (från kurs, sanning) deviate, depart **2**

(vara olik) differ **3** (rymma) abscond **-ande** a4 divergent; deviating; (mening) dissentient **-are** deviant, deviate **-else 1** divergence; digression; deviation, departure **2** (rymning) absconding **3** (kompassens) deviation; tekn. aberration

av|vinna ~ jorden sin bärgning get a living from the soil; ~ ett ämne nya synpunkter evolve new aspects of a subject

avvis|a send (turn) away; (ansökan) dismiss; (förslag, anbud) reject; (beskyllning) repudiate; (invändning) overrule, meet; (anfall) repulse, repel; (leverans) refuse acceptance of; bli ~d be refused [entrance], meet with a rebuff; ~ tanken på reject the idea of **-ande I** s6 sending away etc.; dismissal; rejection; repudiation, repulse **II** a4 repudiating, deprecatory; ställa sig ~ till adopt a negative attitude towards, object to

av|vita oböjligt a 1 jur. insane **2** (dåraktig) preposterous, absurd **-vittra** erode **-vittring** erosion **-väg** (biväg) bypath; byroad, bylane; komma på ~ar go astray

avväg|a (skäl o.d.) weigh [in one's mind], balance [against each other]; (i lantmäteri) take the level of, level; väl -d well-balanced **-ning** weighing etc.

avvägnings|fråga question of priorities **-instrument** levelling instrument

av|vända (misstanke) divert; (olycka) avert; ~ uppmärksamheten från divert attention from **-vänja** (dibarn) wean; jfr vänja av **-vänjning** weaning **-vänjningskur** cure (mot for) **-väpna** disarm **-väpning** disarmament **-värja** ward (fend) off; parry; (olycka) avert **-värjning** warding off etc. **-yttra** dispose of, sell **-yttring** sale, disposal **-äta** eat; have; ~ en finare middag have a grand dinner

ax s7 **1** bot. spike; (sädes-) ear; gå i ~ form ears, ear **2** (nyckel-) bit, web

1 axel ['aks-] s2 **1** (geom.; jord-; polit.) axis (pl axes) **2** (hjul-) axle[tree]; (maskin-) shaft; arbor; spindle

2 axel ['aks-] s2 (skuldra) shoulder; rycka på axlarna shrug one's shoulders; på ~ gevär! shoulder arms!, slope arms!; se ngn över ~n look down on s.b., look down one's nose at s.b.

axel|band shoulder strap; utan ~ (om damkläder) strapless **-bred** broad-shouldered **-bredd** width across the shoulders

axelbrott axle fracture

axelklaff shoulder strap

axelkoppling shaft coupling

axelled shoulder joint

axelmakterna pl the Axis powers

axel|rem carrying (shoulder, satchel) strap **-remsväska** satchel; AE. shoulder bag **-ryckning** shrug [of the shoulders]

axeltryck axle load, shaft pressure

axel|vadd shoulder pad **-väska** se axelremsväska

axi'al, axi'ell a5 axial

axiom [-'å:m] s7 axiom **-atisk** [-'ma:-] a5 axiomatic[al]

axla put on, shoulder; bildl. take over

axplock gleanings (pl); några ~ från a few

examples (facts *etc.*) gleaned from
ayatoll|a [aja*tålla] *-an -or* ayatollah
azalea [asa*le:a] *s1* azalea
azimut *se asimut*
Azorerna [a'så:-] *pl* the Azores
aztek [as'te:k] *s3* Aztec **-isk** *a5* Aztec[an]
azur [*a:sur *el.* 'a:sur, *äv.* a'su:r] *s2* azure **-blå**
azure-blue

B

b *s6* b; *mus.* *(ton)* B flat, *(tecken)* flat sign
babbel ['babb-] *s7*, **babbla** *v1* babble
babelstorn [Tower of] Babel
babi'an *s3* baboon
babord ['ba:-] *s, böjligt endast i genitiv* port;
ligga för ~s halsar be (stand) on the port tack;
land om ~ land to port; *~ med rodret!* helm
aport! **babordslanterna** port light
baby ['be(i)bi *el.* -y] *s2, s3* baby **-kläder** baby
clothes **-lift** carrycot
Babylonien [-'lɒ:-] *n* Babylonia
babylon|ier [-'lɒ:-] Babylonian **-isk** *a5* Baby-
lonian; *~ förbistring* babel, confusion of
tongues; *~a fångenskapen* [the] Babylonian
captivity (*äv. påvarnas*)
baby|sitter *s2* (*ett slags stol*) bouncing cradle
-säng cot **-utstyrsel** layette
ba'cill *s3* bacillus (*pl* bacilli); germ; *AE. vard.*
bug **-bärare** *se smittbärare* **-fri** germ-free
-skräck *ha ~* have a horror of contagion
1 back *s2* **1** (*lådfack*) tray; (*öl-*) crate **2** *sjö.*
(*kärl*) bowl, kid
2 back *s2* **1** *sjö.* forecastle, fo'c's'le
3 back *s2, tekn.* (*broms-*) shoe; (*gäng-*) die
4 back *s2* **1** *sport.* back, fullback **2** (*-växel*) reverse [gear]; *lägga i ~en* put the car in reverse
5 back *adv* back; *brassa ~* brace aback; *gå* (*slå*)
~ back, go astern; *sakta ~!* (slow) easy astern!;
slå ~ i maskin reverse [the engine]
backa back, reverse; (*om fartyg*) go astern; *~*
upp, se uppbacka; ~ ur (*bildl.*) back out
backa'nal *s3* bacchanal **-isk** bacchanalian
backant bacchant, *fem.* bacchante
back|e *s2* **1** (*sluttning*) hill; slope, hillside; *~*
upp och ~ ner up hill and down dale; *sakta i*
-arna! easy does it!; *över berg och -ar* across
[the] country, over hill and dale; *streta uppför*
en ~ struggle (trudge) up a hill; *åka nerför ~n*
go downhill **2** (*mark*) ground; *komma på bar*
~ be left penniless; *regnet står som spön i ~n*
it is raining cats and dogs
backfisch ['back-] *s2* teenage girl, teenager
backhammer (*i brottning*) hammerlock
backhand *s2* backhand **backhandsslag** back-
hander
backhopp|are ski jumper **-ning** ski-jumping
backig *a1* hilly; undulating
backkrön brow [of a hill]
back|ljus, -lykta reversing light **-ning** backing,
reversing
backsippa pasqueflower
back|slag *sjö.* reversing gear **-slagstangent**
backspace [key]
backsluttning slope [of a hill], hillside
backspegel rear-view mirror
back|stuga hut, cabin **-stugusittare** crofter
-svala sand martin **-tävling** ski-jumping competition; (*för bil*) hill climb
backväxel reverse gear

1 bad *imperf. av bedja*
2 bad *s7* bath; (*utomhus*) bathe; *ligga i ~et (äv.)* soak in the bath; *ta sig ett ~* have a bath (bathe)
bada 1 (*ta sig ett bad*) take (have) a bath; (*utomhus*) bathe, take a swim; *~ i svett* be bathed in perspiration; *~ naken* skinny-dip; *gå (åka) och ~* go for a swim **2** (*tvätta*) bath (*ett barn* a child)
bad|balja bathtub **-bassäng** swimming pool; (*inomhus*) swimming bath **-borste** bath brush **-byxor** [swimming] trunks
badda bathe; *~ en svullnad* sponge (dab) a swelling
baddare bouncer, corker; *vard.* whacker; *en ~ till gädda* a whopper of a pike
baddning bathing; sponging
bad|dräkt swimming (bathing) costume, swimsuit; *AE. äv.* bathing suit **-erska** [female] bath attendant **-flicka** bathing beauty **-förbud** bathing ban; (*på skylt*) Bathing Prohibited! **-gäst** (*vid -ort*) visitor; (*vid -inrättning*) bather **-handduk** bath towel **-hotell** seaside hotel; (*vid kurort*) health-resort hotel **-hus** bathhouse, public baths (*pl*) **-hytt** bathing cubicle (hut) **-inrättning** *se -hus* **-kappa** bathrobe **-kar** bath[tub] **-klåda** swimmer's itch **-kur** course of baths; *genomgå en ~ i* take the baths at **-lakan** large bath towel
badminton ['bädd-, *äv.* 'badd-] *n* badminton **-boll** shuttle[cock] **-plan** badminton court **-racket** badminton racket **-spelare** badminton player
bad|mästare bath attendant **-mössa** bathing cap **-ort** seaside resort; (*hälsobrunn*) health resort, spa **-rock** *se badkappa* **-rum** bathroom **-rumsmatta** bath mat **-rumsvåg** bathroom scales (*pl*) **-saker** bathing gear **-salt** bath salts (*pl*) **-sejour** stay at a spa (health resort) **-sko** bathing shoe **-strand** [bathing] beach **-ställe** bathing place **-svamp** [bath] sponge **-säsong** bathing season **-termometer** bath thermometer **-tvål** bath soap **-vatten** bath water; *kasta ut barnet med -vattnet* throw the baby out with the bath water
bag [bägg *el.* bagg] *s2* bag
bagage [-'ga:ʃ] *s7* luggage; *AE. äv.* baggage **-hylla** luggage rack **-hållare** luggage carrier **-inlämning** left-luggage office, cloakroom; *AE.* checkroom **-kärra** [luggage] trolley **-lucka** (*utrymme*) boot; *AE.* trunk **-utlämning** luggage delivery [office]; (*på skylt*) claim baggage here
bagarbarn *bjuda ~ på bröd* (*ung.*) carry coals to Newcastle
bagar|e baker **-mössa** baker's cap
baga'tell *s3* trifle; *det är en ren ~* it's a mere trifle **-artad** [-a:r-] *a5* petty, trivial
bagatelliser|a make light of; belittle; (*överskyla*) extenuate, palliate **-ing** making light of *etc.*
bageri bakery **-arbetare** baker
bagge *s2* ram
baguette [ba'gätt] *s5* baguet[te]
baha'm|an *s3*, **-ansk** [-'a:nsk] *a5* Bahamian
Bahamaöarna [-ˣha:-] [the] Bahamas, [the] Bahama Islands

Bah'rein *n* Bahrain, Bahrein
bahrein|are [-ˣrei-] *s9*, **-sk** [-'rei-] *a5* Bahraini, Bahreini
ba'hytt *s3* bonnet
baisse [bä:s] *s5* decline, fall [in prices], slump; bear market; *spekulera i ~* operate for a fall; *det är ~ på börsen* it is a bear market **-spekulation** bear operation
baja'där *s3* bayadere
Bajern ['baj-] *n* Bavaria **bajersk** ['baj-] *a5* Bavarian
bajo'nett *s3* bayonet **-fattning** bayonet **-fäktning** bayonet drill **-koppling** bayonet **-stöt** bayonet thrust
bajrare Bavarian
bajs *s7* number two **bajsa** do a number two
1 bak *s2* (*rygg*) back; (*ända*) behind, backside
2 bak I *adv* behind, at the back; *~ i boken* at the end of the book; *~ och fram* the wrong way round, back to front; *kjolen knäpps ~* the skirt buttons at the back **II** *prep* behind
3 bak *s7* (*bakning*) baking; (*bakat bröd*) batch
baka bake; *~ ihop sig* cake; *~ in (bildl.)* include; *~ ut en deg* knead and shape dough [into buns (*etc.*)]
bak|axel rear axle; *ledad ~* live rear axle **-ben** hind leg **-binda** pinion
bakbord breadboard
bak|danta *se baktala* **-dantare** *se baktalare* **-del** back, hinder (back) part; (*människas*) buttock[s *pl*]; (*kreaturs*) hindquarter[s *pl*] **-däck** rear tyre **-dörr** back door; (*bils*) rear door **-efter** behind
bake'lit *s3* Bakelite (*varumärke*)
bakelse *s5* pastry, [fancy] cake
bakerst ['ba:k-] **I** *adv* furthest back **II** *superl. a* hind[er]most
bakficka hip pocket; (*restaurangs*) restaurant annexe [with cheaper menu]; *ha ngt i ~n* have s.th. up one's sleeve
bakform baking-tin, patty pan
bak|fot hind foot; *få ngt om ~en* get hold of the wrong end of the stick **-fram** back to front, [the] wrong way round (about) **-full** hung over, crapulous, under the weather; *vara ~* have a hangover; *AE. äv.* be hung over **-gata** backstreet **-grund** background, setting; *teat.* backcloth, backdrop; *mot ~[en] av (äv.)* in [the] light of
bakgrunds|figur background figure **-strålning** background radiation
bak|gård back yard **-hal** slippery, tending to slide backwards **-hasor** *i ~na* hot on the heels; *sätta sig på ~na* dig one's heels in, jib **-hjul** rear (back) wheel **-hjulsdrift** rear [wheel] drive **-huvud** back of the (one's) head **-håll** ambush; *ligga i ~ för ngn* lie in ambush for s.b., waylay s.b.
bak|i I *adv* at the back, behind **II** *prep* behind in, in the back of **-ifrån** from behind
bak|kappa counter **-kropp** (*hos insekt*) abdomen **-laddare** breechloader **-laddningsmekanism** breech mechanism **-land** *geogr.* hinterland **-lucka** (*i bil*) boot cover; *AE.* trunk cover; (*utrymme*) *se bagagelucka* **-lykta**, **-lyse** rear light (lamp); *AE.* taillight, tail lamp **-lås** *dörren har gått i ~* the lock [of the door] has

jammed; *hela saken har gått i* ~ the whole affair has reached a deadlock **-länges** backwards; *falla* ~ fall on one's back; *åka* ~ (*i tåg*) sit (travel) with one's back to the engine, (*i buss etc.*) sit (travel) with one's back to the front (driver, horses) **-läxa** *få* ~ have to do s.th. (homework) [all] over again
bakning [ˣbaːk-] baking
bakom [-å-] behind; *AE. äv.* [in] back of; ~ *knuten* round the corner; *föra ngn* ~ *ljuset* hoodwink s.b.; *klia sig* ~ *örat* scratch one's ear; *känna sig* ~ feel dull (stupid); *vara* ~ [*flötet*] be soft [in the head]; *man förstår vad som ligger* ~ one understands what is at the bottom of it [all] **-liggande** *a4* lying behind [it *etc.*], underlying
bak|plåt baking-sheet **-pulver** baking powder
bakpå I *adv* behind, at (on) the back **II** *prep* at (on) the back
bakre [ˈbaːk-] back; hind
bak|rus *gå i* ~ have a hangover **-ruta** rear window **-sida** back; (*på mynt o.d.*) reverse; *på* ~*n* on the back, overleaf; *medaljens* ~ (*bildl.*) the other side of the coin **-slag** rebound, rebuff; *biol.* atavism; *tekn.* backfire; *bildl.* reverse, setback, recession; *det blev ett* ~ it was a setback **-slug** underhand, sly, crafty **-slughet** slyness **-smälla** hangover **-strävare** reactionary **-sträveri** reaction **-ström** back (backward) current; backwater; (*elström*) reverse current **-stycke** back **-säte** back (rear) seat **-tala** slander, backbite **-talare** slanderer, backbiter, maligner **-tanke** secret (ulterior) motive; *utan -tankar* (*äv.*) unreservedly, straightforwardly; *ha en* ~ have an axe to grind **-tass** hind paw
bakteri'cid *s3* bactericide; germicide
bakterie [-ˈteː-] *s3* bacterium (*pl* bacteria), germ, microbe; *spiralformig* ~ spirochaete **-dödande** germicidal, bactericidal **-fri** germ--free **-härd** colony of bacteria **-krigföring** germ warfare **-kultur** culture [of bacteria] **-stam** strain [of bacteria]
bakterio|log bacteriologist **-logi** *s3* bacteriology **-logisk** *a5* bacteriological; *Statens ~a laboratorium* [the Swedish] national bacteriological laboratory **-ˈstas** *s3* bacteriostasis
baktill behind, at the back
baktråg kneading trough
baktung heavy at the back
bakugn [baker's] oven
bak'ut backwards; behind; *slå* (*sparka*) ~ kick [out]; lash out (*äv. bildl.*)
bak|vagn back of a carriage (*etc.*) **-vatten** backwater; (*bakström*) eddy; *råka i* ~ (*bildl.*) get separated from the main stream [of life]
bakverk [piece of] pastry
bak|väg back way; *gå in* ~*en* go in the back way; *gå* ~*ar* use clandestine methods **-vänd** *a5* the wrong way round; (*befängd*) absurd, preposterous; (*förvrängd*) perverted; (*tafatt*) awkward **-vänt** *adv* the wrong way; *bära sig* ~ *åt* be clumsy, act clumsily
bakåt backward[s]; (*tillbaka*) back **-böjd** *a5* bent back **-böjning** backward bend **-kammad** *a5* combed back **-lutande** leaning (sloping) backward[s]; ~ *handstil* backhand [(hand)writ-

ing] **-riktad** *a5* pointing backward[s]; (*om flygplansvinge*) sweptback **-strävande** reactionary **-strävare** *se baksträvare*
bakända *se bakdel*
1 bal *s2* (*packe*) bale; package
2 bal *s3* (*danstillställning*) ball; *gå på* ~ go to a ball; *öppna* ~*en* open the ball; ~*ens drottning* belle of the ball
balalajka [-ˣlajka] *s1* balalaika
balans [-ˈans *el.* -ˈaŋs] *s3* **1** (*jämvikt*) balance, equilibrium **2** (*saldo*) balance; (*kassabrist*) deficit; *ingående* ~ balance brought forward; *utgående* ~ balans carried forward **3** *tekn.* beam; (*i ur*) balance [wheel]
balanser|a [-ans- *el.* -aŋs-] **1** (*hålla i jämvikt*) balance, poise **2** *hand.* balance **-ad** *a5* balanced, well-balanced; poised; self-controlled **-ing** balancing
balans|gång balancing; *gå* ~ balance [o.s.], walk a tightrope **-hjul** flywheel **-konto** balance account **-organ** organ of equilibrium **-rubbning** disequilibrium **-räkning** balance sheet **-sinne** sense of balance, equilibrium sense **-våg** balance, beam scales
balata [-ˣlaː-] *s1* balata
balda'kin *s3* canopy
baldersbrå *s5, s6* scentless mayweed
ba'lett *s3* ballet; *dansa* ~ *a*) (*vara -dansör*) be a ballet dancer, *b*) (*ta -lektioner*) go to ballet classes **-dansör, -dansös** ballet dancer **-mästare** ballet master **-sko** blocked shoe
1 balja *s1* (*kärl*) tub; bowl
2 balja *s1* **1** *bot.* pod **2** (*fodral*) sheath, scabbard
balj|frukt podded fruit **-växt** leguminous plant
1 balk *s2, jur.* code, section
2 balk *s2, byggn.* beam; (*järn-*) girder
Balkan|halvön [ˈball-] the Balkan Peninsula **-länderna** the Balkans, the Balkan States
balklänning ball dress
balkong [-ˈkåŋ] *s3* balcony **-dörr** balcony door **-låda** balcony flower box, window box **-räcke** balcony parapet
bal'lad *s3* ballad, lay
ballast, ballasta *se barlast, barlasta*
ballerina [-ˣriː-] *s1* ballerina; *prima* ~ prima ballerina
ballist|ik ballistics (*pl, behandlas som sg*) **-isk** [-ˈlist-] *a5* ballistic; ~ *missil* ballistic missile
ballong [-ˈlåŋ] *s3* balloon **-farare** balloonist **-försäljare** balloon seller **-spärr** balloon barrage **-uppstigning** balloon ascent
balloter|a [vote by] ballot **-ing** balloting
balsa *s1* balsa
balsal ballroom
balsam [ball-, *pl* -ˈsaː-] *s3* balsam; *bildl.* balm **-era** embalm **-ering** embalming **-in** [-ˈmiːn] *s3* balsam **-isk** [-ˈsaː-] *a5* balsamic **-poppel** balsam poplar
balsaträ balsa[wood]
balt *s3* Balt; *han är* ~ he is an Estonian (a Latvian, a Lithuanian) **Baltikum** [ˈbalt-] *n* the Baltic States **baltisk** [ˈbalt-] *a5* Baltic
balu'strad *s3* balustrade
bambu [ˈbamm-] *s2* bamboo **-ridån** *polit.* the bamboo curtain **-rör** bamboo **-skott** *kokk.* bamboo shoots (*pl*)
bana I *s1* path; *astr.* orbit; (*projektils*) trajectory;

(*lopp*) course; (*levnads-*) career; (*lärt yrke*) profession; (*järnväg*) line; *sport.* track, ground, rink; *i långa banor* quantities (lots, no end) of; *vid slutet av sin* ~ at the end of one's career; *välja den prästerliga* ~*n* enter the Church, take holy orders **II** *v1,* ~*d väg* beaten track; ~ *väg*[*en*] *för ngn* (*bildl.*) pave the way for s.b.; ~ *väg genom* make (clear) a path (way) through; ~ *sig väg* make one's way

ba'nal *a1* banal, commonplace; ~*a fraser* hackneyed phrases **-isera** reduce to the commonplace **-itet** *s3* banality

ba'nan *s3* banana **-fluga** drosophila (*pl äv.* drosophilae), fruit (vinegar) fly **-kontakt** banana plug **-plantage** banana plantation **-skal** banana skin **-stock** banana stem **-träd** banana

banbryt|ande *a4* pioneering, groundbreaking; ~ *arbete* pioneer[ing] work **-are** pioneer (*för of*)

1 band *imperf. av binda*

2 band *s7* **1** (*ngt som binder*) band; (*remsa, i sht som prydnad*) ribbon; (*linne-, bomulls-*) tape; (*som hopsnör*) tie, string[s *pl*]; (*bindel*) sling; *anat.* ligament; (*bok-*) binding, cover; (*volym*) volume; *tekn.* belt; (*inspelnings-*) tape; *halvfranskt* ~ half-binding; *löpande* ~ assembly line; *ha armen i* ~ have one's arm in a sling; *måla tavlor på löpande* ~ produce (turn out) paintings in a steady stream; *spela in på* ~ record on tape, make a tape recording; *bilen har just lämnat* ~*et* the car has just left the assembly line **2** (*ngt som sammanbinder*) tie, bond; (*boja*) bond; (*för hund*) leash, lead; (*tunn-*) hoop; (*tvång*) restraint; *enande* ~ unifying bond; *kärlekens* ~ the ties of love; *träldomens* ~ the bonds of slavery; *lossa tungans* ~ loosen a p.'s tongue; *lägga* ~ *på ngn* lay restraint upon s.b.; *lägga* ~ *på sig* restrain (control) o.s.; *hunden går i* ~ the dog is on the lead **3** (*följe, anhang*) band, gang **4** (*orkester*) band

banda *radio.* tape[-record], record

bandage bandage

banderoll [-'råll] *s3* banderol[e], banner, streamer

band|hund watchdog; *skälla som en* ~ (*bildl.*) swear the devil out of hell **-inspelning** tape recording

ban'dit *s3* bandit, brigand; *enarmad* ~ (*spelautomat*) one-armed bandit, slot machine **-hövding** brigand chief

band|järn hoop (strip, band) iron **-mask** tapeworm **-rosett** tuft of ribbons; favour **-spelare** tape recorder **-såg** band saw **-traktor** caterpillar [tractor] **-tång** *bot.* eelgrass **-upptagning** tape recording **-vagn** tracked vehicle

bandy ['bandy *el.* -i] *s2* bandy **-klubba** bandy [stick] **-lag** bandy team **-match** bandy match **-spelare** bandy player

1 bane *oböjligt s, bringa å* ~ bring up, set on foot

2 bane *oböjligt s* death; *få sin* ~ meet one's death, perish; *skottet blev hans* ~ the shot proved fatal [to him]

baneman slayer, assassin

ba'ner *s7* banner, standard **-förare** standard-bearer

banesår mortal wound

bang *s2* (*överljudsknall*) sonic boom (bang)

Bangladesh [-'deʃ] *n* Bangladesh

bangladesh|are [-ˣdeʃ-] *s9,* **-isk** [-'deʃ-] *a5* Bangladeshi

bangård [railway, *AE.* railroad] yard

banjo ['banjω] *s5* banjo

1 bank *s2* (*undervattensgrund*) bank, bar; (*vall*) embankment, dyke; (*moln-*) [cloud]bank

2 bank *s3* (*penninginrättning*) bank; banking house; (*blod- etc.*) bank; *pengar på* ~*en* money in (at) the bank; *spränga* ~*en* (*spel.*) break the bank; *sätta in på* ~*en* deposit in the bank, bank; *ta ut från* ~*en* withdraw from the bank

1 banka *se bulta*

2 banka *flyg.* bank

bank|affärer bank[ing] business (transactions) **-automat** *se bankomat* **-bok** bankbook, passbook **-bud** bank messenger **-direktör** bank executive; bank manager

ban'kett *s3* banquet

bank|fack safe-deposit box **-filial** branch [of a bank] **-fridag** bank holiday **-förbindelse** bank (banking) connection; (*i brevhuvud*) bank[er] **-garanti** bank[er's] guarantee **-giro** bank giro service (account) **-inspektion** ~*en* [the Swedish] bank inspection board

ban'kir *s3* [private] banker **-firma** banking house, bankers (*pl*)

bank|kamrer *ung.* chief clerk of a bank department, bank accountant; (*vid filial*) branch manager **-kassör** bank cashier; *AE.* teller **-konto** bank account **-kontor** bank (banking, branch) office **-kort** banker's card, bank card **-kredit** bank credit **-lån** bank loan **-man** banker, bank official; bank clerk

bankofullmäktige the board of governors of the Riksbank (Bank of Sweden)

bankomat automatic cash dispensing machine, cash dispenser **-kort** cash card

bank'rutt I *s3* bankruptcy, failure; *göra* ~ become bankrupt **II** *a4* bankrupt, ruined; *vara* (*bli*) ~ be (go) bankrupt **-era** become bankrupt; go bankrupt **-mässig** *a1, vara* ~ be insolvent, be on the verge of bankruptcy **-ör** bankrupt

bank|rån bank robbery **-rånare** bank robber **-räkning** bank account **-ränta** bank rate **-tillgodohavande** bank balance **-tjänsteman** bank clerk; *AE.* teller **-valv** strongroom; vault **-väsen** ~[*det*] banking

bann *s7* ban; anathema; *jfr bannlysning* **banna** scold

bann|bulla papal bull of excommunication **-lysa** excommunicate, put under a ban; (*friare*) ban, prohibit **-lysning** excommunication; banishment, ostracism **-or** *pl* scolding (*sg*); *få* ~ be scolded, get a scolding **-stråle** anathema; *utslunga en* ~ *mot* condemn vehemently, fulminate against

banrekord track record

banta slim; ~ *ner* reduce (*utgifterna* expenses)

bantamvikt bantamweight

bant'lär *s3* bandoleer, shoulder belt

bantning slimming **bantningskur** [course of] slimming

bantu|neger Bantu **-språk** Bantu **-stan** Bantu-

stan, homeland
ban|vagn *fritt å* ~ free on rail *(förk.* f.o.r.), *AE.*
free on truck *(förk.* f.o.t.) **-vakt** lineman
-vaktsstuga lineman's cottage **-vall** [railway]
embankment, roadbed **-övergång** level *(AE.*
grade) crossing
bapt|ism Baptist faith **-ist** *s3,* **-istisk** *a5* Baptist
baptistsamfund Baptist Church
1 bar *s3 (självservering)* snack bar, cafeteria;
(utskänkningsställe) bar, cocktail lounge
2 bar *s9 (måttenhet)* bar
3 bar *a1* bare; naked; *(blottad)* exposed; *inpå*
~a kroppen to the skin; *under ~ himmel* under
the open sky; *be på sina ~a knän* pray on one's
bended knees; *blomma på ~ kvist* blossom on
a leafless (bare) twig; *ertappa ngn på ~ gär-*
ning catch s.b. red-handed (in the act)
4 bar *imperf. av bära*
bara I *adv* only; merely; *i ~ skjortan* in one's
shirt; *det fattas ~ det!* that would be the last
straw!; *du skulle ~ våga!* just you dare!, do it,
if you dare!; *gör ~ som jag säger* you just do
as I tell you; *hon är ~ barnet* she is a mere
(just a) child; *vänta ~!* just you wait! **II** *konj*
if only; *(för så vitt)* provided, so (as) long as
ba'rack *s3* barracks *(ibl. äv.* barrack); *(skjul)*
shed; *(bostad)* tenement [building]
bar|armad *a5* barearmed **-axlad** *a5* bareshouldered
barb *s3 (fisk)* barbel
barbacka [ˣbaːr-] bareback[ed]
bar'bar *s3* barbarian **barba'ri** *s4* barbarism,
barbarity, barbarousness
barbar|isk [-'baː-] *a5* barbarian, barbaric, barbarous **-iskhet** barbarity, barbarousness **-ism**
barbarism
barbent [ˣbaːrbeːnt] *a4* barelegged
barberare [-ˣbeː-] barber
barbiturat *s7, s4* barbiturate
1 bard [-aː-] *s3 (hos val)* whalebone, baleen
2 bard [-aː-] *s3 (skald)* bard; minstrel
bardi'san *s3* partisan
bardisk [ˣbaːr-] bar [counter]
bar'dun *s3, sjö.* backstay
bardval whalebone (baleen) whale
ba'rett *s3* peakless cap; *(kantig)* biretta
barfota *adv o. oböjligt a* barefoot[ed] **-läkare**
barefoot doctor
bar|huvad *a5* bareheaded **-hänt** *a4* barehanded
barium ['baː-] *s8* barium **-gröt** barium meal
1 bark *s3, s2 (skepp)* barque, bark
2 bark *s2, s3 (på träd)* bark
3 bark *s2, s3, med.* cortex *(pl* cortices)
1 barka ~ *[av] (träd)* bark, strip; *(hudar)* tan;
~de händer horny hands
2 barka ~ *i väg* fly off; ~ *åt helvete* go to pieces
(to the dogs); *det ~r åt skogen för honom* he's
sunk
barkaroll [-'råll] *s3* barcarol[l]e
bar'kass *s3* launch; longboat
bark|borre *s2* bark beetle **-bröd** bark bread
-båt bark boat **-ning** barking, removal of the
bark
bar|last ballast; *bildl.* dead weight **-lasta** ballast
barm *s2* bosom, breast; *bildl. äv.* heart; *nära*

en orm vid sin ~ nourish a viper in one's bosom
barmark [ˣbaːr-] bare (snowless) ground
barmhärtig [-'härt-, *ibl.* ˣbarm-] *a1* merciful
(mot to); *(välgörande)* charitable *(mot* to) **-het**
mercy; *visa ~ mot* show mercy to
barmhärtighetsverk act of mercy (charity)
barmästare bartender
1 barn [-aː-] *r el. n, fys.* barn
2 barn [-aː-] *s7* child *(pl* children); *(späd-)* baby,
infant; *ett stundens ~* a creature of impulse;
samma andas ~ birds of a feather; *med ~ och*
blomma with the whole family, with kith and
kin; *bli ~ på nytt* be in one's second childhood;
vara (bli) med ~ be (become) pregnant; *han*
är som ~ i huset he is like one of the family;
hon är bara ~et she is a mere child; *hon är*
ett ~ av sin tid she is a child of her age; *alla*
~ i början everyone is a fumbler at first; *av*
~s och spenabarns mun out of the mouths of
babes and sucklings; *bränt ~ skyr elden* a once
bitten, twice shy; *kärt ~ har många namn* a
pet child has many names; *lika ~ leka bäst*
birds of a feather flock together
barna|dödlighet infant mortality **-fader** father
[of an illegitimate child] **-föderska** woman in
confinement
barnalstring procreation (begetting) of children
barna|mord infanticide **-mun** *i ~* in the mouth
of a child **-mördare** infanticide
barnarbete child labour
barna|rov kidnapping **-sinne** childlike mind;
det rätta ~t true childlike piety; *ha sitt ~ kvar*
be still young at heart **-skara** *se barnskara*
-tro childlike faith
barnavdelning children's section; *(på sjukhus)*
children's ward
barnavård child welfare (care)
barnavårds|central child welfare clinic; *AE.*
well baby clinic **-man** child welfare officer
-nämnd child welfare committee
barnaår childhood
barn|barn grandchild **-barnsbarn** great-grandchild **-beck** *med.* meconium **-begränsning**
birth control **-bespisning** meals for [poor]
children; *skol.* provision of free meals for
school children **-bidrag** [government] child
benefit **-biljett** child's ticket **-bok** child's
(children's) book **-bördshus** maternity
(lying-in) hospital **-daghem** day nursery,
crèche
barndom childhood; *(späd)* infancy *(äv. bildl.)*
barndoms|hem home of one's childhood
-minne memory from one's childhood **-vän**
friend of one's childhood
barn|dop christening **-familj** family with children **-film** children's film **-flicka** nursemaid,
nurserymaid, nurse **-förbjuden** for adults
only; ~ *film* adult audience (A) film **-förlamning** polio[myelitis], infantile paralysis **-hage**
playpen **-hem, -hus** orphanage **-husbarn** orphanage child **-jungfru** nurse[ry]maid, nurse,
nanny **-kalas** children's party **-kammare**
nursery **-kammarrim** nursery rhyme **-kläder**
children's (baby) clothes **-koloni** [children's]
holiday camp **-konfektion** children's wear

-krubba crèche **-kär** fond of children **-lek** children's game; *bildl.* child's play **-läkare** children's specialist; paediatrician **-lös** childless **-mat** baby food **-misshandel** child abuse **-morska** *s1* midwife **-omsorg** child welfare **-parkering** crèche **-passning** child minding **-piga** *se -jungfru* **-program** children's programme **-psykiater** child psychiatrist **-psykiatri** child psychiatry **-psykolog** child psychologist **-psykologi** child psychology **-puder** baby powder **-radio** radio broadcast for children; children's programme **-rik** *~a familjer* large families **-rumpa** *skämts.* baby, silly fool; *han är en riktig ~* he is a real baby **barns|ben** *från ~* from early childhood **-börd** childbirth, confinement **barn|sjukdom** children's disease (illness); *~ar* (*bildl.*) teething troubles **-sjukhus** children's hospital **-skara** family of children **-sko** child's (baby) shoe; *ha trampat ur ~rna* be out of the cradle **-skrik** child's howling **-sköterska** [child's, children's] nurse **barnslig** *a1* childlike; (*oförståndig*) childish **-het** childishness **barn|stuga** child day-care centre **-säker** childproof **-säng 1** child's bed, cot **2** *med.* childbed, childbirth, confinement; *ligga i ~* be lying-in; *dö i ~* die in childbirth **-sängsfeber** (*puerperal*) fever **-teater** children's theatre **-tillsyn** child minding **-tillåten** for children also; *~ film* universal exhibition (U) film **-trädgård** nursery school, kindergarten **-unge** child, kid; (*neds.*) brat **-uppfostran** education (bringing up) of children **-vagn** perambulator, pram; *AE.* baby carriage **-vakt** baby-sitter; *sitta* (*vara*) *~* baby-sit **-visa** children's song **-vänlig** *~t dörrhandtag* child-adapted door handle; *~ miljö* environment suitable for children
barock [-'råck] **I** *a1* **1** *konst.* baroque **2** (*orimlig*) odd, absurd **II** *s2* baroque **-ornament** baroque ornament **-pärla** baroque (irregularly shaped) pearl **-stil** baroque
barograf barograph
barometer [-'me:-] *s2* barometer; *vard.* glass **-stånd** barometric pressure
ba'ron *s3* baron; (*brittisk titel*) Lord; (*icke brittisk titel*) Baron **-essa** [-*essa] *s1* baroness; (*brittisk titel*) Lady; (*icke brittisk titel*) Baroness
1 barr *s3* (*gymnastikredskap*) (*för herrar*) parallel bars (*pl*), (*för damer*) uneven [parallel] bars (*pl*)
2 barr *s7, bot.* needle
barra shed its needles
barracuda [-*ku:-] *s1* barracuda
barri'kad *s3*, **-era** *v1* barricade
barri'är *s3* barrier
barr|skog coniferous forest (woodland) **-träd**, **-växt** conifer; fir
barservering snack bar, cafeteria
barsk *a1* gruff, harsh, rough **-het** gruffness *etc.*
barskrap|a scrape bare **-ad** *a5, vard.* stony broke; *han är inte ~* he is not badly off
bar|skåp cocktail cabinet **-stol** bar stool
bart [-a:-] *blott och ~* merely, only
bartender *s2* bartender

bartolomeinatten [-*me:i-] *hist.* St. Bartholomew's Day Massacre
barvinter snowless winter
baryon [-'å:n] *s3* baryon
bary'sfär *s3* barysphere
ba'ryt *s3, miner.* barytes
baryton ['barrytån *el.* 'barri-] *s3* baritone
1 bas *s2, mus.* bass; bass voice
2 bas *s2* (*arbetsförman*) foreman, *fem.* forewoman; *vard.* boss
3 bas *s3, mat. o. kem.* base; (*utgångspunkt*) base
4 bas *s3* (*grund*) basis
1 basa (*aga*) whip, smack
2 basa (*ångbehandla*) steam
3 basa *vard.* (*vara ledare*) be the boss (*för* of)
ba'salt *s3* basalt
ba'sar *s3* baza[a]r **-stånd** *s7* stall
basbelopp basic amount
baseball ['beisbå:l] *s2* baseball **-spelare** baseball player
Basedows sjukdom ['ba:-] Graves' disease
basera base; *~ sig på* be based upon; base one's statements upon
basfiol double bass; *vard.* bass [fiddle]
bashyra basic rent
basilika [-'si:- *el.* -*si:-] *s1* **1** (*byggnad*) basilica **2** (*kryddväxt*) [sweet] basil
basi'lisk *s3* basilisk; (*fabeldjur äv.*) cockatrice
basindustri basic industry
basis ['ba:-] *r* basis; *på ~ av* on the basis of
basisk ['ba:-] *a5* basic
basist double-bass player; bassist
bask *s3* Basque
basker ['bask-] *s2* beret
basketboll ['ba:sket-] basketball
bask|isk ['bask-] *a5* **-iska** *s1* (*språk*) Basque
basklav bass clef, F clef
bas|linje baseline **-livsmedel** staple foods **-läger** base camp
basrelief *s3* bas-relief
basröst bass [voice]
basse *s2, vard.* lubber; *mil. ung.* private, Tommy
bassångare bass [singer]
bas'säng *s3* basin; (*bad-*) pool
bast *s7* bast; (*fiber*) bast, bass; (*t. flätning etc.*) raffia
1 basta *och därmed ~!* and there's an end of it!, and that's that!
2 basta *vard.* (*bada bastu*) take a sauna
bas'tant *a1* substantial, solid; (*tjock*) stout
bastard [-'ta:rd] *s3* bastard; *naturv.* hybrid
bastfiber bast fibre
Bastiljen [-'tiljen] the Bastille
bastingering [-iŋ'ge:-] *sjö.* topgallant bulwark
bastion [basti'@:n] *s3* bastion
bast|matta bass (bast) mat **-omspunnen** *a5, ~ flaska* bast-encased bottle
baston [*ba:s-] bass note
basto'nad *s3* bastinado, thrashing
bastrumma bass drum
bastu *s5* sauna; *bada ~* take a sauna
bastuba bass tuba
basun *s3* trombone; (*friare*) trumpet; *stöta i ~ för sig* blow one's own trumpet **-era** *~ ut* noise abroad (about) **-ist** trombonist **-stöt** trumpet blast

B

bas|vara staple commodity **-år** base year
ba'talj s3 battle; (tumult) turmoil, tussle **-mål-ning** painting of battle scene[s]; battlepiece
batal'jon s3 **1** mil. battalion **2** (i kägelspel) slå ~ make a strike, knock down all the pins
batat sweet potato, batata
ba'tik s3 bat[t]ik
batist batiste, cambric, lawn
batong [-'tåŋ] s3 truncheon; AE. äv. blackjack
batteri battery; tekn. o. fys. storage battery, accumulator; mus. rhythm section, drums **-dri-ven** battery operated (powered) **-laddare** [battery] charger **-radio** battery receiver (set)
batterist drummer; timpanist
baty|'sfär bathysphere **-'skaf** s3 bathyscaph[e]
baud [bå:d] r (måttenhet) baud
bautasten [bau-] ung. menhir, old Norse memorial stone
bauxit [bau'ksi:t] s3 bauxite
B-avdrag leave on partial pay
baxa prise; AE. pry
baxna be astounded; han ljuger så man ~r his lies take one's breath away
BB förk. för barnbördshus
B-dur B flat major
be bad bett **1** (anhålla) ask (ngn om ngt s.b. for s.th.); (hövligt) request (ngn att göra ngt s.b. to do s.th.); (enträget) beg, implore, entreat, beseech; får jag ~ om brödet? may I trouble you for the bread?; jag ber att få beklaga sorgen may I express my deep sympathy; jag ber om min hälsning till my kind regards to, please remember me to; jag ber om ursäkt I beg your pardon; litet gladare, om jag får ~ do cheer up a little; nu ber du för din sjuka mor that's one for her (etc.) and two for yourself; se bedjande på ngn look imploringly at s.b.; å jag ber! don't mention it! **2** (förrätta bön) pray **3** (inbjuda) ask, invite
beakt|a [-'akta] pay attention to; notice, observe; (fästa avseende vid) pay regard to, heed; (ta hänsyn t.) consider, take into consideration; att ~ to be noted **-ande** s6 consideration; med ~ av in (with) regard to, considering **-ansvärd** [-ˣakt-] a1 worth (worthy of) attention, noteworthy; (ansenlig) considerable
bearbet|a [ˣbe:-] (gruva o.d.) work; (jord) cultivate; kem. treat, process; tekn. machine, (med verktyg) tool; (bok) revise; (teaterpjäs) adapt; (vetenskapligt material, råmaterial) work up; mus. arrange; (bulta på) pound; bildl. [try to] influence; (väljare, kunder) canvass **-ning** working etc.
bearnaisesås [-ˣnä:s-] Béarnaise [sauce]
bebland|a [-'blanda] rfl **1** (umgås) associate, mix (med with) **2** have sexual intercourse (med with) **-else 1** association **2** sexual intercourse
be'bo inhabit; (hus) occupy, live in **-elig** [-'bo:-] a5 [in]habitable, fit to live in
bebygg|a [-'bygga] (område) build [up]on; (befolka) colonize, settle [down] in; glest -da områden thinly populated (rural) areas; tätt -da områden densely built-up areas **-else 1** konkr. buildings (pl), houses (pl) **2** building up; colonization, settlement
bebåd|a [-'bå:-] (tillkännage) announce, proclaim; (förebåda) herald, betoken; (ställa i ut-

sikt) foreshadow **-else** bibl. Annunciation **-el-sedag** Marie ~ Lady (Annunciation) Day
béchamelsås [beʃaˣmell-] béchamel sauce
beck s7 pitch
becka'sin s3 snipe
beckbyxa (sjöman) Jack Tar
beck|ig pitchy **-mörk** pitch-dark **-mörker** pitch-darkness **-svart** pitch-black
becquerel [beke'räll] r (måttenhet) becquerel
be|dagad [-'da:-] a5 passé; past one's prime **-darra** [-'darra] calm down, lull, abate
bedja [ˣbe:-] se be
be|'dra[ga] deceive, impose upon; vard. dupe, trick; (på pengar) swindle, defraud; (vara otrogen mot) betray; om inte mitt minne -drar mig if [my] memory serves me right; skenet -drar appearances are deceptive; snålheten -drar visheten penny-wise and pound-foolish; världen vill ~s the world likes to be cheated; ~ sig be mistaken (på ngn in s.b.)
bedrag|are, -erska [-'dra:-] impostor, swindler; vard. fraud
be|'drift s3 exploit, achievement, feat **-driva** [-'dri:-] carry on, manage; (studier) pursue; (sysselsättning) prosecute; ~ hotellrörelse run a hotel
bedräg|eri (brott) fraud, imposture, swindle; (bländverk) illusion; lögn och ~ fraud and falsehood **-lig** [-'drä:g-] a1 (om pers.) false, deceitful; (om sak) deceptive, delusive, illusory, fraudulent; ~t förfarande fraudulent proceeding[s pl], deceit; på ~t sätt fraudulently, by fraud
bedröv|a [-'drö:-] distress, grieve; det ~r mig djupt it distresses me deeply **-ad** a5 distressed, grieved (över at, about) **-else** distress, grief, sorrow, affliction; efter sju sorger och åtta ~r after countless troubles and tribulations **-lig** a1 deplorable, lamentable; (svagare) regrettable, sad; (usel) miserable
bedu'in s3 Bed[o]uin
bedyr|a [-'dy:-] protest (inför to; vid on); asseverate; ~ sin oskuld protest one's innocence; edligen ~ swear **-ande** s6 protesting; protestation (om of), asseveration
bedår|a [-'då:-] infatuate, fascinate; enchant **-ande** a4 infatuating etc.; charming
bedöm|a [-'dömma] judge, form an opinion of; (uppskatta) estimate; (betygsätta) mark; (en bok) review, criticize **-ande** s6 judging, judgement; estimate; judgement; mark-setting; review, criticism; efter eget ~ at one's own discretion; det undandrar sig mitt ~ that is beyond my judgment **-are** judge **-ning** se -ande **-ningsfråga** matter of judgment
bedöv|a [-'dö:-] make (render) unconscious; stun, stupefy; med. anaesthetize **-ande** a4 stunning, stupefying; med. anaesthetic; narcotic; (öron-) deafening **-ning** (medvetslöshet) unconsciousness; (narkos) anaesthesia **-nings-medel** anaesthetic [agent]
beediga [-'e:di-] swear to, confirm by oath; ~d sworn [to]; ~t intyg sworn certificate
befall|a [-'falla] v2 **1** (kommendera) order; (högtidligt) command; (tillsäga) tell; (föreskriva) prescribe, direct; (an-) commit, commend; inte låta sig ~s av vem som helst not take orders

from just anybody; *som ni -er* as you choose (please); *vad -s?* I beg your pardon? **2** (*föra befälet*) [have, exercise] command; *~ fram* call for; *~ fram sina hästar* order one's horses; *ni har blott att* ~ you have only to say the word **-ande** *a4* commanding; imperative; imperious **-ning** order, command; *på ngns* ~ by the order of s.b.; *få* ~ *att* receive orders to, be ordered to; *ge* ~ *om ngt* issue orders about s.th. **-ningshavande** *s9, konungens* ~ (*ung.*) County Administration

1 befara [-'fa:-] *v1* (*frukta*) fear; *~ det värsta* expect the worst

2 befar|a [-'fa:-] *befor befarit* (*fara på el. över*) travel through, traverse; (*om fartyg*) navigate; *~ en väg* use (frequent) a road

befaren *a5, sjö.* experienced

befatt|a [-'fatta] *rfl, ~ sig med* concern o.s. with, *vard.* go in for; *sådant ~r jag mig inte med* that is no business of mine **-ning 1** (*beröring*) dealing, connection; *ta ~ med* take notice of; *vi vill inte ha ngn ~ med den saken* we do not want to have anything to do with that **2** (*anställning*) post, appointment, position; office

befattnings|beskrivning job description **-havare** employee; (*ämbetsman*) official; *koll.* staff, *AE.* personnel

befinn|a [-'finna] *rfl* (*vara*) be; (*känna sig*) feel; (*upptäcka sig vara*) find o.s.; *hur -er ni er i dag?* how are you today? **-ande** *s6* [state of] health, condition **-as** prove (turn out) [to be]; *han befanns vara oskyldig* he turned out to be innocent; *vägd och befunnen för lätt* weighed in the balance and found wanting

befintlig [-'fint-] *a5* (*förefintlig*) existing; (*tillgänglig*) available; *i ~t skick* in [its] existing condition **-het** existence; presence

be|fjädrad [-'fjä:d-] *a5* feathered **-flita** [-'fli:-] *rfl, ~ sig om* exert o.s. to maintain, strive after [to attain] **-fläcka** [-'fläcka] stain, defile

befogad [-'fo:-] *a5* (*om pers.*) authorized, entitled (*att* to); (*om sak*) justifiable, justified, legitimate; *det ~e i* the justness (legitimacy) of **befogenhet** [-'fo:-] authority, powers (*pl*), right; *sakna* ~ lack competence; *överskrida sina ~er* exceed one's powers

befolk|a [-'fålka] populate, people; *glest* (*tätt*) *~d trakt* sparsely (densely) populated region **-ning** population

befolknings|explosion population explosion **-förhållanden** *pl* demographic (population) situation (*sg*) **-grupp** group of the population **-lager** stratum (*pl* strata) of the population **-lära** demography **-pyramid** population pyramid **-statistik** vital (population) statistics (*pl*) **-tillväxt** population growth **-täthet** population density **-överskott** surplus population

befordr|a [-'fo:rdra] **1** (*sända*) convey, transport, forward, send; (*skeppa*) ship; (*med post*) send by mail **2** (*upphöja*) promote; *~ ngn till kapten* promote s.b. captain **3** (*främja*) promote, further; *arbete ~r hälsa och välstånd* he that labours and thrives spins gold; *~ matsmältningen* aid digestion **-an r 1** conveyance *etc.*; *för vidare* ~ to be forwarded **2** promotion, advancement, furtherance **-ande** *a4* promotive (*för* of)

befordrings|avgift [-'fo:rd-] forwarding charge[s *pl*], postage, carriage **-gång** system of promotion **-medel** means of conveyance (transport), transportation **-möjligheter** chances of promotion **-sätt** mode of conveyance

befrakt|a [-'frakta] charter, freight **-are** charterer, freighter, shipper **-ning** chartering, freighting **-ningsavtal** freight contract; *sjö.* [time] charter

befri|a [-'fri:a] set free, liberate; (*från löfte o.d.*) release; (*frälsa*) deliver (*från* from; *ur* out of); (*från börda o.d.*) relieve; (*från bojor*) unchain; (*från ansvar o.d.*) exonerate; (*frikalla*) exempt; (*från examensprov*) excuse; (*undsätta*) relieve; *~d från (exempt) from; ~ träd från ohyra* rid trees of blight; *~ från rost* derust, clean of rust; *~ från straff* remit a penalty (punishment); *~ sig från* free o.s. from; *~ sig från ngt obehagligt* shake off s.th. unpleasant **-ande** I *a4* liberating *etc.*; *en ~ suck* a sigh of relief II *adv, verka* ~ have a relieving effect, give relief **-are** liberator; deliverer; rescuer

befrielse [-'fri:-] **1** (*frigörelse*) freeing; liberation; release; *~ns timme* the hour of deliverance **2** (*frikallande*) exemption; *~ från avgift* exemption from duty **3** (*lättnad*) relief **-front** liberation front **-krig** war of liberation **-rörelse** liberation movement

befrukt|a [-'frukta] fertilize, fecundate; *bildl.* stimulate, inspire **-ning** fertilization, fecundation; *konstgjord* ~ artificial insemination

befrynd|a [-'frynda] *rfl* ally o.s. (*med ngn* to s.b.) **-ad** *a5* related (*med* to); allied (*med* to, with) (*äv. bildl.*)

befrämj|a [-'främja] promote, further, stimulate; encourage **-ande** I *s6* furthering; promotion, furtherance; encouragement II *a4* promoting *etc.* **-are** promoter, supporter

befullmäktig|a [-full-] authorize, empower; *en ~d* an attorney, a proxy; *~t ombud* authorized representative, proxy **-ande** *s6* authorization

be'fäl *s7* **1** command; *föra ~ över* be in command of; *inneha högsta ~et* be first in command **2** *pers. koll.* [commissioned and noncommissioned] officers (*pl*) **-havande** *s9, ~ officer* commanding officer, officer in command **-havare** commander (*över* of); *sjö.* master, captain (*på ett fartyg* of a ship)

befäls|föring the exercise of command **-person** *se befäl 2* **-post** command **-tecken** broad pennant

befängd [-'fäŋd] *a1* preposterous, absurd, ridiculous; (*om pers.*) out of his (*etc.*) senses **-het** madness, absurdity

befäst|a [-'fästa] fortify; *bildl.* consolidate, confirm, strengthen; *~ sin ställning* consolidate one's position **-ning** fortification

befästnings|konst [science of] fortification **-verk** fortifications (*pl*), defensive works (*pl*)

begabb|a [-'gabba] scoff [at], mock **-else** scoffing, mockery

begagn|a [-'gaŋna] use, make use of, employ; *~ sig av* (*använda*) make use of, employ, *b*) (*dra fördel av*) profit by, avail o.s. of; *~ sig av tillfället* seize the opportunity **-ad** *a5* used; (*om*

vara) second-hand **-ande** *s6* use, employment
begapa [-'ga:pa] gape at
be|ge [-'je:] *rfl* go, proceed; ~ *sig av* depart (*till*
to, for), set out (off) (*till for*), start (*till for*);
repair (*till* to); ~ *sig på flykt* take to flight; ~
sig till sjöss go (put out) to sea; *på den tiden
det -gav sig* in the good old days; *det -gav sig
inte bättre än att han* as ill-luck would have
it, he
begeistr|ad [-'gei- *el.* -'gai-] *a5* enthusiastic
-ing enthusiasm
begiva [-'ji:-] *se bege*
begiven [-'ji:-] *a3* given (*på* to), fond (*på* of),
keen (*på* on) **-het** (*böjelse*) fondness (*på* for);
(*händelse*) [great] event; (*attraktion*) highlight
begjuta [be'ju:-] pour upon; soak, water
begonia [-'gɔ:-] *s1* begonia
begrav|a [-'gra:-] *v2* bury; *död och -en* dead and
buried; ~ *i glömska* consign to oblivion; *här
ligger en hund -en* I smell a rat **-ning** (*jord-
fästning*) burial; (*ceremoni*) funeral
begravnings|akt funeral ceremony **-byrå** firm
of undertakers (*AE. äv.* morticians) **-entrepre-
nör** undertaker; *AE. äv.* mortician **-hjälp** death
grant **-kassa** funeral expenses fund **-marsch**
dead march **-plats** (*äldre*) burial ground; (*modern*) cemetery **-procession** funeral procession
be'grepp *s7* conception, notion, idea; *filos.* concept, idea; *göra sig* (*ge*) *ett ~ om* form (give)
an idea of; *inte ha det ringaste ~ om* not have
the slightest idea (notion) of, know nothing
whatever about; *stå i ~ att* be on the point of,
be about to
begrepps|analys concept analysis **-bestäm-
ning** concept definition **-förvirring** confusion
of ideas **-vidrig** illogical
begrip|a [-'gri:p-] understand, comprehend;
grasp; see; *få ngn att ~* make clear to s.b.; ~
sig på understand **-lig** *a1* intelligible, comprehensible (*för* to); *av lätt ~a skäl* for obvious
reasons; *göra ngt ~t för ngn* make s.th. clear
to s.b.
begrundan [-'grund-] *r* meditation, reflection
begrundansvärd [-ˣgrunn-] *a1* worth considering
begråta [-'grå:-] mourn, weep for, deplore, lament; (*högljutt*) bewail
begräns|a [-'gränsa] bound, border; *bildl.* de-
fine; (*inskränka*) limit, restrict, circumscribe;
~ *sig* limit (restrict, confine) o.s. (*till* to); *bolag med ~d ansvarighet* limited [liability] company; *ha ~de resurser* have limited resources
(means) **-ning** boundary; *bildl.* limitation, restriction, restraint
begynn|a [-'jynna] *v3* begin **-else** beginning,
outset
begynnelse|bokstav initial [letter]; *stor ~* capi-
tal **-lön** commencing salary **-ord** initial (opening) word **-stadium** initial (first) stage (phase)
be'gå 1 (*göra sig skyldig t.*) commit; ~ *ett fel*
make a mistake; ~ *självmord* (*ett brott*) commit
suicide (a crime) **2** (*fira*) celebrate; ~ *nattvar-
den* go to Communion **-ende** *s6* **1** committing
etc. **2** celebration
begåv|a [-'gå:-] endow **-ad** *a5* gifted, clever,
talented; *klent ~* untalented; *konstnärligt ~* ar-

tistic; *han är konstnärligt ~* (*äv.*) he has artistic
gifts **-ning 1** (*anlag*) talent[s *pl*], gift[s *pl*] **2**
pers. talented (gifted) person; *en av våra största ~ar* one of our best (most brilliant) minds
begåvnings|flykt brain drain **-reserv** unex-
ploited talent
begär [-'jä:r] *s7* desire (*efter* for); (*starkare*)
craving, longing (*efter* for); (*åtrå*) appetite, lust
(*efter* for); *fatta ~ till* conceive a desire for;
hysa ~ efter (*till*) feel a desire for, covet; *tygla
sina ~* restrain one's desires (passions)
begära [-'jä:-] *v2* ask [for], demand; (*anhålla
om*) request; (*ansöka om*) apply for; (*fordra*)
require; (*trakta efter*) covet; (*vänta sig*) expect;
~ *avsked* hand in one's resignation; ~ *ordet* ask
permission to speak; *är det för mycket begärt?*
is it too much to ask?
begär|an [-'jä:r-] *r* (*anhållan*) request (*om* for);
(*anmodan*) demand (*om* for); (*ansökan*) application (*om* for); *på ~* on request; *på egen ~*
at his (*etc.*) own request; *bifalla en ~* grant a
request; *skickas på ~* will be sent on request
(application) **-else** desire **-lig** *a5* (*eftersökt*) in
demand, sought after; (*tilltalande*) attractive;
(*lysten*) covetous **-ligt** *adv* covetously; ~ *gripa
efter* reach greedily for
be'hag *s7* **1** (*belåtenhet*) pleasure, delight; (*tillfredsställelse*) satisfaction; (*tycke*) fancy; *fatta
~ till* take a fancy to; *finna ~ i* [take] pleasure
in, delight in **2** (*gottfinnande*) pleasure, will;
efter ~ at pleasure, at one's own discretion **3**
(*behaglighet*) charm; amenity; *äga nyhetens ~*
have the charm of novelty; *det har sitt ~* it has
a charm of its own **4** (*behagfullhet*) grace,
charm; *åldras med ~* grow old gracefully **5**
(*yttre företräden*) charms (*pl*), allurements (*pl*);
kvinnliga ~ feminine charms
behag|a [-'ha:-] **1** (*tilltala*) please, appeal to;
(*verka tilldragande*) attract; *gör som det ~r er!*
do as you please! **2** (*önska, finna för gott*) like,
choose, wish; *ni ~r skämta* you see fit to make
jokes; *~s det te?* do you wish to have tea?; *vad
~s?* what would you like?; *som ni ~r* as you
please **-full** graceful; charming **-lig** *a1* pleasant; (*tilltalande*) pleasing, attractive; (*starkare*)
delightful; *en ~ röst* a pleasant voice; *~t sätt*
engaging manners **-sjuk** coquettish **-sjuka** co-
quettishness, coquetry
behandl|a [-'hand-] treat; (*handskas med, av-
handla, handla om*) deal with; (*dryfta*) discuss,
consider; (*hantera*) handle, use, manipulate;
(*sår*) dress; *tekn.* process, work; ~ *illa* ill-treat,
treat badly; *~s varsamt* handle with care **-ing**
treatment; dealing [with]; discussion; handling,
usage; process; *parl.* reading, discussion; *jur.*
conduct, hearing **-ingsmetod** method of treatment; procedure
behandskad [-'hand-] *a5* gloved
behaviorism [bihei-] behaviourism
be|hjälplig [be'hjälp-] *a5, vara ngn ~ med* help
s.b. (*att göra ngt* to do s.th., in doing s.th.)
-hjärtad [be'järtad] *a5* brave, courageous
-hjärtansvärd [beˣjärt-] *a1* worth[y of] earnest consideration; *-hjärtansvärt ändamål* deserving cause **-hornad** [-'hɔ:r-] *a5* horned
be'hov *s7* **1** (*brist; krav*) want, need, lack; (*nöd-
vändighet*) necessity; (*förråd*) requirement[s

pl]; *allt efter* ~ as required; *av ~et påkallad* necessary, essential; *för framtida* ~ for future needs; *vid* ~ when necessary; *fylla ett länge känt* ~ supply a long-felt demand; *ha ~ av* need, have need of; *vara i ~ av* be in need of; *tobak är ett ~ för honom* tobacco is a necessity for him **2** (*naturbehov*) *förrätta sina* ~ relieve o.s.
behovsprövning means test
behå *s2* brassiere; *vard.* bra
be'håll *n, i* ~ left intact; *i gott* ~ safe and sound; *undkomma med livet i* ~ escape alive
behåll|a [-'hålla] keep, retain; (*bi-*) preserve; ~ *fattningen* keep one's head; ~ *ngt för sig själv* keep s.th. to o.s.; *inte få* ~ *maten* not be able to keep one's food down; *om jag får* ~ *hälsan* if I am allowed to keep my health **-are** container; (*vatten-*) tank, cistern; (*större*) reservoir **-en** *a5* remaining; (*om vinst*) clear, net **-ning** (*återstod*) remainder, rest, surplus; (*saldo*) balance; (*vinst*) [net] profit (proceeds [*pl*]), yield; (*i dödsbo*) residue; *bildl.* profit, benefit; *ha ~ av ngt* (*bildl.*) profit (benefit) by s.th.
behår|ad [-'hå:-] *a5* covered with hair **-ing** hair growth
be|häftad [-'häft-] *a5,* ~ *med* afflicted with; ~ *med brister* defective; ~ *med fel* marred by errors, defective; ~ *med skulder* in debt **-händig** [-'händ-] *a1* (*flink*) deft, dexterous; (*fyndig*) clever; (*lätthanterlig*) handy; (*näpen*) natty; *ett ~t litet barn* a sweet (*AE.* cute) little child **-hänga** [-'häŋa] hang all over
behärsk|a [-'härs-] **1** (*härska över*) rule over, control; (*vara herre över*) be master of; (*dominera*) command; (*vara förhärskande*) dominate; ~ *marknaden* (*havet*) control the market (the sea); ~ *situationen* be master of the situation **2** (*tygla*) control; ~ *sina känslor* (*sig*) control one's feelings (o.s.) **3** (*vara hemma i*) ~ *franska fullständigt* have a complete mastery of French **-ad** *a5* [self-]controlled, restrained, self-restrained **-ning** control, [self-]restraint
behörig [-'hö:-] *a5* **1** (*vederbörlig*) proper, fitting, due; *i* ~ *ordning* in due course; *på ~t avstånd* at a safe distance **2** (*berättigad*) appropriate, competent, duly qualified; (*om lärare o.d.*) certificated; *icke* ~ unauthorized, incompetent; ~ *domstol* court of competent jurisdiction; ~ *ålder* required age **-en** properly, duly **-het** authority, competence; *domstols* ~ the jurisdiction of a court; *styrka sin* ~ prove one's authority
behöv|a [-'hö:-] *v2* **1** (*ha behov av*) need, be in need of, want, require; *jag -er det inte längre* I have no more use for it; *han -de bara visa sig på gatan för att* he only had to appear in the street to **2** (*vara tvungen*) need, have [got] to; *detta -er inte innebära* this does not necessarily imply (mean); *du hade inte -t komma* you need not have come; *jag har aldrig -t ångra detta* I have never had occasion to regret it **-ande** *a4* needy **-as** *v2, dep* be needed (necessary, wanted); *det -s inte* there's no need [for (of) it]; *om (när) så -s* if (when) necessary; *mer än som -s* more than enough, enough and to spare; *det -des bara att hon sade* all it needed was for her to say **-lig** *a1* necessary

beige [bä:ʃ] *oböjligt s o. a* beige
beivr|a [-'i:v-] denounce, protest against; *lagligen* ~ bring an action against, take legal action (steps) **-an** *r* denunciation
bej *s3* bey
bejak|a [-'ja:-] (*fråga*) answer in the affirmative; (*anhållan*) assent to **-ande I** *s6* answering; affirmative answer; assent (*av* to) **II** *a4* affirmative, assenting
bekajad [-'kaj-] *a5* affected, afflicted (*med* with)
be'kant I *a1* (*känd*) known; *som* ~ as you know, as is well known; *enligt vad jag har mig* ~ as far as I know, to the best of my knowledge; *det är allmänt* ~ it is generally known **2** (*allmänt känd*) well-known; (*omtalad*) noted (*för* for); (*ökänd*) notorious; ~ *för sin skönhet* famous (celebrated) for its (*etc.*) beauty **3** (*personligen* ~) acquainted; *nära* ~ intimate; *hur blev ni ~a?* how did you become acquainted? **4** (*förtrogen med*) familiar with, cognizant of; *han föreföll mig* ~ his face seemed familiar [to me] **II** *subst. a* acquaintance, friend
bekant|a [-'kanta] *rfl* get to know (*med ngn* s.b.), make acquaintance (*med* with) **-göra** [-ˣkant-] announce, proclaim, make known; (*i tidning*) publish, advertise **-skap** *s3* acquaintance; (*kännedom*) knowledge; *vid närmare* ~ on [closer] acquaintance; *göra ~ med* become acquainted with; *stifta ~ med ngn* make a p.'s acquaintance; *säga upp ~en med* cease to be friends with **-skapskrets** [circle of] acquaintances
bekika [-'çi:-] stare (gaze) at
beklag|a [-'kla:-] (*tycka synd om*) be sorry for; (*hysa medlidande med*) pity; (*vara ledsen över*) regret; (*känna ledsnad över*) deplore; (*ta avstånd från*) deprecate; ~ *sorgen* extend one's condolences; ~ *sig* complain (*över* of; *för, hos* to); *jag ~r att jag inte kan komma* I regret I cannot come; *jag ber att få ~ sorgen* I am grieved to hear about your bereavement, please accept my deep sympathy **-ande I** *s6* [expression of] sorrow (regret); *det är med ~ jag måste meddela* I regret to inform you **II** *a4* regretful **-ansvärd** [-ˣkla:-] *a1* (*om sak*) regrettable, deplorable, sad; (*om pers.*) poor, pitiable, to be pitied, wretched **-lig** *a1* regrettable, deplorable, unfortunate; *det är ~t* it is to be deplored **-ligtvis** unfortunately, to my (*etc.*) regret, I (*etc.*) regret to say
bekläd|a [-'klä:-] **1** (*påklädа*) clothe **2** (*täcka*) cover, case; (*med bräder*) board [up]; (*med plattor*) tile [over]; (*invändigt*) line; (*utvändigt*) face **3** (*inneha*) fill, hold; ~ *ngn med ett ämbete* invest s.b. with an office **-nad** *s3* **1** (*beklädande*) clothing, covering **2** (*överdrag*) *tekn.* (*invändigt*) lining, (*utvändigt*) covering, *byggn.* (*utvändigt*) facing, revetment; (*trä-*) boarding, panelling **-nadsindustri** clothing industry
be'kläm|d *a1* oppressed, depressed **-mande** *a4* depressing, distressing; *det är ~ att se* (*äv.*) it is a depressing sight **-ning** oppression, depression
bekomm|a [-'kåmma] **1** (*erhålla*) receive; *valuta -en* value received **2** ~ *ngn väl* (*illa*) agree

(disagree) with s.b.; do s.b. good (harm); *väl -e! (välönskan) (ung.)* it's a pleasure!, *AE.* you're welcome [to it]!, *iron.* serve[s] you right! **3** *(göra intryck på)* concern; *det -er henne ingenting* it has no effect upon her; *utan att låta sig ~* without taking any notice **bekost|a** [-'kåsta] pay for, defray (cover) [the expenses of] **-nad** *r* expense, cost; *på allmän ~* at the public expense; *på egen ~* at one's own expense; *på ngns ~* at a p.'s expense; *på ~ av* at the expense of
be|kransa [-'kransa] wreathe; *(friare)* festoon **-kriga** [-'kri:-] wage war [up]on, fight against
bekräft|a [-'kräfta] **1** *(bestyrka)* confirm, corroborate; *(intyga)* certify; *(erkänna)* acknowledge; *(säga ja)* affirm; *~ en uppgift* confirm a statement, *jur.* corroborate evidence; *~ riktigheten av* bear [s.b.] out; *~ med ed* swear [to]; *undantaget som ~r regeln* the exception that proves the rule; *~ mottagandet av* acknowledge receipt of **2** *(stadfästa)* ratify **-else 1** *(bestyrkande)* confirmation, corroboration; *(intygande)* certification; *(erkännande)* acknowledgment, acknowledgement **2** *(stadfästelse)* ratification, sanction
be'kväm *a1* **1** *(angenäm)* comfortable; *(hemtrevlig)* cosy; *(läglig)* convenient, handy; *göra det ~t för sig* make o.s. comfortable **2** *(maklig)* easy-going, indolent; *vara ~ [av sig]* like to take things easy, be lazy **bekväma** [-'kvä:ma] *rfl, ~ sig till* be induced (bring o.s.) to [do s.th.] **bekvämlighet** [-'kvä:m-] **1** *(bekvämhet)* convenience; *(trevnad)* comfort; *till de resandes ~* for the convenience of the passengers **2** *(maklighet)* love of ease **3** *(komfort)* convenience; *med alla moderna ~er* with every modern convenience
bekvämlighets|flagg flag of convenience **-hänsyn** *av ~ for* the sake of convenience **-inrättning** public convenience **-skäl** reasons of convenience
bekymmer [-'çymm-] *s7 (oro)* anxiety, concern, worry; *(omsorg)* care; *(starkare)* trouble; *ha ~ för* be worried about; *ekonomiska ~* economic worries
bekymmer|fri [-ˣçymm-] free from care, carefree, untroubled **-sam** *a1* anxious, troubled, full of care, distressing; *det ser ~t ut för oss* things look bad for us **-samt** *adv, ha det ~* be having a worrying time
bekymmerslös [-ˣçymm-] light-hearted; *(slarvig)* careless **-het** light-heartedness; carelessness
bekymr|a [-'çymra] trouble, worry; *det ~r mig föga* that doesn't worry me much; *vad ~r det henne* what does she care; *~ sig om* trouble (worry) o.s. about, *äv. care about; ~ sig för framtiden* worry about the future **-ad** *a5* distressed, worried, troubled, concerned *(för, över* about)
bekyttad [-'cytt-] *a5* in a quandary
bekämp|a [-'çämpa] fight against, combat; *(i debatt)* oppose **-ande** *s6* combating **-ningsmedel** [-ˣçämp-] means of control; *~ för skadeinsekter* insecticide; *~ för ogräs* weedkiller
bekänn|a [-'çänna] *(erkänna)* confess; *(öppet ~)* avow, profess; *~ [sig skyldig]* confess, *jur. äv.*

plead guilty; *~ sig till kristendomen* confess the Christian faith; *~ färg* follow suit, *bildl.* show one's hand **-are** confessor **-else** confession; *(religionssamfund)* confession, creed, religion; *avlägga ~* confess, make a confession; *Augsburgska ~n* the Confession of Augsburg
bel *r* bel
be|lacka [-'lacka] slander, backbite **-lackare** [-'lack-] slanderer, backbiter **-lamra** [-'lamra] encumber, clutter up; *(väg)* block up
belast|a [-'lasta] **1** load, charge, burden; *bildl.* saddle **2** *hand.* charge, debit; *ärftligt ~d* with a hereditary taint **-ning** load[ing], charge, stress, pressure; *med.* affliction; *bildl.* strain, burden; *hand.* charge, debit **-ningsprov** load (tolerance) test
beledsag|a [ˣbe:-, *äv.* -ˣle:d-] accompany; *(följa efter)* follow; *(uppvakta)* attend **-are** companion **-ning** *mus.* accompaniment
belevad [-'le:-] *a5* well-bred, polite, mannerly, well-mannered
belgare Belgian **Belgien** ['belg-] *n* Belgium **belg|ier** ['belg-] *s9,* **-isk** ['belg-] *a5* Belgian
beljuga [be'ju:ga] tell lies (a lie) about
belladonna [-'dånna, -ˣdånna] *s1, bot.* deadly nightshade, belladonna, dwale; *med.* belladonna
bellis ['bell-] *s2* daisy
be'lopp [-å-] *s7* amount, sum [total]; *till ett ~ av* amounting to, to the value of; *intill ett ~ av* not exceeding; *överskjutande ~* surplus [amount]
belys|a [-'ly:-] light [up], illuminate; *bildl.* shed light on, illuminate, illustrate **-ande** *a4* illuminating; illustrative, characteristic; *ett ~ exempel* an illustrative example **-ning** lighting; illumination; *(dager)* light; *bildl.* light, illustration; *elektrisk ~* electric light; *i historisk ~* in the light of history; *i ~ av dessa omständigheter* in the light of these circumstances
belysnings|anläggning lighting plant **-armatur** *s3, ej pl* light fittings *(pl)*
belån|a [-'lå:-] **1** *(pantsätta)* pledge, pawn; *(upptaga lån på)* raise (borrow) money on; *(om fastighet)* mortgage; *fastigheten är högt ~d* the estate is heavily mortgaged **2** (ge lån på) lend [money] on; *~ en växel* discount a bill **-ing 1** *(upptagande av lån)* raising a loan, borrowing [on] **2** *(beviljande av lån)* lending **-ingsvärde** loan (collateral) value
belåten [-'lå:-] *a3 (om pers.)* content[ed]; *(om min o.d.)* satisfied, pleased **-het** contentment; satisfaction; *till allmän ~* to everybody's satisfaction; *utfalla till ~* prove satisfactory; *vara till ~* give satisfaction
belägen [-'lä:-] *a5* situated, located; *avsides ~* remote, secluded **-het** situation, position, site, location; *bildl.* situation, state, position; *svår ~* predicament, plight
be|'lägg *s7 (bevis)* proof, evidence *(för* of); *(citat)* quotation **-lägga** [-'lägga] **1** *(täcka)* cover; *(med färg o.d.)* coat; *(plats)* reserve, secure, occupy **2** *(utfästa straff för)* impose upon; *med böter* impose a fine upon, make punishable by a fine; *~ med kvarstad* sequestrate, embargo **3** *(förse med)* put on; *~ med hand-*

bojor handcuff; ~ *med stämpel* stamp **4** ~ *ett hotell med gäster* accommodate guests at a hotel **5** (*med exempel*) support [by examples]; *formen finns inte -lagd före 1500* there is no instance of the form before 1500 **6** *stopp och -lägg!* belay there! **-läggning** (*täckning*) cover[ing]; (*färg- o.d.*) coat[ing]; (*av plats*) reservation; (*på sjukhus*) number of occupied beds; (*gatu- o.d.*) paving, pavement; (*på tungan*) fur

belägr|a [-'lä:-] besiege **-ing** siege; *häva ~en* raise the siege **-ingstillstånd** state of siege; *proklamera* ~ proclaim martial law

be|läsenhet [-'lä:-] wide reading; book-learning **-läst** [-'lä:st] *a4* well-read

beläte [*be:-] *s6* **1** (*avbild*) image, likeness **2** (*avguda-*) idol

belön|a [-'lö:-] reward; (*vedergälla*) recompense; (*med pengar*) remunerate **-ing** reward; recompense; remuneration; (*pris*) award, prize

belöpa [-'lö:-] *rfl*, ~ *sig till* amount (come) to

bemann|a [-'manna] man; ~ *sig* nerve o.s., pull o.s. together; ~ *sig med tålamod* summon up patience; ~ *sig mot* harden o.s. against **-ing** crew

bemedlad [-'me:d-] *a5*, *en* ~ *person* a well--to-do person, a person of means; *mindre* ~ of small means

bemyndig|a [-'mynn-] authorize, empower **-ande** *s6* authorization; (*fullmakt*) authority, power; (*av myndighet*) sanction, warrant

be|mäktiga [-'mäkt-] *rfl* take possession of, seize; *vreden ~de sig henne* wrath took possession of her **-mälde** [-'mä:l-] *oböjligt a*, ~ *man* the said man; *ovan ~ person* the aforesaid [person] **-mänga** [-'mäŋa] *v2*, *-mängd med* mixed [up] (mingled) with, *bildl. äv.* interlarded with

bemärk|a [-'märka] observe, note **-else** sense; *i ordets egentliga* ~ in the strict sense of the word **-elsedag** red-letter (important) day

be'märkt *a4* (*uppmärksammad*) noted, well--known; (*framskjuten*) prominent; *göra sig* ~ make one's mark

be|mästra [-'mästra] master; get the better of, overcome

bemöd|a [-'mö:da] ~ *sig* endeavour, strive; *absol.* try [hard], exert o.s.; ~ *sig om ett gott uppförande* try hard to behave well **-ande** *s6* (*ansträngning*) effort, exertion; (*strävan*) endeavour

bemöt|a [-'mö:ta] **1** (*besvara*) answer; (*tillbakavisa*) refute **2** (*behandla*) treat; (*mottaga*) receive; *bli väl bemött* be treated politely **-ande** *s6* **1** reply (*av* to); refutation (*av* of) **2** treatment; *vänligt* ~ kind treatment, a kind reception

ben *s7* **1** (*i kroppen*) bone; *bara skinn och* ~ only skin and bone; *få ett* ~ *i halsen* have a bone stick in one's throat; *gå genom märg och* ~ pierce to the marrow; *skinna inpå bara ~en* fleece to the very skin **2** (*lem*) leg; *inte veta på vilket* ~ *man skall stå* be at one's wit's end; *bryta ~et* [*av sig*] break one's leg; *dra ~en efter sig* loiter along, dawdle; *hela staden var på ~en* the whole town was astir; *komma på ~en* get on one's feet; *lägga ~en på ryggen* cut and run, make off; *rör på ~en!* stir your

stumps!, get moving!; *sticka svansen mellan ~en* droop away with one's tail between one's legs; *stå på egna* ~ stand on one's own feet; *ta till ~en* take to one's heels; *vara på ~en igen* be up and about again

1 bena I *v1* (*hår*) part **II** *s1* parting

2 bena *v1* (*fisk*) bone; ~ *upp* (*bildl.*) analyze

ben|aska bone ash **-brott** fracture **-byggnad** frame[work], skeleton

benedik'tin[er]|munk Benedictine [monk] **-orden** the Order of St. Benedict, the Benedictine order

ben|fisk bony fish **-fri** off the bone; boneless

Bengalen [ben'ga:-] *n* Bengal **bengal|ier** [ben-'ga:-] *s9*, **-isk** *a5* Bengali, Bengalese; ~ *eld* Bengal light

ben|get *hon är en sån* ~ she's as thin as a rake **-hinna** *med.* periosteum (*pl* periostea) **-hård** [as] hard as bone; *bildl.* rigid, adamant

benig *a1* **1** bony; full of bones **2** (*invecklad*) puzzling

benign [-'niŋn] *a5* benign

ben|kläder trousers; *AE.* pants; (*kalsonger*) pants, undershorts, *AE.* underpants; (*dambyxor*) panties **-knota** *s1* bone **-linda** *s1* puttee, putty **-mjöl** bone meal **-märg** bone marrow **-pipa** *anat.* shaft **-porslin** bone china **-rangel** [-'raŋel] *s7* skeleton **-röta** caries

bensaldehyd [*bens-] *s3* benzaldehyde

ben'sen *s3, s7* benzene

ben'sin *s3, kem.* benzine; (*motorbränsle*) petrol, *AE.* gas[oline]; *fylla på* ~ fill up **-bolag** petroleum (*AE.* oil) company **-bomb** petrol bomb; *vard.* Molotov cocktail **-driven** petrol powered **-dunk** petrol can **-mack** *se -station* **-motor** petrol engine **-mätare** fuel (gas tank) gauge **-pump** petrol pump **-snål** petrol-saving **-station** filling (petrol) station; *AE. äv.* gas station **-tank** petrol tank

ben|skydd *sport.* shin guard, leg pad **-skörhet** brittle-bone disease

bensoe ['bensåe] *s5* benzoin **-syra** benzoic acid

bensol [-'å:l] *s3* (*äldre namn på bensen*) benzol[e]

ben|stomme skeleton **-sår** varicose ulcer **-vit** ivory white **-värmare** leggings (*pl*) **-vävnad** bone tissue

benåd|a [-'nå:da] pardon; (*dödsdömd*) reprieve **-ning** pardon[ing]; (*av dödsdömd*) reprieve

benäg|en [-'nä:-] *a3* **1** (*böjd*) inclined, willing; given; ~ *för att skämta* given (prone) to joking **2** (*välvillig*) kind, [well-]disposed; *med -et tillstånd* by kind permission; *till -et påseende* on approval; *vi emotser Ert -na svar* we await your kind reply **-enhet** inclination (*för* to, for), disposition (*för* to, towards), preference (*för* for), tendency (*för* to, towards), propensity (*för* to, towards, for), proneness (t*för to*)

benämn|a [-'nämna] call, name; (*beteckna*) designate; *-da tal* denominate numbers **-ing** name, denomination (*på* for); designation, term

beordra [-'å:r-] order; direct; (*tillsäga äv.*) instruct

beostare hill myna, Indian grackle

be|pansra [-'pans-] armour **-prisa** [-'pri:-] praise, extol **-pryda** [-'pry:-] adorn **-prövad**

[-'prö:-] *a5* [well-]tried, tested; (*om boteme-del*) approved; *en ~ vän* a staunch friend **-pudra** [-'pu:d-] dust **-rama** [-'ra:-] plan, arrange
berber ['bärr-] Berber
berberis ['bärr-] *s2* barberry
bereda [-'re:-] **1** (*tillreda, för-*) prepare; (*bearbeta*) dress, process; (*hudar*) curry; (*tillverka*) make; (*skaffa*) furnish; (*förorsaka*) cause, give; *~ ngn tillfälle* give s.b. an opportunity; *~ ngn glädje* (*bekymmer*) cause s.b. joy (trouble); *~ plats för ngn* make room for s.b. **2** *rfl* prepare o.s. (*på, till* for), get (make) ready (*för* for); (*skaffa sig*) find, furnish (give, cause, provide) o.s.; *~ sig på avslag* be prepared for a refusal; *~ sig tillträde till* effect (force) an entry to, gain access to
be'redd prepared, ready (*på* for); *vara ~ på det värsta* be prepared for the worst
beredning [-'re:d-] (*bearbetning*) dressing; currying; (*tillverkning*) manufacture; (*förberedelse*) preparation **beredningsutskott** working committee
beredskap [-'re:d-] *s3* [military] preparedness; *i ~* in readiness, ready, prepared; *ha ngt i ~* have s.th. up one's sleeve; *hålla i ~* hold in readiness (store)
beredskaps|arbete relief work **-tillstånd** state of emergency **-tjänst** emergency service
beredvillig [-ˣre:d-] ready, willing **-het** readiness, willingness
berest [-'re:st] *a4* travelled; *vara mycket ~* have travelled a great deal
berg [bärj] *s7* mountain (*äv. bildl.*); (*vid egennamn ofta*) mount; (*klippa*) rock (*äv. geol.*); (*mindre*) hill; *det sitter som ~* it won't budge
bergamott [bärga'mått] *s3* (*päron*) bergamot
berg|art rock **-bana** mountain railway **-bestigare** mountaineer; [mountain] climber **-bestigning** mountaineering; (*med pl*) [mountain] climb, ascent **-borr** jumper; (*maskin*) rock drill **-fast** [as] firm (solid) as a rock; *~ tro* steadfast belief **-grund** bedrock **-häll** rock face; flat rock
bergig [ˣbärjig] *a1* mountainous; rocky; hilly
berg|knalle rocky knoll, hillock **-kristall** [rock] crystal **-landskap** mountainous country; mountain scenery **-massiv** *s7* mountain massif **-och-dalbana** switchback; (*i nöjespark*) roller coaster, big dipper **-olja** rock oil, petroleum
bergs|bo highlander **-bruk** mining **-hantering** mining [industry] **-ingenjör** mining engineer **-kam** mountain crest **-kedja** mountain chain (range) **-knalle** *se bergknalle*
bergskreva crevice **bergslag** *s3* mining district **bergsluttning** mountain slope (side)
bergs|man occupier of a miner's homestead **-pass** mountain pass **-platå** mountain plateau **-predikan** [the] Sermon on the Mount
bergsprängare 1 (*person*) rock blaster **2** (*kassettradio*) boom box
bergs|rygg ridge **-topp** mountain peak **-trakt** mountainous district **-vetenskap** mining and metallurgy, metallurgy and materials technology
berg|säker dead certain **-tagen** *a5* spirited away [into the mountain] **-troll** mountain sprite **-uv** eagle owl **-verk** mining [industry],

mine **-vägg** rock face
beriberi [-'be:ri] *s2* beriberi
berid|are [-'ri:-] horse-breaker; *mil. äv.* riding- -master **-en** *a5* mounted
berika [-'ri:-] enrich
beriktig|a [-'rikti-] correct, rectify; adjust **-ande** *s6* correction, rectification; adjustment
berkelium [-'ke:-] *s8* berkelium
berlinare [bärˣli:-] **1** inhabitant of Berlin, Berliner **2** (*vagn*) berlin **berlinerblått** Prussian blue
berlock [bär'låck] *s3* charm
bermudarigg [-ˣmu:-] Bermuda rig
Bermudasöarna [bärˣmu:-] the Bermudas, Bermuda Islands
be'ro *v4* **1** *~ på* (*ha sin grund i*) be due (owing) to; (*komma an på*) depend on; *det ~r på* that depends, that's all according; *det ~r på tycke och smak* it is a question of taste; *det ~r på vad man menar med dyrt* it all depends on what you mean by expensive; *det ~dde på ett missförstånd* it was due to a misunderstanding **2** (*stå i beroende*) be dependent (*av* on) **3** *låta det ~ vid* be content with; *låta saken ~* let the matter rest **-ende I** *s6* dependence (*av* on) **II** *a4* dependent (*av* on); *~ på* (*på grund av*) ett misstag owing to a mistake; *~ på omständigheterna* depending on circumstances; *vara ~ av andra* be dependent on others
beroende|framkallande *a4* habit-forming **-ställning** dependence
berså [bär'så:] *s3* arbour, bower
berus|a [-'ru:-] intoxicate, inebriate; *~ sig* intoxicate o.s., get drunk (*med* on); *~d* intoxicated, drunk, *vard.* tipsy, tight; *smått ~d* a bit merry **-ande** *a4* intoxicating **-ning** intoxication, inebriation **-ningsmedel** intoxicant
beryktad [-'rykt-] *a5* notorious; *illa ~* of bad repute, disreputable
be'ryll *s3* beryl **beryllium** [-'ryll-] *s8* beryllium
be|'råd *n* **1** (*villrådighet*) hesitation; perplexity **2** *stå i ~ att* intend to **-'rått** *oböjligt a, med ~ mod* deliberately, in cold blood
beräkn|a [-'rä:k-] calculate, compute, reckon; (*noggrant*) determine; (*uppskatta*) estimate (*till* at); (*ta med i beräkningen*) take into account, count (reckon) on; (*debitera*) charge; *~ en planets bana* determine the orbit of a planet; *~ ränta* calculate interest; *~d ankomsttid* scheduled time of arrival; *~d kapacitet* rated capacity; *fartyget ~s kosta 5 miljoner kr att bygga* the cost of building the ship is estimated at 5 million kronor **-ande** *a4* calculating, scheming **-ing** calculation, computation, reckoning; estimate, estimation; *med ~* with a shrewd eye [to the effect]; *ta med i ~en* allow for, take into consideration (account)
berätt|a tell, relate, narrate; *absol.* tell stories; *~nde stil* narrative style; *~ till slut* get to the end of one's story; *det ~s att* it is reported that; *jag har hört ~s* I have been told **-are** storyteller
berättar|glädje *han visar stor ~* he takes great pleasure in storytelling **-talang** gift for telling stories, narrative skill; *pers.* born storyteller **-teknik** narrative technique
berättelse [-'rätt-] tale, short story; narrative;

(redogörelse) report *(om* about, on)*, account *(om* of)*
berättig|a [-'rätt-] entitle, justify; *(kvalificera)* qualify; *(bemyndiga)* empower, authorize **-ad** *a5* entitled, authorized, justified; *(rättmätig)* just, legitimate; well-founded, well-grounded; *~e tvivel* reasonable doubts **-ande** *s6* justification; authorization; *sakna allt ~* be completely unjustified
beröm [-'römm] *s7* praise; *(heder)* credit; *få ~* be praised; *eget ~ luktar illa* self-praise stinks in the nostrils; *med* [*utmärkt*] *~ godkänd* passed with [great] distinction; *icke utan ~ godkänd* passed with credit **be'römd** *a1* famous, well-known **berömdhet** [-'römd-] celebrity **berömlig** [-'römm-] *a1* praiseworthy, laudable; *(betyg)* excellent **berömma** [-'römma] *v2* praise, commend; *(starkare)* laud; *~ sig av* boast of; *i ~nde ordalag* in eulogistic terms **berömmelse** [-'römm-] *(ryktbarhet)* fame, renown; *(anseende)* credit; *det länder honom inte till ~* it reflects no credit on him; *vinna ~* gain distinction **berömvärd** [-ˣrömm-] *a1* praiseworthy, commendable
berör|a [-'rö:ra] touch; *(omnämna)* touch upon; *(påverka)* affect; *ytterligheterna berör varandra* extremes meet; *illa (angenämt) -d* unpleasantly (agreeably) affected; *bagerierna -s inte av strejken* the bakeries are not affected by the strike; *nyss -da förhållanden* circumstances just mentioned **-ing** contact, touch; *(förbindelse)* connection; *komma i ~ med* get into touch with, come into contact with **-ingspunkt** point of contact; *bildl.* interest (point) in common
be|röva [-'rö:-] *~ ngn ngt* deprive (rob) s.b. of s.th.; *~ ngn friheten* deprive s.b. of his liberty; *~ sig livet* take one's own life **-sanna** [-'sanna] verify; *drömmen ~des* the dream came true *-'sats* braiding; ornament
be'satt *a1 (behärskad)* possessed, obsessed; *(förryckt)* absurd; *~ av en idé* obsessed by an idea; *~ av en demon* possessed by a demon; *skrika som en ~* cry like one possessed **-het** possession; absurdity
be|'se see, look at (over); *~ Paris* see the sights of *(vard.* do) Paris **-segla** [-'se:g-] **1** sail, navigate **2** *(bekräfta)* seal; *hans öde var ~t* his fate was sealed
besegr|a [-'se:g-] beat, conquer, vanquish; *(fullständigt)* defeat; *(svårighet o.d.)* overcome, get the better of; *ve de ~de!* woe to the vanquished! **-are** conqueror, vanquisher
besiffr|a [-'siffra] *mus.* figure **-ing** *mus.* figure
besikt|iga [-'sikt-] inspect, survey, examine **-ning** inspection, survey, examination
besiktnings|instrument *(för motorfordon)* registration certificate (book) **-man** surveyor; *(för motorfordon)* motor vehicle examiner; *(för körkortsprov)* driving examiner
besinn|a [-'sinna] **1** consider, think of, bear in mind **2** *rfl (betänka sig)* consider, reflect, stop to think; *(ändra mening)* change one's mind **-ande** *s6* consideration; *vid närmare ~* on second thoughts **-ing 1** *se -ande* **2** *(medvetande)* consciousness; *förlora ~en* lose one's head; *komma till ~* come to one's senses

besinnings|full [-ˣsinn-] calm, deliberate; *(klok)* discreet **-lös** rash; *(hejdlös)* reckless
besitt|a [-'sitta] possess, have, own **-ning** possession; *franska ~ar* French possessions; *komma i ~ av* come into possession of; *ta i ~* take possession of, *(med våld)* seize
besittnings|havare possessor, occupant, owner **-rätt** possession, tenure, seisin *(AE.* seizin) **-skydd** security of tenure **-tagare** possessor, occupant, owner
be|sjunga [-'ʃuŋa] sing [of] **-själa** [-'ʃä:la] animate, inspire
besk I *a1* bitter; *~ kritik* caustic criticism **II** *s2* bitters *(pl)*
beskaff|ad [-'skaff-] *a5* conditioned; constituted; *annorlunda ~* of a different nature **-enhet** nature, character; *(varas)* quality
beskatt|a [-'skatta] tax, impose taxes [up]on; *högt ~d* heavily taxed **-ning** taxation, imposition of taxes; *(skatt)* tax[es *pl*]; *progressiv ~* progressive taxation
beskattnings|bar [-ˣskatt-] *a1* taxable *(inkomst* income) **-år** fiscal year
be'sked [-ʃ-] *s7* answer, reply; *(upplysning)* information; *(bud)* message; *(order)* instructions (pl), order; *ge ~* give an answer, send word; *ge ngn rent ~* tell s.b. straight out; *veta ~ om* know about; *●ed ~* well and good, with a will, properly; *det regnar med ~* it is raining in earnest; *det är aldrig ngt ~ med honom* he doesn't know his own mind
beskedlig [-'ʃe:d-] *a1 (flat)* meek and mild, submissive; *(anspråkslös)* modest; *(snäll)* kind, good[-natured]; *~t våp* milksop **-het** submissiveness; modesty; kindness, good-naturedness
beskhet bitterness
beskickning [-'ʃick-] embassy, legation; diplomatic representation, mission
beskjut|a [-'ʃu:ta] fire at; shell, bombard **-ning** firing; shelling, bombardment
beskriv|a [-'skri:-] describe, depict; *det kan inte ~s* it is indescribable (not to be described); *bollen beskrev en vid båge* the ball described a wide curve **-ande** *a4* descriptive **-ning** description, account *(av, på* of)*; *ge en ~ av* describe, depict; *trotsa all ~* defy description
beskugga [-'skugga] shade
be'skydd [-ʃ-] *s7* protection *(mot* from, against)*; *under kungligt ~* under royal patronage; *ställa sig under ngns ~* take refuge with s.b.
beskydd|a [-'ʃydda] protect, guard, shield *(för, mot* from, against)*; patronize **-ande I** *s6* protection **II** *a4* protective; patronizing **-are** protector; patron
beskyddarmin [-ˣʃydd-] patronizing air
beskyll|a [-'ʃylla] accuse *(för* of)*, charge *(för* with)* **-ning** accusation, charge *(för* of)*
beskåd|a [-'skå:-] look at **-ande** *a6* inspection; *utställd till allmänt ~* placed on [public] view
beskäftig [-'ʃäftig] *a1* meddlesome, fussy important, self-important **-het** meddlesomeness, self-importance
beskällare [-'ʃäll-] stallion, studhorse
be'skänkt [-ʃ-] *a4* tipsy, the worse for drink
1 beskär|a [-'ʃä:-] *v2 (ge)* vouchsafe *(ngn ngt* s.b. s.th.), grant *(ngn ngt* s.th. to s.b.); *få sin*

-**da** *del* receive one's [allotted, due] share
2 beskära [-'ʃä:-] *beskar beskurit, (avskära)*
tekn. trim; *(träd)* prune; *(reducera)* cut [down],
reduce

be|skärma [-'ʃärma] *rfl* lament *(över* over),
complain *(över* of) **-skärning** [-'ʃä:r-] *tekn.*
trimming; *(av träd)* pruning; *(reducering)* cutting, paring

be'slag *s7* **1** *(metallskydd, prydnad)* fittings,
mountings *(pl)*; *koll.* ironwork, furniture; *(på
nyckelhål o.d.)* escutcheon **2** *(kvarstad)* sei-
zure, confiscation; *lägga ~ på* requisition,
seize, vard. bag; *bildl.* secure; *lägga ~ på hela
uppmärksamheten* monopolize everybody's attention **-ta[ga]** confiscate, seize, requisition;
commandeer

be'slut *s7* decision; *(avgörande)* determination;
(av möte) resolution; *(av myndighet o. jur.)*
decision, decree, judgment; *fatta ~* make
(come to) a decision, make up one's mind, *(av
möte)* pass a resolution; *det är mitt fasta ~* it
is my firm resolve; *med ett raskt ~* without [a
moment's] hesitation, at once

besluta [-'slu:-] **1** *(bestämma)* decide *(om, över*
upon); *(föresätta sig)* resolve, determine **2** *rfl*
(bestämma sig) decide *(för* upon), make up
one's mind; *(föresätta sig)* resolve, determine
(för att to) **beslutanderätt** [-ˣslu:-] right of
decision; competence to pass a resolution **besluten** [-'slu:-] *a5* resolved, determined; *fast
~* firmly resolved **beslutför** [-ˣslu:t-] *se be-
slutsmässig*

beslutsam [-'slu:t-] *a1* resolute **-het** resolution
besluts|fattare decision-maker **-mässig** *a1,
vara ~* form a quorum; *~t antal* quorum **-pro-
cess** decision-making process

be|'slå 1 *(förse med beslag)* fit with metal;
mount; *(överdraga)* cover, case; *sjö.* furl **2** *(ertappa) ~ ngn med lögn* catch s.b. lying **-släk-
tad** [-'släkt-] *a5* related, akin *(med* to); *(om
språk o.d.)* cognate; *(om folkslag, anda)* kindred; *andligen ~ med* spiritually allied to **-slö-
ja** [-'slöja] veil; *bildl.* obscure; *~d blick* veiled
glance; *~d röst* husky voice

besman *s7* steelyard

besmitt|a [-'smitta] infect, taint; *bildl. äv.* con-
taminate **-else** infection, contagion; contami-
nation

bespara [-'spa:ra] *(spara)* save; *(förskona)*
spare; *det kunde du ha ~t dig* you might have
spared yourself the trouble **besparing 1** saving; *göra ~ar* effect economies **2** *sömn.* yoke
besparingsåtgärd economy measure

be|speja [-'speja] spy upon, watch **-spetsa**
[-'spetsa] *rfl, ~ sig på* look forward to, set
one's heart on

bespis|a [-'spi:-] feed **-ning** *abstr.* feeding,
konkr. (skol-) dining-hall

bespott|a [-'spåtta] mock [at], scoff at, deride
-else mocking *etc.*

besprut|a [-'spru:-] sprinkle, spray **-ning**
sprinkling, spraying **-ningsmedel** spray [dis-
infectant, insecticide *etc.*]

bessa'rab Bessarabian **Bessarabien** [-'ra:-] *n*
Bessarabia **bessarabisk** [-'ra:-] *a5* Bessarabian

bessemer|process [ˣbess-] Bessemer process

-**ugn** Bessemer converter
besserwisser ['bess-] know-all, wiseacre
best *s2* beast, brute; monster **bestialisk** [-ti'a:-]
a5 bestial, beastly **bestialitet** [-sti-] *s3* bestiality, beastliness

be'stick *s7* **1** *(rit- o.d.)* set of instruments;
(mat-) set of knife, spoon and fork, cutlery **2**
sjö. [dead] reckoning; *föra ~* work out the
[ship's] position

besticka [-'sticka] bribe; corrupt
bestickande [-'stick-] *a4* seductive, insidious;
låta ~ sound attractive enough
bestick|lig [-'stick-] *a1* open to bribes; cor-
ruptible **-ning** bribery; corruption
bestickräkning dead reckoning

bestig|a [-'sti:-] *(tron)* ascend; *(berg)* climb;
(häst; schavott; talarstol) mount; *bildl.* scale
-ning climbing; ascent

bestorma [-'stårma] attack, assault; *bildl.* assail, overwhelm

bestraff|a [-'straffa] punish; *(med ord)* rebuke
-ning punishment; *jur.* penalty; *(i ord)* rebuke

1 bestrida [-'stri:-] *(opponera sig mot)* contest,
dispute; *(förneka)* deny; *(tillbakavisa)* repudiate; *(förvägra)* contest, dispute, deny; *det
kan inte ~s att* it is incontestable that

2 bestrida [-'stri:-] **1** *(sköta)* fill; be responsible
for **2** *(betala)* defray, pay for

1 bestridande *s6 (t. 1 bestrida)* contesting *etc.*;
denial; repudiation

2 bestridande *s6 (t. 2 bestrida)* **1** filling **2** *(betalning)* payment; *till ~ av* in defrayment of

bestryka [-'stry:-] smear, daub; *(med färg o.d.)*
coat; *(beskjuta)* sweep, cover

beströl|a [-'strå:-] irradiate *(äv. med.)*, shine,
illumine **-ning** [ir]radiation, exposure to rays
be'strö strew, sprinkle, dot; *(med pulver)* powder

bestseller ['best-] *s2, s9* best seller **-författare**
author of popular books, best seller
bestyck|a [-'stycka] arm **-ning** armament

be'styr *s7* **1** *(göromål)* work; *(uppdrag)* duty,
task; *(skötsel)* management **2** *(besvär)* cares
(pl), trouble

bestyra [-'sty:-] *(göra)* do; *(ordna)* manage, arrange; *(sköta)* see about, attend to; *ha mycket
att ~* have a great deal to do (attend to)

bestyrelse [-'sty:-] [organizing, managing]
committee

bestyrka [-'styrka] *(bekräfta)* confirm, corrobo-
rate; *(intyga)* attest, certify; *(stödja)* bear out;
(bevisa) prove; *~ riktigheten av en uppgift*
authenticate a statement; *bestyrkt avskrift* attested (certified) copy

be'stå 1 *(vara)* last, continue, remain; *(existera)*
exist, subsist **2** *(utgöras)* consist *(av* of; *i* in);
däri ~r just svårigheten that just constitutes
the difficulty; *svårigheten bestod i* the difficulty lay in **3** *(genomgå)* go through, stand,
endure; *~ provet* stand the test **4** *(bekosta)* pay
for, defray; *(bjuda på)* treat [s.b.] to, stand s.b.;
(skänka) provide, furnish, procure **-ende** *a4*
1 *(varaktig)* lasting, abiding; *av ~ värde* of
lasting value; *den ~ ordningen* the established
order of things **2** *(existerande)* existing

be'stånd 1 *(existens)* existence; persistence;
duration; *äga ~* last **2** *(samling)* stock; *bot.*

B

stand, clump; (*antal*) number; *zool.* population; (*av kreatur*) stock **beståndsdel** constituent, component, part; (*i matvaror*) ingredient **beställ|a** [-'ställa] **1** (*tinga*) order (*av* off, from); (*plats, biljett*) book, reserve; ~ *tid hos* make an appointment with; *får jag* ~ please take my order; *komma som -d* come just when it (one etc.) is wanted; *-da tyger* textiles on order **2** *det är illa -t med henne* she is in a bad way; *ha mycket att* ~ have a great deal to do **-are** (*köpare*) buyer, purchaser, orderer; (*kund*) customer, client **-ning 1** (*rekvisition*) order; *på* ~ [made] to order **2** (*befattning*) appointment **beställnings|blankett, -sedel** order form **-skrädderi** bespoke tailor's; *AE.* custom tailor **beställsam** [-'ställ-] *a1* (*beskäftig*) fussy, officious **bestämbar** [-ˣstämm-] *a1* determinable; definable **be'stämd** *a1* (*besluten*) determined; (*beslutsam*) resolute, determined; (*om tid, ort o.d.*) fixed, appointed, settled; (*viss*) definite; (*tydlig*) clear, distinct; *språkv.* definite; (*avsedd*) meant, intended (*för* for); *på det ~aste* most emphatically **-het** definiteness; determination; *veta med* ~ know for certain **bestämma** [-'stämma] **1** (*fastställa*) fix, settle, determine; (*tid, plats*) appoint, set; ~ *tid* make an appointment, fix a time **2** (*stadga*) decree; provide, lay down **3** (*avgöra*) decide [upon] **4** ~ *sig* decide (*för* [up]on), make up one's mind (*för att* to) **5** (*begränsa, fixera*) determine **6** (*ämna, avse*) intend, mean **7** (*fastställa, konstatera*) establish; (*klassificera*) classify, determine, define **8** *språkv.* modify, qualify **bestämmande** [-'stämm-] **I** *s6* fixing *etc.*; decision; determination; classification **II** *a4* determining, determinative; (*avgörande*) decisive **-rätt** right to decide, right of determination; authority **bestämmelse** [-'stämm-] **1** (*stadga*) provision, regulation; (*i kontrakt*) stipulation, condition **2** (*ändamål*) purpose; (*uppgift*) task, mission **-ort** [place of] destination **bestämning** [-'stäm-] **1** (*bestämmande*) determination **2** *språkv.* qualifying word, adjunct (*till* of); (*friare*) attribute, qualification **bestämningsord** qualifier **be'stämt** *adv* **1** (*med visshet*) definitely; decidedly; resolutely; positively; *veta* ~ know for certain **2** (*högst sannolikt*) certainly; *du mår* ~ *inte bra* you are surely not well; *närmare* ~ more exactly; *det blir* ~ *regn* it's sure to rain **beständig** [-'ständ-] *a1* **1** (*stadig*) settled, steady; (*ståndaktig*) constant, steadfast **2** (*oföränderlig*) impervious, resistant **3** (*bestående*) perpetual, continuous **bestänka** [-'stänka] [be]sprinkle; (*med smuts, färg o.d.*) splash **be'stört** *a4* dismayed, perplexed (*över* at) **-ning** dismay, consternation; perplexity **be|sudla** [-'su:d-] soil, stain; *bildl. äv.* sully, tarnish **-sutten** [-'sutt-] *a5* propertied, landed, well-to-do **besvara** [-'sva:-] **1** (*svara på*) answer, reply to **2** (*återgälda*) return, reciprocate; (*vädjan o.d.*) respond to; ~ *en skål* respond to a toast

besvik|else [-'svi:-] disappointment (*över* at); *vard.* letdown **-en** *a5* disappointed (*på* in; *över* at) **be'svär** *s7* **1** (*olägenhet*) trouble, inconvenience; (*möda*) [hard] work, labour, pains (*pl*); *göra sig ~et att komma hit* take the trouble (make the effort) to come [here]; *gör dig inget ~!* don't bother!; *ha mycket* ~ *med ngn* have no end of trouble with s.b., have a hard time with s.b.; *kärt* ~ no trouble at all; *kärt* ~ *förgäves* love's labour's lost; *tack för ~et!* thank you for all the trouble you have taken; *vara* [*ngn*] *till* ~ be a trouble to [s.b.]; *inte vara rädd för* ~ not mind taking trouble; *vålla* [*ngn*] ~ cause s.b. trouble **2** (*klagan*) appeal; *anföra* ~ complain [of]; *anföra* ~ *hos* appeal to **besvära** [-'svä:-] **1** (*störa*) trouble, bother; *får jag* ~ *er att komma den här vägen* may I trouble you to step this way; *får jag* ~ *om ett kvitto* may I trouble you for a receipt; *förlåt att jag ~r* excuse my troubling you; *värmen ~r mig* I find the heat trying; *hon ~s av allergi* she suffers from an allergy **2** *rfl* (*göra sig omak*) trouble (bother) o.s.; (*klaga*) complain (*över* of), protest (*över* against); *jur.* appeal, lodge a protest **besvär|ad** [-'svä:-] *a5* troubled, bothered (*av ngn* by s.b.); *känna sig* ~ feel embarrassed **-ande** *a4* troublesome, annoying; embarrassing **besvärj|a** [-'svärja] **1** (*frammana*) conjure up **2** (*anropa*) beseech **3** (*gå ed på*) confirm by oath **-else** conjuration, invocation; (*trolldom*) sorcery **-elseformel** spell, charm **besvärlig** [-'svä:r-] *a1* troublesome, tiresome; (*svår*) hard, difficult; (*ansträngande*) trying; (*mödosam*) laborious; *ett ~t barn* a difficult child; *en* ~ *väg* a tiresome road **-het** troublesomeness; (*med pl*) trouble, hardship, difficulty **besvärs|instans** board (court) of appeal **-rätt** right of appeal **-skrift** petition [for a new trial], complaint **-tid** term of appeal **besynnerlig** [-'synn-] *a1* strange, odd, peculiar; (*underlig*) queer; (*märkvärdig*) curious **-het** strangeness *etc.*; (*med pl*) peculiarity, oddity **besynnerligt** [-'synn-] *adv* strangely *etc.*; ~ *nog* strangely enough **be'så** *v4* sow **besätt|a** [-'sätta] **1** (*förse*) set; (*med spik*) stud; (*med spetsar*) trim **2** *mil.* occupy **3** (*upptaga, förse med innehavare*) fill; *väl* (*glest*) *besatt* well (sparsely) filled **-ning 1** *sjö.* crew; *mil.* garrison **2** (*kreatursbestånd*) stock, herd [of cows] **3** (*garnering*) trimming[s *pl*], braiding **-ningsman** one (member) of the crew **be'sök** *s7* visit (*hos, i* to); (*vistelse*) stay (*hos* with; *vid* at); (*kortvarigt*) call (*hos* on); *avlägga* ~ *hos* pay a visit to, call on; *få* ~ have a visitor (caller); *komma på* ~ come to see, visit; *tack för ~et* thank you for calling (coming); *under ett* ~ *hos* while staying with; *väl värd ett* ~ well worth a visit; *vänta* ~ expect visitors **besök|a** [-'sö:-] visit, pay a visit to; (*hälsa på*) call on, go to see; (*bevista*) attend; (*regelbundet*) resort to, frequent; *en mycket -t restaurang* a much frequented restaurant **-ande** *s9, -are* *s9* visitor, caller (*i, vid* to)

besöks|dag visitors' day **-frekvens** (*på möte etc.*) attendance rate **-tid** visiting hours (*pl*)
besörja [-'sörja] ~ [*om*] attend to, deal with, take care of
1 bet *imperf. av bita*
2 bet *s2* **1** (*straffinsats vid spel*) forfeit, loo; (*mark*) counter **2** *gå* (*bli*) ~ (*spel.*) have to pay the game, *bildl.* be stumped (nonplussed); *han gick ~ på uppgiften* the task was too much for him
1 beta I *s1* (*munsbit*) bite, morsel; *efter den ~n* after that experience **II** *v1* (*bryta i stycken*) break
2 beta *v1* (*om djur*) graze; *absol. äv.* browse; ~ *av* graze, crop
3 beta I *v1* (*metaller*) pickle, bate; (*hudar*) soak; (*textilier*) mordant; *biol.* disinfect **II** *s1*, *tekn.* steep; (*färg*) mordant
4 beta *v1* (*agna*) bait
5 beta *s1*, *bot.* beet
6 beta *s6* (*bokstav*) beta
7 be'ta *se betaga*
betacka [-'tacka] *rfl*, ~ *sig* [*för*] decline; *jag ~r mig!* no, thanks, not for me!
beta[ga] [-'ta:(ga)] **1** (*fråntaga*) ~ *ngn ngt* deprive (rob) s.b. of s.th.; *det betog mig lusten att* it robbed me of all desire to **2** (*överväldiga*) overwhelm, overcome **betagande** [-'ta:-] *a4* (*förtjusande*) charming, captivating **betagen** [-'ta:-] *a5* overcome (*av* with); ~ *i* charmed by, enamoured of
betal|a [-'ta:la] pay; (*vara, arbete*) pay for; (*skuld äv.*) pay off, settle; ~ *av* pay off; ~ *fiolerna* foot the bill; ~ *för sig* pay for one's keep; ~ *kontant* pay [in] cash; ~ *sig* pay, be worth while; ~ *tillbaka* pay back; ~*t kvitteras* received with thanks; ~ *ngn med samma mynt* pay s.b. back in his own coin; *få* ~*t* be paid; *få bra* ~*t* get a good price; *det här ska du få* ~*t för!* I'll pay you out for this!; *ge* ~*t för gammal ost* pay [s.b.] out, *AE.* get back at, fix; *svar* ~*t* reply prepaid; *vaktmästarn, får jag* ~*!* Waiter! May I have the bill, please?
betalare [-'ta:-] *payer*
betal|bar [-ˣta:l-] *a5* payable **-kort** charge (debit) card **-kurs** buying price
betalning [-'ta:l-] payment; (*lön*) pay; (*avgift*) charge; (*ersättning*) compensation, remuneration; *förfalla till* ~ be (become, fall) due; *inställa ~arna* stop (suspend) payment[s]; *mot kontant* ~ for ready money, against cash; *som* ~ [*för*] in payment [for]; *utan* ~ free [of charge]; *verkställa ~ar* make payments; *vid kontant* ~ on payment of cash
betalnings|anstånd respite [for payment] **-ansvar** payment liability **-balans** balance of payments **-beredskap** liquidity **-dag** date (day) of payment; due date **-föreläggande** injunction to pay **-förmåga** solvency, ability to pay **-inställelse** suspension of payments **-medel** means of payment; (*ett lands*) currency; *lagligt* ~ legal tender, *AE.* lawful money **-påminnelse** collection letter **-skyldig** liable for payment **-svårigheter** *pl* insolvency (*sg*); *ha* ~ be insolvent **-termin** day (term) of payment **-villkor** *pl* terms of payment
beta|partikel beta particle **-stråle** beta ray

-strålning beta radiation
betatron [-'trå:n] *s3* betatron
betal-TV pay-TV
1 bet|e *s2* (*huggtand*) tusk; *djur med -ar* tusker
2 bete *s6, lantbr.* pasture; pasturage; *gå på* ~ be grazing; *saftigt* ~ verdant pasture[*s pl*]
3 bete *s6* (*agn*) bait
4 be'te *v4, rfl* behave; (*bära sig åt äv.*) act
beteckna [-'teckna] (*symbolisera*) represent; (*utmärka*) indicate, designate; (*markera*) mark; label; (*betyda*) denote, signify, stand for; imply; (*karakterisera*) characterize, describe; *detta ~r höjdpunkten* this marks the peak (culmination); *x och y ~r obekanta storheter* x and y represent (stand for) unknown quantities
beteckn|ande [-'teck-] *a4* characteristic (*för* of); typical, significant (*för* of) **-ing** (*benämning*) designation; term, denomination; (*symbol*) symbol; (*angivelse*) indication **-ingssätt** method of notation
beteende [-'te:en-] *s6* behaviour **-forskare** behavioural scientist **-forskning** behavioural science **-mönster** pattern of behaviour **-rubbning** behavioural disturbance **-vetare** social scientist **-vetenskap** social science
betel ['be:-] *s2* betel **-blad** betel **-nöt** betel nut **-palm** betel palm **-tuggning** betel chewing
betes|hage enclosed grazing **-mark** pasture, grazing land **-vall** pasture[-land]
be'ting *s7* piecework; *på* ~ by contract
betinga [-'tiŋa] **1** (*kosta*) command, fetch; involve **2** (*utgöra förutsättning för*) presuppose; (*utgöra villkor för*) condition; ~*d av* conditioned by, dependent on; ~*d reflex* conditioned response (*särsk. förr* reflex) **3** ~ *sig* stipulate (bargain) for
beting|else [-'tiŋ-] condition; stipulation; (*förutsättning, om pers.*) qualification **-ning** conditioning
betitla [-'titla] *se titulera; den ~de adeln* the titled nobility
betjän|a [-'çä:-] serve; (*passa upp*) attend [on]; (*vid bordet*) wait on; *tekn.* operate, work; ~ *sig av* make use of, avail o.s. of; *vara -t av* (*med*) have use for
betjäning [-'çä:-] service; attendance; waiting on; *tekn.* operation, working; (*tjänare*) attendants, servants (*pl*), staff **betjäningsavgift** tip, service [charge]
betjänt [-'çä:nt] *s3* man[servant], footman; *neds.* flunk[e]y
betmedel seed disinfectant (dressing)
betning [ˣbe:t-] grazing *etc., se 2, 3 o. 4 beta*; (*av utsäde*) dressing **betningsmedel** seed disinfectant
betodl|are beet-grower **-ing** beet-growing
betona [-'tɷ:-] emphasize, accentuate (*att* the fact that); *fonet.* stress; *kulturellt ~de kretsar* cultural circles
betong [-'tåŋ] *s3* concrete **-beläggning** concrete surface **-blandare** concrete mixer **-gjutning** concreting **-konstruktion** concrete structure **-vägg** concrete wall
betoning [-'tɷ:-] emphasis, stress, accent, accentuation
betrakt|a [-'trakta] **1** (*se på*) look at, watch, observe; (*ägna uppmärksamhet åt*) contem-

plate, consider 2 (anse) ~ som regard (look upon) as, consider -ande s6 watching etc.; contemplation; ta i ~ take into consideration; i ~ av considering, in consideration of -are observer, onlooker

betraktelse [-'trakt-] reflection, meditation (över upon); (anförande i religiöst ämne) discourse; (åskådande) regarding; försjunken i ~r lost in contemplation; anställa ~r över meditate upon -sätt outlook, way of looking at things

be|'tro ~ ngn med ngt entrust s.b. with s.th. -'trodd a5 trusted

be'tryck (trångmål) embarrassment; (nöd) distress be'tryckt a4 oppressed; dejected

betrygg|ad [-'tryggad] a5 secure, safe -ande I a4 (trygg) reassuring; (tillfredsställande) satisfactory, adequate; på ett fullt ~ sätt in a way that ensures complete safety II s6, till ~ av for the safeguarding of

beträda [-'trä:-] set foot on; bildl. tread, enter upon; förbjudet att ~ gräset keep off the grass

beträff|a [-'träffa] vad mig ~r as far as I am concerned; vad det ~r as to that, for that matter -ande regarding, concerning, in (with) regard to; (i brevrubrik) re

be'trängd a5 hard pressed, distressed

1 bets [be:-] imperf. av bitas

2 bets s3 (för trä) stain; (för hudar) lye

betsa stain

bets|el ['bets-] s7 bridle -la bridle -ling bridling

betsning staining; konkr. stain

betsocker beet sugar

1 bett sup. av bedja

2 bett s7 1 (hugg, insekts-) bite 2 (på betsel) bit 3 (tandställning) dentition, bite 4 (egg) edge

bettl|a beg -are beggar -eri begging

betung|a [-'tuŋa] burden; overload; ~s av be oppressed by -ande a4 burdensome; oppressive

betuttad [-'tuttad] a5, vara ~ i be sweet on, be enamoured of

betving|a [-'tviŋa] subdue; (underkuva) subjugate; bildl. overpower, overcome, repress, control; ~ sig control (check) o.s. -are subjugator; subduer

betvivla [-'tvi:v-] doubt, question, call in question

betyd|a [-'ty:-] 1 (beteckna) mean, signify, denote; imply, connote; vad skall detta ~? what is the meaning of this? 2 (vara av vikt) be of importance, matter, mean; det -er ingenting that doesn't matter, it makes no difference -ande a4 (betydelsefull) important; (ansenlig) considerable, substantial, large; (framstående) notable, of mark; en ~ man a prominent man

betydelse [-'ty:-] 1 (innebörd) meaning, signification; (ords äv.) sense; i bildlig ~ in a figurative sense 2 (vikt) importance, significance; det har ingen ~ it is of no importance, it doesn't matter; av föga ~ of little consequence -full significant; important, momentous -lära semantics (pl, behandlas som sg) -lös meaningless; insignificant, unimportant

betydenhet [-'ty:-] importance, consequence

betydlig [-'ty:d-] a1 considerable, substantial;

en ~ skillnad (äv.) a great [deal of] difference

be'tyg s7 certificate, testimonial; (arbets-) character; (termins-) report, AE. report card; (vitsord) mark, AE. credit, grade; univ. class; få fina ~ get high marks, do very well; sätta ~ allot marks betyga [-'ty:-] 1 (intyga) certify; testify 2 (bedyra) protest, profess, declare 3 (uttrycka) express; ~ ngn sin vördnad pay one's respect to s.b.

betygs|avskrift copy of testimonial (certificate) -hets examination fever -poäng credit total -skala scale of marks

betygsätt|a [-'ning grading, marking] grade, mark; bildl. pass judgment on -ning grading, marking

betäck|a [-'täcka] cover (äv. göra dräktig); mil. äv. shelter -ning cover[ing]; mil. äv. shelter; (eskort) convoy, escort; ta ~ take cover

betänk|a [-'tänka] consider, think of, bear in mind; när man -er saken when you come to think of it; ~ sig think it over, (tveka) hesitate -ande s6 1 (övervägande) thought, reflection; (tvekan) hesitation, scruple[s pl]; ta ngt i ~ take s.th. into consideration; utan ~ without [any] hesitation 2 (utlåtande) report

betänketid [-'tänke-] time for consideration

betänklig [-'tänk-] a1 (misstänkt) questionable, dubious; (oroande) precarious; hazardous, dangerous; (allvarlig) serious, grave; (vågad) doubtful -het misgiving, doubt, apprehension, scruple; hysa ~er have (entertain) misgivings, hesitate; uttala ~er express doubts

betänksam [-'tänk-] a1 (eftertänksam) deliberate; (försiktig) cautious; (tveksam) hesitant -het wariness

be'tänkt a4, vara ~ på att göra think of doing, contemplate doing

beundr|a [-'und-] admire -an r admiration -ansvärd [-ˣund-] a1 admirable; (friare) wonderful

beundrar|e, -inna admirer -post fan mail

bevak|a [-'va:-] (vakta) guard; (misstänksamt) watch, spy upon; (tillvarataga) look after; ~d järnvägsövergång controlled level (AE. grade) crossing; ~ sina intressen look after one's interests; ~ ett testamente prove a will -ning guard; custody; sträng ~ close custody; stå under ~ be under guard

bevaknings|kedja cordon of patrols -manskap guard -tjänst guard-duty; sjö. patrol-duty

bevandrad [-'vand-] a5 (förtrogen) acquainted, familiar (i with); (skicklig) versed, skilled (i in)

bevar|a [-'va:-] v1 1 (skydda) protect (för, mot from, against); -e mig väl! goodness gracious!; Gud -e konungen God save the King; Herren välsigne dig och -e dig the Lord bless thee and keep thee 2 (bibehålla) preserve; maintain; (hålla fast vid) retain; (förvara, gömma) keep; ~ fattningen retain one's self-possession, keep unruffled; ~ i tacksamt minne keep in thankful remembrance; ~ åt eftervärlden hand down to posterity -ande s6 protection, preserving etc.; preservation, maintenance

be'vars good heavens!, goodnes [, gracious] me!

bevattn|a [-'vatt-] water; (med kanaler o.d.) irrigate -ning watering; irrigation -ningsan-

läggning, -ningssystem irrigation system
bevek|a [-'ve:-] *v3 (förmå)* induce; *(röra)* move; *låta sig ~s* [allow o.s. to] be persuaded **-ande** *a4* moving, persuasive; entreating **-elsegrund** motive, inducement
bevilja [-'vilja] *v1* grant, accord, allow; *parl.* vote
bevill|ning [-'vill-] appropriation, vote of supply, government grant **-ningsutskott** *~et (i USA o. Storbritannien)* the Committee of Ways and Means
bevingad [-'viŋad] *a5* winged; *~e ord* familiar quotations
be'vis *s7* proof *(på* of); *(skäl)* argument; *(vittnesmål)* evidence *(för* of); *(-föring)* demonstration; *(uttryck för känsla o.d.)* proof, evidence, demonstration *(på* of); *(intyg)* certificate; *(kvitto)* receipt; *bindande ~* conclusive proof; *framlägga ~ (jur.)* introduce evidence, *(friare)* furnish proof of; *leda i ~* prove, demonstrate; *vilket härmed till ~ meddelas* which is hereby certified; *frikänd i brist på ~* acquitted in default of proof of guilt; *~ på högaktning* mark (token) of esteem
bevis|a [-'vi:-] *(utgöra bevis på, ge prov på)* prove, demonstrate; *(ådagalägga)* show; *~ riktigheten av* bear [s.b.] out; *vilket skulle ~s* which was to be proved **-ande** *a4* demonstrative; conclusive **-bar** *se bevislig*
bevis|börda burden of proof **-föring** argument, argumentation, demonstration; submission of evidence **-kraft** conclusive power
bevislig [-'vi:s-] *a1* provable, demonstrable **-en** demonstrably
bevis|material evidence **-medel** [means of] evidence
bevisning [-'vi:s-] argumentation, demonstration; *det brister i ~en* there is a flaw in the argument
bevista [-'vista] attend
bevisvärde value as evidence
bevittn|a [-'vitt-] witness; *(intyga äv.)* attest, certify **-ning** witnessing
bevuxen [-'vuxen] *a3* overgrown, covered; *~ med skog* wooded, woody
be'våg *n, endast i uttr.: på eget ~* on one's own responsibility
bevågen [-'vå:-] *a3, vara ngn ~* be kindly disposed towards s.b., favour s.b. **-het** favour, good will
be'vänt *a, n sg, det är inte mycket ~ med honom* he is not up to much
beväpn|a [-'vä:p-] *arm: bildl.* fortify **-ing** arming; *(vapen)* armament, arms *(pl)*
bevärdiga [-'vä:r-] *~ ngn med ett leende* condescend to smile at s.b.
bevär|ing [-'vä:-] *(beväringsman)* conscript, recruit **beväringsmönstring** enrolment of conscripts
be'växt *a4, se bevuxen*
Bhu'tan Bhutan **bhuta'nes** *s3,* **-isk** *a5* Bhutanese
1 bi *adv* 1 *stå ~* hold out, stand the test 2 *sjö., dreja ~* heave to; *ligga (lägga) ~* lie (lay) to
2 bi *s6, zool.* bee; *arg som ett ~* [absolutely] furious, spluttering with rage
1 bi- *(bredvid, intill)* by-

2 bi- *(två-, dubbel-)* bi-
biaccent secondary accent (stress)
biavel beekeeping
bi|avsikt subsidiary purpose; *(baktanke)* ulterior motive **-bana** branch line
bibehåll|a keep; preserve; *(upprätthålla)* maintain, keep up; *(ha i behåll)* retain; *~ gamla seder och bruk* keep up (preserve) old customs; *~ sig (om kläder)* wear, *(om färg)* stand, *(om seder)* last; *~ sin värdighet* maintain one's dignity; *~ sina själsförmögenheter* retain one's faculties; *~ sitt anseende som* keep up one's reputation for; *väl -en* well preserved; *en väl -en byggnad* a building in good repair; *han är väl -en* he is well kept **-ande** *s6* keeping *etc.*; preservation; maintenance; retention; *tjänstledighet med ~ av lönen* leave with full pay
bibel ['bi:-] *s2* bible; *~n* the [Holy] Bible **-citat** biblical quotation **-forskning** biblical research **-konkordans** concordance to the Bible **-kritik** biblical criticism **-kunskap** knowledge of the Bible **-ord** quotation from the Scriptures **-papper** bible (India) paper **-språk** *se -ställe* **-sprängd** *a5* versed in the Bible **-ställe** Bible passage **-tolkning** exegesis **-översättning** Bible translation
bibetydelse subordinate sense, secondary meaning
biblio'fil *s3* bibliophil[e] **-upplaga** de luxe edition
biblio|graf bibliographer **-grafi** *s3* bibliography **-grafisk** [-'gra:-] *a5* bibliographical
biblio'tek *s7* library **-arie** [-'a:rie] *s5* librarian
biblioteks|band library binding **-väsen** libraries [and library organization]
biblisk ['bi:-] *a5* biblical; *~a historien* biblical narratives, Bible stories *(pl)*
bibringa *~ ngn ngt* impart (convey) s.th. to s.b., imbue s.b. with s.th.; *~ ngn en åsikt* impress s.b. with an opinion
biceps ['bi:-] *s3* biceps
bicicleta *s1, sport.* bicycle kick
bida bide; await, wait for; *~ sin tid* bide one's time **bidan** *r* [time of] waiting
bi'dé *s3* bidet
bide'vind *a5* close to (by) the wind; *segla ~* sail close-hauled **-seglare** *zool.* velella; Portuguese man-of-war
bidrag contribution; share; *(penning-)* allowance, benefit; *(stats-)* subsidy; *lämna ~* make a contribution **bidraga** contribute; *(samverka)* combine; *~ med* contribute; *~ till* aid, promote, help; *~ till att förklara* help to explain, be instrumental in explaining **bidragande** *a4* contributory, contributing
bidrags|förskott advance maintenance payment **-givare** contributor
bidrottning queen bee
biedermeierstil ['bidermaier-] Biedermeier style
bieffekt side effect
bi'enn *bient, pl ~a* biennial **bien'nal** *s3* biennial
bifall *(samtycke)* assent, consent; *(godkännande)* sanction; *(medhåll)* approval, approbation; *(applåder)* applause, acclamation; *stormande ~* thunderous applause; *vinna ~* meet with approval; *yrka ~* support **bifalla** approve [of],

assent to; (*godkänna*) sanction; (*bevilja*) grant; ~ **en anhållan** grant a request; **begäran bifölls** the request was granted

bifalls|rop shout of approval **-storm** burst (storm) of applause **-yrkande** motion in favour [of the proposal] **-yttring** applause, acclamation

biff *s2* [beef]steak; *saken är* ~ (*vard.*) everything is all right (okay, O.K.); *jag ska ordna* ~*en* (*vard.*) I'll swing it somehow **-kor** *pl* beef cattle, dual-purpose cattle (*sg*) **-stek** *se biff*

bi|figur subsidiary (minor) character **-flod** tributary, affluent

bifoga attach; (*närsluta*) enclose; (*tillägga vid slutet*) append, subjoin; *betygen skall* ~*s ansökan* testimonials (*etc.*) should be attached to the application, (*friare*) apply with full particulars; ~*d blankett* accompanying form; *härmed* ~*s* enclosed please find; *med* ~*nde av* enclosing, appending; ~*t översänder vi* we are enclosing; *vara* ~*d* (*till dokument o.d.*) be attached, (*i brev etc.*) be enclosed

bifo'kal *a5* bifocal **-glas** bifocals (*pl*)

bifurkation bifurcation

biförtjänst extra (additional) income; incidental earnings (*pl*)

biga crease, bow

biga'm|i *s3* bigamy **-ist** bigamist

bigar'rå *s3* white heart cherry, bigarreau

bigata side street

bigning [*bi:g-] crease, bow

bi'gott *a1* bigoted **-eri** bigotry

bigård apiary

bi|handling episode **-hang** *s7* appendage; (*i bok*) appendix (*pl* append|ixes el. -ices); mask-formiga ~*et* the [vermiform] appendix **-hustru** concubine **-håla** *med.* sinus **-håleinflammation** sinusitis **-hänsyn** secondary consideration **-inkomst** *se biförtjänst* **-intresse** sideline

bijouteri|er [biʃøte'ri:-], **-varor** *pl* jewellery (*sg*), jewellery goods, trinkets

bikarbonat [*bi:-, *äv.* -'a:t] bicarbonate [of soda]

bikini [-'ki:-] *s9, s3* bikini

bi|konkav [*bi:-, *äv.* -'ka:v] biconcave **-konvex** [*bi:-, *äv.* -'vex] biconvex

bikt *s3* confession **bikta** ~ [*sig*] confess

bikt|barn confessant **-fader** confessor **-stol** confessional

bikupa *s1* beehive

bil *s2* [motor]car; *AE.* car, auto[mobile]; *köra* ~ drive a car **1 bila** *v1* travel (go) by car, motor; go motoring **2 bila** *s1* broad-axe

bilaccis car tax

bilaga *s1* (*i brev*) enclosure; (*i bok, tidning*) appendix, supplement

biland dependency

bilate'ral *a1* bilateral

bil|besiktning (*ung.*) [annual] motor vehicle inspection **-buren** motorized **-bälte** seat (safety) belt **-chassi** [motorcar] chassis

bild *s3* picture; (*illustration*) illustration; (*avbildning, äv. bildl. o. opt.*) image; (*spegel-*) likeness, reflection; (*på mynt*) effigy; *språkv.* figure [of speech], metaphor; *ge ngn en* ~ *av*

situationen put s.b. in the picture; *tala i* ~*er* speak figuratively (metaphorically)

bilda 1 (*åstadkomma, grunda, utgöra*) form (*äv. språkv.*), found establish **2** (*uppfostra, förädla*) educate; cultivate **3** *rfl* (*uppstå*) form, be formed; (*skaffa sig bildning*) educate (improve) o.s.; ~ *sig en uppfattning om* form an idea of **bildad** *a5* cultivated; educated; refined, civilized; *akademiskt* ~ with a university education; *bland* ~*e människor* in cultural (intellectual) circles; *en* ~ *uppfostran* a liberal education **bildande** *a4* educative, instructive; ~ *konster* imitative arts

bild|arkiv photo archive **-band** film strip

bildbar *a1* **1** (*formbar*) plastic **2** capable of being educated, educable

bild|erbok picture book **-galleri** [picture] gallery **-huggare** sculptor **-huggarkonst** sculpture **-hållning** *TV* frame hold; *AE.* vertical hold **-konst** visual arts

bild|lig *a1* figurative, metaphorical **-material** illustrative material; illustrations (*pl*)

bildning 1 formation; (*form*) form, shape **2** (*odling*) culture; (*skol-*) education; (*själs-*) cultivation; (*levnadssvett*) breeding, refinement; *en man av* ~ a man of culture (refinement)

bildnings|förbund adult education institute **-grad** degree of culture **-törst** thirst for knowledge

bild|ordbok illustrated (pictorial) dictionary **-redaktör** illustrations editor **-rik 1** (*stil, språk*) picturesque, ornate, flowery **2** (*bok*) richly illustrated

bil|drulle road hog

bild|reportage picture story **-ruta** *film.* frame; *TV* [viewing] screen **-rör** *TV* television (picture) tube, [tele]tube **-serie** comic strip, strip cartoon; *särsk. AE.* comics (*pl*) **-sida** pictorial page; (*på mynt*) obverse, face **-skrift** picture writing, pictography; hieroglyphics (*pl, behandlas som sg*) **-skärm** screen **-skärmsarbete** VDU (Visual Display Unit) work **-skärpa** *foto., TV* definition **-skön** pretty as a picture, of statuesque beauty, well-favoured **-språk** imagery; metaphorical language **-stod** statue **-stormare** iconoclast **-telefon** videophone **-telegrafi** phototelegraphy, telephotography **-text** [picture] caption **-tidning** pictorial, picture magazine **-verk** volume of pictures

bildäck 1 [motorcar] tyre; *AE.* [automobile] tire **2** *sjö.* car deck

bildöverföring transmission of visual matter, picture transmission

bil|ersättning mil[e]age [allowance] **-fabrik** motor works, car factory **-firma** car dealer **-fri** ~ *gata* pedestrian street; ~*tt område* pedestrian precinct **-färd** car drive (trip) **-färja** car ferry **-förare** car driver **-försäkring** motorcar insurance **-försäljare** car salesman **-handlare** car dealer

bilharzios [-tsi'å:s] *s3, med.* schistosomiasis, bilharziasis, bilharziosis

bil|hjul car wheel **-industri** motor (*AE.* automotive) industry

bil|ism motorism, motoring **-ist** motorist, driver

bil'jard [-a:-] *s3, ej pl* billiards (*pl*) **-boll** billiard ball **-bord** billiard table **-kö** [billiard] cue **-salong** billiard room **-spelare** billiard player
bil'jett *s3* ticket; (*brev*) note; *enkel ~* single (*AE.* one-way) ticket; *lösa ~ till* buy (get) a ticket for **-automat** ticket vending machine **-försäljare** booking (ticket) clerk; *AE.* ticket agent **-försäljning** sale of tickets **-häfte** book of coupons **-kontor** ticket office; *järnv.* booking office; *teat. o.d.* box office **-kontrollör** ticket collector (inspector) **-lucka** *järnv.* booking office; *teat. o.d.* box office [window] **-pris** price of admission; (*för resa*) fare
bil'jon *s3* (*1 miljon miljoner*) billion; *AE.* trillion
biljud intruding sound; *med.* accessory sound, (*vid andning*) rale
bil|karosseri car body **-karta** road map **-krock** car crash **-kö** line of cars **-körning** [car] driving; motoring
bill *s2* (*plog*) [plough]share
billig *a1* **1** cheap (*äv. bildl.*); inexpensive; (*om pris äv.*) low, moderate, reasonable **2** (*rättmätig*) fair, reasonable; *det är inte mer än rätt och ~t* it's only fair **-bok** low-price edition **-het 1** (*rättvisa*) justice, fairness **2** (*lågt pris*) cheapness *etc.* **-hetsupplaga** cheap edition
billigt *adv* cheaply; *köpa* (*sälja*) *~* buy (sell) cheap; *komma för ~ undan* be let off too cheaply; *mycket ~* [at] a bargain [price]
billion *s3, se* biljon
bil|lots car pilot **-lån** car theft **-lånare** car thief, joy rider **-mekaniker, -montör** car mechanic (fitter) **-märke** make [of car] **-nyckel** car key **-olycka** motor accident **-park** car fleet **-parkering** car park; *AE.* parking lot **-provning** *AB Svensk B~* Swedish Motor Vehicle Inspection Co. **-radio** car radio **-register** vehicle register **-reparationsverkstad** motorcar repair shop, garage **-reparatör** motor mechanic **-ring 1** *se bildäck* **2** *vard.* (*fettvalk*) spare tyre **-ruta** car window **-salong** *se bilutställning* **-sjuk** travel-sick **-skatt** [motorcar] licence duty **-skola** driving school **-skollärare** driving instructor **-speditionsfirma** road haulage firm, haulier **-sport** motoring; car racing **-stöld** car theft **-tjuv** car thief
biltog *a5* outlawed; *~ man* outlaw
bil|trafik motor traffic **-tur** [motor]drive, ride; (*längre*) motor trip, trip by car **-tvätt** (*anläggning*) car wash; (*-tvättning*) car washing **-tävling** car race **-uthyrning** car rental **-utställning** motor show **-verkstad** *se bilreparationsverkstad* **-vrak** car wreck **-väg** motor road; *AE.* motor highway **-ägare** car owner
bil|läger [royal, princely] nuptials (*pl*) **-lägga 1** *se bifoga* **2** (*åstadkomma förlikning*) settle, make up, reconcile **-läggande** *s6* settlement, adjustment
bimetall bimetal
binamn by-name
bind|a I *s1* roller [bandage]; *elastisk ~* elastic bandage **II** *v, band bundit* **1** bind; (*knyta*) tie; (*fästa*) fasten (*vid* [on] to); (*hålla fästad vid*) confine; (*nät, kvastar o.d.*) make; *~ fast* tie up (*vid* to); *~ för ngns ögon* blindfold s.b.; *~ ihop* tie up, bind together; *~ in böcker* have books

bound, bind books; *~ om* tie up, (*böcker*) rebind; *~ upp* tie up, *kokk.* truss; *~ åt* tie; *~ ngn till händer och fötter* bind s.b. hand and foot (*äv. bildl.*); *~ ris åt egen rygg* make a rod for one's own back; *bunden vid sängen* bedridden, confined to bed **2** (*fästa, sammanhålla*) bind, hold; *limmet -er bra* the glue sticks well **3** *rfl* bind (pledge) o.s.; *tie* o.s. down (*vid, för* to) **-ande** *a4* binding; (*avgörande*) conclusive; *~ bevis* conclusive proof; *~ order* firm order
bindehinna *se bindhinna*
bindel *s2* bandage
binde|medel binder, fixing agent; (*lim o.d.*) adhesive **-ord** conjunction **-streck** hyphen
bind|galen stark [staring] mad **-garn** twine, packthread **-hinna** conjunctiva **-hinneinflammation** conjunctivitis
bindning binding; (*av bok*) binding; (*på skida*) [ski] binding; *språkv.* liaison; *mus.* slur[ring]
bindsle [×binsle] *s6* fastening; (*på skida*) [ski] binding
bind|sula insole **-väv** connective tissue
bingbång ding dong
binge [×biŋe] *s2* bin
bingo ['biŋ(g)ω] *s2* bingo
binjure adrenal (suprarenal) gland **-bark** cortex of the adrenal gland
binnikemask tapeworm
binom *s7* binomial
binomial|fördelning binomial distribution **-teorem** binomial theorem
bi'när *a1* binary, twofold; *~a talsystemet* the binary notation (system)
binäring subsidiary (ancillary) industry (occupation)
bio ['bi:ω] *s9* cinema, motion-picture theatre; *AE.* movies, movie theater; *gå* (*vara*) *på ~* go to (be at) the cinema (the pictures, *sl.* the flicks, *AE.* the movies) **-besök** cinema visit **-besökare** cinemagoer **-biljett** cinema (*AE.* movie) ticket
biobränsle [×bi:ω-] biomass fuel, biofuel **bio'cid** *s3* biocide **biocykel** [×bi:ω-] biocycle
biodl|are beekeeper **-ing** beekeeping, apiculture
bio|dynamik biodynamics (*pl, behandlas som sg*) **-dynamisk** [-'na:-] biodynamic[al]; *~ odling* organic farming
bio|ekologi bioecology
bio|fy'sik biophysics (*pl, behandlas som sg*) **-fysisk** [-'fy:-] biophysical
biogas biogas
bio|gen [-'je:n] *a5* biogenetic[al], biogenous **-ge'nes** [-j-] biogenesis **-genetisk** [-je'ne:-] *se -gen*
biogeografi biogeography
biograf *s3* **1** (*levnadstecknare*) biographer **2** *se bio* **-byrå** *Statens ~* [the Swedish] national board of film censors **-föreställning** cinema performance (show)
bio|grafi *s3* biography **-grafisk** [-'gra:-] *a5* biographical
biograf|publik cinema audience; filmgoers (*pl*); *AE.* moviegoers (*pl*) **-vaktmästare** cinema attendant; (*dörrvaktmästare*) ticket collector
bio|ke'mi biochemistry **-kemisk** [-'çe:-] biochemical **-kemist** biochemist
bio|log biologist **-logi** *s3* biology **-logisk** *a5*

biological; ~ *klocka* biological clock; ~ *krigföring* biological warfare; ~*t nedbrytbar* biodegradable

bio|massa biomass **-medicin** biomedicine **-me'tri** *s3* biometry, biometrics (*pl, behandlas som sg*)

biomständighet minor incident, incidental circumstance

bio'nik *s3* bionics (*pl, behandlas som sg*)

bio'psi *s3* biopsy

biopublik *se biografpublik*

bi|orsak subsidiary reason, incidental cause

bio|'sfär biosphere **-syntes** biosynthesis **-teknik** biotechnology **-teknisk** biotechnological, biotech

bioteknologi ergonomics (*pl, behandlas som sg*); *AE.* biotechnology

biotisk [bi'å:-] *a5* biotic

bio'tit *s3* biotite

bio|top [-'tå:p] *s3* biotope **-'typ** *s3* biotype

bi|person *se bifigur* **-plan** biplane **-po'lär** bipolar **-produkt** by-product; (*avfall*) waste product

birfilare [*bi:r-] fiddler

bi|roll subordinate part, minor role **-sak** matter of secondary importance; side issue; *huvudsak och* ~ essentials and nonessentials (*pl*)

bisam ['bi:-] *s3* musquash (muskrat) fur

bisamhälle colony of bees

bisamråtta muskrat

bi'sarr *a1* bizarre, odd, fantastic

bisats subordinate clause

Biscayabukten [bis*kaja-] Bay of Biscay

bisektris *s3* bisector

bisexu'ell bisexual

bisittare [legal] assessor, member of lower court

biskop [*biskåp] *s2* bishop **-inna** bishop's wife **-lig** *a1* episcopal

biskops|döme *s6* bishopric, episcopate **-mössa 1** mitre **2** *se fingerborgsblomma* **-stav** pastoral [staff] **-stift** diocese, see **-stol** [bishop's] throne; *bildl.* see **-säte** see **-ämbete** episcopate, see, office of a bishop

bis'kvi *s3* macaroon, ratafia (ratafee) [biscuit]

biskölkörtel parathyroid gland

biskötsel beekeeping

bismak [extraneous] flavour; smack; tang; *i sht bildl.* taint

bison ['bi:sån] *r* bison **-oxe** European bison, wisent; *amerikansk* ~ American bison, *AE.* buffalo

bisp *s2, se biskop*

bispringa assist, succour; ~ *ngn med råd och dåd* support s.b. in word and deed (by word and act)

bisser|a give over again, repeat **-ing** encore

bist|er ['bist-] *a2* grim, fierce, forbidding; (*sträng*) stern; (*om köld o.d.*) severe; *-ra tider* hard times

bisting bee sting

bisträck|a ~ *ngn med pengar* advance s.b. money **-ning** pecuniary assistance, financial help

bistå assist, help **bistånd** assistance, help, aid; *med benäget* ~ *av* kindly assisted by

biståndspakt pact of mutual assistance

bisvärm swarm of bees

bi|syfte *se biavsikt* **-syssla** spare-time occupation, sideline

bisätt|a remove to the mortuary; ~ *ngn* remove a p.'s remains to the mortuary **-ning** removal [of a p.'s remains] to the mortuary

bit *s2* piece, bit; (*socker-*) lump [of sugar]; (*fragment*) fragment; (*muns-*) mouthful, morsel; *data.* bit; *följa ngn en* ~ *på vägen* accompany s.b. part of the way; *inte en* ~ *bättre* not a bit (scrap) better; *äta en* ~ [*mat*] have [a little] s.th. to eat; *gå i* ~*ar* go to pieces; *gå i tusen* ~*ar* be smashed to smithereens

bit|a *bet bitit* **1** bite; ~ *huvudet av skammen* be past all sense of shame; ~ *i det sura äpplet* swallow the bitter pill; ~ *i gräset* bite (lick) the dust; ~ *på naglarna* bite one's nails; ~ *sig fast i* (*vid*) cling tight on to; ~ *sig i tungan* bite one's tongue **2** (*vara skarp*) bite; (*om ankare*) hold; (*om kniv*) cut; (*om köld*) nip, be sharp; ~ *av* bite off, (*en sup*) sip; ~ *ifrån sig* hit back, retort; ~ *ihjäl* bite to death; ~ *ihop tänderna* clench one's teeth; ~ *sönder* bite to pieces; *ingenting -er på honom* nothing has any effect on him **-ande** *a4* biting; (*om vind äv.*) piercing; (*om köld*) intense; (*om svar äv.*) stinging, cutting, sharp; (*om smak, lukt*) pungent; (*om kritik äv.*) caustic

bitanke underlying thought; ulterior motive

bitas *bets bitits, dep* bite **bitit** *sup. av bita*

bi|testikel epididymis (*pl* epididymides) **-ton** *språkv.* secondary accent (stress); *mus.* secondary tone

bitring teething ring

bitryck *se biaccent*

biträd|a 1 (*hjälpa*) assist, help; ~ *ngn vid rättegång* appear (plead) for s.b. at trial **2** (*mening, förslag*) accede to, support, subscribe to; (*parti*) join **-ande** *a4* assistant, auxiliary

biträde *s6* **1** (*medverkan*) assistance, help **2** (*medhjälpare*) assistant, hand; *rättsligt* ~ counsel

bitsk *a1* ill-tempered, savage

bitsocker lump (cube) sugar

bitter ['bitt-] *a2* bitter; (*om smak äv.*) acrid; (*plågsam*) acute, severe, sore; ~ *fiende* (*saknad*) bitter enemy (grief); ~ *nöd* dire want (distress); ~*t öde* harsh fate; *till det bittra slutet* to the bitter end **-het** bitterness; (*om smak*) acridity; (*sinnesstämning*) embitterment, bitter feeling **-ligen** bitterly **-ljuv** bittersweet **-mandel** bitter almond **-mandelolja** bitter-almond oil **-salt** Epsom salts (*pl*)

bittersta ['bitt-] *i uttr.: inte det* ~ not in the least, not at all

bittert ['bitt-] *adv, det känns* ~ *att* it feels hard to

bitti[da] early; *i morgon* ~ [early] tomorrow morning

bitum|en [-'tu:-] *-en el. -inet, pl saknas* bitumen **-i'nös** *a1* bituminous

bitvarg curmudgeon

bitvis bit by bit, piecemeal; here and there

biuppgift additional (subsidiary) task

bi'vack *s3,* **bivackera** *v1* bivouac

bivax beeswax

biverk|an, -ning side effect, secondary effect

bivråk honey buzzard

biväg byway, bypath
bjud|a *bjöd bjudit* **1** (*befalla*) bid, order, enjoin; ~ *och befalla* order and command; *anständigheten -er* decency dictates **2** (*säga, hälsa*) bid, say; ~ *farväl* bid farewell **3** (*erbjuda*) offer; (*ge bud på auktion*) [make a] bid; ~ *motstånd* offer resistance; ~ *ngn att sitta ner* ask s.b. to sit down; ~ *ngn spetsen* defy s.b. **4** (*undfägna med*) treat to; ~ *ngn på en god middag* treat s.b. to an excellent dinner; *vad får jag* ~ *dig på?* what may I offer you?; *staden har mycket att* ~ *på* the town has many attractions; *han bjöd alla på drinkar* all drinks were on him, he stood everybody drinks **5** (*inbjuda*) invite; ~ *ngn på lunch* invite s.b. to lunch; ~ *ngn på middag på restaurang* invite s.b. out for dinner, dine s.b. at a restaurant; *det -er mig emot att* it is repugnant to me to; ~ *hem ngn* ask (invite) s.b. home; ~ *igen* invite back; ~ *in* ask in; ~ *omkring* hand round; ~ *till* try; ~ *under* underbid; ~ *upp* ask for a dance; ~ *ut varor* offer goods for sale; ~ *över* outbid
bjud|it *sup. av bjuda* **-ning 1** (*kalas*) party **2** (*inbjudan*) invitation **-ningskort** invitation card
bjäbba (*om hund*) yelp; ~ *emot* answer back
bjäfs *s7* finery; trinkets (*pl*)
bjälk|e *s2* beam; (*stor*) ba[u]lk; (*bärande*) girder; (*stock*) log; *~n i ditt eget öga* (*bibl.*) the beam that is in thine own eye **-lag** *s7* system of joists
bjäll|erklang jingle of sleigh bells **-ko** *se skällko* **-ra** *s1* bell, jingle
bjärt I *a1* gaudy, glaring **II** *adv* glaringly; *sticka av* ~ *mot* be in glaring contrast to
bjässe *s2* colossal man; hefty chap; (*baddare äv.*) whopper
bjöd *imperf. av bjuda*
björk *s2* birch; *av* ~ (*äv.*) birch; *möbel av* ~ birchwood suite [of furniture]
björkna *s2* white (silver) bream
björk|ris birch twigs; (*t. aga*) birch[rod] **-skog** birch wood **-trast** fieldfare **-ved** birchwood
björn [-ö:-] *s2* **1** bear; *Stora* (*Lilla*) *Björn[en]* [the] Great (Little) Bear; *väck inte den* ~ *som sover* let sleeping dogs lie; *sälj inte skinnet innan ~en är skjuten* don't count your chickens before they are hatched **2** (*fordringsägare*) dun **-bär** blackberry, bramble **-hona** she-bear **-jägare** bear hunter **-kloört** *bot.* bear's-breech **-loka** *s1* cow parsnip, hogweed, keck **-mossa** hairy-cap moss **-ram** bear's paw **-skinn** bearskin **-skinnsmössa** bearskin **-tjänst** *göra ngn en* ~ do s.b. a disservice **-tråd** patent strong yarn **-unge** [bear] cub
bl.a. (*förk. för bland annat, bland andra*) *se under bland*
1 black *s2* fetter, iron; *vara en* ~ *om foten för* be a drag on
2 black I *a1* (*smutsgul*) tawny, drab (*äv. bildl.*); (*grå*) gray, dingy; (*urblekt*) faded **II** *s2* cream-coloured horse, dun
blad *s7* (*löv, bok-*) leaf (*pl* leaves); (*kron-, blom-*) petal; (*ark*) sheet; (*tidning*) paper; (*kniv-, år-, propeller- o.d.*) blade; *oskrivet* ~ clean sheet, *bildl.* unknown quantity; *~et har vänt sig* the tide has turned; *spela från ~et* play

at sight; ta ~et från munnen speak out (one's mind)
blad|bagge gold beetle, goldbug **-fjäder** plate spring **-formig** leaf-shaped, foliate[d] **-grönt** chlorophyll **-guld** gold leaf, (*tjockare*) gold foil **-horning** [-ω:-] *zool.* dung beetle (chafer) **-lus** plant louse, aphid, (*grön äv.*) greenfly **-mage** third stomach, psalterium, omasum, manyplies (*pl, behandlas som sg*) **-mossa** [leaf] moss **-mögel** leaf mould, rust [fungus] **-selleri** *se blekselleri* **-veck** axil
B-lag second team (eleven, *särsk. AE.* string); *bildl.* second-raters (*pl*)
blam|age [-'ma:ʃ] *s5* faux pas **-era** bring discredit on; ~ *sig* bring discredit on o.s., put one's foot in it
blanchera blanch
blancmangé [blaŋmaŋ'ʃe: *el.* blammaŋ'ʃe:] *s5* blancmange
blanco *se blanko*
bland among[st]; ~ *andra* among others; ~ *annat* among other things, for instance, inter alia; *programmet upptar* ~ *annat* the programme includes; ~ *det bästa jag vet* one of the best things I know; *en* ~ *tio* one in ten; *många* ~ *läsarna* many of the readers; *omtyckt* ~ *damerna* a favourite with the ladies
blanda mix; (~ *tillsammans*) blend; *bildl.* mingle; *kem.* compound; (*metaller*) alloy; (*kort*) shuffle, mix; ~ *vatten i mjölken* mix water with milk, adulterate milk with water; ~ *bort* muddle away; ~ *bort korten för ngn* confuse s.b., put s.b. out; ~ *ihop* mix up; ~ *in* (*tillsätta*) admix; ~ *in ngn i ngt* get s.b. mixed up in s.th.; ~ *till* mix; ~ *upp ngt med ngt* mix s.th. with s.th.; ~ *ut vin med vatten* dilute wine with water; ~ *sig* mix, mingle; ~ *sig i* meddle in, interfere with; ~ *sig med mängden* mingle in (mix with) the crowd
bland|ad *a5* mixed *etc.*; *~e känslor* mixed feelings; ~ *kör* mixed choir; *-at sällskap* mixed company **-are** mixing machine, mixer
bland|ekonomi mixed economy **-ekonomisk** of (associated with) a mixed economy **-folk** mixed people (race)
blandning mixture; (*av olika kvaliteter el. sorter*) blend; (*legering*) alloy; (*korsning*) hybrid; *med en* ~ *av hopp och fruktan* with mixed hope and fear
bland|ras mixed breed **-skog** mixed forest **-språk** mixed language **-säd** mixed grain; (*växande*) mixed crops (*pl*) **-äktenskap** (*interracial*) marriage
blank *a1* shiny, bright; ~ *sida* blank page; ~ *som en spegel* smooth as a mirror; *med ~a vapen* honourably, with clean hands; *mitt på ~a förmiddagen* right in the middle of the morning; *~t game* (*i tennis*) love game; *ett ~t nej* a flat (curt) no
blanka polish; (*skor*) clean; black
blan'kett *s3* form; blank; *fylla i en* ~ fill in (up) a form **-raseri** mania for form-filling
blanko ['blankω] *se in blanko* **-check** blank cheque **-endossement** *se -överlåtelse* **-fullmakt** blank cheque **-växel** blank bill **-överlåtelse** blank endorsement, endorsement in

blank
blank|polera polish **-skinn** patent leather **-slipa** polish, finish, smooth **-sliten** shiny **-svärta** blacking
blankt *adv* shinily *etc.*; *dra* ~ draw one's sword; *rösta* ~ return a blank vote; *säga* ~ *nej* flatly refuse; *strunta* ~ *i* not give a damn about
blankvers blank verse
blasé *oböjligt a*, **blaserad** [-'se:-] *a5* blasé
blasfe'm|i *s3* blasphemy **-isk** [-'fe:-] *a5* blasphemous
blask *s7* wash, dishwater; *(snö-)* slush
1 blaska *v1* splash
2 blaska *s1*, neds. rag
blaskig *a1 (om potatis)* watery; *(om färg)* washy, washed out; ~ *köttstuvning* slumgullion *(AE..sl.)*
blast *s3, ej pl* tops *(pl)*
blazer ['blä:- *el.* 'blei-] *s2* [sports] jacket; *(skol-, klubb-)* blazer
bleck *s7* **1** *se* -plåt **2** ~*et (mus.)* the brass **-blåsinstrument** brass instrument **-burk, -dosa** tin, *(särsk. AE.)* can **-plåt** [thin] sheet metal, sheet [iron]; tin plate; *av* ~ *(äv.)* tin **-slagare** tinsmith
blek *a1* pale; *(starkare)* pallid; *(svag)* faint; ~ *av fasa* pale with terror; ~ *av raseri* pallid with rage; ~ *om kinden* pale-cheeked; ~ *som ett lik* deathly pale; ~*a döden* pallid Death; ~*a vanvettet* utter madness; ~*t ljus* faint light; *göra ett* ~*t intryck* make a lifeless (tame) impression; *inte ha den* ~*aste aning om* not have the faintest idea of **bleka** *v3* bleach; *(färg)* fade; ~*s* become discoloured
blekansikte paleface
bleke *s6 (stiltje)* calm
blek|fet pasty **-het** paleness, pallor **-lagd** *a5* pale-faced; *(sjukligt)* sallow **-medel** bleach, bleacher; bleaching agent
blekn|a [*ble:-] turn pale *(av* with); *(om färger, kinder, minnen o.d.)* fade, grow paler **-ing** bleaching
blek|nos washed-out little thing **-selleri** selery, blanched celery **-siktig** *a1* chlorotic **-sot** chlorosis, greensickness
blemm|a *s1* pimple **-ig** *a1* pimpled, pimply
bless|era wound **-'yr** *s3* wound
blev *imperf. av* bli
bli (bliva) *blev blivit* **I** *passivbildande hjälpv* be; *vard.* get; *(vid utdragen handling)* become **II** *självst. v* **1** be; ~ *överraskad* be surprised; *festen blev lyckad* the party was a success; *(innebärande förändring)* become; ~ *fattig (soldat)* become poor (a soldier); *(vard., med adjektivisk pred.fylln.)* get, *(långsamt)* grow, *(plötsligt)* fall, turn; ~ *arg (gift, våt)* get angry (married, wet); ~ *blek (katolik)* turn pale (Catholic); ~ *gammal* grow old; ~ *sjuk (kär)* fall ill (in love); ~ *skämd (tokig)* go bad (mad); *vi* ~*r fyra till bordet* there'll be four of us at table; *det skall* ~ *mig ett nöje* it'll be a pleasure; *hur mycket* ~*r notan på?* what does the bill come to? **2** *(förbli)* remain; ~ *sittande* remain seated; *det måste* ~ *oss emellan* this must be between ourselves; *skomakare,* ~*v vid din läst!* let the cobbler stick to his last **3** *det* ~*r tio pund* it makes ten pounds, *(vid betalning)* that'll be ten

pounds; *han* ~*r 20 år i morgon* he will be 20 [years old] tomorrow; *det* ~*r svårt* it will be difficult; *när* ~*r det?* when will it be?; *när jag* ~*r stor* when I grow up **4** *låt* ~*!* don't!; *låt* ~ *att skrika!* stop shouting!; *jag kunde inte låta* ~ *att skratta* I could not help laughing; *låt* ~ *mig!* leave me alone! **5** *(med betonad partikel)* ~ *av* take place, come about; ~*r det ngt av?* will it come to anything?; *festen* ~*r inte av* the party is off; *vad har det* ~*vit av henne?* what has become of her?; ~ *av med (bli kvitt)* get rid of, *(förlora)* lose, *(få sälja)* dispose of; ~ *borta* stay away, *(omkomma)* be lost (missing); ~ *efter* drop (lag) behind; ~ *ifrån sig* be beside o.s.; ~ *kvar (stanna kvar)* remain, stay [behind], (~ *över)* be left [over]; ~ *till* come into existence; ~ *till sig* get excited; ~ *utan* get nothing; ~ *utan pengar* run out of money; ~ *utom sig* be beside o.s. *(av* with); ~ *över* be left [over]
blick *s2* **1** look; *(ihärdig)* gaze; *(hastig)* glance; *kasta en* ~ *på* look (glance) at **2** *(öga)* eye; *sänka (lyfta)* ~*en* lower (raise) one's eyes; *följa ngn med* ~*en* gaze after s.b.; *föremål för allas* ~*ar* focus of attention; *ha* ~ *för* have an eye for
blick|a look; gaze; glance **-fång** eye-catcher **-punkt** focus; *bildl.* limelight **-stilla** calm; [as] smooth as glass
blid *a1* mild; *(om röst o.d.)* soft; *(vänlig)* gentle, kind; *tre grader blitt* three degrees above freezing point **blidhet** [*bli:d-] mildness *etc.* **blidka** [*blidd-] appease, conciliate, placate; *låta* ~ *sig* relent, give in **blidväder** mild weather; thaw
bliga glare, stare *(på* at)
blimp *s2, film.* blimp
blind *a1* blind *(för* to); *(okritisk, obetingad)* implicit; *bli* ~ go blind; ~ *lydnad* implicit (passive) obedience; ~ *på ena ögat* blind in one eye; ~*a fläcken* the blind spot; *den* ~*e* the blind man; *en* ~ *höna hittar också ett korn* a fool's bolt may sometimes hit the mark; *stirra sig* ~ *på (bildl.)* let o.s. be hypnotized by, get stuck at **-bock** blind man's buff
blindering [-'de:-] blindage
blind|flygning instrument (blind) flying **-fönster** blind window **-gångare** dud, unexploded bomb **-het** blindness **-hund** guide dog **-institut** blind school, school for the blind
blindo *i uttr.*: *i* ~ blindly, at random
blind|skola *se* blindinstitut **-skrift** Braille; *trycka i (skriva med)* ~ Braille **-skär** sunken rock **-styre** blind buffer **-tarm** caecum **-tarmsinflammation** appendicitis
bli'ni *s3,* ~*er* blini[s] *(pl)*
blink *s2* **1** (-*ande*) twinkling **2** (-*ning*) wink; *i en* ~ in a twinkling, in the twinkling of an eye
blinka *(med ögat)* blink, wink *(mot, åt* at); *(om ljus)* twinkle; *utan att* ~ without batting an eyelid, unflinchingly
blink|er *s2* blinker, [flashing direction] indicator **-fyr** *se* blänkfyr **-hinna** nic[ti]tating membrane, third eyelid, haw **-ljus** flashing light **-ning** blinking *etc.*; wink
blint *adv* blindly *etc.*, *se* blind; *gatan slutar* ~ it is a blind alley

bliv|a *se bli* **-ande** *a4* (*tillkommande*) future, ... to be; (*tilltänkt*) prospective; ~ *mödrar* expectant mothers **-it** *sup. av bliva*

blixt I *s2* lightning; (*konstgjord o. bildl.*) flash; *en* ~ a flash of lightning; *~en slog ner i huset* the house was struck by lightning; *som en oljad* ~ like a streak of lightning; *som en ~ från klar himmel* like a bolt from the blue; *som träffad av ~en* thunderstruck; *hans ögon sköt ~ar* his eyes flashed **II** *adv, bli* ~ *kär* fall madly in love **-anfall** lightning attack (raid), (*särsk. om flyg*) blitz **-belysning** *i* ~ in a flash **-fotografering** flash photography **-halka** extreme slipperiness **-krig** blitz, lightning warfare **-kub** *foto.* flash bulb; (*med fyra blixtar*) flash cube **-ljus** flashing light; *foto.* flashlight **-ljuslampa** flash bulb, photoflash **-lås** zip [fastener]; *AE.* zipper **-nedslag** stroke of lightning

blixtra lighten (*äv.* ~ *till*); (*friare*) flash, sparkle; *~nde ögon* flashing eyes; *~nde huvudvärk* splitting headache; *~nde kvickhet* sparkling wit

blixt|snabb [as] swift as a lightning **-visit** flying visit

block [-å-] *s7* block; *geol. äv.* boulder; *polit.* bloc; (*skriv-*) pad; (*hissanordning*) block; (*sko-*) shoetree **blocka** [-å-] ~ *ut skor* tree shoes

bloc'kad [-å-] *s3* blockade; *förklara i* ~ impose a blockade; *häva* (*bryta*) *en* ~ raise (run) a blockade **-brytare** blockade runner

block|bildning formation of blocs **-choklad** cooking chocolate

blocker|a [-å-] blockade; (*friare*) block **-ing** block

block|flöjt recorder **-hus** blockhouse **-ämne** subject block

blod *s7* blood; *levrat* ~ clotted blood, gore; *gråta* ~ (*ung.*) cry one's eyes out; *med kallt* ~ in cold blood; *~ är tjockare än vatten* blood is thicker than water; *~et steg mig åt huvudet* the blood went to my head; *det har gått dem i ~et* it has got into their blood; *det ligger i ~et* it runs in the blood; *prins av ~et* prince of the blood; *väcka ont* ~ breed bad blood **bloda** ~ *ner* stain with blood; *få ~d tand* (*bildl.*) acquire the taste

blod|apelsin blood orange **-bad** blood bath, massacre; *anställa* ~ *på* butcher wholesale **-bana** blood vessel **-bank** blood bank **-befläckad** *a5* bloodstained **-bok** copper beech **-brist** anaemia **-cirkulation** circulation of the blood **-drypande** *a4* bloody; ~ *historia* bloodcurdling story **-fattig** anaemic **-fläck** bloodstain **-flöde** flow of blood; haemorrhage **-full** full-blooded **-förgiftning** blood poisoning **-förlust** loss of blood **-givarcentral** blood donor centre **-givare** blood donor **-givning** donation of blood **-grupp** blood group (type) **-gruppsbestämning** blood-group determination **-hosta** *ha* ~ cough blood **-hund** bloodhound

blodig *a1* bloody; bloodstained, gory, sanguinary; (*friare*) deadly; grievous; ~ *biffstek* underdone (*AE.* rare) steak; *det var inte så ~t* (*vard.*) this wasn't too stiff

blod|igel medicinal leech **-korv** black (blood) pudding (*AE.* sausage) **-kropp** blood cell (corpuscle); *röd* ~ red blood cell, erythrocyte; *vit* ~ white blood cell, leucocyte **-kräfta** leukaemia, *AE.* leukemia **-kärl** blood vessel **-lus** apple (American) blight **-lönn** red maple **-omlopp** circulation of the blood, bloodstream **-plasma** blood plasma **-platta**, **-plätt** platelet, (*särsk. förr*) thrombocyte **-propp** thrombus **-proppsbildning** thrombosis **-prov** blood sample; (*-analys*) blood test **-pudding** black (blood) pudding **-röd** blood red; *bli* ~ *i ansiktet* turn crimson

blods|band *pl* ties of blood; *besläktad genom* ~ related by blood **-drama** bloody drama **-droppe** drop of blood **-dåd** bloody deed

blod|serum blood serum

blods|förvant kinsman **-hämnd** blood feud, vendetta

blod|sjukdom blood disease **-skam** incest **-skuld** blood guilt **-socker** *med.* blood sugar; *för högt* ~ hyperglycaemia, *AE.* hyperglycemia; *för lågt* ~ hypoglycaemia, *AE.* hypoglycemia **-sprängd** bloodshot **-spår** track of blood; blood mark **-sten** haematite **-stillande** *a4* haemostatic, styptic; ~ *medel* styptic **-stockning** congestion, engorgement **-störtning** haemorrhage of the lungs; haematemesis; violent haemoptysis **-sugare** bloodsucker; *bildl. äv.* vampire, extortioner

blodsutgjutelse bloodshed

blod|sänka [blood] sedimentation [rate] **-transfusion** [blood] transfusion **-tryck** blood pressure; *för högt* ~ hypertension; *för lågt* ~ hypotension **-törst** bloodthirstiness **-törstig** bloodthirsty **-utgjutning** extravasation [of blood] **-vallning** flush **-vite** *s6* blood wound **-värde** blood count **-åder** blood vessel, [blood] vein **-överföring** *se -transfusion*

blom [blɒmm] *s2* blossom; *koll. äv.* bloom; *slå ut i* ~ [come out in] blossom; *stå i* ~ be in bloom (flower) **-axel** *bot.* receptacle, thalamus **-blad** petal **-bord** plant (flower) stand, flower box **-botten** *bot., se -axel* **-bukett** bouquet, bunch of flowers **-doft** scent of flowers **-fat** flowerpot saucer **-foder** *bot.* calyx **-fäste** *bot., se -axel* **-hylle** *bot.* floral envelope, perianth **-kalk** *bot.* flower cup **-klase** *bot.* raceme **-knopp** [flower] bud **-korg** *se blomsterkorg* **-krona** *bot.* corolla **-kruka** flowerpot **-kål** cauliflower **-kålshuvud** head of cauliflower **-kålsöra** cauliflower ear; boxer's ear **-låda** flower box **-lös** flowerless

blom|ma [ˣblɒmma] **I** *s1* flower; *i ~n av sin ålder* in one's prime **II** *v1* flower, bloom, blossom; ~ *upp* (*bildl.*) take on a new lease of life; ~ *ut* shed its blossoms **-mig** *a1* flowery, flowered

blommografera [blɒmmo-] send flowers by Interflora

blom|ning [ˣblɒmm-] flowering, blooming **-ningstid** flowering season

blomster ['blɒms-] *s7* flower **-affär** florist's [shop] **-arrangemang** flower arrangement **-dekoration** floral decoration **-frö** flower seed **-förmedling** *B~en* Interflora Flower Relay **-försäljare** flower seller **-försäljerska** flower girl **-girland** garland of flowers **-handel** *se -affär* **-hyllning** floral tribute **-korg**

flower basket **-krans** wreath [of flowers]; lei **-kvast** bunch of flowers **-lök** bulb **-odlare** floriculturist, flower grower **-odling** floriculture, flower growing **-prakt** floral splendour, floweriness **-prydd** *a5* flowered, flowery **-rabatt** flowerbed **-skrud** flower array **-språk** language of flowers; *bildl.* flowery language **-säng** flowerbed **-uppsats** flower arrangement **-utställning** flower show; floricultural exposition **-vän** lover of flowers, flower fancier **-äng** flower field; *poet.* flowery mead

blomstr|a [ˣblåms-] blossom, bloom; *bildl.* flourish, prosper **-ing** *bildl.* prosperity **-ingstid** *bildl.* era of prosperity; heyday

blom|ställning inflorescence **-vas** flower vase

blond [-ånd *el.* -åŋd] *a1* blond, *fem.* blonde; fair **-era** bleach **-in** [-'di:n] *s3* blonde

bloss [-å-] *s7* **1** *(fackla)* torch; *(fastsatt)* flare **2** *(på cigarett o.d.)* puff, pull, whiff; *vard.* drag; *ta sig ett* ~ have (take) a smoke **blossa** blaze, flare; *bildl. äv.* burn, flush [up]; ~ *upp (om eld)* flare up; *(om pers.)* flare up, kindle; ~*nde kinder* burning cheeks; ~*nde röd* crimson

blot *s7* sacrificial feast **blota** *v1* sacrifice

1 blott [-å-] **I** *adv* only, but, merely; ~ *och bart* only; *det vet jag* ~ *alltför väl* that I know only too well; *icke* ~...*utan även* not only...but also; *det är ett minne* ~ it is but a memory **II** *konj* if only

2 blott [-å-] *a, mest i best. form* mere; bare; *med* ~*a ögat* with the naked eye; ~*a tanken därpå* the mere thought of it; *slippa undan med* ~*a förskräckelsen* get off with a fright [only]

blotta [-å-] **I** *s1* gap; *bildl.* opening, weak spot **II** *v1* **1** lay bare, expose; ~ *sitt huvud* uncover [one's head]; *med* ~*t huvud* bareheaded; *med* ~*t svärd* with the sword drawn **2** *(röja)* disclose, unveil, expose; ~ *ngns brister* expose a p.'s shortcomings; ~ *sin okunnighet* expose one's ignorance; ~ *sig* uncover, *bildl.* expose (betray) o.s.; ~*d på* destitute (void) of **blottare** exhibitionist **blottställ|a** expose *(för* to); ~ *sig* expose o.s. *(för* to); *familjen är alldeles* -*d* the family is absolutely destitute

bluff *s2* bluff; *sl.* stumer **bluffa** bluff; ~ *sig till en plats* bluff one's way to a job; ~ *sig fram* make one's way by bluff **bluffare, bluffmakare** bluffer

blund *s3, inte få en* ~ *i ögonen* not get a wink of sleep; *ta sig en* ~ take a nap *(vard.* shuteye); *John B~ (ung.)* the sandman **blunda** shut one's eyes *(för* to) **blunddocka** sleeping doll

blunder ['blund-] *s2* blunder; *vard.* boob

blus *s2* blouse **-liv** [lady's] blouse

bly *s7* lead; *av* ~ *(äv.)* lead[en] **-ackumulator** lead accumulator **-dagg** plummet, plumb bob

blyerts [ˣbly:- *el.* 'bly:-] *s2* **1** *(ämne)* black lead, graphite; *(i pennor)* lead **2** *(penna)* lead pencil; *skriva med* ~ write in pencil **-penna** *se blyerts* **2** **-stift** lead **-teckning** pencil drawing

bly|fri lead-free; ~ *bensin* unleaded (lead-free) petrol *(AE.* gasoline) **-förgiftad** [-j-] *a5* lead poisoned **-förgiftning** lead poisoning

blyg *a1* shy *(för* of), bashful **-as** *v2, dep* be ashamed *(för* of); blush *(över* at)

blygd *s3, ej pl* private parts *(pl)* **-ben** pubic bone, pubis **-läppar** *pl* labia [pudendi]

blyghet [ˣbly:g-] shyness, bashfulness

bly|glans galena, galenite **-glas** lead glass **-glete** *s7, s5* lead monoxide, litharge **-grå** livid; leaden

blyg|sam [ˣbly:g-] *a1* modest, unassuming **-samhet** modesty **-sel** ['blygg-] *s2* shame; *känna* ~ *över* feel ashamed of; *rodna av* ~ blush with shame

bly|hagel lead shot **-halt** lead content **-haltig** *a1* lead-bearing, plumbiferous **-infattad** *a5,* ~*e rutor* leaded panes **-infattning** lead mounting **-kula** lead bullet **-malm** lead ore **-mönja** red lead, minium; *(färg)* red-lead paint **-tung** [as] heavy as lead; leaden **-vitt** white lead, lead paint

blå *a1* blue; *ett* ~*tt öga* a black eye; *slå ngn gul och* ~ beat s.b. black and blue; *i det* ~ up in the clouds **-aktig** *a1* blu[e]ish **-anlupen** blue-tempered **-bandist** blue-ribbonist **-blodig** blue-blooded **-byxor** *pl* blue jeans **-bär** whortleberry, blaeberry; bilberry; *AE.* blueberry **-bärsris** whortleberry wire[s] **-bärssylt** bilberry jam **-dåre** madman **-eld** viper's bugloss; *AE.* blueweed **-else** blue, blu[e]ing **-fisk** bluefish, snapper **-frusen** blue with cold **-grå** bluish grey **-grön** bluish green, sea green; ~*a alger* blue-green algae **-gul** blue and yellow **-hake** *zool.* bluethroat **-jacka** *(matros)* blue-jacket **-klint** cornflower, bluebottle **-klocka** harebell, *(i Skottland)* bluebell **-klädd** dressed in blue **-kläder** *pl* overalls; dungarees **-kopia** blueprint, cyanotype **-kopiering** blueprinting **-krage** *se -jacka* **-kråka** European roller

Blåkulla *n* the Brocken **-färd** witches' ride

blå|lera blue clay **-lusern** alfalfa, lucerne, purple medic **-mes** bluetit **-mussla** sea (edible) mussel **-märke** bruise

blåna become blue; ~*nde berg (ung.)* distant blue mountains **blånad** *s3* bruise

blåneka flatly deny

blånor *pl* tow, oakum *(sg)*

blå|penna blue pencil **-räv** blue fox **-röd** purple

1 blås|a *s1, med.* bladder; *(luft-, i glas o.d.)* bubble; *(hud-; i metall)* blister; *full av* -*or* bubbly; blistery; *med.* vesicular, vesiculate

2 blås|a *v3* blow; *det* -*er kallt* there is a cold wind blowing; *det* -*er nordlig vind* the wind is in the north; ~ *[nytt] liv i* infuse fresh life into; ~ *av* blow (call) off, *sport.* stop play; ~ *bort* blow away; ~ *in luft i* inflate [with air]; ~ *ner* blow down; ~ *omkull* blow over; ~ *upp en ballong* inflate (blow up) a balloon; *det* -*er upp* it is blowing up; *fönstret* -*te upp* the window blew open; ~ *upp sig* puff o.s. up; ~ *ut* blow out

blåsare *(musiker)* player of a wind instrument; -*arna (koll. ung.)* the wind[s *pl*]

blåsbildning blistering, bubble formation

blåsbälg bellows *(behandlas som sg el. pl)*; *en* ~ a pair of bellows

blåshalskörtel prostate [gland]

1 blåsig *a1 (t 1 blåsa)* blistery

2 blåsig *a1 (t. 2 blåsa)* windy, breezy

blåsinstrument wind instrument

blåsippa hepatica

blåskatarr cystitis

Blåskägg *riddar* ~ Bluebeard

blåslagen *a3* black and blue
blås|lampa blowlamp; *AE.* blowtorch **-ljud** *med.* [heart] murmur, souffle **-ning** blowing; *åka på en* ~ be taken in **-orkester** (*mässingsorkester*) brass band
blåsprit methylated spirits
blåsrör blowpipe; *AE.* blowgun
1 blåst [-å:-] *s2* wind
2 blåst [-å:-] *oböjligt a, vard.* **1** *se korkad* **2** (*lurad*) bamboozled, taken in
blåstrumpa bluestocking
blåstång bladderwrack
blå|ställ *ung.* [blue] overalls (*pl*) **-svart** blue black
blåsväder windy weather
blåsyra prussic (hydrocyanic) acid
blått *s, best. form: det blåa* blue; *jfr* **blå**
blå|val blue whale **-vinge** (*scout*) Brownie [Guide] **-vit** bluish white **-ögd** *a5* blue-eyed; (*naiv*) dewy-eyed; ~ *optimism* starry-eyed optimism
bläck *s7* ink; *skriva med* ~ write in ink
1 bläcka *v1,* ~ *ner sig* ink one's fingers; get o.s. inky
2 bläcka *v1* (*märka träd*) blaze
3 bläcka *s1, ta sig en* ~ get drunk, have a booze, go on a drinking bout
bläck|fisk cuttle[fish]; squid; (*åttaarmad*) octopus **-fläck** inkstain **-horn** inkpot, inkwell **-penna** pen; (*reservoarpenna*) fountain pen **-plump** blot [of ink] **-svamp** ink cap; *fjällig* ~ shaggy cap **-säck** ink sac
blädderblock flipover
bläddra turn over the leaves (pages) (*i en bok* of a book); ~ *igenom* skim [through], glance through; ~ *tillbaka* turn back a few pages
bländ|a blind, dazzle; *bildl. äv.* fascinate; ~ *av* (*bilstrålkastare*) dip [the headlights]; *foto.* stop down **-ande** *a4* blinding; dazzling, glaring
bländar|e *foto.* diaphragm, stop **-öppning** *foto.* aperture
blände *s6* blende
bländ|fri non-glare **-skydd** *foto.* lens hood; (*på bil*) sun visor (shield) **-verk** delusion, illusion **-vit** dazzlingly white
blänga *v2* glare, stare (*på at*)
blänk *s7, s2* **1** flash **2** *se* **blänke blänka** *v3* shine, gleam, glitter, glisten; ~ *till* flash, flare
blänkare (*i tidning*) short notice
blänk|e *s6,* (*vid pimpelfiske*) lure, jig **-fyr** long-flashing light **-ljus** long-flashing light
bläs *s2* blaze **-and** wi[d]geon
bläster ['blæst-] *s2* blast, blower **-smide** blastfurnace (osmund) iron **-ugn** blast furnace
blästr|a blast **-ing** blasting
blöda *v2* bleed (*äv. bildl.*)
blödar|e bleeder **-sjuka** haemophilia
blödig *a1* soft, timid, chicken-hearted, chicken-livered **-het** softness *etc.*
blödning ['blö:d-] bleeding, haemorrhage
blöj|a ['blöja] *s1* nappy, napkin; *AE.* diaper **-byxor** [plastic] baby pants **-snibb** tie-on **-vadd** *se* cellstoff
blöt I *a1* wet; (*vattnig*) watery, soggy; *bli* ~ get soaked **II** *oböjligt s, ligga i* ~ be in soak; *lägga i* ~ [put...to] soak, steep; *lägga sin näsa i* ~ poke one's nose into everything; *lägg inte nä-*

san i ~! mind your own business!
blöt|a *v3* soak, steep, wet; ~ *ner sig* get o.s. all wet; ~ *upp* soak, sop **-djur** mollusc **-lägga** *se* **blöt II -läggningsmedel** soaking agent **-snö** wet snow; (*sörja*) slush
b-moll B-flat minor
BNP (*förk. för bruttonationalprodukt*) GNP
bo I I *s5* (*i sms.*) inhabitant; *moskva*~ inhabitant of Moscow, *äv.* Muscovite; *london*~ Londoner; *paris*~ Parisian; *newyork*~ New Yorker **2** *s6* (*fågel-*) nest; (*däggdjurs*) den, lair **3** *s6* (*kvarlåtenskap*) estate; (*bohag*) furniture; *sitta i orubbat* ~ retain undivided possession of the estate; *sätta* ~ settle, set up house; *hustrun medförde...i* ~*et* his wife brought...into the home **II** *v4* live; (*vanl. förnämt*) reside; (*tillfälligt*) stay; (*i högre stil*) dwell; ~ *billigt* pay a low rent; ~ *inackorderad hos* board and lodge with; ~ *kvar* stay on; ~ *trångt* have limited living space, be overcrowded; ~ *åt gatan* have rooms facing the street; *du kan få* ~ *hos mig* (*äv.*) I can put you up; *här* ~*r jag* this is where I live; *på Grönland* ~*r eskimåer* there are Eskimos living in Greenland
boa *s1* boa **-orm** boa constrictor
boaser|a panel, wainscot **-ing** panelling, wainscot, wainscot[t]ing
bobb [-å-] *s2* bobsleigh
1 bobba [-å-] *v1* (*håret*) bob
2 bobba [-å-] *s1* **1** bug; (*kackerlacka*) cockroach **2** (*liten bold*) pimple
bo'bin *s3* bobbin
1 bock [-å-] *s2* **1** (*djur*) he-goat, buck; *sätta* ~*en till trädgårdsmästare* set a thief to catch a thief **2** (*gymnastikredskap*) buck **3** (*stöd*) trestle **4** *hoppa* ~ play [at] leapfrog **5** (*fel*) [grammatical] fault (mistake); howler; (*tecken*) cross, tick; *sätta* ~ *för* mark as wrong
2 bock [-å-] *s2* (*bugning*) bow
bocka [-å-] **1** *tekn.* bend **2** (*buga*) bow; ~ *sig för* bow to **3** ~ *för* (*markera*) tick
bockfot *där stack* ~*en fram!* the (your, his *etc.*) cloven hoof is showing!
bockning [-å-] **1** *tekn.* bending **2** (*bugning*) bow
bock|skägg goat's beard; (*hakskägg*) goatee **-språng** caper, gambol
bod *s2* **1** (*affär*) shop **2** (*uthus*) shed; storehouse **-betjänt, -biträde** *se* affärsbiträde
bodega [-ˣde:-] *s1* bodega
bodelning (*vid skilsmässa*) partition (division) of joint property [upon separation]; (*av dödsbo*) partition (division) of the estate (inheritance)
Bodensjön [ˣbå:-] the Lake of Constance
bodknodd counter jumper
bodräkt *jur.* fraud on one's next of kin
boende *a4* living; resident; who lives **-form** type of housing **-kostnad** housing costs (*pl*) **-standard** housing (living) conditions (*pl*)
boer ['boˑ:-] Boer **-kriget** [the] Boer War
bo'ett *s3* watchcase
bofast resident, domiciled, settled
bofink *s2* chaffinch
bog *s2* **1** (*på djur*) shoulder **2** *sjö.* bow; *lägga om på en ny* ~ (*bildl.*) go off on a fresh tack; *slå in på fel* ~ (*bildl.*) take a wrong tack **-ankare** bower **-blad** shoulder blade; *anat.* scapu-

la
boggi ['båggi] *s3* bogie, bogy; truck **-vagn** bogie car[riage]
bogser|a tow, take in tow, tug **-bil** *se bärgningsbil* **-båt** tug[boat], towboat **-ing** towing, towage **-lina, -tross** towrope, towline
bogspröt bowsprit
bohag *s7* household goods (*pl*) (furniture)
bo'hem *s3* Bohemian **-artad** [-a:r-] *a5* Bohemian **-e'ri** *se bohemliv* **-isk** *a5* Bohemian **-liv** Bohemia, Bohemianism
1 boj [båj] *s3* (*tyg*) baize
2 boj [båj] *s2, sjö.* buoy; *förtöja vid ~* moor; *lägga ut en ~* put down a buoy
boj|a [ˣbåja] *s1* fetter, shackle; *bildl.* bond; *slå ngn i -or* put s.b. in irons
bo'jar [-å-] *s3* boyar
bojkott [ˣbåj- *el.* -'kått] *s3*, **bojkotta** [ˣbåj- *el.* -'kåtta] *v1* boycott
1 bok *s2, bot.* beech[tree]; *av ~* (*äv.*) beech[en]
2 bok *-en böcker* **1** book; *häftad ~* paperback; *inbunden ~* hardback; *avsluta böckerna* close the books; *föra böcker* keep books; *föra ~ över* keep a record of; *hänga näsan över ~en* bury one's nose in one's book; *tala som en ~* talk like a book **2** (*24 el. 25 ark papper*) quire
1 boka 1 *hand., se bokföra* **2** (*beställa biljett o.d.*) book, reserve
2 boka (*krossa malm*) stamp, pound
bok|anmälan book review **-anmälare** book reviewer, critic **-auktion** book auction **-band** (*del av bokverk*) volume; (*pärmar etc.*) binding **-bestånd** stock of books **-bindare** bookbinder **-binderi** bookbindery, bookbinder's [workshop] **-buss** mobile library; *AE.* bookmobile **-cirkel** book circle **-flod** season's new books; (*friare*) flood of fiction **-form** *i ~* in book form, as a book
bokför|a book, enter [in the books]; *-t värde* book value **-are** accountant, book-keeper; clerk
bokföring book-keeping, accounts; *dubbel* (*enkel*) *~* book-keeping by double (single) entry
bokförings|lag accounting act (law) **-maskin** accounting (book-keeping) machine **-plikt** obligation (liability) to keep books
bok|förlag publishing company (house), publishers (*pl*) **-förläggare** publisher **-handel** bookshop, bookseller's [shop]; bookstore; *i ~handeln* (*abstr.*) in the book trade; *utgången ur -handeln* out of print **-handlare** bookseller **-hylla** bookcase; (*enstaka hylla*) bookshelf **-hållare** accountant, book-keeper; *vanl.* clerk **-klubb** book club
boklig [ˣbo:k-] *a1* literary, bookish; *~ bildning* book-learning
bok|låda *se bokhandel* **-lärd** well-read; bookish; scholarly **-mal** bookworm **-marknad** book market **-märke** bookmark[er]
bokning [ˣbo:k-] **1** (*bokföring*) posting, posting of items; (*av enskild post*) [book] entry **2** (*biljettbeställning o.d.*) booking, reservation
bokollon beechnut; *koll.* beech mast
bok|omslag dust jacket (cover), [book] jacket, wrapper **-pärm** book cover **-rygg** spine, back of a book **-samlare** book collector, bibliophil[e] **-samling** collection of books, library

bokskog beech woods (*pl*)
bok|skåp bookcase **-slut** balancing of the books; *konkr.* final accounts; *göra ~* close (balance) the books, make up a balance sheet
bokstav *-en bokstäver* letter; character; *grekiska bokstäver* Greek characters; *liten ~* small letter; *stor ~* capital [letter]; *efter ~en* literally; *to the letter* **-era** spell **-lig** [-a:-] *a1* literal **-ligen** [-a:-] *adv* literally; (*rent av*) positively
bokstavs|följd alphabetical order **-gåta** anagram; logogriph **-lås** combination (letter) lock **-ordning** *se -följd* **-trogen** true to the letter
bok|stöd book end **-synt** [-y:-] *a1* well-read **-synthet** book knowledge **-titel** book title, title of a book **-tryck** book printing; (*högtryck*) letterpress [printing] **-tryckare** printer **-tryckarkonst** [art of] printing, typography **-tryckeri** printing-house, printing-office **-verk** book **-ägarmärke** bookplate, ex-libris **-älskare** booklover, bibliophil[e]
bolag *s7* company; *AE.* corporation; *enkelt ~* partnership; *ingå i ~ med* enter into partnership with
bolags|beskattning company (corporate) taxation **-man** partner **-ordning** articles of association (*pl*), corporate bylaws (*pl*) **-styrelse** board of directors **-stämma** annual meeting of shareholders, annual general meeting
bolero [bå'le:rå] *s5* bolero
bo'lid *s3* bolide, fireball
bo'lin *s3, sjö.* bowline; *låta allt gå för lösa ~er* let things go as they please, allow things to slide
Bolivia [-'li:-] *n* Bolivia **bolivi'an** *s3*, **boliviansk** [-'a:-] *a5* Bolivian
boll [-å-] *s2* **1** ball; (*slag i tennis*) stroke; *kasta ~* play catch; *sparka ~* play football; *en hård ~* a hard stroke; *~en ligger hos dig* the ball is in your court **2** *sl.* (*huvud*) nut, loaf; *AE.* bean; *vara tom i ~en* be batty, be off one's nut
boll|a play ball; *~ med ord* play (juggle) with words, split hairs **-kalle** *s2* ball boy **-kastning** ball-throwing **-sinne** ball-sense **-spel** ball game **-spelare** ballplayer **-sport** ball games (*pl*) **-trä** bat
bolma [-å-] (*om sak*) belch out smoke; (*om pers.*) puff; *~ på en pipa* puff away at a pipe
bolmört [-å-] henbane
bolometer [-'me:-] *s2* bolometer
bolsje'v|ik [bålʃe-] *s3* Bolshevik **-ism** Bolshevism **-istisk** *a5* Bolshevist[ic]
bolster ['båls-] *s2, s7* soft mattress; feather bed **-var** *s7* tick; (*tyg*) ticking
1 bom [båmm] *s2* (*stång*) bar, *järnv.* level-crossing (*AE.* grade-crossing) gate; (*väg-*) barrier; (*gymnastikredskap*) [balance] beam; *sjö.* boom; (*last-*) derrick, jib; (*på vävstol*) beam; *inom lås och ~* under lock and key
2 bom [båmm] **I** *s2* (*felskott*) miss, wide **II** *adv,* *skjuta ~* miss [the mark] **III** *interj* boom
bomb [-å-] *s3* bomb; (*fälla ~er* drop bombs, bomb; *slå ner som en ~* (*bildl.*) come as a bombshell
bomb|a [-å-] bomb **-anfall** bombing attack
bombard|emang *s7* bombardment **-era** bomb, bombard; batter; (*friare*) pelt
bom'bas|m [-å-] *s3* bombast **-tisk** *a5* bombas-

tic

bomb|attentat bomb outrage (attempt) **-flyg** bombers; bomb command **-flygplan** bomber **-fällning** bomb dropping, release of bombs **-hot** bomb warning **-krater** bomb crater **-last** bombload **-matta** bomb carpet **-nedslag** impact of a bomb; *ett blont* ~ a blonde bombshell **-ning** bombing **-plan** *se -flygplan* **-rum** (*i flygplan*) bomb bay **-räd** bomb raid **-sikte** bombsight **-stopp** bomb[ing] halt **-säker** bombproof

1 bomma (*missa*) miss [the mark]; ~ *på* miss
2 bomma ~ *för* (*igen, till*) bar, lock up
3 bomma *sl.* (*låna*) cadge, scrounge; *AE.* bum, mooch

bomolja [ˣbɷmm-] industrial olive oil
bomsegel [ˣbɷmm-] boomsail
bomskott [ˣbɷmm-] *se 2 bom I*
bomull [ˣbɷmm-] cotton; (*förbands-*) cotton wool, purified (*AE.* absorbent) cotton; *av* ~ (*äv.*)

bomulls|bal bale of cotton **-band** cotton tape **-buske** cotton shrub **-fabrik** cotton mill **-flanell** flannelette **-frö** cottonseed **-garn** cotton yarn **-klänning** cotton dress **-krut** guncotton **-odlare** cotton grower **-odling** cotton growing **-plantage** cotton plantation **-spinneri** cotton mill **-trikå** cotton stockinet **-tråd** cotton thread; *en rulle* ~ a reel of cotton **-tuss** piece of cotton-wool **-tyg** cotton fabric (cloth) **-vadd** cotton wool **-växt** cotton plant

bomärke [owner's] mark; (*på kreatur*) brand [mark]

1 bona (*polera*) wax, polish
2 bona ~ *om* wrap up well; *se äv. ombona*
bonad *s3* hanging [piece of] tapestry
bonapparat floor polisher
bonbonjär [båŋbånˈjäːr] *s3* sweetmeat dish, bonbonnière

bond|bröllop peasant wedding **-by** farming village **-böna** broad (horse) bean **-dräng** farm hand; ploughboy

bonde *-n bönder* **1** farmer; (*allmogeman*) peasant, countryman **2** (*schack-*) pawn **-befolkning** farming population; [the] farmers (*pl*) **-här** army of peasants **-kultur** peasant culture **-praktika** *s1, ung.* farmers' almanac **-stånd** peasantry **-uppror** peasants' revolt

bond|flicka country girl **-folk** country people **-fångare** con[fidence] man, trickster **-fångeri** confidence trick (*AE.* game), con trick **-förnuft**, **-förstånd** common sense **-försök** *ung.* unblushing (cheeky) attempt; *vard.* try-on **-grann** gaudy, showy **-gubbe** old countryman **-gumma** old countrywoman **-gård** farm; (*boningshus*) farmhouse **-hund** mongrel **-jänta** country wench **-komik** burlesque; lowbrow comedy **-komiker** lowbrow comedian; (*dålig amatör*) ham actor **-kvinna** countrywoman **-land** *~et, se bondvischan* **-lurk** *s2* yokel; *AE.* hick **-neka** stubbornly deny **-permission** French leave **-piga** farm maid; *neds.* country ninny **-pojke** country lad (boy)

bondsk *a1* peasantlike, rustic; boorish
bond|slug sly, shrewd **-spelman** village fiddler **-stuga** farmhouse **-tur** *rena ~en* a real fluke **-tölp** country bumpkin **-vatten** Adam's ale

(wine), [drinking] water **-vischan** the backwoods (sticks) (*pl*); *AE.* Hicksville; *på* ~ in the sticks **-ånger** [maudlin] self-reproach

bong [båŋ] *s2* voucher; (*på restaurang*) bill, *AE.* check; (*vid totalisator*) tote ticket **bonga** *ung.* register

bongotrumma [ˣbåŋgå-] bongo
1 boning (*t. 1 bona*) polishing
2 boning (*bostad*) dwelling [place], abode
bonings|hus dwelling house **-rum** living room
bonjour [båŋˈʃɷːr *el.* -ˈʃuːr] *s3* frock coat
bon'nett *s3* bonnet
bonus [ˈbɷː-] *s2* bonus **-klass** bonus class
bonvax [ˈbɷːn-] floor wax (polish)
bo|plats habitation, dwelling place; site **-pålar** *pl, slå ner sina* ~ settle down

bor [båːr] *s2* boron **-at** [bɷ- *el.* båː-] *s4* borate **-ax** [ˈbɷ:- *el.* ˈbåː-] *s2* borax; (*mineral äv.*) tincal

1 bord [-ɷ:-] *s7* table; (*skriv-*) desk; *tekn.* platform; *duka ~et* lay the table; *gående* ~ buffet; *vi var tio till ~et* we were ten at table; *dricka ngn under ~et* drink s.b. under the table; *föra ngn till ~et* take s.b. in to dinner; *lägga korten på ~et* put one's cards on the table; *passa upp vid ~et* wait at (*AE.* on) table; *sitta (sätta sig) till ~s* sit at (sit down to) table

2 bord [-ɷ:-] *s7, sjö.* board; (*i bordläggning*) plank; *kasta över* ~ jettison; throw overboard; *falla över* ~ fall overboard; *man över* ~! man overboard!; *se äv. ombord*

borda board
bord|beställning table reservation **-dans** table-turning **-duk** tablecloth
borde [ˣbɷ:r-] *imperf. av böra*
bordeaux [bårˈdåː] *s3*, **bordeauxvin** [bårˣdåː-] Bordeaux; (*rött*) claret **bourdeauxvätska** [bårˣdåː-] Bordeaux mixture
bor'dell [-å-] *s3* brothel
1 bordlägga shelve; table; postpone
2 bordlägga *sjö.* plank; (*stålfartyg*) plate
1 bordläggning shelving; tabling; *parl.* first reading
2 bordläggning *sjö.* (*av trä*) [outside] planking; (*av plåt*) shell-plating
bordlöpare [table] runner
bords|bön grace; *läsa* ~ say grace **-dam** [lady] partner at table **-dekoration** table decoration; centrepiece **-duk** *se bordduk* **-granne** neighbour (partner) at table **-kavaljer** [gentleman] partner at table **-kniv** table knife **-lampa** table lamp **-låda** [table] drawer **-salt** table salt **-samtal** table talk **-servis** tableware **-silver** table silver **-skick** table manners (*pl*) **-skiva** tabletop **-tändare** tablelighter **-uppsats** centrepiece **-vatten** mineral water **-vin** table wine **-visa** drinking song **-ända** end of the table; *sitta vid övre ~n* sit at the top (head) of the table; *nedre ~n* the bottom (end, foot) of the table

bordtennis table tennis **-racket** bat
bordåvätska *se bordeauxvätska*
Bore Boreas
bor|en [ˣbåː-] *a5* born; *han är den -ne ledaren* he is a born leader
borg [bårj] *s2* castle; stronghold
borga [ˣbårja] buy (sell) on credit; ~ *för* guar-

antee, warrant, vouch for
borgarbracka [*bårjar-] *s1* narrow-minded bourgeois, Philistine; *AE.* Babbitt
borgar|e [*bårr-] citizen, townsman; commoner; *hist.* burgher; burgess; *-na (äv.)* the bourgeoisie *(sg)* **-klass** *~en* the bourgeoisie, the middle classes *(pl)* **-press** Liberal and Conservative press **-råd** city commissioner **-stånd** *~et* the burghers *(pl)*; *(i Storbritannien)* the commons *(pl)*
borgen ['bårjen] *r* [personal] guarantee, security, warrant; *gå i ~ för* stand surety for, warrant, *(friare)* vouch for, stand (go) bail for; *ställa ~* give surety; *teckna ~* provide a personal guarantee; *frige mot ~* release on bail; *den som går i ~* går i sorgen go bail for a borrower and come home a sorrower
borgens|förbindelse personal guarantee, surety bond, security **-lån** loan against a [personal] guarantee **-man** guarantor; surety, warrantor
borge'när [bårje-] *s3* creditor
borgerlig [*bårjer-] *al* **1** civil; *~ vigsel* civil marriage; *~a rättigheter* civil rights; *~t år* civil (calendar) year **2** *(av medelklass)* middle--class, bourgeois; *~t yrke* ordinary occupation **3** *polit., de ~a partierna* the Liberals and Conservatives **4** *neds.* Philistine, narrow-minded, square **-het** [middle-class] respectability
borgerskap [*bårjer-] *s7, ej pl* burghers *(pl)*
borg|fred party truce **-fru** chatelaine **-gård** castle courtyard
borgis ['bårgis *el.* -jis] *s2, boktr.* bourgeois
borgmästar|e *(kommunal-)* mayor, *(i Skottland)* provost, *(i större engelska städer)* lord mayor **-inna** [lord] mayoress
borgruin ruined castle
boricka [*bɔ:-] *s1* donkey
bornera [-å-] effervesce; *(om vin)* sparkle
bornerad [-år'ne:-] *a5* narrow-minded; Philistine
bor'nyr [-å-] *s3* head, froth; *(i vin)* sparkle
borr [-å-] *s2, s7* borer; *(drill-)* drill; *(navare)* auger; *tandläk.* dental drill, bur; *(liten hand-)* gimlet
borr|a *(i material)* bore, drill; *(brunn, gruva)* bore, sink; *~ efter vatten* bore for water; *~ hål i (äv.)* hole; *~ igenom (äv.)* perforate; *~ i sank* sink; scuttle; *~ [ner] huvudet i kudden* bury one's head in the pillow; *~ upp* bore a hole in, drill; *~ ögonen i ngn* give s.b. a piercing stare **-are** borer **-fluga** fruit fly **-hål** drill hole, bore[hole] **-krona** drill bit **-maskin** drilling (boring) machine **-ning** boring, drilling **-plattform** drilling platform **-stål** drill steel **-sväng** brace; *~ med borr* brace and bit **-torn** derrick, drilling tower
borst [-å-] *s7* bristle; *resa ~* bristle [up]; *försedd med ~* bristled **borsta** brush; *(skor, tänder äv.)* clean
borst|bindare brushmaker; *svära som en ~* swear like a trooper **-binderi** brush factory
borste [-å-] *s2* brush **-ig** *al* bristly
borst|mask chaetopod **-nejlika** sweet william **-ning** brushing; cleaning
borsyr|a boric (orthoboric) acid **-esalva** boracic ointment
1 bort [-ɔ:-] *sup. av böra*

2 bort [-å-] away; *gå ~ a) (på kalas)* go [to a party], go out [to dinner], *b) (dö)* pass away; *~ med er!* away with you!; *~ med tassarna!* hands off!; *långt ~* far away; *längst ~* at the far end
borta [-å-] away; *(försvunnen)* gone; *(frånvarande)* absent; *(ej tillfinnandes)* missing, lost; *(ute)* out; *där ~* over there; *~ bra men hemma bäst* East or West, home is best; *~ från skolan* absent from school; *~ med vinden* gone with the wind; *~ på kalas [out]* at a party; *känna sig alldeles ~* feel completely lost *(förvirrad:* muddled)
bortackordera board out
borta|lag *sport.* away team **-match** *sport.* away game
bortanför *se bortom*
bortaplan *sport.* away ground
bort|arbeta eliminate [by hard work] **-arrendera** lease out
bortaseger *sport.* away win
bort|auktionera sell at (by) auction, auction off **-bjuden** *a5* invited out *(på middag to dinner)* **-blåst** *a4, är som ~* has vanished into thin air **-byting** changeling **-bytt** *a4, få sina galoscher ~a* get s.b. else's galoshes [by mistake]; *mina barn var som ~a* they did not seem like my children at all **-döende** *a4* dying away **-efter** along **-emot** *(i riktning mot)* in the direction of; *(nära)* nearly **-erst** ['bårt-] **I** *adv* farthest off **II** *a, superl.* farthest, farthermost **-fall** falling off; *(försvinnande)* disappearance **-falla** drop (fall) off; *(försvinna)* disappear, be dispensed with, be omitted **-forsla** carry away; *(med t.ex. kärra)* cart away; remove **-frakta** **1** remove **2** *~ ett fartyg* charter a ship, let a ship by charter party **-fraktare** *(rederi)* shipowner, charterer **-fraktning** removal **-färd** **1** outward journey **2** departure **-förklara** explain away **-förklaring** prevarication; trumped-up excuse **-gift** *bli ~* be given away in marriage; *få en dotter ~* marry off a daughter **-glömd** *a5* forgotten **-gång** decease; departure *(ur tiden* from this life) **-gången** *a5* gone away; *(död)* deceased; *den -gångne* the deceased **-ifrån** **I** *prep* from [the direction of] **II** *adv, där ~* from over there; *långt ~* from far off (away) **-igenom** away through **-kastad** *a5* thrown away; wasted; *~ möda* wasted effort **-klemad** *a5* coddled [and spoiled] **-kollrad** [-å-] *a5, bli alldeles ~* have one's head quite turned **-kommen** [-å-] *a5* lost; *(om pers. äv.)* absent-minded, confused; *känna sig ~* feel like a fish out of water **-lovad** [-å-] *a5* promised; *(tingad)* bespoken **-manövrera** eliminate by a [clever] manoeuvre **-om** **I** *prep* beyond; *~ all ära och redlighet* beyond the pale [of civilization] **II** *adv, där ~* beyond that **-operera** remove [by surgery]
bortovaro *s2* absence
bortrationalisera make redundant by efficiency improvement
bortre ['bårt-] *a, komp.* further; *i ~ delen av* at the far end of; *~ parkett* pit stalls
bort|resonera reason away, get over by argument[s *pl*] **-rest** [-e:-] *a4, han är ~* he is (has gone) away **-ryckt** *a4* pulled out; *(av döden)*

bortröva–botövning   80

snatched away by death **-röva** kidnap, run away with; (*kvinna*) abduct **-se** ~ *från* disregard, leave out of account;; ~*tt från* apart from, irrespective of **-skriva** sign away **-skämd** *a1* spoilt (*med* by) **-slarvad** *a5* lost **-slumpa** sell off **-sprungen** *a5* strayed **-stött** *a4* expelled **-trängning** *psykol.* repression **-val** optional exclusion **-väg** *på* ~*en* on the way there **-vänd** *a5* turned away; *med* -*vänt ansikte* with averted face **-åt** ['bårt- *el.* -'å:t] **I** *adv* **1** *där* ~ somewhere in that direction; *en tid* ~ for some time **2** (*nästan*) nearly **II** *prep* towards, in the direction of; ~ *gatan* along the street; ~ *kyrkan* near the church; *hon är* ~ *femtio år* she is going on for fifty **-över** [-'ö:- *el.* 'bårt-] **I** *prep* away over **II** *adv, dit* ~ away over there
bosatt *a4* residing; resident; *vara* ~ *i* reside (live) in
bosch [-å-] *s7* bosh
boskap [ˣbɔ:-] *s2, ej pl* cattle (*behandlas som pl*), livestock (*behandlas som sg el. pl*)
boskaps|avel stockbreeding **-hjord** herd of cattle **-marknad** cattle market **-skötsel** cattlebreeding, cattleraising **-uppfödare** stockbreeder, cattlebreeder **-vagn** cattle truck; *AE.* stock car
bo|skifte *se bodelning* **-skillnad** judicial division of a joint estate
Bosnien ['båsni-] *n* Bosnia **bosnier** ['båsni-] *s9,* **bosnisk** ['båss-] *a5* Bosnian
boson [-'så:n] *s3* boson
Bosporen [bås'på:-] *n* the Bosporus
1 boss [-å-] *s2, polit.* [party] boss
2 boss [-å-] *s7* (*agnar*) chaff
bossa nova ['båssa 'nå:va] *r* bossa nova
bostad -*en* bo*städer* dwelling, habitation, housing [accommodation]; (*våning*) flat, *AE.* apartment; (*hyrda rum*) lodgings (*pl*), *vard.* digs (*pl*); (*hem*) home, house; *jur.* domicile; *fast* ~ permanent address (residence, home); *fri* ~ free housing (accommodation); *utan* ~ homeless; *olämplig som* ~ unfit for habitation
bostads|adress home (private) address; *jur.* domicile **-bidrag** housing allowance **-brist** housing shortage **-byggande** housing construction, house building **-departement** ministry of housing and physical planning **-domstol** ~*en* [the Swedish] rents and tenancies court of appeal **-fastighet** block of flats, residential property, dwelling house **-förening** *se* -*rättsförening* **-förmedling** housing agency, local housing authority **-hus** *se* -*fastighet* **-kvarter** residential quarter **-kö** housing queue **-lån** housing loan **-lägenhet** flat; *AE. äv.* apartment **-lös** homeless **-marknad** housing market **-minister** minister of housing and physical planning **-område** residential area, housing estate (development) **-politik** housing policy **-problem** housing problem **-rättsförening** tenant-owners' society **-standard** housing standard **-styrelse** ~*n* [the Swedish] national housing board **-tillägg** housing allowance **-utskott** ~*et* [the Swedish parliamentary] standing committee on housing **-yta** dwelling space, floor space of a flat
boston|terrier [ˣbåstån-] Boston terrier (bull)

-vals boston
boställe [official] residence
bosätt|a *rfl* settle [down], take up residence **-ning** (*handlingen att sätta bo*) setting up house, starting a home; (*anskaffande av husgeråd m.m.*) housefurnishing; (*bebyggande*) settlement; establishment
bosättnings|affär household equipment store **-lån** government loan for setting up house
bot *s3* **1** (*botemedel*) remedy; cure; *finna* ~ *för* find a cure for; *råda* ~ *för* (*på*) remedy, set right **2** (*gottgörelse*) penance; *göra* ~ *och bättring* do penance, turn over a new leaf **3** *jur.* penalty **bota 1** (*läka*) cure (*för* of) **2** (*avhjälpa*) remedy, set right
botan|ik *s3* botany **-iker** [-'ta:-] botanist **-isera** botanize **-isk** [-'ta:-] *a5* botanic[al]; ~ *exkursion* botanical excursion; ~ *geografi* botanic geography; ~ *trädgård* botanical garden **-ist** botanist
bot|dag day of penance **-emedel** remedy, cure **-färdig** penitent **-färdighet** penitence **-görare** [-j-] penitent **-göring** [-j-] penance **-predikan** penitential sermon
Botswana [båts'va:na] *n* Botswana
botten ['båtten] **I** *s2* bottom; (*mark*) soil; (*på tapet, tyg*) ground; *dricka i* ~ drain (empty) [one's glass]; ~ *opp!* bottoms up!, down the hatch!, no heeltaps!; *det finns ingen* ~ *i honom* there's no limit to his appetite; *gå till* ~ go to the bottom, sink, founder; *gå till* ~ *med ngt* (*bildl.*) get to the bottom of s.th.; *i grund och* ~ at heart (bottom), (*helt o. hållet*) thoroughly; *på nedre* ~ on the ground (*AE.* first) floor; *på svensk* ~ on Swedish soil **II** *oböjligt a, vard.* lousy, rotten **-beskaffenhet** quality of the bottom **-frysa** freeze solid (to the bottom) **-färg** ground [colour]; (*grundningsfärg*) primer, priming; *sjö.* bottom coat
Bottenhavet [ˣbått-] the southern part of the Gulf of Bothnia
botten|hederlig *se* -*ärlig* **-inteckning** first mortgage **-kran** *sjö.* seacock **-kurs** bottom price (quotation) **-känning** grounding; *ha* ~ (*sjö.*) touch bottom (ground) **-lån** first mortgage loan **-läge** lowest point **-lös** bottomless; (*friare*) unfathomable, fathomless, immeasurable; ~*a vägar* roads deep in (impassable for) mud **-pris** rock-bottom price **-rekord** [the] lowest level ever reached **-reva** *sjö.* close-reef; ~*d* close-reeved **-rik** made of (rolling in) money **-sats** sediment; (*i vin, kaffe o.d.*) dregs (*pl*); *bildl. o. kem.* deposit **-skikt** bottom layer; (*geol. o. befolknings-*) lower strata (*pl*); (*drägg*) residuum **-skrap** (*äv. bildl.*) last scraps (*pl*) **-skrapa I** *s1* trawl, dredge **II** *v1* **1** scrape [a ship's bottom] **2** *bildl.,* ~ *sina tillgångar* exhaust one's funds **-skyla** [-ʃ-] *s1* enough to cover the bottom **-våning** ground (*AE.* first) floor **-ärlig** downright honest, honest to the core
bot'tin [-å-] *s3* galosh (snow) boot
bottna [-å-] **1** (*nå botten*) reach (touch) the bottom **2** *det* ~*r i* it originates in, it springs from
Bottniska viken ['bått-] [the] Gulf of Bothnia
botulism botulism
botövning discipline, penance

boudoir [bɒdo'a:r] *s3, se budoar*
bougie [bɒ'ʃi:] *r* bougie
bouillabaisse [bɒja'bä:s] *s3* bouillabaisse
boulevard [bɒle'va:rd] *s3* boulevard; (*i Stor-britannien*) avenue **-kafé** boulevard café
boupteck|ning estate inventory; *förrätta ~* [make an estate] inventory **-ningsman** administrator; (*förordnad i testamente*) executor
bouquet [bɒ'ke:] *s3* flavour; (*t.ex. vin-*) bouquet
bourgeoisie [bɒrʃɒa'si:] *s3* bourgeoisie
bourgogne [bɒr'gånj] *s5,* **bourgognevin** [bɒr*gånj-] Burgundy
boutique [bɒ'tick] *s5* boutique
boutred|ning administration of the estate of a deceased **-ningsman** (*förordnad av domstol*) administrator; (*förordnad i testamente*) executor
bov *s2, eg.* crook; villain (*äv. teat.*); *skämts.* rascal, rogue; *~en i dramat* the villain of the piece **-aktig** *a1* villainous; rascally, roguish **-aktighet** villainy; rascality
bovete buckwheat
bovfysionomi villainous countenance
bowl|a [*båɒ- el.* *båv-] bowl **-are** bowler **-ing** ['båɒ- *el.* 'båv-] [tenpin] bowling; *AE.* tenpins **-bana, -hall** bowling alley **-klot** bowl **-kägla** [ten]pin
bovstreck [piece of] villainy; dirty trick
box [båks] *s2* box, case; (*kol-*) bunker; (*kätte*) box, stall; (*post-*) [post-office] box
box|a [*båksa] *~ till ngn* give s.b. a punch (blow) **-are** boxer, pugilist **-as** *dep* box
boxer ['båkser] *s2* boxer
boxhandske [*båks-] boxing glove
boxkalv [*båks-] box calf
boxning [*båks-] boxing, pugilism
boxnings|match boxing match **-ring** boxing ring **-sporten** boxing, the noble art of self-defence
bra *bättre bäst* **I** *a* **1** good; (*starkare*) excellent; (*som det skall vara*) all right; *~ karl reder sig själv* self-help is a primary virtue, an honest man does his own odd jobs; *blir det ~ så?* will that do?; *det är ~ (tillräckligt)* that'll do, that's enough; *det var ~!* that's good!; *det var ~ att du kom[mer]* it is a good thing (job) you came, I am glad you came; *allt skall nog bli ~ igen* I am sure everything will turn out for the best; *vad skall det vara ~ för?* what is the good (use) of that? **2** (*frisk*) well; *han är ~ igen* he is all right again; *har du blivit ~ från din förkylning?* have you recovered from your cold? **3** (*ganska lång*) good[ish], long[ish] **II** *adv* **1** well; *lukta (smaka) ~* smell (taste) nice; *tack ~* very well, thank you; *jag mår inte riktigt ~* I am not feeling well, I am feeling a bit under the weather; *ha det ~* be well off, (*trivas*) be happy, like it, feel at home; *se ~ ut* be good-looking; *tycka ~ om* like very much **2** (*mycket, ganska mycket*) very; *vard.* jolly; *få ~ betalt* be well paid, get a good price; *det var ~ synd att* what a pity that; *det dröjde ett ~ tag innan* it took quite a while before; *jag skulle ~ gärna vilja veta* I should very much like to know
bracka *s1,* **brackig** *a1* Philistine **brackighet** Philistinism

brackvatten brackish water
bragd *s3* exploit, feat; achievement
bragelöfte boastful vow
bragt [brakt] *sup. av bringa* **bragte** [*brakte] *imperf. av bringa*
brahman *se braman*
brailleskrift [*braj-] Braille
brak *s7* crash; (*om kanon*) boom; (*om åska*) peal **braka** crasch, crack; *~ ihop* (*slåss*) come to blows; *~ lös* break out, get going; *~ ner* come crashing down; *~ samman* collapse
brak|middag *en riktig ~* quite a banquet **-skit** *vard.* fart; loud one **-succé** smash-hit
brakteat *s3* bracteate
brakved *s2, bot.* alder buckthorn
brallis ['brall-] *s2, sl., se brud 2*
brallor *pl, vard.* bags
bra'm|an *s3* Brahman **-anism** Brahmanism **-'in** *s3* Brahman, Brahmin
bramsegel [*bramm-] toppgallant sail
brand *-en bränder* **1** fire; (*större*) conflagration; (*brinnande trästycke*) [fire]brand; *råka i ~* catch fire; *stå i ~* be on fire; *sätta i ~* set fire to, set on fire, (*om känslor*) inflame **2** *med.* gangrene **3** *bot.* blight, mildew
brand|alarm fire alarm **-bil** fire engine **-bomb** firebomb, incendiary [bomb] **-chef** fire [department] chief, head of a fire brigade; *AE.* fire marshal **-damm** fire dam, emergency tank **-fackla** incendiary torch; *bildl.* firebrand **-fara** danger of fire **-fast** fireproof **-försvar** fire fighting, fire prevention; (*brandkår*) fire brigade; *AE.* fire department (company)
brand|försäkra insure against fire **-försäkring** fire insurance **-försäkringsbolag** fire company
brand|gata firebreak, fire line **-gavel** fireproof gable **-gul** orange, flame-coloured **-kår** fire brigade; *AE.* fire department **-larm** *se -alarm* **-lukt** smell of fire (burning) **-man** fireman **-mur** fire wall **-plats** place of fire **-post** fire hydrant; *AE.* fireplug **-redskap** fire-fighting equipment **-risk** fire hazard **-rök** smoke from a fire **-segel** jumping sheet **-skada** fire damage **-skadad** damaged by fire **-skadeersättning** fire indemnity **-skatta** extort contributions from; overtax; *bildl.* plunder, fleece **-skattning** [extortion of] contributions; *bildl.* plundering **-skydd** fire protection **-skåp** fire-alarm [box] **-slang** firehose **-släckare** fire-extinguisher **-släckning** fire fighting **-soldat** fireman **-spruta** fire-extinguisher **-station** fire station; *AE.* firehouse, station house **-stege** fire escape **-stodsbolag** fire-insurance company **-säker** fireproof, flameproof **-tal** inflammatory speech **-talare** fiery speaker **-vakt** fire watcher; *gå ~* (*bildl.*) be compelled to pace the streets all night **-varnare** automatic fire-alarm **-väsen** fire-fighting services (*pl*) **-övning** fire drill
brann *imperf. av brinna*
bransch *s3* line [of business], branch **-känne-dom** knowledge of a (the) trade **-man** expert (specialist) in a line of trade (business) **-or-ganisation** trade association **-vana** experience of a line of business
brant I *s3* precipice; *på ruinens ~* on the verge

brasa–bringa

82

of ruin **II** *al* steep, precipitous, sheer; ~ *udde* (*klippa, strandbank*) bluff **III** *adv* steeply *etc.*; *stupa* ~ *ner* (*äv.*) fall sheer away

brasa *sl* [log-]fire; *lägga in en* ~ lay a fire; *sitta vid* (*framför, kring*) *~n* sit at (in front of, round) the fire; *tända en* ~ make (light) a fire; *göra en* ~ *av* make a bonfire of

brasilianare [-ˣaːn-] *s9*, **brasiliansk** [-ˈaːnsk] *a5* Brazilian **Brasilien** [-ˈsiː-] *n* Brazil

braska (*bli kallt*) be frosty, freeze

braskande *a4* showy, ostentatious; ~ *annonser* ostentatious (showy, blazing) advertisements

brasklapp [ˣbrask-] *s2, ung.* mental reservation

bras|kudde hearth cushion **-redskap** fire irons

brass *s2, sjö.* brace

1 brassa *sjö.* brace; ~ *fullt* (*back*) brace full (aback)

2 brassa ~ *på* (*elda*) stoke up [the fire]; (*eldvapen*) fire away

brasserie [-ˈriː] *s4* brasserie

brast *imperf. av* brista

braständare firelighter

Braunschweig [ˈbraʊnʃvajg] *n* Brunswick

braˈvad *s3* exploit; bravado **bravera** (*utmärka sig*) be brilliant; (*skryta*) boast (*med* of), brag (*med* about)

bravo [ˈbraː-] bravo!, well done! **-rop** cheer

bravur dash; valour; *mus.* bravura **-nummer** star turn

braxen [ˈbraksen] *best. form* =, *pl* braxnar bream **-panka** *sl* young bream

bre *se* breda

bred *al* broad, wide; *på* ~ *front* on a broad front; *brett uttal* broad accent; *de ~a lagren* the masses; *göra sig* ~ assert o.s.; *på* ~ *bas* on a broad scale

breda *v2* spread; ~ *en smörgås* make a sandwich, butter a slice of bread; ~ *på* (*om smörgås*) spread, make, (*överdriva*) pile it on [thick], lay it on; ~ *ut* spread out; ~ *ut sig* spread, extend

bred|axlad *a5* broad-shouldered **-bar** *al* easy-spreading, spreadable **-bent** [-beːnt] *al* straddle-legged; *stå* ~ stand with one's legs wide apart **-brättig** *al* wide-brimmed **-bröstad** *a5* broad-chested

bredd *s3* **1** breadth, width; wideness; *gå i* ~ walk side by side; *i* ~ *med* abreast of, (*i jämförelse med*) compared to; *på* *~en* in breadth; *största* ~ (*sjö.*) overall width, beam **2** *geogr.* latitude

bredd|a broaden, make wider **-grad** [degree of] latitude; *på varmare ~er* in warmer climes **-ning** broadening, widening

bred|flikig *al* broad-lobed **-näsapa** *zool.* New World monkey **-randig** *al* broad-striped **-sida** broadside; *avfyra en* ~ fire a broadside **-spektrumantibiotikum** broad-spectrum antibiotic **-sparig** *järnv.* broad-gauge

bredvid [bre(d)ˈviːd *el.* ˣbreː(d)vid] **I** *prep* beside, at (by) the side of, by; (*intill*) next to; ~ *varandra* side by side; *prata* ~ *munnen* give the game (show) away, blab; ~ *sin fru verkar han obetydlig* beside his wife he looks insignificant **II** *adv* close by; (*-liggande, -stående*) adjacent, adjoining; (*extra*) in addition; *där* ~ close to it; *här* ~ close by here; *rummet* (*hu-*

set) ~ the next (adjacent, adjoining) room (house), *äv.* next door; *hälla* ~ miss the cup (glass *etc.*); *han tjänar en del* ~ he has some additional sources of income, he makes some extra cash in his spare time

breitschwanz [ˈbraitʃvants] *s2* (*pälsverk*) broadtail

bretagnare [-ˣtanjare] Breton **Bretagne** [-ˈtanj] *n* Brittany **bretagnisk** [-ˈtanjisk] *a5* Breton

breˈton *s3* Breton **breˈtonsk** [-ɷ:-] *a5* Breton

brett *adv* broadly, widely; *tala vitt och* ~ talk at great length

brev *s7* letter; (*bibl. o. friare*) epistle; *vard.* line[s *pl*]; *komma som ett* ~ *på posten* [come to] drop straight into one's lap **-befordran** transmission of letters **-bomb** letter bomb **-bärare** postman, *fem.* postwoman; *AE.* mailman **-bäring** mail-delivery service **-censur** postal censorship **-duva** carrier pigeon **-form** *i.~* in the form of a letter **-hemlighet** secrecy of the mails **-huvud** letterhead

breviarium [-viˈaː-] *s4* breviary

brev|kopia carbon copy **-kort** postcard; ~ *med betalt svar* reply postcard **-ledes** by letter **-låda** letter box; *AE. äv.* mailbox; (*pelare, i Storbritannien*) pillar box, post; (*i dörr*) *AE.* [mail] drop **-papper** notepaper, writing paper; stationery; (*med tryck*) letterhead **-porto** [letter] postage **-press** letter-weight, paperweight **-pärm** [letter] file **-remissa** mail remittance **-skola** correspondence school **-skrivare** letter writer, correspondent **-skrivning** letter writing, correspondence **-ställare** guide to letter-writing **-telegram** letter telegram **-våg** letter balance **-vän** pen pal (friend) **-växla** correspond **-växling** correspondence **-öppnare** letter opener

brick|a *sl* tray; (*för visitkort etc.*) salver; (*karottunderlägg*) [table]mat; (*plåt-*) plate; (*igenkänningstecken*) badge; (*spel-*) counter, piece; man; (*nummer-*) tab, check; *tekn.* washer; *en* ~ *i spelet* (*bildl.*) a pawn in the game **-duk** traycloth

bridge [briddʃ] *s2* bridge **-parti** game of bridge **-spelare** bridge player

bridreaktor [ˣbriːd-] breeder [reactor]

briˈgad *s3* brigade **-general** brigadier; *AE.* brigadier general

brigg *s2* brig

briˈkett *s3* briquet[te]

briljans [-ˈans *el.* -ˈaŋs] *s3* brilliance

briljant [-ˈant *el.* -ˈaŋt] **I** *s3* brilliant [cut], diamond **II** *al* brilliant, first-rate **-era** set with brilliants (diamonds), diamond **-ˈin** [-an- *el.* -aŋ-] *s4, s3* brilliantine **-ring** brilliant (diamond) ring **-smycke** set of brilliants, diamond ornament

briljera shine, show off; ~ *med* show off

brillor *pl* specs, spectacles

1 bringa *sl* breast; *kokk.* brisket

2 bringa *bragte bragt el. vl* bring; (*föra t. annan plats*) convey, conduct, carry; ~ *hjälp* render assistance; ~ *i dagen* bring to light; ~ *i oordning* put out of order, make a mess of; ~ *i säkerhet* convey into safety; ~ *klarhet i* throw light upon, make clear; ~ *ngn lycka* bring s.b.

happiness; ~ *ngn om livet* put s.b. to death, do s.b. in; ~ *ngn på fall* bring s.b. to ruin, cause a p.'s ruin; ~ *ngn sin hyllning* pay one's respect to s.b.; ~ *ngn till förtvivlan* reduce s.b. to despair; ~ *olycka över* bring disaster to, bring down ruin on; ~ *ordning i* put in order; ~ *på tal* bring up [for discussion], broach [a matter]; ~ *ur världen* dispose of; ~ *det därhän att man är* come (get) to the point of being
brink *s2* hill; (*älv-*) bank
brinn|a *brann brunnit* burn; be on fire; *det -er i spisen* there is a fire in the stove; *det -er i knutarna* the place is getting too hot [for me (*etc.*)]; *huset -er* the house is on fire; ~ *av iver* be full of enthusiasm; ~ *av nyfikenhet* (*otålighet*) be burning with curiosity (impatience); ~ *av* go off, explode; ~ *inne* be burnt to death; ~ *ner* burn down, (*om brasa*) burn low; ~ *upp* be destroyed by fire, be burnt out; ~ *ut* burn itself out, go out **brinnande** *a4* burning; ~ *bön* fervent prayer; ~ *kärlek* (*hängivenhet*) ardent love (affection); ~ *ljus* lighted candle; *springa för* ~ *livet* run for dear life; *mitt under* ~ *krig* while war is (was) raging (at his height)
brio ['briɷ] *s3* brio, vivacity; *med* ~ with zest (ardour)
bris *s2, s3* breeze; *lätt* ~ light breeze; *god* (*frisk*) ~ gentle (moderate) breeze; *styv* (*hård*) ~ fresh (strong) breeze
bri's|ad *s3,* **brisera** *v1* burst
brist *s3* **1** (*otillräcklighet*) lack, want, shortage, scarcity; (*saknad*) want; (*fel*) defect, flaw, shortcoming; *biol.* deficiency; (*nackdel*) disadvantage, drawback; *lida* ~ *på* be short of, be in want of; *i* (*av*) ~ *på* for want of, failing, lacking; *i* ~ *på bättre* for want of s.th. better **2** (*underskott*) deficit, shortage
brist|a *brast brustit* **1** (*sprängas*) burst; (*gå av, gå sönder*) break, snap; (*ge vika*) give way; (*rämna*) split; ~ *i gråt* burst into tears; ~ *i sömmarna* burst at the seams; ~ *ut i skratt* burst out laughing; *brusten blick* shattered glance; *brusten blindtarm* perforated appendix; *brustna illusioner* shattered illusions; *det varken bär eller -er* the ice holds but won't carry; *det var som om hjärtat ville* ~ my heart was ready to break; *hennes tålamod brast* her patience gave way; *det må bära eller* ~ sink or swim **2** (*vara otillräcklig*) fall short; be lacking (wanting) (*i* in); ~ *i lydnad* be wanting in obedience **2** (*underskott*) deficit, shortage
bristande *a4* (*otillräcklig*) deficient, inadequate, insufficient; (*bristfällig*) defective; ~ *betalning* default, nonpayment; ~ *kunskaper* inadequate knowledge; ~ *lydnad* disobedience; ~ *uppmärksamhet* inattention; *på grund av* ~ *bevis* in default of (for lack of) evidence
bristfällig *a1* defective, imperfect, faulty **-het** defectiveness, imperfection, faultiness
brist|ning burst[ing], break[ing]; *med.* rupture **-ningsgräns** breaking-limit, breaking-point; *fylld till* ~*en* filled to the limit of its capacity, (*friare*) full to overflowing
brist|situation [state of] shortage **-sjukdom** deficiency disease
britanniametall [-'tannia-] Britannia metal **Britannien** [-'tann-] *n* Britain **britannisk** [-'tann-] *a5* Britannic

brits *s2* bunk
britt *s3* Briton; (*i sht AE.*) Britisher; *~erna* the British **-isk** ['britt-] *a5* British; *B~a öarna* the British Isles
brittsommar Indian summer
bro *s2* bridge; *slå en* ~ *över* bridge, throw a bridge across **-avgift** bridge toll **-byggare** bridge-builder **-byggnad** bridge construction
broccoli ['bråkåli] *s2* broccoli
brock *se* bråck
brockfågel [-å-] plover; (*ljungpipare*) golden plover
1 brodd [-å-] *s2, bot.* sprout, shoot
2 brodd [-å-] *s2* (*järnpigg*) spike; (*i hästsko*) calk[in]
brodda calk
broder *-n bröder, se* bror
brodera embroider
broderfolk sister nation
brodergarn [-ˣde:r-] embroidery thread
broderi embroidery
broder|lig *a1* brotherly, fraternal **-mord, -mördare** fratricide **-skap** *s7* brotherhood, fraternity
broderskärlek brotherly love
bro'd|yr *s3* embroidered edging **-ös** embroiderer
bro|fäste [bridge] abutment **-förbindelse** connecting bridge **-huvud** bridgehead
broiler ['bråi-] *s2, s9* broiler
bro'kad *s3* brocade
brokig *a1* motley, multicoloured; variegated; (*grann*) gaudy, gay; *bildl. äv.* miscellaneous; ~ *samling* motley crowd **-het** variegation; diversity
brom [-å:-] *s3* bromine **-'id** *s3* bromide
1 broms [-å-] *s2, zool.* gadfly
2 broms [-å-] *s2, tekn.* brake; *bildl.* check
broms|a [-å-] brake; *bildl.* [put a] check [on] **-anordning** brake mechanism **-are** *järnv., AE.* brakeman **-back** brake shoe **-band** brake band **-belägg** brake lining **-fallskärm** brake parachute **-kloss** *se -back* **-ledning** brake line **-ljus** brake light, stoplight **-ning** braking **-olja** *se -vätska* **-pedal** brake pedal **-prov** brake test **-raket** retrorocket **-rör** *se -ledning* **-skiva** [brake] disc **-sko** drag, skid **-spår** skid mark **-sträcka** braking distance **-system** brake system **-trumma** brake drum **-vagn** *järnv.* brake van; *AE.* caboose **-vätska** brake fluid
bronk|er ['brånker] *pl* bronchi (*sg* bronchus) **-'it** *s3* bronchitis
brons [-åns *el.* -åŋs] *s3* bronze **-era** bronze **-medalj, -märke** bronze medal **-staty** bronze statue **-åldern** the Bronze Age
bropelare pier; pillar; tower; (*för hängbro*) pylon
bror *brodern bröder* brother; (*bibl. o. poet. pl ibl.* brethren); *Bröderna Grimm* the Brothers Grimm; *Bröderna A.* (*firma*) A. Brothers (*förk.* Bros.); *Bäste Bror* (*i brev*) Dear (My dear) (James *etc.*); *vara* (*du och*) ~ *med ngn* (*ung.*) be on familiar terms with s.b.
brors|barn brother's child **-dotter** niece
brorskål *dricka* ~ (*ung.*) drink to the use of Christian names
brorslott lion's share

brorson nephew
broräcke bridge railing (parapet)
brosch [-å:-] *s3* brooch; breastpin
bro'schyr [-å-] *s3* brochure, booklet, pamphlet, folder
brosk [-å-] *s7, anat.* cartilage; (*särsk. i kött*) gristle **-artad** *a5* cartilaginous; gristly **-fisk** cartilaginous fish
bro|slagning bridging **-spann** span of a bridge
brotsch [bråttʃ] *s2* reamer **brotscha** ream
brotschning reaming
brott [-å-] *s7* **1** (*brytande*) break, fracture; (*på rör äv.*) burst; leak; (*brutet ställe*) breach, break[age]; (*ben-*) fracture; (*sten-*) quarry; (*yta äv.*) fracture, break **2** (*straffbar gärning*) crime; (*mindre svårt*) offence; (*förseelse*) breach, infringement, violation; *begå ett* ~ commit a crime; *ett* ~ *mot reglerna* a violation of the rules (regulations)
brottanvisning *tekn.* stress raiser
brott|are [-å-] wrestler **-as** *dep* wrestle; grapple
brott|hållfasthet tensile strength **-mål** criminal case **-målsdomstol** criminal court
brottning [-å-] wrestling; (*friare äv.*) struggle
brottningsmatch wrestling match
brotts|balk criminal code (law) **-förebyggande** *a4*, ~ *rådet* [the Swedish] national council for crime prevention; ~ *åtgärder* crime-prevention measures
brottsjö breaker; heavy sea
brottslig [-å-] *a1* criminal; (*skyldig t. brott*) guilty **-het** crime, criminality; guilt
brottsling [-å-] *s* criminal; (*gärningsman*) culprit
brottsplats scene of [the] crime, venue **-undersökning** scene of crime investigation; on-the-spot crime investigation
brott|stycke fragment **-ställe** fracture **-yta** [area of] fracture
bro|valv bridge-arch **-öppning** (*om klaffbro*) raising of a bridge
brr *interj* brrh!, ugh!
brud *s2* **1** bride; *hemföra ngn som* [*sin*] ~ bring home one's bride; *stå* ~ be married **2** *sl.* (*flicka*) bird, chick; *AE.* broad; *en snygg* ~ a smasher **-bröd** *bot.* dropwort **-bukett** bridal bouquet **-följe** bridal train **-gum** *s2* bridegroom **-kista** *AE. ung.* hope chest **-klänning** wedding dress **-krona** bridal crown **-näbb** (*flicka*) bridesmaid; (*pojke*) page **-par** bridal couple, bride and bridegroom; *~et A.* (*i telegram*) Mr. and Mrs. A- **-rov** bride abduction **-slöja** bridal veil **-sporre** *bot.* fragrant gymnadenia **-stol** *gå* (*träda*) *i* ~ get married **-säng** marriage bed; *träda i* ~ enter into marriage **-tärna** bridesmaid
brugd *s3, zool.* basking shark
bruk *s7* **1** (*användning*) use, employment, usage; *för eget* ~ for personal (one's own) use; *ha* ~ *för* find a use for; *inte ha* ~ *för* have no use for; *komma i* ~ come into use; *komma ur* ~ fall into disuse, go out of use; *ta i* ~ begin using; *till utvärtes* ~ for external application (use) only; *vara i* ~ be used; *vid sina sinnens fulla* ~ in one's right mind **2** (*sed*) custom, usage, practice; *~et att röka tobak* the habit (practice) of smoking tobacco; *seder och* ~ usages and customs **3** (*odling*) cultivation **4**

(*fabrik*) factory, mill; works (*sg o. pl*) **5** (*mur-*) mortar; (*puts-*) grout, plaster
bruka 1 (*begagna*) use, make use of, employ; *han ~r sprit* he will take a drink [occasionally]; ~ *våld* use force **2** (*odla*) cultivate, till; (*gård*) farm **3** (*ha för vana*) be in the habit of; (*ofta omskrivning med adv såsom*) generally, usually; *jag ~r äta lunch kl. 12* I usually have lunch at twelve o'clock; (*endast i imperf.*) *~de* used to **4** (*kunna, pres. o. imperf.*) will, would; *han ~de sitta i timmar utan att göra någonting* he would sit for hours doing nothing
brukas *dep, det* ~ *inte* it is not customary (the fashion)
brukbar [-u:-] *a1* useful, fit for use; *i ~t skick* in working order, in serviceable condition; *försätta ur ~t skick* make useless, disable **-het** usefulness, fitness for use, serviceability, serviceableness
bruk|lig [-u:-] *a1* customary, usual **-ning** tillage
bruks|anvisning directions for use (*pl*) **-artikel** utility article **-disponent** managing director, mill (works) manager **-föremål** *se -artikel* **-patron** *se -ägare* **-samhälle** industrial community **-vara** utility product **-värde** utility value **-ägare** foundry proprietor, mill owner
brulépudding *se brylépudding*
brum|björn [ˌbrumm-] *bildl.* growler, grumbler **-ma** growl; (*om insekt*) hum, buzz, drone **-ning** growl[ing], hum[ming], buzz[ing]
brun *a1* brown; (*läderfärgad*) tan; ~ *bönor* (*maträtt*) brown beans **-aktig** *a1* brownish, browny **-alger** *pl* brown algae **-and** pochard **-björn** brown bear **-bränd** *a5* singed, scorched; (*av solen*) bronzed, tanned
bru'nett *s3* brunette
brun|grön brownish green **-hyad** *a5* brown-complexioned **-hyllt** *a4* swarthy; tanned **-kol** lignite, brown coal
brunn *s2* well; (*hälso-*) [mineral] spring, spa
brunnen *a5* burnt; ~ *gödsel* decomposed manure; *jfr brinna* **brunnit** *sup. av brinna*
brunns|borrning well boring (drilling) **-gäst** health spa visitor **-kur** water cure **-ort** health resort, spa **-vatten** well-water
brunst *s3* (*honas*) heat; (*hanes*) rut **-ig** *a1* in heat; ruttish **-tid** oestrus; heat
brunt [-u:-] *s, best. form det bruna* brown
brunte *s2* dobbin
brunögd *a5* brown-eyed
brus *s7* roar[ing]; (*vindens*) sough[ing]; (*vattnets äv.*) rush, rushing, surge; *mus.* swell[ing]; *tekn.* noise
brus|a roar; sough; swell; *det ~r i mina öron* there's a buzzing in my ears; *det ~nde livet* (*ung.*) the hustle [and excitement] of life; ~ *upp* (*bildl.*) flare up, get into a heat; ~ *ut* (*bildl.*) fly out **-hane** ruff; (*hona*) reeve **-huvud** hotspur, hothead
brusning [-u:-] *se brus*
brustablett effervescent tablet
brusten *a5, se brista* **brustit** *sup. av brista*
bru'tal *a1* brutal **-isera** brutalize **-itet** *s3* brutality
brut|en *a5* broken; *en* ~ *man* a broken man; *-et tak* curb roof; mansard [roof]; *AE.* gambrel [roof]; *jfr bryta* **-it** *sup. av bryta*

brutto *s6* gross; ~ *för netto* gross for net **-be-lopp** gross amount **-inkomst** gross income **-nationalprodukt** gross national product *(förk.* GNP) **-pris** gross price **-prissättning** resale price maintenance **-registerton**, **-ton** gross register ton **-vikt** gross weigh **-vinst** gross profit

bry *v4* **1** ~ *sin hjärna (sitt huvud)* puzzle one's head *(med* over; *med att* over + *ing-form*), cudgel (rack) one's brains *(med att* to + *inf.*) **2** ~ *ngn för ngn (ngt)* tease s.b. about s.b. (s.th.) **3** ~ *sig om (bekymra sig)* mind, *(tycka om)* care; ~ *dig inte om det* don't bother about it; *det är ingenting att* ~ *sig om* that's nothing to worry about; *vad ~r jag mig om det?* what do I care?; *jag ~r mig inte ett dugg om det* I don't care a hang about it; ~ *dig inte om vad han säger* take no notice of what he says; *hon ~r sig inte om honom* she gives him the cold shoulder, she cold-shoulders him

brydd *a1* puzzled *(för* about); embarrassed; confused; abashed

bryd|eri perplexity; embarrassment; *vara i* ~ *hur man skall göra* be puzzled what to do; *försätta ngn i* ~ put s.b. in a quandary; *råka i* ~ get embarrassed; *i* ~ *för pengar* hard up for money **-sam** *a1* awkward; embarrassing; perplexing

brygd *s3, abstr.* brewing; *konkr.* brew

1 brygga *s1* bridge; *(tilläggsplats)* landing stage; *(lastkaj)* wharf; *tandläk.* bridge[work]

2 brygga *v2* brew; *(kaffe)* percolate, make

bryggar|e brewer **-häst** drayhorse

bryggeri brewery **-jäst** brewer's yeast

brygg|hus brewing-house; *(tvättstuga)* wash-house **-kaffe** drip-coffee, percolator coffee **-kar** brewer's vat **-mal|en** *-et kaffe* fine-ground coffee

brylépudding caramel custard

brylling third cousin

bryn *s7* edge, verge, fringe

1 bryn|a *v3 (göra brun)* brown; *kokk.* brown, fry; *-t av solen* tanned

2 bryna *v3 (vässa)* whet, sharpen

bryne *s6* whetstone

1 bryning browning *etc., jfr 1 bryna*

2 bryning whetting *etc., jfr 2 bryna*

brynja *s1* [coat of] mail, hauberk

brynsten whetstone

bryo|log bryologist **-logi** *s3* bryology

brysk *a1* brusque, curt

Bryssel ['bryssel] *n* Brussels

bryssel|kål Brussels sprout **-matta** Brussels carpet **-spets** Brussels lace

bryta *bröt brutit* **1** *(av-, komma att brista)* break; *(elektrisk ström)* break, switch off; *(malm o.d.)* mine, dig for; *(sten)* quarry; *(färg, smak)* modify, vary; *(ljusstråle)* refract; *(brev)* open; *(sigill)* break open; *(servett)* fold; *(telefonsamtal o.d.)* cut off, disconnect, interrupt; *(förlovning)* break [off]; ~ *en blockad* run a blockade; ~ *kön (vard.)* jump the queue **2** *(om vågor)* break; *(avtal, lag o.d. äv.)* infringe, violate, offend; *(begå brott)* offend *(mot* against); ~ *med ngn* break with s.b.; ~ *med en vana* give up a habit; ~ *mot lagen* infringe (violate, break) the law; ~ *på tyska* speak with

a German accent **3** *(med betonad partikel)* ~ *av* break [off]; ~ *av mot* be in contrast to (with); ~ *fram* break out, *(om tand o.d.)* break through; ~ *in (om årstid, natt)* set in; ~ *in i ett land* invade a country; ~ *lös* break loose; *stormen bryter lös[t]* the storm breaks; ~ *samman* break down, collapse; ~ *upp* break up, make a move; *mil.* decamp; ~ *upp en dörr (ett lås)* break open (force) a door (lock); ~ *ut* break out **4** *rfl* break; *(om ljuset)* be refracted; *(om meningar)* diverge

bryt|arspets contact-breaker point **-böna** French (dwarf, kidney) bean, haricot

brytning [-y:-] breaking *etc.; (av kol etc.)* mining; *(av sten)* quarrying; *(ljusets)* refraction; *(i uttal)* accent; *kokk.* relish; *bildl.* breach, break; *(åsikters)* divergence

brytnings|index refractive index **-tid** [period of] transition **-vinkel** [angle of] refraction **-ål-der**, **-år** time of maturity; *(pubertet)* puberty, pubescence

brytärt pea

bråck *s7, med.* hernia, rupture **-band** truss

bråd *a1* hasty; sudden; *(om tid)* busy; *en* ~ *tid* a busy time; *ond*, ~ *död* violent and sudden death **-djup** I *s7* precipice II *a5* precipitous; *här är det ~t* it gets deep suddenly here **-mo-gen** *bildl.* precocious **-rasket** *i* ~ all at once; *inte i* ~ not at the drop of a hat, none too quickly

brådsk|a [ˣbråska] I *s1* hurry; haste; *det är ingen* ~ there is no hurry; *vi har ingen* ~ we needn't hurry; *hon gör sig ingen* ~ she takes her time, she is in no hurry *(med* about). II *v1 (om pers.)* hurry; *(om sak)* be urgent; *det ~r inte med betalningen* there is no hurry about paying **-ande** *a4* urgent, pressing; hasty; *ett* ~ *arbete* a rush job

brådstörtad *a5* precipitate; headlong

1 bråk *s7, mat.* fraction; *allmänt* ~ simple (common, vulgar) fraction; *egentligt (oegentligt)* ~ proper (improper) fraction

2 bråk *s7* **1** *(buller)* noise, disturbance, clamour; *(gräl)* row; *(oro)* fuss **2** *(besvär)* trouble, bother, difficulty; *ställa till* ~ stir up trouble, make a [great] fuss *(för, om* about)

1 bråka 1 *(stoja)* be noisy (boisterous); *(ställa t. uppträde)* make a disturbance; *(kritisera)* crab, carp, nag **2** *(krångla)* make difficulties **3** *se bry 1*

2 bråka *(lin)* break, bruise

bråkdel fraction[al part]

bråkig *a1 (bullersam)* noisy; *(stojande)* boisterous; *(oregerlig)* disorderly; *(om barn)* fidgety, restless; *(besvärlig)* troublesome, fussy; *(gräls|uk)* quarrelsome, cantankerous, contentious **-het** noisiness *etc.*

bråk|makare *s9*, **-stake** *s2* troublemaker; noisy person; *(orostiftare)* disturber of the peace

bråkstreck solidus *(pl* solidi), diagonal, separatrix *(pl* separatrices), shilling mark, stroke

brånad *s3* lust

brås *v4, dep*, ~ *på* take after

bråte *s2* **1** *(skräp)* rubbish, lumber **2** *(timmer-)* log jam

brått *n av bråd o. adv*, **bråttom** [ˣbråttåm *el.* 'brått-] *adv, ha* ~ be in a hurry *(med* for; *med*

att to + *inf*); *det är mycket* ~ it is very urgent, there is no time to lose; *det är* ~ *med leveransen* the delivery is urgent
1 bräcka I *s1* flaw, crack, breach **II** *v3* **1** break, crack; (*övertrumfa*) outdo, surpass, trump; ~ *till* (*av*) snub, flatten **2** (*gry*) break
2 bräcka *v3, kokk.* fry
bräck|age breakage **-järn** crowbar
bräckkorv smoked sausage for frying
bräcklig *a1* fragile, brittle; (*om pers.*) frail, puny **-het** fragility, brittleness; frailness, puniness
bräckt *a4,* ~ *vatten* brackish water
bräda I *s1, se bräde* **II** *v1* (*slå ut rival*) cut out, supplant
brädd *s2* edge, brim; brink; *fylla ett glas till* ~*en* fill a glass to the brim; *floden stiger över sina* ~*ar* the river overflows [its banks]; *stå på gravens* ~ be on the brink of the grave, have one foot in the grave **bräddad** *a5,* **bräddfull** *a5* brimming, brimful
bräd|e *s7, s6* **1** board; *hyvlade* ~*r* planed boards, floorings; *slå ur* ~*t* cut out; *sätta allt på ett* ~ put all one's eggs in one basket **2** *se* **-spel** **-fodra** cover with boards, board, wainscot **-fodring** [-ɷ:-] boarding, wainscot[t]ing **-golv** board[ed] floor **-gård** timberyard; *AE.* lumberyard **-segla** go windsurfing **-segla** go windsurfing **-seglare** windsurfer **-skjul** wooden shed **-spel** backgammon **-stapel** pile of boards
bräk|a *v3* bleat, baa; *bildl.* bray **-ande** *a4* bleating *etc.*
bräken ['brä:-] *s2, bot.* bracken **-växt** fern
bräm *s4* **1** border, edging, edge; (*päls-*) fur trimming **2** *bot.* limb
bränna *v2* **1** burn; (*sveda*) scorch, singe; parch; (*rosta*) calcine; (*tegel*) bake; (*keramik*) fire; (*lik, värdepapper*) cremate; (*i bollspel*) hit out; ~ *hål på* burn a hole in (on); ~ *sina skepp* burn one's boats (bridges); ~ *sitt ljus i båda ändar* burn the candle at both ends; *brända mandlar* burnt almonds; *bränd lera* fired clay; *bränt barn skyr elden* a burnt child dreads the fire; ~ *av ett fyrverkeri* let off fireworks; ~ *upp* burn; ~ *vid* burn **2** (*smärta*) burn **3** *rfl* burn (*på vatten, ånga*: scald) o.s.; (*på nässlor*) get stung; ~ *sig på tungan* burn one's tongue; ~ *fingrarna* burn one's fingers (*äv. bildl.*)
brännande *a4* burning; (*om hetta*) scorching; (*om smärta*) lancinating, sharp; (*om törst*) parching, consuming; (*frätande*) caustic; *bildl.* burning, ardent, intense; (*fråga*) crucial, urgent, vital, burning **brännare** burner **brännas** *v2, dep* burn; *det bränns!* (*i lek*) you are getting warm!; *nässlor bränns* nettles sting
bränn|bar *a1* [in]flammable, combustible; *bildl.* risky, controversial, touchy **-blåsa** blister [from a burn] **-boll** *ung.* rounders (*pl*)
bränneri distillery
bränn|glas burning glass **-het** *a1* burning hot, scorching
1 bränning burning; (*av lik*) cremation
2 bränning (*våg*) breaker, surf
bränn|manet giant jellyfish **-märka** brand; *bildl. äv.* stigmatize **-märke** brand; *bildl. äv.* stigma **-nässla** (*hopskr. brännässla*) stinging nettle **-offer** burnt offering **-olja** fuel oil

-punkt focus; focal point, principal focus **-skada, -sår** burn; ~ *av första* (*andra, tredje*) *graden* first-degree (second-degree, third-degree) burn **-tid** combustion time **-ugn** furnace, kiln **-vidd** focal length (distance) **-vin** *ung.* Scandinavian vodka; schnap[p]s
brännvins|advokat pettifogger **-bränneri** distillery **-glas** dram glass; shot
bränsle *s6* fuel; *fasta och flytande* ~*n* solid and liquid fuels **-behållare** fuel tank **-besparande** *a4* fuel-saving **-cell** fuel cell **-element** (*för kärnreaktor*) fuel element **-flis** fuel chips (*pl*) **-förbrukning** fuel consumption **-insprutning** fuel injection **-mätare** fuel gauge **-påfyllning** fill-up, refuelling **-snål** fuel-saving **-tank** *se* **-behållare** **-tillförsel** (*i motor*) fuel feed **-tillägg** heating surcharge **-upparbetning** (*i kärnteknik*) fuel reprocessing
bräsch [-ä(:)-] *s3* breach; *gå* (*ställa sig*) *i* ~*en för* take up the cudgels for; *skjuta en* ~ breach, batter
bräsera braise
bräss *s2, anat.* thymus; *kokk.* sweetbread
brätte *s6* brim
bröa sprinkle with crumbs
bröd *s7* bread; *franskt* ~ (*långt*) French bread, (*litet*) roll; *hårt* ~ crispbread; *rostat* ~ toast; *förtjäna sitt* ~ earn one's living; *den enes* ~, *den andres död* one man's loss is another man's gain; *ta* ~*et ur munnen på ngn* take the bread out of a p.'s mouth **-bit** piece of bread; *jfr* **brödskiva** **-butik** bakery, baker's [shop] **-fat** bread dish (plate) **-frukt** breadfruit **-fruktträd** breadfruit [tree] **-föda** bread; *slita för* ~*n* struggle to make a living **-kaka** round loaf **-kant** crust [of bread] **-kavel** rolling pin **-korg** breadbasket **-lös** *bättre* ~ *än rådlös* better breadless than witless
brödra|folk [*brö:dra-] sister nations **-skap** *s7* brotherhood, fraternity, fellowship
bröd|rost *s2* toaster **-skiva** slice of bread **-skrin** breadbin, breadbox **-smula** crumb **-spade** peel **-stil** *boktr.* body (text) type **-säd** cereals (*pl*); (*spannmål*) corn, grain
bröllop [-åp] *s7* wedding, spousal (*ofta pl*); *boktr.* (*dubbelsättning*) double[t]
bröllops|dag wedding day; (*årsdag*) wedding anniversary **-gåva** wedding present **-marsch** wedding (bridal) march **-middag** wedding feast (dinner, *i Storbritannien vanl.* breakfast) **-natt** wedding night **-resa** wedding trip, honeymoon **-tårta** *ung.* wedding cake **-vittne** marriage witness
bröst *s7* breast; (*-korg*) chest; (*barm*) bosom, bust; *kokk.* breast, (*av fågel*) white meat; *ha klent* ~ have a weak chest; *ha ont i* ~*et* have a pain in one's chest; *förkylningen sitter i* ~*et* (*etc.*) have a cold on my chest; *ge ett barn* ~*et* give a baby the breast; *kom till mitt* ~*!* come into my arms!; *slå sig för* ~*et* beat one's breast **brösta** ~ *av* (*mil.*) unlimber; ~ *sig över* glory in, boast of (about)
bröst|arvinge direct heir, heir of the body, issue (*sg o. pl*) **-barn** breast-fed baby **-ben** breastbone; *anat.* sternum **-bild** half-length [portrait] **-böld** mammary abscess **-cancer** cancer of the breast, mammary cancer **-droppar** *p*

cough mixture (*sg*) **-fena** pectoral fin **-ficka** breast-pocket **-gänges** [-jäŋes] *gå ~ till väga* act high-handedly, go at it full tilt **-håla** cavity of the chest, thoracic cavity **-hållare** brassiere, bra **-höjd** breast height **-karamell** cough drop **-korg** chest, thorax **-körtel** mammary gland **-ning** *byggn.* breast [wall] **-sim** breaststroke **-sjuk** consumptive **-sjukdom** lung disease, chest disease **-socker** sugar (rock) candy **-ton** chest voice (register); *ta till ~erna* beat the drum, speechify, spout **-vidd** chest measurement **-vårta** nipple, teat, mamilla **-värn** breastwork, parapet

1 bröt *s2* log jam

2 bröt *imperf. av bryta*

B-skatt business profit tax **B-språk** *skol.* second foreign language

bu *interj,* **bua** *v1* boo

bubbel|kammare bubble chamber **-pool** whirlpool bath, jacuzzi (*varumärke*)

bubbla *s1 o. v1* bubble

buckan'jär *s3* buccaneer

buckl|a *1 s1* **1** (*upphöjning*) boss, knob **2** (*inbuktning*) dent, dint; (*på bil*) bodywork damage **II** *v1* buckle; *~ till* dent; batter **-ig** *a1* **1** embossed **2** dented

bud *s7* **1** (*befallning*) command, order; *tio Guds ~* the Ten Commandments; *hederns ~* the dictates of honour; *det är hårda ~* that's a tall order **2** (*an-*) offer; (*på auktion*) bid; *kortsp.* call, bid; *ett ~ på 5 pund* an offer of 5 pounds; *vara många om ~et* be many bidders **3** (*underrättelse*) message; *skicka ~ efter* send for; *skicka ~ att* send word to say that; *få ~ om ngt* receive message about s.th. **4** (*-bärare*) messenger **5** *stå till ~s* be available (at hand); *med alla till ~s stående medel* with all available means

bud|a summon, call in, send for **-bil** courier's van **-bärare** messenger

budd|ism Buddhism **-ist** *s3,* **-istisk** *a5* Buddhist

budfirma couriers'

budget ['buddjet] *s3, s2* budget; *balanserad ~* balanced budget; *göra upp en ~* budget, prepare (draw up) a budget **-chef** (*i finansdepartementet*) budget director **-era** budget **-ering** budgeting **-förslag, -proposition** budget [proposals *pl*] **-år** financial (*AE.* fiscal) year

budgivning [-ji:v-] *kortsp.* bidding

budkavle *hist.* (*i Skottland*) fiery cross; *~n går!* the fiery cross is out! **-tävling** *sport.* relay race

budning [*bu:d-] **1** summoning *etc., se buda* **2** (*om tömning av latrinkärl*) notice to nightmen

budoar [budɷ'a:r] *s3* boudoir

bud|ord commandment **-skap** *s7* message, announcement; address **-skickning** [-ʃ-] messenger service

buffé *s3, se byffé*

buffel ['buff-] *s2* buffalo; *bildl.* boor, lout, churl **-aktig** *a1, bildl.* boorish, loutish, churlish **-hjord** buffalo herd **-hud** buffalo hide

buffert ['buff-] *s2* buffer **-lager** buffer stock **-stat** buffer state **-zon** buffer zone

buga *~* [*sig*] bow (*för* to)

bugg|a (*avlyssna*) bug **-ning** bugging

bugning [-u:-] bow

buk *s2* belly; *neds.* paunch; *anat.* abdomen

Bukarest ['bu:-] *n* Bucharest

bu'kett *s3* bouquet; (*mindre*) nosegay, posy; bunch (*äv. bildl.*)

buk|fena pelvic (ventral) fin **-fylla, -fyllnad** filling food **-hinna** peritoneum **-hinneinflammation** peritonitis **-håla** abdominal cavity

bukig *a1* bulging, bulged

bukland|a belly land **-ning** belly landing

bukolisk [-'kå:-] *a5* bucolic

bukspott pancreatic juice **-körtel** pancreas

bukt *s3* **1** (*böjning*) bend, winding, turn **2** (*större vik*) bay, gulf; (*mindre*) cove, creek **3** (*slinga på tross e.d.*) bight, fake, coil **4** *få ~ med* (*på*) manage, master **bukta** *rfl* bend, curve, wind; *~ sig utåt* bulge

buktalare ventriloquist

bukt|ig *a1* bending, curving, winding **-ning** bend, curve, turn, winding

bula *s1* bump, lump, swelling

bulb *s3* bulb **-'är** *a1* bulbous, bulbaceous

bulevard *se boulevard*

bul'gar *s3* Bulgarian **Bulgarien** [-'ga:-] *n* Bulgaria **bulgarisk** [-'ga:-] *a5* Bulgarian

buli'mi *s3, med.* bulimia

buljong [-'jåŋ] *s3* bouillon, clear soup, meat broth (stock); (*för sjuka*) beef tea **-tärning** meat extract cube

bulk *s2* bulk **-last** bulk cargo

1 bulla *s1* (*påvlig*) bull

2 bulla *v1, ~ upp* make a spread

bull|dogg [-å-] *s2* bulldog **-dozer** *s9* bulldozer

bull|e *s2* bun, roll; *nu ska ni få se på andra -ar* you'll be seeing some changes around here

buller ['bull-] *s7* noise, sound, row, din; racket, clamour; (*dovt*) rumbling; *med ~ och bång* with a great hullabaloo **-bekämpning** noise [nuisance] control **-matta** noise strip **-mätning** noise measurement **-nivå** noise level **-sam** *a1* noisy **-skada** injury caused by noise **-skadad** suffering from noise-induced hearing impairment (loss) **-skydd** noise (sound) protection

bulle'tin *s3* bulletin

bullr|a make a noise; (*mullra*) rumble; (*dåna*) roar, thunder **-ande** *a4* noisy, boisterous **-ig** *a1* noisy

buln|a [*bu:l-] fester; gather **-ad** *s3* swelling; (*böld*) boil, furuncle

bult *s2* bolt; (*gängad äv.*) screw

bult|a 1 (*kött*) pound; beat; *med ~nde hjärta* with a pounding (palpitating) heart **2** (*knacka*) knock (*i, på* on, at); (*om puls*) throb; (*dunka*) thump; *det ~de på dörren* there was a knock at the door **-ning** pound, pounding; knock, knocking

bul'van *s3* decoy; *bildl. äv.* dummy; *köp genom ~* acquisition via ostensible buyer

bumerang boomerang

bums right away, instantly, on the spot

bunden *a5* bound (*äv. om bok*); *bildl.* tied, fettered; (*fästad*) attached (*vid* to); *~ aktie* restricted share; *bundet lån* fixed-term loan; *~ stil* poetry; *bundet värme* latent heat **-het** confinement; (*stelhet*) constraint, stiffness

bundit *sup. av binda*

bundsförvant ally; confederate

bunke *s2* bowl; dish; (*av metall*) pan
bunker ['bunk-] *s2* **1** *sjö.* bunker **2** *mil.* concrete dugout, pillbox **3** bunker, (*särsk. AE.*) sand trap **bunkerkol** bunker coal **bunkra** bunker
bunsenbrännare Bunsen burner
bunt *s2* bundle, pack, truss; (*papper, hö*) sheaf; *hela ~en* the whole bunch (lot) **bunta** ~ [*ihop*] make up into bundles (packs)
buntmakare furrier
buntvis in bundles (packs)
bur *s2* cage; (*emballage*) crate; (*för transport av smådjur, höns-*) coop; (*fotbollsmål o.d.*) goal; (*vard. finka*) clink, cooler, jug, nick, stir; *känna sig som en fågel i* ~ feel cooped up (in) **bura** ~ *in* lock up
bur'dus I *adv* abruptly, slapdash **II** *a1* abrupt; *bildl.* blunt, bluff
burfågel cagebird, cageling
burgen [-j-] *a3* well-to-do, affluent; *han är en* ~ *man* he is very well-off (well-to-do) **-het** affluence
Bur'gund *n* Burgundy **burgunder** [-'gund-] *s9,* **burgundisk** [-'gund-] *a5* Burgundian
burit *sup. av bära*
burk *s2* pot; (*sylt-*) jar; (*bleck-*) tin, *AE.* can; (*apoteks-*) gallipot; *på* ~ tinned, *AE.* canned **-mat** tinned (*AE.* canned) food **-öl** canned beer **-öppnare** tin (*AE.* can) opener
bur'lesk *a1 o. s3* burlesque, burlesk
Burma *n* Burma **bur'man** *s3* Burmese **burmansk** [-'ma:nsk] *a5* Burmese, Burman
bur'mes *s3, se* burman **-isk** *a5, se* burmansk
bur'nus *s2, s3* burnoose, burnous[e]
1 burr *se* brr
2 burr *s7* (*om hår*) frizz[le]
burra ~ *upp* ruffle up; *fågeln ~de upp sig* the bird ruffled up its feathers **burrig** *a1* frizz[l]y, frizzled
burskap [*bu:r-] *s7* **1** *hist.* burghership **2** *vinna* ~ be adopted (*i* into), become established, (*friare*) gain ground
burspråk [*bu:r-] *s7* oriel; (*utbyggt fönster*) bay window
bus *leva* ~ make a nuisance of o.s., (*skämts.*) make mischief, be noisy **busa** make trouble; be noisy **busaktig** *a1* rowdy; mischievous, noisy
buschman Bushman
bus|e *s2* **1** *barnspr.* bogeyman, bogyman **2** (*ruskig karl*) ruffian, rowdy **-fasoner** *pl* rowdy behaviour (*sg*) **-frö** ragamuffin **-ig** *a1, se* busaktig
buskablyg bashful, timid
buskage *s7* shrubbery; thicket; copse, coppice **buske** *s2* bush; (*liten, risig*) scrub; (*större*) shrub; *sticka huvudet i ~en* bury one's head in the sand **buskig** *a1* bushy; shrubby
buskis ['busk-] *s2, vard.* ham acting
busk|skvätta *s1* whinchat **-snår** thicket **-teater** *ung.* farcical open-air play
busliv rowdyness, rowdyism
1 buss 1 *s2* (*krigs-*) old campaigner; *~ar* warriors bold; *se äv.* sjöbuss **2** *oböjligt s o. a, vara* ~ *med ngn* be pals with s.b.
2 buss *s2* (*tugg-*) quid
3 buss *s2* (*fordon*) bus; (*turist-*) coach
4 buss *interj o. adv,* ~ *på honom!* at him!

bussa ~ *hunden på ngn* set the dog on s.b.
bussarong [-'råŋ] *s3* [sailor's] jumper
buss|chaufför bus driver **-fil** bus lane **-förbindelse** bus connection **-hållplats** bus stop, (*med regnskydd*) bus shelter
bussig *a1* (*förträfflig*) capital; (*hygglig*) kind, good; *hon är en* ~ *flicka* she is a good sort
buss|konduktör [bus] conductor **-linje** bus service (line)
bussning *tekn.* bush; (*särsk. AE.*) bushing; sleeve
busstation (*särskr. buss-station*) *se* bussterminal
buss|terminal bus terminal; *AE.* depot **-trafik** bus service
bus|unge *vard.* little blighter (rascal, devil); urchin **-vissling** wolf whistle **-väder** foul (squally) weather
butadi'en *s3, s4* butadiene
bu'tan *s4* butane
bu'telj *s3* bottle; *tappa på ~er* draw off into bottles, bottle **-axlar** champagne shoulders **-era** bottle **-grön** bottle green **-importerad** bottle imported
bu'tik *s3* shop; *AE.* store; *slå igen* (*stänga*) ~*en* shut [up] (close) the shop, (*upphöra med butiken*) shut up shop; *stå i* ~ work (serve) in a shop
butiks|biträde shop assistant; salesman, *fem.* saleswoman; *AE.* [sales]clerk **-centrum** shopping centre (precinct) **-föreståndare** shop manager, shopkeeper **-innehavare** shopkeeper, proprietor **-inredning** shop fittings (*pl*) **-kedja** chain, multiple stores (shops) (*pl*) **-råtta** shoplifter **-snatteri, -stöld** shoplifting
butter ['butt-] *a2* sullen, sulky, morose **-het** sullenness *etc.*
bu'tyl *s3* butyl **-gummi** butyl rubber
buxbom *s2* box; (*träslag*) boxwood
1 by *s2* (*vindstöt*) squall, gust
2 by *s2* (*samhälle*) village; (*mindre*) hamlet
byalag [*by:a-] *s7* village community; (*i modern bet. ung.*) concerned citizens committee
byallmänning land owned in common by a village
byffé *s3* **1** (*för förfriskningar*) buffet, refreshment counter **2** (*skänk*) sideboard
by|fåne village idiot **-gata** village street
bygd *s3* (*nejd*) district, countryside; (*odlad*) settled country; *ute i ~erna* out in the country
bygde|gård community centre **-mål** dialect **-spelman** country fiddler; folk musician
bygel *s2, tekn.* loop, yoke; clamp; (*beslag*) mount[ing]; (*på handväska*) [hand]grip; (*på hänglås*) shackle; (*på sabel*) guard **-häst** (*gymnastikredskap*) pommel horse
bygga *v2* build, construct; (*uppföra*) erect; (*grunda*) base, found; ~ *och bo* set up house, reside; *ingenting att* ~ *på* nothing to build on (upon), not to be relied on; ~ *om* rebuild; ~ *på* (*om hus*) add [a storey] to, (*öka*) add to, increase, enlarge; ~ *till* enlarge; ~ *upp* build up, erect
bygg|ande *s6* building; construction, erection **-branschen** the building trade
bygg|e *s6* building, construction **-element** building unit **-herre** commissioner of a building

project; future owner **-kloss** brick, building block **-kostnader** pl building (construction) costs **-lekplats** adventure playground **-låda** box of bricks **-mästare** building contractor, builder

byggnad s3 **1** se byggande **2** (bildning, konstruktion) construction, structure **3** (hus) building, edifice

byggnads|arbetare building worker **-entreprenör** building contractor **-firma** construction firm **-förbud** building ban **-komplex** block **-konst** structural engineering, architecture **-kreditiv** building credit (loan) **-lov** building permit, planning permission **-lån** building loan **-material** building (construction) materials (pl) **-nämnd** local housing (building) committee **-reglering** building control **-stadga** building bylaws (pl) **-stil** architectural style **-styrelse** ~n [the Swedish] national board of public building **-ställning** scaffold[ing] **-tillstånd** building licence (permit) **-uppvärmning** [domestic] space heating **-verk** structure **-verksamhet** construction (building) [activity]

byggnation construction work

bygg|sats building kit **-stopp** [temporary] prohibition of all building work

byig a1 squally, gusty; flyg. bumpy

byk s2 wash[ing]; han har en trasa med i ~en he has a finger in that pie **byka** v3 wash

byke s6 rabble, pack

bykkar [*by:k-] washtub

byling vard. cop[per]

bylta ~ ihop make into a bundle; ~ på ngn muffle s.b. up **bylte** s6 bundle, pack

byracka s1, vard. mongrel, cur

by'rett s3 buret[te]

1 byrå [*by:- el. 'by:-] s2 (möbel) chest of drawers; AE. bureau

2 byrå [*by:- el. 'by:-] s3 (ämbetsverk etc.) office, department, agency, bureau; division

byrå|assistent senior clerical officer **-chef** head of a division **-direktör** senior administrative officer **-ingenjör** technical officer; förste ~ higher technical officer **-inspektör** executive officer (inspector, accountant etc.); förste ~ higher executive officer etc.

byråkrat bureaucrat; vard. red-tapist, bigwig **byråkra't|i** s3 bureaucracy; vard. red tape **-isera** bureaucratize **-isering** bureaucratization **-isk** [-'kra:-] a5 bureaucratic; vard. red tape **-ism** bureaucratism

byrålåda drawer

byråsekreterare administrative officer; förste ~ higher administrative officer

Bysans ['by:-] n Byzantium **bysan'tin** s3, **bysantinsk** [-'ti:nsk] a5 Byzantine

byst s3 bust **-hållare** brassiere, bra

bysätt|a arrest for debt **-ningshäkte** debtor's prison

byta v3 change; (utbyta) exchange; (vid byteshandel) barter; trade; (utväxla) interchange; vard. swap; ~ buss (spårvagn etc.) transfer; ~ ord med ngn bandy words with s.b.; ~ plats a) change places (med ngn with s.b.) b) (ändra) move c) (byta tjänst) get a new post; ~ sida (uppfattning) tergiversate; ~ av ngn relieve

s.b.; ~ bort exchange (mot for); ~ bort sin rock take s.b. else's coat; ~ in (t.ex. bil) trade in; ~ om change [one's clothes]; ~ till sig get by exchange; ~ ut exchange (mot for)

byte s6 **1** change, exchange; förlora på ~t lose by the exchange; göra ett gott ~ (vard.) make a good swap, gain by the exchange **2** (rov) booty, spoils (pl); (rovdjurs o. bildl.) prey; (jakt-) game, quarry

bytes|affär barter transaction **-balans** balance of current payments **-handel** barter, exchange, trade **-rätt** right to exchange

byting tot, toddler, urchin

bytta s1 firkin; (smör-) tub

byx|a [*byksa] s1, se byxor **-bak** s2 trouser seat **-ben** trouser leg **-dress** trouser suit **-ficka** trouser pocket **-gördel** panty girdle **-kjol** culottes (pl), divided skirt **-linning** trouser waistband

byxor [*byksơr] pl (lång-) trousers; AE. pants; (korta) shorts; (golf-) plus fours; (knä-) knickerbockers, knickers; (lediga lång-) slacks; (damunder-) pants, (långa) knickers, drawers, underdrawers, (korta) panties, briefs

byxångest vard. blue funk

1 båda v1 (förebåda) betoken, foreshadow; (ngt ont) [fore]bode, portend, presage; det ~r inte gott it is a bad omen, it bodes no good; ~ upp, se uppbåda

2 båda pron (betonat) both (äv.: ~ två); (obetonat) the two; vi ~ we two (both), both of us; mina ~ bröder my two brothers; av ~ könen of either sex; i ~ fallen in both cases, in either case; för ~s vår skull for both our sakes; ~s föräldrar the parents of both of them; en vän till oss ~ a mutual friend

3 båda s1, sjö. shoal

bådadera both

både both; ~ han och hon (äv.) he as well as she

båg s7 hoax, confidence trick (AE. game), vard. con trick; det är rena ~et it's all eyewash **båga** bluff, hoax, swindle, hoodwink

båg|e s2 **1** (vapen) bow; ha flera strängar på sin ~ have several strings to one's bow; spänna en ~ draw a bow; spänna ~n för högt aim too high **2** (linje) curve; mat. arc **3** mus. slur; tie **4** arkit. arch **5** (på glasögon) frame, rim **6** (sy-) frame **-fil** hacksaw **-formig** [-å-] a1 curved; arched **-fris** arched moulding **-fönster** arched window **-gång** anat. semicircular canal **-lampa** arc light (lamp) **-linje** curve, curvature **-ljus** arc light **-minut** minute [of arc] **-sekund** second [of arc]

bågna [*bågna el. *bångna] bend; sag, bulge

båg|skytt archer **-skytte** archery **-sträng** bowstring

båk s2 **1** (sjömärke) [tower] beacon **2** (fyrtorn) lighthouse

1 bål s2, anat. trunk, torso; body

2 bål s2 (skål) bowl; (dryck) punch

3 bål s7 (ved- o.d.) bonfire; (lik-) [funeral] pyre; brännas på ~ be burnt at the stake

båld [-å-] a1 dauntless, bold, doughty

bålgeting hornet

bålrullning (kroppsövning) trunk gyration

bålverk s7 bulwark; bildl. äv. safeguard

bångstyrig *a1* refractory, rebellious, unruly; (*om häst, åsna*) stubborn

bår *s2* (*lik-*) bier; (*sjuk-*) stretcher; litter; *ligga på ~* be lying on one's bier **-bärare** (*lik|bår, -kista*) pallbearer; (*sjukbår*) stretcher-bearer

bård [-å:-] *s3* border; (*särsk. på tyg*) edging

bår|hus mortuary, morgue; funeral parlour (*AE.* home) **-täcke** pall

bås *s7* stall, crib, box; (*friare*) compartment, booth

båt *s2* boat; (*fartyg*) ship; (*mindre äv.*) skiff; *sitta i samma ~* (*bildl.*) be in the same boat; *gå i ~arna* take to the boats; *ge ngt på ~en* give s.th. up as a bad job, fling s.th. to the winds; *ge ngn på ~en* throw s.b. over, jilt s.b., *vard.* chuck s.b. [up (in)]

båta *det ~r föga att* it is no use (+ *ing*-form)

båt|ben *anat.* navicular[e] [bone] **-brygga** landing stage **-byggare** boatbuilder **-däck** (*på fartyg*) boat deck **-förbindelse** boat connection **-hus** boathouse **-last** shipload, cargo **-ledes** by boat **-lägenhet** *med första ~* by [the] first [available] ship **-motor** marine engine **-mössa** forage cap

båtnad [-å:-] *s3* advantage; *till ~ för* to the advantage of

båts|hake boathook **-man** boatswain, bosun, bo's'n **-mansstol** boatswain's chair

båtsport|kort yachting chart **-led** yachting course

båtvarv boatyard, boatbuilding yard

bä *interj* baa; bah

bäck *s2* brook, rill, rivulet; *AE.* creek; *många ~ar små gör en stor å* many a little makes a mickle; *det är bättre att stämma i ~en än i ån* a stitch in time saves nine

bäckebölja *s1* (*tyg*) cotton crepe

bäcken ['bäck-] *s7* **1** *anat.* pelvis **2** (*fat*) basin; (*säng-*) bedpan **3** *geol.* basin **4** *mus.* cymbal **-ben** pelvic girdle (arch)

bäckröding brook (speckled) trout

bädd *s2* bed; (*fundament*) foundation; (*maskin-*) bedplate

bädda make a (the, one's) bed; *det är ~t för* (*bildl.*) the ground is prepared for; *som man ~r får man ligga* as you make your bed, so you must lie on it; *~ ner* put to bed; *~ upp* make the (one's) bed

bädd|bar convertible into a bed **-jacka** bed jacket **-ning** bed-making **-soffa** sofa bed; day bed; studio couch

bädeker ['bä:-] *s2* Baedeker

bägare cup, mug; *kyrkl.* chalice

bägge *se 2 båda*

bälg [-j] *s2* bellows (*pl*); *en ~* a pair of bellows **bälga** [-j-] *~ i sig* gulp down **bälgkamera** folding camera

Bält *n, Stora* (*Lilla*) *~* Great (Little) Belt

bält|a *s1,* **-djur** armadillo

bältdäck radial [tyre]

bälte *s6* belt; (*gördel*) girdle; *ett slag under ~t* a blow below the belt **-spännare** *ung.* knife-wrestler

bältros shingles

bända *v2* prise; *AE.* pry (*loss* loose; *upp* open)

bändsel ['bäns-] *s2, sjö.* lashing; seizing **bändsla** [ˣbäns-] *sjö.* lash; seize

bängel [ˣbäŋ-] *s2* (*drasut*) great lout; (*slyngel*) rascal

bänk *s2* seat; (*arbets- o. parl.*) bench; (*kyrk-*) pew; (*skol-*) desk; (*lång*) form; bench; *teat.* row; *sport.* bench

bänk|a *rfl* seat o.s. **-kamrat** *vi var ~er* we sat next to one another at school **-rad** row

bänsel ['bäns-] *se* **bändsel**

bär *s7* berry; *plocka ~* pick (gather) berries, berry; *lika som ~* as like as two peas [in a pod]

bära *bar burit* I **1** (*lyfta o. gå med*) carry; (*friare o. bildl.*) bear; (*kläder*) wear; (*stötta*) support; *~ ansvar för* be responsible for; *~ bud om* bring (take, carry) word (a message) about; *~ frukt* (*vittnesbörd*) bear fruit (witness); *~ hand på ngn* use violence on s.b.; *~ huvudet högt* carry one's head high; *~ sina år med heder* carry one's years well; *~ skulden för* be responsible for, be to blame for; *gå och ~ på ngt* have s.th. on one's mind, be suffering under s.th. **2** (*leda, föra*) lead **3** (*om is*) bear; *det må ~ eller brista* sink or swim **4** (*med betonad partikel*) *~ av* (*sjö.*) bear off; *när bär det av?* when are you going (leaving)?; *det bär* [*mig*] *emot* it goes against the grain [for me]; *bär hit böckerna* bring me the books; *han såg vart det bar hän* he saw what it would lead to; *~ på sig* carry about [with] one, have on one; *han bär upp hela föreställningen* he is the backbone of the whole performance; *han kan ~ upp en frack* he can carry off a dress suit, he looks well in tails; *vägen bär uppför* (*utför*) the road goes uphill (downhill); *bär ut det!* take it out! II *rfl* **1** *det bar sig inte bättre än att han* as ill-luck would have it he **2** (*löna sig*) pay **3** *~ sig åt* behave; *~ sig illa åt* misbehave; *hur bar du dig åt för att* how did you manage to; *hur jag än bär mig åt* whatever I do

bär|ande *a4* carrying *etc.*; *den ~ tanken* the fundamental idea; *~ vägg* load-bearing wall **-are** bearer; (*stadsbud*) porter, *AE. äv.* redcap; (*av idé*) exponent **-bar** [-ä:-] *a1* portable

bär|buske berrybush **-fis** *s2* stink bug

bärga [-j-] I **1** (*rädda*) save; (*bil o.d.*) tow; *sjö.* salvage **2** (*skörda*) harvest, reap **3** (*segel*) take in; furl II *rfl* **1** (*reda sig*) get along **2** (*behärska sig*) contain o.s.

bärgad [-j-] *a5* well-to-do, well-off

bärg|arlön salvage [money] **-ning** **1** (*av bil etc.*) tow; *sjö.* salvage **2** (*av skörd*) harvest **3** (*av segel*) taking-in; furl **4** (*utkomst*) livelihood **bärgnings|bil** breakdown van (truck); *AE.* wrecker, tow truck **-fartyg** salvage ship (vessel, boat)

bärig *a1, se* **bärkraftig** **-het 1** (*lastförmåga*) carrying capacity; (*flytförmåga*) buoyancy **2** (*räntabilitet*) profitability, earning capacity; *tekn.* ultimate bearing resistance

bäring *sjö.* bearing

bärkasse string bag; carrier bag

bärkorg berrybasket

bärkraft *tekn.* bearing capacity; *ekon.* financial strength; (*fartygs*) buoyancy **-ig** strong; *ekon.* economically sound

bärnsten [-ä:-] amber **bärnstenssyra** succinic acid

bärplan *flyg.* aerofoil, plane, wing; *sjö.* hydrofoil **bärplansbåt** hydrofoil [vessel]
bärplock|are berry picker **-ning** berry-picking, berry-gathering
bär|raket carrier rocket **-rem** strap **-stol** palanquin, palankeen; (*hist.*) sedan [chair]
bärsärk [*bä:r-] *s2* berserk[er]; *gå fram som en ~* go berserk, run amuck (amok)
bärvåg *radio.* carrier [wave]
bäst *superl. t. bra, god, väl* **I** *a* best; *~ före (sista förbrukningsdag)* use before [date]; *de allra ~a vänner* the best of friends; *de här skorna har sett sina ~a dagar* these shoes are past praying for; *efter ~a förmåga* to the best of one's ability; *i ~a fall* at [the] best, ideally; *i ~a mening* in the best sense; *det var i ~a välmening* I (he, she *etc.*) only meant well; *i sina ~ år* in the prime of life; *med de ~a avsikter* with the best of intentions; *med ~a vilja i världen* with the best will in the world; *på ~a möjliga sätt* in the best way possible; *vid första ~a tillfälle* at the earliest opportunity; *det är ~ vi går* we had better go; *hon är ~ i engelska* she is best at English; *hoppas på det ~a* hope for the best; *~e bror!, se broder* **II** *adv* best; *vad tyckte du ~ om?* what did you like best?; *jag höll som ~ på med* I was in the middle of; *det vet jag ~ själv* I know best; *du får klara dig ~ du kan* you must manage as best you can; *du gör ~ i att* it would be best for you to **III** *konj, ~ [som]* just as; *~ som det var* all at once; *~ som vi pratade* just as we were talking
bäst|a *s* good, benefit, welfare; *det allmänna ~* the public good; *tänka på sitt eget ~* think of one's own good; *få ngt till ~* have some refreshments; *ta sig för mycket till ~* take a drop too much; *förste -e* the first that comes; *det kan hända den -e* that (it) can happen to the best of us; *göra sitt [allra] ~* do one's [very] best; *göra det ~ möjliga av situationen* make the best of a bad job
bästis ['bästis] *s2, vard.* chum, pal; *AE.* buddy
bättra improve [on]; *~ på* touch (*vard.* brush) up; revamp; *~ sig* mend, improve
bättre ['bätt-] *komp. t. bra, god, väl* **I** *a* better; *bli ~* get better; *få (ha) det ~* be better off; *han har sett ~ dagar* he has seen better days; *~ mans barn* well-born child[ren]; *~ kvalitet* superior quality (*än* to); *komma på ~ tankar* think better of it; *mot ~ vetande* against one's better judgement; *så mycket ~ för mig* so much better for me; *~ upp* one better; *ju förr desto ~* the sooner the better **II** *adv* better; *han förstår inte ~* he doesn't know any better; *han borde veta ~ än att* he ought to know better than to; *det hände sig inte ~ än att han* as ill-luck would have it,- he
bättring improvement; (*om hälsa*) recovery; *relig.* repentance **bättringsvägen** *vara på ~* be on the road to recovery, *vard.* be on the mend
bäva tremble; (*darra*) quiver, shake; (*rysa*) shudder (*för* at) **bävan** *r* dread, fear
bäver ['bä:-] *s2* beaver **-råtta** coypu, nutria
böckling smoked Baltic herring
bödel ['bö:-] *s2* executioner, hangman; *bildl.* tormentor **bödelsyxa** executioner's axe

bög *s2, vard.* gay, queer, fairy
böhmare [*bö:mare] Bohemian **Böhmen** ['bö:men] *n* Bohemia **böhmisk** ['bö:misk] *a5* Bohemian
böja [*böja] *v2* **I 1** bend, curve; (*huvudet*) bow, incline; (*lemmarna äv.*) flex; *~ knä inför* bend the knee to; *knäna böj!* knees bend!; *det skall ~s i tid som krokigt skall bli* best to bend while it is a twig; *~ undan* turn aside, deflect **2** *språkv.* inflect, conjugate **II** *rfl* **1** bend (stoop) [down]; *~ sig undan* turn aside; *~ sig över* bend (lean) over **2** (*foga sig*) bow; *~ sig för det oundvikliga* bow to the inevitable **3** (*ge efter*) yield (give in) (*för* to)
böjbar *a1* bendy, bendable
böjd *a1* **1** bent, bowed; (*om hållning*) stooping; (*krökt*) curved; (*bågformig*) arched; *~ av ålder* bent with age **2** *språkv.* inflected, conjugated **3** (*benägen*) inclined, disposed
böjelse [*böj-] inclination, bent, proneness (*för* for, to[wards]); tendency (*för* to); (*öm känsla*) fancy, liking (*för* for)
böjhållfasthet bending strength
böjlig *a1* flexible; *bildl.* pliable, supple **-het** flexibility; *bildl.* pliability, suppleness
böjning bending; (*krökning*) flexure, curvature; *språkv.* inflection
böjnings|form inflected form **-mönster** paradigm **-ändelse** inflectional ending
bök|a root, grub **-ig** *a1, vard.* tiresome; awkward; messy
böl *s7* bellow **böla** bellow; (*råma*) low, moo
böld *s3* boil; *med.* furuncle; (*svårare*) abscess **-pest** bubonic plague
bölj|a **I** *s1* billow, wave; *bildl.* surge **II** *v1* undulate; (*om sädesfält*) billow **-ande** *a4* (*om hav*) billowy, rolling, swelling; (*om sädesfält*) billowing; (*om hår*) wavy, waving; (*om människomassa*) surging
bömare, bömisk *se böhmare, böhmisk*
bön *s3* **1** (*anhållan*) petition, request (*om* for); (*enträgen*) solicitation, supplication, plea, entreaty (*om* for) **2** *relig.* prayer; *Herrens ~* the Lord's Prayer; *be en ~* say a prayer; *förrätta ~* offer [up] prayer
1 böna *v1, ung.* beseech, implore; *~ för ngn* plead for a p., speak in favour of a p.
2 böna *s1* **1** bean **2** *sl.* (*flicka*) bird, chick; *AE.* broad
bön|bok prayer book **-dag** *ung.* intercession day **böne|hus** chapel; meeting house **-kvarn** prayer wheel **-man** beadsman; wooer's proxy **-matta** prayer rug (mat) **-möte** prayer meeting **-skrift** petition **-timme** hour of prayer
bönfalla plead (*om* for); implore (beseech, entreat) (*ngn om ngt* s.b. for s.th.)
bönhas [*bö:n-] *s2* interloper
bönhör|a *~ ngn* hear a p.'s prayer; *han blev -d* his prayer was heard, (*friare*) his request was granted **-else** hearing (answering) of prayer
bön|syrsa [praying] mantis **-söndag** *B~en* Rogation Sunday
böra *borde bort (pres. o. imperf.)* ought to, should; (*inf. o. sup. översätts genom omskrivning*); *hon bör vara framme nu* she should be there by now; *jag anser mig ~ göra det* I think I ought to do it; *det borde vi ha tänkt på* we

B

ought to have thought of that; *det är alldeles som sig bör* it is quite fitting; *man bör aldrig glömma* one should never (ought never to) forget
börd [-ö:-] *s3* birth; (*härkomst äv.*) ancestry, lineage, descent; *till ~en* by birth; *av ringa ~* of lowly birth
börda [ˣbö:r-] *s1* burden; load; *digna under ~n* be borne down by (droop under) the load; *livet blev honom en ~* life became a burden to him; *lägga sten på ~* increase the burden, add insult to injury
1 bördig [ˣbö:r-] *a1* (*härstammande*) *hon är ~ från* she was born in, she is a native of
2 bördig [ˣbö:r-] *a1* (*fruktbar*) fertile
bördighet fertility
börds|adel hereditary nobility **-stolt** proud of one's birth
börja begin; start; *vard.* kick off; (*mera högt.*) commence; (*~ på med*) set about, enter upon; *det ~r bli mörkt* it is getting dark; *till att ~ med* to begin (start) with; *nu ~s det* here we go, now we are in for it; *~ i fel ända* put the cart before the horse; *~ om* begin again; *~ om från början* start afresh, make a fresh start
början *r* beginning; start; (*av brev*) opening; (*ursprung*) origin; *från första ~* from the very beginning; *från ~ till slut* from beginning to end, from first to last; *i (från) ~* at first; *i ~ av* at the beginning of; *i ~ av åttiotalet* in the early eighties; *till en ~* to begin (start) with
börs 1 *s2* (*portmonnä*) purse **2** *s3* (*fond-*) exchange; *spela på ~en* speculate on the stock exchange (market) **-affärer** exchange business (dealings) **-hus** stock exchange **-jobbare** stockjobber **-kupp** stock exchange manoeuvre **-lista** [stock] exchange list; (*för aktier*) share (*AE.* stock) list **-mäklare** [stock]broker **-notera** list on the stock exchange **-noteringar** [stock] exchange quotations **-spekulant** speculator on the [stock] exchange; stockjobber **-spekulation** speculation on the [stock] exchange; stockjobbery, stockjobbing **-transaktion** stock exchange transaction
böss|a *s1* **1** (*gevär*) gun, rifle; (*hagel-*) shotgun **2** (*penningskrin*) moneybox **-håll** *inom ~* within gunshot **-kolv** butt-end **-mynning** muzzle **-pipa** gun barrel **-skott** (*hopskr. bösskott*) gunshot
böta pay a fine; *~ för* suffer (pay) for **böter** [ˈbö:-] *pl* fine (*sg*); *döma ngn till 10 punds ~* fine s.b. 10 pounds; *belagd med ~* liable to (punishable by) a fine
bötes|föreläggande order to pay fine[s] **-straff** fine, pecuniary penalty
bötfäll|a fine, mulct; *-d till ~* fined
bövel *s2* deuce, devil

C

ca *förk. för cirka*
cabotage [kabⓐˈta:ʃ] *s7* cabotage
cabriolet [kabriⓐˈle:] *el.* -ˈlä:] *s3* drophead coupé; convertible
café-au-lait [kaˈfe: å ˈlä:] coffee with milk
cafeteria [-ˈte:-] *s1* cafeteria
caffè espresso [kaˈfä esˈpresså] *se espresso*
californium [-ˈfå:r-] *s8* californium
calmettevaccination [kalˈmett-] BCG vaccination
calvados [kalvaˈdå:s] *s3* Calvados
calypso *s5* calypso
camembert [kamåŋˈbä:r] *s3* Camembert
camouflage [kamⓐˈfla:ʃ] *s7* camouflage **-färg** camouflage colour
camouflera [kamⓐˈfle:ra] camouflage
camp|a [ˣkam-] camp **-are** camper
camping [ˈkam-] camping **-bil** camper **-plats** camp[ing] site, camping ground
Canada [ˈkann-] *n* Canada
canasta [kaˣnasta] *s1* canasta; (*bud äv.*) meld
cancan [ˣkaŋkaŋ] *r* cancan
cancer [ˈkanser] *s2* cancer **-cell** cancer cell **-forskning** cancer research **-framkallande** cancer-inducing, carcinogenic
cancer|ogen [kanserⓐˈje:n] *a5* cancer-inducing, carcinogenic **-tumör** malignant tumour, cancer
candela [kanˈde:la] *r* candela
cannabis [ˈkann-] *s3* cannabis, hemp
cape [keip *el.* kä:p] *s5* cape
capita [ˈka:-] *per ~ of* (for) each person, per capita
cappuccino [kappⓐˈtɕi:nⓐ] *s9* cappuccino
carci|nogen [karsinⓐˈje:n] **I** *a5* carcinogenic **II** *s4* carcinogen **-nom** [-ˈnå:m] *s3* carcinoma
cardigan [ˈkard-] *s3* cardigan
carnet [karˈnä:] *s4* carnet
CD|-ROM CD-ROM (*förk. för Compact Disc-Read Only Memory*) **--skiva** CD, compact disc (*AE.* disk) **--spelare** CD player
C-dur C major
ceder [ˈse:-] *s2* cedar
cedera cede
cederträ cedar [wood]
ceˈdilj *s3* cedilla
ceˈkal *a5, anat.* caecal
celeber [seˈle:-] *a2* distinguished, famous **celebrera** celebrate **celebritet** *s3* celebrity
ceˈlest *a4* celestial; *~ mekanik* celestial mechanics (*pl, behandlas som sg*)
celesta [seˣlesta] *s1* celesta, celeste
celiaˈki [s-] *s3, med.* sprue; (*hos barn*) coeliac disease
celibat *s7* celibacy
cell *s3* cell; *data.* location **-delning** cell division **-forskning** cytological research; cytology **-fånge** prisoner in solitary confinement **-gift** cytotoxin, cytotoxic drug

cellist cellist
cell|kärna nucleus (*pl äv.* nuclei) **-lära** *se cell-
lära*
cello ['sellɷ] *-n celli* cello
cello'fan *s3, s4* cellophane
cellskräck claustrophobia
cell|stoff ['sell-] cellulose wadding, cellucotton
-ull rayon staple
cellu'lar *a5* cellular
cellu'lit *s3* cellulitis
cellulo'id *s3* Celluloid (*varumärke*)
cellulosa [-ˈlɷːsa] *s1* cellulose **-acetat** cellulose acetate **-fabrik** cellulose plant; pulp mill
-lack cellulose lacquer (enamel) **-nitrat** *se
nitrocellulosa* **-vadd** *se cellstoff*
cell|vägg cell wall **-vävnad** cellular tissue
cellära (*särskr. cell-lära*) cytology
Celsius ['sell-] *r, fem grader* ~ five degrees Celsius (centigrade) **celsiustermometer** Celsius
(centigrade) thermometer
cembalist [çemb-] harpsichordist; cembalist
cembalo [ˈçemb-] *s5* harpsichord; cembalo
cement *s3, s4* cement **-blandare** cement mixer
cementer|a cement **-ing** cementation
cementfabrik cement works (*pl*)
cendré [saŋ'dreː] *oböjligt a* ash-coloured, ash-
-blond
censor [-år] *s3* censor; *skol.* [external] examiner
censur (*censurerande*) censoring; censorship;
sträng ~ strict censorship; *öppnat av* ~*en*
opened by censor **-era** censor **-ering** censoring
census [ˣsens-] *r* census
cen'taur [s-] *s3, se kentaur*
center ['sent-] *s2, s4* centre; *AE.* center **-bord**
sjö. centreboard; daggerboard **-forward** centre forward **-halv** centre half **-halvback** centre halfback
center|ism centrism **-ist** centrist
centerpart|i centre party **-ist** member of the
centre party
centi- centi-
centi|gram [-ˈgramm] centigram[me] **-liter**
[-ˈliː-] centilitre **-long[storlek]** children's
size **-meter** [-ˈmeː-] centimetre
centner ['sent-] *s9* centner, short hundred-
weight
centra (*i bollspel*) centre; *AE.* center
cen'tral I *a1* central; (*väsentlig*) essential **II** *s3*
centre; *AE.* center; central office; (*huvudsta-
tion*) central station; *tel.* [telephone] exchange
Centralamerika *n* Central America
central|antenn communal aerial (antenna)
-bank central bank **-dirigerad** *a5* centrally
controlled **-dirigering** central[ized] control
-dispensär mass radiography centre **-enhet**
data. central processing unit **-figur** central
figure **-förvaltning** central administration
centraliser|a centralize **-ing** centralization
central|kommitté *polit.* Central Committee
-lyrik *ung.* lyrical poetry **-makterna** *pl, hist.*
Central Powers **-postkontor** General Post Office **-station** central station **-stimulerande**
stimulating the central nervous system **-upp-
värmning, -värme** central heating
centrer|a centre; *AE.* center **-ing** centring; *AE.*
centering

centri'fug *s3* centrifuge; (*för tvätt*) spin-dryer
centrifu'gal *a1* centrifugal **-kraft** centrifugal
force
centrifugera centrifuge; (*tvätt*) spin-dry
centripe'tal *a1* centripetal **-kraft** centripetal
force
centrisk ['sent-] *a5* centric[al]
centrum ['sent-] *s8* centre; *AE.* center
cepheid [sefeˈiːd] *s3, astr.* Cepheid variable
cerat *s7, s4* cerate
cere'bral *a1* cerebral, of the brain; ~ *pares* cerebral palsy
cerebrospi'nal *a1* cerebrospinal **-vätska** cerebrospinal fluid
ceremo'ni *s3* ceremony; *AE. äv.* exercises (*pl*);
utan ~*er* (*bildl.*) without ceremony **ceremoni'el** *s7,* **ceremoni'ell** *s7 o. a1* ceremonial
ceremonimästare master of ceremonies;
AE. äv. emcee (M.C.) **ceremoni'ös** *a1* ceremonious
cerise [seˈriːs] *a5* cerise
cerium ['seː-] *s8* cerium
cerner|a *mil.* invest **-ing** *mil.* investment
certepar'ti *s4* charter party
certifikat *s7* certificate
cervelat *kokk.* cervelat
cesium ['seː-] *s8* caesium; *AE.* cesium
cession [seˈʃɷːn] *s3* **1** *jur.* cession **2** (*konkurs*)
bankruptcy
cesur caesura
ce'tan *s4, s3* cetane **-värde** cetane number (rating)
c & f *hand.* c & f (cost and freight)
cha-cha-'cha cha-cha-cha, cha-cha
chagrin [ʃaˈgrän] *s3, s4* shagreen
chalet [ʃaˈläː] *s3* chalet
champagne [ʃamˈpanj] *s5* champagne
champinjon [ʃampinˈjɷːn] *s3* champignon;
(*ängs-*) meadow mushroom; (*snöbolls-*) horse
mushroom
changera [ʃaŋˈʃeːra el.* -'seːra] lose colour,
fade; (*om utseende*) deteriorate, go (run) to
seed
chans [çaŋs *el.* ʃ-] *s3* chance, opportunity (*till
of*); opening (*till for*)
chans|a [ˣçaŋsa *el.* ʃ-] chance, take a chance
-artad [-aːr-] *a5* hazardous; *vard.* dicey **-lös**
han är ~ he does not stand a chance **-ning** venture
chapeau-claque [ʃapåˈklack] *s5* opera hat
charabang [ʃaraˈbaŋ] *s3* charabanc
charad [ʃaˈraːd] *s3* charade; (*lek*) charades (*pl*)
chargé d'affaires [ʃarˈʃeː daˈfäːr] *s3* chargé
d'affaires
chargera [ʃarˈʃeːra] exaggerate
charkuteri [ʃ-] *s4,* **charkuteriaffär** butcher;
delicatessen [shop] **charkuterist** butcher
charkuterivaror cured meats and provisions
charla'tan [ʃ-] *s3* charlatan; quack **-eri** char-
latanism, charlatanry; quackery
charm [ʃ-] *s3* charm; attractiveness **charma**
vard. charm **charmant** [-maŋt, *äv.* -'mant] *a1*
delightful, charming **charmera** charm; ~*d av*
charmed with **charmerande** [-ˈmeː-] *a4*
charming
charmeuse [ʃarˈmöːs] *s5* Charmeuse
charmfull [ʃ-] *a1,* **charmig** *a1* charming

charmlös [ʃ-] without charm, unattractive; dull **charmör** charmer

char'ner [ʃ-] *s7, tekn.* hinge

charter|flyg [*svenskt uttal* 'ça:r-] air charter; charter flight **-resa** charter trip

chartr|a [ˣça:rtra] charter **-ing** chartering; affreightment

chassi [ʃa'si:, *äv.* 'ʃassi] *s4* chassis (*pl* chassis)

chateaubriand [ʃaˣtå:briaŋ *el.* -'aŋ] *s3* Chateaubriand

chaufför [ʃå'fö:r] driver; (*anställd*) chauffeur

chauvin|ism [ʃå-] chauvinism. jingoism **-ist** chauvinist, jingoist **-istisk** *a5* chauvinistic, jingoistic

check [ç-] *s3, s2* cheque; *AE.* check; *en ~ på 100 pund* a cheque for 100 pounds; *korsad ~* crossed cheque; *betala med ~* pay by cheque; *utställa en ~* draw a cheque; *~ utan täckning* uncovered cheque

checka [ç-] *vard.* check; *~ in (på flygplats, hotell o.d.)* check in; *~ ut (från hotell, arbete)* check out

check|bedrägeri cheque forgery (fraud) **-blankett** cheque [form] **-häfte** cheque book **-konto** current (*AE.* checking) account

checklista [ç-] check list

check|lön [ç-] salary (wages) paid by cheque **-räkning** *se checkkonto*

chef [ʃe:f] *s3* head, principal, manager (*för* of); *vard.* boss, chief; (*för stab o.d.*) chief, director; (*för förband*) commanding officer **-konstruktör** chief designer, chief design engineer **-redaktör** editor in chief

chefs|befattning position as head, managerial post (position) **-egenskaper** *pl* executive talent (*sg*)

chefskap [ˣʃe:f-] *s7* headship, leadership

chefs|rådman senior judge **-åklagare** chief district prosecutor; *AE.* district attorney

chevale'resk [ʃ-] *a1* chivalrous

cheviot ['ʃe:viåt] *s3* Cheviot; *blå ~ (äv.)* blue serge

chevreau [ʃev'rå:] *s3* kid[skin], chevrette

chianti [ki'anti] *s5* chianti

chic [ʃick] *a1* chic, stylish

chiffer ['ʃiff-] *s7, s3* **1** code, cipher; *forcera ett ~* break a code **2** (*namn-*) monogram **-skrift** code, cipher **-telegram** code (cipher) telegram

chiffong [ʃi'fåŋ] *s3* chiffon

chiffonjé [ʃiffån'je:] *s3* chiffon[n]ier, bureau

chiffr|era [ʃ-] encode, encipher **-ering** encoding, enciphering **-ör** encoder, encipherer

chi'kan *s3* **1** (*förolämpning*) affront, insult; (*vanheder*) ignominy **2** (*kortsp.*) chicane **-era** affront; offend, insult; humiliate

Chile [ˣçi:le] *n* Chile **chi'len** *s3,* **chilenare** [-ˣle:-] *s9,* **chi'lensk** [-e:-] *a5* Chilean **chilesalpeter** Chile saltpetre (nitre), soda nitre

chili ['çili] *s5* (*rödpeppar*) chi[l]li

chi'mär [ʃ-] *s3* chim[a]era

chinchilla [çinˣçilla] *s1* chinchilla

chinjong [in'jåŋ] *s3* chignon

chintz [çints *el.* -] *s3* chintz

chips [çips] *s7* **1** *kokk.* crisp; *AE.* chip **2** *data.* chip

chock [ʃåck] *s3* **1** (*anfall*) charge; *göra ~ mot*

charge **2** *med.* shock **chocka** [ˣʃåcka] **1** *med.* shock **2** *vard.* (*chockera*) shock

chock|artad [-a:r-] *a5, en ~ upplevelse* a shock **-behandling** shock therapy (treatment)

chocker|a [ʃåck-] (*uppröra*) shock; (*väcka anstöt*) offend **-ande** *a4* (*upprörande*) shocking; (*stötande*) offensive

chock|skadad *a5, bli ~* get a shock **-verkan** shock effect

choka [ˣçå:ka] *v1,* **choke** [çå:k] *s2* choke

chok'lad [ʃå-] *s3* chocolate; (*dryck*) cocoa **-ask** box of chocolates; (*i sht tom*) chocolate box **-bit** piece of chocolate; (*pralin*) chocolate [cream] **-brun** chocolate **-kaka** bar of chocolate **-pralin** chocolate cream **-pudding** chocolate pudding

chosa [ˣʃå:sa] *rfl* show off **choser** [ˣʃå:-] *pl* affectation (*sg*) **chosefri** [ˣʃå:s-] unaffected, natural **chosig** [ˣʃå:-] *a1* affected

chuck [ʃuck *el.* çuck] *s2* chuck

cicero ['si:-] *s9* cicero

cice'ron *s3* cicerone, guide

cider ['si:-] *s2* cider; (*alkoholhaltig*) hard cider

cif [siff] *hand.* cif, c.i.f. (cost, insurance, freight) **-pris** cif-price

ciga'rett *s3* cigarette, *vard.* cig[gy], *sl.* fag, *AE.* butt **-aska** cigarette ash **-etui** cigarette case **-fimp** *vard.* butt; cigarette end **-munstycke** cigarette holder **-märke** brand of cigarettes **-paket** pack[et] of cigarettes **-papper** cigarette paper **-rökning** cigarette smoking **-tändare** (*hopskr. cigarettändare*) [cigarette] lighter

ciga'rill *s3* cigarillo

ci'garr *s3* cigar **-affär** tobacconist **-aska** cigar ash **-cigarett** *se cigarill*

cigarrett *se cigarett*

cigarr|handlare *se -affär* **-låda** cigar box **-snoppare** cigar cutter

cikada [-ˣka:-] *s1* cicada, cicala

cikoria [-ˣko:-] *s1* chicory, succory

cilie ['si:-] *s5* **1** (*flimmerhår*) cilium (*pl* cilia) **2** (*ögonhår*) cilium, eyelash

cimbrer ['simb-] *s9* Cimbrian

cine'ast *s3* cineaste

cinerarium [-'ra:-] *s4* cinerarium (*pl* cineraria)

cinnober [-'nå:- *el.* -'nɷ:-] *s9* cinnabar; (*färg äv.*) vermil[l]ion

cirka about, approximately, roughly **-pris** approximate (standard) price

cirkel *s2, geom.* circle (*äv. friare*); *rubba ngns cirklar (ung.)* upset a p.'s plans **-bevis** vicious circle; *göra ett ~* reason in a circle **-båge** arc **-definition** vicious circle **-formig** *a1,* **-rund** *a1* circular **-segment** segment [of a circle] **-sektor** sector [of a circle] **-såg** circular saw **-yta** area [of a circle]

cirkla circle **cirklad** *a5* (*tillgjord*) affected; formal

cirkulation circulation

cirkulations|organ circulatory organ **-rubbning** circulatory disturbance

cirkulera circulate, go round; *låta ~* circulate, send round

cirku'lär I *s7* circular **II** *a5* circular; *~t resonemang* vicious circle **-skrivelse** circular [letter]

cirkum|'flex *s3* circumflex **-po'lar** *a5, astr.,*

-po'lär *a5* circumpolar
cirkus ['sirr-] *s2* circus **-arena** ring **-artist** circus performer **-direktör** circus manager **-föreställning** circus [performance] **-ryttare** circus rider (equestrian); *(kvinnlig äv.)* equestrienne **-tält** circus marquee; *vard.* big top
cirrocumulusmoln [-'ku:-] *meteor.* cirrocumulus *(pl* cirrocumuli)
cirros [-'å:s] *s3* cirrhosis
cirrostratusmoln [-'stra:-] *meteor.* cirrostratus *(pl* cirrostrati)
cirrusmoln [ˣsirr-] *meteor.* cirrus *(pl* cirri)
cisalpinsk [-'pi:nsk] *a5* cisalpine
cisel|lera chase **-ering** [-'le:-] chasing **-ör** chaser
ciss C sharp **Ciss-dur** C-sharp major **ciss-moll** C-sharp minor
cisterci'ens *s3,* **cisterci'enser** *s9* Cistercian, White Monk **-orden** Cistercian order
cistern [-'ä:rn] *s3* tank; *(särsk. för vatten)* cistern
cita'dell *s7* citadel
citat *s7* quotation **citationstecken** quotation mark; inverted (turned) comma **citera** quote; *(anföra som exempel)* cite
citrat *s7* citrate
ci'tron *s3* lemon **-fjäril** brimstone **-fromage** lemon mousse **-gul** lemon [yellow] **-press** lemon squeezer **-saft** lemon juice **-skal** lemon peel **-syra** citric acid **-syracykeln** Krebs cycle, citric acid cycle **-träd** lemon [tree]
citrusfrukt [ˣsi:-] citrous (citrus) fruit
cittra *s1* zither
city ['sitti *el.* -y] *s6* city centre, business district; *AE.* downtown
ci'vil *a1* civil[ian]; *(ej i uniform)* in plain clothes; *(motsats t. militär)* civil **-befolkning** civilian population **-befälhavare** director [regional civilian defence area] **-departement** ministry of public administration **-ekonom** graduate from a [Swedish] School of Economics; *(i Storbritannien ung.)* Bachelor of Economic Science; *(i USA ung.)* Master of Business Administration **-flyg** civil aviation **-flygare** civil pilot **-försvar** civil defence **-försvarsstyrelse** ~n [the Swedish] civil defence administration **-förvaltning** civil service **-ingenjör** graduate (university-trained) engineer
civilis|ation civilization **-era** civilize; ~d civilized
civilist civilian
civil|klädd in civilian clothes; in mufti; *(om polis etc.)* in plain clothes **-kurage** moral courage **-lista** civil list **-minister** minister of public administration **-motstånd** civil defence **-mål** civil case **-person** civilian **-rätt** civil law **-rättslig** [in] civil law **-stånd** civil status
c-klav *s3* C clef
clair|obscur *se* klärobskyr **-voyance** *se* klärvoajans
cleara [ˣkli:ra] clear **clearing** ['kli:-] clearing **clearingavtal** clearing agreement
clementin *se* klementin
clips *se* klips
clitoris *se* klitoris
clou [klɷ:] *s2* highlight, star turn; showpiece

clown [klaon] *s3* clown **-eri** clownery, clowning
c-moll C minor
c/o c/o, care of
cocktail ['kåckteil] *s2* cocktail **-pinne** cocktail stick
coda [ˣkå:-] *s1* coda
colchicin [kålki'si:n] *s4* colchicine
collage [kå'la:ʃ] *s7* collage
collier [kål'je:] *s3* (smycke) necklace
Colombia [kå'låm-] *n* Colombia **colombi'an** *s3,* **colombi'ansk** [-a:-] *a5* Colombian
columbarium *se* kolumbarium
commando|räd, **-trupp** *se* kommandoräd, -trupp
Comorerna *se* Komorerna
container [kån'teiner] *s2, s9* container **-fartyg** container ship **-hamn** container port
corps-de-logi [kårdölå'ʃi:] *s4* manor [house (seat)], hall
corps diplomatique [kå:r diplåma'tick] *r* diplomatic corps (body), corps diplomatique
cortes ['kårt-] *r* Cortes
cortison *se* kortison
cosinus [ˣkɷ:- *el.* 'kɷ:-] *r, best. form* =, *mat.* cosine
Costa Rica ['kåsta 'ri:ka] *n* Costa Rica **costari'can** *s3,* **costari'cansk** [-a:-] *a5* Costa Rican
cotangent *se* kotangent
coulomb [kɷ'låmb] *s9* coulomb
courtage [kɷr'ta:ʃ] *s4* brokerage
cowboy [ˣkaobåi] *s3* cowboy **-film** cowboy film; Western
crawl [krå:l] *s3* crawl **-a** [ˣkrå:-] crawl **-are** [ˣkrå:-] crawler
crêpe 1 [krä:p] *-n, pl -s (pannkaka)* crepe; ~ Suzette crêpe suzette **2** *se* kräpp
crescendo [kre'ʃendå] *s6 o. adv* crescendo
croquis [krå'ki:] *s3* sketch
croupier [krɷp'je:] *s3* croupier
C-språk *skol.* third foreign language
Cuba *n* Cuba **cu'ban** *s3,* **cubansk** *a5* Cuban
cumulonimbusmoln [-'nimm-] *meteor.* cumulonimbus *(pl äv.* cumulonimbi)
cumulusmoln ['ku:-] *meteor.* cumulus *(pl* cumuli)
cup *[svenskt uttal* kupp] *s3* cup **-final** cup final **-match** cup tie **-tävling** cup competition
curaçao [ˣkyrraså] *s3* Curaçao
curare [kuˣra:-] *s6* curare, curari
curium ['ku:-] *s8* curium
curling ['kölig] curling **-bana** curling rink **-sten** curling stone
curry ['kurry] *s2* curry powder
cy'an *s3, s4* cyanogen
cya'n|id *s3* cyanide **-kalium** potassium cyanide
cyano|s [-'nå:s] *s3* cyanosis **-tisk** [-'nå:-] *a5* cyanotic
cyanväte hydrogen cyanide, hydrocyanic acid
cybernet|ik *s3* cybernetics *(pl, behandlas som sg)* **-iker** [-'ne:-] cyberneticist **-isk** [-'ne:-] *a5* cybernetic
cykel [ˣsyck-] **1** *s3, s2 (serie, följd)* cycle **2** *s2 (fordon)* bicycle, cycle; *vard.* bike; åka ~ ride a bicycle, [bi]cycle **-affär** bicycle dealer **-bana** cycle path (track); *(tävlingsbana)* bicycle-rac-

ing track, velodrome **-belysning** bicycle lights
(*pl*) **-däck** bicycle tyre **-hjul** bicycle wheel
-kedja bicycle chain **-klocka** bicycle bell
-klämma bicycle clip **-korg** pannier, bicycle
basket **-lopp** *se -tävling* **-lykta** bicycle lamp
-pump bicycle pump **-ram** bicycle frame
-slang bicycle [inner] tube **-sport** bicycling
-ställ (*på cykel*) kickstand; (*för cyklar*) bicycle
stand **-tur** bicycling tour; (*kortare*) bicycle
ride **-tävling** bicycle race **-väska** carrier bag;
(*för verktyg*) tool bag **-åkare** bicyclist,
bicycler **-åkning** [-å:k-] bicycling
cykla bicycle; *vard.* ride a bike
cykla'mat cyclamate
cyklamen [-'kla:-] *r* cyclamen
cykling *se cykelåkning*
cyklisk ['syck-] *a5* cyclic
cyklist bicyclist, bicycler; cyclist; *AE.* cycler
cyklo'id I *a* (*i psykiatri*) cycloid **II** *s3, geom.*
cycloid
cyklon [-'å:n] *s3, meteor. o. tekn.* cyclone
cyklop [-'å:p] *s3* Cyclops (*pl* Cyclop[s]es) **-öga**
(*för sportdykare*) skin-diver's mask
cyklotron [-'trå:n] *s3* cyclotron
cylinder [-'linn-] *s2* cylinder; *se äv.* **-hatt -dia-**
meter bore **-formig** [-å-] *a1* cylindrical **-hatt**
top (high) hat; silk hat **-press** flat-bed (cylinder) press **-volym** cylinder capacity
cylindrisk [-'lind-] *a5* cylindrical
cym'bal *s3* cymbal
cyn|iker ['sy:-] cynic **-isk** ['sy:-] *a5* cynical;
(*oanständig*) indecent; (*rå*) coarse **-ism** *s3*
cynicism; indecency; coarseness
Cypern ['sy:-] *n* Cyprus
cy'press *s3* cypress **-lund** cypress grove
cyprier ['sy:-] *s9,* **cypri'ot** *s3,* **cypriotisk**
[-'ꞷ:-] *a5* Cypriot[e]
cysta *s1* cyst **cystisk** ['syss-] *a5* cystic **cys'tit**
s3 cystitis
cysto|skop *s7* cystoscope **-sko'pi** *s3* cystoscopy
cyto|log cytologist **-lo'gi** *s3* cytology **-logisk**
[-'lå:-] *a5* cytological

D

dabba *rfl* make a blunder
dada|ism Dada, Dadaism **-ist** Dadaist **-istisk**
a5 Dadaist[ic]
dadda *s1* nanny; (*amma*) [wet] nurse
dadel ['dadd-] *s2* date **-palm** date palm
dag *s2* **1** day; ~ *efter annan* day after day; ~
för ~ day by day; ~ *ut och* ~ *in* day in, day
out; day after day; ~*en därpå* (*förut*) the following (preceding) day; ~*en efter* the day after,
the following day; *vara* ~*en efter* feel like the
day after the night before; ~*en före anfallet* the
day before (the eve of) the attack; ~*en lång*
all day long; ~*ens rätt* today's special; *en* ~
one day (*om förfluten tid*), some day (*om framtid*); *endera* ~*en* one of these days; *god* ~*!, se*
god [*dag*]; *samma* ~, *se samma*; *varannan* ~,
se varannan; *bestämma* ~ name the day; *den*
~ *som i* ~ *är* this very day; *den* ~*en den sor-*
gen don't meet trouble halfway; *för* ~*en har*
vi inga bananer we have no bananas today; *en*
fråga för ~*en* a question of the day; *han har*
gått för ~*en* he has gone for the day; *leva för*
~*en* live from hand to mouth (from day to
day); *göra sig en glad* ~ make a day of it; *hela*
~*en* [*i ända*] all [the] day; *i* ~ today; *i* ~ *om*
ett år a year today; *i* ~ *[om] åtta* ~*ar* this day
week; *i* ~ *på morgonen* this morning; *i* ~ *röd,*
i morgon död here today and gone tomorrow;
från och med i ~ as from today; *vad är det för*
~ *i* ~*?* what day [of the week] is it?; *vad är*
det för väder i ~*?* what sort of day is it?; *den*
skulle vara färdig till i ~ it was to be ready
[by] today; *just i* ~*arna* just recently (*om för-*
fluten tid), during the next few days (*om kom-*
mande tid); *ännu i denna* ~ to this very day; *i*
forna ~*ar* in the old[en] days; *i sin krafts* ~*ar*
in the full vigour of life, in his (*etc.*) prime; *i*
morgon ~ tomorrow; *i våra* ~*ar* in our days,
nowadays; *i yngre* ~*ar* in his (*etc.*) earlier days
(early life); *kors i all min dar!* well, I never!;
kommer ~ *kommer råd* tomorrow is another
day; *de närmaste* (*senaste*) ~*arna* the next
(last) few days; *om* (*på*) ~*en* (~*arna*) in the
daytime; *två gånger om* ~*en* twice a day; *om*
några ~*ar* in a few days[' time]; *betala per* ~
pay by the day; *på* ~*en ett år sedan* a year ago
to the day; *det var långt lidet på* ~*en* the day
was far advanced; *senare på* ~*en* later in the
day; *på gamla* ~*ar* in one's old age; *på mången*
god ~ for many a [long] day; *sedan ett par* ~*ar*
for some days past; *de sista* ~*arnas heliga* the
Latter-Day Saints; *ta* ~*en som den kommer*
take each day as it comes; *under* ~*ens lopp*
during the course of the day; *en vacker* ~ *på*
sommaren on a fine summer day; *en vacker* ~
slår du dig one fine day you will hurt yourself;
för var ~ *som går* with every day that passes;
var ~ *har nog av sin egen plåga* sufficient unto
the day is the evil thereof (*bibl.*); *var fjortonde*

~ every fortnight; *våra ~ars Paris* present-day Paris **2** (*dagsljus*) daytime; daylight; *full ~* broad daylight; *vacker som en ~* a flame of loveliness; *det ligger i öppen ~* it is obvious to everybody; *bringa (lägga) i ~en* reveal, show; *likna ngn upp i ~en* be the very image of s.b.; *mitt på ljusa ~en* in broad daylight; *klart som ~en* as clear as daylight; *se ~ens ljus* see the light [of day]; *~sens sanning* gospel [truth]

daga *i uttr.*: *ta ngn av ~* put s.b. to death

dagas *dep* dawn; *det ~* day is dawning

dag|barn child in day care in private home **-blindhet** day blindness **-bok** diary; *bokför.* daybook, journal, book of account (original entry) **-boksanteckning** entry in a (one's) diary **-brott** opencast **-brytning** opencast (*särsk. AE.* strip) mining **-bräckning** *i ~en* at dawn (daybreak)

dagdriv|are idler, loafer **-eri** idleness, loafing

dagdröm daydream **-mare** daydreamer

dager ['da:-] *s2* [day]light; (*ljusning*) ray of light; *full ~* full light; *framställa ngt i fördelaktig ~* put s.th. in a favourable light; *framträda i sin rätta ~* stand out in its right light; *skuggor och dagrar* light and shade

dagerro|'typ *s3* daguerreotype **-ty'pi** *s3* daguerreotypy

dagfjäril butterfly

1 dagg *s2* (*straffredskap*) cat-o'-nine-tails; *sjö.* rope's end

2 dagg *s2* dew

daggdroppe dewdrop

daggert ['dagg-] *s2* dagger

dagg|frisk fresh as dew **-ig** *a1* dewy **-kåpa** lady's mantle **-mask** earthworm **-punkt** dew point

dag|gryning dawn, daybreak; *i ~en* at dawn **-hem** day nursery, cräche; *AE.* care center **-jämning** equinox **-jämningspunkt** equinoctial point, equinox

daglig [ˣda:g-] *a1* daily; day-to-day; *fack.* diurnal; *~ tidning* daily [paper]; *~t tal* everyday (colloquial) speech (conversation) **-dags, -en** every day, daily **-varor** *pl* everyday commodities

dag|lönare day-labourer **-mamma** woman providing day-care for other's child[ren]

dagning [ˣda:g-] dawn, daybreak

dag|officer officer of the day, orderly officer **-order** order of the day **-ordning** (*föredragningslista*) agenda; *parl.* order paper; *stå på ~en* be on the agenda; *övergå till ~en* proceed to the business of the day, (*bildl.*) get down to business **-ort** gallery, adit **-rum** (*sällskapsrum*) day room

dags [daks] *i vissa uttr.*: *hur ~?* [at] what time?; when?; *det är ~ nu* it is [about] time now; *det är så ~ nu!* (*iron.*) it is a bit late now!; *så här ~ på natten* at this time of [the] night; *till ~ dato* to date

dags|aktuell topical; of current interest **-behov** daily requirement **-bot** *-en dagsböter* fine assessed on the basis of one's daily income

dagsedel *vard.* biff, sock

dagsens ['daks-] *se dag 2*

dags|förtjänst daily earnings (*pl*), daily pay

-kassa daily takings (*pl*) **-kurs** *hand.* rate of the day, current price **-ljus** daylight; *vid ~* by daylight **-läge** present-day situation

dagslända mayfly, dayfly

dags|marsch day's march **-meja** [-mejja] *s1* noonday thaw **-nyheter** *pl* (*i radio, TV*) today's news (*pl, behandlas som sg*) **-press** daily press; *~en* the press **-pris** current price; *till gällande ~* at the current price **-regn** continuous rain **-resa** day's run (journey, voyage) **-temperatur** day temperature **-tidning** daily [paper] **-tur** day trip **-verke** *s6* day's work; *göra ~* work by the day

dag|teckna date **-tinga** (*kompromissa*) compromise; (*köpslå*) bargain **-tingan** compromise; bargain **-traktamente** daily allowance [for expenses]; *ha 20 pund i ~* be allowed 20 pounds a day for expenses

dahlia ['da:lia] *s1* dahlia

da'jak *s3* Dyak, Dayak

dakapo [-'ka:-] **I** *adv* da capo **II** *s6* (*extranummer*) encore **III** *interj* encore

dak'tyl *s3* dactyl[ic]

dal *s2* valley; dale

dala decline, sink, go down; (*om snö*) fall gently

dalahäst painted wooden horse from Dalarna (Dalecarlia)

Dalarna *n* Dalarna, Dalecarlia

daler ['da:-] *s9, ung.* rix-dollar, rigsdaler

dalgång *s2* glen, valley

dalj *s7* thrashing, licking

dalkulla [ˣda:l-] Dalecarlian woman (girl)

dallr|a tremble, quiver; (*om ljud*) vibrate **-ing** tremble; vibration

dal|mas man from Dalarna (Dalecarlia), Dalecarlian

dalmatiner [-'ti:-] Dalmatian

dalmål Dalecarlian dialect

dal|ripa willow grouse **-sänka** depression [of the ground]

dalt *s7* coddling **dalta** *~ med ngn* coddle (pamper) s.b., (*kela*) fondle s.b.

daltonplanen *skol.* the Dalton plan (system)

1 dam *s3* **1** lady; (*bords- etc.*) partner; *mina ~er och herrar* ladies and gentlemen; *hon är stora ~en nu* she is quite the young lady now **2** *spel.* queen

2 dam *s3* (*-spel*) draughts (*pl, behandlas som sg*); *AE.* checkers (*pl, behandlas som sg*)

da'mask *s3* gaiter; (*herr-*) spat

damask|enerstål [-ˣʃe:- *el.* -ˣske:-] Damascus (damask) steel **-era** damascene, damask

damast [ˣdamm-, 'damm-, *äv.* -'mast] *s3* damask

dam|avdelning ladies' department **-badhus** ladies' baths **-bekant** lady friend **-besök** *ha ~* have a lady visitor **-binda** sanitary towel (*AE.* napkin) **-bjudning** ladies' party; *vard.* hen party **-byxor** (*med ben*) knickers, drawers; (*trosor*) panties, briefs **-cykel** lady's bicycle

damejeanne [damme'ʃann *el.* -'ʃa:n] *s5* demijohn; (*för frätande vätskor*) carboy

damfris|ering ladies' hairdresser's **-ör, -örska** [ladies'] hairdresser

damgambit queen's gambit

dam|lig *a1* ladylike **-kappa** lady's coat **-klocka** lady's watch **-kläder** *pl* women's wear (*sg*)

D

-konfektion ladies' ready-made clothing **-kör** ladies' choir

1 damm *s2* **1** (*vattensamling*) pond **2** (*fördämning*) dam; dyke (*AE*. dike); weir; barrage

2 damm *s7* (*stoft*) dust

1 damma *s2* **1** (*befria från damm*) dust **2** (*avge damm*) make (raise) a dust; *vägarna ~r* (*äv.*) the roads are dusty; *~ av* dust [down], take the dust off; *~ ner* make dusty, cover with dust **2 damma** *vard.*, *~ på* (*till*) ngn hit (clout) s.b.

dammanläggning dam, weir plant

dammborste dust[ing]-brush

dammbyggnad *se dammanläggning*

damm|fri dustless, free from dust **-handduk** *se dammtrasa*

damm|ig *a1* dusty **-korn** grain of dust

dammlucka floodgate, head gate; sluice[gate]

damm|lunga *med.* pneumo[no]coniosis **-moln** (*hopskr.* dammoln) cloud of dust **-påse** dustbag **-suga** vacuum [clean] **-sugare** vacuum cleaner **-sugarpåse** dustbag **-sugning** vacuum cleaning **-torka** dust **-trasa** duster; *AE.* dust cloth **-vippa** feather-duster

damning [ˣdamm-] dusting

damoklessvärd [-ˣmåkles-] Sword of Damocles

damp *imperf. av* dimpa

dam|rum ladies' room, ladies (*pl, behandlas som sg*); *AE.* rest room **-sadel** side-saddle

damspel *se 2 dam*

dam|sällskap *i ~* with ladies (a lady) **-tidning** women's magazine **-toalett** ladies' cloakroom; powder room **-underkläder** *pl* ladies' underwear, lingerie **-väska** handbag, bag; *AE.* purse, pocketbook

dana fashion, shape, form (*till* into); (*karaktär*) mould; (*om skola*) educate, turn out; (*utbilda*) train

danaarv escheat

dandy [-y *el.* -i] *s3* dandy, fop

1 dank *s2* (*ljus*) [tallow (candle)] candle, dip

2 dank *s, i uttr.*: *slå ~* idle, loaf [about]

Danmark ['dann-] *n* Denmark

dans *s3* dance; (*-ande, -konst*) dancing; *damernas ~* ladies' invitation (excuse-me) [dance]; *gå som en ~* go like clockwork; *en ~ på rosor* a bed of roses; *middag med ~* dinner and dancing; *bli bjuden på ~* be invited to a dance; *bjuda upp ngn till ~* ask (invite) s.b. to dance, ask s.b. for a dance; *börja ~en* open the ball

dansa dance; *~ bra* be a good dancer; *~ efter ngns pipa* dance to a p.'s tune; *~ omkull* go tumbling over; *~ på lina* dance on the tightrope; *~ sig varm* dance o.s. warm; *~ ut a*) (*börja dansa*) dance out, *b*) (*sluta dansa*) stop dancing; *~ ut julen* (*ung.*) wind up Christmas with a children's dance (party); *~ vals* waltz; *gå och ~* go dancing; *det ~des hela natten* the dance lasted all night; *när katten är borta ~r råttorna på bordet* when the cat's away, the mice will play

dans|ande *a4* dancing; *de ~* the dancers **-ant** [-'sant, *äv.* -'saŋt] *a1, inte vara ~* be no dancer **-are** dancer **-bana** open-air dance floor; (*med tak*) dance pavilion **-erska** dancer **-golv** dance floor **-högskola** *~n* [the Swedish] national college of dance

dansk I *a1* Danish; *~ skalle* butt with the head **II** *s2* Dane **danska** *s1* **1** (*språk*) Danish **2** (*kvinna*) Danish woman **dansk-svensk** Dano--Swedish

dans|lek dance game **-lektion** dancing lesson **-lokal** dance hall, dancing rooms (*pl*) **-lysten** keen on dancing **-lärare** dancing instructor (*fem.* instructress) **-melodi** dance tune **-musik** dance music **-orkester** dance orchestra **-restaurang** dance restaurant **-sjuka** St. Vitus's dance **-skola** dancing school **-steg** dance step **-tillställning** dance **-visa** dancing song **-ör, -ös** dancer

Dardanellerna [-'nell-] *pl* the Dardanelles

darr *s7* tremble; *med ~ på rösten* with a quiver in the voice **darra** tremble; (*huttra*) shiver (*av köld* with cold); (*skälva*) quiver; (*skaka*) shake; (*om röst, ton*) quaver, tremble; *~ i hela kroppen* tremble all over; *hon ~r på handen* her hands shake; *hon ~de på målet* her voice quavered (trembled)

darr|ande *a4* trembling *etc.*; (*om röst, handstil äv.*) tremulous **-gräs** quaking grass

darrhänt *a1, han är så ~* his hands are so shaky **-het** tremor (shaking) of the hands

darr|ig *a1* trembling *etc.*; (*om pers. äv.*) doddering **-ning** trembling; tremulation, tremor; quiver[ing], shiver **-rocka** (*hopskr.* darrocka) electric ray **-ål** electric eel

darwin|ism Darwinism, Darwinian theory **-ist** Darwinist, Darwinite **-istisk** [-'ist-] *a5* Darwinistic

dask 1 *s7* (*stryk*) spanking **2** *s2* (*slag*) slap, spank **daska** spank, slap

dass *s7, vard.* lav, loo, bog

data *pl* (*årtal*) dates; (*fakta*) data (*vanl. sg*), particulars **-bank, -bas** data bank (base) **-behandla** computerize **-behandling** data processing **-bärare** data carrier; storage device **-central** data processing centre **-inspektion** *~en* [the Swedish] data inspection board **-intrång** hacking; illegal use of computer information **-logi** computer science **-maskin** *se dator* **-medium** data medium **-program** [computer] program; software **-register** computer file **-spel** computer game **-styrd** [-y:-] *a5* computer controlled **-sättning** *boktr.* computer (automatic) typesetting **-teknik** computer technology **-terminal** computer terminal **-virus** computer virus **-ålder** computer age

dater|a date; *~ sig från* date from (back to) **-bar** *a5* dat[e]able **-ing** dating

dativ *s3* dative; *i ~* in the dative **-objekt** indirect object

dato *s6* date; *a ~* from date; *till dags ~* to date

dator *s3* computer

datoriser|a computerize **-ing** computerization

dator|språk computer language **-styrd** [-y:-] *a5* computer controlled **-stödd** *a5* computer-aided **-system** computer system **-tomografi** computer tomography

datoväxel time bill (draft)

datt *se 2 ditt*

datum *s8* date; *poststämpelns ~* date of postmark; *av gammalt ~* of ancient date; *av senare ~* of later date **-gräns, -linje** [international] date line **-märka** mark with date **-märkning**

sell-by-date marking **-parkering** *ung.* night parking on alternate sides of the street according to even or odd date **-stämpel** date stamp; *(poststämpel)* postmark

davidsstjärna Star of David

D-dagen *(6 juni 1944)* D-day

D-dur D major

de I *best. art. pl* the; ~ *flesta människor* most people; *hon är över* ~ *femtio* she is over fifty; ~ *dansande* the dancers; ~ *närvarande* those present **II** *pron* **1** *pers.* they; ~ *själva* they themselves **2** *demonstr.,* ~ *där* those, ~ *här* these **3** *determ.* those, the ones *(som* who); *fören. äv.* the **4** *obest.* they, people; ~ *säger på stan* they say, I hear, people are saying

deaktivera deactivate

debacle [-'backel] *s5, s7* debacle

debarker|a disembark **-ing** disembarkation, disembarkment

de'batt *s3* debate, discussion; *livlig* ~ lively debate; *ställa (sätta) ngt under* ~ bring s.th. up for discussion **-era** debate, discuss **-inlägg** contribution to a debate **-ämne** subject of discussion (debate) **-ör** debater

debet ['de:-] *n* debit; ~ *och kredit* debit and credit; *få* ~ *och kredit att gå ihop* make both ends meet; *införa under* ~ enter on the debit side **-konto** debit account **-saldo** debit balance **-sedel** [income tax] demand note; *AE.* tax bill; ~ *å slutlig skatt* final tax demand note **-sida** debit side

de'bil *a1* mentally retarded **-itet** mental retardation

debiter|a debit *(ngn för* s.b. with); charge *(för* for); *kostnaderna skall* ~*s oss* the costs should be charged to our account **-ing** charge, debit; *för hög* ~ overcharge

debitor [ˣde:- *el.* 'de:-] *s3* debtor; ~*er (bokför.)* *(AE.)* account receivable

de'but *s3* debut **-ant** singer *etc.* making his *(etc.)* debut; *(i societetslivet)* debutante **-bok** first book **-era** make one's debut

deceler|ation deceleration **-era** decelerate

december [-'semm-] *r* December

decennium [-'senn-] *s4* decade

decentraliser|a decentralize **-ing** decentralization

decharge [-'ʃarʃ] *s5,* ~ *beviljades (vägrades) (polit., ung.)* the vote of censure was defeated (passed) **-debatt** *ung.* vote of censure debate

dechiffrer|a decipher, decode **-ing** deciphering, decoding **-ör** decipherer, decoder

deci- deci-

decibel [-'bell] *r, pl* = decibel

deciderad [-'de:-] *a5* pronounced, decided

deci|gram [-'gramm] decigram, decigramme **-liter** [-'li:-] decilitre

deci'mal *s3* decimal **-bråk** decimal [fraction]; *periodiskt* ~ recurring (circulating, repeating) decimal **-komma** decimal point **-system** decimal system **-våg** decimal balance

decimer|a decimate; *(friare)* reduce [in number] **-ing** decimating; ~ *av personalen* depletion of the staff

decimeter [-'me:-] decimetre

deckar|e *(roman)* detective story, mystery; *vard.* whodun[n]it; *(person) vard.* sleuth; *jfr detek-*

tiv, detektivroman

dedi|cera dedicate **-kation** dedication

dedikationsexemplar dedication (inscribed) copy

deducera deduce

deduk|tion [-duk'ʃɒ:n] deduction **-'tiv** *a1* deductive

de facto ['facktɒ] de facto

defait|ism [-fä-] defeatism **-ist** *s3,* **-istisk** *a5* defeatist

de'fekt I *s3* defect; deficiency **II** *a1* defective

defen'siv *s3 o. a1* defensive; *hålla sig på* ~*en* be on the defensive

defibrillator *s3* defibrillator

deficit ['de:-] *s7* deficit

defiler|a defile; ~ *förbi* march past **-ing** defiling; march past

definier|a define **-bar** [-ˣe:r-] *a1* definable

defini|tion definition **-'tiv** *[äv.* 'deff-] *a1* definite, definitive, final; ~*t beslut* final decision

deflagration deflagration

deflation deflation

deflor|ation defloration **-era** deflower

defoliant defoliant

deform|ation deformation, distortion **-era** deform, distort **-itet** *s3* deformity

defroster [-'fråst-] *s2, s3* defroster

deg *s2* dough; *(mör-, smör-)* paste

degel [ˣde:g-] *s2* crucible, melting pot

degenera|tion [-j-] degeneration **-'tiv** *a1* degenerative

degenerer|a [-j-] degenerate; ~*d* degenerate **-ing** degeneration

deg|ig [ˣde:g-] *a1* doughy; pasty **-klump** lump of dough

degrader|a degrade **-ing** degradation

degression [-gre'ʃɒ:n] degression

degsporre pastry wheel

dehumanisera dehumanize

dehydr|ation dehydration **-era** dehydrate

de|ism deism **-ist** deist **-istisk** *a5* deist, deistic[al]

dejlig *a1* fair, lovely

deka ~ *ner sig (vard.)* go to the dogs

deka- deca-, deka-

de'kad *s3* decade

dekadans [-'dans *el.* -'daŋs] *s3* decadence, decline **-period** [period of] decadence

dekadent *a1* decadent

de'kal *s3* decal **dekalkoma'ni** *s3* decalcomania

de'kan *s3* dean

dekanter|a decant **-ing** decanting

dekanus [-'ka:-] *se* dekan

dekis ['de:k-] *s, vard. i uttr.:* *vara på* ~ be down on one's luck; *komma på* ~ go to the dogs **-figur** seedy-looking character

deklam|ation recitation; *(högtravande)* declamation **-atorisk** [-'tɒ:-] *a5* declamatory **-atör** reciter **-era** recite; *(tala högtravande)* declaim

deklar|ant person filing a tax return **-ation** declaration; *(själv-)* tax return

deklarations|blankett tax-return form **-skyldighet** obligation to file a tax return **-uppgift** income-tax statement

deklarera declare; *(förkunna)* proclaim; *(inkomst)* file one's tax return; *han* ~*r för 100 000* he has a taxable income of 100,000

deklasser|a bring down in the world **-ing** decline

deklin|ation *språkv.* declension; *fys.* declination **-era 1** *språkv.* decline **2** *(förfalla)* go off, deteriorate; *(mista sin skönhet)* fade

dekokt [-'kåkt] *s3* decoction *(på* of)

dekollet|age [-å-] *s4* décolletage **-erad** [-'te:-] *a5* décolleté, wearing a low-necked dress; *(om plagg)* low-necked

dekompression decompression **dekompressionskammare** decompression chamber

dekor [-'kå:r] *s3* décor, decor; scenery **-ation** decoration; ornament **-a'tiv** *a1* decorative; ornamental **-atör** decorator; *(för skyltfönster)* window-dresser; *teat.* stage designer **-era** decorate *(äv. med orden)*; ornament

dekorum [-ˣkå:- *el.* -ˣkɷ:-] *n* decorum; *iaktta (hålla på)* ~ observe the proprieties

de'kret *s7* decree **-era** decree; dictate

del *s2* **1** part, portion; *(band)* volume; *(avsnitt)* section; *en* ~ *av eleverna* some of the pupils; *en* ~ *av sändningen* part of the consignment; *en hel* ~ *besvär (s utan pl)* a good deal of trouble; *en hel* ~ *kvinnor (s med pl)* a great (good) many women; *en hel* ~ *fel* quite a lot (a fair number) of mistakes; *större (största)* ~*en av* most of; *för en* ~ *år sedan* a few years ago; *i en* ~ *fall* in some cases; *till* ~*s* partly; *till stor* ~ largely, to a large extent; *till större (största)* ~*en* mostly, to a large extent **2** *(andel)* share, portion; *(lott)* lot; ~ *i kök* part-use of the kitchen; *få* ~ *av* be notified of; *få sin beskärda* ~ receive one's due [share]; *för min (egen)* ~ for my [own] part; *ha (få)* ~ *i* have a share in; *komma ngn till* ~ accrue to s.b., fall to a p.'s lot; *ta* ~ *av* acquaint o.s. with, study **3** *(avseende)* respect; *(punkt)* point; *för den* ~*en* as far as that goes; *till alla* ~*ar* in all respects **4** *för all* ~*!* *(avböjande)* don't mention it!; that's all right!; *ja, för all* ~*!* yes, to be sure!; *nej, för all* ~*!* certainly not!; *gör er för all* ~ *inget besvär* please don't go to any trouble!; *kom för all* ~ *inte hit!* whatever you do, don't come here!

dela 1 *(i delar)* divide [up], split up; ~ *i lika delar* divide into equal parts **2** *(sinsemellan)* share; *(instämma i)* share, participate in; ~ *lika* share evenly, divide fair[ly], *vard.* go shares; ~ *ngns uppfattning* share a p.'s opinion; ~ *rum med ngn* share a room with s.b.; ~ *med 52* divide by 52; ~ *52 med 13* divide 52 by 13, divide 13 into 52; ~ *av, se avdela*; ~ *med sig* share with others; share and share alike; ~ *ut a) (distribuera)* distribute, *(post)* deliver, *b) (order)* issue, *c) (nattvard)* administer **3** *rfl* divide [up], split up; *(gå isär)* part; *vägen* ~*r sig* the road forks

delad *a5* divided *etc.*; ~*e meningar* divergent opinions; *det rådde* ~*e meningar om det* opinions were divided about it; ~ *glädje är dubbel glädje* a joy that's shared is a joy made double

delaktig *a1* participant *(av, i* in); concerned, involved *(av, i* in); *vara* ~ *i* participate in, *(förbrytelse o.d.)* be a party (an accessory) to **-het** participation, share; *(i förbrytelse)* complicity

del|bar *a1* divisible **-betalning** part payment

-betänkande interim report

delcredere [-'kre:-] del credere, guarantor for; *stå* ~ work on a del credere basis

deleatur [-e*ˣ*a:tur] *n* dele

deleg|at delegate **-ation** delegation, mission **-era** delegate; *en* ~*d* a delegate

del'fin *s3* dolphin

del|ge *(delgiva)* inform *(ngn ngt* s.b. of s.th.), communicate *(ngn ngt* s.th. to s.b.) **-givning** [-ji:v-] communication; *jur.* service

delikat *a1* delicate; *(välsmakande)* delicious

delikatess delicacy; ~*er (äv.)* delicatessen **-affär** delicatessen [shop]; *AE., vard.* deli

delinkvent criminal; culprit; delinquent

deliri|um [-'li:-] *s4* delirium; ~ *tremens* delirium tremens **-ös** *a1* delirious

delkredere *se delcredere*

del|leverans part delivery **-likvid** part payment

delning [ˣde:l-] *(uppdelning)* division, partition; *(i underavdelningar)* subdivision; *(sinsemellan)* sharing; *biol.* fission

delo *s, i uttr.*: *komma (råka) i* ~ *med* fall out with, quarrel with

delpension partial pension

dels [-e:-] *dels ... dels...* partly ... partly ...; *(å ena sidan ... å andra sidan)* on [the] one hand ... on the other

del|stat federal (constituent) state **-sträcka** section; *(etapp)* stage; *sport.* leg

1 delta [ˣde:lta] *se deltaga*

2 delta [ˣdelta] *s6, geogr. o. bokstav* delta

deltaga 1 *(i handling)* take part, participate *(i* in); ~ *i en expedition* be a member of an expedition; ~ *i en kurs i franska* attend a course in French; ~ *i konversationen* join in the conversation; ~ *i lunchen* be present at the luncheon; *han deltog i första världskriget* he served in World War I **2** *(i känsla)* share, participate

deltagande I *a4* participant; *de* ~ those taking part *(etc.)*, *(i tävling o.d.)* the competitors **2** *(medkännande)* sympathizing, sympathetic **II** *s6* **1** participation, taking part; *(bevistande)* attendance *(i* at); *(medverkan)* cooperation **2** *(medkänsla)* sympathy; *känna (hysa)* ~ *med (för)* ngn sympathize with s.b., feel sympathy for s.b.; *ert vänliga* ~ *i min sorg* your kind message of sympathy in my bereavement

deltagare participant, participator, sharer; *(i expedition)* member; *(i möte)* attender; *(i idrott)* participant, entrant, competitor

delta|muskel deltoid **-vinge** delta wing

deltid *arbeta på* ~ work part time

deltidsanställ|d part-time employee **-ning** part-time employment

deltidsarbete part-time work (job) **-pension** part-time retirement pension

del|vis [ˣde:l-] **I** *adv* partially, partly, in part **II** *a1* partial **-ägare** partner, joint owner; *passiv* ~ sleeping *(AE.* silent) partner

dem [demm, *vard.* dåmm] *pron (objektsform av de)* **1** *pers.* them; ~ *själva* themselves **2** *demonstr., determ.* those *(som who, which)*

dema|gog [-'gå:g] *s3* demagogue **-go'gi** *s3* demagoguery, demagogy **-gogisk** [-'gå:-] *a5* demagogic[al]

demarkationslinje line of demarcation

de'marsch s3 démarche; approach, action
demaskera ~ [sig] unmask
de'mens s3 dementia
dementera deny, contradict **demen'ti** s3 denial, contradiction
demilitariser|a demilitarize **-ing** demilitarization
demimond [-'må̱ŋd] s3 demimonde
demission resignation **-era** resign
demissionsansökan inlämna sin ~ hand in one's resignation, resign
demobiliser|a demobilize **-ing** demobilization
demodul|ation demodulation **-ator** s3 demodulator **-era** demodulate
demo|graf s3 demographer, demographist **-grafi** s3 demography **-grafisk** [-'gra:-] a5 demographic[al]
demokrat democrat
demokra't|i s3 democracy **-isera** democratize **-isering** democratization **-isk** [-'kra:-] a5 democratic
demoler|a demolish, tear down **-ing** demolition
demon [-'må:n] s3 demon, fiend **-isk** [-'må:-] a5 demoniac[al], fiendish
demonstra|nt [-å-] demonstrator **-tion** demonstration
demonstrations|möte mass meeting **-tåg** demonstration; protest march
demonstra|tiv [-'ti:v, -'månn-, 'de:-] demonstrative **-tris, -tör** demonstrator
demonstrera 1 (förevisa) demonstrate 2 (tillkännage sin mening) demonstrate, make a demonstration
demonter|a dismantle, dismount **-ing** dismantling, dismounting
demoraliser|a demoralize **-ande** a4 demoralizing **-ing** demoralization
den [denn] jfr det, de I best. art. the II pron 1 pers. it; (om djur äv.) he, she; (syftande på kollektiv äv.) they 2 demonstr. that; ~ dåren! that fool!; ~ där a) fören. that, b) självst. (om sak) that one, (om pers.) that man (woman etc.); ~ här a) fören. this, b) självst. (om sak) this one, (om pers.) this man (woman etc.); hör på ~ då! just listen to him (her)! 3 determ. a) fören. the, b) självst., ~ som (om sak) the one that, (om pers.) the man (woman etc.) who, anyone who, whoever; ~ av er som the one of you that, whichever of you; han är inte ~ som ger sig he is not one (the man) to give in; till ~ det vederbör to whom it may concern; ~ som ändå vore rik! would I were rich! 4 obest., ~ eller ~ this or that person; herr ~ och ~ Mr. So and So; på ~ och ~ dagen on such and such a day 5 opers. det, se det II
denaturalis|ation denaturalization **-era** denaturalize
denaturera denature; ~d sprit methylated spirits, metho
dendro|kronologi dendrochronology **-log** dendrologist **-logi** s3 dendrology **-logisk** a5 dendrologic[al], dendrologous
denier [den'je:] r denier
denitrifikation denitrification
denn|e -a, pron 1 fören. (nära den talande) this, (längre bort) that; -a min uppfattning this view of mine; -a min kritik (tidigare gjord) that criticism of mine 2 självst. (om pers.) he, she, this (that) man (woman etc.); (om sak) it; this [one]; (den senare) the latter; förklaringen är -a the explanation is this
dennes (vid datum) instant (förk. inst.)
denot|ation denotation **-era** denote
densamm|e [-'samme] -a the same; (den) it
densitet density
den'tal a1 o. s3 dental
dentist dental technician
denukleariser|a denuclearize **-ing** denuclearization
deodorant deodorant
departement s7 department (äv. franskt distrikt); ministry, office, board
departements|chef head of a department; minister, secretary of state **-råd** assistant undersecretary **-sekreterare** senior administrative officer; principal administrative officer
depensera [-pen'se:- el. -paŋ'se:-] disburse
de'pesch s3 dispatch **-byrå** news-office
depil|ation depilation **-era** depilate
deplacement s7 displacement
deponens [-'på:-] n deponent
deponer|a deposit (hos ngn with s.b.; i en bank at a bank) **-ing** deposit; (av avfall) deposition, controlled tipping
deport|ation [-å-] deportation **-ationsort** penal colony **-era** deport
deposition deposit, deposition; depositing; (nedfall av luftföroreningar) [contaminant] fallout
depositions|bevis (värdehandling) depositary receipt; (pengar) deposit receipt; (kvitto) deposit slip **-räkning** deposit account
depp|a vard. have the blues, be down in the dumps **-ig** a1 down in the dumps
depravera deprave; ~d depraved
deprecier|a depreciate **-ing** depreciation
depress|ion [-e'ʃɵ:n] depression; ekon. äv. slump **-i'v** [-'si:v] a1 depressive
deprimera depress; ~d depressed
deputation deputation **deputerad** [-'te:-] -en, pl -e deputy **deputeradekammare** chamber of deputies
de'på s3 depot **-fartyg** depot ship
derangera [-aŋ'ʃe:-] derange
deras pron 1 poss., fören. their; självst. theirs 2 determ., ~ åsikt som the opinion of those who
derby [svenskt uttal 'därby el. -i] s6 Derby; (lokal-) local Derby
deriv|at s7 derivative **-ata** [-ˣva:-] s1, mat. derivative **-era** derive
derma'tit s3 dermatitis
dermato|log dermatologist **-logi** s3 dermatology **-logisk** a5 dermatological
der'visch s3 dervish; dansande ~er whirling dervishes
desamma [-'samma] the same; (de) they
desarmer|a disarm **-ing** disarming; disarmament
desavouer|a repudiate, disavow **-ing** repudiation, disavowal
desegregation desegregation
desensibiliser|a desensitize **-ing** desensitization

desert|era desert **-ering** desertion **-ör** deserter
design [*svenskt uttal* di'sajn] *s3* design **-er** [*svenskt uttal* di'sajner] designer
designera [-in'ne:- *el.* -in'je:-] designate, name; ~*d* designate[d]
desillusion disillusion **-erad** [-'e:rad] *a5* disillusioned
desinfek|tera disinfect **-tion** [-k'ʃɷ:n] disinfection **-tionsmedel** disinfectant
desinficer|a [-'se:-] disinfect **-ing** disinfection
desinformation disinformation
desintegrator disintegrator
deskalera de-escalate
deskrip'tiv *a1* descriptive
desmanråtta [*ˣ*dess-] Russian desman
desolat *a1* desolate
des|organisera disorganize **-orientera** disorientate; ~*d* disorientated; confused, at a loss
desper|ado [-'ra:-] *s5* desperado **-at** *a1* desperate **-ation** desperation
despot [-'på:t] *s3* despot
despo'ti|i *s3* despotism **-isk** [-'på:-] *a5* despotic[al] **-ism** *se despoti* **-välde** tyrannic rule
1 dess *s7, mus.* D flat
2 dess I *pron* its; *om koll. äv.* their **II** *adv, innan (sedan, till)* ~ before (since, till) then; *till* ~ *att* until, till; *ju förr* ~ *bättre* the sooner the better; ~ *bättre (värre) vaknade jag* fortunately (unfortunately) I woke up
dessa *(de här)* these; *(de där)* those; *(de)* they; *(dem)* them
Dess-dur D-flat major
dessemellan [-*ˣ*mell- *el.* 'dess-] in between; at intervals, every now and then
dessert [de'sä:r] *s3* dessert, sweet; *vid ~en* at dessert **-kniv** dessertknife **-sked** dessertspoon **-tallrik** dessertplate **-vin** dessertwine
dess|förinnan [-*ˣ*inn- *el.* 'dess-] before then **-förutan** [-*ˣ*u:tan *el.* 'dess-] without it
dessinatör pattern designer
dess|likes [-*ˣ*li:-] likewise, also **-utom** [-*ˣ*u:tåm *el.* 'dess-] besides, as well; *(vidare)* furthermore; *(ytterligare)* moreover, in addition
des'säng *s3* **1** *(avsikt)* plan; scheme **2** *(anvisning)* pointer; hint; wink **3** *(mönster)* design, pattern
destill|at *s7* distillate, distillation **-ation** distillation, distilling **-ationsapparat** still; distilling apparatus **-ator** *s3* distiller
destiller|a distil **-ing** *se destillation*
destin|ation destination **-ationsort** [place of] destination **-erad** [-'ne:-] *a5, sjö.* bound *(till* for); ~ *till hemorten* homeward bound
desto ['dess-] *icke* ~ *mindre* none the less, nevertheless; *ju förr* ~ *hellre* the sooner the better; ~ *bättre* all (so much) the better
destruera destruct
destruk|tion [-k'ʃɷ:n] destruction **-'tiv** *a1* destructive
det *(jfr den)* **I** *best. art.* the **II** *pers. pron* **1** it; *(om djur, barn äv.)* he, she; *betonat* that; ~ *har jag aldrig sagt* I never said that; ~ *var* ~, ~*!* that's that!; ~ *var snällt av dig!* that's very kind of you!; ~ *vill säga* that is; *är* ~ *så?* is that so?; *ja, så är* ~ yes, that's [how] it [is]; *är* ~ *där aprikoser? nej,* ~ *är persikor* are those apricots? no, they are peaches; *känner*

du den där pojken (de där pojkarna)? ~ *är min bror (mina bröder)* do you know that boy (those boys)? he is my brother (they are my brothers) **2** *(i opers. uttr.) a) (som eg. subj.; som formellt subj. då det eg. subj. är en inf., ett pres. part. el. en hel sats)* it; *b) (som formellt subj. då det eg. subj. är ett subst. ord)* there; *c) (ibl.) that, this;* ~ *blir storm* there will be a storm; ~ *går tolv månader på ett år* there are twelve months in a year; ~ *regnar (snöar)* it is raining (snowing); ~ *ser ut att bli regn* it looks like rain; ~ *skulle dröja många år innan* it was to be many years before; ~ *står i tidningen att* it says in the paper that; ~ *tjänar ingenting till att försöka* it is no use trying; ~ *tjänar ingenting till att försöka göra* there is no use in trying to do that; ~ *var en gång en prins* once upon a time there was a prince; ~ *var frost i natt* there was a frost last night; ~ *återstår inget annat att göra* there remains nothing to be done; ~ *är bra många år sedan jag* it is a good many years since I; ~ *är* ~ *jag vill* that is what I want; ~ *är fem grader kallt* it is five degrees below freezing point; ~ *är här jag bor* this is where I live; ~ *är ingen brådska* there is no hurry; ~ *är ingenting kvar* there is nothing left; ~ *är jag* it is I *(vard.* me); ~ *är långt till* it is a long way to; ~ *är lätt att säga* it is easy to say; ~ *är mycket folk här* there are a lof of people here; ~ *är synd att* it is a pity that; *när* ~ *gäller att arbeta* when it is a question of working; *så måste* ~ *ha varit* that must have been it; *vad är* ~ *du talar om?* what is it you are (what are you) talking about?; *vad är* ~ *för dag i dag?* what day is it today?; *vem är* ~ *som kommer?* who is [it (that)] coming?; *är* ~ *mig du söker?* is it me you want?, are you looking for me? **3** *(ibl. som pred.fylln. o. obj.)* so; ~ *tror jag,* ~*!* I should just think so!; *jag antar (tror)* ~ I suppose (think; *vard., särsk. AE.* guess) so; *och* ~ *är jag med* and so am I; *var* ~ *inte* ~ *jag sa!* I told you so! **4** *(oöversatt el. annan konstruktion)* ~ *drar här* there is a draught here; ~ *gör ont i fingret* my finger hurts; *och* ~ *gör inte jag heller* nor do I; ~ *knackar* there's a knock; ~ *luktar gott här* there is a nice smell here; ~ *lyckades mig att få* I succeeded in getting, I managed to get; ~ *pratades mycket litet* there was very little talk[ing]; ~ *talas mycket om* there is much talk about; ~ *var mycket varmt i rummet* the room was very hot; ~ *var roligt att höra* I am glad to hear it; ~ *vet jag inte* I don't know; ~ *är inte tillåtet att röka här* smoking is not allowed here; ~ *är mulet* the sky is overcast; *efter middagen dansades* ~ *litet* after dinner we danced a little; *i dag är* ~ *torsdag* today is Thursday; *jag kände* ~ *som om* I felt as if; *jag tror inte jag kan (vågar)* ~ I don't think I can (dare); *nej,* ~ *har jag inte* no, I haven't; *som* ~ *nu ser ut* as matters now stand; *som* ~ *sedan visade sig* as appeared later; *varför frågar du* ~*?* why do you ask?; *vore* ~ *inte bättre med...* wouldn't...be better **5** *subst.* it; *hon har* ~ she has it **III** *demonstr. pron* that; ~ *där (här)* that (this); ~ *eller* ~ this or that; ~ *har du rätt i* you are right there; ~

har jag aldrig hört I never heard that; ~ *är just likt henne* that's just like her; *med ~ och ~ namnet* with such and such a name; *så var ~ med ~* so much for that **IV** *determ. pron a) fören.* the, *betonat that, b) självst.* the person (man *etc.*), the one; ~ *som* that which, what; *allt ~ som* all (everything) that; *vi hade ~ gemensamt att* we had this in common that, one thing we had in common was that

detache|ment *s7* detachment **-era** detach

de'talj *s3* detail; particular; *(maskindel)* part, component; *i ~* in detail, minutely; *i ~ gående* minute; *in i minsta ~* in every detail; *gå in på ~er* enter (go) into details; *närmare ~er* further details; *sälja i ~* retail, sell [by] retail **-anmärkning** criticism in (on points of) detail **-arbete** detail work

detalj|erad [-'je:-] *a5* detailed, circumstantial **-granskning** detailed examination **-handel** retail trade; *(butik)* retail shop **-handelspris** retail price **-handlare** retailer

detalj|ist retailer **-rik** full of details, very detailed, circumstantial **-rikedom** wealth of detail

detek|tera detect **-tion** [-k'ʃɔ:n] detection

detek'tiv *s3* detective, criminal investigator; *~a polisen, se kriminalpolis* **-byrå** detective agency **-författare** author of detective stories, crime writer **-roman** detective story, mystery

detektor [-ˣtektår] *s3* detector

detergent detergent

determin|ativ [-'tärr- *el.* -'ti:v] *a1* determinative **-era** determine **-ism** determinism **-ist** determinist

deton|ation detonation **-ator** *s3* detonator **-era** detonate

detronisera dethrone

detsamma [-'samma] the same [thing]; *(det)* it; *det gör ~* it doesn't matter; *det gör mig alldeles ~* it is all the same to me; *i ~* at that very moment; *med ~* at once, right away; *tack, ~!* thanks, and the same to you!

detta this; ~ *mitt beslut* this decision of mine; ~ *om ~* so much for that; ~ *är mina systrar* these are my sisters; *före ~ (f.d.)* former, late, ex-; *livet efter ~* the life to come

deuterium [dev'te:-] *s8* deuterium

devalver|a devalue **-ing** devaluation

devi|ation deviation **-era** deviate

de'vis *s3* device; motto

devot [-'vå:t] *a1* devout

dex'trin *s4, s3* dextrin[e] **dextros** [-'å:s] *s3* dextrose, grape sugar

di *s2, ge ~* give suck to, suckle; *få ~* be put to the breast

1 dia *v1* suck, suckle

2 dia *s1, se diapositiv*

dia'bas *s3* diabase

diabet|es [-'be:-] *s3* diabetes; *(sockersjuka)* diabetes [mellitus] **-iker** [-'be:-], **-isk** [-'be:-] *a5* diabetic

diabild slide, transparency

diabolisk [-'bå:-] *a5* diabolic

dia'dem *s7* diadem, tiara

diafilm slide film

diafragma [-ˣfragma] *s4, s1* diaphragm

diagnos [-'gnå:s] *s3* diagnosis (*pl* diagnoses); *ställa en ~* diagnose, make a diagnosis **-'tik**

s3 diagnostics *(pl, behandlas som sg)* **-tisera** diagnose **-tisk** [-'gnåss-] *a5* diagnostic

diago'nal I *s3* diagonal; *(tyg)* diagonal [cloth] **II** *a1* diagonal **-däck** cross-ply tyre

diagram [-'gramm] *s7* diagram, chart, graph

diakon [-'kå:n] *s3* deacon; lay worker

diakoniss|a deaconess; lay worker **-anstalt** training school for deaconesses

diakritisk [-'kri:-] *a5* diacritical; *~t tecken* diacritic, diacritical mark

dia'lekt *s3* dialect **-'al** *a1* dialectal

dialekt|ik *s3* dialectics *(pl, behandlas som sg)* **-isk** [-'lekt-] *a5* dialectic[al]; ~ *materialism* dialectical materialism

dialog dialogue **-form** *i ~* in [the form of a] dialogue

dia'ly|s *s3* dialysis; *med.* [haemo]dialysis, extracorporeal dialysis **-sera** dialyse **-tisk** [-'ly:-] *a5* dialytical

diamagnetism diamagnetism

diamant diamond **-borr** diamond drill **-borrning** diamond drilling **-bröllop** diamond wedding **-gruva** diamond mine **-ring** diamond ring **-slipare** diamond cutter **-slipning** diamond cutting

diameter [-'me:-] *s2* diameter; *invändig (utvändig) ~* inside (outside) diameter **diame'tral** *a1* diametrical **diametralt** [-'a:lt] *adv,* ~ *motsatt* diametrically opposed

diaposi'tiv *s7* transparency, slide

diarieföra [diˣa:rie-] enter in a journal, record

diarium [di'a:-] *s4* [official] register; *(dagbok)* diary; *hand.* daybook

diarré *s3* diarrhoea

diater'mi *s3* diathermy, diathermia

diatonisk [-'tɔ:-] *a5* diatonic

dibarn unweaned child; suckling

dibbla *(gruppså)* dibble

didakt|ik *s3* didactics *(pl, behandlas som sg)* **-isk** [-'dakt-] *a5* didactic

diesel|motor [ˣdi:sel-] diesel engine (motor) **-olja** diesel oil (fuel)

di'et *s3* diet; *hålla ~* be on a diet, diet **dietetik** *s3* dietetics *(pl, behandlas som sg)* **dietisk** [-'te:-] *a2* dietetic[al] **dietist** [di'e:-] *a5, se dietetisk* **dietist** dietitian **dietmat** diet food

differens [-'ens *el.* -'aŋs] *s3* difference

differential [-entsi'a:l] *s3* differential **-kalkyl** differential calculus **-växel** differential gear

differentier|a [-tsi'e:ra] differentiate; diversify **-ing** differentiation; diversification

differera differ

diffraktion [-k'ʃɔ:n] diffraction

diffundera diffuse

dif'fus *a1* diffuse **diffusera** diffuse **diffusion** diffusion **diffusor** [diˣfu:går] *s3* diffuser

difte'ri *s3* diphtheria

diftong [-'tåŋ] *s3* diphthong **-era** [-åŋ'ge:ra] diphthongize **-'ering** [-åŋ'ge:r-] diphthongization

dig [*vard.* dejj] *pron (objektsform av du)* you; *bibl. o. poet.* thee; *rfl* yourself; thyself

digel *s2* platen **-press** platen press

diger ['di:-] *a2* thick, bulky; *(om bok äv.)* voluminous **-döden** the Black Death

digestion [-ge'ʃɔ:n *el.* -je-] digestion

digga *vard.* dig

digi'tal *al* digital

digitalis [-gi˟ta:- *el.* -gi'ta:-] *s2* **1** *bot., se fingerborgsblomma* **2** *med.* digitalis

digital|maskin digital computer **-ur** digital watch (clock)

digivning [-ji:-] suckling, breast-feeding

digna [˟diŋna] sink down, succumb; collapse; ~ *under bördan* be borne down by (droop under) the load; *ett ~nde bord* a table loaded with food

digni|tet [diŋni-] *s3* **1** (*värdighet*) dignity **2** *mat.* power **-'tär** *s3* dignitary

digression [-e'ʃɷ:n] digression

dika ditch, drain, trench **dike** *s6* ditch, drain, trench; *han körde i ~t* he drove into the ditch

dikes|kant, -ren ditchside, ditchbank

dikning [˟di:k-] draining, ditching

1 dikt *a4 o. adv, sjö.* close

2 dikt *s3* **1** (*skaldestycke*) poem; *koll.* poetry **2** (*osanning*) fiction, fabrication; invention

1 dikta *sjö.* caulk

2 dikta 1 (*författa*) write [poetry] **2** (*fabulera*) fabricate, invent

diktafon [-'få:n] *s3* dictaphone (*varumärke*); [tape] recorder

dikta|men *-men -mina, n el. r* dictation

diktan *s, endast i uttr.:* ~ *och traktan* aim and endeavour

diktanalys analysis of poetry

dikt|arbegåvning poetic[al] talent **-are** poet, writer

dikt|arskap poetic calling **-art** type of composition (poetry)

diktcykel cycle of poems

diktera dictate (*för* to) **dikteringsmaskin** dictating machine, [tape] recorder

diktion [-k'ʃɷ:n] diction

dikt|konst [art of] poetry **-ning** writing; fiction; (*poesi*) poetry; *hans* ~ his literary production **-samling** collection of poems **-verk** poem; poetical work

dilemma [-˟lemma] *s6* dilemma, quandary

dilettant dilettante; amateur **-isk** *a5, se -mässig* **-ism** dilettantism **-mässig** *al* dilettantish; amateurish

diligens [-'ʃaŋs] *s3* stagecoach

dill *s2* dill

dilla babble **dille** *s6* **1** (*delirium*) D.T.'s **2** (*mani*) craze (*på* for); *ha fått* ~ *på ngt* be crazy (mad, *sl.* nuts) about s.th.

dill|krona head of dill **-kött** boiled mutton (veal) with dill sauce

diluvi'al *al* diluvial

dim|bank fog bank **-bildning** smoke screening **-bälte** belt of fog (mist)

dimension [-n'ʃɷ:n] dimension, size; *~er* (*äv.*) proportions **-era** dimension **-ering** dimensioning

dim|figur phantom, vague shape **-höljd** *a5* shrouded in mist (fog)

diminuendo [-u'endå] *s6 o. adv* diminuendo

diminu'tiv *al o. s4, s7* diminutive **-form** diminutive form **-ändelse** diminutive affix

dim|kammare [Wilson] cloud chamber **-ljus** foglight

dimm|a *s1* mist; (*tjocka*) fog; (*dis*) haze **-ig** *al* misty, foggy; *bildl.* hazy

dimmer ['dimm-] *s2* dimmer

dimpa *damp dumpit* fall, tumble (*i golvet* on to the floor), tumble (*i* in, into)

dimridå smoke screen (*äv. bildl.*)

din [dinn] (*ditt, dina*) pron **1** *fören.* your; *bibl. o. poet.* thy; ~ *toker!* you fool! **2** *självst.* yours; *bibl. o. poet.* thine; *de ~a* your people; *du och de ~a* you and yours

di'nar *s3* dinar

diné *s3* dinner **dinera** dine

dinge *s2* ding[h]y

dingla dangle, swing; ~ *med benen* dangle one's legs

dinosaurie [-'sau-] *s5* dinosaur

diod [-'å:d] *s3* diode

dionysisk [-'ny:-] *a5* Dionysian

diop|'tri *s3* dioptre **-trik** *s3* dioptrics (*pl, behandlas som sg*) **-trisk** [di'åpt-] *a5* dioptric[al]

diorama [-˟ra:ma] *s6* diorama

dioxid dioxide

diplom [-'å:m] *s7* diploma, certificate

diplom|at diplomat **-a'ti** *s3* diplomacy **-atisk** [-'ma:-] *a5* diplomatic[al]; *på* ~ *väg* through diplomatic channels; *~a kåren* the diplomatic corps (body); ~ *immunitet* diplomatic immunity

diplomerad [-'me:-] *a5* holding a diploma; *han är* ~ (*äv.*) he is a diplomate

dipolantenn [-˟pɷ:l-] dipole [aerial]

dippa (*doppa i sås*) dip

di'rekt I *al* direct; (*omedelbar*) immediate; (*rak*) straight; (*trafikterm*) through, nonstop; ~ *anföring* direct speech; ~ *skatt* direct tax; *den ~a orsaken* the immediate cause **II** *adv* (*om tid*) directly, immediately, at once; (*om riktning*) direct, straight; (*avgjort*) distinctly; ~ *från fabrik* direct from factory; *hon var* ~ *oförskämd* she was downright rude; *inte* ~ *utsvulten* not actually starved; *uppgiften är* ~ *felaktig* the information (statement) is quite wrong (incorrect)

direkt|ansluten *data.* on-line, on line **-flyg, -flygning** nonstop flight **-förbindelse** direct connection **-försäljning** direct sale[s *pl*] (selling) **-insprutning** direct injection

direktion [-k'ʃɷ:n] (*styrelse*) board [of directors], management; (*riktning*) direction

direktions|sammanträde management (managers') meeting **-sekreterare** secretary to management

direk'tiv *s7* directions, *ibl.* direction; terms of reference, directive; *ge ngn* ~ (*äv.*) instruct s.b.

direktreferat running commentary

direktris woman manager, manageress; (*mode-*) dress designer, stylist

direkt|sändning live broadcast **-trafik** through traffic

direktör director; (*affärschef*) manager; *AE.* vice president; *verkställande* ~ managing director, *AE.* president **direktörsassistent** assistant manager

dirigent [-'gent *el.* -'ʃent] conductor, (*äv., särsk. AE.*) director **-pult** conductor's platform, podium

diriger|a [-'ge:- *el.* -'ʃe:-] direct; *mus.* conduct, (*äv., särsk. AE.*) direct **-ing** control; direction; *mus.* conducting

dis *s7* haze
discipel [-'sipp, *äv.* -'ʃipp-] *s2* pupil
disciplin [dissi'pli:n] *s3* **1** (*läroämne*) branch of learning (instruction), discipline **2** (*lydnad*) discipline; *hålla* ~ maintain discipline, keep order **-brott** breach of discipline, [act of] insubordination **-era** discipline **-straff** disciplinary punishment **-'är** *a1* disciplinary
disharmo'ni *s3* disharmony, discord **-era** discord; clash **-isk** [-'mɔ:-] *a5* disharmonious, discordant
disig *a1* hazy
disjunk'tiv [*el.* 'diss-] *a1* disjunctive
1 disk *s2* **1** (*butiks-*) counter; (*bar-*) bar **2** *anat.* disc
2 disk *s2* **1** *abstr.* washing-up **2** *konkr.* washing-up, dishes (*pl*); *torka* ~*en* dry the dishes
1 diska (*rengöra*) wash up; *AE.* wash the dishes
2 diska *sport.* disqualify
diskant treble **-klav** treble (G) clef
disk|balja washing-up bowl; *AE.* dishpan **-borste** dishbrush (washing-up) brush
diskbräck slipped disc
diskbänk [kitchen] sink
dis'kett *s3* flexible diskette, floppy disk **-enhet** disc (*AE.* disk) drive
disk-jockey *s3* disc jockey
disk|maskin dishwasher **-medel** washing-up liquid (powder, detergent) **-ning 1** washing-up **2** *sport.* disqualification
disko'fil *s3* discophil[e], gramophone-records collector
diskonter|a discount **-ing** (*transaktion*) discounting of a bill; (*rörelse*) discounting, discount[ing] business
diskontinuerlig [-'e:r-] *a1* discontinuous, intermittent
diskontnota [dis×kånt-] discount note
diskonto [-'kåntɔ] *s6* official discount [rate]; *höja* (*sänka*) ~*t* raise (lower) the official discount rate **-höjning** increase in the official discount rate
diskont|ränta discount rate **-ör** discounter
diskomusik disco music **disko'tek** *s7* **1** (*grammofonarkiv*) record library **2** (*danslokal*) discotheque, disco
diskplockare table clearer
diskreditera discredit; ~*nde för* discreditable to
diskrepans [-'ans *el.* -'aŋs] *s3* discrepancy
disk'ret *a1* discreet, tactful; (*om färg*) quiet **diskretion** discretion
diskrimination discrimination **diskriminera** discriminate **diskriminering** discrimination **diskrimineringsombudsman** *ung.* equal opportunities ombudsman
disk|ställ plate rack **-trasa** dishcloth; *ibl.* dishclout
dis'kurs *s3* discourse
diskus ['dis-] *s2* discus **-kastare** discus thrower **-kastning** throwing the discus; (*idrottsgren*) the discus
diskussion [-u'ʃɔ:n] discussion, debate
diskussions|inlägg contribution to a debate **-ämne** subject of (for) discussion
diskut|abel *a2* debatable **-era** discuss; debate;

argue; *det skall vi inte* ~ *om* we won't argue the point; *det kan ju* ~*s* it is open to discussion
diskvalificera disqualify **diskvalificering, diskvalifikation** disqualification
diskvatten dishwater
disparat *a1* disparate
dis'pasch *s3, sjö.* average statement **-ör** average adjuster
dispens [-'aŋs] *s3* exemption; *kyrkl.* dispensation; *få* ~ be exempted **-era** [-paŋ'se:- *el.* -pen-] exempt **-är** [-aŋ'sä:r] *s3* tuberculosis clinic
dispersion dispersion
disponent [works (factory)] manager
disponer|a 1 ~ [*över*] (*förfoga över*) have at one's disposal (command) **2** (*ordna*) arrange, organize; (*göra mottaglig*) render liable (susceptible) to; ~ *en uppsats* plan (organize) an essay **-ad** *a5* disposed, inclined; ~ *för infektioner* susceptible to infection; *hon kände sig inte* ~ *att sjunga* she did not feel like singing
disponibel [-'ni:-] *a2* available, in hand, disposable **disponibilitet** availability; *i* ~ unattached; (*mil.*) on the inactive list; on half pay
disposition disposition; disposal; (*utkast*) outline; (*arrangemang*) arrangement; (*anlag o.d.*) tendency, predisposition; *ha ngt till sin* ~ have s.th. at one's disposal; *stå till ngns* ~ be at a p.'s disposal (service); *ställa ngt till ngns* ~ place s.th. at a p.'s disposal; *vidtaga* ~*er* make dispositions
dispositions|fond special reserve fund **-rätt** right of disposal
disposi'tiv [*el.* 'diss-] *a1* optional
disproportion disproportion
disput|ation disputation; *univ. äv.* oral defence of a [doctor's] thesis **-era** dispute, argue; *univ.* defend one's thesis; *han* ~*de på* his doctor's thesis was about (on)
dis'pyt *s3* dispute, controversy, argument; altercation; *råka i* ~ get involved in a dispute
diss *s7, mus.* D sharp
dissekera dissect **dissektion** [-k'ʃɔ:n] dissection
dissenter [-'sent-] dissenter, nonconformist
dissimil|ation dissimilation **-era** dissimilate
diss-moll D-sharp minor
dissoci|ation dissociation **-era** dissociate
dissonans [-'ans *el.* -'aŋs] *s3* dissonance
distans [-'ans *el.* -'aŋs] *s3* distance **-era** outdistance, leave behind; beat **-minut** [international] nautical mile
distingerad [-iŋ'ge:-] *a5* distinguished **dis'tinkt** *a1* distinct **distinktion** [-k'ʃɔ:n] distinction
distorsion [-r'ʃɔ:n] distortion
distrahera ~ *ngn* distract a p.'s attention, disturb s.b.; *utan att låta sig* ~*s* without becoming confused **distra'herad** *a5* distraught **distraktion** [-k'ʃɔ:n] distraction (*äv. förströelse*); (*tankspriddhet*) absent-mindedness
distribuer|a distribute **-ing** distribution
distribution distribution; *i* ~ (*om bok*) published (sold) for the author (*hos* by)
distributions|ekonomi marketing [efficiency] **-företag** distribution firm; distributors (*pl*) **-kostnad** distribution (marketing) cost

D

distribu't|iv [*el.* 'diss-] *a1* distributive **-ör** distributor

dis'trikt *s7* district, region, area

distrikts|läkare district medical officer **-mästare** district champion **-mästerskap** district championship **-sköterska** district nurse **-åklagare** district prosecutor (*AE.* attorney)

dis'trä *a1* absent-minded, distrait

disör diseur **disös** diseuse

dit *adv* **1** *demonstr.* there; ~ *bort* (*fram, in, ner, upp, ut, över*) away (up, in, down, up, out, over) there; ~ *hör även* to that category also belong[s]; *det var* ~ *jag ville komma* that's what I was getting at; *hit och* ~ to and fro; (*högre stil*) hither and thither; *är det långt* ~? (*om plats*) is it a long way there?, (*om tid*) is it a long time ahead? **2** *rel.* where; (*varthelst*) wherever **-hän** *se därhän* **-hörande** *a4* belonging to it; (*t. saken*) relevant; *ej* ~ irrelevant **-intills** ['di:t- *el.* ˣdi:t-] till (up to) then

dito ['di:- *el.* ˣdi:-] **I** *oböjligt a* ditto (*förk.* do.) **II** *adv* likewise

ditresa journey (*etc.*) there

1 ditt *se din, sköt du* ~ mind your own business

2 ditt *i uttr.*: ~ *och datt* one thing and another, this and that; *tala om* ~ *och datt* talk about all sorts of things

dittills ['di:t-] till then **-varande** *a4*, *hans* ~ *arbete* his work till then, his previous work

dit|vägen *på* ~ on the way there **-åt** ['di:t-] in that direction, that way; *någonting* ~ something like that

diva *s1* diva **-later** *ung.* airs and graces

di'van *s3* couch, divan

diver'g|ens *s3* divergence **-era** diverge; ~*nde* divergent

diverse [-ˣvärse] **I** *oböjligt a* sundry, various; ~ *utgifter* incidental (sundry) expenses **II** *s pl* sundries, odds and ends; (*rubrik o.d.*) miscellaneous, sundries **-arbetare** odd-jobman, oddjobber; labourer **-handel** general shop (store) **-handlare** general dealer

diversifier|a diversify **-ing** diversification

divi'd|end *s3* dividend; *minsta gemensamma* ~ lowest (least) common multiple **-era 1** *mat.* divide (*med* by; *i* into) **2** (*resonera*) argue (*om* about)

di'vis *s3* hyphen

division division; *flyg.* squadron

divisions|chef divisional commander; *flyg.* squadron leader **-tecken** division sign

divisor [-ˣvi:sår] *s3* divisor

djonk [djånk] *s3* junk

djungel ['juŋel] *s3* jungle **-telegraf** bush telegraph; *vard.* grapevine [telegraph]

djup [ju:p] **I** *s7* depth; *bildl. äv.* profundity; *högt. äv.* depths (*pl*); *kaptenen följde fartyget i ~et* the captain went down with his ship; *gå på ~et med ngt* go to the bottom of s.th.; *på ringa* ~ at no great depth; *ur ~et av mitt hjärta* from the depths of my heart **II** *a1* deep; (*högre stil o. bildl.*) profound; (*fullständig*) complete; (*stor, svår*) great; ~ *tystnad* profound silence; ~*t ogillande* profound disapproval; *en* ~ *skog* a thick forest; *de ~a leden* the rank and file; *den ~aste orsaken till* the fundamental

cause of; *i* ~*a tankar* deep in thought; *i* ~*aste hemlighet* with utmost secrecy; *mitt i* ~*aste skogen* in the very depths of the forest; *ge sig ut på ~t vatten* (*bildl.*) get out of one's depth

djup|blå deep blue **-borrning** deep-drilling **-dykning** deep-sea diving **-frys** deepfreeze **-frysa** deepfreeze **-frysning** deepfreezing **-fryst** ~ *mat* frozen food **-gående I** *a4* deep; *bildl.* profound, deep; *sjö.* deep-drawing **II** *s6*, *sjö.* draught **-hav** ocean **-havsfiske** deep-sea fishing **-havsforskning** oceanography

djup|ing [ˣju:-] *vard.*, *en* ~ a deep one **-kurva** *sjö.* depth contour **-loda** strike deep-sea soundings

djup|na [ˣju:p-] get deeper; deepen **-psykologi** depth psychology **-rotad** *a5* deep-rooted, deep-seated **-sinne** profundity, depth; profoundness **-sinnig** *a1* deep; profound; (*svårfattlig*) abstruse **-skärpa** *foto.* depth of field

djupt [ju:pt] *adv* deeply; profoundly; ~ *allvarlig* very serious (grave); ~ *liggande* (*bildl.*) deep-rooted, deep-seated; ~ *rörd* deeply (profoundly) moved; ~ *sårad* intensely hurt; *buga sig* ~ bow low; *sjunka* (*falla, gräva, ligga*) ~ sink (fall, dig, lie) deep; *känna sig* ~ *kränkt* feel deeply injured; *djupast sett* at bottom

djuptryck photogravure [printing], intaglio

djur [ju:r] *s7* animal; (*större; föraktfullt*) beast; (*boskaps-*) cattle (*behandlas som pl*); *slita som ett* ~ work like a horse; *vilda* ~ (*ej tama*) wild animals, (*farliga för människan*) wild beasts; *de oskäliga* ~*en* the dumb brutes; *reta inte* ~*en* do not tease dumb animals **-art** species (*pl* species) [of animal], animal species **-besättning** [animal] stock **-fabel** [beast] fable **-fabrik** factory farm **-fett** animal fat **-försök** animal experimentation

djur|isk ['ju:-] *a5* animal; (*bestialisk*) bestial; (*rå*) brutal; (*sinnlig*) carnal **-kretsen** the zodiac **-park** zoological garden, zoo **-plågare** tormentor of animals **-plågeri** cruelty to animals **-riket** the animal kingdom **-sjukhus** animal (veterinary) hospital **-skydd** protection of animals **-skyddsförening** society for the prevention of cruelty to animals **-skötare** *lantbr.* cattleman; (*-vårdare*) keeper **-tämjare** animal tamer **-uppfödning** [animal] breeding (farming) **-vårdare** keeper **-vän** *vara stor* ~ be very fond of animals **-vänlig** kind to animals **-värld** animal world

djäkne [ˣjä:k-] *s2*, *ung.* upper-school scholar

djärv [järv] *a1* bold; (*oförvägen*) intrepid, audacious; (*dristig*) daring; (*vågad*) venturesome, venturous; *lyckan står den* ~*e bi* Fortune favours the brave **djärvas** [ˣjärr-] *v2*, *dep* dare, venture **djärvhet** [ˣjärv-] boldness; daring; intrepidity, audacity

djäv|la [ˣjä:vla] *oböjligt a* bloody; damn[ed]; *AE. äv.* goddam[n]; *din* ~ *drummel* you bloody fool **-las** *v1*, *dep* make hell (*med* for); provoke, incite to anger **-lig** *a1*, *se djävulsk* **-ligt** *adv*, *jag är* ~ *trött* I am devilish (desperately) tired; *en* ~ *bra pianist* a damn good pianist

djävul [ˣjä:-] **-en** *djävlar* devil; *djävlar, anamma!* damn [it]!; *jag ska djävlar anamma visa honom* I am bloody well going to show him **djävulsdyrkan** [ˣjä:-] devil-worship **djävulsk**

['jä:-] *a5* hellish, devilish; fiendish **djävulskap** [ˣjä:-] *s7* devilry **djävulsrocka** [ˣjä:-] manta [ray], devilfish, devil ray **djävulstyg** [ˣjä:-] *s7* devilry

d-moll D minor

dobbel ['dåbb-] *s7* gambling **dobbla** [ˣdåbb-] gamble

docent reader, senior research fellow; *AE.* associate professor **docentur** readership *etc.*

docer|a hold forth, pontificate, pontify **-ande** didactic, magisterial; *neds.* lecturing

dock [-å-] (*likväl*) yet, still; (*emellertid*) however; (*ändå*) for all that

1 docka [-å-] *s1* **1** (*leksak, äv. bildl.*) doll; (*marionett o. bildl.*) puppet **2** (*garn-*) skein

2 dock|a [-å-] **l** *s1, sjö.* dock **ll** *v1, sjö. o. rymdfart* dock

dockning docking **dock|skåp** doll's house **-teater** puppet theatre **-vagn** doll's pram

doft [-å-] *s3* scent, odour (*äv. bildl.*); fragrance **dofta** [-å-] **1** smell; *det ~r rosor* there is a scent of roses; *vad det ~r härligt!* what a delicious scent! **2** (*beströ*) dust; ~ *socker på en kaka* dust a cake with sugar

dog *imperf. av* dö

doge [då:ʃ *el.* 'då:dʒe] *s5* doge

dogg [-å-] *s2* bulldog; (*större*) mastiff

dogm [-å-] *s3* dogma **dogmatik** *s3* dogmatics (*pl, behandlas som sg*), dogmatic (doctrinal) theology **dogmatiker** [-'ma:-] dogmatist **dogmatisera** dogmatize **dogmatisk** [-'ma:-] *a5* dogmatic[al] **dogmatism** dogmatism

doktor [ˣdåktår] *s3* doctor; (*läkare*) physician; *medicine* ~ doctor of medicine

dokto'rand [-å-] *s3* candidate for the doctorate (doctor's degree) **-stipendium** postgraduate scholarship

doktor|era [-å-] work for a doctor's degree **-inna** *~n A.* Mrs. A.

doktors|avhandling doctor's thesis (dissertation) **-disputation** oral defence (public examination) of a [doctor's] thesis **-grad** doctorate, doctor's degree **-hatt** doctor's hat **-promotion** conferring of doctor's degrees **-ring** doctor's ring **-värdighet** doctorate

dok'trin [-å-] *s3* doctrine **-'är** *a1* doctrinaire

dokument [-å-] *s7* document; *jur. äv.* deed, instrument **-arisk** [-'ta:-] *a5* documentary **-ation** documentation

dokument|era [-å-] document, substantiate, prove; ~ *sig som* establish o.s. as **-förstörare** paper shredder **-portfölj** document case, briefcase **-samling** file [of documents] **-skåp** filing cabinet

dokumen'tär [-å-] *a1* documentary **-film** documentary [film] **-roman** documentary novel

dold [-å-] *a1* hidden, concealed; *~a reserver* hidden reserves (assets); *illa* ~ ill-concealed, ill-disguised **dolde** [-å-] *imperf. av* dölja

dolk [-å-] *s2* dagger; (*kort*) poniard; *sticka ner ngn med* ~ stab s.b. **-styng, -stöt** stab [with a dagger *etc.*], dagger-thrust

dollar ['dåll-] *s9* dollar; *AE. sl.* buck **-kurs** dollar rate [of exchange] **-prinsessa** dollar princess **-sedel** dollar note (*AE.* bill); *AE. sl.* greenback

dolma [ˣdåll-] *s1* (*plagg*) dolman; (*husars äv.*) dolman jacket

dolo'mit *s3* dolomite **Dolomiterna** [-'mi:-] *pl* the Dolomites

dolsk [-å-] *a1* (*lömsk*) insidious; (*bedräglig*) deceitful; (*lurande*) treacherous

dolt [-å-] *sup. av* dölja

1 dom [då:m, *i sms.* dɷmm] *s3* (*kyrka*) cathedral

2 dom [dɷmm] *s2* judg[e]ment; (*utslag*) verdict; (*i sht i brottmål*) sentence; *~ens dag* Judgment Day, Day of Judgment; *fällande* (*friande*) ~ sentence (verdict) of guilty (not guilty); *yttersta ~en* the Last Judgment; *fälla* ~ *över* pass sentence upon; *sitta till ~s över* sit in judgment upon; *sätta sig till ~s över* set o.s. up as a judge of

Domarboken [ˣdɷmmar-] Judges, the Book of Judges

domarbord [ˣdɷmmar-] judge's (judges') table

domar|e [ˣdɷmmare] judge; magistrate; (*i högre instans*) justice; (*friare o. bildl.*) arbiter; (*i sporttävling*) umpire; (*i fotboll m.m.*) referee **-ed** judicial oath **-kår** judiciary, bench

domdera [-å-] bluster

domedag [ˣdɷmme-] judgment day, doomsday; *till ~[s otta]* until kingdom come

domedags|basun last trump **-predikan** hellfire sermon

domes|ticera domesticate **-tik** *s3* **1** (*fodertyg*) cotton lining, denim; (*underklädestyg*) calico **2** (*tjänare*) servant

domherre [ˣdɷmm-] bullfinch

domi'cil *s4* domicil[e]

domin|ans [-'ans *el.* -'aŋs] *s3* domination; dominance **-ant** *s3 o. a1* dominant **-era** dominate; (*vara förhärskande*) be predominant, prevail; (*behärska, ha utsikt över*) dominate, command; (*tyrannisera*) domineer **-'erande** *a4* dominating *etc.*, predominant; ~ *anlag* dominant

domini'kan *s3* Dominican **-[er]orden** [the] Dominican Order

dominikansk [-'ka:nsk] *a5* Dominican **Dominikanska republiken** Dominican Republic

domino ['dåmm- *el.* 'då:-] **1** *s5* (*dräkt*) domino **2** *s6* (*spelbricka*) domino; (*spel*) *se -spel; spela* ~ play dominoes **-bricka** domino **-spel** dominoes (*pl, behandlas som sg*), game of dominoes **-teori** domino theory

domkapitel [ˣdɷmm-] [cathedral] chapter

domkraft [ˣdɷmm-] *s3* jack

domkyrka [ˣdɷmm-] cathedral; (*i Storbritannien äv.*) minster

domn|a [ˣdåmna] go numb (*äv.* ~ *av, bort*); *foten har ~t* my foot has gone to sleep **-ing** numbness

domprost [ˣdɷmm-] dean

dompt|era [-å-] tame [animals] **-ör** [animal] tamer

domsaga [ˣdɷmm-] *s1* judicial district

domsbasun *se domedagsbasun*

domslut judicial decision

domssöndagen the Sunday before Advent

domstol [ˣdɷmm-] court [of justice (law)]; tribunal (*äv. bildl.*); *vid* ~ in the law court; *dra*

D

ngn inför ~ bring s.b. before the court; *dra ngt inför* ~ go to court (law) about s.th.; *Högsta ~en, ung.* (*i England*) the Supreme Court of Judicature, (*i Skottland*) Court of Justiciary, (*i USA*) the Supreme Court, (*friare*) the supreme court
domstols|förhandlingar court proceedings **-verk** ~*et* [the Swedish] national courts administration
domsöndagen *se domssöndagen*
dom|villa miscarriage of justice **-värjo** *r* jurisdiction; *lyda under ngns* ~ fall under a p.'s jurisdiction
do'män *s3* domain **-styrelse** national board of crown forests and lands **-verk** ~*et* [the Swedish] forest service
don *s7* (*verktyg*) tool; implement; (*anordning*) device; (*grejor*) gear, tackle; ~ *efter person* to every man his due **dona** ~ *med* (*vard.*) busy o.s. with
donation donation, legacy **donationsfond** donation fund **donator** [-ˣna:tår] *s3* donor
Donau ['då:nau] *r* the Danube
donera donate; *den* ~*e summan* the sum presented
doningar *pl, vard.* tools, gear (*sg*), tackle (*sg*)
donjuan [dån'ju:-] *best. form* =, *äv. -en, pl -er* Don Juan
donkeypanna [ˣdåŋki-] *sjö.* donkey boiler
donna [-å-] *s1, sl.* (*särsk. AE.*) dame, broad
dop *s7* baptism; (*barn-, fartygs-*) christening; *bära ngn till* ~*et* present s.b. at the font
dopa dope
dopa'min *s7* L-dopa
dop|attest certificate of baptism **-funt** baptismal (christening) font **-gåva** baptismal gift
doping ['då:p-] doping, drug-taking
dop|klänning christening robe **-namn** Christian name
dopning [ˣdå:p-] *se doping*
dopp [-å-] *s7* **1** (*-ning*) dip[ping]; *ta sig ett* ~ take a swim **2** (*kaffebröd*) buns, cakes (*pl*) **doppa** dip; (*hastigt*) plunge; (*helt o. hållet*) immerse; (*ge ngn ett dopp*) duck; ~ *i grytan* (*ung.*) soak bread in ham broth; ~ *sig* have a dip (plunge) **dopparedagen** Christmas Eve
dopping [-å-] *zool.* grebe
dopplereffekt [ˣdåpp-] Doppler effect (shift)
doppning [-å-] dip, plunge; immersion
doppsko (*beslag*) ferrule
doppvärmare immersion heater
dor[i]er ['då:-] Dorian **dorisk** ['då:-] *a5* Doric, Dorian
dormitorium [dårmi'tå:-] *s4* dormitory
dorn [-å:- *el.* -ɷ:-] *s2* mandrel, arbor
dos *s3* dose; *dödlig* ~ lethal dose; *för stor* ~ overdose
dosa *s1* box; (*för te o.d.*) canister, (*mindre*) caddy
dosekvivalent dose equivalent
1 dosera *med.* dose
2 dosera (*slutta*) slope; ~ *en kurva* superelevate (bank, camber) a curve
1 do'sering *med.* dosage
2 do'sering (*av kurva*) superelevation, bank, camber
dosimeter [-'me:-] *s2* dosimeter, dosemeter

dosis ['då:-] *s3, se dos; en rejäl* ~ a good measure (share)
dosmätare *se dosimeter*
dosrat (*måttenhet*) dose rate
dossera *se 2 dosera* **dossering** *se 2 dosering*
dossié [dåssi'e:] *s3,* **dossier** [dåssi'e:] *s3* dossier, file
dotter [-å-] *-n döttrar* daughter **-bolag** affiliated company, affiliate; subsidiary [company] **-dotter** granddaughter **-lig** *a1* daughterly **-son** grandson **-svulst** metastasis
douglasgran [ˣdåg-] Douglas fir (spruce, hemlock)
dov [-å:-] *a1* (*om ljud*) dull, hollow, muffled; (*om värk*) aching; (*halvkvävd*) stifled, suppressed
dovhjort fallow deer; (*hane*) buck
doyen [*svenskt uttal* doa'jäŋ] *s3* doyen
dra (*draga*) *drog dragit* **I 1** draw; (*kraftigare*) pull, tug; (*släpa*) drag, haul; *drag!* pull!; ~ *en historia* reel off a story; ~ *fullt hus* draw full houses; ~ *ngn i håret* pull s.b. by the hair, pull a p.'s hair; ~ *i* (*ur*) *led* set into (put out of) joint; ~ *ngn inför rätta* bring s.b. before the court; ~ *kniv* draw a knife (*mot* on); ~ *en kopia* run off a copy; ~ *ett kort* draw a card; ~ *lakan* stretch (pull) sheets; ~ *ett tungt lass* pull a heavy load; ~ *lott* draw lots; ~ *en lättnadens suck* breathe a sigh of relief; ~ *olycka över ngn* bring disaster [up]on s.b.; ~ *slutsatser om* draw conclusions on, conclude; ~ *ett streck över* draw a line across, *bildl.* let bygones be bygones; ~ *det kortaste strået* come off worst, get the worst of it; ~ *sitt strå till stacken* do one's part (bit); ~ *uppmärksamheten till* draw attention to; *komma* ~*gandes med* come along with; ~*s* (*känna sig dragen*) *till ngn* feel drawn to (attracted by) s.b. **2** (*driva*) work (*en maskin* a machine); (*vrida*) turn (*veven* the crank) **3** (*subtrahera*) take [away], subtract; (*erfordra*) take; (*förbruka*) use [up]; ~ *kostnader* involve cost (expenses) **4** (*om te o.d.*) draw **5** (*tåga*) march, go; ~ *i fält* take the field; ~ *i krig* go to the wars; ~ *sina färde* take one's departure; ~ *åt skogen* go to blazes; *gå och* ~ hang about (around) **6** ~ *efter andan* gasp for breath; ~ *på munnen* smile; *det* ~*r här* there is a draught here **II** *rfl* **1** (*förflytta sig*) move, pass; (*bege sig*) repair **2** *ligga och* ~ *sig* (*om morgnarna*) lie in; ~ *sig efter* (*om klocka*) lose, be losing; *klockan* ~*r sig tio minuter* [*efter*] *varje dag* the clock loses ten minutes every day; *klockan har* ~*git sig fem minuter* [*efter*] the clock is five minutes slow; ~ *sig före* (*om klocka*) gain, be gaining; *klockan* ~*r sig fem minuter före varje dag* the clock gains five minutes every day; *klockan har* ~*git sig fem minuter före* the clock is five minutes fast; ~ *sig fram* get on (along); ~ *sig för ngt* (*för att* + *inf.*) be afraid of s.th. (of + *ing-form*); *inte* ~ *sig för ngt* (*för att*) (*äv.*) not mind s.th. (not mind + *ing-form*); ~ *sig tillbaka* draw [o.s.] back, retire, *mil.* retreat; ~ *sig undan* move (draw) aside, withdraw; ~ *sig ur spelet* quit the game, (*friare*) back up, give up, *vard.* chuck [up] **III** (*med betonad partikel*) **1** ~ *av a*) (*klä av*) pull (take) off, *b*) (*dra ifrån*) deduct; ~ *av ringen från fingret* slip the ring

from one's finger **2** ~ *bort a*) draw away, (*trupper e.d.*) withdraw, *b*) (*gå bort*) move off, go away, (*om trupper e.d.*) withdraw **3** ~ *fram a*) (*ta fram*) draw (pull) out, (*väg e.d.*) construct, *bildl.* bring up, produce, *b*) (*gå fram*) advance, march; ~ *fram stolen till bordet* draw up the chair to the table; ~ *fram genom* (*äv.*) traverse **4** ~ *för* pull (*gardinerna* the curtains) **5** ~ *förbi* go past, pass by **6** ~ *ifrån a*) draw (pull) back (*gardinerna* the curtains), *b*) (*ta bort*) take away, subtract, *c*) *sport.* draw away (*de andra* from the rest) **7** ~ *igen* (*dörr e.d.*) close, shut **8** ~ *igenom* (*band e.d.*) pull (draw) through; ~ *igenom boken* skim (through) the book **9** ~ *i gång ngt* set s.th. working; ~ *i gång med ngt* get s.th. going **10** ~ *ihop sig* contract, (*sluta sig*) close; *det ~r ihop sig till oväder* a storm is gathering; *det ~r ihop sig till regn* it looks like rain **11** ~ *in* draw in (*äv. bildl.*), (*återtaga, återfordra*) withdraw, (*avskaffa*) abolish, do away with, (*konfiskera*) confiscate; (*underhåll o.d.*) stop, discontinue; (*tidning, körkort*) suspend; ~ *in ett körkort* take away (*på viss tid:* suspend) a driving licence; ~ *in ett flyg* cancel (call off) a flight; ~ *in magen* pull in one's stomach; ~ *in* (*installera*) *vatten* lay on water; ~ *in på* (*inskränka*) cut down **12** ~ *i väg* move off, march away **13** ~ *jämnt* get on (along) (*med ngn* with s.b.) **14** ~ *med* drag along; ~ *med sig a*) eg. take about with one, *b*) *bildl.* bring with it (them), (*innebära*) involve; ~ *med sig ngn i fallet* drag s.b. down with one **15** ~ *ner a*) pull down (*rullgardinen* the blind), *b*) (*smutsa ner*) make dirty **16** ~ *omkull* pull down, (*slå omkull*) knock down **17** ~ *på* (*starta*) start [up], (*öka farten*) speed up; ~ *på sig* pull (put) on, (*bildl.*) catch **18** ~ *till* (*hårdare*) pull tighter, tighten; ~ *till bromsen* apply the brake; ~ *till med en svordom* come out with an oath; ~ *till sig a*) eg. draw towards one, *b*) (*attrahera*) attract (*äv. bildl.*) **19** ~ *tillbaka* draw back, (*trupper äv.*) withdraw **20** ~ *undan* draw (pull) aside, withdraw, remove **21** ~ *upp* draw (pull) up, (*fisk äv.*) land, (*butelj*) uncork, (*klocka*) wind up; ~ *upp ankaret* weigh anchor; ~ *upp benen under sig* curl up one's legs; ~ *upp med roten* pull up by the roots **22** ~ *ur* draw (pull) out **23** ~ *ut a*) draw (pull) out, (*förlänga*) draw out, prolong, (*tänja ut*) stretch out, *b*) (*tåga ut*) go off (*i krig* to the wars), *c*) (*om rök e.d.*) find its way out; ~ *ut en tand* extract a tooth; *det ~r ut på tiden* (*tar lång tid*) it takes rather a long time, (*blir sent*) it is getting late; *det drog ut på tiden innan* it was a long time (a long time elapsed) before **24** ~ *vidare* move (march) on **25** ~ *åt* draw (pull) tight[er], tighten; ~ *åt svångremmen* (*bildl.*) tighten one's belt; ~ *åt sig* (*bildl.*) attract, (*absorbera*) absorb, suck up (*damm* dust) **26** ~ *över på ett konto* overdraw an account; ~ *över tiden* run over [the] time; ~ *över sig* pull over one

drabant 1 (*livvakt*) bodyguard; (*följeslagare*) henchman **2** *astr. o. bildl.* satellite **-stat** satellite state

drabba 1 (*träffa*) hit, strike; (*hända ngn*) happen to, *åld. o. litt.* befall; (*komma på ngns lott*)

fall [up]on; (*beröra*) affect; *förlusten ~r honom ensam* he, alone, bears the loss, the loss falls upon him alone; *~s av en olycka* meet with misfortune; *~s av en svår förlust* suffer a heavy loss; *~s av sjukdom* be stricken with illness **2** ~ *ihop* (*samman*) meet, have an encounter (*om trupper*), come to blows (*om enskilda*), *bildl.* [come into] conflict, clash

drabbning battle; action; (*friare*) encounter

drack *imperf. av* dricka

drag *s7* **1** (*-ande*) pull, tug; (*med penna, stråke etc.*) stroke; *i några snabba* ~ with a few bold strokes **2** (*spel. o. friare*) move; *ett skickligt* ~ a clever move **3** (*luftström*) draught, *AE.* draft; *sitta i* ~ sit in a draught; *det är dåligt* ~ *i spisen* the stove is drawing badly **4** (*bloss*) puff, whiff; *njuta i fulla* ~ enjoy to the full **5** (*drickande*) draught; *tömma glaset i ett* ~ empty the glass at a gulp (draught) **6** (*anletsdrag*) feature; (*karaktärsdrag*) trait; (*anstrykning*) touch, strain; *ett utmärkande* ~ *för* a characteristic [feature] of **7** (*fiskredskap*) spoon[bait], spinner; *fiska med* (*ro*) ~ [*i*] troll **8** *vard., i det ~et* at this juncture

draga *se* dra

dragant *s3, s4* tragacanth

dragare (*lastdjur*) draught animal, beast of burden

dragas *se* dras

drag|band drawstring **-basun** slide trombone **-djur** *se* dragare

dragé [-'ʃeː] *s3* dragée

dragen *a5* (*lindrigt berusad*) tipsy

dragg *s2* drag, dragnet; (*litet ankare*) grapnel **dragga** drag (*efter* for); (*om båt*) drag anchor

draggning dragging

drag|harmonika concertina **-hund** draught dog **-hållfasthet** tensile strength

drag|ig *a1* draughty **-it** *sup. av* dra[ga]

drag|kamp tug of war **-kedja** *se blixtlås* **-kraft** traction force; *järnv. etc.* traction power **-kärra** handcart **-nagel** *vard.* dram, tot

dragning [-aː-] **1** draw (*äv. lott- o. bildl.*); dragging; pull **2** (*böjelse*) tendency, inclination (*till* for); (*dragningskraft*) attraction **3** (*skiftning*) tinge (*åt gult* of yellow)

dragnings|kraft attraction; (*tyngdkraft*) gravity **-lista** lottery prize list

drago'man *s3* dragoman (*pl äv.* dragomen)

dra'gon *s3* **1** (*ryttare*) dragoon **2** *bot.* tarragon, estragon

drag|plåster *bildl.* attraction, *vard.* draw; *AE. äv.* drawing card **-skåp** *kem.* fume cupboard **-snöre** *se* dragband **-spel** accordion; (*mindre*) concertina **-spänning** tension, tensile stress **-stift** drawing pen

drakblod dragon's blood (*äv. harts*) **drakblodsträd** dragon tree; (*släkte*) dracaena

drak|e *s2* dragon (*äv. bildl.*); (*leksak o. meteor.*) kite; (*skepp*) Viking [dragon] ship **-flygning** kite flying

drakma ['drack-] *s3* drachma

drakonisk [-'kɔ:-] *a5* Draconian, Draconic

drak|skepp *se* drake **-sådd** *en* ~ a sowing of dragon's teeth

drama *s4* drama

dramat|ik *s3* drama, dramatics (*pl, behandlas*

vanl. som sg) **-iker** [-'ma:-] dramatist, playwright **-isera** dramatize **-isering** dramatization **-isk** [-'ma:-] *a5* dramatic; *D~a institutet* University College of Film, Television, Radio and the Theatre; *Kungliga Dramatiska teatern* the Royal Dramatic Theatre -'**urg** *s3* dramaturge, dramaturgist
drank *s3* slop[s]
drapa *s1* [bardic] ode *(över* on)
drapera drape, hang **draperi** curtain, drapery, hangings *(pl)*; *AE. äv.* drapes **drapering** draping, drapery
dras *(dragas) drogs dragits, dep, ~ med a) (sjukdom)* be afflicted with, suffer from, *b) (skulder, bekymmer)* be harassed by, *c) (utstå)* put up with
drastisk ['drass-] *a5* drastic
dra'sut *s3* tall ungainly fellow
drav *s2, s4* draff; *(skräp)* rubbishy mess
dravel ['dravv-] *s7* drivel, nonsense
dregl|el ['dre:-, *äv.* 'dregg-] *s7*, **dregla** [*dre:-, *äv.* *dregg-] drivel, slobber
drej|a [*dreja] **1** *tekn.* turn **2** *sjö.:* ~ *bi* heave (lay) to **-skiva** potter's wheel
dress *s3, s2* dress, attire; togs *(pl)*
dresser|a train *(till* for); *(friare)* drill; *(häst, hund äv.)* break **-ing** training *etc.*
dres'sin *s3* trolley
dressing ['dress-] [salad] dressing
dres'syr *s3* [animal] training; *(häst-)* dressage; *i sht bildl.* drill **-ridning** dressage [riding]
dressör trainer [of animals]
1 drev *s7 (blånor o.d.)* oakum
2 drev *s7 (hjul)* [driving] pinion; *(växel)* gear, gearwheel
3 drev *s7, jakt.* drive, beat
4 drev *imperf. av driva*
dreva *(t. 1 drev)* caulk
drev|jakt battue **-karl** beater, driver
dribbl|a dribble **-are** dribbler **-ing** dribbling, dribble
dricka I *s7 (läskedryck)* soft drink, lemonade; *(öl)* beer; *~t* (= *sjön, havet), vard.* the drink **II** *drack druckit* drink; *(intaga)* have, take; *~ brunn* take (drink) the waters; *~ i botten* drain one's glass; *~ kaffe* have coffee; *~ ngns skål* drink a p.'s health, drink the health of a p.; *~ ngn till* pledge s.b.; *~ ngn under bordet* drink s.b. under the table; *~ ur kaffet* finish one's coffee; *~ ur sitt glas* empty (drain) one's glass; *~ sig full* get drunk (intoxicated); *~ sig otörstig* quench one's thirst; *han har börjat ~* he has taken to drinking
drickbar *a1* drinkable, fit to drink
dricks *s3* tip; *ge ~* tip; *ge 1 pund i ~* give a one-pound tip **-fontän** bubbler, drinking fountain **-glas** [drinking] glass; tumbler; *ett ~ ...* a glass[ful] of ... **-pengar** tip *(sg)*; gratuity *(sg)*; service [charge] *(sg)* **-vatten** drinking water
drift *s3* **1** *(drivande)* drifting; *råka (komma i) ~* get adrift; *ungdom på ~* youth (young people) adrift **2** *(skötsel)* management, administration; *(gång)* running, operation; *i (ur) ~* in (out of) operation (service); *billig i ~* economical; *stoppa ~en* stop production; *övergå till elektrisk ~* change to electric power **3** *(trafik)* traffic **4** *(instinkt, böjelse)* instinct, urge;

impulse; *göra ngt av egen ~* do s.th. of one's own accord **5** *(gyckel)* joking
driftig *a1* energetic, enterprising, pushing **-het** energy, enterprise, push
drift|kapital working capital **-kucku** *s2* laughing stock **-liv** instincts *(pl)*
drifts|budget working budget **-ingenjör** production engineer **-inskränkning** production cutback **-inställelse** stoppage, close-down, shutdown **-kostnad** running costs *(pl)*
drift|stopp *se driftsinställelse* **-störning** breakdown, stoppage **-säker** dependable, reliable
1 drill *s2 (exercis)* drill
2 drill *s2 (borr)* drill
3 drill *s2, mus.* trill, quaver; *(fåglars)* warble; *slå sina ~ar* warble
1 drilla *(exercera)* drill
2 drilla *(borra)* drill
3 drilla *mus.* trill, quaver; warble
drillande *a4, mus.* trilling *etc.*
drillborr [spiral] drill, wimble
drilling three-barrel gun
drillsnäppa common sandpiper
drink *s2* drink **-are** drunkard
drista ~ *sig [till] att* be bold enough to, venture to **dristig** *a1* bold, daring **dristighet** boldness, daring
drittel *s2* cask, butter keg
driv|a I *s1* [snow]drift; *snön låg i djupa -or* the snow lay in huge drifts **II** *drev drivit* **1** drive; *(maskin)* work, operate; *(fram-)* propel; *(fabrik o.d.)* run, conduct **2** *(i drivbänk)* force **3** *(täta)* caulk **4** *(metall)* chase **5** *(bedriva)* carry on; *(politik)* pursue **6** *(tvinga)* drive, force **7** *(förmå)* impel, urge, prompt **8** *~ ngn på flykten* rout s.b., put s.b. to flight; *~ ngt i höjden* force (screw) s.th. up; *~ saken för långt* push (carry) things too far **9** *(föras undan)* drive; *(sjö. o. om moln, snö e.d.)* drift; *~ för ankar* drag anchor **10** *gå och ~* walk aimlessly about, loaf [about] **11** *~ med ngn* poke fun at s.b. **12** *(med betonad partikel)* ~ *igenom ett lagförslag* force (push) through a bill; *~ sin vilja igenom* get one's own way; *~ in (pengar, fordran)* collect, call in, *jur.* recover; *~ omkring* drift (walk aimlessly) about; *fartyget drev omkring* the ship was adrift; *~ på* urge on; *~ samman boskapen* herd the cattle; *~ tillbaka* drive back, repel; *~ upp (i höjden)* force up; *(damm e.d.)* raise; *(villebråd)* rouse, raise; *(affär)* work up; *~ ut* drive (push) out, cast out
driv|ande *a4* driving *etc.*; *den ~ kraften* the driving force, *(om pers. äv.)* the prime mover; *~ karl* pushing man; *~ vrak* floating wreck **-ankare** sea (drift) anchor **-axel** shaft, driving shaft **-bänk** hotbed
driv|en *a3* **1** *(skicklig)* clever; *(erfaren)* skilful, skilled, practised; *~ handstil (ung.)* flowing hand **2** *(ciselerad)* chased **-fjäder** mainspring; *bildl. äv.* incentive, motive **-garn** drift net **-hjul** driving wl.eel (gear) **-hus** greenhouse, hothouse **-huseffekt** greenhouse effect **-husplanta** hothouse plant **-is** drift ice
driv|it *sup. av driva* **-kraft** motive power; *(om pers. äv.)* prime mover; *tekn. äv.* propelling force **-medel** *(för fordon)* [motor] fuel; *(för projektil)* propulsive agent, propellant **-mina**

floating (drifting) mine **-ning** [-i:-] driving; (*tätning*) caulking **-raket** booster [rocket], launching vehicle **-rem** driving (transmission) belt **-ved** driftwood

1 drog [-ω:-] *imperf. av dra*[*ga*]

2 drog [-å:-] *s3* drug

drog|a [-å:-] drug **-fri** drug free **-handel** drugstore **-handlare** druggist **-växt** medicinal plant

drome'dar *s3* dromedary, Arabian camel

dropp [-å-] *s7* drip; *med. äv.* infusion

dropp|a [-å-] **1** (*falla i droppar*) drip, fall in drops **2** (*hälla droppvis*) drop (*i* into) **-avskiljare** droplet separator **-boll** *sport.* drop shot

dropp|e [-å-] *s2* drop; globule; (*svett-*) bead; *en ~ i havet* a drop in the bucket (the ocean) **-flaska** drop bottle **-fri** nondrop **-infektion** droplet infection **-skål** *kokk.* drip[ping] pan **-sten** dripstone; (*nedhängande*) stalactite; (*upprättstående*) stalagmite **-torka** drip-dry **-vis** drop by drop

drosk|a [-å-] *s1* cab **-bil** cab, [taxi]cab **-chaufför, -förare** cab (taxi) driver, cabman **-kusk** cabman **-station** cab rank **-ägare** taxi owner (proprietor)

drossel ['dråss-] *s2, radio.* choke [coil]

drots [-å-] *s2, hist.* Lord High Steward

drott [-å-] *s2* king, ruler, sovereign, sire

drottning [-å-] queen; (*bi-*) queen [bee]; *balens ~* belle of the ball; *göra en bonde till ~* (*schack.*) queen [a pawn]

drucken *a3, predik.* drunk; intoxicated, tipsy **druckit** *sup. av dricka*

drulla *~ omkull* sprawl, fall over; *~ i vattnet* tumble into the water **drulle** *s2* oaf **drulleförsäkring** liability insurance **drullig** *a1* clumsy **drullighet** clumsiness

drumla *se drulla* **drumlig** *a1* clumsy, awkward; (*fumlig*) bungling **drummel** ["drummel. 'drumm-] *s2* lout

drunkna be (get) drowned; *bildl.* be (get) swamped (*i* with); *en ~nde* a drowning man (*etc.*) **drunkning** drowning **drunkningsolycka** drowning accident

drupit *sup. av drypa*

druv|a *s1* grape **-blå** grape-purple **-hagel** grapeshot **-klase** bunch (cluster) of grapes **-saft** grape juice **-socker** grape sugar, dextrose

dry'ad *s3* dryad

dryck *s3* drink; beverage; *mat och ~* meat and drink; *alkoholfri ~* nonalcoholic beverage; *starka ~er* strong drinks, liquor (*sg*)

dryckenskap *s3* drunkenness, inebriation

dryckes|broder fellow toper; pot (boon) companion **-horn** drinking horn **-kanna** stoup **-kärl** drinking vessel **-lag** *s7* drinking bout, binge, spree, carousal **-varor** *pl* drinks, beverages **-visa** drinking song

dryckjom [-åmm] *n, r* **1** drinking, carousing **2** *se dryckesvaror*

dryfta discuss, talk over

dryg *a1* **1** (*som räcker länge*) lasting; (*som väl fyller måttet*) liberal, ample, large; (*rågad*) heaped; *en ~ mil* a good mile; *~t mått* full measure; *~ portion* large helping; *~ timme* full (good) hour **2** (*mödosam*) hard; (*betungande*) heavy; *~t arbete* hard work; *~a böter* a heavy

fine **3** (*högfärdig*) stuck-up, self-important **dryga** *~ ut vin med vatten* add water to the wine **dryghet** self-importance **drygt** [-y:-] *adv, ~ hälften* a good half of it (them); *mäta ~* give full measure; *~ mätt* full measure

drypa *dröp drupit* **1** (*hälla droppvis*) drop, pour a few drops of (*på* on to; *i* into) **2** (*ge ifrån sig vätska*) drip; (*rinna ned*) trickle; *han dröp av svett* he was dripping with perspiration

dråp *s7* homicide; *jur.* manslaughter **-are** homicide **-lig** [-å:-] *a1* very funny, killing **-slag** deathblow; *bildl. äv.* staggering blow

dråsa come down in masses; *~ ner* come tumbling down

drägel, drägla *se dregel, dregla*

drägg *s2, ej pl* dregs (*pl*); (*slödder*) scum

dräglig [-ä:-] *a1* tolerable, endurable; fairly acceptable

dräkt *s3* dress; (*jacka o. kjol*) suit costume; (*national-*) costume; (*friare*) attire, garb

dräktig *a1* pregnant, big with young **-het** **1** pregnancy **2** *sjö.* tonnage, capacity

dräll *s3* diaper

dräll|a *v2* **1** spill **2** *gå och ~* hang about (around); *det -er av karlar* it's lousy with men

drämma *v2, ~ näven i bordet* bang one's fist on the table; *~ till ngn* strike s.b., give s.b. a clout

drän *s3* drain (*äv. med.*) **-age** *s7, se drän* **-era** drain **-ering** draining, drainage **-eringsrör** drainpipe

dräng *s2* farm hand; *själv är bästa ~* if you want a thing well done, do it yourself; *sådan herre sådan ~* like master like man **-kammare** farm-hand's room **-stuga** farm-hand's quarters (*pl*)

dränk|a *v3* drown; (*översvämma*) flood; *~ in med olja* [impregnate with] oil; *~ sig* drown o.s. **-ning** drowning

dräpa *v3* kill; *åld. o. litt.* slay; *du skall icke ~* thou shalt not kill; *~nde svar* crushing reply

drätsel|kammare, -nämnd [borough] finance department

dröglapp [-ö:-] *zool.* dewlap

dröj|a ["dröjja] *v2* **1** (*låta vänta på sig*) be late (*med att* in + *ing*-form); (*vara sen*) be long (*med ngt* about s.th.; *med att* about + *ing*-form); *du har -t länge* it has taken you a long time; *svaret -de* the answer was a long time in coming **2** (*låta anstå*) postpone, delay, put off; (*tveka*) hesitate; *~ med svaret* (*att svara*) hesitate to answer, put off answering; *~ på stegen* dawdle **3** (*vänta med*) wait **4** (*stanna kvar*) stop, stay; tarry, linger; *var god och dröj* (*tel.*) hold the line, please; *~ kvar till slutet* stay on (remain) till the end; *~ vid ngt* dwell [up]on **5** *opers., det -er länge innan* it will be a long time before; *det -de inte länge förrän* it was not long before; *det -de en evighet innan* it was ages before **-ande** *a4, ~ steg* dawdling footsteps; *~ blick* lingering gaze; *~ svar* hesitating answer

dröjs|mål *s7* delay; *utan ~* without delay, immediately **-målsränta** penalty interest on arrears

dröm [-ömm] *s2* dream; *bildl. äv.* daydream, reverie, revery; *hon var vacker som en ~* she looked a dream; ~men slog in the dream came true; försjunken i ~mar lost in a reverie (daydreams pl) **-bild** vision **-bok** book of dreams **-jobb** dream job **-lik** dreamlike; dreamy **-lös** dreamless

drömm|a v2 dream; bildl. äv. daydream; muse; ~ sig tillbaka till carry o.s. back in imagination to **-ande** a4 dreamy **-are** dreamer; visionary **-eri** dreaming; ett ~ a reverie

dröm|sk a5 dreamy **-slott** mitt ~ the castle of my dreams **-sömn** REM (rapid eye movement) sleep **-tydning** interpretation of dreams (a dream) **-villa** dream house **-värld** dream world

drön|a drowse, idle **-are 1** (bi) drone [bee] **2** pers. sluggard, snail

dröp imperf. av drypa

dröppel ['dröpp-] s2, se gonorré

drös|a shower (tumble) down **-vis** vard. masses [of]

du you; bibl., poet., dial. thou; ~ själv you yourself; hör ~, kan jag få låna...? I say, can you lend me...?; hör ~, det här går inte! look here, this won't do!; nej. vet ~ [vad]! I never heard of such a thing!; nej, vet ~ vad, nu gör vi ngt annat look here (listen), let's do something else; det skall ~ säga! you've no room to talk!; vi är ~ med varandra we call each other by our Christian names; bli ~ med drop the formalities of address with

dua be on Christian name terms with

dual|ism dualism **-ist** dualist **-istisk** a5 dualistic

dubb s2 stud (äv. på t.ex. fotbollsskor), knob; (is-) [ice] prod; (däck-) stud, (för tävling) spike

1 dubba ~ ngn till riddare dub s.b. a knight

2 dubba (film e.d.) dub

3 dubba (däck) stud

dubbdäck studded tyre

dubbel ['dubb-] **1** a2 double; ~ bokföring double-entry book-keeping; ligga ~ av skratt be doubled up with laughter; vika ~ [fold] double; det dubbla twice as much; dubbla belopp twice the amount; dubbla storleken double the size **2** s2 (i tennis m.m.) doubles (pl) **-agent** double agent **-arbetande** a4 doing two jobs; ~ kvinnor housewives with a paid (an outside) job **-arbete** (samma arbete) duplication of work; (två arbeten) two jobs

dubbel-b mus. double flat

dubbel|beckasin great snipe **-beskattning** double taxation **-betydelse** se -mening **-bindning** kem. double bond **-bottnad** [-å-] a5 (om sko) double-soled; bildl. ambiguous, with double meaning **-bröllop** double wedding **-bössa** double-barrelled gun **-däckare** double-decker **-dörr** double door **-exponering** foto. double exposure **-fel** (i tennis) double fault, double **-fönster** double glazing **-gångare** double **-haka** double chin **-het** doubleness **-knäppt** a4 double-breasted **-kommando** dual control **-kontakt** elektr. two-way plug **-kontroll** double check **-kontrollera** double-check **-kors** mus. double sharp **-liv** double life **-match** (i tennis m.m.) doubles (pl) **-mening** double meaning **-moral** double standard [of morality] **-mord** double murder **-myntfot** bimetallism, gold and silver standard **-namn** double-

-barrelled (hyphenated) name **-natur** split personality **-nelson** (i brottning) full nelson **-park-kera** double-park **-pipig** a1 double-barrelled **-riktad** a5, ~ trafik two-way traffic **-roll** dual role; bildl. double game **-rum** double room **-schack** double check **-seende** s6 double vision **-seger** double win **-sidig** a1 double-sided; ~ lunginflammation double pneumonia **-spel** bildl. double-dealing, double-cross; (i tennis m.m.) doubles (pl) **-spelare** (i tennis m.m.) doubles player **-spion** se -agent **-spår** double track **-spårig** a1 double-track[ed] **-stjärna** double star; (fysisk) binary star; (optisk) optical double star **-säng** double bed

dubbel|t ['dubb-] adv doubly; (två gånger) twice (så as); ~ försiktig doubly careful; ~ så gammal som jag twice my age; bjuda ~ upp bid as much again; se ~ see double **-trampa** (i bil) double-declutch; AE. double-clutch **-trast** mistle (missel) thrush **-tydig** a1, se tvetydig **-verkande** a4 double-acting **-vikt** [-i:-] a4 doubled; ~ av skratt doubled up with laughter; ~ krage turndown collar **-yxa** two-edged axe **-örn** double eagle

dubbla double

dubblé s3 **1** (guldsmedsarbete) gold (silver) plated metal **2** jakt. double hit **3** spel. cushion[ing]

dubbler|a 1 double **2** sjö. round **3** teat. understudy **-ing** doubling etc.

dubb'lett s3 **1** (kopia) duplicate, copy, double **2** (tvårumslägenhet) two-roomed flat **3** (ord-) doublet **-exemplar** duplicate copy **-nyckel** duplicate key

1 dubbning (av riddare) dubbing, accolade

2 dubbning (av film) dubbing

dubi|er ['du:-] pl, ha sina ~ have one's doubts (om about) **-'ös** a1 dubious

ducka duck

du'ell s3 duel (på pistol with pistols) **-ant** dueller, duellist **-era** duel

duenna [-ˣenna] s1 duenna

du'ett s3 duet[te], duo

duffel ['duff-] s2 duffel coat **-knapp** toggle

dug|a v2 el. dög dugt do; be suitable (till for); (komma t. pass) serve; (vara god nog) be good enough (åt for); det -er that will do; det -er inte att it won't do to; -er ingenting till is no use (good); det var en karl som hette ~ that is what I call a man; visa vad man -er till show what one is worth; han dög inte till lärare he was no good as a teacher **-ande** a4 efficient; competent; en ~ kraft a competent person; se äv. duglig

dugg s7 **1** (regn) drizzle **2** inte ett ~ not a bit (scrap), not the least; det är inte värt ett ~ it is not worth a farthing (jot); inte bry sig ett ~ om not care a fig for; hon gör aldrig ett ~ she never does a thing

dugg|a drizzle; det ~r it is drizzling; det ~de [med] ansökningar applications came pouring in **-regn** drizzle **-regna** se dugga

duglig [ˣdu:g-] a1 able; capable (till of; till att of + ing-form); competent, qualified, efficient **-het** competence; capability; ability; efficiency

duk s2 cloth; (bord-) tablecloth; (målar- o. sjö.) canvas; (film-) screen; (flagga) flag, bunting

1 duka ~ [*bordet*] lay the table; *bordet var ~t för två* the table was laid for two; *ett ~t bord* a table ready laid; ~ *av* clear the table; ~ *fram* put on the table; ~ *upp en historia* cook up a story
2 duka ~ *under* succumb (*för* to)
dukat ducat
dukning [-u:-] laying the (a) table
dukt *s3* strand
duktig *a1* **1** (*dugande*) able, capable, efficient (*i att* at + *ing-form*); (*skicklig*) clever, accomplished (*i ngt* at s.th.; *i att* at + *ing-form*) **2** (*käck*) brave **3** (*kraftig*) vigorous, powerful; (*frisk*) strong **4** *ett ~t mål mat* a substantial meal; *en ~ portion* a good-sized helping **5** *han fick en ~ skrapa* he got a good rating (telling-off); *det var ~t!* well done!
duktigt *adv* (*kraftigt*) powerfully; (*ihärdigt*) sturdily; (*med besked*) soundly, thoroughly; (*strängt*) hard; (*skickligt*) efficiently, cleverly; *han har arbetat ~* he has worked hard; *han tjänar ~ med pengar* he earns plenty of money; *äta ~* eat heartily; *få ~ med stryk* get a sound thrashing
dum [dumm] *a1* stupid; *AE. äv.* dumb; (*obetänksam*) silly, foolish; *han är ingen ~ karl* he is no fool; *han är inte så ~ som han ser ut* he is not such a fool as he looks; *så ~ jag var!* what a fool I was!; *det var bra ~t av mig att* I was a fool to; *det vore inte så ~t att* it would not be a bad idea to **-bom** *s2* fool, ass, blockhead; *din ~!* you silly (stupid) [fool]! **-burk** *vard.* goggle box; *särsk. AE.* boob tube **-dristig** foolhardy, rash **-dryg** vain, pompous
dumdumkula dumdum [bullet]
dum|het stupidity, folly; silliness, foolishness; *~er!* rubbish!, nonsense!; *göra en ~* do a foolish thing, (*svagare*) make a blunder; *prata ~er* talk nonsense; *vad är det här för ~er?* what is all this nonsense? **-huvud** blockhead, dolt, *AE. sl.* squarehead
dumma *rfl* make a fool of o.s.
dummerjöns tomfool
dummy [*svenskt uttal* 'dummy] *s5* dummy
dump|a **1** *hand.* dump; undersell **2** (*tippa*) dump **-er** *s2* dumper **-ing** *se dumpning*
dumpit *sup. av dimpa*
dumpning **1** dumping; underselling **2** (*tippning*) dumping
dum|skalle, -snut silly idiot
dumt *adv, bära sig ~ åt* be silly (stupid), act like a fool
dun *s7* down **-bolster** feather bed
dunder ['dunn-] *s7* thunder[ing], rumble; (*kanon-, åsk- äv.*) peal, boom; *väggen föll med ~ och brak* the wall came crashing down **dundra** thunder, rumble, boom; ~ *mot* thunder (fulminate) against; *åskan ~de* there was a clap of thunder **dundrande** *a4*, *en ~ succé* a roaring success; *ett ~ kalas* a terrific party; *sl.* a humdinger of a party
dunge *s2* grove; (*mindre*) clump of trees
dun|ig *a1* downy, fluffy **-jacka** duvet
1 dunk *s2* (*behållare*) can
2 dunk 1 *s2* (*slag*) thump **2** *s7* (*dunkande*) thud, thudding **3** *leka ~* play hide-and-seek (*AE.* hide-and-go-seek); *~ för mig!* I'm in!

dunka thud; (*bulta*) throb, beat; ~ *ngn i ryggen* thump s.b. on the back; ~ *på piano* thump on the piano
dunkel ['dunn-] **I** *a2* dusky, dark; (*hemlighetsfull*) mysterious; (*svårbegriplig*) obscure, abstruse; (*obestämd*) vague; ~ *belysning* (*uppfattning*) dim light (idea); *~t minne* dim (vague) recollection **II** *s7* dusk, shadow; gloom; dimness; *höljd i ~* wrapped in obscurity; *skingra dunklet* clear up the mystery **-blå** dark (darkish) blue
dunkning thump[ing]; throbbing
dunkudde down cushion (pillow)
duns *s2* bump, thud **dunsa** ~ *ner* come down with a thud
dunst *s3* fume, vapour, exhalation; *slå blå ~er i ögonen på ngn* pull the wool over a p.'s eyes
dunsta **1** ~ *av* (*bort, ut*) evaporate **2** *vard.* (*ge sig iväg*) make o.s. scarce, clear off (out)
dun|täcke eiderdown **-unge** fledg[e]ling, (*om pers. äv.*) greenhorn
duo ['du:ɔ] *s5* duet[te], duo
duode'nit *s3* duodenitis
duol [-'ɔ:l *el.* -'å:l] *s3, mus.* duplet
dupera dupe, bluff; *låta sig ~s* [allow o.s. to] be duped
dup'lett *s3, se dubblett*
duplicera duplicate **dupliceringsmaskin** duplicator **dupli'kat** *s7* duplicate **duplikation** duplication **duplikator** [-ˣa:tår] *s3* duplicator **duplo** ['du:plɔ] *in* ~ in duplicate
dur *s3* major; *gå i* ~ be in the major key
durabel *a2* durable; (*präktig*) splendid
durackord major chord
duraluminium duralumin
duration duration
durk *s2, sjö.* floor; (*förvaringsrum*) storeroom; (*ammunitions-, krut-*) magazine
durka bolt, run away
durkdriven (*fullfjädrad*) thoroughpaced, thoroughgoing, cunning, crafty; (*skicklig*) practised
durkslag strainer, colander
duroplast thermosetting plastic
durra *s1, s4* durra, Guinea corn, Indian millet
dur|skala major scale **-tonart** major key
dus *n, se sus 2*
dusch *s2* shower [bath] **duscha** take (have) a shower; (*ge en dusch*) [give a] shower
dusch|draperi shower curtain **-kabin** shower cabin **-rum** shower room
dusk *s7* drizzle **duska** drizzle **duskig** *a1* drizzly **duskväder** drizzly weather
duskål *dricka ~* (*ung.*) drink to the use of Christian names
dussin *s7* dozen; *ett halvt ~* half a dozen; *två ~ knivar* two dozen knives; *tretton på ~et* thirteen to the dozen **-människa** commonplace person **-roman** *vard.* potboiler, penny-dreadful; *AE.* pulp novel **-tal** *s7* dozen; *i ~* by the dozen **-tals** [-a:-] dozens of **-vara** cheap-line article **-vis** by the dozen
dust *s3* (*strid*) tussle, clash, bout; *bildl. äv.* tilt; *ha en ~ med* have a tussle (bout) with; *det blir en hård ~* it will be a tough fight; *utstå många ~er* have many a tussle, take a lot of knocks
dusör gratuity, fee; (*dricks*) tip
duv|a *s1* pigeon; dove (*äv. bildl. o. poet.*); *-or*

och hökar (polit.) doves and hawks **-blå** pigeon-blue

duven *a3 (avslagen)* flat, insipid, vapid; *(dåsig)* drowsy

duv|grå dove-grey **-hök** goshawk **-kulla** *s1, se skogsstjärna*

duvning [-u:-] **1** *(avbasning)* upbraiding, dressing-down; *(handgriplig)* hiding **2** *(inpluggande)* coaching; *ge ngn en ~* coach a p.

duv|slag dovecot[e] **-unge** young pigeon; *hon är ingen ~* she is no chicken

dvala *s1 (halvslummer)* doze, drowse; *(halv medvetslöshet)* trance, coma; *bildl. äv.* torpor, apathy; *ligga i ~ (vintertid)* lie dormant, hibernate

dvaldes [-a:-] *imperf. av dväljas*

dvalliknande [-a:-] lethargic; torpid; trance-like

dvalts [-a:-] *sup. av dväljas*

dvs. *(förk. för det vill säga)* i.e.

dväljas *dvaldes dvalts el. v2, dep* dwell, abide, sojourn

dvärg [-j] *s2* dwarf, *(sagofigur äv.)* gnome; pygmy; *(på cirkus)* midget

dvärg|alåt whining **-björk** dwarf birch **-folk** pygmaean people; pygmies *(pl)* **-hund** miniature (toy) dog **-palm** dwarf fan palm, palmetto **-stjärna** dwarf star **-tall** *se martall* **-träd** dwarf tree **-växt 1** *(dvärgform av växt)* dwarf plant **2** *(förkrympt utveckling)* dwarfishness, dwarfism; *vara av ~* be dwarf-sized, be stunted

d.y. *(förk. för den yngre) se under yngre*

dy *s3* mud, sludge; *bildl.* mire, slough **-blöt** *se dyvåt*

dyckert ['dyck-] *s2* brad

dyft *endast i uttr.: inte ett ~, se dugg* 2

dygd *s3* virtue; *(kyskhet äv.)* chastity; *~ens väg* the path of virtue; *göra en ~ av nödvändigheten* make a virtue of necessity **dygdemönster** paragon of virtue **dygdig** *a1* virtuous

dygn [dyŋn] *s7* day [and night], twenty-four hours; *~et om* throughout the twenty-four hours, twice (all) round the clock; *en gång om ~et* once in twenty-four hours, once a day

dygns|gammal one-day-old **-lång** *en ~ färd* a twenty-four-hour trip **-rytm** daily rhythm

dyig *a1* muddy, sludgy, miry

dyk|a *v3 el.* dök *dykt* dive; *(hastigt)* duck [under the surface]; *(om flygplan äv.)* nose dive; *~ ner* dive down, plunge (*i* into); *~ upp* emerge (*ur* out of), *bildl.* crop (turn) up, *(om tanke e.d.)* suggest itself **-and** diving (sea) duck

dykardräkt diving suit (dress)

dykar|e 1 diver **2** *zool.* diving beetle **-glasögon** diving (scuba) mask **-hjälm** diver's helmet **-klocka** diving bell **-sjuka** decompression sickness (illness), *vard.* the bends **-utrustning** diving outfit (equipment)

dyk'dalb *s3* dolphin

dykläge [-y:-] *(om ubåt)* in the awash position; *(om flygplan)* ready for diving

dykning [-y:-] diving; *konkr.* dive, plunge; *flyg.* nose dive; *(ubåts)* submergence, submersion, *(snabb)* crash dive

dylik *a5* of that kind (sort), like that, such, similar; *eller (och) ~t* or (and) the like, et cetera; *ngt ~t* something of the sort

dymedelst by that (those) means

dymling dowel [pin]

dymmel|onsdag Wednesday in Holy Week **-vecka[n]** [the] Holy Week

dyn 1 *s3 (sand-)* dune **2** *r (kraftenhet)* dyne

dyna *s1* cushion; pad *(äv. stämpel-)*

dynam|ik *s3* dynamics *(pl, behandlas som sg)* **-isk** [-'na:-] *a5* dynamic

dyna'mit *s3* dynamite **-ard** [-'a:rd] *s3* dynamiter **-patron** stick of dynamite, dynamite cartridge

dynamo [ˣdy:-, 'dy:- *el.* -'na:-] *s5* dynamo **-meter** [-'me:-] *s2* dynamometer

dynas'ti *s3* dynasty

dyng|a dung, muck; *(gödsel)* manure **-bagge** dung beetle (chafer) **-grep[e]** *s2* muckrake **-hög** dunghill

dyning swell; *i sht bildl.* backwash

dynt *s2, s4* bladder worm

dypöl [mud] puddle

dyr *a1* **1** dear; *(kostsam)* expensive, costly; *det blir ~t i längden* it comes expensive in the long run; *det är ~t att leva här* living is expensive here; *det kommer att stå dig ~t* I'll make you pay for that **2** *(älskad)* dear; *(högtidlig)* solemn; *svära en ~ ed* swear a solemn oath **3** *nu var goda råd ~a* here was a dilemma, now we were in a pickle **-bar** *a1 (kostsam)* costly, expensive, dear **2** *(värdefull)* valuable; *(högt värderad)* precious **-barhet 1** *abstr.* costliness *etc.* **2** *konkr.* expensive article; *~er* valuables **-grip** *s2* treasure

dyrk *s2* skeleton key, passkey, picklock

1 dyrka *~ upp (lås)* pick

2 dyrka *(tillbedja)* worship; *(starkt beundra)* adore

dyrkan *r* worship; adoration **dyrkansvärd** *a1* adorable

dyrkfri burglar-proof

dyr|köpt [-çö:pt] *a4* dearly-bought; *(om seger o.d.)* hard-earned **-ort** cost-of-living index locality

dyrorts|grupp cost-of-living index region **-gruppering** regional division according to cost of living **-tillägg** area (local) allowance

dyrt [-y:-] *adv* **1** *(om kostnad)* dearly, expensively; *bo ~* pay a high rent; *köpa (sälja) ~* buy (sell) dear; *han fick ~ betala sitt misstag* he paid heavily (dear) for his mistake; *stå ngn ~* cost s.b. dear; *sälja sitt liv ~* sell one's life dearly **2** *(högt)* dearly **3** *(högtidligt)* solemnly; *lova ~* promise solemnly, vow

dyrtid period of high prices **dyrtidstillägg** cost-of-living allowance

dys *s3,* **dysa** *s1* spray nozzle

dyscha *s1,* **dyscha'tell** *s3* couch

dysente'ri *s3* dysentery

dys|funk'tion dysfunction **-le'xi** *s3* dyslexia **-pep'si** *s3* dyspepsia

dysprosium [-'prɔ:-] *s8* dysprosium

dyster ['dyst-] *a2* gloomy, dreary; *(till sinnes)* melancholy, sad; *~ färg* sombre colour **dysterhet** gloominess, dreariness; melancholy, sadness **dystra** *~ till* get down in the dumps

dyvelsträck asafoetida

dyvika *s1, sjö.* plug

dyvåt soaking wet, wet through

då I *adv* **1** *demonstr.* then; at that time, in those days; (*senast vid den tiden*) by then; (*i så fall*) then, in that case; *~ och då* now and then, once in a while; *det var ~ det* things were different then; *~ för tiden* at that time, in those days; *nå, ~ så!* well, then!; *vad nu ~?* what now?; *än sen ~?* what then (next)?, *vard.* so what?; (*har du läst brevet?*) *vilket ~?* which one?; (*sitt inte uppe för länge*) *~ blir du för trött* or you will be too tired **2** *rel.* (*om tid*) when; (*i vilket fall*) in which case; *den tid kommer ~* the time will come when; *nu ~ vi* now that we **II** *konj* **1** (*temporal*) when; (*med participialkonstruktion*) on; *~ jag fick se honom tänkte jag* on seeing him I thought; *just ~* just as **2** (*kausal*) as, since; *~ så är förhållandet* that being the case; *~ vädret nu är vackert* since the weather is fine now, the weather being fine now

dåd *s7* deed, act; (*bragd*) feat, exploit; *med råd och ~* by word and act; *bistå ngn med råd och ~* give s.b. advice and assistance **-kraftig** energetic, active **-lust** eagerness to achieve great things **-lysten** eager to achieve [great things] **-lös** inactive, inert

dåförtiden ['då-] *då för tiden* at that time, in those days

dålig *~t sämre sämst* **1** bad; (*otillräcklig, skral*) poor; (*otillfredsställande*) unsatisfactory; (*sämre*) inferior; (*ond*) evil, wicked; (*usel*) mean, base; *en ~ affär* a bad bargain; *~ andedräkt* bad breath; *~t hjärta* a weak heart; *på ~t humör* in a bad temper; *~ hörsel* bad hearing; *~ kvalitet* poor (inferior, bad) quality; *~ luft* bad air; *han är ingen ~ människa* there is no harm in him; *~t rykte* (*samvete*) a bad reputation (conscience); *~ sikt* poor visibility; *~ smak* bad taste (*äv. bildl.*); *komma i ~t sällskap* get into bad company; *~a tider* bad (hard) times; *~a vanor* bad habits; *det var inte ~t!* that's not bad! **2** (*sjuk*) ill, not quite well; indisposed; poorly; *AE. äv.* mean; *känna sig ~* feel out of sorts, feel bad (*AE. äv.* mean)

dålighet *vara ute på ~er* (*vard.*) be out on the spree, paint the town red

dåligt *adv* badly; poorly; *affärerna går ~* business is bad; *höra ~* hear badly; *ha det ~ [ställt]* be badly off; *det gick ~ för henne i franska* she did badly in French; *det är ~ med respekten* there is a lack of respect; *det blir ~ med päron i år* there will not be many pears this year; *se ~* have poor sight (weak eyes); *äta ~* have a poor appetite

dån *s3, bot.* hemp nettle

dån *s7* noise, roar[ing]; thunder; rumble

dåna (*dundra*) roar, boom; thunder; rumble

dåna (*svimma*) faint [away], swoon [away]

dåndimpen *s i uttr.: få ~* have a fainting-fit

dåra infatuate, bewitch **-aktig** *a1* foolish; (*starkare*) idiotic, insane, mad **-aktighet** foolishness; idiocy, madness; *en ~* a [piece of] folly

dåre *s2* madman (*fem.* madwoman), lunatic; (*friare*) fool **-fink** nut **-hus** lunatic asylum; *AE., vard.* booby-hatch; *ett rent ~* bedlam **-skap** *s3* [piece of] folly; *rena ~en* sheer madness (folly)

dåsa doze, be drowsy **dåsig** *a1* drowsy, half asleep **dåsighet** drowsiness

dåtida *oböjligt a* the...of that time **dåtiden** en-

ligt *~s* sed according to the customs of that time (day)

dåvarande *a4* the...of that time, then; *~ fröken A.* Miss A., as she was then; *i sakernas ~ läge* in the then [existing] state of affairs; *under ~ förhållanden* as things were then

d.ä. (*förk. för den äldre*) *se under äldre*

däck *s7* **1** (*fartygs-*) deck; *alle man på ~!* all hands on deck!; *under ~* below deck; *under hatches* **2** (*bil-*) tyre; *AE.* tire; *slanglöst ~* tubeless tyre **däcka** *sjö.* deck **däckad** *a5* decked

däckel *s2, boktr.* tympan, packing; (*papperstillverkning*) deckle, deckel

däcks|befäl ship's officers (*pl*) **-hus** deckhouse **-last** deck cargo **-personal** deck staff **-stol** deck chair

dädan from there, thence

dägg|a suck[le] **-djur** mammal

däld *s3* dell, glen

dämma *v2* dam, bank up, stem, block; *~ för* (*igen, till, upp*) dam up **dämmare** *mus.* damper

dämp|a moderate, check; (*starkare*) subdue; (*ljud*) muffle, hush; (*färg äv.*) tone down, soften; (*eld*) damp [down], extinguish; (*instrument*) mute; *bildl. äv.* damp, calm; (*vrede e.d.*) subdue, suppress; (*en boll*) trap; *med ~d röst* in a hushed (subdued) voice **-ning** moderation *etc.*

dän [-ä:-] away; *gå ~!* go away!

däng *s7* walloping **dänga** *v2* **1** (*slå*) wallop; smack **2** *~ iväg* rush off; *~ till ngn* strike s.b.

där **1** *demonstr.* there; *~ borta* (*framme, inne, nere, uppe, etc.*) over (on *el.* up, in, down, up *etc.*) there; *~ hemma* at home; *~ har vi det!* there you are!; *~ sa du ett sant ord* you hit the nail on the head there; *~ ser du* I told you so; *så ~* like that, in that way; *vem ~?* who's there?; *det finns ingenting ~* there is nothing there **2** *rel.* where; *ett hus ~ man* a house where (in which) you

där|'an *vara illa ~* be in a bad way; *vara nära ~ att* come near + ing-form **-av** of (by; from; off, out of; with) it (that, them); *~ blev ingenting* nothing came of it; *~ följer att* hence (from that) it follows that; *~ kommer det sig att* that's [the reason] why; *fem barn, ~ tre pojkar* five children, three of them boys; *i anledning (till följd) ~* on that account

där|efter ['dä:r-] after (for; about; according to; by) that (it, them); (*om tid äv.*) afterwards; (*därnäst*) then; *ett par dagar ~* a few days later; *först ~ känner man sig* not until after that will you feel; *resultatet blev ~* the result was as might have been expected; *rätta sig ~* conform to it (that) **-emellan** between them; (*om tid*) in between; (*stundtals*) at times **-emot 1** (*emot det*) against it **2** (*emellertid*) on the other hand; (*tvärtom*) on the contrary; *då ~* whereas, while **-est** if; (*ifall*) in case; *~ icke* unless

därför ['dä:r-] **I** *adv* for (to; of; before; on; in) it (that, them); *han kunde inte ange ngt skäl ~* he could give no reason for this; *till stöd ~* in support of it **II** *konj* therefore; (*i början av sats*) so, consequently, accordingly, for that reason, on that account; *~ att* because; *det var ~ som* that is [the reason] why; *det var just ~*

som it was just on that account that

där'hän 1 (*så långt*) so far, to that point; to such an extent; *det har gått ~ att* it has gone so far that **2** *lämna det ~* leave it at that

där'i in that (it, the matter, the letter *etc.*); (*i detta avseende*) in that respect; (*vari*) in which; *~ ligger skillnaden* that is where the difference is; *~ misslyckades han fullständigt* he failed completely there

där|ibland ['dä:r-] among them (others; other things); including **-ifrån** from there (it, the place *etc.*); *~ och dit* from there to there; *borta* (*bort*) *~* away, gone; *jag reser ~ i morgon* I shall be leaving [there] tomorrow; *han bor inte långt ~* he lives not so far away [from there]; *långt ~* (*bildl.*) far from it **-igenom 1** (*från det*) through it (them, the room *etc.*) **2** (*med hjälp därav, medelst detta*) thereby; by that [means], by this, in this way; *redan ~ är mycket vunnet* even this is a step in the right direction

därjämte ['dä:r-] besides, in addition

därmed ['dä:r-] **1** (*med detta*) by (with) that (it, them, that remark *etc.*); *i enlighet ~* accordingly; *i samband ~* in this connection; *~ gick han sin väg* with that (those words) he departed; *~ var saken avgjord* that settled the matter; *~ är inte sagt att* that is not to say that; *~ är mycket vunnet* that helps a great deal; *~ är vi inne på* that brings us to; *och ~ basta!* and that's that!; *och ~ jämförliga varor* and other similar goods **2** (*medelst detta*) by that (those) means **3** (*följaktligen*) so, consequently

därnäst ['dä:r-] next, in the next place; *den ~ följande* the one immediately following

därom ['dä:r-] **1** *rumsbet.* of it; *norr* (*till höger*) *~* to the north (to the right) of it **2** (*angående den saken*) about (concerning, as to) that (it, the matter *etc.*), on (to, in, of) that; *~ tvista de lärde* on that point the scholars disagree; *~ är vi eniga* we agree about that; *vittna ~* bear witness to that

därpå ['dä:r-, *äv.* -'på] **1** *rumsbet.* [up]on (in; to; at) it (them *etc.*) **2** *tidsbet.* after that; (*sedan äv.*) then, afterwards; (*därnäst*) next; *dagen ~* the following (next) day; *strax ~* immediately afterwards **3** *bildl.* [up]on (of, by, to) it (them *etc.*); *ett bevis ~ är* a proof of it (that) is; *ta miste ~* mistake it

därstädes there

därtill ['dä:r-, *äv.* -'till] **1** to (for; into; of; at; towards) it (that, them *etc.*); *~ behövs pengar* for that money is required; *~ bidrog också* a contributory factor was; *~ hör också* to that category also belong; *~ kommer* to that must be added, then there is; *anledningen ~ är okänd* the reason for that is unknown; *med ~ hörande* with the ... belonging to it (relating thereto); *med allt vad ~ hör* with everything that goes with it; *med hänsyn ~* in consideration of that **2** (*därutöver*) in addition, besides

därunder ['dä:r-, *äv.* -'un-] **1** *rumsbet.* under (beneath, below) it (that *etc.*) **2** (*om tid*) during the time; while it (*etc.*) lasts (lasted); meanwhile; *~ fick han* while doing so he received **3** *barn på sex år och ~* children of six and under; *äpplen till ... och ~* apples at ... and

less

däruppå ['dä:r-] *se därpå*

därur ['dä:r-] out of it

därutöver ['dä:r-] above [that]; *vad ~ är* the rest is; *önskas ngt ~* should you require anything more; *jfr däröver*

därvarande *a4* local; residing (stationed) there

därvid ['dä:r-, *äv.* -'vid] **1** *rumsbet.* at (in; on; along; by; near; close to; beside; of; to; over) it (that, them *etc.*) **2** (*om tid*) at (during) it (the time *etc.*), on that occasion, then; in doing so, when that happens; *~ bör man helst* when that happens it is best to; *~ föll han och* in doing so he fell and; *~ upptäckte man* then (on that being done) it was discovered; *och sade ~* saying in doing so; (*ett sammanträde hölls*) *och* *~ beslöts* during which it was decided **3** *~ blev det* it was left at that; *fästa avseende ~* pay attention to that

därvidlag ['dä:r-] in that respect; on that point (subject); *~ måste man vara försiktig* great care must be taken in this respect

däråt ['dä:r-] at (to; in; [out] of; over) it (that *etc.*); *den kostade 15 pund eller någonting ~* it cost 15 pounds or something like that

däröver ['dä:r-, *äv.* -'över] over (above; across; of; at) it (that, them *etc.*); *~ i USA* over there in the USA; *100 pund och ~* 100 pounds and upwards; *jfr därutöver*

däst [-ä:-] *a1* (*tjock o. fet*) obese; (*övermätt*) full up, gorged

däven *a3* damp, moist

dävert ['dä:-] *s2, sjö.* davit

dö *dog dött* die; *~ av skratt* die with laughter; *~ av svält* (*törst, ålderdom*) die of starvation (thirst, old age); *~ bort* die away; *~ en naturlig död* die a natural death; *~ för egen hand* die by one's own hand; *~ för fosterlandet* die for one's country; *~ i lunginflammation* die o' pneumonia; *~ ifrån hustru och barn* die leaving wife and children; *~ ut* die out (off), (*om ätt äv.*) become extinct; *så nyfiken så jag kan* *~* I am dying of curiosity; *vinden mojnade och dog* the wind died down

döbattang folding door

död I *s2* death; (*frånfälle*) decease, demise; *~en i grytan* (*bibl.*) death in the pot, *vard.* a sure death; *~en inträdde efter några timmar* he (she) died after a few hours; *~en var ögonblicklig* death was instantaneous; *det blir min ~* it will be the death of me; *du är ~ens om* you are a dead man (woman *etc.*) if; *ligga för ~en* be dying, be at death's door; *gå i ~en för* die for; *in i* (*intill*) *~en* unto death; *ta ~ på* kill [off], exterminate; *strid på liv och ~* life and death struggle; *pina ngn till ~s* torture s.b. to death; *vara ~ens lammunge* be done for I *a1* dead; *den ~e* (*~a*) the dead man (woman *etc.*), the deceased; *de ~a* the dead; *~a* (*tidningsrubrik*) deaths; *~a, sårade och saknade* killed, wounded and missing; *~ för världen* dead to the world; *~ mans grepp* dead man's handle (pedal); *~ punkt* (*tekn.*) dead centre (point), (*-läge*) deadlock, *bildl.* dull moment; *~ vinkel* dead (blind) angle; *bollen är ~* the ball is out of play; *falla ~ ner* fall down dead; *Döda havet* the Dead Sea; *dött kapital* (*språk.*) dead

capital (language); *dött lopp* dead heat
döda 1 kill (*äv. bildl.*) **2** (*växel, inteckning, motbok*) cancel; (*konto*) close; (*check äv.*) stop
Dödahavsrullarna [-ˣhavs-] the Dead Sea Scrolls
död|ande I *s6* killing *etc.* **II** *a4* killing; fatal; *ett ~ slag* a mortal blow **III** *adv*, *~ tråkig* deadly dull **-dagar** *pl*, *till ~* till death, to one's dying day **-dansare** bore; *vard.* spoilsport, wet blanket **-full** blind [drunk] **-född** *a5* stillborn; (*friare*) abortive; *-fött förslag* abortive project **-förklara** officially declare...dead **-förklaring** official declaration of death **-grävare 1** gravedigger, sexton **2** *zool.* burying beetle, sexton **-gång** *tekn.* backlash, play **-kött** proud flesh; *med.* granulation tissue
dödlig [ˣdö:d-] *a1* deadly; mortal, fatal, lethal; *~ dos* lethal dose; *sjukdomen fick ~ utgång* the illness was fatal; *en vanlig ~* an ordinary mortal **dödlighet** mortality **dödlighetsprocent** death (*särsk. AE.* mortality) rate
död|ligt [ˣdö:d-] *adv* mortally, fatally; *vara ~ kär* be madly in love **-läge** deadlock, stalemate **-period** slack period
döds|aning premonition of death **-annons** obituary [notice] **-attest, -bevis** death certificate **-blek** deadly pale, livid
dödsbo estate [of a deceased person] **-delägare** party to an estate; (*arvtagare äv.*) heir, inheritor **-förvaltare** estate administrator (executor), trustee
döds|bricka identification (identity) disc **-bringande** *a4* deadly **-bud** news of a p.'s death **-bädd** deathbed; *på ~en* on one's deathbed **-cell** death cell **-dag** *ngns ~* day (anniversary) of a p.'s death **-dans** dance of death; danse macabre **-dom** death sentence **-dömd** *a5* sentenced to death; *bildl.* doomed; (*sjuk*) given up [by the doctors]; *hon är ~* there is no hope for her **-fall** death; (*säljs*) *på grund av ~* owing to decease of owner (*etc.*) **-fara** mortal danger **-fiende** mortal enemy; deadly foe **-fruktan** fear of death **-fälla** deathtrap **-förakt** contempt of death **-föraktande** *a4* intrepid **-förskräckt** *a4* terrified; *vara ~ för ngt* be frightened (scared) to death of s.th. **-hjälp** mercy killing; *med.* euthanasia
dödskalle death's-head, skull **-fjäril** death's--head moth
döds|kamp death struggle, agony **-körning** fatal car accident **-lik** deathlike, deathly **-mask** death mask **-märkt** *a4, vara ~* be marked by death; fey **-mässa** Requiem **-offer** victim, fatal casualty; *olyckan krävde ett ~* the accident claimed one victim **-olycka** fatal accident **-orsak** cause of death **-riket** the kingdom of the dead; Hades, hell **-rossling** death rattle **-runa** obituary [notice] **-ryckningar** *pl* death throes (*äv. bildl.*) **-siffra** death toll **-sjuk** dying, moribund **-skri** dying shriek **-skugga** shadow of death **-stilla** *a4* deathly still **-straff** capital punishment, death penalty; *förbjudet vid ~* forbidden on pain of death **-stråle** death ray **-stöt** deathblow **-synd** mortal (deadly) sin **-trött** *a4* dog-tired, tired to death **-tyst** *a4* silent as the grave **-tystnad** dead silence **-ur** *zool.* deathwatch beetle **-ångest** agony [of

death]; *bildl.* mortal (deadly) fear **-år** *ngns ~* the year of a p.'s death **-ängel** angel of death
död|säsong off-season (slack) period **-vatten** (*bildl.*) deadlock; *råka i ~* reach a deadlock **-vikt** deadweight **-viktton** deadweight ton
döende dying, moribund
dög *imperf. av* duga
dök *imperf. av* dyka
dölja *dolde dolt* hide; conceal (*för* from); (*överskyla*) disguise; *bakom signaturen ... döljer sig ...is* the pen name of
döma [ˣdömma] *v2* **1** (*be-*) judge (*efter* by); *~ andra efter sig själv* judge others by o.s.; *~ ngn för hårt* be too severe in one's judgment of s.b. **2** (*avkunna dom över*) sentence, condemn; *~ ngn till böter* fine s.b.; *~ ngn till döden* sentence s.b. to death; *~ ngn skyldig till stöld* find s.b. guilty of theft; *dömd att misslyckas* doomed to failure **3** (*fälla omdöme*) judge (*om, över* of); *av allt att ~* to all appearances; *av omständigheterna* (*utseendet*) *att ~* judging from circumstances (by appearances); *mänskligt att ~* as far as one can judge; *döm om min förvåning* judge of (imagine) my surprise **4** (*avkunna dom*) pronounce sentence (*över* on); (*friare*) pronounce judgment (*över* on); (*i fotboll, boxning m.m.*) referee; (*i fri idrott*) judge; (*i kricket, baseball, tennis*) umpire
döp|a *v3* baptize; (*barn, fartyg*) christen; *han -tes till John* he was christened (given the name of) John **-are** baptizer, baptist; *Johannes D~n* John the Baptist **-else** baptism
dörj *s2* (*fiskredskap*) handline **dörja** fish by handline
dörr *s2* door; *följa ngn till ~en* see s.b. out; *gå från ~ till ~* go from door to door; *inom lyckta ~ar* behind closed doors, in camera, *parl.* in a secret session; *stå för ~en* (*bildl.*) be imminent ([near] at hand); *visa ngn på ~en* turn s.b. out, show s.b. the door; *öppna ~ens politik* open--door policy **-handtag** [door]knob **-karm** doorframe, doorcase **-klapp** knocker **-klocka** doorbell **-knackare** door-to-door salesman, hawker **-lås** [door] lock **-matta** doormat **-nyckel** latchkey, doorkey **-post** doorjamb, doorpost **-spegel** door panel **-springa** chink of the door **-stopp[are]** doorstop **-stängare** door closer **-tröskel** doorsill; doorstep **-vakt** doorkeeper; (*t.ex. på hotell*) doorman **-vred** *se* -handtag **-öppning** doorway
dös *s2* dolmen
dösnack *s7, vard.* gibberish, chatter, twaddle **dösnacka** talk rubbish (rot), twaddle, chatter
dött *sup. av* dö
döv *a1* deaf (*för* to); *~ på ena örat* deaf in one ear; *tala för ~a öron* talk to deaf ears
döv|a deafen; alleviate; *bildl.* stun, benumb; *~ hungern* still one's hunger; *~ sitt samvete* silence one's conscience; *~ smärtorna* deaden the pains **-het** deafness **-lärare** teacher of the deaf **-skola** school for the deaf **-stum** deaf--and-dumb, deaf-mute; *en ~* a deaf-mute **-stumhet** deaf-muteness, deaf-mutism **-öra** *mest i uttr.: slå ~t till* turn a deaf ear (*för* to)

E

EAN *förk.* för European Article Numbering
eau-de-cologne [ådökå'lånj] *s5* cologne, Cologne water, eau de Cologne
eau-de-vie [ådö'vi:] *s5* brandy
ebb *s3;* ~ *och flod* ebb and flow; *det är* ~ it is low tide; *det är* ~ *i kassan* my (*etc.*) funds are low, I am (*etc.*) short of money **ebba** ~ *ut* ebb [away], peter out
ebenholts [-å-] *s3, s4* ebony **-svart** [as black as] ebony **-trä** ebony
ebo'nit *s3* vulcanite, ebonite; hard rubber
echaufferad [eʃå'fe:-] *a5* hot [and bothered]
ecklesias'tik|departement ~*et* the [Swedish] ministry of education and ecclesiastical affairs, (*i Storbritannien, ung.*) the ministry of education **-minister** minister of education and ecclesiastical affairs, (*i Storbritannien, ung.*) minister of education
Ecuador [ekua'då:r] *n* Ecuador **ecuadori'an** *s3,* **ecuadoriansk** [-'a:nsk] *a5* Ecuador[i]an **e.d.** (*förk. för eller dylikt*) *se under dylik*
ed *s3* oath; *avlägga* ~ take an oath, swear; *gå* ~ *på* take one's oath upon, swear to; *gå* ~ *på att* swear that; *låta ngn gå* ~ *på* take a p.'s oath; *under* ~ on (upon, under) oath
edamerost [ˣe:dam-] Edam
EDB (*förk. för elektronisk databehandling*) E.D.P. (electronic data processing)
edda *s1* Edda; *äldre (poetiska)* E~*n* Elder (Poetic) Edda; *yngre (prosaiska)* E~*n* Younger (Prose) Edda **-diktning** Eddaic poetry **-kväde** Eddaic poem (song)
edelweiss [ˣe:delvais *el.* 'e:del-] *s3* edelweiss
Eden ['e:den] *n* Eden; ~*s lustgård* Garden of Eden
eder ['e:-] *se er*
edera edit
edgång swearing
e'dikt *s7* edict
e'dil *s3* aedile
edition edition
edlig [ˣe:d-] *a1* sworn; *under* ~ *förpliktelse* under oath
eds|avläggelse taking of an oath **-förbund** confederation
edsvuren *a5* sworn
E-dur E major
EEG (*förk. för elektroencefalogram*) EEG (electroencephalogram)
EES-avtal *ung.* European Economic Cooperation Agreement
efe'drin *s3, med.* ephedrin[e]
efeme'rid *s3, astr.* ephemeris **-sekund** ephemeris second **-tid** ephemeris time
efe'mär *a1* ephemeral
efes[i]er [e'fe:-] Ephesian **-brevet** Ephesians (*pl, behandlas som sg*) *eg.* the Epistle of Paul the Apostle to the Ephesians
ef'fekt *s3* **1** (*verkan*) effect; *göra god (dålig)* ~ produce (make, have) a good (bad) effect **2** *tekn.* power, efficiency; (*maskins*) output, capacity **3** (*föremål*) ~*er* goods [and chattels], effects; *kvarglömda* ~ lost property; *expedition för tillvaratagna* ~ lost property office; *jfr reseffekter* **-full** striking, effective **-förvaring** left-luggage office, cloakroom; *AE.* checkroom
effek'tiv *a1* effective, efficient, efficacious, effectual; (*verklig*) actual; ~ *arbetstid* actual working hours; ~ *avkastning* actual yield; ~ *hästkraft* brake horsepower; ~ *ränta* effective (actual) rate [of interest]; ~*t värmevärde* net calorific (*AE.* heating) value **-[is]era** make more effective (efficient), increase the capacity of **-itet** efficiency, effectiveness, capacity **-värde** *elektr.* root mean square value
effektsökeri straining (striving) after effect
effektuera execute, accomplish, fulfil, carry out
effeminerad [-'ne:-] *a5* effeminated
efor [e'få:r] *s3* ephor
efter ['ef-] **I** *prep* **1** after; (*bakom äv.*) behind; [*omedelbart*] ~ on, immediately after; ~ *att ha sett pjäsen* after seeing (having seen) the play; ~ *avslutat arbete* when work is over; ~ *en timme* (*vanl.*) an hour later; ~ *Kristi födelse* (*e.Kr.*) anno Domini (A.D.); ~ *mottagandet av* on receipt of; *den ena* ~ *den andra* one after the other; *göra rent* ~ *sig* clean up after one; *stå* ~ *ngn i kön* stand behind s.b. in the queue (*AE.* line); *stå* ~ *ngn på listan* be after s.b. ón the list; *vara* ~ *de andra* (*äv. bildl.*) be behind the others; *vara* ~ *sin tid* be behind the times; *han lämnade en väska* ~ *sig* he left a bag behind [him]; *hon heter Anna* ~ *sin mamma* she is called Anna after her mother, Anna is named after her mother; *hon är klen* ~ *sjukdomen* she is frail after her illness; *stäng dörren* ~ *dig.* shut the door after (behind) you! **2** (*utmed*) along; (*nedför*) down; (*uppför*) up; ~ *kanten* along the edge; *fukten rann* ~ *väggarna* the walls were glistening with moisture **3** (*beteckande mål el. syfte*) for; *annonsera* (*ringa, skicka, skriva*) ~ advertise (ring, send, write) for; *böja sig* ~ *ngt* stoop to pick up s.th.; *jaga* ~ *popularitet* run after popularity; *sökandet* ~ the search for; *polisen var* ~ *honom* the police were after him **4** (*från*) from; (*efterlämnad av*) of; *arvet* ~ *föräldrarna* the inheritance from one's parents; *märken* ~ *fingrarna* marks of the fingers; *spela* ~ *noter* play from music; *trött* ~ *resan* tired from the journey; *utplåna spåren* ~ obliterate the tracks of; *hon är änka* ~ *en kapten* she is the widow of a captain **5** (*enligt*) according to; (*med ledning av äv.*) by; *from, on, to;* (*efter förebild el. mönster av äv.*) after; ~ *bästa förmåga* to the best of one's ability; ~ *gällande priser* at present prices; ~ *min uppfattning* in (according to) my opinion; ~ *mått* to measure; ~ *vad de säger* according to them; ~ *vad du har gjort så skall du inte klaga* after what you have done, you shouldn't complain; ~ *vad jag har hört* from what I have heard; ~ *vad jag vet* as far as I know; *inga spår att gå* ~ no clues to go by; *gå* ~ *kompass* walk by the compass; *klädd* ~ *senaste modet* dressed after the latest fashion; *ordna* ~ *storlek* arrange according to size; *rätta sig* ~ conform to; *segla*

~ *stjärnorna* sail by the stars; *spela* ~ *gehör* play by ear; *ställa klockan* ~ *radion* set one's watch by the radio; *sälja ngt* ~ *vikt* sell s.th. by weight; *teckna* ~ *modell* draw from a model **6** (*[in]om*) in; (*alltsedan*) since; (*räknat från*) of; ~ *den dagen har jag varit* since that day I have been; ~ *några dagar* in (after) a few days (days' time); *inom ett år* ~ *giftermålet* within a year of the marriage **7** (*i riktning mot*) at; *slå* ~ aim a blow at **8** ~ *hand* (*så småningom*) gradually, little by little, by degrees, (*steg för steg*) step by step; ~ *hand som* [according] as **II** *adv* **1** (*om tid*) after; *dagen* ~ the day after, the following day; *min klocka går* ~ my watch is slow (losing); *kort* ~ shortly after[wards] **2** (*bakom, kvar*) behind; *vara* ~ *med* be behind (*om betalning*: in arrears) with **III** *konj* **1** *vard.* (*eftersom*) since **2** ~ [*det att*] after

efter|apa imitate, ape, mimic **-apning** [-a:-] imitation, mimicry (*äv. konkr.*); (*förfalskning*) counterfeit **-behandling** after-treatment, finishing; curing; follow-up **-besiktning** supplementary (final) inspection **-beskattning** additional (supplementary) taxation **-beställning** reorder, repeat (follow-up) order **-bild** afterimage, aftersensation **-bilda** imitate, copy **-bildning** imitation, copy **-bliven** *a5* (*outvecklad*) backward; retarded; (*föråldrad*) old-fashioned, out of date **-blivenhet** backwardness **-blomstring** after-flowering **-brännkammare** afterburner **-börd** afterbirth **-börs** [exchange] dealings (*pl*) after trading hours **-dyningar** repercussions, consequences, aftereffects; aftermath (*sg*) **-forska** search for, investigate, inquire into (after) **-forskning** search (*efter* for), inquiry (*efter* about, *i* into), investigation (*i* into) **-fråga** inquire (ask) for; *mycket ~d* in great demand **-frågan** *r* **1** (*förfrågan*) inquiry **2** (*eftersökthet*) demand, request (*på* for); *livlig* (*dålig*) ~ brisk (slack) demand; *ha stor* ~ be in great demand; *tillgång och* ~ supply and demand **-följande** *a4* following, succeeding, subsequent **-följansvärd** *a5* worth following, worthy of imitation **-följare 1** (*anhängare*) follower, adherent **2** (*efterträdare*) successor **-följd** *mana till* ~ be worth imitating **-gift** *s3* **1** (*medgivande*) concession **2** (*efterskänkande*) remission **-given** [-j-] *a5* compliant, indulgent, yielding (*mot* to) **-givenhet** [-j-] indulgence, compliance, compliancy (*mot* towards, to) **-gjord** *a5* imitated; (*förfalskad*) counterfeit **-granskning** final examination (scrutiny)

1 efterhand *s, komma i* ~ take second place; *sitta i* ~ be the last player
2 efter'hand *adv, se under hand 1*
efter|hängsen *a3* importunate, persistent; *en* ~ *person* a hanger-on **-härma** imitate, copy; echo **-härmning** imitation, copy; echo **-kalkyl** cost account[ing] **-klang** lingering note, resonance; *bildl.* reminiscence; echo **-klok** *vara* ~ be wise after the event **-klokhet** hindsight **-komma** comply with, obey **-kommande I** *a4* succeeding, following **II** *s pl* (*avkomlingar*) [one's] descendants **-kontroll** supervisory control **-krav** cash on delivery (*förk.* C.O.D.); *sända varor mot* ~ send goods

C.O.D.; *uttaga genom* ~ cash (*AE.* collect) on delivery, charge forward **-krigstid** postwar period **-kälke** *komma på ~n* get behindhand, be outdistanced, (*med betalning*) be in arrears **-känning** aftereffect; *ha ~ar av* suffer from the aftereffects of **-leva** (*rätta sig efter*) observe, obey, act up to **-levande I** *a4* surviving **II** *s9* survivor **-leverans** supplementary delivery **-levnad** observance (*av* of), obedience, adherence (*av* to) **-likna** imitate; (*tävla med*) emulate (*i* in) **-lysa 1** (*person*) search for, notify as missing, send out (*i radio* broadcast) a p.'s description; post s.b. as wanted [by the police]; *vara -lyst av polisen* be wanted by the police; *-lysta arvingar* heirs sought for **2** (*sak*) advertise for, advertise as missing, search for **-lysning 1** (*av pers.*) notification of missing person, circulation (*i radio* broadcasting) of a p.'s description **2** (*av sak*) advertisement of the loss of, search for **-låten** *a5* lenient, indulgent (*mot* to, towards) **-lämna** leave [behind]; (*arv*) leave; ~ *skrifter* posthumous works, literary remains; *hans ~de förmögenhet* the fortune he left; *A:s ~de maka, fru A.* Mrs. A., widow of the late Mr. A. **-längtad** *a5* [eagerly] longed for, eagerly awaited

efter|middag afternoon; *i* ~ this afternoon; *i går* (*i morgon*) ~ yesterday (tomorrow) afternoon; *på ~en* (*~arna*) in the afternoon (afternoons); *på lördag* ~ on Saturday afternoon **-middagskaffe** afternoon coffee **-mäle** *s6* posthumous reputation; *han har fått ett gott* ~ he has been judged favourably **-namn** surname; *AE. äv.* last name **-natt** later part of the night; *på ~en* late at night **-ord** (*i bok*) epilogue, afterword **-prövning** supplementary examination **-rationalisering** hindsight wisdom **-räkning 1** (*tilläggsräkning*) additional bill **2** (*obehaglig påföljd*) unpleasant consequence **-rätt** sweet, dessert; pudding; *vard.* afters (*sg el. pl*) **-rättelse** observance, example; *lända till* ~ serve as an example, be complied with **-satt** *a4* (*försummad*) neglected; *de ~a grupperna i samhället* the underprivileged [social] groups **-siktväxel** *se avisoväxel* **-sinna** think [over], meditate [on] **-sinnande I** *a4* thoughtful, contemplative, reflecting **II** *s6* consideration, reflection; *vid närmare* ~ on second thoughts **-skalv** aftershock **-skicka** send for; *komma som ~d* arrive at the right moment **-skott** [-å-] *s7, i* ~ in arrears; *betala i* ~ pay after (on) delivery **-skrift** appendix, supplement; (*t. brev*) postscript **-skänka** (*straff*) remit, pardon; (*skuld*) remit, release **-skänkning** [-ʃ-] remission **-skörd** aftermath (*äv. bildl.*); gleanings (*pl*) **-släckning** final extinction [of a fire]; *bildl.* day-after party **-släng** *en* ~ *av* another slight bout (attack) of **-släntrare** laggard, straggler; (*sölare*) latecomer, dawdler, lingerer **-släpning** [-ä:-] lag, delay **-smak** aftertaste **-snack** *vard.* postmortem [talk]
eftersom as, seeing [that], since; (*alldenstund*) inasmuch as; (*allteftersom*) [according] as
efter|spana search for; *~d av polisen* wanted by the police **-spaning** search, inquiry; *anställa ~ar* institute a search (*efter* for), make inquiries **-spel 1** *mus.* postlude **2** epilogue;

bildl. sequel, consequences (*pl*); *saken kommer att få rättsligt* ~ the matter will have legal consequences **-sträva** aim at, strive to attain; *det ~de målet* the objective, the target aimed at **-strävansvärd** *a1* worth striving for, desirable **-stygn** backstitch **-synkronisering** playback **-sägare** repeater; echo **-sända 1** (*skicka efter*) send for **2** (*skicka vidare*) forward, send on; *-sändes* (*på brev*) please forward, to be forwarded (redirected) **-sätta** (*försumma*) neglect, disregard **-sättsblad** *bokb.* [back] flyleaf (endpaper) **-sökt** *a4* (*begärlig*) in great demand, popular, sought after; *vara mycket* ~ be in great demand

efter|tanke reflection, consideration; *utan* ~ carelessly, thoughtlessly; *vid närmare* ~ on second thoughts, on further consideration; *~ns kranka blekhet* the pale cast of thought **-tax-era** assess [for arrears] **-taxering** additional assessment [for arrears] **-trakta** *se eftersträva*; *~d* coveted **-trupp** rearguard **-tryck 1** (*kraft*) energy, vigour; *med* ~ energetically **2** (*betoning*) stress, emphasis; *ge* ~ *åt* lay stress on, emphasize; *med* ~ emphatically, with emphasis **3** (*avtryckt upplaga*) reprint; (*olovligt*) piracy; ~ *förbjudes* all rights reserved, copyright **-trycklig** *a1* **1** (*om handling*) energetic, vigorous **2** (*om yttrande*) emphatic **-träda** succeed; (*ersätta*) replace **-trädare** successor; *B:s* ~ (*förk. eftr.*) (*hand.*) Successor[s *pl*] (*förk.* Succ.) to B. **-tänksam** *a1* thoughtful; (*förståndig*) prudent, circumspect **-verkan** aftereffect **-vård** aftercare **-värkar** afterpains **-värld[en]** posterity; *gå till ~en* go (be handed) down to posterity, (*till historien*) go down in history

efteråt 1 (*senare*) afterwards, later **2** (*bakom*) behind, after

EG (*förk. för europeiska gemenskaperna*) EEC (European Economic Community)

e'gal *a1, det är mig ~t* it is all one (all the same) to me **egalisera** make uniform; establish equality

Egeiska havet [e'ge:-] the Aegean Sea

eg|en *a3* **1** (*tillhörande ngn*) own (*föregånget av genitiv el. poss. pron*); *mina -na barn* my own children; *skolans -na elever* the school's own pupils; *bilda sig en* ~ *uppfattning om* form an opinion about; *ha* ~ *bil* have a car of one's own; *ha* ~ *ingång* have a private entrance; *vara sin* ~ be one's own master; *öppna -et* (~ *affär*) start a business of one's own; *av* ~ *erfarenhet* from one's own experience; *av* ~ *fri vilja* of one's own free will; *för* ~ *del* for my (*etc.*) own part, personally; *för -et bruk* for private (personal) use; *i* ~ *hög person* in person; *tala i* ~ *sak* plead one's own cause; *i* [*sitt*] *-et hem* in one's own home; *i sitt -et intresse* in one's own interest; *i -et namn* in one's own name; *med -na ord* in one's own words; *på* ~ *begäran* on his (her) request; *på* ~ *bekostnad* at one's own expense; *på* ~ *hand* by oneself; *på -et initiativ* on one's own initiative; *stå på -na ben* stand on one's own feet **2** (*karakteristisk*) peculiar (*för* to), characteristic (*för* of) **3** (*underlig*) odd, strange

egen|art distinctive character, individuality **-ar-**

tad [-a:r-] *a5* (*säregen*) peculiar, odd **-dom** [-dɷmm] *s2* **1** (*utan pl*) property; *enskild* ~ private property; *fast* ~ real property (estate); *lös* ~ personal property, personalty; (*ägodel[ar]*) possession[s] **2** (*med pl, jordagods*) estate

egendomlig [-dɷmm-] *a1* **1** (*besynnerlig*) peculiar, strange, odd, queer, singular **2** (*utmärkande*) characteristic (*för* of), peculiar (*för* to) **-het 1** (*besynnerlighet*) peculiarity, strangeness, oddity, queerness, singularity **2** (*utmärkande drag*) characteristic [trait], peculiarity **egendoms|agent** estate (house) agent; *AE. äv.* realtor **-brott** crime involving property **-folk** *~et* (*bibl.*) the peculiar people **-gemenskap** (*fleras*) community of property; (*allas*) public (common) ownership **-lös** unpropertied, without property

egen|het peculiarity; *han har sina ~er* he has his own little ways **-händig** in one's own hand[writing], autograph; ~ *namnteckning* own (proper) signature, autograph **-händigt** *adv* with one's own hands; (*friare*) in person, oneself; ~ *bakade kakor* home-made cakes **-kär** conceited; [self-]complacent **-kärlek** conceit; [self-]complacency **-mäktig** arbitrary, high-handed; *~t förfarande* unlawful (unauthorized) interference **-namn** proper noun (name) **-nytta** selfishness, self-interest **-nyttig** selfish, self-interested **-rättfärdig** self-righteous **-rättfärdighet** self-righteousness **-sinne** wilfulness, obstinacy **-sinnig** *a1* wilful, obstinate, headstrong

egenskap *s3* **1** (*beskaffenhet*) quality; *besitta en* ~ possess a quality; *god* (*dålig*) ~ good (bad) quality **2** (*kännetecken*) attribute; (*kännemärke*) characteristic **3** (*särskild ~*) property; *järnets ~er* the properties of iron **4** (*erforderlig ~*) qualification **5** (*persons ställning, roll*) capacity, quality; *i min ~ av lärare* in my capacity of (as a) teacher

egentlig [e'jent-] *a1* **1** (*huvudsaklig, främst*) real; *det ~a syftet med* the chief (real) purpose of **2** (*verklig, sann*) real, true, intrinsic[al]; *i ordets ~a* (*motsats t. bildliga*) *betydelse* in the literal (strict, proper) sense of the word; *~a England* England proper; *~t bråk* (*mat.*) proper fraction **3** *fys.,* ~ (*specifik*) *vikt* specific gravity (weight)

egentligen [e'jent-] (*i själva verket*) really, in fact; (*med rätta*) by right[s]; ~ *borde jag gå och lägga mig* I ought to go to bed, really; ~ *är hon ganska snäll* she is really quite nice

egenvärde intrinsic value

egg *s2* edge

egg|a ~ [*upp*] egg on, incite; (*stimulera*) stimulate **-ande** *a4* inciting, incentive **-else** incitement, incentive; stimulation

egg|vapen cutting weapon; side arms (*pl*) **-verktyg** sharp-edged tool

e'gid *s3* aegis

egna'hem owner-occupied house **egnahems-lån** loan to build one's own home

ego ['e:gɷ] *n* ego, self **-centricitet** egocentricity **-centriker** [-'senn-] egocentric **-centrisk** [-'senn-] *a5* egocentric, self-centred **-ism** egoism **-ist** egoist **-istisk** *a5* egoistic[al], self-

ish **-tism** egotism **-tripp** ego trip
Egypten [e'jypp-] *n* Egypt
egypt|er, -ier [e'jypt(s)[i]er] Egyptian **-isk** *a5*
Egyptian **-iska 1** (*språk*) Egyptian **2** (*kvinna*)
Egyptian woman **-olog** Egyptologist **-ologi** *s3*
Egyptology
e'ho *åld.* whosoever
ehuru [e*hu:-] [al]though, even if
einsteinium [ain'stain-] *s8* einsteinium
ej [ejj] *se inte*; ~ *heller* nor
eja [ˣejja] ~ *vore vi där!* would we were there!
ejakul|at *s7* ejaculate, semen **-ation** ejaculation
-era ejaculate
ejder ['ej-] *s2* eider [duck] **-dun** eiderdown **-ha-
ne** eider drake, male eider **-hona** female eider
ejektor [eˣjektår] *s3* ejector, jet
ek *s2* oak; (*virke*) oak [wood]; *av* ~ (*äv.*) oak[en]
1 eka *s1* skiff, punt
2 eka *v1* echo; reverberate; resound (*äv. bildl.*)
eker ['e:-] *s2* spoke
EKG (*förk. för elektrokardiogram*) E.C.G. (elec-
trocardiogram)
ekip|age *s7* carriage [and horses], turnout; equi-
page **-era** equip, fit out **-ering** equipment,
outfit; *se äv. herrekipering*
ekivok [-'vå:k] *a1* indelicate, indecent, suggestive; dubious
eklat|ant [-'ant *el.* -'aŋt] *a1* striking; brilliant,
startling **-era** announce, make public
e'klatt I *a* official, public **II** *adv* officially, publicly
eklekt|icism eclecticism **-iker** [e'klekt-] *s9,*
-isk [e'klekt-] *a5* eclectic
e'klip|s *s3* eclipse **-tika** [e'klipp-] *s1* ecliptic
eklog [-'lå:g] *s3* eclogue
eklut [ˣe:k-] assay; *gå igenom ~en* (*bildl.*) go
through the mill
eklärera illuminate, light up
eklöv oak leaf
eko ['e:kω] *s6* echo; *ge* ~ [make an] echo
ekobrott economic crime, fraud
eko'cid *s3* ecocide
ekollon acorn
ekolod echo sounder, sonar, asdic **-ning** echo
sounding
ekolog|i *s3* ecology **-isk** *a5* ecological
ekonom economist **ekonomome'tri** *s3*
econometrics (*pl, behandlas som sg*)
ekonomi *s3* economy; (*affärsställning*) financial position, finances (*pl*); (*vetenskap*) economics (*pl, behandlas som sg*); *han har god* ~
his financial position is good **-avdelning** (*i
företag*) economic department; (*på hotell o.d.*)
catering department **-byggnad** (*på lantgård*)
farm building, annex **-chef** financial manager,
accountant **-departement** ministry of economics **-förpackning** economy pack (size)
-klass economy (tourist) class **-minister** minister of economics (for economic affairs)
ekonomisera economize **ekonomisk** [-'nå:-]
a5 economic; (*penning-*) financial; (*sparsam*)
economical; ~ *fråga* economic question; ~ *förening* incorporated (economic) association; ~
geografi economic geography; ~ *livslängd* economic life; ~ *ställning* financial status (position); ~*a svårigheter* financial difficulties; ~
utveckling economic development; ~ *i drift*

economical in operation; *i* ~*t avseende* economically, financially **ekonomiskt** [-'nå:-]
adv economically; ~ *oberoende* financially independent; ~ *sett* from an economic point of
view
ekorr|e [red] squirrel **-hjul** treadwheel, tread-
mill (*äv. bildl.*)
eko|sfär ecosphere **-system** ecosystem **-typ**
ecotype
ekoxe stag beetle
e.Kr. (*förk. för efter Kristus*) A.D. (anno Domini)
ek'sem *s7* eczema **-artad** [-a:r-] *a5* eczematous
ekstock 1 (*stock*) oak log **2** (*eka*) punt, skiff
ekumen|ik *s3* ecumenicalism, ecumenicism
-isk [-'me:-] *a5* ecumenic[al]
ekvation equation
ekvations|lära theory of equations **-system**
compound equation
ekvator [eˣkva:tår] *s3* equator **-i'al** *a5* equa-
torial
ekvecklare *zool.* green oak tortricid
ekvilibrist equilibrist **-isk** *a5* equilibristic
ekvival|ens *s3* equivalence, (*särsk. kem.*) equi-
valency **-ent** *s3 o. a1* equivalent
el- *se äv. elektricitets-, elektrisk*
elaffär electrical appliance shop (store)
elak [ˣe:lak] *a1* (*ond, ondskefull*) evil, wicked,
bad; (*stygg, bråkig*) naughty, mischievous; (*illvillig, illasinnad*) malicious, spiteful, malevolent, (*starkare*) malignant; (*giftig*) venomous;
(*bitande*) cynical, caustic; (*t. karaktären*) ill-
-disposed (*mot* towards); ill-natured (*ovänlig*)
unkind, mean (*mot* to); (*grym*) cruel (*mot* to)
2 (*obehaglig, motbjudande*) nasty, horrid, bad;
~ *lukt* (*smak*) nasty (bad) smell (taste); (*besvärlig*) troublesome; *en* ~ *hosta* a troublesome
(nasty) cough **-artad** [-a:r-] *a5* (*om sjukdom
o.d.*) malignant, virulent, pernicious; (*om
olyckstillbud e.d.*) serious **-het** evilness *etc.*;
malice, spitefulness, malevolence; malignancy;
venom; evil disposition; unkindness, meanness; cruelty
elakt *adv* spitefully, ill-naturedly, unkindly *etc.*;
det var ~ *gjort av honom* it was nasty (spiteful,
horrid) of him to do that
elasticitet elasticity; resilience **elasticitets-
modul** modulus of elasticity, elastic modulus
elastisk [e'last-] *a5* elastic; resilient; ~ *binda*
elastic bandage
el|avbrott power failure (cut) **-behandling**
electroconvulsive (electroshock) therapy **-be-
lysning** electric lighting **-chock** electroshock
-chockbehandling electroconvulsive therapy
eld *s2* **1** fire; *~en är lös!* fire!; ~ *upphör!* cease
fire!; *fatta* (*ta*) ~ catch (take) fire; *ge* ~ fire,
begin firing; *göra upp* ~ make a fire, light a
(the fire); *koka vid sakta* ~ boil over a slow
fire; *sätta* (*tända*) ~ *på* set on fire, set fire to;
vara i ~en be under fire; *öppna* ~ *mot* open
fire on **2** (*för cigarett o.d.*) light; *stryka* ~ *på
en tändsticka* strike a match; *vill du låna mig
lite ~?* may I trouble you for a light? **3** *bildl.*
fire, spirit; (*eldighet*) ardour, fervour; (*entusi-
asm*) enthusiasm; *gå genom* ~ *och vatten* go
through fire and water; *leka med ~en* play with
fire; *mellan två ~ar* between two fires; *vara* ~

och lågor be all aflame, be on fire

elda 1 (*göra upp eld*) light a fire; keep a fire burning; ~ *med kol* (*ved*) burn coal (wood), use coal (wood) for heating; ~ *ordentligt* make a good fire; ~ *på* keep up a good fire; *vi måste* ~ *här* we must light a fire here **2** (*uppvärma*) heat; get hot; (*ångpanna e.d.*) fire; (*egga*) rouse, inspire; *pannan* ~*s med koks* the furnace is fired by coke; ~ *upp a*) (*värma upp*) heat, *b*) (*i maskin e.d.*) get up the fire[s *pl*], *c*) (*förbruka*) burn up, consume; ~ *upp sig* get excited **eld|are** stoker, fireman **-begängelse** [-jäŋ-] cremation **-dop** baptism of fire; *få sitt* ~ (*äv.*) be put to the test for the first time **-fara** danger (risk) of fire, fire risk; *vid* ~ in case of fire **-farlig** inflammable **-fast** fireproof; ~ *form* ovenware, casserole; ~ *glas* heat-resistant glass; ~ *lera* fire clay; ~ *tegel* firebrick **-fluga** firefly **-fängd** [-äŋd] *a1* [in]flammable; *bildl. äv.* fiery **-gaffel** poker **-givning** [-ji:v-] firing **-handvapen** firearm **-hastighet** rate of fire **-hav** sea of fire **-hund** firedog, andiron **-härd** seat of the (a) fire **-härjad** *a5* fire ravaged

eldig *a1* fiery, ardent, passionate

eldistribution distribution of electrical energy **eld|kastare** flame-thrower **-klot** fireball **-kraft** *mil.* fire power **-kula** fireball; *astr. äv.* bolide **-kvast** puff of flame and smoke **-ledning** *mil.* fire control **-linje** *mil.* firing line

eldning firing, heating; lighting of fires; ~ *med ved* wood firing, (*på ångbåt*) stoking **eldningsolja** [domestic] fuel oil, heating oil; *tjock* ~ (*tjockolja*) heavy fuel oil; *tunn* ~ (*villaolja*) light fuel oil

eldorado [-'ra:-] *s6* eldorado

eldprov (*gudsdom*) ordeal by fire; *bildl.* ordeal

eldriven driven (powered) by electricity, electrical

eld|röd red as fire, flaming red **-rör 1** (*på kanon o.d.*) tube, barrel **2** (*i ångpanna*) fire-tube **-salamander** European fire salamander **-själ** dedicated person **-sken** firelight **-skrift** *i* ~ in letters of fire **-skärm** fire screen

Eldslandet Tierra del Fuego

eldsljus *vid* ~ by candlelight (artificial light)

eldslukare fire-eater

eldslåga flame of fire

eldsläck|are fire-extinguisher **-ning** fire fighting

eldsläcknings|apparat *se eldsläckare* **-manskap** fire brigade, firemen (*pl*)

eldsländare Fuegian

eldsmärke *med.* haemangioma

eld|sprutande *a4* fire-spitting; ~ *berg* volcano; ~ *drake* firedrake, firedragon **-stad** *-staden* *-städer* fireplace, hearth; (*kamin, kakelugn*) stove; (*på lok*) firebox; (*på ångbåt*) furnace **-stod** *bibl.* pillar of fire **-strid** gunfight **-stål** steel

eldsvåda *s1* fire; (*större*) conflagration; *vid* ~ in case of fire

eld|säker fireproof, flameproof **-tång** fire-tongs (*pl*) **-understöd** *mil.* fire support **-vapen** firearm, gun **-vatten** firewater **-verkan** *mil.* fire effect

elefant elephant **-bete** elephant's tusk **-gräs** elephant grass **-hane** bull elephant **-hona** cow

elephant

elefantiasis [-ˣti:- *el.* -'ti:-] *r* elephantiasis

elefantunge calf elephant

eleg|ans [-'ans *el.* -'aŋs] *s3* elegance; (*stass*) finery; (*i uppträdande*) refinement, polish; (*smakfullhet*) style; (*prakt*) splendour **-ant** [-'ant *el.* -'aŋt] *a1* (*om stil*) elegant; (*om kläder*) stylish, tasteful, fashionable, smart; (*om uppträdande*) refined

elegi [-'gi: *el.* -'ʃi:] *s3* elegy (*över* on) **elegisk** [-'le:-] *a5* elegiac

elektor [eˣlektår] *s3* elector **elektorskår** electorate

elektrakomplex [eˣlektra-] Electra complex

elektricitet electricity

elektricitets|lära electricity **-mängd** [electric] charge

elektrifier|a electrify **-ing** electrification

elektriker [e'lekt-] electrician

elektrisera electrify; *bildl.* enthuse

elektrisk [e'lekt-] *a5* electric; (*friare o. bildl.*) electrical; ~ *affär* (*anläggning*) electric appliance shop (plant); ~ *belysning* electric light, lighting; ~ *energi* electrical energy; ~ *industri* electrical industry; ~ *laddning* electric charge; ~*a ledningar* electric wiring; ~ *motor* (*spis, uppvärmning*) electric motor (cooker *el.* stove, heating); ~*a stolen* the electric chair, *vard.* the chair; ~ *ström* [electric] current; ~ *urladdning* electric discharge; ~*t värmeelement* electric heater (heating element)

elektrod [-'å:d] *s3* electrode

elektro|dynamik electrodynamics (*pl, behandlas som sg*) **-dynamisk** electrodynamic[al] **-encefalogram** electroencephalogram **-filter** electrofilter; electrostatic filter (precipitator) **-fon** [-'få:n] *s3* electrophone **-for** [-'få:r] *s3* electrophorus **-fo'res** *s3* electrophoresis **-fysiologi** electrophysiology **-ingenjör** electrical engineer **-kardiogram** electrocardiogram **-kemi** electrochemistry **-kemisk** electrochemical **-kirurgi** electrosurgery

elektro|'lys *s3* electrolysis **-lysera** electrolyse **-'lyt** *s3* electrolyte **-lytisk** [-'ly:-] *a5* electrolytic[al]

elektro|magnet electromagnet **-magnetisk** electromagnetic; ~ *strålning* electromagnetic radiation **-magnetism** electromagnetism **elektro|mekanik** electromechanics (*pl, behandlas som sg*) **-mekanisk** electromechanical **-metallurgi** electrometallurgy **-motorisk** electromotive (*kraft* force)

elektron [-'å:n] *s3* electron **-blixt** electronic flash **-fysik** electron physics **-hjärna** *vard.* electronic brain, computer

elektronik *s3* electronics (*pl, behandlas som sg*)

elektronisk [-'trå:-] *a5* electronic; ~ *databehandling* electronic data processing; ~ *musik* electronic music

elektron|kanon electron gun **-mikroskop** electron microscope **-negativitet** electronegativity **-optik** electron optics **-rör** electron tube; [electronic] valve, tube; *AE.* vacuum tube **-ugn** electron oven **-volt** electronvolt

elektro|skop electroscope **-statik** *s3* electrostatics (*pl, behandlas som sg*) **-statisk** elec-

trostatic **-stål** electric steel
elektro|teknik *s3* electrotechnology, electrical engineering **-tekniker** electrical engineer **-teknisk** electrotechnical **-terapi** (*behandling*) electrotherapy; (*vetenskap*) electrotherapeutics (*pl, behandlas som sg*)
elelement [ˣeːl-] heating element, electric heater
element *s7* **1** element; *de fyra ~en* the four elements; *~ens raseri* the fury of the elements; *vara i sitt rätta ~* be in one's element; *ljusskygga ~* shady characters **2** (*första grund*) element, rudiment **3** *tekn.* cell; *galvaniskt ~* galvanic cell (element); *byggn.* unit; (*värme-*) radiator; (*elektriskt*) heating element, electric heater
elementar|analys [-ˣtaːr-] elementary analysis **-bok** primer (*i* of) **-partikel** elementary (fundamental) particle **-skola** secondary school
elementborste radiator brush
elemen'tär *a1* elementary, basic; *~ kunskaper* elementary (fundamental) knowledge; (*enkel, ursprunglig*) simple; rudimentary
elenergi electrical energy
e'lev *s3* pupil; (*vid högskola, kurs o.d.*) student; (*praktikant*) learner, trainee; (*lärling*) apprentice; (*kontors-, bank-*) junior [clerk]; *en av mina f.d. ~er* one of my former pupils; *skolans f.d. ~er* the old boys (girls *etc.*); *AE.* the alumni (*sg* alumnus), *fem.* alumnae (*sg* alumna)
eleva|tion elevation **-tionsvinkel** angle of elevation
elevator *s3* elevator; (*för tungt gods*) hoist
elev|hem [college] hostel; *AE.* dormitory **-kår** body of pupils (students) **-organisation** student (pupil) organization **-råd** student (pupil) council **-skola** *teat.* drama[tic] school **-tid** period of training **-tjänstgöring** probationership; apprenticeship
elfenben ivory; *av ~* (*äv.*) ivory
Elfenbenskusten the Ivory Coast
elfenbens|torn ivory tower **-vit** ivory [white]
elfte eleventh; *Karl XI* Charles XI (the Eleventh); *i ~ timmen* at the eleventh hour **-del** eleventh [part]; *en ~* one-eleventh
el|förbrukning electricity consumption **-gitarr** electric guitar
Elia[s] [eˣliː-] (*profet*) Elijah; (*i Nya testamentet*) Elias
elidera elide
eliminer|a eliminate **-ing** elimination
elinstallatör electrician; (*firma*) electrical contractor
Elisabet [eˣliː-] Elizabeth **elisabe'tansk** [-aː-] *a5* Elizabethan
elision elision
e'lit *s3* elite; pick; flower; choice; *en ~ av* a picked group of; *~en av* the pick (cream) of **-idrott** competitive sports **-ism** elitism **-ist** elitist **-kår** corps d'élite **-trupp** picked troop **-tänkande** elitism
eli'xir *s7* elixir
eljes[t] *se annars*
elkraft electrical power **-försörjning** power supply **-station** [electrical] power plant **-verk** [electrical] power station

eller [ˈell-] **1** or; *~ dylikt* or something like that; *~ hur, se hur* 2; *~ också* or [else]; *antingen ... ~ either ...* or; *en ~ annan person* some person or other; *om en ~ annan timme* in an hour or two (so) **2** (*efter varken*) nor; *varken min bror ~ min syster* neither my brother nor my sister
el'lips *s3* **1** *geom.* ellipse **2** *språkv.* ellipsis (*pl* ellipses) **-formig** *a1* elliptic[al], oval
elliptisk [eˈlipp-] *a5*, *geom., språkv.* elliptic[al]
el|lok electric locomotive **-motor** electric motor
elmseld Saint (St.) Elmo's fire, corposant
el|mängd [electric] charge **-mätare** electricity meter **-nät** electric mains (*pl*), electric supply network
eloge [eˈlåːʃ] *s5* commendation, praise, eulogy; *ge ngn en ~* congratulate s.b. (*för* on), pay a tribute to s.b.
elo'kvens *s3* eloquence
elorgel electric organ; electronic organ
eloxera anodize
el|panna electric boiler **-ransonering** electricity rationing **-reparatör** electrician
elritsa [ˣeːl-, *äv.* ˣell-] *s1* minnow
elräkning electricity bill
Elsass [ˈell-] *n* Alsace **elsassare** [-ˣsass-] *s9*, **elsassisk** [-ˈsass-] *a5* Alsatian
elsevier *se elzevier*
el|spis electric cooker **-ström** [electric] current **-svetsning** arc (electric) welding **-taxa** electricity rate **-transmission** transmission of electrical energy
eludera elude
el|uppvärmning electric heating **-uttag** socket
elva eleven (*för sms. jfr fem-*) **-hundratalet** the twelfth century **-tiden** *vid ~* round (about) eleven **-tåget** the eleven o'clock train
el|verk electric (electricity) works **-visp** electric whisk **-värme** electric heating
elyseisk [-ˈseː-] *a5* Elysian; *E~a fälten* Elysian fields, Elysium
elzevier [-seˈviːr] *s3* Elzevir
elände [ˣeː- *el.* eˈlänn-] *s6* misery; (*nöd*) distress; (*missöde, otur*) misfortune, bad luck; (*obehag*) nuisance; *ett ~ till bil* a scrapheap of a car; *råka i ~* fall on evil days; *störta ngn i ~* reduce s.b. to misery; *vilket ~!* *a*) what misery!, *b*) what a misfortune!, *c*) what a nuisance! **eländig** [ˣeː- *el.* eˈlänn-] *a1* miserable, wretched
e.m. (*förk. för eftermiddagen*) p.m., P.M. (post meridiem)
e'malj *s3* enamel (*äv. tand-*) **-arbete** [a piece of] enamelwork **-era** enamel; *~de kärl* enamelware (*sg*) **-'ering** enamelling **-öga** glass (artificial) eye **-ör** enameller, enamellist
emanation emanation
emancip|ation emancipation **-era** emancipate
emanera emanate
emball|age [emm- *el.* amm-, -ˈaːʃ] *s7* packing, wrapping; *~ återtages* empties (packing) returnable; *exklusive (inklusive) ~* packing excluded (included) **-era** pack, wrap up **-ering** packing, wrapping
embargo [-ˈbarr-] *s6* embargo; *lägga ~ på ett fartyg* lay (put) an embargo on a ship; *lägga ~ på* (*bildl.*) seize; *upphäva ett ~* raise (take

off) an embargo

embarker|a [emm- *el.* amm-] embark **-ing** embarkation **-ingskort** *flyg.* boarding pass

em'blem *s7* emblem; badge

embo'li *s3* embolism

embonpoint [*svenskt uttal* aŋ- *el.* ambåŋpo'äŋ] *s3* plumpness, stoutness

embryo ['emm-] *s6* embryo (*pl* embryos) **-log** embryologist **-logi** *s3* embryology **-'nal** *a1* embryonic, embryonal

emedan [e*me:-] (*därför att*) because; (*eftersom*) as, since, seeing [that]; ~ *jag var upptagen kunde jag inte komma* as I was (being) busy I could not come

emellan [e*mell-] **I** *prep* (*jfr mellan*); (*om två*) between; (*om flera*) among; *man och man* ~ as one man to another; *det stannar oss* ~ it remains strictly between ourselves; *oss* ~ *sagt* between ourselves; *vänner* ~ between friends **II** *adv* between; *trädgårdar med staket* ~ gardens with fences between; *ngt mitt* ~ something in between; *inte lägga fingrarna* ~ not spare s.b.; handle the matter without mittens; *ge 100 pund* ~ give 100 pounds into the bargain (to square the transaction) **-åt** occasionally, sometimes, at times; *allt* ~ from time to time, every now and then

emeller'tid however

emerit|us [e'me:-] **I** *-us -i, r* emeritus (*pl* emeriti) **II** *oböjligt a* emeritus; *professor* ~ professor emeritus

em'fa|s *s3* emphasis **-tisk** *a5* emphatic

emfy'sem *s7, med.* emphysema

emigr|ant emigrant **-ation** emigration **-era** emigrate

emin|ens *s3, Ers (Hans)* ~ Your (His) Eminence (Eminency) **-ent** *a1* eminent

e'mir *s3* emir **emirat** *s7* emirate

emissarie [-'sa:rie] *s5* emissary

emission [emi'ʃɷ:n] (*av värdepapper*) issue

emissions|bank investment bank **-kurs** price (rate) of issue

emittera issue

emk (*förk. för elektromotorisk kraft*) emf, EMF (electromotive force)

emma *s1,* **emmastol** easy chair

emmentalerost [-*ta:-] Emmenthal[er]

e-moll E minor

e'mot I *prep, se mot; mitt* ~ *ngn* opposite [to] s.b.; *alla var* ~ *honom* everybody was against him **II** *adv, mitt* ~ opposite; *för och* ~ for and against; *skäl för och* ~ (*äv.*) pros and cons; *det bär mig* ~ it goes against the grain; *inte mig* ~ I have no objection, it's O.K. by me

emotion emotion **emotio'nell** *a1* emotional **emo'tiv** *a1* emotive

emot|se [*e:mɷ:t-, *äv.* e*mɷ:t-], **-taga** *se motse, mottaga*

empa'ti *s3* empathy

em'pir [emm- *el.* aŋ-] *s3, se empirstil* **-iker** empiricism **-isk** *a5* empirical **-ism** empiricism

empirstil [-*pi:r-] Empire style

emsersalt Ems salt

emu ['e:-] *s3* emu

emulgator *s3* emulsifier

emulger|a emulsify **-ingsmedel** emulsifier

emul|sion emulsion **-sionsfärg** emulsion paint

1 en [e:n] *s2* (*buske*) [common] juniper; (*trä*) juniper [wood]

2 en [enn] *adv* (*omkring*) about, some; *det var väl* ~ *fem sex personer* there were some five or six persons; *han gick för* ~ *tio minuter sedan* he left about ten minutes ago

3 en [enn] (*jfr ett*) **I** *räkn.* one; ~ *och* ~ one by one; ~ *gång* once; ~ *och samma* one and the same; ~ *till* another; ~ *åt gången* (*i taget*) one at a time; ~ *för alla och alla för* ~ one for all and all for one; *det är inte* ~*s fel att två träter* it takes two to make a quarrel; *ta* ~ *kaka till!* help yourself to another biscuit! **II** *obest. art* a, an; *ibl.* one; (*framför vissa, i sht abstr. substantiv*) a piece of; ~ *dag* one day; ~ *upplysning* (*oförskämdhet*) a piece of information (impudence) **III** *obest. pron* one; (*kasusform av man*) one, you, me; *mitt* ~*a öga* one of my eyes; ~*s egen* one's own; ~ *och annan besökare* occasional visitors; ~ *av de bästa böcker jag läst* one of the best books I have read; *den* ~*e av pojkarna* one of the boys; *den* ~*e...den andre* [the] one...the other; *den* ~*a efter den andra* one after another; *det* ~*a med det andra gör att jag* what with one thing and another I; *från det* ~*a till det andra* from one thing to another; *vad är du för* ~*?* who are you[, my boy *etc.*]?; *ingen tycker om* ~ *om man är elak* nobody likes you if you are nasty; *du var just en snygg* ~*!* you are a nice chap, I must say!

ena [*e:na] (*förena*) unite; (*foga samman*) unify; (*förlika*) conciliate; ~ *sig* (*bli enig*) come to an agreement (*om* as to), (*komma överens*) agree (*om* [up]on, about, as to), *AE. äv.* get together

enahanda [*e:na-] **I** *a4* (*alldeles liknande*) identical, same **II** *s7* (*enformighet*) monotony, sameness

enaktare one-act play

enande [*e:n-] **I** *s6* unification, uniting **II** *a4* (*förenande*) uniting, unifying; (*förlikande*) conciliating

enarmad *a5* one-armed; ~ *bandit* one-armed bandit, slot machine

enastående [*e:na-] **I** *a4* unique, unparalleled, exceptional; (*friare*) matchless, extraordinary **II** *adv* exceptionally, extremely

enbart [*e:nba:rt] merely; (*uteslutande*) solely, exclusively

enbent *a4* one-legged

enbuske [*e:n-] juniper [shrub]

enbyggare [*e:n-] *bot.* mon[o]ecious plant

enbär ['e:n-] juniper berry **enbärsbrännvin** gin

encefa'lit *s3* encephalitis

encefalogram [-'gramm] *s7* encephalogram

encellig *a1* unicellular

encykl|ika [-'syk-] *s1* encyclical **-isk** *a5* encyclic[al]

encyklope'd|i [aŋ- *el.* enn-] *s3* encyclop[a]edia **-isk** [-'pe:-] *a5* encyclop[a]edic **-ist** encyclop[a]edist

encylindrig *a5* single-cylinder

end|a *pron* only, single, sole, one; *den* ~*e* the only man; *det* ~ the only thing; *en* ~ *gång* just once; *denna* ~ *vän* this one friend; *ingen* ~ not a single one; *inte en ~ blomma* not a single flower; *hon är ~ barnet* she is an only child; *det blev en ~ röra* it turned into one big muddle

endast *adv* only, but; *~ för vuxna* adults only

endaste *pron* one single

endels in part

ende'mi *s3*, **endemisk** [-'de:-] *a5* endemic

endera ['enn-] **I** *pron* one [or the other] of the two; *~ dagen* one of these days, some day or other; *i ettdera fallet* in either case **II** *konj, se antingen*

en'div *s3*, **endivsallad** (*grönsallad*) endive; *AE.* chicory crown; (*handelsnamn på sallatcikoria*) chicory, succory

endo|ergisk [-'ärg-] *a5* endoergic **-gen** [-'je:n] *a5* endogenous

endo'krin *a5* endocrine; *~ körtel* endocrine (ductless) gland **-ologi** endocrinology **-ologisk** *a5* endocrinologic[al]

endo|skop [-'skå:p] *s7* endoscope **-sko'pi** *s3* endoscopy

endossat [aŋ-, *äv.* enn-] endorsee; transferee

endoss|ement [aŋdåsse'maŋ *el.* enn-] *s7* endorsement **-ent** endorser **-era** endorse **-'ering** endorsement

endo'term[isk] *a5* endothermic, endothermal

endräkt [ˣe:n-] *s3* concord, harmony; (*enstämmighet*) unanimity

energi [-'ʃi:] *s3* energy, *AE. sl.* pizzazz; *elektrisk ~* electrical energy **-analys** energy analysis **-användning** energy application **-balans** energy balance **-bärare** energy carrier **-distribution** energy distribution **-förbrukning** energy consumption; (*elförbrukning*) power consumption **-förlust** loss of energy **-försörjning** energy supply (supplies) **-gröda** energy crop **-hushållning** rational use of energy **-knippe** bundle of energy **-kris** energy crisis **-källa** source of energy **-lagring** energy storage **-omvandling** energy conversion (transformation)

energisk [e'närgisk] *a5* (*full av energi*) energetic (*i* in, at); (*kraftfull*) vigorous

energi|skatt energy tax **-skog** energy forest **-snål** power saving **-sparande** energy saving **-system** energy system **-tillgång** energy supply; (*eltillgång*) power supply **-täthet** volume energy, energy density **-utvinning** energy recovery **-verk** Statens ~ [the Swedish] national energy administration **-åtgång** energy consumption **-överföring** energy transfer

enerver|a enervate, unnerve **-ande** *a4* enervating, trying

en face (*om porträtt*) fullface

enfald [ˣe:n-] *s3* silliness, foolishness; (*starkare*) stupidity; *heliga ~* sancta simplicitas **-ig** *a1* silly, foolish; stupid

enfamiljshus [one-family] house

en famille [aŋfa'mij] with one's family; at home; (*utan formaliteter*) informally

en|fasmotor single-phase motor **-filig** *a5* single-file **-formig** [-å-] *a1* monotonous, tedious, dull **-formighet** [-å-] monotony, dullness **-färgad** one-coloured; plain; (*om ljus, målning*) monochromatic **-född** *relig.*, *den ~e sonen, Hans ~e son* the (His) only begotten Son

engag|emang [aŋgaʃe'maŋ] *s7* **1** (*anställning*) engagement, contract **2** *hand.* (*förpliktelse*) engagement, obligation, commitment; (*penningplacering*) investment **-era 1** (*anställa*) engage **2** (*förplikta*) engage, commit; *vara starkt ~d i* be deeply committed (engaged) in **3** *rfl*, *~ sig i* engage (be engaged) in, concern o.s. with, (*intressera sig för*) interest o.s. in; *~ sig för* stand up for

en garde [aŋ'gard] on guard

engelsk ['eŋ-] *a5* English; British; *~t horn* cor anglais, English horn; *E~a kanalen* the [English] Channel; *~a kyrkan* (*såsom institution*) the Church of England; *~ mil* [English] mile; *~a pund* pound sterling; *~t salt* Epsom salts (*pl*); *~a sjukan* [the] rickets, rachitis; *~a språket* the English language, English

engelska ['eŋ-] **1** (*språk*) English; *på ~* in English; *översätta till ~* translate into English **2** (*kvinna*) Englishwoman, English lady

engelsk|fientlig anti-English, Anglophobe **-född** English-born, British-born **-språkig** *a5* English-speaking; (*om litteratur o.d.*) in English **--svensk** Anglo-Swedish; *~ ordbok* English-Swedish dictionary **-talande** *a4* English-speaking, Anglophone **-vänlig** pro-English, pro-British, Anglophili[a]c

engels|man [ˣeŋ-] Englishman; *-männen a*) (*hela nationen*) the English, Englishmen, *b*) (*några engelsmän*) the Englishmen

engifte [ˣe:n-] monogamy; *leva i ~* be monogamous

England ['eŋ-] *n* England; (*Storbritannien*) [Great] Britain; (*officiellt*) the United Kingdom [of Great Britain and Northern Ireland]

en gros [aŋ'grå:] wholesale

engros|firma [aŋ'grå:-] wholesaler **-handel** wholesale

engångs|belopp non-recurring (non-recurrent) amount **-bägare** (*dricks-*) disposable cup **-företeelse** non-recurrent phenomenon, isolated case **-förpackning** disposable packing (package) **-glas** nonreturnable bottle **-kostnad** non-recurrent charge, once-for-all cost **-lakan** disposable sheet **-servis** disposable tableware

enhet [ˣe:n-] (*enhetlighet*) unity; *mat., mil., sjö. m.m.* unit

enhetlig [ˣe:nhe:t-] *a1* (*om begrepp o.d.*) unitary; (*likartad*) uniform, homogeneous; (*om mode, typ o.d.*) standardized **-het** unity; uniformity, homogeneity; standardization

enhets|front united front **-pris** standard (uniform) price **-rörelse** *italienska ~n* the movement for Italian unity **-strävan** struggle for unity

en|hjärtbladig [ˣe:n-] *a5* monocotyledonous **-hällig** *a1* unanimous **-hänt** *a4* one-handed **-hörning** [-hö:r-] unicorn

enig *a1* (*enad*) united, unanimous; (*ense*) of one opinion, agreed; *bli ~[a]* come to an agreement (*med* with; *om* as to) **-het** unity; unanimity; agreement; concord; *~ ger styrka* unity is strength

enkammarsystem unicameral (single-chamber) system

enkannerligen [en'kann-] [more] particularly

enkel ['enn-] *a2* **1** (*motsats dubbel el. flerfaldig*) single; ~ *biljett* single (*AE*. one-way) ticket **2** (*motsats sammansatt, tillkrånglad o.d.*) simple; (*flärdlös äv.*) plain; *av* ~ *konstruktion* of simple construction; *en vanlig* ~ *människa* just an ordinary person; ~ *uppgift* easy task (job); *av det enkla skälet att* for the simple reason that, simply because; *ju enklare ju simplare* the simpler the easier; *ha enkla vanor* have simple habits; *får jag bjuda på en* ~ *middag?* may I invite you to a simple dinner?; *känna sig* ~ feel very small
enkel|beckasin common (Wilson's) snipe **-het** (*jfr enkel*) singleness; simplicity **-knäppt** *a4* single-breasted **-rikta** ~*d gata* (*trafik*) one-way street (traffic) **-rum** single room **-spårig** *a5* single-track, one-track (*äv. bildl.*); *bildl.* simplistic; *vara* ~ (*bildl.*) have a one-track mind
enkel|t ['enk-] *adv* simply; *helt* ~ [quite] simply **-verkande** single-acting
enkilosburk [one-]kilo tin
en'klav *s3* enclave; enclosure
enkom [ˣenkåm] purposely, expressly, especially; ~ *för att* for the sole purpose of (+ *ing-form*), solely to (+ *inf.*)
enkrona *en* ~ a one-krona [piece]
en'kät [aŋ-, *äv.* enn-] *s3* inquiry, investigation **-undersökning** opinion poll
enkönad [-ç-] *a5* unisexual
enlever|a [aŋle-] run away with; abduct **-ing** abduction
enlighet [ˣe:n-] *i uttr.*: *i* ~ *med* in accordance (conformity) with, according to
enligt [ˣe:n-] according to; *hand. äv.* as per; ~ *faktura* as per invoice; ~ *kontrakt* (*lag*) by contract (law); ~ *min uppfattning* in my opinion
enmans|hytt single cabin **-kanot** single[-seater] canoe **-teater** one-man show **-valkrets** single-member constituency
enmotorig *a5* single-engined
e'norm [-å-] *a1* enormous, immense
enpartivälde one-party rule
en passant [aŋpa'saŋ] *schack.* in passing
en|plansvilla one-storey house, bungalow **-procentig** *a5* one-percent **-pucklig** *a5* single-humped
enquete *se enkät*
enradig *a5* (*om kavaj*) single-breasted; (*om halsband*) single row
enris [ˣe:n-] *s7* juniper twigs (*pl*) **-rökt** *a4* smoked over a fire of juniper twigs
enroller|a [aŋ-] enrol, enlist **-ing** enrolment, enlistment
en|rum [ˣe:n-] *i* ~ in private; *tala med ngn i* ~ have a private interview with s.b. **-rummare, -rumslägenhet** one-room[ed] flatlet; bed-sitter
1 ens *oböjligt a, sjö.* in line with each other
2 ens *adv, inte* ~ not even; *med* ~ all at once; *utan att* ~ *säga* without even saying; *om* ~ *så mycket* if that much
ensak [ˣe:n-] *det är min* ~ it is my [private] affair (my [own] business)
ensam *a1* **1** (*enda*) sole; ~ *innehavare* sole proprietor **2** (*allena*) alone; lonely, lonesome; (*ensamstående*) solitary; ~ *i sitt slag* unique of its kind; *känna sig* ~ feel lonely; *leva ett* ~*t*

liv live a secluded life; *vara* (*bli*) ~ be (be left) alone; *vara* ~ *sökande* be the only applicant; *en olycka kommer sällan* ~ misfortunes seldom come singly; *vi fick en* ~ *kupé* we had a compartment to (for) ourselves **-boende** *a4* living alone (on one's own) **-cell** solitary confinement **-försäljare** sole (exclusive) agent
ensamhet (*jfr ensam*) **1** solitariness **2** loneliness; *i* ~*en* in [one's] solitude; *i min* ~ in my loneliness **ensamhetskänsla** [feeling of] loneliness
ensam|jungfru maid-of-all-work, general [servant] **-rätt** sole (exclusive) right[s *pl*] **-stående** *a4* solitary, isolated; (*om person*) single, living alone; (*fristående*) detached; ~ *förälder* single parent
ensartad *a5* similar, uniform
ense *bli* ~ *om* agree upon, come to an agreement (understanding) about; *vara* ~ be agreed (*om* about), agree (*om att* that); *vi är fullständigt* ~ *med er* we are one (in complete agreement) with you
ensemble [aŋ'sambel] *s5* ensemble **-spel** ensemble playing
ensfyr *sjö.* range (leading) light
ensidig *a1* one-sided (*äv. bildl.*); (*partisk äv.*) partial, prejudiced, biased; (*om avtal o.d.*) unilateral **-het** one-sidedness *etc.*; prejudice, bias
ensiffrig *a5* one-figure; ~*t tal* digit, figure
ensilage [aŋsi'la:ʃ *el.* enn-] *s7, lantbr.* ensilage
ensitsig *a1* ~*t jaktplan* single-seater fighter
enski|ld [ˣe:n,ʃild] *a1* **1** (*privat*) private, personal; ~*t rum* (*område*) private room (property, grounds); *inta* (*stå i*) ~ *ställning* come to (stand at) attention; ~ *väg* private road **2** (*enstaka*) individual; (*särskild*) specific, particular; *i varje* ~*t fall* in each specific case
enskildhet privacy; *gå in på* ~*er* enter into particulars (details)
ensl|ig [ˣe:ns-] *a1* solitary, lonely; ~*t belägen* solitary, isolated **-ing** *se enstöring*
ens|linje [ˣe:ns-] *sjö.* range (leading) line **-märke** *sjö.* range target (marker)
en|språkig *a5* unilingual **-spännare** gig, trap, buggy
enstaka [ˣe:n-] *oböjligt a* (*enskild*) separate, detached; (*sporadisk*) occasional; (*sällsynt*) exceptional; *i* ~ *fall* in exceptional cases; *någon* ~ *gång* once in a while; *på* ~ *ställen* in certain places; *vid* ~ *tillfällen* very occasionally
en|stavig *a5* monosyllabic; ~*t ord* monosyllable **-stämmig** *a5* unanimous; *mus.* unison **-stämmigt** unanimously; *mus.* in unison **-ständigt** persistently; urgently **-störing** solitary, recluse, hermit **-tal 1** *mat.* unit **2** *språkv.* singular
entent[e] [aŋ'taŋt] *s3* [*s5*] entente
ente'rit *s3* enteritis
entita [ˣe:n-] *s1* marsh tit
entitet entity
entledig|a [-'le:-] dismiss, discharge **-ande** *s6* dismissal, discharge
entomo|log [aŋ-] entomologist **-logi** *s3* entomology **-logisk** *a5* entomologic[al]
entonig *a5* monotonous; *mus.* monotone **-het** monotony; *mus.* monotone
entré [aŋ'tre:] *s3* **1** entrance; (*intåg*) entry; *göra*

sin ~ make one's appearance **2** *se -avgift; fri* ~ admission free **-avgift** admission (entrance) fee; *~er* (*vid tävling m.m.*) gate money **-biljett** ticket [of admission]
entrecôte [aŋtre'kå:t] *s5* entrecôte
entrepre'n|ad [aŋtre- *el.* entre-] *s3* contract [by tender]; *ta på* ~ sign a contract for; *utlämna ett arbete på* ~ invite tenders for a job **-ör** contractor
entrérätt entrée, first course
entresol[l] [aŋter- *el.* aŋtre'såll] *s3*, **-våning** mezzanine [floor], entresol
entro'pi *s3* entropy
enträgen [ˣe:n-] *a3* urgent, pressing; earnest; (*efterhängsen*) importunate; (*envis*) insistent; ~ *begäran* urgent request; ~ *bön* earnest prayer **enträget** [ˣe:n-] *adv* urgently *etc.*; *be ngn* ~ *att* implore (entreat) s.b. to
entusi|'asm [aŋ- *el.* enn-] *s3* enthusiasm **-asmera** inspire with enthusiasm, make enthusiastic **-'ast** *s3* enthusiast **-astisk** [-'ass-] *a5* enthusiastic (*för* for), keen (*för* on)
en|tydig *a5* (*om ord o.d.*) univocal; (*otvetydig*) unequivocal, unambiguous; (*klar*) clear-cut, distinct **'-var** everybody; *alla och* ~ each and all **-veten** *a3, se envis* **-vig** [ˣe:nvi:g] *s7* duel, single combat
environger [aŋvi'råŋer] *pl* environs
envis [ˣe:n-] *a1* stubborn, obstinate, *AE.* vard. ornery; (*ihärdig*) dogged; (*om pers. äv.*) pertinacious, headstrong; (*om sak äv.*) persistent; ~ *hosta* persistent cough; ~ *som synden* as obstinate as sin **envisas** *dep* be obstinate *etc.*; ~ [*med*] *att* persist in (+ *ing-form*) **envishet** stubbornness, obstinacy *etc.*
envoyé [aŋvɔa'je:] *s3* envoy
en|våldshärskare absolute ruler, dictator **-våningshus** one-storey house **-välde** [ˣe:n-] absolutism; dictatorship; autocracy **-väldig** [ˣe:n-] absolute; autocratic; sovereign **-värd**, *a5* **-värdig** *a5* monovalent, univalent
enzym [-'(t)sy:m] *s4, s7* enzyme
enäggstvilling identical twin
e'när *se eftersom, emedan*
enögd *a5* one-eyed
e.o. (*förk. för extra ordinarie*) pro tem (pro tempore)
eolsharpa [ˣe:åls-] aeolian (wind) harp
eon [e'å:n] *s3* aeon; *AE.* eon
eo'sin *s4* eosin[e]
epicentrum [-'senn-] epicentre
epide'mi *s3* epidemic **epidemiolo'gi** *s3* epidemiology **epidemisjukhus** isolation hospital, infectious disease unit **epidemisk** [-'de:-] *a5* epidemic
epi|'fyt *s3* epiphyte **-gon** [-'gå:n] *s3* poor imitator **-gra'fik** epigraphy **-gram** [-'gramm] *s7* epigram
e'pik *s3* epic poetry **epiker** ['e:-] epic poet
epikuré *s3* epicurean; (*goddagspilt*) epicure **epikureisk** [-'re:-] *a5* epicurean
epilation epilation
epilep'si *s3* epilepsy **epileptiker** [-'lepp-] *s9*, **epileptisk** [-'lepp-] *a5* epileptic **epileptoid** [-tɔ'i:d] *a5* epileptoid, epileptiform
epilera epilate
epilog epilogue

episk ['e:-] *a5* epic
episko'pal *a5* episcopal **-kyrkan** (*anglikanska kyrkan*) Church of England
epi'sod *s3* episode, incident
epistel [-'pist-] *s2* epistle
epi'taf *s7, s4*, **epitafium** [-'ta:-] *s4* memorial tablet; (*inskrift*) epitaph
epi'tel *s7* epithelium **-cell** epithelial cell
epi'tet *s7* epithet
epizoo'ti *s3* epizootic
epok [e'på:k] *s3* epoch; *bilda* ~ make [a new] epoch; *be* a turning point **-görande** [-j-] *a4* epoch-making
epo'nym *s3* eponym
epos ['e:pås] *s7* epos, epic
e-post e-mail
epoxi|harts [eˣpåksi-] epoxy (epoxide) resin **-plast** epoxy plastic
epsilon ['epsilån] *s7* epsilon
epsomsalt [ˣepsåm-] Epsom salts (*pl*)
epå'lett *s3* epaulet[te]
er *pron* **1** *pers.* you; *rfl* yourself, *pl* yourselves **2** *poss.* a) *fören.* your b) *självst.* yours; *Ers Majestät* Your Majesty; *~a dumbommar!* you fools!; *Er tillgivne* (*i brevslut*) Yours sincerely
era *s1* era
erbarmlig [-'barm-] *a1* (*ömkansvärd, ynklig*) pitiable; (*eländig*) wretched, woeful
erbium ['ärr-] *s4* erbium
erbjud|a [ˣe:r-] **1** (*med personsubj.*) offer; (*mera formellt*) proffer, tender; *jag blev -en att* (*äv.*) I was invited to **2** (*med saksubj.*) (*förete*) present; (*ge, lämna*) afford, provide; ~ *en ståtlig anblick* present an imposing sight; ~ *skydd mot* provide shelter from **3** *rfl* (*med personsubj.*) offer; volunteer; (*med saksubj.*) offer [itself]; present itself; occur, arise **erbjudan** *r* offer **erbjudande** *s6* (*anbud*) offer; *AE.* proposition; (*pris-*) quotation, tender
erektion [-k'fɷ:n] erection
ere'mit *s3* hermit **-age** *s7* hermitage; *E~t* (*i Leningrad*) the Hermitage **-boning** hermitage **-kräfta** hermit crab
erfara [ˣe:r-] **1** (*få veta*) learn (*av* from); learn, get to know **2** (*röna*) experience, feel
erfaren [ˣe:r-] *a3* experienced, practised; (*kunnig*) skilled, versed (*i* in) **-het** experience; *bli en* ~ *rikare* gain by experience, be taught by an experience; *veta av egen* ~ know from [one's own] experience; *vis av ~en* wise by experience; *ha dåliga ~er av ngt* have negative experience of s.th., find s.th. unsatisfactory **-hetsmässig** *al* acquired by experience
erforderlig [ˣe:rfɷ:r-] *a1* requisite, necessary **erfordra** require, need, want; demand, call for; *om så ~s* if required (*etc.*), if necessary
erg (*enhet för energi*) erg
ergo|meter [-'me:-] *s2* ergometer **-nom** ergonomist; *AE.* biotechnologist **-nomi** *s3* ergonomics (*pl, behandlas som sg*); *AE.* biotechnology **-nomisk** *a5* ergonomic; *AE.* biotechnological
erhåll|a [ˣe:r-] (*få*) receive, get; (*bli tillerkänd äv.*) be awarded (granted); (*skaffa sig*) obtain, acquire, procure, secure; *vi har -it Ert brev* we are in receipt of your letter **-ande** *s6* receiving *etc.*, receipt; obtaining; *omedelbart efter ~t av*

[immediately] on receipt of
erigera [-g-] erect
eriksgata [a Swedish] king's tour of the country
erinra 1 (*påminna*) remind (*ngn om ngt* s.b. of s.th.); ~ *sig* remember, recollect, recall; *hon ~r om sin mormor* she resembles her grandmother **2** (*invända*) *jag har ingenting att ~ mot* I have no objection to make to **erinran** *r* **1** (*påminnelse*) reminder (*om* of) **2** (*varning*) admonition (*om* as to) **3** (*invändning*) objection (*mot* to) **erinring 1** *se* **erinran 2** (*hågkomst*) recollection, remembrance
erkänd [ˣeːr-] *a5* acknowledged, recognized, accepted
erkänn|a [ˣeːr-] acknowledge; (*medge äv.*) admit; (*godkänna*) recognize, accept; ~ *mottagandet av ett brev* acknowledge receipt of a letter; ~ *sig besegrad* acknowledge defeat; ~ *sig skyldig* confess o.s. [to be] guilty, *jur. äv.* plead guilty **-ande** *s6* acknowledg[e]ment; admission; recognition **-sam** *a1* appreciative; grateful (*mot* to)
erkänsla [ˣeːr-] gratitude (*mot* to); *mot kontant ~* for a consideration; *som en ~ för* in recognition of
erlägg|a [ˣeːr-] pay; ~ *avgift för* make payment for, pay **-ande** *s6* paying, payment; *mot ~ av* on (against) payment of
ernå [ˣeːr-] attain, achieve **-ende** *s6* attaining, achievement; *för ~ av* in order to attain
erodera erode
erogen [-ˈjeːn] *a5* erogenous; *~a zoner* erogenous zones [of the body]
erosion erosion
erot|ik *s3* eroticism, erotism; sex **-isk** [-ˈrɔ:- *el.* -ˈrå:-] *a5* erotic[al]
eroto|ˈman *s3* erotomaniac **-maˈni** *s3* erotomania
ers [eːrs] *se er*
ersätt|a [ˣeːr-] **1** (*gottgöra*) ~ *ngn för ngt* compensate s.b. for s.th., make up to s.b. for s.th.; ~ *ngn för hans arbete* pay (recompense) s.b. for his work **2** (*träda i stället för, byta ut*) replace, take the place of; supersede **-are** substitute; proxy; (*efterträdare*) successor **-ning 1** compensation; (*skade-*) indemnity, damages (*pl*); (*betalning*) remuneration; ~ *för sveda och värk* damages (*pl*) for pain and suffering; *AE.* smart money **2** (*surrogat*) substitute
ersättnings|anspråk claim for compensation (damages, indemnity) **-belopp** [amount of] compensation (indemnity) **-medel** substitute **-skyldig** liable to pay damages **-skyldighet** liability
ertappa [ˣeːr-] catch; ~ *ngn i färd med att* catch s.b. (+ *ing-form*); ~ *sig med att sitta och stirra* catch o.s. staring; ~ *ngn på bar gärning* catch s.b. red-handed (in the act)
erupt|ion [-pˈʃɔ:n] eruption **-ˈiv** eruptive
erövra [-öːv-] conquer; *bildl. äv.* vanquish; (*intaga*) capture; (*pris, mästerskap o.d.*) win **erövrare** conqueror **erövrarfolk** nation of conquerors **erövring** conquest; capture; *göra ~ar* (*äv. bildl.*) make conquests
erövrings|krig war of conquest (aggression) **-lust[a]** eagerness (thirst) for conquest **-po-**

litik policy of aggrandizement **-tåg** military expedition
Esaias [eˈsai-] Isaiah; (*i Nya testamentet*) Esaias
eskader [-ˈkaː-] *s2, sjö.* squadron; *flyg.* group **-chef** *sjö.* commodore; *flyg.* group captain
eskal|ation escalation **-era** escalate
eska'pad *s3* escapade
eskap|ism escapism **-ist** *s3*, **-istisk** *a5* escapist
es'karp *s3* escarp
eskatolog|i [-låˈgi:] *s3* eschatology **-isk** *a5* eschatological
eski'må *s3* Eskimo **-isk** *a5* Eskimo
eskort [-ˈårt] *s3*, **eskortera** escort **eskortfartyg** escort vessel
esomoftast [esåmˣåff-] (*då o. då*) every now and then; (*för det mesta*) mostly; (*allt som oftast*) very often
esoterisk [-ˈte:-] *a5* esoteric
espad'rill *s3* espadrille
esparto [esˈpartå] *s9*, **-gräs** esparto [grass]
esperan|tist Esperantist **-to** [-ˈrantå] *r* Esperanto
espla'nad *s3* esplanade, avenue
espresso [-ˈpresså] *s3* espresso
e'spri *s3* **1** (*kvickhet*) esprit, wit **2** (*fjäderknippe*) osprey plume, aigret[te]
1 ess *kortsp., se* **äss**
2 ess *s7, mus.* E flat
essay *se* **essä**
Ess-dur E flat major
esse *n, vara i sitt ~* be in one's element
essens [-ˈens *el.* -ˈaŋs] *s3* essence
essentiell [-n(t)siˈell] *a5* essential
esskornett cornet
es'sä *s3* essay **-ist** essayist **-samling** collection of essays
est *s3* Est[h]onian
ester [ˈess-] *s2, kem.* ester
estet *s3* aesthete **esteticism** aestheticism **estetik** *s3* aesthetics (*pl, behandlas som sg*) **estetiker** [-ˈte:-] aesthetician **estetisk** [-ˈte:-] *a5* aesthetic[al] **estetsnobb** aesthete
estimera esteem; *stat.* estimate
Estland [ˈest-] *n* Est[h]onia **estländare** *s9*, **estländsk** *a5* Est[h]onian **estländska 1** (*språk*) Est[h]onian **2** (*kvinna*) Est[h]onian woman
estnisk[a] [ˈest-] *se* **estländsk[a]**
est'rad *s3* platform, dais, rostrum; stand **-debatt** panel [discussion]
e-sträng *mus.* E string
estuarium [-ˈa:-] *s4* estuary
etabler|a establish; ~ *sig* set up [in business] for o.s., (*bosätta sig*) settle down; ~ *sig som* set up as a **-ad** established **-ing** establishment
etablisse'mang *s7* establishment; ~*et* (*det bestående samhället*) the Establishment
etage *s5* storey, floor **-lägenhet** maison[n]ette; *AE.* duplex [apartment]
e'tan *s4, s3* ethane **etanol** [-ˈnå:l] *s3* ethanol, ethyl alcohol
e'tapp *s3* **1** (*förråds- el. rastställe*) halting-place; (*vägsträcka*) day's march; (*friare*) stage, lap; *rycka fram i ~er* advance by stages (*mil., i ansatser* by bounds; *i omgångar* by echelon); *försiggå i ~er* take place in stages **2** (*förråd*) depot **-linje** *mil.* supply route, supply-line, communication zone **-vis** by (in) sta-

ges, gradually
etcetera [-'setra] et cetera (*förk.* etc., &c.)
e'ten *s3,s4* ethylene, ethene
eter ['e:-] *s2* ether, [di]ethyl ether, ethoxy-ethane; ~*n* (*rymden*) the ether **-isera** etherize **-isk** [e'te:-] *a5* ethereal; ~*a oljor* (*äv.*) essential oils
eter'nell *s3* immortelle, everlasting [flower]
eter|rus ether intoxication **-våg** ether wave
e'tik *s3* ethics (*pl, behandlas som sg i betydelsen vetenskap*) **etiker** ['e:-] moral philosopher, ethicist
eti'kett *s3* **1** (*lapp*) label (*äv. bildl.*); *sätta* ~[*er*] *på* label **2** (*umgängesformer, regler*) etiquette **-era** label
etiketts|brott breach of etiquette **-fråga** question of etiquette
etiologi *s3* aetiology
Etiopien [eti'ɷ:-] *n* Ethiopia **etiopier** [eti'ɷ:-] *s9,* **etiopisk** [eti'ɷ:-] *a5* Ethiopian
etisk ['e:-] *a5* ethical, moral
Etna [ˣe:t-] *n* [Mount] Etna
etnisk ['e:t-] *a5* ethnic[al]
etno|centrisk [-'senn-] *a5* ethnocentric **-centrism** ethnocentrism **-graf** *s3* ethnographer **-grafi** *s3* ethnography **-grafisk** [-'gra:-] *a5* ethnographical **-log** ethnologist **-logi** *s3* ethnology **-logisk** *a5* ethnological
eto|log ethologist **-logi** *s3* ethology **-logisk** *a5* ethological
Etrurien [-'tru:-] *n* Etruria
e'trusk *s3,* **etrusker** [e'truss-] *s9,* **etruskisk** [e'truss-] *a5* Etruscan, Etrurian
ets|a etch; ~ *sig in* (*a*) eat its way (*i* into), *b*) *bildl.* make an indelible impression, engrave itself (*i* on) **-are** etcher **-medel** etchant **-ning** etching **-nål** etching-needle **-plåt** etched plate
ett (*se 3 en*); ~, *tu, tre* all of a sudden; hey presto!; ~ *är nödvändigt* one thing is necessary; *vara* ~ *med* be at one with; *klockan är* ~ it is one o'clock; *i* ~ continuously; *betalning i* ~ *för allt* composition (lump sum) payment; *hålla tre mot* ~ lay three to one; *det kommer på* ~ *ut* it is all one, it's as broad as it's long
etta *s1* **1** one; *komma in som god* ~ come in an easy first; ~*n*[*s växel*] [the] first [gear] **2** *se enrumslägenhet*
ettdera ['ett-] *se endera*
etter ['ett-] I *s7* poison, venom; *bildl.* virulence, venom II *adv,* ~ *värre* worse and worse **-myra** fire ant
etthundrafemtio one hundred and fifty
ettiden *vid* ~ about one o'clock
ettrig *a1* poisonous; *bildl. äv.* fiery, hot-tempered, irascible
ett|struken *a5, mus.* one-line, once-accented; *-strukna C* middle C **-tusen** (*hopskr. ettusen*) one (a) thousand **-tåget** (*hopskr. ettåget*) the one o'clock train **-årig** *a5* one year's, one-year; (*årsgammal*) one-year old; (*som gäller för ett år*) annual **-åring** one-year old child (*etc.*), child of one (*etc.*); (*djur äv.*) yearling **-öring** one-öre piece
etu'i *s4* case; étui
e'tyd *s3* étude; study
e'tyl *s3* ethyl **-alkohol** *se etanol*
ety'len *se eten* **-glykol** ethanediol, [ethylene]

glycol
etymo|log etymologist **-logi** *s3* etymology **-logisk** *a5* etymological
eufemis|m *s3* euphemism **-tisk** *a5* euphemistic
eufon|i [evfå'ni:] *s3* euphony **-isk** [-'få:-] *s5* euphonic, euphonious
eufor|i [evfå'ri:] *s3* euphoria **-isk** [-'få:-] *a5* euphoric
eugen|ik [evg- *el.* evj-] *s3* eugenics (*pl, behandlas som sg*) **-isk** [-'ge:- *el.* -'je:-] *a5* eugenic
eukalyptus [evka'lypp-] *s2* eucalypt[us]
Euklides [-'kli:-] Euclid
eu'nuck [ev-] *s3* eunuch
Eurasien [-'a:-] *n* Eurasia
euro|dollar Eurodollar **-kommunism** Eurocommunism
Europa Europe **-marknaden** the European Economic Community, the Common Market
europa|mästare European champion **-mästerskap** European championship
Europarådet the Council of Europe
europaväg European highway
europé *s3* European
europe|isera Europeanize **-isk** [-'pe:isk *el.* -'pejsk] *a5* European; *E~a unionen* the European Union
europium [-'rɷ:-] *s8* europium
Eurovision Eurovision
eutana'si [ev-] *s3* euthanasia, mercy killing
Eva Eve
e'vad whatever; ~ *som* whatsoever
evakostym *i* ~ in the nude (the altogether, *vard.* the raw); *vard.* in one's birthday suit
evakuer|a evacuate; *de* ~*de* the evacuees **-ing** evacuation
evaluera evaluate
evalver|a (*värdera*) estimate, evaluate; (*omräkna*) convert **-ing** estimation, evaluation; conversion
evangel|isation [-j-] evangelization **-isera** evangelize **-isk** [-'je:-] *a5* evangelical **-ist** evangelist **-ium** [-'je:-] *s4* gospel
e'var where[so]ever
evene'mang *s7* [great] event; function
eventualitet *s3* eventuality, contingency; *för alla* ~*er* against (for) an emergency
eventu'ell *a5* [if] any, possible, prospective; ~*a förbättringar* emendations (improvements), if any; ~*a kostnader* any expenses that may arise; ~*a köpare* prospective buyers **eventu'ellt** *adv* possibly, perhaps; if necessary (required); *jag kommer* ~ I may [possibly] come
evertebrat *zool.* invertebrate
evidens *s3, bevisa ngt till full* ~ prove conclusively **evident** *a1* evident, obvious
evig *a1* eternal, everlasting; (*oavbruten*) perpetual; *den* ~*e* the Eternal one; *den* ~*a staden* (*Rom*) the Eternal City; *det* ~*a livet* eternal (everlasting) life; *var* ~*a dag* every single day; *en* ~ *lögn* a confounded lie; *detta* ~*a regnande* this perpetual (everlasting) rain; ~ *snö* perpetual snow; *det tog en* ~ *tid* it took ages **evighet** eternity; *i* [*all*] ~ for ever, in perpetuity; *för tid och* ~ now and for evermore; *det är* ~*er sedan vi sågs* it's ages since we met
evighets|blomma *se eternell* **-göra** never-ending job **-låga** (*gas-*) pilot flame; *relig. e.d.*

eternal flame **-längtan** yearning for things eternal **-maskin** perpetual motion machine **-tro** belief in eternity

evigt *adv* eternally; *för* ~ for ever

evinnerlig [e'vinn-] *a5* eternal, everlasting, endless **-en** eternally; for ever

evolution evolution **-ist** evolutionist

evolutionsteori theory of evolution

evärdlig [e'vä:rd-] *a5* eternal; *för ~a tider* for ever, for all time

ex'akt *a1* exact; precise **-het** exactness; precision

exalt|ation exaltation **-erad** [-'te:-] *a5* exalted; *(friare)* excited, agitated

exam|en *-en -ina, r* examination; *vard.* exam; *avlägga akademisk* ~ take a university degree, graduate; *ta* ~ pass one's examination; *gå upp i* ~ present o.s. for one's examination

examens|betyg examination certificate **-bok** *ung.* examination record book **-feber** exam nerves *(pl)* **-fordringar** examination requirements **-förrättare** examiner **-läsning** reading [up] for an examination **-nämnd** examining board, board of examiners **-uppgift** examination paper **-ämne** examination subject

exami'n|and *s3* examinee **-ation** examination **-ator** *s3* examiner **-era** examine, question; *(växt)* determine **-ering** *(av växt)* determination

excell|ens *s3* excellency; *Ers* ~ Your Excellency **-ent** *a1* excellent **-era** excel *(i* in, at)

excenter [ek'senn-] *s2* eccentric **-skiva** eccentric disc (sheave)

excentr|icitet *s3* eccentricity **-isk** [ek'senn-] *a5* eccentric

exceptio'nell [eksepʃɷ-] exceptional

excerper|a [ekser-] excerpt, make excerpts **-ing** excerpting, excerption

excerpt [ek'särpt] *s7, s3* excerpt

excess [ek'sess] *s3* excess; *~er (utsvävningar)* orgies

excitera excite *(äv. fys.)*; *~d* excited

exdrottning ex-queen

exe|'ges *s3* exegesis **-'get** *s3* exegete, exegetist **-getik** *s3* exegetics *(pl, behandlas som sg)* **-getisk** [-'ge:-] *a5* exegetic[al]

exekution 1 *(avrättning)* execution **2** *(utmätning)* distraint, distress

exekutions|betjänt bailiff **-pluton** firing squad

exeku'tiv *a5 o. s3* executive; ~ *auktion* compulsory auction **exekutor** [-ˣku:tår] *s3* executor; executory officer **exekutör** executor

exekvera execute

exempel [ek'semm-] *s7* example; *(inträffat fall)* instance; *belysande (avskräckande)* ~ illustrative (warning) example; *belysa med* ~ illustrate by examples, exemplify; *föregå med gott* ~ set an (a good) example; *statuera ett* ~ make an example; *till* ~ for instance, say, *(vid uppräkning)* e.g. **-lös** unprecedented, unparalleled; exceptional **-samling** collection of examples **-vis** for instance; by way of example

exem'plar *s7* copy; *naturv.* specimen; *i två (tre)* ~ in duplicate (triplicate); *i fem* ~ in five [identical] copies; *renskrivet* ~ fair copy **-isk** *a5* exemplary; *en ~ ung man* a model (an exem-

plary) young man

exemplifi|era exemplify **-kation** exemplification

exercera drill, train; ~ *beväring* do one's military service; ~ *med* drill, work **exer'cis** *s3* drill; military service **exercisfält** drill-ground

exer'gi *s3* exergy

exhibition|ism exhibitionism **-ist** exhibitionist **-istisk** *a5* exhibitionistic

e'xil *s3* exile **-regering** exile government

exis'tens *s3* **1** *(tillvaro)* existence, life; being; *(utkomst)* living, subsistence **2** *(person)* individual **-berättigande** raison d' tre, right to exist **-minimum** subsistence level **-möjlighet** means of support, possibility of making a living **-villkor** *pl* conditions of existence

existential|ism [-(t)sia-] existentialism **-ist** *s3*, **-istisk** *a5* existentialist

existera exist; live; subsist; *~r fortfarande* is still in existence, is extant

exklamation exclamation

exklu|dera exclude, reject, expel **-'siv** *a1* exclusive **-sive** [-'si:-] excluding, exclusive of; ~ *emballage* excluding packing, packing excluded **-sivitet** exclusiveness, exclusivity

exkommuni|cera excommunicate **-kation** excommunication

exkonung ex-king

exkrementer [-'menn-] *pl* excrements, faeces

ex'kre|t *s7* excreta *(pl)* **-tion** [-e'ʃɷ:n] excretion

ex'kurs *s3* excursus **-ion** [-r'ʃɷ:n] excursion; *göra en* ~ go on an excursion

exlibris [-'li:-] *s7* ex-libris, bookplate

exo|biologi exobiology, astrobiology **-ergisk** [-'ärg-] *a5* exoergic

ex officio [å'fi:siå] ex officio, by right of office (position)

exo|gen [-'je:n] *a5* exogenous **-'krin** *a5* exocrine; ~ *körtel* exocrine gland

exorc|ism exorcism **-ist** exorcist

exo'sfär *s3* exosphere

exo|terisk [-'te:-] *a5* exoteric **-term[isk]** *a5* exothermic, exothermal

exot|isk [ek'så:-] *a5* exotic **-ism** exoticism

expander [-'pann-] *s2* expander **expandera** expand **expanderbult** expansion bolt

expansion [-n'ʃɷ:n] expansion; *stadd i* ~ expanding **-ism** expansionism **-'istisk** *a5* expansionistic

expansions|förmåga capacity of expansion **-kärl** expansion tank

expan'siv *a1* expansive

expatrier|a expatriate **-ing** expatriation

expedier|a 1 *(sända)* send, dispatch, forward; *(per post)* post, mail; *(ombesörja)* carry out, dispatch **2** *(betjäna)* attend to **3** *(göra slut på)* settle **-ing** *(av kunder)* attendance, serving; *jfr äv. expedition*

expe'dit *s3* shop assistant; salesman, *fem.* saleswoman; *AE.* [sales]clerk

expedition 1 *(avsändande)* sending, dispatch, forwarding; *(per post)* posting, mailing; *(ombesörjande)* execution, carrying out **2** *(betjänande)* attendance, serving of customers **3** *(lokal för expediering)* office; department **4** *(forsknings- o. mil.)* expedition

expeditions|avgift service (dispatch) fee **-chef** permanent undersecretary **-ministär** caretaker government **-tid** office (business) hours (*pl*)
expeditör sender, forwarding agent
expenser [-'penn-] *pl* expenses; (*småutgifter*) petty expenditure (*sg*)
experiment *s7* experiment; (*prov*) trial, test; *jfr äv. försök* **experimentator** *s3* experimenter **experimentdjur** *se försöksdjur* **experimen-'tell** *a5* experimental **experimentera** experiment (*på* on) **experimentstadium** experimental stage
ex'pert *s3* expert (*på* in); specialist (*på* on) **exper'tis** *s3* expertise, expertness; (*sakkunniga*) experts (*pl*)
expert|kommission commission of experts **-kommitté** committee of experts, advisory committee **-utlåtande** expert opinion, report of experts **-utredning** [findings of a] specialist investigation
explana'tiv *a5* explanatory, explanative
expli'cit *a4* explicit
explikation (*tolkning*) explication, explanation
exploat|era (*bearbeta*) exploit; (*gruva äv.*) work; (*uppfinning äv.*) develop; (*utsuga*) make money (capital) out of, tap **-ering** exploitation: working **-ör** developer
explodera explode, blow up; (*detonera*) detonate; (*om bildäck*) burst
explor|ation exploration **-era** explore
explosion explosion; detonation; burst
explosions|artad [-a:r-] *a5* explosive **-fri** explosion-proof **-motor** internal-combustion engine **-risk** danger of explosion **-ritning** exploded view
explo'siv *a1* explosive; *~a varor* explosives
exponen|t exponent (*för* of); *mat. äv.* power, index **-tiell** [-tsi'ell] exponential
exponer|a (*utställa*) exhibit, show; (*blottställa o. foto.*) expose; *~ sig* expose o.s. **-ing** *foto.* exposure
exponerings|mätare exposure (light) meter **-tid** [time of] exposure
ex'port *s3* (*utförsel*) export, export trade; exportation; (*varor*) exports (*pl*) **-affär** export business, exportation **-artikel** *se -vara* **-avgift** export duty
export|era export **-firma** export[ing] firm **-förbud** ban on export[s] **-förening** export[ers'] association; *Sveriges allmänna ~* [the] General Export Association of Sweden **-hamn** export port **-handel** export trade **-industri** export[ing] industry **-kreditnämnd** *~en* [the Swedish] export credits guarantee board **-licens** export licence **-marknad** export market **-råd** *Sveriges ~* [the] Swedish Trade Council **-tillstånd** export permit (licence) **-tull** export duty **-underskott** export deficit **-vara** export product; exports, export goods (*pl*); *AE äv.* exportation **-öl** export beer
export|ör exporter **-överskott** export surplus
expos|é *s3* survey; summary **-ition** exhibition
expresident ex-President, former P.
ex'press I *s3, se expressbyrå, expresståg* **II** *adv* express; *sända ~* send by express (special delivery) **-brev** express (special delivery) letter **-bud** express (special) message **-byrå** (*åkeri*) transport firm (agency); (*budcentral*) parcel-delivery agency **-försändelse** (*paket*) express (special delivery) parcel; *se äv. -brev* **-gods** express goods (*pl*); *sända som ~* send by express, express
expression|ism [-preʃɷ-] expressionism **-ist** expressionist **-istisk** *a5* expressionistic
expres'siv *a1* expressive
expresståg express train
expropri|ation expropriation **-era** expropriate
exspir|ation [eksp-] expiration **-era** expire
exsu'dat *s7, med.* exudation, exudate
ex'ta|s *s3* ecstasy; *råka i ~* (*bildl.*) go into ecstasies (raptures) **-tisk** *a5* ecstatic
extemporera extemporize
exten'siv [*äv.* 'eks-] *a1* extensive
exteriör exterior
extern [-'tä:rn] **I** *s3* (*elev*) day scholar, extern **II** *a1* (*yttre*) external
exterritorialrätt [-ˣa:l-] extraterritorial rights (*pl*)
extra *oböjligt a o. adv* extra, additional; (*ovanlig*) extraordinary, special; (*biträdande äv.*) assistant; (*mycket fin*) superior; *~ avgift* surcharge; *~ billig* exceptionally cheap; *~ kontant* prompt cash; *~ tilldelning* supplementary allowance **-arbete** extra work; additional source of income **-förtjänst** extra income; *~er* extras
extrahera extract
extra|inkomst *se extraförtjänst* **-knäck** job on the side; *vard.* moonlighting; *jag tjänar några pund i veckan på ~* (*vard.*) I'm raking in a few quid every week on extra work **-knäcka** *vard.* moonlight **-knäckare** moonlighter
ex'trakt *s7, s4* extract; essence **extraktion** [-k'ʃɷ:n] extraction **extraktor** [-ˣaktår] extractor
extra|lektion extra (private) lesson **-lärare** temporary master **-nummer 1** (*av tidning*) special issue, extra [edition] **2** (*utöver programmet*) extra performance, encore **-ordinarie** [-'na:-] **I** *oböjligt a* temporary-staff, pro tempore, pro tem. **II** *s5* temporary officer (official, clerk); *vara ~* be on the temporary staff **-ordi'när** extraordinary **-personal** extras (*pl*), extra staff (personnel) **-polera** *mat.* extrapolate **-polering** *mat.* extrapolation **-pris** special offer **-säng** spare bed **-tur** special trip; extra service **-tåg** relief (special) [train] **-uppdrag** special assignment **-upplaga** special edition **-utgift** additional expense
extravag|ans [-'ans *el.* -'aŋs] *s3* extravagance **-ant** [-'ant *el.* -'aŋt] *a1* extravagant
ex'trem *a1 o. s7, s3* extreme **-ism** extremism **-ist** extremist **-istisk** *a5* extremist
extremitet *s3* extremity
extrovert [-'värt] *a4* extrovert, extravert

F

fabel ['fa:-] *s3* fable **-aktig** *a1* fabulous **-dikt-ning** writing of fables **-djur** fabulous beast
fabla [*fa:-] ~ *om* romance about, make up fantastic stories about
fabricera manufacture, make, produce; *bildl.* make up, fabricate
fa'brik *s3* factory; works (*pl, behandlas vanl. som sg*); mill, workshop; *AE.* [manufacturing] plant; *fritt* ~ ex works, free at mill **fabrikant** (*fabriksägare*) factory owner, manufacturer; (*tillverkare*) maker, manufacturer **fabrikat** *s7* (*vara*) manufacture, product; (*i sht textil-*) fabric; (*tillverkning*) make **fabrikation** manufacture, manufacturing, making, production **fabrikations|fel** flaw, defect [in manufacture] **-hemlighet** trade secret **fabriks|anläggning** *se fabrik* **-arbetare** factory worker (hand) **-byggnad** factory building **-gjord** *a5* factory-made **-idkare** manufacturer, factory owner **-kontor** factory office **-lokal** ~*er* factory premises **-märke** trademark **-mässig** *a1* factory, large-scale **-mässigt** *adv* on an industrial basis **-ny** brandnew **-skorsten** factory chimney **-tillverkad** factory-made **-vara** factory-made article; *-varor* manufactured goods
fabrikör factory owner, manufacturer
fabuler|a fable; ~ *om* romance (make up stories) about **-ing** fable-making **-ingsförmåga** *ha* ~ have a fertile imagination
fabu'lös *a1* fabulous
fa'cil *a1* (*om pris*) moderate, reasonable **-itet** *s3* facility
facit ['fa:-] **1** *n* answer, result; *bildl.* result **2** *best. form* = *el. -en, r* (*bok*) key
fack *s7* **1** (*förvaringsrum*) partition, box; (*del av hylla e.d.*) compartment, pigeonhole **2** (*gren, bransch*) department, line, branch; (*yrke*) profession, trade; *det hör inte till mitt* ~ it is not in my line **-arbetare** skilled worker **-bok** book of nonfiction; handbook, textbook **fackel|bärare** torchbearer (*äv. bildl.*) **-tåg** torchlight procession
fack|förbund federation [of trade unions] **-förening** trade (*AE.* labor) union
fackförenings|medlem trade unionist, trade-union member **-pamp** union boss **-rörelse** trade unionism, trade-union movement
fack|idiot narrow specialist **-kretsar** *pl* professional circles **-kunnig** experienced, skilled **-kunskap** professional knowledge
fackla *s1* torch, flare
facklig *a1* [trade-]union
fack|litteratur nonfiction **-lärare** teacher specializing in one subject (group of subjects) **-man** professional [man]; specialist, expert; *han är inte* ~ *på området* he is not a specialist in the field **-mannahåll** *i uttr.: på* ~ among experts; *på* ~ *anser man* experts agree **-mässig**

a1 professional **-ord** *se -term* **-press** specialist (professional, technical) press **-skola** continuation school **-språk** technical language **-studier** vocational studies; *bedriva* ~ *i* specialize in **-term** technical term **-tidskrift** trade (professional, technical, scientific) journal **-utbildning** professional (specialized) training **-uttryck** se *-term*
fack|verk framework **-verksbro** truss (lattice) bridge
factoring ['fäktəriŋ] factoring **-bolag** factoring company
fadd *a1* flat, stale; *bildl.* vapid, insipid
fadder ['fadd-] *s2* godfather, godmother; (*friare*) sponsor; *stå* ~ *för* be (act as) [a] godfather (*etc.*) to, *bildl.* stand sponsor to **-barn** godchild; sponsored (adopted) child **-gåva** *i* ~ as a christening gift
fader *-n fäder* (*jfr far*) father (*till* of); (*alstrare äv.*) procreator; (*-djur*) sire; *Gud F~* God the Father; *F~ vår, som är i himmelen* Our Father, which art in Heaven; *stadens fäder* the city fathers; *han har samlats till sina fäder* he has been gathered to this fathers **-lig** *a1* fatherly, paternal **-lös** fatherless **-mördare 1** parricide **2** (*slags krage*) high starched collar, choker
fadersarv patrimony
fader|skap *s7* fatherhood; *i sht jur.* paternity **-skapsmål** affiliation proceedings (*pl*); *AE.* paternity suit **-'vår** *n* the Lord's Prayer; *läsa ett* ~ say the Lord's Prayer
fading ['fejdiŋ] *radio.* fading
fa'däs *s3* foolishness, blunder; faux pas
fager ['fa:-] *a2* fair; (*om löften, ord*) fine; ~ *under ögonen* good-looking, bonny
faggorna *best. form pl, vara i* ~ be imminent (in the offing); *ha ngt i* ~ be in for, (*om sjukdom*) have ... coming on
fago'cyt *s3* phagocyte
fa'gott [-å-] *s3* bassoon **-ist** bassoonist
Fahrenheit ['fa:-] Fahrenheit
faiblesse *s5, se fäbless*
fajans [-'jans *el.* -'jaŋs] *s3* faïence, tin-glazed earthenware
fajt *s3,* **fajtas** *v1* fight
fa'kir *s3* fakir
faksi'mil *s7* facsimile **-tryck** facsimile print **-utgåva** facsimile edition
faktaspäckad crammed with (full of) facts, information-packed
faktisk ['fack-] *a5* real, actual, founded on facts; *det* ~*a förhållandet* the facts (*pl*), the actual situation **faktiskt** ['fack-] *adv* really *etc.*; in fact; (*bekräftande*) honestly
faktor [-år] *s3* **1** factor; *den mänskliga* ~*n* the human element **2** (*tryckeriföreståndare*) foreman, overseer **-analys** factor analysis
fakto'ri *s4* **1** (*varunederlag*) factory, trading settlement **2** (*fabrik*) [manu]factory
faktotum [-*to:-] *n* factotum, right-hand man
fakt|um *s8* fact; ~ *är* the fact is; *konstatera -a* point out facts
faktura [-*tu:-] *s1* invoice, bill (*på ett belopp* for an amount); *det på* ~*n angivna beloppet* the invoice[d] amount; *enligt* ~ as per invoice **-belopp** invoice amount
fakturer|a invoice, bill **-ing** invoicing, billing

-ingsmaskin billing machine
fakulta'tiv [äv. 'fack-] *a1* optional
fakultet *s3* faculty
fal *a1 (om sak)* for sale; *(om pers.)* mercenary, venal
falang phalanx; wing, group; *F~en (i Spanien)* Falange **-ist** Falangist
falk *s2* falcon; *AE.* hawk
falk|a spy out *(efter* for); ~ *efter ngt (att bli ngt)* have one's eye on s.th. (on becoming s.th.) **-blick** *ha* ~ be eagle-eyed (hawk-eyed)
falk|enerare [-ˣne:-] falconer **-jakt** hawking; *(som konst)* falconry
Falklandsöarna [ˣfä:k-] the Falkland Islands
falkög|a *ha -on, se falkblick*
fall *s7* **1** *(av falla)* fall; descent; *(lutning)* slope; *(kläders o.d.)* hang; *bildl.* [down]fall, collapse; *(pris- o.d.)* fall, decline; *(vatten-)* falls *(pl)*, waterfall; *platt* ~ *(brottn.)* [pin]fall, *bildl.* fiasco, *vard.* flop; *hejda ngn i ~et* prevent s.b. from falling; *bringa ngn på* ~ cause a p.'s downfall; *komma på* ~ come to ruin **2** *(händelse, tillfälle, exempel o.d.)* case, instance, event; *ett typiskt* ~ a typical case; *från* ~ *till* ~ in each specific case; *i alla* ~ *a) eg.* in all cases, *b) (i alla händelser)* in any case, at all events, anyhow, anyway, at least; *i annat* ~ [or] else, otherwise; *i bästa* ~ at best; *i de* ~ *då* where, when; *i förekommande* ~ where applicable; *i så* ~ in that case; *i varje* ~ in any case; *i vilket* ~ *som helst* in any case, come what may; *i värsta* ~ if the worst comes to the worst **3** *sjö.* halyard
fall|a *föll fallit* **I** *(störta* [*ner*]) fall; *(om kläder o.d.)* hang; *(om regering)* fall, be overthrown; ~ *av hästen (i vattnet)* fall off one's horse (into the water); *låta* ~ let fall, *(släppa)* let go; *låta frågan* ~ drop the question; *hur föll hans ord?* what were his actual words?; *det -er av sig självt* that is a matter of course; ~ *för frestelsen* yield to temptation; ~ *för ngn* fall for s.b.; ~ *i glömska* be forgotten, fall into oblivion; ~ *i god jord* fall on good ground; ~ *i händerna på ngn* ngn fall into a p.'s hands; ~ *i pris* fall in price; ~ *i sömn* fall asleep; ~ *i ögonen* catch (strike) the eye; ~ *ngn i ryggen* attack s.b. from behind; ~ *ngn i smaken* be to a p.'s taste; ~ *ngn i talet* interrupt s.b.; ~ *ngn om halsen* fling one's arms around a p.'s neck; ~ *till föga* yield, give in; ~ *ur minnet* escape one's memory; ~ *ur rollen* act out of character **II** *(med betonad partikel)* **1** ~ *av* fall off, *(om frukt, löv)* come down, drop off, *bildl.* droop, be in the decline, *sjö.* fall off **2** ~ *ifrån* die, pass away **3** ~ *igen* fall (shut) to **4** ~ *igenom (i examen)* fail, *vard.* be ploughed, *(vid val)* be rejected, be defeated **5** ~ *ihop (om pers.)* collapse **6** ~ *in* fall in, *mus.* strike in, *(om ljus)* come in **7** ~ *ngn in* occur to s.b., enter a p.'s head; *det föll mig aldrig in* it never occurred to me; *det skulle aldrig ~ mig in att* I should never dream of (+ *ing-form*) **8** ~ *in i ledet (mil.)* fall in; get into line **9** ~ *isär, se* ~ *sönder* **10** ~ *ner* fall down *(död* dead, *för en trappa* a flight of stairs) **11** ~ *omkull* fall [over], tumble down **12** ~ *på* come on; *när andan -er på* when one is in the mood **13** ~ *sönder* fall to pieces **14** ~ *tillbaka* fall (drop,

slip) back *(på* on), *(om beskyllning)* come home *(på* to), *(om sparkapital e.d.)* fall back *(på* on) **15** ~ *undan* fall away, *bildl.* give way (yield) *(för* to) **16** ~ *upp (om bok)* open [itself], fall open **17** ~ *ut (om flod o.d.)* fall *(i* into) **18** ~ *ut genom fönstret* fall out of the window **III** *rfl (hända)* chance, happen, fall out; *det föll sig naturligt att* it came natural to; *det föll sig så att* it so happened that
fallande|sjuk epileptic **-sjuka** falling sickness (evil), epilepsy
fall|bila guillotine
fallen *a5* **1** fallen *(äv. bildl.)*; *de fallna* the fallen (slain); *en* ~ *storhet* a fallen star; ~ *efter (om husdjur)* [bred] out of; *stå som* ~ *från skyarna* be struck all of a heap **2** ~ *för studier* have a gift for studying **-het** *(för ngt förmånligt)* gift (talent, aptitude) *(för* for), proneness *(to* för); *(för ngt oförmånligt)* predisposition *(för* to, towards)
fallera *vard. (fattas)* lack, be short of; *(slå fel)* go wrong, miscarry
fall|frukt *koll.* windfall[s *pl*] **-färdig** tumble-down, ramshackle, dilapidated **-grop** pitfall *(äv. bildl.)* **-höjd** [height of] fall, drop
fallisk ['fall-] *a5* phallic
fallissemang *s7, s4* failure, collapse, crash
fallit *sup. av falla*
fallos ['fallås] *s2* phallus
fall|rep 1 *sjö., se fallrepstrappa* **2** *vara på ~et* be at the end of one's tether, be on the brink of bankruptcy **-repstrappa** *sjö.* gangplan, gangway
fallskärm parachute; *hoppa i* ~ make a parachute jump; *landsätta med* ~ [drop by] parachute
fallskärms|avtal golden parachute **-hopp** parachute jump (descent) **-hoppare** parachutist **-jägare** paratrooper; *koll.* paratroop[er]s, parachute troops **-trupper** parachute troops, paratroop[er]s
fallstudie case study
fallucka trap door
falna [ˣfa:l-] *(om glöd o.d.)* die down
fals *s2* **1** *(på bleckplåtar o.d.)* lap; *(på gryta o.d.)* rim **2** *bokb.* guard **3** *snick. (löpränna)* groove **falsa 1** lap **2** fold **3** groove
falsarium [-'sa:-] *s4* forgery; falsification
fal'sett *s3, mus.* falsetto; *fonet.* head voice (register); *sjunga i* ~ sing falsetto; *tala i* ~ talk in a fluting voice **-röst** falsetto voice
falsifiera falsify **falsifi'kat** *s7* counterfeit, forgery **falsifikation** falsification
falsk *a1* false; *(oriktig)* wrong; *(bedräglig)* delusive; *(förfalskad)* forged; *(eftergjord)* fictitious, sham, counterfeit, bogus; *(låtsad)* feigned, pretended; *~t alarm* a false alarm; ~ *blygsamhet* false modesty; *~t pass* forged passport; *~a pengar* counterfeit (bad) money; *~a pärlor* sham (imitation) pearls; *göra sig ~a föreställningar om ngt* fool o.s. about s.th.; *under ~ flagg* under false colours; *under ~t namn* under a false name **-deklarant** tax evader (dodger) **-deklaration** tax evasion (dodging) **-deklarera** make a fraudulent income tax return

F

falsk|eligen falsely *etc.*, *jfr falsk* **-het** falseness; (*hos pers. äv.*) duplicity, deceit; (*oäkthet*) spuriousness, fictitiousness **-myntare** counterfeiter, coiner **-skyltad** *a5* (*om bil*) provided with false [number, *AE.* license] plates **-spel** cheating (swindling) at cards (*etc.*); cardsharping **-spelare** cheat; cardsharp[er] **falskt** *adv* falsely; *spela ~* (*mus.*) play false notes (out of tune)

falukorv *ung.* lightly-smoked bologna (polony) sausage

fa'milj *s3* family; *~en B.* the B. family; *bilda ~* raise a family, marry and have children; *av god ~* of good family; *vara av god ~* come of a good family

familje|angelägenheter *pl* family affairs (matters) **-bibel** family Bible **-bidrag** family allowance; *mil.* separation allowance **-bolag** family business **-daghem** registered child-minding home; pre-school play group **-drama** family tragedy **-far** father of a (the) family; family man **-flicka** girl of good family **-företag** *se* -*bolag* **-förhållanden** *pl* family circumstances **-förpackning** economy pack (size) **-försörjare** breadwinner, supporter of a (the) family **-grav** family grave (vault) **-hotell** *se kollektivhus* **-krets** family circle **-liv** family life **-medlem** member of a (the) family **-namn** family name, surname **-planering** family planning **-rådgivning** family guidance (counselling, *AE.* counseling) **-rätt** family law **-skäl** *av ~* for family reasons **-överhuvud** head of [the] family

famil'jär *a1* familiar; *alltför ~* (*äv.*) too free [and easy] (*mot* with)

faml|a grope (*efter* for); *~ i mörkret* grope about in the dark **-ande I** *s6* groping **II** *a4* groping; *bildl.* tentative

famn *s2* **1** (*ngns* a p.'s) arms (*pl*); (*fång*) armful; *ta ngn i* [*sin*] *~* embrace s.b.; *kom i min ~!* come into my arms! **2** (*längdmått*) fathom; (*rymdmått*) cord (*ved* of firewood) **famna** embrace; (*omsluta*) encompass, encircle **famntag** embrace; (*häftigt*) hug

fa'mös *a1, iron.* [so] famous; (*illa beryktad*) notorious

1 fan *s7* (*på fjäder*) web, vane [of a feather]

2 fan *r* the devil, the deuce; *~ heller!* hell, no!; *fy ~!* hell!, damn it all!; *åh ~!* well, I'll be damned!; *stackars ~!* (*om pers.*) poor devil!; *det vete ~* the devil only knows; *det ger jag ~ i* I don't care a damn; *ta mig ~, om* I'm damned if; *han är full i* (*av*) *~* he is a cunning [old] devil; *har man tagit ~ i båten får man också ro honom i land* in for a penny, in for a pound

3 fan [fänn] *en fan, pl =, äv. -s* (*entusiast*) fan

fan|a *s1* banner, standard, flag (*äv. bildl.*); *mil.* colours (*pl*); *den blågula ~n* the Swedish colours; *med flygande -or och klingande spel* with flags flying and drums beating; *hålla konstens ~ högt* keep the banner of Art flying

fanat|iker [-'na:-] fanatic **-isk** *a5* fanatic[al] **-ism** fanaticism

fan|borg massed standards (*pl*) **-bärare** standard-bearer

fanders ['fann-] *oböjligt s, vard., åt ~ med ...!* ... be hanged!; *dra åt ~!* go to the devil!, go

to hell!, drop dead!

fa'ner *s7*, **fanera** *v1* veneer

fanero'gam I *s3* phanerogam **II** *a5* phanerogamic, phanerogamous

fanerskiva veneer sheet

fan'far *s3* fanfare; *blåsa en ~* sound a fanfare

fanflykt desertion [from the colours] **-ing** deserter [from the colours]

fanjunkare (*vid armén, kustartilleriet*) warrant officer class 1 (class 2); (*vid flottan*) fleet chief petty officer; (*vid flygvapnet*) warrant officer; *AE.* (*vid armén, marinkåren*) master sergeant, (*vid flottan*) senior chief petty officer, (*vid flygvapnet*) senior master sergeant

fanken *r, ta mig ~* I'll be damned

fann *imperf. av finna*

fanskap ['fa:n-] *s7*, **fanstyg** ['fa:ns-] *s7* [piece of] devilry

fanta'si *s3* **1** (*inbillningskraft, föreställningsförmåga*) imagination, imaginative power; (*djärvare*) fancy, fantasy; *livlig ~* vivid imagination; *ge ~n fritt spelrum* give free rein to one's imagination, let one's imagination run away with one **2** (*inbillningsprodukt*) fancy; imagination, fantasy; *~ och verklighet* dreams and reality; *fria ~er* pure fantasy (fabrications), wild imaginings; *försjunken i* [*sina*] *~er* absorbed in reveries (daydreams) **3** *mus.* fantasia

fantasi|eggande stimulating to the imagination; *det är ~* it stirs the imagination **-foster** figment of the imagination **-full** imaginative **-lös** unimaginative **-pris** fancy price **-rik** highly imaginative **-rikedom** wealth of imagination **-värld** world of the imagination; (*barns*) make-believe world

fantasma [-'tass-] *s1* phantasm **-go'ri** *s3* phantasmagoria

fan'tast *s3* fantast, dreamer **-isk** *a5* fantastic[al]; fanciful

fantisera indulge in daydreams (reveries), dream; (*mus. o. friare*) improvise; *~ ihop* concoct, imagine

fantom [-'tå:m] *s7, s3* phantom **-bild** *ung.* identikit **-smärta** *med.* phantom [limb] pain

fanvakt colour guard

far *fadern fäder* (*jfr fader*); *smeks.* dad[dy]; *bli ~* become a father; *han är ~ till* he is the father of

1 fara *s1* danger; (*stor*) peril; (*vågspel*) hazard; (*risk*) risk; *~n över!* (*signal*) all clear!; *ingen ~* [*på taket*]! don't worry!, no harm done!; *med ~ för eget liv* at the risk of one's life; *med ~ att* at the risk of (+ *ing-form*); *utom all ~* [quite] out of danger; *sväva i ~* be in danger; *utsätta för ~* expose to danger; *det är ~ värt att* there is a risk that; *det är ingen ~ med honom* he's all right (out of danger)

2 fara *for farit* **I** go; (*färdas*) travel; (*i vagn*) drive; (*avresa*) leave (*till* for); *~ i luften* (*explodera*) blow up, (*bli rasande*) vard. fly off the handle; *~ illa* fare badly, be badly treated; *hatten far illa av att* it is bad for the hat to; *~ illa med* handle roughly, knock about; *~ med osanning* tell lies; *~ med tåg* go by rail (train); *~ sin väg* go away, depart, leave; *~ till a*) (*en pers.*) go to see, *b*) (*en plats*) go (travel, drive) to; *det är ett annat namn jag far efter* it is another name I am trying to get hold of **II** (*med betonad partikel*) **1** ~ *bort* drive away, (*friare*) leave [home], go away [from home] **2** ~ *efter ngn* (*hämta*) fetch s.b. **3** ~ *fram* (*eg.*) drive up (*till* to); ~ *varligt fram med* treat gently, go gently with; ~ *fram som ett vilddjur* carry (go) on like a wild thing (a madman); ~ *illa fram med* be rough in one's treatment of **4** ~ *förbi* go (drive) past (by), pass **5** ~ *före ngn* go on ahead of s.b. **6** ~ *i*; *vad har farit i honom?* what has taken possession of him (got into him)? **7** ~ *ifrån* go (drive) away from, depart from, leave **8** ~ *igenom* travel (pass) through; *en tanke for igenom honom* a thought flashed through his mind; *jfr genomfara* **9** ~ *in till staden* go (run) up to town; ~ *in från landet* travel in from the country **10** ~ *iväg* go off **11** ~ *med a*) go too (with the others), *b*) (*ngn*) go (*ibl.* come) with s.b. **12** ~ *omkring* travel about (*i* in); ~ *omkring som ett torrt skinn* bustle about **13** ~ *på* fly (rush) at (*ngn* s.b.) **14** ~ *upp a*) (*om pers.*) spring (jump) to one's feet, *b*) (*öppna sig*) fly up, open **15** ~ *ut på landet* go into the country; ~ *ut mot ngn* let fly at s.b. **16** ~ *vilse* lose one's way, go astray **17** ~ *över ngt med handen* pass one's hand over (across) s.th.; ~ *över med blicken* glance over

fa'rad *s3, fys.* farad
farao *s3* Pharaoh
farbar [ˣfaːr-] *a1* (*om väg*) passable, open to traffic, *sjö.* navigable
far|broderlig [ˣfarr-] *a1* avuncular; (*välvillig*) benevolent **-bror** [ˣfarr-] uncle; *eg.* father's brother; (*friare*) [kindly old] gentleman
far|far [ˣfarfar] [paternal] grandfather, *vard.* grandpa[pa] **-farsfar** [-faːr] great-grandfather **-föräldrar** [ˣfaːr-] [paternal] grandparents
fargalt [ˣfaːr-] *s2* boar
farhåg|a [ˣfaːr-] apprehension, fear, misgiving; *hysa -or* entertain (have) apprehensions (*för* about, as to); *mina -or besannades* my fears came true
fa'rin *s4, s3,* **farinsocker** demerara (brown) sugar
faris|é *s3* Pharisee **-'eisk** *a5* Pharisaic[al] **-eism** Pharisaism, Phariseeism
farit *sup. av 2 fara*
far|kost [ˣfaːrkåst] *s3* vessel, boat, craft; *poet.* barque **-led** channel, [navigable] course (passage), track, fairway
farlig [ˣfaːr-] *a1* **1** dangerous (*för* for); (*förenad med stor fara*) perilous; (*äventyrlig*) hazardous, risky; (*kritisk*) critical; ~ *för den allmänna säkerheten* a danger to the public; *det är inte så ~t med honom* there is not much wrong with him; *det är inte så ~t som det låter* it is not so bad as it seems **2** ('*förskräcklig*') awful, dreadful **-het** dangerousness *etc.*
farm *s2, s3* farm
farmaceut [-'sevt] *s3* pharmac[eut]ist, dispenser **-isk** *a5* pharmaceutic[al], pharmacal
farma'ci *s3* pharmacy, pharmaceutics (*pl, behandlas som sg*)
farmako|log pharmacologist **-logi** *s3* pharmacology **-logisk** *a5* pharmacological
farmakopé *s3* pharmacopoeia
farmare farmer

far|mor [ˣfarmɵr] [paternal] grandmother, grandma[ma]; *smeks.* gran[ny] **-morsmor** great grandmother
faro|fylld *a5* fraught with danger **-zon** danger zone
fars *s3* farce
farsa *s1, vard.* dad; pop; *se äv. farsgubben*
farsartad [ˣfarsaːr-] *a5* farcical
fars|arv [ˣfaːrs-] patrimony **-gubben** *vard.* my (*etc.*) [old] dad; the old man, the governor, the guv
farsot [ˣfaːr-] *s3* epidemic; pestilence
farstu *s5, se förstuga*
fart [-aː-] *s3* **1** (*hastighet*) speed; (*i sht vetenskapligt*) velocity; (*takt, tempo*) pace; (*fartygs-o.d.*) headway; *med en ~ av* at a speed of; *i* (*med*) *full* ~ at full speed; *i rasande* ~ at breakneck speed; *alltid i ~en* always on the go; *komma i ~en* get into stride, get going; *medan man är i ~en* while one is at it; *minska ~en* slow down; *öka ~en* speed up; *sätta full* ~ go full speed ahead; *det gick av bara ~en* it went automatically, it happened unintentionally **2** (*ansats*) start, run; *ta* ~ get a start **3** (*livlighet, raskhet*) force, energy, activity; push; *komma riktigt i ~en* get into full swing; *sätta* ~ *på* speed up, get going; *det gick med* ~ *och fläkt* it went with a bang; *det är ingen* ~ *i honom* there is no go (*vard.* dash) about him **4** (*sjö.* trade; *gå i utrikes* ~ be in foreign trade
fart|begränsning speed limit **-blind** speed-blinded **-dåre** scorcher **-gräns** speed limit **-kontroll** speed trap **-syndare** speeder **-vidunder** speedster
fartyg [ˣfaːr-] *s7* ship, vessel; (*mindre o. koll.*) craft; (*linje-*) liner; (*ångare*) steamer
fartygs|befäl ship's officers (*pl*) **-befälhavare** captain, [ship]master, shipman **-register** register of shipping
farvatten [ˣfaːr-] waters (*pl*), sea[s *pl*]; (*farled*) fairway (*se äv. farled*); *i egna* ~ in home waters
far'väl I *interj* farewell!, goodbye! **II** *s7* farewell; *säga* ~ *åt, ta* ~ *av* bid farewell (say goodbye) to
faryn'git *s3* pharyngitis
fas *s3* phase; *bildl. äv.* aspect, appearance; (*avsneddad kant*) bevel, cant; chamfer
1 fasa *v1, tekn.* bevel; chamfer
2 fas|a I *s1* horror; (*stark rädsla*) terror; (*bävan*) dread; *blek* (*stel*) *av* ~ horrified, terrified; *krigets -or* the horrors of war; *väcka* ~ *hos* horrify, terrify; *till min* ~ *fick jag se* to my horror I saw **II** *v1* shudder (*för, över* at); (*rygga tillbaka*) shrink back (*för* at, from); ~ *för tanken* shudder at the thought
fa'sad *s3* face, front; *med ~en åt gatan* facing the street **-beklädnad** facing, cladding **-belysning** floodlighting **-klättrare** cat burglar **-krona** *tandläk.* artificial crown **-tegel** facing brick
fa'san *s3* pheasant **-höna** hen pheasant **-jakt** pheasant shooting
fasansfull horrible; terrible; awful; ghastly
fasantupp cock pheasant
fasaväckande *a4* horrifying, appalling
fascin|ation [faʃi- *el.* fassi-] fascination **-era** fascinate **-'erande** *a4* fascinating

fasc|ism [fa'ʃism] fascism **-ist** fascist **-istisk** a5 fascist[ic]

fa'sett s3 facet **-era** facet **-'erad** a5 faceted; (friare) many-sided **-ering** faceting

fasett|slipning facet cut **-öga** compound eye

fasförskjutning phase shift (displacement)

fashionabel [-ʃɷ'na:-] a2 fashionable

faskin [fa'ʃi:n] s3 fascine

faslig [ˣfa:s-] a1 dreadful, frightful, terrible; (förskräcklig) awful; (avskyvärd) horrid; ha ett ~t besvär have no end of trouble; ett ~t oväsen a terrible row

fasning [ˣfa:s-] (av kant) bevelling; chamfering; elektr. paralleling, phasing

fasomvandling kem. phase transformation (change)

fa'son s3 **1** (form) shape, form; sätta ~ på get into shape **2** (sätt) way; (beteende) manners (pl); är det skick och ~? do you call that good form?; vad är det för ~er? where are your manners?; låta var och en bli salig på sin ~ live and let live **-era** shape, figure; ~d ornamented, figured

1 fast konj though, although

2 fast al **1** (motsats lös) firm, solid, rigid; (fastgjord, fastsatt) fixed, attached; (motsats flyttbar) stationary, fixed; (motsats flytande) solid; (tät) compact, massive, dense; ~ knut tight knot; ~ konduktör stationary conductor **2** (säker) firm; (jur., motsats t. lös) real; (bestämd) fixed; (varaktig) permanent; (fångad) caught; ~ beslut (grepp, övertygelse) firm resolve (hold, conviction); ~ bostad permanent address; ~ egendom real property (estate); ~ kapital (pris) fixed capital (price); ~a kostnader fixed costs, overheads; ~ kund regular customer; ~ ljus (sken) fixed light; ~ utgift fixed charge; ta ~ form assume [a] definite shape; få ~ fot get a firm footing; med ~ hand with a firm hand; känna ~ mark under fötterna be on firm ground (äv. bildl.); köpa (sälja) ngt i ~ räkning give (receive) a firm order for s.th. **3** (i förbindelse med verb) bli ~ be (get) caught; frysa ~ freeze [in]; göra ~ make fast (firm), fasten; hålla ~ hold fast, keep [fast (firm) hold of]; hålla ~ vid maintain, stick (keep) to; hänga ~ a) (fästa) fasten (vid to), b) (vara upphängd) remain hanging (vid from); klistra ~ (på väggen) paste (stick) up; köra ~ get stuck, come to a standstill; sitta ~ (ha fastnat) stick, adhere, (om fordon, pers. o.d.) be stuck, (vara inklämd) be jammed; slå ~ hammer on (down), bildl. se fastslå; spika ~ nail [up, on]; stå ~ a) (om pers.) stand firm (steadfast), b) (om anbud e.d.) hold (stand) good; stå ~ vid sitt löfte abide by (keep) one's promise; sätta ~ fix, fasten, attach (i, vid to); sätta ~ ngn (bildl.) drive s.b. into a corner; sätta sig ~ (om sak) stick, (friare) establish o.s.; ta ~ catch, capture, seize; ta ~ tjuven! stop thief!

3 fast adv firmly; compactly; permanently; vara ~ anställd have a permanent appointment; vara ~ besluten att be firmly resolved (determined) to

1 fasta oböjligt s, ta ~ på bear in mind, seize upon

2 fasta I s1 **1** (fastande) fasting **2** (fastetid) fast; ~n Lent **II** v1 fast; på ~nde mage on an empty stomach

fastedag fast day; fasting day

faster [ˣfass- el. 'fass-] s2 [paternal] aunt

fastetid fast, time of fasting

fast|frusen frozen fast; ~ kredit frozen credit **-grodd** a5, vara ~ have taken root (i in) **-het** firmness etc.; solidity; stability; strength

fasthåll|a se under 2 fast 3 **-ande** s6 holding etc.; persistence (vid in); (vid krav) insistence on; ~t vid principer the adherence to principles

fastighet (hus) house [property]; (jordagods) landed property (estate); (fast egendom) real property (estate)

fastighets|förvaltare property manager **-marknad** property market **-mäklare** estate (house) agent; (i Skottland) house factor; AE. realtor **-skatt** real-estate tax **-skötare** caretaker; AE. janitor **-taxering** real-estate assessment **-ägare** house owner; property owner, estate owner

fast|kedja chain [up] (vid to) **-kila** wedge [fast, tight] **-klämd** a5, sitta ~ sit jammed in; vara ~ be squeezed tight in, be jammed **-knuten** a5 firmly tied (vid to)

fastlagen Lent

fastlags|bulle se semla **-ris** twigs with coloured feathers affixed [used as decoration during Lent] **-söndagen** Quinquagesima [Sunday]

fastland s7 continent; (i motsats t. öar) mainland **fastlandsklimat** continental climate

fast'mer[a] [much] rather

fastna get caught; (om sak) catch; (i ngt klibbigt samt om pers.) stick, get stuck; (i kläm) get jammed; ~ för decide on, choose; ~ i minnet stick (remain) in the (one's) memory; ~ på kroken get hooked; han ~de med handen i his hand got caught in

fast|nagla nail [firmly] (vid, på to); stå som ~d stand riveted to the spot **-nitad** a5 firmly riveted (vid to) **-rostad** a5, är ~ has got rusted in **-rotad** a5 fixed (fastened) [on] (vid to) **-sittande** a4 fixed, attached (vid to) **-skruvad** a5 screwed tight (firmly) (i into; vid onto) **-slå** bildl. lay down; (fastställa) establish; (bestämma) settle, fix

fastställ|a (bestämma) fix, settle; determine, decide; (stadfästa) confirm, ratify, sanction; (konstatera) establish, ascertain; -d i lag prescribed (laid down) by law; på de -da villkoren on the terms approved **-else** fixing; determination; confirmation; establishment

fast|sättning fastening **-tagande** s6 catching etc.; se 2 fast 3 **-vuxen** firmly rooted (vid to)

fastän [ˣfast-, äv. -'änn] although, (even) though

fat s7 **1** (för matvaror) dish **2** (te-, blom-) saucer **3** (bunke, tvätt- o.d.) basin; bowl **4** (tunna) cask, barrel; (kar) vat; öl från ~ draught beer; vin på ~ wine from the wood **5** ligga ngn i ~et stand in a p.'s way

fatabur se fatbur

fa'tal al (ödesdiger) fatal, disastrous; (olycklig) unfortunate; (obehaglig) awkward, annoying; ~ situation awkward situation; det var ~t att låta honom undkomma it was a bad mistake to let him escape

fatal|ism fatalism **-ist** fatalist **-istisk** *a5* fatalistic **-itet** *s3* stroke of bad luck, misfortune
fatbur [ˣfaːt-] *s2* storeroom; *ur egen* ~ out of one's own head
1 fatt *oböjligt a, hur är det* ~*?* what's the matter?, what's up?
2 fatt *adv, få (ta)* ~ *i (på)* get (catch) hold of; *hinna* ~ *ngn* catch s.b. up
fatta 1 (*ta tag i*) grasp, seize; take hold of (*äv. fatta tag i*); ~ *pennan* (*glaset*) take up one's pen (glass) **2** ~ *posto* post o.s., take one's stand **3** (*börja hysa*) conceive (*avsky för* a hatred of; *avsmak för* a distaste for), take (*tycke för* a fancy to; *motvilja för* a dislike to), form (*agg mot* a grudge against); ~ *ett beslut* make (come to, arrive at) a decision; ~ *humör* flare up; ~ *kärlek till* fall in love with; ~ *misstankar* get suspicious, be seized with suspicion; ~ *mod* take (pick up) courage; ~ *motvilja mot ngn* take a dislike to s.b. **4** (*begripa*) understand, comprehend, grasp; ~ *galoppen* catch the drift; ~*r du inte vad jag menar?* don't you see (understand) what I mean?; *jag kan inte* ~ *att* it beats me how; *ha lätt* (*svårt*) [*för*] *att* ~ be quick (slow) on the uptake **5** ~ *sig kort* be brief, make a long story short
fattad *a5* (*lugn*) composed
fatta|s *dep* **1** (*föreligga brist på*) be wanting (short); (*saknas*) be missing; (*brista, med personobj.*) want, lack, be short of; *det* ~ *folk* we (they *etc.*) are short of people; *det* ~ *ett pund i kassan* there is one pound missing from the funds, *vard.* the kitty is a pound short; *det -des ingenting av livets nödtorft i det huset* that household was not wanting in the necessities of life; *det* ~ *bara* (*det skulle bara* ~) *att* we are only waiting for **2** (*felas*) *vad* ~ *dig?* what is the matter [with you]?
fattbar *a1* comprehensible (*för* to); conceivable
fattig *a1* (*motsats rik*) poor; (*medellös*) penniless; (*utarmad*) impoverished, poverty-stricken; (*behövande*) needy, indigent; (*om jordmån o.d.*) meagre; ~*t folk,* ~*a* poor people; *de* ~*a* the poor; *de i anden* ~*a* the poor in spirit; *en* ~ *stackare* a poor wretch; ~*a riddare* (*kokk.*) bread fritters **2** (*friare*) poor; (*usel*) miserable; (*obetydlig*) paltry; *efter* ~ *förmåga* to the best of one's poor ability; *en enda* ~ *brödkant kvar* one miserable crust left
fattig|begravning pauper's funeral **-bössa** poor box
fattigdom *s2* poverty (*på* in, of); (*armod*) penury, indigence; (*nödställdhet*) destitution; (*torftighet*) poorness, meagreness (*på* in); (*social företeelse*) pauperism; (*brist*) deficiency (*på* in, of), lack (want) (*på* of) **fattigdomsbevis** *bildl.* confession of failure
fattig|hjon pauper **-hus** poorhouse; workhouse **-kvarter** slum **-lapp** *s2* pauper **-man** ~*s barn* a poor man's child (*pl* poor people's children)
fattigt *adv, ha det* ~ be badly (poorly) off; ~ *klädd* dressed in poor clothes
fattigvård (*förr*) poor[-law] relief; *se äv. socialvård m.m.* **fattigvårdsunderstöd** (*förr*) poor relief
fattning 1 (*grepp*) hold, grip (*om* on, round) **2** (*för glödlampa*) socket **3** (*avfattning*) version

4 (*besinning*) self-possession, self-control; (*lugn*) composure; *bringa ngn ur* ~*en* discompose s.b.; *förlora* ~*en* lose one's head; *återvinna* ~*en* recover one's composure
fattningsförmåga ability to comprehend (understand); intelligence, capacity; *ha god* ~ (*vard.*) be quick on the uptake
fatöl draught beer
faun *s3* faun
fauna [ˈfau-] *s1* fauna
favoriser|a favour, treat with special favour **-ing** favouring *etc.*
favo'rit *s3* favourite; pet; *hon är allas* ~ she is a favourite with everybody **-författare** favourite writer **-rätt** favourite dish **-system** favouritism
favör favour; (*förmån*) advantage; *till ngns* ~ to a p.'s advantage
fax *s7* fax, telefax, facsimile **faxa** fax, send a fax
f.d. (*förk. för före detta*) se *detta*
F-dur F major
fe *s3* fairy; *god* ~ fairy godmother
feber [ˈfeː-] *s2* fever; (*stegrad kroppstemperatur, vard.*) temperature; (*spänning*) excitement; (*nervös brådska*) flurry; *hög* ~ a high fever; *ha* ~ have a temperature, be feverish; *ligga i 40°* (*Celsius*) ~ be in bed with a temperature of 104° (Fahrenheit) **-aktig** *a1* feverish (*äv. bildl.*); febrile **-anfall** attack of fever **-artad** [-aːr-] *a5, se* -aktig **-fantasier** *pl* delirium (*sg*) **-fri** free from fever; *vara* ~ have no (a normal) temperature **-glänsande** *a4* bright with fever **-gummiträd** *se feberträd* **-het** *a1* very feverish **-kurva** temperature curve (chart) **-nedsättande** *a4*, antipyretic, refrigerant; ~ *medel* antipyretic, refrigerant **-sjukdom** fever **-termometer** clinical thermometer **-träd** blue gum **-yrsel** feverish rambling, delirium
febrig [ˣfeː-] *a1* feverish **feb'ril** *a1* feverish, febrile
februari [-ˈaːri] *r* February **-revolutionen** the February Revolution
fede'ral *a5* federal **-ism** federalism **-ist** federalist **-istisk** *a5* federalistic
feder|ation federation **-a'tiv** *a5* federative; federal **-'erad** *a5* [con]federate[d]
fedrottning fairy queen **feeri** fairy pageant; enchanting scenery
feg *a1* cowardly; (*räddhågad*) timorous, timid; *vard.* wet; *en* ~ *stackare* a coward; *visa sig* ~ show (prove) o.s. a coward **feghet** cowardice, cowardliness *etc.* **fegis** *s2, vard.* funk, mouse; *AE.* milquetoast **fegt** [-eː-] *adv* in a cowardly fashion, timorously *etc.*
feja [ˣfejja] clean
fejd *s3* feud; (*friare*) strife; *bildl. äv.* quarrel, controversy; *ligga i* ~ *med* be at feud with; *litterära* ~*er* literary controversies
fejka fake
fejs *s7, vard.* face; *sl.* mug, kisser
fel I *s7* **1** (*mera stadigvarande*) fault; (*kroppsligt*) defect; (*moraliskt*) imperfection; (*brist*) shortcoming, failing; (*avigsida*) demerit, weak point; *avhjälpa ett* ~ remedy a defect, put a fault right; *det är* ~ *på hissen* the lift is out of order; *det är ngt* ~ *med mitt hjärta* there is s.th.

wrong with my heart **2** (*mera tillfälligt*) fault; error; (*misstag*) mistake; (*grovt fel*) blunder; (*förbiseende*) slip; (*försummelse*) omission; (*fabrikations-* o.d.) flaw (*hos, i, på* in); *begå ett* ~ make a mistake, be at fault; *ha* ~ be [in the] wrong; *hela* ~*et är att* the real trouble is that **3** (*skuld*) fault; *det är hans* ~ he is to blame (*att* for + *ing-form*); *det är inte ens* ~ *att två träter* it takes two to make a quar'rel; *vems är* ~*et?* whose fault is it? **II** *oböjligt a* wrong; *på* ~ *sida* on the wrong side **III** *adv, gissa* ~ guess wrong; ~ *underrättad* wrongly informed; *läsa* (*räkna, höra*) ~ misread (miscalculate, mishear); *klockan går* ~ the clock (watch) is wrong; *slå* ~ *a*) eg. miss [the mark], *b*) (*misslyckas*) go wrong, fail, prove a failure, (*om plan e.d.*) miscarry; *det slår inte* ~ *att han* he cannot fail to; *ta* ~ make a mistake (*på dag* in the day); *ta* ~ *på vägen* miss the way; *jag tog* ~ *på honom och hans bror* I mistook him for his brother; *om jag inte tar* ~ *så* if I am not mistaken
1 fela *v1* (*begå fel*) err; (*brista*) be wanting; (*göra orätt*) do wrong; *det är mänskligt att* ~ to err is human
2 fela *s1, vard.* fiddle
feladressera misdirect
felaktig *a1* (*oriktig*) erroneous, wrong, mistaken; (*behäftad med fel*) incorrect, faulty; (*bristfällig*) defective, faulty; (*osann*) false, misleading **-het** (*utan pl*) faultiness, incorrectness, defect[iveness]; (*med pl*) fault, mistake, error
felande *a4* missing; *den* ~ *länken* the missing link
fel|as *dep, se fattas* **-adressera** misdirect **-bedöma** misjudge **-bedömning** misjudgment **-behandling** malpractice -beräkning miscalculation **-citera** misquote **-datera** misdate **-debitering** mischarge **-dosering** wrong dosage **-drag** wrong move **-expediering** incorrect dispatch; mistake [made by salesman *etc.*] **-fri** faultless, flawless; perfect, impeccable **-grepp** *mus.* false touch; *bildl.* mistake, blunder **-kalkyl** miscalculation **-konstruerad** wrongly constructed **-källa** source of error[s *pl*] **-läsning** (*i text*) misreading; (*vid uppläsning*) slip (fault) in reading **-manöver** mismanoeuvre **-marginal** margin of error **-orienterad** misorientated **-parkerad** wrongly parked **-parkering** (*förseelse*) parking offence **-placerad** *a5* misplaced **-planerad** *a5* miscalculated, wrongly planned **-procent** percentage of error **-räkning** miscalculation (*på* of); miscount **-skriven** *a5* wrongly written **-skrivning** miswriting; *genom* ~ (*äv.*) by an error in writing **-slagen** ~ *skörd* a failure of the crops; *-slagna förhoppningar* disappointed hopes **-slut** false (wrong) conclusion **-sortera** misfile **-spekulation** wrong (bad) speculation **-stava** misspell **-stavad** *a5* wrongly spelt, misspelt **-stavning** misspelling **-steg** false step, slip; *bildl. äv.* lapse **-syn** erroneous point of view **-sägning** [-ä:-] slip of the tongue **-sökning** [-ö:-] fault localization, fault-detecting **-tolka** misinterpret; misconstrue **-tolkning** misinterpretation; misconstruction **-tryck** faulty print; (*frimärke*) printing error

-tända *v2*, **-tändning** *s2* (*om motor*) misfire **-underrättad** *a5* misinformed **-vänd** *a5* back-to-front, upside down; turned the wrong way **-översättning** mistranslation
fem [femm] five; *ha* (*kunna*) *ngt på sina* ~ *fingrar* have s.th. at one's fingertips; *en* ~ *sex stycken* five or six **-dagarsvecka** [a] five-day [working] week **-dubbel** fivefold **-etta** [-ˣetta] bull's-eye **-femma** *ung.* certified mental case; *förklara ngn som* ~ certify a p. **-hundratalet** *på* ~ in the sixth century **-hörning** [-ö:-] pentagon
feminin ['fe:- *el.* -'ni:n] *a1* feminine **femininum** ['fe:-] *s4* **1** (*feminint ord*) feminine [noun] **2** (*honkön*) feminine [gender]
femin|isera feminize **-ism** feminism **-ist** *s3*, **-istisk** *a5* feminist
fem|kamp pentathlon **-kampare** pentathlete **-krona** *en* ~ a five-krona [piece] **-kronesedel** five-kronor note
femling quintuplet, *vard.* quin
femma *s1* (*siffra*) five; (*på tärning, spelkort äv.*) cinque; (*sedel*) fiver; *det var en annan* ~ that is quite another story; *jfr äv. femkronesedel*
fem|mastare five-master **-siffrig** *a5* five-figure
femte fifth; *F~ Mosebok* Deuteronomy; *den* ~ *april* [on] the fifth of April, (*i början av brev o.d.*) April 5 (5th); *för det* ~ in the fifth place, fifthly; *vart* ~ *år* every five years; ~ *hjulet under vagnen* the fifth wheel **-del** fifth [part] **-kolonn** fifth column **-kolonnare** fifth columnist
femti[o] fifty **-elfte** [-ˣelfte] *för* ~ *gången* for the umpteenth time **-elva** [-ˣelva] umpteen **-lapp** fifty-kronor note
femtion|de [-å-] fiftieth **-[de]del** fiftieth [part]
femti[o]|tal [(the) number] fifty; *ett* ~ some (about) fifty; *på* ~*et* in the fifties **-årig** *a5* fifty-year-old **-åring** man (*etc.*) of fifty **-årsdag** fiftieth anniversary (birthday) **-årsjubileum** fiftieth anniversary, jubilee **-årsålder** *i* ~*n* [aged] about fifty **-öring** *en* ~ a fifty-öre [piece]
femto- femto-
femton [-ån] fifteen **-de** fifteenth **-hundratalet** *på* ~ in the sixteenth century **-årig** *a5* fifteen-year-old **-åring** boy (*etc.*) of fifteen; ~*ar* fifteen-year-olds
femuddig *a5*, ~ *stjärna* pentacle, pentagram, pentangle
femår|ig *a5* **1** five-year-old **2** (*för fem år*) five-year child of five, five-year-old
femårs|dag fifth anniversary (birthday) **-plan** five-year plan **-ålder** *i* ~*n* [aged] about five
femöring *en* ~ a five-öre [piece]; *bildl., inte värd en* ~ not worth a penny (cent)
fena *s1* fin; (*AE., på flygplan*) vertical stabilizer; *inte röra en* ~ not move a muscle
fender[t] *s2, sjö.* fender
Fenicien [-'ni:-] *n* Phoenicia **fenicier** [-'ni:-] *s9*, **fenicisk** [-'ni:-] *a5* Phoenician
Fenix ['fe:-] [*Fågel*] ~ [the] Phoenix
fenköl fin keel
fenol [-'å:l] *s3* phenol, carbolic acid; ~*er* phenols
fenolftalein phenolphthalein
fenolharts phenolic resin

fenologi *s3* phenology
feno'men *s7* phenomenon -**'al** *a1* phenomenal, extraordinary -**ologi** *s3* phenomenology
fenoxisyra [-ˣnåksi-] phenoxy acid
feno'typ *s3* phenotype
fenval finback
fe'nyl *s3* phenyl -**ketonuri** [-ˣtå:n-] *s3* phenylketonuria
feo'dal *a5* feudal -**herre** feudal lord -**ism, -väsen** feudalism, feudal system
ferie ['fe:-] *s5, mest i pl* holiday; *AE.* vacation -**arbete** holiday course (task) -**läsning** holiday studies *(pl)* -**skola** summer school
fermat *s3, s7, mus.* pause, fermata
ferment *s7, s4,* **fermentera** *v1* ferment
fermion [-'å:n] *s3* fermion
fermium ['ferr-] *s8* fermium
ferniss|a [-'nissa] *s1 o. v1* varnish -**ning** varnishing
feromon [-'må:n] *s7, s4* pheromone
ferri|förening [ˣfärri-] ferric compound -**magnetism** ferrimagnetism
fer'rit *s3* ferrite -**antenn** ferrite-rod aerial
ferro|förening [ˣfärrɷ-] ferrous compound -**magnetism** ferromagnetism
fer'til *a1* fertile -**itet** fertility
fes *imperf. av fisa*
fesaga fairy tale
fest *s3* festival; celebration; *(munter fest)* festivity, merrymaking; *(bjudning)* party, celebration; *en ~ för ögat* a feast for the eyes; *gå på ~* go [out] to a party; *ställa till ~* give (throw) a party **festa** feast; have a gay time; *~ på färsk potatis* feast on new potatoes; *~ av* throw a farewell party *(ngn* for s.b.); *~ upp* squander on a gay life **festande** *s6* feasting, merrymaking
fest|arrangör organizer of a festival (party) -**dag** festival day; *allmän ~* public holiday -**dräkt** festive attire; evening dress -**föremål** fêted guest, guest of honour -**föreställning** gala performance -**glädje** festivity
festi'v|al *s3* festival -**ivitas** [-'ti:-] *r* [air of] festivity
fest|klädd dressed in evening dress, dressed for a party -**kommitté** [festival] committee
festlig *a1* **1** festive, festival; *(storartad)* grand **2** *se lustig, komisk* -**het** festivity
festmåltid banquet, feast
feston[g] [-'åŋ] *s3* festoon
fest|prisse *s2* gay dog -**skrift** festschrift; *en ~ tillägnad* a publication (volume) dedicated to -**spel** dramatic (musical, opera) festival -**stämning** gay atmosphere, festive mood -**talare** *se högtidstalare* -**våning** reception room, banqueting rooms *(pl)*; functions room
fet *a1* fat; *(fetlagd)* stout; corpulent; *(fyllig)* plump; *(abnormt fet)* obese; *(om kött o. fläsk)* fatty; *(om mat utom kött o. fläsk; om jordmån)* rich; *(flottig)* oily, greasy; *bli ~* fat[ten], *(äv.)* put on weight; *det blir han inte ~ på* he won't get much out of that; *de har det inte ~t* they are none too well off
fe'tisch *s3* fetish, fetich -**dyrkan, -ism** fetishism, fetichism -**ist** fetishist, fetichist
fet|knopp *bot.* stonecrop -**lagd** *a5* inclined to stoutness, [somewhat] stout; *(fyllig)* plump;

(om kvinna äv.) buxom
fetma [ˣfett-] **I** *s1* fatness; *(i sht hos pers.)* stoutness, corpulence **II** *v1, se [bli] fet*
fets *se fez*
fet|sill fat herring -**stil** extra bold type
fett *s4* fat; *(för håret o.d.)* oil, grease; *(smörj-)* grease, lubricant; *(stek-)* dripping; *(späck)* lard; *kokk.* shortening -**bildande** *a4* fattening -**bildning** *konkr.* accumulation (layer) of fat; *sjuklig ~* fatty degeneration -**emboli** *med.* fat embolus (embolism) -**fena** adipose fin -**fläck** grease spot -**fågel** oilbird -**halt** fat content -**haltig** *a1* fatty, containing fat -**hjärta** fatty heart
fettisdag [ˣfe:t-] *~en* Shrove Tuesday, Pancake Day **fettisdagsbulle** *se semla*
fett|klump lump of fat -**körtel** sebaceous gland -**lager** layer of fat -**lever** fatty liver -**löslig** fat-soluble -**sot** *med.* adiposity -**sugning** liposuction -**svansfår** fat-tailed sheep -**svulst** *wen; med.* lipoma -**syra** fatty acid -**valk** roll of fat -**vävnad** fatty tissue -**ämne** fatty substance
fetvadd unrefined cotton wool
fez [fetz *el.* fäss] *s3* fez; tarboosh
fia [ˣfi:a] *s1* ludo
fi'asko *s6* fiasco, failure; *göra ~* be a fiasco, *(om tillställning)* fall flat
fiaspel *se fia*
fibbla *bot.* hawkweed
fiber ['fi:-] *s3* fibre -**kost** roughage -**optik** fibre optics -**platta** fibreboard -**rik** rich in fibres; *~ kost* roughage -**växt** fibre plant
fibrig [ˣfi:-] *a1* fibred
fi'brin *s7, s4* fibrin **fibrinogen** [-'je:n] *s7, s4* fibrinogen **fibri'nös** *a5* fibrinous
fib'rös *a5* fibrous
fick *imperf. av 2 få*
fick|a *s1* pocket; *tekn. äv.* bin, hopper -**almanacka** pocket almanac -**bok** pocket book -**dagbok** pocket diary -**flaska** [hip] flask -**format** pocket size; *i ~* pocket-sized -**kniv** pocketknife -**lampa** torch; *AE.* flashlight -**lock** pocket flap -**ordbok** pocket dictionary -**parkera** park between two cars -**pengar** pocket money *(sg)* -**plunta** *se* -flaska -**räknare** pocket calculator -**spegel** pocket mirror -**stöld** pocket picking -**tjuv** pickpocket -**ur** pocket watch
fideikom'miss *s7* estate in tail, entail -**arie** [-'a:rie] *s5* tenant in tail *(till* to, of), entailer
Fidji Fiji
fiende *s5* enemy *(till* of); *poet.* foe *(till* of); *skaffa sig ~r* make enemies -**hand** *falla för ~* die at the hand of the enemy; *falla i ~* fall into the hands of the enemy -**land** hostile country
fiendskap *s3* enmity; hostility *(mot* towards, to)
fientlig [-'ent-] *a1* hostile, inimical *(mot* to, towards); *attr.* enemy; *stå på ~ fot med* be on bad terms with, be at enmity with -**het** hostility; *inställa ~erna* suspend hostilities
fientligt [-'ent-] *adv* hostilely; *vara ~ stämd mot* be hostile (antagonistic) to (towards)
fiffa *~ upp* smarten up
fiffel [ˣfiff-] *s7* crooked dealings *(pl)*, tricks *(pl)*, manipulations *(pl)*, *vard.* shenanigan
fiffig *a1* smart; *(slug)* shrewd

fiffla cheat, wangle; ~ *med böckerna* cook the books

figur figure; (*i sht neds.*) individual, character; (*ritad*) diagram, design; *göra en slät* ~ cut a poor figure; *vad är det där för en* ~? who on earth (what sort of a specimen) is that?

figur|ant figurant **-ation** embellishment; ornamentation **-a'tiv** *a5* figurative **-era** (*förekomma*) figure; (*uppträda*) appear, pose

figurframställning figure painting

figu'rin *s3* figurine

figurlig [-'gu:r-] *a1* figurative; *i* ~ *betydelse* in a figurative sense

figur|målning figure painting **-nära** closely fitting; hugging the figure **-sydd** *a5* close-fitting; waisted

fik *s7, vard.* café

1 fika *vard.* (*dricka kaffe*) have coffee

2 fika hanker (*efter* after, for)

fikon [-ån] *s7* fig **-löv** fig leaf **-träd** fig tree

fiktion [-k'ʃɷ:n] fiction **fik'tiv** *a1* fictitious, imaginary

fikus ['fi:-] *s2* **1** *bot.* rubber plant **2** (*homosexuell man*) pansy

1 fil *s3* **1** (*rad*) row; *rummen ligger i* ~ the rooms are in a suite **2** (*trafik-*) lane; (*fordons-*) line **3** *data.* file

2 fil *s2* (*verktyg*) file

3 fil *s3, se filmjölk*

fila file; *bildl. äv.* polish; ~ *på en fiol* scrape a fiddle

filan|trop [-'å:p] *s3* philanthropist, philanthrope **-tro'pi** *s3* philanthropy **-tropisk** [-'trå:-] *a5* philanthropic[al]

filate'l|i *s3* philately **-ist** philatelist **-istisk** *a5* philatelic

filbunke [bowl of] processed sour whole milk; *lugn som en* ~ as cool as a cucumber

filé *s3* **1** *kokk.* fillet **2** (*spetsvävnad*) netting, fillet lace **filea** [-'le:a] *kokk.* fillet

filharmonisk [-'mɷ:-] *a5* philharmonic

fili'al *s3* branch [office]; (*-affär*) multiple store (shop) **-affär** multiple store (shop) **-avdelning** branch department **-kontor** branch [office]

filibuster [-'bust-] *s2*, **filibustra** *v1, AE.* filibuster

fili'gran *s7, s3* filigree **-arbete** [a piece of] filigree work

fili'pin *s3, spela* ~ *med ngn* play philippina (philippine) with s.b.

filipper [-'lipp-] Philippian **-brevet** Philippians (*pl, behandlas som sg*); *eg.* the Epistle of Paul the Apostle to the Philippians

filip'pik *s3* philippic

filippinare [-ˣpi:-] Filipino **Filippinerna** [-'pi:-] *pl* the Philippines **filippinsk** [-'pi:nsk] *a5* Philippine, Filipino

filis'té *s3*, **filisteisk** [-'te:-] *a5*, **filister** [-'liss-] *s2*, **filist'rös** *a1* Philistine

filkörning driving in lanes

film *s3* film; (*smal-*) cine (*AE.* movie) film; (*spel-*) film; *AE.* motion (moving) picture, *vard.* movie; ~*en* (*-konsten*) the cinema; *gå in vid* ~*en* go on the films; *spela in en* ~ make a film, film; *sätta in en* ~ *i en kamera* load a camera

film|a [take (make) a] film, shoot; (*uppträda i*

film) act in a film; (*låtsas, vard.*) feign, simulate **-ateljé** film studio

filmatiser|a adapt for the screen **-ing** adaptation for the screen; (*film*) screen version

film|atisk [-'ma:-] *a5* filmic **-bolag** film company **-branschen** the movie business **-censur** film censorship **-festival** film festival **-fotograf** cameraman **-föreställning** cinema performance (show) **-hjälte** hero of the screen **-idol** movie idol **-industri** film industry; ~*n* the screen (cinema) **-inspelning** filming, shooting **-institut** *Svenska F~et* [the] Swedish Film Institute

filmisk ['fill-] *a5* filmic

filmjölk *ung.* processed sour milk

film|kamera film camera, cine (*AE.* movie) camera **-kassett** film cassette **-komiker** screen comedian **-konst** ~*en* [the] art of film, the cinema **-kännare** cineaste **-manuskript** [film] script, screenplay

filmo|gra'fi *s3* filmography **-'tek** *s7* film library

film|premiär first (opening) night [of a film] **-producent** film (*AE.* motion picture) producer **-regissör** film (*AE.* motion picture) director **-roll** [film] role (part) **-rulle** roll of film; (*kassett med film*) reel [of film] **-skådespelare** film actor **-skådespelerska** film actress **-stjärna** film star **-studio** film studio **-upptagning** filming, film shooting

filning [ˣfi:l-] filing; *bildl. äv.* polishing

filo|log philologist, philologer **-logi** *s3* philology **-logisk** *a5* philological

filosof [-'så:f] *s3* philosopher **-era** philosophize (*över* [up]on, about)

filoso'f|i *s3* philosophy; ~*e doktor* Doctor of Philosophy; ~*e kandidat* (*magister*) Bachelor (Master) of Arts (Science, Education) **-isk** [-'så:-] *a5* philosophic[al]; ~ *fakultet* Faculty of Arts and Sciences

filspån filings (*pl*)

filt *s2* **1** (*material*) felt **2** (*säng-*) blanket; (*res-*) rug **filta** felt; ~ *ihop sig* get matted **filtduk** felted cloth, felting

filter ['fill-] *s7, s4* filter **-cigarett** filter-tipped cigarette, filter tip

filt|hatt felt hat, trilby, fedora **-penna** felt tip marker (pen)

filtrat *s7* filtrate

filtrer|a filter, filtrate **-apparat** filtering apparatus **-ing** filtration **-papper** filter paper

filt|sula felt (hair) sole **-toffel** felt slipper **-underlägg** felt pad

filur sly dog

fimbulvinter a bitter winter

fimmelstång shaft, thill

fimp *s2, vard.* fag end, butt **fimpa** stub (put) out

fin *a1* **1** (*motsats grov*) fine; (*tunn, smal*) thin; (*spenslig*) slender, thin; (*späd*) tender; (*skör, ömtålig*) delicate; (*mjuk o. len*) soft; (*slät*) smooth; ~*t damm* fine dust; ~ *stil* small type (handwriting); ~ *tråd* finespun thread **2** (*väl renad*) refined; ~*t silver* refined silver **3** (*motsats enklare, sämre*) fine; (*prydlig*) neat, clean, tidy; (*elegant*) elegant; (*vacker*) handsome; (*utsökt*) choice, exquisite, select; (*läcker*) delicious; (*förnäm*) aristocratic, distinguished; (*be-*

levad) polished, well-bred; (*förfinad*) refined; (*värdig*) dignified; (*försynt*) tactful, considerate; (*omdömesgill*) fine, discriminating; (*känslig*) sensitive; (*skarp*) keen; (*förstklassig*) first--rate, first-class, superior, excellent; *iron.* fine, nice; ~ *hörsel* acute hearing; ~ *och behaglig* well-bred; charming; *en* ~ *affär* a bargain; *en* ~ *dam* an aristocratic lady; *en* ~ *flicka* a girl of good family; *en* ~ *herre* a gentleman; *en* ~ *och hygglig karl* a nice gentlemanly fellow; *en* ~ *vink* a delicate (gentle) hint; *extra* ~ superfine; *klä sig* ~ dress up [in one's best]; *göra* ~*t* (*städa*) tidy up, (*pryda*) make things look nice; *det anses inte* ~*t att* it is not good manners to; *i* ~*t sällskap* in polite society; *det* ~*a i* the best part (the point) of **4** *mus.* (*hög, gäll*) high[-pitched]

fi'nal *s3, mus.* finale; *sport.* final[s *pl*]; *gå till* ~*en* enter the finals **-ist** finalist

finans [-'ans *el.* -'aŋs] *s3* finance; ~*en* (*finansmännen*) high finance; ~*er* finances; *ha dåliga* ~*er* (*äv.*) be in financial difficulties **-departement** ministry of finance; ~*et* (*i Storbritannien*) the Treasury, (*i USA*) department of the treasury **-expert** financial expert **-furste** financial magnate **-geni** financial genius

finansi'ell *a5* financial

finansier|a finance **-ing** financing

finansinstitut *ung.* finance house

finansi'är *s3* financier

finans|man financier **-minister** minister of finance; (*i Storbritannien*) chancellor of the Exchequer; (*i USA*) secretary of the treasury **-politik** financial policy **-rätt** [public] finance **-tull** revenue duty **-utskott** ~*et* [the Swedish parliamentary] standing committee on finance **-världen** the world of finance **-väsen** finance, public finance[s *pl*] **-år** financial (*AE.* fiscal) year

finbageri fancy bakery

finemang *vard.* great

finess finesse; tact; ~*er* refinements; niceties; *bilen har många* ~*er* the car is fitted with a lot of gadgets

finfin splendid, tiptop; exquisite; *vard.* topnotch, crack

finfördel|a grind, pulverize; levigate; (*vätska*) atomize **-ning** grinding, pulverization; levigation; (*av vätska*) atomization

fing|er ['fiŋer] *s7, s2* finger; *ha ett* ~ *med i spelet* have a finger in the pie; *peka* ~ *åt* point one's finger at; *inte röra* (*lyfta*) *ett* ~ not stir (lift, raise) a finger; *sätta* -*ret på den ömma punkten* put (lay) one's finger on the weak (sore) spot; *kunna ngt på sina fem* -*rar* have s.th. at one's fingers ends; *hålla* -*rarna borta från ngt* (*bildl.*) keep one's hands off s.th.; *det kliar i* -*rarna på mig att* my fingers are itching to; *inte lägga* -*rarna emellan* handle the matter without kid gloves; *räkna på* -*rarna* count on one's fingers; *se genom* -*rarna med ngt* turn a blind eye to s.th.; *slå ngn på* -*rarna* (*bildl.*) come down on s.b.

fingera [fiŋ'ge:-] feign, simulate; ~*d* fictitious, imaginary; mock, sham; ~*t namn* assumed (false) name

finger|avtryck fingerprint **-borg** thimble

-borgsblomma foxglove

fingerfärdig nimble-fingered; dexterous **-het** dexterity, manual skill; *mus.* execution, technique

finger|hatt *se fingerborgsblomma* **-krok** *i uttr.*: *dra* ~ *med* (*ung.*) have a locked-fingers tug of war with **-skiva** [telephone] dial **-spets** fingertip **-språk** *se handalfabet* **-svamp** coral fungi **-sättning** *mus.* fingering **-topp** fingertip **-tuta** fingerstall, cot, fingertip **-vante** [woollen (cotton)] glove **-visning** hint, pointer **-övning** *mus.* five-finger exercise

fingra ~ *på* finger

fingransk|a scrutinize **-ning** scrutiny

fin|hacka chop finely **-het** fineness *etc., jfr fin o. finess* **-hyllt** *a4* delicate-complexioned, delicate-hued

fininställ|a calibrate **-ning** precision (fine) adjustment

fi'nit *a4, språkv.* finite

finjustera (*motor*) tune up

fink *s2* finch

finka I *s1* **1** (*polishäkte*) *sl.* quod, jug; clink, nick **2** (*godsvagn*) covered wagon; [luggage] van; *AE.* boxcar; baggage car **II** *v1, sl.* nick

fin|kalibrig [-li:b-] *a1* small-bore **-kamma** comb with a fine-tooth[ed] comb; *bildl.* comb out, examine thoroughly, go over (through) with a fine-tooth[ed] comb

finkel ['finn-] *s2, se finkelolja*; (*dåligt brännvin, vard.*) rotgut **-olja** fusel [oil]

fin|klippa cut up fine **-klädd** dressed up; well--dressed **-kornig** fine-grained; *foto.* fine-grain **-kultur** highbrow culture (*ibl. neds.*)

finkänslig delicate; tactful, discreet **-het** delicacy [of feeling]; tactfulness, discretion

Finland ['finn-] *n* Finland **finlandssvensk I** *s2* Swedish Finn **II** *a5* Finno-Swedish

finlemmad *a5* slender-limbed

finländ|are Finn, Finlander **-sk** *a5* Finnish

fin|mala grind fine (small) **-malen** *a5* finely ground **-maskig** *a5* fine-meshed **-mekaniker** precision-tool maker **-mekanisk** ~ *verkstad* precision-tool workshop

finn|a *fann funnit* **I 1** find; (*upptäcka*) discover, find out, perceive; (*träffa på*) come upon (across); (*röna*) meet with **2** (*erfara*) find, see, learn **3** (*anse*) think, consider; ~ *för gott att* think it best to; ~ *lämpligt* think fit; ~ *på* find out, invent; ~ *på råd* find a way; *den står inte att* ~ it is not to be found **II** *rfl* **1** (*finna sig vara*) find o.s.; (*anse sig*) consider (think) o.s. **2** (*känna sig*) feel **3** (*nöja, foga sig*) be content (*i* with); ~ *sig i* (*äv.*) put up with, submit to, stand **4** (*ge rätta svaret e.d.*) *han* -*er sig alltid* he is never at a loss; *han fann sig snart* he soon collected his wits

finn|ande *i uttr.*: *vara till* ~*s* be to be found, exist **-as** *dep* (*vara*) be; (*stå att finna*) to be found, exist; *det* -*s gott om* there is plenty of; *han* -*s ej mer* he is no longer; *det* -*s inte att få* it is not to be had; -*s det äpplen?* have you [got] any apples?; ~ *kvar a*) (*återstå*) be left, (*i behåll*) be extant, *b*) (*finnas på samma plats*) be still there; ~ *till* exist, be in existence

finnbygd Finnish settlement

1 finne *s2* Finn

2 finne *s2* (*blemma*) pimple
finnig *a1* pimpled, pimply
finnmark (*mynt*) Finnish mark, markka
fin|polera high-polish; ~*d* highly polished **-putsa** *byggn.* plaster; (*friare*) put final touches to **-rum** *ung.* drawing room
finsk *a1* Finnish; *F~a viken* the Gulf of Finland
finsk|a 1 (*språk*) Finnish **2** (*kvinna*) Finnish woman **-språkig** *a5* Finnish-speaking **--ugrisk** [-u:g-] *a5* Finno-Ugric
fin|skuren *a5* **1** *kokk.* finely cut **2** (*om tobak e.d.*) fine-cut **3** *bildl.* finely chiselled **-slipa** polish smooth; *bildl.* put the finishing touches to; ~*d* polished, elegant **-smakare** epicure, gourmet **-smide** whitesmithery **-snickare** cabinet-maker **-stilt** [-i:lt] *a4* in small type; *det ~a* (*i kontrakt e.d.*) the fine (small) print **-stämd** *a1, bildl.* delicate; moving **-stött** *a4* pounded fine
1 fint *s3* feint (*äv. i boxning, fäktning o.d.*); (*knep*) trick, dodge, stratagem
2 fint [-i:-] *adv* finely *etc., jfr fin;* ~ *bildad* [well] educated, cultured; ~ *utarbetad* elaborately worked out
fint|a feint; (*i fotboll ung.*) dribble (*av past*) **-lig** *a1* ingenious, clever
fin|trådig fine-threaded **-tvätt** washing requiring careful handling
finurlig [-'nu:r-] *a1* (*om pers.*) shrewd, knowing; (*om sak*) ingenious, clever
fi'ol *s3* violin; *vard.* fiddle; *spela* ~ play the violin; *spela första* (*andra*) ~[*en*] (*eg.*) play [the] first (second) violin, *bildl.* play first (second) fiddle **-byggare** violin maker **-låda** violin case **-spelare** violinist, fiddler **-sträng** violin string **-stämma** violin part
1 fira 1 (*högtidlighålla*) celebrate; (*minne äv.*) commemorate; (*hedra*) fête, honour; ~ *gudstjänst* hold divine service; *var tänker du ~ jul?* where are you going to spend Christmas? **2** (*skolka från arbetet*) absent o.s.
2 fira (*släppa efter*) ease [away]; (*skot*) slack, ease off; ~ *ner* lower
firma *s1* [business] firm; ~ *Jones & Co.* Messrs. Jones & Co.; *teckna ~n* sign for the firm **-bil** company car
firmament *s7, på ~et* in the firmament
firma|märke trademark **-namn** name of a firm, trade name **-tecknare** person authorized to sign for a (the) firm **-teckning** signing for a (the) firm
firn *s3* névé, firn
firning [ˣfi:r-] *vard.* (*arbetsfrånvaro*) absenteeism
fis *s2, fisa* *fes fisit* fart
fi'schy *s3* fichu
fisit *sup. av fisa*
fisk *s2* fish; *en ful* ~ (*bildl.*) an ugly customer; *vara som en* ~ *i vattnet* take like a fish to water, be in one's element; *fånga några ~ar* catch a few fish; *våra vanligaste ~ar* our commonest fishes; *få sina ~ar varma* be ticked off; *i de lugnaste vattnen går de största ~arna* still waters run deep **fiska** fish; ~ *efter* (*bildl.*) ish (angle) for; ~ *upp* (*bildl.*) fish out; ~ *med drag* troll; ~ *i grumligt vatten* fish in troubled water; *vara ute och* ~ be out fishing

fiskaffär fishmonger
fiskafänge *s6* (*utan pl*) fishing; (*med pl*) catch [of fish]; *Petri* ~ (*bibl.*) the miraculous draught of fishes
fis'kal *s3, ung.* public prosecutor
fiskarbefolkning fishing population
fiskare fisherman
fisk|ben fishbone **-bensmönster** herringbone pattern **-blåsa** sound **-bulle** fishball; fish cake **-damm** fishpond
fiske *s6* fishing; (*näringsgren*) fishery **-bank** fishing bank **-båt** fishing boat **-don** fishing tackle **-fartyg** fishing vessel **-flotta** fishing fleet **-fyr** fishing light **-garn** fishing net **-gräns** fishing-limits (*pl*), limit of the fishing zone **-hamn** fishing port (harbour) **-kort** fishing licence (permit) **-lycka** luck at fishing **-läge** fishing village **-plats** fishing ground, fishery
fiskeri fishery **-intendent** inspector of fisheries **-konsulent** fisheries expert **-näring** fishing industry **-styrelse** ~*n* [the Swedish] national board of fisheries
fiske|rätt piscary, fishery, fishing **-vatten** fishing ground, fishery
fisk|filé fillet of fish **-fjäll** fish scale **-färs** minced fish **-gjuse** [-ju:se] *s2* osprey, fish eagle (*AE.* hawk) **-handlare** fishmonger; ('*fiskgumma'*) fishwife **-konserv** tinned (*AE.* canned) fish **-leverolja** cod-liver oil **-lim** fish glue **-lir** *s7,* **-lira** *v1* play for time **-mjöl** fish meal **-mås** common (mew) gull, [sea] mew **-nät** fish[ing] net **-odling** fishfarm **-pinne** fishfinger; *AE.* fish stick **-redskap** fishing tackle **-restaurang** fish restaurant **-rätt** fish course **-soppa** fish soup (*AE.* chowder) **-stim** shoal [of fish] **-stjärt** fishtail **-sump** corf; crawl **-trappa** fish ladder **-tärna** common tern **-yngel** spawn **-öga** fish eye; *foto.* fish-eye lens
fiss *s7* F sharp
fis'sil *a5* fissile, fissionable **fission** [fi'ʃɷ:n] fission
fissur *anat., med.* fissure
fistel *s2, med.* fistula
fitta *s1, vard.* cunt
fix *a5* **1** (*fast*) fixed; ~ *idé* fixed idea, (*friare*) rooted idea, craze; ~*t pris* fixed price **2** ~ *och färdig* all ready **fixa** *vard.* fix up **fixare** *vard.* fixer
fixa'tiv *s7* fixative
fixer|a 1 (*fastställa*) fix (*till at*) **2** (*se skarpt på*) stare hard at; *AE.* fixate **3** *foto., konst., med.* fix **-bad** *foto.* fixer **-ing** fixing, fixation; (*med blicken*) stare, staring; *foto.* fixing
fixerings|bild puzzle picture **-vätska** *foto.* fixer, hypo; (*för teckning o.d.*) fixative
fixersalt fixing salt
fix|punkt fixed point **-stjärna** fixed star
fixtur fixture, fixing plate
fjant *s2* busybody, officious blighter; twerp, jerk **fjanta** ~ *för* fawn [up]on; ~ *omkring* fuss around **fjantig** *a1* fussy
fjol *i uttr.:* *i* ~ last year; *i* ~ *vinter* last winter; *från i* ~ last year's
fjoll|a [-å-] *s1* foolish (silly) woman (girl) **-ig** *a1* foolish, silly **-ighet** foolishness, silliness
fjol|år ~*et* last year **-årskalv** last year's calf

fjompig [-å-] *a1* dumb, silly
fjor *se fjol*
fjord [-ω:- *el.* -å-] *s2* (*i Norge*) fjord, fiord; (*i Skottland*) firth
fjorton [*fjω:rtån] fourteen; ~ *dagar* [a] fortnight; *i dag* ~ *dagar* today fortnight; *i dag för* ~ *dagar sedan* a fortnight ago today; *med* ~ *dagars mellanrum* at fortnightly intervals **-de** fourteenth; *var* ~ *dag* once a (every) fortnight, fortnightly **-[de]del** fourteenth [part] **-hundratalet** *på* ~ in the fifteenth century **-årig** *etc., se femårig etc.*
fjun *s7* (*dun*) down; (*på växt äv.*) floss; (*på persika*) fur **-ig** *a1* downy; flossy
1 fjäd|er ['fjä:-] *s2* (*på fågel*) feather; *bildl. äv.* plume; *en* ~ *i hatten* a feather in one's cap; *lysa med lånta -rar* strut in borrowed plumes
2 fjäder ['fjä:-] *s2, tekn.* spring
fjäder|beklädd *a5* feathered, plumy **-boll** shuttle[cock] **-buske** plume, panache **-dräkt** plumage, feathering, feathers
fjäderfä poultry **-avel** poultry breeding **-skötsel** poultry farming (keeping)
fjäder|gräs feather grass **-lätt** [as] light as a feather; ~ *papper* featherweight paper **-moln** cirrus
fjäderstål spring steel
fjädervikt featherweight
fjädervåg spring balance (*AE.* scale)
fjädr|a [-ä:-] be elastic, spring; ~ *sig* show off (*för* to), be cocky (*över* about) **-ande** *a4* elastic; (*om gång*) springy **-ing** spring system; (*fjädringsförmåga*) spring, elasticity
1 fjäll *s7* (*berg*) mountain; (*i Skandinavien äv.*) fjeld
2 fjäll *s7* scale
fjälla 1 (*fisk*) scale [off] **2** (*flagna av*) peel; ~ *av* [*sig*] scale (peel) off
fjäll|bestigare mountaineer, alpinist **-bestigning** mountaineering; (*med pl*) [mountain (alpine)] climb **-boskap** mountain cattle
fjäll|ig *a1* scaly, scaled **-ning** scaling; *med.* peeling
fjäll|pipare dott[e]rel **-ripa** ptarmigan **-räddning** mountain rescue [service] **-räv** arctic fox **-sippa** [mountain] avens (*pl, behandlas som sg*) **-sjö** tarn **-skivling** *bot.* parasol mushroom **-topp** summit, peak; mountain top **-vandring** mountain hike (tour) **-vidd** *på ~erna* (*ung.*) on the boundless hills **-vråk** rough-legged buzzard **-växt** alpine plant
fjällämmel (*särskr. fjäll-lämmel*) lemming
fjär *a1* standoffish, distant
fjärd [-ä:-] *s2, ung.* bay
fjärde [-ä:-] fourth; *F~ Mosebok* Numbers **-del** fourth [part], quarter; *tre ~ar* three fourths (quarters) **-delsnot** crotchet; *AE.* quarter note
fjärding [-ä:-] (*kärl o. mått*) *ung.* firkin
fjärdings|man *ung.* country (parish) constable **-väg** *pl* =, *en* ~ a quarter of a [Swedish] mile
fjäril *s2* butterfly; (*natt-*) moth
fjärils|hund papillon **-håv** butterfly net
fjärilsim butterfly [stroke]
fjärilslarv caterpillar
fjärma remove [far off]; *bildl.* estrange, alienate; ~ *sig* draw away (*från* from), remove o.s.
fjärmare *komp. t. fjärran* farther (further)

[off]
fjärran I *adv* afar, far [away, off]; *från när och* ~ from far and near; *komma* ~ *ifrån* come from far off; *det vare mig* ~ *att* far be it from me to **II** *a, fjärmare fjärmast* distant, remote, faraway, far[-off]; *F~ östern* the Far East **III** *oböjligt n* distance; *i* ~ in the distance, afar off; *i ett avlägset* ~ in the [remote] distance
fjärr|kontroll remote control **-manövrera** operate by remote control **-manövrering** remote control **-skrivare** teleprinter **-skådande** *l s6* clairvoyance, second sight **II** *a4* **1** *eg.* far-seeing **2** clairvoyant, second-sighted **-skådare** clairvoyant, seer **-styrd** [-y:-] *a5* remote-controlled; ~ *raket* guided missile **-styrning** remote control **-trafik** long-distance traffic
fjärrvärme distant heating **-nät, -system** district heating system **-verk** district heating plant
fjärsing weever
fjärt *s2, vard.* fart
fjäsa ~ *för* make a fuss of; fawn on
fjäsk *s7* **1** (*brådska*) hurry, flurry; bustle **2** (*krus*) fuss (*för* of; *med* about), servility **fjäska 1** be in a hurry (*etc.*) **2** ~ *för* make a fuss of; fawn on **fjäskig** *a1* fussy, bustling; (*krypande*) fawning
fjät *s7* footstep
fjättra fetter, shackle, bind, chain; *~d till händer och fötter* bound hand and foot; *~d vid sängen* (*äv.*) bedridden **fjättrar** *pl, litt.* fetters, shackles
fjöl *s2* closet seat
f-klav bass clef, F clef
f.Kr. (*förk. för före Kristus*) B.C.
flabb *s7* (*skratt*) guffaw; vulgar laugh **2** *s2* (*pratmakare*) driveller **flabba** guffaw **flabbig** *a1* drivelling
flack *a1* **1** (*jämn o. öppen*) flat, level **2** (*ytlig*) superficial
flacka roam about (around)
flacktång flat pliers (*pl*)
fladder ['fladd-] *s7* flutter; *bildl.* levity; (*flärd*) empty show **-mus** bat
fladdr|a flutter; (*om fågel*) flit; (*om flagga*) stream, flap; (*om ljus, låga*) flicker **-ig** *a1* **1** (*löst hängande*) flapping **2** *bildl.* (*ostadig*) volatile, fickle
flaga I *s1* flake **II** *v1* shed flakes (*äv.* ~ *av* [*sig*]); ~ *sig* flake, scale off
flagell|ant Flagellant **-at** *biol.* flagellate
flageolett [-ʃå'lätt] *s3* flageolet **-ton** (*hopskr. flageoletton*) flageolet tone, fluted note
flagg *s2* flag; colours (*pl*); *föra brittisk* ~ fly the British flag; *segla under falsk* (*främmande*) ~ sail under false colours (a foreign flag); *stryka* ~ strike one's colours
flagga I *s1* flag; *hala ~n* lower the flag; *hissa ~n på halv stång* fly the flag at half-mast **II** *v1* fly flags (the flag, one's flag); *det ~s för* the flags are (the flag is) flying for (in honour of)
flagg|adjutant flag lieutenant **-duk 1** (*tyg*) bunting **2** (*flagga*) flag **-lina** flag halyard **-man** flag officer **-ning** *allmän* ~ a general display of flags **-prydd** *a5* decorated with flags **-signalering** signalling with flags **-skepp** flagship

F

-spel flagstaff, ensignstaff **-stång** flagpole, flagstaff
flag|ig *al* flaky, scaly **-na** [-a:g-] flake [off], scale off, peel
flagrant [-'ant *el.* -'aŋt] *al* flagrant
flak *s7* **1** *se isflak* **2** (*last-*) platform [body]
flakong [-'åŋ] *s3* flacon
flakvagn open-sided waggon
flambera flame
flamenco [-'menn-] *s5* flamenco
flamingo [-'miŋ(g)ω] *s5* flamingo
flam|ländare Fleming; *-ländarna* (*koll.*) the Flemish **-ländsk** *a5* Flemish **-ländska 1** (*språk*) Flemish **2** (*kvinna*) Flemish woman
flamma l *s1* **1** flame (*äv. bildl.*); (*häftig äv.*) blaze, flare **2** (*svärmeri*) flame; *vard.* baby **II** *v1* flame, blaze, flash; *~ för* (*vara entusiastisk*) be enthusiastic for, (*vara förälskad i*) be sweet on; *~ upp* blaze up, flare up **flammig** *a1* flamelike; (*fläckig*) patchy, blotchy **flamning** blaze, flare **flampunkt** flash[ing] point
flams *s7* gabble; giggle; loud chatter **flamsa** fool, monkey about **flamsig** *a1* silly; giggly
flamsk *a5, se flamländsk*
flam|säker flameproof **-ugn** reverberatory furnace
Flandern ['flann-] *n* Flanders **flandrisk** ['flann-] *a5, se flamländsk*
fla'nell *s3, s4* flannel **-byxor** *pl* flannel trousers, flannels
flanellograf *s3* flannel|board, -graph
flanera stroll; *vard.* troll
flank *s3* flank **-angrepp** flank attack, attack in the flank **-era** flank
flanör flâneur, idler, loafer, man about town
flarn [-a:-] *s7, driva som ett ~ på vattnet* drift along like a straw in the stream
flask|a *s1* bottle; (*fick-*) [hip] flask; (*av metall*) can; *ett litet barn ~n* give a baby its bottle; *tappa på -or* put in bottles, bottle; *öl på -or* bottled beer **-barn** bottle-fed baby **-borste** bottlebrush **-hals** bottleneck (*äv. bildl.*) **-post** message sent in a bottle [thrown into the sea] **-propp** stopper
flat *a1* **1** *eg.* flat; *~ tallrik* [shallow] plate; *med ~a handen* with the flat of the (one's) hand **2** (*förlägen*) aghast, dumbfounded, taken aback **3** (*släpphänt*) weak, indulgent (*mot* to)
flat|a *s1, se handflata* **-bottnad** [-å-] *a5* flat--bottomed **-het 1** *eg.* flatness **2** (*förlägenhet*) dumbfoundedness, blank amazement **3** (*släpphänthet*) weakness, indulgence **-lus** crab louse **-skratt** guffaw
flau oböjligt *a* dull, flat, depressed
flax *s2, vard.* [piece of good] luck; *ha ~* be lucky (in luck)
flaxa flutter; *~ med vingarna* flap (flutter) its (*etc.*) wings
flegma ['flegg-] *s1* phlegm; indifference **-tiker** [-'ma:-] phlegmatic person **-tisk** [-'ma:-] *a5* phlegmatic[al]; impassive
flekterande [-'te:-] *a4, ~ språk* (*pl*) inflectional languages
flektion *se flexion*
flenört common figwort
flera ['fle:-] *komp. t. många* **1** (*med jämförelse*) (*mera* [*än*]) more; (*talrikare*) more numerous;

allt ~ och ~ more and more; *mycket ~ människor* many more people; *många ~* many more; *vi blir inte ~* there won't be any more of us **2** (*utan jämförelse*) many; (*talrika*) numerous; (*åtskilliga*) several; *med ~* and others; *~ gånger, vid ~ tillfällen* on several occasions, on more than one occasion; *det blir billigare om vi är ~* the more we are, the cheaper it will be
fler|barnsfamilj large family **-dubbel** multiple, manifold **-dubbla** multiply **-faldig** *a5, ~ vinnare av* several times the winner of; *jfr mångfaldig* **-faldiga** multiply; (*skrift o.d.*) reproduce **-falt** many times, [ever so] much **-familjshus** block of flats; *AE.* apartment building (house) **-filig** *a5* multiple-lane **-färgad** multicoloured **-färgstryck** multicolour process printing; *konkr.* multicolour print **-omättad** polyunsaturated **-sidig** *a5* polygonal **-siffrig** *a5* of several figures **-språkig** *a5* multilingual, polyglot **-stavig** *a5* polysyllabic **-stegsraket** multistage rocket **-städes** in several places **-stämmig** *a5* polyphonous; *~ sång* part song **-stämmigt** *adv, sjunga ~* sing in parts **-tal** *s7* **1** *språkv.* plural **2** (*större delen*) majority; *~et människor* the [great] majority of people, most people; *i ~et fall* in most cases **3** *ett ~* several, a number of **-värd** *kem.* polyvalent **-årig** *a5* of several years[' duration]; *bot.* perennial
flesta *best. superl. t. många, de ~ a*) *fören.* most, *b*) *självst.* (*om förut nämnda*) most of them; *de ~* [*människor*] most people; *de ~ pojkarna* most of the boys; *av vilka de allra ~* by far the greater number of whom (which)
flex|a be on flexitime **-ibel** [-'i:-] *a2* flexible **-ibilitet** flexibility
flexion [-k'ʃω:n] inflection
flex|skiva *data.* floppy disk, flexible diskette **-tid** flexitime, flexible working hours
1 flicka *v1* patch, cobble
2 flick|a *s1* girl; *-orna Jones* the Jones girls
flick|aktig *a1* girlish **-aktighet** girlishness **-bekant** girlfriend **-bok** book for girls; *-böcker* (*äv.*) girls' books **-ebarn** [baby] girl, girl-child **-jägare** skirtchaser **-namn** girl's name; (*frus*) maiden name **-pension** girls' boarding school **-scout** [Girl] Guide; *AE.* Girl Scout **-snärta** young thing **-tjusare** charmer **-tycke** *ha ~* be a favourite with girls **-vän** girlfriend
flik *s2* (*på plagg, kuvert*) flap; (*snibb*) lappet; (*bit*) patch; (*yttersta kant*) edge, end; *bot.* lobe **-ig** *a1, bot.* lobate
flimmer ['flimm-] *s7* flicker **-hår** cilium (*pl* cilia), flagellum (*pl* flagella)
flimra quiver, shimmer, flicker; *det ~r för ögonen* my (*etc.*) eyes are dazzled
flin *s7* grin; (*hångrin*) sneer **flina** grin; sneer
flinga *s1* flake
flink *a1* (*kvick* [*av sig*]) quick, nimble (*i* at); (*färm*) prompt; (*driftig*) active; *~ i fingrarna* nimble-fingered, deft
flint *s3, vard.* **1** (*panna*) *mitt i ~en* full in the (one's) face **2** [bald] crown of the head; *början till ~* first signs of baldness
flint|a *s1* flint **-bössa** *se -låsgevär* **-glas** flint glass, [optical] flint **-kniv** flint knife **-låsgevär** flintlock, firelock **-porslin** flintware **-redskap**

flint implement[s *pl*]
flintskall|e bald head; (*person*) baldhead **-ig** *a1* bald[headed]
flint|vapen flint weapon **-verktyg** *se flintredskap* **-yxa** flint axe
flipperspel pinball machine
flirt [flört] *se flört*
flis *s3* wood chips (*pl*)
flisa I *s1* (*skärva, trä-*) splinter; (*tunn bit*) flake **II** *v1*, ~ [*sig*] splinter
flis|are *s9*, **-hugg** *s7* chipper **-stack** chip pile
flit *s3* **1** diligence; (*arbetsiver*) industry; (*trägenhet*) assiduity **2** *med* ~ (*avsiktligt*) on purpose, purposely, deliberately **-ig** *a1* diligent; (*idog*) industrious; (*arbetsam*) hard-working; (*trägen*) assiduous; (*aldrig sysslolös*) busy; (*ofta återkommande, t.ex.* om besök) frequent; *en* ~ *kyrkobesökare* a habitual churchgoer; *F~a Lisa* busy Lizzie **-pengar** overtime allowance (*sg*)
1 flock [-å-] *s7* (*avfall av ull o.d.*) flock
2 flock [-å-] *s2* **1** (*av fåglar, får o.d.*) flock; (*av renar*) herd; (*av vargar*) pack; (*av fåglar äv.*) flight; (*av människor*) crowd, party **2** *bot.* umbel
flock|a *rfl* flock [together], cluster **-blommig, -blomstrig** [-å-] *a5* umbelliferous **-instinkt** herd instinct
flod *s3* **1** *eg.* river; *bildl.* flood, torrent **2** (*högvatten*) flood, tide **-arm** branch (arm) of a (the) river **-bank** river bank **-bädd** riverbed **-fåra** river channel **-häst** hippopotamus; *vard.* river horse **-mynning** river mouth; (*stor äv.*) estuary **-spruta** fireboat **-system** river system **-våg** tidal wave **-ångare** river steamer
flopp [-å-] *s2*, **floppa** [-å-] *v1* flop
1 flor *s7* (*tyg*) gauze; (*sorg-*) crape; (*slöja*) veil
2 flor *n*, *stå* (*vara*) *i* [*sitt fulla*] ~ be in full bloom
flora *s1* flora
Florens ['flå:-] *n* Florence
florentin|are [-*ti:-] *s9*, **-sk** *a5* Florentine
florer|a flourish, be at its (*etc.*) prime; *neds.* be rife (rampant) **-ande** *a4* widely prevalent
flo'rett *s3* foil **-fäktare** foilsman **-fäktning** foil fencing
flo'rin *s3* florin; *holländska* ~*er* [Dutch] guilders (*förr äv.* florins)
flors|huva [-ⱷ:-] tipsiness **-tunn** thin as gauze; filmy
floskler ['flåsk-] *pl* empty phrases, balderdash (*sg*) **flosku'lös** *a1* inflated, bombastic
flossamatta pile rug (carpet)
1 flott [-å-] *oböjligt a*, *sjö.*, *komma* (*bli*) ~ get afloat
2 flott [-å-] *a1* (*elegant*) stylish, smart; (*frikostig*) generous; (*överdådig*) extravagant; *leva* ~ live in great style, lead a gay life
3 flott [-å-] *s4* grease; (*stek-*) dripping; (*ister-*) lard
1 flotta [-å-] *s1* (*örlogs-, handels-*) navy, fleet; (*fartygssamling*) fleet; *gå in vid* ~*n* join the Navy
2 flotta [-å-] *v1* float, drive, raft
3 flotta [-å-] *v1*, ~ *ner* make all greasy
flottare log-floater, log-driver
flottbas naval base

flottbro pontoon bridge
flotte *s2* raft
flottfläck grease spot
flotthet stylishness; generosity *etc.*
flottig *a1* greasy
flot'tilj [-å-] *s3*, *sjö.* flotilla; *flyg.* wing **-chef** *flyg.* wing commander; *AE.* lieutenant colonel **-enhet** *sjö.* naval unit
flottist [-å-] seaman, sailor
flottled floating channel, floatway
flottmanöver naval manoeuvres (*pl*)
flottning [-å-] floating, log-driving **flottningsränna** log flume (chute)
flottstyrka naval operating force
flot'tyr [-å-] *s3* frying-fat **-koka** deep-fry; *-kokt potatis* [potato] chips, French fried potatoes, *AE.* French fries **-kokning** deep-frying **-stekt** deep-fried
flottör float
flox [-å-] *s2* phlox
fluffig *a1* fluffy
flug|a *s1* **1** fly; *slå två -or i en smäll* kill two birds with one stone **2** (*halsduk*) bow [tie] **3** (*vurm*) craze **-fiske** fly-fishing (*efter forell* for trout) **-fångare** flypaper; flytrap
flugig *a1* cranky
flugit *sup. av flyga*
flug|nät fly net **-smuts** flyspeck **-smälla** fly swatter **-snappare** flycatcher; *grå* (*svart och vit*) ~ spotted (pied) flycatcher **-svamp** amanita; (*röd*) fly agaric; (*lömsk*) death cap (angel) **-vikt** flyweight **-viktare** flyweight [boxer *etc.*]
flu'id *s3* fluid **-isera** fluidize **-isering** fluidization **-istor** [-*istår] *s3* fludistor **-itet** fluidity, fluidness **-um** ['flu:i-] *s4* fluid, liquid
fluktu|ation fluctuation **-era** fluctuate
flum|debatt mixed-up debate **-mig** *a1*, *vard.* spaced out; mixed-up
flundra *s1* flounder, flatfish
fluor [-'å:r] *s3* fluorin[e] **-era** fluoridate **-ering** fluoridation
fluoresc|ens [-e'sens *el.* -'ʃens] *s3* fluorescence **-ent** fluorescent **-era** fluoresce **-erande** fluorescent
fluo'rid *s3* fluoride
fluorider|a, -ing *se fluorera, fluorering*
1 fluss *s3, med., se flytning, inflammation, katarr*
2 fluss *s3, kem.* flux[ing agent]
fluss|glas milk glass **-medel** *se 2 fluss* **-spat** (*hopskr. flusspat*) *s3* fluorspar, fluor; *AE.* fluorite
fluster ['fluss-] *s7* beehive entrance
flutit *sup. av flyta*
flux straight [away], all in a jiffy
1 fly *se ankarfly*
2 fly *se gungfly*
3 fly *s6, zool.* noctuid moth
4 fly *v4* **1** (*ta t. flykten*) fly, flee (*för fienden* before the enemy); (*rymma*) run away; (*undkomma*) escape; (*friare*) vanish, disappear; ~*dda tider* bygone days; *livet hade* ~*tt* he (*etc.*) was dead; *bättre* ~ *än illa fäkta* discretion is the better part of valour **2** (*undfly*) flee from, escape; (*faran*) shun
5 fly *adv, bli* ~ *förbannad* fly into a rage, get absolutely furious

flyg *s7* **1** *se flygvapen* **2** (*-konst*) aviation **3** (*-plan*) aeroplane; *AE.* airplane; *med* ~ by air **flyga** *flög flugit* fly; (*högt, uppåt*) soar (*mot höjden* aloft); (*ila, rusa*) dart, dash, rush; ~ *i luften* (*explodera*) blow (go) up; ~ *på ngn* fly at s.b.; *vad har det flugit i henne?* what [ever] can have possessed (got into) her?, what's bitten her?; *ordet flög ur honom* the word escaped him **flyg|ande** *a4* flying; ~ *besiktning* (*av bil etc.*) roadside inspection (safety check); ~ *fästning* (*mil.*) flying fortress; *F*~ *holländaren* the Flying Dutchman; ~ *hund* flying fox; ~ *mara* flying mare; ~ *start* flying start (*äv. bildl.*); ~ *tefat* flying saucer; *i* ~ *fläng* in a terrific hurry, posthaste **-anfall** air raid (attack) **flygar|e** flier, flyer, aviator, *mil.* airman; (*förare*) pilot **-sjuka** aeroembolism, decompression sickness (illness) **flyg|aska** fly ash, flue dust **-attaché** air attaché **-bas** air base (station) **-bild** *se flygfoto* **-biljett** air ticket **-blad** leaflet, handbill; fly sheet **-bolag** airline [company] **-buren** *a3* airborne **-buss** airbus **-båt** (*flygplan*) flying boat; (*båt*) hydrofoil **-certifikat** pilot's certificate, flying licence **-duglig** airworthy **-däck** (*på hangarfartyg*) flight deck **flygel** *s2* **1** wing; (*stänkskärm*) wing, *AE.* fender; *mil., polit., sport.* flank **2** *mus.* grand piano **-byggnad** wing **-karl** *mil.* pivot [man] **flyg|eskader** group **-fisk** flying fish **-flottilj** wing **-foto** aerial photograph (view) **-fotografera** photograph from the air **-fotografering** aerial photography **-frakt** air freight **-fyr** aeronautical (air) light; (*radiofyr*) [radio] beacon **-fä** winged insect; *förbaskade* ~*n!* blasted flies! **-fält** airfield, landing field, (*mindre*) flying field; *jfr flygplats* **-färd** flight **-färdig** (*om flygare*) ready to fly; (*om fågelunge*) fully fledged, full-fledged **-förband** flying unit **-förbindelse** air service; plane connection **flygg** *a1*, *se flygfärdig* **flyg|hamn** [marine] airport **-haveri** aircraft crash (accident) **-havre** wild oat **-industri** aircraft industry **-kapten** (*vid trafikflyget*) pilot **-korridor** air corridor, airway **-kropp** fuselage **-larm** air-raid alarm (warning) **-ledare** control officer **-ledartorn** [airport] control tower **-ledning** air-traffic control **-linje** airline, air route **-lotta** *ung.* (*i Storbritannien*) member of the Women's Auxiliary Air Force (W.A.A.F.); *vard.* Waaf **-maskin** *se flygplan* **-medicin** aviation medicine **-mekaniker** aircraft mechanic **-motor** aircraft (aero) engine **-myra** winged ant **flyg|ning** [-y:-] flying; aeronautics (*pl, behandlas som sg*); (*-tur*) flight **-officer** air-force officer **-olycka** *se flyghaveri* **-parad** fly-past; *AE.* flyover **-plan** aircraft; aeroplane; *AE.* airplane **flygplans|besättning** aircrew **-kapare** [aircraft] hijacker **-kapning** [aircraft] hijack **flyg|plats** airport, (*mindre*) air station, aerodrome, *AE.* airdrome; *jfr flygfält* **-porto** airmail postage **-post** airmail **-resa** flight, [air] trip **-rutt** air route (service) **-räd** air raid **-rädd** afraid of flying **-sand** shifting sand **-si-**

mulator flight simulator **-sinnad** *a5* air-minded **-sjuk** airsick **-sjuka** airsickness **-skydd** *mil.* air cover (support) **-spaning** air reconnaissance **-stab** air staff **-stridskrafter** air forces **-styrman** first officer **-säker** airworthy **-säkerhet** safety in flight **-säkerhetstjänst** air security service **-terminal** air terminal **-tidtabell** [air service] timetable (schedule) **-trafik** air traffic (service) **-transport** air transport (transportation) **-tur** flying trip, flight **-uppvisning** air show **-vapen** air force; *-vapnet* (*i Storbritannien*) the Royal Air Force (R.A.F., RAF), (*i USA*) United States Air Force (USAF, U.S.A.F.) **-värdinna** air hostess, stewardess **-ödla** pterosaur **flyhänt** *a1* deft; *bildl.* dext[e]rous, quick **-het** deftness; *bildl.* dexterity, quickness **1 flykt** *s3* (*t. flyga*) flight; *fälla en fågel i* ~*en* shoot a bird on the wing; *gripa tillfället i* ~*en* seize the opportunity **2 flykt** *s3* (*t. fly*) flight; (*rymning*) escape; *vara på* ~ be on the run; ~*en från landsbygden* the flight from the land; ~*en till Egypten* (*bibl.*) the flight into Egypt; *jaga på* (*ta till*) ~*en* put (take) to flight **flyktförsök** attempted escape **flykthastighet** *rymdtekn.* escape velocity **flyktig** *a1* **1** (*övergående*) fleeting, passing, fugitive; *en* ~ *bekantskap* a slight acquaintance; *kasta en* ~ *blick på ngt* give s.th. a hasty (passing, cursory) glance; ~ *genomläsning* cursory perusal **2** *kem. o.d.* volatile **3** (*ostadig*) fickle, flighty **flykting** refugee; (*flyende*) fugitive **-hjälp** aid to refugees **-läger** refugee camp **-ström** stream of refugees **flyta** *flöt flutit* **1** (*motsats sjunka*) float (*äv. bildl. och om valuta*); ~ *i land* be washed ashore **2** (*rinna o.d.*) flow (*äv. bildl.*); (*om tårar, svett o.d.*) run; ~ *med strömmen* float down with (be carried along by) the stream (current); *blod kommer att* ~ blood will be shed **3** (*ha flytande konsistens*) be fluid; (*om bläck o.d.*) run **4** ~ *ihop* (*om floder*) flow into each other, (*om färger*) run into each other; ~ *upp* rise to the surface; *han vill gärna* ~ *ovanpå* he likes to be superior **flyt|ande** *a4* **1** (*på vätska*) floating; (*om fartyg*) afloat; *hålla det hela* ~ keep things going **2** (*rinnande*) flowing, running; *bildl. äv.* fluent (*franska French*); *tala engelska* ~ speak English fluently **3** (*i vätskeform*) fluid, liquid; ~ *bränsle* liquid fuel; ~ *föda* liquid nourishment (food); ~ *kristaller* (*t.ex. i fickräknare*) liquid crystal display; ~ *luft* liquid air; ~ *naturgas* liquefied natural gas; ~ *syre* liquid oxygen; (*som raketbränsle äv.*) lox; ~ *tvål* liquid soap; ~ *valuta* floating currency **-docka** floating [dry] dock **-glas** *se floatglas* **-kropp** float **flytning** [-y:-] **1** floating **2** *med.* discharge, flux **flytta 1** (*ändra plats för*) move; remove (*äv. flytta bort*); (*i spel*) move; *bli* ~*d* (*skol., uppflyttad*) be moved up (till [in]to) **2** (*byta bostad*) move (*äv. flytta på* [*sig*]); (*lämna anställning*) leave (*från en plats* a place); (*från hotell etc.*) check out; (*om fåglar*) migrate; ~ *fram klockan* put the clock on (forward); ~

fram resan (resa tidigare) arrange an earlier date for the journey, advance the journey, (uppskjuta) postpone the journey; ~ fram trupperna advance the troops; ~ ihop move [closer] together; ~ ihop med ngn go to live with s.b.; ~ om shift, rearrange; ~ upp (i grad) move up; ~ sig move, change one's place

flytt|bar a5 mov[e]able, portable **-block** geol. erratic [block], boulder **-buss** removal van **-fågel** migratory bird **-fågelssträck** flight of migratory birds **-kalas** house-warming [party] **-karl** furniture remover **-lass** vanload of furniture

flyttning moving etc., removal, transportation; move; (fåglars, nomaders) migration

flyttnings|anmälan notification of change of residence (abode) **-betyg** (utfärdat på pastorsexpedition) certificate of change of address

flyttsaker movables

flytväst life jacket; AE. life preserver

flå v4 flay; (om fisk) skin

flås s7, vard. wind **-a** puff [and blow]; (pusta o. flämta) pant; ~nde av breathless with **-ig** a1 wheezy **-patos** strained pathos

fläck s2 **1** stain, mark, spot; (av färg) smudge; bildl. stain, blot, (fel) blemish; sätta en ~ på duken stain the tablecloth **2** (på djurhud) spot **3** (ställe) spot; på ~en (genast) on the spot, at once; jag får den inte ur ~en I cannot move it; han rörde sig inte ur ~en he did not move (budge); vi kommer inte ur ~en we are not getting anywhere (making any progress)

fläck|a spot, stain (äv. bildl.); (smutsa) smear, besmear; (söla ner) soil; ~ ner sig get o.s. (one's clothes) all stained (soiled) **-borttagning** spot (stain) removal **-borttagningsmedel** spot (stain) remover **-feber** spotted fever **-fri** stainless, spotless; unsoiled; bildl. äv. unspotted, blameless, immaculate

fläck|ig a1 **1** spotted; (nedfläckad) stained, soiled **2** (om djur) spotted **-vis** in spots (places)

fläder ['flä:-] s2 elder[berry] **-buske** elder shrub

flädermus se fladdermus

fläder|märg elder pith **-te** elder tea

fläka v3 slit, split open

fläkt s2 **1** (vindpust) breath [of air]; breeze; puff, blow; (friare o. bildl.) breath, waft; en frisk ~ a breath of fresh air; inte en ~ rörde sig not a breath was stirring **2** (apparat) fan, ventilator, blower

fläkt|a fan; ~ med solfjädern fan the air; det ~r skönt there is a nice breeze blowing **-rem** fan belt **-ventilation** mechanical ventilation

flämt|a 1 pant, puff **2** (fladdra) flicker **-ning 1** pant **2** flicker

fläng s7 bustling; hurry; i flygande ~ in a [flying] hurry **flänga** v2 **1** (rusa) fling (omkring i round); ~ och fara rush to and fro; ~ omkring (i väg) dash about (away) **2** (rycka) strip (av off)

fläns s2 flange **flänsa 1** tekn. flange **2** (valar) flense, flench

flärd [-ä:-] s3 vanity; frivolity **-fri** unaffected, artless, simple; (blygsam) modest **-full** vain; frivolous

fläsk s7 pork; (sid-) bacon; (hull) flesh; magert (randigt) ~ lean (streaky) bacon; rökt (stekt)

~ smoked (fried) bacon; ~ och bruna bönor pork and beans; ärter och ~ yellow pea soup and pork **-ben** ham bone **-filé** fillet of pork **-flott** pork dripping **-hare** kokk. boneless loin of pork

fläsk|ig a1 porky **-karré** loin of pork **-korv** pork sausage **-kotlett** pork chop **-lägg** hand (knuckle) of pork **-läpp** swollen lip **-pannkaka** pancake with diced pork **-svål** pork (bacon) rind (skin) **-änger** s2 larder beetle

flät|a I s1 plait; tress; (nack-) pigtail; (bröd, tobaks-) twist **II** v1 plait; braid; (krans o.d.) twine, wreathe; ~ in (bildl.) intertwine, intertwist; ~ in i (bildl.) weave into; ~ sig entwine itself (omkring round) **-ning** [-ä:-] plaiting etc. **-verk** plaited work

flöda flow; (häftigt) gush, pour, stream; ~ av overflow with; ~ över flow (run) over, bildl. brim over (av with); champagnen ~de the champagne flowed **flödande** a4 flowing etc.; bildl. fluent; abounding, exuberant **flöde** s6 flow; torrent, stream; fys. flux

flödes|diagram, -schema flow chart (sheet)

flög imperf. av flyga

flöjel [*flöjj-] s2 vane, weathercock

flöjt s3 flute **-blåsare, -ist** flute player, flautist; AE. flutist **-lik** flutelike, fluty

flört s3 **1** (flörtande) flirtation **2** pers. flirt **flörta** flirt **flörtig** a1 flirtatious, flirty

flöt imperf. av flyta

flöte s6 float; vara bakom ~t be dull (stupid)

flöts s3, geol. seam

FM (förk. för frekvensmodulering) FM

f.m. (förk. för förmiddagen) a.m.

f-moll F minor

FN (förk. för Förenta nationerna) U.N.

f.n. (förk. för för närvarande) se under närvarande

fnas s7 husk, shuck **fnasa** husk **fnasig** a1 scaly; chapped

fnask s7 **1** (obetydlighet) trifle **2** (grand) jot, scrap **3** (prostituerad) tart **-er** ['fnass-] s2 (pojkvasker) shrimp [of a lad]

fnatt få ~, vard. blow one's top

FN-bataljon United Nations battalion

fnissa v1, **fnissning** s2 titter, giggle

fnitter ['fnitt-] s7, **fnittra** v1, se fnissning, fnissa **fnittrig** prone to giggle, giggly

FN|-kommission United Nations commission **--observatör** United Nations observer

fnoskig [-å-] a1 dotty, silly; (om person) barmy, AE. balmy, loco

FN-stadgan United Nations Charter

fnurra s1, det har kommit en ~ på tråden mellan dem they have fallen out

fnysa v3 el. fnös fnyst, **fnysning** [-y:-] s2 snort

fnös imperf. av fnysa

fnösk|e s6 tinder, touchwood; torr som ~ dry as tinder **-ticka** s1 tinder fungus

foajé s3 foyer

fob [fåbb] f.o.b. (free on board)

fo'bi s3 phobia

fob-pris f.o.b.-price

fock s2, sjö. foresail, forecourse; (på mindre båt) jib

focka [-å-] (avskeda) turn off, [give…the] sack

fock|mast foremast **-skot** foresheet **-stag** fore-

stay
1 foder ['fø:-] *s7 (kreatursföda)* [cattle]food; forage; *(kraft-)* fodder, feed
2 foder ['fø:-] *s7 (i kläder o.d.)* lining; *(hylsa o.d.)* casing; *(dörr-, fönster- o.d.)* architrave; *bot.* calyx
foderbeta mangel[wurzel], mangold[wurzel]
foderblad *bot.* sepal
foder|kaka oil cake **-säd** fodder grain
foderväv lining material
foderväxt fodder (forage) plant
1 fodra [ˣfø:-] *(t. 1 foder)* [give ... a (its *etc.*)] feed, fodder
2 fodra [ˣfø:-] *(t. 2 foder)* line
fod'ral *s7* case; *(låda äv.)* box; *(hölje)* casing, cover
1 fodring [ˣfø:-] *(t. 1 foder)* feeding *etc.*
2 fodring [ˣfø:-] *(t. 2 foder)* lining
1 fog *n (skäl)* justice, [good] reason, justification, right; *med [allt]* ~ with good reason, reasonably; *utan ringaste* ~ without the slightest reason; *ha ~ för sig* be reasonable; *ha [fullt]* ~ *för* have every reason for
2 fog *s2 (skarv)* joint; *(söm)* seam; *med.* suture
foga I 1 *(förena)* join *(till, i* to); *bildl.* add [to], attach [to], affix **2** *(avpassa)* suit, fit **3** *(bestämma)* ordain; *ödet har ~t det så* fate has so ordained (determined) **II** *rfl* **1** *(ansluta)* join [itself *(etc.)*] on *(till* to) **2** *(falla sig) det har ~t sig så att* things have so turned out that **3** *(ge med sig)* give in; ~ *sig efter* accommodate o.s. to; ~ *sig i* resign o.s. to
fogde [ˣføgg-] *s2, ung.* sheriff, bailiff; *AE.* marshal
foglig [ˣfø:g-] *a1* accommodating, compliant; *(medgörlig)* amenable **-het** compliance, compliancy; amenability
fogning [ˣfø:g-] joining *etc., jfr foga*
fogsvans foxtail saw; handsaw
fo'kal *a5* focal **-distans** focal length (distance) **-infektion** focal infection
fokus ['fø:-] *-en el.* =, *pl -ar* focus **-era** focus **-ering** focusing
folder ['fåll-] *s2, s9* folder
foliant [book in] folio [volume]
folie ['fø:-] *s5* foil; *(plast- äv.)* film, sheet
folier|a 1 *tekn.* foliate, foil **2** *hand.* folio **-ing** *tekn. o. hand.* foliation
folio ['fø:-] folio **-band** folio volume **-format** folio size
folk [-å-] *s7* **1** *(folkslag, nation)* people **2** *(underlydande)* servants *(pl)*; *mil., sjö.* men **3** *(människor)* people *(pl)*; *vard.* folks *(pl)*; *F~ets hus* community centre, assembly hall; *göra ~ av ngn* teach s.b. manners; *uppföra sig som* ~ behave properly; *som ~ är mest* like the general run of people; *se ut som ~ gör mest* be ordinary looking; *det var mycket ~ på gatan* there were a lot of people in the street; *det är skillnad på ~ och fä* there are people and people; *har du inte sett ~ förr?* what are you standing there gaping for?
folkbildning *(bildningsnivå)* general level of education; *(undervisning)* adult education
folkbildnings|arbete adult educational activities **-förbund** adult education organization
folk|bok popular book **-bokföring** national reg-

istration
folk|dans folk dance
folkdemokrat|i people's democracy **-isk** of (belonging to) a people's democracy
folk|djup *ur ~et* from the masses **-domstol** people's court **-dräkt** national costume **-etymologi** folk (popular) etymology
folk|fattig sparsely populated **-fest** national holiday; *(folklig fest)* popular festivity **-front** popular front **-församling** national assembly **-försörjning** national food supply
folkgrupp *polit.* national group; *(minoritet)* minority
folk|hem *ung.* welfare state **-hjälte** national hero **-hop** crowd [of people]; *neds.* mob **-humor** popular (folk) humour **-hushållning** national economy **-hälsa** public health **-högskola** residential college for adult education
folkilsken vicious; savage
folk|kommissarie *(i Sovjetunionen)* People's Commissar **-kär** beloved by the people
folk|lager class [of society] **-ledare** popular leader **-lek** national game
folklig [-å-] *a1* **1** *(tillhörande folket)* popular; democratic **2** *(i umgänge)* affable **-het 1** popularity **2** affability
folkliv **1** street life; crowds *(pl)* **2** *(allmogens liv)* life of the people; *svenskt ~* the life and manners of the Swedish people
folklivs|forskning folklore **-skildring** description of the life of the [common] people
folklor|[e] [-'lå:r] *s3* folklore **-ist** folklorist **-istik** *s3* folklore [research] **-istisk** *a5* folkloristic
folklåt folk song
folk|massa *se folkhop* **-medicin** folk medicine **-minnesforskning** folklore research **-mord** genocide **-mun** *i ~* in popular speech, colloquially **-musik** folk music **-mål** dialect **-mängd** population **-mängdsstatistik** population statistics *(pl, behandlas som sg)* **-möte** public (mass) meeting
folk|nykterhet national standard of temperance **-näring** *se folkförsörjning* **-nöje** popular entertainment
folk|omröstning popular vote; referendum; plebiscite **-opinion** public opinion
folk|park amusement park **-parti** liberal party
folkpension national old age pension **-ering** national old age pensions scheme **-är** old-age pensioner
folk|ras race **-representation** parliament, legislature **-republik** people's republic **-resning** insurrection, popular rising **-rik** populous **-räkning** census **-rätt** international law **-rättslig** of (in) international law **-rörelse** popular (national) movement
folk|saga folk tale (story) **-samling** gathering of people, crowd **-sjukdom** endemic disease **-skara** *se folkhop*
folkskola elementary school; *AE.* grade school
folkskole|seminarium training college, elementary-school teacher's training college **-stadga** elementary-education statute
folkskollärar|e, -inna elementary school teacher
folk|skygg shy, retiring; *(om djur)* shy **-slag**

nationality **-spillra** remnant of a nation **-stam** tribe **-storm** mass protest, general uproar **-styre** democracy, representative government **-sång 1** (*folkvisa*) folk song **2** (*nationalsång*) national anthem **-sångare** folk singer **-sägen** popular tradition (legend)

folk|talare popular speaker (orator) **-tandvård** national dental service **-tom** (*om gata o.d.*) deserted, empty; (*om land o.d.*) depopulated **-ton** *visa i ~* song on a folk-song theme **-tribun** tribune **-tro** folklore, popular belief; lay opinion **-trängsel** crowd[s *pl*] [of people] **-tät** densely populated **-täthet** density of population

folk|upplaga popular edition **-upplopp** riot, tumult

folk|vald *a5* popularly elected **-vandring** migration **-vandringstiden** the time of the Great Migration **-vett** [good] manners (*pl*) **-vilja** will of the people **-vimmel** *i -vimlet* in the throng (crowd, crush) [of people] **-visa** folk song **-välde** democracy **-vänlig** democratic (democratically) disposed **-ökning** increase of population, population growth

follik|el [-'lick-] *s2, anat.* follicle **-u'lär** follicular, folliculate

fon [få:n] *s3* **1** *språkv.* phone **2** *fys., se phon* **1 fond** [fånd *el.* få̱ŋd] *s3* (*bakgrund*) background; *teat.* back [of the stage] (*på scenen*), centre (*i salongen*); *första radens ~* the dress-circle centre

2 fond [fånd *el.* få̱ŋd] *s3* (*kapital*) fund[s *pl*], capital; (*stiftelse o.d.*) foundation; (*förråd*) stock, store

fondbörs stock exchange (market)

fonddekoration backcloth, backdrop

fond|emission bonus (scrip) issue; *AE.* stock dividend issue **-era** fund, consolidate **-kommissionär** member of the stock exchange, stockbroker

fondloge *första radens ~* the dress-circle box

fondmäklare stockbroker

fondvägg *teat.* backscene

fondy [få̱ŋ'dy] *s3* fondue

fo'nem *s7* phoneme

fonet|ik *s3* phonetics (*pl, behandlas som sg*) **-iker** [-'ne:-] phonetician **-isk** [-'ne:-] *a5* phonetic

fonograf *s3* phonograph

font [-å-] *s3* fount, (*särsk. AE.*) font

fonta'nell [-å-] *s3* fontanel[le]

fon'tän [-å-] *s3* fountain; jet [of water]

for *imperf. av 2 fara*

fora *s1* (*lass*) [wag(g)on]load; (*vagn*) cart

force majeure [fårs ma'ʒö:r] force majeure

forcer|a [får'se:ra] **1** (*påskynda*) speed up, rush; (*intensifiera*) intensify **2** (*tilltvinga sig tillträde etc.*) force; (*chiffer*) break, cryptanalyse **-ad** *a5* forced, strained; *i -at tempo* at top speed **-ing** speeding up; forcing; (*kryptoanalys*) cryptanalysis

fordom[dags] [*fo:r-] formerly; in times past; in bygone days; *från ~* from former times; *i ~ tid* in former times, in olden days

fordon [*fo:r-] *s7* vehicle; (*last-*) van, truck, cart

fordons|skatt vehicle licence duty **-våg** weigh-

bridge

fordra [-ɷ:-] **1** (*med personsubj.*) demand (*ngt av ngn* s.th. of s.b.; *betalning* payment); (*bestämt yrka på*) insist upon; (*omilt kräva*) exact; (*göra anspråk på*) require (*att ngn skall veta s.b.* to know; *hövlighet av ngn* civility of [*el.* from] s.b.); (*som sin rätt*) claim; *~ räkenskap av ngn* call (bring) s.b. to account; *~ skadeersättning* demand (claim) damages; *ha 10 pund att ~ av ngn* have a claim of 10 pounds on s.b. **2** (*med saksubj.*) *a*) (*erfordra*) require, want, call for, *b*) ([*på*]*bjuda*) prescribe, *c*) (*ta tid i anspråk*) take; *arbetet ~r stor noggrannhet* the work demands great care

fordr|an [*fo:r-] *r, i pl används fordringar* **1** demand (*på ngn* on s.b.); requirement (*på ngn* in s.b.) **2** (*penning-*) claim (*på ngn* on s.b.; *på 10 pund* of 10 pounds) **-ande** *a4* exacting **-as** *dep* be required (needed)

fordring [*fo:r-] *se fordran; ~ar a*) demands, (*förväntningar*) expectations, (*anspråk*) claims, *b*) (*tillgodohavanden*) claims, [active] debts; *osäkra ~ar* doubtful claims, (*friare*) bad debts; *ha stora ~ar på livet* expect a lot of life; *ställa stora ~ar på* demand a great deal of, be exacting in one's demands on; *uppfylla ~arna för godkänd examen* satisfy the examiner[s *pl*]

fordringsägare creditor

fo'rell *s3* trout

form [-å-] **1** *s3* form; (*fason o.d.*) shape, cut; (*tillstånd*) state; *för ~ens skull* for form's sake, as a matter of form; *i ~ av a*) in [the] form of (*en roman* a novel), *b*) in the shape of (*en cirkel* a circle), *c*) in the state of (*is* ice); *i fast* (*flytande*) *~* in solid (fluid) form; *hålla mycket på ~en* stand on ceremony, be a stickler for etiquette; *i många ~er trivs det sköna* beauty appears in many guises **2** *s3, sport. o. bildl.* form; *inte vara i ~* be out of form **3** *s2* (*gjut-*) mould; *kokk.* dish, tin

forma [-å-] form, mould (*äv. bildl.*); (*friare*) shape, model; *~ en mening* frame a sentence

formaldehyd [*fårm-] *s3* formaldehyde

formalia [får'ma:-] *pl* formalitites

forma'lin [-å-] *s4, s3* formalin

formaliser|a [-å-] formalize **-ing** formalization

formal|ism [-å-] formalism **-ist** formalist **-istisk** *a5* formalistic

formalitet [-å-] *s3* formality, matter of form; *utan ~er* without ceremony

forma|t [-å-] *s7* size, format; *bildl.* importance, weight **-tion** formation

formbar [-å-] *a1* formable; mouldable, plastic **-het** mouldability, plasticity, workability

formbröd tin [loaf]

formel ['fårr-] *s3* formula **for'mell** *a1* formal, conventional

formenlig [-e:-] *a5* correct [in form]

former|a [-å-] **1** *mil., ~* [*sig*] form **2** (*vässa*) sharpen **-are** sharpener **-ing** formation; (*vässning*) sharpening

form|fast non-deformable; *~a jerseybyxor* jersey trousers that keep their shape **-fel** error in form **-fulländad** *a5* perfect in form **-fulländning** perfection of form **-förändring** modification of form; *konkr. äv.* deformation

formge design

formgiv|a *se formge* **-are** designer **-ning** [-ji:v-] designing, shaping; *konkr.* [creative] design
formgjut|a die-cast **-ning** die-casting
formi'dabel [-å-] *a2* formidable
formligen [-å-] (*bokstavligen*) literally; (*rentav*) positively; (*helt enkelt*) simply
form|lära *språkv.* accidence **-lös** formless, shapeless; (*obestämd*) vague
form|ning [-å-] shaping, forming **-pressa** die- -cast; press, mould **-pressning** die-casting; moulding **-rik** abundant in forms; (*om språk*) highly inflectional **-sak** matter of form, formality **-skön** beautiful in form, beautifully shaped **-sättning** *byggn.* casing, mould
formuler|a [-å-] formulate, word; ~ *frågor* frame questions **-ing** formulation; (*ordalydelse*) wording
formu'lär [-å-] *s7* form
forn [-ɷ:-] *a5* former, earlier; (*-tida*) ancient **-borg** hillfort **-engelsk** Anglo-Saxon **-engelska** Old English, Anglo-Saxon **-forskare** arch[a]eologist, antiquary **-forskning** arch[a]eology, arch[a]eological research **-fynd** arch[a]eological find **-grekisk, -grekiska** Ancient Greek **-historia** ancient history **-historisk** of ancient history **-högtysk, -högtyska** Old High German **-isländsk, -isländska** Old Icelandic **-kunskap** *se fornforskning* **-lämning** ancient monument; ~*ar* ancient remains **-minne** ancient monument, relic of antiquity **-minnesvård** preservation of ancient monuments **-nordisk, -nordiska** Old Norse **-sak** arch[a]elogical relic **-svensk, -svenska** Old Swedish **-tid** prehistoric age (period); ~*en* antiquity; *i den grå* ~*en* in the dim and distant past **-tida** *oböjligt a* ancient
fors [-å-] *s2* **1** rapids (*pl*), white water; cataract **2** (*friare o. bildl.*) stream, cascade, torrent **forsa** rush; (*friare*) gush; *en* ~*nde bäck* a torrent; *blodet* ~*de ur såret* the blood gushed from the wound; *regnet* ~*r ner* it rains cats and dogs **forsfarare** rapids shooter
forsk|a [-å-] search (*efter* for); *absol.* [carry out] research; ~ *i* (*undersöka*) inquire into, investigate **-ande** *a4* inquiring; (*prövande*) searching
forskar|begåvning gift for research; *pers.* gifted researcher **-bragd** triumph of research, scientific feat
forskar|e [-å-] [research] scientist, researcher; investigator (*i* of) **-flykt** brain drain **-grupp** group of researchers (research scientists) **-gärning** scientific achievement **-möda** painstaking research
forskning [-å-] research (*i* upon); (*naturvetenskap*) science; (*undersökning*) investigation (*i* into, on)
forsknings|anslag research grant **-anstalt** research institute **-arbete** research work **-centrum** research centre **-fält** field of research **-institut** *se -anstalt* **-resa** exploration expedition **-resande** explorer **-resultat** research findings (*pl*)
forsl|a [-å-] transport, convey, carry; ~ *bort* carry away, remove **-ing** carriage, transportation, conveyance
forsränning white water rafting

forst|mästare [-å-] [certified] forester, forest officer **-väsen** forestry organization
forsythia [får'sy:tia] *s1* forsythia
1 fort [-å-] *s7* (*fästning*) fort
2 fort [-ɷ-] **I** *adv* (*i snabbt tempo*) fast; (*på kor* *tid, snabbt*) quickly, speedily; (*raskt*) rapidly; (*i* [*all*] *hast*) hastily; *det gick* ~ *för honom i* didn't take him long, he was quick about it, i was over quickly for him; *det går inte så* ~ *för mig att* I must take my time about (+ *ing-form*), I am rather slow at (+ *ing-form*); *har* *tröttnade* ~ he soon got tired, he tired easily; *gå lika* ~ *som ngn* keep pace with s.b.; *klockan* *går för* ~ the (my *etc.*) watch (clock) is fast **I** *interj* quick!, sharp!
forta [*förr-] *rfl* (*om klocka*) gain
fortbe|stå continue [to exist] **-stånd** continued existence
fortbild|a train (educate *etc.*) further; ~ *sig* continue one's training (education) **-ning** further training (education) **-ningskurs** extension (continuation) course
forte [*fårr-] *adv o. s6* forte **-piano** *adv o. s6* pianoforte
fortfar|a continue, go on (*att sjunga* singing) (*hålla i*) keep on (*med* with); (*fortvara*) last **-ande** still
fortfärdig expeditious; nimble, quick
fortgå go on, proceed; (*fortsätta*) continue **-en-de I** *s6* continuance **II** *a4* continued
fortifikation [-å-] fortification
fortifikations|förvaltning ~*en* [the Swedish] fortifications administration **-officer** military engineer
fortissimo [får'tiss-] *adv o. s6* fortissimo
fortkörning speeding [offence]
fort|leva live on; survive **-löpande** *a4* continuing, continuous; ~ *kommentar* running commentary
fortplant|a *vl* **1** (*om människor, djur, växter* propagate, reproduce **2** (*friare o. bildl.*) transmit **3** *rfl* propagate [o.s., itself] (*äv. om ljud ljus*); *eg. äv.* breed; (*om rykte*) spread; (*on* *sjukdom*) be transmitted, spread **-ning** propagation, breeding; transmission
fortplantnings|drift reproductive (propagative procreative) instinct **-duglig** reproductive, procreative **-förmåga 1** procreative faculty **2** *fys.* power of transmission **-organ** reproductive organ
fortsatt *a4* continued; (*-löpande*) continuous; (*återupptagen*) resumed; (*ytterligare*) further
fortskaff|a transport, convey **-ningsmedel** means (*sg o. pl*) of conveyance (transport transportation)
fortskrida proceed; (*framskrida äv.*) advance
fortsätt|a 1 (*fortfara med*) continue; go on (proceed) with; (*efter uppehåll*) take up, resume; (*fortsätta o. fullfölja*) carry on **2** (*fortgå* go on (continue) (*att spela* playing); (*efter uppehåll*) proceed; *fortsätt bara!* go ahead! **-ning** continuation; proceeding; ~ *följer* (*forts.*) to be continued; *i* ~*en* henceforth, from now or **-ningsvis** (*vidare*) further
fortuna [-*tu:-] *n,* **-spel** bagatelle
fort|vara continue [to exist] **-varo** *s5* continued existence

forum *s8* forum; quarter; *rätt* ~ *för* [the] proper authority for, the right place for

forwardskedja [ˣfåːrvards-] forward line

fosfat [-åˑ-] *s7, s4* phosphate

fosfor [ˣfåssfår] *s2* phosphorus

fosforesc|ens [-ˈsens *el.* -ˈʃens] *s3* phosphorescence **-ent** phosphorescent **-era** phosphoresce [-ˈseː- *el.* -ˈʃeː-] phosphorescent

fosfor|förgiftning phosphorus poisoning **-syra** [orto]phosphoric acid **-tändsticka** phosphorus match

fosgen [fåsˈjeːn] *s3* phosgene

fos'sil [-åˑ-] l*s7* fossil **II** *a5* fossil; ~*t bränsle* fossil fuel **-fynd** fossil find **-kraftverk** fossil-fuelled power station

fostbrödralag *s7* sworn brotherhood

foster [ˈfɶss-] *s7* fetus, foetus; *bildl.* offspring, product, creation

fosterbarn foster child

fosterfördriv|ande *a4* abortive, abortifacient **-are** abortionist **-ning** [criminal] abortion

foster|föräldrar foster parents **-hem** foster home **-hinna** fetal membrane **-jord** native soil **-land** [native] country

fosterlands|förrädare traitor [to one's country] **-förräderi** high treason **-kärlek** patriotism, love of one's country **-vän** patriot

fosterljud fetal heart sound

fosterländsk *a5* patriotic

foster|rörelse fetal movement **-utveckling** development (growth) of the fetus **-vatten** amniotic fluid **-vattensprov** amniocentesis

fostra bring up, rear; *bildl.* foster, breed **fostran** *r* bringing up *etc.*; (*upp-*) education; *fysisk* ~ physical training **fostrare** fosterer; (*friare*) trainer of the young

fot 1 *-en fötter* foot (*pl* feet); (*på glas*) stem; (*lamp-*) stand; *bildl.* footing, terms (*pl*), standing; ~*!* (*t. hund*) heel!; *lätt på* ~*en* light of foot, *bildl.* of easy virtue; *på resande* ~ on the move; *på stående* ~ instantly; *få fast* ~ get a footing; *försätta på fri* ~ set free; *gå till* ~*s* go on foot, walk; *leva på stor* ~ live in grand style, live it up; *stryka på* ~*en* give in (*för* to); *stå på god* ~ *med ngn* be on a friendly footing with s.b.; *inte veta på vilken* ~ *man skall stå* not know which leg to stand on; *han har inte satt sin* ~ *där* he has not set foot there, *neds.* he has not darkened the roof of that home (house *etc.*); *dra fötterna efter sig* drag one's feet (heels); *kasta sig för ngns fötter* fall down at a p.'s feet; *komma på fötter igen* get on to one's feet again, (*bli frisk*) be up and about again; *trampa under fötterna* trample underfoot; *vara kall om fötterna* have cold feet **2** *s9* (*längdmått*) foot

fota base; ~ *sig på* be based on

fotabjälle *s6, från hjässan till* ~*t* from top to toe (head to foot); cap-a-pie

fot|arbete *sport.* footwork **-bad** foot bath **-behandling** pedicure **-beklädnad** (*skor*) footwear, footgear **-boja** fetter, shackle; (*förr*) foot and chain **-boll** football; (*spelet*) [association] football, soccer; *vard.* footer; *AE.* soccer

fotbolls|domare referee **-fantast** football (*AE.* soccer) fan **-lag** football (*AE.* soccer) team **-förbund** football association; *AE.* soccer

league **-match** football (*AE.* soccer) match **-plan** football (*AE.* soccer) ground **-spelare** football (*AE.* soccer) player, footballer **-tröja** *vard.* strip

fot|broms (*i bil*) foot (pedal) brake; brake pedal **-fel** foot fault **-folk** infantry **-fäste** foothold; (*insteg*) footing; *få* (*vinna*) ~ get (gain) a foothold (footing); *förlora* ~*t* lose one's foothold **-gavel** footboard **-gängare** [-jäŋ-] pedestrian **-knöl** ankle **-kurtis** *vard.* footsie **-led** ankle joint **-not** footnote

foto *s6* photo (*pl* photos); *se fotografi* **-affär** camera shop; photograpic dealer's **-album** *se fotografialbum* **-ateljé** photographic studio **-blixt** flashlight, flash **-cell** photocell, photoelectric cell **-elektricitet** photoelectricity **-elektrisk** [-ˈlekt-] photoelectric[al]

fotogen [-ˈʃeːn] *s3, s4* paraffin[e] [oil]; *AE.* kerosene

fotogenisk [-ˈjeː-] *a5* photogenic

fotogen|kök oil (paraffin, *AE.* kerosene) stove **-lampa** paraffin (*AE.* kerosene) lamp

foto'graf *s3* photographer **-era** photograph; *absol. äv.* take photographs; ~ *sig* have one's photo[graph] taken **-ering** photography; (*-erande*) photographing

fotogra'fi *s4, s3* photograph, *vard.* photo; (*som konst*) photography **-album** photograph album

fotografisk [-ˈgraː-] *a5* photographic

fotogramme'tr|i *s3* photogrammetry **-isk** [-ˈmeː-] *a5* photogrammetric

fotogra'vyr photogravure

fotoke'm|i photochemistry **-isk** [-ˈçeː-] photochemical

fotokopi|a print; *se äv. fotostat[kopia]* **-era** photocopy **-ering** photocopying

fotolampa photoflood

foto'ly|s *s3* photolysis **-tisk** *a5* photolytic

foto|meter [-ˈmeː-] *s2* photometer **-me'tri** *s3* photometry **-metrisk** [-ˈmeː-] *a5* photometric

foto|modell photographer's model **-montage** photomontage

foton [-ˈtåːn] *s3* photon

foto'sfär photosphere

foto'stat *s3*, **-kopia** photostat [copy], photocopy

foto|syntes photosynthesis **-sätta** filmset, photoset; *AE.* photocompose **-sättning** filmsetting; *AE.* photocomposition, phototypesetting **-terapi** phototherapy, phototherapeutics (*pl, behandlas som sg*) **-tropism** phototropism **-ty'pi** (*metod*) photoengraving; (*kliché, tryck*) photoengraving, line block

fot|pall footstool, footrest **-riktig** ~*a skor* well-fitting shoes **-sack** *s2* foot muff

fotsdjup one foot deep

fot|sid reaching [down] to the (one's) feet **-soldat** foot soldier, infantryman **-spår** footprint, footmark; (*i sht bildl.*) footsteps (*pl*) **-steg** [foot]step; (*på bil o.d.*) running board **-stöd** (*på t.ex. motorcykel*) footrest **-sula** sole [of a (the, one's) foot] **-svamp** athlete's foot **-svett** *ha* ~ have sweaty feet (*pl*) **-valv** arch of the foot **-vandra** walk; hike **-vandring** walking tour; hike **-vård** pedicure **-vårta** verruca **-vänlig** ~*a skor* comfortable shoes **-ända** foot of the bed

fox|terrier [ˣfåks-] fox terrier **-trot[t]** [ˈfåks-] s3 foxtrot
frack s2 (kostym) dress suit; (rock) tail (dress) coat, tails (pl) **-skjorta** dress shirt **-skört** dress-coat tail
fradga I s1 froth, foam; ~n står om munnen på honom he is frothing (foaming) at the mouth; tugga ~ foam with rage **II** v1, ~ [sig] foam, froth
fragil [-ˈʃiːl el. -ˈgiːl] a1 fragile
frag'ment s7 fragment **-arisk** [-ˈtaː-] a5 fragmentary, fragmental
frakt s3 freight; (t. lands) goods (pl); (skeppslast) cargo, shipload, äv. freight; ~ betald freight (carriage) paid; ~[en] betalas vid framkomsten freight (carriage) forward **frakta** transport, convey; (t. lands äv.) carry; AE. äv. freight
frakt|avgift freight charge **-brev** se fraktsedel **-fart** carrying trade **-fartyg** freighter, cargo vessel **-flyg** cargo plane; air cargo service **-fritt** freight prepaid; järnv. carriage paid; ~ London freight (carriage) paid to London **-gods** goods (pl); AE. [regular] freight; (motsats ilgods m.m.) goods forwarded by goods train
fraktion [-kˈʃɔːn] **1** (grupp) faction, group [of a party] **2** kem. fraction
fraktioner|a kem. fractionate; ~d destillation fractional distillation **-ing** fractioning **-ingskolonn** fractionating column
frakt|kostnad freight [charge, cost] **-sats** freight rate **-sedel** (t. lands) consignment note, waybill; (t. sjöss) bill of lading; flyg. air waybill (consignment note)
fraktur 1 med. fracture **2** boktr. Gothic, black letter **-stil** se fraktur 2
fram [-amm] adv **1** rumsbet. a) (framåt, vidare) on, along, forward, b) (genom) through, c) (i dagen) out, d) (fram t. ngn, ngt) up [to], e) (t. målet) there, f) (framme) further on, g) (motsats bak) in front; ~ med det! out with it!; längre ~ further on; ända ~ all the way there; ända ~ till right up to; få sin vilja ~ get one's own way; gå ~ och tillbaka go there and back, (av o. an) go to and fro; gå rakt ~ go (walk) straight on; gå vägen ~ walk on along the road; hinna ~ i tid get there in time; om sanningen skall ~ to tell the truth, to be quite honest; stig ~! come out (here)!; solen tittar ~ the sun peeps [out] **2** tidsbet. on; litet längre ~ a little later on; ~ på dagen later in the day; till långt ~ på natten until far into the night; ända ~ till våra dagar right up to the present day (to our own time); ~ till 1990 up to 1990
fram|axel front axle **-ben** foreleg, front leg **-besvärja** conjure up **-bringa** bring forth; (skapa) create; (ljud, säd etc.) produce **-bära** take (etc.) [up] (till to); (gåva o.d.) present, offer; (vad ngn sagt) report, pass on; (hälsning) deliver, convey; (lyckönskan, tacksägelse) tender
fram|del forepart, front [part] **-deles** later on; (i framtiden) in the future **-driva** propel; bildl. urge on, drive **-drivning** propulsion
fram|emot [on] towards **-fall** med. prolapse **-faren** a5 past; i -farna dagar in days gone

by **-fart** (friare) rampaging[s pl], sweep; (ödeläggelse) ravaging[s pl]; (körning) reckless driving **-flytta** move forward; (uppskjuta) postpone, put off **-flyttning** postponement **-fot** forefoot; visa -fötterna show one's paces **-fusig** a1 pushing, bumptious, forward **-fusighet** pushingness etc. **-föda** bring forth; give birth to
framför I prep **1** (rumsbet., äv. bildl.) before, in front of; (framom) ahead of; mitt ~ näsan på ngn straight in front of s.b., right under a p.'s nose **2** (om företräde) a) (i vikt, värde) above, ahead of, b) (hellre än) preferably (in preference) to, rather than; ~ allt above all (everything); ~ alla andra of all others, above all the rest; ~ allt gäller detta om this applies particularly to; föredra te ~ kaffe prefer tea to coffee **II** adv in front; ahead
framför|a 1 se föra fram **2** (uppföra, uppvisa) present, produce **3** (överbringa) convey, deliver, give; (anföra) state, put forward **-ande** s6 **1** (av motorfordon) conveyance **2** (anförande) delivery; (av teaterpjäs o.d.) performance
framförhållning 1 (vid skjutning) aim-off **2** bildl. long-term planning
fram|gaffel (på cykel) front fork **-gent** [-jeː-] henceforth, for (in) the future; allt ~ ever after
fram|gå bildl. be clear (evident); härav ~r att from this we conclude that, (friare) it appears from this that; av vad han säger ~r it appears from what he says; av Ert brev ~r att we see (understand) from your letter that; det -gick tydligt att it was made very clear that; **-gång** s2 success; med ~ (äv.) successfully; utan ~ (äv.) unsuccessfully **-gångsrik** successful
fram|hjul front wheel **-hjulsdrift** front-wheel drive **-hjulsinställning** alignment of front wheels
fram|hålla (framhäva) give prominence to (call attention to); (betona) [lay] stress [on], emphasize; (påpeka) declare, say; ~ nödvändigheten av emphasize the necessity of; jfr framhäva **-härda** persist, persevere **-häva** bildl. hold up, bring out; jfr framhålla **-hävande** s6 holding up etc.; med ~ av [in] bringing out
fram|ifrån from the front; ett hus sett ~ the front view of a house **-ilande** s6 rushing forwards
framkall|a 1 (i minnet, för tanken) recall **2** (uppkalla t. försvar o.d.) call up **3** foto. develop **4** bildl. (frambringa) call forth, provoke, evoke; (förorsaka) cause; (åstadkomma) bring about, give rise to; (uppväcka) arouse, raise **-ning** foto. developing, development **-ningsvätska** foto. developer
fram|kant front edge **-kasta** bildl. throw out; (idé) put forward, suggest; (tanke) bring up; (omnämna) mention; ~ beskyllningar bring forward (starkare: hurl) accusations; ett löst ~t påstående a haphazard statement
fram|komlig [-å-] a1 (om väg) passable, trafficable; (om vatten) navigable; (friare) practicable; bildl. feasible **-komma 1** se komma fram **2** (friare o. bildl.) come out, appear; ~ med bring forward, produce; det har -kommit önskemål om att wishes have been expressed that **-komst** [-å-] s3 **1** (fortkomst) advance,

progress **2** (*ankomst*) arrival; *att betalas vid ~en* charges forward, cash on delivery
framkörning driving up
fram|laddare muzzle-loader **-leva** live; *~ sina dagar* pass one's days **-liden** *a5* (*avliden*) past; *den -lidne...* the late... **-locka** bring (draw) forth; (*upplysningar, nyheter*) elicit **-lykta** headlight **-lägga** *bildl.* (*framkomma med*) put (bring) forward; (*anföra*) adduce; (*förete*) present; (*förslag*) table; *~ bevis* produce evidence; *~ för* produce before, submit to **-länges** [-län-] forwards; *åka ~* (*i tåg*) sit (travel) facing the engine, (*i buss etc.*) sit (travel) facing forward (the front)
fram|mana *bildl.* call forth, evoke; (*frambesvärja*) conjure up **-marsch** advance; *bildl.* advancement, progress; *stadd på ~* advancing, making headway **-matning** feed
framme 1 in front **2** (*vid målet*) at one's destination, there; *när vi var ~* when we got there; *nu är vi ~* here we are **3** (*framlagd o.d.*) out; on view; (*ej undanlagd*) about; *låta ngt ligga ~* leave s.th. about; (*till hands*) ready, at hand; *har pojkarna varit ~?* is it the boys who have done it (been at work)?; *när olyckan är ~* when things go wrong **4** *hålla sig ~* push o.s. forward, keep o.s. to the fore
frammumla mutter, mumble
framom I *adv* ahead, in advance **II** *prep* before, ahead of, in advance of
fram|pressa *bildl.* extract (*ur* out of); (*tårar*) squeeze out; (*ljud*) utter, ejaculate **-provocera** provoke **-på I** *prep* **1** (*om rum*) in front of, in (on) the front part of **2** (*om tid*) a little later; *till långt ~ natten* far into the night **II** *adv* in [the] front
fram|rusande *a4* (*om vatten*) gushing; (*framåtrusande*) onrushing **-ryckning** advance
fram|sida front; (*på check, sedel o.d.*) face; (*på mynt*) obverse **-skjutande** *a4* projecting, protruding; prominent **-skjuten** *a5* advanced; *bildl.* prominent **-skrida** (*om tid, arbete o.d.*) progress, advance **-skriden** *a5* advanced; *tiden är långt ~* it is getting late **-skymta** *se skymta fram*; *låta ~* give an intimation **-släpa** *~ sitt liv* drag on one's existence **-smygande** *komma ~* creep along **-springande** *se framskjutande*; *komma ~* come running up **-stamma** stammer out (forth) **-steg** progress, advance[ment]; *göra ~* make progress (headway)
framsteg|fientlig reactionary, anti-progressive **-man** progressive **-parti** progressive party **-vänlig** progressive
fram|stormande *se framrusande* **-stupa** flat, headlong, prostrate
framstå stand (come) out (*som* as); appear **-ende** prominent; (*högt ansedd*) eminent; (*förträfflig*) distinguished
framställa I 1 (*återge, visa*) represent; show; (*konstnärligt*) depict, represent, draw; (*på scen*) [im]personate **2** (*skildra*) describe; (*beteckna*) represent **3** (*framföra, komma fram med*) bring (put) forward; *~ en fråga* put a question; *~ klagomål* lodge complaints; *~ krav* make demands; (*uttala, ge uttryck åt*) express, state; *~ önskemål* express a wish, state requirements **4** (*tillverka*) produce, make; (*fabriks-*

mässigt) manufacture; (*utvinna*) extract; *börja ~* put in hand **II** *rfl* represent o.s.; (*uppstå*) yppa sig) arise
framställan *r, se framställning*; *på ~ av* at the instance of
framställning 1 (*i bild*) representation, picture, depiction **2** (*skildring*) description, rendering; (*redogörelse*) account; (*muntlig*) narration **3** (*framställningssätt*) *a*) (*författares*) style *b*) (*talares*) delivery, *c*) (*talares, konstnärs*) presentation, presentment, *d*) *teat.* rendering, interpretation **4** (*förslag*) proposal, proposition; (*hemställan*) petition, request **5** (*tillverkning*) production; (*fabriksmässig*) manufacture; (*utvinning*) extraction
framställnings|förmåga descriptive power, power of [re]presentation **-kostnad** cost of production **-metod, -sätt** method of production, manufacturing process
fram|stöna [utter] groan[ingly] **-stöt** *mil. o. bildl.* drive, thrust; attack, assault **-synt** [-y:-] *a1* (*förutseende*) far-seeing, far-sighted **2** (*klärvoajant*) gifted with second sight **-synthet** [-y:-] **1** foresight **2** [gift of] second sight **-säga 1** (*uttala, yttra*) articulate, pronounce **2** (*deklamera*) recite **-säte** front seat **-tand** front tooth **-tass** forepaw
framtid future; *för all ~* for all time (evermore); *det får ~en utvisa* time will show; *för ~en måste jag* in (for the) future I shall have to; *ha ~en för sig* have the future before you; *saken får ställas på ~en* it must wait until later, the matter must be postponed; *tänka på sin ~* think of one's [future] career **framtida** *oböjligt a* future
framtids|dröm dream of the future **-forskare** futurologist **-forskning** futurology **-man** coming man **-mål** prospective aim, future goal **-plats** position (job) offering good (excellent) prospects **-studier** futurology **-tro** belief in the future **-utsikter** [future] prospects **-vision** vision of the future
framtill in front
framtoning image
framträd|a 1 *se träda fram* **2** (*uppträda*) appear (*inför offentligheten* before the public; *på scenen* upon the stage) **3** *bildl.* make one's appearance, appear; (*ur det fördolda*) come into sight (view); (*om anlag, egenskap o.d.*) assert (display) itself; (*avteckna sig*) stand out; *låta ~* bring out (into relief) **-ande I** *s6* appearance **II** *a4* prominent, outstanding, salient
fram|tränga penetrate, force one's (its *etc.*) way forward; *flyg.* nose-heavy **-tvinga** extort; [en]force; (*kräva*) necessitate **-vagn** front part of the chassis **-vagnsupphängning** front suspension **-visa** show [up]
framåt ['framm-] **I** *adv* **1** *rumsbet.* ahead; (*vidare framåt*) on[ward], onwards; forward[s]; *fortsätt ~!* keep straight on!; *gå ~ a*) (*promenera*) walk along (*emot* towards; *till* to), *b*) (*utvecklas*) go ahead, [make] progress; *se rakt ~* look straight ahead **2** *tidsbet.* ahead, to come, into the future; *gå raskt ~* make rapid strides; *komma ~ i världen* get on in the world **II** *prep* **1** (*i rummet*) [on] toward[s]; ([*fram*] *längs*)

F

[on] along 2 (*i tiden*) [on] toward[s] III *interj* on!, onward!, forward!; *sjö.* ahead!

framåt|anda go-ahead spirit **-böjd** *a1*, **-lutad** *a5* bent forward[s]; *gå* ~ walk with a stoop **-skridande** I *s6* progress, advance II *a4* progressive **-strävande** *a4, bildl.* pushing, go- -ahead

fram|ända front end **-över** I *prep* out (away) across II *adv* forwards; onwards, ahead

franc [fraŋ] *s9* franc

francis'kan *s3,* **franciskaner** [-'ka:-] *s9* Franciscan [monk] **-orden** Franciscan Order

francium ['frans-] *s8* francium

1 frank *a1* frank, open, straightforward

2 frank *s3* Frank

Franken ['frann-] *n* Franconia

franker|a (*frimärka*) stamp **-ing** stamping **-ingsmaskin** franking machine

frankisk ['frann-] *a5* Frankish, Franconian

franko ['frann-] post-free, postpaid; *hand.* franco, free of charge (carriage) **-stämpel** postage impression **-tecken** postage stamp

Frankrike ['frank-] *n* France

frans *s2,* **fransa** *v1* fringe; ~ *sig* fray **fransad** *a5* fringed **fransig** *a1* (*trasig*) frayed

fransk *a1* French; ~*a fönster* French windows (*AE.* doors); ~ *lilja* (*her.*) fleur-de-lis, *äv.* lily of France **franska 1** (*språk*) French **2** (*bröd*) French roll; (*lång-*) French loaf

fransk|bröd *se franska 2* **--engelsk** Franco- -British; French-English **-klassicism** French classicism **--svensk** Franco-Swedish; French- -Swedish **-talande** French-speaking, Francophone **-vänlig** pro-French, Francophil[e]

fransman Frenchman; -*männen a*) (*hela nationen*) the French, *b*) (*några fransmän*) the Frenchmen **fran'sos** *s3, se fransman* **fran-** '**sysk** *a5* French; ~ *visit* flying visit (call) **fran-syska** [-ˣsyska] **1** (*kvinna*) Frenchwoman **2** *kokk.* rump-steak piece **fran'säs** [fraŋ- *el.* frann-] *s3* contredanse, contradance

frapp|ant [-'ant *el.* -'aŋt] *a1* striking **-era** strike; surprise **-'erande** *a4* striking; surprising

1 fras *s3* (*uttryck*) phrase (*äv. mus.*); *stående* ~ current phrase; *tomma* ~*er* empty phrases, mere twaddle, hollow words

2 fras *s7* (-*ande*) rustle, rustling

frasa rustle

fras|eologi *s3* phraseology **-era** phrase **-ering** phrasing; (*utan omskrivning*) **-fri** without circumlocution; straight-forward; natural

frasig *a1* crisp

fras|makare chatterbox; windbag **-radikal** high-flown (high-sounding) radical

frasvåffla crisp waffle

fraterniser|a fraternize **-ing** fraternization

freak *s2* freak

fred *s3* peace; *hålla* (*sluta*) ~ keep the (conclude) peace; *leva i* ~ *med* live at peace with; *lämna ngn i* ~ leave s.b. alone; *jag får inte vara i* ~ *för honom* he never leaves me in peace

freda protect (*mot, för* from, against); ~ *sitt samvete* appease one's conscience; *med* ~*t samvete* with a clear conscience; ~ *sig för misstanken att* banish the suspicion from one's mind that

fredag ['fre:-] Friday; ~*en den 13 april* on Fri-

day, April 13th, (*i början av brev o.d.*) Friday, April 13th; *om* ~*arna* on Fridays

fredlig [-e:-] *a1* peaceful; (*fridsam*) gentle, inoffensive; *på* ~ *väg* in a peaceful way, by peaceful means **-het** peacefulness

fredlös outlawed; *en* ~ an outlaw

freds|anbud peace offer **-appell** call (appeal) for peace **-domare** justice of the peace **-duva** dove of peace **-forskare** peace researcher **-forskning** peace research **-fot** *ställa krigsmakten på* ~ restore armed forces to peacetime strength **-fördrag** peace treaty **-förhandlingar** peace negotiations **-konferens** peace conference **-kongress** peace congress **-kår** peace corps **-kårist** member of peace corps **-mäklare** peacemaker, mediator **-pipa** peace pipe, calumet **-plikt** peace obligation **-pris** peace prize **-rörelse** peace movement **-slut** conclusion of peace **-strävan[de]** effort to achieve peace **-tid** peacetime, time of peace **-traktat** peace treaty **-trevare** peace feeler **-underhandlingar** peace negotiations **-vilja** willingness to make peace **-villkor** peace terms **-älskande** peaceloving

freestyle (*varumärke*) ~*n* ~*s* personal stereo, walkman (*varumärke*)

fre'gatt *s3* frigate **-fågel** frigate bird, man-of- -war bird

frejd *s3* character, reputation **-ad** *a5* renowned, celebrated

frejdig *a1* spirited; (*oförskräckt*) bold, intrepid, plucky

frek'vens *s3* frequency; (*av besökande etc.*) patronage **-modulering** frequency modulation **-undersökning** activity (work) sampling

frek'vent *a1* frequent, common **-era** patronize, frequent

frene|'si *s3* frenzy **-tisk** [-'ne:-] *a5* frantic, frenzied; frenetic

freno|log phrenologist **-logi** *s3* phrenology

freon [-'å:n] *s4* freon

fresia *s1* freesia

fresk *s3* fresco **freskomålning** painting in fresco; *konkr. äv.* fresco

fresnellins [fre'nell-] Fresnel lens

frest|a 1 (*söka förleda*) tempt **2** (*pröva, försöka*) try; ~ *lyckan* try one's luck **3** (*utsätta för ansträngning*) try, strain; *tekn.* strain **-ande** *a4* tempting **-are** tempter **-else** temptation; *falla för* ~*n* give way (yield) to temptation **-erska** temptress

freudi'an *s3* Freudian

fri *a1* **1** free; (*oavhängig*) independent; (*öppen, oskymd*) open; (*i frihet*) at large; *på* ~ *hand* by hand, (*oförberett*) offhand[ed]; ~ *höjd* headroom, headway; ~ *idrott* athletics (*pl o. sg*); ~ *kost* free board; *i* ~*a luften* (*det fria*) in the open air; ~*tt val* option, free choice; *av* ~ *vilja* of one's own accord (will), voluntarily; *förklara ordet* ~*tt* declare the meeting open [for discussion]; *försätta på* ~ *fot* set free; *gå* ~ *a*) (*vara på fri fot*) be at large, *b*) (*bli frikänd*) be acquitted, *c*) (*undkomma*) escape, *d*) (*från obehag*) get off, dodge [trouble *etc.*]; *gå* ~ *för misstankar* be cleared of suspicion; *göra sig* ~ *från* rid o.s. of; *ha* ~ *tillgång till* have free access to; *lämna ngn* ~*tt spelrum* allow s.b. (let

s.b. have) ample scope; *det står dig ~tt att* you
are free (at liberty) to; *svära sig ~ från* swear
o.s. out of (free from) **2** *(oupptagen)* vacant,
unoccupied
1 fria 1 propose *(till to)* **2** *~ till ngns gunst* court
a p.'s favour, curry favour with
2 fria *(frikänna)* acquit; *~nde dom* verdict of not
guilty, acquittal; *~ sig från misstankar* clear
o.s. of suspicion; *hellre ~ än fälla* give s.b.
the benefit of the doubt
friarbrev written proposal of marriage
friar|e suitor *(till* for the hand of); *ibl.* admirer
-stråt *vara på ~* be courting
fri|biljett *järnv.* pass; *teat. o.d.* free ticket, com-
plimentary ticket **-bord** freeboard **-boren**
freeborn **-brev** *försäkr.* paid-up policy **-brott-
ning** freestyle wrestling; catch-as-catch-can
-bytare freebooter **-bärande** overhung
frid *s3* peace; *(lugn)* tranquillity, serenity; *allting är ~ och fröjd* everything is fine (all se-
rene); *vad i ~ens namn nu då?* whatever's happening now?, what's up now?
fridag free day, day off; *(tjänstefolks)* day out
frid|full peaceful **-lysa** place under the protec-
tion of the law, protect by law **-lysning** protection by law **-sam** *al* peaceable
fridsfurste *F~n* the Prince of Peace
fridstörare disturber of the peace; *(friare)* in-
truder
frielev nonpaying pupil
frieri proposal [of marriage]
fri|exemplar free (complimentary, presentation)
copy **-flykt** *rymdtekn.* free flight
frige liberate, [set] free; release; *(upphäva ran-
sonering)* deration; *(från beslag)* derequisition;
(slav) emancipate; *frigivna varor* free-listed
goods
frigid [-'gi:d] *al, n undviks* frigid **-itet** frigidity
fri|giva *se frige* **-givning** [-ji:-] liberation, set-
ting free, release; derationing; derequisition;
emancipation
frigjord *al* emancipated **-het** *(i sätt)* free and
easy manners *(pl)*; emancipation
frigång *tekn.*, *gå på ~* freewheel
frigör|a liberate, set free *(äv. kem.)*; free, re-
lease; *(göra disponibel)* make available; *(från
slaveri)* emancipate; *~ sig från (etc.)* o.s., *kem.*
[be] disengage[d] **-else** liberation *etc.*; *kvinnans ~* the emancipation of woman **-elsehas-
tighet** *se flykthastighet*
fri|hamn free port **-handel** free trade **-handels-
område** free trade area **-handsteckning**
freehand drawing
friherr|e baron; *(i Storbritannien som titel äv.)*
lord **-inna** baroness; *(i Storbritannien som titel äv.)* lady **-lig** *a5* baronial
frihet 1 freedom; *(motsats tvång, fångenskap)*
liberty; *(från skyldighet)* exemption; *(oavhäng-
ighet)* independence; *(fritt spelrum)* scope, latitude; *~, jämlikhet, broderskap* liberty, equality,
fraternity; *poetisk ~* poetic licence; *skänka ngn
~en* give s.b. his freedom; *återfå ~en* regain
one's freedom (liberty) **2** *(privilegium)* privilege; *(självsvåld)* liberty; *fri- och rättigheter*
rights and privileges; *ta sig ~er mot ngn* take
liberties with s.b.; *ta sig ~en att* take the liberty

of (+ *ing-form*)
frihets|hjälte champion of liberty **-kamp** strug-
gle for liberty **-krig** war of independence **-käm-
pe** fighter for freedom, patriot **-kärlek** love
of liberty **-rörelse** liberty movement; *(mot-
ståndsrörelse)* resistance movement **-straff** imprisonment, detention, confinement **-strävan**
effort to attain independence **-tiden** *hist., ung.*
the Period of Liberty, the period 1718–1772
-älskande freedom-loving, liberty-loving
fri|hjul freewheel **-hult** *s7, s2* fender **-idrott**
athletics *(pl o. sg)*
frika'dell *s3, kokk.* forcemeat ball, quenelle
frikall|a *(från plikt, ansvar)* exempt *(äv. mil.)*;
(från löfte) release **-else** exemption; release
frikassé *s3* fricassee *(på* of)
frikast *sport.* free throw
frikativa ['frikka-] *s1* fricative
frikoppl|a declutch **-ing** declutching, disengage-
ment of the clutch; *konkr.* slipping clutch
frikostig [-å-] *al* liberal, generous; *(om gåva
äv.)* handsome **-het** liberality, generosity
friktion [-k'ʃɷ:n] friction
friktions|fri frictionless; *bildl.* smooth **-koeffi-
cient** friction coefficient **-koppling** friction
clutch **-motstånd** frictional resistance
frikyrk|a Free Church; *(i Storbritannien äv.)*
Nonconformist Church **-lig** Free-Church
frikyrko|församling Nonconformist Church
-predikant Nonconformist (Free-Church)
preacher **-präst** Nonconformist (Free-Church)
minister
frikänn|a acquit *(från* of); find (pronounce) not
quilty **-ande I** *s6* acquittal; *yrka ~* plead not
quilty **II** *a4, ~ dom* verdict of not guilty
frilans *s2* freelance[r] **-a** freelance **-are** freelance[r] **-basis** *på ~* on a freelance basis
frilista *s1* free list
frilla *s1* paramour
frilufts|bad open-air pool; public beach **-guds-
tjänst** open-air service **-liv** outdoor life **-män-
niska** sportsman, lover of open-air life **-tea-
ter** open-air theatre
frilägga lay bare, uncover
frimodig frank, candid; *(modig)* fearless **-het**
frankness *etc.*
fri|murare Freemason **-murarloge** *s3* Masonic
lodge **-murarorden** Free and Accepted Ma-
sons; Masonic order **-mureri** Freemasonry;
bildl. freemasonry
frimärk|a stamp **-e 1** *post.* [postage] stamp **2**
sjö. clearing line
frimärks|album stamp album **-automat**
stamp[-vending] machine **-häfte** book of
stamps **-samlare** stamp collector **-samling**
stamp collection
fri- och rättigheter rights and privileges
fri|passagerare stowaway; *(med fribiljett)* vard.
deadhead **-plats** *(i skola)* free place; *teat. o.d.*
free seat **-religiös** dissenting
1 fris *s3, byggn.* frieze
2 fris *s3 (folkslag)* Fri[e]sian
frisbee ['frissbi:] *s3* Frisbee
frisedel *mil.* exemption warrant
friser|a *bildl.* doctor [up]; *~ ngn* dress a p.'s hair
-ing hairdressing **-salong** hairdresser's, hairdressing saloon

fri|sim freestyle swimming **-sinnad** *a5* liberal, broad-minded; *polit.* Liberal
frisisk ['fri:-] *a5* Fri[e]sian; *F~a öarna* Frisian Islands **frisiska** ['fri:-] **1** (*språk*) Fri[e]sian **2** (*kvinna*) Fri[e]sian woman
frisk *a1* **1** (*sund, felfri*) sound; (*ej sjuklig*) healthy; (*som pred.fylln.: ej sjuk*) well; *~ och kry* hale and hearty; *~ och stark* strong and well; *~ som en nötkärna* [as] sound as a bell **2** (*ny, bibehållen*) fresh; (*kall*) cold; (*uppfriskande*) refreshing; (*bitande*) keen; *~a krafter* renewed strength; *hämta ~ luft* get some [fresh] air; *bevara ngt i ~t minne* have a vivid recollection of s.th.; *~t mod!* cheer up!; *med ~t mod* with a will; *vara vid ~t mod* be of good cheer; *~ smak* a refreshing taste; *~t vatten* cold water; *se ~ ut* look well
friska *vinden ~r* [*i*] the wind is freshening; *~ upp minnet av* refresh one's memory of; *~ upp sina kunskaper* brush up (refresh) one's knowledge
friskara *mil.* free company
frisk|förklara *se friskskriva* **-het** freshness *etc.* **-intyg** certificate of health
frisklufts|intag fresh-air intake **-ventil** fresh-air ventilator
frisk|na *~ till* recover **-skriva** declare fit; *vard.* give a clean bill of health **-sportare** [-å-] fitness freak, health nut
friskt *adv* freshly *etc.*; *vard.* (*duktigt*) ever so [much], like anything; *det blåser ~* there is a fresh (strong) breeze blowing
frisk|us ['friss-] *s2, han är en riktig ~* he is always full of beans **-vård** prophylaxis
friskytt charmed-bullet marksman
fri|slag, -spark *sport.* free hit (kick)
frispråkig *a1* outspoken **-het** outspokenness
frist *s3* respite, grace; time limit, deadline
fri|stad [place of] refuge, sanctuary, asylum; resort (*för* of) **-stat** free state **-stund** spare (leisure) time **-stående** *a4* detached, standing alone; *~ gymnastik* freestanding exercises (*pl*), Swedish drill (exercises *pl*, gymnastics *pl*)
friställ|a release; (*permittera*) lay off; *-d arbetskraft* released manpower, redundant labour **-ning** lay-off
fri'syr *s3* (*dam-*) hairstyle, coiffure; *vard.* hairdo; (*herr-*) haircut **frisör** barber, hairdresser **frisörska** hairdresser
frita[ga] exempt, release; *~ sig från ansvar* disclaim any responsibility
fritera deep-fry
fritid spare (leisure) time; *på ~en* in leisure hours
fritids|aktivitet leisure-time activity **-båt** pleasure boat **-gård, -hem** youth recreation centre **-hus** leisure house (cottage), holiday cottage **-kläder** casual clothes, sportswear **-pedagog** youth worker **-problem** leisure problem **-sysselsättning** spare-time occupation, hobby
fritt *adv* freely; (*öppet*) openly; *tala ~* speak openly (frankly); (*gratis*) free; *~ banvagn* (*kaj, ombord*) free on rail (alongside [ship], on board); *~ fabrik* ex works; *~ förfoga över* have entirely at one's disposal; *huset ligger ~* the house stands on open ground (commands a

free view); *historien är ~ uppfunnen* the story is a pure invention
fri'tyr *s3, se flottyr*
fri|tänkare freethinker **-vakt** *sjö.* off-duty watch; *ha ~* be off duty **-vikt** *flyg.* free luggage allowance
frivillig voluntary, optional; *en ~* (*mil.*) a volunteer **-het** voluntariness; (*fri vilja*) free will **-kår** volunteer corps
frivilligt *adv* voluntarily, of one's own free will; optionally
frivol [-'å:l] *a1* (*lättsinnig*) flippant; (*oanständig*) indecent **-itet** *s3* **1** flippancy; indecency **2** *~er* (*ett slags spets*) tatting (*sg*); *slå ~er* do tatting
frivolt somersault
frivård noninstitutional care
frodas *dep* thrive, flourish; *bildl.* be rife, grow rampant
frodig *a1* (*om växt o. bildl.*) luxuriant; (*om pers. o. djur*) fat, plump **-het** luxuriance *etc.*
from [-ɷmm] *a1* **1** (*gudfruktig*) pious; (*andäktig*) devout, religious; *~ma önskningar* pious hopes, idle wishes **2** (*saktmodig*) quiet, gentle; (*om hund*) good-tempered; *~ som ett lamm* [as] gentle as a lamb
fromage *s5* mousse
fromhet 1 piety **2** quietness *etc.*
froml|a be sanctimonious **-eri** sanctimoniousness, hypocrisy
from|ma *oböjligt s, till ~ för* for the benefit of **-sint** *a1* gentle
fronder|a [fråɳd-] *polit.* oppose authority [of one's party]; rebel **-ing** faction politics; dissention
frondör [fråɳd-] rebel
front [fråɳt *el.* fråɳt] *s3* front; *göra ~ mot* face, *bildl.* stand up against
frontal [-å-] *a5* frontal **-angrepp** frontal attack **-kollision, -krock** head-on collision
fronte'spis [-å-] *s3, byggn.* front gable; frontispiece (*äv. boktr.*)
front|förändring change of front (*bildl.* tactics) **-linje** front [line] **-matad** front-loading **-soldat** combat soldier **-tjänst** active service (*särsk. AE.* duty)
frosch [-å-] *s3* nut, frog (*särsk. AE.*)
1 frossa [-å-] *s1, med.* ague; (*malaria*) malaria; *ha ~* have the shivers
2 frossa [-å-] *v1* **1** *eg.* gormandize; gorge (*på* on) **2** *bildl.* revel (*i* in)
frossare [-å-] glutton (*på* of), gormandizer (*på* on); reveller (*i* in)
frossbrytning [-å-] fit of shivering (ague)
frosseri [-å-] gluttony; gormandizing *etc.*
frost [-å-] *s3* frost **frosta** *~ av* defrost
frost|bildning frost formation **-biten** *a5* frostbitten **-fjäril** winter moth **-fri** frostless **-härdig** frost-resistant, frostproof
frost|ig *a1* frosty **-knöl** chilblain **-natt** frosty night **-skada** frost injury **-skadad** *a5* damaged by frost **-skyddsvätska** antifreeze
frotté [-å-] *s3* towelling, terry cloth **-handduk** Turkish (terry) towel
frotter|a [-å-] rub, chafe; *~ sig med ngn* hobnob with s.b. **-ing** rubbing, chafing
fru *s2* (*gift kvinna*) married woman; (*hustru*)

wife; *(titel)* Mrs.; ~ *Fortuna* Dame Fortune;
Vår ~ Our Lady; *~n i huset* the lady of the
house; *vad önskar ~n?* what would you like,
Madam?, can I help you, Madam?
fruga *s1*, *~n* the (my *etc.*) missis (missus), the
little woman
fru'gal *al* frugal
frukost ['fruckåst] *s2 (morgonmål)* breakfast;
(lunch) lunch; *äta [ägg till]* ~ have [eggs for]
breakfast **-bord** breakfast table **-bricka** breakfast tray **-dags** *adv, det är* ~ it is time for
breakfast; *vid* ~ at breakfast time **-era** have
breakfast **-middag** brunch **-rast** *se lunchrast*
-rum breakfast room
frukt *s3* **1** fruit *(äv. koll.)*; *(jordbruksprodukter
äv.)* yield; *bära* ~ *(äv. bildl.)* [bear] fruit, fruc-
tify; *sätta* ~ *(äv. bildl.)* form fruit **2** *bildl.*
fruit[s *pl*]; *(resultat)* consequence, result; *njuta ~en av sin möda* enjoy the fruits of one's
labour
frukta fear; *(starkare)* dread; *(vara rädd för)* be
afraid of; *en ~d motståndare* a dreaded ad-
versary; ~ *för (hysa fruktan för)* fear, dread,
(dra sig för) be afraid of, shun; *man ~r för
hans liv* they fear for his life
fruktaffär fruit shop, fruiterer's [shop]
fruktan *r* fear *(för* of*)*; *(starkare)* dread *(för* of*)*;
(skrämsel) fright *(för* of*)*; *(oro)* apprehension,
anxiety *(för* about*)*; *av* ~ *för* for fear of; *hysa*
~ *för* be in fear of, *(hysa respekt)* stand in awe
of; *injaga* ~ *hos ngn* inspire s.b. with fear
fruktansvärd *al* terrible, fearful; *(förfärlig)*
dreadful; *(svagare)* formidable; *(friare)* terrific
frukt|assiett fruit plate **-bar** *al* fertile; *bildl.
äv.* fruitful; *(om jordmån)* productive, rich
-barhet fertility; fruitfulness; productivity
-barhetskult fertility cult **-bärande** fruit-
-bearing, fructiferous; *(friare)* fruitful, advantageous **-fluga** *se borrfluga* **-handlare** fruiterer
frukt|ig *al* fruity **-kniv** fruit knife **-konserv**
tinned *(AE.* canned*)* fruit **-kött** pulp **-lös** fruitless; *bildl. äv.* unavailing, futile **-odlare** fruit
grower, orchardman **-odling** **1** *abstr.* fruit
growing **2** *konkr.* fruit farm
frukt|os [-'å:s] *s3* fructose, fruit sugar **-saft** fruit
juice **-sallad** fruit salad **-salt** fruit salts *(pl)*
frukt|sam *al* fruitful *(äv. bildl.)*; *(om kvinna)*
fertile; *(alstringsrik)* prolific, fecund **-het**
fruitfulness; fertility; fecundity
frukt|skål fruit bowl **-socker** *se fruktos* **-träd**
fruit tree, fruiter **-trädgård** [fruit] orchard
-ämne *bot.* ovary
fruntimmer *s7* woman; *neds.* female
fruntimmers|karl ladies' (lady's) man, lady-
killer **-veckan** *ung.* Ladies' Week, the period
July 18–24
frusa gush forward (out)
frus|en *a3* **1** frozen; *(om växt, gröda o.d.)*
blighted by frost, frostbitten; *kokk.* chilled; *-et
kött* cold-storaged meat **2** *(kall)* cold; *(genom-
frusen äv.)* chilled; *vara* ~ *av sig* be sensitive
to cold, *vard.* be a chilly mortal **-it** *sup. av
frysa*
frust|a snort **-ning** snort[ing]
frustr|ation frustration **-era** frustrate **-ering**
frustration

Frygien ['fry:g-] *n* Phrygia **fryg|ier** ['fry:g-] *s9*,
-isk ['fry:g-] *a5* Phrygian; *-isk mössa* Phrygian
cap
fryntlig *al* genial; jovial
frys *s2, se frysbox, frysfack, frysskåp*
frys|a *frös frusit (i bet. frysa matvaror o. frysa
till is äv. v3)* freeze; *(känna kyla)* be (feel)
cold; *(skadas av frost)* get frostbitten; ~ *till is*
freeze [to ice]; ~ *öronen av sig* get one's ears
frostbitten; *jag -er* I am cold; *jag -er om fötterna* my feet are cold (freezing); *det har fru-
sit i natt* there was a frost last night; ~ *fast i*
get frozen fast in; ~ *ihjäl* get frozen to death;
~ *inne* be (get) icebound; ~ *ner (mat)* freeze;
~ *sönder* be (get) split by the frost, burst by
the frost; ~ *till* freeze (get frozen) over; ~ *ut*
cold-shoulder, send to Coventry
frys|box deepfreeze, freezer **-disk** frozen-food
merchandiser (counter) **-eri** freezing plant
-fack freezing compartment **-hus** cold storage
-ning freezing; refrigeration **-punkt** freezing
point **-skåp** freezer **-torka** freeze-dry **-tork-
ning** freeze-drying
fråg|a **I** *s1* question; *(förfrågan)* inquiry; *(sak)*
question, matter, point; *en* ~ *om* a matter of; *i*
~ *om* as to, regarding, in the matter of; *saken
i* ~ the matter in question (at issue); *dagens
-or* current questions (issues); *göra ngn en* ~
ask s.b. a question; *komma i* ~ *som chef* be in
the running for manager's post; *sätta i* ~ *(betvivla)* question, call in question; *det blir en
senare* ~ that will be a matter for later consideration; *det kommer aldrig i* ~ *(på ~n)* it is
quite out of the question; *det är en annan* ~
that is another question (matter); *det är inte
~[n] om det* that is not the point; *det är nog
~[n] om* you never can tell, *vard.* I wouldn't
bank on it; *~n är fri* anybody may ask a question; there is no harm in asking; *vad är det ~n
om? a) (vad står på)* what is the matter?, *b)
(vad gäller frågan)* what is it all about?, *c)
(vad vill ni)* what do you want? **II** *v1* ask *(ngn
om ngt* s.b. about s.th.*)*; inquire *(äv. fråga om,
efter)*; *(förhöra)* question *(ngn om* s.b. about*)*;
absol. äv. ask questions; ~ *efter ngn* ask (inquire) for s.b., *(bry sig om)* ask after s.b.; ~
om (igen) ask again, repeat the (one's) question; ~ *ngn om lov att* ask a p.'s permission
to; ~ *om (efter) priset på* ask (inquire) the price
of; ~ *sig* ask o.s. [the question] *(om* whether*)*;
~ *sig fram* ask one's way; ~ *sig för* make inquiries *(om* about, as to*)*; ~ *ut ngn* question
s.b. *(om* about*)*, interrogate s.b. *(om* as to*)*;
förlåt att jag ~r, men excuse my asking, but
frågande *a4* inquiring; questioning; *se* ~ *ut* look
puzzled (bewildered)
fråge|formulär questionnaire **-sats** interroga-
tive clause **-spalt** questions and answers column **-sport** quiz **-stund** question time **-ställ-
ning** *(formulering av fråga)* framing of a (the)
question; *(problem)* problem, question at issue
-tecken question mark
frågvis [-å:-] *al* inquisitive **-het** inquisitiveness
från **I** *prep* from; *(bort, ner från)* off; *(ända
från)* [ever] since; ~ *och med nu* from now on;
~ *och med 1 april* as from April 1st; ~ *vettet*
out of one's wits; *herr A.* ~ *N.* mr. A. of N.;

från döma–fräta

158

år ~ *år* from year to year; *berättelser* ~ *hans barndom* stories of his childhood; *doften* ~ *en blomma* the scent of a flower; *för att börja* ~ *början* to begin at the beginning; *undantag* ~ *regeln* exceptions to the rule; *jag känner honom* ~ *Paris*[*tiden*] *a*) I got to know him in Paris, *b*) I have known him ever since we were in Paris together **II** *adv, (frånslagen)* off; ~ *och till a*) *(av o. till)* to and fro, *b*) *(då o. då)* off and on; *gå* ~ *och till (som hjälp)* come and go; *det gör varken* ~ *eller till* that is neither here nor there

från|döma ~ *ngn ngt* sentence s.b. to forfeit (lose) **-fälle** *s6* death, decease **-gå 1** *(avgå, avräknas)* to be deducted [from] **2** *(ändra, uppge)* relinquish *(ett tidigare beslut* a previous decision); abandon *(sin ståndpunkt* one's point of view) **-hända** *v2*, ~ *ngn ngt* deprive s.b. of s.th.; ~ *sig* part with, dispose of **-känna** ~ *ngn rätten att* deny s.b. the right to; ~ *ngn talang* deny a p.'s [possession of] talent **-landsvind** offshore wind **-lura** ~ *ngn ngt* wheedle s.th. out of s.b. **-rycka** ~ *ngn ngt* snatch s.th. from s.b. (out of a p.'s hands) **-se** disregard, leave out of account; ~*tt detta (att)* apart from that (the fact that) **-sida** back; *(på mynt o.d.)* reverse **-skild** *(om makar)* divorced **-skilja** detach, separate **-slagen** switched off **-stötande** repellent, repugnant; *(starkare)* repulsive; *(om utseende)* unattractive **-säga** *rfl (avvisa)* decline, refuse; *(ansvar)* disclaim; *(nöje)* renounce **-ta[ga]** ~ *ngn ngt* deprive s.b. of s.th. **-träda** *(befattning)* retire from, resign; *(egendom)* surrender; *(arrende)* leave **-varande** *a4* absent; *bildl.* absent-minded, preoccupied; *de* ~ those absent, *(vid möte o.d.)* the absentees **-varo** *s9* absence *(av of; från* from); *(brist, avsaknad)* lack, want; *lysa med sin* ~ be conspicuous by one's absence

fräck *a1* impudent, insolent; *(oblyg, om pers.)* audacious; *(ogenerad)* cheeky, cool; *vard.* fresh; *(djärv)* daring; *(oanständig)* indecent **-het** impudence, audacity, audaciousness, insolence; *vard.* cheek, gall; *ha* ~*en att* have the impudence to

fräckis *s2, vard.* dirty story (joke)
fräken ['frä:-] *s2*, **-växt** *bot.* horsetail
fräkn|e [ˣfrä:-] *s2* freckle **-ig** *a1* freckled, freckly

frälsa *v1 el. v3* save *(från* from); *relig. äv.* redeem; *(befria)* deliver; *(rädda äv.)* rescue; *fräls oss ifrån ondo* deliver us from evil; *han har blivit frälst* he has found salvation

frälsar|e saviour; *F~n, Vår F~* the (our) Saviour, the Redeemer **-krans** life buoy
frälse I *s6* **1** *(befrielse från skatt)* exemption from land dues to the Crown **2** *(adel ung.)* privileged classes *(pl)* **II** *oböjligt a*, ~ *och ofrälse* [*män*] noblemen and commoners **-hemman** farmstead exempt from land dues **-stånd** *se frälse I 2*
frälsning saving *etc.*; *relig. äv.* salvation; *(räddning)* deliverance
frälsnings|armé *F~n* the Salvation Army **-soldat** Salvationist
främj|a further; *(ngns intresse e.d.)* promote; *(uppmuntra)* encourage; *(understödja)* support

-ande *s6* furtherance; promotion; encouragement; support; *till* ~ *av* for the furtherance *(etc.)* of, in order to promote **-are** supporter; promoter
främling stranger *(för* to); *(utlänning)* foreigner
främlingshat hatred of foreigners (strangers), xenophobia
främlingskap *s7* alienation; *bildl.* estrangement
främlings|legion foreign legion; *[franska] F~n* the Foreign Legion **-pass** alien's passport
främmande I 1 *s9 (främling)* stranger; *(gäst)* guest; *(besökande)* visitor, caller **2** *s7, koll.* company; guests; guests, visitors *(pl)*; *vi skall ha* ~ *till middag* we are having company (guests) to dinner **II** *oböjligt a (utländsk)* foreign, alien; *(okänd)* strange, unknown *(för* to), unfamiliar *(för* with); *(ovidkommande)* extraneous; ~ *språk* foreign languages; *en* ~ *herre* an unknown gentleman, a stranger; *en vilt* ~ *människa* a complete stranger; *förhållande*[*t*] *till* ~ *makter* [our] relationship to foreign powers; *de är* ~ *för varandra* they are strangers to one another; *han är helt* ~ *för tanken* the idea is quite alien to him
främmandegöra alienate *(för* from), estrange *(för* from)
främre ['främm-] *a komp.* fore; front; *fack.* anterior; *F~ Asien (ung.)* southwest Asia; *F~ Orienten, se Mellersta Östern*
främst *adv (om rang, rum)* foremost; *(om ordning)* first; *(framför allt o.d.)* principally, especially; *först och* ~ first and foremost, first of all; ~ *i boken* at the beginning of the book; ~ *i skaran* in the forefront of the crowd; *ligga* ~ *(i tävling)* be ahead (leading); *sitta* ~ sit right at the front, sit in the front row; *stå* ~ *på listan* stand first on the list
främst|a *best. superl. (om rum, rang)* foremost; *(om ordning)* first; *i* ~ *rummet* in the first place, first of all; *vår -e kund* our biggest (most important) customer; *vår -e leverantör* our principal supplier
frän *a1* rank; *(om smak äv.)* acrid; *bildl.* acrimonious, caustic; *(högdragen)* arrogant; *(cynisk, rå)* coarse
fränd|e *s5* kinsman, *fem.* kinswoman, relative **-skap** *s3* kinship, relationship; *bildl.* affinity
fränhet [-ä:-] *s* rankness; acrimony; arrogance
fränka *s1* kinswoman
1 fräs *s7* **1** hissing; frying; *jfr 1 fräsa* **2** *för full* ~ at top speed
2 fräs *s2, tekn.* milling machine, miller
1 fräsa *v3* **1** *(väsa)* hiss; *(stänka o. fräsa)* sputter, splutter; *(om katt)* spit; *(i stekpanna)* sizzle; *fräs! (snyt ut)* blow [your nose]! **2** *(hastigt ss. upp)* kokk. fry, frizzle **3** ~ *fram (förbi)* zoom (rip) along (past)
2 fräs|a *v3, tekn.* mill
fräsare milling-machine operator (worker)
fräsch [-ä:-] *a1* fresh[-looking]; *(obegagnad)* [quite] new; *(ny o. frisk)* fresh, clean
fräsch|a ~ *upp* freshen up **-het** *se fräschör* **-ör** freshness; newness
1 fräsning [-ä:-] *se 1 fräs*
2 fräsning [-ä:-] *tekn.* milling
frästorv milled peat
frät|a *v3* **1** *(om syror o.d.)* corrode; eat *(hål på*

a hole in); ~ *bort* eat (corrode) away; erode; ~ *sig igenom* eat its way through **2** *bildl.* fret, gnaw (*äv. fräta på*) **-ning** corrosion; erosion **-sår** malignant ulcer; *bildl.* canker

frö *s6, pl hand. äv. -er* seed; *koll.* seed[s *pl*]; *bildl.* germ, embryo; *gå i* ~ go to seed

frö|a ~ *sig* go to seed; ~ [*av sig*] shed its seed **-handel** seed shop **-hus** seed capsule, seedcase, seed vessel, pericarp

fröjd *s3* joy, delight; *bordets -er* the delights of the table; *i ~ och gamman* merrily **fröjda** delight, give joy to; ~ *sig* rejoice (*åt, över* at), delight (*åt, över* in) **fröjdefull** joyful, joyous

frö|kapsel *se fröhus* **-katalog** seed catalogue

frök|en ['frö:-] *-en -nar* unmarried woman, young lady; (*som civilstånd*) spinster; (*som titel*) Miss; (*lärarinna*) teacher; (*servitris*) waitress; *F~ Ur* speaking clock; *F~ Väder* telephone weather forecast

frö|kontroll seed testing **-mjöl** pollen **-odling** *abstr.* seed cultivation; *konkr.* seed-cultivation station

frös *imperf. av frysa*

frö|skal seed coat **-träd** seed tree **-vita** endosperm; perisperm **-växt** seed plant **-ämne** ovule

fuchsia ['fuksia] *s1* fuchsia

fuffens ['fuff-] *n* trick[s *pl*], dodge[s *pl*]; *koll. äv.* mischief; *ha* [*ngt*] ~ *för sig* be up to s.th. (mischief)

fuga *s1* fugue

fukt *s3* damp, moisture **fukta 1** (*väta*) moisten, damp[en]; (*med tårar*) wet **2** (*vara fuktig*) be (get) damp **fuktas** *dep* moisten

fukt|bevarare humectant **-drypande** *a4* wet with damp **-fläck** damp stain **-halt** moisture content

fuktig *a1* damp; (*genom-*) moist; (*om luft*) humid **-het** dampness; moisture; humidity

fukt|ighetsmätare hygrometer **-skada** damage caused by damp **-svabb** damp mop **-torka** damp wipe

ful *a1* ugly; *AE. äv.* homely; (*föga tilltalande*) unattractive; (*obehaglig för örat*) harsh; (*om väder*) bad; ~ *i mun[nen]* foul-mouthed; *~a ord* dirty words, bad (foul) language (*sg*); ~ *som stryk* [as] ugly as sin; *en ~ fisk* (*bildl.*) an ugly customer; *ett ~t spratt* a nasty (a dirty, *AE. vard.* an ornery) trick; *hon är inte* ~ she is not bad-looking **-ing** fright; (*om barn*) scamp, rascal

full *a1* **1** full (*av, med* of); filled (*av, med* with); ~ *av idéer* teeming with ideas; ~ *i* (*av*) *skratt* brimming over with laughter; *för ~a segel* in full sail; *ropa med* ~ *hals* roar; *spela för ~a hus* play to crowded houses; *det är ~t med människor på gatan* the street is crowded with people **2** (*hel, fullständig*) full (*fart* speed; *sysselsättning* employment; *verksamhet* activity); complete, whole; ~ *hand* (*kortsp.*) full house; ~ *sommar* full (the height of) summer; ~ *tid* (*sport.*) full time; ~ *tjänstgöring* full-time duty; *~a tre månader* fully three months, a full three months; *dussinet ~t* a full dozen; *med* ~ *rätt* quite rightly; *till* ~ *belåtenhet* to my (*etc.*) entire satisfaction; *vara i sin ~a rätt* have every right **3** *till ~o* in full, fully **4** (*drucken*) drunk;

vard. tight

full|belagd *a5, sjuksalen är* ~ the ward is full up **-blod** *s7* thoroughbred, full blood **-blodshäst** thoroughbred [horse], full blood **-bokad** *a5* booked up; fully booked

fullbord|a [-ɷ:-] complete, accomplish, finish; ~ *sin avsikt* fulfil one's intention; *ett ~t faktum* an accomplished fact; *det är ~t* (*bibl.*) it is finished **-an** *r* **1** completion; accomplishment **2** (*uppfyllelse*) fulfilment; *i tidernas* ~ in the fullness of time; *nalkas* (*nå*) *sin* ~ be approaching (reach) its (*etc.*) completion

full|fjädrad [-ä:-] *a5* fully fledged, full-fledged; *bildl.* full-blown **-följa 1** (*slutföra*) complete; (*föresatser, planer*) carry out; (*fortsätta* [*med*]) continue, carry on, proceed; (*följa upp*) follow up **2** *jur.* prosecute; carry on **-gjord** *efter -gjort uppdrag* on the completion of a mission (an assignment) **-god** [perfectly] satisfactory, perfect, adequate; (*om mynt*) standard; ~ *säkerhet* full security **-gången** *a5* fully developed **-göra** (*utföra*) carry out; (*plikt*) perform; (*uppfylla*) fulfil; ~ *sin militärtjänst* do one's military service **-het** fullness *etc., jfr full*

fullkomlig [-å-] *a1* perfect; (*fullständig*) complete, entire; (*absolut*) utter, absolute **-het** perfection

fullkom|ligt *adv* perfectly; completely *etc., se fullkomlig* **-na** [make] perfect; (*fullborda*) accomplish, finish **-ning** perfection

fullkorns|bröd wholemeal bread **-mjöl** wholemeal

full|makt 1 (*bemyndigande*) power[s *pl*]; (*dokument*) power (letter) of attorney, warrant; (*vid röstning*) proxy; *enligt* ~ as per power of attorney, by proxy; *äga* ~ be authorized, to have authority **2** (*ämbetsmans*) letters (*pl*) of appointment; (*officers*) commission; (*riksdagsmans*) proxy **-måne** full moon **-mäktig** *-en -e* authorized representative, proxy, delegate

full|o *se full 3* **-proppad** [-å-] *a5* stuffed; crammed **-riggare** full-rigged vessel (*etc.*) **-satt** *a4* (*om lokal o.d.*) full, crowded, filled to capacity; (*översållad*) studded; ~ *till sista plats* full up, not a seat left **-skalig** *a1* full--scale **-skriven** *a5* filled with writing **-stoppad** [-å-] *a5* crammed full (*av, med* of), crammed (*av, med* with)

fullständig *a1* complete, entire; total; (*absolut o.d.*) utter, absolute; ~ *avhållsamhet* total abstinence; *med ~a rättigheter* (*spritservering*) fully licensed

fullständig|a make complete; complete **-ande** *s6* (*utan pl*) completing, completion; (*med pl*) supplement; *till* ~ *av* to supplement, as a supplement to **-het** completeness

fullständigt *adv* completely; entirely

fullt *adv* fully; (*alldeles*) quite; (*fullständigt*) completely; *inte* ~ *en timme* not quite an hour; *ha* ~ *upp med pengar* (*att göra*) have plenty of money (to do); *njuta* ~ *och helt av ngt* enjoy s.th. to the full; *tro ngt* ~ *och fast* have absolute faith in s.th., be firmly convinced of s.th.

full|talig *a1* [numerically] complete; full; *är vi ~a?* are we all here? **-teckna** (*lista*) fill with signatures; (*belopp*) subscribe in full; *lånet*

F

~*des snabbt* the loan was fully subscribed quickly **-träff** direct hit; *bildl.* [real] hit **-trä-nad** in peak condition **-vuxen** full-grown, fully grown; *en* ~ a grown-up [person], an adult **-värdig** (*om mynt, vikt*) standard; *bildl.* sound **fulländ|a** complete (*jfr fullborda*); ~*d* perfect, complete; ~*d smak* consummate taste; ~ *sig* perfect o.s. **-ning** completion; perfection **fullärd** (*särskr. full-lärd*) *a5* fully trained (qualified); skilled **fullödig** (*särskr. full-lödig*) *a1* standard; (*gedigen*) sterling; *bildl. äv.* thorough, genuine; ~*t uttryck* fully adequate expression **fult** [-u:-] *adv* in an unsightly (ugly) way; (*för örat*) harshly; (*obehagligt*) disagreeably; (*starkare*) nastily; *det var* ~ *gjort av dig* it was a nasty thing of you to do **fuml|a** fumble (*med* with, at) **-ig** *a1* fumbling **-ighet** fumblingness **fundament** *s7* foundation; (*för maskin*) bed, footing; (*sockel*) base **-'al** *a1* fundamental, basic **-alism** fundamentalism **-alist** fundamentalist **funder|a** (*grubbla*) ponder (*på* upon); muse, meditate (*på* upon, about); think; (*undra*) wonder; ~ *hit och dit* turn the matter over in one's mind; ~ *på att göra ngt* think of (consider) doing s.th.; ~ *på saken* think the matter over; ~ *ut* think (work) out **-are** *ta sig en* ~ have a good think **-ing** ~*ar* thoughts, reflections, speculations, (*idéer*) ideas, notions **fundersam** [-'de:r-] *a1* (*tankfull*) thoughtful, contemplative, meditative; (*tveksam*) hesitative **-het** thoughtfulness *etc.*; hesitativeness **fungera** [-ŋ'ge:-] (*om maskin e.d.*) work, function; (*om pers.*) officiate, serve, act **fungi|'cid** [-ŋgi-] *s3* fungicide **-stat** *s3* fungistat **funkis** ['funkis] *oböjligt s* functional style **-villa** functionalist (*friare* modern-looking) house **funktion** [-ŋk'ʃω:n] function[ing]; (*plikt*) function, duty; *i* (*ur*) ~ in (out of) operation (order), (not) working; *försätta ngt ur* ~ throw s.th. out of gear **funktional|ism** [-ŋkʃω-] functionalism **-ist** *s3, -istisk* *a5* functionalist **funktio'n|ell** [-ŋkʃω-] *a1* functional **-era** *se fungera* **funktions|duglig** serviceable; adequate; *i* ~*t skick* in working order **-duglighet** serviceability; adequacy **-oduglig** inadequate; out of order **-teori** *mat.* theory of functions **funktio'när** [-ŋkʃω-] *s3* functionary, official **funnit** *sup. av finna* **funt** *s2, se dopfunt* **funtad** *a5, se beskaffad* **fur** *s1* **1** (*träd*) *se fura* **2** (*trä*) *se furu* **fura** *s1* pine **furag|e** *s7*, **-era** *v1, mil.* forage **furie** ['fu:-] *s5* fury **furioso** [-'å:så] *adv, mus.* furioso **fu'rir** *s3* corporal; (*vid flottan*) leading rating; *AE.* sergeant, (*vid flottan*) petty officer 2nd class, (*vid flygvapnet*) staff sergeant **furner|a** furnish, supply **-ing** furnishing, supply **furnissör** purveyor **furor** [-'å:r] *r* furore; *göra* ~ create a furore **furste** *s2* prince **-hus** *se furstesätt*

furste|ndöme *s6* principality **-ätt** princely (royal) house **furst|inna** princess **-lig** *a1* princely **-ligt** *adv* like a prince; *belöna ngn* ~ give s.b. a princely reward **furu** *oböjligt s* pine [wood] **-bräda** deal, fir board **furunkel** [-'runn-] *s2* boil; *fack.* furuncle **furu|planka** deal, fir board **-ved** pine firewood **fusion** fusion; *hand. äv.* merger, amalgamation; *kärnfys.* [nuclear] fusion **-era** fuse, amalgamate **fusk** *s7* **1** (*slarv*) scamping; (*illa gjort arbete*) botch **2** (*svek*) cheating; *skol. äv.* cribbing **fuska 1** (*med arbete o.d.*) scamp, botch; ~ *i fotografyrket* dabble in photography; ~ *med ngt* scamp (skimp) s.th. **2** *skol., spel., hand. o.d.* cheat (*i at*); *skol. äv.* crib **fusk|are 1** botcher; dabbler **2** cheat[er], crib, cribber **-bygge** jerry-building **-lapp** crib **-verk** *se fusk 1* **fustanella** [-ˣnella] *s1* fustanella **fu'thark** *s3* futhark **fu'til** *a1* futile **-itet** *s3* futility **futtig** *a1* paltry; (*småaktig, obetydlig*) petty **-het 1** (*utan pl*) paltriness **2** (*med pl*) pettiness **futu'r|al** *a5* future **-ism** futurism **-ist** *s3*, **-istisk** *a5* futurist **futuro|log** futurologist **-logi** futurology **futur|um** [-ˣtu:-] *s8, pl äv. -er* the future, the future tense; ~ *exactum* the future perfect **fux** *s2* bay [horse] **fy** ugh!, oh!, phew!; ~ *sjutton!* confound it!; ~ *skäms!* shame [on you]! **fylka** *hist.* draw up in battle formation; (*friare*) array; ~ *sig* (*fylkas*) draw together, (*friare*) flock (*kring* round), *bildl. äv.* rally (*kring ngn* round s.b., to s.b.) **fylke** *s6, ung.* shire, county **fylking** [-k-] *hist.* wedge-shaped battle formation **fylla I** *s1* booze; *i* ~*n och villan* [when] in a drunken fit; *ta sig en* ~ have a booze; *vara på* ~*n* (*vard.*) be on the booze **II** *v2* **1** fill; (*fullproppa o. kokk.*) stuff; (*utfylla*) fill up; (*behov, brist*) supply; *bildl.* fulfil, serve; ~ *en ballong* inflate a balloon; ~ *ett länge känt behov* supply a long-felt want; ~ *sin uppgift* (*om sak*) fulfil (serve) its purpose; ~ *vin i glasen* pour wine into the glasses **2** (*med betonad partikel*) ~ *i* *a*) (*kärl e.d.*) fill up, (*blankett*) fill in (up), *b*) (*ngt som fattas*) fill in, *c*) (*vätska*) pour in; ~ *igen* fill up (in); ~ *på* *a*) (*kärl*) fill [up], replenish, *b*) (*vätska*) pour [out]; ~ *upp* fill up; ~ *ut* (*t.ex. en rad, kläder*) fill out, (*t.ex. program, brist, äv.*) fill up **3** *han fyller 25 år i morgon* he will be 25 tomorrow, tomorrow is his 25th birthday **4** (*berusa*) intoxicate, make drunk **fyllbult** *s2* boozer **fylleri** drunkenness, intoxication **-förseelse** offence of drunkenness **fyllerist** drunkard, drunk **fyllest** *till* ~ sufficiently; *vara till* ~ be sufficient (satisfactory) **fyll|hicka** drunken hiccup **-hund** boozer **fyllig** *a1* **1** (*om pers.*) plump **2** (*om ljud*) full,

full-toned, rich, mellow; (*om vin*) full-bodied; (*om cigarr*) full-flavoured; (*detaljerad*) detailed **-het** fullness *etc.*; fullness of tone (flavour *etc.*)

fyllkaja boozer

fyllna ~ *till* get tipsy

fyllnad *s3* filling; (*tillägg*) supplement; (*ut- äv.*) complement

fyllnads|material filling [material] **-prövning** supplementary examination **-sten** *koll.* filling stone **-val** *polit.* (*i Storbritannien*) by-election

fyllning filling [material]; (*i tand*) filling, *vard.* stopping; *kokk.* stuffing

fyll|o ['fyllɑ] *s6* drunk **-sjuk** *vara* ~ be sick (ill) after drinking **-skiva** booze, boozing party **-tratt** boozer

fynd *s7* find; finding; (*upptäckt*) discovery; (*oväntad gåva*) godsend; (*lyckat påhitt*) stroke of genius; *göra ett* ~ make a [real] find; find a treasure, (*i affär etc.*) find a [real] bargain; *mannen är ett verkligt* ~ the man is a regular find

fynd|a bargain-hunt **-gruva** *bildl.* mine, treasure house **-jägare** bargain-hunter

fyndig *a1* **1** (*uppfinningsrik*) inventive; (*påhittig, förslagen*) resourceful, ingenious; (*rådig*) ready-witted; *ett ~t svar* a quick-witted reply, a repartee **2** *miner.* metalliferous **-het 1** ingenuity **2** *miner.* deposit, mining find

fynd|ort site [of a find]; *biol.* habitat **-pris** bargain price

1 fyr *oböjligt s, ha ngt ~ för sig* be up to s.th. (mischief)

2 fyr *s2* lad; *en glad (lustig)* ~ a gay spark; a cheerful chap

3 fyr *s2* **1** *mil.*, [*ge*] ~*!* fire! **2** (*eldstad*) stove **3** (*eld i spis e.d.*) fire **4** ~ *och flamma* all afire (aflame)

4 fyr *s2*, *sjö.* light[house]; beacon

1 fyra *v1*, ~ *av se avfyra;* ~ *på a*) (*elda*) keep a fire burning, stoke, *b*) (*skjuta*) fire away

2 fyra I *räkn* (*för sms jfr fem-*) four; ~ *hundra* four hundred; *mellan* ~ *ögon* in private; *på alla* ~ on all fours **II** *s1* four; ~*n*[*s växel*] [the] fourth [gear]; *han går i* ~*n* he is in the fourth form (class)

fyra|hundratalet the fifth century **-rummare** four-room flat **-tiden** *vid* ~ [at] about four o'clock **-årig** *a1* **1** four-year-old **2** (*för fyra år*) four-year **-åring** child of four, four-year-old

fyrbent [-e:-] *a4* (*om djur*) four-footed, quadruped; (*om möbel o.d.*) four-legged

fyr|byggnad lighthouse **-båk** beacon

fyr|cylindrig *a5* four-cylinder **-dela** quarter **-dimensionell** *a5* four-dimensional **-dubbel** fourfold, quadruple **-dubbla** quadruple, multiply by four **-faldig** *a5* fourfold

fyrfat firepan

fyr|fota *a4*, **-fotadjur** quadruped **-färgstryck** four-colour print[ing] **-handsfattning** (*gullstol*) chair grip **-hjulig** *a5* four-wheel[ed] **-hjulsdrift** four-wheel drive **-händig** *a5* four-handed; ~*t pianostycke* duet **-hörning** [-ö:-] quadrangle **-kant** square; quadrangle; *fem yards i* ~ five yards square **-kantig** square; quadrangular **-klöver** four-leaf clover; *bildl.*

quartet[te] **-ling** quadruplet, quad

fyrlista list of lights

fyr|motorig *a5* four-engined **-sidig** *a5* four-sided **-siding** quadrilateral **-siffrig** *a5* four-figure; *in the four figures* **-sitsig** *a5* four-seated; ~ *bil* four-seater

fyr|sken lighthouse beam, light **-skepp** lightship

fyr|spann four-in-hand; *köra* ~ drive a carriage and four **-språng** *i* ~ at a full gallop, (*friare*) at full speed **-stämmig** *a5* four-part **-taktsmotor** four-stroke (AE. four-cycle) engine **-tal** [the number] four; (*i poker*) four of a kind

fyrti[o] [ˣförrti] forty

fyrtion|de [ˣförr-] fortieth **-[de]del** fortieth part

fyrti[o]|talist writer (author) of the forties **-årig** *etc., se femtioårig etc.* **-åttatimmarsvecka** forty-eight-hour week

fyr|torn lighthouse **-vaktare** lighthouse keeper

fyrverkeri fireworks (*pl*) **-pjäs** firework

fyr|väppling *se fyrklöver* **-värd** *kem., vara* ~ have a valency (AE. valence) of four, be tetravalent (quadrivalent)

fyrväsen lighthouse service

fy'sik *s3* **1** (*vetenskap*) physics (*pl, behandlas som sg*) **2** (*kroppsbeskaffenhet*) physique; constitution **-alisk** [-'ka:-] *a5* physical; ~ *behandling* physiotherapeutic treatment; ~ *kemi* physical chemistry

fysik|er ['fy:-] physicist **-laboratorium** physics laboratory **-lektion** physics lesson **-lärare** physics teacher

fysikum ['fy:-] *n* physics institution

fysiokra'ti *s3* physiocracy **-isk** [-'kra:-] *a5* physiocratic **-ism** physiocracy

fysio|log physiologist **-logi** *s3* physiology **-logisk** *a5* physiological **-nom** physiognomist **-nomi** *s3* physiognomy **-nomisk** *a5* physiognomic[al] **-terapeut** [-'pevt] physiotherapist **-tera'pi** physiotherapy, physical therapy; AE. *äv.* physiatrics (*pl, behandlas som sg*)

fysisk ['fy:-] *a5* physical; (*kroppslig äv.*) bodily; ~ *person* natural person; *en* ~ *omöjlighet* a sheer (downright) impossibility

fytotron [-'å:n] *s3* phytotron

1 få *pron* few; (*några få*) a few; *alltför* ~ all too few; *om några* ~ *dagar* in a few days

2 få *fick fått* **I 1** (*erhålla, mottaga*) receive, get; (*lyckas få, skaffa sig*) get, obtain; (*förvärva*) get, acquire; (*få o. behålla*) keep, have; ~ *arbete* get a job; ~ *barn* have a baby; ~ *betalt* be (get) paid; ~ *en fråga* be asked a question; ~ *en gåva* receive a present; ~ *huvudvärk* get a headache; ~ *ett namn* get (*om småbarn* be given) a name; ~ *ro* find peace; ~ *ett slut* come to an end; ~ *snuva* catch [a] cold; ~ *sitt straff* be punished; ~ *tid* get (find) [the] time; ~ *tillträde* be admitted, obtain admission; ~ *torra kläder på kroppen* get dry clothes on; ~ *ngt att tänka på* get s.th. to think about; ~ [*sig*] *en bit mat* get s.th. to eat; ~ *sig ett gott skratt* have a good laugh; *vad ~r vi till middag?* what are we having for dinner?; *vem har du ~tt den av?* who gave you that?; *har blommorna ~tt vatten?* have the flowers been watered?; *den ~r inte plats* there is no room for it; *den va-*

ran går inte att ~ längre that article is no longer obtainable; *då skall du ~ med mig att göra!* then you'll catch it from me!; *det skall du ~ för!* I'll pay you out for that!; *där fick du!* serves you right!; *där fick han så han teg!* that shut him up! **2** *(lyckas göra el. bringa el. laga)* get, have; *~ ngt färdigt* get s.th. finished, finish s.th.; *~ kläderna förstörda* get one's clothes spoilt; *~ ett slut på* put an end to; *~ sin önskan uppfylld* get (have) one's wish; *de har ~tt det bra (ekonomiskt)* they are well off **3** *(förmå, bringa)* make, get, bring; *~ ngn att göra ngt (ngn till ngt)* get s.b. to do (make s.b. do) s.th.; *~ ngt till stånd* bring about s.th. **4** *(ha tillåtelse)* be allowed (permitted) to; *~r* may, can; *fick (i indirekt tal)* might, could; *~r (i indirekt tal: fick)* inte must not; *~r ej vidröras!* do not touch!; *jag ~r inte glömma* I must not forget; *jag ~r inte för min mamma* my mummy won't let me; *du ~r inte bli ond* you must not get angry; *~r jag följa med?* may I come too?; *~r jag komma in? Nej, det ~r du inte* may (can) I come in? No, you may not; *~r jag störa dig ett ögonblick?* could you spare me a minute?; *om jag ~r ge dig ett råd* if I might give you a piece of advice; *huset fick inte byggas* they were not allowed to build the house, permission was not given for the house to be built **5** *(i artighetsuttryck)* be att ~ tala med ask to speak to; *~r jag tala med* can (could) I speak to; *låt mig ~ försöka* let me try; *~r jag be om litet ost? (vid bordet)* may I have some cheese?; *~r det vara en cigarett?* would you like a cigarette?; *vad ~r det lov att vara?* what can I do for you[, Sir (Madam)]?; *jag ~r tacka så mycket* [I should like to] thank you very much; *vi ~r härmed meddela att* we wish to inform you that; *det ~r jag verkligen hoppas* I should hope so **6** *(vara tvungen att, nödgas)* have to, *vard.* have got to; *det ~r duga* that will have to do; *jag ~r lov att gå nu* I must go now; *jag ~r väl försöka då* I shall have to try, then; *du ~r ursäkta mig* you must excuse me; *då ~r det vara* we'll leave it at that, then; *jag fick vänta* I had to wait, I was kept waiting **7** *(kunna, ha möjlighet att)* be able to; *~r* can; *~ höra (veta etc.)* se under *höra, veta etc.*; *vi ~r tala om det senare* we'll talk about that later; *vi ~r väl se* we'll see [about that]; *har du fått sova i natt?* were you able to sleep last night?; *jag fick göra som jag ville* I could do as I liked **II** *(med betonad partikel)* **1** *~ av* get off **2** *~ bort* remove **3** *~ fingrarna emellan* get one's fingers caught **4** *~ fram (ta fram)* get out, *(skaffa)* procure, *(framställa)* produce; *jag fick inte fram ett ord* I could not utter a word **5** *~ för sig (inbilla sig)* imagine, *(få ett infall)* get it into one's head **6** *~ i ngt* I get s.th. into; *~ i ngn ngt* get s.b. to take s.th.; *~ i sig (svälja)* swallow, *(tvinga i sig)* get down **7** *~ igen a) (återfå)* get back, *b) (stänga)* close; *det skall du ~ igen!* I'll pay you back for that, you'll see! **8** *~ igenom* get through **9** *~ ihop a) (stänga)* close, *b) (samla ihop)* get together, *(pengar)* collect **10** *~ in* get in, *radio.* get; *~ in ... i* get ... into; *~ in pengar (samla ihop)*

collect money, *(tjäna)* make money **11** *~ med [sig]* bring [along]; *inte ~ med (lämna kvar)* leave behind, *(utelämna)* omit; *~ med sig (få på sin sida)* get over to one's side, *(få att följa med)* get to come along **12** *~ ner* get down **13** *~ på [sig]* get on **14** *~ tillbaka på 1 pund* get change for 1 pound **15** *~ undan* get out of the way **16** *~ upp (dörr e.d.)* get open, *(lock e.d.)* get off, *(kork e.d.)* get out, untie, *(lyfta)* raise, lift, *(fisk)* land, *(kräkas upp)* bring up; *~ upp farten* pick up speed; *~ upp ögonen för* have one's eyes opened to, *(inse)* realize **17** *~ ur ngn ngt* get s.th. out of s.b. **18** *~ ut* get out, *(arv)* obtain; *~ ut lön* get one's pay, get paid; *jag kunde inte ~ ut ngt av honom* I could not get anything out of him **19** *~ över (kvar)* have left (over)

fåfäng *a1* **1** *(inbilsk)* conceited; *(ytlig)* vain **2** *(fruktlös)* vain, useless **3** *(sysslolös)* idle; *~t (adv) (förgäves; inbilskt)* in vain

fåfäng|a *s1* vanity; *(inbilskhet)* conceit[edness] **-lig** [ˈfåː- *el.* -ˈfäŋ-] *a1* vain **-lighet** vanity

fågel [ˈfåː-] *s2* bird; *(i sht höns-)* fowl, *koll.* poultry; *koll. jakt. o. kokk.* game birds *(pl)*; *varken ~ eller fisk* neither fish, flesh, nor fowl; *bättre en ~ i handen än tio i skogen* a bird in the hand is worth two in the bush **-art** bird species **-bad** birdbath **-berg** bird cliff **-bo** bird's nest *(pl* birds' nests) **-bord** bird table **-bur** birdcage **-bär** sweet cherry **-bössa** fowling-piece **-fri** se *fredlös* **-frö** birdseed, canary seed **-fängare** bird catcher; fowler **-holk** birdhouse **-hund** pointer; setter; *AE. äv.* bird dog **-jakt** bird shooting **-kvitter** bird twitter (chirp) **-kännare** birdman, ornithologist **-näbb** beak, bill **-perspektiv** bird's-eye view; *Paris i ~* a bird's-eye view of Paris **-skrämma** *s1* scarecrow **-skytte** game-bird shooting **-skådare** bird-watcher **-skådning** [-å:-] bird-watching **-spindel** bird spider **-station** ornithological station **-sträck** flight of birds **-sång** [the] singing of [the] birds, bird song **-unge** young bird, nestling **-vägen** as the crow flies **-ägg** bird's egg *(pl* birds' eggs)

fågalåt se *fågelsång*

fåkunnig I *a1* ignorant **II** *s, en ~* an ignoramus **-het** ignorance

fåle *s2* colt; *poet.* steed

fåll *s2* hem

1 fålla *v1, sömn.* hem; *~ upp* hem up

2 fålla *s1* pen, [pin]fold; *stänga in i ~* pinfold

fållbänk *ung.* turn-up bedstead

fåll|ning hemming **-söm** hemstitching

få|mannavälde oligarchy **-mansbolag** close corporation **-mäld** [-ä:-] *a5,* se *fåordig*

fån *s7,* se *fåne* **fåna** *rfl* be silly (asinine); *(prata dumheter)* drivel **fåne** *s2* fool; *(starkare)* idiot

fång *s7* **1** armful; *ett ~ ved* an armful [of] wood; *i stora ~* armful **2** *jur.* acquisition; *laga ~* acquest

1 fånga *i uttr.:* *ta till ~* take prisoner[s *pl*], capture; *ta sitt förnuft till ~* listen to reason, be sensible

2 fånga *v1* catch; *(ta till fånga)* capture; *(med fälla)* trap

fångdräkt prison (convict's) dress

fånge *s2* prisoner, captive

fången *a5* imprisoned, captive; *ge sig ~* surrender; *hålla ~ a)* keep in prison, hold [a] captive (prisoner), *b)* (*om uppmärksamhet e.d.*) hold; *sitta ~* be kept in prison, be imprisoned **-skap** *s3* captivity; (*vistelse i fängelse*) imprisonment; *befria ngn ur ~en* release s.b. from captivity

fång|lina *sjö.* painter **-läger** (*för krigsfångar*) prisoner-of-war camp

fångrin [ˈfåːn-] stupid grin

fångst *s3* **1** (*fångande*) catching *etc.*, capture **2** (*byte*) catch (*äv. bildl.*); (*jakt- o. bildl.*) bag; (*fiskares*) draught, haul **-arm** *zool.* tentacle **-fartyg** fishing boat; (*val-*) whale catcher, whaler; (*säl-*) sealer **-redskap** *koll.* trapping tackle (gear); (*fisk- koll.*) fishing tackle (gear)

fång|vaktare warder, *fem.* wardress (*AE.* matron), jailer, gaoler **-vård** correctional treatment [of prisoners], prison welfare

fångvårds|anstalt prison, penal institution **-styrelse** *f~n, se kriminalvårdsstyrelsen*

fånig *a1* idiotic; (*friare*) silly, stupid **-het** silliness, stupidity; *~er* stupidities

fåntratt *sap;* silly idiot

fåordig [-ɷ:-] *a1* of few words; (*ordkarg*) taciturn, laconic[al], reticent **-het** taciturnity *etc.*

får *s7* sheep (*pl lika*); (*kött*) mutton; *skilja ~en från getterna* separate the sheep from the goats

fåra I *s1* furrow; (*rynka*) line; *bildl. äv.* groove **II** *v1* furrow; line

fåra|herde shepherd, *fem.* shepherdess **-kläder** *pl, en ulv i ~* a wolf in sheep's clothing

får|aktig *a1* (*enfaldig*) sheepish, sheeplike **-avel** sheep breeding **-fiol** leg of mutton **-hjord** flock of sheep **-hund** sheepdog **-klippning** sheepshearing **-kött** mutton **-lus** sheep ked (tick) **-sax** sheep shears (*pl*) **-skalle** *bildl.* num[b]skull, goon **-skinn** fleece, sheepskin **-skinnspäls** sheepskin coat **-skock** flock of sheep **-skötsel** sheep farming **-stek** leg of mutton; (*tillagad*) roast mutton **-stuvning** mutton stew **-styng** [sheep] botfly **-ticka** *s1* sheep polyporus **-ull** sheep's wool

fåt *s3* mistake, error, blunder

fåtal *s7, ett ~ personer* a few people; *i ett ~ fall* in a minority of cases **-ig** *a1* few [in number]; *en ~ församling* a small assembly

fått *sup. av 2 få*

få'tölj *s3* armchair, easy chair

fåvitsk [ˈfåː-] *a5* foolish **fåvitsko** *s i uttr.: i ~* foolishly, witlessly

fåvälde oligarchy

fä *s6* beast; *koll.* cattle; (*bildl. om pers.*) dolt, blockhead; *både folk och ~* [both] man and beast **-aktig** *a1* caddish, doltish

fäbless weakness, partiality

fäbod *ung.* chalet **-vall** *ung.* mountain pasture (grazing)

fäderne *s7, på ~t* on the (one's) father's (the paternal) side **-arv** patrimony **-bygd** home of one's fathers, native place **-gård** family estate **-jord** *~en* one's native soil

fädernesland native country

fäderneärvd *a5* handed down from father to son, hereditary

fä|fluga horsefly **-fot** *ligga för ~* lie uncultivated; *bildl.* lie waste

fägna [ˈfäŋna] *det ~r mig* I am delighted; *~ sig*

rejoice (*över* at) **fägnad** *s3* delight

fägring [-ä:-] beauty

fä|hund *bildl.* cad, blighter, heel, rat, rotter **-hus** cattle shed

fäkta 1 fence (*med florett* with a foil); (*friare*) fight; *bildl.* tilt (*mot* at) **2** *~ med armarna* gesticulate wildly

fäkt|are fencer, swordsman **-mask** fencer's mask **-mästare** fencing master **-ning** fencing (*med, på* with); (*strid*) fight, encounter

fälb *s3* long pile plush

fälg [-j] *s2* rim

fäll *s2* fell; (*djurskinnstäcke*) skin rug

1 fälla *s1* trap; *bildl.* pitfall; *gå i ~n* fall (walk) into the trap, get caught [in the trap]; *sätta ut en ~ för* set a trap for

2 fäll|a *v2* **1** (*nedhugga*) fell, cut [down]; (*slå omkull*) knock down; (*regering*) overthrow **2** (*döda*) kill, slay; *jakt.* bring down **3** (*sänka*) lower; (*låta falla*) drop; (*tårar*) shed; (*bajonett*) level; (*lans*) couch; (*ankare*) cast, drop; *bildl.* lose (*modet* courage) **4** (*tappa*) lose (*håret* one's hair); (*om djur, t.ex. horn*) shed; (*löv, blad*) shed; (*färga av sig*) bleed; *färgen -er* the colour runs **5** *kem.* deposit, precipitate **6** (*uttala, avge*) drop, let fall; *~ ett omdöme* express an opinion **7** (*döma*) condemn, convict, damn, (*avkunna*) pronounce (*dom* a verdict) **8** (*med betonad partikel*) *~ igen* shut [up]; *~ ihop* fold, (*kniv*) shut, clasp; *~ in a)* (*infoga*) let in, inlay, *b)* (*t.ex. landningsställ*) retract; *~ ner* let down, (*lock e.d.*) shut [down], (*krage*) turn down; *~ ut (kem.)* precipitate

fällande I *s6* felling *etc.*; conviction, condemnation; pronouncement **II** *a4, ~ dom, se dom;* *~ vittnesmål* incriminating evidence

fäll|bar *a5* collapsible, foldable, folding **-bord** drop-leaf table **-bro** bascule [bridge], drawbridge **-kniv** clasp knife **-ning 1** *abstr.* felling *etc.* **2** *konkr., kem.* precipitate; (*bottensats*) sediment; *geol.* deposit **-stol** folding chair; (*vilstol*) deck chair; (*på teater o.d.*) tip-up seat **-söm** lap[ped] seam

fält *s7* field; *bildl. äv.* sphere, scope; (*dörr-*) panel; (*vägg-*) bay, panel; *i ~* (*mil.*) in the field; *dra i ~* take the field; *ha ~et fritt* have a free hand; *ligga i vida ~et* be far from being settled; *rymma ~et* quit the field; *över hela ~et* over the whole expanse **-arbete** field work **-artilleri** field artillery **-befästning** *mil.* fieldwork **-biologi** biology in the field **-flaska** canteen **-flygare** *ung.* sergeant pilot; *AE. ung.* second lieutenant **-grå** field-grey **-gudstjänst** field service **-hare** European hare **-herre** general, military commander **-herrebegåvning** strategic talent **-jägare** *ung.* rifleman **-kikare** field glasses (*pl*) **-kök** field kitchen **-lasarett** field hospital **-läkare** army surgeon **-marskalk** field marshal **-mässig** *a1* active-service; *AE.* active-duty **-mätning** [detail] surveying **-post** army postal service, field post (mail) **-präst** army chaplain **-rop** watchword, password **-skjutning** field shooting [practice] **-skär** *s3, hist., ung.* barber-surgeon **-slag** pitched battle **-spat** *s3* felspar; *AE.* feldspar **-säng** camp bed **-tecken** (*fana*) banner **-tjänst** field (active) service **-tjänstövning**

manoeuvres (*pl*) **-tåg** campaign (*mot* against, on) **-tågsplan** plan of campaign **-undersökning** field survey **-uniform** battledress **-väbel** *ung.* sergeant major; *AE.* master sergeant
fänad *s3* livestock
fängelse *s4* **1** (*byggnad*) prison, jail, gaol; *AE. äv.* penitentiary; *sitta i* ~ be in prison; *sätta ngn i* ~ put s.b. in prison, imprison s.b. **2** (*straff*) imprisonment; *livstids* ~ imprisonment for life, life sentence; *dömas till två månaders* ~ be sentenced to two months' imprisonment, get a two months' sentence **-cell** prison cell **-direktör** prison governor; *AE.* warden **-håla** dungeon **-kund** jailbird, gaolbird, lag; *vard.* con **-präst** prison chaplain **-straff** imprisonment
fäng|hål touchhole **-krut** priming [powder]
fängsl|a 1 (*fjättra*) fetter, shackle **2** (*sätta i fängelse*) imprison, arrest **3** *bildl.* fascinate, captivate; (*dra t. sig*) attract **-ande** *a4* fascinating; attractive **-ig** *i uttr.*: *hålla i* ~*t förvar* keep in custody
fänkål [ˈfäŋ-, *äv.* ˣfänn-] fennel
fänrik [ˈfänn-] *s2* (*vid armén, kustartilleriet*) second lieutenant, (*vid flottan*) midshipman, (*vid flygvapnet*) pilot officer; *AE.* second lieutenant, (*vid flottan*) ensign
färd [-ä:-] *s3* **1** journey; (*t. sjöss*) voyage; (*turist-*) trip, tour; (*bil- etc.*) ride; (*flyg-*) flight; (*forsknings-*) expedition; *ställa* ~*en till* make for **2** *bildl.*, *vara i* ~ *med att göra ngt* be busy doing s.th.; *ge sig i* ~ *med ngt* (*att*) set about s.th. (+ *ing-form*) **3** *dra sina* ~*e* take one's departure; *fara på* ~*e* danger ahead; *vad är på* ~*e?* what is up (the matter)?
färd|as [-ä:-] *dep* travel **-bevis** travel document **-biljett** ticket **-broms** foot (pedal) brake
färde [-ä:-] *se* färd 3
färdhandling travel document
färdig [-ä:-] *a5* **1** (*fullbordad*) finished, done; (*avslutad*) complete; (*klar*) ready **2** (*om pers., beredd*) ready (*till* for), prepared; (*slut*) done for, worn-out; *bli* ~ *med ngt* get through with s.th., get s.th. done; *få* ~ get done; *göra* ~ get ready, finish; *vara* ~ have done; *vara* ~ *att* be ready to; *vara* ~ *med* have done [with], have finished (got through); *nu är det* ~*t!* (*vard.*) now the fat's in the fire! **3** (*nära att*) on the point of **4** (*ej ofärdig*) sound
färdig|förpackad *a5* prepacked; *AE.* prepackaged **-gjord** finished, complete; (*om kläder*) ready-made
färdig|het (*kunnighet*) skill, proficiency (*i* in, at); (*händighet*) dexterity (*i* in, at); (*talang*) accomplishment; *övning ger* ~ practice makes perfect **-klädd** *a5* dressed; *jag är inte* ~ I have not finished dressing **-kokt** *a4* cooked, boiled; *är äggen* ~*a?* are the eggs done? **-köpt** [-çö:pt] *a4* bought ready-made **-lagad** *a5* ready-to-eat; ~ *mat, äv.* convenience food **-ställa** get ready, finish, complete **-sydd** *a5* ready-made **-utbildad** fully trained
färd|knäpp *s2, vard.* one for the road **-kost** *ung.* eatables (provisions) for the journey **-ledare** leader [of an expedition], guide **-medel** means of conveyance (transport) **-mekaniker** *flyg.* flight engineer **-riktning** direction

of travel **-riktningsvisare** (*visare*) trafficator; (*blinker*) blinker, [direction] indicator **-skrivare** (*i bil*) tachograph; *flyg.* flight recorder, *vard.* black box **-sätt** method (means) of travel **-tjänst** taxi service for the disabled **-väg** route
färg [-j] *s3* colour (*äv. bildl.*); (*målar-*) paint; (*-ämne*) dye; (*nyans*) shade, tone; (*hy*) complexion, colour; (*klang-*) timbre; *boktr.* ink; *kortsp.* suit; *röd till* ~*en* red in colour; *gå i* ~ *med* match in (for) colour; *nedkladdad med* ~ painty; *i vilken* ~ *skall den målas?* what colour is it to be painted?
färg|a [-j-] colour (*äv. bildl.*); (*textil o.d.*) dye; (*glas, trä o.d.*) stain; (*måla*) paint; ~ *av sig* lose (give off) its colour **-ad** *a5* coloured; *socialistiskt* ~ tinged with socialism **-are** dyer
färg|bad dyeing bath **-band** (*för skrivmaskin*) ribbon, typewriter ribbon **-beständig** colourfast **-bild** *se* färgfoto **-blandning** *konkr.* colour blend **-blind** colour-blind **-blindhet** colour blindness **-borttagningsmedel** paint remover **-brytning** colour refraction **-dia[positiv]** colour transparency (slide) **-dyna** stamp pad
färg|eri [-j-] dye works **-film** colour film **-filter** colour filter **-foto** colour photo **-fotografering** colour photography **-fotografi** colour photograph **-glad** gay, gaily coloured **-glädje** gaiety of colour **-grann** *neds.* gaudy; *se äv.* -glad **-handel** paint (colourman's) shop **-klick** daub (splash) of colour (paint) **-kopp** colour well **-krita** (*vax-*) crayon **-känslig** colour-sensitive **-låda** paintbox, colourbox **-lägga** colour **-läggning** colouring **-lös** colourless (*äv. bildl.*) **-löshet** colourlessness; lack of colour
färg|ning [-j-] dyeing **-penna** coloured pencil **-plansch** (*i bok*) colour plate; coloured illustration **-prakt** display of colour **-prov** colour sample **-pyts** paint pot **-rik** profusely (richly) coloured; *bildl. äv.* vivid **-rikedom** richness (variety) of colour **-sinne** sense of colour **-skala** range of colours; *konkr.* colour chart (guide) **-skiftning 1** (*nyans*) hue, tint; tinge; (*om pärlemor*) iridescence **2** (*-förändring*) changing (change) of colour **-stark** highly coloured, colourful (*äv. bildl.*) **-sätta** decide on colours (a colour scheme) **-sättning** colouration, colouring; colour scheme **-television** colour television **-ton** colour shade, hue, tinge **-tryck** colour printing; *konkr.* colour print **-tub** paint tube **--TV** colour-TV set **-verkan** colour effect **-äkta** colourfast **-ämne** colouring agent, colorant; (*lösligt*) dye, dyestuff
färing *se* färöbo
färj|a **I** *s1* ferry[boat] **II** *v1* ferry (*över* across) **-förbindelse** ferry service **-karl** ferryman **-läge** ferry berth
färla [-ä:-] *s1* ferule
färm *a1* prompt, expeditious **-itet** promptness
färnbock [-ä:-] brazil [wood]
färre [ˈfärre] fewer; less numerous
färs *s3, kokk.* forcemeat, farce[meat] **-era** stuff
färsk *a1* **1** (*nyligen tillagad etc., ej gammal*) new; (*ej skämd, saltad, konserverad*) fresh; (*ej torkad*) green; ~*t bröd* fresh bread; ~ *frukt* fresh fruit; ~*a jordgubbar* fresh strawberries; ~ *potatis* new potatoes; ~*a ägg* new-laid eggs

2 *(som nyligen gjorts, inträffat etc.)* fresh; *av ~t datum* of recent date; *~a spår* fresh tracks; *de ~aste nyheterna* the latest news

färsk|a *tekn.* refine **-ning** oxidation, refining **-ningsprocess** refining process **-rökt** *~ lax* smoked salmon **-varor** perishable goods, perishables **-vatten** fresh water

Färöarna *pl* the Fa[e]roes, the Fa[e]roe Islands **färö|bo, -ing** Fa[e]roese *(pl lika)* **färöisk** *a5* Fa[e]roese **färöiska 1** *(språk)* Fa[e]roese **2** *(kvinna)* Fa[e]roese woman

fästa *v3, v1* **1** *(fastgöra)* fasten, fix, pin *(vid* to, on [to]); attach *(vid* to) **2** *(friare o. bildl.)* *~ blicken på* fix one's eyes upon; *~ uppmärksamheten på* call attention to; *~ vikt vid* attach importance to **3** *(anteckna, överföra)* commit *(på papperet* to paper, to writing) **4** *(fastna, häfta)* affix, stick; *(om spik e.d.)* hold **5** *rfl, ~ sig vid ngn* become attached to s.b.; *~ sig vid ngt* notice, pay attention to; *inte ~ sig vid småsaker* not bother about trifles; *det är inget att ~ sig vid* ignore it, don't take any notice of it, it is nothing to worry about

fäste *s6* **1** *(fast stöd el. grund)* hold; *bildl.* stronghold, foundation; *(rot-)* root; *få ~* get a hold (grip), take root **2** *(skaft, handtag)* shaft, attachment; *(hållare)* holder; *(svärd-)* hilt **3** *bot.* receptacle **4** *(himlavalv)* firmament **5** *(befästning)* stronghold

fäst|ekvinna *hans ~* his betrothed **-folk** engaged couple

fästing *zool.* tick

fäst|man fiancé; *hennes ~ (äv.)* her young man **-mö** fiancée; *hans ~ (äv.)* his young lady

fästning *mil.* fort[ress] **fästningsanläggning** fortification[s *pl*]

fästpunkt [point of] attachment

fäsör hack

föda I *s1* food; *(kost)* diet; *(näring)* nourishment; *(uppehälle)* living; *huvudsaklig ~* mainstay; *arbeta för ~n* work for a living (one's bread); *inte göra skäl för ~n* not be worth one's keep **II** *v2* **1** *(bringa t. världen)* give birth to; bear; *absol.* bear children; *~s* be born **2** *bildl.* bring forth; breed **3** *(ge näring åt)* feed *(på* on); nourish; *(underhålla)* maintain, support; *~ sig* live, earn one's (a) living *(av, på* on; *med* by), *(om djur)* feed **födas** *se föda II* 1

född *a5* born *(av* of); *~a (rubrik)* births; *fru Jones, ~ Smith* Mrs. Jones, née (formerly) Smith; *han är ~ den 1 maj* he was born on the 1st of May; *han är ~ engelsman* he is an Englishman by birth; *han är ~ till musiker* he is a born musician

födelse birth; *alltifrån ~n* from [one's] birth **-annons** birth announcement **-attest** birth certificate **-dag** birthday; *hjärtliga gratulationer på ~en! many happy returns [of the day]!*

födelsedags|barn person celebrating a birthday **-kalas** birthday party (celebration) **-present** birthday present **-tårta** birthday cake

födelse|datum date of birth **-kontroll** birth control **-märke** birthmark **-nummer** birth registration number **-ort** birthplace; *(i formulär e.d.)* place of birth **-siffra, -tal** birth rate **-underskott** excess of deaths over births **-år**

year of birth **-överskott** excess of births over deaths

föd|geni [an] eye to the main chance **-krok** means of livelihood

födo|ämne food[stuff]; *~n (äv.)* comestibles, eatables, provisions **-ämneslära** dietetics *(pl, behandlas som sg)*

födsel ['född-] *s2* **1** *(förlossning)* childbirth; delivery **2** *(födelse)* birth

födslo|vånda travail **-värkar** labour pains **1 föga I** *n* [very] little **II** *oböjligt a* [very (but)] little **III** *adv* [very (but)] little; *(icke just)* not exactly; *(knappast)* scarcely, hardly; *~ angenäm* disagreeable; *~ givande* hardly profitable, rather unprofitable (unfruitful); *~ uppbygglig* unedifying

2 föga *oböjligt s i uttr.: falla till ~* yield, submit *(för* for), give in

fögderi county administrative division; *hist.* bailiwick; *bildl.* domain

föhnvind föhn, foehn

föl *s7* foal; *(unghäst)* colt; *(sto-)* filly **föla** foal

följ|a *v2* **1** *(följa efter)* follow **2** *(ledsaga)* accompany *(äv. bildl.)*; go (come) with; *~ ngn till graven (äv.)* pay one's last honours (respects) to s.b.; *~ ngn hem (äv.)* see s.b. home **3** *(efterträda)* succeed **4** *(förflytta, sträcka sig längs)* follow **5** *(iakttaga, studera, förstå)* follow; *(följa med blicken)* watch; *~ föreläsningar* attend lectures **6** *(rätta sig efter)* follow *(modet* the fashion; *ngns exempel* a p.'s example); obey; comply with; observe **7** *(inträffa efter ngt annat)* follow; *(om tid äv.)* ensue; *brev -er* letter to follow; *brevet lyder som -er* the letter runs as follows; *fortsättning -er* to be continued; *härav -er* hence it follows **8** *(med betonad partikel) ~ efter* follow [on behind]; *~ med a)* *(gå med)* go (come) with s.b., go (come) too, *b)* *(hålla jämna steg med)* keep pace with, keep abreast of *(sin tid* the times), *c)* *(vara uppmärksam)* follow; *~ med [på utfärden]* join the party; *han har svårt att ~ med i engelska* he has difficulty in keeping pace in English; *~ upp (driva vidare)* follow up

följaktligen accordingly, consequently

följande *a4* following, next; successive; *(som konsekvens)* consequent, resulting; *~ dag* [on] the following (the next) day; *i det ~ (nedan)* below, *(senare)* in the sequel; *med därav ~* consequently entailing; *på ~ sätt* in the following way, as follows; *på varandra ~* successive; *ett brev av ~ innehåll* a letter to the following effect; *~ exemplar (boktr.)* run-on copies; *~ 1 000 exemplar (boktr.)* run-on per 1,000 copies

följas *v2, dep, ~ åt* go together, *bildl.* run together, occur at the same time

följd *s3* **1** *(verkan, konsekvens)* consequence; result; *ha till ~ att* have the result that; *till ~ av* in consequence of **2** *(räcka, serie)* succession, line; series *(pl lika)*; *en lång ~ av år* a long succession of years; *i ~* running, in succession; *i löpande ~* consecutively **-företeelse** consequence, sequel **-riktig** logical; *(konsekvent)* consistent **-sats** corollary **-sjukdom** complication **-verkan** resulting effect, aftereffect

följe *s6* **1** (*svit, uppvaktning*) suite, retinue; attendants (*pl*); (*väpnat*) escort; (*pack*) gang, crew **2** (*sällskap*) company; *göra* (*slå*) ~ *med ngn* accompany s.b. **-brev** covering (accompanying) letter **-sedel** delivery note **-slagare** companion; follower

följetong [-åŋ] *s3* serial [story]

följsam *a1* (*med anpassningsförmåga*) adaptable, accommodating; (*smidig*) flexible, pliant

föll *imperf. av falla*

föna blow-dry

fönst|er ['föns-] *s7* window; *kasta ut genom* **-ret** throw out of the window; *sova för öppet* ~ sleep with one's (the) window open; *stå i* **-ret** *a*) (*om pers.*) stand at the window, *b*) (*om sak*) be in the window

fönster|bleck metal [window]sill **-bord** table by the window **-bräde** windowsill, window ledge **-båge** window frame; (*för skjutfönster*) sash **-bänk** window ledge **-glas** window glass **-hake** window catch; *jfr* -krok **-hållare** window stay; *jfr* -hake **-karm** window frame **-krok** window stay; *jfr* -hake **-kuvert** window envelope **-lucka** [window] shutter **-nisch** window bay (recess) **-plats** (*på buss, tåg e.d.*) window seat **-post** mullion **-putsare** window-cleaner **-putsning** window-cleaning **-ruta** windowpane; *jfr isolerruta* **-shoppa** [-ʃäppa] window-shop **-skyltning** window-dressing, window-display **-smyg** *s2* embrasure **-tittare** Peeping Tom

1 för *sjö.* **I** *s2* stem, prow; *från* ~ *till akter* from stem to stern; *i* ~*en* at the prow **II** *adv* fore; ~ *och akter* fore and aft; ~ *om masten* before the mast; ~ *ut* (*över*) ahead, (*inombords*) forward

2 för I *prep* **1** (*framför, inför*) before; *gardiner* ~ *fönstren* curtains before the windows; ~ *öppen ridå* with the curtain up, *bildl.* in public; *hålla handen* ~ *munnen* hold one's hand to one's mouth; *skjuta sig en kula* ~ *pannan* blow one's brains out; *sova* ~ *öppet fönster* sleep with one's window open; *stå* ~ *dörren* (*bildl.*) be at hand, be near **2** (*i tidsuttr.*) ~ *alltid* for ever; ~ *ett år sedan* one (a) year ago; ~ *lång tid framåt* for a long time to come; ~ *länge sedan* long ago; ~ *de närmaste tio åren* for the next ten years **3** (*i förhållande t., med hänsyn t., i stället för, i utbyte mot, på grund av, t. följd av, t. förmån el. skada för, avsedd för*) for; *en almanacka* ~ *1960* an almanac for 1960; *en* ~ *alla och alla* ~ *en* one for all and all for one; *en gång* ~ *alla* once [and] for all; *känd* ~ known for; ~ *våra förhållanden* by our standards; *öga* ~ *öga* an eye for an eye; *arbeta* ~ *ngt* work for s.th.; *göra ngt* ~ *ngn* do s.th. for s.b.; *ha öga* ~ *have an eye for; köpa* ~ *100 pund* buy for £100; *tala* ~ *ngn* speak for (on behalf of) s.b.; *äta* ~ *tre* eat for three; ~ *mig får du* as far as I am concerned you can; *vad tar ni* ~*...?* what do you charge for...?; *det har du ingenting* ~ you won't gain anything by that; *det blir inte bättre* ~ *det* that won't make it any better; *det är bra* ~ *dig* it is good for you; *han är stor* ~ *sin ålder* he is tall for his age; *jag får inte* ~ *mamma* mother won't let me; *jag vill* ~ *mitt liv inte göra det* I don't want to do it for the life of me; *vi betalar var*

och en ~ *sig* each of us will pay for himself **4** (*i dativkonstruktion o. liknande*) to; *en fara* ~ a danger to; *blind* ~ *fördelarna* blind to the advantages; *svag* ~ *ngn* partial to s.b.; *det blev en besvikelse* ~ *henne* it was a disappointment to her; *det var nytt* ~ *mig* it was new to me; *tiden blev lång* ~ *henne* time seemed long to her **5** (*i genitivkonstruktion*) of; *chefen* ~ *armén* the commander in chief of the army; *dagen* ~ *avresan* the day of my (*etc.*) departure; *platsen* ~ *brottet* the scene of the crime; *priset* ~ the price of; *tidningen* ~ *i dag* today's paper; *bli ett offer* ~ be a victim of; *vara föremål* ~ be the object of **6** (*mot, från, hos*) from; *dölja ngt* ~ *ngn* conceal s.th. from s.b.; *gå och dansa* ~ *ngn* take dancing lessons with (from) s.b.; *skydda ngn* ~ *ngt* protect s.b. from s.th.; *ta lektioner* ~ *ngn* take lessons with (from) s.b.; *vi har engelska* ~ *magister A.* we have Mr. A. in English **7** (*i fråga om*) about; *oroa sig* ~ be anxious about **8** (*såsom*) as, for; ~ *det första* in the first place, firstly; *anse* (*förklara, kalla m.fl.*) *ngn* ~ *ngt* consider (declare, call) s.b. s.th.; *hålla ngt* ~ *troligt* regard s.th. as likely **9** (*t. ett pris av*) at; *köpa ngt* ~ *2 kronor kilot* buy s.th. at 2 kronor a kilo **10** (*andra prep*) ~ *egna pengar* with one's own money; *dag* ~ *dag* day by day; *rädd* ~ afraid of; *steg* ~ *steg* step by step; *utmärkande* ~ characteristic of; *intressera sig* ~ take an interest in; *skriva* ~ *hand* write by hand **11** (*utan prep*) *bli värre* ~ *varje dag* (*gång*) get worse every day (each time) **12** *bo* ~ *sig själv* live by oneself; *han går ofta* ~ *sig själv* he often walks alone (by himself); *le* (*tänka*) ~ *sig själv* smile (think) to o.s.; *den kan stå* ~ *sig själv* it can stand by itself **II** *konj* **1** (*ty*) for **2** ~ *att* (*därför att*) because; *nog* ~ *att det finns orsak att* to be sure (it is true) there is reason to; *inte* ~ *att jag bryr mig om det* not that I care [about it]; *jag är glad* ~ *att det är vackert väder* I am happy because the weather is fine **3** *den var för liten* ~ *att passa* it was too small to fit; *den var för tung* ~ *att jag skulle kunna bära den* it was too heavy for me to carry **4** ~ *att* (*uttr. avsikt*) *a*) (*före bisats*) so (in order) that, *b*) (*före inf.*) [in order] to (+ *inf.*), with the intention of (+ *ing-form*); *liksom* ~ *att* as if to; ~ *att inte tala om* not to mention, let alone; ~ *att säga som det är* to tell the truth; *hon har gått ut* ~ *att handla* she has gone out shopping; *han reste* ~ *att aldrig mer återvända* he left, never to return; *man måste stödja den* ~ *att den inte skall falla* one must support it so that it does not fall; *vi kom i tid* ~ *att se flygplanet lyfta* we arrived in time to see the plane take off **5** *vara misstänkt* ~ *att ha* be suspected of having; *jag skäms* ~ *att säga* I am ashamed to say; *han är duktig* ~ *att vara så liten* he's good for such a little boy **6** ~ *såvitt* provided [that]; ~ *såvitt inte* unless **III** *adv* **1** (*alltför*) too; *mycket* ~ *liten* much too small; *hon är* ~ *näpen!* she's just too sweet! **2** *stå* ~ (*dölja*) stand in front; *stå* ~ *ngn* (*skymma*) stand in a p.'s way; *gardinerna är* ~ the curtains are drawn; *regeln är* ~ the bolt is to **3** (*motsats emot*) for (*och emot* and against); *vara* ~ *ett*

förslag (äv.) be in favour of a proposal
föra *v2* **1** *(förflytta)* convey; transport, remove; ~ *ett glas till läpparna* raise a glass to one's lips; ~ *handen över* pass one's hand over **2** *(ta med sig)* a) *(hit)* bring, b) *(dit)* take; *(bära)* carry *(äv. bildl.)*; *(leda)* lead *(äv. bildl.)*; *(ledsaga)* conduct; *(bil e.d.)* drive; *(fartyg)* navigate, sail; ~ *ngn bakom ljuset* hoodwink s.b.; ~ *ngn till bordet* take s.b. in to dinner; ~ *ngt på tal* broach a matter **3** *(ha t. salu)* stock, carry, run, keep *(en vara* a line of goods) **4** *(hantera, manövrera)* handle **5** *bildl. (hän-, räkna)* assign; ~ *krig (ett samtal)* carry on war (a conversation); ~ *oväsen* make a row; ~ *ett fritt språk* talk freely, be outspoken **6** *(skriva, uppgöra)* keep *(böcker* books; *räkenskaper* accounts) **7** *(om väg o.d.)* lead; *det skulle ~ alltför långt* it would take us too far **8** *(med betonad partikel)* ~ *bort* carry (take) away (off), remove; ~ *fram* bring up (forward); ~ *fram en kandidat* launch a candidate; ~ *ihop* bring (put) together; ~ *in a)* bring (take; *om pers. el. djur* lead) in (into a [*resp.* the] room *etc.*), b) *(i protokoll, räkenskaper o.d.)* enter; ~ *med sig a)* carry [along] with one (it *etc.*), b) *(ha t. följd)* involve, entail; ~ *ut* bring (take; *om pers. el. djur* lead) out *(på* into; *ur* of); ~ *vidare (skvaller o.d.)* pass on; ~ *över* convey (bring, carry *etc.*) across, *(varor äv.)* transport **9** *rfl* carry o.s.; *hon för sig väl* she carries herself well (has poise)
för'akt *s7* contempt, scorn *(för* for, of); *(överlägset)* disdain *(för* of, for); *(ringaktning)* disregard *(för* of, for); *hysa ~ för* feel contempt for
förakt|a [-'akta] despise; scorn; *(försmå)* disdain **-full** contemptuous; disdainful, scornful **-lig** *a1* contemptible; *(starkare)* despicable, mean
förandliga [-'and-] spiritualize
föraning premonition
förankr|a [-'ank-] anchor, moor; *bildl.* establish firmly; *fast ~d i* deeply rooted in **-ing 1** anchoring; *konkr.* anchorage **2** *byggn.* abutment
föran|leda *v2* give rise to, bring about, lead to, result in; *känna sig -ledd att* feel impelled (led) to **-låta** *se föranleda*; *se sig -låten att* feel called upon to, think fit to
föranstalt|a ~ *[om]* arrange, organize *(ngt* s.th.) **-ande** *s6* arranging; *på ~ av* thanks to, by direction of **-ning** arrangement; *vidtaga ~ar för ngt* make preparations (arrangements) for s.th.
för|arbeta prepare, work [up] *(till* into) **-arbete** preparatory (preliminary) work
förare *(vägvisare)* guide; *(av bil etc.)* driver; *flyg.* pilot
förarga [-'arja] annoy, provoke; *(reta äv.)* vex; *bli ~d*, ~ *sig* be annoyed (get angry, vexed) *(över* at); *det ~r mig mycket* it makes me so annoyed *(etc.)*
förargelse [-'arj-] annoyance; *(förtrytelse)* vexation; *(anstöt)* offence; *(bannor)* scolding **-klippa** stumbling block **-väckande I** *a4* offensive, intolerable; *(starkare)* scandalous; ~ *beteende* disorderly conduct [in a public place]; disturbing the peace **II** *adv*, *uppträda ~* commit

nuisance
förarglig [-'arj-] *a1* **1** *(förtretlig)* provoking, annoying, vexing; *(brydsam)* awkward; *så ~t! what a nuisance!*, how annoying! **2** *(retsam)* irritating, aggravating
förar|hytt [driver's] cab; *flyg.* cockpit, *(större)* flight deck **-säte** driver's seat
för'band *s7* **1** *med.* bandage, [surgical] dressing; *första ~* first-aid bandage; *lägga ~* apply a bandage *(på* to) **2** *mil.* unit; *flyg.* formation
förbands|artiklar first-aid supplies, dressing materials **-gas** surgical gauze **-låda** first-aid kit (box)
förbann|a [-'banna] curse, damn; *-e mig* I'm (I'll be) damned **-ad** *a5* cursed; *(svordom)* damned; *(svagare)* confounded; *bli ~ på ngn* get furious (mad) with s.b.; *det var då [alldeles] -at!* damn it [all]!; *är du [rent] ~?* are you quite crazy? **-else** curse; *fara ut i ~r mot* curse
förbarm|a [-'barma] *rfl* take pity *(över* on); *Herre,* ~ *dig över ...!* Lord, have mercy on ...! **-ande** *s6* compassion, pity; *bibl.* mercy
förbask|ad [-'bask-] *a5* confounded, blasted, ruddy, *AE. vard.* pesky; *-at också!* botheration!
förbehåll *s7* reserve, reservation; *(begränsning)* restriction; *(villkor)* condition; *(klausul)* proviso, [saving] clause; *med ~* with reservations; *med ~ att* provided that; *med ~ för fel* with reservation for possible errors; *utan ~ (äv.)* unconditionally **förbehålla** ~ *ngn ngt (ngn att)* reserve s.th. for s.b. (s.b. the right to); ~ *sig a) (betinga sig)* reserve for (to) o.s., b) *(kräva)* demand
förbehållsam *a1* reserved, guarded **-het** reserve, reticence
förbehållslös unconditional; unreserved
förbena [-'be:-] *äv. förbenas*, ~ *sig* ossify
förbered|a 1 prepare *(för, på* for), make preparations for **2** *rfl* prepare [o.s.] *(för, på, till* for); *(göra sig redo)* get [o.s.] ready *(för, till* for); ~ *sig på ett tal (för en lektion)* prepare a speech (a lesson) **-ande** *a4 (om skola)* preparatory; *(om möte, arbete, åtgärder)* preliminary **-else** preparation *(för, på, till* for)
för'bi I *prep* past, by **II** *adv* **1** *eg.* past, by **2** *(t. ända)* over; *(borta)* gone; *(avslutad)* done; *min tid är ~* my time is up (over) **3** *(uttröttad)* done in (up), all in
förbid|a [-'bi:-] wait upon (for) **-an** *i (under)* ~ *på* awaiting, while waiting for
förbi|farande [-ˣbi:-] *a4* passing **-fart** ['fö:r-] *i ~en* in (when) passing **-fartsled** bypass
förbi|gå [ˣfö:r-] pass over *(med tystnad* in silence), ignore **-gående I** *s6, i ~ (flyktigt)* incidentally, by the way; *i ~ sagt* by the way; *med ~ av* passing over, omitting **II** *a4* passing; *en (de)* ~ a passer-by ([the] passers-by) **-gången** *bli ~* be passed over; *känna sig ~* feel left out
förbilliga [-'bill-] cheapen
förbimarsch *mil.* march past
1 förbinda [ˣfö:r-] *se binda för*
2 förbind|a [-'binda] **1** *(sår)* bandage, dress **2** *(förena)* join *(med* to); attach *(med* to); connect, combine *(med* with); *(associera)* associate, connect **3** *(förplikta)* bind over, pledge *(till* to) **4** *rfl* bind (pledge) o.s.; *vi -er oss att*

we undertake to
förbindelse [-'bind-] **1** connection; (*mellan personer*) relations (*pl*), relationship; *stå i ~ med* be in communication (touch, contact) with; *sätta sig i ~ med* get in touch (contact) with, contact **2** (*samfärdsel*) communication (*äv. mil.*); (*trafiklinje*) service, line **3** *~r* (*bekantskaper*) connections **4** (*förpliktelse*) obligation, engagement; (*skuldsedel e.d.*) bond; (*skuld*) liability, debt; *utan ~* under no obligation, without engagement, (*om pris*) not binding **-gång** tunnel **-led** connecting link **-officer** liaison officer
förbindlig [-'bind-] *a1* courteous, obliging; *~t leende* engaging smile **-het** courtesy
förbipasserande [*fö:r- el.* -'bi:-] *a4* passing-by; *en* (*de*) *~* a passer-by ([the] passers-by)
förbise [*fö:r-] overlook; disregard **-ende** *s6* oversight; *av* (*rent*) *~* through an (a pure) oversight, [quite] inadvertently
förbistring [-'bist-] confusion
förbittr|a [-'bitt-] **1** (*göra bitter*) embitter **2** (*uppreta*) exasperate **-ad** *a5* bitter, embittered; (*uppretad*) exasperated (*på ngn* with s.b.; *över* at); (*våldsam*) enraged **-ing** bitterness; exasperation; (*starkare*) rage
förbjud|a [-'bju:-] forbid; ban (*kärnvapen* nuclear weapons); (*om myndighet o.d.*) prohibit **-en** *a5* forbidden (*frukt* fruit); prohibited; *~ ingång* (*väg*) no admission (thoroughfare); *-et område* prohibited area, no trespassing; *parkering ~* no parking; *rökning ~* no smoking, smoking prohibited; *tillträde -et* no admittance
för|blanda [-'blanda] mix [up]; confuse **-blekna** [-'ble:k-] fade
förblind|a [-'blinda] blind; *bildl. äv.* infatuate; (*blända*) dazzle; *~d* blind[ed] **-else** infatuation
för'bli[va] remain; (*stanna kvar*) stay; *är och förblir* is and will remain; *den var och förblev borta* it was gone for good [and all]
förbluff|a [-'bluffa] amaze, astound; *vard.* flabbergast **-ande** amazing
förblöda [-'blö:-] bleed to death
förbomma bar [up], barricade
för|borga [-'bårja] conceal (*för* from); *~d* hidden (*för* from) **-borgerliga** [-'bårj-] turn into bourgeois; *~s* become bourgeois **-brinna** [-'brinna] burn; *bildl.* burn out, be consumed **-broskas** [-'bråsk-] turn into cartilage
förbruk|a [-'bru:ka] consume; use [up]; (*pengar, kraft*) spend **-are** consumer; user **-ning** consumption
förbruknings|artikel consumers' article, consumer goods (*pl*), article of consumption **-dag** *sista ~* use before [date] **-material** incidental material[s *pl*], expendable supplies (*pl*) **-ändamål** *för ~* for consumption purposes, for use
förbruten [-'bru:-] *a5, se förverkad*
förbrylla [-'brylla] confuse, bewilder, perplex; *~d, vard.* foxed
för|bryta [-'bry:-] *vanl. rfl* offend, trespass (*mot* against); *vad har han förbrutit?* what wrong has he done? **-brytarband** gang of criminals **-brytare** criminal; (*svagare*) offender; (*dömd fånge*) prisoner, convict **-brytarslang** lingo of the underworld; argot **-brytelse** crime; (*sva-*

gare) offence
förbränn|a [-'bränna] burn [up]; *bildl.* blast; (*sveda*) scorch **-ing** burn[ing]; *fys.* combustion; *ofullständig ~* incomplete combustion
förbrännings|kammare combustion chamber **-motor** internal-combustion engine **-produkt** product of combustion; metabolic waste product; slag
förbrödr|a [-'brö:d-] **1** (*förena*) unite in brotherhood **2** *rfl* fraternize **-ing** fraternization
för'bud *s7* prohibition (*mot* of), ban, embargo (*mot* on); *häva ett ~* raise a ban, repeal a prohibition; *införa ~ för* lay an embargo on
förbuds|anhängare prohibitionist **-fråga** question of prohibition **-lagstiftning** restrictive legislation **-skylt** (*trafikmärke*) prohibition sign
för'bund *s7* **1** (*avtal om samverkan*) compact; *relig.* covenant; (*allians, förbindelse*) alliance, union; *sluta ~ med ngn* make an alliance with s.b.; *stå i ~ med* enter into an alliance with, be allied with **2** ([sammanslutning av] *förening[ar]*) federation, association; *polit.* confederation, league; *hemligt ~* secret society; *Nationernas ~* the League of Nations
1 förbund|en [*fö:r-] *a5, med -na ögon* [with] blindfold[ed eyes]
2 förbund|en [-'bunn-] *a5* **1** (*förenar*) connected (*med* with, to); communicating, in communication (*med* with); (*allierad*) allied (*med* to); *det är -et med stora risker* it involves considerable risks **2** (*förpliktad*) bound (*till* to); *vara ngn mycket ~* be very much obliged to s.b. **3** *med.* dressed, bandaged
förbunds|dagen (*västty. riksdagen*) the Bundestag, the West German parliament **-kansler** federal chancellor **-kapten** *sport.* coach (trainer) of the national team **-nivå** *på ~* at the national level **-president** (*i Västtyskland o. Österrike*) federal president **-regering** federal government; *den tyska ~en* the German federal government **-republik** federal republic; *F~n Tyskland* the Federal Republic of Germany, *före 1990, vard.* West Germany **-råd** national council **-stat** federal state **-styrelse** national executive committee
förbusk|as [-'busk-] *dep, ängarna ~* the meadows are becoming overgrown with bushes **-ning** *~en av* the invasion of woodland into
förbygga [-'bygga] *rfl* overbuild; build beyond one's means
förbyt|a [-'by:-] **1** *se byta bort* **2** (*förvandla*) change, transform (*i, till* into); *han var som -t* he was changed beyond recognition **-as** *dep* change, be turned (*i, till* into)
förbålt [-'å:lt] deuced, confounded[ly]
förbättr|a [-'bätt-] improve; ameliorate; (*rätta*) amend; (*moraliskt*) change for the better, reform; *det ~r inte saken* that does not mend matters; *~ sig, ~s* improve **-ing** improvement; betterment, amelioration; (*av hälsan*) recovery
förbön intercession
fördatera predate, antedate
fördel *s2* advantage (*framför* over; *för* to; *med* of); (*fromma*) benefit; (*nytta*) good; (*vinst*) profit; *dra ~ av* benefit by, derive advantage from; *förändra sig till sin ~* change for the better; *tala till ngns ~* speak (be) in a p.'s

favour; *vara till ~ för ngn* be to a p.'s advantage; *väga för- och nackdelar* weigh the pros and cons; *det kan med ~ göras nu* it may very well be done now

fördela [-'de:-] (*utdela*) distribute (*bland, emellan, på* among[st]); (*genom lottning*) allot; (*uppdela*) divide (*bland, emellan* among[st]; *i* into); (*allmosor*) dispense; (*skingra*) dissipate; *~ på grupper* distribute on groups; *~ rollerna* cast (distribute) the parts; *~ sig* distribute themselves, be distributed

fördelaktig *a1* advantageous (*för* to, for); (*gynnsam*) favourable; (*inbringande*) profitable (*för* to, for); (*tilltalande*) attractive, prepossessing; *ett ~t yttre* a prepossessing appearance

fördelning 1 (*uppdelning*) distribution, division (*bland, emellan, på* among[st]); allotment; *~ av exporten på varuslag* breakdown of exports by commodity **2** *mil.* division **fördelningspolitik** distribution policy

fördetting [-*ˣdett-] has-been; (*gammalmodig*) back number

förde'vind *adv, sjö.* before the wind; *vända ~* veer

fördjup|a [-'ju:-] **1** deepen, make deeper **2** *rfl* (*i ett ämne*) enter deeply (*i* into); (*i studier, sysselsättning*) become (get) absorbed (engrossed) (*i* in) **-ad** *a5* (*om pers.*) absorbed; (*om studier*) deeper **-ning** depression; (*grop*) cavity; (*i marken äv.*) hollow; (*i vägg o.d.*) recess, niche

fördold [-'då:ld] *a5* hidden; secret

fördom *s2* prejudice; *full av ~ar, se fördomsfull*

fördoms|fri unprejudiced, unbias[s]ed; broad-minded; (*skrupelfri*) unscrupulous **-frihet** freedom from prejudice; broad-mindedness; (*skrupelfrihet*) unscrupulousness **-full** prejudiced **-fullhet** prejudice, bias

för'dra *se fördraga*

för'drag *s7* **1** (*överenskommelse*) treaty, pact; agreement; *sluta ~ med* conclude a treaty with **2** (*tålamod*) patience; forbearance

fördrag|a [-'dra:-] bear, stand; (*tåla*) put up with; (*uthärda*) endure **-sam** *al* tolerant, forbearing (*mot* to, towards) **-samhet** tolerance, forbearance

för'drags|brott breach of a treaty **-enlig** [-e:n-] *al* according to (in accordance with) a treaty; *~a förpliktelser* treaty obligations

fördragsgardin [*ˣfö:r-] curtain

för'dragsstridig contrary to the terms of a treaty

fördriv|a [-'dri:-] **1** (*driva bort*) drive away (out); (*driva i landsflykt*) banish **2** *~ tiden* while away the time, kill time **-ning** driving away (out); expulsion

fördröj|a [-'dröja] delay; retard; (*uppehålla*) detain, keep; stall; *-d utlösning* delayed action; *~ sig* be delayed **-ning** delay; retardation; detention

fördubbl|a [-'dubb-] double; *bildl.* redouble; *~ sig, se fördubblas* **-as** *dep* [re]double

fördum|ma [-'dumma] make stupid; *absol.* blunt the intellect **-ning** dulling of the intellect

fördunkla [-'dunn-] darken; obscure (*äv. bildl.*); (*ställa i skuggan*) overshadow; (*överträffa*) eclipse

fördyr|a [-'dy:-] make dearer (more expensive), raise the price of **-ing** *~ av* rise in the price[s *pl*] of

fördystra [-'dyst-] make gloomy; cast a gloom over; *~ stämningen* spoil the [happy] atmosphere

fördäck foredeck

fördäm|ma [-'dämma] dam [up] **-ning** dam; embankment

för|'därv *s7* **1** (*olycka*) ruin; (*undergång*) destruction; *störta ngn i ~et* lead (drive) s.b. to destruction, bring s.b. to ruin **2** (*moraliskt förfall*) corruption, depravation; (*tidens o.d.*) depravity **-därva 1** (*i grund*) ruin; (*tillintetgöra*) destroy; (*skada*) damage; (*skämma*) spoil **2** (*sedligt*) corrupt, deprave; (*försämra*) blight (*ngns utsikter* a p.'s prospects) **-därvad** *a5* **1** ruined *etc.*; *skratta sig ~* die with laughter, burst one's sides with laughing **2** corrupt *etc.*

fördärv|as [-'därv-] *dep* be ruined; (*skadas*) get damaged **-bringande** *a4* fatal, ruinous, destructive **-lig** *al* pernicious; (*skadlig*) injurious, deleterious, destructive

för|dölja *se dölja* **-döma** [-'dömma] condemn; (*ogilla*) blame; *relig.* damn

för'döm|d *a5, relig.* damned; *~t!* hang it [all]! **-else** *s5, relig.* condemnation **-lig** *al* to be condemned, reprehensible

1 före *s6* (*på snö etc.*) surface [for skiing *etc.*]

2 före I *prep* before; in front of; (*framom*) ahead (in advance) of (*äv. bildl.*); *~ detta, se under detta; ~ Kristi födelse* (*f.Kr.*) before Christ (B.C.) **II** *adv* before; *min klocka går ~* my watch is fast (gaining); *ärendet skall ~ i morgon* the matter is to come up tomorrow

förebild prototype (*för, till* of); (*mönster*) pattern, model; *ha som ~* have as a pattern **-lig** *a5* exemplary, ideal, model

förebringa produce, bring in

förebrå *v4* reproach; (*högtidligt*) upbraid; (*klandra*) blame; *~ sig* reproach o.s. (*för* with); *han har ingenting att ~ sig* he has nothing to reproach himself with **-else** reproach; *få ~r* be reproached **-ende** *a4* reproaching, reproachful

förebud 1 *poet.* (*föregångare*) harbinger **2** (*varsel*) presage (*till* of); omen, portent (*till* of)

förebygg|a (*förhindra*) prevent; provide against; (*förekomma*) forestall **-ande I** *s6* preventing *etc.*; prevention; *till ~ av* for the prevention of **II** *a4* preventive

förebåda forebode; portend

förebär|a plead, allege **-ande** *s6, under ~ av* on the plea of

föredra 1 (*framföra*) deliver; (*utantill*) recite; (*musikstycke*) execute **2** (*redogöra för*) [present a] report **3** (*ge företräde åt*) prefer (*framför* to); *det är att ~* it is preferable

föredrag *s7* **1** discourse; (*kåserande*) talk; (*tal*) address; *hålla ~* give (deliver) a discourse (lecture), lecture **2** (*framställningssätt*) delivery, diction; *mus.* execution, interpretation

föredrag|a *se föredra* **-ande I** *s9* person reporting on a case **II** *a4, den ~ a*) the reciter (singer *etc.*), *b*) *se I* **-ning** report, submission **-ningslista** agenda

föredragshållare lecturer
föredöm|e *s6* example; (*mönster*) model, pattern **-lig** *a5* (*efterföljansvärd*) worthy of imitation; (*förebildlig*) ideal, model; *~t uppförande* exemplary conduct
före|falla 1 (*inträffa*) occur, pass **2** (*tyckas*) seem, appear (*ngn* to s.b.) **-finnas** *dep* exist; *de -finns hos* they are to be found in (at) **-fintlig** *a5* existing; available
förege *se föregiva*
föregiv|a pretend, allege **-ande** *s6*, *under ~ av* under (on) the pretext of, pretending **-en** *a5* alleged
föregripa anticipate, forestall
före|gå 1 (*inträffa tidigare*) precede **2** *~ med gott exempel* set an (a good) example **-gående I** *a4* preceding, previous, former **II** *s6* (*tidigare liv*) previous (former) life; antecedents (*pl*) **-gångare** precursor, forerunner; (*företrädare*) predecessor
föregångs|land leading country **-kvinna, -man** pioneer
före|ha[va] have in (on) hand, be doing **-havande** *s6, ngns ~n* a p.'s doings
förehålla point out; *~ ngn ngt* expostulate with s.b. on (for, about) s.th.
förekomm|a 1 (*hinna före*) be in advance of; (*föregripa*) anticipate, forestall; *bättre ~ än ~s* better to forestall than be forestalled **2** (*hindra*) prevent; (*omintetgöra*) frustrate **3** (*anträffas*) be found (met with) **4** (*hända*) occur; *på -en anledning får vi påpeka* it has been found necessary to point out **-ande** *a4* **1** occurring; *i ~ fall* whenever (wherever) applicable; *ofta* (*sällan*) *~* frequent (rare) **2** (*tillmötesgående*) obliging; (*artig*) courteous
förekomst [-å-] *s3* occurrence; presence (*i* in); (*fyndighet*) deposit
föreligg|a be before us (*etc.*); be to hand; (*finnas att tillgå*) be available; *inget bevis -er ännu* no evidence is as yet forthcoming; *här -er ett misstag* this is a mistake; *det -er risk för* there is a risk of **-ande** *a4* in question, before us; *i ~ fall* in the present case
förelägg|a 1 *~ ngn ngt* place (put, lay) s.th. before s.b.; (*underställa*) submit (*ngn ngt* s.th. to s.b.) **2** (*föreskriva*) prescribe; (*ålägga*) enjoin upon; (*pålägga*) impose; (*befalla*) command, order **-ande** *s6* command, order, injunction (*äv. jur.*)
föreläs|a 1 (*uppläsa*) read (*för* to) **2** (*hålla föreläsningar*) lecture (*i, om, över* on; *vid* at) **-are** reader **2** lecturer **-ning 1** reading **2** lecture; *bevista* (*hålla*) *~ar* attend (give) lectures (*över* on)
föreläsnings|sal lecture room **-serie** series of lectures
föremål *s7* **1** (*ting*) object; article, thing **2** (*mål för tanke, känsla e.d.*) object; *vara ~ för ngns medlidande* be an object of pity to s.b. **3** (*ämne*) subject (*för* of); *han blev ~ för stark kritik* he was subjected to severe criticism; *den blev ~ för vårt intresse* it attracted our interest
för|ena [-'e:na] **1** unite (*med* to; *till* into); (*förbinda*) join, connect; *i sht bildl.* associate; (*kem. o. friare*) combine; (*sammanföra*) bring together; (*förlika*) reconcile; *F~de Arabemir-*

aten the United Arab Emirates; *Förenta nationerna* (*staterna*) the United Nations (States [of America]) **2** *rfl* unite (*med* with); associate o.s. (*med* with); (*kem. o. friare*) combine (*med* with); *~ sig med* (*äv.*) join (*ett parti* a party); *floderna ~r sig längre ner* the rivers join (meet) further down **-enad** *a5* united *etc.*; (*om arméer o.d.*) allied; (*om bolag*) associated; (*om stater*) federated; *med ~e krafter* with combined strength (united forces); *vara ~ med a*) eg. be bound up (associated) with, *b*) (*medföra, innebära*) involve, entail
förening 1 (*utan pl*) uniting *etc.* (*till* into); (*av pers., stater*) union, unification; (*friare*) association; *i ~* in combination (*med* with), jointly **2** (*med pl*) (*förbund*) alliance, union, league, federation; (*samfund*) society; (*större*) association; (*mer intim*) club; *kem.* compound
förenings|band bond [of union]; (*friare*) tie **-liv** organizational activities (*pl*) **-medlem** member of a (the) society (an organization) **-rätt** *ung.* freedom (right) of association
förenkl|a [-'enk-] simplify **-ing** simplification
förenlig [-'e:n-] *a1* consistent, compatible; *är inte ~t med* is inconsistent with, does not accord (tally) with **-het** consistency, compatibility
förent [-'e:nt] *a4, se förena*
före|sats purpose, intention; (*beslut*) resolution; *goda ~er* good resolutions; *i den* [*fasta*] *~en att* with the [firm] purpose of (+ *ing-form*) **-skrift** direction, instruction; (*läkares*) prescription, directions (*pl*); (*befallning*) order, command; *meddela ~er angående* issue directions (instructions) as to **-skriva** prescribe (*ngn vad han skall göra* what [s.b. is] to do); direct (*ngn att göra ngt* s.b. to do s.th.); *~ ngn villkor* dictate terms to (lay down conditions for) s.b. **-slå** propose, suggest (*ngn ngt* s.th. to s.b.); *absol.* make a suggestion; (*rekommendera*) recommend; *~ ngn som kandidat* nominate s.b. (*till* for)
förespegl|a *~ ngn ngt* hold out the prospect (promise) of...to s.b.; *~ sig* promise o.s. in advance **-ing** promise, prospect (*om* of); *falska ~ar* false (dazzling) promises
före|språkare 1 (*böneman*) intercessor, pleader (*för* for; *hos* with) **2** (*som förordar*) advocate (*för* of); spokesman (*för* for) **-spå** prophecy, predict **-stava 1** (*säga före*) dictate (*för* to); *~ eden* administer the oath (*för ngn* to s.b.) **2** (*orsaka, föranleda*) prompt; induce
förstå 1 (*handha*) be [at the] head of; (*affär e.d.*) manage, supervise, conduct **2** (*stunda*) be at hand, be near, impend **-ende** *a4* approaching; imminent; *vara* [*nära*] *~* be approaching ([close] at hand, impending)
föreståndar|e manager; principal, director, head; (*för institution*) superintendent; (*för skola*) headmaster, principal **-inna** manageress; principal; (*för anstalt*) matron; (*för skola*) headmistress, principal
föreställa I 1 (*framställa*) represent; (*spela ngns roll*) play the part of; *skall detta ~ konst?* is this supposed to be art? **2** (*presentera*) introduce (*för* to) **II** *rfl* **1** (*tänka sig*) imagine; fancy; envisage, visualize **2** (*presentera sig*)

introduce o.s. (*för* to)

föreställning 1 (*framförande*) representation; *teat. o.d.* performance, show **2** (*begrepp*) conception, notion, idea (*om* of); *bilda* (*göra*) *sig en ~ om* form a conception (*etc.*) of **3** (*erinring, varning*) remonstrance, protest; *göra ngn ~ar* remonstrate (expostulate) with s.b.

föreställnings|ram conceptual framework **-värld** [personal] philosophy

före|sväva *det ~r mig att jag har* I seem to have a dim recollection of having; *det har aldrig ~t mig* such an idea never crossed my mind **-sätta** *rfl* set one's mind [up]on; *~ sig en uppgift* set o.s. a task

företa *se företaga*

företag *s7* **1** (*förehavande, verk*) undertaking, enterprise; (*vågsamt*) venture; *mil.* operation; *det är ett helt ~ att* it is quite an undertaking to **2** (*affärs-*) company, [business] firm, business; *AE. äv.* corporation

företag|a 1 (*utföra*) undertake; get about; (*om t.ex. resa, undersökning*) make **2** *rfl* undertake (*att* to); (*göra*) do (*med* with) **-are** businessman; entrepreneur; *egen ~* self-employed person **-sam** *a1* enterprising **-samhet** enterprise, initiative; *fri ~* free enterprise

företags|demokrati industrial democracy **-ekonom** business economist **-ekonomi** business (industrial) economics (*pl, behandlas som sg*) **-ekonomisk** *~ teori* theory of business economics; *från ~ synpunkt* from the point of view of business economics **-inteckning** floating charge **-jurist** company lawyer **-ledare** manager; executive **-ledning** [company, business] management **-nedläggelse** close--down, shutdown **-nämnd** works council (committee) **-vinst** [company (*AE.* corporate)] profits (*pl*)

företal preface

förete 1 (*uppvisa*) show [up]; (*framtaga*) produce **2** (*förebringa*) present (*bevis* proof) **3** (*ådagalägga*) exhibit, show; *~ tecken på utmattning* show signs of fatigue **-else** phenomenon (*pl* phenomena); (*friare*) fact; (*person*) apparition; *en vanlig ~* a common occurrence **-ende** *s6* showing [up] (*etc.*); production; presentation; *vid ~ av* on the production of

företräd|a 1 (*gå före*) precede; *~ ngn* be a p.'s predecessor **2** (*representera*) represent **-are** (*i ämbete o.d.*) predecessor; (*representant*) representative; (*för idé o.d.*) advocate, leader

företräde *s6* **1** (*audiens*) audience; *begära ~ hos ngn* request s.b. for an audience; *få ~ hos* obtain an audience of **2** (*förmån framför andra*) preference; (*i rang*) precedence; *ge ~ åt* give the preference to; *ha ~ framför* take precedence over **3** (*fördel*) advantage, merit (*framför* over); (*överlägsenhet*) superiority (*framför* to)

företrädes|rätt [right of] priority (precedence) **-vis** preferably; especially, particularly

förevarande *a4* present

föreviga [-'e:vi-] perpetuate (*i* in); immortalize

förevis|a show; (*för pengar äv.*) exhibit; *fack.* demonstrate **-ning** exhibition; demonstration; (*föreställning*) performance

förevändning pretext; (*ursäkt*) excuse; (*undan-*

flykt) evasion; *ta ngt till ~* take s.th. as an excuse, use s.th. as a pretext

förfader forefather, ancestor

1 för'fall (*förhinder*) excuse [for nonattendance], hindrance; *laga ~* lawful excuse; *utan laga ~* without due cause

2 för'fall (*förstöring*) decay, ruin, decline; (*urartning*) degeneration; (*moraliskt*) decadence, degradation

förfalla [-'falla] **1** (*försämras*) [fall into] decay, deteriorate; (*om byggnad o.d.*) go to ruin, fall into disrepair, dilapidate; (*moraliskt*) go downhill, degenerate; *~ till dryckenskap* take to drink[ing] **2** (*bli t. intet*) come to nothing; (*om patent, fordran*) lapse, expire; (*om förslag*) be dropped; (*bli ogiltig*) become invalid; *~ till betalning* fall (be, become) due [for payment], be payable

förfallen [-'fall-] *a5* **1** decayed *etc.*; dilapidated (*äv. om pers.*); (*om byggnad äv.*) in disrepair, tumble-down **2** (*ogiltig*) invalid; (*om skuld*) due, payable, (*om premie*) outstanding; *jur.* forfeited, lapsed

förfallodag [-*fall◌-] expiry (due) date, maturity

förfalsk|a [-'falska] (*räkenskaper o.d.*) falsify; (*dokument, namnteckning*) forge, counterfeit; (*pengar*) counterfeit; (*varor*) adulterate **-are** forger, counterfeiter **-ning** falsification; forgery; counterfeiting; adulteration; *konkr.* imitation, forgery, counterfeit, fake

förfar|a [-'fa:-] *förfor förfarit* proceed; act **-ande** *s6* procedure, proceeding[s *pl*]; *tekn.* process **-as** *förfors förfarits, dep* be wasted; go bad; *låta ~* (*äv.*) waste **-en** *a3* experienced, skilled (*i* in)

förfaringssätt procedure, method of proceeding; *tekn.* process

förfasa [-'fa:-] *rfl* be horrified (*över* at)

författa [-'fatta] write; (*avfatta*) pen

författarbegåvning literary talent; *pers.* gifted (brilliant) author

författar|e [-'fatt-] author (*av, till* of); writer **-honorar** author's fee[s *pl*]; (*royalty*) royalty **-inna** authoress **-namn** (*antaget*) pen name **-rätt** copyright, author's rights **-skap** *s7* author's occupation; (*konkr. produktion*) writings (*pl*)

författning [-'fatt-] **1** (*stats-*) constitution; (*förordning*) statute; ordinance **2** (*tillstånd*) condition, state **3** *gå i ~ om* proceed (take steps) to (*för + ing-form*)

författnings|enlig [-e:-] *a1* constitutional; statutory **-reform** constitutional reform **-rätt** constitutional law **-samling** statute book; code **-stridig** unconstitutional

förfel|a [-'fe:-] miss; *~ sin verkan* fail to produce the desired effect **-ad** *a5* ineffective; *ett ~at liv* a misspent life; *vara ~* prove a failure

förfin|a [-'fi:-] refine; *~de seder* polished manners; *~d smak* cultivated taste **-ing** refinement; polish

förfjol *i ~* [during, in] the year before last

förflack|a [-'flacka] make shallow, vulgarize **-ning** superficial|ity, -ness

för|flugen [-'flu:-] *a3* (*om plan, tanke*) wild, random; (*om ord*) idle; (*om kula*) stray **-fluten** [-'flu:-] *a5* past; (*förra*) last; *det -flutna* the

past **-flyktigas** [-'flykt-] *dep* volatilize, vaporize; (*friare äv.*) evaporate **-flyta** [-'fly:-] pass; (*om tid äv.*) go by, elapse
förflytt|a [-'flytta] **1** [re]move, transport, transfer; (*befolkningsgrupp*) relocate; *bildl.* transplant **2** *rfl* move; *i sht bildl.* transport o.s. **-ning** removal, transfer; transplantation
förfoga [-'fω:-] **1** ~ *över* have at one's disposal, have recourse to **2** *rfl* repair (*till* to); ~ *sig bort* remove o.s.
förfogande [-'fω:-] *s6* disposal; *stå (ställa ngt) till ngns* ~ be (place s.th.) at a p.'s disposal **-rätt** right of disposition
förfrisk|a [-'friska] refresh **-ning** refreshment, refection
förfrusen [-'fru:-] *a5* frostbitten; (*om växt*) blighted with frost
förfrys|a [-'fry:-] get frostbitten; (*om växt*) get blighted with frost; ~ *händerna* get one's hands frostbitten **-ning** frostbite
förfråg|a [-'frå:-] *rfl* inquire (make inquiries) (*hos ngn om ngt* of s.b. about s.th.) **-an** *r, som pl används pl av förfrågning* **-ning** inquiry; *göra -ningar* make inquiries (*om* about; *efter* for)
för|fula [-'fu:-] make ugly **-fuska** [-'fuska] bungle, botch, spoil **-'fång** *n* detriment; (*skada*) damage, injury; *till ~ för* to the prejudice (detriment) of; *vara ngn till* ~ be a hindrance to s.b. **-fäa** [-'fä:a] brutalize; (*förslöa*) stupefy
förfäder *pl* ancestors, forefathers
förfäkta [-'fäkta] defend, uphold; (*förespråka*) advocate; (*hävda*) maintain, assert; (*rättighet*) vindicate
förfär|a [-'fä:-] terrify (*med* with), appal **-an** *r* terror, horror **-ande** *a4, se förfärlig* **-as** *dep* be horror-struck; be appalled (shocked) (*över* at, by)
förfärdiga [-'fä:r-] make (*av* [out] of); (*industriellt*) manufacture, produce; (*konstruera*) construct
förfärlig [-'fä:r-] *a1* terrible; frightful, dreadful; (*hemsk*) appalling; (*vard. oerhörd*) terrific, awful
förfölj|a [-'följa] pursue, chase; (*plåga*) persecute; **-d** *av otur* dogged by misfortune; *tanken -er mig* the idea haunts me **-are** pursuer; persecutor
förföljelse [-'följ-] pursuit; *bildl.* persecution (*mot* of) **-mani** persecution complex (mania), *vard.* paranoia
förför|a [-'fö:-] seduce; (*locka*) allure; (*t. ngt orätt*) corrupt, pervert **-are** seducer
förfördela wrong, injure
förförelse [-'fö:-] seduction; (*lockelse*) allurement; (*t. ngt orätt*) corruption **-konst** art of seduction; seductive trick
förförerska [-'fö:-] seductress; (*friare*) temptress
förförisk [-'fö:-] *a5* seductive; (*om kvinna*) bewitching, fascinating **-het** seductiveness; allurement; fascination
förgapa [-'ga:-] *rfl* go crazy (*i* about)
förgas|a [-'ga:-] gasify; ~*s* become gas **-are** carburettor **-ning** gasification; carburation
förgift|a [-'jifta] poison; (*förbittra*) infect, taint **-ning** poisoning; *bildl.* infection **-ningssym-**

tom toxic symptom
för|'gjord *a5, det är som -gjort* everything is going wrong **-glömma** [-'glömma] forget
förgren|a [-'gre:-] *rfl,* **-as** *dep* ramify, branch off; **-ad** ramified; branchy; *bot.* ramose **-ing** ramification; fork
förgrip|a [-'gri:-] *rfl,* ~ *sig på* (*mot*) outrage, use violence against, violate **-lig** *a1* (*kränkande*) outrageous; (*brottslig*) criminal; (*förolämpande*) injurious
förgrova [-'grω:-] coarsen
förgrund *s3* foreground; *träda i* ~*en* (*bildl.*) come to the fore
förgrunds|figur, -gestalt prominent (outstanding) figure
förgrymm|ad [-'grymm-] *a5* incensed (*på* with; *över* at); (*ursinnig*) enraged (*på with; över* at) **-as** *dep* become incensed
för|gråten [-'grå:-] *a3* (*om ögon*) red (swollen) with weeping; *hon var alldeles* ~ she had been crying her eyes out **-grämd** [-'grä:md] *a1* grieved; (*om min e.d.*) woeful **-gubbning** [-'gubb-] ageing; (*befolkningens*) increasing proportion of old people
förgud|a [-'gu:-] (*avguda*) idolize; (*dyrka*) adore **-ning** idolization; adoration
förgyll|a [-'jylla] *v2* gild; *bildl. äv.* embellish; ~ *upp* (*bildl.*) touch up, embellish; **-d** gilt, gold-plated **-are** gilder **-ning** gilding
för|'gå pass [away, by]; (*försvinna*) disappear, vanish; ~ *sig* forget o.s. (*mot* and insult) **-gången** [-'gåŋen] *a5* past, bygone
förgår *se förrgår*
förgård forecourt; *helvetets* ~ limbo
för|'gås *-gicks -gåtts, dep* (*gå förlorad*) be lost; (*försmäkta, dö*) perish, die (*av* with); [*vara nära att*] ~ *av nyfikenhet* be dying (consumed) with curiosity
förgäng|else [-'jäŋ-] decay, dissolution; *i sht bibl.* corruption **-lig** *a1* perishable; corruptible; (*dödlig*) mortal; (*kortvarig*) fugitive, transient **-lighet** perishability; (*dödlighet*) mortality; (*kortvarighet*) transience
förgäta [-'jä:-] *förgat* (*åld.*) *förgätit* forget
förgätmig'ej *s3, s9* forget-me-not, scorpion grass
förgäves [-'jä:-] in vain
förgöra [-'jö:-] destroy, annihilate; (*bringa om livet*) put to death
förhal|a [-'ha:-] **1** *sjö.* warp **2** (*försena*) delay, retard; ~ *förhandlingarna* drag out the proceedings; ~ *tiden* spin out the time **-ning 1** *sjö.* warping **2** (*försening*) delay, retardation
förhalnings|politik policy of obstruction **-taktik** delaying tactics; *AE. polit.* filibuster[ing]
förhand 1 *kortsp.* elder hand; *ha* ~ have the lead **2** *på* ~ beforehand, in advance
förhandenvarande [-ˣhann-] *a4, under* ~ *omständigheter* under [the] present circumstances
förhandl|a [-'hand-] negotiate (*med* with; *om* about); (*överlägga*) deliberate, discuss **-are** negotiator **-ing** (*överläggning*) deliberation; (*vid domstol, möte e.d.*) proceeding; (*underhandling*) negotiation; *avbryta* (*inleda*) ~*ar* suspend (start) negotiations
förhandlings|basis basis for (of) negotiations **-bord** negotiation table **-delegation** negotia-

tion delegation **-läge** bargaining position **-part** negotiating party **-partner** counterpart in negotiations **-rätt** right to negotiate **-uppgörelse** agreement **-villig** willing to negotiate **förhands|anmälan** advance registration **-avisera** preadvise **-besked** advance notice **-beställning** advance booking **-diskussion** preliminary discussion **-granskning** preliminary examination **-inställning** attitude taken in advance; prejudiced view; *om du redan har en ~ om* if you have already made up your mind about **-löfte** promise in advance **-meddelande** advance notice **-reklam** advance publicity **-rätt** prior right **-visa** preview **-visning** preview, trade show

förhast|a [-'hasta] *rfl* be rash (too hasty) **-ad** *a5* rash; *dra ~e slutsatser* jump to conclusions

förhatlig [-'ha:t-] *a1* hateful, detestable, odious (*för* to)

förhind|er [-'hind-] *få ~* be prevented [from] going (coming); *med ~* with impediments; *i händelse av ~* in case of impediment **-ra** prevent (*ngn från att s.b.* from + *ing*-form); (*stoppa*) stop

förhistor|ia 1 prehistory **2** background **-isk** prehistoric[al]

förhjälpa *~ ngn till ngt* help (assist) s.b. to obtain s.th.

förhoppning [-'håpp-] hope; (*förväntning*) expectation; *~ar* (*utsikter*) prospects; *göra sig ~ar* indulge in expectations; *hysa ~ar om* hope for; *inge ngn ~ar* inspire s.b. with hopes, give s.b. hope; *i ~ om* (*att*) hoping for (to)

förhoppnings|full hopeful; (*lovande*) promising **-vis** hopefully

förhud foreskin

förhyd|a [-'hy:-] *v2, sjö.* sheathe **-ning** *sjö.* sheathing

förhyra [-'hy:-] **1** (*hus o.d.*) rent **2** (*sjöman*) hire

förhåll|a [-'hålla] *rfl* **1** (*om pers.*) *a*) (*uppföra sig*) behave; (*handla*) act, *b*) (*förbli*) keep (*lugn* quiet), remain (*passiv* passive, *likgiltig* indifferent) **2** (*om sak*) *a*) (*kem. o.d.*) behave, *b*) (*mat. o. friare*) be; *hur -er det sig med...?* what is the position as regards...?, how are things with...?; *så -er sig saken* that is how matters stand; *bredden -er sig till längden som 1 till 3* the breadth is to the length as 1 to 3

förhållande [-'håll-] *s6* **1** (*tillstånd*) state of affairs (things), (*pl äv.*) conditions; (*omständigheter*) circumstances; *rätta ~t* the fact [of the matter]; *under alla ~n* in any case; *under inga ~n* under (in) no circumstances, in no case **2** (*inbördes ställning*) relations (*pl*), relationship; (*kärleks-*) intimacy, connection; *spänt ~* strained relations (*pl*), estrangement; *i ~ till* in relation to; *stå i vänskapligt ~ till* be on friendly terms with; *ha ett ~ med ngn* have an affair with s.b. **3** (*proportion*) proportion; *mat.* ratio; *i ~ till hans inkomster* in proportion to his income; *inte stå i ngt rimligt ~ till* be out of all proportion to; *i ~ till sin ålder är han* for his age he is **4** (*uppträdande*) behaviour, conduct **-vis** [-*håll-] proportionately

förhållning [*fö:r- *el.* -'håll-] *mus.* suspension

förhållnings|order [-*håll-] *pl* orders, instrucions, directions **-regel** direction, rule of conduct

för|håna [-'hå:-] scoff at **-hårdnad** [-'hå:rd-] *s3* induration, callus, callosity

förhänge curtain

förhärd|a [-'hä:r-] harden; *~ sig* harden one's heart **-ad** *a5* hardened, obdurate; (*inbiten*) inveterate; *en ~ skurk* a double-dyed villain **-as** *dep* [become] harden[ed] **-else** obduracy, obdurateness

för|härja [-'härja] ravage, devastate, lay waste **-härliga** [-'hä:r-] *i sht bibl.* glorify; (*prisa*) extol, laud

förhärsk|a [*fö:r-, äv. -'härr-] predominate, prevail **-ande** *a4* predominant, prevailing; prevalent; *vara ~, se förhärska*

förhäv|a [-'hä:-] *rfl* pride o.s. (*över ngt* on s.th.); (*skryta*) boast (*över ngt* of s.th.) **-else** arrogance; boasting

förhäx|a [-'häxa] bewitch **-ning** bewitchment

förhöj|a [-'höjja] raise; (*friare*) increase; *bildl.* heighten, enhance **-ning** raising; (*mera konkr.*) increase, rise, *AE.* raise

för|'hör *s7* examination; (*utfrågning*) interrogation; (*rättsligt*) inquest, hearing; *skol.* test, *AE.* quiz **-höra** [-'hö:-] examine; (*fråga ut*) interrogate; *skol.* question (*på* on), test; *AE.* quiz; *~ sig, se höra* [*sig för*]

förhörs|ledare interrogator **-protokoll** statement **-teknik** cross-examination technique

förhöst early autumn

förinta [-'inta] annihilate, destroy; *~nde blick* withering glance

förintelse [-'int-] rannihilation, destruction **-strålning** annihilation radiation **-vapen** weapon of extermination

för|irra [-'irra] *rfl* go astray, lose one's way; wander **-ivra** [-'i:v-] *rfl* get [too] excited; lose one's head (self-control) **-jaga** [-'ja:-] chase (drive) away, expel; *i sht bildl.* dispel

förkalk|a[s] [-'kall-] *fysiol.* calcify **-ning** calcification

förkalkyl preliminary calculation (estimate)

förkasta [-'kasta] **1** (*ogilla, avslå*) reject, repudiate; (*förslag äv.*) turn down, refuse **2** (*fördöma*) denounce; *en ~d människa* a rejected person, an outcast

förkastelse [-'kast-] rejection; repudiation **-dom** condemnation; *uttala en ~ över* pass a condemnation upon, denounce

förkast|lig [-'kast-] *a1* (*fördömlig*) to be condemned; (*friare*) unjustifiable; (*avskyvärd*) abominable **-ning** *geol.* fault **-ningsspricka** *geol.* fault fissure

förklara [-'kla:-] **1** explain; (*klargöra*) make clear, elucidate; (*tolka*) interpret; (*utlägga*) expound **2** (*tillkännage*) declare; (*uppge*) state; (*kungöra*) proclaim; *~ krig* declare war; *~ ngn för segrare* proclaim s.b. [the] victor; *~ ngn sin kärlek* declare one's love for s.b.; *han ~des skyldig till* he was found guilty of **3** (*förhärliga*) glorify **4** *rfl* explain o.s.; *~ sig för* (*mot*) declare for (against); *~ sig om* (*över*) *ngt* declare (state) one's opinion of s.th.

förklar|ad [-'kla:-] *a5* **1** (*avgjord*) declared, avowed **2** (*överjordisk*) glorified, transfigured **-ing 1** explanation (*av, på, till, över* of); elucidation; (*tolkning*) interpretation; *till ~ in* (by

way of) explanation; *utan ett ord till* ~ without a word of explanation **2** (*tillkännagivande*) declaration; statement; *avge* ~ make a declaration **-lig** *a1* explicable; (*lätt insedd*) comprehensible; *av lätt* ~*a skäl* for obvious reasons
för|klena [-'kle:-] disparage, depreciate; *i* ~*nde ordalag* in disparaging terms **-klinga** [-'kliŋa] die away; ~ *ohörd* fall on deaf ears
förklä *s6, se förkläde*
förkläd|a [-'klä:-] disguise (*till* as); *-d till brevbärare* disguised as (in the disguise of) a postman
förkläde 1 apron; (*för barn*) pinafore **2** *bildl.* chaperon
för|klädnad [-'klä:d-] *s3* disguise; *skyddande* ~ (*biol.*) mimicry **-knippa** [-'knippa] associate
förkol|a *rfl*, **-as** [-'kå:-] *dep* char **-na** char, carbonize; *bildl.* cool [down, off]
förkomm|a [-'kåmma] get lost; (*om försändelse*) miscarry **-en** *a5* missing; (*förfallen*) lost
förkonstl|a [-'kånst-] artificialize; ~*d* artificial; sophisticated **-ing** artificiality; sophistication
förkoppra [-'kåpp-] copper
förkort|a [-'kårta] shorten; (*ord e.d.*) abbreviate; (*bok e.d.*) abridge; (*tiden*) while away, beguile; *mat.* reduce, simplify **-ning** shortening; (*av ord e.d.*) abbreviation; (*av bok e.d.*) abridgement; *mat.* reduction
förkovr|a [-'kå:v-] **1** improve; (*öka*) increase **2** *rfl* improve; advance; ~ *sig i engelska* improve one's English **-an** *r* improvement; (*framsteg*) advance
för|krigstiden *under* ~ in the prewar period, *äv.* before the war **-kristen** pre-Christian
förkroma [-'krå:-] chrome
förkroppslig|a [-'kråpps-] embody, incarnate **-ande** *s6* embodiment, incarnation
förkross|a [-'kråssa] crush; overwhelm **-ad** *a5* brokenhearted; (*ångerfull*) contrite **-ande** *a4* crushing; heartbreaking; ~ *majoritet* overwhelming majority **-else** contrition; brokenheartedness
för'krympt *a4* stunted, dwarfed; *fysiol.* abortive
förkunn|a [-'kunna] *v1* announce (*för* to); (*utropa*) proclaim; (*predika*) preach; (*förebåda*) foretell, herald **-are** announcer, preacher; herald **-else** announcement, proclamation; preaching
förkunskaper *pl* previous knowledge (*sg*) (*i* of); *ha goda* (*dåliga*) ~ be well (poorly) grounded (*i* in)
förkväv|a [-'kvä:-] choke, stifle **-as** *dep* stifle
förkyl|a [-'çy:-] *rfl* catch [a] cold; *bli* -*d* catch [a] cold; *vara mycket* -*d* have a bad (severe) cold; *nu är det* -*t!* (*vard.*) that's torn it! **-ning** cold
för|kämpe champion (*för* of) **-känning, -känsla** presentiment, premonition, forewarning **-kärlek** predilection (*för* for), partiality (*för* for, to)
förkättrad [-'çätt-] *a5* decried, run (cried) down
förköp advance booking; *köpa* ~ book in advance
förköpa [-'çö:-] *rfl* spend too much money
för|köpspris advance-booking price **-körsrätt** [-çö:rs-] right of way **-laddning** (*i äldre va-*

pen) wad[ding]; (*i sprängborrhål*) stemming
för'lag *s7* (*bok-*) publishing house (company, firm), publishers (*pl*); *utgiven av A:s* ~ published by A; *utgiven på eget* ~ published by the author
förlaga [*x*fö:r-] *s1* (*original*) original; (*förebild*) model, pattern
förlags|beteckning [publisher's] imprint **-bevis** [subordinated] debenture **-man** sleeping partner, advancer of capital **-redaktör** editor [in a publishing house] **-rätt** publishing right[s *pl*], copyright **-verksamhet** publishing
förlam|a [-'la:-] paralyse (*äv. bildl.*); ~*d av skräck* paralysed with fright (horror) **-ning** paralysis
förled *språkv.* first element
förled|a [-'le:-] entice; seduce (*till* into) **-ande** *a4* enticing; seductive
förlegad [-'le:-] *a5* antiquated, out-of-date, old-fashioned, outmoded; ~ *kvickhet* stale joke
förlid|a [-'li:-] go by, pass **-en** *a5* past, over, spent; (*förra*) last
förlig [*x*fö:r-] *a1, sjö.* forward; ~ *vind* following (favourable) wind
förlik|a [-'li:-] *v3, v1* reconcile (*med* to); ~ *sig* become reconciled (*med* to, with) **-as** *v3, dep* be[come] reconciled; (*sämjas*) agree, get on **-ning** reconciliation; (*överenskommelse*) agreement, settlement; *avgöras genom* ~ be settled out of court; *träffa* ~ come to terms, settle out of court
förliknings|förslag mediation offer; offer of a compromise **-kommission** conciliation board **-man** [official] conciliator, arbitrator, mediator **-mannaexpedition** *Statens* ~ [the Swedish] national conciliators' office
förlis|a [-'li:-] *v3* be wrecked, sink, founder; (*om pers.*) be shipwrecked **-ning** loss, [ship]wreck
förlit|a [-'li:-] *rfl*, ~ *sig på a*) (*ngn*) trust in s.b., *b*) (*ngt*) trust to (rely on) s.th., *c*) (*att få*) rely on obtaining **-an** *r* confidence (*på* in); *i* ~ *på* trusting to, relying on
förljud|ande [-r'ju:-] *s6* report; rumour, hearsay; *enligt* ~ according to what one hears, from hearsay **-as** *förljöds förljudits, dep, det* -*es att* it is reported that
förljugen [-r'ju:-] *a3* mendacious, false **-het** mendacity, inveterate falsity
för|ljuva [-r'ju:-] gladden, sweeten **-lopp** [-'låpp] *s7* **1** (*utgång*) lapse; *efter* ~*et av ett år* after [the lapse of] a year **2** (*utveckling*) course; ~*et av händelsen var följande* the course of events was this
förlor|a [-'lɔ:-] lose; ~ *besinningen* lose one's head; ~ *i styrka* decrease in strength; ~ *i vikt* lose weight; ~ *på affären* lose on the transaction; ~ *på en vara* lose on an article; ~ *sitt hjärta till* lose one's heart to; ~ *sig* lose o.s. (be lost) (*i* in), (*om ljud*) die away **-ad** *a5* lost; (*borta*) missing; (*bortkastad, om möda o.d.*) wasted; *den* ~*e sonen* the Prodigal Son; ~ *ägg* poached eggs; *gå* ~ be lost (*för* to); *ge ngn* ~ (*ngt -at*) give s.b. (s.th.) up for lost **-are** loser
förloss|a [-'låssa] *relig.* redeem **-are** *relig.* redeemer **-ning 1** *relig.* redemption **2** *med.* delivery; childbirth
förlossnings|avdelning maternity ward **-konst**

obstetrics *(pl, behandlas som sg)*; midwifery **-kramp** eclampsia **-tång** [obstetric(al)] forceps *(sg o. pl)*

förlov [-'lå:v, *äv.* ˣfö:r-] *i uttr.: med ~ sagt* with your permission, if I may say so

förlov|a [-'lå:-] *åld.* betroth *(med* to); *~ sig* become engaged *(med* to) **-ad** *a5* **1** *det ~e landet* the Promised Land; *ett -at land för* a promised land (paradise) for **2** engaged [to be married] *(med* to), *högt.* betrothed *(med* to) ; *de ~e* the engaged couple **-ning** engagement, *högt.* betrothal

förlovnings|annons announcement of an (the) engagement **-ring** engagement ring

förlupen [-'lu:-] *a5* runaway; *~ kula* stray bullet

för'lust *s3* loss *(av* of; *för* for; *på* on); *~er (i fältslag)* casualties; *en ren ~* a dead loss; *gå (sälja) med ~* run (sell) at a loss; *göra (lida) stora ~er* sustain heavy (severe) losses; *företaget går med ~* it is a losing concern

förlusta [-'lusta] divert *(sig* o.s.)

förlustbringande *a4* involving a loss, with a heavy loss *(för* to, for); *ett ~ företag* a company running at a loss; *vara ~* be attended with losses

förlustelse [-'lust-] amusement, entertainment

förlust|ig [-'lust-] *a5, gå ~* lose, be deprived of, forfeit **-konto** loss account **-lista** *mil.* casualty list **-sida** debit side; *uppföra på ~n* enter as a debit, *bildl.* write off as a loss

förlyfta [-'lyfta] *rfl, ~ sig på a) eg.* overstrain o.s. by lifting, *b) bildl.* fail to accomplish, overreach o.s. in

förlåt [ˣfö:r-] *s3 (förhänge)* veil; *lyfta på ~en* unveil, uncover, disclose, allow s.b. to catch a glimpse

förlåta [-'lå:-] forgive *(ngn ngt* s.b. for s.th.); pardon; *(ursäkta)* excuse; *förlåt!* *(ursäkt)* [I am] sorry!; *förlåt att jag avbryter* excuse my interrupting; *förlåt, jag hörde inte* I beg your pardon, but I didn't catch what you said; *det tror jag inte, det får du ~ mig* I don't believe it, whatever you may say

förlåt|else [-'lå:-] forgiveness *(för* for); *syndernas ~* remission of [one's] sins; *be [ngn] om ~* ask (beg) a p.'s forgiveness; *få ~* be pardoned (forgiven) **-lig** *a1* pardonable, excusable, forgivable

förlägen [-'lä:-] *a3* abashed; embarrassed *(över* at); *(blyg)* shy; *(brydd)* perplexed; *(förvirrad)* confused; *göra ngn ~* embarrass (disconcert) s.b. **-het** embarrassment, confusion; shyness; *(trångmål)* embarrassment, difficulty, trouble; *råka i ~ för pengar* get into financial difficulties, be hard up for money

förlägg|a [-'lägga] **1** *(slarva bort)* mislay **2** *(placera)* locate *(till* in); *mil.* station *(i, vid* in, at); *(inkvartera)* accommodate, billet; *(förflytta)* remove, transfer *(till* to); *(t. annan tid)* assign, alter the time for; *handlingen är förlagd till medeltiden* the action (story) takes place in the Middle Ages **3** *(böcker o.d.)* publish **-are** *(bok-)* publisher **-ning** accommodation, location; *mil.* station, camp **-ningsort** *mil.* garrison [town]

förläggsgaffel [ˣfö:r-] serving fork

förläna [-'lä:-] **1** *~ ngn ngt* grant s.b. s.th., confer s.th. on s.b., *(begåva)* endow s.b. with **2**

hist., ~ ngn ngt enfeoff s.b. with s.th.

förläng|a [-'läŋa] *v2* lengthen, extend; *(giltighet, i tid)* extend, prolong; *~ ett bråk (mat.)* extend a fraction **-ning** lengthening, extension; *(av giltighet, i tid)* prolongation, extension **-ningssladd** extension flex *(AE.* cord)

för|läning [-'lä:-] *(gods)* fief, fee; *(utdelning av gods)* enfeoffment **-läsa** [-'lä:-] *~ sig* overwork o.s. by reading; study too much **-läst** [-'lä:st] *a4* overworked (strained) by too much study; *(verklighetsfrämmande)* starry-eyed **-löjliga** [-'löjj-] [turn (hold up) to] ridicule

förlöp|a [-'lö:-] *v3 el. förlöpte förlupit* **1** *(förlida)* pass; *(avlöpa)* pass off; *(gå t. ända)* pass away **2** *(rymma från)* run away from; desert, abandon **3** *rfl* lose one's head **-ning** *(överilning)* indiscretion

förlös|a [-'lö:-] *med.* deliver **-ande** *a4, det ~ ordet* the right word at the right time; *ett ~ skratt* a laugh that relieves the tension

förmak [ˣfö:r-] *s7* **1** *(sällskapsrum)* drawing room **2** *anat.* auricle

förmal|a [-'ma:-] grind, mill **-ning** grinding, milling

förman foreman, supervisor; *(överordnad)* superior, *vard.* boss; *kvinnlig ~* forewoman

förman|a [-'ma:-] *(råda o. varna)* warn; *(uppmana t.)* exhort; *(tillrättavisa)* admonish **-ing** warning; exhortation; admonition **-ingstal** admonitory address; *(friare)* mild lecture

för|mast foremast **-match** preliminary (opening) match

förmedelst [-'me:-] *se* medelst

förmedl|a [-'me:-d] mediate, act as [an] intermediary in; *(åstadkomma)* bring about; *(nyheter e.d.)* supply; *(telefonsamtal)* connect, put through; *~ en affär* act as [an] intermediary in a transaction; *~ trafiken mellan* ply between **-ande** *a4* intermediary **-are** intermediary, mediator **-ing** mediation; supplying; *(kontor)* agency, office; *genom ~ av* through the agency of

förmedlings|länk intermediary link, connection **-provision** agent's commission; brokerage

1 förmena [-'me:-] *v1 (hindra, neka)* deny *(ngn ngt* s.b. s.th.); *(förbjuda)* forbid

2 förmen|a [-'me:-] *v1 el. -ade -t (anse)* think, believe, be of opinion; *~ sig ha rätt* consider that one is right

för|menande *s6, enligt mitt ~* in my opinion **-ment** *a4* supposed

för'mer[a] oböjligt *a* better *(än* than), superior *(än* to)

förmera [-'me:-] *se* föröka

förmiddag forenoon; *vanl.* morning; *kl. 8 ~en (förk. f.m.)* at eight o'clock in the morning *(förk.* at 8 [o'clock] a.m.); *i dag på ~en, i ~s* this morning; *i morgon ~* tomorrow morning; *på (om) ~arna* in the mornings

förmiddags|bröllop morning wedding **-dräkt** morning dress

förmildrande [-'mild-] *a4, ~ omständigheter* extenuating circumstances

förminsk|a [-'minska] diminish, lessen, reduce; *foto.* reduce; *i ~d skala* on a reduced scale **-as** *dep* diminish, decrease **-ning** reduction, diminution; *foto.* reduction

förmoda–förnämhet 176

förmod|a [-'mɔ:-] suppose, imagine; *AE. äv.* guess; *(ta för givet)* assume; *(med stor säkerhet)* presume **-an** *r* supposition; *efter ~ as supposed; mot [all] ~* contrary to [all] expectation **-ligen** presumably

förmultn|a [-'mult-] moulder [away]; decay **-ing** mouldering; decay **-ingsprocess** process of decay (mouldering away)

förmyndar|e [-'mynn-, *äv.* *x*fö:r-] guardian *(för* for, of); *stå under ~* be under guardianship; *ställa under ~* place under a guardian **-regering** regency

förmynderskap [-'mynn-, *äv.* *x*fö:r-] *s7* guardianship; *bildl.* authority

för'må *v4* **1** *(kunna, orka)* be able to (+ *inf.*), be capable of (+ *ing-form*); *(i pres.)* can; *(i imperf.)* could; *allt vad jag ~r* all that I can; *allt vad huset ~r* all I (we) can offer you; *jag ~r inte mer* I can do no more, *(orkar äta)* I can't eat any more, I'm quite satisfied, thank you **2** *~ ngn [till] att* induce (prevail upon, get) s.b. to, *(övertala)* persuade s.b. to; *jag kan inte ~ mig [till] att* I can't induce (bring) myself to

förmåga [-'må:-] *s1* **1** *(kraft)* power[s *pl*] *(att* to); *(prestations-)* capacity *(att* for); *(medfödd fallenhet)* faculty *(att* for, of + *ing-form*); *(duglighet)* ability *(att* to); *(begåvning)* gift, talent; *~n att tänka* the power of thought; *efter bästa ~* to the best of one's ability; *uppbjuda all sin ~* tax one's power to the utmost; *det går över min ~* it surpasses (is beyond) my powers (capacity) **2** *pers.* man (woman) of ability (parts); *(talang)* talent, outstanding actor (singer *etc.*)

förmån [*x*fö:r-] *s3* advantage; privilege; *(gagn, nytta)* favour, benefit; *sociala ~er* social benefits; *till ~ för* to the benefit of, in favour of; *ha ~en att* have the privilege of; *detta talar till hans ~* this weighs in his favour **-lig** [-å:-] *a1* advantageous *(för* to); *(gynnsam)* favourable; *(vinstgivande)* profitable; *(välgörande)* beneficial

förmåns|erbjudande special offer, bargain **-rätt** priority [right]; *med ~* preferential, privileged **-ställning** preferential (priority) position **-tagare** *försäkr. jur.* beneficiary

1 förmäl|a [-'mä:-] *v2, v3 (omtala)* state, report, tell; *ryktet -er att* it is rumoured that

2 förmäla [-'mä:-] *v2 (bortgifta)* marry; *~ sig med* wed, marry

förmälning [-'mä:l-] marriage

för|mänskliga [-'männ-] give human form to; *(personifiera)* personify **-märka** [-'märka] notice

förmäten [-'mä:-] *a3* presumptuous; *(djärv)* audacious, bold; *vara nog ~ att* make so bold as to **-het** presumption; arrogance

förmögen [-'mö:-] *a3* **1** *(i stånd)* capable *(att* of + *ing-form)* **2** *(välbärgad)* wealthy, well-to-do; *(predikativt)* well off; *en ~ man (äv.)* a man of means (property); *de förmögna klasserna* the propertied classes **-het 1** *~er* *(andliga o. kroppsliga)* powers **2** *(rikedom)* fortune; *(samlad egendom)* property; *(kapital)* capital

förmögenhets|beskattning taxation of capi-

tal (property) **-brott** crime against property **-fördelning** distribution of wealth **-förhållanden** *pl* financial (economic) circumstances **-rätt** law of property **-skatt** capital levy

förmörk|a [-'mörka] darken; *(himlen o. bildl.)* cloud; *(skymma)* dim; *astr.* eclipse **-as** *dep* [be] darken[ed] **-else** *astr.* eclipse

förna [*x*fö:r-] *s1, biol., geol.* litter

för'nam *imperf. av förnimma*

för|namn Christian (first, given) name; *vad heter hon i ~?* what is her Christian name? **-natt** *på ~en* before midnight

förnedr|a [-'ne:-] **1** *(vanära)* degrade, disgrace, dishonour; *hur kan du ~ dig till sådant?* how can you stoop to that? **2** *bibl. (förringa)* abase, humble **-ing** degradation; humiliation **-ingstillstånd** state of humiliation *(etc.)*

förnek|a [-'ne:-] *(neka t.)* deny; *(bestrida)* dispute; *(t.ex. sitt barn)* disown; *~ sin natur* abnegate (renounce) one's nature; *han ~r sig aldrig* he is always true to type, *iron.* trust him to do such a thing; *hans goda hjärta ~r sig aldrig* his kindness of heart never fails **-else** denial; repudiation; abnegation

förnickl|a [-'nick-] nickel **-ing** nickel plate, nickelling

förnimbar [-'nimm- *el.* -*x*nimm-] *a1* perceptible *(för* to), sensible *(för* to); *(synlig äv.)* perceivable; *(hörbar)* audible

för|nimma [-'nimma] *-nam -nummit* **1** *(uppfatta)* be sensible of; *(höra)* hear; *(se)* perceive; *(andligt)* apprehend **2** *(märka)* notice; *(få veta)* hear [of]

förnimmelse [-'nimm-] **1** *(uppfattning)* perception; apprehension **2** *(känsla)* sense, sensation; *(sinnesintryck o. friare)* impression **-förmåga** power of perception, perceptivity

förning [*x*fö:r-] [guest's] contribution to a (the) meal (party); *ha ~ med sig* bring something to eat and drink

för'nuft *s7* reason *(äv. förnuftet)*; *sunt ~* common sense; *ta sitt ~ till fånga* listen to reason; *tala ~ med* talk sense to

förnuftig [-'nuft-] *a1* reasonable; *(förståndig)* sensible **-het** reasonableness; rationality

förnufts|enlig [-e:-] *a1*, **-mässig** *a1* rational **-skäl** rational argument **-stridig** *a1*, **-vidrig** *a1* contrary to all reason; irrational; *(friare)* unreasonable

förnummit [-'numm-] *sup. av förnimma*

förnumst|ig [-'nums-] *a1* would-be-wise, sapient **-ighet** sapience **-igt** *adv* as one who knows (knew)

förny|a [-'ny:a] renew; *(upprepa)* repeat; *(återuppliva)* refresh; *~ sig* renew o.s.; *~ sitt lager* replenish one's stock **-are** renewer **-bar** *a5* renewable; *~ energi* renewable energy

förnyelse [-'ny:-] renewal; *(upplivande)* revival, regeneration **-bar** *se förnybar*

för'näm *a1* noble, aristocratic, distinguished; *(högättad)* highborn; *(högdragen)* lofty, haughty, *vard.* high and mighty; *(värdig)* dignified; *~ av sig* stately, proud; *med ~ min* with a stately air; *~t folk* people of rank; *i ~ avskildhet* in splendid isolation; *det var värst vad hon är ~ av sig* she certainly puts on airs **-het 1** *(börd)* high breeding **2** *(högdragenhet)* superciliousness **-itet** *s3* **1** *se förnämhet* **2** *(förnäm pers.)* distinguished person, celebrity

förnämlig [-'nä:m-] *a1* distinguished; excellent **-ast** *adv* chiefly, principally

för'nämst [-ä:-] **I** *a superl.* foremost, first; *(om pers.)* greatest, most distinguished **II** *adv, se främst*

för'när *se 2 när I*

för|närma [-'närma] offend; affront; insult; *känna sig ~d av* take offence at **-nödenheter** [-ˣnö:-] *pl* necessities, requirements; *(livs-)* necessities of life, *jur.* necessaries

förnöj|a [-'nöjja] *v2 (roa)* gratify, please; *ombyte -er* variety is the spice of life

för'nöj|d *a1* **1** *(tillfredsställd)* content, satisfied **2** *(glad)* pleased, delighted *(över* at) **-else** *(förlustelse)* amusement, pleasure; *finna sin ~ i* delight in, find pleasure in

förnöjsam [-'nöjj-] *a1* contented **-het** contentedness

förnöta [-'nö:-] *bildl.* use up; *~ tiden* waste one's time *(med att* in + *ing-*form)

förolyck|ad *a5* mortally wounded; *(t. sjöss)* wrecked; *(om flygplan)* crashed; *de ~e* the victims [of the accident], the casualties **-as** *dep* meet with an accident; *(t. sjöss)* be wrecked

förolämp|a insult, offend, affront; *känna sig ~d över (av)* feel very much offended at (by) **-ning** insult, offence, affront *(mot* to)

för|ord 1 *(företal)* preface, foreword **2** *(rekommendation)* [special] recommendation **-orda** recommend *(hos* to; *till* for); *livligt ~* highly recommend

förordn|a [-'å:rd-] **1** *(påbjuda)* ordain, decree; *(testamentariskt)* provide *(om* for) **2** *(ordinera)* prescribe, order **3** *(utse)* appoint, nominate; *(bemyndiga)* authorize, commission **-ande** *s6* **1** *(föreskrift)* ordaining, ordination; *(testamentariskt)* provision **2** *(bemyndigande)* authorization, commission; *(tjänste-)* appointment; *hans ~ utgår* his commission (appointment) expires **-ing** ordinance, decree, order

föroren|a contaminate, defile, pollute **-ing** contamination, defilement, pollution; *konkr.* impurity, pollutant

för|orsaka cause, occasion **-ort** suburb

förorts|bo suburban[ite]; commuter **-område** suburban area

förorätta wrong, injure

förpack|a [-'packa] pack (wrap) [up] **-ning** *abstr.* packing, wrapping up; *konkr.* package, packet; *(ask)* box; *(låda)* case; *(emballage)* packing, wrapping, package; *exklusive (inklusive) ~* packing excluded (included)

förpacknings|dag packing date **-industri** packaging industry **-teknik** packaging technique

för|paktare [-'pakt-] leaseholder; tenant **-panta** [-'panta] pledge, pawn

förpassa [-'passa] *(befordra)* dispatch, send [off]; *~ till evigheten* dispatch into eternity; *~ ur landet* deport; *~ sig bort* take o.s. off

förpesta [-'pesta] poison, pollute, infect *(äv. bildl.)*

förpik *sjö.* forepeak

förpinad [-'pi:-] *a5* harrowed; tortured

förplikt|a [-'plikta] *~ ngn att* put (lay) s.b. under an (the) obligation to, bind s.b. to; *rike-*

dom ~r wealth entails responsibility; *adelskap ~r (äv.)* noblesse oblige; *~ sig* bind (engage) o.s.; *känna sig ~d att* feel [in duty] bound to **-else** *(plikt)* duty, obligation; *(förbindelse)* engagement, commitment, obligation; *ha ~r mot ngn* have obligations towards s.b.; *ikläda sig ~r* assume obligations **-iga** *se förplikta*

förpläg|a [-'plä:-] provide with food and drink, treat *(med* to) **-nad** [-ä:-] *s3* **1** fare, food **2** *(proviantering)* provisioning **-nadstjänst** supply service **-ning** [-ä:-] entertainment; *(utspisning äv.)* feeding

förpost outpost *(mot* against) *(äv. bildl.)* **-fäktning** outpost skirmish

förprick|a tick [off], mark [off], check [off] **-ning** marking (checking) off; tick

förprövning preliminary examination

förpupp|a *rfl,* **-as** [-'pupp-] *dep* change into a chrysalis, pupate **-ning** pupation

förr 1 *(förut)* before; *(fordom)* formerly *(äv. förr i tiden)*; *~ och nu* then and now; *~ låg det en lada här* there used to be a barn here; *~ trodde man* people used to think **2** *(tidigare)* sooner, earlier; *ju ~ dess bättre* the sooner the better **3** *(hellre)* rather, sooner

förre *förra, a komp.* **1** *(förutvarande)* the former; *~ ägaren* the former (late) owner; *([nyss] avgångne)* late; *(motsats senare)* early; *förra hälften av 1800-talet* the first half of the 19th century **2** *(föregående, senaste)* [the] last; *i förra månaden* last month; *mitt förra brev* my last letter; *den förra* the former *(...den senare* the latter)

förresten [-'ress-] *se rest 1*

förr|fjol *se förfjol* **-förra** last but one; *~ veckan* the week before last **-går** *i ~* the day before yesterday

förridare outrider

för|ringa [-'riŋa] *v1* minimize, lessen; *(nedvärdera)* depreciate; *(ngns förtjänst o.d.)* belittle **-rinna** [-'rinna] run (flow) away *(i* into); *i sht bibl.* ebb away

förromant|iken pre-Romanticism **-isk** [-'mant-] *a5* preromantic

förrum anteroom

förruttna [-'rutt-] rot, putrefy, decompose; decay

förruttnelse [-'rutt-] putrefaction, corruption; decay **-bakterie** putrefactive bacteria

förrycka [-'rycka] distort; *(friare)* dislocate

för'ryckt *a4* distracted; mad; *är du [alldeles] ~?* are you [quite] mad? **-het** madness

för'rymd *a5* runaway; *(om fånge e.d.)* escaped

förrysk|a [-'ryss-] Russianize **-ning** Russianization

förråa [-'rå:a] coarsen, brutalize; *verka ~nde* have a brutalizing effect *(på* on)

för'råd *s7, s4* store *(äv. bildl.)*; *(lager)* stock; *(tillgång)* supply, *(lokal)* storeroom, storage room; *lägga upp ett ~ av* lay up a store of, store up

förråda [-'rå:-] betray *(åt* to); *(röja)* reveal *(för* to); *~ sig* betray o.s., give o.s. away

förråds|arbetare store[house]man **-byggnad** storehouse; warehouse **-fartyg** supply ship, store carrier **-förman** storekeeper

förräd|are [-'rä:-] traitor *(mot* to); betrayer *(mot*

of) **-eri** treachery (*mot* to); (*lands-*) [an act of] treason (*mot* to); (*friare*) betrayal (*mot* of) **-isk** *a5* treacherous

förrän [ˣförr-, ˈförr-, *el.* -ˈänn, *vard.* förrn] before; *icke* ~ *a*) (*ej tidigare än*) not before, not earlier than, *b*) (*först*) not until (till); *det dröjde inte länge* ~ it was not long before; *knappt hade de kommit* ~ no sooner had they come than

förränt|a [-ˈränta] (*placera mot ränta*) place at interest, invest; ~ *sig* [*bra*] yield (bring in) [a good] interest **-ning** yield; *dålig* ~ low yield (rate of interest)

förrätt *kokk.* first course

förrätt|a [-ˈrätta] (*utföra*) perform; (*uträtta*) accomplish; *kyrkl.* officiate at, conduct; (*auktion o.d.*) hold; *efter väl* ~*t värv* having accomplished one's task successfully, one's duties done **-ning 1** (*utan pl*) performing, execution, carrying out **2** (*med pl*) function; duty; ceremony; *vara ute på* ~*ar* be out on official duties **-ningsman** executor, executive official

förˈsagd *a1* timid, pusillanimous **-het** timidity, pusillanimity

försak|a [-ˈsa:-] (*vara utan*) go without, give up; (*avsäga sig*) renounce; (*avstå från*) deny o.s., do without **-else** (*umbärande*) privation; (*frivillig*) [act of] self-denial

församl|a [-ˈsamla] **1** assemble, gather **2** *rfl, se församlas* **-as** *dep* assemble; gather together; meet **-ing 1** (*möte*) meeting; (*samling personer*) assembly, convention, body **2** (*kyrka, kyrkosamfund*) church; (*menighet*) congregation; (*administrativ enhet*) parish

församlings|bo parishioner; ~*rna* (*koll.*) the parish **-bok** parish register **-hus** parish hall **-kyrka** parish church **-liv** parish (congregational) life **-rätt** right of public assembly **-syster** *ung.* deaconess

försats *språkv.* antecedent clause

för|ˈse furnish, supply, provide; (*med utrustning*) equip; ~ *med strängar* (*underskrift*) string (sign); ~ *sig* furnish (*etc.*) o.s., (*vid bordet*) help o.s. (*med* to) **-ˈsedd** *a5* furnished (*etc.*) (*med* with); ~ *med* (*äv.*) with; *väl* ~ (*om pers.*) well supplied (*etc.*); *vara* ~ *med* (*äv.*) have

förseelse [-ˈse:-] offence, fault; *jur.* misdemeanour

försegel headsail, foresail

försegl|a [-ˈse:-] seal [up]; ~*de läppar* sealed lips; *med* ~*de order* under sealed orders **-ing** seal; sealing

försen|a [-ˈse:-] delay; retard; hold up; *10 minuter* ~*d* 10 minutes late; *vara* ~*d* be late (delayed) **-ing** delay **-ingsavgift** extra charge for overdue payment

försiggå take place; (*inträffa*) happen, come about; (*avlöpa*) pass (*vard.* come) off; (*pågå*) be going on; *handlingen* ~*r på* (*i*) the scene is laid at (in); *vad* ~*r här?* what is going on here?

försigkommen [-å-] *a3* advanced, forward; precocious; *de mest försigkomna eleverna* the most advanced pupils **-het** maturity; precociousness, precocity

försiktig [-ˈsikt-] *a1* cautious (*med* with); guarded; (*aktsam*) careful (*med* with, of); *var* ~ *med*

vad du säger be careful of what you say, watch your words **-het** caution; guardedness; (*aktsamhet*) care

försiktighets|mått, -åtgärd precaution, precautionary measure; *vidtaga* ~*er* take precautions

försiktigtvis [-ˣsikt-] so as to be on the safe side

försilvr|a [-ˈsilvra] silver, silver-plate **-ing** silver-plating, silvering

för|sinka [-ˈsinka] *se försena* **-sitta** [-ˈsitta] ~ *chansen* miss the chance; ~ *tiden* [be in] default; ~ *tillfället* lose the opportunity **-sjunka** [-ˈʃunka] sink (*i* into); *bildl. äv.* fall (*i* into); ~ *i tankar* be lost in thought; ~ *i tystnad* fall silent **-skaffa** [-ˈskaffa] (*skaffa*) procure, obtain; (*skänka*) afford; *vad* ~*r mig äran av ert besök?* to what do I owe the honour of your visit?

förskans|a [-ˈskansa] entrench; ~ *sig* entrench o.s., *bildl.* take shelter (*bakom* behind) **-ning** entrenchment

förskepp forebody; bow

förskingr|a [-ˈʃiŋra] (*försnilla*) embezzle, defalcate; (*bortslösa*) dissipate, squander **-are** embezzler **-ing 1** (*försnillning*) embezzlement, defalcation **2** *svenskarna i* ~*en* the Swedes scattered abroad; *judarna i* ~*en* the [Jewish] Diaspora

förskinn leather apron

1 förskjut|a [ˣfö:r-] *se skjuta* [*för*]; *regeln är* ~*en* the door is bolted

2 förskjut|a [-ˈʃu:-] **1** (*stöta ifrån sig*) reject; cast [off]; (*barn*) disown **2** (*förstäcka*) advance **3** (*rubba*) displace **4** *rfl, se förskjutas* **förskjut|as** [-ˈʃu:t-] *dep* get displaced, shift; (*om last*) shift **-ning** (*rubbning*) displacement, shifting; (*av last*) shifting; *geol.* fault; (*friare*) change

förskola nursery school; kindergarten

förskol[e]|barn preschool child **-lärare, -lärarinna** nursery school (kindergarten) teacher **-lärarlinje** nursery school teacher training centre

förskon|a [-ˈskɔ:-] ~ *ngn för* (*från*) ngt spare s.b. s.th., preserve s.b. from s.th. **-ing** forbearance, mercy

förskott *s7* advance [payment], payment in advance; ~ *på lön* advance on salary; *betala i* ~ pay in advance **-era** [pay in] advance

förskotts|belopp advance amount **-likvid** payment in advance, advance [payment]

förskrift copy; *skriva efter* ~ write (make) copies

förskriv|a [-ˈskri:-] **I 1** (*rekvirera*) order **2** (*överlåta*) convey, assign (*till, åt* to) **II** *rfl* **1** (*härröra*) come, originate, derive [one's (its) origin] **2** ~ *sig åt satan* sell one's soul to the devil **-ning 1** (*rekvisition*) order, request **2** (*skuldförbindelse*) certificate of debt, bond

förskräck|a [-ˈskräcka] *v3* frighten, scare, startle; *bli* ~*t* be (get) frightened (*etc.*) (*för, över* at); *spåren* ~*er* the footprints frighten me (*etc.*) **-as** *v3, dep* be frightened (*etc.*), *jfr förskräcka* **-else** fright, alarm; consternation; *ta en ända med* ~ come to a tragic end **-lig** *a1* dreadful, frightful; (*ohygglig*) horrible; *vard.* awful; *se*

~ *ut* look a fright

för|'skrämd *a1* frightened, scared [out of one's wits]; (*skygg*) shy, subdued **-skyllan** [-'ʃyll-] r, *utan egen* ~ through no fault of mine (*etc.*); *utan egen* ~ *och värdighet* no thanks to me **-'skämd** [-ʃ-] foul; *bildl. äv.* corrupt

förskärar|e, -kniv carving knife, carver

förskön|a [-'ʃö:-] embellish, beautify; (*med prydnader o. friare*) adorn **-ing** embellishment; adornment

1 förslag [ˣfö:r-] *mus.* grace [note]

2 för'slag 1 proposal; *i sht AE.* proposition; (*anbud*) offer (*om, till* for); (*uppslag*) suggestion, recommendation; *parl.* motion, (*lag-*) bill; *på* ~ *av* at the suggestion of; *antaga* (*förkasta*) *ett* ~ accept (reject) a proposal; *framlägga ett* ~ submit (make) a proposal; *gå in på ett* ~ agree to a proposal; *väcka* ~ *om* move **2** (*plan*) project, scheme (*till* for); (*utkast*) draft (*till* of); (*kostnads-*) estimate [of cost(s)] **3** (*vid besättande av tjänst*) nomination list

förslagen [-'sla:-] *a3* cunning, artful; (*fyndig*) smart

förslags|rum place on the nomination list; *komma i första* ~*met* be the leading candidate (frontrunner) **-ställare** proposer [of a motion], mover **-vis** as a suggestion, [let us] say

förslapp|a [-'slappa] weaken; (*t.ex. seder, disciplin*) relax **-as** *dep* be (become) relaxed **-ning** weakening; (*av moralen*) laxity

förslava [-'sla:-] enslave

förslit|a [-'sli:-] wear out **-ning** wear[ing out]; wear and tear

förslum|mas [-'slummas] *dep, området* ~ the district is becoming (turning into) a slum **-ning** deterioration into slum

förslut|a [-'slu:-] *förslöt förslutit* close, lock; seal **-ning** *konkr.* locking (closing) device; seal

för'slå suffice, be enough; *det* ~*r inte långt* that won't go far (last long); *dumt så* [*att*] *det* ~*r* as stupid as can be

förslö|a [-'slö:a] *bildl.* make apathetic, dull **-as** *dep* grow (get) apathetic (dull)

förslösa [-'slö:-] waste, squander (*på* on); (*friare*) dissipate, use up (*på* in)

försmak foretaste; *få en* ~ *av* have a foretaste of

för'små *v4* disdain; (*förakta*) despise; ~*dd friare* rejected lover

försmäd|lig [-'smä:d-] *a1* (*hånfull*) sneering, scoffing; (*förtretlig*) annoying **-ligt** *adv* sneeringly *etc.*; ~ *nog* provokingly enough

försmäkta [-'smäkta] (*i fängelse e.d.*) pine [away], languish; grow faint (*av törst* of thirst; *av värme* from heat)

försnill|a [-'snilla] embezzle [money] (*för ngn* off s.b.; *ur* from) **-ning** embezzlement

försockra [-'såckra] saccharify, saccharize; (*söta*) sugar

försoff|a [-'såffa] *v1* dull, make apathetic; ~*d* dulled, apathetic **-ning** apathy; sloth[fulness]

försommar early summer

förson|a [-'sɔ:-] **1** (*blidka*) conciliate, propitiate **2** (*förlika*) reconcile (*med* to) **3** (*sona*) atone for; (*friare*) expiate, make amends for **4** *rfl* reconcile o.s. (*med* to); (*inbördes*) make it up, become reconciled **-as** *dep, se försona 4* **-ing** reconciliation; atonement, expiation (*äv. relig.*); *till* ~ *för sina synder* in expiation (atonement) of one's sins

försonings|dag *F*~*en* the Day of Atonement, Yom Kippur **-död** expiatory death **-fest** Feast of Expiation **-offer** propitiatory sacrifice **-politik** policy of reconciliation

försonlig [-'sɔ:n-] *a1* conciliatory, forgiving

för|sorg [-'sårj] r **1** *dra* ~ *om* provide for; take care of **2** *genom ngns* ~ through (by) s.b. **-sova** [-'så:-] *rfl* oversleep [o.s.]

för|spann *s7* leading horses (*pl*) **-spel** prelude (*till* to, of); (*till sexuellt umgänge*) foreplay

förspilla [-'spilla] waste; throw away; (*förslösa*) squander; (*förverka*) forfeit

för|språng start, lead; *bildl. äv.* advantage; *få* ~ *före* get a start over; *ha en timmes* ~ have an hour's start **-spänd** *a5* (*om häst*) in the shafts; *vagnen är* ~ the carriage is ready **-spänt** *adv, ha det väl* ~ have a good start in life, be well off (well-to-do)

först I *konj* when...first **II** *adv* first; (*inte förrän*) not until (till), only; (*i början*) at first; (*för det första*) in the first place; (*vid uppräkning*) first[ly]; ~ *nu* not until now, only now; ~ *och främst* first of all; *den* ~ *anlände* the first arrival, the first to arrive; *lika väl* ~ *som sist* just as well now as later; *komma* ~ be first; *komma* ~ *fram* get there first; *stå* ~ *på listan* [be at the] head [of] the list; *det är* ~ *nyligen som* it is only recently that; *jag hörde det* ~ *i går* I only heard it yesterday; *den som kommer* ~ *till kvarnen får* ~ *mala* first come, first served

första *se förste*

förstad suburb

förstadags|kuvert first-day cover **-stämpel** first day of issue

förstadium preliminary stage

förstads|bo suburban[ite]; commuter **-område** suburban area

förstag *sjö.* forestay

förstagradsekvation equation of the first degree

förstagångs|förbrytare first offender **-väljare** new voter, s.b. voting for the first time

förstahands|kontrakt leaseholding **-uppgift** first-hand information

förstaklass|are first-form boy (*etc.*) **-biljett** first-class ticket

förstamaj|blomma [-ˣmajj-] May-Day flower, [artificial] buttonhole flower worn on May Day **-demonstration** May-Day manifestation (demonstration) **-firande** May-Day celebrations (*pl*)

förstaplacering *sport.* first place

förstatlig|a [-'sta:t-] nationalize; (*socialisera*) socialize **-ande** *s6* nationalization; socialization

förstaupplaga first edition

för|stavelse prefix **-steg** precedence

först|e *-a, a superl.* [the] first; (*i tiden*) earliest; (*i rummet*) foremost; (*i betydenhet, värde e.d.*) principal, chief, head; (*ursprunglig*) original, primary; *-a avbetalning* initial payment; ~ *bibliotekarie* principal librarian; *-a bästa* the first that comes; *-a hjälpen* first aid; *-a juni*

[on] the first of June, (*i brev*) June 1st; *F-a Mosebok* Genesis; *-a raden* (*teat.*) dress circle, *AE.* balcony; *-a öppet vatten* (*hand.*) first open water (*förk.* f.o.w.); *från -a början* from the very beginning; *för det -a, i -a rummet* in the first place; *i -a hand* [at] first hand; *den ~ jag mötte* the first person I met; *det -a jag såg* the first thing I saw

förstelna [-'ste:l-] stiffen, become (get) quite stiff; *bildl.* numb; *fack.* fossilize, petrify

försten|a [-'ste:-] petrify (*äv. bildl.*) **-ing** petrifaction

först|född *a5* first-born; *vår ~e* our first-born (eldest) [child] **-föderska** primipara **-födslorätt** right of primogeniture; birthright; *sälja sin ~* sell one's birthright

förstklassig *a1* first-class, first-rate; crack

först|ling firstling **-lingsverk** first (maiden) work

först|nämnda, -nämnde *a5* the first-mentioned; (*den, det förra*) the former

förstock|ad [-'ståck-] *a5* hardened, obdurate **-else** hardness of heart; obduracy

förstone *s, endast i uttr.: i ~* at first, to begin with

förstopp|a [-'ståppa] constipate **-ning** constipation

förstor|a [-'stɷ:-] enlarge (*äv. foto.*); *opt. o. bildl.* magnify; *starkt ~d* greatly enlarged, highly magnified **-ing** enlargement; magnification

förstorings|apparat enlarger **-glas** magnifying glass, magnifier

förstrykning mark, tick; (*understrykning*) underline, underscore

försträck|a [-'sträcka] **1** (*sträcka för mycket*) strain; *~ sig* strain o.s. (a limb) **2** (*låna*) advance **-ning 1** (*skada*) strain (*i* of) **2** (*lån*) advance

för'strö divert; (*roa*) entertain, amuse; *~ sig* amuse (divert) o.s.

för'strödd *a5* preoccupied **-het** preoccupation

förströelse [-'strö:-] diversion; recreation **-litteratur** light reading

förstubro porch step

förstucke|n [-'stuck-] *a5* concealed, hidden; *-t hot* veiled threat

för|studie pilot study **-studium** preparatory study

förstu|ga [entrance] hall; (*mindre*) passage **-kvist** porch

förstulen [-'stu:-] *a5* furtive, surreptitious

förstumm|a [-'stumma] silence **-as** *dep* become (fall) silent; be struck dumb

för'stå 1 understand (*av* from, by; *med, på* by); (*begripa*) comprehend, grasp; *vard.* dig; (*inse*) see; (*få klart för sig*) realize; (*veta*) know; *~s* (*naturligtvis*) of course; *det ~s!* that is clear!; *~ mig rätt* don't misunderstand me; *låta ngn ~ att* give s.b. to understand that, (*antyda*) intimate (hint) to s.b. that; *åh, jag ~r!* oh, I see!; *~r du inte skämt?* can't you see a joke?; *han ~r inte bättre* he doesn't know any better; *jag förstod på honom att han* he gave me to understand that he, I saw that he **2** *rfl, ~ sig på a*) understand, *b*) (*affärer*) be clever at (skilled in), *c*) (*konst, mat e.d.*) be a judge of; *~ sig på*

att know (understand) how to; *jag ~r mig inte på den flickan* I can't make that girl out

förstå|elig [-'stå:-] *a5* understandable, comprehensible, intelligible (*för* to) **-else** understanding, comprehension (*för* of); *finna ~ för* meet with understanding for **-ende** *a4* sympathetic

för'stånd *s7* understanding, comprehension; (*tankeförmåga*) intellect; (*begåvning*) intelligence; (*sunt förnuft*) [common] sense; (*omdöme*) discretion, judg[e]ment; *vard.* brains; *efter bästa ~* to the best of one's ability; *förlora ~et* lose one's reason; *ha ~ om att göra ngt* have the sense to do s.th.; *tala ~ med* talk sense to; *han talar som han har ~ till* he speaks according to his lights; *mitt ~ står stilla* I am at my wit's end; *det övergår mitt ~* it is beyond me

förståndig [-'stånd-] *a1* intelligent; (*klok*) wise; prudent; (*förnuftig*) sensible

förstånds|gåvor intellectual powers **-handikappad** educationally subnormal **-mässig** *a1* rational

förstås [-'ståss] *se förstå 1*

förståsigpåare [-'på:-] connoisseur, expert; *iron.* would-be authority

förställ|a [-'ställa] disguise (*rösten* one's voice); *~ sig* dissimulate, dissemble; *-d* disguised, (*låtsad*) feigned **-ning** dissimulation

för'stäm|d *a5* **1** *bildl.* out of (in low) spirits, disheartened **2** (*om trumma o.d.*) muffled **-ning** gloom; depression

förståndiga [-'stänn-] *~ ngn att* [*icke*] enjoin (order) s.b. [not] to

förstärk|a [-'stärka] strengthen; *bildl. äv.* fortify; *mil.* reinforce; *tekn.* reinforce; magnify; *elektron.* amplify **-are** *elektron.* amplifier; *utan ~* unplugged; *tekn.* magnifier **-arrör** *elektron.* [pre]amplifier valve; *AE.* vacuum tube amplifier **-ning** strengthening; *i sht mil.* reinforcement; *elektron.* amplification

förstäv *sjö.* stem, prow

förstör|a [-'stö:-] *v2* **1** destroy (*äv. bildl.*); (*ödelägga*) lay waste, devastate, *bildl. äv.* wreck, blast; (*allvarligt skada*) damage, injure; *se -d ut* look a wreck **2** (*totalt*) *fördärva*) ruin (*äv. bildl.*); (*förslösa*) waste, dissipate, squander **3** (*förta, skämma*) spoil **-as** *v2, dep* be destroyed (*etc.*); decay; (*totalt*) perish

förstörelse [-'stö:-] destruction **-lusta** love of destruction, destructive urge **-vapen** weapon of [mass] destruction **-verk** work of destruction

förstöring [-'stö:-] *se förstörelse; Jerusalems ~* the Fall of Jerusalem

försum|bar [-ˣsumm- *el.* -'summ-] *a5* insignificant; trifling **-lig** *a1* negligent; dilatory; (*vårdslös*) neglectful, careless **-lighet** negligence

försumm|a [-'summa] (*underlåta*) neglect; (*utebli från*) miss, let slip; (*vansköta*) neglect, be careless of; *~ att* fail to; *~ tillfället* let the opportunity slip; *känna sig ~d* feel neglected (slighted); *ta igen det ~de* make up for lost ground (time) **-else** neglect, negligence; (*förbiseende*) oversight; (*underlåtenhet*) failure, omission

försump|a [-'sumpa] *bildl.* allow to stagnate **-as**

dep **1** become waterlogged **2** *bildl.* get bogged down **-ning 1** waterlogging **2** *bildl.* stagnation
försupen [-'su:-] *a5* sottish; drunken
försur|a [-'su:-] acidify **-ning** acidification
försutten [-'sutt-] *a5* forfeited, lost
försvag|a [-'sva:-] weaken; enfeeble, debilitate; *(skada)* impair; *(mildra)* soften **-as** *dep* grow (become, get) weak[er], weaken **-ning** weakening; enfeeblement, debilitation
för'svann *imperf. av försvinna*
för'svar *s7* defence; *(berättigande)* justification *(av, för* of); *(beskydd)* protection *(för* of); *det svenska ~et* the Swedish national defence; *till ~ för* in defence of; *andraga ngt till sitt ~* say s.th. for (in justification of) o.s.; *ta ngn i ~* stand up for s.b.
försvar|a [-'sva:-] defend *(mot* from, against); *(rättfärdiga)* justify; *(i ord äv.)* advocate, stand up for **-are** defender; *offentlig ~* [court-appointed] counsel for the defence, *AE.* public defender **-bar** *a5, se försvarlig* 1 **-lig** *a1* **1** *(försvarbar)* defensible; justifiable; *(ursäktlig)* excusable; *(hjälplig)* passable **2** *(ansenlig)* considerable; *(betydande)* respectable, *vard.* jolly big
försvars|advokat counsel for the defence **-allians** defensive alliance **-anläggning, -anordning** *~ar* defences **-attaché** defence attaché **-beredskap** defensive preparedness **-departement** ministry of defence; *AE.* department of defense **-duglig** *sätta i ~t skick* make capable of defence **-fientlig** opposed to national defence **-förbund** defensive alliance **-fördrag** defence treaty **-gren** arm, [fighting] service **-högskola** defence college; *F~n* [the Swedish] national defence college **-krig** defensive war **-linje** line of defence **-lös** defenceless **-löshet** defencelessness **-makt** defence force, national defence **-medel** means of defence **-mekanism** *psykol.* defence mechanism **-minister** minister of defence; *AE.* secretary of defense **-obligation** defence bond **-plan** plan of defence **-politik** defence policy **-skrift** apology **-stab** defence staff **-styrka** defence force (unit) **-ställning** defensive position **-tal** speech for the defence; *(friare)* apology **-talan** *jur.* plea for the defendant **-utgifter** *pl* defence spendings (expenditure *[sg]*) **-utskott** *~et* [the Swedish parliamentary] standing committee on defence **-vapen** defensive weapon **-vilja** will to defend o.s. **-vänlig** in favour of national defence **-åtgärd** defensive measure
försvensk|a [-'svens-] give a Swedish character, make Swedish; *(översätta)* turn into Swedish **-as** *dep* become Swedish **-ning** [the] changing (rendering) *(av* of...) into Swedish; [the] Swedish form
försvinn|a [-'svinna] *försvann försvunnit* disappear *(från, ur* from; *[in] i* into); *(plötsligt)* vanish [away]; *(förflyta)* pass [away]; *(ur sikte)* be lost; *(upphöra att finnas till)* cease to exist; *~ i fjärran* disappear in (vanish into) the distance; *försvinn!* be off with you!, get lost!, clear out!, scram! **-ande I** *s6* disappearance **II** *adv* exceedingly; infinitesimal[ly]
försvunn|en [-'svunn-] *a5* vanished; gone; *(bortkommen)* missing **-it** *sup. av försvinna*

för|svåra [-'svå:-] make (render) [more] difficult; *(förvärra)* aggravate; *(lägga hinder i vägen för)* obstruct; *(trassla till)* complicate **-svär[j]a** [-'svä(:)-] forswear; *~ sig (med ed binda sig vid)* commit o.s. *(åt, till* to); *~ sig åt djävulen* sell one's soul to the devil
för'syn *s3, relig.* providence; *~en* Providence; *genom ~ens skickelse* by an act of providence; *låta det gå på Guds ~* trust to luck, let matters take their own course
för'synd|a *rfl* sin *(mot* against) **-else** sin, offence *(mot* against); *(friare)* breach *(mot* of)
för'synt [-y:-] *a1* considerate, tactful; discreet **-het** considerateness; modesty, discretion
för'såt *s7 (bakhåll)* ambush; *(fälla)* trap; *(svek)* treachery; *ligga i ~* lie in ambush; *lägga ~ för* lay an ambush (set snares) for **-lig** *a1* treacherous; *~a frågor* tricky questions
för|såvida [-˘vi:da], **-så'vitt** *se såvida, såvitt*
försäga [-'säja] *rfl (förråda ngt)* blab out a secret, let the cat out of the bag
försäkra [-'sä:k-] **I 1** *(betyga)* assure *(ngn om* s.b. of), aver; *jag kan ~ dig [om] att* I can assure you that, you can take my word for it that; *du kan vara ~d om att* you may rest assured that **2** *(assurera)* insure; *(om sjö- o. flygförsäkring äv.)* underwrite; *den ~de* the insured, the policyholder; *högt ~d* heavily insured; *för högt ~d* overinsured; *lågt ~d* insured for (at) a low figure **II** *rfl* **1** *(förvissa sig)* secure *(om ngt* s.th.), make sure *(om ngt* of s.th.) **2** *(ta en försäkring)* insure one's life (o.s.)
försäkr|an [-'sä:k-] *r, som pl används pl av försäkring* assurance, declaration; assertion; affirmation **-ing 1** *se försäkran* **2** *(brand-, liv-)* insurance; *(liv- äv.)* life assurance (insurance); *(sjö-)* underwriting; *teckna en ~* take out (effect) an insurance
försäkrings|agent insurance agent **-avgift** insurance contribution (fee) **-avtal** insurance contract **-bar** *a5* insurable **-bedrägeri** insurance fraud **-belopp** sum insured **-besked** insurance statement **-bolag** insurance company **-brev** insurance policy **-domstol** *F~en, se Försäkringsöverdomstolen* **-givare** insurer; *(om brittisk livförsäkring)* assurer **-inspektion** *~en* [the Swedish] private insurance supervisory service **-kassa** *allmän ~* [local] social insurance office **-matematik** actuarial mathematics *(pl, behandlas som sg)* **-polis** *se -brev* **-premie** insurance premium **-rätt** *(domstol)* [regional] social insurance court **-summa** *se -belopp* **-tagare** [the] insured, policyholder **-tjänsteman** insurance officer **-villkor** insurance terms (conditions) **-värde** *(som kan försäkras)* insurable value; *(som är försäkrat)* insured value **-överdomstol** *~en* [the Swedish] supreme social insurance court
försälj|a [-'sälja] sell **-are** salesman, seller, *fem.* saleswoman, salesgirl **-ning** selling; sale[s *pl*]; *till ~* for (on) sale; *utbjuda till ~* offer for sale
försäljnings|bolag trading company; *(-ombud)* broker **-chef** sales manager **-distrikt** sales territory **-främjande** *a4, ~ åtgärder* sales promotion *(sg)* **-kostnad** sales (selling) cost **-omkostnad** selling expense **-organisation** marketing (-sales) organization **-pris** sales (sel-

ling) price **-provision** commission on sales **-villkor** *pl* terms of sale

försämr|a [-'sämra] deteriorate; *(skada, förvärra)* impair, make worse **-as** *dep* deteriorate; get (grow) worse; *(moraliskt)* degenerate **-ing** deterioration, impairment *(i* in, of); *(moralisk)* degeneration *(i* in); *(av hälsotillstånd)* change for the worse

försändelse [-'sänd-] *(varu-)* consignment; *(kolli)* parcel; *(post-)* [postal] packet (package); *assurerad* ~ insured articles

försänk|a [-'sänka] **1** *tekn.* countersink **2** *bildl.* plunge *(i sorg* into grief); put *(i sömn* to sleep); reduce *(i fattigdom* to poverty) **-ning 1** *tekn.* countersink **2** *~ar (bildl.)* influential friends; *ha goda ~ar* have good connections

försätta [-'sätta] **1** *(bringa)* set *(i rörelse* in motion; *på fri fot* free); put *(i raseri* in a rage); ~ *ngn i konkurs* adjudge (declare) s.b. bankrupt **2** *bibl.* remove *(berg* mountains)

försätts|blad *bokb.* [front] flyleaf (endpaper) **-lins** lens attachment

för'sök *s7 (ansats)* attempt *(till* at); *(bemödande)* effort, endeavour *(till* at); *(prov)* trial, test *(med* with, of); *(experiment)* experiment *(med* with; *på* on); ~ *till brott* attempted crime; *på* ~ *a)* by way of [an] experiment, just for a trial, on trial, *b) (på måfå)* at random, at a venture; *våga ~et* risk it, take one's chance [with it]; *det är värt ett* ~ it is worth trying

försöka [-'sö:-] try; *absol. äv.* have a try; *(bemöda sig)* endeavour, seek; *(pröva på)* attempt; ~ *duger* there's no harm in trying; ~ *sig på* try one's hand at, *(våga sig på)* venture on, have a go, *vard.* take a crack at; *försök bara! a) (uppmuntrande)* just try!, *b) (hotande)* just you try it on!; *försök inte!* don't try that on with me!, *AE.* you're kidding!

försöks|anläggning pilot (experimental) plant **-ballong** pilot balloon; *släppa upp en* ~ *(bildl.)* send up a kite **-djur** laboratory animal **-fel** error in [carrying out] an experiment **-heat** qualifying heat **-kanin** *bildl.* guinea pig **-ledare** experimenter; *(vid institut)* research officer **-metod** experimental method **-objekt** subject of experiments (an experiment) **-order** trial order **-person** test subject **-stadium** experimental stage; *på -stadiet* at the experimental stage **-utskriva, -utskrivning** discharge on trial [from mental hospital] **-verksamhet** experimental work; research **-vis** experimentally; by way of experiment

försörj|a [-'sörja] *(underhålla)* support, keep; *(dra försorg om)* provide for; ~ *sig* earn a living (support o.s.) *(genom, med* by) **-are** supporter, breadwinner **-ning** providing *etc.*; support, maintenance; provision

försörjnings|balans balance of resources **-börda** maintenance burden **-inrättning** charitable institution **-plikt** maintenance liability (obligation); ~ *mot* liability for the maintenance of **-skyldig** bound (obliged) to maintain (support) [s.b.]

för'ta[ga] 1 *(hindra)* take away *(verkan* the effect); *(dämpa)* deaden; *(fördunkla)* obscure **2** *(fråntaga)* deprive *(ngn ngt* s.b. of s.th.) **3** ~ *sig* overwork o.s.; *han förtar sig inte* he doesn't overwork himself

för|'tal slander; *(starkare)* calumny *(mot* against, upon); *elakt* ~ foul slander, black calumny **-tala** [-'ta:-] slander; calumniate **-tap-pad** [-'tapp-] *a5* lost; *en* ~ *varelse* a lost soul

förtecken *mus.* key signature

förteckn|a [-'teck-] note down; make a list of **-ing** *(lista)* list, catalogue *(över* of)

förtegen [-'te:-] uncommunicative, reticent **-het** reticence

förtenn|a [-'tenna] *v1 el. förtennade förtent* tin, tin-plate **-ing** tinning

förti *se fyrti[o]*

förtid *i uttr.: i* ~ too early (soon), prematurely; *gammal i* ~ old before one's (its) time

förtidig *(skrivs äv. för tidig)* [*fö:r- el.* -'ti:-] premature

förtidspension early retirement pension; *(invalidpension)* supplementary disability pension **-era** grant early retirement pension, pension off

för|'tiga [-'ti:-] keep secret; *(förbigå med tystnad)* say nothing about **-tjockning** [-'çåck-] thickening; *(utvidgning)* swelling

förtjus|a [-'çu:-] enchant, charm, fascinate **-ande** *a4* charming; delightful **-ning** *(hänryckning)* enchantment *(över* at); *(entusiasm)* enthusiasm *(över* about, at, over); *(glädje)* delight *(över* at, in); *jag kommer med* ~ I shall be delighted to come

förtjust [-'çu:st] *a4 (intagen)* charmed *etc. (i* with); *(betagen, förälskad)* in love *(i* with), enamoured, fond *(i* of); *(mycket glad)* delighted, happy, pleased

förtjäna [-'çä:-] **1** *(förvärva)* earn; *(friare)* make; *(vinna)* gain, [make a] profit *(på en affär* by a bargain, on a transaction; *på en vara* on an article); ~ *en förmögenhet på* make a fortune out of (by); ~ *sitt uppehälle* earn one's living **2** *(vara värd[ig])* deserve; *(med saksubj. äv.)* be worth *(ett besök* a visit); *han ~r inte bättre* he deserves no better; *han fick vad han ~de* he got what he deserved; *det ~r att nämnas att* it is worth mentioning that

för|'tjänst *s3* **1** *(inkomst)* earnings *(pl)*; *(vinst)* profit[s *pl*]; *ren* ~ clear profit; *gå med* ~ be run at a profit **2** *(merit)* merit; *utan egen* ~ without any merit of one's own; *behandla ngn efter* ~ treat s.b. according to his deserts; *det är min* ~ *att* it is thanks (due) to me that **-full** *(om pers.)* deserving; *(om handling)* meritorious **-tecken** badge of merit

förtjänt [-'çä:nt] *a4 (värd)* deserved, merited; *göra sig* ~ *av* show o.s. (be) deserving of, deserve; *göra sig* ~ *om fosterlandet* deserve well of one's country

förton|a [-'tö:-] *(förklinga)* die (fade) away; ~ *sig* stand out *(mot* against) **-ing** *sjö.* view **-ingspunkt** view point

förtork|a [-'tårka] dry [up]; parch; *(vissna)* wither [away] **-ning** drying, parching; withering

förtrampa [-'trampa] trample [upon], tread down; *~d (i sht bildl.)* downtrodden

för'tret *s3* annoyance, vexation *(över* at); *(trassel)* trouble; *(grämelse)* chagrin; *till sin stora* ~ much to his chagrin; *svälja ~en* pocket one's pride; *vara till ~ för* be a nuisance to; *vålla ngn ~* cause s.b. annoyance, give s.b. trouble

förtret|a [-'tre:-] annoy, vex; *med ~d min* with a look of annoyance **-lig** *a1* vexatious, annoying **-lighet** (*med pl*) vexation, annoyance

för'tro confide (*ngn ngt* s.th. to s.b.); *~ sig till* (*åt*) place confidence in

förtroende [-'tro:-] *s6* 1 (*tillit*) confidence; faith, trust; reliance; *i ~ sagt* confidentially speaking, between ourselves; *med ~* confidently; *hysa ~ för* have confidence in; *inge ~* inspire confidence; *mista ~t för* lose confidence (one's faith) in; *åtnjuta allmänt ~* enjoy public confidence 2 (*förtroligt meddelande*) confidence; *utbyta ~n* exchange confidences **-fråga** *göra ngt till ~* put s.th. to a vote of confidence **-full** trusting, trustful; confiding **-ingivande** *a4* (*om uppträdande*) reassuring; *vara ~* inspire confidence **-klyfta** confidence gap **-kris** crisis of confidence **-man** fiduciary; (*ombud*) agent, representative; (*inom fackförening*) appointed representative **-post** position of trust **-uppdrag** commission of trust; *få ~et att* be entrusted with the task of (+ *ing-form*) **-vald** *en ~* an elected representative **-votum** vote of confidence **-väckande** *a4, se -ingivande*

förtrogen [-'tro:-] I *a3* 1 (*förtrolig*) confidential; (*intim*) intimate, close 2 (*hemmastadd med*) familiar with, cognizant of II *s* confidant[e *fem.*]; *göra ngn till sin förtrogne* take s.b. into one's confidence, make s.b. one's confidant[e] **-het** familiarity (*med* with), [intimate] knowledge (*med* of)

förtrolig [-'tro:-] *a1* (*intim*) intimate; close; (*familjär*) familiar; (*konfidentiell*) confidential; *stå på ~ fot med* be on an intimate footing (on familiar terms) with **-het** intimacy; familiarity

förtroll|a [-'trålla] enchant; bewitch (*äv. bildl.*) **-ande** *a4* enchanting, bewitching, fascinating **-ning** enchantment; bewitchment; spell; *bryta ~en* break the spell

förtrupp *mil.* advance guard; (*friare*) van, vanguard

för'tryck oppression; tyranny; *lida ~* be oppressed

förtryck|a [-'trycka] oppress; tyrannize over **-are** oppressor

förtryt|a [-'try:-] provoke, annoy, vex **-else** displeasure, resentment (*över* at); (*starkare*) exasperation, indignation (*över* at) **-sam** *a1* indignant, resentful

förträfflig [-'träff-] *a1* excellent, splendid **-het** excellence; splendid qualities (*pl*)

förträng|a [-'träŋa] (*göra trång*) narrow, constrict, contract; *psykol.* repress **-ning** narrowing, constriction, contraction; *psykol., se bortträngning*

förtröst|a [-'trösta] trust (*på Gud* in God; *på försynen* to Providence) **-an** *r* trust; reliance; confidence (*på* in); *i ~ på* in reliance on

förtröttas [-'tröttas] *dep* tire, [grow] weary

förtull|a [-'tulla] (*låta tullbehandla*) clear, declare [in the customs]; (*betala tull för*) pay duty on (for); *har ni något att ~?* have you anything to declare? **-ning** (*tullbehandling*) [customs] clearance (examination)

förtullnings|avgift customs clearance fee **-kostnad** customs duty

förtunn|a [-'tunna] thin [down]; (*gas*) rarefy; (*utspäda*) dilute **-as** *dep* get thin[ner] **-ing** 1 thinning; rarefaction; dilution 2 (*förtunningsmedel*) thinner

förtur, förtursrätt *ha ~* have priority (right of precedence) (*framför* over)

förtvin|a [-'tvi:-] wither [away] (*av* with); *bildl. äv.* languish [away] **-ing** withering [away]; *med.* atrophy

förtvivl|a [-'tvi:v-] despair (*om ngt* of s.th.; *om ngn* about s.b.) **-ad** *a5* (*om pers.*) in despair (*över* at); (*desperat*) desperate; *ett -at läge* a desperate situation; *vara ~* be in despair (exceedingly sorry) (*över att ha gjort det* at having done it); *det kan göra en ~* it is enough to drive one to despair **-an** *r* despair (*över* at); (*desperation*) desperation (*över* at); *med ~s mod* with the courage of despair

förtvålning [-'två:l-] saponification

förtvätt pre-wash **-medel** pre-washing detergent

för|'ty therefore; *icke ~* nevertheless, none the less **-tycka** [-'tycka] *du får inte ~ om (att) jag* you must not take it amiss if I

förtydlig|a [-'ty:d-] make clear[er]; *bildl. äv.* elucidate **-ande** I *s6* elucidation II *a4* elucidative

för|'täckt *a4* veiled, covert; *i ~a ordalag* circuitously, in a roundabout way **-tälja** [-'tälja] *v2* tell; relate, narrate **-tänka** [-'tänka] *inte ~ ngn att* (*om*) *han* not blame (think ill of) s.b. for (+ *ing-form*)

förtänksam [ˣfö:r-] *a1* prudent; (*förutseende*) far-sighted **-het** forethought, prudence; foresight

förtär|a [-'tä:-] eat; (*göra slut på*) eat up (*äv. bildl.*); (*friare*) consume; (*starkare*) devour; (*fräta på*) gnaw, wear away; *Farligt att ~!* Poison. Not to be taken!; *aldrig ~ sprit* never touch (take) spirits; *~s av svartsjuka* be consumed by jealousy **-ing** consumption; *konkr.* food [and drink], refreshments (*pl*)

förtät|a [-'tä:-] condense (*till* into); (*friare o. bildl.*) concentrate (*till* into); *~d stämning* tense atmosphere **-ning** condensation; concentration

förtöj|a [-ˣtöjja] moor, make fast (*vid* to) **-ning** mooring

förtöjnings|boj mooring buoy **-lina** mooring rope **-plats** moorage, tie-up wharf; berth **-ring** mooring ring

för|'törna [-'tö:r-] provoke, anger; *~d* provoked (angry) (*på* with; *över* at); *~s* (*bli förtörnad*) *över* take offence at **-underlig** [-'under-] wondrous, marvellous; (*underlig*) strange

förundersök|a subject to a preliminary investigation **-ning** preliminary investigation (examination, study); *jur.* preliminary hearing[s *pl*]

förundr|a [-'und-] fill with wonder; astonish; *~d* struck with wonder; *~ sig, se förundras* **-an** *r* wonder (*över* at) **-ansvärd** [-ˣund-] *a1* wondrous, marvellous; astonishing **-as** *dep* wonder, be astonished (*över* at)

förunna [-'unna] *bibl. o.d.* vouchsafe; (*friare*) grant; *det är inte alla ~t att* not everyone gets the chance to

1 förut ['föːr-] *sjö.*, *se 1 för II*
2 förut [ˣföːr- *el.* -'uːt] before, in advance; *(om tid äv.)* previously; *(förr)* formerly
förutan [-ˣuːtan] without
förutbeställ|a [ˣföːr-] order in advance **-ning** advance order
förutbestämm|a [ˣföːr-] settle beforehand; *(predestinera)* predestine, predestinate **-else** predestination
förutfattad [ˣföːr-] *a5* preconceived; ~ *mening (äv.)* prejudice; *ha en* ~ *mening* be prejudiced
förutom [-ˣuːtɷm] besides ([*det*] *att han är his being*)
förutsatt [ˣföːr-] *a i uttr.*: ~ *att* provided [that]
förutse [ˣföːr-] foresee; anticipate; *efter vad man kan* ~ as far as one can see **-bar** *a5* foreseeable **-ende I** *s6* foresight; *(framsynthet)* forethought **II** *a4* foreseeing; provident
förut|skicka [ˣföːr-] premise **-spå** predict
förutsäg|a [ˣföːr-] predict, foretell; *(förespå)* prophesy; forecast **-else** prediction; forecast; prophecy
förutsätt|a [ˣföːr-] *(antaga)* assume, presume, suppose; *(ta för givet)* take it for granted; *log.* postulate; *(bygga på förutsättningen [att])* imply, presuppose **-ning** *(antagande)* assumption, presumption, supposition; *log.* postulation; *(villkor)* condition, prerequisite; *(erforderlig egenskap)* qualification; *ekonomiska* ~*ar* economic prerequisites; *under* ~ *att* on condition that; *skapa* ~*ar för* create the necessary conditions for; *han har alla* ~*ar att lyckas* he has every chance of succeeding **-ningslös** unprejudiced, impartial, unbias[s]ed
förutvarande [ˣföːr-] *a4 (förra)* former; *(föregående)* previous
förvalt|a [-'valta] administer; manage; *(ämbete)* discharge, exercise; ~ *sitt pund väl* put one's gifts to good use **-are** administrator; *(av lantgods)* steward, bailiff; *(av dödsbo)* trustee; *(konkurs-)* receiver; *mil., ung.* sergeant major, **-arskap** *s7* trusteeship **-ning** administration, management; *(stats-)* public (state) administration, government services *(pl)*
förvaltnings|apparat administrative organization **-berättelse** administration report; *(styrelseberättelse)* annual report **-bolag** holding company **-byggnad** administration building **-domstol** administrative court **-kostnad** administration cost **-område** administrative district *(abstr.* sphere) **-organ** administrative body (agency) **-utskott** executive committee **-år** financial year
förvandl|a [-'vand-] transform, turn, convert *(till, i* into); *(förbyta)* change *(till, i* into); *(till ngt sämre)* reduce *(till* to); *jur.* commute *(till* into); *tekn.* convert; *teol.* transsubstantiate **-as** *dep* be transformed *(etc.)*; *äv.* turn, change *(till, i* into) **-ing** transformation; conversion; change; reduction; *teol.* transsubstantiation
förvandlings|konstnär quick-change artist **-nummer** quick-change act
förvansk|a [-'vans-] corrupt, distort; tamper with; misrepresent **-ning** corruption *etc.*
för'var *s7* [safe]keeping, custody; charge; *i säkert* ~ in safe custody; *lämna i* ~ *hos ngn* commit to a p.'s charge (custody); *ta i* ~ take

charge (custody) of; *se äv. under fängslig*
förvar|a [-'vaː-] *v1 (ha i förvar)* keep; *(deponera)* deposit; ~*s kallt (oåtkomligt för barn)* keep in a cool place (out of the reach of children) **-ing** keeping; charge, custody; ~ *på säkerhetsanstalt* preventive detention in prison; *inlämna till* ~ leave to be called for, *järnv.* put in the cloakroom; *AE. äv.* check; *mottaga till* ~ receive for safekeeping
förvarings|avgift storing *(bank. etc.* safekeeping) fee, *järnv.* cloakroom fee **-box** [storage] locker **-kärl** receptacle **-plats** repository, storeroom, storage space **-pärm** [letter] file **-skåp** filing cabinet **-utrymme** storage space
förvarn|a forewarn, warn in advance **-ing** [advance] notice, forewarning
förveckl|a [-'veck-] complicate; entangle **-ing** complication; entanglement
förvedas [-'veː-] *dep* become lignified, lignify
förveklig|a [-'veːk-] emasculate **-as** *dep* become emasculate
förverka [-'verka] forfeit
förverklig|a [-'verk-] *(t.ex. förhoppningar)* realize; *(t.ex. plan, idé)* carry out **-ande** *s6* realization **-as** *dep* be realized; *(om dröm e.d.)* come true
förveten [-'veː-, ˣföːr-] *a3* overcurious, nosy
förvild|ad [-'vild-] *a5 (om djur, växt)* undomesticated, wild; *(vanskött)* that has run wild; ~*e seder* demoralized customs **-as** *dep* return to natural state; *(om människor)* become uncivilized; *(om barn)* be turned into young savages; *(om djur, växter)* run wild; *(om odlad mark)* go out of cultivation
förvill|a [-'villa] *(föra vilse)* lead astray *(äv. bildl.)*; *(vilseleda)* mislead; *(förleda)* deceive; *(förvirra)* bewilder, confuse; ~*nde lik* confusingly like; ~*nde likhet* deceptive likeness; ~ *sig* lose one's way, *bildl.* get bewildered **-else** error, aberration; *(sedlig)* delinquency
förvinter early winter
förvirr|a [-'virra] confuse; *(förbrylla)* bewilder, perplex; *(svagare)* puzzle, embarrass; *(bringa ur fattningen)* disconcert; *(bringa i oordning)* derange, disorder; *tala* ~*t* talk incoherently **-ing** confusion; *(persons äv.)* perplexity, embarrassment, bewilderment; *(om sak äv.)* disorder[ed state]; *i första* ~*en* in the confusion of the moment
förvis|a [-'viː-] banish, exile, send away *(ur* from, out of) *(äv. bildl.)*; *(deportera)* deport; *(relegera)* expel **-ning** banishment, exile; deportation; expulsion **-ningsort** place of banishment (exile)
förvissa [-'vissa] ~ *ngn om ngt (om att)* assure s.b. of s.th. (that); *vara* ~*d* rest assured, *(övertygad)* be convinced; ~ *sig* make sure *(om* of; [*om*] *att* that)
1 förvissning [-'viss-] assurance; conviction; *i* ~ *om* in the assurance of
2 förvissning [-'viss-] *(förvissnande)* withering [away]
förvisso [-ˣvissɷ] *(utan tvivel)* for certain; *(visserligen)* certainly
förvittr|a [-'vitt-] *(på ytan)* weather; *(upplösas)* disintegrate; *(sönderfalla)* crumble, moulder **-ing** weathering; erosion, disintegration; crum-

bling
förvittrings|process weathering process **-produkt** sedimentary material
förvrid|a [-'vri:-] distort, twist; ~ *huvudet på ngn* turn a p.'s head **-en** distorted
förvräng|a [-'vräŋa] distort; *(fakta äv.)* misrepresent **-ning** distortion; misrepresentation
för|vunnen [-'vunn-] *(överbevisad)* convicted *(till* of); *(förklarad skyldig)* found guilty *(till* of) **-vuxen** [-'vuxen] overgrown; *(missbildad)* deformed
förvåll|an [-'våll-] *r, se följande* **-ande** *s6, genom eget* ~ through one's own negligence; *utan eget* ~ by no fault of one's own
förvån|a [-'vå:-] **1** surprise, astonish; *~d* surprised *etc. (över* at); *det ~r mig* I am surprised *(etc.)* **2** *rfl* be surprised *(etc.) (över* at); *det är ingenting att* ~ *sig över* it is not to be wondered at **-ande** *a4*, **-ansvärd** *a1* surprising, astonishing **-as** *dep, se förvåna* 2 **-ing** surprise, astonishment
förvår early spring
förväg *i uttr.: i* ~ in advance, ahead, before, beforehand
för|vägen [-'vä:-] *a3* overbold, rash **-vägra** [-'vä:g-] *(vägra)* refuse; *(neka)* deny; *han ~des rätten att träffa sina barn* he was denied the right to see his children
förväll|a [-'välla] parboil **-ning** parboiling
för'vänd *a1* disguised, distorted; *(dålig, syndig)* perverted
förvänd|a [-'vända] *(förvränga)* distort; disguise; ~ *synen på folk* throw dust in people's eyes **-het** perversity
förvänt|a [-'vänta] ~ *[sig]* expect; look forward to **-an** *r, som pl används pl av förväntning* expectation *(på* of); *efter (mot)* ~ according (contrary) to expectations; *över* ~ *bra* better than expected, unexpectedly good **-ansfull** expectant **-ning** expectation; *motsvara ngns ~ar* come up to a p.'s expectations
för|'värkt *a4* crippled with rheumatism **-världsliga** [-'vä:rds-] secularize; *~d (om pers. äv.)* worldly
förvärm|a preheat **-are** preheater **-ning** preheating
förvärr|a [-'värra] make worse, aggravate **-as** *dep* grow worse, become aggravated
för|'värv *s7* **1** *(förvärvande)* acquisition **2** *(ngt förvärvat)* acquisition; *(genom arbete)* earnings *(pl)* **-värva** [-'värva] acquire; *(förtjäna)* earn; *(komma över)* procure; *(vinna)* gain; ~ *vänner* make friends; *surt ~de slantar* hard--earned money
förvärvs|arbeta have gainful employment; *(om kvinna)* go out to work **-arbetande** *a4* wage--earning, gainfully employed; ~ *kvinnor (äv.)* women out at work **-arbete** gainful employment; *ha* ~ have a job **-avdrag** tax allowance on earnings **-begär** acquisitiveness **-källa** source of income **-liv** *träda ut i ~et* start working [for one's living] **-syfte** *i* ~ with a view to making money
förvätsk|a[s] [-'vätska(s)] liquefy **-ning** liquefaction
förväxl|a [-'växla] confuse, mix up **-ing** confusion; *(misstag)* mistake, mix-up

för'växt *a4, se förvuxen*
föryngr|a [-'yŋra] rejuvenate, make [look] younger; *(skog)* reafforest, *AE.* reforest **-as** *dep* grow young again **-ing** rejuvenation; *(av skog)* reafforestation, *AE.* reforestation
föryngrings|källa source of rejuvenation (fresh vitality) **-medel** rejuvenation tonic
förytliga [-'y:t-] superficialize
förzink|a [-'sinka] coat with zinc; *särsk. AE.* zinc; *(galvanisera)* galvanize **-ning** zinc-plating; galvanizing
föråldr|ad [-'åld-] antiquated, out of date; *~e ord* obsolete words **-as** *dep* get (grow) old; become antiquated *(etc.)*
förädl|a [-'ä:d-] **1** ennoble **2** *biol.* breed, improve **3** *(bearbeta råvara)* refine, work up; *~d smak* refined taste **-ing 1** ennoblement **2** breeding *etc.* **3** refinement, processing
förädlings|anstalt *lantbr.* breeding-centre **-industri** processing industry **-metod** processing technique
föräktenskaplig *a5* premarital; ~ *förbindelse* premarital intimacy
förälder [-'äld-] *s2* parent; *ensamstående* ~ single parent
föräldra|auktoritet parental authority **-förening** parents association **-försäkring** parental insurance **-hem** [parental] home **-ledig** on parental leave **-ledighet** parental leave **-lös** orphan; *hem för ~a barn* orphanage **-möte** parent-teacher association (P.T.A.) meeting **-penning** parent's allowance **-skap** *s7* parenthood, parenting
förälsk|a [-'älska] *rfl* fall in love *(i* with) **-ad** *a5* in love *(i* with); ~ *blick* amorous (loving) glance **-else** love *(i* for); *(kortvarig)* infatuation
förändr|erlig [-'änd-] *a1* variable; *(ombytlig)* changeable; *lyckan är* ~ fortune is fickle **-ra 1** *(ändra)* alter; *(byta [om])* change (till into); *inte* ~ *en min* not move a muscle **2** *rfl, se -ras* **-ras** *dep* change, alter; *tiderna* ~ times change; *hon har -rats till oigenkännlighet* she has changed beyond recognition **-ring** change; alteration; *sjuklig* ~ pathological change
förär|a [-'ä:ra] ~ *ngn ngt* make s.b. a present of s.th. **-ing** present
föräta [-'ä:ta] *rfl* overeat [o.s.] *(på* on), eat too much *(på* of)
föröd|ande [-'ö:dan-] *a4* devastating, ravaging **-else** devastation; *~ns styggelse* (bibl.) the abomination of desolation; *anställa stor* ~ make (play) havoc
förödmjuk|a humiliate *(sig* o.s.) **-else** humiliation
förök|a [-'ö:ka] *(utöka)* increase; *(mångfaldiga, fortplanta)* multiply; ~ *sig* increase, multiply **-ning 1** increase **2** *(fortplantning)* multiplication, propagation
föröv|a [-'ö:va] commit **-are** perpetrator; *~n av brottet* the man guilty of the crime
föröver ['fö:r-] *se 1 för II*
förövning preliminary exercise
förövrigt [-ˣö:v-] *se under övrig*
fösa *v3* drive, *(friare)* shove *(fram* along; *ihop* together)

G

gabar'din *s3, s4* gaberdine
Ga'bon *n* Gabon **gabo'nes** *s3,* **gabonsk** [-'bɔː:-] *a5* Gabonese
gadd *s2* sting; *ta ~en ur (av) ngn* take the sting out of s.b.
gadda *~ ihop sig* gang together (up) (*mot against*); *~ sig samman, se sammangadda sig*
gaddstekel *zool.* aculeate hymenopteran
gadolinium [-'liː-] *s8* gadolinium
gael [ga'e:l *el.* gä:l] *s3* Gael **-isk** *a5* Gaelic **-iska** 1 (*språk*) Gaelic 2 (*kvinna*) Gaelic woman
gaff *s2 (huggkrok)* gaff
gaffel [ˣgaff- *el.* 'gaff-] *s2* 1 fork; *kniv och ~* a knife and fork; *jag har det på ~n* it's in the bag, it's all wrapped up 2 *sjö.* gaff **-antilop, -bock** pronghorn, American antelope **-segel** gaffsail **-truck** fork-lift truck
gaffla babble, jabber
gagat jet
gage [ga:ʃ] *s7, s4 (sångares o.d.)* fee
gagg *s7, vard.* gag
gagg|a babble **-ig** *al* gaga
gagn [gaŋn] *s7 (nytta)* use; (*fördel*) advantage, benefit; *mera till namnet än till ~et* more for show than use; *vara till ~ för* be of advantage to
gagn|a [ˣgaŋna] be of use (advantage) to, benefit; (*ngns intressen*) serve; *det ~r föga* it is of little use (advantage); *vartill ~r det?* what is the use of that? **-elig** *al* useful **-lös** useless, of no use; fruitless, unavailing **-virke** (*värt att förädlas*) merchantable wood **-växt** utility plant
gaj *s2, sjö.* guy
1 **gala** *gol galit el. v2* crow; (*om gök*) call
2 **gala** *s1* gala; *i [full]* ~ in gala (full) dress
galaföreställning gala performance
galaktisk [-'lakt-] galactic
galaktometer [-'meː-] *s2* galactometer
galaktos [-'åːs] *s3* galactose
galamiddag gala banquet
galant [-'lant, -'laŋt] I *al (artig)* gallant II *adv, det gick ~* it went off splendidly
galanteri gallantry **-varor** *pl* fancy goods
Galaterbrevet [-'laː-] [The Epistle of Paul the Apostle to the] Galatians
gala|uniform full-dress uniform **-vagn** state coach
ga'lax *s3* galaxy
gale'as *s3, ung.* ketch
galej [-'lejj] *s7* party, celebration; spree, fling; *gå på ~ (vard.)* paint the town red
galeja [-ˣlejja] *s1* galley
galen *a3* 1 mad; *vard.* crazy, (*oregerlig*) wild; (*överförtjust*) passionately fond (*i of*), crazy (*i* about); *skvatt ~* stark mad, as mad as a hatter; *bli ~* go mad (*etc.*); *det är så man kan bli ~* it is enough to drive one mad 2 (*om sak: orätt*) wrong (*ända* end); (*dåraktig*) mad, wild; (*för-*

ryckt) absurd; *hoppa i ~ tunna* make a blunder, get into the wrong box; *det var inte så galet* [it's] not bad **-panna** madcap **-skap** *s3* 1 (*utan pl*) (*vansinne*) madness; (*dåraktighet*) folly 2 (*med pl*) act of folly; *hitta på ~er (tokerier)* play the giddy goat
galet *adv* wrong; *bära sig ~ åt a) (bakvänt)* be awkward, *b) (oriktigt)* go about in the wrong way; *det gick ~ för henne* things went wrong with her
galgbacke gallows hill
galge [ˣgalje] *s2* gallows (*sg*), gallow[s] tree; (*med en arm*) gibbet; (*klädhängare*) [coat] hanger; *sluta i ~n* come to the gallows
galgenfrist [ˣgalg-, *äv.* ˣgalj-] short respite
galg|fysionomi [-j-] gallows (hangdog) look, sinister face **-fågel** gallows bird **-humor** gallows (grim) humour
galilé *s3* Galilean **Galiléen** [-'leːen] *n* Galilee **galileisk** [-'leː-] *a5* Galilean
galit *sup. av 1 gala*
galjons|bild, -figur [-ˣjɔ:ns-] figurehead (*äv. bildl.*)
gall *oböjligt a* barren
galla *s1* bile (*äv. bildl.*); *åld.* gall; *utgjuta sin ~ över* vent one's spleen upon
gallbildning gall
gallblåsa gall bladder
1 **galler** ['gall-] *s9 (folkslag)* Gaul
2 **galler** ['gall-] *s7 (skydds-)* grating, grate, grill[e]; (*fängelse- o.d.*) bars (*pl*), grating; (*spjälverk*) lattice[work], trellis; *radio.* grid; *sätta ~ för* lattice, grate
galler|fönster lattice window; (*med skyddsgaller*) barred window **-grind** wrought-iron gate
galleri gallery **galle'ria** *s1* shopping mall
gallerverk latticework
gall|feber *få ~* have (get) one's blood up; *reta ~ på ngn* infuriate s.b. **-gång** bile duct
gallicism *s3* Gallicism
Gallien ['gall-] *n* Gaul **gallier** ['gall-] *se 1 galler*
gallimatias [-ˣtiː-] *r* balderdash
gallion- *se galjon-*
gallisk ['gall-] *a5* Gallic
gallium ['gall-] *s8* gallium
gallko barren cow
gallmygga gall midge (gnat)
gallr|a (*plantor*) thin out; (*skog*) thin; *~ bort (ut)* (*ngt onyttigt o.d.*) sort (weed) out **-ing** thinning [out] *etc.*; sorting out
gall|skrik, -skrika yell, howl
gallsprängd *a5* with burst gall bladder; *bildl.* splenetic[al], choleric
gallstekel gallfly
gall|sten gallstone, bilestone **-stensanfall** biliary colic
gallupundersökning Gallup poll; public opinion poll
gallussyra gallic acid
gallväg *~ar* bile ducts
galläpple oakapple, gall
galn|as [ˣga:l-] *dep* act (play) the fool **-ing** madman, *fem.* madwoman, lunatic, maniac; *som en ~ (äv.)* like mad
1 **galon** *s4 (plastväv)* PVC-coated fabric

2 galon *s3* (*uniformsband*) gold (silver) braid; galloon
galonerad [-'ne:-] *a5* braided, gallooned
galopp [-'åpp] *s3* **1** *ridk.* gallop; *i* ~ at a gallop; *i full* ~ [at] full gallop (*friare* speed); *kort* ~ canter, hand gallop; *falla in i* ~ break into a gallop; *fatta* ~*en* (*bildl.*) catch the drift **2** (*dans*) galop **3** *mus.* galop, gal[l]opade **-bana** racecourse; *särsk. AE.* racetrack **-era** gallop; ~*nde lungsot* galloping consumption **-sport** horse racing
galosch [-'låʃ] *s3* galosh, *ibl.* golosh; ~*er, AE. äv.* rubbers **-hylla** rack for galoshes
galt *s2* **1** *zool.* boar **2** (*tackjärn*) pig
galvaniser|a galvanize, electroplate **-ing** galvanization, electroplating
galvanisk [-'va:-] *a5* galvanic, voltaic; ~*t element* primary cell, galvanic (voltaic) cell
galvano|meter [-'me:-] *s2* galvanometer **-plas'-tik** *s3* galvanoplastics (*pl, behandlas som sg*) **-skop** [-'skåp] *s7* galvanoscope
ga'lär *s3* galley **-slav** galley slave
gam *s2* vulture (*äv. bildl.*)
Gambia ['gamm-] *n* [the] Gambia **gamb|ier** ['gamm-] *s9*, **-isk** *a5* Gambian
gambit ['gamm-] *s2, schack.* gambit
gamling old man (woman); ~*ar* old folks (people)
gamma ['gamma] *s6* gamma **-globulin** gamma globulin **-kamera** gamma camera
gammal ~*t äldre äldst* old; (*forn*[*tida*]) ancient; (*antik*) antique; (*som varat länge*) long-established, of long standing; (*åldrig*) aged; (*ej färsk, om bröd o.d.*) stale; (*begagnad äv.*) second-hand; ~*t nummer* (*av tidning o.d.*) back issue; ~ *nyhet* stale [piece of] news; *en fem år* ~ *pojke* a five-year old boy, a boy of (aged) five; ~ *som gatan* as old as the hills; *av* ~*t* of old; *av* ~ *vana* from [long-accustomed] habit; *den gamle* (*gamla*) the old man (woman); *den gamla goda tiden* the good old days; *på gamla dagar* in one's old age; *känna ngn sedan* ~*t* know s.b. of old (for many years); *vara* ~ *och van* be an old campaigner (hand); ~ *är äldst* old folks know best; *låta ngt bli vid det gamla* let s.th. remain as it is
gammal|dags *oböjligt a* old-fashioned, *neds.* oldfangled **-dans** old-time dance; (*dansande*) old-time dancing **-modig** *a1, se gammaldags;* (*omodern äv.*) out of fashion, outmoded; (*uråldrig*) antiquated; ~ *hat* old hat **-stavning** old spelling **-testamentlig** *a5* of the Old Testament **-vals** old-time waltz
gamman *oböjligt s, i* (*med*) *fröjd och* ~ merrily
gammastrål|ar *pl* gamma rays **-ning** gamma radiation
ga'mäng *s3* gamin
ganglie ['gaŋ-] *s5* ganglion (*pl äv.* ganglia)
gangster ['gaŋ-] *s2* gangster; *AE. sl.* mobster **-band, -liga** gang; *AE. sl.* mob **-metoder** ruthless methods **-välde** gang (*AE. sl.* mob) rule
gans *s3* [fancy] braid
ganska (*mycket*) very; (*oftast i positiv betydelse*) quite (*roligt* fun); (*oftast i negativ betydelse*) rather (*tråkigt* boring); (*inte så litet*) pretty; (*tämligen*) fairly, tolerably; ~ *mycket a*) (*som*

adjektiv) a great (good) deal of, [rather] a large (quite a) number of (*folk* people), quite a lot of, *b*) (*som adv*) very much, a great (good) deal, quite a lot; *det var* ~ *mycket folk på teatern* there was quite a good audience at the theatre
gap *s7* mouth; (*djurs o. tekn.*) jaws (*pl*); *bildl.* gape, jaws; (*öppning*) gap, opening **gapa 1** (*om pers. o. djur*) open one's mouth; hold one's mouth open; (*förvånat*) gape (*av* with); (*stirra*) stare; (*skrika*) bawl, yell; *den som* ~*r över mycket mister ofta hela stycket* grasp all, lose all **2** (*om avgrund o.d.*) yawn; (*stå öppen*) stand open
gap|ande *a4* gaping (*folkhop* crowd; *sår* wound); wide-open (*mun* mouth) **-hals** loudmouth; (*pratmakare*) chatterbox **-skratt** roar of laughter, guffaw; *ge till ett* ~ burst out laughing **-skratta** roar with laughter, guffaw
garag|e *s7* garage **-era** put in a garage
garageinfart garage entrance
garan'ti *s3* guarantee; (*ansvarighet*) responsibility; (*säkerhet*) security; *ställa* ~[*er*] *för ngt* give (furnish) a guarantee for s.th. **-belopp** guarantee amount **-sedel** certificate of guarantee
garçon [-'såŋ] *s3* waiter; *en glad* ~ a merry-maker
gard *s3* **1** *sport.* guard; *ställa sig i* ~ take one's guard **2** *kortsp.* guard; *ha* ~ be guarded
garde ['garr-] *s6* guards (*pl*); [*det*] *gamla* ~*t* the old guard
gardenia [-'de:-] *s1* gardenia
garder|a guard, safeguard, cover; (*i tips*) cover, allow [up to] **-ing** guard; *i tips, se hel-* resp. *halvgardering*
garderob [-'å:b] *s3* **1** (*skåp*) wardrobe; (*klädkammare*) clothes closet; (*i offentlig lokal*) cloakroom; *AE.* checkroom **2** (*kläder*) wardrobe, clothes (*pl*) **garderobié** [-åb'je:] *s3*, **garderobiär** [-åb'jä:r] *s3, se garderobsvakt*
garderobs|avgift cloakroom (*AE.* checkroom) fee **-sorg** *ha* ~ have only one's Sunday best to wear **-vakt** cloakroom (*AE.* checkroom) attendant
gar'din *s3* curtain; (*rull-*) [roller] blind; *dra för* (*ifrån*) ~*erna* pull (pull back) the curtains; *dra upp* ~*en* draw up the blind **-kappa** pelmet, valance **-omtag** tie-back **-stång** curtain rod (*av trä:* pole) **-uppsättning** curtain arrangement
gardist guardsman
garfågel [ˣga:r-] great auk, garefowl
garn [-a:-] *s7, s4* yarn; (*bomulls- äv.*) cotton; (*silkes- äv.*) silk; (*ull- äv.*) wool; (*fångst-*) net; *snärja ngn i sina* ~ entangle (catch) s.b. in one's toils **-bod** shop selling yarn
garner|a (*kläder*) trim; (*mat*) garnish **-ing** trimming; garnish
garni'son *s3* garrison; *ligga i* ~ (*äv.*) be garrisoned
garnisons|ort garrison station **-sjukhus** military hospital
garni'tyr *s7* garniture; (*sats, uppsättning*) set
garn|nystan ball of yarn (*etc.*) **-ända** end of yarn, thrum
garrottering [-'te:-] gar[r]otte

G

garv *s7, vard.* horse laugh
1 garva *vard.* (*skratta*) laugh; guffaw
2 garva tan (*äv. bildl.*); dress, curry
garvad *bildl.* (*erfaren*) seasoned
garv|are tanner, leather dresser **-eri** tannery **-ning** tanning **-syra** tannin, tannic acid **-ämne** tanning agent
1 gas *s3* (*tyg*) gauze
2 gas *s3* gas; *ge* ~ (*t. motor*) step on the gas, accelerate; *minska på* ~*en* (*t. motor*) slow down; *släcka* (*tända*) ~*en* turn out (on) the gas
gas|a gas; ~ *på* step on the gas **-betong** porous concrete **-bildning** gas formation
gasbinda gauze bandage
gasbrännare gas burner
gascognare *se gaskonjare* **Gascogne** [-'kånj] *n* Gascony
ga'sell *s3* gazelle
gas|form *i* ~ in the form of gas, in a gaseous state **-formig** [-å-] *a1* gaseous **-förgiftning** gas poisoning
gask *s2, s3* (*fest*) spree, party **gaska** ~ *upp sig* cheer up, buck up; (*rycka upp sig*) pull o.s. together
gas|kamin gas fire (stove) **-kammare** gas chamber (oven) **-klocka** gasholder, gasometer
gaskonjare [-ˣkånja-] Gascon
gas|krig gas war[fare] **-kromatografi** gas chromatography **-kök** gas ring **-lampa** gas lamp **-ledning** gas pipe; (*huvudledning*) gas main **-ljus** gaslight **-lykta** *se -lampa* **-låga** gas jet **-mask** gas mask; respirator **-mätare** gas meter **-ning** [-a:-] gassing
gasol [-'å:l] *s3* liquefied petroleum gas (*förk.* LPG, LP gas) **-driven** *a5* operated on liquefied petroleum gas **-kök** liquid-gas stove **-tub** bottle (cylinder) of liquefied petroleum gas
gas|pedal accelerator, throttle **-pollett** gas-meter disc **-reglage** throttle lever
gass *s7* heat, [full] blaze
gass|a be blazing [hot]; ~ *sig i solen* bask in the sun **-ande** *s6*, **-ig** *a1* blazing, broiling
gas|spis gas cooker (range, stove) **-svetsning** gas welding; oxyacetylene welding
1 gast *s2* (*matros*) hand
2 gast *s2* (*spöke*) ghost
gasta yell, howl
gastera appear as a visiting company (actor)
gastkram|a hug violently; ~*d* ghostridden **-ande** *a4* hair-raising **-ning** iron grip; stranglehold
gastr|ekto'mi *s3* gastrectomy **-isk** ['gast-] *a5* gastric **-'it** *s3* gastritis
gastro|ente'rit *s3* gastroenteritis **-enterologi** gastroenterology **-nom** gourmet; *äv.* gastronome[r], gastronomist **-no|mi** *s3* gastronomy **-nomisk** [-'nå:-] *a5* gastronomic[al] **-skop** [-'skå:p] *s7* gastroscope **-sko|pi** *s3* gastroscopy **-sto'mi** *s3* gastrostomy
gas|turbin gas turbine **-tändare** gas lighter **-ugn** gas oven **-utveckling** gas generation, gasification **-verk** gasworks (*sg o. pl*); gas company
gata *s1* street; (*körbana*) roadway; ~ *upp och* ~ *ner* up and down the streets; *på* ~*n* in the street; *på sin mammas* ~ on one's native heath; *gammal som* ~*n, se gammal; rum åt* ~*n* front

room, room facing the street; *gå och driva på* *gatorna* walk the streets
gat|flicka streetwalker **-hus** part of house facing the street **-hörn** street corner **-lopp** *springa* ~ run the gauntlet **-lykta** streetlamp, streetlight **-sopare** scavenger, street sweeper (*AE.* cleaner) **-sten** paving stone (*koll.* paving stones *pl*), sett
gatt *s7, sjö.* **1** (*hål*) hole **2** (*inlopp*) gut, narrow inlet
gatu|adress [street] address **-barn** street child **-belysning** street lighting **-beläggning** street paving (surface) **-försäljare** street vendor, hawker **-korsning** intersection; crossing **-kök** *ung.* snack bar **-liv** street life **-namn** street name **-nät** street system **-plan** street level **-renhållning** street cleansing **-skylt** street sign **-strid** street fighting (*äv.* ~*er*) **-vimmel** *i gatuvimlet* in the throng of the streets
gaucho ['gaotçå] *s5* gaucho
gav *imperf. av ge* (*giva*)
1 gavel ['ga:-] *i uttr.: på vid* ~ wide open
2 gavel ['ga:-] *s2* gable; (*på säng o.d.*) end; *ett rum på* ~*n* a room in the gable
gavelfönster gable window
gavi'al *s3* gavial, garial
gavott [-'vått] *s3* gavot[te]
g-dräkt *flyg.* G-suit, anti-G suit
G-dur G major
ge (*giva*) *gav givit el. gett* **I 1** (*skänka*) give; (*förära*) present (*ngn ngt s.b. with s.th.*), bestow (*ngn ngt s.th. on s.b.*); (*förläna äv.*) lend (*glans åt* splendour to); (*bevilja äv.*) grant (*tillåtelse* permission; *kredit* credit); (*bispringa med äv.*) render ([*ngn*] *hjälp* help (assistance) [to s.b.]); (*räcka äv.*) hand (*ngn ngt s.b. s.th.*); (*skicka* [*hit, dit*]) pass (*ngn brödet s.b.* the bread); ~ *dricks* tip; ~ *ngn sin hyllning* pay (do) one's homage to s.b.; *jag skall* ~ *dig!* I'll give it you!; *vad* ~*r du mig för det?* what do you say to that?; *Gud give att...!* God grant that...! **2** (*uppföra*) play, perform, give; *vad* ~*r dom i kväll?* what are they giving (what's on) tonight? **3** (*avkasta*) yield; give; ~ *ett gott resultat* yield (give) an excellent result **4** *kortsp.* deal **II** (*med betonad partikel*) **1** ~ *bort* give away **2** ~ *efter* yield, give way (*för* to) **3** ~ *emellan* give into the bargain **4** ~ *hit!* give me!; hand over! **5** ~ *ifrån sig a*) *fys.* emit, give off, *b*) (*ljud, tecken*) give, *c*) (*lämna ifrån sig*) give up, deliver **6** ~ *igen* give back, return, *bildl.* retaliate, pay back **7** ~ *med sig a*) (*ge efter*) yield, (*om pers. äv.*) give in, come [a]round, *b*) (*minska i styrka*) abate, subside, (*om sjukdom äv.*) yield to treatment; *inte* ~ *med sig (äv.*) stand firm, hold one's own **8** ~ *till ett skrik* give a cry, set up a yell **9** ~ *tillbaka a) se ge II 6, b*) (*vid växling*) give [s.b.] change (*på* for); *jag kan inte* ~ *tillbaka* I have no change **10** ~ *upp* give up (*äv. absol.*) **11** ~ *ut a*) (*pengar*) spend, *b*) (*publicera*) publish, *c*) (*utfärda*) issue, emit **III** *rfl* **1** give o.s. (take) (*tid time*) **2** (*ägna sig*) devote o.s. (*åt* to) **3** (*erkänna sig besegrad*) yield; *mil.* surrender; (*friare*) give in **4** (*om sak*) yield, give way (*för* to); (*töja sig*) stretch; (*slakna*) slacken **5** (*minska i styrka*) abate, subside **6** *det* ~*r sig* [*självt*] it goes

without saying; *det ~r sig nog med tiden* things will come right in time **7** ~ *sig i kast med* grapple with, tackle; ~ *sig i samspråk med* enter into conversation with; ~ *sig i strid med* join battle with; tackle **8** *(med betonad partikel)* ~ *sig av a)* set out (start) *(på* on), *b) (bege sig i väg)* be off, take one's departure; ~ *sig in på* embark upon *(ett företag* an enterprise), enter into *(en diskussion* a discussion); ~ *sig in vid teatern* go on the stage; ~ *sig på a) (börja med)* set about, tackle, *b) (angripa)* fly at, attack *(ngn* s.b.); ~ *sig till att skjuta* start (set about) shooting; ~ *sig ut a)* go out *(och fiska* fishing), set out (start) *(på en resa* on a journey), *b) (våga sig ut)* venture out; ~ *sig ut för att vara* pretend (profess [o.s.]) to be

ge'bit [g- *el.* j-] *s7* domain, province
gecko ['geckɷ] *s5, s3,* **-ödla** gecko
gedige|n [je'di:-] *a3* **1** *(metall)* pure; *(massiv)* solid **2** *bildl.* solid, sterling; genuine; ~ *karaktär* sound character; *-t arbete* sterling piece of work, excellent workmanship
gegg|amoja [ˣgeggamåjja] *s1* mess **-ig** *a1* sticky, messy
gehenna [jeˣhenna] *s7* Gehenna
ge'hör [j-] *s7* **1** *mus. o.* språkv. ear; *absolut* ~ absolute (perfect) pitch; *spela efter* ~ play by ear **2** hearing; *(aktning)* respect; *(uppmärksamhet)* attention; *vinna* ~ meet with sympathy; find a ready listener (audience); *skaffa sig* ~ gain a hearing
geigermätare [ˣgajger-] Geiger (Geiger-Müller) counter
geisha [ˣgejʃa *el.* 'gejʃa] *s1* geisha
geist [gajst *el.* gejst] *s3* liveliness, spark; passion
gejd [g-] *s3, tekn.* guide; slide
gejser ['gejj-] *s2* geyser
gel [j-] *s4, kem.* gel
gela'tin [ʃ-] *s4, s3* gelatin[e] **-artad** [-a:-] *a5* gelatinous
gelé *s4, s3* jelly **gelea** [ʃe'le:a] *rfl* jelly, jellify; congeal **geléartad** [-a:-] *a5* gelatinous
gelik|e [je'li:-] *s2* equal; *du och dina -ar* you and your likes; *hennes -ar (äv.)* the likes of her
1 gem [jemm *el.* g-] *s3 (ädelsten)* engraved (inlaid) jewel
2 gem [ge:m] *s7 (pappersklämma)* paperclip
ge'mak [j-] *s7* apartment, stateroom
ge'men [j-] *a1* **1** *(nedrig)* low, mean; *(lågsinnad)* base; *(friare: otäck)* horrid; dirty **2** *~e man a)* the man in the street, *b) mil.* the rank and file; *i* ~ in general **3** *(folklig)* friendly; sociable **4** *boktr.,* ~ *bokstav* lower case, lower-case letter
gemen|het [je'me:n-] *(egenskap)* lowness *etc.*; *(handling o.d.)* [act of] meanness; mean *(vard.* dirty) trick; *(starkare)* infamy **-ligen** commonly, in general
gemensam [je'me:n-] *a5 (i sht för alla)* common *(för* to); *(i sht för två el. flera)* joint *(beslut* resolution); *(ömsesidig)* mutual *(vän* friend); *ett ~t intresse* an interest in common; *två våningar med ~t kök* two flats with shared kitchen; *med ~ma ansträngningar* by united effort; *göra* ~ *sak med* make common cause

with; *ha ngt ~t* have s.th. in common **-het** community *(i* of)
gemensamhetskänsla sense of community
gemen|samt [je'me:n-] *adv* in common, jointly **-skap** *s3* community; fellowship; *(samfund)* communion; *(samband)* connection; *känna* ~ *med* have a fellow feeling for
gemmo|log [j- *el.* g-] gem[m]ologist **-logi** gem[m]ology
gems [g- *el.* j-] *s3* chamois
ge'myt [j- *el.* g-] *s7 (sinnelag)* disposition, temperament; *(godlynthet)* good nature **-lig** [-'my:t-] *a1 (om pers.)* good-natured, good-humoured, genial **2** *(om sak)* [nice and] cosy; comfortable **-lighet 1** good nature (humour), geniality **2** cosiness
ge'mål [j-] *s3* consort; spouse
1 gen [j-] *s3, biol.* gene
2 gen [j-] *a1* short, near, direct
gena take a short cut
genant [ʃe'naŋt *el.* -'ant] *a1* embarrassing, discomfiting, awkward
genast [ˣje:-] *adv* at once, immediately, straight away; *(om ett ögonblick)* directly; ~ *på morgonen* first thing in the morning
genbank *biol.* gene bank
gen'darm [ʃaŋ-] *s3* gendarme **-eri** gendarmerie, gendarmery
gendriva [ˣje:n-] disprove *(ett påstående* a statement); refute *(kritik* criticism)
genea'log [j-] genealogist **-lo|gi** *s3* genealogy **-logisk** [-'lå:-] *a5* genealogic[al]
genera [ʃ-] *(besvära)* bother, trouble, inconvenience; be a nuisance to; *(göra förlägen)* be embarrassing to; *ljuset ~r mig* the light bothers me; *~r det om jag röker?* do you mind if I smoke?; *låt inte mig* ~! don't mind me!; ~ *er inte för att säga mig sanningen* don't hesitate to tell me the truth; *det skulle inte* ~ *honom att* he would never hesitate to; *han ~r sig inte* he is not one to stand on ceremony
generad [ʃe'ne:-] *a5* embarrassed; self-conscious; *jag är* ~ *för honom* I feel embarrassed in his presence
gene'ral [j-] *s3* general, *(vid flygvapnet)* air chief marshal; *AE.* general **-agent** general agent **-agentur** general agency **-bas** *mus.* thorough bass, [basso] continuo **-direktör** director-general **-församling** general assembly **-guvernör** governor general
generaliser|a [ʃ-] generalize, make sweeping statements **-ing** generalization
general|konsul consul general **-löjtnant** *(vid armén, kustartilleriet)* lieutenant general, *(vid flygvapnet)* air marshal; *AE.* lieutenant general **-major** *(vid armén, kustartilleriet)* major general, *(vid flygvapnet)* air vice-marshal; *AE.* major general **-order** general order[s *pl*] **-paus** *mus.* general pause *(förk.* G.P.) **-plan** general plan **-repetition** dress rehearsal **-sekreterare** secretary-general **-stab** general staff
generalstabs|karta ordnance [survey] map **-officer** general-staff officer
general|strejk general strike **-tullstyrelse** ~*n* [the Swedish] board of customs
generation [j-] generation

generations|klyfta, -motsättning conflict between generations; generation gap **-växling** *biol.* alternation of generations, metagenesis
genera'tiv [j-] *a5* generative
generator [jene ̆ ra:tår] *s3* generator **-gas** *se gengas*
genera'tris [j-] *s3* generatrix *(pl generatrices)*
gene'r|ell [ʃ-] *a1* general **-ellt** *adv*, ~ *sett* generally speaking, from a general point of view
generera [j-] generate
generisk [je'ne:-] *a5* generic[al]
gener|ositet [ʃ-] generosity **-'ös** *a1* generous *(mot* to)
gene't|ik [j-] *s3* genetics *(pl, behandlas som sg)* **-iker** [-'ne:-] geneticist **-isk** [-'ne:-] *a5* genetic[al]; ~ *kod* genetic code
ge'nett [j-] *s3, se ginstkatt*
Genève [ʃö'nä:v] *n* Geneva
genever [ʃö'nä:-] *s9* hollands *(sg)*
Genèvesjön the Lake of Geneva
gengas [̆ je:n-] producer (air) gas **-aggregat** producer-gas unit
gen|gångare [̆ je:n-] ghost, spectre **-gåva** gift in return **-gäld** *i* ~ in return *(för* for) **-gälda** ~ *ngn ngt* pay s.b. back for s.th.; *jag kan aldrig* ~ *hans vänlighet* I shall never be able to repay his kindness
ge'ni [ʃ-] *s4, s6* genius *(pl geniuses)*
geni'al [j-, *äv.* ʃ-] *a1*, **-isk** [-'a:-] *a5* brilliant; *(fyndig)* ingenious **-itet** brilliance; *(ngns äv.)* genius
genie ['je:-] *s5, se genius*
geniknöl bump of genius; *gnugga ~arna* cudgel one's brains
geni'tal [j-] *a5* genital **-ier** *pl*, **-organ** genitals, genitalia
genitiv ['je:-] *s3* genitive; *i* ~ in the genitive
geni|us ['je:-] *-en -er* genius *(pl äv. genii)*
gen|klang [̆ je:n-] echo; *bildl. äv.* sympathy, approbation, response; *vinna* ~ meet with response **-ljud** echo, reverberation; *ge* ~ awake an echo **-ljuda** echo, reverberate *(av* with)
genmanipulation genetic manipulation
gen|mäla [̆ je:n-] *v2, v3 (svara)* reply; *(starkare)* rejoin; *(invända)* object *(mot, på* to) **-mäle** *s6* reply; *(starkare)* retort; *(i tidning)* rejoinder)
genom ['je:nåm] **1** *rumsbet.* through; *fara hem* ~ go home by way of (via); *kasta ut* ~ *fönstret* throw out of the window; *komma in* ~ *dörren (fönstret)* come in at the door (window) **2** *tidsbet.* through; ~ *hela* ... all through ..., throughout ... **3** *(angivande mellanhand)* through; *(angivande överbringare)* by; *jag fick veta det* ~ *henne* I got to know it through her; *skicka ett meddelande* ~ *ngn* send a message by s.b. **4** *(angivande medel)* by [means of]; ~ *enträgna böner* by means of persistent prayers **5** *(angivande orsak)* by, owing to, thanks to; ~ *drunkning* by drowning; ~ *hans hjälp* by (thanks to) his assistance; ~ *olyckshändelse* through (owing to) an accident **6** *mat., 12* ~ *4* 12 divided by 4
genom|andad *a5* penetrated, instinct *(av* with) **-andas** *dep* be penetrated *(etc.) (av* with) **-arbeta** deal with thoroughly, work through
genombläddr|a leaf (skim) through **-ing** cursory perusal

genom|blöt soaking wet **-blöta** soak, drench **-borra** *(med svärd o. bildl.)* pierce; *(med dolk)* stab; *(med blicken)* transfix **-brott** breakthrough, breaking through; *mil. o. bildl.* breakthrough, *(bildl. äv.)* triumph **-bruten** broken through; *(nätartad)* latticed, open-work **-bäva** ~*s av* be thrilled with, thrill with **-diskutera** thrash out **-driva** force through, get carried, carry; *AE. vard.* railroad **-dränka** soak *(med* in), saturate *(med* with) **-dålig** thoroughly bad **-fara** *se fara* [igenom]; ~*s av en rysning* experience a sudden thrill, *(av obehag)* shudder **-fart** way through; passage; *ej* ~ no thoroughfare
genomfarts|trafik through traffic **-väg** thoroughfare
genom|forska explore thoroughly **-frusen** chilled through (to the bone)
genomför|a carry through (out), realize; *(utföra)* accomplish, effect **-ande** *s6* carrying through, accomplishment, realization **-bar** *a5* feasible, practicable
genom|gjuten [-ju:-] *a5,* ~ *linoleum* inlaid linoleum **-gripande** *a4* thorough, exhaustive; ~ *förändringar* radical (sweeping) changes **-gräddad** *a5* well-baked
genomgå *se gå* [igenom]; *bildl.* go (pass) through; *(genomlida)* undergo, suffer; *(erfara)* experience; *(undersöka)* go through, examine **-ende I** *a4* [all-]pervading *(drag i* characteristic of); *(ständigt förekommande)* constant *(fel* error); *(grundlig)* thorough; *järnv.* through; ~ *trafik* through (transit) traffic **II** *adv* all through, throughout
genomgång *s2* going through *etc.*; *(väg o.d.)* passage, thoroughfare; *förbjuden* ~! no passage!
genomgångs|rum room giving access to another; in-between room **-trafik** through traffic
genom|hederlig downright (thoroughly) honest *-ila se ila* [igenom]; *bildl.* pass through; ~*s av skräck* shudder with fear, *vard.* be in a blue funk **-kokt** [-ɷ:-] *a4* thoroughly done; *ej* ~ not done **-korsa** cross [and recross] **-kämpa** fight through **-leta** search through, ransack **-leva** live through; *(uppleva)* experience **-lida** ~ *mycket* go through a great deal [of suffering]; ~ *en föreställning (skämts.)* endure a performance to the bitter end
genomlys|a *(med röntgenstrålar)* X-ray, x-ray; *-t av godhet* radiant with goodness **-ande** *a4* translucent **-ning** fluoroscopy
genomlysningsskärm fluorescent screen
genomläs|a read through, peruse **-ning** reading through, perusal
genom|löpa *v3, bildl. äv. -lopp -lupit* **1** *(tillryggalägga)* run through **2** *(genom|gå, -se)* pass through **3** *(genomleva)* live through **-musikalisk** exceedingly musical **-präktig** *en* ~ *flicka* an exceedingly fine girl **-pyrd** [-y:-] *a5* impregnated *(av, med* with); *bildl.* steeped *(av* in), brimming over *(av* with)
genom|resa I *s1* journey through, transit; *vara på* ~ *till* be passing through [the town *etc.*] on one's way to **II** *v3* travel (pass) through, traverse **-resetillstånd** transit permit

genom|rolig exceedingly (awfully) funny **-rutten** rotten all through (to the core)
genomse look through; (*granska*) revise
genomskinlig [-ʃi:-] *a1* transparent; diaphanous; *vard.* seethrough; *bildl. äv.* plain **-het** transparency
genom|skåda see through; (*hemlighet*) penetrate, find out; (*avslöja*) unmask **-skärning 1** (*avskärning*) intersection **2** (*tvärsnitt*) cross section **-slag 1** *se genomslagskopia* **2** (*projektils*) penetration **3** *elektr.* disruptive discharge
genomslags|kopia carbon copy **-kraft** penetration; *mil.* penetrative power
genomsläpplig *a5* pervious, permeable
genomsnitt 1 (*genomskärning*) cross section **2** (*medeltal*) average, mean; *i ~ on* [an] average; *under ~et* below average **-lig** *a5* average
genom|snittshastighet average speed **-stekt** well done **-stråla** irradiate
genomström|ma flow through; *~s av floder* be traversed by rivers **-ning** flowing (running) through
genom|ströva roam through **-svettig** wet through with perspiration **-syn** inspection, perusal **-syra** *bildl.* leaven [all through], permeate **-söka** *se genomleta* **-trevlig** delightful, very pleasing **-tryckt** (*om tyg*) printed right through **-tråkig** insufferably dull, very boring
genomträng|a *se tränga* [*igenom*]; (*genomborra*) pierce (*äv. bildl.*); (*tränga in i*) penetrate (*äv. bildl.*); (*sprida sig i*) permeate (*äv. bildl.*) **-ande** *a4* (*om blåst, blick*) piercing; (*om lukt, röst*) penetrating **-lig** *a5* penetrable (*för by*), pervious (*för* to) **-ning** penetration
genom|trött tired out, *vard.* dog-tired **-tänka** meditate upon, think out; *väl -tänkt* well thought out; *ett väl -tänkt tal* a carefully prepared speech **-vakad** *a5, ~ natt* sleepless night **-våt** wet through; (*om kläder*) soaking wet **-vävd** *a5* interwoven; *-vävt tyg* double-faced cloth
geno'typ [j-] *s3* genotype
genre ['ʃaŋer] *s5* genre **-bild** genre picture **-målning** genre painting
genrep [ˣje:n-] *s7* dress rehearsal
gensaga [ˣje:n-] *s1* protest
gensare [ˣgenn-] guernsey
gen|skjuta [ˣje:n-] (*hinna upp*) [take a short cut and] overtake; (*hejda*) intercept **-stridig** *a1*, **-strävig** *a1*, **-störtig** *a1* (*motsträvig*) reluctant, refractory (*mot* to) **-svar** reply; (*genklang, sympati*) response **-sägelse** contradiction; *utan ~* incontestably, indisputably
genteknologi [ˣje:n-] genetic engineering
gentemot [j-] *prep* (*emot*) against; (*i jämförelse med*) in comparison to (with); (*i förhållande t.*) in relation to
gentiana [g- *el.* j-, -t(s)iˣa:na] *s1* gentian
gen'til [ʃaŋ-] *a1* (*fin*) fine, stylish; (*frikostig*) generous, handsome
gentjänst [ˣje:n-] service in return
gentle|man gentleman **-mannamässig** *a1* gentleman-like, gentlemanly
Genua ['je:-] *n* Genoa **Genuabukten** the Gulf of Genoa
genuafock *sjö.* genoa [jib], *vard.* genny, jenny

genu'es [j-] *s3*, **-isk** *a5* Geno[v]ese
genu'in [j-] *a1* genuine; (*utpräglad*) out-and-out; *en ~ snobb* a real snob
genus ['je:-] *n, språkv.* gender
genväg [ˣje:n-] short cut; *~ar är senvägar* a short cut is often the longest way round
geocentrisk [jeⱺ'senn-] *a5* geocentric
geo|de'si [j-] *s3* geodesy, geodetics (*pl, behandlas som sg*) **-'det** *s3* geodesist **-detisk** [-'de:-] *a5* geodetic[al]; *~ linje* geodesic [line]
geofy|'sik [j-] geophysics (*pl, behandlas som sg*) **-iker** [-'fy:-] geophycisist **-isk** [-'fy:-] *a5* geophysical
geo|graf [j-] *s3* geographer **-grafi** *s3* geography **-grafisk** [-'gra:-] *a5* geographic[al]; *~ bredd* latitude; *~ längd* longitude
geoke'm|i [j-] geochemistry **-isk** [-'çe:-] *a5* geochemical
geokronologi [j-] geochronology
geo|log [j-] geologist, geologer **-logi** *s3* geology **-logisk** *a5* geologic[al]
geome'tr|i [j-] *s3* geometry; *analytisk ~* analytical geometry **-iker** [-'me:-] geometer, geometrician **-isk** [-'me:-] *a5* geometric[al]; *~ serie* geometric progression, (*summa*) geometric series; *~t medium* geometric mean
geo|morfologi [j-] geomorphology **-politik** geopolitics (*sg o. pl*)
georgette [ʃår'ʃett] *s5* georgette [crepe]
Georgien [je'årgien *el.* -ji-] *n* Georgian Soviet Socialist Republic, *vard.* Georgia **georgier** [je'årgier *el.* -ji-] Georgian
geo|statik [j-] geostatics (*pl, behandlas som sg*) **-stationär** *~ satellit* geostationary satellite
geotekn|ik [j-] geotechnics (*pl, behandlas som sg*) **-isk** [-'tekn-] *a5* geotechnical
geoterm|alvatten geothermal (hot) water **-isk** geothermal, geothermic; *~ energi* geothermal energy
geovetenskap [ˣje:ⱺ-] geoscience
gepard [je'pa:rd] *s3* cheetah
ge'päck [g-, *äv.* j-] *s7* luggage
gerani|um [je'ra:-] *-en -er* geranium
geria'tr|i[k] [g-] *s3* geriatrics (*pl, behandlas som sg*) **-iker** [-'a:-] geriatrician, geriatrist **-isk** [-'a:-] *a5* geriatric
gerilla [ge'rilla] *s1* guer[r]illa **-krig** guer[r]illa warfare **-rörelse** guer[r]illa movement
gering [ˣje:-] *fack.* mitre **geringslåda** mitre block (box)
ger'man [j-] *s3* Teuton **-ism** *s3* Germanism **-ist** Germanic philologist
germanium [jer'ma:-] *s8* germanium
germansk [-'a:-] *a5* Germanic; Teutonic
geronto|log [g-] gerontologist **-logi** *s3* gerontology **-logisk** *a5* gerontological
gerundium [-'runn-] *s8* gerund
ges *gavs givits el. getts, dep, det ~* (*finns*) there is (are)
ge'schäft [g- *el.* j-] *s7* business
ge'sims [j-, *äv.* g-] *s3* cornice, moulding
gess [j-, *äv.* g-] *s7* G flat **Gess-dur** G flat major
gest [ʃ-] *s3* gesture
ge'stalt [j-] *s3* figure; (*pers.*) character; (*avbildad ~*) image; (*form*) shape, form; *psykol.* gestalt; *ta ~* take on (assume) shape; *i en tigga-*

res ~ in the guise (shape) of a beggar; *en av vår tids största ~er* one of the greatest figures (characters) of our time

gestalta [je'stalta] **1** shape, form, mould; ~ *en roll (äv.)* create a character **2** *rfl (utveckla sig)* turn out; *(arta sig)* shape; *hur framtiden än kommer att ~ sig* no matter what the future holds

gestalt|ning formation; *(form)* form; shape, configuration; *(av roll e.d.)* creation **-nings-förmåga** power of portrayal (creating) characters

gestaltpsykologi Gestalt psychology

gestikuler|a [ʃ-] gesticulate **-ing** gesticulation

ge'säll [j-] *s3* journeyman **-brev** journeyman's certificate **-prov** apprentice's examination work

get [j-] *-en -ter* goat; *(hona)* she-goat **getabock** [ˣje:-] he-goat, billy goat

geting [ˣje:-] wasp **-bo** wasp's nest; *röra om (sticka handen) i ett* ~ stir up a hornet's nest **-midja** wasp waist **-stick** wasp's sting

get|ost goat's-milk cheese **-ragg** goat's wool **-rams** *s3, bot.* Solomon's seal **-skinn** goatskin, kid; *(getfäll)* goat-fell **-väppling** kidney vetch, ladies' fingers

gett [j-] *sup. av giva (ge)*

getto ['gettɔ] *s6* ghetto

getöga goat's eye; *kasta ett* ~ *på* take a quick look at

ge'vär [j-] *s7 (räfflat)* rifle; *(friare)* gun; *för fot* ~*!* order arms!; *i* ~*!* to arms!; *på axel* ~*!* shoulder arms!; *sträcka* ~ lay down one's arms

gevärs|eld rifle fire **-exercis** rifle drill **-faktori** arms manufacturers (factory) **-kolv** [rifle] butt **-kula** [rifle] bullet **-mynning** muzzle **-pipa** [rifle] barrel **-skott** rifle shot **-skytt** rifleman **-stock** gunstock

Ghana [ˣga:-] *n* Ghana **gha|'nan** *s3,* **-ansk** [-'a:-] *a5* Ghanaian

gibbon [-'å:n] *s3* gibbon

Gibraltar sund [ʃi'brall-] the Straits of Gibraltar

gick [jick] *imperf. av gå*

gid [gidd] *s3* guide

giffel ['g- *el.* 'j-] *s2* croissant

1 gift [j-] *s4* poison *(äv. bildl.)*; *(orm- o.d.)* venom *(äv. bildl.)*; *fack.* toxin

2 gift [j-] *a4* married *(med* to)

gifta [ˣjifta] *gifte gift*; ~ *bort* marry off; give away in marriage; ~ *sig* marry *(äv.* ~ *sig med) (av kärlek* for love), get married; ~ *sig för pengar* marry for money; ~ *sig rikt* marry money; ~ *in sig i en familj* marry into a family; ~ *om sig [med]* remarry

giftas|lysten keen on getting married **-tankar** *gå i* ~ be thinking of getting married **-vuxen** old enough to get married, of marriageable age

gift|blandare, -blanderska poisoner **-blåsa** poison bag, venom sac; *bildl.* venomous person **-bägare** poison cup

gifte [j-] *s6* marriage; *barn i första ~t* children of the first marriage

giftermål [j-] marriage; match

giftermåls|anbud offer (proposal) of marriage **-annons** marriage advertisement **-balk** marriage act

gift|fri nonpoisonous, nontoxic **-gas** poison gas

giftig [j-] *a1* poisonous, mephitic[al]; venomous; toxic **-het** poisonousness; venomousness; toxicity; *~er (bildl.)* venomous remarks

gift|mord murder by poison[ing] **-mördare** poisoner

giftoman [ˣjiftɔmann] *jur.* guardian

giftorm poisonous snake

giftorätt [j-] *jur.* widow's (widower's) right to property held jointly

giftorättsgods property held jointly by husband and wife, matrimonial property

gift|pil poisoned arrow **-skåp** poison cupboard **-stadga** poisons act **-tand** [poison] fang **-tecken** poison sign **-verkan** toxic effect

giga [j-] *s1* fiddle

gigant [g- *el.* j-] giant **-isk** *a5* gigantic

gigg [j-] *s2* gig *(äv. sjö.)*

gigolo ['ji:- *el.* 'jigg- *el.* 'ʃ-] *s5* gigolo

gikt [j-] *s3* gout **-bruten** gouty, gout-ridden

gilj|a [j-] woo; court **-are** wooer

giljar|färd, -stråt *dra på* ~ go wooing

giljo'tin [j-] *s3,* **-era** *v1* guillotine

gill [j-] *a5, gå sin ~a gång* be going on just as usual; *tredje gången ~t!* third time lucky!

gill|a *(godkänna)* approve of; *vard. (tycka om)* like, AE. dig; *det ~s inte! (vid lek)* [that's] not fair!, that doesn't count! **-ande** *s6* approval, approbation; *vinna ngns* ~ meet with a p.'s approval

gille [j-] *s6* **1** *(gästabud)* banquet, feast; party **2** *(skrå)* guild; *(samfund)* guild, society

giller ['jill-] *s7* trap, gin; *bildl. äv.* snares *(pl)*

gille[s]stuga *ung.* informal [basement] lounge; AE. *äv.* rumpus room

gillra [j-] set *(en fälla* a trap)

giltig [j-] *a1* valid, effective; current; *(om dokument, överenskommelse)* effectual; *(om biljett äv.)* available; *bli* ~ become valid (effective), come into force; *inget ~t skäl* no just cause **-het** validity; availability; *äga* ~ be in force

giltighetstid period of validity; *förlängning av ~en* extension of the validity; *~ens utgång* expiry

gimmick ['gimm-] *s2* gimmick

1 gin [ji:n] *se 2 gen*

2 gin [jinn *el.* ji:n] *s3, s4* gin

ginnungagap [ˣjinn-] yawning gulf

ginseng ['ginn-] *s2* ginseng

ginst [g-] *s3, bot.* broom, genista

ginstkatt [g-] genet[te]

ginväg *se genväg*

gip[p] *s2, sjö.* gybe, jibe

1 gipa [j-] *s1, se mungipa*

2 gipa *el. gippa* [j-] *v1, sjö.* gybe, jibe

gips [j-] *s3* **1** *(mineral)* gypsum **2** *(gipsmassa)* plaster of Paris, *vard.* plaster

gips|a *(tak e.d.)* plaster; *(lägga förband [på]) äv.* put in plaster [of Paris] **-avgjutning** plaster cast **-figur** plaster figure **-förband** plaster (plaster-of-Paris) cast (bandage) **-katt** plaster cat **-ning** plastering **-platta** plasterboard

gir [j-] *s2,* **gira** [j-] *v1, sjö.* sheer; *(friare)* turn, swerve

gi'raff [ʃ-] *s3* giraffe

girer|a [j-], **-ing** transfer

girig [j-] *a1* avaricious, miserly; (*lysten*) covetous, greedy (*efter* of); *den ~e* the miser **-buk** miser **-het** avariciousness *etc.*; avarice, greed; (*lystnad*) cupidity (*efter* for); (*vinstbegär*) avidity

girland [g- *el.* j-, -'and *el.* -'aŋ(d)] *s3* garland, festoon

giro ['ji:-] *s6* **1** *se* girering **2** (*jfr äv. postgiro*) *se -konto* **-konto** giro account

giss [j-] *s7* G sharp

gissa [j-] guess; (*förmoda*) conjecture; (*sluta sig t.*) divine; *rätt ~t!* you've got it!, right!; *~ sig till* guess, divine; *det kan man inte ~ sig till* that's impossible to guess

gissel ['jiss-] *s7* scourge; *satirens ~* the sting of the satire **-djur** flagellate **-slag** lash with a scourge

gissla [j-] scourge; *bildl. äv.* lash

gisslan [j-] *r* hostage[s *pl*]; *ta ~* seize hostages (a hostage)

gisslare [j-] scourger

gissning [j-] guess; conjecture, surmise; *bara ~ar* (*äv.*) pure guesswork (*sg*)

gissnings|tävlan guessing competition **-vis** at a guess

gisten [j-] *a3* (*om båt, laggkärl*) leaky, open at the joints; (*om golv*) gaping **gistna** become leaky; open at the joints; begin to gape

gi'tarr [j-] *s3* guitar; *akustisk ~* acoustic guitar; *elektrisk ~* electric guitar; *knäppa på ~* twang the guitar **-ackompanjemang** guitar accompaniment **-ist** guitarist

gitt|a [j-] *v1 el. gitte gittat* (*idas*) *bäst hon -er* as much as ever she likes, to her heart's content; *jag -er inte svara* I can't be bothered to answer

gitter ['g- *el.* 'j-] *s7* **1** *fys.* grating; *radio.* grid **2** *miner.* lattice

giv [j-] *s2* deal; *nya ~en* (*i USA*) the New Deal **giva** [j-] *se* ge

giv|akt [j-] *n, se 3 akt; bildl., ett ~* a [word of] warning

giv|ande [j-] *a4* (*fruktbar*) fertile; *bildl. äv.* fruitful; (*lönande*) profitable, rewarding **-are, -arinna** [j-] giver, donor

givas [j-] *se* ges

giv|en [j-] *a3* given; (*avgjord*) clear, evident; *~na förutsättningar* understood prerequisites; *på ett -et tecken* at an agreed sign (signal); *ta för -et att* take it for granted that; *jag tar för -et att* I assume (take it) that; *det är -et!* of course!; *det är en ~ sak* it is a matter of course

giv|etvis [j-] of course, naturally **-it** *sup. av giva* (*ge*)

givmild [*ji:v-] generous, open-handed **-het** generosity, open-handedness

1 gjord [jɷ:rd] *a5* done; made; (*jfr göra*); *historien verkar ~* the story seems to be made-up

2 gjord [jɷ:rd] *s2* girth

gjorde [*jɷ:r-] *imperf. av göra* **gjort** [jɷ:rt] *sup. av göra*

gjut|a [j-] *göt gjutit* **1** (*hälla*) pour **2** (*sprida, låta flöda*) shed **3** *tekn.* cast; (*metall o. glas äv.*) found; (*glas äv.*) press; (*friare*) mould; *rocken sitter som -en* the coat fits like a glove

gjut|are [j-] founder **-eri** [iron] foundry **-form** mould **-gods** *s7* castings (*pl*)

gjut|it [j-] *sup. av gjuta* **-järn** cast iron **-ning** casting *etc.* **-stål** cast steel

g-klav treble (G) clef

glacéhandske kid glove

glaci'al *a5* glacial **-period** glacial period (epoch), ice age

glacio|log glaciologist, glacialist **-logi** *s3* glaciology **-logisk** *a5* glaciologic[al]

glaci'är *s3* glacier **-spricka** crevasse

glad *a1* (*gladlynt*) cheerful; (*upprymd*) merry, jolly, gay; (*lycklig*) happy; (*belåten*) delighted, pleased (*över* at); *~a färger* gay colours; *en ~ lax* (*bildl.*) a jolly chap; *~a nyheter* good news (*sg*); *~ påsk!* [A] Happy Easter!; *G~a änkan* the Merry Widow; *~ och munter* cheerful and gay; *glittrande ~* radiantly happy; *~ som en lärka* [as] happy as a lark; *med glatt hjärta* with a cheerful heart; *göra sig ~a dagar* make a day of it; *vara ~ i* (*t.ex. mat*) be fond of

glada *s1, zool.* [red] kite

gladde *imperf. av* glädja

gladeligen gladly; (*utan svårighet*) easily

gladiator [-ˣa:tår] *s3* gladiator **-spel** gladiatorial games

gladiol|us [-'di:-] *-usen -us, pl äv.* *-er* gladiolus (*pl äv.* gladioli, gladiolus), sword lily

gladlynt [ˣgla:d-] *a1* cheerful; (*glad t. sitt sinne*) good-humoured **-het** cheerfulness; good humour

glam [glamm] *s7* gaiety, merriment **-ma** talk merrily; (*stimma*) be noisy

glamo[u]r [gla'mɷ:r, *äv.* 'glämmə] *s3* glamour **-isera** glamorize **-'ös** *a5* glamo[u]rous

glans *s3* **1** (*glänsande yta*) lustre; (*tygs o.d. äv.*) gloss; (*guld-*) glitter; (*genom gnidning e.d.*) polish; (*sken*) brilliance, brightness; (*bländande*) glare; (*strål-*) radiance **2** (*härlighet, prakt*) magnificence, splendour; (*ära*) glory; *sprida ~ över* shed lustre over; *visa sig i all sin ~* appear (come out) in all its glory **3** *med ~* (*med bravur*) brilliantly, with flying colours, (*utan svårighet*) with great ease **-dagar** *pl* palmy days; heyday (*sg*) **-full** brilliant

glans|ig *a1* glossy; lustrous; (*om papper*) glazed **-[k]is** glassy ice **-lös** lustreless, lacklustre, dull **-nummer** (*persons*) showpiece; (*aftonens*) star turn **-papper** glazed paper **-period** heyday, golden age **-roll** brilliant (celebrated) role **-tid** *se -period*

glapp **I** *s7* backlash; play **II** *a1* loose; *vara ~* (*äv.*) gape **glappa** be loose, gape; (*om skor o.d.*) fit loosely

glas *s7* **1** glass; (*mängd av en dryck äv.*) glassful; (*-varor*) glasswork; *ett ~ mjölk* a glass of milk; *ta ett ~ med ngn* have a jar with s.b.; *gärna ta sig ett ~* be fond of a drink; *han har tagit sig ett ~ för mycket* he has had a drop too much, *vard.* he has one over the eight; *sätta inom ~ och ram* frame [and glaze] **2** *sjö.* bell

glas|a glaze **-artad** [-a:r-] *a5* glassy, glasslike; *~ blick* a glassy look **-assiett** glass side plate **-berget** *sitta på ~* be left on the shelf **-bit** piece of glass **-björk** downy birch **-blåsare** glassblower **-bruk** glassworks (*pl, behandlas som sg*) **-burk** glass jar

glaser|a glaze; *kokk.* frost, ice **-ing** glazing;

frosting, icing
glasfiber glass fibre **-armerad** *a5* reinforced with glass fibre **-plast** glass-fibre plastic **-ull** glass wool **-väv** fibreglass [fabric]
glas|flaska glass bottle **-hal** slippery as glass **-hus** glasshouse; *man skall inte kasta sten när man sitter i ~* those who live in glasshouses should not throw stones **-iglo[o]** bottle bottle bank **-klar** as clear as glass **-kropp** *anat.* vitreous body **-kupa** glass cover; bell jar (glass); *(på lampa)* glass shade **-massa** melted glass **-målning** *~ar (konkr.)* stained glass *(sg)*; *fönster med ~ar* stained-glass window **-mästare** glazier **-mästeri** glaziery **-putsmedel** glass cleaner **-ruta** pane [of glass] **-rör** glass tube
glass *s3* ice cream **-bomb** bombe [glacée]
glas|skiva glass plate (sheet) **-skärva** glass splinter **-slipare** glass grinder (cutter)
glass|pinne ice [cream] **-strut** *(hopskr. glasstrut)* ice-cream cone (cornet) **-stånd** *(hopskr. glasstånd)* ice-cream stall
glas|ull glass wool **-varor** *pl* glasswork, glassware *(sg)* **-veranda** glassed-in veranda, sun lounge
gla'syr *s3* glazing; *(på porslin)* glaze; *kokk.* frosting, icing
glasål glass eel
glasögon *pl* glasses, spectacles, *vard.* specs; *särsk. AE.* eyeglasses; *(stora)* goggles **-bågar** *pl* spectacle frame *(sg)* **-fodral** spectacle case **-orm** cobra
1 glatt *adv* gaily , merrily *etc.*; *bli ~ överraskad* be pleasantly surprised; *det gick ~ till* we *(etc.)* had a very gay time
2 glatt *a1* smooth; *(glänsande)* glossy, sleek; *(hal)* slippery; *~ muskel* smooth muscle; *springa för ~a livet* run for all one is worth
3 glatt *sup. av* glädja
glattmask oligochaete
glaubersalt Glauber['s]salt
glaukom [-'kå:m] *s4* glaucoma
gled *imperf. av* glida
gles *a1 (ej tät, tätt bevuxen o.d.)* thin *(hårväxt* growth of hair; *fläck* spot); *(om vävnad o.d.)* loose; *~ befolkning* sparse population; *~ skog* open forest; *~a tänder* teeth with spaces in between **-befolkad** [-å-] *a5* sparsely populated **-bevuxen** sparsely covered **-bygd** thinly populated area
glesna [ˣgle:s-] grow thin *(etc.)*; *(om hår äv.)* get thin; become [more] open; *leden ~r* the ranks are thinning
gli *s6* **1** *(fiskyngel)* [small] fry *(pl)* **2** *(barnunge)* brat; *~n* small fry *(pl)*
glid *s7* **1** *(glidning)* glide, slide; *med långa ~* with long strides **2** *(glidförmåga, skidföre)* running **3** *på ~* on the glide, going astray
glida *gled glidit* glide; *(över ngt hårt)* slide; *(halka)* slip; *flyg.* sideslip; *(friare)* pass; *~ ifrån* glide away from; *~ isär* drift apart; *~ undan* slip away, *(slingra sig)* dodge, evade; *låta handen ~ över* pass one's hand over
glid|ande *a4 (rörelse)* gliding; *(skala)* sliding **-bana** [sliding] chute, slide
glidflyg|are glider pilot **-ning** gliding, glide **-plan** glider
glid|flykt glide; gliding flight; *flyg.* volplane,

volplaning; *gå ner i ~* volplane **-form** *byggn.* sliding form
glid|it *sup. av glida* **-lager** plain bearing **-ning** gliding, glide; sliding, slide
glimlampa [ˣglimm-] glowlamp **glimma** gleam; *(glittra)* glitter, glisten; *det är inte guld allt som ~r* all is not gold that glitters **glimmer** ['glimm-] **1** *s7* gleam[ing], glitter[ing] **2** *s2, miner.* mica **glimra** *se glimma*
glimt *s2* gleam *(äv. bildl.)*; *(i ögat)* glint, twinkle; *(skymt)* glimpse; *en ~ i ögat* a glint (twinkle) in the eye; *få en ~ av* catch a glimpse of **glimt|a** glance, glimpse, glint **-vis** by glimpses (flashes)
glindra *se glittra, glimma*
glipa *s1* [narrow] gap
gliring gibe, jibe, sneer; dig; *få en ~* be gibed (sneered) at
glitter ['glitt-] *s7* **1** glitter, lustre; *(daggens etc.)* glistening; *(julgrans- e.d.)* tinsel; *(grannlåt)* gewgaws, baubles *(pl)* **2** *bildl. (tomt empty)* show **glittra** glitter, sparkle, shimmer; *~nde glad, se glad*
glo *v4* stare *(på* at); glare, goggle *(på* at)
glob *s3* globe; *(friare äv.)* ball
glo'bal *a5* global; worldwide **-avtal** global agreement
globetrotter ['glåobtrått-] *~n, pl ~s el. ~* globe-trotter
globin *s4* globin **globulin** *s4* globulin
glop *s2* whippersnapper, whipster, jackanapes; *vard.* puppy
glopp [-å-] *s7, se snöglopp*
gloria ['glɔ:-] *s1* **1** *(strålkrans)* halo, glory; *(helgons äv.)* aureole, nimbus **2** *bildl.* nimbus
glori|fiera glorify **-fiering** glorifying, glorification **-ös** *a5* glorious
glos|a *s1* **1** word; vocable **2** *(glåpord)* gibe, jibe, sneer **-bok** vocabulary [notebook]; *(tryckt)* glossary, vocabulary
glossarium [glås'sa:-] *s4* glossary
glosögd *a5* popeyed, fisheyed
glottis ['glått-] *best. form* = glottis **-stöt** glottal stop
gloxinia [glå'xi:-] *s1* gloxinia
glufsa *~ i sig [maten]* gobble up (down) [one's food]
glugg *s2* hole, aperture
glukagon [-'ga:n] *s4* glucagon
glukos [-'å:s] *s3* glucose **-'id** *s3* glucoside
glunkas *det ~s* there is a rumour *(om* about; *om att* that)
glup|a *se glufsa* **-ande** *a4* ravenous *(aptit* appetite); voracious; *~ ulvar* ravening wolves
glupsk *a1* greedy; *(omättlig)* voracious, ravenous, gluttonous **-het** greed[iness]; voracity, gluttony
glutamat *s4* glutamate
gluten ['glu:-] *best. form* = el. -et gluten
glutta peep, glance
glyce'r|id *s3* glyceride **-'in** *s3, s4, se glycerol*
glycerol [-'å:l] *s3* glycerol, glycerin[e]
glykol [-'kå:l] *s3* ethanediol, [ethylene] glycol
glykos [-'kå:s] *s3, se glukos* **-'id** *s3* glycoside
glytt *s2* lad
glåmig *a1* washed out; *blek och ~* pale and washed out; *~ ansikte* wheyface **-het** washed-out

appearance; sallowness
glåpord taunt, scoff, jeer
gläd|ja [-ä:-] *gladde glatt* **1** give pleasure; make happy, please; (*starkare*) delight; ~ *ngn med ett besök* give s.b. pleasure by visiting him (*etc.*); *det -er mig* I am so glad [of that (to hear it)]; *om jag kan ~ dig därmed* if it will be any pleasure to you **2** *rfl* be glad (delighted) (*åt, över* at, about); rejoice (*åt, över* in, at); *kunna ~ sig åt ngt (åtnjuta)* enjoy s.th.; *jag -er mig mycket åt att få träffa dig* I am looking forward very much to seeing you
glädj|ande [-ä:-] *a4* joyful, pleasant (*nyheter* news [*sg*]); (*tillfredsställande*) gratifying (*resultat* result); ~ *nog* fortunately enough; *en ~ tilldragelse i familjen* a happy event in the family **-as** *gladdes glatts, dep, se* **glädja** 2
glädje [-ä:-] *s3* joy (*över* at); (*nöje*) pleasure (*över* in); (*starkare*) delight (*över* at); ([*känsla av*] *lycka*) happiness; (*munterhet*) mirth; (*tillfredsställelse*) satisfaction; *i ~ och sorg* in joy and sorrow; *med ~* (*äv.*) gladly; *till min stora ~* to my great delight; *bereda ngn ~* give s.b. happiness (*etc.*); *finna ~ i, ha ~ av* find (take) pleasure (*etc.*) in (*att göra* doing); *gråta av ~* weep for joy; *känna ~ över* feel joy (rejoice) at; *vara till ~ för* be a joy (*etc.*) to; *vara utom sig av ~* be beside o.s. with joy; *~n stod högt i tak* [the] mirth ran high; *det var en sann ~ att se* it was a real treat to see; *han har haft mycken ~ av sina barn* his children have been a great joy to him
glädje|bud[skap] good tidings (*pl*); *ett ~* (*friare*) wonderful (a wonderful piece of) news **-dödare** kill-joy; *vard.* wet blanket **-fattig** *se* **-lös** **-flicka** prostitute **-hus** brothel **-källa** source of joy **-lös** joyless; cheerless **-rik** full of joy, joyful **-rop** cry (shout) of joy **-rus** transport of joy, rapture **-spridare** bringer of happiness; (*barn*) ray of sunshine **-språng** leap for joy, caper **-strålande** radiant (beaming) [with joy] **-tjut** shout of joy **-tårar** *pl* tears of joy **-yra** whirl of happiness **-yttring** manifestation of joy **-ämne** subject for (of) rejoicing
gläfs *s7* yelp, yap **gläfsa** *v3* yelp, yap (*på* at)
gläns|a *v3* shine (*av, med* with) (*äv. bildl.*); glitter; (*om tårar, ögon*) glisten; (*om sidan e.d.*) be lustrous **-ande** *a4* shining *etc.*, shiny; (*om ögon*) lustrous; (*om sidan e.d.*) glossy; *bildl.* brilliant, splendid
glänt *s, i uttr.: stå på ~* stand (be) ajar
glänta I *s1* (*skogs-*) glade **II** *v1*, ~ *på* open slightly
glätta smooth; (*papper*) glaze; (*läder*) sleek; (*polera*) polish
glättig *a1* gay; cheerful, light-hearted **-het** gaiety; cheerfulness *etc.*
glättning smoothing; glazing *etc.*
glöd *s7, s3* **1** (*glödande kol*) live coal; (*koll. ofta*) embers (*pl*) **2** (*glödande sken o. bildl.*) glow; (*hetta*) heat; (*lidelse*) passion; *bildl. äv.* ardour, fervour
glöd|a *v2* glow (*av* with); *i sht bildl.* be [all] aglow (*av* with); (*om järn o.d.*) be red-hot; (*brinna*) burn **-ande** *a4* glowing; (*om järn*) red-hot (*äv. bildl.*); (*häftig*) burning, ardent,

fervent; ~ *hat* fiery hatred; *samla ~ kol på ngns huvud* heap coals of fire on a p.'s head
glödg|a [ˣglöddga] make red-hot; (*stål*) anneal; (*vin*) mull; (*göra glödande*) ignite **-ning** (*av järn o.d.*) [the] bringing of...to a red heat; (*av stål*) annealing
glöd|het red-hot, white-hot, glowing **-lampa** [light] bulb; *fack.* incandescent lamp **-steka** grill; fry on the embers **-strumpa** incandescent mantle **-ström** filament current **-tråd** filament **-tändning** ignition by incandescence
glögg *s2, ung.* mulled and spiced wine
glöm|ma *v2* forget; (*försumma*) neglect; (*kvarglömma*) leave [behind], forget; ~ *bort* forget; *man -mer så lätt* one is apt to forget; *jag har -t vad han heter* I forget his name; *jag hade alldeles -t* [*bort*] *det* (*äv.*) it had entirely escaped (slipped) my memory (mind); ~ *sig* (*förgå sig*) forget o.s.; ~ *sig själv* be forgetful of o.s.; ~ *sig kvar* stay on
glöm|sk *a5* forgetful; absent-minded; (*ej aktande på*) unmindful (*av sina plikter* of one's duties); oblivious (*av omgivningen* of one's surroundings); *vara ~* (*av sig*) have a bad memory, be absent-minded **-ska** *s1* **1** forgetfulness; *av ren ~* out of sheer forgetfulness **2** (*förgätenhet*) oblivion; *falla i ~* be forgotten, fall into oblivion
g-moll G minor
gnabb *s7* bickering[s *pl*], wrangling[s *pl*], tiff; *AE.* spat **-as** *dep* bicker, wrangle
gnag|a *v2* gnaw (*på* at); (*knapra*) nibble; ~ *sig* gnaw its (*etc.*) way (*igenom* through) **-ande** *a4* nagging (*oro* worry); *bildl. äv.* fretting, worrying **-are** *zool.* rodent
gnat *s7* nagging (*på* at; *över* about); cavilling (*på, över* at) **gnata** nag, cavil (*på* at) **gnatig** *a1* nagging; ~ *av sig* fretful, peevish
gned *imperf. av* **gnida**
gnejs *s3* gneiss
gnet *-en gnetter* (*lusägg*) nit
gnet|a write in a crabbed hand **-ig** *a1* (*om handstil*) crabbed
gnid|a *gned gnidit* rub; (*friare*) scrape (*äv. ~ på*); (*för att värma*) chafe; (*snåla*) pinch **-are** miser, skinflint **-ig** *a1* stingy, miserly, mean **-it** *sup. av* **gnida** **-ning** rubbing *etc.*; *fys.* friction
gnissel [ˈgnissˈ] *s7* **1** screech[ing] *etc.*, *se* **gnissla 2** *bildl.* (*slitningar*) jars (*pl*); (*knot*) croak, croaking **gnissla** screech; (*om gångjärn e.d.*) creak; (*om hjul e.d.*) squeak; (*knorra*) croak; ~ [*med*] *tänder[na]* grind (gnash) one's teeth; *det ~r i maskineriet* (*bildl.*) things are not working smoothly
gnist|a *s1* **1** spark (*äv. bildl.*); (*genialitet*) spark of genius; *den tändande ~n* (*bildl.*) the igniting spark; *ha ~n* have the spark of genius; *spruta -or* give off sparks, *bildl.* flash **2** (*uns*) vestige, shade, particle; *en ~ hopp* a ray of hope; *en ~ sunt förnuft* a vestige of common sense **-bildning** formation of sparks, sparking **-galler** fireguard, fire screen **-gap** spark gap
gnist|ra emit sparks; (*blixtra*) sparkle; *i sht bildl.* flash (*av vrede* with rage); **-nde kvickhet** sparkling wit; *få ett slag så det ~r för ögonen* get a blow that makes one see stars **-regn** shower of sparks

gno *v4* **1** (*gnugga*) rub **2** (*arbeta*) toil (work) [away] (*med* at) **3** (*springa*) run (*för brinnande livet* for dear life); ~ *på a*) (*arbeta*) work away, *b*) (*springa*) run hard[er], scurry

gnola hum; ~ *på en melodi* hum a tune

gnom [-å:-] *s3* gnome

gnost|icism [-å-] Gnosticism **-iker** ['gnåss-] *s9*, **-isk** ['gnåss-] *a5* Gnostic

gnu *s3* gnu

gnugg|a rub (*sig i ögonen* one's eyes); (*plugga med*) vard. cram **-bild** transfer picture **-bokstav** transfer letter

gnugg|is *s2, se gnuggbild, gnuggbokstav* **-ning** rub[bing]

gnutta *s1* particle, tiny bit

gny I *s6* din; (*vapen-*) clatter; (*brus*) roar; *bildl.* cry-out, disturbance **II** *v4* **1** (*dåna*) roar; (*om vapen*) clatter; (*larma*) clamour **2** (*jämra sig*) whimper

gnägg *s7*, vard. (*skratt*) neigh, whinny **gnägga** neigh; (*lågt*) whinny (*äv. bildl.*) **gnäggning** neigh[ing]

gnäll *s7* **1** (*gnissel*) creak[ing], squeak[ing] **2** (*klagan*) whining, whine, whimper; (*småbarns*) puling; (*knot*) grumbling **gnälla** *v2* **1** (*om dörrar e.d.*) creak, squeak **2** (*klaga*) whine, whimper; (*om småbarn*) pule; (*yttra sitt missnöje med*) grumble (*över* about, at); (*gnata*) nag

gnäll|ig *a1* **1** (*gnisslande*) creaking *etc.*, creaky **2** (*klagande*) whining; (*om röst äv.*) strident, shrill; (*som yttrar sitt missnöje*) grumpy **-måns** *s2* croaker, whiner; (*barn*) crybaby

gnöla vard. grumble (*över* at)

gobe'läng *s3* Gobelin [tapestry], tapestry

god *gott bättre bäst* (*jfr gott*) good (*mot* to); (*vänlig*) kind (*mot* to); (*välvillig*) kindly; (*utmärkt*) excellent, first-rate, (*i ledigare stil*) capital; (*tillfredsställande*) satisfactory; (*välsmakande o.d. äv.*) nice; ~ *dag!* good morning (afternoon, evening)!, (*vid första mötet med ngn*) how do you do!; ~ *morgon!* good morning!; ~ *natt!* good night!; ~ *man* (*boutredningsman*) executor, (*konkursförvaltare*) trustee, (*förordnad av domstol*) administrator, receiver; *en* ~ *vän* a good (great) friend; *denna världens* ~*a* the good things of this world; *av* ~ *familj* of a good family; *för den* ~*a sakens skull* for the good of the cause; *för mycket av det* ~*a* too much of a good thing; *i* ~*an ro* in peace and quiet; *på mången* ~ *dag* for many a long day; *på* ~*a grunder* for good (sound) reasons; *på* ~ *svenska* in good Swedish; *bli* ~ *tvåa* come in a good second; *här finns* ~ *plats* there is plenty of room here; *gå i* ~ *för* vouch for; *ha* ~ *lust att* have a good mind to; *hålla* (*anse*) *sig för* ~ *att* consider it beneath one to; *lägga ett gott ord för* put in a [good] word for; *inte* ~ *att tas med* not easy to deal with; *var så* ~! *a*) (*när man ger ngt*) here you are [Madam (Sir)]!, *b*) (*ta för er*) help yourself, please!, *c*) (*ja, naturligtvis*) by all means!; *var så* ~ *och...*, *vill ni vara så* ~ *och...* please..., will you [kindly]...; *vara* ~ *för 5 000 pund* be good for 5,000 pounds; *vara på* ~ *väg att* be well on the way to; *vara vid gott mod* be of good courage; *han är inte* ~ *på dig* he's got it in for you; *det har det* ~*a med sig att man kan* the advantage of this is that

Godahoppsudden [-*håps-] the Cape of Good Hope

god|artad [-a:r-] *a5* (*lindrig, ej elakartad*) nonmalignant, benign **-bit** titbit (*äv. bildl.*), dainty morsel -'**dag** *se god* [*dag*] **-dagspilt** [*gω:d-] bon vivant, easy-going chap **-het** goodness *etc., jfr god; ha* ~*en att* be kind enough to **-hetsfullt** kindly **-hjärtad** [-j-] *a5* kind-hearted

godis ['gω:-] oböjligt *s, se godsaker*

god|känd *a5* approved (*som* as); *bli* ~ [*i examen*] pass [one's examination] **-känna** approve (*ngn som* s.b. as); (*förslag e.d.*) approve of, sanction; (*i examen*) pass; (*gå med på äv.*) agree to; accept (*en leverans* a delivery; *som bevis* as evidence; *en växel* a bill of exchange) **-kännande** *s6* approval, approbation; sanction; admission; acceptance

god|lynt *a4* good-humoured, good-tempered **-modig** good-natured **-morgon, -natt** *se god* [*morgon, natt*] **-nattkyss** good-night kiss

godo *i uttr.:* *i* ~ amicably, in a friendly spirit; *uppgörelse i* ~ amicable settlement, *jur.* settlement out of court; *mig till* ~ in my favour; *håll till* ~! *a*) (*ta för er*) please help yourself!, *b*) (*svar på tack*) you are welcome [to it]!; *hålla till* ~ *med* [have to] put up with; *komma ngn till* ~ be of use to s.b.; *räkna ngn ngt till* ~ (*äv. bildl.*) put s.th. down to a p.'s credit; *får jag ha det till* ~ *till en annan gång?* can I leave it standing over for some future occasion?, *AE.* can I take a raincheck?

gods [gωtts, *äv.* gωdds] *s7* **1** (*egendom*) property; (*ägodelar*) possessions (*pl*); ~ *och guld* money and possessions **2** (*varor, last*) goods (*pl*); *AE.* freight; *lättare* ~ (*bildl.*) light wares (*pl*) **3** (*material*) material **4** (*jorda-*) estate, manor **5** *sjö., löpande* (*stående*) ~ running (standing) rigging

godsaker *pl* (*sötsaker*) sweets; vard. goodies; *AE.* candy (*sg*)

gods|befordran conveyance of goods, goods traffic **-expedition** goods (*AE.* freight) office **-finka** luggage van; goods waggon; *AE.* boxcar, freight car **-inlämning** goods [forwarding] office; *AE.* freight office **-magasin** goods depot, warehouse **-trafik** goods traffic; *AE.* freight traffic (service) **-tåg** goods (*AE.* freight) train **-vagn** *se godsfinka* **-ägare** estate owner, landed proprietor; ~*n* the landlord

god|ta[ga] accept, approve [of] **-tagande** *s6* acceptance, approval **-tagbar** [-a:g-] *a5* acceptable

godtemplar|e [*gω:d- el. -*temm-] Good Templar **-loge** [-lå:ʃ] Good-Templar lodge **-orden** the [Independent] Order of Good Templars

godtrogen credulous, unsuspecting **-het** credulity

godtrosförvärv *jur.* acquisition made in good faith

godtyck|e 1 (*gottfinnande*) discretion, pleasure, will; *efter eget* ~ at one's own discretion **2** (*egenmäktighet*) arbitrariness; *rena* ~*t* pure arbitrariness **-lig** *a1* **1** (*vilken som helst*) just any, fortuitous **2** (*egenmäktig*) arbitrary; (*nyckfull*) capricious; (*utan grund*) gratuitous **-lighet 1**

fortuitousness **2** arbitrariness *etc.*
godvil|lig voluntary **-ligt** *adv* voluntarily, of one's own free will
goffrer|a [-å-] *v1*, **-ing** *s2* goffer, gauffer
goja [ˣgåjja] *s1* **1** *se papegoja* **2** *vard.* rubbish, bosh; *prata ~* talk through one's hat
gol *imperf. av 1 gala*
1 golf [-å-] *s3* (*havsvik*) gulf
2 golf [-å-] *s3* (*spel*) golf
golf|bana golf course (links *vanl. sg*) **-boll** golf ball **-byxor** *pl* plus fours **-klubb** golf club **-klubba** golf club **-spelare** golfer, golf player
Golfströmmen the Gulf Stream
Golgata [ˈgållgata] *n* Calvary; Golgotha
golv [-å-] *s7* floor; (*-beläggning*) flooring; *från ~ till tak* from floor to ceiling; *falla i ~et* fall to the floor
golv|a [-å-] *sport.* floor **-beläggning** flooring **-bonare** floor polisher **-borste** [floor] brush **-brunn** draining gutter **-bräda** floorboard **-drag** draught along (through) the floor **-lampa** floor lamp **-list** skirting board; *AE.* base-board **-läggare** floor-layer, floorer **-mopp** [floor] mop **-raka** *s1* floor squeegee **-ur** grandfather (longcase) clock **-vård** floor care **-vårdsmaskin** floor-care machine **-växel** (*i bil*) floor[-mounted] gearshift **-yta** floor area (space); surface of a floor
gom [gɔmm] *s2* palate **-segel** soft palate; velum **-spalt** cleft palate
gon [-å:-] *s3* (*nygrad*) grade
gona *rfl* relax to one's heart's content
goˈnad *s3, biol.* gonad
gondol [gån'då:l] *s3* **1** gondola **2** (*ballongkorg*) car **-'jär** *s3* gondolier
gonggong [ˣgåŋgåŋ] *s3, s2* [dinner] gong; *~en har gått* the gong has gone; *räddad av ~en* saved by the bell
gonokock [-'kåck] *s3* gonococcus (*pl* gonococci) **gonor'ré** *s3* gonorrhoea
gordisk [ˈgå:r-] *a5, ~ knut* Gordian knot
gorgonzola [gårgånˣså:la] *s1* Gorgonzola [cheese]
gorilla [-ˣilla] *s1* gorilla (*äv. bildl., vard.*)
gorm|a [-å-] brawl; kick up a row (*för, om* about) **-ande** *s6* brawl, racket, row
gorån [ˣgɔ:-] *s7* wafer
gosa *v1, ~ med* cuddle
gossaktig [-å-] *a1* boyish
gosse [-å-] *s2* boy; lad; *mammas ~* mother's boy; *gamle ~!* old boy (chap, fellow)! **-barn** boy child; [baby] boy **-lynne** youthful outlook, optimism
gosskör boys' choir
got [gɔ:t, *äv.* gå:t] *s3* Goth **-'ik** *s3*, **-isk** [ˈgɔ:-, *äv.* ˈgå:-] *a5*, **-iska** [ˈgɔ:-, *äv.* ˈgå:-] *s2* Gothic
Gotland [ˈgått-] *n* Got[h]land **gotländsk** [ˣgått-] *a5* Got[h]land
gott [-å-] (*jfr god*) **I** *s* (*sötsaker*) *se godsaker* **II** *a o.* oböjligt *s* **1** *varmt och ~* nice and warm; *~ och väl en vecka* at least a week; *det var inte ~ att veta* how could I (he *etc.*) know; *det vore lika ~ att* it would be just as well to; *det är ~ och väl, men* it's all very well, but **2** *göra mycket ~* do a great deal of good; *ha ~ av* [derive] benefit from; *önska ngn allt ~* wish s.b. every happiness **3** *~ om a*) (*tillräckligt*

med) plenty of, *b*) (*mycket*) a great many (deal of), *vard.* lots of; *på ~ och ont* that cuts both ways **III** *adv* well; (*starkare*) capitally, excellently; (*lätt*) easily, very well; (*medgivande*) very well; *kort och ~ a*) (*i korthet*) briefly, *b*) (*helt enkelt*) simply; *så ~ som* practically, almost, all but; *finna för ~* think fit (proper); *göra så ~ man kan* do one's best; *komma ~ överens* get on well; *leva ~* live well (sumptuously); *lukta (smaka) ~* smell (taste) nice; *må så ~!* take care of yourself!; *skratta ~* laugh heartily; *sova ~* sleep soundly, (*som vana*) sleep well; *det kan ~ hända* it may very well happen
gott|a [-å-] *rfl* have a good time; *~ sig åt* thoroughly enjoy **-er** *se godsaker* **-finnande** *s6*, *efter [eget] ~* as one thinks best, according to one's own choice
gottgör|a **1** (*ersätta*) make good (*ngn ngt* to s.b. s.th.), make up (*ngn ngt* to s.b. for s.th.), recompense; (*för skada äv.*) indemnify, compensate **2** (*försona*) make good, make up for; (*reparera*) redress, repair; (*kreditera*) credit **3** *rfl* allow o.s. **-else** [-jö:-] (*ersättning*) compensation, indemnification, recompense; (*betalning*) remuneration, payment; (*skadestånd*) indemnity
gottis [-å-] *oböjligt s, se godsaker*
gottköps|affär bargain store, cut-price shop; *AE.* cut-rate store **-pris** *till ~* at a bargain price **-varor** *pl* cheap-line goods
gottskriv|a credit; *~ ngn ett belopp* credit s.b. with an amount **-ning** credit[ing]
gottsugen *a5*, *vara ~* (*just nu*) feel like s.th. sweet to eat, (*alltid*) have a sweet tooth
gouache [goˈaʃ] *s5* gouache; (*tekniken äv.*) body colour
gourˈmand [gɔrˈmaŋ(d)] *s3* go[u]rmand **-ˈmé** *s3* gourmet
gouterad [gɔˈte:-] *a5* appreciated, acclaimed
grabb *s2* chap; *AE.* fellow
grabba *~ tag i* grab [hold of], lay hands on; *~ åt (för) sig* grab for o.s., appropriate; cop **-tag** *se grabbtag*
grabb|näve [big] fist[ful] **-tag** grab
grace [gra:s] *s5* **1** (*behag*) grace[fulness], charm **2** (*gunst*) favour; *fördela sina ~r* spread one's favours **gracerna** [ˈgra:s-] *de tre ~* the three Graces
graˈci|l [-s-] *a1* gracile, slender **-ˈös** *a1* graceful
1 grad *a, n sg obest. form saknas, tekn.* (*rak*) straight; (*jämn*) even
2 grad *s3, tekn.* burr
3 grad *s3* **1** degree; (*omfattning*) extent; *i hög ~* to a great extent, highly, exceedingly (*intressant* interesting); *i högsta ~* extremely, exceedingly; *till den ~ oförskämd* so terribly insolent **2** (*vinkelmått, temperaturenhet, mat.*) degree; *i 90 ~ers vinkel* at an angle of 90 degrees; *på 90 ~ers nordlig bredd* at 90 degrees North Latitude; *15 ~er kallt* 15 degrees below freezing point (zero) **3** (*rang*) rank, grade; (*doktors-*) [doctor's] degree; *tjänsteman av lägre ~* a minor official, a low-salaried worker; *stiga i ~erna* rise in the ranks
gradbeteckning badge of rank

grader|a *tekn.* graduate; calibrate; (*friare*) grade (*efter* according to) **-ing** *tekn.* graduation; calibration; (*friare*) gradation, grading

gradient *fys., mat.* gradient

grad|indelning division into degrees; graduation **-skillnad** difference of (in) degree **-skiva** protractor **-tal** *mat.* degree; *vid höga ~ (temperaturer)* at high temperature

gradu'al|avhandling doctor's dissertation **-psalm** gradual

gradvis I *adv* by degrees, gradually **II** *a5* gradual

graf *s3, mat.* graph

gra'fem *s7, språkv.* grapheme

graffit|o [-'fi:tå] *-on -i* graffito

gra'f|ik *s3, abstr.* graphic arts (*pl*); *konkr.* prints (*pl*) **-iker** ['gra:-] graphic artist, printmaker **-isk** ['gra:-] *a5* graphic[al]; *~ framställning* graphic representation, (*kurva*) graph, diagram; *~ industri* printing industry

gra'fit *s3* graphite

grafo|log graphologist **-logi** *s3* graphology **-logisk** *a5* graphologic[al]

grahamsmjöl graham flour

gram [-amm] *s7* gram[me] **-atom** gram atom, gramatomic weight **-kalori** [gram] calorie

gramma't|ik *s3* grammar **-ikalisk** [-'ka:-] *a5* grammatical[ly correct] **-iker** [-'matt-] grammarian **-isk** [-'matt-] *a5* grammatical **-iskt** [-'matt-] *adv, det är ~ fel* it is bad grammar

grammofon [-'få:n] *s3* gramophone, record-player; *AE.* phonograph **-inspelning** recording; *konkr.* disc **-musik** gramophone music **-skiva** [gramophone] record, disc **-stift** gramophone needle

grammolekyl gram molecule, grammolecular weight

gramse *oböjligt a, vara ~ på ngn* bear s.b. a grudge

1 gran *s7* (*vikt*) grain

2 gran *s2* **1** (*träd*) fir; spruce; *vanlig ~* Norway spruce **2** (*virke*) fir; spruce

1 granat *bot.* pomegranate [shrub, tree]

2 granat (*ädelsten*) garnet

3 granat *mil.* shell; (*hand-*) [hand] grenade

granat|eld shellfire **-gevär** recoilless antitank rifle **-kastare** trench mortar (gun)

granatsmycke set of garnets

granatsplitter shell splinter

granatäpple pomegranate

granbarr fir (spruce) needle

1 grand *s7* **1** *~et och bjälken* the mote and the beam **2** (*aning*) atom, whit; *litet ~* just a little (wee bit); *inte göra ett skapande[s] ~* not do a [single] mortal thing; *vänta litet ~* wait a little (a minute)

2 grand *s3* (*titel*) grandee

grandezza [-'dessa] *s1* grandeur, dignity

grandios [-i'å:s] *a1* grandiose

gra'nit *s3* granite **-block** granite block **-klippa** granite rock

gran|kotte fir (spruce) cone **-kvist** fir (spruce) twig

1 grann *se 1 grand 2*

2 grann *a1* **1** (*brokig*) gaudy, gay; (*lysande*) brilliant; (*prålig*) gorgeous, showy **2** (*ståtlig*) fine[-looking]; (*om väder*) magnificent **3** (*hög-*

travande) high-flown, high-sounding, fine

grann|e *s2* neighbour **-fru** neighbour['s wife] **-gård** neighbouring house (farm *etc.*); *i ~en* at the next house (*etc.*) [to ours]

grannlag|a *oböjligt a* (*finkänslig*) tactful; considerate; (*ömtålig*) delicate **-enhet** tactfulness *etc.*; discretion, delicacy

grannland neighbouring country; *vårt södra ~* our neighbour-country to the south

grannlåt *s3* show, display; *~[er]* gewgaws, (*floskler*) pretty phrases

grann|skap *s7* neighbourhood, vicinity **-sämja** neighbourliness, [good] neighbourship

granntyckt *a1* fastidious, overparticular (*i, på* in)

gran|ris fir (spruce) twigs (*pl*) **-ruska** fir (spruce) branch

gransk|a examine, scrutinize; scan; (*kontrollera*) check; (*recensera*) review; (*rätta*) correct; *~nde blick* scrutinizing (critical) look **-are** examiner **-ning** examining *etc.*; examination, scrutiny; (*kontroll*) checkup **-nings-arvode** inspection (scrutiny) fee

granskog fir (spruce) forest

granul|at *s7* granulated (granular) material **-era** granulate **-ering** granulation

granvirke fir (spruce) timber; (*sågat*) white deal

grapefrukt [ˣgrejp-] grapefruit

grasser|a (*om sjukdom*) rage, be prevalent (rife); (*om missbruk o.d.*) run (be) rampant **-ande** *a4* rife, prevalent; rampant

gratierna ['gratsi-] *se gracerna*

gratifikation gratuity, bonus

gratin [-'täŋ] *s3, se gratäng* **-era** [-'ti'ne:-] bake in a gratin dish; *~d* au gratin

gratis ['gra:- *el.* ˣgra:-] *adv o. oböjligt a* free [of charge], gratuitous; *~ och franko* delivered free, carriage (postage) paid **-aktie** bonus share **-biljett** complimentary ticket, free ticket (pass) **-emission** bonus issue **-erbjudande** free offer **-exemplar** *se friexemplar* **-föreställning** free performance **-nöje** free entertainment **-prov** free sample, hand-out **-värme** incidental heat gain

grattis ['gratt-] *interj, äv. s, vard.* congratulations! (*pl*)

gratul|ant congratulator **-ation** congratulation; *hjärtliga ~er på födelsedagen* many happy returns [of the day] **-ationskort** greetings card **-era** congratulate (*till* on)

gra'täng *s3* gratin; *~ på fisk* baked fish

1 grav *s2* **1** grave; (*murad e.d.*) tomb; *på ~ens brädd* (*bildl.*) on the brink of the grave; *tyst som i ~en* [as] silent as the grave **2** (*dike*) trench (*i sht mil.*), ditch **3** (*grop*) pit, hole

2 grav *a1* (*svår*) serious

3 grav *a1 ~ accent* grave accent

grava *kokk.* pickle raw

gravallvarlig very solemn

gravand *zool.* common shelduck (*hane äv.* sheldrake)

gravation encumbrance, mortgage

gravations|bevis abstract of the register of land charges; (*i Storbritannien äv.*) certificate of search **-fri** unencumbered, unmortgaged

1 gravera *jur.* encumber; *~nde omständigheter* (*friare*) aggravating circumstances

2 gravera (*inrista*) engrave
graver|ing engraving **-nål** engraving needle
grav|fynd grave find **-fält** grave field **-häll** grave slab **-hög** barrow, mound
gra'vid *a, n sg obest. form undviks* pregnant **-itet** pregnancy **-itetstest** pregnancy test
gravita|tion gravitation, gravity **-tionslagen** the (Newton's) law of gravitation
gravite|ra gravitate (*åt* towards) **-tisk** *a5* grave, solemn; (*friare*) pompous
grav|kammare sepulchral chamber, sepulchre **-kapell** mortuary chapel **-kor** *s7* crypt **-kulle** grave, mound
gravlax *kokk.* raw spiced salmon
grav|lik *a5* sepulchral; *med* ~ *stämma* in a sepulchral voice; ~ *tystnad* deathly quiet **-monument** monument; memorial **-plats** burial ground; [piece of ground for a] grave **-plundrare** grave robber **-plundring** grave robbery
gravrost deep-seated rust
grav|skick burial custom **-skrift 1** (*inskrift*) epitaph **2** (*minnesord*) memorial words (*pl*) **-skändning** grave desecration **-sten** gravestone, tombstone **-sänka** *geol.* rift valley **-sättning** interment **-urna** sepulchral urn **-valv** tomb; crypt **-vård** memorial stone, sepulchral monument; *jfr -sten*
gra'vyr *s3* engraving
gravöl funeral feast
gravör engraver
grede'lin *a5* heliotrope, mauve, lilac
gregoriansk [-'a:-] *a5*, ~*a kalendern* the Gregorian calendar; ~ *sång* Gregorian chant, plainsong, plainchant
grej [-ejj] *s3* thing, article; ~*or* (*vard.*) paraphernalia, tackle (*sg*), gear (*sg*) **greja** fix, put right; ~ *med bilen* work on (tinker with) the car
grek *s3* Greek **-cypriot** Greek Cypriot[e] **-inna** [-ˣinna] Greek woman
grek|isk ['gre:-] *a5* Greek; (*antik äv.*) Grecian **-iska 1** (*språk*) Greek **2** *se grekinna*
grekisk|-katolsk, --ortodox ~*a kyrkan* the Eastern Orthodox Church, the Greek [Orthodox] Church; *en* ~ *trosbekännare* a member of the Eastern Orthodox Church **--romersk** ~ *brottning* Greco-Roman wrestling
Grekland ['gre:k-] *n* Greece
gren *s2* **1** branch (*äv. bildl.*); limb, bough; (*av flod e.d.*) arm **2** (*förgrening*) fork; (*skrev*) crotch, crutch **grena** *rfl* branch, fork
Grenada [-ˣna:-] *n* Grenada **grenadier** [-'na:-] *s9* Grenadian
grena'din 1 (*fruktsaft*) grenadine **2** (*råsilke*) grenadine
grenadisk [-'na:-] *a5* Grenadian
grenad'jär *s3* grenadier
gren|ig *a1* branched; *bot.* ramose **-klyka** fork of a bough **-ljus** branched candle **-rör** branch pipe; manifold
grensla straddle, bestride **grensle** astride (*över* of); *sitta* ~ straddle
grenverk [network of] branches
grep *imperf. av* **gripa**
grep *s2* pitchfork
1 grepe *s2, se* **grep**
2 grepe *s2* (*handtag*) handle

grepp *s7* grasp (*i, om* of); (*vid brottning o. bildl.*) grip (*i, om* of); (*tag äv.*) hold; *mus.* touch; *nya* ~ new methods, moves; *få* ~ *på ett ämne* grasp (get the hang of) a subject; *ha ett gott* ~ (*bildl.*) have the knack **-bräde** *mus.* fingerboard
greve *s2* count; (*i Storbritannien*) earl; ~*n* (*vid tilltal*) Your Lordship, My Lord; *i* ~*ns tid* in the nick of time **-titel** title of count (earl) **-värdighet** countship, earldom
grev|inna countess; ~*n* (*vid tilltal*) Your Ladyship, My Lady **-lig** *a5, ett* ~*t gods* a count's (*etc.*) estate; *upphöjas i* ~*t stånd* be created (made) an earl **-skap** *s7* **1** (*område*) county **2** *se grevevärdighet*
griffel *s2* slate pencil **-tavla** slate
grift *s3* tomb, grave
grifte|ro quiet of the tomb **-tal** funeral oration
griljera grill (roast, fry) after coating with egg and breadcrumbs
grill *s2* grill, gridiron, *vard.* grid; (*-rum*) grill, grillroom; (*på bil*) grill[e]
grill|a grill **-bar** *s3* rotisserie
griller ['grill-] *pl* fads, fancies, whims
grill|korv sausage for grilling **-panna** grill pan **-restaurang** grillroom **-spett** skewer, brochette
gri'mas *s3* grimace; *göra en* ~ pull (make) a [wry] face **-era** pull (make) faces, grimace
grimma *s1* halter
grin *s7* **1** *se* **grimas 2** (*flin*) grin; (*hån-*) leer **3** (*gråt*) whine **grina 1** *se* **grimasera**; ~ *illa* pull faces (*åt* at), *bildl.* sneer (*åt* at) **2** (*gapa*) gape; *armodet* ~*de dem i ansiktet* poverty stared them in the face **3** (*flina*) grin; leer **4** (*gråta*) whine, pule
grind *s2* gate **-slant** gate money **-stolpe** gatepost **-stuga** [gatekeeper's] lodge **-vakt** gatekeeper; (*i kricket*) wicketkeeper
grindval pilot (black) whale, blackfish
grin|ig *a1* **1** (*som gråter*) whining, puling **2** (*missnöjd*) complaining, fault-finding; *AE. vard.* ornery; (*kinkig*) peevish **-olle** *s2* crybaby, whiner
grip *s2* griffin
gripa *grep gripit* **1** (*fatta tag i*) seize (*äv. bildl.*); (*tjuv e.d.*) catch, capture; (*fatta kraftigt tag i*) catch (take) hold of, clasp, clutch; ~ *tag i get* hold of; ~ *tillfället* seize the opportunity; ~ *tyglarna* catch hold of (*bildl.* take) the reins; ~ *ngn på bar gärning* catch s.b. red-handed (in the act); ~ *ngt ur luften* make s.th. up; ~*s av förtvivlan* be seized by despair **2** (*djupt röra*) affect, move **3** ~ *sig an med* set about, (*ett arbete* a job; *att arbeta* working); ~ *efter* catch (grasp) at; ~ *i varandra* (*i mekanism*) interlock, (*om kugghjul*) engage; ~ *in i* interfere with, intervene in; ~ *omkring sig* spread, gain ground
grip|ande *a4* touching, moving; pathetic **-arm 1** *zool.* prehensile arm **2** *tekn.* transferring arm **-bar** *a1* (*fattbar*) comprehensible; (*påtaglig*) palpable, tangible; (*konkret*) concrete
gripen *a3* **1** seized (*av* with) **2** (*rörd*) touched, moved **-het** emotion
grip|it *sup. av* **gripa -klo** *zool.* prehensile claw **-tång** clutching-tongs (*pl*)

gris *s2* **1** pig; *(kött)* pork; *helstekt* ~ sucking pig roasted whole; *köpa* ~*en i säcken* buy a pig in a poke **2** *(om pers.)* pig

gris|a **1** *eg.* farrow **2** ~ *ner (till)* make a mess, muck up; ~ *ner sig* get o.s. in a mess **-aktig** *se* grisig **-eri, -farm** piggery **-fot** pig's foot; **-fötter** *(kokk.)* pig's trotters **-huvud** pig's head

gris|ig *a1* piggish; filthy **-kulting** sucking pig, piglet; *vard.* piggy **-mat** pig feed

grissla *s1* guillemot

grisslybjörn grizzly [bear]

grisöga pig's eye *(äv. bildl.)*

gro *v4* germinate, sprout; *(växa)* grow; *bildl.* rankle; ~ *igen a)* *(om jord)* grass over, *b)* *(om dike e.d.)* get filled up [with grass]; *det [ligger och]* ~*r i ngn* it rankles in a p.'s breast; *medan gräset* ~*r dör kon* while the grass grows the steed starves **-bar** *a5* germinable, germinative **-barhet** germinativeness; fertility

grobi'an *s3* boor, churl; *(starkare)* ruffian

groblad *bot.* [great] plantain

groda *s1* **1** *zool.* frog **2** *bildl.* blunder, howler

grodd *s2* germ, sprout; *koll.* sprouts *(pl)* **-blad** germ layer

grod|djur batrachian **-lår** frog's leg **-man** frogman **-mansutrustning** scuba gear; frogman's equipment; underwater diving kit **-perspektiv** *i* ~ *(bildl.)* from a worm's eye view **-rom** frogspawn **-spott** cuckoo (frog) spit, frog spittle **-yngel** tadpole; *koll.* tadpoles *(pl)*

grogg [-å-] *s2* grog; whisky (brandy) and soda; *AE.* highball

grogg|a [-å-] [drink] grog **-glas** *(hopskr. grogglas)* grog tumbler, whisky glass

grogrund *eg.* fertile soil; *bildl.* hotbed

groll [-å-] *s7* grudge; *gammalt* ~ long-standing grudge; *hysa* ~ *mot ngn* bear s.b. a grudge

groning germination, sprouting

grop *s2* pit; *(större)* hollow, cavity; *(i väg)* hole; *(i hakan, kinden)* dimple; *flyg.* bump, pocket; *den som gräver en* ~ *åt andra faller själv däri* he who diggeth a pit shall fall therein **-ig** *a1* **1** full of holes; *(om golv o.d.)* worn into holes; *(om väg)* bumpy, uneven **2** *(om hav)* rough; *flyg.* bumpy

1 gross [-å-] *s7* *(tolv dussin)* gross; *i* ~ by the gross

2 gross [-å-] *s i uttr.: i* ~ *(i parti)* wholesale

grossess pregnancy; *i* ~ pregnant, big with child

grosshandel wholesale trade

grosshandels|firma wholesale business (firm) **-pris** wholesale price

gross|handlare, -ist wholesale dealer, wholesaler **-istförbund** *Sveriges G*~ Federation of Swedish Wholesalers and Importers

gro'tesk **I** *a1* grotesque **II** *s3, boktr.* sans serif, sanserif, grotesque

grotta [-å-] *s1* cave; *(större)* cavern; *(konstgjord o. måleriskt)* grotto

grottekvarn [-å-] treadmill

grott|forskare cave explorer, speleologist **-forskning** speleology **-målning** cave painting **-människa** *förhist.* caveman, troglodyte

grov *-t grövre grövst* **1** *(motsats fin)* coarse; *(stor)* large; *(storväxt)* big; *(tjock)* thick; *(om röst)* rough, coarse; *(om yta)* rough; ~*t artilleri* heavy artillery; ~*t bröd (salt)* coarse bread

(salt); ~ *sjö* rough sea **2** *bildl.* rough; *(nedsättande)* coarse, gross, crude; *(allvarlig)* grave; *(ohyfsad)* rude, rough; ~*t brott* heinous crime; ~ *förolämpning (okunnighet)* gross insult (ignorance); *i* ~*a drag* in rough outline *(sg)*; *tjäna* ~*a pengar* make big money; *vara* ~ *i munnen* use foul language, be unrefined

grov|arbetare labourer, unskilled worker **-arbete** unskilled labour **-göra** heavy (rough) work; *AE. äv.* chore **-hacka** chop coarsely

grov|het [-ᴏ:-] coarseness *etc., jfr* grov; ~*er* foul language *(sg)* **-huggare** *se grobian* **-huggen** *a5* **1** *(om utseende)* rugged, coarsely chiselled **2** *se* grovkornig **2** **-hyvla** rough-plane **-kalibrig** [-i:b-] *a1* large-bore, large-calibred **-kornig** **1** coarse-grained **2** *bildl.* coarse, gross, rude; ~*t skämt* broad joke **-lek** *s2* thickness **-lemmad** *a5* heavy-limbed **-mala** grind coarsely **-maskig** *a1* wide-meshed, coarse-meshed **-rengöringsmedel** heavy duty cleaner **-sopor** large items of refuse **-sortera** do the first sorting **-sortering** first sorting **-sysslor** *pl* rough jobs

grov|t [-ᴏ:-] *adv* coarsely *etc.*; *tjäna* ~ *på* make a pile of money on; *gissa* ~ make a rough guess; *ljuga* ~ tell barefaced lies **-tarm** colon

grubbel ['grubb-] *s7* *(funderande)* musing[s *pl*], rumination; *relig. äv.* obsession; *(sjukligt morbid)* brooding

grubbl|a *(ängsligt)* brood; *(fundera)* cogitate, muse, ruminate; puzzle [one's head]; ~ *sig fördärvad över* rack one's brains over **-are** brooder, cogitator; *(friare)* philosopher **-eri** *se* grubbel

gruff *s7* row, wrangle; *råka i* ~ *med* get at loggerheads with **gruffa** make *(vard.* kick up) a row, squabble *(för, om* about; *med* with)

grumla *eg.* make muddy, soil, roil *(om vätska)*; *(friare, äv. bildl.)* cloud, dim; *(göra suddig)* blur; *(bildl. smutsa ner)* soil, tarnish; *(fördunkla)* obscure; ~ *själens lugn* disturb the peace of mind grumlas *(om vätska)* roil grumlig *a1* muddy, turbid *(äv. bildl.)*; *(virrig)* muddled, confused; *(dunkel)* obscure; *(om röst)* thick; *fiska i* ~*t vatten* fish in troubled water

grums *s7* grounds *(pl)*, dregs *(pl)*; *(i vatten)* sediment

grumsa grumble

1 grund *s7* *(grunt ställe)* shallow[s *pl*], shoal; *(sand- o.d.)* bank; *(klipp-)* sunken rock; *gå (stöta) på* ~ run aground; *komma av* ~*et* get afloat

2 grund *a1* *(föga djup)* shallow

3 grund *s3* **1** *(botten)* ground; *(mark äv.)* soil; *i* ~ *[och botten]* *(helt o. hållet)* completely, entirely; *i* ~ *och botten, i* ~*en* in reality, *(i själva verket)* at heart, basically, *(på det hela taget)* after all, essentially; *gå från gård och* ~ give up one's house [and lands]; *gå till* ~*en med* go to the bottom of **2** *(underlag)* foundation *(för, till* of); *bildl. äv.* basis; *(hus- äv.)* foundations *(pl)*; *kemins* ~*er* the elements of chemistry; *tillbaka till* ~*erna* back to basics; *brinna ner till* ~ *en* be burnt to the ground; *ligga till* ~ *för* be the basis (at the bottom) of; *lägga* ~*en till* lay the foundation[s *pl*] *(bildl.* basis) of; *lägga ngt till* ~ *för* make s.th. the basis of, base on s.th. **3** (*orsak*) cause; (*skäl*) reason; (*motiv*) motive, ground[s *pl*]; *på ~ av* on account of, because of, owing to; *på goda ~er* for excellent reasons; *på mycket lösa ~er* on very flimsy grounds; *ha sin ~ i* be due to, originate in; *sakna all ~* be groundless (completely unfounded) **grund|a 1** (*-lägga*) found; establish, set up; start; (*friare*) lay the foundation of **2** (*stödja*) base (*ett påstående på* a statement on); *~ sig på* be based on **3** (*-måla o. konst.*) ground, prime **-are** founder **grund|avgift** basic charge (fee, rate) **-begrepp** fundamental principle **-betydelse** basic meaning (sense) **-bok** *bokför.* daybook **-drag 1** (*karakteristiskt drag*) fundamental feature, basic trait **2** (*huvuddrag*) *~en* [*till*] the [main] outlines [of] **-element** essential (basic) element **-enhet** fundamental unit **grund|era** *se* **grunda 3 -falsk** fundamentally wrong **-fel** fundamental fault (error) **-form** primary form; *gram.* common case **-forskning** basic research **-färg 1** *fys.* primary colour **2** (*huvudsaklig färg*) predominating colour **3** (*bottenfärg*) primer, first coat **-förutsättning** primary (fundamental) condition (prerequisite) **-hyra** basic rent **-kurs** basic course **-lag** fundamental law; (*författning*) constitution[al law] **grundlags|beredning** working committee on the constitution (the fundamental laws) **-enlig** [-e:-] *a5* constitutional **-stridig** *a5* unconstitutional **-ändring** constitutional amendment **grundlig** *a1* thorough; (*djup*) profound; (*ingående*) close; (*gedigen*) solid, sound; (*fundamental*) fundamental, radical **-het** thoroughness *etc.* **grund|linje** base[line]; *~rna till* (*bildl.*) the outlines of **-lurad** *a5* thoroughly (completely) taken in **grundlägg|a** found, lay the foundation[s *pl*] (*bildl. äv.* basis) of **-ande** *a4* fundamental, basic **-are** founder **-ning** foundation **grund|lön** basic salary (wages *pl*) **-lös** groundless; baseless; unfounded **-murad** *a5, bildl.* solidly established, firmly rooted **grund|ning** (*-målning*) priming **-orsak** primary cause **-plåt** nucleus (*till* of); first contribution **-polish** sealer **-princip** fundamental (basic) principle **-regel** fundamental (basic) rule **-ritning** ground plan (*äv. bildl.*) **-sats** principle **-skola** comprehensive (*AE.* elementary, grade) school **-skott** *bildl., ett ~ mot* a death blow to **-slag** (*i tennis*) ground stroke **-sten** foundation stone **-stomme** groundwork (*till* of); *bildl. äv.* nucleus (*till* of) **-stämning** keynote **-stöta** run aground **-stötning** grounding **-syn** basic view **-tal** cardinal number (numeral) **-tanke** fundamental (basic, leading) idea **-tema** main theme **-text** original [text] **-ton 1** *fys.* fundamental tone **2** *mus. o. bildl.* keynote **-tillstånd** *fys.* ground state (level) **-utbildning** basic education (training) **-val** *s2* foundation; *bildl. äv.* basis, groundwork; *på ~ av* on the basis of **-valla** (*för skidor*) tar primer **-vatten** subsoil water **-villkor** fundamental (basic) condition **-ämne** element **grunka** *s1, se* **grej**

grunna cogitate, ponder; *~ på* (*äv.*) turn over in one's mind; *sitta och ~* sit musing, sit and think **grupp** *s3* group; (*klunga*) cluster; *polit. o.d. äv.* section; *mil. äv.* squad, section; *flyg.* flight **-arbete** teamwork **-bild** group picture **-bildning** group formation; grouping **-biljett** party ticket **-chef** *mil.* squad commander (leader) **-dynamik** group dynamics (*pl, behandlas som sg*) **grupper|a** group **-ing** grouping; *mil.* deployment **grupp|försäkring** group [accident, life] insurance **-ledare** (*sport- e.d.*) group leader **-livförsäkring** group insurance **-resa** conducted tour **-samtal** *tel.* conference call **-sex** group sex **-terapi** group therapy **-vis** in (by) groups **grus** *s7* gravel (*äv. med.*) **grusa 1** gravel **2** *bildl.* dash [to the ground], spoil; (*gäcka*) frustrate; *~de förhoppningar* dashed hopes **grus|grop** gravel pit **-gång** gravel walk **-hög** gravel heap; *bildl.* heap of ruins **-tag** *s7,* **-täkt** *s3* gravel pit **1 gruva** *v1, rfl, ~ sig för* (*över*) dread **2 gruva** *s1* mine; (*kol- äv.*) pit **gruv|arbetare** miner; (*i kolgruva äv.*) collier, pitman **-arbete** mining; colliery **-brytning** *se* **-drift -distrikt** mining district **-drift** mining [operations *pl*] **-fält** mining area, (*kol-*) coalfield **-gas** firedamp **-gång** heading, gallery **-industri** mining industry **-ingenjör** mining engineer; (*i kolgruva*) colliery engineer **-lampa** miner's (safety, Davy) lamp **gruv|lig** [-u:-] *a1* dreadful, horrible **-olycka** pit (mining) accident **-ras** *s7* caving-in of a mine, fall **-samhälle** mining community **-schakt** shaft **-stötta** *s1* pit prop **-öppning** mouth of a mine **1 gry** *s7, det är gott ~ i honom* he has [got] grit **2 gry** *v4* dawn (*äv. bildl.*); break; *dagen ~r* day is breaking **gryende** *a4* dawning; *~ anlag* (*äv.*) budding talents **grym** [-ymm] *a1* cruel (*mot* to); (*bestialisk*) fierce, ferocious; *ett ~t öde* a cruel (harsh) fate **-het** cruelty (*mot* to); (*begången äv.*) atrocity **1 grymt** *adv, bli ~ besviken* be terribly disappointed **2 grymt** *s7* grunt **grymta** grunt **grymtning** grunt[ing] **gryn** *s7, s4* [hulled] grain; (*havre-, vete- äv.*) groats (*pl*) **-ig** *a1* grainy, granular **gryning** dawn (*äv. bildl.*); daybreak; *i ~en* at dawn; *i första ~en* at first light **gryningsljus** light of early dawn **grynmat** farinaceous food **grynna** *s1* sunken rock, reef **grynvälling** *bildl.* mess of pottage **gryt** *s7* **1** (*lya*) earth, burrow **2** (*stenrös*) pile of stones **gryt|a** *s1* pot; (*med lock*) casserole; (*maträtt*) casserole; *små -or har också öron* little pitchers have long ears **grythund** burrower **gryt|lapp** saucepan (kettle) holder **-lock** casserole (pot) lid **-stek** pot roast; braised beef **-vante** oven glove **grå** *a1* grey; *i sht AE.* gray; (*gråsprängd äv.*)

grizzled; (*om väder*) overcast; (*dyster*) dull, drab, dreary, gloomy; ~ *eminens* grey eminence; ~ *marknad* grey market; *i den* ~ *forntiden* in the hoary past; *tillbaka till den* ~ *vardagen igen* back into harness again, back to the humdrum of every day **-aktig** *a5* greyish **-al** grey alder **-berg** granite **-blek** ashen grey **-blå** greyish blue **-bo** *bot.* mugwort **-broder** Grey Friar **-brödrakloster** Franciscan monastery **-dask** *s7* greyness **-daskig** *a5* dirty grey **-gam** black vulture **-gosse** elderly messenger **-gås** greylag [goose]; *AE.* graylag **-hårig** grey--haired; (*gråsprängd*) grizzled **-kall** bleak, chill, raw **-kråka** hooded (*i Skottland* hoodie) crow

grålle *s2* grey horse

grå|na turn grey; (*om pers.*) go (get) grey; ~*d* (*om hår*) grey, grizzled, (*åldrig*) grey-headed **-papper** (*för växtpressning*) pressing paper **-päron** butter-pear **-sej** [-sejj] *s2* coalfish, saithe, coley **-sparv** house (*AE.* English) sparrow **-sprängd** *a5* grizzled; (*om skägg äv.*) grizzly **-sten** granite **-sugga** woodlouse **-säl** grey seal

gråt *s3* crying, weeping; (*snyftande*) sobbing; *brista i* ~ burst into tears; *ha* ~*en i halsen* be on the verge of tears, have a lump in one's throat; *kämpa med* ~*en* fight back tears

gråt|a *grät* -*it* **1** cry (*av glädje* for joy; *av ilska* with rage); weep (*av* for); ~ *ut* have a good cry; ~ *över spilld mjölk* cry over spilt milk; *det är ingenting att* ~ *för* (*över*) it is nothing to cry about; *det är så man kan* ~ it is enough to make one cry; *hon har lätt för att* ~ she cries easily **2** ~ *sina ögon röda* cry one's eyes red **3** *rfl* cry o.s. (*till sömns* to sleep) **-attack** fit of crying

gråt|erska [professional] mourner, weeper **-färdig** on the verge of tears, ready to cry

gråt|it *sup. av gråta* **-mild** tearful; (*sentimental*) maudlin

gråtrut herring gull

grått *s, best. form det grå[a]* grey

gråverk squirrel fur

gråväders|dag grey (*bildl.* cheerless) day **-stämning** gloom, gloomy atmosphere (mood)

1 grädda *v1* bake; (*uppe på spisen*) fry, make

2 grädda *s1,* ~*n av* the cream of (*societeten* society)

gräddbakelse cream cake, éclair

grädd|e *s2* cream; (*vispad* ~ whipped cream **-fil** *s3* sour[ed] cream **-glass** ice cream **-gul** cream-coloured, creamy **-kanna** cream jug; *AE.* creamer **-kola** cream caramel

gräddning baking; frying

grädd|snipa, -snäcka *se gräddkanna* **-tårta** cream-layer cake **-visp** whisk, beater

gräl *s7* (*tvist*) quarrel; (*ordväxling äv.*) squabble, wrangle; *råka i* ~ fall out, clash (*med ngn* with s.b.); *söka* ~ pick a quarrel (*med ngn* with s.b.)

gräla quarrel; squabble, wrangle; ~ *på ngn* scold s.b. (*för att han är* for being)

gräll *a1* loud, glaring; garish

gräl|makare quarreller; squabbler, wrangler **-sjuk** quarrelsome, cantankerous; (*som bannar*) scolding

gräm|a *v2* grieve, vex; ~ *sig* grieve (*över* at, for), fret (*över* about); ~ *sig till döds* fret one's heart out **-else** grief; worry

gränd *s3* alley, [by-]lane; (*ruskig*) slum

gräns *s3* **1** (*-linje*) *geogr.* boundary; *polit.* frontier, *AE.* border; (*friare*) borderline; *dra* ~*en* (*polit.*) fix the boundary, *bildl.* draw the line; *stå på* ~*en till* (*bildl.*) be on the verge of **2** (*slutpunkt*) limit (*för* of); *bildl. äv.* bounds (*pl*); *inom vissa* ~*er* within certain limits;; *sätta en* ~ *för* a) (*begränsa*) set bounds (limits) to, *b*) (*stävja*) put an end (a stop) to; *det finns ingen* ~ *för hans fåfänga* his vanity knows no bounds; *det här går över alla* ~*er!* [no really,] that's the limit! **3** ([*område utmed*] *gränslinje*) confines (*pl*), border[s *pl*]; *vid belgiska* ~*en* on the Belgian border

gräns|a ~ *till* border [up]on (*äv. bildl.*); (*om land, område*) be bounded (*till by*); (*om ägor*) adjoin, abut on; *med en till visshet* ~*nde sannolikhet* with a probability almost amounting to certainty; *det* ~*r till det otroliga* it borders on the incredible **-befolkning** border (frontier) population **-befästning** frontier fortification **-bevakning** frontier patrol[ling] **-bo** borderer **-bygd** border country **-dragning** delimitation **-fall** borderline case **-intäkt** marginal revenue **-kontroll** border checkpoint **-kostnad** marginal cost **-kränkning** violation of the frontier **-land** border country

gränsle *se grensle*

gräns|linje boundary line; *bildl.* borderline, dividing line **-lös** boundless, limitless; *bildl.* unbounded; (*ofantlig*) tremendous, immense **-märke** boundary mark; landmark **-nytta** marginal utility **-område** border district; *bildl.* borderland, confines (*pl*) **-oroligheter** *pl* border fighting (disturbances) **-postering** frontier outpost **-påle** boundary post **-station** frontier station **-trakt** *se -område* **-värde** limit

gräs *s7* grass; *i* ~*et* a) (*på gräset*) on the grass, *b*) (*bland gräset*) in the grass; *bita i* ~*et* lick the dust; *ha pengar som* ~ have a mint of money **-and** mallard **-bevuxen** *a5* grass-grown, grassy **-frö** grass seed[s *pl*] **-grön** grass-green **-hoppa** grasshopper; locust **-klippare** lawn mower

gräslig [-ä:-] *a1* atrocious, horrid (*mot* to); terrible, shocking; (*friare*) awful, frightful **-het** atrociousness *etc.*; ~*er* atrocities

gräs|lök chive; *kokk.* chives **-matta** lawn; grass; green **-rot** *bildl.* grass roots (*pl*) **-rotsdemokrati** grassroot democracy **-rotsnivå** *på* ~ at grass-roots level **-slätt** grassy plain; prairie **-strå** blade [of grass] **-stäpp** *se stäpp o. grässlätt* **-torv** turf **-torva** sod, turf **-tuva** tuft [of grass] **-växt** gramineous plant **-änka** grass widow **-änkling** grass widower **-ätare** graminivorous animal, grass-eater

grät *imperf. av gråta*

grätten *a3* fastidious; squeamish

gräva *v2* dig (*efter* for); (*t.ex. kanal, tunnel*) cut; (*om djur*) grub, burrow; (*friare o. bildl.*) delve (*i en byrålåda* in a drawer); (*rota*) rummage (*i fickorna* in one's pockets); ~ *fram* dig up, unearth; ~ *igen* fill up; ~ *ner* dig down (*i* into), bury (*i* in); ~ *ner sig i* dig (burrow) one's way down into, (*begrava sig*) bury o.s. in; ~ *ut* dig out, excavate

grävling [-ä:-] [Eurasian] badger

grävmaskin excavator, power shovel **-ist** excavator operator

gräv|ning [-ä:-] digging; *fack.* excavation **-skopa** bucket, dipper; *jfr grävmaskin*

gröda *s1* (*växande*) crops (*pl*); (*skörd*) harvest, crop

grön *a1* green (*av* with) (*äv. bildl.*); ~ *våg* (*trafik*) synchronized [green] traffic lights (*pl*); ~*a ön* (*Irland*) the Emerald Isle; *i det* ~*a* in the [green] fields (the country); *i min* ~ *ungdom* in my callow youth, *vard.* in my salad days; *komma på* ~ *kvist* be in clover, do well for o.s. **-aktig** *a5* greenish **-alg** green alga (seaweed) **-bete** [grass] pasture; *vara på* ~ (*bildl.*) be in the country **-fink** greenfinch **-foder** green forage **-gräset** *i* ~ on the grass **-göling** [-j-] **1** *zool.* green woodpecker, yaffle **2** *bildl.* greenhorn **-kål** kale, borecole

Grönköping *n* Little Puddleton **grönköpingsmässig** *a1* Puddletonian; parochial

Grönland ['grö:n-] *n* Greenland; *på* ~ in Greenland

grönlandsval Greenland whale

grönländ|are Greenlander **-sk** *a5* Greenlandic **-ska 1** (*språk*) Greenlandic **2** (*kvinna*) Greenland woman

grön|mögelost blue cheese **-område** green area **-peppar** green pepper **-sak** *s3* vegetable

grönsaks|affär greengrocer's shop, greengrocery **-handlare** greengrocer **-land** vegetable patch **-soppa** vegetable soup

grön|sallad (*växt*) lettuce; (*rätt*) green salad **-siska** *s1* siskin

grönska I *s1* **1** (*vårens*) verdure; *ängarnas* ~ the green of the meadows **2** (*trädens etc.*) greenery, green foliage **II** *v1* be (become) green

grönsåpa soft soap

grönt [-ö:-] *s, best. form det gröna* **1** green **2** (*grönfoder, grönsaker*) greenstuff **3** (*prydnad*) greenery

gröpa *v3*, ~ *ur* hollow out

gröpe *s7* groats (*pl*); (*mindre grovt*) grits (*pl*)

gröt *s2, kokk.* porridge; (*risgryns-*) rice pudding; *tekn.* pulp, pap; (*friare*) mush; *med.* poultice; *gå som katten kring het* ~ beat about the bush; *vara het på* ~*en* be overeager **-ig** *a1* porridge- -like; pulpy; mushy, pappy; (*om röst*) thick **-myndig** pompous, high and mighty **-rim** doggerel [rhyme]

grövre ['grö:v-] *komp. t.* grov **grövst** [-ö:-] *superl. t.* grov

g-sträng G-string

guano [gu'a:nå] *s2, s7* guano; *bildl.* rubbish, nonsense

Guatemala [-ˣma:-] *n* Guatemala **guatema-'l|an** *s3*, **-ansk** [-'a:nsk] *a5* Guatemalan

gubbaktig *a1* old-mannish, old man's...; senile

gubbe *s2* **1** old man; ~*n A.* old A.; *min* ~ *lille!* my lad! **2** (*bild*) picture; (*grimas*) face; ~ *eller pil* (*på mynt*) heads or tails; *rita gubbar* (*klottra*) doodle **3** (*tabbe*) blunder **4** *den* ~*n*

går inte! that won't wash!, tell that to the marines!; *för hundra gubbar!* by all the saints!

gubb|ig *a1, se gubbaktig* **-strutt** *s2* old buffer, dodderer

gube'vars ['gu:-, -'vars] **I** *interj* goodness me! **II** *adv* of course, to be sure

guckusko *s5* lady's-slipper

gud *s2* god; *G~ Fader* God the Father; *G~ bevare oss!* God preserve us!; *G~ nåde dig!* God have mercy upon you!; *G~ vet* Heaven knows; *om G~ vill* God willing; *ta G~ i hågen* take one's courage in both hands; *för G~s skull* for the love of God, (*utrop*) for goodness' (God's, Heaven's) sake!; *inte G~s bästa barn* no angel; *det vete* ~*arna!* Heaven only knows!

guda|benådad *a5* divinely gifted; *en* ~ *konstnär* a real artist **-bild** image of a god, idol **-dryck** drink of the gods, nectar **-god** divine **-gåva** godsend, gift of the gods **-lik** godlike **-lära** *se mytologi* **-saga** myth **-skymning** Twilight of the Gods, Ragnarök **-skön** divinely beautiful **-sänd** *a5* god-sent **-väsen** god

gud|barn godchild **-dotter** goddaughter **-fa-[de]r** godfather **-fruktig** *a1* god-fearing, devout; *jfr gudlig*

gudi *i uttr.*: *en* ~ *behaglig gärning* a pious deed; ~ *lov* God be praised; *ha* ~ *nog av* have enough and to spare of

guding eider drake, male eider

gud|inna goddess **-lig** [-u:-] *a1* godly, pious; (*gudsnådelig*) goody-goody **-lös** godless; impious; (*hädisk*) blasphemous; ~*t leverne* wicked life; ~*t tal* profane language, blasphemy **-mo[de]r** godmother

gudom [ˣgudɷmm] *s2* divinity; ~*en* the Godhead

gudomlig [-'dɷmm-] *a1* divine; (*underbar*) superb, magnificent **-het 1** (*gudomlig natur*) divineness *etc.* **2** (*gud*) divinity; god

guds|begrepp concept of God **-bevis** proof of God's existence **-dom** ordeal **-dyrkan** worship [of God], religion **-fruktan** piety, godliness **-förgäten** *a5* **1** (*om plats*) godforsaken **2** *se gudlös* **-förnekare** atheist **-förnekelse** denial of God; atheism **-förtröstan** trust in God **-gemenskap** communion with God

gudskelov [ˣguʃe-, 'guʃe- *el.* -'lå:v] thank goodness (Heaven)

guds|man man of God **-nåd[e]lig** [ˣguts-, -ˣnå:- *el.* -'nå:-] *a1* sanctimonious; (*salvelsefull*) unctuous

gudson godson

gudstjänst [divine] service; *bevista* ~*en* (*äv.*) attend church (chapel); *förrätta* ~ officiate [at the service], conduct [the] service; *hålla* ~ hold divine service **-förrättare** officiating clergyman **-ordning** order for divine service, liturgy

gudstro faith (belief) [in God]

guida [ˣgaj-] *v1*, **guide** [gajd] *s5* guide

Guinea [gi'ne:a] *n* Guinea **Guinea-Bis'sau** *n* Guinea-Bissau

guine|an [gine'a:n] *s3*, **-ansk** [-'a:nsk] *a5* Guinean

gul *a1* yellow; *slå ngn* ~ *och blå* beat s.b. black and blue; ~*a febern* yellow fever; ~*a pressen* the gutter (yellow) press

gul|a *s1* yolk **-aktig** *a5* yellowish

gu'lasch *s3* **1** *kokk.* [Hungarian] goulash **2** [war] profiteer; *vard.* spiv **-baron** *se gulasch 2*
gul|blek sallow **-brun** yellowish brown
guld *s7* gold; *trogen som* ~ [as] true as steel; *gräva* ~ dig for gold; *lova ngn* ~ *och gröna skogar* promise s.b. the moon; *skära* ~ *med täljknivar* make a mint of (coin) money **-arm-band** gold bracelet **-brun** golden brown **-bröllop** golden wedding **-bågad** *a5* (*om glasögon*) gold-rimmed **-dubblé** rolled (filled) gold; gold plate
guld|en ['guld-] *r, pl* =, guilder **-feber** gold fever **-fisk** goldfish **-fyndighet** gold deposit **-färgad** gold-coloured, golden **-förande** *a4* gold-bearing, auriferous **-galon** gold braid **-galonerad** *a5* gold-braided **-glans** gold (*bildl.* golden) lustre **-glänsande** shining like gold **-gruva** gold mine (*äv. bildl.*) **-grävare** gold-digger **-gul** golden **-halt** percentage of gold, gold content **-kalven** the golden calf **-kantad** *a5* gilt-edged; (*om servis e.d.*) gold--rimmed; ~*e papper* gilt-edged securities **-klimp** gold nugget **-klocka** gold watch **-korn** grain of gold; *bildl.* pearl **-krog** *vard.* plush (posh) restaurant **-krona** gold[en] crown
Guldkusten (*förutvarande namn på Ghana*) the Gold Coast
guld|lamé *s3* gold lamé **-lock** (*blond pers.*) Goldilocks **-lockig** with golden curls **-makare** alchemist **-medalj** gold medal **-mynt** gold coin (piece) **-myntfot** gold standard **-plomb** gold filling **-ring** gold ring **-rush** *s3* gold rush **-skiva** (*grammofon-*) golden disc **-slagare** gold-beater **-smed** goldsmith; (*som butiksägare vanl.*) jeweller **-smedsaffär** jeweller's [shop]; *AE.* jewelry store **-smide** goldsmith's work **-snitt** (*på bok*) gilt edge[s *pl*] **-stämpel** hallmark **-tacka** gold ingot (bar) **-tand** gold tooth **-vaskning** gold washing, placer-mining **-våg** assay balance; *väga sina ord på* ~ weigh one's words carefully **-åder** gold (auriferous) vein **-ålder** golden age
gul|filter yellow filter **-ing** *vard.* **1** (*mongol*) yellowman **2** (*strejkbrytare*) blackleg; *AE.* scab **-kroppen** *anat.* (*lat.*) corpus luteum
gull|gosse [spoilt] darling; blue-eyed (white--headed; *AE.* fair-haired) boy; *en lyckans* ~ a lucky beggar (dog) **-höna** *se nyckelpiga*
gull|ig *a1* sweet; *AE.* cute **-regn** *bot.* laburnum **-ris** *bot.* goldenrod **-stol** *bära ngn i* ~ chair s.b. **-viva** *s1* cowslip
gul|metall brass, yellow metal **-måra** *s1* lady's bedstraw
gul|na [-u:-] [turn (grow)] yellow **-sot** jaundice **-sparv** yellowhammer
gult [-u:-] *s, best. form det gula* yellow
gumaktig [ˣgumm-] *a1* old womanish, old woman's ...; senile
gumma *s1* old woman; *min* ~ (*maka*) the wife, my old woman; *min* ~ *lilla!* my pet!
gummer|a gum, rubberize **-ing** gumming
gummi *s6* **1** (*växtämne*) rubber; gum **2** (*kautschuk*) [India] rubber **3** (*preventivmedel*) French letter, rubber; *AE.* safe **-band** rubber (elastic) band **-boll** rubber ball **-båt** rubber boat **-gutta** [-ˣgutta, -'gutta] *s1* gamboge **-handske** rubber glove **-hjul** rubber-tyred

wheel **-lacka** [-ˣlacka, -'lacka] *s1* lac **-lösning** rubber solution **-madrass** rubber mattress **-plantage** rubber plantation **-ring** rubber ring (tyre) **-sko** rubber shoe **-slang** rubber hose (tube, pipe) **-snodd** rubber band **-stövel** rubber boot; *-stövlar* (*äv.*) Wellington boots, gum-boots **-sula** rubber sole **-träd 1** (*Eucalyptus*) gumtree **2** (*Ficus elastica*) rubber plant **-va-ror** *pl* rubber products (articles) **-verkstad** vulcanizing [work]shop
gump *s2, zool.* uropygium; (*friare*) rump
gumse *s2* ram
gung|a I *s1* swing **II** *v1* swing; (*på -bräde o. friare*) seesaw; (*i vagga, -stol; om vågor*) rock; (*ett barn på foten e.d.*) dandle; ~ *på stolen* tilt the chair; ~ *på vågorna* float up and down (*om pers.* be tossed) on the waves; *marken -de under deras fötter* the ground quaked (rocked) beneath their feet **-bräde** seesaw **-fly** *s6* quagmire (*äv. bildl.*) **-häst** rocking horse
gung|ning swinging *etc.*; *sätta ngt i* ~ (*bildl.*) set s.th. rocking, rock the boat **-stol** rocking chair; *AE. äv.* rocker
gun[n]rum wardroom, gun room
gunst *s3* favour; *stå* [*högt*] *i* ~ *hos ngn* be in high favour with s.b., be in a p.'s good books **-ig** *a1* **1** (*välvillig*) well-disposed, friendly (*mot* towards, to); (*om lyckan*) propitious; (*gynnsam*) favourable **2** *vard. vanl. oböjt: min* ~ *herre* my fine friend (fellow, Sir); *det passade inte* ~ *herrn* it didn't suit his lordship **-ling** favourite **-lingssystem** favouritism
gu'nås alas; worse luck
gupp *s7* **1** bump; (*grop*) hole, pit; (*i skidbacke*) jump **2** (*knyck*) jolt, jog **guppa** jolt, jog; (*om åkdon äv.*) bump; (*om flytande* [*mindre*] *före-mål*) bob [up and down] **guppig** *a1* bumpy
guppy *s3, zool.* guppy
gurgel ['gurr-] *s7, vard.* row, squabble **-vatten** gargle, gargling fluid
gurgl|a ~ *halsen* gargle, gargle one's throat; ~ *sig* [*i halsen*] gargle [one's throat]; *ett* ~*nde ljud* a gurgling sound **-ing** gargling, gargle; (*om ljud*) gurgling
gurk|a *s1* cucumber; (*inläggnings-*) gherkin **-meja** [-ˣmejja, *äv.* ˣgurk-] *s1* curcuma, turmeric **-säng** cucumber bed
guru ['gu:-] *s3* guru
gustavi|'an *s3*, **-ansk** [-'a:nsk] *a5* Gustavian
gut [gutt] *s3, s4* (*till metrev*) gut
gute *s2* inhabitant of Gotland
guterad *se gouterad*
gutt *se gut*
guttaperka [-ˣperr-, -'perr-] *s1* gutta-percha
guttu'ral *a5* guttural
gu'tår *åld., ung.* cheers!
guvernant [-'ant *el.* -'a<ng>t] governess (*för* to)
guvern|ement *s7* province; colony **-ör** governor
Guyana [gai'änna] *n* Guyana
guyan|an [gaiänn'a:n] *s3*, **-ansk** [-'a:nsk] *a5* Guyanese, Guyanian
gyckel ['jyck-] *s7* (*skoj*) play, sport; (*skämt*) fun; (*upptåg*) joking, jesting, larking, joke[s *pl*]; *bli föremål för* ~ be made a laughing stock of; *driva* ~ *med ngn, se gyckla med ngn* **-makare**

joker, jester, wag **-spel** (*-bild*) illusion; (*task-speleri*) jugglery, hocus-pocus
gyckl|a [*jyck-] jest, joke (*med, över* at); ~ *med ngn* make fun of (poke fun at) s.b. **-are** joker, jester, wag; *neds.* buffoon, clown
gylf [j-] *s2* fly [of the trousers]
gyllen|e [*jyll-] *oböjligt a* golden; (*av guld*) gold, golden; *G~ Horden* the Golden Horde; ~ *snittet* the golden section (mean); *den ~ friheten* glorious liberty; *den ~ medelvägen* the golden mean, the happy medium **-blond** golden haired **-läder** gilt leather
gym [jymm] *~met ~men* gym
gymnasie|elev [jym'na:-] *se gymnasist* **-ingenjör** *ung.* technical college graduate **-lärare** *ung.* upper secondary school teacher; *AE.* senior high school teacher **-skola** *ung.* upper secondary school; *AE.* senior high school
gymnas|ist [j-] *ung.* pupil of upper secondary school; *AE.* senior high school student **-ium** [-'na:-] *s4, ung.* upper secondary school; *AE.* senior high school
gym'nast [j-] *s3* gymnast
gymnastik [j-] *s3* gymnastics (*pl, behandlas som sg*); *skol. äv.* physical training, drilling; *vard.* gym; *...är en bra ~ ...is* [an] excellent [form of] exercise **-direktör** certified physical training instructor **-dräkt** gymnasium (*vard.* gym) suit **-högskola** university college of gymnastics, physical training college; *Gymnastik- och idrottshögskolan i Stockholm* [the] Stockholm college of physical education **-lärare** physical training master (mistress) **-redskap** gymnastics apparatus (*koll.* appliances *pl*) **-sal** gymnasium; *vard.* gym **-sko** gym (gymnasium) shoe; ~*r, AE. vard.* sneakers **-uppvisning** gymnastic display
gymnast|isera [j-] do gymnastics **-isk** [-'nass-] *a5* gymnastic; ~*a övningar* physical exercises
gymping [j-] *ung.* workout
gyneko|log [j-, *äv.* g-] gynaecologist **-logi** *s3* gynaecology **-logisk** *a5* gynaecologic[al]
gynn|a [j-] favour, (*bistå äv.*) support; (*främja äv.*) further, promote **-are 1** supporter *etc.*; patron **2** *skämts.* fellow, chap, customer **-sam** *al* favourable, advantageous (*för* to); *i ~maste fall* (*äv.*) at best, ideally; *ta en ~ vändning* take a favourable turn (a turn for the better)
gyro ['gy:- *el.* 'jy:rå] *s6* gyro **-horisont** artificial (gyro) horizon **-kompass** gyrocompass **-skop** [-'skå:p] *s7* gyroscope **-stabilisator** gyrostabilizer
gytter ['jytt-] *s7* conglomeration
gyttja [j-] *s1* mud; slough; (*blöt*) ooze; (*smörja*) mire, slush **gyttjebad** [j-] mud bath **gyttjig** [j-] *a1* muddy; oozy; miry, slushy
gyttr|a [j-] ~ *ihop* [*sig*] cluster together **-ig** *a1* conglomerate[d], clustered together
gå *gick gått* **I** *eg. bet.* **1** (*motsats åka, stå e.d.*) walk; (*om t.ex. hund*) trot; (*om t.ex. anka*) waddle; (*stiga*) step (*åt sidan* to one side); (*med långa steg*) stride; (*gravitetiskt*) stalk; ~ *rak* walk upright **2** (*motsats stanna kvar, stå stilla*) go; (*tyst e.d. äv.*) pass; (*röra sig äv.*) move; (*förfoga sig, komma*) get; (*bege sig av*) go away, leave, *absol.* be off; ~ *hemifrån kl. 8* leave home at 8 o'clock; ~ *ur fläcken* move

from the spot; ~ *ur vägen för ngn* get out of a p.'s way; ~ *och sätta sig* (*hämta*) go and sit down (to fetch); *jag måste ~ nu* (*äv.*) I must be off now; *vart skall du ~?* where are you going? **3** (*om sak*) go, pass; (*om t.ex. båt, flygplan tåg äv.*) travel; (*regelbundet*) run, ply; (*segla äv.*) sail; ~ *med en hastighet av* (*om bil o.d.*) travel at a speed of; *bussar ~r varje timme* buses run every hour **4** (*avgå, avresa*) start (*till* for), leave (*äv.* gå *från*) **5** (*röra sig* [*på visst sätt*], *äv. om sjön, vågorna*) run; ~ *på hjul* run on wheels; *lådan ~r lätt* the drawer runs easily; *sjön ~r hög* the sea runs high **6** (*vara i gång*) go; (*om fabrik, maskin*) run, work; ~ *med elektricitet* be worked by electricity; ~ *varm* run hot; *klockan ~r fel* the clock is wrong **II** (*friare o. bildl.*) **1** go; ~ *i kyrkan* go to church; ~ [*omkring*] *i trasor* go about in rags; ~ *på föreläsningar* attend (go to) lectures; ~ *och gifta sig* go and get married; *se vad ngn ~r för* put s.b. through his paces, see what sort of a fellow s.b. is; *får jag komma som jag ~r och står?* may I come as I am?; *jag har ~tt hos tandläkaren* I have been going to the dentist's; *det ~r inte* it won't work (is out of the question) **2** (*avgå, lämna sin tjänst*) retire; (*om regering*) resign **3** (*vara*) be (*i första klassen* in the first form); (*rymmas*) go (*i* into); ~ *arbetslös* be out of work; *dansen ~r* the dancing is on; *påssjukan ~r* there is an outbreak of mumps; *det ~r två liter i flaskan* the bottle holds two liters; *det ~r 100 pence på ett pund* there are 100 pence in a pound **4** (*om tiden*) pass [away], go [by] **5** (*sträcka sig*) go, extend; (*nå*) reach; (*om flod, väg e.d.*) run; (*om väg äv.*) go, lead; (*om dörr, trappa e.d.*) lead **6** (*om varor*) sell, be sold, go **7** (*belöpa sig*) amount (*till* to); *det ~r till stora pengar* it runs into a lot of money **8** (*avlöpa*) turn out, go off; *hur det än ~r* whatever happens; *så ~r det när* that's what happens when; *hur ~r det med...?* what about...?, how is...going?; *hur ~r det för dig?* how are you getting on?; *hur ~r det för barnen om...?* what will happen to the children if...?; *det får ~ som det vill* let it ride; *det gick bra för honom* he got on well **III** *rfl,* ~ *sig trött* tire o.s. out [with] walking **IV** (*med betonad partikel*) **1** ~ *an* (*passa sig*) do, be all right; *det ~r inte an* it won't do; *det ~r väl an för dig som* it is all right for you who **2** ~ *av a*) (*stiga av*) get out (off), *b*) (*nötas av*) wear through, break off, (*om färg e.d.*) wear off, (*brista*) break, *c*) (*om skott, vapen*) go off **3** ~ *bort a*) (*gå ut*) go out (*på middag* to dinner), *b*) (*avlägsna sig*) go away, *c*) (*dö*) die, pass away, *d*) (*om fläck o.d.*) disappear, come out **4** ~ *därifrån* leave [there, the place], go away [from there] **5** ~ *efter a*) walk behind, *b*) (*om klocka*) be slow (behind [time]), *c*) (*hämta*) go and fetch, go for **6** ~ *emot a*) (*möta*) go to meet, *b*) (*stöta emot*) go against, walk into, *c*) (*vara motigt*) go against, *d*) (*motsätta sig*) oppose; *allting ~r mig emot* everything goes wrong for me **7** ~ *fram a*) go (walk) forward (on), *b*) *se konfirmeras;* ~ *fram med stor försiktighet* proceed with great care; ~ *fram till* go up to **8** ~ *framför a*) go (walk) in front [of],

G

b) (*ha företräde framför*) rank before **9** ~ *före a*) *se gå framför*, *b*) (*om klocka*) be fast **10** ~ *för sig, se gå an* **11** ~ *hem till ngn* go to a p.'s home, call on s.b. at his home **12** ~ *i a*) go in[to], *b*) *se rymmas*; *det* ~ *inte i mig!* that won't go down with me! **13** ~ *ifrån* leave; *båten gick ifrån mig* I missed the boat **14** ~ *igen a*) (*dörren* ~*r inte igen* the door doesn't (won't) shut [to], *b*) (*spöka*) haunt, *c*) (*upprepa sig*) reappear, recur **15** ~ *igenom a*) go (walk) through, *b*) (*utstå*) pass (go) through; *jfr genomgå*, *c*) (*om förslag o.d.*) be passed, (*efter omröstning*) be carried, *d*) (*om begäran*) be granted; ~ *igenom i examen* pass one's examination **16** ~ *ihop* (*mötas*) meet, (*förenas*) join, unite, *bildl.* agree, (*passa ihop*) correspond, match; *få debet och kredit att* ~ *ihop* make both ends meet; *det* ~*r inte ihop med* it doesn't tally (fit in) with **17** ~ *in* go in[side]; ~ *in för* go in for, set one's mind upon; ~ *in i a*) enter, *b*) (*förening e.d.*) join, become a member of; ~ *in på a*) (*ge sig in på*) enter upon, *b*) (*bifalla*) agree to, accept; ~ *in vid teatern* go on the stage **18** ~ *inåt* (*om fönster e.d.*) open inwards; ~ *inåt med tårna* be pigeon-toed, turn one's toes inward **19** ~ *isär* come apart, (*om åsikter e.d.*) diverge **20** ~ *löst på a*) (*anfalla*) go for, *b*) (*uppgå till*) run into (up to) **21** ~ *med a*) *se följa med*; *absol.* go (come) too (as well), *b*) (*vara med*) join in (*i, på* at); ~ *med på ett förslag* agree to a proposal **22** ~ *ner* go down, (*t. nedre våning*) go downstairs, (*om flygare, flygplan äv.*) descend, (*om ridå äv.*) fall, drop, (*om himlakropp äv.*) set; ~ *ner sig på isen* go through the ice **23** ~ *om* (*skolklass*) repeat a year, be kept down; ~ *om ngn* overtake s.b. [in walking], (*vid tävling*) pass s.b., get (go) ahead of s.b.; ~ *om varandra* (*om pers.*) pass each other, (*om brev*) cross in the post **24** ~ *omkring* (*hit o. dit*) walk about, go round; *jfr kringgå* **25** ~ *omkull* (*om företag*) go bankrupt, come to grief **26** ~ *sönder* be (get) broken (smashed), (*om maskin o.d.*) break down, have a breakdown **27** ~ *till a*) (*hända*) happen, come about, *b*) (*om sill e.d.*) come in; ~ *till och från* come in for a few hours; *hur gick det till?* how did it happen?, what happened?; *hur skall det* ~ *till?* how is that to be done?; *det gick livligt till* things were lively **28** ~ *tillbaka a*) go back, return, *b*) (*i tiden*) date back (*till* to), (*t. ursprunget*) originate (*till* in, from), have its origin (*till* in), *c*) (*avtaga*) recede, subside, abate, *d*) (*försämras*) deteriorate, *e*) (*om avtal*) be cancelled, be broken off **29** ~ *undan a*) (*ur vägen*) get out of the way, *b*) (*gå fort*) get on (progress) fast (rapidly) **30** ~ *under* (*om fartyg*) go down, be lost, (*om pers. o. friare*) be ruined **31** ~ *upp a*) go up, (*om pris, temperatur äv.*) rise, ascend, *b*) (*stiga upp*) rise, (*om pers. äv.*) get up, (*ur vattnet*) get (come) out, *c*) (*öppnas*) [come] open, (*om is*) break up, (*om knut*) come undone, (*om plagg i sömmarna*) give [way]; *det gick upp för mig att* it dawned upon me that; ~ *upp mot* come up (be equal) to; *ingenting* ~*r upp mot* there is nothing like (to compare with); ~ *upp i sitt arbete* be absorbed in one's

work; ~ *upp i* (*om företag*) be (become) incorporated in; ~ *upp och ner* (*om priser*) fluctuate **32** ~ *ur a*) get out [of], (*klubb e.d.*) leave, (*tävling*) withdraw, *b*) (*om fläck*) come out, disappear, (*om knapp e.d.*) come (fall) out **33** ~ *ut och* ~ go for (take) a walk; ~ *ut och äta* eat out; ~ *ut på* (*avse*) be aimed at, have as its aim, amount to; *låta sin vrede* ~ *ut över* vent one's anger upon **34** *hon* ~*r utanpå allesammans* she is superior to them all **35** ~ *utför* go downwards (downhill); *det* ~*r utför med dem* they are going downhill **36** ~ *utåt* (*om fönster e.d.*) open outwards; ~ *utåt med tårna* turn one's toes outward **37** ~ *vidare* go on; *låta ngt* ~ *vidare* pass s.th. on **38** ~ *åt a*) (*ta slut*) be consumed (used up), (*behövas*) be needed, (*finna åtgång*) sell, *b*) (*förgås*) perish, be dying (*av* with); *vad* ~*r åt dig?* what is the matter with you?; ~ *illa åt, se fara* [*illa med*]; *det* ~ *åt mycket tyg till den här klänningen* this dress takes a lot of material **39** ~ *över a*) go (walk) over, cross [over], *b*) (*se igenom*) look through (over), (*maskin äv.*) overhaul, *c*) *se övergå*, *d*) (*om smärta*) pass [over], subside

gåborts|kläder [-ˣbårts-] *pl* party clothes **-kostym** best suit

gå|ende *a4 o. s6* walking, going *etc.*; *en* ~ a pedestrian; ~ *bord* buffet, stand-up meal **-gata** pedestrian street

1 gång *s3* **1** (*levande varelsers*) walking; (*sätt att gå*) gait, walk; (*hästs*) pace; *spänstig* ~ springy step (gait); *känna igen ngn på* ~*en* recognize s.b. by his walk (step) **2** (*rörelse*) going, moving; (*motors o.d.*) running, working, motion, action; (*lopp*) run; (*fortgång*) progress; (*förlopp*) course; *i full* ~ well under way, (*om arbete äv.*) in full swing; *under samtalets* ~ in the course of the conversation; *få i* ~ get going (started), start; *hålla i* ~ keep going; *komma i* ~ get started, (*om maskin*) begin running (working); *sätta i* ~ start (set) going (running), start; *vara i* ~ be running (working, going, in operation), (*om förhandlingar e.d.*) be in progress, be proceeding

2 gång *s2* **1** (*väg*) path[way], walk **2** (*korridor*) passage, corridor; (*i kyrka*) aisle; (*i teater, i buss*) gangway, *AE.* aisle; (*under gata*) subway **3** *anat.* duct, canal

3 gång *s3* **1** (*tillfälle*) time; *en* ~ *a*) once (*om dagen* a day), *b*) (*om framtid*) some time, some (one) day, *c*) (*ens*) even; *en* ~ *för alla* once and for all, for good; *en* ~ *är ingen* ~ once is no custom; *en* ~ *till* once more, [over] again; *en halv* ~ *till så mycket* half as much again; *en och annan* ~ once in a while, every now and then, occasionally; *en åt* ~*en* one at a time; *för en* ~*s skull* for once [in a while]; *bara för den här* ~*en* just [for] this once; *förra* ~*en* last time; *inte en* ~ *hans barn* not even his children; *med en* ~ all at once; *ngn* ~ some time, (*ibland äv.*) now and then, from time to time; *ngn enda* ~ very rarely, on some rare occasion; *nästa* ~ next time; ~ *på* ~ time and again, time after time, over and over [again]; *på en* ~ *a*) (*samtidigt*) at the same time, *b*) (*i en omgång*) in one go, *c*) (*plötsligt*) all at once, suddenly; *på en och samma* ~ at one and the same time;

det var en ~ once upon a time there was; *det är nu en* ~ *så att* the fact is that **2** *två* ~*er två är fyra* twice two is four; *tre* ~*er* three times; *ett par tre* ~*er* two or three times; *rummet är tre* ~*er tre meter* the room is three by three metres (three metres square)

gång|are (*häst*) steed; *sport.* walker **-art** (*hästs*) pace **-avstånd** walking distance **-bana** pavement; *AE.* sidewalk **-bar** *a1* (*om väg*) negotiable **2** (*gällande, gängse*) current **3** (*kurant*) saleable, marketable **-bro** footbridge

gång|en *a5* gone; (*förfluten*) gone by; *långt* ~ far advanced (*sjukdom* disease); *-na tider* the past, past time; *den -na veckan* the past week **-grift** chambered barrow **-järn** hinge **-kläder** *pl* wearing-apparel (*sg*), clothing (*sg*) **-låt** marching tune **-matta** runner **-sport** [long--distance] walking **-stig** footpath, footway **-trafik** pedestrian traffic **-trafikant** pedestrian **-tunnel** [pedestrian] subway **-väg** footpath

gåpåaraktig [-ˣpå:-] *a5* hustling, go-ahead **gåpåar|e** [-ˣpå:-] pusher, go-getter **-fasoner** *pl* go-getting (*sg*)

går *i uttr.: i* ~ yesterday; *i* ~ *kväll* yesterday evening, (*senare*) last night; *i* ~ *morse* yesterday morning; *i* ~ *för en vecka sedan* a week [ago] yesterday; *tidningen för i* ~ yesterday's paper

gård [-å:-] *s2* **1** (*kringgärdad plats*) yard; (*bak-*) backyard; (*vid bondgård*) farmyard; (*framför herrgård o.d.*) courtyard; *rum åt* ~*en* back room; *två trappor upp åt* ~*en* on the second floor at the back **2** (*bond-*) farm; (*större*) estate; (*man-*) farmstead, homestead

går|dagen yesterday **-dagstidning[en]** yesterday's paper

gårdfarihand|el [-å:-] house-to-house peddling **-lare** [itinerant] pedlar, hawker

gårds|hus back-yard house **-karl** odd-jobman, odd-jobber; caretaker **-musikant** itinerant musician **-plan** courtyard **-sida** *åt* ~*n* at the back [of the house]

gårdvar [-å:-] *s2* watchdog

gås *-en gäss* goose (*pl* geese); *vitkindad* ~ barnacle goose; *ha en* ~ *oplockad med ngn* have a bone to pick with s.b.; *det är som att hälla vatten på en* ~ it's like [pouring] water on a duck's back; *det går vita gäss på havet* there are white horses on the sea **-hud** goose flesh (bumps *pl*, pimples *pl*, skin); *få* ~ get goose pimples **-karl** gander **-lever** goose liver **-leverpastej** pâté de foie gras; goose-liver paste **-krås** goose giblets (*pl*) **-marsch** *i* ~ in single file **-penna** quill **-ögon** (*citationstecken*) French quotation marks, guillemets **-ört** *bot.* silverweed

gåt|a *s1* riddle; (*friare*) enigma, puzzle, mystery **-full** mysterious, puzzling, enigmatic[al]

gått *sup. av gå*

gåva *s1* gift; present (*till* for, to); (*genom testamente*) bequest; *en man med stora gåvor* (*äv.*) a man of great parts

gåvo|brev deed of gift **-paket** gift parcel **-skatt** capital transfer (gift) tax

gäck [j-] **1** *s7, driva* ~ *med, se gäckas* [*med*] **2** *s2, slå* ~*en lös* let o.s. go **gäcka** (*svika*) baffle; disappoint; frustrate; *bli ~d i sina förhoppningar* have one's hopes dashed; *bli ~d i kär-*

lek be crossed in love **gäckande** *a4* roguish, elusive **gäckas** *dep,* ~ *med* mock (scoff) [at], deride; (*gyckla med*) make fun of, poke fun at **gäckeri** mocking, derision (*med* at)

gädd|a [j-] *s1* [northern] pike (*pl äv.* pike) **-drag** (*hopskr. gäddrag*) [trolling] spoon[bait]

gäl [j-] *s2* gill; *djur som andas med* ~*ar* gill--breathing animals

gälbgjutare [ˣjälb-] brazier

gäld [j-] *s3* debt[s *pl*] **gälda 1** (*betala*) pay; (*bestrida kostnad*) defray **2** (*försona*) atone for; (*återgälda*) requite

gäld|e|när *s3* debtor **-ränta** debt interest **-stuga** debtor's prison

gäll [j-] *a1* shrill; (*genomträngande*) piercing **gäll|a** [j-] *v2* **1** (*vara giltig*) be valid; (*om lag e.d.*) be in force, *AE.* be effective; (*om biljett äv.*) be available; (*om mynt*) be current; (*om påstående*) be true (*om* of; *ännu* still); (*äga tillämpning*) apply, be applicable (*för, på* to) **2** (*vara värd*) be worth **3** (*väga* [*tungt*], *betyda*) have (carry) weight **4** (*anses*) pass (*för, som* as); be looked (regarded) upon (*för, som* as) **5** (*avse*) be intended for; (*åsyfta*) have as its object; (*röra*) concern, have reference to; *vad -er saken?* what is it about?; *samma sak -er om* the same thing may be said of **6** *opers., det -er livet* it is a question of life or death; *nu -er det att* now we have got to; *när det verkligen -er* when it really comes to the point (*att of* + *ing-form*); *han sprang som om det -de livet* he ran for dear life **-ande** *a4* **1** (*giltig*) valid (*för* for), in force, *AE.* effective; (*tillämplig*) applicable; ~ *priser* current (ruling) prices **2** *göra* ~ (*påstå*) assert, maintain; *göra sina kunskaper* ~ bring one's knowledge to bear; *göra sina anspråk* ~ establish one's claims; *göra sitt inflytande* ~ assert one's influence; *göra sig* ~ (*om pers.*) assert o.s., (*om sak*) manifest itself, make itself felt

gällen [j-] *a5* on the turn

gällock gill cover (lid)

gäms *se gems*

gäng [j-] *s7* ([*arbets*]*lag*) gang; (*klick*) set **gäng|a** [j-] **I** *s1* [screw] thread; *gå i de gamla -orna* be in the old groove; *komma ur -orna* get out of the gear; *vara ur -orna* be off colour, be under the weather **II** *v1* **1** thread **2** *sl.* (*ha samlag*) screw **3** *rfl, vard.* get spliced **-kloppa** [-å-] *s1* diestock

gänglig [j-] *a1* lank[y] **-het** lank[i]ness

gängning [j-] *s2* [screw] threading

gängse [j-] *oböjligt a* current; (*rådande*) prevalent

gäng|snitt [j-] die **-tapp** tap

gärd [jä:rd] *s3* tribute; token (*av tacksamhet* of gratitude)

gärda [ˣjä:r-] fence

gärde [ˣjä:r-] *s6* (*fält*) field; ~*t är upprivet* (*bildl.*) the game is lost

gärds|gård [*vard.* ˈjärs-] fence **-gårdsstör** hurdle pole

gärdsmyg [ˣjä:rd-] *s2, zool.* wren; *AE.* winter wren

gärna [ˣjä:r-] *hellre helst, adv* **1** (*med nöje*) gladly; (*villigt*) willingly; (*utan hinder*) easily, readily; *ja,* ~ [*för mig*]! by all means!; *lika* ~

just as well; *en ~ sedd gäst* an ever-welcome guest; *hur ~ jag än vill* though nothing can give me more pleasure; *jag erkänner ~ att* I am quite prepared (ready) to admit that; *jag kommer mer än ~* I shall be delighted to come; *jag skulle ~ vilja* I should be glad to; *jag skulle ~ vilja veta* I should like to know; *du får ~ stanna här* you are quite welcome to stay here; *du kan ~ läsa högt* you may just as well read aloud; *han talar ~ om* he likes (is fond of) talking of; *han kan inte ~ hinna fram i tid* he will hardly get there in time **2** (*ofta*) often; *följden blir ~ den att* the result is liable to be that

gärning [*jä:r-] **1** (*handling*) act, deed; *goda ~ar* good deeds, kind actions; *i ord och ~* in word and deed; *tagen på bar ~* caught red-handed (in the act) **2** (*syssla*) work

gärningsman criminal, culprit, pertetrator

gärs [j-] *s2, zool.* ruff[e], pope

gäsp|a [j-] yawn **-ning** yawning; *en ~* a yawn

gässling [j-] gosling

gäst [j-] *s3* guest; (*besökande*) visitor; (*hotell-*) resident; (*restaurang-*) guest, patron

gästa [j-] *~ ngn* be a p.'s guest; *~ ngns hem* be a guest at a p.'s home **-bud** feast; banquet **-budssal** banqueting hall

gäst|bok guest book **-dirigent** visiting conductor **-fri** hospitable **-frihet** hospitality **-föreläsare** visiting lecturer

gästgiv|are [*jäst-, *vard.* *jäʃi-] innkeeper **-ar-gård, -eri** inn, hostelry

gäst|hamn guest harbour **-handduk** guest towel **-rum** spare (guest) room **-spel** special performance **-spela** give a special performance **-vänlig** *se gästfri*

göd|a [j-] *v2* **1** (*djur*) fatten; (*människor äv.*) feed up; *slakta den -da kalven* kill the fatted calf **2** (*jord, växter*) fertilize **3** *rfl* feed (fatten) [o.s.] up **-boskap** beef (fat[tening]) cattle (*pl*) **-kalv** beef (fatted) calf, fatling; *kokk.* prime veal **-kyckling** broiler

gödning [*jö:d-] **1** fattening *etc.* **2** fertilizing, fertilization **gödningsmedel** fertilizer, fertilizing substance

gödsel ['jödd-] *s9* manure, dung, muck; (*konst-*) fertilizer[s *pl*] **-grep** muckrake **-spridare** manure spreader **-stack** dunghill

gödsl|a [j-] manure, dung; (*konst-*) fertilize **-ing** manuring; fertilizing

gödsvin [j-] fattening (fatted) pig

gök [j-] *s2* **1** *zool.* [European] cuckoo **2** *bildl. o. skämts.* fellow, chap **3** *vard., se kaffekask* **-blomster** ragged robbin, cuckooflower **-otta** *ung.* dawn picnic to hear first birdsong **-tyta** *s1* wryneck **-unge** young cuckoo **-ur** cuckoo clock **-ärt** bitter vetch

göl [j-] *s2* pool; (*mindre sjö äv.*) mere

gömfröig [*jömm-] *a5* angiospermous; *~ växt* angiosperm

göm|ma [j-] **I** *s1* hiding place; place where one keeps things; *gravens tysta ~* the silent harbourage of the grave; *leta i sina -mor* search in one's drawers (cupboards) **II** *v2* **1** (*dölja*) hide [away], conceal (*för* from); (*begrava*) bury (*ansiktet i händerna* one's face in one's hands) **2** (*förvara*) keep (*till, åt* for); save [up]; (*låta ligga*) keep back, put by; *~ undan* put

away; *~ sig* hide, conceal o.s.

gömme [j-] *s6* **1** *se gömma I* **2** *bot.* pericarp

göm|sle *s6*, **-ställe** *s6* hiding place, hide-out, hideaway

1 göra [j-] *gjorde gjort* **I 1** (*syssla med, ombesörja*) do (*affärer med* business with; *ett gott arbete* good work; *sin plikt* one's duty; *ngn en tjänst* a favour); perform (*en uppgift* a task); (*utföra*) carry out, execute; *gör det själv* do it yourself **2** (*åstadkomma, avge o.d.*) make (*ngns bekantskap* a p.'s acquaintance; *intryck på* an impression upon; *ett misstag* a mistake; *slut på* an end of; *en uppfinning* an invention; *en överenskommelse* an agreement); (*åstadkomma*) bring about (*en förändring* a change); *~ underverk* work wonders **3** (*obj. är ett neutralt pron el. a*) do; *~ sitt bästa* do one's best; *sitta och ~ ingenting* sit doing nothing; *vad gör du i kväll?* what are you doing (going to do) this evening?; *vad är att ~?* what is to be done?; *det är inget att ~ åt saken* nothing can be done about it (in the matter), it cannot be helped **4** (*bereda*) give, afford, do (*ngn den glädjen att* s.b. the pleasure of + *ing-form*); (*tillfoga*) do, inflict upon; (*skapa, utgöra*) make; (*betyda*) be of importance, matter; (*företaga resa e.d.*) go; *~ en resa* go on a journey; *~ ngn skada* do s.b. harm; *det gör ingenting a*) (*har ingen betydelse*) it is of no importance, *b*) (*är alldeles detsamma*) it doesn't matter!, never mind!, *c*) (*avböjande ursäkt*) not at all!, don't mention it!; *det gör mig ont att höra* I am sorry to hear; *kläderna gör mannen* clothes make the man **5** (*tillverka*) make; (*konstnärligt äv.*) do; (*göra färdig*) do, finish **6** (*bese*) do; *~ Paris* do Paris **7** (*i vissa förbindelser*) make (*ngn lycklig* s.b. happy; *ngn till kung* s.b. [a] king; *det klart för ngn att* it clear to s.b. that; *saken värre* matters worse); do (*ngn gott, orätt* s.b. good, wrong); *~ ngn tokig* drive s.b. crazy; *~ det möjligt för ngn att* enable s.b. to; *~ det till sin plikt* make it one's duty; *det gjorde att jag bestämde mig för* this made me decide to (+ *inf.*) **8** (*handla*) act; do; *inte veta hur man bör ~* not know how to act; *gör som jag säger* do as I tell you **9** (*uppföra sig*) behave **II** (*i stället för tidigare nämnt verb*) do; be; shall; will; *han läser mer än jag gör* he reads more than I do; *han sprang, och det gjorde jag med* he ran, and so did I; *om du inte tar den gör jag det* if you don't take it I shall; *skiner solen? ja, det gör den* is the sun shining? yes, it is **III** (*med betonad partikel*) **1** *~ av; var skall jag ~ av...?* where am I to put...?, what am I to do with...?; *~ av med* (*mörda*) bump off; *AE.* waste; *~ av med pengar* spend (run through) money; *inte veta var man skall ~ av sig* not know what to do with o.s. **2** *~ bort sig* drop a brick **3** *~ efter* imitate, copy **4** *~ ngn emot* cross (thwart) s.b. **5** *~ fast* make fast, fasten **6** *~ färdig* get finished, finish, (*i ordning*) get ready **7** *~ ifrån sig ett arbete* get a piece of work off one's hands; *~ bra ifrån sig* give a good account of o.s. **8** *~ om a*) (*på nytt*) do over again, *b*) (*upprepa*) repeat, *c*) (*ändra*) alter **9** *~ rent efter sig* clean (*AE.* fix) up before leaving **10** *~ till; om det kan ~ ngt* *till* if that can help matters at all; ~ *sitt till för att det skall lyckas* do one's part to make it a success; *det gör varken till eller från* it makes no difference **11** ~ *undan* get done (off one's hands) **12** ~ *upp a*) (*eld, planer o.d.*) make, *b*) (*förslag, program o.d.*) draw up, *c*) (*räkning*) settle, *d*) (*ha en uppgörelse*) agree, settle, come to terms (*med* with; *om* about) **13** ~ *ngt åt saken* do s.th. about it (the matter) **IV** *rfl* **1** make o.s. (*omtyckt* popular; *förtrogen med* acquainted with); (*låtsas vara*) make o.s. out (pretend) to be (*bättre än man är* better than one is) **2** (*ta sig ut*) look (come out) (*bra* well) **3** (*tillverka åt sig*) make o.s. (*en klänning* a dress); (*låta göra*) have made; (*förvärva*) make (*en förmögenhet* a fortune); (*bilda sig*) form (*ett begrepp om* a conception of) **4** ~ *sig av med* get rid of; ~ *sig till* be affected, give o.s. airs, (*förställa sig*) dissimulate, sham; ~ *sig till* *för* make up to

2 göra [j-] *s6* (*arbete*) task, work; (*göromål*) business; (*besvär*) trouble
görande [j-] *s6*, ~*n och låtanden* doings
gördel [ˣjö:r-] *s2* girdle **-däck** radial [tyre]
gör|lig [ˣjö:r-] *a1* feasible, practicable; (*möjlig*) possible; *i ~aste mån* as far as possible **-ning-en** *best. form i uttr.: ngt är i* ~ s.th. is brewing
göromål [j-] *s7* (*arbete*) work, business; (*syssla*) occupation; (*åliggande*) duty
1 gös [j-] *s2* (*fisk*) pikeperch
2 gös [j-] *s2, sjö.* jack
gösstake jack staff
1 göt [j-] *s2, s3* (*om forntida svenskar*) Geat
2 göt [j-] *s7, tekn.* casting, billet, bloom, ingot
3 göt [j-] *imperf. av gjuta*
Göteborg [jöte'bårj] *n* Göteborg, Gothenburg
götisk [ˈjö:-] *a5* Geatish
göt|stål [j-] ingot (cast) steel **-valsverk** cogging (*AE.* blooming) mill

H

h s6 **1** h; *stumt* ~ silent h; *utelämna* ~ drop one's h's (aitches) **2** *mus.* B [natural]
1 ha *interj* ha[h]!
2 ha (*hava*) *hade haft* I *hjälpv* have II *huvudv* **1** have; (*mera vard.*) have got; (*äga*) possess; (*få, erhålla*) get; ~ *det bra* be well off; ~ *ledigt* be free; ~ *roligt* have a good time [of it]; ~ *rätt* be right; ~ *stort behov av* be in great need of; ~ *svårt för ngt* find s.th. difficult; *här ~r ni!* here you are!; *här ~r ni mig!* here I am!; *nu ~r jag det!* now I've got it!; *var ~r vi söder?* where is [the] south?; *vad vill ni ~?* a) what do you want?, b) (*att förtära*) what would you like?, what will you take?, c) (*i betalning*) what do you want (is your charge)?; *allt vad jag äger och* ~*r* everything I possess; *hur* ~*r du det nu för tiden?* how are things [with you] nowadays?; *hur mycket pengar* ~*r du på dig?* how much money have you got [on you]?; *jag vet inte var jag* ~*r honom* I don't know where he stands **2** (*förmå, låta*) get, have, make; ~ *ngn att lyda* make (have) s.b. (get s.b. to) obey **III** (*med betonad partikel*) **1** ~ *bort a*) (*tappa*) lose, (*förlägga*) mislay, b) (*ta bort*) have removed, take away **2** ~ *emot, inte* ~ *ngt emot* have nothing against **3** ~ *för sig a*) (*ha framför sig*) have before one, b) (*vara sysselsatt med*) be doing (up to), c) (*föreställa sig*) be under the impression, have an idea **4** ~ *ngn hos sig* (*som gäst*) have s.b. staying with one **5** ~ *i* put in **6** ~ *inne* (*varor*) have in stock; ~ *åldern inne* have reached the right age **7** ~ *kvar a*) (*ha över*) have left, b) (*ha i behåll*) have still **8** ~ *med sig* have with one **9** ~ *på sig* (*kläder o.d.*) have on; ~ *hela dagen på sig* have the whole day before one; ~ *bara en timme på sig* have only one hour left (to spare) **10** ~ *sönder* break, *vard.* smash **11** ~ *över* (*ha kvar*) have left
Haag [ha:g] *n* the Hague
habegär acquisitiveness
ha'bil *a1* (*skicklig*) clever; (*smidig*) adroit; (*duglig*) able; (*förbindlig*) suave
ha'bit *s3* attire
habitu|'é *s3* habitué **-'ell** *a5* habitual
habitus [ˈha:-] *oböjligt s, r* (*hållning*) bearing
1 hack *i uttr.: följa ngn* ~ *i häl* follow hard on the heels of s.b.
2 hack *s7* **1** (*skåra*) jag[g], notch, hack **2** (*lätt hugg*) peck
1 hacka 1 *kortsp.* small (low) card **2** (*liten summa*) *en* ~ a little cash; *en rejäl* ~ a tidy sum **3** *han går inte av för hackor* he is not just a nobody, he's a competent chap
2 hacka I *s1* pick[axe]; (*bred*) mattock; (*för jordluckring*) hoe II *v1* **1** hoe **2** *kokk.* chop; (*fin-*) mince; *det är varken* ~*t eller malet* it is neither one thing nor the other **3** (*om fåglar*) peck (*på* at) **4** *han* ~*de tänder* his teeth were

chattering **5** (*i bord, mark med t.ex. kniv*) hack, pick **6** (*klanka*) find fault (*på* with); (*gnata*) nag (*på* at) **7** (*tala med avbrott*) stammer, stutter
hackelse chopped (cut) straw, chaff **-maskin** chaff cutter
hackhosta hacking cough
hack|ig *a1* **1** (*full med hack*) jagged **2** (*stammande*) stuttering **-kyckling** *hon är deras* ~ they are always picking on her **-mat** *bildl.* mincemeat
hack|ning hoeing *etc., se 2 hacka* **II -spett** *s2* woodpecker
hade *imperf av ha*[*va*]
haffa nab, cop, nick, collar
hafnium ['haff-] *s8* hafnium
hafs *s7* (*slarv*) slovenliness; (*brådska*) scramble
hafs|a do things in a hurry; ~ *ifrån sig* scramble through **-ig** *a1* slapdash, slovenly **-verk** scamped (slovenly) work
haft *sup av ha*[*va*]
hagalen [ˣha:-] avaricious
hage *s2* **1** (*betesmark*) enclosed pasture[-land]; (*lund*) grove **2** (*för småbarn*) [baby's] playpen **3** *hoppa* ~ play hopscotch
hagel ['ha:-] *s7* **1** (*iskorn, koll.*) hail (*sg*); *ett* ~ a hailstone **2** (*blykula*) [small] shot (*sg o. pl*) **-by** hailstorm **-bössa** shotgun, fowling piece **-korn** hailstone **-patron** shot cartridge **-skott** shot from a shotgun **-skur** hailshower, hailstorm **-svärm** *jakt.* charge [of shot]
hagga *s1* hag
hagla [ˣha:g-] hail; *bildl. äv.* rain, come thick and fast
hagtorn [ˣhagg-] *s2* hawthorn, may [tree]
Haiti [ha'i:ti] *n* Haiti **haiti|'an** *s3*, **-ansk** [-'a:nsk] *a5* Haitian, Haytian
haj [hajj] *s2* shark
haja [ˣhajja] (*förstå*) get, dig; ~ *till* give a start; be startled (scared)
hajfena shark's fin
hajk *s2* hike
hak *s7* notch; hack, dent
1 haka *v1* hook (*i, vid* to); ~ *av* unhook; ~ *fast a*) hook [on], fasten, *b*) (*fastna*) get caught (*i* by, on), catch (*i* in); ~ *i, se haka fast b*); ~ *upp a*) (*fästa upp*) loop up, *b*) (*öppna*) unhook, unfasten; ~ *upp sig a*) get caught, *b*) *bildl.* get stuck; ~ *upp sig på småsaker* stick at (worry about) trifles; ~ *sig* get stuck; ~ *sig fast* (*äv. bildl.*) cling (*vid* to)
2 haka *s1* chin; *tappa* ~*n* be taken aback; *stå i vatten upp till* ~*n* be in water up to one's chin
hakband string; (*brett*) cheek band
hake *s2* **1** hook; (*fönster-*) catch **2** *det finns en* ~ (*bildl.*) there is a snag in it; [*för*] *tusan hakar!* the deuce! **-bössa** [h]arquebus, hackbut, hagbut
hak|formig [-å-] *a5* hooked, hooklike **-kors** swastika
haklapp bib, feeder
hakmask hookworm **-sjuka** hookworm disease
hak|rem chin strap **-spets** point of the chin
hal *a1* slippery; *bildl. äv.* evasive; (*glatt*) oily, sleek; ~ *tunga* smooth tongue; ~ *som en ål* [as] slippery as an eel; *på* ~ *is* (*bildl.*) on treacherous ground, on thin ice; *sätta ngn på det* ~*a*

drive s.b. into a corner; *det är* ~*t på vägarnc* the roads are slippery
hala 1 *sjö.* haul; pull, tug; ~ *flaggan* lower the flag; *hissa och* ~ hoist and lower; ~ *an* haul (tally) aft; ~ *in* haul in; ~ *fram* haul (*friare* draw, drag) forwards **2** *bildl.*, ~ *ut på tider* drag out the time **3** *rfl*, ~ *sig ner* lower o.s. let o.s. down
halka I *s1* slipperiness; *svår* ~ very slippery roads (road surface) **II** *v1* slip [and fall], slide glide; (*slira*) skid; ~ *förbi* (*bildl.*) skim past skilfully elude; ~ *omkull* slip over (down), slip and fall; *ordet* ~*de över mina läppar* the word escaped me (my lips)
halk|bana (*för träningskörning*) skidpan **-fri** *se* **-säker -ig** *a1* slippery **-säker** nonskid, nonslip
hall *s2* (*förrum*) lounge; (*pelar-*) colonnade
halleluja [-'ja:, *äv.* -ˣlu:-] hallelujah!
hallick ['hall-] *s2* pimp, ponce
hallon [-ån] *s7* raspberry **-buske** raspberry bush (shrub); **-buskar** (*äv.*) raspberry canes **-saft** raspberry juice (syrup) **-sylt** raspberry jam **-änger** *s2* raspberry fruitworm
hallstämpel hallmark
hallucin|ation hallucination **-atorisk** [-'tɷ:-] *a5* hallucinatory **-era** be subject to hallucinations **-ogen** [-'je:n] *s3* hallucinogen
hal'lå I *interj* hello, hallo[o], hullo **II** *s6* (*ovätsen*) hullaba[l]oo
hallå|a *vard.* **I** [-ˣlå:a] *s1, se -kvinna* **II** [-'lå:a] *v1, radio.* announce **-kvinna** [woman] announcer **-man** announcer
halm *s3* straw; *av* ~ (*äv.*) straw
halma *n* halma; *spela* ~ play halma
halm|arbete article made of straw; *abstr. o. koll.* straw work **-gul** straw[-coloured] **-hatt** straw hat; (*platt*) boater **-kärve** sheaf **-madrass** straw mattress (bed) **-stack** straw stack (rick) **-strå** straw; *gripa efter ett* ~ (*bildl.*) catch at a straw **-tak** thatched roof **-täckt** *a4* straw-covered, thatched
halo ['ha:-] *s5, meteor.* halo
halogen [-'je:n] *s3* halogen **-lampa** halogen lamp **-ljus** halogen light
hals *s2* **1** neck; (*strupe o. tekn.*) throat; ~ *över huvud* head over heels; *med* (*av*) *full* ~ at the top of one's voice; *bryta* ~*en av sig* break one's neck; *falla ngn om* ~*en* fall on a p.'s neck; *få ngn på* ~*en* get saddled with s.b.; *få nya bekymmer på* ~*en* be saddled with new adversities; *ge* ~ *a*) (*om hund*) give tongue, *b*) (*om pers.*) raise a cry; *ha ont i* ~*en* have a sore throat; *sitta ända upp till* ~*en i* be immersed up to the neck in; *sätta ett ben i* ~*en* have a bone stick in one's throat; *det står mig upp i* ~*en* it makes me sick, I am fed up with it; *orden fastnade i* ~*en på mig* the words stuck in my throat; *skjortan är trång i* ~*en* the shirt is tight round the neck **2** (*på instrument*) neck; (*på nottecken*) stem **3** *sjö.* tack; *ligga för babords* ~*ar* be (stand) on the port tack
hals|a 1 (*dricka*) take a swig **2** *sjö.* wear, tack **-band** necklace; (*hund-*) collar **-bloss** *dra* ~ inhale [the smoke] **-brytande** *a4* breakneck **-bränna** *s1* heartburn **-böld** quinsy **-duk** scarf, neckerchief; (*tjock*) muffler; (*fischy*) fichu; (*kravatt*) tie, *AE.* necktie; *vit* ~ a white

tie **-fluss** s3 tonsillitis **-grop** ha hjärtat i ~en have one's heart in one's mouth (throat) **-hugga** behead, decapitate **-huggning** beheading, decapitation **-järn** iron collar **-katarr** pharyngitis **-kedja** chain [round the neck] **-kota** cervical vertebra **-krås** ruff, frill **-linning** neckband **-mandlar** pl [palatine] tonsils **-ont** sore throat **-pulsåder** carotid [artery] **-smycke** necklace **-starrig** al stubborn, obstinate **-tablett** throat lozenge, cough drop

halst|er ['hals-] s7 gridiron, grill **-ra** grill
1 halt s3 **1** (proportion, kvantitet) content; percentage; (i guldarbeten o. mynt) standard **2** bildl. substance; worth, value
2 halt I s3 (uppehåll) halt **II** interj halt!; (stanna) stop!
3 halt al lame (på ena benet in one leg)
halta limp (på ena foten with one foot); ~ iväg limp along; jämförelsen ~r the comparison does not hold good; versen ~r the [rhythm of the] verse halts
halv a5 half; ~ biljett half fare; ~ lön half pay; ~a året half the year; ett ~t dussin half a dozen; ett ~t löfte a half-promise; en ~ gång till så stor half as big again; en och en ~ månad six weeks; ett och ett ~t år eighteen months; till ~a priset at half price, half-price; hissa flaggan på ~ stång fly the flag at half-mast, half-mast; mötas på ~a vägen meet halfway; klockan är ~ ett it is half past twelve
halv|a s1 **1** half; en ~ öl half a (a small) bottle of beer; de tog var sin ~ they took one half each **2** (andra sup) second glass **-annan** [-ˣann-] n = halvtannat one and a half **-apa** zool. prosimian **-automatisk** semiautomatic **-back** sport. halfback **-bildad** half-educated **-blod** s7 **1** (människa) half-breed **2** (häst) half-blood **-bra** so-so; indifferent; middling **-bror** half-brother **-butelj** half-bottle **-cirkel** semicircle **-cirkelformig** semicircular **-dager** twilight **-dagsplats** part-time job **-dan[n]** a5 mediocre, middling **-dunkel I** s7 dusk, semi-darkness **II** a5 dusky, dim **-dussin** half-dozen; ett ~ (äv.) half a dozen **-däck** half-deck; (på örlogsfartyg) quarter-deck **-död** half-dead
halver|a halve, divide into halves; geom. bisect; absol. äv. go halves **-ing** halving etc.
halv|eringstid kärnfys. half-life **-fabrikat** semi-manufacture, semi-manufactured product **-fet** low-fat (ost cheese); boktr. bold; ~ stil bold face **-figur** porträtt i ~ half-length [portrait] **-fransk** ~t band half-binding; i ~t band half-bound **-full** half full; (om pers.) tipsy **-färdig** half-finished; vara ~ be half ready (finished, done) **-gammal** no longer young **-gardering** (i tips) 2-ways [forecast] **-genomskinlig** semitransparent **-gräs** sedges (pl) **-gud** demigod; (friare) hero
halv|het (halvmesyr) half measure (ljumhet) half-heartedness **-hjärtad** [-j-] a5 half-hearted **-hög** of medium height; med ~ röst in an undertone, in a loud whisper **-klot** hemisphere **-klädd** a5 half-dressed **-kokt** half boiled; underdone; AE. rare **-kombi** hatchback **-kväden** i uttr.: förstå ~ visa be able to take a hint **-kvävd** [-ä:-] a5 half-choked **-ledare** elektron. semiconductor **-lek** sport. half; under första

~ during the first half **-ligga** recline **-liter** en ~ half a litre **-ljus I** s7 half-light; (på bilar) dipped (AE. dimmed) headlights **II** a5 semi-transparent **-mesyr** s3 half measure **-mil** en ~ half a [Swedish] mile; den första ~en the first half-mile **-måne** half-moon **-månformig** [-år-] a5 shaped like a half-moon, semilunar **-mätt** half full **-mörker** semidarkness, half-light **-naken** half naked, seminude **-nelson** (i brottning) half-nelson **-not** minim; AE. half note **-officiell** semiofficial **-part** half share, half **-pension** half board, demi-pension **-professionell** semiprofessional **-profil** i ~ in semi-profile **-ras** half-breed **-rund** semicircular **-sanning** half-truth **-sekel** half-century **-sekelgammal** half-a-century (fifty-year) old **-sida** half-page **-skugga** half-shade **-slag** half-hitch; dubbelt ~ clove hitch **-slummer** drowse **-sluten** half-closed **-sova** doze, be half asleep **-statlig** partly owned by the state (government) **-stekt** [-e:-] half roasted; (ej tillräckligt stekt) underdone; AE. rare **-stor** medium-sized **-strumpa** sock **-sula** s1 o. v1 sole, half-sole **-sulning** [-u:-] soling **-syskon** half-brothers and half-sisters **-syster** half-sister **-söt** medium sweet
halv|t adv half; ~ om ~ lova more or less promise **-tid** sport. half-time; arbeta ~ work half (part) time
halvtids|anställd part-timer, part-time employee **-tjänst** part-time work
halv|timme half-hour; en ~ half an hour; en ~s resa half an hour's (a half-hour's) journey; om en ~ in half an hour['s time]; varje ~ every half-hour, half-hourly **-timmeslång** en ~ ... a[n] ... of half an hour, a half-hour... **-ton** mus. semitone; AE. half step **-torr** (om vin o.d.) medium dry **-trappa** en ~ half a flight [of stairs] **-vaken** half-awake **-vild** (om folkstam) semibarbarian; (om tillstånd) half-wild **-vokal** semivowel **-vuxen** (om pers.) half grown-up, adolescent; (om djur, växt) half-grown **-vägs** halfway **-år** six months, half-year; ett ~ [a] half-year, six months; varje ~ semiannually **-årig** a5 half-year's, six months'; (som återkommer varje halvår) half-yearly, semiannual
halvårs|gammal six months old; of six months **-ränta** half-yearly interest **-vis** semiannually, every six months, half-yearly
halvädelsten semiprecious stone
halv|ö peninsula **-öppen** half-open, (på glänt) ajar; med ~ mun with lips parted
hambo ['hamm-] s5 Hambo; dansa ~ dance the Hambo
hamburg|are hamburger **-erkött** smoked salt horseflesh
ha'mit s3 Hamite **-isk** a5 Hamitic
hammar|e hammer; mallet; anat. malleus; ~n och skäran the hammer and sickle **-haj** hammerhead **-skaft** hammer handle **-slag** hammer blow (stroke) **-tå** med. hammertoe
hammock ['hammåk] s2 hammock settee
1 hamn s2 **1** (skepnad) guise **2** (vålnad) ghost, apparition
2 hamn s2 harbour; (hamnstad, mål för sjöresa) port; bildl. o. poet. haven; inre ~ inner harbour (port); yttre ~ outer basin (harbour); anlöpa en

~ call at a (make) port; *löpa in i en* ~ enter a port; *söka* ~ seek harbour; *äktenskapets lugna* ~ the haven of matrimony
hamn|a land [up]; ~ *i en soffa* come to rest on (be placed on) a sofa; ~ *i galgen* end up on the gallows; *-de i vattnet* landed in the water **-anläggning** harbour; docks (*pl*) **-arbetare** docker, stevedore; *AE.* longshoreman **-arbetarstrejk** dock strike **-avgifter** harbour dues, port charges **-bassäng** dock **-fyr** harbour light **-förvaltning** (*myndighet*) port authorities (*pl*) **-inlopp** harbour entrance **-kapten** harbour master **-kontor** port authority; harbour master's office **-kvarter** dock district; dockland **-område** dockyard **-plats** berth, wharf **-stad** port; seaport
1 hampa *v1, det -de sig så* it so turned out
2 hampa *s1* hemp; *ta ngn i -n* (*vard.*) collar s.b., *bildl.* take s.b. to task
hamp|frö hempseed **-rep** hemp rope
hamr|a hammer (*på* at); *tekn. äv.* forge, beat; (*friare o. bildl.*) drum (*på bordet* on the table); pound (*på piano* [on] the piano); (*om hårt föremål*) pound, beat **-ad** *a5* hammered; beaten **-ing** hammering *etc.*
hamster ['hamm-] *s2* hamster
hamstr|a hoard; pile up **-are** hoarder **-ing** hoarding
han [hann] he; (*om djur, sak*) it, *äv.* he, she; ~ *som står där borta är* the man standing over there is
hanblomma [ˣhaːn-] male flower
hand *-en händer* **1** hand; *-en på hjärtat!* cross your heart!; *ngns högra* ~ (*bildl.*) a p.'s right--hand man; *efter* ~ gradually, little by little; *efter* ~ *som* [according] as; *för* ~ by hand; *i första* ~ in the first place, first of all, above all, (*omedelbart*) immediately; *i andra* ~ [at] second-hand, in the second place; *köpare i andra* ~ second-hand buyer; *i sista* ~ in the last resort, in the end, finally; *med varm* ~ readily, gladly, of one's own free will; *på egen* ~ a) (*självständigt*) by o.s., b) (*utan hjälp*) by o.s.; *på fri* ~ a) (*utan hjälpmedel*) by hand, b) (*oförberett*) off-hand; *på tu man* ~ by ourselves (*etc.*); *under* ~ privately; *anhålla om ngns* ~ ask for a p.'s hand; *byta om* ~ change hands; *bära* ~ *på ngn* lay hands on s.b.; *bära ngn på sina händer* make life a bed of roses for s.b.; *börja med två tomma händer* start empty--handed; *dö för egen* ~ die by one's own hand; *få ngt ur händerna* get s.th. off one's hands; *ge ngn fria händer* give s.b. a free hand; *ge vid -en* indicate, show, make it clear; *gå* ~ *i* ~ *med* go (walk) hand in hand with; *gå ur* ~ *i* ~ go from hand to hand; *ha* ~ *om* be in charge of; *ha* [*god*] ~ *med barn* be able to manage (have a way with) children; *ha ngn helt i sin* ~ have s.b. entirely in one's hands (pocket); *ha ngt helt i sin* ~ have complete control over s.th.; *ha ngt för händer* have s.th. on (in) hand; *ha ngt på* ~ have the option of s.th.; *hyra ut i andra* ~ (*äv.*) sublet; *hålla sin* ~ *över* hold a protecting hand over; *komma i orätta händer* get into the wrong hands; *kyssa ngn på -en* kiss a p.'s hand; *leva ur* ~ *i mun* live from hand to mouth; *låta ngt gå sig ur händerna* let s.th.

slip through one's fingers; *inte lyfta en* ~ *för att* not lift a hand to; *lägga sista -en vid* put the finishing touches to; *räcka ngn -en* hold out one's hand to s.b.; *räcka ngn en hjälpande* ~ lend s.b. a [helping] hand; *sitta med händerna i kors* sit with folded hands, sit idle; *skaka* ~ *med* shake hands with; *stå på händerna* do a handstand; *sätta händerna i sidan* put one's arms akimbo; *ta* ~ *om* take in hand, take charge of; *ta emot med uppräckta händer* be only too pleased to receive; *ta mig i* ~ *på* [give me] your hand on; *ta ngn i* ~ take a p.'s hand, (*hälsa*) shake hands with s.b., shake a p.'s hand; *ta sin* ~ *ifrån* (*bildl.*) withdraw one's support from, drop, abandon; *två sina händer* wash one's hands of it; *tvätta händerna* wash one's hands; *upp med händerna!* hands up!, stick'em up!; *vara för -en a*) (*finnas*) exist, *b*) (*vara nära*) be close at hand; *vinka med kalla -en* turn s.th. down flat, refuse point-blank, blankly refuse; *äta ur -en på ngn* (*bildl.*) eat out of a p.'s hands; *de kan ta varann i* ~ it's six of one and half a dozen of the other, it's six and two threes; *det var som att vända om en* ~ it was a complete right about face; *hon var som en omvänd* ~ she was quite a different person; *allt gick honom väl i händer* fortune smiled on him, everything he touched succeeded **2** (*sida*) hand, side; *på höger* ~ on the right[-hand] side **3** *till -a* (*på brev*) to be delivered by hand; *gå ngn till -a* assist (wait) on s.b.; *komma ngn till -a* come to hand, reach s.b. **4** *till -s* at hand; *ligga nära till -s* be close (near) at hand, be handy; *nära till -s liggande* (*om förklaring o.d.*) plausible, reasonable
hand|alfabet manual alphabet **-arbete** (*sömnad o.d.*) needlework; (*broderi*) embroidery; (*stickning*) knitting; (*motsats maskinarbete*) handwork; *ett* ~ a piece of needlework **-bagage** hand luggage (*AE.* baggage) **-boja** handcuff, manacle (*båda äv.* = *belägga med handbojor*) **-bok** handbook; (*lärobok äv.*) manual, guide **-boll** handball **-brev** personal (private) letter **-broderad** *a5* hand-embroidered **-broms** handbrake **-diskmedel** manual dishwashing detergent **-duk** towel; (*köks-*) [tea] cloth **-dusch** hand shower
handel ['hann-] *s9* **1** trade; (*i stort, i sht internationell*) commerce; (*handlande*) trading, dealing; (*affärstransaktion*) transaction; (*köp*) bargain; (*bytes-*) barter; (*i sht olaglig*) traffic; (*butik*) shop; ~ *och industri* trade (commerce) and industry; *-n med utlandet* foreign trade; *i* [*allmänna*] ~ on (in) the [open] market; *driva* (*idka*) ~ carry on trade (business); *driva* (*idka*) ~ *med a*) (*land, pers.*) trade with, carry on trade with, *b*) (*vara*) trade (deal) in **2** ~ *och vandel* dealings (*pl*), conduct
handeldvapen firearm; *pl äv.* small arms; *AE. äv.* handgun
handels|agent commercial (trade) agent **-anställd** commercial employee **-attaché** commercial attaché **-avtal** trade agreement **-balans** (*lands*) balance of trade; (*firmas*) trade balance **-balk** commercial code **-bod** shop; *särsk. AE.* store **-bolag** trading company

-bruk trade (business) custom **-departement** ministry of commerce; *~et* (*i Storbritannien*) the Department of Trade, (*i USA*) the Department of Commerce **-fartyg** merchant vessel (ship) **-flagga** merchant flag **-flotta** merchant navy (*i sht AE.* marine) **-förbindelser** *pl* trade relations; (*firmor*) business connections **-gymnasium** higher commercial (business) school **-hus** business house (firm) **-högskola** school of economics and business administration **-idkare** tradesman (*pl äv.* tradespeople, tradesfolk) **-institut** business institute, institute of commerce **-järn** commercial iron, ordinary steel **-kammare** chamber of commerce **-kontor** [Swedish] trade office **-korrespondens** commercial (business) correspondence **-lära** commercial science; (*lärobok*) textbook in commerce **-lärare** teacher of commerce **-man** shopkeeper, storekeeper **-minister** minister of commerce; (*i USA*) secretary of commerce **-politik** trade (commercial) policy **-politisk** of trade (commercial) policy **-resande** travelling salesman, commercial traveller (*för* representing; *i* in); *AE.* traveling salesman **-räkning** commercial arithmetic **-rätt** commercial law **-rättighet** trader's licence **-sekreterare** trade commissioner **-skola** business (commercial) school, school of commerce **-stad** commercial (trading) city (town) **-teknik** trading technique **-teknisk** commercial, business, trade **-trädgård** market garden; *AE.* truck farm **-utbildning** commercial (business) training **-utbyte** trade, exchange of commoditites **-vara** commodity; *pl äv.* merchandise (*sg*), goods **-vinst** trading (business) profit **-väg** trade route

hand|fallen nonplussed, taken aback **-fast** sturdy, stalwart **-fat** washbasin, washbowl **-flata** palm, flat of the (one's) hand **-full** *oböjligt s, en ~* a handful of, (*friare*) a few **-gemäng** [-j-] *s7, mil.* hand-to-hand fighting; (*friare*) scuffle, affray; *råka i ~* (*mil.*) come to close quarters, (*friare*) come to blows **-gjord** handmade **-granat** hand grenade **-grepp** manipulation, grip; *mil.* motion; *invanda ~* practised manipulation[s *pl*]

handgriplig [-i:p-] *a1* **1** (*som utförs med händerna*) *ett ~t skämt* a practical joke; *~ tillrättavisning* corporal punishment **2** (*påtaglig*) obvious, palpable, tangible; *~t bevis* tangible proof **-en** *adv, gå ~ till väga* use [physical] force **-heter** *pl, gå* (*komma*) *till ~* take (come) to blows

hand|gången *a5, ngns -gångne man* a p.'s henchman **-ha** (*ha vård om*) have (be in) charge of, be responsible for; (*ämbete*) administer; (*hantera*) handle **-havande** *s6* administration, management, handling

handikapp ['hand-] *s7*, **handikappa** *v1* handicap

handikapp|ad *a5* handicapped, disabled **-lägenhet** apartment designed for disabled person **-råd** *Statens ~* [the Swedish] national council for the disabled **-tävling** handicap competition

hand|kammare still room, storeroom, pantry **-kanna** water-jug; (*vattenkanna*) watering-can

-klappning clapping of hands; *~ar* applause (*sg*) **-klaver** accordion; concertina **-klove** *se handboja* **-kraft** manual power; *drivas med ~* be worked by hand **-kyss** kiss on the (a p.'s) hand **-kärra** handcart

handla **1** (*göra uppköp*) shop, do shopping, make one's purchases; *gå ut och ~* go shopping; *handla ~* buy milk **2** (*göra affärer*) trade, deal, do business (*i, med* in; *med ngn* with s.b.) **3** (*bete sig*) act (*efter sitt samvete* according to one's conscience; *i god tro* in good faith; *mot ngn* towards s.b.); *~ orätt* act wrongly, do wrong **4** (*vara verksam*) act; *tänk först och ~ sen!* think before you act! **5** *~ om a*) (*ha t. innehåll*) deal with, be about, treat of, *b*) (*vara fråga om*) be a question of

handlag *s7, ngns ~ med ngt* a p.'s way of doing (handling) things; *det rätta ~et* the right knack; *ha gott ~ med barn* have a good hand with (be good at managing) children

handl|ande **1** *s6* acting *etc.* **2** *s9* (*handelsman*) shopkeeper, storekeeper; (*köpman*) tradesman (*pl äv.* tradespeople, tradesfolk), dealer **-are** *se handlande 2*

handled *s3* wrist

handled|a *v2* (*i studier*) guide, tutor; (*vid uppfostran e.d.*) have oversight over, superintend; (*undervisa*) instruct **-are** instructor, teacher, tutor, supervisor; guide **-ning** supervision, guidance; (*lärobok*) guide; *ge ngn ~ i* give s.b. guidance in

handling **1** (*gärning*) action; (*bedrift*) act, deed; *en ~ens man* a man of action; *goda ~ar* good deeds; *gå från ord till ~* translate words into deeds **2** (*i roman o.d.*) action, scene; (*intrig*) story, plot **3** (*dokument*) document, deed; *lägga till ~arna* put aside

handlings|frihet freedom of action; *ha full ~* (*äv.*) be a free agent **-kraft** energy, drive **-kraftig** energetic, active **-människa** man (woman) of action **-sätt** conduct, line of action; behaviour

hand|lov[e] *s2* wrist **-lån** temporary loan

handlägg|a deal with, handle; *jur.* hear **-ning** dealing (*av* with), handling; *jur.* hearing; trial; *målets ~* the hearing of the case

hand|löst headlong, precipitately, violently **-målad** *a5* hand-painted **-penning** down payment, deposit **-plocka** (*utvälja*) hand-pick **-påläggning** *relig.* imposition (laying on) of hands **-rengöringsmedel** hand cleaner **-räckning** **1** assistance (*äv. jur.*); *ge ngn en ~* give (lend) s.b. a [helping] hand **2** *mil.* fatigue duty **-rörelse** motion (movement) of the (one's) hand

handsbredd handbreadth

handsekreterare private secretary

handskaffär [*hansk-] gloveshop, glover's shop

handskakning handshake

handskas [*hanskas] *dep, ~ med a*) (*hantera*) handle, *b*) (*behandla*) treat, deal with; *~ varligt med* (*äv.*) be careful about, handle with care

handskbeklädd [*hansk-] *a5* gloved

handsk|e [*hanske] *s2* glove; (*krag-*) gauntlet; *kasta ~n åt ngn* (*bildl.*) throw down the gauntlet to s.b.; *ta upp [den kastade] ~n* take up the

gauntlet, accept the challenge **-fack** (*i bil*) glove compartment **-makare** glover
hand|skrift 1 (*stil*) hand[writing]; (*motsats maskinskrift äv.*) [manu]script **2** (*manuskript*) manuscript (*förk.* MS., *pl* MSS.) **-skriven** *a5* written by hand, handwritten
handskskinn [ˣhansk-] glove-leather
hand|slag handshake **-stickad** *a5* hand-knit, hand-knitted **-stil** [hand]writing **-stöpt** [-ö:-] *a4*, ~ *ljus* hand-dipped candle **-svett** excessive sweating of the hands; *ha* ~ have clammy hands **-sydd** *a5* hand-sewn; handmade **-såg** handsaw **-sättare** *boktr.* hand-compositor **-sättning** *boktr.* hand-composition **-tag 1** (*fäste*) handle (*på, till* of); (*på kniv etc. äv.*) haft; (*runt*) knob **2** (*tag med handen*) grip, grasp, hold; *ge ngn ett* ~ give s.b. a [helping] hand **-tryck** block printing, hand-printing; *konkr.* block-print **-tryckning 1** pressure (squeezing) of the hand **2** (*dusör*) tip; *ge ngn en* ~ tip s.b., grease a p.'s palm **-uppräckning** show of hands; *rösta genom* ~ vote by show of hands **-vapen** hand weapon; *pl* (*eldvapen*) small arms, firearms **-volt** handspring **-vändning** *i en* ~ in a twink[ling] (trice), in [next to] no time; *AE. äv.* in short order **-väska** handbag, bag; *AE. äv.* purse, pocketbook **-vävd** hand-woven
1 hane *s2* (*djur*) male; (*fågel- äv.*) cock
2 hane *s2* **1** (*tupp*) cock; *den röda ~n* the fire fiend **2** (*på handeldvapen*) cock, hammer; *spänna ~n på* cock
hanegäll [-j-] *s7*, *i ~et* at cockcrow
hangar [-ŋ'ga:r] *s3* hangar **-fartyg** aircraft carrier
hanhund [he-]dog
hank *s2*, *inom stadens* ~ *och stör* within the bounds (confines) of the town
hanka *gå och* ~ be ailing (puling), go about looking poorly; ~ *sig fram* manage to get along somehow
hankatt tomcat
hankig *a1* ailing, off-colour
han|kön male sex **-lig** *a5* male
hann *imperf. av* hinna
hanne *se 1* hane
hanrej [ˣha:n-] *s2, s3* cuckold
hans his; (*om djur*) its
Hansan *s, best. form* the Hanseatic League
hansestad Hanseatic city (town)
hantel *s2* dumbbell
hanter|a handle; (*sköta*) manage; (*racket, svärd e.d.*) wield; (*använda*) use, make use of; (*behandla*) treat **-ing 1** (*hanterande*) handling *etc.* **2** (*näring*) trade, business; (*sysselsättning*) occupation **-lig** *a1* handy; manageable
hantlangare helper, assistant; (*murar-*) hodman; *neds.* henchman, tool
hantverk *s7* [handi]craft; trade **-are** craftsman, artisan; (*friare*) workman
hantverks|mässig *a1* manual; handicraft; (*schablonmässig*) mechanical **-produkt** handicraft product **-skicklighet** skill of craftsmanship
harakiri [-'ki:-] *s6, s7* harakiri
harang long speech; harangue; *hålla en lång ~ om* produce a long rigmarole about **-era** [-ŋg-]

harangue
hare *s2* hare; (*vid hundkapplöpning*) electric hare; *bildl.* coward, *vard.* funk; *ingen vet var ~n har sin gång* (*ung.*) there's no knowing what the upshot will be
harem ['ha:-] *s7* harem **haremsdam** lady of a (the) harem
harhjärtad [-j-] *a5* chicken-hearted, chicken-livered
haricots verts [arrikå'vä:r] *pl* haricots, French beans
harig *a1* timid; *vard.* funky; (*försagd*) pusillanimous
harkl|a hawk; ~ *sig* clear one's throat **-ing** hawk, hawking
harklöver *bot.* hare's-foot
harkrank [ˣha:r-] *s2* crane fly, daddy-longlegs
harlekin [ˣha:r-, *äv.* 'ha:r-] *s3* harlequin
harm *s3* indignation (*mot* against, with; *över* at); (*svagare*) resentment; (*förtret*) annoyance, vexation
harm|a vex, annoy, fill with indignation; *det ~r mig att han* (*äv.*) I am annoyed at his (+ *ing-form*) **-as** *dep* get (be) annoyed (*över* at); feel indignant (*på* with; *över* at) **-lig** *a1* provoking, vexatious, annoying **-lös** (*oförarglig*) inoffensive; innocuous; (*ofarlig*) harmless **-löshet** inoffensiveness; innocence
harmo'ni *s3* harmony; (*samstämmighet*) concord **-era** harmonize; ~ *med* (*äv.*) be in harmony with
harmo'n|ik *s3, se* harmonilära **-ika** [-'mɔ:-] *s1* harmonica
harmon|ilära theory of harmony; harmonics (*pl o. sg*) **-isera** harmonize **-isk** [-'mɔ:-] *a5* harmonious; *mat. o. mus.* harmonic; ~*t medium* harmonic mean **-ium** [-'mɔ:-] *s4* harmonium
harmsen *a3* indignant, angry; vexed, annoyed (*på* with; *över* at)
harmynt [ˣha:r-] *a4* harelipped **-het** harelip
harnesk ['ha:r-] *s7* cuirass; armour (*äv. bildl.*); *bringa ngn i* ~ *mot* rouse s.b. to hostility against, set s.b. up against; *vara i* ~ *mot* be up in arms against
1 harpa *s1* **1** *mus.* harp **2** *vard.* (*om kvinna*) old hag, witch
2 harpa *s1, lantbr.* sifting machine; (*såll*) riddle
harpest rabbit fever, tularaemia
harpist harper, harpist **harpolekare** harp player, harper
har'pun *s3* harpoon
harpuner|a harpoon **-are** [-ˣne:-] harpoone[e]r **-ing** harpooning
harpunkanon harpoon gun
harpya [-ˣpy:a *el.* -'py:a] *s1* *zool.* harpy eagle **2** *myt.* Harpy
harr *s2, zool.* grayling
harskla *se* harkla
har|skramla beater's rattles (*pl*), harestop **-spår** hare's track, pricks (*pl*); *ett* ~ a prick **-syra** *bot.* [wood] sorrel
hart [-a:-] *adv*, ~ *när* well-nigh; almost; ~ *när omöjligt* well-nigh impossible
hartass hare's foot; *stryka över med ~en* smooth it over, set things straight again
harts *s4* resin; (*renat, hårt*) rosin **hartsa** rosin; (*stråke äv.*) resin; (*flaska o.d. äv.*) seal up [with

resin]
harv *s2*, **harva** *v1* harrow **harvning** harrowing
harvärja [ˣhaːr-] *i uttr.*: *ta till ~n* take to one's heels
has *s1*, *s2* hock; ham; *dra ~orna efter sig* loiter along; *rör på ~orna!* stir your stumps! **hasa** shuffle, shamble; *~ ner* (*om strumpa e.d.*) slip down; *~ sig fram* shuffle (*etc.*) along; *~ sig nedför* slither (slide) down
hasard [-ˈaːrd] *s3* (*slump*) chance, luck; *se äv. hasardspel* **-artad** [-aːr-] *a5* accidental, chance **-era** hazard
hasardspel game of chance; (*~ande*) gambling; (*vågspel*) hazard; *ett ~* a gamble **-are** gambler
hasch[isch] [ˈhaʃ(iʃ)] *s2*, *s7* hashish, hasheesh **-rökning** hashish smoking
hasp *s2*, **haspa** *v1* hasp
haspel *s2* reel; spool; (*härvel*) coiler; *gruv.* [hauling] windlass **-fiske** fishing with spinning rod **-rulle** spinning reel **-spö** spinning rod
haspla reel, coil; *~ ur sig* (*bildl.*) reel off
hassel [ˈhass-] *s2* hazel, cob; *koll.* hazels, hazel trees (*pl*) **-buske** hazel shrub **-mus** dormouse **-nöt** hazelnut, filbert, cob[nut] **-snok** smooth snake
hassena [ˣhaːs-] hamstring
hast *r* haste, hurry; *i* [*all*] *~* in a hurry, hastily, (*plötsligt*) all of a sudden; *i största ~* in great haste, in a great hurry **hasta** hasten, hurry; *saken ~r* the matter is very urgent; *tiden ~r* time is short; *det ~r inte med betalningen* there is no hurry about the payment
hastig *a1* (*snabb*) rapid, quick; (*påskyndad*) hurried; (*plötslig*) sudden; (*skyndsam, överilad*) hasty; *i ~t mod* unpremeditatedly, *jur.* without premeditation **-ast** *som ~* in a great hurry; *titta in som ~* look (*vard.* pop) in for a moment **-het 1** (*fart*) speed; rate; *fys.* velocity; *med en ~ av* at a rate (speed) of; *med hög ~* at a high (great) speed; *högsta tillåtna ~* speed limit, maximum [permitted] speed; *minska ~en* (*äv.*) slow down, decelerate; *öka ~en* (*äv.*) speed up, accelerate **2** (*snabbhet*) rapidity; quickness **3** (*brådska*) hurry, haste, hastiness; *i ~en glömde jag* in my hurry (haste) I forgot
hastighets|begränsning speed limit **-kontroll** speed check-up; (*plats*) speed trap **-minskning** deceleration, slowing down **-mätare** speedometer; *flyg. äv.* airspeed indicator **-rekord** speed record **-åkning** (*på skridskor*) speed-skating **-ökning** acceleration, speeding up
hast|igt *adv* (*snabbt*) rapidly, quickly, fast; (*brådskande*) hastily; *~ och lustigt* without more ado, straight away; *~ verkande* of rapid effect; *helt ~* all of a sudden, (*oväntat*) quite unexpectedly **-verk** *det är bara ett ~* it's just been thrown together
hat *s7* hatred; *poet.* hate; (*agg*) spite; (*avsky*) detestation; *bära ~ mot* (*till*) *ngn* cherish hatred towards s.b., loathe s.b. **hata** hate; (*avsky*) detest, abhor, abominate; *~ som pesten* hate like poison
hat|full full of hatred (*mot* towards), spiteful (*mot* towards); *~ blickar* malignant glances **-isk** [ˈhaː-] *a5*, *se hatfull o. hätsk* **-kärlek** love-hate relationship **-propaganda** propaganda

of hatred
hatt *s2* hat; (*på svamp*) cap, pileus (*pl* pilei); *tekn.* cap, hood, top; *vara i ~en* (*vard.*) have had a drop too much; *vara karl för sin ~* stand up for o.s., hold one's own
hatt|a dilly-dally, shillyshally **-affär** hat shop, hatter's [shop] **-ask** hatbox; (*kartong*) bandbox **-brätte** hat brim **-hylla** hatrack **-kulle** crown of a hat **-makare** hatter, hat manufacturer **-nummer** size, head-fitting **-nål** hatpin **-skrålla** *s1* wreck of a hat **-stomme** hat shape, felt hood **-svamp** mushroom
haubits [ˈhau- *el.* -ˈbitts] *s3*, *s2* howitzer
hausse [håːs] *s5* rise, boom; bull market **-artad** [-aːr-] *a5* bullish, boom-like **-spekulant** bull [operator]
hautrelief [åːrelˈjeff] *s3* high relief
hav *s7* sea (*äv. bildl.*); (*världs-*) ocean; *till ~s a*) (*riktning*) to sea, *b*) (*befintlighet*) at sea; *vid ~et a*) (*vistas*) at the seaside, by the sea, *b*) (*vara belägen*) on the sea [coast]; *öppna ~et* the open sea, the high seas (*pl*); *höjd över ~et* altitude above sea level; *mitt ute på ~et* right out at sea, in the middle of the ocean; *som en droppe i ~et* like a drop in the ocean
hava *se 2 ha*
havande *a4* pregnant **-skap** *s7* pregnancy
havanna [-ˣvanna] *s1*, **-cigarr** Havana [cigar]
haverera be wrecked; *bildl. äv.* get (be) shipwrecked; (*om el. med flygplan*) crash, have a breakdown
haveri (*förlisning*) shipwreck, loss of ship; *flyg.* crash, breakdown; (*skada*) damage, loss; *jur.* average; *enskilt ~* particular average; *gemensamt ~* general average **-kommission** commission of inquiry; *Statens ~* [the Swedish] board of accident investigation
haveri|st 1 (*fartyg*) disabled (shipwrecked) vessel; *flyg.* wrecked (crashed) aeroplane **2** (*pers.*) shipwrecked man; *flyg.* wrecked airman **-utredning** average statement (adjustment)
havre [ˣhaːv-] *s2* (*växten*) oat; (*säd*) oats (*sg o. pl*); *av ~* (*äv.*) oat **-gryn** *koll.* hulled oats, oatgroats (*pl*); *vanl.* rolled oats (*pl*) **-grynsgröt** oatmeal porridge **-mjöl** oatmeal
havs|anemon [ˣhaffs-] sea anemone **-arm** arm of the sea **-bad 1** [a] sea bathe **2** (*badort*) seaside resort, watering place **-band** *i ~et* on (among) the seaward skerries **-borstmask** polychaete **-botten** sea (ocean) bed; *på -botten* at (on) the bottom of the sea **-bris** sea breeze **-djup** depth of the sea **-fisk** marine (sea) fish **-fiske** deep-sea fishing **-forskning** oceanography, marine research **-gud** sea god **-gudinna** sea goddess **-katt** *zool.* wolffish, catfish **-kryssare** cruising yacht, ocean racer **-kräfta** Norway lobster **-kust** seacoast, seashore; *särsk. AE.* seaboard **-orm** sea snake **-sköldpadda** sea turtle **-ström** ocean current **-sula** gannet **-trut** great black-backed gull **-tulpan** acorn barnacle (shell) **-vatten** sea water **-vik** (*bred*) bay; (*långsmal*) gulf; (*i Skottland*) loch, (*i Irland*) lough **-växt** seaweed **-yta** surface of the sea; *under (över) ~n* below (above) sea level **-ål** conger **-öring** sea trout **-örn** European sea eagle, white-tailed eagle

H

havtorn sea buckthorn
H-dur B major
hebré *s3* Hebrew
Hebreerbrevet [-*bre:er-] Hebrews (*pl, behandlas som g*)
hebre|isk [-'bre:-] *a5* Hebrew, Hebraic[al] **-iska** *s1* (*språk*) Hebrew; *det är rena ~n för mig* it's [all] Greek to me
Hebriderna [-'bri:-] *pl* the Hebrides
hed *s2* moor[land]; (*ljung- äv.*) heath; (*särsk. i södra England*) downs (*pl*), downland
heden *a5* heathen; (*från hednisk tid*) pagan **-dom** [-dɷmm] *s2* (*hednatid*) heathendom; (*hednisk tro*) heathenism, heathenry; (*mångguderi o.d.*) paganism **-hös** *oböjligt s, från ~* from time immemorial
heder ['he:-] *s2* honour; (*berömmelse äv.*) credit; (*oförvitlighet*) honesty; *på ~ och samvete* [up]on my (*etc.*) honour; *göra ~ åt anrättningarna* do justice to the meal, *vard.* eat with gusto; *komma till ~s igen* be restored to its place of honour; *lända ngn till ~* do s.b. credit; *ta ~ och ära av ngn* calumniate (defame) s.b.; *den pojken har du all ~ av* that boy is a credit to you
hederlig [*he:-] *a1* **1** honourable; (*ärlig*) honest; (*ärbar*) respectable **2** (*anständig*) decent; (*frikostig*) handsome; *få ~t betalt* be paid handsomely **-het** honourableness; honesty; respectability; decency; *han är ~en själv* he is honesty itself
hedersam *a1* honourable; flattering
heders|begrepp concept of honour **-betygelse** mark (token) of honour (respect); *under militära ~r* with full military honours **-bevisning** *se* **-betygelse** **-doktor** honorary doctor **-gåva** testimonial, token of respect **-gäst** guest of honour **-knyffel** *s2, en riktig ~* a real brick, a card **-kodex** code of honour **-kompani** guard of honour **-känsla** sense of honour **-ledamot** honorary member **-legionen** the Legion of Honour **-man** *en ~* an honest man, a man of honour **-omnämnande** honourable mention **-ord** word of honour; *frigiven på ~* liberated on parole **-pascha** *se* **-knyffel** **-plats** place of honour; (*sitt-*) seat of honour **-prick** *se* **-knyffel** **-pris** special prize **-sak** point of honour **-skuld** debt of honour **-tecken** sign (mark) of distinction, badge of honour **-titel** honorary title **-uppdrag** honorary task **-vakt** guard of honour
hedervärd *a1* (*aktningsvärd*) estimable, creditable; (*redbar*) honourable, honest
hedlandskap moorland, heath country
hedna|folk [*he:d-] heathen people **-mission** *~en* foreign missions (*pl*)
hed|ning [*he:d-] heathen; (*från förkristen tid*) pagan; *bibl.* Gentile **-isk** *a5* heathen; pagan
hedr|a [*he:d-] honour; show honour to; (*göra heder åt*) do honour (credit) to; *~ sig* do o.s. honour (credit), (*utmärka sig*) distinguish o.s. **-ande** *a4, se* **hedersam**; *~ uppförande* honourable conduct
hegemo'ni *s3* hegemony
hej [hejj] hallo!; (*adjö*) cheerio!; *hej* [*då*]*!* bye-bye!, so long; *~ hopp!* heigh-ho!; *man skall inte ropa ~ förrän man är över bäcken* do not

halloo until you are out of the wood, don't crow too soon
heja I ['hejja] *interj* hurrah!, *vard.* 'rah!; *sport.* come on! **II** [*hejja] *v1, ~ på* cheer [on], (*hålla på*) support, *AE. äv.* root [for]
1 hejare [*hejj-] *tekn.* drop forge (hammer); (*pålkran*) pile-driver
2 hejare [*hejj-] *se baddare*
heja|rklack claque [of supporters]; cheer section **-rop** cheer
hejarsmide drop forging
hejd *r, utan ~* inordinately, *vard.* no end; *det är ingen ~ på* there are no bounds to
hejd|a stop; (*ngt abstr. äv.*) put a stop to, check; *~ sig* stop (check) o.s., (*om talare e.d.*) break off **-lös** (*ohejdad*) uncontrollable; (*ohämmad*) violent; (*måttlös*) inordinate, excessive
hejduk [*hejj- el.* 'hejj-] *s2* henchman; tool
hej|dundrande [-*dunn-] *a4* tremendous **-san** ['hejj-] *interj, se hej*
hekatomb [-'tåmb] *s3* hecatomb
hekt'ar *s7, s9* hectare; *ett ~* (*ung.*) two and a half acres
hektisk ['hekt-] *a5* hectic
hekto ['hektɷ] *s7* hectogram[me]; *ett ~* (*ung.*) three and a half ounces **-graf** *s3,* **-grafera** hectograph **-gram** [-'gramm] *se hekto* **-liter** [-'li:-] hectolitre; *en ~* (*ung.*) twenty-two gallons
hel *a1* **1** (*odelad, total*) whole; entire; complete; *~a dagen* all (the whole) day; *~a namnet* (*äv.*) the name in full; *~a Sverige* (*landet*) the whole of Sweden, (*folket*) all Sweden; *~a tal* whole (integral) numbers; *en ~ del* a great deal of; *en ~ förmögenhet* quite a fortune; *tre ~a och en halv* three wholes and a half; *det ~a a*) *eg.* the whole (total), *b*) (*friare*) the whole matter (affair, thing); *i det stora ~a* on the whole; *i ~a två veckor* for a whole fortnight; *på det ~a taget* on the whole, in general; *som en ~ karl* like a man; *varje ~ timme* every hour on the hour; *över ~a Sverige* throughout Sweden; *det blir aldrig något ~t med* nothing satisfactory ever comes of; *det är inte så ~t med den saken* things are not all they should be in that respect; *jag var vaken ~a natten* I was awake all night **2** (*oskadad*) whole, unbroken; (*om glas o.d. äv.*) uncracked; (*om plagg*) not in holes, not worn through (out); (*hålla barnen ~a och rena* keep the children neat and clean
1 hela *s1* (*helbutelj*) whole (large) bottle; (*första sup*) first dram; *~n går!* (*ung.*) now for the first!
2 hela *v1* heal
hel|afton *göra sig en ~* make a night of it **-ark** folio **-automatisk** fully automatic
helbrägda [-j-, *äv.* -g-, *äv.* *hell-] *oböjligt a* whole **-görare** [-j-] [faith-]healer **-görelse** [-j-] [faith-]healing; *~ genom tron* saved by faith
hel|butelj whole (large) bottle **-fet 1** full-cream (*ost* cheese) **2** *boktr.* extra bold **-figur** full figure; *porträtt i ~* full-length portrait **-flaska** *se* **-butelj** **-försäkring** (*för motorfordon*) comprehensive motour insurance
helg [-j] *s3* (*kyrklig högtid*) festival; (*friare*) holiday[s *pl*]; *i ~ och söcken* [on] high days

and working days alike

helga [-g-] sanctify; (*inviga*) consecrate, dedicate; (*hålla helig*) keep holy, hallow; *~t varde ditt namn!* hallowed be thy name!; *~ vilodagen* (*bibl.*) remember the Sabbath day to keep it holy; *ändamålet ~r medlen* the end justifies the means

helgarder|ad *a5* fully covered **-ing** (*i tips*) 3-ways [forecast]

helgd [-j-] *s3* (*okränkbarhet*) sanctity; (*t.ex. löftes, ställes*) sacredness; *hålla i ~* hold sacred

helgdag holy day; (*ledighetsdag*) holiday; *allmän ~* public (bank) holiday

helgdags|afton [the] day (evening) before a public holiday **-kläder** *pl* holiday (best) clothes

helgedom [ˣhelgedɷmm] *s2* sanctuary; (*byggnad äv.*) sacred edifice, temple; (*relik*) sacred thing

helgeflundra [ˣhellje-] *se hälleflundra*

helgelse [-g-] (*helgande*) sanctification

helg|erån [-g-, *äv.* -j-] sacrilege **-fri** [-j-] *~ dag* ordinary business (normal working) day

helgjuten [-j-] *a5, bildl.* [as if] cast in one piece, sterling; (*harmonisk*) harmonious

helgmålsringning [the] ringing in of a (the) Sabbath

Helgoland *n* Heligoland

helgon [-gån] *s7* saint **-dyrkan** saint worship **-förklarad** *a5* canonized **-gloria** halo; aureole **-legend** legend of saints (a saint) **-lik** *a5* saint-like, saintly

helhet entirety, whole; completeness, wholeness; totality; *i sin ~ a*) in its entirety, as a whole, *b*) (*helt o. hållet*) entirely

helhets|bild general picture **-intryck** general impression **-syn** comprehensive view **-verkan** total effect

helhjärtad [-j-] *a5* wholehearted

helig *a1* holy; (*-gjord*) sacred; (*högtidlig*) solemn (*försäkran* assurance); *~a alliansen* (*landet*) the Holy Alliance (Land); *~a tre konungar* (*bibl.*) the three Magi; *ett ~t löfte* a sacred (solemn) promise; *Erik den ~e* Saint Eric; *den ~a natten* the Night of the Nativity; *den ~a staden* (*om Jerusalem*) the Holy City; *den ~a stolen* the Holy See; *det allra ~aste* (*bibl.*) the holy of holies, (*friare*) the inner sanctum; *svära vid allt vad ~t är* swear by all that one holds sacred

helig|förklara canonize **-het** holiness; *Hans H~* (*om påven*) His Holiness **-hålla** keep (hold) sacred

helikopter [-'kåpp-] *s2* helicopter; *vard.* chopper **-landningsplats** heliport

helinackordering 1 full board and lodging **2** *pers.* boarder; lodger

helio|centrisk [-'senn-] heliocentric **-graf** *s3* heliograph **-stat** *s3* heliostat **-trop** [-'å:p] *s3* heliotrope

helium ['he:-] *s8* helium

helix ['he:-] *s2* helix

hel|konserv fully-sterilized tinned goods **-kväll** *se helafton*

hell [all] hail!; *~ dig!* hail to thee!

hel'len *s3* Hellene, Hellenian **-ism** Hellenism **-ist** Hellenist **-istisk** *a5* Hellenistic[al]

hellensk [-'e:nsk] *a5* Hellenic

heller ['hell-] (*efter negation*) either; *ej ~* nor, neither; *och det hade inte jag ~* nor had I, and I hadn't either, neither had I; *du är väl inte sjuk ~?* you are not ill, are you?

hel|linne pure linen; (*i sms.*) all-linen **-ljus** (*på bil*) *köra med ~* drive with headlights full on

hellre ['hell-] *adv, komp. t. gärna* rather; sooner; *ju förr dess ~* the sooner the better; *så mycket ~ som* [all] the rather as; *~ dö än ge sig* rather die than surrender; *jag vill ~* I would rather; *jag dricker ~ kaffe än te* I prefer coffee to tea; *jag önskar ingenting ~* I wish no better

hel|lång full-length **-not** semibreve; *AE.* whole note **-nykter** teetotal **-nykterist** teetotaller, total abstainer **-omvändning** about-turn; *AE.* about-face; *jfr* *sht* *bildl.* volte-face **-pension 1** *se* helinackordering **2** (*skola*) boarding school **-sida** full (whole) page **-siden** pure silk; (*i sms.*) all-silk **-sidesannons** full-page advertisement

helsike [ˣhell-] *s6* hell; *i ~ heller!* hell, no!

hel|skinnad [-∫-] *a5, komma ~ ifrån ngt* get off scot-free, escape unhurt, *vard.* save one's bacon **-skägg** full beard **-spänn** *i uttr.: på ~ a*) (*om gevär o.d.*) at full cock, *b*) *bildl.* on tenterhooks; *med alla sinnen på ~* with all one's senses at full stretch (on the qui vive)

helst I *adv, superl. t. gärna* preferably, by preference; *hur som ~ a*) (*sak samma hur*) anyhow, no matter how, *b*) (*i varje fall*) anyhow, in any case, *c*) (*som svar*) [just] as you like (please); *när som ~* [at] any time, whenever you (*etc.*) like; *vad som ~* anything [whatever]; *vem som ~* anybody, anyone; *hur liten som ~* no matter how small; *hur länge som ~* any length of time, as long as you like; *ingen som ~ risk* no risk whatever; *i vilket fall som ~* anyhow, in any case; *allra ~ skulle jag vilja* most (best) of all I should like; *därmed må vara hur som ~* be that as it may, however that may be; *jag kan betala hur mycket som ~* I can pay any amount (as much as you like) **II** *konj* especially (all the more) (*som* as; *då* when)

hel|stekt roasted whole; (*om större djur äv.*) barbecued **-svart** all black **-syskon** full brothers and sisters

helt [-e:-] *adv* entirely, wholly; completely, totally; (*alldeles*) altogether, quite; (*ganska*) quite, rather; *~ enkelt* simply; *~ igenom* all through; *~ och fullt* to the full; *~ och hållet* altogether, completely; *~ om!* about turn! (*AE.* face!); *~ säkert* quite sure, no doubt [about it]; *en ~ liten* quite a small; *gå ~ upp i* be completely engrossed (absorbed) in; *göra ~ om a*) *mil.* about-turn, *AE.* about-face, *b*) (*friare o. bildl.*) turn right about

hel|tal integer, whole number **-tid** *adv* full time; *arbeta ~* work full time

heltids|anställd full-time employee **-arbete** full-time job (work) **-tjänst** *se -arbete*

hel|ton whole tone (*AE.* step) **-tonsskala** whole-tone scale **-täckande** *a4, ~ matta* wall-to-wall carpet **-täckningsmatta** (*i metervara*) broadloom carpet **-täckt** *a4, ~ bil* closed car **-veckad** *a5, ~ kjol* [knife-]pleated skirt

helvete [ˣhell-] *s6* hell; (*dödsrike[t]*) Hell; *ett riktigt ~* sheer hell; *ett ~s oväsen* a hell of a row, an infernal row; *av bara* ~ for very hell, like blazes; *i* ~ *heller!* hell, no!; *dra åt* ~*!* go to hell!, drop dead!; *barka åt* ~ go to pieces **helvetes|hund** hellhound **-maskin** infernal (clockwork) machine **-straff** eternal damnation **1 helvetisk** [-'ve:-] *a5* (*schweizisk*) Helvetic **2 helvetisk** [-'ve:-] *a5* (*helvetes-*) infernal, hellish **hel|ylle** pure wool; (*i sms.*) all-wool **-år** whole year **helårs|prenumeration** annual subscription **-vis** yearly, annually **helägd** *a5* wholly-owned **hem** [hemm] **I** *s7* home (*äv. institution*); (*bostad äv.*) house, place; *i* ~*met* in the (one's) home, at home; (*i* ~*mets härd* at the domestic hearth; *lämna* ~*met* leave home **II** *adv* home; *bjuda* ~ *ngn* invite s.b. to one's home; *gå* ~ (*i spel*) get home, (*i bridge*) make the contract; *gå* ~ *och lägg dig!* (*vard.*) make yourself scarce!; *hälsa* ~*!* remember me (kind regards) to your people!; *låna ngt med sig* ~ borrow s.th. and take it home [with one]; *ta* ~ *ett spel* win a game; *det gick* ~ the point (it) went home **hem|arbetande** *a4,* ~ *kvinna* [a] woman working in the home **-arbete** homework; (*hushållsarbete*) housework **-bageri** small-scale bakery **-bakad** *a5* home-made **-besök** home visit (call) **-biträde** [domestic] servant, maid **-bjuda 1** *se hem II 2 jur.* offer to those having the right of first refusal **-bränd** *a5* home-distilled; (*olagligt*) illicitly distilled **-bränning** home-distilling; (*olaglig*) illicit distilling **-buren** *a5, fritt* ~ delivered free; *få ngt -buret* have s.th. delivered at one's home **-bygd** native place, home district **hembygds|gård** folk museum **-kunskap** local geography and history **-museum** *se -gård* **hem|bära** *bildl.* (*framföra*) present, offer; (*vinna*) carry off (*ett pris* a prize), win (*segern* the day) **-dator** home computer **-dragande** *a4, komma* ~ *med a*) (*sak*) come home lugging, *b*) *pers.* come home bringing (with) [...in one's train] **-falla 1** (*åter tillfalla*) devolve (*till* upon), revert (*till* to) **2** (*förfalla*) yield, give way (*åt dryckenskap* to drinking); (*hänge sig*) give o.s. up; (*drabbas*) fall a victim (*åt* to) **-fallen** addicted (*åt* to) **-fridsbrott** unlawful entering of a p.'s residence (house) **-färd** homeward journey, journey home **-föra** take (*hit* bring) home; (*gifta sig med*) marry **-förhållanden** home background (*sg*) **-förlova** *mil.* disband, demobilize; *parl.* prorogue; adjourn; (*skolungdom*) dismiss **-försäkring** householder's comprehensive insurance **-försäljare** door-to-door salesman (saleswoman) **-försäljning** door-to-door sales (*pl*) **-gift** [-j-] *s3* dowry **-gjord** home-made **-hjälp** domestic (home) help **-ifrån** from home **-inredning** home furnishing, interior decoration **-inredningsarkitekt** interior decorator (designer) **hemi'sfär** hemisphere **hem|kalla** summon home; *polit.* recall **-kommen** [-å-] *a5, nyligen* ~ just back [home] **-kommun** home municipality, (*friare*) city (town), borough) where s.b. is registered

-komst [-å-] *s3* return [home], homecoming **-konsulent** domestic science adviser **-kunskap** domestic science **-känsla** homely atmosphere **-kär** home-loving **-körd** delivered **-körning** delivery **-lagad** *a5* home-cooked, home-made **-land** native country, country of birth; (*i Sydafrika*) homeland, Bantustan **-landstoner** *pl, det är verkligen* ~ this is quite like home **hemlig** *a1* secret (*för* from); (*dold*) hidden, concealed (*för* from); (*motsats offentlig*) private; (*i smyg*) clandestine; ~ *agent* secret agent; ~*t förbehåll* mental (tacit) reservation; *strängt* ~ strictly confidential, top secret **-het 1** (*med pl*) secret; *offentlig* ~ open secret **2** (*utan pl*) secrecy, privacy; *i* [*all*] ~ in secret (private), secretly, *vard.* strictly on the q.t. **hemlighets|full** mysterious; (*förtegen*) secretive **-makare** mystery maker **-makeri** mystery making, *vard.* hush-hush **hemlig|hus** privy **-hålla** keep secret, conceal (*för* from) **-stämpla** stamp as secret, classify as strictly (top) secret; ~*d* (*äv.*) classified **hem|lik** homelike **-liv** home life; domesticity **-lån** (*om bok*) for home reading **-längtan** homesickness, longing for home; *ha* ~ feel homesick **-läxa** homework **-lös** homeless **-löshet** homelessness **hemma** at home; ~ *från skolan* away from school; ~ *hos mig* at my place (home); *höra* ~ *i* (*om sak*) belong to; *han hör* ~ *i Stockholm* his home is in Stockholm; *känna sig som* ~ feel at ease (home); *vara* ~ *i* (*kunnig*) be at home in (on, with) **-bruk** *för* ~ for domestic use **-dotter** daughter living at home **-front** home front **-fru** housewife **-hörande** *a4,* ~ *i a*) (*om pers.*) native of, domiciled in, with one's home in, *b*) (*om fartyg*) of, belonging to, hailing from **-kvinna** woman not working outside the home **-kväll** evening at home **-lag** home team **-man** house husband **-marknad** home (domestic) market **-match** *sport.* home game **hemman** *s7* homestead; [freehold] farm **hemmansägare** yeoman [farmer], freeholder; *vanl.* [small] farmer **hemma|plan** home ground; *match på* ~ home game **-stadd** *a5* at home; *vara* ~ *i* be at home in (familiar with, versed in) **-varande** *a4,* ~ *barn* children [living] at home **hemmiljö** home environment (atmosphere) **hemoglo'bin** *s4* haemoglobin **hemorrojder** [-'råjd-] *pl* haemorrhoids **hem|ort** legal domicile, place of residence; *sjö.* home port, port of registry **-ortskommun** municipality of residence **-ortsrätt 1** *jur.* domiciliary rights **2** *bildl., vinna* ~ *i* gain recognition in **-permanent** home perm **-permittera** grant home leave; ~*d* on home leave **-resa** *s1* journey (voyage, return) home, home (homeward) journey; *på* ~*n* while going (*etc.*) home, on the way home **-samarit** health visitor; home help **hemsk** *a1* **1** ghastly; (*skrämmande*) frightful, shocking; (*kuslig*) uncanny, weird, gruesome; (*hisklig*) grisly; (*dyster*) dismal, gloomy; (*olycksbådande*) sinister **2** *vard.* (*väldig*) aw-

ful, frightful, tremendous; *det var ~t!* how awful! **-het** ghastliness *etc.*
hemskillnad judicial separation
hemskt *adv (väldigt)* awfully, frightfully; *~ mycket folk* an awful lot of people
hem|slöjd hand[i]craft; domestic (home) crafts (industries) *(pl)* **-språksundervisning** immigrant language teaching **-stad** home town; *(födelsestad)* native town **-ställa** *(föreslå)* propose, suggest; *~ om* request (ask) for; *~ till ngns prövning* submit to a p.'s consideration **-ställan** *oböjligt s* request, proposal, suggestion **-syster** trained home help, home aide **-sända** send home; *(varor äv.)* deliver; *(fångar äv.)* repatriate **-söka** *(om högre makter)* visit *(med krig* with war); *(om rövare, pest)* infest; *(om spöke)* haunt; *(om sjukdom)* attack, inflict **-sökelse** visitation; scourge; infliction **-sömmerska** home dressmaker **-tagningskostnader** delivery costs **-tam** domesticated **-trakt** home district; *i min ~ (äv.)* near my home **-trevlig** nice and comfortable (cosy), homelike **-trevnad** homelike atmosphere, domestic comfort **-vist** *s7, s9* residence, domicile address; *jack.* habitat; *bildl.* abode; *vara ~ för (äv.)* be a seat (centre) of **-vårdare** health visitor; home help **-väg** way home; *(-färd)* homeward journey; *bege sig på ~* start for home; *vara på ~* be on the way home, *(om fartyg)* be homeward bound **-värn** home defence; *konkr.* home guard[s *pl*] **-värnsman** home guard **-vävd** handwoven; *-vävt tyg (äv.)* homespun **-åt** homewards, towards home
henna *s9* henna
henne *pron (objektsform av hon) (om pers., fartyg)* her; *(om djur, sak)* it **hennes 1** *fören.* her; *(om djur, sak)* its, *ibl.* her **2** *självst.* hers
henry ['henn-] *r (måttenhet)* henry
hepa|'rin *s4* heparin **-'tit** *s3, med.* hepatitis
heral'd|ik *s3* heraldry **-iker** [-'rall-] heraldist, herald **-isk** [-'rall-] *a5* heraldic
herbarium [-'ba:-] *s4* herbarium
herbi'cid [-s-] *s3* herbicide
herdabrev [*he:r-] pastoral letter
herde [*he:r-] *s2* shepherd; *bildl. o. poet. äv.* pastor **-diktning** pastoral poetry **-stund** amorous interlude
herdinna shepherdess
Herkules ['härr-] Hercules
herkul|esarbete [*härr-] Herculean task **-isk** [-'ku:-] *a5* Herculean
hermafro'dit *s3* hermaphrodite
herme'lin *s3* stoat; *(i vinterdräkt)* ermine
hermelinsmantel ermine cloak
hermet|isk [-'me:-] *a5* hermetic[al] **-iskt** *adv, ~ tillsluten* hermetically sealed
hero [-'rå:] *s3, el. heros, pl heroer* hero
Herodes [-'rω:-] Herod
hero'in *s4* heroin **-ist** heroin addict
hero|isk [-'rå:-] *a5* heroic[al] **-ism** *s4* heroism
heros ['he:rås] *se hero*
herostratisk [-'stra:-] *a5, ~ ryktbarhet* notoriety
herpes *s2* herpes
herr [-ä-] **1** *(framför namn)* Mr. *(pl Messrs.) (förk. för* Mister, *pl* Messieurs); *(på brev o.d., efter namnet, i Storbritannien)* Esq. *(förk. för*

Esquire); *~arna J. och R. Mason* Messrs. J. and R. Mason, the Messrs. Mason; *unge ~ Tom (vanl.)* Master Tom; *er ~ fader (ung.)* your respected father **2** *(framför titel) ~ professor (doktor) Jones* Professor (Doctor) Jones **3** *(vid tilltal) ~ domare!* Your Honour!; *ja, ~ general* yes, General (Sir); *~ greve (baron)!* Count! (Baron!), *(i Storbritannien)* Your Lordship!; *~ ordförande!* Mr. Chairman!, Sir!
herradöme *s6* dominion
Herran *se herre 5*
herr|avälde 1 *(makt)* domination *(över* over); *(välde)* dominion, supremacy *(över over, of); (styrelse)* rule, sway *(över* over, of) **2** *(kontroll, övertag)* control, mastery, command *(över* of); *förlora ~t över* lose control of; *ha ~t till sjöss* have the mastery of the seas, have supremacy at sea; *vinna ~ över sig själv* gain control of o.s., get o.s. under control **-bekant** gentleman friend **-betjänt** stand for men's clothes **-bjudning** men's *(vard.* stag) party **-cykel** man's bicycle
herr|e *s2* **1** gentleman **2** *(i tilltal) a) (framför namn, titel) se herr, b) (utan titel, namn)* you; *vad önskar -n?* what do you want, sir?, may I help you, sir?; *förlåt -n, kan ni säga mig excuse* me, sir, can you tell me **3** *(förnäm, adlig)* nobleman; *i Storbritannien* lord; *andliga och världsliga -ar* lords spiritual and temporal **4** *(härskare)* lord, ruler; *(friare o. husbonde)* master; *min ~ och man* my lord and master; *situationens ~* master of the situation; *bli ~ över* gain the mastery of (over), get the better of; *spela ~* lord it; *vara ~ på täppan* rule the roost; *vara sin egen ~* be one's own master **5** *H~n* the Lord; *~ gud!* Good heavens (God)!; *i -ans namn (vard.)* for goodness' sake; *för många -ans år sedan* years and years ago, ages ago; *vilket -ans oväder!* what awful weather!
herrefolk master race
herrekipering[saffär] [gentle]men's outfitter's, outfitter
herre|lös without a master; *(om egendom)* ownerless, abandoned; *(om hund äv.)* stray **-man** gentleman; *(godsägare)* country gentleman, squire **-säte** country seat, manor
herr|frisör barber **-gård** manor (country) house, mansion, estate, hall **-gårdsvagn** estate car; *AE.* station wagon **-kläder** *pl* men's (gentlemen's) wear *(sg)* (clothes) **-konfektion** men's [ready-made] clothing **-kostym** [man's] suit **-middag** [gentle]men's dinner party **-mode** *s6, s4* [gentle]men's fashion
herrnhutare *pl* Moravians, Moravian Brethren
herrskap *s7* **1** *(fin familj)* gentleman's family; *(herre o. fru)* master and mistress; *det höga ~et* the august couple *(om fler än två personages); det unga ~et* the young couple; *spela ~* play the gentlefolks; *~et är bortrest* the family (Mr. and Mrs. Y.) are (have gone) away **2** *(vid tilltal) mitt ~!* ladies and gentlemen!; *hos ~et Jones* at the Jones's; *skall ~et gå redan?* are you leaving already?
herrskaps|aktig *a5* genteel **-folk** gentry; gentlefolk[s]
herr|sko man's shoe **-skräddare** [gentle]men's

H

tailor **-skrädderi** gentlemen's tailor **-sällskap** *i* ~ in male company, *(bland herrar)* among gentlemen **-toalett** [gentle]men's lavatory; *AE.* men's room **-tycke** sex appeal
hertig *s2* duke **-döme** *s6* duchy, dukedom **-inna** duchess **-lig** *a5* ducal **-titel** ducal title
hertz *r* hertz *(pl* hertz)
hes *a1* hoarse; *(om röst äv.)* husky **-het** hoarseness; huskiness
het *a1* hot; *(om klimat äv.)* torrid *(zon* zone); *bildl. äv.* ardent, fervent; *(hetsig)* heated, excited; *~a linjen* the hot line; *~ potatis* hot potato; *kvävande* ~ suffocatingly *(vard.* stifling) hot; *vara* ~ *på gröten* be overeager; *var inte så* ~ *på gröten* hold your horses
het|a *-te -at* **1** *(kallas)* be called (named); *allt vad böcker -er* everything in the way of books; *allt vad karlar -er* anything that goes by the name of man, the whole tribe (race) of men; *jag -er Kate* my name is Kate; *det var en yxa som -te duga* that was a fine axe; *vad -er det på tyska?* what is the German for it (is it in German)?; *vad -er det i pluralis?* what is the plural of it?; *vad -er hon i sig själv?* what was her maiden name?; *vad han nu -er* whatever he's called **2** *opers.*, *som det -er på engelska* as it is called (as one says) in English; *det -er att* it is said (people say) that; *det -er att han* he is said to
hetat *sup av heta*
hetero|dox [-'dåcks] *a5* heterodox **-gen** [-'je:n] *a1* heterogeneous **-'nym** **I** *s3* heteronym **II** *a5* heteronymous
heterosexu|ali'tet heterosexuality **-'ell** heterosexual
het|levrad [-e:v-] *a5* hot-headed, hot-tempered; *(kolerisk)* choleric, irascible **-luft** hot air
hets *s2* **1** *(förföljelse)* baiting, persecution *(mot* of) **2** *(iver)* bustle
hets|a *(förfölja)* bait, worry *(t. döds* to death); *(bussa)* hound *(på* on to); *(uppegga)* incite *(till* to), egg on; ~ *upp sig* get excited **-ande** *a4* inflammatory; *(om dryck)* fiery, heady; *(om kryddor)* fiery, hot **-hunger** bulimia
hetsig *a1* hot, fiery; passionate, vehement; heated *(diskussion* discussion) **-het** hotness *etc.*; impetuosity, vehemence
hetsjakt hunt[ing], chasing *(på* of); *(efter nöjen o.d.)* chase *(efter* after), eager pursuit *(efter* of)
hetsporre hotspur
hets|propaganda inflammatory propaganda **-ätande** *s6* compulsive eating
hett *adv* hotly *etc., se het*; *ha det* ~ *om öronen* be in hot water; *det börjar osa* ~ the place is getting too hot to hold me *(etc.)*; *det gick* ~ *till (blev slagsmål)* it was a real roughhouse, *(i diskussion etc.)* feelings ran high; *när striden stod som hetast* in the very thick of the struggle (fight)
hetta **I** *s1* heat; *bildl. äv.* ardour; passion; *(häftighet)* impetuosity; *i stridens* ~ in the heat of the struggle *(bildl.* debate) **II** *v1* emit heat; ~ *upp* heat, make hot; *det* ~*r om kinderna* my cheeks are burning
hette *imperf av heta*
hetvatten high-temperature hot water
he'tär *s3* hetaera, hetaira; *(friare)* courtesan

heuristik *s3* heuristics *(pl, behandlas som sg)*
hexa|decimalsystem [-ˣma:l-] hexadecimal [notation] **-meter** [-ˣxa:- *el.* -'xa:-] *s2* hexameter
hibiskus [-'biss-] *s2* hibiscus
hick|a **I** *s1* hiccup, hiccough; *ha* ~ have the hiccups **II** *v1* hiccup **-ning** hiccup; *(-ande)* hiccuping
hickory ['hick-] *s9* hickory
hierar'k|i *s3* hierarchy **-isk** [-'rark-] *a5* hierarchic[al]
hiero'glyf *s3* hieroglyph[ic] **-isk** *a5* hieroglyphic[al]
hihi he, he!
hillebard [-'a:rd] *s3* halberd, halbert
Himalaya [-'ma:-] *n* the Himalayas *(pl)*
himla **I** *v1, rfl* turn (roll) up one's eyes [to heaven] **II** *oböjligt a, vard.* awful **-kropp** heavenly (celestial) body; *särsk. poet.* orb **-päll** *se -valv* **-stormare** *se himmelsstormare* **-valv** *~et* the vault (canopy) of heaven, the heavens *(pl)*, the sky, *poet.* the welkin
him|mel *-meln, -len el. -melen, pl -lar* **1** sky; firmament; *under bar* ~ in the open [air]; *allt mellan* ~ *och jord* everything under the sun; *röra upp* ~ *och jord* move heaven and earth, *(friare)* make a tremendous to-do **2** *(Guds boning, paradis)* heaven, Heaven; *o, ~!* good heavens!; *i sjunde -len* in the seventh heaven; *uppstiga till -len* ascend into heaven
himmelrike heaven; *~t* the kingdom of heaven; *ett* ~ *på jorden* a heaven on earth
himmels|blå sky blue, azure **-ekvator** celestial equator, equinoctial [circle] **-färd** *Kristi* ~ the Ascension **-färdsdag** *Kristi* ~ Ascension Day
himmelsk ['himm-] *a5* heavenly; celestial *(sällhet* bliss); *bildl. äv.* divine; *~t tålamod* angelic patience; *det ~a riket (Kina före republiken)* the Celestial Empire
himmels|pol celestial pole **-sfär** celestial sphere **-skriande** crying, glaring *(orättvisa* injustice); atrocious *(brott* crime) **-stormare** [-å-] heaven-stormer, titan **-säng** canopied bed, four-poster [bed] **-vid** huge, immense, enormous; *en* ~ *skillnad* all the difference in the world
hin [hi:n, *äv.* hinn] the devil; Old Harry; ~ *håle* the Evil One; *han är ett hår av* ~ he is a devil of a man
hind *s2* hind
hinder ['hinn-] *s7* obstacle *(för, mot* to); impediment *(för* to); *(ngt som fördröjer o.d.)* hindrance; *(avsiktligt utsatt)* obstruction; *sport.* hurdle; fence; *(dike, grav)* ditch, bunker; *(spärr)* bar, barrier *(äv. bildl.)*; *lägga* ~ *i vägen för ngn* place obstacles in a p.'s way, obstruct s.b.; *ta ett* ~ *(sport.)* jump (take, clear) a hurdle (fence); *vara till* ~*s för ngn* be in a p.'s way; *övervinna alla* ~ surmount every obstacle, overcome all difficulties; *det möter inga* ~ *från min sida* there is nothing to prevent it if as far as I am concerned, I have no objection to it **-bana** steeplechase course **-hoppning** *ridk.* hurdle-jumping **-löpning, -ritt** steeplechase **-sam** *a1, vara* ~ be a hindrance, *(besvärande)* be cumbersome
hindersprövning application for a marriage

licence
hindra (*för-*) prevent (*ngn från att göra ngt* s.b. from doing s.th.); (*avhålla äv.*) deter, restrain, keep, withhold; (*hejda*) stop; (*störa*) hinder; (*lägga hinder i vägen för*) impede, hamper, keep back, stand in the way of; (*trafik, utsikt*) obstruct, block; (*fördröja*) delay; *stå ~nde i vägen* be an obstacle (a hindrance), get in the way; *det ~r inte att du försöker* there's nothing to stop you trying; *han låter inte ~ sig* nothing can stop him

hin'du *s3*, **-isk** *a5* Hindu **-ism** Hinduism **-stani** [-'sta:-] *r* Hindustani

hingst *s2* stallion

hink *s2* bucket; (*mjölk-, slask-*) pail

1 hinna *s1*, *biol.* membrane; (*friare*) coat; (*mycket tunn*) film

2 hinna *hann hunnit* **1** (*uppnå*) reach, get as far as; (*upp-*) catch up; (*komma*) get, (*mot den talande*) come; *hur långt har du hunnit?* how far have you got? **2** (*komma i tid*) be in time; (*ha el. få tid*) have (find) time; (*få färdig*) get done; *allt vad jag hinner* as fast as [ever] I can; *jag har inte hunnit hälften* I haven't got half of it done **3** (*med betonad partikel*) *~ fatt* catch up with, (*pers. äv.*) catch up, overtake; *~ fram* arrive (*till* at, in), *absol. äv.* reach one's (its) destination; *~ fram i tid* arrive (get there) in time; *~ förbi* manage to get past; *~ med a*) (*följa med*) keep up (pace) with, *b*) (*tåget etc.*) [manage to] catch, *c*) (*hinna avsluta*) [manage to] finish (get done); *inte ~ med tåget* miss (not catch) the train

1 hipp *interj, ~, ~, hurra!* hip, hip, hurrah!

2 hipp *det är ~ som happ* it's neither here nor there, it amounts to the same thing

hippa *s1*, *vard.* party

hippodrom [-'å:m] *s3* hippodrome

hird [-i(:)-] *s3* housecarls **-man** housecarl

hirs *s3*, *bot.* millet

hisklig *a1* horrid, horrible; (*skräckinjagande*) terrifying; (*avskyvärd*) abominable; (*hemsk*) gruesome

hisna *se hissna*

hiss *s2* lift; *AE.* elevator; (*varu-*) hoist, *AE.* freight elevator

hiss|a hoist; (*pers.*) toss; *~ en flagga* hoist (run up) a flag; *~ segel* (*äv.*) set sail; *~ upp* hoist (run) up **-konduktör** liftman, liftboy **-korg** lift cage (car), elevator cage

hissna feel dizzy (giddy); *~nde avgrund* appalling abyss; *~nde höjd* dizzy height[s]; *en ~nde känsla* a feeling of dizziness (giddiness)

hisstrumma lift shaft (well)

hista'min *s4* histamine

histo|gram [-'amm] *s7* histogram **-log** histologist **-logi** *s3* histology **-logisk** *a5* histologic[al]

histori|a [-'tɔ:-] *-en* (*i bet. 2 o. 3 vard. äv. -an*) *-er* **1** history; (*lärobok*) history book; *~ med samhällslära* history and civics; *gamla (nyare) tidens ~* ancient (modern) history; *gå till -en* become (go down in) history **2** (*berättelse*) story **3** (*sak, händelse*) story, thing, business, affair; *en ledsam ~* a sad (unpleasant) business (affair); *en snygg ~* a fine (pretty) business **-citet** historicity

historie|berättare storyteller **-bok** history

book **-skrivning** (*som vetenskap*) historiography

histo'r|ik *s3* history **-iker** [-'tɔ:-] historian **-isk** [-'tɔ:-] *a5* historical; (*historiskt betydande*) historic; *H~a museet* museum of national antiquities

hit here; *~ och dit* here and there, hither and thither, to and fro; *ända ~* as far as this; *fundera ~ och dit* cast about in one's mind; *prata ~ och dit* talk of one thing and another; *det hör inte ~* that has nothing to do with this (is not relevant) **-hörande** *a4* in (of) this category, pertinent, relevant **-intills** *se hittills*

hitlista [*ʰitt-] hit list

hitom [on] this side [of]

hitta 1 (*finna*) find; (*påträffa*) come (light) on (upon); *det var som ~t* it was a real godsend (bargain) **2** (*hitta vägen*) find the (one's) way; (*känna vägen*) know the (one's) way **3** *~ på* (*komma på*) hit upon, (*upptäcka*) find [out], discover, (*uppfinna*) invent, (*dikta upp*) make up; *vad skall vi ~ på* [*att göra*]? what shall we do?

hittebarn foundling

hittegods lost property **-magasin** lost property office

hittelön reward

hittills up to now, hitherto, till now; (*så här långt*) so far **-varande** *a4* hitherto (*etc.*) existing (*etc.*); (*nu avgående*) retiring, outgoing

hit|vägen *på ~* on the (my *etc.*) way here **-åt** ['hi:t-, *äv.* -'å:t] in this direction, this way

hiva heave

hiv|positiv, -smittad HIV positive **--virus** HIV virus

hjon [jɔ:n] *s7* (*tjänare*) servant; (*på inrättning*) inmate **hjonelag** *s7* connubial union

hjord [jɔ:rd] *s2* herd; (*får- o. bildl.*) flock **-instinkt** herd instinct

hjort [jɔ:rt] *s2* deer (*pl äv.* deer); *se äv. dovhjort, kronhjort* **-horn 1** antler **2** (*ämne*) hartshorn **-hornssalt** ammonium carbonate, sal volatile **-kalv** fawn

hjortron [*jɔ:rtrån el. *jɔrr-] *s7* cloudberry **-sylt** cloudberry jam

hjul [ju:l] *s7* wheel; (*utan ekrar*) trundle; (*under möbel o.d.*) caster, castor; (*på ångare*) paddle wheel **hjula** [*ʰju:la] turn cartwheels

hjul|axel axle[tree] **-bas** wheelbase **-bent** [-e:-] *a4* bow-legged, bandy-legged **-nav** hub **-spår** wheel track; (*djupare*) rut **-tryck** wheel pressure **-upphängning** wheel suspension **-ångare** paddle steamer, (*med skovelhjul på sidan*) sidewheeler

hjälm [j-] *s2* helmet **-buske** crest

hjälp [j-] *s3* **1** help; (*bistånd*) assistance, aid; (*undsättning*) rescue; (*understöd*) support; *första ~en* first aid; *med ~ av* with the help of; *få ~ av* be helped (assisted) by; *komma ngn till ~* come to a p.'s assistance; *tack för ~en!* thanks for your [kind] help!; *ta ngt till ~* make use of (have recourse to) s.th.; *vara ngn till stor ~* be a great help to s.b. **2** (*biträde*) help, assistant **3** (*botemedel*) remedy (*mot* for) **4** *ridk., ~er* aids

hjälp|a [j-] *v3* **1** help; (*bistå*) assist, aid; (*bota*) remedy; (*om läkemedel e.d.*) be effective; relieve, ease; (*rädda*) save, rescue; *Gud -e mig!* Goodness gracious!; *så sant mig Gud -e!* so help me God!; *det -er inte hur mycket jag än* it makes no difference however much I; *det -te inte* it had no effect (was of no avail); *hos honom -te inga böner* he turned a deaf ear to our (*etc.*) pleas; *jag kan inte ~ att* (*äv.*) it is not my fault that; *vad -er det att han* what is the use (good) of his (+ *ing-form*); ~ *sig själv* help o.s., (*reda sig*) manage **2** (*med betonad partikel*) ~ *ngn av med kappan* help s.b. off with his (*etc.*) coat; ~ *fram ngn* help s.b. [to get] on (*etc.*); ~ *till hjo* (*med att göra ngt* to do s.th.), *absol. äv.* make o.s. useful; ~ *upp a*) (*ngn på fötterna*) help s.b. on to his feet (to get up, to rise), *b*) (*förbättra*) improve

hjälpaktion relief action

hjälp|ande [j-] *a4* helping *etc.*; *träda ~ emellan* come to the rescue **-are** helper *etc.*; supporter **-as** *v3, dep, det kan inte ~* it can't be helped; ~ *åt* help each other (one another); *om vi -s åt* if we do it together (make a united effort)

hjälp|behövande *a4, de* ~ those requiring (in need of) help, the needy **-klass** class for backward children **-lig** *a1* passable, tolerable, moderate **-lös** helpless; (*tafatt äv.*) shiftless **-medel** aid, help, means (*sg o. pl*) [of assistance]; (*utväg*) expedient, shift; (*källa*) resource, (*litterär*) work of reference **-motor** auxiliary engine (motor) **-präst** assistant priest; *i Storbritannien ung.* curate **-reda** *s1* **1** (*biträde*) helper, assistant **2** (*bok*) guide

hjälpsam [j-] *a1* helpful, ready (willing) to help **-het** helpfulness

hjälp|sökande I *s9* applicant [for assistance (relief)] **II** *a4* seeking relief **-trupp** auxiliary force; ~*er* auxiliary troops, auxiliaries **-verb** auxiliary verb

hjälte [j-] *s2* hero **-dikt** heroic poem **-dåd** heroic achievement (deed) **-död** heroic death; *dö ~en* die the death of a hero **-mod** valour, heroism **-modig** heroic **-tenor** Heldentenor

hjältinna [j-] heroine

hjärn|a [ˣjäː-] *s1* brain; (*förstånd*) brains (*pl*); *lilla ~n* [the] cerebellum; *stora ~n* [the] cerebrum; *bry sin ~* rack one's brains **-bark** cerebral cortex **-bihanget** *undre ~, se hypofysen*; *övre ~, se tallkottkörteln* **-blödning** cerebral haemorrhage **-död I** *s2* brain death **II** *a5* brain dead **-feber** *se -inflammation* **-flykt** *vard.* brain drain **-gymnastik** mental gymnastics **-hinna** cerebral membrane **-hinneinflammation** meningitis **-inflammation** inflammation of the brain **-kontor** *skämts.* upper storey **-skada** brain injury **-skakning** concussion [of the brain] **-skål** brainpan **-spöke** *det är bara ~n* they are idle imaginings **-stammen** the brain stem **-trust** brains trust **-tumör** brain tumour **-tvätt** brainwashing **-tvätta** brainwash

hjärta [ˣjärta] *s6* **1** heart; *ett gott ~* a kind heart; *av allt* (*hela*) *mitt ~* with all my heart, from [the bottom of] my heart; *i ~t av* in the heart (very centre) of (*staden* the town); *med glatt* (*tungt*) ~ with a light (heavy) heart; *given med gott ~* given out of the goodness of one's heart,

given gladly; *med sorg i ~t* with grief in one's heart; *lätt om ~t* light of heart; *ha ngt på ~t* have s.th. on one's mind; *ha ~t på rätta stället* have one's heart in the right place; *lätta sitt ~* unburden o.s., get s.th. off one's chest; *rannsaka ~n och njurar* search the hearts and reins; *säga sitt ~s mening* speak one's mind; *tala fritt ur ~t* speak straight from the heart; *trycka ngn till sitt ~* clasp s.b. to one's bosom; *det ligger mig varmt om ~t* it is very close to my heart; *det skär mig i ~t* it cuts me to the quick; *en sten föll från mitt ~* a weight was lifted off my mind; *hon hade inte ~* [*till*] *att göra det* she hadn't [got] the heart for (to do) it; *jag känner mig varm om ~t* my heart is warmed **2** ~*ns gärna a*) with all my (*etc.*) heart, *b*) (*för all del*) by all means; *av ~ns lust* to one's heart's content **3** *kära ~n*[*d*]*es!* dear me!, well, I never!

hjärt|anskär sweetheart, truelove **-attack** heart attack **-besvär** heart trouble; cardiac complaint **-blad** *bot.* cotyledon; *vard.* seed leaf **-block** heart block **-död I** *s2* cardiac death **II** *a5* cardiac dead

hjärte|angelägenhet affair of the heart **-god** very kind-hearted **-krossare** [-å-] heartbreaker **-lag** *s7* disposition

hjärter [ˈjärt-] *s9, kortsp., koll.* hearts (*pl*); *en ~* a heart; ~ *ess* ace of hearts; ~ *fem* five of hearts; ~ *knekt* the jack of hearts

hjärte|rot *ända in i ~en* to the very marrow **-sak** *det är en ~ för honom* he has it very much at heart **-sorg** poignant (deep) grief; *dö av ~* die of a broken heart **-vän** bosom (best) friend

hjärt|fel [organic] heart disease **-flimmer** fibrillation **-formig** [-å-] *a5* heart-shaped **-förlamning** heart failure **-förmak** auricle **-förstoring** cardiac enlargement, hypertrophy of the heart **-infarkt** myocardial infarction (*AE.* infarct) **-innerlig** [*mest* -ˈinn-] most fervent **-kammare** ventricle **-klaff** cardiac valve **-klappning** palpitation [of the heart]

hjärtlig [ˣjärr-] *a1* hearty; (*svagare*) cordial; (*friare*) kind, warm; ~*a hälsningar* kind regards; ~*a lyckönskningar* sincere congratulations, good wishes; ~*t tack* hearty thanks **-het** heartiness, cordiality

hjärt-lungmaskin heart-lung machine

hjärtlös heartless; unsympathetic, unfeeling **-het** heartlessness

hjärt|massage heart massage **-medicin** heart drug; (*stimulerande*) cardiac stimulating agent; (*lugnande*) cardiac depressant (depressive agent) **-mur** *byggn.* main partition-wall **-muskel** heart muscle **-nupen** *a3* sentimental; (*om pers. äv.*) tenderhearted **-punkt** *bildl.* centre, heart; core **-sjukdom** heart disease **-skärande** heart-rending; heartbreaking **-slag 1** (*pulsslag*) heartbeat, heart-throb **2** *se hjärtförlamning* **3** (*innanmäte*) pluck **-slitande** *a4, se -skärande* **-specialist** cardiologist **-stock** *sjö.* rudderpost, rudderstock **-svikt** heart failure **-säck** heart sac **-trakten** *i ~* in the region of the heart **-transplantation** heart transplant **-verksamhet** action of the heart **-åkomma** heart trouble **-ängslig** nervous and frightened (*över*

hjäss|a [ˣjässa] *s1* crown; *kal* ~ (*äv.*) bald pate; *från ~n till fotabjället* from top to toe (head to foot); *cap-a-pie* **-ben** parietal bone

H.K.H. (*förk. för Hans* [*el. Hennes*] *Kunglig Höghet*) H.R.H.

hm hem!, h'm!

h-moll B minor

1 ho *interr. pron, åld.* who

2 ho *s2* trough

hobby ['håbbi *el.* -y] *s3* hobby **-arbete** hobby work-**rum** home workshop, hobbyroom **-verksamhet** hobby activity

hockey ['håcki *el.* -y] *s2* (*is-*) ice hockey; (*land-*) field hockey **-klubba** hockey stick

hoj [håjj] *s2, vard.* bike

hojta [ˣhåjj-] shout, yell (*till* to, at)

hokuspokus ['hɷ:-, 'pɷ:-] **I** *n* hocus-pocus **II** *interj* hey presto!

holdingbolag holding company

holis|m holism **-tisk** *a5* holistic

holk [-å-] *s2* **1** (*fågel-*) birdhouse **2** *bot.* epicalyx, calycle **-fjäll** *bot.* bract

Holland ['håll-] *n* Holland

hollandaise [hållan'dä:s] *s5*, **-sås** hollandaise sauce

holländare [ˣhåll-] Dutchman; *-arna* (*koll.*) the Dutch

holländ|sk [ˣhåll-] *a5* Dutch **-ska 1** (*språk*) Dutch **2** (*kvinna*) Dutchwoman

holm|e [ˣhåll-] *s2* islet, holm[e] **-gång** *s2, ung.* single combat

holmium ['håll-] *s8* holmium

holo|gra'fi *s3* holography **-gram** [-'amm] *s7* hologram **-kaust** ['hållɷ-] *s3* holocaust

homeo|pat hom[o]eopath, hom[o]eopathist **-pa'ti** *s3* hom[o]eopathy **-patisk** [-'pa:-] *a5* hom[o]eopathic

homerisk [-'me:-] *a5* Homeric, Homerian

Homeros [-'me:-] *Homer*

homi'nid *s3* hominid

homo'fil *s3* homosexual

homogen [-'je:n] *a1* homogen[e]ous **-isera** homogenize **-itet** homogeneity

homo'nym I *a1* homonymic, homonymous **II** *s3* homonym

homosexu|alitet homosexuality **-'ell** homosexual; *en* ~ a homosexual

hon [hɷnn] (*om pers.*) she; (*om djur, sak*) it, *ibl.* she; ~ *som sitter där borta är* the woman sitting over there is

hon|a *s1* female; *jfr björnhona etc.* **-blomma** female flower **-djur** female animal

hondu'r|an *s3*, **-ansk** [-'a:nsk] *a5* Honduran

Honduras [-'du:-] *n* Honduras

hon|katt she-cat **-kön** female sex **-lig** *a5* female

hon'nett *a1, åld.* honest, fair, straightforward

honnör 1 (*hälsning*) salute (*äv.* göra honnör [*för*]); (*hedersbevisning*) honours (*pl*) **2** (*erkännande*) honour **3** *kortsp.* honour

honnörs|bord table of honour **-ord** prestige word

honom [ˣhånnåm, *äv.* ˣhɷ:-] *pron* (*objektsform av han*) (*om pers.*) him; (*om djur*) it, *ibl.* him; (*om sak*) it

hono'rar *s7* fee, remuneration; (*författares äv.*)

royalty

honor|atiores [-atsiˣå:res] *pl, stadens* ~ the notabilities of the town **-era** (*betala*) remunerate; (*skuld*) settle, pay off; ~ *en växel* take up (honour, pay) a bill **-'är** *a1* honorary

honung [ˣhå:-] *s2* honey

honungs|bi honeybee, hive bee **-kaka** honeycomb **-len** honeyed, honied (*röst* voice) **-slungare** honey extractor

1 hop *adv, se ihop*

2 hop *s2* **1** (*hög*) heap (*med* of); (*uppstaplad*) pile (*med* of) **2** (*av människor*) crowd, multitude; *höja sig över ~en* rise above the common herd **3** (*mängd*) lot; heap, multitude

hopa heap (pile) up; (*friare o. bildl.*) accumulate; ~ *sig a*) (*om levande varelser*) crowd together, *b*) (*om saker*) accumulate, (*om snö*) drift

hop|biten *a5, med -bitna läppar* with compressed lips **-diktad** *a5* made-up, concocted **-fantisera** compose out of one's own imagination **-foga** join; (*med fog*) joint; *snick. äv.* splice **-fällbar** folding; collapsible, collapsable **-fälld** *a5* shut-up **-gyttra** conglomerate, cluster together **-klibbad** *a5*, stuck together **-klämd** *a5* squeezed together **-knycklad** *a5* crumpled up **-knäppt** *a4* buttoned up; (*om händer*) folded, clasped **-kok** hotchpotch **-kommen** [-å-] *a5, bra* ~ (*om bok o.d.*) well put together (composed) **-krupen** *a5*, **-kurad** *a5* hunched up; *sitta* ~ sit crouching (crouched up, huddled up) **-lagd** *a5* folded [up] **-lappad** *a5* pieced together, patched [up]

1 hopp [-å-] *s7* (*förhoppning*) hope (*om* of); *ha* (*hysa*) ~ *om* have (entertain) hopes of (*att kunna* being able to); *ha gott* ~ (*absol.*) be of good hope; *låta ~et fara* abandon hope; *sätta sitt* ~ *till* pin one's faith on; *uppge ~et* give up hope; *i* ~ *om att snart få höra från dig* hoping to hear from you soon; *det är föga* ~ *om hans tillfrisknande* there is little hope of his recovery

2 hopp [-å-] *s7* (*språng*) jump (*äv. bildl.*); (*djärvt*) leap; (*elastiskt*) spring; (*skutt*) bound; (*lekfullt*) skip; (*fågels, bolls etc.*) hop; (*sim-*) dive; (*stav-, gymnastik-*) vault

hoppa [-å-] jump; leap; spring; bound; skip; hop; dive; vault; *se 2 hopp*; ~ *med fallskärm* make a parachute jump (descent), bale (bail) out; ~ *och skutta* hop about, caper; ~ *av* jump off (out [of]), *polit.* seek (ask for) political asylum; defect; ~ *på a*) (*ta sig upp på*) jump on (on to, in, into), *b*) (*inlåta sig på*) seize upon, grasp at; ~ *till* give a start (jump); ~ *över* (*eg.*) jump over, *bildl.* skip (*några rader* a few lines)

hoppas [-å-] *dep* hope (*på* for); ~ *på ngn* be hoping in (pin hopes on) s.b.; *jag* ~ *det* I hope so; *det skall vi väl* ~ let us hope so; *bättre än man hade hoppats* better than expected

hoppbacke ski jump

hoppetossa [ˣhåppetåssa] *s1* flibbertigibbet

hopp|full hopeful; confident **-fullhet** hopefulness **-ingivande** [-j-] *a4* hopeful, promising

hoppjerk|a [-å-] *s1* rolling stone; *-or* (*äv.*) migratory workers

hoppla ['håpp-] houp la!

hopplock [ˣhɷ:p-plåck] *s7* miscellany

hopplös hopeless; (*om pers. äv.*) devoid of hope; (*desperat*) desperate; *ett ~t företag* (*äv.*) a forlorn hope **-het** hopelessness
hopp|ning [-å-] jump[ing] **-rep** skipping-rope; *AE.* jump rope; *hoppa ~ skip* **-rätvinge** orthopteran, orthopteron
hoppsan ['håpp-] upsy-daisy!, upsadaisy!, whoops!
hopp|ställning *sport.* take-off **-torn** *sport.* diving-tower **-tävling** jumping (diving) competition
hop|rafsad *a5* scrambled together **-rullad** *a5* rolled up; (*om rep, orm*) coiled up **-sjunken** *a5* shrunken **-skrynklad** *a5* creased, crumpled
hopslag|en *a5* **1** (*om bord e.d.*) folded-up; (*om bok*) shut-up, closed; (*om paraply*) rolled up **2** (*hopspikad*) nailed (fastened) up together **3** (*sammanhälld*) poured together **4** *bildl.* combined, united; (*om bolag e.d.*) amalgamated **-ning** folding up *etc.*; (*av bolag e.d.*) amalgamation, fusion; (*av skolklasser*) uniting
hop|slingrad *a5* intertwined **-snörd** [-ö:-] *a5* **1** laced up **2** (*friare o. bildl.*) compressed, constricted **-sparad** *a5*, *~e slantar* savings **-sättning** putting together; (*av maskin*) assembly, mounting **-tagning** [-a:-] (*vid stickning*) decreasing, narrowing **-trängd** *a5* crowded (packed, cramped) together; (*om handstil*) cramped **-tvinning** twining **-vikbar** foldable, collapsible, collapsable **-vikt** [-i:-] *a4* folded up
hor *s7* adultery; (*otukt*) fornication; *bedriva ~* commit adultery
hor|a *s1 o. v1* whore **-bock** *se horkarl*
hord [-å:-] *s3* horde
horhus whorehouse
horisont [-ånt] *s3* horizon; skyline; *från vår ~* (*bildl.*) from our viewpoint; *vid ~en* on the horizon; *avteckna sig mot ~en* stand out against the horizon; *det går över min ~* it is beyond me
horison'tal *a5* horizontal **-plan** horizontal plane
horison'tell *a5, se horisontal*
horkarl [ˣhɷ:rka:r] fornicator; whore|master, -monger
hormon [-'å:n *el.* -'ɷ:n] *s7, s4* hormone **-avsöndring** hormone secretion **-behandling** hormone treatment **-'ell** *a5* hormonal
horn [-ɷ:-] *s7* horn (*äv. ämne o. mus.*); (*på hjortdjur*) antler; (*jakt-*) [hunting] horn; (*signal-*) bugle; (*bil-*) car horn, hooter; *blåsa* (*stöta*) *i ~* sound the bugle; *stånga ~en av sig* (*bildl.*) sow one's wild oats; *ha ett ~ i sidan till ngn* bear s.b. a grudge; *ta tjuren vid ~en* (*äv. bildl.*) take the bull by the horns **-artad** [-a:r-] *a5* hornlike, horny **-blåsare** horn|player, -blower; *mil. äv.* bugler **-blände** *s6, miner.* hornblende **-boskap** horned cattle **-bågad** *a5, ~e glasögon* horn-rimmed spectacles **-hinna** cornea **-musik** horn (brass) music **-orkester** brass band **-stöt** *mus.* bugle blast **-uggla** long-eared owl **-ämne** horny substance, keratin
horoskop [-'å:p] *s7,* *ställa ngns ~* cast a p.'s horoscope
horribel [-'ri:-] *a2* horrible
horsgök [ˣhårs-] *zool., se enkelbeckasin*

horst [-å-] *s2, geol.* horst
hortensia [-'tensia] *s1* hydrangea
hort|ikultur [-å-] horticulture **-onom** horticulturist
horunge 1 bastard **2** *boktr.* widow
hos 1 (*i ngns hus, hem o.d.*) at; with; *~ juveleraren* at the jeweller's [shop]; *hemma ~ oss* in our home; *inne ~ mig* in my room; *bo ~ sin syster* live at one's sister's [place *etc.*] (with one's sister); *göra ett besök ~* pay a visit to, call on **2** (*bredvid, intill*) by, beside, next to; *kom och sätt dig ~ mig* come and sit down by (beside) me **3** *adjutant ~ kungen* A.D.C. to the king; *anställd ~* employed by; *arbeta ~ ngn* work for s.b.; *göra en beställning ~* place an order with, order from; *han var ~ mig när* he was with me when; *jag har varit ~ henne med blommorna* I have been to her with the flowers; *jag har varit ~ tandläkaren* I have been to the dentist **4** (*i uttr. som anger egenskap, utseende, känsla o.d.*) in; about; with; *en ovana ~ ngn* a bad habit with s.b.; *ett vackert drag ~ ngn* a fine trait in s.b.; *det finns ngt ~ dem som* there is s.th. about them that; *det finns ~ Shakespeare* it is in Shakespeare; *felet ligger ~ mig* the fault lies with me, the mistake is mine
hosianna [-'anna] *interj o. s6* hosanna
hospi'tal *s7* [lunatic] asylum
host|a I *s1* cough; *ha ~* have a cough **II** *v1* cough; (*om motor*) splutter; *~ blod* cough up blood; *~ till* give a cough (hem) **-attack** attack of coughing
hostia ['håss-] *s1* Host
host|ig *a5* troubled with a cough; (*om motor*) spluttering **-medicin** cough mixture **-ning** cough; (*-ande*) coughing
hot *s7* threat[s *pl*] (*mot against*; *om* of); (*-ande fara*) menace (*mot* to), threatening; [*ett*] *tomt ~* empty threats (*pl*)
hot|a threaten; (*i högre stil*) menace; (*vara överhängande äv.*) be impending, impend; *~ ngn till livet* threaten a p.'s life **-ande** *a4* threatening *etc.*; (*överhängande äv.*) impending, imminent
hotchpotchsoppa ['håtʃpåtʃ-] hotchpotch [soup]
ho'tell [hå- *el.* hɷ-] *s7* hotel; *H~ Baltic* the Baltic Hotel; *ta in på ~* put up at a hotel **-betjäning** hotel staff (attendants *pl*) **-gäst** resident **-reception** hotel reception desk **-rum** hotel room; *beställa ~* make a reservation (book a room) at a hotel **-räkning** hotel bill **-rörelse** hotel business **-ägare** hotel proprietor, hotelier
hotelse threat (*mot* against); menace (*mot* to); *sätta sin ~ i verket* carry out a (one's) threat; *utslunga ~r mot* utter threats against **-brev** threatening letter
hotfull menacing
hottentott [ˣhått- *el.* -'tått] *s3* Hottentot
1 hov [-ɷ:-] *s2* (*på djur*) hoof; *försedd med ~ar* (*äv.*) hoofed
2 hov [-å:-] *s7* (*regerande furstes*) court; *vid ~et* at court; *vid ~et i* at the court in (of); *hålla ett lysande ~* keep court with great splendour
hovdam lady-in-waiting (*hos* to)
hovdjur [ˣhɷ:v-] *~en* the hoofed animals

hovdräkt [ˣhå:v-] court dress
hovera [-ө-] *rfl* swagger, strut about
hov|folk [ˣhå:v-] courtiers (*pl*) **-fotograf** photographer to H.M. the King (*etc.*) **-fröken** maid of honour **-funktionär** court functionary (official) **-kapell** *mus.* royal orchestra; *Kungl. ~et* the Royal Opera House Orchestra **-kapellmästare** *förste ~* master of the king's (*etc.*) music **-lakej** royal footman **-leverantör** purveyor to H.M. the King (*etc.*) **-man** courtier **-marskalk** marshal of the court; *i Storbritannien ung.* Lord Chamberlain [of the Household] **-mästare 1** (*på restaurang*) head waiter **2** (*i privathus*) butler **-narr** court jester **-nigning** reverence, court curts[e]y **-predikant** court chaplain
hovra [ˣhå:v- *el.* -ө:-] hover
hovrätt [ˣhå:v-] court of appeal
hovrätts|assessor associate judge of appeal **-fiskal** reporting clerk [to a (the) court of appeal] **-lagman** head of division [to a (the) court of appeal] **-notarie** law clerk [of a (the) court of appeal] **-president** president [of a (the) court of appeal]; *i Storbritannien* Lord Chief Justice **-råd** judge of appeal
hovsam [ˣhө:v-] *a1* moderate; *i ~ma ordalag* in measured terms
hovslagare [ˣhө:v-] farrier, blacksmith
hov|sorg [ˣhå:v-] court mourning **-stall** *~et* the royal stables (*pl*) **-stallmästare** crown equerry **-stat** *~en* the royal household **-sångare, -sångerska** court singer
hovtång [ˣhө:v-] [large (heavy)] pincers (*pl*); *en ~* a pair of [large (heavy)] pincers
hu ugh!, whew!; *~, så du skrämde mig!* oh, what a shock you gave me!
huckle *s6* kerchief
hud *s2* skin; (*av större djur*) hide; *anat.* (*överhud*) cuticle, epidermis; *~ar och skinn* hides and skins; *ge ngn på ~en* give s.b. a good hiding (rating) **-cancer** skin cancer **-flänga** *v2, äv. bildl.* scourge, horsewhip **-färg 1** (*hudens färg*) colour of the skin; (*hy*) complexion **2** (*köttfärg*) flesh colour **-färgad** *a5* flesh-coloured **-kräm** skin cream; face cream, cold cream **-sjukdom** skin disease **-specialist** dermatologist **-veck** fold of the skin **-transplantat** skin graft **-transplantation** skin grafting; *en ~* a skin graft
hugad *a5, ~e spekulanter* prospective buyers
hugenott [-ge'nått] *s3* Huguenot
hugfäst|a [ˣhu:g-] commemorate; celebrate (*minnet av* the memory of) **-else** *till ~ av* in commemoration of
hugg *s7* **1** (*med vapen el. verktyg*) cut; (*vårdslöst*) slash; (*med spetsen av ngt*) stab (*äv. bildl.*); (*träff*) hit; (*slag*) blow, stroke; (*med tänder e.d.*) bite; *~ och slag* violent blows; *med kniven i högsta ~* with one's knife ready to strike; *ge ~ på sig* lay o.s. open to attack (criticism); *rikta ett ~ mot* aim a blow at **2** (*märke efter*) cut; (*häftig smärta*) spasm; twinge; (*håll*) stitch
hugga *högg huggit* **1** (*med vapen el. verktyg*) cut; (*vårdslöst*) slash; (*med spetsen av ngt*) stab; (*fälla*) cut down, fell; (*skog, sten*) hew; (*ved*) chop; (*om bildhuggare*) carve; *~ i sten*

(*bildl.*) go wide of the mark; *det kan vara hugget som stucket* it doesn't make much difference **2** (*om djur*) (*med tänder*) bite, (*med klor e.d.*) grab, clutch, (*om orm*) sting **3** *bildl.* (*gripa*) seize (catch) [hold of] **4** (*med betonad partikel*) *~ för sig* help o.s. (*av* to), grab; *~ i* (*gripa sig an*) set to; *hugg i och dra!* pull away! (*med* at); *~ in på a*) *mil.* charge, *b*) (*mat e.d.*) fall to; *~ tag i a*) (*om pers.*) seize (catch) hold of, *b*) (*om sak*) catch [in]; *~ till a*) (*ge hugg*) strike, deal a blow, *b*) (*svara på måfå*) hazard, make a guess, *c*) (*ta betalt*) ask an exorbitant price
huggare 1 *pers., se skogs-, stenhuggare etc.* **2** (*vapen*) cutlass; *en ~ till karl* (*vard.*) a topper (corker, humdinger)
hugg|järn chisel **-krok** gaff **-kubb[e]** chopping-block **-orm** adder; viper (*äv. bildl.*) **-sexa** grab-and-scramble meal **-tand** (*bete*) tusk; (*hos orm, rovdjur*) fang **-vapen** cutting-weapon **-värja** rapier
hugn|a [ˣhuŋna] favour; gladden **-ad** *s3, till ~ för* to the comfort of **-esam** *a1* comforting
hug|skott [-u:-] passing fancy; (*nyck*) whim, caprice **-stor** (*om pers.*) magnanimous; (*om sak*) sublime **-svala** *v1* comfort; solace, soothe **-svalelse** comfort; solace; consolation
huj [hujj] *oböjligt s o. interj, i ett ~* in a flash; *~, vad det gick!* whew (oh), that was fast!
huk *oböjligt s, sitta på ~* squat, sit on one's heels **huka** *rfl* crouch [down]
huld *a1* (*ljuv*) fair; (*välvillig*) benignant, kindly; (*bevågen*) propitious (*mot* towards, to); (*nådig*) gracious; *om lyckan är mig ~* if fortune smiles on me
huldra *s1* lady of the woods
hull *s7* flesh; *med ~ och hår* completely, bodily, (*svälja ngt* swallow s.th.) whole; *lägga på ~et* put on weight
huller om buller ['hull-, 'bull-] pell-mell, higgledy-piggledy
hulling barb; (*på harpun o.d.*) fluke
hum [humm] *oböjligt s, n el. r, ha litet ~ om* have some idea (notion) of
hu'man *a1* (*människovänlig*) humane; (*friare*) kind, fair, considerate; *~a priser* reasonable prices **-biologi** human biology
humaniora [-ˣå:ra] *oböjligt s, pl* [the] humanities, the arts
human|isera humanize **-ism** humanism **-ist** humanist; arts student (*etc.*) **-istisk** *a5* humanistic; humane; *~ fakultet* faculty of arts; *~a vetenskaper* [the] humanities, the arts **-itet** humanity **-i'tär** humanitarian
humbug ['hummbugg] *s2* humbug; fraud (*äv. pers.*)
humla *s1* bumblebee
humle *s9, s7* (*planta*) hop; (*som handelsvara*) hops (*pl*) **-ranka** hopbine, hopbind **-stör** hop-pole; *lång som en ~* lanky as a beanpole
hummer ['humm-] *s2* lobster **-tina** lobster pot (trap)
humor ['hu:-] *s9* humour **-'esk** *s3* humorous story (sketch) **-ist** humorist **-istisk** *a5* humorous **-lös** devoid of humour
humus ['hu:-] *s2* humus **-syra** humic acid
humör *s7* temperament; (*lynne*) temper; (*sin-*

nesstämning) humour, mood, spirits (*pl*); *på dåligt* ~ in a bad humour (temper, mood), out of spirits; *på gott* ~ in a good temper (humour), in good spirits; *fatta* ~ flare up, take offence (*över* at); *hålla* ~*et uppe* keep up one's spirits; *tappa* ~*et* lose one's temper; *visa* ~ show bad temper; *är du på det* ~*et?* is that the mood you are in?

hund *s2* dog; (*jakt- äv.*) hound; *röda* ~ German measles; *frysa som en* ~ be chilled to the marrow; *leva som* ~ *och katt* lead a cat-and-dog life; *slita* ~ work like a horse, rough it; *inte döma* ~*en efter håren* not judge the dog by its coat; *här ligger en* ~ *begraven* I smell a rat here; *lära gamla* ~*ar sitta* teach an old dog new tricks **-aktig** *a1* doglike; **-ben** dogbone **-biten** *a5* dog-bitten **-göra** [a piece of] drudgery **-halsband** dog collar **-huvud** *bära* ~*et för* be made the scapegoat for **-kapp-löpning** greyhound racing **-kex** dog biscuit **-koja** kennel; *AE. äv.* doghouse **-koppel** leash, lead **-käx** *s3*, **-käxa** *s1*, *se* -*loka* **-liv** *leva ett* ~ lead a dog's life **-loka** *s1, bot.* cow parsley, keck **-lort** dog's dung **-mat** dog food

hundra ['hund-] hundred; *ett* ~ a (*betonat* one) hundred; *många* ~ many hundreds of; ~ *tusen* a (one) hundred thousand

hundracka *s1* cur, mongrel

hundra|de I *s6* hundred; *i* ~*n* in hundreds **II** (*ordningstal*) hundredth **-[de]del** one hundredth part **-faldig** *a5*, **-falt** *adv* hundredfold **-kronesedel**, **-kronorssedel** hundred-kronor note **-lapp** *se* -*kronesedel* **-procentig** *a5* one-hundred per cent

hundras breed of dog

hundra|tal *tiotal och* ~ tens and hundreds; *ett* ~ a hundred or so, about a (some) hundred; *i* ~ in hundreds; *på* ~*et e.Kr.* in the second century A.D. **-tals** [-a:-] hundreds (*böcker* of books) **-tusentals** hundreds of thousands **-årig** *a5* a (one) hundred years old; one-hundred-year-old **-åring** centenarian

hundra|årsdag centennial day, centenary; hundredth anniversary **-jubileum**, -minne centenary

hundsfott [*ˣ*hundsvått] *avdelat hunds-fott, sjö.* becket **-era** *avdelat hunds-fottera* bully

hund|skall barking of dogs (a dog); *jakt.* cry of hounds; *ett* ~ a dog bark **-skatt** dog licence **-skattemärke** dog-licence plate **-släde** dog sledge **-släktet** the canine genus **-spann** dog team **-utställning** dog show **-vakt** *sjö.* middle watch **-valp** pup[py] **-väder** vile (dirty) weather **-vän** dog lover (fancier) **-år** *pl* years of struggle (of hard life) **-ägare** dog owner **-öra** dog['s]-ear (*äv. bildl.*)

hunger ['huŋ-] *s2* hunger (*efter* for); (*svält*) starvation; *dö av* ~ die of hunger (starvation), starve to death; *lida* ~*ns kval* suffer from [the pangs of] hunger; *vara nära att dö av* ~ be [on the point of] starving; ~*n är den bästa kryddan* hunger is the best sauce

hungersnöd famine

hunger|strejk, **-strejka** hunger strike

hungr|a [*ˣ*huŋ-] be hungry (starving); *bildl.* hunger (*efter* for); ~ *ihjäl* starve to death **-ig** *a1* hungry; (*svulten*) starving; ~ *som en varg*

(*äv.*) ravenously hungry

hunner ['hunn-] Hun; ~*na* the Huns

hunnit *sup. av hinna*

hunsa bully; browbeat

hur 1 (*frågande*) how; what; ~ *sa?* what did you say?, I beg your pardon?; ~ *så?* why?; ~ *blir det med...? (äv.)* what about...?; ~ *mår du?* how are you?; ~ *menar du?* what do you mean?; ~ *ser han ut?* what does he look like? **2** *eller* ~? (*inte sant*) isn't that so?, don't you think?, am I not right?; *du tycker inte om det, eller* ~? you don't like it, do you?; *du kan simma, eller* ~? you can swim, can't you? **3** ~...*än* however; ~ *hon än gör* whatever she may do; ~ *mycket jag än arbetade* however [much] I worked, work as I might; ~ *trött han än är* however tired (tired as) he may be; ~ *det nu kom sig* whatever happened; ~ *det nu var* somehow or other; ~ *gärna jag än ville* however much I should like to **4** ~ *som helst, se helst*

hurdan ['hu:r-, -*ˣ*da:n, -'dann] *a5*, ~ *är han som lärare?* what kind (sort) of a teacher is he?; ~*t vädret än blir* whatever (no matter what) the weather may be

hurra I [-'ra:] *interj* hurrah! **II** [*ˣ*hurra] *s6, s7 o. v1* hurrah; ~ *för ngn* cheer s.b., give s.b. a cheer; *det är ingenting att* ~ *för* it is nothing to write home about **-rop** [*ˣ*hurra-] cheer

hurr|il *s2*, **-ing** *s2* box [of the ear]

hurt|bulle *vard.* hearty **-frisk** hearty

hurtig *a1* (*livlig*) brisk, keen; (*käck*) dashing; (*frimodig*) frank; (*rapp*) smart; (*spänstig*) alert **-het** briskness *etc.*; dash

hurts *s2* [drawer] pedestal

huru *se hur* **-dan** *se hurdan* **-ledes** how, in what way (manner) **-som** that **-vida** [-*ˣ*vi:da] whether

hus *s7* house; (*byggnad*) building, block; (*familj*) house, family; ~ *och hem* house and home; *en vän i* ~*et* a friend of the family; *frun i* ~*et* the lady of the house; *habsburgska* ~*et* the House of Hapsburg; *föra stort* ~ keep [up] a large establishment; *gå man ur* ~ turn out to a man; *göra rent* ~ make a clean sweep; *spela för fullt* ~ play to a full house; *allt vad* ~*et förmår* all I (we) can offer you; *var har ni hållit* ~? where have you been?

hus|a *s1* housemaid; (*som passar upp vid bordet*) parlourmaid **-aga** domestic chastisement **-apotek** family medicine chest

hu'sar *s3* hussar **-regemente** hussar regiment

hus|arrest house arrest **-behov** *till* ~ for household use; *kunna ngt till* ~ know s.th. just passably, have a rough knowledge of s.th. **-bil** caravanette, dormobile; *AE.* camper, winnebago, mobile home **-bock** *zool.* old house borer **-bonde** master; ~*ns röst* his master's voice **-bondfolk** master and mistress **-bygge** house under construction **-båt** houseboat **-djur** domestic animal; ~*en (på lantgård)* the livestock (*sg*) **-djursavel** livestock breeding

husera (*hålla till*) haunt; (*härja*) ravage, make havoc; (*fara fram*) carry on; (*fara vilt fram*) run riot; ~ *fritt* run riot

hus|esyn *förrätta* ~ *i* carry out the prescribed inspection of; *gå* ~ *i* make a tour of inspection of **-fader** father (head) of a (the) family **-fluga** housefly **-frid** domestic peace **-fru** mistress of a (the) household; (*på hotell*) [head] housekeeper, matron **-föreståndare, -föreståndarinna** housekeeper **-förhör** parish catechetical meeting **-geråd** [-j-] *s7* household utensils (*pl*) **-gud** *~ar* household gods; *bildl.* idol **hushåll** *s7* **1** (*arbetet i ett hem*) housekeeping; *ha eget ~* do one's own housekeeping; *sköta ~et åt ngn* do a p.'s housekeeping for him, keep house for s.b. **2** (*familj*) household, family; *ett fyra personers ~* a household of four [persons] **hushåll|a** *v1* **1** keep house **2** (*vara sparsam*) economize; *~ med* be economical (careful) with **-erska** housekeeper **-ning 1** housekeeping **2** (*sparsamhet*) economizing; economy **3** (*förvaltning*) economic administration (management) **-ningssällskap** [county] agricultural society **hushålls|apparat** household appliance **-arbete** housework **-göromål** *pl* household (domestic) duties, housework; (*skolämne*) household management, domestic science **-kassa** *se -pengar* **-lärare** domestic science teacher **-maskin** household appliance (*vanl. pl*) **-pengar** housekeeping [money (allowance)] **-rulle** kitchen roll **-skola** domestic science school **hus|katt** domestic cat **-knut** corner of a (the) house **-kors** *skämts.* shrew **-kur** household remedy **huslig** [*ˣhu:s-*] *a1* **1** (*familje-*) domestic, household; *~ ekonomi* household economy; *~t arbete* domestic work, housework **2** (*intresserad av hushåll*) domesticated, house-proud **-het** domesticity **hus|läkare** family doctor **-länga** (*rad av hus*) row of houses; (*långsträckt hus*) long low house, wing **-man** crofter **-manskost** homely fare, plain food **-moder** housewife; (*matmor*) mistress of a (the) household; (*på institution*) matron **-modersförening** housewives' association; (*i Storbritannien*) Women's Institute **-mor** *se -moder* **-mus** house mouse **-ockupation** squatting **-rannsakan** *se husundersökning* **-rum** accomodation, lodging; (*tak över huvudet*) shelter **husse** *s2* master **hus'sit** *s3* Hussite **hus|svala** house martin **-tomte** brownie **hustru** *s5* wife **-byte** wife swapping **-misshandel** wife batting **-plågare** *han är en ~* he is a torment (devil) to his wife **hus|tyrann** family tyrant **-undersökning** domiciliary visit, search [of a house] **-vagn** caravan; *AE.* trailer **-vill** homeless **-värd** landlord **-ägare** house owner **hut 1** *interj,* ~ *människa!* how dare you! **II** *r, lära ngn veta* ~ teach s.b. manners; *vet ~!* none of your insolence!; *han har ingen ~ i kroppen* he has no sense of shame (no decency) **huta** ~ *åt ngn* tell s.b. to mind his manners, (*läxa upp*) snub s.b., take s.b. down a peg [or two] **hutch** *se hurts* **hutlös** shameless (*äv. om pris*), impudent **hutt** *s2* spot, snort[er] **huttel** [*'hutt-*] *s7* shillyshallying **huttla** [*ˣhutt-*]

(*tveka*) shillyshally; (*vara undfallande*) yield (*med* to); (*driva gäck*) trifle; *jag låter inte ~ med mig* I am not to be trifled with **huttra** shiver (*av* with) **huv** *s2* hood; cap; (*skrivmaskins- etc*) cover; (*motor-*) bonnet, *AE.* hood; (*rök-*) cowl; (*te-*) [tea] cosy; (*på reservoarpenna*) cap, top **huva** *s1* hood; ('*kråka' äv.*) bonnet **huvud** *s7, pl äv. -en* head; (*förstånd äv.*) brains (*pl*), intellect; *efter mitt ~* my own way; *med ~et före* headfirst; *upp med ~et!* (*bildl.*) keep your chin up!; *över ~ taget* on the whole, (*alls*) at all; *bli ett ~ kortare* (*bildl.*) get one's head blown off; *få ngt i sitt ~* get s.th. into one's head; *ha ~et fullt av* have one's head full of; *ha ~et på skaft* have a head on one's shoulders, be all there; *ha gott ~* be clever (brainy); *hålla ~et kallt* keep cool, keep one's head; *köra ~et i väggen* (*bildl.*) bang one's head against a brick wall; *slå ~et på spiken* hit the nail on the head, strike home; *stiga ngn åt ~et* go to a p.'s head; *ställa allting på ~et* make everything topsy-turvy; *sätta sitt ~ i pant på* stake one's life on; *tappa ~et* lose one's head; *vara ~et högre än* (*bildl.*) be head and shoulders above; *växa ngn över ~et a*) eg. outgrow s.b., *b*) bildl. get beyond a p.'s control; *om vi slår våra kloka ~en ihop* if we put our heads together **huvud-** (*i sms., bildl.*) (*förnämst*) principal, main, head, chief; (*ledande*) leading; (*i första hand*) primary **huvud|accent** primary accent (stress) **-ansvar** main responsibility **-bangård** central (main) station, main terminus **-beståndsdel** principal (main) ingredient **-bok** *hand.* [general] ledger **-bonad** headgear *s7, göra sig mycket ~* puzzle a great deal; *vålla ngn ~* be a worry (puzzle) to s.b. **-byggnad** main (central) building **-del** main (greater) part, bulk **-drag** main (principal) feature; *~en av engelska historien* the main outlines of English history **-duk** kerchief, headscarf **-däck** main deck **-figur** *se -person* **-form 1** *anat.* shape of the head **2** (*-art*) principal (main) form **3** *språkv.* voice **-förhandling** *jur.* main session, trial, hearing **-förutsättning** first (principal) prerequisite **-gata** main street, thoroughfare **-gavel** headboard [of a bed] **-gärd** bed's head; (*kudde*) pillow **-ingång** main entrance **-innehåll** principal (main) contents (*pl*); *redogöra för ~ et i* give a summary of **-intresse** principal (chief, main) interest **-intryck** principal (main) impression **-jägare** head-hunter **-kontor** head (main, central) office **-kudde** pillow **-led** (*väg*) major road **-ledning** (*för gas, vatten*) main [pipe]; *elektr.* main circuit **-lus** head louse **-lös** (*tanklös*) thoughtless; (*dåraktig*) foolish; (*dumdristig*) foolhardy **-man** (*för familj*) head (*för* of); (*uppdragsgivare*) principal, client; (*i sparbank o.d.*) trustee; (*ledare*) leader, head **-motiv** principal motive, main reason **-mål 1** *se huvudsyfte* **2** (*måltid*) principal meal **-nummer** principal item **-nyckel** master (pass) key **-näring 1** (*föda*) principal nutriment **2** (*yrkesgren*) principal (main, chief) industry **-ord 1** (*nyckelord*) key word **2** språkv. headword **-orsak** principal (main, chief) cause

-part *se -del* **-person** principal (leading) figure; (*i roman o.d.*) principal (leading) character; protagonist **-post** main (general) post office **-princip** main principle **-punkt** main (principal) point; (*i anklagelse*) [principal] count **-redaktör** editor in chief **-regel** principal (chief) rule **-riktning** general direction **-roll** leading (principal) part **-rubrik** main heading **-räkning** mental arithmetic **-rätt** *kokk.* main course **-rörelse** movement of the head

huvudsak *~en* the main (principal) thing; *i ~* in the main, on the whole **-lig** *a1* principal, main, chief, primary; (*väsentlig*) essential; *~ föda* mainstay **-ligen** principally *etc.*; (*för det mesta*) mostly, for the most part

huvud|sanning primary (cardinal) truth **-sats 1** (*i logiken*) [the] main proposition **2** *språkv.* main clause **-skyddsombud** senior safety delegate **-skål** cranium **-stad** capital; (*stor o. bildl.*) metropolis **-stadsbo** inhabitant of the capital **-stupa** headfirst; (*friare*) headlong; (*brådstörtat*) precipitately **-styrka** *mil.* main body **-svål** scalp **-syfte** main purpose (aim) **-synpunkt** main point of view **-sysselsättning** main (principal) occupation **-säte** centre; headquarters (*behandlas äv. som sg*) **-tanke** main (principal) idea **-tema** main theme **-tes** principal thesis **-titel** (*i riksstat*) *ung.* section (classification) of government estimates (budget); *första ~n* the Royal Household and Establishment, (*i Storbritannien*) the Civil List **-ton 1** *mus.* keynote **2** *språkv.*, *se huvudaccent* **-tonart** principal key **-uppgift** main task (function) **-verb** main verb **-vikt** *lägga ~en vid* lay the main stress upon, attach primary importance to **-villkor** principal (essential) condition **-vittne** chief witness **-väg** trunk road **-värk** headache **-värkstablett** headache tablet **-ämne** chief (principal) subject; *univ.* major subject **-ändamål** main (chief) purpose

hux flux (*med detsamma*) straight away; (*plötsligt*) all of a sudden

hy *s3* complexion; skin

hya'cint *s3, bot. o. miner.* hyacinth

hy'brid *s3 o. a1* hybrid **-isera** hybridize

hybris ['hy:-] *best. form* =, *äv. -en* arrogance

hyckl|a (*ställa sig from*) play the hypocrite (*inför* before); (*förställa sig*) dissemble (*inför* to); (*låtsas*) simulate, feign; palter **-ad** *a5* (*låtsad*) mock, sham, pretended, simulated **-ande** *a4* hypocritical **-are** hypocrite **-eri** hypocrisy; (*i tal*) cant[ing]

hydda *s1* hut, cabin

hydra [*hy:-] *s1* hydra (*äv. bildl.*)

hydrat *s7, s4,* **-isera** *v1* hydrate

hydraul|ik *s3* fluid mechanics, hydraulics (*pl, behandlas som sg*) **-isk** [-'drau-] *a5* hydraulic

hydrer|a hydrogenate, hydrogenize **-ing** hydrogenation, hydrogenization

hy'drid *s3* hydride

hydro|dynamik hydrokinetics, hydrodynamics (*pl, behandlas som sg*) **-dynamisk** [-'na:-] *a5* hydrokinetic[al] **-fon** [-'få:n] *s3* hydrophone **-for** [-'få:r] *s3* pressure tank, air-loaded water storage **-graf** *s3* hydrographer **-grafi** *s3* hydrography **-grafisk** [-'gra:-] *a5* hydrographic[al] **-kinon** [-çi'nå:n] *s3, s7* hydroquinone, hydroquinol **-kopter** [-'kåpp-] *s2* airboat, swamp boat **-log** hydrologist **-logi** *s3* hydrology **-logisk** *a5* hydrologic[al]; *~ cykel* water (hydrologic) cycle **-lys** *s3* hydrolysis **-mekanik** hydromechanics (*pl, behandlas som sg*) **-mekanisk** [-'ka:-] *a5* hydromechanical **-meter** [-'me:-] *s2* hydrometer **-me'tri** *s3* hydrometry **-metrisk** [-'me:-] *a5* hydrometric[al] **-'plan** *s7* seaplane **-'sfär** hydrosphere **-statik** hydrostatics (*pl, behandlas som sg*) **-statisk** [-'sta:-] *a5* hydrostatic[al] **-teknik** hydrotechnology

hydrox|'id *s3* hydroxide **-'yl** *s3* hydroxyl

hyena [-*e:na] *s1* hy[a]ena (*äv. bildl.*)

hyende [*hy:en-] *s6* cushion; *lägga ~ under lasten* (*bildl.*) bolster up vice

hyfs *r, se hyfsning; sätta ~ på, se hyfsa*

hyfs|a 1 (*äv. ~ till*) trim (tidy) up, make tidy; *bildl.* teach manners; *~t uppträdande* proper behaviour; *en ~d ung man* a well-behaved (well-mannered) young man **2** *mat.* simplify, reduce **-ning** trimming up *etc.*; (*belevenhet*) good manners (*pl*)

hygge *s6* cutting (felling) area

hygglig *a1* **1** (*väluppfostrad*) well-behaved; (*vänlig*) kind, good, *vard.* decent; (*tilltalande*) nice; *en ~ karl* a nice (decent) fellow (chap) **2** (*anständig*) respectable **3** (*skälig*) decent; (*moderat*) fair, reasonable, moderate

hygi'en [-g-] *s3* hygiene; *personlig ~* personal hygiene **-iker** hygienist **-isk** *a5* hygienic; sanitary

hygro|graf *s3* hygrograph **-meter** [-'me:-] *s2* hygrometer **-metrisk** [-'me:-] *a5* hygrometric **-skop** *s7* hygroscope **-skopisk** [-'skå:-] *a5* hygroscopic **-stat** *s3* humidistat, hygrostat

1 hylla *s1* **1** shelf (*pl* shelves); (*möbel*) set of shelves; (*bagage-, sko-, tallriks- o.d.*) rack; *lägga ngt på ~n* (*bildl.*) put s.th. on the shelf, shelve s.th. **2** *teat., vard.* (*översta rad*) *~n* the gods (*pl*)

2 hylla *v1* **1** (*svära tro*) swear allegiance to; (*erkänna*) acknowledge **2** (*uppvakta, hedra*) congratulate; pay (do) homage to; honour **3** (*omfatta*) embrace, favour **4** *rfl, ~ sig till ngn* attach o.s. to s.b.

hylle *s6, bot.* involucre, perianth

hyllning congratulations (*pl*); homage; (*ovation*) ovation; *bringa ngn sin ~* pay (do) homage to s.b. **hyllningsdikt** complimentary poem

hyll|papper shelf (lining) paper **-remsa** shelf-edging, shelf-strip **-värmare** *hand., vard.* sticker, drug [on the market]

hyls|a *s1* case, casing; *tekn.* socket, sleeve; *bot.* shell, hull **-nyckel** box spanner

hymen ['hy:-] *r* **1** *myt.* Hymen; *knyta ~s band* tie the nuptial knot **2** *anat.* hymen

hymla *vard.* (*hyckla*) pretend; (*smussla* [*med*]) try to shuffle away

hymn *s3* hymn; (*friare*) anthem **-diktning** hymn writing, hymnody

hynda *s1* bitch

hyperaktiv [*hy:-] hyperactive

hyperbel [-'pärr-] *s3* hyperbola **-formig** [-å-] *a5* hyperbolic[al]

hyper|bolisk [-'bå:-] *a5* hyperbolic[al] **-bo'ré**
s3 Hyperborean
hyper|elegant [ˣhy:-] very stylish **-korrekt**
meticulously correct **-kritisk** hypercritical
-känslig hypersensitive **-modern** ultramodern
-nervös extremely nervous
hyperon [-'å:n] *s3* hyperon
hyper|snabb high-velocity; high-speed **-venti-
lation** hyperventilation
hypnos [-'å:s] *s3* hypnosis (*pl* hypnoses)
hypnot|isera hypnotize **-isk** [-'nå:-] *a5* hyp-
notic **-ism** hypnotism **-isör** hypnotist
hypo'fys *s3* hypophysis (*pl* hypophyses), pitui-
tary gland (body)
hypoidväxel [-pøˣi:d-] hypoid gear
hypokond|er [-'kånn-] *s3* hypochondriac **-'ri** *s3*
hypochondria **-risk** [-'kånn-] *a5* hypochon-
driac[al]
hypo'tek *s7* mortgage; encumbrance; (*säkerhet*)
security
hypoteks|bank, -inrättning, -kassa mortgage
bank (institution); building society; *AE.* building and loan [association] **-lån** mortgage loan
hypotenusa [-ˣnu:-] *s1* hypotenuse
hypo'te|s *s3* hypothesis (*pl* hypotheses) **-tisk**
a5 hypothetic[al]; (*tvivelaktig*) doubtful
hyra I *s1* **1** rent; (*för bil, båt e.d.*) hire, rental;
betala 50 pund i ~ pay a rent of 50 pounds **2**
sjö. (*tjänst*) berth; (*lön*) [seaman's] wages (*pl*);
ta ~ ship (*på* on board, aboard) **II** *v2* rent; (*bil,
båt e.d.*) hire, take on hire; *att* ~*!* to let!, *AE.*
for rent!, (*om bil etc.*) for hire; ~ *av ngn* rent
from s.b.; ~ *in sig hos ngn* take lodgings in a
p.'s house; ~ *ut* (*rum*) let, *AE. äv.* rent, (*fastighet äv.*) lease, (*bil etc.*) hire out, let out on
hire; ~ *ut i andra hand* (*äv.*) sublet
hyrbil hire[d] (rental) car
hyres|bidrag rent allowance **-fri** *bo* ~*tt* live
rent-free **-förmedling** housing rental agency
-gäst tenant; (*för kortare tid*) lodger; *AE. äv.*
roomer **-haj** rack-renter **-hus** block of flats;
AE. apartment house (building) **-kasern** tenement [building] **-kontrakt** lease, tenancy
agreement; (*för lösöre*) hire contract **-kontroll**
rent control **-marknad** housing market
-nämnd [regional] rent tribunal **-reglering**
rent control **-värd** landlord
hyr|kusk [hackney] coachman **-verk** car-hire
service; (*för häst o. vagn*) livery stable
hysa *v3* **1** (*bereda rum åt*) house (*äv. bildl.*),
accommodate; (*pers. äv.*) put up, take in; (*in-
rymma*) contain **2** (*nära, bära*) entertain, have;
~ *betänkligheter* have (entertain) misgivings,
hesitate; ~ *förhoppningar om* entertain (cherish) hopes for, hope for; ~ *förtroende för* have
confidence in; ~ *illvilja mot ngn* bear s.b. ill
will, have a grudge against s.b.
hyska *s1* eye; ~ *och hake* hook and eye
hyss *s7, ha ngt* ~ *för sig* be up to [some] mischief
hyssj [hyʃ] hush!,shsh! **hyssja** [ˣhyʃa] cry hush
(*på, åt* to); ~ [*på*] hush
hysta *ung.* toss
hysterekto'mi *s3* hysterectomy
hyste'r|i *s3, s4* hysteria; *med. äv.* hysterics (*pl*)
-ika [-'te:-] *s1* hysterical woman **-iker** [-'te:-]
hysterical person, hysteric **-isk** [-'te:-] *a5* hys-

teric[al]; *bli* ~ go into hysterics; *få ett* ~*t anfall* have a fit of hysterics
hytt *s3, sjö.* berth, cabin; (*telefon- etc.*) booth,
box
1 hytta *v3, se höta*
2 hytta *s1, tekn.* smeltery, foundry; (*masugn*)
blast furnace
hytt|plats *sjö.* berth **-ventil** porthole
hyvel *s2* plane; (*-maskin*) planer **-bänk** carpenter's (planing) bench **-spån** *koll.* shavings (*pl*)
hyvl|a [ˣhy:v-] plane; (*ost e.d.*) slice; *bildl.* po-
lish up; ~*t virke* planed boards (*pl*); ~ *av* plane
smooth, smooth off **-ing** planing; (*friare*) slic-
ing
hå oh!; ~ ~*!* oho!; ~ ~, *ja ja!* oh, dear, dear!
håg *s3* **1** (*sinne*) mind; thoughts (*pl*); *glad i* ~*en*
gay at heart, carefree; *slå ngt ur* ~*en* dismiss
s.th. from one's mind, give up all idea of s.th.;
ta Gud i ~*en* trust to Providence (one's lucky
star); *det leker honom i* ~*en* his mind is set on
it (*att göra* on doing) **2** (*lust*) inclination; (*fallenhet*) bent, liking; *hans* ~ *står till* he has an
inclination towards
håg|ad *a5* inclined; disposed; *vara* ~ *att göra
ngt* feel like doing s.th. **-komst** *s3* remembrance, recollection **-lös** listless; (*oföretagsam*)
unenterprising; (*loj*) indolent **-löshet** listlessness; indolence
håkäring *s2* Greenland shark
hål *s7* hole; (*öppning äv.*) aperture, mouth; (*lucka*) gap; (*läcka*) leak; (*rivet*) tear; *tandläk.* cavity; *nöta* (*bränna*) ~ *på* wear (burn) a hole
(holes) in; *ta* ~ *på* make a hole in, (*sticka hål
äv.*) pierce, perforate, *med.* lance; *hon har* ~
på armbågarna her dress (*etc.*) is out at the
elbows; *det har gått* ~ *på strumpan* there is a
hole in the (my etc.) stocking
hål|a *s1* cave, cavern; (*vilda djurs o. bildl.*) den;
(*rävs, grävlings o.d.*) earth; *anat.* cavity;
(*landsorts-*) *vard.* hole **-fot** arch of the foot
-fotsinlägg arch support
hål|ig *a1* full of holes; (*ihålig, äv. bildl.*) hollow;
(*pipig*) honeycombed **-ighet** hollow, cavity
-kort punch[ed] card **-kortsmaskin** punched-
-card machine
håll *s7* **1** (*tag*) hold, grip; *få* ~ *på ngn* get a hold
(grip) on s.b. **2** (*avstånd*) distance; *på långt* ~
at a long distance, (*skjutning*) at a long range;
släkt på långt ~ distantly related; *på nära* ~
close at hand, near by (at hand); *sedd på nära*
~ seen at close quarters (range) **3** (*riktning*)
direction; (*sida*) quarter, side; *från alla* ~ [*och
kanter*] from all directions (quarters); *från så-
kert* ~ from a reliable quarter (source); *på annat* ~ in another quarter, elsewhere; *på sina* ~
in places; *åt andra* ~*et* the other way; *åt vilket* ~*?* which way?; *åt mitt* ~ my way; *de gick
åt var sitt* ~ they went their separate ways **4**
jakt. station; stand; (*skott-*) range, [rifle] shot
5 (*häftig smärta*) stitch
hålla *höll hållit* **I 1** (*ha tag i; fasthålla*) hold
(*sin hand över* a protecting hand over; *ngn i
handen* a p.'s hand; *andan* one's breath); ~
hårt om hold tight; ~ *ngn kär* hold s.b. dear; ~
stånd hold out, keep one's ground, stand firm
2 (*bibehålla; hålla sig med*) keep (*dörren öppen* the door open; *maten varm* the dinner

H

hållare–hård

[*etc.*] hot; *ngt för sig själv* s.th. to o.s.; *hemligt* secret); (*upprätt-*) maintain; ~ *ett löfte* keep a promise; ~ *i minnet* keep (bear) in mind; ~ *värmen* (*om kamin e.d.*) retain its heat; ~ *öppet hus* (*två tjänare*) keep open house (two servants); *den håller vad den lovar* it fulfils its promise **3** (*förrätta*) hold (*auktion* an auction; *möte* a meeting) **4** (*debitera*) charge (*höga priser* high prices) **5** (*slå vad om*) bet, lay, wager, stake (*tio mot ett på att* ten to one that) **6** (*anse; hålla för*) consider, regard, look upon [as]; ~ *ngt för troligt* think s.th. likely **7** (*rymma*) hold; (*inne-*) contain; ~ *måttet* be full measure, come up [the] standard **II 1** (*ej gå sönder*) hold, not break; (*om kläder*) wear, last (*i evighet* for ever); (*om bro, is*) bear; *allt vad tygen håller* at [the] top [of one's] speed, (*springa*) for dear life **2** (*styra sina steg*) keep (*t. höger* to the right); (*sikta på*) aim, hold (*för högt* too high) **3** ~ *på sin värdighet* stand on one's dignity; ~ *styvt på sin mening* stick to one's opinion; ~ *till godo, se godo*; *hon håller på sig* she stands by her virtue **4** (*stanna*) stop **III** (*med betonad partikel*) **1** ~ *av a*) (*tycka om*) be fond of, *b*) (*väja*) turn [aside] **2** ~ *efter* (*övervaka*) keep a close check (tight hand) on **3** ~ *emot* (*ta spjärn*) put one's weight against, (*hindra att falla*) hold (bear) up, (*motarbeta*) resist, set o.s. against it **4** ~ *i a*) hold [*vard.* on to], (*stödja*) hold on to, *b*) (*fortfara*) continue, go on, persist **5** ~ *igen* (*bildl.*) act as a check **6** ~ *igång* keep swinging, live it up **7** ~ *ihop* hold (keep, *vard.* stick) together **8** ~ *in a*) (*hålla indragen*) hold in, *b*) (*häst*) pull up, rein in **9** ~ *med ngn a*) (*vara av samma mening*) agree with s.b., *b*) (*ställa sig på ngns sida*) support s.b., back s.b. up, side with s.b. **10** ~ *om ngn* hold one's arms round s.b. **11** ~ *på a*) (*vara sysselsatt*) be busy (at work) (*med ngt* with s.th.), *b*) (*vara nära att*) be on the point of (*kvävas* choking); *vad håller du på med?* what are you doing [now]? **12** ~ *till; var håller du till?* where are you [to be found]?, *vard.* where do you hang out?; (*om djur*) be found, have its (their) haunts **13** ~ *tillbaka* keep back, withhold **14** ~ *upp a*) (*hålla upplyft*) hold up, *b*) (*hålla öppen*) hold (keep) open, *c*) *sjö.* (*hålla upp i vinden*) go (sail) close to the wind, *d*) (*göra uppehåll*) [make a] pause (*med* in), stop, cease; *när det håller upp[e]* when it stops raining **15** ~ *uppe a*) *eg.* hold upright, *b*) (*ovan vattenytan*) keep afloat (above water), *c*) *bildl.* keep up (*modet* one's courage) **16** ~ *ut a*) hold out, *b*) (*ton*) sustain; ~ *ut med* stand, put up with **IV** *rfl* **1** hold o.s. (*beredd* in readiness; *upprätt* upright); keep [o.s.] (*ren* clean; *vaken* awake); keep (*i sängen* in bed; *borta* away; *ur vägen* out of the way); ~ *sig* (*i fråga om naturbehov*) hold o.s.; ~ *sig väl med ngn* keep in with s.b.; ~ *sig framme* keep to the fore; ~ *sig hemma* stay at home; ~ *sig kvar* keep (stick) (*i* to); ~ *sig uppe* keep [o.s.] up, keep afloat **2** (*om pjäs*) retain its place (*på repertoaren* in the repertory) **3** (*om mat e.d.*) keep; ~ *sig för skratt* keep o.s. from laughing; *jag kunde inte* ~ *mig för skratt* I couldn't help laughing **4** ~ *sig för god att* consider o.s. above; ~ *sig med bil* keep a car; ~ *sig med tidning* take (have) a paper; ~ *sig till a*) keep (*vard.* stick) to (*fakta* facts), *b*) (*ngn*) hold (*vard.* stick) to

håll||are holder; clip, cramp, hook, buckle **-as** *dep* **1** (*vistas*) be, spend one's time **2** *låt dem* ~*!* leave them alone!, let them have their way! **hållbar** *a1* **1** (*som kan hållas*) tenable; *mil. äv.* defensible; (*om argument o.d. äv.*) valid **2** (*varaktig*) durable, lasting; (*färg*) fast; (*om tyg o.d.*) that wears well (will wear); (*om födoämnen*) that keeps well (will keep) **-het 1** tenability; validity **2** durability, lastingness; wearing (keeping) qualities (*pl*) **håll||en** *a5* (*skött*) kept; (*avfattad*) written; (*målad*) painted; *hel och* ~ the whole [of], all over; *strängt* ~ strictly brought up **-fasthet** strength, firmness, tenacity, solidity **-fasthetslära** *s1* mechanics (*pl, behandlas som sg*) of materials **-hake** check; hold (*på* on) **-i'gång** *s7* jamboree **håll||it** *sup. av* hålla **-ning 1** (*kropps-*) carriage; (*uppträdande*) deportment; *militärisk* ~ military deportment; *ha bra* ~ (*äv.*) hold o.s. well **2** (*beteende*) attitude (*mot* towards); *intaga en avvaktande* ~ take up a wait-and-see attitude; *intaga en fast* ~ make a firm stand (*mot* against) **3** (*stadga*) firmness, backbone **hållningslös** vacillating, vacillant; *vard.* wobbly, flabby; (*utan ryggrad*) spineless; unstable, unprincipled **-het** vacillation; spinelessness; instability **håll||plats** stop, halt **-punkt** basis; grounds (*pl*) **hål||remsa** paper (punch[ed]) tape **-rum** cavity **-slag** punch; perforator **-slagning** perforation **-slev** perforated ladle **-slå** punch; perforate **-stans** punch[ing machine] **-söm** drawn (drawn-thread) work; *sy* ~ hemstitch **-tegel** airbrick **-timme** *skol.* free period **-ven** vena cava (*pl* venae cavae) **-väg** gorge, ravine **-ögd** *a5* hollow-eyed

hån *s7* scorn; (*spe*) derision, mockery; (*i ord äv.*) scoffing, taunting, sneering, jeering; *ett* ~ *mot* an insult to, a mockery of

hån||a (*förlöjliga*) deride, make fun of; (*förakt-fullt*) put to scorn; (*i ord äv.*) scoff (sneer, jeer) at, mock, taunt **-flin** *se* hångrin **-full** scornful; scoffing *etc.*, derisive

hång||el ['håŋ-] *s7* petting; necking **-la** pet; neck

hån||grin mocking grin **-grina** grin contemptuously **-le** smile scornfully, sneer, jeer (*åt* at) **-leende** scornful smile **-skratt** derisive (scornful, mocking) laugh[ter] **-skratta** laugh derisively (*etc.*), jeer (*åt* at)

hår *s7* hair; *kortklippt* ~ short hair; *inte kröka ett* ~ *på ngns huvud* not touch (injure) a hair on a p.'s head; *skaffa ngn gråa* ~ give s.b. grey hairs; *slita sitt* ~ *i förtvivlan* tear one's hair in despair; ~*et reste sig på mitt huvud* my hair stood on end; *det var på* ~*et att jag* I was within a hair's-breadth (an ace) of (+ *ing-form*)

hår||a ~ *av sig* shed (lose) its hair; ~ *ner* cover with hair[s *pl*] **-band** fillet **-beklädnad** hairy coat; *zool.* pelage **-bevuxen** hairy **-borste** hairbrush **-borttagningsmedel** depilatory **-botten** capillary matrix; (*friare*) scalp

hård [-å:-] *a1* hard; (*fast äv.*) firm, solid;

(sträng, svår äv.) severe *(mot towards, to, on); (bister)* stern; *(högljudd)* loud; *(om ljud, barsk)* harsh; *(påfrestande)* tough; *hårt klimat* severe climate; *~ konkurrens* keen (fierce) competition; *~ i magen* constipated; *ett hårt slag* a hard (severe, serious) blow; *~a tider a) (arbetsamma)* tough times, *b) (nödtider)* hard times, times of hardship; *~a villkor* severe conditions, tough terms; *sätta hårt mot hårt* give as good as one gets; *vara ~ mot ngn* be hard on s.b.; *det vore hårt för dem om* it would be hard on them, if

hård|arbetad *a5* hard to work (shape, mould); *-arbetat material* difficult material **-bränd** *a5* **1** *(svår att bränna)* difficult to burn **2** *(hårt bränd)* hard-burnt, hard-baked **-disk** hard disc *(AE.* disk) **-exploatera** exploit mercilessly **-fjällad** *a5, bildl.* hard-boiled; *en ~ brottsling* a hardened criminal; *en ~ fisk* a difficult fish to scale **-flörtad** *a5* standoffish **-frusen** frozen hard; hard-frozen *(is ice)* **-för** *a1* hardy, tough **-förhet** hardiness, toughness **-gummi** hard rubber; vulcanite, ebonite **-handskarna** *ta i med ~* take drastic action (a hard line) **-het** hardness *etc.*; severity **-hetsgrad** degree of hardness **-hjärtad** [-j-] *a5* hardhearted; *(känslolös)* callous **-hudad** *a5, bildl.* thick-skinned **-hänt** I *a1, bildl.* rough, heavy-handed *(mot* with); *(friare)* severe II *adv, gå ~ till väga* be rough *(med* with) **-hänthet** heavy-handedness; severity

hård|ing [-å:-] *s2, han är en riktig ~* he's as hard as nails **-knut** tight knot **-kokt** hard--boiled **-körning** *bildl.* tough programme

hård|na [-å:-] harden; become (get, grow) hard; *(bli okänslig)* get callous (hardened) **-nackad** *a5, bildl.* stubborn *(motstånd* resistance); obstinate *(nekande* denial) **-porr** hard-porn

hårdrag|a [ˣhå:r-] *bildl.* strain **-en** *a5, bildl.* forced, strained, far-fetched

hård|rock metal (hard) rock **-smält** *a1* **1** *(om föda)* difficult (hard) to digest; *(friare)* indigestible **2** *(om metall)* refractory **-träna** train hard **-valuta** hard currency (exchange) **-vara** hardware

hår|fin 1 *(om tråd o.d.)* [as] thin (fine) as a hair **2** *bildl.* exceedingly fine, subtle **-frisör** barber, hairdresser **-frisörska** hairdresser **-färg** colour of the hair; *(färgämne)* hair-dye **-fäste** edge of the scalp; *rodna upp till ~t* blush to the roots of one's hair

hår|ig *a1* hairy **-klippning** haircut[ting] **-klyveri** hairsplitting *(äv. ~er)* **-kors** cross wires *(AE.* hairs), retic[u]le **-lock** lock of hair; *(kvinnas äv.)* tress **-nål** hairpin **-nålskurva** hairpin bend **-nät** hairnet **-olja** hair oil **-piska** pigtail; *(stång-)* queue **-pomada** pomade [for the hair] **-resande** *a4* hair-raising, appalling, bloodcurdling, shocking; *en ~ historia (äv.)* a story to make one's hair stand on end **-rör** capillary tube **-rörskärl** capillary vessel **-slinga** strand of hair

hårsmån *r* hair's-breadth; *(friare)* trifle, shade

hår|sprej *s3, s2* hairspray **-spänne** hair slide **-strå** hair **-svall** thick wavy hair **-säck** hair follicle

hårt [-å:-] *adv* hard; *(fast, tätt)* firm, firmly,

tight, tightly; *(högljutt)* loud; *bildl.* severely; *en ~ prövad man* a severely tried man; *arbeta ~* work hard; *fara ~ fram med* be rough with; *gå ~ åt* handle roughly, be hard on; *ta ngt ~* take s.th. very much to heart; *tala ~ till ngn* speak harshly to s.b.; *det känns ~ att* it feels hard to; *det satt ~ åt* it was a job

hår|test *s2* wisp of hair **-tork[ningsapparat]** hair dryer **-tuss** tuft of hair **-uppsättning** *konkr.* hairstyle, coiffure **-vatten** hair tonic (lotion) **-växt** growth of hair; *missprydande ~* superfluous hair

håv *s2 (fiskares)* landing net; *(sänk-)* dip-net; *(insekts-)* butterfly net; *(kollekt-)* collection bag; *gå med ~en (bildl.)* fish [for compliments] **håva** *~ in* gather (rake) in; *~ upp* land

håvor *pl* gifts, bounties; *jordens ~* the fruits of the earth

1 häck *s2* **1** hedge; *bilda ~ (om människor)* form a lane **2** *sport.* hurdle; *110 m ~* 110 metres hurdle

2 häck *s2* **1** *(foder-)* hack, rack **2** *(vagns-)* rack **3** *(låda)* crate

3 häck *s2, vard.* bottom, behind, backside; *ha ~en full* have one's plate full

häcka *(om fåglar)* breed

häckl|a I *s1* heckle II *v1* **1** *(lin)* hackle, heckle **2** *bildl.* cavil (carp) at, find fault with **3** *polit.* heckle **-ing 1** *(av lin)* hackling, heckling **2** *polit.* heckling

häcklöp|are hurdler **-ning** hurdle-racing, hurdle-race, hurdling

häckning breeding

häcknings|plats breeding ground (place) **-tid** breeding season

häda blaspheme *(äv. ~ Gud)*

hädan hence; *skiljas ~* depart this life; *vik ~!* get thee hence!, begone! **-efter** henceforth, from now on **-färd** passing, departure [from this life] **-gången** *a5, se avliden* **-kalla** *(om Gud)* call unto Himself

häd|are blasphemer **-else** blasphemy; *utslunga ~r* hurl blasphemies, blaspheme **-isk** ['hä:-] *a5* blasphemous; *(friare)* profane, impious; *(grovt respektlös)* irreverent

häfta I *s1, se häftplåster* II *v1* **1** *bokb.* sew, stitch; *~d bok* sewn (stitched) book, paperback **2** *(hålla fäst)* fasten, fix *(blicken vid* one's gaze on) **3** *(fastna)* stick, adhere *(vid* to) **4** *misstanken ~r vid honom* suspicion attaches to him **5** *~ i skuld till ngn* be in a p.'s debt

häftapparat stapler, stapling machine

häfte *s6 (tryckalster)* folder, booklet, brochure, pamphlet; *(del av bok)* part, instalment; *(nummer av tidskrift)* number, issue; *(skrivbok)* exercise book

häftig *a1* **1** *(våldsam)* violent; *(obehärskad)* vehement; *(impulsiv)* impetuous *(människa individual); (hetsig)* heated *(diskussion* discussion); *(om smärta)* sharp, acute; *ett ~t regn* a heavy downpour; *~ törst* violent thirst; *ett ~t uppträde* a scene **2** *(temperamentsfull)* impulsive, hasty; *(hetlevrad)* hot-headed, hot-tempered **3** *(förstärkande) vard.* hot, groovy

häftighet violence; vehemence; impetuosity; impulsiveness; hot-headedness *etc.*; irascibility; hot temper

häftigt adv violently etc.; vard. groovy; andas ~ breathe quickly, pant; gräla ~ quarrel violently; koka ~ boil fast; hjärtat slog ~ the (my etc.) heart beat excitedly

häft|klammer [paper] staple **-ning 1** bokb. sewing, stitching **2** (-ande) fastening, fixing; sticking, adherence; attaching **-plåster** [sticking] plaster; AE. adhesive tape **-stift** drawing pin; AE. thumbtack

häger ['hä:-] s2 heron

hägg s2 bird cherry

hägn [häŋn] s7, i ~ av under the cover of; vara i ngns ~ be under a p.'s protection (aegis) **hägna** [*häŋna] protect, guard

hägr|a [*hä:g-] loom (äv. bildl.) **-ing** mirage; bildl. äv. illusion

häkta I s1 hook **II** v1 **1** (fästa) hook (fast [vid] on [to]); ~ av unhook; ~ upp sig catch, get caught up **2** (arrestera) arrest, take into custody; den ~de the man (etc.) under arrest, the prisoner; ~ ngn i hans frånvaro issue a warrant for s.b.'s arrest

häkt|e s6 custody; jail, gaol **-ning** arrest

häktnings|förhandlingar court proceedings for issue of arrest warrant **-order** [arrest] warrant

häl s2 heel; följa ngn tätt i ~arna follow close upon a p.'s heels

hälare receiver [of stolen goods], vard. fence

hälben heel bone

häleri receiving [of stolen goods]

hälft s3 half; äkta ~ (vard.) better half; ~en av månaden half the month; ~en så mycket half as much; ~en så stor half as large (som as), half the size (som of); på ~en så kort tid in half the time; till ~en dold half hidden; göra ngt till ~en do s.th. by halves

hälftenbruk métayage

hälgångare zool. plantigrade

häll s2 (klippa) flat rock; (sten) slab [of stone]; (i öppen spis) hearthstone

1 hälla s1 (under foten) strap; (för bälte o.d.) loop

2 hälla v2 pour; ~ i pour in (el. upp out); ~ i ett glas vin pour out a glass of wine; ~ ur pour out; ~nde regn pouring rain

hälle|berg [bed]rock, solid rock **-flundra** halibut

hällkista arkeol. cist

hällre se hellre

häll|regn pouring rain, downpour **-regna** pour [with rain]

hällristning rock-carving, petroglyph

1 hälsa s1 health; vid god ~ in good health

2 hälsa v1 **1** (välkomna, mottaga) greet; (högtidligt) salute; ~ ngn välkommen bid s.b. welcome, welcome s.b.; ~ ngn som sin kung salute s.b. as one's king **2** (säga goddag e.d.) say good morning (good afternoon, good evening, vard. hello) [to s.b.], (ta i hand) shake hands [with s.b.], (buga) bow [to s.b.], (lyfta på hatten) raise one's hat [to s.b.]; mil. salute (på ngn s.b.); ~ god morgon på ngn wish s.b. good morning **3** (upptaga) receive (ett förslag med glädje a proposition with delight) **4** (framföra hälsning) send (ngn s.b.) one's regards (compliments, respects, love); ~ hem! remember me to your people!; ~ på (besöka) go

(come) and see; ~ henne så hjärtligt! give her my best regards (etc.)!; låta ~ send word; nu kan vi ~ hem! (vard.) now it's all up with us!; jag kan ~ [dig] från I can give you news from; jag skulle ~ från fru A. att hon Mrs. A. asked me to tell you that she; vem får jag ~ ifrån? what (may I have your) name, please?, (i telefon) who is speaking[, please]?

hälsena Achilles tendon, heel string

hälsning 1 greeting; (högtidlig) salutation **2** (översänd e.d.) compliments (pl); (bud) message, word; hjärtliga ~ar kind regards, love (sg); byta en ~ pass the time of day; får jag be om min ~ till please remember me to **3** (bugning) bow; (honnör) salute

hälsnings|anförande address of welcome, opening speech **-ord** pl words of welcome (greeting); se äv. -anförande

hälso|bringande a4 healthy, health-giving **-brunn** spa **-farlig** injurious to one's health, unhealthy **-kontroll** [health] checkup **-kost** health food **-kostbutik** health [food] store **-källa** mineral spring **-lära** (skolämne) hygiene **-risk** health hazard **-sam** a1 wholesome; (om klimat) salubrious, healthy; bildl. äv. salutary; (välgörande) beneficial **-skäl** av ~ for reasons of health **-tecken** healthy sign, sign of wellbeing **-tillstånd** state of health; mitt ~ [the state of] my health **-undersökning** medical examination **-vådlig** (ohygienisk) insanitary; (om klimat) unhealthy **-vård** (enskild) care of one's health; (allmän) public health, health service[s pl] **-vårdsinspektör** environmental health officer **-vårdsnämnd** public health committee **-vårdsstadga** public health act[s pl]

hälta s1 [form of] lameness

hämm|a (hejda) check, curb, arrest, stop; (blodflöde äv.) sta[u]nch; (hindra) obstruct, block (trafiken the traffic); (ngns rörelser) impede, hamper; (fördröja) retard; psykiskt ~d inhibited; ~ ngt i växten stunt the growth of s.th. **-ande** a4 checking etc.; verka ~ på have a checking (etc.) effect on, act as a check on, curb, depress

hämn|a avenge, revenge; slöseri ~r sig waste brings woe **-are** avenger, revenger **-as** dep avenge (revenge) o.s., wreak one's vengeance (på on), retaliate; ~ ngn avenge s.b., take vengeance for s.b.

hämnd s3 revenge; högt. vengeance; retaliation; ~en är ljuv revenge is sweet **-begär** desire for vengeance

hämnd|eaktion reprisal **-girig** revengeful; vindictive **-girighet** revengefulness; vindictiveness **-lysten** se -girig **-lystnad** se hämndbegär

hämning 1 checking etc., se hämma **2** psykol. inhibition

hämningslös uninhibited; unrestrained

hämpling zool. linnet

hämsko drag (äv. bildl.)

hämta fetch; (av-, komma o. hämta) collect, call for; (ta, skaffa sig e.d.) take, gather; (opt abstr.) draw, derive; data. retrieve, open;~ ngn med bil fetch s.b. by car; ~ frisk luft get fresh air; ~ mod (styrka) från draw (derive) courage (strength) from; ~ *nya krafter* recover (get up) one's strength; *låta* ~ send for; *uppgiften är* ~*d ur* I have the information from; ~ *sig* recover (*efter, från* from); *jag har inte* ~*t mig än (äv.)* I haven't got over it yet

hämtpris cash-and-carry price

hän away; ~ *mot* towards; *vart skall du* ~*?* where are you going?

hända *v2* happen; *(förekomma)* occur, take place; ~ *sig* happen, chance, come about (to pass); ~ *vad som* ~ *vill* happen what may; *det kan* ~ *att jag går ut i kväll* I may go out this evening; *det kan nog* ~ that may be [so]; *det hände sig inte bättre än att jag* as ill luck would have it I; *det må vara hänt* it can't be helped

händelse 1 occurrence; *(betydelsefull)* event, happening; *(episod)* incident **2** *(tillfällighet)* coincidence; *(slump)* chance; *av en ren* ~ quite by chance, by a pure coincidence **3** *(fall)* case; *i* ~ *av* in case of; *i alla* ~*r* at all events; *för den* ~ *att han skulle komma* in case he comes, in the event of his coming **-fattig** uneventful **-förlopp** course of events **-lös** uneventful **-rik** eventful **-utveckling** development of [the] events; trend of affairs **-vis** by chance; accidentally; *(apropå)* casually; *du har* ~ *inte en penna på dig?* you don't happen to have a pencil [on you], do you?; *jag träffade henne* ~ I just happened to meet her, I ran across her

händig *a1* handy, dext[e]rous *(med* with) **-het** handiness, dexterity

hänföra *(föra...till)* assign, refer, relate *(till* to); *(räkna)* class[ify] *(till* among), range *(till* under) **2** *(tjusa)* carry away, transport; *(gripa äv.)* thrill; *låta sig* ~*s av* allow o.s. to be carried away by **3** *rfl* have reference *(till* to); *(datera sig)* date back *(från* to)

hänför|ande *a4* ravishing; enchanting **-bar** *a5* assignable *(till* to); classifiable *(till* as) **-else** rapture; exultation; *(entusiasm)* enthusiasm **-lig** *a5, se* **-bar**

hänga *v2* **1** *(uppfästa o.d.)* hang *(äv. avrätta)*; *(tvätt)* hang up; *(låta hänga)* droop; *(t.ex. taklampa)* suspend; ~ *läpp* pout, sulk, be bad-tempered; ~ *näsan över boken* pore over (bury one's nose in) the book[s *pl*] **2** *(vara upphängd)* hang; *(hänga fritt)* be suspended; *(om kjol)* hang down *(bak* at the back); *(sväva)* hover; ~ *ngn i kjolarna* cling to a p.'s skirt; ~ *ngn om halsen* cling round a p.'s neck; ~ *och dingla* hang loose, dangle; *stå och* ~ loiter about; *hela företaget hänger i luften* the whole enterprise is hanging in the air; *slagsmålet hänger i luften* there's a fight in the air **3** *(be-ro)* depend *(på* [up]on); *(komma sig)* be due (owing) *(på* to) **4** *(med betonad partikel)* ~ *efter ngn* run after (hang around) s.b.; ~ *fram (kläder)* put out; ~ *för* hang in front; ~ *i (vard.)* keep at it; ~ *ihop*; *jag hänger knappt ihop* I can scarcely keep body and soul together; *så hänger det ihop* that's how it is; ~ *med a)* keep up with *(i klassen* the rest of the class), *b) (förstå)* follow, catch on, *c) (följa med)* go along with; ~ *upp sig på (bildl.)* take exception to **5** ~ *sig* hang o.s.; ~ *sig fast vid* hang on firm to; ~ *sig på ngn* hang on (attach o.s.) to s.b.

häng|ande *a4* hanging; *(fritt)* suspended *(i taket* from the ceiling); *bli* ~ *i* get caught (hooked) on **-are** *(krok)* hook; *(pinne)* peg; *(med flera krokar)* rack; *(i kläder)* hanger, loop; *(galge)* [coat] hanger **-björk** weeping birch **-bro** suspension bridge

1 hänge [*ˣhäŋe] *s6, bot.* catkin

2 hänge [*ˣhä:nje:] *rfl* surrender o.s., give o.s. up *(åt* to); *(ägna sig)* devote (apply) o.s. *(åt* to); *(hemfalla)* abandon o.s. *(åt* to); *(försjunka)* fall *(åt* into)

häng|färdig *se* ~ *ut (vard.)* look down in (at) the mouth *a1* limp; out of sorts

hänggiv|a *se* 2 **hänge** **-else** [the] surrendering of o.s.

hängiven *(tillgiven)* devoted, affectionate **-het** devotion, attachment *(för* to)

häng|lås padlock; *sätta* ~ *för* padlock **-mapp** suspended pocket (file) **-matta** hammock **-ning** hanging **-ränna** gutter

hängs|elstropp brace end **-le** *s6* brace; *ett par* ~*n* a pair of braces *(AE.* suspenders)

häng|smycke pendant **-torr** drip-dry **-växt** hanging plant

hän|rycka ravish, enrapture **-ryckning** rapture[s *pl*]; ecstasy **-ryckt** *a4* rapturous; *vara* ~ be in raptures

hänseende *a6, i tekniskt* ~ from a technical point of view; *i vissa* ~*n* in certain respects; *med* ~ *till* in consideration of, with respect (regard) to

hän|skjuta refer, submit **-syfta** allude *(på* to); *(mera förtäckt)* hint *(på* at) **-syftning** allusion *(på* to); hint *(på* at)

hänsyn *s9* consideration; regard, respect; *av* ~ *till* out of consideration for; *med* ~ *till* with regard (respect) to, as regards, *(i betraktande av)* in view of, considering; *utan* ~ *till* without [any] consideration (regard) to, regardless of, disregarding; *låta alla* ~ *fara* throw discretion to the winds; *ta* ~ *till* take into consideration, pay regard to

hänsynsfull considerate *(mot* to, towards) **-het** considerateness; consideration

hänsynslös regardless of other people[s' feelings]; inconsiderate; *(skoningslös)* ruthless; ~ *framfart (bildl.)* reckless impetuosity; ~ *upp-riktighet* brutal frankness **-het** inconsiderateness, lack of consideration; ruthlessness

häntyd|a ~ *på a)* *(tyda på)* suggest, indicate, *b) se* **hänsyfta** **-ning** allusion *(på* to), hint *(på* at)

hänvis|a *(visa till)* direct; *(ge anvisning, referera)* refer; *(åberopa)* point; *jur.* assign, allot; *vara* ~*d till* be obliged to resort to, be reduced to *(att* + ing-form); *vara* ~*d till sig själv* be thrown upon one's own resources **-ning** reference; direction; *(i ordbok e.d. äv.)* cross--reference **-ningston** *tel.* special information tone

hänvänd|a *rfl* apply *(till* to) **-else** application; *(vädjan)* appeal; *genom* ~ *till* by applying (making application) to

häpen *a3* amazed *(över* at); *(bestört)* startled *(över* at) **-het** amazement; *i* ~*en över* in his *(etc.)* amazement at; *i första* ~*en* in the confusion of the moment

häpn|a ['hä:p-] be amazed (*inför, vid, över* at); *hör och* ~! who'd have thought it! **-ad** *s3, se häpenhet*; *slå ngn med* ~ strike s.b. with amazement **-adsväckande** *a4* amazing, astounding
1 här *s2* army; *bildl. äv.* host
2 här *adv* here; ~ *borta* (*nere, uppe*) over (down, up) here; ~ *och där* here and there; ~ *och var* in places; ~ *i staden* in this town; *så* ~ *års* at this time of the year; ~ *bor jag* this is where I live; ~ *har vi det!* here we are!, here it is!; *nu är han* ~ *igen!* here he is again!
härad *s7, s4, s6, ung.* jurisdictional district; *hist.* hundred
härads|domare *ung.* senior juryman, foreman of a jury **-hövding** *ung.* circuit judge
härav ['hä:r-] from (by, of, out of) this; hence; ~ *följer att* [hence] it follows that, (*friare*) this means that
härbre *s6, ung.* wooden storehouse
härbärg|e [-je] *s6* shelter, accommodation, lodging; (*för husvilla*) [common] lodging house; (*Frälsningsarméns o.d.*) [night] refuge **-era** lodge; put up
härd [-ä:-] *s2* **1** (*eldstad*) hearth (*äv. tekn.*); *hemmets* ~ the domestic hearth **2** *bildl.* seat, centre, focus (*för* of); (*näste*) nest, hotbed
härd|a [-ä:-] **1** *tekn.* anneal, temper; (*plast*) set, cure **2** (*göra motståndskraftigare*) harden (*mot* against); *bildl. äv.* inure (*mot* to) **3** *rfl* harden o.s.; inure o.s.; (*stålsätta sig*) steel o.s. (*mot* against) **-are** hardener
härdig *a1* hardy; inured to hardship[s *pl*]; (*mot frost äv.*) hardened **-het** hardiness
härd|ning hardening, tempering; (*av plast*) setting, curing **-plast** thermosetting plastic
härdsmälta (*i kärnreaktor*) core meltdown
här|efter (*efter denna händelse, tidpunkt*) after this; (*från denna tid*) from now (this date), hence; (*hädanefter*) from now on, from this time forth **-emot** against this (it)
härflyta spring, emanate (*ur, från, av* from); (*ha sitt ursprung*) originate (*ur, från, av* from)
härfågel hoopoe
härförare army leader, general
härförleden [-'le:-] some time ago; (*nyligen*) recently
här|i in this (that); (*i detta avseende*) in this (that) respect **-ibland** among these (those) **-ifrån** from here; *bildl.* from this **-igenom** through here; *bildl.* owing to this (that), on this (that) account; (*medelst detta*) by this (that, these, those) means, in this (that) way
härj|a **1** ravage (*i ett land* a country); (*ödelägga*) devastate, lay waste; (*om skadedjur*) wreak havoc; ~ *svårt* make [great] havoc; *se* ~*d ut* look worn and haggard **2** (*om sjukdom*) be rife (prevalent); rage **3** (*väsnas*) make a row, run riot **-ning** ravaging, devastation, havoc; ~*ar* ravages **-ningståg** ravaging expedition
härjämte in addition [to this]
härkomst [-å-] *s3* extraction, descent; (*ursprung*) origin; *av borgerlig* ~ of middle-class extraction (origin)
härled|a *v2* derive (*äv. språkv.*); (*sluta sig t.*) deduce; ~ *sig* be derived (*från, ur* from); **-d enhet** derived unit

1 härledning *språkv.* derivation; deduction
2 härledning *mil.* [the] army command; *konkr.* army staff
härlig ['hä:r-] *a1* glorious; (*präktig*) magnificent, splendid; (*ljuvlig*) lovely; (*vacker*) fine (*äv. iron.*); *så det står* ~*a till* like anything **-het** glory; magnificence, splendour; *hela* ~*en* the whole business
härma imitate; (*naturv.; förlöjliga*) mimic; (*efterapa*) copy
härmed with (by, at, to) this; *hand.* herewith, hereby; *i enlighet* ~ accordingly; *i samband* ~ in connection herewith; ~ *vill vi meddela* (*hand.*) we wish to inform you; *vi sänder* ~ (*hand.*) we are sending you enclosed, we enclose herewith
härm|fågel mockingbird **-ning** imitation; mimicry **-ningsdrift** mimicry instinct
härnad ['hä:r-] *s3, draga i* ~ *mot* take up arms against **härnadståg** war[like] expedition
härnäst next; (*nästa gång*) next time
härold [-å-] *s3* herald
härom (*norr* north) from here; (*angående denna sak*) about (concerning, as to this) **-dagen** the other day **-kring** all round here, in this neighbourhood **-sistens** a little while ago; (*nyligen*) recently **-året** a year or so (two) ago
härpå *rumsbet.* on this (that); *tidsbet.* after this (that)
härröra ~ *från* (*av*) come (arise) from, originate in (from)
härs ~ *och tvärs* to and fro, in all directions; hither and thither
härsk|a **1** (*styra*) rule; (*regera*) reign **2** (*om sak*) predominate; (*vara förhärskande*) prevail, be prevalent **-ande** *a4* ruling; (*om parti*) dominating; (*gängse*) prevalent, prevailing
härskara host
härskar|e ruler; monarch, sovereign; (*herre*) master (*över* of) **-inna** ruler *etc.*; (*som behärskar ngn*) mistress **-natur** masterful character, domineering nature; *pers.* man (*etc.*) of despotic nature
härsken *a3* rancid
härsklyst|en with a thirst for power; domineering, imperious **-nad** thirst for power; masterfulness *etc.*
härskna go (become, turn, get) rancid; *bildl.* sour
härskri war cry; (*friare*) outcry
härsmakt armed force, army; *med* ~ by force of arms
härstam|ma ~ *från* be descended from, (*om pers. o. sak*) derive one's (its) origin from, (*datera sig från*) date from **-ning** descent; (*ursprung*) origin; (*ords*) derivation
härstädes here, in this place
härtapp|ad *a5* bottled in this country (by the importers) **-ning** local bottling (*äv. konkr.*)
här|till to this (that, it); ~ *kommer att vi måste* besides (in addition to this) we must **-under** *rumsbet.* under this; *tidsbet.* during the time this was (is) going on (lasted; lasts) **-ur** out of this **-utav** *se härav* **-utinnan** in this (that) respect **-utöver** *bildl.* beyond this, in addition to this
härva *s1* skein; (*virrvarr*) tangle

här|varande *a4, en* ~ a[n]...of this place, a local **-vid** at (on, to) this **-vidlag** in this respect; (*i detta fall*) in this case **-åt 1** *rumsbet., se hitåt* **2** (*åt den här saken e.d.*) at this

hässja [ˣhäʃa] **I** *s1* hay fence **II** *v1,* ~ *hö* pile hay on fences to dry

häst *s2* **1** horse; *sitta till* ~ be on horseback; *sätta sig på sina höga ~ar* ride the high horse; *man skall inte skåda given* ~ *i munnen!* don't look a gift-horse in the mouth! **2** *gymn.* [vault-ing-]horse, buck, (*bygel-*) pommel horse; *schack.* knight, *vard.* horse **-ansikte** *bildl.* horse-face **-avel** horse-breeding **-djur** *pl* [the] horses **-droska** horse-drawn cab **-fluga** horse-fly **-gardist** trooper (*officer* officer) in the Horse Guards **-handlare** horse-dealer **-hov 1** horse's hoof **2** *bot.* coltsfoot **-kapplöpning** horse-racing; *en* ~ a horse-race **-kastanj[e]** horse chestnut **-kraft** (*beräknad, effektiv, bromsad* indicated, effective, brake) horse-power; *vard.* horse **-krake** hack, jade **-kur** *bildl.* drastic cure **-kött** (*livsmedel*) horseflesh **-lass** cartload **-lort** horse dung **-längd** *sport.* [horse-]length **-minne** *vard.* phenomenal memory **-polo** polo **-ras** breed [of horses] **-rygg** horse's back; *sitta på ~en* be on horse-back **-skjuts** horse-drawn conveyance **-sko** horseshoe **-skojare** horse-swindler, coper, horse-coper **-skosöm** horseshoe nail **-skötare** groom **-spillning** horse dung **-sport** equestrian sport; *~en* (*kapplöpningssporten*) horse-racing, the turf **-styng** botfly **-svans** horse's tail; (*frisyr*) ponytail **-tagel** horsehair **-täcke** horse-cloth **-väg** *det var något i* ~ that's really something

hätsk *a1* rancorous, spiteful (*mot* towards); (*bitter*) bitter, fierce **-het** spitefulness; rancour

hätta *s1* hood; (*munk-*) cowl; (*barn-*) bonnet

häva *v2* **1** heave; (*kasta*) toss, chuck; *på tå häv!* on your toes!; ~ *sig* raise o.s., (*om bröst o.d.*) heave **2** (*undanröja*) remove; raise (*en belägring* a siege); (*bota*) cure; *jur.* cancel; (*bilägga*) settle **3** ~ *ur sig* come out with

häv|arm lever **-as** *v2, dep* heave

hävd *s3* **1** *jur.* prescription; (*besittningsrätt*) usage; *urminnes* ~ immemorial prescription **2** (*tradition*) tradition, custom **3** (*historia*) history, chronicled history; *~er* (*äv.*) annals of the past; *gå till ~erna* go down in history **4** *lantbr.* (*gott tillstånd o.d.*) cultivation

hävda 1 (*försvara*) vindicate, maintain (*sina rättigheter* one's rights); (*vidmakthålla*) maintain (*sin ställning* one's position), uphold (*sina intressen* one's interests) **2** (*påstå*) maintain, assert, state **3** *rfl* hold one's own, vindicate o.s. **-teckning** *se historieskrivning*

hävdvunnen time-honoured, established; *jur.* prescriptive

hävert [ˈhä:-] *s2* siphon

häv|ning [ˣhä:v-] heaving *etc, se häva* **-stång** lever

häx|a [ˣhäksa] *s1* witch; (*ondskefull kvinna*) old hag **-brygd** witch-broth **-dans** witches' dance; *bildl.* welter **-eri** witchery, witchcraft; sorcery **-kittel** *bildl.* maelstrom **-mästare** wizzard; *eg. bet. äv.* sorcerer **-process** witch-trial **-ring** *bot.* fairy ring

hö *s4* hay **-bärgning** haymaking **1 höft** *s, i uttr.: på en* ~ (*efter ögonmått*) roughly, approximately, (*på en slump*) at random **2 höft** *s3* hip; *~er fäst!* hands to hips!

höft|ben hipbone **-benskam** iliac crest **-hållare** girdle; foundation garment **-kam** *se -benskam* **-led** hip joint **-skynke** loincloth

1 hög *s2* **1** heap (*av, med* of); (*uppstaplad*) pile (*av, med* of); (*trave*) stack (*av, med* of); *samla* (*lägga*) *på* ~ pile (heap) up, accumulate; *ta ett exempel ur ~en* take an example at random; *kläderna låg i en* ~ the clothes were lying [all] in a heap **2** (*kulle*) hillock; mound (*äv. konstgjord*)

2 hög *-t -re -st* **1** high; (*reslig*) tall; (*högt liggande*) elevated; (*tung, svår*) heavy, severe; (*högt uppsatt*) exalted; (*om furstlig pers.*) august; (*-dragen*) haughty; *~[a] och låg[a]* high and low, the exalted and the lowly; *~a böter* a heavy fine; *~t gräs* long grass; ~ *militär* high-ranking officer [in the army *etc.*], *vard.* brass hat; ~ *panna* high (lofty) forehead; *H~a Porten* the Sublime Porte; *i egen* ~ *person* in person; *vid* ~ *ålder* at an advanced age; *ha ~a tankar om* think highly of; *spela ett ~t spel* (*bildl.*) play a risky game; *det är* ~ *tid* it is high time; *diskussionens vågor gick ~a* the debate was heated **2** (*-ljudd*) loud; *mus.* high, high-pitched; *med* ~ *röst* in a loud voice **3** (*om luft*) clear **4** *skrika i ~an sky* scream to high heaven **5** (*upprymd; narkotikaberusad*) high

högad|el *~n* the higher nobility, *vard.* the upper crust **-lig** belonging to the higher nobility

högaffel hayfork, pitchfork

högakt|a esteem; (*svagare*) respect; think highly of, value **-ning** esteem; respect; *med utmärkt* ~, *se högaktningsfullt*

högaktnings|full respectful **-fullt** *adv* (*i brev*) Yours faithfully, ĄE. Very truly yours

hög|aktuell of great current (immediate) interest; topical **-altare** high altar **-avlönad** highly paid **-barmad** *a5* full-bosomed, bosomy **-borg** *bildl.* stronghold **-borgerlig** upper middle class **-bröstad** *a5, se -barmad* **-buren** *a5, med -buret huvud* with one's head held high **-djur 1** *koll.* high game **2** *bildl., sl.* bigwig, big shot, *vard.* V.I.P. (*förk. för* very important person) **-dragen** haughty, lofty, arrogant **-effektiv** (*om pers.*) very efficient; *en* ~ *maskin* a high-efficiency (high-production, high-capacity) machine

högeligen exceedingly; highly

höger [ˈhö:-] **I** *a, best. form högra* right; right, right-hand; *min högra hand* (*bildl.*) my right--hand man; *på min högra sida* on my right (right-hand side) **II** *adv,* ~ *om! fäst!; göra* ~ *om* turn by the right **III** *s9* **1** right; *från* ~ from the right; *till* ~ *om* to the right of **2** *polit., ~n* the Right, the Conservative Party, the Conservatives (*pl*) **3** *sport., en rak* ~ a straight right **-back** *sport.* right [full]back **-extremist** right-wing extremist **-halvback** *sport.* right half[back] **-hand** right hand **-handske** right--hand glove **-hänt** *a4* right-handed; dextral **-inner** *sport.* inside right **-kurva** right-hand curve (bend) **-man** conservative **-parti** *se höger III* **2 -sida** *boktr.* recto **-styrd** [-y:-] *a5* (*om* *bil*) right-hand driven **-sväng** right turn **-tra-fik** right-hand traffic **-vriden** *polit.* rightist **-vridning** *polit.* rightism **-ytter** *sport.* outside right

hög|fjäll high mountain; ~*en* the High Alps **-fjällshotell** mountain hotel **-form** *i* ~ in great form **-frekvens** high frequency **-frekvent** high-frequent; *bildl.* occurring often, of high frequency

högfärd [ˣhö:g- *el.* ˣhögg-] pride (*över* in); (*fåfänga*) vanity; (*inbilskhet*) [self-]conceit **-ig** proud (*över* of); cocky (*över* about); (*fåfäng*) vain; (*inbilsk*) [self-]conceited, *vard.* hoity-toity, stuck-up

högfärds|blåsa *vard.* swank[pot] **-galen** bursting with self-importance

högförräderi high treason

högg *imperf. av hugga*

hög|gradig *a5* (*av hög halt*) high-grade; (*ytterlig*) extreme; (*svår*) severe; (*intensiv*) intensive **-halsad** *a5* high-necked **-hastighetståg** high-speed train

höghet [ˣhö:g-] **1** (*upphöjdhet*) loftiness; sublimity; ([*världslig*] *storhet*) greatness **2** (*högdragenhet*) haughtiness, high-and-mightiness **3** (*titel*) highness; *Ers H*~ Your Highness

höghus high-rise [building], tower block; multistorey building **-bebyggelse** high-rise development **-område** high-rise area (development)

hög|inkomsttagare high-income earner **-intressant** highly interesting **-kant** *på* ~ on end **-klackad** *a5* high-heeled **-klassig** *a1* high-class **-konjunktur** [business, trade] boom; ~*en inom* the boom [period] in **-kultur** *lantbr.* high farming **-kvarter** headquarters (*pl*) **-kyrka** High Church **-kyrklig** High-Church **-land** upland; *Skotska -länderna* the Highlands

höglast high load

högljudd [-judd] *a1* loud; (*högröstad*) loud-voiced, vociferous; (*bullersam*) noisy **-het** loudness; vociferousness; noisiness

hög|ländare Highlander **-länt** *a1* upland; *ön är* ~ the island is elevated (lies high) **-läsning** reading aloud **-lönegrupp** high-income category (group) **-mod** pride; (*överlägsenhet*) haughtiness, loftiness, airs (*pl*); (*övermod*) arrogance; ~ *går före fall* pride goeth before destruction **-modern** absolutely up-to-date **-modig** proud; haughty, lofty; arrogant **-målsbrott** [high] treason, lese-majesty **-mäld** [-ä:-] *a1, se högljudd* **-mält** *adv* in a loud voice **-mässa** morning service; *kat.* high mass **-nivåspråk** *data.* high-level language **-oktanig** *a5* high-octane **-platå** tableland **-prosa** literary prose

högre ['hö:g-] *komp. t. 2 hög* higher *etc., se 2 hög; de* ~ *klasserna* the upper classes (*skol.* forms); *en* ~ *makt* a higher power; *den* ~ *matematiken* higher (advanced) mathematics (*pl*); *en* ~ *officer* a high-ranking officer; *den* ~ *skolan* the upper (*friare* advanced) school, *ridk.* the higher mange; *ett* ~ *väsen* a superior being; *i allt* ~ *grad* to an ever-increasing extent; *i den* ~ *stilen* in the lofty style (*iron.* sublime manners); *på* ~ *ort* in high quarters; *intet* ~ *önska än att* desire nothing better than to; *tala* ~ speak louder

hög|relief high relief **-renässans** ~*en* the Mid-Renaissance **-rest** [-e:-] *a4* tall **-röd** vermil-[l]ion, scarlet, bright red **-röstad** *a5, se högljudd* **-sint** *al* high-minded; (*storsint*) magnanimous **-sjöflotta** ocean-going fleet **-skola** university college; (*friare*) academy; *teknisk* ~ institute (college) of technology **-skoleutbildning** university (college) education **-slätt** tableland, plateau **-sommar** *på* ~*en* at the height of the summer **-spänd** *a5*, elektr. high-tension, high-voltage **-spänn** *i uttr.: på* ~ (*bildl.*) at high tension, agog **-spänning** high tension (voltage) **-spänningsledning** high-tension (high-voltage) [transmission] line

högst [höckst] **I** *superl. t. 2 hög* highest *etc., se 2 hög;* ~*a tillåtna hastighet* speed limit, maximum [permitted] speed; *H*~*a domstolen* [the] supreme court; *H*~*a sovjet* Supreme Soviet; *min* ~*a önskan* my most fervent wish; *i* ~*a laget* as high (*etc.*) as it ought to be, (*äv.*) a little too high (*etc.*) if anything; *på* ~*a ort* at top level; *när solen står som* ~ when the sun is at its height (highest [point]) **II** *adv* highest *etc.*; most highly; (*mest*) most; (*i* ~*a grad*) in the highest degree; (*ytterst*) exceedingly, extremely; (*mycket*) very (*avsevärd* considerable); (*på sin höjd*) at most, at the [ut]most; *allra* ~ at the utmost (very most)

högstadium advanced (higher, senior) stage; (*i grundskola*) senior level

högstbjudande *a4, den* ~ the highest bidder

hög|stämd *bildl.* elevated, high-pitched, lofty **-säsong** height of the season, peak **-säte** high settle; (*förnämsta plats*) seat of honour

högt [höckt] *adv* high; highly; (*om ljud*) loud, loudly; (*motsats för sig själv*) aloud; (*högeligen*) highly; ~ *belägen* on high ground, (*situated*) high up; ~ *ställda fordringar* great (exacting) demands; ~ *uppsatt person* person of high station; ~ *älskad* dearly beloved; *lova* ~ *och dyrt* promise solemnly; *spela* ~ (*spel.*) play for high stakes; *stå* ~ *över* (*bildl.*) be far above, be far removed from

högtalare loudspeaker

högtflygande high-flying, high-soaring; ~ *planer* ambitious plans

högtid [ˣhöck-, *äv.* ˣhö:g-] *i sht bibl.* feast; *i sht kyrkl.* festival

högtidlig [ˣhöck-, *äv.* -'ti:d-, *äv.* ˣhö:g-] *a1* solemn; (*ceremoniell*) ceremonious, ceremonial; *vid* ~*a tillfällen* on state (formal, ceremonious) occasions; *se* ~ *ut* look solemn; *ta det inte så* ~*t!* don't be so solemn about it! **-het 1** solemnity; (*stått*) state, pomp **2** (*med pl*) ceremony; solemn **-hålla** celebrate, commemorate **-hållande** *s6* celebrating; celebration

högtids|blåsa *vard.* Sunday best **-dag** festival (commemoration) day; red-letter day **-dräkt** festival attire; (*frack*) evening dress **-firande I** *a4* festive **II** *s6* celebration, festival **-klädd** *a5* in festival attire; (*i frack*) in full dress **-sal** ceremonial room (hall), stateroom **-stund** time of real enjoyment, precious moment; *en musikalisk* ~ a musical treat **-talare** the speaker at a function (ceremony, festival *etc.*)

hög|trafik heavy (peak) traffic **-travande** *a4*

bombastic, high-flown; (*om pers.*) grandiloquent, pompous **-tryck** high pressure; *boktr.* letterpress, relief printing
högtrycks|aggregat high-pressure unit **-område** area of high pressure **-rygg** ridge of high pressure **-tvättning** high-pressure (jet) cleaning
högt|stående *a4, kulturellt* ~ on a high level of culture **-svävande** high-soaring; (*om planer*) ambitious
hög|tyska High German **-vakt 1** (*manskap*) main guard **2** (*vakthållning*) main guard duty **-varv** *s, arbeta på* ~ work full out **-varvig** *a5* high-speed **-vatten** high water; (*tidvatten*) high tide **-vilt** big game **-vinst** top lottery prize
högvis in heaps (piles, stacks); ~ *med* piles of
hög|välboren *Högvälborne Greve A.* The Right Honourable Earl A., *i Storbritannien* The Earl [of] A. **-växande** tall-growing **-växt** *a4* tall **-vördighet** *hans* ~ *biskopen* the Right Reverend the Lord Bishop; *Ers* ~ *torde* you will ..., My Lord **-ättad** *a5* of noble lineage, highborn **-önsklig** *mest i uttr.: i* ~ *välmåga* in the best of health, *vard.* in the pink
höj|a [ˣhöjja] *v2* raise; make higher, put up; (*för-*) heighten; (*förbättra*) improve; (*öka*) increase; ~ *priset på* raise (put up) the price of, mark up; ~ *ngn till skyarna* praise (exalt) s.b. [up] to the skies; ~ *upp* raise; ~ *sig* (*äv. bildl.*) rise above, raise o.s.; *-d över alla misstankar* above suspicion; *-d över allt tvivel* beyond all doubt; *det -des röster för* voices were raised in favour of **-bar** *a5, höj- och sänkbar* vertically adjustable
höjd *s3* **1** (*kulle o.d.*) height; hill **2** height; (*högsta* ~) top, summit; (*nivå*) level; *fack.* altitude; *geogr.* latitude; *mus.* pitch; *fri* ~ [free] headroom, [overhead] clearance; *största* ~ maximum height; *vishetens ~er* the pinnacles of wisdom; *~en av oförskämdhet* the height of impudence; *i* ~ *med* on a level with; *på sin* ~ at the [ut]most; *driva i ~en* intensify, force up, boost; *flyga på en* ~ *av* fly at an altitude (a height) of; *stå på ~en av sin bana* be at the height of one's career; *det är väl ändå ~en!* that's really the limit!
höjd|are *sl.* bigwig, big shot; *vard.* V.I.P. (*förk. för* very important person); *mil.* brass hat; *-arna* (*vard.*) the higher-ups **-hopp** high jump **-hoppare** high jumper **-led** *i* ~ vertically **-läge** *mus.* upper register **-mätare** altimeter **-punkt** highest point; peak; *bildl.* height, maximum; (*kulmen*) climax; *~en i hans diktning* the height of his literary production **-roder** *flyg.* elevator **-skillnad** difference in altitude (height) **-vind** upper wind
höjning (*höjande*) raising; (*av pris*) rise, increase; (*av lön*) rise, AE. raise; ~ *och sänkning* raising and lowering, (*i pris äv.*) rise and fall, *geol.* elevation and depression
hök *s2* hawk; *duvor och ~ar* (*polit.*) doves and hawks; ~ *och duva* (*lek*) tig
hökare *ung.* grocer
hö|lada hay barn **-lass** [cart]load of hay
hölj|a *v2* cover; (*insvepa*) wrap [up], envelop; (*friare*) coat; *-d i dunkel* veiled (wrapped) in obscurity, nebulous; ~ *sig med ära* cover o.s.

with glory
hölje *s6* envelope; (*fodral*) case, casing
höll *imperf. av hålla*
hölster ['höls-] *s7* **1** (*pistol-*) holster **2** *bot.* spathe
höna *s1* **1** hen; *kokk.* chicken **2** (*våp*) goose
höns *s7* **1** *pl* [domestic] fowls; (*hönor*) hens; *koll. äv.* poultry (*sg*); *springa omkring som yra* ~ rush around like a hen on a hot griddle; *vara högsta ~et* [*i korgen*] be cock of the roost, be top dog **2** *kokk.* chicken **-avel** poultry rearing **-buljong** chicken broth **-bur** hencoop **-bär** *bot.* dwarf cornel
höns|eri poultry (chicken) farm, hennery **-foder** chicken (poultry) feed **-fåglar** *pl* gallinaceous birds **-gård 1** poultry yard, hen (chicken) run **2** *se hönseri* **-hjärna** *bildl.* addle-pate (*äv. pers.*) **-hud** goose flesh (skin) **-hus** poultry house, henhouse **-minne** memory like a sieve **-nät** chicken wire **-skötsel** poultry keeping (farming) **-ägg** hen's egg
1 höra *v2* (*räknas*) belong (*till* to); ~ *hemma* belong (*i* to); ~ *ihop* belong together; ~ *ihop med* be connected with, (*bero på*) be dependent on; *det hör till yrket* it is part of the profession (job); *han hör till familjen* (*äv.*) he is one of the family; *det hör inte hit* it has nothing to do with this; *det hör till att* it is the right and proper thing that (*to* + *inf.*)
2 höra *v2* **1** (*uppfatta ljud*) hear; *han hör illa* (*äv.*) he is hard of hearing; *det hörs bra härifrån* you can hear well from here; *hör nu!* come now!; *hör du, kan du* I say (look here), can you; *han lät* ~ *en djup suck* he gave a deep sigh **2** (*erfara, få* ~) hear, learn; be told; (*fråga efter*) hear, inquire, ask, find out; *så snart han fick* ~ *om* directly he heard (was told) of; *jag har just fått* ~ *att* I have just heard that; *jag har hört sägas att* I have heard it said that; *jag vill inte* ~ *talas om det* I will not hear of it (such a thing); *gå och hör om han har rest* go and find out if he has gone; *har man hört på maken!* did you ever hear the like?; *låt* ~! out with it! **3** (*lyssna*) listen; (*åhöra*) hear (*en predikan* a sermon), attend (*en föreläsning* a lecture); ~ *ngns mening* ask a p.'s opinion; *jag vill* ~ *din mening om* I would like your opinion on (about); *han ville inte* ~ *på det* orat he just wouldn't listen **4** (*för-*) hear; (*vittne äv.*) examine **5** *rfl, det låter* ~ *sig!* that's s.th. like!; ~ *sig för* make inquiries (*om* about); ~ *sig för hos ngn* (*på en plats*) inquire of s.b. (at a place) **6** (*med betonad partikel*) ~ *av* hear from; *låta* ~ *av sig* send word; ~ *efter a*) (*lyssna till*) listen to, *b*) (*fråga efter*) inquire (*hos ngn* of s.b., *om ngt* for s.th., about s.th.), *c*) (*ta reda på*) hear, inquire, find out; ~ *fel* hear amiss, mishear; *hör in i morgon!* look in and inquire tomorrow!; ~ *på* listen; *hör upp ordentligt!* mind you pay proper attention!
hör|apparat hearing aid **-bar** *a5* audible **-central** hearing-aids centre **-fel** (*missuppfattning*) mishearing **-håll** *i uttr.: inom* (*utom*) ~ within (out of) earshot **-lur 1** (*för lomhörda*) ear trumpet **2** (*t. telefon*) receiver, earpiece; (*t. radioapparat*) earphone; *~ar* headphones, *vard.* cans

H

hörn [-ö:-] *s7* corner; (*vrå äv.*) nook; (*vinkel*) angle; *i ~et* at (*om inre hörn* in) the corner; *bo om ~et* live round the corner; *vara med på ett ~* join in; *vika om ~et* turn the corner

hörn|a *s1* **1** *vard., se hörn* **2** *sport.* corner **-hus** corner house **-pelare** corner pillar; *bildl.* pillar of strength **-skåp** corner cupboard **-sten** cornerstone (*äv. bildl.*) **-tand** eyetooth, canine [tooth], dogtooth

hör|propp earphone **-sal** lecture hall, auditorium

hörsam [ˣhö:r-] *a1* obedient **-ma** obey; (*kallelse e.d.*) respond to; (*inbjudan*) accept; (*uppmaning*) pay heed to

hörsel ['hörs-] *s2* hearing **-ben** auditory bone (ossicle) **-gång** auditory canal (meatus) **-klinik** hearing clinic **-minne** auditive memory **-nerv** auditory nerve **-organ** organ of hearing **-sinne** [sense of] hearing, auditory sense **-skada** impairment of hearing **-skadad** *a5* with impaired hering **-skydd** ear protection (guard); (*öronpropp*) earplug

hör|spel radio play **-sägen** (*enligt* from) hearsay **-telefon** [telephone] receiver, earpiece

hö|räfsa hayrake **-skrinda** haycart **-skulle** haymow **-skörd** hayharvest; *konkr. äv.* haycrop **-snuva** hay fever

höst *s2* autumn; *AE.* fall; *i ~ a*) (*nu*) this autumn, *b*) (*nästkommande*) next autumn; *i ~as* last autumn; *om ~en* (*~arna*) in the autumn; *på ~en 1966* in the autumn of 1966

höstack haystack, hayrick

höst|dag autumn day, day in the autumn **-dagjämning** autumnal equinox **-kanten** *i uttr.: på ~* around the beginning of the autumn **-lig** *a5* autumnal **-löv** autumn leaf **-mörker** autumn darkness **-storm** autumn[al] gale **-säd** autumn-sown grain **-säsong** autumn season **-termin** autumn term

hösäck (*tom*) haysack; (*full*) sack of hay

höta *v3, ~ åt ngn* (*med näven*) shake one's fist at s.b., (*med käpp*) brandish one's stick at s.b.

hö|tapp wisp of hay **-tjuga** [-çu:-] *s1* hayfork, pitchfork **-torgskonst** *ung.* trashy art

hövan *best. form sg i uttr.: över ~* beyond measure, excessively **hövas** *v2, dep* be befitting for

hövding chief[tain]

hövisk ['hö:-] *a5* (*anständig*) decent, seemly; (*ärbar*) modest; (*artig*) courteous; (*belevad*) refined; (*ridderlig*) chivalrous **-het** decency, seemliness; modesty; courteousness, courtesy; refinement; chivalry

hövitsman captain; *bibl. äv.* centurion

hövlig [-ö:-] *a1* civil, polite (*mot* to); (*belevad*) courteous; (*aktningsfull*) respectful (*mot* to) **-het** civility, politeness, courtesy; respect **-hetsvisit** courtesy (polite) call

hövligt [-ö:-] *adv* civilly *etc.*; *bli ~ bemött* be treated with civility; *svara ~* give a polite reply (*på* to)

hövolm [-å-] *s2* haycock

1 i *s6* i; *pricken över ~* the dot over the i, *bildl. äv.* the finishing touch

2 i *prep* **I** *rumsbet. o. bildl.* **1** (*befintl.*) in (*världen* the world; *Sverige* Sweden; *London* London); at (*Cambridge* Cambridge; *skolan* school); (*vid genitivförhållande vanl.*) of; (*på ytan av*) on (*soffan* the sofa); *~ en bank* in (at) a bank; *~ brödbutiken* at the baker's; *~ gräset* on the grass, (*bland grässtråna*) in the grass; *~ trappan* on the staircase; *~ ena änden av* at one end of; *freden ~ B.* the peace of B.; *högsta berget ~* the highest mountain in; *professor ~ engelska* professor of English; *det roliga ~ historien* the amusing part of the story; *uttrycket ~ hans ansikte* the expression on his face; *han bor ~ Bath* he lives at Bath; *jag bor här ~ Bath* I live here in Bath; *pojken satt ~ trädet* the boy was sitting in the tree; *katten sitter ~ fönstret* the cat is in the window; *pojken står ~ fönstret* the boy is standing at the window **2** (*friare*) among (*buskarna* the bushes); over (*högtalaren* the loudspeaker); through (*kikaren* the binoculars); in (*litteraturen* literature); at (*arbete* work); *~ frihet* at liberty; *~ stor skala* on a large scale; *för trång ~ halsen* too tight round the neck; *blåsa ~ trumpet* blow a trumpet; *göra ett besök ~* pay a visit to; *sitta ~ en styrelse* be on a board; *tala ~ näsan* talk through one's nose; *tala ~ radio* (*TV*) speak on the radio (on TV); *lampan hänger ~ taket* the lamp is hanging from the ceiling; *6 går ~ 30 fem gånger* 6 goes into 30 five times **3** (*vid rörelse, förändring*) into; in; *dela ngt ~ fyra delar* divide ngt. into four parts; *falla ~ vattnet* fall into the water; *få ngt ~ sitt huvud* (*bildl.*) get s.th. into one's head; *klättra upp ~ ett träd* climb up a tree; *placera ngt ~* place s.th. in; *resultera ~* result in; *stoppa ngt ~ fickan* put s.th. in[to] one's pocket; *störta landet ~ krig* plunge the country into war; *titta ~ taket* look up at the ceiling **4** (*gjord av*) of, in; (*medelst*) by (*bil* car); (*om hastighet o.d.*) at (*full fart* full speed); (*i o. för*) on; (*i form av*) in; (*såsom*) as; *en kjol ~ bomull* a skirt of cotton, a cotton skirt; *gjuten ~ brons* cast in bronze; *~ lag förbjudet* forbidden by law; *~ regel* as a rule; *~ stor utsträckning* to a large extent; *bortrest ~ affärer* away on business; *inte ~ min smak* not to my taste; *dra ngn ~ håret* pull s.b. by the hair, pull a p.'s hair; *dö ~ cancer* die of cancer; *få ~ present* get as a present; *gripa ngn ~ kragen* seize s.b. by the collar; *ligga ~ influensa* be down with the flu; *ta ngn ~ armen* take s.b. by the arm; *vad har du ~ lön?* what wages (salary) do you get? **5** *duktig* (*dålig*) *~* good (bad) at; *förtjust ~* fond of, delighted with; *tokig ~* crazy about; *ha ont ~ magen* have a stomach ache; *jag är trött ~ fötterna* my feet are tired **II** *tidsbet.* **1** (*tid-*

punkt) in (*maj* May; *medelåldern* the middle age); at (*jul* Christmas; *början av* the beginning of; *solnedgången* sunset); last (*höstas* autumn); next (*vår* spring); (*före*) to; ~ *en ålder av* at the age of; ~ *natt a*) (*som är el. kommer*) tonight, *b*) (*som var*) last night; *förr* ~ *tiden* in earlier times, formerly; *en kvart* ~ *åtta* a quarter to eight **2** (*tidslängd*) for (*åratal* years); ~ *trettio år* (*de senaste trettio åren*) [for] the last thirty years, (*om framtid*) [for] the next thirty years; *vi stannade* ~ *två veckor* we stayed [for] two weeks **3** (*per*) a[n], per; *två gånger* ~ *månaden* twice a month; *60 miles* ~ *timmen* 60 miles per (an) hour **III** (*i adverbiella, prepositionella o. konjunktionella förbindelser*) ~ *och för utredning* for the purpose of investigation; ~ *och för sig* in itself; ~ *och med detta* with this; ~ *och med att han gick var han* in going he was;~ *det att* [just] as; ~ *det att han gick* as he went, in going; *han gjorde rätt* ~ *att komma* he was right in coming **3 i** *adv, en skål med choklad* ~ a bowl with chocolate in it; *hoppa* ~ jump in; *hälla* ~ *kaffe åt ngn* pour [out] coffee for s.b.; *hälla* ~ *vatten i en vas* pour water into a vase

iaktta[ga] 1 (*observera*) observe; (*lägga märke t. äv.*) notice; (*uppmärksamt betrakta äv.*) watch **2** *bildl.* observe (*tystnad* silence); exercise (*största försiktighet* the greatest caution); (*fasthålla vid äv.*) adhere to, keep (*reglerna* the rules)

iakttag|ande *s6* observance, observation; *under* ~ *av* observing **-are** observer **-else** observation **-elseförmåga** powers of observation

I-balk I-beam

i'ber *s3,* **-isk** [i'be:-] *a5* Iberian; *I~a halvön* Iberian Peninsula

ibis ['i:-] *s2* ibis

i'bland I *prep, se bland; mitt* ~ amid[st], in the midst of **II** *adv* (*stundom*) sometimes; (*då o. då*) occasionally; (*vid vissa tillfällen äv.*) at times, now and then

icke not; no; none; ~ *desto mindre* nevertheless, nonetheless; *i* ~ *ringa grad* in no small degree

icke|- *i sms.* non- **-angreppspakt** nonaggression pact **-rökare** nonsmoker **-spridningsavtal** nonproliferation treaty **-våld** nonviolence **-våldsmetoder** passive resistance (*sg*)

1 id *s2, zool.* ide

2 id *s2* (*verksamhet*) occupation[s *pl*], pursuit[s *pl*]; (*flit*) industry

i'dag *se dag*

idas *iddes itts, dep* have enough energy (energy enough) (*göra ngt* to do s.th.); *han iddes inte ens svara* he couldn't even be bothered to answer

ide *s6* hibernation-den; winter quarters (*pl*), winter lair; *gå i* ~ go into hibernation, *bildl.* shut o.s. away (up in one's den); *ligga i* ~ (*äv.*) hibernate, lie dormant (*äv. bildl.*)

idé *s3* idea (*om* about, as to, of); *få en* ~ get (have) an idea; *det är ingen* ~ *att göra* it is no use (good) doing, there is no point in doing; *hur har du kommit på den ~n?* what put that idea into your head?; *han har sina ~er* he has some odd ideas

ide'al *s7 o. a1* ideal (*av, för* of) **-bild** ideal im-

age **-figur** ideal figure; (*-mått*) ideal measurements (*pl*) **-gestalt** ideal figure

ideal|ism idealism **-ist** idealist **-istisk** [-'ist-] *a5* idealistic **-itet** ideality

ideal|samhälle ideal society; Utopia **-tillstånd** ideal state; ideal existence

idé|association association of ideas **-drama** problem play; ideological drama

ide'ell *a1* idealistic; ~ *förening* non-profit-making association

idé|fattig unimaginative **-givare** inspirer, brain

idegran yew [tree]

idé|historia history of ideas **-historisk** ideo-historical, pertaining to the history of ideas **-innehåll** idea-content (*i* of)

idel ['i:-] *oböjligt a* (*uteslutande*) mere, nothing but; (*ren*) pure, sheer; *vara* ~ *öra* be all ears; ~ *glädje* pure joy; *han var* ~ *solsken* he was all sunshine

idelig *a5* perpetual; continual, incessant **-en** perpetually *etc.*; over and over again; *han frågar* ~ he keeps on asking

idé|lära (*Platons*) doctrine of ideas **-man** (*i reklambranschen*) visualizer, *BE. äv.* visualiser

identifi|era identify **-ering, -kation** identification

identi|sk [i'dent-] *a5* identical **-tet** *s3* identity; *fastställa ngns* ~ establish a p.'s identity; *styrka sin* ~ prove one's identity

identitets|bricka *mil.* identity disc **-kort** identity card **-kris** identity crisis

ideo|log ideologist, ideologue **-logi** *s3* ideology **-logisera** ideologize **-logisk** *a5* ideologic[al]

idé|rik full of ideas **-skiss** draft, rough sketch **-utbyte** exchange of ideas **-värld** [personal] philosophy

idiom [-'å:m] *s7* idiom **-atisk** [-'ma:-] *a5* idiomatic[al]

idiosynkra|'si *s3* idiosyncrasy; (*motvilja*) aversion **-tisk** [-'kra:-] *a5* idiosyncratic

idi'ot *s3* idiot; (*svagare*) imbecile

idio't|i *s3* idiocy; imbecility **-isk** [-'⍵:t-] *a5* idiotic **-säker** foolproof

idissl|a ruminate, chew the cud; *bildl.* repeat, harp on **-ande** *s6* rumination; repetition **-are** ruminant

idka carry on; (*yrke, idrott äv.*) practise; (*yrke äv.*) follow; ~ *familjeliv* devote o.s. to one's family; ~ *handel* carry on business

ID-kort ID card

idog *a1* industrious; laborious; (*trägen*) assiduous **-het** industriousness *etc.*; industry

idol [-'å:l] *s3* idol **-dyrkan** idol worship

idrott [-å-] *s3* sport; [athletic] sports (*pl*); *skol., univ.* games (*pl*); *allmän* (*fri*) ~ athletics (*pl o. sg*) **idrotta** go in for sport; *skol. o.d. äv.* play games

idrotts|anläggning stadium, sports arena **-dag** sports day **-evenemang** sporting event **-förening** athletic (sports) club **-gren** branch of athletics (sport) **-intresse** sporting interest **-klubb** *se -förening* **-kvinna** woman athlete, sportswoman **-lig** *a5* athletic **-lov** *skol.* time off (holiday) for sports **-man** athlete, sportsman **-märke** athletics (sports) badge **-plats** sports ground (field), athletic ground[s *pl*] **-tävling** sports (athletics) meeting

ids [i:-, *vard.* iss] *se* idas
i'dyll *s3* idyll; (*plats*) idyllic spot **-iker** idyllist **-isk** *a5* idyllic
i'fall 1 if, in case; (*förutsatt*) supposing (provided) [that] **2** (*huruvida*) if, whether
i'fatt *gå* (*köra, simma*) ~ *ngn* catch s.b. up
i|'fjol *se* fjol **-'fred** *se* fred
ifråga|komma [i*frå:-] *se fråga I*; ~ *vid en befordran* be considered (a possible choice) for a promotion; *brukar sådant ~?* do such things usually happen? **-sätta 1** (*föreslå*) propose, suggest **2** (*betvivla*) question, call in question **-varande** *a4* in question, at issue
ifrån I *prep, se från I*; *söder* ~ from the south; *vara* ~ *sig* be beside o.s. **II** *adv, komma* ~ (*bli fri el. ledig*) get off (away); *man kommer inte* ~ *att* there is no getting away from the fact that
iföra *rfl, se* ikläda
igel *s2* leech
igelkott [-å-] *s2* hedgehog
igen [i'jenn] **1** (*ånyo*) again; *om* ~ over again; (*en gång till*) once more **2** (*tillbaka*) back; *slå* ~ hit back; *ta* ~ (*om tid*) make up for; *jag kommer snart* ~ I shall (will) soon be back **3** (*kvar*) left **4** (*tillsluten*) to; *dörren slog* ~ the door slammed to **5** *fylla* ~ fill in
igen|bommad *a5, huset var* -*bommat* the house was barred (shut) up; *dörrarna är* ~*e* the doors have been fastened **-grodd** *a5* choked up, (*om stig e.d.*) overgrown (*av ogräs* with weeds) **-känd** *a5* recognized **-kännande** *s6* recognition **-känningstecken** distinctive (distinguishing) mark **-kännlig** *a5* recognizable (*för* to; *på* by) **-mulen** *a5* overclouded, overcast, clouded over
igenom [i'je:-] *prep o. adv* through; *rakt* ~ right (straight) through; *tvärs* ~ right across; *natten* ~ all through (throughout) the night, all night long; *hela livet* ~ all (throughout) one's life; *han har gått* ~ *mycket* he has suffered (gone through) a great deal
igen|proppad [-å-] *a5* clogged up **-snöad** *a5* (*om väg*) snowed-up; (*om spår*) obliterated by snow **-stängd** *a5* shut up, closed **-växt** *a4* (*om gångstig*) overgrown; (*om sjö o.d.*) choked-up
iglo[o] ['i:glɷ] *s5* igloo
ignor|ans [iŋnå'rans *el.* injå- *el.* -'aŋs] *s3* ignorance **-ant** ignorant person **-era** ignore, take no notice of; disregard
i'gång *se 1* gång **2 -sättning** starting, start **-sättningstillstånd** building start permit
i'går *se* går
ihjäl [i'jä:l] to death; *skjuta* ~ *ngn* (*äv.*) shoot s.b. dead; *slå* ~ kill; *slå* ~ *tiden* kill time; *svälta* ~ (*äv.*) die of hunger, starve to death; *arbeta* ~ *sig* work o.s. to death; *skratta* ~ *sig* die of laughing; *slå* ~ *sig* get (be) killed **-frusen** *a5* frozen to death **-skjuten** [-ʃu:-] *a5* shot dead **-skrämd** *a5* frightened (*etc.*) to death **-slagen** *a5* killed **-sparkad** *a5* kicked to death **-trampad** *a5* trampled to death
i'hop 1 (*tillsammans*) together; *passa* ~ go well together, (*om pers.*) suit each other **2** *fälla* ~ shut up; *krympa* ~ shrink [up]; *sätta* ~ *en historia* make up a story
i'håg *komma* ~ remember, (*erinra sig äv.*) rec-

ollect, (*lägga på minnet*) bear (keep) in mind; *jag kommer inte* ~ (*äv.*) I forget **-komma** *se ihåg; det bör* ~*s att* it should be borne in mind that
ihålig *a1* hollow (*äv. bildl.*); (*tom*) empty **-het** *konkr.* cavity; hole; hollow; *abstr.* hollowness, emptiness
ihållande *a4* prolonged (*applåder* applause; *kyla* frost); continuous, steady (*regn* rain)
ihärdig *a1* (*om pers.*) persevering; (*trägen*) assiduous, tenacious; (*om sak*) persistent; ~*t nekande* persistent denial **-het** perseverance; assiduity, tenacity; persistence
i'kapp (*i tävlan*) in competition; *hinna* ~ *ngn* catch s.b. up; *springa* ~ *med ngn* run a race with s.b.; *de rider* ~ *med varandra* they are racing each other on horseback
ikläda dress in; clothe in (*äv. bildl.*); ~ *sig* (*påtaga sig*) take upon o.s., assume, make o.s. responsible for
ikon [i'kå:n] *s3* icon **-ografi** *s3* iconography
ikraftträdande [i*kraft-] *a4* coming into force; ~ *av lag* passing into law
i'kring *se* kring, omkring
iktyo|log ichthyologist **-logi** *s3* ichthyology **-logisk** *a5* ichthyologic[al]
i'kull *se* omkull
i'kväll *se* kväll
1 il *s2* (*vind-*) gust [of wind]; squall
2 il *s7, se* -gods, -samtal *o.d.*; (*påskrift på telegram o.d.*) urgent
1 ila *det* ~*r i tänderna på mig* I have a shooting pain in my teeth
2 ila *litt.* speed; fly, dart, dash; (*mera vard.*) hurry; *tiden* ~*r* time flies [apace]
i-land *se* industriland
ilast|a load **-ning** loading
il|bud urgent message (*efter* for); *pers.* express messenger **-fart** *med* ~ at full (top) speed **-gods** *koll.* express goods, goods sent by express train; *sända som* ~ send by express **-godsförsändelse** express parcel
illa *komp.* värre *el.* sämre, *superl.* värst *el.* sämst; *adv* (*dåligt*) badly; (*låta* sound) bad; (*klent*) poorly; (*på tok*) wrong; (*elakt, skadligt*) ill, evil; (*svårt*) badly, severely; (*mycket*) very (*trött* tired); ~ *behandlad* ill-treated; ~ *berörd* unpleasantly affected; ~ *dold avundsjuka* ill-concealed envy; ~ *kvickt* pretty (damn) quick; ~ *till mods* sick at heart, downhearted; *behandla ngn* ~ treat s.b. badly; *göra ngn* ~ hurt s.b.; *göra sig* ~ *i foten* hurt one's foot; *må* ~ feel poorly (out of sorts), (*vilja kräkas*) feel sick; *ta* ~ *upp* take it amiss; *ta* ~ *vid sig* be very upset (grieved) (*av* about); *tala* ~ *om ngn* run s.b. down, speak ill of s.b.; *tycka* ~ *vara* take it amiss, mind; *det går* ~ *för mig* things are going badly (*på tok* wrong) for me; *den* ~ *gör han* ~ *far* who evil does, he evil fares; *man ligger* ~ *i den här sängen* this bed is uncomfortable; *den luktar (smakar)* ~ it has a nasty smell (taste); *hon ser* ~ her sight is bad; *hon ser inte* ~ *ut* she is not bad-looking; *det var* ~! that's a pity!; *det var inte* ~! that is not bad!, that is pretty good!; *det var inte så* ~ *menat* no offence was intended (meant); *är det så* ~? is it as bad as all that?

illa|luktande *a4* nasty-smelling, evil-smelling **-mående** *a4* poorly, out of sorts, unwell; indisposed; *känna sig ~ (ha kväljningar)* feel sick

illande *a4*, *~ röd* flaming red

illa|sinnad *a5* ill-disposed; *(om handling)* malicious **-sittande** badly fitting **-smakande** *a4* with a nasty (disagreeable) taste; *(om mat äv.)* unsavoury **-varslande** *a4* evil-boding, ill-boding; ominous

illdåd wicked (evil) deed; outrage *(mot* on)

ille'g|al *a1* illegal **-i'tim** *a5* illegitimate

iller ['ill-] *s2* polecat

ill|fundig *a1*, *se* -listig **-fänas** *dep* **1** *(väsnas)* pester **2** *(envisas)* bother *(med* with) **-gärning** malicious (evil, wicked) deed; outrage *(mot* on) **-gärningsman** evil-doer; malefactor **-listig** *(hopskr. illistig)* cunning, wily; insidious *(påhitt* device); *(listig äv.)* crafty **-listighet** *(hopskr. illistighet)* malicious cunning (craftiness)

illitte'rat *a1* illiterate, unlettered

illmarig *a1* sly, knowing; *(slug)* cunning; *(skälmsk)* arch

illo'jal *a1* disloyal; *~ konkurrens* unfair competition **-itet** disloyalty

ill|röd glaring red **-tjut** piercing yell; *ge till ett ~* make a hell of a row **-tjuta** scream

illudera produce an illusion of

illumin|ation illumination **-era** illuminate

illusion illusion; *(falsk föreställning)* delusion; *göra sig ~er om* cherish illusions about; *ta ngn ur hans ~er* disillusion s.b.

illusionist illusionist **-isk** *a5* illusionistic

illusions|fri, -lös free from all illusion[s *pl*]; absolutely disillusioned

illusorisk [-'sɷ:-] *a5* illusory; *(bedräglig)* illusive; *(inbillad)* imaginary

illust|er [-'lust-] *a2* illustrious **-ration** illustration **-ra'tiv** *a5* illustrative; *boktr. äv.* illustrational **-ratör** illustrator **-rera** illustrate

ill|vilja *(ont uppsåt)* spite, ill will *(mot* towards); *(elakhet)* malevolence; *(djupt rotad)* malignity **-villig** spiteful, malicious, malevolent *(mot* towards) **-vrål** *se* illtjut

ilmarsch forced march

ilning [ˈiːl-] thrill *(av glädje* of joy); *(av smärta)* shooting pain

il|paket express parcel **-samtal** *tel.* express call

ilsk|a *s1* [hot] anger, [boiling] rage, [intense] fury *(över ngt* at s.th.); *i ~n in his (etc.)* anger, for very rage; *göra ngt i ~n* do s.th. in a fit of anger **-en** *a3* angry; *(ursinnig)* furious; *(om djur)* savage, ferocious; *bli ~* get angry *(på ngn* with s.b.); *över ngt* at s.th) **-na ~ till** fly *(så småningom* work o.s.) into a rage (fury); *~ till mer och mer* get angrier and angrier

iltelegram express telegram (wire, cable)

imagi'när [-ʃi-] *a5* imaginary *(äv. mat.)*; unreal, fancied

i'mam *s3* ima[u]m

imbe'cill *a5* imbecile **-itet** imbecility

imit|ation imitation **-a'tiv** *a5* imitative **-atör** imitator; *(varietéartist o.d.)* mimic **-era** imitate; copy; *(människor äv.)* take off, mimic; *~t läder* imitation leather

imma I *s1 (ånga)* mist, vapour; *(beläggning)* steam, moisture; *det är ~ på fönstret* the window is steamed (misted) over **II** *v1* get misted [over]

imman|ens *s3* immanence, immanency **-ent** *a4* immanent

immateri'ell *a5* immaterial

immatrikulera matriculate

immersion immersion

immig *a1* misty, steamy

immigr|ant immigrant **-ation** immigration **-era** immigrate *(till* into)

im'mun *a1* immune *(mot* against, from, to) **-globulin** immunoglobulin **-isera** immunize **-isering** [-'seː-] immunization **-itet** immunity

immuno|log immunologist **-logi** *s3* immunology **-logisk** *a5* immunologic[al]

immunserum serum

imorgon *se* morgon 2

impala[antilop] ['imp-] impala

impedans [*äv.* -'aŋs] *s3, elektr.* impedance

imperativ I *s3 (i* in the) imperative **II** *a5* imperative **-isk** *a5* imperative

imperator *s3* imperator **-isk** [-'tɷ:-] *a5* imperial; *(om gest o.d.)* imperious

imperfekt *s7, s4* **-um** *s4* imperfect; *i ~* in the past tense

imperial|ism imperialism **-ist** imperialist **-istisk** *a5* imperialist[ic]

imperium [-'peː-] *s4* empire

impertin|ens *s3* impertinence **-ent** *a1* impertinent

implant|at *s7* implant **-ation** implantation **-era** implant

implic|era implicate **-'it** *a4* implicit

implo|dera implode **-sion** implosion

imponer|a make an impression *(på* on); impress; *jag blev mycket ~d* I was very much impressed *(av* by) **-ande** *a4* impressive; imposing; *ett ~ antal* a striking[ly large] number of; *en ~ gestalt* an imposing figure; *~ siffror* striking figures

impopul|aritet unpopularity **-'är** *a1* unpopular *(bland, hos* with)

im'port [-å-] *s3 (-erande)* import[ation]; *(varor)* imports *(pl)* **-avgift** import duty

import|era import *(till* [in]to); *~de varor (äv.)* imports **-firma** import[ing] firm; importers *(pl)* **-förbud** import prohibition (ban) **-licens** import licence **-restriktioner** import restrictions **-tillstånd** import permit (licence) **-tull** import duty **-underskott** import deficit **-vara** imported article, import[ation]

import|ör importer **-överskott** import surplus

imposant [-'ant *el.* -'aŋt] *a1*, *se* imponerande; *(storslagen)* grand

impot|ens *s3* impotence, impotency **-ent** *a4* impotent

impregner|a [-eŋ'neː- *el.* -en'jeː-] impregnate; *(mot väta)* waterproof; *(trä)* creosote **-ing** impregnation; *(mot vatten)* waterproofing; *(av trä)* creosoting **-ingsmedel** impregnating agent

impressario [-'saː-] *s3* impresario

impression|ism [-eʃɷ-] impressionism **-ist** impressionist **-istisk** [-'ist-] *a5* impressionist[ic]

improduk'tiv *a1* unproductive; *(oräntabel)* unprofitable **-itet** unproductiveness; unprofitability

impromptu [-'åmp-] s6 impromptu

improvis|ation improvisation **-atör** improviser **-era** improvise; (om talare äv.) extemporize

im'puls s3 impulse; (utifrån kommande äv.) stimulus, incentive, spur, impetus (till to); elektr. excitation **-givare** elektr. exciter

impul'siv a1 impulsive **-itet** impulsiveness

impulsköp (-ande) impulse buying; ett ~ a purchase made on [the] impulse; göra ett ~ buy on [the] impulse

imrör vent

in [inn] in; (~ i huset o.d.) inside; hit (dit) ~ in here (there) ~ i into; ~ till staden in (äv. up) to town; till långt ~ på natten until far [on] into the night

inackorder|a board and lodge (hos with); vara ~d board and lodge, be a boarder; ~ sig arrange to board and lodge (hos with) **-ing 1** abstr. board [and lodging], board-and-lodging accommodation **2** pers. boarder; ha ~ar take in boarders **-ingsrum** rented room

inadekvat a4 inadequate

inadvertens s3 inadvertence

inak'tiv [el. 'inn-] inactive; inert **-itet** inactivity

inaktu'ell (förlegad) out of date; problemet är ~t the problem does not arise (is not pertinent)

inalles [-'all-] in all, altogether

inand|as inhale; breathe in **-ning** inhalation

inarbeta 1 work in **2** (förtjäna tillbaka) work off (en förlust a loss) **3** (skaffa avsättning för) push [the sale of], find a market for; en väl ~d firma a well-established firm

i'natt se natt

inaugurera inaugurate

in|avel inbreeding **-begripa** comprise, comprehend; (innesluta) include; (medräkna) take into account; ...ej -begripen not including ...; -begripen i samtal engaged in conversation **-beräkna** include, take into account; allt ~t everything included **-berätta** report (ngt för ngn s.th. to s.b.) **-bespara** save **-besparing** saving **-betala** pay [in, up]; ~ till en bank (på sitt konto) pay into a bank (one's account); -betalda avgifter paid-up fees **-betalning** paying [in, up], payment; in- och utbetalningar receipts and disbursements, in- and outgoing payments **-betalningskort** post. paying-in form

inbilla ~ ngn ngt make s.b. (get s.b. to) believe s.th.; ~d imagined, fancied, imaginary; vem har ~t dig det? whoever put that into your head?; det kan du ~ andra! tell that to the marines!; ~ sig imagine, fancy; ~ sig vara imagine that one is; ~ sig vara ngt think a great deal of o.s.

inbillning imagination; (falsk föreställning) fancy; det är bara ~[ar]! that is pure imagination (all fancy)!

inbillnings|foster figment of the imagination **-sjuk** en ~ an imaginary invalid, a hypochondriac; vara ~ suffer from an imagined complaint **inbilsk** a1 conceited; vard. toffee-nosed **-het** conceit

in|binda (böcker) bind **-bindning** binding; lämna till ~ leave to be bound **-biten** a5 con-

firmed (ungkarl bachelor); inveterate (rökare smoker)

inbjud|a invite; ~ till kritik invite criticism; ~ till teckning av aktier invite subscription[s] to a share issue; har äran ~ ... till middag request the pleasure of the company of...to dinner **-ande** a4 inviting; (lockande) tempting **-ning** invitation **-ningskort** invitation card

inbland|a se blanda; bli ~d i ngt become (get) involved (implicated, mixed up) in s.th. **-ning** bildl. interference, meddling; (ingripande) intervention

in blanko ['blann-] in blank; in blanco

in|blick insight (i int); få en ~ i (äv.) catch a glimpse of **-boka** book **-bokning** booking; reservation **-bringa** yield, bring [in] **-bringande** a4 profitable; lucrative **-bromsning** braking, application of the brake[s pl]

inbrott 1 (början) setting in; vid dagens ~ at the break of day, at daybreak (dawn); vid nattens ~ at nightfall; vid mörkrets ~ at the approach of darkness **2** (under dagen) housebreaking; (under natten) burglary; göra ~ hos ngn break into (commit a burglary at) a p.'s house

inbrotts|försäkring burglary insurance **-tjuv** (under dagen) housebreaker; (under natten) burglar

in|brytning mil. break-in (i in) **-buktning** inward bend **-bunden** a3 **1** (om bok) bound **2** bildl. uncommunicative, reserved **-bundenhet** uncommunicativeness etc.; reserve **-burad** a5 locked up **-byggare** (bebyggare) settler; se äv. invånare **-byggd** a5 built in; en ~ veranda a closed-in veranda[h] **-byte** trading-in **-bytesbil** trade-in car; vi använder vår gamla Morris som ~ när vi köper Buicken we trade in our old Morris for the Buick **-bytesvärde** trade-in value **-bäddad** a5 embedded

inbördes [-ö:-] **I** adv (ömsesidigt) mutually; reciprocally; (med varandra) with one another; (inom sig själva) among[st] themselves **II** oböjligt a mutual; reciprocal; deras ~ avstånd their relative distance; sällskap för ~ beundran mutual admiration society; ~ testamente mutual ([con]joint) will **-krig** civil war

in'cest s3 incest

incheck|a se checka in **-ning** checking-in **-ningsdisk** check-in [counter]

incident s3 incident

incitament s7 incentive; incitement

indata data. input

indefi'nit [äv. 'inn-] a4 indefinite

indel|a divide (i into); (uppdela) divide up (i into; efter according to); (i klasser) classify, group; (i underavdelningar) subdivide **-ning** dividing [up]; division; classification, grouping; subdivision **-ningsgrund** principle (basis) of division (etc.)

indelt [-e:-] a4, mil. ung. tenement (soldat soldier)

index ['inn-] s7, s9 index (pl äv. indices); mat. subscript **-reglerad** a5 index-linked **-tal** index [number (figure)] **-tillägg** index increment

indi'an s3 [American] Indian **-bok** Red-Indian storybook **-dräkt** Red-Indian costume **-höv-**

ding [Red-]Indian chief **-krasse** *bot.* nasturtium, Indian cress
indi'an|sk [-a:-] *a5* [Red-]Indian **-ska** [Red-]Indian woman **-sommar** Indian summer **-stam** Indian tribe **-tjut** Indian war whoop
indicera *se indikera*
indici|ebevis [-ˣdi:-] circumstantial evidence **-um** [-'di:-] *s4* indication (*på* of); *jur.* circumstantial evidence; *bildl.* criterion; *starka -er* weighty evidence; *döma ngn på -er* convict s.b. on circumstantial evidence
indiefarare person (ship) bound for (sailing from) India; *(fartyg äv.)* Indiaman
Indien ['inn-] India; *Bortre ~* Farther India **indier** ['inn-] Indian
indiffe'rens *s3* indifference **-ent** *a4* indifferent
indign|ation [-diŋna-, *äv.* -dinja-] indignation **-erad** [-'e:-] *a5* indignant (*över* of)
indigo ['inn-] *s5* (*växt*) indigo; *(färgämne)* indigo, indigotin **-blå** indigo [blue]
indikation indication
indikativ *s3 o. a1* indicative; *stå i ~* be in the indicative
indikator *s3* indicator
indiker|a indicate **-ing** indication, indicating
indirekt ['inn-, *äv.* -'ekt] *a4* indirect; *~ anföring* indirect (reported) speech, *AE.* indirect discourse; *~ belysning* indirect (concealed) lighting; *~ bevis* indirect proof; *~ skatt* indirect tax; *~ val (ung.)* election by ad hoc appointed electors
indi|sk ['inn-] *a5* Indian **-ska** Indian woman; *I~a oceanen* [the] Indian Ocean
indis'kre|t *a1* indiscreet; tactless; *(lösmynt)* talkative **-tion** indiscretion
indis|ponerad [-'ne:-] *a5* indisposed, out of sorts; *(om sångare)* not in good voice **-ponibel** [-'ni:-] unavailable **-position** indisposition
indium ['inn-] *s8* indium
indi'vid *s3* individual; *(om djur äv.)* specimen; *(neds. om pers. äv.)* specimen, character
individual|isera individualize **-ism** individualism **-ist** individualist **-istisk** *a5* individualistic **-itet** individuality
individu'ell *a5* individual
indoeurop|é *s3*, **-eisk** [-'e:-] *a5* Indo-European
Indokina Indochina, Indo-China, Farther India
indoktriner|a indoctrinate **-ing** indoctrination
indol|ens *s3* indolence; idleness **-ent** *a1* indolent; idle, lazy
indo|log Indologist **-logi** *s3* Indology
indo'nes *s3, se indonesier*
Indonesien [-'ne:-] *n* Indonesia
indones|ier [-'ne:-] *s9*, **-isk** *a5* Indonesian
indrag indentation, indent
indrag|a *se dra [in]*; *(friare)* draw in; *(inveckla)* involve, implicate (*i* in) **-ning** drawing in; involvement, implication; withdrawal; stoppage, discontinuation; confiscation; suspension
indriv|a *(inkassera)* collect, call in; *(på rättslig väg)* recover **-are** debt collector **-ning** collection; recovery
indräktig *a1* lucrative
indränka soak, saturate
inducera induce
induk|tans *s3* inductance **-tion** [-k'ʃɷ:n]

induction
induktions|spole inductance coil **-ström** induction (induced) current
indunstning [concentration by] evaporation
indus'tri *s3* industry; *~ och hantverk* the crafts and industries
industrial|isera industrialize **-isering** industrialization **-ism** industrialism
industri|arbetare industrial (factory) worker **-departement** ministry (*AE.* department) of industry
industri|'ell *a5* industrial **-förbund** *Sveriges I~* [the] Federation of Swedish Industries **-företag** industrial enterprise (concern, company) **-gren** [branch of] industry **-idkare** industrialist, manufacturer **-land** industrialized country **-man** industrialist **-minister** minister (*AE.* secretary) of industry **-mässa** industrial fair **-nedläggelse** close-down of a factory **-område** industrial region (area); *(planerat område)* industrial estate (*AE.* park) **-produktion** industrial production **-robot** industrial robot **-semester** general industrial holiday **-spionage** industrial espionage **-stad** industrial town **-varor** *pl* industrial goods (products), manufactured goods **-verk** *Statens I~* [the Swedish] National Industrial Board
ineffek'tiv *a1* ineffective; *(om pers. äv.)* inefficient **-itet** ineffectiveness; inefficiency
inemot ['inn-] *(om tid)* towards; *(om antal o.d.)* nearly, close on
in'ert *a1* inert
inex'akt *a1* inexact, inaccurate **-het** inaccuracy; inexactitude
in extenso [-'tenn-] in full
in|fall *s7* **1** *(angrepp)* invasion (*i* of); incursion (*i* into) **2** *(påhitt)* idea, fancy; *(nyck)* whim; *jag fick ett ~* I had a bright idea (a brain wave) **3** *(kvickhet)* sally **-falla 1** *(om vattendrag o.d.)* fall (*i* into) **2** *~ i ett land* invade a country **3** *(inskjuta yttrande)* put in **4** *(inträffa)* fall *(på en söndag* on a Sunday) **-fallen** *a5, infallna kinder* sunken (hollow) cheeks
infallsvinkel angle of incidence (*bildl.* approach)
in'fam *a1* infamous; abominable; *vara ~t påpassad* be under close surveillance **infa'mi** *s3* infamy
infanteri infantry **-avdelning, -förband** infantry unit **-regemente** infantry regiment
infanterist infantryman
infan'til *a1* infantile **-ism** infantilism
in'farkt *s3, med.* infarct[ion]; *AE.* infarct
infart [-a:-] *s3* approach (*äv. sjö.*); *~ förbjuden!* No Entry!; *under ~en till* when approaching (entering)
infarts|led arterial road **-parkering** commuter parking **-väg** drive[way], approach
infatt|a *(kanta)* border; *(juveler e.d.)* set, mount; *~ i ram* frame **-ning** *(kant)* border; edging; *(ram)* frame[work]; *(för juveler o.d.)* setting, mounting; *(t. glasögon e.d.)* rim; *(t. fönster e.d.)* trim
infek|tera infect **-tion** [-k'ʃɷ:n] infection
infektions|härd focus of infection **-sjukdom** infectious disease **-ämne** infectious organism; germ

infektiös [-k'ʃö:s] infectious; contagious
infernalisk [-'na:-] *a5* infernal
inferno [-'fä(:)rnå] *s6* inferno
infiltr|at *s7* infiltrate **-ation** infiltration **-atör** infiltrator **-era** infiltrate
infi'nit *a4* infinite
infinitiv *s3* (*i* in the) infinitive **-märke** sign of the infinitive, infinitive marker
infinna *rfl* appear, make one's appearance; put in an appearance; turn up; ~ *sig hos ngn* present o.s. (appear) before s.b.; ~ *sig vid en begravning* (*på sammanträdet*) attend a funeral (the meeting)
inflamm|ation inflammation (*i* in, of) **-atorisk** [-'tɔ:-] *a5* inflammatory **-era** inflame
inflation inflation **-istisk** [-'ist-] *a5* inflationary
inflations|drivande inflationary **-fara** risk of inflation **-skydda** inflation-proof **-spiral** inflationary spiral
inflatorisk [-'tɔ:-] *a5* inflationary
infli[c]ka put in, interpose
influ'ens *s3* influence
influensa [-ˣenn-] *s1* influenza, *vard.* flu **-epidemi** influenza epidemic **-virus** influenza virus
in|fluera ~ [*på*] influence **-flygning** (*mot flygplats*) approach **-flyta** (*om pengar*) come (be paid) in; (*publiceras*) appear, be inserted
inflyt|ande *s6* (*inverkan*) influence (*på ngn* with s.b.); (*om sak*) impact, effect, power; *göra sitt* ~ *gällande* make one's influence felt, use one's influence; *röna* ~ *av* be influenced by; *öva* ~ *på* exert influence on **-elserik** influential
inflytt|a (*invandra*) immigrate (*i* into) **-ning** moving in, taking possession; (*immigration*) immigration **-ningsklar** ready for occupation
in|fläta *se* fläta II **-flöde** influx, inflow (*i* into)
in|fo (*kortform för information*) *vard.* info **-foga** fit in; insert (*bildl.*) **-fordra** (*anmoda*) demand; *i sht hand.* solicit, request; (*återkräva*) demand back; (*lån*) call in; ~ *anbud* invite tenders (*på* for)
informa|nt [-å-] informant **-'tik** informatics (*pl, behandlas som sg*) **-tion** information; (*underrättelse*) intelligence; *mil.* briefing
informations|behandling data processing **-möte** meeting to give information **-sekreterare** information officer **-teori** data processing theory
informa't|iv *a5* informative **-or** *s3* [private] tutor **-ör** person who gives information, informant; (*angivare*) informer
infor'm|ell *a5* informal **-era** inform (*om* of); *mil.* brief; *hålla ngn* ~*d* keep s.b. posted
infra|grill infrared grill **-lampa** infrared lamp **-ljud** infra sound **-röd** infrared; ~ *strålning* infrared radiation **-struktur** infrastructure **-värme** infrared heating
in|fria 1 redeem; (*förbindelse äv.*) meet; (*skuld äv.*) discharge **2** (*uppfylla*) redeem, fulfil (*ett löfte* a promise) **-frusen** frozen in; *bildl.* frozen; ~ *i isen* icebound; *-frusna tillgodohavanden* frozen assets **-frysning** freezing; (*av matvaror äv.*) refrigeration
infusion infusion
infusionsdjur ciliate, infusorian
infånga catch; (*rymling o.d. äv.*) capture

infäll|a *tekn.* let into; *sömn.* insert; *boktr.* inset **-bar** *a5* retractable, retractile **-ning** letting into; *konkr.* inlay; *sömn.* insertion, inset
in|född native; *en* ~ *stockholmare* a native of Stockholm **-föding** native
inför ['inn-] **1** *rumsbet.* before; (*i närvaro av*) in the presence of; ~ *domstol* in court; *finna nåd* ~ *ngn* find favour with s.b.; *ställas* ~ *problem* be brought face to face (confronted) with problems **2** *tidsbet.* (*nära*) on the eve of; (*friare*) at (*underrättelsen om* the news of); ~ *julen* with Christmas [near] at hand
inför|a *se föra* [*in*]; (*importera*) import; (*friare o. bildl.*) introduce; (*annons*) insert; ~ *förbud för* lay embargo on, prohibit **-ing** introduction; (*i protokoll e.d.*) entry, entering; (*av annons*) insertion
införliv|a incorporate (*med* with, in[to]); ~ *en bok med sina samlingar* add a book to one's collection **-ande** *s6* incorporation
införsel *s2* **1** *se import o. sms.* **2** ~ *i lön* attachment of wages (*etc.*)
inför|skaffa procure (*upplysningar om* particulars about) **-stådd** *a5*, *vara* ~ *med* agree with, be in agreement with
inga [ˣiŋa] *se ingen* **-lunda** by no means; not at all
inge [ˣinje:] **1** (*inlämna*) send (hand) in **2** *bildl.* inspire (*ngn respekt* s.b. with respect)
ingefära [ˣiŋe-] *s1* ginger
ingefärs|dricka ginger ale; (*alkoholhaltig*) ginger beer **-päron** *pl* pear ginger (*sg*)
ingen [ˣiŋen] **1** *fören.* no (*lätt sak* easy matter); ~ *människa* (*vanl.*) nobody, (*starkare*) not a soul; *det var* ~ *dum ide!* that's not a bad idea! **2** *självst.* nobody, no one, none; ~ (*inga*) *av dem* none of them; *inga* none; ~ *alls* nobody (no one) at all, not a single person; ~ *mindre än* no less [a person] than; *nästan* ~ hardly any (*etc.*) **-dera** neither [of them (the two)]
ingenium [in'je:-] *s4* understanding; brains (*pl*); (*snille*) genius; wit
ingenjör [inʃen'jö:r] engineer
ingenjörs|firma engineering firm **-kår** *mil.* corps of engineers **-trupper** *pl* engineers, sappers; ~*na* (*i Storbritannien*) the Royal Engineers **-vetenskap** [science of] engineering **-vetenskapsakademi** *I~en* [the Swedish] Academy of Engineering Sciences
ingenmansland no-man's-land
ingen|stans, -städes nowhere; *AE. vard.* no place
ingenting nothing; *nästan* ~ hardly anything, next to nothing; *det blir* ~ *av med det!* that's off!, *vard.* there's nothing doing!; *det gör* ~ it does not matter; *det säger jag* ~ *om!* I have nothing to say to that!
ingeny [änʃe'ny:] *s3* ingénue
in|gift *a4*, *bli* ~ *i* marry into **-gifte** intermarriage
ingiv|a *se inge* **-else** inspiration; (*impuls*) idea, impulse; *stundens* ~ the spur of the moment
in|gjuta *bildl.* infuse (*nytt mod hos ngn* fresh courage into s.b.) **-gravera** engrave
ingredi'ens [ing-] *s3* ingredient; component
ingrepp 1 *kir.* [surgical] operation **2** *bildl.* interference; (*intrång*) encroachment, infringement **3** *tekn.* engagement; (*av kuggar*) mesh,

meshing
in'gress *s3* preamble, introduction
ingrip|a *bildl.* intervene; *(hjälpande)* step in, come to the rescue; *(göra intrång)* interfere **-ande I** *s6* intervening *etc.*; intervention; interference **II** *a4* far-reaching; radical, thorough; ~ *förändringar* radical changes
ingrodd *a5* **1** ingrained *(smuts* dirt) **2** *(inrotad)* inveterate *(ovana* bad habit); deep-rooted *(misstro* suspicion)
ingå 1 ~ *i den eviga vilan* enter into the everlasting peace **2** *(om tid)* set in, come, begin; *dagen ingick strålande klar* the day dawned radiantly clear **3** *(inkomma)* arrive; *(om underrättelse)* come to hand; *(om pengar)* come in **4** *(inlåta sig)* enter *(på* into); *(utgöra del)* be (become) [an integral] part *(i* of); *(medräknas)* be included; ~ *i allmänna medvetandet* become part of the public consciousness; *det ~r i hans skyldigheter* it is part (one) of his duties **5** *(avtal, förbund e.d.)* enter into; ~ *fördrag* conclude (make) a treaty; ~ *förlikning* come to terms, arrive at a compromise; ~ *ett vad* make a bet (wager); ~ *äktenskap* [*med*] marry
ingående I *a4* **1** *(ankommande)* arriving; *(om brev o.d.)* incoming; ~ *balans* balance brought forward **2** *(grundlig)* thorough, close *(granskning* scrutiny); ~ *kännedom om* intimate knowledge of; ~ *redogörelse för* detailed report of **II** *adv* thoroughly *etc.*; *diskutera* ~ discuss in detail; ~ *redogöra för* give a full and detailed account of **III** *s6* **1** *fartyget är på* ~ the vessel is inward bound **2** *(av fred o.d.)* conclusion; *(av äktenskap)* contraction
ingång 1 entrance; *(port* door, gate; *förbjuden* ~! No Admittance! **2** *(början)* commencement, beginning; *(gryning)* dawn
ingångs|psalm opening hymn **-värde** initial (opening) value
inhal|ation inhalation **-ator** *s3* inhalator **-era** inhale
in|handla buy **-hav** inland sea
inhemsk *a5* **1** *(motsats utländsk)* home, domestic; *äv.* English, Swedish *(etc.)* **2** *biol.* indigenous, native
inhiber|a inhibit; cancel, call off **-ing** inhibition; cancellation
inhopp *bildl.* sudden initiative
inhu'man inhuman
in|hysa house; accommodate; *vara -hyst hos ngn (om sak)* be stored at a p.'s house **-hyseshjon** dependent tenant **-hägna** [-häŋna] enclose; ~ *med plank (staket)* board (fence) in **-hägnad** [-häŋnad] *s3* *(område)* enclosure; *(fålla)* fold, pen; *(staket)* fence
inhämta 1 *(skaffa sig)* gather, pick up; procure, secure; *(lära sig)* learn; ~ *kunskaper* acquire knowledge; ~ *ngns råd* ask a p.'s advice, consult s.b.; ~ *upplysningar* obtain information, make inquiries **2** *(nå fatt)* catch up; ~ *ett försprång* gain on, reduce a lead
inhöst|a *bildl.* reap; *(poäng)* score **-ande** *s6* harvesting; scoring
ini *se inuti, inne i* **-från I** *adv* from within; from [the] inside **II** *prep* from the interior of; from inside (within)
initi'al [-tsi-] *s3* initial **-kostnad** initial cost

-ord initialism **-skede** initial phase **-svårigheter** initial difficulties, teething troubles
initia'tiv [-tsia-] *s7* initiative; *på eget* ~ on one's own initiative; *ta* ~ *till ngt* take the initiative in doing s.th. **-förmåga** power of initiative **-rik** full of initiative, enterprising **-rikedom** abundance of initiative **-tagare** initiator, originator, promoter *(till* of)
initier|a [-tsi-] initiate **-ad** *a5* initiated *(i* into); well-informed *(i* on); *i ~e kretsar* in well-informed circles
injaga ~ *respekt hos ngn* command respect in s.b.; ~ *skräck hos ngn* strike terror into (intimidate) s.b.
injek|tera inject **-tion** [-k'ʃɷ:n] injection; *vard.* shot
injektions|nål [hypodermic] needle **-spruta** hypodermic syringe; *vard.* needle
injic[i]era inject
injustering adjustment
inka *-n -s* Inca **-folket** the Incas
inkall|a call in; *(möte e.d.)* summon *(äv. jur.)*, convoke, convene; *mil.* call up, AE. draft *(t. militärtjänst* for military service); *en ~d (mil.)* a conscript, AE. a draftee **-ande** *s6* calling in; summoning, convocation, convening
inkallelse summons; *mil.* call-up, AE. draft [call] **-order** calling-up papers (order), AE. induction papers
inkapabel [-'pa:-] incapable
inkapsl|a enclose, encase **-ing** enclosure; encapsulation
inkariket the Inca Empire
inkarn|ation incarnation **-era** incarnate **-erad** [-'e:-] *a5* incarnate
inkasser|a collect, recover; *bildl.* receive **-ing** collector **-ing** *se inkasso*
inkasso [-'kassɷ] *s6* collection [of debts], collecting, recovery **-avgift** collecting (collection) fee **-byrå** debt-collecting agency (firm) **-uppdrag** collection (encashment) order
in|kast 1 *sport.* throw-in **2** *(invändning)* objection, observation **-kilad** [-çi:-] *a5* wedged *(i* into; *mellan* in between)
inklarer|a *(fartyg)* clear (enter) inwards **-ing** clearance (entry) inwards
inklin|ation inclination; *(om magnetnål äv.)* dip **-era** incline; dip
inklu|dera include **-sive** [-'si:-] included; including, inclusive of
inklämd *a5* squeezed (jammed) in; *med.* strangulated
inkognito [-'kåŋni-] *adv o. s6* incognito, *fem.* incognita
inkokning preserving; bottling; canning; *jfr koka* [*in*] **inkokt** *a4* preserved *etc.*; *(i socker)* candied; ~ *fisk* poached fish
inkomm|a ~ *med (anbud, redogörelse etc.)* hand in, submit; ~ *med klagomål* lodge complaints **-ande** *a4* incoming
inkommendera call up
inkommensurab|el [-'a:bel] *-la storheter* incommensurable quantities
inkompatib|el [-'ti:-] incompatible **-ilitet** incompatibility
inkompet|ens incompetence; incapacity; disability **-ent** incompetent; *(om platssökande)*

unqualified
inkomplett incomplete
inkomst [-å-] *s3* income; earnings (*pl*) (*av, på* from); (*stats-*) revenue[s *pl*]; (*avkastning*) yield, proceeds (*pl*); ~ *av arbete* earned income; ~ *av kapital* unearned income; *fast* ~ settled income; *-er och utgifter* income and expenditure; *ha goda -er* have a good income; *hur stora -er har han?* what is his income?
inkomst|baserad earnings-related **-beskattning** income taxation **-bortfall** loss of income; income shortfall **-bringande** [-briŋ-] *a4* profitable, remunerative, rewarding **-fördelning** distribution of income **-klass** income bracket **-källa** source of income **-läge** income bracket **-politik** incomes policy **-prövning** means test **-sida** *på ~n* on the income (credit) side **-skatt** income tax **-tagare** wage earner **-år** income year
inkongru|ens incongruity **-ent** incongruous; *geom. äv.* incongruent
inkonsekv|ens inconsistency **-ent** inconsistent
inkontin|ens *s3* incontinence **-ent** *a4* incontinent
inkonvertibel [-'i:bel] *a5* inconvertible
inkoppl|a 1 couple, connect; *elektr.* switch in (on), turn on **2** inform, advice, get in touch with; *polisen är ~d* the police have been called in **-ing** coupling, connection; *elektr.* switching in (on), turning on
inkorporer|a [-'e:ra *el.* ˣinn-] incorporate (*i, med* in[to]) **-ing** incorporation
in|kor'rekt *a1* incorrect **-krupen** *a5, sitta ~ i* sit huddled-up in **-kråm** *s7* **1** (*av bröd*) crumb **2** (*av fågel o.d.*) entrails (*pl*)
inkräkt|a encroach, trespass, intrude (*på* on, upon) **-are** trespasser, intruder; (*i ett land*) invader
inkrökt [-ö:-] *a4, bildl.* egotistic[al], egocentric
inkubationstid incubation period
inkunabel [-'na:-] *s3* incunabulum (*pl* incunabula)
inku'rant *a1* unsaleable, unmarketable
inkvarter|a *mil.* billet, quarter (*hos* on); (*friare*) accommodate **-ing 1** billeting; accommodation **2** (*plats*) quarters (*pl*), billet
inkvisi|tion *-en* the Inquisition **-tionsdomstol** court of inquisition; *-en* the Court of the Inquisition **-tor** [-ˣi:tår] *s3* inquisitor **-torisk** [-'tɷ:-] *a5* inquisitorial
inköp purchase; *göra ~* (*i butik*) do shopping, shop; *den kostar ... i ~* the cost price is ...
inköp|a buy, purchase **-are** buyer, purchaser
inköps|anmälan notification of purchase **-avdelning** buying department **-chef** chief (head) buyer **-lista** shopping list **-pris** cost price
inkör|d [-çö:-] *a5* (*om bil*) run-in; (*om häst*) broken[-in]; *~a fraser* well-drilled phrases **-ning** (*av hö e.d.*) bringing in; (*av motor*) running-in; *bilen är under ~* the car is being run (driven) in
inkörsport entrance [gate]; *bildl.* gateway
in|laga *s1* **1** (*skrift*) petition, address, memorial **2** (*i cigarr e.d.*) filler **3** (*boks inre*) body **-lagd** *a5* **1** (*i ättika*) pickled; (*i olja*) put down; (*i flaska*) bottled; (*i bleckburk*) tinned, canned **2** *-lagt arbete* inlaid work, inlay **-lagring** *geol.*

inclusion **-land** interior, inland parts (*pl*); *i in-och utlandet* at home and abroad
inlands|is inland ice **-klimat** inland climate
inlast|a *sjö.* ship; *järnv.* load **-ning** shipping; loading
inleda *v2* **1** (*förbindelser, förhandlingar, möte, samtal*) open, enter into (upon); (*diskussion e.d.*) introduce, begin, start off; (*undersökning e.d.*) initiate, set on foot, institute; usher in, initiate (*en ny epok* a new epoch); ~ *en offensiv* launch an offensive **2** (*locka*) lead (*i frestelse* into temptation)
inled|ande *a4* introductory, opening (*anförande* address); (*förberedande*) preparatory, preliminary **-are** opening (first) speaker **-ning** introduction; (*friare*) opening, beginning
inlednings|anförande introductory address, opening speech **-skede** initial stage **-vis** by way of introduction; to start (begin) with
inlemma incorporate
inlevelse feeling insight, vivid realization (*i* of) **-förmåga** ability to enter into
in|leverera deliver, hand in (over) **-lopp 1** (*infartsled*) entrance, [sea] approach **2** (*inflöde*) inflow, inlet **3** *tekn.* inlet, intake
inlån borrowing; (*av ord äv.*) adoption **-ing** borrowing; (*i bank*) [bank] deposits (*pl*), receiving on deposit; *affärsbankernas ~* the deposits of the commercial banks **-ingsränta** interest on deposit[s *pl*]; deposit rate
in|låta *rfl*, ~ *sig i* (*på*) enter into; ~ *sig i strid* engage (get involved) in a fight; ~ *sig med ngn* have dealings (take up) with s.b. **-lägg** *s7* **1** (*ngt inlagt*) inlay, inset; (*bilaga*) enclosure, insert; (*i sko*) insertion; *sömn.* tuck **2** (*i diskussion*) contribution (*i* to)
inlägg|a 1 *se lägga* [*in*] **2** *bildl.* put in (*ett gott ord för* a word for); (*införa*) insert (*i* in); *jur.* enter, lodge; ~ *känsla i* put feeling into **3** *konst. o.d.* inlay **-ning 1** *abstr.* putting in; insertion; (*av grönsaker e.d.*) bottling, preserving, tinning, AE. canning; *konst.* inlaying **2** *konkr.* bottled (tinned) fruit (*etc.*); *konst.* inlay
inläggssula insole, inner sole
inlämn|a hand (send) in; (*deponera*) leave, deposit; ~ *ansökan* make (lodge, hand in) an application **-ning 1** handing (sending) in; (*deponering*) leaving, depositing **2** (*inlämningsställe*) cloakroom **-ningskvitto** *post.* certificate of posting; (*för postanvisning*) certificate of issue; *järnv.* cloakroom receipt (ticket, check)
in|ländsk *a5* internal, domestic, home **-länka** insert
inlär|a learn; (*lära andra*) teach, instruct **-ning** learning; (*utantill*) memorizing; instruction
inlärnings|förmåga learning capacity **-kurva** learning curve **-maskin** teaching machine **-psykologi** psychology of learning **-studio** learning laboratory
inlöpa 1 *sjö.* put in; ~ *i hamn* put into (enter) port **2** (*om underrättelse o.d.*) come in (to hand), arrive
inlös|a (*betala*) pay; (*check e.d.*) cash; (*växel*) honour, take up; (*fastighet*) buy [in]; (*pant*) redeem **-en** *oböjligt s*, **-ning** *s2* payment; cashing; honouring, taking up; (*av lån, pant e.d.*)

redemption; (*av sedlar*) withdrawal

in|malning mixing [of certain percentage] of home-grown with foreign grain in flour-milling **-marsch** march in, entry

inmat|a *tekn.* feed **-ning** *tekn.* feeding (*i* into); *data.* input

in|montera install, set up, put in **-mundiga** consume, eat, partake of

inmur|a (*i vägg e.d.*) wall (bond) in; (*inspärra*) immure (*i* in) **-ning** walling in *etc.*

inmut|a take out a mining concession for, [put in a] claim **-ning** *konkr.* mining concession (claim)

innan I *konj o.* prep before II *adv* 1 *utan och ~* inside and out[side]; *känna ngn utan och ~* know s.b. thoroughly (inside out) 2 *tidsbet.* before; *dagen ~* the day before **-döme** *s6* inside, interior; *jordens ~* the bowels (*pl*) of the earth **-fönster** inner window **-för** I *prep* inside, within; (*bakom*) behind II *adv, den ~ belägna...* the...within (on the inside) **-hav** *se inhav* **-lår** *kokk.* (*av oxe o.d.*) thick flank; (*av kalv*) fillet **-läsning** reading [aloud] **-mäte** *s6* (*av djur*) entrails (*pl*), guts (*pl*), bowels (*pl*); (*av frukt e.d.*) pulp **-till** *läsa ~* read from the book (*etc.*)

in natura [-ˣtu:-] in kind

inne 1 (*motsats ute*) inside; (*motsats utomhus*) indoors, in the house; (*hemma*) in 2 (*på lager*) in stock, on hand; (*i kassan*) in hand; *sport., kortsp.* in play; (*hemmastadd*) up, at home (*i* in); *vara ~ (insatt) i* be familiar with, be well versed in 3 *tiden är ~ att* the time has come to 4 (*på modet*) trendy, in

inne|bana *se inomhusbana* **-boende** 1 *oböjligt s, alla i huset ~* all the people living in the house; *en ~* a lodger, *AE. äv.* a roomer; *vara ~ hos* lodge (live) with s.b. 2 *a4, bildl.* inherent (*anlag* talent); intrinsic (*värde* value) **-bruk** *för ~* for indoor use **-bränd** *a5, bli ~* be burnt to death in a house (*etc.*) **-bära** imply, mean, denote; (*föra med sig*) involve **-börd** signification, meaning; implication; *av [den] ~en att* to the effect that; *av följande ~* of the following purport **-fatta** (*inbegripa*) include, comprise; (*omfatta*) embrace; (*bestå av*) consist of **-ha** (*äga*) be in possession of, have in one's possession; (*aktier, ämbete, titel*) hold

inne|hav *s7* possession; *konkr.* holding (*av guld* of gold) **-havare** possessor; owner; (*av firma e.d.*) proprietor; (*av värdepapper, ämbete*) holder; (*av prästämbete*) incumbent; *~ av ett patent* patent owner (holder), patentee **-havarpapper** bearer bond

inne|håll *s7* contents (*pl*); *geom., filos. o.d.* content; (*ordalydelse äv.*) tenor; (*kontrakts o.d. äv.*) terms **-hålla** 1 contain; (*rymma äv.*) hold; (*om tidning äv.*) carry 2 (*ej utbetala*) withhold, keep back, retain

innehålls|deklaration declaration of contents **-förteckning** table of contents, index **-lös** empty, inane **-mässigt** as regards contents; *AE.* contents-wise **-rik** containing a great deal; (*omfattande*) comprehensive; *en ~ dag* an eventful day; *ett ~t liv* a full life, a life rich in experience

inneliggande *a4* (*på lager*) in hand; (*bifogad*) enclosed; *~ beställningar* orders on hand; *~ varulager* (*äv.*) stock in trade

inner ['inn-] *-n inrar, sport.* inside forward **-bana** inside track **-belysning** (*i bil*) courtesy light **-dörr** inner door **-ficka** inside (inner) pocket **-fil** inside lane **-kurva** inside curve

inner|lig *a1* (*djupt känd*) ardent (*kärlek* love), fervent (*önskningar* desires); intimate (*vänskap* friendship); (*hjärtlig*) heartfelt; (*uppriktig*) sincere; *min ~aste önskan* (*äv.*) my dearest wish; *dikten har en ~ ton* the poem has a warm sincerity **-ligen**, **-ligt** ardently *etc.*; (*friare*) heartily, utterly (*trött på* tired of)

inner|sida inner side; (*handens äv.*) palm **-skär** *sport., åka ~* do the inside edge **-slang** inner tube

inner|st ['inn-] *adv, ~ [inne]* farthest (furthest) in; *~ inne* (*bildl.*) at heart **-sta** I *a, best. form superl.* innermost, inmost (*tankar* thoughts), (*friare*) deepest II *n, i sitt ~* in one's heart [of hearts]

inner|stad city (town) centre; *AE.* downtown **-tak** ceiling

innerv|ation innervation **-era** innerve

inner|vägg interior (inside) wall; (*mellanvägg*) partition [wall] **-öra** internal (inner) ear, labyrinth

innesko indoor shoe

inneslut|a enclose; (*omge*) encompass, encircle, shut in; (*innefatta*) include **-ning** kärntekn. containment

inne|stående *a4* (*outtagen*) still due; (*i bank*) deposited, on deposit; *~ fordringar* claims remaining to be drawn; *~ lön* salary (wages) due **-ställe** in-place **-varande** *a4* present; *~ år* this year; *den 6:e ~ månad* on the 6th inst. (of this month) **-vånare** *se invånare*

innov|ation innovation **-atör** innovator **-era** innovate

in|nästla *rfl* insinuate (wheedle) o.s. (*hos* into the confidence of) **-nöta** drum in

inoffici|ell unofficial; informal

inokulera inoculate

inom [ˣinnåm] *prep* 1 *rumsbet.* within; (*inuti*) in; *~ sig* inwardly, in one's heart (mind); *vara ~ synhåll* keep within sight; *~ sitt område är han* in his speciality (field) he is; *styrelsen utser ~ sig* the directors elect from among their number 2 (*om rörelse*) within, into; *komma ~ hörhåll* get within hearing 3 *tidsbet.* within; (*om*) in (*ett ögonblick* a moment); *~ kort* shortly, before long; *~ loppet av* [with]in the course of; *~ den närmaste tiden* in the immediate future; *~ mindre än en timme* in less than an hour

inombordare [-ɷ:r-] boat with inboard motor

inombords [-ɷ:r-] *sjö.* (*ombord*) on board, aboard; *bildl.* (*invärtes*) inside; *han har mycket ~* he has got a lot in him **-motor** inboard motor

inomeuropeisk intra-European

inomhus indoors **-antenn** indoor aerial (antenna) **-bana** *sport.* covered (indoor) court; (*ishockey-*) indoor rink **-sport** indoor sports

inom|skärs [-ʃä:rs] in the skerries, inside the belt of skerries (islands) **-statlig** intrastate **-äktenskaplig** marital, matrimonial

inoppor'tun *a5* inopportune

in|ordna range, arrange, adapt; ~ *i ett system* arrange according to a system, systematize; ~ *sig under* conform to **-packning 1** packing [up], wrapping **2** *med.* pack **-pass** *s7* interjection, remark; observation **-passa 1** fit in (into), adapt **2** (*inflicka*) put in

inpisk|ad *a5* thoroughpaced, out-and-out; *en ~ lögnare* a consummate liar; *en ~ skojare* an out-and-out rogue **-are** whip **-ning** whipping up

inplacer|a place **-ing** placing

in|planera schedule, plan the organization of **-planta** implant

inplanter|a **1** (*i krukor*) transplant **2** (*från annat land e.d.*) naturalize **-ing** (*av växter*) transplanting; (*av fiskyngel äv.*) introduction, putting out; (*av skog*) afforestation

inpricka dot, plot

inprägl|la engrave (*ngt i sitt minne* s.th. on one's mind); impress (*i* on) **-ing** engraving *etc.*

in|pränta impress (*hos* on); bring home (*hos* to); *få ngt ~t i sig* have s.th. drummed into one **-pyrd** [-y:-] *a5* reeking, stuffy, choked; *bildl.* impregnated, steeped in

inpå I [*inn el. 'inn-] prep **1** *våt ~ bara kroppen* wet to the [very] skin; *för nära ~ varandra* too close to one another (together) **2** *till långt ~ natten* until far into the night II [-'på:] *adv, för nära ~* too close [to it, him *etc.*]

inram|a frame **-ning** framing; *konkr.* frame, framework; (*friare*) setting

in|rangera *se inordna* **-rapportera** report; (*friare*) give a report of

inre ['inn-] I *a, komp.* **1** inner; interior; internal; (*inom familj, hus, land äv.*) domestic, home; *~ angelägenheter* domestic (home) affairs; *~ diameter* inside (inner, internal) diameter; *~ energi* internal energy; *~ mission* home mission; *~ organ* internal organ; *~ oroligheter* civil (internal) disturbances; *~ säkerhet* public safety **2** *bildl.* intrinsic (*värde* value); essential (*sanning* truth); innate (*egenskap* quality); (*andlig*) inner (*liv* life); *~ öga* inward eye II *n* (*saks*) interior; inside; (*ngns*) inner man; *i sitt ~* inwardly, deep down; *det ~ av landet* the inland (upcountry); *hela mitt ~ är upprört över* my whole soul (being) is revolted at

inred|a fit up, equip (*till* as); (*med möbler*) furnish **-ning 1** fitting up *etc.*; equipment **2** *konkr.* fittings (*pl*), appointments (*pl*); interior decoration **-ningsarkitekt** interior decorator (designer)

inregistrer|a register; enter; *hand.* file, docket; (*friare*) score (*en framgång* a success) **-ing** registering *etc.*; registration; enrolment

inresa *s1* journey up (*till staden* [in]to town); (*t. annat land*) entry, arrival

inresekretorisk internal-secretion

inrese|tillstånd entry permit **-visum** entry visa

inrid|en *a5* broken[-in], broken to the saddle **-ning** breaking[-in]; horse-breaking

inrikes I *adv* [with]in the country II *oböjligt a* inland (*porto* postage); home (*angelägenheter* affairs); domestic, internal **-departement** ministry of the interior; (*i Storbritannien ung.*) Home Office; *AE. ung.* department of the interior **-flyg** domestic (inland) aviation; domes-

tic airlines **-handel** domestic (home) trade **-minister** minister of the interior; (*i Storbritannien ung.*) Home Secretary; *AE. ung.* secretary of the interior **-nyheter** *pl* home news (*sg*) **-politik** domestic policy; ~[*en*] home (internal) politics **-politisk** [of] domestic [policy] **-porto** inland postage

inrikt|a put in position, adjust; (*vapen*) aim (*mot* at); *bildl.* direct (*mot, på* towards, *fientligt* against); ~ *sig på* direct one's energies towards, concentrate upon, (*sikta på*) aim at **-ning** putting in position, adjusting; (*av vapen*) aiming; *bildl.* [aim and] direction, concentration

in|rim assonance **-ringa** encircle, surround; *bildl. äv.* close (hedge) in **-ringning** encircling *etc.* **-rista** engrave; carve, cut **-ristning** engraving *etc.* **-rop** (*på auktion*) bid; *konkr.* [auction] purchase **-ropa 1** *teat., bli ~d* be called before the curtain **2** (*på auktion*) buy [at an (the) auction] **-ropning** [-ⱺ:-] curtain call **-rotad** *a5, bildl.* deep-rooted, deep-seated, inveterate, ingrained **-rusning** rushing in; inrush **-ruta** chequer [out], divide up into squares **-rutad** *a5, bildl.* regular, dictated by routine **-rutning** [-u:-] chequering *etc.* **-ryckning 1** *mil.* reporting for active service **2** *boktr.* indentation, inden[tion] **-rymma 1** (*rymma*) accommodate; (*innehålla*) contain; (*innefatta*) include **2** (*bevilja*) accord, grant

inrådan *r, på* (*mot*) *min* ~ on (contrary to) my advice (recommendation)

inrätt|a **1** (*anlägga*) establish, set up; (*skola e.d.*) found; (*ämbete*) create; (*inreda*) equip **2** (*ordna*) arrange **3** *rfl* settle down (*bekvämt* comfortably); (*rätta sig*) adapt (accommodate) o.s. (*efter* to) **-ning 1** (*anstalt*) establishment; (*allmän, social äv.*) institution **2** (*anordning*) device, appliance, apparatus

insalta salt [down], cure; (*gurkor, sill*) pickle

insaml|a collect, gather **-ing** collection; (*av pengar äv.*) subscription; *starta en* ~ start (get up) a subscription (*för* for, in aid of)

insamlings|aktion fundraising (collection) drive **-lista** subscription list

insats **1** *tekn.* lining, inset **2** (*i spel, företag o.d.*) stake[s *pl*]; (*i affär*) deposit; (*i bolag*) investment **3** (*prestation*) achievement, effort; (*bidrag*) contribution (*i* to; *för* towards); (*andel*) share, part; *göra en* ~ make a contribution (an effort) **-lägenhet** owner (freehold) flat; *AE.* cooperative apartment

in|satt *a4,* ~ *i* initiated in, well-informed on, familiar with **-scenera** stage **-se** see, perceive; (*förstå*) realize; (*vara medveten om*) be aware of **-seende** *s6, ha* ~ *över* supervise, superintend **-segel** seal

insegl|ing *under* ~ *till* inward bound for; *under* ~*en till Stockholm* while sailing into Stockholm **-ingsränna** [navigable] channel, waterway

insekt *s3* insect; *AE. äv.* bug

insekti'cid *s3* insecticide

insekt|[s]|art species of insect **-bett** insect bite **-forskare** entomologist **-larv** larva (*pl* larvae) **-medel** insect repellent; insecticide **-samling** entomological collection **-ätare** insect eater,

insectivore
insemin|ation insemination **-era** inseminate
insida inside; inner side; (*hands äv.*) palm; (*friare o. bildl.*) interior
insignier [-'siɲi-] *pl* insignia
insikt *s3* **1** (*förståelse*) understanding (*i* of); (*inblick*) insight (*i* into); (*kännedom*) knowledge (*i, om* of); *komma till ~ om* realize, see, become aware of **2** (*kunskap*) *~er* knowledge (*sg*); *~er och färdigheter* knowledge and practical attainments
insiktsfull well-informed; (*sakkunnig*) competent
insinu|ant [-'ant *el.* -'aŋt] *al* insinuating **-ation** insinuation **-era** insinuate
insistera insist (*på* on)
insjukna [-ʃu:-] fall (be taken) ill (*i* with); *hon har ~t i mässlingen* she has caught the measles
insjung|en [-ʃuŋ-] *a5* (*på grammofon, band*) recorded **-ning** recording
insjö lake **-fisk** freshwater fish
inskepp|a (*varor*) import by ship, ship; (*pers., hästar e.d.*) embark; *~ sig* go on board, embark (*på* on; *till* for) **-ning** (*av varor*) importing by ship; (*av pers. etc.*) embarkation **-ningshamn** (*för varor*) port of shipment; (*för pers. etc.*) port of embarkation
in|skjuta 1 *se inflicka* **2** (*föra*) insert, interpolate **-skolningsperiod** period of adjustment to school **-skott** insertion
in|skrida intervene, step in (*mot* to prevent; *t. förmån för* on behalf of) **-skridande** *s6* intervention, stepping in **-skrift** inscription; (*på grav*) epitaph; (*på mynt*) legend, inscription **-skription** [-p'ʃɔ:n] inscription; legend
inskriv|a 1 enter; *geom. o. bildl.* inscribe; (*pers.*) enrol (*äv. mil.*); *mil.* enlist; *jur.* register **2** *rfl*, [*låta*] *~ sig* enter one's name, enrol o.s.; *univ.* register **-ning** entering *etc.*, entry; inscription; enrolment; enlistment; registration
inskrivnings|avgift admission fee **-bok** *mil.* enrolment book **-domare** *ung.* court registrar **-område** registration area
inskränk|a *v3* (*begränsa*) restrict, confine; limit; (*minska*) reduce, cut down, curtail; *~ sig* restrict o.s., economize, cut down one's expenses; *~ sig till* confine o.s. to, (*om sak*) be confined (restricted) to, (*ej överstiga*) not exceed **-ning** restriction; limitation; reduction; curtailment; (*förbehåll*) qualification
inskränkt *al* **1** restricted *etc.*; *i ~ bemärkelse* in a restricted (limited) sense; *~ monarki* constitutional (limited) monarchy **2** (*trångsynt*) stupid; narrow-minded **-het** (*trångsynthet*) stupidity; narrowness of outlook
inskärning *konkr.* incision; cut, notch; (*i kust o.d. samt bot.*) indentation
inskärp|a inculcate (*hos* in); (*klargöra*) bring home (*hos* to); (*med eftertryck*) enforce, enjoin, impress (*hos* upon) **-ning** inculcating *etc.*, inculcation
inslag 1 (*i väv*) weft, filling, woof **2** *bildl.* element; feature; streak (*av humor* of humour), strain (*av grymhet* of cruelty) **-en** *a5* (*om paket*) wrapped up; (*om fönster*) smashed, broken **-ning** (*av paket*) wrapping up; (*av fönster*) smashing, breaking; (*av spik*) knocking (driv-

ing) in
inslagsgarn weft thread (yarn)
insmickr|a *rfl* ingratiate o.s. (*hos* with) **-ande** *a4* ingratiating
in|smord smeared **-smuggla** smuggle [into] **-smyga** *rfl* (*om fel e.d.*) creep (slip) in [unnoticed] **-smörjning** greasing [up], oiling **-snärja** entangle; *~ sig* get [o.s.] entangled **-snöad** *a5* **1** *bli ~* get (be) snowed up, (*blockeras*) get (be) held up by snow **2** *bildl., vard.* narrow-minded
insolv|ens insolvency **-ent** insolvent
insomn|a go off to sleep; fall asleep; (*avlida*) pass away, die; *djupt ~d* fast asleep **-ande** *s6* going off to sleep
insorter|a sort, assort **-ing** sorting, assortment
inspark *sport.* goal kick
in spe future, to be
inspek|tera inspect **-tion** [-k'ʃɔ:n] inspection **-tionsresa** tour of inspection **-tor** *s3* **1** [-*spektår] inspector (*för, över* of); (*för skola o. univ.*) inspector **2** [-'tɔ:r] *lantbr.* steward; bailiff **-tris** inspectress, woman inspector **-tör** inspector; surveyor, superintendent, supervisor
inspel|a (*på band, skiva*) record; (*film*) produce, shoot; *~t program* recorded programme **-ning** recording; (*grammofon- äv.*) record; (*film-*) production; *filmen är under ~* the film is being shot (is in production)
inspelnings|apparat recorder **-bil, -buss** outside broadcast car (unit)
inspicient *teat.* stage manager; *film.* studio manager
inspir|ation inspiration **-ationskälla** source of inspiration **-atör** inspirer **-era** inspire; *~d* inspired; *~nde* inspiring
insprut|a inject (*i* into) **-ning** injection **-ningsmotor** fuel-injection motor
insprängd *a5* **1** blasted (*i berget* into the mountain) **2** (*inblandad*) disseminated; interspersed, intermixed
inspärr|a shut up: *pers. äv.* lock up **-ning** shutting up *etc.*; confinement, imprisonment
insta'bil unstable **-itet** instability
installation installation; *univ.* inauguration; (*av präst*) induction; (*av biskop*) enthronement
installations|firma electrical fitters (*pl*); (*för värme o. sanitet*) sanitary engineers (*pl*) **-fö-reläsning** inaugural (inauguration) lecture
install|atör electrician; installation engineer **-era 1** install: *univ. äv.* inaugurate; (*präst*) induct; (*biskop*) enthrone **2** *tekn.* install, fit [in], set up, mount **3** *rfl* install (establish, settle) o.s.
instans [-'ans *el.* -'aŋs] *s3, jur.* instance; (*myndighet*) authority [in charge]; *högsta ~* final (highest) court of appeal; *lägsta ~* court of first instance
insteg *få* (*vinna*) *~* get (obtain, gain) a footing (*i* in; *hos* with); gain ground
instift|a institute (*en orden* an order); *relig. äv.* ordain; (*grunda*) found, establish **-are** founder; institutor **-else** institution; foundation
instinkt [*inn-, *äv.* -'inkt] *s3* instinct **-'iv** [*äv. *inn-] *a5* instinctive **-ivt** [-'i:vt, *äv. *inn-] *adv*, instinctively, by instinct **-mässig** *a5* instinctive; intuitive

insti'tut *s7* institute; institution (*äv. jur.*); (*skola*) school, college
institution institution, institute **-alisera** institutionalize **-'ell** *a5* institutional
instruera instruct; *mil.* brief
instruk|tion [-k'ʃɷːn] instruction; (*föreskrift, äv. konkr*) instructions (*pl*); *mil. äv.* briefing **-tionsbok** instruction book, manual **-'tiv** [*äv.* 'inn-] *a1* instructive **-tör** instructor
instrument *s7* instrument
instrumen'tal *a5* instrumental **-ist** instrumentalist **-musik** instrumental music
instrument|ation instrumentation, orchestration **-bräda, -bräde** *se instrumentpanel*
instrumen't|ell *a5* instrumental **-era** orchestrate, instrument
instrument|flygning instrument flying **-landning** instrument landing **-makare** instrument maker **-panel** instrument panel (board); (*i bil äv.*) dashboard **-tavla** instrument board (panel); switchboard
in|strödd *a5, bildl.* interspersed **-strömmande** *a4* inpouring
instuder|a study; rehearse **-ing** studying *etc.*; rehearsal
instundande *a4* coming, approaching (*måndag* Monday)
inställa 1 (*avpassa*) adjust, set; (*kamera, kikare e.d.*) focus; (*radio, TV*) tune in; (*rikta*) point, direct 2 (*upphöra med*) cancel, call off; (*arbete*) discontinue, cease, stop; (*betalningar*) suspend, stop; ~ *fientligheterna* suspend hostilities, cease fire; ~ *förhandlingarna* discontinue (suspend) negotiations 3 *rfl* (*infinna sig*) appear (*inför rätta* in court); *mil.* report [for duty]; (*vid möte*) put in an appearance, turn up; (*om sak*) make its appearance; (*om känsla*) make itself felt (*hos* in); (*uppenbara sig*) present itself; ~ *sig på* (*bereda sig på*) prepare o.s. for, (*räkna med*) count on
inställ|ande *s6* 1 adjustment *etc.* 2 (*inhibering*) cancellation, discontinuance, suspension **-bar** *a5* adjustable; (*om radio*) tunable
inställd *a5* adjusted *etc.*; *fientligt* ~ inimically disposed; *vara* ~ *på* be prepared for; *vara* ~ *på att* intend to
inställelse *jur.* appearance (*inför* before) **-order** *mil.* calling-up papers (order)
inställ|ning 1 adjustment; setting; (*tids-*) time--setting, timing; *foto. äv.* focusing; *radio.* tuning in 2 *bildl.* attitude (*till* to, towards); outlook (*till* on) **-sam** *a1* ingratiating, cringing **-samhet** ingratiation, obsequiousness
1 instämma *jur.* summon to appear; call (*som vittne* as a witness)
2 instämm|a *bildl.* agree (*i* with), concur (*i* in); ~ *med ngn* agree with s.b.
instämmande *s6* concurrence, agreement
instängd *a5* shut up; (*inlåst*) locked up; confined; (*unken*) stuffy, close **-het** (*unkenhet*) stuffiness; closeness
insubordina|tion insubordination **-tionsbrott** case of insubordination, breach of discipline
insufficiens *s3* insufficiency
insug|a suck in; (*inandas*) inhale; (*friare, om sak*) suck up, absorb, imbibe; *bildl.* drink in (*beröm* praise); (*tillägga sig*) acquire, pick up

-ning sucking in *etc.*; absorption, imbibition; *tekn.* intake, suction
insugnings|rör (*i motor*) inlet pipe **-ventil** inlet valve
insu'lin *s4* insulin **-behandling** insulin treatment **-chock** insulin reaction (shock) **-koma** insulin coma
insu'lär *a5* insular
insupa (*frisk luft e.d.*) drink in, inhale; (*uppsuga*) absorb; *bildl.* imbibe
insurgent insurgent, rebel
insvepa envelop, enwrap; ~ *sig i* wrap o.s. up (*envelop o.s.*) in
insväng|d *a5* curved inwards; ~ *i midjan* shaped at the waist **-ning** curving inwards; *en* ~ an inward curve
in|sydd *a5, vard.* placed behind bars, doing time **-syltad** *a5, bildl.* involved, mixed up **-syn 1** observation; view; *skyddad mot* ~ protected from view 2 *bildl.* insight; public control (*i* of)
insändar|e 1 *pers.* sender[-in]; (*t. tidning*) correspondent 2 (*brev t. tidning*) letter to the editor **-spalt** letters-to-the-editor column
insätta put in; (*inbetala*) pay in; (*i bank*) deposit; (*i företag*) invest; (*förordna*) appoint, install; (*ngn i hans rättigheter*) establish; ~ *ngn som sin arvinge* make s.b. one's heir
insätt|are (*i bank*) depositor **-ning** putting in *etc.*; (*av pengar*) deposition, investment; *konkr.* deposit **-ningskvitto** deposit receipt (ticket)
insöndr|ing endocrine secretion **-ingsorgan** endocrine gland
insöva *bildl., se invagga*
inta *se intaga*
intag *tekn.* intake; *elektr.* lead-in; (*friare*) inlet
intaga 1 take in; (*förtära*) take; (*måltid*) eat, have; (*på sjukhus, i skola etc.*) admit; (*i tidning*) insert, publish 2 (*ta i besittning*) take; occupy (*äv. mil.*); (*upptaga*) take up, occupy; ~ *sin plats* take one's seat; ~ *en avvaktande hållning* take up a wait-and-see attitude; ~ *en framskjuten ställning* hold (occupy) a prominent position 3 (*betaga*) captivate
intag|ande *a4* attractive, charming **-ning** taking in *etc.*; taking; admission; insertion; *mil. äv.* capture
intagnings|nämnd admissions board **-poäng** admission credits
in'takt *a4* intact, whole
intala 1 (*på band o.d.*) record 2 ~ *ngn ngt* put s.th. into a p.'s head; ~ *ngn att göra ngt* persuade s.b. to do (into doing) s.th.; ~ *ngn mod* inspire s.b. with courage; ~ *sig* persuade o.s.; ~ *sig mod* give o.s. courage
intarsia [-'tarsia] *s1* inlaid wood, intarsia
inte not; no; ~ *för* ~ not for nothing; ~ *en enda gång* (*äv.*) never once; ~ *mig emot* I have no objection, *vard.* OK by me; ~ *sant?* don't you think so?, isn't that so?; ~ *senare än* not (no) later than; ~ *för att jag klagar* not that I'm complaining; *jaså,* ~ *det?* oh, you don't (aren't *etc.*)?; *det var* ~ *för tidigt* that was none too early; *det är* ~ *utan att jag tycker* I must say I think
inteckn|a mortgage **-ing** mortgage; encumbrance, security; *ha en* ~ *i* have a mortgage on **-ingslån** mortgage loan

inte'gral *s3* integral **-kalkyl** integral calculus
-tecken [symbol denoting an] integral
integration integration
integrer|a integrate; ~*d krets* integrated circuit
-ande *a4* integral, integrant; *utgöra en ~ del
av* form an integral part of **-ing** integration
integritet integrity
intele|fonera dictate over a telephone, send in
by telephone **-grafera** send in by telegram
(wire, cable)
intel'lekt *s7* intellect; *ett rörligt ~* a lively intellect
intellektu|alisera intellectualize **-alism** intel-
lectualism **-'ell** *a5* intellectual
intelli'gens *s3* intelligence **-aristokrati** intellectual aristocracy **-fri** unintelligent, stupid
-kvot intelligence quotient *(förk.* I.Q.) **-mät-
ning** intelligence measurement **-prov** intelligence test **-snobb** intellectual snob **-test**
intelligence test **-ålder** mental age
intelligent *al* intelligent; *(starkare)* clever
intelligentia [-'gentsia] *s1* intelligentsia
intendent *(föreståndare)* manager, superintendent; *(förvaltare)* steward; *(vid museum)* keeper, curator; *(i ämbetsverk)* comptroller, controller; *(polis-)* superintendent; *mil.* commissary,
quartermaster, *AE.* quartermaster supply officer
intendentur *mil.* commissariat [service] **-för-
band** quartermaster unit **-kår** ~*en* (*i Storbritannien*) the Army Supply Corps, (*i USA*) the
Quartermaster Corps
intensifier|a intensify **-ing** intensification
intensitet intensity
inten'siv [*äv.* 'inn-] *al* (*motsats extensiv*) intensive; *(stark, kraftig)* intense; *(ivrig)* keen,
energetic **-kurs** crash course **-vård** intensive
care **-vårdsavdelning** intensive care unit
intention intention
inter|agera [-a'ge:ra] interact **-aktion** [-ak-
'ʃɷ:n] interaction **-ak'tiv** interactive
inter'dikt *s7* interdict; injunction
interdiscipli'när interdisciplinary
interferens *s3* interference **-fenomen** interference phenomenon
interferera interfere
interferon [-'å:n] *s3* interferon
interfolier|a interleave; *(friare)* intersperse **-ing**
interleaving *etc.*
inter|galaktisk [-'lakt-] *a5* intergalactic **-gla-
ci'al** interglacial
interimistisk [-'mist-] *a5* provisional, temporary
interims|bevis [ˣinn-] scrip; *AE.* interim cer-
tificate **-regering** caretaker government **-sty-
relse** provisional (interim) board
interkontinen'tal intercontinental **-robot** intercontinental ballistic missile *(förk.* ICBM)
inter|lokutör interlocutor **-ludium** [-'lu:-] *s4*
interlude **-messo** [-'messɷ], **-mezzo** [-'met-
så] *s6* (*mus. o. friare*) intermezzo; *(uppträde)*
interlude **-mit'tent** *a4* intermittent; ~ *ljus* (*i
fyr*) occulting light
intern [-'tä:rn] **I** *s3* internee; (*i fängelse*) inmate
II *a5* internal; domestic *(angelägenhet* matter)
-alisera internalize
internat *s7, se* internatskola

internatio'nal *s3* **1** *polit.* International **2** *I~en*
The Internationale **-isera** internationalize **-ise-
ring** internationalization **-ism** internationalism
-ist internationalist **-istisk** *a5* international
internatio'nell international
internatskola boarding school; (*i Storbritannien*) public school
interner|a shut up, confine; (*krigsfånge* e.d.)
intern, detain; *de ~de* the internees (inmates)
-ing shutting up, confinement; internment, detention **-ingsläger** internment (detention)
camp
internist internist
internordisk [-'nɷ:r-] inter-Nordic
intern|rekrytering internal (inside) recruit-
ment **-TV** closed-circuit television (CCTV)
interpella|nt questioner, interpellator **-tion**
question, interpellation; (*i Storbritannien
vanl.*) question [in debate] **-tionsdebatt** debate on question raised in parliament
interpellera interpellate; (*i Storbritannien
vanl.*) ask a question, question
inter|planetarisk [-'ta:-] *a5* interplanetary **-po-
lera** interpolate **-polering** interpolation **-'pret**
s3 interpreter
interpunk|tera punctuate; point **-tion** [-punk-
'ʃɷ:n] punctuation **-tionstecken** punctuation
mark
inter|regnum [-ˣräŋn- *el.* -'räŋn-] *s7* interreg-
num **-rogativ** ['inn- *el.* -'i:v] *a5* interrogative
interur'ban *a5* interurban **-samtal** trunk call;
AE. long-distance call
inter'vall *s3, s7* interval
interven|era intervene; *(medla)* mediate **-tion**
intervention; mediation
inter'vju *s3* interview
intervju|a [-'vju:a] interview **-are** interviewer
intervju|objekt interviewee, person inter-
viewed **-offer** *skämts.* interviewee **-undersök-
ning** field survey (investigation) **-uttalande**
statement made during an interview
intet I *pron, se ingen*; ~ *ont anande* unsuspecting, suspecting no mischief **II** *n* **1** nothing;
gå om ~ come to naught (nothing), miscarry;
därav blev ~ nothing came of it, it came to
nothing **2** *(intighet)* *(tomma* empty*)* nothing-
ness **-dera** *se ingendera* **-sägande** *a4 (tom)*
empty; *(obetydlig)* insignificant; *(uttryckslös)*
vacant
intig *a5 (tom)* empty; *(fåfänglig)* vain **-het** emptiness; vanity
intill I [ˣinn-, 'inn- *el.* -'till] *prep* **1** *rumsbet.*
up to, to; next to; *(emot)* against; *nära ~* close
(near) to; *strax ~* quite close to **2** *tidsbet.* until,
up to **II** [-'till] *adv* adjacent, adjoining; *nära
~* close (near) by **-liggande** [-ˣtill-] *a4 (hopskr. intilliggande)* adjacent, adjoining
in'tim *al* intimate, close **-itet** intimacy
intjäna earn, make; ~*d lön* salary earned in advance
intoler|abel *a2* intolerable **-ans** [-'ans *el.* -'aŋs]
intolerance **-ant** [-'ant *el.* -'aŋt] intolerant
inton|ation intonation **-era** intone
intramusku'lär *a5* intramuscular
intransitiv [ˣinn- *el.* 'inn-] *a5* intransitive
intrave'nös *a5* intravenous
intressant [-'ant *el.* -'aŋt] *al* interesting

intresse [-ˣtresse] *s6* interest; *av ~ för saken* out of interest in the matter; *fatta ~ för, finna ~ i* take an interest in; *tappa ~t för* lose interest in; *tillvarataga sina ~n* protect one's interests; *vara av ~* be of interest *(för* to); *det ligger inte i hans ~* it is not in his interests **-ge-menskap** community of interests **-grupp** interest (pressure) group **-inriktning** main interest **-konflikt** conflict of interests **-lös** without interest; uninteresting *(äv. om pers.)* **-mot-sättning** conflict of interests
intressent interested party; participant; *(delägare)* partner
intresseområde *se intressesfär*
intressera interest; *~de parter* interested parties, parties concerned; *musikaliskt ~d* with musical interests; *~d av (för)* interested in; *~ ngn för ngt* interest s.b. in s.th.; *~ sig för* take [an] interest in, be interested in; *det ~r mig mycket* it is of great interest to me, I take [a] great interest in it
intresse|sfär sphere of interest **-väckande** *a4* interesting
in'trig *s3* intrigue; *(stämpling äv.)* plot *(äv. i drama e.d.);* *(friare)* scheme **-ant** [-'ant *el.* -'aŋt] *a1* intriguing; plotting; scheming **-era** intrigue, plot; scheme **-makare** intriguer; *(ränksmidare)* plotter, schemer **-spel** plotting, scheming; intrigues *(pl)* **-ör** *se -makare*
intrikat *a1* intricate, complicated
intrimma trim, run in
introducera introduce *(hos* to)
introduktion [-k'ʃɷ:n] introduction
introduktions|brev letter of introduction **-er-bjudande** introductory offer **-kurs** introductory course
introduktör introducer
introspek|tion [-k'ʃɷ:n] introspection **-'tiv** *a5* introspective
intro'vert *a4* introvert
intrumfa *se trumfa*
intryck 1 *(märke)* impress, mark *(efter* from, of) **2** *bildl.* impression; *mottaglig för ~* susceptible to impressions, impressionable; *göra ~ av att vara* give the impression of being; *göra ~ på* make an impression on; *ta ~ av* be influenced by; *jag har det ~et att* I have the impression that
in|trång *s7* encroachment, trespass *(i, på* on); *göra ~ på* encroach (trespass) on **-träda 1 ~** *[i]* enter **2** *bildl. (om pers.)* step in *(i ngns ställe* to a p.'s place); *(om sak)* set in; *(börja)* begin, commence; *(följa)* ensue; *(uppstå)* arise **-träde** *s6* entrance *(i* into); *i sht bildl.* entry *(i into);* admission, admittance; *(början)* commencement, setting in; *vid mitt ~ i rummet* on my entering the room; *göra sitt ~ i (vanl.)* enter; *söka ~* apply for admission
inträdes|ansökan application for admission **-avgift** entrance (admission) fee **-biljett** admission (entrance) ticket *(till* for) **-fordringar** entrance requirements, qualifications for admission **-prov** entrance examination **-spärr** *(t. utbildning)* restricted admission **-sökande** *s9* applicant [for admission]
in|träffa 1 *(hända)* happen; occur, come about **2** *(-falla)* occur, fall *(i slutet av maj* at the end

of May) **3** *(anlända)* arrive, turn up *(i* at, in) **-träna** drill
inträng|a penetrate; *(med våld)* intrude **-ande** I *s6* penetration; intrusion II *a4* penetrating; penetrative *(förstånd* intelligence) **-ling** intruder
intui|tion intuition **-'tiv** *a5* intuitive
in|tvåla soap; *(haka äv.)* lather **-tyg** *s7 (i sht av myndighet)* certificate *(om* of); *(i sht av privatpers.)* testimonial *(om, på, över* respecting, as to); *jur.* affidavit **-tyga** *(skriftligen)* certify; *(bekräfta)* affirm; *härmed ~s att* this is to certify that; *rätt avskrivet ~r* true copy certified by **-tåg** entry *(i* into); march (marching) in; *hålla sitt ~* make one's entry **-tåga** march in; *~ i* march into **-täkt** *s3* **1** *~er* income *(sg),* receipts, *(statens, kommuners)* revenue *(sg), (avkastning)* yield *(sg), (biljett-)* takings, *vard.* take *(sg)* **2** *ta ngt till ~ för* use s.th. as a justification for **-under** [-'und-] underneath; *i våningen ~* in the flat below **-uti** inside; within **-vadera** invade **-vagga ~** *ngn i säkerhet* lull s.b. into a sense of security, throw s.b. off his guard; *~ sig* lull o.s. *(i* into) **-val** *s7* election *(i* into)
inva'lid *s3* disabled person (soldier *etc.);* invalid **-bil, -fordon** invalid car
invalidi|sera disable **-tet** disability; *fullständig ~* total disability (disablement)
invalid|itetsersättning disablement benefit **-pension** disability pension, disablement annuity **-vagn** invalid car
invand [-a:-] *a5* habitual; *~a föreställningar* ingrained ideas (notions, opinions)
invandra immigrate *(till* into); *(om djur, växter)* find (make) its way in (into the country)
invandrar|e immigrant **-verk** *Statens ~* [the] Swedish immigration board
invandring immigration
invandrings|förbud ban on immigration **-kvot** immigration quota **-tillstånd** immigration certificate (permit)
invasion invasion **invasionsarmé** army of invasion, invading army
inveckl|a involve; *~ sig* get [o.s.] involved (entangled) *(i* in) **-ad** *a5* involved *(i i* in); *(svårlöst)* complicated, intricate
invek'tiv *s7* invective
inventarie|bok inventory (stock) book **-förteckning** inventory **-konto** fittings and fixtures account
inventar|ium [-'ta:-] *s4* **1** *(förteckning)* inventory **2** *(fast)* fixture; *~er* effects, movables, *(i hus, på kontor e.d.)* furniture (fittings) and fixtures, *(i fabrik e.d.)* equipment, *hand. o. lantbr.* stock *(sg)* **3** *pers.* fixture
inventer|a make an inventory of, inventory; *hand.* take stock of **-ing** inventory; *hand.* stocktaking
inven|tionssoffa [-n'ʃɷ:ns-] sofa bed **-tiös** [-'ʃö:s] *a1* ingenious; ingeniously planned
inverk|a have an effect (influence) *(på* on); *~ på (äv.)* influence, affect **-an** influence, effect; *utsatt för luftens ~ (äv.)* exposed to the air; *röna ~ av* be influenced (affected) by; *utöva ~ på* influence, affect
inversion inversion

invertebrat invertebrate [animal]
invert|era invert **-socker** [-ˣvärt-] invert sugar
invester|a invest **-are** investor **-ing** investment
investerings|avgift investment tax (duty) **-bo-lag** investment company **-kostnad** investment cost **-objekt** investment object (project) **-vo-lym** volume of investment
investitur investiture
investmentbolag investment trust company
invid I [ˣinn-, 'inn- el.· -'viːd] *prep* by; (*utefter*) alongside; *tätt ~ vägen* close to the road II [-'viːd] *adv* close (near) by (*äv. tätt ~*)
invig|a 1 (*t.ex. kyrka, flagga, biskop*) consecrate; (*t.ex. skolhus, bro*) inaugurate, open; (*präst*) ordain; (*använda första gången*) put on (wear, use) for the first time 2 (*göra förtrogen med*) initiate (*i* into) 3 (*helga*) consecrate, dedicate **-ning** 1 consecration; dedication; inauguration, opening; ordination 2 initiation
invignings|fest inaugural (opening) ceremony **-tal** inaugural (dedicatory) address (speech)
invikning [-viːk-] turning (folding) in; *konkr.* inward fold
in'vit *s3* (*inbjudan*) invitation; (*påstötning*) intimation; (*vink*) hint **-ation** invitation **-era** invite
invokation invocation
involvera involve
invån|arantal number of inhabitants, [total] population **-are** inhabitant; (*i hus äv.*) inmate; (*i stadsdel o.d.*) resident; *per ~* (*äv.*) per head (capita)
invägla weigh in **-ning** weighing in
invälja elect; return
invänd|a object, raise (make) objections (*mot* to, against); *jag har ingenting att ~* [*mot det*] I have no objection; *har du ngt att ~?* have you any objection to make (anything to say against)?; *nej, -e hon* no, she protested (demurred) **-ig** *a5* internal, inside **-igt** *adv* internally; (*på insidan*) [on the] inside; (*i det inre*) in the interior **-ning** objection (*mot* to); *göra ~ar, se invända* **-vändningsfri** unobjectionable
invänta wait for; (*avvakta*) await
invärtes *oböjligt a* (*om sjukdom o.d.*) internal; inward (*suck* sigh); *för ~ bruk* for internal use; *~ medicin* internal medicine
invävd *a5* woven in[to] (*äv. bildl.*)
inymp|a inoculate; *i sht bildl.* implant (*hos ngn* in s.b.) **-ning** inoculation; engraftment
inåt ['inn-] I *prep* towards the interior of; into; *~ landet* up country II *adv* inwards; *gå längre ~* go (move) further in; *dörren går ~* the door opens inwards
inåt|buktad *a5*, **-böjd** *a5* bent inwards; in-bent, inward-bent **-gående** I *s6* (*om fartyg*) *på ~* inward bound II *a4* (*om dörr e.d.*) *vara ~* open inwards **-riktad** *a5* pointing (that points) inwards; *bildl. se följande* **-vänd** *a5* turned inwards; (*om blick, tanke e.d. äv.*) introverted, introspective; *psykol.* introvert **-vändhet** introspectiveness
inägor *pl* infields
inälvor *pl* bowels, intestines; (*hos djur*) viscera, entrails; *vard.* guts
inälvsparasit intestinal parasite

inöv|a practise; (*repetera*) rehearse; train **-ande** *s6* practising; rehearsal; training
iordning|gjord [iˣåːrd-] *a5, är ~* has been got ready **-ställa** put in order
I'rak *n* Iraq **irak|ier** [i'raː-] *s9*, **-isk** *a5* Iraqi
I'ran *n* [Islamic Republic of] Iran **iran|ier** [i'raː-] *s9*, **-sk** [i'raː-] *a5* Iranian
irer ['iː-] *Irish Celt, Gael
iridium [i'riː-] *s8* iridium
iris ['iː-] *s2, anat. o. bot.* iris **-bländare** *foto.* iris diaphragm
irisk ['iː-] *a5* Irish **iriska** ['iː-] (*språk*) Irish Gaelic
Irland ['iːr-] *n* (*ön*) Ireland; (*republiken*) [Republic of] Ireland, Irish Republic, Southern Ireland
irländ|are [ˣiːr-] Irishman; *skämts.* Paddy, Milesian; *-arna* (*äv.*) the Irish **-sk** *a5* Irish; *skämts.* Milesian; *I~a fristaten* Irish Free State; *I~a republiken, se Irland* **-ska** 1 (*språk*) Irish [Gaelic] 2 (*kvinna*) Irishwoman
iro'n|i *s3* irony **-iker** [i'rɷː-] ironic[al] person **-isera** speak ironically (*över* of, about) **-isk** [i'rɷ:-] *a5* ironic[al]
irra ~ [*omkring*] wander (rove) about
irratio'nell *a1* irrational; *~a tal* irrational numbers
irrbloss will-o'-the-wisp, friar's lantern, jack-o'-lantern
ir|re'ell unreal **-regul'jär** irregular **-relevant** [-'ant *el.* -'aŋt] irrelevant **-religiös** [-'ʃöːs *el.* -gi'öːs] irreligious **-reparabel** [-'aːbel] irreparable **-reversibel** [-'iːbel] irreversible
irr|färd roving (rambling) expedition; *~er* wanderings [hither and thither] **-gång** maze; labyrinth
irrita|bel [-'aːbel] *a2* irritable **-'ment** *s7* excitant; stimulus **-tion** irritation **-tionsmoment** source of irritation
irriter|a irritate; *bildl. äv.* annoy, harass **-ande** irritating *etc.*, nettlesome; raspish
irrlära false doctrine, heresy
irrlärig *a5* heretical **-het** heresy
iråkad *a5, hans ~e svårigheter* the difficulties he has got into
is *s2* ice; *under ~en* (*bildl.*) (*moraliskt*) done for, (*ekonomiskt*) down on one's luck; *bryta ~en* (*bildl.*) break the ice; *frysa till ~* freeze [in]to ice; *gå ner sig på ~en* go through the ice [and get drowned]; *ha ~ i magen* (*bildl.*) keep one's cool; *lägga på ~* (*bildl.*) postpone, defer; *~arna är osäkra* the ice on the lakes is not safe; *~en har inte lagt sig än* the lake is not frozen yet; *~en låg till i i april* the lake[s] remained frozen until April; *varning för svag ~* (*på anslag, ung.*) Notice: Ice unsafe here
isa cover with ice; (*drycker*) ice, put in ice; (*mat*) store on ice
isabellafärgad [-ˣbella-] Isabella [coloured]
is|ande *a4, bildl.* icy; *~ kyla a*) eg. biting (severe) frost, *b*) *bildl.* icy coldness **-as** *dep, blodet -ades i mina ådror* my blood ran cold
is|bana *sport.* ice track; (*skridskobana*) skating rink **-bark** coating of ice **-belagd** *a5* icy, covered with ice **-berg** iceberg **-bergssallad** iceberg lettuce **-bildning** *abstr.* formation of ice; *konkr.* ice formation **-bill** *s2* ice pick, ice chisel

-bit piece (lump) of ice **-björn** polar bear **-blomma** (*på fönster*) ice fern; *-blommor* frostwork **-blåsa** ice bag; (*omslag*) ice pack **-brytare** icebreaker **-brytning** icebreaking **-bälte** ice belt

iscensätt|a [i*se:n-] stage, produce; *bildl.* stage, engineer **-ning** staging (*äv. bildl.*), production

ischias ['iʃ-] *s3* sciatica **-nerv** sciatic nerve

is|dubb ice proʼd **-flak** ice floe **-fri** ice-free; (*om hamn äv.*) open **-gata** ice-coated (ice-glazed) road **-glass** water ice **-hav 1** *geogr., Norra (Södra) I~et* the Arctic (Antarctic) Ocean **2** *geol.* glacial sea **-hinder** ice obstacle (obstruction) **-hink** ice pail

ishockey ice hockey **-hjälm** ice-hockey helmet **-klubba** ice-hockey stick **-rink** ice-hockey rink **-rör** ice-hockey skate **-spelare** ice-hockey player

is|ig *a5* icy **-jakt** ice yacht **-kall** ice-cold, as cold as ice; (*friare*) icy cold; icy (*blick* gaze; *ton* tone of voice) **-kalott** icecap **-konvalj** [late--flowering] lily of the valley **-kristall** ice crystal **-kyld** ice-cold, iced

i|skänka fill the glasses **-slagen** *en snett ~ spik* a nail driven in askew; *kaffet är islaget* coffee has been poured out

isʼlam *r* Islam **-isk** [-'la:-] *a5*, **-itisk** [-'i:t-] *a5* Islamic

Island ['i:s-] *n* Iceland

islands|lav Iceland moss **-sill** Iceland herring[s *pl*] **-tröja** Iceland sweater

is|lossning break-up of the ice, clearing of ice **-läggning** freeze-up

isländ|are Icelander **-sk** *a5* Icelandic **-ska 1** (*språk*) Icelandic **2** (*kvinna*) Icelandic woman

islänning *se isländare*

ism *s3* ism

isoʼbar *s3* isobar

isolat *s7* isolate

isolation isolation; *tekn.* insulation **-ism** isolationism **-istisk** *a5* isolationist

isolator *s3* insulator; (*ämne*) insulant, insulating material

isoler|a isolate; *tekn.* insulate; *bo ~t* live in a house isolated from others; *leva ~t* lead an isolated life, isolate o.s. from others **-band** insulating tape **-ing** isolation; *tekn.* insulation

isolerings|förmåga insulating capacity **-material** insulating (nonconducting) material

iso|ʼmer I *s3* isomer **II** *a5* isomeric **-meʼri** *s3* isomerism

isometrisk [-'me:-] *a5*, *~ träning* isometrics (*pl, behandlas som sg*)

isomorf [-'årf] *a5* isomorphic, isomorphous **isomorʼfi** [-å-] *s3* isomorphism

isop [*isåp el.* 'isåp] *s2, bot.* hyssop

iso|ʼterm *s3* isotherm **-top** [-'tå:p] *s3* isotope

is|period glacial period **-pigg** icicle **-pik** ice stick **-prinsessa** ice princess

Israel ['i:s-] *n* Israel

israʼel *s3*, **-ier** *s9*, **-isk** *a5* Israeli

israeʼlit *s3* Israelite **-isk** *a5* Israelitic, Israelite

is|ranunkel glacier crowfoot **-rapport** ice report **-ränna** channel through the ice **-situation** ice situation **-skorpa** ice crust **-skruvning** [-u:-] [rotatory] ice pressure **-skåp** icebox **-stack** ice store **-sörja** (*på land*) ice slush; (*i vatten*) broken ice

istadig *a1* restive, refractory **-het** restiveness

istapp icicle

ister ['ist-] *s7* lard **-buk** potbelly **-flott** lard

istid glacial period; *~en* (*äv.*) the Great Ice Age

iståndsätt|a put in order; restore **-ning** refitting; restoration

istället *se ställe 2*

is|tärning ice cube **-vatten** icy water; (*kylt med is*) ice[d] water **-vidd** icy expanse

isänder *se sänder*

iʼsär (*åtskils*) apart; (*från varandra*) away from each other **-tagbar** [-a:g-] *a5* dismountable

isättika glacial acetic acid

isätt|ning 1 (-*ande*) putting in (*etc.*) **2** *konkr.* insertion

italer [i'ta:-] *~na* the Itali **Italien** [i'ta:-] *n* Italy

italien|are [-*e:n-] *s9*, **-sk** *a5* Italian **-ska 1** (*språk*) Italian **2** (*kvinna*) Italian woman

iter|ation iteration **-aʼtiv** *a5* iterative **-era** iterate

iʼtu 1 in two; in half (halves); (*i bitar*) in pieces; *falla ~* fall to pieces; *gå ~* go to pieces **2** *ta ~ med ngn* take s.b. in hand; *ta ~ med ngt* set about (set to work at) s.th.

ituta *jag blev alltid ~d att* they always kept on at me about

iʼty *~ att* inasmuch as, since, as

iver ['i:-] *s2* eagerness; keenness; (*nit*) ardour, zeal; (*brinnande*) fervour, enthusiasm; *i ~n (hettan)* in one's ardour (enthusiasm); *med ~* (*äv.*) with great zest, with alacrity

ivra [*i:v-] *~ för ngt* be a zealous (keen) supporter (an ardent advocate) of s.th.; *~ för att* be eager (keen) on (*ngt görs* s.th. being done)

ivr|are [*i:v-] eager supporter, champion (*för* of) **-ig** *a1* eager; (*nitisk*) zealous; (*brinnande av iver*) ardent, fervent, avid; (*angelägen*) anxious; keen (*efter* on)

iögon[en]fallande [i*ö:gån-] *a4* striking; conspicuous, noticeable; obvious

J

ja I *interj* **1** yes; *(dröjande, betänksamt e.d.)* well; *(vid upprop)* here!; *ack ~!* yes, worse luck!; *just det, ~!* that's just it!; *så ~! (lugnande)* there (come) now!, *(uppmuntrande)* so there!; *~ då* oh, yes; *~, det är det* yes, it is; *~, gör det!* yes, do!; *~ ~, jag kommer! (lugnande)* all right *(irriterat:* yes, yes) I'm coming!; *~, varför inte?* [yes, (well,)] why not! **2** *(stegrande)* indeed; even, nay; *~ visst!, se visst; dagar, ~ veckor* days, even weeks **II** *s7, s6* yes; *få ~ a)* receive a favourable answer, *b) (vid frieri)* be accepted; *rösta ~* vote in favour [of the proposition]; *säga ~ till* say yes to, answer in the affirmative, agree to; *frågan är med ~ besvarad* the answer is in the affirmative

jabb *s2* jab

1 jack *s7 (hack)* gash, cut

2 jack *s2, tel.* jack

jacka *s1 (dam-)* jacket; *(herr- äv.)* coat

jacketkrona jacket crown

jac'kett [ʃ-] *s3 (mansrock)* morning coat

jackpott ['jackpått] *s3* jackpot

jade [jeid, jä:d, *äv.* ja:d] *s5, miner.* jade

jag I *[vard.* ja] *pron* I; *~ själv* I myself; *det är ~* it is me **II** *s7,* self; *filos.* ego; *ngns bättre ~* a p.'s better self; *visa sitt rätta ~* show one's true colours

jag|a 1 hunt; *(hare, högvilt, fågel äv.)* shoot **2** *(förfölja)* chase, pursue; *(driva, fösa)* drive; *~ ngn på dörren* turn s.b. out; *~ ngn på flykten* put s.b. to flight; *~ livet ur ngn* worry the life out of s.b. **3** *(ila)* drive, chase; *(skynda)* hurry, dash **-are** *sjö.* **1** *mil.* destroyer **2** *(segel)* flying jib

jag|betonad *a5* egocentric **-form** *s3, i ~* in the I-form (the first person singular) **-medvetande** awareness of self, self-knowledge

jagu'ar *s3* jaguar

jaha well; *(jaså)* oh, I see

jaja well, well; *~ dig!* you just look out!, mind what you are doing!

jak *s2* yak

jak|a say 'yes' *(till* to), answer in the affirmative **-ande** *s6* affirmative; *~ sats* affirmative clause; *svara ~* answer in the affirmative

jakaranda [ʃ- *el.* j-, -ˣranda] *s1 (trä)* jacaranda

jako'b|in *s3* Jacobin **-insk** [-'bi:nsk] *a5* Jacobinic[al]

jakobsstege Jacob's ladder

1 jakt *s3, sjö.* yacht

2 jakt *s3* hunting; *(med gevär)* shooting; *(-tillfälle)* day's shooting; *(förföljande)* pursuit, chase; *(letande)* hunt *(efter* for); *~en efter lyckan* the pursuit of happiness; *gå på ~* go out hunting; *vara på ~ efter* be hunting (on the hunt) for *(äv. bildl.)*

jakt|bombplan fighter-bomber **-byte** *(jägares)* bag; *(djurs)* prey, game; *(dagens äv.)* kill **-falk**

zool. gyrfalcon, gerfalcon **-fasan** ring-necked pheasant **-flyg** fighter-aircraft; fighters *(pl)* **-flygare** fighter-pilot **-gevär** sporting gun **-horn** hunting horn **-hund** sporting (hunting, gun) dog; *~arna (äv.)* the hounds **-kniv** hunting knife **-lag** *s2* game act **-licens** hunting licence **-lycka** the luck of the chase; *har ~n varit god?* have you had a good day's sport? **-mark** hunting (shooting) ground; *(inhägnad)* preserve; *(ej inhägnad)* chase; *de sälla ~erna* the happy hunting grounds **-plan** interceptor, fighter **-robot** *mil.* air-to-air missile; *målsökande ~* homing missile **-rätt** shooting (hunting) rights *(pl)* **-slott** hunting seat **-stig** *ge sig ut på ~en* go out hunting **-stuga** shooting box (lodge), hunting lodge **-sällskap** *koll.* hunting (shooting) party; *~et (äv.)* the hunt (field) **-säsong** hunting (shooting) season **-vapen** hunting (sporting) weapon **-vård** game management **-vårdare** gamekeeper; *AE.* game warden **-väska** game bag

ja'lu [ʃ-] *oböjligt a* jealous *(på* of)

jalu'si [ʃ-] *s3* **1** *(svartsjuka)* jealousy **2** *(fönsterskärm)* jalousie; Venetian blind **3** *(på skrivbord o.d.)* roll-top; *(på skåp o.d.)* roll-front

jama mew, miaow; *~ med (bildl.)* acquiesce [in everything]

Jamaica [-ˣmaika] *n* Jamaica **jamai|'can** [-a:-] *s3,* -'**cansk** *a5,* -'**kan** [-a:-] *s3,* -'**kansk** [-a:-] *a5* Jamaican

jamande *s6* mew, miaow

jamb *s3* iamb[us] **-isk** ['jamm-] *a5* iambic

jams *s3* yam

jamsa drivel

jamsrot yam

janitsjar [-t'ʃa:r] *s3* janissary, janizary **-musik** Turkish music

januari [-'a:ri] *r* January

janusansikte Janus face

Japan ['ja:-] *n* Japan

ja'pan *s3* Japanese; *vard.* Jap **-lack** [ˣja:-] japan

japan|sk [-'pa:nsk] *a5* Japanese **-ska** *s1* **1** *(språk)* Japanese **2** *(kvinna)* Japanese woman

jardin'jär [ʃ-] *s3* jardinière; flower stand

jargong [ʃar'gåŋ] *s3* lingo, jargon; slang; *(svada)* jabber; *(rotvälska)* gibberish

jarl [-a:-] *s2* jarl

ja|rop cry of 'yes' **-röst** vote in favour, aye

jas'min [ʃ-] *s3* jasmine, jessamine

jaspis ['jass-] *s2, miner.* jasper

jass *se jazz*

jaså [ˣjasså, 'jasså] oh!, indeed!, is that so?, really!; *~ inte det!* no?, not?

jasägare yes man

Java *n* Java

ja'van|sk [-'es a3, -'es** *s3,* **-esisk** [-'ne:-] *a5* Javan[ese]

javanesiska [-'ne:-] *(kvinna)* Javan[ese] woman

javan|sk [-'va:nsk] *a5* Javan[ese] **-ska** *(kvinna)* Javan[ese] woman

javisst *se visst*

jazz [jass] *s3* jazz

jazz|a dance [to jazz music], jazz **-balett** jazz (modern) ballet **-musik** jazz music **-orkester** jazz band

jeep [ji:p] *s2* jeep

je'hu *i uttr.: som ett ~* like a hurricane

Jemen ['je:-] *n* Yemen [Arab Republic]

jeme'nit *s3*, **-isk** [-'ni:-] *a5* Yemeni
Jeremia [-*mi:a] Jeremiah
jeremi'ad *s3* jeremiad, lamentation
Jeremias *se Jeremia*
Jeriko ['je:-] *n* Jericho
jersey ['jö:rsi] *textil.* jersey
Jesaja [-*sajja *el.* -'sajja] Isaiah
jesu'it *s3* Jesuit **-isk** *a5* Jesuitic; *neds.* Jesuitical **-orden** the Society of Jesus
Jesus [*je:- *el.* 'je:-] Jesus **-barnet** the Infant Jesus, the Holy Child
1 jet [jett] *s3, miner.* jet
2 jet [jett] *s3, tekn.* jet
jet|aggregat jet propulsion unit **-bränsle** jet fuel **-drift** jet propulsion **-driven** *a5* jet-propelled **-flygplan** *se jetplan* **-motor** jet engine
jetong [ʃe'tåŋ] *s3* (*spelmark*) counter; (*belöning*) medal
jet|plan jet plane (aircraft) **-set** *el.* jet set jet set **-ström** jet stream **-åldern** the jet age
jiddisch ['jidd-] *s2* Yiddish
jigg *s2* (*dans o. tekn.*) jig
jippo ['jippɷ] *s6* [publicity] stunt
jiu-jitsu [-'jitsu] *s5* jujitsu, jujutsu
JK [*ji:kå:] *förk. för justitiekanslern*
JO [*ji:ɷ:] *förk. för justitieombudsmannen*
jo yes, oh yes, why yes; (*eftertänksamt*) well, why; ~ *då* yes, to be sure; oh yes; ~ *visst vill jag det!* oh yes, certainly I will!, to be sure I will!
jobb [-å-] *s7* **1** work, job; (*knog*) job **2** *se jobberi*
jobb|a [-å-] **1** work, be on the job; (*knoga*) go at it; (*syssla*) dabble (*med* in) **2** (*spekulera*) speculate, do jobbing **-are 1** jobber, worker **2** (*som gör tvetydiga affärer*) profiteer **-eri** speculation; profiteering **-ig** *a1* (*mödosam*) laborious; (*besvärlig*) bothersome; *det är ~t* it's hard work
jobspost [*jåbs-] *s3*, *en* ~ evil tidings (*pl*), [a piece of] bad news
jock|ej [ʃå'kej] *s3*, **-ey** ['djåcki] *s3* jockey
jod [jådd] *s3* iodine **jodda** [*jådda] iodize
joddel ['jådd-] *s7* yodel
joddl|a [*jådd-] yodel **-are** yodeller **-ing** yodelling
jod|haltig *a1* iodic **-sprit** tincture of iodine
jogg|a [-å-] jog **-are** jogger **-ing** jogging
Johannes [-'hann-] ~ *evangelium* the Gospel according to St. John, John; ~ *döparen* John the Baptist
johannes|bröd (*träd*) carob; (*frukt*) carob, St. John's bread **-ört** St. John's wort
johannit|orden [-*ni:t-] Knights Hospitallers, Knights [of the Hospital] of St. John of Jerusalem **-riddare** Hospitaller
John Blund (*ung.*) the Sandman
joho oh yes, to be sure
jojk [-å-] *s2* Lappish song
1 jojo [*jɷjjɷ] *interj* why, yes to be sure!
2 jojo [*jɷjjɷ] *s5* yo-yo
joker ['jå:-] *s2* joker
jolle [-å-] *s2* ding[h]y, skiff; yawl
joller ['jåll-] *s7* babble; (*småbarns äv.*) crowing, prattle **jollra** [*jåll-] (babble); crow, prattle
jolmig [*jåll-] *a1* mawkish, vapid; *vard.* wishy-washy

jolt [-å-] *s7* silly talk, twaddle
jon *s3* ion **-bytare** ion exchange [resin]
jongl|era ['jåŋ- *el.* 'ʃåŋ-] juggle (*äv. bildl.*) **-ering** [-'e:riŋ] juggling; jugglery **-ör** juggler
jonier ['jɷ:-] Ionian
jonisa|tion ionization **-tionskammare** ionization chamber
joniser|a ionize; ~*nde strålning* ionizing radiation **-ing** ionization
jonisk ['jɷ:-] *a5* Ionic; (*om invånare o.d.*) Ionian
jonkammare ionization (ion) chamber
jono'sfär ionosphere
jord [-ɷ:-] *s2* **1** earth; (*värld*) world; *Moder J~* Mother Earth; *här på ~en* here on earth; *på hela ~en* in the whole world; *resa ~en runt* travel round the world **2** (*-yta*) ground; soil; earth; *ovan* ~ above ground; *på svensk* ~ on Swedish soil; *förbinda med* ~ (*elektr.*) connect to earth (*särsk. AE.* ground), earth; *gå under ~en* go underground; *komma ner på ~en igen* come back (down) to earth; *sjunka genom ~en* (*bildl.*) sink into the ground **3** (*ämne, -art o.d.*) earth; (*mat-*) soil; (*stoft*) dust; *falla i god* ~ fall into good ground **4** (*-område*) land; *odlad* ~ cultivated land
jorda [*jɷ:r-] **1** (*begrava*) bury **2** *elektr.* earth
jorda|balk *s2* code of land laws, land law **-gods** landed estate (property)
jordande *s2* earth spirit
Jordanien [-'da:-] *n* Jordan **jordan|ier** [-'da:-] *s9*, **-sk** *a5* Jordanian
jord|art 1 *geol.* earth deposit **2** *lantbr.* soil **3** *kem.* earth **-artsmetall** earth metal **-axel** axis of the earth
jordbruk *s7* **1** *abstr.* farming, agriculture; *bedriva* ~ do farming, farm, be a farmer **2** *konkr.* farm
jordbruk|arbefolkning agricultural population **-are** farmer, agriculturist
jordbruks|arbetare farm hand (worker) **-arbete** farming, agricultural work **-bygd** agricultural district **-departement** ministry (*AE.* department) of agriculture **-fastighet** farm property **-maskin** agricultural machine **-minister** minister (*AE.* secretary) of agriculture **-nämnd** *Statens* ~ [the Swedish] national agricultural market board **-näring** farming [industry], agriculture **-politik** agricultural policy **-produkt** agricultural product **-redskap** agricultural (farming) implement **-utskott** ~*et* [the Swedish parliamentary] standing committee on agriculture
jord|bunden *bildl.* earthbound, earthy **-bävning** [-ä:-] earthquake **-egendom** landed property
jordeliv life upon earth; ~*et* (*äv.*) this life
jordenrunt|farare [-*runt-] globetrotter **-resa** round-the-world trip
jord|fräs rotary cultivator **-fästa** inter, read the burial service over **-fästning** burial (funeral) service **-förbättring** soil improvement **-geting** ground-dwelling wasp **-glob** globe **-golv** earthen floor **-gubbe** [garden] strawberry **-gubbssylt** strawberry jam **-håla** cave in the earth **-hög** earth mound, mound of earth **-höjd** earth-covered hill

jord|ig [ˈjɔ:r-] *a1* (*-aktig*) earthy; (*nersmutsad*) soiled with earth **-isk** [ˈjɔ:r-] *a5* earthly; terrestrial; (*världslig*) worldly; mundane; (*timlig*) temporal; *~a kvarlevor* mortal remains; *lämna detta ~a* depart this life
jord|kabel underground cable **-klot** earth; *~et* (*äv.*) the globe **-koka** *s1* clod [of earth] **-kula** den; (*djurs äv.*) cavern **-källare** underground storehouse, mattamore **-lager** earth layer; stratum [of earth] **-lapp** patch (plot) of ground **-ledning 1** *elektr.* earth (*särsk. AE.* ground) connection; *konkr.* earthing wire **2** (*underjordisk ledning*) underground conduit **-loppa** flea beetle **-lott** plot, allotment **-löpare** *zool.* ground beetle **-magnetism** terrestrial magnetism **-mån** *s3* soil (*äv. bildl.*)
jord|ning [ˈjɔ:rd-] *elektr.* earthing; *AE.* grounding **-nära** down-to-earth **-nöt** peanut, groundnut **-reform** land reform **-register** land register **-ränta** ground (land) rent **-satellit** earth satellite **-skalv** earthquake **-skorpa** [earth] crust; *~n* the earth's crust **-skred** landslide (*äv. polit.*); landslip **-skredsseger** landslide [win] **-slå** earth up **-stöt** earthquake [shock]; (*i Sydamerika*) temblor **-svin** aardvark **-värme** ground heat; geothermal energy **-yta** surface of the ground; (*ytområde*) area of ground; *på ~n* on the earth's surface, on the face of the earth **-ägare** landowner **-ärtskocka** [-å-] *s1* Jerusalem artichoke
jos *se* **juice**
jota 1 *s6* (*grekisk bokstav*) iota **2** *n, inte ett ~* not a jot (an iota)
joule [jɔ:l] *s9, elektr.* joule
jour [ʃɔ:r] *s3* **1** *ha ~[en]* be on call (duty) **2** *hålla ngn à ~ med* keep s.b. informed on (as to); *hålla sig à ~ med* (*äv.*) keep [o.s.] abreast of (up to date on) **-havande** *a4, ~ läkare* doctor on duty (emergency call); *~ officer* duty (orderly) officer, officer of the day **-läkare** doctor on duty
jour'nal [ʃɔr-] *s3* **1** *bokför.* journal, diary; (*läkar-*) case book; (*sjukhus-*) case record; (*för enskild patient*) case sheet; *föra ~* keep a journal **2** *film.* newsreel **3** (*tidskrift*) journal, magazine **-film** newsreel **-föring** keeping a journal
journalism [ʃɔr-] journalism
journalist [ʃɔr-] journalist; newspaperman, *fem.* newspaperwoman; pressman **-högskola** college of journalism
journalis't|ik [ʃɔr-] *s3* journalism **-isk** *a5* journalistic
jourtjänst on-call duty
jovi'al *a1*, **-isk** *a5* jovial **-itet** joviality
jovisst *se under* **jo**
jox [jɔks] *s7* stuff, rubbish **joxa** [ˈjɔksa] peddle; *~ ihop* (*mat e.d.*) concoct, (*trassla till*) muddle up; *~ med ngt* mess about with s.th.
ju I *adv* why; (*som du vet*) you know (see); (*naturligtvis*) of course; (*visserligen*) it is true; (*som bekant*) as we [all] know; (*det förstås*) to be sure; *du vet ~ att* you know of course that; *där är du ~!* why, there you are!; *jag har ~ sagt det flera gånger* I have said (told you) so several times, haven't I?; *du kan ~ göra det a*) (*om du vill*) there's nothing to prevent you doing so, *b*) (*uppmanande*) you may [just] as

well do it **II** *konj* the; *~ förr desto bättre* the sooner the better
jubel [ˈju:-] *s7* (*hänförelse*) jubilation, rejoicing, exultation; (*glädjerop*) shout[s] of joy, enthusiastic cheering (cheers *pl*) (*över* at); (*bifall*) shouts of applause (*över* at); *allmänt ~* general rejoicing; *jublet brast löst* a storm of rejoicing broke out **-doktor** person who has held a doctorate for fifty years **-idiot** arch idiot **-rop** shout of joy **-år** [year of] jubilee
jubi'l|ar *s3* person celebrating an anniversary **-era** celebrate
jubileum [-ˈle:-] *s4* jubilee
jubileums|fest anniversary celebration **-firande** celebration of a jubilee **-skrift** anniversary issue **-utställning** jubilee exhibition
jubl|a [ˈju:b-] shout for joy; (*inom sig*) rejoice, exult **-ande** *a4* shouting for joy; jubilant, exultant
jucka *vard.* bump
Juda Judah
juda|folket the Jewish people; the Jews (*pl*) **-konung** *~en* the King of the Jews
Judas Judas **judaskyss** Judas (traitor's) kiss
jude *s2* Jew; Hebrew, Israelite; *vandrande ~n a*) (*Ahasverus*) the Wandering Jew, *b*) *bot.* spiderwort, tradescantia **-fientlig** anti-Jewish, anti-Semitic **-förföljelse** persecution of [the] Jews **-hat** hatred of the Jews; anti-Semitism **-kristen** Jewish Christian **-kvarter** Jewish quarter, ghetto **-körs** [-ç-] *s3* strawberry tomato, Cape gooseberry
juden|dom [-dɔmm] *s2* Judaism **-heten** the Jews, the Jewish people
judetyska Yiddish
judici'ell *a5* judicial
jud|inna Jewish woman, Jewess **-isk** [ˈju:-] *a5* Jewish
judo [ˈju:-] *s5* judo
jugendstil [ˈjɔ:gent-] Art-Nouveau style
jugo'slav *s3* Jugoslav[ian], Yugoslav[ian] **Jugoslavien** [-ˈsla:-] *n* Jugoslavia, Yugoslavia **jugoslavisk** [-ˈsla:-] *a5* Jugoslav[ian], Yugoslav, Yugoslavian
juice [jɔ:s] *s5* juice
jujutsu *se* **jiujitsu**
jul *s2* Christmas (*fork.* Xmas); (*hednisk jul o. poet.*) Yule[tide]; *god ~!* A Merry Christmas!; *i ~* at (this) Christmas; *i ~as* last Christmas; *fira ~[en]* keep (spend) [one's] Christmas
jul|a *se* [*fira*] **jul** **-afton** Christmas Eve **-bock** Christmas goat **-boksfloden** the Christmas-book inundation **-bord** Christmas smorgasbord (buffet) **-brådska** *i ~n* in the Christmas rush **-bön** Christmas Eve service (evensong) **-dag** Christmas Day **-evangeliet** the Gospel for Christmas Day **-ferier** *pl* Christmas holidays (vacation *sg*) **-fest** Christmas party (celebration) **-firande** *s6* [the] keeping (celebration) of Christmas **-glädje** Christmas cheer **-gran** Christmas tree
julgrans|belysning Christmas-tree illumination **-fot** Christmas-tree stand **-karamell** Christmas-tree decoration filled with sweets **-plundring** party when the Christmas tree is stripped of decorations
jul|gris Christmas pig **-gröt** boiled rice pudding

J

julgåva–jycke   258

-**gåva** Christmas gift -**handel** Christmas trade -**handla** do one's Christmas shopping -**helg** *under* ~*en* during Christmas (*ledighet* the Christmas holidays), at Christmas -**hälsning** Christmas greeting
juli ['ju:-] *r* July
juliansk [-'a:nsk] *a5* Julian
jul‖kaktus Christmas (crab) cactus -**klapp** Christmas present; *önska sig i* ~ want for Christmas -**klappsvers** rhymed inscription written on a Christmas present -**kort** [-ɷ:-] Christmas card -**krubba** [Christmas] crib
julle *s2, se jolle*
jul‖lek Christmas game -**lik** *a5* Christmassy -**lov** Christmas holidays (*pl*) (vacation) -**natt** Christmas night -**otta** early service on Christmas Day
julp *s2, se gylf*
jul‖prydnader *pl* Christmas decorations -**ros** Christmas (winter) rose, hellebore -**rush** Christmas rush -**skinka** Christmas ham -**stjärna** 1 *hist.*, ~*n* the Star of Bethlehem 2 (*i julgran*) Christmas-tree star 3 *bot.* poinsettia -**stämning** Christmas spirit (atmosphere) -**stök** preparations (*pl*) for Christmas -**sång** Christmas carol (song) -**tid** (*äv.* ~*en*) Christmas time, *poet. äv.* Yuletide -**tomte** Christmas gnome; ~*n* Santa Claus, Father Christmas
Julön Christmas Island
jumbo ['jumm-] *s5, sport., komma* ~ come last -**jet** *vard.* jumbo [jet] -**pris** booby prize
jumpa jump from one sheet of floating ice to another
jumper ['jump-] *s2* jumper -**set** twin-set
jungfru *s5* 1 (*ungmö*) virgin; maid[en]; *J~ Maria* the Virgin Mary, the Blessed Virgin, Our Lady; *J~n av Orléans* the Maid of Orléans 2 *se hembiträde* 3 (*för gatläggning*) [paving] beetle, punner; *sjö.* deadeye -**bur** maiden's (lady's) bower -**dom** [-dɷmm] *s2* virginity, maidenhood -**födsel** *teol.* Virgin Birth; *biol.* parthenogenesis, virgin birth -**kammare** servant's [bed]room
jungfrulig [ˣjuŋ-, *äv.* -'fru:-] *a1* maidenly, maidenlike, maiden; *bildl.* virgin (*mark* soil) -**het** maidenliness; virginity
jungfru‖lin [common] milkwort -**resa** maiden voyage -**tal** maiden speech
jungman [ˣjuŋ- *el.* 'juŋ-] ordinary seaman; deck hand
juni ['ju:-] June
junior ['ju:niår, *sport.* -'å:r] *oböjligt a o. s3* junior; *univ. ung* undergraduate -**lag** junior team
junker ['junk-] *s2* 1 *hist.* (*titel ung.*) squire; (*tysk godsägare*) Junker 2 *gunstig* ~ young gentleman
junonisk [-'nɷ:-] *a5* Junoesque; (*friare*) majestic
junta *s1* 1 *polit.* junta 2 (*klubb o.d.*) junta, junto; *AE. äv.* bee
jura *s1*, -**perioden** the Jurassic [period]
juri'd‖ik *s3* law; (*vetenskap äv.*) jurisprudence; *studera* ~ study [the] law -**isk** [-'ri:-] *a5* 1 juridical; (*friare*) legal; *den* ~*a banan* the legal profession; ~ *fakultet* faculty of law; ~*t ombud* legal representative; ~ *person* juridical (juristic) person; ~ *rådgivare* legal adviser; ~*a*

uppdrag legal (lawyer's, law) work 2 (*rättslig*) judicial; ~*t förfarande* judicial procedure 3 (*om rättsvetenskap*) jurisprudential
juris ['ju:-] ~ *doktor* Doctor of Laws (*förk.*, *efter namnet* LL.D.); ~ *kandidat* (*licentiat*) (*ung.*) Bachelor (Master) of Laws (*förk.*, *efter namnet* LL.B., LL.M.) -**diktion** [-kˈʃɷ:n] jurisdiction -**pru'dens** *s3* jurisprudence
jurist lawyer; (*ngns äv.*) legal adviser; (*rättslärd*) jurist -**eri** lawyer's quibbling, juridical formalism
jury ['jurry, *äv.* -i] *s3* jury; *sitta i en* ~ be (serve) on a jury -**man**, -**medlem** juryman, juror
1 **just** *adv* just; (*precis äv.*) exactly, precisely; (*alldeles*) quite; (*egentligen*) really; ~ *det* [, *ja*]! that's exactly it!; ~ *ingenting* nothing in particular; ~ *så* [, *ja*]! exactly (precisely, quite)!; *ja*, ~ *han!* yes, the very man!, to be sure, he and no other!; *jag vet* ~ *inte det!* I am not so sure!; *det var* ~ *snyggt!* oh, very nice, I must say!; *det var* ~ *det jag trodde* that was (is) just (exactly) what I thought; *varför välja* ~ *mig?* why choose me of all people?
2 **just** [ʃyst] *a1* (*rättvis*) fair; (*oklanderlig*) correct, right; (*som sig bör*) seemly, åld. meet; (*noggrann*) exact, accurate; *vara* ~ *mot* (*äv.*) treat s.b. fairly (justly)
juster‖a 1 (*inställa, korrigera*) adjust; (*avhjälpa fel*) correct; (*friare*) put right (to rights); (*instrument*) regulate, set right, rectify; (*mått o. vikt*) verify, inspect; (*granska o. godkänna*) revise; ~ *protokollet* sign the minutes [as correct] 2 *sport.* injure; *vard.* nobble -**are** adjuster; (*av mått o. vikt*) inspector [of weights and measures]; (*av instrument*) regulator -**bar** *a5* adjustable -**ing** adjustment; correction; regulation; inspection; revision
justerings‖man person who checks minutes -**skruv** adjusting (adjustment) screw
justitie‖departement [-ˣti:tsie-] ministry (*AE.* department) of justice; (*i England och Wales*) Lord Chancellor's Office -**kansler** chancellor of justice; ~*n* (*ämbetet*) [the] office of the chancellor of justice -**minister** minister of justice; (*i England och Wales*) Lord Chancellor; (*i USA*) attorney general -**mord** judicial murder; miscarriage of justice -**ombudsman** [the Swedish] parliamentary ombudsman -**råd** justice of the supreme court; (*i Storbritannien*) Lord Justice of Appeal; (*i USA*) associate justice of the supreme court -**utskott** ~*et* [the Swedish parliamentry] standing committee on justice
1 **jute** *s2* Jute; (*jyllänning*) Jutlander
2 **jute** *s2, s7* (*spånadsämne*) jute
juteväv jute cloth; *AE. äv.* gunny
ju'vel *s3* jewel (*äv. bildl.*); gem; ~*er* (*koll.*) jewellery -**armband** jewelled bracelet -**besatt** *a4* jewelled
juvelerar‖affär [-ˣle:-] jeweller's [shop] -**arbete** jeweller's work, jewellery
juvelerare [-ˣle:-] jeweller
juvel‖prydd *a5* [be]jewelled -**skrin** jewel case -**smycke** jewelled ornament
juve'nil *a1* juvenile
juver ['ju:-] *s7* udder
jycke *s2* dog; *neds.* cur; (*"kurre"*) beggar, john-

Jylland ['jyll-] *n*, **jylländsk** [ˣjyll-] *a5* Jutland
jädrans [ˣjä:d-] *oböjligt a* darned, confounded
jägar|e hunter, shooter; sportsman; *bildl.* huntsman, hunter; *(anställd)* huntsman; *mil.* commando [soldier], light infantryman, *AE.* ranger **-folk** nation of hunters **-hatt** huntsman's hat; *(mjuk mössa med brätte fram o. bak)* deerstalker **-horn** hunter's horn, hunting horn
jägmästare [ˣjä:g-] forester, forest officer (supervisor)
jäkel *s2* devil; *jäklar!* damn! **-skap** *s3, s4, på ~* just for the hell of it
jäk|la [ˣjä:k-] *oböjligt a o. adv* blasted **-las** *dep,* ~ *med* be nasty to, provoke **-lig** *a1* rotten; damn[ed]
jäkt *s7 (brådska)* hurry, haste; *(hets)* drive, hustle **jäkta 1** *(driva på* [*ngn*]*)* hurry on, keep [s.b.] on the drive (run) **2** *(hasta)* be constantly on the go (move), be in a hurry **jäktad** *a5* hurried, worried **jäktig** *a1* bustling, hectic **jäktigt** *adv, ha det ~* have a hectic time of it
jäm|bredd *i uttr.: i ~ med* side by side with **-bördig** *eg.* equal in birth; *bildl.* equal [in merit] *(med* to), of equal merit *(med* with) **-fota** *hoppa ~* jump with both feet together
jämför|a *v2* compare; ~ *med* compare with, *(likna vid)* compare to; *jämför* compare *(förk.* cp.)*, confer *(förk.* cf.); ~*nde språkvetenskap* comparative philology **-bar** *a1* comparable; *fullt* ~ *med (hand.)* quite up to the standard of
jämförelse comparison; *göra ~r* make comparisons *(mellan* between); *det är ingen ~!* there is no comparison! **-material** comparison material **-vis** comparatively; relatively
jämförlig [-ö:-] *a1* comparable (to be compared) *(med* with, to); *(likvärdig)* equivalent *(med* to)
jämförpris unit price
jäm|gammal of the same age *(med* as) **-god** *se jämngod*
jämk|a *(flytta)* move, shift; *bildl.* adjust, adapt, modify; ~ *på* adjust, *(ändra)* modify, *(pruta på)* give way (in), *(pris)* knock off; ~ *ihop (bildl.)* adjust; ~ *ihop sig* move closer together **-ning** [re]adjustment, modification; *(kompromiss)* compromise; *(av skatt)* tax adjustment
jäm|lik *a5* equal *(med* to) **-like** equal **-likhet** equality **-likt** [-i:-] *adv* according to, in accordance with
jämmer ['jämm-] *s9* groaning; *(kvidande)* moaning; *(missnöje)* complaint; *(veklagan)* lamentation; *(elände)* misery **-dal** vale of tears **-lig** [ˣjämm-] *a1* miserable, deplorable; wretched; *(jämrande)* mournful, wailing **-rop** plaintive cry, cry of pain (distress)
jämn *a1* **1** *(om yta)* level, even; *(slät)* smooth **2** *(likformig)* uniform *(värme* heat); even; equable *(klimat* climate; *lynne* temperament); *(oavbruten)* continuous, steady; *(regelbunden)* regular; *med ~a mellanrum* at regular intervals; *hålla ~a steg med* keep in step with, *bildl.* keep pace with **3** *(motsats udda)* even; ~*a hundratal kronor* even hundreds of kronor; ~*a par* an equal number of men and women; ~*a pengar* even money, the exact sum; *en ~ summa (äv.)* a round sum

jämna level, make level (even, smooth), even out; *(klippa jämn)* trim; *bildl.* smooth; ~ *med marken* level with the ground; ~ *ut* level off; ~ *väg*[*en*] *för ngn (bildl.)* pave the way for s.b.; *det ~r ut sig* it evens itself out
jämn|a *i uttr.: för ~* for always **-god** *vara ~a* be equal to one another, be equals; ~ *med* equal to, as good as **-grå** of an even grayness; overcast **-het** levelness; evenness, smoothness; equality; uniformity **-hög** of [a] uniform height; *två ~a* two equally tall **-höjd** *i uttr.: i* ~ *med* on (at) a level with; *vara i* ~ *med* be of the same level as **-mod** equanimity, composure **-mulen** entirely overcast **-stor** of [a] uniform size; *vara ~a* be equal in size
jämnt [*vard.* jämt] **1** level; evenly *etc.*; even; *(lika)* equally; *(regelbundet)* regularly, steadily; *dra* ~ *med ngn* get on with s.b.; *väga* ~ *(om t.ex. våg)* [just] balance, *bildl.* be even; *det är* ~*!* (*kan behållas som dricks*) keep the change!; *och därmed* ~ and there's an end of it **2** *(exakt)* exactly; ~ *så mycket som* exactly (just) so (as) much as; *inte tro ngn mer än* ~ only half believe s.b.; *3 går* ~ *upp i 9* nine is divisible by three
jämn|tjock of [a] uniform thickness, equally thick **-varm** ~*a djur* warm-blooded *(fack.* homoiothermic) animals **-årig** *a1* of the same age *(med* as); *(samtidig)* contemporary; *mina ~a* persons of my [own] age, my contemporaries
jämra *rfl* wail, moan; *(gnälla)* whine; *(klaga)* complain *(över* about); *(högljutt)* lament; *(stöna)* groan
jäms ~ *med* at the level of, level with; *(längs)* alongside [of]
jäm|sides side by side *(med* with), abreast *(med* of)*, *(vid tävling äv.)* neck and neck; alongside [of]; ~ *med sina studier* alongside [of] his studies; *fartygen ligger* ~ the ships lie alongside each other **-spelt** *a1* evenly matched, even *(med* with) **-ställa** place side by side (on a level) *(med* with), juxtapose *(med* to); place on an equal footing *(med* with); *(jämföra)* draw a parallel between; *-ställd med* on a par (an equality) with **-ställdhet** equality, parity **-ställdhetsombudsman** equal opportunities ombudsman; ~*nen (ämbetet)* [the] office of the equal opportunities ombudsman
jämt always; *(gång på gång)* constantly; *(oupphörligt)* incessantly, perpetually; ~ *och ständigt (samt)* always, for ever, everlastingly
jämte together with, in addition to; *(förutom)* besides; *(och även)* and [also]
jämvikt *s3* balance *(äv. bildl.)*; *fys.* equilibrium; *i* ~ *(bildl.)* [well-]balanced; *förlora ~en* lose one's (its *etc.*) balance; *åstadkomma* ~ *mellan* establish equilibrium between, equipoise; *återställa ~en* restore equilibrium (the balance)
jämvikts|läge position (state) of equilibrium; balanced position **-organ** organ of balance (equilibrium) **-rubbning** disturbance of equilibrium; disequilibrium
jämväl [ˣjämm-, *äv.* -'vä:l] likewise; *(även)* also
jänkare *vard.* Yankee
jänta *s1* lass
järn [-ä:-] *s7* iron; *ge ~et (vard.)* go in for s.th., give one's all; *ha många ~ i elden* have several

irons in the fire; *smida medan ~et är varmt* strike while the iron is hot; *ta sig ett ~ (vard.)* take a schnapps **-affär** *se -handel* **-beslag** iron mounting **-beslagen** iron|sheathed, -bound **-brist** iron deficiency **-bro** iron bridge **-bruk** ironworks (*sg o. pl*); foundry **-ek** *bot.* holly **-fil** iron file **-filspån** iron filings (*pl*) **-fysik** *se -hälsa* **-förande** *a4* iron-bearing, ferriferous **-förening** *kem.* iron compound **-grepp** iron grip **-gruva** iron mine **-halt** iron content **-haltig** *a5* containing iron, ferriferous **-hand** *styra med ~* rule with an iron hand **-handel** *konkr.* ironmonger's [shop], ironmongery; *AE.* hardware store **-handlare** ironmonger; *AE.* hardware dealer **-hantering** iron industry (trade) **-hård** [as] hard as iron, iron-hard; *bildl.* iron, iron-hard; *~ disciplin* iron discipline **-hälsa** iron constitution **-industri** iron industry **-kamin** iron stove **-korset** (*orden*) the Order of the Iron Cross **-malm** iron ore **-malmsfält** iron-ore field **-manufaktur** hardware **-medicin** iron tonic **-natt** frosty night **-näve** *bildl.* iron fist **-oxid** (*med tvåvärt järn*) ferrous oxide; (*med trevärt järn*) ferric oxide **-plåt** sheet iron **-ridå** *teat.* safety curtain; *polit.* iron curtain **-skrot** scrap iron **-smide** hammered ironware **-spis** iron range **-stång** iron bar **-säng** iron bedstead **-tråd** [iron] wire **-tvåa** *golf.* mid-iron **-varor** *pl* iron goods; ironware (*sg*); hardware (*sg*) **-verk** ironworks (*sg o. pl*) **-vilja** iron will **-väg** railway; *AE.* railroad; *Statens ~ar (SJ)* Swedish State Railways; *anställd vid ~en* employed on the railway; *fritt å ~* free on rail (*AE.* truck); *resa med ~* go by rail (train); *underjordisk ~* underground, tube, *AE.* subway **järnvägs|arbetare 1** (*-byggare*) navvy **2** (*vid färdig järnväg*) railway worker **-bank** [railway] embankment **-bro** railway bridge **-förbindelse** train service, railway connection **-karta** railway map **-knut** railway junction **-linje** railway line, track **-man** railwayman, railway employee **-nät** railway system (network) **-olycka** railway accident **-resa** railway journey (trip) **-restaurang** railway-station refreshment room, railway restaurant; (*mindre*) buffet **-skena** rail **-spår** railway (*AE.* railroad) track **-station** railway station; (*änd-*) terminus, *AE.* terminal **-trafik** railway traffic (service) **-tunnel** railway tunnel **-tåg** [railway] train **-vagn** railway carriage; *AE.* railroad car; (*godsvagn*) goods waggon, *AE.* freight car **-övergång** railway crossing; (*plankorsning*) level (*AE.* grade) crossing; *bevakad* (*obevakad*) *~* guarded (ungated) level crossing
järnåldern the Iron Age
järpe *s2* hazelhen
järtecken ['jä:r-] omen, portent, presage
järv *s2* wolverine
jäs|a *v3* ferment; (*om sylt o.d.*) go fermented; *bildl. a*) (*om missnöje o.d.*) ferment, *b*) (*vara uppblåst*) swell up; *låta degen ~* let the dough rise; *~ upp* (*om deg*) ferment, rise; *~ över* ferment and run over; *han -te av vrede* he boiled with fury; *det -te i sinnena* people's minds were in a ferment **-ning** fermentation; *bildl.* ferment; *bringa i ~* bring to fermentation, *bildl.* work up into a ferment

jäsnings|process fermentation (fermentative) process **-ämne** ferment
jäst *s3* yeast **-pulver** baking powder **-svamp** yeast [fungus]
jätte *s2* giant **-arbete** gigantic (herculean) [piece of] work **-bra** super, topnotch; *AE.* great **-fin** first-rate, terrific; *AE.* dandy **-format** gigantic size **-glad** pleased as punch **-gryta** *geol.* giant's kettle, pothole **-kvinna** giantess, female giant; (*storväxt kvinna*) enormous woman, (*på cirkus*) fat woman **-lik** *a5* gigantic; giant-like **-panda** [giant] panda **-planet** giant planet **-skön** very comfy (comfortable) **-steg** giant stride; *gå framåt med ~* (*bildl.*) make tremendous progress, progress by leaps and bounds **-stjärna** giant star **-stor** gigantic, enormous, huge **-tanker** mammoth tanker, supertanker **-trevlig** awfully nice, delightful, charming **-ödla** great saurian, dinosaur
jättinna *se jättekvinna*
jäv *s7, jur.* challenge (*mot* to); *anmäla ~ mot* challenge, make (lodge) a challenge to; *laga ~* lawful disqualification
jäva 1 *jur.* take exception to; (*testamente e.d.*) challenge the validity of **2** (*bestrida*) belie
jävig *a5* (*om vittne*) challengeable, exceptionable; (*inkompetent, partisk*) disqualified, non-competent **-het** challengeability; non-competence
jäv|la, -las, -lig, -ligt *se djävla, djävlas, djävlig, djävligt*
jökel ['jö:-] *s2* glacier **-älv** glacier stream
jöns *s2* johnny; ninny
jösse *s2, ung.* Jack hare
jösses good heavens!; *vad i jösse namn!* what on earth!

K

ka'bal *s3* cabal
kaba'ré *s3* cabaret **-artist** cabaret artiste
kabbal|a ['kabb-] *s1* cab[b]ala **-ist** cab[b]alist **-istisk** [-'ist-] *a5* cab[b]alistic
kabb[e]leka *s1* marsh marigold
kabel ['ka:-] *s2* cable; *sjö. äv.* hawser **-bro** cable suspension bridge **-brott** cable breakdown
kabeljo [ˣkabb-] *s5* dried [cured] cod
kabel|ledning cable **-längd** cable, cable['s] length **-sko** *elektr.* [cable] socket **--TV** cable television, cablevision
ka'bin *s3* (*för passagerare*) cabin; (*för pilot äv.*) cockpit **-bana** cablecar **-båt** cabin (family) cruiser
kabi'nett *s7*, *s4* cabinet (*äv. polit.*); (*budoar*) boudoir
kabinetts|fråga vote of confidence; *ställa* ~ demand a vote of confidence **-kammarherre** lord-in-waiting **-medlem** cabinet member, member of the cabinet **-sekreterare** undersecretary of state for foreign affairs
kabla [ˣka:-] cable
kabrio'lett *s3* cabriolet, convertible
ka'byl *s3* Kabyle
ka'byss *s3*, *sjö.* [cook's] galley, caboose
kackalorum [-ˣlɷ:-] *s7* to-do, hullabaloo
kackel ['kack-] *s7*, *se kacklande*
kackerlacka *s1* cockroach
kackl|a cackle; (*om höna äv.*) cluck **-ande** *a4 o. s6* cackling; cluck-clucking
kadaver [-'da:-] *s7* carcass; (*lik*) corpse **-disciplin** blind discipline
ka'dens [*el.* -'aŋs] *s3*, *mus.* (*slutfall*) cadence, fall; (*solo-*) cadenza
kader ['ka:-] *s2*, *s3*, *mil.* cadre
ka'dett *s3* cadet; *sjö.* [naval] cadet **-skola** military academy (school)
kadmium ['kadd-] *s8* cadmium
ka'drilj *s3* (*dans*) quadrille
kafé *s4* café; coffee bar (shop, house); teashop, tearoom; *AE. äv.* cafeteria
kafeteria [-'te:-] *se cafeteria*
kaffe *s7* coffee; *koka* ~ make coffee; ~ *med grädde* (*mjölk*) white coffee; ~ *utan grädde* (*mjölk*) black coffee **-automat** coffee machine **-blandning** blend of coffee **-bricka** coffee tray **-bryggare** percolator, coffee maker (machine) **-bröd** *koll.* buns, cakes **-buske** coffee shrub (bush) **-böna** coffee bean **-dags** coffee time, time for coffee **-grädde** coffee cream **-gök** *se* -*kask* **-junta** coffee club (party) **-kanna** coffeepot **-kask** *s2* coffee laced with schnapps **-kokning** coffee-making **-kopp** coffee cup; (*mått*) coffee-cupful **-kvarn** coffe mill (grinder) **-panna** coffeepot **-paus** coffee break **-plantage** coffee plantation
kaffer ['kaff-] *s3*, *åld. el. neds.* Kaf[f]ir
kafferast coffee break
kafferbuffel African buffalo

kaffe|rep *s7* coffee party **-rosteri** coffee-roasting factory **-servering** *se kafé* **-servis** coffee set **-sked** coffee spoon **-sump** coffee grounds (*pl*) **-surrogat** coffee substitute, ersatz coffee **-träd** coffee tree **-tår** drop of coffee
kaf'tan *s3* (*prästrock*) cassock; (*österländsk*) kaftan, caftan
kagge *s2* keg, cask
kainsmärke [ˣka:ins-] mark (brand) of Cain
kaj [kajj] *s3* quay; wharf, dock, (*hamngata*) embankment; (*utskjutande*) jetty; *fritt vid* (*å*) ~ free at (on) quay
kaja [ˣkajja] *s1* jackdaw
ka'jak *s3* kayak
kajavgift quayage; wharfage; quay-dues (*pl*)
kajennpeppar [-ˣjenn-] cayenne [pepper]
kajka row around (mess about) in an old boat
kaj'man *s3* cayman
kajplats quay berth
kajuta [-ˣju:-] *s1* cabin; (*liten*) cuddy
kaka *s1* cake, pastry; (*små-*) biscuit, *AE.* cookie; (*av hårt bröd*) round; ~ *söker maka* birds of a feather flock together
kakadu[a] [-'du:, -ˣdu:a] *s3* [*s1*] cockatoo
kakao *s9* cacao; (*dryck, pulver*) cocoa **-böna** cocoa bean **-fett** cocoa butter **-likör** crème de cacao
kakburk biscuit tin
kakel *s7* [Dutch, glazed] tile **-klädd** *a5* tiled **-platta** *se kakel* **-ugn** tiled stove
kak|fat cake dish **-form** baking tin
kaki ['ka:-] *s9* khaki **-färgad** khaki [coloured]
kak|mix [ready-made] cake mix **-mått** pastry cutter
kakofo'ni *s3* cacophony
kakskrin biscuit tin
kakt|é *s3* cactaceous plant **-us** ['kakt-] *s2* cactus
kaktång pastry tongs (*pl*)
kal *a1* bare; (*om kust*) naked; (*om gren*) leafless; (*om pers.*) bald
kalaba'lik *s3* uproar, fracas, tumult
kalamitet (*missöde*) mishap, (*starkare*) calamity; (*olycka*) misfortune
ka'las *s7* party; feast; (*friare o. bildl.*) treat; *få betala* ~*et* have to pay for the whole show; *ställa till med stort* ~ *för* throw a big party for
kalas|a feast **-kula** paunch, potbelly **-mat** delicious food; a real delicacy
kalcedon [-se'då:n *el.* -'dɷ:n] *s3* chalcedony
kalciner|a calcine **-ing** calcining; calcination **-ingsugn** kiln, calcining furnace
kalcium ['kall-] *s8* calcium **-fosfat** calcium phosphate **-hydroxid** calcium hydroxide **-karbid** [calcium] carbide **-karbonat** calcium carbonate **-klorid** calcium chloride **-oxid** calcium oxide
kaldé *s3* Chaldean **Kaldéen** [-'de:en] *n* Chaldea; *Ur i* ~ Ur of the Chaldees **kaldeisk** [kal-'de:-] *a5* Chaldean
kale'bass *s3* calabash
kaledonisk [-'dɷ:-] *a5* Caledonian; *K~a bergskedjan* the Caledonian folding
kalejdoskop [-'å:p] *s7* kaleidoscope **-isk** *a5* kaleidoscopic
kalendarium [-'da:-] *s4* calendar
kalender [-'lenn-] *s2* calendar; almanac; (*årsbok*) annual, yearbook **-bitare** *han är* ~ he is

a who's-who specialist **-dag** calendar (civil) day **-månad** calendar month **-år** calendar (civil) year
kalesch [-'ä(:)ʃ] *s3* barouche; calash, calèche
kalfaktor [-ˣfaktår] *s3* batman, officer's servant
kalfatra [ˣkall- *el.* -'fa:-] **1** *sjö.* caulk **2** *bildl.* find fault with
kall|fjäll bare mountain **-hugga** deforest **-huggning** deforestation **-hygge** deforestation
kali ['ka:-] *s7* potash
kaliber [-'li:-] *s2, s3* calibre (*äv. bildl.*)
kalibrer|a calibrate **-ing** calibration
ka'lif *s3* caliph, calif -'**at** *s7* caliphate
Kalifornien [-'få:r-] *n* California
kaligödsel potassic fertilizer
kali'kå [ˣkall-, 'kall- *el.* -'kå:] *s3* calico
kali|lut lye **-salpeter** potassium nitrate, saltpetre
kalium ['ka:-] *s8* potassium **-cyanid** potassium cyanide **-hydroxid** potassium hydroxide, caustic potash **-karbonat** potassium carbonate, potash *-klorid* potassium chloride
1 kalk *s2* **1** (*bägare*) chalice; *bildl.* cup: *tömma den bittra ~en* drain the bitter cup **2** *bot.* perianth
2 kalk *s3* lime; (*bergart*) limestone; *osläckt ~* quicklime, unslaked lime; *släckt ~* slaked lime
kalk|a whitewash, limewash; (*göda*) lime **-avlagring** lime deposit
kalk|brott limestone quarry **-brist** (*i kost*) calcium deficiency **-bruk 1** (*-bränneri*) lime works (*sg o. pl*) **2** (*murbruk*) lime mortar
kalker|a trace; *bildl.* copy **-ing** tracing **-papper** tracing (carbon) paper
kalk|fattig lime-deficient; (*om kost*) deficient in calcium **-gruva** lime pit **-halt** lime content **-haltig** *a1* calcareous, calciferous; limy **-kväve** calcium cyanamide **-målning** fresco (mural) painting
kal'kon *s3* turkey **-rulle** *film.* turkey film (*AE.* movie)
kalk|salpeter nitrate of lime **-sten** limestone **-stensbrott** limestone quarry **-stryka** limewash **-tablett** calcium tablet
kal'kyl *s3* calculation; *hand.* cost estimate; *mat.* calculus **-ator** *s3* (*person*) cost accountant, calculator; (*maskin*) calculator, calculating machine
kalkyler|a calculate, estimate, work out **-ing** (*-ande*) calculating, estimating; *se äv.* kalkyl **-ingsmaskin** calculating machine; (*elektronisk*) [electronic] computer
1 kall *a1* cold (*äv. bildl.*); (*om t.ex. zon*) frigid; (*kylig*) chilly; (*sval*) cool; *två grader ~t* two degrees below zero; *det ~a kriget* the cold war; *bli ~ om fötterna* get cold feet; *hålla huvudet ~t* keep cool; *han håller huvudet ~t* he has a cool head; *vinka med ~a handen* dismiss s.b. coldly; *jag blev alldeles ~ (av förskräckelse)* I went cold all over
2 kall *s7* calling, vocation; (*uppgift*) task, mission
1 kalla *s1, bot.* calla, calla (arum) lily
2 kalla call; name, designate; (*ropa [på], till-*) summon; (*utnämna*) appoint, nominate; ~ *på läkare* send for (call in) the doctor; *det kan man ~ tur!* that is what you may call luck!; ~

sig call o.s., (*antaga namnet*) take the name of
kallad *a5* called *etc.*; *så ~* so-called; *även ~* alias, otherwise called; *känna sig ~ till* feel fitted for (called upon to); *han blev ~ till president* he was called to be president (to the presidency)
kall|bad cold bath; (*ute-*) bathe **-blodig** cold-blooded; *bildl. äv.* cool; ~*a djur, se* växelvarma djur **-blodigt** *adv* coolly, in cold blood **-blodighet** cold-bloodedness **-brand** gangrene **-dragen** *a5, tekn.* cold-drawn **-dusch** cold shower (douche) (*äv. bildl.*)
Kalle Anka Donald Duck
kallelse 1 (*t. möte e.d.*) summons, notice; *univ.* call; *kyrkl.* invitation; (*utnämning*) nomination **2** *se 2 kall*
kall|front *meteor.* cold front **-garage** unheated garage **-grin** sneer **-grina** sneer [superciliously] (*åt* at) **-hamra** cold-hammer; ~*d* (*bildl.*) hard-boiled
kalli|graf *s3* calligrapher, calligraphist **-grafi** *s3* calligraphy **-grafisk** [-'gra:-] *a5* calligraphic
kall|jord *på ~* in cold soil, outdoors **-lim** (*hopskr. kallim*) cold-water glue **-mangel** mangle
kall|na cool; (*om mat e.d.*) get cold **-prat** small talk **-prata** talk about trivialities **-sinnig** *a1* cold, cool; (*likgiltig*) indifferent **-sinnighet** coldness *etc.*; indifference **-skuret** *n, best. form: det -skurna, litet ~* a few cold-buffet dishes **-skänk** *s2* cold buffet **-skänka** [-ʃ-] *s1* cold-buffet manageress **-start** cold start **-sup** involuntary gulp of cold water **-svett** cold sweat (perspiration) **-svettas** *dep* be in a cold sweat **-svettig** *vara* ~ be in a cold sweat
kall|t *adv* coldly *etc.*; *förvaras* ~ keep in a cool place; ~ *beräknande* coldly calculating; *ta saken* ~ take the matter coolly, keep cool about **-valsning** cold-rolling **-vatten** cold water **-vattenskran** cold-water tap
kal'muck *s3* **1** Kalmuck, Kalmyk **2** (*tyg*) kalmuck
kalops [-'åps] *s3, ung.* spiced beef stew
kalo'ri *s3* calorie **-behov** calorie requirement **-fattig** low calorie
kalorimet|er [-'me:-] *s2* calorimeter -'**ri** *s3* calorimetry **-risk** [-'me:-] *a5* calorimetric[al]
kalorivärde calorific (calorie) value
kalott [-'ått] *s3* (*huvudbonad*) calotte, skullcap
kalsonger [-'såŋ-] *pl* (*korta*) underpants, undershorts; (*långa*) long underpants
ka'lufs *s3* forelock
ka'luv *s3* **1** *se* kalufs **2** *på nykter ~* (*bildl.*) in one's sober senses
kalv *s2* calf (*pl* calves); *kokk.* veal
kalv|a calve **-bräss** sweetbread **-dans** *kokk.* curds (*pl*) **-filé** fillet of veal **-frikassé** fricassee of veal **-färs** minced veal
kalvin|ism Calvinism **-ist** Calvinist **-istisk** *a5* Calvinistic[al]
kalv|kotlett veal chop (cutlet) **-kätte** calf's crib (pen) **-kött** veal **-lever** calf's liver
kalv|ning calving **-skinn** *hand.* calfskin **-stek** *slaktar.* joint of veal; *kokk.* roast veal
kam [kamm] *s2* comb; (*berg-, tupp-, våg-*) crest; (*excenter-*) cam; *skära alla över en* ~ judge

(treat) all alike
kamarilla [-ˣrilla, -'rilla] *s1* camarilla; clique
kamaxel camshaft
Kambodja [-ˣbådja] *n* Cambodia
kambrik ['kamm-] *s3* cambric
kambr|isk ['kamb-] *a5* Cambrian **-ium** *s8* Cambrian **-osi'lur** *s3* Cambro-Silurian
kamé *s3* cameo
ka'mel *s3* camel; *enpucklig* ~ dromedary **-drivare** camel driver
kameleont [-'ånt] *s3* chameleon **-isk** *a5* chameleonic
kamel|hår camel's hair, camelhair **-hårskappa** camelhair coat
kamelia [-'me:-] *s1* camellia
kamera ['ka:-] *s1* camera **-jakt** hunt for [sensational] photographs
kame'ral *a5* fiscal; financial
kameraman cameraman
Kame'run *n* Cameroon
kamfer ['kamm-] *s9* camphor **-liniment** camphor embrocation **-olja** camphorated oil **-sprit** camphorated spirits (*pl*)
kamgarn worsted [yarn]; (*tyg*) worsted [fabric]
ka'min *s3* [heating] stove; (*fotogen- e.d.*) heater; *elektrisk* ~ electric fire (heater)
kamkofta dressing jacket, peignoir
kamma comb; ~ *håret* comb (do) one's hair; ~ *noll* (*vard.*) draw a blank
kammar|e -[e]*n* *kamrar, äv. s9* room; *polit., tekn., biol.* chamber; (*hjärt-*) ventricle; (*i Storbritannien, polit.*) house; *första ~n* (*förr i riksdagen*) the First Chamber, (*i Storbritannien*) the House of Lords; *andra ~n* (*förr i riksdagen*) the Second Chamber, (*i Storbritannien*) the House of Commons
kammar|herre chamberlain (*hos* to) **-jungfru** lady's maid **-kollegiet** [the Swedish] national judicial board for public lands and funds **-lärd** *en* ~ a bookish person **-musik** chamber music **-opera** chamber opera **-orkester** chamber ensemble **-rätt** administrative court of appeal
kammarrätts|assessor associate judge [of the administrative court of appeal] **-fiskal** reporting clerk [of the administrative court of appeal] **-president** president [of the administrative court of appeal]
kammar|spel *teat.* chamber play **-tjänare** valet **-åklagare** district prosecutor
kam|mussla pecten **-ning** combing; (*frisyr*) coiffure, hairstyle
kamo'mill *s3* wild (German) camomile **-te** camomile tea
kamouflage, kamouflera *se camouflage, camouflera*
1 kamp *s2* (*häst*) jade
2 kamp *s3* (*strid*) struggle (*om* for); fight, combat (*om* for) (*äv. bildl.*); (*drabbning*) battle (*äv. bildl.*); (*brottning*) wrestle, wrestling; *~en för tillvaron* the struggle for existence; *en* ~ *på liv och död* a life-and-death struggle
kampa *se campa*
kampanda fighting spirit
kampa'nil *s3* campanile
kam'panj *s3* campaign; (*reklam- äv.*) drive
kamp|are *se campare* **-era** be (lie) encamped (in camp); ~ *ihop* (*tillsammans*) share the same

tent (room *etc.*), be fellow workers **-ing** ['kamp-] *se camping*
kamp|lust fighting spirit **-sång** camp song **-vilja** will to fight
Kampuchea [-ˣtçe:a] *n* Kampuchea
kamrat comrade, fellow; (*vän*) friend; (*följeslagare*) companion; (*arbets-*) fellow worker; (*skol-*) schoolmate, schoolfellow; (*studie-*) fellow student; (*kollega*) colleague; *en god* ~ a good chap; *mina ~er på kontoret* my colleagues at the office; *vi är ~er från skoltiden* we are old schoolmates **-anda** comradeship, fellowship **-förening** society of fellow students (schoolmates *etc.*); *mil.* service club **-krets** *i ~en* among [one's] friends (*etc.*)
kamratlig [-'ra:t-] *a1* friendly (*mot* towards) **-het** friendliness
kamrat|skap *s7* companionship, comradeship **-äktenskap** companionate marriage
kam'rer *s3*, **-are** [-ˣre:-] *s9* accountant (*i, på* at, in)
1 kan [ka:n] *s3* khan
2 kan [kann] *pres av kunna*
kana I *s1* slide; *åka* ~ slide, go sliding **II** *v1* slide, go sliding
Kanaan *n* Canaan
Kanada ['kann-] *n* Canada
kanadagås Canada goose
kanadens|are [-ˣdens-] Canadian (*äv. kanot*) **-isk** [-'dens-] *a5* Canadian **-iska** [-'dens-] Canadian woman
ka'nal *s3* (*naturlig*) channel (*äv. elektron. o. bildl.*); (*grävd samt anat. o. naturv.*) canal; *tekn.* channel, duct; *Engelska K~en* the [English] Channel **-avgift** canal dues (*pl*)
kanaliser|a canalize, channel (*äv. bildl.*) **-ing** canalization
kanalje [-'nalje] *s5* blackguard, villain; *din lille* ~ you little rascal
kanal|system canal system, network of canals **-väljare** channel selector
Kanalöarna *n* the Channel Islands
kanané *s3* Canaanite **kananeisk** [-'ne:-] *a5* Canaanitic
kanapé *s3* **1** (*soffa*) settee, canapé **2** (*bakelse*) pig's ear [of puff pastry]
kanarie|fågel [-ˣna:-] canary **-gul** canary yellow
Kanarieöarna [-ˣna:-] the Canary Islands, the Canaries
kancer, kancerogen *se cancer, cancerogen*
kandelaber [-'la:-] *s2* candelabra
kander|a candy; *~d* candied, preserved in sugar **-ing** candying
kandidat 1 (*sökande*) candidate, applicant (*till* for) **2** *univ.* Bachelor; *filosofie* ~ Bachelor of Arts (*förk.* B.A.); *medicine* ~ graduate in medicine, medical student **-examen** *ta* ~ take one's B.A. degree **-lista** list of candidates; *polit. äv.* nomination list; *AE. äv.* ticket **-nominering** nominations (*pl*) [of candidates]
kandid|a'tur *s3* candidature **-era** set [o.s.] up as a candidate; *polit.* stand (*AE.* run) for
kandisocker sugar candy
ka'nel *s3* cinnamon **-stång** bark cinnamon
kanfas ['kann-] *s3* canvas, duck
kanhända [-ˣhänn-] perhaps; *jfr kanske*

ka'nik *s3* canon
ka'nin *s3* rabbit **-avel** rabbit breeding **-bur** rabbit hutch **-hanne** buck rabbit **-hona** doe rabbit **-pest** myxomatosis **-skinn** *hand.* rabbit skin **-unge** young rabbit
kanister [-'nist-] *s2* canister, can, tin
kanjon ['kanjån] *s3* canyon
kanna *s1* (*kaffe- etc.*) pot; (*grädd-*) jug
kannel|era flute; ~*d* fluted **-ering** [-'le:-] fluting -'**yr** *s3* flute
kanni'bal *s3* cannibal **-isk** *a5* cannibal[istic] **-ism** cannibalism
kannring *tekn.* piston ring
kannstöp|a talk politics without having any real knowledge **-are** armchair politician, political windbag **-eri** [airing of] uninformed political opinions
1 kanon ['ka:nån] *s3, s9* **1** (*rättesnöre o.d.*) canon **2** *mus.* canon, round
2 kanon [ka'nɔ:n] *s3* (*artilleripjäs*) gun; (*äldre*) cannon; *som skjuten ur en* ~ like a shot
kano'n|ad *s3* cannonade **-båt** gunboat **-dunder** thunder (roaring) of guns **-eld** gunfire **-form** *sport.* great form **-fotograf** street photographer **-gjuteri** cannon foundry
kanon|isation canonization **-isera** canonize **-isk** [-'nɔ:-] *a5* canonical; ~*a böcker* canon (*sg*); ~ *rätt* canon law
kanon|kula cannonball **-lavett** gun carriage **-lockar** cannon curls **-mat** *bildl.* cannon fodder **-mynning** gun muzzle **-port** gun port, porthole **-skott** gunshot **-torn** gun turret
ka'not *s3*, **kanota** [-'nɔ:-] *v1* canoe
kanot|färd canoe trip **-ist** canoeist **-sport** canoeing
kanske [ˣkanʃe] perhaps; (*måhända*) maybe; ~, ~ *inte* maybe, maybe not; *han kommer* ~ he may (might) come; *du skulle* ~ *vilja hjälpa mig?* would you mind helping me?; ~ *vi skulle gå ut?* what about going out?
kansler [ˣkann-, *äv.* 'kann-] *s3* chancellor
kanslersämbete chancellorship
kans'li *s4, s6* (*vid ämbetsverk o.d.*) secretariat, [secretary's] office; (*i Storbritannien äv.*) chancery; *AE. äv.* chancellery; *univ.* registrar's office; *teat.* general manager's office; *Kungl. Maj:ts* ~ the Government Offices (*pl*) **-biträde** clerical officer **-chef** (*vid ambassad*) head of chancery; (*vid HD, regeringsrätten*) senior judge referee; (*vid riksdagens utskott*) secretary; (*vid kommun, landsting*) chief executive; (*vid nämnd m.m.*) administrative director **-råd** deputy assistant undersecretary **-sekreterare** administrative officer [second (third) secretary] **-skrivare** clerk **-språk** official (civil service) English (*etc.*); official jargon, officialese; *vard.* gobbledygook
kanslist clerical officer **kansli|stil, -svenska** *se kanslispråk*
kant *s3* **1** (*bård o.d.*) border; (*marginal*) margin; (*på kläder e.d.*) edging, selvage; (*på kärl*) rim, brim; (*på huvudbonad*) brim **2** (*bröd-*) crust; (*ost-*) rind **3** *hålla sig på sin* ~ keep one's distance, hold aloof; *komma på* ~ *med ngn* get at cross-purposes with s.b., fall out with s.b.
kanta edge; (*omge*) border, line; (*kantskära*) trim

kanta'rell *s3* chanterelle
kantat cantata
kantband edging, trimming
kantele [ˣkann-, 'kann-] *s5* kantele
kantig *a1* angular; (*om anletsdrag o. bildl.*) rugged; (*till sättet äv.*) unpolished, abrupt **-het** angularity; ruggedness *etc.*
kan'tin *s3* canteen
kan'ton *s3* canton
kantor [ˣkann-, 'kanntår] *s3* cantor, precentor
kantr|a turn over, capsize, [be] upset; (*om vind o. bildl.*) veer [round] **-ing** capsizal, upset; veering [round]
kant|sten kerbstone; *AE.* curbstone **-ställd** placed on edge **-stött** chipped [at edge]; (*om anseende o.d.*) damaged
kantänka [-ˣtänn-] no doubt; of course; (*försmädligt*) if you please
ka'nyl *s3* cannula (*pl* cannulae)
kao'lin *s4, s3* kaolin, china clay (stone)
kao|s ['ka:ås] *s7* chaos **-tisk** [ka'ɔ:-] *a5* chaotic
1 kap *s7* (*udde*) cape
2 kap *s7* (*fångst*) capture; *ett gott* ~ a fine haul
1 kapa (*uppbringa*) capture, take; (*flygplan*) hijack; skyjack
2 kapa *sjö.* cut away; (*lina äv.*) cut; (*timmer etc.*) crosscut; ~ *av* cut off
kapabel [-'pa:-] *a2* capable
kapaci|'tans *s3, elektr.* capacitance **-tet** capacity; (*pers. äv.*) able man
kapar|e privateer; (*flygplans-*) hijacker; skyjacker **-fartyg, -kapten** privateer
1 ka'pell *s7* (*överdrag*) cover, cap, hood
2 ka'pell *s7* **1** (*kyrkobyggnad*) chapel **2** *mus.* orchestra, band
kapellmästare conductor [of an orchestra]; bandmaster
kaperi privateering; piracy
kapillaritet capillarity
kapil'lär *s3 o. a5* capillary **-kraft** capillarity **-kärl** capillary **-rör** capillary tube
1 kapi'tal *a1* downright; ~*t misstag* capital mistake, flagrant error
2 kapi'tal *s7* capital; (*pengar äv.*) funds, money
kapital|behållning capital [in hand] **-bildning** capital accumulation (formation) **-brist** lack of capital **-budget** capital budget **-flykt** flight of capital **-försäkring** endowment assurance (insurance) **-intensiv** capital-intensive
kapitaliser|a capitalize **-ing** capitalization
kapital|ism capitalism **-ist** capitalist **-istisk** *a5* capitalist[ic]; ~*t samhälle* capitalist society **-konto** capital account **-marknad** capital market **-placering** [capital] investment **-räkning** [long-term] deposit account **-samlingsräkning** [long-term] deposit account, capital accumulation account **-stark** financially strong
kapitalt [-'a:lt] *adv* downright, radically; (*fullständigt*) completely, totally
kapital|varor capital goods **-värde** capital value
kapitel [ka'pittel] *s7* chapter; *ett helt annat* ~ (*bildl.*) quite another story; *när man kommer in på kapitlet om* (*bildl.*) when you get on to the topic of **-indelning** division into chapters **-rubrik** chapter heading

kapitul|ation capitulation **-ationsvillkor** terms of surrender **-era** capitulate, surrender
kapi'täl 1 *s7, s3, arkit.* capital **2** *s3, boktr.* small capital
kap'lan *s3* chaplain
kapning [ˣkaːp-] **1** (*uppbringande*) capture; (*av flygplan*) hijacking; skyjacking **2** *sjö.* cutting [away] **3** (*av timmer etc.*) crosscutting
kapock [-'påck] *s3* kapok
kapp *se* **ikapp**
kapp|a *s1* **1** coat; cloak; (*akademisk, domares, prästs*) gown; *vända ~n efter vinden* trim one's sails according to the wind, veer with every wind **2** (*gardin-*) pelmet, valance; (*volang*) flounce **-affär** coat shop
kappas *dep* vie (compete) [with one another]
kappe *s2, ung.* half-peck
kappkörning racing; *en ~* a race
kapplöp|ning racing (*efter* for); *en ~* a race **-ningsbana** racetrack; (*häst-*) racecourse, *AE.* racetrack **-ningshäst** racehorse, racer
kapprak bolt upright
kapprodd boat-racing; *en ~* a boat race **-are** member of a boat-race crew; single sculler
Kapprovinsen [ˣkaːp-] *r* [the] Cape Province
kapprum cloakroom
kapprustning arms (armaments) race
kappsegl|a compete in sailing-races (yacht--races) **-ing** yacht-racing; *en ~* a sailing-match (sailing-race), a yacht-race **-ingsbåt** racing--boat, racing-yacht, racer
kappsimning competition swimming; *en ~* a swimming-race (swimming-competition)
kappsäck suitcase; portmanteau; (*mjuk*) bag
kapriciös [-si'öːs] *a1* capricious
kapri'fol *s3*, **kaprifoli|um** [-'fœ:-] *-en -er, best. form äv. -er* honeysuckle
kapri'ol *s3* capriole
1 kap'ris *s3* (*nyck*) caprice, whim
2 kapris ['kaː-] *s2* (*krydda*) capers (*pl*)
kapsejs|a [-'sejsa] capsize; (*om bil etc.*) turn over **-ning** capsizal
kaps|el *s2* capsule; *bot.* [seed] capsule, seedcase, pericarp **-la** *tekn.* enclose, encase
kap'son *s3* cavesson
Kapstaden *r* Cape Town
kap'syl *s3* [bottle] cap, capsule; (*skruv-*) screw cap **-öppnare** bottle opener
kapsåg crosscut saw
kap'ten *s3* captain; *sjö. äv.* master, *vard.* skipper; (*vid flottan*) lieutenant; (*vid flyget*) flight lieutenant; *AE.* captain, (*vid flottan*) lieutenant
kapu'cin *s3* Capuchin
kapucin[er]|apa capuchin [monkey] **-munk** Capuchin [monk]
ka'pun *s3* capon
kapuschong [-'ʃåŋ] *s3* hood
ka'putt *oböjligt a, vard.* done for
Kap Verde ['värr-] *n* (*staten*) Cape Verde; (*ögruppen*) Cape Verde Islands
kar *s7* vat; (*bad-*) bathtub, bath
karabin'jär *s3* car[a]bineer
ka'raff *s3* decanter; *hand. äv.* carafe; (*vatten-*) water bottle **karaf'fin** *s3* carafe
karakteriser|a characterize **-ing** characterizing; characterization

karakteris'tik *s3* characterization, descriptive account (*över* of)
karakterist|ika [-'riss-] *s1* index, characteristic **-ikon** *best. form -ikon, äv. -ikonet, pl -ikon, äv. -ika* characteristic [feature] **-isk** *a5* characteristic, typical (*för* of)
karak'tär *s3* character; (*beskaffenhet, natur äv.*) quality, nature; (*karaktärsfasthet*) strength of character
karaktärs|danande *a4*, **-daning** *s2* character--building **-drag**, **-egenskap** characteristic [feature, trait]; trait of character **-fast** firm (steadfast) in character; of [a] firm character **-fasthet** firmness (strength) of character **-fel** flaw in character **-lös** lacking in character, unprincipled **-löshet** lack of character (principle) **-roll** character part **-skildring** portraiture of a character (person) **-skådespelare** character actor **-studie** character study (*över* of) **-styrka** strength of character **-svag** weak [in character]; spineless **-svaghet** weakness [of character]; spinelessness **-teckning** character-drawing; characterization
karam|bolage [-'laːʃ] *s7* (*slags biljardspel*) cannon; *särsk. AE.* carom **-boll** [-'båll] *s3, se* karambolage
kara'mell *s3* sweet, candy **-fabrik** confectionery, sweet factory **-färg** colouring essence **-påse** bag of sweets (*etc.*)
karan'tän *s3* quarantine; *ligga i ~* be in quarantine
karantäns|flagga quarantine flag, yellow jack **-tid** quarantine period
ka'rat *s9, s7* carat
karate [-ˣraː-] *s2* karate
kara'van *s3* caravan **-seraj** *s3, s4* caravanserai **-väg** caravan route
kara'vel[l] *s3* caravel
karbad bath
karba'mid *s3* urea **-plast** urea-formaldehyde resin
kar'bas *s3* cane
kar'bid *s3* [calcium] carbide **-lampa** carbide lamp
kar'bin *s3* carbine **-hake** snap-hook, spring-‑hook, snaplink, (*vid klippklättring*) karabiner, snap ring
karbol [-'åːl] *s3, tidigare namn på fenol* **-kalk** carbolic lime **-syra** *se* karbol
karbon [-'åːn] *s3* carbon **-'at** *s7, s4* carbonate **-isera** carbonize **-papper** carbon paper
karborundum [-ˣrund-] *s8* carborundum **-skiva** carborundum wheel
karbunkel [-'bunk-] *s2* carbuncle
karburator *s3* carburettor **-sprit** carburettor spirit
karcinogen, karcinom *se* carcinogen, carcinom
karda [ˣkaːr-] **I** *s1* card[ing-brush] **II** *v1* card
kar'dan *s3* cardan **-axel** propeller (cardan) shaft **-knut** universal joint (coupling), cardan joint
kardansk [-'daː-] *a5*, *~ upphängning, se* kardanupphängning
kardan|upphängning cardanic suspension **-växel** cardan drive
kardborr|e (*växt*) burdock; (*blomhuvud*) bur **-band** velcro closing

K

kar'del s3 strand
kardemumma [-ˣmumma] s1 cardamom
kardigan se cardigan
kardi'nal s3 cardinal
kardinalfel cardinal error
kardinal[s]|kollegium the Sacred College, the College of Cardinals -rött cardinal [red]
kardinal|streck cardinal point -synd se dödssynd -system sjö. cardinal marking system -tal cardinal number (numeral)
kardio|graf s3 cardiograph -grafi s3 cardiography -gram [-'gramm] s7 [electro]cardiogram -log cardiologist -logi s3 cardiology -logisk a5 cardiological
kardning [ˣka:-] carding
kar'dus s3 (omhölje) cartridge, cartouche -papper cartridge paper
Karelen [-'re:-] n Karelia
karens|dag [-ˣrens-] försäkr. day of qualifying period for benefit -tid qualifying (waiting) period
karess s3 caress
ka'ret s3 coach; (gammalmodig vagn) shandrydan
karg [-j] a1 1 (om pers.) chary, sparing (på of) 2 (om natur) barren
Karibiska havet [-'ri:-] n the Caribbean [Sea]
karibo ['ka:-] s5 caribou
karies [ˣka:-] r [dental] caries
karika'tyr s3 caricature; polit. äv. cartoon -isk a5 caricatural -tecknare caricaturist; polit. äv. cartoonist
karikera caricature, make a caricature of; (friare) overdraw, burlesque
karisma ['ka:-, äv. -'risma] s3 charisma -tisk [-'ma:-] a5 charismatic
Karl [-a:-] Charles; ~ den store Charlemagne, Charles the Great; ~ XII Charles XII (the Twelfth)
karl [ka:r] s2 man; fellow; (mansperson) male; vard. chap, AE. guy; som en hel ~ like a man; vara ~ för sin hatt hold one's own; han är stora ~en nu he is quite the man now; bra ~ reder sig själv an honest man does his own odd jobs
karlakarl [ˣka:rakar] en ~ a man of men
karlaktig [ˣka:r-] a1 manly; (om kvinna) mannish -het manliness etc.
karlatag [ˣka:ra-] det var ~! that was man-size effort!
Karlavagnen [ˣka:rla-] the Plough, Charles's Wain; AE. the Big Dipper
karl|avulen [ˣka:ra-] a5 manly -göra det är ~ it is a man's job -hatare man-hater
karljohans|stil [-ˣjø:-] Swedish Empire style -svamp cep
karlsbadersalt [ˣka:rls-, äv. -ˣba:-] Carlsbad salts (pl)
karl|tokig [ˣka:r-] man-mad -tycke ha ~ be attractive to men, have sex appeal
karm s2 (armstöd) arm; (ram) frame
karma ['karr-] s1 karma
karme'lit s3, karmeliter s9 Carmelite
karmelit[er]|munk Carmelite monk, white friar -nunna Carmelite nun -orden the Carmelite Order
kar'min s4, s3 carmine -röd carmine[-red]

karmo'sin s4, s3 crimson -röd crimson[-red]
karmstol armchair
karnaubavax [-ˣnauba-] carnauba [wax]
karneol [-'ω:l el. '-å:l] s3 carnelian
karne'val s3 carnival
karnevals|dräkt carnival costume -upptåg carnival escapade -yra riotous revelry [of the carnival]
kar'nis s3 cornice
karnivor [-'vå:r] s3 carnivore
karo'lin s3 soldier of Charles XII of Sweden
karolingisk [-'liŋ-] a5 Carolingian, Carlovingian
kaross [-'råss] s3 chariot -eri [car] body, coachwork
karo'ten s4 carotene, carotin
1 karott [-'rått] s3 (morot) carrot
2 karott [-'rått] s3 deep dish, vegetable dish
karottunderlägg table mat
karp s2 carp
Karpaterna [-'pa:-] pl the Carpathian Mountains, the Carpathians
karpdamm carp pond
karré se fläskkarré
karri'är s3 1 i full ~ at (in) full career 2 (levnadsbana) career; göra ~ make a career for o.s., get on in the world -ist careerist, [social] climber
karsk a1 plucky; bold; cocky
karsk|a ~ upp sig pluck up [one's] courage -het pluck; cocksureness
karstbildning karst formation
kart [-a:-] s2, s9 green (unripe) fruit
karta [ˣka:r-] s1 map (över of); komma på överblivna ~n be on the shelf, become an old maid
kartagisk [-'ta:-] a5 Carthaginian
Kartago [-'ta:-] n Carthage
kart|blad map sheet -bok atlas
kar'tell s3 cartel; (val- o.d.) [com]pact -bildning cartelization
kartera se kartlägga
kartesch [-'e(:)ʃ] s3 cartouche, case shot
kartfodral map case (cover)
kartig [ˣka:r-] a1 unripe, green
kartlagd mapped [out]
kartlägg|a map [out], chart, make a map of; delineate -ning mapping, survey
kart|läsare (i bilsport) codriver -läsning map reading -mätare cartometric wheel pen
kartnagel [ˣka:rt-] deformed nail
karto|graf s3 cartographer -grafi s3 cartography -grafisk [-'gra:-] a5 cartographic[al] -gram [-'gramm] s7 cartogram
kartong [-'åŋ] s3 1 (styvt papper) cardboard 2 (pappask) cardboard box, carton 3 konst. cartoon
kartonn|age [-'a:ʃ] s7 (papparbete) cardboard article; (pappband) [binding in] paper boards -era bind in paper boards
karto'tek s7 card index (file); föra ~ över keep a file (card index) of
kartotekskort index card
kart|projektion [ˣka:-] map projection -ritare cartographer -tecken map symbol
kartusi'an s3 Carthusian -kloster Carthusian monastery
kartverk [ˣka:-] 1 (ämbetsverk) map[-issuing]

office 2 (*atlas*) atlas
karu'sell *s3* roundabout, merry-go-round; *AE.
äv* car[r]ousel; *åka* ~ ride on the roundabout
(merry-go-round) **-svarv** vertical boring and
turning mill
karva whittle, chip (*på* at); (*skära äv.*) cut (*äv.*
~ *i*)
karya'tid *s3* caryatid
kaschmir ['kaʃ- *el.* -'iːr] *s3, s4* cashmere **-sjal**
cashmere shawl **-ull** cashmere wool
kase *s2* beacon fire
kase'in *s4* casein **-lim** casein glue
kase'matt *s3* casemate
kasern [-'äːrn] *s3* barracks (*pl*) **-förbud** confinement to barracks **-gård** barrack square
(yard) **-liv** barrack life
kasino [-'siː-] *s6* casino
1 kask *se kaffekask*
2 kask *s2* casque, helmet
kas'kad *s3* cascade; torrent
kaskelott [-'ått] *s3* cachalot, sperm whale
kas'kett *s3* [brimmed] cap
kaskoförsäkring hull insurance; (*fordons-*)
insurance against material damage to a motor
vehicle
kasper ['kass-] *s9* Punch **-teater** Punch-and--
Judy show
Kaspiska havet ['kass-] *n* the Caspian Sea
kass *a1, vard.* (*dålig*) poor, miserable, wretched,
(*starkare*) lousy, rotten
kassa *s1* **1** (*penningförråd*) cash, purse; money;
(*-låda*) cash box, till; (*intäkt*) takings (*pl*),
receipts (*pl*); *per* ~ (*hand.*) for cash; *brist i* ~*n*
deficit in the cash [account]; *ha hand om* ~*n*
keep the cash; *vara stadd vid* ~ be in funds;
~*n stämmer* the cash account balances; *min* ~
tillåter inte my purse will not allow **2** (*fond*)
fund **3** (*-avdelning*) cashier's department; (*i
butik*) cash (cashier's) desk, checkout; (*i bank*)
cashier['s desk], *AE. äv.* teller['s desk]; (*tea-
ter-*) box office
kassa|apparat cash register **-behållning** cash
balance, cash in hand **-bok** cash-book **-brist**
deficit; (*förskingring*) defalcation **-fack** safe-
-deposit box **-förvaltare** cashier, treasurer
-kista strongbox **-kladd** rough cash-book
-konto cash account **-kontor** pay-office,
cashier's office **-kvitto** sales slip, cash receipt
-kvot cash ratio **-låda** cash box (drawer) **-pjäs**
box-office play **-rabatt** cash discount; *minus
2 %* ~ less 2 % discount [for cash] **-register**
cash register **-skrin** cash box **-skåp** safe
-skåpstjuv safe-breaker, safe-cracker
kassations|domstol supreme court of appeal
-procent rejection percentage
kassava [-ˣsaː-] *s9* cassava, manioc
kassavalv strongroom, safe-deposit vault
kasse *s2* string bag; (*pappers-*) paper carrier
[bag]
kassera reject; (*förslag äv.*) turn down; (*ut-
döma*) condemn; (*kasta bort*) discard
kas'sett *s3, foto.* film holder, cartridge, cassette,
magazine; (*bok-*) slipcase **-bandspelare**
cassette [tape] recorder **-däck** cassette deck
-däck radio cassette recorder
kassler ['kass-] *s9* smoke-cured loin of pork
kas'sun *s3* caisson **-sjuka** decompression

sickness, caisson disease
kassör cashier; (*AE. bank-*) teller; (*förenings-*)
treasurer **-ska** [lady] cashier (*etc.*)
1 kast *s3, boktr.* case
2 kast *s3* (*klass*) caste
3 kast *s7* **1** throw; (*slungande*) fling, pitch, toss;
(*häftigt*) jerk; (*med metspö e.d.*) cast; *stå sitt*
~ put up with the consequences **2** (*hastig rörelse*) toss, jerk (*på huvudet* of the head); *tvära*
~ *i vinden* sudden [chops and] changes in (of)
the wind **3** *ge sig i* ~ *med* grapple with, tackle
kasta I 1 throw; fling, pitch, toss; jerk; cast **2**
veter. abort **3** (*sy*) overcast, whip[stitch] **4** (*om
vind*) chop about, veer [round] **5** (~ *bort*) throw
away; *kortsp.* discard; ~ *pengarna i sjön*
(*vard.*) throw (chuck) money down the drain
6 *rfl* throw (*etc.*) o.s.; ~ *sig av och an i sängen*
toss about in bed; ~ *sig in i* fling o.s. (plunge)
into; ~ *sig om halsen på ngn* throw o.s. round
s.b.'s neck; ~ *sig upp i sadeln* fling o.s. into
the saddle; ~ *sig upp på cykeln* jump on to
one's bicycle; ~ *sig över* fling o.s. upon, fall
upon **II** (*med betonad partikel*) **1** ~ *av throw
off* **2** ~ *bort* throw away, (*slösa äv.*) waste,
squander **3** ~ *i sig maten* bolt one's food **4** ~
loss a) (*lösgöra*) let go, *b*) (*lägga ut*) cast off,
bildl. äv. cut adrift **5** ~ *om a*) (*ändra om*)
change [round], rearrange, *b*) (*en gång till*)
throw again, *c*) (*om vind*) change [round] (*äv.
bildl.*), veer [round] **6** ~ *omkull* throw (knock)
down (over); *bildl. se kullkasta* **7** ~ *på sig* fling
on (hurry into) (*kläderna* one's clothes) **8** ~
tillbaka a) throw back, *mil. äv.* repulse, *b*)
(*ljus*) reflect, (*ljud*) re-echo; ~ *huvudet tillbaka*
toss one's head back
kastanj[e] [-'anj(e)] *s3, s5* chestnut [tree];
krafsa ~[*e*]*rna ur elden åt ngn* be a p.'s
cat's-paw **-brun** chestnut [brown]
kastan'jett *s3* castanet
kastby gust [of wind], squall
kas'tell *s7* citadel **-'an** *s3* caretaker; (*förr*)
castellan
kastfiske spinning; *AE.* baitcasting
kastili|'an *s3*, **-ansk** [-'aːnsk] *a5* Castilian
Kastilien [-'tiː-] *n* Castile
kastlek throwing-game
kastlös outcaste; *de* ~*a* (*äv.*) the untouchables
kastmaskin 1 *mil.* catapult **2** *lantbr.*
winnowing-machine, winnower
kastmärke caste mark
kastning 1 throwing *etc.* **2** *veter.* abortion
kastor [-'åːr] *s3* beaver
kastrat eunuch **-sångare** castrato
kastrer|a castrate, neuter; (*djur äv.*) geld **-ing**
castration; gelding
kast'rull *s3* saucepan
kast|sjuka *se kastning* **2 -spjut** javelin **-spö**
casting rod; (*för flugfiske*) fly rod **-söm** over-
casting; (*stygn*) whipstitch **-vapen** missile
-vind *se kastby*
kastväsen caste system
kasu'ar *s3, zool.* cassowary
kasus ['kaː-] *n, best. form och pl* =, case **-form**
case form **-ändelse** case ending
kata|bolism catabolism **-'falk** *s3* catafalque
-komb [-'åmb] *s3* catacomb
kata'l|an *s3*, **-ansk** [-'aːnsk] *a5* Catalan **-anska**

[-'a:nska] **1** (*språk*) Catalan **2** (*kvinna*) Catalan woman
katalog catalogue
katalogiser|a catalogue **-ing** cataloguing
katalogpris list (catalogue) price
kata'lys *s3* catalysis (*pl* catalyses) **-ator** *s3* catalyst **-era** catalyse
katalytisk [-'ly:-] *a5* catalytic
katama'ran *s3* catamaran
kata'pult *s3* catapult **-stol** ejection (ejector) seat
kata'rakt (*vattenfall o. med.*) cataract
ka'tarr *s3* catarrh **-'al** *a5* catarrhal, catarrhous
katastrof [-'å:f] *s3* catastrophe; *ekon. äv.* crash; (*olycka*) disaster **-'al** *a5* catastrophic; disastrous **-fall** emergency case **-läge** emergency (catastrophic) situation **-situation** state of disaster
kateder [-'te:-] *s2, skol.* teacher's desk; *univ. o.d.* lecturer's desk, rostrum
kated'ral *s3* cathedral
katego'ri *s3* category; class, group; *alla ~er* all types (kinds) (*av* of) **-klyvning** classification by category, grouping
kategoriser|a categorize **-ing** categorization
kategor|isk [-'gɔ:-] *a5* categoric[al]; (*obetingad*) unconditional; *~ vägran* categorical (flat) refusal **-iskt** *adv, neka ~ till ngt* flatly deny s.th.
katekes [-'çe:s] *s3* catechism
katek|et [-'ke:t, *äv.* -'çe:t] *s3* catechist **-isation** catechizing
ka'tet *s3* cathetus (*pl* catheti)
katet|er [-'te:t-] *s2* catheter **-risera** catheterize
katgut *se kattgut*
katjon [*x*katt-] *s3* cation
katod [-'ɔ:d *el.* -'å:d] *s3* cathode **-rör** cathode tube (valve) **-stråle** cathode ray **-strålerör** cathode-ray tube
katolicism [Roman] Catholicism
kato'lik *s3* [Roman] Catholic
katolsk [-'ɔ:lsk] *a5* [Roman] Catholic; *~a kyrkan* (*vanl.*) the Roman Catholic Church
katrinplommon [-*x*tri:n-] (*torkat*) prune
katzenjammer [*x*katt-] *s9* caterwauling
katt *s3* cat; *BE. sl.* mog[gy]; *för ~en!* confound it!; *jag ger ~en i det!* I don't care a fig for that!; *jag kan ge mig ~en på* I'll swear; *arga ~er får rivet skinn* quarrelsome dogs come limping home; *i mörkret är alla ~er grå* all cats are grey in the dark; *när ~en är borta dansar råttorna på bordet* when the cat's away the mice will play
katt|a *s1* female cat, she-cat **-aktig** *a1* catlike, cattish; feline **-djur** feline **-fot** *bot.* cat's-foot **-guld** *miner.* yellow mica; *bildl.* glitter
kattgutt ['katt- *el.* *x*katt-] *s3* catgut
katt|hane tom[cat] **-ost** *bot.* mallow **-rakande** *s6* hullabaloo **-skinn** catskin **-uggla** tawny owl
kat'tun [*el.* *x*katt-] *s4, s3* printed calico
katt|unge kitten **-öga** (*reflexanordning*) cat's-eye (*äv. miner.*), reflector
Kaukasien [-'ka:-] *n* Caucasia
kaukas|ier [-'kas:-] *s9,* **-isk** *a5* Caucasian
Kaukasus ['kau-] *n* the Caucasus
kaurisnäcka ['kauri-] cowry
kaus [-au-] *s3, sjö.* [stay] thimble, eyelet

kaus'al *a5* causal **-itet** causality **-sammanhang** causal nexus **-sats** causal clause
kausativ [*x*kau-, 'kau-, *äv.* -'i:v] *s7, s4 o. a5* causative
kaus'tik *a5* caustic
kautschuk ['kau-] *s2* caoutchouc, [India] rubber; (*radergummi*) eraser, rubber
kav *~ lugnt* absolutely (dead) calm
kavaj [-'ajj] *s3* jacket, coat; (*på bjudningskort*) informal dress **-kostym** lounge (*AE.* business) suit **-skutt** informal dance
kava'lett *s3* revolving chassis
kaval'jer *s3* cavalier; (*bords-, dans- e.d.*) partner; (*ledsagare*) escort
kaval'kad *s3* cavalcade
kavalleri cavalry **-anfall** cavalry charge **-regemente** cavalry regiment
kavallerist cavalryman, trooper
ka'vat *a1* game, spirited; plucky
kavatina [-*x*i:na] *s1* cavatina (*pl* cavatine)
kavel *s2* roller; (*för bakning äv.*) rolling pin **-dun** *bot.* bulrush, reed mace
kavern [-'vä:rn] *s3* cavity
kaviar ['kavv- *el.* *x*kavv-] *s9* caviar[e]
kavi|tation cavitation **-tet** cavity
kavla [*x*ka:v-] roll; *~ ner* (*äv.*) unroll; *~ upp* (*äv.*) tuck up (*ärmarna* one's sleeves); *~ ut* roll out (*degen* the dough)
kavle [*x*ka:v-] *s2, se kavel*
kavring [*x*ka:v-] *ung.* black rye bread
kax|e *s2* bigwig, big shot (gun); panjandrum **-ig** *a1* cocky, high and mighty (*över* about); (*översittaraktig*) overbearing (*mot* to[wards])
kebab [-'babb] *s3* [shish] kebab
kedj|a [*x*çe:-] **I** *s1* chain; *sport.* forward line; *slå ngn i -or* put s.b. into chains, chain s.b. **II** *v1* chain (*vid* to); fasten with chains
kedje|brev chain letter **-bråk** continued fraction **-butik** multiple store (shop), chain store **-byte** (*t.ex. om lägenhet*) multiple exchange **-driven** chain-driven **-hus** link house **-reaktion** chain reaction (*äv. bildl.*) **-röka** chain-smoke **-rökare** chain smoker **-rökning** chain-smoking **-skydd** chain guard **-såg** chain saw **-söm** chain-stitch embroidery
kejsardöme [*x*çejj-] *s6* empire
kejsar|e [*x*çejj-] emperor **-inna** empress **-krona 1** imperial crown **2** *bot.* crown imperial **-pingvin** emperor penguin **-snitt** Caesarean section **-tiden** *under, ~* under (in the time[s] of) the Emperors; *~s romare* the Romans of the Empire **-värdighet** emperorship
kejserlig [*x*çejj-] *a5* imperial; *de ~a* the Imperialists
kel|a [*x*çe:-] pet; *~ med* (*äv.*) fondle, dandle **-en** *a3, se kelig* **-gris** pet, favourite **-ig** *a1* loving **-sjuk** wanting to be cuddled
kelp [k-] *s3* kelp
kelt [k-] *s3* Celt **-isk** ['kelt-] *a5* Celtic
kelvin ['kelv-] *oböjligt s, fys.* kelvin
ke'mi [ç-] *s3* chemistry **-graf** *s3* photoengraver **-grafi** *s3* photoengraving
kemikal|ieaffär [-*x*ka:-] paint and chemicals shop **-ier** [-'ka:-] *pl* chemicals, chemical preparations
kem|isk ['çe:-] *a5* chemical; *~ förening* chemical compound; *~ industri* chemical

industry; ~ *reaktion* chemical reaction; ~ *tvätt, se kemtvätt* **-iskt** *adv* chemically; *tvätta* ~ dry-clean

kemisk-teknisk chemicotechnical, chemical; ~ *industri* chemical industry

kemist [ç-] chemist

kemotera'pi [ç-] chemotherapy

kem|tvätt [ˣçe:-] dry-cleaning; (*lokal*) dry-cleaner's **-tvätta** dry-clean

ken'taur [k-] *s3* centaur

Kenya ['ke:-] *n* Kenya

keny|'an [k-] *s3*, **-ansk** [-'a:nsk] *a5* Kenyan

keps [k-] *s2* cap

kera'm|ik [ç-, *äv.* k-] *s3* ceramics (*pl, behandlas som sg*); (*artiklar*) pottery, ceramic ware **-iker** [-'ra:-] ceramist, potter **-isk** [-'ra:-] *a5* ceramic

kerrcell [k-] Kerr cell

ke'rub [ç-] *s3* cherub **-ansikte** cherubic face

kesa [ç-] (*om kreatur*) rush around

keso [k-] curd (cottage) cheese

ketch [k-] *s3* ketch

ketchup ['ketʃupp] *s3* [tomato] ketchup, catchup

keton [ke'tå:n] *s3* ketone

kex [k-, *äv.* ç-] *s7*, *s6* biscuit; cracker (*äv. AE.*)

KFUK [kåäffˣu:kå:] (*förk. för Kristliga Föreningen av Unga Kvinnor*) YWCA, *se under kristlig* **KFUM** [kåäffˣu:ämm] (*förk. för Kristliga Föreningen av Unga Män*) YMCA, *se under kristlig*

kibbutz [ki'bɒtts] *s3* kibbutz

1 kick [k-] *oböjligt s i uttr.: på ett litet* ~ in a tick

2 kick [k-] *s2* (*spark*) kick; *få ~en* (*vard.*) get the sack

1 kicka [k-] *s1* lassie, girlie

2 kick|a [k-] *v1* kick; ~ *boll* play football

kickstart kick-starter

kid [ç-] *s7* fawn

kidnapp|a [k-] kidnap **-are** kidnapper **-[n]ing** kidnapping

Kielkanalen [ˣki:l-] the Kiel Canal

kika [ç-] peep, peer (*på* at)

kikar|e [ˣçi:-] binoculars (*pl*); field glasses; (*större*) telescope; *ha ngt i ~n* have one's eye on s.th., have s.th. in view; *vad har du nu i ~n?* what are you up to now? **-sikte** telescopic sight

kikhosta [ˣçi:k-] whooping cough

kikkran [ˣçi:k-] [stop]cock, tap

kikna [ˣçi:k-] whoop; ~ *av skratt* choke with laughter

kikärt [ˣçi:k-] chickpea

kil [ç-] *s2* wedge; *sömn.* gusset, gore; (*på strumpa*) slipper heel

1 kila [ç-] (*springa*) scamper; ~ *stadigt* (*vard.*) go steady; *jag ~r nu!* now I'm off!

2 kila [ç-] (*med kil*) wedge

kil|ben sphenoid [bone] **-formig** [-å-] *a5* wedgeshaped, wedgelike

kili'asm [k-, *äv.* ç-] *s3* chiliasm, millenarianism

killa [k-] *se kittla*

kille [k-] *s2* boy; chap; *AE.* guy

killing [ç-] kid

kilo ['çi:- *el.* 'ki:-] *s7* kilo

kilogram [-'gramm] kilogram[me] **-kalori** kilogram calorie, kilocalorie, Calorie **-meter** kilogram metre

kilo|'hertz kilohertz **-joule** [-'jɷ:l] kilojoule **-kalori** *se kilogramkalori*

kilometer [-'me:-] kilometre **-lång** a kilometre long

kilo|pond [-'pånd] *s7* kilopond **-pris** price per kilogram **-ton** [-'tånn] kiloton **-'watt** kilowatt **-wattimme** *särskr. kilowatt-timme* kilowatt--hour **-vis** by the kilo[gram] **-volt** [-'vålt] kilovolt

kil|rem V-belt **-skrift** cuneiform [writing]

kilt *s2* kilt

kimbrer ['kimm-] *s9* Cimbrian

kimono ['kimm-] *s5* kimono

kimrök [ˣçimm-] carbon black; lampblack

Kina [ˣçi:-] *n* [People's Republic of] China

kina [ˣçi:-] *s9* quinine **-bark** cinchona bark

kind [ç-] *s3* cheek **-ben** cheekbone

kindergarten [ˣkinn-] *r* kindergarten, nursery school

kind|k[n]ota cheekbone **-påse** cheek pouch **-tand** molar

kinematograf [ç-, *äv.* k-] *s3* cinematograph

ki'nes [ç-] *s3* Chinese; Chinaman; *~erna* the Chinese

kines|a [çi'ne:-] *han ~de hos oss* we put him up for the night **-eri 1** (*pedanteri*) pedantry; red tape **2** *konst.* Chinese ornamentation, chinoiserie **-isk** *a5* Chinese; *K~a muren* Chinese wall **-iska** *s1* **1** (*språk*) Chinese **2** (*kvinna*) Chinese woman **-ögon** *pl* slanting eyes

kine't|ik *s3* kinetics (*pl, behandlas som sg*) **-isk** [-'ne:-] *a5* kinetic; ~ *energi* kinetic energy

ki'nin [ç-] *s4*, *s3* quinine

1 kink [ç-] *s2* (*ögla*) kink, catch-fake

2 kink [ç-] *s7* (*gnäll*) petulance, fretfulness

kink|a [ç-] fret, whimper **-ig** *a1* petulant, fretful; (*fordrande*) particular, hard to please, exacting; (*om fråga o.d.*) delicate, ticklish, *vard.* tricky

kiosk [ki'åsk, *äv.* çi-, *vard.* çåsk] *s3* kiosk; (*tidnings-*) newsstand, bookstall, newspaper stall

1 kippa [ç-] ~ *efter andan* gasp (pant) for breath

2 kippa [ç-] *skon ~r* the shoe slips up and down

kippskodd *a5, gå* ~ walk about in shoes without stockings on

kir'gis [k-] *s3* Kirg[h]iz **-isk** *a5* Kirg[h]iz[ian]

Kiribati [-'ba:-] *n* Kiribati

kiro|man'ti [ç-] *s3* palmistry, chiromancy **-praktiker** [-'prakt-] *s9*, **-praktor** [-ˣpraktår] *s3* chiropractor

kirra *vard.* fix

kirsch[wasser] [k-] *r* Kirsch[wasser]

ki'rurg [ç-] *s3* surgeon

kirur'g|i *s3* surgery **-isk** [-'urg-] *a5* surgical

kis [ç-] *s3, miner.* pyrites (*pl*)

kisa [ç-] screw up one's eyes; ~ *mot solen* screw up one's eyes in the sun; *~nde ögon* screwed up eyes

kisel ['çi:-] *s2*, *s7* silicon **-alg** [ˣçi:-] diatom **-gur** [ˣçi:-] *s3* kieselguhr **-haltig** *a5* siliceous, siliciferous **-sten** pebble

1 kiss [k-] *interj*, ~ ~*!* puss puss!

2 kiss [k-] *s7* wee, pee

kissa [k-] wee, pee

kisse|'katt [k-] *s3*, **-'miss** *s2* pussy[cat]

K

kist|a [ç-] *s1* chest; *(penning-)* coffer; *(lik-)* coffin **-botten** *ha pengar på* ~ have money saved up **-lock** coffin lid

ki'tin [ç-] *s4, s3* chitin

kitslig [ç-] *a1* *(snarstucken)* touchy; *(retsam)* annoying; *(småaktig)* petty; *(om sak) jfr besvärlig, kinkig* **-het** touchiness; annoyance; pettiness

kitt [ç-] *s7* cement; *(fönster-)* putty **kitta** cement; putty

kittel [ç-] *s2* boiling-pot; *(stor)* ca[u]ldron *(äv. bildl.)*; *(fisk-, te-)* kettle *(äv. bildl.)*; *(tvätt-)* copper **-dal** basin **-flickare** tinker

kittl|a [ç-] tickle; *det ~r i fingrarna på mig att (bildl.)* my fingers are itching (tingling) to **-as** *dep* tickle; ~ *inte!* don't tickle! **-ig** *a1* ticklish **-ing** tickling; tickle

kiv [ç-] *s7* strife, contention; quarrelling **-as** *dep* contend [with each other] *(om* for); *(träta)* quarrel, wrangle *(om* about, as to)

kivi ['ki:-] *s5*, **-fågel** kiwi

kiwi ['ki:-] *s5*, **-frukt** kiwi, Chinese gooseberry

kjol [çɔ:l] *s2* skirt; *hänga ngn i ~arna* be tied to s.b.'s apron strings **-linning** waistband **-längd** skirt length **-regemente** petticoat government **-tyg** *vard.* skirt

kjortel [ˣçɶ:r-] *s2, se kjol*

1 klabb *s2* *(trästycke)* chunk of wood

2 klabb *s7* **1** *(snö-)* sticky snow **2** *hela ~et* the whole lot

klabb|a *(om snö)* cake **-ig** *a1* sticky

1 klack *imperf av 1* klacka

2 klack *s2, jfr* hejarklack

3 klack *s2* *(på sko etc.)* heel; *tekn.* boss; *slå ihop ~arna* click one's heels; *slå ~arna i taket* kick up one's heels; *snurra runt på ~en* turn on one's heel

klack|a heel **-bar** heel bar **-järn** heel iron **-ning** heeling **-ring** signet ring

1 kladd *s2* *(utkast)* rough copy

2 kladd *s7* *(klotter)* scribble

kladd|a mess about, dabble; *(med färg)* daub; ~ *ner sig* mess o.s. up, get o.s. mucky (sticky) **-ig** *a1* smeary; *(degig)* doughy; *(klibbig)* sticky

klaff *s2* flap; *(bords-)* drop leaf; *(på blåsinstrument)* key; *anat.* valve; *hålla ~en* shut up

klaffa *(gå ihop)* tally; *allting ~de* everything fitted in

klaff|bord gate-leg[ged] (drop-leaf) table **-bro** drawbridge; *(med rörlig sektion)* bascule [bridge] **-fel** *(hopskr. klaffel)* valvular disorder **-stol** folding chair

klafsa splash, squelch

klaga complain *(för* to; *över* about, of); *absol.* make complaints; *(jämra)* lament, wail; *gudi ~t* worse luck; *uppassningen var inte att ~ på* the service left no room for complaint

klag|an *r* complaint *(äv. jur.)*; *(jämmer)* lament[ation], wail[ing] **-ande I** *s9, jur., ~n* the complainant, the lodger of the complaint **II** *a4* complaining, plaintive; *(sorgsen)* mourning

klago|låt wailing, moaning, lamentation **-mur** wailing wall **-mål** complaint; *jur. äv.* protest; *(reklamation)* claim; *anföra ~ mot* complain of; *inge ~ mot (hos)* lodge a complaint against (with) **-skri** wail; outcry **-skrift** written complaint (protest); *jur.* bill of protest **-tid** *~en*

utgår i morgon the time for appeal expires tomorrow **-visa** lamentation, jeremiad

klammer ['klamm-] *s9, pl äv. klamrar* [square] bracket; *sätta inom* ~ put in brackets

klammeri altercation, wrangle; *råka i* ~ *med* be at cross-purposes with; *råka i* ~ *med rättvisan* fall foul of the law

1 klamp *s2* *(trästycke)* block of wood

2 klamp *s7* *(-ande)* tramping, tramp

klampa tramp

1 klamra *rfl* cling *(intill* on to); ~ *sig fast vid (bildl.)* cling firmly to

2 klamra *bokb.* stitch

klan *s3* clan

klander ['klann-] *s7* blame; censure; *(kritik)* criticism *(mot* of); *(bestridande)* contesting, dispute **-fri** blameless, irreproachable, impeccable **-värd** blameworthy, reprehensible, censurable

klandr|a blame; censure, find fault with, criticize; *(bestrida)* contest, dispute **-ande** *a4* fault-finding, censorious

klang *s3* ring; sound, clang; *(av glas)* clink; *(ton)* tone; *hans namn har god* ~ he has a good name; *rösten har fyllig* ~ it is a resonant voice **-full** sonorous; *(om röst äv.)* full, rich **-färg** timbre, quality **-lös** thin, flat **-tid** *klang- och jubeltid* time of glee and rejoicing

klank *s7*, **klanka** *v1* grumble *(på* at)

klant|a *rfl, vard.* put one's foot in it **-ig** *a1, vard.* clumsy **-skalle** *vard.* clumsy clot

klapp *s2* tap; *(smeksam)* pat

klappa *(ge en klapp)* tap; pat; *(om hjärtat)* beat, *(häftigt)* palpitate, *(hårdare)* throb; ~ *[i] händerna* clap [one's hands]; ~ *ihop (vard.)* go to pieces

klapper ['klapp-] *s7* clattering *etc., se* klappra

klappersten cobblestone

klappjakt battue; *bildl.* witch-hunt; *anställa* ~ *på (friare)* start a hue and cry after

klappmyts *s2, zool.* hooded seal, bladdernose

klappra clatter; rattle; *(om träskor e.d.)* clip-clop

klapprä beater, batlet

klar *a1* clear; *(om färg, solsken)* bright; *(genomskinlig)* transparent; *(om vatten)* limpid; *bildl.* clear, lucid, *(tydlig)* plain, *(bestämd)* definite, *(avgjord)* decided, distinct; *(färdig)* ready; *sjö.* clear, ready; *~t besked* definite orders, [a] plain answer; *~t väder* fair weather; *~t till London!* *(tel.)* [you are] through to London!; *bilda sig en* ~ *uppfattning om* form a clear conception of; *bli* ~ *över* realize; *få ~t för sig* get a clear idea of; *göra ~t för ngn att* make it clear to s.b. that; *göra ~t skepp* clear the ship (decks) for action; *ha ~a papper* have one's paper in order; *komma på det ~a med* be clear on (about), see one's way clearly in; *den saken är* ~ *nu* that is settled now (cleared up)

klara 1 *i sht tekn.* clarify, clear *(äv. bildl.)*; *(rösten)* clear; *(reda upp)* settle, clear up, solve; *(gå i land med)* manage, cope with, tackle successfully; ~ *begreppen* make things clearer; ~ *en examen* pass (get through) an exam[ination] **2** *rfl* get off, escape; *(reda sig)* manage, get on (along); ~ *sig undan* get off, escape; ~ *sig utan* do without; *han ~r sig all-*

tid he always falls on his feet; *han ~r sig nog (äv.)* he'll do all right **3** ~ *av* clear off, *(skuld e.d. äv.)* settle [up]; ~ *upp* clear up, settle

klar|blå bright blue **-bär** sour cherry

klarer|a *sjö.* clear **-are** *(fartygs-)* shipping agent, shipbroker; *se äv. tågklarerare* **-ing** clearance, clearing

klargöra make clear, bring home *(för* to); *(förklara äv.)* explain

klarhet clearness *etc.*; clarity; *jfr klar*; *(upplysning)* enlightenment, light; *bringa ~ i ngt* throw (shed) light on s.th., elucidate s.th.; *gå från ~ till ~ (friare)* go from strength to strength; *komma till ~ om (i) ngt* get a clear idea of (understand) s.th.

klari'nett *s3* clarinet **-ist** clarinet player, clarinet[t]ist

klarlägg|a make clear, explain; elucidate **-ande** *s6* elucidation

klarmedel clarifier

klar|na [ˣkla:r-] *tekn.* clarify; *(om kaffe äv.)* settle; *(om himlen)* [become] clear; *(om vädret äv.)* clear up; *bildl.* become clear[er]; *(ljusna)* brighten [up] **-signal** go-ahead signal; *få ~* get the go-ahead **-språk** straight talking; *tala ~ (AE., vard.)* talk turkey **-syn** clear vision; sharp perception; *(klärvoajans)* clairvoyance **-synt** [-y:-] *a1* clear-sighted; *(skarp-)* perspicacious **-synthet** clear-sightedness, clarity of vision; *(skarp-)* perspicacity **-tecken** road (line) clear sign; *jfr -signal* **-text** text en clair; *bildl.* plain language **-tänkt** *a1* clear-headed, level-headed **-vaken** wide awake **-ögd** *a5* bright-eyed, clear-eyed

klase *s2* bunch *(druvor* of grapes); *(klunga)* cluster; *bot.* raceme

klass *s3* class; *skol. äv.* form, *AE.* grade; *den bildade ~en* the educated classes *(pl)*; *tredje ~ens hotell* third-rate hotel; *indela i ~er* arrange in classes, classify; *stå i ~ med* be of the same class as, be classed with; *åka tredje ~* travel third class

klass|a class, classify **-anda** class spirit **-delningstal** class division index, statutory maximum class size **-fest** class party **-föreståndare** form teacher; *AE.* homeroom teacher **-hat** class hatred

klassic|ism classicism **-ist** classicist **-istisk** *a5* classicistic

klassifi|cera classify **-cering** [-'se:-], **-kation** classification; breakdown

klassiker ['klass-] classic; *(filolog)* classical philologist (scholar)

klassindelning *(klassificering)* classification; *skol.* division into forms (classes); *(social)* class division

klassisk ['klass-] *a5* classical; *(mönstergill)* classic; ~ *musik* classical music; *~a språk* classical languages

klass|kamp class struggle **-kamrat** classmate, classfellow; *mina ~er* the fellows (boys *etc.*) in my form; *vi är gamla ~er* we were in the same form at school **-lärare** form master **-lös** classless **-medvetande** class-consciousness **-motsättning** *~ar* differences between classes

klass|ning *sjö.* classification **-rum** classroom

-samhälle *(hopskr. klassamhälle)* class society **-skillnad** *(hopskr. klasskillnad)* class distinction **-stämpel** *(hopskr. klasstämpel) polit.* class mark **-träff** class reunion **-utjämning** levelling out of classes **-vis** by (in) classes

klatsch I *interj* crack! **II** *s2* lash; crack, smack

klatscha 1 *(med piska)* give a crack (flick); *(om piska)* crack; *(klå upp)* smack **2** *(färg)* daub *(på* on to) **3** ~ *med ögonen åt* ogle, make eyes at **-ig** *a1* striking; *(schvungfull)* dashing; *(med kraftig färg)* bold

klaustrofo'bi *s3* claustrophobia

klau'sul *s3* clause

klav *s3* key; *mus. äv.* clef

klavbinda tie down; shackle

klave *s2, se krona 5*

klave'cin *s3* harpsichord, clavecin

kla'ver *s7, mus.* keyboard instrument; *trampa i ~et (bildl.)* drop a brick, put one's foot in it **-tramp** blunder, faux pas

klaviatur keyboard

klema ~ *med* pamper, coddle

klematis ['kle:-, *äv.* -'ma:-] *s9* clematis

klemen'tin *s3* clementine

klemig *a1* pampered, coddled; effeminate, soft

klen *a1 (svag, kraftlös)* feeble; delicate, frail, *(tillfälligt)* poorly, ailing; *(om muskelstyrka)* weak; *(tunn)* thin *(planka* plank); *(motsats dryg)* meagre *(bidrag* contribution); *bildl. (dålig)* poor; *(om resultat äv.)* meagre, slender; *en ~ ursäkt* a poor (feeble) excuse; ~ *till förståndet* of feeble intellect; ~ *till växten (om pers.)* of delicate frame

klen|het feebleness *etc.*; *(t. hälsan äv.)* delicacy, frailty **-mod** timidity, pusillanimity **-modig** timid, pusillanimous

kle'nod *s3* jewel; gem; *(friare)* treasure

klen|smed jobbing blacksmith, *äv.* village blacksmith **-smedja** small smithy

klent [-e:-] *adv* feebly *etc.*; ~ *begåvad* poorly gifted; *det är ~ beställt med* it is a poor lookout as regards..., ...leaves much to be desired

klentrogen incredulous, sceptical **-het** incredulity, scepticism; lack of faith

kle'nät *s3, ung.* cruller

klepto|man [-'a:n] *s3* kleptomaniac **-ma'ni** *s3* kleptomania

kleri'kal *a5* clerical

klerk *s3* cleric

klet *s7* daub **-a** daub, smear; scribble **-ig** *a1* messy, mucky

klev *imperf. av kliva*

kli *s7* bran

klia *(förorsaka klåda)* itch; *(riva)* scratch; *det ~r i fingrarna på mig att (bildl.)* my fingers itch to; ~ *sig* scratch o.s.; ~ *sig på benet* scratch one's leg

klibb|a *(vara klibbig)* be sticky (adhesive); *(fastna)* stick *(vid* [on] to); ~ *ihop* stick together **-al** *bot.* [common] alder **-ig** *a1* sticky *(av* with); adhesive; *(limaktig)* gluey

kliché *s3* cliché *(till* for); *boktr. äv.* block, cut, plate; *bildl.* cliché, stereotyped phrase, tag **-anstalt** process engraving works **-artad** [-a:r-] *a5* stereotype **-avdrag** block pull, engraver's

proof
klicher|a stereotype, electrotype **-ing** stereotyping, electrotyping
1 klick *s2* (*sluten krets*) clique, set; *polit.* faction
2 klick *s2* (*klimp*) pat; (*mindre*) dab (*sylt of* jam); (*färg-*) daub, smear; *få en ~ på sig* (*bildl.*) get a blot on one's reputation, vard. blot one's copybook
3 klick I *interj* click!; *det sa ~ för oss* we clicked **II** *s2* (*av vapen*) misfire; (*kameras*) click
klicka (*om vapen*) misfire; (*mankera*) go wrong; be at fault
klickvälde clique rule
klient client **-'el** *s7, s9* clientele
klimakter|isk [-'te:-] *a5* climacteric **-ium** *s4* menopause, climacteric
kli'mat *s7* climate **-bälte** climatic region (zone) **-isk** *a5* climatic **-kammare** grow chamber; *tekn.* phytotron
klimatolog|i *s3* climatology **-isk** *a5* climatologic[al]
klimat|ombyte change of climate **-område, -zon** *se klimatbälte*
klimax ['kli:-] *s2* climax
klimp *s2* lump; *kokk.* [small] dumpling
klimp|a *rfl* get (go) lumpy **-ig** *a1* lumpy
1 kling|a *s1* blade; *korsa sina -or* cross swords
2 klinga *v1* ring, have a ring; (*ljuda*) sound, resound; (*om mynt o.d.*) jingle, chink; (*om glas*) clink; *~ i glaset* (*för att begära tystnad*) tap one's glass
kling|ande *a4* ringing (*skratt* laughter); *på ~ latin* in high-sounding Latin; *~ mynt* hard cash **-e'ling** *interj* jingle, jangle!
klin|ik *s3* clinic; [department of a] hospital; (*privat sjukhem*) nursing home **-iker** ['kli:-] clinical instructor; clinician **-isk** ['kli:-] *a5* clinical
klink *s7* (*dåligt spel*) strum[ming]
1 klinka *v1* strum (*på piano* [on] the piano)
2 klinka *s1* (*dörr-*) latch
klinkbyggd *a5* clinker-built
klinker ['klinn-] *s9* (*tegel*) clinker [brick]; (*slagg*) clinkers (*pl*) **-platta** clinker slab
klint *s2* (*höjd*) hill; (*bergskrön*) brow of a (the) hill; (*bergstopp*) peak
klipp *s7* **1** clip, cut; (*tidningsurklipp*) cutting, clipping (*AE.*) (*ur* out of) **2** *göra ett ~* (*en god affär*) make a killing
1 klipp|a *v3* cut; (*gräsmatta o.d.*) mow; (*naglar*) pare; (*får*) shear; (*biljett*) punch; (*häck, skägg*) trim; *~ itu* cut in two (half); *~ kuponger* clip coupons; *~ med ögonen* blink (wink) (*mot ngn* at s.b.); *~ med öronen* twitch one's ears; *~ till* cut out; *~ till ngn* (*vard.*) land s.b. one; *som -t och skuren till* just cut out for; *~ sig* have one's hair cut
2 klipp|a *s1* rock (*äv. bildl.*); (*hög, brant*) cliff, crag
klipp|avsats ledge **-block** [piece of] rock, boulder
klippbok book for cuttings
klippbrant precipice
klippdocka cut-out doll
klippduva rock dove (pigeon)
klipper ['klipp-] *s2,* **-skepp** clipper [ship]

klippfisk split cod (*sg o. pl*)
klippfyr isophase light
klipp|grav rock tomb **-hylla** ledge **-ig** *a1* rocky; *K~a bergen* the Rocky Mountains, the Rockies **-klättring** crag (rock) climbing, cragging
klipp|ljus isophase light **-ning** cutting *etc.*; (*hår-*) haircutting, [a] haircut; (*av film*) cutting, editing
klipp|rev ledge **-tempel** rock temple **-vägg** rock wall **-ö** rocky island
klips *s7* clip; (*öron-*) ear clip
klipsk *a1* shrewd; quick-witted
klirr *s7* jingling *etc., se klirra* **klirra** jingle; (*om glas, is*) clink; (*om mynt*) chink; (*om porslin*) clatter
klister ['klist-] *s7* **1** paste **2** *råka i klistret* get into a scrape; *sitta i klistret* be in the soup **-burk** paste pot **-märke** sticker, sticky label **-remsa** adhesive tape
klistr|a paste, cement, glue, stick (*fast vid* on to); *~ igen* (*till*) stick down; *~ upp* (*på väggen*) paste (stick) up; *~ upp på väv* mount on cloth **-ing** pasting
klitoris ['kli:-] *r* clitoris
klitter ['klitt-] *pl* dunes, sandhills
kliv *s7* stride; *med stora ~* in (with) long strides
kliva *klev klivit* stride, stalk; (*stiga*) step; (*klättra*) climb; *~ fram* step (walk) up (*till* to); *~ ner* step down, descend; *~ upp* climb up (*för trapporna* the stairs); *~ över* (*dike e.d.*) step across; (*gärdesgård e.d.*) climb over
klivit *sup. av kliva*
klo *s5* claw; *friare o. bildl. äv.* clutch; (*kräftdjurs*) pincers (*pl*); (*på gaffel e.d.*) prong; *få ngn i sina ~r* get s.b. into one's clutches; *råka i ~rna på* get into the clutches of; *slå ~rna i* get one's claws into; *visa ~rna* be up in arms (*mot* against)
klo'ak *s3* **1** (*avloppsledning*) sewer; drain **2** *zool.* cloaca (*pl* cloacae) **-brunn** cesspool, cesspit **-djur** monotreme **-ledning** [main] sewer, conduit **-rör** sewer **-system** sewage system **-vatten** sewage
1 klocka [-å-] *s1* (*kyrk-, ring-*) bell
2 klocka [-å-] *s1* (*vägg- o.d.*) clock; (*fick-*) watch; *hur mycket är ~n?* what time is it?, what is the time?; *~n är fem* it is five o'clock; *~n är halv sex* it is half past five, it is five thirty; *går den här ~n rätt?* is this clock (watch) right?; *~n är bara barnet* (*vard.*) it's early days yet, there's bags of time; *~n är mycket* it is getting late; *~n närmar sig åtta* it is getting near eight o'clock; *förstå vad ~n är slagen* understand the situation, know what to expect
3 klocka [-å-] *v1* (*ge klockform åt kjol*) gore, flare
4 klocka [-å-] *v1, sport.* (*ta tid på*) clock
klockar|e [-å-] parish clerk and organist; (*kyrkomusiker*) precentor **-katt** *kär som en ~* be madly in love **-kärlek** fondness, affection (*för* for)
klockarmband watchstrap; *AE.* watchband; (*av metall*) [watch] bracelet
klockboj bell buoy
klock|fjäder clock (watch) spring **-fodral**

watchcase
klock|formad [-fårm-] *a5* bell-shaped **-gjutare**
bell-founder
klockkedja watch chain
klock|kjol flared skirt **-klang** ringing of a bell
(of bells) **-ljung** bell heather **-malm, -metall**
bell metal
klockradio clock radio
klock|ren [as] clear as a bell-ringing (tolling)
-ringning bell-ringing
klock|skojare clock-and-watch hawker **-slag** *på*
~et on the stroke [of the clock]; *på bestämt ~*
at a definite time
klock|spel chime (peal) of bells, carillon **-sta-
pel** detached bell tower, bell frame **-sträng**
bell pull **-torn** bell tower, belfry
klok *a1* **1** *(förståndig)* wise, judicious; *(intelligent)* intelligent, clever; *(förnuftig)* sensible;
(försiktig) prudent, discreet; *(tillrådlig, lämplig)* advisable; *~ gubbe, se kvacksalvare; de
slog sina ~a huvuden ihop* they put their heads
together; *jag är lika ~ för det* I am none the
wiser [for that]; *jag blir inte ~ på det* I cannot
make it out, I can make neither head nor tail
of it **2** *(vid sina sinnens fulla bruk)* sane, in
one's senses; *inte riktigt ~* not in one's right
senses, not all there, *AE.* nuts
klokhet [-ʊ:-] wisdom, judiciousness, prudence, sagacity
klokoppling clutch coupling, jaw clutch
klokskap [-ʊ:-] *s3* overwiseness; *(självklokhet)*
self-sufficiency; *jfr äv. klokhet*
klokt [-ʊ:-] *adv* wisely *etc.*; *det var ~ gjort* it
was the sensible thing to do; *du gjorde ~ i att*
you would be wise to
klon [-ʊ:n] *s3* clone **klona** [ˣklʊ:-] clone **klo-
ning** [ˣklʊ:-] cloning
klor [-å:r] *s3* chlorine **-amin** [ˣklå:r- el. -'i:n]
chloramine **-at** *s7, s4* chlorate **-era** chlorinate
-gas chlorine [gas] **-haltig** *a5* chlorinous **-'id**
s3 chloride **-kalk** chloride of lime, bleaching
powder
kloroform [-'fårm] *s3*, **-era** *v1* chloroform
klor|o'fyll *s4, s3* chlorophyll **-syra** chloric acid
-väte hydrogen chloride **-vätesyra** hydro-
chloric acid
klo'sett *s3* closet; *(vatten-)* toilet, lavatory **-bor-
ste** lavatory brush
kloss [-å-] *s2* block; clump
kloster ['klåss-] *s7* abbey, priory; *(munk-)*
monastery; *(nunne-)* convent, nunnery; *(fran-
ciskan-, dominikan-)* friary; *(mindre)* community; *gå i ~* enter a monastery **-arbete**
bildl. [extremely] fine needlework **-broder**
monk **-cell** monastery (convent *etc.*) cell **-löf-
te** *avlägga ~* take [the] vows **-regel** monastic
(conventual) rule **-ruin** ruined abbey *(etc.)*
-skola monastery (convent) school **-väsen**
~det monasticism, the monastic system
1 klot *s7 (kula)* ball; *sport. äv.* bowl; *(jord-)*
globe; *fack.* sphere
2 klot *s3 (t. foder)* sateen; *(t. bokband)* cloth,
buckram
klotband cloth binding; *i ~* in cloth, clothbound
klot|blixt fireball **-formig** [-år-] *a5* ball-shaped;
globular; spherical **-rund** round like a ball;
(om pers. äv.) rotund, tubby

klots [-å-] *s2 (rit-)* model
klotter ['klått-] *s7* scrawl, scribble **-plank** [pu-
blic] scribble board
klottr|a [-å-] *s7* scrawl, scribble **-ig** *a5* scrawling
klove *s2, tekn.* vice; *AE.* vise
klubb *s2* club
klubba I *s1* club; *sport. äv.* stick; *(krocket-)*
mallet; *(ordförande-)* gavel, hammer; *(slick-
epinne)* lollipop; *föra ~n* hold the chair; *gå
under ~n* go under the hammer **II** *v1* club;
knock on the head; *~ ner (talare)* call to order; *boken ~des för 100 kronor (vid auktion)*
the book was knocked down for 100 kronor
klubb|hus clubhouse **-jacka** blazer **-kamrat**
fellow club member; *vi är ~er (äv.)* we belong
to the same club **-lokal** club premises *(pl)*
-medlem club member **-märke** club badge
-mästare 1 master of ceremonies; *AE. äv.*
emcee **2** *sport.* club champion **-rum** club-
room; *univ. ung.* common room
klubbslag stroke with a (the) club; *(vid auktion)*
blow of the hammer; *sport.* shot; *bildl.* knockout blow
kluck *s7* cluck
kluck|a cluck; *(skvalpa)* gurgle **-ande** *a4*
clucking *etc.*; *ett ~ skratt* a chuckle
kludd *s7*, **-a** *v1* daub **-ig** *a1* dauby
klump *s2* lump; *(jord-; pers.)* clod; *i ~* in the
lump, wholesale; *sitta som en ~ i bröstet* lie
like a lump on the chest
klumpa *rfl, se klimpa sig*
klump|e'duns *s2* clodhopper **-fot** club foot
klumpig *a1 (otymplig)* lumbering, unwieldy;
(tung) heavy; *(ovig o. tafatt)* clumsy, awkward;
(ohyfsad) churlish **-het** clumsiness
klump|summa lump sum **-vis** in clumps
klunga *s1* cluster; bunch; group; *(hop)* crowd
klunk *s2* draught, gulp *(vatten* of water); *(liten)*
sip; *ta [sig] en ~* have (take) a swig **klunka**
gulp
kluns *s2* lump **-ig** *a1* lumpy
klurig *a1* artful; ingenious
klu'sil *s3*, språkv. plosive
klut *s2* patch; *(trasa)* rag; *sätta till alla ~ar* clap
on all sail, *(friare)* do one's level best
kluven *a3* split *(i* into); *bot.* cleft; *(om läpp)* slit;
(om stjärt) forked; *~ gom* cleft palate; *~ personlighet* split personality **-het** *bildl.* duality;
dualism
kluvit *sup. av klyva*
klyfta *s1* **1** *(bergs-)* gorge; cleft; *(ravin)* ravine;
(rämna) fissure, crevice; *bildl.* breach; gap,
gulf **2** *(vitlöks-)* clove; *(apelsin-)* segment;
(äppel-, ägg-, tomat-) wedge, slice
klyftig *a1* shrewd, bright, clever; *inte så värst
~* not overbright **-het** shrewdness *etc.*
klyka *s1 (träd- o.d.)* fork; *(år-)* rowlock, *AE.*
oarlock; *(telefon-)* receiver rest, hook
klys *s7, sjö.* hawse[hole]
klyscha *s1* cliché, hackneyed phrase
klyva *klöv kluvit* split; *(dela)* divide, split up *(i*
into); *(ved)* chop, cleave; *fys.* break up, split,
disintegrate; *~ sig* split
klyv|arbom jib boom **-are** *sjö.* jib **-bar** *a5*
cleavable; *(del-)* divisible; *(kärnfys.)* fissionable; *~t material (kärnfys.)* fissile material
-frukt schizocarp **-ning** splitting *etc.*; split;

K

fissure; (kärn-) fission; fack. division, disintegration -ningsprodukt kärnfys. fission product

klå v4 1 (ge stryk) thrash, beat; ~ upp ngn give s.b. a [good] thrashing 2 (pungslå) fleece, cheat

klåda sl itch[ing]

klåfing|er pers. person who fingers everything -rig a5, vara ~ be unable to let things alone -righet inability to let things alone

klåpare bungler, botcher, fumbler (i at)

klä v4 1 (förse med kläder) clothe; (iföra kläder) dress; (pryda) array, deck; som man är ~dd blir man hädd a man is measured by the cut of his coat 2 bildl. clothe; ~ sina tankar i ord clothe one's thoughts in words, put one's thoughts into words 3 (möbler) cover; (julgran) dress; (fodra) line 4 rfl dress [o.s.]; put on one's clothes; (om naturen) clothe itself; ~ sig fin dress up; ~ sig varmt put on warm clothes, wrap [o.s.] up well 5 (med betonad partikel) ~ av [sig] undress; ~ om (möbler) re-cover; ~ om sig change (till middagen for dinner); ~ på ngn help s.b. on with his (etc.) clothes; ~ på sig dress, put one's clothes on; ~ ut sig dress [o.s.] up (till as) 6 (passa) suit; become; be becoming; hon ~r i blått blue suits her, she looks well in blue

1 kläcka klack, opers. vard.: det klack till i mig när jag såg honom the sight of him gave me quite a start

2 kläck|a v3 (ägg) hatch; ~ fram (bildl.) hatch, hit on; ~ ur sig en dumhet come out with a stupid remark

kläckning hatching

kläcknings|maskin [poultry] incubator, brooder -tid hatching (incubation) period

kläda v2, se klä

kläde s6 broadcloth -dräkt costume, dress

kläder ['klä:-] pl clothes; koll. clothing, apparel; bli varm i ~na (bildl.) [begin to] find one's feet; jag skulle inte vilja vara i dina ~ I wouldn't be in your shoes

klädes|borste clothes brush -plagg article of clothing, garment; pl äv. outfit (sg)

kläd|hängare coat hanger; (väggfast) clothes rail; (fristående) hat and coat stand -kammare clothes closet -konto clothing account -korg clothes basket -loge dressing room -lus body louse -lyx extravagance in dress -mal clothes moth -medveten clothes-conscious -mod fashion

kläd|nad [-ä:-] s3 1 (utan pl) dress 2 (med pl) garment[s pl], vestment[s pl] -nypa clothes peg

kläd|sam [-ä:-] a1 becoming (för to) -sel ['klädd-] s2 1 (utan pl) dressing, attiring 2 (dräkt) dress, attire 3 (möbels) covering, upholstery

kläd|skåp wardrobe -snobb dandy -streck clothesline -sömnad dressmaking -visning fashion show -vård [the] care of clothes -väg i ~ in the way of clothes

kläm [klämm] s2 1 komma i ~ a) eg. get jammed, b) bildl. get into a scrape; få foten i ~ get one's foot caught 2 (fart) go, dash, push, pep; (kraft) force, vigour; med fart och ~ with

vigour and dash 3 (sammanfattning) [summarized] statement (declaration); (slut-) summing-up 4 få ~ på ngt get the hang of s.th.; ha ~ på ngt be well up in s.th. -dag working day between holidays

klämma I sl 1 (knipa) pinch; straits (pl); komma i ~ get into a scrape (tight corner, fix) 2 (hår-, pappers- e.d.) clip; (fjädrad) spring-holder II v2 1 squeeze; (trycka) press; (nypa, äv. om sko) pinch; (absol., om sko e.d.) be tight; ~ fingret (foten) get one's finger pinched (foot jammed) 2 rfl get pinched (squeezed) 3 (med betonad partikel) ~ fast fasten, squeeze together; ~ fram squeeze out; ~ fram med come out with; ~ i strike up (med en sång a song); ~ ihop squeeze up, jam; ~ sönder squeeze (crush) to pieces; ~ till (slå till) go at it, give a good one; ~ ur sig (vard.) bring out, come out with; ~ åt ngn clamp down on s.b., badger (pester) s.b.

kläm|mare clip -mig a1 (om t.ex. melodi) dashing; (stilig) tiptop -skruv clampscrew

klämt|a toll (i klockan the bell) -ning toll, tolling

klänga [ˣkläŋa] v2, ~ [sig] climb (uppför up); ~ sig fast vid cling on to

kläng|e [ˣkläŋe] s6, bot tendril -ros rambler [rose] -växt climbing plant, climber; creeper

klänning dress; frock; (gala- o.d.) gown

klänningstyg dress material

kläpp s2 1 (klock-) clapper, tongue 2 (i ljuskrona) drop

klärobskyr [-'sky:r] s3 chiaroscuro

klärvoaj|ans [-'jaŋs] s3 clairvoyance -ant [-'jant el. -'jaŋt] a4 clairvoyant

klätter|fot zool. scansorial foot -skor climbing shoes -ställning climbing frame -växt climbing plant, creeper

klättr|a climb (nedför down; uppför, upp [i] up); (klänga) scramble -ing climbing; en ~ a climb

klös|a v3 scratch; ~ ut ögonen på ngn scratch a p.'s eyes out -as v3, dep scratch

1 klöv imperf. av klyva

2 klöv s2, zool. hoof (pl hooves), cloven hoof (foot)

klöv|bärande a4 hoofed -djur cloven-hoofed (cloven-footed) animal

1 klöver ['klö:-] s9, kortsp., koll. clubs (pl); jfr hjärter

2 klöver ['klö:-] s9, bot. o. lantbr. clover; bot. äv. trefoil

klöver|blad cloverleaf; arkit. trefoil; (tre pers.) trio -vall field of clover

klövja [ˣklö:v-] transport on packhorses (a packhorse)

klövje|djur pack animal -sadel packsaddle

knacka (bulta) rap; (svagare) tap; (på dörren) knock; (sten) break; ~ bort rost från chip the rust off; ~ hål på ett ägg crack an egg; ~ ner ngt på skrivmaskin tap s.th. out on the typewriter; ~ på„ knock [at the door]; ~ sönder knock to pieces; det ~r! there's a knock!

knack|ig a1, vard., ~ svenska poor Swedish -igt adv, vard., ha det ~t have a job to make ends meet -ning knock (äv. i motor); rap; tap

knagg|la ~ fram push on to; ~ sig fram (igenom) struggle along to (through) -lig a1 rough, bumpy, uneven; (*om stil*) rugged, laboured; ~ *engelska* broken English -**ligt** *adv, det gick ~ för honom a*) (*i tentamen*) he didn't do too well, *b*) (*med studierna*) it was tough going for him

knak|a crack; creak (*i alla fogar* in every joint) -**ande** *a4* cracking *etc.*

knal *a1, det var ~t med maten* food was scarce

knall *s2* report; (*smäll*) crack, bang; (*vid explosion*) detonation; (*åsk-*) peal, clap; (*duns*) bang; ~ *och fall* on the spot, all of a sudden **1 knalla** (*gå*) trot; ~ *vidare* (*äv.*) push on; ~ *sig iväg* trot off; *det ~r och går* I am (*etc.*) jogging along

2 knalla (*explodera*) detonate; (*smälla*) bang, pop; (*om åskan*) crack

knallblå bright blue

knalle *s2* (*bergs-*) hill, hillock

knall|effekt sensational effect -**gas** oxyhydrogen gas -**hatt** percussion cap -**pulver** fulminating powder -**pulverpistol** toy pistol -**röd** scarlet

knalt [-a:-] *adv, ha det ~* be hard up

knap *s2, sjö.* cleat

knapadel petty nobility; (*i Storbritannien ung.*) baronetage

knapert ['kna:-] *adv, ha det ~* be badly off

1 knapp *s2* **1** button; (*lös skjort-*) stud; *försedd med ~ar* buttoned **2** (*på käpp, lock e.d.*) knob; (*prydnads- äv.*) boss; (*på svärd*) pommel

2 knapp *a1* scanty; (*knappt tillmätt äv.*) short; (*röstövervikt, utkomst e.d.*) bare; (*seger äv.*) narrow; (*om omständigheter e.d.*) reduced, straitened; (*ord-*) sparing, chary (*på* of); *~a tre veckor senare* barely three weeks later; *i ~aste laget* hardly sufficient; *på sin ~a lön* on his (*etc.*) meagre salary; *ha det ~t* be poorly off (in straitened circumstances); *ha ~t om* be short of; *rädda sig med ~ nöd* narrowly escape, have a narrow escape; *tillgången på...är ~* ...are in short supply

knapp|a ~ *av* (*in*) *på* reduce, cut down -**ast** scarcely, hardly -**het** scantiness *etc.*; scarcity (*på* of); shortage (*på* of)

knapphål buttonhole

knapphåls|blomma buttonhole; *AE.* boutonniere -**silke** buttonhole silk -**stygn** buttonhole stitch

knapphändig *a1* meagre, scant; (*förklaring, ursäkt e.d. äv.*) curt, scantily worded

knappnål pin

knappnåls|brev sheet of pins -**dyna** pincushion -**huvud** pinhead -**stick** pinprick

knappolo'gi *s3* trifle, pedantry

knapp|rad row of buttons -**slagning** [-a:g-] button-making

knappt *adv* **1** scantily *etc.*; *leva ~* live sparingly; *mäta ~* give short measure **2** *vinna ~* win by a narrow margin **3** (*nätt o. jämnt*) barely; *jfr äv. knappast*; *~...förrän* scarcely...before (when), no sooner...than

knapptelefon push-button telephone

knapr|a [*kna:-] nibble (*på* at); ~ *i sig* munch (chew) up; ~ *på en skorpa* crunch (munch) a rusk -**ig** *a1* crisp

knark *s7* dope; *AE. äv.* junk

knark|a use (take) dope -**are** dope [fiend];

(*särsk. marijuana*) pothead; *AE. äv.* junkie

knark|arkvart dope nest, pad -**hund** sniffer dog -**langare** [dope] peddler (pusher), drug pusher

knarr 1 *s7* (*-ande*) creak[ing]; (*i dörr etc.*) squeak **2** *s2, s7, ha ~ i skorna* have creaking (squeaky) shoes **3** *s2* (*knarrig människa*) old growler (croaker)

knarr|a (*om trappa, skor e.d.*) creak; (*om dörr, gångjärn e.d.*) squeak; (*om snö*) crunch -**ig** *a1* (*om pers.*) cross, morose; (*grinig*) peevish, grumpy

knasig *a1* (*tokig*) (*vard.*) daft

knast *s2* knot, knag

1 knaster ['knass-] *s9* (*tobak*) canaster

2 knaster ['knass-] *s7* crackling *etc.*; [a] crackle

knast|ertorr as dry as a stick -**ra** crackle; crepitate; (*krasa äv.*) [s]crunch; (*om tobak i pipa*) rustle; *~de mellan tänderna* grated between my (*etc.*) teeth; *gruset ~de under hans fötter* the gravel crunched under his feet

knata *vard., ~ iväg* trot off

knatte *s2* nipper

knatter ['knatt-] *s7,* **knattra** [*knatt-] *v1* rattle, clatter

kneg|a toil; *vard.* slog -**are** *vard.* wage-slave

knekt *s2* (*soldat*) soldier; (*i Storbritannien ung.*) redcoat; (*bildl., 'verktyg'*) myrmidon; *kortsp.* jack, knave

1 knep *imperf. av 1 knipa II*

2 knep *s7* trick, device; (*list*) stratagem, ruse; (*fuffens*) dodge; (*konstgrepp*) artifice

knepig *a1* (*listig*) artful, cunning; (*sinnrik*) ingenious, clever **2** (*svår*) hard, ticklish, tricky

knesset *r* Knesset[h]

knip *s7, ~ i magen* stomachache

1 knip|a I *s1, komma i en svår ~* get into a fix; *vara i ~* be in straits (in difficulties, in a tight place) **II** *knep knipit* **1** pinch; ~ *en applåd* elicit a cheer; ~ *ihop* pinch together; ~ *ihop läpparna* compress one's lips; ~ *ihop ögonen* screw up one's eyes **2** *om det -er* (*bildl.*) at a pinch, if need be; *det -er i magen på mig* I have [got] a griping pain in my stomach

2 knipa *s1* (*fågel*) goldeneye

knipit *sup. av 1 knipa II*

knippa *s1* bunch

knippe *s6* cluster, fascicle; bundle; *bot.* cyme

knipsa clip (*av* off)

knip|slug knowing, shrewd; (*listig*) sly -**tång** pincers (*pl*), nippers (*pl*) -**tångsmanöver** pincer movement

knirk *s7* grating (creaking) [sound] **knirka** grate; (*knarra*) creak, [s]crunch

knittelvers doggerel [verse]

kniv *s2* knife (*pl* knives); *med ~en på strupen* with the knife at one's throat; *strid på ~en* war to the knife; *dra ~* draw one's knife; *ränna ~en i* run one's knife into -**blad** knife blade, blade of a knife -**drama** knifing tragedy -**hugg** stab [with a knife] -**hugga** stab [with a knife]; *bli -huggen* be stabbed [with a knife]

kniv|ig *a1* (*om sak*) delicate, tricky; (*om pers.*) shrewd, crafty -**kastning** *bildl.* altercation

knivsegg knife edge

kniv|skaft knife handle -**skarp** [as] sharp as a razor -**skuren** *a5* knifed, gashed with a knife

K

-**skära** knife -**spets** knife-point -**styng** stab [with (of) a knife]
knivsudd knife-point; *en ~ salt* a pinch of salt
knix *s2* curts[e]y; *göra en ~ för* drop a curts[e]y
knixa bob, curts[e]y
knock|a [ˣnåcka] knock *s.b.* out -**out** [nåck'aot] *s3* knockout [blow]; *slå ngn ~* knock *s.b.* out; *vinna på ~* win by a knockout
knodd [-å-] *s2, vard.* bounder -**aktig** *a1* slick
knog *s7* work, toil; *vard.* fag **knoga** labour (work, plod) *(med* at); *~ på„ a)* trudge (plod) along, *b) bildl.* peg away
knoge *s2* knuckle
knogig *a1* fagging, strenuous
knogjärn knuckle-duster
knollr|a [-å-] *rfl* curl -**ig** *a1* curly, frizzy
knop *sjö.* 1 *s9 (hastighet)* knot; *med åtta ~* at [a speed of] eight knots; *göra tolv ~* do twelve knots 2 *(knut)* knot; *slå en ~* tie (make) a knot
knopp [-å-] *s2* 1 *bot.* bud; *skjuta ~* bud 2 *(knapp)* knob 3 *(huvud-)* nob, nut; *klar i ~en* clear-headed; *vara konstig i ~en* be a bit cracked -**as** *dep* bud -**ning** budding
1 **knorr** [-å-] *s2 (krökning)* curl; *ha ~ på svansen* have a curly tail
2 **knorr** *s7, se* 2 *knot*
knorr|a *se* 2 *knota* -**hane** *zool.* grey gurnard (gurnet)
1 **knot** *s2 (fisk) se knorrhane*
2 **knot** *s7 (-ande)* murmuring *(mot* against); grumbling *(mot, över* at)
1 **knota** *s1, anat.* condyle; *(friare)* bone
2 **knota** *v1* murmur; grumble *(över* at)
knotig *a1 (om träd)* knotty; *(om trädrot)* twisted; *(om pers.)* bony, *(mager)* scraggy
knott [-å-] *s7, s9* black fly
knottr|a [-å-] I *s1* [goose] pimple II *v1, rfl* become granulated -**ig** *a1* granular; *(om hud)* rough; *(kinkig)* touchy; *jag blev alldeles ~* I got goose flesh all over
knubb|ig *a1* plump; chubby -**säl** harbour seal
knuff *s2* push, shove; *(med armbågen)* elbowing, nudge; *(i sidan)* poke, dig **knuffa** push, shove, shoulder *etc.*; *~ omkull* push (shove, knock) over, upset; *~ till* push (bump, knock) into; *~ undan* push *(etc.)* out of the way; *~ sig fram* shoulder one's way along **knuffas** *dep, ~ inte!* don't push (shove)!
knull *s7, vard.,* **knulla** *v1, vard.* fuck
knussel ['knuss-] *s7* niggardliness; *(svagare)* parsimony; *utan ~* without stint
knuss|la be niggardly *(etc., se -lig) (med* with) -**lig** *a1* niggardly, stingy, sparing; parsimonious, mean
knut *s2* 1 *(hörn)* corner; *bakom ~en* round the corner; *inpå ~arna* at our *(etc.)* very doors 2 knot; *(hår- äv.)* bun; *(ögle-)* tie; *knyta (slå) en ~* tie (make) a knot *(på* in); *~en har gått upp* the knot has come untied (undone); *det har blivit ~ på tråden* the thread has got into a knot 3 *bildl.* point; *det var just ~en!* that's just the [crucial] point! 4 *fack.* node
knut|a I *s1 (förhårdnad i vävnad)* node II *v1, rfl* snarl, become entangled (knotted) -**en** *a5* tied *(äv. bildl.)*, knotted; clenched *(näve* fist); *bildl.* bound up *(vid* with); *vara ~ vid (till) a)* *(verksamhet)* be bound up (associated) with,

b) (läroanstalt, tidning) be on the [permanent] staff of -**ig** *a1* knotty, nodose -**it** *sup. av knyta* -**piska** knout -**punkt** junction, intersection; *(friare)* centre -**timra** *~d stuga* cabin built of logs dovetailed at corners
knyck *s2* jerk; twitch
knyck|a *v3* 1 jerk, twitch *(på* at); *~ på nacken* toss one's head, *(friare)* turn up one's nose *(åt* at) 2 *(stjäla)* pinch, bone -**ig** *a1* jerky
knyckla crease; *~ ihop* crumple up
knyppel|dyna lace-pillow -**pinne** lace-bobbin
knyppl|a make lace; *~d spets* pillow (bobbin) lace -**erska** lacemaker -**ing** lacemaking
knyst *n* sound; *inte säga ett ~* not breathe a word *(om* about)
knysta utter a sound; *utan att ~* without uttering a sound, *(utan att mucka)* without murmuring
knyta *knöt knutit* 1 tie *(igen, till* up); *(fästa)* fasten; *(näven)* clench; *bildl.* attach; bind, unite *(vid* to), connect *(till* to); *~ bekantskap med ngn* make a p.'s acquaintance; *~ förbindelser* establish connections; *~ upp* untie, undo, *(öppna)* open, *(fästa upp)* tie up; *~ åt* tie tight 2 *rfl* knot, get knotted; *(om sallad o.d.)* head; *(gå t. sängs)* turn in; *~ sig i växten* become stunted
knyt|e *s6* bundle *(med* of) -**kalas** Dutch treat -**näve** fist -**nävsslag** punch -**nävsstor** as big as a fist -**skärp** sash
knåd|a knead -**ning** kneading
knåp *s7* finicky job **knåpa** *~ med* potter [about] at; *~ ihop ett brev* patch together at letter **knåpgöra** *s6* finicky job
knä *s6* 1 knee; *tekn. äv.* elbow; *~na böj!* knees bend!; *byxor med [stora] ~n* trousers with [great] baggy knees; *på sina bara ~n* on one's bended knees; *falla på ~ för* kneel [down] to, go down on one's knees to; *ha ett barn i ~t* have a child on one's knee[s] (on [in] one's lap); *ligga på ~ för* kneel to; *tvinga ngn på ~ (bildl.)* bring *s.b.* to his knees 2 *bot.* articulation; *(krök)* bend, elbow
knä|a bend one's knees; *~ fram* walk with bended knees -**byxor** *pl* short trousers; breeches -**böja** bend the knee, kneel *(för* to; *inför* before, to); *relig.* genuflect
1 **knäck** *s2, kokk.* toffee, butterscotch
2 **knäck** *s2* 1 *(-ning)* crack 2 *(nederlag)* blow; *ta ~en på* do for, ruin
knäck|a *v3* crack; *(bryta av)* break; *(gåta, problem)* scotch, floor; *en hård nöt att ~* a hard nut to crack; *~ till* give a crack; *det -te honom* that broke him
knäckebröd crispbread, hard bread
knäckform toffee cup
knä|fall kneeling, genuflection -**hund** lap dog -**höjd** knee-height -**kort** *~ kjol* knee-length skirt -**led** knee-joint -**liggande** *a4* kneeling
1 **knäpp** 1 *s2 (-ning)* click; *(finger-)* flip, flick 2 *s7 (ljud)* sound
2 **knäpp** *a1, vard. (tokig)* daft, bananas
1 **knäpp|a** *v3* 1 *det -te i klockan* the clock gave a click; *det -er i väggarna* there's a ticking in the walls 2 *(fotografera)* snap; *(i sht film)* shoot 3 *(med fingrarna)* flip, flick, snap; *~ ngn på näsan* rebuke *s.b.* 4 *mus., ~ [på]* twang, pluck *(på gitarren* one's guitar) 5 *~ nötter*

crack nuts
2 knäppa *v3* **1** button; (*spänne*) buckle, clasp; ~ *av* (*upp*) unbutton; ~ *igen* button [up]; ~ *på* (*elektr.*) switch on **2** ~ *händerna* fold (clasp) one's hands
knäppe *s6* clasp, snap
knäppinstrument plucked string instrument
knäpp|känga button boot **-ning** (*till 2 knäppa*) buttoning
knä|skydd kneepad **-skål** kneecap; *anat.* panatella **-strumpa** knee sock **-stående** *a4, sport.* crouching; ~ *ställning* kneeling position **-svag** weak in the knees **-sätta** adopt **-veck** hollow of the knee; *darra i ~en* tremble at the knees; *hänga i ~en* hang by the knees
knävelborr [-å-] *s2* military moustache (*sg*)
knöl *s2* **1** bump; (*upphöjning e.d.*) boss, knob, knot; (*utväxt*) tuber, protuberance; *fack.* node; *bot.* bulb **2** (*drummel*) swine, cad
knöl|a ~ *ihop* crumple up; ~ *till* batter, knock out of shape **-aktig** *a1* loutish; caddish **-begonia** tuberous begonia **-ig** *a1* **1** bumpy (*väg* road); (*om madrass e.d.*) lumpy; (*om träd e.d.*) knotty; (*om finger, frukt*) knobbly; *fack.* nodose, nodular **2** *se -aktig* **-påk** thick knotted stick; (*vapen*) cudgel **-ros** *med.* traumatic erysipelas **-svan** mute swan
knös *s2* swell, nob; *en rik* ~ a [rich] nabob
knöt *imperf. av knyta*
KO *se konsumentombudsman*
ko *s5* cow
koaff|era *se frisera* **-'yr** *s3* coiffure **-ör** hairdresser
koagulation coagulation
koaguler|a coagulate, clot **-ing** coagulation
koala [-'a:la] *s1* koala [bear]
koalition coalition
koalitionsregering coalition government
koaxialkabel [-ˣa:l-] coaxial cable
kobbe [-å-] *s2* islet [rock], rock
kobbel ['kåbb-] *s2* cobbler
kobent [-e:-] *a1* knock-kneed
kobolt ['kɷ:bålt *el.* 'kå:-] *s3* cobalt **-blå** cobalt blue **-bomb** cobalt bomb **-glans** cobaltite **-kanon** gammatron
kobra [ˣkå:-] *s1* cobra
1 kock [-å-] *s3* (*bakterie*) coccus (*pl* cocci)
2 kock [-å-] *s2* [male] cook; (*kökschef*) chef; *ju flera ~ar dess sämre soppa* too many cooks spoil the broth
kock|a [-å-] *s1* [female] cook **-mössa** chef's hat
kod [-å:-] *s3*, **koda** [-å:-] *v1* code **kodbeteckning** code notation
kode'in *s4, s3* [kå-] codeine
kodex ['kɷ:- *el.* 'kå:-] *s2* **1** (*handskrift*) codex (*pl äv.* codices) **2** (*lagsamling*) code **3** (*norm*) code
kodi'cill *s3* codicil
kodifier|a codify, code **-ing** codification
kod|meddelande code message **-ning** coding
koefficient coefficient
koexis'tens *s3* coexistence
koff [-å-] *s2, sjö.* koff
koffe'in [kå-] *s4, s3* caffeine
koffer'dikapten [kå-] captain in the merchant navy
kofferdist [kå-] **1** (*sjöman*) merchant seaman **2**

(*fartyg*) merchantman, trader, trading vessel
koffert ['kåff-] *s2* trunk; (*på bil*) boot, *AE.* trunk
kofot (*bräckjärn*) crowbar; *vard.* jemmy, *AE.* jimmy
kofta [-å-] *s1* (*stickad*) cardigan
kofångare *se stötfångare*
koger ['kɷ:-] *s7* quiver
kognat [kåg'na:t *el.* kåŋ'na:t] cognate **-isk** *a5* cognate
kogni'tiv [*äv.* 'kåggn- *el.* 'kåŋn-] *a5* cognitive
kogubbe cowherd
kohandel *polit.* logrolling, party-bargaining, vote-bartering
kohe|'rens *s3* coherence **-'rent** *a4* coherent **-sion** cohesion
kohort [-'hårrt] *s3, hist.* cohort
koj [kåjj] *s3* (*häng-*) hammock; (*fast*) bunk; *gå* (*krypa*) *till ~s* turn in
1 koja [ˣkåjja] *s1* cabin, hut
2 koja [ˣkåjja] *v1, se under koj*
kojplats *sjö.* bunk, [sleeping] berth
kok *s7* boiling; *ett* ~ *stryk* a good hiding
1 kok|a *v1, v3* **1** (*bringa i -ning*) boil; (*tillreda mat*) cook; (*t.ex. gröt, kaffe, karameller*) make; ~ *ihop a*) (*koncentrera genom -ning*) boil down, *b*) *bildl.* concoct, make up, fabricate; ~ *in* (*frukt o.d.*) preserve; (*i glasflaska*) bottle; *jfr inkokt*; ~ *upp* bring to the boil **2** (*befinna sig i -ning*) boil, be boiling; ~ *upp* come to the boil; ~ *över* boil over; ~ *av vrede* foam with rage
2 koka *s1* clod
koka'in *s4, s3* cocaine **-ist** cocainist
kokard [-'a:rd] *s3* cockade
kokbok cookery book; *i sht AE.* cookbook
kokerska [female] cook
ko'kett I *a1* coquettish **II** *s3* coquette **-era** coquet (*för, med* with) **-eri** coquetry
kok|fru hired cook **-het** boiling (steaming) hot; *-hett vatten* (*vanl.*) boiling water
ko'kill *s3* **1** (*gjutform*) chill [mould] **2** (*parerplåt*) coquille
kok|konst cookery, culinary art; (*ngns*) culinary skill **-kärl** cooking-vessel; *pl äv.* pots and pans; (*soldats*) mess kit (gear), billy[can] **-ning** boiling; cooking; making
kokong [-'kåŋ] *s3* cocoon
kokoppor *pl* cowpox
kokos ['kɷ:-] *s2* coconut **-fett** coconut butter (oil) **-fiber** coconut fibre, coir **-flingor** *pl* shredded coconut **-matta** coir mat **-mjölk** coconut milk **-nöt** coconut **-nötsolja** coconut oil **-palm** coconut palm (tree), coco palm
kokott [-'kått] *s3* cocotte; *vard.* demirep
kok|platta hotplate **-punkt** *på ~en* at boiling point (*äv. bildl.*)
koks [-å-] *s3*, **koksa** [-å-] *v1* coke
koksalt (*vanligt* common) salt **-lösning** salt solution
koks|ning [ˣkåks-] coking **-verk** coke-oven plant
kok|t [-ɷ:-] *a4* boiled; *nu är det ~a fläsket stekt!* now the fat's in the fire! **-tid** *ngts* ~ the time required for boiling s.th. **-vagn** *mil.* field kitchen **-vrå** kitchenette
kol [-å:-] *s7, kem.* carbon; (*trä-, rit-*) charcoal; (*bränsle*) coal; *utbrända* ~ cinders; *samla glö-*

dande ~ *på ngns huvud* heap coals of fire on a p.'s head
1 **kola** [ˣkå:-] *s1* caramel, toffee
2 **kola** [ˣkå:-] *v1* **1** (*bränna* [*t.*] *kol*) make charcoal out of, burn to charcoal; *kem.* carbonize **2** (*ta in kol*) coal; *sjö.* bunker
3 **kola** [ˣkɔ:-] *v1* (*dö, vard.*) kick the bucket
kolar|e [ˣkå:-] charcoal-burner **-tro** implicit (blind) faith
kol|atom carbon atom **-box** coal box; *sjö.* [coal] bunker
kolchos [kåll'ʃå:s] *s3* kolkhoz, collective [farm]
kol|dammslunga *med.* anthracosis, coalminer's lung **-dioxid** carbon dioxide **-distrikt** coal-mining district, coalfield **-disulfid** carbon disulphide **-eldad** *a5* coal-fired, coal-heated
kolera [ˈkɔ:-] *s9* [epidemic] cholera **-epidemi** cholera epidemic
koler|iker [-'le:-] choleric (irascible) person **-isk** *a5* choleric, irascible
koleste'rin *s3, s4,* **kolesterol** [-'å:l] *s3* cholesterol, cholesterin
kol|filter charcoal filter **-fyndighet** coal deposit **-fält** coalfield **-förande** *a4* coal-bearing, carboniferous **-förening** *kem.* carbon compound **-gruva** coal mine (pit); (*stor*) colliery **-gruvearbetare** collier, [coal] miner **-gruveindustri** coal mining **-halt** carboncontent **-haltig** *al* carboniferous, carbonaceous, carbonic **-hydrat** carbohydrate
kolibakterie [ˣkɔ:-] coli bacillus
kolibri [ˣkåll-, *äv.* 'kåll-] *s3* hummingbird
ko'lik *s3* [the] colic **-smärtor** *pl* colicky pains
koling *ung.* [out-of-work] longshoreman
ko'lit *s3* colitis
kolja *s1* haddock
koljé *s3, se collier*
kolka [ˣkåll-] ~ [*i sig*] gulp (swill) down
koll [-å-] *s3, s2, vard.* check **kolla** [-å-] *vard.* (*kontrollera*) check; (*titta* [*på*]) dig [in]
kollabor|atör [kåll-] collaborator **-era** collaborate
kollage *se collage*
kollagen [kålla'je:n] *s3, s4* collagen
kollager *geol.* coal seam (bed)
kol'laps *s3, -a v1* collapse
kollast coal cargo, cargo of coal
kollationera [kå-] collate; (*t.ex. räkenskaper*) check (tick) [off]
kolleg|a [-'le:-, *äv.* -ˣle:-] *s3* colleague; confrère; (*tidning e.d.*) contemporary **-i'al** *al* collegial, collegiate; friendly **-ialitet** friendliness; comradeship
kollegie|block student's note pad **-rum** *skol.* staff committee-room; (*lärarrum*) staff [common] room
kollegium [-'le:-] *s4* **1** (*myndighet*) corporate body, board **2** (*lärar-*) [teaching] staff **3** (*lärarsammanträde*) staff meeting **4** *univ.* course; (*anteckningar*) lecture notes (*pl*)
kol'lekt *s3* collection **-bössa** collection box **-håv** collection bag
kollektion [-k'ʃɔ:n] collection
kollektiv [ˈkåll-, *äv.* -'i:v] **I** *s7, s4* collective **II** *a5* collective **-ansluta** affiliate as a body **-anslutning** affiliation as a body **-avtal** collective [labour] contract, collective wage agreement

-fil public-transport lane **-förhandlingar** p collective bargaining (*sg*) **-hus** block o service-flats; *AE.* apartment hotel
kollektiviser|a collectivize **-ing** collectivizatioi
kollektivis|m collectivism **-tisk** *a5* collectiv istic
kollektiv|jordbruk *abstr.* collective farming *konkr.* collective farm **-trafik** public transpor
kollektor [-ˣläktår] *s3* collector, commutator
koller [ˈkåll-] *s9* [blind] staggers (*pl*)
kolli [ˈkålli] *s7, s6* package, parcel; (*fraktgod. äv.*) piece [of goods]; (*resgods äv.*) piece [o luggage]
kolli|dera come into collision, collide; ~ mee *a*) *eg. äv.* run into, *sjö.* fall foul of, *b*) bildi (*om pers.*) get across, (*om förslag, plikter etc.* clash (conflict, interfere) with, run counter t **-sion** collision; *bildl. vanl.* clash
kollisionskurs collision course; *ha råkat på* ~ *med* be on [a] collision course with
kollodium [-'lɔ:-] *s4* collodion, collodium
kollo'id *s3* colloid, colloidal solution, suspen sion **-al** *a5* colloid[al]
kollokvium [kå'låck-] *s4* colloquium
kollr|a [-å-] ~ *bort ngn* turn a p.'s head **-ig** *a* mad, crazy
kol|lämpare coal trimmer **-mila** charcoal stac▮
kolmonoxid carbon monoxide
kolmörk pitch-dark **-er** pitch-darkness
kolna [ˣkå:l-] get charred; ~*d* charred; *se äv. för kolna*
kolofon [-'få:n] *s3* colophon
kolofonium [-'fɔ:-] *s4* rosin, colophony
kolon [ˈkɔ:lån] *s7* colon
kolo'ni *s3* colony; (*nybygge äv.*) settlement (*skollovs-*) holiday camp
koloni'al *a5* colonial **-ism** colonialism
kolonial|makt colonial power **-minister** ▮ *Storbritannien*) Colonial Secretary, Secretar of State for the Colonies **-politik** colonial po licy **-varor** *pl* imported groceries **-varu handel** (*affär*) grocer's [shop] **-välde** coloni▮ rule
kolonis|ation colonization **-atör** colonizer **-er▮** colonize
koloni|st colonialist **-stuga** allotment-garde▮ cottage **-trädgård** allotment [garden]
kolonn [-'lånn] *s3* column; *femte* ~ fifth colum▮ -'**ad** *s3* colonnade
kolorado[skal]bagge [-ˣra:-] Colorado (po tato) beetle
koloratur coloratura **-aria** coloratura aria **-so▮ pran** coloratura soprano
kolorer|a colour; ~*d veckopress* illustrate▮ weekly magazines (*pl*) **-ing** colouring, col oration
kolorimet|er [-'me:-] *s2* colorimeter, tintom eter **-'ri** *s3* colorimetry
kolor|ist colourist **-istisk** *a5* colouristic -'it *s* (*färgton*) colouring; (*färgbehandling*) colou treatment
kolos [ˣkå:lɔ:s] fumes (*pl*) from burning coa (coke, wood) **-förgiftning** poisonin (asphyxia resulting) from the inhalation of coa (*etc.*) fumes
koloss [-'låss] *s3* colossus; (*friare*) hulk, mons ter; *en* ~ *på lerfötter* a monster with feet o

clay -'al *a1* colossal; (*friare*) enormous, tremendous, immense, huge -**alt** [-'a:lt] *adv* enormously *etc.*; awfully

Kolosserbrevet [-ˣlåss-] [the Epistle of Paul the Apostle to the] Colossians (*pl, behandlas som sg*)

kolosto'mi *s3* colostomy

koloxid carbon monoxide -**förgiftning** carbon monoxide poisoning

kolportage [kålpår'ta:ʃ] *s7* colportage, book hawking -**roman** cheap novel

kolportör [kålpår-] book hawker; (*i sht av religiös litteratur*) colporteur; (*predikant*) lay-preacher

kol|stybb coal dust; cinders (*pl*), [charcoal] breeze -**stybbsbana** cinder track -**svart** coal (jet) black -**svavla** *s1, se koldisulfid*

kolsyra carbonic acid; ~*d* carbonated -**assimilation** carbonic-acid assimilation, photosynthesis

kolsyre|haltig *a5* aerated; *kem.* containing carbon dioxide -**snö** carbon dioxide snow

kolt [-å-] *s2* frock

kol|tablett charcoal tablet -**teckning** charcoal drawing -**tetraklorid** carbon tetrachloride -**tjära** coal tar -**trast** blackbird

kolugn [ˣkɷ:-] [as] cool as a cucumber

kolumbarium [-'ba:-] *s4* columbarium

ko'lumn *s3* column -**ist** columnist -**titel** *levande* ~ running head (title)

kolupplag coal depot

kolv [-å-] *s2* **1** (*på gevär*) butt **2** *tekn.* piston; (*pump-*) plunger **3** (*glas-*) flask **4** *bot.* spadix (*pl spadices*) **5** (*lås-*) bolt -**motor** piston engine -**ring** piston ring -**slag** piston stroke -**stång** piston rod

kol|väte hydrocarbon -**ångare** [steam] collier

kom [kåmm] *imperf. av 2 komma*

1 koma ['kå:-] *s6* (*medvetslöshet*) coma (*pl comas*)

2 koma ['kå:-] *s6, astr., fys.* coma (*pl comae*)

kombattant [-å-] combatant

kombi ['kåmbi] *s9*, **kombibil** [ˣkåmbi-] estate car; *AE.* station wagon

kombination [kåmb-] combination

kombinations|förmåga power (faculty) of combination -**lås** combination lock -**tång** combination pliers (*pl*)

kombinato'r|ik [kå-] *s3* combinatorial analysis -**isk** [-'tɷ:-] *a5* combining, combinatory

kombinera [-å-] combine; ~*d* combined, in one

kome'di *s3* comedy; *spela* ~ (*bildl.*) act a part, put on an act -**ant** play-actor -'**enn** *s3* comedienne -**författare** comedy (comic) writer

ko'met *s3* comet -**bana** comet's orbit -**huvud** comet's head (nucleus) -**lik** cometlike; *en* ~ *karriär* a meteoric career -**svans** comet's tail

komfort [kåm'fårt, *äv.* 'kåmm-] *s3* comfort -**abel** [-'a:bel] comfortable

komi'håg [kå-] *s7, skämts.* memory

ko'mik *s3* comic art; (*t.ex. i en situation*) comedy -**er** ['kɷ:-] comic actor, comedian

Komin|form [kåmin'fårm] [the] Cominform -**tern** [-'tärn] [the] Comintern (Komintern)

komisk ['kɷ:-] *a5* comic[al]; (*lustig*) funny, droll; (*löjlig*) ridiculous

komjölk cow's milk

1 komma [-å-] *s6* comma; (*decimal-*) [decimal] point

2 komm|a [-å-] *kom kommit* **I 1** come; (*ta sig fram, anlända*) arrive (*till at*, in), get; (*infinna sig äv.*) appear, vard. turn up; ~ *och gå* come and go; ~ *gående* come walking along (*på vägen* the road); ~ *för sent* be (come, arrive) too late; -*er strax!* coming!; *i veckan som* -*er* in the coming week; *inte veta vad som* ~ *skall* not know what is [going] to come (happen); *vart vill du* ~*?* what are you driving at?; *ta det som det* -*er* take things as they come; *här* -*er han* here he comes (is); *här* -*er Eva* here comes Eva; -*er det många hit?* will there be many people [coming] here?; *vilken väg har du* -*it?* which way did you come?; *kom och hälsa på oss* come and see us; *påsken* -*er sent i år* Easter comes (is) late this year; -*er dag* -*er råd* tomorrow will take care of itself; *planet skulle* ~ *kl.* 6 the plane was due at 6; ~ *av* (*bero på*) be due to; ~ *efter* (*efterträda*) come after, succeed; ~ *från en fin familj* come of a fine family; ~ *i* (*ur*) *balans* regain (get out of) balance; ~ *i beröring med* come in contact with; ~ *i fängelse* be put into (sent to) prison; ~ *i olag* get out of order; ~ *i ropet* become the fashion, (*om pers.*) become popular; ~ *i tid* be in time; ~ *i tidningen* get into the paper; ~ *i vägen för* get in the way of; ~ *med* (*medföra*) bring; ~ *med ursäkter* make excuses; *ha ngt att* ~ *med* have s.th. to say (*visa* show; *bjuda på* offer); *kom inte med några invändningar!* none of your objections!; ~ *på benen igen* get on one's legs again; ~ *på besök till* call at; ~ *på fest* be at a party; *det* -*er på räkningen* it will be put down on the bill; *jag* -*er sällan på teatern* I seldom go to the theatre; ~ *till ett beslut* come to a decision; ~ *till heders* come into favour; ~ *till korta, se 2 kort I*; ~ *till nytta* be of use, come in useful; ~ *till ro* settle down, get some rest; ~ *till synes* appear; ~ *till tals med ngn a*) (*få träffa*) get a word with s.b., *b*) (*komma överens med*) reach agreement with s.b.; ~ *till uttryck i* find expression in, show itself in **2** ~ *att a*) -*er att* (*uttr. framtid*) shall (*1:a pers.*), will (*1:a, 2:a o. 3:e pers.*), *b*) (*råka*) happen (come) to, *c*) (*uttr. försynens skickelse*) *han kom aldrig att återse henne* he was never to see her again; *jag kom att nämna* I happened to mention; *jag har* -*it att tänka på* it has occurred to me **3** (*tillkomma, tillfalla*) *det kom på min lott att* it fell to my lot to; *den gästfrihet som* -*it mig till del* the hospitality shown to me (I have received); *av utgifterna* -*er hälften på* half of the expenses refer to **4** (*betecknande tillägg*) *härtill* -*er att vi måste* in addition to this we must; *till övriga kostnader* -*er* other costs include **5** (*lända*) ~ *ngn till godo* be of use to s.b.; ~ *väl till pass* come in handy **6** (*uppgå t.*) *det hela* -*er på 4 pund* it amounts altogether to £4 **7** *opers., kom till ett uppträde* there was a scene **II** *rfl* **1** (*bero på*) come from, be due to; (*ske*) happen, come about; *det* -*er sig av att* it is due to the fact that; *hur* -*er de„t sig?* how is that?, how come?; *hur kom det sig att du...?* how is it (did it come about) that you...? **2** (*tillfriskna*) recover, get better (*efter* from) **III** (*föranleda*) make (*ngn att skratta* s.b. laugh); (*förmå*) induce (*ngn att göra ngt* s.b. to do s.th.); ~ *ngn på fall* cause a p.'s downfall (ruin) **IV** (*med betonad partikel*) **1** ~ *an på, se bero*; *kom an!* come on! **2** ~ *av sig* stop [short], (*tappa tråden*) lose the thread **3** ~ *bort* (*avlägsna sig*) get away, (*försvinna*) disappear, (*gå förlorad*) get lost **4** ~ *efter* (*bakom*) come (go) behind, (*följa*) follow, (*bli efter*) get behind, (*senare*) come afterwards **5** *fingrarna kom emellan* my (*etc.*) fingers got caught; *det kom ngt emellan* (*bildl.*) s.th. intervened **6** ~ *emot* (*t. mötes*) come (go) towards, (*stöta emot*) bump against (into) **7** ~ *fram a*) (*stiga fram*) come (go) up (along), (*från gömställe*) come out (*ur* of), *b*) (*förbi*) get past (*igenom* through; *vidare* on), (*på telefon*) get through, *c*) (*hinna fram, nå fram*) get there (*hit* here), (*anlända*) arrive, *d*) (*framträda*) come out, appear, *e*) (~ *t. rätta*) turn up; (*vinna framgång*) get on; *kom fram!* come here!; ~ *fram med ett förslag* make a suggestion; ~ *fram med sitt ärende* state one's business; *jag har -it fram till att* I have come to the conclusion that **8** *det kom för mig att* it occurred to me that; ~ *sig för med att* bring o.s. to **9** ~ *förbi* get round (past), *eg.* pass **10** *saken -er före i morgon* the case comes on tomorrow **11** ~ *ifrån* (*absol.*) get away, (*bli ledig*) get off; ~ *ifrån varandra* get separated; *man kan inte* ~ *ifrån att* there is no getting away from the fact that **12** *kom snart igen!* come back soon! **13** ~ *igenom* come (get) through **14** ~ *ihop sig* fall out (*om* about) **15** ~ *in i a*) (*rum etc.*) come (get) into, enter, *b*) (*skola*) be admitted to, *c*) (*tidning*) be inserted in, *d*) (*ämne e.d.*) become familiar (acquainted) with; ~ *in i bilden* come in; ~ *in med a*) (*uppgifter o.d.*) hand in, *b*) (*ansökan*) make, present, *c*) (*klagomål*) lodge; ~ *in på a*) (*sjukhus e.d.*) be admitted to, (*ämne*) get on to; ~ *in vid posten* be taken on in the Post Office **16** ~ *loss a*) (*om ngt*) come off, *b*) (*om ngn*) get away **17** ~ *med a*) (*följa med*) come along, come with (us, me *etc.*), *b*) (*deltaga*) join in (*i kriget* the war), *c*) (*hinna med*) catch (*tåget* the train), *d*) (*tas med*) be brought along; *han kom inte med på bilden* he didn't get into the picture; *han kom inte med bland vinnarna* he wasn't among the winners **18** ~ *ner på fötterna* alight (*bildl.* fall) on one's feet **19** ~ *vida omkring* travel far and wide; *när allt -er omkring* after all **20** ~ *på a*) (*stiga på*) get (come) on, *b*) (*erinra sig*) think of, recall, remember, *c*) (*upptäcka*) find out, discover, *d*) (*hitta på*) think of, hit on, (*ertappa*) come upon; *det kom hastigt på* it was sudden **21** ~ *till a*) (*anlända till*) come and see (*ngn see* s.b.), *b*) (*uppstå*) come about, arise, (*grundas*) be established, (*skrivas*) be written, (*komponeras*) be composed, *c*) (*födas*) be born, *d*) (~ *som tillägg*) be added, *e*) (*hända*) come about, happen; *frakten -er till* carriage is extra; *ytterligare kostnader har -it till* additional costs (expenses) have been incurred **22** ~ *undan* get away, escape **23** ~ *upp a*) come up, (*stiga upp*)

get up, *b*) (*i nästa klass*) be moved up; *frågan kom upp* the question came (was brought) up (*till diskussion* for discussion); ~ *upp i en hastighet av* reach a speed of; ~ *sig upp* make one's way, get on **24** ~ *ut a*) *eg.* come out (*ur* of), (*lyckas* ~ *ut*) get out, (*utomlands*) get (go) abroad, *b*) (*utges*) come out, be published, appear, *c*) (*utspridas*) get about (abroad), *d*) (*förmå betala*) afford to pay; *hans nya bok -er ut i vår* his new book will appear (come out, be published) this spring; *man vet aldrig vad som kan* ~ *ut av det* you never know what can come out of it; *det -er på ett ut* it is all one, it's as broad as it's long **25** *det -er inte mig vid* that is no business of mine **26** ~ *åt a*) (~ *över*) get hold of, secure, (*nå*) reach, *b*) (*ansätta*) get at, *c*) (*stöta emot, röra vid*) touch, come in contact with, (*få tillfälle t.*) get an opportunity (a chance) **27** ~ *över a*) *eg.* come over, (*lyckas* ~ *över*) get over, *b*) (*få tag i*) get hold of, come by (across), *c*) (*överraska, om oväder e.d.*) overtake, *d*) (*drabba*) come upon, befall, *e*) (~ *förbi*) get past (round), (*övervinna*) get over; *han har -it över från USA* he has come over from the States; *jag -er över i morgon* I'll come round tomorrow

kommande *a4 o. s6* coming; (*t.ex. dagar, generationer*) ...to come; *för* ~ *behov* for future needs; ~ *släkten* (*äv.*) succeeding generations

kommanditbolag [kåmman*di:t-] limited partnership

kommando [kå'mandå] *s6* **1** command; order; *föra* ~ *över* be in command of, command; *rösta på* ~ vote to order; *stå under ngns* ~ be under a p.'s command; *ta* ~[*t*] *över* take command of **2** (*trupp*) body of troops

kommando|brygga [captain's (navigation)] bridge **-ord** [word of] command **-rop** shouted order (command) **-räd** commando raid **-ton** tone of command; *i* ~ in a commanding (an imperious) tone **-trupp** commando unit, task force; *AE.* ranger [unit]

kommater|a [-å-] punctuate; put the commas in **-ing** punctuation

kommateringsregel punctuation rule

kommend|ant [-å-] commandant **-antur** commandantship

kommender|a [-å-] (*föra befäl*) be in command (*över* of); (*befalla*) command, order; (*beordra*) appoint; ~ *halt* give the order 'Halt' **-ing** (*-ande*) commanding *etc.*; *få en* ~ be given a command (*sjö.* an appointment)

kommendör [-å-] **1** captain; (*i Frälsningsarmén*) commissioner; ~ *av 1. graden* commodore **2** (*ordensriddare*) knight commander **-kapten** commander

kommensurabel [-å-, -'a:bel] *a5* commensurable, commensurate

kommen't|ar [-å-] *s3* commentary (*till* to; *över* on); ~*er* comment (*sg*); *utan några* ~*er* without [any] comment; *kortfattad* ~ brief notes (annotations) **-ator** *s3* commentator **-era** comment [up]on; (*förse med noter*) annotate; ~*d upplaga* annotated edition

kommers [kå'märs] *s3*, *livlig* ~ brisk trade; *sköta* ~*en* run the business (show); *hur går* ~*en?* how's business?

kommerseråd head of division of the [Swedish] national board of trade
kommersial|isera [-å-] commercialize **-isering** commercialization **-ism** commercialism
kommers|i'ell [-å-] *a5* commercial **-kollegium** [the] [Swedish] national board of trade
komminister [-å-, -'ister] *s2* (*i Storbritannien ung.*) assistant vicar
kommiss ['kåmm-, *äv.* -'miss] *s3* (*tyg*) uniform cloth
kommissari'at [-å-] *s7* commissioner's office
kommissarie [-å-, -'sa:-] *s5* **1** (*ombud*) commissary; (*polis-*) superintendent, inspector **2** (*utställnings-*) commissioner **3** (*i Sovjetunionen*) commissar
kommission [kåmmi'ʃɷ:n] **1** *hand.* commission; *i* ~ on commission **2** (*utskott*) commission, board, committee; *tillsätta en* ~ appoint (set up) a commission **3** (*uppdrag*) commission
kommissions|arvode commission [fee] **-handel** commission business (trade)
kommissionär [kåmmiʃɷ'nä:r] *s3* **1** *hand.* commission agent (merchant, dealer) **2** (*vid ämbetsverk e.d.*) *ung.* official agent
kommit [-å-] *sup. av 2 komma*
kommitté [-å-] *s3* committee; *sitta i en* ~ be on a committee **-betänkande** report of a committee, committee report **-ledamot** committee member
kommitt|ent [-å-] (*uppdragsgivare*) principal; ~*er* (*väljare*) constituents **-erad** [-'e:rad] *s9* committee member
kommod [kå'mɷ:d] *s3* washstand
kom'mun [-å-] *s3* (*administrativ enhet*) *ung.* municipality; *AE.* township; (*stads-*) urban district, city; (*lands-*) rural district; (*myndigheterna*) municipality, local authority (*AE.* government)
kommu'nal [-å-] *a5* municipal, local-government; local (*utskylder* rates); ~*a myndigheter* local authorities; ~ *självstyrelse* local government **-anställd** municipal employee **-arbetare** municipal worker **-förvaltning** local government, municipal administration **-hus** city (*AE.* town) hall
kommunal|isera [-å-] municipalize **-kontor** municipal office[s] **-lagstiftning** local government legislation **-man** local politician **-nämnd** local-government committee **-politik** local-government politics (*pl*) **-politiker** local politician **-råd** municipal commissioner **-skatt** local taxes (*i Storbritannien äv.* rates) **-tjänsteman** municipal officer **-val** local-government election
kommun|block municipal union **-fullmäktige** *koll.* municipal (city) council **-förbund** *Svenska* ~*et* [the] Swedish Association of Local Authorities
kommuni|cera [-å-] communicate; ~*nde kärl* communicating vessels **-kation** communication
kommunikations|departement ministry (*AE.* department) of transport and communications **-medel** means (*sg o. pl*) of communications (transportation) **-minister** minister (*AE.* secretary) of transport and communi-

cations **-radio** radio; (*bärbar*) walkie-talkie **-satellit** communications satellite **-tabell** railway (steamboat and airline) timetable **-väsen** system of communications
kommuniké [-å-] *s3* communiqué, bulletin
kommunindelning division into local-government areas
kommunism [-å-] communism (*ofta* Communism)
kommunist [-å-] communist (*ofta* Communist) **-isk** *a5* communist[ic] **-parti** Communist Party **-stat** Communist state
kommun|minister minister of local government **-styrelse** municipal executive board; city executive board
kommut|ator [-å-] commutator **-era** commutate
komocka [ˣkɷ:måcka] *s1* cowpat
Komorerna [kå'må:-] *pl* Comoro Islands; *eg.* the Federal and Islamic Republic of the Comoros
kom'pakt [-å-] *a1* compact; solid (*massa* mass); dense (*mörker* darkness) **-skiva** compact disc (*AE,* disk)
kompa'ni [-å-] *s4* company **-chef** company commander
kompan'jon [kå-] *s3* partner; joint owner; *bli* ~*er* go into partnership [with each other] **-skap** *s7* partnership
kompar|abel [-å-, -'a:bel] *a5* (*jämförlig*) comparable **-ation** comparison **-ativ** ['kåmp-, *äv.* -'i:v] **1** *a5* comparative **2** *s3* comparative; *i* ~ in the comparative [degree] **-era** compare, form the comparative forms of
kom'pass [-å-] *s3* compass; *segla efter* ~ sail by the compass **-hus** compass bowl **-kurs** compass course **-nål** compass needle **-ros** compass card
kompatib|el [-'ti:-] *a5* compatible **-ilitet** compatibility
kompendium [-å-, -'pend-] *s4* compendium; summary
kompensation [-å-] compensation
kompensationsledig on compensatory leave **-het** compensatory leave
kompensera (*gottgöra*) compensate; (*uppväga*) compensate [for], make up for
kompe'tens [-å-] *s3* competence; competency; qualifications (*pl*) **-bevis** certificate of qualifications (competency)
kompe'tent [-å-] *a1* competent (*för, till* for; *till att* to); ~ *för en plats* [fully] qualified for a post
kompil|lat [-å-] *s7*, **-ation** *s3* compilation **-ator** *s3* compiler **-era** compile
kompis ['kåmp-] *s2* **1** *göra ngt i* ~ do s.th. in partnership **2** (*kamrat*) pal; *AE. äv.* buddy
komple'ment [-å-] *s7* complement (*till* to, of) **-färg** complementary colour **-vinkel** complementary angle **-'är** *a5* complementary
kom'plett [-å-] **I** *a1* complete; absolute, downright **II** *adv* absolutely
kompletter|a [-å-] **1** complete; supplement; make up; ~ *varandra* complement each other; ~*nde uppgifter* supplementary details **2** ~ *i matematik* sit for a supplementary examination in mathematics **-ing 1** completing; supplemen-

ting; (*en* ~) completion; (*utvidgning*) amplification; (*av förråd äv.*) replenishment; *till* ~ *av vårt brev* to supplement our letter **2** *skol. o.d.* supplementary examination
kom'plex [-å-] **1** *a5* complex; *~a tal* complex numbers **2** *s7* (*av hus o.d.*) block, group of buildings; *psykol.* complex **-itet** complexity
kompli|cera [-å-] complicate **-kation** complication
kompli|mang [-å-] compliment; *ge ngn en ~ för* compliment s.b. on; *säga ~er* pay compliments **-mentera** compliment (*ngn för* s.b. on)
komplott [kåm'plått] *s3* plot; conspiracy
kompon|ent [kå-] component, constituent **-era** (*sammansätta*) put together; (*skapa*) create; (*balett, tavla*) design; (*maträtt*) concoct; (*tonsätta, författa*) compose **-ist** composer
komposant [kå-] *fys.* component
kompo'sit [kå-] *s3* composite [material]
komposition [kå-] design; creation; concoction; (*tonsättning*) composition
kompositmaterial composite [material]
kompositör [kå-] composer
kompost [kåm'påst] *s3*, **-era** *v1* compost **-ering** composting
kompott [kåm'pått] *s3* compote (*på* of); *blandad ~* (*bildl.*) a very mixed dish
kom'press [-å-] *s3* compress **-ion** [-pre'ʃɔ:n] compression **-or** [-'*pressår] *s3* compressor
komprimer|a [-å-] compress; *~d luft* compressed air **-ing** compressing; compression
kompromettera [kå-] compromise; ~ *sig* compromise o.s.
kompro'miss [kå-] *s3* compromise
kompromiss|a [kå-, -'missa] compromise **-förslag** proposed compromise **-lösning** compromise solution
kon *s3* cone; *stympad ~* frustum of a cone
kona *s1, tekn.* cone, taper; (*på bil*) clutch
koncentrat [-å-] *s7* concentrate; *bildl.* epitome; *i ~* (*bildl.*) in a concentrated form
koncentration [-å-] concentration
koncentrations|förmåga power of concentration **-läger** concentration camp
koncentrera [-å-] concentrate (*på* on); *i sht bildl.* focus, centre (*på* on); ~ *sig* concentrate (*på* on); ~ *sig på ngt* (*äv.*) focus (centre) one's attention on s.th.
koncentr|icitet [-å-] concentricity **-isk** [-'sent-] *a5* concentric
kon'cept [-å-] *s7, s4* [rough] draft (*till* of); (*kladd*) first outline, rough copy; *tappa ~erna* (*bildl.*) be disconcerted (put out)
konception [kånsep'ʃɔ:n] conception
konceptpapper scribbling-paper
koncern [kån'sä:rn, *äv.* -'sö:rn] *s3* group [of companies]; concern
konces|sion [kånse'ʃɔ:n] [parliamentary] sanction (*på* for); licence; concession; *bevilja ngn ~* grant s.b. a concession; *söka ~ på en järnväg* apply for powers for constructing a railway **-sionsnämnd** *K~en för miljöskydd* the [Swedish] national franchise board for environment protection
koncessiv ['kånn-, *äv.* -'si:v] *a5* concessive
konciliant *se konsiliant*
koncipiera [-å-] **1** (*befruktas*) conceive **2** (*göra*

utkast t.) make concepts; (*författa*) compose
kon'cis [-å-] *a1* concise; succinct
kon'dens [-å-] *s7, s3*, -'at *s7* condensate
kondensa|tion [-å-] condensation **-tionsstrimma** vapour (condensation) trail, contrail
kondensator [-å-] *s3, tekn.* condenser; *elektr.* capacitor
kondenser|a [-å-] condense **-ing** condensation; condensing
kondens|or [-å-, -*densår] *s3* [steam] condenser **-vatten** condensation [water]
kondis ['kånn-] *s7 o. s2, vard., se konditori resp. kondition 1*
kondition [-å-] **1** (*tillstånd*) condition, state; *i utmärkt ~* (*sport. äv.*) splendidly fit **2** (*tjänst*) situation **3** *~er* (*hand.*) conditions, terms of account
konditio'n|al [-å-] *a5* conditional **-alis** [-*a:lis, *äv.* -'a:lis] *r* (*i* in the) conditional [mood]
konditioner|a [-å-] condition; *väl* (*illa*) *~d in* [a state of] good (bad) repair, *se äv. beskaffad* **-ing** conditioning
konditions|test fitness test **-träning** fitness training
konditor [kån*di:tår] *s3* confectioner, pastry cook
kondito'ri *s4* confectioner's [shop]; (*serveringsställe*) coffee house (bar), café, teashop, tearoom **-varor** *pl* confectionery (*sg*), cakes and pastries
kondoleans [kåndåle'ans, *äv.* -'aŋs] *s3* condolence **-brev** letter of condolence (sympathy)
kondolera [kåndå-] express one's condolence[s] (sympathy) (*ngn med anledning av* with s.b. on)
kondom [kån'då:m] *s3* condom; *vard.* French letter
kondominium [kåndå'mi:-] *s4* condominium
kondor [kån'då:r] *s3, zool.* condor
kondotti'är [kå-, -å-] *s3* condottiere
konduk't|ans [kå-] *s3, elektr.* conductance **-ivitet** conductivity **-or** [-*duktår] *s3, fys.* conductor
kondukt|ris [-å-] *se* [*kvinnlig*] *konduktör* **-ör** (*för spårvagn e.d.*) ticket collector, conductor; *järnv.* guard; *kvinnlig ~* conductress, *vard.* clippie
konfeder|ation [kå-] confederation **-erad** [-'e:rad] *a5* confederate[d]
kon'fekt [-å-] *s3* assorted sweets and chocolates, confectionery; *engelsk ~* liquorice all-sorts; *bli lurad på ~en* be thwarted; *variera ~en* (*bildl.*) ring the changes **-ask** box of assorted sweets and chocolates (confectionery)
konfektion [kånfek'ʃɔ:n] ready-made clothing (clothes *pl*)
konfektionskläder *pl* ready-made (*AE. äv.* ready-to-wear) clothes
konfektskål sweet-dish
konfek'tyr [-å-] *~er* (*pl*) confectionery (*sg*) **-affär** confectioner's [shop]
konferenc|ié [kånferaŋsi'e:] *s3*, **-ier** [-si'e:] *s3* compere; *AE.* emcee (master of ceremonies)
konfer|ens [kånfe'rens, *äv.* -'raŋs] *s3* conference, meeting; (*större*) congress; (*rådplägning äv.*) consultation, parley **-era** confer, consult (*med ngn om* with s.b. about); discuss

konfession [kånfe'ʃɷ:n] confession, creed -**'ell** a5 confessional

konfessionslös (om undervisning o.d.) non--confessional; (om pers.) adhering to no particular confession

konfetti [kån'fetti] s9 confetti

konfidenti|ell [kånfiden(t)si'ell] a5 confidential -**'ellt** adv confidentially, in confidence

konfigura|tion [kå-] configuration -**'tiv** a5 configurational, configurative

konfir'm|and [kå-] s3 candidate for confirmation -**ation** confirmation

konfirmations|kostym confirmation suit -**undervisning** preparation for confirmation

konfirmera [-å-] confirm

konfiskation [-å-] confiscation

konfisker|a [-å-] confiscate -**ing** confiscation

konfityrer se konfektyr

kon'flikt s3 conflict; dispute; (i roman o.d. äv.) problem; komma i ~ med get into conflict with -**situation** [state of] conflict

konformad [ˣkɷ:n-] a5 conic[al]

konform|ism [kånfår-] conformism -**ist** conformist

konfront|ation [kånfrånt- el. -frånt-] confrontation; vid ~ med (vanl.) on being confronted with -**era** confront, bring face to face (med with)

kon|fundera [-å-] confuse, bewilder -**'fys** al confused, bewildered

kongeni'al [kånje-] al congenial; en ~ översättning a translation true to the spirit of the original -**itet** congeniality; inherent affinity

kongeni'tal [kånje-] a5 congenital

konglome'rat [kånglå-] s7 conglomerate; conglomeration

Kongo ['kångɷ] 1 r (flod) [the] Congo 2 n (land) [Republic of the] Congo

kongo'les [kångɷ-] s3, -**isk** a5 Congolese

kongregation [kångre-] congregation

kongress [kåŋ'gress] s3 congress; (mindre) conference

kongress|a [kåŋˣgressa] [hold a] congress -**deltagare** participant in (member of) a congress -**ledamot** AE. Congressman, fem. Congresswoman -**val** Congressional election

kongruens [kångru'ens] s3 congruity, congruence (äv. mat.); språkv. agreement, concord -**fall** geom. case of equality in all respects

kongruent [kångru'ent] a4 congruous, congruent (äv. mat., geom.); språkv. agreeing, concordant

kon|icitet conic[al] form -**isk** ['kɷ:-] a5 conic, conical; ~ sektion conic [section]

konjak ['kånn-] s3 cognac; vanl. brandy

konjakskupa brandy glass

konjug|ation [-å-] conjugation -**era** conjugate

konjunktion [kånjuŋ(k)'ʃɷ:n] conjunction

konjunktiv [ˣkånn-] s3 (i in the) subjunctive [mood] -**isk** a5 subjunctive -**'it** s3 conjunctivitis

konjunktur [kånn-] business activity, economic situation; trade (business) cycle; ~er business (market) conditions; goda ~er boom (sg), prosperity (sg); dåliga ~er [trade] depression (sg), slump (sg); avmattning i ~en slowdown in business activity; uppåtgående ~er business upturn (sg), improving markets; vikande ~er [trade] recession -**avmattning** slowdown in business activity -**betingad** a5 cyclical (arbetslöshet unemployment) -**institut** K~et the [Swedish] national institute of economic research -**läge** economic situation, state of the market -**nedgång** decline in business activity -**politik** economic policy -**politisk** ~a åtgärder action taken to steer business activity -**svacka** slump -**uppgång** period of economic recovery, business upturn -**utveckling** business (economic) trend (development)

konkarong [kåŋka'råŋ] s3, hela ~en the whole lot

kon'kav [-å-] a5 concave -**itet** concavity

kon'klav [-å-] s3 conclave

konklu|dera [-å-] conclude, infer -**sion** conclusion, inference -**'siv** a5 conclusive

konkord|ans [kånkår'dans el. -'daŋs] s3 (bibel-) concordance -**'at** s7 concordat

kon'kret I al concrete; (om förslag äv.) tangible; ~ musik (poesi) concrete music (poetry) II s4, språkv. concrete

konkre|tion [-å-] 1 (utan pl) concreteness 2 miner. concretion -**tisera** give a concrete form to

konku'bin [-å-] s3 concubine

konkurrens [-å-, äv. -'aŋs] s3 competition (om for); rivalry (om about); hård (illojal) ~ fierce (unfair) competition; utan ~ (äv.) unchallenged; stå sig i ~en hold its (etc.) own in competition -**begränsning** restriction of competition; restraint-of-trade practices (pl) -**kraft** competitiveness, competitive strength -**kraftig** able to compete; competitive (priser prices)

konkurrent [-å-] competitor, rival (om for) -**företag** rival (competing) company, competitor

konkurrera [-å-] compete (om for; med with), enter into competition; ~ ut outdo, outrival; ~ ut en firma oust a competitor (competing firm)

kon'kurs [-å-] s3 bankruptcy; failure; begära ngn i ~ file a bankruptcy petition against s.b.; försätta ngn i ~ declare s.b. bankrupt; gå i ~ file one's (a) petition; göra ~ fail, go (become) bankrupt -**ansökan** petition in bankruptcy, bankruptcy petition -**bo** bankrupt's (bankruptcy) estate -**förvaltare** (utsedd av enskild pers. el. firma) trustee; (utsedd av domstol) [official] receiver -**gäldenär** bankrupt -**lager** bankrupt's stock -**mässig** a5 insolvent

konnot|ation [kå-] connotation -a'**tiv** a5 connotative, connotive -**era** connote

konnässör [-å-] connoisseur (av, på of)

konosse'ment [kånnå-] s7 bill of lading

konsekutiv ['kånn- el. -'i:v] a5 consecutive

konse'kv|ens [-å-] s3 (logisk följd) consequence; (följdriktighet) consistency; (påföljd) consequence, sequel; det får allvarliga ~er it (this) will have serious consequences -'**ent** I al consistent II adv consistently; (genomgående) throughout

kon'selj [-å-] s3 cabinet meeting -**president** prime minister

konsert [-'sä:r, äv. -'särt] s3 concert -**era** give a concert ([a series of] concerts) -**estrad** concert platform -**flygel** concert grand -**hus** concert hall -**mästare** leader [of an orchestra];

K

AE. concertmaster -**program** *äv.* concert bill -**sal** *se -hus*
kon'serv [-å-] *s3*, *~er* tinned (canned [*särsk. AE.*]) goods (food *sg*), preserved provisions
konservat|ism [-å-] conservatism -'**iv** [*el.* 'kånn-] *a1* conservative
konservator [kå-] *s3* (*djuruppstoppare*) taxidermist; (*av tavlor s3.d.*) restorer; (*vid museum*) curator, keeper
konservatorium [kå-, -'tɔ:-] *s4* academy of music, conservatoire, conservatory
konserv|brytare tin-opener, can-opener -**burk** tin, can (*särsk. AE.*); (*av glas*) preserving-jar
konserver|a [-å-] **1** (*bevara*) preserve **2** (*matvaror*) preserve; (*i glasflaska*) bottle; (*i burk*) can; (*i bleckburk*) tin; *~t kött* (*vanl.*) corned (canned) beef **3** (*restaurera*) restore -**ing** preservation, bottling *etc.* -**ingsmedel** preservative
konserv|fabrik cannery, canning (tinned-foods) factory -**öppnare** *se konservbrytare*
konsign|ation [kånsiŋna- *el.* -sinja-] consignment; *i ~* on consignment -**era** consign
konsiliant [-å-, -'ant *el.* -'aŋt] *a1* conciliatory (*mot* towards)
konsilium [kån'si:-] *s4* synod
konsis'tens [-å-] *s3* consistency; *till ~en* in consistency; *antaga fast ~* (*äv.*) acquire substantial form, materialize -**fett** heavy (lubricating) grease, [cup] grease -**givare** gelling agent
konsistor|i'ell [kå-] *a5* **1** *kyrkl.* consistorial **2** *univ.* of (pertaining to) a university court -**ium** [-'tɔ:-] *s4* **1** *kyrkl.* consistory **2** *univ.* university council (court)
konsol [-'å:! *el.* -'såll] *s3* bracket, support; *byggn.* console, cantilever -**hylla** bracket-shelf
konsolider|a [kå-] consolidate -**ing** consolidation
konsom'mé [kånn-, *äv.* kåŋ-] *s3* consommé
konson|ans [kånså'nans *el.* -'naŋs] *s3* consonance -**ant** [-'ant] *s3 o. a4* consonant -**antisk** [-'ant-] *a5* consonantal
konsortium [kån'sårtsium] *s4* syndicate, consortium
konspir|ation [-å-] conspiracy, plot -**atorisk** [-'tɔ:-] *a5* conspiratorial -**atör** conspirator, plotter -**era** conspire, plot
konst [-å-] *s3* art; (*skicklighet*) skill; (*knep*) trick, artifice; *~en* fine art, the arts (*pl*); *de sköna* (*fria*) *~erna* the fine (liberal) arts; *efter alla ~ens regler* according to all the recognized rules; *förstå sig på ~* know about art; *göra ~er* do (perform) tricks; *han kan ~en att* he knows how to (the trick of...-ing); *är det ngn ~?* what's difficult about that?; *det var väl ingen ~!* that's easy enough!; *det är ingen ~ för mig att* it's easy [enough] for me to; *~en är lång, livet är kort* art is long, life is short -**akademi** academy of art ([fine] arts); *K~en* [the] royal [Swedish] academy of fine arts -**alster** work of art
kon'st|ans [-å-] *s3* constancy -**ant I** *a1* constant; fixed, given (*förhållande* ratio); (*oföränderlig*) invariable; (*beständig*) permanent, perpetual **II** *s3, mat.* constant
konstapel [kån'sta:-] *s2* **1** (*polis*) [police] constable **2** *mil. ung.* bombardier

konstart form of art, art genre
konstater|a [-å-] (*fastställa*) establish (*att* the fact that); (*ådagalägga*) demonstrate, prove (*betyga*) certify; (*påpeka*) point out, draw attention to (*att* the fact that); (*framställa som faktum*) state, assert; (*iaktta*) notice, observe (*upptäcka, utröna*) find out, discover, ascer tain; *~ faktum* state a fact -**ande** *s6* estab lishment; certification; ascertainment; (*påstå ende*) statement, assertion
konst|befruktning artificial insemination -**be ridare** circus-rider, equestrian -**bevattning** irrigation
konstellation [-å-] constellation
konstern|ation [-å-] consternation -**erad** [-'e:rad] *a5* nonplussed, dumbfounded, taken aback
konst|fackskola college of arts, crafts and de sign -**fiber** synthetic (man-made) fibre -**flit** arts and crafts (*pl*) -**flygning** stunt flying aerobatics (*pl, behandlas som sg*) -**frusen** arti ficial[ly frozen] (*is* ice) -**full** skilled; (*sinnrik* ingenious -**färdig** skilful -**föremål** object o1 art -**förfaren** skilled; *med -förfarna händer* with the hands of a skilled artist -**galleri** ar gallery -**gjord** *a5* artificial; man-made; (*falsk* imitation; *~ andning* artificial respiration; *~ dimma* smoke screen; *på ~ väg* by artificia means -**gjutning** statue-casting -**grepp** (*yrkesgrepp*) trick [of the trade] **2** (*knep* [crafty] device, artifice -**gödning 1** (*artificiel gödning*) artificial manuring **2** (*-gödsel*) arti ficial manure, fertilizer -**hall** art gallery -**han del** (*butik*) art dealer's [shop] -**handlare** ar dealer -**hantverk** [art] handicraft; (*varor*) ar wares, handicraft products (*pl*) -**hantverkare** [arts] craftsman -**harts** artificial (synthetic) resin, plastic -**historia** history of art (*äv. -his torien*) -**historiker** art historian -**historisk** of art history, art history -**högskola** college of fine arts
konstig [-å-] *a1* **1** (*besynnerlig*) strange, pe culiar, odd, curious, queer; *en ~ kropp* (*vard.* an odd customer **2** (*svår*) intricate; (*kinkig* awkward; *~are än så var det inte* that is all there was to it
konst|industri art industry; arts and crafts (*pl* -**industriell** of applied (industrial) art -**intres serad** *a5* interested in art (*etc.*); *den ~e all mänheten* art lovers, the art-loving public
konstituera [-å-] constitute; *mötet har ~t sig* the meeting has appointed its executive com mittee; *~nde bolagsstämma* statutory meeting; *~nde församling* constituent assembly
konstitution constitution -'**ell** *a5* constitution al; *~ monarki* constitutional (limited) mon archy
konstitutionsutskott *~et* [the Swedish parlia mentary] standing committee on the consti tution
konst|kritiker art critic -**kännare** connoisseur [of the fine arts], art expert
konstlad [-å-] *a5* (*tillgjord*) affected (*sätt* manners *pl*); (*konstgjord*) artificial; (*tvungen* forced; (*låtsad*) assumed
konst|läder artificial leather, Leatherette (*va rumärke*) -**lös** artless; (*okonstlad*) unaffected;

(enkel) simple **-museum** art museum (gallery), museum of art **-mässig** *al* **1** *(konstnärlig)* artistic **2** *(konstgjord)* artificial **-njutning** artistic treat (enjoyment)

konstnär [-å-] *s3* artist **-inna** [woman] artist

konstnärlig [*ˣ*kånst-, *äv.* -'näːr-] *al* artistic; *det ~a i* the artistry of **-het** artistry

konstnärs|ateljé artist's studio (workshop) **-bana** artistic career, career as an artist **-blick** eye of an artist

konstnärskap [-å-] *s7 (det att vara konstnärlig)* one's *(etc.)* being an artist; *(konstnärlig begåvning)* artistic ability

konstnärs|koloni colony of artists **-krets** *i ~ar* in artists' circles, among artists **-liv** *~et* the (an) artist's life **-natur** artistic temperament; *pers.* artist; *en sann ~* a true artist

konstpaus pause for [the sake of] effect

konst|ra [-å-] *(krångla)* be awkward; *(om pers. äv.)* make a fuss; *(om häst)* jib **-rik** *(-färdig)* skilful; *(konstnärlig)* artistic **-riktning** tendency (style) in art; school [of art]

konstruer|a [-å-] **1** *(göra ritning t.)* design; *(uppbygga)* construct **2** *språkv.* construe **3** *mat.* draw **-ad** *a5* constructed; *(uppdiktad)* fabricated

konstruktion [kå-, -kˈʃoːn] **1** *(konstruerande)* designing *etc.*; construction *(äv. språkv.)*; *(uppfinning)* invention; *(tanke-)* conception **2** *konkr.* construction; design

konstruktions|fel 1 *tekn.* constructional error (fault, defect); *abstr.* error in design **2** *språkv.* construing error **-lära** theory of constructions **-ritning** constructional drawing

konstruk't|iv *a5* constructive **-ör** constructor, designer; *(byggmästare)* constructional builder

konst|salong art gallery **-samlare** art collector **-samling** art collection **-siden**, **-silke** artificial silk; rayon **-skatt** art treasure **-skicklig** skilled in art (handicraft) **-skojare** art fraud **-smide** art metalwork (forging) **-stoppning** invisible mending **-stycke** *(ngt svårt)* feat, achievement; *(trick)* trick, tour de force **-ull** artificial wool **-uppfattning** conception of art **-utställning** art exhibition **-verk** work of art; *(mästerverk)* masterpiece **-åkare** figure skater **-åkning** figure skating **-älskare** art lover

konsul [*ˣ*kånn- *el.* 'kånn-] *s3* consul; *engelsk ~ i* British consul in (at) **-'at** *s7* consulate

konsulent [-å-] consultant, adviser

konsulinna [-å-] consul's wife; *~n X.* Mrs. X.

kon'sult [-å-] consultant, adviser; *se äv. under konsultativ* **-ation** consultation **-a'tiv** [*äv.* 'kånn-] *a5* consultative; *~t statsråd (ung.)* minister without portfolio

konsult|era consult **-firma** firm of consultants **-uppdrag** commission for a consultant

konsu'lär [-å-] *a5* consular

konsumbutik [-å-] cooperative shop

konsument [-å-] consumer **-förening** [consumer's] cooperative society **-kooperation** consumer's cooperation **-ombudsman** consumer ombudsman **-prisindex** consumer price index **-upplysning** consumer information **-verk** *~et* [the Swedish] national board for consumer policies

konsum|era [-å-] consume **-tion** consumption

konsumtions|förening *se konsumentförening* **-samhälle** consumption (affluent) society **-skatt** consumption tax, excise **-varor** *pl* consumer goods, non-durable goods; *varaktiga ~* consumer durables

kont [-å-] *s2, s3* basket of birch bark carried on the back, pannier

kon'takt [-å-] *s3* **1** *abstr.* contact; *bildl. äv.* touch; *få ~ med* get into touch with; *förlora ~en med* lose (get out of) touch with **2** *konkr., elektr.* contact; *(strömbrytare)* switch; *(vägg-)* socket, *vard.* point, plug, *AE.* outlet

kontakt|a [-å-] contact, get into touch with **-kopia** contact print **-lim** contact (pressure-sensitive) adhesive **-lins** contact lens **-man** contact [man]; *(med allmänheten)* public relations man **-mina** contact mine

kontakt|or [kånˣtaktår] *s3* contactor **-person** *se kontaktman* **-svårigheter** *pl* difficulty *(sg)* in making contacts

kontamin|ation [-å-] contamination **-era** contaminate

1 kon'tant [-å-] *a4 (sams)* on good terms

2 kon'tant [-å-] *a4 o. adv (i reda pengar)* cash; *~ betalning* cash payment, payment in cash; *mot ~ betalning* for cash, for ready money; *per [extra] ~* for [prompt] cash; *betala ~* pay [in] cash; *köpa ~* buy for cash

kontant|affär cash transaction (deal) **-belopp** cash amount, amount in cash

kontant|er [-å-] *pl* cash *(sg)*, ready money *(sg)* **-insats** down payment, amount [to be paid] in cash, cash amount **-köp** cash purchase **-likvid** cash settlement

kontempla|tion [-å-] contemplation **-'tiv** [*äv.* 'kånn-] *a5* contemplative

kontenans [kånte'nans *el.* -'naŋs] *s3, behålla ~en* keep one's countenance; *förlora ~en* be disconcerted (put out)

kontenta [kånˣtenta] *s1, ~n av* the gist of

konteramiral [-å-] rear admiral

konter'fej [-å-] *s7* portrait

kon'text [-å-] *s3* context **-u'ell** *a5* contextual

konti'nens [-å-] *s3, med.* continence

kontinent [-å-] *s3* continent; *~en (Europas fastland)* the Continent

kontinen'tal [-å-] *a5* continental **-drift** continental drift **-klimat** continental climate **-sockel** continental shelf **-systemet** the Continental System

kontingent [kåntiŋ'gent *el.* -in'jent] *s3* **1** *mil.* contingent; *(grupp)* group **2** *(avgift)* subscription; *(andel)* quota

kontinu|erlig [-å-, -'eːr-] *a5* continuous **-itet** continuity

konto *s6* account; *(löpande räkning)* current account; *avsluta ett ~* close an account; *ha ~ i en affär* have an account at a shop; *insätta på ett ~* pay into an account; *skriva på ngns ~ (bildl.)* put down to a p.'s account **-kort** credit card **-kurant** *s3* account current; *(-utdrag)* statement of account

kontor [kån'tcoːr] *s7* office; *(bolags, firmas äv.)* offices *(pl)*; *på ~et* at the office; *sitta på ~ be* [employed] in an office

kontoriser|a [kå-] turn residential property into offices **-ing** process of turning residential

property into offices
kontorist [kå-] clerk, office employee; *kvinnlig* ~ lady (girl) clerk
kontors|anställd *se kontorist* -**arbete** office (clerical) work -**artiklar** *pl* office accessories (equipment *sg*) -**chef** office manager, head clerk -**göromål** office duties (*pl*) (work) -**landskap** open-plan office -**maskin** business (office) machine; (*skrivmaskin*) typewriter -**materiel** office supplies (*pl*); (*pappersvaror*) stationery -**personal** office (clerical) staff -**tid** office (business) hours (*pl*)
kontoutdrag statement of account
kontra [-å-] **I** *prep* contra; (*friare*) versus **II** *v1, sport.* break away -**alt** contralto -**band** contraband -**bas** double bass -**bok** *se motbok* -**dans** contredance, contradance; (*friare*) square dance; *dansa* ~ square-dance -**diktion** contradiction -**diktorisk** [-'tɷ:-] *a5* contradictory
kontrah|ent [-å-] [contracting] party (*i, vid* to) -**era 1** *hand.* make a contract, contract **2** *språkv.* contract
kontraindikation contraindication
kon'trakt [-å-] *s7* contract, agreement; (*hyres-*) lease; *enligt* ~ as per contract; *enligt detta* ~ under this contract; *avsluta ett* ~ *med ngn om ngt* conclude (make) a contract with s.b. about s.th. -**era** contract; ~*de varor* goods contracted for
kontraktion [kåntrak'ʃɷ:n] contraction
kontrakts|bestämmelse provision (stipulation) of a contract (an agreement) -**bridge** contract [bridge] -**brott** breach of contract -**enlig** [-e:n-] *a5* contractual, as contracted [for] -**formulär** contract form -**förslag** draft contract -**prost** rural dean
kontra|mandera countermand; cancel -**märke** check -**order** counterorder, contrary order
kontrapunkt *mus.* counterpoint -**isk** [-'punkt-] *a5* contrapuntal
kontrarevolution counter-revolution -'**är** *a5 o. s3* counter-revolutionary
kontrasigner|a countersign -**ing** countersign, countersignature
kontraspion counterspy -**age** counterespionage
kon'trast [-å-] *s3* contrast (*till, mot*); *stå i skarp* ~ *till* be in sharp contrast to; *utgöra en* ~ *till* form a contrast to, contrast with -**era** contrast (*med, mot* with)
kontras't|iv [-å-] contrastive -**medel** contrast medium -**verkan** contrast[ing effect]
kontribu|era [-å-] contribute -**tion** contribution; (*skatt*) tax, levy
kontring [-å-] *sport.* breakaway
kontroll [kån'tråll] *s3* control (*över* over, of); check; (*tillsyn*) supervision, inspection; (*-ställe*) checkpoint, control station; *ha läget under* ~ control the situation -**anordning** control[ling device]
kontroll|ant [-å-, -å-] controller, supervisor -**besiktning** *se bilbesiktning o. veterinärbesiktning* -**bord** observation (control) desk (panel)
kontroller|a [-å-, -å-] check; verify, control; make sure (*att* that); (*ha tillsyn över*) exercise (have) control over; ~*t silver* hallmarked silver -**bar** *a5* controllable

kontroll|grupp control group -**kommission** control commission -**lampa** (*hopskr. kontrollampa*) pilot lamp (light) -**läsa** (*hopskr. kontrolläsa*) read through for the purpose of checking -**märke** check, controlling-mark -**mäta** check the measure (*ngt* of s.th.), remeasure -**nummer** (-*märke*) check; (*kodnummer*) key number -**rum** control room -**räkna** re-count, check [off], verify -**siffra** check digit -**station** checkpoint, control station -**stämpel** control stamp; (*för guld etc.*) hallmark -**torn** *flyg.* control tower -**uppgift** (*löneuppgift*) salary (wage) statement -**åtgärd** control [measure]
kontrollör [-å-, -å-] controller; comptroller; checker, supervisor, inspector; (*biljett-*) ticket inspector; *post.* assistant superintendent
kontro'vers [kåntrå-] *s3* controversy -**i'ell** *a5* controversial
kon'trär [-å-] *a5* contrary
kontur [-å-] contour [line]; (*friare o. bildl.*) outline -**era** contour -**fast** firmly outlined -**karta** outline map -**lös** vague[ly outlined]; undefined -**teckning** outline drawing
kontusion [-å-] contusion, bruise
konung [-å-] *s2* (*jfr kung*) king; *Gud bevare* ~*en!* God save the King!; ~*arnas* ~ the King of Kings; *Till K~en* (*i skrivelse*) To His Majesty the King
Konungaböckerna [the] Kings
konungs|lig [kå'nuŋs-, *äv.* 'kå-] *a5* kingly (*hållning* deportment); regal (*makt* power) -**man** courtier
konvalescens [kånvale'sens *el.* -'ʃens] *s3* convalescence
konvalescent [kånvale'sent] convalescent -**hem** convalescent home
konvalje [kån'valje] *s5* lily of the valley
konvektion [kånvek'ʃɷ:n] convection
konvenans [kånve'naŋs] *s3* propriety, convention; (*starkare*) decorum; *brott mot* ~*en* breach of etiquette -**parti** marriage of convenience
konvenera [-å-] suit, be convenient (*ngn* to s.b., for s.b.)
kon'vent [-å-] convention
konventikel [kånven'tick-] *s2* conventicle -**plakatet** *ung.* the Conventicle Act
konvention [-å-] convention -'**ell** *a1* conventional
konverg|ens [-å-] *s3* convergence -**ent** *a4* convergent, converging -**era** converge (*mot* towards)
konversa|bel [-å-] *a2* conversable -**tion** conversation
konversationslexikon encyclop[a]edia
konvers|atör [-å-] conversationalist -**era** converse (*om* about, on)
konversion [-å-] conversion
konverter [kån'värt-] *s2, tekn.* converter
konverter|a [-å-] convert; (*t. annan religion*) become a convert -**ing** conversion -**ingsanläggning** converter plant (equipment)
konver|tibel [-å-, -'ti:-] *a5* convertible -'**tit** *s3* convert
kon'vex [-å-] *a5* convex -**itet** convexity
konvoj [kån'våj] *s3*, -**era** *v1*, -**ering** *s2* convoy
konvojfartyg (*som konvojerar*) escort vessel;

(*som konvojeras*) convoy vessel
konvo'lut [kånvå-] *s7* envelope, wrapper, cover
konvul|sion [-å-] convulsion **-sivisk** [-'si:-] *a5* convulsive
kooper|ation [kⱷåpe-] cooperation **-a'tiv** *a5* cooperative; *K~a förbundet* [the] Swedish cooperative union and wholesale society; *~ förening* cooperative [society], *vard.* coop, co-op **-atör** cooperator, member of a cooperative society **-era** cooperate
koordinat [kⱷår-] coordinate **-axel** coordinate axis
koordination [kⱷår-] coordination
koordinat|or [kⱷårdin*a:tår] coordinator **-system** system of coordinates
koordinera [kⱷår-] coordinate
ko'pek *s9* kope[c]k
kopia [-*pi:a] *s1* copy; duplicate; (*avskrift*) copy, transcript; *foto.* print; (*av konstverk o. bildl.*) replica; *neds.* imitation; *ta ~ av* copy, make a copy of
kopiator *s3, se kopieringsmaskin*
kopie|bläck copying ink **-papper** copying paper; (*karbon-*) carbon [paper]; *foto.* printing paper
kopier|a copy; transcribe; *foto.* print **-ing** copying; *foto. o. boktr.* printing
kopierings|anläggning printing (processing) laboratories (*pl*) **-maskin** copying machine, copier
kopist copying clerk; copyist; *foto.* printer; (*av konstverk*) imitator
kopi'ös *a5* copious; enormous
kopp [-å-] *s2* cup (*kaffe* of coffee); (*som mått*) cupful [of...]
koppa [-å-] *s1* pock
koppar [-å-] *s9* copper; (*-slantar*) coppers (*pl*) **-bleck** copper plate **-förande** *a4* cupriferous **-förhydning** [-y:d-] copper-sheathing **-glans** *miner.* chalcocite **-gruva** copper mine **-halt** copper content **-haltig** *a5* cupreous **-kis** *miner.* chalcopyrite, copper pyrites **-mynt** copper [coin] **-orm** *se kopparödla* **-oxid** copper oxide; (*med envärd koppar*) cuprous oxide; (*med tvåvärd koppar*) cupric oxide **-plåt** (*för taktäckning e.d.*) [plate of] copper-sheeting; (*enstaka*) copper-sheet; (*för gravyr*) copper plate **-röd** copper-coloured, [as] red as copper; (*om hår*) coppery **-slagare 1** *eg.* coppersmith **2** (*bakrus*) hangover **-stick** (*konstverk*) copperplate, print; (*konstart*) copper engraving, copper-plate engraving **-sulfat** copper (cupric) sulphate **-tryck** copperprint **-ödla** *zool.* slowworm, blindworm
koppel ['kåpp-] *s7* **1** (*hund-*) lead, leash **2** (*jakthundar*) leash **3** *tekn.* coupling **4** *mil.* shoulder belt **5** (*hop, skara*) pack
koppla [-å-] **I 1** (*hund*) put on the lead, leash **2** (*jakt. o. friare*) leash **3** *tekn.* couple up (*till* to); *elektr.* connect (*i serie* in a series); *radio., tel.* connect up (*till* to); *var vänlig ~ mig till* please put me through to **II** (*med betonad partikel*) **1** *~ av a*) *järnv., radio., tel.* switch off, *b*) (*vila*) relax, unwind, slack off **2** *~ ifrån* disconnect, *järnv.* uncouple **3** *~ ihop* (*elektr.*) connect, join up, *radio., tel.* connect up **4** *~ in* connect, throw in, *elektr.* switch in **5** *~ till* (*järnv.*) put

on, attach **6** *~ ur* disengage, disconnect, *elektr.* interrupt, (*motor*) declutch
koppl|are [-å-] procurer **-eri** procuring **-erska** procuress, bawd **-ing 1** (*-ande*) *tekn.* connection **2** *konkr., tekn.* coupling; (*i bil*) clutch; *tel.* switch
kopplings|anordning coupling (connecting) device; *flyg. äv.* release mechanism **-dosa** *elektr.* coupling box **-lamell** clutch disc **-pedal** clutch pedal **-schema** *elektr.* wiring diagram **-ton** *tel.* dialling (*AE.* dial) tone
kopp|or [*kåppⱷr] *se koppa, smittkoppor o. vattkoppor* **-ärrig** pockmarked
kopra [*kå:p-] *s1* copra
kopt|er ['kåpp-] Copt **-isk** *a5* Coptic; *~a kyrkan* Coptic Church **-iska** (*språk*) Coptic
kopul|ation copulation **-ativ** ['kⱷ:-, 'kåpp- *el.* -'i:v] *a5, språkv.* copulative **-era** copulate
kor *s7* choir; (*hög-*) chancel; (*där altaret står*) sanctuary; *jfr gravkor*
kora [*kå:-] choose, select (*till* as)
ko'ral *s3* chorale **-bok** hymn book with tunes
ko'rall *s3* coral **-djur** anthozoan (*pl* anthozoa) **-orm** coral snake **-rev** coral reef **-röd** coral [red] **-ö** coral island; atoll
ko'ran *s3* [the] Koran
kord [-å:-] *s3* cord
korda [*kå:r-] *s1, mat.* chord
korderoj [kårde'råj] *s3* corduroy
kordi'al [-å-] *a1* cordial **-itet** cordiality
kordong [kår'dåŋ] *s3* cord[on]; *bot.* cordon
kordväv cord [fabric]
Korea [-*re:a] *n* Korea
kore'an *s3,* **-sk** *a5,* **-ska** (*språk*) *s1* Korean
koreo'graf *s3* choreographer
koreografi *s3* choreography **-isk** [-'gra:-] *a5* choreographic
korg [kårj] *s2* basket; (*större*) hamper; (*i självbetjäningsbutik*) wire basket; *få ~en* (*bildl.*) be refused, get the brushoff; *ge ngn ~en* (*bildl.*) refuse s.b., give s.b. the brushoff **-arbete** wicker[work], basketwork **-blommig** *bot.* composite **-boll** basketball **-flätning** [-ä:t-] basketry **-makare** basket-maker **-möbel** [set of (*ett föremål* piece of)] wicker[work] furniture
korgosse server, acolyte; (*i kör*) choirboy
korgstol wicker[work] chair
koriander [-'ann-] *s9* coriander
ko'rint *s3* currant
korint[i]er [-'int(si)er] Corinthian **-brev** *K~* [the] Corinthians (*pl, behandlas som sg*); *första K~et* the First of Corinthians (*eg.* the First Epistle of Paul the Apostle to the Corinthians)
korintisk [-'rint-] *a5* Corinthian
korintkaka currant cake
korist chorister; (*opera- äv.*) member of the chorus; (*kyrko- äv.*) choir-member
kork [-å-] *s2* **1** (*ämne*) cork **2** (*propp*) cork, stopper; *dra ~en ur* uncork; *sätta ~en i* cork **3** *styv i ~en* cocky, swollen-headed **korka** cork; *~ igen* (*till*) cork; *~ upp* uncork
kork|ad [-å-] *a5* (*dum*) stupid **-bälte** cork [life] belt **-bössa** popgun **-dyna** cork pillow **-ek** cork oak **-matta** linoleum; *hand. äv.* lino **-skruv** corkscrew
korn [-ⱷ:-] *s7* **1** (*frö, kornformig smådel*) grain

(äv. bildl.); *ett ~ av sanning* a grain of truth **2** *(sädesslag)* barley **3** *(riktmedel)* bead; *mil. äv.* front sight; *få ~ på* get sight of, *bildl. äv.* spot, *vard. äv.* get wind of; *ta ~ på* draw a bead on; *ta...på ~et* get (hit off)...to the life **4** *se under skrot*

korn|a [-ɷ:-] ~ [*sig*] granulate **-ax** ear of barley **-blixt** flash of summer lightning **-blå** cornflower blue **-bod** granary

kor'nell *s3, bot.* cornel

kor'nett [-å-] *s3, mus. o. mil.* cornet **-ist** cornetist, cornet player

korn|gryn barley grain; *koll.* hulled barley **-grynsgröt** barley porridge

kornig [-ɷ:-] *a1* granular **-het** granularity; granulation; *foto.* graininess

kor'nisch [-å-] *s3* cornice

korn|knarr *s2* corncrake **-mjöl** barley meal (flour)

korollarium [kårå'la:-] *s4* corollary

korona [kå'rå:-] *s1, astr.* corona

korp [-å-] *s2* **1** *zool.* raven **2** *(hacka)* pickaxe, mattock

korp|a [-å-] ~ *åt sig* grab [for o.s.] **-gluggar** *pl (ögon)* giglamps

korporation [kårpå-] corporate body, body corporate; association

korporationstävling intercompany (interworks) tournament

korpora'tiv [*äv.* 'kårpå-] *a5* corporative **-ism** corporative system of society

kor'pral [-å-] *s3 (vid armén)* lance corporal; private, *(vid flottan)* ordinary rating, *(vid flyget)* leading aircraftman; *AE. (vid armén)* corporal, *(vid flottan)* petty officer 3. class, *(vid flyget)* sergeant

korpsvart raven [black]

korpul|ens [-å-] *s3* stoutness, corpulence **-ent** *a1* stout, corpulent

korpus ['kårr-] *s2* **1** *boktr.* long primer **2** *(kropp)* body **-kel** [-'puss-] *s3* corpuscle

korr [-å-] *s7, vard., se korrektur*

kor'rek|t [-å-] *a1* correct; *(felfri)* faultless, impeccable **-tion** [-k'ʃɷ:n] correction **-'tiv** *s7* corrective

korrektur [-å-] *s7* proof [sheet], printer's proof; *första ~* first proof[s], *(spalt-)* galley proof; *ombrutet ~* page proof; *tryckfärdigt ~* clean proof; *läsa ~ på* read the proofs of, proofread **-avdrag** pull[ed proof], proof leaf **-fel** error in a (the) proof **-läsa** read in proof, proofread; *dåligt -läst* badly proofread **-läsare** proofreader **-läsning** proofreading **-tecken** proofreader's mark **-ändring** alteration in [the] proof

korrel|at [-å-] *s7 o. a4* antecedent **-ation** correlation **-era** correlate

korrespondens [kårrespån'dens, *äv.* -'aŋs] *s3* correspondence **-institut** correspondence school **-kort** correspondence card **-kurs** correspondence course **-undervisning** postal tuition

korrespond|ent [kå-, -å-] correspondent; correspondence clerk **-era** correspond

korridor [kårri'då:r] *s3* corridor; *AE. äv.* hallway; *(i hus äv.)* passage; *AE. äv.* hall; *polit.* lobby **-politik** lobby politics *(pl)*, lobbying

korriger|a [kårri'ʃe:-] correct; *(revidera)* revise **-ing** correction; revision

korro|dera [kårrå-] corrode **-sion** corrosion

korrosions|beständig corrosion-resistant, noncorrodible **-skyddsmedel** corrosion preventing agent

korrugera [kårru'ge:-] corrugate; *~d plåt* corrugated sheet [metal]

korrumpera [-å-] corrupt

kor'rup|t [-å-] *a4* corrupt **-tion** [-p'ʃɷ:n] corruption; *AE. polit. äv.* graft

kors [-å-] **I** *s7* **1** cross; *i ~* crosswise; *Röda K~et* the Red Cross; *krypa till ~et* eat humble pie; *lägga armarna i ~* fold one's arms; *lägga benen i ~* cross one's legs; *sitta med armarna i ~* (*bildl.*) sit idle (doing nothing); *inte lägga två strån i ~* not lift a finger **2** *mus.* sharp **II** *adv,* ~ *och tvärs* crisscross, in all directions **III** *interj* well, I never!, Oh, my!, bless me!

korsa [-å-] cross; *(~ varandra)* intersect; *bildl.* thwart, *(ngns planer a p.'s plans); (om tankar)* traverse, run counter to *(varandra each other);* ~ *sig* cross o.s.

kor'sar [-å-] *s3* corsair

kors|as [-å-] *dep* cross [each other], intersect; *bildl.* traverse each other, crisscross **-band** *post., skicka som ~* send as printed matter **-befruktning** cross-fertilization **-ben** *anat.* sacrum **-blommig** cruciferous **-drag** through (cross) draught **-eld** crossfire

kor|se'lett [-å-] *s3* cors[e]let **-'sett** *s3* corset; *åld.* stays *(pl)*

kors|farare crusader **-formig** [-å-] *a5* cross-shaped, cruciform **-fästa** crucify **-fästelse** crucifixion **-förhör** cross-examination **-förhöra** cross-examine **-förlamning** *se korslamhet* **-gång** cloister **-hänvisning** cross-reference

Korsika ['kårs-] *n* Corsica

korsi'ka|n [-å-] *s3,* **-nsk** *a5* Corsican

kors|kyrka cruciform church **-lagd** *a5* laid crosswise; *(om ben)* crossed; *(om armar)* folded; *~a benknotor* crossbones **-lamhet** paraplegia

korsning [-å-] **1** *(väg- e.d.)* crossing, intersection; *planskild ~* flyover, overpass **2** *biol.* crossing, crossbreeding; *konkr.* cross

korsningsfri without crossroads

kors|näbb crossbill **-ord** crossword [puzzle]: *lösa ett ~* do (solve) a crossword **-riddare** crusader **-rygg** *~en* the small of the back **-spindel** diadem spider **-stygn** cross-stitch **-tecken** *göra -tecknet* cross o.s., make the sign of the Cross

korstol ['ˣkɷ:r-] [choir] stall

kors|tåg crusade **-virkeshus** half-timbered (framework) house **-vis** crosswise, traversely **-väg** crossroad; *vid ~en* at the crossroads **-ört** groundsel

1 kort [-ɷ-] *s7* card; *klätt ~* court (picture) card; *ett parti ~* a game of cards; *spela ~* play [at] cards; *blanda bort ~en för ngn (bildl.)* confuse s.b., put s.b. out; *lägga ~en på bordet (bildl.)* put (lay) all one's cards on the table; *sköta sina ~ väl* play one's cards well (right); *sätta allt på ett ~* stake everything on one card, put all one's eggs in one basket; *titta i ngns ~* peep

at a p.'s cards, *bildl.* be up to a p.'s little game
2 kort [-å-] **I** *al* short; (*tidsbet. äv.*) brief; *bildl.*
short; (*avmätt äv.*) abrupt, curt; ~ *om huvudet*
short-tempered; ~ *till växten* short [in stature];
~*a varor* haberdashery (*sg*), small wares, *AE.*
notions; *en* ~ *stund* a little while; *efter en* ~
tid in a short time, shortly afterwards; *inom* ~
before long, shortly; *göra* ~*are* (*äv.*) shorten;
göra processen ~ *med* make short work of; *gör*
pinan ~*!* don't prolong the agony!; *komma till*
~*a* fall short (*med* in), (*i tävling e.d.*) fail; *re-*
dogöra för ngt i ~*a drag* give a short (brief,
concise) account of s.th. **II** *adv* shortly, briefly; (*t.ex. uttala* ~, ~ *tillmätt*) short; ~ *efter* soon
after; ~ *sagt* (*och gott*) in short, in so many
words, (*i själva verket*) in fact, to make a long
story short; *andas* ~ take short breaths; *hålla*
ngn ~ keep s.b. on a tight rein
korta [-å-] *v1*, ~ [*av*] shorten
kortbrev [-ɷ:-] letter card; *AE.* double postal
card
kort|byxor [-å-] *pl* shorts **-distanslöpare**
sprinter
kortege [kår'te:ʃ *el.* -'tä:ʃ] *s5* cortege
kort|eligen [-å-] in short **-fattad** *a5* brief; *K~*
lärobok i A Short (Concise) Textbook of **-film**
short film; short **-form** *språkv.* abbreviated
form **-fristig** *a1* short-term **-het** shortness *etc.*;
brevity; *i* ~ briefly; *i* ~ *redogöra för* outline,
summarize **-huggen** *a5, bildl.* abrupt
kort|hus [-ɷ-] house of cards **-hög** pile of cards
kortison [kårti'så:n] *s4* cortisone
kortklippt [-å-] *a4* [cut] short; (*om hår äv.*)
closely cropped, bobbed
kort|konst [kɷ-] card trick **-lek** pack [of cards]
kort|kort [-å-å-] ~ *kjol* miniskirt, *vard.* mini **-li-**
vad *a5* short-lived
kort|oxe [-ɷ-] inveterate card player **-register**
card index (file) (*över* of)
kort|sida [-å-] *n* the short side (end) **-siktig** *a5*
short-range, short-term **-skallig** brachycephalic
-sluta *-slöt -slutit* short-circuit **-slutning** [-u:-]
short circuit
kortspel [-ɷ-] **1** (*-ande*) playing cards, card-
-playing; *fuska i* ~ cheat at cards **2** (*ett* ~) card
game **-are** card player
kortsynt [*kårtsy:nt] *a1* short-sighted
kortsystem [-ɷ-] card[-index] system
korttids|anställning [-å-] short-time (tempo-
rary) employment **-minne** short-term memory
kort|tänkt [-å-] *a1* short-witted, short-sighted,
unthinking **-varig** *a1* [of] short [duration];
short-lived, transitory (*framgång* success); ~*t*
straff short-term penalty **-varor** *se korta va-*
ror under 2 kort I **-varuhandlare** haberdasher
-våg short wave
kortvågs|behandling short-wave treatment
-radio short-wave radio **-sändare** short-wave
transmitter
kort|växt [-å-] *a1* short [in stature] **-ända** *se*
kortsida **-ärmad** *a5* short-sleeved
korum [*kɷ:-] *best. form o. pl* =, *äv. s7* [regi-
mental] prayers (*pl*)
ko'rund *s3* corundum
korus ['kɷ:-] *i uttr.: i* ~ in chorus
korv [-å-] *s2* sausage **korva** *rfl* (*om strumpa*)
wrinkle

kor'vett [-å-] *s3* corvette
korvgubbe hot-dog man
korv|ig [-å-] *a1* rucked-up, wrinkly **-kiosk** hot-
-dog stand **-skinn** sausage-skin **-spad** *klart*
som ~ (*bildl.*) as plain as a pikestaff **-stopp-**
ning sausage-making, sausage-filling; *bildl.*
cramming **-stånd** hot-dog stand **-öre** *inte ett*
~ not a brass farthing
kory'fé *s3* coryphaeus (*pl* coryphaei), (*friare*
äv.) leader; *iron.* bigwig
kos *r, springa sin* ~ run away; *har flugit sin* ~
has disappeared (flown)
kosa *s1* course, way; *ställa* ~*n* steer (direct)
one's course (steps) (*mot* to), make for
ko'sack *s3* Cossack **-dans** Cossack dance
kosing *vard.* dough (*särsk. AE.*)
kosinus *se cosinus*
ko|skälla cowbell **-skötare** cowherd, cowman
kosmet|ik *s3* **1** (*skönhetsvård*) beauty care **2**
(*skönhetsmedel*) cosmetic **-iker** [-'me:-] cos-
metician **-isk** [-'me:-] *a5* cosmetic; ~*t medel*
cosmetic [preparation] **-olog** cosmetologist;
beautician
kosmisk ['kåss-] *a5* cosmic; ~ *strålning* cosmic
rays (radiation)
kosmo|drom [kåsmå'drå:m] *s3* cosmodrome
-go'ni *s3* cosmogony **-log** cosmologist **-logi**
s3 cosmology **-logisk** *a5* cosmologic[al]
-'naut *s3* cosmonaut **-po'lit** *s3*, **-politisk**
[-'li:-] *a5* cosmopolitan
kosmos ['kåsmås] *r, best. form* =, cosmos
kospillning cow dung
kossa [-ɷ-] *s1* [moo-]cow
kost [-å-] *s3* (*föda*) food, diet; (*förplägning*)
fare; *blandad* ~ mixed diet; *mager* ~ poor diet,
scanty fare; ~ *och logi* board and lodging, bed
and board
1 kosta [-å-] *det* ~*r på a*) it is a trial, *b*) (*är*
pinsamt) it is very painful (trying); *det* ~*r på*
krafterna it saps one's (*etc.*) strength
2 kosta [-å-] cost; (*belöpa sig t.*) amount to; ~
ngn möda give s.b. trouble; ~ *mycket pengar*
cost a great deal of money; ~ *på* pay for, meet
the expenses of; ~ *på ngn en god uppfostran*
[find the money to] give s.b. a good education;
~ *på sig* treat o.s. to; *kunna* ~ *på sig* be able
to afford; ~ *vad det* ~ *vill* no matter what it
costs, cost what it may, at all costs; *vad* ~*r det?*
how much is it?, what is the price [of it]?, what
do you want for it?; *vad får det* ~*?* how much
are you prepared to pay for it?; *det* ~*r mer än*
det smakar it is more trouble than it is worth;
han har ~*t sina föräldrar mycket pengar* he
has been a great expense to his parents
kostbar [-å-] *a1* costly, precious
kost|föraktare *ingen* ~ no despiser of good
food **-håll** fare, diet
kostlig [-å-] *a1* **1** (*dyrbar*) precious **2** (*löjlig*)
priceless
kostnad [-å-] *s3* cost (*äv.* ~*er*); (*utgift*) expense;
(*utlägg*) outlay, expenditure; (*avgift*) charge;
(*arvode*) fee; *utan* ~ free of charge; *diverse* ~*er*
sundry expenses; *fasta* ~*er* overheads, fixed
costs; *rörliga* ~*er* prime (variable) costs; *stora*
~*er* heavy expenses; *för en ringa* ~ at a trifling
cost; *inklusive alla* ~*er* all costs included; *med-*
föra ~*er* involve expenditure; *stå för* ~*erna* pay

(bear, stand) the expenses (costs); *ådraga sig* *~er* incur expenses

kostnads|analys costs analysis **-beräkna** cost **-beräkning** costing, computation of costs **-fri** free [of cost (charge)] **-fråga** question of costs **-förslag** quotation, estimate [of costs], tender **-kalkyl** cost estimate, statement of costs **-krävande** costly, expensive **-skäl** financial reason; *av ~* costwise **-ökning** increase in costs **-övervältring** transfer of costs

kostpengar *pl* food allowance (*sg*), board wages

kostsam [-å-] *a1* costly, expensive

kostvanor *pl* eating habits

kos'tym *s3* 1 suit; *mörk ~* dark lounge suit 2 *teat. o.d.* costume, dress **-bal** fancy-dress ball

kostymer|a dress up **-ing** (*-ande*) dressing up; (*dräkt*) dress

kostym|pjäs *teat.* costume piece **-tyg** suiting

kota *s1* vertebra (*pl äv.* vertebrae)

kotangent [ˣkɔ:-] *s3, mat.* cotangent

kotiljong [-'jåŋ, *äv.* ˣkått-] *s3* cotillion

kotknackare [ˣkɔ:t-] *vard.* chiropractor

kot'lett [-å-] *s3* cutlet; (*med ben*) chop **-fisk** catfish, wolffish **-rad** [the] ribs (*pl*)

kotpelare [ˣkɔ:t-] spinal (vertebral) column, spine; *vard. o. bildl.* backbone

kotte [-å-] *s2* cone

kotteri [-å-] *coterie*, set; (*klandrande*) clique **-väsen** cliquism

kottfjäll cone scale

kotyledon [kåtyle'då:n] *s3* cotyledon

ko'vall *s3* cow-wheat

kovänd|a veer, wear **-ning** *sjö.* veering, wearing; *en ~* (*äv.*) a veer, a volte-face

kpist [ˣkå:-] *s2, se kulsprutepistol*

krabat fellow; young beggar, rascal

krabb *a1, sjö.* choppy, short

krabba *s1* crab

krack|a *kem.* crack **-bensin** cracked petrol (*AE.* gasoline)

krackeler|a, -ing crackle

krack|er ['krack-] **-ning** [ˣkrack-] cracking **-ningsanläggning** cracking plant

krafs *s7* (*skräp*) trash

krafs|a scratch **-ning** scratching

kraft *s3* 1 force; (*förmåga, elektr.*) power; (*styrka*) strength; (*energi*) energy; *AE. sl.* pizzazz; (*livaktighet*) vigour, vitality; (*verkan*) effect; (*intensitet*) intensity; *drivande ~* driving force, prime mover; *fysisk ~* physical power (strength); *av alla ~er* with all one's strength, (*t.ex. ropa*) with all one's force, (*t.ex. springa*) as hard as ever one can; *i sin fulla ~, i sin ~s dagar* in one's prime; *med ~* (*t.ex. uttala sig, uppträda*) with vigour (energy); *ge ~ åt* lend (give) power to, (*ngns ord*) lend (give) force to; *hushålla med sina ~er* conserve one's strength (energy); *pröva sina ~er* try one's strength; *samla ~er* regain (build up) one's strength; *spänna alla sina ~er för att* strain every nerve to; *ägna hela sin ~ åt att* apply the whole of one's energy to (+ *ing*-form); *hans ~er avtog* his strength was failing 2 *konkr.* (*arbetare*) worker, (*medarbetare*) helper, cooperator; *den drivande ~en inom the* leading force in; *duglig ~* capable man (wom-

an); *yngre ~er* younger men; *förvärva nya ~er* get new people 3 *jur.* (*gällande ~*) force; *i ~ av* by (in) virtue of, on the strength of; *träda i ~* come into force, take (come into, go into) effect; *vinna laga ~* gain legal force; *äga ~* hold good, be in force; *till den ~ och verkan det hava kan* for what it is (may be) worth

kraft|ansträngning exertion, effort; *göra en ~* make a real effort, put on a spurt **-besparing** saving of power **-centrum** centre of force **-foder** concentrated feed (fodder) **-full** powerful, forceful; (*fysiskt*) vigorous, strong; (*om t.ex. vilja*) energetic **-fält** field of force; *elektriskt* (*magnetiskt*) ~ electric (magnetic) field **-förbrukning** expenditure of energy; *elektr.* power consumption **-förlust** *med.* loss of strength; *tekn.* power loss **-försörjning** power supply

kraft|ig *a1* 1 powerful; (*livlig o. ~*) vigorous; (*energisk*) energetic; (*verksam*) effective; (*stark*) strong (*äv. bildl.*); (*t. hälsan*) robust; (*eftertrycklig*) emphatic; (*våldsam*) violent; (*intensiv*) intense, acute; *~ protest* strong protest; *~ ökning* sharp (substantial) increase; *ett ~t slag i huvudet* a violent (heavy) blow on the head 2 (*stor*) big, great, considerable; tremendous 3 (*om mat*) nourishing; (*mäktig*) rich; (*bastant*) substantial (*måltid* meal) **-kabel** power cable **-karl** strong man **-källa** source of power (energy); *bildl. äv.* source of strength **-ledning** power [transmission] line **-lös** powerless; weak, feeble; (*orkeslös*) effete **-mätning** *bildl.* trial of strength **-nät** grid **-papper** kraft [paper] **-prestation** *en verklig ~* a really great achievement, a real feat **-prov** trial of strength **-reaktor** power reactor **-station** power station (plant) **-tag** *ett verkligt ~* a really strong pull (*vard.* big tug), *bildl.* a real effort **-uttryck** oath, expletive; *använda ~* use strong language **-utveckling** generation of power **-verk** power station (plant) **-värmeverk** combined power and heating plant **-åtgärd** strong (drastic) measure **-överföring** power transmission

krag|e *s2* collar; *ta ngn i ~n* criticize s.b. sharply; *ta sig i ~n* pull o.s. together **-handske** gauntlet **-knapp** collar stud **-nummer** size in collars **-snibb** collar point **-stövel** top boot **-ödla** frilled lizard

krake *s2* (*häst-*) jade, hack; (*stackare*) weakling; (*kräk*) wretch

kra'kel *s7* (*gräl*) squabble, row; (*med slagsmål*) brawl

krakmandel [ˣkra:k-] dessert almond

kral *s3* kraal

1 kram *s7* (*varor*) small wares (*pl*)

2 kram *a1* (*om snö*) wet, cloggy

3 kram *s2* (*-ning*) hug

krama 1 (*pressa*) squeeze (*saften ur* the juice out of) **2** (*omfamna*) embrace, hug

kramhandel fancy-goods (small-ware) shop

kramp *s3* cramp; (*konvulsion*) convulsion, spasm; *få ~* get (be seized with) cramp

krampa *s1* clincher, clamp, cramp [iron]

kramp|aktig *a1* spasmodic; (*konvulsivisk*) convulsive (*gråt* crying); *~t försök* desperate effort **-anfall** attack of cramp **-artad** [-a:r-] *a5* cramp-like **-lösande** antispasmodic (*äv. ~ me-*

del) **-ryckning** spasm, twitch **-stillande** *se*
-lösande **-tillstånd** spasmodic condition; spas-
ticity
kramsfågel *koll.* [edible] small birds *(pl)*
kramsnö wet snow
kran *s2* **1** *(tapp-)* tap; *särsk. AE.* faucet; *(ven-
til-)* stopcock **2** *(lyft-)* crane **-arm** jib **-balk**
sjö. cathead **-bil** crane lorry
kranium ['kra:-] *s4* cranium
krans *s2* **1** wreath; *(blomster- äv.)* garland **2**
bildl. ring, circle **3** *kokk.* ring-shaped bunloaf
(biscuit)
krans|a *se bekransa* **-artär** coronary artery
-formig [-å-] *a5* wreath-shaped **-kärl** coro-
nary vessel
kranskötare crane operator
krans|list cornice, ornamental moulding **-ned-
läggning** laying of wreaths
kranvagn crane truck; *AE.* derrick car
krapp *s3*, **-rot** *bot.* madder **-röd** madder red
-rött *best. form det* **-röda** madder [lake]
kras *s7, gå i* ~ go to (fly into) pieces **krasa**
[s]crunch
krasch *s3* crash *(äv. bildl.),* smash; *bildl. äv.*
collapse, failure **krascha** go crash; *(om företag, vard.)* go smash
kra'schan *s3* grand star
kraschlanda *flyg.* crash-land
krass *a1* crass; *(utpräglad äv.)* gross; *(grovkor-
nig)* coarse
krasse *s2, bot.* cress; *se äv. indian-, kryddkrasse*
krasslig *a1* ailing, seedy, poorly; *vard.* under the
weather; *AE. vard.* mean
krater ['kra:-] *s2* crater **-lik** craterous **-sjö** crater
lake
krats *s2, tekn.* scraper **kratsa** scrape; scratch
kratta I *s1* **1** *(redskap)* rake **2** *(ynkrygg)* coward, funk **II** *v1* rake [over]; ~ *ihop* rake together
krav *s7* **1** demand *(på ngt* for s.th.; *på att* to +
inf.; på livet of life); *(anspråk)* claim *(på* to);
requirement; *rättmätigt* ~ legitimate claim;
resa ~ bring claims, claim; *ställa höga* ~ be
exacting; *ställa stora* ~ *på a)* make great
(heavy) demands upon, *b) (ngns förmåga)* put
to a severe test **2** *(anmodan att betala)* dem-
and *(hövligare:* request) for payment; *(skuld-
fordran)* monetary claim
kra'vall *s3, vanl. pl,* ~*er* riots; *(gatu-)* street
disturbances **-polis** riot police (squad) **-sta-
ket** crowd control barrier, crush barrier
kra'vatt *s3* necktie **-nål** tiepin
kravbrev letter requesting payment; *(påminnelse)* reminder; *AE.* collection letter
kravellbyggd [-*vell-] *a5* carvel-built
kravla ~ [*sig*] crawl
krax, krax|a croak **-ande** *s6* croaking
krea|tion *(modeskapelse)* creation **-'tiv** [*äv.*
'kre:a-] *a1* creative **-tivitet** creativity
kreatur [*kre:a-] *s7* animal; *(fä)* beast; *koll.*
cattle *(pl); bildl.* creature, tool
kreaturs|avel cattle breeding, stockbreeding
-besättning stock [of cattle], livestock **-fo-
der** cattle feed (fodder) **-handlare** livestock
dealer **-lös** ~*t jordbruk* crop farming **-ras**
breed of cattle **-skötsel** stockraising
kreatör creator, designer

1 kredit ['kre:-] *n (tillgodohavande)* credit; *debet och* ~ debits and credits
2 kre'dit *s3 (förtroende, betalningsanstånd)*
credit; *på* ~ on credit; *få (ha)* ~ get (have)
credit; *köpa på* ~ *(vard.)* buy on tick
kredit|avtal credit agreement **-behov** credit
requirements *(pl)* **-bevis** *se kreditkort*
krediter|a credit; ~ *ngn för ett belopp (äv.)*
credit an amount to a p.'s account **-ing** credit,
entry on the credit side
kredit|förening credit association (society)
-givning [-ji:v-] granting of credit[s *pl*], credit
facilities *(pl);* lending **-institut** finance company (house)
kredi'tiv *s7* **1** *bank.* letter of credit **2** *(diplo-
mats)* credentials *(pl),* letters of credence
-brev *se kreditiv 2*
kredit|kort credit card **-köp** purchase on credit,
credit purchase **-marknad** credit market
kreditor [*kre:- el.* 'kre:-] *s3* creditor; ~*er (bokför.) (AE.)* account payable
kreditpost ['kre:-] credit item (entry)
kre'ditrestriktioner *pl* credit restrictions
kreditsida ['kre:-] credit side
kre'dit|stopp credit freeze **-stöd** credit aid
-upplysning credit report **-värdighet** credit
rating **-åtstramning** credit squeeze (restraint)
kreera [kre'e:ra] create
krematorium [-'tɔ:-] *s4* crematorium
kremer|a cremate **-ing** cremation
Kreml *n* the Kremlin
kremla *s1, bot.* russula
kreneler|ad [-'le:-] *a5, arkit.* crenellated **-ing**
crenellation
kreol [-'å:l] *s3* Creole **kreolsk** [-'å:lsk] *a5*
creole
kreosot [-'så:t] *s3, s4* creosote
krepera *(krevera)* burst, explode
Kreta *n* Crete
kretens|are [-*tens-] *s9,* **-isk** [-'tens-] *a5* Cretan
kre'tin *s3* cretin **-ism** cretinism
kreti och pleti ['kre:-, 'ple:-] Tom, Dick and
Harry
kretong [-'tån] *s3* cretonne; *(blank)* chintz
krets *s2* circle; ring; *tekn.* circuit; *(område)* district; *i* ~*en av sin familj* in the bosom of one's
family; *i diplomatiska* ~*ar* in diplomatic circles; *i välunderrättade* ~*ar* in well-informed
circles (quarters)
krets|a circle, fly (go) in circles; *(sväva äv.)*
hover; *(om tankar e.d.)* revolve, circulate
(kring round) **-gång** circle; cyclic motion
-lopp circulation, rotation; *(jordens)* orbit; *(av
nöjen e.d.)* round; *(årstidernas)* cycle **-lopps-
samhälle** *ung.* green community (society)
kre'v|ad *s3* explosion, burst **-era** explode, burst
kria [*kri:a] *s1* [written] composition **-bok**
composition book **-rättning** correction of
compositions
kricka *s1, zool.* common teal
kricket ['krick-] *s2* cricket **-grind** wicket **-plan**
cricket ground **-spelare** cricketer
krig *s7* war; *(-föring)* warfare; *det kalla* ~*et* the
cold war; *för det moderna* ~*et* for modern
warfare; *befinna sig i* ~ be at war; *börja* ~ start
a (go to) war *(mot* against); *föra* ~ make
(wage) war; *förklara* ~ *mot (friare)* proclaim

K

war against; *förklara ett land (ngn)* ~ declare war on a country (against s.b.); *vara med i* ~ see active service **kriga** make war **krigar|e** soldier; *poet.* warrior **-folk** nation of soldiers **-liv** military life; *~et (äv.)* soldiering **-yrke** *~t* the military profession **krigför|ande** *a4* belligerent; *icke* ~ nonbelligerent **-ing** [form of] warfare; *(-förande)* waging of war **krigisk** ['kri:-] *a5* warlike *(anda* spirit; *folk* nation); martial *(utseende* appearance) **krigs|arkiv** [*kricks-] military record office **-artiklar** *pl* articles of war **-barn** war baby **-beredskap** preparedness for war; general alert **-brand** war conflagration **-buss** *en gammal* ~ an old campaigner **-byte** war trophy; *som* ~ as booty **-dans** war dance **-domstol** military tribunal (court) **-fara** danger of war, war risk[s *pl*] **-fartyg** warship, man-of-war **-flotta** navy; battle fleet **-fot** war-footing; *komma på* ~ *med (bildl.)* get at loggerheads with; *stå på* ~ be on a war-footing; *sätta på* ~ mobilize **-fånge** prisoner of war **-fångeläger** prisoner-of-war camp **-fångenskap** captivity **-förbrytare** war criminal **-förbrytelse** war crime **-förklaring** declaration of war **-förnödenheter** *pl* military supplies, munitions **-handling** act of war **-herre** warlord **-hetsare** warmonger, agitator for war; jingoist **-historia** military history **-händelser** *pl* war incidents **-här** army, military force **-härjad** *a5* war-ravaged **-högskola** military academy **-industri** war (armaments) industry **-invalid** disabled soldier **-ivrare** *se -hetsare* **-konjunkturskatt** excess profits tax **-konst** art of warfare; *(ngns)* strategy **-korrespondent** war correspondent **-list** stratagem *(äv. bildl.)* **-lycka** fortune[s *pl*] of war; *med skiftande* ~ with varying success in the field **-makt** military power; *~en* the armed forces; *...vid ~en* military... **-man** member of the armed forces; *pl äv.* armed service personnel **-materiel** war material, munitions **-minister** minister of war; *(i Storbritannien)* minister of defence; *AE.* secretary of defense **-mål** war aim **-målning** war paint **-operation** military operation **-orsak** cause of war **-placering** war posting **-plan** plan of campaign, military plan **-risk** risk of war; *försäkr.* war risk **-råd** *hålla* ~ hold a council of war **-rätt** *(domstol)* court martial; *ställa ngn inför* ~ court-martial s.b. **-sjukhus** military hospital **-skada** *(ngns)* injury sustained in war, war injury; *(materiell* ~*)* war damage (loss) **-skadestånd** war indemnity, reparations [for war damages] **-skola** military academy **-skådeplats** theatre of war, front; *bildl.* scene **-stig** *på ~en* on the warpath **-styrka** war strength **-tid** *i (under)* ~*[er]* in (during) wartime, in times of war **-tillstånd** state of war; *när landet befinner sig i* ~ when the country is at war **-tjänst** active service; *göra* ~ be on active service **-trött** war weary **-tåg** military expedition **-utbrott** outbreak of war **-vetenskap** military science **-veteran** ex-serviceman; *AE.* veteran **-viktig** [of] military [importance] **krikon** [-ån] *s7, bot.* bullace **krill** *s2, zool.* krill

Krim [-imm] *n* the Crimea **krimi'nal** *s3 o.* *a5* criminal **-fall** criminal case **-film** crime film, thriller **-inspektör** detective inspector; *(chef)* detective chief inspector **kriminaliser|a** make (declare to be) criminal, outlaw **-ing** criminalization **kriminal|itet** criminality **-kommissarie** detective chief inspector; *(chef)* detective superintendent **-konstapel** detective [constable] **-lagstiftning** penal legislation **-polis** *~en* the criminal police; *(i Storbritannien)* the Criminal Investigation Department *(förk.* C.I.D.) **-politik** penal policy **-reportage** crime reporting; article[s] on criminal case[s] **-roman** detective novel **-vård** treatment of offenders **-vårdsnämnden** [the Swedish] national paroles board **-vårdsstyrelsen** [the Swedish] national prisons and probation administration **krimi'nell** *a1* criminal **krimino|log** criminologist **-logi** *s3* criminology **krimskrams** *s7 (grannlåt)* knickknacks *(pl)*, gewgaws *(pl)* **kring** *rumsbet.* round, around; *tidsbet.* [round] about; *(friare, bildl.)* round; *(om, angående)* about, concerning **-boende** *a4, de* ~ those (the people) living all around **-byggd** *a5* surrounded by buildings **-farande** *a4* itinerant **-flackande** *a4* roving; travelling about **-fluten** *a5* washed, surrounded *(av* by) **-gå** *bildl.* get round, circumvent, bypass; *(undvika)* evade; *en ~ende rörelse* a flanking movement; *ett ~ende svar* an evasive answer **-gärda** [-jä:r-] fence in *(äv. bildl.)*; enclose **kringla** *s1, ung.* figure-of-eight biscuit, twist-biscuit **kring|liggande** *a4* surrounding, neighbouring **-resande** *a4* travelling; *(om t.ex. predikant)* itinerant; ~ *teatersällskap* touring (itinerant) theatre company **-ränna** *mil.* surround, envelop **-ränning** surrounding, envelopment **-segla** sail round **-skuren** *a5* restricted, cut down, curtailed **-skära** circumscribe, curtail, restrict, limit **-smygande** *a4* prowling, lurking; *en* ~ *person* a lurcher **-spridd** *a5, ligga* ~ be scattered about (around) **-strykande** *a4* strolling; *(i smyg)* prowling **-stråla** bathe in light, shine round about **-stående** *a4* the people *(etc.)* standing round, the bystanders **-synt** [-y:-] *a1* broad-minded **-värva** *v2* envelop; *vara -värvd av* be enveloped in **krino'lin** *s3* crinoline; hoops *(pl)* **1 kris** *s2 (dolk)* kris, creese **2 kris** *s3* crisis *(pl* crises) **kris|artad** [-a:r-] *a5* critical **-läge, -situation** crisis, critical situation **kris'tall** *s3* crystal **-glas** crystal; cut glass **kristal'lin** *a5,* **-isk** *a5* crystalline **kristall|isation** crystallization **-isera** crystallize **-isk** [-'tall-] *a5* crystalline **kristall|klar** crystal clear, crystalline **-krona** cut-glass chandelier **-kula** crystal ball **-mottagare** *radio.* crystal set (receiver) **kristall|ografi** *s3* crystallography **-olja** white spirit **-socker** granulated sugar **-system** crystal system **-vas** cut-glass vase **-vatten** crystal water **kristen** *a5* Christian; *den kristna läran* the

Christian doctrine; *den kristna världen (äv.)* Christendom; *vara ~* be a Christian **-dom** [-dɷmm] *s3* **1** Christianity **2** *skol.* religion, scripture
kristendoms|fientlig Antichristian **-kunskap** *se kristendom 2* **-lärare** teacher of religious knowledge **-undervisning** religious instruction
kristenhet Christendom *(äv. ~en)*
kristid time of crisis; *ekon.* depression, slump; *~en (äv.)* the crisis
kristids|nämnd rationing board **-vara** *s1* wartime product
Kristi himmelsfärdsdag Ascension Day
kristillstånd critical state, [state of] crisis
krist|lig *al* Christian; *(lik Kristus)* Christlike; *(from)* pious; *ett ~t byte (vard.)* a fair exchange (swop); *K~a Föreningen av Unga Kvinnor (Män)* Young Women's (Men's) Christian Association *(förk. se KFUK o. KFUM)* **-ligt** *adv* like Christians (a Christian)
krist|na 1 *(omvända)* Christianize **2** *(döpa)* christen **-torn** *se järnek*
Kristus Christ; *efter ~* anno Domini *(förk. A.D.)*; *före ~* before Christ *(förk. B.C.)*
kristus|barn *~et* the Christ-child; *Madonnan med ~et* the Madonna with the Infant Christ **-bild** image of Christ **-gestalt** figure of Christ
krit|a I *s1* chalk; *(färg-)* crayon; *ta på ~ (vard.)* buy on tick; *när det kommer till ~n* when it comes to it **II** *v1* chalk; *(skor e.d.)* whiten, pipeclay **-avlagring** chalk bed (stratum) **-bit** piece of chalk **-brott** chalkpit
kriterium [-'te:-] *s4* criterion *(pl* criteria) *(på of)*
kritig *al* chalky
kri'tik *s3* **1** criticism *(över, av* on, of); *nedgörande ~ (BE., vard.)* slating;*under all ~* beneath contempt, miserable; *inbjuda till ~* invite criticism; *läsa med ~* read critically; *möta stark ~* encounter severe criticism **2** *(recension)* review, notice; *~en (~erna)* the critics *(pl)*; *få god ~* be favourably reviewed
kritiker ['kri:-] critic; *(recensent)* reviewer
kritik|lysten critical; fault-finding **-lös** uncritical; *(utan urskillning)* indiscriminate
krit|isera 1 *(klandra)* criticize; comment adversely on, censure, find fault with; *vard.* run down, slate **2** *(recensera)* review **-isk** ['kri:-] *a5* critical; *(avgörande äv.)* crucial *(punkt* point)
krit|klippa chalk cliff **-perioden** the Cretaceous [period] **-pipa** clay pipe **-streck** chalk line **-strecksrandig** pinstriped **-teckning** chalk (crayon) drawing **-vit** as white as chalk, snow white; *~ i ansiktet* as white as a sheet
kroat [krɷ'a:t] *s3* Croat **Kroatien** [-'a:tsien] *n* Croatia **kroatisk** [-'a:tisk] *a5* Croatian
krock [-å-] *s2 (bil-)* collision, crash, smash [up]; *(i krocketspel)* croquet **krocka** *(om fordon)* collide, crash, smash; *vard.* go smash; *(i krocketspel)* croquet **krockera** *(i krocketspel)* croquet
krocket ['kråck-] *r* croquet **-klot** croquet ball **-klubba** croquet mallet
krockkudde air bag
krog *s2* restaurant; *(värdshus)* inn **-gäst** patron

-rond pub-crawl **-rörelse** *idka ~* keep a restaurant (an inn) **-sväng** pub-crawl **-värd** innkeeper
krok *s2* **1** hook; *(fönster- e.d.)* catch; *få på ~en (äv. bildl.)* hook; *lägga ut sina ~ar för* spread a net for, try to catch; *nappa på ~en a)* eg. bite at the bait, *b) bildl.* swallow the bait; *sätta mask på ~en* bait the hook with a worm **2** *(krökning)* bend, curve; *gå en stor ~* go a long way round; *slå sina ~ar kring* prowl round **3** *boxn.* hook **4** *(vrå)* nook, corner; *här i ~arna* in these parts, about here
kroka hook; *~ av* unhook; *~ fast* hook on
kro'kan *s3* ornamented (pagoda-shaped) cake
krokben *sätta ~ för ngn a)* eg. trip s.b. up, *b) bildl.* upset a p.'s plans
kro'kett *s3, kokk.* croquette
kro'ki *s3* sketch
krok|ig *al* crooked; *(böjd)* bent; *(i båge)* curved; *gå ~* walk with a stoop; *sitta ~* sit hunched up **-linje** curve[d line]
krok|na [-ɷ:-] get bent *(etc.)*, bend; *(falla ihop)* collapse **-näsa** hooknose; *vard.* beak **-näst** [-ä:-] *a4* hooknosed
kroko'dil *s3* crocodile **-skinn** crocodile skin **-tårar** *pl* crocodile tears
krok|ryggig *al* with a crooked back, stooping, bent **-sabel** scimitar
krokus ['krɷ:-] *s2* crocus
krokväg roundabout (circuitous) way: *~ar (bildl.)* devious paths, underhand methods
krollsplint [-å-] *s2* vegetable fibres *(pl)*
krom [-å:-] *s3, s4* chromium, chrome **kroma** chrome
kromatisk [-'ma:-] *a5, mus. o. fys.* chromatic
krom|dioxid chromium dioxide **-garva** chrome tan **-grönt** *best. form det -gröna* chrome green **-gult** *best. form det -gula* chrome yellow **-haltig** *a5* chromiferous
kromosom [-'så:m] *s3* chromosome
krom|oxid chromium oxide **-stål** chrome (chromium) steel
krona *s1* **1** crown; *(adels-)* coronet; *(påve-)* tiara; *skapelsens ~* the crowning work of creation; *en ~ bland städer* a pearl among cities; *nedlägga ~n* abdicate [the throne]; *sätta ~n på verket* put on the finishing touch, crown the work, *iron.* cap (beat) everything **2** *~n (staten)* the State (Crown); *en ~ karl (ung.)* a soldier of the King; *i ~ns tjänst* in the service of the Crown; *på ~ns mark* on Crown (government) land (property); *vara klädd i ~ns kläder* wear the King's uniform **3** *(träd-)* top, tree-top, crown; *(blom-)* corolla; *anat.* crown; *(tand-)* crown; *(ljus-)* chandelier **4** *(mynt)* krona, [Swedish *etc.*] crown **5** *~ eller klave?* heads or tails?; *spela ~ och klave* toss *(om* for)
kron|belopp kronor (crown) amount, amount in kronor (crowns) **-brud** bride who wears the parish bridal crown at her wedding **-hjort** red deer; *(hane äv.)* stag
kroniker ['krɷ:-] chronic invalid **-hem** home for chronic invalids
kron|isk ['krɷ:-] *a5* chronic **-iskt** *adv* chronically; *~ sjuk, se kroniker*
kron|jurist law officer of the Crown; *(i Storbritannien äv.)* Attorney (Solicitor) General

K

-juvel crown jewel **-koloni** crown colony **krono|assistent** assistant bailiff **-direktör** director of an enforcement district **-fogde** senior enforcement officer; *(chef)* head of an enforcement district **-fogdemyndighet** enforcement service **-gods** Crown property **kronograf** *s3* chronograph **krono|gård** Crown farm **-häkte** local prison **-jord** Crown land **-jägare** *ung.* state forester; *AE.* forest ranger **kronolog|i** *s3* chronology **-isk** *a5* chronologic[al]; *i ~ ordning* in chronological order **kronometer** [-ˈme:-] *s2* chronometer **krono|park** *se -skog* **-skatt** state [income] tax; *AE.* federal (national income) tax **-skog** Crown (State) forest **kron|prins** crown prince **-prinsessa** [-ˣsessa] crown princess **-vittne 1** *(huvudvittne)* principal witness **2** *(vittne mot medbrottsling) bli ~* turn king's (queen's; *AE.* state's) evidence **-vrak** *vard.* army washout, reject **-ärtskocka** [-skåcka] *s1* [globe] artichoke **kropp** [-å-] *s2* body; *(bål)* trunk *(och lemmar* and limbs); *(slaktad)* carcass; *flyg.* body, fuselage; *fasta och flytande ~ar* solid and fluid bodies; *främmande ~ar* foreign bodies; *en konstig ~* (vard.) a rum chap (customer); *i hela ~en* all over; *till ~ och själ* in mind and body; *våt inpå bara ~en* wet to the skin; *bära väl närmast ~en* wear wool next to one's skin; *darra i hela ~en* tremble all over; *inte ha en tråd på ~en* be without a stitch of clothing, not have a stitch on; *inte äga kläderna på ~en* not own the clothes on one's back **kroppkaka** [-å-] potato dumpling with chopped pork filling **kropps|aga** corporal punishment **-ansträngning** physical exertion **-arbetare** labourer, manual worker **-arbete** manual labour (work) **-byggare** body builder **-bygge** body building **-byggnad** bodily (physical) structure; *(fysik)* physique; *(-beskaffenhet)* constitution **-del** part of the body **-hydda** body **-konstitution** physical constitution **-krafter** *pl* physical strength *(sg)* **kropps|lig** [-å-] *a5* bodily, physical; *(om t.ex. straff)* corporal **-pulsåder** *stora ~n* aorta **-rörelse** movement of the body; *(motion)* physical exercise **-språk** body language **-storlek** *målning i ~* life-size painting **-straff** corporal punishment **-styrka** physical strength **-temperatur** body temperature **-tyngd, -vikt** weight of the body **-visitation** [personal] search **-visitera** search [from head to foot] **-värme** heat (temperature) of the body **-övning** *~ar* physical exercises **kross** [-å-] *s2, tekn.* crushing mill, crusher **kross|a** crush *(äv. bildl.)*; *(slå sönder)* smash; shatter, wreck *(äv. bildl.)*; *(finfördela)* pound, grind down; *~ fienden (äv.)* rout the enemy; *~ ngns hjärta* break a p.'s heart; *~ allt motstånd* crush all resistance **-skada** *(hopskr. krosskada)* bruise, contusion **-sår** *(hopskr. krossår)* [severe] bruise (contusion) **kroton** [ˈkrå:tån] *best. form o. pl* = croton **krubb** *s7, vard.* grub, feed **1 krubba** *v1, vard.* grub, feed

2 krubba *s1* manger, crib **krubbitare** *(särsk. krubb-bitare)* crib-biter **krucifix** [-ˈficks] *s7* crucifix **kruka** *s1* **1** pot; *(burk)* jar; *(med handtag)* jug, pitcher **2** *(ynkrygg)* coward, funk **kruk|makare** potter **-makeri** pottery **-skärva** potsherd **-växt** pot plant **krull|a** ~ *[sig]* curl; *~ ihop sig* curl itself up **-hårig** curly-haired **-ig** *a1* curly **krum** [-umm] I *a1* curved, crooked; *(böjd)* bent, *(i båge)* arched II *s2, s4, i ~* arched **krumbukt|a** [-ˈbukta] *(göra -er)* twist and turn; *(slingra sig)* hem (hum) and haw; *buga och ~* bow and scrape **-er** *pl* **1** *(krökar)* curves, bends; *(bugningar)* obeisances **2** *(omsvep)* circumlocutions; *(undanflykter)* subterfuges, prevarication *(sg)*; *(invändningar)* humming and hawing *(sg)* **krumelur 1** *(släng)* flourish, curl; *rita ~er* doodle **2** *pers.* oddity **krum|språng** caper; gambol; *göra ~* cut capers, gambol **-stav** crosier, crozier **krupit** *sup. av krypa* **krupp** *s3, med.* croup **1 krus** *s7 (dryckeskärl)* jar; *(vatten-)* pitcher **2 krus** *s7* **1** *(på sömnad o.d.)* ruff[le]; *koll.* frilling **2** *(-ande)* ceremony; *(fjäsk)* fuss; *utan ~* without [any] ceremony **krusa 1** *(göra krusig)* crisp, curl; *(rynka)* ruffle; *(vattenyta)* ripple **2** *(fjäska för)* cringe, truckle *(för* to); stand on ceremony *(för* with); *jag ~r ingen!* I go my own way regardless of everybody! **krusbär** [ˈkru:s-] gooseberry **krusbärs|buske** gooseberry [shrub] **-kräm** gooseberry cream (fool) **krusiduller** [-ˈdull-] *pl, eg.* curls; *bildl.* frills; *(i skrift)* flourishes **krus|ig** *a1* curly; *(om kål e.d. äv.)* crisp; *(vågig)* wavy; *(om t.ex. blad)* wrinkled **-kål** kale, borecole **-lockig** curly-haired **-mynta** [ˣkru:s-, *äv.* -ˣmynn-] *s1, bot.* mint **krusning** [-u:-] *(på vatten)* ripple **krus'tad** *s3* croustade **krut** *s7* gunpowder; *(energi)* spunk; *han var inte med när ~et uppfanns* he'll never set the world (the Thames) on fire; *ont ~ förgås inte så lätt* ill weeds grow apace **-durk** powder magazine *(äv. bildl.)* **-gubbe** *vard.* tough old boy **-hus** powder house **-laddning** powder charge **krutong** [-ˈån] *s3* crouton **krut|rök** gunpowder smoke **-stänkt** *a4* powder-stained **-torr** bone-dry **-tunna** powder barrel **krux** [krucks] *s7* crux **kry** *a1* well; hale [and hearty]; *pigg och ~* fit and well **krya** ~ *på sig* get better, recover, come [a]round **krycka** *s1* crutch; *(handtag)* handle, crook **kryd|a** I *s1* spice *(äv. bildl.)*; *kokk.* seasoning, flavouring II *v1* season, flavour, spice *(äv. bildl.)*; *starkt (svagt) ~d* highly (slightly) seasoned *(etc.)* **-bod** *(speceriaffär)* grocer's shop **-doft** *(hopskr. kryddoft)* smell of spice[s *pl*] **-grönt** green herbs *(pl)* **-krasse** garden cress **-kvarn** spice mill **-nejlika** clove **krydd|ning** seasoning, flavouring **-ost** clove-spiced cheese **-peppar** allspice **-skorpa**

spiced rusk **-smak** flavour of spice **-smör** butter mixed with herbs **-stark** highly seasoned, hot **-växt** aromatic plant, herb
Kryddöarna *pl* [the] Spice Islands
krylla *se myllra*
krymp|a *v3* shrink (*i tvätten* in the wash); ~ *ihop* shrink [up] **-behandlad** *a5* antishrink treated **-fri** unshrinkable, preshrunk, nonshrinking; Sanforized **-ling** cripple **-mån** shrinkage [allowance] **-ning** shrinkage
kryo|kirurgi [ˣkry:ɷ-] cryosurgery **-'lit** *s3* cryolite **-teknik** cryogenics (*pl, behandlas som sg*)
kryp *s7* [small] creeping (crawling) thing (creature); *vard.* creepy-crawly; *ett litet ~* (*om barn*) a little mite
krypa *kröp krupit* **1** creep (*äv. om växt*); (*kräla*) crawl; ~ *på alla fyra* crawl on all fours; ~ *bakom ngn* (*bildl.*) shield o.s. behind s.b.; *det kryper i mig när jag ser* it gives me the creeps to see; *bilen kröp uppför backen* the car crawled up the hill **2** (*bege sig*) go (*till kojs* to bed; *i fängelse* to prison); ~ *i kläderna* get into one's clothes **3** (*svansa*) cringe, grovel **4** (*med betonad partikel*) *nu kröp sanningen fram* now the truth came out; ~ *ihop a*) (*om en*) huddle up, (*om flera*) huddle together, *b*) (*huka sig*) crouch (cower) down
kryp|ande *a4* (*inställsam*) servile, cringing; *bot.* procumbent **-byxor** *pl* crawlers **-eri** cringing, obsequiousness **-fil** crawler lane **-hål** *bildl.* loophole **-in** [-'inn] *s7* nest, hole, retreat; (*vrå*) nook, corner **-skytt** stalker; (*tjuvskytt*) poacher; *mil.* sniper
krypta *s1* crypt
krypt|era write in cipher (code) **-isk** ['krypt-] *a5* cryptic
krypto ['kryptɷ] *s6* cipher, code **-'gam I** *s3* cryptogam **II** *a5* cryptogamic **-grafera** cipher, code **-grafi** *s3* cryptography **-gram** [-'gramm] *s7* cipher, code, cryptograph
krypton [-'å:n] *s4, s3* krypton
kryptoteknik cryptography
krysantem|um [-ˣsann-] *s9 el. -en -er* [-'te:-] chrysanthemum
kryso'lit *s3* chrysolite
kryss 1 *s7* (*kors*) cross **2** *s2, sjö.* beating, cruising; *ligga på* ~ be tacking
kryssa 1 (*korsa*) cross; ~ *för* put a cross against **2** *sjö.* beat (*mot vinden* [up] against the wind), beat to windward, tack; (*segla fram o. tillbaka*) cruise; ~ *över gatan* zigzag across the street
kryss|are 1 *sjö., mil.* cruiser **2** (*jakt*) cruising vessel, yacht; *se äv. havskryssare* **-faner** plywood **-ning** cruise
kryssnings|fartyg cruise liner **-robot** cruise missile
kryss|prick *sjö.* spar buoy **-valv** cross vault[ing]
kryst|a (*vid avföring*) strain [at stool]; (*vid förlossning*) bear down **-ad** *a5* strained, laboured; (*om kvickhet äv.*) forced **-ning** strain **-värkar** *pl* labour [pains]
kråk|a *s1* **1** *zool.* crow; *hoppa* ~ hop; *elda för -orna* let all the heat from the fire go up the chimney **2** (*tecken*) tick; (*utmärkande fel*) error mark **3** (*huvudbonad*) bonnet **-bo** crow's-nest **-bär** crowberry **-fötter** *pl, bildl.* pothooks;

scrawl (*sg*) **-slott** *skämts.* rookery **-spark** *sömn.* featherstitch **-sång** *det fina i ~en* the beauty of it **-vinkel** *skämts.* one-horse town, hole
kråma *rfl* prance [about]; (*om pers. äv.*) strut (swagger) [about]; (*om häst äv.*) arch its neck
krångel ['kråŋel] *s7* bother, trouble; (*svårighet*) difficulty; *AE. vard.* bug[s]; *ställa till* ~ make a fuss (difficulties) **-makare** [ˣkråŋel-] troublemaker
krångla [ˣkråŋla] **1** make a bother (a fuss, difficulties) (*med betalningen* about the payment); ~ *till ngt* get s.th. into a muddle, make a muddle of s.th. **2** (*ej fungera*) be troublesome; (*förorsaka krångel*) give (cause) trouble; *låset ~r* the lock has jammed **3** (*fumla med*) fiddle with **4** (*göra undanflykter*) quibble, beat about the bush; (*bruka knep*) be up to tricks **5** *rfl,* ~ *sig fram till* muddle one's way through to; ~ *sig ifrån* manage to get out of; ~ *sig igenom* get through somehow **krånglig** *a1* troublesome, tiresome; (*kinkig*) awkward; (*invecklad*) difficult, complicated
1 krås *s7* giblets (*pl*); *smörja ~et* feast, do o.s. well (*med on*)
2 krås *s7* (*hals- o.d.*) frill, ruffle
kråsnål tiepin
1 kräfta *s1* **1** *zool.* crayfish, crawfish ; *röd som en kokt* ~ as red as a boiled lobster **2** *K~n* (*astr.*) Cancer
2 kräfta *s1* (*med.*) cancer
kräft|bur crayfish pot **-djur** crustacean **-fiske** crayfishing **-gång** backward movement **-kalas** crayfish party **-pest** crayfish disease **-skiva** *se -kalas*
kräft|svulst cancerous tumour (growth) **-sår** cancerous ulcer; *bildl.* canker
kräk *s7* **1** *se kryp* **2** *se kreatur* **3** (*neds. om människa*) miserable beggar (wretch); *ett beskedligt* ~ (*äv.*) a milksop; *stackars* ~ poor thing (wretch)
kräkas *v3, dep* be sick, vomit; ~ *upp* vomit, bring up
kräkla [ˣkräck-, *äv.* ˣkrä:k-] *s1* crosier, crozier
kräk|medel emetic **-ning** [-ä:-] vomiting; *häftiga ~ar* violent attacks of vomiting **-rot** *bot.* ipecac[uanha]
kräl|la crawl; ~ *i stoftet* (*bildl.*) grovel [in the dust] (*för* to) **-djur** reptile
kräm *s3* cream; *jfr hud-, sko-*
krämaraktig *a1* mercenary
krämar|e shopkeeper, tradesman; *neds.* huckster **-folk** *ett* ~ a nation of shopkeepers **-själ** *pers.* mercenary soul
krämfärgad cream-coloured
krämp|a *s1* ailment; *-or* aches and pains
kräng|a *v2* **1** (*luta åt ena sidan*) cant, list, heel (heave) [over]; roll; *flyg.* bank **2** (*lägga på sidan*) cant, heave down **3** *se vända* [*ut och in på*]; ~ *av sig en skjorta* struggle out of a shirt **-ning** canting, heel[ing]; lurch, roll; *flyg.* banking **-ningshämmare** stabilizer
kränk|a *v3* (*lag e.d.*) violate, infringe; (*överträda*) transgress; (*förorätta*) wrong; (*förolämpa*) insult, offend; (*såra*) hurt, outrage **-ande** *a4* insulting, offensive; ~ *tillmälen* abusive treatment **-ning** (*jfr kränka*) violation, in-

fringement; transgression; wrong; insult, offence; outrage; ~ *av privatlivets helgd* violation of privacy
kräpp *s3, s4* crepe, crape
kräpp|a, -era crinkle; *(hår e.d.)* wave **-nylon** stretch nylon **-papper** *(hopskr. kräppapper)* crepe paper
kräs|en *a3* fastidious, particular, choosy *(på* about); *vara* ~ be hard to please **-lig** [-ä:-] *a1 (om mat)* choice, delicious; sumptuous **-magad** *a5* fussy; squeamish
1 kräva *s1* crop
2 kräva *v2* **1** *(fordra)* demand, [lay] claim [to] **2** *(erfordra)* call for; *(behöva)* require, need; *(nödvändiggöra)* necessitate; *(ta i anspråk)* take; ~ *mycket tid* take up much time **3** *olyckan krävde flera dödsoffer* the accident cost the lives of several people (claimed several victims) **4** *(anmana att betala)* apply to for payment, demand payment of, *(skriftligt)* dun *(på* for); ~ *ngn på pengar* press s.b. for money, request s.b. to pay
krävande *a4* exacting; *(prövande)* trying; *(påkostande)* severe; *en* ~ *uppgift (äv.)* an arduous task
krögare innkeeper
krök *s2* bend; *(flod-, väg- e.d.)* curve, wind, winding
krök|a *v3* bend; *(göra krokig)* make crooked; *(armen, fingret)* crook; ~ *[på] läpparna* curl one's lips; ~ *rygg (om djur)* arch its back; *inte* ~ *ett hår på ngns huvud* not hurt a hair of a p.'s head; *det skall ~s i tid som krokigt skall bli* best to bend while it is a twig **-ning** [-ö:-] *(-ande)* bending *etc.*; *(en* ~) *se krök*
krön *s7* crest; *(allmännare)* top, ridge, crown; *(mur- o.d.)* coping **kröna** *v3* crown *(ngn till kung* s.b. king); *~s med framgång* be crowned with success, be successful
krönika ['krö:-] *s1* chronicle; annals *(pl)*, records *(pl)*; *(tidnings- e.d.)* review, column
krönike|böcker *K~na* [the] Chronicles **-skrivare** chronicler, annalist **-spel** chronicle play; *(hist. festspel)* pageant [play]
krönikör chronicler, annalist; *(i tidning)* columnist
kröning coronation
kröningsceremoni coronation ceremony
kröp *imperf. av krypa*
krösus ['krö:-] *s2* Croesus
kub *s3* cube; *upphöja i* ~ raise to the third power, cube
Kuba *n* Cuba
ku'b|an *s3,* **-ansk** [-'a:nsk] *a5* Cuban
1 kubb *s2 (hatt)* bowler [hat]; *AE. äv.* derby [hat]
2 kubb *s2 (hugg- etc.)* block
kubbe *s2, se 2 kubb*
kubera cube
ku'bik *s9* cubic **-fot** cubic foot **-innehåll** cubic contents, cubature, cubage **-meter** cubic metre **-mått** cubic measure **-rot** cube root **-tum** cubic inch
kub|isk ['ku:-] *a5* cubic **-ism** Cubism **-ist** Cubist **-istisk** [-'iss-] *a5* Cubist[ic]
kuckel ['kuck-] *s7* hanky-panky; hocus-pocus
kuckeli'ku I *interj* cock-a-doodle-doo! **II** *s6*

cock-a-doodle-doo call
kuckla fiddle
kudd|e *s2* cushion; *(säng-)* pillow **-krig** pillow fight **-var** *s7* pillowcase
kuf *s2* queer (odd, rum) customer **-isk** ['ku:-] *a5,* vard. odd, queer
kugga 1 *(underkänna)* reject, fail, plough; *hon blev ~d* she failed (was ploughed) **2** *(lura)* take in
kugg|bana rack *(särsk. AE. cog)* railway **-drev** gear drive; pinion
kugge *s2* cog *(äv. bildl.),* gear tooth
kuggfråga poser, catch question
kugg|hjul gear[wheel], cogwheel *(äv. bildl.)* **-stång** rack **-växel** gear, gearing
ku'jon *s3* coward, funk **-era** domineer, bully
kuk *s2,* vard. cock, prick
kukeli'ku *se kuckeliku*
ku'ku I *interj* cuckoo! **II** *s6* cuckoo call
kul *oböjligt a* funny, amusing; *ha* ~ have fun; *det var* ~ *att träffas* it was nice meeting you
1 kula *s1 (håla)* cave, hole; *(lya)* lair, den; *(bostad, vard.)* digs *(pl)*
2 kula *s1* **1** ball; *(gevärs- äv.)* bullet; *(pappers-, bröd- e.d.)* pellet; *(vid omröstning)* ballot; *skjuta sig en* ~ *för pannan* blow one's brains out; *den ~n visste var den tog (bildl.)* that shot went home **2** *sport.* shot; *stöta* ~ put the shot **3** *(leksak)* marble; *spela* ~ play marbles **4** *(bula)* bump *(i pannan* on the forehead) **5** *börja på ny* ~ start afresh
kul|bana *(projektils)* trajectory **-baneprojektil** ballistic missile **-blixt** fireball
kulen *a3* raw [and chilly], bleak
kul|formig [-å-] *a5* ball-shaped, spherical, globular **-gevär** rifle **-hammare** ball-peen hammer **-hål** bullet hole
kuli ['ku:-] *s3* coolie
kulinarisk [-'na:-] *a5* culinary
kuling half-gale; *styv (hård)* ~ moderate (fresh) gale **-varning** small craft warning
ku'liss *s3* coulisse; wing; *bakom ~erna (bildl.)* behind the scenes; *i ~erna (vanl.)* in the wings
kulkärve volley of bullets
1 kull *s2 (av däggdjur)* litter; *(av fåglar)* hatch; covey; brood; *(av grisar)* farrow; *(friare)* batch
2 kull *se omkull*
3 kull I *interj* you're "it" **II** *s7, leka* ~ play tag
1 kulla *s1 (dal-)* Dalecarlian woman (girl)
2 kulla *v1,* ~ *ngn* tag s.b.
kullager [ˣku:l-] ball bearing
kullbyttera 1 *(tumla överända)* topple over **2** *(om fordon)* turn over *(i diket* into the ditch); *(göra konkurs)* fail, come a cropper
1 kulle *s2 (hatt-)* crown
2 kulle *s2 (höjd)* hill; *(liten)* hillock; *(grav-)* mound; *de sju kullarnas stad* City of the Seven Hills
kulled [ˣku:l-] ball-and-socket joint
kullerbytta *s1* somersault; *göra en* ~ *a)* eg. turn a somersault, *b) (falla)* tumble, go tumbling over
kullersten cobble[stone]; *koll.* cobbles *(pl)*
kullerstens|gata cobbled street **-ås** cobble esker
kullfallen *a5* that has fallen over (down)
1 kullig *a1* hilly; *(kuperad)* undulating

2 kullig *a5* (*om boskap*) hornless, polled
kull|kasta 1 *bli* ~*d* be thrown down (off one's
legs); *jfr kasta* [*omkull*] **2** *bildl.* upset (*planer*
plans), overthrow; (*upphäva*) reverse, set aside
-körning (*med cykel, på skidor*) fall, tumble
-ridning fall
kullrig *a1* (*buktig*) bulging, convex; (*rundad*)
rounded; (*om stenläggning*) cobbled
kull|slagen *a5, bli* ~ be knocked over (down)
-stjälpt [-ʃ-] *a4, glaset låg* ~ the glass had
been knocked over
kulmage potbelly
kulmen ['kull-] *r, best. form* =, culmination,
climax; (*mera eg.*) summit, highest point,
acme; *ekon.* peak, maximum; *nå* ~ reach its
climax (*etc.*)
kulmin|ation *astr.* culmination **-era** culminate,
reach its climax (*etc.*)
kul|penna *se* -spetspenna **-ram** abacus **-regn**
rain (hail) of bullets **-sinter** pellets (*pl*) **-sin-
terverk** pelletizing plant **-spel** marbles (*pl*)
-spetspenna ballpoint [pen]; (*i Storbritannien
äv.*) Biro **-spruta** machine gun
kulsprute|gevär light machine gun **-pistol** sub-
-machine-gun **-skytt** machine gunner **-torn**
gun turret
kulstöt|are *sport.* shot-putter **-ning** putting the
shot
kult *s3* cult **-föremål** appurtenance of a cult
-handling cult ceremony, rite
kultiv|ator *s3* cultivator **-era** cultivate **-erad**
[-'e:rad] *a5* cultivated, cultured, refined
kultplats cult centre (site)
kultur 1 (*civilisation*) civilization; *västerländsk*
~ Western civilization **2** (*bildning*) culture;
(*förfining*) refinement; *han saknar* ~ he lacks
refinement, he is a rough diamond **3** (*odlande*)
cultivation **4** (*bakterie-, fisk- o.d.*) culture **-ar-
betare** cultural worker **-artikel** article on a
cultural subject **-arv** cultural heritage **-atta-
ché** cultural attaché **-bygd** *en gammal* ~ a district with cultural traditions **-centrum** cultural centre **-chock** culture shock **-debatt**
open debate on cultural matters
kultu'r|ell *a1* cultural **-epok** cultural epoch
-fara threat to culture **-fientlig** hostile to cultural progress **-folk** civilized people **-geografi**
social and economic geography, human geography **-gärning** cultural achievement **-histo-
ria** social history **-hus** arts (cultural) centre
-insats contribution to [the spread of] culture
-institut cultural institution **-knutte** *s2* culture vulture **-krock** cultural clash **-land** civilized (culturally progressive) country **-liv** cultural life **-minne, -minnesmärke** (*byggnad
o.d.*) historical monument; relic of ancient culture **-nation** civilized nation **-nämnd** arts
committee; cultural affairs committee **-per-
sonlighet** leading personality in the world of
culture; *vard.* lion **-politik** cultural policy **-re-
servat** nature reserve **-revolution** cultural revolution **-samhälle** civilized society **-råd** (*institution*) national council for cultural affairs;
(*pers.*) counsellor for cultural affairs **-sam-
hälle** civilized society **-sida** arts page **-språk**
de stora ~*en* the principal languages of the
civilized world **-strömning** cultural influence

-tradition cultural tradition **-utskott** ~*et* [the
Swedish parliamentary] standing committee on
cultural affairs **-växt** cultivated plant
kulvert ['kull-] *s2* culvert; conduit
kulör colour; *bildl. äv.* shade **kulört** [-ö:-] *a1*
coloured; ~*a lyktor* Chinese lanterns
1 kummel ['kumm-] *s7* **1** (*stenrös, gravrös*)
cairn; (*grav- äv.*) barrow **2** (*sjömärke*) heap of
stones
2 kummel ['kumm-] *s2, zool.* [European] hake
kummin [ˣkumm-] *s9, s7* caraway; [*spis-*]
cum[m]in **-ost** seed-spiced cheese
kum'pan *s3* companion, crony; (*medbrottsling*)
accomplice
kumul|a'tiv [*äv.* 'kumm-] *a5* [ac]cumulative
-era [ac]cumulate
kund *s3* customer; client; (*på krog e.d.*) patron;
fasta ~*er* regular customers; *gammal* ~ old
customer; *vara* ~ *hos* shop at, patronize; *han
är* ~ *hos oss* (*vanl.*) he is a customer of ours
kunde *imperf. av* kunna
kund|krets [regular] customers, clients, clien-
tele **-vagn** trolley
kung *s2* (*jfr* konung) king; *gå till* ~*s* appeal to
the highest authority
kunga|döme *s6* (*statsform*) monarchy; (*rike*)
kingdom **-familj** ~*en* the Royal Family **-för-
säkran** *avge* ~ make a declaration, sign a charter **-hus** royal house (family) **-krona** king's
crown **-makt** royal power **-mord** regicide
-par King and Queen, royal couple **-rike** kingdom **-värdighet** dignity of a sovereign, royalty
kunglig *a5* royal; *Hans K~ Höghet* His Royal
Highness; *K~ Majestät* (*förk. Kungl. Maj:t*) the
Government, the King [in Council]; *de* ~*a* the
royal personages (family *sg el. pl*); *K~a bib-
lioteket* [the Swedish] Royal Library **-het** royalty
kungligt *adv* royally; *roa sig* ~ have a right
royal time, enjoy o.s. immensely
kungs|blått royal blue **-fiskare** *zool.* kingfisher
-fågel goldcrest **-gambit** king's gambit **-gård**
demesne of the Crown (State) **-ljus** *bot.* (*koll.*)
mullein; (*art*) common mullein, Aaron's rod
-tanke leading (basic) idea **-tiger** Bengal tiger **-vatten** aqua regia **-väg** *bildl.* royal road
-ängslilja snake's head **-örn** golden eagle
kungör|a [-j-] announce, make known; (*utropa*)
proclaim; ~ *för allmänheten* (*äv.*) give public
notice of; *härmed* -*es att* notice is hereby given that **-else** announcement, publication;
(*högtidlig*) proclamation; (*förordnande e.d.*)
public notice
kun|na *kunde kunnat* **I** *huvudv* (*veta, känna t.*)
know; ~ *engelska* know English; ~ *ett hantverk* know a craft (trade); ~ *sin läxa* know
one's lesson; ~ *utantill* know by heart; *han kan
ingenting* he knows nothing **II** *hjälpv* **1** *inf.*
kunna, sup. kunnat (*vara i stånd att*) be (*resp.*
been) able to (capable of), (*förstå sig på att*)
know (*resp.* known) how to; *inte* ~ (*äv.*) be
unable to; ~ *läsa och skriva* know how to read
and write; *vilja men inte* ~ be willing but unable; *skulle* ~ (= *kunde*), *vanl.* could, might
(*jfr II 2 o. 3*); *skulle ha* ~*t* (= *kunde ha*), *vanl.*
could, might (*jfr II 2 o. 3*); *jag har gjort så*

K

gott jag har ~t I have done as well as I could, I have done my best; *det har inte ~t undvikas* it has been unavoidable **2** (*uttryckande förmåga, tillfälle, uppmaning*) *kan* can, *kunde* could; *visa vad man kan* show what one can do; *jag kan* [*göra det*] *själv* I can do it myself; *han kan sjunga* he can sing; *hon kan åka skridskor* she can (knows how to) skate; *materialet kan köpas från* the material can (is to) be had from; *vi kan ta sextåget* we can take the six o'clock train; *det kan inte beskrivas* it cannot be described; *jag kan inte få upp dörren* I can't open the door; *han kan inte komma* he can't (*är ej i stånd att* is not able to) come; *spring så fort du kan* run as fast as you can; *hur kan du vara så lättlurad?* how can you be so easily taken in?; *kan du säga mig* can you tell me; *kan ni inte vara tysta?* can't you be quiet?; *hur -de du?* how could you?; *vi -de ju försöka* we could try; *om det bara -de sluta regna* if only it could stop raining; *hur kan det komma sig att* how is it that; *vad kan klockan vara?* I wonder what the time is?; *du kan väl komma!* (*bönfallande*) do come, please!; *nu kan det vara nog!* that's enough [from you]!; *man kan vad man vill* where there's a will there's a way **3** (*uttryckande oviss möjlighet, tillåtelse, försäkran*) *kan* may, *ibl.* can, *kunde* might, *ibl.* could; *de kan komma vilket ögonblick som helst* they may come (be here) any moment now; *det kan man lätt missförstå* that may (can) easily be misunderstood; *han kan ha misstagit sig* he may have been mistaken; *det kan så vara* maybe; *du kan gå nu* you may go now; *kan jag få litet mjölk?* may (can, might, could) I have some milk, please?; *som man kan se* as you may (can) see; *kan jag få se?* may (can) I see?; *nej, det kan du inte* no, you can't (may not); *du kan göra det om du vill* you may do it if you want; *jag kan försäkra dig att* I may (can) assure you that; *det kan du ha rätt i* you may be right there; *du kan vara säker på att* you may (can) rest assured that; *du kan lika väl göra det själv* you may as well do it yourself; *hur underligt det än kan låta* strange as it may sound; *man kan lugnt påstå att* it may (can) safely be maintained (said) that; *du -de gärna ha givit mig den* you might have given it to me; *den kan väl kosta omkring 20 kronor* I should think it costs about 20 kronor; *du kan tro att det blev bra* you bet it was good; *det kan väl inte ha hänt någonting* I hope there is nothing wrong, surely nothing has happened; *det kan vara på tiden* it's about time **4** (*brukar, har en benägenhet att*) *kan* will, can, *kunde* would, could; *sådant kan hända* such things happen; *de kan vara svåra att ha att göra med* they can be difficult to deal with; *de -de sitta där i timmar* they would sit there for hours; *på våren -de floden svämma över* in spring the river could overflow its banks **5** (*annan konstruktion*) *man kan bli galen för mindre* it's enough to drive one crazy; *det är så man kan gråta* it's enough to make one cry; *det kan göra detsamma* it doesn't matter, it makes no difference; *man kan inte förneka att* there's no

denying that; *det kan man kalla tur!* that's what I call luck!; *man kan aldrig veta om* there's no knowing if; *det kan du säga!* that's easy for you to say! **6** (*med betonad partikel*) *jag kan inte med dem* I can't stand them

kun|nande *s6* skill, ability; (*kunskap*) knowledge; *tekniskt* ~ technical know-how (expertise) **-nat** *sup. av kunna* **-nig** *a1* skilful, capable, competent; (*styv*) proficient; (*som har reda på sig*) well-informed **-nighet** *se kunnande*

kunskap *s3* knowledge (*äv. ~er*) (*i* of, on; *om* about, of); (*vetskap äv.*) cognizance (*om* of); (*inhämtad*) information; *~er och färdigheter* knowledge and proficiency; *K~ens träd* [*på gott och ont*] the tree of knowledge [of good and evil]; *ha goda ~er i* have a thorough knowledge of

kunskap|a *mil.* reconnoitre, scout **-are** *mil.* [military] scout

kunskaps|begär craving for knowledge **-källa** *min ~* my source of information **-nivå** educational level **-område** branch (field) of knowledge **-prov** proficiency test **-teori** theory of cognition **-test** knowledge test, **-törst** thirst for knowledge

kupa I *s1* (*lamp-*) shade; (*globformig*) globe; (*glas-*) glass cover, bell jar (glass); (*bi-*) hive **II** *v1* **1** cup (*händerna* one's hands) **2** *lantbr.* earth (bank) up

kupé *s3* **1** *järnv.* compartment **2** (*vagn*) coupé

kuper|a 1 (*svans o.d.*) dock, crop **2** *kortsp.* cut **-ad** *a5* (*om landskap o.d.*) hilly; (*vågformig*) undulating

kupévärmare car heater

kupidon [-'å:n *el.* -'o:n] *s3* cupid

kupig *a1* convex[ly rounded]; (*utstående*) bulging (*ögon* eyes)

ku'plett *s3* music-hall (revue) song; comic song **-författare** writer of revue songs

kupol [-'å:l] *s3* cupola, dome **-formig** [-år-] *a5* dome-shaped, domed **-grav** *arkeol.* dome--crowned tomb **-tak** dome, cupola roof

kupong [-'åŋ] *s3* coupon; (*mat- äv.*) voucher; (*på postanvisning e.d.*) counterfoil, (*särsk. AE.*) stub; *klippa ~er* (*skämts.*) be one of the idle rich **-häfte** book of coupons **-skatt** tax on share dividends

kupp *s3* coup; *en djärv ~* a bold stroke, a daring move; *på ~en* (*vard*) as a result [of it], at it **-försök** *polit. o.d.* attempted coup; (*rån-*) attempted robbery **-makare** perpetrator of a (the) coup; (*stats-*) instigator of a coup d'état

1 kur *s2* (*skjul*) shed, hut

2 kur *s3, med.* [course of] treatment (*mot* for); cure (*mot* for) (*äv. bildl.*)

3 kur *s3, göra ngn sin ~* court s.b., pay court to s.b.

kura *sitta och ~* sit huddled up, (*ha tråkigt*) sit around moping

kurage pluck, nerve; *vard.* guts (*pl*), spunk

kuranstalt spa, hydro[pathic establishment]; *fysikalisk ~* physical therapy clinic

ku'rant *a1* **1** *hand.* marketable, saleable **2** (*gångbar*) current **3** *se frisk*

kurare *se curare*

kura'tiv *a5* curative

kurator *s3* **1** *univ.* curator, president [of a student's club] **2** (*övervakare*) curator, supervisor; (*sjukhus-*) almoner; (*social-*) [social] welfare officer; (*skol-*) school (educational) welfare officer
kurbits *s2, s3, bot.* pumpkin
kurchatovium [-'tå:-] *s8* kurchatovium; *AE. äv.* rutherfordium
kurd *s3,* **kurder** ['kurr-] *s9* Kurd **kurdisk** ['kurr-] *a5* Kurdish
kurera cure (*för* of)
kurfurste elector **kurfurstendöme** *s6* electorate
kuria ['ku:-] *s1* curia
kurialstil [-i*x*a:l-] official (departmental) style
kuriosakabinett [-i*x*ω:sa-] curio cupboard
kuriositet curiosity; *konkr. äv.* curio; *~er* (*äv.*) bric-a-brac; *som en ~* as a curious fact (coincidence) **kuriositetsintresse** *bara ha ~* be interesting only as a curiosity
kurios|um [-i*x*ω:-] *-umet -a* curiosity; (*om pers. äv.*) odd specimen
ku'rir *s3* courier **-post** courier's bag (pouch); *med ~* by diplomatic (courier's) bag (*etc.*)
kuri'ös *a1* curious, strange, odd
Kurland ['ku:r-] *n* Courland, Kurland
kurländsk [*x*ku:r-] *a5* Courland
kurort [-ω:-] spa, health resort
1 kurra *v1* **1** *det ~r i magen på mig* my stomach is rumbling **2** (*om duvor*) coo
2 kurra *s1* (*finka*) gaol, quod
kurragömma [-*x*jömma] *i uttr.: leka ~* play hide-and-seek
kurre *s2* chap, fellow; *en underlig ~* a rum chap, an odd fish
kurry *se curry*
kurs *s3* **1** (*läro- o.d.*) course [of instruction] (*i* in, on); (*skol- o.d.*) curriculum **2** *sjö.* course; (*-linje*) track; *flyg.* heading; *bildl. äv.* [line of] policy, tack; *hålla ~ på a*) (*hamn*) stand in for, (*udde*) stand (make, head) for, *b*) (*flyg. o. friare*) steer (head) for, bear down upon; *komma ur ~en* (*sjö.*) fall away out of course; *ändra ~* veer, (*friare äv.*) change one's course **3** *hand.* (*valuta-*) rate [of exchange] (*på* for); (*på värdepapper*) quotation (*på* of); (*på aktier*) price (*på* of); *efter gällande ~* at the current rate of exchange; *lägsta ~* (*vanl.*) [the] bottom price; *stå högt i ~* be at a premium, *bildl. äv.* be in great favour; *stå lågt i ~* be at a discount
kursa *vard.* sell
kurs|avgift course fee **-bok** textbook **-deltagare** course participant; student **-fall** fall (decline, drop) in prices (rates); *starkt ~* sharp break in prices (rates) **-förändring** change of course (policy)
kur'siv **I** *a5* italic **II** *s3* italics (*pl*); *med ~ in* italics **-era** print in italics, italicize; (*bildl., understryka*) underline; *~t av mig* my italics **-läsning** reading at sight **-stil** *se kursiv II*
kursivt [-'i:vt] *adv, läsa ~* read at sight (without preparation)
kurs|kamrat fellow student [in a course] **-lista** [stock] exchange list, list of stock exchange quotations; (*över utländsk valuta*) list of exchanges rates **-litteratur** study literature [for a course] **-plan** curriculum, syllabus **-stegring**

rise in prices, upward tendency; (*stark*) boom **-verksamhet** (*vid univ.*) extramural activity **-värde** market value (price, rate); (*valutas*) exchange value **-ändring** change of course; (*valuta-*) change of rate
kurtage *s7, hand.* brokerage, commission
kur'tis *s3* flirtation **-'an** *s3* courtesan **-era ~ ngn** carry on a flirtation with s.b. **-ör** flirt, philanderer
kurva *s1* curve; (*krök*) bend; *i ~n* at the curve; *ta en ~ för snävt* take a curve too sharp, cut a corner
kurv|ig *a1* curving, with many curves **-linje** curving (curved) line **-tagning** cornering, [the] rounding of curves
kuscha [*x*ku(:)ʃa] **1** (*om hund*) lie down **2** (*kujonera*) browbeat, cow
ku'sin *s3* [first] cousin **-barn** second cousin; *ett ~ till mig* my first cousin once removed
kusk *s2* coachman; driver
kusk|a ~ landet runt tour round the country; *~ omkring* travel about **-bock** [coachman's] box, driver's seat
kuslig [-u:-] *a1* dismal, gloomy, dreary; (*hemsk*) uncanny, gruesome; *känna sig ~ till mods* feel creepy, have a creepy sensation
kust *s3* coast; (*havsstrand*) shore; *vid ~en on* the coast, (*för semester*) at the seaside; *~en är klar* the coast is clear **-artilleri** coast artillery **-band** *i ~et* on the seaboard (seacoast) **-batteri** shore battery **-befolkning** coastal population **-bevakning 1** *abstr.* coast protection **2** *konkr., ~en* the coastguard **-bevakningsstation** coastguard station **-fart** coastal traffic, coasting trade **-flotta** *~n* the Coastal (*i Storbritannien ung.* Home) Fleet **-jägare** *mil., ung.* commando, commando soldier **-klimat** coastal climate **-land** coastal land **-linje** coastline **-radiostation** coastal radio station **-remsa** coastal strip (belt) **-stad** coastal (seaside) town **-sträcka** stretch of coast, littoral **-trakt** coastal region
1 kut *s2, zool.* seal pup
2 kut *s2* (*krökt rygg*) stoop
kut|a 1 walk with a stoop **2** *vard.* (*springa*) dart (*iväg* away) **-ig** *a1, se krokryggig*
kutrygg hunchback, humpback **-ig** *a1, se krokryggig*
1 kutter ['kutt-] *s7* (*duv-*) cooing (*äv. bildl.*)
2 kutter ['kutt-] *s2* (*båt*) cutter
kuttersmycke belle of the boat
kutterspån cutter shavings (*pl*)
kutting small keg
kuttra coo **-sju** [-'ʃu:] **I** *oböjligt s* flirting, spooning **II** *oböjligt a* intimate, thick as thieves
ku'tym *s3* custom, usage, practice
kuva subdue; (*under-*) subjugate; (*uppror o.d.*) suppress; (*betvinga*) check, curb; (*kujonera*) cow
Ku'wait *n* Kuwait
kuwait|ier [-'vait-] *s9,* **-isk** *a5* Kuwaiti
kuvert [-'ä:r, *äv.* -'ärt] *s7* **1** (*för brev*) envelope **2** (*bords-*) cover **-avgift** cover charge **-bröd** [dinner] roll **-era** put into an envelope (*resp.* envelopes) **-väska** pochette
kuvös incubator
kvacksalv|a quack **-are** quack [doctor], char-

K

latan **-eri** quackery, charlatanry
kvad *imperf. av kväda*
kvadda (*t.ex. bil*) smash
kvader ['kva:-] *s2* ashlar, freestone
kvadrant quadrant
kvadrat square; *~en på* the square of; *fem i ~* five squared (raised to the second power); *två tum i ~* two inches square; *dumheten i ~* stupidity at its height **-fot** square foot
kvadratisk [-'dra:-] *a5* **1** (*geom. o. friare*) square **2** *mat.* quadratic
kvadrat|meter square metre **-rot** *~en ur* the square root of
kvadra'tur quadrature; *cirkelns ~* (*vanl.*) the squaring of the circle
kvadrera square, raise to the second power
kvadril'jon *s3* quadrillion; *AE.* septillion
kval *s7* (*smärta*) pain; (*lidande*) suffering; (*plåga*) torment; (*ångest*) anguish; (*vånda*) agony; *svartsjukans* (*hungerns*) *~* (*pl*) the pangs of jealousy (hunger); *i valet och ~et* in two minds (*om* whether), on the horns of a dilemma **-full** agonizing; torturing; (*om död*) extremely painful; (*om smärtor e.d.*) excruciating
kvalificer|a qualify (*för* for); *~ sig* qualify o.s. **-ad** *a5* qualified (*till* for); *-at brott* aggravated crime; *~ majoritet* [a] two-thirds majority **-ing** qualification **-ingsmatch** qualifying match
kvalifikation qualification
kvalita'tiv [*el.* 'kvall-] *a5* qualitative
kvalité *s3*, **kvalitet** *s3* quality; *hand. äv.* sort, type; grade; (*märke*) brand (line) [of goods]; *vinna* (*förlora*) *~* (*schack.*) win (lose) the exchange
kvalitets|beteckning description [of quality] **-kontroll** quality check (control) **-medveten** quality conscious **-märke** mark of quality; quality brand **-vara** superior (high-class) article; quality product
kvalm *s7* closeness, stuffy atmosphere; heavy scent **-ig** *a1* suffocating, stifling, close
kvalmatch *sport.* qualifying match
kvalster ['kvall-] *s7* mite, acarid
kvantfysik quantum physics (*pl, behandlas som sg*)
kvantifiera quantify
kvantita'tiv [*el.* 'kvann-] *a5* quantitative
kvantitet quantity; (*mängd äv.*) amount **kvantitetsrabatt** quantity rebate (discount)
kvant|kemi quantum chemistry **-mekanik** quantum mechanics (*pl, behandlas som sg*) **-teori** quantum theory
kvant|um *-umet el. -um, pl -um el. -a* quantum
kvar *adv, se äv. under olika verb*; (*igen, i behåll, -lämnad, -glömd*) left; (*till övers*) left over; (*efter de andra o.d.*) behind; (*bevarad*) preserved; *han stannade ~* he stayed behind; *jag vill bo ~ här* I want to go on living here; *hon kan inte ha långt ~* [*att leva*] she cannot have long left [to live]; *han var ~ när vi gick* he was still there when we left; *under den tid som är ~ till påsk* during the time remaining to Easter
kvar|blivande *a4* remaining, permanent **-bliven** *a5* left over; (*-lämnad*) left behind; *-blivna biljetter* unsold tickets **-dröjande** *s6 o. a4* lingering

kvarg *s3* curd (cottage) cheese
kvarglömd *a5*, *~a effekter* lost property (*sg*)
kvarhåll|a keep; *-en på polisstationen* detained at the police station
kvark *s2*, *fys.* quark
kvarka *s1*, *veter.* the strangles (*pl*)
kvar|leva *s1* remnant; *bildl. äv.* relic, survival; *-levor* (*äv.*) remains (*efter* of); *ngns -levor* a p.'s mortal remains **-ligga** remain, stay on; (*~ med*) retain, keep **-låtenskap** *s3, ngns ~* property left by s.b.; (*litterär*) remains (*pl*) **-lämnad** *a5* left behind
kvarn [-a:-] *s2* mill **-damm** millpond **-hjul** millwheel **-industri** flour-mill (milling) industry **-sten** millstone **-vinge** windmill sail **-ägare** owner of a mill, miller
kvar|sittare pupil who has not been moved up; *bli ~ i ettan* stay down in the first form **-skatt** tax arrears (*pl*), back tax **-stad** *-en -er* sequestration (*på of*); *sjö.* embargo (*på* on); (*på tryckalster*) impoundage, (*tillfällig*) suspension; *belägga med ~* sequester, sequestrate, *sjö.* embargo, (*tryckalster*) impound **-stå** remain
1 kvart *s2, i bet. 2 s9* **1** (*fjärdedel*) quarter; *med hatten på tre ~* with one's hat cocked over one eye **2** (*fjärdedels timme*) quarter of an hour; *en ~ i två* a quarter to two; *en ~ över två* a quarter past two **3** (*format*) quarto **4** *mus.* fourth **5** (*i fäktning*) quarte, carte
2 kvart *s2* (*rum*) pad (*äv. tillhåll för narkomaner*)
kvarta *vard.* (*sova över*) doss down
kvar'tal *s7* quarter [of a year]
kvartals|avgift quarter's fee **-hyra** quarter's rent **-skifte** beginning of the new quarter **-vis** by the quarter, quarterly
kvar'ter *s7* **1** block; (*distrikt*) quarter, district **2** *mil.* quarters (*pl*); billet **3** (*mån-*) quarter **-mästare** quartermaster
kvarte'ron *s3* quadroon
kvarters|butik neighbourhood (local) shop **-krog** *ung.* local pub (restaurant) **-polis** local policeman
kvar'tett *s3* quartet
kvar'til *s3* quartile
kvarting *en ~* a small bottle
kvarto ['kvarr-] quarto **-format** quarto [size]; *i ~* in quarto
kvarts *s3, miner.* quartz
kvarts|final *sport.* quarterfinal **-format** *se kvartoformat*
kvarts|glas quartz glass **-lampa** ultraviolet lamp
kvartssekel quarter of a century; *ett ~* (*äv.*) twenty-five years
kvartsur quartz clock (watch)
kvar'tär *a5* Quaternary **-perioden** the Quaternary [period]
kvarvarande *a4* remaining
kva'sar *s3* quasar
kvasi|- quasi-, pseudo-; (*låtsad*) sham- **-elegant** flashy **-filosofi** pseudo-philosophy **-litterär** pseudo-literary **-vetenskap** quasi-science
kvast *s2* broom; *nya ~ar sopar bäst* new brooms sweep clean **-bindare** broommaker **-fening** *zool.* crossopterygian **-prick** *sjö.* broom--head, perch with broom **-skaft** broomstick

kvav I *a1* close; (*instängd*) stuffy; (*tryckande*) oppressive, sultry **II** *s, i uttr.* **gå i ~** founder, go down, *bildl.* be wrecked, come to nothing
kved *imperf. av kvida*
kverul|ans *s3* querulousness, grumbling **-ant** querulous person, grumbler **-antisk** [-'ant-] *a5* querulous **-era** complain, croak, grumble
kvick *a1* **1** (*snabb*) quick; rapid, swift; (*rask*) ready, prompt (*svar* answer) **2** (*snabbtänkt*) clever (*äv. iron.*) **3** (*spirituell*) witty; smart (*replik* retort); **göra sig ~ på andras bekostnad** crack jokes at other people's expense **kvicka ~ på** hurry up (*äv. ~ sig*)
kvicke *s2* (*i horn*) [horn] core; (*i hov*) [sensitive] frog
kvick|het 1 (*snabbhet*) quickness *etc., se kvick* **2** (*spiritualitet*) wit **3** (*kvickt yttrande*) witticism, joke; *AE. vard.* [wise]crack **-huvud** wit, witty chap **-lunch** quick-lunch
kvick|na ~ till revive, (*efter svimning*) come round, rally, *bildl.* chirp up **-rot** *bot.* couch [grass] **-sand** quicksand
kvicksilver mercury, quicksilver **-betning** mercury disinfection **-förening** mercury compound **-förgiftning** mercurialism, mercurial poisoning **-haltig** *a1* mercurial **-termometer** mercury thermometer
kvick|tänkt I *a1* quick-witted, ready-witted, clever **II** *adv* with ready wit, cleverly **-ögd** *a1* quick-sighted; (*om iakttagelseförmåga*) rapid, swift
kvida *kved kvidit* wail; (*klaga*) whine, whimper **kvidan** *r, best. form =,* wail[ing] *etc.* **kvidit** *sup. av kvida*
kvidd *s3* minnon
kvig|a *s1* heifer, stirk **-kalv** cow calf
kvillajabark [-ˣlajja-] soapbark, quillai bark
kvinn|a *s1* woman; *~ns frigörelse* the emancipation of women (woman) **-folk 1** *koll.* womankind; (*kvinnor*) women; *vard.* womenfolk **2** (*ett ~*) woman **-folksgöra** a woman's job
kvinnlig *a1* **1** female (*kön* sex; *organ* organ); ~ *arbetskraft* female labour; ~ *idrott* women's athletics; ~ *läkare* woman doctor; ~ *polis* policewoman; *~a präster* women clergymen; ~ *rösträtt* woman suffrage, votes for women; *familjens ~a medlemmar* the feminine members of the family **2** (*som karakteriserar kvinnor*) womanly, feminine; (*om man*) womanish, effeminate; ~ *fägring* feminine beauty; *det evigt ~a* the eternal feminine; ~ *ungdom* young women (*pl*), girls (*pl*) **-het** womanliness, womanhood, femininity; (*veklighet*) effeminacy
kvinno|bröst female breast **-emancipation** emancipation of woman **-fråga[n]** [the] woman question **-fängelse** prison for women, women's prison **-förening** women's club (association, society) **-hatare** woman hater, misogynist **-hjärta** *~t* (*ett ~*) a woman's heart **-ideal** woman ideal, ideal of a woman **-klinik** gynaecological clinic **-kön** *~et* the female sex; (*-släktet*) womankind **-linje** *på ~n* on the distaff side **-läkare** gynaecologist **-präst** woman clergyman (minister) **-rörelse** women's-rights (feminist) movement **-sakskvinna**

[-saːks-] woman advocate of feminism; (*rösträtts-*) suffragette **-sjukdom** woman's disease **-tjusare** [-çuː-] lady-killer **-tycke** *ha ~* be a lady's man, have a way with women **-överskott** excess (surplus) of women
kvinnsperson woman, female
kvint *s3* (*intervall*) fifth **-essens** [-'sens *el.* -'saŋs] quintessence **-'ett** *s3, mus.* quintet
kvintilera (*på fiol*) scrape; (*på flöjt*) tootle
kvissl|a *s1* pimple **-ig** *a1* pimply
kvist *s2* **1** twig, sprig; (*i sht avskuren*) spray; *på bar ~* on a leafless (bare) twig; *komma på grön ~* come into money **2** (*i trä*) knot, knag
1 kvista (*avkapa*) lop the twigs off
2 kvista *vard.,* ~ **in till stan** run into town
kvist|fri free from knots, clean **-hål** knothole **-ig** *a1* **1** twiggy, spriggy; (*om trä*) knotty, knaggy **2** (*brydsam*) awkward, puzzling; *en ~ fråga* a tricky question **-ning** pruning **-såg** pruning saw
kvitt *oböjligt a* **1** *bli ~ ngn* get rid of s.b. **2** *~ eller dubbelt* double or nothing (quit[s]); *vara ~* be quits **kvitta 1** offset, set off, countervail; settle **2** *det ~r mig lika* it is all one (makes no difference) to me
kvitten ['kvitt-] *r el. n, bot.* quince
kvittens *s3* receipt **-blankett** receipt form
kvitter ['kvitt-] *s7* chirp[ing], twitter
kvitt|era receipt; (*t.ex. belopp*) acknowledge; (*lämna kvitto på*) give a receipt for; (*återgälda*) repay; *sport.* equalize; *~d räkning* receipted invoice; *betalt ~s* payment received, received with thanks **-ning** offset, setoff; *bokför.* settlement per contra
kvitto *s6* receipt (*på* for); (*spårvägs- e.d.*) ticket
kvittra chirp, twitter, chirrup
kvot *s3* (*vid division*) quotient; (*friare*) quota
kvoter|a allocate quotas **-ing** allocation of quotas
kväda *kvad kvädit* sing; (*dikta*) compose, write **kväde** *s6* lay, poem, song **kvädit** *sup. av kväda*
kväk|a *v3* croak **-ande** *a4* croaking
kväkare Quaker, member of the Society of Friends
kvälj|a *v2, det -er mig a*) absol. I feel sick, *b*) (*friare*) it makes me sick (to + *inf.*) **-ande** *a4* sickening, nauseating **-ning** *få ~ar a*) absol. be sick, *b*) (*av ngt*) be nauseated (*av* by)
kväll *s2* evening; (*motsats t. morgon*) night; *i ~* this evening, tonight; *i morgon ~* tomorrow evening (night); *på ~en (~arna)* in the evening (evenings)
kväll|as *dep, det ~* the evening (night) is drawing (coming) on **-ningen** *i ~* at nightfall, at eventide
kvälls|arbete evening (night) work **-bris** evening breeze **-gymnasium** *ung.* evening secondary school **-kurs** evening class (course), night school **-kvisten** *på ~* towards evening **-mat** supper **-människa** night owl (hawk) **-nyheter** *pl* late news (*sg*) **-sömnig** *vara ~* be sleepy in the evenings **-tidning** evening paper **-vard** [-aː-] *s3* supper, evening meal
kväsa *v3* take down, teach a thing or two; *~ ngns högmod* humble s.b., take the wind out of s.b.'s sails; (*undertrycka*) suppress

kväv|a *v2* choke, stifle, suffocate (*äv. bildl.*); (*undertrycka o.d.*) quell, suppress; ~ *elden* smother the fire; ~ *i sin linda* (*bildl.*) nip in the bud; *han var nära att ~s* he was almost suffocated (*av* by); ...*så att man var nära att ~s* ...to suffocation **-ande** *a4* choking (*känsla* sensation); (*om luft*) suffocating, stifling, *vard.* choky
kväve *s6* nitrogen **-gödsel** nitrogenous fertilizer **-haltig** *a1* nitrogenous **-oxid** nitric oxide
kvävgas nitrogen
kväv|matt *schack.* smothered mate **-ning** suffocation, choking; smothering; *bildl. äv.* quelling, suppression
kvävnings|anfall choking fit **-död** death by suffocation (asphyxiation)
kybernetik *s3* cybernetics (*pl, behandlas som sg*)
kyckling [ç-] chicken; (*nykläckt äv.*) chick **-kull** brood of chickens
kyff|e [ç-] *s6* hovel, hole **-ig** *a1* poky
1 kyl [ç-] *s2* (*lårstycke*) knuckle
2 kyl [ç-] *s2, se -rum, -skåp*
kyla [ç-] **I** *s1* cold [weather]; (*kylighet*) chilliness (*äv. bildl.*); *bildl.* coldness, coolness **II** *v2* chill, cool down (*äv. bildl.*); *tekn.* refrigerate; ~ *näsan* get one's nose frostbitten
kyl|aggregat refrigerating machine, refrigerator **-anläggning** refrigerating plant
kylar|e [ç-] cooler, chiller; (*på bil*) radiator **-grill** (*på bil*) [radiator] grille **-huv** (*på bil*) bonnet; *AE.* hood **-vätska** [motorcar] antifreeze
kyl|d [çy:-] *a5* (*förfrusen*) frostbitten **-disk** refrigerated display case **-fartyg** cold-storage ship **-hus** cold store **-ig** *a1* chilly, cold (*äv. bildl.*) **-knöl** chilblain
kyller ['kyll-] *s7* buff coat
kyl|medel cooling agent, refrigerant **-ning** cooling, chilling; *tekn.* refrigeration **-rum** cold-storage room **-skada** frostbite; (*kylknöl*) chilblain **-skåp** refrigerator; *vard.* fridge **-slagen** *a5* (*om dryck*) slightly warm, tepid; (*om luft*) chilly **-system** cooling system **-vatten** cooling water **-väska** cool bag (box)
kymig [k-, *äv.* ç-] *a1* nasty, mean
kymr|er ['kymm-] [the] Cymry (Kymry) **-isk** ['kymm-] *a5* Cymric, Kymric
kyndel ['çynn-] *s2, bot.* [summer] savory
kyndels|mässa [ç-] Candlemas **-mässodag** Candlemas [Day]
kyniker *se* cyniker
kynne [ç-] *s6* [natural] disposition; character, temperament
kypare [ç-] waiter
kypert ['çy:-] *s2* [cotton] twill, twilled cotton
kypra [*çy:-] twill
ky'rass *s3* cuirass **-i'är** *s3* cuirassier
kyrk|a [ç-] *s1* church; (*fri-*) chapel; *engelska ~n* the Church of England, the Anglican Church; *gå i ~n* go to (attend) church (chapel) **-backe** *på ~n* in the open space round the church **-bok** *se* kyrkobok **-bröllop** church wedding **-båt** church boat **-bänk** pew **-folk** churchgoers (*pl*) **-fönster** church window **-kaffe** after-church coffee **-klocka** church bell; (*tornur*) church clock

kyrklig [ç-] *a1* (*om fråga, konst, ändamål e.d.*) church; (*om t.ex. myndighet*) ecclesiastical; (*om t.ex. intressen*) churchly; (*prästerlig*) clerical; ~ *angelägenhet* ecclesiastical affair; ~ *begravning* Christian burial; *~t intresserad* with church interests, interested in church affairs
kyrko|adjunkt curate **-besökare** churchgoer **-bok** parish register **-bokförd** ~ *i* registered in the parish of **-bokföring** parish registration **-byggnad** church building **-fader** Father of the Church; *-fäder* Fathers of the early Church, Apostolic Fathers **-fullmäktig** *ung.* vestryman, member of a select vestry **-fullmäktige** *ung.* select vestry **-furste** prince of the Church **-gård** cemetery, burial ground; (*kring kyrka äv.*) churchyard **-handbok** service (prayer) book **-herde** *Engl. ung.* vicar; rector; parson; *kat.* parish priest; ~ *N.* (*titel*) Rev. (the reverend) **-herdeboställe** vicarage; rectory **-historia** church (ecclesiastical) history **-kör** church choir **-lag** canon law **-musik** church music **-möte** synod, council
kyrkorgel church organ
kyrko|råd parish council **-samfund** denomination **-skatt** church rate **-staten** the Papal States (*pl*), the States (*pl*) of the Church **-stämma** common vestry; (*sammanträde äv.*) parochial church meeting **-år** ecclesiastical year
kyrk|port church doorway (porch) **-råtta** church mouse **-sam** *a1* regular in one's attendance at church; *vara ~* (*äv.*) be a regular churchgoer **-silver** church plate **-socken** church parish **-torn** church tower, steeple **-tupp** church weathercock (vane) **-vaktmästare** sexton, verger **-värd** churchwarden **-ängel** cherub
kysk [ç-] *a1* chaste; (*jungfrulig*) virgin; *leva ~t* lead a chaste life **-het** chastity; virginity
kyskhets|bälte girdle of virginity, virgin knot **-löfte** vow of chastity
kyss [ç-] *s2* kiss **kyssa** *v3* kiss **kyssas** *v3, dep* kiss [each other], exchange kisses
kyss|täck kissable **-äkta** kiss-proof
kåd|a *s1* resin **-ig** *a1* resinous
kåk *s2* **1** ramshackle (tumble-down) house, shack; *skämts.* house; (*fängelse*) clink, jug **-farare** *vard.* jailbird **-stad** shanty-built (shackle) town **2** *kortsp., vard.* full house
kål *s3* **1** *bot.* cabbage **2** *göra ~ på* make mincemeat; *ta ~ på* do for; *värmen kommer att ta ~ på mig* this heat will be the death of me **-dolma** [*kå:ldålma] *s5* stuffed cabbage roll **-fjäril** large white **-huvud** [head of] cabbage **-mask** caterpillar **-rabbi** *s3* kohlrabi, turnip cabbage **-rot** swede, Swedish turnip **-soppa** cabbage soup **-supare** *de är lika goda ~* each is as bad as the other, they are tarred with the same brush
kånka ~ *på* struggle (toil) along with
kåpa *s1* **1** (*plagg*) gown, robe; (*munk-*) cowl; (*narr-*) [jester's] cloak; (*kor-*) cope **2** *tekn.* hood, cap, cover, mantle
kår *s3* (*sammanslutning*) body; (*förening*) union; *mil. o. dipl.* corps **-anda** esprit de corps **-chef** corps commander

kår|e *s2* **1** (*vind-*) breeze **2** *det går kalla ~ar efter ryggen på mig* cold shivers go down my back

kårhus students' union building

kås|era discourse (*över* on), chat, talk (*över* about, [up]on); *~nde föredrag* informal lecture **-eri** causerie, informal talk; (*tidnings-*) chatty (topical) article, column **-ör** writer of light (conversational) articles; (*tidnings- äv.*) columnist **-ös** (*soffa*) settee

kåt *a1* randy, horny

kåta *s1* [coneshaped] hut, Laplander's tent

käbbel ['çäbb-] *s7* bickering, squabble; wrangling **-la** [ˣçäbb-] bicker, squabble; wrangle; *~ emot* answer back

käck [ç-] *a1* dashing (*yngling* young man); (*oförfärad*) bold, intrepid; (*tapper*) brave, gallant, plucky, sporting; (*vågsam*) daring; (*hurtig*) spirited; (*munter*) sprightly; *en ~ melodi* a sprightly tune; *det var ~t gjort av dig* it was a sporting thing of you to do, it was sporting of you; *med mössan ~t på sned* with one's cap cocked on one side **-het** dashingness *etc.*; dash; gallantry, intrepidity; daring spirit, pluck

käft [ç-] *s2* **1** jaws (*pl*); *tekn.* jaw; *dödens ~ar* the jaws of death; *ett slag på ~en* a blow on the chaps; *håll ~en!* shut up!; *vara slängd i ~en* have the gift of the gab, (*slagfärdig*) be quick at repartee; *vara stor i ~en* shoot off one's mouth **2** (*levande själ*) living soul **käfta** (*prata*) jaw; (*gräla*) wrangle; *~ emot* answer back

kägel ['çä:-] *s2, boktr.* body [size] **-bana** skittle (*särsk. AE.* ninepin) alley **-formig** [-å-] *a1* conical, coneshaped **-spel** (*-spelande*) skittles, *särsk. AE.* ninepins (*pl, behandlas som sg*)

kägl|a [ˣçä:g-, ˣçägg-] *s1* **1** cone **2** (*i kägelspel*) skittle, ninepin; *slå* (*spela*) *-or* play skittles (*särsk. AE.* ninepins)

käk [ç-] *s7, vard.* grub, feed **käka** *vard.* grub, feed

käkben [ç-] jawbone; *fack.* mandible

käk|e [ç-] *s2* jaw; *fack.* mandible **-håla** maxillary sinus (antrum) **-led** maxillary joint

kälkbacke toboggan run

kälkborgare [ç-] Philistine

kälkborgerlig [ç-] Philistine **-het** Philistinism, narrow-mindedness

kälk|e [ç-] *s2* sledge; *sport. vanl.* toboggan; *åka ~* sledge, toboggan **-åkning** tobogganing

källa [ç-] *s1* spring; well, (*flods äv.*) source (*äv. bildl.*) (*till* of); *från* (*ur*) *säker ~* from a reliable source, on good authority

källar|e [ç-] **1** cellar; (*-våning*) basement **2** *se krog* **-glugg** cellar air hole **-mästare** restaurant keeper, restaurateur **-trappa** cellar stairs (*etc.*) **-valv** cellar vault **-våning** basement

käll|beskattning taxation at [the] source; pay-as-you-earn system **-flod** river source **-flöde** source-tributary **-forskning** study of original sources (manuscripts) **-förteckning** list of references, bibliography **-hänvisning** reference to sources **-kritik** criticism of the sources **-sjö** springlake; (*som källa t. flod*) source-lake **-skatt** tax at [the] source, pay-as-you-earn (P.A.Y.E.) tax **-skrift** original text, source **-språng** fountain **-vatten** spring water **-åder**

vein of water

kält [ç-] *s7* nagging **kälta** nag

kämpa [ç-] (*strida*) contend, struggle (*om* for); (*slåss*) fight (*om* for); *~ med svårigheter* contend with difficulties; *~ mot fattigdomen* struggle against poverty; *~ mot vinden* battle against the wind; *~ sig fram* fight one's way (struggle) along (*till* to); *~ sig igenom en sjukdom* (*äv.*) pull through [from] an illness **-hög** giant-size **-lek** tournament-game **-tag** gigantic effort **-visa** ballad of heroes (a hero)

kämpe [ç-] *s2* fighter; (*stridande*) combatant; (*krigare*) warrior; (*för-*) champion (*för* of)

kän|d [ç-] *a* **1** (*bekant*) known; (*väl-*) well-known; (*som man är förtrogen med*) familiar; (*ryktbar*) famous, noted; *ett -t ansikte* a well-known (familiar) face; *en ~ sak* a well-known fact, a fact familiar to all, common knowledge; *det är allmänt -t att* it is generally known (*neds.* notorious, a notorious fact) that; *vara ~ för att vara* be known as being; *~ för prima varor* (*hand.*) noted for first-quality goods; *vara ~ under namnet* go by the name of; *vara illa ~* be of bad (evil) repute, have a bad reputation; *~a och okända* the well-known and the anonymous **2** (*förnummen*) felt; *frambära ett djupt -t tack* proffer one's heartfelt thanks

kändis ['çänn-] *s2, vard.* celebrity; (*manlig*) lion

käng|a [ç-] *s1* boot **-snöre** bootlace

känguru ['käng-, 'ç-] *s5* kangaroo

känn [ç-] *s, i uttr.: på ~* by instinct; *ha på ~ att* have a feeling (an inkling) that

1 känna [ç-] *s, i uttr.: ge till ~, se tillkännage; ge sig till ~* make o.s. known (*för* to); (*om ngt*) manifest itself

2 känn|a [ç-] *v2* **I 1** (*förnimma*) feel; (*erfara*) experience [feelings (a feeling) of]; (*märka*) notice (*smak av* a taste of); (*pröva, smaka*) try [and see]; *~ besvikelse* (*trötthet*) feel disappointed (tired); *~ för* (*ha lust med el. till*) feel like; *~ för ngn* (*ha medkänsla med*) feel for (sympathize with) s.b. **2** (*beröra med handen*) feel **3** (*~ till*) know; *känn dig själv!* know thyself!; *på sig själv -er man andra* one judges others by o.s.; *lära ~ ngn* get to know s.b., get acquainted with s.b.; *lära ~ varandra* (*äv.*) become acquainted [with each other]; *om jag -er dig rätt* if I know you at all **II** (*med betonad partikel*) **1** *~ av* feel; *få ~ av* be made to feel **2** *~ efter* feel; *~ efter om dörren är låst* [try the handle to] see whether the door is locked **3** *~ igen* know (*ngn på rösten* s.b. by his voice), (*ngn el. ngt man sett förr*) recognize; *~ igen sig* know one's way about (where one is) **4** *få ~ på* have to experience, come in for; *~ på sig* have a feeling, feel instinctively (in one's bones) **5** *~ till* know, be acquainted with, (*veta av, äv.*) know of, (*vara hemma i, äv.*) be up in **III** *rfl* feel; *~ sig för* feel one's way [about], (*sondera äv.*) sound

kännande [ç-] *a4* feeling; sentient (*varelse* being)

kännar|e [ç-] connoisseur; (*sakkunnig*) expert, authority (*av, på* on, in) **-min** *med ~* with the air of a connoisseur (*etc.*)

känn|as [ç-] *v2, dep* feel; be felt; *hur -s det?* how do you feel?, what does it feel like (*att* to)?; *det -s lugnande att veta* it is a relief to know; *det -s angenämt att (äv.)* it is a pleasant feeling to; ~ *vid (tillstå)* confess, acknowledge, (*erkänna som sin tillhörighet*) acknowledge; *inte vilja* ~ *vid* refuse to acknowledge, disown **-bar** *a1* to be felt (*för* by); (*förnimbar*) perceptible, noticeable (*för* to); (*svår*) severe, serious (*för* for); *en* ~ *förlust* a heavy (severe) loss; *ett* ~*t straff* a punishment that hurts

känne|dom [ç-] *s2* (*vetskap*) knowledge, cognizance (*om* of); (*underrättelse*) information (*om* about, as to); (*kunskap*) knowledge; (*bekantskap*) acquaintance, familiarity (*om* with); *bringa till ngns* ~ bring to a p.'s notice (attention); *få* ~ *om* receive information (be informed) about, get to know; *ha* ~ *om* be aware (cognizant) of; *för* [*er*] ~ for [your] information; *till allmänhetens* ~ *meddelas* for the information of the public, notice is given **-mär- ke, -tecken 1** *konkr.* [distinctive] mark, token, sign **2** (*egenskap*) characteristic, distinctive feature, criterion (*på* of) **-teckna** characterize; be a characteristic of; (*särskilja*) distinguish **-tecknande** *a4* characteristic (*för* of); distinguishing, distinctive

känning [ç-] **1** (*förnimmelse*) feeling, sensation; *ha* ~ *av sin reumatism* be troubled by one's rheumatism **2** (*kontakt*) touch; *få* ~ *med fienden* get in touch with the enemy; *ha* ~ *av land (sjö.)* be within sight of land

känsel ['çänn-] *s9* feeling; perception of touch **-nerv** sensory nerve **-organ** tactile organ **-sin- ne** (*för tryck*) sense of touch, tactile sense; (*för smärta, köld, värme*) sense of feeling **-spröt** feeler, palp

känsl|a [ç-] *s1* feeling (*för ngt* for s.th.; *för ngn* towards s.b.); (*kroppslig förnimmelse*) sensation (*av köld* of cold); (*sinne, intryck, uppfattning*) sense (*för* of), sentiment (*av tacksamhet* of gratitude); (*i hjärtat*) emotion; (*med-*) sympathy; *psykol.* affect; *mänskliga -or* human feelings (sentiments); *instinktiv* ~ gut feeling; *hysa varma -or för* feel affection for, be fond of; *i* ~*n av* feeling (*att* that) **-ig** *a1* **1** sensitive (*för* to), (*för drag, smitta, smärta o.d.*) susceptible (*för* to); (*om kroppsdel o. äv. om pers.*) sensible (*för* to) **2** (*-ofull*) feeling; sympathetic; (*rörande*) feeling, moving; (*ömtålig*) delicate; (*lättretlig*) touchy; ~ *för kritik* sensitive to (touchy as regards) criticism **-ighet** sensitivity, sensitiveness; susceptibility; sensibility; delicacy; touchiness

känslo|betonad *a5* emotionally tinged (coloured) **-full** full of feeling, emotional; *se äv. känslosam* **-kall** frigid **-kyla** frigidity **-laddad** ~ *stämning* explosive atmosphere **-liv** emotional life; ~*et (äv.)* the sentient life **-läge** affect **-lös** (*kroppsligt*) insensitive, insensible, numb (*för* to); (*själsligt*) unfeeling (*för ngn* towards s.b.), unemotional, callous; (*likgiltig*) indifferent (*för* to); (*apatisk*) apathetic **-löshet** insensitiveness *etc.*; insensibility; indifference **-människa** man (*etc.*) of feeling (sentiment); emotionalist **-mässig** *a1* emotional **-sak** matter of sentiment **-sam** *a1* sentimental; emotional; (*överdrivet*) mawkish **-samhet** sentimentality; (*överdriven*) emotionality **-skäl**

sentimental reason **-tänkande** *a4 o. s6* emotional thinking **-utbrott** outburst of feeling

käpp [ç-] *s2* stick; (*rotting*) cane; *få smaka* ~*en* be given a taste of the stick (cane); *sätta en* ~ *i hjulet för ngn (bildl.)* put a spoke in a p.'s wheel **-häst** hobbyhorse (*äv. bildl.*); cockhorse **-rak** bolt upright **-rapp** blow with a stick (cane)

kär [ç-] *a1* **1** (*förälskad*) in love (*i* with); *bli* ~ fall in love; *få ngn* ~ become attached to (fond of) s.b.; *hålla ngn* ~ hold s.b. dear **2** (*avhållen*) dear (*för* to); (*älskad*) beloved (*för* by); *en* ~ *gäst* a cherished (welcome) guest; *en* ~ *plikt* a privilege; ~*a barn!* my dear[s]!, my dear child (children)!; *K*~*e vän!* (*i brev*) Dear (My dear) Bill (*etc.*)!; *mina* ~*a* my dear ones, those dear to me; *i* ~*t minne* in fond (cherished) remembrance; *om livet är dig* ~*t* if you value your life; ~*t barn har många namn* we find many names for s.o. we love

kärande [ç-] *s9* plaintiff; suer

käresta [ç-] *s1* sweetheart; (*ngns*) darling, beloved

käring ['çä-, 'çärr-] old woman; *hon är en riktig* ~ she is a real shrew **-aktig** *a1* old womanish **-knut** granny, granny['s] knot **-tand** *bot.* birdsfoot-trefoil

kärkommen *a3* welcome

kärl [çä:-] *s7* vessel; (*förvarings-*) receptacle, container; *biol.* vessel, duct

kärlek [ˣçä:r-] *s2* love (*till ngn* for s.b.; *till ngt* for *el.* of s.th.); (*kristlig äv.*) charity; (*tillgivenhet*) affection (*till* for); (*hängivenhet*) devotion (*till* to); (*passion*) passion (*till* for); *av* ~ *till* out of love for; *den stora* ~*en* the great passion; *dö av olycklig* ~ die of a broken heart; *förklara ngn sin* ~ make s.b. a declaration of love; *gammal* ~ *rostar inte* love does not tarnish with age; *gifta sig av* ~ marry for love **kärleks|affär** love affair **-brev** love letter **-dikt** love poem **-dryck** love potion **-full** loving, affectionate; (*öm*) tender **-förbindelse** love affair **-förklaring** declaration (confession) of love **-gud** god of love **-gudinna** goddess of love **-historia 1** (*-berättelse*) love story **2** (*-affär*) love affair **-krank** lovesick **-kval** *pl* pangs of love **-liv** love life **-lyrik** love poetry **-lös 1** (*hårdhjärtad*) uncharitable **2** (*fattig på kärlek*) loveless, unloving **-löshet** lack of love **-ro- man** love story, romance **-scen** love scene **-sorg** disappointment in love, a broken heart

kärl|förändring vascular change **-kramp** vascular spasm **-sammandragande** *a4,* ~ *medel* vasoconstrictor **-vidgande** *a4,* ~ *medel* vasodilator

1 kärna [ˣçä:r-] **I** *s1* (*smör-*) churn **II** *v1* churn
2 kärn|a [ˣçä:r-] **I** *s1.* **1** (*i frukt*) pip; (*i bär, druva, melon o.d.*) seed; (*i stenfrukt*) stone; *AE. äv.* pit; (*i nöt*) kernel **2** (*i säd*) grain **3** (*i låga*) core, body; (*jordens*) kernel; *fys. o. naturv.* nucleus (*pl äv.* nuclei); *tekn.* core; (*i träd*) heartwood **4** *bildl.* kernel, nucleus; (*det viktigaste*) core, heart, essence **II** *v1,* ~ *ur* seed, stone, core; *AE. äv.* pit

kärn|avfall nuclear waste **-bränsle** nuclear fuel **-energi** nuclear energy **-energianläggning** nuclear power plant **-familj** nuclear family

-forskning nuclear research **-fri** pipless, seedless, stoneless **-frisk** sound to the core **-frukt** pome **-full** *bildl.* vigorous; (*kraftfull*) racy, pithy **-fysik** *fys.* nuclear physics **-fysiker** nuclear physicist **-hus** core **-ig** *a1* full of pips (*etc.*); stony, seedy **-kemi** nuclear chemistry **-klyvning** nuclear fission **-kraft** nucler power **-kraftinspektion** *Statens* ~ the [Swedish] nuclear-power inspectorate **-kraftverk** nuclear power station **-kraftvärmeverk** nuclear power station for production of heat and electricity **-laddning** nuclear charge **-minne** *data.* core store, memory

kärnmjölk buttermilk

kärn|partikel nuclear particle **-punkt** ~*en i* the principal point (the gist) of **-reaktion** nuclear reaction **-reaktor** nucler reactor **-skugga** true shadow; umbra (*pl* umbrae) (*äv. astr.*) **-sönderfall** nuclear disintegration **-trupp** picked troops **-vapen** nuclear weapon **-vapenfri** nuclear-free **-vapenförbud** ban on nuclear weapons, nuclear ban **-vapenkrig** nuclear war, (warfare) **-vapenprov** nuclear test **-ved, -virke** heartwood **-värmeverk** nuclear power station for production of heat

käromål [ç-] plaintiff's case

kärr [ç-] *s7* marsh; (*sumpmark*) swamp

kärra [ç-] *s1* cart; (*drag-, skott-*) barrow

kärr|hök *brun* ~ marsh harrier; *blå* ~ hen harrier **-mes** marsh tit

kärv [ç-] *a1* harsh (*i smaken* in (to the) taste; *för känseln* to the feel); (*om ljud äv.*) strident, rasping; (*bitande, äv. bildl.*) acrid, pungent (*humor* humour); (*om natur*) austere; (*om pers. o. språk*) harsh, rugged

1 kärva [ç-] *v1* (*om motor o.d.*) seize, jam; *det ~r till sig* it's getting tougher

2 kärva [ç-] *v1* sheaf, sheave

kärve [ç-] *s2* sheaf (*pl* sheaves)

kärvhet harshness *etc.*; acridity, pungency; austerity

kärvänlig [-'vänn-, *äv.* ˣçä:r-] fond, affectionate

kättar|bål [ç-] heretic's pile, stake **-domstol** court of inquisition

kättare [ç-] heretic

kätte [ç-] *s2* pen, pinfold, [loose] box

kätteri [ç-] heresy **kättersk** ['çätt-] *a5* heretical

kätting [ç-] chain[-cable]

kättja [ç-] *s1* lust[fulness] **kättjefull** lustful, lecherous

1 käx [k-, ç-] *s7, s9, se kex*

2 käx [ç-] *s7, se tarmkäx*

3 käx [ç-] *s7* persistent asking, nagging

käxa [ç-] nag; ~ *sig till ngt* get s.th. by nagging for it

1 kö *s3* (*biljard-*) cue

2 kö *s3* queue; *AE.* line-up; (*av bilar o.d. äv.*) line, file, string; *mil. o. sport.* rear; *bilda* ~ form a queue; *stå bakom ngn i* ~*n* stand behind s.b. in the queue; *ställa sig i* ~ queue up, take one's place in the queue, *AE.* line up

kö|a queue [up], *AE.* line up **-bildning** queuing-up; *om det blir* ~ if there is a queue **-bricka** [queue] ticket

kök [ç-] *s7* kitchen; (*kokkonst*) cuisine; (*kokapparat*) stove; *ett rum och* ~ one room and kitchen; *med tillgång till* ~ with kitchen facilities **köksa** *s1* cook, kitchen-maid

köks|avfall kitchen-refuse, garbage **-bord** kitchen-table **-dörr** kitchen (back) door **-fläkt** kitchen fan **-handduk** tea towel (cloth), *AE.* dishtowel **-ingång** back door **-inredning** kitchen fittings **-latin** dog Latin **-maskin** kitchen machine **-mästare** chef, chief cook **-personal** kitchen staff **-redskap** kitchen utensils (*pl*) **-regionerna** *pl* the kitchen quarters **-rulle** kitchen roll **-spis** kitchen range; (*elektr. el. gas-*) cooker, stove **-trappa** kitchen stairs (*pl*), backstairs (*pl*) **-trädgård** kitchen (vegetable) garden **-vägen** *gå* ~ go through (by way of) the kitchen **-växt** vegetable; potherb

köl [ç-] *s2* keel; *sträcka* ~*en till ett fartyg* lay [down] the keel of a vessel; *ligga med* ~*en i vädret* be bottom up; *på rätt* ~ (*bildl.*) straight on the right track (tack)

kölapp *se köbricka*

köld [ç-] *s3* **1** cold; cold weather; *sträng* ~ a severe (keen) frost; *darra av* ~ shiver with cold **2** (*kallsinnighet*) coldness; (*starkare*) frigidity **-blandning** freezing mixture **-grad** degree of frost **-härdig** winter-hardy (*växt* plant) **-knäpp** cold spell **-period** cold period **-rysning** chill

köl|fena fin of a (the) keel **-hala** careen, heave down; (*som straff*) keelhaul **-halning** [-a:-] careening; (*straff*) keelhauling

Köln *n* Cologne

köl|sträckning laying of keel **-svin** keelson, kelson **-vatten** wake (*äv. bildl.*), wash, track

kön [ç-] *s7* sex; *av manligt* ~ of the male sex **-lig** [-ö:-] *a1* sexual **-lös** sexless; asexual (*fortplantning* reproduction)

köns|akt sexual act; coitus **-cell** sex cell, gamete **-delar** *pl* sexual organs, genitals **-diskriminering** sex discrimination, sexism **-drift** sex instinct, sexual desire **-hormon** sex hormone **-kromosom** sex chromosome **-kvotering** quota allocation by sex **-körtel** gonad **-liv** sex[ual] life **-mogen** sexually mature **-mognad** sexual maturity **-organ** sexual organ **-roll** sexual role **-rollsdebatt** debate on the role of the sexes **-sjukdom** venereal disease **-umgänge** sexual intercourse, sex

könummer number in queue

köp [ç-] *s7* purchase; (*fördelaktigt*) bargain, deal; *avsluta ett* ~ make a purchase; *ett gott* ~ a bargain; ~ *i fast räkning* outright purchase; *på* ~*et* into the bargain; *på öppet* ~ on a sale-or-return basis, with the option of returning the goods; *till på* ~*et* what's more, to boot, in addition, ... at that

köp|a [ç-] *v3* buy, purchase (*av* from); ~ *billigt* buy cheap[ly]; ~ *kontant* buy for cash; ~ *kakor för ett pund* buy a pound's worth of cakes; ~ *in* (*upp*) buy up; ~ *upp sina pengar* spend all one's money [in buying things]; ~ *ut en delägare* buy out a partner **-are** buyer, purchaser **-centrum** shopping centre

köpe|avtal contract of sale (purchase) **-brev** bill of sale; purchase deed **-kontrakt** *se -avtal*

Köpenhamn [ç-] *n* Copenhagen

köpenicki'ad *s3* hoax

K

köpenskap [ç-] *s3* trade, trading; *idka* ~ do business
köpeskilling [ç-] purchase-price
köping [ç-] urban district, market town; *hist.* borough
köp|kort credit card **-kraft** purchasing power **-kraftig** with great purchasing power, able to buy **-kurs** bid (buying) price; *(för valutor)* buying-rate **-man** merchant, dealer, businessman; *(handlande)* tradesman; *(grosshandlare)* wholesaler **-mannaförbund** merchants' (tradesmen's) association (union) **-motstånd** buyers' (consumers') resistance **-rush** buying rush **-slagan** *r* bargaining **-slå** bargain *(om for)*; *(kompromissa)* compromise **-stark** with great purchasing power, with [plenty of] money to spend **-tvång** obligation to buy
1 kör *s3, pers.* choir; *(sång)* chorus *(äv. bildl.)*; *i* ~ in chorus; *en* ~ *av ogillande röster* a chorus of disapproval
2 kör [ç-] *i uttr.: i ett* ~ unceasingly, without stopping, *(tätt på varandra)* in a stream
kör|a [ç-] *v2* **I 1** drive *(bil* a car; *en häst* a horse; *ngn t. stationen* s.b. to the station); *(föra i sin bil e.d.)* take (run) [in one's car *etc.*]; *(åka)* ride, go, *(i bil äv.)* motor; *(motorcykel)* ride; *(transportera)* convey, carry, take; *(skjuta)* push; *(motor e.d.)* run *(med bensin* on petrol); *kör sakta!* slow down!, dead slow!, *AE.* drive slow! **2** *(stöta, sticka)* thrust *(ngt i s.th.* into); run *(fingrarna genom håret* one's fingers through one's hair); *(film)* reel, run **3** ~ *med ngn* worry s.b.; ~ *med ngt* keep on about s.th. **4** *kör för det!* right you are!, yes let's!; *kör till (i vind)!* agreed!, a bargain!, done! **5** *(kuggas)* fail, be ploughed **II** *(med betonad partikel)* **1** ~ *bort* drive away, *(avskeda)* dismiss, turn out, send packing **2** ~ *emot (kollidera med)* run into **3** ~ *fast* get stuck, *(om förhandlingar o.d.)* come to a deadlock **4** ~ *ifatt* catch up **5** ~ *ihjäl ngn* run over s.b. and kill him; ~ *ihjäl sig* be killed in a driving (car *etc.*) accident **6** *det har -t ihop sig för mig* things are getting on top of me **7** ~ *in a) (hö e.d.)* cart (bring) in, *b) (tid)* save on the schedule, make up for, *c) (en ny bil)* run in **8** ~ *om* overtake *(en bil* a car) **9** ~ *omkull* have a driving accident, have a fall [from one's bicycle] **10** ~ *på a) (vidare)* drive on, *b) se* ~ *emot* **11** ~ *sönder* drive into and smash it, *(vagn e.d.)* have a smash-up, *(väg)* damage badly by driving on it **12** ~ *upp (för körkort)* take one's driving test; ~ *upp ngn ur sängen* rout s.b. out of bed **13** ~ *ut ngn* turn s.b. out of the room *(etc.)* **14** ~ *över a) (bro e.d.)* cross, drive across
kör|bana roadway, carriageway **-bar** *a1 (trafikduglig)* roadworthy **-fil** [traffic] lane **-förbud** driving ban
körig [ç-] *a1, vard.* hectic
kör|karl driver **-kort** driving (driver's) licence **-kortsprov** driving test **-kunnig** able to drive
körledare choirmaster
kör|lektion driving lesson **-ning** [ˣçö:r-] driving *etc.*; *(av varor)* haulage; *en* ~ *a* drive, *(taxi-)* a fare **-riktning** direction of travel; *förbjuden* ~ no thoroughfare **-riktningsvisare**

[direction] indicator
körsbär [ç-] cherry
körsbärs|brännvin kirsch[wasser] **-likör** cherry brandy **-träd** cherry
körskola driving school, school of motoring
körs'när [ç-] *s3* furrier
körsven [ˣçö:r-] driver
körsång choir-singing; *(komposition)* chorus
körteknik [ˣçö:r-] driving technique
körtel [ç-] *s2* gland **-vävnad** glandular tissue
körtid driving (running) time
körvel [ç-] *s2, bot.* sweet cicely
körväg roadway, carriageway; *(i park e.d.)* drive; *(rutt)* route
kösamhälle society with many queues [for housing, services *etc.*]
kött [ç-] *s7* **1** flesh; *(som födoämne)* meat; *(frukt-)* flesh, pulp **2** *mitt eget* ~ *och blod* my own flesh and blood **-affär** butcher's [shop] **-ben** meaty bone **-bulle** [force]meat ball **-extrakt** meat extract, essence of meat **-färs** minced meat, ground beef; *AE.* ground meat; ~ *i ugn* meat loaf **-ig** *a1* fleshy; *(om frukt)* pulpy, pulpous; ~ *blad* fleshy leaves **-konserv** tinned (canned) meat **-kvarn** meat-mincer; *(större)* minching-machine **-rätt** meat course (dish) **-saft** meat juice, gravy **-skiva** slice of meat **-sky** gravy meat **-slamsa** scrap of flesh (meat)
köttslig [ç-] *a1* **1** *min* ~*e bror* my own brother, my brother-german **2** *(sinnlig)* fleshy
kött|soppa meat broth, beef soup **-spad** stock **-stuvning** stew, ragout; *AE. sl. (blaskig* ~*)* slumgullion **-sår** flesh wound **-varor** meat products **-yxa** butcher's axe, meat-chopper **-ätande** *a4 o. s6* flesh-eating, carnivorous **-ätare** *pers. vanl.* meat-eater; *(djur)* flesh-eater, carnivore

L

la [la:] *vard., imperf. av lägga*
1 labb *s2, vard.* paw
2 labb *s2, zool.* skua
3 labb *vard.* lab[oratory]
laber ['la:-] *a2, sjö.* light
labi'al *a1 o. s3* labial **-isering** [-'se:-] labialization **-pipa** *mus.* flue [pipe]
la'bil *a1* unstable **-itet** instability
labor|ation laboratory experiment (work) **-a'tiv** *a1* laboratory, experimental **-ator** [-ˣa:tår] *s3, univ.* reader; *Am.* associate professor
laboratorie|assistent laboratory assistant; medical technician **-försök** *se laboration*
labor|atorium [-'tɷ:-] *s4* laboratory **-era 1** do laboratory work **2** *(friare)* ~ *med* work with; ~ *med färg* play about with colours
laby'rint *s3* labyrinth (*äv. bildl.*); maze **-isk** *a5* labyrinthine
lack *s7, s3* **1** *(sigill-)* sealing wax **2** *(fernissa)* varnish, lacquer; *(färg)* enamel
1 lacka *svetten ~r av honom* he is dripping with sweat
2 lacka *(försegla)* seal [with sealing wax]; ~ *igen* seal up
3 lacka *(framskrida)* approach [slowly]; *det ~r mot jul* Christmas is approaching
lack|arbete lacquer work **-era** lacquer, japan; *(fernissa)* varnish; *(måla)* enamel **-ering** lacquering, japanning; varnishing; *(bils etc. äv.)* paint **-färg** enamel [paint]; *syntetisk ~* synthetic paint (enamel)
lackmus ['lakk-] *s2* litmus **-papper** litmus paper
lacknafta ligroin
lack|röd vermilion **-skinn** patent leather **-sko** patent-leather shoe **-stång** stick of sealing wax **-viol** wallflower, gillyflower
lada *s1* barn
ladd|a load; *elektr. o. bildl.* charge; ~ *om* reload, recharge; ~ *en kamera* load a camera; *vara ~d med energi (om pers. äv.)* be a live wire; *en ~d roman* a novel packed with action; ~ *ur* discharge; ~ *ur sig (om batteri)* run down, *bildl.* get out of one's system, relieve o.s. **-ning 1** *abstr.* loading, charging **2** *konkr.* load, charge
lade [*vard.* la:] *imperf av lägga*
ladugård ['la:gård, *äv.* 'lagg-] cowhouse, cowshed; *AE. äv.* barn
ladugårds|förman farm foreman **-karl** cowman **-piga** dairymaid
ladusvala common (barn) swallow
lafs|a slop, shuffle **-ig** *a1* slack, sloppy
1 lag *s2 (avkok)* decoction; *(lösning)* solution; *(spad)* liquor; *(socker-)* syrup
2 lag *s7* **1** *(lager)* layer **2** *(sällskap)* company; *(krets)* set; *(arbets-)* gang, team; *sport.* team; *i glada vänners ~* in convivial company; *gå ~et runt* go the round; *låta gå ~et runt* pass round; *ge sig i ~ med ngn* begin to associate

---

with s.b.; *ha ett ord med i ~et* have a voice in the matter; *över ~ a) (över hela linjen)* all along the line, *b) (över huvud taget)* in general; *komma ur ~* get out of order **3** *göra ngn till ~s* please (suit, satisfy) s.b. **4** *i hetaste ~et* too hot for comfort; *i minsta ~et* a bit on the small side; *i senaste ~et* at the last moment, only just in time; *vid det här ~et* by now, by this time, at this stage
3 lag *s2* law; *(av statsmakterna antagen)* act; *~ar och förordningar (ung.)* rules and regulations; ~ *och rätt* law and justice; *likhet inför ~en* equality before the law; *ta ~en i egna händer* take the law into one's own hands; *upphäva en ~* repeal an act; *läsa ~en för (bildl.)* lay down the law to, lecture; *enligt ~* by (according to) law; *i ~ förbjuden* prohibited by law; *i ~ens hägn* under the protection of the law; *i ~ens namn* in the name of the law
1 laga *vl* **1** *(till-)* prepare *(middagen the dinner)*; make; *AE. äv.* fix; ~ *mat* cook; ~ *maten* do the cooking; ~ *god mat* be an excellent cook; ~ *sin mat själv* do one's own cooking; *~d mat* cooked food **2** *(reparera)* mend, fix, repair **3** *(ombesörja)* ~ *[så] att* arrange (manage) things so that, see to it that; ~ *att du kommer i tid* make sure you are (take care to be) there in time **4** ~ *sig i ordning* get [o.s.] ready *(till for)*; ~ *sig i väg* get going (started); ~ *dig härifrån!* be off with you!
2 laga *oböjl. a* legal; ~ *förfall* lawful absence, valid excuse; *vinna ~ kraft* gain legal force, become legal; *i ~ ordning* according to the regulations prescribed by law; *i ~ tid* within the time prescribed [by law]; *vid ~ ansvar* under penalty of law
laga'kraftvunnen *a5* having gained (acquired) legal force
lag|anda team spirit **-arbete** teamwork
lag|beredning *(delegation)* law-drafting committee **-bestämmelse** legal provision **-bok** statute book, code of laws **-brott** breach (infringement, violation) of the law, offence **-brytare** lawbreaker, offender **-bunden** *a5* regulated by law; *(som följer vissa ~ar)* conformable to law **-bundenhet** conformity to law
lagd *a5, vara ~ för språk* have a bent for languages; *romantiskt ~* romantically inclined
lagenlig [-e:-] *a1* by (according to) law, statutory
1 lag|er ['la:-] *s2, bot.* [bay] laurel, bay; *skörda -rar* win laurels; *vila på sina -rar* rest on one's laurels
2 lager ['la:-] *s7* **1** *(förråd)* stock, *AE.* inventory; *(rum)* store (storage) room; *(magasin)* warehouse; *från ~ ex stock; förnya sitt ~* replenish one's stock, restock; *ha på ~* have in stock, stock, *AE. äv.* carry; *lägga på ~* lay (put) in stock; *lägga upp ett ~* lay in (set up) a stock **2** *(varv)* layer; *geol. äv.* stratum *(pl strata)*, bed; *(avlagring)* deposit; *(färg-)* coat; *bildl.* stratum; *de breda lagren* the masses, the populace **3** *tekn.* bearing
lager|arbetare storeman **-behållning** stocks [on hand] *(pl)*
lagerblad bay leaf

lager|bokföring stock (inventory) accounting **-byggnad** storehouse, warehouse
lager|bär bay berry **-bärsblad** bay leaf
lager|chef warehouse (stores) manager **-hylla** storage rack, storing shelf **-hållning** stock- -keeping **-inventering** stocktaking **-katalog** catalogue of goods stocked; (*för bokhandel*) publisher's list
lager|krans laurel crown, laurel wreath; *vinna* ~*en* win the laurel wreath **-kransa** crown with laurel (*univ.* the laurel wreath)
lager|lokal storeroom, warehouse **-minskning** stock (inventory) reduction **-utrymme** storage space
lageröl lager beer
lag|fara have legally registered (ratified) **-faren** *a5* (*om pers.*) knowledgeable in legal matters **-fart** entry into the land register, legal confirmation of one's title; *ansöka om* ~ apply for the registration of one's title to a property; *det hindrar inte* ~*en!* (*vard.*) that needn't stand in the way! **-fartsbevis** certificate of registration of title **-föra** sue, proceed against **-förslag** [proposed] bill; draft [law]; *framlägga ett* ~ present a bill
lagg *s2* (*panna*) [flat] frying pan, griddle; *en* ~ *våfflor* a round of waffles **-kärl** barrel, cask
lag|kapp *s3, sport.* relay **-kapten** *sport.* captain of a (the) team
lagklok versed in the law; *en* ~ (*bibl.*) a lawyer
lagledare *sport.* manager of a team
lag|lig [*la:g-] *a1* lawful; (*rättmätig*) legitimate, rightful; (*-enlig*) legal; ~*t betalningsmedel* legal tender, *AE.* lawful money; ~ *ägare* rightful (legal, lawful) owner; *på* ~ *väg* by legal means **-ligen** legally; lawfully; ~ *beivra* bring an action against, take legal steps against; ~ *skyddad* protected by law **-lighet** lawfulness; legitimacy; legality **-lott** lawful (legitimate) portion (share) **-lydig** law-abiding **-lydnad** obedience to the law **-lös** lawless **-löshet** lawlessness **-man** chief judge (*vid tingsrätt* of a district court, *vid länsrätt* of a county administrative court)
lagning [-a:-] repairing, mending, fixing
lagom [-åm] **I** *adv* just right (enough); (*tillräckligt*) sufficiently; (*med måtta*) moderately, in moderation; *precis* ~ exactly right (enough); ~ *stor* just large enough; *i* ~ *stora bitar* in suitably-sized pieces; *en* ~ *lång promenad* a walk of suitable length; *skryt* ~*!* stop blowing your own trumpet!; *det var så* ~ *roligt!* it was anything but fun! **II** *oböjl. a* just right; (*nog*) enough; (*tillräcklig*) sufficient, adequate; (*passande*) fitting, appropriate, suitable; *på* ~ *avstånd* at the (an) appropriate distance; *blir det här* ~*?* will this be enough (about right)?; ~ *är bäst* there is virtue in moderation, gently does it; *det var* ~ *åt dig!* that served you right!
lagparagraf section (paragraph) of a law, enactment
lagr|a [*la:g-] **1** *geol.* stratify; dispose in layers (strata) (*äv. bildl.*) **2** (*lägga på lager*) store (*äv. data.*), stock; (*spara*) put by , hoard; (*vin*) lay down **-ad** *a5* (*om ost*) ripe; (*om sprit o.d.*) matured; (*om virke*) seasoned **-ing 1** stratifying *etc.*; stratification **2** storing, storage; (*för*

kvalitetsförbättring) seasoning, maturing
lag|rum *se -paragraf* **-råd** council on legislation **-samling** body of laws, code **-språk** *på* ~ in legal language **-stadgad** *a5* statutory, laid down (prescribed) by law **-stifta** make laws (a law), legislate; ~*nde församling* legislative body, legislature; ~*nde makt* legislative power **-stiftare** legislator, lawmaker **-stiftning** *konkr.* legislation **-stridig** *a1* contrary to (at a variance with) [the] law; (*olaglig*) illegal **-söka** sue, proceed against **-sökning** [legal] action (proceedings *pl*)
lagt [lakkt] *sup. av lägga*
lagtima *oböjl. a* held in the ordinary course; ~ *riksdag* ordinary parliamentary session
lagtävling *sport.* team competition
la'gun *s3* lagoon
lag|utskott ~*et* [the Swedish parliamentary] standing committee on civil-law legislation **-vigd** *a5* lawfully wedded; *min* ~*a* (*vard.*) my better half **-vrängare** perverter of the law; (*neds. om advokat*) pettifogger
lagård ['la:-] *se ladugård*
lag|ändring revision (amendment) of the law **-överträdelse** transgression of the law, misdemeanour; offence
laka ~ *ur* soak
lakan *s7* sheet lakansväv sheeting
1 lake *s2* (*salt-*) brine, pickle
2 lake *s2, zool.* burbot
lakej [-'kejj] *s3* [liveried] footman; lackey (*äv bildl.*); (*föraktligt*) flunk[e]y; (*ngns lydige tjänare*) henchman **-själ** servile soul
lakon|isk [-'kω:-] *a5* laconic **-ism** laconicism
lakrits ['la:-, 'lakk-, -ri(t)s] *s3* liquorice **-pastill** BE. ung. pomfret-cake, Pontefract cake **-rot** *bot.* liquorice root
lakt|at *s4, kem.* lactate **-os** [-'å:s] *s3, kem.* lactose
laktuk ['lakk, -'u:k] *s3, bot.* lettuce
la'kun *s3* lacuna (*pl* lacunae); (*friare*) gap, pause
lalla babble; mumble
lam *a1* **1** (*förlamad*) paralysed **2** *bildl.* lame, feeble
1 lama *s1, zool.* llama (*äv. tygsort*)
2 lama *s1 el. -n -er* (*munk*) lama
lama|ism lamaism **-kloster** lama monastery
la'mell *s3, naturv. o. biol.* lamella (*pl* lamellae); *geol. äv.* scale, flake; *tekn.* wafer, lamina (*pl* laminae); (*i koppling*) disc; *elektr.* segment **-artad** [-a:r-] *a5* lamellar, lamellate; scaly, flaky; disc-like **-glas** laminated glass **-koppling** [multiple] disc-clutch **-trä** laminated wood
lamhet [-a:-] **1** (*förlamning*) paralysis (*i* of, in) **2** *bildl.* lameness
lami'nat *s7* laminera laminate
lamm *s7* lamb lamma lamb
lamm|bringa *kokk.* breast of lamb **-kotlett** *vanl.* lamb chop **-kött** *kokk.* lamb **-stek** *kokk.* roast lamb **-ull** lamb's wool **-unge** young lamb, lambkin
lamning [*lamm-] lambing
lamp|a *s1* lamp; (*glöd-*) bulb **-borste** lamp-brush ~'ett *s3* bracket candlestick, sconce **-fot** lamp foot (stand) **-glas** [lamp] chimney **-hållare** electric light socket **-kupa** [lamp] globe **-skärm** lampshade

lam|slagen a5 paralysed (äv. bildl.); ~ av fasa paralysed with terror **-slå** paralyse
land -et länder (i bet. 4 o. 5 s7) **1** (rike) country; det egna ~et one's native country; vårt ~ (vanl.) this country, Sweden (etc.); i hela ~et in the whole (throughout the) country; inne i ~et inland; Johan utan ~ John Lackland **2** (mots. sjö e.d.) land (äv. geol. o. bildl.); ~ i sikte! (sjö.) land ahoy (in sight)!; se hur ~et ligger see how the land lies (wind blows); gå i ~ go ashore, land; gå i ~ med (bildl.) accomplish, manage, succeed in; inåt ~et landward[s]; långt inåt ~et far inland; på ~ (mots. t. sjöss) on shore, ashore, (mots. i vattnet) on land; till ~s by land; Sverige är starkt till ~s Sweden is powerful on land **3** (mots. stad) country; in the country; livet på ~et (äv.) country life; resa ut till ~et go out to (go into) the country **4** (odlad mark) land **5** (trädgårds-) plot
land|a land; flyg. äv. touch down **-amären** pl, åld., inom våra ~ within our borders **-avträdelse** cession of territory (land) **-backen** på ~ ashore, on shore on dry land **-bris** land breeze **-djur** land animal **-fäste** (bros) abutment **-förbindelse** connection with the mainland **-förvärv** acquisition of territory (land) **-gång** gangway; flyg. entrance ladder **-hockey** hockey, (särsk. AE.) field hockey **-höjning** land elevation **-krabba** bildl. landlubber **-känning** få ~ have a landfall, sight land **-mina** land mine **-märke** sjö. landmark **-ning** landing; flyg. äv. alighting
landnings|bana airstrip, landing strip, runway **-förbud** det är ~ på flygplatsen the airport is closed for landing **-ljus** landing light **-plats** landing place; flyg. äv. landing ground **-sträcka** landing run **-ställ** undercarriage; AE. landing gear **-tillstånd** permission to land
land|område territory **-permission** sjö. shoreleave; liberty **-remsa** strip of land
lands|arkiv county records office **-bygd** country[side]; rural area[s pl] **-del** part of the country; province **-fader** beloved monarch **-fiskal** ung. district police superintendent [and public prosecutor]; AE. district attorney, sheriff **-flykt** exile **-flyktig** exiled **-flykting** exile; refugee **-förrädare** traitor [to one's country] **-förräderi** treason **-förrädisk** treasonable, traitorous **-församling** rural parish **-förvisa** banish [from the country], exile, expatriate **-förvisning** banishment, exile, expatriation **-hövding** county governor **-kamp** international match
landskap s7 **1** (landsdel) [geographical] province, county, shire **2** (ur natur- o. konstsynpunkt) landscape; (sceneri) scenery
landskaps|arkitekt landscape architect **-gräns** provincial (county) boundary **-målare** landscape-painter, landscapist **-vapen** coat of arms of a province
lands|kommun rural district **-lag 1** s2, jur. national law code **2** s7, sport. [inter]national team **-lagsspelare** international, member of a country's team **-man** fellow countryman, compatriot; vad är han för ~? what nationality is he? **-maninna** fellow countrywoman **-mål** dialect **-omfattande** nationwide **-orga-**
nisation L~en i Sverige [the] Swedish Trade Union Confederation; Brittiska ~en the Trades Union Congress (förk. TUC); Amerikanska ~en American Federation of Labor and Congress of Industrial Organizations (förk. AFL-CIO)
landsort i ~en in the provinces (pl)
landsorts|bo man (etc.) from the provinces, provincial **-stad** provincial town **-tidning** provincial newspaper
lands|plåga national scourge; vard. nuisance **-sorg** national mourning
landstig|a land **-ning** landing; göra en ~ land, effect a landing
landstigningstrupper pl landing forces
lands|ting ung. county council **-tingsman** county councillor **-tingsråd** county commissioner
land|storm ung. veteran reserve **-stormsman** militiaman **-stridskrafter** pl land forces **-strykare** tramp **-ställe** (sommarställe) place in the country, country house (cottage)
lands|väg [*lanns-, 'lanns-] highway, main road; allmän ~ public highway **-vägsbro** road bridge **-vägsriddare** se luffare **-ända** part of the country; (avlägsen) remote district
land|sänkning subsidence [of the earth's crust] **-sätta** land, put on shore; ~ med fallskärm [drop by] parachute **-sättning** landing etc. **-tunga** tongue of land, spit **-vind** land wind (breeze) **-vinning** reclamation of land; bildl. advance, achievements; vetenskapens ~ar achievements in the field of science **-vägen** fara ~ go by land
lan'då [-n-, -ŋ-] s3 landau
langa 1 pass [from hand to hand]; vard. shove over **2** ~ sprit carry on an illicit trade in liquor (etc.), bootleg **langare** bootlegger; AE. moonshiner; (narkotika-) dope pedlar, pusher
lan'gett [-ŋg-] s3 buttonhole stitching; sy ~ do buttonhole stitching **-era** buttonhole stitch
langning 1 (vid brand) bucket-passing **2** (sprit-) bootlegging
lango'bard [-ŋg-] s3 Lombard **-isk** a5 Lombard
lan'gust [-ŋg-] s3, zool. spiny lobster
lank s3 (tunn dryck) wish-wash
lanka s1, kortsp. small (low) card
lano'lin s3, s4 lanolin[e]
lans s2 lance; bryta en ~ take up the cudgels (för for)
lansera launch, bring out, introduce; ~ ngt på marknaden put s.th. on the market
lan'sett s3 lancet **-fisk** lancelet **-formig** [-å-] a1 lancet-shaped **-lik** biol. lanceolate
lansi'är [laŋ-, lan-] s3, mil. lancer
lant|adel ~n the county **-arbetare** farm worker (hand, labourer) **-befolkning** country (rural) population **-brevbärare** country (rural) postman **-bruk** agriculture, farming industry; jfr jordbruk **-brukare** se jordbrukare; Lantbrukarnas Riksförbund Federation of Swedish Farmers
lantbruks|högskola agricultural college **-maskin** agricultural (farm) machine (pl machinery) **-nämnd** county agricultural board **-produkt** agricultural (farm) product; ~er (äv.) agricultural (farm) produce (sg) **-redskap** agricultural implement, farm tool **-skola** agri-

cultural school **-styrelse** L~n [the Swedish] national board of agriculture **-sällskap** agricultural society **-universitet** Sveriges L~ [the] Swedish university of agricultural sciences **-utställning** agricultural show

lantegendom estate

lantern|a [-ˣtä:r-, ˣlann-] s1 lantern; light; flyg. navigation light **-'in** s3 lantern; skylight [turret], clerestory

lant|gård farm, [agricultural] holding **-handel** country shop, general store **-handlare** country (village) shopkeeper **-hushåll** farm (country) household **-hushållning** husbandry, agronomy **-hushållsskola** rural domestic school **-is** ['lann-] s2, vard. country bumpkin; AE. äv. hick **-junkare** country squire **-lig** al rural (behag charm; enkelhet simplicity); country (liv life); neds. rustic (sätt manners pl); (mots. stadsaktig) provincial **-liv** country (rural) life

lant|lolla vard. country wench **-man** farmer **-mannaparti** agrarian (farmer's) party **-mannaskola** agricultural college (school) **-mästare** farm foreman **-mätare** [land] surveyor **-mäteri** [land] surveying **-mäteriverk** Statens ~ central office of the [Swedish] national land survey **-ras** jordbr. native breed **-vin** home-grown wine **-värn** militia

laotier [la'ω:t(s)i-, la'å:-] Laotian **laotisk** [-'ω:-] a5 Laotian

lapa lap; lick up; bildl. drink in, imbibe

lapidar|isk [-'da:-] a5 lapidary; (kortfattad) brief, laconic **-stil** lapidary style

lapis ['la:-] s2 lunar caustic, silver nitrate; ~ lazuli lapis lazuli **-lösning** silver-nitrate solution

1 lapp s2 (folk) Laplander, Lapp

2 lapp s2 (tyg-) piece; (påsydd) patch; (pappers-) slip, scrap; (remsa) strip, slip, label

lappa patch; (laga äv.) mend; ~ ihop patch up

lapp|hund Lapland dog **-kast** sport. reverse (kick turn) on skis **-kåta** Laplander's hut

Lappland ['lapp-] n Lapland

lapplisa s1 [woman] traffic warden; vard. meter maid

lapp|ländsk a5 Lappish, Lapland **-mark 1** L~en Lapland **2** nomadic Laplander's territory

lappri ['lapp-] s6, sådant ~ such trifles (pl)

lappsjuka melancholia induced by isolated life

lapp|skomakare cobbler

lapp|skrivning AE. skol. pop quiz

lapp|skräddare repairing-tailor **-täcke** patchwork quilt **-verk** [ett] ~ [a piece of] patchwork

lapsk al Lappish, Lapp; se lappländsk **lapska** s1 **1** (kvinna) Laplander (Lapp) woman **2** (språk) Lapp, Lappish

lapskojs ['lapskåjs, ˣlap-] s3, kokk. lobscouse

lapsus ['lapp-] s9, s2 lapse, slip

larm s7 **1** (buller) noise; din, row; (oväsen) clamour, uproar **2** (alarm) alarm; slå ~ sound the alarm (äv. bildl.)

larm|a 1 (bullra) clamour (över about), make a noise (över at, about) **2** alarm, sound the alarm **-ande** a4 clamouring, clamorous; noisy **-beredskap** alert **-klocka** alarm-bell **-signal** alert

1 larv s3 larva (pl larvae), caterpillar, grub

2 larv vard. nonsense, rubbish

1 larva (traska) tramp, trudge, trot

2 larva rfl behave flippantly; ~ dig inte! don't be silly!

larvfötter pl, tekn. caterpillars, caterpillar treads

larvig al (enfaldig) foolish; (dum) silly

larvstadium larval stage

laryn'g|it [-ŋg-] s3 laryngitis **-oskop** s7 laryngoscope

lasa'rett s7 [general] hospital

lasaretts|fartyg hospital ship **-läkare** hospital doctor; resident physician (surgeon)

lasciv [la'ʃi:v] al lascivious

laser ['la:-] s2, fys. laser (förk. för Light Amplification by Stimulated Emission of Radiation) **laser|a** glaze, paint over with transparent colour[s] **-ing** glazing

laserstråle [ˣla:-] laser beam

lask s2, tekn. scarf [joint], fish joint; (på handske, sko) rib **laska** scarf; rib

lass s7 [wagon]load; bildl. äv. burden; (friare) cartload (med of); fullt ~ a full load; få dra det tyngsta ~et (bildl.) do the lion's share [of the work] **lassa** load; ~ på ngn för mycket (bildl.) overload s.b.; ~ på ngn ngt load s.b. with s.th.

lasso ['lassω] s3 lasso; kasta ~ throw a lasso **-kast** ett ~ a lasso cast

1 last s3 cargo, freight; (belastning) load; (börda) burden; med ~ av carrying (with) a cargo of; lossa ~en unload, discharge one's (its) cargo; stuva ~en trim the hold, stow the cargo; ligga ngn till ~ be a burden to s.b. lägga ngn ngt till ~ lay s.th. to a p.'s charge blame s.b. for s.th.

2 last s3 (fördärvlig vana) vice

1 lasta (klandra) blame; (starkare) censure

2 lasta load (på on to); sjö. äv. ship, take in cargo; djupt ~d deep-laden; ett skepp kommer ~t (lek) the mandarins

lastageplats [-ˣta:ʃ-] loading site; sjö. wharf

lastbar al vicious, depraved **-het** viciousness, depravity

last|bil lorry, truck; AE äv. freight car **-bilschaufför** lorry (truck) driver, trucker (särsk. AE.) **-bilstrafik** road transport (haulage) **-brygga** loading ramp (gangway) **-båt** cargo ship, freighter **-djur** beast of burden **-dryghet** dead weight capacity **-fartyg** se -båt **-flak** platform [body] **-fordon** goods vehicle, van truck **-förmåga** carrying (loading) capacity **-gammal** ancient, old as the hills **-kaj** loading dock, wharf **-lucka** cargo hatch; (öppningen) [cargo] hatchway **-märke** load (Plimsoll) line **-ning** loading; lading **-pall** se pall **-pråm** lighter; (större) lump **-rum** hold, cargo space **-ångare** cargo steamer, freighter

lasur 1 miner. lapis lazuli, lazurite **2** (äv. lasyr) painting in transparent (glazing) colour[s]

lat al, n sg obest. f. obruklig lazy; (maklig) indolent; (sysslolös) idle **lata** rfl be lazy (idle); gå och ~ sig laze, take it easy

lat|ens s3 latency **-ent** al latent

later pl, stora ~ high-and-mightiness (sg), grand airs; ha ~ give o.s. airs

latex s3, s4 latex

lathund 1 (lätting) lazybones, slacker **2** (rad

papper) lined paper; (*moja*) crib, cab; (*för räk-ning*) ready reckoner
la'tin *s7* Latin
La'tinamerika *n* Latin America **la'tiname-rikansk** Latin American
latinare [-ˣti:-] **1** Latin **2** *skol. ung.* classical student **latiner** [-'ti:-] Latin
latin|isera latinize **-linje** *gå* ~*n* read classics **-segel** lateen sail
latinsk [-'ti:-] *a5* Latin; ~*a bokstäver* Roman letters
lati'tud *s3* latitude
lat|mansgöra *ett* ~ a soft (an easy) job **-mask** *s2* lazybones
la'trin *s3* **1** (*avträde*) latrine, privy **2** (*spillning*) excrement[s *pl*]
latsidan *i uttr.*: *ligga på* ~ be idle (lazy), take things easy
latta *s1* (*träribba*) lath, slat; (*i segel*) batten
laudatur [-ˣda:-] *n* honours (*pl*)
laura *s1, vard.* jaywalker
lav *s2, bot.* lichen
lava *s1* lava **-ström** stream of lava
lave *s2* **1** (*i bastu*) bench, ledge **2** (*gruv-*) head frame, pitgear head
lave'mang *s7* enema (*pl äv.* enemata) **-spruta** rectal (enema) syringe
la'vendel *s9* lavender **-blå** lavender blue
laver|a *konst.* wash; tint **-ing** *konkr.* wash (tinted) drawing
la'vett *s3* gun carriage
la'vin *s3* avalanche (*äv. bildl.*) **-artad** [-a:r-] *a5* avalanche-like, like wildfire; *en* ~ *utveckling* an explosive development **-fara** avalanche danger (hazard)
lavoar [-ɷ'a:r, ˣlavv-] *s3* washstand
la'vyr *s3, se lavering*
lax *s2* salmon; *en glad* ~ a lively spark
laxa'tiv *s7* purgative; laxative, aperient **laxera** take an aperient (*etc.*) **laxermedel** *se* **-ativ**
lax|fiske salmon fishing **-färgad** salmon coloured (pink) **-rosa I** *n el. r* salmon pink **II** *oböjligt a* salmon pink **-stjärt** *snick.* dovetail **-trappa** salmon ladder **-öring** salmon trout
layout [läj'aut] *s3* layout **-man** layout man
le *log lett* smile (*åt* at); *lyckan log mot dem* fort-une smiled on them
lealös *vard.* loose-limbed, loose-jointed
leasa [ˣli:-] lease **leasing** ['li:-] leasing
lebeman ['le:-] man about town, roué
leci'tin *s4, kem.* lecithin
1 led *s3* **1** (*väg o.d.*) way, track; (*riktning*) di-rection **2** (*far-*) passage, channel; (*rösad*) [mountain] track, trail, footpath
2 led 1 *s3, anat.* joint; (*finger-, tå- äv.*) phalanx; *darra i alla* ~*et* tremble in every limb; *dra en arm i* ~ [*igen*] put an arm back into joint; *gå ur* ~ get dislocated; *känna sig ur* ~ feel out of sorts; *ur* ~ *är tiden* the time is out of joint **2** *s7, s4* (*länk*) link (*äv bildl.*); (*etapp*) stage; (*i ekvation*) term, side; (*beståndsdel*) part, ele-ment; (*rad av pers.*) row, line; *mil.* rank; *ingå som ett* ~ *i* be a component (part) of (an ele-ment in); *de djupa* ~*en* the rank and file of the people, the masses; *en man i* (*ur*) ~*et* a com-mon soldier; *stå i främsta* ~*et* be in the front rank (*bland* of) **3** *s3, s7* (*släkt-*) generation;

degree; line; *språkv.* element; *i rätt nedsti-gande* ~ in a direct line (*från* from)
3 led *a1* **1** (*trött*) tired (sick, weary) [to death] (*på, vid* of); *vard.* fed up (*på, vid* with) **2** *den* ~*e* the Evil One **3** (*elak*) wicked, evil
4 led *imperf. av 1, 2 lida*
1 leda *s1* (*avsmak*) disgust; (*motvilja*) repug-nance; (*vedervilja*) loathing; (*trötthet*) weari-ness; *känna* ~ *vid* feel disgust at; *få höra ända till* ~ hear till one is sick to death of it
2 leda *v1* (*böja i leden*) bend [at the joint], flex; ~ *mot* be articulated to; ~*d axel* (*tekn.*) articulated shaft
3 leda *v2* **1** (*föra*) lead; (*väg-*) guide; *fys. o. elektr.* conduct **2** (*om dörr, väg o.d.*) lead, go, take one; ~ *till a*) lead to, b) (*medföra*) bring about, c) (*ge upphov t.*) give rise to, bring on **3** (*anföra*) conduct; (*affärsföretag*) manage, direct, be in charge of; (*anfall*) lead; ~ *för-handlingarna* be in the chair, preside **4** ~ *sitt ursprung från* trace one's (its) origin from (back to), originate from **5** (*med betonad par-tikel*) ~ *bort* lead off, (*vatten, ånga o.d.*) carry off; ~ *in vatten* lay on water; ~ *in samtalet på* turn the conversation on to
ledad *a5, se 2 leda*
ledamot *-en ledamöter* member; (*av lärt säll-skap*) fellow; *ständig* ~ life-member
ledande *a4* leading; (*t.ex. princip äv.*) guiding, ruling; *fys.* conductive; *de* ~ *inom* the leaders of, those in a leading position within; *i* ~ *ställ-ning* in a leading (key, prominent) position
ledarbegåvning gift as a leader; *pers.* brilliant leader
ledar|e 1 *pers.* leader; (*väg-*) guide, conductor; (*företags-*) manager, executive, director, head, principal, AE. president; (*idrotts-*) manager, organizer **2** *fys.* conductor (*för* of) **3** (*tidnings-artikel*) leader, editorial **-egenskaper** *pl* qualities of leadership **-gestalt** *en* ~ a born leader **-hund 1** (*i hundspann*) leader [dog] **2** (*för blinda*) guide dog **-inna** [woman *etc.*] leader **-plats 1** (*ngns*) position as a leader **2** (*i tidning*) *på* ~ in the leader (editorial) column **-skap** *s7* leadership; (*för företag*) managership **-skribent** leader writer **-spalt** leader column **-stick** *ung.* subsidiary leader **-ställning** *vara i* ~ be in a leading position (at the head), hold the lead
ledas *v2, dep* (*känna leda*) be (feel) bored (*åt* by; *ihjäl* to death)
ledband (*koppel*) leading-strings (*pl*); *gå i* ~ be in leading-strings; *gå i ngns* ~ be lead by the nose by s.b.
ledbar [-e:-] *a1* jointed; (*böjlig*) flexible
led|brosk *anat.* articular cartilage **-bruten** stiff in the (one's) joints **-djur** arthropod
ledfyr *sjö.* range (leading) light; beacon (*äv. bildl.*)
ledgångsreumatism rheumatoid arthritis
ledig *a1* (*lätt o.* ~) easy; (*om hållning, rö-relse o.d.*) free, effortless, unhampered; (*om sätt att vara*) free and easy; *en* ~ *gång* an agile (easy) gait; *en* ~ *handstil* a flowing hand (handwriting); *ett* ~*t uppträdande* an easy manner, free and easy manners (*pl*); *känna sig* ~ *i kläderna* feel at one's ease (feel easy) in

one's clothes; *skriven i* ~ *stil* written in a natural style; *~a!* (*mil.*) [stand] at ease! **2** (*ej upptagen om pers.*) free, at leisure; (*sysslolös*) idle, unoccupied; (*om t.ex. kapital*) idle, uninvested; (*om sittplats o.d.*) unoccupied; (*om tjänst o.d.*) vacant; (*att tillgå*) available; (*om taxi*) disengaged, (*på skylt*) vacant, (*på taxi*) for hire; *bli* ~ *a*) (*från arbetet*) get, (be let) off [work, duty], *b*) (*få semester*) get one's holiday, *c*) (*om hembiträde*) have her evening out; *~a platser* vacancies; *på ~a stunder* in [one's] leisure (spare) moments (time) **-förklara** declare vacant, announce (advertise) as vacant

ledighet 1 (*i rörelser*) freedom, ease; (*i uppträdande*) easiness, ease of manner **2** (*från arbete*) time off [work, duty]; (*semester*) holiday, *AE.* vacation; (*ledig tid*) free (spare) time, leisure

ledighets|kommitté *tillhöra ~n* (*vard.*) be a member of the leisured classes **-tid** leisure time

ledigt *adv.* **1** easily *etc., se ledig*; *röra sig* ~ move with ease; *sitta* ~ (*om kläder*) fit comfortably; *tala* ~ be a fluent speaker; *du hinner* ~ you get there in time easily; *vi får* ~ *plats i bilen* we'll have an empty (a free) seat in the car **2** *få* (*ge, ha, ta*) ~ get (give, have, take) time off; *ta sig* ~ *några dagar* take a few days off

ledkapsel *anat.* joint-capsule

ledljus guiding light

ledlös jointless; (*friare*) loose-jointed

ledmotiv *mus.* leitmotif, recurrent theme; *bildl.* leading (guiding) principle

ledning [ˣleːd-] **1** (*väg-*) guidance; (*-tråd*) clue, lead (*till* to); (*skötsel*) management, conduct, direction; (*krigs-*) [war] command; *fys.* conduction; *sport.* lead; *ta ~en* (*äv. sport.*) take the lead; *överta* ~ *en av* take charge of; *med* ~ *av* guided by, with the aid of; *med* ~ *av dessa upplysningar* on the basis of this information; *till* ~ *för* for the guidance of; *under* ~ *av* under the guidance (*etc.*) of **2** *konkr., ~en* the managers (directors) (*pl*), the management, (*för parti*) the leaders (*pl*), *mil.* the commanders (*pl*) **3** *elektr.* wire, line, cable; (*rör-*) pipe, conduit, duct; *dragning av elektriska ~ar* electric wiring

lednings|brott *tel.* line breakdown **-förmåga** conductivity **-motstånd** line (conductor) resistance **-nät** electric supply mains; (*högspännings-*) distribution system **-stolpe** pylon, telegraph pole **-tråd** electric wire

ledsag|a [ˣleːd-] *v1* accompany; (*beskyddande*) escort **-are** *se följeslagare*

ledsam [*vanl.* ˣlessam] *a1* **1** (*tråkig*) boring, tiresome, tedious **2** (*sorglig*) sad; *det var ~t!* how sad!, I am so sorry! **3** (*obehaglig*) disagreeable, unpleasant; (*förtretlig*) annoying; *en* ~ *historia* a disagreeable (sad) story **-het** boringness *etc.*; boredom; *få ~er för* have trouble on account of; *råka ut för ~er* meet with unpleasantness; *här vilar inga ~er!* not a dull moment here!

ledsen [ˣlessen] *a3* sorry (*för, över* about); (*bedrövad*) grieved (*för, över* at, about); (*olyck-*)

lig) unhappy (*för, över* at, about); (*sorgsen*) sad (*över* about); (*förargad*) annoyed, angry (*för, över* at; *på* with); *jag är mycket* ~ *över* I am very sorry about, I deeply regret; *var inte~!* don't be sad!, cheer up!; *han är inte* ~ *av sig* he doesn't let anything get him down

ledskena guide-rail

ledsna [ˣlessna] get (grow) tired (*på* of); *ha ~t på ngn* (*ngt*) have had enough of (be fed up with) s.b. (s.th.)

ledsnad [ˣless-] *s3* (*bedrövelse*) sorrow, distress, grief (*över* at); *med uppriktig* ~ with sincere regret

ledstjärna lodestar (*äv. bildl.*), guiding star

ledstyv stiff-jointed

led|stång handrail; banisters (*pl*) **-syn** *med.* locomotor vision; *han har* ~ he can only just see his way about **-tråd** clue

ledung *s2, hist.* maritime (predatory) raid

leende I *a4* smiling; (*om natur o.d. äv.*) pleasant; *vänligt* ~ with a kindly smile; *med ett* ~ smilingly; *lev livet ~!* keep smiling! **II** *s6* smile

1 lega *s1* (*rävs*) lodge; (*hares*) form; (*björns*) cache

2 lega *s1, jur.* hire; (*lejning*) hiring, hire

le'gal *a1* legal

legaliser|a legalize **-ing** legalization

legalitet legality

1 le'gat *s3* (*sändebud*) legate

2 le'gat *s7, jur.* legacy, bequest

3 legat [ˣleː-] *sup. av ligga*

legation legation **legationssekreterare** secretary of (to) [a] legation

le'gend *s3* legend

legend|arisk [-'daː-] *a5* legendary **-artad** [-aːr-] *a5* like a legend **-bildning** *abstr.* legend--making, legend-creation; *konkr.* legend **-omspunnen** legendary

leger|a *v1*, **-ing** *s2* alloy

legio [ˈleː-] *oböjl. a pl, de är* ~ their number is legion **legion** [-giˈoːn] *s3* legion **legio'när** *s3* legionary [soldier]

legi'tim *a1* legitimate

legitimation identification; (*för yrkesutövning*) authorization, certification; *mot* ~ upon identification, on proof of identity

legitimations|handling, -kort identity card **legitimera** legitimate, legitim[at]ize; *~d* legitimated *etc.,* (*om läkare*) registered, fully qualified, authorized, (*om apotekare*) certifi[cat]ed; ~ *sig* prove (establish) one's identity, identify o.s. **legitimitet** legitimacy

lego|arbete piecework **-soldat** mercenary [soldier] **-tillverkning** contract manufacture **-trupper** *pl* mercenary troops

legu'an *s3, zool.* iguana

le'gymer *pl* vegetables

leidnerflaska [ˣlejd-] Leyden jar

leja [ˣlejja] *v2* engage, hire; *sjö. äv.* charter

lejd *s3* safe-conduct

lejdare 1 *sjö.* [sea] ladder **2** *gymn.* rope-ladder

lejon [ˣlejån] *s7* lion; *en men ett ~!* one, but what a one! **-gap** *bot.* snapdragon **-grop** lion's den **-hjärta** *Rikard L~* Richard Coeur de Lion ([the] Lion-Heart) **-inna** lioness **-klo** *visa ~n* (*bildl.*) show one's mettle **-parten** the lion's share **-tämjare** lion-tamer **-unge** lion cub

lek *s2* **1** game; (*-ande*) play (*med dockor* with dolls), playing (*med döden* with death); (*t.ex. kattens* ~ *med råttan*) toying, dallying; ~ *och idrott* games (*pl*); *en* ~ *med ord* playing with words; *den som sig i* ~*en ger får* ~*en tåla* once you must take the consequences; *på* ~ in play; *vara ur* ~*en* be out of the game (the running) **2** (*fiskars*) spawning; (*fåglars*) pairing, mating **3** (*kort-*) pack [of cards]

lek|a *v3* **1** play (*en lek* [at] a game); (*friare o. bildl.*) *äv.* toy, dally; ~ *med döden* (*äv.*) treat death lightly; ~ *med ngns känslor* trifle with a p.'s feelings; *livet -te för henne* life was a game for her; *inte att* ~ *med* not to be trifled with; *han är inte att* ~ *med* (*äv.*) he won't stand any nonsense; *vara med och* ~ join in [the game] **2** (*om fiskar*) spawn; (*om fåglar*) pair, mate

lekam|en [-'ka:-] *r* body **-lig** *a1* bodily; corporeal; ~*en* bodily *etc.*, in the body

lek|ande *a4*, ~ *lätt* as easy as winking **-boll** *bildl.* plaything, toy **-dräkt 1** (*fisks*) spawning array **2** (*barns*) playsuit; rompers (*pl*) **-full** playful (*äv. bildl.*), full of fun **-kamrat** playmate, playfellow

lek|man layman; (*ej fackman*) nonprofessional, amateur **-mannamässig** *a1* lay; amateur

lekmogen (*om fisk*) ready to spawn, mature

leko'tek *s7* toy-lending library

lek|park playground **-plats** playground

leksak toy

leksaks|affär toyshop **-bil** toy (model) car **-djur** toy animal

lek|skola nursery school, kindergarten **-stuga** play house **-terapi** play therapy **-tid** (*fisks, fågels*) spawning (*etc.*) time (season); *jfr leka 2*

lektion [-k'ʃɷ:n] *s2* lesson; *ge* ~*er i* give lessons in; *ta* ~*er för ngn* have lessons with (from) s.b.

lektor [*lektår, 'lekt-] *s3* (*vid läroverk*) senior master; *univ.* lecturer; ~ *i engelska* senior master of English **-at** *s7* (*vid läroverk*) post as senior master; *univ.* lectureship

lektris [woman] reader **lek'tyr** *s3* reading [matter]; things to read (*pl*) **lektör** (*manuskriptläsare*) [publisher's] reader

lekverk *det är ett* ~ *för mig* it is child's play (a simple matter) for me

lem [lemm] *s2* limb, member **-lästa** maim, mutilate; (*göra ofärdig*) cripple, disable

lemo'nad *s3* lemonade

len *a1* **1** (*mjuk*) soft; (*slät*) smooth **2** (*om ljud o.d.*) bland (*röst* voice) **lena** soothe (*i halsen* the throat) **lenhet** softness; smoothness; blandness

leninism Leninism

leo'pard [-a:-] *s3* leopard **-hona** leopardess

lepra [*le:p-] leprosy

ler|a *s1* clay; (*sandig*) loam; (*dy*) mud; *bränd* ~ fired clay; *eldfast* ~ fire clay; *hänga ihop som ler och långhalm* stick together through thick and thin **-botten** (*i sjö*) clayey bottom **-duva** clay pigeon **-duvskytte** clay-pigeon shooting **-fötter** *i uttr.: en koloss på* ~ a colossus with feet of clay **-gods** earthenware, pottery **-golv** earth (mud) floor **-gök** toy ocarina

ler|ig *a1* clayey, loamy; (*om t.ex. väg*) muddy **-jord** clay[ey] soil **-koka** *s1* clod [of clay]

-krus stone (earthenware) jar **-kärl** earthen[ware] vessel; *koll.* earthenware, crockery, pottery **-skiffer** shale **-skärva** *arkeol.* potsherd **-välling** mass (sea) of mud

lesbisk *a5* lesbian

less *a1, vard.* fed up (*på* with)

leta search, hunt, look (*efter* for); ~ *efter ord* be at a loss for words; ~ *i minnet* cast about in (ransack) one's memory; ~ *igenom* search, ransack; ~ *reda på* try to find; ~ *upp* hunt up; ~ *ut* pick out; ~ *sig fram* find (make) one's way

le'tal *a1* lethal; mortal

letar'g|i *s3* lethargy **-isk** [-'tarr-] *a5* lethargic

1 lett *s3* Lett, Latvian

2 lett 1 *sup. av le* **2** *sup. av leda*

lett|isk ['lett-] *a5* Lettish; *geogr.* Latvian **-iska** ['lett-] *s1* **1** (*språk*) Lettish **2** (*kvinna*) Lettish woman

Lettland ['lett-] *n* Latvia

leukemi [levke'mi:] *s3, med.* leukaemia

lev *s3* loaf

lev|a *v2, sup. äv. -at* **1** live; (*existera*) exist, be in existence; ([*ännu*] *vara vid liv*) be alive; (*kvar-*) survive; (*väsnas*) be noisy, make a noise; ~ *ett glatt liv* lead a gay life; *så sant jag -er!* as sure as I stand here!; *-e konungen!* long live the King!; *-e friheten!* Liberty for ever!; *den som -er får se* he who lives will see; *ja, må han* ~ (*ung.*) for he is a jolly good fellow; *om jag får* ~ *och ha hälsan* if I am spared and keep well; *om han hade fått* ~ if he had lived; ~ *högt* live sumptuously; *hur -er världen med dig?* how is the world treating you?; ~ *som man lär* practise what one preaches; ~ *som om man var den sista* take thought for the morrow; *låta ngn veta att han -er* give s.b. a hot time [of it]; ~ *i den tron att* be under the impression that; ~ *kvar* live on, survive, exist still; ~ *med a*) (*i skildring o.d.*) take a great interest in, *b*) (*i stora världen*) go [out] into society, be a man (*etc.*) of fashion; ~ *om a*) (*sitt liv*) live over again, relive, *b*) (*svira*) lead a fast life, be a fast liver; ~ *på* live [up]on, (*om djur*) feed on; ~ *på stor fot* live in great style; ~ *upp a*) (*förmögenhet*) run through, use up, *b*) (*på nytt*) revive; ~ *vidare* go on living **2** (*om segel*) flap, slap, shake **3** ~ *sig in i* enter into (*ngns känslor* a p.'s feelings)

levande *a4* **1** living; animate (*väsen* being); (*predik. om pers.*) alive; (*mots. död, uppstoppad, slaktad e.d.*) live; (*livfull*) lively (*hopp* hope); (*livlig*) vivid (*skildring* description); (*om t.ex. porträtt*) lifelike; *en* ~ *avbild av* the very image of; ~ *blommor* real (natural) flowers; ~ *djur* living animals; ~ *eld* burning fire; ~ *ljus* lighted candles; *teckna efter* ~ *modell* draw from life; *ett* ~ *exempel på* a living example of; *ett* ~ *intresse för* a living (live) interest in; ~ *kraft* (*fys.*) kinetic energy; *på ett* ~ *sätt* in an animated (a vivid) way; *som föder* ~ *ungar* viviparous; *inte en* ~ *själ* not a [living] soul **2** *inte veta sig ngn* ~[*s*] *råd* be at one's wits ends; *inte få ngn* ~[*s*] *ro* get no peace anywhere **-göra** make lifelike (live)

levang [*le:-] deck brush

Levanten [-'vann-] *n* [the] Levant

levan'tinsk [-i:-] *a5* Levantine

leve *s6* cheer; viva[t]; *utbringa ett fyrfaldigt ~ för* give four (*Storbritannien* three) cheers for

levebröd livelihood, living

lever ['le:-] *s2* liver

leverans [-ans, -aŋs] *s3* **1** (*tillhandahållande*) furnishing, supplying (*av* of); (*avlämnande*) delivering, delivery **2** *konkr.* delivery; goods delivered (*pl*); (*sändning*) consignment; *vid ~* on delivery **-avtal** delivery agreement **-dag** day (date) of delivery, delivery date **-förmåga** ability to deliver **-klar** ready for delivery **-tid** time (date) of delivery **-villkor** *pl* terms (conditions) of delivery **-vägran** refusal to supply

leverantör [-an-, -aŋ-] supplier, deliverer; contractor; (*livsmedel*) purveyor

levercirrhos *s3, med.* cirrhosos of the liver

leverera (*tillhandahålla*) supply, furnish; (*avlämna*) deliver; *fritt ~t* carriage free

lever|fläck mole; birthmark **-korv** liver sausage, liverwurst

leve|rne *s6* **1** (*levnadssätt*) life; *hans liv och ~* his life [and way of living] **2** (*oväsen*) hullabaloo **-rop** cheer

lever|pastej liver paste **-sjukdom** liver (hepatic) disease **-tran** cod-liver oil

le'vit *s3* Levite

levnad [-e:-] *s3* life

levnads|bana career **-beskrivning** biography; curriculum vitae **-förhållanden** *pl* conditions of living; circumstances **-glad** [high-]spirited, light-hearted, buoyant **-konstnär** adept in the art of living, s.b. who gets the best out of life **-kostnader** *pl* cost of living (*sg*), living costs **-kostnadsindex** cost-of-living index **-lopp** life span; *ngns ~* [the course of] a p.'s life **-regel** rule of conduct **-standard** standard of living **-sätt** manner (way) of living (life) **-tecknare** biographer **-teckning** biography, life (*över* of) **-trött** weary of life **-vanor** *pl* habits (ways) of life (living) **-villkor** *pl* conditions of life **-år** year of life

levra [-e:-] *rfl* coagulate, clot; *~t blod* clotted blood, blood clot, gore

lexikalisk [-'ka:-] *a5* lexical

lexiko|graf *s3* lexicographer **-grafi** *s3* lexicography **-grafisk** [-'gra:-] *a5* lexicographical

lexik|on ['leksikån] *s7, pl äv. -a* dictionary; (*för dött språk vanl.*) lexicon

li'an *s3* liana, liane

liba'nes *s3* Libanese **-isk** *a5* Libanese

Libanon ['li:-ån] *n* Lebanon

libe'ral I *a1* liberal **II** *s3, polit.* Liberal

liberaliser|a liberalize **-ing** liberalization

liberalis|m liberalism **-tisk** *a5* liberalist[ic]

liberalitet liberality

libero ['li:-] *s5*, (*fotboll*) sweeper

librettist librettist **libretto** [-'brettⱺ] *s9, s7* libretto

Libyen ['li:-] *n* Libya

libyer ['li:-] *s9* Libyan **libysk** ['li:-] *a5* Libyan

licens *s3* licence; permit **-ansökan** application for a licence **-avgift** licence fee **-era** license **-innehavare** licensee, licence-holder **-tillverkning** manufacture on licence

licentiat [-n(t)si-] licentiate; *filosofie ~* (*ung.*) master of arts, doctor of philosophy; *medicine ~* (*ung.*) bachelor of medicine **-avhandling** licentiat [examination] treatise **-examen** licentiate examination

1 lid|a *led -it; tiden -er* time is getting on, time is passing; *det -er mot kvällen* it is getting [on] towards evening, night is drawing on; *det -er mot slutet med honom* his life is ebbing out, his life is drawing towards its close; *vad det -er* sooner or later, (*så småningom*) by and by

2 lid|a *led -it* **1** (*utstå*) suffer; (*uthärda*) endure; (*drabbas av*) sustain, incur; *~ brist på* be short of; *~ skada* (*äv.*) be injured (damaged), take harm, (*om pers.*) be hurt **2** (*pinas*) suffer (*av* from); (*ha plågor*) be in pain **3** (*tåla*) bear, stand, endure

lidande I *s6* suffering **II** *a4* suffering (*av* from); afflicted (*av* by); *bli ~ på* be the loser by (from), lose by

lidelse passion **-fri** dispassionate, passionless **-full** passionate; impassioned (*tal* speech) **-fullhet** passion; (*glöd*) enthusiasm, fervour, vehemence

lider ['li:-] *s7* shed

liderlig *a1* lecherous, lewd **-het** lechery, lewdness

lidit *sup. av 1, 2 lida*

lie [*'li:e] *s2* scythe **-mannen** the grim reaper, Death

liera *rfl* ally o.s. (*med* to, with) **lierad** *a5* allied, connected

lift *s2* lift **lifta** hitchhike **liftare** hitchhiker

liga *s1* **1** (*förbrytarband*) gang, set **2** *sport.* league **3** *hist.* league, [con]federation **-match** *sport.* league match

ligament *s7, anat.* ligament

ligatur *boktr.* ligature

ligg|a *låg legat* **I 1** (*om levande varelser*) lie, be lying [down]; (*befinna sig, vara*) be (*på sjukhus* in hospital); *bildl.* be; *~ och läsa* lie reading, read in bed; *~ och sova* be asleep (sleeping); *han -er redan* he is in (has gone) to bed; *~ länge på morgnarna* lie (stay) in bed late of a morning, get up late; *~ i underhandlingar* be engaged in negotiations; *~ med ngn* sleep (go to bed) with s.b.; *~ på ägg* brood, sit on eggs; *~ vid universitet* be at the university; *~ lågt* (*avvakta*) lie low; wait and see; *bide one's time* **2** (*om sak o. bildl.*) lie, be; (*vara belägen, i sht geogr.*) be [situated]; *kyrkan -er vid vägen* the church stands (is) at the roadside; *var skall huset ~?* where will the house be built?; *åt vilket håll -er skolan?* in which direction is the school?; *-er alldeles härintill* is quite near (close to) here; *häri -er skillnaden* this is where the difference lies; *avgörandet -er hos mig* the decision lies (rests) with me; *det -er i sakens natur* it is in the nature of the case; *det -er i blodet (släkten)* it runs in the blood (family); *~ på* keep [possession of] (*vard.* sit tight on) s.th.; *det -er i luften* it is in the air **II** (*med beton. part.*) **1** *~ av sig* get out of practise (form), *vard.* get rusty **2** *~ bi (sjö.)* lie to (by) **3** *~ efter a)* (*vara på efterkälken*) be behind (in arrears), *b)* (*ansätta*) press **4** *det -er inte för mig* it is not in my line, it does not come natural to me **5** *~ i* *a*) *eg.* be in (*vattnet* the water), *b*) *bildl.* stick at it, keep on (*o. arbeta* working) **6** ~ *kvar över natten* stay the night **7** ~ *nere* be at a standstill **8** *solen -er på här hela eftermiddagen* we get the sun here the whole afternoon; *vinden -er på* the wind is driving at us (*etc.*) **9** *hur -er saken till?* how does the matter stand?; *så -er det till* those are the actual facts, that is how things are; ~ *till sig* improve by keeping **10** ~ *under* (*bildl.*) be inferior to **11** ~ *över a*) (*övernatta*) stay the night (overnight), *b*) (*vara överlägsen*) be [the] superior

liggande *a4* lying; reclining, recumbent (*ställning* position); *en avsides* ~ *plats* an out-of--the-way spot (*etc.*); *den närmast till hands* ~ *förklaringen* the explanation nearest to hand; *djupt* ~ (*äv.*) deep-lying, (*om ögon*) deep-set; *bli* ~ (*bli kvar*) be left [lying]

igg|are register; *bokför. äv.* ledger **-dags** bedtime

igge|dagar *pl* lay days **-dagspengar** *pl* demurrage (sg)

igg|plats berth **-sjuk** *som en* ~ *höna* like a broody hen **-soffa** *ung.* bed-sofa **-stol** lounge--chair; deck chair **-sår** bedsore **-underlag** sleeping mat (pad); ground sheet **-vagn** (*barnvagn*) perambulator; *vard.* pram

igist hooligan **-dåd** [act of] hooliganism; (*friare*) wanton destruction, vandalism

ig'nin [-ŋn-] *s4* lignin

iguster [-'gust-] *s2, bot.* privet **-svärmare** *zool.* privet hawk

lik *s7* **1** corpse; [dead] body; *blek som ett* ~ deathly pale; *stå* ~ lie laid out; *segla med* ~ *i lasten* (*bildl.*) be doomed to failure; *ett* ~ *i lasten* (*hand.*) a dead loss, dead weight, a dud line **2** *boktr.* out flag

lik *s7, sjö.* leech; (*tross*) boltrope

lik *a5* like; (*om två el. flera*) alike; (*liknande*) similar; (*i storlek, värde e.d.*) the same; *identiskt* ~*a* identical[ly alike]; *vi är alla* ~*a inför lagen* all men are equal in the eye of the law; ~*a barn leka bäst* like draws to like, birds of a feather flock together; *porträttet är mycket* ~*t* the portrait is a very good likeness; *han är sig inte* ~ he is not at all himself; *du är dig då* ~*!* that's just like you!

ika I *oböjl. a* (*i storlek, värde o.d.*) equal (*med* to); (*likvärdig*) equivalent; (*identiskt* ~) identical; *är* ~ *med* is equal to (the same as); *två plus tre är* ~ *med fem* two plus three makes five; *tillsätta* ~ *delar av* add in equal portions; ~ *mot* ~ measure for measure; *30* ~ (*tennis.*) thirty all **II** *adv* in the same way (manner) (*som* as); (*jämnt; i samma grad o.d.*) equally; ~ ... *som* just as ... as, (*både ... och*) both ... and; *klockorna går inte* ~ the clocks don't keep the same time; ~ *bra a*) just as good (*förklaring* an explanation), *b*) (*sjunga* sing) as well (*som någonsin* [as ever]); *i* ~ [*hög*] *grad* to the same extent, equally; ~ *många som vanligt* [just] as many as usual, the usual number; *de är* ~ *stora* they are the same (are equal in) size, (*om abstr. förhållanden*) they are equivalent (equally great *etc.*)

ika|berättigad *vara* ~ have equal rights, be of equal standing (*med* with) **-berättigande** *s6*

equality of status (rights) **-dan** [ˣli:ka-, -'dann]*a5* of the same sort (kind); *de är precis* ~*a* they are exactly alike (just the same, all of a piece) **-dant** [ˣli:ka-, -'dant] *adv* the same **-fullt** nevertheless, all the same **-ledes** likewise, similarly **-lydande** *a4* of identical (the same) wording (tenor); *i två* ~ *exemplar* in two identical copies **-lönsprincipen** the principle of equal pay

likare standard, gauge

likartad [-a:r-] *a5* similar in character (nature) (*med* to), similar

lika|sinnad *a5* like-minded, of the same way of thinking **-så** also; *jfr likaledes* **-väl** just as well (*som* as)

likbegängelse [-jäŋ-] funeral [ceremony]; obsequies (*pl*)

likbent [-e:-] *a4, geom.* isosceles

lik|besiktning postmortem examination **-bil** motor hearse **-bjudarmin** funereal expression, gloomy mien **-blek** ghastly, deathly pale, livid **-bärare** pallbearer

lik|e *s2* equal; *söka sin* ~ be without an equal, be unequalled (unmatched); *en ... utan* ~ an unparalleled (unprecedented) ... **-formig** [-å-] *a1* uniform; (*alltigenom* ~) homogeneous; *geom.* similar (*med* to)

lik|färd funeral procession **-förgiftning** cadaverous poisoning

likgiltig 1 indifferent (*äv. om sak*); (*betydelselös*) unimportant, insignificant, trivial; *det är mig fullständigt* ~*t* it is all the same (makes no difference [whatever]) to me **2** (*ointresserad*) indifferent (*för* to); (*liknöjd*) listless, apathetic; impassive **-het 1** (*saks*) unimportance, insigni ficance **2** (*brist på intresse*) indifference (*för* to) listlessness, apathy

likhet [-i:-] resemblance, similarity (*med* to); (*porträtt-*) likeness; (*fullständig*) identity (*med* with); ~ *inför lagen* equality before the law; *äga en viss* ~ *med* have (bear) a certain resemblance to; *i* ~ *med* in conformity with, on the lines of, (*liksom*) like

likhetstecken sign of equality, equal[s] sign

lik|kista coffin; *AE. äv.* casket **-lukt** smell of death

likmätigt [-i:-] *sin plikt* ~ pursuant to (in pursuance of) one's duty

likn|a [-i:-] **1** (*vara lik*) resemble, be like; look like **2** (*jämföra*) compare (*vid* to) **-ande** *a4* similar; *eller* (*och*) ~ or (and) the like; *av* ~ *slag* [of a] similar [kind]; *eller ngt* ~ *namn* or some name of the sort (some such name); *på* ~ *sätt* in much the same (a similar) way, similarly **-else** *bibl.* parable; (*bildlig jämförelse*) simile, metaphor; *tala i* ~*r* speak in metaphors (*bibl.* parables)

lik|nöjd indifferent; *jfr likgiltig* **-rikta** *elektr.* rectify; (*friare*) unify; standardize; ~*d opinion* regimented opinion **-riktare** *elektr.* rectifier **-riktning** *elektr.* rectification; (*friare*) regimentation, standardization **-sidig** *a1* equilateral **-som** [ˈli:k-] **I** *konj* like; (*ävensom*) as well as; (~ *om*) as if **II** *adv* as if; (*så att säga*) as it were, so to say; *jag* ~ *kände på mig* I somehow (*vard.* sort of) felt

likstelhet *med.* rigor mortis

lik|ström direct current (*förk.* D.C.) **-ställa** place on an equal footing (a level) (*med* with) **-ställd** *a5* equal, of the same standing; *vara* ~ rank equal, be on a par **-ställdhet, -ställighet** equality **-stämmighet** agreement **lik|tal** funeral sermon (oration) **-torn** [-ɷ:-] *s2* corn **-tornsplåster** corn-plaster

lik|tydig synonymous (*med* with), equivalent in meaning (*med* to) (*friare*) tantamount (*med* to) **-tänkande** *a4* of the same way of thinking **lik|vagn** hearse **-vaka** vigil by a corpse before burial, wake

lik'vid I *s3* payment (*för* of, for); (*insänd* ~) remittance; *full* ~ payment in full; *som* ~ *för Er faktura* in settlement of your invoice **II** *a1, n sg obest.* form undviks liquid, available; (*om ställning*) solvent; *~a medel* ready money, cash (*sg*); liquid funds (assets)

likvida ['li:k-] *s1*, *språkv.* liquid

likvid|ation liquidation; (*bolags äv.*) winding up; *träda i* ~ go into liquidation **-era 1** (*avveckla*) liquidate, wind up **2** (*betala*) liquidate, settle, discharge **3** (*upplösa*) eliminate; (*döda*) liquidate **-itet** liquidity; (*firmas äv.*) solvency

likvinklig *a1* equiangular

lik|väl ['li:k-, -'vä:l] nevertheless; all the same **-värdig** *a1* equivalent (*med* to); of equal value (importance) **-värdighet** equivalence

likör liqueur; *är inte min* ~ (*vard.*) is not my cup of tea

lila ['li:-, *ˣ*li:-] *s1 o. oböjl. a* lilac, mauve

lilja *s1* lily

lilje|konvalje lily of the valley **-vit** lily-white **-växt** lily

lilla *a, best. form sg* (*jfr liten*) small; little; *barn ~!* my dear child!; *minsta* ~ *bidrag* the smallest contribution; *det* ~ *jag äger* what little I possess; *hur mår den* ~ (*lille*)? how is the (your) little girl (boy)? **lillan** *s, best. form sg* the little girl in the family **lillasyster** our (*etc.*) little sister **lillebror** *jfr lillasyster* **lillen** the little boy in the family; *L~* Tiny **lilleputt** *s2, s3* Lilliput, Lilliputian; dwarf, pygmy

lill|finger little finger **-gammal** precocious **-hjärnan** [the] cerebellum **-slam** *s2, kortsp.* little slam **-tå** little toe

lim [limm] *s7* glue, (*för papper*) size **-färg** distemper

li'mit *s3, hand.* limit; (*högsta el. lägsta pris*) maximum (minimum) price **-era** limit

lim|ma glue; (*papper, väv o.d.*) size; (*mur*) lime **-ning** (*-mande*) gluing *etc.*; *gå upp i* ~*en* (*vard.*) fly off the handle

limno|log limnologist **-logi** *s3* limnology

limousin[e] [-mɷ'si:n] *s3* limousine

limpa *s1* **1** ryemeal bread, loaf **2** *en* ~ *cigarretter* a carton of cigarettes

lim|panna gluepot **-ämne** glue-stock; (*för papper o.d.*) sizing agent

lin *s4* flax

lin|a *s1* rope; (*smalare*) cord; (*stål-*) wire; *sjö.* line; *löpa* ~*n ut* (*bildl.*) keep on to the bitter end, go the whole hog; *visa sig på styva* ~*n* (*bildl.*) show off **-bana** [aerial] ropeway (cableway); (*för skidåkare*) ski lift

lin|beredning flax-dressing **-blå** flax-blue

lind *s2* lime [tree]; *AE.* linden, basswood

linda I *s1* swaddling clothes (*pl*); *i sin* ~ (*bildl.*) in its infancy, in its initial stage; *kväva i sin* ~ (*bildl.*) nip in the bud **II** *v1* **1** wire, tie (*omkring* round); (*slingra*) twine; *hon kan* ~ *honom runt sitt* [*lill*]*finger* she can twist him round her [little] finger; ~ *in* wrap up (*äv. bildl.*), envelop; ~ *upp* unwind; ~ *upp på* (*t.ex rulle*) wind on to **2** *med.* bind up, bandage **3** (*barn*) wrap in swaddling clothes, swaddle

lindans|are, -erska tightrope walker (dancer)

lind|ebarn baby (infant) in arms **-ning** *tekn.* winding

lindr|a (*mildra*) mitigate, appease; (*lugna*) soothe, mollify; (*nöd o.d.*) alleviate, relieve **-ig** *a1* (*obetydlig*) slight; (*ej svår*) light; (*mild*) mild; (*human*) easy; (*om straff o.d.*) lenient **-igt** *adv* slightly *etc.*; *~t sagt* to put it mildly; *slippa ~t undan* get off lightly **-ing** mitigation, appeasement; (*förbättring*) amelioration; (*av t.ex. straff*) reduction (*i* of); (*lättnad*) relief (*för* to, for)

linearritning [line*ˣ*a:r-] linear drawing **line'är** *a1* linear

linfrö flaxseed; *kem., med.* linseed

linfärja cable ferry

lingarn linen thread

lingon [-ŋån] *s7* cowberry, red whortleberry; *inte värd ett ruttet* ~ not worth a straw **-ris** cowberry (*etc.*) twigs (*pl*)

lingul flax-coloured; (*om hår*) flaxen

lingv|ist [-ŋ(g)v-] linguist **-is'tik** *s3* linguistics (*pl, behandlas som sg*)

linhårig flaxen-haired

lini'ment *s7* liniment, embrocation

lin'jal *s3* ruler

linje ['li:n-] *s5* line; (*buss- o.d. äv.*) route, service; *mil. äv.* rank; *skol. o.d.* side, stream; *rät* ~ straight line; *den slanka* ~*n* the slender figure; ~ *4 Nr.* 4 buses (trams *etc.*) (*pl*); *uppställa på* ~ (*mil.*) draw up in line, line up; *över hela* ~*n* (*bildl.*) all along the line **-arbetare** line[s]man **-buss** coach **-domare** *sport.* linesman **-fart** liner traffic **-fartyg** liner **-fel** *tekn.* line disturbance

linje|ra 1 = [*upp*] rule; ~*t papper* ruled (lined) paper **2** (*stå på linje*) range; **-rederi** shipping line, liner company **-regemente** line regiment

linje|ring [-'je:-] ruling **-sjöfart** liner shipping **-skepp** line-of-battle ship **-spel** lines (*pl*); line-pattern **-trafik** intercity (interurban) traffic **-trupper** *pl* line troops **-val** *skol.* choice of line **-väljare** *tel.* series telephone set

lin'jär *a1* linear

linka limp, hobble

linne *s6* (*tyg*) linen; *koll.* linen; (*plagg*) vest

linnea [-*ˣ*ne:a] *s1, bot.* linnaea

linne|skåp linen cupboard (press) **-utstyrsel** (*bruds*) stock of household linen, *vard.* bottom drawer, *AE.* hope chest **-varor** *pl* linen goods, linens

linning band

linodling flax-growing

linoleum [-'nɷ:-] *s7, s9* linoleum; *hand. äv.* lino **-matta** linoleum flooring **-snitt** linoleum block, linocut

linolja linseed oil

1 lins *s3, bot.* lentil

2 lins *s3, fys., anat.* lens
lintott flaxen-haired child (person)
lip *s2, ta till ~en* start crying, *vard.* turn on the waterworks **lipa** cry, sob; blubber **lipsill** crybaby
1 lir|a *-an -e (mynt)* lira (*pl* lire)
2 lira *vard.* play
lirare player
lirka work [it]; ~ *med ngt* turn s.th. this way and that; ~ *med ngn* coax (wheedle, cajole) s.b.
lisa *s1* relief; *(tröst)* comfort, solace; *en ren* ~ a real mercy
lisma fawn, wheedle **lismande** *a4* fawning, bland; ~ *tal* bland (honeyed) speech **lismare** fawner; *(smickrare)* flatterer; *vard.* bootlicker
lispund lispound; *ett* ~ *(ung.)* a stone
Lissabon ['lissabån] *n* Lisbon
1 list *s3* *(-ighet)* cunning, craft[iness]; *(knep)* artifice, stratagem; *kvinnans* ~ *övergår mannens förstånd* the female of the species is more deadly than the male
2 list *s3 (bård)* border, edging; *(remsa)* strip; *byggn.* band, fillet; *(på fotpanel)* ledge
1 lista *s1* list *(på, över* of); *svart* ~ black list; *sätta ngn på svarta ~n* blacklist s.b.; *göra upp en* ~ draw up a list
2 lista *v1, rfl,* ~ *sig in i* steal (sneak) into; ~ *sig till ngt* get s.th. by trickery
listig *a1* cunning, artful, crafty **-het** cunningness *etc.*
listverk moulding[s *pl*]
lisös bed-jacket
lit *r, sätta [sin]* ~ *till* put (place) one's confidence in, *vard.* pin one's faith on **lita** ~ *på* have confidence in, trust [in], *(för- sig på)* depend (rely) [up]on, trust to; *det kan du* ~ *på!* you may depend on that!
litania [-^ni:a] *s1* litany
Litauen [-'tau-] *n* Lithuania
litau|er [-'tau-] *s9* Lithuanian **-isk** *a5* Lithuanian
lit de parade [li: dö pa'radd] *i uttr.: ligga på* ~ lie in state
lite *(i talspråk o. ledigt skriftspråk) se litet*
liten *litet mindre minst (jfr äv. litet)* small, little; *(ytterst* ~) minute, tiny; *(obetydlig)* slight, insignificant; ~ *till växten* small, short; *som* ~ as a child; *när jag var* ~ when I was small (a little boy *etc.*); *få en* ~ have a baby; *stackars* ~ poor child; ~ *bokstav* small letter; *boktr.* lower-case [letter] **-het** smallness *etc.*
liter ['li:-] *s9* litre; *AE.* liter **-butelj** litre bottle **-mått** litre measure **-vis** *(t.ex. säljas ~)* by the litre; *(~ efter ~)* litre by litre
litet I *adv* little; *(ngt [~])* a little, somewhat, a bit; *(obetydligt)* slightly; *han blev inte ~ förvånad* he was not a little astonished; *sova* ~ sleep [for] a little while; *jag är ~ förkyld* I have got a slight cold; *för* ~ *sedan* a little while ago; ~ *var (till mans) har vi* pretty well every one of us has; ~ *varstans* here and there, *(nästan överallt)* almost everywhere; ~ *då och då* every now and then **II** *a, n till liten* a little, some; *(föga)* little; *det var ovanligt* ~ *folk där* there were unusually few people there; *vi behöver* ~ *blommor* we need a few flowers; *bra* ~ *intresse* very little interest **III** *oböjl. s* a little;

something; a trifle; *(föga)* little; ~ *men gott* little but good; ~ *roar småbarn* anything will amuse a child, little things please little minds; *det vill inte säga* ~! that's saying a good deal!; *om än aldrig så* ~ be it ever so little; ~ *av varje* a little of everything
litium ['li:t(s)-] *s8, kem.* lithium
lito|graf *s3* lithographer **-grafera** lithograph **-grafi** *s3* lithography; *konkr.* lithograph **-grafisk** [-'gra:-] *a5* lithographic
littera ['litt-] *s1* [capital] letter **litte'rat** *a1 o. s3* literate
litteratur literature **-anmälan** review **-förteckning** bibliography, list of references **-historia** history of literature **-historiker** literary historian **-historisk** of the history of literature **-hänvisning** recommended literature; *L~ar* Further Reading *(sg)* **-kritiker** literary critic **-sökning** literature search, information retrieval, documentary research **-vetenskap** comparative literature
litteratör writer, author **litte'rär** *a1* literary; *(om pers. äv.)* of a literary turn; ~ *äganderätt* copyright
li'turg *s3* officiating priest (clergyman) **litur'gi** *s3* liturgy **liturgisk** *a5* liturgical
1 liv *s7* **1** *(kropp)* body; ~ *och lem* life and limb; *veka ~et* the waist; *gå (komma) ngn inpå ~et* get (come) close to s.b., get to know s.b. intimately; *med* ~ *och själ* wholeheartedly; *till* ~ *och själ* to the backbone **2** *(midja)* waist; *smal om ~et* slender-waisted **3** *(klädesplagg)* bodice **4** *få sig ngt till* ~*s* have s.th. to eat *(some food), bildl.* be treated to s.th.
2 liv *s7* **1** *(levande, levnad, leverne)* life; *(tillvaro)* existence; *börja ett nytt* ~ turn over a new leaf; *musik är mitt* ~ music is what I live for; *sådant är ~et!* such is life!; *få* ~ *i* get some life into, *(avsvimmad)* bring round; *få nytt* ~ get a new lease of life; *gjuta nytt* ~ *i* revive, resuscitate; *det gäller ~et* it is a matter of life and death; *hålla* ~ *i* keep alive (going); *sätta ~et till* lose one's life; *ta ~et av ngn* take a p.'s life, make away with s.b.; *berättelser ur levande ~et* stories from [real] life; *ett helt ~s arbete* the work of a lifetime; *leva ~ets glada dagar (vard.)* be having the time of one's life; *för hela ~et* for life; *frukta för sitt* ~ go in fear for one's life; *inte för mitt ~!* not for the life of me!; *i hela mitt* ~ all my life; *han har inte ngn släkting i ~et* he has no living relatives; *det är hopp om ~et (skämts.)* where there's life there's hope; *en strid på* ~ *och död* a life-and-death struggle; *trött på ~et* tired of [one's] life; *väcka till* ~ wake to life, *(friare)* awaken [to life], arouse **2** *bildl.* life, vitality; *(kläm)* spirit, mettle; *(fart)* go; *AE. vard.* pep; *det var* ~ *och rörelse överallt* there was a bustling throng everywhere; *med* ~ *och lust* with enthusiasm, very heartily **3** *(oväsen)* commotion, row; *föra ett förfärligt* ~ make (kick up) a terrible row **4** *(levande varelse)* living being; thing; *det lilla ~et!* the little darling!; *inte ett* ~ not a soul
liva 1 animate, enliven; *(muntra upp)* liven (cheer) up **2** *(egga)* stimulate; *(öva pennalism)* rag, bully **livad** *a5* **1** *(munter)* jolly, merry **2**

L

(*hågad*) inclined (*för* for)
liv|aktig *a1* lively; (*-full*) animated **-boj** life buoy **-båt** lifeboat **-båtsövning** boat drill **-bälte** life belt; cork jacket; *AE.* life preserver **-dömd** *a5* sentenced to death **-egen** I *a3* in villeinage (serfdom) II *s, pl -egna*, villein, serf **-egenskap** *s3* villeinage, serfdom **-full** full of life (animation), vivid, vivacious
livförsäkr|a insure (*ngn* a p.'s life; *sig* one's life) **-ing** life insurance (*BE. äv.* assurance)
livförsäkrings|agent life insurance agent **-brev** life insurance policy **-premie** life insurance premium
liv|garde life-guards; (*truppförband*) Life Guards (*pl*) **-gardist** Life-Guardsman **-givande** *a4* life-giving; vivifying; animating; *bildl. äv.* heartening **-hanken** *vard. i uttr.: rädda ~* save one's skin
Livius ['li:-] Livy
livklädnad *bibl.* tunic
livlig [*'li:v-] *a1* lively; (*-full*) animated, spirited; (*rörlig*) active; (*t. temperamentet*) sprightly, vivacious; (*levande*) vivid; ~ *debatt* keen debate; *röna ~ efterfrågan* meet with a keen (brisk, lively) demand; ~ *fantasi* lively (vivid) imagination; ~ *trafik* heavy (busy) traffic; ~*t trafikerad gata* busy (crowded) street; ~ *verksamhet* lively (intensive) activity **-het** liveliness *etc.*; animation; vivacity; activity
liv|lina lifeline **-lös** lifeless; (*död*) dead; *bildl. äv.* dull; ~*a ting* inanimate things **-medikus** *s, best. form = el. -medikusen, pl -medici* physician in ordinary (*hos* to) **-moder** *anat.* uterus (*pl* uteri); womb **-moderhals** cervix **-nära** support, maintain; feed
Livorno [-'vårnå] *n* Leghorn
livré *s4* livery **-klädd** liveried
liv|rem belt **-rustkammare** *L~n* [the] Royal Armoury **-rädd** terrified, frightened to death **-räddare** life-saver, rescuer **-räddning** life-saving **-räddningsbåt** lifeboat **-ränta** life annuity **-rätt** favourite dish
livs [lifs] *se 1 liv 4* **-andar** *pl, ngns* ~ a p.'s spirits **-avgörande** *a4* vital, of decisive importance **-bejakande** *a4* positive **-bejakelse** positive attitude to life **-cykel** life cycle **-duglig** capable of survival; healthy **-elixir** elixir of life **-erfaren** experienced, with experience of life **-erfarenhet** experience [of life] **-fara** deadly peril, danger (peril) to life [and limb]; *sväva i ~* be in mortal danger (peril) **-farlig** highly dangerous, perilous; (*om sjukdom*) grave; ~ *spänning!* (*elektr.*) Danger! High Voltage **-filosofi** philosophy [of life] **-form** form of life **-föring** way of life **-förnödenheter** *pl* necessaries of life **-glädje** joy of living **-gnista** spark of life, vital spark **-hotande** ~ *skador* grave injuries **-intresse** chief interest in life **-kraft** vital force (power); vitality **-kraftig** vigorous, robust **-kvalitet** quality of life **-leda** weariness of life **-ledsagare, -ledsagarinna** life companion **-levande** lifelike; in person (the flesh) **-lust** zest for life **-lång** lifelong **-längd** length (term) of life; (*t.ex. lampas*) life **-lögn** lifelong deception
livsmedel *pl* provisions, food[s], foodstuffs
livsmedels|butik food shop, grocer's (grocery)

[store]; (*snabbköp*) self-service shop **-försörjning** food supply [system] **-industri** food [manufacturing] industry **-teknologi** food technology **-verk** *Statens* ~ [the Swedish] national food administration
livs|mod will to life **-nerv** *bildl.* vital nerve **-oduglig** unfit to live **-rum** *polit.* lebensraum; living-space **-stil** way of life **-tecken** sign of life; *han har inte givit ngt ~ ifrån sig* there is no news from him, he has not written
livstid *i* (*under*) *vår* ~ in our lifetime; *på* (*för*) ~ for life; ~*s straffarbete* penal servitude for life
livstids|fånge prisoner serving life sentence; *vard.* lifer **-straff** lifelong punishment; imprisonment for life
livstycke (*för barn*) under-bodice
livs|uppgift task (mission) in life **-verk** life's work, life-work **-viktig** vitally important, of vital importance **-vilja** will to life **-villkor** vital condition **-åskådning** view (conception) of life; philosophy
livtag *sport.* waist lock; *ta* ~ apply a waist lock, *bildl.* wrestle
livvakt bodyguard
ljud [ju:d] *s7* sound (*äv. ~et*); *inte ge ett ~ ifrån sig a*) not make a (the slightest) sound, *b*) (*tiga*) not say a single word **ljud|a** *ljöd -it* (*språkv. v1*) sound; (*klinga*) ring; (*brusa*) peal; *det ljöd röster i trappan* voices were heard on the stairs; *ett skott ljöd* a shot rang out
ljud|arkiv sound archive **-band** recording tape; *film.* sound track **-bang** *s2* sonic bang (boom) **-boj** whistling buoy **-dämpande** *a4* sound-absorbing **-dämpare** [exhaust] silencer, *särsk. AE.* muffler **-effekt** sound effect **-film** soundfilm, *AE.* talkie **-härmande** *a4* sound-imitating; onomatopoe[t]ic; ~ *ord* (*äv.*) imitative word **-isolera** soundproof **-isolering** sound insulation
ljud|it *sup. av ljuda* **-kuliss** *radio.* background sound effect **-lag** *s2* sound (phonetic) law
ljud|lig [-u:-] *a1* loud[-sounding]; resounding (*kyss* kiss) **-lära** *fys.* acoustics (*sg*); *språkv.* phonetics (*sg*), phonology **-lös** soundless, noiseless **-nivå** sound level **-radio** sound-broadcasting **-signal** sound-signal **-skridning** [-i:d-] *språkv.* sound shift **-skrift** phonetic transcription (notation) **-spår** *film.* soundtrack **-styrka** sound; (*volym*) [sound] volume **-tät** soundproof **-upptagning** sound recording **-vall** sound (sonic) barrier **-våg** sound wave **-återgivning** sound reproduction **-överföring** sound transmission
ljug|a [*'ju:-] *ljög -it* lie (*för* to); tell lies (a lie, falsehood); ~ *för ngn* tell s.b. a lie (*etc.*); ~ *ngn full* tell s.b. a tissue of lies; ~ *som en häst travar* lie like a horse-coper; ~ *ihop ngt* trump up (fabricate) s.th. **ljugit** *sup. av ljuga*
ljum [jumm] *a1* tepid, lukewarm (*äv. bildl.*); *bildl. äv.* half-hearted; (*om väder*) warm **ljumma** warm [up], take the chill off
ljumsk|brock [*'jumsk-] inguinal hernia **ljumske** *s2* groin
ljung [juŋ] *s3* heather, ling
ljung|a [*'juŋa] lighten; flash (*äv. bildl.*); *bildl. äv.* fulminate **-ande** *a4* flashing (*ögon* eyes);

bildl. fulminating; (*om protest o.d.*) vehement **-eld** flash of lightning
ljung|hed [j-] heatherclad moor (heath) **-pipare** *zool.* golden plover
ljus [ju:s] **I** *s7* **1** light (*äv. ~et*); *tända ~et* switch on the light; *stå i ~et för ngn* stand in a p.'s light; *se dagens ~* see the light of the day; *föra ngn bakom ~et* pull the wool over a p.'s eyes, take s.b in; *nu gick det upp ett ~ för mig* now the light has dawned on me **2** (*stearin- etc.*) candle; *bränna sitt ~ i båda ändar* burn the candle at both ends; *söka efter ngt med ~ och lykta* search high and low [for s.th.]; *han är just inte något ~* he is no great light, he is not on the bright side **II** *a1* light; light-coloured; (*lysande*) brilliant (*idé* idea), bright (*färger* colours; *framtid* future); (*om hy, hår*) fair; *det är redan ~an dag* it is day[light] already; *mitt på ~a dagen* in broad daylight; *stå i ~an låga* be ablaze; *~a ögonblick* lucid moments; *i ~aste minne bevarad* cherished in happy remembrance
ljus|bild slide; *föredrag med ~er* lantern lecture **-blå** light (pale) blue **-brytning** [light] refraction **-båge** electric arc **-dunkel** *konst.* chiaroscuro **-effekt** light (lighting) effect **-flöde** luminous flux **-glimt** gleam of light, *bildl. äv.* ray of hope **-gård I** *byggn.* well, light-court **2** (*-fenomen*) corona **3** *astr.* halo, *foto. äv.* halo **-huvud** *bildl.* bright boy **-hyllt** a1 light-complexioned, fair-complexioned **-hårig** fair[-haired] **-kopiering** light printing; (*blåkopiering*) blueprinting **-knippe** light beam **-krona** chandelier; (*kristall-*) lustre **-kägla** cone of light **-källa** source of light **-känslig** sensitive to light; (*elektriskt*) photosensitive; *~t papper* sensitized paper **-lagd** *se -hyllt* **-lockig** with fair curly hair **-låga** candle-flame **-manschett** candle-ring **-mätare** light meter, photometer
ljus|na [-u:-] get (grow) light; (*dagas äv.*) dawn; *bildl.* brighten [up], get (become) brighter **-ning 1** *se gryning* **2** (*glänta*) clearing, glade **3** *bildl.* brightening[-up], change for the better, improvement **-punkt** lighting (luminous) point; *elektr.* focus; *bildl.* bright spot, consolation **-reflex** reflected light, reflection of light **-reklam** illuminated [advertisement] sign, neon sign (light) **-sax** *en ~* a pair of snuffers **-signal** light signal, signal light **-sken** shining (bright) light **-skimmer** shimmer of light **-skygg** *med.* photophobic; *bildl.* shady **-skygghet** *med.* photophobia; *bildl.* shadiness **-skylt** electric sign **-stake** candlestick, candleholder **-stark** (*om stjärna e.d.*) of great brilliance; (*om lampa e.d.*) bright **-strimma** streak of light **-stråle** ray (*kraftigare:* beam) of light **-stump** candle-end **-styrka** intensity of light; (*i normalljus*) candlepower **-stöpning** [-ö:-] candle-making
ljuster ['just-] *s7* [fishing-]spear, [fish]gig **ljustra** spear
ljus|veke candlewick **-våg** light-wave **-år** light year **-äkta** light-proof; *~ färg* fast colour
ljut|a [*ˣju:-] *ljöt -it, num. end. i uttr.:* *~ döden* meet one's death **ljutit** *sup. av ljuta*
ljuv [ju:v] *a1* sweet; (*om doft, sömn, vila äv.*)

delicious; (*behaglig*) delightful (*syn* sight); *dela ~t och lett med ngn* share the fortunes (the ups and downs) of life with s.b. **ljuvhet** sweetness *etc.* **ljuvlig** *a1* sweet *etc., jfr ljuv*
ljöd [jö:d] *imperf. av ljuda*
ljög [jö:g] *imperf. av ljuga*
ljöt [jö:t] *imperf. av ljuta*
LO [*ˣällɔ:] *förk. för Landsorganisationen*
lo *s2, zool.* lynx (*pl äv.* lynx)
lob *s3* lobe
lobb [-å-] *s2, sport.* lob **lobba** *v1, sport.* lob
lobbyverksamhet lobbying
loboto'mi *s3* lobotomy
1 lock [låck] *s2, (hår-)* lock [of hair]; (*ringlad*) curl
2 lock [låck] *s7* (*på kärl o.d.*) lid; (*löst äv.*) cover; *det slog ~ för öronen på mig* I was deafened
3 lock [låck] *s7 (-ande) med ~ och pock* by hook or [by] crook; *varken med ~ eller pock* neither by fair means nor foul
1 locka [-å-] (*göra lockig*) curl, do up in curls; *~ sig* curl
2 lock|a [-å-] **1** (*förleda*) entice, allure ([*till*] at into + *ing-form*); (*fresta*) tempt, entice ([*till*] *att* into + *ing- form*); (*fängsla*) attract; *~ ngn i fällan* trap s.b.; *~ fram* draw out (*ur* of); *~ fram tårar* draw tears (*ur* from) **2** *jakt. o.d.* call (*äv. ~ på*); (*om höna äv.*) cluck (*på* to)
lock|ande *a4* enticing *etc.*; tempting, attractive **-bete** lure (*äv. bildl.*); bait; *bildl. äv.* decoy **-else** enticement, allurement; attraction; temptation **-fågel** decoy bird
lockig [-å-] *a1* curly
lockout [låkk'aut] *s3* lockout; *varsla om ~* give advance notice of a lockout **lockouta** [-'auta] *v1* lock out
lock|pris price to catch customers; special offer **-rop** mating call **-sång** call **-ton** callnote; *~er* (*bildl.*) siren call **-vara** bait, loss leader
locktång curling irons (tongs) (*pl*)
lod *s7* weight; (*sänk-*) plummet; *sjö.* lead
1 loda *sjö.* sound; *bildl.* plumb, fathom
2 loda (*ströva*) stroll [about]; *neds.* mooch [about]
lodenrock loden coat
lodjur *se lo*
lod|lina *sjö.* lead (sounding) line **-linje** vertical line **-ning** sounding (*äv. bildl.*) **-rät** plumb; vertical; perpendicular; *~a ord* (*i korsord*) clues down; *~t 5 5* down
loft [låft] *s7* loft
log *imperf. av le*
loga'ritm *s3* logarithm **-isk** *a5* logarithmic **-tabell** table of logarithms
logdans barn dance
1 loge [*ˣlɔ:ge] *s2* barn
2 loge [lå:ʃ] *s5* **1** *teat.* box **2** (*ordens-*) lodge
logement [låʃe-, -lɔ-] *s7* barrack room
logera [lå-] **1** (*inhysa*) put up, accomodate, lodge **2** (*vara inhyst*) put up (*hos ngn* at a p.'s house *etc.*), lodge (*hos ngn* with s.b.)
logg [lå-] *s2, sjö.* log **logga** log **loggbok** logbook
loggert ['lågg-] *s2, sjö.* lugger
loggia ['lɔggia, -ja, 'låddja] *s1* loggia
logg|lina log line **-ning** logging

L

logi ['ʃi:] *s4, s6* accommodation, lodging; *konkr.* lodging house; *kost och* ~ board and lodging, full board

lo'g|ik *s3* logic **-iker** ['lå:-] logician **-isk** ['lå:-] *a5* logical

logistik *s3* logistics (*behandlas som sg el. pl*)

logo'|ped *s3* speech therapist (pathologist) **-pe-'di** *s3* speech pathology **-'typ** *s4* logotype

loj [låjj] *a1* (*trög*) inert; (*slö*) slack; (*håglös*) listless; (*indolent*) indolent

lo'jal *a1* loyal (*mot* to[wards]) **-itet** loyalty

lok *s7, se lokomotiv*

lo'kal I *s3* place; (*rum*) room; (*sal*) hall; (*kontors-*) premises (*pl*) **II** *a1* local **-avdelning** local branch **-bedöva** give a local anaesthetic (*ngn* to s.b.) **-bedövning** local anaesthesia **-färg** local colour (*äv. bildl.*) **-hyra** rent (of premises *etc.*)

lokaliser|a localize, locate. place; *vara väl ~d* be thoroughly at home in (*äv. bildl.*) **-ing** localization, location

lokaliserings|politik industrial location policy **-stöd** industrial location grant

lokal|itet *s3* locality **-kännedom** local knowledge **-patriot** local patriot **-patriotism** local patriotism, regionalism **-plan** *på ~et* on the local level **-samtal** local call **-sinne** *ha ~* have a good sense of direction **-telefon** internal (interoffice) telephone **-trafik** local traffic **-tåg** local (suburban) train **-vård** cleaning **-vårdare** cleaner; (*pl*) cleaning staff

lokatt *se lo*

lokbiträde engine-driver's assistant **lokförare** engine driver; (*på ellok*) motorman; (*på diesellok*) engineer **lokomo'tiv** *s7* engine; locomotive **lokstall** engine shed

lolla [-å-] *s1* country wench

lom [lɔmm] *s2, zool.* diver, *AE.* loon

loma *se lomma*

lombardlån [låm'ba:rd-, ˣlåmm-] loan against security

lomhörd [ˣlɔmmhö:rd] *a1* hard of hearing, deaf

londonbo [ˣlånndånbɔ] *s5* Londoner; (*infödd, vard. äv.*) cockney

longi'tud [lån(g)i-] *s3* longitude **-i'nell** *a1* longitudinal

longör [lån'gö:r] tedious passage; (*friare*) dull period

lopp [-å-] *s7* **1** *sport.* running; (*ett ~*) run; (*tävling*) race; *dött ~* a dead heat **2** (*rörelse, gång*) course; *flodens övre ~* the upper reaches of the river; *ge fritt ~ åt* (*bildl.*) give vent to; *efter ~et av ett år* after [the lapse of] one year; *i det långa ~et* (*bildl.*) in the long run; *inom ~et av* within (the course of]; *under dagens ~* (*äv.*) during the day; *under tidernas ~* in the course of time **3** (*gevärs- o.d.*) bore

lopp|a [-å-] *s1* flea; *leva ~n* (*vard.*) have a gay time, go out on the spree **-bett** fleabite **-cirkus** flea circus **-marknad** flea (junk) market; jumble sale

lord [-å-] *s3* lord; ~ *A.* Lord A.; *~en* his Lordship **-kansler** *L~n* the Lord Chancellor

lorn'jett *s3* lorgnette

lort *s2* (*smuts*) dirt, filth, muck **lorta** ~ *ner* get all dirty (*etc.*). **lortgris** little (dirty) pig **lor-**

tig *a1* dirty, filthy, mucky

loss [-å-] *oböjl. a o. adv* loose; off, away; *kasta* ~ (*sjö.*) cast off, let go; *skruva* ~ (*äv.*) unscrew **lossa 1** (*lösa upp*) loose[n]; (*ngt hårt spänt äv.*) slack[en]; *bildl.* relax; (*knyta upp*) untie, unfasten, undo; (*bryta loss*) detach **2** (*urlasta*) unload, discharge; (*fartyg äv.*) unship, land; *~ lasten* discharge one's (its) cargo **3** (*skott*) discharge, fire [off] **lossna** come loose (off, untied *etc.*); (*om t.ex. tänder*) get loose; (*om färg o.d.*) loosen **lossning** unloading, discharging, discharge; landing **lossningsplats** (*för fartyg*) discharging berth; (*lossningshamn*) place (port) of discharge

lots *s2* pilot **lotsa** pilot (*äv. bildl.*); conduct **lots|avgift** pilotage **-båt** pilot-boat **-distrikt** pilotage district **-ning** pilotage, piloting **-station** pilot station **-verket** [the Swedish] Pilotage Service

lott [-å-] *s3* **1** lot; (*andel äv.*) share, portion; (*öde*) lot, fate, destiny; (*jord-*) lot, plot; *dra ~ om* draw lots for; *falla på ngns ~ att* fall to a p.['s lot] to; *olika falla ödets ~er* fate apportions her favours unevenly **2** (*-sedel*) lot, lottery ticket

1 lotta [-å-] *s1* member of [the Swedish] Women's Voluntary Defence Service

2 lott|a [-å-] *v1, se [dra] lott*; ~ *bort* (*ut*) dispose of by lottery

lott|ad *a5, lyckligt* ~ well off (situated) **-dragning** drawing [of lots] (*om* for) **-eri** lottery (*äv. bildl.*); *spela på* ~ take part in a lottery; *vinna på* ~ win in a lottery **-eridragning** lottery draw **-lös** portionless; *bli* ~ be left without any share, be left out **-nummer** lot-number **-sedel** lottery ticket

lotus ['lɔ:-] *s2* lotus

1 lov [lå:v] *s7* **1** (*tillåtelse*) permission, leave; *be [ngn] om* ~ ask [a p.'s] leave; *får jag* ~ *att hjälpa till* may I ([will you] allow me to) help you (*etc.*); *får jag* ~? shall we dance?; *vad får det* ~ *att vara?* what can I show (get for) you? **2** *nu får jag* ~ *att gå* I must leave now **3** (*ferier*) holiday[s *pl*]

2 lov [lɔ:v] *s2* **1** *sjö.* (*göra en* make a) tack **2** *bildl., slå sina ~ar kring* hover (prowl) round; *ta ~en av ngn* get the better of s.b., take the wind out of a p.'s sails

3 lov [lå:v] *s7* (*beröm*) praise; *sjunga ngns* ~ sing a p.'s praises; *Gud vare* ~! thank God!, God be praised!

1 lova [ˣlå:-] (*ge löfte* [*om*]) promise; (*högtidligt*) vow; ~ *runt och hålla tunt* promise a lot, fulfil ne'er a lot; ~ *gott* promise well, be promising; *det* ~*r gott för framtiden* it promises well for the future; *det vill jag* ~! I should say so!, rather!, *AE. vard.* I'll say!; *jag har redan* ~*t bort mig till i kväll* (*äv.*) I have got another engagement this evening

2 lova [ˣlɔ:-] *sjö.* luff

3 lova [ˣlå:-] (*prisa*) praise; ~*d vare Gud!* blessed be God!

lovande [ˣlå:-] *a4* (*hoppingivande*) promising; (*om sak äv.*) auspicious; *det ser inte vidare* ~ *ut* (*äv.*) it doesn't look very hopeful

lovart ['lɔ:-] *r, i* ~ to windward, on the windward side

lov|dag holiday; *ha en ~* have a day's holiday **-lig** [*ˣlå:v-] *a1, den ~a tiden för (jakt.)* the open season for; *änderna blir ~a snart* duck-shooting begins soon
lov|ord [word of] praise **-orda** commend, praise **-prisa** eulogize; *~ ngn (äv.)* sound a p.'s praises **-sjunga** sing praises unto; *(friare)* sing the praise of **-sång** song of praise; *(jubel-)* paean **-tal** panegyric, eulogy *(över* upon); encomium **-värd** *a1* praiseworthy, commendable; *(om företag, försök o.d.)* laudable
LP-skiva [*ˣellpe:-] LP (long-playing) record
lucia|dagen Lucia Day *(December 13)* **-firande** [-ˣsi:a-] *s6, ~t* Lucia Day celebrations *(pl)*
lucka *s1* **1** *(ugns- o.d.)* door; *(fönster-)* shutter; *(damm-)* gate; *(källar-)* flap; *(titthålls-)* [spy-hole] hatch; *sjö.* [hatchway] lid **2** *(öppning)* hole, aperture; *sjö.* hatch **3** *(i skrift)* lacuna *(pl äv.* lacunae); *bildl.* gap; *(i minnet)* blank
lucker ['lukk-] *a2* loose; light, mellow **luckra** loosen, break up, mellow; *~ upp* loosen up
ludd *s3, s7* fluff; nap **ludda** *~ [sig]* cotton, rise with a nap **luddig** *a1* fluffy, cottony, nappy **luden** *a3* hairy; *bot. äv.* downy
luff *s2, vara på ~en* be tramping **luffa** tramp; lumber; *(springa)* run **luffare** tramp, vagabond
luffarschack *ung.* noughts and crosses *(pl)*
lufsa go lumbering; walk (run) clumsily **lufsig** *a1* clumsy
1 luft *s3, en ~ gardiner* a pair of curtains
2 luft *s3* air; *(friare äv.)* atmosphere; *fria ~en* the open air; *få [litet] frisk ~* get a breath of air; *ge ~ åt (bildl.)* give vent to, vent; *behandla ngn som ~* treat s.b. as though he did not exist; *han var som ~ för henne* he was beneath her notice; *det ligger i ~en* it is in the air; *gripen ur ~en* imaginary, made up
luft|a air; *~ på sig* go out for a breath of air; *(däck)* let down **-affär** bogus transaction; fraud **-angrepp** air attack (raid) *(mot* on) **-ballong** [air-]balloon **-bevakning** air defence warning service **-bro** airlift, air bridge **-broms** *flyg.* air brake **-bubbla** air-bubble **-buren** *a5, -burna trupper* airborne (parachute) troops **-buss** *(flygplan)* airbus **-bössa** air gun; *(leksak)* popgun **-cirkulation** air circulation **-drag** air current, draught; *AE.* draft **-fart** *(äv. ~en)* flying, aviation; *(flygtrafik)* air traffic **-farts-myndighet** civil aviation authority **-farts-verket** *L~* [the Swedish] board of civil aviation **-fartyg** aircraft *(sg o. pl.)* **-flotta** air fleet **-fuktare** humidifier **-fuktighet** humidity of the atmosphere (air) **-färd** air (aerial) trip **-förorening** air pollution; *(ämne)* air pollutant **-försvar** air defence **-gevär** air gun (rifle) **-grop** *flyg.* air pocket **-hål** air (ventilation) hole; *(-utsläpp)* air-escape
luft|ig *a1* airy; *(om t.ex. klänning)* billowy **-in-tag** air-intake **-konditionerad** *a5* air-conditioned **-konditionering** air conditioning **-kudde** air cushion; *(i bil)* air bag **-kudde-farkost** cushioncraft, hovercraft **-kyld** *a5* air-cooled **-kylning** air-cooling **-lager** air stratum, layer of air **-landsättning** landing of airborne troops **-led** air corridor, airway **-led-ning** overhead [power transmission] line **-ma-drass** air bed **-maska** chain stitch **-massa** air

mass **-motstånd** air resistance (friction, drag)
luft|ning airing, ventilation **-ombyte** change of air **-pistol** air gun **-post** air mail **-pump** air pump, pneumatic pump; *(för cykeldäck o.d.)* tyre-inflator **-renare** air filter (cleaner) **-re-ning** air purification **-rum** airspace; *flyg.* air territory **-räd** air raid **-rör** *anat.* windpipe, trachea **-rörskatarr** bronchitis **-skepp** airship; dirigible **-skydd** air raid precautions service **-slott** castle in the air (in Spain) **-språng** *(glädje-)* caper; *göra ~* cut capers **-streck** climate **-strid** aerial combat **-strupe** *se -rör* **-ström** current of air, air current, airflow **-tillförsel** air supply **-tom** airless; *~t rum* vacuum, void **-torka** air-dry **-trumma** *tekn.* air shaft **-tryck** atmospheric pressure **-tät** airtight, hermetic **-täthet** air density **-va-pen** *se flygvapen* **-ventil** air valve **-vägs-infektion** respiratory infection **-värn** anti-aircraft defence **-värnsartilleri** anti-aircraft artillery **-värnskanon** anti-aircraft gun **-växling** ventilation
1 lugg *s2 (ludd)* nap, *(på sammet)* pile
2 lugg *s2* **1** *(pann-)* fringe; *titta under ~* look furtively, keep the (one's) eyes lowered **2** *(-ning)* wigging **lugga** *~ ngn* pull a p.'s hair
luggsliten threadbare; shabby *(äv. bildl.)*
lugn [luŋn] **I** *s7* calm; *(egenskap äv.)* calmness; *(upphöjt ~)* serenity; *(stillhet)* quiet; *(ro)* tranquillity; *(sinnes-)* equanimity, composure ; *i ~ och ro* in peace and quiet; *återställa ~ och ordning* restore peace and order; *~et före stormen* the calm before the storm **II** *a1* calm; *(jämn)* smooth *(yta* surface); *(fridfull, ej upp-rörd)* tranquil; *(stilla)* quiet; *(mots. ängslig)* easy *(för* about); *(med bibehållen fattning)* composed; *med ~t samvete* with an easy conscience; *aldrig ha en ~ stund* never have a moment's peace; *hålla sig ~ (ej bråka)* keep quiet; *var bara ~!* don't you worry!
lugna calm, quiet[en]; *(farhågor, tvivel o.d.)* set at rest; *~ sig* calm o.s. (down); *~ dig!* don't get excited!, take it easy!; *~ dina upprörda känslor!* calm down!; *känna sig ~d* feel reassured **lugnande** *a4* calming *etc.*; *(om nyhet o.d.)* reassuring; *med.* sedative; *~ medel* sedative, tranquillizer **lugnt** *adv* calmly *etc.*; *ta det ~* take it (things) easy
luguber [-'gu:-] *a5* lugubrious, gloomy, dismal
Lukas ['lu:-] Luke; *~ evangelium* the Gospel according to St. Luke, Luke
lukrativ [-'ti:v, 'lukk-] *a1* lucrative, profitable
lukt *s3* smell; odour; *(behaglig äv.)* scent, perfume
lukt|a smell; *~ gott (illa)* smell nice (nasty); *det ~r vidbränt här* there's a smell of burning here; *det ~r tobak om honom* he smells of tobacco **-flaska** smelling-bottle **-fri** free from smell; odourless; scentless **-organ** organ of smell **-salt** smelling salts *(pl)*, sal volatile **-sinne** sense of smell, olfactory sense; *ha fint ~ (äv.)* have a keen sense of smell **-vatten** liquid scent **-viol** sweet violet **-ärt** sweet pea
lukullisk [-'kull-] *a5* Lucullan, Lucullian; *(fri-are)* sumptuous, luxurious
lull *adv, vard., i uttr.: stå ~* stand on its *(etc.)* own, stand without support

L

lulla *gå och* ~ shamble along
lullull *s7, koll.* gewgaws (*pl*), tinsel
lumbal|punktion lumbar puncture **-vätska** cerebrospinal fluid
lumberjacka windcheater, lumberjacket
lumin|ans *s3* luminance **-iscens** [-'sens, -'ʃens] *s3* luminescence **-ös** *a1* luminous; (*snillrik*) brilliant
lummer ['lumm-] *s9, bot.* club moss
lummig *a1* thickly foliaged; spreading
lump *s1* **1** rags (*pl*) **2** *vard.* *göra* ~*en* do one's military service **-bod** rag-and-bone[] shop, junk shop
lumpen *a3* paltry; (*småaktig*) petty, mean, shabby
lump|or *pl* rags **-papper** rag-paper **-samlare** rag-and-bone man, ragman
lunch *s3* lunch; luncheon **luncha** have [one's] lunch, lunch (*på* on)
lunch|bar *s3* lunch (snack) bar **-rast** lunch break; *skol.* lunch hour (recess) **-rum** (*i företag*) dining (lunch) room; (*självservering*) canteen
lund *s2, s3* grove; copse
lung|a *s1* lung; *blodpropp i* ~*n* pulmonary embolism **-blåsa** pulmonary vesicle **-blödning** haemorrhage of the lungs, pulmonary haemorrhage **-cancer** lung cancer, cancer of the lung **-fisk** lungfish **-inflammation** pneumonia; *dubbelsidig* ~ double (bilateral) pneumonia **-mos** *kokk.* hashed [calf's] lights (*pl*) **-siktig** *a1* consumptive **-sot** *s3* [pulmonary] consumption, phthisis **-säck** pleural sack **-säcksinflammation** pleurisy **-tuberkulos** pulmonary tuberculosis **-ört** *bot.* lungwort
lunk *s2* trot; *i sakta* ~ at a slow jog trot **lunka** jog along
lunnefågel [common] puffin
luns *s2* boor, bumpkin **lunsig** *a1* (*om pers.*) loutish, hulking; (*om plagg*) baggy, ill-fitting
lunta *s1* **1** (*bok*) tome, [big] volume; *nådiga* ~*n* the Budget Bill **2** (*för antändning*) match
lu'pin *s3* lupin
lupp *s3* magnifying glass, pocket lens
1 lur *s2* (*instrument*) horn, trumpet
2 lur *s2* (*slummer*) nap, doze; *ta sig en* ~ take a nap, have forty winks
3 lur *s, i uttr.: ligga på* ~ lie in wait, *bildl.* lurk; *stå på* ~ stand in ambush
1 lura (*slumra*) drop off [to sleep], doze off
2 lura 1 (*ligga på lur*) lie in wait (*på* for), *bildl.* lurk **2** (*bedra*) take in; cheat (*på* in, over); (*dupera*) impose upon, dupe; (*övertala*) coax, wheedle, cajole (*ngn att göra* s.b. into doing); (*överlista*) get the better of; *bli* ~*d* be taken in; *mig* ~*r du inte!* (*äv.*) you dont catch me!; ~ *av ngn ngt* wheedle (coax) s.th. out of s.b.; ~ *till sig ngt* secure s.th. [for o.s.]; *låta* ~ *sig* [allow o.s. to] be taken in (cheated *etc.*)
lurendrej|are fraud, trickster **-eri** cheating; fraud
lurifax ['lu:-, -'aks] *s2* sly dog (fox) **lurpassa 1** *kortsp.* lie low **2** *bildl.* [lie in] wait **lurt** [-u:-] *vard., ngt* ~ s.th. suspect
lurvig *a1* rough; (*rufsig*) tousled; (*om hund o.d.*) shaggy
lus -*en löss* louse (*pl* lice)

lu'sern [-ä:-] *s3* lucerne, purple meddick, alfalfa
lusig *a1* lousy
luska *se snoka*
luspank stony-broke
lussa *v1, vard.* celebrate Lucia Day
lust *s2* **1** (*håg*) inclination, mind; (*benägenhet, håg*) bent, disposition; (*smak*) taste, liking; *få* ~ *att* (*äv.*) take it into one's head to; *kom när du får* ~*!* come when you feel inclined [to]!; *ha* ~ *att a*) feel inclined (have a mind) to, *vard.* feel like (*sjunga* singing), *b*) (*bry sig om*) care to; *tappa* ~*en för* lose all desire for **2** (*glädje*) delight, pleasure; *i nöd och* ~ in weal and woe, (*i vigselformulär*) for better for worse **3** (*åtrå*) desire
lust|a *s5* lust; desire **-barhet** [-a:-] amusement **-betonad** pleasurable; ~*e känslor* feelings of pleasure **-eld** bonfire **-gas** laughing gas, *fack.* nitrous oxide **-gård** *Edens* ~ the garden of Eden **-hus** summerhouse
lustig *a1* **1** (*roande*) amusing, funny; (*munter*) merry, jolly; *göra sig* ~ *över* make fun of, poke fun at; *hastigt och* ~*t* all of a sudden, straight away **2** (*löjlig*) funny, comic[al]; (*underlig*) odd, strange, peculiar **-het** *säga en* ~ say s.th. amusing, make an amusing remark, crack a joke **-kurre** joker, wag
lust|jakt [pleasure] yacht **-känsla** sense (*-förnimmelse:* sensation) of pleasure **-mord** sex murder **-resa** pleasure trip (excursion) **-slott** royal out-of-town residence, pleasure palace **-spel** comedy **-spelsförfattare** comedy writer **-vandra** stroll about for pleasure
1 lut *s2* (*tvätt-*) lye
2 lut *s3, s7 stå* (*ligga*) *på* ~ be aslant; *ha* [*ngt*] *på* ~ have s.th. in reserve (up one's sleeve)
1 luta *s1* lute
2 luta *v1* (*lutlägga*) soak (steep) in lye
3 luta *v1* **1** lean (*äv.* ~ *sig*); incline; (*slutta*) slope, slant; ~ *sig ner* stoop; ~ *sig ut* lean out **2** (*tendera*) incline (*åt* towards); *jag* ~*r åt den åsikten att* I am inclined to think that; *det* ~*r nog ditåt* that is what it is coming to; *se vartåt det* ~*r* see which way things are going; ~ *mot sitt fall* be on the road to ruin **lutad** *a5* leaning (*mot* against); inclined, sloping (*bakåt* backwards); *gå* ~ walk with a stoop **lutande** *a4* leaning; inclined (*plan* plane); (*om bokstäver o.d.*) sloped, slanted; (*framåt-*) stooping; ~ *tornet i Pisa* the leaning tower of Pisa; ~ *stil* [a] sloping hand
luteran, luterdom, lutersk *se lutheran, lutherdom, lutersk*
lutfisk [dried] stockfish
luthe'r|an *s3* Lutheran **lutherdom** [ˣlutt-] *s2*, ~[*en*] Lutheranism **lutersk** ['lutt-] *a5* Lutheran
lutning [-u:-] inclination; (*sluttning*) slope
lutningsvinkel angle of inclination, pitch
lut|spelare lute player, lutenist **-sångare** singer to the lute
lutter ['lutt-] *oböjl. a* sheer, pure; downright **luttra** *bildl.* try, purify, chasten; ~*d* tried, chastened **luttring** trying *etc.*; purification
luv *s2, ligga i* ~*en på varandra* be at loggerheads [with each other]; *råka i* ~*en på varandra* fly at each other, fall foul of each other

luva *sl* [woollen] cap
luxu'ös *al* luxurious, sumptuous
lya *sl* lair, hole; den (*äv. bildl.*)
1 lyck|a *v3, inom -ta dörrar* behind closed doors
2 lyck|a *sl* (*levnads-*) happiness; (*sällhet*) bliss; (*tur*) luck, good fortune; (*framgång*) success; (*öde*) fortune; *bättre ~ nästa gång!* better luck next time!; *~ till* good luck!; *du ~ns ost!* you lucky beggar!; *göra stor ~* be a great success; *en stor ~ fyllde honom* he was filled with great joy, he was brimming over with happiness; *göra sin ~* make one's fortune; *ha ~ med sig* a) (*ha framgång*) be successful (fortunate), b) (*medföra ~*) bring [good] luck; *ha den ~n att* have the good fortune to, be fortunate enough to; *pröva ~n* try one's fortune; *sin egen ~s smed* the architect of one's own fortunes **lyckad** *a5* successful; *vara mycket ~* be a great success; *påståendet var mindre ~at* the statement was hardly a happy one **lyckas** *dep* succeed, be successful (*göra* in doing); (*gå bra*) be (turn out) a success; (*om pers.*) manage, contrive (*hitta* to find); *det ~ades inte alls* (*äv.*) it proved to be a complete failure; *allt ~ för honom* everything he touches prospers, he is successful in everything **lycklig** *al* (*uppfylld av lycka*) happy; (*gynnad av lycka*) fortunate; (*tursam*) lucky; *~ resa!* a pleasant journey!, bon voyage!; *i ~aste fall* at best; *av* (*genom*) *en ~ slump* by a lucky (happy) chance; *en ~ tilldragelse* a happy event **lyckligen** safely (*anländ* arrived) **lyckliggöra** make happy **lyckligt** *adv* happily *etc.*; *~ okunnig om* blissfully ignorant of; *komma ~ och väl hem* get home safely; *om allt går ~* if everything goes favourably (well, successfully); *leva ~* live happily **lyckligtvis** fortunately, luckily; happily
lycko|bringande *a4* lucky, bringing fortune (*etc.*) [in its train] **-dag** lucky day **-hjul** wheel of fortune **-kast** lucky throw (hit) **-klöver** four-leaf (four-leaved) clover **-moral** eudaemonism; ethics of happiness **-piller** tranquillizer **-sam** *al* prosperous; successful **-slant** lucky coin **-stjärna** lucky star **-tal** lucky number
lycksalig supremely happy, blissful **-het** bliss, supreme happiness (felicity)
lycksök|are -erska fortune hunter, adventurer
lyckt *se 1* lycka
lyck|träff lucky shot, stroke of luck; *en ren ~ a* mere chance **-önska ~ ngn** congratulate s.b. (*till ngt* on s.th.) **-önskan** congratulation **-önskningstelegram** greetings telegram
1 lyda *v2, imperf äv. löd* (*åt-*) obey; (*råd äv.*) follow, take; (*lyssna t.*) listen to (*förnuftets röst* the voice of reason); *ej ~ order* (*äv.*) disobey orders; *~ roder* answer [to] the helm; *~ under* a) (*om land o.d.*) be subject to, b) (*om ämbetsverk o.d.*) be under (subordinate to), be under the jurisdiction of, c) (*tillhöra*) belong to
2 lyd|a *v2, imperf äv. löd* **1** (*ha viss -else*) run, read; *hur -er frågan?* how does the question read?; *..., löd svaret ...*, was the reply; *domen -er på* the sentence is **2** *en räkning ~nde på 200 pund* a bill for £200; *~nde på innehava-*

ren made out to bearer
lydelse wording, tenor
lydfolk tributary people **lydig** *al* obedient; (*lag-*) loyal; (*foglig*) docile; (*snäll*) good **lydnad** [-y:-] *s3* obedience (*mot* to); loyalty **lydstat** tributary (vassal) state
lyft *s7* lift, hoist, heave **lyfta** *v3* **1** lift; (*höja*) raise (*på hatten* one's hat); (*häva*) heave; *bildl.* lift, elevate **2** (*uppbära*) draw, collect (*sin lön* one's salary); (*uttaga*) withdraw, take out (*pengar på ett konto* money from an account) **3** (*om fågel*) take wing (flight); *flyg.* take off, lift; (*om dimma o.d.*) lift
lyft|anordning hoist, gin **-kran** [hoisting] crane **-ning** lift; *bildl.* elevation, uplift
lyhörd [-ö:-] *al* **1** (*om pers.*) with a sensitive (sharp) ear; keenly alive (*för* to) **2** (*om rum o.d.*) insufficiently soundproof **-het** sensitiveness of hearing (ear) (*för* for); sensitive ear (*för* to); inadequacy of soundproofing
1 lykta *vl, se* sluta
2 lykta *sl* lantern; (*gat-, bil- o.d.*) lamp
lykt|gubbe *se* irrbloss **-stolpe** lamppost **-tändare** lamplighter
lymf|a *sl* lymph **-kärl** lymphatic [vessel] **-knuta** lymph node (gland) **-körtel** *se* -knuta
lymmel *s2* blackguard; scoundrel, villain **-aktig** *al* blackguardly; villainous
lynch|a lynch **-ning** lynching
lynn|e *s6* **1** (*läggning*) temperament; (*sinnelag*) disposition, temper; *ha ett häftigt ~* have a hasty temper **2** (*sinnesstämning*) humour; temper, mood; *vara vid dåligt ~* (*äv.*) be in low spirits **lynneskast** *tvära ~* temperamental ups and downs **lynnesutbrott** outburst of temper **lynnig** *al* capricious
1 lyr|a *sl* (*kast*) throw; *ta -or* catch balls
2 lyra *sl* (*mus. o friare*) lyre
lyr|formig [-å:-] *al* lyre-shaped **-fågel** lyrebird **ly'rik** *s3* lyrics (*pl*); lyric poetry **lyriker** ['ly:-] lyric poet **lyrisk** ['ly:-] *a5* lyric; *bli ~* (*vard.*) grow lyrical
lys|a *v3* **1** (*avge ljus*) shine (*klart* bright[ly]); give (shed) light; (*glänsa*) gleam, glitter; (*glöda*) glow; *det -er i köket* the light is (lights are) on in the kitchen **2** *bildl.* shine (*av* with); *ansiktet -te av lycka* his (*etc.*) face was alight with happiness; *glädjen -te i hans ögon* joy shone in his eyes; *~ inför andra* show off before other people; *~ med sina kunskaper* (*äv.*) make a display of one's knowledge; *~ med sin frånvaro* be conspicuous by one's abscence; *~ med lånta fjädrar* (*äv.*) strut in borrowed plumes; *~ upp* light up, (*illuminera*) illuminate, (*friare äv.*) lighten, brighten [up] **3** *~ ngn* light s.b. (*nedför en trappa* down a staircase) **4** *det -er för dem* the banns are to be published for them
lysande *a4* **1** shining *etc.*; (*klar*) bright; (*själv-*) luminous; (*strålande*) radiant; (*om t.ex. dräkter*) resplendent (*i granna färger* in gay colours) **2** *bildl.* brilliant; (*storartad*) splendid; (*bländande*) dazzling (*framgång* success); (*frejdad*) illustrious; (*~ resultat* (*äv.*) spectacular result; *ett ~ undantag* (*äv.*) an outstanding exception; *gick allt annat än ~* was by no means a brilliant success

L

lysboj–långods   324

lys|boj light buoy **-bomb** flare
lys|e *s6* light[ing] **-färg** luminous paint **-gas** coal (town, city) gas **-kraft** luminosity **-mask** glow-worm
lysning [-y:-] banns (*pl*) **lysningspresent** wedding present
lysol [-'så:l] *s3, kem.* lysol
lys|olja lamp oil **-rör** fluorescent tube **-rörsarmatur** fluorescent tube fittings, neon light fittings (*pl*)
lyssna listen (*efter* for; *på* to) **lyssnarapparat** *mil.* sound detection apparatus, sound locator **lyssnare** listener **lyssnarpost** *mil.* listening post; (*radio. etc.*) listeners' mail
lysten *a3* (*glupsk*) greedy (*efter* for); (*girig*) covetous (*efter* for); (*ivrig*) eager (*på* for)
1 lyster ['lyss-] *s3, s2* lustre
2 lyster ['lyss-] *pres sg, imperf. lyste, vanl. opers., det ~ mig att* I have a good mind to
lystmäte *s6, få sitt ~* have one's fill (*på* of)
lystnad *s3* greediness *etc.*; greed
lystra pay attention; obey (*äv. ~ till*); (*spetsa öronen*) prick up one's (its) ears; *~ till ett namn* answer to a name **-ing** response; obedience; *~!* (*mil.*) attention! **-ingsord** word of command, call to attention
lystråd [ˣly:s-] filament
lyte *s6* defect; deformity; *bildl.* fault, vice
1 lytt *a1* maimed, crippled, disabled
2 lytt *a, n, se lyhörd*
lyx *s3* luxury; (*i fråga om mat o. dryck*) sumptuousness; (*överdåd*) extravagance **-artikel** luxury **-bil** luxury car, de luxe model **-hotell** luxury (first-class) hotel
lyx|ig *a1* luxurious **-kryssare** luxury cruiser **-liv** life of luxury **-skatt** luxury tax **-telegram** greetings telegram **-upplaga** de luxe edition
låd|a *s1* **1** box; (*större äv.*) case; (*byrå- o.d.*) drawer; (*maträtt*) dish cooked in a baking-dish **2** *hålla ~* talk the hind leg(s) off a donkey **-kamera** box camera
1 låg *imperf. av ligga*
2 låg *~t lägre lägst* low; *bildl.* low, mean, base; *hysa ~a tankar om* have a poor opinion of
låg|a I *s1* flame (*äv. bildl.*); (*starkare*) blaze; *bli -ornas rov* perish in [the] flames; *stå i ljusan ~* be [all] ablaze; *föremålet för hans ömma ~* the object of his tender passion **II** *v1* blaze; flame (*äv. bildl.*); (*glöda*) glow (*av* with)
lågad|el *~n* the lesser nobility, (*i Storbritannien ung.*) the gentry **-lig** of (belonging to) the lesser nobility (*etc.*)
lågande *a4* blazing; flaming; burning (*hat* hatred); *med ~ kinder* (*äv.*) with cheeks afire
låg|avlönad low-paid **-frekvens** low frequency **-halsad** *a5* low-necked **-halt** *vara ~* have one leg shorter than the other **-het** lowness *etc.* **-hus** low-rise building **-inkomsttagare** low-income earner **-klackad** *a5* low-heeled **-konjunktur** depression, economic (business) recession, slump **-kyrklig** Low-Church **-land** lowland[s *pl*] **-länt** *a1* low-lying **-lönegrupp** low-income category (group) **-mäld** [-ä:-] *a1* low-voiced, low-key (*äv. bildl.*); *bildl.* quiet, unobtrusive **-mäldhet** [-ä:-] *bildl.* quietness *etc.* **-mält** [-ä:-] *adv* in a low voice **-nivåspråk** *data.* low-level language **-sinnad** *a5 se*

-sint -sint *a1* base, mean **-skor** shoes **-slätt** lowland plain **-spänning** low voltage **-stadielärare** junior level teacher **-stadium** beginning stage, junior stage; *-stadiet* (*skol.*) primary department **-säsong** off season
lågt [-å:-] *lägre lägst, adv* low; *bildl.* basely, meanly; *~ räknat* at a low estimate
låg|tryck 1 *meteor.* depression, low **2** *fys.* low pressure **-trycksområde** low pressure area
lågtstående *a4* (*om kultur o.d.*) primitive
låg|tyska Low German **-vatten** low water; (*vid ebb*) low tide **-vattenmärke** *bildl.* low-water mark **-växt** *a1* short
lån *s7* loan (*mot ränta* at interest; *mot säkerhet* on security); *ordet är ett ~ från engelskan* the word has been borrowed from the English; *ha ngt till ~s* have s.th. on loan, have borrowed s.th.
låna 1 (*ut-*) lend (*åt* to); *AE. äv.* loan; (*förskottera*) advance; *~ ut* lend [out]; *~ sitt namn åt* allow one's name to be used by; *~ sig till* lend o.s. to **2** (*få t. låns*) borrow (*av* from); *~ upp* borrow; *~ pengar på* raise money on
låne|ansökan loan application **-belopp** amount of the loan, loan (credit) amount **-bibliotek** lending library; circulating library **-handling** loan (credit) document **-verksamhet** lending operations (*pl*) **-villkor** *pl* terms of a loan, loan terms
lång *~t längre längst* **1** (*om tid o. rum*) long; (*väl ~, -randig etc.*) lengthy; (*tämligen ~*) longish; (*stor*) great (*avstånd* distance), big (*steg* stride); *lagens arm är ~* the arm of the law is far-reaching; *lika ~* of equal length; *hela ~a dagen* all day long; *inte på ~a vägar så bra* not by a long way (not anything like) so good; *han blev ~ i ansiktet* his face fell; *det tar inte ~ tid att* it won't take long to; *tiden blir ~ när* time seems long when; *på ~ sikt* in the long run, on the long term, long-range ... **2** (*om pers.*) tall
långa *s1, zool.* ling
lång|bent [-e:-] *a1* long-legged **-bord** long table **-byxor** *pl* long trousers, (*fritids-*) slacks **-dans** long-line dance **-distanslöpning** long-distance race **-distansrobot** long-range [guided] missile **-dragen** *a3, bildl.* protracted (*debatt* debate); lengthy; (*tröttsam*) tedious **-film** long (full-length) film **-finger** middle finger **-fingrad** *a5, bildl.* light-fingered **-franska** *s1, s7, ung.* tin loaf **-fredag** Good Friday (*äv. ~en*) **-fristig** *a1* long-term **-färd** long trip (expedition, voyage) **-färdssegling** long-distance sailing **-färdsskridsko** long-distance skate **-grund** (*om strand*) shelving; (*om vatten*) shoaling **-hårig** long-haired
långivare lender; granter of a loan
lång|kalsonger *pl* long underpants, *vard.* long johns **-kok** long, slow cooking **-körare** pjäsen har blivit en ~ the play has had a very long run **-körning** long-distance run
lång|lig *a1* longish; *på ~a tider* for ever so long, for ages **-livad** *a5* long-lived; *inte bli ~* not last long, (*om pers.*) not be long for this world **-mjölk** processed sour milk **-modig** patient, forbearing, long-suffering
långgods borrowed (loaned) property

lång|promenad *ta sig en ~* go for a long walk **-randig** *bildl.* long-winded, tedious[ly long] **-resa** long journey (*sjö.* voyage) **-rev** long line **långsam** *a1* slow (*i, med* in, at, over); (*trög, äv. om puls*) sluggish; (*maklig*) leisurely; (*senfärdig*) tardy **långsamt** *adv* slowly; *~ men säkert* slow[ly] but sure[ly]; *ett ~ verkande gift* a slow[-working] poison; *det går ~ för dem att* it is a slow business their (+ *ing-form*), they are so slow in (+ *ing-form*) **långsamhet** slowness *etc.*

lång|sida long side **-sides** alongside **-siktig** *a1* long-range, long-term **-siktsplanering** long-range planning **-sint** *a1* resentful **-sjal** *vard.* one grand (= 1 000 kronor bill) **-skallig** dolichocephalic, dolichocephalous **-skepp 1** *byggn.* nave **2** (*drakskepp*) longship **-skepps** [-ʃ-] *sjö.* fore-and-aft **-skjutande** *a4* long-range **-skäggig** long-bearded **-sluttande** *a4* gradually sloping **-smal** long and narrow **-spelande** *a4* long-playing (*skiva* record) **-strumpa** stocking **-sträckt** *a1* of some length, longish **-synt** [-y:-] *a1* long-sighted **-sökt** [-ö:-] *a4* far-fetched; strained

långt *längre längst, adv* **1** *rumsbet.* far (*härifrån* [away] from here); a long way (*dit* there; *till* to); *gå ~* (*bildl.*) go far, rise high [in life]; *gå för ~* (*bildl.*) go too far; *nu går det för ~!* this is too much of a good thing!; *hon hade inte ~ till tårarna* her tears were not far off; *man kommer inte ~ med fem shilling* you don't get far with five shillings; *så ~* thus (so) far; *så ~ ögat når* as far as the eye can see; *resa ~ bort* go a long journey; *vi har ~ till affären* we have a long way to go to the shop; *det är ~ mellan bra filmer* good films are few and far between; *det är ~ mellan gårdarna* the farms are far apart; *det är ~ mellan blixtarna* the lightning flashes come at long intervals; *~ inne i tunneln* far (well) down the tunnel **2** *tidsbet.* long (*efteråt* afterwards); far (*in på det nya året* into the new year); *~ innan* long (a long while) before; *~ om länge* at long last; *så ~ jag kan minnas tillbaka* as far back as I can remember **3** (*vida*) far (*bättre* better; *överlägsen* superior to); (*mycket äv.*) much, a great deal, a lot; *~ ifrån* (*ingalunda*) by no means **-gående** *a4* far-reaching, extensive, considerable **-ifrån** ['lånt-] *se långt* 3

lång|tidsprognos long-term (long-range) forecast **-tradare** transport (long- distance) lorry; *AE.* freight truck; *vard.* juggernaut **-tråkig** very tedious (*etc.*) **-varig** *a1* long; of long duration; (*utdragen*) lengthy, protracted; (*om t.ex. förbindelse*) long-standing **-varighet** lengthiness, protractedness **-våg** *radio.* long wave **-vård** long-term treatment, long-stay care **-vårdsklinik** long-stay ward **-väga** *oböjl. a o. adv* from a [long] distance; *en ~ gäst* a guest [who has come] from afar; *~ ifrån* from far away **-ärmad** *a5* long-sleeved

lån|ord loan word **-tagare** borrower

1 lår *s2* (*låda*) [large] box; (*pack-*) case, chest

2 lår *s7* thigh

lår|ben thighbone, *fack.* femur **-bensbrott** fractured thigh[bone] **-benshals** neck of the femur

låring *sjö.* quarter

lås *s7* lock; (*häng-*) padlock; (*knäppe*) clasp, catch; *inom ~ och bom* under lock and key; *gå i ~* (*bildl.*) go without a hitch

lås|a *v3* lock; *~ in* lock up; *~ upp* unlock; *~ sig* (*om sak*) get locked, jam, (*fastna*) get stuck; *~ sig ute* lock o.s. out **-anordning** locking device **-bar** *a1* lockable, lock-up **-kolv** spring (latch) bolt **-mekanism** lock device (mechanism) **-smed** locksmith **-vred** door handle

låt *s2* (*melodi*) melody, tune, song; (*ljud*) sound, *bildl.* tune

1 låt|a *lät -it* (*ljuda, lyda*) sound (*som* like); *det -er misstänkt* it sounds suspicious; *maskinen -er illa* the machine makes a row; *det -er oroväckande* the news is alarming; *jo, det -er något det!* (*iron.*) tell me another one!; *det -er som om han tänkte komma* [from what I (*etc.*) hear] it seems as if he would come; *du -er inte vidare glad* you don't sound very cheerful

2 låt|a *lät -it* **I** *hjälpv* **1** let; allow to; permit to; *~ bli* leave (let) s.th. alone; *~ ngt ligga* (*stå*) leave s.th. alone (where it is); *~ nyckeln sitta kvar i låset* leave the key in the lock; *ingen lät märka något* no one let on about it; *~ saken bero* let the matter rest, drop the matter; *~ vara* leave alone; *låt vara att* even though, although; *låt så vara, men* that may be so, but **2** (*laga att*) have (*hämta ngt* s.th. fetched); get (*göra ngt* s.th. done); (*föranstalta att*) cause (*ngn göra ngt* s.b. to do s.th.); (*förmå*) make (*ngn göra ngt* s.b. do s.th.); *~ sömmerskan sy en klänning* get the dressmaker to make a dress; *låt se att* see to it that; *låt tala om sig* he gave people cause to talk [about him], he got himself talked about; *~ ngn förstå* give s.b. to understand; *~ ngn vänta* keep s.b. waiting, let s.b. wait **3** *det -er göra sig* it is possible, it can be done; *det -er höra sig!* that's s.th. like!; *~ sig väl smaka* tuck in; *det -er säga sig* it can (may) be said; *inte ~ säga sig ngt två gånger* not need to be asked twice; *~ övertala sig* allow o.s. to (let o.s.) be persuaded **4** *~ sitt vatten* pass one's water

låt|gåsystem [-ˣgå:-] laissez-faire [system]

låtit *sup. av 1, 2 låta*

låtsad [ˣlå(t)ss-] *a5* pretended *etc.*; (*falsk*) sham, mock, make-believe

låtsa|s [ˣlå(t)ss-] *dep* pretend; feign; make pretence of, simulate (*vara* being); *~ att* (*äv.*) make believe that; *han -des att han inte såg mig* he pretended not to see me; *~ som om det regnar* behave as if nothing were the matter; *~ inte om det!* don't let on about it!; *skall det här ~ vara ...?* is this supposed to be ...?

låtsaslek make believe

lä *n* lee; *i ~* to leeward, on the lee[ward] side; *komma i ~ för land* get under the lee of the land; *i ~ för vinden* sheltered from the wind, in the lee of the wind; *ligga i ~* (*bildl.*) fall short, be behindhand

läck *oböjligt a* leaky; *springa ~* spring a leak; *vara ~* leak, be a leak **läcka I** *s1* leak; *bildl.* leakage **II** *v3* leak (*om fartyg äv.*) make water; *~ ut* leak out (*äv. bildl.*) **läckage** *s7* leakage

läcker ['läck-] *a2* dainty, delicious **-bit** dainty, morcel; titbit **-gom** gourmet **-het** daintiness;

delicacy, dainty

läder ['lä:-] *s7* leather; *en ... av ~ (äv.)* a leather ... **-arbete** leather-work **-artad** [-a:r-] *a5* leather-like; leathery **-fåtölj** leather armchair **-hud** *anat.* leather-skin, corium, dermis **-imitation** imitation leather, leatherette **-lapp** *se fladdermus* **-plastik** embossed (raised) leather--work **-rem** leather strap **-varor** *pl* leather goods **-väska** leather bag

läge *s6* situation; position; *(plats)* place; *(nivå)* level; *(belägenhet)* site, location; *(tillstånd)* state, condition; *i soliga ~n (träd g.)* in a sunny location; *hålla ngt i ~* hold s.th. in position; *i nuvarande ~* as things stand at present; *i rätt ~* in place; *saken har kommit i ett nytt ~* the matter has entered a new phase, the situation has changed; *som ~t nu är* as matters now stand

lägel *s2* bottle; *(fat ung.)* puncheon

lägenhet 1 *se våning* **2** *efter råd och ~* according to one's means **3** *(transport- o.d., resetillfälle)* opportunity; means of transport; *(båt- äv.)* sailing, ship; *med första ~ (sjö.)* by the first ship [sailing]

läg|er ['lä:-] *s7* **1** *(tält- o.d.)* camp *(äv. bildl.)*; *slå ~* pitch [one's] camp, encamp; *det blev oro i -ret (bildl.)* everybody was upset **2** *(parti)* party; *ur olika ~* belonging to various parties **3** *(liggplats)* bed; *(djurs äv.)* lair; *reda sig ett ~* make a bed **-eld** camp fire **-liv** camp life **-plats** camp site, camping ground

lägervall *i uttr.: ligga i ~* be in a state of decay, lie waste

läges|bestämning determination of position **-energi** potential energy

1 lägg *s2, anat.* shank

2 lägg *s7 (pappers-, tidnings-)* file

lägga *lade lagt* **I** put; *(i vågrätt ställning äv.)* lay *(äv. bildl.)*; *(placera på viss plats, på visst sätt e.d.)* place; *(t. sängs)* put to bed; *(ordna sängplatser för)* put to sleep; *(anbringa)* apply *(på* to); *~ grundstenen till* lay the foundation stone of; *~ håret* have one's hair set; *~ ägg* lay eggs **II** *(med betonad partikel)* **1** *~ an (gevär o.d.)* level, point, aim *(på* at); *~ an på a)* *(eftersträva)* aim at, *b)* *(söka vinna)* make up to, make a dead set at **2** *~ bi (sjö.)* lay (heave) to **3** *~ bort (upphöra med)* give up, drop, *(ovana äv.)* leave off **4** *~ fram* put out; *jfr fram-* **5** *~ för ngn (vid måltid)* help s.b. to **6** *~ ifrån sig* put (lay) down **7** *~ ihop* put (place) together **8** *~ in (jfr in-) a)* *(ngt i)* put into, *b)* *se konservera*; *~ in ansökan* file (submit) an application; *~ in en brasa* lay a fire; *~ in golv* put down a floor, floor; *~ in hela sin själ i ngt (äv.)* do s.th. wholeheartedly **9** *~ ner a) se ned-, b)* *(pengar, möda o.d.)* spend, expend *(på* in, on), *c) (sin röst vid omröstning)* abstain [*sin röst* from voting], *d) (klänning)* let down, *e) (teaterpjäs)* withdraw **10** *~ om a) (ändra)* change, alter, *b) med.* bandage, bind up, dress; *~ om rodret* shift the helm **11** *~ på a)* put on, *b) (brev o.d.)* post; *~ på luren* hang up [the receiver] **12** *~ till a) (tillfoga)* add [on], *b) sjö.* put in *(vid* at) **13** *~ undan* put away, put aside **14** *~ under sig (bildl.)* subdue **15** *~ upp a)* put up *(på* on), *b) (mat)* dish up, *c) (klänning)*

shorten, put a tuck in, *d) (hår)* dress, *AE. äv.* fix up, *e) (maskor)* cast on, *f) (fartyg, förråd)* lay up, *g) (an-)* start, set up, *h) (upphöra med)* give up; *~ upp håret på rullar* set one's hair on rollers **16** *~ ut a)* lay out *(äv. pengar)*, *b) (klädesplagg)* let out, *c) sjö.* put off (out) *(från* from), *d) (bli tjock)* put on weight **III** *rfl a) (äv. ~ sig ner)* lie down, *(gå t. sängs)* go to bed, *(om sjuk)* take to one's bed, *b) (om sak)* settle, *(sänka sig)* descend, *(isbeläggas)* freeze, get frozen over, *c) bildl.* abate, subside, *(försvagas)* lie down (away), *(om svullnad)* go down; *~ sig i* interfere, meddle *(ngt* in s.th.); *lägg dig inte i det!* mind your own business!, *(äv.)* keep clear of that!; *~ sig till med (skägg o.d.)* grow, *(glasögon)* take to, *(titel e.d.)* adopt, *(bil e.d.)* acquire, *(tillägna sig)* appropriate; *~ sig ut för ngn* take up a p.'s cause, *(hos ngn)* intercede (put in a good word) for s.b. *(hos* with)

lägg|dags bedtime **-ning 1** *bildl.* disposition, character; *(håg)* bent, turn **2** *(hår-)* setting; *tvättning och ~* shampoo and set **-spel** jigsaw puzzle

läglig [*läg-] *a1* opportune, timely; *(passande)* suitable, convenient; *vid första ~a tillfälle* at your earliest convenience

lägra [*lä:g-] *rfl* encamp; *(om dimma, damm o.d.)* settle

lägre ['lä:g-] *komp. t. låg, lågt* **I** *a* lower; *(i rang, värde o.d.)* inferior *(än to)* **II** *adv* lower

lägst [-ä:-] *superl. t. låg, lågt* lowest; *~a växeln (på bil)* the low gear; *till ~a möjliga pris* at the lowest possible price, at rock-bottom price; *i ~a laget* too low; *som ~* at its (their) lowest

läk|a *v3* heal *(igen* over, up) *(äv. bildl.)*; *(bota)* cure; *tider -er alla sår* time heals all wounds **läkande** *a4* healing; curative

läkar|arvode medical (doctor's) fee **-behandling** medical treatment **-besök** visit to a doctor **-bok** medical book

läkar|e doctor; physician; *(kirurg)* surgeon; *praktiserande ~* general practitioner; *kvinnlig ~* woman doctor; *gå till ~* see (consult) a doctor, seek medical advice; *tillkalla ~* call in a doctor **-hus** health centre **-intyg** doctor's (medical) certificate **-kår** *~en* the medical profession **-mottagning** surgery; consulting rooms *(pl)* **-recept** [doctor's] presription **-sekreterare** medical secretary **-undersökning** medical examination (inspection), physical examination **-vetenskap** medical science *(äv. ~en)* **-vård** medical attendance (care)

läkas *v3, dep* heal [up]

läke|dom [-dɷmm] *s3* cure **-konst** [the] art of healing; *utöva ~en* practise medicine **-medel** medicine; pharmaceutical preparation; drug; *(botemedel)* remedy **-medelsindustri** pharmaceutical industry **-medelsmissbruk** drug abuse

läk|kött *ha gott ~* have flesh that heals quickly **-ning** [-ä:-] healing **-ningsprocess** process of healing

läkt *s3 (ribba)* lath, batten

1 läktare *(åskådar-)* gallery; *(utomhus)* platform, stand; *(utan tak) AE. äv.* bleachers

2 läktare *sjö.* lighter

läktarvåld *ung.* football hooliganism

läm [lämm] *s2* (*lucka*) flap

lämmel *s2* lemming **-tåg** lemming migration

lämn|a 1 leave; (*ge sig av*) quit; (*överge äv.*) give up; (*befattning äv.*) retire from; ~ *mycket övrigt att önska* leave a great deal to be desired; ~*r mig ingen ro* gives me no peace; ~ *i arv åt ngn* leave to s.b. **2** (*över-*) hand (*ngn ngt* s.b. s.th., s.th. [over] to s.b.); leave; (*in-*) hand in; *hand äv.* render; (*ge, skänka*) give; (*hjälp äv.*) render; (*bevilja*) grant; (*avkasta*) yield **3** ~ *ifrån sig* hand over; ~ *igen* return, give back; ~ *kvar* leave [behind] **-ing** *se kvarleva*

lämp|a I *s1*, *-or* gentle means; *gå fram med -or* go gently, use velvet gloves; *bruka -or med ngn* coax s.b.; *ta ngn med -or* coax s.b. into [doing] s.th. II *v1* **1** (*anpassa*) adapt, accommodate, suit (*efter* to); (*justera*) adjust (*efter* to); ~ *sig* (*foga sig*) adapt (accommodate, suit) o.s. (*efter* to); ~ *sig för* be adapted (suited) for **2** *sjö.* trim; ~ *över bord* jettison

lämp|ad *a5* adapted (*efter* to); suited (*för* for) **-lig** *a1* suitable, fitting; (*som duger, äv.*) fit; (*om anmärkning, behandling äv.*) appropriate; (*lagom*) adequate; (*tillbörlig*) due, proper; (*rådlig*) advisable, expedient; (*läglig*) opportune, convenient; *vidtaga ~a åtgärder* take appropriate action; *vid ~t tillfälle* at a suitable (convenient) opportunity **-ligen** suitably *etc.*; *det görs* ~ it is best done **-lighet** suitability; fitness

lämpor *se lämpa I*

län *s7, ung.* county, administrative district, province

länd *s3* loin; (*på djur*) hind quarters (*pl*); *omgjorda sina ~er* gird up one's loins

lända *v2*, ~ *ngn till heder* redound to a p.'s honour; ~ *ngn till varning* serve as a warning to s.b.

länga [-ŋ-] *s1* (*rad*) row, range; *jfr huslänga*

längd [-ŋd] *s3* **1** (*i rum*) length; (*människas*) height, tallness, stature; *geogr.* longitude; *tre meter på ~en* three metres in length; *i hela sin* ~ full length; *resa sig i hela sin* ~ draw o.s. up to one's full height; *på ~en* (*äv.*) lengthways, lengthwise; *största* ~ (*sjö.*) length over all **2** (*i tid*) length; *i ~en* in the end, in the long run; *dra ut på ~en* be prolonged **-axel** longitudinal axis **-grad** [degree of] longitude **-hopp** long (*AE.* broad) jump **-hoppare** long-jumper **-löpning** long-distance racing **-mått** linear (long) measure **-riktning** longitudinal direction; *i ~en* lengthwise, longitudinally; *i papperets* ~ lengthways of the paper

läng|e [-ŋ-] *-re -st, adv* long; (*i påståendesats*) [for] a long time (while); (*lång stund äv.*) for long; *ganska* ~ [for] quite a long time (while); *både ~ och väl* no end of a time; *hur ~ till?* how much longer?; *för ~ sedan* a long time (while) ago, long ago; *på* ~ for a long time, for ever so long; *sitt ner så* ~! take a seat while you wait!; *så ~ som* as (*nekande:* so) long as; *så ~ jag kan minnas* ever since I can remember; *än så* ~ for the present (the time being)

längesedan long (a long time) ago; *vard.* ages ago

längre ['läŋ-] *komp. t.* lång, långt, länge I *a* **1** longer; (*rumsbet. äv.*) farther, further; (*högre*) taller; *göra* ~ (*äv.*) lengthen; *för* ~ *avstånd än* (*äv.*) for distances greater than **2** (*utan jämförelse*) long; (*om t.ex. tal, paus, äv.*) longish, lengthy, of some length; *någon* ~ *tid kan jag inte stanna* I cannot stay very long; *under en* ~ *tid* for a considerable time, for quite a long time II *adv* (*om rum, tid*) further, farther; (*om tid äv.*) longer; *det går inte* ~ *att* it is no longer possible to; *det finns inte* ~ it does not exist any longer; ~ *bort* farther away; ~ *fram* further on, (*senare*) later on

längs [-ŋs] ~ [*efter* (*med*)] along; (~ *sidan av*) alongside **-efter** [-'efter, 'läŋs-] along **-gående** *a4* longitudinal **-'med** along

längst [-ŋst] *superl. t.* lång, långt, länge I *a* longest; (*högst*) tallest; *i ~a laget* too long if anything; *i det ~a* as long as possible, (*t.ex. hoppas att*) to the [very] last II *adv* farthest, furthest (*bort* away); ~ *bak* rearmost; ~ *ner* (*upp*) at the [very] bottom (top) (*i* of); ~ *till vänster* (*äv.*) at the extreme left

längta [-ŋ-] long, yearn (*efter* for; *efter att* to); ~ *efter att ngn skall komma* (*äv.*) be looking forward to a p.'s coming; ~ *bort* long to get away; ~ *hem* be homesick, long for home

längtan *r* longing (*efter* for); *förgås av* ~ *att ngn skall* be dying [with longing] for s.b. to (+ *inf.*) **längtande** *a4*, **längtansfull** longing, yearning; (*om blick äv.*) wistful

länk [-ŋk] *s2* link (*äv. bildl.*); *felande* ~ missing link **länka** chain (*fast vid* on to); (*foga*) join, link on ('*till* to) (*äv. bildl.*); *bildl. äv.* guide

1 läns *oböjl. a*, *pumpa* ~ pump dry, drain; *hålla en båt* ~ (*äv.*) keep the water out of a boat; *ösa en båt* ~ bail out a boat

2 läns *s2*, *sjö.* following wind

1 länsa 1 *se pumpa läns under 1 läns* **2** (*friare*) empty; *bildl.* drain (*på* of); *vard.* clear out; (*förråd äv.*) make a clean sweep of

2 länsa *sjö.* run [before the wind]

läns|arbetsnämnd county labour (employment) board **-bokstav** (*på bil*) county registration letter **-bostadsnämnd** county housing board **-herre** *hist.* feoffor, feudal lord **-man** ['läns-] *ung.* constable; head of the county constabulary **-polischef** county police commissioner

läns|pump bilge-pump **-pumpa** *se under 1 läns*

läns|råd county director **-rätt** county administrative court **-skolnämnd** county board of education **-styrelse** county administrative board

länstol ['lä:n-, 'länn-] armchair, easy chair

läns|åklagare county prosecutor **-åklagarmyndighet** county public prosecution authority

läpp *s2* lip; *falla ngn på ~en* be to (suit) a p.'s taste; *hänga* ~ (*bildl.*) sulk; *melodin är på allas ~ar* the song is on everybody's lips **läppja** ~ *på* sip [at], just taste, *bildl.* have a taste of **läppstift** lipstick

lär *v, end. i pres* **1** (*torde*) *han* ~ *nog* he is likely to; *jag* ~ *väl inte få se honom mer* I don't expect to see him again **2** (*påstås*) *han* ~ *vara* he is said (supposed) to be

lära I *s1* doctrine; (*tro*) faith; (*vetenskap*) science, theory; (*hantverks-*) apprenticeship; *gå i ~ hos* be apprenticed (an apprentice) to **II** *v2* **1** (*~ andra*) teach (*ngn franska* s.b. French); (*undervisa äv.*) instruct (*ngn engelska* s.b. in English); *~ bort till ngn* let s.b. into; *~ ut* teach (*ngt t. ngn* s.th. to s.b.) **2** (*~ sig*) learn; *ha svårt för att ~* be slow at learning **3** *rfl* learn (*att skriva* [how] to write); (*tillägna sig äv.*) acquire, pick up; *~ sig uppskatta* come (grow) to appreciate
läraktig *a1* ready (willing) to learn, docile, quick at learning; apt (*elev* pupil) **-het** readiness to learn, teachability
lärarbana teaching career
lärar|e teacher (*för* of, for; *i franska* of French); instructor; (*t. yrket äv.*) schoolmaster; (*i sht vid högre skola*) master **-fortbildning** teacher in-service training **-högskola** college of education, teacher training college
lärarinna [woman] teacher, [school]mistress; *vard.* schoolmarm **lärarinneaktig** *a1* schoolmarmish
lärar|kandidat student teacher **-kår** teaching staff **-rum** staff room **-tjänst** teaching post **-yrket** the teaching profession
lärd [-ä:-] *a1* learned; (*grundligt*) erudite; (*vetenskaplig*) scholarly; *en ~* [*man*] a learned (*etc.*) man, a man of learning; *gå den ~a vägen* go in for (take up) an academic career
lärdom [ˣlä:rdɷmm] *s2* **1** (*kunskaper*) learning; erudition; scholarship **2** *dra ~ av* learn from
lärdoms|grad academic degree **-historia** history of learning **-högfärd** pride of learning **-prov** test of scholarship
lärft *s4, s3* linen
lärjung|e [ˣlärr-] pupil; scholar; (*friare*) disciple; *Jesu -ar* the Disciples of Christ
lärk|a *s1* [sky]lark **-falk** hobby
lärkträd larch [tree]
lärkving|e *gå som -ar* (*bildl.*) twinkle, flash
lär|ling [-ä:-] apprentice; trainee **-lingstid** apprenticeship [period]
läro|anstalt educational institution **-bok** textbook; manual; (*nybörjarbok*) primer **-byggnad** (*-system*) doctrinal system **-dikt** didactic poem **-fader** *kyrkl.* father of the Church; (*friare*) master **-medel** *pl* educational (teaching) materials **-mästare** master; *ta ngn till ~* take s.b. as one's teacher **-plan** curriculum **-rik** instructive; informative; *föga ~* not very instructive **-sal** *univ.* lecture room, (*större*) lecture theatre **-sats** precept, thesis, doctrine **-spån** *s7, göra sina första ~* make one's first tentative efforts, serve one's apprenticeship **-stol** [professor's, professorial] chair **-säte** seat of learning, educational centre **-verk** [-värk] *s7* secondary [grammar] school; *AE. ung.* high school and junior college; *tekniskt ~* technical college
läroverks|adjunkt assistant master [at a secondary (grammar) school] **-lärare** secondary school master (teacher)
läroår apprenticeship year, (*friare*) training year
lär|pengar *betala ~* pay for one's experience **-pojke** boy apprentice
läsa *v3* **1** read (*för ngn* to s.b.; *hos, i* in; *om*

about; *ur* from; *på läpparna* from the lips); (*genom-*) peruse; *~ en bön* say a prayer; *~ korrektur* proofread; *~ ut en bok* finish [reading] a book **2** (*studera*) read (*juridik* law; *på en examen* for an examination), study; *~ in* learn (study up) thoroughly; *~* [*på sina*] *läxor* prepare (do) one's homework **3** (*få undervisning* [*i*]) take (have) lessons (*franska för* in French from); (*för privatlärare äv.*) coach (*för* with); *gå och ~* (*för prästen*) be prepared for one's confirmation **4** (*ge undervisning i*) teach, give lessons in; *~ latin med en klass* take Latin with a class; *~ läxor med ngn* help s.b. with his (*etc.*) homework
läs|are 1 reader **2** *relig.* pietist **-art** reading, version **-bar** *a1* readable **-barhet** readability **-drama** chamber drama
läse|bok reader; (*nybörjar- äv.*) reading-book **-cirkel** reading-circle **-krets** readers (*pl*), public; *stor ~* wide readership **-sal** reading room
läs|glasögon reading glasses **-hunger** appetite for reading **-hungrig** eager to read; *vara ~* (*äv.*) be an avid reader **-huvud** *ha gott ~* have a good head for study (studying)
läsida leeward side; *på ~n* leewards
läsk *s2, vard.* soft drink, *AE.* pop
läsk|a 1 (*med -papper*) blot, dry with blotting paper **2** (*släcka törsten*) quench; (*svalka*) cool; (*uppfriska*) refresh (*äv. bildl.*); *~ sig* refresh o.s.
läskedryck [flavoured] mineral water, lemonade, soft drink
läsklass remedial reading class (form)
läskpapper (*ett* a sheet of) blotting paper
läs|kunnig able to read **-lampa** reading lamp; (*säng-*) bedside lamp
läslig [-ä:-] *a1* legible, readable **-het** legibility, readability
läs|lust inclination for (love of) reading (study) **-ning** [-ä:-] reading; (*lektyr äv.*) reading matter **-- och skrivkunnighet** literacy **-- och skrivsvårigheter** *pl* problems in reading and writing **-ordning** timetable, curriculum
läsp|a lisp **-ning** lisp[ing]
läst *s3* (*sko-*) last **lästa** *~* [*ut*] last
läs|värd worth reading **-år** school year; *univ.* academic year **-ämne** (*motsats övningsämne*) theoretical subject **-övning** reading exercise (practice)
lät *imperf. av 1, 2 låta*
läte *s6* [inarticulate] sound; (*djurs*) call, cry
lätt I *a1* (*motsats tung*) light (*äv. bildl.*); (*om t.ex. cigarr, öl*) mild; *med ~ hand* lightly, gently; *~ om hjärtat* light of heart; *känna sig ~ om hjärtat* feel light-hearted; *~ på foten* light of foot, *bildl.* of easy virtue **2** (*lindrig*) slight (*förkylning* cold); easy (*rullning* roll); gentle (*bris* breeze); (*svag*) faint; *ett ~ arbete* (*äv.*) a soft job **3** (*motsats svår*) easy; (*enkel*) simple; *göra det ~ för sig* make things easy for o.s.; *han har ~ för språk* languages come easy to him, he finds languages easy; *ha ~* [*för*] *att* find it easy to **II** *adv* **1** (*motsats tungt*) light; (*ytligt, nätt o. jämnt*) lightly, gently; (*mjukt*) softly; *väga ~* (*äv. bildl.*) weigh light; *sova ~* sleep lightly; *ta ngt ~* take s.th. lightly, make light of s.th. **2** (*lindrigt*) slightly; (*ngt litet*)

somewhat **3** (*motsats svårt*) easily; readily; *vard.* easy; ~ *fånget*, ~ *förgånget* easy come, easy go; *man glömmer så* ~ *att* one is so apt to forget (one so easily forgets) that **lätt|a 1** (*göra -are, lyfta*) lighten; (*samvete, tryck o.d.*) ease; (*spänning*) relieve, alleviate; ~ *ankar* weigh anchor; ~ *sitt hjärta* unburden one's mind (*för ngn* to s.b.) **2** (*ge -nad*) be (give) a (some) relief; (*bli -are*) become lighter (*etc.*); (*minska i vikt*) go down in weight **3** (*om dimma o.d.*) lift, become less dense; *det börjar* ~ it is beginning to clear up **4** (*bildl., bli mindre svår*) ease; *det har* ~*t litet* things have eased a little **5** (*lyfta*) lift; *flyg. äv.* rise, take off; ~ *på förlåten* lift the smoke screen, abandon secrecy; ~ *på restriktionerna* ease the restrictions; ~ *på pungen* lighten one's purse **lätt|ad** *a5, bildl.* eased, relieved **-antändlig** *a1* [highly] inflammable **-are** *komp. t. lätt* **I a** lighter *etc.*, *se lätt I*; (*utan jämförelse*) light *etc.* **II** *adv* more lightly *etc.*, *se lätt II*; ~ *sagt* än *gjort* easier said than done **-bearbetad** *a5* easy to work **-begriplig** easily understood; obvious **-betong** porous concrete **-fattlig** *a1* easily comprehensible, easy to understand; intelligible **-flytande** (*om vätska*) of low viscosity; (*om skrivsätt, tal*) fluent, flowing **-fotad** *a5* **1** light-footed **2** *se lättfärdig* **-framkomlig** (*om skog o.d.*) [easily] penetrable; (*om väg o.d.*) easy to go (walk *etc.*) along (on) **-funnen** *a5* easily found **-fångad** *a5* easily caught (come by) **-färdig** frivolous; (*osedlig*) of lax morals; (*lösaktig*) wanton **-färdighet** frivolousness *etc.* **-förklarlig** *av* ~*a skäl* for obvious reasons **-förståelig** easy to understand **-förtjänt** easily earned (*etc.*) **-hanterlig** easy to handle, easily handled; *bildl.* easily manageable **lätthet 1** lightness *etc.* **2** easiness; simplicity; (*t.ex. att lära sig*) ease; (*t.ex. att uttrycka sig*) facility; *med* ~ (*äv.*) easily **lätting** idler, slacker **lättja** *s1* laziness; idleness, indolence **lättjefull** lazy; indolent **lätt|köpt** [-çö:-] *a1, bildl.* easily won, cheap **-lagad** *a5* **1** (*om mat*) easy to prepare **2** (*-reparerad*) easy to repair **-ledd** *a1* easily guided (led); (*om pers. äv.*) tractable **-lurad** *a5* easily taken in (duped *etc.*); *han är* ~ he's a sucker (*vard.*) **-läslig** (*om handstil*) legible **-läst** [-ä:-] *a4* **1** *se lättläslig* **2** (*om bok, författare*) easy to read **-löslig** easily dissolvable **-manövrerad** *a5* manageable, handy; *flyg.* manoeuvv[e]rable **-matros** ordinary seaman **-metall** light metal **-mjölk** low-fat milk **lättna** become (get) lighter; *bildl.* lighten, become brighter; *det börjar* ~ (*äv.*) things are looking up **lättnad** *s3, bildl.* relief (*för* for, to), alleviation; (*i restriktioner*) relaxing (*i* of), relaxation (*i* in, of); (*förenkling*) simplification; *det känns som en* ~ it is a relief; *dra en* ~*ens suck* breathe a sigh of relief **lätt|påverkad** *a5* easily influenced (affected), impressionable **-retlig** irritable; touchy **-road** *a5* easily amused **-rökt** lightly smoked **-rörd** (*bildl. om pers.*) easily moved (*etc.*); (*om sinne*) excitable; (*om hjärta*) responsive; (*känslosam*) emotional **-rörlig** mobile; *bildl.* very

active **-saltad** *a5* slightly salted **-sam** *a1* easy **-sinne** (*obetänksamhet*) thoughtlessness, recklessness; (*slarv*) carelessness; (*-färdighet*) frivolousness, wantonness **-sinnig** *a1* light-hearted, happy-go-lucky, easy-going; (*om handling äv.*) thoughtless; (*-färdig*) wanton, loose **-sjungen** *a3* that sings well **-skrämd** *a5* easily frightened; fearful **-skött** [-ʃött] *a1* easy to handle, easily operated (worked) **-smält** *a1* **1** (*om födoämne*) easily digested, digestible **2** (*om bok o.d.*) *se lättläst* **-stekt** [-e:-] *a1* lightly done, underdone; *AE. rare* **-stött** *bildl.* ready to take offence, touchy **-såld** marketable, readily sold; *en* ~ *vara* (*äv.*) a product with ready sale **-sövd** *a5, vara* ~ be a light sleeper **-tillgänglig** (*hopskr. lättillgänglig*) that can easily be got at; accessible; (*om pers. äv.*) responsive, easy to get on with **-trogen** (*hopskr. lättrogen*) credulous, gullible **-vikt** *sport.* lightweight **-viktare** *sport.* lightweight **-vin** wine **-vindig** *a1* (*ej svår*) easily made, simple; (*bekväm*) handy; (*utan omsorg*) easy-going; (*slarvig*) careless **-vunnen** *a5* easily won **-åtkomlig** easy to get at, easily accessible (*vard.* get-at-able) **-öl** light lager beer **läx|a 1** *s1* lesson (*till* for); *ge ngn en* ~ give (*bildl.* teach) s.b. a lesson; *ha i* (*till*) ~ have as homework **II** *v1*, ~ *upp ngn* read s. b. a lesson, lecture s.b., *vard.* read the riot act to s.b. **-bok** lesson-book, textbook **-förhör** questioning on homework **-läsning** preparation (learning) of one's homework **löd** *imperf av 1, 2 lyda* **löda** *v2* solder; (*hård-*) braze **lödder** ['lödd-] *s7* lather; (*tvål- äv.*) soapsuds (*pl*); (*fradga äv.*) foam, froth **löddra** lather (*äv.* ~ *sig*) **löddrig** *a1* lathery; (*om häst vanl.*) foaming **lödig** *a1* (*om silver*) standard; *bildl.* sterling **-het** [standard of] fineness; *bildl.* sterling character (quality) **löd|kolv** soldering iron **-lampa** blowlamp, soldering lamp **-ning** [-ö:-] soldering **-pasta** solder [paste] **-tenn** soldering [tin], soft (tin) solder **-vätska** soldering-fluid **löfte** *s6* promise (*om* of; [*om*] *att* to + *inf.*, of + *ing-* form); (*högtidligare*) vow; *avlägga ett* ~ make a promise; *bunden av ett* ~ (*äv.*) under a vow; *ha fått* ~ *om* have had a promise of, have been promised; *ta* ~ *av ngn* exact a promise from s.b.; *hålla sitt* ~ keep one's promise; *mot* ~ *om* on the promise of **löftes|brott** breach of one's promise **-brytare** promise-breaker **-rik** promising, full of promise **löga** *rfl, åld.* bathe **lögn** [löŋn] *s3*,lie; falsehood; (*liten*) fib; (*stor, vard.*) whopper; *fara med* ~ tell a lie (lies); *det var* ~ *att få ngt ur henne* (*vard.*) it was impossible to get anything out of her **-aktig** *a1* lying; (*om historia o.d.*) mendacious; (*om påstående*) untruthful **-aktighet** untruthfulness, mendacity **-are** liar **-detektor** lie detector, polygraph **-hals** liar **löja** *s1* bleak **löje** ['löjje] *s6* (*leende*) smile; (*åt-*) ridicule **-väckande** *a4* ridiculous; *verka* ~ have a

L

ridiculous (comic) effect
löjlig *a1* ridiculous; *(lustig)* funny, comic[al]; *(orimlig)* absurd; *göra en* ~ *figur* cut a ridiculous (sorry) figure; *göra sig* ~ *över* make fun of **-het** ridiculousness *etc.*; absurdity
löjrom whitefish roe
löjtnant [ˣlöjt-] *s3 (vid armén)* lieutenant, *AE.* first lieutenant; *(vid flottan)* sublieutenant, *AE.* lieutenant junior grade; *(vid flyget)* flying officer, *AE.* first lieutenant
löjtnantshjärta *bot.* bleeding heart
lök *s2* **1** *(blom-)* bulb **2** *(som maträtt)* onion **3** *lägga* ~ *på laxen (bildl.)* make matters worse **-formig** [-å-] *a1* onion-shaped, bulbous **-kupol** onion dome **-soppa** onion soup **-växt** bulb[ous plant]
lömsk *a1* insidious; *(bedräglig)* deceitful; *(illistig)* sly, wily; *(bakslug)* underhand; *(försåtlig)* treacherous, *AE. vard.* ornery
lön *s3* **1** *(belöning)* reward; recompense; *(ersättning)* compensation; *få* ~ *för mödan* be rewarded for one's pains; *få sina gärningars* ~ get one's deserts **2** *(arbetares)* wages *(pl)*, pay, remuneration; *(tjänstemans o.d.)* salary
lön|a *(be-)* reward; *(vedergälla)* recompense; *jfr äv. avlöna; ~ ont med gott* return good for evil; ~ *mödan* be worth while **2** *rfl* pay; *(om företag)* be profitable (lucrative); *det ~r sig inte* it is no use, it is not worth while (the trouble) **-ande** *a4 (om företag)* profitable; *(om sysselsättning äv.)* remunerative; *bli* ~ *(äv.)* become a paying proposition
löne|anspråk *pl* salary requirements; *svar med* ~ replies stating salary expected (required) **-avdrag** deduction from wages (salary), payroll deduction **-avtal** wage contract; *koll.* wages (pay) agreement **-förhandlingar** *pl* wage negotiations, pay talks; *centrala* ~ collective bargaining *(sg)* **-förhöjning** increase (rise, *AE.* raise) in salary (wages) **-förmån** emolument; ~*er (äv.)* payments in kind, fringe benefits **-glidning** wage drift **-grad** salary grade **-klass** subdivision of salary grade **-läge** wage situation **-nivå** wage level **-rörelse** wage negotiations *(pl)*, collective bargaining **-skala** *(glidande moving)* wage *(etc.)* scale **-stegring** rise of wages *(etc.)* **-stopp** wage freeze **-sänkning** wage *(etc.)* cut **-sättning** setting of wage *(etc.)* rates, wage determination **-tillägg** bonus, increment **-villkor** *pl* salary (wage) terms, terms of remuneration **-ökning** wage *(etc.)* increase
lönlös [ˣlö:n-] *(gagnlös)* useless, futile
1 lönn *s2, bot.* maple [tree]
2 lönn *r, i* ~, *se* [i] *lönndom*
lönn|brännare illicit distiller **-bränning** illicit distilling **-dom** *i uttr.: i* ~ secretly, in secret, clandestinely **-dörr** secret door **-gång** secret (underground) passage **-krog** unlicensed gin--shop **-lig** *a1* secret; clandestine; *jfr hemlig* **-mord** assassination **-mörda** assassinate **-mördare** assassin
lönsam [ˣlö:n-] *a1* profitable, remunerative, lucrative **-het** profitability, earning capacity **-hetsberäkning** cost-benefit analysis (calculation)
lönsparande save as you earn

lönt [-ö:-] *oböjl. a, det är inte* ~ *att du försöker* it is no good (use) your trying
löntagar|e *(arbetare)* wage earner; *(tjänsteman)* salary earner; employee **-fond** wage-earners' investment fund **-organisation** labour organization
löp|a *v3* **1** run *(ett lopp* a race); *jfr 2 springa 1; låta* ~ let go; ~ *fara* be in danger; ~ *risk att* run the risk of (+ *ing-form*) **2** *(sträcka sig)* extend, run, go *(längs* along); *en mur -er runt ... (äv.)* a wall encircles ... **3** *(om drivrem, kran o.d.)* run, travel, go; *(hastigt äv.)* fly, dart; *nålen -er lätt* the needle goes through easily; *låta fingrarna* ~ *över* run one's fingers over **4** *(om ränta o.d.)* run; *lånet -er med 5 % ränta (äv.)* the loan carries interest at 5 % **5** *(om tik)* be in heat **6** ~ *till ända (om tidsfrist o.d.)* run out; ~ *ut (om tid)* expire, run out; ~ *ut ur hamnen* leave (put off from) [the] harbour
löpande *a4* running *(äv. hand.)*; *i sht hand.* current; *i* ~ *följd (bokför. o.d.)* in consecutive order; ~ *konto* open (current) account; ~ *order* standing order; ~ *rigg (sjö.)* running rigging; *i* ~ *räkning* on current (running) account; ~ *utgifter* running (working) expenses; ~ *band* assembly line; *(transportband)* conveyor belt; *producera på* ~ *band* mass-produce
löparbana running track **löpare 1** runner **2** *(bord-)* table-runner **3** *(schackpjäs)* bishop
löpe *s6* rennet
löp|eld 1 *(skogseld)* surface-fire **2** *sprida sig som en* ~ spread like wildfire **-grav** *mil.* sap; ~*ar* parallels; approaches **-knut** *(running)* noose
löpmage *zool.* abomasum, fourth stomach
löp|maska ladder, run **-meter** running-metre, linear metre **-ning 1** running; *(en* ~*)* run; *(kapp-)* race **2** *mus.* run, roulade **-sedel** placard; [news]bill **-snara** loop **-tid** *(växels o.d.)* currency; *(låns o.d.)* life; duration, [period of] validity (maturity)
lördag [ˈlö:r-] Saturday; *jfr fredag*
lös I *a1* **1** loose; *(rörlig)* movable; *(flyttbar äv.)* portable; *(-tagbar)* detachable; *(ej hårt spänd)* slack; ~*a blommor* cut flowers; ~*a delar (reservdelar)* spare parts; ~ *och fast egendom* real and movable estate; *i* ~ *vikt (hand.)* by weight **2** *(ej tät* [*t. konsistensen*]) loose *(snö* snow); *(mjuk)* soft *(blyerts* lead); *(grötig)* pappy; *vara* ~ *i magen* have loose bowels **3** *(konstgjord)* false *(tand* tooth); *(motsats skarp)* blank *(skott* shot) **4** *(om häst o.d.)* untethered, at large; *(om hund)* unleashed, off the lead; *(om seder)* loose, lax; *(om förbindelse)* irregular; *(om antagande, misstanke)* vague; *(om prat o.d.)* empty, idle; ~*t folk* people on the loose, drifters; *gå* ~ be at large; ~*a påståenden* unfounded statements; *på* ~*a grunder* on flimsy grounds **5** *bli (komma)* ~ get loose; *nu brakar det* ~! *(om oväder o.d.)* now we are in for it!; *slå sig* ~ take a day off; *(bland vänner e.d.)* let o.s. go **II** *adv, gå* ~ *på (angripa)* attack, go for *(ngn* s.b.), go at *(ngt* s.th.)
lösa *v3* **1** *(tjudrat djur)* untether, unloose; *(hund)* let off the leash, unleash; *(friare)* release, set free *(från, ur* from) **2** *(lossa på)* loose[n]; *(boja, knut o.d.)* undo, unfasten, untie **3** *(i vätska)*

dissolve **4** (*gåta, problem o.d.*) solve **5** (*ut-*) redeem; (*biljett e.d.*) buy, take, pay for; ~ *ut ngn ur* (*firma e.d.*) buy s.b. out of **6** *rfl* (*i vätska*) dissolve, be dissolvable; (*om problem o.d.*) solve
lös|aktig *a1* loose, dissolute **-ande** *a4*, ~ [*medel*] laxative
lös|as *v3, se lösa* **6 -bar** *a1* [dis]soluble **-bladsystem** loose-leaf system **-bröst** (*skjortbröst*) shirt front **-drivare** vagrant, vagabond **-driveri** vagrancy **-egendom** personal property (estate), movable property; chattels (*pl*)
lösen ['lö:-] *r* **1** (*för stämpel e.d.*) stamp fee (duty) **2** (*för brev e.d.*) surcharge **3** (*igenkänningsord*) password; catchword; *dagens* ~ the order of the day **-ord** *se* **lösen 3**
lösesumma ransom
lös|fläta false plait **-gom** dental plate **-göra 1** (*djur*) set free, release; (*hund*) let off the leash, unleash, unchain **2** (*sak*) detach, unfasten, unfix, disengage; (*ur nät, snara e.d.*) extricate **3** *bildl.* free, liberate; (*kapital*) liberate **4** *rfl* set o.s. free, free (release) o.s. **-hår** false hair **-häst 1** loose horse **2** *bildl.* gentleman without lady; (*friare*) gentleman at large **-kokt** lightly boiled, soft-boiled **-krage** [loose] collar **-lig** [-ö:-] *a1* **1** (*i vätska*) soluble, dissolvable **2** (*om problem*) solvable, soluble **3** (*lös*) loose; (*om t.ex. moral*) lax, slack **-manschett** loose cuff **-mustasch** false moustache **-mynt** *a4* blabbing **-ning** [-ö:-] **1** *konkr.* solution **2** (*förklaring*) solution (*på* of); (*frågas äv.*) settlement; *gåtans* ~ (*äv.*) the answer (key) to the riddle **-ningsmedel** [dis]solvent **-nummer** single copy **-nummerpris** single-copy price **-näsa** false nose **-peruk** wig, toupee **-ryckt** *a4* torn loose (*från* off, from); (*om ord, mening o.d.*) disconnected, isolated
löss (*pl av lus*) lice
lössjord loess
lös|skägg false beard **-släppt** *a4*, let loose (*etc*); (*otyglad*) unbridled; (*uppsluppen*) wanton, unrestrained
löst [-ö:-] *adv* loosely *etc.*; (*lätt*) lightly; (*obestämt*) vaguely; *sitta* ~ (*om plagg*) fit loosely; *gå* ~ *på 100 pund* (*vard.*) run into £ 100
lös|tagbar [-a:g-] *a5* detachable **-tand** false tooth **-öre** *se* **lösegendom**
löv *s7* leaf **löva** adorn with leafy branches **lövas** *dep* leaf, leave, burst into leaf
löv|biff leaf-thin slice[s] of beef **-fällning** [the] fall of the leaves; defoliation (*äv. ~en*) **-groda** tree frog **-hyddohögtid** *relig.* Feast of Tabernacles, Sukkoth **-jord** leaf mould (soil)
lövkoja *s1, bot.* stock
löv|rik leafy, full of leaves **-ruska** leafy branch **-sal** arbour, bower **-skog** deciduous forest; *AE.* hardwood forest **-sprickning** leafing **-såg** fret saw **-sångare** willow warbler **-trä** hardwood **-träd** deciduous (*AE.* hardwood) tree **-tunn** as thin as a leaf **-verk** foliage **-äng** forest meadow

Maas [-a:-] *r* the Meuse
Macedonien [-ke-, -se-, -'dɷ:-] *etc., se* **Makedonien** *etc.*
machiavellisk [makia'vell-] *a5* machiavellian
machtal [*ˣ*mack-] Mach number, Mach
mack *s2* (*pump*) petrol pump; (*bensinstation*) filling (*AE.* gas[oline]) station; (*med service*) petrol (service) station
macka *s1, vard.* sandwich
mackab|é *s3* Maccabe **-eisk** [-'be:isk] *a5* Maccabean
macka'pär *s3, vard.* gadget
mad *s3* marsh (bog) meadow
Madagaskar *n* (*ön*) Madagascar; (*republiken*) Madagascar (1958—75 Malagasy)
madagaskisk [-'gask-] *a5* Madagascan, Malagasy
madam [-'damm] *s3, åld.* woman
madonna [-ˣdånna, -'dånna] *s1* Madonna **-bild** Madonna, madonna
mad'rass *s3* mattres **-era** pad; quilt **-var** *s7* [bed] tick
madri'gal *s3* madrigal
maffia ['maff-] *s1* Maf[f]ia **-medlem** mafioso
maga'sin *s7* **1** (*förrådshus*) storehouse; *hand.* warehouse; (*förvaringsrum*) depository; (*skjul*) shed **2** (*butik*) shop **3** (*på eldvapen*) magazine **4** (*tidskrift*) magazine **-era** store [up]; *hand.* warehouse; (*möbler äv.*) store **-ering** storing; (*möbel- äv.*) [furniture] storage
magasinshyra (*för magasin*) warehouse rent; (*för magasinering*) storage [charges *pl*]
mag|besvär stomach (digestive) trouble; upset stomach **-blödning** [an] attack of bleeding in the stomach; *med.* gastric haemorrhage **-dans** belly dance
mage *s2* stomach; (*buk*) belly; *anat. äv.* abdomen; (*matsmältning*) digestion; *vard.* tummy; *ha dålig* ~ suffer from indigestion; *ha ont i ~n* have [a] stomachache (a pain in one's stomach); *vard.* have a belly ache; *vara hård i ~n* be constipated; *vara lös i ~n* have diarrhoea; *få en spark i ~n* (*äv.*) get a kick in the guts; *min* ~ *tål inte* my stomach won't stand, I can't take; *ligga på ~n* lie on one's face
1 mager ['ma:-] *s9* (*österländsk vis*) magus (*pl magi*)
2 mager ['ma:-] *a2, eg. o. bildl.* lean; (*om pers., kroppsdel äv.*) thin; (*knotig*) bony; (*friare, bildl.*) meagre; (*klen*) slender; (*knapp*) scanty; ~ *jord* poor (meagre, barren) soil; ~ *kassa* scanty funds (*pl*); ~ *ost* low-fat cheese; ~ *stil* (*boktr.*) lean face; *sju magra år* seven lean years; ~ *som ett skelett* a mere skeleton
magerhet leanness *etc.*
magerlagd *a5* rather thin; on the thin side
mag|grop pit of the stomach **-gördel** *med.* abdominal support; (*på cigarr*) band
ma'gi *s3* magic **-ker** ['ma:-] magician

maginfluensa gastric flu
magisk ['ma:-] *a5* magic[al]
magister [-'jist-] *s2, filosofie* ~ *(ung.)* Master of Arts *(förk. M.A.)*; *(lärare)* schoolmaster; *ja ~n!* yes, Sir! **-examen** *ung.* Master-of-Arts examination
magis'tral *a1* magistral; *(friare)* authoritative; *(mästerlig)* masterly
magistrat [-j-] civic (city, town) administration; municipal authorities *(pl)*
mag|katarr catarrh of the stomach, gastric catarrh **-knip** pains *(pl)* in the stomach; gripes *(pl)*
magma *s1* magma
magmun orifice of the stomach
magnat [-ŋn-] magnate; *AE. vard.* tycoon
magnesium [-ŋ'ne:-] *s8* magnesium **-blixt** magnesium flash[light]
magnet [-ŋ'ne:t] *s3* magnet *(äv. bildl.)*; *(tändapparat)* magneto; *naturlig* ~ *(äv.)* loadstone **-band** magnetic tape **-fält** magnetic field **-isera** magnetize **-isering** magnetization **-isk** *a5* magnetic; *bildl. äv.* magnetical **-ism** magnetism **-'it** *s3* magnetite **-kompass** magnetic compass **-mina** magnetic mine **-nål** magnetic needle **-ofon** [-'få:n] *s3* magnetophone, tape recorder **-pol** magnetic pole
magnetron [maŋne'trå:n] *s3, tekn.* magnetron
magnet|spole magnetic coil **-tändning** magneto ignition
magnificus [maŋ'ni:fikus] *rector* ~ vice-chancellor
magni'fik [-ŋni-, -nji-] *a1* magnificent; grand, splendid
magni'tud [-ŋn-] *s3* magnitude
magnumbutelj [ˣmaŋn-] magnum
mag|plask belly flop **-plågor** *pl* stomach pains **-pumpa** ~ *ngn* empty a p.'s stomach of its contents; *bli ~d* have one's stomach pumped out **-pumpning** pumping-out of the stomach
magra [-a:g-] become (get, grow) thinner, lose weight; ~ *tre kilo* lose three kilos [in weight]
mag|saft gastric juice **-sjuk** suffering from a stomach disorder **-sjukdom** disease of the stomach **-stark** *det var väl ~t!* *(vard.)* that's a bit too thick! **-stärkande** *a4* stomachic *(äv. ~ medel)* **-sur** suffering from acidity in the stomach; *bildl.* sour[-tempered], sardonic **-syra** acidity in the stomach; *bildl.* sourness of temper **-sår** gastric ulcer **-säck** stomach
magyar [-'dja:r] *s3* Magyar
magåkomma stomach complaint (trouble)
maharadja [-'radja] *s1* maharaja[h]
mahogny [-'håŋni, -y] *s9, s7* mahogany
maj [majj] *r* May; *första* ~ May Day, the first of May **-blomma** May-Day flower
majes'tät *s7, s4* majesty; *Hans M~* His Majesty; *Ers M~* Your Majesty **-isk** *a5* majestic; *(friare)* stately
majestäts|brott lese-majesty **-förbrytare** person guilty of lese-majesty
majolika [-'jɷ:-] *s1* majolica
majon'näs *s3* mayonnaise
ma'jor *s3* major; *(vid flottan)* lieutenant commander; *(vid flyget)* squadron leader; *AE.* major, *(vid flottan)* lieutenant commander
majoritet *s3* majority; *ha* ~ have (be in) a ma-

jority; *absolut (relativ, kvalificerad)* ~ absolute (relative, [a] two-thirds *etc.*) majority
majoritets|beslut majority resolution **-ställning** *vara i* ~ be in [a] majority **-val** elections conducted on the majority [voting] system
majorska [-ˣjɷ:r-] *s1* major's wife (widow)
majs *s3* maize, Indian corn; *AE.* corn **-ena** [-ˣse:-, -'se:-] *s1* cornflour; *AE.* cornstarch **-flingor** *pl* cornflakes **-kolv** ear of maize (corn), corncob **-mjöl** cornflour; *AE.* cornstarch
majsmörblomma goldilocks
majsolja maize oil
majstång maypole
majuskel [-'jusk-] *s3, boktr.* majuscule, capital letter
mak *oböjl. s i uttr.: i sakta* ~ at an easy pace, *(t.ex. arbeta)* slow but sure
1 maka *v1* move, shift *(äv.* ~ *på)*; ~ *sig* move o.s.; ~ *sig till rätta* settle o.s. comfortably; ~ *åt sig* make room, give way
2 maka I *s1* wife; *poet. äv.* spouse; *hans äkta* ~ his wedded wife **II** *oböjl. a (som bildar ett par)* that match, that are fellows (a pair)
makaber [-'ka:-] *a2* macabre
makadam [-'damm] *s3* macadam, road metal
maka|lös matchless, unmatched; incomparable; peerless **-löst** *adv* peerlessly; incomparably; *(ytterst)* exceedingly, exceptionally
makaroner [-'rɷ:-] *koll.* mac[c]aroni
mak|e *s2* **1** *(äkta ~)* husband; *poet. äv.* spouse; *(om djur)* mate; *-ar* husband and wife; *-arna A.* Mr. and Mrs. A. **2** *(en av ett par)* fellow, pair; *~n till den här handsken* the other glove of this pair **3** *(like)* match; *~n till honom finns inte* his match (the like of him) does not exist, you will not find his peer; *jag har då aldrig hört på ~n!* I never heard the like (such a thing)!, well, I never!
Makedonien [-'dɷ:-] *n* Macedonia
makedon|ier [-'dɷ:-] *s9* Macedonian **-isk** *a5* Macedonian
maklig [-a:-] *a1* easy-going; *(bekväm)* comfortable; *(loj)* indolent; *(sävlig)* leisurely
makramé *s3* macramé
makrill *s2* mackerel **-moln** mackerel sky
makro|biotik macrobiotics *(pl, behandlas som sg)* **-ekonomi** macroeconomics *(pl, behandlas som sg)* **-kosmos** [-'kåsmås] *r* macrocosm **-molekyl** macromolecule **-skopisk** [-'skå:-] *a5* macroscopic
makt *s3* power; might; *([tvingande] kraft)* force; *(herravälde)* dominion, rule; *([laglig] myndighet)* authority; *(kontroll)* control; ~ *går före rätt* might goes before right; *vanans* ~ the force of habit; *ingen ~ i världen kan* no power on earth can; *sätta* ~ *bakom orden* back up one's words by force; *få* ~ *över* obtain power over, make o.s. master of; *ha (sitta vid) ~en* be in (hold) power; *en högre* ~ superior force; *genom omständigheternas* ~ by force of circumstances; *av (med) all* ~ with all one's might; *med all* ~ *söka att* do one's utmost to; *ha ordet i sin* ~ be eloquent, have the power of expressing o.s., *vard.* have the gift of the gab; *det står inte i min* ~ *att* it is beyond my power to; *komma till ~en* come into (obtain)

power; *vädrets* ~*er* the weather gods
makt|balans balance of power **-befogenhet** authority; powers (*pl*) **-begär** [the] lust for power **-faktor** factor of power **-fullkomlig** despotic, dictatorial **-fördelning** distribution of power **-förskjutning** shift of power **-havande** *s9,* **-havare** *s9* ruler; *de* ~ those in power **-kamp** struggle for power **-koncentration** concentration of power **-lysten** greedy for power **-lystnad** lust for power **-lös** powerless; impotent; (*svag*) weak; (*matt*) faint **-medel** instrument of force; forcible means (*pl*) **-missbruk** abuse of power **-påliggande** *a4* (*viktig*) important, urgent; (*ansvarsfull*) responsible **-sfär** sphere of influence **-spel** gamble for power; ~*et* the power game **-språk** language of force **-ställning** position of power, powerful position **-övertagande** *s6* assumption of power
makul|atur wastepaper, spoilage **-era** (*kassera*) destroy, obliterate, reject as waste[paper]; (*göra ogiltig*) cancel; ~*s!* cancelled! **-ering** (*destruction, obliteration; cancellation*)
1 mal *s2* (*insekt*) moth
2 mal *s2* (*fisk*) European catfish, sheatfish
mala *v2* **1** grind (*till* into); (*säd äv.*) mill; (*kött äv.*) mince; ~ *på ngt* (*bildl.*) keep on repeating s.th.; ~ *om samma sak* (*bildl.*) keep harping on the same string **2** (*om tankar*) keep on revolving
Malackahalvön [-ˣlakk-] the Malay Peninsula
malaj [-'lajj] *s3* Malay[an]; *skämts. mil.* C3 (C—3) man **-isk** *a5* Malay[an]
mala'kit *s3* malachite
malapro'på *adv* malapropos
malaria [-'la:-] *s1* malaria **-mygga** mosquito
malaw|ier [-'la:-] *s9* Malawian **-isk** *a5* Malawian
malays|ier [-'laj-] *s9* Malaysian **-isk** *a5* Malaysian
malen *perf. part. av mala* ground; *fin~* finely ground; *grov~* coarsely ground
malhål moth-hole
malici'ös *a1* malicious; spiteful
malign [-'liŋn] *a1, med.* malignant
ma'lis *s3,* ~*en påstår* malicious rumour has it that
mall *s2, tekn.* mould; (*friare äv.*) pattern, model; (*rit-*) [French] curve
malla *v1,* ~ [*upp*] *sig, vard.* be cocky (stuck-up)
mallig *a1* cocky, stuck-up **-het** cockiness
Mallorca [maˣjårka] *n* Majorca
malm *s3* **1** *miner.* ore; (*obruten*) rock **2** (*legering*) bronze **3** *ljudande* ~ sounding brass; *han har* ~ *i stämman* his voice has got a ring in it **-berg** metalliferous rock **-brytning** ore-mining
malmedel antimoth preparation, mothproofing agent
malm|fyndighet ore deposit **-fält** ore deposit (field) **-förande** *a4* ore-bearing, metalliferous **-förekomst** *se -fyndighet* **-gruva** ore mine **-halt** content of ore **-haltig** *a1* containing ore **-klang** metallic ring **-letning** [-e:-] ore prospecting **-åder** metalliferous vein
malning [-a:-] grinding *etc., se mala*
malplacerad [mallpla'se:-] *a5* misplaced, out

of place; (*om anmärkning o.d.*) ill-timed
malpåse mothproof bag; *stoppa* (*lägga*) *i* ~ put in mothballs
malström [ˣma:l-] maelstrom
malsäker mothproof
malt *s4, s3* malt **-dryck** malt liquor
Malta *n* Malta
maltesare [-ˣte:-] Maltese
malteserkors Maltese cross
malteserriddare knight of [the Order of] Malta, knight hospitaller
maltesisk [-'te:-] *a5* Maltese
maltos [-'tå:s] *s3* maltose, malt sugar
malträtera maltreat, ill-treat
malva *s1, bot.* mallow **-färgad** mauve, mauve-coloured
malva'sir *s3* (*vinsort*) malmsey
maläten *a5* moth-eaten, mothy; (*luggsliten*) threadbare; (*om pers.*) haggard
malör mishap; (*starkare*) calamity
malört *bot.* wormwood (*äv. bildl.*); ~ *i glädjebägaren* a fly in the ointment
malörts|bägare *bildl.* cup of bitterness **-droppar** *pl* tincture (*sg*) of wormwood
mamelucker *pl* pantalet[te]s; knickers
mamma *s1* mother (*till* of); *vard.* ma, mum; *barnspr.* mummy; ~*s gosse* mother's boy; *på sin* ~*s gata* on one's native heath **-klänning** maternity dress
mammalier [-'ma:-] *pl, zool.* mammals
mammig *a1* who clings to his (her) mother's skirts
mammografi *s3* mammography
mammon [-ån] *r* mammon; (*rikedom*) riches (*pl*); *den snöda* ~ filthy lucre
mammonsdyrkan [the] worship of mammon
mammut ['mamm-] *s2, zool.* mammoth
mam'sell *s3* Miss
Man [mann] *r* [*ön*] ~ the Isle of Man; *invånare på* ~ Manxman
1 man [ma:n] *s2* (*häst- o.d.*) mane
2 man [mann] *-nen män, mil. o.d. pl man* man (*pl men*); (*som motsats t. kvinna äv.*) male; (*arbetskarl, besättnings- e.d. äv.*) hand; (*äkta* ~) husband, man; *en styrka på fyrtio* ~ a force of forty men; *sjunka med* ~ *och allt* go down with all hands; *det skall jag bli* ~ *för!* I'll make sure that's done!; *tredje* ~ third person (party); ~ *och* ~ *emellan* from one to another; *per* ~ a head, per man, each; *på tu* ~ *hand* by ourselves, on our own (*etc.*); *som en* ~ to a man, one and all; *litet till* ~*s har vi* pretty well every one of us has; *var* ~ everybody
3 man [mann] *pron* one, you; we; (*vem som helst ibl.*) anyone; (*folk*) people, they, *vard.* folks; ~ *trodde förr* people used to think; ~ *kan aldrig veta vad som* one (you) can never know what; *det kan* ~ *aldrig veta!* one never knows!; *när* ~ *talar till dig* when people speak to you, when you are spoken to; *om* ~ *delar linjen* if you (we) bisect the line; ~ *påstår att han är* they (people) say that he is, he is said to be; *har* ~ *hört på maken!* did you ever [hear the like]!; *eller, om* ~ *så vill* or, if you like (prefer [it]); *ser* ~ *på!* well, well!
mana (*upp-*) exhort; (*befalla*) bid; (*uppfordra*) call upon; (*driva på*) incite, urge, admonish;

exemplet ~r inte till efterföljd his (*etc.*) example hardly invites imitation; *~ till försiktighet* call for caution; *känna sig ~d att* feel called upon (prompted) to; *~ fram* call forth (out); *~ på ngn* urge on s.b.; *~ gott för ngn* put in a good word for s.b.

manager ['männidjer, 'mann-] (*för idrottsman*) manager; (*för artist*) impresario, publicity agent

manbar [ˣmann-] *a1* pubescent **-het** manhood

manbyggnad [ˣmann-] manor house

manchestersammet [ˣmannçester-, -'çest-] ribbed velvet, corduroy

manchu [-'ʃuː] *s3* Manchu

Manchuriet [-'riet] *n* Manchuria

manchu[r]isk [-'ʃuː-] *a5* Manchurian

1 manda'rin *s3* (*ämbetsman*) mandarin; (*högkinesiska*) Mandarin

2 manda'rin *s3* (*frukt*) mandarin[e]

man'dat *s7* **1** *jur.* authorization, authority **2** (*som riksdagsman*) mandate; commission; (*riksdagsmannaplats*) seat; *nedlägga sitt ~* resign one's seat, *britt. parl.* accept [the Stewardship of] the Chiltern Hundreds; *få sitt ~ förnyat* be returned again for one's constituency **3** (*förvaltarskap*) mandate **-fördelning** distribution of seats **-tid** term of office

manda'tär *s3* mandatary **-stat** trusteeship nation; (*förr*) mandatory nation (power)

mandel [ˣmann-] *s2* **1** almond; *brända mandlar* burnt almonds **2** *anat.* tonsil **-blomma** white meadow saxifrage **-formad** [-åː-] *a5* almond--shaped **-kvarn** almond grinder **-massa** almond paste, marzipan **-olja** almond oil **-träd** almond [tree]

mando'lin *s3* mandolin[e]

man|dom [ˣmanndɷmm] *s2* (*tapperhet*) bravery, valour; (*-barhet*) manhood; (*mänsklig gestalt*) human form (shape) **-domsprov** (*tapperhetsprov*) test of courage; (*vuxenhetsprov*) trial of manhood; initiation rite

mandråpare [ˣmann-] manslayer

mandsju *se* **manchu**

manege [-'neːʃ, -'näːʃ] *s5* manège, manege

1 maner ['maː-] *pl* (*avlidnas andar*) manes

2 ma'ner *s7* (*sätt*) manner; (*stil*) style; (*förkonstling*) mannerism; (*tillgjordhet*) affectation; *förfalla till ~* become affected

ma'net *s3* jellyfish

man|fall [ˣmann-] *det blev stort ~* there were a great many [men *etc.*] killed, (*i examen e.d.*) a great many failed (were rejected **-folk** *ett ~* a man; *koll.* men, menfolk

mangan [-ŋ'gaːn] *s3, s4* manganese **-'at** *s7, s4* manganate

mangel ['maŋel] *s2* mangle; *dra ~n* drive (*bords-*: turn) the mangle **-bod** mangle-house **-duk** mangling-sheet

mangl|a mangle; *absol. äv.* do [the] mangling **-ing** mangling; *bildl.* draw-out negotiations (*pl*) **-ingsfri** noniron

mangofrukt [ˣmaŋgɷ-] mango [fruit]

mangold ['maŋgåld] *s2, bot.* [Swiss] chard, white-beet

mangoträd [ˣmaŋgɷ-] mango [tree]

man|grann [ˣmann-] full-muster; in full force **-grant** *adv, samlas ~* assemble to a man (in

full force) **-gårdsbyggnad** mansion, manor house; (*på bondgård*) farmhouse **-haftig** *a1* stouthearted; (*karlaktig*) manly; (*om kvinna*) mannish **-hål** manhole

ma'ni *s3* mania; *vard.* craze (*på att* for + *ing-form*)

ma'nick *s3* gadget

manier|erad [-'reː-] *a5* mannered, affected **-ism** mannerism

mani'fest I *s7* manifesto **II** *a4, med.* manifest **-ation** manifestation **-era** manifest; (*ådagalägga äv.*) display

mani'kyr *s3* manicure **-era** manicure; *absol. äv.* do manicuring **-ist** manicurist

manillahampa [-ˣnilla-] Manil[l]a hemp

man|ing exhortation; (*vädjan*) appeal; *rikta en ~ till* address an appeal to **-ingsord** word of exhortation; admonitory word, word of warning

maniok [-ni'åk, -'åck] *s3, bot.* [bitter] cassava, manioc

manipul|ation manipulation **-era** manipulate; handle; *~ med* (*äv.*) tamper with, (*göra fuffens med*) juggle with; (*räkenskaper*) cook

manisk ['maː-] *a5* manic

manke *s2* withers (*pl*); *lägga ~n till* (*bildl.*) put one's shoulder to the wheel, *AE. vard.* dig [in]

mank|emang [-ŋ] *s7, s4* (*fel*) fault, hitch, breakdown; *AE. vard.* bug[s] **-era** (*komma för sent t.*) fail [to come, to turn up]; (*fattas*) want, be missing

man|kön [ˣmann-] *~et* the male sex; *koll. äv.* mankind; *av ~* of the male sex **-lig** *a1* **1** (*av mankön*) male; masculine **2** (*som anstår en man*) manly, virile **-lighet** manliness, virility **-ligt** *adv* like a man, manfully **-lucka** manhole [cover]

1 manna *v1, sjö., ~ reling!* man the bulwarks!

2 manna *s1, s7* manna; *som ~ i öknen* like manna in the wilderness

mannagryn semolina

manna|kraft man's (manly) strength; *i sin fulla ~* in the full vigour of his manhood **-minne** (*i* within) living memory **-mod** [manly] courage, prowess **-mån** *r* favouring; *utan ~* (*äv.*) without respect of persons **-ålder** manhood

manne'käng [-ŋ] *s3* [fashion] model, mannequin; (*skyltdocka*) [tailor's] dummy

mannekänga [-ˣkäŋa] model

mannekänguppvisning fashion show (parade)

manodepres'siv *a1* manic-depressive

manometer [-'meː-] *s2* pressure gauge, manometer

mans *se* **2 man**

mansardtak [-ˣsaːrd-] mansard (curb) roof

mans|bot wer[e]gild **-chauvinism** male chauvinism **-chauvinist** male chauvinist

man'schett *s3* cuff; (*linning äv.*) wristband; *tekn.* sleeve; *fasta* (*lösa*) *~er* attached (detachable) cuffs; *darra på ~en* (*bildl.*) shake in one's shoes **-brott** white-collar crime **-knapp** cuff link **-proletariat** white-collar workers (*pl*) **-yrke** white-collar job

mans|dräkt man's (male) attire **-gris** [*mullig*] *~* male chauvinist pig **-göra** *s7* men's ([a] man's) work **-hög** as tall as a man

manskap *s7, mil.* men (*pl*); (*värvat äv.*) enlisted

men (*pl*); (*servis-*) [gun] personnel; *sjö.* crew, hands (*pl*)

mans|kör male (men's) choir -lem penis -linje *på ~n* on the spear side

manslukerska vamp

mans|namn male (man's) name -person man; male person

manspillan [ˣmann-] *r* loss of men; *stor ~* heavy losses (*pl*)

mans|roll male role -samhälle male-dominated society

man|stark strong in number, numerically strong -starkt *adv, infinna sig ~* muster strong

mansålder generation

mantal *s7* assessment unit of land

mantals|blankett population census questionnaire -längd population register (schedule) -skriva register for census purposes; take a census -skrivning registration for census purposes -uppgift census registration statement

mant|el *s2* 1 (*plagg*) cloak; (*kunga- o.d. o. bildl.*) mantle 2 *tekn.* casing, jacket; *geom. o.d.* mantle; (*aktie-*) [share] certificate -'ilj *s3* mantilla -lad *a5, tekn.* jacketed

manu|'al *s3* (*handbok, mus.*) manual -'ell *a1* manual

manufaktur|affär [-ˣtu:r-] draper's shop; *AE.* dry-goods store -varor *pl* (*textil-*) drapery [goods], *AE.* dry goods; (*järn-*) hardware

manusförfattare scriptwriter

manu'skript *s7* manuscript; *boktr. äv.* copy, matter; (*film-, radio-*) script; *maskinskrivet ~* (*äv.*) typescript, typed copy

manår man-year

ma'növer *s3, mil. o. bildl.* manoeuvre; (*knep äv.*) dodge, trick; (*rörelse*) *mil.* movement, *sjö.* *mil.* exercise -bord console -duglig manoeuvrable, in working order; *sjö. äv.* steerable -fel *flyg.* pilot's error -förmåga manoeuvrability -oduglig unmanageable; out of control -spak *flyg.* control lever

manövrer|a manoeuvre (*äv. bildl.*); *sjö äv.* steer; (*friare*) handle, manage, operate -bar *a1* manoeuvrable -ing manoeuvring *etc.*

maoism Maoism

mapp *s2* file, folder

mara *s1* nightmare; (*plåga*) bugbear; *ridas av ~n* be hag-ridden

marabustork [ˣma:-, -ˣbu:-] marabou

maraton|lopp [-ån-] marathon race -löpare marathon runner

mardröm nightmare (*äv. bildl.*)

mareld phosphorescence [of the sea]

marga'rin *s4* margarine

margi'nal [-g-, -j-] *s3* margin; *boktr. äv.* border; *börs äv.* difference -anteckning marginal note -kostnad marginal cost -skatt marginal income tax -väljare floating voter

margi'nell marginal

Mar'ie bebådelsedag [-'bå:-] Lady (Annunciation) Day

marig *a1* 1 (*förkrympt*) dwarfed, stunted 2 (*besvärlig*) *vard.* tricky, ticklish, knotty

mariju'ana *s1* marijuana, marihuana

ma'rin I *s3* 1 (*sjömakt*) navy; *~en* the Marine, the Navy 2 (*-målning*) marine, seascape II *a1* marine

marina [-ˣri:-] *s1* marina

mari'nad *s3, kokk.* marinade

marin|attaché navy attaché -blå navy blue

marinera marinade

marin|flyg naval air force -lotta (*Storbritannien*) [a] member of the Women's Royal Naval Service (*förk.* W.R.N.S.), *vard.* [a] Wren; *AE.* [a] member of the Women Accepted for Volunteer Emergency Service (*förk.* WAVES), *vard.* [a] Wave -läkare naval medical officer -målare marine painter -målning *se marin I* 2 -soldat marine -stab naval staff

mario'nett *s3* marionette, puppet (*äv. bildl.*) -regering puppet government -teater (*hopskr.* marionetteater) puppet theatre (*föreställning:* show)

mari'tim *a1* maritime

1 mark *s3* (*jordyta, jordområde o.d.*) ground (*äv. bildl.*), land; (*åker-*) field; (*jordmån*) soil; *klassisk ~* classical ground; *förlora* (*vinna*) *~* lose (gain) ground; *känna ~en bränna under sina fötter* (*bildl.*) feel the place beginning to get too hot for one; *på svensk ~* on Swedish soil; *ta ~* land (alight) [on the ground]

2 mark *s9* (*mynt*) mark

3 mark *s3* [*pl* 'marr-] (*spel-*) counter, marker, fish

markant [-'kant, -'kaɳt] 1 *a1* striking, marked, conspicuous; (*märklig*) remarkable 2 *adv* strikingly *etc.*

markasit *miner.* marcasite

markatta 1 *zool.* guenon 2 (*vard.* '*häxa*') shrew, bitch; *jfr* ragata

markeffektfarkost (*svävare*) hovercraft

marker|a mark; (*vid spel äv.*) score; (*ange*) indicate; (*visa*) show; (*sittplats e.d.*) put s.th. in (on) to mark it; *sport.* mark; (*betona*) accentuate, emphasize -ad *a5* marked; (*utpräglad äv.*) pronounced -ing marking *etc.*

marketent|are [-ˣtent-] canteen-keeper -eri canteen

markförsvar land defence[s]

markgreve margrave

1 mar'kis *s3* (*solskydd*) sun blind, awning

2 mar'kis *s3* (*adelstitel*) Storbritannien marquess, marquis

markisinna Storbritannien marchioness

markkontroll *flyg., rymd.* ground control

marknad *s3* market; (*i samband med folknöjen*) fair; *introducera en vara på ~en* introduce (launch) an article on the market; *i ~en* on (in) the market

marknads|andel share of the market -dag market day -domstol *~en* the [Swedish] market court -ekonomi market economy -föra market, launch, merchandise -föring marketing *etc.* -läge market situation (position), state of the market -nöje sideshow -plats (*-område*) marketplace, fairground -pris market price -stånd market stall, stand -undersökning market[ing] research (analysis) -värde market (trade) value

mark|personal *flyg.* ground personnel (staff, crew) -robot surface-to-surface missile -sikt ground visibility -strid ground fighting, warfare on land -stridskrafter *pl* ground forces

Markus ['marr-] Mark; *~ evangelium* the Gos-

pel according to St. Mark, Mark
mark|värdestegring rise in the value of land
-värdinna ground stewardess **-ägare** land-
owner, landlord; ground owner
markör marker, scorer; *data.* cursor; *flyg.* plotter
marme'lad *s3* marmalade; *(konfekt ung.)* fruit
jellies **-burk** pot of marmalade
marmor *s9* marble; ... *av* ~ *(äv.)* [a] marble ...
-brott marble quarry **-era** marble; vein
-ering marbling **-kula** marble **-skiva** marble
slab; *(på bord)* marble top **-stod** marble monument
maroc'kan *s3* Moroccan **-sk** [-a:-] *a5* Moroccan, of Morocco
Marocko [-'råckɷ] *n* Morocco
marodör marauder, exploiter
maro'käng *s3* *(läder)* morocco; *(tyg)* marocain
mars *r* March
Mars *r, astr.* Mars
marsch [marʃ] I *s3* march; *vanlig* ~ march in
step; *vara på* ~ be on the march *(äv. bildl.)* II
interj march!; *framåt (helt om)* ~! forward
(right about face) march!; ~ *i väg! (vard.)* be
off with you!; *göra på stället* ~ *(gymnastik
o.d.)* mark time
marschall [-'ʃall] *s3* cresset
marsch|era [-'ʃe:-] march; *(skrida)* pace *(fram
o. tillbaka* to and fro); *det var raskt* ~*t! (bildl.)*
[jolly] quick work, that! **-fart, -hastighet**
[marching] pace; *flyg.* cruising speed **-kolonn**
(trupp) march[ing] column; *(formering)* column of route **-känga** marching-boot **-order**
marching order; *ha fått* ~ be under marching
orders **-takt 1** *mil.* marching step; *gå i* ~ walk
in marching step **2** *mus.* march-time
Marseille [mar'säjj] *n* Marseilles
marseljäsen [-'jä:-] *r, best. f.* the Marseillaise
Marshallplanen [the] Marshall Plan, *(officiellt)*
European Recovery Programme
marsin[ne]vånare Martian
marsi'pan *s3* marzipan
1 marsk *s3, geogr.* marshland
2 marsk *s2, hist., rikets* ~ *(Engl. ung.)* the Lord
High Constable
marskalk [ˣmarʃalk, -'ʃalk] *s2* **1** *mil.* marshal
2 *(platsvisare)* usher, *AE. äv.* floor manager;
univ. o.d. steward; *(vid bröllop)* groomsman,
(förste ~) best man
marskalksstav marshal's baton
marskland marshland
marsvin *zool.* guinea pig
martall dwarfed (stunted) pine [tree]
mart|er ['ma(:)r-] *pl* torments, tortures **-era**
torment, torture
martialisk [-tsi'a:-] *a5* martial
martin|process [-ˣtäŋ-] open-hearth process
-ugn open-hearth furnace
martorn [ˣma:rtɷ:rn] *s7, s2 bot.* sea holly
mar'tyr *s3* martyr *(för* for, to); *(offer äv.)* victim
-död *lida* ~*en* suffer martyrdom (the death of
a martyr) **-gloria** martyr's halo **-ium** *s4* [pe-
riod of] martyrdom; *ett verkligt* ~ *(friare)* a
veritable affliction **-krona** martyr's crown
-skap *s7* martyrdom
mar|ulk *s2, zool.* angler [fish] **-vatten** *ligga i*
~ be waterlogged **-viol** sea rocket

marxism Marxism **--leninism** Marxism-Lenin-
ism
marxist *s3* **-isk** *a5* Marxist, Marxian
ma'räng *s3* meringue **-sviss** *s3* cream-filled
meringue-shells
masa saunter; ~ *[sig] i väg* slope (shuffle) off;
~ *sig upp [ur sängen]* drag o.s. out of bed; *gå
och* ~ be idling (lazing)
mascara [-ˣka:-] *s1* mascara
maser ['ma:-] *s3* maser (microwave amplification by stimulated emission of radiation)
-stråle maser beam
1 mask *s2, zool.* worm; *(larv)* grub; *(kål-)* caterpillar; *(i kött, ost)* maggot; *full av -ar* alive
with worms *(etc.)*; *vrida sig som en* ~ wriggle
like a worm
2 mask *s3,* mask *(äv. bildl.)*; *(kamouflage)*
screen; *bildl. äv.* guise; *(-erad pers.)* masked
person; *låta -en falla (bildl.)* throw off one's
mask, unmask o.s.; *hålla ~en (spela ovetande)*
not give the show away, *(hålla sig för skratt)*
keep a straight face
3 mask *s3, kortsp.* finessing; *(en* ~ *äv.)* finesse
1 maska *v1* **1** *kortsp.* finesse **2** *(sänka arbets-
takten)* go slow, work to rule; *(låtsas arbeta)*
pretend to work; *sport.* play for time
2 maska *v1* *(sätta mask på)* bait with worms
(a worm); ~ *på* bait the hooks
3 maska I *s1* mesh; *(virkad, stickad)* stitch; *(på
strumpa)* ladder; *tappa en* ~ drop a stitch II
v1, ~ *av* cast off; ~ *upp på en strumpa* mend a
ladder
maskara *se mascara*
maskbo nest of grubs
maskera mask; *(klä ut)* dress up *(till* for); *teat.
äv.* make up; *(friare o. bildl., i sht mil.)* mask,
camouflage; *(dölja)* hide; *(t.ex. avsikter)* disguise; ~ *sig* mask o.s., *(friare)* dress o.s. up,
make up, disguise o.s.; *~d person (äv.)* mas-
querader; *vara ~d till (äv.)* impersonate
maske'rad *s3* masquerade; mummery **-bal** fancy-dress ball **-dräkt** fancy dress
maskering masking *etc.*; *(mera konkr.)* mask,
screen; *i sht mil.* camouflage; *(förklädnad)*
disguise; *teat.* make-up
maskerings|konst [the] art of make-up **-tejp**
masking tape
mask|formig [-å-] *a1* vermiform *(äv. anat.)*;
worm-shaped **-gång** worm burrow (track) **-hål**
wormhole
maskin [-'ʃi:n] *s3* machine *(för, till* for); *(större)*
engine; *(mera allm.)* apparatus, device; *(skriv-)*
typewriter; *~er (koll.)* machinery; *gjord (sydd)
på* ~ done (sewn, made) on a (by) machine,
machine-made; *full* ~ *[framåt]! (sjö.)* full speed
[ahead]!; *för egen* ~ by its own engines, *bildl.*
on one's own; *för full* ~ *(bildl.)* at full tilt
(steam); *skriva [på]* ~ type **-bokföring** machine accounting (bookkeeping) **-driven** *a5*
power-driven
maski'nell *a1* mechanical; ~ *utrustning* machinery, mechanical equipment; *~a hjälpmedel* machine aids
maskin|eri machinery *(äv. bildl.)*; *~et (på far-
tyg)* the engines *(pl)*; *(på fabrik)* the plant **-fa-
brik** engineering (engine) works **-fel** engine
trouble **-gevär** machine gun **-gjord** *a5* ma-

chine-made; -*gjort papper* machine paper **-industri** mechanical engineering industry **-ingenjör** mechanical engineer **-ist** engine (machine) man, mechanic; *sjö.* engineer, machinist **-mässig** *a1* mechanical **-park** machinery, machine equipment, plant **-rum** engine room **-satt** *a4, boktr.* machine-composed; linotyped, monotyped **-skada** engine trouble, breakdown **-skrift** typescript **-skrivare, -skriverska** typist **-skrivning** typing, typewriting **-skötare** [machine] operator; machine tender **-språk** *data.* machine (computer) language (code) **-sydd** *a5* machine-sewn; (*om klänning e.d.*) machine-made **-stickning** machine-knitting **-sätta** *boktr.* compose by monotype (linotype) **-sättning** *boktr.* machine composition **-söm** machined seam **-teknik** mechanical engineering **-telegraf** *sjö.* engine-room telegraph **-tvätta** wash by (in a) machine **-vara** *data.* hardware **-verkstad** machine (engineering) shop

maskning go-slow; work-to-rule; *AE.* slowdown

masko'pi *s3, s4, vara i ~ med* be in collusion with

maskot ['maskått] *s2, s3* mascot

mask|ros dandelion **-rosbarn** *ung.* born survivor **-stungen** *a5* worm-eaten

masksäker (*om strumpa*) ladder-proof, non-run

maskulin ['mask-, -'li:n] *a1* masculine; male **-um** [ˣmass-] *s4* **1** (*-t ord*) masculine [noun]; *i ~* (*gram.*) in the masculine [gender] **2** (*karl*) male

maskäten *a5* worm-eaten, wormy

maskör *teat. o.d.* make-up man

masoch|ism masochism **-ist** masochist

maso'nit *s3* masonite

mass|a *s1* **1** mass, volume; (*stort oformligt stycke*) lump **2** (*grötlik ~*) pulp; *kokk.* paste; (*deg-*) dough; *tekn.* composition; *bli till en fast ~* become a firm mass, solidify **3** (*mängd*) mass, [large] quantity; heap, pile; lot; *en ~ saker* lots (heaps) of things; *prata en ~ dumheter* talk a lot of nonsense; *-or med folk* crowds of people; [*den stora*] *~n* the masses (*pl*), the rank and file; (*flertalet*) the great majority; ... *i -or* (*-or med* ...) lots (heaps, quantities) of ...

massafabrik pulp mill

massage [-'sa:ʃ] *s5* massage

massak|er [-'sa:-] *s3* massacre, slaughter **-rera** massacre, slaughter; (*lemlästa*) mutilate; *svårt ~d i ansiktet* with his (*etc.*) face terribly mutilated

mass|arbetslöshet mass unemployment **-artikel** mass-produced article

massaved pulpwood

mass|avrättning mass-execution **-beställning** bulk bookings (orders) (*pl*) **-demonstration** mass demonstration **-död** wholesale death

massera massage; treat with massage

mass|fabrikation large-scale manufacture, mass production **-flykt** mass desertion[s *pl*] **-grav** mass (common) grave

mas'siv I *s7* massif **II** *a1* solid; massive **-itet** solidity; massiveness

mass|kommunikation mass communication **-korsband** bulk posting (mail); *AE.* bulk third class [mail] **-media** *pl* mass media **-mord**

mass murder, multicide; massacre **-mördare** mass murderer, slaughterer **-möte** mass meeting; *AE. äv.* rally **-producera** mass-produce **-produktion** mass production **-psykologi** mass psychology **-psykos** mass psychosis **-slakt** (*hopskr. masslakt*) wholesale (mass) slaughter **-tillverkning** *se -produktion* **-uppbåd** *mil.* levy in mass, mass levy; (*friare*) large muster [of people] **-verkan** mass effect **-vis** in large (vast) numbers, in great quantities; *jfr massa 3*

massör masseur

massös masseuse

mast *s3* mast; (*radio- o.d. äv.*) pylon; (*signal-*) post; (*flagg-*) pole

mastix ['mast-] *s3* mastic

mast|korg top **-kran** derrick (mast) crane

mastodont [-'dånt] *s3* mastodon (*äv. bildl.*)

masttopp masthead

masturb|ation masturbation **-era** masturbate

masugn blast furnace

masur *s9* curly-grained wood

masurka [-ˣsurr-, -'surr-] *s1* maz[o]urka

mat *s9* food; (*-varor äv.*) eatables, provisions (*pl*); *vard.* grub; *en bit ~* s.th. to eat, a bite, a snack; *~ och dryck* food and drink; *~ och husrum* board and lodging; *intages efter ~en* to be taken after meals; *vila efter ~en* rest after dinner (*etc.*); *det är ingen ~* (*eg. näring*) *i* there is no nourishment in; *~en står på bordet!* the (your) dinner (*etc.*) is on the table!; *hålla ~en varm åt ngn* keep a p.'s dinner (*etc.*) hot; *vad får vi för ~ i dag?* what are we going to have for dinner (*etc.*) today?; *dricka öl till ~en* have beer with one's dinner (*etc.*); *ha ngn i ~en* board s.b.; *vara liten i ~en* be a small eater **mata** feed (*äv. bildl.*); *~ ngn med kunskaper* stuff s.b. with knowledge; *~d* (*om säd*) full, full-eared

matador [-'då:r] *s3* matador (*äv. bildl.*); *bildl. äv., vard.* big noise, bigwig; *AE.* big shot

matarbuss feeder bus

matar|e *tekn.* feeder **-ledning** feeder [cable]

mat|beredare food processor **-bestick** knife, fork and spoon set; [a set of] eating implements (*pl*); *koll.* table cutlery; *AE.* table set, flatware **-bit** [a] bite of food (s.th. to eat), snack **-bord** dining table **-bröd** [plain] bread

match [matʃ] *s3* match; *en enkel ~* (*bildl.*) child's play; *givna ~er* (*tips.*) bankers

matcha (*låta tävla*) match

matchboll match point

matdags *det är ~* it is time for a meal

matelass|é [mattla'se:] *s3* matelassé **-era** quilt

matema't|ik *s3, ej pl* mathematics (*pl, behandlas som sg*); *vard.* maths (*pl*) **-iker** [-'ma:-] mathematician **-ikmaskin** [electronic] computer **-isk** [-'ma:-] *a5* mathematical

materi|a [-'te:-] *s3* matter (*äv. -en*); (*ämne äv.*) substance

materi'al *s7, pl äv. -alier* material (*till* for); (*i bok o.d. äv.*) matter **-fel** defect (fault) in material[s *pl*] **-förråd** store of materials **-förvaltare** storekeeper **-isation** materialization **-isera ~** (*sig*) materialize **-ism** materialism **-ist** materialist **-istisk** [-'ist-] *a5* materialistic **-kontroll** inventory control **-kostnad** cost of

M

material[s] **-lära** science of engineering and building materials **-provning** materials testing **-samling** collection of material **-återvinning** material recovery, recycling

materi|e [-'te:-] *s3, se materia* -'el *s9, ej pl* materials *(pl); elektr.* equipment; *mil.* munitions *(pl); rullande* ~ rolling stock -'ell *al* material; *~a tillgångar (äv.)* tangible assets

mat|fett cooking fat **-friare** sponger **-frisk** with a good appetite **-förgiftad** *a5* poisoned by food **-förgiftning** food poisoning **-gaffel** [table] fork **-gäst** boarder **-hållning** catering [service]

matiné *s3* matinée [performance]

mat|jord topsoil **-kniv** [table] knife **-korg** hamper **-kupong** food (dinner) check **-källare** food cellar **-lag** *s7* sitting; *mil.* mess **-lagning** cooking, cookery, preparation of food **-lust** appetite **-mor** mistress [of a (the) household]; *vard.* missis **-ning** feeding, supply **-nyttig** suitable as food, edible **-olja** cooking oil **-ordning** dietary **-os** smell of cooking (of food being cooked); cooking fumes **-pengar** *pl* housekeeping [money *(sg)*] **-pinne** chopstick **-plats** dining space **-ranson** food ration **-rast** food break; *mil. o.d.* halt for refreshment[s *pl*] **-recept** [cooking] recipe **-rester** *pl* remains [of food]; *vard.* leftovers

matriar|kalisk [-'ka:-] *a5* matriarchal -'kat *s7* matriarchate, matriarchy

matrikel [-'trick-] *s2* list (roll) [of members]; *(kår- äv.)* calendar, directory

ma'tris *s3* matrix *(pl* matrices), mould

matro peace at mealtimes

ma'trona *s1* matron

ma'tros *s3* able[-bodied] seaman; *vard.* sailor **-jacka** bluejacket, sailor's jacket **-kostym** sailor suit **-krage** sailor-suit collar

mat|rum *se matsal* **-rätt** dish

mats *r, i uttr.: ta sin ~ ur skolan* withdraw altogether, beat a retreat

mat|sal dining room **-salong** *sjö.* dining saloon **-sedel** menu, bill of fare **-servering** *(-ställe)* eating house; dining-rooms *(pl)* **-servis** dinner service **-silver** table silver **-sked** tablespoon **-skribent** cookery writer **-smältning** digestion; *ha dålig* ~ suffer from indigestion (a bad digestion)

matsmältnings|apparat digestive system (tract) **-besvär** indigestion, dyspepsia **-organ** digestive organ **-process** process of digestion **-rubbning** ind igestion; digestive upset

mat|strejka refuse to eat **-strupe** oesophagus, gullet **-ställe** *se matservering* **-säck** [˟ma:t-, *vard.* ˟massäk] [bag of] provisions *(pl)*, package of food, packed meal (lunch); *vard.* grub, tommy; *rätta munnen efter ~en* cut one's coat according to one's cloth **-säckskorg** provision basket; *(vid utfärd äv.)* picnic hamper

1 matt *al* **1** *(kraftlös o.d.)* faint *(av* from, with); *(klen, svag)* weak, feeble; *(slö, slapp)* languid; *(utan kläm)* spiritless, tame; *hand.* dull; *(livlös)* lifeless; *känna sig* ~ feel exhausted (washed out) *(efter* after) **2** *(färgsvag)* mat[t], dead; *(glanslös)* dull, lustreless; *(dunkel)* dim; *bli* ~ *(äv.)* get tarnished, tarnish

2 matt *oböjl. a o. s3 (i schack)* mate; *schack*

och ~! checkmate!; göra ngn ~ checkmate s.b.; *förhindra ~en* prevent [the] [check]mating

1 matta *s1* carpet; *(mindre)* rug; *(dörr-, korko.d.)* mat; *(grövre)* matting; *heltäckande* ~ fitted carpet; *hålla sig på ~n (bildl.)* toe the line

2 matta *v1* weaken, enfeeble; *(trötta)* tire; weary

mattaffär rug and carpet dealer

mattas *dep* get (become, grow) weak[er]; *(om sken)* get *(etc.)* dim[mer]; *(om pers.)* get *(etc.)* [more] tired; *(om färg)* fade; *ekon.* weaken

mattblå dull blue

1 matte *s2, vard.* mistress

2 matte *s7 (paraguayte)* maté, mate

3 matte *vard.* maths, *AE.* math

Matteus [-'te:-] Matthew; ~ *evangelium* the Gospel according to St. Matthew, Matthew

mattförgylla gild with a mat[t] surface

matt|handlare *se mattaffär*

matt[ig]het lassitude; faintness, feebleness *etc.*

mattpisk|are carpet-beater **-ning** carpet-beating

mattpolerad *a5* matt-finished

mattram *s3, bot.* feverfew

mattrasor *(särskr. matt-trasor) pl* rag-strips for hand-woven rugs

matt|sam *al* fatiguing; tiresome **-skiva** *foto.* focusing screen, ground glass **-slipad** *a5* ground, frosted

mattsopare carpet sweeper

mattvarp carpet warp

mat|tvång *(på restaurang)* [the] no-drinks--without-food system **-varor** *pl* provisions, eatables, foodstuff **-varuaffär** provision-dealer's [shop], food sho **-vrak** gormandizer, glutto **-vrå** dining recess; *AE.* dinett **-väg** *i uttr.: ngt i* ~ s.th. in the way of foo **-vägran** refusal to ea **-vägrare** person (child) who refuses to ea **-äpple** cooking-apple

Mauretanien [-'ta:-] *n* Mauritania

mauret|anier [-'ta:-] *s9* Mauritania **-ansk** [-'ta:-] *a5* Mauritanian

mausergevär Mauser [rifle]

mausoleum [-˟le:-, -'le:-] *s4* mausoleum

ma'xim *s3* maxim

maxi'm|al *al* maximu **-era** *(göra så stor som möjligt)* maximize; *(bestämma högsta gräns för)* put an upper limit on, fix a ceiling for; ~ *räntan till 5 %* set (fix) interest at a maximum of 5 **-ering** fixation of the limits; *räntans* ~ *till 5 %* the fixing of the interest at 5 % as a maximum

maximi|belopp maximum [amount **-gräns** upper limit, ceilin **-hastighet** maximum spee **-pris** maximum price, ceiling pric **-termometer** maximum thermometer

maximum ['maks-] *s8* maximum *(pl* maxima)

mayafolk [˟majja-] *~en* the Maya peoples, the Mayas

MBL *se medbestämmandelagen*

mecenat patron of the arts (sciences)

Mecka *n* Mecca

1 med *s2 (kälk- o.d.)* runner; *(gungstols- o.d.)* rocker

2 med [*vard. me:, mä:*] **I** *prep* **1** with; ~ *all aktning för* with all respect to, however much one may respect; ~ *eller utan* with or without; ~ *nöje* with pleasure; ~ *omsorg* with care, carefully; ~ *rätta* rightly, with good reason; ~ *säkerhet* certainly; ~ *öppna armar* with open arms; *diskutera (leka)* ~ *ngn* discuss (play) with s.b.; *felet* ~ the trouble with; *fylld* ~ *sand* filled with sand; *färdig* ~ ready with; *jämföra* ~ compare with, *(likna vid)* compare to; *kriget* ~ *Spanien* the war with Spain; *ned* ~ ...! down with ...!; *nöjd* ~ content with; *skriva* ~ *en penna* write with a pencil; *tillsammans* ~ together with; *tävla* ~ *ngn* compete with s.b.; *vara* ~ *barn* be pregnant (with child); *äta* ~ *sked* eat with a spoon; *en man* ~ *långt skägg* a man with a long beard; ~ *de orden lämnade han mötet* with these words he left the meeting; *ordet stavas* ~ *e* the word is spelt with an e; *vi bor granne* ~ *dem* they are our neighbours, we live next door to them; *han kom* ~ *ett brev* he came with a letter; *han stod där* ~ *hatten i hand (händerna i fickorna)* he stood there [with his] hat in [his] hand (with his hands in his pockets); *vad är det* ~ *dig?* what is the matter with you?; *det är samma sak* ~ *mig* it is the same [thing] with me 2 *([kommunikations]medel)* by; ~ *tåg* by train; *betala* ~ *check* pay by cheque; *höja priset* ~ *5 öre* raise the price by 5 öre; *skicka* ~ *posten* send by post; *vinna* ~ *10 poäng* win by ten points; *börja* ~ *att förklara* begin by explaining; *vad menar du* ~ *det?* what do you mean by that? 3 *(släktskap, jämförelse)* to; *gift* ~ married to; *lika* ~ equal to; *släkt* ~ related to, a relative of; *bo vägg i vägg* ~ live next door to; *vara god vän* ~ be good friends with (a good friend of) 4 *(innehållande)* containing, of, with; *en ask* ~ *choklad* a box of chocolate[s]; *massor* ~ *folk* lots of people; *tre säckar* ~ *kaffe* three bags of coffee 5 *(trots)* with, in spite of; ~ *alla sina fel är hon dock* with (in spite of) all her faults she is 6 *(och)* and; *biffstek* ~ *lök* steak and onions; *Stockholm* ~ *omnejd* Stockholm and [its] environs; *herr S.* ~ *familj* Mr. S. and family; *det ena* ~ *det andra* one thing and another; ~ *flera* and others; ~ *mera* et cetera, and so on 7 *(inberäknat)* with, including; ~ *rabatt är priset* the price less discount is 8 *(genitivförhållande)* of; with, about; *det bästa* ~ *boken är* the best thing about the book is; *fördelen (nackdelen)* ~ the advantage (disadvantage) of; *vad är meningen* ~ *det?* what is the meaning of that?; *det roliga* ~ the funny thing about 9 *(annan prep)* ~ *andra ord* in other words; ~ *avsikt* on purpose; ~ *en gång* at once; ~ *en hastighet av* at a speed of; ~ *full fart* at full speed; ~ *små bokstäver* in small letters; ~ *tre minuters mellanrum* at intervals of three minutes; *noga* ~ particular about; *tala* ~ *ngn* speak to s.b.; *ha tid* ~ have time for; *kapplöpning* ~ *tiden* a race against time; *skrivet* ~ *bläck* written in ink *(jfr 1)*; *det är ngt egendomligt* ~ *honom* there is s.th. strange about him; *hur är det* ~ *den saken?* what have you got to say about that?, what's the actual position?; *vad är det för roligt* ~ *det?* what's so funny about that?; *han har tre barn* ~ *henne* he has three children by her; *så var det* ~ *den*

saken so much for that; *tillbringa kvällen* ~ *att sy* spend the evening sewing 10 *(annan konstr.)* ~ *början kl. 9* commencing at 9 o'clock; ~ *eller mot min vilja* whether I like it or not; ~ *åren* as the years pass[ed], over the years; *adjö* ~ *dig!* bye bye!; *ajöss* ~ ... there goes ...; *bort* ~ *tassarna!* hands off!; *fara* ~ *osanning* tell lies; *försök* ~ *bensin!* try petrol!; *jämnårig* ~ of the same age as; *springa* ~ *skvaller* gossip, tell tales; *tyst* ~ *dig!* be quiet!; *ut* ~ *dig!* get out!; *betalning sker* ~ *100 kronor i månaden* payment will be made in monthly instalments of 100 kronor; *det är ingen fara* ~ *pojken* the boy is all right; *jag gör det* ~ *glädje* I'll do it gladly; *räcker det* ~ *detta?* will this do (be sufficient)?; *hur står det till* ~ *henne?* how is she?; *tidskriften utkommer* ~ *10 nummer om året* the journal appears 10 times a year; ~ *sin artikel vill han* the purpose of his article is to II *adv* 1 *(också)* too; as well; *det tror jag* ~ I think so too; *han är gammal han* ~ he is old too 2 *(i förening med verb)* du *får inget* ~ *om du inte* you won't get anything (your share) unless you; *vill du följa* ~? will you come with us (me)?; *det håller jag* ~ *dig om* I agree with you there; *ta* ~ *dig ngt att äta* bring s.th. to eat; *vara* ~ *a) (vara närvarande)* be present, *b) (vara medlem e.d.)* be a member; *får jag vara* ~ *och leka?* can I join in the game?, may I play too?; *han har varit* ~ *om mycket* he has seen a great deal in his days, he has been through a great deal; *jag är* ~ *på det* I agree to that

me'**dalj** *s3* medal *(för* for; *över* in commemoration of); *prägla en* ~ strike (cast) a medal; *tilldela ngn en* ~ award a medal to s.b **-era** award a meda **-ong** [-'jåŋ] *s3* medallion; *(med hårlock e.d.)* locke **-utdelning** presentation of medal **-ör** medallist
medan while; *(just då äv.)* as; *sitt ner* ~ *du väntar* sit down while [you are] waiting; ~ ... *på-går (äv.)* during ...
medansvarig jointly responsible *(med* with; *för* for); *vara* ~ share the responsibility
medarbeta cooperate, collaborate; *(i tidning)* contribute *(i* to)
medarbetar|e fellow worker, co-worker, colleague; *(litterär o.d.)* collaborator *(i* in); *(i tidning)* staff member, contributor; *(-hjälpare)* assistant; *från vår utsände* ~ from our special correspondent; *konstnärlig* ~ art[istic] contributor (adviser **-skap** *s7* collaboratio **-stab** staff
medbestämmande|lagen *(MBL)* the act on employee participation in decision-making **-rätt** *(i bolag o.d.)* right of co-determination; *polit.* right of participation in decision-making
medbjuden *a5*, *var också* ~ was also invited
medborgaranda [-årj-] civic spirit
medborgar|e citizen *(i* in, of); *(i sht i monarki)* subject; *utländsk* ~ foreign national, *(ej svensk)* non-Swedish subject; *akademisk* ~ member of a universit **-kunskap** civics *(pl, behandlas som sg)* **-plikt** civic duty, duty as a citizen **-rätt** civil rights *(pl)*; *beröva ngn* ~*en (äv.)* deprive s.b. of his franchise, disfranchise s.b. **-skap** *s7* citizenship

med|borgerlig [-årj-] civil (*rättighet* right); civic (*skyldighet* duty; *fest* festival) **-broder** companion; *relig.* brother **-brottslig** *vara ~ i* be implicated in (accessory to) **-brottsling** accomplice; accessory
meddel|a 1 (*omtala*) communicate (*ngn ngt* s.th. to s.b.), tell, let ... know, inform (notify, *i sht hand.* advise) of; *härmed ~s att* notice is hereby given that; *vi ber att få ~ att* we wish to inform you that; *vi ber Er ~ när* please let us know when **2** (*uppge*) state; (*kungöra e.d.*) announce, notify, report; (*bevilja, lämna*) give, grant, furnish; *jur. äv.* pronounce; *det ~s att* it is announced that, information has been received to the effect that **3** ~ *undervisning* give tuition (*åt* to) **4** *rfl* communicate (*med* with); ~ *sig med varandra* (*brevledes*) correspond [with each other] **meddelande** *s6* communication; (*budskap*) message; (*brev e.d.*) letter, note, notification; (*underrättelse*) information; (*kort skriftligt*) memorandum (*förk.* memo); *hand. äv.* advice; (*uppgift*) statement; (*officiellt*) announcement; (*anslag*) notice; *lämna ett ~ deliver* a message, (*offentligt e.d.*) make a statement; *få ~ om* be notified of, receive information about; *anslå ett ~ post* a notice **meddelare** informant **meddelsemedel** means of communication **meddelsam** [-e:l-] *a1* communicative; ready to impart information
mede *s2, se 1 med*
medel ['me:-] *s7* **1** means (*sg o. pl*); (*om sak*) medium; (*utväg*) expedient; (*verktyg äv. bildl.*) instrument; (*bote-*) remedy (*mot* for, against); *lugnande ~* tranquillizer, sedative; *antiseptiskt ~* (*äv.*) antiseptic **2** (*pengar*) means, funds, resources (*pl*); *allmänna ~* public funds; *avsätta ~ till* allocate (set aside) funds for; *egna ~* private means
medel-| [ˣme:-] medium, standard; *i sht vetensk.* mean; (*genomsnittlig*) average, mean **-antal** average (mean) number **-avstånd** mean distance
medelbar *a1* indirect
medel|betyg average mark (grade) **-distans** *sport.* middle-distance **-distansrobot** intermediate-range ballistic missile **-djup** *s7* mean depth **-engelska** Middle English **-god** medium, of medium quality **-hastighet** average speed
Medelhavet *n* the Mediterranean
medel|högtyska Middle High German **-inkomst** middle (average) income **-klass** *~en* the middle classes (*pl*) **-livslängd** average [length of] life **-längd** *av* (*under, över*) ~ of (below, above) medium (average) length (height); *av ~* (*om pers.*) of medium height
medellös without means, impecunious; (*behövande*) indigent **-het** lack of means; indigence
medel|måtta *s1* average; medium; (*om pers.*) mediocrity **-måttig** *a1* medium, average; (*måttlig*) moderate; *neds.* mediocre, middling **-proportional** *mat.* mean proportional **-punkt** (*cirkels etc. o. bildl.*) centre (*av, för, till* of); (*friare äv.*) focus, central point
medelst ['me:-] (*genom*) by; (*genom förmedling av*) through, by means of
medel|stor of medium (average) size, medium-sized **-storlek** medium size; *av ~, se medelstor* **-svensson** *vard.* the average Swede **-svår** of medium (average) difficulty, moderately difficult; (*om artilleri*) of medium calibre **-tal** average (*för* for, of); *mat.* mean; *beräkna ~et* strike an average (*av* of); *i ~* on an average; *i ~ uppgå till* (*kosta etc.*) average **-temperatur** mean temperature; *årlig ~* mean annual temperature
1 medeltid *s3* **1** *astr.* mean [solar] time **2** (*genomsnittstid*) average time
2 medeltid *s3, ~en* the Middle Ages; *Sveriges ~* Sweden's medieval period
medeltida *oböjligt a* medieval; *ibl.* Middle-Age
medel|tidskyrka medieval church **-vattenstånd** mean sea level **-väg** middle course (way) **-värde** mean value **-ålder 1** (*mellan ungdom o. ålderdom*) middle life; *en ~s man* a middle-aged man, a man in middle life; *över ~n* past middle-age **2** (*genomsnitts-*) average (mean) age
med|faren *a5, illa ~ a*) (*sliten*) much the worse for wear, in poor condition, *b*) (*bucklig e.d.*) badly knocked about **-fånge** fellow prisoner **-född** *a5* inborn, innate (*hos* in); *i sht med.* congenital (*hos* in); (*friare*) native (*hos* to); (*livlighet* vivacity); *det tycks vara -fött hos henne* it seems to come natural to her **-följa** *se följa* [*med*]; (*om bilaga*) be enclosed **-följande** *a4* accompanying; (*bifogad*) enclosed **-föra 1** (*-bringa*) take (bring) with one; (*ha med sig*) have (carry) with one; (*ha på sig*) have (carry) on one; (*om tåg, buss e.d.*) bring, take, convey **2** (*friare o. bildl.*) bring [about] (... in its train); (*förorsaka*) cause, occasion; (*ge upphov t.*) give rise to, lead to; (*ha t. följd*) result in, entail, involve; ~ *kostnader* involve expenditure; *detta -förde att vi blev* this led to our being **-författare** coauthor
med|giva 1 (*tillåta*) admit, permit, allow; (*bevilja*) grant, (*rättighet äv.*) accord; (*samtycka t.*) consent to; *tiden -ger inte att jag* time does not allow me to; *-ger inget undantag* admits of no exception **2** (*erkänna*) admit, confess (*för ngn* to s.b.); *det -ger jag gärna* I willingly (am quite ready to) admit that; *det måste -ges att* it must be confessed (admitted) that **-givande** *s6* **1** (*tillåtelse*) permission, consent; *tyst ~* tacit consent **2** (*erkännande*) admission; (*eftergift*) concession
med|gång *s2* prosperity, good fortune; (*fram-*) success; *i med- och motgång* for better for worse **-görlig** [-jö:r-] *a1* accommodating, tractable, complaisant (*mot to; i* in); amendable, easy to get on with **-görlighet** tractability; complaisance **-havd** *a5, de ~a smörgåsarna* the sandwiches one has brought [with one] **-hjälp** *jur.* complicity (*till* in) **-hjälpare** assistant **-håll** (*gillande*) approval; (*stöd*) support, *vard.* backing-up; (*gynnande*) favour, favouring; *finna ~* meet with approval; *ha ~ hos* be in favour with **-hårs** [-å:-] with the furs; *stryka ngn ~* (*bildl.*) rub s.b. up the right way
media ['me:-] *s1, språkv.* media (*pl* mediae)
mediaforskning media research
medi'al *a1* medial

medi'an *s3* median **-värde** median value
medi'cin *s3* **1** (*läkarvetenskap*) medicine; *studera* ~ study medicine **2** (*läkemedel*) medicine; (*preparat äv.*) drug
medicinal|styrelse [-ˣnaːl-] *se socialstyrelse* **-vikt** apothecaries' weight **-växt** medicinal herb
medicinare [-ˣsiː-] medical student; (*läkare*) physician
medicine ~ *doktor* Doctor of Medicine (*förk. M.D. efter namnet*); ~ *kandidat* graduate in medicine; ~ *licentiat* Bachelor of Medicine (*förk. M.B. efter namnet*); ~ *studerande* medical student
medicin|era take medicine[s *pl* **-flaska** medicine bottle; (*liten*) phial **-förråd** store of medicines; (*skåp*) medicine cupboard **-låda** medicine chest **-man** medicine man
medicin|sk [-'siː-] *a5* medical; ~ *fakultet* faculty of medicine **-skåp** medicine cupboard
medika'ment *s7, s4* medicament, medicine
med|inflytande *ha* ~ have some influence (*över* on), have a voice (say) in **-intressent** co-partner **-intresserad** *vara* ~ *i* have a part--interest in
medio ['meː-] *prep o.* oböjligt *s* middle, in the middle of; ~ *januari* (*äv.*) by (in) mid-January
medioker *a1* mediocre
medit|ation meditation **-a'tiv** *a1* meditative, contemplative **-era** meditate, ponder (*över* upon, over)
mediter'ran *a5* Mediterranean
medi|um ['meː-] *s4* **1** (*mitt*) *se medio* **2** *fys.* medium; *mat.* mean; *beräkna det aritmetiska -et av* calculate the arithmetical mean of **3** (*medel för spridning av ngt*) medium, agent, vehicle **4** *språkv.* middle voice **5** (*spiritistiskt*) medium
med|kandidat fellow candidate **-kämpe** comrade-in-arms; (*friare*) fellow combatant **-kännande** *a4* sympathetic **-känsla** sympathy (*för* for; *med* with)
medl|a [-eː-] mediate; act as [a] mediator; (*vid arbetskonflikt o.d.*) arbitrate, negotiate; (*mellan stridande äv.*) intervene **-are** mediator (*vid arbetskonflikt o.d.*) conciliator, arbitrator; *AE. äv.* troubleshooter
medlem [-eː-] *s2* member; (*av lärt sällskap äv.*) fellow; *icke* ~ non-member; *vara* ~ *av* (*i*) (*kommitté e.d.*) serve (sit, be) on
medlems|antal membership, number of members **-avgift** membership fee (subscription); *AE.* dues (*pl*) **-förteckning** list of members
medlemskap [-eːd-] *s7* membership (*i* of)
medlems|kort membership card; (*i parti*) party card **-stat** member state; (*i federation*) constituent state
medlid|ande *s6* compassion; (*medömkan*) pity; (*deltagande*) sympathy; (*skonsamhet*) mercy; *ha* ~ *med* (*äv.*) pity, have (take) pity on **-sam** [-iː-] *a1* compassionate; pitying (*leende* smile); *med en* ~ *blick* with a look full of pity
medling [-eː-] mediation; (*uppgörelse*) settlement, arrangement; (*förlikning*) conciliation; (*i äktenskap*) reconciliation
medlings|förslag proposal for settlement, draft settlement **-försök** attempt at mediation

-kommission mediation (arbitration) committee
med|ljud consonant **-lut** downhill slope **-löpare** *polit.* fellow traveller; opportunist **-människa** fellow creature (being) **-mänsklighet** human kindness **-passagerare** fellow passenger **-regent** co-regent **-resenär** travelling companion **-ryckande** *a4* exciting, stirring; captivating **-räkna** count in, include; *ej* ~*d* excluded; *däri* -*räknat* included, inclusive of **-skyldig** accessory (*i* in) **-sols** [-ʊː-] clockwise, sunwise, with the sun **-spelare** *teat. o.d.* fellow actor; *kortsp., film.* partner **-ströms** with the current **-syster** sister **-sända** send along [with], enclose **-taga** *se ta* [*med*]; *bör* ~*s* (*om uppgift e.d.*) should be given (included); *hundar får ej* ~*s* dogs [are] not admitted **-tagen** *a5* (*utmattad*) tired out, done up (*av* with); *känna sig* ~ feel used up (run down) **-trafikant** fellow passenger (road user) **-tävlare** [fellow] competitor (*om, till* for); rival **-urs** [-uːrs] clockwise
medusahuvud [-ˣduː-] Medusa's (Gorgon's) head
medverka (*samverka*) cooperate (*i, vid* in); (*vid fest, konsert o.d.*) assist, lend one's services (*vid* at); (*deltaga*) participate, take part (*i, vid* in); (*bidraga*) contribute (*till* towards, in)
medverkan cooperation (*i, vid* in; *till* towards); (*deltagande*) participation (*i, vid* in); (*hjälp*) assistance, support (*vid* in, at); *under* ~ *av* with the cooperation of, assisted by, (*i samarbete med*) in collaboration with **medverkande** *a4* cooperating *etc.*; (*bidragande*) contributory (*orsak* cause); *de* ~ the performers (actors), those taking part
medvetande *s6* consciousness (*om* of, as to); *förlora* (*återfå*) ~*t* lose (regain) consciousness; *vara vid fullt* ~ be fully conscious; *ingå i det allmänna* ~*t* be part of the public consciousness; *i* ~ *om* in the consciousness (aware) of
medveten *a3* conscious (*om* of); *vara* ~ *om* (*inse*) be aware (sensible) of **-het** consciousness, awareness
medvetet *adv* (*fullt* quite) consciously *etc.*; (*med vett o. vilja*) wittingly, deliberately
medvetslös unconscious **-het** unconsciousness
medvind tailwind, fair (following) wind; *i* ~ with a favourable (*etc.*) wind; *segla i* ~ sail before the wind, (*om företag*) be prospering
medvurst *s2* German sausage
medömkan commiseration, compassion
mefa *s1, se markeffektfarkost*
mefistofelisk [-'feː-] *a5* Mephistophelean
mega|cykler [-'sykk-] *pl* megacycles **-fon** [-'fåːn] *s3* megaphone **-hertz** [-'härts] *r* megacycles per second, megahertz
megalitisk [-'liː-] *a5* megalithic
megaloma'ni *s3* megalomania
megära [-ˣgäː-, -'gäː-] *s1* shrew, termagant, vixen
mej [mejj] *vard., se mig*
meja [ˣmejja] (*gräs*) mow (*äv. bildl.*); (*säd, åker*) cut; ~ *ner* mow down (*äv. bildl.*)
mejeri dairy; (*butik*) creamery, dairy [shop] **mejerihantering** dairying, dairy farming **mejeriprodukt** dairy product **mejerist**

dairyman
mejka *v1, rfl, vard.* make o.s. up, make up one's face
mejning mowing *etc.*
mejram [ˣmejj-, 'mejj-] *s3* [sweet] marjoram
mejsel *s2* chisel **mejsla** chisel (*äv. bildl.*), cut [with a chisel]; ~ *ut* (*äv. bildl.*) chisel out; *~d* chiselled; (*om anletsdrag o.d. äv.*) clear-cut
mekanik *s3, ej pl* **1** mechanics (*pl, behandlas som sg*) **2** *se mekanism*
mekaniker [-'ka:-] mechanic, mechanician
mekaniser|a mechanize **-ing** mechanizing, mechanization
mekan|isk [-'ka:-] *a5* mechanical; ~ *verkstad* engineering shop **-ism** *s3* mechanism; (*i ur äv.*) works (*pl*)
melanesier [-'ne:-] Melanesian
melanko'l|i *s3* melancholy; *med. äv.* melancholia **-iker** [-'kɷ:-] melancholic; melancholy person **-isk** [-'kɷ:-] *a5* melancholy; *ibl.* melancholic; (*dyster äv.*) gloomy; *vara* ~ [*av sig*] (*äv.*) be of melancholy turn (temperament)
melanom *s7, med.* melanoma; *benignt (malignt)* ~ benign (malignant) melanoma
me'lass *s3* molasses
melerad [-'le:-] *a5* mixed; mottled; (*om tyg*) pepper-and-salt
mellan (*vanl. om två*) between; (*om flera*) among; (*mitt ibland*) in the midst of; *ibl.* inter-; ~ *sina besök hos* (*äv.*) in between his (*etc.*) visits to; *titta fram* ~ *träden* peep out from behind (among) the trees; ~ *femtio och sextio personer* some fifty or sixty persons; *det inbördes förhållandet* ~ the mutual relations of; ~ *fyra ögon* in private **-akt** interval [between the acts], intermission **-aktsmusik** entr'acte [music], interlude
Mellanamerika *n* Central America
mellan|blond ashblond **-blå** medium blue **-dagarna** *pl, under* ~ during the days between Christmas and New Year **-däck** *sjö.* between-decks (*pl*), *förk.* 'tween-decks (*pl*)
Mellaneuropa *n* Central Europe **mellaneuropeisk** Central European
mellan|foder interlining **-folklig** international **-form** intermediate (intermediary) form **-fot** metatarsus (*pl* metatarsi) **-fotsben** metatarsal [bone] **-gärde** [-j-] *s6* diaphragm **-hand 1** *anat.* metacarpus (*pl* metacarpi) **2** *kortsp.* second (third) hand; *i* ~ in between, *bildl.* between two fires **3** *hand.* intermediary, middleman; *gå genom flera* -*händer* go via several middlemen **-handsställning** in-between position; intermediary position **-havande** *s6* (*affär*) account; (*skuld*) balance, debt; (*tvist*) dispute, difference; *ekonomiska* ~*n* financial transactions; *göra upp ett* ~ settle a matter (an account) **-instans** intermediate authority (court of law) **-klass** *skol.* middle (intermediary) form **-klänning** semi-evening (afternoon) dress **-kommande** *a4* intervening **-komst** [-å-] *s3* intervention **-krigsgeneration** interwar generation **-krigsperiod** interwar period (years *pl*) **-landa** make an intermediate landing, touch down **-landning** intermediate landing; *flygning utan* ~ nonstop flight **-led 1** *s3, anat.* intermediate (middle) joint; *bot.* internode **2** *s7* (*förmed-*

lande led) intermediate link, medium **-liggande** *a4* [situated] in between, interjacent; *den* ~ *tiden* the time in between, the intervening time **-läge** intermediate (middle) position **-lägg** *s7, tekn.* spacer; (*tunt*) shim, diaphragm; (*av tyg*) interlayer, interlining **-mjölk** semi-skimmed milk **-mål** snack [between meals]; *jag äter aldrig* ~ I never eat between meals **-rum** *boktr. o. allm.* space; (*friare*) interval, interspace, gap; *med jämna* ~ at regular intervals; *med två minuters* ~ at intervals of two minutes, at two-minute intervals **-rätt** *kokk.* intermediate course; extra dish **-skikt** intermediate layer (*etc.*) **-skillnad** difference; *betala* ~*en* pay the extra (difference) **-skola** *ung.* middle (intermediate) school **-slag** *boktr.* space; (*mellan rader*) blank (white) line; (*mellan stycken*) space line, leads (*pl*); (*på skrivmaskin*) spacing; *utan* ~ *solid* **-slagstangent** (*på skrivmaskin*) spacebar, spacer **-sort** *i sht hand.* medium [sort, quality] **-spel** *teat., mus.* interlude; intermezzo; *sällsamt* ~ strange interlude **-stadielärare** intermediate level teacher **-stadium** intermediate (middle) stage **-station** intermediate station **-statlig** international; interstate **-stick 1** insertion **2** *se ledarstick* **-stor** medium[-sized] **-storlek** medium size **-ställning** intermediate position **-sula** mid-sole
Mellansverige *n* Central Sweden
mellan|säsong off-season **-tid** interval; *under* ~*en* in the meantime (meanwhile) **-ting** *ett* ~ *mellan* something between, a compromise between **-vikt, -viktare** *sport.* middleweight **-våg** *radio.* medium wave **-vägg** partition (division, interior) wall **-öl** medium-strong beer **-öra** middle ear
Mellanöstern *n* the Middle East
mellerst ['mell-] *adv* in the middle **mellersta** ['mell-] *a, superl.* middle; *geogr.* central, centre, middle; *M~ Östern* [the] Middle East; ~ *Wales* (*äv.*) Mid-Wales; *i* ~ *England* (*äv.*) in the Midlands
melo'di *s3* melody; tune, air **-lära** melodics (*pl, behandlas som sg*)
melodi|sk [-'lo:-] *a5* melodious, melodic **-stämma** melody **-'ös** *a1, se melodisk*
melo'dram *s3* melodrama **-atisk** [-'ma:-] *a5* melodramatic
me'lon *s3* melon
mem'bran *s3, tekn. äv. s7* membrane, diaphragm
memoar|er [-ɷ'a:-] *pl* memoirs **-författare** writer of memoirs
memo'r|andum *s8* memorandum (*pl äv.* memoranda; *förk.* memo), note **-era** memorize, commit to memory **-ering** [the] learning of ... by heart, memorization **-i'al** *s7* memorandum
1 men [menn] *konj* but; only; (~ *ändå*) yet, still; ~ *så förtjänar han också bra* but then he earns a lot of money [too]; ~ *det var inte allt* (*äv.*) nor was that all; *jag vill inte höra några* ~! I'll have no buts!; *efter många om och* ~ after a lot of shillyshallying
2 men [-e:-] *s7* disadvantage, detriment; (*skada*) injury; (*lyte*) disability; *vara till* ~ *för* be detrimental to; *få* ~ *för livet* be marked for life

men|a *v1, vard. o. poet. äv. v3* **1** (*tro, anse*) think, be of [the] opinion; *det ~r du väl inte, eller hur?* you don't think that, do you? *vad ~r du om ...?* what is your opinion about ...? **2** (*åsyfta*) mean; (*avse*) intend; *~ väl med ngn* mean well by s.b.; *~ allvar* be in earnest (*med* about); *det var inte så illa -t* (*~t*) no offence was intended; *säga ett och ~ ett annat* say one thing and mean another; *vad ~r han med ...?* what does he mean by ...?; *vad ~s med logik?* what is meant by logic?

menageri [-na:ʃe-] menagerie

menande I *a4* meaning, significant; knowing (*blick* look) **II** *adv* meaningly *etc.*; *blinka ~ åt ngn* give s.b. a knowing wink; *se ~ ut* look knowing

mened perjury; *begå ~* commit perjury, perjure o.s. **-are** perjurer

menig *a1, äv. anv. som s, mil.* private, common soldier; *AE.* enlisted man; (*i flottan*) rating; *~e man* (*allm.*) the common people **-het** the public; (*församling*) congregation

mening 1 (*uppfattning*) opinion (*om* about, of), idea, view (*om* about); *den allmänna ~en* public opinion; *avvikande ~* dissenting opinion; *bilda sig en ~ om* form an opinion about; *inhämta ngns ~ om* get a p.'s opinion (hear a p.'s views) about; *säga sin ~* give one's opinion, speak one's mind **2** (*betydelse, innebörd*) meaning, sense; (*idé, förnuft*) reason, sense; *i lagens ~* within the meaning of the law, in the legal sense; *i viss ~* (*äv.*) in a sense; *det vore ingen ~ i* (*för mig*) *att* there would be no point (sense) in (+ *ing-form*) (in my + *ing-form*) **3** (*avsikt*) intention; (*syfte*) purpose; *det var inte min ~ att* I had no intention of (+ *ing-form*); *vad är ~en med det?* what is the sense (point) of that? **4** *språkv.* sentence; (*kort*) clause; (*längre*) period

menin'git [-ŋg-] *s3* meningitis

menings|byggnad sentence structure **-byte** debate; dispute **-frände** *mina ~r* those who share my opinion[s] (views); *vi är ~r* we hold the same views **-full, -fylld** meaningful **-lös** meaningless; void of sense; senseless, useless; (*fånig*) nonsensical; *det är ~t att* there is no sense (point) in (+ *ing-form*); *deras ~a prat* (*äv.*) the nonsense they talk **-löshet** meaninglessness *etc.* **-motståndare** opponent; antagonist **-motsättning** conflict of opinion **-skiljaktighet** difference of opinion; disagreement **-utbyte** exchange of opinions **-yttring** expression of opinion

me'nisk *s3, anat.* meniscus

menlig [ˣme:n-] *a1* injurious, prejudicial, detrimental (*för* to) **menligt** *adv* injuriously; *inverka ~ på* have an injurious effect on, prejudice

menlös [ˣme:n-] innocent, harmless; (*klandrande*) puerile; *M~a barns dag* Holy Innocents' Day **-het** innocence, harmlessness

meno'paus *s3* menopause

mens *s3, vard.* period; *ha ~* have one's period **-skydd** sanitary protection

menstru|ation menstruation; menses (*pl*) **-ationsbesvär** menstrual pain **-era** menstruate

men'tal *a1* mental **-hygien** mental hygiene **-hygienisk** of mental hygiene **-itet** *s3* mentality **-patient** mental patient **-sjuk** mentally ill (deranged) **-sjukhus** mental hospital **-[sjuk]vård** mental care; mental health services (*pl*)

mentol [-'tå:l] *s3* menthol

mentor [-år] mentor, adviser

menu'ett *s3* minuet

me'ny *s3* menu

mer *komp. t. mycken, mycket* **I** *a* more; *mycket vill ha ~* much will have more; *klockan är ~ än jag trodde* it is later than I thought; *han kommer inte någon ~ gång* he will not come again (any more); *vill du ha ~ te?* would you like some more tea?; *och, vad ~a är* and, what is more; *någon ~ gång* again some time; *med ~a* (*m.m.*) et cetera (etc.), and such like; *inte ~ än a*) (*bara*) no more than, *b*) (*ej över*) not more than **II** *adv* more; *~a känd under namnet* better known as; *~ eller mindre* more or less; *det händer ~a sällan* it happens [quite] rarely; *tycka ~ om* like ... better; *~ än nog* (*äv.*) enough and to spare; *aldrig ~* never again; *han förstår sig inte ~ på ... än* he has no more idea of ... than; *det är inte ~ än rätt att* it is only fair that; *han vet ~ än väl* he knows perfectly well; *det räcker ~ än väl* that'll be more than enough; *så mycket ~ som* especially (all the more) as

merarbete extra work

merceriser|a [-s-] mercerize **-ing** mercerizing; mercerization

merendels [-de:-] mostly; (*vanligtvis*) usually, generally

meridi'an *s3* meridian

merinkomst additional (extra) income

merinofår [-ˣri:-] merino

me'rit *s3* merit; (*kvalifikation*) qualification (*för* for) **-era** qualify (*för* for); *~ sig* qualify o.s. **-förteckning** list of qualifications, personal record **-okra'ti** *s3* meritocracy **-värdering** assessment of qualifications, merit rating

merkan'til *a1* commercial; mercantile **-ism** mercantilism **-systemet** the mercantile system, mercantilism

merkostnad additional (extra) cost

Merkurius [-'ku:-] Mercury

mer|part greater part **-smak** *ge ~* whet the appetite **-värde** added value **-värde[s]skatt** value-added tax

1 mes *s2, zool.* tit[mouse]

2 mes *s2* (*ställning för ryggsäck*) rucksack frame

3 mes *s2* (*ynkrygg*) coward, funk

mesaktig *a1* faint-hearted, timorous

mesallians [-'aŋs] *s3* misalliance; *ingå en ~* marry beneath one

me'san *s3, sjö.* spanker, mizzen **-mast** mizzenmast

mesig *a1, se mesaktig*

meska'lin *s4* mescalin[e]

meson [-'så:n] meson, *åld.* mesotron

Mesopotamien [-'ta:-] *n* Mesopotamia **mesopotamisk** [-'ta:-] *a5* Mesopotamian; *~a* (*abrakadabra*) double Dutch, gibberish

mesost whey-cheese

mesotron [-'trå:n] *s3, se meson*

M

mesozoisk [-sɷ'så:-] *a5, geol.* Mesozoic; *den ~a eran* the Mesozoic

messi'ansk [-a:-] *s5* Messianic

Mes'sias Messiah

mest *superl. t. mycken, mycket* **I** *a* most, the most; [*den, det, de*] *~a* most, most of; *det ~a* most, most things; *~a delen* most [part] of it; *det allra ~a* by far the greater part, the very most; *göra det ~a möjliga av* make the very most of; *vilken av dem gjorde ~?* which of them did [the] most? **II** *adv* most; (*för det -a o.d.*) for the most part, mostly; (*huvudsakligen*) principally, chiefly, mainly; *de ~ efterfrågade* ... the ... most in (in the greatest) demand; *tycka ~ om* like most (best); *han är som folk är ~* he is quite an ordinary chap, he is not unusual in any way **-adels** [-de:-] mostly; for the most part; (*i de flesta fall*) in most cases; (*vanligen*) generally **-gynnadnationsklausul** most-favoured-nation clause

mes'tis *s3* mestizo

meta angle, fish (*abborre* [for] perch)

meta|bolism metabolism **-don** [-'då:n] *s4* methadone **-for** [-'få:r] *s3* metaphor **-fy'sik** *s3* metaphysics (*pl, behandlas som sg*) **-fysisk** [-'fy:-] metaphysical

metaldehyd [ˣme:t-] *s3* metaldehyde

me'tall *s3* metal; *av ~* (*äv.*) metal ... **-arbetare** metalworker **-glans** metallic lustre **-haltig** *a1* metalliferous **-industri** metal industry **-isk** *a5* metallic **-klang** metallic ring **-ografi** *s3* metallography **-o'id** *s3* metalloid **-skrot** [metal] scrap **-tråd** [metal] wire **-trådsnät** wire netting **-'urg** *s3* metallurgist **-ur'gi** *s3* metallurgy

metamorfos [-mår'få:s] *s3* metamorphosis (*pl* metamorphoses)

me'tan *s4* methane; marsh gas **-ol** [-'nå:l] *s3* methanol, methyl alcohol, wood alcohol

metare angler; (*med fluga*) [fly-]fisherman

meta'stas *s3* metastasis

meta'tes *s3* metathesis (*pl* metatheses)

metdon fishing tackle

mete *s6* angling; [fly-]fishing

meteor [-'å:r] *s3* meteor **-'it** *s3* meteorite; (*järn-*) siderite; (*sten-*) aerolite **-liknande** meteoric **-olog** meteorologist **-ologi** *s3* meteorology **-ologisk** *a5* meteorological **-sten** meteorite

meter ['me:-] *s9, versl. s2* metre; *AE.* meter **-hög** *a* (one) metre high **-mått** (*redskap*) metre-measure; (*hopfällbart*) folding rule **-system** metric system **-varor** *pl, ung.* yard (piece) goods **-vis** (*per meter*) by the metre; (*meter på meter*) yards and yards, metres and metres

met|krok fish-hook **-mask** angling worm **-ning** [-e:-] *se mete*

me'tod *s3* method; (*tillvägagångssätt äv.*) procedure; (*tillverknings-*) process; (*sätt*) way, manner **-'ik** *s3* methodology; (*friare*) methods (*pl*), system **-isk** *a5* methodical **-iskt** *adv* methodically; *gå ~ till väga* proceed methodically; *gå ~ till väga med ngt* (*äv.*) do s.th. methodically

metod|ism Methodism **-ist** Methodist

metod||lära methodology **-studie** methods study, study of methods **-tidmätning** methods

time measurement (*förk.* MTM)

metony'mi *s3* metonymy

metrev [fishing] line

metr|ik *s3* prosody **-isk** ['me:-] *a5* prosodic; metrical

metronom metronome

metropol [-'på:l] *s3* metropolis **-'it** *s3, kyrkl.* metropolitan

metspö fishing rod; *med ~* (*äv.*) with rod and line

me'tyl *s3* methyl **-alkohol** methyl alcohol, methanol **-enblått** [-ˣle:n-] methylene blue

Mexico ['meksikɷ] *n* Mexico

mexi|'kan *s3* Mexican **-'kansk** [-a:-] *a5* Mexican

mezzosopran [ˣmetså-, -'pra:n] *s3* mezzo-soprano

m.fl. *förk. för med flera* and others

mi'au miaow!

mickel ['mikk-] *s2* fox; *M~ räv* Reynard the Fox

middag ['midda:g, *vard.* 'midda] *s2* **1** (*mitt på dagen*) noon; midday; *god ~!* good afternoon!; *i går ~* yesterday noon; *framemot ~en* towards midday; *på ~en* (*~arna*) in the middle of the day **2** (*måltid*) dinner; (*bjudning*) dinner party; *äta ~* have dinner; *äta ~ kl. 7* dine at seven o'clock; *~en är serverad* dinner is served (ready); *bjuda ngn på ~* invite s.b. to dinner; *vad får vi till ~?* what are we going to have for dinner?; *vara borta på ~* be out to (for) dinner; *sova ~* have (take) an afterdinner nap **middags|bjudning** dinner party; (*inbjudan*) invitation to a dinner party **-bord** dinner table; *duka ~et* lay the table for dinner **-gäst** dinner guest, guest for dinner **-hetta** midday heat **-höjd** meridian altitude; *bildl.* meridian **-klänning** dinner gown (dress) **-mat** dinner food **-rast** break for dinner **-sällskap** company of dinner guests **-tid** *vid ~[en]* at (about) noon (dinner time)

midfastosöndag [-i:-] mid-Lent Sunday; *Storbritannien* Mothering Sunday

midja [ˣmi:-] *s1* waist; *om ~n* round the waist **midje|kjol** waist slip **-mått** waist-measurement

midnatt [-i:-] midnight

midnatts|sol midnight sun **-tid** *vid ~* at midnight

midskepps [ˣmi:dʃepps] amidships

midsommar [ˣmi:d-, *vanl.* ˣmiss-] midsummer **-afton** Midsummer Eve **-blomster** wood cranesbill **-dag** Midsummer Day **-firande** *s6* Midsummer celebration **-stång** *se majstång*

midströms [-i:-] in mid-current

midvinter [-i:-] midwinter

mig [mi:g, *vard.* mejj] *pron* (*objektsform av jag*) me; *rfl* myself; *jag gjorde ~ i foten* I hurt my foot; *en vän till ~* a friend of mine; *vad vill du ~?* what do you want me for?; *kom hem till ~* come round to my place; *när det gäller ~ själv* [speaking] for myself, as far as I am concerned; *jag tror ~ veta att* I think I know that

mi'grän *s3* migraine

mikrob [-'krå:b] *s3* microbe

mikro|biologi microbiology **-dator** microcomputer **-fiche** [ˣmi:kråfiʃ, -'fiʃ, -ɷ-] *s5* microfiche **-film** microfilm **-fon** [-'få:n] s3 microphone; *vard.* mike **-fotografering** photomicrography, micrography; (*nedfotografering*) microphotography **-fotografi** photomicrograph; microphotograph **-kosmos** microcosm, microcosmos **-meter** [-'me:-] s2 micrometer **mikro|n** [-'krå:n] s9, s3 micron **-organism** microorganism **-processor** *data.* microprocessor **-skop** s7 microscope **-skopisk** [-'skå:-] a5 microscopic[al] **-teknik** microtechnology **-våg** microwave **-vågsugn** microwave oven

mil s9 ten kilometres; *eng. motsv.* about six miles; *engelsk* ~ mile; *nautisk* ~ nautical mile **mila** s1 (*kol-*) charcoal stack (kiln, pit); (*atom-*) atomic pile, nuclear reactor

mild a1 mild (*i* (*till*) *smaken* in taste); (*mjuk*) soft (*färg* colour; *svar* answer); (*dämpad*) mellow; (*lugnande*) soothing (*röst* voice); (*ej sträng*) lenient (*dom* sentence; *mot* to[wards]); (*lindrig, saktmodig*) gentle; ~*a vindar* gentle winds; *med milt våld* with gentle compulsion; ~*a makter!* Holy Moses!; *du* ~*e!* Good Lord!; *så till den* ~*a grad* so utterly, so awfully **-het** mildness *etc.*; leniency, lenience; (*barmhärtighet*) mercy **-ra** mitigate; temper; (*lätta* [*på*]) alleviate, relax; (*dom, straff äv.*) reduce **-ras** *dep* grow milder (*etc.*); soften **-väder** *det är* ~ a thaw has set in

mi'lis s3 militia **-soldat** militiaman **mili'tant** a1 militant
militariser|a militarize **-ing** militarization **militar|ism** militarism **-ist** militarist **-istisk** [-'riss-] a5 militaristic
militieombudsman [-'li:tsie-, -ˣlittsie-] *hist.*, ~*en* the [Swedish] Parliamentary Commissioner for Military Affairs
mili'tär I s3 (*krigsman*) military man, soldier; (*krigsmakt*) military force[s *pl*]; *högre* ~*er* officers of high rank; ~*en* the military (*pl*); (*hären*) the army **II** a1 military **-allians** military alliance **-attaché** military (service) attaché **-befälhavare** general officer commanding [, military command area south *etc.*] **-diktatur** military dictatorship **-domstol** military tribunal, court martial **-flygplan** army plane **-förläggning** garrison, military camp **-högskola** *M~n* [the Swedish] armed forces staff and war college **-isk** a5 military; army; (*soldatmässig*) soldierly; militant **-junta** military junta **-ledning** ~*en* the military council **-läkare** military (army, naval, air force) medical officer **-makt** military power **-marsch** military march **-musikkår** military band **-område** military command [area]; *AE.* military district **-polis** military police **-sjukhus** military hospital **-tjänst** military service **-utbildning** military training **-väsen** military (service) affairs (*pl*) **-yrket** the military profession

miljard [-'ja:rd] s3 milliard; *AE.* billion; *en* ~ (*vanl.*) one thousand million
mil'jon s3 million; *fem* ~*er pund* five million pounds **-affär** transaction involving millions [of pounds (*etc.*)] **-belopp** *pl* millions **-förlust** loss involving millions [of pounds (*etc.*)]; [*a*] loss of a million **-stad** city (town) with [over] a million inhabitants **-tals** [-a:-] millions of **-te** [-ˣjɷ:n-] (*ordningstal*) millionth **-'är** s3 millionaire

mil'jö s3 environment; *ibl.* milieu; (*omgivning*) surroundings (*pl*); background, general setting **-förstöring** pollution [of the environment] **-minister** secretary of state for the environment **-påverkan** environmental influence **-rörelse** environmental movement **-skadad** a5 maladjusted **-skildring** description of social milieu **-skydd** environmental protection **-station** recycling centre **-vård** control of the environment **-vårdsproblem** environmental problem **-vänlig** non-polluting

milliard *se* **miljard**
milli|'bar s9 millibar **-gram** [-'gramm] milligramme **-liter** [-'li:] millilitre **-meter** [-'me:-] millimetre **-meterpapper** graph paper **-meterrättvisa** absolute fairness
millopp *sport.* mile race
milslång *en* ~ *promenad* a walk of a mile, a mile walk; ~*a köer* queues miles and miles long
mil|sten, -stolpe milestone (*äv. bildl.*)
mils|vid stretching (extending) for miles; *-vitt omkring* for miles around
milt *adv t.* mild mildly; ~ *uttryckt* to put it mildly
miltals [-a:-] for miles
mim s3 mime **-ik** s3 mimicry, miming **-iker** ['mi:-] mimic **-isk** ['mi:-] a5 mimic
mimosa [-ˣmå:-, -ɷ:-] s1 mimosa

1 min [mi:n] s3 air; mien; (*ansiktsuttryck*) (*facial*) expression; (*utseende*) look; *göra fula* ~*er* (*en ful* ~) pull an ugly (make a wry) face; *inga sura* ~*er!* no long faces!; *ge sig* ~ *av att vara* pretend to be, put on an air of [being]; *hålla god* ~ [*i elakt spel*] put a good face on it, make the best of a bad job; *vad gjorde hon för* ~? what was the expression on her face?; *utan att förändra en* ~ without moving a muscle

2 min [minn] *mitt, mina, pron, fören.* my; *självst.* mine; *de* ~*a* my people (*vard. folks*); *denna* ~ *åsikt* this view of mine; ~ *dumbom!* fool that I am!; *nu har jag gjort mitt* I have done my part (bit) now; *skilja mellan mitt och ditt* know the difference between mine and thine

min|a s1 mine; *gå på en* ~ hit a mine; *lägga ut* -*or* lay mines; *låta -an springa* (*äv. bildl.*) spring the mine
mina'ret s3 minaret
minder|värdeskomplex inferiority complex **-värdeskänsla** feeling of inferiority **-värdig** a1 inferior **-värdighet** inferiority **-årig** a1 underage, minor, infant; ~*a barn* minors, young children **-årighet** minority, infancy
mindetektor mine detector
mindre ['minn-] *komp. t. liten* I a **1** (*vid jämförelse*) smaller (*till* in); less[er], minor; (*kortare*) shorter (*till* in); (~ *t. antalet*) fewer; (*lägre*) lower; *bli* ~ grow (get) smaller (*etc.*); *ett* ~ *antal än tidigare* fewer (a smaller number) than before; *med hänsyn till* ~ ~ *orsak* ... all the less reason for (+ *ing-form*); *på* ~ *än en timme* in less than (in under) an hour; *ingen* ~ *än kungen själv* no less [a person] than the

king himself; *ingenting* ~ *än* nothing short of **2** (*utan eg.* jämförelse) small[-sized]; (*yngre*) younger; (*obetydlig*) slight, insignificant; (*oviktig*) unimportant; (*smärre*) minor, lesser; *av* ~ *betydelse* of less importance; *i* ~ *grad* in (to) a minor degree, on a smaller scale; *man kan bli tokig för* ~ (*vard.*) it's more than enough to send one crazy; *inte* ~ *än* no fewer (less) than **3** *med* ~ [*än att*] unless; *det går inte med* ~ [*än att*] *du kommer själv* nothing less than your personal attendance will do, you must be there yourself (in person) **II** *adv* less; not very much; *mer eller* ~ more or less; *så mycket* ~ *som* the less so as; ~ *välbetänkt* ill--advised

Mindre Asien *n* Asia Minor

minera mine; lay mines; *~t område* mined area

mine'ral *s7, åld. pl äv.* -ier mineral **-fyndighet** mineral deposit **-haltig** *a1* containing mineral[s *pl*]; mineral **-isk** *a5* mineral

minera|log mineralogist **-logi** *s3* mineralogy **-logisk** *a5* mineralogical

mineral|olja mineral oil, petroleum **-riket** the mineral kingdom **-ull** mineral (rock) wool **-vatten** mineral water **-ämne** mineral substance

min|ering mining **-fara** danger from mines **-fartyg** minelayer **-fält** minefield

minia'tyr *s3* miniature **-format** *i* ~ in miniature **-golf** *se minigolf* **-isera** miniaturize **-målare** miniaturist **-målning** miniature painting; *konkr.* miniature

mini|buss minibus **-cykel** small-wheel folding bicycle **-dator** minicomputer **-golf** miniature golf **-kjol** miniskirt

mini'm|al *a1* minimal, minimum; diminutive, infinitesimal **-era** (*göra så liten som möjligt*) minimize; (*bestämma lägsta gräns för*) fix the lower limit for

minimi|avgift minimum fee **-belopp** minimum [amount] **-gräns** lower limit, floor **-krav** minimum requirements **-lön** minimum salary (wage[s]) **-pris** minimum price, price floor

minimum ['mi:-] *s8* minimum (*pl äv.* minima)

miniräknare pocket calculator

minister [-'nist-] *s2* minister; *Storbritannien äv.* secretary of state; *svenske ~n i London* the Swedish ambassador in London; *brittiske ~n i Sverige* (*äv.*) Her Britannic Majesty's minister to Sweden **-ium** [-'te:-] *s4* ministry; *Storbritannien äv.* government department **-portfölj** *bildl.* office of minister of state, portfolio **-post** minister's appointment, ministerial duties **-president** *ung.* prime minister, premier **-råd** council of ministers; *Storbritannien* cabinet

minis'tär *s3* ministry, government, cabinet; *bilda* ~ form a government (*etc.*)

mink *s2* mink **-päls** mink coat

min|nas *v2, dep* remember, recollect; *om jag -ns rätt* if I remember rightly, if my memory does not fail me; *jag vill* ~ *att* I seem to remember that; *så långt tillbaka jag kan* ~ as far back as I can remember; *nu -des hon alltsammans* now it all came back to her; *han kunde inte* ~ *att han gjort det* he couldn't remember having done it; *inte på den dag jag -ns* it's so long

ago I can't remember

minne *s6* **1** (*-sförmåga*) memory; mind; *tappa ~t* lose one's memory; *bevara* (*hålla*) *i ~t* keep in mind; *hålla ngt i ~t* bear s.th. in mind; ago *ett upp och ett i* ~ one down and one to carry; *återkalla i ~t* recall, recollect; *med detta i färskt* ~ with this fresh in my (*etc.*) memory; *lägga på ~t* commit to memory, remember; *dra sig ngt till ~s* remember (recollect) s.th., call s.th. to mind; *det har fallit mig ur ~t* it has escaped my memory (slipped my mind); *återge ur ~t* repeat from memory **2** *med ngns goda* ~ with a p.'s approval (consent) **3** (*hågkomst*) memory, remembrance; (*åminnelse äv.*) commemoration; (*minnesbild*) recollection; (*händelse i det förgångna*) memorable event; *ett* ~ *för livet* an unforgettable experience; *uppliva gamla ~n* revive old memories; *hans* ~ *skall leva* his memory will never fade; *till* ~ *av* in memory of; *vid ~t av* at the recollection of **4** (*memoarer o.d.*) recollections, memoirs **5** (*-sgåva, suvenir*) remembrance, souvenir, keepsake **6** *data.* store; *AE.* storage; *yttre* ~ external store (storage)

minnes|album remembrance book **-anteckning** memorandum **-beta** *s1, en* ~ s.th. not easily forgotten **-bild** picture in one's mind **-dag** memorial day **-förlust** loss of memory **-god** with a good memory **-gudstjänst** memorial service **-gåva** keepsake, souvenir **-högtid** memorial ceremony, commemoration **-lista** check list; list of engagements **-märke** memorial, monument; (*fornlämning*) relic, ancient monument **-ord** *pl* words of remembrance **-regel** mnemonic rule **-rik** rich in memories; (*oförglömlig*) unforgettable **-runa** obituary **-sak 1** (*som beror av minnet*) *en* ~ a matter of memory **2** *se suvenir* **-skrift** memorial publication **-sten** monument **-tal** commemoration speech, memorial address **-tavla** commemorative (memorial) tablet **-teckning** biography (*över* of) **-utställning** commemorative exhibition **-värd a1** memorable (*för* to), worth remembering

minnesång minnesong **-are** minnesinger

minoisk [-'nå:-] *a5* Minoan

minoritet *s3* minority; *vara i* ~ be in the (a) minority

minoritets|problem minority problem **-regering** minority government **-ställning** *vara i* ~ be a minority

minröjning mine clearance, removal of land mines

min'sann to be sure; I can tell (assure) you; I'm blessed (blowed); *det är* ~ *inte så lätt* it is not at all that easy; ~ *om jag det begriper* I'm blessed if I understand that; *jag skall* ~ *ge dig!* my word, I'll let you have it!

minsk|a reduce (*med* by; *till* to); diminish, decrease, lessen; (*förkorta*) shorten; (*dämpa*) abate (*ngns iver* a p.'s zeal); (*nedskära*) cut [down] (*utgifterna* the expenses); (*lätta på*) relieve (*spänningen* the tension); ~ *hastigheten* reduce speed, slow down, decelerate; ~ *i betydelse* become less important; ~ *i vikt* go down in (lose) weight; ~ *ngt på sina anspråk* not demand quite so much, reduce one's claims **minskad** *a5* reduced *etc.* *(med by)* **minskas** *dep* grow (become, get) less; diminish, decrease; be reduced *(i in; med by)*; *(avtaga)* fall off; *(dämpas)* abate; *(sjunka)* fall, go down, sink; *(i värde)* depreciate **minskning** reduction, diminution, decrease; *(nedskärning)* curtailment, cut; *(i värde)* depreciation **minspel** changes in facial expression; mimicry **min|spränga** blow up by mines (a mine); *bli -sprängd* be blown up by mines (a mine) **-sprängning** *(-sprängande)* [the] blowing up *(av of)* by mines; *(med pl)* mine-explosion **-spärr** mine barrage **minst** *superl. t. liten* I *a* smallest; least; *(yngst)* youngest; *(kortast)* shortest; *(minimalast)* minimum, minutest; *~a motståndets lag* the law of least resistance; *~a gemensamma nämnare* [the] lowest common denominator; *utan ~a tvekan* without the slightest (least) hesitation; *han hade ~ fel* he had [the] fewest mistakes; *med ~a möjliga* with a (the) minimum of; *in i ~a detalj* [down] to the smallest (minutest) detail; *det ~a a)* *(som substantiv)* the least, *b)* *(som adv)* the least [*vard.* little bit]; *inte det ~a trött* not [in] the least tired; *inte bry sig det ~a om* not care twopence about II *adv* least; the least, at least; *(~ av allt)* least of all; *inte ~ viktig var frågan om* the question of ... was as important as any; *~ sagt* to say the least [of it] **minsvep|a** sweep for mines **-are** minesweeper **-ning** minesweeping **minsökare** mine detector **minus** ['mi:-] I *s7* minus [sign]; *(friare)* minus quantity, minus; *(brist)* deficit, shortage II *adv* minus; *~ 10 grader* 10 degrees [Centigrade] below zero; *~ 3 % kassarabatt* less 3 % discount; *plus ~ noll* plus minus naught **-grad** degree of frost (below zero) **minuskel** [-'nusk-] *s3* minuscule **minustecken** minus sign **mi'nut** *s3* **1** minute; *tio ~ers promenad* ten minutes' walk; *fem ~er över tre* five minutes past three; *en gång i ~en* once a minute; *på ~en* to the minute; *om (på) några ~er* in a few minutes; *i sista ~en* at the last minute, in the nick of time **2** *hand.* retail; *i ~* by *(AE.* at) retail; *köpa i ~* buy retail; *sälja i ~* retail, sell [by] retail **-handel** retail business **-handelspris** retail price **minutiös** [-tsi'ö:s] *a1* meticulous, scrupulous; minute **minutläggare** minelayer **minut|pris** retail price **-visare** minute hand **minör** sapper **mirakel** [-'ra:-] *s7, s4* miracle **-spel** miracle play **miraku'lös** *a1* miraculous **misan|trop** [-'trå:p] *s3* misanthrope **-tro'pi** *s3* misanthropy **-tropisk** [-'trå:-] *a5* misanthropic[al] **mischmasch** *s7* mishmash, hotchpotch, hodgepodge **miserabel** *a2* wretched, miserable; *(ömklig)* pitiable **miss** *s2* *(misslyckande)* miss; *(felslag o.d.)*

missed shot (hit, stroke) **missa** *(bomma)* miss, fail to hit (strike); *(misslyckas)* miss one's shot (hit, stroke, aim); *bildl. äv.* fail; *(om sak)* miss its mark **miss|akta** *(ringakta)* disdain; *(förakta)* despise **-aktning** disrespect, disdain; *(förakt)* contempt **-anpassad** *a5* maladjusted **-belåten** displeased *(med at, about)*; dissatisfied *(med with)* **-belåtenhet** displeasure, dissatisfaction **-bildad** *a5* malformed, misshapen **-bildning** malformation; defect; deformity **missbruk** *(oriktigt bruk)* misuse; *(skadligt bruk)* abuse **missbruka** *(använda fel)* misuse; *(alkohol, förtroende, makt o.d.)* abuse; *kan lätt ~s* lends itself to abuse[s]; *~ ngns godhet* take undue advantage of a p.'s kindness; *~ Guds namn* take the name of God in vain **missbrukare** misuser; abuser **miss|dåd** misdeed; evil deed **-dådare** malefactor, evil-doer **-fall** miscarriage; *få ~* *(äv.)* miscarry **-firma** *v1* insult; abuse **-firmelse** *s5* insult; abuse **-foster** abortion *(äv. bildl.)*; *äv. bildl.* monstrosity **-färga** discolour, stain **-färgning** discoloration **-förhållande** disproportion, disparity *(mellan between)*; *(friare)* incongruity, anomaly; *sociala ~n* social evils **-förstå** misunderstand; *som lätt kan ~s* that is liable (likely) to be misunderstood **-förstånd** misunderstanding; *(misstag)* mistake **-grepp** mistake, bad move **-gynna** treat unfairly; *exporten har ~ts av utvecklingen* development has been unfavourable to exports **-gärning** evil deed; *(svagare)* misdeed **-hag** *s7* displeasure *(med ngn with s.b.; med ngt at s.th.)*; dislike *(med of)* **-haga** displease, be displeasing to; *det ~r mig* *(äv.)* I dislike it **-haglig** [-a:-] *a1* displeasing; *(starkare)* offensive, objectionable; *(förhatlig)* obnoxious; *(impopulär)* unpopular; *~ person* *(äv.)* undesirable person **-handel** maltreatment *(av of)*; *jur.* assault [and battery]; cruelty; *bli utsatt för ~* be assaulted **-handla** maltreat; *jur.* assault; *bildl.* handle roughly; *(t.ex. språk)* murder **-hugg** *i ~* by mistake **-humör** *på ~* in a bad temper **-hushålla** *~ med* mismanage, be uneconomical with **-hushållning** mismanagement, misuse **-hällighet** discord, dissension; *~er* *(äv.)* quarrels **mis'sil** *s3* missile **mission** [mi'ʃo:n] **1** *(beskickning)* mission; *(kall äv.)* vocation; *ha en ~ att fylla* have a vocation (call) **2** *relig.* missions *(pl)*; *inre (yttre) ~* home (foreign) missions *(pl)* **-era** preach [the Gospel] **missions|förbund** *Svenska M~et* the Swedish Mission Covenant Church **-föreståndare** mission superintendent **-hus** mission hall, chapel **-station** mission station, mission **-sällskap** missionary society **missio'när** [-ʃo-] *s3* missionary **mis'siv** *s3* **1** *(skrivelse)* missive; *(följebrev)* covering letter **2** *kyrkl.* ordination as a temporary curate **miss|klä[da]** be unbecoming to, misbecome, not suit; *ingenting -klär en skönhet* *(ung.)* everything becomes a beauty **-klädsam** unbecoming; *(ej smickrande)* unflattering; *(-pry-*

M

dande) disfiguring **-kreditera** discredit **-krediterande** *a4* discreditable (*för* to) **-kund** *r,* *se förbarmande*; *utan ~* (*äv.*) without [any] compassion **-kunda** *rfl* have mercy (compassion) (*över* upon) **-kundsam** *a1* merciful; (*medlidsam*) compassionate, pitying **-känd** *a5* misjudged; unappreciated, underrated **-känna** misjudge, underestimate

miss|leda mislead; *jfr vilse-* **-ljud** jarring sound; *mus.* dissonance (*äv. bildl.*)

miss|lyckad (*som -ats*) unsuccessful; (*förfelad, felslagen*) abortive; *~e existenser* failures; *vara ~* be a failure, have gone wrong **-lyckande** *s6* failure; fiasco **-lyckas** *dep* fail (*i, med* in); be (prove, turn out) unsuccessful (a failure)

miss|lynt *a4* ill-humoured; cross; *göra ngn ~* put s.b. out [of humour], upset s.b., make s.b. cross **-lynthet** ill (bad) humour; crossness **-minna** *rfl, om jag inte -minner mig* if I remember rightly **-mod** downheartedness, depression (dejection) [of spirit[s]]; (*nedslagenhet*) discouragement **-modig** downhearted, depressed, despondent

missne *s9, s7, bot.* calla, arum lily

miss|nöjd (*i sht tillfälligt*) dissatisfied; (*i sht varaktigt*) discontented, displeased; *vara ~ med* (*ogilla*) disapprove of **-nöje** dissatisfaction; discontent; displeasure; (*ogillande*) disapproval (*med* of); *allmänt ~ råder bland* discontent is rife among; *väcka ~ mot en dom* give notice of appeal against a verdict **-nöjesyttring** signs (murmurs) (*pl*) of discontent **-pryda** disfigure, spoil the look of **-riktad** *a5* misdirected; (*oklok*) misguided, ill-advised

missroman sentimental novel

miss|räkna *rfl* miscalculate; *bildl.* make a miscalculation **-räkning** (*fel-*) miscalculation; *bildl.* disappointment (*för* for, to; *över* at) **-sköta** (*hopskr. missköta*) mismanage; (*försumma*) neglect; *~ sig a*) (*sin hälsa*) neglect one's health, *b*) (*sitt arbete e.d.*) neglect one's duties (work) **-stämning** (*hopskr. misstämning*) feeling (sense) of discord (discontent, disharmony) **-sämja** (*hopskr. missämja*) dissension, discord

miss|tag mistake; (*fel*) error; (*förbiseende*) oversight, blunder, slip; *det var ett ~ av mig* it was a mistake on my part, it was my mistake; *göra e tt svårt ~* make a bad mistake, commit a serious blunder; *av ~* by mistake, inadvertently **-taga** *rfl* make a mistake; be wrong; *~ sig på* (*äv.*) misjud ge, get a wrong idea of (about); *man kan ju ~ sig* (*äv.*) one can of course be mistaken; *man kunde inte ~ sig på* there was no mistaking; *om jag inte -t* ar mig if I am not mistaken

miss|tanke suspicion; (*förmodan*) supposition; (*ond aning*) misgiving; *hysa -tankar* entertain suspicions (*mot ngn för ngt* about s.b. for s.th.; *om* as to); *fatta -tankar* become suspicious (*mot ngn* of s.b.; *om* about); *väcka -tankar* arouse suspicion (*hos* in; *om* about, as to) **-tolka** misinterpret; (*ngns avsikter äv.*) misconstrue

misstro I *s9* distrust (*mot* of); (*starkare*) disbelief (*till* in) **II** *v4* distrust, mistrust, be suspicious of; (*tvivla på*) doubt

misstroende *s6, se misstro I*; lack of confidence (*mot* in) **-votum** vote of censure (*mot* on)

misstrogen distrustful, mistrustful (*mot* of); (*skeptisk*) incredulous **-het** distrustfulness *etc.*; incredulity

miss|trösta despair (*om* of); give up hope (*om* of) **-tröstan** *r* despair (*om* of) **-tycka** take it amiss, be offended [at]; *om du inte -tycker* (*äv.*) if you don't mind **-tyda** misinterpret; misconstrue

misstänk|a suspect; *~ ngn för ngt* (*för att ha*) suspect s.b. of s.th. (of having); be suspicious of; (*befara*) apprehend; (*svagare äv.*) fancy, guess **-liggöra** cast (throw) suspicion upon **-sam** *a1* suspicious (*mot* of); full of suspicion (*mot* against) **-samhet** suspiciousness

misstänkt *a1* suspected (*för* [*att*] of [+ *ing--form*]); (*tvivelaktig*) doubtful, dubious; (*som inger misstro*) suspicious; *den ~e* the suspect; *som ~ för* (*äv.*) on [a] suspicion of; *vara ~ för* (*för att ha*) be under suspicion for (for having); *göra ngn ~ för* direct suspicion on s.b. for

miss|unna [be]grudge; (*avundas*) envy **-unnsam** *a1* grudging (*mot* towards); (*avundsam*) envious (*mot* of) **-uppfatta** misunderstand, misconceive; (*-tyda*) misread, put a wrong interpretation on, get a wrong idea of **-uppfattning** misunderstanding, misconception **-visande** *a4* misleading **-visning** (*kompassnålens*) deviation, variation; *ostlig ~* easterly magnetic declination **-växt** *s3* failure of the crop[s]; [a] bad harvest **-växtår** year of crop failure **-öde** mishap, misadventure; *råka ut för ett ~* have a slight accident; *genom ett ~* (*äv.*) by mischance; *tekniskt ~* technical hitch

mist *s3* mist; fog

mista *v1, v3* lose; be deprived of

miste *adv* wrong; *gå ~ om* miss, fail to secure; *ta ~ på a*) (*ngn*) mistake for s.b. else, *b*) (*ngt*) make a mistake about, misjudge; *du kan inte ta ~ på vägen* you cannot miss the road; *det är inte att ta ~ på* there is no mistaking

mistel *s2, bot.* mistletoe

mist|lur foghorn **-signal** fog signal **-signalering** fog signalling **-siren** fog siren

mi'sär *s3* destitution; penury; (*kortspel.*) misery

mitella [-ˣtella] *s1* triangular bandage; sling

mitra [ˣmi:] *s1* mitre

1 mitt *pron, se 2 min*

2 mitt I *s3* middle; *i* (*på*) *~en* in the middle; *i deras ~* in their midst; *från ~en av mars* (*äv.*) from mid-March **II** *adv* **1** *bryta ~ av* break right in two **2** *~ emellan* midway (somewhere) between; *~ emot* right (just, exactly) opposite, opposite; *~ fram* right in front; *~ framför* right (just, straight) in front of; *~ för ögonen på ngn* right in front of a p.'s eyes; *~ för näsan på ngn* under a p.'s very nose; *~ i* in the [very] middle of; *~ i ansiktet* full in the face; *~ ibland* in the midst of, amidst; *~ igenom* through the centre (middle) of, (*rakt igenom äv.*) right (straight) through; *~ inne i* right in the middle (centre) of, (*landet e.d.*) in the interior of; *~ itu* in two equal parts; *dela ~ itu* (*äv.*) halve; *gå ~ itu* break right in two; *~ på* in the middle of; *~ under a*) *rumsbet.* exactly (directly) under, *b*) *tidsbet.* during, just while; ~ *upp i* in the [very] middle of; *skratta ngn ~ upp i ansiktet* laugh in a p.'s face; ~ *uppe i* up in the middle of, (*friare*) right in the midst of (*arbetet* one's work); ~ *ut i* out into the [very] middle of, right out into; ~ *ute i* out in the middle of, right out in; ~ *över* exactly above (over); *bo ~ över gatan* live straight across the street

mitt|bena *ha* ~ have one's hair parted in the middle **-emellan** [-ˣmell-], **-e'mot** *se 2 mitt II 2*

mitten|parti centre party **-politik** centrist policies

mitterst ['mitt-] *adv* in the centre (*i* of) **mittersta** ['mitt-] *superl. a* middle, central

mitt|fältare, -fältsspelare *sport.* midfielder **-linje** centre (central, median) line; *sport.* halfway line **-parti** central part, centre; *polit.* centre party **-punkt** centre; (*på måltavla*) bull's-eye **-remsa** (*på t.ex. motorväg*) central reserve (reservation); *AE.* median strip **-skepp** (*i kyrka*) nave **-sträng** *se mittremsa* **-söm** middle seam **-uppslag** centre spread **-'åt** *mil.* [eyes] front!

mix *s3, s2* cakemix

mixer ['miks-] *s2* mixer

mixtra ~ *med* potter (meddle) with, (*göra fuffens*) juggle with **mixtur** mixture

mjau *se miau*

mjugg *i uttr.*: *i* ~ covertly; *le i* ~ laugh up one's sleeve

mjuk *a1* soft (*till i* in); (*om färgton e.d.*) softened, mellow; *bildl.* gentle (*om konturer e.d.*) sweeping, gentle; (*böjlig*) limp; (*smidig*) supple; lithe, limber; (*om rörelse o.d.*) graceful; (*eftergiven, smidig*) pliable, flexible; (*spak*) meek, mild; *~t bröd* soft bread; *ha ~t anslag* (*mus.*) have a light touch; *bli ~, se mjukna*; *göra ~* make soft, soften **-delar** *pl, anat.* soft parts **-glass** soft ice cream **-görare** softener, plasticizer **-het** softness *etc.*; pliancy; flexibility **-landa** softland **-landning** soft landing

mjukna [-u:-] soften, get (become) soft[er]

mjuk|ost cream cheese, cheese spread **-plast** non-rigid plastic **-porr** soft-porn **-valuta** soft currency **-vara** *data.* software

mjäkig *a1* mawkish; sloppy, sentimental

1 mjäll *s7, s9* dandruff, scurf

2 mjäll *a1* **1** (*mör*) tender **2** (*ren, vit*) transparently white

mjältbrand *veter.* anthrax

mjält|e *s2, anat.* spleen **-hugg** stitch [in the (one's) side] **-sjuk** splenetic (*äv. bildl.*); *bildl. äv.* hypochondriac **-sjuka** *bildl.* spleen; *med.* hypochondria

mjärde [ˣmjä:r-] *s2* osier basket; (*ståltråds-*) wire cage

mjöd *s7, s4* mead

mjöl *s7* flour; (*osiktat*) meal; (*pulver*) flour, powder, dust; *sammalet ~* (*äv.*) wholemeal (*AE.* whole-wheat) flour; *inte ha rent ~ i påsen* (*bildl.*) not be on the level

mjöl|a flour, sprinkle over with flour **-bagge** flour-beetle **-dagg** mildew, blight **-dryga** *s1, bot.* ergot **-ig** *a1* floury, mealy

mjölk *s3* milk; *fet* (*mager*) ~ rich (thin) milk

mjölk|a 1 milk **2** (*ge mjölk*) give (yield) milk **3** (*utsuga*) milk, pump dry **-affär** dairy **-bar** *s3* milk bar; *AE.* drugstore **-bil** milk (milk-collecting) lorry **-bud** milkman **-choklad** milk chocolate

1 mjölke *s2, zool.* milt, soft roe

2 mjölke *s2, bot.* rosebay willowherb, fireweed

mjölk|erska milkmaid **-flaska** (*av glas*) milk-bottle; (*av bleck*) milk-can **-förpackning** milk carton **-ko** milch cow (*äv. bildl.*), milker **-körtel** lactiferous gland **-maskin** milking machine **-ning** milking **-pall** milking stool **-pulver** powdered milk **-socker** milk sugar, lactose **-syra** lactic acid **-syrabakterier** *pl* lactic-acid bacteria **-tand** milk tooth, deciduous tooth **-utkörare** milkman **-vit** milky (milk) white **-ört** *se 2 mjölke*

mjölmat farinaceous food

mjöln|ardräng [-ö:-] miller's man **-are** [-ö:-] miller

mjölon [-ån] *s7, bot.* bearberry

mjölsäck (*tom*) flour (meal) sack; (*fylld*) sack of flour

m.m. (*förk. för med mera*) etc.

mnemotekn|ik *s3* mnemonics (*sg*) **-isk** [-'teck-] *a5* mnemonic, mnemotechnic

MO [ˣämmɷ] *förk. för militieombudsmannen*

mo *s2* (*sand*) fine sand; (*mark*) sandy plain, heath

moaré *s3, s4* moiré; watered silk (fabric)

moatjé [-'tçe:] *s3* partner

mobb [-å-] *s2* mob **mobba** mob **mobb[n]ing** mobbing

mo'bil I *a1* mobile **II** *s3* mobile **-ier** *pl, se lösegendom, bohag*

mobiliser|a mobilize; (*friare äv.*) muster **-ing** [-'se:-] mobilization

mobiltelefon [-ˣbi:l-] cellular telephone

moçambik|ier [-'bi:k-] Mozambican **-isk** *a5* Mozambican

1 mocka [-å-] *v1* clear of dung, clean out; ~ *gräl med* (*vard.*) pick a quarrel with

2 mocka [-å-] *s9* (*kaffesort*) mocha

3 mocka [-å-] *s9* (*skinn*) suede [leather]

mockajacka suede jacket

mockakopp [small] coffee cup, demitasse

mockaplysch moquette

mocka'sin [-å-] *s3* moccasin

mockasked [small] coffee spoon

mockaskor suede shoes

1 mod *s7* **1** (*-ighet*) courage; intrepidity; (*moraliskt äv.*) fortitude; *hans ~ sjönk* (*svek honom*) his courage (heart) sank (failed him); *med förtvivlans ~* with the courage of despair; *hålla ~et uppe* keep up one's courage; *hämta nytt ~* take fresh courage; *ta ~ till sig* pluck up courage; *tappa ~et* lose heart, be discouraged **2** (*sinne, humör*) spirits (*pl*); mood; *vara väl* (*illa*) *till ~s* be at ease (ill at ease); *vara vid gott ~* be in good spirits; *i hastigt ~* without premeditation; *med berått ~* deliberately, wilfully, in cold blood

2 mod *s4* fashion; style; *bestämma ~et* set the fashion; *är högsta ~* is all the fashion (rage); *läkare på ~et* fashionable doctor; *vara* (*komma*) *på ~et* be in the (come into) fashion

mo'dal *a1* modal; *~t hjälpverb* auxiliary of

mood
modd [-å-] *s3* slush **moddig** *a1* slushy
moddlare [-å-] flat brush
mode *s6, se* 2 *mod* **-affär** *(hatt-)* milliner's [shop] **-docka** dressmaker's dummy *(äv. bildl.)*; *bildl. äv.* fashion plate **-färg** fashionable colour **-hus** fashion house **-journal** fashion magazine **-kung** king (dictator) of fashion **-lejon** dandy, fop
mo'dell *s3* **1** *(mönster)* model; *tekn. o. bildl. äv.* pattern; *i sht hand.* style; *(hatt-, sko-)* shape **2** *pers.* [artist's] model; *sitta (stå)* ~ sit (stand) as a model *(för, åt* to); *teckna efter levande* ~ draw from living models **-bygge** *abstr.* construction of models; *konkr.* model **-era** model *(efter* from; *i* in) **-ering** modelling **-flygplan** model aeroplane **-järnväg** model railway **-klänning** model gown **-lera** *(hopskr. modellera)* modelling clay, plasticine
mo'dem *s7* modem
mode|nyck freak (whim) of fashion **-ord** vogue word
moder *-n* mödrar *(jfr mor)* mother; *bildl.* parent; *blivande mödrar* expectant mothers
mode'rat *a1* *(måttfull)* moderate; *(skälig)* reasonable, fair; *~a priser* reasonable prices; *M~a samlingspartiet (i Sverige)* [the] moderate party **-ion** moderation; restraint **-or** [-ˣra:tår] *s3, atomfys.* moderator
moderbolag parent company
moderer|a moderate **-ing** moderation
moderfartyg mother ship
mode|riktig in fashion, fashionable, trendy **-riktning** fashion trend
moder|kaka *anat.* placenta **-land** mother country **-lig** *a1* motherly; *(om t.ex. känslor, oro)* maternal **-lighet** motherliness; maternity **-liv** womb **-lös** motherless
modern [-ˈdä:rn] *a1* *(nutida)* modern, contemporary; *(fullt* ~) [quite] up-to-date; *(nu på modet)* fashionable; *bli* ~ come into fashion; ~ *dans* ballroom dancing **-isera** modernize **-isering** modernization **-ism** modernism **-ist** *s3* modernist **-istisk** [-ˈnist-] *a5* modernist **-itet** *s3* modernity; *~er* innovations, *neds.* novelties
moder|näring principal (primary) industry; *(jordbruk)* agriculture **-planta** mother plant
moders|bröst *barnet vid ~et* the child at its mother's breast **-bunden** *vara* ~ have a mother fixation **-famn** *i ~en* in the maternal (one's mother's) embrace **-glädje** maternal (a mother's) joy **-instinkt** maternal (a mother's) instinct
moderskap *s7* motherhood, maternity
moderskaps|försäkring maternity insurance **-penning** maternity allowance
moders|känsla *~n hos henne* the mother in her **-kärlek** maternal (a mother's) love **-mjölk** *med ~en* with one's mother's milk, *(friare)* from earliest infancy **-mål** mother tongue, native language; *(som skolämne)* Swedish, English *etc.* **-målslärare** teacher of (in) Swedish *(etc.)*; *vår* ~ *(vanl.)* our Swedish *(etc.)* master
modersugga mother-sow
mode|sak *konkr.* fashionable (fancy) article; *abstr.* [a] matter of fashion **-skapare** fashion designer

mo'dest *a1* modest
mode|tecknare fashion designer, stylist **-teckning** fashion drawing (design) **-tidning** *se modejournal* **-visning** fashion show
modfälld *a5* discouraged, disheartened *(över* at); *bli ~ (äv.)* lose courage
modifi|era modify; *(dämpa)* moderate **-kation** modification, moderation
modig *a1* **1** courageous; *(tapper)* brave, plucky; *(djärv)* bold; *(oförvägen)* gallant; *(oförskräckt)* valiant, intrepid **2** *kosta sina ~a slantar* cost a pretty penny; *väga sina ~a 100 kilo* weigh all of 100 kilos
modist milliner, modiste
mod|lös dispirited; spiritless **-löshet** dispiritedness **-stulen** *a5* downhearted
mo'dul *s3* module; *mat. o. fys.* modulus
modul|ation modulation **-era** modulate
modus ['mɔ:-] *n, r, språkv.* mood
mog|en *a3* ripe *(för, till* for; *(om frukt äv.)* mellow; *(friare o. bildl.)* mature; *bildl. äv.* ready; ~ *ålder* maturity, mature age; *efter -et övervägande* after careful consideration; *när tiden är* ~ when the time is ripe (has come) **mogen|het** ripeness *etc.*; maturity **-hetsexamen** matriculation
mogn|a [-ɔ:-] ripen *(äv. bildl.)*; *eg. äv.* get ripe; *(bildl. o. friare)* mature, come to maturity **-ad** *s3* ripeness *(äv. bildl.)*; *i sht bildl.* maturity
mognads|grad degree of ripeness *(etc.)* **-process** process of maturing (growing up)
mogul ['mɔ:-,'må:-, *pl* '-gu:-] *s3* Mogul; *Stora* ~ the [Great] Mogul
mohair [-ˈhä:r] *s3* mohair
mohamme'dan *s3, se muhammedan*
mohi'kan *s3* Mohican; *den siste ~en* the last of the Mohicans
mojna [-å-] *sjö.* slacken, lull; ~ *av (äv. bildl.)* fall dead, die down; *när det ~r* when the wind slackens *(etc.)*
mo'jäng *s3*, *~er* gear *(sg)*, gadgets
1 mol *s9 (grundenhet)* mole
2 mol *adv*, ~ *allena* entirely (all) alone, all by o.s.
mol|a ache slightly; *(friare)* chafe; *det ~r i tänderna på mig* my teeth are aching a little **-ande** *a4* aching; *(om värk)* dull; *(ihållande)* persistent
mole'kyl *s3* molecule **-'ar** *a1* molecular **-massa** *relativ* ~ relative molecular mass, molecular weight **-vikt** *se -massa* **-'är** *a1, se -ar*
1 moll [-å-] *r, mus., gå i* ~ be in a minor key
2 moll [-å-] *s3 (tyg)* mull; light muslin
molla [-å-] *s1, bot.* goosefoot
mollskinn [-å-] moleskin
mollton *mus.* minor note **-art** *mus.* minor key **mol'ton** *s3, zool.* mollusc, mollusk; *(om pers.)* jellyfish
moln [-å:-] *s7* cloud *(äv. bildl.)*; *solen går i* ~ the sun is going behind a cloud; *ett ~ låg över hans panna* his brow was [over]clouded **-bank** *s2* cloudbank **-bildning** cloud formation *(äv. konkr.)* **-bädd** bed of clouds **-fri** cloudless, free from clouds; *bildl. äv.* unclouded **-höjd** height of cloud; *flyg.* ceiling **-höljd** *a5* cloud-enveloped **-ig** *a1* cloudy; clouded, overcast **-ighet** cloudiness; *meteor.* [amount of] cloud **-tapp**

wisp of cloud **-täcke** cloud-cover **-täckt** *a4* cloud-covered, overcast **-vägg** cloud-wall
moloken [ˣmɔ:-] *a3* cast down, dejected; down in (at) the mouth
molotovcocktail [ˣmåll-] Molotov cocktail
mol|tiga [ˣmɔ:l-] not utter a sound **-tyst** absolutely silent, [as] quiet as a mouse
Moluckerna [-'luck-] *pl* [the] Molucca (*förr* Spice) Islands, Moluccas
molvärka [ˣmɔ:l-] *se mola*
molyb'den *s3, s4, miner.* molybdenum
momang instant, moment; *på ~en* instantly, this instant
moment *s7* **1** (*tidpunkt*) moment, instant **2** (*beståndsdel*) moment, element; factor; (*i lagtext*) subsection, clause; (*stycke*) paragraph; (*punkt*) point; *ett störande ~* a disturbing factor **-'an** *a1* momentary
moms [måms] *s3, se mervärdeskatt*
mo'nad *s2, filos.* monad
mo'nark *s3* monarch **monar'ki** *s3* monarchy; *inskränkt ~* constitutional (limited) monarchy
monarkism monarchism **monarkist** *s3* monarchist **monarkistisk** [-'kist-] *a5* monarchist
mon'dän [-å-] *a1* fashionable, sophisticated, elegant; *~a människor* (*äv.*) the fashionable set
mone'gask *s3* Monacan, Monegasque **-isk** *a5* Monacan, Monegasque
mone'tär *a1* monetary
mongol [måŋ'gɔ:l] *s3* Mongol[ian]
Mongoliet [måŋgɔ'li:-] *n* Mongolia
mongol|isk [måŋ'gɔ:-] *a5* Mongolian **-[o]'id** mongoloid **-veck** epicanthus, epicanthic fold
monism [-å-] *filos.* monism
monokel [må'nåkk-] *s2, s3* monocle
mono|kotyledon [månå-'då:n] **I** *s3* monocotyledon **II** *a5* monocotyledonous **-krom** [-'krå:m] **I** *s3* monochrome **II** *a5* monochrome **-kromatisk** [-'ma:-] *a5* monochromatic **-kultur** monoculture **-'lit** *s3* monolith **-log** *s3* monologue; soliloquy **-man** [-'ma:n] **I** *s3* monomaniac (*på* as regards) **II** a1 monomaniac[al] **-ma'ni** *s3* monomania **-'plan** *s7, flyg.* monoplane
monopol [-'på:l] *s7* monopoly; exclusive privilege[s *pl*]; *ha ~ på* have the monopoly of, *bildl. äv.* have the sole right to **-isera** monopolize **-isering** monopolization
monoteis|m monotheism **-tisk** *a5* monotheistic[al]
mono|ton [-'tå:n] *a1* monotonous **-toni** [-'ni:] *s3* monotony
monst|er ['måns-] *s7, -rum s4* monster (*till far* of a father); monstrosity **-ru'ös** *a1* monstrous
mon'strans [-å-] *s3, kyrkl.* monstrance
mon'sun [-å-] *s3* monsoon **-regn** monsoon rain
montage [mån'ta:ʃ, måŋ-] *s7, film.* montage
monter ['månn-, 'måŋ-] *s2, s3* showcase; exhibition case
montera [mån-, måŋ-] **1** (*sätta upp*) mount, fit (set) up (*på* on); (*sätta ihop*) assemble, put together; (*installera*) install; (*t.ex. hus, radiomast*) erect; *~ ner* dismantle **2** (*hatt e.d.*) trim
monter|bar [-ˣte:r-] *a1* mountable **-ing** mounting *etc.*; assembly, assemblage; installation; erection

monterings|färdig prefabricated **-hall** assembly shop
montör fitter, mechanic; *elektr.* electrician; *flyg.* rigger
monu'ment *s7* monument; *resa ett ~ över* erect (put up) a monument to
monumen'tal *a1* monumental; (*friare äv.*) grand **-figur** monumental figure **-itet** grandness **-konst** monumental art **-verk** monumental work
mo'ped *s3* moped, *åld.* autocycle **-ist** mopedist, *åld.* autocyclist
mopp [-å-] *s2* mop **moppa** mop, go over with a mop
1 moppe [-å-] *vard. i uttr.: ge ngn (få) på ~* give s.b. (get) a wigging
2 moppe [-å-] *vard.* moped
mops [-å-] *s2* pug[-dog] **mopsa** *rfl* be saucy (*mot* to) **mopsig** *a1, se* näsvis
1 mor [-ɔ:-, -å:-] *s3* (*folk*) Moor
2 mor [-ɔ:-] *modern mödrar* (*jfr moder*) mother; *bli ~* become a mother; *M~s dag* Mother's Day, *Storbritannien äv.* Mothering Sunday; *vara som en ~ för ngn* be like a mother to s.b., mother s.b.
mo'ral *s3, ej pl* (*ngns*) morals (*pl*); (*trupp- o.d.*) morale; (*-isk uppfattning*) morality; (*sedelära*) moral law, ethics (*pl, behandlas som sg o. pl*); (*sens-*) moral; *predika ~ för* preach morality to **-begrepp** moral concept **-isera** moralize (*över* [up]on) **-isk** *a5* moral; (*etisk*) ethical; *~t stöd* moral support; *M~ Upprustning* Moral Rearmament **-ist** moralist **-itet** *s3* morality **-kaka** *se* -predikan **-lära** ethics (*pl, behandlas som sg*) **-predikan** homily, moral lecture; *hålla ~* (*äv.*) sermonize **-predikant** sermonizer, moralizer
mo'ras *s7* morass, swamp
morator|ium [-'tɔ:-] *s4* moratorium (*pl äv. -ia*)
mor'bid *a1* morbid
morbror [ˣmɔrr-, 'mɔrr-] [maternal] uncle, uncle on the (one's) mother's side
mord [-ɔ:-] *s7* murder (*på* of); *jur. äv.* homicide; *begå ~* commit murder **-brand** arson, incendiarism; *anlägga ~* commit arson **-brännare** incendiary, fire raiser **-försök** attempted murder; *~ mot ngn* attempt on a p.'s life **-isk** ['mɔ:-r-] *a5* murderous, homicidal **-kommission** murder squad; *AE.* homicide squad **-lysten** bloodthirsty **-lystnad** bloodthirstiness **-plats** scene of a murder **-redskap** murderous implement **-vapen** murder weapon; (*-iskt vapen*) deadly weapon **-ängel** destroying angel
mo'rell *s3, bot.* morello [cherry]
mores [ˣmå:-] *i uttr.: lära ngn ~* teach s.b. good manners
mor|far [ˣmɔrr-, 'mɔrr-] [maternal] grandfather **-farsfar** great grandfather [on the mother's side]
mor'fem [-å-] *s7, språkv.* morpheme
mor'fin [-å-] *s4, s3* morphine, morphia **-injektion** morphia injection **-ism** morphinism, morphine addiction **-ist** morphinist, morphine (morphia) addict
morfo|logi [-å-å-å-] *s3* morphology **-logisk** *a5* morphological
morföräldrar *mina ~* my [maternal] grand-

M

parents, my mother's parents
morganatisk [mårga'na:-] *a5* morganatic
morgon [ˣmårgån, *vard.* ˣmårrån] (*vard. morron*) *-en morgnar* (*vard. mornar*) **1** *motsats t. kväll*) morning; *poet.* morn; *tidernas* ~ (*äv.*) the beginning of time; *god* ~*!* good morning!; *på* ~*en* in the morning; *på* ~*en den 1 mars* on the morning of the 1st of March; *i dag på* ~*en* this [very] morning; *tidigt följande* ~ early next morning **2** *i* ~ tomorrow; *i* ~ *åtta dagar* tomorrow week; *i* ~ *bitti*[*da*] tomorrow morning **-bön** morning prayers (*pl*); *skol. äv.* morning assembly **-dag** tomorrow; morrow; *uppskjuta till* ~*en* put off until tomorrow **-gymnastik** early-morning exercises (*pl*) **-gåva** morning gift **-humör** [early-]morning temper **-kaffe** early-morning coffee **-kvisten** *vard. i uttr.: på* ~ early in the morning **-luft** [*börja*] *vädra* ~ begin to see one's chanse **-mål** breakfast **-människa** early bird (riser) **-pigg** alert (lively) in the morning **-rock** dressing gown; *AE. äv.* bathrobe **-rodnad** ~*en* aurora, the red sky at dawn **-samling** *skol.* morning assembly **-sol** *rum med* ~ room that gets the morning sun **-stjärna** morning star **-stund** morning hour; ~ *har guld i mun* the early bird catches the worm **-sömnig** drowsy in the morning **-tidig** *vara* ~ [*av sig*] be up and about early, be an early bird **-tidning** morning paper **-toalett** morning toilet
mori'an *s3* blackamoor
moring (*förtöjningsring*) mooring
morisk [ˈmɒ:-, ˈmå:-] *a5* Moorish, Moresque
morkulla [-ɒ:-] *s1* woodcock
mor'mon *s3* Mormon **mormonsk** [-ˈmɒ:nsk] *a5* Mormon
mor|mor [ˣmɒrr-, ˈmɒrr-] maternal grandmother **-morsmor** great grandmother [on the mother's side]
morna [ˣmå:r-] *rfl* get o.s. awake, rouse o.s.; *inte riktigt* ~*d* not quite awake
morot *-en morötter* carrot
morots|färgad carrot-coloured, carroty **-saft** carrot juice
morr|a [-å-] growl, snarl (*åt* at) **-hår** *koll.* [cat's *etc.*) whiskers (*pl*) **-ning** growl, snarl
mors [-å-] *interj* hello!; *AE.* hi!
1 morsa [-å-] *v1, vard.* say hello
2 morsa [-ɒ-] *s1, vard.* mum
morse [-å-] *i uttr.: i* ~ this morning; *i går* ~ yesterday morning
morse|alfabet [ˣmårse-] [international] Morse code **-signal[ering]** Morse signal[ling] **-tecken** Morse symbol
morsgris mother's darling
morsk *a1* (*orädd*) bold, daring; (*käck*) dashing; (*karsk*) stuck-up, fierce; (*manhaftig*) stout-hearted; *visa sig* ~ make the most of o.s.
morska ~ *upp sig* pluck up courage; ~ *upp dig!* take heart! **morskhet** boldness *etc.*
mortalitet [-å-] mortality
mortel [ˣmɒ:r-] *s2* mortar; *stöta i* ~ grind (crush) in a mortar **-stöt** pestle
mortifi[c]era cancel
mo'rän *s3* moraine **-bildning** *abstr. o. konkr.* moraine formation
mos *s4* (*massa*) pulp; *kokk.* paste, mash; *jfr äv.*

äppel-, potatis-; *göra* ~ *av* make mincemeat of **mosa** reduce to pulp, pulp; (*potatis o.d.*) mash
mosa'ik *s3* mosaic; *lägga* ~ mosaic **-arbete** mosaic work; tesselation **-golv** mosaic (tesselated) pavement (floor) **-inläggning** inlaying with mosaic; incrustation, tesselation
mosaisk [-'sa:-] *a5* Mosaic; (*judisk äv.*) Jewish; *en* ~ *trosbekännare* a Jew
mose|bok *de fem -böckerna* the Pentateuch; *Första* (*Andra, Tredje, Fjärde, Femte*) ~ [the book of] Genesis (Exodus, Leviticus, Numbers, Deuteronomy)
Mosel [ˈmå:-] *r* the Moselle **moselvin** [ˣmå:-] moselle [wine]
1 mosig *a1* (*-ad*) pulpy
2 mosig *a1* (*i ansiktet*) red [and bloated]; (*rusig*) fuddled, tipsy
moské *s3* mosque
mos'kit *s3* mosquito **-nät** mosquito net[ting]
mosko'vit *s3* Muscovite **-isk** *a5* Muscovite
Mosk'va *n* Moscow
moss|a [-å-] *s1* moss **-belupen** *a5* moss-covered, mossy **-djur** bryozoan, *vard.* sea mat
moss|e [-å-] *s2* peat moss, bog **-grön** moss green **-ig** *a1* mossy **-täcke** covering of moss
moster [ˣmɒss-, ˈmɒss-] *s2* [maternal] aunt
mot I *prep* **1** (*riktning*) towards (*äv. om tid*); to; *gå* ~ *staden* walk towards the town; *färden gick* ~ *söder* they (*etc.*) headed south; *hålla upp ngt* ~ *ljuset* hold s.th. up to the light; *rusa* ~ *utgången* dash to the exit; *se upp* ~ *bergen* look up to the hills; *komma springande* ~ *ngn* come running towards s.b. (in a p.'s direction); *vara vänd* ~ (*vanl.*) face; ~ *kvällen* towards the evening; ~ *slutet av året* towards (near) the end of the year **2** (*beröring*) against; *gränsen* ~ *Norge* the Norwegian border; *med ryggen* ~ *väggen* with one's back to the wall; *segla* ~ *strömmen* sail against the current; *vågorna slog* ~ *stranden* the waves lapped [on] the shore; *bilen törnade* ~ *en sten* the car bumped into a stone **3** (*uppträdande, sinnelag*) to, towards; *vänlig* ~ kind to; *hysa agg* ~ bear a grudge against; *misstänksam* ~ suspicious of; *sträng* ~ severe on, strict with; *uppriktig* ~ honest with; *i sitt uppträdande* ~ in his (*etc.*) manner (behaviour) towards **4** (*motsättning, kontrast*) against; (*jämförelse äv.*) compared to (with); *jur. o. sport. äv.* versus; *skydd* ~ protection against (from); *strida* ~ fight against; *grönt är vackert* ~ *blått* green is beautiful against blue; *väga* ~ *varandra* weigh one against the other; *det kom 10 svar* ~ *4 förra gången* there were 10 answers compared to (with) 4 last time; *brott* ~ *en förordning* breach of a regulation; *ett medel* ~ *snuva* a remedy for colds; *det hjälper* ~ *allt* it is good for everything; *det är ingenting* ~ *vad jag kan* that is nothing to what I can do; *hålla 2* ~ *1 på att* bet 2 to 1 that; *förslaget antogs med 20 röster* ~ *10* the proposal was adopted with 20 votes to 10 **5** (*i utbyte mot*) for, against; ~ *kvitto* against receipt; ~ *legitimation* on identification; ~ *skälig ersättning* for a reasonable fee (remuneration); *byta ngt* ~ *ngt* exchange s.th. for s.th.; *göra ngt* ~ *att ngn gör* do s.th. in

exchange for a p.'s doing; *i utbyte* ~ in exchange for **II** *adv, se emot*
mot|a 1 (*hejda*) block (bar) the way for; check; head off; (*avvärja*) ward off; (*förekomma*) forestall; ~ *Olle i grind* nip s.th. in the bud, ward off impending trouble **2** (*driva*) drive; ~ *bort* drive off (away from); ~ *ihop* (*boskap*) drive (herd) together
mot|aktion counteraction, countermeasure **-angrepp** counterattack **-arbeta** (*ngn, ngt*) work against; counteract; (*söka hindra*) check; (*ngns planer*) seek to thwart (traverse); (*bekämpa*) oppose **-argument** counterargument, objection **-bevis** counterproof, counterevidence **-bevisa** refute; belie **-bjudande** *a4* repugnant, repulsive (*för* to); (*otäck*) disgusting **-bok** (*kontra-*) [customer's] passbook; (*sparkasse-*) bankbook; (*för spritinköp*) liquor-ration book **-drag** countermove (*äv. friare*) **-eld** *mil.* counterfire, returnfire
mo'tell *s4* motel
mo'tett *s3, mus.* motet
mot|fordran counterclaim **-fråga** counterquestion **-förslag** counterproposal **-gift** antidote, antitoxin **-gång** *s2* (*med pl*) reverse, setback; (*utan pl*) adversity, misfortune **-hugg** counterblow, counterthrust, counterstroke; *få* ~ meet with opposition **-håll** *ha* ~ be in disfavour (*för* with) **-hårs** [-å:-] (*stryka en katt* stroke a cat) the wrong way
motig *al* adverse, contrary; (*besvärlig*) awkward; *det har varit* ~*t* things have not been easy (*för mig* for me) **-het** reverse, setback, adversity
1 motion [måt'ʃɷ:n] (*kroppsrörelse*) exercise; *få* (*ta*) ~ get (take) exercise
2 motion [måt'ʃɷ:n] (*förslag*) motion (*i* on; *om* for); *väcka* ~ *om* submit a motion for; *väcka* ~ *i* introduce a bill in (*riksdagen* the Riksdag)
1 motionera [måtʃɷ-] (*ge motion*) give exercise, exercise; (*skaffa sig motion*) take exercise
2 motionera [måtʃɷ-] (*väcka förslag*) move (*om* for; *om att* that)
motions|cykel exercycle **-gymnastik** physical (gymnastic) exercises (*pl*), callisthenics (*pl o. sg*), keep-fit exercises (*pl*)
motionär [måtʃɷ'nä:r] *s3* mover [of a resolution]; introducer of a bill
mo'tiv *s7* **1** motive (*för, till* for, of); (*anledning, skäl*) reason, cause (*för, till* of); *vad hade du för* ~ *till att* what was your motive for (+ *ing-form*) **2** *konst., mus. o.d.* motif (*till* for, of); (*t. tavla äv.*) subject; *mus. äv.* theme **motivation** motivation **motivera** (*ange skälen för*) state [the] reasons (grounds) for, account for; (*utgöra tillräckligt skäl för*) be the motive of, motivate; (*berättiga*) warrant; (*rättfärdiga*) justify; *en föga* ~*d* ... a[n] ... for which there is little justification **motivering** justification, explanation (*för* of, for); (*bevisföring*) argumentation; *psykol.* motivation; *med den* ~*en att* on the plea that **-forskning** motivation research **-val** choice of subject (*etc.*)
mot|kandidat rival [candidate] **-kultur** counterculture **-ljus** *foto.* direct light **-ljusskydd** *foto.* lens hood (shade) **-lut** upgrade, ascent **-läsa** *boktr.* checkread; *bokför.* call over **-of-**

fensiv counteroffensive **-offert** counteroffer
motor [ˣmɷ:tår] *s3* motor; engine; *stark* (*svag*) ~ high-powered (low-powered) motor **-bränn-olja** *se dieselolja* **-bränsle** motor fuel **-båt** motorboat; *AE. äv.* powerboat **-cykel** motorcycle; *vard.* motorbike; ~ *med sidvagn* [motorcycle] combination **-cyklist** motorcyclist **-drift** motor operation **-driven** *a5* **-driven-fartyg** motor ship (vessel) **-fel** engine trouble **-fordon** motor vehicle **-förare** motorist, driver **-gräsklippare** power lawnmower **-haveri** engine breakdown **-hotell** *se motell* **-huv** (*bil-*) bonnet, *AE.* hood; *flyg.* cowl[ing] **-'ik** *s3* mobility **-isera** motorize; ~*de trupper* (*biltransporterade*) lorry-borne troops, (*mekaniserade*) mechanized troops **-isk** [-'tɷ:-] *a5* motor[y] **-ism** motorism, motoring **-ist** motorist **-krångel** engine trouble **-man** motorist; (*-vagnsförare*) motorman **-olja** motor (engine) oil **-sport** motoring, motor sport[s] **-sprit** motor spirit **-stopp** engine (motor) failure, breakdown **-styrka** engine power **-såg** chain (power) saw **-torpedbåt** [motor] torpedoboat **-trafik** motor[ing] traffic **-tävling** motor race **-vagn** rail motorcoach, railcar; (*spårvagn*) motorcar **-vagnståg** multiple-unit train **-verkstad** motor works (*sg o. pl*); (*bil- ofta*) garage **-väg** motorway; *i sht AE.* motor highway, express highway, freeway **-värmare** engine preheater
mot|part opposite party, counterparty, opponent **-pol** antipole (*äv. bildl.*) **-prestation** service in return; (*friare*) something in return **-reformation** counter-reformation **-replik** rejoinder **-revolution** counter-revolution **-sats** contrast (*mot, till* to); opposite, contrary, antithesis (*till* of); (*i logiken*) contradictory; *bevisa* ~*en* prove the contrary; *raka* ~*en* the very (exact) opposite (*till* of); *utgöra* (*stå i*) ~ *till* be opposed to; *i* ~ *till* contrary (in contrast) to; *de är varandras* ~*er* they are absolute opposites **-satsförhållande** contrast[ing relationship]; *stå i* ~ *till* be at variance with (in opposition to) **-satt** *a4* **1** *allm. o. bildl.* opposite, contrary, opposing, conflicting; (*omvänd*) reverse; *i* ~ *fall* in the contrary case, (*i annat fall*) otherwise; *i* ~ *riktning* in the opposite direction; *på* ~*a sidan a*) on the opposite side (*av* of; *mot* to), *b*) (*i bok o.d.*) on the opposite page; *förhållandet var det rakt* ~*a* the situation was quite the opposite **2** *bot., med.* ~*a blad* oppositifolious **-se** (*se fram emot*) look forward to; (*vänta*) expect; *vi* ~*r med intresse Ert svar* (*hand.*) we look forward to your reply **-sida** opposite (other) side (*äv. bildl.*) **-skäl** counter-reason; *skäl och* ~ arguments for and against, [the] pros and cons **-sols** [-sɷ:-] anticlockwise, *AE.* counterclockwise **-spelare** (*i spel*) opponent, adversary; *vara* ~ *till ngn* (*teat. o.d.*) play opposite s.b. **-spänstig** refractory; (*olydig*) insubordinate **-stridig** *al* conflicting, contradictory **-strävig** *al* (*-spänstig*) refractory; (*-villig*) reluctant; (*om t.ex. hår*) intractable **-ström** counter-current **-ströms** against the current, upstream **-stycke** *bildl.* counterpart; (*like*) parallel, match, equal; *sakna* ~ be unparalleled (unique) **-stå** resist, withstand; (*an-*

grepp etc. äv.) stand up against; *en ... som man inte kan ~ (äv.)* an irresistible ... **-stående** *a4* opposite; *på ~ sida* on the opposite page **motstånd** *s7* **1** resistance (*äv. fys., elektr., mil.*); *flyg. äv.* drag; *göra ~ mot* resist, offer resistance to; *möta ~* meet with resistance (*bildl.* opposition; *väpnat ~* armed resistance **2** *konkr. elektr.* resistor, resistance box **-are** adversary; opponent; antagonist; (*fiende*) enemy; *~ till* adversary (*etc.*) of **motstånds|ficka** pocket of resistance **-kraft** [power of] resistance (*mot* to); resisting-power; (*fysisk*) resistance, staying power **-kraftig** resistant (*mot* to, against); strong **-man** member of the resistance **-rörelse** resistance movement **motstöt** counterattack; *bildl. äv.* counterthrust **motsvar|a** (*ha sin -ighet i, passa ihop med*) correspond (answer) to; (*vara lika mycket värd som*) be equivalent to; (*tillfredsställa*) satisfy, meet; (*uppfylla*) fulfil; *vinsten ~r inte insatsen* the profit is not in proportion to the 'investment; *~ ngns förväntningar* come up to a p.'s expectations **motsvarande** *a4* corresponding; (*analog*) analogous; (*liknande*) equivalent, similar; *~ värde* the equivalent; *i ~ grad* correspondingly **motsvarighet** (*överensstämmelse*) correspondence; proportionateness; (*full ~*) equivalence; (*analogi*) analogy; (*motstycke*) counterpart, opposite number; *närmaste ~ till* the closest (nearest) equivalent to (of); *sakna ~* have nothing corresponding to it (*etc.*) **motsäg|a** contradict; oppose; (*bestrida*) contest; (*strida emot*) be contradictory to, conflict with; *~ sig* contradict o.s. (itself); be [self-]contradictory **-ande** *a5* contradictory; (*mot varandra stridande*) conflicting **motsäg|else** contradiction; (*brist på överensstämmelse*) incompatibility, discrepancy; (*inkonsekvens*) inconsistency; *inte tåla några ~r* not tolerate contradiction **-full** full of contradictions **-lusta** love of contradictions **motsätt|a** *rfl* oppose, stand out against **-ning** opposition; antagonism; (*motsatsförhållande*) contrast, discrepancy, incongruity; *stå i skarp ~ till* be in striking contrast to **mott** [-å-] *s9, s7, zool.* moth **mottag|a** (*acceptera*) accept; (*besökande*) receive, see; *alla bidrag -es med största tacksamhet* all contributions gratefully received; *vi har -it Ert brev* we have received (are in receipt of) your letter **mottagande** *s6* reception; *i sht hand.* receipt; (*accepterande*) acceptance; *betala vid ~t* pay on receipt (delivery), cash on delivery (*förk. C.O.D.*); *erkänna ~t av ett brev* acknowledge receipt of a letter **mottagarapparat** *radio.* receiving set **mottagare 1** *pers.* receiver; (*av postförsändelse*) addressee; (*av varuförsändelse*) consignee; (*betalnings-*) payee, beneficiary; (*av gåva*) donee; *sport.* striker-out **2** *konkr. radio.* receiver, receiving set **mottaglig** [-a:-] *a1* susceptible (*för* to); (*känslig*) sensitive (*för* to); *~ för förkylning (äv.)* liable to catch cold; *~ för skäl* amenable to reason; *~ för nya idéer* receptive (open) to new ideas **mottaglighet** [-a:-] susceptibility; sensitiveness **mottagning** recep-

tion; (*läkares*) consultation rooms (*pl*), surgery; (*vid hovet äv.*) audience **mottagnings|bevis** advice of receipt (delivery); *post. äv.* post office receipt **-kommitté** reception committee **-rum** reception room; (*läkares*) consulting room **-tid** reception hours (*pl*); (*läkares*) consultation (consulting) hours (*pl*) **motto** [ˣmåtto] *s6* motto **mot|urs** [-u:-] anticlockwise, *AE.* counterclockwise **-vallskäring** cussed (contradictory) person **-veck** *sömn.* box pleat **-verka** (*-arbeta*) work against, run (go) counter to; (*upphäva verkan av*) counteract, offset, neutralize; (*söka hindra*) try to put a stop to, obstruct **-verkan** counteraction **-vikt** counterweight, counterbalance (*mot* to) **-vilja** dislike (*mot* of, to), distaste (*mot* for); (*starkare*) repugnance (*mot* against), antipathy (*mot* for, against, to); *ha (hysa) ~ mot* have a dislike (*etc.*) of, dislike **-villig** reluctant; (*starkare*) averse **-villighet** reluctance; averseness **-vind** headwind, contrary wind; *bildl.* adverse (contrary) wind; *ha ~* have the wind against one; *segla i ~* sail against the wind, *bildl.* be out of luck **-väga** [counter]balance (*äv. ~ varandra*) **-värde** equivalent; (*bank o.d. äv.*) countervalue **-värn** defence, resistance; *sätta sig till ~* offer resistance, fight back **-åtgärd** countermeasure; *vidtaga ~er* take countermeasures **mountainbike** [ˈmaontinbaik] *~n ~s* mountain bike **moussera** [moˈse:-] sparkle, effervesce **mu** moo! **mua** moo **1 muck** *n* **1** *han sade inte ett ~* he didn't say a word; *jag begriper inte ett ~* I don't understand an iota (a thing) **2** *utan ett ~* without a murmur **2 muck** *oböjligt s, vard.* demob[ilization] **1 mucka** *vard. mil.* demob **2 mucka** (*bråka*) growl, grumble (*över* at, about); *~ gräl* pick a quarrel **mudd** *s2* wristlet, loose cuff **mudder** [ˈmudd-] *s7* mud **mudderverk** dredger, dredge **muddra** dredge; *~d farled (sjö.)* dredged channel **muddringsarbete** dredging work **muff** *s2* **1** (*klädespersedel*) muff **2** *tekn.* sleeve, socket [end] **muffin** [ˈmuff-] *s7* muffin **muffkoppling** sleeve (box) coupling **mugg** *s2* (*liten*) mug; (*större*) jug; (*tenn- o.d.*) pot; *för fulla ~ar* (*vard.*) at top speed **Muhammed** [moˈhamm-] Mohammed, Mahomet **muhamme'd|an** [mo-] *s3* Mohammedan, Moslem, Muslim **-anism** Mohammedanism, Islam **-ansk** [-ˈda:-] *a5*, Mohammedan, Moslem, Muslim **mula** *s1* mule **mulatska** [-ˣlatt-] *se mulattkvinna* **mulatt** *s3* mulatto (*pl* -os, -oes) **-kvinna** mulatto woman **mule** *s2* muzzle; snout **mul|en** *a3* overcast; clouded (*äv. bildl.*); *bildl.* gloomy; *det är -et* the sky is overcast **muljer|a** *fonet.* palatize **-ing** palatization **mull** *s2* earth; mould; (*stoft*) dust (*äv. bildl.*) **-bänk** *vard.* quid (cud) of snuff

mull|bär mulberry **-bärsträd** mulberry tree
mulle *s2, zool.* red mullet
muller ['mull-] *s7* rumbling, rumble, rolling
mullig *al* plump
mullra rumble, roll
mulltoalett [type of] earth closet
mullvad *s2, zool.* mole
mullvads|arbete underground work **-grå** mole-coloured **-gång** mole track (run) **-hög** mole-hill **-skinn** (*som handelsvara*) moleskin
mulna [ˣmu:l-] cloud over, become overcast; *bildl.* darken; *det ~r [på]* it (the sky) is clouding over
mul- och klövsjuka foot-and-mouth (hoof-and-mouth) disease
multe *s2, zool.* grey mullet
multen *se murken*
multinationell multinational
multipel [-'tipp-] *s3, s2* multiple; *~ skleros* multiple sclerosis
multiplicera multiply (*med* by) **multipli'kand** *s3* multiplicand **multiplikation** multiplication
multiplikations|tabell multiplication table **-tecken** multiplication sign
multiplikator *s3* multiplier
multna moulder (rot) [away]
mulåsna mule; hinny
mumi|e ['mu:-] *s5* mummy **-fiera** mummify **-fikation** mummification
mumla (*tala otydligt*) mumble; (*knota*) mutter, murmur; *~ i skägget* mutter under one's breath
mummel ['mumm-] *s7* mumble; mutter, murmur
mumrik ['mumrikk] *s2* odd fish, old fogey
mums I *interj* yum-yum! **II** *n, det var ~* that was delicious (lovely) **mumsa** munch; (*knapra*) nibble
mun [munn] *s2* mouth; (*-full*) [a] mouthful (*vatten* of water); *ur hand i ~* from hand to mouth; *i var mans ~* the talk of the town; *med en ~* with one voice; *med gapande ~* open-mouthed, with a wide open mouth; *dra på ~* smile; *gå från ~ till ~* pass from mouth to mouth, be bandied about; *ha många ~nar att mätta* have many mouths to feed; *har du inte mål i ~?* haven't you got a tongue in your head?; *hålla ~* keep one's mouth shut; *håll ~!* (*äv.*) shut up!; *hålla ngt för ~nen* hold s.th. to one's mouth; *prata bredvid ~[en]* let the cat out of the bag; *ta ordet ur ~nen på ngn* take the words out of a p.'s mouth; *ta ~nen full* (*bildl.*) talk big; *ta bladet från ~nen* speak one's mind; *alla talar i ~[nen] på varandra* all speak at the same time **-art** dialect
mundering (*soldats*) equipment
mun|full *en ~* a mouthful (*vatten* of water) **-giga** [-ji:ga] *s1, mus.* jew's-harp **-gipa** [-j:-] *s1* corner of the (one's, its) mouth; *dra ner -giporna* draw down the corners of one's mouth
mungo ['mungɷ] *s3, zool.* mongoose (*pl* mongooses)
mun|harmonika mouth organ **-huggas** *-höggs -huggits, dep* wrangle, bicker, bandy words **-håla** oral (mouth) cavity **-häfta** *med.* trismus, *vard.* lockjaw
municipalsamhälle [-ˣpa:l-] *ung.* municipality, urban district

1 munk *s1* monk; (*tiggar-*) friar
2 munk *s2, kokk.* doughnut; (*äppel- o.d.*) fritter
munkavle muzzle, gag; *sätta ~ på* muzzle
munk|kloster monastery **-kåpa** monk's frock, cowl **-latin** monk's (mediaeval) Latin **-likör** Benedictine **-löfte** monk's vow **-orden** monastic order
munkorg muzzle (*äv. bildl.*); *förse med ~* (*äv. bildl.*) muzzle
munkväsen *~det* monachism
mun|läder *ha gott ~* have a glib tongue (the gift of the gab) **—mot-mun-metoden** the mouth-to-mouth method; *vard.* kiss of life
munsbit morsel; *sluka ngt i en ~* eat s.th. in one mouthful; *det var bara en ~ för honom* (*bildl.*) it was small beer for him
mun|skydd mask **-skänk** *s2* butler; cupbearer **-spel** harmonica, mouth organ **-stycke** mouthpiece; *mus. äv.* embouchure; (*cigarett-*) [cigarette] holder; (*på cigarett*) tip; *tekn.* nozzle, jet; *cigarett med* (*utan*) *~* tipped (untipped, plain) cigarette **-sår** sore on the lips
munta *s1, vard.* oral [exam], viva [voce]
munter ['munn-] *a2* merry, cheerful; (*uppsluppen*) hilarious; *vard.* chirpy; *ett ~t lag* a merry party; *en ~ melodi* a lively tune **-gök** jolly fellow **-het** merriness; gaiety; hilarity; *uppsluppen ~* hilarious mirth (spirits *pl*)
muntlig *al* (*om översättning, prövning o.d.*) oral; (*om meddelande o.d.*) verbal; *~ prövning* oral [examination], *univ.* viva voce [examination]; *~ överläggning* (*vanl.*) personal conference **muntligen** orally; verbally; by word of mouth
muntra *~ upp* cheer up, exhilarate **-tion** amusement, entertainment; jollification
mun|vatten mouthwash; gargle **-vig** glib [with one's tongue]; (*slagfärdig*) quick-witted **-väder** empty (mere) talk; blether, balderdash **-öppning** orifice of the mouth
mur *s2* wall (*äv. bildl.*); *omge med ~ar* (*äv.*) wall in **mura** brick, build [of brick (masonry)]; *~ igen* brick (wall) up, *bildl.* bung up (*ngns ögon* a p.'s eyes); *~ in* build into a wall, immure; *~ med cement* wall (line) with cement, cement **murad** *a5* walled *etc.*; bricked; *i sht bildl.* built
mur|arbas foreman bricklayer (*etc.*) **-are** bricklayer; (*sten-*) mason **-bruk** mortar **-bräcka** *s1* battering ram (*äv. bildl.*) **-gröna** *s1, bot.* ivy
murken *a3* decayed; (*starkare*) rotten
murkla *s1* morel, moril
murkna decay, get (become) rotten
murkrön coping (top) of a wall
murmeldjur *zool.* marmot; *sova som ett ~* sleep like a log
murning [-u:-] bricklaying, masonry
murrig *al* gloomy, dull, sullen
mur|slev trowel **-tegel** [building] brick
murvel *s2, vard.* hack journalist
mur|verk masonry, brickwork, brickwall **-yta** surface [of a wall]
muräna *s1, zool* moray
mus *~en möss* mouse (*pl* mice); *vard.* beaver
mus|a *s3* muse; *de nio -erna* the nine Muses
musch *s3* beauty spot (patch)
muse'al *al* museum; *har bara ~t intresse* is

M

only of interest to museums
mus'ei|föremål museum specimen, exhibit; museum piece (äv. bildl.) **-intendent** curator; Storbritannien keeper of a museum **-man** museum official, museologist **-värde** museum value
musel|'man s3 Muslim, Moslem **-mansk** [-a:-] a5 Muslim, Moslem
museum [-'se:-] s4 museum
musicera play (have) [some] music, make music
mu'sik s9 **1** music; sätta ~ (komponera ~en) till write (compose) the music for; det är som ~ för mig it is music to my ear; detta skall hädanefter bli min ~ that will be my tune in the future **2** (-kår) band **-afton** musical evening
musi'k|al I a1 musical **II** s3 musical [comedy] musical **-alisk** [-'ka:-] a5 musical; (om pers. äv.) music-loving; vara ~ be musical, have a musical ear; M~a akademien the [Royal] Academy of Music **-alitet** musicality, feeling for music
musik|ant musician; fiddler **-begåvad** with a gift (talent) for music **-begåvning** gift (talent) for music; pers. [a] gifted musician **-direktör** graduate of the [Royal] Academy of Music; mil. bandmaster
musik|er ['mu:-] s9 musician; bli ~ (vanl.) go in for music [as a profession] **-estrad** bandstand; (i konserthus) concert platform **-film** musical [film] **-förlag** music publishers (pl) (publishing firm) **-handel** music shop **-historia** history of music **-historiker** authority on the history of music **-högskola** school (college) of music **-instrument** musical instrument **-kapell** orchestra, band **-konservatorium** conservatory, conservatoire **-kritiker** music critic **-kår** band, orchestra; medlem av en ~ (äv.) bandsman **-liv** musical life **-lära** theory of music **-lärare** music teacher (master) **-program** musical programme **-recensent** music reviewer **-studier** pl musical studies; bedriva ~ study music **-stycke** piece of music **-teori** musical theory **-verk** musical composition, work of music **-vetenskap** musicology **-älskare** lover of music, music lover **-öra** musical ear, ear for music
musivguld [-*si:v-] mosaic gold
musjik [-'ʃi:k] s3 m[o]ujik, muzhik
muskat|druva [-a:] muscat [grape] **-'ell** s3 muscatel [wine]
muskedunder [-'dund-] s7, s2 blunderbuss
musk|el ['musk-] s3 muscle; spänna -lerna tense one's muscles; utan -ler muscleless
muskel|ansträngning muscular exertion **-arbete** work done by the muscles **-bristning** rupture of a muscle **-knippe** bundle of muscles **-knutte** s2, vard. muscleman **-spel** play of the muscles **-spänning** muscular tension **-stark** muscular, muscularly strong **-sträckning** [the] spraining of a muscle; sprain **-styrka** muscular strength **-stärkare** muscle developer **-svag** weak-muscled, myasthenic **-värk** muscular pain **-vävnad** muscular tissue
musketör musketeer
muskot [-åt] s2 nutmeg **-blomma** (krydda) mace **-nöt** nutmeg

muskulatur musculature; (ngns) muscles (pl) **musku'lös** a1 muscular
mus'köt s3 musket
mus'lim s3 Muslim, Moslem
mus'lin s3, s4 (tyg) muslin
mussel|bank s2 mussel-bank **-djur** lamellibranch, bivalve **-skal** mussel shell
mussera [-ᴓ-] se moussera
musse'ron s3 tricholoma
mussla s1 **1** (djur) [sea-]mussel (äv. kokk.), clam; bivalve; (hjärt-) cockle **2** (endast skalet) [mussel] shell
must s3 (dryck) must; (i jorden) sap; hand., kokk. concentrated preparation [of ...]; bildl. pith; koka ~en ur köttet boil the goodness out of the meat; arbetet tog (sög) ~en ur mig the work took (sucked) the life out of me; en tavla med ~ i färgen a picture strong in colour
mustasch [-'ta:ʃ] s3 moustache; ha ~er wear a moustache **-prydd** moustached
mustig a1 juicy (äv. bildl.); bildl. äv. racy (anekdot anecdote), salty (svordom oath); en ~ soppa a tasty (nourishing) soup
mut|a I s1 bribe; ta -or take (receive) bribes (a bribe) (av from); -or (vard.) hush money; palm oil sg **II** v1 bribe (med with, by); polit. äv. corrupt
mutant naturv. mutant **mutation** mutation **mutera** mutate
mut|försök attempt to bribe [s.b.] **-kolv** receiver of bribes **-system** system of bribery and corruption
mutter ['mutt-] s2, tekn. nut **-bricka** washer
muttra mutter (för sig själv to o.s.); bildl. äv. grumble (över about, at)
mycelium [-'se:-] s4 mycelium
myck|en -et mer[a] mest much, a great deal of; (stor äv.) great, big; det -na arbetet the great amount of work he (etc.) has had [to do]; det -na regnandet the heavy rain[s pl], the [great] quantity of rain [that has come down]; det -na talet om all the talk about
myckenhet en ~ a) a multitude of, a large (great) number of (bilar cars), b) a large (great) quantity of, plenty of (socker sugar)
mycket I (subst. anv.) much; a great (good) deal of; a great amount (quantity; vard. a lot) of; (gott om) plenty of; (många) a great many, many, a great (large) number of, vard. a lot of; (känslobetonat) ever so much; ~ nöje! enjoy yourself!; för ~ möbler too much furniture; ~ pengar a great deal (a lot) of money; ~ vill ha mer the more you have the more you want; ~ väsen för ingenting much ado about nothing; ganska ~ a good deal (vard. quite a lot) [of], (före pl) a great many; hur ~? how much?; ha ~ att göra have a great deal (a great many things) to do; det är inte ~ med honom he is not up to much; det är inte för ~ att du säger tack you might at least say thank you; det blev för ~ för honom it became too much for him; det är väl ~ begärt! that's expecting a great deal!; hälften så ~ half as much; lika ~ som as much as; så ~ är säkert att one thing is certain, that; så ~ so much as that, that (this) much **II** mer[a] mest, adv (framför a o. adv i positiv) very (liten small; fort fast); (vid komp.

o. vid part. som betraktas som rena verbformer) [very] much (*mindre* smaller; *efterlängtad* longed for); (*framför afraid alike ashamed*) very much; (*djupt*) deeply, greatly (*imponerad* impressed), profoundly; (*högeligen*) exceedingly, highly; (*svårt*) badly; (*synnerligen*) most; ~ *hellre* much rather; ~ *möjligt* very (quite) likely; ~ *riktigt* quite right, very true; *inte* ~ *till sångare* not much of a singer; *vara* ~ *för kläder* be a great one for (be very keen on) clothes; *hur* ~ *jag än tycker om* much as I like; *en gång för* ~ once too often; *ta 25 pence för* ~ *av ngn* charge s.b. 25 pence too much; *det gör inte så* ~ it doesn't matter [very] much; *så* ~ *bättre* so much the (all the) better; *så* ~ *mer som* all the more as; *så* ~ very much, (*med betonat så*) all that much; *så* ~ *du vet det!* and now you know!; *utan att säga så* ~ *som* without saying so much as **III** *a, se mycken*

mygel *s7* string-pulling

mygg *s9, koll.* midges, mosquitoes (*pl*); *sila* ~ *och svälja kameler* strain at a gnat and swallow a camel

mygg|a *s1* midge, gnat; mosquito **-bett** mosquito-bite **-medel** antimosquito preparation **-nät** mosquito net (netting) **-svärm** swarm of gnats (*etc.*)

mygla pull strings **myglare** string-puller

mykensk [-'ke:nsk] *a5* Mycenaean

mykolog mycologist

mylla I *s1* mould; (*humus*) humus; (*matjord*) topsoil **II** *v1,* ~ *ner* (*frön*) cover [up] with earth (soil); ~ *igen* fill in with earth

myller ['myll-] *s7* throng, swarm **myllra** *v1* throng, swarm

München ['mynçen] *n* Munich

myndig *a1* **1** *jur. ...* of age; *bli* ~ come of age, attain one's majority; *vara* ~ be of age, be legally competent **2** (*som vittnar om makt*) powerful, commanding; (*befallande*) authoritative, masterful; *i* ~ *ton* in a peremptory tone **-het 1** (*maktbefogenhet*) authority **2** (*-t uppträdande*) powerfulness, authority **3** *jur.* majority, full age **4** (*samhällsorgan*) authority; *kommunala ~er* local government (authorities); *statliga ~er* central government (authorities)

myndighets|dag coming-of-age day **-förklaring** declaration of majority **-person** person in authority **-ålder** majority, full age

myndling ward

mynn|a (*om flod o.d.*) fall, debouch, discharge [its waters]; (*om väg, korridor etc.*) open out, emerge (*i* into); *bildl.* issue, end (*i* in) **-ing** mouth; (*flod- äv.*) estuary; (*öppning äv.*) opening; (*rör- o.d. äv.*) orifice; (*på vapen*) muzzle

mynnings|arm arm of an estuary **-laddare** muzzle-loader

mynt *s7* **1** coin; piece [of money]; (*valuta*) currency; *slå* (*prägla*) ~ coin money; *betala i klingande* ~ pay in hard cash; *betala ngn med samma* ~ (*bildl.*) pay s.b. back in his own coin; *slå* ~ *av* (*bildl.*) make capital out of **2** (*institution*) mint

1 mynta *s1, bot.* mint

2 mynta *v1* mint, coin (*äv. bildl.*); (*prägla äv.*) stamp

mynt|enhet monetary unit, unit of currency

-fot [monetary] standard, standard of currency **-inkast** slot **-kunskap** numismatics (*pl, behandlas som sg*) **-ning** coinage, mintage **-samling** collection of coins; *konkr. äv.* numismatic collection **-slag** currency; species of coin **-stämpel** die, coin stamp **-verk** mint; *M~et* the [Swedish] Mint **-väsen** monetary system

myokar'dit *s3* myocarditis

myom [-'å:m] *s7* myoma

myr *s2* bog; swamp; *geol.* mire

myr|a *s1* ant; *flitig som en* ~ as busy as a bee; *sätta -or i huvudet på ngn* set s.b. puzzling, mystify s.b.

myri'ad *s3* myriad; *~er* (*äv.*) countless multitude [of ...]

myr|kott [-å-] *s2, zool.* pangolin **-lejon** *zool.* antlion, *AE.* doodlebug **-lejonslända** *zool.* antlion

myr|malm bog ore **-mark** boggy (*etc.*) ground

myrra *s1* myrrh

myr|slok *s2, zool.* anteater **-stack** ant hill **-syra** formic acid

myrten ['myrr-] *best. f. =, pl myrtnar* [common] myrtle **-krona** myrtle crown

mysa *v3* (*belåtet*) smile contentedly (*mot ngn* on s.b.; *åt ngt* at s.th.); (*strålande*) beam (*mot* on) **mysig** [nice and] cosy; (*om pers.*) nice

mysk *s3* musk **-djur, -hjort** musk deer **-oxe** musk ox

myst|eriespel [-'te:-] mystery play **-erium** [-'te:-] *s4* mystery **-eri'ös** *a1* mysterious

mysticism mysticism **mystifiera** mystify **mystifikation** mystification **mys'tik** *s3* mysticism **mystiker** ['myss-] mystic **mystisk** ['myss-] *a5* (*som rör mystik e.d.*) mystic; (*hemlighetsfull*) mysterious, mystical **mys'tär** *s3* mystery

myt *s3* myth (*om* of) **-bildning** creation of myths

myteri mutiny; *göra* ~ raise a mutiny, mutiny **myterist** mutineer

mytisk ['my:-] *a5* mythical; fabled, fabulous **myto|logi** *s3* mythology **-logisk** *a5* mythological **-'man** *s3* compulsive liar

myxö'dem *s7, med.* myxoedema

1 må *v4* (*känna sig*) feel; get on, thrive; *hur ~r du?* how are you?, how are you getting on?; *jag ~r mycket bra* I am (feel) very well; *jag ~r inte så bra* I am not quite well; *jag ~r inte bra av choklad* chocolate doesn't agree with me; *du skulle* ~ *bäst av att* (*äv.*) it would be best for you to; ~ *så gott!* keep well!; ~ *som en prins* be as happy as a king; *nu ~r han!* now he is happy (enjoying himself)!

2 må *imperf måtte* (*jfr måtte*) *hjälpv* may; (*uttryckande uppmaning*) let; (*i samband med negation*) must [not]; *jur.* may; *jag* ~ *då säga att* I must say that; *det* ~ *vara hänt* all right, then; *därom* ~ *andra döma* as to that let others judge; *några exempel* ~ *anföras* a few instances may be cited; *man* ~ *säga vad man vill, men* says what you like, but; *du* ~ *tro att jag var trött* you can imagine how tired I was; *ja, det* ~ *jag säga!* well, I must say!; ~ *så vara att* may be that; *vem det än* ~ *vara* whoever it may be; *av vad slag det vara* ~ of whatever kind it is; *vad som än* ~ *hända* whatever happens (may happen)

måbär ['må:-] alpine currant
måfå i uttr.: på ~ at random, haphazard
måg s2 son-in-law
måhända [-ˣhänn-] maybe, perhaps
1 mål s7 **1** (talförmåga) speech, way of speaking; (röst) voice; har du inte ~ i mun[nen]? haven't you got a tongue in your head?; sväva på ~ et falter, hum and haw **2** (dial.) dialect; tongue
2 mål s7, jur. o.d. case; cause, lawsuit; fakta i ~et case history (record); nedlägga ~et withdraw the case; i oträngt ~ without due (legal) cause
3 mål s7 (-tid) meal; ett ordentligt ~ mat a square meal
4 mål s7 **1** sport. goal; (vid löpning) winning post; (i lek) home; (vid skjutning) mark; mil. target, objective; från start till ~ (vanl.) from start to finish; skjuta i ~ shoot a goal; stå i ~ be in goal; vinna med två ~ mot ett win [by] two [goals to] one; kasta till ~s throw at a target; skjuta till ~s practise target-shooting; skjuta över ~et (bildl.) overshoot the mark **2** (friare, bildl.) goal; (destination) destination, end; (syfte) aim, object, purpose, end; utan bestämt ~ with no definite aim (object); aimlessly; sätta sitt ~ högt (bildl.) aim high
måla paint (efter from; i in; med with, in; på on); bildl. äv. depict; ~ av paint a portrait (picture) of; ~ om repaint, give a coat of paint; ~ över paint out (over); ~ sig, se sminka sig **målande** a4 (uttrycksfull) graphic, vivid; (om gest, ord o.d.) expressive
målar|e 1 (hantverkare) painter [and decorator], house painter; (konstnär) painter, artist **2** kortsp. court (AE. face) card **-färg** paint; ~er (konst.) artist's colours **-inna** [woman] artist (painter) **-konst** [art of] painting **-lärling** painter's apprentice **-mästare** master [house] painter; house-painter employer **-pensel** paintbrush **-skola** school of painting **-skrin** paintbox **-verkstad** [house-]painter's workshop
målbrott han är i ~et his voice is just breaking
mål|bur sport. goal **-domare** sport. judge; referee
måleri painting **målerisk** [-'le:-, 'må:-] a5 picturesque
målforskning applied research
målfoto avgörande genom ~ photo finish
målföre s6, förlora (återfå) ~et lose (recover) one's power of speech
mål|grupp target group **-görare** [-j-] sport. [goal] scorer **-inriktad** targeted **-kamera** finishing-line camera **-kast** goal throw **-kvot** goal average
målla s1 orache
mållinje (vid löpning o.d.) winning post, finishing line; fotb. o.d. goal line
1 mållös (stum) speechless (av with); göra ngn ~ strike s.b. dumb, dumbfound s.b.
2 mållös sport. goalless; bildl. aimless
målmedveten purposeful; (om pers. äv.) resolute **-het** purposefulness; (ngns äv.) fixity of purpose (aim)
målning [ˣmå:l-] abstr. painting; (färg) paint; (tavla) picture, painting
målrelaterad a5 (betygssättning) criterion-ref-

erenced
målro hålla ~n vid makt keep the conversation going, keep the ball rolling
mål|siffra fotb. o.d. score **-skjutning** target-shooting **-skott** shot at goal
målsman ['må:ls-] **1** jur. next friend; (förmyndare) guardian; skol. person standing in loco parentis; (förälder) parent **2** (talesman) champion, spokesman, sponsor
mål|snöre tape **-språk** target language **-stolpe** goal post
måls|ägande s9 [the] person injured **-ägare** plaintiff; injured party
mål|sättning objective, aim, purpose, goal **-sökande** homing **-sökningsrobot** homing missile **-tavla** target [board]
måltid meal; (högtidligt) repast
måltids|dryck table drink (beverage) **-kupong** luncheon voucher, AE. meal ticket
målvakt goalkeeper
1 mån r (utsträckning) extent; (grad) degree, measure; i viss ~ to some extent; in some degree; i görligaste ~ as far as possible; i ~ av behov as need arises; i ~ av tillgång as far as supplies admit, as long as supplies last
2 mån a1 (aktsam) careful (om of); (noga) particular (om sitt yttre about one's personal appearance); (ivrig) eager (om att to); (angelägen) anxious (om about, for)
måna ~ om take care of; nurse; look after
månad s3 month; förra ~en last month; [i] nästa ~ next month; innevarande ~ this month; två gånger i ~en twice a month
månads|biljett monthly (season) ticket **-hyra** monthly (month's) rent **-lång** lasting for months (a month), [a] month-long **-lön** monthly salary (pay, wages) **-skifte** vid ~t at the turn of the month **-smultron** cultivated everbearing wild strawberry **-sten** birthstone **-vis** monthly
månatlig [ˣmå:-, -'na:t-] a1 monthly
mån|bana lunar orbit, orbit of the moon **-belyst** [-y:-] a4 moonlit **-berg** lunar mountain
måndag ['månn-] s2, best. f. vard. äv. måndan Monday; jfr fredag
månde oböjligt v, vad ~ bli av det barnet? what is to become of that child?; vem det vara ~ whoever it is (may be)
mån|e s2 **1** (himlakropp) moon; gubben i ~n the man in the moon; ta ner ~n get hold of the moon, get blood from a stone **2** se flintskalle **-farkost** lunar vehicle **-färd** trip to the moon **-förmörkelse** eclipse of the moon, lunar eclipse
många jfr mången **1** fören. many; (starkare) a good (great) many; (talrika) numerous, a large number of, vard. lots (a lot) of; (ganska ~ quite a number of, not so few; ~ gånger many times (om over), often; hälften så ~ half as many; lika ~ (t.ex. vardera) the same number of, (t.ex. som förra gången) just as many; så ~ böcker! what a lot of books! **2** självst. many; (talrika) numerous; (~ människor) many people, a great number (vard. lots, a lot) of people; en bland ~ one among many; vi var inte ~ there were not many of us; enligt ~s åsikt är det many people are of the opinion (many hold the view)

that it is
mång|ahanda *oböjligt a* multifarious; many
kinds (sorts) of; *av ~ slag* of many various
kinds **-byggare** *bot.* polygamous [plant] **-dub-**
bel multifold; many times greater; *en ~ över-*
makt an overwhelming superiority (force); *~*
verkan multiple effect **-dubbelt** *adv* many
times over; *en ~ överlägsen fiende* a vastly
superior enemy **-dubbla** double many times
over; *(friare)* multiply
mången *månget (äv. mångt) många, komp.*
fler(a), superl. flest(a) many a[n]; *på ~ god*
dag for many a day; *i mångt och mycket* in
many respects, on very many matters **-städes**
in many places
mång|fald *s3* **1** multiplicity, great variety **2** *mat.*
multiple **-faldig** *a1* manifold, multifold; *(va-*
rierande) diverse; *~a gånger* many times
[over], over and over [again]; *vid ~a tillfällen*
on numerous (frequent) occasions **-faldiga**
duplicate, manifold **-faldigt, -falt** *adv* many
times; many times over **-fasetterad** full of
nuances; *(om problem)* very complex **-fres-**
tare versatile person **-gifte** polygamy **-guda-**
dyrkan polytheism **-hundraårig** many centuries old; *(av ~ varaktighet)* for many hundreds of years **-hörning** [-ö:-] polygon **-höv-**
dad *a5* many-headed **-kulturell** multicultural
-kunnig of great and varied learning; versatile
mång|la sell from a market stall; hawk **-are**
coster[monger], hawker **-erska** [woman] coster[monger]
mång|miljonär multimillionaire **-ordig** [-ɷ:-]
a1 verbose, wordy **-ordighet** [-ɷ:-] verbos-
ity; wordiness **-sidig** *a1* many-sided; *bildl. äv.*
diversified, varied; *(om pers.)* versatile, all-
-round; *geom.* polygonal **-sidighet** manysided-
ness *etc.*; versatility **-skiftande** *a4* diversified;
variegated **-stavig** *a1* many-syllabled; multi-
syllabic **-stavighet** multisyllabicity **-stäm-**
mig *a1* many-voiced **-sysslare** versatile person; *vard. s.b.* with many irons in the fire; jack
of all trades
mångt *se* mycken
mång|talig *a1* numerous **-tusende** many thou-
sand[s of] **-tydig** *a1* of (with) many meanings;
(friare) ambiguous, equivocal
mångård lunar halo (corona)
mångårig *a1* of many years[' duration (standing)]; *bot.* perennial
mån|landare lunar module **-landning** moon
landing **-landskap** lunar landscape **-ljus I** *s7,*
se månsken **II** *a1* moonlight, moonlit; *bildl.*
vard. brilliant, just fine
månn|e, -'tro I wonder; do you think?
mån|raket moon rocket **-sken** moonlight **-skif-**
te change of the moon **-skott** moon shot
-skugga shadow of the moon **-skära** *s1* crescent moon; *~n (äv.)* the crescent **-sten** moon-
stone **-stråle** moonbeam **-varv** moon's revolution, lunation **-år** lunar year
måra *s1* bedstraw
mård [-å:-] *s2* marten **-skinn** marten [fur];
(handelsvara) marten [pelt]
mårtens|afton [ˣmå:r-, -ˣaff-] Martinmas Eve
-gås Martinmas dinner (celebration)
mås *s2* [sea] gull

måste *måste måst; pres.* must; *(på grund av*
yttre tvång äv.) have to; *(i samtalsspråk äv.)*
have (has) got to; *(är tvungen)* am (is, are)
obliged to; *(kan inte låta bli att)* cannot but;
(innebärande naturnödvändighet) am *(etc.)*
bound to; *imperf.* had to, was obliged to *etc.*;
om det ~ så vara if it must be so; *han såg så*
rolig ut att jag ~ skratta he looked so funny I
couldn't help laughing; *vi ~ till staden* we must
(i morgon: shall have to) go to town; *priserna*
~ snart gå upp prices are bound to rise soon;
allt vad jag har måst gå igenom all that I have
had to go through
måsunge young gull
mått *s7* **1** measure *(för* for; *på* of), gauge *(äv.*
konkr.); (abstr. äv.) measurement[s *pl*]; *(kak-)*
pastry-cutter; *ett ~ grädde* a decilitre *(Storbri-*
tannien ung. a quarter of a pint) of cream; *ta*
~ hos en skräddare till be measured by a tailor
for; *hålla ~et (om kärl e.d.)* hold the prescribed
quantity, *(i längd e.d.)* be full measure *(äv.*
bildl.), bildl. äv. be (come) up to standard,
make the grade **2** *(friare o. bildl.)* measure;
(storlek äv.) size, dimension, proportion;
(grad) degree; *(mängd)* amount; *(skala)* scale;
(-stock) standard; *en diktare av stora ~* a great
poet; *av internationella ~* of international standard; *efter ~et av min förmåga* as far as I am
able; *efter den tidens ~* according to the
standards of that time; *ett visst ~ av respekt* a
certain amount (degree) of respect; *i rikt ~* in
ample measure; *vidtaga ~ och steg* take measures (steps)
1 mått|a *s1* **1** moderation; mean; *hålla (med)*
~ exercise (in) moderation **2** *i dubbel -o* in a
double sense (degree); *i så -o* to that extent,
in that degree; *i så -o som* in as (so) far as
2 måtta *v1* aim *(mot* at)
måttagning *(särskr. mått-tagning)* measuring
mått|angivelse [details of] measurements *(pl)*
-band tape measure, measuring tape **-beställd**
a5 made to measure; *AE.* custom[-made]
måtte *imperf av må* **1** *(uttryckande önskan)*
may; I [do] hope; *det ~ väl inte ha hänt henne*
något I [do] hope nothing has happened to her;
du ~ väl förstå ...! you will understand ...,
won't you! **2** *(uttryckande visshet)* must; *jag*
~ väl få göra vad jag vill! surely I can do as I
like, can't I!; *det ~ väl du veta!* you of all
people must know that!; *han ~ ha gått och lagt*
sig he must have gone to bed
måttenhet unit of measurement
mått|full *(återhållsam)* moderate; *(behärskad)*
measured, restrained **-fullhet** moderation; mo-
derateness; restraint; sobriety **-lig** *a1* moderate;
(i fråga om mat o. dryck äv.) temperate; *(blyg-*
sam) modest; *det är inte ~t vad han äter*
there's no limit to what he eats **-lighet** moderation; temperance **-lös** measureless, unmeas-
ured
måtto *se 1* måtta 2
mått|sats set of measures *(tekn. gauge blocks)*
-stock measure, measuring-rod; *bildl.* gauge,
standard, criterion, yardstick *(på* of) **-system**
system of measurement **-tagning** *(hopskr.*
måttagning) measuring
Mähren ['mä:-] *n* Moravia

M

mähä *s6, vard.* milksop
mäkla [ˈmä(:)k-] act as a broker; (*medla*) mediate; ~ *fred* negotiate (restore) peace mäklararvode brokerage, broker's commission mäklare broker; (*börs- äv.*) stockbroker; (*medlare*) mediator; *auktoriserad* ~ authorized broker mäklarfirma brokerage (broker's) firm mäklarrörelse brokerage (broker's) business mäkling mediation, conciliation
1 mäkta *adv* tremendously, immensely; highly; *vard.* mighty, jolly
2 mäkta *v1* be capable of (*göra ngt* doing s.th.); be able to manage
mäktig *a1* 1 powerful; (*starkare*) potent; (*känslobetonat*) mighty 2 (*väldig*) immense, huge; (*storartad*) majestic, grandiose 3 (*i stånd t.*) capable of 4 (*mättande*) substantial, heavy -het powerfulness *etc.*
Mälaren *r* Lake Mälaren
mäld *s3* grist
män *se 2 man*
mänga mix; mingle
mängd *s3* (*stor* ~) large amount (quantity), lot; (*stort antal*) large (great) number, multitude, lot[s *pl*]; (*skara*) crowd, multitude; *en hel* ~ a good deal of, a great many; *i riklig* ~ in ample (abundant) quantity, in abundance; *höja sig över* ~*en* stand out from the crowd; *i små* ~*er* in small qu antities -lära set theory, theory of sets -rabatt quantity discount
människ|a [-iʃa] *s1* 1 man (*äv.* ~*n*); (*mänsklig varelse*) human being, mortal; (*individ*) person, individual; (*varelse*) creature; *ingen* ~ no one, nobody; *den moderna* ~*n* modern man; *bli* ~ *igen* (*vard.*) be o.s. again; *känna sig som en ny* ~ feel like a new person;j*jag är inte* ~ *att komma ihåg* I can't for the life of me remember; *jag är inte mer än* ~ I am only human 2 -*or* men, (*folk*) people; *AE. vard.* folks; *alla* -*or* (*vanl.*) everybody, everyone (*sg*); -*or emellan* man to man
människo|ansikte *ett* ~ a man's (a human) face -apa anthropoid [ape] -barn [human] child; (*mänsniska*) human being -boning human habitation -fientlig hostile to man -föda *inte lämplig som* ~ not fit for human consumption -förakt contempt of man[kind] -gestalt *en* ~ the figure of a man -hamn *i uttr.: ett odjur i* ~ a beast in human shape -hand *av* ~ by human hand -hatare manhater, misanthrope -hjärta human heart -jakt manhunting -kropp human body -kännare judge of character -kännedom knowledge of human nature -kärlek love of mankind (humanity); (*välgörenhet*) philanthropy -lik *a1* resembling a human being; manlike -liv *ett* ~ a human life; *förlust av* ~ loss of life; *ett helt* ~ a whole lifetime -massa crowd [of people] -natur human nature (*äv.* ~*en*) -offer human sacrifice -ras human race -rov kidnapping -skildring character study -skygg shy, timid -släktet mankind; the human race (species) -son *M*~*en* Son of Man -spillra wreck -vän humanitarian; philanthropist -vänlig humane; philanthropic[al] -värde human dignity -värdig fit for human beings; ~*a bostäder* (*äv.*) decent houses (*etc.*); *föra ett* ~*t liv* lead a worthwhile life

-ätare man-eater -öde human destiny
mänsklig *a1* human; (*rimlig*) reasonable; *förklaringen om de* ~*a rättigheterna* the Declaration of Human Rights; *allt som står i* ~ *makt* everything [that is] humanly possible; *det är inte* ~*t att* (*äv.*) it is inhuman to -het 1 (*humanitet*) humanity, humaneness 2 *konkr.* (*människorna*) mankind (*äv.* ~*en*); *hela* ~*en* all (the whole of) mankind
märg [märj] *s3* marrow (*äv. bildl.*); *vetensk.* medulla (*pl äv.* medullae); *bot., zool. o. bildl.* pith; *förlängda* ~*en* (*anat.*) the medulla [oblongata]; *det gick* (*skar*) *genom* ~ *och ben på mig* it pierced the very marrow of my bones; *jag frös ända in i* ~*en* I was chilled to the marrow -ben marrowbone
märgel [-j-] *s9* marl
märg|full full of marrow; *bildl. äv.* pithy -lös marrowless; pithless -pipa *se märgben*
märk|a *v3* 1 (*sätta -e på*) mark (*med* with; *med bläck* in ink); (*med bokstäver, namn*) letter, name; -*t av sjukdom* marked by illness; *han är -t för livet* he is marked for life; ~ *ngn* (*med slag e.d.*) scotch s.b. 2 (*lägga -e t.*) notice, observe, be (become) aware of; (*känna*) feel, perceive; (*se*) see; *låt ingen* ~ *att* don't let it be noticed (anyone notice) that; *härvid är att* ~ *att* in this connection it should be noted that; *märk väl att* [please,] observe that; *väl att* ~ observe ..., ... be it noted; *det -tes knappt* it was hardly noticeable; *bland gästerna -tes* among the guests were to be seen -bar *a1* noticeable, perceptible, observable; (*synbar*) visible; (*iakttagbar*) appreciable; (*påtaglig*) marked, evident -bläck marking ink -bok sampler book -duk sampler
märke *s6* 1 (*ej avsiktligt*) mark (*efter* of); (*spår*) trace (*efter* of); (*efter tryck*) impression; (*efter slag o.d.*) dent; (*rispa*) scratch (*efter* from); *om inte gamla* ~*n slår fel* unless all the time-honoured signs play us false 2 *bot.* stigma 3 (*avsiktligt*) mark; (*idrotts-, klubb- e.d.*) badge; *hand.* brand, trademark; (*fabrikat*) make
märkes|dag red-letter day -man man of distinction -vara branded product; (*patentskyddad*) proprietary article -år memorable year
märkgarn marking thread märklig *a1* notable; (*beaktansvärd*) noteworthy; (*starkare*) signal; (-*värdig*) remarkable, striking; *det* ~*a* [*med saken*] *är att* the remarkable (striking) thing [about the matter] is that märkligt *adv* notably *etc.*; ~ *nog* remarkably enough märkning marking märkvärdig remarkable; (*besynnerlig*) curious, strange; (*förvånande*) astonishing, surprising; *göra sig* ~ be self-important (pompous); *det var* ~*t!* how extraordinary (odd)!; ~*are* *än så var det inte* it wasn't more remarkable than that, it was that simple märkvärdighet remarkableness *etc.*; wonder; singularity; (*med pl*) marvel, remarkable feature
märla [-ä:-] *s1* staple, clincher
märlspik [-ä:-] marlinespike
märr *s2* mare; *vard.* jade
märs *s2, sjö.* top -segel topsail
mäsk *s3* mash
mäss *s2* (*lokal*) messroom; *sjö.* (*befäls-, offi-*

cers-) officers' mess; *abstr.* mess
mäss|a I *s1* **1** *kyrkl.* mass; *stilla* ~ low mass; *gå i* ~*n* go to (attend) mass **2** *hand.* fair **II** *v1* say (sing) mass; (*sjunga*) chant; (*läsa entonigt*) drone **-bok** missal **-fall** *det blev* ~ *i söndags* there was no service held last Sunday **-förrättare** celebrant **-hake** chasuble **-hall** exhibition hall
mässing brass
mässings|beslag brass mountings (*pl*) **-bleck** brass-sheet, plate brass **-instrument** brass (wind) instrument; ~*en* (*i orkester*) the brass (*sg*) **-musik** brass-band music **-orkester** brass band **-tråd** brass wire
mässling *s2, ej pl* [the] measles (*pl*); *få* ~*[en]* get (catch) the measles
mässpojke cabin boy, messroom boy
mäss|offer [the] Eucharist Sacrifice **-skjorta** (*hopskr. mässkjorta*) alb **-skrud** (*hopskr. mässkrud*) mass vestments
mässuppassare messman
mästarbrev *ung.* mastership diploma (certificate); *Storbritannien äv.* diploma (certificate) of the freedom of a guild
mästar|e I (*sport. o. friare*) champion; (*sakkunning o.d.*) expert, master-hand; ~ *på fiol* master of the violin; ~ *i tennis* champion at tennis **2** (*hantverkare, upphovsman t. konstverk o.d.*) master (*i* of); *de gamla* -*na* the Old Masters; *övning gör* ~*n* practise makes perfect **3** (*om Jesus*) *M*~ Master; *svära på* ~*ns ord* have blind faith in the experts **-hand** *av* (*med*) ~ by (with) a master's hand **-inna** *sport.* champion **-klass** master's (*sport.* champion) class **-prov** *bildl.* masterpiece
mäster ['mäss-] (*titel*) Master **-katten** *M*~ *i stövlar* Puss in Boots **-kock** master cook **-lig** *a1* masterly; (*skickligt utförd*) brilliant[ly executed]; *vard.* champion **-lots** senior pilot **-man** (*bödel*) headsman **-skap** *s7* masterhood, mastership, master's skill; (*fulländning*) perfection; *sport.* championship **-skytt** champion marksman, crack shot **-stycke** *se mästerverk o. mästarprov* **-sångare** Meistersinger **-verk** masterpiece (*av, i* of); masterstroke
mästra (*anmärka på*) criticize; find fault with
mät *i uttr.: ta i* ~ seize, distress
mät|a *v3* **1** (*eg. o. bildl.*) measure (*efter, med* by; *på millimetern* to the millimetre); (*med instrument äv.*) gauge; ~ *ngn med ögonen* look s.b. up and down, size s.b. up; ~ *djupet av* (*bildl.*) fathom; ~ *knappt* (*väl*) give short (full) measure; ~ *sig* measure o.s. (*med* with, against); ~ *sina krafter med ngn* pit one's strength against another's; *kunna* ~*s med ngn* come up to (match, compare with) s.b.; ~ *upp a*) take the measure[ments] (size) of, *b*) (*mjöl e.d.*) measure out (*åt* for, to) **2** (*ha en viss storlek*) measure; ~ *två meter i längd* measure two metres in length
mätaravläsning meter reading
mätar|e (*el-, gas- e.d.*) meter; (*automat*) slot meter; (*instrument*) gauge, indicator **-fjäril** geometrid moth **-larv** measuring worm, geometer **-tavla** meter panel
mät|bar [-ä:-] *a1* measurable **-glas** graduated glass **-instrument** measuring instrument,

gauge **-metod** method of measurement **-ning** [-ä:-] measuring *etc.*; measurement
mätress mistress; *neds.* paramour
mätsticka measuring stick; (*för vätska*) dipstick; (*med krympmått*) shrinkage rule
mätt *a1* satisfied (*äv. bildl.*) (*av* with); *vard.* full up; *bildl.* full (*av år* of years); *äta sig* ~ have enough to eat, satisfy one's hunger; *jag är* ~ I have had enough, *vard.* I am full up; ~ *på* (*äv. bildl.*) satiated with; *se sig* ~ *på* gaze one's fill at
mätt|a satisfy; appease; (*förse med mat*) fill; *kem., elektr.* saturate; *ha många munnar att* ~ have many mouths to feed; *sådan mat* ~*r inte* that kind of food is not satisfying (is not filling) **-ande** *a4* satisfying *etc.*
mätteknik measurement
mätthet *se mättnad* **mätthetskänsla** feeling of being satisfied; satisfied feeling **mättnad** *s3* (*-het*) state of being satisfied, satiation; *kem.* saturation **mättning** *kem.* saturation **mättsam** *a1, se mättande*
mätverktyg measuring tool
mö *s5* virgin, maid[en]; *gammal* ~ old maid
möbel ['mö:-] *s3* piece of furniture; (*möblemang*) suite of furniture (*sg*); *stoppade möbler* upholstered furniture (*sg*) **-affär** furniture shop, furnisher['s] **-arkitekt** furniture designer **-fabrik** furniture factory **-handlare** furniture dealer **-klädsel** upholstery **-magasin** furniture warehous e **-polityr** furniture polish **-snickare** cabinet-maker **-tyg** furnishing fabric **-vagn** furniture van
möble'mang *s7, s4* [suite (set) of] furniture
möbler|a furnish; *AE. äv.* fix up; ~ *om* (*flytta om*) rearrange the furniture (*i* in, of) **-ing** furnishing
möd|a *s1* (*tungt arbete*) labour, toil; (*besvär*) trouble, pains (*pl*); (*svårighet*) difficulty; *lärda -or* a scholar's labour; *göra sig mycken* ~ take (give o.s.) a great deal of trouble; *det lönar inte* ~*n* it isn't worth while (the trouble); *inte lämna någon* ~ *ospard* spare no pains
möderne *s6, på* ~*t* on the (one's) mother's (the maternal) side **-släkt** mother's family
mödom *s2* virginity, maidenhood **mödomshinna** maidenhead, hymen
mödo|sam *a1* laborious, toilsome; (*om arbete o.d. äv.*) hard; (*svår*) difficult **-samt** *adv* laboriously, with difficulty; ~ *förvärvade slantar* hard-earned money
mödra|gymnastik antenatal exercises (*pl*) **-hem** home for mothers **-vård** maternity welfare **-vårdscentral** maternity clinic; (*för havande kvinnor*) prenatal clinic; (*för nyblivna mödrar*) postnatal clinic
mögel ['mö:-, 'mögg-] *s7* mould; (*på papper o.d.*) mildew-spot **-hund** snifferdog **-svamp** mould (mildew) fungus
mög|la [ˣmö:g-, ˣmögg-] go (get) mouldy **-lig** *a1* mouldy, mildewy; (*förlegad*) fusty, rusty
möhippa *ung.* hen party for bride-to-be; *AE. äv.* shower
möjlig *a1* possible; (~ *att göra*) feasible, practicable; *allt* ~*t* all kinds of things; *det är mycket* ~*t* it is quite possible; *så vitt* ~*t* provided it is possible; *det är inte* ~*t annat* it

M

simply must be so; *det är ~t att vi behöver* we may need; *skulle det vara ~t för dig att ...?* would you be able to ...?; *göra det bästa ~a av ngt* make the best (most) of s.th.; *på kortaste ~a tid* as fast as possible; *8 poäng av 10 ~a* (*sport. o.d.*) 8 points out of a possible 10; *med minsta ~a* with a minimum of **möjligast** *i ~e mån* as far as possible **möjligen** possibly; (*kanske*) perhaps; *har du ~ ...?* do you happen to have ...?, have you by any chance [got] ...?; *skulle man ~ kunna få träffa ...?* I wonder if it is possible to see (speak to) ...? **möjliggöra** make possible; (*underlätta*) facilitate; *~ för ngn att* enable s.b. to **möjlighet** possibility; (*utsikt*) prospect, chance; (*eventualitet*) eventuality; (*tillfälle*) opportunity; (*utväg*) means (*pl*); *det finns ingen annan ~* (*äv.*) there is no alternative **möjligtvis** *se* möjligen
mönja I *s1* red lead **II** *v1* redlead
mönster ['möns-] *s7* pattern (*till* for, of) (*äv. bildl.*); *tekn.* design (*till* for, of); (*friare o. bildl.*) model (*av* of); (*urbild*) archetype, prototype; *sy efter ~* sew from a pattern; *efter ~ av* on the pattern of; *ta ngn till ~* take s.b. as one's pattern; *efter amerikanskt ~* on the American model, as in America **-gill** model, ideal; exemplary **-gillt** [-j-] *adv* in a model way; exemplarily **-jordbruk** model farm **-skydd** protection of designs, trade mark protection **-stickning** patterned knitting **-vävd** [-ä:-] *a5* with woven patterns, figured **-vävning** patterned weaving
mönstr|a 1 (*göra mönster*) pattern **2** (*granska*) look over; scrutinize, examine closely **3** *mil.* (*hålla -ing med*) inspect, review; (*inskrivas som värnpliktig*) enlist, conscript **4** *sjö.* (*ta hyra*) sign on; *~ av a*) (*besättningsman*) pay off, *b*) (*avgå*) sign off **-ing 1** (*granskning*) critical examination, scrutiny **2** (*inspektion av trupp*) inspection, muster; (*inskrivning av värnpliktiga*) conscription; (*på-*) signing on
mör *a1* (*om skorpa o.d.*) crisp, crumbly; (*om kött*) tender; *känna sig ~ i hela kroppen* ache all over (in every limb); *då blev han ~ i mun* that changed his tune **möra** tenderize **mörbulta** *bildl.* beat black and blue
mörda [-ö:-] murder; (*lönn-*) assassinate; *om blickar kunde ~* if looks could kill **mördande** *a4* murdering; (*friare*) murderous; *bildl.* killing, crushing; (*om blick*) withering; *~ konkurrens* cut-throat competition; *~ kritik* crushing criticism; *~ tråkig* deadly dull **mördare** murderer; (*lönn-*) assassin **mördarhand** *falla för ~* be murdered
mördeg short crust pastry
mörderska [-ö:-] murderess
mörk *a1* dark (*till färgen* in colour); (*om färg, ton o.d.*) deep; (*något ~*) darkish; (*svagt upplyst*) dim; (*dyster*) sombre, gloomy; *~ choklad* plain chocolate; *~ kostym* dark lounge suit; *det ser ~t ut* things look bad **-blå** dark (deep) blue
mörker ['mörr-] *s7* darkness (*äv. bildl.*); dark; *bildl.* obscurity; *när mörkret faller* when darkness falls; *till mörkrets inbrott* until nightfall; *mörkrets gärningar* dark deeds **-döden** the night-driving toll
mörk|hyad *a5* dark-skinned **-hårig** dark-haired

-lockig having dark curly hair, with dark curls **-lägga** black out (*äv. bildl.*); (*hemlighålla*) keep secret **-läggning** blackout **-man** obscurant[ist]
mörk|na get (become, grow) dark; darken; (*om blick*) grow darker; *det ~r fort* it gets dark quickly; *utsikterna har ~t* prospects are (have become) less promising **-rostad** *-rostat kaffe* dark-roasted coffee **-rum** *foto.* darkroom **-rädd** afraid of the dark **-rädsla** fear of the dark **-ögd** *a1* dark-eyed
mörsare mortar
mört *s2* roach; dace; *pigg som en ~* [as] fit as a fiddle
möss (*pl av mus*) mice (*sg* mouse)
möss|a *s1* cap; *ta av sig ~n för ngn* raise one's cap to s.b.; *stå med ~n i hand* stand cap in hand **-märke** cap badge **-skärm** (*hopskr. mösskärm*) cap peak
möt|a *v3* **1** meet; (*råka på*) come (run) across; (*röna*) meet with, encounter, come in for; (*svårighet e.d.*) face, confront; *sport.* meet, encounter; *en hemsk syn -te oss* a terrible sight met us (our eyes); *~ stark kritik* encounter severe criticism; *det -er inget hinder* there is no objection **2** (*invänta*) meet s.b.; *jag -er med bil* I'll meet you with the (a) car; *~ upp* assemble, muster up **mötande** *a4* (*om t.ex. pers., fordon*) that one meets; (*som kommer emot en*) oncoming; (*som närmar sig*) approaching, coming the other way; (*som -er varandra*) that pass each other **mötas** *v3, dep* meet; encounter one another; (*gå förbi varandra*) pass one another; *våra blickar -tes* our eyes met
möt|e *s6* **1** (*sammanträffande*) meeting; (*tåg- etc. äv.*) crossing, passing; (*avtalat*) appointment; (*tillfälligt, fientligt*) encounter; *stämma ~ med* make an appointment (*AE.* a date) with; *gå* (*komma*) *ngn till ~s* go to meet s.b., *bildl.* meet s.b. halfway **2** (*sammankomst*) meeting; (*mera tillfälligt*) assembly, gathering; (*konferens*) conference; *~ på högsta nivå* summit meeting **mötes** *se* möte 1
mötes|beslut resolution of (passed at) a meeting **-deltagare** participant in a meeting (conference) **-frihet** freedom of assembly **-förhandlingar** *pl* proceedings at a meeting (conference) **-lokal** assembly (conference) hall **-plats** meeting place; (*för två pers.*) rendezvous; (*på väg*) passing point **-talare** speaker at a meeting (conference) **-tid** time of a meeting

N

nabb *s2* projection, stub; (*på bildäck*) tread block; (*på sko*) stud
nabo *s5* neighbour
nachspi[e]l ['na:ʃspi:l] *s7* follow-up party
nacka chop the head off, behead
nackbena back-parting
nackdel disadvantage, drawback; (*skada*) detriment; *fördelar och ~ar* (*äv.*) pros and cons; *till ~ för framåtskridandet* detrimental to progress
nack|e *s2* back of the head, nape [of the neck]; *bryta ~en av sig* break one's neck; *klia sig i ~en* scratch the back of one's head; *med mössan på ~n* with one's cap at the back of one's head **-grop** nape [of the neck] **-hår** back-hair **-skinn** *ta ngn i ~et* seize s.b. by the scruff of the neck **-skott** shot through the neck **-spegel** hand-mirror **-spärr** wryneck; *med.* torticollis **-styv** *eg.* stiff in the neck; *bildl.* stiff-necked, haughty **-stöd** headrest **-sving** *brottn.* headlock
nadir ['na:-] *oböjl. s, astr.* nadir
nafs *s7* **1** snap; (*hugg*) grab **2** *i ett ~* in a flash
nafsa snap (*efter* at); *~ åt sig* snap up, grab hold of
nafta *s1* naphtha **nafta'len, nafta'lin** *s4, s3* naphthalene
1 nag|el ['na:-] *s2* (*på finger*) nail; *klippa* (*peta*) *-larna* cut (clean) one's nails; *bita på -larna* bite one's nails; *vara en ~ i ögat på* be a thorn in the flesh to
2 nagel ['na:-] *s2* (*nit*) rivet; (*trä-*) treenail, trunnel
nagel|band cuticle **-borste** nailbrush **-bädd** nailbed
nagelfara scrutinize (scan) closely; criticize
nagel|fil nailfile **-lack** nail varnish (polish) **-petare** nail cleaner **-pinne** orange stick **-rot** root of a (the) nail **-sax** nail scissors (*pl*) **-trång** *s7* ingrowing [toe] nail
nagg *s2* (*bröd-*) [bread] pricker **nagga 1** prick **2** *~* [*i kanten*] notch; *porslinet var ~t i kanten* the china was chipped; *~ sparkapitalet i kanten* nibble at one's savings **3** (*oroa*) chafe, fret **4** *se gnata* **naggande** *a4*, *~ god* jolly good
nagla [ˣna:g-] nail, rivet (*vid* to)
na'iv *a1* naive, naïve, simplistic; (*enkel*) simple; unsophisticated; (*barnslig*) childish; (*enfaldig*) silly **-ism** *se -itet*; (*konstriktn.*) naïvism **-ist** naïvist **-itet** *s3* naivety, naïveté, naiveness; simplicity; childishness
naja *sjö., v1* lash
na'jad *s3* naiad
naken *a3* naked; *konst.* nude; (*bar*) bare (*äv. bildl.*); *bildl. äv.* hard, plain; *klä av ngn ~* strip s.b. to the skin; *med ~ överkropp* stripped to the waist; *nakna fakta* bare (hard) facts; *den nakna sanningen* the plain (naked) truth **-badare** nude swimmer, *AE. sl.* skinny-dipper

-dans nude dancing **-dansös** nude dancer **-fröig** *a1, bot.* gymnospermous; *~ växt* gymnosperm **-het** nakedness; *konst.* nudity; *avslöjad i all sin ~* (*bildl.*) revealed in all its nakedness **-kultur** nudism **-modell** nude [life] model **-måleri** nude painting
nakterhus *s7, sjö.* binnacle
nalkas *dep* approach, draw near [to]; (*om tid äv.*) come on, be at hand
nalla *vard.* pinch, swipe, bone
nalle *s2* bruin; (*leksak*) teddy [bear]
namib|ier [-'mi:-] *s9* Namibian **-isk** *a5* Namibian
namn *s7* name; *hur var ~et?* what is your name please?; *byta ~* change one's name; *fingerat ~* assumed (false) name, pseudonym; *fullständigt ~* name in full; *ett stort ~ inom* a big name in; *ngns goda ~ och rykte* a p.'s good name; *hennes ~ som gift* (*vanl.*) her married name; *ha ~ om sig att vara* have the reputation of being; *skapa sig ett ~* make a name for o.s.; *göra skäl för sitt ~* live up to (merit) its name; *i eget ~* in one's own name; *i lagens ~* in the name of the law; *i sanningens ~* to tell the truth; *till ~et* by (in) name; *blott till ~et* in name only; *mera till ~et än till gagnet* only nominally; *under ~et ...* by the name of ...; *vid ~ A.* named A., of the name of A.; *nämna ngn vid ~* mention s.b. by name; *nämna ngt vid dess rätta ~* (*äv.*) call a spade a spade
namna name
namnam yum-yum!
namn|byte change of name **-chiffer** monogram
namn|e *s2* namesake (*till mig* of mine) **-ge** name; *en icke -given person* a person unnamed **-insamling** collection of names; petition **-kunnig** renowned, celebrated, famous **-lös** nameless (*äv. bildl.*); (*outsäglig*) unspeakable (*sorg* grief) **-plåt** nameplate **-register** index, list of names
namns|dag name day **-dagsfirande** *s6* name-day celebration
namn|sedel name slip **-skydd** protection of family (company) names **-skylt** *se namnplåt* **-stämpel** [signature] stamp, stamped signature **-teckning, -underskrift** signature **-upprop** roll call
nankin[g] ['naŋkin, -ŋ] *s2, s7* nankeen, nankin
napalm *s3* napalm **-bomb** napalm bomb
1 napp *s2* (*di-*) teat, nipple; (*tröst-*) dummy [teat], comforter, *AE.* pacifier
2 napp *s7* (*fiske*) bite; *bildl.* nibble; *få ~* have a bite (*bildl.* nibble)
1 nappa *s1* (*skinn*) nappa
2 nappa *v1* bite; *bildl.* nibble; *~ på ett erbjudande* jump at an offer; *~ åt sig* snatch, snap up
nappa|s *dep* tussle (*med* with; *om* for) **-tag** tussle (*äv. bildl.*); *ta ett ~ med* have a tussle (brush) with
nappflaska feeding (nursing) bottle, baby's bottle
naprapat *s3* naprapath
nar'ciss *s3* narcissus
nardus ['narr-, 'na:r-] *s2* [spike]nard
nar[e] *s2* crossbar
nare *s2* (*blåst*) biting wind

narig *a1* (*om hud*) chapped, rough
narko'man *s3* drug addict (fiend); *vard.* dope fiend; *AE. sl.* junkie **narkoma'ni** *s3* drug addiction, narcomania **narkomanvård** care (treatment) of drug addicts
narkos [-'kå:s] *s3* narcosis, anaesthesia; *ge* ~ anaesthetize, administer an anaesthetic **-appa-rat** anaesthetic apparatus **-läkare** anaesthetist, *AE.* anesthesiologist **-medel** anaesthetic [agent]
narkotika [-'kå:-] *pl* narcotics, drugs; *vard.* dope (*sg*) **-handel** drugs traffic **-langare** drug peddler **-missbruk** abuse of narcotics
narkotisk [-'kå:-] *s5* narcotic
narr *s2* fool; (*hov-* *äv.*) jester; (*lättlurad pers.* *äv.*) dupe; *beskedlig* ~ silly fool; *inbilsk* ~ conceited fool, coxcomb; *spela* ~ play the fool; *göra* ~ *av* make fun of, poke fun at **narra** (*bedraga*) deceive, take in; (*lura*) cheat; (*på skoj*) fool; (*locka*) beguile; ~ *ngn att tro* delude s.b. into believing; ~ *ngn att skratta* make s.b. laugh [against his (*etc.*) will]
narraktig *a1* (*löjlig*) ridiculous; (*fjollig*) foolish, silly; (*dåraktig*) vain **-het** ridiculousness *etc.*
narras *dep* tell fibs (a fib) **narri** ['narri] *s6, på* ~ in jest, in (for) fun
narr|kåpa fool's cap [and bells] **-spel** foolery, tomfoolery; buffoonery; *bildl.* farce, folly **-streck** (*spratt*) practical joke, prank
narv *s2* (*på läder*) grain
narval ['na:r-] *s2, zool.* narwhal[e], unicorn fish (whale)
narvsida hair side
na'sal I *a1* nasal **II** *s3* nasal [sound] **-era** nasalize **-konsonant** nasal consonant **-ton** [nasal] twang **-vokal** nasalized vowel
nasare hawker, dorr-to-door salesman
nasaré *s3* Nazarene **Nasaret** *n* Nazareth
nasse *s2* porker; piggy
nasus ['na:-] *s2, vard.* beak
nate *s2, bot.* pondweed
nation [-t'ʃɑ:n] nation; *univ.* student society (association); *Förenta ~erna* the United Nations; *N~ernas förbund* the League of Nations
natio'nal|budget [-tʃɑ-] budget, national budget **-dag** national holiday (commemoration day) **-dräkt** national costume **-egendom** national property **-ekonom** economist **-ekonomi** economics (*sg*), political economy **-ekonomisk** economic, of political economy; *av* ~ *betydelse* important to the country's economy **-epos** national epic **-flagga** national flag **-församling** *franska ~en* the French National Assembly **-hjälte** national hero **-inkomst** national income
nationaliser|a [-tʃɑ-] nationalize **-ing** nationalization
national|ism [-tʃɑ-] nationalism **-ist** nationalist
nationalitet [-tʃɑ-] *s3* nationality
nationalitets|sadjektiv adjective of nationality **-beteckning** nationality mark (sign) **-principen** the principle of national self-determination
natio'nal|karaktär [-tʃɑ-] national character **-känsla** national feeling **-monument** national monument **-museum** national museum

-park national park; *i Storbritannien äv.* National Trust property (reserve) **-produkt** national product **-socialism** National Socialism **-socialist** *s3* National Socialist **-socialistisk** *a5* National Socialist; *ty. äv.* Nazi **-stat** nation-state **-sång** national anthem
natio'nell [-tʃɑ-] *a1* national
nativitet birth rate
nativitets|ökning increase in the birth rate **-överskott** excess of births over deaths
natrium ['na:-] *s8* sodium **-bikarbonat** sodium bicarbonate, baking soda **-klorid** sodium chloride, salt
natron ['na:trån] *s7* [caustic] soda, sodium hydroxide **-lut** soda lye, caustic soda [solution]
natt *-en nätter* night; *god ~!* good night!; *hela ~en* all night; *varje ~* every night, nightly; *~en till lördagen* Friday night; *i* ~ *a*) (*som kommer*) tonight, *b*) (*föregående*) last night; *om* (*på*) *~en* at (by) night, in the night; *sent på ~en* late at night; *till ~en a*) (*t.ex. ta medicin*) for the night, *b*) *se följ.*; *under ~en* during (in) the night; *stanna över ~en hos* (*på*) stay the night at
natt|a *vard.* put [a child] to bed **-arbete** night work **-blind** night blind **-blindhet** night blindness **-djur** nocturnal animal **-dräkt** nightdress, nightgown; *vard.* nightie **-duksbord** bedside table
natt|etid at (by) night **-fack** *bank.* night safe (depository) **-fjäril** *zool.* moth **-flygning** night flying **-frost** night frost **-gammal** ~ *is* ice formed overnight **-gäst** guest for the night **-him-mel** night sky **-härbärge** lodging [for the night]; *konkr.* hostel
natt|iné *s3* [mid]night performance **-kafé** all-night café **-klubb** nightclub **-kräm** night cream **-kröken** *vard. i uttr. på ~n* in the small hours **-kvarter** quarters (*pl*) for the night, night quarters (*pl*) **-kärl** chamber pot **-lampa** night lamp **-lig** *a1* nocturnal; (*under -en*) in the night; (*som sker varje natt*) nightly **-linne** *se nattdräkt* **-logi** *se -kvarter* **-mangling** all-night negotiations (*pl*) **-mara** nightmare **-mörker** night darkness **-mössa** nightcap; *prata i ~n* talk through one's hat, drivel, blether **-parkering** night parking **-pass** night duty **-permission** night leave **-portier** night porter **-ro** night's rest **-rock** dressing gown **-skift** night shift **-skjorta** nightshirt **-skärra** *zool.* nightjar; *AE.* whippoorwill **-sköterska** night nurse **-stånden** *a5* (*om dryck*) flat **-sudd** *s7* night-carousing **-svart** [as] black as night, nightblack (*äv. bildl.*) **-söl** staying up late at nights **-sömn** night's sleep **-taxa** (*hopskr. nattaxa*) night rate **-trafik** (*hopskr. nattrafik*) night traffic **-tåg** (*hopskr. nattåg*) night train **-uggla** night owl (*äv. bildl.*) **-vak** *s7* night-watching; vigils, night vigils (*pl*) (*friare*) late hours (*pl*) **-vakt** night watch; *pers.* night watchman, *mil.* night guard **-vandrare** nocturnal rambler **-vard** [-va:-] *s3* Eucharist, Holy Communion, Blessed Sacrament
nattvards|bröd sacramental bread **-gång** communion **-gäst** communicant **-vin** sacramental wine
nattviol butterfly orchis

natur nature; *(kynne äv.)* character; *(läggning)* disposition, temperament; *(beskaffenhet)* kind; *(landskap)* nature, scenery; *pers.* person[ality], character; *Guds fria* ~ the open country, wide-open spaces *(pl)*; *vild* ~ wild nature *(på en plats:* scenery); *~en tar ut sin rätt* nature takes its toll; *av ~en* by nature, naturally, inherently; *till sin* ~ *är han* ... he is ... by nature; *det ligger i sakens* ~ it is quite natural; *av privat* ~ of a private character (nature)

natura [-ˣtu:-] *s, i uttr.*: *betalning i[n]* ~ payment in kind (goods, merchandise) **-förmån** payment in kind, perquisite **-hushållning** primitive (natural, barter) economy

natural|ier [-'na:-] *pl* natural-history objects **-isation** naturalization **-isera** naturalize **-ism** naturalism **-ist** naturalist **-istisk** *a5* naturalistic

natur|barn child of nature **-begåvning** natural gifts *(pl)*; *pers.* man *(etc.)* with great natural talent **-behov** *förrätta sina* ~ relieve o.s. **-dyrkan** nature-worship **-'ell I** *s3* nature, disposition **II** *a1* natural **-enlig** [-e:n-] *a1* natural **-fenomen** natural phenomenon **-folk** primitive people **-forskare** [natural] scientist, naturalist **-färg** natural colour **-företeelse** *se -fenomen* **-förhållanden** natural conditions (features); nature *(sg)* **-gas** natural gas **-gudomlighet** nature deity **-gummi** natural rubber **-hinder** natural obstacle **-historia** natural history **-historisk** of natural history; natural-history; *N~a riksmuseet* [the] museum of natural history **-katastrof** natural catastrophe **-kraft** natural force **-kunnighet** knowledge of nature; *skol.* nature study **-lag** law of Nature; physical law

naturlig [-'tu:r-] *a1* natural; *(medfödd)* inherent, innate; *(ursprunglig)* native; *(okonstlad)* unaffected, ingenuous; *(äkta)* genuine; *dö en* ~ *död* die from natural causes; *~t urval* natural selection; *av ~a skäl* for natural (obvious) reasons; *i* ~ *storlek* full-size, *(om porträtt o.d. äv.)* life-size; *i ~t tillstånd* in a state of nature; *det är helt ~t att* it is a matter of course that **naturlighet** naturalness; unaffectedness *etc.* **naturligtvis** of course, naturally; *(visst, säkert)* to be sure, certainly

natur|lyrik nature poetry **-läkare** nature-healer **-lära** natural science; *(som lärobok)* natural--science textbook **-makt** elemental force **-nödvändighet** physical (natural) necessity; *med* ~ with absolute necessity **-park** nature--park; national park **-produkt** natural (primary) product **-reservat** nature reserve; national park; *AE.* wildlife sanctuary **-rike** *~t* the natural kingdom **-rikedom** *~ar* natural resources **-sceneri** natural scenery **-siden** real (natural) silk **-skildring** description of [natural] scenery **-skydd** protection (preservation) of nature **-skyddsområde** *se -reservat* **-skön** of great natural beauty; *en* ~ *plats (äv.)* a beauty spot **-skönhet** beauty of nature, natural beauty; *berömd för sin* ~ noted for the beauty of its scenery **-tillgång** natural asset (source of wealth); *~ar (äv.)* natural resources **-tillstånd** natural state; *i ~et* in the state of nature **-trogen** true to life; lifelike **-vetare** scientist **-vetenskap** [natural] science **-veten-**

-skaplig scientific **-vetenskapsman** scientist **-vidrig** contrary to (against) nature **-vård** nature conservation **-vårdsverk** *statens* ~ [the Swedish] national environment protection board **-vän** nature lover **-väsen** elemental being **-älskare** *se -vän*

naur|uer [-'ɷrɷer] Nauruan **-isk** *a5* Nauruan

nautisk ['nau-] *a5* nautical; ~ *mil* nautical mile

nav *s7* hub; *(frihjuls-)* freewheel hub; *(propeller-)* boss

navare *s9 el. -n navrar (borr)* auger

navel *s2* navel **-binda** umbilical bandage **-sträng** umbilical cord, navel string

navigation navigation; *astronomisk* ~ celestial navigation, astronavigation; *terrester* ~ terrestrial navigation

navigations|hytt chart-room **-skola** school of navigation; nautical college

navigatör navigator **navigera** navigate *(efter, med* by) **navigering** navigation

navkapsel hub cap

naz|ism [-'sism] Nazism **-ist** Nazi **-istisk** *a5* Nazi

neandertal|are, -människa Neanderthal man

Neapel [-'a:-] *n* Naples **neapolitansk** [-'ta:nsk] *a5* Neapolitan

nebul|osa [-ˣlɷ:-] *s1* nebula *(pl* nebulae) **-'ös** *a1* nebulous

neces'sär *s3* dressing (toilet) case

ned down; *(-åt)* downwards; *(-för trappan)* downstairs; *(vända* turn) upside down; *uppifrån och* ~ from top to bottom; *längst* ~ *på sidan* at the bottom of the page

nedan I *s7, månen är i* ~ the moon is on the wane (is waning) **II** *adv* below; *se ~!* see below!; *jämför ~!* compare the following! **-för I** *prep* below **II** *adv* [down] below **-nämnd** *a5* mentioned (stated) below **-stående** *a4* stated (mentioned) below, following

ned|bantad *a5* reduced **-blodad** *a5* blood-stained **-bringa** reduce, lower; bring down **-brunnen** *a5* burnt down **-bruten** *a5, bildl.* broken down **-brytande** *a4* destructive *(krafter* forces); subversive *(idéer* ideas) **-brytning** breaking down; demolition; subversion **-busning** rowdyism **-bädda** put to bed; *ligga ~d (inbäddad) i* lie tucked up in **-böjd** *a5* bent down, stooping **-dekad** *a5* gone to the dogs **-dragen** *a5 (om gardin)* drawn [down], lowered

nederbörd [-ö:-] *s3* precipitation; rainfall; snowfall

nederbörds|mätare rain gauge, pluviometer, udometer **-område** *(regn- etc.)* precipitation area; *(avrinningsområde)* catchment area **-rik** with high precipitation (abundant rainfall)

neder|del lower part **-kant** lower edge (side)

1 nederlag *s7* defeat; *(förkrossande)* disaster; *lida* ~ suffer defeat, be defeated

2 nederlag *s7 (magasin)* warehouse, depot, storage

nederländare Netherlander **Nederländerna** *pl* the Netherlands **nederländsk** *a5* Dutch; Netherlands

nederst ['ne:-] *adv* at the bottom (*i, på, vid* of); *allra* ~ farthest *(etc.)* down [of all], at the very

bottom; ~ *på sidan, se under ned*; ~ *till höger* bottom right **nedersta** *a, superl. best. form* lowest; bottom; ~ *våningen* the ground (*AE. äv.* first) floor
nedervåning ground (*AE. äv.* first) floor
ned|fall radioaktivt ~ radioactive fallout **-fart** descent; way down **-fläckad** *a5* stained all over **-frysa** freeze **-frysning** freezing; *med.* hypothermia **-fällbar** *a5* that can be let down; folding, collapsible **-färd** journey (way) down **-för** ['ne:d-] **I** *prep* down; ~ *trappan* downstairs **II** *adv* downwards **-försbacke** (*en lång* a long) downhill slope; *bildl.* downhill; *vi hade* ~ it was downhill [for us] **-gjord** *a5* destroyed; annihilated; (*av kritik e.d.*) picked (torn) to pieces **-gående I** *a4* (*om sol o.d.*) setting; (*om pris o.d.*) declining, falling **II** *s6, vara på* ~ be going down, (*om sol o.d.*) be setting **-gång 1** *konkr.* way (road, path, steps (*pl*), stairs (*pl*)) down **2** *abstr.* descent; (*solens*) setting; (*i temperatur o.d.*) fall, drop; (*minskning*) decrease, reduction; *bildl.* decline **-gången** worn, shabby **-gångsperiod** period of decline (*ekon.* depression) **-göra** *mil.* destroy; *bildl.* annihilate; (*genom kritik*) pull (pick) to pieces; ~*nde kritik* scathing criticism, slating **-hala** haul down; (*flagga o.d.*) lower **-hopp** *sport.* landing **-hukad** *a5* crouched, crouching **-hängande** *a4* pendant, suspended; hanging down **-ifrån** (*gatan* in the street) **-ifrån I** *prep* from down (*gatan* in the street) **II** *adv* from below (underneath); ~ *och ända upp* from below upwards; *femte raden* ~ fifth line from the bottom **-isad** *a5* (*överisad*) covered with ice, iced up; *geol.* glaciated **-isning** [-i:s-] covering with ice; *geol.* glaciation **-kalla** invoke (*över* on), call down (*över* upon) **-kippad** [-ç-] *a5* (*om sko*) down-at-heel **-klad- da** smear (daub) all over; ~*d med färg* painty **-klassa** degrade **-komma** ~ *med* give birth to (be delivered of) (*en son* a son) **-komst** [-å-] *s3* delivery **-kyla** chill, refrigerate **-kylning** chilling, refrigeration **-kämpa** fight down, defeat; (*batteri*) silence, reduce **-lagd** *a5* **1** *eg.* laid down; (*om pengar o.d.*) laid out, spent **2** (*om verksamhet*) discontinued, (*om fabrik, gruva o.d.*) closed [down], shut down **-legad** *a5* (*om säng o.d.*) with broken springs, sagging **-lusad** lousy; *vard. bildl., ~ med pengar* lousy (*AE. sl.* dirty) with money **-låta** *rfl* condescend (*till att* to) **-låtande** *a4* condescending **-låtenhet** condescension **-lägga** (*jfr lägga* [*ner*]) **1** let down; place, deposit; (*villebråd, fiende*) kill, shoot; ~ *vapnen* lay down one's arms **2** (*upphöra med*) give up, relinquish, discontinue; (*fabrik o.d.*) close [down], shut down; ~ *arbetet* stop work; go on strike, strike **3** (*använda*) ~ *pengar i ett företag* invest (put) money into a company; ~ *sin röst* abstain from voting; ~ *stor omsorg på* put a lot of care (work) into **-meja** mow down (*äv. bildl.*) **-montera** dismount, dismantle **-mörk** pitch- -dark **-om** below **-omkring I** *prep* round the base (foot) of **II** *adv* round the bottom **-plöja** *bildl.* plough back **-prutning** reduction, lowering
nedre ['ne:d-] *a, superl. nedersta* lower; *i ~ vänstra hörnet* in the left-hand bottom corner;

i ~ våningen on the ground (*AE. äv.* first) floor
nedrig ['ne:d-] *a1* (*skändlig*) heinous, mean; (*skamlig*) infamous, shameful; *det var ~t av dig att* it was (is) beastly of you to **nedrig-het** *se gemenhet* **nedrigt** *adv, det gjorde* ~ *ont* it hurt terribly
ned|ringd *bli* ~ be showered with telephone calls **-rusta** disarm, cut down armaments **-rustning** disarmament, reduction of armaments **-rustningskonferens** disarmament conference **-räkna** (*addera*) total, add up **-räkning** totalling; (*av raket o.d.*) countdown **-rökt** *a4* smoke-laden **-rösta** vote down **-sablad** [-sa:-] *a5* (*av kritiken*) pulled (picked) to pieces **-sabling** [-a:-] *bildl.* dressing-down, slating **-salta** *kokk.* salt down; pickle in salt **-satt** *a4* (*minskad*) reduced, diminished; (*sänkt*) lowered; ~ *arbetsförmåga* reduced working capacity; *till ~ pris* at a reduced (cut) price (*AE. äv.* cut rate); *få ~a betyg* have one's marks reduced (lowered) **-sjunken** *a5, sitta* ~ *i* be reclining in **-skjutning** shooting down **-skriva** write down; *bokför. äv.* depreciate **-skrivning** writing down; depreciation **-skrotning** [-@:-] scrapping **-skräpning** [-ä:-] littering up **-skuren** *a5* (*minskad*) reduced, curtailed **-skälld** [-ʃ-] *a5* abused **-skärning** (*minskning*) reduction, curtailment, cut **-slag 1** *sport.* landing, alighting; (*vid kast o.d.*) pitch; (*vid simning*) entry, dive-in **2** (*fågels*) descent; (*flygplans*) alighting; *vid ~et* in taking ground **3** (*projektils*) impact, percussion **4** (*på skrivmaskin*) stroke **-slagen** *a5, bildl.* downhearted, low-spirited, dejected **-slagenhet** downheartedness; low spirits (*pl*), dejection **-slaktning** slaughter[ing ... off] **-slående** *a4, bildl.* disheartening, discouraging, depressing; (*beklämmande*) distressing **-släpp** *sport.* face-off **-smittad** *a5, bli* ~ become infected **-smutsad** *a5* dirtied, soiled; (*-smetad*) plastered [over] with dirt **-smutsning** pollution; contamination; defilement **-snöad** *a5* covered with snow, snowed over **-stiga** (*se stiga* [*ner*]); *flyg.* alight; descend (*i, till* into) **-stigning** alighting; descent **-ströms** downstream **-stämd** *a1, bildl.* depressed, downhearted, dejected **-stämdhet** depression, downheartedness, dejection **-stänkt** *a4* splashed all over **-summering** adding up, addition **-sutten** *a5* with worn-out (sagging) springs **-svärta** *bildl.* blacken the character of, defame **-sänka** immerse **-sänkning** immersion, submergence **-sätta** (*jfr sätta* [*ner*]) (*sänka*) put down, reduce; lower (*äv. bildl.*); ~ *straffet* reduce the sentence; ~ *priset* (*äv.*) mark down **-sättande** *a4* (*förklenande*) disparaging, derogatory, depreciatory **-sättning** (*sänkning*) reduction; (*av pris äv.*) lowering; (*av hörsel o.d.*) impairment **-tagning** taking down **-teckna** write down **-till** down in the lower part (half) (*på* of); at the bottom (foot) **-tona** tone down **-toning** toning down; dampening **-trampad** *a5* trampled down **-trappa** de-escalate **-trappning** de-escalation **-tryckt** *a4, bildl.* low-spirited; oppressed **-tyngd** *a5* weighed (*bildl. äv.* borne) down (*av* with) **-tysta** reduce to silence, silence **-vikbar** [-i:-] that can be

turned down; (*om krage e.d. äv.*) ... to turn down **-vikt** [-i:-] *a4* turned-down **-vissnad** *a5* faded, withered **-väg** *på* ~*en* on the way (road, journey) down [south] **-värdera** depreciate; *bildl.* disparage, belittle **-värdering** depreciation; *bildl.* disparagement

nedåt ['ne:d-] **I** *prep* down **II** *adv* downward[s], in a downward direction; *var går gränsen* ~*?* what is the bottom limit? **-böjd** *a5* that is bent downwards; down-bent **-gående I** *s6, vara i* ~ be on the down grade (the downward trend) **II** *a4* downward[-trending]; (*om tendens o.d. äv.*) falling; ~ *konjunkturer* declining business (*sg*), falling markets **-riktad** *a5* directed downwards, declining **-vänd** *a5* turned downwards

ned|järvd *a5* passed on by heredity, hereditary **-över I** *prep* down over (across) **II** *adv*, *hela vägen* ~ all the way down [south]

nef'rit *s3* **1** *med.* nephritis **2** *miner.* nephrite

neg *imperf. av niga*

negation negation; (*nekande ord äv.*) negative **negativ** ['negg-, -'ti:v] **I** *s7* negative **II** *a1* negative **negativism** negativism **negativist** negativist, negationist **negativistisk** *a5* negativist[ic] **negativt** [-i:-] *adv* negatively (*äv. elektr.*), in a (the) negative sense

neger ['ne:-] *s3* Negro (*pl* Negroes), black [man]; coloured person; *neds.* darky, nigger **negera** (*förneka*) deny; ~*d sats* (*vanl.*) clause (*etc.*) containing a negative

neger|barn Negro child **-befolkning** Negro (coloured) population **-by** Negro village, kraal **-folk** Negro people **-hydda** Negro['s] hut **-hövding** Negro chief **-kvarter** Negro quarter **-kvinna** Negress **-slaveri** Negro slavery **-stam** Negro tribe

neglig|é [-i'ʃe:] *s3* negligee, negligé[e], undress, dishabille; *AE.* negligee **-era** neglect; disregard; ~ *ngn* ignore s.b.

negociera negotiate

negr|ess Negress **-o'id** *a1, n sg obest. form undviks* Negroid

nej [nejj] **I** *interj* no; ~, *visst inte!* oh no [certainly not]!; ~, *nu måste jag gå!* well, I must go now!; ~, *men så roligt!* oh, what fun!, oh, how nice!; ~ ~ (*vard. nänä*) *män!* [no], certainly not!; ~, *vad säger du?* you don't say so?; ~, *det menar du väl inte!* oh no, surely not! **II** *s7* no; *ibl.* nay; (*avslag äv.*) refusal; *svara* ~ answer in the negative; *säga* ~ *till ngt* say no to (decline) s.th.; *rösta* ~ vote against [a proposal]; *få* ~ be refused; *frågan är med* ~ *besvarad* (*vid sammanträde*) *o.d.* the noes have it

nejd *s3* (*trakt*) district; (*omgivning*) surroundings (*pl*), neighbourhood

nejlika *s1* carnation, pink; (*krydd-*) clove

nejonöga [-å-] *zool.* lamprey

nej|rop cry (shout) of 'no' **-röst** 'no'-vote, vote against **-sägare** *en* ~ one who [always] says no, a negationist

neka 1 (*vägra*) refuse (*ngn ngt* s.b. s.th.; *att* to); ~ *ngn hjälp* refuse s.b. help (to help s.b.); *han* ~*des tillträde* he was refused admission **2** (*förneka*) deny (*till att ha gjort* having done); (*säga nej*) say no; *han* ~*r bestämt till att ha* he definitely denies having; *jag* ~*r inte till att*

I won't deny that; ~ *till en anklagelse* (*jur.*) plead not guilty **3** *rfl* deny o.s.; *han* ~*r sig ingenting* he never denies himself anything; *jag kunde inte* ~ *mig nöjet att* I couldn't forgo the pleasure of (+ *ing-form*) **nekande I** *a4* negative (*svar* answer); *ett* ~ *svar* (*äv.*) a refusal (denial) ; *om svaret är* ~ if the answer is in the negative **II** *adv, svara* ~ answer in the negative, give a negative answer **III** *s6* denial; (*vägran*) refusal; *döma ngn mot hans* ~ condemn s.b. in spite of his denial

nekrolog obituary [notice]

nek'ros [-å:s] *s3, med.* necrosis

nektar ['nekk-] *s9* nectar (*äv. bildl.*) **-'in** *s3* nectarine

nematod [-'tå:d] *s3* nematode

nemesis ['ne:-] *r* nemesis; (*hämndens gudinna*) Nemesis

neo|klassicism neoclassicism **-kolonialism** neocolonialism **-litisk** [-'li:-] *a5* Neolithic **-logi** *s3* neologism

neon [-'å:n] *s7* neon **-ljus** neon light **-rör** neon tube **-skylt** neon sign

nepa'les *s3* Nepalese **-isk** *a5* Nepalese

nepotism nepotism

ner *se ned* **nere 1** down; *längst* ~ *i* at the very bottom (end) of; *priset är* ~ *i* 2 *pund* the price is down to £2; ~ *på* down on (at) **2** (*friare o. bildl.*) low; *ligga* ~ (*om verksamhet e.d.*) be (have been) stopped, be at a standstill **3** (*kroppsligt o. andligt*) run down; (*deprimerad*) depressed, down in the dumps

neri|um ['ne:-] *-en -er, bot.* oleander

nermörk pitch-dark, pitch-black

nerts [nä-] *s2* mink **-päls** mink coat

nerv [nä:-] *s3* nerve (*äv. bildl.*); *bot. äv.* vein; *han har goda* ~*er* (*äv.*) he doesn't know what nerves are; *gå ngn på* ~*erna* get on a p.'s nerves **-bana** *anat.* nerve circuit; *fysiol.* nerve path **-cell** nerve cell, neuron **-centrum** nerve centre **-chock** nervous shock **-feber** *se tyfoidfeber* **-gas** nerve gas

nerv|ig *a1* **1** *se nervös* **2** *bot.* veined, nerved **-impuls** nerve impulse **-klen** *se nervsjuk* **-knippe** *anat.* nerve bundle; *bildl.* bundle of nerves **-knut** ganglion **-krig** war of nerves **-lugnande** *a4* nerve-soothing; ~ *medel* tranquillizer, sedative **-läkare** nerve specialist, neurologist

nerv|ositet nervousness, nervous tension **-pirrande** *a4* thrilling, exciting **-press** nervous strain **-påfrestande** *a4* nerve-racking, trying to the nerves **-retning** nervous impulse; innervation **-ryckning** nervous spasm **-sammanbrott** nervous breakdown **-sjuk** neurotic **-sjukdom** nervous disorder, neurosis **-slitande** *a4* nerve-racking **-spänning** nervous strain **-stillande** *a4*, *se nervlugnande* **-svag** nervous, neurasthenic **-system** nervous system; *centrala* ~*et* central nervous system (*förk.* CNS) **-tråd** nerve fibre **-vrak** nervous wreck **-värk** neuralgia

ner'vös *a1* nervous; (*för tillfället*) agitated, flurried, excited; (*orolig*) uneasy, restless; (~ *av sig*) highly-strung (*AE.* high-strung), *vard.* nervy, jumpy **ner'vöst** [-ö:-] *adv* nervously *etc.*; *skruva sig* ~ fidget uneasily

nes|a *s1* ignominy, shame, dishonour, disgrace **-lig** [ˣne:s-] *a1* (*vanärande*) ignominious; (*skamlig*) shameful, disgraceful; (*nedrig*) infamous

nestor ['nestår] *s3* doyen; *vard.* grand old man

netto I *adv* net [cash]; (*utan emballage*) without packing **II** *s6* [net] profit; *rent* ~ net without discount; *förtjäna i rent* ~ net, clear; *i* ~ [in] net profit **-avkastning, -behållning** net proceeds (*pl*), net yield **-belopp** net amount **-lön** net wages (*pl*) **-pris** net price **-resultat** net result **-vikt** net weight **-vinst** net gain (profit)

neural'g|i [nev-, neu-] *s3* neuralgia **-isk** [-'rall-] *a5* neuralgic

neuraste'n|i [nev-, neu-] *s3* neurasthenia **-iker** [-'te:-] neurasthenic [patient]

neu'rit [nev-, neu-] *s3, med.* neuritis

neuro|kirurgi [nev-, neu-] neurosurgery; neurotomy **-log** neurologist **-logi** *s3* neurology **-logisk** *a5* neurological

neuron [nev'rå:n, neu-] *s7, s4* neuron **neuros** [-'rå:s] *s3* neurosis (*pl* neuroses)

neurot|isk [nev'rå:-, neu-] *a5* neurotic **-iker** neurotic

neu'tral *a1* neutral; *språkv.* neuter **-isera** neutralize (*äv. bildl.*); (*motväga*) counteract **-isering** neutralization **-itet** neutrality **-itetspolitik** policy of neutrality **-läge** neutral position; *elektr.* neutral plane

neutrino [-'tri:-] *s5, pl äv. neutriner* neutrino

neutron [-'trå:n] *s3* neutron **-bestrålning** neutron radiation **-bomb** neutron bomb **-infångning** neutron capture **-strålning** neutron radiation

neutrum ['neut-, 'ne:u-] *s4* (*i* in the) neuter

newfoundlandshund Newfoundland [dog]

nevö *s3* nephew

ni *pron* you; ~ *själv* [you] yourself

1 nia *v1, ung.* use the formal mode of address

2 nia *s1* nine

nicaragu|'an *s3* Nicaraguan **-ansk** [-'a:nsk] *a5* Nicaraguan

nick *s2* nod **nicka 1** nod (*åt* to); ~ *bifall* nod approval; ~ *till* (*somna*) drop off [to sleep] **2** *sport.* head **nickedocka** *bildl.* yes man

nickel ['nikk-] *s9, s7* nickel **-gruva** nickel mine **-stål** nickel steel

nickning *en* ~ *a)* a nod [of the (one's) head], *b) sport.* a header

nidbild caricature

niding miscreant, vandal **nidingsdåd** villainy, act of vandalism, outrage

nid|skrift lampoon, libellous pamphlet **-skrivare** lampooner, scurrilous pamphleteer **-visa** rhymed lampoon

niece [ni'ä:s, -'e:s] *s5* niece

nieller|a inlay with niello **-ing** niello work

niga *neg nigit* curts[e]y (*djupt* low; *för* to), drop [s.b.] a curts[e]y

nigerer [-'ge:-] *s9* Nigerien

nigeri|'an *s3* Nigerian **-'ansk** [-a:-] *a5* Nigerian

nigerisk [-'ge:-] *a5* Nigerien

nig|it *sup. av niga* **-ning** [-i:g-] curts[e]y[ing]

nihil|ism nihilism **-ist** nihilist **-istisk** *a5* nihilistic

niko'tin *s4, s3* nicotine **-förgiftning** nicotine poisoning **-halt** nicotine content **-haltig** *a1* containing nicotine **-ism** nicotinism **-ist** nicotine addict **-missbruk** excessive smoking

nikt *s4, s3* lycopodium powder

Nilen ['ni:-] *r* the Nile

nimbus ['nimm-] *s2* nimbus (*äv. bildl.*)

nio [*vard.* ˣni:e] nine; *en* ~ *tio stycken* some nine or ten; *jfr fem o. sms.* nionde [-å-] ninth **nion[de]del** [-å-] ninth [part] **niosvansad** *a5, den ~e katten* the cat-o'-nine-tails

nipa *s1* steep sandy river bank

nippel ['nipp-] *s2* nipple

nipper ['nipp-] *pl* trinkets; (*dyrbarare*) jewels, jewellery (*sg*) **-skrin** jewellery case

nippertippa *s1* pert miss, saucy girl

nipprig *a1, vard.* nuts, cracked

nisch *s3* niche (*äv. bildl.*)

nisse *s2* **1** *se tomte* **2** *se smörgåsnisse*

1 nit *s7* (*brinnande iver*) zeal, ardour, fervour; (*flit*) diligence, application; *ovisst* ~ injudicious zeal; *för* ~ *och redlighet* for zealous and devoted service

2 nit *s2, s3* (*-lott*) blank [ticket]; *dra en* ~ draw a blank

3 nit *s2, tekn.* rivet; ~ *med försänkt huvud* flush rivet

nit|a rivet (*vid* [on] to); ~ *fast* rivet [firmly]; ~ *ihop* rivet together **-are** riveter **-hammare** riveting hammer **-huvud** rivet head

nitisk ['ni:-] *a1* zealous, ardent, fervent; (*flitig*) diligent

nit|nagel rivet **-ning** [-i:-] riveting; *konkr. äv.* riveted joint

nitlott *se 2 nit*

nitrat *s7, s4* nitrate **nitrera** nitrify, nitrate **nitrering** nitration **nitrifikation** nitrification **ni'trit** *s7, s3* nitrite

nitro|cellulosa cellulose nitrate, nitrocellulose **-glyce'rin** nitroglycerin[e]

nittio [*vard.* 'nitti] ninety; *jfr femtio o. sms.* **nittionde** [-å-] ninetieth **nittion[de]del** ninetieth [part] **nittiotal** *på ~et* in the nineties **nittioåring** (*äv.*) nonagenarian

nitton [-ån] nineteen **nittonde** nineteenth **nittonhundratal** *på ~et* in the twentieth century

nitvinst consolation prize

nitälska be zealous (eager) (*för* for) **nitälskan** *r* zeal

niveller|a level out, equalize, reduce to one (a uniform) level; (*i lantmäteri*) level **-ing** levelling

nivå *s3* level (*äv. bildl.*); *bildl. äv.* standard; *i* ~ *med* on a level with; *konferens på högsta* ~ (*äv.*) summit (top-level) conference **-karta** contour map **-kurva** contour line **-skillnad** difference in altitude (of level)

nix *interj* not a bit of it!, no!

Nizza [ˣnissa] *n* Nice

njugg *a1* parsimonious, niggardly (*på, med* with, of; *mot* towards, to); (*på ord o.d.*) sparing (*på* of) **-het** parsimoniousness *etc.*

njurbäcken [-u:-] renal pelvis (*pl* pelves)

njur|e *s2* kidney **-formig** [-å-] *a1* kidney-shaped **-sjukdom** kidney disease, disorder of the kidney[s] **-sten** kidney stone, renal calculus **-talg** suet **-transplantation** kidney

transplant
njut|a *njöt -it* enjoy (*livet* life); *absol.* enjoy o.s., have a good time; ~ *av* enjoy, delight (*starkare:* revel) in **njutbar** *a1* (*ätbar*) eatable, edible; (*smaklig*) palatable; (*om t.ex. musik*) enjoyable **njutit** *sup av njuta* **njutning** [-u:-] enjoyment; pleasure, delight; feast (*för ögat:* for the eye)
njutnings|full full of enjoyment, highly (very) enjoyable **-lysten** pleasure-seeking, pleasure-loving **-lystnad** craving for (love of) pleasure **-medel** means of enjoyment (*etc.*); (*stimulerande medel*) stimulant **-människa** epicurean; hedonist **-rik** *se -full*
njöt *imperf. av njuta*
N.N. [ˣännänn] (*beteckning för obekant pers.*) so-and-so
Noak [ˣnɷak] *r* Noah
nobb [-å-] *s2* brushoff, turndown; *få ~en* be given the brushoff, be turned down **nobba** [-å-] turn down, give the brushoff
nobel ['nå:-] *a2* noble, distinguished; (*storsint*) generous
nobelpris [nɷˣbell-] Nobel prize **-tagare** Nobel prize winner
nobless [nå-] nobility; *~en* (*vard.*) the upper ten [thousand]
nock [nåkk] *s2* **1** *sjö.* (*gaffel-*) [gaff] end; (*rå-*) [yard]arm **2** *byggn.* ridge **3** *tekn.* cam
nod *s3, astr., bot., fys.* node; *uppstigande ~* ascending node
nog 1 (*tillräkligt*) enough, sufficiently; *jag har fått ~* (*äv. bildl.*) I have had enough (my fill, all I want); *det är ~* that is enough (sufficient); *nära ~* almost, nearly, all but, well-nigh, practically; *mer än ~* (*äv.*) enough and to spare; *hälften kunde ha varit ~* half would have been enough; *vara sig själv ~* be sufficient unto o.s.; *nu kan det vara ~!* that'll do!, enough of that now!; *inte ~ med att han glömmer* he not only forgets; *och inte ~ med det* and that is not all; *hur skall jag ~ kunna tacka dig!* how can I thank you sufficiently!; *den kan inte ~ berömmas* it cannot be too highly praised; *förklarligt ~* as was only natural; *jag var dum ~ att* I was stupid enough to; *märkvärdigt ~* remarkably enough; *nära ~* practically; *underligt ~* strange to say; *det vore ~ så intressant att* it would be exceedingly (*vard.* ever so, jolly) interesting to **2** (*sannolikt*) probably; I expect, I dare say, I suppose; (*säkerligen*) no doubt, doubtless; (*visserligen*) I (you) [must] admit, certainly, to be sure, it is true; *du förstår mig ~ du* you will understand me[, I am sure (no doubt)]; *du har ~ träffat honom här* you have probably met him here; ~ *vet ni att* you must know (you know of course) that; *han kommer ~* he will come all right; *jag skall ~ se till att* I'll see to it that; *det tror jag ~!* I should think so!; *det kan jag ~ tänka mig!* I can (very well) imagine that!; *det är ~ sant, men* that is probably true, but, that is true enough, but; ~ *för att du har gjort dig förtjänt av det* not but what you have deserved it **3** (*tämligen*) fairly (*bra* good)
noga I *adv* (*exakt*) exactly, precisely; accurately; (*ingående*) closely, minutely, narrowly; (*om-*

sorgsfullt) carefully; (*uppmärksamt*) attentively; (*strängt*) strictly (*bevarad hemlighet* guarded secret); *akta dig ~ för att* take great (good) care not to; *hålla ~ reda på* keep an accurate account of; *lägga ~ märke till* note carefully; *det behöver du inte ta så ~!* you needn't be too particular about that!; ~ *räknat* strictly speaking **II** *a1* (*noggrann*) careful; (*precis*) exact, precise; (*nogräknad*) scrupulous; (*kinkig*) particular; (*petig*) meticulous; (*fordrande*) exacting; *vara ~ med a*) be very exact in (about), *b*) be very particular about (make a point of) (*att passa tiden* being in time); *det är inte så ~ med det!* it doesn't matter very much!, it's not all that important!
nog|grann (*jfr noga II*) (*exakt*) accurate, exact; (*ingående*) close; (*detaljerad*) elaborate, minute; (*sträng*) strict; (*omsorgsfull*) careful, particular **-grannhet** accuracy, exactitude, precision; carefulness *etc.* **-räknad** [-ä:-] *a5* particular, scrupulous; (*granntyckt*) dainty **-samt** (*i högsta grad*) extremely, exceedingly; (*mycket väl*) well enough; *det är ~ känt att* it is a [perfectly] well-known fact that
noj|a [ˣnåjja] *s1, vard.* **paranoia -ig** *a1, vard.* paranoid
nojs [nåjs] *s7, se skämt, flört* **nojsa** *se skämta, flörta*
noll [-å-] nought, naught; *vard.* aught (*på termometer etc.*) zero; *sport. äv.* none, nil; (*i tennis*) love; ~ *komma åtta* (*0,8*) nought point eight (0.8); *mitt telefonnummer är två ~ nio ~ åtta* my telephone number is two o[h] nine o[h] eight; ~ ~ (*sport.*) nil-nil, *tennis.* love all; *plus minus ~ a*) *mat.* plus minus nought, *b*) (*friare*) absolutely nothing (nil); *av ~ och intet värde* of no value what[so]ever, absolutely worthless
noll|a *s1* nought, naught; *vard.* aught; *åld.* cipher; *vetensk.* zero; *en ~* (*om pers.*) a nobody, a nonentity **-gradig** *a1* at freezing temperature, freezing **-korrektur** *boktr.* reader's (first) proof **-läge** (*hopskr. nolläge*) mättekn. mechanical zero; (*friläge*) neutral [position] **-lösning** (*hopskr. nollösning*) zero option **-meridian** prime (datum) meridian **-punkt** zero; freezing point; *absoluta ~en* absolute zero; *stå på ~en* be at zero (*äv. bildl.*) **-ställd 1** set to zero **2** *bildl.* expressionless, blank **-ställning** zero [position] **-taxa** free travel **-tid** *på ~* in no time **-tillväxt** zero growth
no'mad *s3* nomad **-folk** nomadic people **-isera** nomadize; *~nde folk* (*äv.*) migratory people **-isk** *a5* nomad[ic] **-liv** nomadic (*friare:* roving, migratory) life
nomen ['nå:-] *s7, pl äv. nomina, språkv.* noun [and adjective] **-klatur** nomenclature
nomi'nal|form *språkv.* noun form **-lön** nominal wage[s]
nominativ ['nɷmm-, 'nɷ:-, 'nåmm-] *s3* (*i* in the) nominative
nomi'n|ell *a1* nominal; *~t värde* (*äv.*) face value; *~t lydande på* at the face (nominal) value of **-era** nominate **-ering** nomination
nomo|grafi *s3* nomography **-gram** [-'gramm] *s7* nomogram
nonaggressionspakt nonaggression pact

nonchal|ans [nåɲʃa'laŋs, nån-, -'nans] s3 nonchalance, carelessness; offhandedness; (försumlighet) negligence -ant [-'laŋt, '-lant] a1 nonchalant; careless; negligent; offhand[ed] -era pay no attention to, neglect
nonfigurativ [-'i:v, äv. 'nånn-, 'nå:n-] a1 nonfigurative
nonie ['nɒ:-] s5, mättekn. vernier
non|intervention [nån-] nonintervention -kombattant noncombatant -konformism nonconformism
nonsens ['nånn-] n nonsense, rubbish
nopp|a [-å-] I s1 burl, knot II v1 1 tekn. burl 2 (om fågel) pluck, preen; (ögonbryn) pluck; ~ sig (om fågel) preen its feathers -ig a1 burled, knotty
nor s7 narrow passage, sound
noradrenalin noradrenalin[e]
nord [-ɒ:-] I s2 north; N~en the Nordic (Northern, Scandinavian) countries (pl); i höga N~ in the Far North II adv north (om of); vinden var ~ till väst the wind was north by west
Nord|afrika n North Africa -amerika n North America
nordamerikansk North American
nordan ["no:r-] I adv, se norr II II r, se följ. -vind north wind
Nordatlanten r the North Atlantic
nordbo northerner, inhabitant of the North
Norden ["nɒ:r-] n el. r the Nordic countries
Nord|england n Northern England, the North [of England] -europa n Northern Europe
nord|isk ['nɒ:r-] a5 northern; (i etnografin) Nordic; de ~a länderna the Nordic (Northern) countries; N~a ministerrådet [the] Nordic Council of Ministers; N~a rådet [the] Nordic Council; ~a språk Scandinavian (Nordic) languages -ism efforts (pl) to promote Nordic unity -ist Scandinavian philologist
Nord|kalotten ["nɒ:rd-] r the Scandinavian (Baltic) Shield (arctic regions of Norway, Sweden, Finland and Kola Peninsula) -kap n the North Cape
nord|lig ["nɒ:rd-] a1 (i norr) northern; (från norr) north[erly]; ~ bredd north latitude; det blåser ~ vind the wind is in (is blowing from) the north -ligare I a, komp. more northerly II adv further (more to the) north -ligast I a, superl. northernmost II adv farthest north -man hist. Norseman -nordost north-northeast (förk. NNE) -nordväst north-northwest (förk. NNW) -'ost I s2 (~lig vind) northeast wind; (väderstreck) northeast (förk. NE) II adv northeast (om of) -ostlig [-'ɒst-] a1 northeast[ern]; jfr nordlig -ost-passagen the Northeast Passage -pol ~en the North Pole -polsexpedition expedition to the North Pole
Nordsjön r the North Sea
nord|sluttning north[ern] slope -'väst I s2 (~lig vind) northwest wind; northwester; (väderstreck) northwest (förk. NW) II adv northwest (om of) -västlig [-'väst-] a1 northwest, northwestern; jfr nordlig -västra [-'väst-] northwest[ern] -östra [-'össt-] northeast[ern]
Norge ['nårje] n Norway
norgesalpeter Norwegian saltpetre

norm [-å-] s3 standard (för of; för ngn for s.b.); (måttstock äv.) norm; (regel) rule; code; (mönster) model, type (för for); gälla som ~ serve as a standard
nor'mal [-å-] I a1 normal; standard, regular; under ~a förhållanden (äv.) normally; han är inte riktigt ~ (äv.) he is not quite right in his head II s3 standard; type -begåvad a5 normally gifted; average -fördelning stat. normal frequency distribution -isera normalize; standardize -ljus standard candle[power] -mått standard[ized measure] -pris standard price -prosa ordinary (plain) prose -skolekompetens diploma of secondary education for girls -spårig a1 [of] standard gauge -storlek standard (normal, regular) size -studietid normal length of time needed to complete a study program[me] -tid standard (mean) time -ton mus. concert pitch -vikt regular (standard) weight -år mean (normal, average) year
normand [når'mand, -'maŋd] s3 Norman
Normandie [når'man'di:, -maŋ-] n Normandy
normandisk [når'mandisk, -'maŋ-] a5 Norman; N~a öarna the Channel Islands
norm|ativ ['nårm-, -'ti:v] a1 normative -era standardize, gauge; (reglera) regulate -ering standardization -givande a4 normative, standard-forming; vara ~ för (äv.) be a rule (a standard) for
norn|a ["nɒ:r-] s1 Norn; -orna (vanl.) the Weird Sisters, the Fates (Destinies)
norpa [-å-] v1, vard. pinch, bone, swipe, snaffle
norr [-å-] I n the north; mot ~ to the north; rätt i ~ due north II adv [to the] north (om of)
norra best. a the north (sidan side); the northern (delarna av parts of); ~ England Northern England, the North [of England]; N~ ishavet the Arctic Ocean
norr|gående a4 (om tåg o.d.) northbound -ifrån ['nårr-] from the north
norr|ländsk a5 [of] Norrland -ländska (språk) Norrland dialect -länning Norrlander -man Norwegian -sida bergets ~ the north side of the mountain -sken s7 aurora borealis; ~et (äv.) the northern lights (pl) -ut ['nårr-], -över ['nårr-] northward[s], towards [the] north; (i norr) in (to) the north; längst ~ northernmost
nors [-å-] s2, zool. smelt; jag vill vara skapt som en ~ om I'll be blowed if
norsk [-å-] a5 Norwegian; hand. o.d. äv. Norway; hist. Norse norska s1 1 (språk) Norwegian; hist. Norse 2 (kvinna) Norwegian woman
nos s2 nose (äv. friare); (hos hästar, nötkreatur) muzzle; (hos fiskar, kräldjur) snout; blek om ~en green about the gills nosa smell, scent; ~ på sniff (smell) at; ~ reda på ngt ferret s.th. out, find out s.th.
nos|grimma muzzle -hörning [-ö:-] rhinoceros
noshörnings|hanne bull rhinoceros -hona cow rhinoceros
nos|ig a1 cheeky, pert (mot towards, to) -kon nose cone -ring nose ring; cattle leader -spets tip of the nose
nostal'g|i s3 nostalgia -isk [-'tall-] a5 nostalgic
1 not s2 (fisk-) [haul (drag)] seine; dra ~ fish with a seine

2 not *s3* **1** (*anmärkning*) note, annotation; (*fot-*) footnote **2** *polit.* [diplomatic] note, memorandum **3** *mus.* note; *~er* (*-häfte*) music (*sg*); *spela efter ~er* play from music; *skriva ~er* write music; *ge ngn stryk efter ~er* give s.b. a good thrashing; *vara med på ~erna* catch on (the drift), fall in with the idea

nota *s1* (*räkning*) bill, account; *AE. äv.* check; (*förteckning*) list (*på* of); *jfr tvättnota*

notab|el [-'ta:-] *a2* of note **-ilitet** *s3* notability

notariatavdelning [-ˣa:t-] trust department **notarie** [-ˣta:, -'ta:-] *s5* [recording] clerk, notary; (*vid domsaga äv.*) law clerk, deputy judge **notarius publicus** [nɷ'ta:rius 'publikus] *r, pl notarii publici* [-si] notary public

notblad sheet of music

noter|a 1 (*anteckna*) note (write) down, make a note of; (*lägga på minnet*) note; (*bokföra äv.*) enter, book **2** (*fastställa pris på, äv. börs.*) quote (*till* at) **-ing 1** noting (*etc.*) down; (*mera konkr.*) note, notation; (*bokföringspost*) entry, item; *enligt våra ~ar* (*hand.*) according to our records **2** *hand. börs.* quotation

notes|block [ˣnɷ:tes-, ˣnå:ts-] [scribbling] pad **-bok** notebook

not|häfte sheets (*pl*) of music; (*större*) music--book **-ifikation** notification

no'tis *s3* (*underrättelse*) notice; (*tidnings-*) news-item, paragraph; *ta ~ om* take notice of, pay attention to **-byrå** news (press) agency **-jägare** newshawk, newshound

not|linje *boktr.* note rule

notorisk [-'tɷ:-] *a5* notorious

not|papper music paper **-skrivare** music copyist **-skrivning** copying of music **-ställ** music stand (rack) **-system 1** staff **-tecken 1** *mus.* note **2** *boktr.* reference mark

notvarp *s7* seine sweep; *bildl.* crush

not|vändare person who turns pages of music for a pianist **-växling** *dipl.* exchange of notes

nougat [nɷ'ga:t] *s3* nougat, almond paste

nova [ˣnå:-] *s1, astr.* nova (*pl äv.* novae)

no'vell *s3* short story **-ist** short-story writer **-is'tik** *s3* short-story writing **-samling** collection of short stories

november [-'vemm-] *r* November

no'vis *s3* novice; (*friare*) *se nybörjare*

nu I *adv* now; *AE. äv.* presently; (*vid det här laget*) by now (this time); *från och med ~* from now on[wards]; [*ända*] *tills ~* up till now; *~ då* now that; *den ~ rådande* (*äv.*) the present (existing); *vad ~ då?* what's up (the matter) now?; *för att ~ ta ett exempel* just by way of example; *vad var det han hette ~* [*igen*]? whatever was his name? **II** *s7, ~et* the present [time]; *i detta ~* at this moment

nubb *s2* tack **nubba** tack (*vid* on to); *~ fast* tack on, fasten with tacks

nubbe *s2* dram, schnap[p]s

Nubien ['nu:-] *n* Nubia

nubi|er ['nu:-] Nubian **-isk** *a5* Nubian

nuck|a *s1* frump **nuckig** *a1* frumpish

nudda brush; *~ vid* brush against

nudel *s2, kokk.* noodle

nud|ism nudism **-ist** nudist **-istläger** nudist camp

nuförtiden ['nu:-] nowadays; *vard.* these days

nugat *s3, se nougat*

nukle'in *s7, s4* nuclein **-syra** nucleic acid

nukle'är *a1* nuclear; *~a vapen* nuclear weapons

nu|läge present situation **-mer[a]** ['nu:-] now, nowadays

numerisk [-'me:-] *a5* numeric[al] **numeriskt** *adv, en ~ överlägsen* a numerically superior, a[n] ... superior in numbers **numerus** ['nu:-] *n* number **nume'rär I** *s3* number; (*armés o.d.*) [numerical] strength **II** *a5, se numerisk*

numisma'tik *s3* numismatics (*pl, behandlas som sg*) **-iker** [-'ma:-] numismatist **-isk** [-'ma:-] *a5* numismatic

nummer ['numm-] *s7* number; (*exemplar*) copy; (*tidnings- o.d.*) issue; (*storlek*) size; (*programpunkt e.d.*) item; (*av tidning o.d.*) back issue; *göra ett stort ~ av* make a great feature (fuss) of; *behandlas som ett ~* (*om pers.*) be treated as no more than a number **-byrå** *tel.* directory enquiries [office] **-följd** number sequence; *ordna i ~* arrange consecutively **-lapp** queue [number] ticket **-ordning** numerical order **-plåt** (*på motorfordon*) numberplate, *AE. äv.* license plate **-skiva** *tel.* dial

numrer|a number; *~de platser* numbered seats; *~d från 1 till 100* numbered 1 to 100 **-ing** numbering, numeration

numro *s, ingen böjning* number (No.)

nuna *s1, vard.* phiz, dial

nunna *s1* nun; *bli ~* (*äv.*) take the veil

nunne|dok nun's veil **-fjäril** nun moth **-kloster** nunnery, convent **-orden** order of nuns, [religious] sisterhood **-ört** corydalis

nuntie ['nuntsie] *s5* nuncio

nupit *sup. av nypa*

nusvenska present-day Swedish

nutid present times (*pl*); [the] present day; *forntid och ~* past [times] and present; *~ens människor* present-day people, people of today **nutida** *oböjl. a* present-day; modern

nutids|diktning modern poetry **-historia** contemporary (present-day) history **-människa** modern man **-orientering** knowledge of present-day (contemporary) life and events

nutria ['nu:-] *s1* nutria, coypu

nu|varande *a4* present; (*rådande*) existing; (*om pris*) ruling, current; *i ~ läge* as things stand at present, in (under) the present circumstances, as it is; *i ~ ögonblick* at the present moment **-värde** present value; *försäkr.* capitalized value

ny I *a1* new (*för* to); (*förnyad*) fresh; (*färsk*) recent (*böcker* books); (*~ o. ovanlig*) novel (*erfarenhet* experience); (*annan*) [an]other; (*ytterligare*) additional, extra (*börda* burden), further (*order* orders); *bli en ~ människa a*) (*t. hälsan*) become a new man, *b*) (*i åskådning e.d.*) become a different person; *~tt mod* fresh courage; *~tt stycke* (*boktr.*) new paragraph; *~a tiden* modern times, the modern age; *Gott ~tt år!* a Happy New Year!; *det ~a i* the novelty in (of), what is new in **II** *s6, s7* (*-tändning*) new phase of the moon; *månen är i ~* the moon is new; *jfr nymåne*

Nya Guinea [ˣny:a giˣne:a] *n* New Guinea

ny|anläggning new plant (establishment) **-an-**

länd a5 newly (just) arrived; *de ~a* (*äv.*) the newcomers, the new arrivals
nyans [-'ans, -'aŋs] s3 shade; nuance, tone; (*anstryckning*) tinge; (*om uttryck*) shade of meaning; *hans röst saknar ~er* his voice lacks modulation (variation) **nyansera** shade off; *mus.* modulate; (*variera*) vary **nyansering** shading[-off] *etc.*
ny|anskaffning replacement; new acquisition [of equipment] **-anställd** new employee
nyare a, *komp.* newer *etc.*; more modern; *i ~ tid* in modern (recent) times (*pl*) **nyast** a, *superl.* newest; most modern (*etc.*); (*senast*) latest
Nya Zeeland [ˣny:a 'se:-] n New Zealand
ny|bakad a5 **1** fresh from the oven, newmade, newbaked **2** *bildl.* newly fledged **-bildad** a5 newly (recently) formed (founded) **-bildning** new (recent) formation (creation, establishment); *språkv. äv.* neologism, coinage; *med.* new growth, neoplasm **-bliven** a5 (*om student e.d.*) newly fledged; (*om professor e.d*) newly appointed; *hon är ~ mor* she has just become a mother **-byggare** settler, colonist; pioneer **-byggd** a5 new[built], newly constructed (built) **-bygge** house (ship *etc.*) under construction **-byggnad** new construction (house, building *etc.*) **-börjarbok** primer (*i* of) **-börjare** beginner; novice, tyro, tiro, new hand **-börjarkurs** beginners' course
nyck s3 whim; fancy; caprice; *genom en ödets* (*naturens*) *~* by a freak of fate (Nature)
nyckel s2 key; *bildl.* clue; (*kod*) code, cipher; *vrida om ~n* turn the key; *~n till framgång* the key to success **-ax** key bit **-barn** latchkey child **-ben** *anat.* collarbone, clavicle **-blomster** orchis **-figur** key figure **-harpa** *mus.* keyed fiddle **-hål** keyhole **-industri** key industry **-knippa** bunch of keys **-ord** key word; (*t. korsord*) clue **-person** key person **-piga** ladybird; *AE.* ladybug **-ring** key ring **-roll** key role **-roman** roman à clef **-ställning** key position **-ämne** *tekn.* key blank
nyckfull capricious; (*om pers. äv.*) whimsical; (*om väderlek*) changeable, fickle; (*ostadig*) fitful **-het** capriciousness *etc.*; whimsicality
nydan|a fashion anew; reorganize **-are** refashioner; reorganizer, regenerator; (*pionjär*) pioneer, breaker of new ground **-ing** refashioning; reorganization, regeneration
ny|edition new edition **-emission** issue of new shares, new [share] issue **-etablering** new business starts (*pl*) **-examinerad** a5 newly qualified **-fallen** a5 (*om snö*) newly (fresh) fallen **-fascism** neofascism **-fascistisk** neofascist **-fiken** a3 curious (*på* about, as to); (*alltför ~*) inquisitive, prying **-fikenhet** curiosity; inquisitiveness; *av ren ~* out of sheer curiosity; *väcka ngns ~* arouse a p.'s curiosity, make s.b. all agog **-född** newborn; *barnet är alldeles -fött* the baby has just been born **-förlovad** *hon är ~* she has just got engaged [to be married]; *de ~e* the newly engaged couple **-förvärv** ett *~* a new (recent) acquisition **-förvärvad** a5 newly (recently) acquired **-gift** newly married, newlywed; *de ~a* the newly-married couple **-gjord** newly mad **-gotik** neo-Gothic

(*äv. ~en*) **-grad** centesimal degree **-grekiska** Modern Greek **-grundad** a5 newly founded **-gräddad** freshly-baked
nyhet (*egenskap att vara ny*) newness; (*ngt nytt*) novelty, s.th. new; (*ny sak*) novelty; (*nymodighet*) novelty, innovation; (*underrättelse*) news (*sg*); *~ens behag* the charm of novelty; *förlora ~ens behag* become stale; *en ~* (*i tidning e.d.*) a news-item, a piece of news; *en viktig ~* (*äv.*) a piece of important news; *inga ~er är goda ~er* no news is good news; *det var en ~ för mig* this is news to me; *~erna för säsongen* the novelties of the season, (*kläder*) the season's new fashions
nyhets|byrå news (press) agency **-förmedling** news service **-utsändning** *radio.* newscast
ny|inflyttad a5, *vara ~* have just (recently) moved in, (*i område o.d.*) be a newcomer [to the district] **-inkommen** a5 just (recently) arrived **-inredd** a5 recently refitted (fitted up) **-inrättad** a5 newly established (created) **-inskriven** a5 newly enrolled; *mil.* newly enlisted **-instudering** [preparing of a] new production; *hans ~ av Fidelio* his new characterization of Fidelio **-klassicism** neoclassicism **-klippt** a4 newly cut; *han är ~* he has just had his hair cut **-kläckt** a4 newly hatched **-kokt** [-ɷ:-] a4 freshly-boiled **-kolonialism** neocolonialism **-komling** [-å-] newcomer, fresh arrival; (*i skola e.d.*) new boy (girl) **-konstruktion** new construction (design)
nykter ['nykk-] a2 **1** sober; (*måttlig*) temperate **2** *bildl.* sober[-minded]; level-headed **-het** (*äv. bildl.*) sobriety, soberness; temperance
nykterhets|organisation temperance organization **-rörelse** temperance movement **-vård** treatment of alcoholics **-vän** advocate of temperance
nykterist total abstainer, teetotaller
nyktra *~ till* become sober [again], sober up, *bildl.* sober down
ny|kärnad [-çä:r-] a5 newly churned; fresh from the dairy **-lagd** a5 (*om ägg*) new-laid; *håret är -lagt* my (*etc.*) hair has just been set
nyligen recently; lately; (*på sista tiden äv.*) latterly, of late; *helt ~* quite recently
nylon [-'lå:n] s4, s3 nylon **-skjorta** nylon shirt **-strumpor** *pl* nylon stockings (*herr-*: socks) nylons
nymf s3 nymph **nymfo'man** s3 nymphomaniac **nymfoma'ni** s3 nymphomania
ny|modig a1 new-fashioned, modern; *neds.* newfangled **-modighet** modernity; *en ~* newfangled thing (idea, notion) **-mornad** [-å:-] a5 newly awakened; hardly awake **-målad** a5 freshly painted; *är ~* has just been painted; *-målat!* wet paint! **-måne** new moon **-nazism** neonazism
nynna hum
nynorsk I a1 Modern Norwegian **II** s1, *språkv.* New Norwegian
ny|odling 1 *abstr.* land reclamation **2** *konkr.* reclaimed land; (*i skog*) clearing **-omvänd** a5 newly converted; *en ~* a new convert, neophyte **-ordna** reorganize, reform **-ordning** reorganization, rearrangement; new order **-orientering** reorientation, readjustment

nyp *s7* pinch **nypa I** *s1* **1** (*fingrar*) fingers (*pl*); *vard.* paw **2** (*det man tar i ~n*) pinch [of ...]; *en ~ luft* a breath of air; *med en ~ salt* (*bildl.*) with a pinch (grain) of salt **II** *nöp nupit, äv. v3* pinch, nip; *det nyper i skinnet* there is a nip in the air **nypas** *nöps nupits, äv. v3, dep* pinch; *nyps inte!* don't pinch me!

ny|planterad *a5* newly (recently) planted; replanted **-plantering** new plantation, newly planted flowerbed (*etc.*) **-platonism** Neo--Platonism

nypon [-ån] *s7* rosehip **-blomma** dog-rose [flower] **-buske** dog-rose bush **-soppa** rosehip cream **-te** rosehip tea

ny|premiär (*på film*) rerun, revival **-pressad** *a5* newly pressed, (*om byxor äv.*) newly creased **-produktion** new production; *~ av bostäder* newly constructed dwellings **-på-stigen** *a5* who has just entered the bus (train *etc.*) **-rakad** *a5* freshly-shaved **-rekrytera** recruit new man (staff) **-reparerad** *a5* newly repaired **-rik** new-rich; *en ~* a nouveau riche; *de ~a* the new-rich

Nürnberg ['nyrn-] *n* Nuremberg **-processen** the Nuremberg trials (*pl*)

ny|romantik neoromanticism; *~en* (*äv.*) the Romantic Movement **-romantiker** neoromanticist **-rostad** [-å-] *a5* freshly-roasted

nys *s, i uttr.: få ~ om ngt* get wind of s.th.

nysa *v3, imperf. äv.* nös sneeze

ny|silver silver-plated ware; *gafflar av ~* silver-plated forks **-skapa** create anew; *~d* newly created **-skapande** *s6, ~t av* the creating of new **-skapare** innovator, creator of new; *flottans ~* the creator of the new navy **-skapelse** new creation, innovation **-slagen** *a5* (*om hö o.d.*) new-mown

nysning [*ny:s-] sneezing; *en ~* a sneeze

ny|snö newly-fallen snow **-språklig** *a1, ~ linje* modern language side

nyspulver sneezing powder

nyss just [now], a moment ago; *en ~ inträffad olycka* a recent accident **-nämnd** *a5* just mentioned (*etc.*)

nysta wind; *absol. äv.* make up into balls (a ball) **nystan** *s7* ball, spool

ny|startad *a5* (*om företag*) newly established (founded *etc.*) **-stavning** new (reformed) spelling **-struken** *a5* newly ironed

nystvinda reel, hasp, spindle

ny|stärkt *a4* freshly-starched **-svenska** Modern Swedish **-teckna** *~ aktier i* subscribe to new shares in; *~de aktier* newly subscribed shares; *~de försäkringar* new insurance business (*sg*) **-teckning** (*av aktier*) new subscription

nyter ['ny:-] *a2* cheery, bright; *pigg och ~* bright and cheery

ny|tillskott new addition; new influx **-tryck** reprint

nytt *n, någonting ~* something new; *~ och gammalt* new things and old; *på ~* anew, once more; *börja på ~* start (begin) afresh; *försöka på ~* try again, have another try, make a new attempt

nytt|a I *s1* (*användning*) use, good; (*fördel*) advantage, benefit, profit; (*-ighet*) utility, usefulness; *förena ~ med nöje* combine business

with pleasure; *~n med det* the use[fulness] (advantage) of it; *dra ~ av* benefit from, profit by, utilize, (*med orätt*) take advantage of; *göra ~* do some good, be of some use; *ha ~ av* find useful (of use); *vara till ~* be of some help, do some good; *till ~ för* of use to, serviceable for; *till ingen ~* of no use **II** *v1, se gagna; det ~r inte* it is no use (*att göra det* doing it) **nyttig** *a1* useful (*för* for); of use (service) (*för* to); good (*för* for); (*hälsosam*) wholesome; *det blir ~t för mig* it will do me good **nyttiggöra** utilize, use **nyttighet** (*med pl*) utility; (*utan pl äv.*) usefulness

nyttja use, employ; *jfr använda* **nyttjanderätt** usufruct, right of (to) use; *ha ~ till* hold in usufruct, have the use and enjoyment of

nytto|betonad *a5* utility; utilitarian **-föremål** useful article **-konst** applied art **-moral** utilitarian morality **-synpunkt** *ur ~* from the utility (utilitarian) point of view **-trafic** commercial traffic **-varor** utility products (articles) **-växt** useful plant

ny|tvättad *a5* just washed; newly washed; (*om fönster*) newly cleaned **-tändning** appearance of a new moon **-uppfunnen** *a5* recently invented **-upptäckt** *a4* rediscovered **-utgåva** new edition **-utkommen** *a5* just (recently) published, that has just appeared **-utnämnd** *a5* newly appointed **-utslagen** *a5* (*om blomma*) that has just come out **-val** *s7* new election; *utlysa ~* appeal to the country, publish notices of a new election **-vald** *a5* newly elected **-vunnen** *a5* newly won **-värdesför-säkring** reinstatement value insurance **-zee-ländare** [-*se:-] New Zealander **-zeeländsk** [-*se:-] *a5* New Zealand **-år** new year; *fira ~* celebrate New Year

nyårs|afton New Year's Eve **-dag** New Year's Day **-gåva** new-year['s] gift **-löfte** New Year resolution

nyöppnad *a5* newly started (*affär* shop); newly opened (*konto* account)

1 nå *interj* well!; (*ju*) why!; *~ då så!* oh, in that case!

2 nå *v4* (*komma fram t.*) reach (*äv. bildl.*), get (come) to, arrive at; (*upp-*) attain, achieve (*äv. bildl.*); (*räcka*) reach, attain; *~ mogen ålder* reach maturity; *enighet har ~tts om* agreement has been reached on; *jag ~ddes av nyheten* the news reached me; *han ~r mig till axeln* he comes up to my shoulder; *jag ~r inte dit* I cannot reach as far as that, it is beyond my reach; *~ fram till* reach as far as [to]; *~ ner till* reach down to; *~ upp till* reach [up to], come up to **nåd** *s3* **1** (*misskund*) grace; (*barmhärtighet*) mercy; (*ynnest*) favour; *av Guds ~e* (*om kung*) by divine right, (*om t.ex. skald*) divinely gifted; *i ~ens år 1931* in the year of grace 1931; *av ~* out of mercy; *ansöka om ~* apply for a (sue for) pardon; *få ~* be pardoned; *ge sig på ~ och onåd* surrender unconditionally, make an unconditional surrender; *i ~er* graciously; *leva på ~er hos ngn* live on a p.'s charity; *låta ~ gå före rätt* temper justice with mercy; *synda på ~en* (*eg.*) presume on God's grace, *vard.* take advantage of a p.'s generosity; *finna ~ inför ngns ögon* find favour with s.b.; *ta ngn till ~er* *igen* take s.b. back into one's favour **2** (*höghet*) Grace; *Ers* ~ Your Grace, (*Storbritannien äv.*) Your Lordship (Ladyship), my Lord (Lady); *lilla* ~*en* (*skämts.*) her little ladyship; *två gamla* ~*er* two old (elderly) ladies

nåda|skott *se* -*stöt* **-stöt** coupe de grâce, deathblow; *ge* ~*en* finish off, put out of misery **-tid** time of grace, respite

nåde I *s, se nåd 1* **II** *v, i uttr. såsom:* Gud ~ dig! God have mercy upon you!; *Gud* ~ *om ...!* God help me if ...! **-ansökan** petition for pardon **-gåva** gift of grace; (*friare*) bounty, gratuity **-hjon** [-jɔ:n] *s7* receiver of charity **-medel** means of grace **-rik** abounding in grace; (*friare*) gracious, merciful **-skott, -stöt** *se* nådastöt **-vedermäle** mark of favour

nådig *a1* gracious; merciful; *Gud vare mig* ~*!* God be merciful to me (have mercy upon me)!; *på* ~[*a*]*ste befallning* by His (Her) Majesty's Command; ~ *frun* her (*vid tilltal:* Your) Ladyship; *min* ~*a* your Ladyship, my Lady, [my dear] Madam

någ|on [-ån] (*jfr något, några*) (*en viss*) some, *subst.* someone, somebody; (*en el. ett par*) a[n] ... or two (so); (~ *alls,* ~ *som helst*) any, *subst.* anyone, anybody; (*en, ett*) a[n]; (*en enda*) one, a single; *har du* ~ *bror?* have you a brother?; -*ra egna barn har de inte* they have no children of their own; *har du* -*ra pengar?* a) (*på dig*) have you any money?, b) (*att låna mig*) have you got some money?; *om* ~ *vecka* in a week or two (so); *är det* ~ *här?* is there anyone here?; *jag har inte berättat det för* ~ I haven't told anyone; *kan* ~ *av er ...?* can one (any [one]) of you ...?; ~ *av dem måtte ha* one of them must have; *inte i* ~ *större utsträckning* not to any great extent; *utan* ~ [*som helst*] *svårighet* without any difficulty [whatsoever]; *inte på -ot vis!* by no means!, not at all!; *på -ot sätt* somehow (in some way) [or other]; *vi var -ra och trettio* we were thirty odd; *hon är -ra och trettio* she is thirty odd (something); ~ *annan* someone else; ~ *annan gång* some other time; *bättre än* ~ *annan* better than anyone else; ~ *annanstans* somewhere else; -*ot eller -ra år* one year or more; ~ *sådan har jag inte* I have nothing like that (of that kind); *en ... så god som* ~ as good a[n] ... as any; *denne* ~ this somebody; *du om* ~ you if anybody; *tala svenska med* ~ *brytning* speak Swedish with a slight accent; *kära nån* [*då*]*!* goodness me!

någon|dera *fören.* one ... or the other; *självst.* one or other (*av dem* of them) **-sin** [-inn] ever; [at] any time; *aldrig* ~ never **-stans, -städes** (*jfr någon*) somewhere; anywhere; *AE. vard.* some place, any place **-ting** (*jfr något*) something; anything

någorlunda fairly, tolerably, pretty

någ|ot [-ått] **I** *pron* (*jfr någon*) something; anything; (*-on del*) some, any; (~ *litet*) a little; *det är* ~ *mycket vanligt* that (it) is [a] very common [thing]; *vad för* ~*?* what?; *vad är det för* ~*?* what is that?; *det var* ~ *visst med honom* there was [a certain] something about him; ~ *sådant har aldrig hänt förut* such a thing has never (no such thing has ever) happened before; *han är* ~ *av en konstnär* he is some-

thing of an artist; *vill du mig* ~*? a*) (~ *särskilt*) is there something you want to see me about?, *b*) (~ *över huvud taget*) is there anything you want to see me about? **II** *adv* somewhat; a little, a bit, rather; ~ *mindre än en timme* a little less than (somewhat under) an hour; *han är* ~ *till fräck!* he's pretty (a bit) impudent!

någotså'när *se någorlunda* **några** [ˣnå:g-] (*jfr någon*) some; any; *subst.* some (any) people; (~ *få*) a few [people *etc.*]; *om* ~ *dagar* in a few (in two or three) days

nåja [ˈnå:-] oh well!

nål *s2* needle; (*hår-, knapp-*) pin; *sitta som på* ~*ar* (*bildl.*) be on pins and needles (on tenterhooks)

nål|a ~ [*fast*] pin on (*på* to), fasten on (*på* to) **-brev** packet of needles **-dyna** pincushion **-pengar** *pl* pin money (*sg*) **-påträdare** needle threader **-rasp** *s7* (*på grammofon*) scratching **-spets** needle-point, pinpoint **-stick** pinprick (*äv. bildl.*)

nålsöga eye of a (the) needle

nål|vass [as] sharp as a needle **-ventil** needle valve

nåt *s2, s7, sjö. o. fack.* seam

nåtla [ˣnå:t-] *fack.* close, bind

nå'väl well; all right

näbb *s2, s7* bill; (*i sht rovfågels*) beak; *var fågel sjunger efter sin* ~ every bird pipes its own lay; *försvara sig med* ~*ar och klor* defend o.s. tooth and nail **-djur** *zool.* duckbill [platypus] **-gädda 1** *zool.* garfish **2** *bildl.* pert (saucy) girl

näbb|ig *a1, bildl.* pert, saucy, impudent **-mus** shrew[mouse]; *vanlig* ~ common shrew **-val** *s2* bottle-nosed whale

näck *s2* water-sprite; *N~en* Neck[an], *Skottl.* Kelpie **-ros** water lily

näktergal *s2* [thrush] nightingale

nämligen (*framför uppräkning*) namely, *skriftspr.* viz.; (*det vill säga*) [and] that is, which is; (*emedan*) for, because; ('*ser ni*') you see; *sak en är* ~ *den att* the fact is, you see, that, it's like this, you see

nämn|a *v2* (*om-*) mention (*för* to); (*säga*) say; (*omtala*) tell; (*be-*) name, call; ~ *var sak vid dess rätta namn* call a spade a spade; *ingen -d och ingen glömd* all included; *under -da förutsättning* on the given assumption **-are** *mat.* denominator

nämnd *s3* (*jury*) jury, panel; (*utskott*) committee, board

nämndeman juror, juryman

nämn|värd [-vä:-] *a1* worth mentioning (speaking of); considerable, appreciable; *i* ~ *grad* materially; *ingen* ~ *förändring* no change to speak of

nännas *v2, dep* have the heart to

näpen *a3* engaging; sweet (dear) little (*flicka* girl); *i sht AE.* cute

näppe *s i uttr.: med nöd och* ~ only just **-ligen** *se knappast*

näpsa *v3* (*tillrättavisa*) rebuke; (*straffa*) chastise, punish **näpst** *s3* rebuke; chastisement

1 när I *konj* **1** when; (*just som*) [just] as; (*medan*) while; (*-helst*) whenever; ~ *han kom in i rummet såg han* on entering the room he saw **2** *se emedan* **II** *adv* when, at what time; ~ *som*

helst at any time (moment)
2 när I *adv* near, [near (close)] at hand; *från ~ och fjärran* from far and near; *inte göra en fluga för ~* not hurt a fly; *det gick hans ära för ~* it hurt his pride; *jag hade så ~ sagt* I [very] nearly said, I was on the point of saying; *så ~ som på* except [for], but; *inte på långt ~* not by a long way; not anything like; *det var på ett hår ~* it was within an ace of **II** *prep* (*hos*) with, near
1 nära *närmare närmast o. näst* I *oböjl. a* near (*äv. om tid*); close; *bildl.* close, intimate; *på ~ håll* at close quarters; *inom en ~ framtid* in the near future **II** *adv* near; (*i tid äv.*) at hand; close to, nearby; *bildl.* closely, intimately; (*nästan*) almost; *~ förestående* impending, imminent; *vara ~ att* be on the point of (*falla* falling), *AE. äv.* be near to (+ *inf.*); *~ skjuter ingen hare* a miss is as good as a mile; *~ inpå* near at hand; *affären ligger ~ till för oss* the shop is handy for us
2 när|a *v2* nourish, feed (*äv. bildl.*); (*hysa*) cherish, entertain; *~ en orm vid sin barm* nourish a viper in one's bosom; *ett länge -t hopp* a long-cherished hope; *en länge -d misstanke* a long-harboured suspicion
närande *a4* nourishing; nutritious, nutritive
när|apå almost, pretty near[ly]; (*så gott som*) practically **-belägen** (situated *etc.*) near (close) by (at hand); adjacent, neighbouring; *i sht AE.* nearby **-besläktad** closely related (akin) (*med* to) **-bild** close-up [picture] **-butik** neighbourhood shop (*AE.* store) **-demokrati** grassroots democracy **-gränsande** *a4* adjacent, adjoining, neighbouring **-gången** *a3* intrusive; forward; (*taktlös*) indiscreet; (*om fråga o.d.*) inquisitive; *AE. sl.* fresh **-'helst** whenever **-het** nearness; (*grannskap*) neighbourhood, vicinity; *i ~en av* (*äv.*) near [to]; *här i ~en* near (round about) here
närig *a1* (*snål*) greedy, stingy; (*'om sig'*) thrifty **-het** greediness *etc.*
näring 1 (*föda*) nourishment (*äv. bildl.*); *eg. äv.* nutriment; *bildl. äv.* fuel (*åt* to); *ge ~ åt* give (afford) nourishment to, *bildl.* add fuel to; *ge ny ~ åt* (*bildl.*) give new life to **2** (*närings-fång*) industry; *handel och ~ar* commerce and industry
närings|behov nutritional requirement **-fattig** of low food value; (*om jord*) poor **-frihet** freedom of (liberty to pursue a) trade **-frihetsombudsman** Competition Ombudsman **-fysiologi** nutritional physiology **-fång** *s7, äv. yrke* **-gren** [branch of] business (industry) **-idkare** tradesman, industrialist **-kedja** food chain **-liv** economic (industrial) life; trade and industry **-lära** nutrition **-lösning** *fysiol.* nutrient solution; (*för bakterieodling*) culture medium **-medel** food[stuff] **-politik** economic policy **-rik** nutritious, of high food value **-riktig** nourishing; of nutritional value **-ställe** restaurant; refreshment rooms (*pl*), eating house **-tillförsel** nutrient input (supply) **-utskott** *~et* [the Swedish parliamentary] standing committee on industry and commerce **-värde** nutritive (food) value **-ämne** nutritive (nutritious) substance

när|kamp *s3, sport.* infighting **-köp** *se närbutik* **-liggande** *a4, bildl.* close at hand, kindred; *ett ~ problem* a kindred (closely allied) problem; *mera ~* more immediate
närma bring (draw, push) near[er], approach; *~ sig* approach, draw near[er] [to ...]; *~ sig sitt färdigställande* near completion; *klockan ~r sig 10* it is getting on towards 10 o'clock; *slutet ~de sig* the end was approaching, it was drawing near the end **närmande** *s6* approach, advance; renewal of friendly relations; *polit. etc.* rapprochement; *otillbörliga ~n* [improper] advances
närmare *komp. t. nära* I *a* nearer, closer; (*om väg*) shorter; (*ytterligare*) further (*detaljer* particulars) **II** *adv* nearer, closer, more closely; in [greater] detail; *gå ~ in på frågan* go into the question in detail; *bli ~ bekant med ngn* become better acquainted with s.b., get to know s.b. better; *förklara ~* explain in detail, give further particulars; *studera ~* examine in detail; *ta ~ reda på* find out more about; *jag skall tänka ~ på saken* I shall think the matter over more carefully; *eller, ~ bestämt* or, more exactly **III** *prep* nearer [to], closer to; (*nästan*) nearly, close [up]on **närmast** *superl. t. nära* I *a* nearest (*äv. bildl.*); (*omedelbar*) immediate; (*om vän e.d.*) closest, most intimate; (*~ i ordningen*) next; *~e anhörig[a]* next of kin, nearest relative[s]; *mina ~e* those nearest and dearest to me, my people, *vard.* my folks; *mina ~e planer* my plans for the immediate future; *de ~e dagarna* the next few days; *inom den ~e framtiden* in the immediate future; *var och en är sig själv ~* every man for himself; *i det ~e* [very] nearly, almost, practically, as good as **II** *adv* nearest (closest) [to]; *bildl.* most closely (intimately); immediately; next; (*främst*) in the first place; (*huvudsakligast*) principally; *de ~ sörjande* the principal (chief) mourners; *~ föregående år* the immediately preceeding year; *~ på grund av* mainly because (owing to); *han ser ~ ut som en...* he looks more like a[n] ... than anything **III** *prep* nearest (next) [to]
närmevärde approximate value
närsalt nutritive salt
när|sluta *-slöt -slutit* enclose, attach **-strid** close combat, hand-to-hand fighting **-stående** *a4* close, near; (*-besläktad*) kindred; *~ företag* associated company, *AE.* affiliated corporation; *i regeringen ~ kretsar* in circles close to the Government **-synt** [-y:-] *AE.* short-sighted; *med.* myopic **-synthet** short-sightedness; *med.* myopia **-vara** *-var -varit* be present (*vid* at); *~ vid* (*äv.*) attend **-varande** *a4* present (*vid* at); *de ~* those present; *för ~* for the present (time being), at present, *AE. äv.* presently **-varo** *s9* presence; (*vid möte o.d. äv.*) attendance; *i ~ av* in the presence of, before
näs *s7* (*landremsa*) isthmus, neck of land; (*landtunga*) point, headland; *se äv. udde*
näs|a *s1* nose; *peta* [*sig i*] *~n* pick one's nose; *tala i* (*genom*) *~n* talk through the nose, have a nasal twang; *dra ngn vid ~n* lead s.b. by the nose, take s.b. in; *det gick hans ~ förbi* it passed him by; *ha ~ för* have a flair for; *han lå-*

ter ingen sätta sig på ~n på sig he lets no one sit on him; *lägga ~n i vädret (dö)* turn up one's toes [to the daisies]; *mitt för ~ på ngn* right in front of a p.'s nose; *räcka lång ~ åt* cock a snook at, thumb one's nose at; *inte se längre än ~n räcker* not see further than the end of one's nose; *ha skinn på ~n* have a will (mind) of one's own; *stå där med lång ~* be left pulling a long face; *stå på ~n* take a header, come a cropper; *sätta ~n i vädret* toss one's head, be stuck-up (cocky) **-ben** nasal bone **-blod** nose-bleeding; *blöda ~* have an attack of nose-bleeding **-borre** [-å-] *s2* nostril **-bränna** *s1 (tillrättavisning)* rebuke; *(minnesbeta)* lesson **-droppar** nose drops **-duk** handkerchief **-håla** nasal cavity **-knäpp** *s2, vard.* rebuke, snub, reprimand **-pärla** *se näbbgädda* 2 **-rot** root of the nose **-rygg** bridge of the nose

nässel|djur cnidarian **-feber** nettle rash, hives, *fack.* urticaria **-fjäril** tortoiseshell [butterfly] **-kål** *kokk.* nettle soup (broth) **-utslag** nettle rash

nässla *s1* nettle

näs|spets *se nästipp*

näst *superl. t. nära, adv* next *(efter, intill* to); *den ~ bästa* the second (next) best; *den ~ sista* the last but one; *~ äldste sonen* the second son

1 nästa I *s1* neighbour; *kärleken till ~n* love for one's neighbour **II** *a, superl.* next; *(påföljande)* the next, *(påföljande gång)* the next time; *den 1:a ~ månad (hand. äv.)* on the first prox.

2 nästa *v1, sömn.* stitch

nästan almost; *AE. äv. (i sht om tid)* just on; *(ej långt ifrån)* nearly; *(starkare)* all but; *~ aldrig (ingen)* hardly ever (anybody); *jag tror (tycker) ~ att* I rather (almost) think that

näste *s6* nest; *bildl. äv.* den

näst|följande next; the immediate following **-in'till I** *prep* next to **II** *adv* nearest (next) to this (it *etc.*)

nästipp tip of the nose

nästkommande *a4* next; *(nästa månad)* proximo *(förk.* prox.); *~ maj* in May next; *under ~ år (äv.)* during the coming year

nästla *~ sig in, se innästla*

näs|täppa *jag har ~* my nose is stopped up **-vinge** wing of the nose (nostril) **-vis** *a1* impertinent, cheeky; pert, saucy **-vishet** [-i:-] impertinence, cheekiness *etc.*

nät *s7* net; *(spindel- äv.)* web; *(-verk)* network *(äv. bildl.); tel. o.d. äv.* system **-ansluten** *a5, tel. o.d.* connected to the main system **-boll** tennis. *o.d.* net **-hinna** *anat.* retina **-hinneinflammation** inflammation of the retina **-kasse** string bag **-mage** reticulum *(pl* reticula) **-maska** [net] mesh **-planering** network planning **-spänning** mains voltage

nätt I *a1* **1** pretty; dainty; *(prydlig)* neat; *en ~ summa* a tidy (nice little) sum **2** *(knapp)* scanty, sparing **II** *adv* **1** prettily *etc.* **2** scantily *etc.; ~ och jämnt* barely, only just **-upp** ['nätt-] just [about]

nät|verk network; netting **-vinge** *zool.* neuropteran

näva *s1* cranesbill

näv|e *s2* fist; *(handfull)* fistful (handful) [of ...]; *slå ~n i bordet (bildl.)* put one's foot down;

spotta i -arna spit on one's hands, buckle down to work

näver ['nä:-] *s2* birch bark

näv|kamp fisticuffs *(pl)* **-rätt** *hist.* fist (club) law; *(våld)* jungle law

nöd *s3* distress; trouble; *(brist)* need, want; *(trångmål)* straits *(pl); fartyg i ~* vessel in distress; *lida ~* be in need; *den tysta ~en* uncomplaining poverty; *~en har ingen lag* necessity knows no law; *~en är uppfinningarnas moder* necessity is the mother of invention; *när ~en är störst är hjälpen närmast* it is always darkest before dawn; *i ~en prövas vännen* a friend in need is a friend indeed; *det går ingen ~ på honom* he's well provided for; *vara av ~en* be needed (necessary); *med knapp ~* only just; *till ~s* if need be, at a pinch **-bedd** *a5, vara ~* have to be pressed **-bostad** emergency housing (flat *etc.*) **-broms** emergency brake; *dra i ~en* pull the communication cord

nödd *a5, vara ~ och tvungen* be forced [and compelled]

nöd|dop emergency baptism **-fall** *i ~* in case of need (necessity), in an emergency, *(friare)* if necessary **-fallsåtgärd** emergency measure; makeshift **-flagg** distress signal

nödga constrain; *(tvinga)* force, compel; *(truga)* press, urge **nödgas** *v1, dep* be compelled (forced) to

nöd|hamn port (harbour) of refuge **-hjälpsarbete** relief work

nödig *a1 (nödvändig)* necessary; *(erforderlig)* needful, requisite, required

nöd|landa forceland, be forced down **-landning** forced (emergency) landing **-lidande** *a4* necessitous; *(utarmad)* needy, destitute **-läge** distress, critical position; emergency; extremity **-lögn** white lie **-lösning** makeshift (temporary) solution **-mynt** emergency coin **-raket** distress rocket **-rim** halting (makeshift) rhyme **-rop** cry (call) of distress (for help) **-saka** *se nödga; bli (vara) ~d att* be obliged (compelled, forced) to; *se sig ~d att* find o.s. compelled to **-signal** distress signal; S.O.S.; *radiotel.* mayday **-slakt** emergency slaughter **-ställd** *a5* distressed; in distress **-tid** *i ~er* in times of dearth (distress, scarcity) **-torft** [-å-] *s3, livets ~* the bare necessities of life **-torftig** scanty, meagre **-tvungen** *a5* enforced; compulsory **-tvång** *av ~* out of necessity **-utgång** emergency exit

nödvändig [ˣnö:d-, -'vänn-] *a1* necessary **-göra** necessitate, make (render) necessary **-het** necessity; *tvingande ~* imperative (urgent) necessity; *med ~ (-vändigt)* of necessity **-hetsartikel** necessity, necessary [of life] **-tvis** necessarily; of necessity; absolutely; *måste ~ leda till* is (are) bound to lead to; *han ville ~ komma* he would come, he insisted on coming

nöd|värn self-defence **-år** year of famine

nöj|a [ˣnöjja] *v2, rfl* be satisfied (content), content o.s.; *~ sig med att (inskränka sig t. att, äv.)* restrict (confine) o.s. to **-aktig** *a1* satisfactory **-aktigt** *adv, ~ besvara* give a satisfactory answer **-aktighet** satisfactoriness

nöjd *a1* satisfied *(äv. mätt); (för-)* content[ed]; *(belåten)* pleased; *~ med litet* satisfied with a little, easily satisfied; *vara ~ på ngt (ha fått nog av ngt)* have had enough of s.th.

nöje [ˣnöjje] *s6* pleasure; *(starkare)* delight; *(förströelse)* amusement, entertainment; *(tidsfördriv)* diversion, pastime; *ha ~ av, finna ~ i* derive pleasure from, find (take) pleasure in, enjoy; *för sitt höga ~s skull* for one's own sweet pleasure, just for fun; *vi har ~t att meddela* we have the pleasure of informing you; *det skall bli mig ett sant ~ att* I shall be delighted to; *jag skall med ~ göra det (äv.)* I shall be glad to do it, I'll do it gladly; *du får det med ~ (äv.)* you are very welcome to it; *mycket ~!* have a good time!, enjoy yourself!; *offentliga ~n* public amusements **nöjes|branch** entertainment industry **-etablissemang** pleasure ground, amusement park **-fält** fair (pleasure) ground; *AE. äv.* carnival **-industri** entertainment industry **-liv** entertainments *(pl)*; life of pleasure **-lysten** fond of amusement **-lystnad** fondness for (love of) amusement **-resa** pleasure trip **-skatt** entertainment tax
nöjsam *a1, se* rolig
nöp *imperf. av* nypa
nös *imperf. av* nysa
1 nöt *-en nötter, bot.* nut; *en hård ~ att knäcka (bildl.)* a hard nut to crack, a poser
2 nöt *s7* **1** *se* nötkreatur **2** *bildl.* ass, blockhead; *ditt ~!* you silly ass *(etc.)*!
nöta *v3 (slita)* wear; *(gnida)* rub; *~ hål på* wear through; *~ skolbänken* grind away at one's classroom desk; *tyget tål att ~ på* the material will wear [well] (will stand [hard] wear); *du får ~ på dina gamla kläder* you must wear out your old clothes [first]; *~ ut* wear out; *~s* get worn (rubbed)
nötboskap [neat] cattle *(pl)*
nöt|brun nutbrown, hazel **-frukt** nut [fruit]
nöthår cowhair
nöt|knäckare, -knäppare [[a] pair of] nutcrackers *(pl)*
nötkreatur *pl* cattle; *sju ~* seven head of cattle **nöt|kråka** *zool.* nutcracker **-kärna** kernel of a nut
nötkött beef
nötning [ˣnö:t-] wear, use; *bildl.* wear and tear **nöt|skal** nutshell *(äv. bildl.)*; *(om båt äv.)* cockleshell **-skrika** *s1, zool.* jay
nött *a1* worn *(i* at); *(om kläder äv.)* the worse for wear, threadbare, shiny; *~a fraser* hackneyed phrases
nötväcka *s1, zool.* nuthatch

o *interj* oh!; *~ ve!* alas!
oaktat I *prep* notwithstanding; *jfr* trots *II; det[ta] ~* for all that, all the same **II** *konj* [al]though, even though
o|aktsam careless *(med* about) **-aktsamhet** carelessness, negligence **-amerikansk** *~ verksamhet* un-American activities *(pl)* **-anad** *a5* unsuspected; unimagined; *~e möjligheter* undreamed-of (undreamt-of) possibilities **-angenäm** unpleasant, disagreeable **-angripbar** [-i:p-] *a1* **-angriplig** [-i:p-] *a1* unassailable *(äv. bildl.)*; *(om vittnesbörd e.d.)* unimpeachable; *~ bevisföring* unexceptionable argumentation **-anmäld** [-ä:-] *a5* unannounced **-anmärkt** *a4* unchallenged; *låta ngt passera ~* let s.th. pass without comment **-ansenlig** [-e:n-] insignificant; *(ringa)* humble; *(om t.ex. lön)* meagre, modest; *(enkel)* plain *(utseende* looks); *(ej iögonfallande)* inconspicuous **-ansenlighet** insignificance; humbleness *etc.* **-anständig** indecent; *(anstötlig)* shocking; improper; *(slipprig)* obscene; *(otillbörlig)* disgraceful, shameful **-anständighet** indecency; impropriety; obscenity; shockingness *etc.*; *(i ord)* indecent remark, obscenity **-ansvarig** irresponsible **-antagbar** *a5,* **-antaglig** *a5* unacceptable, that cannot be accepted **-antastlig** *a1* unassailable, inviolable; *jur.* unimpeachable **-anträffbar** unavailable; untraceable; not in (at home); engaged **-använd** *a5* unused; *(om plagg äv.)* unworn; unemployed; *(om kapital)* idle **-användbar** unusable, useless, of no use, unfit for use; *vard.* no good
o|aptitlig unappetizing *(äv. bildl.)*; *i sht bildl.* unsavoury; *(otäck)* disgusting **-art** bad habit **-artig** impolite, uncivil, discourteous **-artighet** impoliteness, incivility; *en ~* a discourtesy **-artikulerad** *a5* inarticulate
o'as *s3* oasis *(pl* oases)
o|avbruten *a5* uninterrupted; unbroken *(tystnad* silence); continuous *(verksamhet* activity); *(oupphörlig)* incessant **-avgjord** undecided; unsettled; *spel., sport.* drawn; *-avgjort lopp* dead heat; *~ match* draw; *ärendet lämnades -avgjort* the matter was left unsettled (pending) **-avgjort** *adv, sluta ~* end in a draw; *spela ~* draw, tie **-avhängig** independent; *(autonom)* autonomous, self-governing **-avhängighet** independence; autonomy, self-government **-avhängighetsförklaring** declaration of independence **-avkortad** [-årt-] *a5 (om text)* unabridged, unabbreviated; *(om t.ex. lön)* uncurtailed **-avlåtlig** [-å:-] *a1* incessant, unceasing, continuous; *(ständig)* constant **-avlönad** unpaid, unsalaried; *äv.* honorary **-avsedd** unintended; *-avsett att* irrespective of (apart from) the fact that; *-avsett hur (äv.)* no matter how **-avsiktlig** unintentional, unintended **-avslutad** unfinished, uncompleted; *(om räken-*

skaper) not closed **-avsättbar** *a5* irremovable **-avvislig** [-i:s-] *a1* not to be rejected (refused), unrejectable; imperative; *ett ~t krav* a claim that cannot be refused, an imperative demand **-avvänt** *adv* unremittingly; ~ *betrakta* watch intently

o|**balans** imbalance, disequilibrium **-balanserad** unbalanced; *äv. bildl.* ill-balanced **-banad** *a5* untrodden; unbeaten; pathless; ~*e vägar* unbeaten tracks **-barmhärtig** unmerciful, uncharitable; merciless **-barmhärtighet** mercilessness *etc.*

obduc|ent [åbdu'sänt] postmortem examiner **-era** perform (make) a postmortem [examination] (*ngn* on s.b.) **-ering** *se obduktion*

obduktion [-kʃɷ:n] *s3* postmortem [examination], autopsy

o|**beaktad** *a5* unnoticed; *lämna* ~ leave unheeded, disregard, (*genom förbiseende*) overlook **-bearbetad** *a5* (*om råvara*) raw, crude; (*om metall*) unwrought; (*i maskin*) rough, unmachined **-bebodd** *a5* uninhabited; unoccupied; (*om hus*) untenanted; ~*a trakter* uninhabited regions

obedd *a5* unasked; uninvited

o|**befintlig** nonexistent; that does not exist; missing **-befläckad** *a5* immaculate; (*om namn, ära o.d.*) unsullied, stainless, spotless **-befogad** unwarranted, unjustified (*anmärkning* remark) **-befolkad** [-å-] *a5* uninhabited **-befäst** unfortified; (*om stad äv.*) open; *bildl.* unstable **-begagnad** unused, unemployed; (*i reserv*) spare **-begriplig** incomprehensible; (*dunkel*) unintelligible; (*ofattlig*) inconceivable **-begriplighet** incomprehensibility *etc.* **-begränsad** unlimited; boundless (*förtroende* confidence); *jfr gränslös* **-begåvad** untalented; unintelligent **-behag** discomfort, uneasiness; (*otrevlighet*) annoyance; ('*trassel*') trouble; *få* ~ *av* have trouble from; *känna* [*ett visst*] ~ feel [slightly] ill at ease **-behaglig** disagreeable, unpleasant (*för* to; *mot* towards, to); *en* ~ *situation* (*äv.*) an awkward situation **-behandlad** untreated **-behindrat** *adv* smoothly, easily; unimpededly; (*fritt*) freely; *tala engelska* ~ speak English fluently **-behärskad** uncontrolled; lacking in self-control **-behörig** (*inkompetent*) incompetent; (*av behörig, oberättigad*) unauthorized; ~*a äga ej tillträde* no admittance [except on business]; (*på enskilt område*) trespassers will be prosecuted, no trespassing **-behövlig** unnecessary; not necessary (required) **-bekant I** *a* (*okänd*) unknown (*för* to); (*med ngn, ngt*) unacquainted (*med* with); (*okunnig* [*om*]) ignorant (*med* of); *det torde inte vara Er* ~ *att* you will be aware that **II** *s, pl* -*bekanta, mat., ekvation med flera* ~*a* equation with several unknowns **-bekräftad** *a5* unconfirmed; unverified **-bekväm** uncomfortable; (*ej passande*) inconvenient (*arbetstid* working hours *pl*); (*besvärlig*) awkward **-bekymrad** unconcerned (*om, för* about, as to); heedless (*om* of) **-belevad** unmannerly, ill-mannered

obe'lisk *s3* obelisk

o|**belyst** [-y:-] *a4* unlighted, unlit, not lit up **-belönad** *a5* unrewarded; unremunerated **-be-**

mannad *a5* unmanned **-bemedlad** without means **-bemärkt I** *a4* unobserved, unnoticed; (*anspråkslös*) humble **II** *adv* in obscurity **-bemärkthet** obscurity; *leva i* ~ live in seclusion (obscurity) **-benägen** disinclined (*för* for); unwilling, reluctant **-benägenhet** disinclination; unwillingness, reluctance **-benämnd** *a5* (*om tal*) indenominate **-beprövad** untried **-beroende I** *s6* independence **II** *a4* independent (*av* of) **-beräknelig** [-ä:-] *a1* incalculable; unpredictable; (*nyckfull*) fickle, capricious; (*ofantlig*) immense **-beräknelighet** [-ä:-] incalculability; fickleness *etc.* **-berättigad** unentitled (*till* to); (*orättvis*) unjustified, unwarranted **-berörd** [-ö:-] *a1* untouched; (*opåverkad*) unaffected; (*okänslig*) impassive, unconcerned; (*likgiltig*) indifferent **-berördhet** [-ö:-] unconcern; indifference

o|**besatt** unoccupied; (*ledig*) vacant **-besedd** unseen, unexamined; uninspected **-besegrad** [-se:-] *a5* unconquered; *sport.* undefeated, unbeaten **-beskrivlig** [-i:v-] *a1* indescribable; (*outsäglig*) inexpressible **-beskuren** *a5* uncut; *bildl.* unabridged (*upplaga* edition) **-beslutsam** irresolute; undecided (*om* about); *vara* ~ (*äv.*) hesitate, waver **-beslutsamhet** irresolution; indecision; hesitation **-beslöjad** [-öjj-] *a5* unveiled; (*ohöljd*) undisguised **-besmittad** *a5* undefiled, uncontaminated, unsullied **-besticklig** incorruptible, unbribable **-bestridd** *a5* uncontested, undisputed; (*om t.ex. välde*) unchallenged **-bestridlig** [-i:d-] *a1* indisputable; incontestable; (*otvivelaktig*) undoubted; (*oneklig*) undeniable **-bestridligen** [-i:d-] indisputably; unquestionably **-bestyrkt** *a4* unverified; (*om avskrift*) unattested **-bestånd** insolvency; *komma på* ~ become insolvent **-beställbar** *a1* undeliverable (*försändelse* item of mail) **-bestämbar** indeterminable; (*om känsla o.d.*) indefinable **-bestämd** undecided; (*om antal, tid o.d.*) indefinite; (*om känsla*) undefined; (*vag*) vague; (*oviss*) uncertain; (*otydlig*) ill-defined; ~*a artikeln* the indefinite article; *uppskjuta på* ~ *tid* put off indefinitely **-beständig** inconstant; (*växlande*) changeable; (*ovaraktig*) impermanent, transient; *kem.* unstable **-besudlad** *se obefläckad* **-besvarad** *a5* unanswered; unreturned; (*om kärlek äv.*) unrequited **-besvärad** untroubled, undisturbed; (*otvungen*) unconstrained, [free and] easy

o|**betagen** *det -r honom obetaget att* he is free (welcome, at liberty) to **-betalbar** (*komisk*) priceless, irresistible **-betald** [-a:-] *a5* unpaid; unsettled; (*om växel*) dishonoured **-betingad** *a5* unconditional; (*oinskränkt*) unrestricted, absolute; (*om förtroende, lydnad o.d.*) implicit **-betingat** unconditionally *etc.*; (*utan all fråga*) unquestionably **-betonad** unstressed, unaccented **-betvinglig** *a1* (*okuvlig*) unsubduable; (*oövervinnelig*) invincible, inconquerable; (*oemotståndlig*) irresistible **-betydlig** insignificant; inconsiderable; (*oviktig*) unimportant; (*ringa*) slight **-betydlighet** insignificance; triviality; (*med pl*) insignificant (*etc.*) matter (affair); *en ren* ~ a mere trifle (nothing) **-betydligt** *adv* slightly; a little **-betäckt** *a4* uncovered, bare **-betänksam** thoughtless; (*mot andra*) inconsiderate; (*förhastad*) rash; (*oklok*) imprudent, unadvised, ill-advised **-bevakad** unguarded; unattended; ~ *järnvägsövergång* ungated [railway] level crossing; *i ett -bevakat ögonblick* in an unguarded moment; *en ~ fordran* an unproved claim **-bevandrad** unfamiliar (*i* with); unversed (*i* in) **-beveklig** [-e:k-] *a1* implacable, inexorable; (*om lag, logik*) inflexible **-bevittnad** *a5* unwitnessed; (*om avskrift e.d.*) unattested **-bevuxen** bare **-beväpnad** unarmed; *med -beväpnat öga* with the naked eye **o|bildad** uneducated; (*obelevad*) rude, ill-bred **-bildbar** uneducable **-billig** (*oskälig*) unreasonable; (*orättvis*) unfair **objekt** [åb'jäkt] *s7* object **objektiv I** [-'ti:v] *s7, fys.* objective; *opt.* lens **II** ['åbb-, -'ti:v] *a1* objective; (*saklig*) factual **objektivism** objectivism **objektivitet** objectivity; detachment **objektsform** objective form **o|bjuden** *a5* uninvited; (*obedd*) unasked; ~ *gäst* (*neds.*) intruder, gate-crasher **-blandad** unmixed, unmingled; (*ogrumlad*) unalloyed (*lycka* happiness) **oblat** [sacramental] wafer **-tallrik** paten **o|blekt** [-e:-] *a4* unbleached **-blid** unpropitious, unfavourable; *se med ~a ögon* regard with disapproval; *ett oblitt öde* a harsh (an adverse) fate **-blidkelig** *a1* implacable, inexorable; unappeasable **obli'gat** *a4* obbligato **obliga|tion** [å-] bond **-tionslån** bond loan **obligatorisk** [-'tå:-] *a5* compulsory; (*oumbärlig*) indispensable **o|blodig** bloodless (*revolution* revolution); unbloody (*offer* sacrifice) **-blyg** unblushing, unabashed; (*skamlös*) shameless; (*fräck*) barefaced **oboe** [*å:*båe, å'bå:] *s5* oboe **-spelare** oboist **obol** [å'bå:l] *s3* obol **o|borstad** *a5* unbrushed; (*om sko*) unpolished; (*smutsig*) dirty; (*ohyfsad*) rough, rude, uncouth **-botfärdig** impenitent, unrepentant; *de ~as förhinder* cooked-up excuses **-botlig** [-å:t-] *a1* incurable; (*om skada*) irreparable; (*ohjälplig*) incorrigible (*ungkarl* bachelor) **-botligt** [-å:t-] *adv, en ~ sjuk* an incurable **-brottslig** unswerving (*trohet* loyalty); (*osviklig*) strict (*neutralitet neutrality*) **-brukad** *a5, se oförbrukad*; (*om jord*) uncultivated, untilled **-brukbar** unfit for use, useless **-bruklig** *a1* obsolete **-bruten** unbroken, intact; (*oöppnad*) unopened; ~ *mark* (*äv. bildl.*) unbroken (virgin) ground ; *-brutna krafter* unimpaired force **obs** [åpps] [*förk. för observera*] *s7* [please] note, N.B. (*förk. för* nota bene) **obscen** [åb'se:n, -'ʃe:n] *a1* obscene **obscenitet** *s3* obscenity **observandum** [å-*å*vann-] *s8* thing to be observed; *ett ~* (*äv.*) a pointer **observans** [-'vans, -'vaŋs] *s3* observance; (*av regler*) [the] keeping (*av* of) **observation** observation **observations|förmåga** power of observation **-klass** separate class for pupils with behavioural problems **-punkt** observation spot **observator** *s3* (*iakttagare*) observer; (*vid ob-*

servatorium) astronomer **observatorium** [-*tå:-, -'tå:-*] *s4* observatory **observatör** observer **observera** observe, notice (*iakttaga äv.*) watch; *det bör ~s att* it should be noted that **observerbar** [-*ve:r-] observable **obskurant** obscurant[ist] **ob'skyr** [å-] *a1* obscure; ('*skum*') dubious, shady **obso'let** [å-å-] *a4* obsolete **obstetr|ik** [å-] *s3* obstetrics (*pl, behandlas som sg*) **-iker** [-'te:-] obstetrician **obstinat** [å-] *a1* obstinate, stubborn **obstru|ktion** [-k'ʃå:n] obstruction (*mot* to); *AE. parl.* filibustering **-era** obstruct **o|bunden** *eg.* unchained; (*om bok*) unbound; (*om pers.*) unfettered, unbound, free; *i ~ form* in prose **-bygd** undeveloped (wild) country (district); wilderness **-bäddad** *a5* unmade **-bändig** *a1* (*svårhanterlig*) intractable; (*svår att tygla*) irrepressible; (*våldsam*) unruly **-böjlig** inflexible; *språkv.* indeclinable; (*fast*) rigid; (*orubblig*) uncompromising **-bönhörlig** [-bö:nhö:r-] *a1* implacable, inexorable **-bönhörligen** [-ö:-ö:-] implacably *etc.*; (*oåterkalleligen*) irrevocably **occidenten** [åksi'denn-] *best. form* the Occident **oce'an** *s3* ocean; *bildl. vanl.* sea **-fart** ocean trade; transoceanic traffic **-gående** *a4* ocean-going **Oceanien** [-'a:-] *n* Oceania **oceano|graf** *s3* oceanographer **-grafi** *s3* oceanography **oceanångare** ocean liner **ocensurerad** *a5* uncensored **och** [åkk, *vard. å*] and; ~ *dylikt* and the like; ~ *så vidare* and so on, etc.; *ligga (sitta, stå)* ~ *läsa* lie (sit, stand) reading; *klockan tickar* ~ *tickar* (*äv.*) the clock keeps on ticking; *två* ~ *två* two by two; *5 pund per vecka* ~ *person* 5 pounds per week per person; *försök* ~ *låt bli att* try not to **ociviliserad** *a5* uncivilized **ock** [åkk] *se också, även* **ocker** ['åkk-] *s7* usury; profiteering; *bedriva* ~ practise usury **-hyra** exorbitant rent, rack-rent **-pris** exorbitant (extortionate) price **-ränta** extortionate interest **1 ockra** [*å*kk-] *v1* practise usury; ~ *på ngns godhet* trade upon a p.'s goodwill **2 ockra** [*å*kk-] *s1* ochre **-brun** ochreous **-gul** ochre yellow **ockrare** [*å*kk-] usurer, moneylender; profiteer **också** [*å*kk-] also; as well, too; (*till och med*) even; *eller* ~ or else; *om* ~ even though; *och det gjorde (betonat) jag* ~ and so I did; *och det gjorde jag (betonat)* ~ and so did I; *det var ~ en fråga!* that's quite a question!, what a question!; *men så är de* ~ *vackra* but then they are beautiful **ockult** [å'kult] *a1* occult **-ism** occultism **ockupant** [å-] occupier **ockupation** occupation **ockupations|armé** army of occupation **-makt** occupying power **-trupper** *pl* occupation troops **ockupera** occupy

O

o.d. (*förk för och dylikt*) and the like, and suchlike
odalbonde yeoman
oda'lisk *s3* odalisque
odaterad *a5* undated
odds [å-] *s7* odds (*pl*); *~en stod tio mot ett* the odds were ten to one; *ha ~en emot sig* have the cards stacked against one
ode *s6* ode
o|deciderad undecided, wavering **-definierbar** indefinable, undefinable; (*om t.ex. charm*) subtle **-dekorerad** [-å-] *a5* undecorated; plain **-delad** undivided (*äv. bildl.*); (*hel*) whole, entire; (*enhällig*) universal, unanimous; *-delat nöje* unalloyed pleasure; *väcka ~ beundran* arouse universal admiration; *~ uppmärksamhet* undivided attention **-delbar** indivisible **-demokratisk** undemocratic
Oden ['ω:-] *myt.* Woden
o|diplomatisk undiplomatic **-disciplinerad** [-isi-] *a5* undisciplined **-diskutabel** *a2*, **-disputabel** *a2* indisputable
odi'ös *a1* invidious
odjur monster; beast
odl|a [*ω:d-] cultivate (*äv. bildl.*); (*blommor, grönsaker*) grow; *AE. äv.* raise; (*jorden äv.*) till; *~ sin själ* cultivate (improve) one's mind; *~ en bekantskap* cultivate (foster) an aquaintanceship **-are** cultivator, grower; (*kaffe- o.d.*) planter **-ing** cultivation; culture; (*kaffe- o.d.*) plantation **-ingsbar** *a1* cultivable; (*om jord*) arable
odogmatisk undogmatic[al]
odon [*ω:dån] *s7* bog whortleberry
odonto|logi [ådåntå'lå:g] odontologist **-logi** *s3* odontology; *~e kandidat* Bachelor of Dental Surgery; *~e studerande* dental surgery student **-logisk** *a5* odontological
o|dramatisk undramatic **-drickbar** undrinkable **-dryg** uneconomical **-dräglig** unbearable; unsufferable, intolerable; (*tråkig*) boring; *en ~ människa* (*äv.*) an awful bore **-duglig** (*om pers.*) incompetent, inefficient, unqualified, unfit (*till* for), incapable (*till* of); (*om sak*) useless, of no use, worthless **-dugling** [-u:-] good-for-nothing, incompetent **-dygd** mischief; naughtiness **-dygdig** naughty; mischievous **-dygdspåse** *en riktig ~* a real little mischief (imp)
o.dyl. *se o.d.*
odyssé *s3* Odyssey **Odysseus** [ω'dyssevs] Ulysses
o|dåga *s1* good-for-nothing, waster **-dödlig** immortal; (*oförgätlig*) imperishable (*ära* glory), deathless **-dödliggöra** immortalize **-dödlighet** immortality **-döpt** [-ö:-] *a4* unchristened
odör [bad, nasty] smell
odört [*ω:d-] [poison] hemlock
OECD, O.E.C.D. (*förk. för Organization for Economic Corporation and Development*)
o|eftergivlig [-ji:v-] *a1* irremissable (*krav* demand); indispensable, imperative, absolute (*villkor* condition) **-efterhärmlig** *a1* inimitable **-efterrättlig** *a1* (*oförbätterlig*) incorrigible; (*oresonlig*) unreasonable; (*olidlig*) insufferable **-egennytta** disinterestedness; altruism **-egen-**

nyttig disinterested, altruistic **-egentlig** (*oriktig*) improper; (*bildlig*) figurative (*betydelse* sense); *~t bråk* (*mat.*) improper fraction **-egentlighet** [-je-] impropriety; *~er* (*i bokföring*) irregularities, (*förskingring*) embezzlement (*sg*) **-ekonomisk** uneconomic[al]; (*om pers. äv.*) unthrifty **-elastisk** inelastic **-eldad** *a5* unheated **-emballerad** *a5* unpacked
oemot|sagd *a5* uncontradicted; (*obestridd*) unchallenged **-ståndlig** *a1* irresistible **-säglig** [-ä:-] *a1* irrefutable, incontestable **-taglig** unsusceptible, inaccessible (*för* to); *~ för* (*äv.*) immune to, (*okänslig*) impervious to **-taglighet** insusceptibility; immunity
oengelsk un-English
o|enhetlig nonuniform; (*oregelbunden äv.*) irregular; (*friare*) heterogeneous **-enig** disunited; *se äv. oense* **-enighet** disagreement; dissension; discord **-ense** *vara ~ med* disagree with, be at variance with
o|erfaren inexperienced (*i* in); (*omogen*) callow, green **-erfarenhet** inexperience (*i* in, of) **-erhörd** [-ö:-] *a1* (*exempellös*) unprecedented; (*enorm*) tremendous, enormous **-ersättlig** irreplaceable; irreparable (*skada* damage); irretrievable (*förlust* loss)
o|estetisk unaesthetic **-etisk** unethical
o|fantlig [-'fant-] *a1* enormous, immense; tremendous; huge; (*vidsträckt*) vast **-farbar** untrafficable, impassable; impracticable **-farlig** not dangerous, safe, involving no danger; harmless; (*oskadlig*) innocuous; (*om tumör e.d.*) benign **-fattbar** incomprehensible, unbelievable, inconceivable (*för* to) **-felbar** [-e:-] *a1* infallible; (*osviklig äv.*) unerring **-felbarhet** [-e:l-] infallibility
offensiv I [å-, -'i:v] *s3* offensive; *övergå till ~en* take the offensive **II** ['åff-, -'i:v] *a1* offensive; aggressive **-anda** aggressive spirit
offentlig [å'fent-] *a1* public; (*officiell*) official; *det ~a livet* public life; *~ hemlighet* open secret; *~a myndigheter* public authorities; *~ plats* public place; *den ~a sektorn* the public sector; *~t uppträdande* public appearance **-göra** [-*fent-] announce; (*i tryck*) publish; (*förordning e.d.*) promulgate **-het** publicity; (*allmänhet*) [general] public; *framträda inför ~en* appear before the public **-hetsprincip** principle of public access to official records
offentligt *adv* publicly, in public
offer ['åff-] *s7* (*slakt- o. bildl.*) sacrifice; (-*gåva*) offering; (-*djur; byte, rov*) victim; (*i krig, olyckshändelse*) victim, casualty; *falla ~ för* fall a victim to; *inte sky några ~* shun no sacrifice **-altare** sacrificial altar **-djur** victim
offerera [å-] offer; (*lämna prisuppgift*) quote
offer|gåva offering **-källa** holy well **-lamm** sacrificial lamb; *bildl. äv.* innocent victim
offert [å'färt] *s3* offer (*på* of, for); (*pris*) quotation (*på* for); (*anbud*) tender, *AE.* bid (*på* for); *inkomma med ~* submit an offer; *lämna en ~* make an offer
offer|vilja spirit of self-sacrifice **-villig** self-sacrificing
offi'cer [å-] [-*e*]*n -are* officer (*i* in; *vid* of); *vakthavande ~* officer of the guard; *värnpliktig ~*

conscript officer
officers|aspirant cadet, probationary officer
-grad [officer's] rank **-kår** body of officers
-mäss officers' mess; *sjö.* wardroom
offici|ant [å-] officiating clergyman; officiant
-'ell *al* official **-era** officiate
offi'cin [å-] *s3* (*tryckeri*) printing-office; (*i apotek*) dispensary
offici'ös [å-] *al* semiofficial
offra [å-] (*genom slakt*) sacrifice (*äv. bildl.*);
(*bära fram offergåva*) offer [up]; *bildl. äv.*
victimize; (*avstå från*) give up; ~ *livet för* give
one's life for; ~ *pengar* (*tid*) *på* spend (waste)
money (time) on; *inte* ~ *en tanke på* not give
(pay) a thought to; ~ *åt fåfängan* pay tribute
to vanity; ~ *sig* sacrifice o.s. (*för* for)
offset ['åff-] *s3* offset **-tryck** offset print[ing]
offside [åf'sajd] *s5 o. oböjl. a o. adv, sport.* offside
o|fin (*taktlös*) indelicate; (*ohyfsad*) ill-mannered,
ill-bred; (*opassande*) indecorous; (*lumpen*)
coarse **-finkänslig** tactless, indelicate **-fodrad**
[-ɷ:-] *a5* unlined **-fog** *s7* mischief; *göra* ~ do
(be up to) mischief **-formlig** formless, shapeless **-framkomlig** (*om väg*) impassable;
impracticable (*äv. bildl.*) **-frankerad** *a5*
unstamped, unpaid **-fred** (*krig*) war; (*osämja*)
discord, dissension **-freda** molest **-fredstid**
time of war[fare] **-fri** unfree; (*bunden*) fettered; *på* ~ *grund* on leasehold property **-frihet**
lack of freedom **-frivillig** involuntary; (*oavsiktlig*) unintentional
ofrukt|bar infertile, barren; *bildl.* barren; sterile; (*om t.ex. försök, plan*) unfruitful **-barhet**
infertility; barrenness *etc.* **-sam** barren, sterile
-samhet barrenness, sterility
o|frånkomlig [-åm-] *al* inevitable, unavoidable;
inescapable **-frälse I** oböjligt *s* commoner **II**
oböjligt *a* untitled; *de* ~ *stånden* the commoner
estates
ofta [å-] *al* often; (*upprepade gånger*) frequently; *rätt så* (*ganska*) ~ ever so often; *en* ~
återkommande a frequent[ly recurring]; *så* ~
jag ser whenever I see; ~*st* in most cases, most
often; *allt som* ~*st* every now and then
oftalmia'tri[k] [å-] *s3, se oftalmologi*
oftalmo|log ophthalmologist **-logi** *s3*
ophthalmology **-skop** *s7* ophthalmoscope
o|fullbordad [-ɷ:-] *a5* unfinished, incomplete,
uncompleted **-fullgången** abortive; *bildl.* immature **-fullkomlig** imperfect **-fullkomlighet**
imperfection; ~*er* (*äv.*) shortcomings **-fullständig** incomplete; (*bristfällig*) defective;
(*otillräcklig*) insufficient (*adress* address);
imperfect (*kunskaper* knowledge) **-fullständighet** incompleteness; incompletion; imperfection
o|fyndig (*om bergart*) nonmetalliferous **-färd**
[-ä:-] *s3* calamity; (*olycka*) misfortune; (*fördärv*) ruin; *bringa* ~ *över* bring down calamity
(ruin) upon **-färdig** (*lytt*) crippled, disabled;
(*halt*) lame; (*ej färdig*) unfinished **-färdstid**
period of calamity; *i* ~*er* in times of stress and
calamity **-färgad** (*om t.ex. glas*) uncoloured;
(*om t.ex. tyg*) undyed; natural-coloured **-född**
unborn
o|förarglig harmless, inoffensive **-förbehåll-**

sam unreserved, frank; open **-förberedd**
unprepared, unready **-förblommerad** unreserved; (*rättfram*) blunt; (*osminkad*) unvarnished **-förbränn[e]lig** *al, bildl.* inexhaustible; unquenchable **-förbätterlig** *al* incorrigible (*optimist* optimist); inveterate, confirmed
(*ungkarl* bachelor) **-fördelaktig** disadvantageous, unfavourable; unprofitable (*investering* investment); *i en* ~ *dager* in an unflattering light; *säg inget* ~*t om honom!* don't run
him down! **-fördragsam** intolerant (*mot*
towards, to) **-fördragsamhet** intolerance
-fördröjligen without delay, immediately
-fördärvad unspoiled; (*om smak, moral o.d.*)
undepraved, uncorrupted **-förenlig** incompatible, inconsistent (*med* with); irreconcilable
(*åsikter* opinions)
oföretagsam unenterprising **-het** lack of
enterprise (initiative)
o|förfalskad *a5* (*äkta*) genuine, pure; unadulterated **-förfärad** *a5* undaunted, fearless
-förglömlig *al* unforgettable; never-to-be-forgotten; *en för mig* ~ *...* (*äv.*) a[n] *...* I shall
never forget **-förgriplig** unassailable (*rättighet* right); *säga sin* ~*a mening* state one's
definite opinion **-förgänglig** imperishable,
unfading (*ära* glory); (*odödlig*) immortal **-förgätlig** [-jä:-] *al, se oförglömlig* **-förhappandes** accidentally, by chance; (*oförmodad*)
unexpectedly **-förhindrad** *a5* at liberty (*att
komma* to come), unprevented (*att komma
from coming*) **-förklarlig** inexplicable, unexplainable; *av* ~ *anledning* for some unaccountable reason **-förkortad** [-å-] *a5, se oavkortad* **-förliknelig** [-i:k-] *al* incomparable; (*utan
like*) matchless, unrivalled; (*enastående*)
unique **-förlåtlig** unforgivable, inexcusable,
unpardonable **-förmedlad** *a5* abrupt, sudden;
unexpected **-förminskad** *a5* undiminished,
unabated (*iver* eagerness) **-förmodad** *a5*
unexpected; (*-förutsedd*) unforeseen; *det kom
så -förmodat* it was so unexpected (sudden)
-förmåga inability (*att* to); incapability (*att
göra* to do); incompetence **-förmånlig** *se -fördelaktig* **-förmärkt I** *a4* unnoticed, unobserved; (*som sker i smyg*) stealthy **II** *adv* (*i
smyg*) stealthily; *avlägsna sig* ~ depart
unnoticed (unobserved), take French leave
-förmögen incapable (*till* of; *att* of +
ing-form); unable (*att göra* to do); ~ *till arbete* unable to work, unfit for work **-förneklig**
[-e:-] *al* undeniable **-förnuftig** unreasonable,
irrational; (*dåraktig*) foolish **-förnöjsam** hard
to please (satisfy) **-förnöjsamhet** discontent[edness] **-förrätt** *s3* wrong, injury; *begå
en* ~ *mot* do [an] injury to, wrong **-förrättat**
i uttr.: *återvända med* ~ *ärende* return unsuccessful (*tomhänt:* empty-handed)
o|försiktig imprudent; incautious; (*obetänksam*)
indiscreet; (*vårdslös*) careless **-försiktighet**
imprudence; incautiousness; indiscretion; carelessness **-förskräckt** *a4* undaunted, dauntless,
fearless, intrepid **-förskräckthet** undauntedness *etc.*; intrepidity **-förskuren** unblemished
(*äv. i oförskuret skick*) **-förskylld** [-ʃ-] *a5*
undeserved **-förskämd** [-ʃ-] *al* insolent;
impudent; *AE. sl.* fresh; (*fräck*) audacious;

(*näsvis*) saucy; *en ~ lymmel* (*äv.*) a shameless rogue **-förskämdhet** [-ʃ-] [a] piece of] insolence (impudence); *en ~* (*äv.*) an impertinence **-försonlig** implacable (*fiende* foe); unforgiving (*sinne* spirit) **-försonlighet** implacability **-förstådd** *a5* misunderstood; (*ej uppskattad*) unappreciated **-förståelig** incomprehensible; unintelligible **-förståelse** lack of understanding (appreciation) (*för* of) **-förstående** unsympathetic, inappreciative; *ställa sig ~ till* take up an unsympathetic attitude towards; *titta ~ på* look blankly at **-förstånd** lack of judgement; imprudence **-förståndig** (*oklok*) imprudent, unwise, foolish; (*omdömeslös*) injudicious **-förställd** *a5* undisguised, unfeigned; unaffected (*glädje* joy); (*uppriktig*) sincere **-förstörbar** indestructible, undestroyable **-försvagad** *a5* unimpaired (*kraft* force); unabated (*intresse* interest) **-försvarlig** indefensible; unwarrantable **-försynt** *se oförskämd* **-försäkrad** [-ä:-] *a5* uninsured **-försökt** [-ö:kt] *a4* untried **-försörjd** *a5* unprovided for **-förtjänt** undeserved, unmerited; *~ värdestegring* unearned increment **-förtruten** *a3*, **-förtröttad** *a5* indefatigable; untiring, unwearied **-förtröttlig** *a1* indefatigable **-förtullad** *a5* duty unpaid, uncleared **-förtäckt** unveiled, undisguised; *i ~a ordalag* in plain words **-förtövad** *a5* prompt, immediate **-förutsebar** *a1* unforeseeable **-förutsedd** *a5* unforeseen; unexpected; *~a utgifter* unforeseen expenses, contingencies **-förvanskad** *a5* unadulterated; uncorrupted (*text* text) **-förvillad** *a5* unconfused, not let astray; unbiassed (*omdöme* judgement) **-förvitlig** [-i:t-] *a1* unimpeachable, irreproachable **-förvållad** *a5* unprovoked **-förvägen** daring; undaunted; bold **-förytterlig** *a1* inalienable; *~ egendom* perpetuity **-föränderlig** unchangeable, unalterable; unvarying, invariable; (*bestående*) constant **-förändrad** *a5* unchanged, unaltered; unvaried; *på i övrigt ~e villkor* (*äv.*) all other terms and conditions remaining unaltered; *i oförändrat skick* in its original form, unchanged, unaltered

o|**gemen** (*utomordentlig*) extraordinary; (*oerhörd*) immense **-gement** *adv*, *~ rolig* immensely funny **-generad** free [and easy], unconstrained; (*oblyg*) offhand, jaunty; (*fräck*) cool **-generat** *adv* freely *etc.*; *uppträda ~* behave naturally, be at one's ease

ogenom|**förbar** infeasible; (*om plan äv.*) impracticable, unworkable **-skinlig** not transparent; opaque **-släpplig** *a1* impervious; impermeable **-tränglig** (*om skog, mörker o.d.*) impenetrable (*för* to); *~ för vatten* (*ljus*) impermeable (impervious) to water (light) **-tänkt** that has (*etc.*) not been thoroughly thought out; (*om förslag äv.*) crude

o|**gift** unmarried, single; *~ kvinna* (*jur.*) spinster; *en ~ moster* a maiden aunt; *en ~ farbror* a bachelor uncle; *som ~ before her* (*etc.*) marriage (getting married); *hennes namn som ~* (*äv.*) her maiden name **-gilla** disapprove of; dislike; (*klandra*) find fault with; *jur.* disallow, overrule; *talan ~des* the action was dismissed **-gillande I** *a4* disapproving; deprecating; *med*

en ~ blick (*äv.*) with a frown **II** *s6* disapproval, disapprobation **-giltig** invalid, [null and] void; *göra ~* nullify, vitiate **-giltigförklara** declare nugatory (void); nullify; (*upphäva*) cancel, annul, invalidate **-giltigförklaring** nullification *etc.* **-giltighet** invalidity **-gin** [-ji:n] *a1* disobliging, unaccommodating (*mot* towards) **-gjord** undone; *vara ute i -gjort väder* go on a fool's errand **-glättad** *a5* (*om papper*) uncalendered, antique **-graciös** ungraceful **-grannlaga** untactful, indelicate; (*indiskret*) inconsiderate **-graverad** *a5* (*om fastighet e.d.*) unencumbered; (*orörd*) intact, untouched **-gripbar** *bildl.* impalpable, intangible; elusive **-grumlad** *a5* unpolluted (*äv. bildl.*); (*om lycka, glädje*) unclouded **-grundad** unfounded; (*oberättigad*) unjustified **-gräs** weed; *koll.* weeds (*pl*); *rensa ~* (*äv.*) weed **-gräsbekämpning** weed control (killing) **-gräsmedel** weedkiller; herbicide **-gudaktig** *a1* ungodly; impious **-gudaktighet** ungodliness; impiety **-gulden** *a5* unpaid, unsettled; due **-gynnsam** unfavourable (*för* for, to); disadvantageous; unpropitious **-gärna** unwillingly; (*motvilligt*) grudgingly, reluctantly; *det gör jag högst ~* I am very much against doing it; *jag skulle ~ se att du gjorde det* I should be sorry if you did it **-gärning** misdeed **-gärningsman** malefactor, evildoer **-gästvänlig** inhospitable **-gästvänlighet** inhospitality **-görlig** unfeasible; impracticable

o|**hanterlig** (*om sak*) unwieldy, cumbersome, clumsy; (*om pers.*) unmanageable **-harmonisk** unharmonious **-hederlig** dishonest **-hejdad** *a5* unchecked, unrestrained, uncontrolled; *av ~ vana* by force of habit **-hemul** *a1* unwarranted, unjustified **-herrans** [-ä-] *a* awful **-historisk** unhistorical; historically untrue **-hjälplig** hopeless; (*obotlig*) incurable; (*oförbätterlig*) incorrigible; (*om t.ex. förlust*) irretrievable **-hjälpligt** *adv* hopelessly; *~ förlorad* irretrievably lost **-hjälpsam** unhelpful (*mot* to)

ohm [å:m] *s9* ohm

ohoj [å'håjj] *skepp ~!* ship ahoy!

o|**hyfsad** (*slarvig*) untidy, unkempt; (*plump*) ill-mannered, uncivil, rude, coarse **-hygglig** [*ˣω*:-, *ω*'hygg-] horrible, gruesome, ghastly; (*om t.ex. brott*) atrocious, hideous; *en ~ syn* (*äv.*) a horrid (appalling, bloodcurdling) sight **-hygienisk** insanitary **-hyra** *s1, koll.* vermin (*pl*; *äv. bildl.*) **-hyvlad** [-y:-] *a5* unplaned; (*om bräda o.d. äv.*) rough **-hågad** disinclined; unwilling **-hållbar** (*om t.ex. tyg*) unserviceable, flimsy; (*om ståndpunkt, åsikt*) untenable; *mil.* indefensible; (*om situation*) precarious **-hägn** (*skada*) damage; (*åverkan*) trespass; *göra ~ på* do damage to, trespass on **-hälsa** ill (bad) health; (*sjukdom*) illness **-hälsosam** (*om föda*) unwholesome; (*om klimat o. bildl.*) unhealthy, bad for one's health **-hämmad** unchecked **-hämmat** *adv* unrestrainedly, without restraint **-hämnad** *a5* unavenged, unrevenged **-hängd** *a1, vard.* unhanged, saucy **-höljd** *a1* (*naken*) naked; (*rättfram*) undisguised, unabashed, frank; (*öppen*) open **-hörbar** inaudible **-hörd** [-ö:-] *a5* unheard;

jur. untried; *hans rop förklingade ~a* his cries were unheeded **-hörsam** disobedient **-hövlig** impolite, discourteous (*mot* to) **oidipuskomplex** [ˣåjd-] Oedipus complex **o|igenkännlig** unrecognizable **-igenkännlighet** unrecognizability; *intill ~* beyond recognition **-inbunden** unbound **-inskränkt** unlimited; unrestricted; (*om härskare e.d.*) absolute **-inspirerad** *a5* uninspired **-intaglig** [-a:-] *a1* impregnable, inexpugnable **-intelligent** unintelligent **-intressant** uninteresting; (*tråkig*) dull **-intresse** lack of interest **-intresserad** uninterested (*av* in); *vara ~ av* not be interested in **-invigd** [-i:gd] *a5* uninitiated (*i* in[to]); (*om kyrka o.d.*) unconsecrated; *den ~e* (*äv.*) an outsider **-isolerad** *a5* uninsulated **oj** [åjj] [oh], dear me! **oja** *rfl, ~ sig över* moan (complain) about **o|just** [ˣⲱ:ʃyst] incorrect; unfair; *~ spel* foul play **-jämförlig** incomparable; (*makalös*) unmatched, unparalleled **-jämförligt** [-ö:-] *adv* incomparably, beyond comparison; *den ~ bästa* by far the best; *~ mycket bättre* much better by far **-jämn** uneven (*antal* number; *kvalitet* quality); (*skrovlig*) rough, rugged; (*inte lika*) unequal; (*om klimat, lynne*) inequable; (*oregelbunden*) irregular; (*om väg*) bumpy; *kämpa en ~ strid* fight a losing battle **-jämnhet** unevenness; inequality, irregularity **-jävig** unchallengeable, competent (*vittne* witness); (*opartisk*) unbiased **ok** *s7* yoke; (*träldom äv.*) bondage; *kasta av sig ~et* cast off the yoke; *bringa under ~et* put under the yoke, enslave **o|kammad** *a5* uncombed **-kamratlig** disloyal **okapi** [-'ka:-] *s3, zool.* okapi **okarina** [å-ˣri:-] *s1* ocarina **okben** *anat.* zygomatic bone **o'kej** *interj* OK, okay **o|klanderlig** *a1* irreproachable; (*felfri*) faultless; (*moralisk*) blameless, exemplary **-klar 1** *eg.* obscure, dim; (*om vätska*) turbid, muddy; (*om färg*) indistinct; (*suddig*) blurred; (*molnig*) cloudy **2** *bildl.* unclear, unlucid, vague; (*oredig*) muddled, confused; (*dunkel*) obscure (*föreställning* idea); (*otydlig*) indistinct **3** *sjö.* foul; (*tilltrasslad*) entangled **-klarhet 1** obscurity; turbidity, muddiness *etc.* **2** unclearness *etc.*; confusion; (*osäkerhet*) uncertainty **-klok** unwise, imprudent, injudicious; (*dåraktig*) foolish; (*ej tillrådlig*) inadvisable **-klokhet** unwisdom, imprudence, injudiciousness **-klädd** (*ej färdigklädd*) undressed; (*naken*) naked, without any clothes on; (*om möbel*) unupholstered **-knäppt** *a4* (*om plagg*) unbuttoned; (*om knapp*) undone **-kokt** [-ⲱ:-] *a4* unboiled; (*rå*) raw **-kommenterad** [-å-] *a5* (*om upplaga*) unannotated, not furnished with any commentary (notes) **-komplicerad** uncomplicated; (*om pers. äv.*) simple **-koncentrerad** unconcentrated **-konstlad** (*ej tillgjord, naturlig*) unaffected, natural **-kontrollerad** [-å-å-] uncontrolled, unchecked, unverified **-kontrollerbar** [-å-å-] *a1* uncontrollable **-kontroversiell** uncontroversial **-konventionell** unconventional **-krigisk** peace-loving **-kristlig** ungodly **-kristligt** *adv, ~ tidigt* at an

ungodly hour, outrageously early **-kritisk** uncritical **-kroppslig** incorporeal, immaterial **-krossbar** [-å-] *a1* (*om glas o.d.*) unbreakable **-kryddad** *a5* unseasoned **-kränkbar** *a1* inviolable **-krönt** [-ö:-] *a4* uncrowned **oktaeder** [-'e:der] *s2* octahedron **oktan** [åk'ta:n] *s7, s3* octane **oktant** [å-] octant **oktan|tal, -värde** octane number (rating) **oktav** [åk'ta:v] *s3* **1** (*format*) octavo, eightvo (8vo) **2** *mus.* octave **oktett** [åk'tett] *s3, mus.* octet[te] **oktober** [åk'tⲱ:-] *r* October **oktroj** [åk'tråjj] *s3* charter; (*friare*) licence; *meddela ~* confer a charter **oku'lar** *s7* eyepiece, ocular **okuler|a** *trädg.* bud, graft **-ing** budding, grafting **okultiverad** uncultivated, uncultured; unrefined **oku'lärbesiktning** ocular (visual) inspection **o|kunnig** ignorant (*om* of); *absol. äv.* unlearned; *~ om* (*om att*) (*äv.*) unaware of ([of the fact] that); *~ i engelska* with no knowledge (ignorant) of English **-kunnighet** ignorance (*i, om* of); *lämna ngn i ~ om* leave s.b. in the dark as to; *sväva i ~ om* be unaware (ignorant) of **-kurant** unsaleable, unmarketable **-kuvlig** [-u:-] *a1* indomitable; irrepressible **-kvald** [-a:-] *a5, i ~ besittning av* in undisputed possession of **-kvalificerad** unqualified **-kvinnlig** unwomanly **-kväda** abuse **-kvädin[g]sord** abusive word; *~ (pl)* abusive language (*sg*) **-kynne** [-ç-] *s6* naughtiness, mischief; *på (av)* [*rent*] *~* out of [pure] mischief **-kynnig** [-ç-] *a1* naughty, mischievous **-kysk** unchaste **-känd** unknown (*för* to); unfamiliar; (*främmande*) strange; *av ~ anledning* for some unknown reason; *den ~e soldatens grav* the tomb of the unknown warrior; *en för mig ~ erfarenhet* (*äv.*) an experience new to me; *ta språnget ut i det ~a* take a leap into the unknown **-känslig** insensible, insusceptible (*för* to); (*hårdhjärtad*) unfeeling; (*utan känsel*) numb **-laddad** *a5* unloaded, uncharged **olag** *i uttr.: (råka get) i ~* out of order **olag|a** *oböjl. a* (*lagstridig*) unlawful; (*illegal*) illegal **-lig** unlawful, illegal; (*smyg-*) illicit; *förfarandet är ~t* the proceeding is contrary to [the] law **olat** *s3* vice; *~er* bad habits **oldboy** ['å:ldbåj] *s3, pl äv. -s, sport.* veteran, old boy **oldboystävling** old-boy competition **oleander** [-'ann-] *s2* oleander, rosebay **oledad** *anat.* inarticulate; jointless **olein** [åle'i:n] *s4, s3* [tri]olein **-syra** oleic acid **olidlig** [-i:d-] *a1* insufferable, unbearable, intolerable **oligar'ki** [å-] *s3* oligarchy **oligofre'ni** *s3* mental retardation **oligopol** [-'på:l] *s7* oligopoly **olik** *a5* unlike, different from (to); *vara ~a varandra* be unlike [each other], differ from one another

olika I *oböjl. a* different; (*skiftande*) varying; (*växlande*) various; (*i storlek*) unequal; *av ~ slag* of different (various) kinds; *det är så ~ hur man är* (*äv.*) it all depends [on] how you are; *smaken är ~* tastes differ **II** *adv* differently;

unequally; ~ *långa* of different (unequal, varying) lengths; ~ *stora* unequal in size; ~ *faller ödets lotter* life is a lottery

o|likartad heterogeneous, disparate -likformig diversiform, nonuniform; (*heterogen*) heterogeneous; (*som växlar form*) varying, unequal; ~*a* differing in shape -likformighet irregularity of form -likfärgad (*fler-*) variegated, of different colours; (*av annan färg*) differently coloured -likhet unlikeness (*med* to), dissimilarity (*i* in; *med* to); (*t.ex.* i antal, ålder) disparity (*i* of); (*skillnad*) difference; (*skiljaktighet*) diversity, divergence (*i smak* in tastes); *i ~ med henne* unlike (in contrast to) her -liksidig with unequal sides, unequal-sided; *en ~ triangel* a scalene triangle; ~*t papper* duplex paper -liktänkande *a4, en ~* a dissident, a person holding a different opinion from one's own

olinjerad *a5* unruled

o'liv *s3* olive -grön olive-green -lund olive grove -olja olive oil

olja [å-] I *s1* oil; *måla i ~* paint in oils; *sardiner i ~* sardines in oil; *byta ~* change the oil; *gjuta ~ på elden* (*bildl.*) add fuel to the fire; *gjuta ~ på vågorna* (*bildl.*) pour oil on troubled waters II *v1* oil, grease, lubricate

oljeaggregat oil burner

Oljeberget [å-] the Mount of Olives

olje|blandad mixed with oil -borrning drilling for oil -borrplattform oil-rig -borrtorn derrick -byte change of oil -duk oilcloth, oilskin -eldad oilfired -eldning oil-heating, oil-burning -fat oil drum -fläck oil slick -fyndighet oil deposit -fält oilfield -färg oil paint (colour) -förbrukning oil consumption -grus oil gravel -halt oil content -haltig *a1* containing oil; (*om frö e.d.*) oleaginous -härdad [-ä:-] *a5* oil-hardened, oil-tempered -kaka oil cake -kanna oilcan, oiler -kopp oilcup, oiler -källa oil well -lampa oil lamp -ledning oil pipe; (*transportledning*) oil pipeline -målning oil painting -mätare oil gauge -palm oil palm -plattform oil rig -producerande oil-producing -prospektering prospecting for oil -pump oil pump -raffinaderi oil refinery -rigg oil rig -rock oilskin coat -skiffer oil shale -sticka dipstick -ställ set of oilskins -tank oil tank (cistern) -tanker oil tanker, oiler -tryck 1 *konst.* oil printing, oleography; *konkr.* oleograph 2 *tekn.* oil pressure -utsläpp oil slick (discharge) -växt oil-yielding plant, oil plant

oljig [ˣåll-] *a1* oily; *bildl. äv.* unctuous

oljud noise, din, racket; *föra ~* make a noise

olle *s2* (*tröja*) sweater

ollon [ˣållån] *s7* (*ek-*) acorn; (*bok-*) beechnut, (*koll.*) beech mast; *anat.* glans (*pl* glandes) -borre cockchafer

o|logisk illogical -lovandes [-å:-] without permission (leave) -lovlig forbidden; (*olaglig*) unlawful (*jakt* shooting; *ärende* errand); (*som sker i smyg*) illicit; ~ *underrättelseverksamhet* illegal intelligence activities (*pl*) -lust (*obehag*) [feeling of] discomfort (uneasiness) (*över* at); (*missnöje*) dissatisfaction; (*obenägenhet*) disinclination, unwillingness, reluctance (*för*

for; *för att* to) -lustbetonad unpleasant -lustig uncomfortable, ill at ease; unpleasant -lustkänsla feeling of discomfort (uneasiness) olvon [ˣålvån] *s7, bot.* guelder-rose

olycka *s1* (*ofärd*) misfortune, ill fortune, bad luck; (*bedrövelse*) unhappiness; (*ont*) adversity; (*katastrof*) disaster, calamity; (*elände*) misery; (*-shändelse*) accident; (*missöde*) mishap; *till all ~* as ill luck would have it; *till råga på ~n* to make matters worse; *när ~n är framme* when things go wrong; *hon har råkat i ~* she has got into trouble; *det är ingen ~ skedd* there's no harm done; *en ~ kommer sällan ensam* it never rains but it pours

o|lycklig 1 (*utsatt för -a*) unfortunate, unlucky; (*misslyckad*) unsuccessful (*försök* attempt) 2 (*om människa, liv, tid, äktenskap e.d.*) unhappy; (*eländig*) miserable, wretched -lyckligtvis unfortunately, unhappily -lycksalig [most] unhappy; (*friare*) fatal, disastrous, calamitous

olycks|barn *samhällets ~* (*ung.*) the failures of society, the down and outs -bringande *a4* ill-fated; (*ödesdiger*) fatal, disastrous -broder brother in misfortune -bådande *a4* ill-omened, ominous, sinister -dag unlucky day -fall accident; casualty; ~ *i arbetet* industrial accident; ~ *i hemmet* accident in the home -fallsersättning [industrial] injury benefit, accident compensation -fallsförsäkring [personal] accident insurance; *AE.* casualty insurance -fågel *bildl., vara en ~* be born under an unlucky star -händelse accident; *råka ut för en ~* meet with an accident -korp *bildl.* croaker, Cassandra, *AE.* calamity-howler -plats scene of the accident -profet prophet of calamity -risk accident hazard, risk of accident -tillbud near-accident -tillfälle *vid ~t* at the [time of the] accident -öde unlucky fate

o|lydig disobedient (*mot* to) -lydnad disobedience (*mot* to)

olymp|i'ad *s3* Olympiad -ier [ɒ'lymm-] Olympian -isk [ɒ'lymm-] *a5, O~a spelen* the Olympic Games

o|låst [-å:-] *a4* unlocked -låt noise, din -lägenhet inconvenience, nuisance; (*besvär*) trouble; (*svårighet*) difficulty; (*nackdel*) drawback; *det medför stora ~er för mig* it causes me great inconvenience; *sanitär ~* public nuisance -läglig inopportune, inconvenient; (*illa vald*) ill-timed; *om det inte är ~t för dig* if it is not inconvenient to you -läkt [-ä:-] *a4, ett ~ sår* an open wound -lämplig unsuitable, unfit, unfitted, inappropriate; (*oläglig*) inconvenient; (*inkompetent*) unfit; ~ *som bostad* unfit for habitation -lämplighet unsuitability; unfitness; inconvenience -ländig *a1* rough, rugged -läraktig unteachable -lärd unlearned; unlettered -läslig illegible (*handstil* handwriting) -lönsam unprofitable -löslig *kem. o. bildl.* insoluble -löst [-ö:-] *a4* (*i vätska*) undissolved; (*om problem o.d.*) unsolved

om [åmm] I *konj* 1 (*villkorlig*) if; ~ *du går följer jag med* if you go I will come with you; ~ *du bara vore här!* if only you were here!; *du bör ~ möjligt komma i väg före åtta* you should, if possible, leave before eight; ~ *väd-*

ret tillåter (*äv.*) weather permitting; ~ *så är if so, if that is the case;* ~ *inget oförutsett inträffar* if nothing (unless something) unexpected happens; ~ *inte if not, unless;* ~ *inte han hade varit hade vi inte klarat det* but for him we should not have managed **2** *som* ~ as if; *även* ~, ~ *också* even though (if); *det skall bli färdigt* ~ *jag så skall göra det själv* it will be ready even if I have to do it myself; *det tycks som* ~ (*äv.*) it seems that; *som* ~ *det skulle vara så bra* as though that's any good **3** (*frågande*) if, whether; *de undrade* ~ *de fick komma* they wondered if they could come; *hade ni trevligt? - Om!* did you have a nice time? - Rather!, You bet! **4** ~ *vi skulle gå på bio?* what about going to the cinema? **II** *s* if; ~ *inte* ~ *hade varit* if ifs and ans were pots and pans; *efter många* ~ *och men* after a lot of shillyshallying **III** *prep* **1** (*omkring*) [a]round; about; *en snara* ~ *halsen* a snare round one's neck; *falla ngn* ~ *halsen* fall on a p.'s neck; *försvinna* ~ *hörnet* disappear round the corner; *hålla ngn* ~ *livet* hold s.b. by the waist **2** (*annan konstr.*) *vara kall* ~ *fötterna* have cold feet; *lätt* ~ *hjärtat* light at (of) heart; *tvätta sig* ~ *händerna* wash one's hands; *torka sig* ~ *munnen* wipe one's mouth; *ha mycket* ~ *sig* have a lot [of work] on one's hands; *låsa* ~ *sig* lock o.s. in; *vara* ~ *sig* look after number one, be a pusher **3** (*om läge*) of; *söder* ~ to the south of; *till vänster* ~ to the left of; *vid sidan* ~ *vägen* at the side of the road **4** *lova halvt* ~ *halvt* give a half--and-half promise; *par* ~ *par* two by two, in couples; *de ramlade* ~ *varandra* they tumbled over one another **5** (*om tid: under, inom*) in; ~ *dagen* (*dagarna*) in the daytime, during the day, by day; *långt* ~ *länge* at long last; ~ *lördagarna* on Saturdays; *vara ledig* ~ *lördagarna* have Saturdays off; ~ *lördag åtta dar* a week on Saturday; *vakna tidigt* ~ *mornarna* wake up early in the morning; ~ *natten* (*nätterna*) at (by) night, in the night; ~ *vintern* (*vintrarna*) in winter[time]; *två gånger* ~ *året* twice a year; *förr* ~ *åren* in former years; *året* ~ all the year round **6** (*angående*) about, of; (*över ett ämne*) on; (*beträffande*) as to; *berättelsen* (*drömmen*) ~ *the story* (dream) of; *fråga ngn* ~ ask s.b. about; *fråga ngn* ~ *vägen* ask s.b. the way; *förvissa sig* ~ make sure of; *boken handlar* ~ the book is about (deals with); *kännedom* ~ knowledge of; *slaget* ~ the battle of; *uppgift* ~ information about (on, as to); *en bok* (*föreläsning*) ~ a book (lecture) on; *vi var fem* ~ *lotten* five of us shared the lottery ticket; *de sade ingenting* ~ *när de skulle komma* they said nothing as to when they would come **7** (*efter adj.*) *se adjektivet* **8** (*vid begäran, tävlan*) for; *be* ~ *ursäkt* apologize; *begäran* (*önskan*) ~ request (wish) for; *förslaget* ~ the proposal for; *kämpa* ~ *segern* fight for victory; *spela* ~ *pengar* play for money; *tävlan* ~ competition for **9** (*innehållande, uppgående t.*) of; *ett brev* ~ *fyra sidor* a letter of four pages; a four-page letter; *en säck* ~ *50 liter* a bag holding 50 litres; *en truppstyrka* ~ *500* man a force of 500 men **IV** *adv* **1** (*omkring*) round; *en ask med papper* ~ a box wrapped in paper

(with paper round it); *binda ett snöre* ~ *ngt* tie a string round s.th.; *runt* ~ *i landet* all over the country; *röra* ~ *i gröten* stir the porridge **2** (*tillbaka*) back; *se sig* ~ look back; *vända* ~ turn back **3** (*förbi*) past; *gå* (*köra*) ~ *ngn* walk (drive) past s.b., overtake s.b. **4** (*på nytt*) [over] again; ~ *igen* over again, once more; ~ *och* ~ *igen* over and over again, time after time, time and again; *många gånger* ~ many times over; *göra* ~ make (do) again, remake, redo; *läsa* ~ *en bok* reread a book; *måla* ~ repaint; *se* ~ *en film* see a film again

o|**magnetisk** nonmagnetic **-mak** *s7* trouble, bother **-maka** *oböjl. a* odd; *bildl.* ill-matched; *en* ~ *handske* an odd glove; *skorna är* ~ the shoes are not a pair (do not match) **-manglad** *a5* (*om tvätt*) rough-dry **-manlig** unmanly; effeminate

om|**arbeta** remodel; rework; (*plan*) revise; alter; (*bok e.d.*) revise, rewrite; (*för film e.d.*) adapt **-arbetning** [-e:-] remodelling; reworking; revision, alteration; rewriting; adaptation **-bedja** *han -bads* (*blev -bedd*) *att* he was requested (asked, called upon) to **-besörja** see (attend) to, effect **-bilda** transform (convert, turn) (*till* into); (*t.ex. ministär*) reconstruct **-bildning** transformation, conversion; reconstruction **-bonad** *a5* warm and cosy, snug

ombord [-'bo:rd] on board (*på fartyget* the ship); *fritt* ~ free on board (*förk.* f.o.b.); *gå* ~ (*äv.*) embark; *föra* ~ ship, take on board **-anställd** [person] employed on board a ship **-läggning** [-'bo:rd-] collision **-varande** [-'bo:rd-] *de* ~ those on board

ombryt|a *boktr.* make up [into pages]; *-brutet korrektur* page proof **-ning** making up, make-up

ombud representative; *hand. äv.* agent; (*enl. fullmakt*) proxy, authorized representative; (*juridiskt* ~) solicitor, counsel, attorney, legal adviser **ombudsman** representative, commissioner; (*för bank, verk etc.*) solicitor; (*för bolag äv.*) company lawyer; (*för organisation etc.*) secretary; (*med offentligt uppdrag*) ombudsman, parliamentary commissioner

om|**bunden** *vara* ~ wear a bandage, be tied up **-byggnad** rebuilding; reconstruction; *huset är under* ~ the house is being rebuilt **-byta** *nu är det -bytta roller* now the tables are turned **-byte** change (*underkläder* of underwear); (*omväxling*) variety; ~ *förnöjer!* there's nothing like change! **-bytlig** [-y:-] *a1* changeable, variable; (*nyckfull*) inconstant, fickle; (*ostadig*) unsteady, unstable

omdan|**a** remodel; transform **-are** remoulder; transformer **-ing** remoulding; transformation

om|**debatterad** *a5* much discussed (debated); *en* ~ *fråga* a controversial question **-destinera** divert; reroute **-dirigera** redirect, reroute, divert **-diskuterad** *a5, se -debatterad* **-disponera** rearrange; redistribute **-disponering** rearrangement; redistribution

omdöme *s6* (*-sförmåga*) judg[e]ment; (*urskillning*) discrimination, discernment; (*åsikt*) opinion; *visa gott* ~ show sound judgment; *bilda sig ett* ~ *om* form an opinion of

omdömes|fråga [a] question of judgment (opi-

nion) **-gill** [-j-] *al* discerning; judicious **-lös** undiscerning, undiscriminating; injudicious **o|medelbar** immediate; (*naturlig*) natural; (*spontan*) spontaneous **-medelbarhet** naturalness; spontaneity **-medelbart** *adv* immediately *etc.*; directly; at once, straight off; ~ *efter mottagandet av* immediately on receipt of **-medgörlig** unaccommodating; (*obeveklig*) unyielding; (*motspänstig*) intractable; (*envis*) unreasonable **-medveten** unconscious (*om* of); (*instinktiv*) instinctive
ome'lett *s3* omelette, *särsk. AE.* omelet
omen ['oː-] *s7, pl äv. omina* omen, augury; *det är ett gott ~* (*äv.*) that augurs well
ometodisk unmethodical, unsystematic
om|famna *v1* embrace; *vard.* hug **-famning** embrace; *vard.* hug **-fatta 1** (*gripa om*) clasp, grasp; (*omsluta*) enclose, encircle **2** (*innefatta*) comprise, include; (*täcka*) cover, extend over; (*rymma*) contain; (*ansluta sig t.*) embrace (*en lära* a doctrine); ~ *ngn med sympati* extend sympathy to s.b., regard s.b. sympathetically **-fattande** *a4* extensive; comprehensive; (*utbredd*) widespread, far-reaching; (*stor*) big, great, large **-fattning** extent, scope, compass, range; *av betydande* ~ (*äv.*) of considerable proportions; *i allt större* ~ on an increasing scale, to an increasing extent; *i hela dess* ~ to the whole of its extent, (*i stor skala*) on a large scale **-fattningsrörelse** *mil.* envelopment operation **-fluten** *a5, se kringfluten* **-flyttning** transposition; transfer, removal; *mat.* inversion **-forma** transform; *elektr.* convert **-formare** [-å-] *elektr.* converter; *AE.* generator **-formulera** redraft, reword; (*problem e.d.*) restate
omfång *s7* extent; (*storlek*) size, bulk dimensions (*pl*); (*boktr., beräknat* ~) castoff; (*röst-*) range; *till ~et* in size (scope)
omfångs|beräkna cast off (*ett manuskript* a copy) **-rik** extensive; (*voluminös*) voluminous; (*skrymmande*) bulky
om|fördelning redistribution **-ge** *se -giva* **-gestalta** remould; transform (*ngns liv* a p.'s life) **-gift** remarried **-giv** *kortsp.* re-deal **-giva** surround; ~ *ngt med en mur* (*ett staket*) (*äv.*) wall (fence) in s.th. **-givning** [-ji:v-] surroundings (*pl*); (*miljö*) environment; *han är en fara för sin* ~ he is a source of danger to those around him; *i stadens ~ar* (*äv.*) in the environs of the town **-gjord** remade; reconstructed **-gjorda** [-joːr-] ~ *sina länder* gird up one's loins; ~ *sig* gird o.s. **-gruppera** regroup **-gruppering** regroupment **-gående I** *a4* immediate, prompt; ~ *svar* (*äv.*) reply by return; *per* ~ by return [of post] **II** *adv* by return **-gång** *s2* **1** (*varv*) round, turn, spell **2** (*uppsättning*) set (*kläder* of clothes) **-gärda** [-jä:r-] fence round (*bildl. äv.: about*) **-hulda** cherish, foster; (*om pers. äv.*) make much of
omhänder|ha [-ˣhänd-] have charge of, supervise, manage **-taga** take charge of; *bli -tagen* (*av polis*) be taken in charge; *bli väl -tagen* be taken good care of
om|hölja envelop; wrap round **-hölje** envelope, cover, wrapping
omigen ['åmmijen] again, once more
omild ungentle, harsh (*behandling* treatment);

(*om klimat o.d.*) ungenial; (*om omdöme äv.*) severe
omintetgöra [åmˣinn-] (*gäcka*) frustrate; (*korsa*) thwart
omi'nös *al* ominous; fatal
omiss|känn[e]lig [-ç-] *al* unmistakable; (*otvivelaktig*) undoubted; (*påtaglig*) palpable **-tänksam** unsuspicious, unsuspecting
omistlig *al* inalienable (*rättighet* right); (*oumbärlig*) indispensable; (*oskattbar*) precious; *~a värden* priceless treasures
om|kast *sport.* re-throw **-kastare** *tekn.* [change over] switch (key) **-kastning** sudden change; (*av ordningen*) inversion; (*av bokstäver o.d.*) transposition; (*i vinden*) veer[ing]; *elektr. o. bildl.* reversal; *polit. o.d.* turnabout; (*i stämning*) veering round **-klädning** [-ä:-] changing [of clothes]; (*av möbler*) re-covering **-klädningsrum** changing-room **-komma** die; be killed; *de -komna* those who were killed (lost their lives), the victims **-koppla** *tekn.* switch over; commute **-kopplare** *se -kastare* **-koppling** changing over; reconnection; switching **-kostnad** *~er* costs, expenses, overheads; outlay, expenditure (*sg*) **-kostnadskonto** expense[s] account **-krets** circumference; *i* ~ in circumference, round; *inom en* ~ *av fem kilometer* within a radius of five kilometres
omkring [åmˣkriŋ] round; around; (*ungefär*) about (*trettio* thirty), some (*10 shilling* 10 shillings); at about (*klockan 7* seven); *springa* ~ *på gatorna* run about [in] the streets; *när allt kommer* ~ after all, all things considered; *vida* (*vitt*) ~ far and wide **-liggande** *se kringliggande*
om'kull (*falla* fall) down (over)
om|kväde *s6* refrain **-körning** overtaking **-körningsförbud** *ung.* overtaking prohibited, no passing **-laddning** recharge **-lasta** transship, reship; (*på järnväg*) shift, reload **-lastning** transshipment *etc.*; shifting *etc.* **-ljud** mutation, umlaut **-lokalisera** relocate
omlopp *astr.* revolution, circuit; (*rörelse*) circulation; *sätta i* ~ *a*) (*pengar*) put into circulation, *b*) (*blodet*) set circulating; *ett rykte kom i* ~ a rumour started circulating
omlopps|bana *astr.* orbit **-hastighet** orbital velocity **-tid** period of revolution; (*pengars*) circulation period; *data.* major cycle
om|'lott wrapover **-läggning** (*drift-*) rearrangement, reorganization; (*skatte-*) revision; (*förändring*) change, alteration; (*trafik-*) diversion; ~ *till högertrafik* changeover (switch) to right--hand traffic **-möblera** refurnish; rearrange furniture **-möblering** refurnishing; *bildl.* re-shuffle (*i regeringen* of the Cabinet) **-nejd** *se omgivning*
omnibus[s] [ˣåmm-] [omni]bus; *jfr buss*
om|nämna mention (*för* to) **-nämnande** *s6* mention
o|modern unmodern; out of date (fashion), outmoded; *bli* ~ go out of fashion **-mogen** unripe (*äv. bildl.*); *bildl. äv.* immature; (*grön*) green **-mogenhet** unripeness; immaturity **-moral** (*brist på*) unmorality; (*osedlighet*) immorality **-moralisk** (*sedligt förkastlig*) unmoral; (*osedlig*) immoral

omorganis|ation reorganization **-era** reorganize; *AE. äv.* revamp

o|mornad [-å:-] *a5* drowsy, half awake, sleepy **-motiverad** *a5* unwarranted; (*oberättigad*) unfounded; (*obefogad*) uncalled-for

om|placera put in other positions, rearrange; (*ämbetsman*) transfer; (*pengar*) reinvest **-plantera** replant; transplant (*äv. bildl.*) **-pröva** reconsider; review (*äv. jur.*) **-prövning** reconsideration; review; *ta ngt under* ~ reconsider s.th. **-redigera** (*bok o.d.*) revise **-registrera** reregister **-ringa** *v1* surround; *mil. äv.* encircle **område** *s6, eg.* territory; (*trakt*) district, area, region; (*gebit*) domain, sphere, department, province; (*gren*) branch; *han är expert på sitt* ~ he is an expert in his field **om|räkna** *se räkna* [*om*]; (*valutor*) convert (*t. svenska kronor* into Swedish kronor) **-rörning** [-ö:-] stirring **-röstning** voting, vote; *parl. äv.* division; (*med röstsedlar*) ballot voting; *anställa* ~ put to the vote; *skrida till* ~ take a vote; *sluten* ~ secret ballot, ballot vote

oms [åms] *s3, förk. för omsättningsskatt*

omsedd *få ett sår omsett* have a wound attended to

omsider [åm'si:-] by degrees; (*till sist*) finally, at last; *sent* ~ at long last

om|skaka shake up; ~*s väl!* shake well before use! **-skakad** *a5* shaken (*äv. bildl.*); *bildl. äv.* shocked **-skapa** transform (*till* into) **-skiftare** [-ʃ-] (*på skrivmaskin*) shift key **-skola** *v1* re-educate, retrain; rehabilitate; (*plantor*) transplant **-skolning** re-education, retraining; rehabilitation; (*av plantor*) transplantation **-skolningskurs** retraining (rehabilitation) course **-skriva 1** *mat.* circumscribe **2** (*återge med andra ord*) paraphrase **-skriven** *a5, mycket* ~ often written about, much-discussed **-skrivande** *a4* periphrastic (*verb* verb) **-skrivning 1** *mat.* circumscribing **2** (*återgivande med andra ord*) paraphrase, periphrasis, circumlocution; (*fonetisk* phonetic) transcription; ~ *med 'do'* a 'do'-periphrasis **3** (*omarbetning*) rewriting **-skära** circumcise **-skärelse** [-ʃ-] circumcision

omslag *s7* **1** (*emballage*) wrapping, wrapper; (*bok-*) [dust (book)] jacket, cover **2** (*förändring*) change (*i vädret* in the weather), alteration **3** (*förband*) compress

omslags|bild cover picture (drawing, design) **-papper** wrapping (brown) paper **-revers** promissory note [with collateral security]

om|slut *bokför.* second balancing-up **-sluta** (*omge*) surround, encompass; (*innesluta*) enclose **-slutning** [-u:-] *hand.* total assets **-sorg** care (*om* for, of); (*möda*) trouble, pains (*pl*); *lägga ner* ~ *på* take pains (trouble) with, bestow care upon; *slösa sina* ~*er på* lavish one's care and attention on **-sorgsfull** careful; (*grundlig*) thorough, painstaking; (*i klädsel*) neat; (*i detalj utarbetad*) elaborate (*utförande* workmanship) **-sorgslag** *o~en* [the Swedish] Act on provisions for certain mentally retarded persons **-spel** *sport.* replay; play-off **-spunnen** *a5,* ~ *ledningstråd* wound (taped) wire **-spänna** *bildl.* cover, extend (stretch, range) over; embrace, span (*stora*

områden vast areas) **-stigning** change **-stridd** *a5* contested, disputed, at issue; *en* ~ *fråga* a vexed (controversial) question **-strukturering** change in the structure; (*av industri*) [structural] reorganization **-strålad** *a5,* ~ *av ljus* circumfused (bathed in) light; ~ *av ära* covered with glory **-'styr** *se överstyr* **-stående** *oböjl. a, på* ~ *sida* overleaf **-ställbar** adjustable, convertible **-ställning** adjustment; (*t.ex. t. fredsförhållanden*) adaptation, changeover **-ständighet** circumstance; (*faktum*) fact; *efter* (*alltefter*) ~*erna* according to the circumstances; *de närmare* ~*erna* further particulars (details), the immediate circumstances; *i knappa* ~*er* in reduced (straitened) circumstances; *under inga* ~*er* in (under) no circumstances; *under nuvarande* ~*er* (*äv.*) as it is, this being the case; *utan vidare* ~*er* without more ado (any further ceremony); *den* ~*en att jag har* [the fact of] my having; *befinna sig efter* ~*erna väl* be well considering [the circumstances] **-ständlig** *a1* circumstantial, detailed; (*långrandig*) long-winded, prolix **-störta** overthrow, upset; subvert (*ett samhälle* a society) **-störtande** *a4* subversive (*verksamhet* activity) **-störtning** overthrow, subversion **-störtningsförsök** attempt to subvert **-susa** ~*s av västanfläktar* be fanned by zephyrs; ~*d av sägner* wreathed in legend **om|svep** *s7* circumlocution[s *pl*], roundabout way[s *pl*]; *utan* ~ straight out, candidly; *komma med* ~ beat about the bush **-svängning** swing (veer) round; sudden change (alteration) **-svärma** flock (swarm) around; *en* ~ *flicka* a favourite with the boys **-sänder** [-'sänn-] at a time **-sätta 1** (*växel o.d.*) renew, prolong **2** (*omvandla*) convert, transform (*i* into); ~ *sina planer i handling* put one's plans into action; ~ *i praktiken* put into practice; ~ *ngt i pengar* turn s.th. into cash **3** (*avyttra*) sell, market, turn over; *aktierna -sattes till* the shares changed hands at **-sättning 1** (*av växlar, lån*) renewal, prolongation **2** (*sammanlagt försäljningsvärde*) turnover, sales; (*allm. varuutbyte*) business [volume], trade; (*av arbetskraft*) turnover (*på lärare* of teachers); *börs.* transactions (*pl*), business **3** *boktr.* recomposition **-sättningsskatt** purchase (*AE.* sales) tax **-sättningstillgångar** *pl* current (floating) assets **-sättningsväxel** renewal (continuation) bill **-tag** *AE.* (*gardin-*) tie-back **-tagning** repetition; *mus.* repeat; *foto.* retake **-tala 1** (*-nämna*) mention **2** (*berätta*) tell (*ngt för ngn* s.b. s.th., *s.th. to s.b.*) **-tanke** (*-tänksamhet*) consideration (*om* for); (*-sorg*) solicitude (*om* for) **-tryck** *boktr.* reprint **-tumlad** *a5* giddy, dizzy **-tvistad** *a5* disputed; *en* ~ *fråga* a matter of dispute (at issue), a moot question **-tyckt** *a4* popular, liked; *illa* ~ disliked, unpopular **-tänksam** *a1* considerate (*om* for, of; *mot* towards); thoughtful (*om, mot* for, of); (*försiktig*) prudent **-tänksamhet** considerateness *etc.* **-töckna** darken; (*genom alkohol o.d.*) daze, muddle, fuddle; ~*t tillstånd* state of confusion, daze

o|musikalisk unmusical **-mutlig** [-u:-] *a1* unbribable; incorruptible; (*friare*) inflexible, uncompromising **-mutlighet** [-u:-] incorruptibility; inflexibility

om|val *s7* re-election **-vald** re-elected **-vandla** transform, convert, change *(till* into) **-vandling** transformation, conversion, change **-vittna** give evidence of; *(betyga)* testify **-vittnad** *a5* testified to, vouched for; *ett -vittnat faktum* a certified fact **-vårdnad** care; *ha ~ om* be in (have) charge of **-väg** roundabout (circuitous) way *(äv. bildl.);* *ta en ~* make a detour; *en stor ~ (äv.)* a long way round; *få veta på ~ar* get to know in a roundabout way (indirectly) **-välja** re-elect **-välvande** *a4* revolutionary **-välvning** revolution, upheaval **-vänd** *a5* **1** reversed, turned round (upside down, inside out); *(motsatt)* reverse, opposite; *mat.* inverse; *~ ordning* reverse order; *förhållandet är det rakt ~a* the case is exactly the reverse (opposite); *han var som en ~ hand* he was a changed man **2** *relig.* converted; *en ~* a convert **-vända** *relig.* convert; *~ sig* be converted **-vändelse** conversion **-vänt** inversely; *och ~* and vice versa **-värdera** revalue, reassess **-värdering** revaluation **-värld** *~en* the world around [one *etc.*] **-värva** *v2* envelop; encompass; *vara -värvd av* be enveloped in *(rök* smoke), be encompassed by *(fiender* enemies) **-växlande I** *a4* alternating; alternate; varying *(lycka* fortune); varied *(program* programme); *(olikartad)* diversified **II** *adv* alternatingly *etc.;* *(turvis)* by turns **-växling** alternation; *(förändring)* change; *(olikhet)* variety; *(motsats enformighet)* variation; *som ~* for a change; *för ~s skull* for the sake of variety

omyndig under (not of) age; *en ~* a minor **-förklara** declare incapable of managing his *(etc.)* own affairs **-het** *(minderårighet)* minority; *(fastslagen av domstol)* legal incapacity **-hetsförklaring** declaration of [legal] incapacity **-hetstid** minority

o|målad *a5* unpainted **-måttlig** immoderate; *(om pris, krav äv.)* exorbitant; *(överdriven)* excessive; *(om fåfänga)* inordinate **-måttlighet** immoderation; excess[iveness]; exorbitance **-mänsklig** inhuman; *(mildare)* inhumane; *(barbarisk)* barbarous **-mänsklighet** inhumanity; barbarity **-märklig** imperceptible; *(osynlig)* indiscernible **-märkt** *a4* unmarked; *~ av åren* untouched by the passage of time **-mätbar** *a1,* **-mätlig** [ˣ˞ɷ:-, -'mä:t-] *a1* immeasurable; *(gränslös)* boundless **-mättad** *kem.* unsaturated **-mättlig** *a1* insatiable **-möblerad** *a5* unfurnished

o|möjlig [ˣ˞ɷ:-, -'möjj-] impossible; *(ogörlig)* unfeasible, impracticable; *han är ~ att komma åt* there's no getting at him; *göra sig ~* make o.s. impossible **-möjligen** *se omöjligt* **-möjliggöra** make impossible **-möjlighet** impossibility **-möjligt** *adv, jag kan ~* I cannot possibly

omönstrad unpatterned, plain

onanera masturbate **ona'ni** *s3* masturbation, onanism

o|natur *(tillgjodhet)* affectation **-naturlig** unnatural; *(tillgjord)* affected; *(abnorm)* abnormal

ond *ont värre värst el. a1 (i bet.* 2) **1** *(illvillig)* evil; *(elak)* wicked; *(dålig)* bad *(dröm* dream; *samvete* conscience); *~ aning* misgiving; *i ~ avsikt* with evil intent[ion]; *~ cirkel* vicious circle; *aldrig säga ett ont ord* never say an ill (unkind) word; *väcka ont blod* create ill feeling **2** *(förargad)* angry, vexed, annoyed, cross *(på* with; *över* at; *över att* that); *AE. äv.* mad *(på* at; *över* about); *bli ~* get angry *(etc.)* **3** *(som gör ont)* sore *(ben* leg); *~ tand* aching tooth **4** *det onda a) (t.ex. som ngn gjort)* the evil, *b) (sjukdomen)* the malady (complaint), *c) (smärtorna)* the pain[s *pl*], the ache; *ta det ~a med det goda* take the good with the bad; *den ~e* the Evil One **5** *vara av ~o* be of evil; *fräls oss från ~o!* deliver us from evil!

ondgöra *rfl* take offence *(över* at); *~ sig över att (äv.)* take it amiss that **ondo** *se ond 5* **ondsint** *a1 (argsint)* ill-tempered; *(illvillig)* malevolent **ondska** *s1 evil; (sedefördärv)* wickedness; *(elakhet)* malice, malignity **ondskefull** malignant, malevolent, spiteful

ondul|a [å-] wave **-ing** waving; *en ~* a wave

oneklig [-e:-] *a1* undeniable **onekligen** undeniably, without doubt; *(obestridligen)* indisputably

onjutbar unenjoyable; *(oaptitlig)* unpalatable

onkel ['åŋkel] *s2* uncle

online [ån'lain] *adv* on-line, on line

onomatopoetisk [ånɷ-,-ɷ'e:t-] onomatopoe-[t]ic

onormal abnormal

onoterad *a5* unquoted; *(om värdepapper)* unlisted

onsdag ['ɷns-] *s2* Wednesday; *jfr fredag*

ont *n* **1** evil; *(skada)* harm; *(smärtor)* pain, ache; *ett nödvändigt ~* a necessary evil; *på gott och ~* that cuts both ways; *intet ~ anande* unsuspecting; *göra ~ (orsaka smärta)* give pain; *det gör mig ~ att* it grieves me that; *det gör mig ~ om honom* I feel so sorry for him; *det gör ~ när du nyps* it hurts when you pinch; *ha ~ i huvudet (magen)* have a headache (stomachache); *ha ~ i sinnet* have evil designs; *jag har ~ i ryggen* I have a pain in my back, my back aches (hurts); *jag har inget ~ gjort* I have done no wrong *(skada:* harm); *vad har jag gjort dig för ~?* what harm have I done you?; *vi hade inget ~ av* we were not disturbed (troubled) by *(oväsendet* the noise); *det ligger ingenting ~ i det* there is nothing wrong (no harm) in that; *löna ~ med gott* return good for evil; *jag ser inget ~ i det* there is no wrong (harm) in that; *slita ~* have a rough time of it; *tro ngn om ~* believe the worst of s.b.; *det är inte ngt ~ i honom* there's no harm in him; *inget ~ som inte har ngt gott med sig* it's an ill wind that blows nobody any good **2** *ha ~ om* be short of; *ha ~ om pengar* be hard up [for money]; *ha ~ om tid* be pressed for time; *det är ~ om kaffe* coffee is scarce, there is a shortage of coffee; *det börjar bli ~ om kaffe* coffee is running short

onumrerad *a5* unnumbered; unreserved

onus ['ɷ:-] *s7, pl äv. onera* encumbrance, burden

o|nyanserad without nuances; *(friare)* undifferentiated; *bildl.* oversimplified, superficial **-nykter** drunk[en], intoxicated **-nykterhet** drunkenness; insobriety **-nyttig** useless, of no use; unprofitable, futile

onyx ['ɷ:-] *s2, miner.* onyx

onåd disgrace; disfavour; (*misshag*) displeasure; *komma i ~ hos ngn* fall out of favour with s.b., get into a p.'s bad books **onådig** ungracious; (*ogynnsam*) unfavourable **onådigt** *adv* ungraciously, with a bad grace; *upptaga ngt ~* take umbrage (offence) at s.th.

o|**nämnbar** *a1* unmentionable **-nämnd** *a5* unmentioned; (*anonym*) anonymous **-nödan** *i uttr.*: *i ~* unnecessarily **-nödig** unnecessary; needless **-nödigtvis** unnecessarily; needlessly **-ombedd** [ˣɷ:åm-] *a5* unasked; uninvited **-omkullrunk[e]lig** [ˣɷ:åm-] *a1* irrefutable (*åsikt* opinion); impregnable, invincible (*sanning* truth) **-omtvistlig** [ˣɷ:åm-] *a1* indisputable **-ordentlig** (*om pers.*) careless, (*vårdslös*) slovenly, (*i klädsel*) untidy; (*om sak*) disorderly, (*ostädad*) untidy **-ordnad** disordered; (*om förhållanden o.d.*) unsettled **-ordning** [state of] disorder; (*röra*) mess, muddle; (*förvirring*) confusion; *bringa i ~* throw into confusion, get into a mess **-organiserad** [ˣɷ:år-] *a5* unorganized; (*klandrande*) unordered; *~ arbetare* nonunionist **-organisk** inorganic

o'**pak** *a1* opaque

o'**pal** *s3, miner.* opal **opaliserande** [-'se:-] *a4* **-skimrande** [-ˣpa:lʃim-] *a4* opalescent

o|**partisk** impartial, unbiassed, unprejudiced; *polit.* nonparty **-passande** (*otillbörlig*) unbecoming; (*ej på sin plats*) improper, indecorous; (*anstötlig*) objectionable **-passlig** *a1* indisposed; *vard.* out of sorts, under the weather

OPEC OPEC (*förk. för Organization of Petroleum-Exporting Countries*)

opedagogisk unpedagogic[al]

opera ['ɷ:-] *s1* opera; (*-hus*) opera house **-ballett** opera ballet **-föreställning** opera performance **-musik** opera music **-sångare, sångerska** opera singer

oper|**ation** operation (*äv. mil.*)

operations|**analys** operations (operational) research (analysis) **-bas** operation base **-bord** operating table **-kniv** operating knife **-sal** operation theatre **-sköterska** theatre nurse

opera'tiv *a1* operative **operatris** [woman, girl] operator **operatör 1** (*kirurg*) operating surgeon **2** (*maskin-*) operator **operera 1** *mil. o. allm.* operate **2** *med.* operate (*ngn för magsår* on s.b. for gastric ulcer); carry out an operation; *bli ~d* be operated on; *cancer kan inte alltid ~s* it is not always possible to operate for cancer; *~ bort* remove, have removed by an operation

ope'rett *s3* musical comedy; light opera, operetta

opersonlig impersonal

opiat *s7, s4* opiate

opini'on *s3* opinion; *den allmänna ~en* public opinion; *skapa en ~ för* rouse public opinion in favour of

opinions|**bildande** *a4* that moulds public opinion **-bildare** moulder (creator) of public opinion **-bildning** moulding of public opinion

-mätning *se -undersökning* **-möte** *ung.* public meeting **-undersökning** public opinion survey, [opinion] poll **-yttring** expression of opinion; manifestation, demonstration

opium ['ɷ:-] *s4* opium **-droppar** *pl* laudanum, tincture of opium (*sg*) **-handel** opium traffic **-håla** opium den **-pipa** opium pipe **-rökare** opium smoker **-vallmo** opium poppy

o|**placerad** *a5, sport.* unplaced **-plockad** [-å-] *a5, ha en gås ~ med ngn* have a crow to pluck with s.b. **-plogad** *a5* uncleared by the snowplough **-plöjd** *a5* unploughed **-poetisk** unpoetical **-polerad** *a5* unpolished; *bildl. äv.* unrefined, rough **-politisk** unpolitical, nonpolitical; (*oklok*) impolitic

opossum [ɷˣpåss-] *s3, zool.* (*pungråtta*) opossum; (*pungräv*) [brush-tailed] phalanger

opp [åpp] *se upp*

opponent [å-] opponent **opponera** object (*mot* to); oppose; *~ sig* make (raise) objections (*mot* to); *~ sig mot* (*äv.*) object to, oppose

oppor'tun [å-] *a1* opportune, timely; (*lämplig*) expedient **opportunist** opportunist, timeserver **opportunistisk** [-'niss-] *a5* opportunist **opportunitetsskäl** [-ˣte:ts-] *av ~ for reasons of expediency

opposition [å-] opposition **oppositio'nell** *a1* oppositional (*mot* towards)

oppositions|**ledare** leader of the opposition **-lust** love of opposition **-lysten** oppositional; dissentious **-parti** opposition party; *~et* (*äv.*) the Opposition

o|**praktisk** unpractical; *AE.* impractical **-pressad** *a5* unpressed **-pretentiös** unpretentious **-prioriterad** *a5* unsecured, unprivileged; nonessential, nonpriority **-pris** *det är inget ~* it is not too expensive (quite reasonable) **-privilegierad** *a5* unprivileged **-proportionerlig** disproportionate; *vara ~* (*äv.*) be out of [all] proportion **-prövad** untried, inexperienced; (*ej utprovad*) untested **-psykologisk** unpsychological

op'**tik** [å-] *s3* optics (*pl, behandlas som sg*) **optiker** ['åpp-] optician

opti'**mal** [å-] *a1* optimum **optimera** optimize **optimering** optimization **optimism** optimism; *försiktig ~* guarded optimism **optimist** optimist **optimistisk** [-'miss-] *a5* optimistic **optimistjolle** optimist pram **optimum** ['åpp-] *best. f. optimum, äv. optimet* optimum

option [åp'ʃɷ:n] option **optionstid** option period

optisk ['åpp-] *a5* optical; (*om t.ex. axel, vinkel äv.*) optic; *~ villa* optical illusion

opublicerad *a5* unpublished

opus ['ɷ:-] *s7, pl äv. opera* work, production; *mus.* opus, composition

o|**putsad** *at* unpolished; (*om fönster*) uncleaned **-påkallad** *at* uncalled for **-pålitlig** unreliable; untrustworthy, not to be depended upon; (*farlig*) unsafe **-pålitlighet** unreliability; undependability **-påräknad** [-ä:-] *a5* unexpected **-påtalt** [-a:-] *a4* unnoticed; without remonstrance (a protest) **-påverkad** *a5* unaffected, uninfluenced **-påverkbar** unimpressionable; immovable; unyielding

or *s7, zool.* mite

o|raffinerad unrefined, crude **-rakad** *a5* unshaved, unshaven
orakel [-'ra:-] *s7, s4* oracle **-mässig** *a1* oracular **-svar** oracle
orange [ɷ'ranʃ, -'raŋʃ] **I** *s5* orange **II** *a4* orange **-färgad** orange-coloured
orange|ri [-nʃ-, -ŋʃ-] orangery, hothouse **-röd** orange-red
orangutang [ɷraŋgu'taŋ, ɷraŋu-] orang-utan, orang-outang
oransonerad *a5* unrationed
oration oration **orator** *s3* orator **oratorisk** [-'tɷ:-] *a5* oratorical **oratorium** [-'tɷ:-] *s4* oratorio
ord [ɷ:rd] *s7* word; ~ *för* ~ word for word, verbatim; *ett sanningens* ~ a home truth; *~et är fritt* (*vid möte e.d.*) the meeting is open for discussion; *det ena ~et gav det andra* one word led to another; *det är* ~ *och avsked med honom* he is a plain-speaking man; ~ *och inga visor* plain speaking, no beating about the bush; *använda fula* ~ use bad language; *begära ~et* request permission to speak; *bryta* (*hålla*) *sitt* ~ break (keep) one's word; *få ~et* (*äv.*) get the floor; *få ett* ~ *med i laget* get a voice in the matter; *få sista ~et* have the last word; *ge sitt* ~ *på att* give one's word that; *ha* ~ *om sig att vara* have the reputation of being; *... har ~et ...* is speaking; *ha ~et i sin makt* never be at a loss for words; *i* ~ *och gärningar* in word and deed; *vara stor i ~en* talk big; *lägga ett gott* ~ *för ngn* put in a good word for s.b.; *med andra* ~ in other words, *med egna* ~ in one's own words; *med ett* ~ [*sagt*] in a word, briefly; *märka* ~ catch at words, quibble; *du sa ett ~!* you are right there!; *inte skräda ~en* not mince matters; *stå vid sitt* ~ stick to one's word; *ta ngn på ~en* take s.b. at his word; *ta till ~a* begin to speak; *tala några* ~ *med ngn* have a word with s.b.; *tro ngn på hans* ~ believe a p.'s word; *du måste tro mig på mitt* ~ you must take my word for it; *vi visste inte ~et av förrän* before we knew where we were; *innan man visste ~et av* before you could say Jack Robinson; *välja sina* ~ choose one's words; *överlämna ~et* åt call upon s.b. to speak
orda talk (*om* about) **-grann** literal; word for word **-lag** *pl* words, terms; *i väl valda* ~ in appropriate (well-chosen) terms (phrases) **-lydelse** wording, text
ord|behandling word processing **-behandlare** word processor **-bildning** word-formation **-blind** word-blind **-bok** dictionary **-boksförfattare** lexicographer, dictionary compiler **-byte** dispute, altercation **-böjning** word inflection
orden ['å:r-] *best. f. orden, pl ordnar* order; *få en* ~ have an order conferred upon one
ordens|band ribbon of an order **-behängd** *a5* covered with decorations **-brev** diploma of an order **-broder** brother of an order **-förläning** award of an order **-insignier** *pl* insignia of an order **-kapitel** chapter of an order (the Order) **-regn** shower of decorations (honours) **-sällskap** order [fraternity] **-tecken** badge of an order **-utdelning** bestowal of orders **-väsen** [the] system of orders

ordentlig [år'dent-] *a1* (*noggrann*) careful, accurate (*med* about, as to); (*ordningsam*) well-behaved, well-conducted, orderly (*ung man* young man); (*proper, städad*) tidy, neat; (*riktig*) proper, regular, real, decent; (*rejäl*) thorough, downright, sound (*avbasning* thrashing); *ett ~t mål mat* (*äv.*) a square meal **-het** carefulness *etc.*; orderliness *etc.*; regularity *etc.*
ordentligt *adv* in a careful (*etc.*) way; properly; thoroughly; *sova ut* ~ sleep one's fill
order ['å:r-] order (*om, på* for) (*äv. hand.*); (*uppdrag*) commission; (*instruktion*) instructions (*pl*); *mil.* order, command; *ge* ~ *om* (*äv.*) order; *lyda* ~ obey orders; *på* ~ *av* by order of; *i* ~ on order; *närmare* ~ further instructions; *betala till herr A. eller* ~ pay [to] Mr. A. or order **-bekräftelse** *se -erkännande* **-blankett** order form **-bok** order book **-erkännande** acknowledgement of order, confirmation of an order **-givning** [-ji:v-] *mil.* issuing of orders (an order); *flyg.* briefing **-mottagare** incoming orders clerk **-sedel** order sheet (slip) **-stock** *s2* backlog [of orders], [volume of] orders on hand
ord|fattig (*om språk*) with a small vocabulary **-fläta** *se korsord* **-flöde** flow of words **-följd** word order
ordförande *s9* (*i förening o.d.*) president; (*vid möte*) chairman (*vid* at, of); *sitta som* ~ act as chairman, be in the chair, preside **-klubba** chairman's gavel **-skap** *s7* presidency; chairmanship; *under* ~ *av* under the presidency (*etc.*) of **-stol** president's chair; chairman's seat
ord|förklaring explanation of words (a word); *~ar* (*äv.*) explanatory notes, glossary **-förråd** vocabulary **-hållig** *a1* true (loyal) to one's word
ordi|nand [å-] *s3* candidate for ordination, ordinand
ordinarie [-'na:-] *oböjl. a* ordinary; (*regelmässig*) regular; (*om tjänst*) permanent; (*fast anställd*) on the permanent staff, (*inom förvaltn.*) established; *icke* (*extra*) ~ unestablished; ~ *professor* full professor; ~ *priser* usual (normal) prices
ordinata [-ˣna:-] *s1, mat.* ordinate
ordination 1 *med.* prescription **2** (*prästvigning*) ordination **ordinera 1** *med.* prescribe **2** (*prästviga*) ordain
ordi'när *a1* ordinary; common; average
ord|karg of few words, sparing of words; taciturn **-klass** part of speech **-knapp** *se -karg* **-lek** pun **-lista** list of words, glossary, vocabulary (*över* of)
ordn|a [ˣå:rd-] arrange; *AE. äv.* fix; (*bringa -ing i*) put in order, tidy [up]; adjust (*sin klädsel* one's dress); (*affärer o.d.*) settle; (*reda ut*) get into order; (*reglera*) regulate, order; (*sortera*) sort; ~ *efter storlek* arrange according to size; ~ *med* arrange [for], provide for, attend to; ~ *upp* settle, put to rights; ~ *sig* arrange itself; *det ~r sig nog* things will sort themselves out, it will come out all right **ordnad** *a5* arranged *etc.*; settled; *ordnat arbete* regular work; *~e förhållanden* settled conditions
ordning 1 order; (*ordentlighet*) orderliness,

tidiness; *(metod)* method, plan; *(föreskrift)* regulations *(pl)*; *i god* ~ in an orderly manner; *för ~ens skull* as a matter of form, just in case; *den allmänna ~en* law and order; *få ~ på ngt* get s.th. straight; *hålla ~ i* keep in good order; *hålla ~ på* keep in order; *i ~* in order, *(färdig)* ready, all set ; *alldeles i sin ~* quite right (in order); *i vederbörlig ~* in due course; *göra i ~* get ready, prepare; *göra sig i ~* get ready *(till* for); *höra till ~en för dagen* be quite in the regular course of things; *kalla till ~en* call to order; *återgå till ~en* return to the normal [state of things] **2** *(följd)* course, order; *alfabetisk ~* alphabetical order; *i tur och ~* in turn; *den tredje i ~en* the third **3** *naturv.* order; *stjärna av första ~en* star of the first magnitude **4** *(typ, figur)* specimen
ordningsam *a1, se ordentlig*
ordnings|betyg order mark **-fråga** point of order **-följd** order, succession, sequence **-makt** police; constabulary **-man** *skol.* monitor; prefect **-människa** man *(etc.)* of method **-nummer** serial number **-polis** uniformed *(i storstad*: metropolitan) police **-regel** rule **-sinne** sense of order (method) **-stadga** regulations *(pl)* **-tal** ordinal [number] **-vakt** watchman, patrol; doorkeeper; *jfr -man*
ordonnans [årdå'nans, -'naŋs] *s3* orderly; *(motorcykel-)* dispatch rider **-officer** orderly officer; *(adjutant)* aid[e]-de-camp
ord|rik *(om språk)* with a large vocabulary; *(om pers.)* verbose, wordy **-rytteri** cavilling, quibbling **-slut** word-ending **-språk** proverb **-språksbok** *O~en* [the Book of] Proverbs **-stam** word-stem **-strid** wrangle, verbal dispute **-ström** stream of words **-stäv** *s7* saying **-svall** torrent of words **-val** choice of words **-vändning** phrase **-växling** altercation
o|realiserbar unrealizable, unworkable; *(friare)* utopian **-realistisk** unrealistic **-reda** disorder; *(förvirring)* [state of] confusion; *(röra)* muddle, mess; *bringa ~ i* throw into disorder, get into a muddle (mess); *ställa till ~* cause confusion **-redig** confused; *(om framställning o.d.)* entangled, muddled; *(virrig)* muddleheaded; *(oklar)* vague **-redlig** dishonest **-reflekterad** *a5* unreflecting, rash, hasty
oregano [o're:-, -'ga:-] *s5* oregano, origanum
o|regelbunden irregular; anomalous **-regelbundenhet** irregularity; anomaly **-regerlig** [-je:r-] *a1* unmanageable; *bli ~* *(äv.)* get out of hand **-registrerad** [-j-] *a5* unregistered **-reglerad** *a5* unregulated
oren unclean; *(starkare)* filthy; *(förorenad)* impure *(äv. mus.)*; *mus. äv.* false; *(grådaskig)* muddy; *(syndfull)* unchaste **orena** pollute **orenhet** impurity **orenlig** uncleanly **orenlighet** uncleanliness; *konkr.* dirt, filth
o|rensad *(om trädgårdsland)* unweeded; *(om bär o.d.)* unpicked; *(om fisk)* ungutted **-reparerbar** [-e:r-] *a1* irreparable *(äv. bildl.)*
orera speechify
o|reserverad unreserved; unqualified *(beundran* admiration) **-resonlig** unreasonable; *(halsstarrig)* stubborn, obstinate **-retuscherad** *a5* not touched-up, unretouched
orfisk ['årf-] *a5* Orphic, Orphean

or'gan [å-] *s7* organ *(för* of); *(redskap)* instrument; *(institution e.d.)* institution, body; authority
organ'di [å-] *s3* organdie, organdy
organisation [å-] organization; *facklig ~* trade union (organization)
organisations|förmåga organizing ability **-plan** organization chart (plan) **-tvång** [the principle of the] closed shop, the obligation to join a trade union
organis|atorisk [-'tɑ:-] *a5* organizing, organizational **-atör** organizer **-era** organize
organ|isk ['ga:-] *a5* organic **-ism** *s3* organism
organist [å-] organist, organ player
orgasm [å-] *s3* orgasm
orgel [ˣårjel] *s2* organ **-harmonium** organ harmonium **-konsert** organ recital **-läktare** organ loft **-musik** organ music **-pipa** organ pipe **-register** organ stop **-spelare** organist, organ player **-trampare** organ blower
orgiastisk [årgi'ast-] *a5* orgiastic **orgie** ['årgie, 'årjie] *s5* orgy; *(dryckes- äv.)* revel, carousal; *~r (äv.)* revelry *(sg)*, excesses; *en ~ av färger* a riot of colour
orien'tal [å-] **I** *s3* Oriental **II** *a1* Oriental; Eastern **-isk** *a5* oriental; *(om matta äv.)* Turkish, Persian **-ist** Orientalist
Orienten [åri'enn-] *best. f., r* the Orient; *Främre ~* the [Near and] Middle East
orientera [å-] **1** *(inrikta)* orient[ate] **2** *(underrätta)* inform, brief **3** *sport.* orienteer **4** *rfl (ta reda på var man är)* orient[ate] o.s., get one's bearings; *(göra sig bekant med)* inform o.s. *(i, om* about), acquaint o.s. *(i* with)
orienterad *a5 (inriktad)* oriented *(i norr o. söder* north and south); *polit.* sympathetic *(mot* to); *(informerad)* informed *(i, om* about), familiar *(i* with) **orienterande** *a4* introductory, explanatory *(redogörelse* statement) **orienterare** *sport.* orienteer **orientering 1** *(inriktning)* orientation *(mot* towards); location; *(tendens)* trend, tendency **2** *(införande)* introduction, information; *(översikt)* survey **3** *sport.* orienteering
orienterings|förmåga sense of locality (direction) **-löpare** *se orienterare* **-punkt** checkpoint **-tavla** *(vägmärke)* advance direction sign **-tävling** orienteering race **-ämne** general subject
original [år[i]gi'na:l, -ji-] *s7* original; *pers.* eccentric [person], character; *boktr.* camera-ready copy, mechanical **-förpackning** original packing; *i ~* as packed by the producer *(etc.)* **-handling** original [document, deed]
originalitet originality; *(ngns äv.)* eccentricity **originalitetsjakt** pursuit of originality
original|manuskript original manuscript **-språk** original language **-tappning** *vin i ~* chateau bottled wine **-upplaga** first (original) edition
originell [år[i]gi'nell, -ji-] *a1* original; *(säregen)* eccentric, odd, peculiar
origo ['ri:-] *s9, mat.* origin; *i ~* at the origin
o|riktig incorrect, erroneous, wrong **-riktighet** incorrectness, error **-rimlig** preposterous, absurd; *(obillig)* unreasonable; *det ~a i* the absurdity of; *begära det ~a* demand the impos-

sible **-rimlighet** preposterousness; absurdity **-rimmad** *a5* unrhymed; blank
ork [å-] *s3* energy, strength, stamina **orka** [*årr-] have the strength (power) (*ngt* for (to do) s.th.); *jag ~r inte mer a*) I cannot go on any longer, I am exhausted, *b*) (*äta mer*) I cannot eat any more; *jag ~r inte höra på dig längre* I can't listen to you any longer; *allt vad man ~r a*) (*arbeta* work) one's hardest, *b*) (*skrika* shout) as loud as one can, at the top of one's voice, *c*) (*springa* run) as fast as one can, at the top of one's speed
orkad|ier [-'ka:-] (*inv. på Orkneyöarna*) Orcadian **-isk** Orcadian
or'kan [å-] *s3* hurricane **-artad** [-a:r-] *a5* hurricane-like
orkeslös [*årr-] infirm; (*kraftlös*) effete, enfeebled; (*svag*) feeble **-het** infirmity; feebleness
orkester [å-,-;kest-] *s2* orchestra; (*dans-*) band **-dike** orchestra [pit] **-dirigent** conductor; (*dans-*) bandmaster, bandleader **-ledare** *se* **-dirigent** **-musik** orchestral music **-verk** orchestral work
orkest'r|al [å-] *a1* orchestral **-era** orchestrate **-ering** orchestration
orkide [årki-, -çi-] *s3* orchid
orm *s2* snake; *bibl. o. bildl.* serpent **orma** *rfl* (*ringla*) wind (*fram* along); (*om pers.*) crawl (*fram* along)
orm|bett snakebite **-biten** *a5* snakebitten **-bo** snake's (*bildl.* serpent's) nest **-bunke** *s2* fern **-bär** herb Paris **-gift** snake venom **-grop** snake pit **-lik** *a5* snaky, serpentine **-människa** contortionist **-serum** antivenin **-skinn** (*material*) snakeskin; (*urkrupet*) slough **-slå** *s5* slowworm, blindworm **-spott** cuckoo (frog) spit **-tjusare** [-ç-] snake charmer **-vråk** buzzard
ornament *s7* ornament **ornamental** *a1* ornamental **ornamentera** ornament **ornamentering** ornamentation **ornamen'tik** *s3* ornamental art, ornamentation
ornat official vestments (*pl*); (*ämbetsmans*) robes (*pl*) of office; *i full ~* in full canonicals (*om biskop*: pontificals) (*pl*)
orne [*ω:r-] *s2* boar
orner|a ornament, decorate **-ing** ornamentation
ornito|log ornithologist **-logi** *s3* ornithology **-logisk** *a5* ornithological
oro *s9* **1** [state of] agitation; unrest, restlessness; (*sinnesrörelse*) uneasiness, perturbation; (*farhåga*) anxiety, concern, (*starkare*) alarm; (*nervositet*) nervousness, fidgets (*pl*); *hysa ~ för* feel concern for, be anxious about; *känna ~ i kroppen* feel restless all over, *vard.* have the fidgets **2** (*i ur*) balance wheel **oroa** (*störa*) disturb, trouble, bother; *~ sig* worry (*för, över* about) **oroande** *a4* disturbing, disquieting
orolig *a1* **1** (*rastlös*) restless; (*upprörd o.d.*) agitated, disturbed; troubled (*sömn* sleep); *~a tider* unsettled (troubled) times **2** (*ängslig*) anxious, uneasy, worried, (*starkare*) alarmed; (*bekymrad*) concerned; *vara ~ över* (*äv.*) worry about; *du behöver inte vara ~!* you needn't worry! **-het** *~er* disturbances, troubles, unrest (*sg*)

oromantisk unromantic
oros|ande restless person, rolling stone **-centrum** centre of disturbance **-element** disturbing element **-faktor** element of unrest; disturbing element **-härd** trouble spot **-moln** storm cloud **-stiftare** disturber of the peace, troublemaker; *polit.* agitator
oroväckande *a4* alarming, disquieting
orr|e [*årre] *s2, zool.* black grouse; (*orrtupp*) blackcock **-höna** greyhen **-spel** blackcocks' courtship display **-tupp** blackcock
orsak [*ω:r-] *s3* (*grund*) cause (*till* of); (*skäl*) reason (*till* for); *~ och verkan* cause and effect; *av den ~en* for that reason; *ingen ~!* don't mention it!, not at all!, *AE.* you're welcome!
orsaka cause; occasion
orsaks|förhållande causal relationship, causality **-sammanhang** causal connection
ort [ω:rt] *s3* **1** place; (*trakt*) locality, district; *på ~ och ställe* on the spot; *på högre ~* in higher quarters; *på högsta ~* at top level **2** (*gruv.*) gallery, heading **-namn** place name **-namnsforskning** place-name research, toponymy
orto|cera'tit [å-] *s3* orthoceratite **-don'ti** *s3* orthodontia, orthodontics **-dox** [-'dåkks] *a2* orthodox **-doxi** [-dåk'si:] *s3* orthodoxy **-grafi** *s1* orthography **-grafisk** [-'gra:-] *a5* orthographic[al]
ortolan *s3*, **-sparv** ortolan
orto|'ped *s3* orthopaedist, orthopaedic surgeon **-pe'di** *s3, ej pl* orthopaedics (*pl, behandlas som sg*) **-pedisk** [-'pe:-] *a5* orthopaedic
ortoptist orthoptist **ortoptris** orthoptist
orts|avdrag basic regional tax allowance **-befolkning** *~en* the local population (inhabitants) **-pressen** the local press **-tidning** local [news]paper
o|rubbad *a5, sitta i -rubbat bo* remain in sole possession **-rubblig** *a1* immovable; *bildl.* unshakeable, imperturbable (*lugn* composure); (*fast*) firm, steadfast **-rutinerad** inexperienced; unskilled **-rygglig** *a1* irrevocable (*beslut* decision); unswerving (*trohet* fidelity)
oråd *s7, ana ~* take alarm, *vard.* smell a rat; *utan att ana ~* unsuspectingly; *ta sig det ~et före att* take it into one's head to
o|rädd fearless; (*djärv*) intrepid, daring **-räddhet** fearlessness; intrepidity **-räknelig** [*ω:-, -'rä:k-] *a1* innumerable, countless, numberless **-räntabel** unprofitable, unremunerative
orätt I *s3* wrong, injustice; *med rätt eller ~* rightly or wrongly; *göra ngn ~* wrong s.b., do s.b. an injustice; *ha ~* be in the wrong **II** *a4* wrong; *komma i ~a händer* fall into the wrong hands **-färdig** unjust; unrighteous, iniquitous **-färdighet** injustice; unrighteousness, iniquity **-mätig** unlawful, wrongful, illegitimate **-rådig** unrighteous, iniquitous **-vis** unjust (*mot* to, towards); unfair (*mot* to) **-visa** injustice; (*oförrätt*) wrong; *de -visor som begåtts* the injustices (the wrongs) of the past
o|rörd untouched; intact; (*ej flyttad*) unmoved; *~ natur* unspoiled countryside **-rörlig** immovable; (*stå* stand) motionless (*om ansikte, trupper*) immobile; (*fast*) fixed, stationary
1 os *s7* mouth, estuary

2 os *s7* smell [of smoke]; fumes (*pl*)
osa smell; *det ~r* there's a smell of smoke; *det ~r bränt (äv.)* the fat's in the fire; *~ ihjäl* suffocate by smoke
o.s.a. *(förk. för om svar anhålles)* R.S.V.P., *se under* **anhålla**
o|sagd unsaid; *det vill jag låta vara -sagt* I will leave that unsaid **-sakkunnig** non-expert, incompetent **-saklig** irrelevant; not objective **-salig** *(fördömd)* unredeemed, damned; *en ~ ande* a lost soul **-saltad** *a5* unsalted; fresh *(smör butter)* **-sammanhängande** disconnected; *(lösryckt)* disjointed; *(förvirrad)* incoherent **-sammansatt** uncompounded; *(okomplicerad)* uncomplicated **-sams** *(jfr oense)* bli *~* quarrel *(med* with); *bli ~ med ngn (äv.)* fall out (get at loggerheads) with s.b. **-sann** untrue **-sannfärdig** untruthful, false **-sanning** untruth, lie; *fara med ~* be untruthful, tell untruths; *tala ~* tell lies (a lie), not speak the truth **-sannolik** improbable, unlikely; *det är ~t att han* he is unlikely to
oscill|ator [åʃiˣlaːtår] *s3* oscillator **-era** oscillate
oscillo|graf *s3* oscillograph **-gram** [-ˈgramm] *s7* oscillogram **-skop** *s7* oscilloscope
o|sed bad practice *(hos en pers.:* habit) **-sedd** *a5* unseen, without being seen; unobserved **-sedlig** immoral; *(stötande)* indecent **-sedlighet** immorality **-sedvanlig** not customary; unusual, uncommon **-sentimental** unsentimental **-signerad** [-iŋn-, -inj-] *a5* unsigned **-sinnlig** immaterial; spiritual; *(okroppslig)* incorporeal
osis [ˈoː-] *s3, vard.* bad luck
o|självisk unselfish **-själviskhet** unselfishness **-självständig** dependent on others; *(om produkt)* imitative, unoriginal **-självständighet** lack of independence, unoriginality **-skad[a]d** *a5* unhurt, uninjured; *(om sak äv.)* undamaged; *(om pers. äv.)* safe and sound **-skadlig** harmless; innocuous *(botemedel* remedy) **-skadliggöra** render harmless *(etc.)*; *(gift e.d.)* neutralize; *(kanon o.d.)* put out of action; *(bomb o.d.)* disarm **-skarp** *(slö)* blunt; *(suddig)* blurred, unsharp **-skattbar** *a1* priceless, inestimable, invaluable **-skick** [ˣoːʃikk] *s7* *(dåligt uppförande)* bad behaviour, misconduct; *(oart)* bad habit; *det är ett ~* it is obnoxious **-skicklig** unskillful; *(fumlig)* awkward, clumsy **-skicklighet** unskilfulness; lack of skill **-skiftad** [ˣoːʃif-] *a5* undivided *(dödsbo* estate [of a deceased person]) **-skiljaktig, -skiljbar** *a1* inseparable **-skolad** *a4* untrained; untutored **-skriven** *a5* unwritten *(lag* law); *(som inget skrivits på)* blank *(äv. bildl.)*; *han är ett -skrivet blad* he is an unknown quantity **-skrymtad** *a5* unfeigned, undissembled; sincere, genuine
oskuld *s3* **1** innocence; *(jungfrulighet)* virginity **2** *(orörd flicka)* virgin; innocent; *en ~ från landet* a country cousin **oskuldsfull** innocent; pure
o|skummad *a5, ~ mjölk* whole milk **-skyddad** [ˣoː-ʃyd-] *a5* unprotected *(mot* against, from); *(om läge o.d.)* unsheltered; *(försvarslös)* open **-skyldig** innocent; not guilty *(till* of); *(ej stö-*

tande) inoffensive, harmless; *förklara ngn ~ (jur.)* find s.b. not guilty **-skälig 1** *(orimlig)* unreasonable; excessive, exorbitant **2** *(förnuftslös)* dumb; *~t djur* dumb animal, brute **-skära** [ˣoːʃäː-] *v1* *(besudla)* pollute; *(vanhelga)* desecrate, profane **-skön** *(ful)* ugly; *(ej tilltalande)* unlovely; *(om ansikte o.d.)* plain; *(frånstötande)* unsightly **-slagbar** [-aːg-] *a1, sport. (om pers.)* undefeatable; *(om rekord)* unbeatable **-slipad** *(om verktyg)* unground; *(om glas äv.)* uncut; *(om kniv)* dull; *(om ädelsten)* rough, uncut; *bildl.* unpolished **-släcklig** *a1* inextinguishable; *bildl. äv.* unquenchable **-släckt** *a4, ~ kalk* quicklime, unslaked lime **-smaklig** unsavoury *(äv. bildl.)*; *(obehaglig)* distasteful, disgusting *(äv. bildl.)*
osman [åsˈmaːn] *s3* Osmanli, Ottoman **os-'mansk** [-aː-] *a5* Osmanli, Ottoman
o|smidig unsupple; *bildl.* inelastic; clumsy; *(om pers.)* unadaptable, gauche **-sminkad** *a5* unpainted; *bildl.* unvarnished, plain *(sanning* truth) **-smord** [-oː-] *a5* unoiled, ungreased
osmo|s [åsˈmoːs] *s3* osmosis **-tisk** [-ˈmoː-] *a5* osmotic; *~t tryck* osmotic pressure
o|smyckad *a5* unadorned, plain **-smält** *a4 (om föda o. bildl.)* undigested **-smältbar** *(om föda)* indigestible; *(tekn.* infusible **-snuten** *a3, eg.* snotty; *en ~ lymmel* an unlicked rascal **-snygg** unclean, slovenly, dirty **-sockrad** [ˣoːsåkk-] *a5* unsweetened **-solidarisk** disloyal **-sorterad** un[as]sorted **-spard** [-aː-] *a5, ha all möda ~* spare no pains **-specificerad** *a5* unspecified **-spelbar** [-eː-] *a1* unperformable; *(om musik äv.)* unplayable; *(om pjäs äv.)* unactable **-sportslig** unsportsmanlike, unsporting
oss [åss] us; *rfl* ourselves; *~ alla (andra)* all (the rest) of us; *~ själva* ourselves
1 ost *s2* cheese; *helfet (mager) ~* high-fat (low-fat) cheese; *få betalt för gammal ~* get paid out; *en lyckans ~* a lucky beggar
2 ost I *s2 (väderstreck)* east, East **II** *adv* east; East; *jfr nord*
ostadig unsteady, unstable; *(om väder o.d.)* unsettled, variable; *börs.* unsettled, fluctuating; *bildl.* unstable, volatile
ostan I *r* [the, an] east wind, easterly [wind] **II** *adv* easterly; *jfr nord*
ostasiatisk Far East[ern], East Asiatic
ost|beredning cheesemaking **-bit** piece of cheese **-bricka** cheeseboard
ostenta'tiv *a1* ostentatious
osthyvel cheese slicer (cutter)
ostindiefarare East-Indiaman **Ostindien** *n* the East Indies *(pl)* **ostindisk** East Indian; *~t porslin* old Chinese porcelain
ost|kaka curd cake **-kant** [a piece of] cheese rind **-kniv** cheese cutter (knife) **-kupa** cheese-dish cover
ost|kust *~en* the east coast **-lig** *a1* east[erly]; *jfr nordlig*
ostmassa curd[s *pl*]
ostnordost east-northeast
ostracism ostracism
ostraffad *a5* unpunished; *vara ~* have no police-record **ostraffat** *adv* with impunity
ostron [-ån] *s7* oyster **-bank** oyster bed (bank) **-odling** *abstr.* oyster farming; *konkr.* oyster

O

farm

o|struken *a3* **1** (*om kläder*) unironed; (*om tvätt*) rough-dry **2** *mus.*, *-strukna oktaven* the small octave **-strängad** *a5* unstrung **ost|skiva** slice of cheese **-smörgås** cheese sandwich **ost|sydost** east-southeast **-vart** eastward[s] **ostvassla** whey

o|styckad *a5* (*om egendom*) undivided; (*om djurkropp*) unquartered **-styrig** *a1* unruly; (*oregerlig*) unmanageable **-städad** untidy **-stämd** *a1* out of tune **ostämne** casein

o|stämplad *a5* unstamped; (*om frimärke*) uncancelled; (*om guld, silver*) not hallmarked **-störd** [-ö:-] *a1* undisturbed, untroubled; *i ~ ro* in unbroken peace **-stört** *adv* undisturbedly; *arbeta ~* work in peace **-sund** unhealthy, insanitary; *bildl. äv.* unwholesome, unsound; *~a affärsmetoder* unfair business methods **osv.** (*förk. för och så vidare*) *se under och*

o|sviklig unerring (*precision* accuracy); unfailing (*punktlighet* punctuality); infallible (*botemedel* remedy) **-svuren** *a5*, *-svuret är bäst* better not swear to it **-symmetrisk** asymmetrical, unsymmetrical **-sympatisk** unattractive, disagreeable; distasteful **-synlig** invisible; *göra sig ~* (*försvinna*) make o.s. scarce **-syrad** *a5* unleavened (*bröd* bread) **-systematisk** unsystematic; (*friare*) unmethodical **-såld** unsold **-sårbar** invulnerable **-säker** uncertain, not sure (*om* about; *på* of); (*ostadig*) unsteady, shaky (*hand* hand), faltering (*röst* voice); (*otrygg*) unsure, insecure; (*vansklig*) precarious, risky (*situation* situation); (*tvivelaktig*) doubtful; *vara ~ på sig själv* be unsure of o.s.; *-säkra fordringar* bad (doubtful) debts **-säkerhet** uncertainty; unsteadiness *etc.*; insecurity **-säkerhetskänsla** feeling of uncertainty (insecurity) **-säkra** (*vapen*) cock **-säljbar** unsaleable, unmarketable **-sällskaplig** unsociable **-sämja** *se oenighet* **-sänkbar** *a1* unsinkable **-sökt** unsought; (*otvungen*) natural, spontaneous **-sötad** unsweetened

o|tack ingratitude; *~ är världens lön* the world's reward is ingratitude **-tacksam** ungrateful (*mot* to); (*om arbete, uppgift o.d. äv.*) thankless **-tacksamhet** ingratitude **-tadlig** [-a:-] *a1* blameless; (*oklanderlig*) irreproachable **-takt** *i ~* out of time (step) **-tal** *ett ~* [*av*] a vast (an immense) number of **-talig** [ˈω:-, -ˈta:-] *a1* innumerable, countless **-talt** [-a:-] *i uttr.: ha ngt ~ med ngn* have a bone to pick with s.b.

o|tid *i uttr.: i ~* at the wrong moment; *i tid och ~* (*eg.*) in season and out of season; *fråga inte i tid och ~* don't keep asking questions all the time **-tidig** *a1* (*ovettig*) abusive **-tidighet** abusiveness; *~er* abusive remarks, abuse (*sg*) **-tidsenlig** out of fashion (date); unfashionable **otillbörlig** undue; (*opassande*) improper **otillfreds|ställande** unsatisfactory; unsatisfying **-ställd** unsatisfied; dissatisfied **-ställdhet** unsatisfiedness; dissatisfaction **otill|förlitlig** unreliable; undependable **-gänglig** inaccessible, remote; *vard. äv.* unget-at--able; (*reserverad*) reserved; (*okänslig*) insusceptible, unamenable (*för* to) **-låten** (*hopskr.*

otillåten) forbidden, not permitted; (*olovlig*) unlawful; *sport.* foul **-låtlig** (*hopskr. otillåtlig*) impermissible, inadmissible **-räcklig** insufficient, inadequate **-räcklighet** insufficiency, inadequacy **-räknelig** not responsible for one's actions **-räknelighet** irresponsibility; insanity **-ständig** *a1* unwarrantable, unjustifiable

oting *s7* nuisance, horror

o'tit *s3* otitis

otium [ˈω:tsi-] *s4* leisure; *njuta sitt ~* enjoy one's well-earned leisure (retirement)

o|tjänlig unserviceable; (*olämplig*) unsuitable, unfit (*till* for) **-tjänst** disservice; *göra ngn en ~* do s.b. a bad turn **-tjänstvillig** disobliging **-trampad** *a5* untrodden **-trevlig** disagreeable, unpleasant; (*besvärlig*) awkward, uncomfortable **-trevlighet** unpleasantness **-trevnad** discomfort **-trivsam** cheerless; (*om hem o.d.*) unhomely **-trivsel** discomfort

o|tro disbelief, lack of faith; (*klentrogenhet*) incredulity; (*tvivel*) scepticism **-trogen** unfaithful; (*trolös*) faithless; (*falsk*) false; (*icke rättrogen*) unbelieving, disbelieving; *~ mot* unfaithful (*etc.*) to; *de -gna* the unbelievers **-trohet** unfaithfulness, infidelity (*mot* to) **-trolig** incredible, unbelievable; (*häpnadsväckande*) amazing; *det gränsar till det ~a* it is almost incredible; *~t men sant* strange but true

o|tryckbar *a1* unprintable **-trygg** insecure, unsafe **-trygghet** insecurity, unsafeness **-tränad** *a5* untrained; (*för tillfället*) out of practice (training) **-trängd** *i -trängt mål* without due cause **-tröstlig** *a1* inconsolable (*över* for); disconsolate (*över* at)

otta *i, i ~n* in the early morning; *vara uppe i ~n* get up early; *vänta till domedags ~* wait till doomsday **ottesång** mat[t]ins (*sg el. pl*)

otto'man *s3* **1** (*soffa*) couch, ottoman **2** (*turk.*) Ottoman

o|tukt fornication, lewdness; (*med minderårig*) child assault, *AE.* statutory rape **-tuktig** *a1* indecent, obscene **-tur** bad luck; *ha ~* be unlucky (*i kortspel* at cards); *vilken ~!* what bad luck! **-turlig** [-u:-] *a1* **-tursam** unlucky **-tursdag** unlucky day **-tursförföljd** dogged by misfortune **-tvetydig** unmistakable; (*om uttalande o.d.*) unambiguous, unequivocal **-tvivelaktig** indubitable, undoubted **-tvivelaktigt** *adv* undoubtedly; no doubt **-tvungen** unconstrained, unrestrained; (*ledig*) free and easy **-tvu♦genhet** spontaneity, ease **-tvättad** unwashed **-tydbar** undecipherable **-tydlig** indistinct; (*om uttal äv.*) inarticulate; (*svävande*) vague; (*om t.ex. handstil*) illegible **-tyg** *s7* (*trolltyg*) witchcraft; (*elände*) abomination, nuisance **-tyglad** [-y:-] *a5* unbridled, uncurbed (*fantasi* imagination); unrestrained (*vrede* anger); (*hejdlös*) unchecked, uncontrolled **-tymplig** *a1* ungainly, clumsy **-tålig** impatient (*att göra ngt* to do s.th.; *på ngn* with s.b.; *över* at); (*ivrig*) anxious, eager **-tålighet** impatience **-täck** *a1* nasty, horrid; *AE. vard.* mean; (*ful*) ugly; (*avskyvärd*) abominable; (*besvärlig*) awful (*hosta* cough) **-täcking** ruffian; devil **-tämd** *a1* untamed **-tänkbar** inconceivable,

unimaginable; *det är ~t att (äv.)* it is out of the question to **-tät** not [water-, air- *etc.*]tight; *(om kärl, tak o.d.)* leaky **-täthet** leak **-törstig** *dricka sig ~* drink one's fill *(på* of) o|**umbärlig** indispensable **-undgänglig** [-jä-] *a1* unavoidable; *(nödvändig)* necessary **-undviklig** [-i:k-] *a1* inevitable, unavoidable **-uppfostrad** badly brought up; ill-bred **-uppfylld** *a5* unfulfilled **-uppgjord** *a5* unsettled **-upphörlig** [-ö:-] *a1* incessant; *(idelig)* constant, continual **-upphörligen** [-ö:-] constantly, continually, incessantly **-uppklarad** *a5* unexplained; unsettled; *~e mord* unsolved murder cases **-upplyst** unlit, unilluminated; *bildl.* unenlightened, uninformed, ignorant **-upplöslig** indissoluble, insoluble **-uppmärksam** inattentive, unobservant *(mot* to) **-uppmärksamhet** inattentiveness, inattention; *(förbisende)* inadvertence; *(förströddhet)* preoccupation **-uppmärksammad** *a5* unnoticed **-uppnåelig** *a1* unattainable **-upptäckt** *a4* undiscovered **-uppvärmd** unheated **-ursäktlig** inexcusable **-utbildad** *a5 (outvecklad)* undeveloped; *(för yrke e.d.)* untrained **-utforskad** [-å-] *a5* unexplored **-utförbar** impracticable, unfeasible; *AE. äv.* impractical; *(om plan o.d.)* unrealizable, unworkable **-utgrundlig** *a1* unfathomable; *(outrannsaklig)* inscrutable; *(gåtfull)* enigmatic; *ett ~t leende* an inscrutable smile; *av ngn ~ orsak* for some mysterious reason **-uthyrd** [-y:-] *a5* unlet **-uthärdlig** [-ä:-] *a1* unendurable; intolerable, unbearable **-utlöst** [-ö:-] *a4 (om pant)* unredeemed; *(om postpaket o.d.)* undischarged; *bildl.* unreleased **-utnyttjad** *a5* unused, unemployed; *~ kapacitet* idle capacity **-utplånlig** [-å:-] *a1* ineffaceable; *(om intryck, fläck, skam)* indelible **-utrannsaklig** [-a:k-] *a1, se -utgrundlig* **-utredd** *a5, bildl.* not cleared up; unelucidated *(orsaker* reasons); uninvestigated **-utrotlig** [-ω:-] *a1* ineradicable; *(om ogräs)* inextirpable
outsider [ˣaωtsajder] *s9, pl äv. -s* outsider
out|sinlig [-i:n-] *a1* inexhaustible, unfailing **-slitlig** [-i:t-] *a1* that will not wear out; hard-wearing; indestructible **-spädd** undiluted **-säglig** [ˣω:-, -'sä:g-] *a1* unspeakable **-talad** *a5* unuttered, unexpressed; unspoken *(tanke* thought) **-tröttlig** *a1* indefatigable, inexhaustible; *(friare)* untiring, unremitting *(nit* zeal) **-tömlig** *a1* inexhaustible **-vecklad** *a5* undeveloped; *(om pers.)* immature
ouver'tyr [ωv-] *s3* overture
ovaksam unwatchful
o'val I *s3* oval **II** *a1* oval
1 ovan [ˣå:van] *adv o. prep* above; *som ~* as above
2 ovan [ˣω:va:n] unaccustomed *(vid* to; *(oerfaren)* inexperienced *(vid* at); *(oövad)* unpractised *(vid* in); *(ovanlig)* unfamiliar *(för* to)
ovana 1 *(bristande erfarenhet)* unfamiliarity; lack of practise **2** *(osed)* bad habit
ovan|del upper part; top **-för I** *prep* above **II** *adv* above, higher up **-ifrån** from above
ovanlig unusual, uncommon; *(sällsynt)* rare; *(exceptionell)* exceptional; *det är ~t att ngn* it is unusual for anyone to; *det ~a i situationen* the unusual feature of the situation **-het**

unusualness *etc.*; *(sällsynthet)* rarity; *för ~ens skull* for once, by way of a change; *höra till ~en* be quite unusual, be out of the ordinary
ovanligt *adv* unusually; *(friare)* exceptionally, extraordinarily; *~ nog* for once in a way, extraordinarily enough
ovan|läder *(på sko)* vamp, upper **-nämnd** *a5* above-mentioned **-på I** *prep* on, on [the] top of **II** *adv* on [the] top; *flyta ~ (bildl.)* be superior **-sida** top, upper side
ovansklig [ˣω:-, -'vann-] everlasting; imperishable *(ära* glory)
ovanstående *a4* the above; *av ~ framgår att (äv.)* it will be seen from the foregoing that
ovarium [-'va:-] *s4* ovary
ovarsam *(oaktsam)* heedless; *(vårdslös)* careless
ovation ovation, acclamation **ovationsartad** [-a:r-] *a5* ovationary; *~e applåder* enthusiastic applause *(sg)*
oveder|häftig unreliable; untrustworthy **-lägglig** *a1* irrefutable **-säglig** [-ä:-] *a1* incontrovertible, undeniable
overall [åver'å:l] *s3* overalls *(pl)*; *(småbarns-)* zip suit; *(dam-)* cat suit
overhead|kostnad[er] overheads *(pl)* **-projektor** [åver'hedd-] overhead projector
o|**verklig** unreal; immaterial; phantasmal, phantasmic; *(diktad)* imaginary, fictitious **-verklighet** unreality **-verksam** inactive; inert, passive; *(sysslolös)* idle; *(utan verkan)* ineffective **-verksamhet** inactivity; inertness, passivity; idleness **-vetande** unknowing *(om* of; *om hur* how); *mig ~[s]* without my knowledge **-vetenskaplig** unscientific **-vetskap** *i ~ om ngt (om huruvida)* in ignorance of s.th. (as to whether) **-vett** *(bannor)* scolding; *AE. vard.* calling down; *(skäll)* abuse; *ge ngn ~* give s.b. a scolding, scold s.b.; *en skopa ~* a torrent of abuse; *överösa ngn med ~* heap abuse on s.b. **-vettig** scolding; abusive
o|**vidkommande** [-i:-å-] *a4* irrelevant **-vig** *(i rörelser)* cumbersome; *(klumpig)* heavy, unwieldy, clumsy **-vigd** [-i:-] *a5* unconsecrated *(jord* ground) **-vighet** cumbersomeness *etc.* **-viktig** unimportant, insignificant; *inte helt ~* not altogether immaterial **-vilja** *(motvilja)* aversion *(mot* to), repugnance *(mot* to[wards]); *(avsky)* detestation *(mot* of); *(vrede)* indignation *(mot* with) **-villig** unwilling; *(om pers. äv.)* disinclined, reluctant **-villkorlig** unconditional *(kapitulation* surrender); unqualified, implicit *(lydnad* obedience) **-villkorligen** [-å:-] absolutely, positively; *(obetingat)* unconditionally; *~ vilja veta* absolutely insist on knowing; *han kommer ~ att bli* he is bound to be **-vis** unwise **-viss** uncertain *(om* about, as to); *(villrådig)* doubtful, dubious *(om* about, of); *(obestämd)* indefinite, vague **-visshet** uncertainty; doubtfulness *etc.*; *sväva i ~ om* be in doubt about ; *hålla ngn i ~ om* keep s.b. in suspense as to **-vårdad** neglected; *(om utseende äv.)* untidy; *(om språk)* careless
oväder storm; tempest; *det kommer att bli ~* we are in for a stor
oväders|centrum centre of depression; storm centre **-moln** storm cloud *(äv. bildl.)* **-stäm-**

ning stormy atmosphere
o|**vädrad** [-ä:-] *a5* unaired, unventilated; (*instängd*) close, stuffy **-väld** *s3* impartiality **-väldig** *al* impartial, unbias[s]ed, unprejudiced **-välkommen** unwelcome; (*ej önskad*) undesired, unwanted **-vän** enemy **-vänlig** unkind (*mot* to); unfriendly; (*fientlig*) hostile (*mot* to) **-vänlighet** unkindness *etc.* **-vänskap** enmity **-väntad** *a5* unexpected; *detta kom[mer] alldeles -väntat* (*äv.*) this comes quite as a surprise **-värderlig** [-de:r-] *al* invaluable, inestimable, priceless **-värdig** unworthy (*ngn* of s.b.; *ngt* of s.th.); (*oförtjänt*) undeserving (*ngn* to s.b.); *det är dig ~t* it is beneath you **-världslig** unworldly **-väsen** noise, din; (*bråk*) row **-väsentlig** unessential, unimportant (*för* to); immaterial (*skillnad* difference) **-väsentlighet** *~er* unessential things, unessentials, trifles
oxalsyra [åk*sa:l-] oxalic acid
ox|bringa brisket of beef **-drivare** ox-driver
oxe *s2* ox (*pl* oxen)
oxel ['ɷksel] *s2, bot.* whitebeam
oxeltand molar [tooth], grinder
oxfilé fillet of beef
oxfordgrupprörelsen [*åksfård-] the Oxford Group Movement; Moral Rearmament
oxhud oxhide
oxid [åk'si:d] *s3* oxide **oxidation** oxidation **oxidationsmedel** oxidizer, oxidant **oxidera** oxidize **oxidering** oxidization, oxidation **oxi'dul** *s3* protoxide, suboxide
ox|kärra ox-cart **-kött** beef **-rulad** beef roll **-stek** joint (sirloin) of beef **-svanssoppa** oxtail soup **-tunga 1** oxtongue **2** *bot.* alkanet **-öga** *teat.* bull's eye
ozelot [ɷse'lått] *s3, zool.* ocelot
ozon [ɷ'så:n, å-] *s3, s4, kem.* ozone **-haltig** *al* ozonic **-lager, -skikt** ozone layer
oår *se missväxtår, nödår*
o|**återhållsam** incontinent; (*i mat o. dryck*) immoderate; (*omåttlig*) intemperate **-återkallelig** *al* irrevocable **-återkalleligen** irrevocably, beyond recall **-åtkomlig** inaccessible (*för* to); *vara ~ för* (*äv.*) be unassailable by, be out of reach of
o|**ädel** ignoble, base, mean; (*om metall*) base, nonprecious **-äkta** *oböjl. a* false, not genuine; (*imiterad*) imitation, mock, artificial; (*hycklad*) spurious; (*förfalskad*) counterfeit; *~ barn* illegitimate child; *~ diamanter* imitation (false) diamonds **-ändlig** [-'änd-, *ɷ:-] *al* endless, interminable; (*utan gräns äv.*) boundless; (*mat. o. friare*) infinite; *i det ~a* ad infinitum, for ever and ever, indefintely **-ändlighet** [-'änd-, *ɷ:-] endlessness; infinity (*äv. ~en*); *han pratade i all ~* he talked endlessly (for no end of a time) **-ändlighetstecken** infinity sign (symbol) **-ändligt** [-'änd-, *ɷ:-] *adv* endlessly *etc.*; *~ liten* (*äv.*) infinitesimal **-ärlig** dishonest **-ärlighet** dishonesty **-ätbar** uneatable *etc. se -ätbar*; (*om svamp*) inedible **-även** *a3, inte ~* not bad (amiss) (*som* as); *inte så ~* (*vard.*) not half bad
o|**öm** robust, tough; (*hållbar*) durable (*tyg* cloth) **-önskad** unwanted **-öppnad** *a5* unopened **-övad** unpractised *etc.* (*jfr öva*); (*otränad*) untrained, (*för tillfället*) out of practice; (*om

trupper) undisciplined
o|**över|komlig** insurmountable, insuperable; (*om pris*) exorbitant, prohibitive **-lagd** unpremeditated; (*-tänkt*) ill-considered; (*obetänksam*) rash, hasty **-satt** *a4* untranslated; *en ännu ~ bok* a book not yet translated (*till* into) **-skådlig** incalculable, unforeseeable (*följder* consequences); (*oredig*) badly arranged (*uppsats* essay); (*enorm*) immense, boundless **-stiglig** [-i:g-] *al* unsurmountable; *bildl. äv.* insuperable **-sättlig** untranslatable **-träffad** *a5* unsurpassed **-träffbar** *al* unsurpassable; (*fulländad*) perfect, consummate **-tänkt** *a4, se -lagd* **-vinn[e]lig** *al* invincible; unconquerable; (*ointaglig*) impregnable; (*om svårighet*) insuperable

P

p [pe:] *s6, s7* p; *sätta ~ för* put a stop to
pacemaker ['pejsmejker] *s2, s9, med., sport.*
pacemaker, pacer
pacificer|a pacify **-ing** pacification
pacif|ism pacifism **-ist** pacifist **-istisk** *a5* pacifist
1 pack *s7* (*slödder*) mob, rabble; *ett riktigt ~ a* lot of riffraff, a pack of scoundrels
2 pack *se pick och pack*
packa pack; (*~ full*[*t*]) cram; *~ ihop a*) pack together, *b*) (*dra sig tillbaka*) shut up shop, close down; *~ ihop sig a*) (*om pers.*) squeeze (crowd) together, *b*) (*om snö o.d.*) pack, get packed; *~ in* pack up (*i en låda* in a box); *~ ner ngt i* pack s.th. into; *~ om* repack; *~ upp* unpack; *rummet var ~t med folk* the room was packed (crammed) with people; *stå som ~de sillar* be packed like sardines; *~ sig* (*om snö*) pack; *~ sig av* (*i väg*) make (pack, bundle) off; *~ dig i väg!* be off with you!, clear out!
packad packed; (*berusad*) tight, stoned, loaded
packdjur beast of burden, pack animal
pack|e *s2* package; bundle; (*hög*) pile, heap **-hus** warehouse; (*tull-*) custom-house **-huspengar** warehouse charges **-häst** packhorse **-is** pack ice **-lår** packing-case **-ning 1** (*-ande*) packing *etc., se packa* **2** *mil. o.d.* pack, kit; (*bagage*) luggage; *med full ~* (*mil.*) in full marching kit **3** *tekn.* packing; gasket **-sadel** packsaddle **-sedel** packing list, delivery note **-åsna** pack-ass; *bildl.* beast of burden
padda *s1* toad
paddel ['padd-] *s2* paddle **-kanot** canoe **-åra** paddle
paddl|a paddle **-ing** paddling, canoeing
paff I *interj* pop!, bang!, **II** *oböjl. a, bli ~* be dumbfounded
page [pa:ʃ] *s5* page [boy] **-hår** page-boy coiffure
pagin|a ['pa:-] *s1* page **-era** paginate, page **-ering** paging, pagination
pagod [-'gå:d, -ɷ:-] *s3* pagoda
pain riche *s9, s7* French loaf
paj [pajj] *s3* pie
paja [ˣpajja] *vard.* break down
pajas ['pajj-] *s3, s2* clown, buffoon, merry--andrew; *spela ~* play the fool **-konster** *pl* clown's tricks; buffoonery (*sg*)
paj|botten piecrust **-form** pie plate **-kastning** throwing pies **-skal** pie shell
pa'ket *s7, s3* parcel, packet; package; *slå i ett ~* wrap (do) up a parcel; *slå in ngt i ~* make a parcel of s.th.; *ett ~ cigaretter* a packet (*AE.* pack) of cigarettes; *skicka som ~* send by parcel-post **-bil** delivery van **-cykel** carrier cycle **-era** pack[et], parcel up **-ering** packeting, packaging **-gods** *koll.* parcel-goods (*pl*) **-hylla** luggage rack **-hållare** [luggage] carrier

-inlämning (*post-*) parcel counter; (*för förvaring*) receiving office **-lösning** package solution **-post** parcel-post **-resa** package tour **-utlämning** delivery office
pakist|anare [-ˣta:-] Pakistani **-'ansk** [-a:-] *a5* Pakistani
pakt *s3* pact, treaty; covenant; *ingå en ~* conclude (make) a pact **paktum** *s8, se pakt*; (*äktenskapsförord*) marriage articles (*pl*)
pala'din *s3* paladin
palan'kin *s3* palanquin, palankeen
pala'tal I *a1* palatal **II** *s2* palatal **-isera** palatalize
palats *s7* palace **-liknande** palatial **-revolution** palace revolution
pa'laver *s3* palaver
paleo|'graf [-å-] *s3* palaeographer **-gra'fi** *s3* palaeography **-litisk** [-'li:-] *a5* palaeolithic
paleonto|log [-ånto-] palaeontologist **-logi** *s3* palaeontology **-logisk** *a5* palaeontological
Palestina [-ˣsti:-] *n* Palestine
palest|inier [-'ti:-] Palestinian **-insk** [-'ti:-] *a5* Palestinian
pa'lett *s3* palette; pallet **-kniv** palette knife
pale'tå *s3* overcoat, paletot
palim'psest *s3* palimpsest
palindrom [-'drå:m] *s3* palindrome
palis'sad *s3* palisade; fencing
pal'jett *s3* spangle, paillette **-era** spangle
pall *s2* stool; (*fot-*) footstool, footrest; (*last-*) pallet; (*gruv-*) stope; *stå ~* (*vard.*) stand up to, cope **palla** *~ under* wedge up; *~ upp* trestle, block up
pallia'tiv *s7* palliative
pallra *rfl, ~ sig av* (*i väg*) toddle off; *~ sig upp ur sängen* get o.s. out of bed
palm *s3* palm **-i'tinsyra** palmitic acid **-liknande** palmaceous **-olja** palm oil **-söndag** Palm Sunday (*äv. ~en*) **-vin** palm wine
palpera palpate
palsternacka *s1* parsnip
palta *~ på ngn* (*sig*) wrap s.b. (o.s.) up well
paltbröd blood bread
paltor *pl* rags
pam'flett *s3* libel[lous pamphlet], lampoon **-ist** libeller, lampoonist
pamp *s2* **1** *pers.* bigwig, tycoon, big gun (*AE.* shot) **2** (*huggvärja*) straight sword, broadsword
pampas ['pamm-] *pl* pampas (*pl*)
pampig *a1* grand, magnificent; *vard.* swell
pam'pusch *s3* overshoe; *~er* (*äv.*) rubbers, *AE.* galoshes
panafri'kansk [-a:-] Pan-African
panamahatt [-ˣma:-, 'pann-] panama [hat]
Panamakanalen [-ˣma:-, 'pann-] the Panama Canal
pana'm|an *s3* Panamanian **-'ansk** [-a:-] *a5* Panamanian
panamerikanism Pan-Americanism
panasch [-'naʃ] *s3* crest; panache
panegy'r|ik *s3* panegyric **-isk** [-'gy:-] *a5* panegyric[al]
pa'nel *s3* **1** (*vägg- o.d.*) wainscot, panel [work]; (*golvlist*) skirting [board], *AE.* baseboard **2** (*grupp av pers.*) panel
pa'nel|a panel; wainscot **-debatt** panel discussion; *deltagare i ~* panellist **-höna** wallflower

panera coat (dress) with egg and bread crumbs
panflöjt [ˣpaːn-] panpipe[s *pl*], syrinx
pang bang!, crack! **panga** *vard.* smash **panggrej** *vard.* smasher **-pangsuccé** smash-hit
pa'nik *s3* panic; *gripas av* ~ be seized with panic **-artad** [aːr-] *a5* panic[ky]; ~ *flykt* (*äv.*) stampede **-känsla** sense (feeling) of panic **-slagen** panic-stricken, panic-struck **-stämning** atmosphere (feeling) of panic **-unge** minor panic
panisk ['paː-] *a5*, ~ *förskräckelse för* terror of
pank *oböjl. a* broke, penniless
pankreas[körtel] [ˣpaŋk-] *s3* [*s2*] pancreas
pankromatisk [-'maː-] panchromatic
1 panna *s1* **1** (*kokkärl*) pan **2** (*värme-*) furnace; (*ång-*) boiler
2 panna *s1*, *anat.* forehead; brow; *rynka ~n* knit one's brow[s *pl*]; *med rynkad* ~ (*äv.*) frowning; *skjuta sig en kula för ~n* blow out one's brains; *ta sig för ~n* strike one's brow in dismay; *stöta ngn för ~n* mortally offend s.b.; *ha* ~ (*fräckheten*) *att* have the cheek to
pannben frontal bone
pannbiff *ung.* hamburger
pannbindel frontlet; (*bandage*) forehead bandage
pannkak|a pancake; *grädda -or* fry (make) pancakes; *det blev* ~ *av alltsammans* it all fell flat [as a pancake] **pannkakssmet** pancake batter
pann|lampa head torch (lamp) **-lob** frontal lobe **-lugg** fringe, forelock
pannrum boiler room; furnace room; *sjö.* boiler room, stokehold
pannsmycke diadem, frontlet
pannsten [boiler] scale
pan'nå *s3* panel
panoptikon [-'nåptikån] *s7* waxworks (*sg*), waxwork show
panorama [-åˈraː-, -ˣraː-, *äv.* -ɷ-] *s7, s9* panorama
pansar *s7* **1** armour (*äv. bildl.*) **2** (*vissa djurs*) carapace **-bil** armoured car **-fartyg** armoured vessel; *hist.* ironclad **-förband** armoured unit **-hinder** dragon's teeth **-kryssare** armoured cruiser **plåt** armour plate; *koll.* armour plating **-skepp** *se -fartyg* **-skjorta** shirt (coat) of mail **-trupper** *pl* armoured troops **-vagn** *se -bil*; (*stridsvagn*) tank **-värnskanon** antitank gun
panslavism Pan-Slavism
pansra armour[plate]
pant *s3* pledge; (*säkerhet*) security; (*under-, inteckning*) mortgage; (*i -lek*) forfeit; *lämna* ~ give security; *lämna* (*ta*) *i* ~ give in (take) pledge; *lösa in en* ~ redeem a pledge; *sätta sin heder* (*sitt huvud*) *i* ~ *på* stake one's honour (head) on; *förfallna -er* forfeited pledges; *ställda -er* pledged securities
pantalonger [-'låŋ-] *pl* pantaloons, pants
pantbank pawnshop, pawnbroker's [shop]; *~en* (*vard. äv.*) uncle's
pante|ism pantheism **-ist** pantheist **-istisk** *a5* pantheistic[al]
panteon ['panteån] *n* pantheon
panter ['pann-] *s2* panther **-hona** female panther
pant|förskriva mortgage, pledge **-förskrivning**

mortgage deed, pledge, hypothecation **-kvitto** pawn ticket **-lek** game of forfeits **-lånare** pawnbroker; *~n* (*vard. äv.*) uncle **-lånekontor** *se pantbank*
panto'mim *s3* pantomime, dumb show **-isk** *a5* pantomimic
pant|rätt lien **-sedel** *se pantkvitto* **-sätta** pledge; give as [a] security, mortgage, hypothecate; (*i -bank*) pawn
papegoj|a [-ˣgåjja, ˣpapp-] *s1* parrot **-sjuka** parrot fever, psittacosis **-tulpan** parrot tulip
papier-maché [pap'je:ma'ʃeː] *s3* papier-mɳché
papil'jott [-å-] *s3* curler; *lägga upp håret på ~er* put one's hair in curlers
pa'pill *s3* papilla (*pl* papillae)
pap|ism papism **-ist** papist **-istisk** *a5* papistic[al]
papjemaché [papjema'ʃeː] *s3* papier-mɳché
papp *s3, s7* [paste]board; (*kartong*) cardboard
pappa *s1* father (*till* of); *vard.* dad[dy], pa[pa], *AE. äv.* pop
pappask cardboard box; carton
pappenheimare [-j-] *jag känner mina ~!* I know my customers!
papper *s7* **1** paper; *ett* ~ a piece of paper; *sätta på -et* (*nedteckna*) put down on paper; *det finns endast på -et* it exists only on paper **2** (*dokument, skriftlig handling*) document; *gamla* ~ ancient documents; *kunna visa* ~ *på att* have papers to show that, be able to show documentary evidence that; *lägga ~en på bordet* put one's cards on the table; *ha klara* ~ have the necessary documents [in order] **3** (*värde-*) security; *koll. äv.* stock; (*legitimations-*) [identification] papers (*pl*)
pappers|ark sheet of paper **-avfall** waste paper **-bruk** paper mill **-bägare** paper drinking-cup **-docka** paper doll **-exercis** paperwork, red tape **-fabrik** *se -bruk* **-handduk** paper towel **-handel** stationer's [shop] **-industri** paper industry **-kasse** paper carrier **-klämma** paperclip **-kniv** paperknife **-korg** wastepaper basket (bin); *AE.* wastebasket; (*utomhus*) litter bin **-kvarn** *bildl.* bureaucratic machinery, red tape **-lapp** scrap (slip) of paper **-massa** [papermaking] pulp **-mugg** paper drinking-cup **-näsduk** paper handkerchief **-pengar** *pl* paper money (currency) (*sg*) **-påse** paper bag **-remsa** slip of paper **-rulle** roll (reel) of paper **-servett** paper napkin **-svala** paper dart **-tallrik** paper plate **-tiger** paper tiger **-tillverkning** papermaking, manufacture of paper **-tuss** paper pellet (ball) **-varor** *pl* paper articles (goods); (*som säljs i -handel*) stationery (*sg*)
papp|kartong cardboard box **-skiva** piece of cardboard (*etc.*) **-slöjd** cardboard modelling
paprika ['paː-, 'papp-] *s1* paprika
papyrus [-'py:-] *best. f. -en el. papyren, pl papyrer* papyrus **-rulle** papyrus roll
par *s7* **1** (*två sammanhörande*) pair; (*äkta, älskande* ~ *e.d.*) couple; *ett* ~ *skor* (*glasögon, byxor*) a pair of shoes (glasses, trousers); *ett äkta* (*nygift*) ~ a married (newly-married) couple; *ett älskande* ~ a pair of lovers; *ett omaka* ~ *a*) (*om pers.*) an ill-matched couple *b*) (*om saker*) two odd shoes (gloves *etc.*); *2 pund ~et* 2 pounds a (per the) pair, 2 pounds

the two of them; *gå ~ om ~* walk in pairs (couples), walk two and two; *gå i ~* go in couples (together) **2** *(några) ett ~* a couple of, a few; *ett ~ gånger* once or twice, a couple of times; *ett ~ tre gånger* two or three times; *om ett ~ veckor* in a few (a couple of) weeks, in a week or two; *ett ~ och tjugo* twenty odd **para** *biol.* mate, pair; *bildl.* unite, couple; *~ ihop* pair, mate; *avund ~d med beundran* envy coupled with admiration; *~ sig* mate, pair, copulate
parabel *s3* **1** *mat.* parabola **2** *(liknelse)* parable
parabol|antenn [-ˣbå:l-] paraboloidal aerial, satellite disc *(AE.* disk) **-isk** [-'bå:-] *a5, mat.* parabolic
pa'rad *s3* **1** *(truppmönstring)* parade; *stå på ~* be on show **2** *(-dräkt)* full dress, full-dress uniform **3** *fäktn.* parry **-era** parade; *(ståta äv.)* show off
para'digm *s7* paradigm **-skifte** paradigmatic shift
paradis *s7* paradise; *~et* Paradise; *~ets lustgård* the Garden of Eden; *ett ~ på jorden* a heaven on earth **-dräkt** *i ~* in one's birthday suit **-fågel** bird of paradise **-isk** [-'di:-] *a5* paradisiac[al]; heavenly **-äpple** *bot.* crab [apple]
parad|marsch parade march **-nummer** showpiece
paradox [-'dåks] *s3* paradox **-'al** *a1* paradoxical
parad|säng bed of state **-uniform** full-dress uniform
paraf'fin *s4, s3* solid paraffin, paraffin wax **-era** paraffin **-olja** liquid paraffin; *AE.* paraffin oil
para'fras *s3* paraphrase **-era** paraphrase
paragraf *s3* paragraph; *(i lagtext* [*o.* numrerad]) section; *(i traktat o.d.)* article, clause **-ryttare** formalist; red-tapist **-tecken** section mark
paraguay|'an *s3* Paraguayan **-are** [-uˣajare] Paraguayan **-'ansk** [-a:-] Paraguayan
parallaktisk [-'lack-] *a5* parallactic **paral'lax** *s3* parallax
paral'lell I *s3* parallel ; *dra en ~ mellan* draw a parallel between **II** *a1* parallel **-epi'ped** *s3* parallelepiped **-fall** parallel case **-gata** parallel street **-ism** parallelism **-klass** parallel class (form) **-koppling** parallel connection **-ogram** [-'gramm] *s3* parallelogram
parallell|t *adv, gå ~ med* be parallel with (to) **-trapets** trapezium, *AE.* trapezoid
para|lysera paralyze **-ly'si** *s3* paralysis **-lytiker** [-'ly:-] *s9* paralytic **-lytisk** [-'ly:-] *a5* paralytic
paramagnetism paramagnetism
parameter [-'me:-] *s2* parametr
paranoia [-ˣnåja] *s1* paranoia **paranoid** [-å'i:d] *a5, n sg obest. f. undviks* paranoiac **paranoiker** [-'nå:i-] paranoiac
parant [-'rant, -'raŋt] *a1* very elegant, striking, smart, stylish
paranöt brazil nut
paraplegiker [-'ple:-] paraplegic
para'ply *s7, s3* umbrella; *spänna upp (fälla ner) ~et* put up (close) the umbrella **-fodral** umbrella cover (case) **-organisation** umbrella organization **-ställ** umbrella stand
parapsyko|logi [-'gi:, ˣpa:-] parapsychology **-logisk** *a5* parapsychological
para'sit *s3* parasite **-era** live as a parasite,

sponge *(på* on) **-steklar** [-e:-] *pl* ichneumon flies
para'soll [-å-] *s7, s3* parasol, sunshade
parat *a1* ready, prepared
paratyfus [ˣpa:-, -'ty:-] paratyphoid [fever]
para'van *s3 mil.* paravane
parbladig *a1, bot.* pinnate[d]
par'cell *s3 (jordområde)* site, plot
pardans couple dance; ballroom dancing
par'don *s3 (i krig e.d.)* quarter; *(misskund)* mercy; *det ges ingen ~* no quarter is given; *utan ~* without mercy
parentation *hålla ~ över* deliver an oration to the memory of
parente|s [-en'te:s, -aŋ'te:s] *s3* parenthesis *(pl* parentheses); *(klammer)* bracket; *sätta ngt inom ~* put s.th. in brackets; *inom ~ sagt* incidentally, by the way **-tisk** *a5* parenthetic[al]
parer|a parry, ward off; *(besvara äv.)* retort **-ing** parrying
pa'res *s3* paresis
parflikig *bot.* pinnately lobed
parforcejakt [-ˣfårs-] hunt[ing]
par'fym *s3* perfume; scent **-era** scent; perfume; *~d tvål* scented soap; *starkt ~d* highly scented; *~ sig* use perfume **-eri** perfumery **-flaska** perfume (scent) bottle
parhäst pair-horse *(äv. bildl.);* *köra med ~ar* drive in a carriage and pair; *de hänger ihop som ~ar* (*bildl.*) they are inseparable
pari ['pa:-] *s7* par; *i (till) ~* at par; *under (över) ~* below (above) par
paria ['pa:-] *s1* pariah *(äv. bildl.);* *bildl. äv.* outcast
parig *a1, zool. o.d.* paired
parikurs *(för valuta)* par of exchange, par value; *(för aktier)* face (nominal) value
Pa'ris *n* Paris **parisare** [-ˣri:-] Parisian
pariser|hjul [-ˣri:-] giant wheel **-smörgås** *ung.* hamburger sandwich
parisisk [-'ri:-] *a5* Parisian **parisiska** [-'ri:-] Parisian
parismod Paris fashion
paritet parity; *i ~ med* on a par with
park *s3* park; *Folkets ~* communal park; *stadens ~er* the borough parks **-anläggning** *konkr.* park
parkas ['parr-] *s2, s3* parka
parkera park **parkering** parking; *konkr.* car park, *AE.* parking lot; *~ förbjuden* no parking **parkerings|automat** parking meter **-avgift** parking fee **-böter** *pl* parking fines **-ficka** narrow parking space **-förbud** *det är ~* parking is prohibited **-hus** multistorey carpark **-lapp** parking ticket **-ljus** parking light **-plats** parking space; *(område)* carpark, *AE.* parking lot **-vakt** carpark attendant
par'kett *s3* **1** *teat.* stalls *(pl);* *främre ~* orchestra stalls; *bakre ~* pit; *på ~* in the stalls **2** *(golvbeläggning)* parquet **-golv** parquet floor (flooring) **-läggning** parquet-floor laying **-plats** seat in the stalls, stall **-publik** stalls audience **-stav** parquet block
parksoffa park bench
parkum [ˣparr-, 'parr-] *s3, s7 (tygsort)* fustian
parkvakt park keeper
parlament *s7* parliament; *bli medlem av ~et*

(*äv.*) enter parliament; *sitta i ~et* be a member of parliament (*förk.* be an M.P.) **-ariker** [-'ta:-] parliamentarian **-arisk** [-'ta:-] *a5* parliamentary **-arism** parliamentarism **-era** negotiate, parley **-erande** [-'te:-] *s6* negotiation, parley **-ering** *se -erande*
parlaments|akt act of parliament **-beslut** decision (resolution) of parliament **-byggnad** parliament building; *Storbritannien* [the] Houses of Parliament **-ledamot, -medlem** member of parliament (*förk. M.P.*) **-session** session of parliament **-val** general election
parlamen'tär *s3* negotiator, parleyer **-flagg** flag of truce
parlör phrase-book
parmesanost [-*sa:n-] Parmesan cheese
par'nass *s3, P~en* Mount Parnassus; *bestiga ~en* (*bildl.*) embark on a literary career; *den svenska ~en* the Swedish Helicon
parning [*pa:r-] mating, pairing, copulation
parnings|akt act of mating (*etc.*) **-drift** mating instinct **-dräkt** courtship (mating) plumage **-lek** courtship **-läte** mating call **-tid** mating season
paro'di *s3* parody (*på* on) **parodiera** parody **parodisk** [-'rɔ:-] *a5* parodic[al]
parodon'tit *s3* parodontitis
pa'roll [-å-] *s3* parole, password; (*parti-*) slogan
parox'ysm [-å-] *s3* paroxysm
part [-a:-] *s3* **1** *se huvud-, halv-* **2** *jur.* party, side; *alla berörda ~er* all parties concerned; *~erna i målet* the parties litigant **3** *sjö.* (*kardel*) strand
partenoge'nes [-j-, -g-] *s3* parthenogenesis
parterr [-'tärr] *s3, trädg. o. teat.* parterre **-brottning** ground wrestling
par'ti *s4* **1** (*del*) part, section; (*av bok o. mus.*) passage **2** *hand.* parcel, lot, consignment; *köpa* (*sälja*) *i ~* buy (sell) wholesale; *i ~ och minut* [by] wholesale and [by] retail; *i stora ~er* in bulk **3** *polit.* party; *gå i in i ett ~* join a party **4** *ta ~ för* (*emot*) take sides for (against); *ta sitt ~* make one's decision, make up one's mind **5** *spel.* game; *ett ~ schack* a game of chess **6** (*gifte*) match; *göra ett gott ~* make a good match **-anda** party spirit **-ansluten** enrolled in a party, party member **-beteckning** party label, [party] denomination **-bildning** formation of parties **-biljett** *järnv. ung.* commutation ticket
parti'cip *s7* participle
parti|ell [-tsi'ell] *a1* partial (*solförmörkelse* eclipse [of the sun]) **-ellt** *adv* partially; *~ arbetsför* partially disabled
parti|funktionär party official **-färg** party (political) colour **-grupp** faction, section of a party **-gängare** [-jä-] partisan **-handel** wholesale trade **-kamrat** fellow partisan; *vi är ~er* (*äv.*) we belong to the same party
partikel [-'tick-] *s2* particle **-accelerator** *kärnfys.* particle accelerator
parti|kongress party congress (*AE.* convention) **-ledare** party leader; *AE. vard.* boss **-ledning** party executive (leaders *pl*) **-lös** nonparty; independent **-medlem** party member **-ordförande** party chairman (*AE.* president) **-poli-**

tik party politics (*pl*) **-politisk** of party politics **-pris** *hand.* wholesale price **-program** party program[me] (*AE.* platform)
parti'san *s3* partisan **-krig** guerilla war
partisekreterare party secretary, secretary general
partisk ['pa:r-, 'parr-] *a5* partial; bias[s]ed, prejudiced **-het** partiality; bias
parti|strid party strife (*äv. ~er*) **-styrelse** party executive **-tagande** *s6* taking of sides; showing of partiality (*för* for)
partitiv ['parr-] *a1* partitive
parti'tur *s7* score
parti|vis *adv, hand.* wholesale, in lots, by the lot **-vän** fellow member of a party **-väsen** party system
partner ['pa:rt-] *s9, pl äv. -s* partner
partsinlaga petition
partåig [*pa:r-] *a1, zool.* even-toed, artiodactylous
parvel *s2* [little] lad, youngster
parve'ny *s3* parvenu, upstart
par|vis [*pa:r-] **I** *a1, bot.* conjugate **II** *adv* in pairs (couples), two by two **-åkning** *sport.* pair-skating
pascha *s1* pasha
pas'kill *s3* pasquil, pasquinade
pasma *s1* lea, skein
1 pass *s7* (*bergs-*) pass, defile, gorge
2 pass *s7* (*legitimationshandling*) passport; *falskt ~* forged passport; *utställa* (*förlänga*) *ett ~* issue (renew) a passport
3 pass *s7* (*jakt. o. patrulleringsområde*) beat; *stå på ~* be on guard (the lookout); *polisen på sitt ~* the policeman on his beat
4 pass *s7* **1** *kortsp.* pass, no bid **2** *nej ~!* no such thing!, no thank you!
5 pass *i vissa uttr.: komma väl till ~* come in handy, be serviceable; *vara till ~* satisfy, suit; *vid ~ 10* about 10, 10 or thereabouts (so); *hur ~ mycket* about how much; *kostar den så ~ mycket?* does it cost as much as [all] that?; *det fanns så ~ mycket att jag kunde* there was enough for me to be able to
6 pass *interj, ~ för mig!* I'm out of it!; *~ för den!* bags I!
1 passa *kortsp.* pass
2 passa I 1 (*av-*) fit, adjust; adapt, suit (*efter* to) **2** (*stå på pass, vänta på*) wait for; *~ tiden* be punctual (in time) **3** (*sköta*) attend to; mind, watch; look after (*barn* children); *~ telefonen* answer the telephone **4** *sport.* pass (*äv. absol.*) **II 1** (*i storlek o.d.*) fit; (*i färg, utseende o.d.; vara lämplig*) suit, be suited (*till, som* as, for); (*duga*) do; *nyckeln ~r* the key fits (*till låset* [in] the lock); *klänningen ~r mig precis* the dress fits me perfectly; *grönt ~r honom* green suits him; *handskarna ~r till kappan* the gloves go well with the coat; *han ~r inte till lärare* he is not cut out to be a teacher; *tisdag skulle ~ mig bäst* Tuesday would suit me best; *kom när det ~r dig* come when it suits you; *de ~r bra för varandra* they are well suited to each other **2** (*anstå*) become, be becoming; *det ~r inte en dam att* it does not become (is not becoming for) a lady to **3** *~ på tillfället* take (avail o.s. of) the opportunity **III** *rfl* **1** (*jfr II*)

2); *det ~r sig inte* it is not proper (good form); *komma när det ~r sig* come when [it is] convenient **2** *(akta sig)* take care; look out *(för hunden* for the dog) **IV** *(med betonad part.)* **1** ~ *ihop a) (med obj.)* fit together, *b) (utan obj.)* fit (go) together, *c) (överensstämma)* fit in; *de ~r bra ihop* they are well matched **2** ~ *in a) (med obj.)* fit in, *b) (utan obj.)* fit [in]; *beskrivningen ~r in på honom* the description fits him **3** ~ *på* look out, be ready; ~ *på när du är i stan* take the opportunity (chance) when you are in town; *pass på!* look out! **4** ~ *upp* wait *(på ngn* on s.b.; *vid bordet* at table), attend

passabel *a2* passable, tolerable

pas'sad[vind] *s3* [*s2*] trade wind

passage *s5* passage; *(under gata, järnväg e.d.)* subway; *astr.* transit; *hindra ~n* block the way; *lämna ngn fri* ~ leave (give) s.b. the right of way; *lämna fri* ~ leave the way free *(för fordon* for traffic)

passagerar|avgift [passenger] fare **-befordran** passenger transport

passagerar|e [-ˣʃeː-] passenger **-fartyg** passenger ship **-lista** passenger list **-plan** passenger airliner (plane) **-trafic** passenger traffic

passande *a4 (lämplig)* suitable, appropriate, fit *(för* for); *(läglig)* convenient; *(anständig)* proper, decent; *(tillbörlig)* becoming; *det ~ (det anständiga)* decorum, good form, *allm.* the done thing

passar|e *s9* compasses *(pl)*; *en* ~ a pair of compasses **-spets** *med ~en* with the point of the compass leg

passbyrå passport office

passbåt tender

passepartout [passparˈtɔː] *s3* passe-partout

passera 1 *(genom-, förbi- el. överfara)* pass *(äv. bildl.)*; *(korsa)* cross; *ett ~t stadium* a passed stage; ~ *revy* pass in review **2** *kokk.* strain, pass through a sieve **3** *(gå el. komma förbi)* pass; *bussen hade redan ~t* the bus had already passed (gone by) **4** *(hända)* happen, take place; *det får* ~ *för den här gången* we will overlook it (let it pass) this time **5** *(förflyta)* pass, elapse

passerad *a5 (vissen)* faded, withered *(skönhet* beauty) **passersedel** pass, permit

passform *(klädesplaggs)* fit

pass|foto passport photograph **-frihet** *inom Skandinavien råder nu* ~ no passport is now required for inter-Scandinavian travel

passgång amble **-are** ambler

passion [paˈʃɔːn] passion **passionerad** [-ˈneː-] *a5* passionate; impassioned

passions|blomma passionflower **-frukt** passion fruit **-historien** the Story of the Passion **-veckan** Holy Week

passiv ['pass-] *a1* passive *(motstånd* resistance; *medlem* member); ~ *delägare (äv.)* sleeping partner; *förhålla sig* ~ remain passive **passiva** ['pass-] *pl, hand.* liabilities, debts; *aktiva och* ~ assets and liabilities **passivera** make passive **passivism** passivism **passivitet** passivity **passivum** ['pass-, ˣpass-] *-um -er el. s4 (i* in the) passive [voice]

pass|kontroll *abstr.* passport inspection; *konkr.* passport desk (office) **-myndighet** passport-issuing authority

pass|ning 1 *(tillsyn)* tending, care **2** *tekn.* fit, fit-up; *dålig* ~ poor alignment **3** *sport.* pass **-opp** [-ˈåpp] *s3, s2* attendant

passpoal [-ɷˈall] *s3* piping

passtvång compulsory passport system

passus ['pass-] *s2* passage

pasta *s1* paste

pastej [-ˈtejj] *s3* pie; *(mindre)* pasty, patty; *(t. soppa)* pastry puff

pas'tell *s3* pastel **-färg** pastel colour **-krita** pastel crayon **-målare** pastel[l]ist **-målning** pastel drawing (painting)

pas'till *s3* lozenge, pastille

pas'tisch *s3* pastiche *(på* of)

pastor [ˣpastår, 'past-] *s3* vicar, parson; *(frikyrklig)* minister, pastor; *(vid institution)* chaplain; *(i brevadress o.d.)* Rev. *(förk. för* [the] reverend) **pasto'ral I** *s3* pastoral **II** *a1* pastoral **pastorat** *s7 (befattning)* living, benefice; *(församling)* parish

pastors|adjunkt curate **-expedition** parish [registration] office

pastorska [-ˣtɷ:r-] vicar's *(etc.)* wife

pastorsämbete parish office; *meddelanden från ~t* notices issued by the clergy of the parish

pastöriser|a pasteurize **-ing** pasteurization

pa'ten *s3* paten

patent *s7* patent; *bevilja (få, söka, ta)* ~ *på* grant (obtain, apply for, take out) a patent for **-ansökan** application for a patent **-brev** letters patent *(sg o. pl)* **-byrå** patent agency

patenter|a patent **-bar** *a1* patentable

patent|innehavare holder of a patent, patentee **-kork** patent stopper **-lås** safety (Yale, snap) lock **-lösning** ready-made solution **-medicin** patent (proprietary) medicine **-rätt 1** *jur.* patent law **2** *(rätt t. patent)* patent rights *(pl)* **-skyddad** *a5* patented, protected by patent **-smörgås** *ung.* ham-and-egg sandwich **-verk** Patent Office

pater ['pa:-] *s2* father, pater **paternoster** [-ˈnåss-] *n (läsa ett* say a) paternoster **paternosterverk** paternoster lift, multibucket dredger; *(för vatten)* noria

patetisk [-ˈteː-] *a5 (högtravande)* high-flown; *(rörande)* pathetic

patiens [passiˈaŋs] *s3* [a game of] patience, *AE.* solitaire; *lägga* ~ play [at] patience **-kort** *pl* patience cards

patient [-a(t)si-] patient

patina ['pa:-] *s1* patina *(äv. bildl.)* **patinera** patinate, patine **patinering** patination, patining

pato|log pathologist **-logi** *s3* pathology **-logisk** *a5* pathological; *(sjuklig)* morbid

patos ['pa:tås] *s7* pathos

pa'trask *s7* rabble, mob

patri'ark *s3* patriarch **patriarkalisk** [-ˈka:-] *a5* patriarchal **patriar'kat** *s7* patriarchate **patriarkkors** patriarchal cross

patric|ier [-ˈtri:-] patrician **-isk** *a5* patrician

Patrik Patrick; *St. ~'s Day (Irlands nationaldag 17 mars)*

patri'ot *s3* patriot **-isk** *a5* patriotic **-ism** patriotism

1 pa'tron *s3, best. form vard. patron (gods-*

ägare) squire; (*husbonde*) master; *vard.* boss; (*skyddshelgon*) patron saint

2 pa'tron *s3* (*gevärs-*) cartridge; (*hagel-*) shot cartridge; (*t. kulspetspenna e.d.*) refill; *lös* (*skarp*) ~ blank (ball) cartridge **-bälte** cartridge belt **-hylsa** cartridge [case] **-väska** cartridge case (pouch)

pa'trull *s3* patrol; party; *stöta på* ~ (*bildl.*) meet with opposition **-båt** patrol boat

patruller|a patrol; *~nde polis* policeman on patrol duty, *AE. äv.* patrolman; *~nde vakt[man]* roundsman; *~de polisbil* cruising car **-ing** patrolling

patrulltjänst patrol duty, patrolling

patt *oböjl. a o. r, schack.* stalemate; *ställa sig* ~ be stalemated

pau'lun *s3* (*säng*) four-poster bed; (*omhänge*) tester

Paulus ['pau-] *aposteln* ~ St. Paul

paus ['pa:-] *s3* pause; lull; *mus. äv.* rest; *teat.* interval, *AE.* intermission; (*i samtal o.d.*) break; *ta sig en* ~ take a rest

pauser|a pause, make a pause **-ing** pausing

paus|signal *radio.* interval (call) signal **-tecken** *mus.* rest

paviljong [-'jåŋ] *s3* pavilion; (*lusthus*) summerhouse

pax [paks] *se 6 pass*

PC *förk. för personal computer*

peang h[a]emostatic forceps

pechblände [*peç-] *s6* pitchblende

pedagog *s3* education[al]ist; (*lärare*) teacher, schoolmaster **-ik** *s3* pedagogy, pedagogics (*pl, behandlas som sg*) **-isk** *a5* pedagogic[al]; educational

pe'dal *s3* pedal **-stämma** *mus.* pedal [point]

pedant pedant **-eri** pedantry **-isk** *a5* pedantic

pe'dell *s3, univ.* beadle; *vard.* proctor's dog

pedia'tr|ik *s3* p[a]ediatrics (*pl, behandlas som sg*) **-iker** [-i'a:-] p[a]ediatrician **-isk** [-i'a:-] *a5* p[a]ediatric

pedi'kyr *s3* pedicure

pe'gas *s3* Pegasus

pegma'tit *s3, miner.* pegmatite

pejl|a 1 (*bestämma riktning*) take a bearing on; *absol.* take bearings; ~ *land* set the land **2** (*loda*) sound (*djupet* the depth) (*äv. bildl.*) **-apparat** direction finder **-ing 1** bearing; *radio.* radio location; *ta en* ~ take a bearing **2** sounding **-signal** directional signal **-skiva** pelorus

pejorativ ['pejj-, -'ti:v] *a1* pejorative

pek|a 1 point (*på, mot* at, to); *kompassnålen ~r på norr* (*äv.*) the compass needle indicates north; ~ *finger åt* point one's finger at; *gå dit näsan ~r* follow one's nose; *han får allt han ~r på* he gets everything he asks for; *allting ~r på att* everything points to the fact that; ~ *ut* point out **-finger** forefinger, index finger

pekin[g]'es [-ki(ŋ)'e:s] *s3* (*hund*) Pekin[g]ese [dog]

peko'ral *s7* pompous trash, worthless literary production **-ist** writer of pompous trash

pekpinne pointer

pek'tin *s7, s3* pectin

pekuni'är [-i-, -j-] *a1* pecuniary, financial

pelare pillar; column

pelar'gon[ia] [-'gɔ:n(ia)] *s3* ([*s1, s3*]) geranium, pelargonium

pelar|gång *s2* colonnade; peristyle; (*kring klostergård*) cloister; (*portik*) portico **-helgon** stylite, pillar saint **-huvud** capital **-rad** row of pillars, colonnade **-sal** pillared hall

pele'rin *s3* cape, pelerine

peli'kan *s3* pelican

pelle'jöns *s2* merry-andrew

peloponnesisk [-'ne:-] *a5* Peloponnesian

Peloponnesos [-'ne:sås] *n* the Peloponnese, Peloponnesus

pemmikan ['pemm-] *s3* pem[m]mican

pen [pe:n] *s2* (*på hammare*) peen

penater [-'na:-] *pl* penates; household gods; *flytta sina* ~ move one's lares and penates, move house

pendang [paŋ'daŋ] companion [piece], counterpart

pendel *s2* pendulum **-rörelse** oscillation **-svängning** swing of a pendulum **-trafik** commuter service **-tåg** commuter train; shuttle service train **-ur** pendulum clock

pendla oscillate, pendulate, swing to and fro; (*åka fram o. tillbaka, t.ex. om förortsbo*) commute **pendlare** (*förortsbo som varje dag åker till o. från arbetet*) commuter **pendling** *se pendelrörelse*

pen'dyl [pen-, paŋ-] *s3* ornamental clock (timepiece)

penetr|ation penetration **-era** penetrate; ~ *ett problem* (*äv.*) get to the bottom of a problem

peng *s2* coin **pengar** ['peŋ-] *pl* money (*sg*); (*reda* ~ *äv.*) cash, ready money; *sl.* brass, dough; ~ *eller livet!* your money or your life!; *det kan inte fås för* ~ it is not to be had for money; *förlora* ~ *på* lose money over (by, on); *förtjäna stora* ~ make big money (*på* by); *göra ngt för ~[s skull]* do s.th. for the money; *ha gott om* ~ have plenty of money, be well off; *ha ont om* ~ be short of money, be hard up [for money]; *det har jag inte* ~ *till* I haven't got the money (enough money) for that; *ha* ~ *som gräs* be rolling in money; *i* ~ *räknat* in terms of money; *jämna* ~ even money, the exact amount; *leva på* ~ have private means; *låna* ~ *på* raise money on; *låta ~na rulla* spend money like water

penibel [-'ni:-] *a2* painful, awkward

penicil'lin *s4* penicillin

penis ['pe:-] *s2* penis (*pl äv. penes*)

peni'tens *s3* penance

penjo'ar *s2* peignoir, dressing gown

penna *s1* **1** pen; (*blyerts-*) pencil; (*stål-*) nib; *fatta ~n* put pen to paper; *leva av sin* ~ live by one's pen; *en skarp* ~ (*bildl.*) a formidable pen **2** *zool.* quill

pennal|ism bullying **-ist** bully

penn|drag stroke of the pen **-fat** pen tray **-fodral** pen[cil] case **-formerare** [-å-] pencil sharpener **-fäktare** scribbler **-förlängare** pencil holder

penning piece of money, coin; *~ar* (*koll.*) money (*sg*); *för en ringa* ~ at a small cost **-affär** financial transaction **-angelägenhet** *~er* money matters (affairs) **-aristokrati** plutocracy **-begär** craving for money **-behov** need for money; money requirements (pl) **-bekymmer** pl money worries **-brist** lack (shortage) of money **-fråga** matter of money **-förlust** loss of money, financial loss **-gräs** bot. pennycress **-gåva** money gift **-hushållning** money economy **-inrättning** finance institution **-knipa** råka i ~ get into money difficulties **-lotteri** lottery with money prizes **-marknad** money market **-medel** pl means, funds **-placering** investment of funds (money) **-politik** monetary policy **-pung** purse **-skrin** cash (money) box **-stark** financially strong; vara ~ (äv.) be in a strong financial position **-stinn** made of (rolling in) money **-summa** sum of money **-tillgång** supply of money **-transaktion** se -affär **-understöd** pecuniary aid, benefit payment; (statligt) subsidy, subvention **-värde** value of money; (värde i pengar) money (monetary) value; ~ts fall the fall in the value of money **-värdesförsämring** depreciation of money **-väsen** monetary system

penn|kniv penknife **-skaft** penholder; (kvinnlig journalist) woman journalist, penwoman **-skrin** pen[cil] box (case) **-spets** point of a pen (etc.) **-stift** lead **-stump** pencil stump **-teckning** line (pencil) drawing **-torkare** [-å-] pen wiper **-vässare** se pennformerare

penny ['penni] -n pence [pens] penny (pl pence; -slantar pennies)

pensé [paŋ'se:] s3 pansy

penséer [paŋ-] pl, gå i sina ~ be absorbed in thought, be in a brown study

pensel s2 [paint]brush; bot. egret **-drag** stroke of the brush **-föring** brushwork

pension [paŋ'ʃɔ:n, pen-] **1** (underhåll) pension; avgå med ~ retire on a pension **2** (skola) boarding school; sätta i ~ send to a boarding school **pensionat** s7 boarding house **pensionera** pension [... off], grant a pension to; ~d pensioned, retired **pensionering** pensioning, superannuation, retirement

pensions|anstalt pensions office **-avdrag, -avgift** pension contribution (charge) **-berättigad** entitled to a pension **-fond** Allmänna ~en (AP-fonden) the National [Swedish] Pension Insurance Fund **-försäkring** old age pension insurance **-grundande** ~ inkomst income on which pension is assessed, pensionable income **-kassa** pension (benefit) society **-mässig** a1 pensionable **-poäng** pension credits (pl) **-tagare** pensioner **-ålder** pensionable (retirement) age

pensio'när [paŋ-, pen-] s3 **1** (pensionstagare) pensioner **2** (inackorderingsgäst) boarder **pensionärs|förening** (nationell) pensioners' association; (lokal) pensioners' club **-hem** pensioners' home

pensl|a paint; pencil; fint ~de ögonbryn finely pencilled eyebrows **-ing** painting

pensum s8 task; AE. assignment

penta|gram [-'gramm] s7 pentagram **-meter** [-*ta:-] s2 pentameter

pentry ['pentri, -y] s6 pantry

penultima [-'nult-] s1, best. form äv. penultima penultimate [syllable]

pep imperf. av 1 pipa

peppar s9 pepper; spansk ~ cayenne [pepper];

önska ngn (dra) dit ~n växer send s.b. (go) to Jericho; ~ ~! touch wood!; ~ och salt (textil.) pepper-and-salt **-kaka** gingerbread biscuit; (mjuk) gingerbread cake **-kakshjärta** ung. heart-shaped gingerbread biscuit **-korn** peppercorn **-kvarn** pepper mill **-mynta** s1 peppermint **-myntspastill** peppermint [lozenge] **-rot** horseradish **-rotskött** boiled beef with horseradish sauce **-ströare** pepper pot

peppra ~ [på] pepper (äv. bildl.) **pepprad** a5 peppery; en ~ räkning (vard.) a stiff bill

pep'sin s4, s3 pepsin

per [pärr] (~ båt, post e.d.) by; bokför. as on; ~ person per person, a head, each, a piece; ~ styck apiece, each, per unit; ~ timme by the hour; ~ år a year, yearly, annually, per annum; ~ omgående by return [of post]; ~ capita per capita; ~ kontant [in] cash

perborat [pärbå'ra:t] s4, kem. perborate

percep|tion [pärsep'ʃɔ:n] perception **-tiv** a1 perceptive

pe'renn I a1 perennial **II** s3 perennial [plant]

1 per'fekt [pär-] a1 perfect

2 perfekt ['pärf-, 'pä:r-] s7, s4, språkv. [the] perfect [tense]; ~ particip past participle

perfektion [pärfek'ʃɔ:n] perfection **-ism** perfectionism **-ist** perfectionist

perfekt|um ['pärf-, 'pä:r-] best. form -et el. -um, pl -er, språkv., se 2 perfekt

per'fid [pärr-] a1, n sg obest. f. undviks perfidious **-itet** s3 perfidiousness, perfidy

perforer|a [pärr-] perforate; punch; med. pierce **-ing** perforation

perga'ment [pärr-] s7, s4 parchment; (t. bokband äv.) vellum **-artad** [-a:r-] a5 parchment--like, parchmenty **-band** parchment (vellum) binding **-handskrift** parchment [manuscript] **-rulle** roll (scroll) of parchment

pergola ['pärgå-] s1 pergola

peri'fer a1 peripheral; bild. outlying; frågan var av ~ art the question was of secondary importance **perife'ri** s3 periphery; (cirkels) circumference; (stads) outskirts (pl) **periferisk** [-'fe:-] a5, se perifer **periferivinkel** circumferential angle

peri'fras s3 periphrasis (pl periphrases) **perigeum** [-*ge:-] s4, astr. perigee **perihelium** [-'he:-] s4, astr. perihelion (pl perihelia)

period s3 period **periodicitet** periodicity **periodisk** [-'ɔ:d-] a5 periodic[al]

period|supare dipsomaniac, periodical drinker **-tal** frequency **-vis** periodically

peri|pe'ti s3 peripet[e]ia **-skop** s7 periscope **-skopisk** [-'skå:-] a5 periscopic **-staltik** s3 peristalsis (pl peristalses) **-staltisk** [-'stall-] a5 peristaltic; ~a rörelser peristaltic movements **-'styl** s3 peristyle **-toneum** [-*ne:um] s8 peritoneum **-to'nit** s3 peritonitis

perkussion [pärku'ʃɔ:n] med. percussion

perma'n|ens [pärr-] s3 permanence **-'ent I** a1 permanent **II** s3, se permanentning

permanent|a [pärma'nenta] **1** (hår) permanent--wave; vard. perm; AE. äv. fix up; ~ sig have a perm **2** (väg) lay with a permanent surface (metalling); ~d väg (äv.) tarmac[adam] (metalled) road **-ning** permanent [wave]; vard. perm

permeab|el [pärme'a:-] *a2* permeable **-ilitet** permeability

permission [pärmi'ʃɑ:n] leave [of absence]; *(för längre tid äv.)* furlough; *begära (få)* ~ ask for (get) leave *(etc.)*; *ha* ~ be on (have) leave; *på* ~ on leave

permissions|ansökan application for leave *(etc.)* **-förbud** suspension of leave; *mil.* confinement to barracks **-sedel** pass

permitt|ent [pärr-] person (soldier) on leave **-era 1** *(ge permission)* grant leave to **2** *(entlediga)* lay off *(arbetare* workers), dismiss temporarily **-ering** lay-off

permut|ation [pärr-] *mat.* permutation **-era** permute

pernici'ös [pärr-] *a1, med.* pernicious *(anemi* anaemia)

perpendik|el [pärr-, -'dick-] *s2* perpendicular **-u'lär** *a1* perpendicular

perpetu'ell [pärr-] *a1* perpetual

perpetuum mobile [pär'pe:tuum 'må:-] *n (maskin)* perpetual motion machine

per'plex [pärr-] *a1* perplexed, taken aback

perrong [pä'råŋ] *s3* platform **-biljett** platform ticket

persed|el [pär'se:-] *s2 (sak)* thing, article; *mil.* item of equipment; *-lar (mil.)* accoutrements, equipment *(sg)*, kit *(sg)*

persedel|inspektion *mil.* kit inspection **-vård** *mil.* care of kit

perser ['pärr-] Persian

persi'an [pärr-] *s3* Persian lamb, karakul **-päls** Persian lamb coat

Persien ['pärr-] *n* Persia

persi'enn [pärr-] *s3* Venetian blind

persika ['ˣpärr-] *s1* peach **persikohy** peach complexion

persilja ['ˣpärr-, -'sill-] *s1* parsley; *prata* ~ talk rubbish

persimon [pärsi'må:n] persimmon

persisk ['pärr-] *a5* Persian; *P~a viken* the Persian Gulf **persiska** *s1* **1** *(språk)* Persian **2** *(kvinna)* Persian woman

per'son [pärr-] *s3* person; *(i pl äv.)* people; *(i drama, roman e.d.)* character; *(betydande ~)* personage; *~er (teat.)* dramatis personae, the cast *(sg)*; *fysisk* ~ natural person; *juridisk* ~ artificial person; *enskild* ~ private person, individual; *offentlig* ~ person in public life, public figure; *han kom i egen hög* ~ he came in person (himself); *min ringa* ~ my humble self; *kunglig* ~ royal personage; *i första* ~ *pluralis* in the first person plural **personage** *s5* personage

perso'nal [pärr-] *s3* staff; personnel; employees **-administration** personnel management **-avdelning** staff (personnel) department **-brist** shortage of staff **-chef** staff (personnel) manager

personal|ier [pärsɑ'na:-] *pl* biographical data; personals **-konferens** staff committee **-politik** staffing policy **-tidning** staff magazine **-union** personal union

person|befordran passenger service (conveyance) **-bevis** birth certificate **-bil** private (passenger) car **-dator** personal computer, PC

perso'n|ell [pärr-] *a1, se personlig* **-förteck-**

ning list of persons **-galleri** collection of characters **-historia** personal history

personifiera [pärr-] personify; impersonate; *den ~de blygsamheten* modesty personified (itself) **personifikation** personification; impersonation

person|kort identity card **-kult** personality cult **-kännedom** knowledge of people

personlig [pär'sɑ:n-] *a1* personal; *~t (på brev)* private; *för min ~a del* for my [own] part; *min ~a åsikt* my private opinion; *~t samtal* personal talk (conversation), *tel.* personal call; *utan ~t ansvar* limited, without personal liability; *P~t (spalt i tidning)* the agony column **personligen** personally, in person; *känna ngn* ~ know s.b. personally; *inställa sig* ~ appear in person

personlighet [-'sɑ:n-] **1** *(människans väsen)* personality **2** *(karaktär)* personality; *(framstående person äv.)* personage, person; *en historisk* ~ a historical person; *en framstående* ~ an outstanding personality (personage); *gå (komma) in på ~er* become personal, make personal remarks

personlighets|klyvning *lida av* ~ have a dual personality **-typ** type of personality

person|namn personal name **-nummer** civic registration number, personal code number **-skada** personal injury **-sökare** staff locator **-trafik** passenger traffic (service) **-tåg** *(motsats godståg)* passenger train; *(motsats snälltåg)* ordinary (slow) train **-undersökning** enquiry into personal circumstances

perspek'tiv [pärr-] *s7* perspective; *(utsikt, framtids-)* prospect; *vidga ~et (bildl.)* broaden the outlook **-fönster** picture (vista) window **-isk** *a5* perspective **-ritning** perspective drawing

Pe'ru *n* Peru **peru'an** *s3* Peruvian **peru'ansk** [-a:-] *a5* Peruvian

pe'ruk *s3* wig; *(enl. 1600- o. 1700-talets mod)* periwig, peruke; *vard.* mop **-makare** wig-maker; *teat. äv.* theatrical hairdresser **-stock 1** wig block **2** *bildl.* [old] fogey

pervers [pär'värrs] *a1* perverted **-itet** *s3* sexual perversion

pes'sar *s4* diaphragm, pessary, Dutch cap

pessim|ism pessimism **-ist** pessimist **-istisk** *a5* pessimistic

pest *s3* plague; pestilence; *avsky ngt som ~en* hate s.th. like sin; *sky ngt som ~en* shun s.th. like the plague **-artad** [-a:r-] *a5* pestilential **-böld** bubo **-härd** source of plague; *bildl.* plague-spot

pest|ilensrot [-ˣlens-] *bot.* butterbur **-smittad** *a5 (om pers.)* plague-stricken; *(om område)* plague-infested

pet *s7, se petgöra* **peta 1** poke, pick *(på at)*; ~ *på allt* poke one's finger[s] into everything; ~ *hål i (på)* poke a hole in; ~ *naglarna* clean one's nails; ~ *tänderna* pick one's teeth; *sitta och* ~ *i maten* be pecking at one's food; ~ *omkull* push over, upset **2** *vard. (tränga undan)* oust; *sport.* drop

Peterskyrkan St. Peter's Basilica

peterspenningen Peter's pence *(pl)*

petgöra finicky job

petig *a1 (noga)* finical, finicking; *(om pers. äv.)*

particular, meticulous **-het** finicalness *etc.*
petimäter [-'mä:-] *s2* cockscomb, coxcomb, fop
petit [-'ti:(t)] *s2, boktr.* brevier
petita [-*ˣti:-] *se petitum*
petit-chou [peti'ʃɷ:] *s3* cream puff
petitess *s3* trifle
petition petition (*om* for); *inlämna en* ~ hand in a petition **petitio'när** *s3* petitioner
petitum [-*ˣti:-] *s8* request for a [money] grant; estimate of expenditure
pet|moj [*ˣpe:tmåj] *s2, vard.* telephone [dial] **-noga** *vard.* pernickety, fussy
petrifiera petrify **petrifi'kat** *s7* petrification, fossil
petro|gra'fi *s3* petrography **-kemi** petrochemistry **-kemisk** petrochemical
petroleum [-'trɷ:-] *s3, s7* petroleum, mineral oil
Petrus ['pe:-] *aposteln* ~ Peter the Apostle, St. Peter
petunia [-'tu:-] *s1, bot.* petunia
Pfalz [pfalts] *n* the Palatinate
pfalz|greve Count Palatine **-isk** ['pfalts-] *a5* Palatine
p.g.a. (*förk. för på grund av*) *se under 3* grund *3*
phon [få:n] *s3, fys.* phon
pH-värde [*ˣpe:hå:-] pH value, index of pH
pi *s6, s7, mat.* pi
pi'aff *s3, ridk.* piaffe
pianino [-'ni:-] *s6* pianino, upright piano **pianissimo** [-'niss-] **I** *s6* pianissimo **II** *adv* pianissimo **pianist** pianist, piano player
piano [-'a:nɷ] **I** *s6* piano; *spela* ~ play the piano; *ackompanjera ngn på* ~ accompany s.b. on the piano **II** *adv* piano; *ta det* ~ take it easy **-ackompanjemang** piano accompaniment **-konsert** concert given by a pianist; (*komposition*) piano concerto
piano|la [-*ˣnå:-] *s1* pianola, player piano **-lektion** piano lesson **-skola** piano conservatory; piano-playing manual **-spel** piano-playing **-stol** music stool **-stämma** piano part **-stämmare** piano tuner
piassava [-*ˣsa:-] *s1* piassava, piassaba **-kvast** besom
piccola *se pickola* **piccolo** *se pickola*
picka (*om fågel*) peck (*hål i* a hole in; *i, på* at); (*om hjärtat*) go pitapat; ~ *i sig* peck up
pickelhuva spiked helmet
pickels ['pikk-] *s2* pickles (*pl*)
picknick ['pikk-] *s2, s3* picnic **picknicka** picnic, go picnicking **picknickkorg** picnic basket
pick och pack belongings (*pl*); *ta sitt* ~ *och gå* clear out bag and baggage
pickola ['pickå-] *s1,* **-flöjt** [*ˣpickå-] *s3* piccolo (*pl* piccolos)
pickolo ['pick-] *s5* page [boy], buttons, footboy; *AE.* bellboy, *vard.* bellhop
pickup[p] [pick'app] *s3* pick-up
piedes'tal [pie-, pje-] *s3* pedestal
pietet reverence (*mot* to; *för* for)
pietets|full reverential, reverent **-lös** irreverent **-löshet** lack of reverence, irreverence
piet|ism pietism **-ist** pietist **-istisk** *a5* pietis-

tic[al]
piff I *interj* bang! **II** *s2, sätta* ~ *på a*) *kokk.* give relish to, *b*) *bildl.* smarten up, put style into **piffa** ~ *upp* smarten up; *AE.* revamp **piffig** *a1* (*om mat*) piquant, tasty; (*stilig*) chic, smart
piga *s1* maid; *vard. neds.* slavey
1 pigg *s2* (*metall-*) spike; (*tagg*) spine, quill
2 pigg *a1* (*kry*) fit (*som en mört* as a fiddle); (*rask, livlig*) brisk, spry; *AE. s1* peppy; ('*vaken*') alert, bright, sharp; ~ *och kry* bright and breezy; *känna sig* ~ feel very fit; *vara* ~ *för sin ålder* be spry for one's years; ~ *på* keen on
pigga ~ *upp* cheer up; *AE. s1* pep up **pigge'lin** *oböjl. a* bright and cheery
pigghaj spiny dogfish
piggna ~ *till* come round
pigg|svin porcupine **-svinstagg** quill **-var** *s2* turbot
pigkammare maid's room
pigment *s7* pigment **-erad** [-'te:-] *a5* pigmented **-ering** pigmentation
pig|syssla servant's job **-tjusare** [-ç-] would-be ladykiller
pik *s2* **1** (*spets*) point; (*stickord*) gibe, dig (*åt* at); *jag förstod* ~*en* I got the message **2** (*bergstopp*) peak **3** *sjö.* (*akter-, för-*) peak; ~ *på en gaffel* peak of a gaff **4** *mil.* pike **5** *sport., hopp med* ~ jackknife dive **pika** gibe [at], taunt (*för* with)
pikador [-'då:r] *s3* picador
pikant [-'kant, -'kaŋt] *a1* piquant; spicy, highly seasoned; (*om historia o.d.*) racy, spicy **-eri** piquancy
pikareskroman [-*ˣresk-] picaresque novel
1 piké *s3* (*tyg*) piqué
2 piké *s3* (*kortspel*) piquet; *spela* ~ play at piquet
pikerad [-'ke:-] *a5* (*förnärmad*) piqued (*över* at)
pi'ket *s3* riot squad, picket **-bil** police van
pikrinsyra [-*ˣkri:n-] picric acid
piktur handwriting
1 pil *s2* (*träd*) willow
2 pil *s2* (*vapen*) arrow; (*t. armborst*) bolt; (*att kasta*) dart; *bildl.* arrow, shaft; *kasta* ~ throw darts; *snabb som en* ~ [as] swift as an arrow; *Amors* ~*ar* Cupid's darts (shafts)
pila ~ *i väg* dash away, rush off
pi'laff *s3, kokk.* pilau, pilaw
pilaster [-'lass-] *s2* pilaster
pilbåge bow
pilfink tree sparrow
pilgift poison applied to tips of arrows
pilgrim *s3* pilgrim
pilgrims|falk peregrine falcon **-fäderna** *pl* the Pilgrim Fathers **-färd** pilgrimage; *göra en* ~ go on a pilgrimage **-ort** [place of] pilgrimage; *bildl. äv.* Mecca **-stav** pilgrim's staff
pilka dib (*torsk* for codfish)
pil|kastning dart-throwing; (*som spel*) darts (*pl*) **-koger** quiver
pilla pluck, pick (*på* at); ~ *på* (*äv.*) finger; *sitta och* ~ *med ngt* sit fiddling with s.th.; ~ *bort* pick off
piller ['pill-] *s7* pill; *svälja det beska -ret* (*bildl.*) swallow the bitter pill **-dosa** pillbox **-trillare** *skämts.* pillmaker

P

pillra *se pilla*
pilot [-'ω:t] *s3* pilot
pil|regn, -skur shower (hail) of arrows **-snabb** [as] swift as an arrow
pilsner ['pils-] *s9* Pils[e]ner beer
pilspets arrowhead
pilt *s2* lad[die]
pimpelfiske jigging
pimpi'nell *s3, bot.* [salad] burnet
1 pimpla (*dricka*) swig; (*supa äv.*) tipple
2 pimpl|a jig (*efter abborre* for perch)
pimpling *se pimpelfiske*
pimpsten pumice [stone]
pin *på ~ kiv* out of sheer devilry; *det var ~ livat* it was hilarious; *~ kär* desperately in love
pina I *s1* torment, pain, torture; (*kval*) agony; *död och ~!* torments everlasting!; *för själ och ~!* for mercy's sake!; *göra ~n kort* not prolong the agony, make short work of it **II** *v1* torment, torture; *~ livet ur ngn* (*bildl.*) worry the life out of s.b. (s.b. to death); *~ i sig maten* force down the food; *han hade ett ~t uttryck i ansiktet* his face had a pained expression; *~ fiolen* scrape away at the violin; *~ sig in* (*om blåst, snö o.d.*) worry [its way] through
pi'nal *s3* thing; *inte en ~* nothing whatever, not an atom; *jfr grejor*
pin|ande *a4* tormenting, torturing; racking (*huvudvärk* headache); searching, piercing (*blåst* wind) **-bänk** rack
pincené [päŋs'ne:] *s3* pince-nez
pin'cett tweezers (*pl*); *en ~* pair of tweezers
pinfärsk quite (absolutely) fresh
pingis *s3, se pingpong*
pingla I *s1* [small] bell **II** *v1* tinkle; jingle; (*telefonera*) give a ring **pinglande** *s6* tinkle, jingle
pingpong [-å-] *s2* ping pong, table tennis
pingst *s2* Whitsun[tide], Pentecost (*äv. ~en*); *annandag ~* Whit Monday **-afton** Whitsun Eve, Whit Saturday (*äv. ~en*) **-dag** Whit Sunday, Whitsunday **-helg** Whitsuntide (*äv. ~en*) **-lilja** narcissus **-rörelse** *~n* the Pentecostal Movement **-veckan** Whit[sun] week **-vän** Pentecostalist
ping'vin *s3* penguin
pinje ['pinn-, 'pi:-] *s5* stonepine
pin|lig [*pi:n-] *a1, se pinsam; ~t förhör* examination under torture
pinna *~ fast* peg (*vid* to) **pinnbult** *tekn.* stud
pinn|e *s2* (*trä-, tält-, hatt-*) peg; (*ved-*) stick; (*steg-*) rung; (*höns-*) perch; *styv som en ~* [as] stiff as a poker; *ben smala som -ar* legs as thin as sticks; *hon är smal som en ~* she is as thin as a rake; *rör på -arna!* stir your stumps!; *livet på en ~* high life; *trilla av pinn* peg out **pinnhål** peghole; *komma ett par ~ högre* (*bildl.*) rise a step or two
pinnmo *s2* till
pinn|soffa rib-backed settee **-stol** Windsor chair **-ved** stick firewood
pino|läger *bildl.* bed of torment **-redskap** instrument of torture
pinsam [*pi:n-] *a1* painful; (*besvärande*) awkward, embarrassing (*situation* situation; *tystnad* silence); scrupulous (*noggrannhet* carefulness)

pinuppa [-*nuppa] *s1* pin-up [girl]
pi'on *s3* peony
pion'jär *s3* **1** *mil.* sapper, engineer **2** (*föregångsman*) pioneer **-arbete** pioneer work **-trupp** *se ingenjörstrupper*
1 pip *s2* **1** (*på kanna*) spout **2** *bot.* tube
2 pip *interj* peep!
3 pip *s7* (*ljud*) peep; (*fågels*) chirp; (*råttas*) squeak, cheep; (*gnäll*) whine, whimper
1 pip|a *pep -it* (*om fågel*) chirp; (*om barn, mus*) squeak; (*jämra sig*) whine, whimper; (*om vind, ångvissla*) whistle; *det -er i bröstet på mig* my chest is wheezy
2 pip|a *s1* **1** (*rök-*) pipe; *röka ~* smoke a pipe; *knacka ur ~n* knock the ashes out of one's pipe **2** (*att blåsa i*) pipe; (*vissel-*) whistle; *dansa efter ngns ~* dance to a p.'s tune; *skära -or i vassen* know what tune to dance to, jump at an opportunity **3** (*rör*) pipe, tube; (*gevärs-*) barrel; (*skorstens-*) flue **4** *det här går åt ~n* this is all going wrong (is a mess)
pipare *zool.* plover
pi'pett *s3* pipette
piphuvud [pipe] bowl
1 pipig *a1* (*gäll*) squeaky (*röst* voice); (*gnällig*) whining, whimpering
2 pipig *a1* (*porös*) porous
pipit *sup. av 1 pipa*
pipkrage fluted ruff
piplera pipeclay
piplärka pipit
pip|olja tobacco juice **-orgel** pipe organ
1 pippi *s2* (*fågel*) dickybird
2 pippi *s9, ha ~ på* be crazy about; *det är rena ~n* it is pure folly
pip|rensare pipe cleaner **-rök** pipe smoke **-rökare** pipe smoker
pipsill [*pi:p-] *s2* crybaby
pipskaft pipe stem
pipskägg imperial, pointed beard, goatee
piptobak pipe tobacco
pir *s2, s3* pier, groyne, groin; (*mindre*) jetty; (*vågbrytare äv.*) groyne, AE. groin; mole
pirat pirate **-sändare** pirate transmitter **-upplaga** piratical edition
piraya [-*rajja] *s1* piranha, piraya
pirk *s2* jig
1 pirog [-'rå:g] *s3* (*kanot*) pirogue
2 pirog [-'rå:g] *s3, kokk.* Russian pasty
pirra tingle **pirrande I** *s6* tingling **II** *a4* tingling
piru'ett *s3* pirouette **-era** pirouette
pirum *oböjl. a* tipsy
pirål hagfish
pisk *s7* whipping **piska I** *s1* whip; (*hår-*) pigtail; *klatscha* (*smälla med*) *~n* crack the (one's) whip; *låta ngn smaka ~n* give s.b. a taste of the whip **II** *v1* whip; flog, lash; (*mattor, kläder o.d.*) beat; *regnet -de mot rutorna* the rain was beating against the panes; *hunden ~de med svansen* the dog was swishing its tail; *vara ~d att göra ngt* be forced to do s.th.; *~ på* whip [on]; *~ upp* whip up
pisk|balkong balcony for beating [mats *etc.*] **-käpp** carpet beater **-rapp** lash; *bildl.* whiplash **-smäll** crack of the whip **-snärt** whiplash **-ställning** carpet-beating rack
piss *s7, vard.* piss **pissa** *vard.* piss **pisso'ar** *s3*

urinal
pist *s3, fäktn.* piste; (*cirkus-*) ring fence
pistasch [-'ta:ʃ] *s3* pistachio **-mandel** pistachio [nut]
pis'till *s3* pistil; *~ens märke* the stigma [of the pistil]
pis'tol *s3* **1** (*vapen*) pistol **2** (*mynt*) pistole **-hot** *under ~* at gunpoint **-hölster** [pistol] holster **-man** gunman **-mynning** pistol muzzle **-skjutning** pistol shooting **-skott** pistol shot
pistong [-'tåŋ] *s3* piston
pitprops ['pitpråps] *s2, koll.* pitprops (*pl*)
pitt *s2, vard.* cock, prick, dick
pitto'resk *a1* picturesque
pi'vå *s3* pivot
pizz|a ['pittsa] *s1* pizza **-eria** [-ˣri:a] *s1* pizzeria, pizza parlor
pjosk [-å-] *s7* (*klemande*) coddling; (*klemighet*) mawkishness, squeamishness **pjoska** *~ med* coddle **pjosker** ['pjåss-] *s2* milksop, mollycoddle **pjoskig** *a1* mawkish, effeminate
pjåkig *a1, inte så ~* not half bad
pjåsk *etc., se pjosk etc.*
pjäs *s3* **1** *mil.* piece **2** (*möbel, prydnadsföremål e.d.*) piece, article **3** (*schack-*) man; (*motsats t. bonde*) piece **4** *teat.* play **-författare** playwright
pjäxa *s1* ski-boot
placenta [-ˣsenn-] *s1, anat.* placenta
placera place, put; (*skaffa anställning e.d.*) station; (*gruppera*) seat (*sina gäster* one's guests); (*pengar*) invest; (*insätta i sitt sammanhang*) place, locate; *~ en beställning hos en firma* place an order with a firm; *jag känner igen honom men kan inte ~ honom* I know his face but cannot place him; *~ sig a*) (*sätta sig*) seat o.s., *b*) *sport.* get a place; *~ sig som tvåa* come second **placering** placing; (*vid bord äv.*) seating; (*investering*) investment; (*läge samt sport.*) position, location **placeringskort** place card
pla'dask *falla ~* fall flop down (*i smutsen* into the dirt)
pladder ['pladd-] *s7* babble, chatter; *sl.* yackety-yak **pladdra** babble, chatter **pladdrig** *a1* garrulous
plafond [-'fåŋd] *s3* plafond **-målning** *konkr.* painted ceiling
plage [pla:ʃ] *s5* beach
plagg *s7* garment; article of clothing
plagi|'at *s7* plagiarism **-ator** *s3* plagiarist **-era** plagiarize
1 plakat *s7* (*kungörelse*) proclamation; (*affisch*) placard, poster
2 plakat *oböjl. a* (*full*) dead drunk
pla'kett *s3* plaquette, plaque
plan I 1 *s7* (*yta*) plane; (*nivå*) level; *ett lutande ~* an inclined plane; *i* (*på*) *samma ~ som* (*äv.*) on a level with; *på ett högre ~* on a higher level; *roll i andra ~et* second-grade part; *det ligger på ett helt annat ~* it is on quite another plane; *på det sluttande ~et* (*bildl.*) on the down grade **2** *s7* (*flyg-*) plane **3** *s3* (*öppen plats*) open space, area, (*fyrkantig*) square; *sport.* ground; (*jfr äv. gräs-, tennis- etc.*) **4** *s3* (*projekt, förslag*) plan, scheme (*för, på, till* for, of); (*intrig*) plot; *göra upp ~er* make plans, plan;

ha (*hysa*) *~er på ngt* (*på att*) have plans for s.th. (*for ... -ing*); *det ingår inte i mina ~er* it is not part of my plans; *det finns inga ~er att hinna dit* there's not the faintest chance of getting there in time **II** *al* plane, level
plana 1 (*jämna*) level **2** (*om bil, båt*) plane
planekonomi planned economy **planenlig** [-e:-] *al* according ⚫ plan
planer|a 1 (*jämna*) level **2** (*-lägga*) plan, project; (*ha för avsikt*) intend, *AE. äv.* (+ *inf.*) **-ing 1** (*jämnande*) levelling **2** (*-läggning*) planning, projection
pla'net *s3* **1** *astr.* planet **2** *mitt i ~en* slap in the face **planetarisk** [-'ta:-] *a5* planetary **planetarium** [-'ta:-] *s4* planetarium
planet|bana orbit of a planet **-system** planetary system
plan|geometri plane geometry **-hushållare** planner **-hushållning** economic planning, planned economy
plani|me'tri *s3* planimetry **-metrisk** [-'me:-] *a5* planimetric[al]
plank 1 *s9, s7, koll.* deals (*pl*), planking **2** *s7* (*stängsel*) wood[en] paling (fence); (*kring bygge e.d.*) hoarding[s *pl*]
1 planka *s1* deal; (*större*) plank
2 planka *v1, vard.* **1** (*smita in*) gate-crash **2** (*kopiera*) crib
plankorsning level (*AE.* grade) crossing
plank|strykare *skämts.* dauber **-stump** plank stump
plankton ['planktån] *s7* plankton
plan|lägga plan, make plans for, project; *-lagt mord* premeditated (wilful) murder **-läggning** planning; projection **-lös** planless; unmethodical, indiscriminate; (*utan mål*) aimless, desultory; *irra omkring ~t* wander about aimlessly **-löshet** aimlessness *etc.*, lack of plan **-lösning** *byggn.* plan[ning], design **-mässig** *al* methodical, systematical; according to plan **-mässighet** method[icalness] **-ritning** *konkr.* [ground] plan (*till* for, of); (*som läroämne*) plan-drawing
plansch *s3* plate, illustration; (*vägg-*) chart **-verk** volume of pictures, picture book
planskild *~ korsning* grade-separated intersection
planslip|a grind smooth **-ning** [sur]face grinding
plant|a *s1* plant; (*uppdragen ur frö*) seedling; (*träd*) sapling; *sätta -or* set plants **plantage** [-'ta:ʃ] *s5* plantation **plantageägare** planter, plantation owner **plantera** plant; (*i rabatt äv.*) bed out; *bildl.* plant, set; *~ om* transplant; *~ ut* plant out **plantering** *konkr.* plantation, park; *abstr.* planting **planteringsspade** planting trowel **plantskola** nursery (*för* of, for) (*äv. bildl.*)
plask *s7 o. interj* splash **plaska** splash; (*om vågor, åror*) lap (*mot stranden* on the shore; *mot båtens sidor* against the sides of the boat); (*vada*) paddle; *~ omkring* splash about **plaskdamm** [children's] paddling-pool **plaskvåt** soaking wet
plasma *s9, s7, pl plasmer* plasma **-fysik** plasma physics (*pl, behandlas som sg*)
plast *s3* plastic; *härdad ~* thermosetting plastic;

mjuk ~ nonrigid plastic
plast|a, -behandla coat (spray) with plastic **-behandlad** *a5* plastic-coated **-behandling** plastic treatment **-belagd** plastic-coated **-blomma** plastic flower **-båt** plastic boat **-bägare** plastic beaker
plastel'lin *s3, s4,* **plastellina** [-ˣli:-] *s1* Plasticine (*varumärke*)
plast|fabrik plastics plant **-flaska** plastic bottle **-folie** plastic sheeting (film) **-hink** plastic bucket
plasticitet plasticity
plastik *s3* **1** (*bildhuggarkonst*) plastic art **2** *med.* plastic surgery **3** (*konsten att föra sig väl*) deportment **-kirurgi** plastic surgery
plastisk ['plass-] *a5* plastic; (*formbar*) ductile; (*behagfull*) graceful; *~t trä* wood cement, plastic wood
plast|laminat *s7* laminated plastic sheet **-material** plastic material **-påse** plastic (polythene) bag
pla'tan *s3* plane [tree]
platina [-ˣti:-, 'pla:-] *s9* platinum **-blond** platinum-blonde
Platon ['pla:tån] Plato
platon|iker [-'tɒ:-] Platonist **-[i]sk** [-'tɒ:-] *a5* Platonic (*kärlek* love)
plats *s3* **1** (*ställe, ort, bestämd ~*) place; (*lokalitet*) locality; (*fläck*) spot; (*öppen ~*) space, area, (*fyrkantig*) square; (*skåde-*) scene (*för* of); *veta sin ~* know one's place; *var sak på sin* [*rätta*] ~ everything in its [right] place; *offentliga* (*allmänna*) *~er* public places; *här på ~en* here, in this town, on the spot; *läkaren på ~en* (*äv.*) the local doctor; *vara den förste på ~en* be the first on the spot (to arrive); *sätta ngn på ~* (*bildl.*) take a p. down [a peg or two]; *det vore inte på sin ~ att* it would be out of place (inappropriate) to **2** (*sitt-, äv. i riksdag o.d.*) seat; (*säng-*) bed; *numrerade ~er* numbered seats; *ta ~* take a (one's) seat; *tag ~!* take your seats!; *fylld till sista ~* packed, filled to capacity **3** (*utrymme*) room; space; (*husrum*) accommodation; *lämna ~ för* (*åt*) make room for; *ta liten* (*för stor*) ~ take up little (too much) room; *gott om ~* plenty of room; *den får nätt och jämnt ~* there is only just room for it; *ha ~ för 100 personer* have room (*husrum:* accommodation) for 100 persons **4** (*anställning*) place, situation, job; (*befattning*) position, post; (*ställning*) position; *fast ~* permanent situation; *ha ~ hos* be in the employment of; *söka ~* apply for a situation; *utan ~* unemployed, out of work; *lediga ~er* vacancies, (*tidn.rubrik*) appointments and situations vacant; *intaga en framträdande ~* occupy (take up) a prominent position
plats|annons *~er* situations wanted (vacant) advertisements **-ansökan** application for a situation (*etc.*) **-beställning** seat reservation (booking) **-biljett** seat reservation [ticket] **-brist** lack of room; (*på sjukhus*) shortage of beds **-chef** local manager **-förmedling** employment bureau (agency) **-ombud** local agent **-ombyte** change of job **-siffra** *sport.* place number **-sökande** *s9* applicant [for a situation]; (*tidn.rubrik*) appointments and situations

wanted
platt I *a1* **1** flat (*tak* roof; *som en pannkaka* as a pancake); *ha ~ bröst* be flat-chested; *~ fall* (*sport. o. bildl.*) flop **2** (*banal*) commonplace (*kvickhet* witticism) **II** *adv* flat; *falla ~ till marken* (*bildl.*) fall flat; *trycka sig ~ mot väggen* press one's body flat against the wall; *~ intet* nothing at all, absolutely nothing
platta I *s1* plate; (*spis-*) hotplate; (*sten-*) slab; (*rund*) disc; (*vägg-*) tile; (*grammofon-*) record, disc **II** *v1* flatten (*till* out); *~ till* (*bildl.*) squash
platt|fisk flatfish **-form** *s2* platform **-formsbiljett** platform ticket **-fot** flatfoot **-fotad** *a5* flat-foot[ed] **-het 1** (*utan pl*) flatness **2** *bildl.* platitude
platt|i'tyd *s3, se platthet* **2 -järn** flat steel (iron); *koll.* flats (*pl*) **-mask** *zool.* flatworm **-näst** [-ä:-] *a4* flat-nosed
plattsätt|are [floor-]tiler, tile-layer **-ning** tiling, tile-laying
platt|söm *sömn.* satin stitch **-tyska** (*hopskr. plattyska*) Low German **-tång** (*hopskr. plattång*) flat[-nosed] pliers (*pl*)
pla'tå *s3* plateau, tableland **-sko** platform shoe
plausibel [-'si:-] *a2* plausible; (*rimlig*) reasonable
plebej [-'bejj] *s3* plebeian **plebejisk** [-'bejj-] *a5* plebeian
plebiscit [- 'si:t, -'ʃi:t] *s7* plebiscite
ple'jad *s3* **1** *astr., P~erna* the Pleiades **2** *litt. hist., P~en* the Pleiad[e]
plektr|on ['plektrån] *-et -er,* **plektrum** ['plekt-] *s4* plectrum (*pl* plectra), plectron
plenar|församling [-ˣna:r-], **-möte** plenary meeting
plenum [ˣple:-] *s8* plenary sitting (assembly)
pleo'nas|m *s3* pleonasm **-tisk** *a5* pleonastic[al]
pleti ['ple:-] *se kreti*
pleu'rit *s3* pleurisy
plexiglas plexiglass
pli *s9, s7* manners (*pl*), bearing; *sätta ~ på ngn* (*vard.*) lick s.b. into shape
pligg *s2* peg **pligga** peg (*fast* down)
1 plikt *s3* (*skyldighet*) duty (*mot* to, towards); (*förpliktelse*) obligation; *~en framför allt* duty first; *göra sin ~* do one's duty; *vi har den smärtsamma ~en att meddela* ours is the painful duty to announce
2 plikt *s3* (*böter*) fine
plikta pay a fine (*för* for); *han fick ~ 2 pund* he was fined 2 pounds; *~ med livet* pay with one's life (*för* for)
plikt|förgäten [-j-] *a3* forgetful of one's duty (obligations); negligent **-förgätenhet** [-j-] dereliction (neglect) of duty **-ig** *a1* [in duty] bound, obliged **-känsla** sense of duty **-kär** devoted to duty **-människa** person with a strong sense of duty **-skyldig** dutiful; obligatory (*leende* smile) **-skyldigast** *superl. adv* dutifully, in duty bound; *skratta ~* laugh dutifully **-trogen** faithful, dutiful **-tro[gen]het** faithfulness, dutifulness **-uppfyllelse** fulfilment of one's duty
plimsollmärke [ˣplimsåll-] *sjö.* Plimsoll mark (line), load line
plint *s2* **1** *gymn.* vaulting box (horse) **2** *byggn.* plinth; *elektr.* test terminal box

plio'cen *al, geol.* Pliocene
plira peer, screw up one's eyes (*mot* at) **plirig**
al peering, narrowed (*ögon* eyes)
pliss|é *s3* pleating **-era** pleat, plait **-ering**
pleating
plister ['pliss-] *s2, bot.* dead-nettle
plit *s7* (*knåp*) toil
1 plita (*skriva*) write busily
2 plita *sl* pimple, pustule
plock [-å-] *s7, ej pl* gleanings, odds and ends
(*pl*); (*-ande*) picking **plocka 1** pick, gather
(*blommor* flowers; *frukt* fruit); lift (*potatis*
potatoes); ~ *av* (*bort*) pick off; ~ *fram* bring
(take) out; ~ *ihop* gather together, collect; ~
in (*t.ex. från trädgården*) gather (pick) and
bring in, (*i skåp e.d.*) put away in[to]; ~ *ner*
(*t.ex. äpplen*) get (take) down; ~ *sönder* take
to pieces; ~ *undan* clear away; ~ *upp* pick up;
~ *ut* take out (*ur* of), (*utvälja*) pick out **2** pluck
(*en fågel* a fowl; *ögonbrynen* one's eyebrows)
3 *sitta och* ~ *med* sit and fiddle with; ~ *på la-
kanet* pluck at the sheet **plockning** picking
etc.
plog *s2* plough; *gå bakom* ~*en* follow the
plough; *spänna hästen för* ~*en* put the horse
before the plough; *lägga under* ~*en* put under
the plough
plog|a (*väg*) clear from (of) snow; (*med skidor*)
stem, snowplough **-ben** *anat.* vomer **-bill**
ploughshare-point **-fåra** furrow **-land** (*jord-
mått*) ploughland **-ning** ploughing
ploj [plåjj] *s2, s3* ploy
plomb [-å-] *s3* **1** (*blysigill*) lead [seal], seal **2**
tandläk. filling, stopping **-era 1** (*försegla*) seal
[up], lead **2** *tandläk.* fill, stop **-ering 1** sealing;
konkr. seal **2** filling, stopping
plommon [-ån] *s7* plum **-kärna** plum stone
-stop *s7* bowler (*AE.* derby) [hat] **-träd** plum
[tree]
plotta [-å-] plot
plotter ['plått-] *s7, ej pl* (*krafs*) trifles (*pl*)
plottingbord plotting table
plottra ~ *bort* fritter (*tid äv.:* trifle) away **plott-
rig** *al* jumbled, disjointed
plufsig *al* flabby
plugg 1 *s2* (*tapp*) plug, stopper; (*i tunna*) tap **2**
s2, vard. (*potatis*) spud **3** *s7* (*-läsning*) swotting, cramming; (*skola*) school
plugg|a 1 (*slå in plugg i*) plug, stop up; ~ *igen*
clog **2** (*läsa*) swot (*latin* Latin); *AE. sl.* dig
[in]; ~ *på en examen* cram for an examination;
~ *engelska med ngn* coach s.b. in English
-häst swot[ter] **-ning 1** plugging *etc.* **2**
swotting *etc.*
1 plump *al* coarse, rude
2 plump *s2* blot
plumpa make blots; blot (*äv.* ~ *ner*); ~ *i protokollet* (*bildl.*) make a blunder
plumphet coarseness, rudeness
plumpudding [ˣplumm-] plum pudding
plums *s2, s7, interj, adv* plop, flop **plumsa** [go]
splash, flop (*i vattnet* into the water); *gå och*
~ *i leran* splash about in the mud
plundr|a rob (*ngn på* s.b. of); plunder, pillage,
sack (*en stad* a town); strip (*julgranan* the
Christmas tree) **-ing** robbing; plundering,
pillage, sack **-ingståg** plundering expedition,

raid, foray
plunta *sl* pocket flask; *vard.* pocket pistol
plural|bildning formation of the plural **-böj-
ning** plural inflection
pluralis *s3* (*stå i* be in the) plural **pluralism**
pluralism **pluralitet** *s3* plurality
pluraländelse plural ending
plurr *s7, ramla i* ~*et* fall into the water
plus [pluss] **I** *s7* (*-tecken*) plus [sign]; (*tillägg*)
addition; (*överskott*) [sur]plus; (*fördel*) advantage; *termometern visar* ~ the temperature is
above zero **II** *adv* plus; *2* ~ *2 är 4* two plus
two make four; *det är 1 grad* ~ it is one degree
above zero; ~ *minus noll* zero, nil, absolutely
nothing **-fours** ['plussfårs, -'få:rs] *pl* plus fours
-grad degree above zero **-kvamperfektum**
(*i in the*) past perfect (pluperfect) [tense] **-sida**
positive (credit) side
plussig *al* bloated
plus|tecken plus [sign] **-värde** added value
pluta ~ [*med munnen*] pout
Plutarchos [-'tarkås] Plutarch
pluto|krat plutocrat **-kra'ti** *s3* plutocracy
-kratisk [-'kra:-] *a5* plutocratic
plu'ton *s3* platoon **-chef** platoon leader
plu'tonium *s8* plutonium
plym *s3* plume **plymasch** [-'a:ʃ] *s3* bunch of
feathers; plumage
ply'må *s3* sofa cushion
plysch [-y:-] *s3* plush
plywood ['plajjvɒd] *s3* plywood
plåg|a 1 *sl* pain; torment; (*-oris*) plague,
nuisance; *ha -or* have (be in) pain, be suffering; *vara en* ~ *för sin omgivning* be a plague
to those around one **II** *vl* pain; torment; (*oroa*)
worry; (*besvära*) bother; ~*s av gikt* (*dåligt
samvete*) be tormented by gout (a bad conscience); *se* ~*d ut* look pained
plågo|ande tormentor **-ris** scourge; torment,
plague
plågsam *al* painful
plån *s7* (*skiva*) tablet; (*på tändsticksask*) striking
surface; *tända endast mot lådans* ~ strike only
on the box **-bok** wallet; *AE. äv.* billfold,
pocketbook
plåster ['plåss-] *s7* plaster; *lägga* ~ *på såret* put
plaster on a wound, *bildl.* pour balm into the
wound **plåsterlapp** piece of plaster **plåstra**
plaster; ~ *ihop* patch up; ~ *om ngn* dress a p.'s
wounds, (*sköta om*) tend s.b.
plåt *s2* **1** (*metall*) sheet metal; sheet[-iron] **2**
(*skiva*) plate (*äv. foto-*); *korrugerad* ~ corrugated sheeting
plåt|a *vard.* photograph **-arbete** platework,
sheet-metal work **-beslag** plate covering,
plating **-burk** tin, can **-rör** sheet-metal pipe
(tube) **-sax** plateshears (*pl*) **-skada** sheet damage **-slagare** sheet-metal worker, plater **-sla-
geri** *abstr.* metal-plating; (*-verkstad*) sheet-
-metal [work]shop, plate works **-tak** tin roof
pläd *s3, s2* [travelling] rug; (*skotsk*) plaid
pläder|a plead **-ing** (*slut-*) summing-up of the
defence; *en* ~ (*äv.*) a plea
pläga *se bruka* **plägsed** custom
pläter ['plä:-] *s2* plate **plätera** plate
plätt *s2* **1** (*fläck*) spot **2** *kokk.* small pancake
-lagg pancake iron, griddle

plöja–politisk 410

plöj|a [ˣplöjja] v2 plough (äv. bildl.); ~ igenom en bok plough through a book; ~ ner plough in, (vinst) plough back; ~ upp (åker o.d.) plough up -ning ploughing
plös s2 tongue
plötslig a1 sudden, abrupt; unexpected plötsligen, plötsligt adv suddenly; all of a sudden
PM, P.M. s9, s7 (förk. för promemoria) memo
pneumatisk [pnevˈmaː-] a5 pneumatic pneumo'ni s3 pneumonia
pochera poach
pock [påkk] s7, se 3 lock pocka ~ på [urgently] insist [up]on; frågan ~r på sin lösning the problem craves (demands) a quick solution pockande a4 importunate, pressing, urgent (behov need); (om pers.) importune
pocketbok [ˣpåkk-] paperback; AE. äv. pocketbook
podager [-ˈdaː-] s2 podagra, gout
podium [ˈpɔː-] s4 podium (pl äv. podia); platform
po'em s7 poem poe'si s3 poetry poesialbum poetry album poet s3 poet poe'tik s3 poetics (behandlas vanl. som sg) poetisera poetize poetisk [pɔˈeː-] a5 poetical; poetic (frihet licence)
pogrom [-ˈgråːm] s3 pogrom
pointer [ˈpåjn-] s2 pointer
pointillism [pɔäŋ-] pointillism
pojk|aktig [ˣpåjk-] a1 boyish -aktighet boyishness -bok book for boys -byting little chap, urchin
pojk|e [ˣpåjke, ˈpåjke] s2 boy; (känslobetonat) lad -flicka 1 (-aktig flicka) tomboy 2 (omtyckt av ~ar) girl for the boys -liga street gang -namn boy's name -scout boy scout -spoling young scamp (rascal), hobbledehoy -streck boyish prank -vasker s2, se -spoling -år under ~en during [his etc.] boyhood; alltifrån ~en ever since I (he etc.) was a boy
po'kal s3 (bägare) goblet; sport. cup, trophy
poker [ˈpåː-] s9 poker -ansikte poker (deadpan) face
pokulera drink, tipple, booze
pol s3 pole
po'lack s3 Pole
polardag [-ˣlaːr-] polar day
polare vard. chum, pal, mate, AE. buddy
polar|expedition [-ˣlaːr-] polar (arctic, antarctic) expedition -forskare polar (arctic, antarctic) explorer -hav polar sea -is polar ice
polarisation polarization polarisator s3 polarizer polarisera polarize polaritet polarity
polar|kalott [-ˣlaːr-] polar cap -natt polar night
polaro'id s3 polaroid
polarräv [-ˣlaːr-] arctic fox
polcirkel polar circle; norra (södra) ~n the Arctic (Antarctic) circle
pole'mi|k s3, ej pl polemics (pl, behandlas som sg) polemiker [-ˈleː-] polemic, controversialist polemisera polemize polemisk [-ˈleː-] a5 polemic[al], controversial
Polen [ˈpåː-] n Poland
poler|a polish (äv. bildl.); (metall) burnish; ~t ris polished rice -ing polishing; burnishing

-medel polish; abrasive -skiva polishing wheel (disc)
polhöjd altitude of the pole
policy [ˈpålːisi] s3 policy
polikli'nik s3 outpatient department
polio [ˈpɔː-] s9 polio[myelitis] -vaccin antipolio vaccin -vaccinering polio vaccination
1 po'lis s3, försäk. policy
2 po'lis s3 1 (ordningsmakt) police; koll. [the] police; gå in vid ~en join the police force; anmäla för ~en report to the police; efterspanad av ~en wanted by the police; göra motstånd mot ~ resist arrest; ridande ~ mounted police, AE. äv. (i lantdistrikt) ranger; ropa på ~ shout for the police; ~en har gjort chock the police have charged 2 (-man) policeman, [police] officer; constable; AE. patrolman; vard. i Storbritannien bobby; sl. cop[per]; kvinnlig ~ policewoman
polis|anmäla, -anmälan report to the police -assistent ung. police sergeant -bevakning police surveillance; huset står under ~ the house is being watched by the police -bil police (patrol, squad) car -bricka policeman's badge -chef police commissioner, chief constable, head of a police force; AE. chief of police, marshal -chock police charge -distrikt police district -domare police magistrate -domstol police court -eskort police escort -förhör interrogation by the police; anställa ~ med ngn hold a police interrogation with s.b. -förordning police regulation -förvar i ~ in custody; tas i ~ be taken in charge by the police -hund police dog -hus police headquarters (pl), police station -intendent assistant chief constable
polis|i'är a1 police -kammare administrative police authority; Storbritannien ung. police commissioners (pl) -kedja police cordon -kommissarie police superintendent; AE. captain; biträdande ~ chief inspector -konstapel se 2 polis 2 -kontor sub-police-station -kund old offender; vard. jailbird -kår, -makt police force -man se 2 polis 2 -myndigheter police authorities -mästare chief constable, [police] commissioner
polisonger [-ˈsåŋer] pl sideboards, side whiskers; AE. sideburns
polis|piket riot squad; (bil) police van -pådrag det var fullt ~ the police was there in full force -rapport police report -razzia police raid -sak police matter -spärr police cordon; (väg-) roadblock -stat police state -station police station -syster policewoman -undersökning police investigation -uniform policeman's (policewoman's) uniform -utredning se -undersökning -vakt police guard -väsen police [system, organization; authorities (pl)]
politbyrå [-ˣliːt-] Politburo
polit|ik s3, ej pl 1 (statsangelägenheter, statskonst) politics (sg o. pl); syssla med ~ be engaged in politics; tala ~ talk politics 2 (-isk princip, handlingssätt, slughet) policy; line of action; den öppna dörrens ~ open-door policy; föra en fast ~ take a firm line; avvaktande ~ wait-and-see policy -iker [-ˈliː-] politician -isera politicize -isering politicization -isk

[-'li:-] *a5* political
politruk [-'truck] *s3* political commissar
poli'tyr *s3* [French] polish; *bildl.* polish
polka [ˣpåll-] *s1* polka **-gris** peppermint rock **-hår** pageboy cut
pollare [ˣpåll-] *sjö.* bollard
pollen ['påll-] *s7* pollen **-analys** pollen analysis, palynology **-korn** pollen grain
pol'lett *s3* (*av metall*) check, counter, token; (*av papper*) ticket; (*gas-*) disc
polletter|a label, register; *AE.* check; ~ *sitt bagage* have one's luggage labelled (registered); *AE.* check one's baggage **-ing** [luggage] registration **-ingskvitto** luggage ticket; *AE.* baggage check
pollin|ation [på-] pollination **-era** pollinate
pollution pollution
polo ['pɷ:-] *s6* polo **-krage** turtleneck
polo'näs *s3* polonaise
polo|spel polo **-tröja** turtleneck sweater
polsk [-å(:)-] *a5* Polish; *~a korridoren* the Polish Corridor; ~ *riksdag* (*bildl.*) bedlam
1 polska [-å(:)-] *s1* **1** (*språk*) Polish **2** (*kvinna*) Polish woman
2 polska [ˣpåls-] *s1* (*dans*) reel
pol|spänning terminal voltage **-stjärna** P~n Polaris, the North (Pole) Star
poly|a'mid [på-, pɷ-] *s3* polyamide **-an'dri** *s3* polyandry **-eder** [-'e:d-] *s2* polyhedron (*pl äv.* polyhedra) **-ester** [-'es-] polyester **-e'ten** polythene, polyethylene **-fo'ni** [-få-] *s3* polyphony **-'gam** *a1* polygamous **-ga'mi** *s3* polygamy **-gamist** polygamist **-glott** [-'glått] *s3* polyglot **-gon** [-'gå:n] *s3* polygon **-krom** [-'krå:m] *a1* polychrome **-'mer I** *s3* polymer **II** *a5* polymeric **-merisation** polymerization **-morf** [-'mårf] *a1* polymorphous
Polynesien [pålly'ne:-] *n* Polynesia
polynes|ier [pålly'ne:-] *s9* Polynesian **-isk** *a5* Polynesian
polynom [påly-] *s7, s3* polynomial
po'lyp *s3* **1** *zool.* polyp **2** *med.* polyp, polypus (*pl* polypi); *~er bakom näsan* adenoids **-djur** hydrozoan
poly|semi *språkv.* polysemy **-teism** [pålly-] polytheism **-teist** polytheist **-teknisk** ~ *skola* polytechnic school **-vinylklorid** polyvinyl chloride
po'lär *a1* polar
pomad|a [-ˣma:-] *s1* pomade **-era** pomade
pomerans [-'ans, -aŋs] *s3* Seville (bitter) orange **-skal** Seville-orange peel
Pommern ['påmm-] *n* Pomerania **pommersk** ['påmm-] *a5* Pomeranian
pommes frites [påmm'fritt] *pl* chips, chipped potatoes; *AE.* French fried potatoes, French fries
pomo|log pomologist **-logi** *s3* pomology
pomp [-å-] *s9* pomp (*och ståt* and circumstance)
pompe'jansk [-å-a:-] *a5* Pompeian **Pompeji** [påm'peji] *n* Pompeii
pom'pös [-å-] *a1* pompous; (*högtravande*) declamatory
pondus ['pånn-] *s9* authority, impressiveness; (*eftertryck*) emphasis, weight
ponera [pɷ-, på-] suppose
ponny ['pånni] *s3* pony

pontifi'kat [-å-] *s7* pontificate
ponton [pån'tɷ:n, -'tå:n] *s3* pontoon **-bro** pontoon (floating) bridge
1 pop [på:p] *s3* (*grek.-kat. präst*) pope
2 pop [påpp] *s3* pop
pop|artist [ˣpåpp-] pop musician (singer) **-band** pop group **-konst** pop art
pop'lin [på-] *s3, s4* poplin
pop|musik pop [music] **-orkester** pop orchestra
poppel ['påpp-] *s2* poplar
popsångare pop singer
populariser|a popularize **-ing** popularization
popularitet popularity **popularitetsjakt** popularity hunting
populasen [-'la:-] *best. f.* the populace
populism populism
popu'lär *a1* popular (*bland* among, with) **-press** popular press **-vetenskap** popular science
por *s3* pore
por'fyr [-å-] *s3* porphyry
porig *a1* porous
porla [ˣpå:r-] murmur, babble; *~nde skratt* rippling laugh
pormask blackhead
porno|grafi *s3* pornography; *vard.* smut **-grafisk** [-'gra:-] *a5* pornographic
porositet porosity, porousness
porr *s3* porno **-tidning** porno magazine
pors [pårs] *s3, bot.* sweet gale, bog myrtle
pors'lin [-å-] *s4* (*ämne*) china; (*äkta*) porcelain; *koll.* china, crockery
porslins|affär china shop **-blomma** wax plant **-fabrik** porcelain (china) factory **-figur** porcelain (china) figure **-krossning** [-åss-] (*tivolinöje*) crockery shy **-lera** china clay, kaolin **-målning** porcelain (china) painting **-servis** set of china **-varor** *pl* chinaware, crockery (*sg*); (*finare*) porcelain ware (*sg*)
port [-ɷ(:)-] *s2* (*-gång*) gateway, doorway; (*ytterdörr*) [street, (front)]door; (*t. park, stad samt bildl.*) gate; *köra ngn på ~en* turn s.b. out [of doors]; *fienden stod framför ~arna* the enemy was at the gates; *stå och prata i ~en* stand talking in the doorway (gateway); *den trånga ~en* (*bildl.*) the strait gate; *Höga P~en* the Sublime Porte
portabel [-å-] *a2* portable
por'tal *s3* portal, porch **-figur** *bildl.* outstanding (prominent) figure (personality)
portativ ['pårr-, -'ti:v] *a1* portable
porter ['pår:r-] *s9* stout; (*svagare*) porter
port'följ [-å-] *s3* briefcase; (*av värdepapper*) portfolio; *minister utan* ~ minister without portfolio
port|förbjuda forbid to enter the house (country); (*utestänga*) exclude, keep out; (*bannlysa*) ban **-gång** *s2* gateway, doorway; *köra fast redan i ~en* (*bildl.*) get stuck at the very start (outset) **-halva** half-door, half-gate
portier [pårt'je:] *s3* hall-porter, receptionist; *AE. äv.* [room]clerk **-loge** [-lå:ʃ] *s5* reception desk
por'tik *s3* portico
portion [pårt'ʃɷ:n] portion; (*mat- äv.*) helping, serving; *mil.* rations (*pl*); *i små ~er* in small

P

portions (doses); *en stor ~ kalvstek* a large helping of veal; *en god ~ tur* a great deal of luck; *en viss ~ sunt förnuft* a certain amount of common sense; *i små ~er* in small doses **-era** portion (*ut* out)
portiär [pårt'jä:r] *s3* portire, curtain
portklapp knocker
portmonnä [pårtmå'nä:] *s3* purse; *AE. äv.* pocketbook
portnyckel latchkey
porto [ˣpårr-] *s6* postage; (*för postanvisning, Storbritannien*) poundage; (*för telegram*) charge[s *pl*]; *gå för enkelt ~* pass at the single[-postage] rate **-fri** free of postage, post-free **-kostnad** postage **-sats** rate of postage, postal rate
port'rätt *s7* portrait; *~et är mycket likt* the portrait is a good likeness **-album** family album **-byst** [portrait] bust **-era** portray **-ering** portrayal **-galleri** portrait gallery **-lik** like the original, lifelike *~likhet* likeness to the original **-målare** portrait painter **-måleri** portrait painting
porttelefon hall (house) telephone
Portugal ['pårr] *n* Portugal
portu'gis [-å-] *s3* Portuguese (*pl* Portuguese) **-isk** *a5* Portuguese **-iska** *s1* **1** (*språk*) Portuguese **2** (*kvinna*) Portuguese woman
portvakt porter (*fem.* portress), doorkeeper, gatekeeper; (*i hyreshus*) caretaker, concierge; *AE.* janitor (*fem.* janitress)
port|vin [ˣpå:rt-] port [wine] **-vinstå** *ha ~* have a gouty big toe
portör [-å-] botanical tin, vasculum
porös *a1* porous; (*svamplik*) spongy
pose [på:s] *s5* pose, attitude, posture; *intaga en ~* strike an attitude, adopt a pose **posera** pose (*för* to); strike an attitude; *~ med ngt* make a show of s.th. **poserande** [-'se:-] *a4* posing, attitudinizing
position position; *bildl. äv.* status, standing; *uppge sin ~* (*i fråga o.d.*) give up one's ground **positionsljus** *sjö.* running light
1 positiv ['pɷ:s-, 'pɷss-] **I** *a1* positive **II** *s3* (*i* in the) positive
2 posi'tiv *s7* (*musikinstrument*) barrel organ
positivhalare organ-grinder
positiv|ism positivism **-ist** positivist
positivspelare organ-grinder
positron [-'trå:n] *s3* positron, positive electron
possession [-e'ʃɷ:n] [landed] property (estate) **possessionat** estate owner, landed proprietor **possessiv** ['påss-, -'si:v] *a1* possessive (*pronomen* pronoun)
1 post [-å-] *s3* (*bokförings-*) item, entry; (*belopp*) amount, sum; (*varuparti*) lot, parcel; (*värdepapper*) block, parcel; *bokförd ~* entry; *bokföra en ~* make an entry, post an item
2 post [-å-] *s3* **1** *se dörr-, fönster-* **2** *se brand-, vatten-*
3 post [-å-] *s3* **1** (*-ering; plats, befattning*) post; *stå på ~* stand sentry, be on guard; *stupa på sin ~* be killed at one's post; *bekläda en viktig ~* hold an important post (position) **2** (*vakt-*) sentry, sentinel
4 post [-å-] *s3* (*brev o.d.*) post, *AE.* mail; (*-anstalt*) post office; *jfr äv. postverk; ankommande*

(*avgående*) ~ inward (outward) mail; *med dagens* (*morgonens*) ~ by today's (the morning) post; *per ~* by post; *sortera ~en* sort the mail; *skicka med ~[en]* send by post; *lämna ett brev på ~en* take a letter to the post [office]
post|a post, mail, send by post (mail) **-abonnemang** postal subscription **-adress** postal (mailing) address **-'al** *a1* postal
postament [på-] *s7* postament, pedestal
post|anstalt post office **-anvisning** money order (*förk.* M.O.); (*på fastställt belopp*) postal order (*förk.* P.O.); *hämta ut en ~* cash a money order **-befordran** forwarding (conveyance) by post (mail); *avlämna till ~* post, mail **-befordringsavgift** postage **-box** post office box (*förk.* P.O.B.) **-båt** mailboat, packet [boat]
postdater|a [-å-] postdate **-ing** postdating
post|diligens mailcoach, stagecoach, *AE.* mailcar **-distrikt** postal region (district)
postera [-å-] **1** (*ställa ut post*) station, post **2** (*gå, stå på post*) stand sentry, be on sentry duty
poste restante [påst re'staŋt, -'stant] poste restante, *AE.* general delivery
postering [-å-] picket, outpost
post|expedition [branch] post office **-expeditör** post-office clerk **-fack** *se postbox* **-förande** *a4* mail-carrying; ~ *tåg* mail train **-förskott** cash on delivery (*förk.* C.O.D.); *ett ~ a* cash-on-delivery parcel (*etc.*); *sända ngt mot ~* send s.th. cash on delivery **-försändelse** postal article (matter, item)
postgiro postal giro service **-blankett** postal giro form **-konto** postal giro account **-nummer** postal giro account number
postgymnasi'al [-å-] ~ *utbildning* post-secondary [college (university)] education
postgång postal service
postil'jon [på-] *s3* sorting clerk; (*förr*) mailcoach driver
postilla [-ˣtilla] *s1* collection of sermons (homilies)
postindustriell post-industrial
postisch [pås'tiʃ] *s3* hairpiece, postiche
post|kontor post office **-kort** postcard, postal card **-kupé** mailcoach, *AE.* mailcar **-lucka** post-office counter (window)
postludium [-å-'lu:-] *s4* postlude
postlåda *se brevlåda*
postmodern|ism post-Modernism **-istisk** post-modernistic
post|mästare postmaster (*fem.* postmistress) **-nummer** postcode; *AE.* zip code
posto [ˣpåstɷ] *i uttr.: fatta ~* take one's stand, post o.s.
post|order mail order **-orderfirma** mail-order company **-paket** postal parcel; *skicka som ~* send by parcel post **-papper** notepaper, letter paper **-remissa** *se postväxel* **-röst** (*vid val*) postal vote **-rösta** vote by post **-röstning** postal voting
postskriptum [påst'skripp-] *s8* postscript (*förk.* P.S.)
post|sparbank post-office savings bank **-sparbanksbok** post-office bankbook **-station** sub-post-office **-stämpel** postmark; *~ns datum* date as postmark **-säck** mailbag, postbag, mailsack **-taxa** postage rates (*pl*) **-tjänste-**

man post-office employee (clerk) **-tåg** mail train
postu'l|at [-å-] *s7* postulate **-era** postulate
postum [pås'tu:m] *a1* posthumous
post|utdelning postal delivery **-vagn** mailcoach, *AE.* mailcar **-verk** *~et* [the] Post Office **-väsen** postal services (*pl*), postal system **-växel** money order, bank[er's] draft
posör posturer *etc., jfr posera*
potatis [-'ta:-] *s2* potato; *koll.* potatoes (*pl*); *färsk (oskalad, kokt, stekt)* ~ new (unpeeled, boiled, fried) potatoes; *skala* ~ peel (skin) potatoes; *sätta (ta upp)* ~ plant (lift) potatoes; *han har satt sin sista* ~ (*ung.*) he has cooked his goose **-blast** potato haulm **-bullar** *pl, kokk.* potato cakes **-kräfta** potato wart **-land** *s7* potato plot (patch) **-mjöl** potato flour **-mos** mashed (creamed) potatoes (*pl*) **-näsa** pug nose **-odling** *abstr.* potato-growing; *konkr.* potato field **-plockning** [-å-] potato-picking **-puré** *se* -mos **-sallad** potato salad **-skal** potato peel (skin); (*avskalat*) potato peelings (*pl*) **-skalare** potato-peeler **-åker** potato field
po'tens *s3 (förmåga)* potency; *med. äv.* sexual power, potence; *mat.* power **po'tent** *a4* potent **potentat** potentate **potential** [-n(t)si'a:l] *s3* potential **potentialskillnad** potential difference **potentiell** [-n(t)si'ell] *a1* potential **potentiera** [-n(t)si'e:ra] intensify **potentiometer** [-n(t)siɷ'me:-] *s2* potentiometer
potkes, potkäs [påt'çe:s, -'çess] *s3* cheese creamed with spices and brandy
potpur'ri [-å-] *s3* potpourri; *mus. äv.* medley
pott [-å-] *s3, spel.* pool, kitty
pott|a [-å-] *s1* chamber [pot] **-aska** potash, potassium carbonate
po'äng *s3 (värdeenhet s9)* point; (*skol.*) mark; *få* ~ get a point (points); *få två* ~ (*äv.*) score two; *vinna (förlora) på* ~ win (lose) on points; *livet har sina ~er* life has its points; *historien saknar* ~ the story lacks point (is pointless) **-bedömning** marking **-beräkning** *sport. o. spel.* scoring **-besegra** outpoint **-jakt** *ung.* collecting credits **-plats** points-winning place **-seger** victory (win) on points **-ställning** score **-summa** final (total) score **-sätta** award points to; *skol.* mark, assign marks to **-sättning** [the] awarding of points; *skol. äv.* [the] marking **-tal** [total] points (*pl*), score **-tera** emphasize **-tips** treble chance pool
p-piller [ˣpe:-] contraceptive tablet; *vard.* the pill
PR *förk. för public relations*
pracka ~ *på ngn ngt* foist s.th. [up]on s.b.
Prag *n* Prague
pragmat|iker [-'ma:-] pragmatist **-isk** *a5* pragmatic[al]
prakt *s3* magnificence, grandeur; splendour; *visa sig i all sin* ~ appear in all one's splendour; *sommaren stod i sin fulla* ~ summer was in all its glory **-band** de luxe binding **-exemplar** magnificent (spendid) specimen **-full** magnificent, splendid **-fullhet** *se prakt* **-gemak** state apartment
praktik *s3* **1** practice; (*övning*) experience; *i ~en* in practice; *omsätta i ~en* put into practice; *skaffa sig* ~ get practice ([practical] experi-

ence) **2** (*läkarverksamhet etc.*) practice; *öppna egen* ~ open one's own practice **praktikant** trainee, probationer, learner **praktikant-tjänstgöring** work (*etc.*) as a trainee (*etc.*) **praktiker** ['prakk-] practician; (*om läkare*) practitioner **praktikfall** case study
praktisera 1 (*tillämpa*) put into practice; (*lära sig ett yrke*) get experience **2** (*som läkare etc.*) practise [as a doctor]; *~nde läkare* general practitioner (*förk.* G.P.) **praktisk** ['prakk-] *a5* practical; (*användbar*) useful, serviceable; (*lätthanterlig*) handy; *i det ~a livet* in practical life; ~ *erfarenhet* working experience **praktiskt** ['prak-] *adv* practically, in a practical way; ~ *användbar* practical, useful; ~ *genomförbar* (*utförbar*) practicable; ~ *taget* practically, as good as
prakt|möbel magnificent piece (suite) of furniture **-pjäs** showpiece, museum piece **-verk** magnificent volume (edition), de luxe edition **-älskande** fond of display, splendour-loving
pra'lin *s3* chocolate, chocolate cream
prassel ['prass-] *s7* rustle **prassla** rustle (*äv. med, i*)
prat *s7 (samspråk)* talk, chat; (*strunt-*) nonsense; (*skvaller*) gossip, tittle-tattle; *tomt (löst)* ~ idle talk; [*å*] ~*!* rubbish!, nonsense!; *vad är det för* ~*!* what's all this rubbish!; *inte bry sig om ~et* take no notice of gossip **prata** talk (*med* to, with; *om* about, of); chat; ~ *för sig själv* talk to o.s.; ~ *i sömnen* talk in one's sleep; ~ *affärer (kläder)* talk business (clothes); [*vad*] *du ~r!* nonsense!, rubbish!, fiddlesticks!; ~ *strunt* talk nonsense (rubbish); *folk ~r så mycket* people will talk; ~ *omkull ngn* talk s.b. down [to a standstill]; ~ *på* talk away, go on talking; ~*s vid om saken* talk it over
prat|bubbla (*i serie*) balloon **-ig** *a1 (om pers.)* talkative; (*om stil*) chatty; verbose **-kvarn** chatterbox **-makare** talker, chatterbox, rattler **-sam** *a1* talkative, loquacious **-samhet** talkativeness, loquacity **-sjuk** fond of talking; loquacious **-stund** chat; *ta sig en* ~ have a chat **-tagen** *best. f. pl:* vara *i* ~ be in a talkative mood
praxis ['praks-] *best. f.* praxis *el.* -en practice, custom, usage; *enligt vedertagen* ~ by usage; *bryta mot* ~ depart from practice; *det är* ~ *att* it is the custom to
prebenda [-ˣbenn-, -'benn-] *s6* prebendary's benefice
precedensfall [-ˣdens-] precedent
preceptor [-ˣseptår] *s3, ung.* reader, associate professor
preciosa [-esiˣɷ:-] *pl* valuables; bric-a-brac (*sg*)
preciositet [-siɷsi-] preciosity, affectation
pre'cis I *a1* precise, exact; (*om pers. äv.*) particular; (*punktlig*) punctual **II** *adv* precisely; exactly; *inte* ~ not exactly; *komma* ~ *kl 9* arrive at 9 o'clock sharp (on the dot); *komma* ~ [*på minuten*] be punctual, come on the dot; ~ *som förut* just as before; *just* ~*!* exactly!
preciser|a specify, define exactly; (*i detalj*) particularize; ~ *närmare* state more precisely

-ing defining, specification
precision precision, exactitude, accuracy
precisions|arbete precision work **-instrument** precision instrument **-våg** precision balance (scales)
preci'ös *a1* affected, precious
predestin|ation predestination **-era** predestinate
predika [-'di:-] preach (*för* to; *om, över* on); ~ *bra* preach a good sermon **predika'ment** *s7, s4* predicament
predik|an [-'di:-] *best. f.* *-an, pl predikningar* sermon (*över* on); (*straff-*) lecture; *hålla en* ~ deliver a sermon (*för* to) **-ant** preacher; (*frikyrko-*) minister **-are** preacher; *P~n* [the Book of] Ecclesiastes
predikat *s7* predicate **predika'tiv** I *s7, se predikatsfyllnad* II *a1* predicative **predikatsfyllnad** predicat[iv]e complement
predikning [-'di:k-] *se predikan*
prediko|samling [-ˣdi:-] book of sermons **-text** [sermon] text **-ton** sermonizing tone
predik|stol [ˣpredd-, ˣpre:-] pulpit; *bestiga ~en* go up into the pulpit; *stå i ~en* stand (be) in the pulpit **-stolspsalm** hymn just before the sermon
predispo|nera predispose (*för* to) **-sition** predisposition (*för* to)
pre|dominera predominate **-exis'tens** preexistence **-fabricera** prefabricate **-fabrikation** prefabrication
pre'fekt *s3* (*fransk ämbetsman*) prefect; *univ.* head **prefektur** (*ämbete, lokal*) prefecture
preferens [-'raŋs, -'rens] *s3* preference **-aktie** preference share
pre'fix *s7* prefix
pregn|ans [preŋ'nans, preg-, -'aŋs] *s3* pregnancy **-ant** [preg'nant, -'aŋt] *a1* pregnant
1 preja [ˣprejja] (*skinna*) surcharge, fleece
2 preja [ˣprejja] *sjö.* hail
prejning [ˣprejj-] *sjö.* hailing
prejudicerande [-'se:-] *a4* precedential; ~ *rättsfall* test case **prejudi'kat** *s7* precedent; *skapa ett* ~ create a precedent; *utan* ~ (*äv.*) unprecedented
pre'kär *a1* precarious (*situation* situation)
prelat prelate
prelimi'när *a1* preliminary; provisional; ~ *skatt* preliminary tax, (*källskatt*) pay-as-you-earn tax; *överskjutande* ~ *skatt* preliminary tax paid in excess **preliminärskattesedel** preliminary tax card
preludiera prelude **preludium** [-'lu:-] *s4* prelude
premie ['pre:-] *s5* **1** *försäkr. o.d.* premium (*på* on, for) **2** (*belöning*) prize, reward; (*extra utdeln. på lån e.d.*) bonus; (*export- etc.*) bounty, subsidy; *fast* ~ uniform premium; *inbetalda ~r* paid-up value (*sg*) **-lån** premium bond (lottery) loan **-obligation** premium (lottery) bond
premier|a (*belöna*) reward; (*boskap o.d.*) award a prize to; *~d tjur* prize bull **-ing** (*av boskap o.d.*) awarding of prizes
pre'miss *s3* premise
premi|um ['pre:-] *s4* prize, premium; *dela ut -er* give prizes

premi'är *s3* first (opening) night **-biograf** first-run cinema **-dag** *på ~en* on the first night **-dansör** principal dancer **-dansös** leading ballerina **-lejon** *ung.* first-night habitué **-minister** prime minister, premier **-publik** first-night audience
prenumerant subscriber (*på* for) **prenumeration** subscription (*på* for, to) **prenumerationsavgift** subscription [fee] **prenumerera** subscribe (*på* for, to); ~ *på en tidning* (*äv.*) take a paper
prepa'randkurs preparatory course [of study] **preparat** *s7* preparation; *mikroskopiskt* ~ specimen, slide **preparation** preparation **preparator** *s3* preparator **preparatris** *ung.* medical technical assistant **preparera** prepare (*äv. skol.*)
preposition preposition **-'ell** *a1* prepositional **prepositionsuttryck** prepositional phrase
prerafae'lit *s3, konst.* Pre-Raphaelite
preroga'tiv *s7* prerogative
presbyter ['press-] *s3* [*pl* -'e:rer] presbyter; (*lekmannaäldste*) elder **presbyteri'an** *s3* Presbyterian **presbyteri'ansk** [-a:-] *a5* Presbyterian
presenning [-'senn-, ˣpress-] tarpaulin
presens ['pre:-] *n* (*i* in the) present [tense]; ~ *particip* the present participle
1 present *a4* present
2 present *s3* present, gift; *få ngt i* ~ get s.th. as (for) a present
presenta [-'senta] *se skänka*
presentabel *a2* presentable
presentartiklar *pl* gifts, souvenirs
presentation 1 (*föreställande*) introduction (*för* to); (*mer formellt*) presentation (*för* to) **2** (*uppvisande*) presentation **presentatör** compere
presentbok gift-book
presentera 1 (*föreställa*) introduce (*för* to); (*mer formellt*) present (*vid hovet* at court; *för* to); *får jag* ~ ...? may I introduce ...?, meet ...; ~ *sig* introduce o.s. **2** (*framvisa*) present (*äv. växel e.d.*), show
presentkort gift voucher (token)
preserv|a'tiv *s7* preservative **-era** preserve
preses ['pre:-] *r* president; moderator
president president; (*ordförande äv.*) chairman; (*hovrätts-*) Chief Justice **-kandidat** candidate for the presidency **-skap** *s7* presidency **-tid** (*ngns*) time as president, presidential term
president|ur *se presidentskap* **-val** presidential election
presidera preside (*vid* at, over) **presidium** [-'si:-] *s4* presidency, chairmanship; (*i Sovjet*) presidium; (*styrelse*) presiding (administrative) officers (*pl*)
preskribera *~s* be statute-barred, be barred by the statute of limitations, lapse; *AE. äv.* outlaw; *~d fordran* (*skuld*) statute-barred claim (debt) **preskription** [-p'ʃɷ:n] [statutory] limitation, negative prescription **preskriptionstid** period of limitation
1 press *s3* (*om tidningarna*) press; *~ens frihet* the freedom of the press; *figurera i ~en* appear in the papers; *få god* (*dålig*) ~ get (have) a good (bad) press

2 press *s2* **1** *konkr., tekn.* press; *jfr brev-, frukt-, tryck-* etc.; *gå i* ~ go to press **2** (*tryck, påtryckning*) pressure; *ligga (lägga) i* ~ be pressed; *utöva [stark]* ~ *på* exert [great] pressure [up]on; *leva under en ständig* ~ be living under a constant strain **3** *det är fin* ~ *på byxorna* these trousers have a good crease

press|a 1 press (*kläder* clothes; *blommor* flowers); (*klämma*) squeeze (*apelsiner* oranges); (*med strykjärn äv.*) iron **2** (*tvinga, föra*) press, force; ~ *ngn till [att göra] ngt* force s.b. to (into doing) s.th. **3** (*med betonad partikel*) ~ *fram* press (squeeze; *bildl.* force) out (*ur, av* of); ~ *sig fram* press forward, force one's way along; ~ *ihop* compress; ~ *in* squeeze in; ~ *ner* press (force; *vard.* cut) down (*priserna* [the] prices) **-ande** *a4* oppressive (*hetta* heat); trying (*arbetsförhållanden* working conditions) **press|attaché** press attaché **-byrå** press agency **-censur** censorship of the press **-debatt** debate in the press **-etik** press ethics **-fotograf** press photographer

press|gjuta die-cast **-gjutning** die-casting **-järn** flat iron **-jäst** compressed yeast

press|kampanj press (newspaper) campaign **-klipp** press cutting **-kommentar** press comment[s *pl*] **-konferens** press conference **-lägga** send to [the] press **-läggning** going to [the] press **-läggningsögonblicket** *i* ~ at the moment of going to press **-man** pressman, journalist **-meddelande** press release **-mottagning** *hålla* ~ receive (invite) the press

pressning pressing; squeezing; *jfr pressa*
presspolemik newspaper polemics (*pl*)
press|release [-rili:s] *s5* press release **-revider** press revise (proof) **-stöd** (*hopskr. presstöd*) [state] assistance to newspapers **-uttalande** announcement (statement) in the press
pressveck crease
pressylta (*särskr. press-sylta*) pork brawn
pressöversikt press review
prestanda [-'tann-, -ˣtann-] *pl* (*åligganden*) obligations; *tekn.* performance characteristics, performances **prestation** achievement; performance
prestations|förmåga performance, output [capacity], capacity **-lön** se ackordslön **-mätning** performance measurement
pre'stav *s3* (*stav*) staff at the head of a procession; (*-bärare*) staff bearer
prestera achieve, accomplish; perform
prestige [-'ti:ʃ] *s5* prestige **-fråga** matter of prestige **-förlust** loss of prestige
presum'tiv *a1* presumptive; ~ *arvinge* heir presumptive
preten|dent pretender (*till* to) **-dera** [*äv.* -aŋ'de:-] pretend (*på* to) **-tion** [-taŋ'ʃo:n] pretension (*på* to) **-tiös** [-taŋ'ʃö:s] *a1* pretentious
preteritum [-'te:-] *s8, s4* (*i* in the) preterite
pretiosa [-(t)siˣɷ:-] se preciosa **pretiositet** [-(t)si-] se preciositet **pretiös** [-(t)si'ö:s] se preciös
preussare [ˣpröjs-, ˣpråjs-] Prussian **Preussen** [ˣpröjs-, ˣpråjs-] *n* Prussia **preusseri** [pröjs-, pråjs-] Prussian drill **preussisk** [ˣpröjs-, pråjs-] *a5* Prussian
prevalens *s3* prevalence

preven'tiv I *a1* preventive **II** *s7* preventive **-medel** contraceptive
Priamos Priam
prick *s2* **1** dot, spot, point; (*på måltavla*) bull's eye; (*vid förprickning*) mark, tick; *till punkt och ~a, på ~en* exactly, to a tee (T); *sätta ~en över i-t* (*bildl.*) add the finishing touch; *träffa* ~ hit the mark (*äv. bildl.*); ~ *kl. 6* at six sharp **2** *sport.* penalty point **3** *sjö.* [spar] buoy, perch **4** *en trevlig* (*hygglig*) ~ a nice (decent) fellow (chap, *AE. äv.* guy)
prick|a 1 (*förse med -ar*) dot; (*skjuta prick*) hit; (*sticka hål i*) prick; ~ *av* tick [off], check off, tally; ~ *för* check (mark) off; ~ *in* dot in **2** (*brännmärka*) reprove, reprimand **3** *sjö.* buoy (*en farled* a fairway) **-fri** *sport.* without penalty points **-ig** *a1* spotted, dotted **-ning 1** dotting etc. **2** (*brännmärkning*) reproof, reprimand **3** *sjö.* buoyage **-skytt** sharpshooter; *mil.* sniper **-säker** *en* ~ *skytt* an expert shot
prim [-i:-] *s3, mus. o. fäkt.* prime
prima [ˣpri:-, 'pri:-] *oböjl. a* first-rate, first-class), choice, prime; *vard.* A1, *AE.* dandy
primadonna [-ˣdånna] *s1* prima donna; *teat.* leading lady **primadonnelater** *pl* prima donna airs
primas ['pri:-] *r* primate
primat 1 *s7* primacy **2** *s3, zool.* primate
primfaktor *mat.* aliquot part, prime factor
primitiv [-'ti:v, 'primm-, 'pri:-] *a1* primitive **-itet** primitiveness
primo ['pri:-, ˣpri:-] *pro* ~ firstly, in the first place
primtal prime number
primula ['pri:-] *s1* primula
primus ['pri:-] **I** *r, skol.* top of the class **II** *oböjl. a,* ~ *motor* the prime mover
primuskök [ˣpri:-] primus (*varumärke* [stove])
pri'mär *a1* primary; (*grundläggande*) elementary; (*ursprunglig*) primordial **-lån** first mortgage loan **-val** primary [election]
primör early vegetable (fruit); firstling
prin'cip *s3* principle; *av* (*i*) ~ on (in) principle; *det strider mot mina ~er* it is against my principles; *en man utan ~er* an unprincipled man
princi'pal *s3* principal, proprietor, employer
princi'pat *s7* principate
princip|beslut decision in principle **-fast** strong-principled; *en* ~ *man* (*äv.*) a man of principle **-fråga** question (matter) of principle **-förslag** proposal on guiding principles (guidelines)
principi'ell *a5* founded (based) on principle; (*grundväsentlig*) fundamental; *av ~a skäl* on grounds of principle; *~a hänsyn* considerations of principle **principi'ellt** *adv* on (as a matter of) principle
princip|lös unprincipled **-människa** person (etc.) of principle **-ryttare** doctrinaire **-rytteri** doctrinairism **-uttalande** declaration of principle
prins *s2* prince; *må som en* ~ feel on top of the world **-essa** [-ˣsessa] *s1* princess **-gemål** prince consort **-korv** chipolata sausage **-regent** prince regent
prior [ˣpri:år] *s3* prior (*i* of) **priorinna** prior-

P

ess
prioritera give priority to **prioriterad** *a5* priority, preferential; *AE.* preferred **prioritering** *genom* ~ *av* by giving priority to **prioritet** priority **prioritetsrätt** right of priority
1 pris *s3* (*uppbringat fartyg*) prize, capture; *ta ngt som god* ~ take s.th. as lawful prize
2 pris *s2* (*nypa* [*snus*]) pinch [of snuff]
3 pris *s7, s4* (*värde, kostnad*) price (*på* of); (*begärt* ~) charge; *högt* (*lågt*) ~ high (low) price; *nedsatt* ~ reduced price, cut price (*AE.* rate); *gängse* (*gällande*) ~*er* ruling (current) prices; *höja* (*sänka*) ~*et på* raise (lower) the price of; *höja* ~*et med 6 pence* raise the price by 6 pence; ~*erna stiger* prices are rising; *stiga i* ~ advance (rise) in price, go up; *det i fakturan* (*prislistan*) *angivna* ~*et* the invoiced (listed) price; *vara värd* ~*et* be worth the price, be good value; *komma överens om* ~*et* agree on the price; *sätta stort* ~ *på att få* set great store on getting; *för gott* ~ at a moderate price; *till ett* ~ *av* at the (a) price of; *till halva* ~*et* at half-price, at half the price; *till varje* ~ (*bildl.*) at any cost, at all costs
4 pris *s7, s4* (*belöning*) prize; *få första* ~ be awarded the first prize; *tar i alla fall* ~*et* (*bildl.*) takes first prize (the cake); *sätta ett* ~ *på ngns huvud* set a price on a p.'s head
5 pris *s7* (*lov, beröm*) praise; *Gud ske* ~ glory to God; *sjunga ngns* ~ sing a p.'s praises
prisa praise, glorify; ~ *sig lycklig* consider o.s. fortunate, count o.s. lucky
prisbelöna award a prize to; ~*d* (*vanl.*) prize (*roman* novel), prize-winning
pris|bildning fixing (determination) of prices **-billig** cheap, inexpensive
pris|boxare prizefighter **-domare** judge
pris|elasticitet price elasticity **-fall** decline (fall) in prices; (*kraftigt*) slump **-fluktuation** fluctuation in (of) prices **-fråga** matter (question) of price
prisgiv|a give up, abandon, expose (*åt* to); *vara* -*en åt* (*äv.*) be left at the mercy of **-ning** [-i:v-] abandonment, exposure
prishoppning *ridk.* showjumping
pris|höjning rise (advance) in price[s *pl*] **-index** price index **-klass** price range **-konkurrens** price competition **-kontroll** price control **-kontrollerad** *a5* price-controlled **-krig** price war **-kurant** *s3* price list **-känslig** ~*a varor* goods whose saleability is susceptible to rising prices **-lapp** price label (ticket, tag) **-lista** price list **-läge** price range (level); *i alla* (*olika*) ~*n* at (all different) prices; *i vilket* ~? at about what price?
prisma [ˣpriss-] -*t prismer el. s1* prism; (*i ljuskrona*) drop **-kikare** prism binoculars (*pl*) **-tisk** [-ˈma:-] *a5* prismatic
pris|medveten price-conscious **-märka** mark with prices, put prices on **-nedsättning** price reduction, markdown **-nivå** price level **-notering** quotation **-pengar** *sjö. hist.* prize money **-politik** prices policy **-reglering** price control (regulation)
prisse *s2* fellow, chap
pris|skillnad difference in price **-stegring** *se prishöjning* **-stopp** price freeze; *införa* ~

freeze prices **-summa** prize money **-sänkning** price reduction (decrease) **-sätta** price, fix the price[s *pl*] of **-sättning** pricing, fixing of prices
pris|tagare prize winner **-tävlan** prize competition
prisuppgift [price] quotation (*på* for)
prisutdelning distribution of prizes
prisutveckling price trend
1 prisvärd (*värd sitt pris*) worth its price; good value [for money]
2 prisvärd (*lovvärd*) praiseworthy
privat I *a1* private, personal; ~ *område* private grounds (premises) (*pl*); *den* ~*a sektorn* the private sector; *i det* ~*a* in private life; *jag för min* ~*a del* I for my part **II** *adv* privately, in private; *undervisa* ~ (*äv.*) give private lessons **-angelägenhet** personal matter; *mina* ~*er* my private affairs **-anställd** person in private employment **-bil** private car **-bilism** private motoring **-bostad** private residence **-chaufför** private chauffeur **-detektiv** private detective; *AE.* private eye **-finansierad** privately financed **-flyg** private aviation
privatim [-ˣva:-] privately, in private
privatiser|a privatize **-ing** privatization
privatist external candidate
privat|kapital private capital **-lektion** private lesson **-lärare** private teacher, tutor **-lärd** *en* ~ an independent scholar **-man, -person** private person; *som* ~ in private life **-praktik** private practice **-rätt** civil law **-sekreterare** private secretary **-skola** private school **-ägd** [-ä:-] *a5* privately-owned
privilegi|ebrev [-ˈle:-] charter **-era** privilege **-um** *s4* privilege; (*monopol*) monopoly (*på* of)
PR-man [ˣpe:ärr-] PR (public relations) officer (*förk.* P.R.O.)
pro pro; ~ *forma* pro forma; ~ *primo* (*secundo*) firstly (secondly)
prob|abel *a2* probable **-era** try; (*guld o.d.*) assay; *tekn.* test **-ersten** [-ˣbe:r-] touchstone
pro'blem *s7* problem; *framlägga* (*lösa*) *ett* ~ pose (solve) a problem **problema'tik** *s3* [set of] problems (*pl*) **problematisk** [-ˈma:-] *a5* problematic[al]
problem|barn problem child **-komplex** group of problems **-lösning** solution of problems (a problem) **-ställning** problem, presentation of a problem
proboxning professional boxing
procedur procedure; process
procent *s9* (*hundradel*) per cent, percent; (-*tal*) percentage; *löpa med 5* ~*s ränta* run at 5 per cent interest; *hur många* ~ *är det?* what percentage is that?; *2-*~*ig lösning* a two-per-cent solution; *mot* (*till*) *hög* ~ at a high percentage; *i* ~ *av* as a percentage of; *ökningen i* ~ *räknat* the percentage increase; *vi lämnar 10* ~[*s rabatt*] *vid kontant betalning* 10% cash discount
procent|a [-ˈsenn-] practise usury **-are** [-ˣsenn-] usurer
procent|enhet percentage point **-halt** percentage **-räkning** calculation of percentages **-sats, -tal** percentage **-u'ell** *a1* expressed as a percentage (in percentages)

process 1 (*rättstvist*) lawsuit, action; legal proceedings (*pl*); *öppna ~ med* (*mot*) bring an action against; *ligga i ~ med* be involved in a lawsuit with; *förlora* (*vinna*) *en ~* lose (win) a case; *göra ~en kort med* make short work of, put an end to **2** (*förlopp*) process; procedure **processa** [-'sessa] carry on lawsuits (a lawsuit); *~ om* litigate
processindustri processing industry
procession [-se'ʃɷ:n] procession; *gå i ~* march (walk) in procession, procession **processionsordning** processional order
process|kontroll *tekn.* process control **-makare** litigious person **-rätt** law of [legal] procedure **-teknik** processing technique
producent producer; manufacturer; grower **-kooperation** producer's cooperation **-varor** *pl* producer[s'] goods
producera produce; manufacture; *~ sig* appear [in public]
pro'dukt *s3* product (*äv. mat.*); *~er* (*koll., jordbruks- e.d., äv.*) produce (*sg*); *inhemska ~er* domestic products, home manufacture (*sg*) **produktion** [-k'ʃɷ:n] production; (*framställda varor*) output; (*författares el. konstnärs*) work[s], output; *öka ~en* increase [the] production
produktions|apparat productive apparatus, machinery of production **-faktor** factor of production, productive factor **-främjande** *a4* promoting production **-förmåga** productive power (capacity), productivity **-hämmande** *a4, ~ faktorer* factors holding back production **-kostnad** cost of production **-led** stage of production **-medel** means (*sg o. pl*) of production **-metod** method of production **-siffra** production (output) figure **-tid** production time **-utveckling** trend of production **-volym** volume of production **-ökning** increase (rise) in production
produktiv [-'ti:v, 'prådd-, 'prɷ:-, 'prɷdd-] *a1* productive; (*om författare*) prolific **-itet** productivity
produktutveckling product development
pro'fan *a1* profane; (*världslig*) secular **-era** profane **-ering** profanation
profession [-e'ʃɷ:n] profession; (*näringsfång*) trade; *till ~en* by profession (trade) **-alism** professionalism **-'ell** *a1* professional; *bli ~* turn professional; *~ idrottsman* professional
professor [-ˣfessår] *s3* professor (*i historia* of history); *AE. äv.* full professor; *~ emeritus* professor emeritus **professorsinstallation** ceremonial installation of a professor **professorska** [-ˣsɷ:r-] professor's wife; *~n A.* Mrs. A.
professorskompetens qualifications (*pl*) for a professorship **professur** professorship (*i historia* in history), chair (*i historia* of history); *inneha en ~* hold a professorship (chair); *inrätta en ~* found (establish) a chair
pro'fet *s3* prophet; *de större* (*mindre*) *~erna* the major (minor) prophets; *ingen är ~ i sitt fädernesland* no one is a prophet in his own country **profetera** prophesy; (*förutsäga*) predict **profetia** [-tˣsi:a] *s1* prophecy **profetisk** [-'fe:t-] *a5* prophetic[al] **profetissa** prophetess

proffs [-å-] *s7, s9, sport.* pro (*pl* pros); *bli ~* turn pro
pro'fil *s3* profile (*äv. tekn.*) **-era** profile **-ering** profiling **-järn** section[al] (structural) iron
pro'fit *s3* profit, gain; *för ~ens skull* for the sake of profit **-era** profit (*av* by, from) **-haj** profiteer **-hunger** thirst for gain **-ör** profiteer
pro forma [-'fårr-] pro forma **proformafaktura** pro-forma invoice
profylaktisk [-'lack-] *a5* prophylactic **profy'lax** *s3* prophylaxis (*pl* prophylaxes)
progesteron [-'rå:n] *s4* progesterone
prognos [-g'nå:s] *s3, med.* prognosis (*pl* prognoses); (*väderleks- m.m.*) forecast; *ställa en ~* make a prognosis (forecast) **-karta** (*väderlek*) weather map **-ticera** prognosticate; forecast
program [-'gramm] *s7* programme; *AE.* program (*parti- äv.*) platform; (*plan, förslag*) plan; *göra upp ett ~* draw up a programme; *det hör till ~met* it is part of the programme; *stå på ~met* be on (in) the programme **-enlig** [-e:n-] *a1* according to [the] programme; scheduled **-enligt** [-e:n-] *adv* in accordance with [the] programme; as arranged **-förklaring** *polit.* [election] manifesto **-ledare** *radio.* (*vid underhållning*) compere; (*i debatt*) chairman **-matisk** *a5* [-'ma:-] programmatic
programmer|a *data.* program; *AE.* program; *~d undervisning* programmed instruction **-are** [-ˣme:-] programmer **-ing** programming
program|musik programme music **-punkt** item [in (on) a programme] **-skrift** manifesto **-vara** *se mjukvara* **-värd** *s2, radio. o.d.* compere
progress|ion [-e'ʃɷ:n] progression **-'iv** *a1* progressive (*beskattning* taxation) **-ivitet** progressiveness
prohibi'tiv *a1* prohibitive
projekt [-ʃ-, -j-] *s7* project; plan, scheme **-era** project; plan; *~d* projected **-ering** projecting, projection; planning
projek'til [-ʃ-, -j-] *s3* projectile, missile **-bana** trajectory [of a projectile]
projek|tion [-k'ʃɷ:n] projection **-tionsapparat** projector; projecting apparatus **-tionsritning** projection drawing **-'tiv** *a1* projective
projekt|ledare leader (head) of a project **-makare** projector; schemer
projektor [-ˣjektår] *s3* projector **projicera** project
prokansler vice chancellor
proklam|a [-'kla:-] *s1* [public] notice **-ation** proclamation **-era** proclaim
prokonsul proconsul
prokrustes|bädd, -säng [-ˣkrustes-] Procrustes' bed
prokur|a [-ˣku:-] *s1* procuration, proxy; *teckna per ~* sign per pro (by procuration) **-ator** *s3* procurator **-ist** holder of procuration; managing clerk
proletariat *s7* proletariat
prole'tär I *s3* proletarian **II** *a1* proletarian **-författare** proletarian author **-roman** proletarian novel
prolog prologue
prolong|ation [-långa-] prolongation, extension

P

-era [-låŋ'ge:-] prolong, extend
promemoria [-'mɷ:-] *s1* memorandum (*över* on); memo
prome'nad *s3* **1** (*spatsertur*) walk; (*flanerande*) stroll; (*åktur*) ride; *ta* [*sig*] *en* ~ take a walk; *gå på* ~ go for a walk; *ta ngn med ut på en* ~ take s.b. out for a walk **2** *se -plats* **-dräkt** suit **-däck** promenade deck **-konsert** promenade concert; *vard.* prom **-käpp** walking stick **-plats** promenade; esplanade **-sko** walking shoe **-väg** promenade; (*stig*) walk
promener|a walk; *gå ut och* ~ go [out] for a walk **-ande** *a4, de* ~ the promenaders, people out walking
promille [-ˣmille] per mil[l] (thousand) **-halt** *blodet hade en* ~ *av 0,5* the concentration [of alcohol] in the blood was 50 mg. per cent **-tal** permillage
prominent *a1* prominent
promiskuitet promiscuity **promiskuös** *a1* promiscuous
promotion conferment of doctors' degrees **promotor** [-ˣmɷ:tår] *s3, univ.* person conferring doctors' degrees; *sport.* promoter **pro-mo'vend** *s3* recipient of a doctors' degree **promovera** confer a doctor's degree on
prompt [-å-] **I** *a4* prompt, immediate **II** *adv* (*genast*) promptly, immediately; (*ovillkorligen*) absolutely
promulg|ation promulgation **-era** promulgate
pronom|en [-'nå:-, -'nɷ:-] *best. f. -enet, pl -en el. -ina* pronoun **-i'nell** *a1* pronominal
prononcerad [-nåŋ'se:-] *a5* (*utpräglad*) decided, strong
propaganda [-ˣgann-] *s1* propaganda; *göra* ~ *för* make propaganda for **-avdelning** propaganda department (division, section) **-syfte** *i* ~ for propaganda purposes (*pl*) **-verksamhet** propaganda activities (*pl*)
propag|andist propagandist **-era** propagate, make propaganda (*för* for)
pro'pan *s4, s3* propane
propedeu't|ik [-ev-] *s3* propaedeutics (*pl, behandlas som sg*) **-isk** [-'devv-] *a5* propaedeutic, preparatory j*kurs* course)
propeller [-ˣpell-] *s2* propeller, screw; *flyg. äv.* airscrew **-axel** propeller shaft **-blad** propeller blade **-driven** *a5* propeller-driven **-plan** propeller aircraft **-turbin** turboprop
pro'pen *s4, s3* propene, propylene
proper ['prå:-] *a2* tidy, neat, clean
proponera propose, suggest
proportion [-rt'ʃɷ:n] proportion; *stå i* ~ *till* be in proportion to; *i* ~*en* 2 *till* 3 in the proportion of 2 to 3; *ha sinne för* ~*er* have a sense for (of) proportion; *står inte alls i* ~ *till* is out of all proportion to; *ha vackra* ~*er* be beautifully proportioned (well-proportioned) **proportio'nal** *s3* proportional **proportio-'nell** *a1* proportional; *direkt* (*omvänt*) ~ directly (inversely) proportional (*mot* to) **pro-portionerad** [-'ne:-] *a5* proportioned (*efter* to) **proportionerlig** [-'ne:r-] *a1* (*väl avpassad*) well-proportioned; (*i visst förhållande*) proportionate (*till* to) **proportionsvis** proportionately; comparatively
proposition 1 (*förslag*) proposal, proposition;

(*regerings-*) government bill; *framlägga en* ~ present a bill to Parliament **2** *mat., log.* proposition
propp [-å-] *s2* stopper, plug; (*kork*) cork; *elektr.* fuse; *det har gått en* ~ a fuse has blown
propp|a [-å-] cram, stuff (*med* with); ~ *igen* (*till*) plug up; ~ *i sig mat* stuff o.s. with food **-full** cram-full (*av, med* of) **-mätt** *vara* ~ be full up
proprieborgen [ˣprå:-] personal surety, suretyship
props [-å-] *s9* pitprops
propsa [-å-] ~ *på ngt* (*på att få*) insist on s.th. (on getting)
propå [prå'på:] *s3* proposal
prorektor prorector, pro-vice-chancellor
prosa *s1* prose; *på* ~ in prose **-dikt** prose poem **-författare** prosaist, prose writer **-isk** [-'sa:-] *a5* prosaic; (*opoetisk*) unimaginative (*arbete* work) **-stil** prose style **-tör** *se -författare*
prosektor [-ˣsektår] *s3* associate professor, demonstrator [in anatomy]
prose'lyt *s3* proselyte, convert
proseminarium ['prɷ:-, ˣprå-] proseminar
prosit ['prɷ:-] [God] bless you!
proskri|bera proscribe **-ption** [-p'ʃɷ:n] proscription
proso'di *s3* prosody **prosodisk** [-'sɷ:-] *a5* prosodic[al]
pros'pekt *s7* prospectus (*över* of) **-era** prospect (*efter malm* for ore) **-ering** prospecting
prost *s2* [rural] dean
prostaglan'diner [-å-] *pl* prostaglandins
prostata ['pråss-, -ˣsta:-] *s9* prostate [gland]
prostinna dean's wife; ~*n* A. Mrs. A.
prostitu|era prostitute; *en* ~*d* a prostitute **-tion** prostitution
proteg|é [-'ʃe:] *s3* protégé, *fem.* protégée **-era** (*beskydda*) patronize; (*gynna*) favour
prote'in *s4* protein **-halt** protein content
protektion [-k'ʃɷ:n] protection; patronage **-ism** protectionism **-ist** protectionist **-istisk** *a5* protectionist
protektorat *s7* protectorate
pro'tes *s3* prosthesis (*pl* prostheses); artificial limb (arm, leg); (*löständer*) denture
pro'test *s3* protest; *avge* (*inlägga*) ~ *mot* make (enter, lodge) a protest against; *under* ~[*er*] under protest; *utan* ~[*er*] without a protest **-aktion** protest action
protestant Protestant **-isk** *a5* Protestant **-ism** Protestantism (*äv.* ~*en*)
protest|era protest (*mot* against; *en växel* a bill of exchange); *jag* ~*r* (*äv.*) I object **-möte** protest (indignation) meeting **-skrivelse** letter of protest **-storm** storm of protest **-sång** protest song
protokoll [-'kåll] *s7* minutes (*pl*) (*över* of); *dipl.* protocol; (*domstols- o.d.*) report of the proceedings; (*poäng-*) score, record; *föra* ~*et* keep (take) the minutes, keep the record; *justera* ~*et* verify (check) the minutes; *ta till* ~*et* enter in the minutes; *sätta upp* ~ *över* draw up a report of; *yttra ngt utom* ~*et* say s.th. off the record **-chef** chief of protocol **-föra** enter in the minutes, record **-förare** keeper of the minutes; recorder; (*vid domstol*) clerk [of the

court]; *sport.* scorer
protokollsutdrag extract from the minutes
proton [-'tå:n] *s3* proton **-stråle** proton beam
protoplasma [-*plass-] *s9, s7* protoplasm **proto'typ** *s3* prototype **protozo** [-'så:] *s3* protozoan, protozoon; *~er* protozoa
protuberans *s3, astr.* prominence
prov 1 *s7 (försök, experiment)* trial, test, experiment; *(examens-)* examination; *(-skrivning)* [examination] paper; *anställa ~ med* try, test, give a trial; *efter avlagda ~* after passing the examination[s *pl*]; *avlägga godkänt ~ i* pass the test (examination) in; *bestå ~et* stand the test; *på ~* on trial, *(om pers. äv.)* on probation, *(om varor äv.)* on approval; *sätta ngn på ~* put s.b. to the test; *sätta ngns tålamod på hårt ~* try a p.'s patience very severely; *undergå ~* undergo a test; *visa ~ på sinnesnärvaro* give proof of presence of mind **2** *s7, s4 (varu-)* sample; *(-exemplar, exempel)* specimen; *~ utan värde* sample of no value, trade sample; *ett fint ~ på konsthantverk* a fine specimen of handicraft
prov|a test, try [out]; *(kläder)* try on **-bit** sample, specimen **-borrning** test drilling **-docka** *(skyltdocka)* [tailor's] dummy; *(modelldocka)* lay figure
proveniens *s3* provenance; origin
provensalsk [-vaŋ'sa:lsk, -ven-] *a5* Provençal **provensalska** *s1 (språk)* Provençal
prov|erska fitter **-exemplar** sample, specimen **-filma** have a screen test **-filmning** screen test **-flaska** tester **-flyga** test [fly] **-flygare** test pilot **-flygning** test flight **-frukost** *med.* test meal **-föreläsning** trial lecture **-förpackning** tester
proviant *s9* provisions, supplies, victuals (*pl*); *förse med ~* provision, victual **-era** take in stores, provision **-ering** provisioning, victualling **-fartyg** supply ship **-förråd** stores (*pl*)
pro'vins *s3* province **-ialism** *s3* provincialism **-ialläkare** [-*a:l-] district medical officer **-i'ell** *a1* provincial
provision commission *(på* on); *(mäklarearvode)* brokerage; *fast ~* flat (fixed) commission; *~ på omsättningen* turnover commission
provisor|isk [-'so:-] *a5* provisional; *(tillfällig)* temporary **-ium** *s4* temporary (provisional) arrangement, makeshift
prov|kandidat student teacher **-karta** *hand.* pattern (sample) card; *en ~ på (bildl.)* a variety of **-kollektion** [collection of] samples **-kropp** test piece **-kök** experimental kitchen **-köra** test **-körning** trial (test) run **-ning** [-ɷ:-] testing, checking; *konkr.* test, trial; *(av kläder)* trying on, fitting **-ningsanstalt** testing (research) station **-nummer** specimen copy
provocera provoke; incite
provoka|tion provocation **-torisk** [-'tɷ:-] *a5* provocative **-tör** [agent] provocateur
prov|predikan probationary sermon **-rum** *tekn.* test room; *(för kläder)* fitting room; *(på hotell o.d.)* showroom **-ryttare** commercial traveller; *vard.* bagman **-räkning** *skol.* arithmetic test (paper) **-rör** test tube **-rörsbarn** test-tube baby **-skjutning** artillery practice **-skrivning** written test; *konkr.* test paper **-smaka** taste

-spela have an audition *(för ngn* before s.b.); *(pröva instrument)* try out **-stopp** *s7 (för kärnvapen)* test ban **-stoppsavtal** test-ban treaty **-sändning** *(av varor)* trial consignment; *radio.* trial (test) transmission **-tagning** [-a:g-] sampling; taking of specimens **-tjänstgöring** probationary period (service) **-tryck** *boktr.* proof, pull **-tur** trial trip (run) **-år** year of probation; *(lärares)* student-teacher year **-årskandidat** *se* provkandidat
prudentlig [-'dent-] *a1* prim, finical
prunk|a be resplendent (blazing, dazzling); make a display *(med* of) **-ande** *a4* blazing, dazzling, gaudy, showy
prut *s7, se -ande; utan ~* without demur **pruta** bargain, haggle, palter, beat down the price; *~ på ngt* try to get s.th. cheaper; *få ~ ett pund på ngt* get a pound knocked off s.th.; *~ av på sina fordringar* temper (moderate) one's demands; *regeringen ~de ner anslaget* the government reduced the subsidy **prutande** *s6* bargaining, haggling
prutgås brent [goose]
prut|mån margin for bargaining (haggling) **-ning** [-u:-] *se prutande*
prutt *s2, vard.* fart **prutta** *vard.* fart, **lett off**
pryd *a1, n sg obest.* form undviks prim, prudish
pryd|a *v2* adorn; *(försköna)* embellish; *(dekorera)* decorate; *den -er sin plats* it is decorative where it is (stands *etc.*)
pryderi prudishness, prudery
prydlig [-y:-] *a1* neat; *(om pers. äv.)* trim, smart **-het** neatness *etc.*
prydnad *s3* adornment, decoration, embellishment; *(-nadssak)* ornament; *vara en ~ för* be an ornament (credit) to *(sitt land* one's country)
prydnads|föremål ornament; *pl äv.* fancy goods, bric-a-brac **-växt** ornamental plant
prydno [-y:-] *i uttr.: i sin ~ (i sht iron.)* in its (his *etc.*) glory
prygel ['pry:-] *s7* whipping, flogging; *vard.* hiding; *få ~* get a whipping *etc.* **prygelstraff** flogging, corporal punishment **prygla** [-y:-] whip, flog
pryl *s2* pricker, punch, awl; *~ar (vard.)* odds and ends
pryo ['pryɷ] *skol. (förk. för praktisk yrkesorientering)* introduction to working life
prål *s7* ostentation, parade; *(grannlåt)* finery **påla** *(prunka)* dazzle, blaze; *(ståta)* show off *(med* with), make a show (parade) *(med* of) **prålig** *a1* gaudy, showy; flaunting **prålighet** gaudiness *etc.*
pråm *s2* barge; *(hamn-)* lighter **-dragare** *(båt)* barge (lighter) tug; *pers.* barge tower **-skeppare** bargeman, bargee; lighterman
pråmg *s7* [narrow] passage (space)
prångla *~ ut* utter *(falska sedlar* counterfeit banknotes)
prägel [*prä:-, 'prä:-] *s2 (stämpel)* stamp; *(avtryck)* impression, impress; *bildl.* stamp, impress; *bära äkthetens ~* bear the stamp (impress) of authenticity; *sätta sin ~ på ngt* leave one's stamp (mark) on s.th. **prägla** [-ä:-] strike [off] *(en medalj* a medal); *(mynta)* mint, coin *(mynt* money; *ett nytt ord* a new word);

emboss; *bildl.* stamp, impress, imprint; (*karakterisera*) characterize; *personligt ~de arbeten* works with the stamp of a p.'s personality **prägling** [-ä:-] stamping; (*av mynt*) coining, coinage; (*av nya ord*) coinage
präktig *a1* (*ståtlig*) splendid, magnificent; (*utmärkt, förträfflig*) excellent, good, fine
pränt *s7, på ~* in print **pränta** (*texta*) print; write carefully; *~ i ngn ngt, se inpränta*
prärie ['prä:-] *s5* prairie **-hund** prairie dog **-varg** prairie wolf, coyote
präst *s3* priest; (*i anglikanska kyrkan, prot.*) clergyman; (*frikyrklig, skotsk*) minister; *vard.* parson; *bli ~* become a clergyman (*etc.*), take holy orders; *läsa för ~en* prepare for confirmation; *kvinnliga ~er* women clergymen; *~en i församlingen* the parish clergyman (*etc.*) **-betyg** extract from the parish register **-dräkt** *i ~* in canonicals (clerical attire)
präster|lig *a1* clerical (*stånd* order); sacerdotal, priestly (*värdighet* dignity) **-skap** *s7* clergy; priesthood
präst|fru clergyman's (*etc.*) wife **-gård** parsonage, rectory, vicarage; *kat.* presbytery; (*frikyrklig, skotsk*) manse **-inna** priestess **-kappa** clergyman's gown **-krage 1** *eg.* clerical collar; bands (*pl*) **2** *bot.* oxeye daisy, marguerite **-man** *se präst* **-rock** cassock **-seminarium** theological seminary **-viga** ordain **-vigning** [-i:g-] ordination **-ämbete** ministry
pröjsa *vard.* fork out, foot the bill
pröva 1 (*prova, sätta på prov*) try; (*testa*) test; (*undersöka, examinera*) examine; (*överväga*) consider; *~ lyckan* try one's luck; *~ ett mål* (*jur.*) try a case; *~ ett räkneexempel* check a sum; *~ om den håller* try and see if it holds; *~ själv!* try for yourself!; *i nöden ~s vännen* a friend in need is a friend indeed; *~ sig fram* proceed by trial and error; *~ sina krafter på* try one's strength on; *~ en ansökan* consider an application; *vi har fått ~ på mycket* we have had to put up with a great deal; *~s av ödet* be tried by Fate **2** (*underkasta sig -ning*) be examined (*i* in); *~ in* sit for an entrance examination (*vid en skola* at a school) **3** *jur.* (*anse, finna*) deem, judge (*skäligt* reasonable) **prövad** *a5* (*hårt* sorely) tried (afflicted) **prövande** *a4* (*besvärlig*) trying (*för ngn* to s.b.); (*granskande*) searching (*blick* look) **prövning** [-ö:-] **1** (*undersökning, förhör*) examination, test; *förnyad ~* reconsideration, re-examination; *ta upp ett ärende till förnyad ~* reconsider a matter **2** (*motgång, lidande*) trial, affliction **prövningsnämnd** board of examiners; (*för beskattning*) tax appeal board (committee)
prövo|sten touchstone **-tid** (*provtid*) trial (probationary) period; (*svår tid*) difficult time, time of testing
PS *förk. för postskriptum* P.S. (postscript)
psalm [s-] *s3* (*kyrkosång*) hymn; (*i Psaltaren*) psalm; *Davids ~er* [the Book of] Psalms **-bok** hymn book **-diktning** hymn writing **-ist** psalmist
psalm|odikon [sal'mɵdikån] *s7, ung.* monochord **-sång** hymn singing **-vers** verse of a hymn
psaltare [s-] (*instrument*) psaltery; *P~n* [the Book of] Psalms

pseudo|händelse ['psev-] pseudo-event, pseudo-happening **-'nym** *s3* pseudonym, pen name **-vetenskaplig** pseudoscientific
psoriasis [-ˣri:a-] *s3* psoriasis
pst here!
psyke *s6* psyche, mind **psykedelisk** [-'de:-] *a5* psychedelic **psykförsvar** psychological defence **psykiater** [-i'a:t-] *s3* psychiatrist; *AE.* therapist **psykia'tri** *s3* psychiatry **psykiatrisk** [-ki'a:t-] *a5* psychiatric; *~ behandling* (*AE.*) therapy **psykisk** ['psy:-] *a5* psychic[al]; *~a störningar* psychical (mental) disturbances **psykiskt** ['psy:-] *adv* psychically; *~ efterbliven* mentally retarded
psyko|analys psychoanalysis **-analysera** psychoanalyse **-analytiker** [-'ly:-] psychoanalyst **-analytisk** [-'ly:-] psychoanalytic[al] **-drama** psychodrama **-farmaka** [-'farr-] *pl* psychopharmacological drugs **-gen** [-'je:n] *a1* psychogenic **-log** psychologist **-logi** *s3* psychology **-logisera** psychologize **-logisk** *a5* psychologic[al] **-pat** psychopath **-pa'ti** *s3* psychopathy **-patisk** [-'pa:-] *a5* psychopathic
psyko|s [-'kå:s] *s3* psychosis (*pl* psychoses) **-somatisk** [-'ma:-] *a5* psychosomatic **-tek'nik** psychotechnology **-teknisk** [-'tekk-] psychotechnical **-tera'peut** psychotherapist **-tera'pi** psychotherapy **-tisk** [-'kå:-] *a5* psychotic
Ptolemaios [-'majås] *n* Ptolemy
ptro whoa!
pub [pubb] *s2* pub
pubertet puberty, pubescence **pubertetsålder** [age of] puberty
public|era publish **-ering** publishing, publication **-ist** publicist **-itet** publicity; *få bra ~* get good publicity
pub'lik I *s3* (*åhörare*) audience; (*åskådare*) spectators (*pl*); (*antal närvarande*) attendance; (*teater-*) house; *sport. äv.* fans (*pl*), crowd; (*allmänhet*) public; *den breda ~en* the public at large; *ta ~en med storm* bring down the house **II** *a1* public
publi'kan *s3, bibl.* publican
publik|anslutning (*stor* large) attendance, crowd **-ation** publication **-dragande** *a4* popular, attractive **-favorit** popular favourite **-framgång** success [with the public]; (*boks*) best seller **-friare** *ung.* showman **-frieri** *ung.* playing to the gallery, showmanship **-rekord** attendance record **-siffra** attendance; *sport.* gate **-um** ['pubb-] *n* the audience **-undersökning** [opinion] poll
puck *s2* (*ishockey-*) puck
1 puckel ['pukk-] *s7, se stryk, smörj*
2 puckel ['pukk-] *s2* hump; (*hos människa äv.*) hunch
puckel|oxe zebu **-rygg** hunchback **-ryggig** *a1* hunchbacked
puckla *~ på ngn* thrash s.b.
pudding pudding
pudel ['pu:-] *s2* poodle; *~ns kärna* the heart of the matter
puder ['pu:-] *s7* powder **-dosa** powder compact **-socker** icing (*AE.* confectioners') sugar **-underlag** foundation [cream] **-vippa** powder puff

pudr|a [ˣpu:d-] powder; ~ *sig* powder [o.s.] **-ing** powdering, dusting
pue'ril *a1* puerile **-itet** *s3* puerility
puff *s2* **1** (*svag knall*) pop **2** (*knuff*) push **3** (*rök-*) puff **4** (*pall*) pouf[fe]; (*soffa*) box ottoman **5** (*på ärm*) puff **6** (*reklam*) puff **puffa 1** (*knalla*) pop **2** (*knuffa*) push; ~ *ngn i sidan* dig (poke) s.b. in the ribs **3** (*göra reklam*) ~ *för* puff, give a puff **puffärm** puff[ed] sleeve
pugilist pugilist
puh phew!
puk|a *s1* kettledrum; *med -or och trumpeter* (*bildl.*) with drums beating and flags flying **-slag** beat on the kettledrum **-slagare** kettledrummer
pulka *s1* reindeer (Lapland) sleigh
pull ~ ~*!* chick chick!
1 pulla *s1* (*höna*) chick, pullet; (*tös*) lass, chickabiddy
2 pulla *s1* (*för spelmarker*) pool
pullover [-'å:-] *s2* pullover
pulpa *s1* pulp
pul'pet *s3* desk
puls *s2* pulse; *oregelbunden* (*regelbunden*) ~ irregular (normal) pulse; *ta ~en på ngn* take (feel) a p.'s pulse; *känna ngn på ~en* (*bildl.*) sound s.b., assess a p.'s intentions
pulsa plod, plough (*i snön* through the snow)
pul'sar *s3, astr.* pulsar
pulser|a (*eg. o. friare*) pulsate, throb, beat **-ing** pulsation
puls|frekvens, -hastighet pulse rate **-slag** beat of the pulse; *livets* ~ the pulse of life **-åder** artery; *stora ~n* the aorta
pul'tron *s3* poltroon, coward
pulver ['pull-] *s7* powder **-form** *i* ~ powdered **-isera** pulverize; *~d* (*äv.*) powdered **-isering** pulverization **-kaffe** instant coffee
puma *s1* puma
pump *s2* pump
1 pumpa *s1* **1** *bot.* pumpkin **2** (*kaffe-*) coffee-flask
2 pump|a *v1* pump (*äv. utfråga*); ~ *läns* pump dry, drain; ~ *upp a*) (*vatten*) pump up, *b*) (*cykelring e.d.*) pump up, inflate
pumpkolv pump piston
pumps *pl* court shoes; *AE.* pumps
pump|station pumping-station **-stång** pump handle
pund *s7* **1** (*vikt*) pound (*förk. lb.*) **2** (*myntenhet*) pound (*förk. £*); *engelska* ~ pound sterling **3** *bildl.* talent, pound; *gräva ner sitt* ~ not use one's talents; *förvalta sitt* ~ *väl* make the most of one's talents **-huvud** blockhead **-kurs** pound (sterling) rate of exchange **-sedel** pound note
pung *s2* **1** (*börs*) purse; *lossa på ~en* loosen the purse strings **2** (*tobaks- e.d.*) pouch **3** *anat.* scrotum; *zool.* pouch, marsupium
pung|a ~ *ut med* fork (shell) out, part with **-björn** koala **-djur** marsupial **-råtta** opossum **-slå** fleece, bleed, skin (*på* of)
punisk ['pu:-] *a5* Punic; *~a krigen* the Punic wars
punkt *s3* point (*äv boktr.*); (*prick äv.*) dot; (*skiljetecken*) [full] stop, *AE.* period; (*i kontrakt, på dagordn. e.d.*) item; ~ *och slut!* and there's

an end of it!; *den springande ~en* the crux of the matter; *en öm* ~ a sore point; *här sätter vi* ~ we'll stop here; *sätta* ~ *för* put a stop to; *tala till* ~ have one's say, finish what one is saying; *på alla ~er* at (*bildl.* in) all points **-beskattning** specific taxation
punkter|a 1 (*pricka*) dot ; *konst.* stipple; *~de noter* dotted notes **2** (*sticka hål på*) puncture **-ing 1** dotting; stipple **2** puncture; (*på bilring äv.*) blowout, *AE.* flat tyre; *få* ~ have a puncture
punkt|hus point (tower) block **-lig** *a1* punctual, on time, on the dot; *vara* ~ *med* be punctual in **-lighet** punctuality **-strejk** selective strike, spot strike **-strejka** go on spot strike **-svetsning** spot welding **-öga** *zool.* ocellus (*pl* ocelli)
puns *s2* punch **punsa** punch
punsch *s3* Swedish punch
pu'pill *s3* **1** (*i ögat*) pupil **2** (*myndling*) pupil, ward
pupp|a *s1* chrysalis (*pl äv.* chrysalides), pupa **-artad** *a5* pupal **-skal** cocoon **-stadium** pupal stage
pur *a1* pure; *bildl. äv.* sheer; *av* ~ *nyfikenhet* out of sheer (pure) curiosity
puré *s3* purée; soup
purgatorium [-'tɷ:-] *s4* purgatory **purgera** purge **purgermedel** [-ˣge:r-] purgative, purgative medicine
pur|ism purism **-ist** purist **-istisk** *a5* puristic
puri'tan *s3, hist.* Puritan; *bildl.* puritan **puritanism** Puritanism (*äv. ~en*) **puri'tansk** [-a:-] *a5* Puritan; puritanic[al]
purjolök leek
purken *a3* peevish, sulky (*över* about); huffy (*på ngn* with s.b.)
purpur *s9* purple **-brämad** *a5* edged with purple **-färga** colour (*tekn.* dye) purple **-färgad** purple[-coloured] **-röd** purple **-snäcka** purple shell
purra (*väcka*) call, rouse
purser ['pö:r-] *s2* purser
purung [ˣpu:r-] very young
1 puss *s2* (*pöl*) puddle, pool
2 puss *s2* (*kyss*) kiss
pussa kiss, give a kiss **pussas** *dep* kiss
pussel ['puss-] *s7* puzzle; (*läggspel*) jigsaw puzzle; *lägga* ~ do a puzzle, *bildl.* fit the pieces together **-bit** piece of a [jigsaw] puzzle
pussig *a1* bloated, puffy
pussla do a puzzle; ~ *ihop ngt* put s.th. together
pust *s2* **1** (*bälg*) [pair of] bellows **2** (*vind-*) puff, breath
1 pusta *s1* (*grässtäpp*) *~n* the Hungarian steppe
2 pust|a *v1* **1** (*blåsa*) puff **2** (*flåsa*) puff, wheeze; (*flämta*) pant; ~ *och stånka* puff and blow; ~ *ut* take a breather; *låta hästarna* ~ *ut* rest the horses
1 puta *s1* pad; pillow
2 puta *v1,* ~ *med läpparna* (*munnen*) pout; *skjortan ~de ut* the shirt stuck out
1 puts *s7* (*upptåg*) prank, trick
2 puts *adv,* ~ *väck* gone completely, vanished
3 puts *s3* **1** (*rappning*) plaster; grout **2** (*-medel*) polish **3** (*prydlighet*) tidiness; (*renlighet*) cleanliness
putsa 1 (*rappa*) plaster **2** (*fönster*) clean; (*skor*)

polish, *AE.* shine; *(metall)* polish; *(häck, naglar e.d.)* trim; *~t och fint* neat and tidy **3** *bildl.* *(uppfiffa)* polish; *(förbättra)* improve, better
puts|lustig droll, comic[al] **-makare** [practical] joker
puts|medel polish, cleaning agent **-ning 1** plastering **2** cleaning; polishing; trimming **3** polishing; improvement, betterment **-trasa** polishing rag (cloth)
putt *s2, golf.* putt **putta** shove; *~ till ngn* give s.b. a shove, *(ofrivilligt)* knock into s.b.; *golf.* putt
putte'fnask *s2* whippersnapper, brat, shrimp
putten ['putt-] *i uttr.:* *gå i ~* go smash, *(gå om intet)* come to naught
puttra *(koka)* simmer, bubble [gently]; *(grumsa)* grumble
puzzle ['pussel] *se pussel*
pygmé *s3* pygmy **pygmeisk** [-'me:-] *a5* pygmyish
pyjamas [-'ja:-] *s2, s9* pyjamas *(pl); AE.* pajamas *(pl); en ~* a pair of pyjamas **-byxor** pyjama trousers (pants) **-jacka** pyjama jacket
pykn|iker ['pykk-] pyknic **-isk** ['pykk-] *a5* pyknic
pynt *s7 (grannlåt)* finery; *(julgrans- etc.)* decorations, adornments *(pl)* **pynta** *(göra fint)* titivate things up; *(smycka)* decorate; *(klä fin)* smarten up; *~ sig* dress o.s. up, make o.s. smart; *~d och fin* smartened up
pyra *v2* smoulder
pyra'mid *s3* pyramid; *(biljard-)* pyramids *(pl); stympad ~* truncated pyramid **-'al** *a1 (ofantlig)* huge *(succé* success) **-form** pyramidal shape **-formig** [-å-] *a1* pyramidal
pyre *s6, ett litet ~* a tiny mite
Pyrenéerna *pl* the Pyrenees **pyreneisk** [-'ne:-] *a5* Pyrenean; *P~a halvön* the Iberian Peninsula
pyrola ['py:-] *s1* wintergreen
pyro'man *s3* pyromaniac; incendiary; fire raiser, *vard.* firebug **-ma'ni** *s3* pyromania **-teknik** pyrotechnics *(sg el. pl)* **-tekniker** [-'teck-] pyrotechnist **-teknisk** [-'teck-] pyrotechnic[al]
pyrrusseger Pyrrhic victory
pys *s2* little boy, youngster, brat
pysa *v3* give off steam; *(väsa)* hiss
pyss|el ['pyss-] *s7* pottering **pyssla** busy o.s. *(med* about); *gå och ~ i trädgården* potter about in the garden; *~ om* look after, make comfortable
pyssling 1 pixie, manikin **2** *(femmänning) de är ~ar* they are fourth cousins
Pytagoras [-'ta:-] Pythagoras; *~ sats* the theorem of Pythagoras **pytagoreisk** [-'re:isk] *a5* Pythagorean
pyton ['py:tån] **1** *r* python **2** *adv, vard., det luktar ~* there is a ghastly (horrible) smell; *jag mår ~* I feel awful **-orm** python
pyts *s2* bucket **pytsa** swill, drench **pytsspruta** bucket fire-extinguisher
pytt *[jo] ~!* bah!, pooh!, nothing of the sort!
pyttipanna [-ˣpanna] *s1, ung.* bubble and squeak; *bildl.* hotchpotch
pyttsan ['pytt-] *se pytt*
på I *prep* **A** *rumsbet.* **1** *allm.* on; *~ balkongen* on the balcony; *~ bordet (huvudet)* on the ta-

ble (head); *ärter ~ burk* tinned peas; *~ golvet* on the floor; *han har fått det ~ hjärnan* he has got it on the brain; *~ jorden* on the earth; *~ kartan* on the map; *stå ~ knä* be on one's knees, be kneeling; *~ land* on land; *~ ort och ställe* on the spot; *stå ~ post* be on guard; *ligga ~ rygg* lie on one's back; *klia sig ~ ryggen* scratch one's back; *~ sid. 9* on page 9 *(jfr 3); ~ andra sidan gatan* on the other side of the street; *inte ha någonting ~ sig* have nothing on; *vad hade hon ~ sig?* what did she wear?; *hade hon några pengar ~ sig?* did she have any money on (about) her?; *~ sjön* on the lake, *(~ havet)* at sea; *~ slagfältet* on the battlefield *(jfr 2); göra sig illa ~ en spik* hurt o.s. on a nail; *~ svarta tavlan* on the blackboard *(jfr 2); gå ~ tå* walk on one's toes; *~ en liten ö* on a small island; *~ Björkö* on (at) Björkö *(jfr 2); behålla hatten ~* keep one's hat on; *en kaka med grädde ~* a cake with cream on [top] **2** *(vid gata, gård, torg, fält, land i motsats t. stad, större ö m.m.)* in; *~ bilden (tavlan)* in the picture *(jfr 1); utan ett öre ~ fickan* without a penny in one's pocket; *~ fältet (åkern)* in the field *(jfr 1); ~ gatan* in *(AE.* on) the street; *~ High Street* in the High Street *(jfr 3); ~ gården* in the yard (garden, court); *~ himlen* in the sky; *~ Irland* in Ireland *(jfr 1); hon arbetar ~ kontor* she works in (at) an office; *~ landet* in the country; *~ den här platsen* in this place; *~ sitt rum* in one's room; *ligga ~ sjukhus* be in hospital; *ha hål ~ strumpan* have a hole in one's stocking; *kaffe ~ sängen* coffee in bed; *~ torget* in the [market] square *(jfr 3); ~ vinden* in the attic **3** *(vid hotell, restaurang, teater, möte, tillställning m.m.)* at; *~ banken* at (in) the bank; *~ bio (teater, konsert)* at the cinema (theatre, a concert); *~ 200 m djup (höjd)* at a depth (height) of 200 metres; *vara ~ fest (sammanträde)* be at a party (meeting); *~ High Street 19* at 19 High Street *(jfr 2); bo ~ hotell* stay at a hotel; *~ Hötorget* at Hötorget *(jfr 2); äta middag ~ restaurang* dine at a restaurant; *nederst (överst) ~ sidan* at the bottom (top) of the page; *slå upp böckerna ~ sid. 9!* open your books at page 9! *(jfr 1); ~ slottet* at the palace **4** *(vid sysselsättning)* for, on; *vara ~ besök* be on a visit; *vara ute ~ jakt* be out hunting; *vara ute ~ promenad* be out for a walk **5** *(~ en sträcka av)* for; *vi såg inte en människa ~ flera mil* we didn't see a soul (anybody) for several miles **6** *(uttr. riktning, rörelse)* on, on to, onto; into; to; at; *falla ner ~ golvet* fall on to the floor; *gå ~ besök till ngn* visit s.b.; *gå ~ styltor* walk on stilts; *kliva upp ~ en pall* get on a stool; *lägga ngt ~ bordet* put s.th. on the table; *gå upp ~ vinden* go up into the attic; *kasta ngt ~ elden* throw s.th. into the fire; *lägga ett brev ~ lådan* drop a letter into the box; *resa ut ~ landet* go out into the country; *rusa ut ~ gatan* rush out into the street; *stiga upp ~ tåget* get into (on to) the train; *bli bjuden ~ bröllop* be invited to a wedding; *gå ~ banken (posten)* go to the bank (post office); *gå ~ bio (teater, konsert)* go to the cinema (theatre, a concert); *lyssna ~* listen to; *kasta ngt ~ ngn* throw s.th. at s.b.;

knacka ~ dörren knock at the door; *ringa ~ klockan* ring the bell; *trycka ~ knappen* press the button **7** *(per)* in; *tretton ~ dussinet* thirteen to the dozen; *de fick en krona ~ man* they had one krona per man; *det går 100 pence ~ ett pund* there are a hundred pence in a pound; *en ~ tusen* one in a thousand **8** *(vid transportmedel)* by; *han kom ~ motorcykel* he came by motorcycle; *skicka ~ posten* send by post **B** *tidsbet.* **1** *(tidpunkt)* at; on; in; *~ samma dag* [on] the same day; *~ utsatt dag* on the appointed day; *~ min födelsedag* on my birthday; *~ samma gång* at the same time; *~ kvällen den 1 maj* on the evening of the 1st of May; *~ lördag* on Saturday; *~ morgonen (kvällen, dagen)* in the morning (evening, day[time]); *~ natten* at (in the) night; *~ 1700-talet* in the 18th century; *~ olika tider* at different times; *~ utsatt tid* at the appointed time; *~ våren (hösten)* in [the] spring (autumn) **2** *(under)* on, during; *~ sin fritid* in one's leisure time; *hon arbetar ~ jullovet* she is working during her Christmas holiday; *~ vägen hit* on the way here **3** *(inom)* in; *det gör jag ~ en timme* it will take me [no more than] an hour to do it; *jag kommer ~ ögonblicket* I'll be with you in a moment **4** *(~ en tid av)* for; *jag har inte sett dig ~ evigheter* I haven't seen you for ages; *resa bort ~ en månad* go away for a month; *vi hyrde våningen ~ ett år* we rented the flat for a year; *jag har inte varit hemma ~ tio år* I haven't been home for ten years **5** *(efter)* after; *brev ~ brev* letter after (upon) letter; *den ena dagen följde ~ den andra* one day followed the other; *gång ~ gång* time after time, over and over again; *kaffe ~ maten* coffee after dinner **C** *(friare)* **1** *(i prep.attr.)* of; *namnet ~ boken* the name of the book; *kaptenen ~ fartyget* the captain of the ship; *slutet ~ historien* the end of the story; *färgen ~ huset* the colour of the house; *priset ~ mjöl* the price of flour; *en familj ~ fyra personer* a family of four [persons]; *ett bevis ~ uppskattning* a proof of appreciation; *den regnigaste tiden ~ året* the rainiest time of the year; *en pojke ~ tre år* a boy of three **2** *(med subst.) ~ allvar* in earnest; *förlora ~ bytet* lose by the exchange; *~ engelska* in English; *läsa ~ sin examen* read for one's degree; *~ egen risk* at one's own risk; *rakt ~ sak* straight to the point; *~ skämt* for a joke; *~ sätt och vis* in a way; *komma ~ tal* come (crop) up; *~ vers (prosa)* in poetry (prose); *det stämmer ~ öret* it tallies to the öre **II** *adv, ~ med kläderna!* on with your clothes!; *kör ~!* drive on!; *spring ~ bara!* just keep running! **III** *~ det att* [in order] that; *~ det att inte* lest

på|annons *radio.* introductory announcement **-bjuda** order; command *(tystnad* silence); impose *(skatter* taxes; *straff* a penalty) **-brå** *s6* inheritance, stock; *ha gott (dåligt) ~* come of good (bad) stock **-bröd** *få ngt som ~* get s.th. as an extra [treat] (into the bargain) **-bud** decree, edict **-budsmärke** mandatory (compulsory) sign **-byggnad** superstructure, addition, enlargement **-bättring** touching up, improvement **-börda** [-ö:-] charge *(ngn ngt s.b*

with s.th.) **-börja** begin, start, commence; *för varje ~d timme* for each hour or part of hour **-drag** *tekn.* starter; *bildl.* mobilization of effort; *ha fullt ~ (bildl.)* be working at full speed; *värmen stod på fullt ~* the heating was full on; *polisen har fullt ~* the police are out in full force **-drivare** instigator, prompter **-dyvla** [-y:-] *se* **-börda** **-fallande** *a4 (slående)* striking, remarkable **-fartssträcka** acceleration lane, slip road **-flugen** *a3 (påträngande)* obtrusive; *(framfusig)* forward **-fordra** *(kräva)* demand; *(erfordra)* require; *om så ~s* if required **-frestande** *(mödosam)* arduous, taxing; *(besvärlig)* trying **-frestning** strain, stress **-fund** *s7* invention; *(knep)* device **-fyllning** filling-up, refilling, replenishment; *vill du ha ~?* would you like some more? **-fyllningshål** filler **-fyllningstratt** [feed] hopper

påfågel *s2* peacock
påfågels|blå peacock blue **-höna** peahen **-stjärt** peacock's train **-öga** peacock butterfly

på|följande following, next; *~ dag* [the] next (on the following) day **-följd** consequence; *jur.* sanction, punishment awarded; *vid ~ av* on pain of; *vid laga ~* under penalty of law **-föra** *~ grus på vägarna* spread gravel on the roads; *~ ngn ngt i räkning* debit (charge) s.b. with s.th. **-gå** be going on; *(fortsätta)* continue, be in progress; *~ för fullt* be in full progress; *medan programmet -gick som bäst* right in the middle of the programme **-gående** *a4* in progress; *under ~ förhandlingar* while negotiations are (were) going on; *under [nu] ~ krig* during the present war; *under ~ krig (i krigstid)* in time of war; *den ~ högkonjunkturen* the current (present) boom **-hitt** *s7 (-fund)* idea, invention, device; *(knep)* trick; *AE.* gimmick; *(lögn)* fabrication **-hittad** *a5* invented **-hittig** *a1* ingenious **-hittighet** ingenuity **-hopp** *bildl.* attack **-hälsning** visit, call; *få ~ av tjuvar* be visited by burglars **-häng** *s7, pers.* hanger-on, encumbrance **-hängsvagn** trailer

påk *s2* cudgel; *rör på ~arna!* get moving!; stir your stumps!

på|kalla *(tillkalla)* summon; *(kräva)* demand, call for; attract *(uppmärksamhet* attention); *av behovet ~d* essential, necessary **-klädd** dressed **-kläderska** *teat.* dresser **-klädning** [-ä:-] dressing **-kommande** occurring; *hastigt ~ illamående* a sudden indisposition **-kostad** [-ås-] *a5* expensive, lavish **-kostande** [-ås-] *a4 (mödosam)* hard; *(prövande)* trying **-känning** stress, strain **-körd** [-çö:-] *a5* run into, knocked down **-körning** *(kollision)* smash[-up] **-körnings-ramp** slip road

påla pile; *absol.* drive piles
på|laga *s1* tax, duty, imposition **-landsvind** onshore wind **-lastning** loading

pålbro pile bridge **pålbyggnad** lake dwelling, pile dwelling **påle** *s2* pole, stake, post; *byggn.* pile; *en ~ i köttet* a thorn in the flesh

pålitlig [-i:t-] *a1* reliable, trustworthy **-het** reliability, trustworthiness

pålkran pile-driver
pålle *s2* gee-gee
pål|ning ['på:l-] piling, pile-driving **-nings-**

arbete piling-work, pilework **-stek** *sjö.* bowline [knot] **-verk** pilework, piling
på|lägg *s7* **1** (*på smörgås*) meat (cheese *etc.*) for sandwiches; (*som kan bredas*) sandwich spread **2** *hand.* extra charge (cost), increase **-läggskalv** **1** *lantbr.* stock calf **2** *bildl.* up--and-coming man
påmin|na *-de -t, v3* remind (*ngn om ngt* s.b. of s.th.*); hon -ner [mig] om sin mor* she reminds me of her mother; *det -ner mig [om] att jag måste* that reminds me, I must; *hungern började göra sig -d* hunger began to make itself felt; *~ sig* remember, recollect **-nelse** reminder (*om* of); (*anmärkning*) remark
på|mönstra (*manskap*) engage, take on; *jfr mönstra [på]* **-mönstring** signing on **-nyttföda** [ˣpå:-, -ˣnytt:-] regenerate; *-nyttfödd* regenerate[d], reborn **-nyttfödelse** regeneration, rebirth **-passad** *a5* watched **-passlig** *a1* (*vaken*) alert, watchful; (*uppmärksam*) attentive **-passlighet** alertness *etc.* **-peka** point out (*för* to); *det bör ~s att* it should be observed that; *jag ber att få ~* I should like to point out **-pekande** *s6* reminder; observation **-pälsad** *a5* (*väl* well) wrapped up **-ringning** call, ring **-räkna** count [up]on; expect
pås|e *s2* bag ([*med*] *skorpor* of rusks); *ha -ar under ögonen* have pouches (bags) under the (one's) eyes; *ha rent mjöl i ~n* have nothing to hide; *det har varit i säck innan det kom i ~* that's cribbed from s.b. else
på|seende *s6* inspection, examination; *vid första ~t* at the first glance, at first sight; *vid närmare ~* on closer inspection; *till ~* for inspection, on approval **-segla** run into, collide with **-segling** collision
påsig *a1* baggy; *~a kinder* drooping cheeks
påsk *s2* Easter (*äv. ~en*); (*judisk ~*) Passover; *annandag ~* Easter Monday; *glad ~!* Happy Easter!; *i ~* at Easter; *i ~as* last Easter; *när infaller ~en i år?* on what date does Easter Sunday come this year? **-afton** Holy Saturday, Easter Eve **-alamm** *-et* the paschal lamb **-dag** Easter Sunday (*äv. ~en*) **-helg** *~en* Easter
påskina *end. i uttr.*: *låta ~* (*antyda*) intimate, hint, (*låta märka*) pretend
påsk|käring *ung.* Easter witch **-lilja** daffodil, Lent lily **-lov** Easter vacation (holidays *pl*)
påskrift (*underskrift*) signature; (*utanskrift*) address; (*inskrift*) inscription, notation
påskris twigs decorated with coloured feathers
på|skriven *a5* signed; *få -skrivet* get a reprimand (scolding) **-skruvad** *a5* screwed on; (*om kran e.d.*) [turned] on; *med ~e bajonetter* with bayonets fixed
påskveckan (*veckan före påskdagen*) Holy Week
påskynda hasten (*avfärden* the departure); quicken (*sina steg* one's steps); speed up, urge on (*arbetet* the work); hurry on (*studierna* one's studies; expedite (*saken* the matter)
påskägg Easter egg
påslag increase, rise
påslakan quilt cover (bag)
påspädning increase
pås|sjuka [the] mumps (*pl*) **-te** tea made with a tea bag

på|stigande *a4 o. s6, ~* [*passagerare*] passenger boarding a train (*etc.*); *tåget stannar endast för ~* the train stops only to take up passengers **-stridig** *a1* headstrong, stubborn **-struken** *a3* (*rusig*) tipsy, merry **-strykning** application
påstå (*yttra*) declare, say, state; (*~ bestämt*) assert, maintain; (*göra gällande*) allege; *det ~s att* it is said that; *~ motsatsen* assert the contrary; *jag vågar ~ att* I venture to say that; *det kan jag inte ~* I can't say that; *ni vill väl inte ~ att* you don't surely mean to say that; *han ~r sig vara sjuk* he says he is ill; *han påstod sig bestämt ha sett* he insisted that he had seen; *den ~dda förlusten* the alleged loss **-ende** *s6* statement, assertion; (*förklaring*) declaration **-endesats** declarative sentence; *jakande ~* (*äv.*) affirmative declaration
påstötning [-ö:-] reminder; *trots upprepade ~ar* despite repeated reminders
påta poke [about] (*i jorden* in the soil)
påtag|a ~ sig take on (*en uppgift* a task), assume (*ansvaret* the responsibility) **-lig** [-a:-] *a1* obvious, manifest; palpable; tangible **-ligen** [-a:-] obviously
på|tala comment [up]on, criticize **-tryckargrupp** pressure group **-tryckning** pressure; *utöva ~ar på* bring pressure to bear [up]on **-tryckningsmedel** means of exerting pressure **-trädning** [-ä:-] *nålens ~* the threading of the needle **-träffa** *se träffa på* **-trängande** *a4* (*trängande*) urgent (*behov* need[s *pl*]); (*påflugen*) obtrusive, pushing **-tvinga** *~ ngn ngt* force s.th. [up]on s.b. **-tår** second cup [of coffee *etc.*] **-tänkt** *a4* contemplated, intended, considered
påve *s2* pope; *tvista om ~ns skägg* argue about trivialities, split hairs **-döme** *s6* papacy **-krona** tiara
påver [ˈpå:-] *a2* poor; (*om resultat o.d. äv.*) meagre
på|verka influence, affect; *låta sig ~s av* be influenced by; *~d av starka drycker* under the influence of strong drink **-verkan** influence, effect; *röna ~ av* be influenced by **-verkbar** *a1, lätt ~* easily influenced, impressionable
påve|stol *~en* the Holy See, the Papal Chair **-val** papal election
påvis|a (*påpeka*) point out, indicate; (*bevisa*) prove, demonstrate **-bar** [-i:-] *a1* (*bevisbar*) demonstrable; (*påtaglig*) palpable, noticeable
påvlig [ˣpå:v-] *a1* papal
på|yrka demand, urge **-öka** increase; *få* [*5 pund*] *-ökt* get a [five pound] rise (*på lönen* in salary) **-ökning** increase
päls *s2* (*på djur*) fur, coat; (*plagg*) fur coat; *få* [*ordentligt*] *på ~en* (*få stryk*) get a [thorough] hiding, (*få ovett*) get a [good] telling-off; *ge ngn på ~en* (*klå upp*) give s.b. a good hiding, (*läxa upp*) give s.b. a good slating
päls|a *~ på* wrap up **-affär** fur shop, furrier's [shop] **-brämad** *a5* fur-trimmed **-djur** furred animal **-fodrad** [-ɷ:-] *a5* fur-lined **-handlare** furrier **-jacka** fur jacket **-jägare** trapper **-kappa** fur coat **-krage** fur collar **-mössa** fur cap **-varor** *pl* furs; furriery (*sg*) **-verk** *se -varor* **-änger** *s2* carpet beetle (*AE.* bug)

pär *s3* peer; *utnämna ngn till* ~ create s.b. a peer, raise s.b. to the peerage
pärl|a [ˣpä:r-] **I** *s1* pearl; *(glas- etc.*; *svett-)* bead; *(klenod)* treasure, gem; *(sup)* drop; *äkta (oäkta, odlade) -or* real (artificial, cultured) pearls; *kasta -or för svin* cast pearls before swine; *en ~ bland kvinnor* a pearl among women **II** *v1* sparkle, bubble; *svetten ~de på hans panna* perspiration beaded his forehead; *~nde skratt* rippling laughter; *~nde vin* sparkling wine **-band** string of pearls (beads) **-besatt** *a4* studded with pearls **-broderad** *a5* embroidered with beads (pearls) **-broderi** beadwork; *(med äkta -or)* pearl embroidery
pärlemoknapp [ˣpä:r-] pearl button **pärlemor** *s9* mother-of-pearl **pärlemoskimrande** [-ʃ-] *a4* nacreous, iridescent
pärl|fiskare pearl fisher **-garn** pearl cotton **-grå** pearl grey **-halsband** pearl necklace **-hyacint** grape hyacinth **-höna** guinea hen **-höns** guinea fowl **-koljé** *se -halsband* **-mussla** pearl mussle (oyster) **-** **socker** pearl -höna guinea hen **-höns** guinea fowl **-koljé** *se -halsband* **-mussla** pearl mussle (oyster) **-socker** pearl sugar **-uggla** Tengmalm's owl **-vit** pearl[y] white
pärm *s2* *(bok-)* cover; *(samlings-)* file, folder; *från ~ till ~* from cover to cover
päron [-ån] *s7* pear **-blom** pear-blossom **-formig** [-å-] *a1* pear-shaped **-träd** pear tree
pärs *s3, en svår ~* a severe test, a trying ordeal
pöbel ['pö:-] *s2* mob, riffraff, rabble **-aktig** *a1* mobbish, vulgar **-hop** *en ~* a mob **-välde** mob rule, mobocracy
1 pöl *s2* *(vatten-)* pool, puddle
2 pöl *s2* *(kudde)* bolster
pölsa *s1, kokk.* hashed lights *(pl)*, tripe
pö om pö *(så småningom)* little by little
pörte *s6* [Finland] log cabin
pös|a *v3* swell; *(om deg)* rise; *~ över* brim (swell) over; *~ av stolthet* be puffed up (swell) with pride **-ig** *a1* *(om kudde e.d.)* puffed; *kokk.* spongy; *(om deg)* rising; *(skrytsam)* puffed-up **-munk** *kokk.* puffed fritter, doughnut

q [ku:] *s6, s7, det är* [allt] *fina ~* that's A1
quatre mains [kattröˈmäŋ] *spela à ~* play duets
quilta *se kvilta*
quisling [ˣkviss-] quisling; traitor

R

rabalder [-'ball-] *s7* fuss, hullaballoo; (*uppståndelse*) commotion, stir; *det blev ett väldigt ~* there was a tremendous commotion
rabarber [-'barr-] *s9* rhubarb -**paj** rhubarb pie
1 ra'batt *s3* (*blomster-*) flowerbed; (*kant-*) [flower] border
2 ra'batt *s3, hand.* discount; (*avdrag*) deduction; (*nedsättning*) reduction; *lämna ~* allow a discount (deduction); *3% ~ på priset* 3% discount off (on) the price; *med 3% ~ vid kontant betalning* at 3% cash discount; *sälja med ~* sell at a discount
rabatt|biljett cheap-rate ticket -**era** allow a discount (deduction); reduce -**häfte** book of reduced-rate tickets -**kort** season ticket -**kupong** discount ticket; *AE. äv.* trade stamp -**varuhus** discount house
rab'bin *s3* rabbi
rabbla rattle off; *~ upp* rattle (reel) off
rabiat *al* (*ursinnig*) raving; (*fanatisk*) fanatical, frenzied
rabies ['ra:-] *r* rabies; hydrophobia
rabulist rabid radical, agitator
racer ['rä:-, 'rejs-] *s2, s9* racer -**bil** racer, racing car -**båt** speedboat, racer -**förare** racing driver
racing ['rejsiŋ] *s2* racing
racka *~ ner på* (*skälla ut*) fall foul of; (*kritisera*) run down
rackar|e (*skurk*) scoundrel, wretch; (*kanalje*) rascal; (*lurifax*) rogue; leva *~* kick up a row -**tyg** mischief; *vard.* shenanigan; (*starkare*) devilry; *hitta på ~* be up to some mischief; *på rent ~* out of pure mischief -**unge** mischievous [young] imp, young rascal
racket ['rack-] *s2* racket; (*bordtennis-*) bat
1 rad *s3* 1 row; line; file; string (*pärlor* of pearls); series (*missöden* of misfortunes); *fyra i ~* four in a row; *fyra gånger i ~* four times running (on end); *under en ~ av år* for a number of years 2 *teat. o.d.* circle; *AE.* balcony; *första* (*andra*) *~en* the dress (upper) circle, *AE.* the first (second) balcony; *översta ~en* the gallery, *vard.* the gods 3 (*skriven, tryckt ~*) line; *läsa mellan ~erna* read between the lines; *skriv ett par ~er!* drop me a few lines (a line)!; *~ för ~* line by line; *få betalt per ~* get paid by the line; *ny ~* (*anvisning*) new paragraph
2 rad (*måttenhet*) rad
rada place in rows (a row); *~ upp* expose, display; (*uppräkna*) enumerate
radar ['ra:-] *s9* radar -**anläggning** radar unit (installation) -**antenn** radar aerial (scanner, *AE.* antenna) -**fyr** radar beacon, racon -**kontroll** radar control -**navigering** radar navigation -**reflektor** radar reflector (*vard.* dish) -**signalist** radar operator -**skärm** radarscope, radar screen -**station** radar station -**sändare** radar transmitter -**utrustning** radar equipment -**varnare** [-va:r-] interception receiver
rad|avstånd (*i skrift el. tryck*) spacing, line space; *dubbelt ~* double spacing -**band** rosary; [string of] beads (*pl*)
rader|a 1 (*skrapa bort*) erase, rub (*med kniv:* scratch) out; *data.* delete, erase; *~ i böckerna* cook the books; *~ ut* (*utplåna*) wipe (blot) out 2 (*konst*) etch -**gummi** eraser, [India] rubber -**ing** 1 erasure 2 *konst.* etching -**kniv** erasing knife -**nål** etching needle
radhus terrace (*AE.* row) house
radi'al *al* radial -**däck** radial (radial-ply) tyre
radi|'an *s3* radian -**ator** *s3* radiator
radi|e ['ra:-] *s5* radius (*pl* radii, *äv.* radiuses) -'**ell** *al* radial
1 radiera (*utstråla*) radiate, beam
2 radiera (*utsända i radio*) broadcast
radi'kal I *al* radical; (*genomgripande äv.*) thoroughgoing, sweeping II *s3, polit.* radical; *kem.* radical -**isera** radicalize -**ism** radicalism -**medel** radical (drastic) remedy
radio ['ra:-] *s5, pl vanl.* radioapparater radio, wireless; (*-apparat*) radio (wireless) set (receiver); *i ~* on the radio (wireless, air); *lyssna på ~* listen in (to the radio) -**affär** radio shop
radioak'tiv [*äv.* 'ra:-] radioactive; *~t avfall* (*nedfall*) radioactive waste (fallout); *~ strålning* atomic (nuclear) radiation; *~t sönderfall* radioactive decay, disintegration -**itet** radioactivity
radio|amatör radio amateur -**antenn** [radio] aerial (*AE.* antenna) -**apparat** radio (wireless) set (receiver) -**astronomi** radio astronomy -**bil** (*polis-*) radio patrol car; (*på tivoli*) bumper car, Dodgem (*varumärke*) -**biologi** radiobiology -**bolag** broadcasting company (corporation); *Britiska ~et* the British Broadcasting Corporation (*förk.* BBC) -**fyr** radio beacon -**fysik** radio physics (*pl, behandlas som sg*) -**förbindelse** radio contact -**föredrag** radio talk -**grammofon** radiogram[ophone]
radioisotop radioisotope
radio|kommunikation radio communication -**kompass** radio compass, homing device -**konsert** radio concert -**licens** radio (wireless) licence
radio|log radiologist -**logi** *s3* radiology -**logisk** *a5* radiological
radio|lur earphone, headphone -**lyssnare** listener -**länk** radio relay station (tower) -**mast** radio pylon (tower) -**mottagare** radio (wireless) receiver (receiving set) -**nämnd** *~en* [the Swedish] broadcasting commission -**orkester** radio orchestra -**pejl** *s3* direction finder -**pejling** direction finding -**pjäs** radio play -**polis** police equipped with radio -**program** radio (broadcasting) program[me] -**reparatör** radio serviceman -**reporter** radio commentator -**rör** radio valve (*AE.* tube) -**signal** radio signal -**sond** radiosonde -**station** radio (broadcasting) station -**stjärna** radio source (star) -**styrd** [-y:-] *a5* radio-controlled, radio-guided -**styrning** radio control (guidance) -**störning** interference; (*avsiktlig*) jamming -**sändare** radio (wireless) transmitter -**sändning** broadcast, radio transmission -**teater** radio

theatre **-teknik** radio engineering **-telefoni** radiotelephony **-telegraf** radiotelegraph **-telegrafera** wireless, radio **-telegrafi** wireless telegraphy, radiotelegraphy **-telegrafist** radio operator **-telegram** radiogram **-teleskop** radio telescope
radiotera'pi radiotherapy
radio|utrustning radio (wireless) equipment **-utsändning** broadcasting, radio transmission; *en* ~ a broadcast **-våg** radio wave
radium ['ra:-] *s8* radium **-behandling** radium treatment **-strålning** radium radiation
radi'är *a1* radial
radom [-'då:m] *s3* radome
radon [-'då:n] *s4, s3, kem.* radon
rad|skrivare line printer **-såningsmaskin** seed (*AE*. grain) drill **-vis** in rows
raffel ['raff-] *s7* (*rafflande innehåll*) thrills (*pl*)
raffi'nad *s3* refined sugar **raffinaderi** refinery **raffine'mang** *s7* refinement; elegance, sofistication **raffinera** refine **raffinerad** [-'ne:-] *a5, bildl.* refined; (*utsökt*) exquisite, consummate **raffinering** refining
rafflande *a4* thrilling, exciting
rafräschissör scent spray, atomizer
rafs|a ~ *ihop* rake (scrape) together, (*brev. o.d.*) scribble off **-ig** *a1* (*slarvig*) slapdash
ragata [-*ˣ*ga:-] *s1* vixen, shrew
ragg *s2* goat's hair; (*friare*) shag; *resa* ~ bristle [up], get one's back up
ragga pick up casual partners **raggarbil** neckmobile, cruisemobile; (*trimmad*) hot rod **raggare** hot-rod teenager (driver)
ragg|ig *a1* shaggy; (*om hår, skägg äv.*) rough, coarse **-munk** *kokk.* potato pancake **-socka** thick sock, skiing-sock
ragla stagger, reel
raglan ['ragg-] *s3, best. form o. pl äv. raglan* raglan [coat] **-ärm** raglan sleeve
ragnarök [*ˣ*raŋŋa-] *r el. n* twilight of the gods
ra'gu *s3* ragout; ~ *på ... (äv.)* stewed ...
raja [*ˣ*rajja] *s1* raja[h]
rajd *s3* reindeer drive
rajgräs [*ˣ*rajj-] rye-grass
rak *a1* **1** straight (*linje* line; *rygg* back); (*upprätt*) erect, upright; *gå* ~ [*i ryggen*] walk erect; *gå* ~*a vägen hem* go straight home; *stå* ~ stand straight; *bildl.* straight[forward] **2** *sport.*, ~*a hopp* plain high-diving; *en* ~ *vänster* a straight left; *ta tre* ~*a set* win three straight sets **3** ~ *ordföljd* normal word order; ~*a motsatsen* exactly the reverse; *på* ~ *arm* at arm's length, *bildl.* offhand, straight off; *det enda* ~*a (vard.)* the only right thing
1 raka I *s1* rake; (*för vatten*) squeegee **II** *v1* rake
2 raka *v1* (*rusa*) dash, dart, rush (*i väg* off); ~ *i höjden* shoot up
3 raka *v1* (*barbera*) shave (*äv.* ~ *sig*); *låta* ~ *sig* get shaved (a shave); ~*s eller klippas?* a shave or a haircut?
rak|apparat safety razor; (*elektrisk*) electric shaver (razor) **-blad** razor blade **-borste** shaving brush **-don** shaving things
ra'ket *s3* rocket; (*robot*) [guided] missile; *han for iväg som en* ~ he was off like a shot (lightning) **-bana** trajectory of a rocket **-bas** rocket (missile) base **-drift** rocket (jet) propulsion

-driven *a5* rocket-propelled, rocket-powered **-flygplan** rocket[-propelled] aircraft **-gevär** rocket launcher, bazooka **-hylsa** rocket cylinder **-motor** rocket engine (motor) **-steg** rocket stage **-vapen** missile [weapon]
rakhyvel safety razor
rakitis [-'ki:-] *s3* rickets, rachitis
rak|kniv razor **-kräm** shaving cream
raklång (*ligga* lie) full length; *falla* ~ *på marken* fall flat on [to] the ground
rakmaskin *se rakapparat*
rakna [*ˣ*ra:k-] straighten, become (get) straight; (*om hår*) go out of (lose its) curl
rakning [*ˣ*ra:k-] shaving; *en* ~ a shave
rakryggad *a5* straight-backed; *bildl.* upright, uncompromising
rak|salong barber's [shop], barber shop **-spegel** shaving mirror **-strigel** razor strop
raksträcka straight, stretch
rakt [-a:-] *adv* **1** straight, direct; *gå* ~ *fram* walk straight on; ~ *upp och ner* straight up and down; ~ *österut* due east; *ljuga ngn* ~ *i ansiktet* tell s.b. a lie straight to his face; *det bär* ~ *åt skogen* it is going straight to the dogs; *i* ~ *nedstigande led* in a direct line; *gå* ~ *på sak* come straight to the point; *som går* ~ *på sak* straightforward **2** (*absolut*) absolutely; (*precis*) just; (*riktigt*) downright; *sälja för* ~ *ingenting* sell for next to nothing; *det gör* ~ *ingenting* it does not matter in the least; *till* ~ *ingen nytta* of absolutely no (of no earthly) use
rak|tvål shaving soap **-vatten** shaving water; (*efter -ning*) aftershave lotion
ralj|ans [-'jaŋs, -'jans] raillery, banter **-ant** [-'jaŋt, -'jant] *a1* bantering; (*spefull*) teasing **-era** banter; ~ *med ngn* chaff (tease) s.b. **-eri** raillery, banter
rall *s2, zool.* rail
rallare navvy
rally ['ralli] *s6* rally **-förare** rally driver
1 ram *s2* (*tavel-, cykel-* etc.) frame (*äv. boktr.*); *bildl.* framework, setting; (*omfattning*) scope, limits (*pl*); *inom glas och* ~ framed; *inom* ~*en för* within the limits (scope, framework) of; *falla utom* ~*en för* be outside the scope of
2 ram *s2* (*björntass*) paw; *suga på* ~*arna (bildl.*) live on one's hump
3 ram *superl. -aste, oftast i best. form, på rena* ~*a allvaret* in dead[ly] earnest; *på rena* ~*a bondlandet* in the country pure and simple; *rena* ~*a sanningen* the plain (naked) truth
ram|a ~ *in* frame **-antenn** loope(frame) aerial
ramaskri outcry; *höja ett* ~ raise an outcry (*mot* against)
ram|avtal general (basic) agreement; *uppgöra* ~ *för* draw up the general framework for **-berättelse** frame story
ramla (*falla omkull*) fall (tumble) down; ~ *av hästen* fall off the horse; ~ *nedför trappan* fall down the stairs; *illusionerna* ~*de* my illusions were shattered
ramm *s2, sjö.* ram **ramma** ram; *bildl. äv.* strike
rammakare [*ˣ*ra:m-] frame-maker, carver and gilder
rammelbuljong *få* ~ get a thrashing
ramp *s3* **1** *teat.* footlights (*pl*) **2** (*uppfartsväg*) ramp, slope **3** *se avskjutningsramp* **-feber**

R

stage fright **-ljus** footlights *(pl)*; *bildl.*, *stå i ~et* be (appear) in the limelight
ramponera damage, batter
rampris bargain [price]; *till (för)* ~ at bargain prices
rams|a *s1* string; *(osammanhängande)* rigmarole; *(rimmad)* doggerel; *svära långa -or* swear like a trooper
ramsvart raven (jet) black
ram|såg frame saw **-verk** framework, framing
rand *-en* **ränder 1** *(kant o.d.)* edge, verge; *(bryn)* fringe; *(brädd)* brim; *bildl.* verge, brink; *vid gravens* ~ on the brink of the grave **2** *(på tyg)* stripe; *(strimma)* streak **randa** *(förse med ränder)* stripe, streak **randanmärkning** marginal note; *(friare)* comment; *förse med ~ar* annotate in the margin **randas** *dep* dawn; *när dagen* ~ at daybreak; *svåra tider* ~ hard times are in the offing **randhav** marginal sea **randig** *a1* striped; *(om fläsk)* streaky; *det har sina ~a skäl* there's a very good reason for it **randning** striping; stripes *(pl)*
randomisera randomize
randstat border state **randsydd** *a5* welt *(sko shoe)*
rang *s3* rank; *(social äv.)* standing, status; *företräde i* ~ precedence; *ha högre* ~ *än* take precedence of; *ha samma* ~ *som* rank with; *stå över (under) ngn i* ~ rank above (below) s.b.; *ambassadörs* ~ ambassadorial rank; *en första ~ens* a first-rate, first-class; *en vetenskapsman av* ~ an eminent scientist; *göra ngn ~en stridig* compete with s.b. for precedence, challenge a p.'s position
ranger|a [raŋ'ʃe:ra] **1** range, rank **2** *järnv.* shunt, marshal **-ad** *a5 (välsituerad)* well-to-do; *(stadgad)* established **-bangård** shunting (marshalling) yard
ranglig *a1 (gänglig)* lanky; *(ostadig)* rickety, ramshackle
rang|lista ranking list **-ordna** rank **-ordning** order of precedence, ranking order; *i sträng* ~ in strict [order of] precedence **-plats** leading place; *inneha en* ~ hold an eminent position **-rulla** gradation list **-skala** *se -ordning*; *den sociala ~n äv.* the social ladder **-skillnad** difference in rank
1 rank *a1 (smärt)* slim; tall and slender
2 rank *a1 (om båt)* crank[y]
1 ranka *i uttr.: rida* ~ ride a cockhorse
2 ranka *s1, bot.* runner, creeper; *bildl.* clinging vine
3 ranka *v1 (rangordna)* rank
rankig *a1, se 2 rank*; *(skraltig)* rickety *(trilla surrey)*
rankinglista, rankningslista ranking list
rann *imperf. av rinna*
rannsak|a *jur.* try; *(förhöra)* examine, hear; *(pröva)* search, ransack *(sitt minne* one's memory); *~d och dömd* tried and found guilty; ~ *hjärtan och njurar* search one's hearts **-ning** [-a:k-] *jur.* trial; *(förhör)* examination, hearing; *(prövning)* searching, ransacking; *utan dom och* ~ without either judicial trial or sentence; *hålla* ~ *med* conduct the trial (hearing) of **-ningsdomare** judge conducting the trial **-ningsfängelse** remand prison

ran'son *s3* ration; *ta ut sin* ~ draw one's ration[s *pl*] **-era** ration; *(utportionera)* portion out **-ering** rationing; *~[en] av matvaror (äv.)* food rationing; *upphäva ~[en]* deration **-eringskort** ration card
ranta run *(i trapporna* up and down the stairs; *omkring* about)
ranunkel [-'nuŋkel] *s2, s3* ranunculus
rapa, rapning [-a:-] belch
1 rapp *s2 (häst)* black horse
2 rapp *s7 (slag)* blow; *(med piska o.d.)* lash
3 rapp **l** *s7, i ~et* in a moment, at once, in the twinkling of an eye **ll** *a1* quick, swift, prompt; *(i fingrarna)* nimble; ~ *i munnen* ready-tongued
1 rappa ~ *till ngn* slap s.b.
2 rappa ~ *på, ~ sig* be quick, get a move on
3 rappa *(kalkslå)* plaster, roughcast
rappakalja *s1* rubbish, bunkum
rapp|höna, -höns partridge
rappning plastering; *konkr.* plaster
rap'port [-å-] *s3* report; account; *avlägga* ~ *om* report on, give a report on (of) **-era** report, make a report of **-karl** *mil.* orderly **-system** reporting system **-tjänst** *mil.* dispatch service **-ör** reporter; informant; *(angivare)* informer
raps *s3* rape, colza **-kaka** rape cake
rapso'd|i *s3* rhapsody **-isk** [-'sɷ:-] *a5* rhapsodic[al]
rapsolja rapeseed (colza) oil
rar *a1* **1** *(sällsynt)* rare, uncommon **2** *(älskvärd)* nice, kind, sweet **-ing** darling, honey **-itet** *s3* rarity; *konkr.* rare specimen; curiosity, curio
1 ras *s3 (människo-)* race; *(djur-)* breed, stock
2 ras *s7* **1** *(skred)* [earth] slip, slide; *(jord-)* landslide; *(av byggnad)* collapse **2** *(vild lek)* romp, romping, frolic[king]
rasa 1 *(falla ner)* give way; fall down; collapse; *(om tak o.d.)* fall in; *(om jord o.d.)* slide **2** *(stoja)* romp, rampage, frolic; *(om hav, storm o. bildl.)* rage; *(vara ursinnig)* fume, rave; *ungdomen ~r* youth is having (must have) its fling; *stormen har ~t ut* the gale has spent its fury **rasande l** *a4* raging *(storm* gale; *lidelser* passions); *(ursinnig)* furious *(på* with; *över* at); *AE. äv.* mad *(på* at; *över* about); *bli* ~ get into a rage (passion); *i (med)* ~ *fart* at a furious (breakneck) pace, at lightning speed **ll** *adv (väldigt)* awfully *(stilig* smart); ~ *hungrig* ravenously (furiously) hungry
ras|biologi human genetics *(pl, behandlas som sg)*, racial biology **-blandning** miscegenation; mixture of races *(om djur:* breeds) **-diskriminering** racial discrimination, colour bar **-djur** *(häst)* thoroughbred; *(katt, hund etc.)* pedigree cat (dog) *etc.*
rasera demolish, dismantle; raze, pull down
raseri rage, fury; frenzy; *gripas av* ~ be seized with frenzy; *råka i* ~ fly into a rage **-anfall** fit of rage; *få ett* ~ fly into a rage
rasering demolition, dismantling; pulling down
ras|fördom racial prejudice **-förföljelse** racial persecution **-hat** racial hatred **-hygien** *s3, ej pl* eugenics *(pl, behandlas som sg)* **-häst** thoroughbred **-ism** racism **-ist** racist **-istisk** [-'siss-] *a5* racistic
1 rask *s7* refuse, thrash; *hela ~et* the whole lot

2 rask *a1* **1** quick, speedy, rapid, swift; *(flink)* nimble; *(fortfärdig)* prompt, expeditious; *(hurtig)* brisk; *(käck)* brave; *i ~ takt* at a rapid (brisk) pace (rate); *i ~ följd* in rapid succession **2** *(frisk)* well, healthy; *~ och kry* hale and hearty **raska** *~ sig*, *~ på* hurry up, make haste; *~ på ngn* hurry s.b. on

raskrig racial war

raskt *adv* quickly *etc.*; *det måste gå ~* it must be done quickly; *handla ~* take prompt action

ras|minoritet racial minority **-motsättning** racial antagonism

1 rasp *s2* *(verktyg)* rasp, grater

2 rasp *s7* *(skrap)* rasp[ing sound]; *(pennas)* scratching

raspa rasp, grate; *pennan ~r* the pen scratches **raspig** *a1* raspish

ras|problem racial problem **-ren** purebred; thoroughbred; pedigree

rassel ['rass-] *s7* clatter; *(av vapen)* rattle, clank; *(prassel)* rustle; *med.* rale **rassla** clatter; rattle, clank; *(prassla)* rustle

rast *s3* *(vila)* rest, repose; *(uppehåll)* pause, rest; *mil.* halt; *skol.* break, recess; *utan ~ eller ro* without a pause (breather), nonstop **rasta 1** *(ta rast)* rest, have a break; *mil.* halt **2** *(motionera)* take out for exercise

raster ['rass-] *s7, boktr.* screen; *(TV-)* raster; *förse med ~* screen **-täthet** screen ruling; *(i TV)* scanning density

rast|lös restless; agitated, fidgety **-löshet** restlessness; agitation, fidgetiness **-ning** exercising; airing **-plats** halting place; *(vid bilväg)* lay-by, pull-up

rasåtskillnad *se rasdiskriminering*

rata *(försmå)* despise; *(förkasta)* reject

rate [rejt, rät] *s5 (fraktsats)* rate; *(delbetalning)* instalment

ratificer|a ratify **-ing** ratification

rationaliser|a [-tʃɔ-] rationalize; improve efficiency **-ing** rationalization; efficiency improvement **-ingsexpert** [business] efficiency expert

rational|ism rationalism **-ist** rationalist **-istisk** *a5* rationalist[ic]

ratio'n|ell *a1* rational **-'ellt** *adv* rationally; *~ utformad* scientifically outlined (designed)

ratt *s2 (bil-)* [steering] wheel; *tekn.* hand wheel; *(radio-)* knob **ratta** *vard.* drive

ratt|fylleri drunken driving **-fyllerist** drunken driver **-kälke** bobsleigh **-lås** steeringwheel lock **-onykterhet** drunken driving **-stång** steering column **-växel** steering-column gear change **-växelspak** steering-column [gear] lever

ravaillac [ˣravvajak, 'ravv-] *s2* rogue; reveller

ra'vin *s3* ravine

rayon [-'jå:n] *s4 (tyg)* rayon

razzia ['rattsia, 'rassia] *s1* raid; roundup; *göra ~* raid, round up

1 rea *se jet*

2 rea *s1, vard., se realisation 1*

rea'gens *s7, s3* reagent, test *(på* for) **reagenspapper** test (indicator) paper **reagera** react *(för* to; *mot* against; *på* on); *~ alkaliskt* give an alkaline reaction; *hur ~r han inför ...?* what is his reaction to ...?

reajaktplan jet fighter

reak'tans *s3* reactance

reaktion [-k'ʃɔ:n] reaction; response

reaktions|drift jet propulsion **-driven** *a5* jet-propelled **-förmåga** reactivity **-hastighet** reaction rate (speed) **-motor** jet engine **-tid** reaction time

reaktio'när [-kʃ-] **I** *s3* reactionary **II** *a1* reactionary

reaktiver|a reactivate **-ing** reactivation

reaktor [-ˣaktår] *s3* reactor **-anläggning** reactor plant (installation) **-härd** *s3* reactor core

re'al *a1* real, actual; *(saklig)* factual **-examen** *ung.* intermediate school-leaving examination; *BE. motsv.* General Certificate of Education, ordinary level *(förk. G.C.E., O level)* **-genus** common gender **-gymnasium** *ung.* secondary modern school

real|ia [-'a:l-] *pl* facts, realities; *(-vetenskaper)* concrete (exact) sciences **-inkomst** real income

realisation 1 *hand.* sale **2** *(förverkligande)* realization; *(förvandling i reda pengar äv.)* conversion

realisations|vara cut-price article **-vinst** capital gain **-värde** bargain (clearance) value, sale price

realiser|a 1 *hand.* sell off (out), clear stock[s] **2** *(förverkliga)* realize; *(tillgångar äv.)* convert into cash **-bar** *a1* **1** *(utförbar)* practicable, feasible **2** *(säljbar)* salable, realizable

real|ism realism **-ist** realist **-istisk** *a5* realistic; *('nykter')* matter-of-fact **-iter** [re'a:-] in reality (fact), actually **-itet** *s3* reality; *i ~en* in reality, practically speaking

real|kapital real capital **-linje** *skol.* science (modern) side **-lön** real wages *(pl)* **-politik** practical politics *(pl)* **-skola** *ung.* secondary modern school **-tid** *data.* real time **-tillgångar** *pl* tangible assets **-union** legislative union **-värde** real (actual) value; *(mynts)* intrinsic value

rea|motor jet engine **-plan** jet plane

reassur|ans [-'raŋs] *s3* reinsurance **-era** reinsure

re'bell *s3* rebel, insurgent **-isk** *a5* rebellious, insurgent

rebus ['re:-] *s2* picture puzzle, rebus

recens|ent reviewer, critic **-era** review **-ion** [-n'ʃɔ:n] review **-ionsexemplar** review[er's] (advance) copy

recentior [-ˣsentsiår, -'sent-] *s3 [pl* -'å:-] *univ.* freshman

re'cept *s7, med.* [doctor's] prescription *(på* for); *kokk., tekn., bildl.* recipe *(på* for); *expediera ett ~* make up a prescription; *skriva ut ~ på ngt (äv.)* prescribe s.th.; *endast mot ~* on doctor's prescription only **receptarie** [-'ta:-] *s5* dispenser

recept|belagd *a5* subject to prescription; *~a läkemedel* drugs sold on prescription only **-fri** sold without a doctor's prescription

reception [-p'ʃɔ:n] reception **-ist** receptionist

recep'tiv *a1* receptive **-itet** receptivity

receptur dispensary

recess|ion recession **-'iv** *a1* recessive

R

re'cett *s3* box-office returns *(pl)* **-föreställning** benefit performance

reci'div *s7* relapse, return, recurrence; *få* ~ have a relapse

recipi|'end *s3 (inom orden)* recipiendary **-ent** *tekn.* container **-era** *(intas i orden)* be initiated *(i* into); *(inta i orden)* conduct the initiation of

reciprocitet reciprocity **reciprok** [-å:-] *a1* reciprocal

recit|ation recitation; reading **-a'tiv** *s7* recitative **-atris, -atör** reader **-era** recite

rector ['rekk-] ~ *magnificus* vice-chancellor, *AE.* president

red *imperf. av* **rida**

1 reda *s1* **1** *(ordning)* order; *ordning och* ~ order and method; *det är* [*ingen*] ~ *med honom* he is [not] to be counted upon; *bringa (få)* ~ *i* bring (get) into order; *hålla* ~ *(ordning) på* keep in [good] order *(jfr äv.* 2) **2** *få* ~ *på (få veta)*, get to know, find out, *(finna)* find; *göra* ~ *för* account for; *ha* ~ *på* know [about], be aware of; *ha väl* ~ *på sig* be well informed; *hålla* ~ *(rätt) på* keep count of *(jfr äv.* 1); *ta* ~ *på (skaffa kännedom om)* find out, *(söka rätt på)* find *(åt ngn* for s.b.)

2 reda *oböjl. a, i* ~ *pengar* in cash, in ready money

3 red|a *v2* **1** *(be-)* make, prepare *(ett bo* a nest; *ett läger* a bed); *(*~ *ut)* comb *(ull* wool); *(klargöra)* clear up, sort out *(sina intryck* one's impressions) **2** *(av-)* thicken *(en soppa* a soup) **3** *rfl (om sak) det -er sig nog* things will come out all right; *(om pers.)* get on, manage; ~ *sig själv* help o.s.; *han -er sig nog* he will manage all right **4** ~ *upp* settle, fix, *(svårighet)* clear up; ~ *ut (ngt tilltrasslat)* unravel, *(klargöra)* explain

redaktion [-k'ʃɔ:n] **1** *(utgivande)* editing; *(utgivarskap)* editorship; *(avfattning)* wording; *under* ~ *av* edited by **2** *(personal)* editorial staff; *(lokal)* editorial office (department) **-'ell** *a1* editorial

redaktions|chef editor-in-chief, managing editor **-kommitté** editorial committee **-sekreterare** *ung.* assistant editor-in-chief

redaktör editor

redan *(som bestämning t. predikatsverbet)* already; *(i övriga fall)* as early as, even, *(just, själva)* very; *är du hemma* ~? are you home already?; ~ *på 1600-talet* as early (long ago, far back) as the 17th century; ~ *då* even then, as early as that; ~ *förut* even before this; ~ *efter tre gånger* after only three times; ~ *i dag* this very day; ~ *samma dag* [on] the very same day; ~ *länge* [for] a long time (ever so long); ~ *som barn* while still (even as) a child; ~ *tanken på* the mere thought of

redare shipowner

redbar [ˣre:d-] *a1 (rättrådig)* honest, upright; *(samvetsgrann)* conscientious **-het** honesty, uprightness; conscientiousness

1 redd *s3* road[stead]; *ligga på* ~*en* lie (be) in the roads (roadstead)

2 redd *a5* thick[ened] *(soppa* soup)

rede *s6* nest

rederi shipping company, shipowners *(pl)*;

carrier **-näring** shipping [business]

redig *a1* **1** *(ej trasslig)* orderly; *(om handstil)* clear, legible; *(lätt begriplig)* intelligible, lucid; *(vid full sans)* in one's right senses; *ett* ~*t huvud* a clear intellect **2** *en* ~ *portion* a substantial helping; *en* ~ *karl* a reliable chap, a good sort; *en* ~ *förkylning* a severe cold

rediger|a [-'ʃe:-] edit, redact; draft, formulate **-ing** editing, redaction

redighet clarity, lucidity

redingot ['reddingåt] *s3* frock coat

rediskonter|a rediscount **-ing** rediscount[ing]

redlig [ˣre:d-] *a1, se redbar* **-en** honestly, loyally; ~ *sträva* make honest efforts

redlös 1 *sjö.* disabled **2** *(drucken)* blind (helplessly) drunk

redning [ˣre:d-] *kokk.* thickening *(äv. konkr.)*

redo *oböjl. a* ready, prepared; *var* ~*!* be prepared! **-bogen** *a3* ready, willing **-göra** ~ *för a) (redovisa)* account for, report on *b) (beskriva)* describe, give an account of; ~ *närmare för* give details (a detailed description) of; *i korthet* ~ *för* outline, give a brief outline (summary) of **-görelse** [-j-] account *(för* of), report *(för* of, on)

redovis|a *bokf.* record; ~ *för* account for, give an account of; *bolaget* ~*r vinst* the company shows (reports) a profit **-ning** account; *(räkenskapsbesked)* statement of accounts; *brista i* ~ fail to render an account

redovisningsskyldig accountable, required to render accounts **-het** accountability, obligation to render accounts

redskap [ˣre:d-] *s7, koll.* s9 instrument *(äv. bildl.)*; *(verktyg)* tool, implement *(äv. bildl.)*; *(utrustning)* equipment, tackle; *gymn.* apparatus

redskapsbod tool shed

reducer|a reduce; cut (bring) down **-bar** *a1* reducible **-ing** reduction **-ingsventil** reducing (back pressure) valve

reduktion [-k'ʃɔ:n] reduction **reduktionstabell** conversion table

redund|ans *s3* redundancy **-ant** *a5* redundant

redupli|cera reduplicate **-kation** reduplication

re'dutt *s3, mil.* redoubt

reell [re'ell] *a1* **1** *(verklig)* real, actual; *(påtaglig)* tangible **2** *se rejäl*

referat *s7* account, report; *(sammandrag)* summary

referendum [-ˣrenn-] *s8* referendum *(pl äv.* referenda)

refe'rens *s3* reference; *lämna* ~*er* give references; *svar med* ~*er* reply stating references **-bibliotek** reference library **-grupp** reference group **-ram** frame of reference

referent reporter **referera** *(ge referat av)* report, give an account of; ~ *till* refer to; ~*nde till Ert brev* with reference to (referring to) your letter

reflekt|ant *(spekulant)* prospective buyer **-era 1** *(återspegla)* reflect, throw back **2** *(tänka)* reflect, cogitate *(över* upon); ~ *på (anbud, förslag)* consider, entertain, *(en vara)* be open (in the market) for, be buyer of; ~ *på en plats* think of applying for a post **-ion** [-k'ʃɔ:n] *se reflexion* **-or** [-ˣflektår] *s3* reflector

re'flex *s3* reflex **-band** luminous tape
reflexion [-ek'ʃɷ:n] **1** *fys.* reflection, reflecting; (*av ljud*) reverberation **2** *bildl.* reflection, meditation; (*slutsats*) deduction; (*uttalad*) comment **reflexionsförmåga** reflective powerer
reflexiv ['reff-, 're:-] *a1* reflexive
reflex|rörelse reflex movement (action) **-verkan** reflex effect
reform [-'fårm] *s3* reform; *införa ~er* introduce reforms **-anda** reform spirit **-ation** reformation; *~en* the Reformation **-ator** *s3* reformer **-atorisk** *a5* [-'tɷ:-] reformatory, reforming
reformera reform **reformert** [-'märt] *a4, den ~a kyrkan* the Reformed Church; *en ~* a member of the Reformed Church, Presbyterian, Calvinist; *de ~a* the Reformed
reform|fiende anti-progressive **-fientlig** anti-progressive **-ism** reformism **-iver** reforming zeal **-strävande** *s9, ~n* reforming efforts, struggle for reform **-vänlig** favourable to reform
refraktion [-k'ʃɷ:n] *fys.* refraction
re'fräng *s3* refrain, chorus; *falla in i ~en* join in the chorus; *tänka på ~en* (*vard.*) think about leaving
re'fug *s3* refuge, traffic island
refuser|a refuse, reject **-ing** refusal, rejection
re'gal *s3, boktr.* composing frame
regalera regale **regalier** [-'ga:-] *pl* regalia **regalskepp** [-ˣga:l-] man-of-war, ship of the line
regatta [-ˣgatta] *s1* regatta
1 regel [ˣre:-] *s2* (*för dörr*) bolt; *skjuta för ~n* bolt the door
2 reg|el ['re:-] *s3* (*norm etc.*) rule, regulation; *-ler och anvisningar* rules and regulations; *ingen ~ utan undantag* no rule without an exception; *uppställa -er för* draw up rules for; *enligt -lerna* according to rule (the rules, the book), by the book; *mot -lerna* against the rules; *i (som) ~* as a rule, usually; *göra det till en ~* make it a rule
regel|bunden *a3* regular; *~ puls* normal pulse **-bundenhet** regularity **-lös** (*utan regler*) lawless; (*oordentlig*) irregular; (*tygellös*) licentious **-mässig** *a1, se -bunden* **-rätt** *a4* regular; (*korrekt*) correct; (*sannskyldig*) regular, proper **-vidrig** contrary to the rule[s]
regemente [-je'mente, -g-] *s6* **1** *mil.* regiment **2** (*regering*) government, rule; *föra ett strängt ~* rule with severity
regements|chef regimental commander **-kamrat** *vara ~er* be in the same regiment **-läkare** army (regimental) doctor **-officer** field officer **-pastor** regimental chaplain, padre
regener|ation [-j-] regeneration **-a'tiv** *a1* regenerative **-ator** *s3* regenerator **-era** regenerate
regent [-j-] ruler, sovereign; (*ställföreträdare*) regent **-längd** table of monarchs (rulers) **-skap** [-ˣjent-] *s7* regency
reger|a [-j-] **1** (*styra*) govern; (*härska*) rule; (*vara kung*) reign; *medan han ~de* (*äv.*) during his reign **2** (*behärska*) rule, govern; *~s av sina lidelser* be dominated by one's passions **-ing** (*regeringstid*) rule, reign; (*-ande*) rule, government; (*verkställande myndighet*) government;

AE. vanl. administration; *tillträda ~en* (*om kung*) accede to the throne, (*om myndighet*) take office; *bilda ~* form a government; *den sittande ~en* the government in power
regerings|beslut government decision **-bildning** formation of a government **-bänken** the government (*Storbritannien* treasury) bench **-chef** head of the (a) government; prime minister **-fientlig** anti-government; oppositional **-form 1** (*statsskick*) form of government **2** (*grundlag*) constitution; *1809 års ~* the 1809 Constitution Act **-förslag** government proposal (proposition) **-kris** cabinet crisis **-ledamot** minister of state, cabinet minister **-organ** government organ **-parti** government party **-råd** justice of the supreme administrative court; *Storbritannien* Lord Justice **-rätt** *~en* the [Swedish] supreme administrative court **-ställning** *vara i ~* be in power (office) **-tid** (*regents*) reign; (*regerings*) period of office **-år** year of reign
regi [-'ʃi:] *s3* management; *teat.* stage management; *film.* direction; (*iscensättning*) production; *i egen ~* under private management; *i statlig ~* under government auspices **-anvisning** *~ar* acting (stage) directions
regim [-'ʃi:m] *s3* management, administration, regime; *ny ~* (*hotell- e.d.*) new management **-förändring** change of management
region *s3* region; district, area **-'al** *a1* regional **-alpolitik** regional policy **-plan** regional plan
regissera [reʃi-] produce; (*film*) direct **regissör** producer; (*film., radio. o. AE.*) director
register [-'jiss-] *s7* **1** register, roll, record; (*ord-, sak-*) index **2** (*orgel-*) [organ] stop; (*tonomfång*) range **-kort** index card **-ton** *sjö.* register ton
registrator *s3* registrar, recorder, registry clerk
registratur *s7, s9* copies (*pl*) of public documents; registrar's office
registrer|a register, record **-ing** registration
registrerings|avgift registration fee **-bokstav** (*på bil*) index mark **-nummer** registration number **-skylt** (*på bil*) numberplate, *AE.* license plate
regla [ˣre:g-] bolt
reglage [-'la:ʃ] *s7* control, lever
reglementarisk [-'ta:-] *a5* in conformity with regulations
reglement|e [-'mente] *s6* regulations, rules (*pl*); *~t föreskriver* the regulations prescribe **-era** regulate
reglements|enlig [-e:nl-] *a1* according to regulations **-vidrig** contrary to regulations
regler|● regulate; (*justera*) adjust; (*arbetstid, skuld etc.*) settle; *~d befordringsgång* statutory system of promotion **-bar** [-e:r-] *a1* adjustable **-ing 1** regulation; adjustment; settlement **2** *med.* menstruation
re'glett *s3, boktr.* lead; reglet
regn [reŋn] *s7* rain; *bildl. äv.* shower, hail; *ett stritt ~* a heavy rain, a downpour; *i ~ och rusk* in chilly wet weather; *efter ~ kommer solsken* (*bildl.*) every cloud has a silver lining; *det ser ut att bli ~* it looks like rain
regn|a [ˣreŋna] rain; *bildl. äv.* shower, hail; *det ~r* it is raining; *det ~r in* it is raining in (*ge-*

nom fönstret at (through) the window); *det ~r småsten* it is raining cats and dogs; *låtsas som det ~r* look as if nothing were (was) the matter **-blandad** ~ *snö* rain mingled with snow **-by** rain squall **-båge** rainbow **-bågshinna** iris **-dis** rainy mist **-droppe** raindrop **-fattig** with little rain, dry **-ig** *al* rainy; wet **-kappa** raincoat, mackintosh, w aterproof **-moln** rain cloud **-mätare** rain gauge, pluviometer **-område** area with rainfall **-rock** *se* -*kappa* **-skog** rainforest **-skur** shower [of rain] **-stänk** *pl* spots of rain; *det kom bara några* ~ there were only a few spots **-tid** rainy season; *~en* (*äv.*) the rains (*pl*) **-tung** rain-laden **-vatten** rainwater **-väder** rainy weather; *vara ute i* -*vädret* be out in the rain

regress (*återgång*) retrogradation **-ion** [-e'ʃɷ:n] regression **-'iv** *al* regressive **-rätt** right of recourse

regulade'tri *s3* rule of three

regul|ator *s3* regulator **-'jär** *al* regular

regummera retread, *AE.* recap; (*slitbana*) topcap

rehabiliter|a rehabilitate **-ing** rehabilitation

reine claude [rä:n 'klå:d] *s5, se renklo*

reinkarn|ation [re-in-] reincarnation **-era** reincarnate

re'jäl *al* (*pålitlig*) honest, reliable; (*ordentlig, bastant*) proper, jolly good; *ett ~t mål mat* a good square meal

rek *s7* registered post

rekambioräkning [-'kamm-] re-exchange account

rekapituler|a recapitulate **-ing** recapitulation, summing-up

re'klam *s3* advertising; (*publicitet*) publicity; *konkr.* advertisement; *braskande* ~ loud (showy) advertising; *göra ~ för* advertise, *vard.* boom, puff; *göra ~ för sig själv* blow one's own trumpet **-affisch** advertising poster (bill) **-anslag** publicity allocation **-artikel** publicity device; advertising gift

reklama|tion (*återfordran*) reclaim; (*klagomål*) complaint, claim; *post.* inquiry [about a missing letter (parcel)] **-tionsnämnd** *allmänna ~en* [the Swedish National] board for consumer complaints

reklam|avdelning publicity (advertising) department **-broschyr** publicity (advertising) leaflet **-byrå** advertising agency **-chef** advertising manager

1 reklamera (*klaga*) complain of; *post.* inquire for (about); ~ *en leverans* reject (complain of) a delivery

2 reklamera (*göra reklam för*) advertise, *vard.* boom, puff

reklam|erbjudande bargain (special) offer **-film** advertising film, commercial **-jippo** advertising gimmick, publicity stunt **-kampanj** advertising (publicity) campaign **-konsulent** advertising consultant **-ljus** neon light **-man** publicity (advertising) expert **-material** promotion material **-pris** bargain price **-skylt** advertising sign **-tecknare** commercial artist **-teckning** *konkr.* advertisement designing; *abstr.* commercial art **-text** [advertising] copy **-tryck** advertising matter **-ändamål** *för* ~ for

advertising purposes

rekognos[c]er|a [-kåŋnå-] reconnoitre; scout; ~ *terrängen* (*bildl.*) see how the land lies **-ing** reconnaissance, reconnoitre **-ingstur** reconnoitring tour

rekommend|ation [-å-] **1** recommendation **2** *post.* registration **-ationsbrev** letter of recommendation (introduction) **-era 1** recommend (*ngn* (*ngt*) *för ngn* s.b. (s.th.) to s.b.); ~ *ngn på det varmaste* heartily recommend s.b.; *som kan ~s* recommendable; ~ *sig* take one's leave **2** *post.* register; *~s* (*påskrift på brev*) registered (*förk.* reg[d].); *i* (*som*) *~t brev* by registered post

rekonstruera [-å-] reconstruct **rekonstruktion** [-k'ʃɷ:n] reconstruction

rekonvalesc|ens [-'sens, -'ʃens] *s3* convalescence **-ent** convalescent

rekord [-'kå:rd] *s7* record; *inneha ett* ~ hold a record; *slå ~*[*et*] break the record; *sätta* ~ set up a record **-anslutning** *det blev* ~ there was a record number of participants **-artad** [-a:r-] *a5* unparalleled, unprecedented; record (*hastighet speed*) **-fart** record speed **-försök** attempt at the record **-hållare** record holder **-jakt** record-chasing **-siffra** record figure **-skörd** bumper harvest (crop) **-tid** *ny* ~ new record time; *göra ngt på* ~ do s.th. in record time

rekreation recreation; relaxation

rekreations|ort health resort **-resa** recreation trip

rekreera [-e'e:-] refresh; ~ *sig* refresh o.s., rest, recuperate

re'kryt *s3* recruit; *göra ~en* (*vard.*) do first training period as a conscript **-era** recruit, enlist **-ering** recruiting, recruitment **-tid** first period of compulsory military training **-utbildning** training of recruits

rektang|el [-'taŋ-] *s2* rectangle **-u'lär** [-ŋg-] *al* rectangular

rektascension [-asen'ʃɷ:n] *astr.* right ascension

rektor [ˣrekktår, 'rekk-] *s3* headmaster, principal; (*kvinnlig*) headmistress; (*vid univ.*) vice-chancellor, *AE.* president; (*vid fackhögskola*) principal, rector, warden **rektorat** *s7* headmastership *etc.*

rektors|befattning headmastership *etc.* **-expedition** *~en* the headmaster's (*etc.*) office

rektorska [-'tɷ:rs-] *s1* headmaster's (*etc.*) wife

rekviem ['re:-, 'reck-] *s7, best. form äv. rekviem* requiem

rekvirera 1 (*beställa*) order; *kan ~s genom* obtainable through **2** *mil.* requisition

rekvisi|ta [-ˣsi:-] *pl, äv. s9* (*förnödenheter*) requisites; *teat. o.d.* properties **-tion 1** (*beställning*) order **2** *mil.* requisition **-tions-blankett** requisition form **-tör** *teat.* property man, *vard.* propman

re'kyl *s3* recoil, kick **-era** recoil, kick

relatera relate, give an account of

1 relation (*berättelse*) narration; *i hans* ~ in his account (version)

2 relation 1 (*förbindelse*) relation, connection; (*förhållande*) relationship; *sätta* (*ställa*) *ngt i* ~ *till* relate s.th. to; *stå i* ~ *till* be related to **2**

~er (*inflytelserika förbindelser*) connections; *skaffa sig fina ~er* get influential connections, climb the social ladder; *sakna ~er (äv.)* have no friends at court

relativ ['re:-, 'rell-, -'ti:v] **I** *a1* relative *(äv. språkv.)*; comparative *(lugn* quiet); *allting är ~t* everything is relative **II** *s7, s4* relative **-ism** relativism **-istisk** *a5* relativistic **-itet** relativity **-itetsteori** theory of relativity **-sats** relative clause

releg|ation expulsion **-era** expel; *univ. äv.* send down, *(för kortare tid)* rusticate

relev|ans [-'ans, -'aŋs] relevance **-ant** [-'ant, -'aŋt] relevant

reliabilitet reliability

relief [reli'eff, rel'jeff] *s3* relief *(äv. bildl.)*; *ge ~ åt* bring out in relief; *i ~* in relief **-karta** relief map **-verkan** relief effect

religion [-li'(j)ɷ:n, -'giɷ:n] *s3* religion; *(friare)* faith, belief *(läroämne äv.)* divinity

religions|fientlig antireligious **-filosofi** philosophy of religion **-frihet** religious freedom **-förföljelse** religious persecution **-förkunnelse** preaching of a religion **-historia** religious studies *(pl)*, comparative religion, history of religion[s] **-krig** religious war **-kunskap** religious education **-stiftare** founder of a religion **-undervisning** religious instruction **-utövning** religious worship (practices); *fri ~* freedom of worship **-vetenskap** religious science; *se äv. -historia*

religi|ositet [-i(j)ɷ-, -ligiɷ-] religiousness, piety **-ös** [-i'ʃö:s, -gi'ö:s] *a1* religious; sacred *(bruk* custom)

re'lik *s3* relic **-skrin** reliquary, shrine

re'likt *s3, s4* relict **-form** survival form

reling gunwale, gunnel, rail; *manna ~* man the rail; *fritt vid ~ (hand.)* ex ship

re'lä *s4* relay **reläa** relay, pipe **relästation** relay (repeating) station

rem [remm] *s2* strap; *(smal)* thong; *(driv-)* belt; *ligga som ~mar efter marken* go flat out

remarkabel *a2* remarkable, notable

remb[o]urs [raŋ'burs] *s3* documentary credit; AE. letter of credit, commercial credit

remdrift belt-drive, belt-driving

re'mi *s3, schack.* draw; *det blev ~* the game was drawn; *uppnå ~* achieve a draw

reminiscens [-i'sens, -i'ʃens] *s3* reminiscence

re'miss *s3, abstr.* commitment [for consideration]; *konkr.* [committee] report; *(läkar-)* doctor's letter of introduction, *(t. sjukhus)* admission note; *vara (utsända) på ~* be circulated (circulate) for comment

remissa [-'ˣmissa] *s1* remittance **-brev** remittance letter

remiss|debatt debate on the estimates *(i Storbritannien* Address) **-instans** body to which a proposed [legislative] measure is referred for consideration

remitt|ent I *s3 (växel-)* payee **II** *a4, med.* remittent **-era 1** *hand.* remit **2** *(hänskjuta)* commit (refer) for a pronouncement **3** *med.* refer, send

1 remmare *sjö.* perch, stick

2 remmare *(glas)* hock-glass, rummer

remont [-'månt-, -'måɳt-] *s3* remount [horse]

-depå remount depot

remontera [-mänt-, -måɳt-] bloom twice in one season

remplacer|a [raŋ-, ram-] replace **-ing** replacement

remsa *s1* strip, tape; *(pappers-)* slip; *(tyg)* shred

remskiva [belt] pulley

remu'ladsås remoulade [sauce]

1 ren *s2 (dikes-)* ditch-bank; *(åker-)* headland; *(landsvägs-)* verge

2 ren *s2 (djur)* reindeer *(pl* reindeer[s])

3 ren *a1 (ej smutsig)* clean; *(prydlig)* tidy; *bildl.* pure; *(idel)* pure, sheer, mere; *(oblandad, äkta)* pure, unadulterated; *(klar)* clear; *~t samvete* a clear conscience; *göra ~t* clean *(i köket* in the kitchen); *göra ~t hus (bildl.)* make a clean sweep [of everything]; *~a galenskapen* sheer madness; *av en ~ händelse* by pure (sheer) accident; *av ~ nyfikenhet* out of sheer curiosity; *~t nonsens* sheer nonsense; *~ choklad* plain chocolate; *~a sanningen* plain truth; *säga sin mening på ~ svenska* speak one's mind in plain Swedish; *ett ~t hjärta* a pure heart; *~t spel* fair play; *~ infinitiv* the simple infinitive; *en ~ förlust* a dead (total) loss; *~ vinst* net (clear) profit, net proceeds; *~t netto* net without discount, no discount

rena 1 clean; purify; *(socker)* refine **2** *bildl.* purify; cleanse, purge **renare** filter

ren|avel reindeer breeding **-bete** reindeer pasture

rendera [ren'de:-, raŋ-] *(inbringa)* bring in, yield; *(ådraga)* bring down upon *(ngn* s.b.)

rendezvous [raŋde'vɷ:] *s4* rendezvous *(sg o. pl)*; appointment

renegat renegade; apostate

renfana [ˣre:n-] *bot.* tansy

renframställa produce in pure form

rengör|a clean **-ing** [-j-] cleaning; *(städning äv.)* house-cleaning, cleanup

rengörings|kräm cleansing cream **-medel** detergent, cleaner, cleaning-agent

renhet [ˣre:n-] cleanness *etc. (jfr ren)*; purity *(äv. bildl.)*; *hög ~ (kem.)* high purity **renhetsivrare** puritan

renhjord reindeer herd

renhjärtad [ˣre:njär-] *a5* pure-hearted, pure in heart

ren|hud reindeer skin (hide) **-hudshandske** reindeer glove

ren|hållning cleaning; *(sophämtning)* refuse collection [and disposal]; *(gatu-)* scavenging, street-sweeping, street-cleaning **-hållningsverk** sanitary (scavenging) department **-hårig** *bildl.* honest, fair **-ing** cleaning, cleansing; *(kem. o.d.)* purification **-ingsverk** purifying (sewage-treatment) plant

renklo [reŋ'klɷ:, 'reŋ-, 're:ŋ-] *(plommonsort)* greengage [plum]

renko reindeer doe, doe reindeer

renkultur pure culture

ren|kött reindeer meat **-lav** reindeer moss

ren|levnad chastity, continence **-levnadsman** continent man; ascetic **-lig** [ˣre:n-] *a1* cleanly **-lighet** [ˣre:n-] cleanliness **-lärig** *a1* orthodox **-lärighet** orthodoxy **-odla** isolate, cultivate in isolation **-odlad** [-ɷ:-] *a5, bildl.* absolute,

R

downright (*egoism* egotism)
renommé [-å-] *s4* reputation, repute; *ha gott* ~ have a good name, be well reputed; *par* ~ by repute (hearsay)
renons [-'nåŋs, -'nåns] I *s3* void II *oböjligt a*, *vara* ~ *i spader* be without (have no) spades; *vara fullständigt* ~ *på* be absolutely devoid of, have no ... whatever
renover|a renovate; *AE. äv.* revamp; (*byggnad, tavla o.d.*) restore; (*våning o.d.*) do up, repair **-ing** renovation; restoration; repair
ren|rakad *a5* **1** *se* slätrakad **2** (*barskrapad*) cleaned out, broke **-rasig** *a1* purebred; *se äv. rasren* **-rita** draw fair, make a fair copy of
rens *s7* trimmings (*pl*)
rens|a 1 (*rengöra*) clean; (*bär, grönsaker*) pick over; (*fisk*) clean, gut; (*fågel*) draw; (*ogräs*) weed; (*magen*) purge; (*tömma*) evacuate; ~ *ogräs* weed **2** (*befria*) clear (*havet från ubåtar* the sea of submarines); *åskan* (*samtalet*) ~*de luften* the thunderstorm (conversation) cleared the air; ~ *bort* clear away; remove **-brunn** soakaway, sinkhole **-hacka** weeding--hoe
renskiljning reindeer separation (roundup)
ren|skrift *konkr.* fair (clean) copy **-skriva** make a fair (clean) copy of, write (*på maskin:* type) out **-skrivning** making a fair (clean) copy, (*på maskin*) copy-typing
renskötsel reindeer breeding (husbandry)
rens|ning cleaning *etc.* (*jfr rensa*) **-ningsaktion** *mil.* mopping-up operation[s *pl*]; *polit.* purge **-nål** cleaning-needle
renstek joint of reindeer; (*maträtt*) roast reindeer
rent [re:-] *adv* **1** *eg.* cleanly *etc.* **2** *sjunga* ~ sing (keep) in tune; *skriva* ~ *åt ngn* do a p.'s fair--copying [for him *etc.*]; *tala* ~ talk properly **3** ~ *omöjlig* utterly (absolutely) impossible; ~ *praktiska detaljer* purely practical details; ~ *av* simply, absolutely, downright; *jag tror* ~ *av* I really believe; ~ *ut* plainly, straight [out]; ~ *ut sagt* to put it plainly, not to mince matters; *jag sade honom* ~ *ut* I told him frankly (in so many words) **-av** ['re:nt-] *se rent 3*
rentier [raŋ'tie:] *s3* [*pl* -'e:er] gentleman of independent means
rentjur bull reindeer
rentré [raŋ-] *s3* re-entry, reappearance
ren|tryck clean proof **-två** *bildl.* clear, exonerate; ~ *sig* clear o.s. (*från misstanke of* suspicion)
rentut ['re:nt-] *se rent 3*
renässans [-'saŋs, -'sans] *s3,* ~*en* the Renaissance (Renascence); *uppleva en* ~ experience renaissance **-furste** Renaissance prince **-stil** Renaissance (*etc.*) style **-tiden** the Age of the Renaissance (*etc.*)
reol [re'å:l] *s3* bookcase; shelves (*pl*)
reorganis|ation [reå-] reorganization **-era** reorganize
reostat rheostat
rep *s7* rope; (*smalt*) cord; *hoppa* ~ skip; *tala inte om* ~ *i hängd mans hus* name not a rope in the house of him that was hanged, avoid painful topics
1 repa I *s1* scratch, tear II *v1* scratch, tear; ~

eld på en tändsticka strike a match; ~ *upp* unravel, (*stickning*) undo [one's knitting]; ~ *upp sig* get unravelled
2 repa *v1*, ~ *gräs* pluck handfuls of grass; ~ *vinbär* string currants; ~ *löv* strip leaves
3 repa *v1*, ~ *mod* take heart; ~ *sig* recover, improve, get better
repar|abel *a2* (*-erbar*) repairable; (*möjlig att gottgöra*) reparable **-ation** repair[ing]; *vara under* ~ be under repair, be being repaired
reparations|arbete repairs (*pl*), repair work **-kostnader** *pl* cost (*sg*) of repairs, repair costs **-utrustning** repair kit **-verkstad** repair shop, (*bil- vanl.*) garage
repar|atör repair man; (*bil-*) mechanic **-era** repair; *AE. äv.* fix; (*kläder o.d.*) mend; *våningen skall* ~*s* the flat is to be done up; *kan ej* ~*s* (*äv.*) is past repair
repartisera go shares (*om* for)
repatrier|a repatriate **-ing** repatriation
repe *s6, bot.* darnel
repellera repel
reperto'ar *s3* repertoire, repertory
repeter|a repeat; *teat., mus.* rehearse; *skol.* revise **-gevär, -ur** repeater
repetition repetition; *teat., mus.* rehearsal; *skol.* revision
repetitions|kurs, -övning refresher course
repetitorium [-'tⱷ:-] *s4* **1** *se repetitionskurs* **2** (*lärobok*) synopsis (*i* of)
rephoppning skipping
repig *a1* scratched, full of scratches
re'plik *s3* **1** (*genmäle*) rejoinder, retort, repartee; *teat.* line, speech; *vara snabb i* ~*en* have a quick tongue **2** *konst.* replica **-era** reply, retort **-föring** way of arguing **-skifte** exchange (bandying) of words
replipunkt [-'pli:-] *mil.* base; *bildl.* basis
report|age [-år'ta:ʃ] *s7* (*nyhetsanskaffning*) reporting; (*referat o.d.*) report[age] **-er** [-'på:r-] *s2* reporter; (*radio-*) [radio] commentator
representant representative (*för* of); deputy; (*delegat*) delegate; (*handelsresande*) traveller **-huset** the House of Representatives **-skap** *s7* representation; (*representantsamling*) representative assembly
representation representation
representations|kostnader *pl* entertainment (representation[al]) expenses **-middag** official dinner **-skyldighet** *ha* ~*er* have to entertain **-våning** reception rooms (*pl*)
represent|a'tiv *a1* representative (*för* of) **-era 1** (*företräda*) represent, act for **2** (*utöva värdskap*) entertain
repress|alier [-'sa:-] *pl* reprisals; *utöva* ~ *mot* retaliate (make reprisal) on, take reprisals against **-'iv** *a1* repressive
reprimand [-'mand, -'maŋd] *s3* reprimand
re'pris *s3* **1** *mus.* repeat; *teat.* revival; (*av film e.d.*) rerun, second presentation; *radio., TV.* repeat; (*TV i slowmotion*) action (instant) replay **2** (*omgång*) turn, bout **-era** repeat; revive; rerun **-tecken** *mus.* repeat mark
repro|ducera reproduce **-duktion** [-k'ʃⱷ:n] reproduction (*äv. konkr.*)
reproduktions|anstalt process-engraving establishment (laboratory) **-avdrag** reproduc-

tion proof (pull)
reproduk'tiv *a1* reproductive
rep|slagare rope maker **-slageri** (*-slagning*) rope-making; *konkr.* rope yard, rope works **-stege** rope ladder **-stump** rope's end, short piece of rope
rep'til *s3* reptile
repub'lik *s3* republic **-'an** *s3* republican **-'ansk** [-a:-] *a5* republican
repulsion [-l'ʃɷ:n] repulsion
reput|ation reputation **-erlig** [-'te:r-] *a1* reputable; respectable
repända rope's end
repövning military refresher course
1 res|a *v3* (*höja*) raise (*invändningar* objections); erect (*en gravsten* a gravestone); set up (*en stege* a ladder; *krav* claims); ~ *ett tält* pitch a tent; *taket är -t* the rafters are in place; ~ *talan* (*jur.*) lodge a complaint; ~ *sig* rise, (*stiga upp äv.*) get up; ~ *sig på bakbenen* rear [on its (*etc.*)] hind legs]; ~ *sig över omgivningen* rise above its environment; *håret -te sig på mitt huvud* my hair stood on end; ~ *sig ur sin förnedring* raise o.s. from degradation
2 resa *s1, jur., första* ~*n* first offence, *tredje* ~*n stöld* third conviction for theft
3 res|a I *s1* journey (*äv. bildl.*); (*sjö-*) voyage; (*över-*) crossing, passage; (*kortare*) trip; (*rund-*) tour; (*-ande*) travel; *lycklig* ~*! pleasant journey!; enkel* ~ one-way trip (journey); *fri* ~ free passage; *vad kostar en enkel* ~*?* what is the single fare?; *jag har långa -or till arbetet* I have a long journey to work; *vara [ute] på* ~ be [out] travelling; *bege sig ut på* ~ start (set out) on a journey; *på* ~*n hit såg jag* coming (on my way) here I saw **II** *v3* travel, go (*med tåg* by train; *till lands* by land); (*av-*) leave, depart (*till* for); (*om handelsresande*) travel, *vard.* be on the road; *han har -t mycket* he has travelled a great deal; ~ *bort* go away; *han -te från London i går* he left London yesterday; ~ *för en firma* (*i affärer*) travel for a firm (on business); ~ *hem* go home; *han har -t härifrån* he has left [here] (gone away from here); ~ *igenom* pass through; ~ *in till staden* go up to town; ~ *omkring* travel round (about); ~ *ut på landet* go [out] into the country
resande I *a4* travelling; (*kring*) touring, itinerant; *ett* ~ *teatersällskap* a touring company; *vara på* ~ *fot* be travelling (on the move) **II** *s9* travelling salesman, [commercial] traveller; (*passagerare*) passenger; ~ *i tyger* traveller in fabrics; *rum för* ~ lodgings (*pl*) **-bok** hotel register, visitors' book
res|dag day of travel; (*avrese-*) day of departure **-damm** *tvätta* ~*et av sig* wash off the dust of one's journey
rese *s2* giant
rese|berättelse account of a journey; travel book **-bidrag** travelling allowance **-byrå** travel agency (bureau) **-check** traveller's cheque
reseda [-*se:-, -'se:-] *s1* mignonette
reseffekter *pl* luggage (*sg*); *AE.* baggage (*sg*); personal effects
rese|förbud injunction against leaving the jurisdiction; *åläggas* ~ be forbidden to travel

-försäkring travel insurance **-grammofon** portable gramophone **-handbok** guide[book] **-kostnader** *pl* travel[ling] expenses **-kreditiv** traveller's (circular) letter of credit **-ledare** [tour] conductor, guide **-'när** *s3* traveller; (*passagerare*) passenger **-radio** portable radio
re'serv *s3* reserve; *pers.* extra hand (man); *mil.* reserve; *sport.* reserve, substitute; *i* ~ in reserve (store); *dolda* ~*er* hidden reserves (assets); *överföras till* ~*en* (*mil.*) be put on the reserved list
reservant dissentient **reservare** [-*särr-] *mil.* reservist **reser'vat** *s7* reserve; (*natur-*) national park; (*djur-*) game reserve; (*fågel-*) bird sanctuary; (*infödings-*) reservation **reservation** reservation; (*tillbakadragenhet*) reserve; *ta ngt med en viss* ~ accept s.th. with some reservation; *med* ~ *för förändringar* subject to alteration **reservationslös** unreserved; without reservation
reserv|del spare part **-däck** spare tyre
reservera 1 reserve; set (put) aside; (*rum e.d.*) reserve, make reservations for, book [in advance] **2** ~ *sig* make a reservation (*mot* to); (*protestera*) protest (*mot* against); *vi* ~*r oss för förseningar* we make reservation for delays **reserverad** [-'ve:-] *a5* (*beställd*) reserved, booked; (*förbehållsam*) reserved, guarded
reserv|fond reserve fund **-förråd** reserve [supply, stock] **-hjul** spare wheel **-nyckel** spare key
reservo'ar *s3* reservoir; cistern, tank **-penna** fountain pen
reserv|officer officer of (in) the reserve **-proviant** *s9, ej pl* emergency rations (*pl*) **-tank** reserve tank **-utgång** emergency exit, fire escape
rese|räkning travelling-expenses account **-skildring** travel book; (*föredrag e.d.*) travelogue **-skrivmaskin** portable typewriter **-stipendium** travel[ling] scholarship (grant) **-valuta** travel (tourist) allowance
res|feber (*längtan att resa*) longing to travel; *ha* ~ have the jitters before a journey **-filt** travelling rug **-färdig** ready to start (for departure)
resgods luggage; *AE.* baggage **-expedition** luggage [registration] office **-försäkring** luggage insurance **-förvaring, -inlämning** cloakroom, left-luggage office; *AE.* checkroom
resi'dens *s7* residence **-stad** seat of provincial government; *i Storbritannien* county town
residera reside
residuum [-*si:-] *s4* residue
resignation [-iŋn-, -inj-] resignation **resignera** resign o.s. (*inför* to) **resignerad** [-'ne:-] *a5* resigned; *med en* ~ *min* with an air of resignation
resist|ans [-'ans, -'aŋs] *s3, elektr.* resistance **-ens** *s3* resistance **-ent** *a1* resistant
res|kamrat fellow traveller; (*-sällskap*) travelling companion **-kassa** cash for a journey; travelling funds (*pl*) **-klädd** dressed for a journey
reskontra [-'kånn-, *ress-] *s1* personal ledger; (*kund-*) accounts receivable ledger; (*leverantörs-*) accounts payable ledger
res|kost provisions (*pl*) for a journey **-lektyr**

R

light reading for the journey; *skaffa sig litet ~* get s.th. to read on the journey

reslig [ˣreːs-] *a1* tall

res|lust wanderlust **-lysten** eager to travel

resning [ˣreːs-] **1** (*uppresande*) raising, erection **2** (*höjd, ställning*) build, imposing proportions (*pl*); (*gestalt*) stature; *en man av andlig ~* a man of great moral stature **3** (*uppror*) rising, rebellion, revolt **4** *jur.* review, new trial; *ansöka om ~ i målet* bring a bill of review, lodge a petition for a new hearing

resningsansökan petition for a new trial

reso'lu|t *a1* resolute; prompt **-tion** resolution; (*beslut äv.*) decision; *antaga en ~ pass* (adopt) a resolution; *kunglig ~* royal ordinance, *i Storbritannien* order in council

resolutionsförslag draft resolution

resolvera [-å-] decree, decide

re'son *r* reason; *ta ~* be reasonable, listen to reason, come round **resonabel** *a2* (*om pers.*) amenable; (*om pris, argument etc.*) reasonable

resonans [-ˈnaŋs, -ˈans] *s3* resonance **-botten** sounding board, soundboard

resone'mang *s7, s4* (*diskussion*) discussion; (*samtal*) talk; (*sätt att -era*) reasoning **resonemangsparti** marriage of convenience

reson|era (*jfr resonemang*) discuss; talk over; reason; *~ bort* explain (argue) away **-erande** [-ˈneː-] *a4* (*om framställning e.d.*) reasoned, discursive, argumentative **-lig** [-ˈsɔ:n-] *a1* reasonable; sensible

resorbera [-å-] resorb **resorption** [-pˈʃɔ:n] resorption

respass *bildl., få ~* get sacked, be dismissed; *ge ngn ~* give s.b. the sack, dismiss s.b.

res'pekt *s3* respect; (*högaktning*) esteem; (*fruktan*) awe; *förlora ~en för* lose one's respect for; *ha ~ med sig* command respect; *sätta sig i ~ hos* make o.s. respected by; *visa ~ för* show consideration (respect) for; *med all ~ för* with all (due) deference to **respektabel** *a2* respectable; (*oantastlig*) irreproachable **respektabilitet** respectability

respekt|era respect, have respect for; (*åtlyda äv.*) adhere to **-full** respectful **-ingivande** *a4* that inspires respect **-injagande** *a4* awe-inspiring

respektive [-ˈtiː-, ˈress-] **I** *oböjligt a* respective **II** *adv* respectively; *de kostar 2 ~ 3 pund* they cost 2 and 3 pounds respectively

respektlös disrespectful **-het** disrespect

respengar *pl* money (*sg*) for a journey

respir|ation respiration **-ator** *s3* respirator **-atorisk** [-ˈtɔ:-] *a5* respiratory **-era** respire

res'pit *s3* respite; *en månads ~* a month's grace **-tid** respite, term of grace

res|plan itinerary, travelling plan **-pläd** travelling rug

respondent [-å-] respondent, defendant **respons** [-ˈåns] *s3* response **responsorium** [-ˈsɔ:-] *s4* responsory

res|rutt route, itinerary **-sällskap** *abstr.* company on a journey; *konkr.* travelling companions (*pl*), (*turistgrupp*) conducted party; *få ~ med ...* have the company of ... on the (one's) journey

rest *s3* **1** rest, remainder; *AE. äv.* balance; (*kvar-*

leva) remnant (*äv. tyg-*); *mat.* remainder; *hand.* balance, remainder; *~er* (*kvarlevor*) remains, (*matrester äv.*) leftovers, leavings; *~en* the rest (remainder), what is left, (*de andra*) the others; *för ~en* (*för övrigt*) for the rest, (*dessutom*) besides, moreover, (*i själva verket*) indeed, in fact **2** *vara på ~ med skatterna* be in arrears with taxes; *få ~ på en del av ämnet* (*i tentamen*) have to sit part of an examination again

restantier [-ˈtantsier] *pl* arrears, outstanding debts

restaurang [-auˈraŋ, -tuˈraŋ] restaurant; (*hotellmatsal*) dining room **-besök** visit to a restaurant **-branschen** catering trade (business) **-chef** restaurant manager **-nota** bill; *AE.* check **-vagn** dining (restaurant) car, diner

restauration [-au-] **1** (*restaurering*) restoration **2** (*matställe*) refreshment room, dining saloon **restaurator** *s3* restorer **restauratris** restaurant proprietress **restauratör** restaurant proprietor, restaurateur, caterer

restaurer|a restore **-ing** restoration

restera remain, be left; (*vara på rest med*) be in arrears (*med hyran* with the rent) **resterande** *a4* remaining, leftover; outstanding (*skulder* debts); *~ belopp* balance, outstanding amount, remainder; *~ skatter* arrears of taxes; *~ skulder* (*äv.*) arrears

restid travelling (running) time

restitu|era 1 (*återbetala*) repay, refund, pay back **2** (*återställa*) restore **-tion 1** (*återbetalning*) refund, repayment; (*tull-*) drawback **2** (*återställande*) restoration

rest|lager surplus (remainder) stock **-likvid** final payment **-längd** tax-arrears schedule; *komma på ~* get in arrears with one's taxes **-lös** entire, absolute; unquestioning (*hängivenhet* devotion) **-par** odd pair **-parti** remnant, odd lot

restrik|tion [-kˈʃɔ:n] restriction; *införa* (*upphäva*) *~er* introduce (lift) restrictions **-'tiv** *a1* restrictive **-tivitet** restrictivity

restrött travel-weary

rest|skatt back tax, tax arrears (*pl*) **-upplaga** remainder [of an edition]; *hela ~n* all the rest of the edition

resultant *fys.* resultant

resultat *s7* result; (*verkan*) effect; (*följd*) consequence; (*utgång*) issue; (*behållning*) proceeds (*pl*); *ge till ~* result in; *utan ~, se resultatlös* **-lös** fruitless; *blev ~* was without result (in vain, of no avail) **-räkning** profit and loss account

resultera result (*i* in); *det ~de i att* the result was that

resum|é *s3* résumé, summary, précis; *jur.* brief **-era** sum up, summarize

re'surs *s3* resource; *~er* (*äv.*) means, assets; *utnyttja sina ~er* make full use of (exploit) one's assets (resources)

res|van used (accustomed) to travelling **-vana** experience in travelling **-väg** route [of travel], travelling distance **-väska** suitcase; (*liten*) *AE. vanl.* grip

re'sår *s3* (*spiralfjäder*) spring; (*gummiband*) elastic **-band** elastic **-botten** springbase **-gördel** roll on [girdle] **-madrass** spring mattress

-stickning ribbed knitting, ribbing
reta 1 (*framkalla retning*) irritate (*nerverna* the nerves); (*stimulera*) stimulate, whet (*aptiten* the appetite); (*egga*) excite (*ngns nyfikenhet* a p.'s curiosity); ~ *ngns begär* rouse a p.'s desire (passion) **2** (*förarga*) provoke, annoy, vex; (~*s med*) tease; ~ *upp sig* work o.s. up (*på* at); ~ *sig* get angry (*på, över* at)
retard|ation retardation, deceleration **-era** retard, decelerate
ret|as *dep* tease, chaff (*med ngn* s.b.; *för ngt* about s.th.) **-bar** *a1* (*om organ e.d.*) reactive to stimuli; (*friare*) irritable, excitable
reten|tion retention **-tionsrätt** right of retention
ret|full irritating; (*-sam*) provoking, annoying **-hosta** hacking cough
retina ['re:-] *s1* retina
retirera retire, retreat; (*rygga tillbaka*) recoil
ret|lig [ˣre:t-] *a1* (*lättretad*) irritable, fretful; (*snarstucken*) touchy; (*vresig*) irascible **-lighet** irritability; touchiness; irascibility **-medel** irritant; (*stimulerande medel*) stimulant **-ning** irritation; stimulation; (*känsel-, nerv-* etc.) stimulus, impulse **-ningströskel** stimulation (stimulus) threshold
retor [ˣre:-, 're:tår] *s3* rhetor **-ik** [-ɵ'ri:k] *s3* rhetoric **-iker** [-'tɵ:-] rhetorician **-isk** [-'tɵ:-] *a5* rhetorical
re'tort [-å-] *s3* retort **-flaska** spherical flask **-kol** retort (gas) carbon
retro|aktiv [-'ti:v, 're:-, 'retrɵ-] *a1* retroactive; ~ *verkan* retroaction; *ha* ~ *verkan* retroact **-'grad** *a4, n sg obest. form saknas* retrograde **-spektiv** *a1* retrospective
re'trätt *s3* retreat; (*tillflykt*) refuge; *slå till* ~ beat a retreat; *ta till* ~[*en*] retreat; *ha* ~*en klar* keep a line of retreat open, *bildl.* have a loophole ready; *på* ~ in retreat, retreating **-plats** *bildl.* a job for one's (*etc*) retirement
retur return; ~*er* (*-sändningar*) returned goods, returns; *sända varor i* ~ return goods, send goods back; *första klass tur och* ~ *London* first class return London; *vad kostar tur och* ~ *till ...?* what is the return fare to ...?; *vara på* ~ be abating (on the wane) **-biljett** return (*AE.* round-trip) ticket **-fiber** recycled fibre, secondary fibre **-glas** returnable bottle **-gods** returned goods **-match** return match (game) **-nera** return, send back **-papper** waste paper **-porto** return (reply) postage **-rätt** right of (to) return; *med* ~ on sale or return
re'tusch *s3* retouch[ing]; *ge ngt en lätt* ~ (*bildl.*) touch s.th. up a little **-era** retouch, touch up **-ering** retouching, touching up
reumat|iker [reu'ma:-, rev-] rheumatic **-isk** *a5* rheumatic **-ism** rheumatism **-ologi** *s3* rheumatology
rev *s2* (*met-*) fishing line
rev *s7* (*sand-*) sandbank, spit; (*klipp-*) reef
rev *s7, sjö.* reef
rev *imperf. av riva*
reva *v1, sjö.* reef, shorten; *gå för* ~*de segel* go under reefed sails

reva *s1* (*rispa*) tear, rent, rip; (*skråma*) wound
reva *s1, bot.* runner
revalver|a revaluate **-ing** revaluation
revansch [-'vanʃ, -'vaŋʃ] *s3* revenge; *ta* ~ take one's revenge, revenge o.s. **-era** *rfl, se* [*ta*] *revansch* **-lysten** eager for revenge; implacable, vengeful **-tanke** thought of revenge
rev|ben rib **-bensspjäll** *slaktar.* square rib[s *pl*]; *kokk.* ribs (*pl*) of pork
revel *s2, se 2 rev*
re'velj *s3* reveille; *blåsa* ~ sound (beat) the reveille; ~*en går* the reveille is sounding
reve'ny *s3* profit, gain; yield
reve'rens *s3* reverence
re'vers *s3* **1** (*skuldebrev*) note [of hand], promissory note; IOU (*förk. av* I owe you) **2** (*på mynt*) reverse **-'al** *s7* (*formulär*) promissory note form; (*från ämbetsverk*) notification of the dispatch of a document (sum of money) **-lån** promissory note loan
reveter|a roughcast, lath-and-plaster **-ing** lath-and-plastering; *konkr.* roughcast coating
revi'd|er *s7* clean (revised) proof **-era** (*bearbeta*) revise, review; (*räkenskaper*) audit; ~*d upplaga* revised edition
re'vir *s7* forest district; (*djurs*) territory
revision revision; (*av räkenskaper*) audit **-ism** revisionism **-ist** revisionist
revisions|berättelse auditor's report **-firma** firm of auditors; *auktoriserad* ~ firm of chartered accountants
revisor [-ˣvi:sår] *s3* auditor, accountant; *auktoriserad* ~ authorized public accountant, *i Storbritannien* chartered accountant
revolt [-'vålt] *s3* revolt, insurrection **-era** revolt **-försök** attempted revolt
revolution revolution **-era** revolutionize **-erande** [-'ne:-] revolutionary; (*epokgörande*) epoch-making
revolutionskrig revolutionary war
revolutio'när I *s3* revolutionary **II** *a1* revolutionary
revolver [-'våll-] *s2* revolver **-man** gunman, *AE. sl.* gunslinger **-skott** revolver shot **-svarv** capstan (turret) lathe
revorm *med.* ringworm
re'vy *s3, mil. o. bildl.* review; *teat.* revue, show; *passera* ~ march (file) past **-artist** show artiste
re'vär *s3* stripe
Rhen [re:n] *r* the Rhine
rhen|sk [re:nsk] *a5* Rhine, Rhenish **-vin** Rhine wine, hock **-vinsglas** hock glass, rummer
rhesus|apa [ˣre:-] rhesus monkey **-faktor** rhesus (*förk.* Rh) factor
Rh-faktor [ˣärrhå:-] Rh factor
Rhodos ['rå:dås] *n* Rhodes
ribb|a *s1* lath, batten; *sport.* [cross]bar **-ad** *a5* ribbed (*strumpa* stocking) **-stickad** *a5, se ribbad* **-stol** wall bars (*pl*) **-verk** rails (*pl*)
ricinolja [-ˣsi:n-] castor oil
rid|a *red -it* ride (*barbacka* bareback); *han -er bra* (*äv.*) he is a good rider (horseman); ~ *i galopp* (*skritt, trav*) gallop (pace, trot); ~ *på ngns rygg* (*äv.*) be carried piggyback (pickaback); ~ *in en häst* break a horse in; ~ *ut stormen* (*bildl.*) weather the storm; ~ *för ankaret* ride at anchor; ~ *på ord* split hairs, quibble

R

-ande *a4* riding; on horseback; ~ *polis* mounted police, *AE. äv.* (*i lantdistrikt*) ranger **-bana** riding ground **-byxor** *pl* [riding] breeches, jodhpurs **riddar|borg** feudal castle **-diktning** chivalrous poetry

riddar|e knight; *bli* ~ become (be made) a knight; *vandrande* ~ knight errant; ~*n av den sorgliga skepnaden* the knight of the sorrowful countenance; *en damernas* ~ un chevalier des dames; *fattiga* ~ (*kokk.*) bread fritters **-hus** *R~et* the House of the Nobility **-orden** order of knighthood (chivalry), knightly order **-sporre** *bot.* larkspur **-tiden** the age of chivalry **-väsen** chivalry

ridder|lig *al* chivalrous; *litt.* chivalric; (*chevaleresk*) gallant, courteous **-lighet** chivalry; gallantry **-skap** *s7, abstr.* chivalry, knighthood; *konkr.* Knighthood, (*under medeltiden*) Knights of the Realm; ~*t och adeln* the Nobility

ridder|sman (*riddare*) chevalier, knight; (*-lig man*) man of honour

rid|dräkt riding dress; (*dams*) riding habit **-hus** riding school **-häst** saddle horse, saddler **-it** *sup. av rida* **-konst** horsemanship **-lärare** riding master **-ning** riding **-piska** *se -spö* **-skola** riding school **-sport** riding, equestrian sport **-spö** [horse] whip; (*kort*) [riding] crop **-stövel** riding boot **-sår** saddle sore **-tur** ride

ri'då *s3* curtain **-fall** *vid* ~*et* at the fall of the curtain **-slutare** curtain shutter

riff *s7, mus.* riff

rigg *s2* rig[ging]; *löpande* ~ running rigging; *stående* ~ standing rigging **rigga** rig [out]; (*t.ex. metspö*) rig up; ~ *upp sig* (*vard.*) rig o.s. out

ri'gid *al, n. sg obest. form används ej* rigid **-itet** rigidity

rigorös *al* rigorous

rik *al* **1** (*förmögen*) rich, wealthy; *de ~a* the rich; *bli* ~ get (become) rich; *den ~e mannen* (*bibl.*) Dives **2** (*ymnig*) rich (*på* in); (*fruktbar*) fertile; (*-lig*) abundant, ample, plentiful; ~ *på minnen* full of memories; ~*t urval* wide range, varied assortment; *ett ~t förråd av* a plentiful (an abundant) store (stock) of; *ett ~t liv* a full (vivid) life; *bli en erfarenhet ~are* learn by experience, be that much wiser; *i* ~*t mått* amply, abundantly

rike *s6* (*stat*) state, realm; (*kungadöme*) kingdom; (*kejsardöme*) empire; *bildl.* kingdom, realm, sphere; *det tusenåriga ~t* the millennium; *tredje ~t* the Third Reich; *tillkomme ditt* ~ (*bibl.*) Thy kingdom come

rikedom *s2* **1** (*förmögenhet*) wealth; riches (*pl*) **2** *bildl.* richness (*på* in); (*-lighet*) wealth, abundance (*på* of) **rikeman** rich man **rikemansbarn** *pl* children of rich parents

rik|haltig *al* rich, plentiful, abundant **-lig** [*ˣ*ri:k-] *al* abundant (*skörd* crop); ample, plentiful; *få* ~ *användning för* have plenty of opportunity of using; *det har fallit ~t med snö* snow has fallen in abundance; *i* ~ *mängd* in abundance, in profusion

riko'schett *s3* ricochet; (*-erande projektil*) ricochetting bullet (*etc.*) **-era** ricochet

riks|angelägenhet [*ˣ*riks-] national affair **-antikvarie** director-general of the central board of [the Swedish] national antiquities **-arkiv** ~*e* [the Swedish] national archives (*pl*); (*i Storbritannien*) Public Record Office **-arkivarie** director-general of the [Swedish] national archives **-bank** central (national) bank; *R~en* (*Sveriges* ~) [the] Bank of Sweden **-banksdirektör** director of the Bank of Sweden **-banksfullmäktige** the board of governors of the Bank of Sweden **-bekant** known all over the country; (*ökänd*) notorious **-bibliotekarie** national librarian **-dag** ['riks-] *s2, R~en* the Swedish Parliament, the Riksdag; (*i Storbritannien*) Parliament; *lagtima* ~ ordinary parliamentary session

riksdags|beslut Riksdag (parliamentary) resolution; Act of Parliament **-debatt** Riksdag (parliamentary) debate **-hus** Riksdag (Parliament) Building; (*i Storbritannien*) Houses of Parliament; *AE.* Capitol **-ledamot**, **-man** member of parliament (the Riksdag); (*i Storbritannien*) member of parliament (*förk.* M.P.) *AE.* Congressman, *fem.* Congresswoman **-mandat** seat in parliament (the Riksdag), (*i Storbritannien*) seat in Parliament **-motion** bill **-ordning** Parliament (Riksdag) Act **-parti** Riksdag (parliamentary) party **-sammanträde** sitting of parliament (the Riksdag) **-val** general (parliamentary) election

riks|daler [riks'da:-] *s9, s2* rix-dollar **-drots** [-å-] *s2, ung.* Lord High Chancellor **-förening** national federation (association, union) **-föreståndare** regent **-försäkringsverket** the [Swedish] National Social Insurance Board **-gräns** international boundary, frontier of country **-gäldskontoret** [-jä-] the [Swedish] National Debt Office

riksha ['rikʃa] *s1* rickshaw, jinri[c]k[i]sha

riks|idrottsförbund *Sveriges R~* [the] Swedish Sports Confederation **-kansler** chancellor **-likare** national standard **-marsk** constable of the realm; *i Storbritannien ung.* Lord High Constable **-marskalk** marshal of the realm; *Storbritannien* Lord High Steward **-marskalksämbetet** office of the marshal of the realm **-museum** national museum (gallery) **-möte** parliamentary session, session of the Riksdag **-olycka** national disaster **-omfattande** nationwide **-plan** *på* ~*et* at a national level **-polischef** national police commissioner **-polisstyrelsen** [the Swedish] national police board **-regalier** *pl* regalia **-revisionsverke[t]** [the Swedish] national audit bureau **-råd** (*konselj*) council of the realm; *pers.* councillor **-rätt** court of impeachment; (*BE. motsv.* House of Lords; (*AE. motsv.*) Senate **-rös[e]** frontier cairn **-samtal** trunk call; *AE.* long-distance call **-skatteverket** [the Swedish] national tax board **-språk** standard language **-svenska** (*språk*) standard Swedish **-teater** *ung.* national touring theatre **-telefo[n]** trunk (*AE.* toll) exchange **-vapen** national coat of arms **-viktig** of national importance; (*almännare*) vitally important, momentous **-väg** national highway **-åklagare** prosecutor-general; *i Storbritannien* director of public prose[cutions]

cutions; *AE.* attorney general **-äpple** orb
rikta 1 (*vända åt visst håll*) direct (*mot* towards); aim (*ett slag mot* a blow at); (*skjutvapen*) aim, level, point (*mot* at); (*framställa*) address (*en anmärkning till* a remark to); ~ *en anklagelse mot* bring a charge (make an accusation) against; ~ *en fråga till* put a question to; ~ *misstankar mot* direct suspicion on; ~ *några ord till* say a few words to; ~ *uppmärksamheten på* draw attention to; ~ *sig till a*) (*om pers.*) address [o.s. to], *b*) (*om bok e.d.*) be intended for; ~ *sig mot* (*om tal e.d.*) be directed at **2** (*räta*) straighten; (*bräda, hjul e.d.*) true up
riktig *a1* (*rätt*) right; (*korrekt*) correct; (*verklig*) real; (*äkta*) true; (*regelrätt*) proper, regular; *det ~a* the right (proper) thing; *det var ett ~t nöje att* it was a real pleasure to; *ett ~t kräk* a poor wretch; *en ~ snobb* a regular snob; *han är inte ~* he is not right in his head **riktighet** rightness; correctness; (*noggrannhet*) accuracy; (*tillbörlighet*) propriety; *det äger sin ~ att* it is quite true (a fact) that; *avskriftens ~ intygas* we (I) certify this to be a true copy
riktigt *adv* right[ly]; correctly; (*som sig bör*) properly; (*verkligen*) really; (*ganska*) quite; (*mycket*) very; *mycket ~* quite right, sure enough; ~ *bra* really (very, quite) well, really (very) good; *jag mår ~ bra nu* I feel really well now; *pjäsen var ~ bra* the play was very good; *det anses inte ~ fint att* it is considered not quite the thing to; *jag mår inte ~ bra* I am not feeling quite well; *jag förstår inte ~ vad du säger* I don't quite understand what you say; *jag litar inte ~ på dem* I don't quite trust them; *han blev också ganska ~ förkyld* and sure enough he caught a cold
rikt|linje guideline; policies (*pl*); *uppdraga ~er för* (*bildl.*) lay down the general outline (guiding principles) for; *ge ~* (*äv.*) outline **-märke** target **-ning 1** (*inriktande*) directing, pointing; aiming; (*uträtande*) straightening **2** (*kurs, håll*) direction, course; *bildl.* direction, (*tendens*) tendency, trend, line; (*rörelse*) movement; *i ~ mot* in the direction of; *i vardera ~en* in each (either) direction, each way; *i vilken ~ gick hans uttalande?* what line did he take in his remarks; *ge samtalet en annan ~* (*äv.*) lead the conversation into another track **-nummer** *tel.* exchange code, code number **-pris** standard [retail] price, recommended retail price **-punkt** objective, aim (*för* of); *mil.* aiming point
rim *s7* [rimm] rhyme; *utan ~ och reson* without rhyme or reason **-flätning** [-ä:-] rhyme arrangement
rimfrost [ˣrimm-] hoarfrost, white (rime) frost; *täckt med ~* rimy
rimlexikon rhyming dictionary
rimlig *a1* (*skälig*) reasonable; (*sannolik*) likely, probable; (*måttlig*) moderate; *hålla kostnader inom ~a gränser* keep costs within reason (resonable bounds); *det är inte mer än ~t att* it is only reasonable that **rimlighet** reasonableness *etc.*; *vad i all ~s namn?* what in the name of common sense? **rimligtvis** reasonably

1 rimma rhyme (*på* with; *med* to, with); *absol.* *äv.* make rhymes; *kan du ~ på tänka?* can you supply a rhyme to think?; *ha lätt för att ~* find rhyming easy; *det ~r illa med* (*bildl.*) it doesn't tally (fit in) with
2 rimma *se* rimsalta
rimsalta salt slightly
rimsmidare rhymer, versifier
ring *s2* **1** ring; (*däck*) tyre, *AE.* tire **2** (*krets*) circle, ring; *meteor.* halo, (*kring solen äv.*) corona; *biol.* collar **3** (*i boxning*) boxing ring; *~ar* (*gymn.*) rings **4** *skol.* form in the upper secondary school
1 ring|a *v2* ring; *det -er i telefonen* the telephone is ringing; ~ *av* ring off; ~ *på dörren* ring (press) the [door] bell; ~ *på betjäningen* ring for room service; ~ *till ngn* give s.b. a ring, call s.b. up, phone s.b.; ~ *ett samtal* make a phone call; *det -er och susar för mina öron* there is a ringing in my ears
2 ringa *v1* **1** *jakt., lantbr.* ring **2** (*måltavla*) draw rings on; *se äv.* inringa **3** (*klänning e.d.*) ~ *ur* cut low [at the neck]
3 ringa I *oböjl. a* **1** small, little; (*obetydlig*) insignificant (*roll* part); slight (*ansträngning* effort); *ett ~ bevis på* small proof (token) of; ~ *efterfrågan* little (weak) demand; ~ *tröst* poor consolation; *på ~ avstånd* at a short distance; *till ~ del* to a small extent; *ytterst ~* infinitesimal **2** (*låg, enkel*) humble, lowly; *av ~ börd* of humble origin; *min ~ person* my humble self (person) **II** *adv* little
ringakt|a (*ngt*) make light of; (*ngn*) look down upon; (*förakta*) despise **-ande** *a4* despising *etc.*; contemptuous, disdainful **-ning** disregard; (*förakt*) contempt, disdain; *visa ~ för ngt* hold s.th. in contempt
1 ringare *s9* bell-ringer
2 ringare I *a, komp. t.* ringa smaller *etc.*; (*underlägsen*) inferior (*än* to) **II** *adv* less
ringast I *a, superl. t.* ringa least *etc.*; *utan ~e anledning* without the slightest provocation; *inte den ~e aning* not the slightest idea **II** *adv* least; *inte det ~e* not [in] the least, not at all
ring|blomma pot marigold; (*torkad*) calendula **-brynja** ring (chain) mail **-dans** round dance; *dansa ~* dance in a ring **-domare** *sport.* referee **-duva** wood pigeon, ringdove **-finger** ring finger **-formig** [-å-] *a1* ring-shaped, annular **-förlovad** officially engaged, betrothed
ringhet smallness, insignificance; (*låghet, enkelhet*) humbleness, lowliness
ringhörna *sport.* corner of a [boxing] ring
ringklocka bell
ringla curl; coil; (*om väg e.d.*) wind, meander; ~ *ihop sig* (*om orm*) coil itself up; ~ *sig* coil, wind, (*om lockar*) curl; *kön ~r sig* the queue winds **ringlar** *pl* (*av hår*) curls; (*av orm, rep*) coils
ringledning electric bell installation
ring|lek ring (round) game **-mask** annelid[an], ringed worm **-mur** encircling wall; town wall **-muskel** sphincter **-märka** ring, *AE.* band **-märkning** bird banding
ringning ringing
rink *s2* rink
rinna *rann runnit* run; (*flyta*) flow, stream;

(*droppa*) drip, trickle; (*om ljus*) gutter; (*läcka*) leak; *hennes tårar rann* her tears were flowing; *det kom mina ögon att ~* it made my eyes water; *sinnet rann på mig* I lost my temper; *~ av* drain off; *~ till* (*äv. bildl.*) begin to flow; *~ upp* (*om flod*) rise, have its source; *saken rann ut i sanden* it came to nothing; *~ ut* run out; *~ över* flow over; *det kom bägaren att ~ över* that was the last straw **rinnande** *a4* running

ripa *s1* grouse; (*fjäll-*) ptarmigan; (*dal-*) willow grouse

ri'post [-p-] *s3* ripost[e]; *bildl.* repartee, retort **-era** riposte; *bildl.* retort

rips *s3, s4* rep[p]

1 ris *s7* (*papper*) ream

2 ris *s7* (*sädesslag*) rice

3 ris *s7* **1** (*kvistar*) twigs (*pl*); (*buskvegetation*) brushwood **2** (*straffredskap*) rod, birch, birch rod; (*straff äv.*) birching; *få smaka ~et* have a taste of the birch (rod); *ge ngn ~* whip (birch) s.b.; *binda ~ åt egen rygg* make a rod for one's own back

ris|a 1 (*ärter e.d.*) stick **2** (*ge -bastu*) birch; (*klandra*) blame, criticize **-bastu** birching

ris|fält paddy [(rice) field] **-gryn** (*ett ~*) grain of rice; *koll.* rice (*sg*) **-grynsgröt** [boiled] rice pudding

rishög 1 *eg.* heap of twigs **2** *vard.* (*bil*) jalop[p]y

risig *a1* **1** (*om träd*) with dry twigs; (*-bevuxen*) scrubby **2** *vard.* (*om ting*) rotten, of low quality; (*om pers.*) in bad shape

risk *s3* risk (*för* of); *det är ingen ~ att ... (att jag ...)* there is no risk in (+ *ing-form*) (of my + *ing-form*); *löpa ~[en] att* run the risk of (+ *ing-form*); *med ~ att bli* at the risk of being; *på egen ~* at one's own risk; *ta ~er* take risks (chances); *utan ~* safely

riska *s1, bot.* edible agaric

risk|abel *a2* risky, dangerous, hazardous **-era** risk, run the risk of; hazard, (*äventyra*) jeopardize **-fri** safe **-fylld** hazardous, perilous, dangerous **-laboratorium** high-security laboratory

ris|knippa bundle of twigs, faggott **-koja** hut of twigs

riskorn grain of rice

riskvast besom

risk|tillägg danger money **-villig** *~t kapital* risk (venture) capital **-zon** danger zone; *i ~en* (*bridge.*) vulnerable

risodling *abstr.* rice cultivation; *konkr.* rice plantation, paddy [(rice) field]

ri'soll [-å-] *s3, kokk.* rissole **risotto** [-'åttå] *s9, kokk.* risotto

rispa I *s1* scratch; (*i tyg*) rent, rip **II** *v1* scratch; *~ upp* rip up; *~ sig* scratch o.s., (*om tyg*) fray, get frayed

rispapper rice paper

1 rista *v1* (*inskära*) cut, carve (*i* on); *bildl.* engrave, inscribe

2 rist|a *v3* (*skaka*) shake (*på huvudet* one's head); *det -er i armen* [*på mig*] I have shooting pains in my arm

rit *s3* rite

rit|a draw (*efter* from); (*göra -ning t.*) design (*ett hus* a house; *ett mönster* a pattern); *~ av* make a drawing (sketch) of, (*kopiera*) copy

-are draughtsman, designer **-bestick** set of drawing instruments **-block** sketch block, drawing pad **-bord, -bräde** drawing board **-kontor** drawing office **-ning** [ˣriːt-] **1** *abstr.* drawing, sketching **2** *konkr.* drawing, sketch, blueprint; (*t. byggnad e.d. äv.*) design **-papper** drawing paper

rits *s2, s3* scribed line **ritsa** mark [off], scribe

rit|sal [ˣriːt-] *art* [class]room **-stift 1** (*-penna*) drawing pen[cil] **2** (*häftstift*) drawing pin, *AE.* thumbtack

ritt *s3* ride, riding tour

ritu'al *s3, s4* ritual **-mord** ritual murder (*på* of)

ritu'ell *a1* ritualistic (*dans* dance); ritual (*ändamål* purposes)

riv *s7, bildl.* struggle, demand (*efter* for)

riv|a *rev -it* **1** (*klösa*) scratch; (*ihjäl-*) kill, tear to pieces; *~ hål på* tear a hole in; *~ sönder* tear to pieces, (*klädesplagg*) tear to rags (tatters); *~ ner* (*stöta till*) knock down; *~ upp* (*gata e.d.*) pull (take) up; *~ upp ett sår* tear open a wound; *~ ut* tear out; *~ åt sig* grab; *~ sig* (*klia sig*) scratch o.s., (*rispa sig*) get o.s. scratched **2** *kokk.* grate **3** (*rasera*) pull (*AE.* tear) down, demolish; *AE. äv.* wreck; (*kolmila*) rake out **4** (*rota*) rummage (poke) about (*bland in*) **5** (*svida i halsen*) rasp **6** *sport.,* *~* [*ribban*] knock the bar off

ri'val *s3* rival (*om* for; *till ngn* of s.b.); (*konkurrent*) competitor (*t. en plats* for a situation) **rivalisera** compete (*med ngn* with s.b.; *om* for); *~ med varandra* be rivals (*om att* in + *ing-form*) **rivaliserande** [-'seː-] *a4* rival[ling] **rivalitet** rivalry (*om* for)

rivande *a4, bildl.* tearing (*fart* pace); (*om pers.*) go-ahead, pushing **rivas** *revs* rivits, dep (*om katt e.d.*) scratch **rivebröd** [grated] bread crumbs (*pl*)

Rivieran [-ˣäːran] *r, best. f.* the Riviera

rivig *a1, vard.* go-ahead, pushing **rivit** *sup. av riva*

rivjärn grater; *bildl.* shrew **rivning** (*av byggnad e.d.*) demolition, pulling down

rivnings|hus house to be demolished (pulled down) **-kontrakt** short-term lease [in a house which is to be demolished]

riv|start (*av motorfordon*) flying start; *han startade med en ~* he tore off **-styrka** tearing resistance

1 ro *s9* **1** (*frid*) peace; (*ostördhet*) tranquillity; (*stillhet*) quiet[ness]; *få ~* have (be left in) peace; *aldrig få ngn ~ för* get no peace from; *inte få ngn levande ~* have no peace (rest); *han har ingen ~ i kroppen* he is so restless; *i godan ~, i lugn och ~* in peace and quiet; *ta det med ~* take things (it) easy; *det tar jag med ~* that doesn't worry me; *slå sig till ~* (*slå sig ner*) make o.s. comfortable, (*dra sig tillbaka*) retire, (*bosätta sig*) settle down, (*låta sig nöja*) be satisfied (*med* with) **2** *för ~ skull* for fun; *inte för ~ skull* not for nothing

2 ro *v4* row; pull; (*med vrickåra*) scull; *~ ut och fiska* go out fishing [in a rowing boat]; *~ hit med ...!* (*vard.*) hand over ...!, out with ...!; *~ iland med ngt* bring home the bacon, succeed i doing s.th.; *~ upp sig* (*vard.*) better o.s.

roa amuse; (*underhålla*) entertain; *vara ~d av*

be interested in *(politik* politics), be fond of, enjoy *(musik* music); *inte vara ~d av* not care about (for); *~ sig* amuse o.s. *(med* with), *(ha roligt)* enjoy o.s., have a good time
rob[e] [rå:b] *s3* [*s5*] robe
robot ['råbbåt] *s2* robot; *(-vapen)* [guided] missile; *målsökande ~* homing missile **-bas** guided-missile base **-vapen** [guided-]missile weapon; *koll.* missilery
ro'bust *al* robust
1 rock [-å-] *s2* coat; *(kavaj)* jacket; *(över-)* overcoat; *(skydds-)* overall; *för kort i ~en* be too short, not pass muster
2 rock [-å-] *s2 mus.* rock, rock-and-roll, rock--'n'-roll
1 rocka [-å-] *s1* ray
2 rocka [-å-] *(dansa)* rock, rock-and-roll, rock--'n'-roll
roc'k|ad [-å-] *s3, schack.* castling **-era** castle
rockhängare coat hanger
rock|musik rock [music] **-ring** hula-hoop *(varumärke)*
rock|skört coat-tail **-uppslag** lapel **-vaktmästare** cloakroom attendant
rockvideo rock video
rodd *s3* rowing **roddarbänk** *(toft)* thwart
roddare rower, sculler; oarsman; *(t. yrket)* boatsman
rodd|båt rowing boat; *AE.* rowboat; *sport.* crew racing boat **-sport** rowing **-tur** row, pull, boating trip **-tävling** boat race, rowing match
rodel ['rå:-] *s2* toboggan, bobsleigh
roder ['rɷ:-] *s7* rudder; *(ratt, rorkult)* helm *(äv. bildl.); flyg.* control surface; *lyda ~* obey (answer) the helm; *lägga om -ret* shift the helm; *sitta vid -ret* be at the helm **-blad** rudder blade **-skada** damage to the rudder *(etc.)*
rodna [ˣrå:d-] *(om sak)* turn red, redden; *(om pers.)* blush *(av* for; *över* at) **rodnad** *s3 (röd färg)* redness; flush; *(hos pers.)* blush
rododend|ron [rådåˈdendrån] *-ronen -ron, pl äv. -rer* rhododendron
roff|a [ˣråffa] rob; *~ åt sig* grab, lay hands on **-are** robber; grabber **-eri** robbery
ro|fylld peaceful; *(stilla)* serene **-givande** [-j-] *a4* soothing
rojal|ism [rå-] royalism **-ist** *s3* royalist **-istisk** *a5* royalist[ic]
rokoko [råkåˈkå:] *s9* rococo **-möbel** rococo furniture **-tiden** the Rococo Period
rolig *al (roande)* amusing; *(underhållande)* entertaining, interesting; *(trevlig)* nice, jolly; *(lustig)* funny; *~a historier* funny stories; *det var ~t att höra* I am glad (pleased) to hear; *det var ~t att du kunde komma* I'm so glad you could come; *så ~t!* how nice!, what fun! **-het** *säga ~er* make (crack) jokes **-hetsminister** joker, wag
roligt *adv* funnily *etc.*; *ha ~* have a nice time, have fun, enjoy o.s.; *ha ~ åt* laugh at, *(på ngns bekostnad)* make fun of
1 roll [-å-] *s3* part *(äv. bildl.)*; character; *(om sak)* role; *spela Romeos ~* play the part of Romeo; *spela en viktig ~ (bildl.)* play an important part (role); *det spelar ingen ~* it doesn't matter, it makes no difference; *det spelar mycket liten ~* it matters very little; *han*

har spelat ut sin ~ he is played out, he has had his day; *falla ur ~en (bildl.)* let one's mask slip; *leva sig in i ~en* lose o.s. in one's part; *det blev ombytta ~er* the tables were turned
2 roll [-å-] *s2, flyg.* roll
1 rolla [-å-] *flyg.* roll
2 rolla [-å-] *(måla)* roll on
roller ['råll-] *s2* roller
roll|fack character part **-fördelning** [role] casting **-häfte** *mitt ~* my script **-innehavare** actor playing a (the) part, member of the cast **-lista** *(hopskr. rollista)* cast **-skapelse** creation of a character **-spel** role-playing
rolös restless
Rom [rɷmm] *n* Rome
1 rom [råmm] *s9 (fisk-)* spawn, [hard] roe; *lägga ~* spawn; *leka ~men av sig (bildl.)* sow one's wild oats
2 rom [råmm] *s9 (dryck)* rum
ro'man *s3* novel **-cykel** cycle novel **-diktning** novel writing
roma'nesk *a5* romantic
roman|författare novelist, novel writer **-hjälte** hero of (in) a novel
romani ['råmm-, 'rɷmm-, 'rå:-] *s9* Rom[m]any
romanist Romanist, Romance philologist
romanlitteratur fiction
romans [-'mans, -'maŋs] *s3* romance *(äv. mus.)*
ro'mansk [-a:-] *a5 (om språk, kultur)* Romance, Romanic; *(om konst)* Romanesque, *i Storbritannien* Norman; *(om folk)* Latin
romanssångare ballad singer
romant|ik *s3* romance; *(kulturriktning)* Romanticism **-iker** [-'mann-] romantic; Romanticist **-isera** romanticize **-isk** [-'mann-] *a5* romantic
Romarbrevet [ˣrɷmm-] [the Epistle of Paul the Apostle to the] Romans
romar|e Roman **-inna** Roman woman **-riket** the Roman Empire **-tiden** the Roman Period
romb [-å-] *s3* rhomb[us] **-isk** ['rɷmm-] *a5* rhombic[al] **-o'id** *s3* rhomboid
romersk ['rɷmm-] *a5* Roman; *~ rätt* Roman Law; *~a ringar (gymn.)* [hand] rings **--katolsk** Roman Catholic
rom|korn roe corn **-läggning** spawning **-stinn** [hard] roed
rond [rånd, råŋd] *s3* round; *(vakts äv.)* beat; *gå ~en* go the rounds, *(om läkare)* do the round **-'ell** *s3 (trafik-)* [traffic] roundabout; *AE.* rotary, traffic circle
rondo ['råndå] *s6, mus.* rondo
rondskål *med.* kidney dish
rondör stoutness; plumpness
rop *s7* **1** call, cry *(av* of; *på* for); *(högt)* shout *(av* of, for; *på* for); *(gällt)* yell; *(-ande)* calling, clamour; *ett förtvivlans ~* a cry of despair **2** *(vissa djurs)* call, cry **3** *(auktions-)* bid **4** *i ~et* fashionable, in vogue, popular
ropa call *(äv. om djur)*; *(högljutt)* call out, cry, shout; *som man ~r i skogen får man svar* as the question so the answer; *~ på a)* *(ngn)* call, *b) (ngt)* call for *(hjälp* help), cry out *(på hämnd* for vengeance), *c) (på auktion)* bid on; *~ in a)* *(skådespelare)* call before the curtain, *b) (på auktion)* buy [at an (the) auction]; *~ upp* call over (out) *(namnen* the names) **ropare**

(*megafon*) speaking trumpet, megaphone
ror *s7*, **stå till ~s** be at the helm; *se äv.* **roder**
rorgängare [ˣrɷ:rjäŋ-] steersman; helmsman
(*äv. bildl.*) **rorkult** *s2* tiller **rorsman** *se rorgängare*
1 ros *s1*, *bot.* rose; *ingen ~ utan törnen* no rose
without a thorn; *ingen dans på ~or* not all beer
and skittles; *med ~or på kinderna* with rosy
cheeks
2 ros *s3*, *med.* erysipelas
3 ros *s7* (*lovord*) praise; *~ och ris* praise and
blame
1 rosa [ˣrɷ:-] *v1* praise, sing the praises of; *den
~r inte marknaden precis* it's not exactly a
dazzling success
2 rosa [ˣrå:-] **I** *n el.* *r* rose[-colour] **II** *oböjl. a*
rose-coloured, rosy
rosafärgad *se* 2 *rosa II*
rosen|blad rose leaf **-bröd** kokk. roll **-buske**
rose bush **-böna** bot. scarlet runner [bean]
-doft scent of roses **-gård** rose garden **-kindad** [-ç-] *a5* rosy-cheeked **-knopp** rosebud
-krans rose wreath; (*radband*) rosary **-kål**
Brussels sprout **-odling** *abstr.* rosegrowing;
konkr. rose plantation **-olja** oil of roses **-rasande** raging, furious **-röd** rosy, rosy red; *se
allt i -rött* see everything through rose-coloured spectacles **-sten** rose diamond **-trä**
rosewood **-vatten** rose-water
ro'sett *s3* bow; rosette; (*fluga*) bow [tie], butterfly **-fönster** rose window
rosévin rosé
rosig *a1* rosy
rosmarin [-'ri:n, ˣrɷ:s-] *s3* rosemary
rossla [ˣråss-] rattle; *det ~r i bröstet på honom*
there is a rattle in his chest, he has a wheezy
chest **rosslande** *a4* rattling, wheezing **rosslig** *a1* rhonch[i]al, wheezing **rossling** rattle,
wheeze
1 rost [-å-] *s3* **1** (*på järn*) rust; *angripen av ~*
corroded by rust; *knacka ~* chip the rust off **2**
bot. rust; mildew, blight
2 rost [-å-] *s2* (*galler*) grate, grid
1 rosta [ˣråss-] (*bli rostig*) rust, get rusty,
oxidize; *~ fast* rust in; *gammal kärlek ~r aldrig* an old love is hard to forget
2 rosta [ˣråss-] **1** *kokk.* roast (*kaffe* coffee);
toast (*bröd* bread); *~t bröd med smör* buttered
toast; *~t vete* puffed wheat **2** *tekn.* roast
rostbeständig rustproof, rust-resisting
rostbiff roast beef
rost|bildning formation of rust, corrosion
-brun rusty brown
rosteri roasting house (factory), roastery
rostfläck (*på järn*) spot of rust; (*på tyg*) spot
of iron-mould; (*på säd o.d.*) speck of rust
rostfri stainless (*stål* steel); *~ diskbänk*
stainless steel sink **rostig** *a1* rusty, corroded
1 rostning [-å-] (*järns*) rusting
2 rostning [-å-] *kokk.* roasting; toasting
rost|röd rust-red **-skydd** rust proofing **-skyddsmedel** anticorrosive agent **-svamp** rust fungus
rosväxter *pl* rosaceous plants
rot *-en rötter* root (*på, till* of); *språkv. äv.* base,
radix; (*liten*) rootlet, radicle; *~en till allt ont*
the root of all evil; *dra ~en ur* (*mat.*) extract

the square root of; *~en och upphovet till* the
root and origin of; *gå till ~en med* get to the
root (bottom) of; *ha sin ~ i* (*bildl.*) have its
origin in; *skog på ~* standing forest (timber);
rycka upp med ~en pull up by the roots, *bildl.*
root up, uproot; *slå ~* strike (take) root (*äv.
bildl.*)
1 rota (*böka*) poke about; *~ fram* dig up; *~ i*
rout about in, poke into
2 rota root; *~ sig* strike (take) root; *djupt ~d*
deeply rooted, deep-rooted
rotation rotation; revolution
rotations|axel axis of rotation **-hastighet**
speed of rotation **-press** rotary press
rot|blad radical leaf **-blöta** *s1* soak[er], drench,
drencher **-borste** scrubbing brush
rote *s2*, *mil.* file; *gymn.* squad **rotel** *s2* (*i ämbetsverk*) department, division; *jur.* section
roter|a rotate; revolve **-ande** *a4* rotating (*hjul*
wheel); revolving, rota[to]ry (*rörelse* movement; *motor* engine)
rot|fast [firmly] rooted; *bildl. äv.* securely established **-frukt** root; *~er* (*äv.*) root crops **-fylla**
fill a root cavity in **-fyllning** root filling; *AE.*
root canal **-fäst** *a4*, *bildl.* ingrained **-fästa**
root; *~ sig* (*bildl.*) establish itself (*etc.*) **-kanal** root canal **-knöl** tuber, bulb **-lös** rootless
-löshet rootlessness **-mos** mashed turnips and
potatoes (*pl*) **-märke** *mat.* radical sign
rotogravyr [-'vy:r, ˣrɷ:-, ˣrå:-] *s3* rotogravure
rotor [ˣrɷ:tår] *s3* rotor, armature
rots [-å-] *s3* glanders
rot|saker *pl* roots **-selleri** celeriac **-skott**
sucker **-stock** rhizome, rootstock **-tecken** *se
rotmärke*
rotting [ˣrått-] rattan, cane **-stol** cane (rattan)
chair
rottråd root fibre
rotunda [-ˣtunn-] *s1* rotunda
rotvälska [ˣrɷ:t-] *s1* double Dutch, lingo; *prata
~* (*äv.*) talk gibberish
roué [rɷ'e:] *s3* roué, rake
rouge [rɷ:ʃ] *s4*, *s3* rouge
roulad [rɷ'la:d] *s3*, *se rulad*
roulett [rɷ'lett] *s3* roulette; *spela* [*på*] *~* play
roulette; *vinna på ~* win at roulette
rov *s7* **1** (*om djur: byte*) prey; *gå på ~* be on
the prowl; *leva av ~* live [up]on prey **2** (*om
människor: röveri*) robbing, robbery; (*byte*)
booty, spoil[s *pl*]; *bildl.* prey; *bli ett ~ för* fall
a prey (victim) to; *vara ute på ~* be out
plundering; *icke akta för ~ att* (*bibl.*) not deem
it robbery, (*friare*) think nothing of (+ *ing--form*)
rova *s1* **1** (*rotfrukt*) turnip **2** (*klocka*) turnip;
sätta en ~ fall on one's behind
rov|djur beast of prey, predator **-drift** ruthless
exploitation, overexploitation **-fågel** bird of
prey, raptor [bird] **-girig** rapacious; predatory
-girighet rapacity **-jakt** *bedriva ~* exhaust the
stock of game **-lysten** *se -girig*
rovolja rape (colza) oil
rov|riddare robber baron **-stekel** digger wasp;
mud dauber
rubank ['ru:-] *s2*, *snick.* trying plane
rubb *i uttr.: ~ och stubb* lock, stock and barrel,
the whole lot

rubba 1 (*flytta på*) dislodge, move **2** *bildl.* (*störa*) disturb, upset; (*ändra*) alter; (*bringa att vackla*) shake; *han låter inte ~ sig* there is no moving him; *~ inte mina cirklar!* don't upset my calculations! **rubbad** *a5* (*sinnes-*) deranged; crazy **rubbning 1** dislodging, moving **2** disturbance; alteration, change; (*nervös*) derangement; *mentala ~ar* mental disorders

rubel ['ru:-] *s9, om myntstycken s3* r[o]uble

rubidium [-'bi:-] *s8, kem.* rubidium

ru'bin *s3* ruby **-röd** ruby red

rubricer|a 1 (*förse med rubrik*) give a heading to, headline **2** (*beteckna*) classify, characterize **-ing 1** heading **2** classification, characterization

rub'rik *s3* heading, title; (*tidnings-*) headline, caption **-stil** *boktr.* display type

rucka (*rubba*) move; (*klocka*) regulate, adjust; *~ på ngns vanor* change a p.'s habits

1 ruckel ['rukk-] *s7* (*kyffe*) ramshackle house, hovel

2 ruck|el ['rukk-] *s7* (*svirande*) revelry, debauchery

ruckl|a revel, lead a dissolute life **-are** rake, fast liver

rucklig *a1* (*fallfärdig*) ramshackle, tumble-down

ruckning (*klockas*) regulation, adjustment

ruda *s1* crucian

rudiment *s7* rudiment **-'är** *a1* rudimentary

rudis ['ru:-] *oböjl. a, vard.* ignorant

ruelse *s5* remorse, compunction

1 ruff *s2, sjö.* deckhouse, cabin

2 ruff *s9, s7 sport.* rough play

3 ruff *s2, golf.* rough

ruffa play a rough game, foul

ruffad *a5, sjö., vara ~* have a cabin

1 ruffig *a1, sport.* rough

2 ruffig *a1* (*sjaskig*) shabby, seedy-looking; dilapidated

rufs *s7* tousle **rufsa** *~ till* ruffle, tousle **rufsig** *a1* tousled; *vara ~ i håret* (*äv.*) have untidy hair

rugby ['ruggbi, -y] *s9* rugby [football]; *vard.* rugger; *AE. ung.* football

rugga 1 (*ylle e.d.*) tease[l]; *~ upp* buff, nap **2** (*om fåglar*) moult **rugge** *s2* (*vass- o.d.*) clump; (*tuva*) tuft **ruggig** *a1* **1** (*uppruggad*) teaselled **2** (*fransig*) raw; *bok med ~t snitt* a raw-edged book **3** (*uppburrad*) ruffled (*sparv* sparrow) **4** (*sjaskig*) shabby, frowzy, frowsy; (*gråkall*) bleak, raw; (*kuslig*) gruesome **ruggning** (*fåglars*) moulting

ru'in *s3* ruin; *bildl. äv.* wreck; *det blev hans ~* it brought about his ruin; *på ~ens brant* on the verge of ruin

ruiner|a ruin (*äv. bildl.*), bring to ruin (bankruptcy); *bli ~d* be ruined, go bankrupt, *vard.* go broke; *~ sig* ruin o.s., go bankrupt **-ande** *a4* ruinous

ruin|hög heap of ruins **-stad** ruined city (town)

ru'lad *s3* **1** *kokk.* roll **2** *mus.* roulade, run

ru'lett *se* roulett

ruljangsen [-'jaŋ-] *best. form, vard., sköta* [*hela*] *~* run the [whole] show (business)

1 rull|a *s1, mil.* roll, list, register; *införa i -orna* (*äv.*) enrol; *avföra ur -orna* remove from (strike off) the list, *mil. äv.* disenrol

2 rulla *v1* **1** (*förflytta*) roll; (*linda äv.*) reel,

wind; (*på hjul*) wheel; (*rep*) coil; *data.* scroll; *~ tummarna* twirl one's thumbs **2** (*förflyttas*) roll (*äv. om fartyg, dimma, åska*); *låta pengarna ~* make the money fly; *~ med ögonen* roll one's eyes **3** (*med betonad partikel*) *~ av* unroll, unwind, uncoil; *~ ihop* roll up, make a roll of, scroll; *~ ihop sig* roll up, (*om orm o.d. äv.*) coil; *~ upp* roll up, wind (coil) [up], (*gardin*) pull up, *bildl.* unfold **4** *rfl* roll [over]; *~ sig i stoftet* cringe, grovel

3 rulla *i frasen: leva ~n* go on a spree

rullager (*särskr. rull-lager*) roller bearing

rull|ande *a4* rolling (*material* stock); *~ klinik* mobile clinic; *~ planering* ongoing planning; *~ reform* continuous reform **-bana** (*transport-*) roller conveyor; *flyg.* taxi strip, runway **-band** rolling hoop **-bord** tea (service) trolley **-bräde** skateboard **-bälte** inertia-reel seat-belt, inertia safety belt

rull|e *s2* roll; (*film-, pappers-*) reel; (*rep-*) coil; (*spole*) bobbin; (*dikterings-*) cylinder; (*skrift-*) scroll **-fåll** *sömn.* rolled hem **-gardin** [roller] blind; *AE.* shade **-lager** *se rullager* **-ning** rolling; *sjö. äv.* roll; *sätta i ~* start rolling **-skridsko** roller skate **-sten** boulder **-stens-ås** boulder ridge **-stol** wheelchair, invalid chair **-sylta** collared brawn **-trappa** escalator; moving staircase **-tårta** Swiss roll **-verk** *konst.* scroll

rulta I *s1* podgy woman; (*flicka*) roly-poly, dumpling **II** *v1* waddle, joggle **rultig** *a1* podgy, dumpy

1 rum [rumm] *s7* **1** (*bonings-*) room; *~ åt gatan* (*gården*) front (back) room; *beställa ~ på ett hotell* reserve a room at a hotel; *ett ~ och kök* one room and [a] kitchen **2** (*utrymme*) room; (*plats*) place; *hur många får ~ i soffan?* how many is there room for on the sofa?; *den får inte ~ här* there is no room for it here; *i främsta ~met* in the first place; *komma i första ~met* come first; *lämna ~ för* leave room for (*äv. bildl.*); *lämna* (*bereda*) *~ åt* make room for; *ta stort ~* be bulky, take up a lot of room; *äga ~* take place; (*om möte o.d.*) be held **3** (*rymd*) space; *tid*[*en*] *och ~*[*met*] time and space; *lufttomt ~* vacuum **4** *sjö.* (*last-*) hold

2 rum [rumm] *a1, i ~ sjö* in open water (the open sea)

rumba *s1* rumba

rumla go on a spree, revel **rumlare** reveller, carouser **rummel** ['rumm-] *s7* revelry

rump|a *s1* buttocks (*pl*), posterior, behind; *vard.* backside, rump **-huggen** *a3* tail-docked; *bildl.* truncated, with an abrupt end

rums|adverb adverb of place **-arrest** *mil.* open arrest **-beställning** booking of rooms (a room); (*på skylt*) receptionist **-brist** shortage of accommodation **-förmedling** room agency **-kamrat** roommate; *vara ~er* share a room **-last** hold (inboard) cargo **-lig** *a1* spatial, spacial **-ren** (*om hund e.d.*) house-trained (house-broken) **-temperatur** room temperature

rumstera rummage about (round)

rums|uppassare room attendant **-växt** indoor plant

ru'män *s3* Ro[u]manian

Rumänien [-'mä:-] *n* Ro[u]mania

rumän|ier [-'mä:-] *s9* Ro[u]manian **-[i]sk** *a5* Ro[u]manian **-ska 1** (*kvinna*) Ro[u]manian woman **2** (*språk*) Ro[u]manian
run|a *s1* **1** (*skrivtecken*) rune; *rista -or* carve (cut) runes **2** (*minnes-*) obituary **-alfabet** runic alphabet
rund I *s3* circle, ring; *poet.* round **II** *a1* round; (*cirkel-*) circular; (*klot-*) spherical; (*cylindrisk*) cylindrical; (*fyllig*) plump, chubby; *en ~ summa* a round (lump) sum; *i runt tal* in round figures, roughly **rund|a I** *s1* round; *gå en ~* go for a stroll **II** *v1* **1** round (*av* off) **2** *sjö.* double
rund|a'bordskonferens round-table conference **-båge** round arch **-bågsstil** Romanesque (*Storbritannien* Norman) style
rund|el *s2, trädg.* round [flower]bed; (*rund plats*) circus; (*vindling*) circle **-fil** round file **-flygning** sightseeing flight **-fråga** inquiry, questionnaire **-horisont** *teat.* cyclorama **-hult** *s7, sjö.* spar **-hänt** *a1* generous, liberal **-järn** round [bar-]iron **-kindad** [-ç-] *a5* round--cheeked, chubby-cheeked **-kullig** *a1, ~ hatt* bowler [hat] **-kyrka** round church **-lagd** *a5* plump, rotund **-lig** *a1* ample; (*-hänt*) generous, liberal; *en ~ summa* a good round sum; *en ~ tid* a long[ish] time **-mask** roundworm **-munnar** *pl, zool.* cyclostomes **-målning** panorama (*äv. bildl.*) **-ning** (*-ande*) rounding; (*-het*) roundness, curvature; (*utbuktning*) bulge, swell **-nätt** small and plump **-radio** broadcasting **-radiostation** broadcasting station **-resa** tour, round trip **-skrivelse** circular letter, circular **-smörja** grease **-smörjning** lubrication, greasing **-stav** *pl* billets **-såg** fret saw, circular saw **-tur** sightseeing tour (trip) **-vandring** tour; *göra en ~ i* make a tour of **-ögd** *a5* round-eyed
runforsk|are runologist **-ning** runology
runga resound **rungande** *a4* resounding; *ett ~ hurra* a ringing cheer; *ett ~ skratt* a roar of laughter
runinskrift runic inscription
runka 1 (*gunga*) rock, wag; (*skaka*) shake (*på huvudet* one's head) **2** *vard.* jerk off, masturbate
runnit *sup. av rinna*
run|olog runologist **-ologi** *s3* runology **-ristare** rune cutter (carver) **-skrift** runic characters (letters) (*pl*); (*inskription*) runic inscription **-slinga** runiform ornament **-stav** rune-staff **-sten** runestone, runic stone
runt I *adv* round; *~ om[kring]* round about; *det går ~ för mig* my head is in a whirl; *lova ~ och hålla tunt* promise a lot, fulfil ne'er a jot **II** *prep* round (*hörnet* the corner); *~ om* around, all round; *resa jorden ~* travel round the world; *~ hela jorden* the world over; *året ~* all the year round
runtecken runic character
rupie ['ru:-] *s5* rupee
ruptur rupture, breach
rus *s7* intoxication (*äv. bildl.*); *bildl.* ecstasy, transport; *ett lätt ~* a slight intoxication; *sova ~et av sig* sleep o.s. sober; *ta sig ett ~* get drunk; *under ~ets inverkan* under the influence of drink

rusa 1 (*störta fram*) rush, dash; (*flänga*) tear; *~ fram* rush up (*framåt:* forwards); *~ i väg* rush (dash, dart) off; *~ i fördärvet* plunge into ruin; *~ på dörren* rush for the door; *~ på ngn* rush (fly) at s.b.; *~ upp från* spring (jump) up from; *blodet ~de upp i ansiktet på honom* the blood rushed to his face; *~ upp ur sängen* spring (dash) out of bed **2** (*om motor, ånga*) race; *~ en motor* race (rev up, gun) an engine
rusch *s3* rush; drive **-ig** *a1* energetic; go-ahead
rus|dryck intoxicating liquor, intoxicant **-drycksförbud** prohibition
rush [ruʃ] *s3, sport.* rush
rusig *a1* (*berusad*) drunk; intoxicated (*av vin* with wine; *av lycka* with happiness)
rusk *s7* wet (bad) weather; *i regn och ~* in rain and storm
1 ruska *v1, det regnar och ~r* it's wet and windy
2 rusk|a *s1* tuft; (*träd-*) bunch of twigs
3 ruska *v1* (*skaka*) shake; *~ liv i* shake into life, (*ngn*) rouse; *~ på huvudet* shake one's head; *~ om ngn* give s.b. a shaking
ruskig *a1* (*om väder*) nasty, unpleasant; (*om pers.: sluskig*) disreputable, shady; (*om t.ex. kvarter*) squalid; (*otäck*) horrid; *känna sig litet ~* feel a little out of sorts (seedy) **ruskighet** (*vädrets*) nastiness *etc.*; (*otäckhet*) gruesomeness; *~er* gruesome things, horrors **ruskigt** *adv, vard. äv.* terribly, awfully
ruskprick *sjö.* broom-beacon, broom-perch
ruskväder *se rusk*
rus|ning [ˣru:s-] rush (*efter* for); (*av motor*) racing, overspeeding **-ningstid** rush hour[s *pl*], peak period
russ *s7* Gotland pony
russifi[c]era Russify, Russianize
russin *s7* raisin **-kärna** raisin seed
rusta 1 arm (*till krig* for war); (*utrusta*) equip **2** (*göra i ordning*) prepare, make preparations (*för, till* for); *~ upp (reparera*) do up, repair **3** *rfl* (*göra sig färdig*) get ready, make preparations (*till* for); (*väpna sig*) arm o.s. **rustad** *a5* (*ut-*) equipped; (*beväpnad*) armed **rusthåll** *s7, stå för ~et* (*bildl.*) be responsible for the whole affair, run the show
rustibus[s] *s2* lively child
rustik *a1* rustic; (*bondaktig*) countrified; (*grov*) boorish
rust|kammare armoury **-mästare** staff sergeant 1st class
rustning 1 (*krigsförberedelse*) armament **2** *konkr.* armour, coat of mail; *fullständig ~* (*äv.*) panoply **rustningsindustri** armament industry
ruta I *s1* square; (*i mönster*) check; (*fönster-*) [window]pane; (*TV-*) screen **II** *v1* (*göra rutig*) check; *~t papper* cross-ruled (squared) paper
1 ruter ['ru:-] *s9, kortsp., koll.* diamonds (*pl*); *jfr hjärter*
2 ruter ['ru:-] *r, det är ~ i henne* she has got pluck; *det är ingen ~ i honom* he has no go in him
rutformig [-å:-] *a1* square-shaped **rutig** *a1* check[ed]; chequered
ru'tin *s3* routine; (*färdighet*) professional experience, practical knowledge; *~er* (*äv.*) pro-

cedures **-arbete** routine work **-erad** [-'ne:-]
a5 experienced, practised, skilled **-kontroll**
routine checkup **-mässig** *a1* routine **-mäs-
sighet** routine **-mässigt** *adv* by routine; *neds.*
mechanically
rut|mönster check (*snedvinkligt:* diamond)
pattern **-papper** cross-ruled paper
rutsch|a ['*rutʃa] slide; (*slira*) skid **-bana**
chute, slide; (*vatten-*) water chute
rutt *s3* route
rutten *a3* rotten (*äv. bildl.*); putrid; (*om tänder*) decayed; (*moraliskt äv.*) corrupt, depraved
ruttenhet rottenness *etc.*; *bildl. äv.* corruption
ruttna become (get) rotten, rot; (*om virke äv.*)
decay; (*om kött äv.*) decompose
ruva sit [on eggs], brood; ~ *på* (*bildl.*) brood
on; ~ *över* jealously safeguard (*sina skatter*
one's treasures) **ruvning** [-u:-] sitting, brooding
1 rya ['*ry:a] *v1* shout
2 rya ['*ry:a] *s1* long-pile rug, hooked rug
ryamatta *se 2 rya*
ryck *s7* **1** (*knyck*) jerk, tug, pull **2** (*sprittning*)
start; (*nervöst*) twitch, spasm; *vakna med ett
~* wake up with a start; *snabba ~* fast going,
good going **3** *bildl.* (*anfall*) fit, flicker; (*nyck*)
whim, freak **4** (*i tyngdlyftning*) snatch
ryck|a *v3* **1 1** (*dra*) pull, jerk; (*hastigt*) snatch;
(*våldsamt*) wrench; (*slita*) tear; ~ *ngn i armen*
pull s.b. by the arm **2** (*lin, hampa*) pull **3** (*ruska, dra hit o. dit*) pull, tug, jerk; ~ *i dörren*
pull at the door; ~ *i klocksträngen* pull the
bell[cord]; ~ *på axlarna* shrug one's shoulders
(*åt* at); *det -te i mungiporna på henne* the
corners of her mouth twitched **4** *mil.* march,
move (*mot fienden* against the enemy; *mot
målet* towards the objective); ~ *närmare* approach; ~ *ngn in på livet* press s.b. hard; ~ *till
ngns undsättning* rush to a p.'s rescue **II** (*med
betonad partikel*) **1** *han -tes bort vid unga år*
he was snatched away in early life **2** ~ *fram*
(*mil. o.d.*) push forward, advance **3** ~ *in a*)
boktr. inset, *b*) (*om trupper*) march into, *c*) (*om
värnpliktig*) join up; ~ *in i en stad* march into
(enter) a town; ~ *in i ngns ställe* take a p.'s
place **4** ~ *loss* wrench (jerk) loose **5** *hon -tes
med av hans berättelse* she was carried along
by his story; ~ *med sig* carry away **6** ~ *till* give
a start, start; ~ *till sig* snatch **7** ~ *upp a*) (*ogräs*)
pull up, *b*) (*dörr e.d.*) pull open; ~ *upp sig* pull
o.s. together **8** ~ *ut a*) pull out, (*tand*) extract,
b) *mil.* (*om trupp*) move out, break camp, (*om
värnpliktig*) be furloughed home (released), (*om
brandkår o.d.*) turn out
rycken ['rykk-] *i uttr.:* *stå* ~ stand it, hold one's
own; *stå* ~ *för* stand up to **ryckig** *a1* jerky;
spasmodic; disjointed **ryckning** pull, jerk;
(*nervös*) twitch, spasm; *nervösa* ~*ar* (*äv.*) a
nervous tic (*sg*) **ryckvis** by jerks, by fits and
starts; (*då o. då*) intermittently
rygg *s2* back; *falla ngn i* ~*en* attack s.b. from
the rear; *gå bakom* ~*en på ngn* (*bildl.*) go
behind a p.'s back; *ha* ~*en fri* have a line of
retreat open; *hålla ngn om* ~*en* (*bildl.*) support
s.b., back s.b. up; *skjuta* ~ (*om katt*) arch its
back; *stå med* ~*en mot* stand with one's back
to; *tala illa om ngn på hans* ~ speak ill of s.b.

behind his back; *vända ngn* ~*en* (*bildl.*) turn
one's back on s.b.; *så snart man vänder* ~*en
till* as soon as one's back is turned
rygg|a **1** (*om häst*) back; (*om pers.*) step (*häf-
tigt* start) back; (*dra sig tillbaka*) withdraw
(*från* from); (*frukta för*) shrink, recoil (*inför*
at, before) **2** *ridk.* back (*en häst* a horse) **-be-
dövning** spinal anaesthesia **-fena** dorsal fin
-kota vertebra **-läge** *intaga* ~ lie down on
one's back **-märg** spinal cord **-märgsprov**
lumbar puncture **-rad** spine, spinal column;
bildl. backbone **-radsdjur** vertebrate **-radslös**
invertebrate; *bildl.* without backbone, spineless
-sim backstroke **-skott** lumbago **-stöd** *eg.*
support for the back; (*på stol e.d.*) back; *bildl.*
backing, support **-säck** rucksack, backpack
-tavla back **-ås** ridgepole **-åsstuga** *ung.* timber cottage open to the roof
ryk|a *imperf. rök, äv. v3* **1** smoke; reek; (*pyra*)
smoulder; (*ånga*) steam; (*om damm*) fly about;
det -er in the chimney is smoking; *rågen -er*
the rye is smoking; *slåss så det -er om det*
fight so the feathers fly **2** *där rök hans sista
slantar* there goes the last of his money; ~ *ihop*
fly at each other, (*slåss*) come to blows; ~ *på*
(*anfalla*) assault, (*med fråga e.d.*) attack **-ande**
a4 smoking *etc.*; ~ *varm mat* piping hot food;
i ~ fart at a tearing pace
rykt *s3* (*av häst*) dressing; grooming; *språkets
~ och ans* the cultivation and improvement of
the language **rykta** dress; groom, curry
rykt|as *opers. dep, det* ~ *att* it is rumoured
(there is a rumour) that **-bar** *a1* famous, renowned; *neds.* notorious; ~ *person* (*äv.*) celebrity **-barhet** fame, renown; *neds.* notoriety;
pers. celebrity
ryktborste grooming-brush
rykte *s6* **1** (*kringlöpande nyhet*) rumour; report; (*hörsägen*) hearsay; (*skvaller*) gossip; *det
går ett ~ att* there is a rumour that; *lösa* ~*n*
vague rumours **2** (*ryktbarhet*) fame, renown;
(*allmänt omdöme om ngn*) reputation, name,
repute; *bättre än sitt* ~ better than a p.'s reputation; *upprätthålla sitt goda namn o.* ~ uphold
one's fair name and fame; *åtnjuta det bästa* ~
be in the highest repute; *ha dåligt* ~ [*om sig>*
have a bad reputation; *ha* ~ *om sig att vara* be
reputed to be, have the reputation of being
ryktes|flora crop of rumours **-smidare** scan-
dalmonger **-spridare** spreader of rumours
-spridning spreading of rumours **-vis** (*som ett
rykte*) by [way of] rumour; (*genom hörsägen*)
by hearsay
ryl *s2, bot.* wintergreen, shinleaf
rymd *s3* **1** (*volym*) volume, capacity **2** (*världs-*)
space; *bildl.* region, sphere; *tomma* ~*en* va-
cancy, vacuity; *yttre* ~*en* outer space; *tavlan
har* ~ the picture gives a feeling of space **-bio-
logi** astrobiology, exobiology **-dräkt** spacesuit
-farare spaceman (*fem.* spacewoman), astro-
naut **-farkost** spacecraft **-flygning** space flight
-forskare space scientist **-forskning** space research **-färd** space trip (flight) **-färja** space
shuttle **-geometri** stereometry; solid geom-
etry **-kapsel** space capsule **-medicin** space
medicine **-mått** cubic measure **-promenad**
spacewalk **-raket** space rocket **-skepp** space-

R

ship **-sond** space probe **-station** space station (platform) **-teknik** space technique (technology) **-åldern** the Space Age
rymlig *al* (*stor*) spacious, roomy; (*som rymmer mycket*) capacious; ~*t samvete* accommodating conscience
rymling fugitive, runaway; *mil.* deserter
rymma *v2* **1** (*innehålla*) contain, hold; (*ha plats för*) take, have room for, accommodate **2** (*fly*) run away; (*om fånge*) escape; (*om kvinna:* ~ *från hemmet*) elope; ~ *fältet* quit the field
rymmar|e *se rymling;* ~ *och fasttagare* (*lek*) cops and robbers **-färd, -stråt** *vara på* ~ be on the run
rymmas *v2, dep, det ryms mycket i den här lådan* this box holds a great deal; *det ryms mycket på en sida* there is room for a great deal on one page; *det ryms många i rummet* the room holds many people
rym|ning escape, flight; *mil.* desertion **-ningsförsök** attempted escape (*etc.*)
rynka I *s1* (*i huden*) wrinkle; (*på kläder*) crease, *sömn.* gather **II** *v1* **1** *sömn.* gather, fold, shirr; ~ *pannan* knit one's brows; ~ *ögonbrynen* frown; ~ *på näsan* wrinkle one's nose, *bildl.* turn up one's nose (*åt at*) **2** *rfl* wrinkle, get wrinkled; (*om tyg*) crumple, crease **rynkig** *al* wrinkled, furrowed **rynktråd** drawing thread
rys|a *v3, imperf. äv. rös* shiver, shake (*av köld* with cold); shudder (*av fasa* with terror); *det -er i mig när* I shudder when **-are** thriller
rysch *s7* r[o]uche, frill
rysk *al* Russian
rysk|a *s1* **1** (*språk*) Russian **2** (*kvinna*) Russian woman **-fientlig** anti-Russian **-språkig** *al* (*-talande*) Russian-speaking; (*på ryska*) in Russian **-svensk** Russo-Swedish **-vänlig** pro-Russian
ryslig [ˣry:s-] *al* terrible, dreadful; *vard.* awful **ryslighet** ~*er* horrors, (*begångna*) atrocities **rysligt** *adv* terribly *etc.*; *vard.* awfully (*snällt av dig* nice of you)
rysning [ˣry:s-] shiver; shudder
ryss *s2* Russian
ryssja [ryʃa] *s1* fyke (hoop) net
Ryssland [ˈryss-] *n* Russia
ryssläder Russia leather
ryta *röt rutit* roar (*åt at*); (*om pers. äv.*) shout, bawl (*åt at*) **rytande** *s6* roar[ing]
rytm *s3* rhythm **rytˈmik** *s3, ej pl* rhythmics (*pl, behandlas som sg*) **rytmisk** [ˈrytt-] *a5* rhythmic[al]
ryttar|e rider, horseman; (*i kortsystem*) tab, signal **-inna** horsewoman, woman rider **-staty** equestrian statue **-tävling** horse-riding competition
rytteri cavalry
ryttla hover
ryttmästare cavalry captain
RÅ [ärrå] *förk. för riksåklagare*
1 rå *s5, sjö.* yard
2 rå *s5, s4* (*gränslinje*) boundary, borderline
3 rå *s6, s5, myt.* sprite, fairy
4 rå *al* **1** (*okokt*) raw (*fisk* fish); fresh (*frukt* fruit) **2** (*obearbetad*) crude (*malm* ore); (*ogarvad*) raw **3** (*om klimat*) raw, damp and chilly **4** (*primitiv*) primitive; (*grov*) coarse; (*simpel*)

vulgar; (*ohövlig*) rude; (*brutal*) brutal; *den* ~*a styrkan* brute force; *en* ~ *sälle* a ruffian; *ett* ~*tt överfall* a brutal assault
5 rå *v4* (*jfr råda*) **1** (*orka*) manage, have the strength (power) to; (*vara starkare, längre*) be the stronger (taller); *jag* ~*r inte med det* I cannot manage it, it is too much for me; *människan spår, men Gud* ~*r* man proposes, God disposes; ~ *sig själv* be one's own master, have one's time to o.s. **2** (*med betonad partikel*) *jag* ~*r inte för att* it is not my fault that; *jag* ~*r inte för det* I cannot help it; *du* ~*r själv för att* it is your own fault that; ~ *med* manage [to carry (lift *etc.*)]; ~ *om* be the owner of, possess; ~ *på* be stronger than, get the better of, be able to beat
råbalans *hand.* proof sheet
råbandsknop reef (square, flat) knot
rå|barkad *a5, bildl.* coarse, rough-mannered **-biff** scraped raw beef
råbock roebuck
råd *s7, i bet. 2 o. 5 äv. r* **1** (*tillrådan*) advice; (*högtidligare*) counsel; *ett* [*gott*] ~ a piece of [good] advice, *AE. äv.* a pointer; ~ *och anvisningar för* hints and directions for; *be ngn om* [*ett*] ~ ask s.b. for advice; *bistå ngn med* ~ *o. dåd* give s.b. advice and assistance; *fråga ngn till* ~*s* ask a p.'s advice, consult s.b.; *få många goda* ~ receive a lot of good advice; *följa* (*lyda*) *ngns* ~ follow (take) a p.'s advice; *ge* ~ give advice, counsel; *ge goda* ~ give good advice; *den* ~ *lyder är vis* he who listens to counsel is wise **2** (*utväg*) means (*sg o. pl*), expedient, way; *finna på* ~ find a way out; *veta* ~ *för* know a remedy for; *det blir väl ngn* ~ s.b. is sure to turn up, we shall manage somehow; *det blir ingen annan* ~ *än att* there is no other alternative than to; *nu vet jag* [*mig*] *ingen levandes* ~ now I am at my wits end (completely at a loss) **3** (*församling*) council **4** (*person*) councillor **5** (*tillgång*) means (*sg o. pl*); *ha god* ~ *till ngt* have ample means for s.th., be able to afford s.th.; *jag har inte* ~ *att* (*till det*) I haven't got the money to (for it), I cannot afford to (it); *efter* ~ *och lägenhet* according to one's means
råd|a *v2* **1** (*ge råd*) advise, give advice, counsel; *om jag får* ~ *dig* if you take my advice; *jag skulle* ~ *dig att låta bli* I should advise you not to do it; *jag -er dig att inte* I warn you not to **2** ~ *bot för* (*på*) find a remedy (cure) for **3** (*härska*) rule; *om jag finge* ~ if I had my way; *han vill alltid* ~ he always wants to be master; ~ *över* have control of **4** (*förhärska*) prevail, be prevalent; be, reign; *tystnad -er överallt* (*äv.*) silence reigns everywhere; *det -er inget tvivel* there is no doubt; *det -er ett gott förhållande mellan dem* they are on good terms [with each other] **-ande** *a4* prevailing; current (*priser* prices); *under* ~ *förhållanden* in the circumstances, under present conditions
rådbråka 1 *hist.* break on the wheel **2** *bildl.* (*ett språk*) mangle, murder; *på* ~*d engelska* in broken English; ~ *franska* speak broken French; *känna sig alldeles* ~*d* be aching in every joint, be stiff all over
råd|fråga consult; seek advice from; ~ *advokat*

take counsel's opinion **-frågning** [-:å-] consultation; inquiry **-givande** advisory, consulting, consultative **-givare** adviser; *jur.* counsel; (*dipl. e.d.*) counsellor **-givning** [-ji:-] guidance, counselling (*AE.* counseling); advisory service **-givningsbyrå** advisory bureau, information office **-göra** ~ *med* confer with; ~ *med ngn om ngt* (*äv.*) discuss s.th. with s.b. **-hus** town (*AE.* city) hall **-husrätt** municipal court; (*i Storbritannien*) magistrates' court; (*för svårare brottmål*) central criminal court; *jfr tingsrätt*

rådig *a1* (*fyndig*) resourceful; resolute (*handling* act) **-het** resourcefulness; resolution, presence of mind

rådjur roe [deer]

rådjurs|blick *bildl.* fawnlike glance **-sadel** saddle of venison **-stek** [joint of] venison

råd|lig [ˣrå:d-] *a1* (*klok*) wise; (*till-*) advisable; *inte* ~ (*äv.*) inadvisable **-lös** perplexed, at a loss; *bättre brödlös än* ~ better breadless than headless **-löshet** perplexity; irresolution **-man** [borough] magistrate, alderman; (*vid tingsrätt*) judge of a district court; (*vid länsrätt*) judge of a county administrative court **-pläga** deliberate (*om* about) **-plägning** [-ä:-] deliberation, conference **-rum** respite; (*betänketid*) time for reflection (consideration)

råds [-å:-] *se råd 1*

råds|församling council, board **-herre** councillor

råd|slag *se rådplägning;* *hålla* ~ *se -slå* **-slå** take counsel (*med varandra* together), consult (*med ngn* with s.b.) **-snar** resourceful

råds|republik Soviet republic **-sal** council hall

råd|sturätt *se rådhusrätt* **-vill** *a1* (*villrådig*) irresolute; (*-lös*) perplexed, at a loss **-villhet** irresolution; perplexity

råg *s2* rye

råg|a I *s1* (*se råge*); *till* ~ *på allt* to crown everything; *till* ~ *på eländet* to make matters worse II *v1* heap, pile (*faten* the dishes); (*fylla t. brädden*) fill up [to the brim]; *~d* full, brimful; *en ~d sked* a heaped spoonful; *nu är måttet ~t* this is the last straw

råg|ax ear of rye **-blond** light-blond **-bröd** rye bread

råge *s2* full (good) measure

rågas crude glass

råg|mjöl rye flour **-sikt** sifted rye flour

rågummi crude rubber **-sula** crepe-rubber sole

rågåker rye field

rågång boundary [line], (*i skog äv.*) boundary clearing; *bildl.* demarcation line

råhet rawness; *bildl.* coarseness; (*brutalitet*) brutality

1 råk *s2* (*is-*) crack, rift

2 råk *s7, s3, ej pl* (*fisk-*) guts (*pl*)

1 råka *s1, zool.* rook

2 råka *v1* **1** (*träffa rätt*) hit (*målet* the mark) **2** (*möta*) meet; encounter, come across (*äv.* ~ *på*) **3** (*händelsevis komma att*) happen (*göra* to do) **4** ~ *i bakhåll* fall into an ambush; ~ *i fara* get into danger, *bildl.* be endangered; ~ *i gräl* fall out, start quarreling; ~ *i händerna på* fall into the hands of; ~ *i olycka* come to grief; ~ *i raseri* fly into a rage; ~ *i slagsmål* come to

blows; ~ *på avvägar* go astray; ~ *ur gängorna* (*bildl.*) get out of gear, be upset **5** (*med betonad partikel*) ~ *fast* get caught; ~ *in i* get into, (*bli invecklad i*) be involved in; ~ *illa ut* get into trouble; ~ *på* come across; ~ *illa ut för* fall into the hands of (*en bedragare* an imposter), get caught in (*oväder* a storm), meet with (*en olycka* an accident)

råkall raw and chilly, bleak

råkas *dep* meet

rå|kopia proof **-kost** raw vegetables and fruit **-kostare** [-ås-] vegetarian **-kurr** *vard.* punch-up, brawl

råma moo; *bildl.* bellow

rå|material raw material **-mjölk** beestings (*pl*), *AE.* beastings (*pl*)

råmärke boundary mark; *~n* (*bildl.*) bounds, limits; *inom lagens ~n* within the pale of the law

1 rån *s7* (*bakverk*) wafer

2 rån *s7* (*brott*) robbery; (*överfall*) mugging

rån|a rob **-are** robber; mugger **-försök** attempted robbery **-kupp** [daring] robbery **-mord** murder with robbery **-mördare** person who has committed murder with robbery

rånock *sjö.* yardarm

rå|olja crude oil **-raka** *s1* potato pancake

råriggad *a5, sjö.* square-rigged

rå|ris brown rice **-riven** *a5* grated raw **-rörd** *a5* (*sylt*) preserved by combining with sugar **-saft** raw juice

rå|segel *sjö.* square sail **-seglare** *sjö.* square-rigger

rå|siden raw silk, shantung **-skala** peel raw; *~d potatis* potatoes peeled before boiling **-skinn** [-ʃ-] *s7, bildl.* tough, brute **-skälla** *vard.* rave gainst s.b., shout at s.b. **-socker** raw (unrefined) sugar **-sop** *s2, vard.* swipe; *ge ngn en* ~ swing out wildly at **-sprit** crude alcohol **-steka** (*grönsaker*) fry [without previously boiling]; *-stekt potatis* fried potatoes **-sten** raw limestone

rått|a *s1* rat; (*mus*) mouse (*pl* mice) **-bo** mouse (rat's) nest; *bildl.* rat-infested hovel **-fångare** rat-catcher **-fälla** mousetrap, rattrap **-gift** rat-poison **-hål** mouse (rat) hole **-jakt** *vara ute på* ~ (*om katt*) be out mouse-hunting **-lort** rat-dung **-svans** rat's tail; (*hårfläta*) pigtail **-unge** young rat (mouse) **-utrotningsmedel** rat exterminator **-äten** *a5* gnawed by rats (mice)

rå|vara raw material **-varukälla** raw-material source **-varuproduktion** primary production **-varutillgång** supply of raw materials

räck *s7, gymn.* [horizontal] bar

räck|a I *s1* row, line, range; (*serie*) series, succession II *v3* **1** (*över-*) hand, pass; ~ *ngn handen* give s.b. one's hand; ~ *en hjälpande hand* extend a helping hand; ~ *varandra handen* shake hands; *vill du* ~ *mig brödet?* would you pass me the bread, please? **2** (*nå*) reach; (*gå ända t.*) extend, stretch; (*fortgå*) last, go on (*i evighet* for ever); *jag -er honom till axeln* I reach (come up) to his shoulder; *kön -te ut på gatan* the queue stretched out to the street; *jag -er inte dit* it is beyond my reach; *dra så långt vägen -er* go to blazes **3** (*förslå*) be enough

R

(sufficient), suffice ; *oljan -er en vecka* there is enough oil for one week; *det -er inte långt* that won't go far; *det -er (äv.)* that will do **4** (*med betonad partikel*) ~ *till* be enough (sufficient), suffice; *få pengarna att ~ till (äv.)* make both ends meet; *tiden -er aldrig till för mig* I can never find enough time; *inte ~ till (äv.)* fall short; ~ *upp* put (stretch) up, (*nå upp*) reach up; ~ *upp handen* raise (put up) one's hand; ~ *ut handen* (*i trafiken*) make a hand signal; ~ *ut tungan* put out one's tongue (*åt at*)

räcke *s6* rail[ing], barrier; (*trapp-*) ba[n]nisters (*pl*)

räck|håll reach; *inom* (*utom*) ~ *för ngn* within (beyond) a p.'s reach **-vidd** *eg.* reach; (*skjutvapens e.d.*) range; *bildl. äv.* scope, extent

räd *s3* raid (*mot* on); (*bomb- äv.*) blitz

räd|as *-des -its, dep* fear, dread (*varken fan el. trollen* neither the devil nor his dam)

rädd *a1, n sg obest.* form undviks afraid (*för* of); (*skrämd*) frightened, scared, alarmed; (~ *av sig*) timid, timorous; (*bekymrad*) anxious (*för* about); *mycket* ~ very much afraid; *vara* ~ *för* be afraid (frightened) of, (*sitt liv e.d.*) be in fear of; *vara* ~ *om* be careful with, take care of; *var* ~ *om dig!* take care!

rädda save; (*befria ur fara*) rescue, deliver (*från att* from + ing-form; *ur* out of); *R~a barnens riksförbund* Swedish Save the Children Federation; *den stod inte att* ~ there was no saving (rescuing) it, it was beyond saving; ~ *ngt undan glömskan* rescue s.th. from oblivion; ~ *undan ngt* save (salvage) s.th.; *~nde ängel* angel of mercy **räddare** rescuer, (*ur nöd*) deliverer

rädd|hågad *a5*, **-hågsen** *a5* fearful, timid, timorous

räddning rescue; (*ur trångmål*) deliverance; (*frälsning*) salvation; *fotb.* save

räddnings|ankare *bildl.* sheet anchor **-arbete** rescue work **-båt** lifeboat **-löst [-ö:-]** *adv, ~ förlorad* irretrievably lost **-kryssare** rescue cruiser **-manskap** rescue party **-planka** last resort **-stege** fire escape

rädisa [ˣrädd-, ˣrä:-] *s1* radish

rädsla [ˣrädd-, ˣrä:-] *s1* fear, dread (*för* of)

räffl|a I *s1* groove; (*ränna*) channel; (*i eldvapen*) rifle **II** *v1* groove, channel; (*eldvapen*) rifle; *~d kant* (*på mynt*) milled edge

räfsa I *s1* rake **II** *v1* rake

räfst *s3* inquisition; (*bestraffning*) chastisement; *hålla skarp ~ med* call rigorously to account; *hålla ~ och rättarting med* take severely to task, call to account

räjong [-'jåŋ] *s3* district, area; *bildl.* range, scope

räka *s1* shrimp; (*djuphavs-*) prawn

räkel *s2, lång* ~ lanky fellow

räkenskap *s3* account; *~er* accounts, books, records; *avfordra ngn ~ för* call s.b. to account for; *avlägga ~ för ngn* render (give) an account to s.b. of; *~ens dag* the day of reckoning; *avsluta* (*göra upp*) *~erna* close (settle) the accounts **räkenskapsår** financial year

räkfiske shrimp-fishing

räkna [ˣrä:k-] **1** (*hop-, upp-*) count; (*göra uträkningar*) do sums (arithmetic); (*be-*) cal-

culate, reckon; *lära sig läsa, skriva och* ~ learn reading, writing and arithmetic; ~ *till tio* count up to ten; ~ *ett tal* do a sum; ~ *i huvudet* do mental arithmetic; ~ *med bråk* do fractions; ~ *fel* miscalculate, *bildl.* be mistaken; *det ~s inte* that doesn't count; *hans dagar är ~de* his days are numbered; ~ *tvätt* count the laundry; *högt* (*lågt*) *~t* at a high (low) estimate, at the most (least); *i pengar ~t* in terms of money; *i procent ~t* on a percentage basis; *förändring i procent ~t* percentage change; *noga ~t* to be exact; ~ *med* count (reckon) [up]on, (*ta med i beräkningen*) reckon with, allow for; ~ *på ngn* count (rely) on s.b. **2** (*hänföra t.*) count (*till* among); (*anse*) regard, consider, look upon; ~ *det som en ära att* count (consider) it an honour to; ~ *ngn ngt till godo* (*last*) put s.th. down to a p.'s credit (discredit) **3** (*uppgå till*) number; *hären ~de 30 000 man* the army numbered 30,000 men **4** (*med betonad partikel*) ~ *av* deduct, subtract; ~ *efter* count over; ~ *efter vad det blir* see what it makes; ~ *ihop* add (sum) up; ~ *ned* (*ange återstående tid*) count down; ~ *upp* (*pengar*) count out, (*nämna i ordning*) enumerate; ~ *ut* (*ett tal*) work out, (*fundera ut*) think (figure) out

räknare calculator

räkne|bok arithmetic book **-exempel** arithmetic example, sum [to be worked out] **-fel** mistake in calculation, arithmetical error **-färdighet** numeracy **-konst** *~en* arithmetic **-maskin** calculating machine, calculator **-operation** calculating operation **-ord** numeral **-sticka** slide rule **-sätt** method of calculation; *de fyra ~en* the four rules of arithmetic **-tal** sum **-verk** counter, counting mechanism

räkning [ˣrä:k-] **1** (*hop-*) counting; (*ut-*) calculation; (*upp-*) enumeration; (*skolämne*) arithmetic; *duktig i* ~ good at figures (arithmetic); *hålla* ~ *på* keep count of; *tappa ~en* lose count (*på* of); *gå ner för* ~ (*boxn.*) take the count **2** (*konto*) account (*hos* with); (*nota*) bill, *AE.* check; (*faktura*) invoice; ~ *på* bill (invoice) for; *kvitterad* ~ receipted invoice (bill); *löpande* ~ current account; *specificerad* ~ itemized account; *för ngns* ~ on a p.'s account (behalf); *köp i fast* ~ outright purchase; *köpa i fast* ~ buy firm (outright); *skriva ut en* ~ make out a bill (invoice); *sätt upp det på min ~!* put it down to my account!; *ta på* ~ take on account (credit) **3** *göra upp ~en utan värden* reckon without one's host; *göra upp ~en med livet* settle one's account with life; *hålla ngn* ~ *för ngt* put s.th. down to a p.'s credit; *ta med i* (*lämna ur*) *~en* take into (leave out of) account; *ett streck i ~en för* a disappointment to; *det får stå för din* ~ that is your responsibility; *vara ur ~en* be out of the running

räksallad shrimp sallad

räl *s3* rail

räls *s2, s3* rail **-buss** railcar **-skarv** rail joint **-spik** rail (dog) spike

rämna I *s1* (*spricka*) fissure, crevice; (*i tyg*) rent, slit; (*i moln*) break, rent **II** *v1* crack; (*om tyg*) rend, tear

ränk|er *pl* intrigues, machinations, plots; *smida*

~ intrigue, plot **-lysten** intriguing, scheming **-smidare** intriguer, plotter, schemer

1 ränna *s1 (fåra)* groove, furrow; *(segel-, is-)* channel; *(flottnings-)* flume; *(transport-)* chute

2 ränna *v2* **1** *(springa)* run; ~ *i väg* run away, dash off; ~ *med skvaller* run about gossiping; ~ *i höjden* shoot up fast **2** *(stöta)* run, thrust *(kniven i ngn* one's knife into); ~ *huvudet i väggen (bildl.)* run one's head against the wall

rännande *s6* running; *det har varit ett förfärligt* ~ *här idag* people have been running in and out all day

rännil rill, rivulet

ränn|ing warp **-snara** running noose

ränn|sten gutter, gully **-stensunge** guttersnipe

ränsel *s2* knapsack, kitbag

1 ränta *s1 (inälvor)* offal

2 ränt|a I *s1* interest; *(räntesats)* rate [of interest]; ~ *på* ~ compound interest; *bunden (fast, rörlig)* ~ restricted (fixed, flexible) rate of interest; *upplupen* ~ accrued interest; *hög (låg)* ~ high (low) interest (rate); *årlig* ~ annual interest; *ge 4 %* ~ give (yield) 4 %; *löpa med 4 %* ~ carry 4 % interest; *räkna ut ~n* compute the interest; *leva på -or* live on the interest on one's capital; *låna (låna ut) mot* ~ borrow on (lend at) interest; *ge betalt för ngt med* ~ *(bildl.)* pay back s.th. with interest **II** *v1, rfl, se förränta sig*

räntabel *a2* profitable; remunerative, lucrative

räntabilitet earning power (capacity); remunerativeness

ränte|avdrag tax relief on the interest on a loan **-avkastning** [interest] yield **-belopp** amount of interest **-beräkning** calculation (computation) of interest **-betalning** payment of interest **-bärande** interest-bearing, interest-carrying **-eftergift** interest remission **-fot** rate of interest, interest rate **-fri** free of interest **-frihet** exemption from interest **-förlust** loss of interest **-garanti** fixed interest rate **-höjning** increase in interest rate **-inkomst** income from interest **-kostnader** *pl* interest costs (charges) **-räkning** *se -beräkning* **-sats** *se -fot* **-sänkning** lowering (reduction) of interest rates **-termin** date of payment of interest

rät *a1* straight *(linje* line); right *(vinkel* angle); *bilda* ~ *vinkel med* form a right angle with, be at right angles to; ~ *maska* knit [stitch] **räta I** *s1* right side, face **II** *v1* straighten *(äv.* ~ *på)*; ~ *på ryggen* straighten one's back

rätisk *a5* Rhaetian

rätlinjig *a1* rectilinear, straight-lined; *bildl.* straightforward

räto|ro'man *s3* Rhaeto-Roman **-ro'mansk** [-a:-] *a5* Rhaetian, Rhaeto-Romanic **-romanska** [-'ma:n-] *s9 (språk)* Rhaetian, Rhaeto-Romanic

rätsida right side, face; *(på mynt o.d.)* obverse; *inte få ngn* ~ *på ngt* not be able to get a proper hold (make head or tail) of s.th.

1 rätt *s3 (mat-)* dish; *(del av måltid)* course; *en middag med tre ~er* a three-course dinner; *dagens* ~ today's special

2 rätt I *s3* **1** *(-ighet)* right *(till* to, of); *(-visa)* justice; ~ *till ersättning* right to compensation; ~ *till fiske* right to fish; *lag och* ~ law and justice; *få* ~ prove (be) right, *(inför domstol)* win the case; *ge ngn* ~ admit that s.b. is right; *ge ngn* ~ *till* entitle (authorize) s.b. to; *du ger mig nog* ~ *i att* I think that you will agree that; *göra* ~ *för sig* do one's full share, *(ekonomiskt)* pay one's way; *du gör* ~ *i att* you are right in (+ *ing-form*); *ha* ~ be right, *(ha ~en på sin sida)* be in the right; *det har du* ~ *i* you are right there; *ha* ~ *till att* have a (the) right to, be entitled to; *komma till sin* ~ *(bildl.)* do o.s. justice, show to advantage; *med* ~ *eller orätt* rightly or wrongly; *med full* ~ with perfect justice (good reason); *ta ut sin* ~ claim one's due; *vara i sin fulla* ~ be quite within one's rights **2** *få* ~ *på* find **3** *(rättsvetenskap)* law; *romersk* ~ Roman law **4** *(domstol)* court [of justice]; *inför högre* ~ before a superior court; *inställa sig inför ~en* appear before the court; *sittande* ~ court [in session]; *inför sittande* ~ in open court **II** *a1* **1** *(riktig)* right; *(korrekt äv.)* correct; *(vederbörlig)* proper; *(sann)* true; *det ~a* what is right, *(vid visst tillfälle)* the right thing; *det enda ~a* the only right thing; *~a ordet* the right (appropriate) word; *~e ägaren* the rightful owner; *den ~e (i fråga om kärlek)* Mr. Right; *du är just den ~e att (iron.)* you are just the right one (person) to; *det var ~!* that's right!; *det är ~ åt dig!* it serves you right!; *det är inte mer än* ~ *och billigt* it is only fair; *komma på* ~ *bog (bildl.)* get on the right tack; *i ordets ~a bemärkelse* in the proper sense of the word; *i ~an tid* at the right moment; *ett ord i ~an tid* a word in season **2** *sticka avigt och* ~ knit purl and plain **III** *adv* **1** *(riktigt) a) (före verbet)* rightly, *b) (efter verbet vanl.)* right; ~ *gissat* rightly guessed; *gissa* ~ guess right; *om jag minns* ~ if I remember right[ly]; *går klockan* ~? is the clock right?; *förstå mig* ~! don't misunderstand me!; *när man tänker* ~ *på* saken when you come to think of it; *eller ~are sagt* or rather **2** ~ *och slätt förneka* simply deny; ~ *och slätt en bedragare* a swindler pure and simple **3** *(ganska)* pretty; quite, rather; *vard.* jolly; *jag tycker* ~ *bra om (äv.)* I quite like; ~ *många* a good number of, quite a lot; ~ *så ofta* ever so often **4** ~ *som det var* all at once (of a sudden) **IV** *adv (t. rät)* straight; right; ~ *fram* straight on (ahead); ~ *upp i ansiktet* straight to one's face; ~ *upp och ner* straight up and down

rätt|a I *oböjl. s, i vissa uttr.* **1** *dra ngn inför* ~ bring s.b. before the court; *ställa (stämma) ngn inför* ~ bring s.b. to trail, arraign s.b.; *stå inför* ~ be brought before the court; *gå till* ~ *med ngn för ngt* rebuke s.b. for s.th. **2** *finna sig till* ~ accommodate (adapt) o.s. *(med* to), *(trivas)* feel at home; *hjälpa ngn till* ~ set (put) s.b. right, lend s.b. a hand; *komma till* ~ be found, turn up; *komma till* ~ *med* manage, handle, *(pers. äv.)* bring round; *tala ngn till* ~ talk s.b. into being sensible, get s.b. to see reason **3** *med* ~ rightly, justly; *det som med* ~ *tillkommer mig* what right[ful]ly accrues to me; *och det med* ~ and right[ful]ly so **II** *v1* **1** *(räta upp)* straighten *(på ryggen* one's back); *(ordna till)* adjust, put straight **2** *(korrigera)* correct *(fel*

R

mistakes); ~ *till* (*äv.*) set right; ~ *en skrivning* mark a paper **3** (*avpassa*) adjust, accommodate (*efter* to); ~ *sig efter a*) (*om pers.*) obey (*befallningar* orders), comply with, follow (*ngns önskningar* a p.'s wishes), accommodate (adapt) o.s. to (*omständigheterna* circumstances), conform to, observe (*reglerna* the rules), *b*) (*om sak*) agree with, follow; *det är ingenting att ~ sig efter* it is nothing to go by; *veta vad man har att ~ sig efter* know what one has to go by; *det -er och packer eder efter!* those are the orders you have to obey

rättare *jordbr.* [farm] foreman

rättegång *s2* action; legal proceedings (*pl*); [law]suit; (*rannsakning*) trial; (*rättsfall*) case; *anställa ~ mot* take legal proceedings (bring an action) against; *förlora en ~* fail in a suit, lose a case; *ha fri ~* be entitled to the services of a solicitor and a counsel free of charge

rättegångs|balk code of procedure, rules of court **-biträde** counsel **-fullmakt** power of attorney **-förfarande** course of law **-förhandlingar** *pl* court proceedings **-handlingar** *pl* documents of a case; court records **-kostnader** *pl* court (legal) costs, legal expenses **-protokoll** minutes (*pl*) of [court] proceedings **-sak** legal matter **-sal** courtroom

rätteligen by rights, rightly **rättelse** correction, amendment, adjustment; *~r* (*som rubrik*) errata, corrigenda **rättesnöre** *bildl.* guiding principle, guide; *ta ngt till ~* take s.th. as a guide **rättfram** *a1* straightforward; (*ärlig*) upright; (*frispråkig*) outspoken

rätt|färdig *a1* righteous, just; *sova den ~es sömn* sleep the sleep of the just **-färdiga** (*urskulda*) excuse (*ngns handlingssätt* a p.'s conduct); (*fritaga*) exculpate, vindicate (*ngn från* s.b. from); (*berättiga*) justify; ~ *sig* justify (vindicate) o.s. (*inför* to) **-färdiggöra** justify, vindicate **-färdiggörelse** justification (*genom tron* by faith) **-färdighet** righteousness; justness, justice; *uppfylla all[an]* ~ fulfil all righteousness

rätthaveri *se* rättshaveri

rättighet right; privilege; *ha ~ till* have a (the) right to, be entitled to; *beröva ngn medborgerliga ~er* deprive s.b. of civil rights; *ha fullständiga ~er* (*om restaurang*) be fully licensed

rättika *s1* black (turnip) radish

rättmätig *a1* (*laglig*) rightful, lawful; (*befogad*) legitimate (*harm* indignation); *det ~a i* the legitimacy of; ~ *ägare* rightful (lawful) owner

rättning *mil.* alignment, dressing; ~ *höger!* right dress!

rättrogen (*särskr. rätt-trogen*) faithful; (*renlärig*) orthodox; *en ~ kristen* a true believer **-het** faithfulness; orthodoxy

rättrådig honest, upright; (*rättvis*) just **-het** honesty, uprightness; justice

rätts|anspråk legal (lawful) claim; *göra sina ~ gällande* assert one's legal claims **-begrepp** concept (idea) of justice; *stridande mot alla ~* contrary to all ideas of right and justice **-fall** legal case **-filosofi** legal philosophy **-fråga** legal question **-förhållande** legal relations (*pl*) (*mellan* between); (*i stat*) judicial system (*sg*) **-handling** legal act (transaction) **-haveri** dog-

matism **-haverist** litigious, dogmatic person **-historia** history of law, legal history **-hjälp** legal aid

rätt|sinnad *a5, se* rättrådig

rättsinnehavare assignee, assign

rätt|sinnig *a1* honest, upright **-skaffenhet** honesty, uprightness **-skaffens** *oböjligt a, se -sinnig*

rätts|kapabel legally competent **-kapacitet** legal capacity (competence) **-kemi** forensic chemistry **-kemisk** of forensic chemistry; *~t laboratorium* forensic laboratory

rättskipning [-ʃi:-] administration of justice

rättskriv|ning orthography; (*skolämne*) spelling; *ha ~* do dictation **-ningsregler** *pl* rules for spelling

rätts|kränkning (*civilrätt*) tort, violation of a p.'s rights; (*straffrätt*) criminal offence **-känsla** sense of justice **-lig** *a1* (*laglig*) legal; (*domstols-*) judicial; (*juridisk*) juridical; *på ~ väg* by legal means; *medföra ~ påföljd* involve legal consequences; *vidtaga ~a åtgärder* institute judicial proceedings **-läkare** medicolegal practitioner **-lärd** jurisprudent **-lös** without legal rights (protection) **-medicin** forensic medicine, medical jurisprudence **-medicinsk** medicolegal **-medvetande** legal conscience, sense of justice **-ordning** legal system **-praxis** case law, legal usage **-psykiater** forensic psychiatrist **-röta** *ung.* corrupt legal practice **-sak** case, lawsuit **-sal** courtroom **-samhälle** law-governed society **-skipning** *se rättskipning* **-stat** constitutional state **-stridig** unlawful, illegal, contrary to law **-säkerhet** legal security; law and order

rättstavning [correct] spelling; orthography

rätts|tjänare court usher **-tvist** legal dispute, litigation **-uppfattning** conception of justice **-vetenskap** jurisprudence, legal science **-vetenskaplig** jurisprudential, forensic **-väsen** judicial system, judiciary

rättvis *a1* just (*dom* sentence; *sak* cause; *mot* to[wards]); (*opartisk*) impartial (*domare* judge; (*skälig*) fair; *det är inte mer än ~t* it is only fair; *hur mycket är en ~ klocka?* what is the right time?

rättvisa *s1* justice; (*opartiskhet*) impartiality; (*skälighet*) fairness; (*lag*) law; *för ~ns skull* for the sake of justice; *i ~ns namn* (*bildl.*) in all fairness; *låta ~n ha sin gång* let justice take its course; *skipa ~* do justice; *göra [full] ~ åt* do ... [full] justice to; *för [full] justice to; *överlämna i ~ns händer* deliver into the hands of the law

rättvisande *a4* (*om klocka o.d.*) correct; *sjö.* true (*bäring* bearing) **rättvisekrav** demand for justice **rättvisligen** justly, in justice (fairness)

rättvänd *a5* turned right way round (side up) **rättänkande** (*särskr. rätt-tänkande*) right-minded, fair-minded

rät|vinge *zool.* orthopteron (*pl äv.* orthoptera), orthopteran **-vinklig** *a1* right-angled

räv *s2* fox; *ha en ~ bakom örat* always have some trick up one's sleeve; *han är en riktig ~* he is a sly customer; *surt, sa ~en om rönnbären* sour grapes, said the fox; *svälta ~* (*kortsp.*)

beggar-my-neighbour **-aktig** *al* foxy, foxlike; *bildl.* cunning, sly, wily **-farm** fox farm **-gryt** fox earth (den) **-hanne** dog fox, he-fox **-hona** she-fox, vixen **-jakt** fox-hunting; *(en ~)* fox hunt **-lya** *se -gryt* **-rumpa** *bot.* common horsetail **-sax** fox trap **-skinn** fox skin **-spel** *eg.* fox-and-geese; *bildl.* jobbery, deep game; *politiskt ~ (äv.)* political intrigue **-svans** foxtail, foxbrush **-unge** fox cub

rö *s6, s7* reed

röd *al* red; *(hög-)* scarlet, crimson; *~a hanen* the fire fiend; *~a hund (sjukdom)* German measles, rubella; *den ~a tråden* the main thread, theme; *bli ~ i ansiktet* go red in the face; *det var som ett rött skynke* it was like a red rag to a bull; *i dag ~ i morgon död* here today, gone tomorrow; *inte ett rött öre* not a bean (brass farthing); *köra mot rött ljus* jump the lights; *se rött* see red; *R~a halvmånen* the Red Crescent; *R~a havet* the Red Sea; *R~a korset* the Red Cross

röd|akorssyster [-ˣkårs-] Red Cross nurse **-aktig** *al* reddish **-alg** red alga **-bena** *sl, zool.* redshank **-beta** beetroot; *AE.* red beet **-blindhet** red-blindness **-blommig** *bildl.* rosy *(kind cheek)* **-blå** reddish blue, purple **-bok** *bot.* beech **-brokig** *~ svensk boskap* Swedish red--and-white cattle **-brun** reddish brown **-brusig** *al* red-faced **-flammig** *~ hy* blotchy complexion **-fläckig** red-spotted **-fnasig** *al, ung.* red and chapped **-färg** red paint; red ochre **-förskjutning** red shift **-gardist** red guard **-glödga** make red-hot **-gråten** *a5 (om pers)* red-eyed; *-gråtna ögon* eyes red with weeping **-gul** orange[-coloured] **-hake** robin [redbreast] **-hårig** redhaired; *(om pers.)* red-headed

röding char

röd|kantad *a5* red-bordered *~e ögon* red--rimmed eyes **-kindad** *a5* red-cheeked, rosy--cheeked **-klöver** red clover **-krita** red chalk (crayon) **-kål** red cabbage **-luva** *R~n* Little Red Riding Hood **-lätt** ruddy **-lök** red onion **-mosig** red bloated **-näst** [-ä:-] *al* red-nosed -- **och vitrandig** with red-and-white stripes **-ockra** red ochre **-penna** red pencil **-prickig** dotted red **-randig** striped red, red-striped **-rutig** red-chequered, red-check **-räv** red fox **-skinn** redskin; American (Red) Indian **-skäggig** red-bearded **-sot** dysentery **-spotta** *sl* plaice **-sprit** methylated spirit **-sprängd** *al* bloodshot *(ögon* eyes) **-spätta** *sl, se -spotta* **-stjärt** redstart **-vin** red wine; *(Bordeaux)* claret; *(Bourgogne)* burgundy **-vinge[trast]** redwing **-vinstoddy** mulled claret **-ögd** *al* red-eyed

1 röja [ˣröjja] *v2* **1** *(förråda)* betray; *(yppa)* reveal, disclose; *~ sig* betray o.s., give o.s. away **2** *(ådagalägga)* display, show

2 röj|a [ˣröjja] *v2 (bryta, odla upp)* clear *(mark* land); *(gallra)* thin; *~ väg för* clear a path for, *bildl. äv.* pave the way for; *~ undan* clear away, remove; *~ upp* tidy up; *~ ngn ur vägen* make away with s.b.

röjdykare frogman

röjning clearance; *konkr.* clearing **röjningsarbete** clearance work **röjningsmanskap** clearance squad

1 rök *imperf. av ryka*

2 rök *s2* smoke; *(ånga)* steam; *(i sht illaluktande)* fume[s *pl*]; *gå upp i ~* go up *(bildl. äv.* end) in smoke; *ingen ~ utan eld* no smoke without fire; *vi har inte sett ~en av honom* we have not seen a trace of him

rök|a *v3* **1** *(om tobak)* smoke; *generar det dig om jag -er?* do you mind my smoking?; *~ cigaretter* smoke cigarettes; *~ in en pipa* break in a pipe **2** *(om matvaror)* smoke[-cure]; *(sill äv.)* bloat **3** *(mot ohyra, smitta)* fumigate; *~ ut* smoke out

rök|are smoker; *icke ~ (ej -kupé)* nonsmoker **-avvänjning** antidotal treatment for smokers **-bildning** smoke generation (production) **-bomb** smoke bomb **-bord** smoker's table **-dykare** smoke-helmeted fireman

rökelse incense **-kar** censer, thurible

rök|eri smokehouse, curing house **-fri** free from smoke; smokeless *(bränsle* fuel) **-fylld** smoke-filled **-fång** [fume] hood, smoke bonnet **-förbud** ban on smoking **-förgiftad** *a5* poisoned by smoke, asphyxiated **-gas** flue gas; fumes *(pl)* **-gång** *s2* [smoke] flue **-hosta** smoker's cough (hack) **-huv** chimney cowl; smoke hood

rök|ig *al* smoky **-kupé** smoking compartment, smoker; *(anslag)* for smokers **-lukt** smell of smoke **-moln** cloud of smoke

rök|ning [-ö:-] smoking; *(desinfektion)* fumigation; *~ förbjuden* no smoking; *~ tillåten* smoking, for smokers **-paus** smoking break **-pelare** column of smoke **-ridå** smoke screen **-ring** smoke ring **-rock** smoking jacket **-rum** smoking (smoke) room **-smak** *få ~* get a smoky taste **-sugen** dying for a smoke **-svag** *(om krut)* smokeless **-svamp** puffball

rökt [-ö:-] *a4* smoked; *(om träslag)* fumed *(ek* oak); *~ sill (ung.)* bloater, kippered herring; *~ sidfläsk* bacon

rök|topas smoky topaz **-verk** *s7, ej pl* smokes *(pl)*; *har du ~?* have you anything to smoke?

rölleka *sl* yarrow, milfoil

rön *s7 (erfarenhet)* experience, *(pl äv.* findings); *(iakttagelse)* observation **röna** *v3* meet with *(förståelse* understanding); experience *(motgång* a setback); *~ livlig efterfrågan* be in great demand

rönn *s2* [European] mountain ash, rowan **-bär** rowanberry

röntga X-ray, take an X-ray

röntgen ['rönt-] *r* roentgen **-anläggning** X-ray equipment (unit) **-apparat** X-ray machine (apparatus) **-avdelning** X-ray (radiotherapy) department **-behandling** X-ray treatment, radiotherapy **-bestrålning** X-raying **-bild** X-ray picture, radiograph **-diagnostik** X-ray (radio) diagnostics *(pl, behandlas som sg)* **-fotografering** X-ray photography, radiography **-genomlysning** fluoroscopy, radioscopy **-läkare, -olog** radiologist, roentgenologist **-plåt** X-ray plate **-stråle** X-ray **-strålning** emission of X-rays, X-ray emission **-terapi** radiotherapy **-undersökning** X-ray (radiograph) examination

rör *s7* **1** *tekn.* tube; *koll.* tubing; *(lednings-)* pipe, *koll.* piping; *elektron.* valve; *AE.* tube **2**

R

bot. reed; (*bambu-, socker-*) cane; *spanskt* ~ Spanish reed **3** *se rörskridsko*

rör|a I *s1* mess; mishmash; (*virrvarr*) confusion, muddle; *en enda* ~ a fine (regular) mess **II** *v2* **1** (*sätta i -else, rubba*) move, stir (*i gröten* the porridge; *en lem* a limb); *inte* ~ *ett finger* not lift (stir) a finger; ~ *på sig* move, (*motionera*) get some exercise; *rör på benen!* hurry up!, get going! **2** (*be-*) touch; *se men inte ~!* look but don't touch [anything]!; *allt han rör vid tjänar han pengar på* he makes money out of everything he touches **3** (*framkalla -else hos*) move (*till tårar* to tears) **4** (*angå*) concern, affect; *den här saken rör dig inte* this is none of your business; *det rör mig inte i ryggen* it doesn't affect me (I don't care) in the least **5** (*med betonad partikel*) ~ *i* stir in, stir into; ~ *ihop* (*kokk. o.d.*) stir (mix) together; *han -de ihop alltsammans* (*bildl.*) he got it all muddled up; ~ *om i brasan* poke (rake, stir) up the fire; ~ *upp damm* raise (stir up) dust; ~ *upp himmel och jord* move heaven and earth; ~ *ut med vatten* thin down (dilute) with water **6** *rfl* move; stir; *inte* ~ *sig ur fläcken* not stir (budge) from the spot; ~ *sig med grace* carry o.s. gracefully; *inte en fläkt -de sig* not a breath of wind was stirring; *det -de sig om stora summor* it was a question of large sums, a lot of money was involved; *ha mycket pengar att* ~ *sig med* have a lot of money at one's disposal; *vad rör det sig om?* what is it all about? **rörande I** *a4* touching, moving, pathetic **II** *prep* concerning, regarding, as regards, as (in regard) to

rör|arbetare plumber **arbete** pipefitting

rörd [-ö:-] *a5* moved (*äv. bildl.*); *kokk.* stirred; (*be-, vid-*) touched; *rört smör* creamed butter; *djupt* ~ deeply moved (touched)

rördrom [-åmm] *s2* bittern

rörelse 1 (*ändring av läge el. ställning*) movement; (*åtbörd äv.*) gesture, motion (*med handen* of the hand); (*motion*) exercise; (*oro, liv*) commotion, bustle, agitation; (*gång*) motion; *mycket folk var i* ~ a lot of people were on the move (were about); *sätta en maskin i* ~ set a machine in motion (moving), start a machine; *sätta sig i* ~ begin to move; *sätta fantasin i* ~ stimulate (excite) the imagination; *starka krafter är i* ~ *för att* (*bildl.*) strong forces are at work to **2** (*affärs-*) business, firm; (*verksamhet*) activity **3** (*strömning, folk-*) movement **4** (*själs-*) emotion **-energi** motive (kinetic) energy **-frihet** freedom of movement, liberty of action **-förmåga** locomotive faculty; ability to move **-hindrad** disabled **-idkare** owner of a firm, businessman **-kapital** working capital **-riktning** direction of movement

rörformig [-å-] *a1* tubular

rörig *a1* muddled, confused

rörled|ning piping, conduit; (*större*) pipeline **-ningsentreprenör** plumbing contractor

rörlig [ˣrö:r-] *a1* **1** (*om sak*) movable; moving; (*lätt-*) mobile; *~a delar* movable (*i maskin:* moving) parts; *~a kostnader* variable costs; ~*t kapital* working capital **2** (*om pers.*) (*snabb*) agile, brisk; (*livlig*) alert; (*verksam*) active; ~*t intellekt* versatile intellect; *vara på* ~ *fot* be

moving about, be on the move; *föra ett* ~*t liv* lead an active life **-het 1** mobility; (*räntas e.d.*) flexibility; ~ *på arbetsmarknaden* mobility of labour **2** agility, briskness; alertness; activity

rörlägg|are pipe-layer **-eri** pipe-laying **-nings-arbete** pipefitting

rörmok|are plumber **-eri 1** (*-installation*) plumbing **2** *se rörledningsentreprenör*

rör|post pneumatic dispatch (tube system) **-skridsko** tubular skate **-socker** cane sugar **-sopp** [-å-] *s2* boletus **-tång** pipe wrench

1 rös *imperf. av rysa*

2 rös *s7, se röse*

rösa mark [with boundary-stones] **röse** *s6* cairn, mound of stones

röst *s3* **1** (*stämma*) voice; *ha* (*sakna*) ~ have a good (have no) voice; *med hög* (*låg*) ~ in a loud (low) voice; *känna igen ngn på* ~*en* recognize s.b. by his (*etc.*) voice; ~- *och talvård* voice and speech care **2** (*vid -ning*) vote; *avge sin* ~ cast one's vote (*för* for); *ge sin* ~ *åt* give one's vote to; *nedlägga sin* ~ abstain from voting

röst|a vote (*för, på* for); ~ *blankt* hand in a blank voting paper; ~ *ja* (*nej*) vote for (against); ~ *öppet* (*slutet*) vote by yes and no (by ballot); ~ *om ngt* put s.th. to the vote; ~ *på högern* vote Conservative

röst|ande *a4* voting; *de* ~ the voters **-berätti-gad** entitled to vote

röstetal number of votes; *vid lika* ~ if the votes are equal

röst|fiske *polit.* angling for votes **-kort** poll card **-läge** pitch [of the voice] **-längd** electoral register **-ning** voting, vote; (*sluten*) ballot[ing] **-omfång** voice range (compass) **-plikt** voting duties (*pl*) **-resurser** *pl* vocal powers **-räkning** counting of votes **-rätt** right to vote; franchise; suffrage; *allmän* (*kvinlig*) ~ universal (woman's, women's) suffrage; *fråntaga ngn* ~*en* disfranchise s.b, deprive s.b. of the right to vote

rösträtts|reform franchise reform **-ålder** voting age

röst|sedel ballot (voting) paper **-siffra** number of votes, poll **-skolning** voice training **-springa** *anat.* glottis **-styrka 1** strength (power) of the (one's) voice **2** *polit.* voting strength **-värvning** canvassing [for votes] **-övervikt** majority [of votes]

röt *imperf. av ryta*

röt|a I *s1* **1** rot, decay; putrefaction **2** *vard.* luck **II** *v1, v3* **1** (*skadas av* ~) rot **2** (*lin, hampa*) ret **-månad** ~*en* the dog days (*pl*) **-månads-historia** silly-season story **-ning** [-ö:-] rotting; retting **-skada** decay damage **-slam** sludge **-svamp** mould fungus

rött *s, best. form det röda* red; *se* ~ see red; *jfr röd*

rötägg *bildl.* bad egg, failure

röv *s2, vard.* arse, *AE.* ass

röva rob (*ngt från ngn* s.b. of s.th.); ~ *bort* abduct **rövarband** gang of robbers

rövar|e robber; *leva* ~ (*leva vilt*) lead a dissolute life, (*fara vilt fram*) play havoc, raise hell; *leva* ~ *med ngn* lead s.b. a dance **-historia**

cock-and-bull story **-händer** *pl, falla i* ~ be captured by bandits, *bildl.* fall among thieves **-hövding** robber chief **-näste** haunt of robbers, den of thieves **-pris** daylight robbery; *betala ett* ~ pay through the nose; *få ngt för* ~ get s.th. dirt cheap
röveri robbery, plundering

S

Saar [sa:r] *n* the Saar, Saarland **-området** the Saar territory
sabbat ['sabb-] *s3* Sabbath; *fira* ~ observe (keep) the Sabbath
sabbats|brott breach of the Sabbath **-dag** Sabbath [day] **-år** sabbatical [year]
sabel *s2* sabre **-balja** scabbard, sabre sheath **-fäktning** fencing with sabre **-fäste** sabre hilt **-hugg** sabre cut **-skrammel** clank of swords; *bildl.* sabre rattling
sa'bin *s3* Sabine **sabinsk** [-i:-] *a5* Sabine
sabla [ˣsa:-] **I** *v1,* ~ *ner* (*bildl.*) slash, tear to pieces **II** *oböjligt a* cursed, blasted
sabotage *s7* (*göra* commit) sabotage **sabotagegrupp** *mil.* sabotage unit **sabotera** sabotage **sabotör** saboteur
sachsare [ˣsaksare] Saxon **Sachsen** ['saksen] *n* Saxony **sachsisk** ['saksisk] *a5* Saxon
sacka ~ *efter* lag behind, straggle
sacka'rin *s4* saccharine
sadducé *s3* Sadducee
sade *vard. sa, imperf. av säga*
sadel ['sa:-] *s2* **1** saddle; *bli kastad ur* ~*n* be unseated; *sitta säkert i* ~*n* sit one's horse well, *bildl.* sit firmly in the saddle; *stiga i* ~*n* mount one's horse; *utan* ~ bareback **2** *slaktar. o. kokk.* saddle **3** (*på fiol*) nut **-bom** (*stomme*) saddletree; (*hög kant*) saddlebow **-brott** saddle-gall **-bruten** saddle-sore **-gjord** saddle-girth, bellyband **-knapp** pommel [of a saddle] **-makare** saddler, harness-maker **-makeri** saddlery **-plats** (*på kapplöpningsbana*) paddock **-täcke** saddle-blanket **-väska** saddlebag
sad|ism sadism **-ist** sadist **-istisk** *a5* sadistic
sadla [ˣsa:d-] saddle, put the saddle on; ~ *av* unsaddle; ~ *om* (*byta åsikt*) change one's opinion, (*byta yrke*) change one's profession
SAF [ˣessa:eff] *förk. för Svenska Arbetsgivareföreningen* the Swedish Employers' Confederation
safari [-'fa:-] *s3* safari
saffi'an *s3, s4* saffian; morocco
saffran *s3, s4* saffron **saffransgul** saffron [yellow]
sa'fir *s3* sapphire **-blå** sapphire [blue]
saft *s3,* juice; (*kokad med socker*) [fruit] syrup; (*växt-*) sap; (*kött-*) gravy; *bildl.* pith
saft|a make fruit syrup (*etc.*) out of; ~ *sig* make sap, run to juice **-flaska** bottle of juice (*etc.*) **-ig** *a1* juicy (*äv. bildl.*); (*om ört*) succulent; (*om kött*) juicy; *bildl.* highly flavoured, spicy; ~*a eder* juicy oaths **-lös** juiceless, dry **-ning** juice-making, syrup-making **-press** juice squeezer **-sås** *ung.* fruit sauce
sag|a *s1* fairy tale (story); (*nordisk*) saga; *berätta* -*or* tell fairy stories (*äv. bildl.*); *dess* ~ *är all* it is finished and done with, that's the end of it
sag|d *a5* said; *det är för mycket* -*t* that is saying

too much; *det är inte -t* it is not so certain; *bra -t!* well put!; *nog -t* suffice it to say, *-t och gjort* no sooner said than done; *som -t var as* I said [before]

sagen ['sa:-] *i uttr.: den bär syn för* ~ it tells its own tale, it speaks for itself **sagesman** informant, spokesman, authority

sago|berättare storyteller **-bok** storybook, fairy-tale book **-djur** fabulous animal **-figur** character (figure) from a fairy tale

sagogryn *koll.* pearl sago *(sg)*

sago|kung legendary king; *(i barnsaga)* fairy-tale king **-land** wonderland, fairyland **-lik** fabulous; *en* ~ *tur* [a] fantastic [piece of] luck **-prins** fairy[-tale] prince **-slott** fairy castle

sagt *sup. av säga*

Sahara ['sa:hara] *n* the Sahara

sak *s3* **1** *konkr.* thing; *(föremål äv.)* object, article; ~*er (tillhörigheter)* belongings; *en sällsynt* ~ *(äv.)* a curiosity **2** *abstr. o. bildl.* thing; *(angelägenhet)* matter, affair, subject; *(uppgift)* task; *(omständighet)* circumstance; *(rättegångs-)* cause *(äv. friare)*; ~*en i fråga* the matter in question; ~*en är den att* the fact is that; *det är en* ~ *för sig* that is another story (matter); *det är en annan* ~ that is quite a different matter; *det är hela* ~*en* there is nothing more to it, that's all there is to it; *det är min* ~ it is my business; *det är inte min* ~ *att* it is not for me to; *det är* ~ *samma* it makes no difference, it doesn't matter; *för den goda* ~*ens skull* for the good of the cause; *göra* ~ *av ngt (jur.)* take s.th. to court; *hålla sig till* ~*en* keep (stick) to the point; *som hör till* ~*en* pertinent; *som inte hör till* ~*en* irrelevant; *i* ~ essentially; *ha rätt i* ~ be right in the main; *kunna sin* ~ know one's job; *det är inte så farligt med den* ~*en* that is nothing to worry about, it is not so bad after all; *säker på sin* ~ sure of one's point; *söka* ~ *med ngn* try to pick a quarrel with s.b.; *till* ~*en!* to the point!; *han tog* ~*en kallt* he took it calmly, it left him cold

saka *kortsp.* discard, throw away

saker ['sa:-] *oböjligt a, jur.* guilty *(till of)* **-förklara** ~ *ngn* find s.b. guilty

sak|fel factual error **-fråga** point at issue **-förare** lawyer, solicitor, attorney, counsel **-förhållande** fact, state of affairs **-granska** check facts

sak|kunnig expert; competent; *en* ~ an expert (a specialist) *(på* in); *från* ~*t håll* in expert (authoritative) circles; *tillkalla* ~*a* call in experts **-kunnighet** *se* -*kunskap* **-kunnigutlåtande** expert opinion (report) **-kunskap** expert knowledge; ~*en (de -kunniga)* the experts, competent advisers *(pl)*

saklig [-a:-] *a1 (t. saken hörande)* to the point, pertinent; *(grundad på fakta)* founded on facts; *(objektiv)* objective, unbiased; *(nykter)* matter-of-fact **-het** pertinence; objectivity

saklöst [-ö:-] *(ostraffat)* with impunity; *(utan skada)* easily, safely

sakna [ˣsa:k-] **1** *(inte äga)* lack; *(vara utan)* be devoid of *(mänskliga känslor* human feelings); be without *(mat* food); ~ *humor* have no sense of humour; ~ *all grund* be totally groundless;

~ *ord* be at a loss for words; *det torde inte* ~ *intresse* it will not be without interest **2** *(märka frånvaron el. förlust av)* miss, not find, *(starkare)* feel the loss of; ~*r du ngt?* do you miss anything?, *(har du förlorat ngt?)* have you lost anything?

saknad [ˣsa:k-] **I** *a5* missed; *(borta)* missing **II** *s3* **1** *(brist)* lack, want *(på* of); *(frånvaro)* absence *(av* of); *i* ~ *av* in want of, lacking **2** *(sorg, längtan)* regret; *känna* ~ *efter* miss; ~*en efter henne är stor* her loss is deeply felt

sakna|s [ˣsa:k-] *dep (fattas)* be lacking; *(böra finnas)* be wanting; *(vara borta)* be missing; *tio personer -des* ten persons were missing (reported lost)

sakprosa ordinary prose

sa'kral *a1* sacred

sakrament *s7* sacrament **sakramen'tal** *a1* sacramental **sakramentskad** [-'ment-] *a5, vard.* damned, confounded

sakregister subject (analytical) index

sakristia *s1* sacristy, vestry **sakrosankt** [-'saŋkt] *a1* sacrosanct

sakskäl practical reason, positive argument

sakta I *adv (långsamt)* slowly; *(tyst)* low; *(dämpat)* softly, gently; ~ *men säkert* slow but sure; ~ *i backarna!* gently!, take it easy!, gently does it!; *klockan går för* ~ the clock is slow; ~*!* *(sjö.)* easy ahead! **II** *a1 (långsam)* slow; *(tyst, svag)* low *(mumlande* murmur), soft *(musik* music), gentle *(bris* breeze); *vid* ~ *eld* over a slow fire **III** *v1 (minska farten [hos])* slacken; *(dämpa)* muffle, hush; ~ *farten (äv.)* slow down; ~ *sig (minska)* decrease, abate; *klockan* ~*r sig* the clock is losing [time]

sakt|eligen *se sakta I* **-färdig** slow, tardy **-mod** meekness **-modig** meek; *saliga äro de* ~*a* blessed are the meek

sak|uppgift fact **-ägare** *jur. (målsägare)* plaintiff; *(part)* party to a case

sal *s2* hall; *(på sjukhus)* ward; *allmän* ~ public ward

sala *vard.* club together *(till* for)

salad'jär *s3* salad bowl

salamander [-'mann-] *s2* salamander

salami [-'la:-] *s3* salami

saldera strike a balance, balance [up]

saldo ['sall-] *s6* balance; *ingående (utgående)* ~ balance brought (carried) forward; ~ *mig till godo* balance in my favour **-besked** advice of the balance of an account, balance certificate

salicylsyra [-ˣsy:l-] salicylic acid

salig *a1* **1** *(frälst, säll)* blessed **2** *(om avliden)* late; ~ *kungen* the late [lamented] king; *i* ~ *åminnelse* of blessed memory; *var och en blir* ~ *på sin fason* everybody is happy in his own way **-en** ~ *avsomnad* dead and gone to glory **-förklara** beautify **-görande** [-j-] *a4* saving; *den allena* ~ *(vard.)* the one and only **-het** blessedness; *(stor lycka)* bliss, felicity

sa'lin *s3* saline; saltworks *(pl, behandlas som sg)*

sa'liv *s3* saliva **-avsöndring** salivary secretion **-sugare** salivary extractor

sallad [ˣsall-, 'sall-] *s3, bot.* lettuce; *(maträtt)* salad

sallads|bestick salad servers *(pl)* **-huvud**

lettuce **-skål** salad bowl
salmiak ['sall-] *s3* sal ammoniac
salmonella [-ˣnella] *s1* salmonella
salning [ˣsa:l-] *sjö.* crosstrees *(pl)*
Salomo Solomon; ~*s Höga Visa* the Song of Solomon **salomonisk** [-'mɔ:-] *a5* Solomonic, Solomonian
salong [-'låŋ] *s3* saloon; *(i hem)* drawing room, parlour; *(teater- etc.)* auditorium; ~*en (publiken)* the audience
salongs|berusad *a5* tipsy, merry **-fähig** *se -mässig* **-mässig -gevär** small-bore rifle **-kommunist** parlour communist **-lejon** society lion **-mässig** *a1* fit for the drawing room; *(om pers.)* polite; *inte* ~ *(om pers.)* not presentable **-uppassare** *sjö.* waiter **-vagn** saloon (*AE.* parlor) car
salpeter *s2* saltpetre; nitre; *(kali-)* potassium nitrate **-syra** nitric acid
salsmöbel dining-room furniture
salt I *s4* salt; *attiskt* ~ Attic salt (wit) **II** *a1* salt, salty; ~ *fläsk* salt[ed] pork
salt|a ~ *[på]* salt, sprinkle with salt; ~*d* salted, pickled; *en ~d räkning* a stiff bill; ~ *in* salt, brine **-gruva** salt mine **-gurka** pickled gherkin **-halt** salinity, salt content **-haltig** *a1* saline, briny **-kar** saltcellar **-korn** grain of salt **-kött** salt *(konserverat:* corned*)* beef **-lake** brine, pickle; *lägga i* ~ pickle **-lösning** saline solution **-ning** salting; pickling
saltomor'tal *s3* *(göra en* turn a*)* somersault
salt|sjö salt lake **-stod** pillar of salt **-ströare** salt shaker **-stänk** salt spray **-syra** hydrochloric acid **-vatten** salt water, brine **-vattensfisk** saltwater fish, sea fish
salu *s, endast i uttr.: till* ~ for (on) sale **-bjuda** offer for sale **-föra** *se -bjuda*; *(torgföra)* market, deal in **-hall** market hall **-stånd** booth, stand, stall
sa'lut *s3* salute **-era** salute
salu|torg market[place] **-värde** market value
1 salva *s1* *(gevärs- etc.)* volley; salvo
2 salva *s1* ointment, salve
salvburk ointment jar
salvelse unction, pathos **-full** unctuous; *vard.* soapy
salvia ['sall-] *s1, bot.* sage
sam [samm] *imperf. av simma*
sam|arbeta [ˣsamm-] collaborate; *(samverka)* cooperate **-arbete** collaboration; cooperation
samarbets|avtal [ˣsamm-] agreement for cooperation, collaboration agreement **-man** collaborator **-nämnd** cooperation council (committee, commission) **-vilja** cooperativeness; *visa* ~ show that one is willing to cooperate **-villig** cooperative
sama'rit *s3* Samaritan; *(sjukvådare)* first-aid man; *den barmhärtiga* ~*en* the good Samaritan **-kurs** first-aid course
samba *s1* samba; *dansa* ~ samba
sam|band [ˣsamm-] connection; *ställa (sätta) ngt i* ~ *med* connect (relate, associate) s.th. with **-bandsofficer** liaison officer **-beskattning** joint taxation (assessment)
sambo [ˣsamm-] *s5, vard.* *(som jämställs med make/maka)* common law husband (wife)
same ['sa:-] *s5* Lapp, Laplander **-slöjd** Lapp handicrafts
samexistens [ˣsamm-] coexistence
sam|fund [ˣsamm-] *s7* association; *(lärt)* [learned] society, academy; *(religiöst)* denomination, communion **-fälld** *a5* **1** *(gemensam)* joint, common; *(enhällig)* unanimous **2** *jur.* joint *(egendom* property*)* **-fällighet** *abstr.* relationship; *konkr.* association, society
samfärds|el *s9* communication[s *pl*], intercourse; *(trafik)* traffic **-led** route [of communication] **-medel** means of communication; *(transportmedel)* means of transport
sam|förstånd concert, concord; *(enighet)* unity; *(hemligt* secret*)* understanding; *(i brottslig bemärkelse)* collusion; *komma till [ett]* ~ come to an understanding **-förståndspolitik** policy of compromise
samgående fusion, cooperation
samhälle [ˣsamm-] *s6* **1** society; community; ~*t* society, the community **2** *(kommun, by, tätort)* municipality, village, urban district **3** *biol.* colony **-lig** *a1* social; *(medborgerlig)* civil, civic *(rättigheter* rights*)*
samhälls|anda public spirit **-arbete** community work **-bevarande** *a4* conservative **-debatt** public debate on problems of modern society **-ekonomi** national economy **-ekonomisk** economic **-fara** social danger, danger to society **-farlig** dangerous to society **-fientlig** antisocial **-form** social structure (system); *(statsform)* polity **-förhållanden** *pl* social conditions **-grupp** social group **-hygien** public and environmental health **-intresse** public interest **-klass** class [of society] **-kontrakt** social contract (compact) **-kunskap** civics *(pl, behandlas som sg)* **-lära** civics *(pl, behandlas som sg)*, sociology **-medicin** community and environmental health **-nytta** commonweal **-nyttig** of service to society; *ett* ~*t företag* a public utility undertaking **-omstörtande** subversive **-ordning** social order **-orienterande** ~ *ämnen (förk. SO-ämnen)* social subjects **-planering** national planning; planning of society **-problem** problems of society **-satir** social satire **-sektor** social sector **-skick** social order (conditions *pl*) **-skikt** *se -klass* **-struktur** social structure **-ställning** social position (status) **-tillvänd** socially aware **-vetare** sociologist, social scientist; student of sociology (social sciences) **-vetenskap** social science **-vård** social welfare
sam|hörande [ˣsamm-] *a4,* **-hörig** *a1* associated; *(inbördes förenade)* mutually connected, interlinked; *(om frågor o.d.)* pertinent, kindred **-hörighet** solidarity; *(frändskap)* affinity, kinship **-hörighetskänsla** feeling of affinity (kinship)
samisk ['sa:-] *a5* Lapp, Lappish **samiska** *s1* *(språk)* Lappish
sam|klang accord, harmony; *i* ~ *med* in harmony with **-kostnader** *pl* common costs **-kväm** *s7* social [gathering] **-könad** [-ç-] *a5* androgynous, hermaphrodite
samla 1 collect *(frimärken* stamps; *pengar* money); gather *(fakta* facts; *snäckor* seashells); *(så småningom)* amass *(en förmögenhet* a fortune); *(lagra)* store up; *(för-)* assemble, bring

together; ~ *på hög* accumulate, hoard up; ~ *på sig* accumulate (*arbete* work; *en massa skräp* a lot of rubbish); ~ *sina krafter* get up one's strength (*till* for); ~ *sina tankar* collect one's thoughts, *vard.* pull o.s. together **2** *rfl* collect (gather) [together]; gather (*kring* round); (*hopas*) accumulate; *bildl.* collect o.s., *vard.* pull o.s. together

samlad *a5* collected; *ge en* ~ *bild av* give a concise picture of; ~ *skoldag* integrated schoolday; *hålla tankarna ~e* keep one's thoughts composed; *i* ~ *trupp* in a body; *~e skrifter* complete works

samlag [*samm-] *s7* sexual intercourse; *med.* coitus, coition

samlar|e collector **-vurm** collecting mania **-värde** value to the collector

samlas *dep* **1** (*om pers.*) collect, gather, come together; (*skockas*) congregate **2** *allm.* gather [together]

sam|lastning [*samm-] groupage traffic; collective consignment **-levnad** *fredlig* ~ peaceful coexistens

samlevnads|problem *pl* problems in personal relations **-frågor** personal relationship matters **-undervisning** sex education, instruction in marital and personal relationships

samling 1 *abstr.* collection, gathering, meeting; *mil. äv.* rallying; *inre* ~ composure **2** *konkr.* collection; (*av pers.*) meeting, crowd

samlings|lins convex lens **-lokal** assembly (community) hall **-ministär** coalition ministry **-plats** meeting place **-pärm** file, binder **-regering** coalition government **-sal** *se -lokal* **-verk** compilation, collection [of articles]

samliv [*samm-] life together, cohabitation; *det äktenskapliga ~et* married life

samma [the] same (*som* as); (*liknande*) similar (*som* to); *på* ~ *gång* at the same time, (*samtidigt*) simultaneously; *på* ~ *sätt* (*äv.*) similarly; *redan* ~ *dag* that very day; *det är en och* ~ *sak* it comes to the same thing **-ledes** likewise, in the same manner (way)

sammalen [*samm-] *a5* (*om mjöl*) coarse

sammalunda *se sammaledes*

samman ['samm-, *i sms.* *samm-] together; *jfr ihop, tillsammans* **-binda** join, connect **-biten** *a5, se* ~ *ut* look resolute, have a dogged expression; ~ *beslutsamhet* dogged determination **-blanda** *se blanda* [*ihop*]; (*förväxla*) confuse **-blandning** *bildl.* confusion **-bo** cohabit, live together [as husband and wife] **-boende** *I a4* cohabiting **II** *s6, ung.* common law husband (wife) **-brott** collapse, breakdown **-drabbning** *mil.* encounter, engagement; *bildl.* conflict, clash **-drag** summary, condensation, synopsis, precis; *redogörelse i* ~ abridged (concise) report **-draga 1** (*samla*) assemble; *mil.* rally, concentrate **2** (*hopdraga*) contract; *fack.* constrict; *~nde medel* astringent **3** (*förkorta*) abridge **4** *rfl* contract; *som kan* ~ *sig* contractible **-dragning 1** concentration (*av trupper* of troops) **2** contraction (*av muskler* of muscles) **3** (*förkortning*) abridgement **-falla** (*vara samtidig*) coincide (*med* with); *~nde* coincident, congruent; *-fallna kinder* shrunken cheeks **-fatta** sum up, summarize **-fattning**

summary, summing up, recapitulation **-fattningsvis** to sum up **-flyta** flow together; (*om floder äv.*) meet; (*om färger*) run together **-fläta** interlace **-flöde** confluence, junktion **-foga** join [together]; *bildl.* unite, combine **-fogning** [-ω:-] **1** *konkr.* joint **2** *abstr.* joining [together] **-föra** bring together; (*förena*) combine, unite **-gadda** *rfl* conspire, plot (*mot* against)

samman|hang *s7* (*förbindelse*) connection, relation; (*följdriktighet*) coherence; (*i text*) context; *det har ett bra inre* ~ it is well integrated; *brist på* ~ incoherence; *fatta ~et* grasp the connection; *i ett* ~ without interruption; *ryckt ur ~et* detached from the context; *tala utan* ~ talk incoherently, ramble; *utan* ~ *med* independent of **-hållning** (*enighet*) unity, concord, harmony **-hänga** (*ha sambamd med*) be connected (united) (*med* with); *jfr hänga* [*ihop*] **-hängande** *a4* connected, coherent (*tal* speech); (*utan avbrott*) continuous **-jämka** *se jämka* [*ihop*] **-jämkning** *bildl.* conciliation, compromise (*av åsikter* of views) **-kalla** call together; summon, convene (*ett möte* a meeting); ~ *parlamentet* convoke Parliament **-kallande 1** *s6* calling together *etc.* **2** *s9* (*person*) convener, convenor **-komst** [-å-] *s3* gathering, meeting, conference; (*av två pers.*) interview **-koppla** *se koppla* [*ihop*] **-lagd** *a5* total; *våra ~a inkomster* our combined income[s]; *-lagt 50 pund* a total of 50 pounds, 50 pounds in all; *utgifterna uppgår -lagt till* the expenses total **-läggningsavhandling** doctoral thesis [consisting of previously published articles by candidate, with a summary] **-länka** chain together; *bildl.* link [together] **-packa, -pressa** compress **-räkna** add (sum) up **-räkning** addition, summing up; (*av röster*) count, counting

samman|satt *a4* compound (*ord* word); (*av olika delar, äv. tekn.*) composite (*tal* number); (*invecklad*) complicated (*natur* nature); ~ *av* composed (made up) of; *vara* ~ *av* (*äv.*) consist of **-slagning** [-a:g-] (*förening*) unification, union; (*fusion*) merger, amalgamation, fusion (*av bolag* of companies) **-sluta** *-slöt -slutit, rfl, bildl.* join (*i* in), unite **-slutning** [-u:-] (*förening*) association, alliance, union; (*koalition*) coalition **-slå** (*hopslå*) nail up (together); *bildl.* turn into one, unite **-smälta 1** (*hop-*) fuse, melt together; *bildl.* amalgamate, merge **2** (*förenas, förminskas*) melt down; *bildl. äv.* coalesce; (*om färger*) blend, run together **-smältning** fusion, melting (*etc.*); (*av färger*) blending; *bildl.* coalescence, amalgamation **-snöra** *mitt hjärta -snördes av ängslan* anxiety wrung my heart; ~ *sig* compress, (*om strupe*) be constricted **-stråla** converge; *vard.* meet **-ställa** put (place) together; make up (*en tablå* a schedule); compile (*en diktsamling* a collection of poems) **-ställning** placing together *etc.*; (*förteckning*) list, specification; (*uppställning*) statement **-stötning** [-ö:-] collision; (*konflikt*) conflict; *mil.* encounter **-svetsa** weld together **-svuren** *-svurne -svurna, mest i pl* conspirator, plotter **-svärja** *rfl* conspire (*mot against*) **-svärjning** conspiracy, plot **-sätta** (*hopsätta*) join, put together, compound; (*av* *flera delar*) compose (*en matsedel* a menu) **-sättning** putting together, joining, composition; (*blandning*) mixture; (*struktur*) structure; (*konstitution*) constitution; språkv. compound **-sättningsled** element

samman|träda meet, assemble **-träde** *s6* [committee] meeting, conference; (*session*) session; *han sitter i* ~ he is at a meeting (in conference); *extra* ~ [a] called session **-trädesrum** assembly (meeting, conference) room **-trädesteknik** technique of running a meeting; conference technique **-träffa** meet; (*om omständighet*) coincide, concur **-träffande** *s6* (*möte*) meeting; *bildl.* concurrence, *ett egendomligt* ~ a curious coincidence **-trängd** *a1* compressed; concentrated **-vuxen** grown together, consolidated; *bot.* accrete

samme *se* **samma**

sammelsurium [-'su:-] *s4* conglomeration, jumble, omnium-gatherum

sammet *s2* velvet

sammets|band velvet ribbon **-len** as soft as velvet, velvety

samnordisk [ˣsamm-] Nordic

samojed *s3* Samoyed **-isk** *a5* Samoyedic

samordn|a [ˣsamm] coordinate; ~*de satser* coordinate clauses **-ande** *a4* coordinating **-ing** coordination

samo'var *s3* samovar

samp|el ['sa:m-] *s7* sample **-ling** ['sa:m-] sampling

sam|realskola [ˣsamm-] *ung.* coeducational junior secondary school **-regent** co-regent **-råd** consultation, conference; *efter* ~ *med* having consulted; *i* ~ *med* in consultation with **-råda** consult, confer **-röre** *s6* collaboration

sams *oböjligt a, bli* ~ be reconciled, make it up; *bli* ~ *om ngt* agree upon s.th.; *vara* ~ be friends; *vara* ~ *med ngn* be on good terms with s.b. **samsas** *dep* agree (*med* with); get on well together; ~ *om utrymmet* share the space

sam|segling [ˣsamm-] joint (combined) service **-sikt** coarse meal **-skola** coeducational (*vard.* co-ed) school **-spel** teamwork, ensemble [playing]; *bildl.* interplay, combination (*av färger* of colours) **-spelt** [-e:-] *a1*, *vara* ~*a* play well together; *bildl.* be in accord **-språk** conversation, talk; (*förtroligt*) chat **-språka** converse, talk; *vard.* have a chat **-stämmig** *a1* in accord; unanimous **-stämmighet** accord, concordance; (*enighet*) unanimity **-sändning** radio. joint broadcast; simulcast

samt I *konj* and [also], [together] with **II** *adv*, ~ *och synnerligen* each and all, all and sundry; *jämnt och* ~ always, constantly, (*oupphörligt*) incessantly

samtal [ˣsamm-] conversation, talk; (*småprat*) chat; (*lärt*) discourse; (*överläggning*) conference; (*telefon-*) call; ~ *mellan fyra ögon* tête-a--tête, private interview; *bryta* ~*et* (*tel.*) interrupt the call; ~ *pågår* (*tel.*) call in progress **samtala** converse (*om* about), talk (*om* about, of); (*småprata*) chat; (*överlägga*) confer **samtals|avgift** *tel.* call charge **-form** *i* ~ in dialogue form **-rum** (*i kloster*) parlour; (*läkares*) consultation room **-räknare** [-ä:-] *tel.* telephone-call meter **-terapi** conversation

therapy **-ton** *i* ~ in conversational tone **-ämne** topic (subject) of conversation; *det allmänna* ~*et i staden* the talk of the town

samtaxer|a [ˣsamm-] assess jointly **-ing** joint taxation

sam|tid [ˣsamm-] ~*en* the age in which we (*etc.*) live, our (*etc.*) age (time) **-tida** *oböjligt a* contemporary **-tidig** contemporaneous; (*sammanfallande*) coincident; (*inträffande -tidigt*) simultaneous **-tidighet** simultaneousness, comtemporaneousness **-tidigt** *adv* at the same time (*med mig* as I; *som* as)

samtliga ['samt-] *pl a* all; the whole body of (*lärare* teachers); ~ *skulder* the total debts

samtrafik [ˣsamm-] joint (combined) service

samtyck|a [ˣsamm-] agree, give one's consent (*till* [att] to; *nicka* ~*nde* nod assent; *den som tiger han* -*er* silence gives consent **samtycke** consent, assent; (*tillåtelse*) permission, leave; *ge sitt* ~, *se samtycka; med hans* ~ by his leave

sa'mum *s3* simoom, simoon

samundervisning [ˣsamm-] coeducation

samu'raj *s3* samurai (*pl* samurai)

sam|variera vary in correlation **-varo** *s9* being (time) together; *tack för angenäm* ~*!* I have enjoyed your company very much! **-verka** cooperate, work (act) together; *bildl.* concur, conspire (*till att* to) **-verkan** cooperation, united action; concurrence

samvete [ˣsamm-] *s6* conscience; *dåligt* ~ a bad conscience; ~*t slog honom* his conscience pricked him; *inte ha* ~ *att göra ngt* not have the conscience to do s.th.; *på heder och* ~*!* on my honour!; *det tar jag på mitt* ~ I shall answer for that

samvets|agg twinge (prick) of conscience; compunction **-betänkligheter** *pl* scruples **-fråga** delicate (indiscreet) question **-förebråelse** remorse; self-reproach; *göra sig* ~*r* reproach o.s. **-grann** conscientious; (*skrupulös*) scrupulous; (*minutiös*) meticulous **-grannhet** conscientiousness *etc.* **-kval** *pl* pangs of conscience **-lös** unscrupulous, unprincipled; (*om pers. äv.*) remorseless **-löshet** unscrupulousness *etc.* **-pengar** *pl* conscience money (*sg*) **-sak** matter of conscience **-äktenskap** *ung.* free union **-öm** overscrupulous; *en* ~ (*om värnpliktsvägrare*) a conscientious objector

samvälde [ˣsamm-] *Brittiska* ~*t* the British Commonwealth [of Nations]

samåka car pool

sanatori|evård [-ˣtɷ:-] treatment at a sanatorium **-um** *s4* sanatorium; *AE. äv.* sanitarium

sand *s3* sand; *byggd på lösan* ~ built upon the sand; *rinna ut i* ~*en* (*bildl.*) come to nothing **sanda** sand

san'dal *s3* sandal; *klädd i* ~*er* sandalled **-'ett** high-heeled sandal

sand|bank sandbank **-blästra** sandblast **-blästring** sandblasting **-botten** sand[y] bottom **-dyn** sand dune (hill)

sandelträ sandalwood

sand|grop sandpit **-gång** gravel walk **-hög** heap (mound) of sand

sand|ig *a1* sandy **-jord** sandy soil **-kaka** (*av sand*) sand pie; (*bakverk*) sand cake **-korn** grain of sand **-låda** (*för barn*) sandpit, sandbox -**ning** sanding -**papper** sandpaper; *ett* ~ a piece of sandpaper -**pappra** sandpaper -**rev[el]** shoal [of sand]; bar of sand -**slott** sand castle -**sten** sandstone -**storm** sandstorm -**strand** sandy beach (shore) -**säck** sandbag -**tag**, -**täkt** sandpit

sandwich [ˣsändvitʃ, ˣsand-] *ung*. canapé -**man** sandwich man

sandöken sand desert

saner|a (*göra sund*) make healthy; *mil*. degas; (*slumkvarter o.d.*) clear; (*finanser o.d.*) refinance; (*företag*) reorganize, reconstruct -**ing** sanitation; degassing; slum clearance; refinancing; reorganization, reconstruction

sanforiser|a sanforize -**ing** sanforizing

sang *s9, kortsp*. no trumps

sangvin|iker [-'vi:-] sanguine person -**isk** *a5* sanguine

sanitets|binda [-ˣte:ts-] sanitary towel -**gods** sanitary ware -**teknik** sanitary technology

sani'tär *a1* sanitary

sank I *oböjligt s, borra i* ~ sink, scuttle **II** *a1* swampy, waterlogged -**mark** marsh

sankt *mask. äv.* -*e, fem.* -*a* saint; *S~e* Per St. Peter -'**bernhardshund** St. Bernard [dog]

sanktion [-k'ʃɷ:n] sanction; (*bifall äv.*) assent, approbation -**era** sanction, approve of

sanktpaulia [-'pau-] *s1* African violet, saintpaulia

sann *a1* true (*mot* to); (*sanningsenlig*) truthful; (*verklig*) real; (*uppriktig*) sincere; (*äkta*) genuine; *en* ~ *kristen* a true Christian; *där sa du ett sant ord!* you are right there!; *inte sant?, se [eller] hur; det var så sant!* by the way!, that reminds me!; *så sant mig Gud hjälpe!* so help me God!; *det är så sant som det är sagt* quite true, how true

sann|a ~ *mina ord!* mark my words! -**dröm** *ha* ~*mar* have dreams that come true

sann|erligen indeed, really; truly; ~ *tror jag inte att de* I do believe they; *det var* ~ *inte för tidigt* it was certainly not too soon -**färdig** truthful, veracious -**färdighet** truthfulness, veracity

sanning truth; (-*färdighet*) veracity; *tala* ~ speak the truth; *hålla sig till* ~*en* stick to the truth; *den osminkade* ~*en* plain (naked) truth; *säga ngn obehagliga* ~*ar* tell s.b. a few home truths; ~*en att säga* to tell the truth; *säga som* ~*en är* tell (speak) the truth; *komma* ~*en närmare* be nearer the truth; *i* ~ in truth, truly; *det är dagsens* ~ it is God's truth

sannings|enlig [-e:-] *a1* truthful, veracious -**enlighet** [-e:n-] truthfulness, veracity -**försäkran** statutory declaration -**halt** veracity -**kärlek** love of truth -**serum** truth drug (serum) -**sökare** seeker after truth -**vittne** witness to the truth -**älskande** veracious, truth-loving

sannolik *a1* probable, likely; *AE. äv.* apt; (*plausibel*) plausible (*version* version); *det mest* ~*a är* the most probable thing is; *det är* ~*t att de gör det* they are likely to do so -**het** probability, likelihood (*för att* that); (*rimlighet*) plausibility; *med all* ~ in all probability -**hetskalkyl** calculus of probability -**hetslära** probability theory

sann|saga true story -**skyldig** true, veritable

-**spådd** *a5, bli* (*vara*) ~ be proved a true prophet

1 sans [saŋ] *s9, kortsp., se sang*

2 sans [sanns] *s3, ej pl* senses (*pl*); *jfr medvetande, besinning*

sansa *rfl* calm down **sansad** *a5* sober; (*moderad*) moderate; (*klok*) sensible, prudent; *lugn och* ~ calm and collected **sanslös** senseless, unconscious

sant *adv* truly, sincerely; *tala* ~ tell (speak) the truth

sapfisk ['sapp-] *a5* Sapphic

sapon|ifikation saponification -'**in** *s4* saponin -**lack** [-ˣpå:n-] silver [zapon] lacquer

sappör *mil*. engineer, sapper

sapro'fyt *s3* saprophyte

sara'c|en *s3* Saracen -'**ensk** [-e:-] *a5* Saracenic[al]

sar'd|ell *s3* sardelle, anchovy -'**in** *s3* sardine

sardinare [-ˣdi:-] Sardinian **Sardinien** [-'di:-] *n* Sardinia **sardinsk** [-'di:nsk] *a5* Sardinian

sardonisk [-'dɷ:-] *a5* sardonic (*leende* smile)

sarg [-j] *s3, s2* border, edging; (*ram*) frame; (*på farkost*) coaming; (*ishockey*) boards (*pl*)

sarga [-ja] lacerate; *bildl*. harrow

sari *s3* sari

Sargassohavet [-ˣgassɷ-] the Sargasso Sea

sar'kas|m *s3* sarcasm; *konkr*. sarcastic remark -**tisk** *a5* sarcastic[al]

sarko'fag *s3* sarcophagus (*pl äv*. sarcophagi)

sarkom [-'kå:m] *s7* sarcoma

sarong [-'råŋ] *s3* sarong

sars *s3, s4* serge

sarv *s2* (*fisk*) rudd, redeye

satan *r* Satan; *ett* ~*s oväsen* the devil (deuce) of a row **satanisk** [-'ta:-] *a5* satanic[al] **sate** *s2* devil; *stackars* ~ poor devil

satel'lit *s3* satellite -**bana** orbit of a satellite -**navigering** satellite navigation -**stat** satellite state -**sändning** satellite transmission --**TV** satellite TV

satin [-'täŋ] *s3, s4, se satäng* -**era** [-ti-] (*glätta*) glaze, polish

sa'tir *s3* satire (*över* upon) -**iker** satirist -**isera** satirize -**isk** *a5* satiric[al]

satis|faktion [-k'ʃɷ:n] satisfaction -**fiera** satisfy

satkär[r]ing [ˣsa:t-] bitch, vixen

1 sats *s3* **1** *mat., log*. proposition; (*tes*) thesis, theme; *språkv*. clause, sentence **2** *mus*. movement

2 sats *s3* **1** (*dosis*) dose; *kokk*. batch **2** (*uppsättning*) set **3** *boktr*. type; *stående* ~ standing type

3 sats *s3, sport. o.d.* run; take off; *ta* ~ take a run, run up

1 satsa 1 (*i spel*) stake, wager, gamble; ~ *på fel häst* back the wrong horse **2** (*investera*) invest **3** ~ *på* (*inrikta sig på*) go in for, concentrate on

2 satsa *se 3 sats*

sats|accent sentence stress -**analys** parsing -**bindning** compound sentence

satsbord *koll*. nest of tables

sats|byggnad sentence structure -**del** part of [a] sentence; *ta ut* ~*ar* analyse a sentence -**fogning** [-ɷ:-] complex sentence -**förkortning** contracted sentence -**lära** syntax -**lösning**

parsing
satsning (*i spel*) staking; (*investering*) investment; (*inriktning*) concentration
satsuma [-'su:-] *s1 bot.* satsuma
1 satt *a1* stocky, thickset
2 satt *imperf. av sitta*
3 satt *sup. av sätta*
satte *imperf. av sätta*
sat|tyg [ˣsa:t-] *s7* devilry **-unge** imp; brat
saturera *kem.* saturate
saturnalier [-'na:-] *pl* saturnalia
Saturnus [-'turr-] *r* Saturn
sa'tyr *s3* satyr
sa'täng *s3, s4* satin; (*foder*) satinet
saudi|arab Saudi **-arabisk** Saudi [Arabian]
Saudi-Arabien [ˣsau-] *n* Saudi Arabia
sauna ['sau-] *s1* sauna
sav *s3* sap (*äv. bildl.*); *~en stiger* the sap is rising
sa'vann *s3* savanna
sava'räng *s3* savarin
savojkål [-ˣvåjj-] savoy
1 sax [sakks] *s2* scissors (*pl*); (*plåt-, ull- etc.*) shears (*pl*); (*fälla*) trap; *en ~* (*två ~ar*) a pair (two pairs) of scissors (*etc.*); *den här ~en* these scissors (*pl*), this pair of scissors
2 sax *s2, vard.* saxophone, sax
saxa (*korsa*) cross; (*klippa*) cut (*ur en tidning out of a paper*); *sport.* scissor; (*skidor*) herringbone
sax|are *s9* Saxon **-isk** ['saks-] *a5* Saxon
saxofon [-'få:n] *s3* saxophone **-ist** saxophonist
saxprint split pin, cotter [pin]
scanner ['skänn-] *~n ~s* scanner
scarf [ska:(r)f] *s2, pl äv. scarves* scarf
scen [se:n] *s3* scene; (*skådebana*) stage; *gå in vid ~en* go on the stage **-anvisning** stage direction **-arbetare** stagehand
scen|ario [-'na:-] *s6, pl äv. -arier* scenario **-bild** set, scene **-eri** scenery **-förändring** change of scenery **-ingång** stage door **-isk** ['se:-] *a5* scenic, theatrical **-konst** dramatic (scenic) art **-ograf** *s3* set designer **-skola** drama school **-vana** stage experience **-öppning** proscenium opening
sch be quiet!, shush!
schaber ['ʃa:-] *pl, vard.* brass, dough
scha'blon *s3, i måleri etc.* stencil; *gjut.* template; (*modell*) model, pattern; *bildl.* cliché **-avdrag** standard deduction **-mässig** *a1* stereotyped **-regel** standard rule
scha'brak *s7* housing
schack I 1 *s7* (*spel*) chess; *spela* (*ta ett parti*) *~* play (have a game of) chess **2** *s2, s7* (*hot mot kungen i schack*) check; *hålla i ~* keep in check **II** *interj,* *~!* check!; *~ och matt!* checkmate!
schack|a check **-bräde** chessboard **-drag** move [in chess]; *ett slugt ~* (*äv. bildl.*) a clever (sly) move
schakel ['ʃakk-] *s2* shackle
schack|'matt *a4* checkmate; *bildl.* worn out, exhausted **-ningsperiod** *sport.* temporary failure of strength **-parti** game of chess **-pjäs** chessman, chess piece
schackra (*driva småhandel*) peddle, hawk; (*friare o. bildl.*) chaffer, haggle (*med* with); traffic (*med* in); (*om ngt*) bargain

schack|ruta square of a chessboard **-spel** *abstr.* chess; *konkr.* chessboard and [set of] men **-spelare** chessplayer
schagg *s3* plush **-soffa** plush sofa
schah [ʃa:] *s3* shah
scha'kal *s3* jackal
1 schakt *s7* (*gruv-*) shaft, pit
2 schakt *s4, s3* ([*jord*]*skärning*) excavation, cutting
schakt|a excavate; *~ bort* (*undan*) cut away, remove **-maskin** excavator **-ning** excavation
schal *s2, se sjal*
schalottenlök [-ˣlått-] shallot, scallion
scha'man *s3* shaman **-ism** shamanism
schampo *s6, s9* shampoo **-nera** shampoo **-nering** shampoo[ing] **-neringsmedel** shampoo
schanker ['ʃann-] *med.* chancre; sore; *mjuk ~* soft sore
schappa *se sjappa*
scharlakan [-ˣla:-, 'ʃa:r-, 'ʃarr-] *s7* scarlet
scharlakans|feber scarlet fever; *fack.* scarlatina **-röd** scarlet
schas *se sjas*
schatter|a shade, shadow [out]; shade (tone) off **-ing** shading, gradation [of colours]; *konkr.* shade **-söm** *ung.* satin stitch
scha'tull *s7* casket
schavott [-'vått] *s3* scaffold; (*skampåle*) pillory **-era** stand in the pillory; *låta ngn ~ i pressen* pillory s.b. in the press
schejk *s3* sheik[h] **-roman** *ung.* romantic novel of desert life
schellack ['ʃell-] shellac
schema ['ʃe:-, ˣʃe:-] *s6* (*timplan*) timetable, AE. [time] schedule; (*uppgjord plan*) schedule, plan; (*över arbetsförlopp*) process chart; (*formulär*) form, AE. blank; *filos.* scheme, outline; *göra upp ett ~* draw up a timetable (*etc.*); *utanför ~t* extracurricular **-lagd** *a5* timetabled, scheduled **-läggning** timetabling, scheduling **-tisera** schematize; (*skissera*) sketch, outline **-tisk** [-'ma:-] *a5* schematic; diagrammatic; *~ teckning* skeleton sketch (drawing)
schers'min *s3, bot.* mock orange, syringa
schimpans *s3* chimpanzee
schism *s3* schism **-atisk** [-'ma:-] *a5* schismatic[al]
schizo|fren [skitså'fre:n] *a1* schizophrenic **-fre'ni** *s3* schizophrenia
schlager ['ʃla:-] *s2, s9* hit song **-musik** popular music
schlaraffenland [-'raff-] Cockaigne, Cockayne
Schleswig ['ʃle:s-] *n* Schleswig
schottis ['ʃått-] *s2* schottische
Schwarzwald ['ʃvarts-] *n* the Black Forest
Schweiz [ʃvejts] *n* Switzerland
schweizare [ˣʃvejts-] Swiss
schweizer|franc [ˣʃvejts-] Swiss franc **-ost** Swiss cheese
schweiz|isk ['ʃvejts-] *a5* Swiss, Helvetian **-iska** *s1* Swiss woman
schvung *s2* go, pep; verve
schäfer ['ʃä:-] *s2,* **-hund** Alsatian; *AE.* German shepherd [dog]
schäs *s2* chaise **-long** [-'lån] *s3* chaise longue
scout [skaut] *s3* scout; (*flick-*) [girl] guide, girl scout; (*pojk-*) boy scout **-chef** chief scout **-för-**

bund scout association **-kår** scout troop **-ledare** scoutmaster **-läger** scout camp **-rörelsen** the Scout movement

screentryck [silk-]screen printing

scripta [ˣskripp-] *s1, se skripta*

se *såg sett* **1** see; (*titta*) look; (*bli varse*) perceive, catch sight of; (*urskilja*) distinguish; (*betrakta*) look at, regard; *AE. sl.* dig; (*möta, träffa*) meet, see; *vi ses i morgon* see you tomorrow; *vi ses* see you later; ~ *bra (illa)* see well (badly), have good (bad) eyesight; ~ *en skymt av* catch a glimpse of; *jag tål inte ~ henne* I cannot stand the sight of her; *vi får väl ~* we shall see; *få ~!* let me see!; *som jag ~r det* as I see it; *väl (illa) ~dd* popular (unpopular); *låt ~ att det blir gjort!* see [to it] that it is done!; *... ~r du ...*, you see (know); ~ *där (här, hit)!* look there (here)!; ~ *så!* now then!; ~ *så där [ja]!* well I never!, (*gillande*) that's it (the way)!; ~ *gäster hos sig* have guests; ~ *ngn på en bit mat* have s.b. to dinner (a meal) **2** (*med prep.-uttr.*) *härav ~r man att* from this it may be concluded that; ~ *efter a*) (*ngt bortgående*) gaze after, *b*) (*leta*) look for; ~ *in i framtiden* look into the future; ~ *på* look at, (*noggrant*) watch, observe; *inte ~ på besväret* not mind the trouble; ~ *på slantarna* take care of the pence; *man ~r på henne att* you can see by her looks that; ~ *åt ett annat håll* look away; ~ *ngn över axeln* look down upon s.b. **3** (*med betonad partikel*) ~ *tiden an* wait and see, bide one's time; ~ *efter a*) (*ta reda på*) [look and] see, *b*) (*passa*) look after, take care of (*barnen* the children); ~ *efter i* look in, (*lexikon e.d.*) look up in; ~ *igenom* (*granska*) look through (over); ~ *ner på* look down upon; ~ *på* look on; *~r man på!* just look!, why [did you ever]!; ~ *till att* see [to it] that; ~ *till att du inte* be careful not to, mind you don't; *jag har inte ~tt till dem* I have seen nothing of them; ~ *upp!* look sharp!; ~ *upp för* look out for, mind; ~ *upp med ...!* be on your guard against ...!; ~ *upp till* look up to, respect; ~ *ut a*) look out (*genom fönstret* of the window), *b*) (*förefalla*) look, seem; *han ~r bra ut* he is good-looking; *det ~r bra ut* it looks fine; *det ~r så ut* it looks like it; *det ~r bara så ut* it only appears so; *hur ~r det ut?* what does it look like?; *så du ~r ut!* what a fright you look!; *det ~r ut att bli snö* it looks like snow; ~ *över* look over, inspect, go through **4** *rfl,* ~ *sig för* be careful, look out; ~ *sig om a*) (*tillbaka*) look back, *b*) (*omkring*) look round, *c*) (*i världen*) see the world; ~ *sig om efter* (*söka*) look out for

seans [-'ans, -'aŋs] *s3* seance

seborré *s3, med.* seborrhoea

sebra [ˣse:-] *s1* zebra

sebu ['se:-] *s3* zebu

sed *s3* custom; *~er* (*moral*) morals, habits; *~er och bruk* manners and customs; *som ~en är bland* as is customary with; *ta ~en dit man kommer* when in Rome do as the Romans do **1 sedan** [ˣse:-, 'se:-] *förk. se* [senn] **I** *adv* **1** (*därpå*) then; (*efteråt*) afterwards; (*senare*) later **2** (*tillbaka*) *det är länge ~* it is a long time ago; *för tio år ~* ten years ago **3** *vard., än sen*

då? what of it?, so what?; *kom sen och säg att* don't dare to say that; *och så billig sen!* and so cheap too! **II** *prep* (*från, efter*) since; ~ *dess* since then; ~ *många år tillbaka* for many years **III** *konj* since (*jag såg honom* I saw him); (*efter det att*) after (*han gått* he had gone); ~ *han gjort det* gick *han* when he had done that he left; *först ~ de gått* not until after they had left

2 sedan [-'daŋ, -'dann] *s3* sedan

seda'tiv I *a1* sedative **II** *s7* sedative

sede|betyg conduct mark; *få sänkt ~* get lower marks for good conduct **-fördärv** corruption; immorality

sed|el ['se:-] *s2* (*betalningsmedel*) bank note; *AE.* bill; *i -lar* in notes (paper money; *AE.* bills)

sedelag moral law, ethical code

sedel|bunt bundle of bank notes **-förfalskare** forger of bank notes **-omlopp** note circulation **-press** printing press for bank notes **-reserv** reserve of bank notes **-tryckeri** note-printing works **-utgivning** note issue, issue of bank notes

sedelär|a moral philosophy; ethics (*pl, behandlas som sg*) **-ande** *a4* moral; ~ *berättelse* story with a moral

sedermera *se sedan I 1*

sede|roman novel portraying life and manners **-sam** *a1* modest, decent; (*tillgjort*) prudish

sedeslös immoral, unprincipled **-het** immorality; (*fördärv*) depravity

sedig *a1* gentle (*häst* horse)

sediment *s7* sediment **-era** (*sjunka*) settle **-'är** *a1* sedimentary

sedlig [ˣse:d-] *a1* (*moralisk*) moral; (*etisk*) ethical; *föra ett ~t liv* lead a virtuous life; *i ~t hänseende* morally, from a moral point of view **-het** morality; decency

sedlighets|brott sexual offence, indecent assault **-förbrytare** sexual offender **-polis** vice squad **-sårande** indecent, offensive

sed|vana custom, practice **-vanerätt** customary law **-vanlig** customary, usual **-vänja** *s1* custom; practice

seeda ['si:da] *sport.* seed

seende *a4* seeing *etc.*; (*mots. blind*) sighted

sefardisk [-'farr-] *a5* Sephardic

sefyr [-'fy:r, 'se:-] *s3* zephyr

seg *a1* tough (*äv. bildl.*); (*om kött äv.*) leathery; (*trögflytande*) viscous; (*limaktig*) gluey, sticky; *bildl.* tenacious; *~t motstånd* tough (stubborn) resistance **sega** *rfl,* ~ *sig upp* struggle up

segel ['se:-] *s7* sail; *hissa* (*stryka*) ~ set (strike) sail; *segla för fulla ~* go with all sails set; *sätta till alla ~* crowd on sail **-bar** *a1* navigable, sailable **-båt** sailing boat, *AE.* sailboat **-duk** sailcloth, canvas **-fartyg** sailing ship (vessel) **-flygare** glider [pilot] **-flygning** gliding, soaring, sailplaning **-flygplan** sailplane, soaring-plane; (*glid-*) glider **-garn** [sailmaker's] twine, packthread **-jakt** sailing yacht **-kanot** sailing canoe **-led** fairway, channel **-makare** sailmaker **-ränna** channel **-sport** yachting **-sällskap** yacht[ing] club **-yta** sail area

seger ['se:-] *s2* victory (*över* over; *vid* of, at); (*erövring*) conquest; *sport.* win; *avgå med ~n* come off victorious; *en lätt* ~ an easy conquest, *sport.* a walkover; *vinna* ~ win a victory **-byte** spoils of victory, booty **-herre** victor, conqueror **-hjälte** conquering hero **-huva** caul **-hymn** hymn of victory **-jubel** triumph, jubilation over a victory **-krönt** [-ö:-] *a4* crowned with victory **-rik** victorious, triumphant **-rop** triumphant shout **-rus** intoxication of victory **-tåg** triumphal progress (march) **-vilja** determination to win **-viss** sure (certain) of victory **-yra** flush of victory

seghet [ˣseːg-] toughness *etc.*; tenacity

segla [ˣseːg-] sail; make sail (*till* for); ~ *i kvav* founder, go down; ~ *i motvind* sail against the wind; ~ *omkull* capsize; ~ *på* run into, collide with; ~ *på grund* run aground; ~ *på havet* sail the sea **seglare** (*fartyg*) sailing vessel; *pers.* sailor; (*kapp-*) yachtsman

seglation sailing, navigation **seglationsperiod** sailing (navigation) period **seg'lats** *s3* sailing trip (tour); (*överfart*) crossing, voyage

segling sailing; *sport. äv.* yachting **seglingsbeskrivning** sailing directions

seglivad *a5* tough; hard to kill; *vard.* die-hard; *en* ~ *fördom* a deep-rooted prejudice

segment *s7* segment **-era** segment

segna [ˣseŋna] ~ [*ner*] sink down, collapse

segr|a [ˣseːg-] win; be victorious; *bildl.* (*i omröstning*) be carried; ~ *över, se besegra* **-ande** *a4* victorious, winning; *gå* ~ *ur striden* emerge victorious from the battle **-are** victor, conqueror; (*i tävling*) winner

segreg|ation segregation **-era** segregate **-ering** segregating; segregation

segsliten tough; *en* ~ *fråga* a vexed question; *en* ~ *tvist* a lengthy dispute

seismisk ['sejs-] *a5* seismic

seismo|graf *s3* seismograph **-log** seismologist **-logisk** *a5* seismologic[al]

sej [sejj] *s2, se gråsej*

sejdel [ˣsejj-] *s2* (*av glas*) beer mug, glass; (*av silver, tenn etc.*) tankard

sejour [se'ʃɷːr] *s3* sojourn, stay

sejsning *sjö.* lanyard, seizing

sekant *mat.* secant

sekatör *s3* pruning shears, secateurs (*pl*); *en* ~ a pair of pruning shears (*etc.*)

sekel ['seː-] *s7, s4* century **-gammal** centuries old; (*hundraårig*) centenary **-jubileum** centenary **-skifte** *vid* ~*t* at the turn of the century

se'kin *s3* sequin; *-er, vard.* dough, bread

sekond [-'kånd] *s3* **1** *sjö.* second-in-command, mate **2** *boxn.* second

1 se'kret *s7* secretion

2 se'kret *a1* secret

sekretari'at *s7* secretariat

sekreter|arbefattning [-ˣteː-] secretarial post **-are** secretary (*hos* to) **-arfågel** secretary bird

sekretess (*under* in) secrecy **-belägga** classify [as secret] **-plikt** (*läkares etc.*) [obligation to observe] professional secrecy **-skydd** (*hopskr.* *sekretesskydd*) secrecy safeguards (*pl*)

sekret|ion secretion **-orisk** [-'tɷ:-] *a5* secretory

sekre'tär *s3* writing desk, bureau, escritoire

sekt *s3* sect **sekterism** sectarianism **sekterist** sectarian

sek|tion [-k'ʃɷ:n] **1** *geom.* section **2** (*avdelning*) section **3** *med.* resection **-tor** [-år] *s3* sector

sekulariser|a secularize **-ing** secularization

seku'lär *a1* secular

se'kund *s3* **1** second; *jag kommer på* ~*en!* just a second! **2** *mus.* supertonic

sekunda [-ˣkunn-] *oböjl. a* second-rate; (*om virke*) seconds; ~ *växel* (*hand.*) second of exchange

sekundant second

sekundchef second-in-command, colonel

sekundera second

sekund|meter metre per second **-visare** second hand

sekun'där *a1* secondary **-lån** loan secured by a second mortgage **-minne** *data.* secondary storage

sekvens *s3, mus.* sequence

sel|a ~ [*på*] harness; ~ *av* unharness **-bruten** galled **-don** harness

sele harness; (*barn-*) reins (*pl*); *en* ~ (*barn-*) a pair of reins; *ligga i* ~*n* (*bildl.*) be in harness

selekt|ion [-k'ʃɷ:n] selection **-'iv** *a1* selective **-ivitet** selectivity

se'len *s3, s4, kem.* selenium

selkammare harness room

selleri [-'riː, 'sell-] *s4, s3* celery **-botten** *kokk.* [filled] celeriac

se'lot *s3* zealot

selters|glas small tumbler **-vatten** Seltzer [water]

semafor [-'få:r] *s3* semaphore **-era** semaphore **-ering** semaphore

seman't|ik *s3, ej pl* semantics (*pl, behandlas som sg*) **-isk** [-'mann-] *a5* semantic

semester [-'mess-] *s2* holiday[s *pl*]; *AE.* vacation; *ha* ~ be on holiday, have one's holiday[s *pl*] **-by** holiday (vacation) settlement (camp, village) **-dag** day of one's (*etc.*) holiday **-ersättning** holiday (*etc.*) compensation **-firare** holiday-maker; *AE.* vacationist, vacationer **-hem** holiday home **-lag** holidays law (act) **-lista** holiday schedule (rota) **-lön** holiday pay (*etc.*) **-månad** holiday month **-resa** holiday trip **-vikarie** holiday relief (substitute)

semestra [-'mess-] *se* [*ha*] *semester;* ~ *vid havet* spend one's holiday by the sea

semi|final [-'naːl, ˣseːmi-] semifinal **-kolon** [-'kɷ:-, 'seːmi-] semicolon

seminarie|uppsats [-ˣnaː-] seminar essay (paper) **-övning** seminar

seminar|ist student at a training college **-ium** [-'naː-] *s4* (*lärar-*) teacher's training college; (*präst-*) [theological] seminary; *univ.* seminar

semin|ation insemination **-förening** [-ˣmiːn-] artificial insemination society (association)

semiotik *s3* semiotics (*pl, behandlas som sg*)

se'mit *s3* Semite **-isk** [-'miː-] *a5* Semitic

semla *s1* cream bun eaten during Lent

1 sen [senn] *adv, se sedan*

2 sen [seːn] *a1* **1** late; *det börjar bli* ~*t* it is getting late; *vara* ~ be late; *vid denna* ~*a timme* at this late (advanced) hour **2** (*långsam*) slow; tardy; *han är aldrig* ~ *att hjälpa* he is always ready to help; ~ *till vrede* slow to anger

sena *s1* tendon, sinew

senap *s3* mustard

senaps|gas mustard gas **-korn** mustard seed

S

senare I *a, komp. t.* 2 *sen* **1** later; (*kommande*) future; (*följande*) subsequent; (*motsats förra*) latter; *de*[n] ~ the latter; *det blir en ~ fråga* that will be considered later; *på ~ tid* of later years, (*nyligen*) recently; *vid en ~ tidpunkt* at a future date **2** (*långsammare*) slower; (*senfärdigare*) tardier **II** *adv, komp. t. sedan* later [on] (*på dagen* in the day); *förr eller ~* sooner or later; *inte ~ än* not later than, by **-lägga** postpone; put forward **-läggning** postponement

senast I *a, superl. t.* 2 *sen* latest; (*sist förfluten*) last; (*nyligen inträffad*) recent; *i ~e laget* at the last moment; *på ~e tid*[en] lately **II** *adv, superl. t. sedan* **1** (*i tid*) latest; (*i följd*) last; *jag såg honom ~ i går* (*i lördags*) I saw him only yesterday (last Saturday); *tack för ~!* I enjoyed my stay (the evening I spent) with you very much! **2** (*ej senare än*) at the latest; *~ på lördag* by Saturday at the latest; *~ den 1:a maj* by May 1, on May 1 at the latest

senat senate **senator** *s3* senator

sendrag cramp

sen|färdig slow, tardy **-född** late-born **-grekisk** late Hellenic **-gångare** *zool.* sloth

senhinna sclerotic coat

senhöst late autumn; *på ~en* late in the (in the late) autumn

senig *a1* sinewy; (*om kött*) tough, stringy; (*om pers.*) wiry

se'nil *a1* senile; *~ demens* (*med.*) senile dementia **-dement** *a4, med.* suffering from senile dementia **-itet** senility

senior I ['se:niår] *oböjligt. a* senior, elder **II** ['se:-, *sport.* -'å:r] *s3* senior member; *sport.* senior

sen|komling [-å-] latecomer **-kommen** [-å-] *a5* (*alltför sen*) tardy, belated **-latin** late Latin

sensation sensation **-'ell** *a1* sensational, thrilling

sensations|lysten *vara ~* be a sensation hunter (out after a thrill) **-makare** sensationalist **-press** yellow (sensational) press

sensib|el [-'si:-] *a2* sensitive **-ilisera** sensitize **-ilitet** sensitivity, sensitiveness

sensi'tiv *a1* sensitive **sensitivitet** sensitivity **sensitivitetsträning** sensitivity training

sensmo'ral [sens-, saŋ(s)-] *s3, ~en är* the moral is

sensommar late summer; *jfr senhöst*

sensorisk [-'sɒ:-] *a5* sensory, sensorial

senstäckning strain of a tendon

sensu|alism sensualism **-alitet** sensuality **-'ell** *a1* sensual, sensuous

sent [-e:-] *adv* late; *bittida och ~* early and late; *bättre ~ än aldrig* better late than never; *komma för ~* be late (*till skolan* for school); *som ~ skall glömmas* that will not be forgotten in a hurry; *~ omsider* at long last; *till ~ på natten* till far into the night

sentens *s3* maxim

sentera [saŋ'te-, senn-] (*uppskatta*) appreciate; (*sätta värde på*) value

sentida of today, of our days

sentimen'tal [sent-] *a1* sentimental; (*gråtmild*) maudlin **-itet** sentimentality

separat I *a4* separate; (*fristående*) detached **II** *adv* separately; *~ sänder vi* we are sending you under separate cover **-fred** separate peace

separation separation **separatist** *s3* separatist **separatistisk** [-'tiss-] *a5* separatist **separator** *s3* separator

separat|tryck offprint **-utställning** one-man show

separer|a separate **-ing** separation

september [-'temm-] *r* September

sep'tett *s3* septet[te]

sept|iktank septic tank **-isk** *a5* septic (*tank* tank)

septima ['sepp-] *s1, mus.* seventh

se'raf *s3* seraph

serafimer|orden [-*ˣ*fi:-] the Order of the Seraphim **-riddare** Knight of the Order of the Seraphim

serafisk [-'ra:-] *a4* seraphic

se'ralj *s3* seraglio

serb [-ä-] *s3* Serb[ian] **Serbien** ['särr-] *n* Serbia **serbisk** ['särr-] *a5* Serbian **serbokroatisk** [-'krɒa:-] *a5* Serbo-Croatian

sere'nad *s3* serenade; *hålla ~* [*för*] serenade

sergeant [-r'ʃant] *s3* sergeant; staff sergeant; *AE.* sergeant first class; (*vid flottan*) chief petty officer; (*vid flygvapnet*) flight sergeant, *AE.* master sergeant

serie ['se:-] *s5* **1** series; (*följd*) succession; (*om värdepapper*) issue; (*skämt-*) comic strip, cartoons (*pl*), *AE. vard.* funny; *i ~* (*äv.*) serially **2** *sport.* division **3** *mat.* series, progression **-figur** character in a comic strip **-koppla** *elektr.* connect in series **-krock** multiple collision; *vard.* pile-up **-magasin** comic [paper]; funny paper **-match** league match **-nummer** serial number **-tidning** comic [paper]; funny paper **-tillverkning** series (long-line) production

serigrafi *s3* serigraphy

seriös *a1* serious

serologi *s3* serology

serpen'tin *s3* serpentine; (*pappersremsa*) streamer **-väg** serpentine road

serum ['se:-] *s8* serum

serv|a [*ˣ*sörva] *sport.* serve; *vard.* service (*en bil* a car); (*hjälpa*) serve, back up **-boll** *s2* service **-linje** service line

serve [sörv] *s2, sport.* service, serv **-ruta** service court

server|a serve; (*passa upp vid bordet*) wait at table; *~ ngn ngt* help s.b. to s.th.; *middagen är ~d!* dinner is served (ready)! **-ing 1** *abstr.* service; *sköta ~en vid bordet* do the waiting **2** *konkr., se matservering*

serverings|bord service table **-lucka** service hatch **-rum** pantry

ser'vett *s3* napkin, serviette; *bryta ~er* fold napkins; *ta emot ngn med varma ~er* (*bildl.*) give s.b. a warm reception **-ring** napkin ring **-väska** napkin case

service ['sö:r-, *ˣ*sörv-] *s9* service **-hus** block of service flats; *AE.* apartment hotel **-man** (*reklamman*) agency representative; (*på -station*) petrol-station attendant **-verkstad** car service station **-yrke** service occupation

ser'vil *a1* servile; (*krypande*) cringing **-itet** servility; (*fjäsk*) cringing

ser'vis *s3* **1** (*mat-*) service, set **2** *mil.* gun crew

-avgift service charge; *(dricks)* tip **-ledning** service line, feeder
servitris waitress; *(på fartyg)* stewardess
servi'tut *s7* easement, encumbrance; *belagd med ~* encumbered with an easement
servitutsrätt right to an easement
servitör waiter; *(på fartyg)* steward
servo|broms servo[-assisted] brake **-motor** servomotor **-styrning** power steering, servo control **-teknik** servo technique
se'rös *a1* serous
ses *sågs setts, dep* see each other, meet; *vi ~!* I'll be seeing you!
1 sesam ['se:-] *s3, bot.* sesame
2 sesam ['se:-] *n, ~ öppna dig!* open sesame!
session [se'ʃɷ:n] *parl.* session, sitting; *(domstols-)* session, court; *(sammanträde)* meeting; *avsluta ~en (vid domstol)* close the court
sessions|dag *(vid domstol)* court day **-sal** session (assembly) room; *(vid domstol)* courtroom; *parl.* chamber
se|'så now then!; *(gillande)* that's it!; *(tröstande)* come, come!
set [sett] *s7, sport. o. allm.* set **-boll** set point
sett *sup. av se*
setter *s2* setter
sevärd worth seeing, notable **-het** sight; *(byggnad e.d. äv.)* monument
1 sex [seks] *räkn* six; *(för sms. jfr fem-)*
2 sex *s7* sex
1 sexa ['ˣseksa] *s1 (måltid)* light supper
2 sexa ['ˣseksa] *s1 (siffra)* six
sex|cylindrig *a1* six-cylinder *(motor engine)* **-dubbel** sixfold
sex|dåre sex maniac **-film** sex film (movie), blue movie **-galning** sex maniac
sex|hundratalet the seventh century **-hörnig** [-ö:-] *a1* hexagonal **-hörning** [-ö:-] hexagon
sexig *a1* sexy **sexism** sexism
sexkant hexagon
sex|klubb sex club **-liv** sex life **-ologi** sexology
sexsiffrig *a1* of six figures; *ett ~t tal* a six-figure number
sext|ant sextant **-'ett** *s3* sextet[te]
sex|tio [ˣseks-, 'seks-, *vard.* ˣseksti, 'seksti] sixty **-tionde** sixtieth **-tioåring** sexagenarian
sex|ton [ˣsekstån] sixteen **-tonde** sixteenth **-tondelsnot** *s3* semiquaver, *AE.* sixteenth note
sextrakasserier *(pl)* sex harassment *(sg)*
sexual|brott [-ˣa:l-] sex[ual] crime **-drift** sexual instinct (urge) **-förbrytare** sex criminal, sexual offender **-hygien** sexual hygiene **-itet** sexuality **-liv** sex[ual] life **-rådgivning** advisory service on sexual matters **-system** *bot.* sexual system **-undervisning** sex instruction **-upplysning** information on sexual matters
sexu'ell *a1* sexual
sfinkter ['sfiŋk-] *s2, anat.* sphincter
sfinx [-iŋks] *s3* sphinx **-artad** [-a:r-] *a5* sphinxlike
sfär *s3* sphere; *bildl. äv.* province **-isk** ['sfä-] *a5* spheric[al]; *~ triangel (mat.)* circular triangle
shah *se schah*
shaman *se schaman*
shampoo *se schampo*

shantung ['ʃann-] *s2* shantung
sherry ['ˣʃärri, -y] *s9* sherry
shetlandsull [ˣʃett-] Shetland wool
shiamuslim [ˣʃi:a-] *s3*, **shiit** [ʃi:t] *s3* Shiit, Shiah
shilling ['ʃill-] *s9* shilling *(förk.* s[h].*)*; *det gick 20 ~ på ett pund* there were 20 shillings to the pound
shingla [ˣʃiŋla] shingle
shoppa [ˣʃåppa] go shopping
shopping|center shopping centre **-vagn** shopping trolley **-väska** shopping bag
show [ʃåo, ʃåvv] *s3* show
shunt [ʃunt] *s2, elektr.* shunt, bypass **-ledning** shunt lead **-ventil** shunt valve
1 si *interj* look!; *(högtidligare)* behold!
2 si *adv, ~ och så* only so-so; *det gick ~ och så* it wasn't up to much
sia prophesy *(om* of*)*
sia'mes *s3* Siamese **-isk** [-'me:-] *a5* Siamese
siar|e seer, prophet **-gåva** second sight
Sibirien [-'bi:-] *n* Siberia **sibirisk** [-'bi:-] *a5* Siberian
sibyll|a [-ˣbylla] *s1* sibyl **-insk** [-'li:nsk] *a5* sibylline
sicili|'an *s3*, **-anare** [-ˣa:na-] *s9* Sicilian **-'ansk** [-a:-] *a5* Sicilian
Sicilien [-'si:-] *n* Sicily
sicka'tiv *s7* siccative
sicken *~ en!* what a character!
sickl|a *fack.* scrape **-ing** *konkr.* scraper, scraping iron
sicksack zigzag; *gå i ~* zigzag **-linje** zigzag [line]
sid *a1* long [and loose]
sid|a *s1* 1 side; *(mil., byggn.; djurs)* flank; *(bok-)* page; *geom. (yta)* face; *~ upp och ~ ner* page after page; *~ vid ~* side by side; *anfalla från ~n* attack in (on) the flank; *sedd från ~n* seen side-face; *med händerna i ~n* with arms akimbo; *på båda -or (äv.)* on either side *(av* of*)*; *åt ~n* to the [one] side, *(gå* step*)* aside **2** *bildl.* side, part; *(synpunkt)* aspect, point of view; *visa sig från sin fördelaktigaste ~* show o.s. at one's best; *från hans ~* on (for) his part; *från regeringens ~* from (on the part of) the Government; *se saken från den ljusa ~n* look on the bright side of things;*jdet har sina -or att* there are drawbacks to; *hon har sina goda -or* she has her good points; *problemet har två -or* there are two sides to the problem; *stå på ngns ~* side (take sides) with s.b.; *han står på vår ~* he is on our side; *när han sätter den ~n till* when he makes up his mind to; *vid ~n av (bildl.)* beside, next to, *(jämte)* along with; *å ena (andra) ~n* on one (the other) hand; *vi å vår ~* we for (on) our part, as far as we are concerned; *är inte hans starka ~* is not his strong point **-antal** number of pages **-bena** side parting **-byte** change of ends
siden *s7* silk **-band** silk ribbon **-glänsande** satiny, silky **-klänning** silk dress **-sko** satin shoe **-svans** *zool.* waxwing **-tyg** silk [material (cloth, fabric)] **-varor** *pl* silk goods **-väveri** silk-weaving mill
siderisk [-'de:-] *a5, astr.* sidereal
sid|fläsk bacon **-hänvisning** page reference **-led**

i ~ lateral[ly], sideways

sido|apparat extension [phone] **-blick** sidelong glance; *utan* ~ *på* (*bildl.*) without a thought for **-byggnad** annex, wing **-dörr** side door **-fönster** side window **-gata** side street, bystreet **-gren** side branch; (*av släkt*) collateral branch **-linje** (*parallell-*) sideline; *järnv.* junction line, branch; (*släktled*) collateral line (branch); *fotb.* touchline; *barn på ~n* natural children **-replik** aside **-skepp** (*i kyrka*) lateral aisle **-spår** sidetrack (*äv. bildl.*); *järnv.* siding **-vinkel** adjacent angle **-vördnad** irreverence, disrespect

sid|roder *flyg.* rudder **-siffra** page number **-steppa** *vard.* sidestep **-söm** side seam **-vagn** (*på motorcykel*) sidecar **-vind** crosswind; *landa i* ~ (*flyg.*) make a crosswind landing **-vördnad** *se sidovördnad*

sierraleonier [-le'å:-] Sierra Leonean

sierska seeress, prophetess

siesta [-ˣess-] *s1* siesta, [after dinner] nap

siffer|beteckning number **-granskare** checking-clerk, auditor of accounts **-granskning** checking of accounts **-mässig** *a1* numeral, numeric[al] **-räkning** numerical calculation **-skyddsmaskin** checkwriter **-system** numerical system **-tips** correct score forecasting **-värde** numerical value

siffr|a *s1* figure; *konkr. äv.* numeral; (*entalssiffra äv.*) digit; (*tal*) number; *romerska* -*or* Roman numerals; *skriva med* -*or* write in figures

sifon [-'få:n] *s3* siphon; soda fountain (siphon)

sig [sejj, *äv.* si:g] oneself; himself, herself, itself, themselves; *han anser* (*säger*) ~ *vara frisk* he thinks (says) he is well; *tvätta* ~ *om händerna* wash one's hands; *man skall inte låta* ~ *luras* don't let yourself be deceived (led up the garden path); *det låter* ~ *inte göra*[*s*] it can't be done; *vara häftig av* ~ be hot-tempered by nature; *det är en sak för* ~ that's another story; *var för* ~ one by one; *i och för* ~ in itself; *det för med* ~ ... it involves ... (brings ... in its train); *ha ögonen med* ~ keep one's eyes open; *han tog med* ~ *sin bror* he took his brother [along] with him; *ha pengar på* ~ have some money on one; *inte veta till* ~ *av glädje* be overjoyed; *han är inte längre* ~ *själv* he is no longer himself; *av* ~ *själv*[*t*] by itself (*etc.*); *för* ~ *själv* by o.s. (itself *etc.*); *behålla ngt för* ~ *själv* (*för egen räkning*) keep s.th. for o.s., (*hemlighålla*) keep s.th. to o.s.

sightseeing ['saitsiiŋ] sightseeing; *vara på* ~ be sightseeing

sigill [-'jill] *s7* seal; *sätta sitt* ~ *under* (*på*) affix one's seal to, seal **-bevarare** (*stor-*) Keeper of the [Great] Seal; *Storbritannien* Lord Privy Seal **-lack** (*hopskr. sigillack*) sealing wax **-ring** signet (seal) ring

signa [siŋna] *se välsigna*; *den ~de dag* the blessed day

signal [siŋ'na:l] *s3* signal; *ge* ~ make a signal, (*i bil*) sound the horn; *ge* ~ *till* give the signal for **-anläggning** signalling equipment **-anordning** signalling device **-bok** code of signals, signal book

signalement *s7* description **signalera** signal; (*med signalhorn äv.*) sound the horn

signal|flagga signal flag **-horn** [signal] horn;

[*car*] horn, hooter **-ist** *mil.* signaller, signalman **-raket** signal rocket **-regemente** signal regiment **-skola** *mil.* signal[ling] school **-spaning** signal (communication) intelligence **-system** signalling system **-tjänst** communications (*pl*)

signatur [siŋn-] signature; (*författares äv.*) pen name **-melodi** signature tune, *AE.* theme song

signatärmakt [-ˣtä:r-] signatory power

signer|a [siŋn-, sinj-] sign; initial, mark **-ing** signing

signetring [siŋˣne:t-] signet ring

signifik|ant [-'ant, -'aŋt] *a1* significant **-a'tiv** [*äv.* 'siŋni-] *a1* significative, significant

sik *s2, zool.* whitefish

1 sikt *s2* (*redskap*) sieve

2 sikt *s3* **1** visibility; view; *dålig* (*ingen*) ~ poor (zero) visibility **2** *hand.* sight, presentation **3** (*tidrymd*) term, run; *på* ~ in the long run; *on the long term*

1 sikta (*sålla*) sift, pass through a sieve; (*mjöl*) bolt

2 sikta 1 (*med vapen*) take aim, aim (*på, mot* at) (*äv. bildl.*); point (*på, mot* at); ~ *högt* (*bildl.*) aim high **2** *sjö.* sight

sikt|e *s6* **1** (*på gevär o.d.*) sight **2** (*synhåll*) sight, view; (*mål*) aim; *få ngt i* ~ get s.th. in sight, *sjö.* sight s.th.; *i* ~ in sight, *bildl.* in prospect (view); *land i* ~! land ahoy; *med* ~ *på* with a view to; *ur* ~ out of sight; *förlora ngt ur* ~ lose sight of s.th. **-punkt** point of aim (sight) **-skåra** [sighting] notch **-växel** sight draft (bill)

sil *s2* **1** strainer, sieve **2** *sl.* fix, hit, shot

sil|a 1 (*filtrera*) strain, sieve, filter; ~ *ifrån* strain off; ~ *mygg och svälja kameler* strain at a gnat and swallow a camel **2** (*sippra*) trickle; (*om ljus*) filter **-ben** *anat.* ethmoid [bone] **-duk** straining cloth, screen

sileshår *bot.* sundew

silhuett [silu'ett] *s3* silhouette

silikat *s7, s4* silicate **silikon** [-'kå:n] *s3, s4* silicone **silikos** [-'kå:s] *s3* silicosis

silke *s6* silk; *av* ~ (*äv.*) silken; *mjuk som* ~ silky **silkes|apa** marmoset **-fjäril** silk[worm] moth **-len** as soft as silk; silken (*röst* voice) **-mask** silkworm **-maskodling** sericulture; *konkr.* silkworm farm **-papper** tissue paper **-snöre** silk cord; *ge ngn* ~*t* politely dismiss s.b. **-strumpa** silk stocking **-trikå** silk tricot **-tråd** silk thread, (*från kokong*) silk filament **-vante** *använda* -*vantar* (*bildl.*) use kid gloves **-vävnad** silk fabric

sill *s2* herring; *inlagd* ~ pickled herring; *salt* ~ salt[ed] herring; *som packade* ~*ar* packed together like sardines **-bulle** *kokk.* herring rissole **-burk** tin of herrings **-grissla** guillemot **-mjölke** *s2* milksop **-sallad** *s3* mixture of pickled herring, beetroot, cooked meat and potatoes **-stim** shoal of herring **-trut** *s2* lesser black-backed gull **-tunna** herring barrel **-val** *s2* rorqual, finback

silning [ˣsi:l-] straining; filtering

silo ['si:-] *s5, s3* silo

silu'ett *s3, se silhuett*

si'lur *s3* Silurian **-isk** *a5* Silurian

silver ['sill-] *s7* silver; *förgyllt* ~ silver-gilt **-beslag** silver-mount[ing] **-bröllop** silver wedding **-bägare** silver cup (goblet) **-fat** silver dish (plate) **-fisk** (*insekt*) silverfish **-gran** silver fir **-gruva** silver mine **-halt** silver content, fineness **-haltig** *a1* argentiferous, silver-bearing **-medalj** silver medal **-mynt** silver coin; *i* ~ in silver **-penning** *sälja ngn för 30* ~*ar* betray s.b. for 30 pieces of silver **-poppel** white poplar, abele **-räv** silver fox **-sak** silver article; ~*er* (*koll.*) silverware (*sg*) **-sked** silver spoon **-skål** silver bowl **-smed** silversmith **-smide** wrought silver **-stämpel** hallmark **-te** hot water with sugar [and cream] **-tärna** arctic tern **-vit** silvery

sim|bassäng [ˣsimm-] swimming pool **-blåsa** (*hos fisk*) sound, air (swim) bladder **-byxor** *pl* swimming trunks **-dyna** swimming float **-fena** *zool.* fin **-fot** *zool.* webbed foot; *-fötter* (*för dykare*) [diving] flippers **-fågel** web-footed bird, swimmer **-hall** indoor swimming bath **-hopp** dive **-hud** web; *med* ~ *mellan tårna* with webbed feet

simili [ˈsi:-] *s9, s7* imitation **-diamant** paste diamond **-pärla** artificial pearl

sim|kunnig [ˣsimm-] able to swim **-kunnighetsprov** swimming test **-lärare** swimming instructor

simma *v1 el. sam* summit swim; *bildl. äv.* be bathed (*i* in); (*flyta*) float [on the water]; ~ *bra* be a good swimmer **simmare, simmerska** swimmer **simmig** *a1* well thickened (*sås* sauce); treacly (*punsch* punch); hazy (*blick* look) **simning** swimming; *litt.* natation

simo'ni *s3* simony

simpa *s1* bullhead

simpel [ˈsimm-] *a2* **1** (*enkel*) simple; plain (*arbetskläder* working clothes); common (*soldat* soldier); (*lätt*) easy **2** (*tarvlig*) common, vulgar; (*föraktlig*) low, base; (*om kläder*) mean, shabby **simpelt** *adv* **1** *helt* ~ simply **2** (*tarvligt*) low, mean[ly], shabbily; *det var* ~ *gjort* it was a mean (shabby) thing to do

simplifier|a simplify **-ing** simplification

simsalabim [-ˈbimm] *interj* hocus pocus

sim|skola [ˣsimm-] swimming school **-sätt** (*fritt* free) style **-tag** stroke **-tur** swim **-tävling** swimming competition

simul|ant malingerer **-ator** *s3* simulator **-era** simulate; (*om soldat*) malinger

simul'tan *a1* simultaneous **-schack** simultaneous chess-playing **-tolk** simultaneous interpreter **-tolka** interpret [speech] simultaneously

1 sin [sinn] (*sitt, sina*) *pron* one's; *fören.* his, her, its, their; *självst.* his, hers, its, theirs; ~ *nästa* one's neighbour; *i sitt och* ~ *familjs intresse* in his own interest and that of his family; *de* ~*a* his (*etc.*) relations (people), his (*etc.*) own family; *bli* ~ *egen* be[come] one's own master (boss); *det kan göra sitt till* that can help matters; *ha sitt på det torra* not stand to lose anything; *kärleken söker inte sitt* (*bibl.*) love seeketh not its own; *vad i all* ~ *dar* what on earth; *i* ~*om tid* in due [course of] time; *på* ~ *tid* formerly; *på* ~*a ställen* in places; *hålla på sitt* watch one's own interest; *gå var och en till sitt* all go back home

2 sin [si:n] *s, i uttr.: stå* (*vara*) *i* ~ be dry **sina** dry; *brunnen har* ~*t* the well has dried up;

ett aldrig ~*nde ordflöde* a never-ceasing flow of words

Sinai *n* Sinai **-halvön** the Sinai Peninsula

sinekur [-ˈku:r, ˣsi:-] *s3* sinecure

singa'les [singa-] *s3* Sin[g]halese **-isk** *a5* Sin[g]halese

1 singel [ˈsin-] *s9* (*grus*) shingle

2 singel [ˈsin-] *s2* **1** *sport.* singles (*pl*) **2** *kortsp.* singleton

singel|olycka accident involving one vehicle only **-skiva** single

singla 1 (*kasta*) toss [up]; ~ *slant om* toss for **2** (*dala*) float

singular [ˣsingu-, ˈsingu-] *s3, se singularis* **singularform** [ˣsingu-] singular form **singular|is** [ˣsingu-, ˈsingu-] *-en -er* (*stå i* be in the) singular **singul'jär** *a1* singular

1 sinka *v1* (*fördröja*) delay; (*söla*) waste time

2 sinka I *s1* (*metallkrampa*) rivet; (*hörntapp*) dovetail **II** *v1* (*porslin*) rivet; (*bräder*) dovetail

sinka'dus *s3* **1** (*örfil*) biff **2** (*slump*) toss-up, chance; *en ren* ~ a pure toss-up

sinnad *a5* (*andligt* spiritually) minded; (*vänskapligt* amiably) inclined

sinne *s6* **1** *fysiol.* sense; *de fem* ~*na* the five senses; *ha ett sjätte* ~ have a sixth sense; *med alla* ~*n på helspänn* with all one's wits about one; *från sina* ~ out of one's senses (mind); *vid full possession of one's senses* **2** (*-lag*) mind, temper, nature; (*väsen, hjärta*) soul, heart; (*håg*) taste, inclination, turn; *ett häftigt* ~ a hasty temper; *ha ett vaket* ~ *för* be alert (open) to; ~*t rann på honom* he lost his temper (flew into a passion); *en man efter mitt* ~ a man to my mind (taste); *han har fått i sitt* ~ *att* he has got it into his head to; *ha* ~ *för humor* have a sense of humour; *ha* ~ *för språk* have a talent for languages; *ha i* ~*t* contemplate; *ha ont i* ~*t* have evil intentions; *i mitt stilla* ~ in my own mind, inwardly; *sätta sig i* ~*t att göra ngt* set one's mind [up]on doing s.th.; *till* ~*s* in mind; *sorgsen till* ~*s* in low spirits; *det gick honom djupt till* ~*s* he felt it deeply **-bild** symbol, emblem **-bildlig** symbolical, emblematic[al] **-lag** *s7* temperament, disposition; *vänligt* ~ friendly disposition

sinnes|frid peace of mind **-frånvaro** absence of mind **-förnimmelse** sensation **-förvirrad** *a5* distracted **-förvirring** mental aberration; *under tillfällig* ~ while of unsound mind **-intryck** sensation, impression **-jämvikt** equanimity **-lugn** tranquillity (calmness) of mind **-närvaro** presence of mind **-organ** sense organ **-rubbad** mentally deranged **-rubbning** mental disorder, derangement **-rörelse** emotion; mental excitement **-sjuk** mentally ill, insane; *en* ~ a mentally ill person **-sjukdom** mental disease; insanity **-sjukhus** mental hospital; (*förr*) lunatic asylum **-slö** mentally deficient (retarded) **-slöhet** mental deficiency **-stämning** frame of mind **-svag** feeble-minded **-tillstånd** mental condition (state) **-undersökning** mental examination **-villa** hallucination **-ändring** change of attitude

sinnevärlden the material (external) world

sinn|lig *a1* **1** (*som rör sinnena*) pertaining to the

S

sense **2** (*köttslig*) sensual; *en ~ människa* a sensualist **-lighet** sensuality **-rik** ingenious (*påhitt* device) **-rikhet** ingenuity

sino|log Sinologue, Sinologist **-logi** *s3* Sinology

1 sinom [*ˣsinnåm] *se 1 sin*

2 sinom [*ˣsinnåm] *i uttr.:* *tusen ~ tusen* thousands and thousands

sinsemellan [-*ˣmell-] between (*om sak:* among) themselves

sinter *s2* sinter **sintra** sinter; *~de plattor* sintered slabs

sinu'it *s3, med.* sinusitis

sinus ['si:-] *r* **1** *mat.* sine **2** *anat.* sinus **-funktion** *mat.* sinusoidal function **-'it** *se sinuit* **-kurva** sine curve, sinusoid

sion|ism Zionism **-ist** Zionist

sipp *a1* prim, prudish

sippa *s1, bot.* anemone, windflower

sippra trickle, drop, percolate; *~ fram* ooze out; *~ ut* (*bildl.*) transpire, leak out

sira decorate, ornament, deck

sirap *s3* **1** treacle, golden syrup; *AE.* molasses **2** *med.* syrup; *AE.* sirup

sirat ornament, decoration **-lig** *a1* (*ceremoniös*) ceremonious

si'ren *s3* (*myt. o. signalapparat*) siren

sirlig [*ˣsi:r-] *a1* graceful, elegant; (*om pers.*) ceremonious, formal; (*fin*) dignified

sisalhampa [*ˣsi:-, -*ˣsa:l-] sisal hemp

siska *s1, zool.* siskin

sist I *adv* last; *till ~* (*som det ~a*) at last, (*slutligen*) finally, in the end; *spara det bästa till ~* save the best until last (till the end); *allra ~* last of all; *först och ~* from first to last; *först som ~* just as well now as later; *näst ~* the last but one; *~ men inte minst* last but not least; *den ~ anlände* the last arrival (comer); *han blev ~ färdig* he was the last to get ready; *~ i boken* at the end of the book; *stå ~ på listan* be the last on the list **II** *konj.* *~ jag såg honom var han* the last time I saw him he was

sist|a *-e, superl. a* last; (*senaste*) latest; (*slutlig*) final; *den ~ juni* [on] the last of June; *~ anmälningsdag* closing date for entries; *~ gången* (*sidan*) the last time (page); *~ modet* the latest fashion; *~ skriket* all the rage (go); *~ smörjelsen* the extreme unction; *~ vagnen* (*järnv.*) tail (rear) wagon; *hans ~ vilja* his [last] will [and testament]; *den -e* (*av två*) the latter; *han var den -e som kom* he was the last to arrive; *de två ~ månaderna* the last two months; *lägga ~ handen vid* put the finishing touch to; *utandas sin ~ suck* breathe one's last; *för ~ gången* (*för all tid*) for ever (good); *i ~ instans* (*jur.*) in the court of highest instance, *bildl.* in the last resort; *i ~ det ~* to the very last; *på ~ tiden* lately, of late; *sjunga på ~ versen* draw to its close; *till ~ man* to a man

sist|an *s, best. form, leka ~* play tag (touchlast) **-liden** *a5* last **-nämnda** *a, best. form* [the] last-mentioned, last-named; (*av två*) the latter **-one** [-å-] *s, i uttr.:* *på ~* lately

sisu ['si:-] *s9* perseverance, endurance

sisyfosarbete Sisyphean task (labour)

si'tar *s3* (*indiskt stränginstrument*) sitar

sits *s2* **1** (*stol-, stjärt o.d.; ridk.*) seat; *ha bra ~* (*ridk.*) have a good seat **2** *kortsp.* lie, lay; *dra*

om ~en draw for partners; *bildl., en svår ~* a tricky situation, a sensitive position

sitt *se 1 sin*

sitt|a *satt suttit* **1** (*om levande varelse*) sit; (*på -plats äv.*) be seated; (*motsats stå, ligga*) be sitting; (*om fågel*) perch; (*befinna sig*) be (*i fängelse* in prison); (*om regering*) be in office; *~ bekvämt* be comfortably seated; *sitt [ner]!* sit down, please!; *~ för en målare* sit as a model; *~ och prata* sit talking; *~ still* sit still, (*friare äv.*) keep quiet; *~ trångt* be jammed, *ekon.* be in a tight place; *få ~ a*) get (obtain) a seat, *b*) (*ej bli uppbjuden*) sit out, be a wallflower; *inte ~ i sjön* not be stranded; *~ inom lås och bom* be under lock and key; *~ med goda inkomster* have a large income; *~ vid makten* be in power; *nu -er vi där vackert!* we are in for it now!, now we are in the soup! **2** (*om sak*) be [placed]; (*hänga*) hang; (*om kläder*) sit, fit; *kjolen -er bra* the skirt is a good fit (fits well); *~ på sned* be (*hänga:* hang) askew; *mitt onda -er i* my trouble (the pain) is in; *inte veta hur korten -er* not know how the cards lie **3** (*med betonad partikel*) *~ av* dismount, alight; *~ emellan* (*få obehag*) have trouble, (*bli lidande*) be the sufferer (loser); *~ fast, se 2 fast 3*; *~ hemma* stay at home; *en färg som -er i* a fast colour; *lukten -er i* the smell clings; *nyckeln -er i* the key is in the lock; *ovanan -er i* I (*etc.*) can't free mysolf of the [bad] habit; *~ inne a* (*inomhus*) keep in[doors], *b*) (*i fängelse*) be in prison, do time; *bekännelsen satt långt inne* the confession was hard to get: *~ inne med upplysningar* be in possession of information; *~ kvar a*) remain sitting (seated), *b*) (*stanna*) remain, stay, *c*) (*efter skolan*) stay (be kept) in [after school]; *låt kappan ~ på!* keep your coat on!; *locket -er på* the lid is on; *~ sönder* wear out by sitting on; *jag -er inte så till att* I am not in a position to, from where I am sitting I can't; *~ illa till* (*bildl.*) be in a bad spot; *~ upp a*) (*på häst*) mount, get on, *b*) (*räta upp sig*) sit up; *~ uppe och vänta på* wait up for; *~ åt* (*om plagg*) be tight; *det -er hårt åt* (*bildl.*) it's tough; *~ över a*) (*dans e.d.; i spel*) sit out, *b*) (*arbeta över*) work overtime

sitt|ande *a4* seated; sitting (*ställning* posture); (*om regering*) in office, present; (*om domstol*) in session; *inför ~ rätt* in open court **-bad** hip (sitz) bath **-ben** *anat.* ischium **-brunn** cockpit **-bräde** seat [board] **-möbler** chairs and sofas **-ning** sitting **-opp** *s2* (*slag*) clout **-pinne** perch **-plats** seat **-platsbiljett** seat reservation (ticket) **-riktig** designed for comfortable sitting **-strejk** sit-down strike; shop-floor protest **-vagn** *järnv.* day-carriage; (*barnvagn*) pushchair, *AE.* stroller

situation situation; *sätta sig in i ngns ~* put o.s. in a p.'s place; *vara ~en vuxen* be equal to the occasion

situations|komik comedy; (*i film o.d.*) slapstick **-plan** *byggn.* layout, site plan

situerad [-u'e:-] *a5, väl* (*illa*) *~* well (badly) off

Sixtinska kapellet [-'ti:n-] the Sistine Chapel

SJ [*ˣessji:] *förk. för Statens Järnvägar* the Swedish State Railways

sjabbig [ʃ-] *a1* shabby

sjabbla [ʃ-] *vard.* muff it
sja'kal [ʃ-] *se skakal*
sjal [ʃ-] *s2* shawl -'**ett** *s3* kerchief; head scarf
sjanghaja [ʃaŋ'hajja] shanghai
sjappa [ʃ-] bolt, scram **sjappen** ['ʃapp-] *s, i uttr.: ta till ~* take to one's heels
sjas [ʃ-] scat!, be off!; *~ katta* shoo! **sjasa** shoo away
sjaskig [ʃ-] *a1* slovenly; mucky; shabby
sjava [ʃ-] shuffle **sjavig** *a1* slovenly, slapdash
sjok [ʃ-] *s7* lump, chunk
sju [ʃu:] seven; *(för sms. jfr fem-)* **sjua** *s1* seven **sjuarmad** *a5* seven-branched *(ljusstake* candlestick)
sjubb [ʃ-] *s2* [North American] rac[c]oon
sjud|a [ʃ-] *sjöd -it* simmer; seethe *(äv. bildl.*); *~ av vrede* seethe with anger; *~nde liv* seething life **-it** *sup. av sjuda*
sju|dubbel [ˣʃu:-] sevenfold **-dundrande** [-ˣdund-] *a4* terrific **-falt** sevenfold; seven times *(värre* worse) **-jäkla** [-ˣjä:k-] *a4, ett ~ liv* a hell of a life
sjuk [ʃ-] *a1* **1** *(predikativt)* ill; *(attr. o. illamående)* sick; *(dålig)* indisposed, unwell; *den ~e* the sick person, *(på sjukhus)* the patient; *de ~a* the sick; *bli ~* get (fall, be taken) ill; *mitt ~a knä* my bad knee; *svårt ~* seriously ill; *ligga ~ i mässling* be down with the measles; *äta sig ~* eat o.s. sick; *~ av (i)* suffering from, *bildl.* sick with; *jag blir ~ bara jag tänker på det* the mere thought of it makes me sick **2** *bildl., saken är ~* it's a shady business; *ett ~t samvete* a guilty conscience; *han ber för sin ~a mor* that's one for her and two for himself; *~ efter (på)* eager *(vard.* dying) for
sjuk|a [ʃ-] *s1, se sjukdom; engelska ~n* rickets; *spanska ~n* the Spanish flu; *det är hela ~n* that's the whole trouble **-anmäla** *~ ngn (sig)* report s.b. (report) sick (ill); *-anmäld* reported sick (ill) **-anmälan** notification of illness **-avdelning** ward, infirmary **-avdrag** deduction for sickness **-besök** visiting the sick; *(läkares)* visit to a patient, sick visit **-bädd** sickbed; *vid ~en* at the bedside **-dom** [-dɔmm] *s2* illness, ill-health; *(speciell o. bildl.)* disease; *(ont)* complaint, disorder; *ärftlig ~* hereditary disease
sjukdoms|alstrande *a4* pathogenic **-bild** pathological picture, picture of the (a) disease **-fall** case [of illness] **-orsak** cause of a (the) disease **-sym(p)tom** sympton of a (the) disease
sjuk|ersättning sickness benefit (allowance) **-försäkring** health insurance **-försäkringsbesked** health insurance card **-gymnast** physiotherapist **-gymnastik** physiotherapy, remedial exercises *(pl)* **-hem** nursing home
sjukhus hospital **-direktör** hospital manager **-dräkt** hospital uniform **-läkare** hospital physician (surgeon) **-vård** hospital treatment (care)
sjuk|intyg medical (doctor's) certificate **-journal** case record; *(för en patient)* case sheet **-kassa** *(allmän* regional) health insurance office **-kassekort** health insurance card **-ledig** *vara ~* be on sick leave **-ledighet** sick leave **-lig** [-u:-] *a1* infirm, weak in health; sickly;

bildl. morbid *(misstänksamhet* suspiciousness) **-lighet** [-u:-] infirmity, ill-health; morbidity **-ling** [-u:-] sick person, patient; invalid **-lista** sick list **-lön** sick pay
sjuk|na [-u:-] fall (be taken) ill *(i* with); sicken **-penning** sickness benefit (allowance) **-penningsklass** sickness benefit category (group) **-pension** disablement pension **-permission** sick leave **-rapport** medical report **-rum** sick room **-sal** [hospital] ward **-skriva** *~ ngn* put s.b. on the sick list; *~ sig* report sick (ill); *-skriven* sick-listed, reported sick **-skötare** [male] nurse **-sköterska** nurse; *(examinerad)* trained (staff, *AE.* graduate) nurse
sjuksköterske|elev student nurse **-skola** nurses' training school **-uniform** nurse's uniform **-utbildning** nursing training
sjuk|stuga cottage hospital **-syster** *se sjuksköterska* **-säng** *se sjukbädd* **-transport** conveyance of patients **-vård** medical care (attendance), nursing; care of the sick; *fri ~* free medical attention (treatment) **-vårdare** male nurse, paramedic; *mil.* medical orderly
sjukvårds|artiklar *pl* sanitary (medical) articles **-biträde** assistant nurse, [hospital] orderly **-ersättning** medical expenses allowance **-kunnig** trained in nursing the sick
sjumila|steg *gå med ~* walk with seven-league strides **-stövlar** *pl* seven-league boots
sjunde [ʃ-] seventh; *i ~ himlen* in [the] seventh heaven **-dagsadventist** Seventh-Day Adventist **-del** seventh [part], one seventh
sjunga [ʃ-] *sjöng sjungit* sing; *(om fågel äv.)* warble; *~ falskt* sing out of tune; *~ rent* sing in tune; *~ ngns lov* sing a p.'s praises; *~ på sista versen* be on one's last legs, draw to its close; *~ in (på grammofon)* record; *~ ut* sing out, *bildl.* speak out, speak one's mind **sjungit** *sup. av sjunga*
sjunk|a [ʃ-] *sjönk -it* sink; *(om fartyg äv.)* founder, go down; *(falla)* drop, fall *(t. botten* to the bottom); *(minska)* decrease *(i antal* in numbers); *(i värde)* depreciate, decline, sink, fall; *febern -er* the fever is abating; *kaffet står och -er* the coffee is settling; *priserna -er* prices are falling (declining), prices show a downward tendency; *solen -er* the sun is setting; *termometern -er* the temperature is falling; *önska att man kunde ~ genom jorden* wish one could sink through the floor; *känna modet ~* lose courage (heart); *~ i ngns aktning* go down in a p.'s estimation; *~ i glömska* sink into oblivion; *~ i vanmakt* faint away; *~ ihop (bildl.)* break down, collapse; *~ ner på en stol* sink down on to a chair; *~ till marken* drop to the ground; *~ till ngns fötter* fall at a p.'s feet; *~ undan* sink, subside; *han är djupt -en* he has sunk very low
sjunkbomb depth charge (bomb) **sjunkit** *sup. av sjunka*
sju|rygg *zool.* lumpfish, lumpsucker **-sovare** [-å-] **1** *zool.* dormouse **2** *pers.* lie-abed, sluggard **-stjärnan** *sg, best. form,* **-stjärnorna** *pl, best. form* the Pleiades *(pl)* **-särdeles** [-ˣsä:r-] *vard.* terrific **-tillhållarlås** mortise (mortice) lock
sjuttio [ˣʃuttiⓞ, ʃutt-, *vard.* ˣʃutti, ʃutti]

seventy **sjuttionde** [ˣʃuttiå-] seventieth **sjuttioåring** septuagenarian
sjutton [ˣʃuttån] seventeen; *aj som ~!* by Jove!, Good Lord!; *det var dyrt som ~* it cost a packet; *full i ~* full of mischief; *för ~ gubbar* for goodness sake; *nej för ~!* Good Lord, no!; *ge ~ i att (låta bli)* stop, leave off, *(strunta i)* not bother; *ge sig ~ på att* bet your life that; *det vore väl ~ om* it would be a wonder if **sjuttonde** seventeenth **sjuttonhundratalet** the eighteenth century
sjå [ʃ-] *s7, vard.* big (tough) job **-are** docker longshoreman, stevedore
sjåp [ʃ-] *s7* [silly] goose, ninny **sjåpa** *rfl* be silly, act the ninny **sjåpig** *al* silly, foolish; *vard.* namby-pamby **sjåpighet** silliness *etc.*
själ [ʃ-] *s2* 1 *filos., psykol., rel.-hist.* soul; *(ande)* spirit; *~ens behov* spiritual needs 2 *(sinne)* soul, mind; *det skar mig in i ~en* it cut me to the heart (quick); *få ro i sin ~* get peace of mind; *i ~ och hjärta* at heart, in one's heart of hearts; *med liv och ~* body and soul; *två ~ar och en tanke* two minds with but a single thought; *~arnas sympati* spiritual affinity; *min ~ tror jag inte* upon my soul if it's not 3 *pers.* soul; *vara ~en i ngt* be [the life and] soul of s.th.; *där fanns inte en ~* there wasn't a soul; *en glad ~* a jolly fellow; *varenda ~ (vard.)* every man jack
själa|glad overjoyed, delighted **-herde** pastor, shepherd of souls **-mässa** requiem **-nöd** anguish of the soul, spiritual agony **-ringning** [death] knell, passing (death) bell **-sörjare** spiritual guide **-tåget** *ligga i ~* be dying, be breathing one's last **-vandring** transmigration [of souls] **-vård** cure of souls, spiritual charge of a parish
själfull soulful *(ansikte* face); *(anderik)* animated *(föredrag* lecture) **-het** soulfulness; animation
Själland [ˈʃäll-] *n* Zealand
själlös soulless; spiritless; *(livlös)* inanimate **-het** soullessness *etc.*
själs|adel nobility of mind **-dödande** soul-destroying, deadly **-egenskap** mental quality **-fin** refined, noble **-frånvarande** absent-minded **-frände** kindred spirit; *vara ~r (äv.)* sympathize **-frändskap** congeniality of mind, spiritual affinity **-förmögenhet** faculty, mental ability **-gåvor** *pl* intellectual (mental) gifts **-kval** mental suffering, agony **-lig** [-ä:-] *al* mental; *(andlig)* spiritual **-liv** intellectual (spiritual) life **-sjuk** *(sinnessjuk)* mentally ill; *(hypokondrisk)* hypochondriac[al] **-strid** mental struggle **-styrka** strength of mind
själv [ʃ-] 1 myself, yourself, himself, herself, itself, oneself; *pl* ourselves, yourselves, themselves; *det har jag gjort* ~ I did it myself; *han har ~ skrivit ...* he has written ... himself; *~ är bästa dräng* if you want a thing done well, do it yourself; *bli sig ~ igen* be oneself again; *komma ~* come personally (in person); *om jag får säga det ~* if I may say so myself; *tack ~!* thank you!; *vara sig ~ nog* be self-sufficient; *det kan du vara ~! (vard.)* so are you!; *av sig ~* of oneself, spontaneously, *(frivilligt)* voluntarily; *för sig ~ (avsides)* aside; *tala för*

sig ~ talk to oneself; *i sig ~* in itself; *hon heter A. i sig ~* her maiden name is A.; *på sig ~ känner man andra* one judges others by o.s. 2 *hon är blygsamheten* ~ she is modesty itself; *~e (~aste) kungen* the king himself (in person); *på ~a födelsedagen* on the very birthday; *i ~a verket* as a matter of fact; *han gör ~a grovarbetet* he does the real heavy (ground) work
själv|aktning self-respect **-antändning** spontaneous ignition, self-ignition **-bedrägeri** self-deception, self-delusion **-befruktning** self-fertilization; *bot.* self-pollination **-behärskning** self-control, self-command, self-restraint **-bekännelse** confession **-belåten** self-satisfied; complacent **-bestämmanderätt** right of self-determination, autonomy **-betjäning** self-service **-betjäningsbutik** self-service store **-betraktelse** self-contemplation, introspection **-bevarelsedrift** instinct of self-preservation **-bindare** *lantbr.* [reaper] binder **-biografi** autobiography **-biografisk** autobiographical **-deklaration** income tax return *(AE.* report) **-disciplin** self-discipline **-dö** die out of itself; *ett ~tt djur* an animal that has died from natural causes **-fallen** *a3* obvious, apparent **-fallenhet** matter of course **-förakt** self-contempt **-förbränning** spontaneous combustion **-förebråelse** self-reproach **-förgudning** self-glorification **-förhävelse** presumption **-förnekelse** self-denial **-försakelse** self-denial **-försvar** *(till* in) self-defence **-försörjande** *a4* self-supporting **-försörjning** self-sufficiency **-förtroende** self-confidence, self-reliance **-förverkligande** self-realization, self-fulfilment **-förvållad** *a5* self-inflicted
själv|gjord self-made **-god** self-righteous **-godhet** self-righteousness **-hjälp** self-help; *hjälp till ~* assistance supplementary to one's own efforts **-hushåll** *ha ~* do one's own housekeeping **-hushållning** economy based on domestic production [of necessities] **-häftande** *a4* [self-]adhesive **-härskare** autocrat **-hävdelse** self-assertion **-hävdelsebegär** urge to assert o.s. **-ironi** irony directed against o.s. **-ironisk** ironic at one's own expense
självisk [ˈʃäll-] *a5* selfish, egoistic[al] **-het** [ˈʃäll-] selfishness, egoism
själv|klar obvious; *det är ~t* it is a matter of course, it goes without saying **-kontroll** self-command **-kopierande** *a4* self-copying **-kostnad** prime (production) cost **-kostnadspris** cost price; *till ~* at cost [price] **-kritik** self-criticism **-kritisk** self-critical **-kännedom** self-knowledge **-känsla** self-esteem **-ljud** vowel [sound] **-lockig** naturally curly **-lysande** luminous *(färg* paint) **-länsande** *a4* self-bailing **-lärd** self-taught; *en ~* an autodidact
själv|mant [-a:-] *adv* of one's own accord, voluntarily **-medlidande** self-pity **-medvetande** self-assurance **-medveten** self-assured **-mord** *(begå* commit) suicide **-mordsförsök** attempted suicide **-mordskandidat** would-be suicide **-mål** *sport., göra ~* shoot the ball *(etc.)* into one's own goal **-mördare** suicide **-plågeri** self-torture **-porträtt** self-portrait **-påtagen** *a5* self-assumed **-rannsakan** self-ex-

amination **-registrerande** [-j-] *a4* self-recording **-reglerande** *a4* self-regulating, self--adjusting **-renande** self-cleaning **-risk** *försäkr.* excess, [deductible] franchise **-rådig** self--willed, wilful

själv|servering self-service [restaurant], cafeteria **-skriven** *a3*, *han är ~ som ordförande* he is just the man for chairman; *han är ~ till platsen* he is sure to get the post **-smörjande** *a4* self-lubricating (*lager* bearing) **-spelande** *~ piano* pianola (*varumärke*), *AE.* player piano **-spricka** *s1* chap; *få -spricckor på händerna* get chapped hands **-start** self-starter **-studium** self-instruction, self-tuition, private study **-styre[lse]** self-government, autonomy; *lokal ~* local [self-]government **-ständig** *a1* independent; self-governed **-ständighet** independence **-ständighetsförklaring** declaration of independence **-suggestion** autosuggestion

självsvåld self-indulgence; self-will **-ig** *a1* undisciplined; self-willed

själv|svängning self-oscillation **-sådd** *a5* self--sown **-säker** self-confident, self-assured **-tagen** *a5* self-assumed (*makt* power); usurped (*rätt* right) **-tillräcklig** self-satisfied; self-sufficient **-tillit** self-reliance **-tryck** gravity **-tvätt** self-service laundry, Launderette (*varumärke*), *AE.* Laundromat (*varumärke*) **-uppdragande** *a4* selfwinding **-uppfyllande** *a4* self-fulfilling **-uppoffrande** self-sacrificing **-uppoffring** self-sacrifice **-upptagen** self--centred **-utlösare** *foto.* self-timer **-utnämnd** *a5* self-styled **-utplånande** *a4* self-effacing **-vald** (*-utnämnd*) self-elected; (*frivillig*) self--chosen **-verkande** automatic, self-acting **-verksamhet** self-activity **-ägande** *a4, ~ bönder* owner-farmers, freeholders **-ändamål** end in itself **-övervinnelse** self-mastery; *det kostade mig verklig ~ att* it was hard to bring myself to

själätte [ʃ-] sixth **-del** sixth [part]

själö [ʃö:] *s2* **1** (*in-*) lake; (*hav*) sea; *gå i ~n* (*dränka sig*) drown o.s.; *~n går upp* the ice breaks up; *~n ligger* the lake is coated with ice; *på öppna ~n* on the open sea; *sätta en båt i ~n* put out a boat; *till ~ss* at sea; *gå till ~ss* (*om pers.*) become a sailor, go to sea, (*om fartyg*) put [out] to sea; *till lands och ~ss* on land and sea; *ute till ~ss* in the open sea; *kasta pengarna i ~n* throw money away; *kasta yxan i ~n* throw up the sponge; *regnet bildade ~ar på gatorna* the rain lay in great pools in the streets **2** (*-gång*; *stört-*) sea, wave; *hög ~* high (heavy) sea; *få en ~ över sig* ship a sea; *tåla ~n* stand the sea, be a good sailor

själö|befäl ship's officers (*pl*) **-befälsskola** school of nautical studies **-björn** *bildl., se sjöbuss 1* **-bod** boathouse **-borre** [-å-] *s2, zool.* sea urchin **-bris** sea breeze **-buss 1** *bildl.* sea dog, salt **2** (*farkost*) ferryboat

själöd *imperf. av sjuda*

själö|duglig seaworthy **-elefant** elephant seal, sea elephant **-farande** *a4* seafaring (*folk* nation); *en ~* a mariner (seafaring man, seafarer) **-farare** seafarer **-fart** (*skeppsfart*) navigation; (*sjöhandel*) shipping [business, trade]; *handel och ~* commerce (trade) and shipping **-farts-**

bok discharge book **-fartsmuseum** maritime (nautical) museum **-fartsverket** the Swedish national administration of shipping and navigation **-flygplan** seaplane, hydroplane **-folk** *pl* (*-män*) seamen **-fågel** aquatic bird, sea bird (fowl) **-förklaring** [captain's] protest; *avge ~* enter (make) a protest **-försvar** naval defence **-försäkring** marine insurance **-gräs** seaweed **-grön** sea-green **-gurka** *zool.* sea cucumber **-gång** roll[ing], [heavy, high] sea **-hjälte** naval hero **-häst** sea horse **-jungfru** mermaid

själö|kadett naval cadet, midshipman **-kapten** [sea] captain, master mariner **-ko** sea cow **-kort** [nautical, marine] chart **-krig** naval war, (warfare) **-krigshögskola** naval staff college **-krigsskola** naval college **-lag** maritime law **-ledes** by water (sea) **-lejon** sea lion **-lilja** sea lily **-lägenhet** *med första ~* by the first boat **-lök** sea squill (onion) **-makt** sea power; (*örlogsflotta*) naval force **-malm** bog-iron ore **-man** sailor, seaman; mariner

själömans|biff *ung.* casserole of beef, potatoes and onions **-blus** sailor's blouse **-hem** seamen's home

själömanskap *s7* seamanship

själömans|kista seaman's (sea) chest **-kostym** sailor suit **-krage** sailor collar **-mission** seamen's mission **-mössa** sailor's cap **-präst** seamen's chaplain **-uttryck** nautical expression **-visa** sailor's song, shanty

själö|mil nautical mile **-militär I** *a1* naval **II** *s3* naval man **-märke** navigation mark, seamark; buoy beacon

själönk [ʃ-] *imperf. av sjunka*

själö|nöd distress **-odjur** sea monster **-officer** naval officer **-olycka** accident at sea **-orm** sea serpent **-penna** *zool.* sea pen **-ranunkel** great spearwort **-rapport** weather forecast for sea areas **-reglering** regulation of water level in lakes **-resa** [sea] voyage **-räddning** sea rescue; (*organisation*) lifeboat service (institution), *AE.* coastguard **-räddningsfartyg** rescue launch; lifeboat **-rätt** maritime law; (*domstol*) maritime court **-rövare** pirate **-röveri** piracy **-scout** sea scout **-seger** naval victory, victory at sea **-sidan** *från ~* from the sea[ward side]; *åt ~* towards the sea **-sjuk** seasick **-sjuka** seasickness **-skadad** *a5* seadamaged **-skum 1** *eg.* sea foam **2** *miner.* meerschaum **-skumspipa** meerschaum **-slag** naval battle, action at sea; *bildl.* wet party **-stad** seaport [town] **-stjärna** starfish **-strid** naval encounter **-stridskrafter** *pl* naval forces **-stövel** sea boot **-säker** seaworthy **-sätta** launch **-sättning** launch[ing] **-term** nautical term **-tomt** beach lot, lakeside site **-tunga** *zool.* [European] sole **-van** used (accustomed) to the sea; *bli ~* (*äv.*) find one's sea legs **-vana** familiarity with the sea **-vatten** lake (sea) water **-väg** sea route, seaway; *ta ~en* go by sea **-värdig** seaworthy **-värnskår** auxiliary naval corps

s.k. *förk. för så kallad* so-called

ska *vard. för skall, se* 1 *skola*

skabb *s3* [the] itch; scabies; (*hos djur*) mange **-ig** *a1* scabious, scabby; *neds.* mangy

skab'rös *a1* scabrous, indecent, obscene

skad|a I *s1* injury (*på* to); *med. äv.* insult; (*för-*

skadeanmälan–skallskada 470

ödelse) damage; *(motsats nytta)* harm, mischief; *(förlust)* loss; *('synd')* pity; *anställa ~* cause (do) damage; *avhjälpa en ~* repair an injury; *av ~n blir man vis* once bitten, twice shy; *bli vis av ~n* learn by painful experience; *det är ingen ~ skedd* there is no harm done; *det är ngn ~ på maskinen* s.th. has gone wrong (there is s.th. the matter) with the machine; *det är ~ att* it is a pity that; *det var ~!* what a pity!; *erhålla lätta (svåra) -or* be slightly (seriously) injured (hurt); *ta ~* suffer *(av* from), *(om sak)* be damaged *(av* by); *ta ~n igen* make up for it; *tillfoga ...* ~ inflict damage on ... **II** *v1, pers.* hurt, injure; *(såra)* wound; *(sak)* damage; *abstr.* damage, injure *(ngns rykte* a p.'s reputation); *det ~r inte att försöka* there is no harm in trying; *det skulle inte ~ om* it would do no harm if; *~ sig* be (get) hurt, hurt o.s.; *~ sig i handen* hurt one's hand
skade|anmälan notification of damage **-djur** noxious animal; *koll.* vermin *(pl)* **-ersättning** compensation [for damage], indemnification; indemnity **-glad** spiteful, malicious **-glädje** malicious pleasure, malice **-görelse** [-j-] damage **-insekt** noxious insect **-reglering** settlement [of claims], claims adjustment
skadeslös *hålla ngn ~* indemnify s.b.
skade|stånd *s7* damages *(pl); begära ~* claim damages **-ståndsanspråk** compensation claim, claim for damages **-ståndsskyldig** liable to pay damages **-verkan** damage; deleterious effect
skad|lig [ˣska:d-] *a1* injurious, harmful *(för* to); noxious, unwholesome *(mat* food); *(menlig)* detrimental *(för* to); *ha ~ inverkan på* have a detrimental effect on **-skjuta** wound
skaffa 1 *(an-)* get, procure *(åt* for); *(finna)* find *(arbete* work), furnish *(bevis* proofs); *(förse med)* provide with; *(skicka efter)* send for; *(~ hit)* bring; *~ barn till världen* bring children into the world; *~ ngn bekymmer* cause s.b. anxiety; *~ kunder* attract customers; *~ sig fiender* make enemies; *jag skall ~ pengarna åt dig* I'll find (raise) the money for you; *~ ur världen* do away with; *~ fram* produce; *~ undan* remove, get out of the way **2** *(göra)* do; *jag vill inte ha med honom att ~* I don't want to have anything to do with him **3** *sjö. (äta)* eat **4** *rfl* procure *(etc.)* [for] o.s.; *(köpa)* buy o.s., acquire *(nya kläder* new clothes); make *(vänner* friends); obtain *(upplysningar* information), attain *(kunskaper* knowledge); *(ådraga sig)* contract *(en förkylning* a cold; *skulder* debts); *(förse sig med)* furnish (provide) o.s. with; *(finna)* find *(tillfälle* an opportunity)
skafferi larder, pantry **skaffning** *sjö. (måltid)* meal; food
ska[f]föttes [ˣska:-, ˣskaff-] *ligga ~* lie head to foot
skaft *s7* **1** *(handtag)* handle *(på verktyg o.d. äv.)* shaft; *(på stövel, strumpa)* leg; *sätta ~ på* furnish with a handle, fix handle to **2** *bot.* stalk, stem **3** *bildl., ha huvudet på ~* have one's head screwed on the right way; *med ögonen på ~* with one's eyes starting (popping) out of one's head
Skagen ['ska:-] *n* the Skaw

Skagerack ['ska:-] *n* the Skagerrak
skaka 1 *(försätta i skakning)* shake; *(friare o. bildl.)* agitate *(sinnena* the senses), convulse; *~ hand med* shake hands with; *berättelsen ~de henne djupt* she was deeply shaken by the story; *~ ngt ur ärmen (bildl.)* do s.th. offhand (straight off) **2** *(häftigt röras)* shake *(av* with); *(darra)* shiver *(av köld* with cold); *fys.* vibrate ; *(vagga)* rock; *(om åkdon)* jog, bump *(fram* along); *samhället ~de i sina grundvalar* society was shaken to its [very] foundations; *~ av skratt* shake (rock) with laughter; *~ på huvudet* shake one's head **3** *(med betonad partikel) ~ av [sig]* shake off; *~ om* shake up, stir **skakande** *a4* shaking; *(upp-)* harrowing *(skildring* description)
skak|el ['skack-, 'ska:-] *s2* shaft; *hoppa över -larna (bildl.)* kick over the traces, run riot
skak|is ['ska:-] *oböjligt a, vard., känna sig ~* feel shaky (jittery) **-ning** [-a:-] shake *(på* of); shaking; *(darrning)* trembling; *~ar i motorn* vibrations in the engine
skal *s7 (hårt ~)* shell; *(skorpa äv.)* crust; *(apelsin-, äppel- etc.)* peel; *(banan-, druv-, potatis-)* skin; *(gurk-, melon-)* rind; *(på ris)* husk; *(avskalat)* peelings, parings *(pl); sluta sig inom sitt ~* retire into one's shell
1 skala *v1* [un]shell; *(apelsin, potatis)* peel; *(äpple)* pare; *~ av* peel *(etc.)* off
2 skala *s1, mat., mus.* scale; *(på radio)* dial; *i stor (liten) ~* on a large (small) scale; *en karta i ~ 1:50 000* a map on the scale of 1:50,000; *ordnad efter fallande ~* arranged on a descending scale
skalbagge beetle; *AE. äv.* bug; *fack.* coleopteran, coleopteron
skald *s3* poet **skalda** make poetry
skalde|gåva poetic gift, poetic[al] talent **-konst** poetry, poesy **-stycke** poem, piece of poetry
skaldinna poetess
skaldjur shellfish, crustacean
skalenlig [-e:n-] *a1* made to scale
1 skalk *s2 (brödkant)* crust; *(ostkant)* rind
2 skalk *s2 (skälm)* rogue, wag; *ha en ~ i ögat* have a twinkle in one's eye
skalka *sjö.* batten down *(luckorna* the hatches)
skalkaktig *a1* roguish, waggish **-het** roguishness *etc.*
skalkas *dep* joke, jest
skalkniv skinning knife
1 skall *pres. av 1 skola*
2 skall *s7 (hund-)* bark; *(ljud)* clang, ring, ringing; *ge ~* bark
skalla 1 *(genljuda)* clang, ring; *(eka)* resound; *ett ~nde skratt* a peal of laughter **2** *sport.* head
skallbas base of the skull
skalle *s2* skull; *anat.* cranium; *tekn.* head; *vard.* pate; noddle; *dansk ~* butt with the head
skallerorm rattlesnake
skallfraktur fracture of the skull
skall|gång *s2* chase, search; *gå ~ efter* search for, organize a search for **-gångskedja** searchers *(pl); jakt.* beaters *(pl)*
skallig *a1* bald **-het** baldness
skallra I *s1* rattle **II** *v1* rattle; *(klappra)* clatter; *(om tänder)* chatter
skallskada skull injury

skalm *s2* **1** (*skakel*) shaft **2** ~*ar* (*på glasögon*) bows, (*på sax*) scissor-blades
skalmeja [-ˣmejja] *s1* shawn
skalmodell model built to scale, scale model
skalp *s3* scalp
skal'pell *s3* scalpel
skalpera scalp, take s.b.'s scalp
skalv *s7* quake; (*jord-*) earthquake
ska'lär *a1* scalar (*storhet* quantity)
skalömsning shedding of the shell
skalövning *mus.* scale practice
skam [skamm] *s2* **1** (*blygsel*) shame; (*ngt -ligt*) dishonour; (*skändlighet*) infamy; ~ *till sägandes* to my (*etc.*) shame; *fy ~!* shame on you!; *det var inte fy ~* that was not bad at all; *för ~s skull* for very shame; *bita huvudet av ~men* be past (lost to) shame; *nu går ~[men] på torra land* that's the last straw **2** (*vanära*) shame; disgrace (*för* for, to); ~ *den som ...!* shame on him that ...!; *det är ingen ~* there is no disgrace (*att förlora* in losing); *komma på ~* be frustrated; *få stå där med ~men* be put to shame **-bud** *ung.* extraordinarily low initial bid (offer) **-fila 1** *möblerna var ~de* the furniture was the worse for wear; *med ~t rykte* with a tarnished reputation **2** *sjö.* chafe **-fläck** stain, taint; *vara en ~ för* be a disgrace to **-grepp** *eg.* grabbing of the opponent's genitals; *bildl.* hit below the belt **-känsla** sense of shame **-lig** *a1* shameful, disgraceful; (*vanhedrande*) dishonourable; *det är verkligen ~t att* it is really disgraceful that **-ligen, -ligt** *adv* outrageously **-lös** shameless; (*fräck*) impudent **-löshet** shamelessness; impudence **-påle** pillory; *stå vid ~n* (*bildl.*) be publicly disgraced **-sen** *a3* ashamed (*över* of) *AE. vard.* mean **-senhet** shame **-vrå** *stå i ~n* stand in the corner
skan'dal *s3* scandal; *ställa till ~* cause a scandal; *vard.* kick up a row **-artad** [-a:r-] *a5* scandalous **-hungrig** fond of scandal
skandal|isera disgrace **-omsusad** *a5, ung.* scandal-prone **-tidning** scandal sheet **-unge** potential scandal
skandalös *a1* scandalous
skander|a scan **-ing** scanning, scansion
skandi'nav *s3* Scandinavian **Skandinavien** [-'na:-] *n* Scandinavia
skandinav|isk [-'na:-] *a5* Scandinavian **-ism** Scandinavianism
skandium ['skann-] *s8, kem.* scandium
skank *s2, s1, vard.* shank, leg
skans *s2* **1** *mil.* redoubt; (*kastell*) fortlet; *siste man på ~en* (*bildl.*) the last survivor, the last one out **2** *sjö.* forecastle, fo'c's'le
skapa create, make; (*alstra*) produce; (*framkalla*) cause, give rise to, engender; ~ *förutsättningar för* pave the way for; ~ *sig en förmögenhet* make a fortune; *du är som ~d för uppgiften* you are just the man (*etc.*) for the job; ~ *om sig* transform o.s. (*till* into) **skapande I** *a4* creative (*konstnär* artist); constructive (*sinne* mind); *inte ett ~ grand* not a mortal thing **II** *s6* creation, creating *etc.*
skapar|e creator **-förmåga** creative ability **-glädje** creative joy **-kraft** creative force
skapelse creation; ~*n* (*världen*) creation; ~*ns krona* the crown of creation **-berättelse**

creation narrative (myth)
skap|lig [-a:-] *a1* passable, tolerable, not too bad **-ligt** [-a:-] *adv*, ~ [*nog*] tolerably well, well enough **-lynne** character, disposition **-nad** *s3* shape, form, figure
skar *imperf. av 2 skära*
skar|a *s1* crowd, multitude; *mil.* troop, band (*soldater* of soldiers); *en ~ arbetare* a team (gang) of workmen; *en brokig ~* a motley crowd; *en utvald ~* a select group; *samla sig i -or kring* flock round
skarabé *s3* scarab
skare *s2* crust [on the snow]; ~*n bär* the snow surface is hard enough to bear
skarp I *a1* (*om kniv, spets, vinkel, sluttning o.d.*) sharp; (*om egg, rakkniv, blåst o.d.*) keen; (*besk*) strong (*smak* taste); ~*t angrepp* sharp attack; ~*a hugg* (*äv. bildl.*) hard blows; *en ~ intelligens* a keen intelligence, *pers.* a man of keen intelligens; ~*a konturer* (*gränser*) distinct (clear-cut) outlines (limits); ~ *kritik* sharp criticism; ~ *köld* piercing cold; ~*t ljus* glaring light; ~ *ammunition* live ammunition; *en ~ tunga* a sharp tongue **II** *s2*, *hugga i på ~en* set to work with a will; *ta itu med ngn på ~en* take s.b. really in hand; *säga till på ~en* give s.b. a ticking-off
skarp|blick acute perception, penetration **-ladda** load with live cartridges **-rättare** executioner **-sill** sprat **-sinne** acumen, penetration, ingenuity; (*klarsyn*) perspicacity **-sinnig** *a1* keen, acute; (*klarsynt*) perspicacious, shrewd **-skjutning** firing with live ammunition **-skuren** *a5*, *-skurna drag* clear-cut features **-skytt** sharpshooter **-slipa** sharpen, whet; ~*d* (*äv.*) sharp-edged **-synt** [-y:-] *a1* sharp-sighted **-sås** *kokk.* sauce piquante **-ögd** *a1*, *se -synt*
skarsnö crusty snow
1 skarv *s2, zool.* cormorant
2 skarv *s2* (*fog*) joint; (*söm*) seam; (*-bit*) lengthening-piece; *bildl.* interval
skarv|a 1 (*hopfoga*) join; *tekn.* joint, splice; (*förlänga*) lengthen; ~ *till* add, *sömn.* let in **2** (*ljuga*) stretch a point, embroider the truth **-sladd** *elektr.* extension flex (cord) **-yxa** *adz[e]*
skat|a *s1* magpie **-bo** magpie's nest
skatt *s3* **1** (*klenod*) treasure (*äv. bildl.*) **2** (*t. staten*) tax; (*t. kommun*) local taxes, *i Storbritannien* [town] rate, *AE.* city (municipal) taxes; (*på vissa varor*) duty; ~*er* (*allm.*) [rates and] taxes; *direkt ~* direct tax; *indirekt ~* indirect tax
skatta 1 (*betala skatt*) pay taxes (*etc.*); *han ~r för 30 000 om året* he is assessed at 30,000 a year **2** (*plundra*) plunder, rifle; ~ *en bikupa på honung* take honey from a beehive **3** (*upp-*) estimate, value; *min högt ~de vän* my highly esteemed friend **4** (*betala tribut*) pay tribute to; ~ *åt förgängelsen* pay the debt to nature, go the way of all flesh **5** ~ *sig lycklig* count o.s. fortunate (lucky)
skatte|avdrag tax deduction (allowance) **-belopp** amount of tax **-betalare** taxpayer **-börda** tax burden **-flykt** tax evasion **-fri** tax-free; (*om vara*) duty-free, free of duty **-frihet** exemption from taxes **-fusk** tax evasion **-fuskare** tax dodger **-förmåga** tax-paying ability

S

-höjning increase in taxation **-inkomst** revenue from taxation **-krona** tax rate; *i Storbritannien ung.* rate poundage **-kvitto** *(för fordon)* motor tax disc **-lagstiftning** fiscal (tax) legislation **-lättnad** tax relief **-medel** *pl* tax revenue *(sg)* **-myndighet** tax[ation] authority **-paradis** tax haven **-planering** tax avoidance **-pliktig** *(om pers.)* liable to pay tax[es]; *(om vara etc.)* taxable; *~ inkomst* taxable (assessable) income **-politik** fiscal policy **-rätt** taxation law **-sats** tax rate **-skala** tax scale **-skolk** tax evasion **-smitare** tax dodger **-sänkning** tax reduction (relief) **-tabell** table of tax rates **-teknisk** fiscal **-termin** tax payment period **-uppbörd** tax collection, collection of taxes **-utskott** *~et* [the Swedish Parliamentary] standing committee on taxation **-verk** tax department (division); *i Storbritannien ung.* Board of Inland Revenue, *AE. ung.* Inland Revenue Service **-återbäring** tax refund

skatt|grävare treasure hunter **-gömma** [treasure] cache **-kammare** treasury **-kammarväxel** treasury bill **-mas** tax collector **-mästare** treasurer **-ning** *fack.* approximation, estimate **-pliktig** *se skattepliktig* **-sedel** income-tax demand note; *AE.* tax-bill **-skriva** tax **-skyldig** liable to pay tax[es] **-sökare** treasure hunter

skava *v2* chafe *(äv. ~ på)*; scrape; gall *(hål på skinnet* one's skin)*; *~ hål på* rub a hole in

skavank [-'vaŋk] *s3* flaw, fault; *(krämpa)* ailment

skavsår sore

ske [ʃe:] *v4* happen, occur; *(verkställas)* be done; *~ Guds vilja!* God's will be done!; *skall ~!* [all] right!; *ingen skada ~dd* no harm done; *allt som händer och ~r* all that is going on; *vad stort ~r det ~r tyst* noble deeds are done in silence

sked [ʃ-] *s2* spoon; *en ~ ... (som mått)* a spoonful of ...; *ta ~en i vacker hand* make the best of it

skeda [ʃ-] *kem.* separate, segregate

sked|and [ʃ-] *zool.* shoveller **-blad** bowl of a spoon **-drag** spoon[bait]

skede [ʃ-] *s6* phase, period; stage

sked|full spoonful *(soppa* of soup)* **-skaft** handle of a spoon

skedvatten [ʃ-] *kem.* aqua fortis

skedvis by the spoonful

skeende [ʃ-] *s6* course of events

skela [ʃ-] squint *(på vänster öga* in the left eye)*

ske'lett *s7* skeleton; *bildl. äv.* framework

skel|ning [ˣʃe:l-] squint **-ögd** *a1* squint-eyed, squinting;; *vara ~ (äv.)* have a squint

skelört [ʃ-] greater celandine, swallowwort

1 sken [ʃ-] *s7* **1** *(ljus)* light; *(starkt äv.)* glare **2** *(falskt yttre)* appearance[s *pl*], semblance, guise; *~et bedrar* appearances are deceptive; *han har ~et emot sig* appearances are against him; *hålla ~et uppe* keep up appearances; *ge sig ~ av att vara* make a show of being; *under ~ av vänskap* under the semblance (cloak) of friendship

2 sken [ʃ-] *n (vilt lopp)* bolting; *falla i ~* bolt

3 sken *imperf. av skina*

1 skena [ʃ-] *v1* bolt, run away; *en ~nde häst* a runaway horse

2 skena [ʃ-] *s1* bar, band; *(järnvägs-)* rail; *med.* splint

sken|anfall [ʃ-] feigned attack; *mil. äv.* diversion **-bar** *a1* apparent, seeming **-barligen** [-a:-] obviously **-bart** [-a:-] *adv* apparently, seemingly

skenben [ʃ-] *anat.* shinbone, tibia

sken|bild [ʃ-] phantom, distorted picture **-död I** *a1* apparently dead **II** *s2* apparent death **-frukt** pseudocarp, false fruit **-helig** hypocritical, canting **-helighet** hypocrisy, cant **-köp** sham (mock) purchase **-liv** semblance of life **-manöver** diversion, feint

skenskarv *järnv.* rail joint

skepnad [ˣʃe:p-] *s3* **1** *(gestalt)* figure; shape, guise **2** *(spöke)* phantom

skepp [ʃ-] *s7* **1** *(fartyg)* ship; vessel, craft; *bränna sina ~ (bildl.)* burn one's boats **2** *arkit.* nave; *(sido-)* aisle **3** *boktr.* galley **skeppa** ship

skepparle master; skipper **-brev** master's certificate **-historia** sailor's yarn **-krans** Newgate fringe (frill)

skeppning shipping, shipment

skepps|brott shipwreck; *lida ~* be shipwrecked **-bruten** shipwrecked; *bildl.* derelict **-byggare** shipbuilder **-byggnad** shipbuilding **-byggnadskonst** shipbuilding engineering, naval architecture **-båt** ship's boat, launch **-dagbok** ship's log[book] **-docka** dock **-gosse** ship's boy; *(kajutvakt)* cabin boy **-handlare** ship chandler, marine-store dealer **-handlingar** ship's papers **-katt** ship's cat; *(straffredskap)* cat-o'-nine-tails **-klarerare** shipping agent, shipbroker **-klocka** ship's bell, watch bell **-kock** ship's cook **-kök** caboose **-last** cargo, shipload **-läkare** ship's doctor **-mask** shipworm **-mäklare** shipbroker **-papper** *pl* ship's papers (documents) **-präst** chaplain **-redare** shipowner **-skorpa** hardtack, ship's (sea) biscuit **-sättning** *arkeol.* ship barrow (tumulus) **-varv** shipyard, shipbuilding yard

skep|sis ['skepp-] *s2*, **-ticism** scepticism **-tiker** ['skepp-] sceptic **-tisk** ['skepp-] *a5* sceptic[al]

sket [ʃ-] *imperf. av skita*

sketch [sketʃ] *s3* sketch

skev [ʃ-] *a1* warped; *bildl.* wry; distorted *(uppfattning om* notion of)* **skeva** **1** *(vara skev)* warp; *(vinda)* squint **2** *(ställa snett)* slope, slant; *flyg.* bank; *~ en åra* feather an oar **skevning** [-e:-] warping; *flyg.* bank[ing] **skevningsroder** aileron **skevt** [-e:-] *adv* askew

skick [ʃ-] *s7* **1** *(tillstånd)* condition, state; *i befintligt ~* with all faults, in condition as presented; *i färdigt ~* in a finished state; *i gott ~* in good condition (repair, order); *i oförändrat ~* unchanged, unaltered; *i oskadat ~ (hand.)* intact, in good condition; *försätta ur stridbart ~* put out of action **2** *sätta ngt i ~* igen put s.th. in order again **3** *se bruk* **2**, *sed* **4** *(uppträdande)* manners *(pl)*, behaviour; *är det ~ och fason det?* do you call that good form?

skicka 1 *(sända)* send *(efter* for; *med* by; *till* to); dispatch; remit *(pengar* money); *~ polisen på ngn* set the police on [to] s.b.; *vill du ~ mig brödet?* will you pass me the bread, please?; ~ *bort* send away, dismiss; ~ *i förväg* send on before (ahead); ~ *hit* send here, send to me (us); ~ *med* send [... with him (*etc.*)], (*bifoga*) enclose; ~ *omkring* circulate, (*cirkulär*) circularize; ~ *tillbaka* send back, return; ~ *vidare* send on (forward) **2** *rfl* (*uppföra sig*) behave [o.s.] **skickad** *a5* (*lämpad*) fitted, qualified (*för* for)

skickelse 1 (*bestämmelse*) decree, ordinance; *ödets* ~ [the decree of] Fate, destiny; *genom en försynens* ~ by an act of providence, providentially **2** (*skepnad*) apparition **-diger** fateful, eventful

skicklig *a1* skilful, clever; good (*i* at); (*duglig*) able, capable; (*händig*) dexterous; *en* ~ *arbetare* an able (a capable) workman **-het** skill, skilfulness, cleverness; ability, capability; dexterity

1 skida [ʃ-] *s1* **1** *bot.* siliqua **2** (*slida*) sheath, scabbard; *sticka svärdet i ~n* sheathe one's sword

2 skid|a [ʃ-] *s1* (*snö-*) ski; *åka -or* ski, go skiing **skid|backe** ski slope **-bindning** ski binding (strap) **-byxor** ski[ing] trousers **-dräkt** ski (skiing) suit **-färd** skiing tour **-före** ski ~ *bra* ~ good skiing surface **-glasögon** goggles **-lift** ski lift **-lärare** ski instructor **-löpare** skier **-löpning** cross-country skiing **-pjäxa** ski[ing] boot **-skytte** biathlon **-spets** ski tip **-sport** skiing **-spår** ski track **-stav** ski stick (pole) **-terräng** skiing country **-tävling** skiing competition, ski race **-utrustning** skiing equipment (outfit) **-valla** ski wax **-åkare** skier **-åkning** skiing

skiffer [ˈʃiff-] *s2* slate; schist; (*ler-*) shale; (*som vara*) slating; *täcka med* ~ slate **-olja** shale oil **-grå** slate-gray **-tak** slate (slated) roof, slating

skiffrig [ˈʃiff-] *a1* slaty

skift [ʃ-] *s7* (*arbetsomgång*) shift; turn; (*arbetslag*) shift, gang; *i* ~ in shifts **skifta 1** (*fördela*) divide (*arv* an inheritance); ~ *boet* distribute the estate **2** (*utbyta*) exchange (*hugg* blows); (*byta*) change; ~ *gestalt* shift form; ~ *ord med bandy* (exchange) words with **3** (*förändra sig*) shift, change; (*omväxla* [*med varandra*]) alternate; ~ *i grönt* be shot (tinged) with green

skift|ande *a4* changing, varied; eventful (*liv* life); *med* ~ *innehåll* with a varied content **-arbete** shift work

skifte *s6* **1** (*fördelning*) distribution, division (*av arv* of an inheritance) **2** (*jorddelning*) parcelling[-out]; (*jordområde*) parcel, field **3** (*växling*) vicissitude; (*ombyte*) change, turn; *i livets alla ~n* in the ups and downs of life

skiftes|bruk rotation farming **-rik** eventful, chequered **-vis** by turns, alternately

skift|ning (*förändring*) change; (*nyans*) nuance, shade, tinge; *inte en* ~ *i hans ansiktsuttryck* not the slightest change in his expression; *med en* ~ *i grönt* with a tinge of green **-nyckel** adjustable spanner; *AE.* [monkey] wrench

skikt [ʃ-] *s7* layer; (*tunt*) film; *geol.* stratum (*pl* strata); *bildl.* layer, stratum **skikta** stratify

skild [ʃ-] *a1* **1** (*olika*) separate; different, divers; *vitt ~a intressen* widely differing interests; *gå ~a vägar* (*bildl.*) go separate ways, split **2** (*från-*) divorced

skildr|a [ʃ-] describe, depict; (*förlopp*) relate

-ing description; relation, account

skilj|a *v2* **1** (*från-*) separate, part (*från* from); (*hugga av*) sever (*huvudet från bålen* the head from the body); (*sortera*) sort out (*renar* reindeer); ~ *agnarna från vetet* sift the wheat from the chaff; ~ *ngn från ett ämbete* dismiss s.b. from his office **2** (*åt-*) divide; (*ngt sammanhörande*) disunite, disconnect; *pers. äv.* separate, part; divorce (*äkta makar* married people) **3** ~ *mellan* (*på*) distinguish between; ~ *mellan höger och vänster* know the difference between right and left; *jag kan inte* ~ *dem från varandra* I cannot tell them apart **4** *rfl* part (*från* with); ~ *sig* divorce (*från sin make* one's husband); ~ *sig från mängden* stand out in a crowd; ~ *sig med heder från sin uppgift* acquit o.s. creditably of one's task

skiljaktig *a1* different; ~ *mening* divergent opinion **-het** difference; disparity (*i åsikter* of opinions)

skilj|as *v2, dep* part (*från* from, with); (*om äkta makar*) divorce, be divorced; ~ [*åt*] split; *här skils våra vägar* this is where our ways part **-bar** *a1* separable

skilje|dom *s2* arbitration; award **-domare** arbitrator **-domsförfarande** arbitral (arbitration) procedure **-domstol** court of arbitration; *Internationella ~en i Haag* Permanent Court of Arbitration, the Hague Tribunal **-mur** partition [wall]; barrier (*äv. bildl.*) **-mynt** change, [small] coin **-nämnd** arbitration board **-tecken** *språkv.* punctuation mark **-väg** crossroad; *vid ~en* at the crossroads (*pl*)

skillingtryck [ʃ-] chapbook

skillnad [ʃ-] *s3* difference (*i* in; *på* between); (*avvikelse*) distinction, divergence; *det är det som gör ~en* that's what makes all the difference; *göra* ~ *på* make a distinction between, treat ... differently; *till* ~ *från* in contrast to, unlike

skilsmässa [ʃ-] **1** (*äktenskapsskillnad*) divorce; *ta ut* ~ sue (apply) for a divorce **2** (*uppbrott*) separation; parting (*från* with); *kyrkans* ~ *från staten* the disestablishment of the Church

skilsmässo|ansökan petition for divorce **-barn** child of divorced parents **-orsak grounds** (*pl*) for divorce **-process** divorce suit (proceedings *pl*)

skiltvakt [ʃ-] *s3* sentry

skimmel [ˈʃimm-] *s2* roan

skimmer [ˈʃimm-] *s7* shimmer, gleam; (*glans*) lustre; *sprida ett löjets* ~ *över* throw an air of ridicule over **skimra** shimmer, gleam

skin|a *sken -it* shine; (*stråla*) beam; *solen -er* the sun is shining; ~ *av välmåga* glow with wellbeing; ~ *igenom* show through; *han sken upp* he brightened up; *han är ett klart ~nde ljus* he is a shining light

skingra [ʃ-] disperse; scatter; (*förjaga*) dispel; ~ *ngns bekymmer* banish (drive away) a p.'s cares; ~ *tankarna* divert one's mind (thoughts); ~ *ngns tvivel* dispel a p.'s doubts **skingras** *dep* disperse, be dispersed (scattered); *folkmassan ~des* the crowd dispersed **skingringsförbud** *jur.* injunction against alienation (sale) of property

skinit *sup. av* skina

S

skinka [ʃ-] *s1* **1** (*rimmad*) ham; (*färsk*) pork; *bräckt* ~ fried ham; *kokt* ~ ham **2** (*kroppsdel*) buttock

skinn [ʃ-] *s7* **1** (*hud*) skin; (*päls*) fur, pelt; (*fäll*) fell; (*läder*) leather; *hudar och* ~ hides and skins; *kylan biter i* ~*et* the cold is biting (piercing); *inte sälja* ~*et förrän björnen är skjuten* don't count your chickens before they are hatched; *Gyllene* ~*et* the Golden Fleece; *ha* ~ *på näsan* (*bildl.*) have a will (mind) of one's own; *hålla sig i* ~*et* (*bildl.*) control o.s., keep within bounds, behave o.s.; *vara bara* ~ *och ben* be nothing but skin and bone **2** (*på mjölk e.d.*) film, skin

skinn|a *bildl.* skin, fleece (*ngn på* s.b. of) **-band** leather binding; [*bunden*] *i* ~ leather-bound **-beredning** dressing of fur skins **-byxor** *pl* leather breeches **-fodrad** [-ω:-] *a5* lined with leather **-jacka** leather jacket **-klädd** leather-covered **-knutte** *s2* rocker, leather jacket **-krage** fur collar **-mössa** leather cap — *och benfri* skinned and boned (*ansjovis* anchovy) **-rygg** *bokb.* leather back **-soffa** leather-covered sofa **-torr** skinny, dry as a bone **-varor** *pl* skins, furs, leather articles

skioptikon [ski'åpp-, ʃi-] *s7* magic lantern; slide projector **-bild** slide

skipa [ʃ-] ~ *rättvisa* do justice; ~ *lag och rätt* administer justice

skippa (*slopa*) skip

skir [ʃ-] *a1* **1** (*florstunn*) gossamer; *bildl.* ethereal **2** (*klar*) clear (*honung* honey) **skira** melt (*smör* butter)

skiss *s3* sketch, outline (*till* of) **-artad** [-a:r-] *a5* sketchy **-block** sketchblock **-bok** sketchbook **-era** sketch [out], draw up outline

skit [ʃ-] *s2, vard.* shit **skita** [ʃ-] *sket -it, vard.* shit; *det skall du* ~ *i* (*bildl.*) that's none of your bloody business; *det* -*er jag i* to hell with it **skitig** [ʃ-] *a1, vard.* dirty **skitit** *sup. av skita* **skitsnack** *sl.* crap, bull[shit] **skitviktig** uppity

skiv|a [ʃ-] **I** *s1* **1** plate, slab; (*rund*) disc, disk; (*bords-* etc.) top; (*tunt lager*) flake, lamina **2** (*grammofon-*) record; (*skuren* ~) slice; *spela in en* ~ cut a record, make a gramophone recording **3** (*fest*) party **4** *klara* ~*n* (*bildl.*) manage it (the job), bring it off **II** *v1* slice, cut in slices **-broms** disc brake **-bytare** record changer **-formig** [-å-] *a1* disc-shaped **-ling** [-i:v-] *bot.* agaric **-minne** *data.* disk memory **-pratare** disc jockey **-rem** pulley belt **-samlare** discophil[e] **-samling** collection of records **-spelare** record-player **-stång** disc bar **-tallrik** (*på grammofon*) turntable

skjort|a [ˣʃω:r-, ˣʃorr-] *s1* shirt **-blus** shirt blouse **-bröst** shirt front **-linning** neckband **-ärm** shirtsleeve; *gå i* ~*arna* be in one's shirtsleeves; *kavla upp* ~*arna* roll up one's shirtsleeves

skjul [ˣʃu:l] *s7* shed, hovel

skjut|a *sköt -it* **I** **1** (*med -vapen*) shoot; (*avlossa*) fire (*ett skott* a shot); ~ *bra* shoot well, be a good shot; ~ *skarpt* shoot with live cartridges; ~ *efter* shoot at; ~ *till måls* practise target-shooting; ~ *över målet* overshoot the mark; ~ *på* (*uppskjuta*) put off, postpone; *hennes ögon sköt blixtar* her eyes flashed **2** (*förflytta*)

push, shove, move (*undan* away); (*i bollspel*) shoot (*i mål* a goal); ~ *en båt i sjön* launch a boat **3** ~ *knopp* bud; ~ *skott* sprout; ~ *som svampar ur jorden* spring up like mushrooms; ~ *i höjden a*) (*växa*) shoot up, grow tall, *b*) (*om priser*) soar [up] **II** (*med betonad partikel*) **1** ~ *fram* push (move) forward, (*om föremål*) project, stand out, (*ila*) dash (dart) forward **2** ~ *för* push to (shoot) (*en regel* a bolt) **3** ~ *ifrån* push (shove) off; ~ *ifrån sig* push (shove) away, *bildl.* shift off **4** ~ *igen* shut, close **5** ~ *ihjäl* shoot dead **6** ~ *in sig* (*med -vapen*) find the range **7** ~ *ner* push down, lower, (*döda*) shoot down, (*flygplan*) shoot (bring) down **8** ~ *på* push **9** ~ *till a*) *se* ~ *igen*, b) (*bidraga med*) contribute **10** ~ *upp a*) (*om växter*) shoot up, *bildl.* put off, postpone, b) (*raket*) launch **11** ~ *ut* push (shove) out, (*båt*) launch, (*om föremål*) project, protrude

skjut|bana shooting range; *mil.* rifle range **-bar** *a1* sliding **-dörr** sliding door **-fält** range **-fönster** sash (sliding) window **-galen** trigger-happy

skjut|it *sup. av skjuta* **-järn** gun **-järns-journalistik** hard-hitting journalism, rapid-fire interviewing **-lucka** sliding shutter **-läge** shooting position **-mått** vernier calliper **-skjutning** [ʃu:t-] shooting, firing; *mil.* fire

skjuts [ʃuss, ʃuts] *s2* **1** (-*ning*) conveyance; *få* ~ get a lift; *ge ngn* ~ give s.b. a lift **2** (*förspänt åkdon*) [horse and] carriage

skjuts|a a drive, take **-håll** stage; (-*station*) relay, station **-häst** post horse

skjut|skicklighet markmanship, skill in shooting **-tävling** shooting competition (match) **-vapen** firearm **-övning** shooting practice

skjuv|a [ˣʃu:-] *tekn.* shear **-ning** shearing

sklero|s [-'rå:s] *s3* sclerosis **-tisk** [-'rå:-] *a5* sclerotic

sko I *s5* shoe; (*grövre*) boot; *det är där* ~*n klämmer* (*bildl.*) that is where the shoe pinches **II** *v4* **1** (*häst*) shoe **2** (*med beslag*) mount; (*kanta*) line **3** *rfl* line one's pocket (*på ngns bekostnad* at a p.'s expense) **-affär** shoe shop **-block** shoetree **-borste** shoebrush **-borstning** [-å-] shoecleaning; *AE.* shoeshining

skock [-å-] *s2* crowd, herd **skocka** *rfl* crowd (cluster) [together], gather together; (*om djur äv.*) flock [together]

sko|dd *a5* shod; (*kantad*) lined **-don** *pl* shoes, footwear (*sg*) **-fabrik** shoe factory

skog *s2* wood; (*större*) forest; (*plantera* ~ afforest; ~ *på rot* standing forest (timber); *fälla* ~ cut (fell) timber (trees); *det går åt* ~*en* it is all going wrong (to pieces); *i* ~ *och mark* in woods and fields, (*friare*) in the countryside, out in the country; *dra åt* ~*en!* go to blazes!, (*starkare*) go to hell!; *inte se* ~*en för bara träd* not see the wood for the trees **-bevuxen** wooded, forested, forest-clad **-fattig** poorly wooded

skogig *a1* wooded, woody **skoglig** [-ω:-] *a1* forestry, silvicultural **skogrik** well-wooded, well-forested, rich in forests (woods)

skogs|arbetare wood[s]man, lumberjack **-areal** forest[ed] area **-avverkning** felling; *AE.* logging, lumbering **-backe** wooded hillside

-brand forest fire; *fara för* ~ danger of forest fire **-bruk** forestry, silviculture **-bruksskola** college of forestry **-bryn** edge of a (the) wood **-bygd** woodland **-bälte** forest belt **-dunge** grove; *(mindre)* copse **-duva** stock dove **-död** irreparable damage to forests **-forskning** forestry research **-fågel** forest bird; *koll.* grouse, black game **-gud** silvan god, faun **-hantering** forestry, forest management **-huggare** woodcutter; *AE.* lumberman, lumberjack **-högskola** college of forestry **-industri** forest industry **-mark** wooded ground **-mus** field mouse **-mård** pine marten **-nymf** wood nymph, dryad **-plantering** afforestation **-rå** wood--spirit **-skövling** deforestation, devastation of forests **-stig** forest path **-stjärna** *bot.* chickweed wintergreen **-styrelse** ~*n* [the Swedish] national board of forestry **-trakt** woodland, lumberland, wooded region **-troll** woodland troll **-viol** common violet **-vård** forestry, silviculture **-väg** forest road **-äng** woodland meadow

skogvaktar|boställe forester's house **skogvaktare** forester, gamekeeper, forest keeper; *AE.* [forest] ranger

sko|handlare shoe (footwear) dealer **-horn** shoehorn **-hylla** shoe-rack **-industri** footwear industry

skoj [skåjj] *s7* **1** *(skämt)* joke, jest; *(fuffens)* frolic, lark, shenanigan; *göra ngt för* ~*s skull* do s.th. for the fun of it; *på* ~ for fun; *göra* ~ *av ngn* make fun of (poke fun at) s.b. **2** *(bedrägeri)* fraud, swindle, racket **skoja 1** *(skämta)* joke, jest, lark; ~ *med ngn* pull a p.'s leg **2** *(bedraga)* swindle, cheat **skojare 1** *(skämtare)* joker, jester; *(kanalje)* scamp **2** *(bedragare)* cheat, fraud; *AE.* racketeer **skojarfirma** swindling (bogus) firm **skojfrisk** mischievous, full of fun **skojig** *a1* funny; *jfr lustig*

sko|kartong shoebox **-kräm** shoe polish (cream)

1 skola *skulle -t, pres. skall* **I** *inf. skola; sup. skolat; han sade sig* ~ *bli glad om* he said that he would be glad if; *de lär* ~ *resa i morgon* they are said to be leaving tomorrow; *han lär* ~ *komma* it is thought that he will come; *han hade* ~*t (bort) inställa sig inför rätta i går* he should have appeared in court yesterday **II** *pres. skall, vard. ska; imperf. skulle* **1** *(ren framtid) pres.* shall(*1:a pers.*), will (*2:a o. 3:e pers.) imperf., äv. konditionalis* should *resp.* would; *vad skall det bli av henne?* what will become of her?; *du skall få dina pengar tillbaka* you will get your money back; *jag skall aldrig glömma honom* I shall never forget him; *han och jag skall gå och bada* he and I are going swimming; *jag skall gärna hjälpa dig* I shall be pleased to help you; *han skall resa nästa vecka* he will leave (is leaving) next week; *det går nog bra skall du se* that will be all right, you'll see; *som vi snart skall få se* as we shall soon see; *vi skall träffas i morgon* we shall meet tomorrow; *jag var säker på att jag inte skulle glömma det* I was sure I should not forget it; *jag skulle gärna hjälpa dig om jag kunde* I should be pleased to help you if I could; *jag skulle ha hunnit om jag hade givit*

mig av genast I should have been in time if I had started at once; *vad skulle hända om vi blev upptäckta?* what would happen if we were found out?; *han trodde inte att jag skulle lyckas* he didn't think I should succeed; *skulle han känna igen henne nu om han såg henne?* would he recognize her now if he saw her?; *i ditt ställe skulle jag ha stannat hemma* in your place I should have stayed at home; *det skulle jag inte tro* I shouldn't think so; *jag frågade om han skulle vara närvarande* I asked if he would be present; *de visste att de alltid skulle vara välkomna* they knew they would always be welcome; *skulle du vilja ha en kopp kaffe?* would you like a cup of coffee?; *jag skulle vilja visa dig* I should (would) like to show you **2** *(om ngt nära förestående el. avsett) pres.* am *(etc.)* going to; am *(etc.)* + *ing-form; imperf.* was *(etc.)* going to, was *(etc.)* + *ing-form; vi skall börja snart* we are going to start (are starting) soon; *jag skall gå och bada i eftermiddag* I am going swimming (to swim) this afternoon; *just som tåget skulle gå* just as the train was going to leave (was leaving); *han skulle just resa när jag kom* he was about to leave when I arrived; *hon sade att hon skulle resa till Paris* she said she was going to Paris; *vi skulle just sätta oss till bords* we were just going to sit down to dinner (lunch *etc.*) **3** *(egen vilja)* will *resp.* would; *(annans vilja)* shall *resp.* should; *(efter tell, want m.fl.) inf.-konstr.; jag skulle hellre dö än* I would rather die than; *vi skall väl fara, eller hur?* we will go, won't we?; *jag skulle ge vad som helst för att få se* I would give anything to see; *jag skall göra det åt dig* I will do it for you; *jag lovade ju att jag skulle göra det* I did promise that I would do it; *vad skall du med alla pennorna till?* what do you want with all those pens?; *jag skall ta med mig några skivor* I will bring some records; *jag skulle önska jag var död!* I would I were dead!; *du skall få så många du vill* you shall have as many as you want; *vad skall det här föreställa?* what is this supposed to be?; *skall vi gå på bio?* what about going (shall we go) to the cinema?; *vad vill du att jag skall göra?* what do you want me to do?; *de vill att vi skall komma* they want us to come; *de bad oss att vi skulle komma* they asked us to come; *du skall rätta dig efter vad jag säger* you are to do as I tell you; *det skall han få sota för* he shall smart (pay) for that; *du skall icke stjäla (bibl.)* thou shalt not steal; *han frågar om han skall ta sin bror med* he asks if he shall (should) bring his brother; *jag skulle inte få tala om det för dig* I was not supposed to tell you; *vad skall det tjäna till?* what is the use of that?; *jag vet inte vad jag skall tro* I don't know what to think; *jag lovar att det inte skall upprepas* I promise that it shall not happen again; *han gör det för att det skall så vara* he does it because that's how it is supposed to be; *skall det vara så skall det vara* one may as well do the thing properly or not at all; *skall jag öppna fönstret?* shall I open the window? **4** *(förutbestämt) pres.* am *(etc.)* to; *imperf.* was *(etc.)* to; *han skulle bli borta i*

S

många år he was to be away for many years; *planet skall komma kl. 6* the plane is due at 6; *när skall jag vara tillbaka?* when am I to be back?; *de skulle aldrig återse varandra* they were never to see each other again **5** (*pres. bör, imperf. borde*) should, ought to; (*måste*) must, have (*imperf.* had) [got] to; *du skulle gå på den utställningen* you should go to that exhibition; *du skulle ha sett honom* you should have seen him; *jag vet inte vad jag skall ta mig till* I don't know what to do; *du skall inte tala illa om honom* you should not speak ill of him; *jag skulle ha varit försiktigare* I should (ought to) have been more careful; *vi skall alla dö* we must all die; *jag skall gå nu* (*jfr II 1, 2 o. 3*) I must go now; *du skall inte hålla boken för nära ögonen* you must not hold the book too close to your eyes; *att ni alltid skall gräla!* why must you always quarrel!; *naturligtvis skulle det hända just mig* of course it would happen to me of all people; *han skall då alltid klaga* he is always complaining, he must always complain; *det skall vara en läkare som skall kunna se det* it needs a doctor to (only a doctor can) see that **6** (*sägs, lär*) *pres.* am (*etc.*) said to; *imperf.* was (*etc.*) said to; *skulle det verkligen förhålla sig så?* I wonder if that is really the case?; *det skall vara ett bra märke* it is said to be a good make; *han skall vara mycket rik* he is supposed to be very rich; *det sägs att han skall vara rik* they say he is rich **7** (*retoriskt*) should; *varför skulle någon frukta honom?* why should anybody be afraid of him?; *vem skulle han träffa på om inte sin egen syster* whom should he meet but his own sister?; *hur skall jag kunna veta det?* how should I know? **8** (*i vissa bisatser*) should; *att det skulle gå därhän!* that it should have come to this!; *om vi skulle missa tåget får vi ta taxi* if we should (were to) miss the train we must take a taxi; *om han skulle kunna räddas måste något göras snart* if he is to be saved something must be done soon; *de gick närmare så att de skulle se bättre* they went closer so that they should see better; *om vi skulle ta en promenad?* what (how) about going for a walk?; *det är synd att det skall vara så kallt* it is a pity that it should be so cold; *jag är ledsen att det skall vara nödvändigt* I am sorry that this should be necessary; *hon gick tyst så att hon inte skulle väcka honom* she walked quietly so that she should (might) not wake him **9** (*annan konstr.*) *vad skall det betyda?* what is the meaning of that?; *vi väntade på att någon skulle komma* we were waiting for s.b. to come; *det är för kallt för att någon skall kunna gå ut* it is too cold for anyone to go out; *det var för dåligt väder för att tävlingen skulle kunna äga rum* the weather was too bad for the race to take place; *vad skall jag med det till?* what am I to do with that?; *det skall du säga som aldrig har försökt!* that's easy for you to say who have never tried!; *jag längtar efter att dagen skall ta slut* I am longing for the day to come to an end; *han skall naturligtvis tränga sig före!* of course, he would push in front!; *du skulle bara våga!* just you

dare! **10** (*med betonad partikel*) *jag skall av här* I'm getting (*t. konduktör*: I want to get) off here; *jag skall bort* (*hem, ut*) I'm going out (home, out); *jag skall in på posten* I'm going to call in at the post office; *jag skall iväg nu* I must be off (be going) now; *det skall mycket till för att hon skall ändra på sig* it takes a lot to make her change; *det skall så litet till för att glädja henne* it takes so little to make her happy

2 skol‖a I *s1* school; *~n* (*undervisningen*) school, (*-byggnaden*) the school; *gå i ~n* go to school; *vara i ~n* be in (at) school; *sluta ~n* leave school; *när ~n slutar* (*för dagen*) when school is over for the day, (*för terminen*) when school breaks up; *bilda ~* found a school; *den högre ~n* (*ridk.*) haute école; *ta sin mats ur ~n* back out **II** *v1* **1** school, teach, train **2** (*omplantera*) transplant

skol‖ad *a5* trained, educated; cultivated (*röst* voice) **-arbete** schoolwork

skolast‖ik *s3* scholasticism **-iker** [-'lass-] scholastic **-isk** [-'lass-] *a5* scholastic

skolat *sup. av 1 skola*

skol‖atlas school atlas **-avgift** school fees (*pl*) **-avslutning** breaking-up; *AE.* commencement **-barn** schoolchild **-bespisning** school meal service **-betyg** school report **-bildning** schooling, education **-bok** schoolbook, textbook **-buss** school bus **-bänk** desk; *sitta på ~en* (*bildl.*) be at school **-dag** schoolday **-direktion** local education authority **-exempel** object lesson, typical example **-fartyg** training ship **-ferier** *pl* [school] holidays (vacation *sg*) **-flicka** schoolgirl **-flygning** training flight **-flygplan** trainer, training aircraft **-frukost** school lunch **-fröken** schoolmistress **-gång** *s2* school attendance, schooling **-gård** playground, school yard **-hem 1** boarding school **2** reform school **-inspektör** schools inspector

skolk [-å-] *s7* truancy, nonattendance **skolka** shirk; *skol.* play truant (*vard.* hookey)

skol‖kamrat schoolfellow, schoolmate; (*vän*) schoolfriend; *vi var ~er* we were at school together **-klass** [school] class **-kunskaper** *pl* knowledge (*sg*) acquired at school; schooling (*sg*) **-kurator** *BE.* school (educational) welfare officer, *AE.* attendance officer **-kök** (*ämne*) domestic science; (*lokal*) school kitchen **-kökslärarinna** domestic science teacher; *AE.* home economics teacher

skolla [-å-] *se skålla*

skol‖leda school fatigue **-ljus** shining light at school **-lov** [-å:v] *s7* holiday[s *pl*] **-lovskoloni** holiday camp **-lunch** school dinner **-läkare** school doctor **-lärare** schoolmaster, schoolteacher **-lärarinna** schoolmistress, schoolteacher **-materiel** school materials (supplies) **-matsal** [school] canteen **-mogen** ready to start school **-mognadsprov** test of readiness for school attendance **-måltid** school dinner (meal) **-mästaraktig** pedantic **-ning** [-o:-] training, schooling, education **-peng** school voucher system **-plikt** compulsory school attendance **-pliktig** of school age **-pojke** schoolboy **-psykolog** educational (school) psychologist **-radio** school radio; broadcasting for schools **-reform** school (educational) reform **-resa** school trip; (*kortare*) outing **-ridning** manège riding, haute école **-ryttare** equestrian, manège rider **-sal** classroom **-sjuk** *vara* ~ feign illness to avoid going to school **-skepp** training ship **-skjuts** school transport **-skrivning** written test **-sköterska** schoolnurse **-slips** schooltie (*bärs av f.d.* elever vid public school*) **-styrelse** local education board **-tandvård** school dental service **-television** school television **-tid** (*tid på dagen*) schoolhours (*pl*); (*period då man går i -an*) schooldays (*pl*) **-underbyggnad** [educational] grounding, [previous] schooling **-undervisning** school teaching, schooling **-ungdom** school children (*pl*) **-vaktmästare** school caretaker, *AE.* school custodian **-väg** way to school **-vägran** refusal to attend school **-värd[inna]** school help **-väsen** educational system **-väska** schoolbag; satchel **-ålder** school age **-år** school year; (*-tid*) schooldays (*pl*) **-överstyrelse** ~*n* [the Swedish] national board of education

skomak|are shoemaker; shoe-repairer **-eri** shoemaker's workshop

skona spare; ~ *ögonen* save one's eyes; ~ *sin hälsa* take care of one's health; ~ *sig* spare o.s.

skonare *s9*, **skonert** [-'närt, 'skɔ:-] *s3*, *pl äv.* *-ar* ['skɔ:-] *sjö.* schooner

skoning (*doppsko*) ferrule; (*fåll*) false hem

skon|ingslös unsparing; merciless **-sam** *a1* (*mild*) lenient; (*överseende*) indulgent; (*fördragsam*) forebearing **-samhet** leniency; indulgence; forebearance

skonummer size in shoes

skopa *s1* scoop, dipper; *sjö.* bailer; (*på grävmaskin e.d.*) bucket, ladle; *en* ~ *ovett* a good telling-off

skopola'min *s4*, *kem.* scopolamine

sko|putsare bootblack, shoeblack; *AE.* shoeshine [boy] **-putsning** cleaning (polishing) of shoes; *AE.* shoeshining **-reparation** shoe repair **-rem** shoelace

skorpa [-å-] *s1* **1** (*hårdnad yta*) crust; (*sår-*) scab **2** (*bakverk*) rusk

skorpion [-å-'ɔ:n] *s3* scorpion

skorp|mjöl, **-smulor** *pl* golden breadcrumbs

skorr|a [-å-] **1** (*rulla på r-et*) speak with a burr, burr **2** (*låta illa*) grate, jar **-ande** *a4* burred (*r* r) **-ning 1** burr **2** jarring sound

skorsten ['skårr-] *s2* chimney; (*på fartyg, lok*) funnel; (*fabriks-*) smokestack

skorstens|eld chimney fire **-fejare** chimney sweep (sweeper) **-mur** chimney breast **-pipa** chimneypot

1 skorv [-å-] *s2* (*gammalt fartyg*) old tub
2 skorv [-å-] *s2*, *med., bot.* scurf

skorvig *a1* scurfy

sko|skav *s7*, *ej pl* chafed feet (*pl*) **-smörja** *se* skokräm **-snöre** shoelace, shoestring **-spänne** shoe buckle **-sula** sole [of a shoe] **-svärta** shoeblacking

skot *s7*, *sjö.* sheet **skota** sheet (*hem* home)

skoter ['skɔ:-] *s2* [motor] scooter

skotillverkning shoe manufacture

skotsk [-å-] *a1* Scotch; (*i Skottl.*) Scottish, Scots; *S~a högländerna* the [Scottish] Highlands **skotska** *s1* **1** (*språk*) Scotch, Scottish;

(*i Skottl.*) Scots **2** (*kvinna*) Scotchwoman, Scotswoman

skotstek sheet bend

skott [-å-] *s7* **1** (*gevärs-* etc.; *sport.*) shot; (*laddning*) charge; *ett* ~ *föll* a shot was fired; *jag kommer som ett* ~ I'll come like a shot **2** *bot.* shoot, sprout; *skjuta* ~ sprout **3** *sjö.* bulkhead; *vattentätt* ~ watertight bulkhead

skotta [-å-] shovel (*snö* away the snow); ~ *igen* fill in (*en grav* a grave)

skottavla (*särskr. skott-tavla*) target; *vara* ~ *för* (*bildl.*) be the butt of

skottdag [-å-] leap day, intercalary day

skott|e [-å-] *s2* **1** Scotchman; (*i Skottl.*) Scot, Scotsman; *-arna* (*koll.*) the Scotch (Scots) **2** (*hund*) Scottish terrier

skott|fri 1 *se* skottsäker **2** (*obeskjuten*) shot-free; *gå* ~ (*bildl.*) go scot-free **-fält** field of fire **-glugg** loophole; (*för kanon*) embrasure; *komma i* ~*en* (*bildl.*) come under fire **-hål** bullet hole **-håll** range; *inom* (*utom*) ~ within (out of) range (*för* of) **-kärra** wheelbarrow

Skottland ['skått-] *n* Scotland

skott|linje line of fire **-lossning** firing, discharge **-pengar** *pl* bounty (*sg*) **-rädd** gun-shy **-salva** round, volley **-skada** (*på sak*) damage caused by gunshot; *jfr* -*sår* **-spole** shuttle **-sår** gunshot wound **-säker** bulletproof **-tavla** *se* skottavla **-vidd** range of fire **-växling** exchange of shots; (*-lossning*) firing, shooting **-år** leap year

skovel ['skåvv-, 'skå:-] *s2* **1** (*redskap*) shovel, scoop **2** (*på vattenhjul, mudderverk etc.*) bucket; (*på ångturbin*) blade **skovelhjul** paddle wheel; (*på ångturbin*) blade wheel

skovla shovel

skraffera *konst.* hatch

skraj [-ajj] *a1*, *vard.*, *vara* ~ have the wind up, be in a [blue] funk (*för* about), *AE.* have the jitters

skrake *s2*, *zool.* merganser

skral *a1* **1** (*underhaltig*) poor, inferior; (*krasslig*) poorly, seedy; *AE. vard.* mean **2** *sjö.*, *vinden är* ~ the wind is slight (scant) **skralt** [-a:-] *adv* badly **skraltig** ['skrall-] *a1*, *se* skral 1

skramla I *s1* rattle **II** *v1* **1** rattle, clatter **2** *vard.* club together (*till* for) **skramlig** *a1* rattly **skrammel** ['skramm-] *s7* (*-lande*) rattling *etc.*; (*ett* ~) rattle, clatter, clank

skranglig *a1* **1** (*gänglig*) lank; (*om pers. äv.*) loose-limbed **2** (*ranglig*) rickety (*stege* ladder)

skrank *s7* barrier, railing; (*domstols-*) bar **skrank|a** *s1* barrier; *-or* (*bildl.*) limits, restraints, bounds; *sociala* -*or* social barriers

skrap *s7*, *se* skrapning

skrap|a I *s1* **1** (*redskap*) scraper, rake **2** (*skråma*) scratch **3** (*tillrättavisning*) scolding; *få en ordentlig* ~ get a good rating **II** *v1* scrape; (*om katt, penna*) scratch; ~ *med fötterna* scrape one's feet; (*om häst e.d.*) paw [the ground]; ~ *ihop pengar* scrape together money; ~ *sig på knät* graze [the skin of] one's knee **-ning** [-a:-] **1** scraping *etc.*; (*en* ~) scrape **2** *med.* curettage **-nos** (*spel*) spillikins (*pl*)

skratt *s7* laughter; (*ett* ~) laugh; *brista i* ~ burst out laughing; *vara full av (i)* ~ be bursting (ready to burst) with laughter; *få sig ett gott* ~

have a good laugh; *ett gott ~ förlänger livet* mirth prolongeth life and causeth health

skratta laugh (*åt* at); *det är ingenting att ~ åt* it is no laughing matter; *~ ngn rakt upp i ansiktet* laugh in a p.'s face; *~r bäst som ~r sist* he laughs best who laughs longest; *~ till* give a laugh; *~ ut a)* (*förlöjliga*) laugh at, turn to ridicule, *b)* (*~ ordentligt*) have a good laugh; *~ sig fördärvad åt* split one's sides laughing at

skratt|are laugher; *få -arna på sin sida* have the laugh on one's side **-grop** dimple **-muskel** risible muscle **-mås** black-headed gull **-paroxysm** fit of laughter **-retande** *a4* laughable, droll; (*löjlig*) ridiculous **-salva** burst (roar) of laughter **-spegel** distorting mirror

1 skred *imperf. av* skrida

2 skred *s7* [land]slide, [land]slip

skrek *imperf. av* skrika

1 skrev *imperf. av* skriva

2 skrev *s7* crotch, crutch

1 skreva *s1* crevice, cleft

2 skreva *v1*, *~ med benen* straddle

skri *s6* **1** scream, yell, shriek; (*rop*) cry **2** (*djur-*) shriek; (*ugglas*) hoot **skria** scream *etc.*; cry out **skriande** *a4* crying (*nöd* need); flagrant (*orättvisa* injustice); glaring (*missbruk* abuse)

skribent writer, author

skrid|a *skred -it* (*röra sig framåt*) advance [slowly], proceed; (*med stora steg*) stride; (*glida*) glide; *arbetet -er framåt* the work advances; *~ till huvudförhandling* (*jur.*) open the hearing; *~ till verket* set (go) to work **skridit** *sup. av* skrida

skridsko ['skrisskω] *s5* skate; *åka ~r* skate, go skating **-bana** skating-rink **-is** ice for skating **-prinsessa** girl figure skater **-segel** skating sail, handsail **-segling** skate sailing **-tävling** skating competition **-åkare** skater **-åkning** skating

1 skrift *s3* **1** (*skrivande*) writing; (*skrivtecken*) [written] characters (*pl*); (*handstil*) handwriting; *i tal och ~* verbally and in writing **2** (*-alster*) paper; (*broschyr*) booklet; (*tryckalster*) publication; *samlade ~er* collected works; *den heliga ~* the Scriptures (*pl*), Holy Scripture (Writ)

2 skrift *s3* **1** (*förberedelse t. nattvardsgång*) shriving **2** *se bikt*

skrifta 1 shrive **2** confess **skriftermål** *s7* **1** (*nattvardsgång*) communion **2** (*bikt*) confession

skrift|expert handwriting expert **-lig** *a1* written; *~ bekräftelse* (*äv.*) confirmation in writing **-ligt** *adv* in writing; (*genom brev*) by letter; *ha ~ på ngt* have s.th. in black and white **-lärd** versed in the Scriptures; *bibl.* scribe **-prov** *konkr.* specimen of a p.'s handwriting **-rulle** scroll **-språk** written language **-ställare** writer, author **-växling** *dipl.* exchange of notes

skrik *s7* cry (*på hjälp* for help; *av förtjusning* of delight; *gällt* scream, shriek, yell; (*rop*) shout; (*oväsen*) clamour (*äv. bildl.*); *bildl. äv.* outcry; *sista ~et* all the rage, the latest craze

skrik|a 1 *s1* jay; *mager som en ~* [as] thin as a rake **II** *skrek -it* cry out (*på hjälp* for help);

shout, scream (*åt* at); (*om småbarn*) howl, squeal; *~ i himlens höjd* shout to high heaven; *~ till* cry out; *~ sig hes* shout o.s. hoarse **-hals** screamer; (*om barn*) crybaby

skrikig *a1* screaming *etc.*; (*bjärt*) glaring (*färg* colour); (*om röst*) shrill **skrikit** *sup. av* skrika

skrin *s7* box, case, casket; (*för bröd*) bin

skrinda *s1* haycart, haywagon

skrinlägga (*inställa*) relinquish; (*uppskjuta*) postpone, shelve

skrinna skate

skripta *s1* continuity girl

skritt *s3*, *i ~* at a walking pace **skritta** walk

skriv|a *skrev -it* **I** write; (*författa äv.*) compose; (*stava*) spell; *hur -er man ...?* how do you spell ...?; *han -er på en roman* he is writing a novel; *~ sitt namn* sign one's name; *~ i en tidning* write for (be a contributor to) a paper; *~ på maskin* type; *~ rent* make a fair copy of, copy out; *i ~nde stund* at the time of writing; *~ firman på sin hustru* settle one's firm on one's wife; *får ~s på hans sjukdom* must be ascribed to his illness; *han är -en i Stockholm* he is registered in Stockholm; *~ ngn ngt på näsan* tax s.b. with s.th.; *~ ngn ngt till godo* put s.th. down to a p.'s credit **II** (*med betonad partikel*) **1** *~ av a*) (*kopiera*) copy, *b*) *se avskriva* **2** *~ in* enter; *~ in sig* (*på hotell*) register, *AE.* check in; (*i klubb o.d.*) enrol[l] o.s. **3** *~ om* rewrite **4** *~ på a*) (*lista*) put down one's name [on], *b*) (*växel o.d.*) stand surety **5** *~ under* sign [one's name], *bildl.* subscribe (*på ngt* to s.th.) **6** *~ upp* write (note, put) down, *bokför.* write up; *~ upp ngns namn* take down a p.'s name; *~ upp på ngns konto* charge to a p.'s account **7** *~ ut a*) (*renskriva*) copy out, *b*) (*utfärda*) make (write) out (*en räkning* a bill), draw up (*ett kontrakt* a contract), *c*) (*skatter, trupper*) levy, *d*) (*~ t. slut*) fill up, *e*) (*läkemedel*) prescribe, *f*) (*från sjukhus*) discharge

skriv|arbete writing, desk work **-are** writer; scribe; *data.* printer **-biträde** clerk **-block** writing pad **-bok** *skol.* exercise book; (*för välskrivning*) copybook **-bord** desk; writing table

skrivbords|lampa desk lamp **-produkt** drawing-board product **-underlägg** *se -underlägg*

skriv|byrå typewriting bureau (agency) **-don** writing materials **-else** (*brev*) letter; *jur.* writ; *polit.* address **-eri** writing; *neds.* scribbling **-fel** error (mistake) in writing; typing error; clerical error **-göromål** desk work

skriv|it *sup. av* skriva **-klåda** itch to write **-konst** art of writing; penmanship **-kramp** writer's cramp **-kunnig** able to write **-kunnighet** ability to write **-maskin** typewriter; *skriva på ~* type **-maskinsbord** typewriter (typist's) table **-maskinspapper** typing paper **-ning** [-i:v-] writing; *skol.* written examination; *rätta ~ar* mark papers, correct exercises **-papper** writing paper **-penna** [writing] pen **-pulpet** writing desk; (*hög*) writing stand **-stil** (*tryckstil*) cursive script **-ställ** writing set, inkstand **-tecken** [written] character; graphical sign **-underlägg** writing (blotting, desk) pad **-vakt** *BE.* invigilator, *AE.* proctor **-övning** writing exercise

skrock [-å-] *s7* superstition
skrocka [-å-] cluck; (*om pers.*) chuckle
skrockfull superstitious **-het** superstition, superstitiousness
skrodera swagger, bluster, brag
skrof|ler ['skråff-, 'skrœff-] *pl* scrofula **-u'lös** *a1* scrofulous
skrot *s7* scrap; (*järn-*) scrap [iron]; *de är av samma ~ och korn* they are birds of a feather
1 skrota *sjö., vinden ~r* [*sig*] the wind is veering
2 skrot|a (*förvandla t. skrot*) scrap, reject; (*fartyg e.d.*) break up; *gå och ~* (*vard.*) moon about
skrot|bil junk heap **-handlare** scrap [iron] merchant, junk dealer **-hög** scrapheap **-upplag** scrap yard **-värde** scrap value
skrov [-å:-] *s7* **1** (*kropp*) body; (*djurskelett*) carcass; *få litet mat i ~et* get some food inside one **2** *sjö.* hull
skrovlig [ˣskrå:v-, ˣskråvv-] *a1* rough, raspish; (*om klippa*) rugged; (*hes*) hoarse, raucous
skrovmål [-å:v-] *få sig ett ~* have a square meal
skrubb *s2* (*utrymme*) closet, cubbyhole, boxroom
skrubb|a (*skura*) scrub; (*skrapa*) rub **-hyvel** rough (scrub) plane **-sår** graze, abrasion
skrud *s2* attire, garb **skruda** deck, dress
skrump|en *a3* shrunk[en], wrinkled **-lever** cirrhosis [of the liver] **-na** shrivel, shrink
skrupelfri [ˣskru:p-. ˣskrupp-] unscrupulous
skrupler *pl* scruples **skrupu'lös** *a1* scrupulous
skrutinium *s4* scrutiny
skrutit *sup. av skryta*
skrutt *vard.* **1** *s2* (*person*) good-for-nothing **2** *n* (*sak*) rubbish **3** *du ser ut som en ~* you look awful **-ig** *a1, vard.* wretched, miserable
skruv *s2* screw; (*på fiol*) [turning] peg; *dra åt* (*lossa på*) *en ~* tighten (slacken) a screw; *högergängad ~* right-hand screw; *ha en ~ lös* have a screw loose; *det tog ~* (*bildl.*) that did it (went home)
skruv|a screw; *~* [*på*] *sig* fidget, squirm; *~ av* (*loss*) unscrew; *~ fast* screw up (on), fasten; *~ i* screw in (on); *~ ner* lower, turn down (*gasen* the gas); *~ till* screw up (down); *~ upp* screw up, (*öppna*) unscrew, open, (*gasen*) turn up, (*priser*) push (force) up **-boll** *sport.* spin ball **-borr** helical auger **-bult** screw bolt **-gänga** screw thread **-hål** screw hole **-is** pack ice **-lock** screw lid (cap) **-mejsel** screwdriver **-mutter** nut **-nyckel** spanner, *AE.* wrench **-stycke, -städ** vice; *AE.* vise **-tving** screw clamp
skrymm|a *v2* take up [a great deal of] space; be bulky **-ande** *a4* bulky, voluminous
skrymsla *s1*, **skrymsle** *s6* corner, nook
skrymt *s7, se skrymteri* **skrymta** be a hypocrite, dissemble **skrymtare** hypocrite, dissembler **skrymteri** hypocrisy; cant[ing]
skryt *s7* boast[ing], brag[ging], swaggering; *tomt ~* [*an*] empty (idle) boast; *säga ngt på ~* say s.th. just to show off **skryta** *skröt skrutit* boast, brag (*med, över* of); *~ med* (*äv.*) show off
skrytsam *a1* boastful, bragging **-het** boastfulness, bragging
skrå *s6* [trade] guild; livery company; (*friare*)

fraternity, corporation **-anda** guild spirit; *neds.* cliquishness
skrål *s7* bawl[ing], bellow **skråla** bawl, bellow; *make a noise* **skrålig** *a1* bawling *etc.*; noisy
skråma *s1* scratch, cut; superficial wound
skråordning guild statutes (*pl*)
skråpuk *s2* scarecrow; repulsive mask
skrå|tvång obligation to belong to a guild **-väsen** guild system
skräck *s3* terror (*för* of, to); (*fasa*) horror; (*skrämsel*) fright, dread; (*plötslig*) scare, panic; *sätta ~ i* fill (strike) ... with terror, terrify **-bild** frightful image; *bildl.* terrifying picture **-exempel** hair-raising example **-figur** fright, bugbear **-film** horror film, bloodcurdler all **-fylld** horror-filled **-injagande** *a4* horrifying, terrifying **-kabinett** chamber of horrors **-propaganda** atrocity (terror) propaganda **-regemente** reign of terror, terrorism **-slagen** panic-stricken, horror-struck **-stämning** atmosphere of terror **-välde** terrorism **-ödla** dinosaur
skräda *v2* (*malm*) pick, separate; (*mjöl*) bolt; *inte ~ orden* not mince matters (one's words)
skräddar|e tailor **-gesäll** journeyman tailor **-krita** French chalk **-mästare** master tailor **-räkning** tailor's bill **-sydd** *a5* bespoke, tailor--made, tailored; *AE.* custom-made; *bildl.* tailor-made, custom-made, custom-built
skrädderi (*yrke*) tailoring [business]; *konkr.* tailor's shop, *AE.* tailor shop
skräll *s2* crack, bang; (*åsk-*) clap of thunder; *bildl.* crash, sensation **skrälla** *v2* **1** crack *etc.* **2** score a surprise win, win against all odds **skrällande** *a4* cracking *etc.*; *~ hosta* hacking cough; *~ högtalare* blaring loudspeaker
skrälle *s6, ett gammalt ~* (*om piano*) a cracked old piano, (*om pers.*) a decrepit old body; *ett ~ till vagn* a rickety old car
skräll|ig *a1, se skrällande*
skräm|ma *v2* frighten; (*plötsligt*) scare, startle; *bli -d* be frightened (scared); *låta ~ sig* be intimidated; *~ upp* frighten, terrify, (*fågel*) beat up; *~ livet ur ngn* scare the life out of s.b.; *ge en ~nde bild av* give a terrifying picture of **-sel** ['skrämm-] *s9* fright, scare **-skott** warning shot; *bildl.* empty menace
skrän *s7* yell, howl **skräna** yell, howl; (*gorma*) bluster **skränfock** [-å-] *s2* blusterer, bawler **skränig** *a1* vociferous, noisy
skränka *v3, tekn.* set the teeth (*en såg* of a saw)
skräp *s7* rubbish, trash; junk; (*avskräde*) litter; *prata ~* talk nonsense; *det är bara ~ med honom* he is in a bad way **skräpa** *ligga och ~* lie about and make the room (*etc.*) [look] untidy; *~ ner* litter, *absol.* make a litter **skräphög** heap of rubbish **skräpig** *a1* untidy, littered **skräpkammare** lumber room **skräpsak** trifle, trifling matter
skrävel ['skrä:-, 'skrävv-] *s7* bragging; *vard.* bounce **skrävla** [ˣskrä:v-, ˣskrävv-] brag, bluster **skrävlare** [ˣskrä:v-, ˣskrävv-] braggart, blusterer
skröna *s1* tall tale
skröplig [ˣskrö:p-, ˣskröpp-] *a1* frail, fragile; (*orkeslös*) decrepit **-het** frailty, fragility; decreptitude

S

skröt *imperf. av skryta*

skubba 1 (*gnugga*) rub, chafe **2** (*springa*) be off, clear out

skudda ~ *stoftet av sina fötter* shake the dust off one's feet

skuffa push, shove **skuffs** *dep* jostle

skugg|a I *s1* (*motsats ljus*) shade; (*av ngt*) shadow (*äv. bildl.*); *-or och dagrar* light and shade; *ställa i ~n* (*bildl.*) put in the shade; *en ~ av sitt forna jag* a mere shadow of one's former self **II** *v1* **1** shade **2** (*följa o. bevaka*) shadow; *vard.* tail **-bild** (*silhuett*) silhouette; *bildl.* phantom, shadow **-boxning** shadow-boxing **-ig** *a1* shady, shadowy **-kabinett** *i Storbritannien* shadow cabinet *-lik a5* shadowy **-liv** shadowy existence **-ning** shading; *konkr.* shade, shadow; (*övervakning*) shadowing **-sida** shady (*bildl. äv.* dark, seamy) side **-spel** shadow play

skuld *s3* **1** (*penning-*) debt; *ha stora ~er* be heavily in debt; *infria sina ~er* meet one's liabilities; *stå i ~ hos* be indebted to; *sätta sig i ~, se* skuldsätta; *resterande ~er* arrears; *tillgångar och ~er* assets and liabilities **2** (*förvållande*) fault, blame; (*synd*) guilt; *vems är ~en?* whose fault is it?, who is to blame?; *jag bär största ~en för detta* I am most to blame in this matter; *fritaga ngn från ~* exculpate s.b.; *kasta ~en för ngt på ngn* lay (put) the blame for s.th. on s.b.; *ta hela ~en på sig* take the entire blame [on o.s.]; *vara ~ till* be to blame for; *vara utan ~* not be responsible (to blame); *förlåt oss våra ~er* (*bibl.*) forgive us our trespasses **-belastad** burdened with debt; guilty (*samvete* conscience) **-börda** burden of debt; guilt **-ebrev** *se* skuldsedel

skulderblad shoulder blade; *anat.* scapula

skuld|fri free from debt; (*om egendom*) unencumbered; (*oskyldig*) guiltless, innocent **-förbindelse** *se* skuldsedel **-känsla** sense of guilt **-medveten** guilty (*min* look)

skuldr|a *s1* shoulder; *vara bred över -orna* be broad-shouldered

skuld|regleringsfond debt adjustment fund **-satt** *a4* in debt, indebted; (*om egendom*) encumbered **-sedel** instrument of debt, [promissory] note, note of hand, I.O.U. (= I owe you) **-sätta** (*egendom*) encumber; ~ *sig* run into debt, incur (contract) debts

skull i *uttr.: för din ~* for your sake; *gör det för min ~* (*äv.*) do it to please me; *för vädrets ~* (*t. följd av*) because (on account) of the weather; *för Guds ~!* for God's sake!; *för en gångs ~* for once; *för skams* (*syns*) ~ for the sake of appearances, for form's sake; *för skojs ~* for fun; *för säkerhets ~* for safety['s sake]

1 skulle *imperf. av 1 skola*

2 skulle *s2* (*hö-*) hayloft

skulor *pl* swill (*sg*)

skulpter|a sculpture; carve in stone (*etc.*); *vard.* sculp **-ing** sculpturing

skulptris sculptress **skulptur** sculpture **skulptu'ral** *a1* sculptural **skulptör** sculptor

1 skum [skumm] *a1* dusky, dim, misty; (*beslöjad*) veiled (*blick* look); (*ljusskygg*) shady (*individ* individual)

2 skum [skumm] *s7* foam; (*fradga*) froth,

spume; (*lödder*) lather; (*på kokande vätska*) scum; *vispa till ~* beat (whip) to a froth

skum|bad foam bath **-bildning** frothing **-gummi** foam rubber

skumma 1 (*bilda skum*) foam, spume, froth; (*om vin*) sparkle; (*om öl*) foam, froth; (*om läskedryck e.d.*) fizz; ~ *av ilska* foam with rage **2** (*avskilja skum*) skim; ~ *grädden av mjölken* skim the cream off the milk; ~ *en tidning* skim through a paper **skummjölk** skim[med] milk

skumpa *v1,* ~ [*i väg*] scamper off (away); (*om åkdon*) jog, bump **skumpig** *a1* bumpy (*väg* road)

skumplast foam plastic

skumrask *s7* dusk [of the evening] **-affär** shady business (transaction) **-figur** suspicious individual

skumsläckare foam extinguisher

skumögd *a1* purblind, dim-sighted; bleary-eyed

skunk *s2* [striped] skunk

skur *s2* shower; (*regn- äv.*) downpour, drencher; *spridda ~ar* scattered showers

skur|a scour, scrub; (*polera*) polish, burnish (*mässing* brass) **-borste** scrubbing brush **-duk** scouring cloth **-golv** plain deal floor **-gumma** charwoman **-hink** bucket, pail

skurit *sup. av 2 skära*

skurk *s2* scoundrel, villain; (*skojare*) rascal, blackguard **-aktig** *a1* villainous, scoundrelly **-aktighet** villainy **-streck** evil deed; dirty trick

skur|lov *skol., vi har ~* our shcool is closed for cleaning **-pulver** scouring powder **-trasa** scouring cloth

skut|a *s1* small cargo boat; *vard.* boat, old ship **-skeppare** skipper

skutt *s7* leap, bound **skutta** leap, *etc., jfr* hoppa

skvad'ron *s3* squadron of cavalry

skval|a stream (*äv. bildl.*); pour, spout **-ande** *s6* pouring

skvaller ['skvall-] *s7* gossip; (*lösa rykten*) town-talk; (*förtal*) slander; *skolsl.* sneaking **-aktig** *a1* gossipy; (*förtalande*) slanderous **-bytta** *s1* gossip, gossipmonger, telltale; *skolsl.* sneak **-historia** piece of gossip **-krönika** chronicle of scandal **-käring** [old] gossip, scandalmonger **-rör** overflow pipe **-spegel** window mirror **-tacka** *s1, vard., jfr* -bytta

skvallr|a gossip, tattle; *skolsl.* sneak; ~ *för mamma* tell mother; ~ *på ngn* report s.b.; ~ *ur skolan* tell tales out of school; *hans min ~de om* his looks betrayed **-ig** *a1, se* skvalleraktig

skvalmusik nonstop popular music [on the radio]; (*bakgrundsmusik*) muzak (*varumärke*)

skvalp *s7* splash[ing], lap[ing] **skvalpa** (*om vågor*) lap, ripple; (*skvimpa*) splash to and fro; (*spilla*) spill

1 skvatt *n, inte ett ~* not a thing (scrap)

2 skvatt *adv,* ~ *galen* clean crazy, mad as a hatter

skvattram [-amm] *s3, bot.* wild rosemary

skvimpa ~ [*över*] splash over

skvätt *s2* drop, splash (*mjölk* of milk); *gråta en ~* shed a few tears **skvätta** *v3* splash, spill; (*småregna*) drizzle **skvättbord** *sjö.* waterboard, washboard

1 sky [ʃy:] *s2* (*moln*) cloud; (*himmel*) sky,

heaven; *lätta ~ar* light clouds; *stå som fallen från ~n (~arna)* be struck all of a heap; *skrika i högan (himmelens)* ~ cry blue murder; *höja till ~arna* praise to the skies

2 sky [ʃy:] *s3 (köttsaft)* gravy, meat juice; *AE.* pan gravy

3 sky [ʃy:] *v4* shun, avoid; *(frukta)* dread; *inte ~ ngn möda* spare no pains; *inte ~ några kostnader* spare no expense; *~ som pesten* shun like the plague; *bränt barn ~r elden* once bitten, twice shy

skydd [ʃ-] *s7* protection *(mot* against, from); *(försvar)* defence; *(av växel)* protection, honour; *(mera konkr.)* shelter; *(tillflykt)* refuge; *i ~ av* under cover of *(mörkret* darkness); *söka ~ a) (mot)* take (seek) shelter *(mot vinden from the wind); b) (hos)* seek protection, take refuge *(hos* with); *till ~ för* for the protection of

skydda protect; *(försvara)* preserve, defend *(mot* against, from); *(värna)* shield; *(trygga)* safeguard; *(mera konkr.)* cover, shelter; *~d från insyn* screened off from people's view; *lagligen ~d* protected by law; *~d verkstad* sheltered workshop

skydds|ande guardian spirit **-anordning** safety device (contrivance) **-dräkt** protective suit **-färg** protective colouring **-galler** [protective] grating **-glasögon** *pl* protective goggles **-handskar** protective gloves **-helgon** patron [saint] **-hem** reformatory [school]; *BE.* approved school; *AE.* institution for juveniles **-hjälm** hard hat, crash (protective) helmet **-häkte** preventive arrest, protective custody **-ingenjör** safety engineer **-kläder** protective clothing **-kommitté** safety committee **-konsulent** chief probation [and parole] officer **-kräm** barrier cream **-ling** ward, protegé **-lös** defenceless **-mask** *s3* respirator **-medel** protective agent; *med.* prophylactic **-märke** trademark **-nät** safety net **-ombud** safety controller (representative) **-omslag** *(på bok)* dust jacket (cover) **-område** *mil.* restricted area **-patron 1** *se* **-helgon 2** *(gynnare)* patron, favourer **-rum** [air-raid] shelter; *mil. äv.* dugout **-tillsyn** probation **-tull** protective duty **-uppfostran** correctional education **-vall** *(mot havet)* sea defence work **-ympning** vaccination **-åtgärd** protective measure, preventive **-ängel** guardian angel

sky|drag waterspout, tornado **-fall** cloudburst

skyffel [ˈʃyff-, ˈʃyff-] *s2* shovel; *(sop-)* dustpan **skyffla** [ˈʃyff-] shovel; *~ ogräs* hoe weeds; *~ snö* shovel (clear) snow

skygg [ʃ-] *a1* shy *(för* of); *(blyg)* timid; *(rädd)* frightened; *(tillbakadragen)* reserved; *(ängslig)* timorous; *(om häst)* skittish **skygga** start, take fright *(för* at); *(om häst)* shy *(för* at); *~ för (vara rädd för)* shy of, shrink from **skygghet** shyness etc.; timidity, fear; reserve **skygglappar** blinkers, *AE.* blinders

skyhög towering, colossal; sky-high

skyl [ʃ-] *s2* shock, stook

1 skyla [ʃ-] *v2 (hölja)* cover; hide *(sitt ansikte* one's face); *~ över* cover [up], *bildl.* veil, hide

2 skyla [ʃ-] *v1 (säd)* shock, stook

skyldig [ʃ-] *a1* **1** *(betalnings-)* in debt; *vara ~ ngn ngt* owe s.b. s.th.; *vad är jag ~?* what do

I owe [you]?, *(vid uppgörelse)* how much am I to pay?; *vara ngn tack ~* be indebted to s.b.; *inte bli ngn svaret ~* have a reply ready **2** *(som bär skulden t. ngt)* guilty *(till* of); *jur.* convicted, found guilty *(till* of); *den ~e* the culprit (offender); *erkänna sig ~* plead guilty; *förklara ngn ~* find s.b. guilty, convict s.b.; *göra sig ~ till* commit, be guilty of *(ett brott* a crime) **3** *(pliktig)* bound, obliged; *vara ~ att* have to; *han är inte ~ att (äv.)* he is under no obligation to **-het** duty, obligation *(mot* towards); *ikläda sig ~er* assume liabilities; *rättigheter och ~er* rights and obligations

skyldra [ʃ-] ~ *gevär* present arms

skylla [ʃ-] *v2, ~ ngt på ngn* blame s.b. for s.th.; *~ på otur* plead bad luck; *du får ~ dig själv* you only have yourself to blame; *~ ifrån sig* put (lay) the blame on s.b. else

skylt [ʃ-] *s2* sign[board]; *(reklam-)* advertisement board, poster **skylta** display [one's goods]; *~ med* put on show, display, *bildl.* show off, display; *~ om* redress a shop window **skylt|docka** dummy, lay figure **-fönster** shop window; *AE.* show (store) window **-låda** showcase **-ning** *(-ande)* displaying, window-dressing; *konkr.* window-display **-ställ** display stand (rack)

skyltvakt [ʃ-] sentry

skymf [ʃ-] *s3* insult, affront, offence; *(kränkning)* outrage **skymfa** insult, affront, offend; *(kränka)* outrage **skymflig** *a1* ignominious *(död* death); outrageous *(behandling* treatment) **skymford** insulting (abusive) word; *koll.* abusive language *(sg)*, insults *(pl)*

skym|ma [ʃ-] *v2* **1** *(fördunkla)* stand in the way (light) of; *(dölja)* conceal, hide; *du -mer mig* you are [standing] in my light; *hennes blick -des av tårar* her eyes were dimmed (blinded) by tears **2** *(mörkna)* det -mer it is getting dark (dusk); *det -de för ögonen på henne* her eyes grew dim **-ning** twilight, dusk, nightfall; *hålla (kura)* ~ sit in the twilight

skymt [ʃ-] *s2* glimpse; *(aning)* idea, suspicion; *(spår)* trace; *fånga (se) en ~ av* catch a glimpse of; *en ~ av hopp* a gleam of hope; *utan ~en av bevis* without a trace of evidence; *inte en ~ av intresse* not the slightest interest; *inte en ~ av tvekan* not a trace of hesitation

skymta 1 *(se en skymt av)* catch a glimpse of **2** *(skönjas)* be dimly seen (visible); *~ fram* peep out; *sjön ~r [fram] mellan träden* the lake glitters through the trees; *solen ~r fram* the sun peeps out [from behind the clouds]; *~ förbi* be seen flitting past

skymundan [ʃ-, -ˈunn-] *n, i ~* in the background (shade); *hålla sig i ~* keep o.s. out of the way

skynd|a [ʃ-] hurry, hasten *(t. ngns hjälp* to a p.'s rescue); *~ långsamt!* hasten slowly!; more haste, less speed!; *~ ngn till mötes* hasten to meet s.b.; *~ på* hurry up (on); *~ på med* hurry on with; *~ sig* hurry [up] **-sam** *a1* speedy; prompt *(hjälp* help); *(rask)* quick, hurried *(steg* steps) **-samhet** speed[iness], promptness etc.

skynke [ʃ-] *s6* cover[ing], cloth; *... är för honom ett rött ~* for him ... is like a red rag to a bull

S

skyskrapa skyscraper
skyt [ʃ-] *s3* Scythian **-isk** ['ʃy:-] Scythian **-iska** ['ʃy:-] *s1* (*språk*) Scythian
skytt [ʃ-] *s2* shot, marksman; *S~en* Sagittarius, the Archer
skytte [ʃ-] *s6* shooting **-förening** rifle (shooting) club **-grav** trench
skyttel [ʃ-] *s2* shuttle
skyttelinje firing line
skytteltrafik shuttle service
skåda behold, see; (*varsebli*) perceive; *~ dagens ljus* see the light of day
skåde|bana *s1* stage; scene **-bröd** showbread **-lysten** eager to see; (*nyfiken*) curious **-penning** medal **-plats** *bildl.* scene [of action] **-spel** spectacle, sight; *teat.* play, drama **-spelare** actor; *bli ~* go on the stage **-spelarkonst** art of acting, histrionic art **-spelartrupp** theatrical company **-speleri** *se -spelarkonst*; (*förkonstling*) artificiality **-spelerska** actress **-spelsförfattare** playwright, dramatist
skål *s2* **1** (*kärl*) bowl; (*spilkum*) basin **2** (*välgångs-*) toast; *dricka ngns ~* drink [to] a p.'s health; *utbringa en ~ för ngn* propose a toast to s.b.; *~!* here's to you!, cheers! **skåla 1** *~ för* propose a toast to; *~ med* drink to (*varandra* one another) **2** (*urholka*) scoop (gouge) [out] **skålformig** [-å-] *a1* cup-shaped, bowl--shaped
1 skålla *s1* (*tunn platta*) scale, lamina
2 skålla (*med hett vatten*) scald
skållhet scalding (boiling, *vard.* piping) hot
skållning scalding
skål|pund *ung.* pound **-tal** toast; after-dinner speech
Skåne *n* Scania **skånsk** *a1* Scanian
skåp *s7* cupboard; *AE. äv.* closet; (*med lådor*) cabinet; (*i omklädningsrum*) locker; *bestämma var ~et skall stå* wear the breeches **-bil** [delivery] van, *AE.* panel truck **-dörr** cupboard (*etc.*) door **-mat** (*rester*) remnants (*pl*); *bildl.* stale stuff **-supa** drink in private (on the sly) **-supare** secret drinker
skåra *s1* score; (*inskärning*) notch; (*spår*) groove, slot; (*sår*) cut
skäck [ʃ-] *s2* piebald horse **-ig** *a1* piebald, pied
skädda [ʃ-] *s1* (*fisk*) dab
skägg [ʃ-] *s7* **1** beard; *ha ~* have (wear) a beard; *låta ~et växa* grow a beard; *tala ur ~et* speak out; *tvista om påvens ~* split hairs **2** *biol.* barb; (*på mussla*) beard **-botten** *mörk ~* a blue chin **-dopping** great crested grebe
skägg|ig *a1* bearded; (*orakad*) unshaved **-lös** beardless **-strå** [a] hair [out] of one's beard **-stubb** bristles (*pl*); (*eftermiddagsskägg*) five--o'clock shadow **-svamp** barber's itch (rash) **-töm** (*på fisk*) barbel **-växt** [growth of] beard[s *pl*]; *han har kraftig ~* his beard grows fast
skäkta [ʃ-] **I** *s1* swingle **II** *v1* (*lin*) swingle, scutch
skäl [ʃ-] *s7* reason (*till* of, for); (*orsak*) cause, ground; (*bevekelsegrund*) motive; (*argument*) argument (*för och emot* for and against); *så mycket större ~ att* so much more the reason to; *vägande ~* weighty arguments; *av principiella ~* on ground of principle; *göra ~ för sig*

give satisfaction; *ha allt ~ att* have every reason to; *det har sina* [*randiga*] *~* there are very good reasons for it; *med* [*fullt*] *~ kan man säga* one is [fully] justified in saying; *det vore ~ att* it would be well to; *det vore ~ i att du försökte* you would do well to (you had better) try; *väga ~en för och emot* weigh the pros and cons **skälig** *a1* reasonable, fair; *finna ~t* find it proper **skäligen** (*tämligen*) pretty (*enkel* simple); (*rimligtvis*) reasonably, fairly
skäll [ʃ-] *s7*, *se ovett*
1 skälla [ʃ-] *v2* bark; (*om räv*) yelp, cry; (*vara ovettig*) scream, bellow; *~ ngn för bracka* call s.b. a Philistine; *~ på* (*bildl.*) abuse, scold; *~ ut* blow up, tell off
2 skälla [ʃ-] *s1* bell; *nu blev det annat ljud i ~n* then things took on a new note
skällko bell-cow
skällsord word of abuse; *pl koll.* foul language (*sg*), invectives
skälm [ʃ-] *s2* rogue; (*lymmel*) rascal; (*-unge*) monkey, trot; (*spjuver*) wag; *en inpiskad ~* an arch rogue; *med ~en i ögat* with a roguish twinkle **-aktig** *a1* roguish; mischievous; *~ blick* arch look **-roman** picaresque novel
skälm|sk [ʃ-] *a1*, *se skälmaktig* **-stycke** piece of roguery; (*spratt*) practical joke
skälv|a [ʃ-] *v1* shake, quake; (*darra*) tremble, quiver (*av* with) **-ande** *a4* shaking *etc.*; tremulous **-ning** shaking *etc.*; (*en ~*) tremor; (*rysning*) thrill
skämd [ʃ-] *a5* (*om kött*) tainted; (*om frukt*) rotten; (*om luft, ägg*) bad **skämma** *v2* (*fördärva*) spoil; (*vanpryda*) mar; *för mycket och för litet skämmer allt* too much and too little spoils everything; *~ bort* spoil; *~ ut* dishonour, put to shame; *~ ut sig* disgrace o.s. **skämmas** *v2*, *dep* be ashamed; *det är inget att ~ för* that is nothing to be ashamed of; *boken skäms inte för sig* the book does itself credit; *~ ögonen ur sig* die of shame; *fy -s!* shame on you!
skämt [ʃ-] *s7* joke, jest; *dåligt ~* bad (poor) joke; *grovt ~* coarse joke; *förstå ~* understand (be able to see) a joke; *säga ngt på ~* say s.th. in fun; *~ åsido!* joking apart! **skämta** joke, jest; *~ med* make fun of, poke fun at **skämtare** joker, jester, wag
skämt|artikel party novelty **-historia** funny story **-lynne** humour **-sam** *a1* jocular; (*humoristisk*) humourous; (*rolig*) funny, comical, droll; *ta ngt från den ~ma sidan* take s.th. as a joke **-samhet** jocularity, humour **-serie** comic strip; *AE.* funny **-tecknare** comic artist, cartoonist **-teckning** cartoon **-tidning** comic magazine (paper)
skänd|a [ʃ-] defile, pollute; desecrate (*gravar* graves) **-lig** *a1* infamous (*handling* deed); (*neslig*) nefarious, atrocious (*brott* crime) **-lighet** infamy, atrocity, outrage
1 skänk [ʃ-] *s2* (*skåp*) sideboard, buffet; cupboard
2 skänk [ʃ-] *s3* (*gåva*) gift, present; *till ~s* as a gift
skänka *v3* **1** give (*äv. bildl.*); present (*ngn ngt* s.b. with s.th.); *~ bort* give away **2** *~ i* [*glasen*] fill the glasses
skänkel [ʃ-] *s2* shank, leg (*äv. tekn.*)

skäppa [ʃ-] *s1* (*rymdmått*) bushel; *ge ngn ~n full* let s.b. have it; *sätta sitt ljus under en ~* hide one's light under a bushel
1 skär [ʃ-] *a1* (*ren*) pure, clean; (*obefläckad*) immaculate; [*ren och*] *~ lögn* a downright lie
2 skär [ʃ-] *a1* (*ljusröd*) pink, light red
3 skär [ʃ-] *s7* (*ö*) skerry, rocky islet
4 skär [ʃ-] *s7* **1** (*egg*) [cutting] edge **2** (*skåra*) notch **3** (*med skridsko*) stride
1 skära [ʃ-] *s1* **1** sickle **2** (*mån-*) crescent
2 skära [ʃ-] *skar skurit* **1** cut (*äv. bildl.*); (*kött*) carve; *~* (*korsa*) *varandra* intersect, (*om gator*) cross; *~ halsen av sig* cut one's throat; *~ i bitar* cut up (... to pieces); *~ i remsor* shred; *~ i skivor* slice; *~ i trä* carve; *fartyget skär* [*genom*] *vågorna* the ship cleaves the waves; *~ tänder*[*na*] gnash (grind) one's teeth; *~ alla över en kam* treat all alike; *~ guld med täljknivar* coin money; *~ pipor i vassen* have a big income and little to do for it; *det skär i öronen* it jars (grates) upon my ears **2** (*med betonad partikel*) *~ av* (*bort*) cut off; *~ för* carve; *~ ihop* (*tekn.*) seize; *~ in* incise; *~ in i* cut into; *~ till* cut out; *~ upp* cut up, (*öppna*) cut open; *~ ut* carve **3** *rfl* cut o.s.; *kokk.* curdle; *~ sig i tummen* cut one's thumb; *det skar sig mellan dem* they clashed with one another
skär|ande *a4* cutting *etc.*; (*om ljud*) piercing, shrill **-bräde** cutting (chopping) board; (*för bröd*) breadboard **-brännare** cutting blowpipe, fusing burner **-bönor** French beans
skärgård [ˈʃä:r-, ˈʃä:r-] archipelago, fringe of skerries; *i ~en* in the archipelago (skerries) [off Stockholm *etc.*]
skärm [ʃ-] *s2* screen; *tekn.* shield; (*på huvudbonad*) peak **skärma** *~* [*av*] screen, shield; *~ för* screen off
skärmaskin cutting machine; (*för matvaror*) slicer
skärm|bild mass radiograph, fluoroscopic image **-bilda** *v1* mass-radiograph **-bildsfotografering** mass radiography, X-ray screening
skärmmössa peaked cap
skärmytsl|a [ˈʃä:r-] skirmish **-ing** skirmish
skär|ning [ˈʃä:r-] cutting **-ningspunkt** [point of] intersection
skärp [ʃ-] *s7* belt; (*broderat o. uniforms-*) sash
skärpa [ʃ-] **I** *s1* sharpness, keenness *etc.* (*jfr skarp*); *foto., TV* definition; (*klarhet*) exactness, stringency; (*i ton*) acerbity; *det är ~ i luften* there's a nip in the air **II** *v3* sharpen (*äv. bildl.*); *bildl. äv.* strengthen, quicken; (*öka*) increase, heighten; *konflikten har skärpts* the conflict has deepened (been aggravated); *~ kontrollen* increase (tighten) the control; *~ sina sinnen* sharpen one's senses; *~ straffet* increase (raise) the penalty; *~ tonen* sharpen one's (*etc.*) tone; *~ uppmärksamheten* be more vigilant; *~ sig* sharpen up, pull o.s. together, pull one's socks up; *nu får du ~ dig* pull yourself together now **skärpedjup** *foto.* depth of field (definition) **skärpning** sharpening *etc.*; aggravation
skärpt *a1, vard.* sharp, smart, bright
skärra *~ upp* frighten, worry; *~ inte upp dig* don't get excited **skärrad** *a5, vard.* in a state, all of a dither
skärseld [ˈʃä:rs-] purgatory; *bildl.* ordeal

skärskåd|a [ʃ-] view, examine; scrutinize; scan **-ande** *s6* viewing, examination; *ta i ~* inspect, examine
skärslipare knife grinder
skärsår cut, gash
skärtorsdag [ʃ-] Maundy (Holy) Thursday
skärv [ʃ-] *s2, bibl.* mite; *min sista ~* my last farthing
skärva [ʃ-] *s1* (*kruk- o.d.*) shard, sherd; (*glas-, granat- o.d.*) splinter; (*friare*) fragment, bit
sköka [ʃ-] *s1* harlot
sköld [ʃ-] *s2* shield; (*vapen- äv.*) [e]scutcheon; *zool.* scutellum; (*på sköldpadda*) shell; *bildl.* shelter **-brosk** *anat.* thyroid cartilage **-emärke** [heraldic] bearing **-körtel** thyroid gland **-mö** Amazon **-padd** *s3* tortoise (turtle) shell **-padda** (*land-*) tortoise; (*vatten-*) turtle **-paddsskal** tortoise shell **-paddssoppa** turtle soup
skölj|a [ʃ-] *v2* rinse; (*spola*) wash; *vågorna -er stranden* the waves wash the shore; *~s överbord* be washed overboard; *~ av* rinse off; *~ bort* wash away; *~ sig i munnen* rinse one's mouth **-kopp** finger bowl **-ning** rinsing *etc.*; (*en ~*) rinse, wash; *med.* douche **-skål** (*på matbord*) finger bowl **-vatten** rinsing water
1 skön [ʃ-] *n* discretion; *efter eget ~* at one's own discretion
2 skön [ʃ-] *a1* beautiful; fair; (*angenäm*) nice; (*behaglig*) comfortable; *den ~a* the fair lady (one); *ha sinne för det ~a* have a sense of beauty; *~t!* that's fine!; *en ~ historia* (*iron.*) a pretty story
skön|ande lover of the arts **-het** [-ö:-] beauty (*äv. konkr.*); *konkr. äv.* belle
skönhets|behandling beauty treatment **-drottning** beauty queen **-expert** cosmetologist; *AE. äv.* beautician **-fel, -fläck** flaw **-ideal** idea of beauty **-medel** cosmetic, beauty preparation **-salong** beauty salon (parlour); *AE.* beauty shop (parlor) **-sinne** sense of beauty **-sömn** *vard.* beauty sleep **-tävling** beauty contest (competition) **-vård** beauty care **-värde** aesthetic value
skönj|a [ʃ-] *v2* discern; *inte ~ ngn ljusning* see no signs of improvement **-bar** *a1* discernible; (*synlig*) visible; (*fattbar*) perceptible
skön|litteratur [ʃ-] fiction, belles-lettres **-litterär** literary; *~t arbete* work of fiction **-målning** *bildl.* idealization, gilding **-skrift** calligraphy
sköns|mässig [ˈʃö:ns-] *a1* discretionary, optional **-taxering** discretionary (arbitrary) [tax] assessment
skör [ʃ-] *a1* brittle (*nagel* nail); (*spröd*) fragile, frail; *tyget är ~t* the cloth tears easily
skörbjugg [ˈʃö:r-] *s2* scurvy
skörd [ʃö:rd] *s2* harvest (*äv. bildl.*); (*gröda*) crop; *av årets ~* of this year's growth; *en rik ~ av erfarenheter* a rich store of experience
skörda harvest; reap (*äv. bildl.*); (*bär*) pick; *som man sår får man ~* as you sow, so shall you reap
skörde|fest harvest festival (home) **-maskin** harvester, harvesting machine **-tid** harvest time **-tröska** *s1* combine [harvester] **-utsikter** *pl* harvest prospects

skörhet [ˣʃöːr-] brittleness; fragility, frailty
skörlevnad [ˣʃöːr-] loose living
skört [ʃ-] *s7* tail, flap **skörta** ~ *upp a*) (*bedraga*) fleece, overcharge, *b*) (*fästa upp*) tuck up
1 sköt [ʃ-] *imperf. av* skjuta
2 sköt [ʃ-] *s2* drift net
sköt|a [ʃ-] *v3* **1** (*vårda*) nurse, tend (*sjuka sick people*); (*om läkare*) attend [to]; ~ *sin hälsa* look after one's health; ~ *om* take care of, attend to, nurse; ~ *om ett sår* dress a wound; *sköt om dig väl!* take good care of yourself! **2** (*förestå*) manage; run (*en affär* a shop); (*ombesörja*) attend (see) to; (*se efter*) look after, take care of; ~ *sitt arbete* do one's work; ~ *hushållet* do the housekeeping; ~ *kassan* (*räkenskaperna*) keep the cash ([the] accounts); ~ *korrespondensen* handle the correspondence; ~ *sina kort* (*äv. bildl.*) play one's cards well; *inte kunna ~ pengar* not be able to handle money; ~ *sina plikter* discharge one's duties; *den saken -er jag* I'll attend to that; *sköt du ditt!* mind your own business! **3** *rfl* (*uppföra sig*) conduct o.s. (*bra* well); (~ *om sig*) look after o.s.; *han har måst ~ sig själv* he has had to manage by himself **-are** tender, keeper **-bord** nursing table
sköte [ʃ-] *s6* **1** lap; bosom (*äv. bildl.*) **2** vagina **3** (*moderliv*) womb **-barn** *bildl.* darling, favourite
sköterska [ʃ-] nurse
sköterske|biträde assistant nurse **-elev** pupil nurse, probationer **-uniform** nurse's uniform **-utbildning** training of nurses
skötesynd [ʃ-] besetting sin
skötsam [ˣʃöːt-] *a1* well-behaved; orderly; (*plikttrogen*) conscientious
skötsel [ˈʃött-] *s9* care, tending (*av* of); (*tillsyn*) attention, attendance; (*av maskin*) operation, running; (*förvaltning*) management; (*odling*) cultivation; *kräva* ~ need (require) attendance (care) **-anvisning** operating instructions (*pl*)
skövl|a [ˣʃöːv-, ˣʃövv-] devastate; (*ödelägga*) ravage; wreck (*ngns lycka* a p.'s happiness); (*skog*) damage by reckless cutting **-ing** devastation; ravage
slabba splash about **slabbgöra** mucky job **slabbig** *a1* sloppy, splashy
slacka slacken
1 sladd *s2* **1** (*tågända*) [rope's] end **2** (*ledningstråd*) flex[ible cord]; *AE.* cord **3** *bildl., komma på ~en* bring up the rear; *komma med på ~en* slip in with the rest
2 sladd *s2* (*med fordon*) skid
sladda lurch, skid, slip sideways
sladdbarn child born several years after the other[s] [in a family]; *vard.* afterthought
sladder [ˈsladd-] *s7* chatting, babbling; gossip **-tacka** *s1* gossipmonger
sladdlampa portable worklamp
sladdra chatter, babble; gossip
sladdrig *a1* (*slapp*) flabby, limp; (*om tyg*) flimsy
slafs *s7* sloppiness **slafsa** ~ *i sig* lap up, gobble up
1 slag *s7* (*art, sort*) kind, sort; (*typ*) type; *fack.*

species; (*kategori*) category, class; *alla ~s* all kinds of; *böcker av alla* [*de*] ~ all sorts (kinds) of books, books of every description; *allt ~s* every kind of; *han är något ~s direktör* he is a manager of some sort (some kind of manager); *i sitt* ~ of its kind, in its way; *vad för* ~? what?
2 slag *s7* **1** (*smäll*) blow (*äv. bildl.*), stroke, hit; (*lätt*) pat, dab; (*rapp*) lash, cut; (*knytnävs-; knackning*) knock; *ge ngn ett* ~ deal s.b. a blow; *ett* ~ *för örat* (*bildl.*) a knockout blow; *ett* ~ *i luften* (*äv. bildl.*) a shot in the dark; *hugg och* ~ biffs and blows; ~ *i* ~ in rapid succession; *göra* ~ *i saken* clinch the matter; *i* (*med*) *ett* ~ all at once, straight off; *slå ett* ~ *för* strike a blow for **2** (*rytmiskt* ~) beat; *koll.* beating; (*hjärtats äv.*) throbbing; (*puls- äv.*) throb; (*pendel-*) oscillation **3** (*klock-*) stroke; *på ~et sex* at six o'clock sharp, on the stroke of six; *komma på ~et* arrive on the dot **4** (-*anfall*) [apoplectic] stroke; *få* ~ have a stroke; *jag höll på att få* ~ (*vard.*) I nearly had a fit; *skrämma* ~ *på ngn* frighten s.b. out of his wits **5** (*fält-*) battle (*vid of*) **6** (*varv*) turn, round; (*kolv-*) stroke; (*tag*) moment, while; *ett* ~ *trodde jag* at one time I thought **7** *sjö.* tack; *göra ett* ~ tack, beat **8** (*fågeldrill*) warbling **9** (*på plagg*) facing; (*rock- äv.*) lapel; (*på ärm*) cuff; (*byx-*) turn-up, *AE.* cuff
slag|a *s1* flail **-anfall** apoplectic stroke **-björn** killer bear **-bom** lift gate; (*i vävstol*) batten **-bord** gate-leg[ged] table **-dänga** *s1* hit, street ballad
slag|en *a5* struck (*av förvåning* with surprise); (*besegrad*) defeated, beaten, *AE. äv.* beat; *en* ~ *man* a broken man **-fast** impact resistant **-fält** battlefield battleground **-färdig** eg. ready for battle (fight); *bildl.* quick at repartee, quick-witted **-färdighet** eg. readiness for battle; *bildl.* ready wit, quickness at repartee
slagg *s3, s4* slag, cinder[s *pl*], clinkers (*pl*), dross, scoria **slagga** (*avlägsna slagg*) take off the slag; (*bilda slagg*) form slag
slagg|artad [-aːr-] *a5* slaggy, cindery; scoriaceous **-bildning** slag formation; scorification **-hög** slag heap
slag|hållfasthet impact strength, shock resistance **-hök** goshawk **-instrument** percussion instrument
slag|it *sup. av 2* slå **-kraft** striking power (*äv. bildl.*); effectiveness **-kraftig** effective **-krysare** battle cruiser **-linje** line of battle **-längd** *tekn.* [ram] travel, [piston] stroke **-löda** braze **-man** (*i bollspel*) batsman **-nummer** hit **-ord** catchword, slogan **-ordning** battle array **-påse** punching bag; *bildl.* whipping boy **-regn** downpour, pelting rain **-ruta** *s1* divining (dowsing) rod **-sida** *sjö.* list; *bildl.* preponderance; *få* ~ heel over; *ha* ~ have a list **-skepp** battleship **-skugga** projected shadow
slags|kämpe [ˣslaks-] fighter; rowdy **-mål** *s7* fight; *råka i* ~ come to blows; *ställa till* ~ start a fight
slag|stift *mil.* striker; firing pin **-svärd** large [two-handed] sword **-trä** (*i bollspel*) bat **-tålig** knock resistant **-uggla** Ural owl **-vatten** *sjö.* bilge water **-verk 1** (*i ur*) striking

mechanism **2** *mus.* percussion instruments (*pl*) **-växling** exchange of blows

slak *a1* slack (*lina* rope), loose; (*kraftlös*) limp; ~ *i benen* wobbly at the knees **slakna** [ˣsla:k-] slacken, flag

slakt *s3, s7* slaughter[ing] **slakta** slaughter; (*döda*) kill; (*människor*) massacre; *bildl.*, ~ *en bil* strip down a car

slakt|arbutik butchery, butcher's shop **-are** butcher, slaughterer **-avfall** offals (*pl*) **-boskap** beef (slaughter) cattle **-bänk** slaughterer's block; *leda till ~en* (*bildl.*) be led to the slaughter **-eri**, **-hus** slaughterhouse **-mask** slaughtering mask **-offer** sacrifice, victim

slalom ['sla:låm] *s3* slalom; *åka ~* do slalom-skiing **-backe** slalom slope **-byxor** *pl* slalom pants **-skida** slalom ski **-tävling** slalom

1 slam [slamm] *s2, kortsp.* slam

2 slam [slamm] *s4* mud, ooze; slime

slam|avlagring siltration, silt deposit **-bildning** sludge (slime) formation

slamma (*rena*) wash, purify; (*kalkstryka*) limewash; *~d krita* precipitated chalk, whiting; ~ *igen* get filled with mud

slammer ['slamm-] *s7* rattle, clatter; (*vapen-* etc.) jangle

slam|mig *a1* muddy, slimy **-ning** elutriation; desludging

slampa *s1* slut, slattern, hussy **slampig** *a1* sluttish, slatternly, slipshod

slamra ~ [*med*] rattle, clatter

slams *s7* slovenliness **slamsa I 1** *s1* (*av kött*) scrap **2** (*kvinna*) *se* slampa **II** *v1* **1** (*slarva*) scamp **2** (*sladdra*) babble, chatter **slamsig** *a1* **1** *se* slampig **2** (*om kött*) flabby

slana *s1* pole

1 slang *s2* tube (*äv. inner-*), hose

2 slang *s3* (*språk*) slang

3 slang *i uttr.: slå sig i ~ med* strike up an acquaintance with

slang|båge catapult; *AE.* slingshot **-gurka** cucumber **-klämma** hose clip (clamp) **-koppling** hose coupling (coupler) **-lös** *~a däck* tubeless tyres

slang|ord slang word **-uttryck** slang expression

1 slank *imperf. av* 2 slinka

2 slank *a1* slender, slim

slankig *a1* limp, lank[y]

1 slant *imperf. av* slinta

2 slant *s2* coin; (*koppar-*) copper; *för hela ~en* (*bildl.*) for all one is worth; *ha en sparad ~* have some money saved; *en vacker ~* a nice sum; *slagen till ~* fit for nothing; *vända på ~en* (*bildl.*) be economical, look at every penny

1 slapp *imperf. av* slippa

2 slapp *a1* slack, loose; (*sladdrig*) flaccid; (*kraftlös*) soft, limp; (*matt*) languid; (*löslig*) lax (*moral* morals *pl*)

slappa *vard.* laze around **slapphet** slackness *etc.*; flaccidity; laxity; lack of energy **slappna** ~ [*av*] slack, slacken, relax

slarv *s7* carelessness, negligence; (*oreda*) disorder **slarva I** *s1* careless (negligent, slovenly) woman (girl), slattern **II** *v1* be careless; ~ *med* scamp, (*klädsel o.d.*) neglect; ~ *bort* lose; ~ *ifrån sig* do by halves **slarver** ['slarr-] care-

less fellow; *en liten ~* a slapdash boy **slarvfel** careless mistake **slarvig** *a1* careless, negligent; (*hafsig*) slovenly; (*osnygg*) untidy **slarvsylta 1** *kokk.* minced meat **2** *bildl.* mincemeat

slashas [ˣsla:s-] *s2* ragamuffin, good-for-nothing

slask *s7* **1** (*-ande*) splashing; (*-väder*) slushy weather **2** (*väglag*) slush **3** *se* slaskvatten **4** *se* slasktratt

slask|a 1 splash about; ~ *ner* splash **2** *det ~r* it is slushy weather **-hink** slop pail **-spalt** light column **-tratt** [kitchen] sink **-vatten** slops (*pl*), dishwater

slatt *s2* drop

1 slav *s3* (*folk*) Slav

2 slav *s2* (*träl*) slave (*äv. bildl.*); *vara ~ under* be a slave to (the slave under)

slav|a slave; (*friare*) drudge **-arbete** slave labour **-binda** make a slave of **-drivare** slave--driver **-eri** bondage, slavery **-göra** slavery; *bildl.* drudgery **-handel** slave trade; *vit ~* white-slave traffic **-handlare** slaver, slave--trader **-inna** [female] slave

1 slavisk ['sla:-] *a5* (*t. 1 slav*) Slav[ic], Slavonic; *~a språk* Slav[on]ic languages

2 slavisk ['sla:-] *a5* (*t. 2 slav*) slavish; *bildl. äv.* servile

slaviskhet servility

slav|ism Slavism **-ist** Slavist

slav|kontrakt contract which binds one hand and foot (*äv. bildl.*) **-marknad** slave market **-piska** slave-driver's whip; *ha ~n över sig* (*bildl.*) be slave-driven **-skepp** slave ship **-ägare** slave owner

slejf *s3, s2* strap **-sko** strap-shoe

slem [slemm] *s7* slime; *fack.* mucus; (*vid hosta*) phlegm **-avsöndrande** *a4* mucus-secreting **-bildning** *abstr.* formation of mucus; *konkr.* mucus secretion **-hinna** mucous membrane **-lösande** *a4* expectorant **-mig** *a1* slimy; *fack.* mucous; (*klibbig*) viscous

slentri'an *s3* routine; *fastna i ~* get into a rut **-mässig** *a1* routine; *undersökningen var ~* the investigation was a matter of routine

slet *imperf. av* slita

slev *s2* ladle; *få en släng av ~en* (*bildl.*) come in for one's share **sleva** ~ *i sig* shovel into one's mouth

slick *s2* lick **slicka** lick; ~ *i sig* lap [up]; ~ *på* lick; ~ *sig om munnen* lick one's lips; *~t hår* sleek hair

slicke|pinne *s2* lollipop **-pott** [-å-] *s2* **1** (*pekfinger*) forefinger **2** (*hushållsskrapa*) dough--scraper

slid *s3, tekn.* slide; (*i ångmaskin*) [slide] valve **slida** *s1* sheath (*äv. bot.*); *anat.* vagina **sliddersladder** ['slidd-] *s7* fiddle-faddle; *~!* fiddlesticks!

slid|hornsdjur bovid animal **-kniv** sheath knife **slik** *a1* such like; *~t* that sort of thing

slimmad *a5,* ~ *skjorta* slim-fit shirt

slinga *s1* coil, loop; *sjö.* sling; (*ornament*) arabesque; (*blad-*) creeper; (*rök-*) wisp

slinger|bult *s2* **1** (*undanflykt*) dodge, prevarication **2** *pers.* dodger **-växt** creeper, trailing plant

slingra 1 (*linda*) wind, twine; (*sno*) twist **2** (*om*

S

fartyg) roll **3** *rfl* wind [in and out]; *(sno sig)* twist, twine; *(om flod äv.)* meander; *(om orm)* wriggle; *(om växt)* trail, creep; *bildl.* dodge, hedge; ~ *sig om varandra (äv.)* intertwine; ~ *sig från ngt (bildl.)* wriggle out of s.th.; ~ *sig undan (bildl.)* get out of, tergiversate **slingrande** *a4* winding; *(om flod, väg äv.)* meandering, serpentine **slingrig** *a1* sinuous, tortuous, winding **slingring** wind; twine, wriggle; *sjö.* roll

1 slinka *s1* wench, hussy

2 slinka *slank slunkit* **1** *(smyga)* slink *(i väg, undan* away, off); ~ *om hörnet* slip round the corner; ~ *igenom (förbi)* slip through (past); ~ *in (äv.)* steal (sneak) in **2** *(hänga lös)* dangle, hang loose

slint *s, i uttr.:* *slå* ~ come to nothing, fail **slinta** *slant sluntit* slip; *jag slant med foten* my foot slipped; *glaset slant ur handen på mig* the glass slipped out of my hand

slip *s2* slipway; *ta upp ett fartyg på* ~ take up a vessel on to the slips

slip|a *(skärpa)* grind, whet, sharpen; *(glätta)* grind; *(polera)* polish; *(glas e.d.)* cut **slipad** *a5, bildl.* smart; cunning **slipare** grinder; cutter **slipduk** abrasive cloth

sliper ['sli:-] *s2* [railway] sleeper; *AE.* [railroad] crosstie, tie

slip|eri grindery **-maskin** grinding machine **-massa** mechanical wood pulp **-ning** [-i:p-] grinding *etc., jfr slipa*

slipp|a *slapp sluppit* **1** *(undgå)* escape [from]; *(besparas)* be spared [from]; *(inte behöva)* not need [to] (have to); *(undgå)* avoid; *du -er [göra det]* you needn't [do it]; *du -er inte [ifrån det]* you cannot get out of it; *kan jag få ~?* can I be excused (let off)?; *låt mig ~ se det!* I don't want to see it!; *jag ser helst att jag -er* I would rather be excused (rather not); ~ *besvär* save (be spared) trouble; *han slapp göra det* he did not have to do it; *för att ~ straff* to avoid punishment **2** *(med betonad partikel)* ~ *ifrån* get away [from], escape; ~ *in* be admitted (let in); ~ *lös* break loose, *(bli släppt)* be set free; *elden slapp lös* a fire broke out; ~ *undan* escape, *absol.* get out of it; ~ *undan med blotta förskräckelsen* get off with a fright; ~ *upp i sömmen* come apart at the seams; *det slapp ur mig* it escaped me; ~ *ut* get (be let) out, *(sippra ut)* leak out

slipprig *a1* slippery; *(oanständig)* indecent, obscene

slips *s2* tie

slip|skiva grinding wheel **-sten** grindstone

slira slip, slide; *(om fordon)* skid; *(om hjul)* spin **slirig** *a1* slippery **slirning** [-i:r-] sliding, slide; *(fordons)* skidding; *(kopplings)* slipping

sliskig *a1* sickly sweet; *bildl.* oily

slit *s7* toil, drudgery **slita** *slet slitit* **1** *(nöta)* wear *(hål på a hole in)*; *den håller att ~ på* it stands a great deal of wear; *slit den med hälsan!* you're welcome to it!; ~ *ut* wear out; ~ *ut sig* wear o.s. out with [over]work **2** *(knoga)* toil, drudge; ~ *och släpa* toil and moil; ~ *have a rough time of it* **3** *(rycka)* pull *(i at)*; tear *(av off; sönder* to pieces); ~ *sitt hår* tear one's hair **4** *rfl* get loose, *(om båt)* break adrift

(loose) **slitage** *s7* wear [and tear] **slitas** *slets slitits, dep,* ~ *mellan hopp och fruktan* be torn between hope and dread **slitbana** *(på däck)* [tyre] tread **sliten** *a3* worn [out]; *(lugg-)* threadbare, shabby, shiny; *bildl.* hackneyed *(fras* phrase) **slitit** *sup. av slita* **slitning** [-i:t-] wear; *bildl.* discord, friction

slits *s2* slit; *(på kläder)* vent **slitsa** slit

slit|sam [-i:-] *a1* strenuous, hard; *ha det ~t* have a hard time [of it] **-stark** hardwearing, durable, lasting **-styrka** durability, wearing qualities **-sula** outsole **-varg** *han är en* ~ he is hard on his clothes

slockn|a [-å-] go out; lie down; *(somna)* drop off; *~d vulkan* extinct volcano; *~d blick* dull (lifeless) look **-ande** *a4* expiring; dying down

slog *imperf. av 2* slå

slogan ['slɔ:-, 'slå:-] *s3, äv. best. f. slogan, pl slogan* slogan, catch phrase

slok|a slouch, droop; ~ *med svansen* drag one's tail **-hatt** slouch hat **-örad** *a5* lop-eared; *bildl.* crestfallen

slopa *(avskaffa)* abolish, reject; ~ *tanken på* abandon (give up) the thought of

slott [-å-] *s7* palace; *(befäst)* castle; *(herresäte)* manor [house], hall

slotts|fogde warden of a castle **-fru** chatelaine **-herre** lord of a (the) castle (manor) **-kapell** chapel of a palace, chapel royal **-lik[nande]** palatial **-park** castle (palace) park **-ruin** ruined castle **-tappning, -vin** château wine **-väbel** *s2* superintendent of a royal palace

slo'vak *s3* Slovak **-isk** *a5* Slovak

slo|'ven *s3* Slovene **-'vensk** [-e:-] *a5* Slovenian, Slovene

sludder ['sludd-] *s7* slurred speech **sluddra** slur one's words; *(om drucken)* talk thick **sluddrig** *a1* slurred; thick

slug *a1* shrewd; *(listig)* cunning, sly, wily; *(finurlig)* resourceful

slugga *vard.* slog, *AE.* slug **slugger** ['slugg-] *s2, vard.* slogger, *AE.* slugger

slughuvud *ett* ~ a sly dog

sluka *v1, imperf. äv.* slök swallow *(äv. bildl.)*; devour *(böcker* books); ~ *maten* gobble up (bolt) one's food

slum [slumm] *s3* slum **-kvarter** slum[s *pl*], slum district

slummer ['slumm-] *s9* slumber; *(lur)* doze, nap

slump *s2* **1** *(tillfällighet)* chance; luck, hazard; *av en* ~ by chance, accidentally; *en ren* ~ a mere chance (toss-up); *~en gjorde att jag* it so happened that I; *~en gynnade oss* fortune favoured us **2** *(återstod)* remnant **slumpa 1** ~ *[bort]* sell off (at bargain prices); *vard.* dirt cheap) **2** *det ~de sig så att* it so happened that **-artad** [-a:r-] *a5*, **-mässig** *a1* haphazard, chance, random **-urval** random sample **-vis** *adv (på en slump)* at random (haphazard)

slumr|a slumber, be half-asleep; *(ta en lur)* doze, nap; ~ *in* doze off [to sleep] **-ande** *a4* slumbering; *bildl.* dormant, undeveloped

slumsyster woman Salvationist working in slums

slung|a 1 *s1* sling **II** *v1* sling; *(honung)* extract; *(friare)* fling, hurl; ~ *ngt i ansiktet på ngn* throw s.th. in a p.'s face **-boll** sling ball

slunkit *sup. av 2 slinka*
sluntit *sup. av slinta*
slup *s2 (skeppsbåt)* launch, pinnace; *(enmastad)* sloop
sluppit *sup. av slippa*
slurk *s2* drink; swig; a few drops
slusk *s2* shabby[-looking] fellow; *(lymmel)* ruffian **sluskig** *a1* shabby
sluss *s2* lock; *(dammlucka)* sluice; *(luft-)* airlock
sluss|a *(gå igenom sluss)* pass through a lock; *(låta gå genom sluss)* take through a lock **-avgift** lock dues *(pl)*, lockage **-bassäng** lock chamber **-ning** lockage, passing [a ship] through a lock **-port** lock gate **-trappa** flight of locks
slut I *s7* end; *(avslutning)* ending, termination, close, finish; *(utgång)* result; *när ~et är gott är allting gott* all's well that ends well; *~et blev att han* the end of it (result) was that he; *~et på visan blev* the end of the story was; *få ett ~* come to an end; *få ~ på* get to the end of, see the end of; *göra ~ med ngn* break it off with s.b.; *göra ~ på a)* (*göra av med*) use up, consume, *b)* (*stoppa*) put an end to; *i (vid) ~et* at the end; *känna ~et nalkas* feel that the end is near; *dagen lider mot sitt ~* the day is drawing to a close; *läsa ~ en bok* finish reading a book; *till ~* at last, finally; *ända till ~et* (*vard.*) to the bitter end; *från början till ~* from beginning to end; *låt mig tala till ~* let me finish what I was saying II *oböjligt predik. a* at an end, [all] done (over), finished; *det måste bli ~ på* there must be an end to (*ofoget* this mischief); *är ~ a)* (*i tid*) is at an end, is over *b)* (*om vara o.d.*) is used up, (*slutsåld*) sold out, *c)* (*om krafter, tålamod e.d.*) is exhausted; *kaffet är ~* there is no more coffee; *jag är alldeles ~* I am dead beat; *det är ~ mellan oss* it is all over between us; *ta ~, se sluta II 2;* ... *har tagit ~ (hand.)* we are [sold] out of ..., there is no more ...; *bensinen håller på att ta ~* we are getting (running) short of petrol; *aldrig tyckas ta ~ (äv.)* seem endless (interminable)
slut|a *I slöt -it* **1** *(till-)* close, shut; *~ leden* close the ranks; *~ ngn i sin famn* lock s.b. in one's arms; *~ en cirkel kring* form a circle round; *~ ögonen för (bildl.)* shut one's eyes to; *~ till* shut, close; *~ upp* gather, assemble **2** *(göra upp)* conclude *(fred* peace); *~ avtal* make (conclude, come to) an agreement **3** *(dra -sats)* conclude *(av* from) **II** *v1, imperf. äv. slöt* **1** *(av-)* end, bring to an end; *(säga t. slut)* conclude; *(göra färdig)* finish; *~ skolan* leave school **2** *(upphöra, ta slut)* end *(med* with; *på konsonant* in a consonant); come to (be at) an end, stop, cease; *AE. äv.* quit; *(~ sin anställning)* leave, quit; *~ gråta* stop crying; *han ~de läsa på sidan* ... he left off reading on page ...; *~ röka* give up (stop) smoking; *~ där man börjat* come full circle; *det kommer att ~ illa* it will end badly; *hon har ~t hos oss* she has left us; *hans liv ~de i fattigdom* he ended up in poverty; *~ i en spets* end in a point; *han ~de med några uppskattande ord* he wound up (concluded) with a few appreciative words; *~ upp* stop *(med ngt doing s.th.)* **III** *slöt -it, rfl*

1 *(stänga sig)* shut, close; *~ sig inom sig själv* retire into one's shell **2** *~ sig till ngn (ngt)* join s.b. (s.th.); *~ sig tillsammans (om pers.)* unite **3** *~ sig till ngt (komma fram t.)* conclude (infer) s.th.
slut|akt *teat.* last (final) act **-anmärkning** closing remark, final observation **-are** *foto.* shutter **-avräkning** final settlement (account) **-behandla** conclude *(ett mål* a case); *saken är ~d* the matter is settled **-betalning** final payment (settlement) **-betyg** final (leaving) certificate **-betänkande** final committee report
slut|en *a3* **1** *(till-)* closed; *(förseglad)* sealed *(försändelse* package); *~ omröstning* secret ballot, ballot vote; *[tätt] -na led* serried ranks; *ett -et sällskap* a private company; *~ vokal* close vowel; *~ vård* inpatient care, institutional care; *~t TV-system* closed-circuit television **2** *(inbunden)* reserved; *vard.* buttoned-up **-examen** final (leaving) examination; *vard.* finals **-fall** *mus.* cadence **-föra** bring to an end, conclude **-försäljning** clearance sale **-förvaring** kärntekn. landfill[ing], deposition, controlled tipping **-giltig** definitive, final
slut|it *sup. av sluta I o. III* **-kläm** closing remark, final comment; *(sammanfattning)* summing-up **-körd** *a5, vard.* exhausted, deadbeat **-ledning** conclusion, deduction, inference; *(i logiken)* syllogism **-leverans** final delivery
slutlig [-u:-] *a1* final, ultimate; *~ skatt* final tax
slutligen [-u:-] finally; *(till sist)* in the end, ultimately, eventually; *(omsider)* at last
slut|likvid final (full) payment (settlement) **-lön** terminal (severance) pay **-muskel** *anat.* sphincter **-mål** ultimate objective **-omdöme** final verdict **-plädering** concluding speech **-poäng** total points *(pl)* **-produkt** end product (item), finished product **-prov** final test **-punkt** extremity; terminal point **-redovisning** final statement of account **-replik** closing rejoinder; *(i pjäs)* closing lines **-resultat** final result **-sats** conclusion, inference; *dra sina ~er* draw one's conclusions **-scen** final (closing) scene **-sedel** *hand.* contract note, bill of sale **-signal** *sport.* final whistle **-skattesedel** final [income-tax] demand note **-skede** final stage (phase) **-spel** *sport.* finals; *(i schack)* endgame **-spurt** final spurt; finish **-stadium** final stage **-station** terminus; *AE.* terminal **-steg** *(i raket)* last (final) stage **-stycke** *(på eldvapen)* bolt **-summa** total [amount], sum total **-såld** sold out, out of stock; *(om bok)* out of print
slutta decline, slope [downwards]; descent; *~ brant* slope abruptly
sluttamp *s2, i sht AE.* tag end
sluttande *a4* inclined (plan plane); sloping *(axlar* shoulders); slanting *(tak* roof); *komma på det ~ planet (bildl.)* be on the downgrade
sluttentamen final examination
sluttning slope, descent
slut|uppgörelse final settlement **-vinjett** *(i bok e.d.)* tailpiece; *bildl.* concluding remark, (höjdpunkt) peak, culmination
slyna *s1* hussy, minx
slyngel *s2* young rascal; scamp **-aktig** *a1*

S

ill-mannered **-åldern, -åren** the awkward age **1 slå** *s2* crossbar, slat, rail **2 slå** *slog slagit* I **1** (~ *till, äv. bildl.*) strike (*ett slag* a blow; *ngn med häpnad* s.b. with amazement); hit; smite, knock; (*flera slag; besegra*) beat (*ngn gul o. blå* s.b. black and blue; *på trumma* the drum; *fienden* the enemy); (*om hjärta, puls*) beat, throb; (*om segel*) flap; *han slog henne* he beat (hit, struck) her; *samvetet slog mig* my conscience smote me; *det slog mig att* it struck me that; ~ *en bonde* (*schack.*) take a pawn; ~ *broar* throw bridges (*över* across); ~ *kana* slide, go sliding; *fönstret står och ~r* the window keeps banging [to and fro]; *gäddan ~r* the pike is splashing about; *klockan ~r* the clock strikes; *en vara som ~r* a product that catches on; ~ *fel nummer* dial the wrong number; ~ *för en flicka* court (*AE. äv.* date) a girl; ~ *i dörrarna* bang the doors; ~ *en spik i väggen* knock (drive) a nail into the wall; *regnet ~r mot fönstret* the rain is beating against the window; *vågorna ~r mot stranden* the waves are beating on the shore; ~ *armarna om* put (throw) one's arms round; ~ *papper om* wrap up in paper; ~ *ett snöre om* tie up with string; ~ *en knut* make a knot; ~ *en ring omkring* form a circle round; ~ *på stort* lay it on, do the thing in style; ~ *ngn till marken* knock s.b. down **2** (*meja*) mow, cut (*hö* hay) **3** (*hälla*) pour (*i, upp* out) **4** (*om fåglar*) warble II (*med betonad partikel*) **1** ~ *an a*) (*en sträng*) touch, strike, *b*) (*en ton*) strike up; ~ *an* catch on with, captivate (*åhörarna* the audience); ~ *av a*) knock off, *b*) (*koppla ifrån*) swi tch off, *c*) (*hälla av*) pour off **2** ~ *av på priset* reduce (knock down) the price; ~ *av* sig get flat, lose strength **3** ~ *bort* throw away, (*tankar e.d.*) chase away, drive (shake) off; ~ *bort tanken på* ... dismiss the thought of ... from one's mind; ~ *bort med ett skämt* pass off with a joke **4** ~ *emellan* (*boktr.*) lead [out], space out **5** ~ *i a*) (*spik*) knock (drive) in, *b*) (*hälla i*) pour out (in); ~ *i ngn ngt* drum s.th. into a p.'s head, (*lura*) talk s.b. into believing s.th. **6** ~ *igen a*) (*smälla igen*) slam, bang (*dörren* the door), (*stänga*) shut (*locket* the lid), close, shut down (*butiken* the shop), (*stängas*) shut [with a bang], *b*) (~ *tillbaka*) hit (strike) back **7** ~ *igenom a*) (*tränga igenom*) penetrate, soak through, *b*) (*lyckas*) succeed, make a name for o.s. **8** ~ *ihjäl* (*äv. tiden*) kill **9** ~ *ihop a*) (*händerna e.d.*) clap, (*smälla ihop*) clash together, *b*) (*fälla ihop*) fold [up], (*slå igen*) shut, *c*) (*förena*) put together, unite, combine **10** ~ *in a*) (*krossa*) smash, break, (*dörr*) force, *b*) (*paket e.d.*) wrap up (*i* in), *c*) (*besannas*) come true; ~ *in på en annan väg* turn into (take) another road, *bildl.* branch off, take another course **11** ~ *ner a*) (*t. marken*) knock down, *b*) (*driva ner*) beat (hammer) down (*en stolpe* a pole), *c*) (*fälla ner*) let down, (*ögonen* lower, (*krage e.d.*) turn down, *d*) (*om åskan*) strike, *e*) (*om rovfågel o. bildl.*) swoop down, pounce; *röken ~r ner* the smoke is driving down[wards]; *nyheten slog ner som en bomb* the news broke like a bomb **12** ~ *om* (*bildl. o. om väder*) change **13** ~ *omkull* throw (knock)

over (down) **14** ~ *runt* somersault, overturn, (*festa*) go on the spree; ~ *sönder* break [to pieces] **15** ~ *till a*) strike, (*ngn äv.*) hit, *b*) (*inkoppla*) switch on, turn on, *c*) (*om relä e.d.*) pull up **16** ~ *tillbaka* hit (beat, strike) back, beat off (*ett anfall* an attack) **17** ~ *upp a*) (*öppna*) open, (*dörr e.d.*) throw (fling) open, (*ord i ordbok e.d.*) look up, *b*) (*fästa upp*) stick up, (*affisch e.d.*) post up, *c*) (*fälla upp*) turn up (*kragen* the collar), pitch (*ett tält* a tent, *d*) (*förlovning*) break off, *e*) (*om lågor*) flare up; ~ *upp sidan 5* turn to (open at) page 5; ~ *upp en artikel på första sidan* splash an article over the front page; *hon har slagit upp med honom* she has broken it off with him **18** ~ *ut a*) knock (beat) out, (*fönster*) smash, *b*) (*breda ut*) open (*vingarna* its (*etc.*) wings), *c*) (*om träd, växt*) burst into leaf, come out, (*om knopp*) open, *d*) (*hälla ut*) pour out, (*spilla*) spill [out], *e*) (*fördela*) spread over (*kostnaderna* the costs); *lågorna slog ut från taket* the flames burst through the roof; *försöket slog väl ut* the experiment turned out well; *många kommer att ~s ut i konkurrensen* many will go under in the competition **19** ~ *över* (*gå t. överdrift*) overdo it; *vågorna slog över båten* the waves washed over the boat III *rfl* **1** (*göra sig illa*) hurt o.s.; ~ *sig fördärvad* smash o.s. up **2** ~ *sig för sitt bröst* beat one's breast; ~ *sig för pannan* strike one's forehead; *du kan ~ dig i backen på att han kommer* you bet he will come **3** (*bli krokig*) warp, cast **4** (*i prep. uttryck*) ~ *sig fram* (*bildl.*) make (fight) one's way [in the world]; ~ *sig ihop* (*för att köpa*) club together; ~ *sig ihop med* (*äv.*) join [forces with]; ~ *sig lös, se lös*; ~ *sig ner* sit down, (*bosätta sig*) settle [down]; ~ *sig på* (*ägna sig åt*) go into (*affärer* business); *sjukdomen slog sig på lungorna* the disease went to (affected) the lungs

slående *a4* striking (*likhet* resemblance)
slån *s9, s7* blackthorn, sloe **-bär** sloe
slåss *slogs slagits, dep* fight (*om* about; *med ngn* [with] s.b.)
slåtter ['slått-] *s2* haymaking **-gille** hay-harvest festival **-karl** haymaker **-maskin** mower
1 släcka *v3, sjö.,* ~ [*på*] slacken, ease [off]
2 släcka *v3* (*få att slockna*) extinguish, put out; (*elektr. ljus*) switch off; put out; (*gaslåga*) turn out; (*kalk; törst*) slake
släckning extinction *etc.*
släcknings|arbete fire-fighting [work] **-manskap** fire-fighting squad; fire-fighters (*pl*) **-redskap** fire[-fighting] appliance
släd|e *s2* sleigh; sledge; *åka* ~ sleigh, go sleigh-riding **-färd** sleigh ride **-före** *bra* ~ good snow for sleighing **-parti** sleigh excursion (ride)
slägg|a *s1* sledge[hammer]; *sport.* hammer; *kasta* ~ (*sport.*) throw the hammer **-kastare** hammer-thrower **-kastning** throwing the hammer
släkt I *s3* (*ätt*) family; (*-ingar*) relations, relatives (*pl*); *det ligger i ~en* it runs in the family; ~ *och vänner* friends and relations; *tjocka ~en* (*vard.*) near relations II *oböjligt pred. a* related (*med* to), of the same family (*med* as); *jag är* ~ *med honom* I am a relative of his; ~ *till ~en*

related to one's relations; *vara nära* ~ be closely related; ~ *på långt håll* distantly related **-drag** family trait (characteristic) **släkt|e** *s6* (*-led*) generation; (*ätt, ras*) race; *biol.* genus; *det manliga ~t* the male species **-fejd** family feud **-forskare** genealogist **-forskning** genealogy **-ing** relative, relation (*till mig* of mine) **-klenod** [family] heirloom **-kär** fond of (attached to) one's family **-led** generation **-möte** family gathering **-namn** family name, surname; *biol.* generic name **-skap** *s3, s4* relationship; *bildl.* affinity, kinship **-skaps-förhållande** relationship **-tavla** genealogical table **-tycke** family likeness

1 slända *s1* (*redskap*) distaff

2 slända *s1, zool.* dragonfly; neuropter[an]

släng *s2* **1** (*häftig rörelse*) toss, jerk (*med huvudet* of the head) **2** (*snirkel*) flourish **3** (*slag*) lash, cut **4** (*lindrigt anfall*) touch (*av influensa* of the flu); dash (*av galenskap* of madness)

slänga *v3* **1** (*kasta*) toss, jerk, fling; dash; ~ *av sig rocken* throw off one's coat; ~ *i sig maten* gulp down the food; ~ *på sig kläderna* throw one's clothes on **2** (*dingla*) dangle (*hit o. dit* to and fro); (*svänga*) swing; ~ *i dörrarna* slam the doors; ~ *med armarna* wave one's arms about

släng|d *a1* (*skicklig*) clever, good (*i* at) **-gunga** swing **-kappa** [Spanish] cloak

släng|ig *a1* (*ledlös*) loose-limbed; (*om handstil*) careless **-kyss** *kasta en* ~ *till ngn* blow s.b. a kiss **-kälke** merry-go-round on the ice **-polska** swinging reel **-skott** pot shot

slänt *s3* slope

släntra saunter, stroll

släp *s7* **1** (*på klädesplagg*) train **2** (*-vagn*) trailer; *ha* (*ta*) *på* ~ have (take) in tow **3** (*slit*) toil, drudgery; *slit och* ~ toil and moil

släpa I *v1* **1** (*dra efter sig*) drag, trail; (*bogsera*) tow, tug; ~ *fötterna efter sig* drag one's feet; ~ *med sig* drag about with one; ~ *sig fram* drag o.s. along, *bildl.* drag [on] **2** (*hänga ner*) drag, trail (*i golvet* on the floor) **3** (*slita*) toil, drudge **II** *s1* sled, sledge

släp|ig *a1* trailing, shuffling (*gång* gait); drawling (*röst* voice) **-kontakt** trailing (sliding) contact **-lift** ski tow **-logg** patent log

släpp|a *v3* **1** (*låta falla*) let go; (*tappa*) drop, let slip **2** (*frige, lösa*) release, let loose; (*överge*) give up (*tanken på* the thought of); ~ *taget* release one's hold, let go **3** (*lossna*) come loose; leave hold **4** (*med betonad partikel*) ~ *efter* release one's hold, *bildl.* get lax; ~ *efter på disciplinen* relax the discipline; ~ *fram* (*förbi*) let pass; ~ *ifrån sig* let go, part with, (*avstå från*) give up; ~ *in* let in, admit; ~ *lös* release, let loose; ~ *ner* (*sänka; lägga ner*) let down; ~ *på vatten* turn the water on; ~ *till pengar* contribute (furnish) money; ~ *ut* let out (*äv. sömn.*), (*fånge*) release **-hänt** *a1* butter-fingered; *bildl.* indulgent, easy-going (*mot ngn* towards, with) **-hänthet** indulgence; laxity

släp|räfsa hay sweep, sweeping rake **-sko** *elektr.* trailing (sliding) contact **-skopa** drag[line] bucket **-tåg** *ha i* ~ (*bildl.*) have in tow, bring in one's (its) wake **-vagn** trailer

slät *a1* **1** smooth; (*jämn*) even, level; (*om mark*

äv.) flat; *~t hår* smooth (sleek) hair **2** (*enkel*) plain; (*-struken*) mediocre; (*usel*) poor; *göra en* ~ *figur* cut a poor figure **släta** ~ [*till*] smooth [down]; (*platta till*) flatten; ~ *ut* smooth out [the creases in]; ~ *över* (*bildl.*) smooth over

slät|fila smooth-file **-hugga** cut smooth **-hyvla** smooth-plane **-hårig** straight-haired; (*om hund*) smooth-haired **-kamma** comb smooth; *~d* (*äv.*) sleek-haired **-löpning** flat-race **-prick** *sjö.* spar buoy, marker **-rakad** *a5* clean-shaven **-struken** *a3, bildl.* mediocre, indifferent

1 slätt *adv* **1** smoothly; *ligga* ~ be smooth **2** *rätt och* ~ [quite] simply; *stå sig* ~ cut a poor figure, come off badly

2 slätt *s3* plain; (*hög-*) plateau

slätt|bygd, -land plain, flat country

slät|var [-ä:-] *s2* brill **-välling** thin gruel

slö *a1* blunt, dull (*äv. bildl.*); (*dåsig*) inert; (*loj*) indolent, listless **slöa** idle; *sitta och* ~ sit idle, be dawdling; ~ *till* get slack; (*dåsa till*) get drowsy

slödder ['slödd-] *s7* mob, rabble

slö|fock [-å-] *s2* dullard, mope **-het** bluntness *etc.*; indolence, lethargy

slöja [ˣslöjja] *s1* veil

slöjd *s3* handicraft; (*skolämne*) handicraft (woodwork, carpentry; needlework) instruction **slöjda** do woodwork (*etc.*) **slöjdalster** hand-made article

slöjdans dance of the veils

slöjd|lärare craft teacher **-sal** manual workshop **-skola** handicraft (arts and crafts) school

slöjmoln cirrostratus

slök *imperf. av* sluka

slör *s2, sjö.* free (large) wind **slöra** sail (go) large

slösa **1** (*använda t. övermått*) squander, be wasteful (lavish) (*med* with) **2** (*ödsla*) waste (*pengar* money), spend [lavishly], squander; (*beröm, omsorg o.d.*) lavish; ~ *bort* waste, squander **slösaktig** *a1* lavish (*med* with), wasteful (*med* with, of), squandering; extravagant **slösaktighet** lavishness *etc.*; extravagance **slösande** *a4, jfr -aktig*; ~ *prakt* lavish splendour **slösare** spendthrift, squanderer **slöseri** wastefulness, extravagance; waste (*med tiden* of time)

slöt *imperf. av* sluta

smack *n, inte ett* ~ not a bit

smack|a smack; ~ *med tungan* click one's tongue; ~ *åt* (*häst*) gee up **-ning** smack[ing noise], click

smak *s3* taste (*av* of; *för* for) (*äv. bildl.*); (*arom*) flavour (*av vanilj* of vanilla); *~en är olika* tastes differ; *om tycke och* ~ *skall man inte diskutera* there is no accounting for tastes; *falla ngn i ~en* please s.b., strike a p.'s fancy; *få* ~ *för* take a liking to, get a taste for; *jag har förlorat ~en* I have lost my sense of taste; *ha god* (*säker*) ~ have an unerring taste; *en person med god* ~ a person of [good] taste; *äta med god* ~ eat with gusto (a relish); *i min* ~ to my taste; *den är inte i min* ~ (*äv.*) I don't fancy it; *sätta* ~ *på* give a flavour to, season; *ta* ~ *av ngt* take on the taste of s.th.

smak|a **1** (*av-, eg. o. bildl.*) taste, have a taste

of (*äv. få ~, ~ på*); (*erfara*) experience; ~ *av, se avsmaka*; [*få*] ~ *riset* get a taste of the rod; *han ~r aldrig starkt* he never touches strong drink **2** (*ha viss smak*) taste, have a taste (*tomat* of tomato); ~ *gott* (*illa*) taste nice (bad), have a nice (bad) taste; *hur ~r det? a)* what does it taste like?, *b)* (*tycker du om det?*) is it to your taste?; *nu skall det ~ med te* tea will be welcome; ~ *på* taste; *låta sig ngt väl ~* eat s.th. heartily, help o.s. liberally to; *det kostar mer än det ~r* it costs more than it is worth; *~r det så kostar det* you won't get something for nothing; *han ~de knappt på maten* he hardly touched the food **-bit** bit to taste; (*prov*) sample **-domare** arbiter of taste **-full** tasteful; (*elegant*) stylish, elegant **-fullhet** tastefulness; style, elegance **-förbättring** improvement in taste **-försämring** impairment of taste
smak|lig [-a:-] *a1* (*aptitlig*) appetizing; (*läcker*) delicate, dainty; tasty **-lök** *anat.* taste bud **-lös** tasteless (*äv. bildl.*); *eg. äv.* flat, insipid; *bildl. äv.* in bad taste **-löshet** tastelessness *etc.*; insipidity; *bildl.* bad taste **-nerv** gustatory nerve **-prov** sample **-riktning** taste; tendency, style **-råd** advice (*pers.*: adviser) in matters of taste **-sak** matter of taste **-sensation** taste sensation **-sinne** [sense of] taste **-sätta** flavour, season **-sättning** seasoning **-ämne** flavouring
smal *a1* (*motsats bred, vid*) narrow; (*motsats tjock*) thin; (*om pers. äv.*) lean; (*slank*) slender; *vara ~ om midjan* have a slender waist; *det är en ~ sak* (*bildl.*) it is a small matter (a trifle) **-axlad** *a5* narrow-shouldered **-ben** lower shin **-bent** [-e:-] *a1* slender-legged, thin-legged **-film** substandard (8 (16) mm) film **-films-kamera** cine (*AE.* movie) camera
small *imperf. av* smälla
smal|na [-a:l-] narrow [off, down]; (*magra, bli tunnare*) grow thinner; (*t. en spets*) taper **-randig** narrow-striped **-spårig** *a1* narrow--gauge[d]; *bildl.* narrow-minded
sma'ragd *s3* emerald **-grön** emerald-green
smart [-a:-] *a1* smart
smash smash **smasha** smash
smaska slurp **smaskens** ['smask-] (*endast pred.*) *vard.* delicious, yummy **smaskig** *a1, vard.* delicious, yummy
smatt|er ['smatt-] *s7* clatter; patter, rattle; (*av (om) trumpet*) blare **smattra** clatter; patter, rattle; (*av (om) trumpet*) blare
smed *s3* [black]smith **smedja** [-e:-] *s1* smithy; forge
smek *s7* caressing; (*kel*) fondling; (*ömhetsbety-gelser*) caresses (*pl*) **smeka** *v3* caress; (*kela med*) fondle; (*klappa*) pat **smekande** *a4* caressing; gentle, soft (*toner* tones)
smek|as *v3, dep* caress [each other] **-månad** honeymoon **-namn** pet name **-ning** [-e:-] caress, endearment **-sam** [-e:-] *a1* caressing, fondling
1 smet *imperf. av 1, 2 smita*
2 smet *s3* (*sörja*) sludge; *kokk.* paste, [cake] mixture; (*pannkaks-*) batter
smeta daub, smear (*på* on); ~ *fast* stick; ~ *av sig* make smears, (*om färg*) come off; ~ *ner* [be]smear, bedaub; ~ *ner sig* make a mess of o.s. **smetig** *a1* smeary, sticky

smicker ['smick-] *s7* flattery; (*inställsamt*) blandishment; (*grovt*) blarney; *vard.* soft soap **smickra** flatter, cajole; ~ *sig med* flatter o.s. upon (*att ha gjort ngt* having done s.th.), plume o.s. on (*att vara* being) **smickrande** *a4* flattering; *föga ~* hardly flattering **smick-rare** flatterer
smida *v2* forge (*äv. bildl.*); hammer; *bildl.* devise, concoct (*planer* schemes); ~ *ihop* forge together, weld; ~ *medan järnet är varmt* strike while the iron is hot
smidbar [-i:-] *a1* forgeable, malleable; *~t järn* malleable (wrought) iron **-het** [-i:-] malleability, forging quality
smidd *a5* forged; wrought, hammered **smide** *s6* forging; *~n* hardware (*sg*), iron goods, forgings
smides|järn forging steel (iron), wrought iron **-verkstad** forge, smithy
smidig *a1* (*böjlig*) ductile, flexible; pliable, supple (*äv. bildl.*); (*vig*) lithe; *~a tyger* soft materials **-het** flexibility; suppleness
smil *s7* smile; (*hångrin*) grin; (*självbelåtet*) smirk
smil|a smile; grin; smirk **-band** *dra på ~et* smile [faintly] (*åt* at) **-fink** sycophant, toady **-grop** dimple
smink *s4* make-up; (*rött*) rouge; *teat. äv.* grease paint **sminka** make up, paint; paint o.s.; *teat.* make up
smink|loge [-lå:ʃ] *s5* dressing room **-ning** making up; (*en ~*) make-up **-stång** stick of grease paint **-ör** make-up man
smisk *s7* smack[ing] **smiska** smack
1 smita *smet smitit* make off, run away; *vard.* hook it; (*från bilolycka*) hit and run; ~ *från betalningen* dodge payment
2 smita *smet smitit, ~ åt* (*om plagg*) be tight
smitit *sup. av 1, 2 smita*
smitta I *s1* infection, contagion (*äv. bildl.*); *överföra ~* transmit infection **II** *v1, ~* [*ner*] infect (*äv. bildl.*); *bli ~d* catch the infection (*av ngn* from s.b.; *han ~de henne* (*äv.*) she caught it from him; *exemplet ~r* the example is infectious **smittande** *a4* catching, infectious; ~ *skratt* infectious laughter
smitt|bärare [disease] carrier **-fara** danger of infection **-fri** noninfectious, noncontagious **-förande** *a4* (*om pers.*) infectious; infected, contaminated; disease-carrying **-härd** focus (source) of infection **-koppor** *pl* smallpox (*sg*) **-källa** source of infection **-risk** risk of infection **-sam** *a1* catching; infectious; contagious (*äv. bildl.*) **-spridare** [disease] carrier **-sprid-ning** transmission of infection **-ämne** infectious matter, contagion
smock [-å-] *s3* (*rynkning*) smocking **smock|a** [-å-] **I** *s1* biff **II** *v1,* ~ *till ngn* sock s.b. **-full** crammed full (*med* of), chock-full
smoking ['små:-] dinner jacket; *AE.* tuxedo; *vara klädd i ~* (*äv.*) wear a black tie **-skjorta** evening (*vard.* boiled) shirt
smolk [-å-] *s7* mote; some dirt (*i ögat* in one's eye); *det har kommit ~ i mjölken* (*bildl.*) there is a fly in the ointment
smor|d [-ɷ:-] *a5* greased; oiled; *Herrans ~* the Lord's anointed; *det går som -t* it goes like

491 smorde–smått

clockwork **smorde** *imperf. av smörja II*
smorläder grain-leather **smort** *sup. av smörja II*
smuggel|gods smuggled goods (*pl*), contraband; *vard.* run goods (*pl*) **-trafik** smuggling
smuggl|a smuggle **-are** smuggler; (*sprit-*) bootlegger **-ing** smuggling
smugit *sup. av smyga*
1 smul *a1, sjö.* smooth
2 smul *r el. n, inte ett* ~ not a scrap
smul|a I *s1* **1** (*bröd- etc.*) crumb; *-or* (*äv.*) scraps; *små -or är också bröd* better half a loaf than no bread **2** *bildl.* particle, fragment, atom; *en* ~ a bit (trifle, little); *den* ~ *franska han kan* the little French he knows **II** *v1,* ~ [*sönder*] crumble; ~ *sig* crumble **smulig** *a1* crumbly, full of crumbs
smultron [-ån] *s7* wild strawberry **-ställe** *eg.* place where wild strawberries grow
smussel ['smuss-] *s7, ej pl* underhand practices (*pl*); *vard.* hanky-panky **smussla** practice underhand tricks, cheat, swindle; ~ *in* smuggle (slip) in; ~ *till ngn ngt* slip s.b. s.th.; ~ *undan* smuggle out of the way
smuts *s3* dirt, filth (*äv. bildl.*); (*gat- etc.*) mud, soil; *dra* (*släpa*) *i* ~*en* drag through the mire **smutsa** ~ [*ner*] make dirty, soil; (*smeta ner*) muck up; (*fläcka*) stain; ~ *ner sig* get dirty; ~ *ner sig om händerna* get one's hands dirty **-brun** dirty brown **-fläck** blotch, smudge **-gam** Egyptian vulture **-gris** (*om barn*) dirty [little] grub
smuts|ig *a1* dirty; filthy; (*äv. bildl.*); *bildl. äv.* foul; (*om gator etc.*) muddy; *bli* ~ get dirty; *vara* ~ *om händerna* have grubby hands **-kasta** *bildl.* throw mud at; defame **-kastning** mud-throwing; defamation **-kläder** *pl* dirty linen (*sg*) **-litteratur** gutter literature **-säck** dirty-clothes bag **-titel** *boktr.* half-title, bastard title **-tvätt** *se -kläder* **-vatten** slops (*pl*)
smutta ~ [*på*] sip
smycka adorn, ornament; (*dekorera*) decorate **smycke** *s6* piece of jewellery, trinket; *bildl.* ornament; ~*n* jewellery (*sg*) **smyckeskrin** jewel box (case)
smyg 1 *s2, se fönstersmyg* **2** *i uttr.: i* ~ stealthily, furtively, on the sly **smyga** *smög smugit* **1** (*smussla*) ~ [*in*] slip (*ngt i handen på ngn* s.th. into a p.'s hand) **2** (*oförmärkt glida*) sneak (*som en indian* like an Indian); *gå och* ~ [go] sneak[ing] about; *komma* ~*nde* come sneaking **3** *rfl* steal, sneak (*bort* away); ~ *sig intill ngn* snuggle up to s.b.; ~ *sig på ngn* steal up to s.b.
smyg|ande *a4* sneaking; lurking (*misstanke* suspicion); insidious (*sjukdom* illness; *gift* poison) **-handel** illicit trade **-läsa** read on the sly **-premiär** *AE.* sneak preview **-propaganda** insidious propaganda **-röka** smoke on the sly **-supa** drink on the sly **-väg** secret path; ~*ar* (*bildl.*) underhand means
små *smått smärre; i stället för felande former används liten* (*jfr liten*) little; small; *bildl. äv.* petty; ~ *barn* little (small) children; ~ *bokstäver* small letters; *de* ~ (*barnen*) the little ones; *stora och* ~ great and small, (*om pers. äv.*) old and young **-aktig** *a1* petty, mean; *AE. äv.*

picayune **-aktighet** pettiness, meanness **-barn** little children; infants **-barnsaktig** *a1* childish **-barnsfamilj** family with small children **-barnsåldern** infancy; childhood **-belopp** *pl* small amounts (sums) **-bil** small car; (*mycket liten*) mini-car **-bildskamera** miniature camera, minicamera **-blommig** with small flowers **-bord** small tables **-borgerlig** [petit] bourgeois **-bruk** smallholding, small farm **-brukare** smallholder, small farmer **-bröd** *koll.* biscuits (*pl*); *AE.* cookies (*pl*) **-båtar** *pl* small boats **-båtshamn** harbour for small boats **-delar** *pl* particles, small parts
små|fel *pl* petty faults (errors); *tekn.* small (minor) defects **-fisk** *koll.* [small] fry **-flickor** *pl* little girls **-folk** humble folk, ordinary people **-franska** French roll **-frusen** chilly **-fräck** cheeky **-fågel** small bird[s] **-företagare** *pl* owners of small firms (businesses, companies) **-gata** bystreet **-gnola** hum **-grisar** piglets, young pigs **-gräla** bicker **-handlare** *eg.* small dealer; *bildl.* small fry **-husbebyggelse** area of one-family houses **-kaka** *se småbröd* **-klasser** first three forms in primary school **-koka** simmer **-krafs** odds and ends (*pl*) **-kryp** insect; *vard.* bug **-krämpor** *pl* aches and pains **-le** smile (*mot* at) **-leende I** *a4* smiling **II** *s6* smile **-mynt** *se småpengar* **-mönstrad** small-patterned
småningom [-åm] [*så*] ~ (*efter hand*) gradually, little by little, (*med tiden*) by and by
små|näpen, -nätt sweet little **-ord** *pl* small words; *språkv.* particles **-paket** *post.* small packet **-pengar** *pl* small change (*sg*) **-planet** asteroid, planetoid **-plock** *koll.* odds and ends (*pl*) **-pojkar** little boys **-potatis** *det var inte* ~ (*bildl.*) that wasn't to be sneezed at, *AE.* that wasn't small potatoes **-prat** chat, small talk **-prata** chat **-prickig** with small dots **-påve** *neds.* big noise **-randig** narrow-striped **-regna** drizzle **-rolig** [quietly] amusing, droll **-rutig** small-checked **-rätter** *pl ung.* hors d'oeuvres
små|sak trifle, small (little) thing; *hänga upp sig på* ~*er* worry about little (unimportant) things; *det är inte* ~*er* it is no light matter **-sint** *a1, se småaktig* **-skog** brushwood **-skola** junior school **-skol[e]lärare** junior school teacher **-skratta** chuckle **-skrift** pamphlet, booklet **-skulder** *pl* small (petty) debts **-skuren** *a3* fine[ly] cut; *bildl. se småaktig* **-slantar** *se -pengar* **-slug** shrewd, artful **-snål** cheeseparing **-sparare** small saver **-springa** half run, trot **-stad** small town; (*landsorts-*) country (provincial) town **-stadsaktig** *a1* provincial **-stadsbo** inhabitant of a small town (*etc.*), provincial **-sten** *koll.* pebbles (*pl*) **-summor** *pl* small (petty) sums **-sur** sulky **-svära** swear under one's breath **-syskon** *pl* small (younger) sisters and brothers **-timmarna** *pl* the small hours; *fram på* ~ in the small hours of the morning **-tokig** scatty **-trevlig** cosy; (*om pers.*) pleasant
smått I *a, jfr små* little, small; ~ *och gott* a little of everything; *ha det* ~ be badly off; *ha* ~ *om* be short of; *hacka ngt* ~ chop s.th. small **II** *adv* a little; slightly, somewhat (*förälskad* in love) **III** *s, i vissa uttr.: vänta* ~ expect a baby; *i* ~

in little [things], in a small way, on a small scale; *i stort som* ~ in great as in little things **-ing** baby, youngster, kid
småtvätt *s2, ej pl* smalls *(pl)*
små|varmt *best. form det -varma, koll.* hot snack **-vilt** *koll.* small game **-vägar** *pl* byroads **-växt** *a4 (om pers.)* short [of stature]; *(om djur)* small; *(om växt)* low
smäcka *vard.* **1** *(slå)* slam, hit **2** *(ljuga)* lie, brag
smäcker ['smäck-] *a2* slender
smäda abuse; *(ärekränka)* defame; ~ *Gud* blaspheme **smädedikt** lampoon, libellous poem **smädelse** abuse; defamation; *~r* invectives **smädeskrift** libel[lous pamphlet], lampoon **smädlig** [-ä:-] *a1* abusive
smäkt|a languish **-ande** *a4 (trånande)* languishing; *(ljuv)* melting
smälek *s2* disgrace, ignominy; *lida* ~ suffer (be put to) shame
smäll 1 *s7, få* ~ get a spanking (smacking) **2** *s2 (knall, skräll)* bang, crack; *dörren slog igen med en* ~ the door shut with a bang (slammed to) **3** *s2 (slag)* smack, slap; *(med piska)* lash
smäll|a *v2, imperf. i intransitiv betydelse äv. small* **1** *(slå)* slap; *(ge ngn smäll)* spank, smack **2** *(frambringa en smäll)* crack; ~ *i dörrarna* bang (slam) the doors; ~ *med piskan* crack the whip; *nu -er det!* off it goes!; ~ *igen* shut [...] with a bang, *([om] dörr)* bang, slam **-are** cracker **-fet** immensely fat **-kall** bitterly cold **-karamell** cracker **-kyss** smack
smält|a I *s1, tekn.* [s]melt **II** *v3* **1** *(göra flytande)* melt; *(metall äv.)* smelt, fuse; *(mat o.d.; bildl.)* digest; *bildl. äv.* put up with, swallow *(förtreten* one's annoyance); *smält smör* drawn butter **2** *(övergå t. flytande form)* melt *(äv. bildl.)*; *(om is, snö äv.)* thaw; *(lösa sig)* dissolve; *(vekna)* soften; ~ *ihop* fuse *(äv. bildl.)*; *(minskas)* twindle [down]; *-er i munnen* melts in the mouth; ~ *ner* [s]melt down; ~ *samman* fuse *(äv. bildl.)*; ~ *samman med (äv.)* merge into **-ande** *a4* melting (toner tones); *bildl. äv.* liquid **-degel** crucible, melting pot **-hytta** smelting works **-ning** [s]melting *etc.*; liquefaction; dissolution; fusion; *(av mat)* digestion **-ost** processed cheese **-punkt** melting (fusing) point **-säkring** [safety] fuse **-ugn** [s]melting furnace **-vatten** melted snow (ice), meltwater **-värme** fusion (melting) heat
smärgel ['smärjel, 'smärr-] *s9* emery **-duk** emery cloth **-skiva** emery wheel
smärgla [-j-] emery, grind (polish) with emery
smärre *komp. t. små* smaller; minor *(fel* faults)
smärt *a1* slender, slim
smärt|a I *s1* pain; *(häftig, kort)* pang, twinge [of pain]; *(pina)* agony, torment; *(lidande)* suffering; *(sorg, bedrövelse)* grief, affliction, distress; *känna* ~ feel (be in) pain, *(själsligt)* be grieved (pained) *(över* at); *med* ~ *hör jag att* I am grieved to hear that **II** *v1* pain; *(själsligt äv.)* grieve *(djupt* deeply) **-fri** painless; *(smidig)* smooth **-förnimmelse** sensation of pain **-gräns** pain threshold
smärting canvas
smärt|lindring pain relief **-punkt** focus of pain **-sam** *a1* painful; *(själsligt äv.)* sad, grievous, distressing; *ytterst ~ma plågor (äv.)* extreme

pain *(sg)* **-stillande** *a4* pain-relieving, analgesic; *(lugnande)* sedative; ~ *medel* analgesic, anodyne, sedative
smög *imperf. av smyga*
smör *s7* butter; *breda* ~ *på* spread with butter, spread butter on, butter; *gå åt som* ~ *i solsken* sell like hot cakes; *inte för allt* ~ *i Småland* not for all the tea in China; *se ut som om man sålt ~et och tappat pengarna* look as though one has made a fortune and lost it; *komma [sig] upp i ~et* be in clover, be in high favour **smöra** *v1* butter
smör|ask butter box **-bakelse** puff-pastry cake **-blomma** buttercup **-boll** *bot.* globeflower **-deg** puff paste **-dosa** butter dish **-fett** butterfat; butyrin
smörgås [ˣsmörr-] *s2* [piece (slice) of] bread and butter; *(med pålägg)* open sandwich; *kasta* ~ *(lek)* play ducks and drakes **-bord** smorgasbord; hors d'oeuvres *(pl)* **-mat** sliced meats (cheese *etc.*) used on open sandwiches *(pl)* **-nisse** *s2* assistant waiter; *AE.* bus boy
smörj *s7* thrashing, licking **smörja I** *s1* *(-medel)* grease, lubricant **2** *(skräp)* rubbish, trash; *prata* ~ talk nonsense (rubbish) **II** *smorde smort* **1** grease, lubricate; *(med olja)* oil; *(med salva)* salve; *(kung e.d.)* anoint; *(bestryka)* smear; ~ *in a)* *(ett ämne)* rub in *b)* *(ngn, ngt) dets. som smörja* **2** ~ *ngn (smickra)* butter s.b. up, *(muta)* grease (oil) a p.'s palm **smörjare** greaser, oiler **smörjelse 1** *(-ning)* anointing **2** *(salva)* ointment; *(helig olja)* chrism; *sista ~n* the extreme unction
smörj|fett [lubricating] grease (fat) **-grop** greasing pit **-hall** greasing bay **-hål** lubricating (oil) hole **-ig** *a1 (smutsig)* greasy, smeary **-kanna** oilcan, lubricating can **-kopp** oilcup, lubricating cup **-medel** *tekn.* lubricant **-ning** greasing *etc.*; lubrication **-nippel** oil (grease) nipple **-olja** lubricating oil **-spruta** grease (lubricating) gun
smör|klick pat of butter **-kniv** butter knife **-kräm** butter cream **-kärna** churn **-papper** greaseproof paper **-sopp** *s2* ringed boletus **-syra** butyric acid
snabb *a1* rapid, swift *(rörelse* motion); speedy; fast *(löpare* runner); prompt, quick *(svar* reply); ~ *i vändningarna* nimble, alert, agile; *~t tillfrisknande* speedy recovery
snabb|a ~ *på* hurry up **-behandla** *(hopskr. snabbehandla)* ~ *ett ärende* take prompt action on (deal quickly with) a matter **-eld** *mil.* rapid firing **-fotad** *a5* fleet-footed, swift-footed **-förband** adhesive plaster **-gående** *a4* fast, high-speed **-het** swiftness *etc.*; rapidity; speed **-kaffe** instant coffee **-kurs** short (concentrated) course **-köp[sbutik]** self-service shop *(AE.* store) **-läsning** speed reading **-seglande** [-e:-] *a4* fast[-sailing] **-seglare** fast[-sailing] vessel **-simmare** fast (racing) swimmer **-skjutande** [-ʃ-] *a4* quickfiring **-skrift** shorthand [writing] **-skrivare** *data.* high-speed printer **-stål** high-speed steel **-telefon** intercom [telephone] **-tänkt** *a1* quick-witted, ready-witted **-tänkthet** quickness of wit **-växande** fast-growing
snabel ['sna:-] *s2* trunk

snack *s7, vard., se prat, strunt* **snacka** chatter, chat **snacksalig** *vard.* garrulous

snagg *s3* crew cut **snagga** crop **snaggad** *a5* cropped

snappa snatch, snap (*efter* at); ~ *bort* snatch away; ~ *upp* snatch (pick) up; ~ *upp några ord* catch a few words

snapphane *s2, hist.* pro-Danish partisan in Scania (17th C)

snaps *s2* schnap[p]s **-visa** drinking song

snar *a1* speedy (*bättring* recovery); quick (*t. vrede* to anger); *inom en* ~ *framtid* in the immediate (near) future

snar|a I *s1* snare; (*fälla*) trap; (*fågel-*) springe; (*ränn-*) noose; *lägga ut -or för* set (lay) traps for; *fastna i* ~*n* fall into the trap (*äv. bildl.*) **II** *v1* snare

snar|are *adv* **1** (*hellre*) rather; ~ *kort än lång* short rather than long; *det är* ~ *så att* ... the fact is that ... if anything; *jag tror* ~ *att* I am more inclined to think that **2** (*snabbare*) sooner **-ast** *adv* **1** ~ [*möjligt*] as soon as possible, at one's earliest convenience, without delay **2** (*egentligen*) if anything **-fager** pretty-pretty

snark|a snore **-ning** snore; ~*ar* (*äv.*) snoring (*sg*)

snar|lik rather like; ~ *i form* much of the same shape; *en* ~ *historia* an analogous (similar) story **-likhet** close similarity **-stucken** *a5* quick to take offence; touchy, susceptible **-stuckenhet** touchiness

snar|t [-a:-] *adv* soon; (*inom kort*) shortly, before long; *alltför* ~ only too soon; ~ *sagt* well-nigh, not far off; *så* ~ [*som*] as soon as, directly; *så* ~ *som möjligt, se snarast 1* **-tänkt** *a1* ready-witted, quick-witted

snask *s7* sweets (*pl*); *AE.* candy **snaska 1** eat sweets; ~ *i sig* munch **2** ~ *ner* make a mess on (of); ~ *ner sig* mess o.s. up **snaskig** *a1* messy, dirty

snatta pilfer, pinch, filch

snatter ['snatt-] *s7* quack[ing]; gabble (*äv. bildl.*); *bildl. äv.* jabber

snatteri petty theft, *jur.* petit (petty) larceny; (*butiks-*) shoplifting

snattra (*om fågel*) quack; gabble (*äv. bildl.*); *bildl. äv.* jabber

snava stumble, trip (*på* over)

sned I *a1* (*om linje, vinkel e.d.*) oblique; (*lutande*) slanting, sloping, inclined; (*skev*) askew, warped; (*krokig*) crooked (*rygg* back); *kasta* ~*a blickar på* look askance at **II** *s i uttr.: sitta* (*hänga*) *på* ~ be (hang) askew (on one side, awry); *gå på* ~ (*bildl.*) go [all] wrong (awry); *komma på* ~ (*bildl.*) go astray; *lägga huvudet på* ~ put one's head on one side **-belastning** uneven weight distribution **-bena** side parting

snedda 1 (*gå snett* [*över*]) edge; ~ *förbi* pass by; ~ *över gatan* slant across (cross) the street **2** (*avskära på -en*) slant, slope; *tekn.* bevel

snedden *s best. form i uttr.: på* ~ obliquely, diagonally; *klippa ett tyg på* ~ cut a piece of cloth on the cross (bias)

sned|gången *a5* (*om sko*) worn down on one side **-het** [-e:d-] obliqueness, obliquity; (*krokighet*) crookedness **-hugga** bevel **-klaff** sloping top **-rekrytering** biased (unequal) recruitment **-remsa** bias strip (band) **-skuren**

a5 cut obliquely (*om tyg:* [on the] bias) **-språng** sideleap; *bildl.* slip, lapse, escapade **-steg** *jfr -språng* **-streck** slanting line, oblique [stroke], solidus, *vard.* slash **-tak** sloping roof **-vinklig** *a1* oblique-angled **-vriden** distorted (*äv. bildl.*), warped **-ögd** *a1* slanteyed

snegla [ˣsne:-, ˣsnegg-] ogle; ~ *på* ogle, look askance at, (*lömskt*) leer at

snett *adv* obliquely; awry, askew; *bo* ~ *emot* live nearly opposite; *gå* ~ *över gatan* cross the street diagonally; *gå* ~ *på skorna* wear one's shoes down on one side; *hänga* ~ hang awry (crooked); *se* ~ *på ngn* look askance at s.b.

snibb *s2* corner, point; (*spets äv.*) tip; *se äv. blöjsnibb* **snibbig** *a1* pointed

snickarbänk joiner's bench

snickar|e (*möbel-*) joiner, cabinet-maker; (*byggnads-*) carpenter **-glädje** *skämts.* ornate decorative carving **-lim** joiner's glue **-verkstad** joiner's (carpenter's) workshop

snickeri 1 (*snickrande*) joinery, carpentry **2** *se snickarverkstad* **3** (*snickararbete*) piece of carpentry [work] **-arbete** *se snickeri 3* **-fabrik** joinery (carpentry) shop

snickra do joinery (carpentry) work, do woodwork; ~ *en möbel* make a piece of furniture

snicksnack *s7 vard.* rubbish, nonsense

snid|a carve [in wood] **-are** woodcarver **-eri** carving; *konkr. äv.* carved work

sniff|a sniff (*äv. om missbruk*) **-ning** sniffing

snigel *s2* slug; (*med hus*) snail **-fart** *med* ~ at a snail's pace

snigla [-i:-] ~ *sig fram* creep along (forward)

sniken *a3* avaricious, greedy (*efter, på* of) **-het** greed[iness]

snille *s6* genius; *han är ett* ~ he is a man of genius **-blixt** brain wave, flash of genius

snillrik *a1* brilliant (*uppfinnare* inventor); (*om pers. äv.*) of genius **-het** genius

snip|a *s1* (*båt*) gig **-ig** *a1* pointed, peaked

snirk|el *s2, byggn.* volute; (*släng*) flourish **-lad** *a5* (*krystad*) ornate

snits *s2* chic, style; *sätta* ~ *på ngt* give s.th. style

snitsel *s2* **1** (*pappersremsa*) paper strip **2** (*av sockerbetor*) beet slices (*pl*) **-jakt** paper chase

snitsig *a1* elegant, chic

snitsla mark path with paper strips

snitt *s7* **1** (*skärning*) cut, section; *kir.* incision; *gyllene* ~*et* (*mat.*) the golden section **2** (*preparat*) section cutting **3** (*tvär-*) section **4** (*trä-*) [wood]cut **5** (*på kläder*) cut, pattern **6** (*bok-*) edge **-blomma** cut flower **-yta** cut, section (*etc.*) surface

sno *v4* **1** (*hopvrida*) twist; (*tvinna*) twine; (*vira*) twirl (*tummarna* one's thumbs); (*linda*) turn, wind; ~ *ett rep om* wind a rope round **2** (*springa*) scamper, run; ~ *runt på klacken* turn on the heel; ~ *om hörnet* dash round the corner **3** *rfl* twist, get twisted (*hoptrasslad:* entangled); (*skynda sig*) hurry [up] **4** *vard.* steal, lift

snobb [-å-] *s2* snob; (*kläd-*) dandy, fop **snobba** ~ [*med*] show off, swank about **Snobben** *r* (*seriefigur*) Snoopy **snobberi** snobbery, dandyism **snobbig** *a1* (*sprättaktig*) snobbish, *vard.* stuck up; (*överdrivet elegant*) foppish

snodd *s3, s2, konkr.* string, cord; (*t. garnering*) lace

snofsig [-å-] *a1, vard.* dapper, spiffing
snok *s2* grass snake
snok|a spy, pry; poke, ferret; *gå och* ~ go prying about, *vard.* snoop; ~ *efter* hunt for; ~ *i* poke [one's nose] into; ~ *igenom* rummage; ~ *reda på* hunt up, ferret out **-ande** *a4, vard.* snoopy
snopen *a3* baffled, crestfallen; *se* ~ *ut* (*äv.*) look blank (foolish); *han blev ngt* [*till*] ~ he was struck all of a heap
snopp [-å-] *s2* **1** (*ljus-*) snuff, trim; (*bär-*) tail **2** *vard., barnspr.* (*penis*) willy **snoppa** (*ljus*) snuff; (*bär e.d.*) top and tail; (*cigarr*) cut; ~ *av ngn* (*bildl.*) snub s.b., take s.b. down a peg or two
snor *s7, vard.* snot **snora** snivel **snorfana** *sl.* (*näsduk*) nose rag **snorgärs** [-j-] *s2* **1** *zool.* ruff[e], pope **2** *se snorunge* **snorig** *a1* snivelling, snotty
snorkel [-å-] *s2* snorkel
snorkig [-å-] *a1* snooty, toffee-nosed
snor|unge, -valp *vard.* snotty kid, whelp
snubbeltråd tripwire **snubbla** stumble [and fall]
snubbor *pl* snubbing, rating (*sg*)
snudd *s2* light touch; ~ *på skandal* little short of a scandal; ~ *på seger* on the verge of victory **snudda** ~ *vid* graze, brush against, *AE.* sideswipe, *bildl.* touch [up]on
snugga *sl* (*pipa*) cutty [pipe]
snurr *s7* (*-ande*) whirl, rotation; *rena ~en* (*galenskapen*) sheer madness **snurra I** *sl* (*leksak*) top **II** *v1* **1** (*rotera*) whirl, spin; ~ *runt* go round and round, rotate; *det ~r runt i huvudet på mig* my head is spinning **2** (*låta rotera*) spin, whirl **snurrig** *a1* dizzy; (*virrig*) confused, muddled
snus *s4* snuff; *en pris* ~ a pinch of snuff **snusa 1** (*använda snus*) take snuff **2** (*lukta*) sniff (*på* at); (*under sömnen*) breathe heavily **snusande** *a4* snuff-taking **snusdosa** snuffbox **snusen** ['snu:-] *s best. form, vard., vara på* ~ be tipsy
snusförnuft knowingness -ig would-be-wise; (*om barn*) precocious; *en* ~ *person* a wiseacre, a know-all
snusk *s7* dirt[iness]; uncleanness, squalor; obscenity **snuska** ~ *ner* mess up, soil **snuskhummer** *vard.* [old] lecher, dirty old man **snuskig** *a1* dirty, squalid; filthy, smutty (*historia* story) **snuskpelle** *s2* dirty [little] pig
snus|malen *a5, -malet kaffe* finely ground (pulverized) coffee **-näsduk** bandan[n]a **-torr** [as] dry as dust (*äv. bildl.*); *vard.* bone-dry
snut *s2, vard.* **1** (*trut*) snout **2** (*polis*) cop[per]; *~en* the fuzz, *AE.* the heat
snutit *sup. av snyta*
snutt *s2* short piece [of music *etc.*], snatch; tag end
snuva *sl* head cold; *få* ~ catch (get) a cold **snuvig** *a1, vara* ~ have a cold in the head
snyft|a sob (*fram* out); ~ *till* give a sob **-ning** sob
snygg *a1* tidy; (*ren*) clean; (*vacker, om man*) handsome; (*vacker, om kvinna*) pretty; *iron. äv.* fine, pretty; *det var en* ~ *historia!* that's a pretty story! **snygga** ~ *upp* make tidy, tidy up; ~ *till sig* make o.s. presentable **snygghet** tidiness; cleanliness **snyggt** *adv* tidily; (*pryd-*

ligt) neatly; ~ *klädd* nicely (well) dressed
snylt|a be a parasite (sponge) (*på* on) **-gäst** parasite, sponger **-rot** *bot.* broomrape
snyt|a *snöt snutit* **1** wipe a p.'s nose; (*ljus*) snuff; *det är inte snutet ur näsan* it's not just a case of pressing a button; ~ *sig* blow one's nose **2** (*snatta*) pinch, snatch; (*lura*) cheat **-ing** punch on the nose **-ning** [-y:-] blowing (wiping) of the nose
snål *a1* **1** stingy; (*knusslig*) parsimonious, mean, cheeseparing **2** (*bitande*) cutting (*blåst* wind) **snåla** be stingy *etc.*, pinch and screw; ~ *in på ngt* save on s.th.
snål|blåst bitter wind **-het** [-å:-] stinginess *etc.*; *~en bedrar visheten* penny wise pound foolish **-jåp** *s2* miser, skinflint **-skjuts** *åka* ~ get a lift, *bildl.* take advantage [of] **-varg** *se -jåp* **-vatten** *-vattnet rinner på honom* his mouth waters
snår *s7* thicket; brush **-ig** *a1* brushy **-skog** brushwood, undergrowth
snäck|a *s1* **1** *zool.* gast[e]ropod; (*trädgårds-*) helix; (*-skal*) shell; *anat.* cochlea **2** *tekn.* worm; (*på fiol e.d.*) scroll **-formig** [-å-] *a1* spiral, helical **-linje** scroll **-skal** [sea]shell **-växel** worm gear
snäll *a1* good; (*av naturen*) good-natured; (*vänlig*) kind, nice (*mot* to); *~a du!* my dear!; vara ~ a) (*om barn*) be good, b) (*om vuxen*) be kind; *var ~ och stäng dörren* please shut the door; *har barnen varit ~a?* have the children behaved themselves? **-het** goodness *etc.*
snäll|press high-speed (cylinder) press **-tåg** express [train], fast train
snälltågs|biljett supplementary express [train] ticket **-fart** *med* ~ at express speed
snäppa *sl, zool.* sandpiper
snärj *s9* (*jäkt*) hectic time **snärja** *v2* [en]snare, entangle (*i* in) (*äv. bildl.*); *bildl. äv.* catch; ~ *in sig i* get entangled in **snärjande** *a4, bildl.* insidious (*frågor* questions) **snärjig** *a1, eg.* tangled; (*jäktig*) hectic; (*jobbig*) laborious
snärt *s2* **1** (*på piska*) lash, thong **2** (*slag*) lash **3** (*stickord*) gibe, taunt **snärta I** *v1*, ~ [*till*] lash; (*pika*) gibe at, make a crack at **II** *sl, se flicksnärta* **snärtig** *a1* cutting (*svar* reply)
snäs|a I *v3* speak harshly to, snap at **II** *sl* snub[bing], rating, rebuff **-ig** *a1* snappish, brusque **-ning** [-ä:-] *se snäsa II*
snäv *a1* **1** (*trång*) narrow; (*om plagg*) tight, close **2** (*ovänlig*) stiff, cold; curt (*svar* answer)
snö *s3* snow; *tala inte om den* ~ *som föll i fjol* let bygones be bygones; *det som göms i* ~ *kommer upp i tö* there is no secret time will not reveal
snö|a snow; *det ~r* it is snowing; *vägen har ~t igen* the road is blocked (covered) with snow **-blandad** *-blandat regn* sleet **-blind** snowblind **-boll** snowball **-bollskrig** snowball fight **-by** snow squall **-bär** snowberry
snöd *a1* sordid, vile
snö|drev spin-drift **driva** snowdrift **-droppe** *bot.* snowdrop **-fall** snowfall, fall of snow **-fattig** with little snow **-flinga** snowflake **-fästning** snow castle **-glopp** [-å-] *s7* sleet **-grotta** igloo **-gräns** snow line **-gubbe** snowman **-hinder** snow obstruction **-ig** *a1* snowy **-kedja** tyre chain, non-skid chain **-klädd** snowclad

-kristall snow crystal **-lykta** lantern made of snowballs **-man** abominable snowman, yeti **-mos** *bildl.* boloney

snöp|a *v3* geld **-ing** gelding

snöplig [-ö:-] *a1* ignominious, inglorious; *få ett ~t slut* come to a sad (sorry) end

snöplog snowplough **-ning** [-ɔ:-] snowploughing

snöra *v2* lace [up]; *~ fast* fasten [with a lace]; *~ till* lace up *(ett par skor* a pair of shoes); *~ på sig* put on *(skridskorna* the skates); *~ upp* unlace; *~* draw together, *(hårdare)* tighten; *~ sig* lace o.s. up

snör|e *s6* string, cord; *(segelgarn)* twine; *(prydnads-)* braid **-hål** lace hole, eyelet

snöripa *se dalripa*

snör|liv stays *(pl)*, corset; *ett ~* a pair of stays **-makare** lacemaker **-makeri** *(hantverk)* lacemaking; *(-verkstad)* passementerie workshop; *~er (tränsar m.m.)* lace *(sg)*, braids and trimmings **-ning** [-ö:-] lacing

snörp|a *v3* purse *(ihop* up); *~ på (med) munnen* purse (screw up) one's mouth **-vad** *s2* purse seine (net)

snör|rem lace; *(läder-)* strap **-rät** [as] straight as an arrow **-sko** laced shoe **-stump** piece of string

snörvl|a snuffle, speak through one's (the) nose **-ing** snuffling; *(en ~)* snuffle

snö|skata *se björktrast* **-sko** snowshoe **-skoter** snowmobile, snow scooter **-skottare** [-å-] snow clearer (shoveller) **-skottning** [-å-] snow clearing **-skovel** *se -skyffel* **-skred** avalanche **-skydd** snowbreak **-skyffel** snow shovel **-slask** sleet; slush **-slunga** snow thrower **-smältning** melting (thawing) of [the] snow **-sparv** snow bunting **-storm** snowstorm; blizzard **-sväng** *s2, vard.* snow-clearance squad **-sörja** slush, melting snow

snöt *imperf. av snyta*

snö|tjocka snow fog **-täcke** covering of snow **-täckt** *a4* snow-covered **-vidd** snowfield **-vit** snowy, snow-white; *S~* Snow White **-yra** whirling snow, snowstorm

so *best. form son, som pl används suggor* sow

soaré *s3* soiree, evening entertainment; *musikalisk ~* musical evening

sobel ['så:-] *s2* sable **-päls** sable coat

sober ['så:-] *a2* sober; subdued

soci'al *a1* social **-antropologi** cultural (social) anthropology **-arbetare** social (welfare) worker **-arbete** social (welfare) work **-assistent** social welfare officer **-bidrag** social *(AE.* public) assistance; supplementary benefit **-byrå** welfare office **-demokrat** social democrat **-demokrati** social democracy **-demokratisk** social democratic; *Sveriges ~a arbetareparti* [the] Swedish social democratic party **-departement** *~et* [the] ministry for health and social affairs, *BE. ung.* the ministry of pensions and national insurance, *AE. ung.* the department of health, education and welfare **-ekologi** human ecology **-fall** s.b. receiving social assistance **-försäkring** national (social) insurance **-försäkringsutskott** *~et* [the Swedish] [parliamentary] standing committee on social insurance **-förvaltning** *ung.* [local

authority] social services department **-grupp** social group; *~ 1* [the] upper class; *~ 2* [the] middle class; *~ 3* [the] working (lower) class **-hjälp** [public] assistance allowance; *få ~* receive public assistance, be on welfare (relief) **-högskola** school of social studies

social|isera socialize; nationalize **-isering** socialization; nationalization **-ism** socialism *(äv. ~en)* **-ist** socialist **-istisk** *a5* socialist[ic]

social|kunskap social studies **-lagstiftning** social *(AE.* security) legislation **-liberal** liberal social reformer **-medicin** social[ized] medicine **-minister** minister of health and social affairs **-nämnd** social welfare committee **-politik** social [welfare] policy; social politics *(pl, behandlas som sg)* **-politisk** sociopolitical, of social policy **-styrelse** *~n* [the Swedish] national board of health and welfare **-utskott** *~et* [the Swedish] [parliamentary] standing committee on social questions **-vetenskap** social science[s *pl*] **-vetenskaplig** of social science[s] **-vetenskapsman** sociologist **-vård** social welfare (assistance) **-vårdare** welfare officer, social worker **-vårdsbyrå** [local] social welfare office (bureau)

societet *s3* society

societets|dam socialite **-hus** clubhouse; casino **-lejon** social lion

socio|ekonomisk socioeconomic **-gram** [-'gramm] *s7* sociogram **-log** sociologist **-logi** *s3* sociology **-logisk** *a5* sociological **-nom** graduate from a school of social studies **-pat** sociopath

socka ['ˣsåcka] *s1* sock

sockel ['såck-] *s2 (byggn.; postament)* base, plinth; *(fattning)* holder, mounting; *(lamp-)* socket

socken ['sɔck-] *socknen socknar* parish **-bo** parishioner; *~r (äv.)* the inhabitants of a parish **-dräkt** *ung.* peasant costume **-kyrka** parish church **-stämma** parish meeting

socker ['såck-] *s7* sugar **-bagare** confectioner **-beta** sugar beet **-bit** lump of sugar **-bruk** sugar mill (refinery) **-dricka** *ung.* lemonade **-fri** sugar-free **-haltig** *a1* containing sugar **-kaka** sponge cake **-kulör** caramel **-lag** *s2* syrup [of sugar] **-lönn** sugar maple **-lösning** sugar solution **-piller** sugar-coated pill **-plantage** sugar plantation **-pulla** sugarplum **-raffinaderi** sugar refinery **-rör** sugar cane **-sjuk** diabetic **-sjuka** diabetes **-skål** sugar basin **-ströare** sugar sifter (castor) **-söt** [as] sweet as sugar; *bildl. äv.* sugary, honeyed **-topp** sugar loaf **-tång** sugar tongs *(pl)* **-vatten** sugared water **-ärtor** sugar peas

sockra ['ˣsåckra] sweeten [with sugar], sugar; *~ på* put sugar in (on); *~ sig* sugar, crystallize

soda *s9* soda **-lut** soda lye **-vatten** soda water

sodo'mi *s3* sodomy

soff|a [-å-] *s1* sofa; *(liten)* settee; *(trädgårds-)* seat **-bord** coffee table **-grupp** three-piece suite **-kudde** sofa cushion **-liggare** idler; *(vid val)* abstainer **-lock** sofa seat (top); *ligga på ~et* take it easy, idle

sof|ism *s3* sophism **-ist** sophist **-istikerad** [-'ke:-] *a5* sophisticated **-istisk** *a5* sophistic[al]

soignerad [sɔan'je:-] *a5* soigné[e]; *en ~ herre*

(*äv.*) a well-groomed gentleman
soja [ˣsåjja] *s1* soya; soy **-böna** soya bean; *AE.*
 soybean **-sås** soy (soya) sauce
sokratisk [så'kra:-] *a5* Socratic
sol *s2* sun
sol|a expose to the sun; ~ *sig* sun o.s., sunbathe,
 bildl. bask **-aktivitet** solar activity **-altan** sun
 balcony (terrace)
so'lar *a1* solar **solarium** [-'la:-] *s4* solarium
solarplexus [-ˣla:r-, 'sɷ:-] *s2* solar plexus
solaväxel [ˣså:-] sole (single, only) bill [of
 exchange]
sol|bad sun bath **-bada** sunbathe, take a sun
 bath **-bana** ecliptic, solar orb **-batteri** solar
 battery **-belyst** [-y:-] *a4* sunlit, sunny **-blekt**
 [-e:-] *a4* sun-bleached **-blind** sun-blind, blind-
 ed by the sun **-blindhet** sun-blindness **-bränd**
 a5 sunburnt, tanned **-bränna** *s1* sunburn, tan
 -cell solar cell
sold [-å-] *s3, mil.* pay
soldat soldier; *bli* ~ enlist, join the army; *den
 okände ~ens grav* the tomb of the Unknown
 Soldier **-ed** military oath **-'esk** *s3* [licentious]
 soldiery **-hop, -hord** rabble of soldiers **-liv**
 [a] soldier's (military) life **-rock** soldier's
 tunic **-torp** tenement soldier's smallholding
sol|dis heat haze **-dräkt** sunsuit **-dyrkan** sun
 worship **-eksem** sun rash **-el[ektrisk en-
 ergi]** solar electric power, solar electricity
 -energi solar energy
so'lenn *a1* solemn **-itet** *s3* solemnity
sol|eruption solar flare **-fattig** not very sunny;
 en ~ trakt a district with little sun[shine] **-fjä-
 der** fan **-fjäderformad** [-å-] *a5* fan-shaped
 -fläck sunspot **-fångare** solar collector **-föl-
 jare** sun tracker **-förmörkelse** eclipse of the
 sun, solar eclipse **-gass** blazing (blaze of the)
 sun **-glasögon** sunglasses **-glimt** glimpse of
 the sun **-glitter** (*på vatten*) sparkle **-gud**
 sun-god **-gård** [solar] halo **-höjd** altitude of
 the sun
so'lid *a1* solid; *ekon. äv.* sound, well-established, respectable; *~a kunskaper* [a] thorough
 (sound) knowledge
solidar|isera *rfl* identify o.s. (*med* with) **-isk**
 [-'da:-] *a5* loyal, solidary; joint; ~ *med* loyal
 to; *förklara sig* ~ *med* declare one's solidarity
 with **-itet** solidarity
soliditet solidity; (*ekonomisk*) solvency,
 soundness; (*persons*) respectability
soliditets|byrå credit information agency; *AE.*
 mercantile agency **-upplysning** credit[worthi-
 ness] report
solig *a1* sunny (*äv. bildl.*)
solist soloist, solo performer
soli'tär *s3* solitaire
solk [-å-] *s7* soil **solka** [-å-] ~ *ner* soil
solkatt reflection of the sun
solkig [-å-] *a1* soiled
sol|klar clear and sunny; *bildl.* as clear as
 noonday (daylight) **-konungen** the Sun King
 -korona solar corona, corona of the sun
 -kraftverk solar power station **-kurva** *en ~
 hade uppstått* the rails had buckled in the sun
 -ljus I *s7* sunlight **II** *a5, se* **-klar -månad** solar month **-mättad** sun-drenched **-nedgång**
 sunset, sundown; *i ~en* at sunset

solo ['sɷ:-] **I** *s6* solo (*pl äv.* soli) **II** *oböjl. a o.
 adv* solo
solochvåra [-ˣvå:-] obtain valuables by false
 promise of marriage; *bli ~d* be cheated by false
 promise of marriage **solochvårare** con man
 [who cheats women out of money by false
 promises of marriage]
solo|dansös solo dancer, prima ballerina **-flyg-
 ning** solo flight
sololja suntan oil (lotion)
solo|nummer solo **-stämma** solo part **-sång**
 solo singing
sol|ros sunflower **-rosolja** sunflower seed oil
 -rök haze **-segel** awning **-sida** *på* (*åt*) *~n* on
 the sunny side **-sken** sunshine; *det är* ~ the
 sun is shining **-skensdag** sunny day **-skens-
 historia** charming little story **-skenshumör**
 sunny mood **-skiva** sun's disk **-skydd** (*i bil*)
 sun shield (screen) **-skärm** sunshade **-spek-
 trum** solar spectrum **-sting** (*få* have) sunstroke **-strimma** ray of sunshine **-stråle**
 sunbeam **-strålning** solar radiation **-styng** *se*
 -sting **-stånd** solstice **-system** solar system
 -tak awning; (*på bil*) sliding roof (top) **-tek-
 nik** solar technology **-torka** dry [...] in the
 sun; **~d** sun-dried **-tält** awning **-uppgång**
 sunrise; *AE. äv.* sunup; *i ~en* at sunrise **-upp-
 värmning** solar heating **-ur** sundial
solution rubber solution
solv [-å-] *s7, väv.* heddle
sol|varg *han är en riktig* ~ he's as happy as a
 sandboy **-vargsleende** dazzling smile **-varv**
 revolution of the sun
solv|ens [-å-] *s3* solvency; reliability **-ent** *a1*
 solvent; reliable
solvera [-å-] *mat.* solve
sol|vind solar wind **-vända** *s1, bot.* rockrose
 -värme heat of the sun; *fack.* solar heat **-vär-
 mekraftverk** solar thermal power station **-år**
 solar year **-'är** *a1* solar
som [såmm] **I** *pron* (*om pers.*) who (*som obj.
 o. efter prep äv.* whom); (*om djur el. sak*)
 which; (*i nödvändig rel. sats om djur, sak o.
 ibl. pers., äv.*) that; (*efter such o. vanl. the
 same*) as; *pojken ~ kommer här* the boy who
 comes here; *den ~ lever får se* he who lives
 will see; *den ~ köper en bil måste* anyone who
 buys (anyone buying) a car must; *det är en
 dam ~ söker dig* there is a lady [who wants]
 to see you; *han frågade vem det var ~ kom* he
 asked who came (had come); *vem är det ~ du
 pratar med?* who is that you are talking to?;
 det är ngn ~ gråter s.b. is crying; *huset ~ de
 bor i* the house where (in which) they live; *han
 brukade berätta sagor, något ~* he used to tell
 stories, which; *allt* (*mycket, litet*) ~ *all* (much,
 little) that; *det är saker ~ vi sällan talar om*
 these are things [that] we seldom speak of; *den
 största konstnär ~ någonsin levat* the greatest
 artist that ever lived; *mannen och hästen ~ gick
 förbi* the man and the horse that passed; *vem
 ~ än kommer* whoever comes; *vad ~ än händer* whatever happens; *det var på den tiden ~*
 it was at the time when; *de var de sista ~ kom*
 they were the last to arrive; *så dum jag var ~
 sålde den!* what a fool I was to sell it!; *jag
 kom samma dag ~ han reste* I arrived on the

[same] day [as] he left; *det är samme man ~ vi såg i går* that is the same man [that, whom] we saw yesterday ; *hon var en sådan skönhet ~ man sällan ser* she had the kind of beauty one seldom sees **II** *konj* **1** *såväl ... ~* as well ... as; *unga ~ gamla* young and old alike **2** *(såsom, i egenskap av)* as; *(såsom, i likhet med)* like; *redan ~ pojke* even as a boy; *L ~ i London* L as in London; *säg ~ det är* tell me (him *etc.*) exactly how things stand; *kom ~ du är* come as you are, don't dress up, don't bother to change; *~ vanligt* as usual; *han är lika lång ~ jag* he is as tall as I am; *~ tur var* as luck would have it, luckily; *~ läkare måste han* as (being) a doctor he must; *~ sagt* as I (*etc.*) said before; *gör ~ du vill* do as you like; *gör ~ jag* do as I do, do like me; *vara ~ en mor för ngn* be [like] a mother to s.b.; *vara ~ förbytt* be changed beyond recognition; *om jag vore ~ du* if I were you; *det är bara ~ du tror* that's only your idea **3** *han lever ~ om var dag var den sista* he lives as though each day was his last; *det verkar ~ om* it seems as if (though) **4** *(när)* when; *just (bäst) ~* [just] as, at the very moment [when]; *rätt ~ det var* all of a sudden, all at once **5** *(eftersom)* as, since; *~ han är sjuk kan han inte komma* as (since) he is ill he cannot come **III** *adv, när jag ~ bäst höll på med att* while I was in the midst of (+ *ing-form*); *du kan väl titta in ~ hastigast* you can surely pop in for just a moment; *när solen står ~ högst* when the sun is at its height; *vi skulle resa ~ på måndag* we were to leave on Monday **IV** *interj, ~ vi skrattade!* how we laughed!

so'mal|ier Somalian **-isk** *a5* Somalian

somatisk [-'ma:-] *a5* somatic

somlig [ˣsåmm-] some; *~a* (*om pers.*) some [people]; *~a andra* some other people; *~t* some things (*pl*); *i ~t* in some parts (respects)

sommar [ˣsåmm-] *s2* summer; *i ~* this (next) summer; *i somras* last summer; *om ~en* (*somrarna*) in the summer; *på ~en 1968* in the summer of 1968; *en svala gör ingen ~* one swallow does not make a summer **-dag** summer['s] day **-gäst** summer visitor **-kappa** summer coat **-klänning** summer dress **-kostym** summer suit **-kväll** summer evening **-lov** summer vacation (holidays) (*pl*), long vacation **-nöje** *se -ställe* **-sjuka** summer diarrhoea **-solstånd** summer solstice **-stuga, -ställe** weekend cottage, summer cottage (villa); *vårt ~* (*äv.*) the place where we spend our summers **-tid** summertime; *(framflyttning av klockan)* daylight-saving time **-värme** summer warmth; heat

somna [-å-] *~ [in]* fall asleep, go to sleep; *vard.* drop off; *~ från lampan* go to sleep and leave the light on; *~ om* go to sleep again; *~ vid ratten* fall asleep when driving; *min fot har ~t* my foot has gone to sleep

somnam'bul [-å-] **I** *s3* somnambulist **II** *a1* somnambulistic **-ism** somnambulism, noctambulism

somt [-å-] some things (*pl*); *~ föll på hälleberget* some fell on stony ground

son [så:n] *-en söner* son (*till* of)

sona expiate; make amends for

sonant sonant

sonar ['så:-] *s3* echo sounder, sonar, asdic

sonat sonata **-form** sonata form **-'in** *s3* sonatina

sond [sånd, såŋd] *s3, kir.* probe, sound; *rymd.* probe **sondera** probe, sound; *~ terrängen* reconnoitre, see how the land lies **sondering** [-'de:-] probing, probe, sounding **sondmata** *med.* tubefeed **sondmatning** nasogastric feeding

sondotter granddaughter; *~s barn* great-grandchild

so'nett *s3* sonnet

sonhustru daughter-in-law

sonika ['sɷ:-] *helt ~* [quite] simply, without ceremony

son|lig [ˣså:n-] *a1* filial (*vördnad* piety) **-namn** family name ending in -son

sonor [-'nå:r] *a1* sonorous **-itet** sonority

son|son grandson **-sonsson** great-grandson

sop|a sweep (*gatan* the street); *~ rent* sweep [...] clean (*från* of); *~ upp* sweep up; *~ rent för egen dörr* put one's own house in order; *~ igen spåren efter* (*bildl.*) cover up one's tracks after **-backe** refuse tip **-bil** refuse [collection] lorry, dustcart; *AE.* garbage truck **-borste** brush, broom **-hink** refuse bucket **-hämtare** dustman; *AE.* garbage collector **-hämtning** refuse collection; *AE.* garbage removal **-hög** rubbish heap **-kvast** broom **-kärl** dustbin **-lår** *se soptunna* **-nedkast** refuse (*AE.* garbage) chute **-ning** [-ɷ:-] sweeping **-or** *pl* sweepings; *(avfall)* refuse, waste, *AE.* garbage (*sg*)

sopp|a [-å-] *s1* soup; *(kött-)* broth; *koka ~ på en spik* (*bildl.*) make s.th. from nothing **-ben** *pl* bones for soup **-kittel** soup cauldron **-rötter** *pl* vegetables for soup, potherbs **-skål** [soup] tureen **-slev** soup ladle **-tallrik** soup plate **-terrin** *se -skål*

so'pran *s3* soprano; *(-stämma äv.)* treble

sop|skyffel dustpan **-säck** refuse sack **-tipp** refuse (*AE.* garbage) dump **-tunna** dustbin; *AE.* garbage (trash) can **-åkare** dustman

sorbet [-'be:(t)] *s3* sorbet, sherbet

sor'din *s3, mus.* sordino, mute; *lägga ~ på* (*bildl.*) put a damper on

sorg [sårj] *s3* **1** sorrow (*över* at, for, over); grief (*över* for, of, at); distress; *(bedrövelse)* affliction; *(bekymmer)* trouble, care; *med ~ i själen* with sorrow in one's heart; *den dagen den ~en* cross your bridges when you come to them; *efter sju ~er och åtta bedrövelser* after much trial and tribulation **2** *(efter avliden)* mourning; *bära ~* be in (wear) mourning (*efter* for); *djup ~* full (deep) mourning; *beklaga ~en* express one's sympathy; *få ~* have a bereavement, lose a relative **-band** mourning (crape) band **-dräkt** mourning

sorge|barn problem child; black sheep **-bud** sad news, news of a death **-hus** house of mourning **-högtid** funeral ceremony **-musik** funeral music **-spel** tragedy **-tåg** funeral procession

sorg|flor mourning crape **-fri** carefree, free from care **-fällig** *a1* careful; conscientious, solicitous **-fällighet** care[fulness]; solicitude **-kant** black edge (border); *kuvert med ~* black-edged envelope **-klädd** [dressed] in

S

mourning **-kläder** *pl* mourning [attire] (*sg*)
sorglig [ˣsårj-] *a1* sad; (*bedrövlig*) deplorable (*syn* sight); (*ömklig*) pitiful; *~t men sant* sad but true; *en ~ historia* a sad (deplorable, tragic) story **sorgligt** *adv* sadly; *~ nog* unfortunately
sorg|lustig tragicomic **-lös 1** *se sorgfri* **2** (*obetänksam*) careless; (*lättsinnig*) happy-go-lucky, improvident; (*tanklös*) unthinking, heedless **-löshet** carelessness *etc.* **-mantel** *zool.* Camberwell beauty, *AE.* mourning cloak **-marsch** funeral march **-modig** melancholy
sorgsen [ˣsårj-] *a3* sad; (*bedrövad*) grieved (*över* at); (*nedslagen*) depressed; (*betryckt*) melancholy, gloomy **-het** sadness *etc.*; melancholy, gloom
sork [-å-] *s2* vole; (*förr*) fieldmouse
sorl [-å:-] *s7* (*vattenbrus*) ripple; (*bäcks äv.*) murmur, purl; (*av röster*) murmur, hum; *det gick ett ~ av bifall genom publiken* a murmur of approval went through the house (theatre, hall *etc.*) **sorla** [-å:-] ripple, purl; murmur, hum
sort [-å-] *s3* sort, kind; species, description; (*märke*) brand, mark; *mat.* denomination; *den ~ens människor* people of that kind (sort), that sort of people; *av bästa ~* first-rate **sortera 1** (*dela upp*) [as]sort; classify, grade; (*efter storlek*) size **2** *~ under* belong to, (*ämbetsverk*) come under the supervision of **sorterad** [-'te:-] *a5* (*välförsedd*) well-stocked (*i* in); *vara ~ i* (*äv.*) have a large assortment of **sortering** (*-erande*) [as]sorting, assortment; (*sortiment*) selection; *första ~* first[s *pl*] **sorteringsmaskin** sorting (grading) machine
sor'ti *s3* exit
sortiment *s7* (*varulager*) assortment, range; product mix; (*uppsättning*) set; *fullständigt ~ av* full line of, complete range of
SOS *ett ~* an SOS
sosse *s2, vard.* social democrat
1 sot *s7* **1** soot; (*i motor*) carbon **2** (*på säd*) brand, blight
2 sot *s3* (*sjukdom*) sickness, disease
1 sota (*umgälla*) *~ för* smart (suffer) for
2 sot|a 1 (*befria från sot*) sweep (*en skorsten* a chimney); decarbonize (*en motor* a motor) **2** (*svärta*) *~* [*ner*] soot, cover with soot; *~ ner sig* get o.s. sooty **3** (*~ ifrån sig*) soot, give off soot
sotar|e chimney sweep[er] **-murre** *s2, vard., se -are* **-mästare** master sweep
sotdöd *dö ~en* die a natural death
sot|eld chimney fire **-fläck** smudge, smut **-höna** coot
sot|ig *a1* **1** sooty; (*om skorsten*) full of soot; (*fläckig*) smudgy, smutty **2** (*om säd*) smutty, blighted **-lucka** soot door **-ning** [-ɷ:-] (*av skorsten*) chimney-sweeping; (*av motor*) decarbonization **-svamp** common smut of wheat **-svart** sooty [black]
sotsäng *ligga på ~en* lie on one's deathbed
sotviska flue brush
souschef [ˣsɷ:ʃe:f] deputy chief
souve'nir [sɷve-] *s3* souvenir, keepsake
sov [-å:-] *imperf. av sova*
sov|a [-å:-] *sov -it* sleep; (*ligga o. ~*) be asleep; *lägga sig att ~* go to sleep (bed); *~ gott* sleep

soundly, be fast asleep, (*som vana*) sleep well; *sov gott!* sleep well!; *har du -it gott i natt?* did you have a good night?; *~ oroligt* have a troubled sleep; *mitt ben -er* my leg has gone to sleep; *~ på saken* sleep on it; *~ ut* have enough sleep **-alkov** bed recess **-ande** *a4* sleeping; *bildl.* dormant; *en ~ a sleeper* **-dags** bedtime **-dräkt** sleeping suit
sovel [ˣså:-] *s7* meat, cheese *etc.*
sovit [-å:-] *sup. av sova*
sov'jet [-å-] *s3* soviet; *högsta ~* Supreme Soviet **-isk** *a5* Soviet, of the Soviet Union **-republik** Soviet Republic **-rysk** Soviet Russian
Sovjet|ryssland Soviet Russia **-unionen** the Soviet Union
sov|kupé sleeping-compartment, sleeper **-plats** sleeping-place; (*på tåg, båt*) berth **-påse** sleeping bag
sovr|a [-å:-] pick over; sift, winnow; (*malm e.d.*) dress **-ing** picking *etc.*
sov|rum bedroom **-sal** dormitory **-stad** dormitory suburb; *AE.* bedroom suburb (town) **-säck** sleeping bag **-vagn** sleeping car, sleeper **-vagnsbiljett** sleeper ticket **-vagnskonduktör** sleeping-car attendant
spackel ['spack-] *s7* putty [knife] **spackla** putty **spackling** puttying
spad *s7, sg best. form vard.* spat liquid; (*kött-*) broth; (*grönsaks- äv.*) water; *trilla i spat* (*vard.*) fall into the water
spade *s2* spade
spader ['spa:-] *s9, kortsp., koll.* spades (*pl*); *en ~ a spade*; *~ kung* the king of spades; *dra en ~* (*vard.*) have a game of cards
spadtag cut (dig) with a spade; *ta det första ~et* throw up the first sod; *inte ta ett ~* (*vard.*) not lift a finger
spagat *s3, gå ner i ~* do the splits
spagetti [-'getti] *s9* spaghetti **-västern** *r, vard.* spaghetti western
1 spak *s2* lever; bar; *flyg.* control stick
2 spak *a1* manageable, tractable; docile; *bli ~* relent, soften
spaljé *s3* espalier, trelliswork, latticework **-träd** trained fruit tree
spalt *s3* column; *figurera i ~erna* appear in the papers
spalt|a 1 (*dela i -er*) put into columns **2** (*klyva*) split, cleave **-bredd** column width **-fyllnad** padding **-korrektur** galley proof **-vis** (*i - er*) in columns; (*spalt efter spalt*) columns of, column after column
spana watch, look out (*efter* for); scout; *mil.* reconnoitre, observe; *~ efter* (*äv.*) search (be on the lookout) for; *~ upp* spy out; *~ ut över* gaze out over (*vidderna* the expanses); *~nde blickar* searching looks **spanare** scout; *flyg.* observer
spaniel ['spanjel] *s2* spaniel
Spanien ['spannjen] *n* Spain
spaning search; *mil.* reconnaissance; *få ~ på ngt* (*vard.*) get wind of s.th.
spanings|arbete *~t har pågått* the search has been on **-flygplan** reconnaissance aircraft scout **-ledning** search coordination headquarters **-patrull** search party; *mil.* reconnaissance [party] **-uppbåd** search party

span'jor *s3* Spaniard **-ska** [-ˣjɷːr-] Spanish woman
spankulera stroll, saunter
1 spann *s7, byggn.* span
2 spann *s2, s7, pl äv.* **spänner** (*hink*) pail, bucket
3 spann *s9* (*mått*) span
4 spann *s7* (*av dragdjur*) team [of horses *etc.*]; *köra* (*med*) *i* ~ drive a team of [horses *etc.*]
5 spann *imperf. av* spinna
spannmål *s3* grain, corn; (*brödsäd*) cereal[s *pl*]
spannmåls|förråd corn (*etc.*) store **-handel** corn (grain) trade (business) **-magasin** granary, corn (grain) store **-produkt** grain (corn) product **-skörd** grain (corn) crop
spansk *a1* Spanish; ~*a sjukan* the Spanish flu, *med.* rachitis; ~ *peppar* red pepper; ~*a ryttare* (*mil.*) chevaux-de-frise
spansk|a *s1* (*språk*) Spanish **--amerikansk** Spanish-American **-fluga** *zool.* Spanish fly; (*drog*) cantharis **-gröna** *s1* verdigris **-rör** rattan [cane]
spant *s7, sjö.* frame, rib
spara save (*pengar* money; *sina krafter* one's strength; *tid* time; *arbete* work); spare (*hästarna* the horses); (*för framtiden*) reserve (*till* of); (*uppskjuta*) put off; ~ *på* save, economize, use sparingly; ~ *in* save; *den som spar han har* waste not want not; *snål spar och fan tar* ever spare, ever bare; *inte* ~ *på beröm* be lavish in praise; *det är inget att* ~ *på* it is not worth saving (keeping); ~ *sig* spare o.s., husband one's strength ; *du kunde ha* ~*t dig den mödan* you could have spared yourself the trouble
sparande *s6* saving; thrift; *det privata* ~*t* private saving[s *pl*]; *frivilligt* ~ voluntary saving **sparare** saver; depositor
spar|bank *s3* savings bank **-banksbok** savings book, savings-bank book **-bössa** money-box **-gris** piggy bank
spark *s2* **1** kick; *få* ~*en* (*avsked*) get the sack, be fired (sacked) **2** kick-sledge
sparka kick; ~ *av sig skorna* kick off one's shoes; ~ *av sig täcket* kick off one's bedclothes; ~ *bakut* (*om häst*) kick [out behind]; ~ *fram* (*bildl.*) thrust forward; ~ *ngn* [*snett*] *uppåt* (*vard.*) kick s.b. upstairs; ~ *till* give a kick; ~ *ut ngn* kick s.b. out
sparkapital savings (*pl*), saved capital
sparkas *dep* kick
sparkassa savings association
sparkasseräkning savings account
spark|boll football **-byxor** *pl* rompers **-cykel** scooter **-dräkt** rompers (*pl*)
spar|klubb thrift (savings) club **-konto** thrift account; *jfr äv.* sparkasseräkning
sparkstötting kick-sledge
spar|lakan bed curtain **-lakansläxa** curtain lecture
spar|låga low heat; *ställa på* ~ put on a low heat, simmer gently **-medel** *pl* savings **-obligation** savings bond
sparra *sport.* spar
sparre *s2* small square timber; (*tak-*) rafter, baulk
sparris ['sparr-] *s2* asparagus **-knoppar** aspara-

gus tips **-kål** broccoli
sparsam [ˣspaːr-] *a1* (*ekonomisk*) economical (*med* with, in); thrifty; sparing (*på* (*med*) *beröm* of one's praise); (*enkel*) frugal; (*gles*) sparse, scanty; (*sällsynt*) rare (*förekomst* occurrence) **-het** economy; thrift; (*sparsam förekomst*) scantiness
sparsamhets|kampanj economy drive (campaign) **-skäl** *av* ~ for reasons of economy
sparsamt *adv* economically *etc.*; *förekomma* ~*t* occur rarely, be scarce
sparsmakad *a5* fastidious
spar't|an *s3* Spartan **-'ansk** [-aː-] *a5* Spartan
sparv *s2* sparrow **-hök** sparrowhawk **-uggla** pygmy owl
spasm *s3* spasm; convulsion, cramp **spasmodisk** [-ˈmɷː-] *a5* spasmodic
spast|iker ['spass-] *s9* spastic **-isk** ['spass-] *a5* spastic
spat *s3, miner.* spar
spatel *s2* spatula
spatiös [-tsiˈöːs] *a1* spacious; roomy
spatser|a walk; strut **-käpp** walking stick
spatt *s3* spavin **-ig** *a1* spavined; (*om pers.*) stiff
spe *n* (*narr*) derision, ridicule; (*hån*) sneer[s *pl*], gibe[s *pl*]
speaker ['spiːker] *s2* (*utropare*) compere; *AE. äv.* emcee; (*hallåman*) announcer
spece'riaffär grocer's [shop], grocery [store]
speceri|er [-ˈriː-] *pl* groceries **-handlare** grocer
speci'al|affär specialized shop **-arbetare** specialist worker **-arbete** *skol.* special project **-begåvning** special gift **-byggd** *a5* specially built, *AE.* custom-made **-erbjudande** special offer **-fall** special case **-intresse** special interest; hobby
special|isera *rfl* specialize (*på* in) **-isering** specialization, specializing **-ist** specialist (*på* in); expert (*på* on) **-itet** *s3* special[i]ty
special|klass *skol.* remedial class **-kunskaper** *pl* specialist knowledge **-lärare** remedial teacher **-pedagogik** special education, remedial teaching **-stål** special steel **-tillverkad** *a5* specially made, *AE.* custom-made **-uppdrag** special task (charge, mission) **-utbildning** special training **-utrustning** special equipment
speci'ell *a1* special, particular; (*konstig*) odd, peculiar
specificer|a specify, itemize, detail, particularize **-ing** specification, specifying
specifik *a1* specific (*vikt* gravity, weight) **-ation** specification, detailed description
specimen ['speː-] *n, pl äv.* specimina [-ˈsiː] specimen
spedi|era forward, dispatch **-tion** forwarding (dispatch) [of goods] **-tionsfirma** forwarding (shipping) agency **-tör** forwarding (shipping) agent
spe|full (*hånfull*) mocking, derisive; (*gäcksam*) quizzical; (*om pers.*) given to mockery **-fågel** wag, tease
spegel *s2* mirror, looking glass; *se sig i* ~*n* look into the mirror; *själens* ~ the mirror of the soul; *sjön ligger som en* ~ the lake is as smooth as glass **-bild** reflected image, reflection; *bildl.* image **-blank** glassy (*yta* surface); like a mir-

S

ror; (om sjö) [as] smooth as glass **-fäktning** dissimulation, dissembling **-galleri** gallery of mirrors **-glas** mirror (plate) glass **-reflexkamera** reflex camera **-sal** hall of mirrors **-skrift** reversed (mirror) script **-teleskop** reflecting telescope **-vänd** a5 reversed

spegl|a [ˣspe:g-] reflect, mirror; ~ sig (avspegla sig) be reflected (i vattnet in the water), (om pers.) look at o.s. in the mirror **-ing** reflection

speglosa gibe, scoff

spej|a [ˣspejja] spy (efter about (round) for); mil. scout **-ande** a4 spying; searching (blick look) **-are** spy; mil. [reconnaissance] scout

spektakel [-'ta:-] s7 **1** (oväsen) row; (skandal) scandal; (förtret) mischief, trouble; ställa till ~ make a scene; ett sånt ~! what a nuisance! **2** (åtlöje) ridicule; göra ~ av ngn make a fool of s.b. **spektaku'lär** al spectacular

spek'tral|analys spectrum (spectral) analysis **-färg** spectral colour **-klass** astr. spectral type (class)

spektro|graf s3 spectrograph **-skop** s7 spectroscope

spektrum ['spekt-] s8 spectrum (pl spectra); [dis]kontinuerligt ~ [dis]continuous spectrum

spekulant 1 (reflektant) prospective (would-be) buyer; hugade ~er prospective buyers; vara ~ på be [a] prospective buyer of **2** (börs-) operator, speculator **spekulation** speculation, venture; (börs- äv.) operation; på ~ on speculation **spekulationsvinst** speculative profit (gain) **spekulativ** [-'ti:v, 'speck-] speculative **spekulera 1** speculate (på on; i baisse (hausse) for a decline (rise)) **2** (tänka) ponder, think (på, över about)

1 spel s7 (vinsch) winch, windlass; (gruv-) winder; (-rum) clearance, play

2 spel s7 **1** (-ande) play[ing]; (musikaliskt -sätt) execution; teat. acting; (lek; idrott) game (äv. bildl.); ~ om pengar playing for money; ~et är förlorat the game is up; dra sig ur ~et quit [the game]; övernaturliga makter driver sitt ~ supernatural powers are abroad; förlora (vinna) på ~ lose (win) at play (by gambling); det är en kvinna med i ~et there is a woman in the case; ha ett finger med i ~et have a finger in the pie; otur i ~ tur i kärlek unlucky at cards, lucky in love; rent ~ fair play; spela ett högt ~ play for high stakes, bildl. play a high game; stå på ~ be at stake; sätta på ~ put at stake, stake; ta hem ~et win; tillfällighheternas ~ pure chance **2** (parningslek) courtship **3** kortsp. trick

spela 1 play (fiol the violin; ett spel a game; om pengar for money); (musikstycke äv.) execute, perform; gå och ~ piano för take piano lessons from; ~ falskt play out of tune, kortsp. cheat [at cards]; ~ hasard gamble; ~ sina kort väl play one's cards well; ~ ngn i händerna play into a p.'s hands **2** teat. act, play; ~ herre play the gentleman; ~ sjuk pretend to be ill; ~ teater (låtsas) make pretence **3** (med betonad partikel) ~ av ngn ngt win s.th. off s.b.; ~ bort gamble away; ~ in a) (inöva) rehearse, b) (på grammofonskiva e.d.) make a recording, record; det är många faktorer som ~r in many factors come into play; ~ upp till dans strike

up; ~ ut ett kort play a card; ~ ut ngn mot ngn play s.b. off against s.b.; han har ~t ut sin roll he is played out (finished); ~ över a) (öva) practise, b) (överdriva) overdo it, overact

spelande a4 playing; sparkling (ögon eyes); de ~ the players, mus. the musicians, teat. the actors **spelarbyte** (fotboll) exchange of player for reserve; (ishockey) change of players

spel|are player; (hasard-) gambler **-automat** gambling (slot) machine, fruit machine **-bank** casino **-bar** al, teat., mus. performable; sport. (om spelare) unmarked **-bord** card (gambling) table **-djävulen** gripas av ~ be gambling-mad **-dosa** music[al] box

speleologi s3 speleology

spelevink [-'viŋk] s2 irresponsible youngster

spel|film feature (full-length) film **-hall** amusement arcade **-håla** gambling den **-kort** playing card **-lektion** music lesson **-lista** teat. list of performances, repertory **-man** musician; (fiolspelare) fiddler **-mark** counter; (-penning) jetton

spel|ning engagement, vard. gig **-passion** gambling fever **-regel** rule of the game **-rum** bildl. scope, margin, freedom to act; lämna fritt ~ give free scope **-skuld** gambling debt **-säsong** theatrical season **-sätt** mus. [way of] execution; sport. style of play **-teori** företagsekon. game theory **-tid** (för film) screen (running) time; (för grammofonskiva) playing time **-vinst** winnings (pl) [at cards (from gambling)] **-år** teat. theatrical year **-öppning** schack. o. bildl. gambit; sport. opening [of the game]

spenabarn suckling

spenat spinach

spender|a spend [... liberally], bestow (på upon) **-byxorna** pl, ha ~ på sig be in a generous (lavish) mood **-sam** [-'de:r-] al generous, liberal **-samhet** [-'de:r-] generosity, liberality

spene s2 teat, nipple

spenslig al [of] slender [build]; slim

spenvarm ~ mjölk milk warm from the cow

sperm|a [ˣspärr-] s9, s7 sperm **spermaceti** [-'se:-] s9 spermaceti **spermatozo** [-tå'så:] s3, **spermie** ['spärr-] s5 spermatozoon (pl spermatozoa)

speta 1 (spreta) stick up (out) **2** (kliva) stalk about **spetig** al **1** (spretande) straggly **2** (tunn) skinny; ~a ben spindly legs

1 spets s2 **1** (udd) point (äv. bildl.); (på finger, tunga o.d.) tip; (berg-) peak, top; geom. apex; bildl. äv. head; bjuda ngn ~en stand up to s.b., defy s.b.; driva ngt till sin ~ carry s.th. to extremes; gå i ~en walk at the head, lead the way, bildl. äv. be the prime mover (för of); stå i ~en för be at the head of, head; samhällets ~ar the leaders of society (a nation) **2** (betyg) with distinction

2 spets s2, text. lace; (sydd) needlepoint

3 spets s2 (hund) spitz; Pomeranian

spets|a 1 (göra -ig) point; sharpen (en blyertspenna a pencil); ~ öronen prick up one's ears **2** (genombora) pierce; (på nål) pin, nail; (på spjut etc.) spear etc. **3** (en dryck) lace, vard. spike

Spetsbergen Spitsbergen
spets|bov arch rogue **-byxor** *pl* [riding-]breeches **-båge** pointed (Gothic, lancet) arch **-bågstil** pointed (Gothic) style **-fundig** *a1* subtle; hairsplitting **-fundighet** subtlety; ~*er* (*äv.*) sophistry, quibbling (*sg*) **-gavel** pointed gable **-glans** *s3, miner.* stibnite, antimony glance **-glas** tapering dram-glass **-hacka** pickaxe
spetsig *a1* pointed (*äv. bildl.*); (*avsmalnande*) tapering; pointed (*skägg* beard); *bildl. äv.* cutting, sarcastic; ~ *vinkel* acute angle **-het** pointedness *etc.*; ~*er* (*sarkasmer*) sneers, sarcasms
spets|krage lace collar **-krås** lace frill **-näst** [-ä:-] *a4* sharp-nosed **-vinklig** *a1* acute-angled
spett *s7* crowbar; pinch bar; (*stek-*) spit **-[e]kaka** cake baked on a spit
spetälsk *a5* leprous; *en* ~ a leper **spetälska** *s9* leprosy
spex *s7* students' farce; (*friare*) farce **spexa** *ung.* rollick **spexhumör** rollicking mood **spexig** *a1* farcial; comical
spicke|n *a5* salt-cured **-sill** salt herring
spigg *s2* stickleback
1 spik *adv,* ~ *nykter* [as] sober as a judge
2 spik *s2* nail; *slå huvudet på* ~*en* hit the nail on the head; *den* ~*en drar* (*bildl.*) that strikes home
spik|a nail; spike; (*med nubb*) tack; *bildl.* peg, fix; ~ *fast* fasten with nails, nail (*ngt vid s.th.* on to); ~ *igen* nail down; ~ *upp* nail [... up], placard **-huvud** head of a nail, nailhead **-hål** nail hole **-klubba** *hist.* mace **-matta** bed of nails
spiknykter *se 1 spik*
spikpiano tinny [old] piano
spikrak [as] straight as an arrow (a poker)
spiksko *sport.* track shoe
spilkum *s2* bowl, basin
spill *s7* wastage, waste; *radioaktivt* ~ radioactive fallout **spilla** *v2* **1** (*hälla ut*) spill, drop; ~ *på sig* spill (drop) s.th. on one's clothes; ~ *ut* spill [out], shed; *spill inte!* don't spill it! **2** (*för-*) waste, lose; *-d möda* labour thrown away, (*friare*) waste of energy; *-da människoliv* lost lives; *det var många -da människoliv* the loss of life was very great
spillkråka black woodpecker
spillning 1 (*avfall*) refuse **2** droppings (*pl*); (*gödsel*) dung
spillo *oböjligt s, ge ... till* ~ give ... up [as lost], abandon; *gå till* ~ get (be) lost, go to waste
spillolja waste oil
spillr|a *s1* (*flisa*) splinter; *-or* (*bildl.*) remaining fragments, scattered remnants, wreckage (*sg*); *falla* (*gå*) *i -or* fly (break) into splinters, fall to pieces; *slå i -or* break into fragments, *bildl.* shatter
spill|tid lost (waste[d]) time **-vatten** waste water; overflow; (*avloppsvatten*) sewage **-värme** surplus heat
spillånga [ˣspi:llåŋa, ˣspill-] (*fisk*) stockfish
spilta *s1* stall; (*för obunden häst*) loose box
spinalanestesi [-ˣna:l-] *kir.* spinal anaesthesia
1 spindel *s2, tekn.* spindle
2 spindel *s2, zool.* spider
spindelben spider's leg, *bildl.* spindleleg
spindelbult steering pivot pin, kingpin, swivel pin
spindel|nät, -väv cobweb[s *pl*]; (*tunnare*) gossamer
spi'nett *s3, mus.* spinet
spinkig *a1* very thin, spindly **-het** thinness
1 spinn *r, flyg.* spin; *råka i* ~ get into a spin
2 spinn *s7* (*fiske*) *se -fiske*
spinna *spann spunnit* **1** spin; twist (*tobak* tobacco); (*rotera*) spin, twirl **2** (*om katt*) purr
spinnaker [ˈspinn-, ˣspinn-] *s2* spinnaker
spinnare *s9* (*fiskedrag*) troll
spinnarfjäril bombycid
spinneri spinning (cotton) mill **spinnerska** [female] spinner
spinn|fiske spinning; *AE.* bait-casting **-hus** spinning-house **-maskin** spinning machine **-rock** spinning wheel **-rulle** *fisk.* casting reel **-sida** distaff side **-spö** spinning (casting) rod
spi'on *s3* spy **spionage** *s7* espionage, spying **spionera** spy (*på* [up]on) **spioneri** *se spionage* **spionliga** spy ring
1 spira *v1,* ~ [*upp*] sprout, germinate; ~*nde kärlek* budding love
2 spira *s1* (*torn-*) spire; (*trä-*) spar (*äv. sjö.*); (*stång*) pole; (*värdighetstecken*) sceptre
spi'ral *s3* **1** spiral, helix; (*vindling*) whorl; *gå i* ~ turn spirally **2** (*livmoderinlägg*) coil, intrauterine device (*förk.* I.U.D.) **-block** spiral notebook **-fjäder** coil spring; (*plan*) spiral spring **-formig** [-å-] *a1* spiral, helical; ~ *bakterie* spirochaete **-rörelse** spiral motion (movement) **-trappa** spiral (winding) staircase
spirant *fonet.* fricative [sound]
spirea [-ˣre:a] *s1, bot.* spiraea
spirit|ism spiritism **-ist** spiritist **-istisk** *a5* spiritistic
spiritual|ism spiritualism **-ist** spiritualist **-istisk** *a5* spiritualistic **-itet** *s3* wit, esprit
spiritu'ell *a1* brilliant; witty
spirituosa [-tuˣⱺ:sa] *s1* spirits; spirituous liquors **spiritus** [ˈspi:-] *r* spirit, alcohol
spiroket *s3* spirochaete
1 spis *s2, boktr.* rising space; *AE.* work-up
2 spis *s2* (*eldstad*) fireplace; (*köks-*) stove, range; *öppen* ~ [open] fireplace; *stå vid* ~*en* stand over the stove, be cooking
3 spis *s3* (*föda*) food (*äv. bildl.*); *bildl. äv.* nourishment
spis|a eat **2** *vard.* listen intently (*jazz* to jazz); dig **-bröd** crispbread
spisel *s2, se 2 spis* **-häll** hearth[stone] **-krans** mantelpiece
spis|krok poker **-kupa** [range, ventilating] hood **-platta** hotplate **-vrå** chimney (fireside) corner
spjut *s7* spear; (*kort*) dart; *sport.* javelin; *kasta* ~ (*sport.*) throw the javelin **-formig** [-å-] *a1* spear-shaped; lanciform (*blad* leaf) **-kast** throw of a (the) spear (*etc.*) **-kastare** *sport.* javelin-thrower **-kastning** *sport.* javelin-throwing **-skaft** shaft of a (the) spear (*etc.*) **-spets** spearhead, spearpoint (*etc.*)
spjuver [ˈspju:-] *s2* rogue **-aktig** *a1* roguish
spjäl|a *s1* lath; (*i jalusi*) rib, slat **ll** *v1* splint; *med. äv.* put in splints **-förband** splint dressing
spjälk|a split **-ning** splitting; (*atom-*) fission

S

spjäll *s7* damper, register; (*på motor*) throttle; *öppna ~et* open the damper (*etc.*) **-snöre** cord of a (the) damper (*etc.*)
spjäll|låda [-ä:-] crate **-ning** [-ä:-] *med.* splinting **-staket** pale fence **-säng** cot with bars **-verk** trelliswork, latticework
spjärn [-ä:-] *n, ta* ~ brace one's feet (*mot* against) **spjärna** ~ *emot* kick against, resist
splines [splajns] *pl, tekn.* splines
splint *s3, bot.* sapwood; *koll.* (*flisor*) splinters (*pl*)
split *s7* discord, dissension; *utså* ~ sow dissension
splits *s2, sjö.* splice **splitsa** splice **splitsning** splicing; *konkr.* splice
1 splitter ['splitt-] *adv,* ~ *ny* brand-new
2 splitt|er ['splitt-] *s7, koll.* (*flisor*) splinters (*pl*); (*granat- etc.*) splinter
splitterfri ~*tt glas* safety glass **splittra I** *s1* splinter, shiver **II** *v1* splinter, break into splinters; *bildl.* divide [up]; *känna sig ~d* feel at sixes and sevens; ~ *sig* (*bildl.*) divide (split) one's energy **splittring** *bildl.* split, division; (*söndring*) disruption
1 spola (*skölja*) flush, rinse, wash; *vågorna ~de över däcket* the waves washed the deck; ~ *av* a) wash down (*en bil* a car), b) rinse, swill (*disken* the dishes); ~ *bort* wash away; ~ *gatorna* sprinkle (water) the streets; ~ [*på toaletten*] flush the toilet; ~ *en skridskobana* flood a skating rink
2 spola (*garn*) spool, reel, wind [up]; (*film*) reel
spolarvätska washer fluid **spole** *s2* **1** (*garn-; på* [*sy*]*maskin*) bobbin; (*för film*) spool; *elektr.* coil, spiral **spolformig** [-år-] *a1* spool-shaped
spolier|a spoil, wreck **-ing** spoliation
spoling *vard.* stripling; whippersnapper
spolmask ascarid
1 spolning [-ω:-] (*t. 1 spola*) flushing *etc.*
2 spolning [-ω:-] (*t. 2 spola*) reeling, winding
spondé [-å-] *s3* spondee **spondeisk** [-'de:-] *a5* spondaic[al]
sponsor ['spånsår] *s3* sponsor, backer **sponsra** [ˣspånsra] sponsor **sponsring** [ˣspåns-] sponsoring
spont [-å-] *s3* groove, tongue, rebate **sponta** [-å-] groove, tongue, rebate; ~*de bräder* match (matched) boards; ~*d och notad* tongued and grooved
spon'tan [-å-] *a1* spontaneous **-ism** abstract expressionism **-ist** painter of the abstract expressionist school **-itet** spontaneity
spor *s3* spore
sporadisk [-'ra:-] *a5* sporadic; isolated
sporde [-ω:-] *imperf. av spörja*
sporra [-å-] spur (*hästen* one's horse); *bildl. äv.* incite (*ngn till att* s.b. into + *ing-form*), stimulate
sporr|e *s2* spur (*äv. bildl.*); (*på hund äv.*) dewclaw; *bildl. äv.* incentive, stimulus; *försedd med -ar* spurred;*vinna sina -ar* (*bildl.*) win one's spurs **-sträck** *i* ~ at full gallop (speed) **-trissa** rowel
1 sport [-ω:-] *sup. av spörja*
2 sport [-å-] *s3* sport[s *pl*]; games (*pl*)
sport|a go in for sports (games) **-affär** sports shop (outfitter) **-artiklar** *pl* sports (sporting)

equipment (*sg*) **-bil** sports car **-dräkt** sports suit (*dams* costume); tweeds (*pl*) **-dykare** skin-diver, free diver **-fiskare** angler **-fiske** angling **-flygare** private pilot **-flygning** private flying **-flygplan** private (sports) plane **-journalist** sports writer
sport|ig [-å-] *a1* sporty; keen on sport[s] **-kläder** sportswear
sportler ['spårt-] *pl* perquisites
sport|lov winter sports holidays (*pl*) **-sida** (*i tidning*) sports page
sports|lig [-å-] sporting (*chans* chance) **-man** sportsman **-mannaanda** sportsmanship **-mässig** *a1* sportsmanlike
sportstuga weekend cottage, log-cabin
spotmarknad spot market
spotsk [-å-] *a1* contemptuous, scornful **-het** contempt, scorn
spott [-å-] *s3, s7* **1** (*saliv*) spittle, saliva **2** (*hån*) scorn
spott|a [-å-] spit; ~ *i nävarna och ta nya tag* spit in one's hands and have another go [at it] **-kopp** spittoon; *AE.* cuspidor **-körtel** salivary gland **-strit** froghopper, spittle insect, spittlebug **-styver** *för en* ~ for a song, for next to nothing
spov *s2* curlew
sprack *imperf. av spricka II*
sprak|a sparkle, emit sparks **-ande I** *a4* sparkling; crackling (*ljud* sound); ~ *kvickhet* sparkling wit **II** *s6* sparkling **-fåle** frisky colt; *bildl.* scapegrace **-galler** fireguard
sprallig *a1* frisky, lively
sprang *imperf. av 2 springa*
1 spratt *s7* trick; hoax; *spela ngn ett* ~ play a trick on s.b., trick (hoax) s.b.
2 spratt *imperf. av spritta*
sprattel ['spratt-] *s7* flounder, struggle **-gubbe** jumping jack
sprattla flounder, struggle; (*om fisk*) frisk (flap) about; (*med benen*) kick about
spray [sprejj] *se sprej*
spred *imperf. av sprida*
sprej *s3* spray **spreja** spray **sprejflaska** spray bottle; atomizer
spret|a sprawl **-ig** *a1* sprawling, straggling
spri *s6, sjö.* sprit
sprick|a I *s1* crack, fissure; (*större*) crevice; (*hud-*) chap; *bildl.* breach, schism, rift **II** *sprack spruckit* **1** crack; (*brista*) break, burst; (*rämna*) split; ~ *av ilska* burst with rage; *äta tills man är färdig att* ~ eat till one is ready to burst; *spruckna läppar* chapped lips; ~ *ut* (*om knopp*) open, (*om löv*) come out **2** (*bli kuggad*) fail, be ploughed **-bildning** cracking, formation of cracks **-fri** crack-proof **-färdig** ready to burst; (*om knopp*) ready to open
sprickig *a1* cracked; chapped
sprida *v2, imperf. äv. spred* spread; distribute (*reklam* advertisements); circulate (*ett rykte* a report); (*utströ*) scatter; ~ *en doft av* give off a smell of; ~ *glädje* bring joy; ~ *ljus över* shed light on; ~ *ut* (*semestrar, arbetstid*) stagger; ~ *sig* spread, (*skingras*) be scattered, scatter, be dispersed, disperse, (*utbreda sig*) extend; *en rodnad spred sig över hennes ansikte* a blush suffused her face; *ryktet spred sig* the rumour

got abroad
spridare spreader (*äv. sjö.*), sprayer; (*vatten-*) sprinkler
sprid|d *a5* spread; scattered; dispersed; *en allmänt ~ uppfattning* a widespread view (conception); *~a fall* isolated cases; *några ~a hus* a few scattered houses; *i ~ ordning* in scattered (*mil.* extended) order; *på ~a ställen* here and there **-ning** [-i:d-] spreading *etc.*; spread (*av en växt* of a plant; (*av tidning*) circulation, distribution; *boken har vunnit stor ~* (*äv.*) the book has become very popular
1 spring *s7* (*-ande*) running; *det är ett ~ dagen i ända* people are coming and going all day
2 spring *s7, sjö.* sheer; (*på kabel*) spring
1 springa *s1* chink, fissure; slot, slit
2 spring|a *sprang sprungit* **1** run (*hit o. dit* to and fro); (*fly*) make off; (*hoppa*) spring, jump (*i sadeln* into the saddle); *vi måste ~ allt vad vi orkade* we had to run for it; *~ sin väg* run away, make off, *vard.* skedaddle; *~ ärenden* run errands; *~ efter flickor* run after girls; *~ efter hjälp* run for help; *~ hos läkare* keep running to the doctor; *~ i affärer* go shopping; *~ i höjden* (*om pris*) soar; *~ på dörren* make for the door; *~ på bio* keep going to the cinema **2** (*brista*) burst; (*om säkring e.d.*) blow; *~ i dagen* come to light, (*om källa*) spring forth; *~ i luften* [be] blow[n] up, explode **3** (*med betonad partikel*) *~ av* (*brista*) burst; *~ fram* rush out, (*om sak*) stand out, project; *~ ifatt* overtake, catch up; *~ ifrån* run away from, desert; *~ om* pass [... running], run past; *~ omkring* run around; *~ omkull* run down; *~ upp a*) (*rinna upp*) spring up, *b*) (*om dörr*) fly open
spring|ande *a4* running; *den ~ punkten* the crucial point **-are** (*häst*) courser, steed; (*i schack*) knight **-brunn** fountain **-flicka** errand girl **-flod** spring tide **-mask** pinworm, threadworm **-pojke** errand boy, messenger **-vikarie** (*lärare*) supply teacher
sprinkler ['spriŋ-] *s9, pl äv. -s* sprinkler **-anläggning** sprinkler plant (installation) **-system** sprinkler system
sprint *s2* split pin, peg
sprinter ['sprinn-] *s2* sprinter **-lopp** sprint[race]
sprisegel spritsail
sprit *s3* spirits (*pl*); alcohol; liquor; *denaturerad ~* methylated spirits; *ren ~* pure alcohol
sprita (*ärter*) shell, hull, pod
sprit|begär craving for spirits (liquor) **-bolag** company selling alcoholic liquors **-drycker** *pl* spirits, alcoholic liquors (beverages) **-duplicering** spirit duplication **-dupliceringsapparat** spirit duplicator **-fabrik** [alcohol] distillery **-förbud** prohibition **-haltig** *a1* spirituous, alcoholic **-kök** spirit stove **-langare** bootlegger **-missbruk** abuse of alcohol **-påverkad** *a5* under the influence of drink **-rättigheter** *pl, ha ~* be fully licensed
sprits *s2* forcing (piping) bag **spritsa** pipe
sprit|skatt duty on spirits, liquor tax **-smugglare** liquor smuggler, bootlegger
spritt *adv, ~ galen* stark (raving) mad; *~ naken* stark-naked
spritt|a *spratt spruttit, ~* [*till*] give a start, start, jump (*av förskräckelse* with fright); *det -er i*

benen I want to dance so much I can't keep still **-ande** *a4, ~ glad* ready to jump for joy; *en ~ melodi* a lively tune **-ning** start, jump
spritärter shelling peas
spruck|en *a5* cracked (*tallrik* plate; *röst* voice) **-it** *sup. av spricka II*
sprudl|a [-u:-] bubble, gush **-ande** *a4* bubbling over (*av* with); sparkling (*kvickhet* wit); *~ fantasi* exuberant imagination; *~ humör* high spirits (*pl*)
sprund *s7* (*i plagg*) slit, opening; (*på laggkärl*) bung[hole]
sprungit *sup. av 2 springa*
sprut|a *s1* spray[er], squirt; (*finfördelande*) atomizer; (*brand-*) fire engine; (*injektions-*) syringe; *få en ~* get an injection, have a shot **II** *v1* spray, squirt; (*spola*) wash, flush; *~ eld* spit (*om vulkan* emit) fire; *hennes ögon ~de eld* her eyes flashed fire; *~ vatten på* throw water on, hose; *~ in* (*med.*) inject; *~ ut* eject, spout, throw out **-lackera** spray[-paint] **-lackering** spraying, spray painting **-munstycke** spray nozzle, jet pipe **-måla** *se -lackera* **-ning** [-u:-] spraying, squirting; (*med brandspruta*) playing the hose[s] **-pistol** spray gun
spruttit *sup. av spritta*
språk *s7* language; idiom, tongue; (*tal*) speech; manner of speaking, style; *föra ett bildat ~* speak in an educated manner; *lärare i ~* teacher of languages; *skriva ett ledigt ~* have an easy (natural) style of writing; *inte vilja ut med ~et* beat about the bush; *slå sig i ~ med* enter into conversation with **språka** talk, speak (*om* about); (*förtroligt*) chat **språkas** *dep, ~ vid* talk to each other; *~ vid om* (*äv.*) discuss
språk|begåvad *vara ~* have a gift for languages **-bruk** usage; *gällande ~* current usage **-centrum** (*i hjärnan*) speech areas **-familj** family of languages **-fel** linguistic error **-forskare** linguist **-forskning** linguistics (*pl, behandlas som sg*), linguistic research; *jämförande ~* (*äv.*) comparative philology **-färdighet** language proficiency **-förbistring** confusion of tongues (languages) **-geni** genius for languages **-gräns** linguistic frontier **-historia** history of languages **-kunnig** skilled in languages; *en ~ person* a good linguist **-kunskap** knowledge of language[s] **-kurs** language course **-känsla** feeling for language **-laboratorium** language laboratory **-lektion** language lesson
språk|lig [-å:-] *a1* linguistic (*studier* studies); philological (*problem* problem); *i ~t avseende* from a linguistic point of view **-ljud** speech sound **-låda** *slå upp ~n* start talking **-lära** grammar **-lärare, -lärarinna** teacher of languages **-man** linguist **-melodi** intonation **-nämnd** *Svenska ~en* [the] Swedish language committee **-riktighet** grammatical correctness **-rör** *bildl.* spokesman (*fem.* spokeswoman), mouthpiece **-sam** [-å:-] *a1* talkative; (*prat-*) loquacious; (*meddel-*) communicative **-samhet** [-å:-] talkativeness *etc.* **-sinne** talent for languages; *jfr äv. språkkänsla* **-studier** *pl* study (*sg*) of languages, linguistic studies **-störningar** speech disabilities (defects) **-svå-**

righeter *pl* difficulties in speaking and/or understanding a language **-undervisning** language teaching **-vetare** linguist; student of languages **-vetenskap** linguistics *(pl, behandlas som sg)* **-vetenskaplig** philological; linguistic **-vård** preservation of terminology and usage [in a language] **-öra** *ha ett gott* ~ have an ear for languages

språng *s7* leap, spring; *(skutt)* bound, skip; *ta ett* ~ take a leap, make a jump; *i fullt* ~ at full speed; *på* ~ on the run; *ta ~et ut i det okända* take a leap in the dark **-bräda** springboard *(äv. bildl.)* **-marsch** *i* ~ [at] double quick [time], *mil.* at a run **-segel** jumping sheet, canvas **-vis** by leaps *(etc.)*

spräcka *v3* crack; break; ~ *skallen* fracture one's skull

spräcklig *a1* speckled; mottled

spräng|a *v2* burst; *(med -ämne)* blast, blow up, explode; *(skingra)* scatter, *mil.* put to the rout; ~ *banken* break the bank; ~ *en häst* break a horse's wind; *det -er i örat* my (his *etc.*) ear is throbbing; ~ *fram* gallop along (forward) **sprängas** *v2, dep* burst, break

spräng|bomb high-explosive bomb **-deg** explosive paste **-granat** high-explosive shell **-kil** wedge **-kraft** explosive force **-laddning** blasting (explosive) charge; *(i robot o.d.)* warhead **-lista** *(vid val)* splinter list **-lärd** brimful of learning, erudite **-läsa** cram, swot **-ning** bursting *etc.*; explosion; *(skingring)* dispersion **-ningsarbete** blasting work **-skiss** exploded view **-skott** blast **-sten** blast stone, broken rock **-verkan** explosive (blast) effect **-ämne** explosive **-ämnesexpert** explosives expert

sprätt *s2* **1** dandy, fop, *AE.* dude **2** *sätta* ~ *på a) (ngn)* ginger up, *b) (pengar)* throw around

1 sprätta *v1, v3 (skära upp)* rip [open] *(en söm* a seam), unpick *(en klänning* a dress); ~ *upp* rip up; ~ *ur* rip out *(en knapp* a button)

2 sprätta *v3, bet. 1 äv. v1* **1** *(snobba)* show off, swank **2** *(om höns)* scratch **3** *(sprida)* scatter **4** *(stänka)* spatter; *(om penna)* spurt

sprättbåge *som en* ~ *(bildl.)* like a drawn bow

sprättig *a1* smart[ly dressed], dandified, foppish

spröd *a1* brittle; short; *(klen)* fragile **-het** [-ö:-] brittleness; shortness; fragility

spröjs *s2* bar

spröt *s7* **1** *(paraply-)* rib **2** *zool.* antenna, feeler

spunnit *sup. av* spinna

spurt *s3, sport.* spurt **spurta** *sport.* spurt

spy *v4* vomit *(äv. rök* smoke); *(om kanon)* belch out **spyor** [ˣspy:ɔr] *s, pl* vomit

spydig *a1* malicious, sarcastic, ironic[al] **-het** malice, sarcasm; *AE. äv.* wisecrack

spyfluga blowfly, bluebottle; *bildl.* caustic person

spygatt [ˣspy:-, -'gatt] *s7, sjö.* scupper

spå *v4, absol.* tell fortunes *(i kort* by the cards); ~ *ngn* tell s.b. his *(etc.)* fortune; *jfr äv. förutsäga;* ~ *i händer* practise palmistry, read hands; *jag ~dde rätt* my prediction came true; *människan ~r och Gud rår* man proposes, God disposes **-dom** *s2* prophecy; prediction; soothsaying **-domskonst** art of divination **-kvinna** [female] fortune-teller; sibyl **-man** fortune--teller; soothsayer

spån *s7, s1 (trä-, metall-)* chip; *(hyvel-)* shaving; *koll.* chips, shavings *(pl); dum som ett* ~ as stupid as they come

spånad *s3, abstr.* spinning; *konkr.* spun yarn

spånads|lin [fibre] flax **-växt** textile plant

spån[fiber]platta chipboard, fibreboard

spång *s2, pl äv.* spänger footbridge, plank

spån|korg chip basket **-tak** shingled roof **-täcka** shingle

spår *s7* **1** *(märke)* mark *(efter* of); *(fot-)* step, footstep *(äv. bildl.)*, footprint; *(djur-)* track, trail; *bildl. äv.* trace, vestige; *inte det minsta* ~ *av tvivel* not the faintest doubt; *inte ett* ~ *intresserad* not a bit interested; *följa i ~en* be fast on the heels of, *bildl.* follow in the footsteps of; *förlora ~et* lose the track *(om jakthund:* scent); *komma på ~en* get on the track of, *bildl. äv.* find out; *sopa igen ~en efter sig* obliterate one's tracks; *sätta djupa* ~ *(bildl.)* make a profound impression; *vara inne på rätt* ~ be on the right track **2** *(skenor)* rails *(pl); järnv.* track; *vagnen hoppade ur ~et* the carriage (wagon) ran off the track (left the rails)

spåra 1 *(söka spår av)* track, trace *(äv. bildl.); jakt. äv.* scent; ~ *upp* track down, *(friare o. bildl.)* hunt out, discover **2** *(gå upp ett [skid-]spår)* make a track **3** ~ *ur a) (järnv.)* run off the rails, derail, *b) (om pers.)* go astray, *c) (om diskussion)* sidetrack, get off the track

spår|bunden trackbound **-element** trace[r] element **-hund** sleuthhound; bloodhound *(äv. bildl.)* **-korsning** *järnv.* rail crossing **-ljus** tracer **-löst** [-ö:-] *adv* leaving no trace, without leaving any tracks; *den är* ~ *försvunnen* it has vanished into thin air **-sinne** scent; nose **-snö** [new-fallen] snow in which tracks are visible **-vagn** tram[car]; *AE.* streetcar, trolley [car]

spårvagns|biljett tram ticket **-förare** tram driver; *AE.* motorman **-konduktör** tram conductor

spår|vidd [track] gauge **-väg** tramway **-vägslinje** tramline; *AE.* streetcar line **-vägsstall** tram depot; *AE.* carbarn **-växel** point[s *pl*]; *i sht AE.* switch[es *pl*] **-ämne** trace[r] element

späck *s7* lard; *(val-)* blubber

späck|a lard; *bildl.* interlard; *en ~d plånbok* a bulging (fat) wallet **-huggare** *zool.* killer [whale], grampus **-nål** larding needle **-strimla** lardon

späd *a1 (mycket ung)* tender *(grönska* verdure; *ålder* age); *(spenslig)* slender *(växt* growth); *bot. äv.* young *(löv* leaves); *från sin ~aste barndom* from one's earliest infancy; ~ *röst* feeble (weak) voice

späda *v2,* ~ *[ut]* dilute, thin down; ~ *på (öka, utöka)* add, mix in

späd|barn infant, baby **-barnsdödlighet** infant mortality **-barnsvård** infant welfare **-gris** sucking pig **-het** [-ä:-] tenderness *etc.* **-kalv** sucking calf

späk|a *v3* mortify *(sitt kött* one's flesh); *(friare)* castigate; ~ *sig* mortify o.s. **-ning** [-ä:-] mortification *etc.*

spän|d *a1 (jfr* spänna*)* tight *(rep* rope); stretched; *(styv)* taut; *bildl.* tense, highly strung *(nerver* nerves), intense, intent; *(om båge)* drawn; *-t förhållande* strained relations (*pl*) (*till* with); *högt ~a förväntningar* eager expectations; *lyssna med ~ uppmärksamhet* listen with strained (tense) attention; *jag är ~ på hur det skall gå* I am eager to see how things go **spänn** *s, sätta ngt i ~* put s.th. in a press; *sitta på ~* be on tenterhooks

spänna *v2* **1** (*sträcka*) stretch (*snören* strings); strain (*musklerna* one's muscles); tighten (*ett rep* a rope); *~ en fjäder* tighten a spring; *~ hanen på en bössa* cock a gun; *~ en båge* draw (bend) a bow; *~ bågen för högt* (*bildl.*) aim too high; *~ sina krafter till det yttersta* muster up all one's strength, *bildl.* strain every nerve; *~ ögonen i* fasten (rivet) one's eyes on; *~ öronen* prick up one's ears **2** (*med spänne*) clasp, buckle; (*med rem*) strap **3** (*om kläder*) be tight, pull **4** *rfl* strain (brace) o.s. **5** (*med betonad partikel*) *~ av a*) unstrap, unfasten, undo, *b*) *vard.* relax, lean back, *~ av sig skridskorna* take off one's skates; *~ fast* fasten, buckle (strap) on (*vid* to); *~ för* (*ifrån*) (*absol.*) harness (unharness) the horse[s]; *~ på sig* put on (*skridskorna* one's skates), strap on (*ryggsäcken* one's knapsack); *~ upp* undo, unfasten, (*rem*) unstrap, (*paraply*) put up; *~ ut* stretch, (*magen*) distend, (*bröstet*) expand; *~ åt* tighten **spännande** *a4, bildl.* exciting, thrilling; *en ~ bok* (*äv.*) a thriller **spänne** *s6* buckle, clasp, clip **spänning** tension; *tekn. äv.* strain, stress; *elektr.* voltage; *bildl.* tension, excitement, stress, strain; *livsfarlig ~* (*på anslag*) live wire; *hållas i ~* be kept on tenterhooks; *vänta med ~* wait excitedly (eagerly) **spännings|fall** *elektr.* voltage (potential) drop **-förande** *a4, elektr.* live, under tension **-tillstånd** state of strain **spänn|kraft** tension, elasticity, resilience, *bildl.* tone **-ram** tenter **-skruv** turnbuckle **-vidd** span; *stat.* range; *bildl.* scope **spänsband** waistband **spänst** *s3* vigour, elasticity; *bildl.* buoyancy **spänstig** *a1* elastic, springy; (*kraftig*) vigorous; *bildl.* buoyant; *gå med ~a steg* walk with a springy gait **-het** elasticity, spring[iness]; vigour; *bildl.* buoyancy **spänt** *adv* (*jfr spänd*), *iakttaga ngn ~* observe s.b. intently **spänta** split (*stickor* wood) **1 spärr** *i uttr.: rida ~ mot* tilt against (at); *bildl.* resist, struggle against **2 spärr** *s2, boktr.* spaced-out type (letters *pl*) **3 spärr** *s2, tekn.* catch, stop, barrier; *järnv.* gate, barrier; (*hinder*) block, obstacle; (*väg-*) roadblock; *skol.* restricted intake **4 spärr** *s2,* (*i bowling*) spare **1 spärra 1** (*ut-*) spread out, stretch open; *~ upp ögonen* open one's eyes wide **2** *boktr.* space out; *~d stil* spaced-out type (letters *pl*) **2 spärra 1** (*avstänga*) bar; block [up]; obstruct (*vägen för ngn* a p.'s passage); blockade, close (*en hamn* a port) **2** *hand.* block (*ett konto* an account); *~ en check* stop [payment of] a cheque **spärr|ballong** barrage balloon; *vard.* blimp **-eld** barrage [fire] **-hake** [locking] pawl; (*på kugghjul*) click, catch **-konto** blocked (frozen)

account **-ning 1** barring *etc.*; obstruction; blockade **2** (*av konto e.d.*) blocking, freezing **-vakt** *järnv.* ticket collector **spätta** *s1, zool.* plaice **-filé** fillet of plaice **spö** *s6* **1** (*kvist*) twig; (*käpp*) switch; (*ridpiska*) whip; (*met-*) rod; *regnet står som ~n i backen* it's pouring rain, *vard.* it is raining cats and dogs **2** *slita ~* be publicly flogged (whipped) **spöa** flog, whip **spök|a** (*visa sig som -e*) haunt a place, walk the earth; *det ~r i huset* the house is haunted; *gå uppe och ~ om nätterna* be up and about at night; *~ ut sig* make a fright of o.s. **-aktig** *a1* ghostlike; (*hemsk*) weird, uncanny **-bild** TV ghost **spök|e** *s6* ghost, spectre; *vard.* spook; *bildl.* scarecrow, *se ~n på ljusa dagen* be haunted by imaginary terrors **-eri** *~r* ghostly disturbances **-historia** ghost story **-lik** ghostlike, ghostly, phantasmal, phantasmic; (*kuslig*) uncanny, weird; *ett ~t sken* a ghostly light **spöknippe** bundle of rods **spök|rädd** afraid of ghosts **-skepp** phantom ship **-skrivare** ghostwriter **-slott** haunted castle **-timme** witching hour **spöregn** downpour, pouring rain **spöregna** pour, pelt **spörja** *sporde sport* **1** (*fråga*) ask, inquire **2** (*erfara*) learn **spörsmål** *s7* question, matter, problem; *ett intrikat ~* an intricate problem **spöstraff** whipping, flogging **squaredance** [*ung.* ˈskwäːrdaːns] *i sht AE.* square dance; *dansa ~* square-dance **squash** *s3* (*spel*) squash; (*grönsak*) squash, zucchini **stab** *s3* staff; *tjänstgöra på ~* be on the staff **sta'bil** *a1* stable; *en ~ firma* a sound firm; *~a priser* stable prices **-isator** *s3, sjö.* stabilizer; (*flygplans-, ubåts-*) tailplane **-isera** stabilize; *förhållandena har ~t sig* conditions have stabilized (become more settled) **-isering** stabilization **-itet** stability **stabs|chef** chief of staff **-officer** staff officer **1 stack** *imperf. av sticka II o. stinga* **2 stack** *s2* stack, rick; (*myr-*) ant hill (heap); *dra sitt strå till ~en* do one's share (*vard.* bit) **stacka** stack, rick **stackare** [poor] wretch; (*ynkrygg*) coward, funk; *en ~ till ... a* wretch of a ...; *en fattig ~* a beggar; *den ~n!* poor thing (devil)!; *en svag ~* a weakling, a pitiable creature; *var och en är herre över sin ~* everybody is s.b.'s master **stackars** *oböjligt a* poor (*krake* wretch); *~ du* (*dig*)*!* poor you!; *~ liten!* poor little thing! **stackato** [-ˈkaː-] *s6 o. adv, mus.* staccato **stackmoln** cumulus **1 stad** *s3* (*på väv*) selvage, selvedge; *AE.* selvage **2 stad** *r* (*ställe*) stead; abode; *var och en i sin ~* each in his own place **3 stad** *-en städer, best. form vard.* stan (*samhälle*) town; (*större o. katedral-*) city; *~en Paris* the city of Paris; *den eviga ~en* the Eternal City; *land och ~* town and country; *han har blivit en visa för hela stan* he is the talk of the town; *bo i ~en* live in [the] town; *gå ut på*

S

stan go into town; *lämna ~en* leave town; *resa till ~en* go up to town; *springa stan runt efter* rush round town for; *över hela ~en* all over the town

stadd *a5*, *~ i fara* in [the midst of] danger; *vara ~ i upplösning* be disintegrating; *~ på resa* on the move; *~ vid kassa* in funds

stadde *imperf. av städja*

stadfäst|a confirm (*en dom* a sentence); establish (*en lag* a law); legalize, sanction (*en förordning* a decree); ratify (*ett fördrag* a treaty) **-else** confirmation; establishment; legalization, sanction; ratification

stadga I *s1, i bet. 2 äv. s5* **1** (*stadighet*) consistency; steadiness, firmness (*äv. bildl.*) **2** (*förordning*) regulation, statute; *föreningens ~r* the charter (*sg*) (rules) of the association **II** *v1* **1** (*ge fasthet*) consolidate, steady **2** (*föreskriva*) direct, prescribe, enact; (*bestämma*) decree **3** *rfl* consolidate, become firm[er] (steadier); (*om vädret*) become settled; (*om pers.*) settle down

stadg|ad *a5* steady, staid; *en ~ herre* a staid (reliable) man; *komma till ~ ålder* arrive at a mature age; *ha -at rykte för att vara* have a well-established reputation of being

stadge|enlig [-'e:n-] *a1* according to regulation (rules *pl*), statutory **-ändring** alteration of [the] rules (statutes)

stadig *a1* steady; (*fast*) firm; (*stabil*) stable; (*grov o. stark*) square built, sturdy; (*tjock*) stout; (*kraftig*) substantial (*mat* food), thick (*gröt* porridge); *bildl.* (*varaktig*) permanent (*kund* customer); *~ blick* firm look; *~ hand* steady (firm) hand; *ett ~t mål mat* (*äv.*) a square meal; *ha ~t arbete* have a steady job (regular work) **stadigt** *adv* steadily *etc.*; *sitta ~* (*om sak*) be firmly fixed; *stå ~* stand steady (firm) **stadigvarande** *a4* permanent (*anställning* employment); constant; *~ inkomst* steady income

stadion ['sta:djån] *n* stadium

stadium ['sta:djum] *s4* stage; (*skede*) phase; *befinna sig på ett förberedande ~* be at a preparatory (an initial) stage

stads|antikvarie city (town) antiquarian **-arkitekt** town (city) architect **-arkiv** municipal (city, town) archives (*pl*) (records office) **-barn** town (city) child **-befolkning** urban (town) population **-bibliotek** public (town, city) library **-bo** town dweller; (*borgare*) citizen; *~r* townspeople **-bud** [town] messenger; (*bärare*) porter **-budskontor** messengers' (porters') office **-del** quarter of a city (town), district **-fiskal** public prosecutor; *AE. ung.* district attorney **-fogde** [court] bailiff; *AE.* sheriff, marshal **-fullmäktig** city (town) councillor; *~e* city (town) council (*sg*) **-förvaltning** civic (city, town) administration **-gas** town (coal) gas **-gräns** city (town) boundary **-hotell** principal hotel in a town **-hus** town (city) hall **-kärna** [the old] city centre **-lag** urban code **-liv** town (city) life **-läkare** municipal (city, town) medical officer **-mur** town (city) wall **-plan** town plan **-planerare** town planner **-planering** town (city) planning **-port** town (city) gate **-rättigheter** *pl* town charter (*sg*) **-teater** municipal theatre **-vapen** city arms

(*pl*)

sta'fett *s3* **1** (*kurir*) courier **2** *se -pinne*; *springa ~* run in a relay race **-löpning** relay race **-pinne** [relay-race] baton

staffage *s4* figures (*pl*) in a landscape **-figur** *eg.* foreground figure; *bara en ~* (*bildl.*) just an ornament

staf'fli *s4, s6* easel **-målare** painter who uses an easel

stafylokock [-'kåck] *s3* staphylococcus (*pl* staphylococci)

stag *s7, sjö.* stay; *gå över ~* go about **staga** *sjö.* stay (tack) ship; *allm.* stay

stagn|ation [-ŋn-] stagnation; (*stopp*) stoppage, standstill **-era** stagnate

stag|ning [-a:-] staying **-vända** tack, go about **1 staka** *rfl* stumble, hesitate; *~ sig på läxan* stumble over one's lessons

2 staka 1 punt, pole ([*fram*] *en båt* a boat [along]) **2** mark (*en väg* a road); *~ ut, se utstaka*

stake *s2* pole, stake; (*ljus-*) candlestick

sta'ket *s7* fence, railing[s *pl*], paling

stal *imperf. av stjäla*

sta|lag'mit *s3* stalagmite **-lak'tit** *s3* stalactite

1 stall *s7* (*på fiol*) bridge

2 stall 1 (*för hästar*) stable; *AE. äv.* barn; (*uppsättning hästar*) stud **2** (*lok- etc.*) depot, garage

stall|a stable **-backe** stable yard **-broder** companion; *vard.* chum **-dräng** stableman, groom **-knekt** stableman **-lykta** (*hopskr. stallykta*) hurricane lamp, storm lantern **-pojke** stableboy

stam [stamm] *s2* **1** (*träd-*) stem, trunk (*äv. bildl.*); *språkv.* stem, radical **2** (*i checkbok o.d.*) counterfoil, stub **3** (*släkt[e]*) family, lineage; (*folk-*) tribe; *en man av gamla ~men* a man of the old stock **-aktie** ordinary (*AE.* common) share; *~r* (*koll.*) stock (*sg*), equities; *utdelning på ~r* ordinary dividend **-anställd** *a o. s* regular **-bana** main line [railway]; *norra ~n* the main northern line **-bok** (*över djur*) pedigree book; (*över hästar*) studbook; (*över nötkreatur*) herd-book **-bord** regular table **-fader** [first] ancestor; progenitor **-form** (*med avseende på härstamning*) primitive (original) form **-gäst** regular [frequenter] (*på en restaurang* of a restaurant), habitué **-kund** regular customer

1 stamma *se härstamma*

2 stamma (*tala hackigt*) stutter; (*svårare*) stammer; *~ fram* stammer out

stammanskap regulars (*pl*)

stammare stutterer, stammerer

stammoder [first] ancestress

stamning stuttering, stammering

stam|ord radical word **-ort** place of origin

stamp 1 *s7, se stampning* **2** *s2, tekn.* (*hål-*) punch; (*stämpel*) stamp

1 stampa *s1* stamp (*i golvet* [on] the floor); (*om häst*) paw the ground; *stå och ~ på samma fläck* (*bildl.*) be still on the same old spot, be getting nowhere; *~ takten* beat time with one's feet; *~ av sig snön* stamp the snow off one's shoes; *~ till jorden* trample down the earth **2** *sjö.* pitch, heave and set **3** stamp, punch (*hål i* a hole in); (*kläde*) mill, full **2 stamp|a** *vard.*, ~ *på* (*pantsätta*) hock, pop **stampen** ['stamm-] *endast best. form, vard.* (*pantlånekontor*) *på* ~ at uncle's, in hock **stamp|kvarn** stamp[ing] mill **-maskin** stamp, stamping machine **-ning** stamping; pawing; *tekn.* punching, pounding **stam|ros** standard rose **-tavla** genealogical table; pedigree (*äv. om djur*) **-tillhåll** [favourite] haunt **-träd** genealogical (family) tree **stan'dar** *s7* standard **standard** ['stand-] *s3* standard **-avvikelse** *stat.* standard deviation, standard error **-brev** form letter **-format** standard size **-hus** house of standard design; (*monteringsfärdigt*) prefabricated house **-höjning** rise in the standard of living; *en allmän* ~ a general rise in the living standard **-isera** standardize **-isering** standardization **-modell** standard design **-mått** standard size; (*likare*) standard measure[ment] **-prov** *skol.* standardized achievement test **-sänkning** lowering of one's standard [of living] **-utförande** standard design **-verk** standard work **standert** ['stann-] *s2, sjö.* [broad] pennant **1 stank** *s3* stench, stink **2 stank** *imperf. av stinka* **stanna 1** (*upphöra att röra sig*) stop, stand still; (*av-*) come to a standstill; (*upphöra äv.*) cease; *hjärtat har ~t* the (his *etc.*) heart has stopped (ceased to beat); *klockan ~de* the (my *etc.*) watch stopped; ~ *i växten* stop growing; ~ *på halva vägen* stop halfway; *han lät det* ~ *vid hotelser* he went no further than threats; *reformerna ~de på papperet* the reforms never got past the paper stage; *det ~de därvid* it stopped at that **2** (*om vätska*) cease to run; (*stelna*) coagulate; *kokk.* set **3** (*dröja kvar*) stay [on], stop; (*slutgiltigt förbli*) remain; ~ *hemma* stay [at] home; ~ *hos ngn* stay with s.b.; ~ *kvar* stay [on]; remain; ~ *till middagen* stay for dinner; ~ *över natten* stay the night (*hos* with); *låt det* ~ *oss emellan!* this is between you and me! **4** (*hejda*) stop; (*fordon äv.*) bring to a standstill; (*maskin*) stop **stannfågel** sedentary (nonmigratory) bird **stanniförening** stannic compound **stanniol** [-'jo:l, -'jå:l] *s3* tinfoil **-papper** tinfoil **1 stans** *s3, versl.* stanza **2 stans** *s2* punch **stans|a** ~ [*ut*] punch **-maskin** punching machine **-ning** punching **-operatris** puncher, punching-machine operator **stapel** *s2* **1** (*trave*) pile, stack **2** *skeppsb.* stocks (*pl*); *gå* (*löpa*) *av ~n* leave the stocks, be launched, *bildl.* take place, come off **3** (*på bokstav*) stem; *nedåtgående* (*uppåtgående*) ~ downstroke (upstroke) **-avlöpning** launch, launching **-bar** *a1*, **~a stolar** nesting (stacking) chairs **-bädd** stocks (*pl*), shipway, slip, slipway **-diagram** histogram, bar graph **-stad** staple town (port) **-vara** staple [commodity] **stapl|a** [ˣsta:-] ~ [*upp*] pile [up], heap up, stack **-ingsbar** stackable **stappl|a** (*gå ostadigt*) totter; (*vackla*) stagger; ~ *sig fram* stumble along; ~ *sig igenom läxan* stumble through one's lesson **-ande** *a4* totte-

ring; staggering; *de första* ~ *stegen* the first stumbling steps **stare** *s2* starling **stark** *a1* strong; (*kraftfull*) powerful (*maskin* engine); (*om maskin äv.*) high-powered; (*hållbar*) solid, durable; (*fast*) firm (*karaktär* character); (*utpräglad*) pronounced, mighty; (*intensiv*) intense; ~ *blåst* high wind; ~*a drycker* strong drinks; ~ *efterfrågan på* great (strong) demand for; ~ *fart* great speed; ~ *färg* strong colour; ~*t gift* virulent poison; ~*t inflytande* powerful influence; ~ *kyla* bitter (intense) cold; ~*a misstankar* grave (strong) suspicions; ~ *motvilja* pronounced aversion; ~*a skäl* strong reasons; ~*a verb* strong verbs; *är inte min* ~*a sida* is not my strong point; *en sex man* ~ *deputation* a deputation of six men; *med den* ~*ares rätt* with the right of might **-sprit** spirits (*pl*); *AE.* hard liquor **-ström** high-tension current **starkt** *adv* strongly *etc.*; ~ *kryddad* highly seasoned; *lukta* ~ *av* smell strongly of; *jag misstänker* ~ *att* I very much suspect that; *det var väl* ~ that's a bit thick (much) **stark|varor** *pl* spirits **-vin** dessert wine **-öl** strong beer **1 starr** *s3, bot.* sedge **2 starr** *s2* (*sjukdom*) [*grå*] ~ cataract; *grön* ~ glaucoma **starrblind** *bildl.* purblind **start** [-a(:)-] *s3* start; *AE. vard.* kickoff; *flyg.* takeoff; (*av företag*) starting, launching **start|a** [-a(:):-] start; *AE. vard.* kick off; *flyg.* take off; (*företag*) start, launch; ~ *en affär* open a business **-anording** starter **-avgift** entry fee **-bana** *flyg.* runway; tarmac (*varumärke*) **-block** starting block **start|er** ['sta:r-] *s2, sport.* starter **-förbud** *flyg.*, *det råder* ~ all planes are grounded **-grop** starting hole; *ligga i* ~*arna* (*äv. bildl.*) be waiting for the starting signal **-kablar** jump leads, *AE.* jumper cables **-kapital** initial capital **-klar** ready to start **-knapp** starter button **-kontakt** starter **-linje** starting line **-motor** starting motor **-nyckel** ignition key **-pedal** starting pedal; (*på motorcyckel*) kick-starter **-pistol** starting pistol **-platta** (*för robot e.d.*) launch[ing] pad **-raket** booster, launching vehicle **-signal** starting signal **-skott** *sport.* starting shot; ~*et gick* the pistol went off **-snöre** starting strap **-vev** starting handle, crank **stas** *s3, med.* stasis **stass** *s3* finery **1 stat** *s3* (*samhälle; rike*) state; ~*en* the State; *Förenta* ~*erna* the United States [of America]; ~*ens finanser* Government finance (*sg*); *S~ens Järnvägar* the Swedish State Railways; ~*ens tjänst* public (government) service; *i* ~*ens tjänst* in the service of the State; ~*ens verk* Government (civil service) departments; *på* ~*ens bekostnad* at public expense **2 stat** *s3* **1** (*tjänstemannakår*) staff; (*förteckning*) list of persons belonging to the establishment **2** *föra* [*stor*] ~ live in [grand] style; *dra in på* ~*en* cut down expenses **3 stat** *s3* **1** (*avlöningsanordning*) establishment; *officer på* ~ permanent officer **2** (*budget*) esti-

S

mates (*pl*), budget
statare farm labourer, cotter
statera walk on, be a super (extra)
statik *s3, ej pl* statics (*pl, behandlas som sg*)
station [-(t)'ʃɷ:n] station; *ta in en ~ (radio.*)
tune in a station **-era** station **-ering** stationing
stations|inspektor stationmaster **-samhälle**
town (village) around a railway station **-skri-**
vare railway clerk **-vagn** (*bil*) estate car; *AE.*
station wagon
stationär [-tʃɷ'nä:r] *al* stationary
statisk ['sta:-] *a5* static; ~ *elektricitet* static
electricity
statist *teat.* walker-on, supernumerary, *vard.* super; *film.* extra
statist|ik *s3, ej pl* statistics (*pl, behandlas som*
sg) **-iker** [-'tiss-] statistician **-isk** *a5* statistic,
statistical; *S~a centralbyrån* Statistics Sweden;
~a uppgifter statistical data (*sg*), statistics; ~
årsbok statistical yearbook
sta'tiv *s7* stand, rack; (*stöd*) support; (*trebent*)
tripod
statlig [ˣsta:t-] *al* state (*egendom* property);
government (*verk* office); national (*inkomst-*
skatt income tax), public (*institution* institution); *~t ingripande* government (state) intervention; *i ~ regi* under government auspices,
run by the State
stats|angelägenhet affair of state **-anslag**
government (state, public) grant (subsidy) **-an-**
ställd *a5* employed in government service; *en*
~ a government (state) employee **-arkiv** [pub-
lic] record office **-bana** state (state-owned)
railway **-besök** state (official) visit **-bidrag**
se statsunderstöd **-budget** national budget
-chef head of a (the) state **-egendom** state
(national, public) property; *göra till ~* nation-
alize **-fientlig** subversive (*verksamhet* activity)
-finanser *pl* public (government) finances **-fi-**
nansierad *a5* state-financed **-form** form of
government, polity **-fru** lady of the bedcham-
ber **-fängelse** state prison **-förbrytare** political offender **-förbrytelse** political crime,
high treason **-förbund** association (union,
[con]federation) of states **-författning** constitution **-förvaltning** public (state) administration **-gräns** state boundary, frontier
stats|hemlighet state secret **-historia** politi-
cal history **-inkomster** *pl* public (national)
revenue (*sg*) **-kalender** official yearbook (directory) **-kassa** treasury, exchequer **-klok**
politic, versed in state affairs **-klokhet** political wisdom **-konst** statesmanship, statecraft;
diplomacy **-kontoret** [the Swedish] agency
for administrative development **-kontrollerad**
a5 state (government) controlled **-kunskap**
political science **-kupp** coup d'état **-kyrka**
established (national, state) church; *engelska*
~n the Church of England, the Anglican
Church; *svenska ~n* the Lutheran State Church
of Sweden; *avskaffa ~n* disestablish the
Church **-kyrklig** state-church **-lån** government
(state) loan **-lära** sociology **-lös** stateless
-makt state authority, power of the state; *~er*
(*äv.*) government authorities; *den fjärde ~en*
(*pressen*) the fourth estate **-man** statesman;
(*politiker*) politician **-minister** prime minis-

ter, premier; *ställföreträdande* ~ deputy prime
minister **-obligation** government bond; *~er*
(*äv.*) government securities, consols **-papper**
pl government securities, treasury bills **-polis**
national (state) police **-revision** auditing of
public (state, national) accounts
stats|råd 1 *pers.* [cabinet] minister, councillor
of state; *Storbritannien äv.* secretary of state;
konsultativt ~ minister without portfolio **2** (*mi-*
nistär) council of state cabinet **3** (*sammanträ-*
de) cabinet council (meeting); *konungen i ~et*
the king in council **-rådinna** [cabinet] minister's wife **-rådsberedning** *~en* [the] cabinet
office **-rätt** constitutional law **-sekreterare**
under-secretary of state **-skatt** national (state)
tax **-skick** constitution **-skuld** na-tional debt
-teater national theatre **-tjänst** public (civil)
service **-tjänsteman** civil servant, government employee **-understöd** government subsidy, state aid **-understödd** *a5* state-sub-
sidized **-utgifter** *pl* state (government) expenditure (*sg*) **-verksproposition** budget bill
(proposals *pl*) **-vetare** *vard.* political scientist,
expert in (student of) political science **-veten-**
skap political science **-vetenskaplig** of political science **-vetenskapsman** expert on political science **-välvning** [political] revolution
-överhuvud *se statschef*
statt *sup. av städja*
statuera ~ *ett exempel* make an example
status ['sta:-, ˣsta:-] *s2, s7* (*ställning*) status;
(*affärsföretags*) standing; ~ *quo* status quo;
rättslig ~ legal status **-symbol** status symbol
statuter [-'tu:-] *pl* rules, regulations, statutes
sta'ty *s3* statue **-'ett** *s3* statuette
stav *s2* staff; *sport.* pole; (*skid-*) ski stick (pole);
(*i tunna*) stave; *bryta ~en över ngn* (*bildl.*)
condemn s.b. [outright]
stava spell; *hur ~s ...?* how do you spell ...?; ~
och lägga ihop put two and two together; ~
sig igenom spell one's way through
stavbakterie rod-shaped bacterium, bacillus
stav|else syllable **-fel** spelling mistake; ortho-
graphical error
stav|hopp pole vault; (*-hoppning*) pole-vaulting;
hoppa ~ pole-vault **-hoppare** pole-vaulter
-kyrka stave church **-lampa** electric torch
-magnet bar magnet
stav|ning [-a:-] spelling; (*rättskrivning*) ortog-
raphy
stavrim alliteration
stearin *s4, s3* stearin[e], candle-grease **-ljus**
candle **-syra** stearic acid
1 steg *imperf. av stiga*
2 steg *s7* **1** step (*äv. bildl.*); (*gång äv.*) gait,
pace; *små ~* short steps; *ta stora ~* take great
(long) strides; *gå framåt med stora ~* (*bildl.*)
advance with rapid strides; ~ *för ~* step by
step, *bildl. äv.* gradually; *hålla jämna ~* keep
pace (*med* with); *med långsamma ~* at a slow
pace; *med stänstiga ~* with a springy gait; *följa*
på några ~s avstånd follow a few paces
behind; *styra (ställa) sina ~ till* direct one's
steps to; *ta första ~et till försoning* make the
first move towards conciliation; *ta ~et fullt ut*
(*bildl.*) go the whole way (*vard.* hog); *vidtaga*
sina mått och ~ take measures **2** *tekn.* stage

stega 1 ~ [*upp*] step out, pace **2** ~ *i väg* stride out (along)
stege *s2* ladder
stegel *s7* wheel **stegla** [-e:-] break upon the wheel
stegjärn (*klippklättring*) crampon
steglitsa [*ˣste:-, -'litt-] *s1* goldfinch
steg|längd pace **-löst** *adv*, ~ *variabel* infinitely variable
stegpinne rung
1 stegra [-e:-] *rfl* rear; *bildl.* rebel; object
2 stegr|a [-e:-] raise, increase; (*förstärka*) intensify, heighten
stegring rise, increase; intensification, heightening
stegräknare pedometer
stegvagn ladder truck
stegvis step by step, by steps; (*gradvis äv.*) gradually, by stages (degrees)
1 stek *s7, sjö.* hitch; bend
2 stek *s2* joint; *kokk.* roast meat, joint [of roast meat]; *ösa en* ~ baste a joint
steka *v3* **1** roast (*kött* meat; *kastanjer* chestnuts); (*i stekpanna*) fry; (*i ugn*) roast (*potatis* potatoes); (*halstra*) broil **2** *bildl.*, *solen steker* the sun is broiling; ~ *sig i solen* broil (bake) in the sun **stekande** *a4* broiling, roasting (*hett* hot; *sol* sun) **stekas** *v3* roast, be roast, broil, be broiling
stekel *s2, zool.* hymenopteran, hymenopteron
stek|fat meat dish **-fett** frying fat **-flott** dripping **-fläsk** sliced pork **-gryta** braising-pan **-het** broiling, roasting **-hus** steakhouse **-ning** [-e:-] roasting *etc., jfr* steka **-nål** [meat] skewer **-os** smell of frying (*etc.*) **-panna** frying pan, *AE.* fry-pan **-spade** slice, spatula **-spett** spit **-sås** [pan] gravy
stekt [-e:-] *a4* roast (*kött* meat); fried (*potatis* potatoes); baked (*äpplen* apples); *för mycket* (*litet*) ~ overdone (underdone); *lagom* ~ well done **-ugn** [roasting] oven **-vändare** turnspit, roasting jack
stel *a1* stiff (*äv. bildl.*); (*styv*) rigid (*äv. bildl.*); (*av köld*) numb; *bildl.* formal, reserved (*sätt manners pl*); ~ *av fasa* paralysed (frozen) with horror; *vara* ~ *i ryggen* have a stiff back; *en* ~ *middag* a very formal dinner **-bent** [-be:-] *a1* stiff-legged; *bildl.* stiff, formal **-frusen** (*om pers.*) stiff with cold, frozen stiff; (*om kött, mark e.d.*) [hard]frozen **-het** stiffness *etc.*; rigidity; *bildl. äv.* formality, constraint **-kramp** tetanus, *vard.* lockjaw
stellarastronomi [-ˣla:r-] stellar astronomy
stelna [-e:-] get (grow) stiff; stiffen; (*övergå i fast form*) solidify; (*om vätska*) congeal, coagulate, (*om blod äv.*) clot; *kokk.* set; ~*de metaforer* frozen metaphors; ~ *till is* be congealed into ice; *man* ~*r till med åren* one stiffens up as one gets older; *han* ~*de till när han fick se oss* he froze when he caught sight of us
sten *s2* stone (*äv. i frukt o. med.*); *AE. äv.* rock; (*liten*) pebble; (*stor äv.*) boulder, rock; *bryta* ~ quarry stone; *en* ~ *har fallit från mitt bröst* that's a load off my mind; *hugga i* ~ (*bildl.*) bark up the wrong tree; *kasta* ~ *på* throw stones at; *lägga* ~ *på börda* increase the bur-

den; *inte lämna* ~ *på* ~ not leave one stone upon another; *det kunde röra en* ~ *till tårar* it is enough to melt a heart of stone
sten|a stone (*till döds* to death) **-art** variety of stone **-beläggning** paving **-bit** *zool.* lumpfish, lumpsucker **-block** boulder [stone], block of stone **-bock 1** *zool.* ibex; steinbok **2** *astr.*, *S~en* Capricorn **-brott** quarry **-bräcka** *bot.* saxifrage **-bumling** boulder **-bär** stone bramble
sten'cil *s3* stencil; *skriva en* ~ cut a stencil **-era** stencil **-ering** stencil copying
sten|dammlunga silicosis **-död** stone dead; *vard.* [as] dead as a doornail **-döv** stone deaf, [as] deaf as a post **-flisa** chip of stone **-fot** *byggn.* stone base **-frukt** stone fruit; *fack.* drupe **-get** chamois **-gods** stoneware **-golv** stone floor **-gärdsgård** *se stenmur* **-huggare** stonemason **-huggeri** stonemasonry **-hus** stone house; (*tegel-*) brick house **-hård** [as] hard as stone (flint); (*bildl.*) adamant **-häll** stone slab; (*platta*) flagstone; (*i öppen spis*) hearthstone
sten|ig *a1* stony; rocky (*bergsluttning* hillside); (*mödosam*) hard **-kaka** *vard.* 78 [record] **-kast** (*avståndsmått*) stone's throw **-kista** caisson **-kol** [pit] coal, mineral (hard) coal
stenkols|formation *geol.* carboniferous formation **-förande** *a4* carboniferous **-gruva** coal mine, colliery **-tjära** coal tar
sten|kross stone crusher **-kruka** stoneware (earthenware) jar **-kula** (*leksak*) [stone] marble **-kummel** cairn [of stones] **-lägga** pave **-läggning** *abstr.* paving; *konkr.* pavement **-mur** stone wall; (*tegel-*) brick wall **-murkla** turban-top
steno|graf *s3* shorthand writer, stenographer; ~ *och maskinskriverska* shorthand ty pist **-grafera** take down in shorthand; *absol.* write shorthand **-grafi** *s3* stenography, shorthand **-grafisk** [-'gra:-] stenographic, shorthand, in shorthand
stenogram [-'gramm] *s7* stenograph, shorthand notes; *skriva ut ett* ~ transcribe shorthand notes **-block** shorthand pad
sten|parti rock garden, rockery **-platta** stone slab, flagstone **-rik** *bildl.* rolling in money **-riket** the mineral kingdom **-rös[e]** mound (heap) of stones **-skott** flying stone [hitting a motorcar] **-skvätta** *s1* wheatear **-slipare** stone polisher, lapidary **-sliperi** stone polisher's workshop **-sopp** *s2* cep **-stil** lapidary style **-sätta** *se stenlägga* **-sättare** paver **-sättning** *arkeol.* circle (row) of stones, cromlech **-söta** *s1, bot.* polypody **-tavla** *bibl.* table of stone
stentorsröst [*ˣstentårs-] stentorian voice
sten|tryck lithography, lithographic printing; *konkr.* lithograph **-ull** mineral (rock) wool **-yxa** stone axe **-åldern** the Stone Age; *yngre* (*äldre*) ~ the neolithic (palaeolithic) period **-åldersmänniska** Stone Age man **-öken** stony (rocky) desert; (*bildl. om stad*) wilderness of bricks and mortar
stepp *s3* tap dance **steppa** tap-dance **-dansör** tap-dancer
stereo ['ste:-] *s5* stereo, stereophonic sound **-anläggning** stereo [equipment] **-foni** [-å'ni:]

s3 stereophony **-fonisk** [-'få:-] *a5* stereophonic **-fotografi** stereophotography **-me'tri** *s3* stereometry **-metrisk** [-'me:-] *a5* stereometric **-skop** *s7* stereoscope **-skopisk** [-'skå:-] *a5* stereoscopic **-'typ** I *a5* stereotyped, set (*leende* smile) II *s3* stereotype, cliché **-ty'pi** *s3* stereotyping

ste'ril *a1* sterile; (*ofruktbar*) barren (*mark* ground) **-isera** sterilize **-isering** sterilization **-itet** sterility; barrenness

sterling ['stö:r-, 'stä:r-] *pund* ~ pound sterling **-blocket** the sterling area (bloc)

steroid [-ɷ'id] *s3* steroid; *anabola* ~*er* anabolic steroids

stetoskop *s7* stethoscope

stia [*sti:a] *s1* [pig]sty, *AE.* pigpen

stick I *s7* 1 stick[ing]; (*nål-*) prick; (*med vapen*) stab, thrust; (*insekt-*) sting, bite 2 *lämna ngn i ~et* leave s.b. in the lurch 3 (*gravyr*) engraving, print 4 *kortsp.* trick II *adv, ~ i stäv* (*sjö.*) dead ahead, *bildl.* directly contrary (*mot* to)

stick|a I *s1* (*flisa*) splinter, split; (*pinne*) stick; *få en ~ i fingret* run a splinter into one's finger; *mager som en ~* [as] thin as a rake 2 (*strump-*) [knitting] needle II *stack stuckit* 1 (*med nål e.d.*) prick, stick; (*med kniv e.d.*) stab; (*slakta*) stick; (*om insekt*) sting, bite; (*stoppa*) put (*handen i fickan* one's hand into one's pocket), (*häftigare*) thrust; *bildl.* sting; *~ kniven i* stab [... with a knife]; *~ eld på* set fire to, set on fire; *~ hål på* prick (make) a hole in, puncture; *~ en nål igenom* run a pin through; *~ in huvudet i* pop one's head into; *hans ord stack mig i själen* his words cut me to the heart 2 (*gravera*) engrave 3 (*med -or*) knit; (*på symaskin*) stitch; (*vaddera*) quilt 4 *det -er i bröstet* I have a pain in my chest; *lukten -er i näsan* the smell makes my nose itch; *ljuset stack mig i ögonen* the light dazzled me; *~ till sjöss* put out (*om pers.* run off) to sea; *kom så -er vi!* (*vard.*) come on, let's go (get out of here)!; *~ sin väg* clear out, hit the road 5 *rfl* prick o.s.; *jag stack mig i fingret* I pricked my finger 6 (*med betonad partikel*) *~ av* (*kontrastera*) contrast (*mot, från* to); *~ emellan med* fit in; *~ fram a*) stretch (stick) out (*nosen* its (*etc.*) nose) *b*) (*skjuta fram*) project, protrude; *månen -er fram* the moon is peeping out; *~ ner* (*ihjäl*) stab [to death]; *det stack till i foten* I had a sudden twinge in my foot; *det stack till i honom* (*bildl.*) he felt a pang; *~ upp a*) stick up (*huvudet* one's head), *b*) (*framträda*) stick up (out), (*träda i dagen*) crop up, *c*) *vard.* be cheeky; *~ ut* stick out; *~ ut ögonen på ngn* put out a p.'s eyes; *~ över a*) *kortsp.* take, *absol.* take it, *b*) (*kila över*) pop over

stickande *a4* shooting (*smärta* pain); pungent (*lukt* smell); piercing (*blickar* looks); *~ smak* pungent (biting) taste

stick|as *stacks stuckits, dep* prick, sting (*jfr* *sticka II 1*) **-beskrivning** knitting instructions **-bäcken** bedpan

stickel ['stick-] *s2, tekn.* graving tool

stickelhår (*i päls*) bristles (*pl*)

stick|garn knitting yarn (wool) **-ig** *a1* prickly **-kontakt** (*-propp*) plug; (*vägguttag*) point, wall socket

stickling cutting, slip

stick|maskin knitting machine **-ning** 1 knitting (*äv. konkr.*) 2 (*-ande känsla*) pricking [sensation] **-ord** 1 (*gliring*) sarcasm, taunt 2 (*uppslagsord*) entry, headword 3 *teat.* cue **-propp** plug **-prov** sample (spot) test; *ta ett ~* take a sample **-provsförfarande** sample-test procedure **-provsundersökning** random sampling **-replik** *se -ord 1 o. 3* **-spår** *järnv.* dead-end siding (track) **-såg** padsaw **-vapen** pointed (stabbing) weapon

1 **stift** *s7* 1 (*att fästa med*) pin, brad, tack; (*rit-*) drawing pencil, crayon; (*penn-*) pencil lead; (*grammofon-*) needle 2 *bot.* style

2 **stift** *s7, kyrkl.* diocese

stift|a (*in-*) found; establish (*en fond* a fund); institute (*regler* rules); form (*ett förbund* an alliance); *~ bekantskap med ngn* make a p.'s acquaintance; *~ fred* conclude (make) peace; *~ lagar* institute laws, legislate **-ande** *s6* founding *etc.*; foundation; establishment **-are** founder; originator

stiftelse foundation; institution, establishment **-urkund** charter of foundation; (*bolags*) memorandum of association; *AE.* articles of incorporation, corporate charter

stiftpenna propelling (automatic) pencil

stifts|adjunkt diocesan curate **-jungfru** [secular] canoness **-stad** cathedral city, diocesan capital

stifttand pivot (pin) tooth

stig *s2* path; *bildl. äv.* track

stig|a *steg -it* 1 (*kliva*) step (*fram* forward); walk (*in i rummet* into the room); *jag kan inte ~ på foten* I can't put my weight on my foot; *~ i land* go ashore; *~ miste* make a false step; *~ närmare* step nearer 2 (*höja sig*) rise; (*om pris äv.*) increase, go up, (*från säljarsynpunkt*) advance, improve; *flyg.* climb, ascend; (*öka*) rise, increase; *aktierna -er* shares are going up; *barometern -er* the barometer is rising; *febern -er* his (etc.) temperature is going up; *~ i ngns aktning* rise in a p.'s esteem; *~ i pris* advance (rise) in price; *~ i rang* acquire a higher rank, advance; *~ i värde* rise in value; *tårarna steg henne i ögonen* tears rose to her eyes; *~ till a*) (*nå*) rise to, attain, *b*) (*belöpa sig t.*) amount to; *~ ur sängen* get out of bed; *framgången steg honom åt huvudet* success went to his head 3 (*med betonad partikel*) *~ av* get off, (*häst*) dismount, (*tåg*) get off; *~ fram* step forward, approach; *~ in* step (walk) in; *stig in!* please come in!, (*som svar på knackning*) come in!; *~ ner* descend; *~ på* (*absol.*) come in; *~ på tåget* get on the train, take the train (*vid* at); *~ upp* rise, *vard.* get up; *~ upp från bordet* (*äv.*) leave the table; *~ upp i en vagn* get into a carriage; *stig upp!* get up!; *en misstanke steg upp inom henne* a suspicion arose within her; *~ upp på* mount, ascend; *~ ur* get (step) out (*en vagn* of a carriage); *~ ur sängen* get out of bed; *~ ut* step out; *~ över* step over (across)

stigande *a4* rising; (*ökande äv.*) increasing, growing; (*om pris*) rising, advancing; *~ konjunkturer* rising tendency; *~ kurva* upward

curve; *efter en* ~ *skala* on an ascending scale, progressively; *vara i* ~ be on the rise
stigarledning *se stigrör*
stigbygel stirrup; (*i örat*) stirrup-bone; *fack.* stapes (*pl*)
stigfinnare pathfinder
stig|hastighet *flyg.* rate of climb **-höjd** ceiling **-it** *sup. av stiga*
stigma [ˣstigg-] *s6* stigma
stigman highwayman, brigand; footpad
stigmatiser|a stigmatize **-ing** stigmatization
stig|ning [-i:g-] rising, rise, ascent; (*ökning*) increase; (*i terräng*) incline, slope; *flyg.* climb **-ort** *gruv.* raise **-rör** ascending pipe, riser **-vinkel** *flyg.* angle of climb
stil *s2* **1** (*hand-*) hand[writing] **2** (*konstnärlig* ~, *stilart*; *bildl.*) style; touch, manner; *det är* ~ *på honom* he has style; *det är hennes vanliga* ~ it is her usual way; *hålla* ~*en* observe good form; *i* ~ *med* in keeping with; *ngt i den* ~*en* s.th. in that line; *i stor* ~ on a large scale **3** *skol.* [written] exercise **4** (*trycktyp*) type; *spärrad* ~ spaced-out letters (*pl*) **5** (*tideräkning*) style **-art** style **-bildande** style-forming **-blomma** *ung.* unsuccessful attempt at rhetorical brilliance **-brott** breach of style **-brytning** *ung.* clash of styles **-drag** characteristic of a style **-enlig** [-e:-] *a1* in keeping with the style [of the period]
sti'lett *s3* stiletto **-klack** stiletto (spike) heel
stil|full stylish, tasteful, in good style **-gjuteri** *boktr.* type foundry **-grad** *boktr.* type size, size of type
stilig *a1* stylish, elegant, chic, *vard.* smart; *det var* ~*t gjort av henne* it was a fine thing of her to do
stiliser|a 1 (*förenkla*) stylize, conventionalize **2** (*formulera*) word, compose **-ing 1** formalizing *etc.* **2** wording
stil|ist stylist; *en god* ~ a master of style **-is'tik** *s3* stylistics (*pl el. sg*) **-istisk** *a5* stylistic; *i* ~*t avseende* as regards style **-känsla** feeling for style, artistic sense (taste)
still *se stilla I*
stilla I *oböjligt a o. adv* (*utan rörelse, äv. bildl.*) still; (*lugn*) calm; (*svag*) soft (*bris* breeze); (*tyst*) quiet; *S~ havet* the Pacific [Ocean]; ~ *vatten* calm (unruffled) waters; *S~a veckan* Holy Week; *tyst och* ~ quiet and tranquil; *föra ett* ~ *liv* lead a quiet life; *det gick ett* ~ *sus genom salen* a gentle murmur went through the room (hall); *ligga* (*sitta, stå, vara*) ~ lie (sit, stand, be) still; *vi sitter för mycket* ~ we lead a too sedentary life; *smedjan stod* ~ the forge was at a standstill; *stå* (*var*) ~*!* keep still (quiet)!; *luften står* ~ the air is not stirring; *det står alldeles* ~ *för mig* just can't remember, it's gone completely out of my head; *tiga* ~ be silent **II** *v1* (*dämpa*) appease; (*lugna*) quiet; (*lindra*) soothe, alleviate (*smärtan* the pain); ~ *sin hunger* appease one's hunger; ~ *sin nyfikenhet* satisfy one's curiosity; ~ *sin törst* slake (quench) one's thirst
stillahavskusten the Pacific Coast
stilla|sittande I *a4* sedentary (*arbete* work) **II** *s6* sedentary life **-stående I** *a4* stationary (*luft* air); stagnant (*vatten* water); (*utan utveckling*)

unprogressive **II** *s6* standstill; stagnation **-tigande** *a4* silent; in silence; ~ *finna sig i ngt* accept s.th. in silence
stillbild still
stilleben ['still-, -'le:-] *s7* still life (*pl* still lifes)
stille|stånd *s7* **1** *mil.* armistice, truce **2** (*vid industri o.d.*) standstill **-ståndsavtal** truce
still|film film strip **-het** calm, quiet; stillness, tranquillity; *begravningen sker i* ~ the funeral will be strictly private; *i all* ~ quite quietly, in silence; *leva i* ~ lead a quiet life
stillna quieten down; (*mojna*) abate, drop **stillsam** *a1* quiet, tranquil; *vara* ~ *av sig* be of a quiet disposition
still|lös without style, in bad style **-löshet** lack of style **-möbler** *pl* period furniture **-prov** (*handstils-*) specimen of a p.'s handwriting; *boktr.* type specimen **-ren** [of] pure [style] **-sort** *boktr.* kind of type; *fel* ~ wrong fo[u]nt (*förk. w.f.*)
stiltje [ˣstiltje] *s9* calm; lull
stilvidrig at variance with the style [of the whole]
STIM [stimm] *ung.* ASCAP (*förk. för American Society of Composers and Performers*)
stim [stimm] *s7* **1** (*fisk-*) shoal; (*av småfisk*) fry **2** (*stoj*) noise, din **stimma 1** (*om fisk*) shoal **2** (*stoja*) be noisy, make a noise
stimul|ans [-'lans, -'laŋs] *s3* stimulation (*till* of); stimulus; (*medel*) stimulant **-antia** [-'lantsia] *pl* stimulants, stimuli **-era** stimulate; ~*nde medel* stimulant **-ering** stimulation **-us** ['sti:-] *r, pl stimuli* stimulus (*pl* stimuli)
sting *s7* (*stick*) prick, sting (*äv. bildl.*); *bildl. äv.* pang (*av svartsjuka* of jealousy); (*kraft*) bite, go; *det är inget* ~ *i det här* there is no punch in this **stinga** stack *stungit* sting; *jfr sticka*
stingslig *a1* touchy, irritable
stink|a *stank* (*sup. saknas*) stink; ~ *av ngt* smell strongly of s.th., *vard.* stink of s.th.; ~*nde* (*äv.*) mephitic[al] **-djur** skunk **-näva** *s1, bot.* herb Robert
stinn *a1* (*uppblåst*) inflated; (*utspänd*) distended; (*av mat*) full [up]; *en* ~ *penningpung* a bulging (fat) purse
stins *s2* stationmaster
stint *se* ~ *på ngn* look hard at s.b.; *se ngn* ~ *i ögonen* look s.b. straight in the eye
stipel ['sti:-] *s3, bot.* stipel; stipule
stipendiat holder of a scholarship
stipendie|ansökan application for a scholarship (grant) **-fond** scholarship fund **-nämnd** scholarship committee
stipendium [-'penn-] *s4* scholarship; (*bidrag*) grant, award
stipul|ation stipulation **-era** stipulate; state
stirra stare, gaze (*på* at); ~ *som förhäxad på* stare as one bewitched at; ~ *sig blind på* (*bildl.*) have eyes for nothing else but **stirrande** *a4* staring; ~ *blick* (*äv.*) fixed look **stirrig** *a1* scatterbrained; nervous
stjäla [ʃ-] *stal stulit* steal (*äv. bildl.*); ~ *sig till att göra ngt* do s.th. by stealth; ~ *sig till en stunds vila* snatch a short rest
stjälk [ʃ-] *s2* stalk; stem **-blad** stem leaf **-stygn** stem stitch
stjälp|a [ʃ-] *v3* **1** (*välta*) overturn; tip; upset (*äv.*

S

bildl.); ~ *av* (*ut*) tip out; ~ *i sig* gulp down; ~ *upp* turn out **2** (*falla över ända*) [be] upset, turn (topple, tip) over **-ning** tipping, upsetting
stjärn|a [ˣʃäː r-] *s1* star **-baneret** the Star--Spangled Banner, the Stars and Stripes **-be-strödd** *a5* starred, starry **-bild** constellation **-fall 1** (*-skott*) [swarm of] shooting star[s *pl*] **2** (*ordensregn*) shower of decorations **-formig** [-å-] *a1* star-shaped; *fack.* stellar, stelliform **-fysik** astrophysics (*pl, behandlas som sg*) **-himmel** starry sky **-karta** star chart **-kikare** [astronomic] telescope **-klar** starlit (*natt* night); starry (*himmel* sky); *det är ~t* the stars are out (shining) **-lös** starless **-skott 1** *se -fall l* **2** (*underhållare*) shooting star **-smäll** *vard., ge ngn en* ~ make s.b. see stars, knock s.b. into the middle of next week **-system** stellar (star) system **-tydare** astrologer **-år** sidereal year
stjärt [ʃ-] *s2* tail (*äv. tekn.*); (*på pers.*) behind, bottom **-fena** tail (caudal) fin **-fjäder** tail feather **-lanterna** *flyg.* tail (rear) light **-mes** long-tailed tit
sto *s6* mare; (*ungt*) filly
stock [-å-] *s2* **1** (*stam*) log; *sova som en* ~ sleep like a log; *över* ~ *och sten* up hill and down dale, across country; *sitta i ~en* be (sit) in the stocks **2** (*på gevär*) stock **3** *tryck från ~ar* (*boktr.*) block printing
1 stocka [-å-] (*hattar*) block
2 stocka [-å-] *rfl* clog; stagnate (*äv. om trafik*); *orden ~r sig i halsen* the words stick in my throat
stock|blind stone-blind **-bro** pole bridge **-eld** log fire **-fisk** stockfish
stockholmare [-å-å-] inhabitant of Stockholm, Stockholmer
stock|hus log house **-konservativ** *en* ~ a die--hard conservative
stockning [-å-] (*avbrott*) stoppage; (*försening*) delay; (*blod-*) [blood] stasis; (*trafik-*) traffic jam, block, congestion; *bildl.* deadlock
stock|ros hollyhock **-ved** logwood
1 stod *imperf. av stå*
2 stod *s3* (*bildl-*) statue
stoff [-å-] *s7, om tyger o.d.* *s4* stuff (*till* for) (*äv. bildl.*); material[s *pl*]; (*ämne*) [subject] matter **-era** hem
sto'fil *s3* odd fish; *gammal* ~ (*äv.*) old fogey
stoft [-å-] *s7* dust; (*puder*) powder; (*jordiska kvarlevor*) ashes, remains (*pl*); *kräla i ~et för* crawl in the dust before **-hydda** mortal clay **-korn** grain of dust
sto|icism [-å-] stoicism **-iker** [ˈstå:-] stoic **-isk** [ˈstå:-] *a5* stoic[al]
stoj [ståjj] *s7* noise, din **stoja** make a noise, be noisy; (*om barn äv.*) romp **stojig** *a1* noisy, boisterous; romping
stokastisk [-ˈkass-] *a5* stochastic; *stat. äv.* random
stol *s2* chair; (*utan ryggstöd*) stool; *sticka under* ~ *med* hold back, conceal; *sätta sig mellan två ~ar* (*bildl.*) fall between two stools
stola [ˣstå:-] *s1* stole
stolgång *s2* (*ändtarmsmynning*) anus **2** (*av-föring*) stools (*pl*), motion
stoll [-å-] *s2, gruv.* gallery; *AE.* adit
stolle [-å-] *s2* fool, silly person

stollift chair lift
stollig *a1* cracked, crazy
stolpe [-å-] *s2* post; pole; (*stötta*) prop, stanchion; (*i virkning*) treble; (*minnesanteckning*) brief note, jotting
stolpiller suppository
stolpskor *pl* climbing irons
stols|ben chair leg, leg of a chair **-karm** arm of a chair **-rygg** back of a chair **-sits** [chair] seat
stolt [-å-] *a1* proud (*över* of); (*högdragen*) haughty; *med en* ~ *gest* with a proud gesture; *vara* ~ *över* (*äv.*) pride o.s. on, take pride in **-het** pride (*över* in); (*högdragenhet*) arrogance; *berättigad* ~ legitimate pride; *sårad* ~ (*äv.*) pique, *sätta sin* ~ *i* take pride in **-sera** *absol.* swagger; (*gå o.* ~) swagger about; (*om häst*) prance; ~ *med* parade
stoma'tit *s3* stomatitis
stomme *s2* frame[work], shell; skeleton (*äv. bildl.*)
stomp [-å-] *s2* stump
stop *s7* **1** (*kärl*) stoup, pot **2** (*rymdmått*) quart
1 stopp [-å-] I *s7* (*stockning*) stoppage (*i röret* in the pipe); (*stillastående*) stop, standstill (*äv. bildl.*); *sätta* ~ *för* put an end (a stop) to; *säg* ~! (*vid påfyllning*) say when! II *interj* stop!
2 stopp [-å-] *s2* **1** (*på strumpa e.d.*) darn **2** (*pip-*) fill
1 stoppa [-å-] **1** (*hejda*) stop, bring to a stand-still; stem (*blodflödet* the flow of blood) **2** (*stanna*) stop, come to a standstill **3** (*förslå*) suffice, be enough **4** (*orka*) stand the strain; *han ~r nog inte länge till* he can't stand the strain much longer
2 stoppa [-å-] **1** (*laga hål*) darn (*strumpor* socks) **2** (*fylla*) fill (*pipan* one's pipe); stuff (*korv* sausages; *med tagel* with horsehair); upholster (*möbler* furniture); (*proppa*) cram; ~ *fickorna fulla med* fill one's pockets with **3** (*sticka in*) put (*ngt i fickan* s.th. into one's pocket; tuck **4** (*med betonad partikel*) ~ *i ngn ngt* stuff s.b. with s.th.; ~ *i sig* put away; ~ *ner* put (tuck) down; ~ *om ett barn* tuck a child up [in bed]; ~ *om en madrass* re-stuff a mat-tress; ~ *på sig* put into one's pocket, pocket; ~ *undan* stow away
stopp|boll *sport.* drop shot **-förbud** (*på skylt*) No waiting; ~ *gäller* waiting is prohibited
stoppgarn darning wool (cotton, worsted)
stopp|gräns stopping limit **-knapp** stop button **-plikt** (*hopskr. stopplikt*) obligation to stop
stoppljus stoplight
stopp|ning [-å-] (*jfr 2 stoppa*) darning; filling; stuffing *etc.* **-nål** darning needle
stopp|signal halt signal, red light **-skruv** set (stop) screw **-skylt** stop sign
stoppsvamp darning egg (mushroom)
stopp|ur stopwatch **-volley** *sport.* stop volley
stor *-t större störst* **1** (*i sht om ngt konkr.*) large (*hus* house; *förmögenhet* fortune); (*i sht i kroppslig bet.*) big (*näsa* nose), (*starkare*) huge; (*reslig*) tall; (*i sht om ngt abstr.*) great (*skillnad* difference); *bildl. äv.* grand; *Alexander den ~e* Alexander the Great; *Karl den ~e* Charlemagne; *dubbelt så* ~ *som* double the size of, twice as large (*etc.*) as; *lika* ~ *som* the same

size as, as large (*etc.*) as; *hur ~ är han?* how big is he?; *en ~ beundrare av* a great admirer of; *~ bokstav* capital [letter]; *~ efterfrågan* great (large, heavy) demand; *ett ~t antal* a great (large) number (*barn* of children); *hon är ~a flickan nu* she is a big girl now; *den ~a hopen* the crowd; *han är ~a karlen nu* he is quite a man now; *en ~ man* a great man; *vara ~ i maten* be a big eater; *ett ~t nöje* a great pleasure; *~a ord* big words; *bruka ~a ord* talk big; *du ~e tid!* good heavens!; *i ~a drag* in broad outline; *i det ~a hela* on the whole, by and large; *till ~ del* largely, to a great extent **2** (*fullvuxen*) grown-up, adult; *de ~a* grown-up people; *när jag blir ~* when I grow up

storartad [-aːr-] *a5* grand; magnificent, splendid; *på ett storartat sätt* (*äv.*) magnificently, splendidly

storasyster big sister

stor|belåten highly satisfied **-blommig 1** *bot.* large-flowered **2** (*om mönster*) with a large floral pattern **-bonde** farmer with extensive lands **-boskap** cattle

Storbritannien *n* Great Britain

stor|cirkel great circle **-dia** *s1, s6* overhead transparency **-drift** large-scale production (*jordbr.* farming) **-dåd** great (noble) achievement **-ebror** big brother

stor|en [ˈstɔː-] *best. form, sjö.* the main **-familj** extended family **-favorit** main favourite **-finans** high finance **-främmande** distinguished guest[s *pl*] **-furste** grand duke **-furstendöme** grand duchy **-förbrukare** bulk (big) consumer **-företag** large[-scale] enterprise (company) **-gods** large landed estate **-gråta** cry copiously **-hertig** grand duke **-het** [-ɔː-] **1** *abstr.* greatness; *fack.* magnitude **2** *mat.* quantity **3** (*om pers.*) great man (personage); (*berömdhet*) celebrity; *en okänd ~* an unknown celebrity (quantity)

storhets|tid (*lands*) era of greatness **-vansinne** megalomania, illusions (*pl*) of grandeur

stor|hjärna *~n* [the] cerebrum **-industri** big (large[-scale]) industry

stork [-å-] *s2* stork

storkapital big capital

storkbo stork's nest

storkna [-å-] choke, suffocate

stor|kommun big (large) municipal district **-konflikt** major conflict **-kornig** coarse-grained **-kors** (*av orden*) grand cross (*förk.* G.C.) **-kök** catering [service] **-lek** *s2* size; dimensions (*pl*); (*omfång*) extent, width, vastness; (*rymd*) volume; *fack.* magnitude; *av betydande ~* of large dimensions; *i ~* in size (*etc.*); *i naturlig ~* life-size; *stora ~ar* (*av plagg e.d. äv.*) outsizes; *upplagans ~* number of copies printed **-leksordning** magnitude, order; size; *av ~en* in the region of (*500 pund* 500 pounds), of the order of (*5% 5%*); *av första ~en* of the first order (magnitude); *i ~* in order of size **-ligen** [-ɔː-] greatly; highly; very much **-ljugare** arrant liar **-lom** black-throated diver

storm [-å-] *s2* **1** (*vind*) storm (*äv. bildl.*); gale; (*oväder*) tempest; *det blåser upp till ~* a storm is brewing; *~ i ett vattenglas* a storm in a teacup; *lugn i ~en!* calm down now!; *rida ut ~en* (*bildl.*) ride out the storm **2** *mil., ta med ~* (*äv. bildl.*) take by storm; *gå till ~s mot* make an assault upon **3** *se stormhatt 1*

storma [-å-] **1** (*blåsa*) storm; *det ~r* storm is raging, it is stormy, a gale is blowing **2** *bildl.* (*rasa*) storm, rage; (*rusa*) rush; *~ fram* rush forward **3** *mil.* assault, force, storm

stor|makt great power **-maktspolitik** power (great-power) politics (*pl*) **-man** great man; magnate; (*berömdhet*) celebrity

storm|ande [-å-] *a4* **1** eg., *se stormig* **2** *bildl.* thunderous (*applåder* applause); tremendous, enormous (*succé* success); *göra ~ succé* (*om skådespelare äv.*) bring down the house

stor|marknad hypermarket, out-of-town superstore **-maskig** *a1* wide-meshed, coarse-meshed **-mast** mainmast

storm|by heavy squall **-centrum** storm centre **-driven** *a5* storm-tossed **-flod** flood [caused by a storm] **-fågel** fulmar **-förtjust** absolutely delighted **-gräla** quarrel furiously (*med* with); *~ på ngn* storm at s.b. **-hatt 1** (*hög hatt*) top (high) hat **2** *bot.* monkshood

storm|ig *a1*, eg. o. *bildl.* stormy; tempestuous (*känslor* emotions); *bildl. äv.* tumultuous (*uppträde* scene); *~t hav* rough sea **-klocka** alarm bell **-lykta** hurricane lamp, storm lantern **-ning** *mil.* assault, storming **-plugga** swot; read hard, cram **-rik** immensely rich **-segel** storm sail **-steg** *med ~* by leaps and bounds **-styrka** gale force **-svala** storm[y] petrel **-trupp** *mil.* storming party **-tändsticka** fusee **-varning** gale warning **-vind** gale [of wind] **-virvel** violent whirlwind, tornado

stor|märs *sjö.* maintop **-mästare** grandmaster **-mönstrad** large-patterned **-möte** general meeting **-ordig** [-ɔː-rd-] *a1* grandiloquent; (*skrytsam*) boastful **-pamp** *vard.* big noise (shot), bigwig, VIP **-politik** top-level politics (*pl*) **-politisk** *~t möte* summit meeting **-rengöring** spring-cleaning **-rutig** large-checked **-rysk, ryss** Great Russian **-rökare** heavy smoker **-segel** mainsail **-sint** *a1* magnanimous, generous **-sinthet** magnanimity, generosity **-skarv** *zool.* cormorant **-skifte** amalgamation of smallholdings into large production units **-skog** large forest **-skojare** big swindler **-skrake** goosander; *AE.* merganser **-skratta** roar with laughter, guffaw **-skrika** yell (scream) [at the top of one's voice] **-skrävlare** swaggerer, big braggart **-slagen** *a3* magnificent, grand **-slagenhet** magnificence, grandeur **-slalom** giant slalom **-slam** *kortsp.* grand slam **-slägga** *ta till ~n* (*bildl.*) go at s.th. with hammer and tongs **-spov** curlew **-stad** big town, city; metropolis **-stadsaktig** *a1* metropolitan, fitting to a big town **-stadsbo** inhabitant of a big town (*etc.*), city dweller **-stilad** *a5* grand, fine

Stor-Stockholm Greater Stockholm

stor|strejk general strike **-ståtlig** majestic, grand, magnificent **-städning** *se storrengöring* **-stövlar** *pl* high boots **-säljare** best seller

stort [-ɔː-] **I** *adv* largely *etc.*; *inte ~ mer än* not much more than; *det hjälper inte ~* it won't help much; *tänka ~* think nobly **II** *a, i ~* on a large scale; *i ~ sett* on the whole; *slå på ~* make a splash, do the thing big **stor|ting** Storting, Norwegian Parliament **-tjuta** howl **-tjuv** masterthief **-tvätt** big wash **-tå** big (great) toe **-verk** *se stordåd* **-vesir** grand vizier **-vilt** big game **-vulen** *a3, se storstilad* **-vuxen** tall [of stature] **-ätare** big eater; *(frossare)* glutton **-ögd** *a1* large-eyed **-ögt** *adv, titta ~ på* gaze round-eyed at

straff *s7* punishment *(för* for); *jur.* penalty, *avtjäna sitt ~* serve one's penalty; *milt ~* light (mild) punishment; *strängt ~* severe sentence; *lagens strängaste ~* the maximum penalty; *ta sitt ~* take one's punishment; *till ~ för* as (for) [a] punishment for **straffa** punish *(för* for); *(näpsa)* reprove; *~s med böter eller fängelse* carries a penalty of fines or imprisonment; *synden ~r sig själv* sin carries its own punishment **straffad** *a5* punished; *jur.* convicted; *tidigare ~* previously convicted

straff|arbete penal servitude; *livstids ~* penal servitude for life; *ett års ~* one year's hard labour **-bar** *a1* punishable; *(brottslig)* criminal; *(friare)* condemnable **-dom** *Herrens ~* divine judgement **-eftergift** remission [of penalty] **-exercis** punishment drill **-fri** *(hopskr. straffri)* exempt from punishment **-friförklara** *(hopskr. straffriförklara)* discharge without penalty, exempt from punishment **-frihet** *(hopskr. straffrihet)* impunity, exemption from punishment **-fånge** *(hopskr. straffånge)* convict **-fängelse** *(hopskr. straffängelse)* penitentiary, convict prison **-föreläggande** *(hopskr. strafföreläggande) ung.* order [of summary punishment] **-kast** *sport.* penalty [throw] **-koloni** penal settlement **-lag** criminal (penal) code (law) **-lindring** reduction [of penalty] **-område** *sport.* penalty area **-predikan** hellfire sermon; *(friare)* severe lecture **-påföljd** penalty, [punitive] sanction; *vid ~ on* penalty **-register** criminal (police) records *(pl)* **-ränta** penal interest, interest on arrears **-rätt** *jur.* penal (criminal) law **-rättslig** criminal, penal **-slag** *sport.* penalty [shot] **-spark** *sport.* penalty [kick] **-tid** term of punishment; *avtjäna sin ~ (äv.)* undergo one's sentence, *vard.* do one's time

stram *a1 (spänd)* tight, strained; *bildl.* stiff *(uppträdande* bearing); *(reserverad)* distant; *en ~ livsföring* an austere way of life; *en ~ kreditpolitik* a stiff (restrictive) credit policy **strama** *(sträckas)* be tight, pull; *~ åt* tighten, stiffen

stra'malj *s3* canvas [for needlework] **stramhet** [-a:-] tightness *etc.; bildl.* stiffness **stramt** [-a:-] *adv* tightly *etc.; sitta ~* be (fit) tight; *hälsa ~* give a stiff greeting **strand** *-en stränder* shore; *(havs- äv.)* seashore; *(sand-)* beach; *(flod-)* bank **strand|a** run ashore, be stranded; strand *(äv. bildl.); bildl. äv.* fail, break down **-aster** sea aster **-brink** [steep river] bank **-brädd** waterside; brink of the water **-fynd** flotsam, jetsam **-hugg** *göra ~ (om sjörövare)* raid a coast, *(om seglare)* go ashore **-ning** stranding *etc.; bildl. äv.* failure **-pipare** *zool., större ~* ringed plover **-promenad** *(väg)* promenade, *AE.*

boardwalk **-remsa** strip of shore, foreshore **-råg** lyme grass **-rätt** right to use the beach; *(rätt att bärga vrakgods)* salvage right **-satt** *a4, bildl.* stranded, at a loss *(på* for) **-skata** oystercatcher **-sätta** *bildl.* fail, leave in the lurch **-tomt** beach lot, lakeside site **-vallmo** yellow horned poppy **-ägare** riparian [owner] **stra'pats** *s3* hardship **-rik** adventurous **strass** *s3* paste, strass; rhinestones *(pl)* **stra'teg** *s3* strategist **-te'gi** *s3* strategy **-tegisk** [-'te:-] *a5* strategic[al] **stratifier|a** stratify **-ing** stratification **strato'sfär** stratosphere **strax I** *adv* **1** *(om tid)* directly, immediately; *(med ens)* at once; *(om ett ögonblick)* in a moment; *[jag] kommer ~!* just a moment (minute)!; *klockan är ~ 12* it is close on twelve o'clock; *~ efter* just (immediately) after **2** *(om rum)* just *(utanför* outside); *~ bredvid* close by; *följa ~ efter* follow close on **II** *konj, ~ jag såg dig* directly (the moment) I saw you **streber** ['stre:-] *s2* pusher, climber, thruster; *AE. vard.* go-getter **-aktig** *a1* pushing **streck** *s7* **1** *(penndrag)* stroke; *(linje)* line; *(grad-)* mark; *(kompass-)* point; *munnen smalnade till ett ~* his *(etc.)* mouth became a thin line; *vi stryker ett ~ över det (bildl.)* let's forget it; *ett ~ i räkningen* a disappointment; *hålla ~ (bildl.)* hold good, be true; *artikel under ~et* feature article **2** *polit.* qualification **3** *(kläd-)* cord, line **4** *(spratt)* trick; *ett dumt ~* a stupid trick **streck|a** mark with lines; *(skugga)* hatch; *~ för* check (tick) off; *~ under* underline; *~d linje* broken line **-kliché** line block **-kod** bar-code **-ning** *(i ritning e.d.)* streaking; *(skuggning)* hatching **-teckning** line drawing **stred** *imperf. av* strida **strejk** *s3* strike; *gå i ~* go (come out) on strike; *vild ~* wildcat strike **strejk|a** strike, go (come out) on strike **-ande** *a4* striking; *de ~* those (the workers *etc.*) on strike, the strikers; *~ hamnarbetare* dock strikers **-brytare** strikebreaker, non-striker; *neds.* blackleg, *AE.* scab **-hot** strike threat **-kassa** strike fund **-rätt** right to strike **-vakt** picket **-varsel** strike notice, notice of a strike; *utfärda ~* serve notice of strike **strepto|kock** [-'kåck] *s3* streptococcus *(pl* streptococci) **-my'cin** *s4* streptomycin **stress** *s3* stress **stressa 1** put under pressure **2** *vard., han ~de iväg till jobbet* he dashed off to work; *han ~de som en galning för att hinna i tid* he rushed off his feet to make it on time **stressad** *a5* under stress (tension); overstrained **stressande** *a4* stressful **stressfaktor** stress factor **streta** strive, struggle *(med* with; *mot* against); *~ emot* resist, struggle against *(äv. bildl.); ~ uppför backen* struggle up the hill **1 strid** *a1* rapid, violent *(ström* current); torrential *(regn* rain); *gråta ~a tårar* weep bitterly **2 strid** *s3* struggle *(för* for; *mot* against; *om* about); *(kamp, äv. mil.)* fight, combat, battle; *(dispyt)* dispute, altercation; *inre ~* inward struggle; *livets ~* the struggle (battle) of life;

en ~ på liv och död a life and death struggle; öppen ~ open war; en ~ om ord a dispute about mere words; det står ~ om honom he is the subject of controversy; i ~ens hetta in the heat of the struggle (bildl. äv. debate); stupa i ~ be killed in action; i ~ med (mot) in opposition to, in contravention of; inlåta sig i ~ med get mixed up in a fight with; råka i ~ med get into conflict with; stå i ~ mot be at variance with; göra klar[t] till ~ prepare for action; gå segrande ur ~en emerge victorious from the battle; ge sig utan ~ give up without a fight

strid|a stred -it, v2 **1** fight (om for); battle (för for); (friare) struggle, strive (för for); (tvista) contend (om about) **2** (stå i motsats [till]) be contrary (opposed, in opposition) to; det -er mot lagen it is contrary to (against) the law **stridande** a4 **1** mil. combatant, fighting; (friare) contending, opposing; de ~ the fighters, mil. the combatants **2** (oförenlig) adverse, opposed (mot to), contrary (mot to), incompatible (mot with) **stridbar** a1 fighting (skick trim); (stridslysten) battling (sinne spirit **stridig** a1 **1** se stridslysten **2** (omstridd) disputable, disputed; göra ngn rangen ~ contend for precedence with s.b., bildl. run s.b. close **3** (motstridig) contradictory; conflicting; ~a känslor conflicting feelings **stridighet 1** (motsättning) opposition, antagonism **2** (tvist) dissension, dispute **stridit** sup. av strida

strids|anda fighting spirit **-beredskap** readiness for action **-domare** umpire **-duglig** in fighting trim; fit for fight **-duglighet** fighting efficiency **-flygare** fighter pilot **-flygplan** fighter aircraft **-fråga** controversial question (issue), point at issue **-gas** war gas **-handling** act of war[fare] **-handske** gauntlet **-häst** charger **-humör** fighting mood **-iver** i ~n in the heat of the battle **-krafter** pl military [armed] forces **-kämpe** warrior, combatant **-laddning** warhead **-ledning** supreme command **-linje** battle line, front **-lust** fighting spirit **-lycka** fortune[s pl] of war **-lysten** eager for battle; (friare) aggressive, quarrelsome; argumentative **-lystnad** pugnacity, fighting mood **-medel** weapon **-robot** guided missile with warhead **-rop** war (battle) cry **-skrift** [polemical] pamphlet **-spets** warhead **-tupp** gamecock, fighting cock **-vagn** tank, armoured car **-vagnsförband** armoured unit **-vapen** combat weapon **-vimmel** confusion of battle; mitt i -vimlet in the thick of the battle **-yxa** battle-axe; (indians) tomahawk; gräva ner ~n bury the hatchet (äv. bildl.) **-åtgärd 1** mil. action **2** (på arbetsmarknaden) industrial action **-äpple** apple of discord, bone of contention **-övning** tactical exercise, manoeuvre

strig|el s2 strop **-la** [-i:-] strop
strike [strajk] s2 (bowling) strike
strikt a1 strict; (sträng) severe; ~ klädd soberly dressed
stril s2 spray nozzle **strila** spray; (spruta) sprinkle; ~ in filter in; ~ ner come down steadily
strimla I s1 strip, shred II v1 cut in strips, shred
strimm|a s1 streak; (rand) stripe; (i marmor) vein; bildl. gleam **-ig** a1 streaked, striped
string|ens [-ŋ'gens] s3 stringency; cogency

-ent a1 stringent; logical
strip|a I s1 wisp of hair II v1 strip **-ig** a1 lank, straggling (hår hair)
strippa vard. I v1 strip II s1 stripper **striptease** s5 striptease
strit s2, zool. cicada (pl äv. cicadae)
strof [-å:-] s3 stanza
strong [-å-] a1 (fin) fine; (stram) strict
strontium ['stråntsium] s8 strontium
stropp [-å-] s2 **1** strap, strop; sjö. äv. sling; (på skor) loop **2** pers. snooty devil **-ig** a1 snooty, stuck-up
strosa stroll around; mooch about
struk|en a5, en ~ tesked a level teaspoonful (salt of salt) **-it** sup. av stryka
struktur structure; bildl. äv. texture **-alism** structuralism **-'ell** a1 structural **-era** structure **-formel** structural formula **-omvandling** structural change (transformation) **-rationalisering** structural rationalization
strul s7, vard. muddle, trouble **-ig** vard. trying, difficult, bothersome
struma s1 struma, goitre
strump|a s1 stocking; (kort) sock; -or (koll.) hose (sg) **-byxor** pl [stretch] tights, pantyhose (behandlas som pl); var är mina ~? where are my tights (pantyhose)?
strumpe|band suspender; (ringformigt o. AE.) garter **-bandshållare** suspender (AE. garter) belt **-bandsorden** the Order of the Garter
strump|fabrik hosiery, stocking manufactures (pl) **-läst** i ~en in one's stockinged feet **-sticka** knitting needle **-stoppning** darning of stockings (etc.)
strunt s3, s4 rubbish, trash; det vore väl ~ om it would be the limit if; å ~! bosh!, poppycock!; ~ i det! never mind!; prata ~ talk nonsense (rubbish)
strunt|a i ~ not care a bit about (a fig for) **-förnäm** would-be refined **-prat** nonsense, rubbish; AE. boloney **-sak** trifle **-summa** trifle, trifling sum
strup|e s2 throat; (svalg) gorge; (luft-) windpipe; anat. trachea; (mat-) gullet; få ngt i galen ~ have s.th. go down the wrong way; ha kniven på ~n have no alternative, be at bay **-grepp** stranglehold **-huvud** larynx **-katarr** laryngitis **-ljud** guttural sound, guttural **-lock** epiglottis **-mikrofon** throat microphone **-tag** se -grepp
strut s2 cornet, cone
struts s2 ostrich **-fjäder** ostrich feather **-plym** ostrich plume **-politik** bedriva ~ be unwilling to face unpleasant facts
strutta strut, trip
stryk s7 (ge ngn give s.b.) a beating (whipping); (i slagsmål) a thrashing; få ~ be beaten (äv. bildl.); ett kok ~ a good thrashing; han tigger ~ (bildl.) he is asking for a thrashing; ful som ~ ugly as sin
stryk|a strök strukit **1** (med handen e.d.) stroke; (släta) smooth **2** (med -järn) iron **3** (be-, med färg e.d.) paint, coat; ~ salva på ett sår smear ointment on a wound; ~ smör på brödet spread [a piece of] bread with butter **4** (bryna) whet **5** ~ eld på en tändsticka strike a match **6** (utesluta) cut out, delete (ngt i en text s.th. from a

text); (~ över) cross (strike) out; *stryk det icke tillämpliga!* cross out what does not apply!; ~ *ngn ur medlemsförteckningen* strike s.b. off the list of members; ~ *ett streck över* draw a line through, *bildl. se streck 1 7 sjö.* strike (*flagg* one's colours; *segel* sail) **8** (*ströva*) roam, ramble (*omkring* about); *flygplanet strök över taken* the aeroplane swept over the roofs **9** ~ *askan av en cigarr* knock the ash off a cigar; ~ *handsken av handen* strip the glove off the hand; ~ *håret ur pannan* brush one's hair from one's forehead; ~ *på foten* give in (för to) **10** *rfl* rub (*mot* against); ~ *sig om munnen* wipe one's mouth (*med* with); ~ *sig över håret* pass one's hand over one's hair **11** (*med betonad partikel*) ~ *bort* sweep off (away); ~ *fram* pass; ~ *för* mark, check off; ~ *förbi* sweep past; ~ *in* rub in (*salvan* the ointment); ~ *med a*) (*gå åt*) go [too], (*om pengar*) be spent, *b*) (*dö*) die, perish; ~ *omkring* rove [about], (*om rovdjur*) prowl about; ~ *omkring på gatorna* wander about the streets; ~ *på* spread, lay on; ~ *tillbaka* stroke back; ~ *under* underline, *bildl.* emphasize, stress; ~ *ut* (*utplåna*) strike out, (*utradera*) scratch out, erase, (*torka bort*) rub out; ~ *över* (*med färg*) give another coat of paint

stryk|ande *a4*, ~ *aptit* ravenous appetite; *ha ~ åtgång* (*hand.*) have a rapid sale **-bräda** ironing board **-erska** ironing woman **-filt** ironing cloth **-fri** noniron **-inrättning** ironing workshop **-järn** [flat]iron **-mangel, -maskin** ironing machine
stryk'nin *s4, s3* strychnine
stryk|ning [-y:-] **1** (*smekning*) stroke, stroking; (*gnidning*) rubbing **2** (*med -järn*) ironing **3** (*med färg e.d.*) painting, coating **4** (*uteslutning*) deletion, cancellation **5** *geol.* strike, course
stryk|pojke *bildl.* whipping boy, scapegoat **-rädd** afraid of getting thrashed
stryk|tips results pool **-torr** ready for ironing
stryk|tålig tough, durable **-täck** cheeky, impudent
stryp|a *v3, imperf. äv. ströp* strangle; throttle (*äv. bildl. o. tekn.*); (*friare o. tekn.*) choke **-ning** [-y:-] strangling *etc.*; strangulation; *bildl. äv.* constriction **-sjuka** croup; (*hos djur*) strangles (*pl*) **-ventil** throttle valve
strå *s6* straw (*äv. koll.*); (*hår-*) hair; (*gräs-*) blade; *ett ~ vassare* a cut above; *dra det kortaste ~et* get the worst of it, come off worst; *dra sitt ~ till stacken* do one's part (bit); *inte lägga två ~n i kors* not lift a finger **-hatt** straw hat
stråk *s7* (*samfärdsled*) passage, course; thoroughfare
stråk|drag stroke of the bow
stråk|e *s2* bow **-ensemble** string ensemble **-föring** bowing; *ha en bra ~* have a good bow hand **-instrument** string[ed] (bow) instrument **-kvartett** string quartet **-orkester** string orchestra (band)
stråkväg highroad, thoroughfare; *den stora ~en* (*bildl.*) the beaten track
strål|a beam, be radiant (*av glädje* with joy); (*skina*) shine (*äv. bildl.*); (*sprida -ar*) radiate,

emit rays **-ande** *a4* beaming, radiant; brilliant (*solsken* sunshine); (*lysande*) brilliant (*äv. bildl.*); ~ *glad* radiantly happy; ~ *ögon* sparkling eyes
strål|behandling radiation treatment, radiotherapy **-ben** *anat.* radius **-blomma** ray flower **-blomstrig** [-å-] *a1* radiate **-brytning** refraction **-dos** radiation dose
strål|e *s2* **1** ray, beam; *bildl.* gleam (*av hopp* of hope) **2** (*vätske-*) jet, spray; (*fin*) squirt **3** *bot.* radius **-form** *i* ~ in the form of rays **-formig** [-å-] *a1* radiate[d], radiating **-glans** radiance (*äv. bildl.*); (*friare*) brilliance **-kamin** radiation heater **-kastare** searchlight; (*på bil*) headlight; (*för fasadbelysning*) floodlight; *teat.* spotlight **-kastarljus** searchlight; *teat.* spotlight; (*fasadbelysning*) floodlight **-kirurgi** radiation surgery **-knippe** bunch (pencil) of rays **-ning** [-å-] beaming *etc.*; (*ut-*) radiation; (*be-*) irradiation
strålnings|biologi radiation biology **-detektor** radiation detector **-energi** radiant energy, emissive power **-kemi** radiation chemistry **-källa** source of radiation **-mätare** *kärnfys.* radiation meter, radiac dosimeter **-olycka** radiation accident **-risk** [ionizing] radiation risk **-skydd** protection against radiation **-värme** radiant heat **-värmare** radiant heater
strål|sjuka radiation sickness **-skada** radiation damage (*på pers.* injury) **-skydd** *se strålningsskydd* **-svamp** *koll.* actinomycete **-svampsjuka** *veter.* actinomycosis, *vard.* lumpy jaw
stråt *s2* path, way **-rövare** highwayman, brigand; footpad
sträck 1 *n, utan pl, i* [*ett*] ~ at a stretch, on end; *vara borta månader i* ~ be away for months on end; *läsa fem timmar i* ~ read for five hours without stopping; *sova hela natten i ett* ~ sleep all night through **2** *s7* (*flyttfågels-*) flight (track) of migratory birds
sträck|a I *s1* stretch; (*väg-*) length, distance, way; (*järnvägs-*) section, run **II** *v3* **1** (*räcka ut; tänja; spänna*) stretch (*händerna mot* one's hand to[wards]; *på benen* one's legs; *en lina* a rope); (*ut-*) extend; (*för-*) strain (*en sena* a tendon); ~ *på sig* straighten (pull) o.s. up, stretch **2** ~ *kölen till ett fartyg* lay [down] the keel of a vessel **3** ~ *vapen* lay down one's arms, surrender **4** (*om fåglar*) migrate **5** *rfl a*) (*ha utsträckning*) stretch, extend, *b*) (~ *ut kroppen*) stretch o.s., *c*) (*räcka*) stretch [out], reach; ~ *sig längs kusten* run along the coast; *längre än till 10 pund -er jag mig inte* I will go no farther than £ 10; ~ *sig över 10 år* extend over a period of ten years; ~ *ut sig på sängen* stretch out on the bed **6** (*med betonad partikel*) ~ *fram handen* hold out one's hand; ~ *upp sig a*) *se sträcka* [*på sig*], *b*) (*klä sig fin*) dress up; ~ *ut a*) extend, stretch out, *b*) (*förlänga*) prolong (*äv. bildl.*), *c*) (*gå fort*) stride (step) out; ~ *ut huvudet genom fönstret* put one's head out of the window; *låta hästen* ~ *ut* give one's horse its head **-bänk** rack; *ligga på ~en* be on the rack; *hålla ngn på ~en* (*bildl.*) keep s.b. on tenterhooks **-förband** traction bandage **-läsa** read without stopping **-muskel** *anat.* tensor **-ning** (*-ande*) stretching *etc.*; (*ut-*) extension;

(riktning) direction; *(för-)* strain
1 sträng *a1* severe *(kyla* cold); *(ytterst nog-grann)* strict *(disciplin* discipline), rigorous *(rättvisa* justice), rigid *(uppsikt* supervision); *(allvarlig)* stern *(min* look), austere *(uppsyn* countenance); *~t arbete* exacting work; *hålla ~ diet* be on a strict diet; *vara ~ mot* be severe *(mot barn:* strict) with
2 sträng *s2 (mus.; båg-)* string *(äv. bildl.)*; *bildl. äv.* chord; *ha flera ~ar på sin lyra (båge) (bildl.)* have more than one string to one's bow
stränga string; *~ sin lyra (bildl.)* tune one's harp (lyre)
strängaspel playing upon a stringed instrument
sträng|eligen strictly, severely; *jfr strängt* **-het** severity; strictness, rigour
stränginstrument stringed instrument
strängt *adv* **1** severely *etc.*; *arbeta ~* work hard; *~ förbjudet* strictly forbidden (prohibited); *~ hållen (om barn)* strictly brought up; *~ konfidentiellt* strictly confidential; *~ upptagen* fully occupied, pressed for time **2** *(noga)* hålla *~ på* observe rigorously; *~ taget* strictly speaking
sträv *a1* rough; *(i smak o. bildl.)* harsh; *(barsk)* stern, gruff; *~ smak (äv.)* acerbity; *under den ~a ytan (bildl.)* under the rough (rugged) surface
1 sträva *s1, byggn.* strut, shore; *(sned)* brace
2 sträva *v1* strive; *(knoga)* toil; *~ att* endeavour to; *~ efter* strive for; *~ mot himlen (om torn e.d.)* soar aloft; *~ med* work hard at, struggle with; *~ till* aspire to; *~ uppåt* strive upwards, *bildl.* aim high
strävbåge *byggn.* flying buttress
sträv|het [-ä:-] roughness, harshness *etc. (jfr sträv.)*; *(i smak)* acerbity, asperity **-hårig** rough-haired; *(om hund)* wire-haired
strävpelare *byggn.* buttress
strävsam [-ä:-] *a1* **1** *(arbetsam)* assiduous, industrious, hard-working **2** *(mödosam)* laborious, strenuous; *föra ett ~t liv* lead a strenuous life **-het** industriousness; thrift
strävt *adv, ha det ~* have a hard time of it
strö I *s7* litter **II** *v4* strew; sprinkle *(socker på* sugar on; *över* over); *~ ... omkring sig* scatter [... about]; *~ pengar omkring sig* splash money around; *~ rosor för ngn (bildl.)* flatter s.b.
ströare castor, dredger **ströbröd** breadcrumbs **strödd** *a5, ~a anmärkningar* casual remarks; *~a anteckningar* odd notes
strög *s7* main street, boulevard
strök *imperf. av stryka*
strökund odd (stray) customer
ström [-ömm] *s2* **1** *(flod)* stream; river *(äv. bildl.)*; *(flöde)* flood *(av tårar* of tears), flow *(av ord* of words); *(häftig)* torrent *(äv. bildl.)*; *en ~ av folk* a stream of people; *en ~ av blod* a stream of blood; *gästerna kom i en jämn ~* the guests arrived in a steady stream; *vinet flöt i ~mar* wine flowed freely **2** *(i luft, vatten; äv. elektr.)* current; *bildl. äv.* tide; *följa med ~men*

(äv. bildl.) follow the tide, drift with the current; *gå mot ~men* go against the current *(friare o. bildl.:* tide); *stark ~ (i vatten)* rapid current; *sluta ~men* switch on the current, close the circuit **-avbrott** power failure; *(avstängning)* power cut **-brytare** switch; *(för motor e.d. äv.)* circuit breaker **-drag** current; race **-fåra** stream *(äv. bildl.)*; *(flodbädd)* bed **-förande** *a4* live, charged; *vara ~* be alive **-förbrukning** power (current) consumption **-fördelare** *(i bil)* distributor **-försörjning** power (current) supply **-kantring** *bildl.* turn of the tide *(äv. om tidvatten)*, changeover **-karlen** [-ka:ren] *se* näcken **-krets** circuit **-linje** streamline **-linjeform** streamlining, streamlined shape **-linjeformad** [-å-] *a5* streamlined **-lös** *elektr.* dead **-löshet** absence of current
strömma stream, flow; *(om regn, tårar)* [come] pour[ing]; *(häftigt)* gush, rush; *den välvilja som ~de emot mig* the goodwill that met me; *~ fram* pour out; *~ in* rush in, [come] pour[ing] in; *folk ~de till* people came flocking; *~ ut* stream *(etc.)* out, *(om gas e.d.)* escape; *folk ~de ut ur teatern* people came pouring out of the theatre; *~ över* overflow
strömming Baltic herring
ström|mätare *elektr.* amperemeter, ammeter; *se äv. elmätare* **-ning** current, flow, stream; *bildl.* current, tide **-riktning** direction of current **-skena** conductor rail **-snål** electricity-saving **-stare** dipper, water ouzel **-styrka** *elektr.* current [intensity], amperage **-stöt** current rush, impulse
ström|t *a4, end. i n, ~ vatten* rapid-flowing water **-virvel** whirl[pool], eddy
ströp *imperf. av strypa*
ströppla *fack.* stipple
strö|skrift pamphlet, tract **-socker** granulated (castor) sugar
strössel ['ströss-] *s9, s7, ej pl, fack.* hundreds and thousands *(pl)*
ströv|a stroll, ramble; wander; *vard.* troll; *(~ hit o. dit)* stray; *~ omkring* range, rove; *~nde renar* stray reindeer **-område** rambling area **-tåg** ramble, excursion; *pl äv.* wanderings; *bildl.* excursion
1 stubb *se* rubb [*och* stubb]
2 stubb *s2 (av säd e.d.)* stubble; *(skägg-)* bristles *(pl)*
stubb|a crop *(håret* the hair); dock *(svansen på en hund* a dog's tail) **-brytare** *(hopskr. stubbrytare)* [stump] grubber (puller) **-brytning** *(hopskr. stubbrytning)* stump pulling
stubb|e *s2* stump, stub **-ig** *a1* stubbed, stubb[l]y **-svans** bobtail, docked tail **-åker** stubble field
stu'bin *s3,* **-tråd** fuse
stuck *s3* stucco **-atur** stucco [work] **-atör** stucco worker, stuccoer
stuck|en *a5, bildl.* nettled, offended **-it** *sup. av* sticka II
student [university, college] student, undergraduate; *ta ~en* qualify for entrance to a university **-betyg** higher school certificate; *Storbritannien* General Certificate of Education at Advanced level (A level) **-bostad** room in [student] hall of residence, student flat **-examen** higher school examination; *Storbritan-*

S

nien [examination for the] General Certificate of Education at Advanced level *(förk.* G.C.E. at A level) **-förening** student association **-hem** students' hostel; *AE.* dorm[itory] **-ikos** [-'kå:s] *a1* student-like; carefree, high-spirited **-kamrat** fellow student **-kår** students' union **-liv** university (college) life **-mössa** student's cap **-rabatt** student reduction **-revolt** student uprising **-rum** room in [student] hall of residence **-ska** girl student; undergraduate; *AE. vard. äv.* co-ed **-skrivning** written examination for entrance to a university

studer|a study *(språk* languages; *till läkare* to be a doctor); *~ medicin (äv.)* be a student of medicine; *~ juridik* study (read) law; *låta sina barn ~* let one's children go to college (the university); *~ vid universitetet* study (be) at the university, go to college; *en ~d karl* a scholar, a man with a university education **-ande I** *s9* student *(vid* at); *(vid univ. o. högskola)* undergraduate; *(skolelev)* pupil; *ekonomie ~* student of economics; *juris ~* law student, student of law; *medicine ~* medical student; *odontologie ~* dental surgery student; *teknologie ~* student of engineering (technology); *teologie ~* divinity student, student of theology (divinity) **II** *a4, den ~ ungdomen* schoolboys and schoolgirls, [the] young people at college (the university) **-kammare** study

studie ['stu:-] *s5* study *(över, av* of); *(konstnärs äv.)* sketch *(av* of); *(litterär)* essay *(över* on) **-begåvning** aptitude for studies; *han är en ~* he is a gifted student **-besök** [educational (study)] visit **-cirkel** adult education class, study circle **-dag** teachers' seminar **-finansiering** study support **-grupp** workshop **-handbok** guide for students **-intyg** proof of registration **-kurs** course of studies **-ledare** leader of a study circle **-ledighet** study (educational) leave **-lån** study loan **-material** study material **-medel** study support **-objekt** object of study **-plan** plan of studies, curriculum; *(för visst ämne)* syllabus **-rektor** *ung.* director of studies **-resa** study trip **-rådgivare** educational adviser **-rådgivning** educational guidance **-skuld** study debt, debt incurred for higher education **-stöd** study support **-stödsnämnd** *centrala ~en* [the Swedish] national board for educational assistance **-syfte** *i ~* for purposes of study **-teknik** study technique **-år** *pl* years of study

studio ['stu:-] *s5* studio **studiosus** [-ˣɷ:-, -ˣå:-] *r* student

studi|um ['stu:-] *s4* study; *bli föremål för ett ingående ~* be the subject of close study; *bedriva -er* study; *lärda -er* advanced studies; *musikaliska -er* the study *(sg)* of music; *vetenskapliga -er* scientific research

studs [stuts] *s2* rebound, bounce **studsa** rebound, bounce *(mot väggen* off the wall); *(om kula)* ricochet; *bildl.* start, be taken aback **studsare** sporting rifle

studs|matta trampoline **-ning** rebounding *etc.*; repercussion

stug|a *s1* cottage; *(vardagsrum)* living room **-by** holiday village **-knut** cottage corner **-sittare** home-body

1 stuka *s1* potato *(etc.)* clamp

2 stuka *v1* **1** *(kroppsdel)* sprain **2** *(deformera)* batter, knock out of shape; *bildl.* browbeat, crush, humiliate **3** *tekn.* upset, jump

stukning [-u:-] **1** spraining; *en ~* a sprain **2** battering *etc.;* browbeating, humiliation **3** upsetting

stul|en *perf. part. av stjäla* **-it** *sup. av stjäla*

stulta *v1 (om barn)* toddle

stum [stumm] *a1* **1** dumb; *(mållös)* mute *(beundran* admiration); *(som inte uttalas)* silent, mute; *~ av förvåning* dumb with astonishment; *bli ~* be struck dumb *(av* with) **2** *(ej fjädrande)* rigid **-film** silent film **-fin** *~ linje (boktr.)* obtuse (blunt) line **-het** dumbness; muteness

stump *s2* stump, [tag] end; *sjunga en ~* sing a tune **stumpa** *s1* toddler; poppet

stund *s3* while; *(ögonblick)* moment, instant, minute; *(eg. timme)* hour; *en god ~* quite a while; *det dröjde en ~ innan* it was some little time before; *en liten ~* a few minutes, a short while; *han har sina ljusa ~er* he has his bright moments; *när ~en är kommen* when one's hour has come; *min sista ~* my last hour; *från första ~[en]* from the [very] first moment; *för en ~ sedan* a [little] while (few minutes) ago; *i denna ~* [at] this [very] moment; *ännu i denna ~ vet jag inte* I don't know to this [very] moment; *i farans ~* in the hour of danger; *i samma ~* at the same moment *(som* when); *i sista ~[en]* at the [very] last moment, just in time; *om en liten ~* in a little while, presently; *på lediga ~er* in one's spare (leisure) moments; *adjö på en ~!* so long!

stund|a approach, be at hand **-ande** *a4 (nästkommande)* next; *(in-)* coming **-ligen** constantly **-om** [-åm] at times; *se äv. ibland* **-tals** [-a:-] now and then; at intervals

stungit *sup. av stinga*

stup *s7* precipice, steep **stupa** **1** *(falla omkull)* fall; *hästen ~de under honom* his horse went down under him; *~ i säng* tumble into bed; *~ på en uppgift (bildl.)* fail in a task; *jag var nära att ~ av trötthet* I was ready to drop [with fatigue], was tired to death **2** *(i strid)* fall, die, be killed; *de ~de (subst.)* the killed (fallen) **3** *(brant sänka sig)* descend abruptly, incline sharply **4** *(luta)* tip *(en balja* a tub)

stup|full reeling drunk **-rör** drainpipe **-stock** block

sturig *a1* sullen, sulky

stursk *a1 (uppstudsig)* insolent, impudent; *(fräck)* brazen; *(högfärdig)* stuck-up; *vara ~ (äv.)* give o.s. airs, show off **-het** insolence; bumptiousness

stuss *s2* seat; *vard.* bottom, behind

stut *s2* steer **-eri** stud [farm]

stuv *s2* remnant [of cloth]; *~ar (äv.)* oddments

1 stuva *kokk.* cook in white sauce; *~d potatis* potatoes in white sauce

2 stuva *(inlasta)* stow; *(kol, säd äv.)* trim; *~ om* shift, rearrange; *~ undan* stow away

stuvare stevedore, longshoreman

stuvbit *se stuv*

stuveri|arbetare *se stuvare* **-förman** stevedore's foreman

1 stuvning [-u:-] *(kött-)* stew; *(vit sås)* white

sauce
2 stuvning [-u:-] (*inlastning*) stowage, stowing
stybb *s3, s4* coal dust; *sport.* cinders (*pl*)
styck *oböjligt* s piece; *per* ~ each, a piece; *1 krona* [*per*] ~ 1 krona each (a piece); *kostnad per* ~ piece cost, cost each; *pris per* ~ price each
stycka 1 *slaktar.* cut up **2** (*uppdela*) divide up; (~ *sönder*) cut into pieces; ~ *till tomter* parcel out in plots
stycke *s6* **1** (*bit, del*) piece (*bröd* of bread); (*avsnitt*) part; (*lösryckt*) fragment; *ett* ~ *land* a piece of land; *bestå av ett enda* ~ consist of one single piece; *jag har hunnit ett bra* ~ I have made considerable progress (*på* with); *i ett* ~ all [in] one piece, all of a piece; *slå i* ~*n* smash, knock to pieces **2** (*avdelning*) part, section (*av en bok* of a book); (*ställe*) passage; (*i skrift*) paragraph; (*musik-*) piece [of music]; (*teater-*) play; *tredje* ~*t nedifrån* third paragraph from below; *sjunga ett* ~ sing a song; *valda* ~*n* selected pieces (passages) **3** (*hänseende*) respect, regard; *i många* ~*n* in many respects **4** (*exemplar*) piece; specimen, *vi var tio* ~*n* we were ten, there were ten of us; *kan jag få tio* ~*n* may I have ten; *ett par* ~*n* a couple of; *en tjugo, trettio* ~*n* twenty, thirty or so **5** (*väg*) way; (*sträcka*) distance; *det är bara ett litet* ~ *dit* it is only a short distance, it is not far from here; *ett gott* ~ *in på nästa år* well on into next year **6** (*neds. om kvinna*) *elakt* ~ nasty piece of work; *lättfärdigt* ~ trollop **-bruk** gun foundry (factory) **-gods** (*t. sjöss*) general (mixed) cargo; (*t. lands*) part loads; *järnv.* part-load traffic, parcels (*pl*) **-pris** price each (a piece, per unit) **-vis** (*per styck*) by the piece; (*en efter en*) piece by piece, piecemeal
styckjunkare *mil.* sergeant-major of artillery; *AE.* warrant officer
styck|mästare *slaktar.* butcher **-ning 1** cutting up **2** dividing up; partition; (*sönderdelning*) dismemberment
styckvis se styckevis
stygg *al* bad, wicked; (*om barn*) naughty; (*otäck*) nasty, ugly **-else** abomination **-het** wickedness; naughtiness **-ing** naughty (nasty) thing
stygn [-ŋn] *s7* stitch; *sy med långa* ~ tack
stylt|a *sl* stilt; *gå på* -*or* walk on stilts
stymp|a maim, mutilate; (*friare o. bildl.*) mangle; (*förvanska text e.d.*) mutilate; *geom.* truncate; ~*d kon* (*äv.*) frustum of a cone **-are** (*klåpare*) bungler **-ning** maiming *etc.*, mutilation; truncation
1 styng *s7, sömn.,* se stygn
2 styng *s7,* se sting
3 styng *s7* (*insekt*) botfly
styr *r, hålla* ~ *på, hålla i* ~ keep in order (in check); *hålla sig i* ~ keep a hold on o.s., restrain o.s.; *över* ~, se överstyr
styr|a *v2* **1** (*föra*) steer (*ett fartyg* a ship; *en bil* a car), (*fartyg äv.*) navigate; (*stå vid rodret*) be at the helm; ~ *i hamn* bring into port **2** (*rikta*) direct (*sina steg* one's steps); (*leda*) guide; (*behärska*) control, dominate; ~ *sina begär* control one's desires; ~ *sin tunga* curb

one's tongue; ~ *sig* control (master) o.s.; ~ *allt till det bästa* arrange things for the best, see things through **3** (*bestämma över*) govern, rule (*landet* the country); ~ *och ställa i huset* manage the house; ~ *och ställa som man vill* have a free hand, *vard.* be cock of the roost **4** *språkv.* govern (*genitiv* the genitive) **5** (*med betonad partikel*) ~ *om* (*bildl.*) see to (about); ~ *om att* see to it that; *det skall jag* ~ *om* I will see to it that; ~ *till, se ställa* [*till*]; ~ *till sig get* [o.s.] into a mess; *vad du har* -*t till dig!* what a fright you look!; ~ *ut från land* stand off shore; ~ *ut till sjöss* make for the open sea; ~ *ut sig* dress up
styr|ande *a4* governing (*myndighet* body); *de* ~ those in power, *vard.* the powers that be **-bar** *al* steerable, dirigible **-bord** ['sty:r-] *s,* böjligt *endast i genitiv, sjö.* starboard; *för* ~*s halsar* on the starboard tack **-bordslanterna** starboard light
styre *s6* **1** (*fartygs*) helm; (*-stång*) handlebar[s *pl*] **2** rule; *sitta vid* ~*t* be in power (at the helm)
styrelse 1 *abstr.* government; administration, regime **2** *konkr.* (*bolags-*) board [of directors]; (*förenings-*) council, committee; *sitta i* ~*n* be on the board **-berättelse** annual report, report of the board **-ledamot** director, member of the board (council, committee); *han är* ~ *i* he is on the board [of directors] of **-ordförande** chairman of the board (committee) **-sammanträde** board (committee) meeting **-sätt** system (form) of government
sty'renplast polystyrene
styr|esman governor; (*föreståndare*) director **-fart** *sjö.* steerage-way **-förmåga** manoeuvrability **-hytt** *sjö.* pilot house, wheelhouse **-inrättning** steering gear
styrk|a I *sl* **1** strength (*hos, i* of); (*kropps- äv.*) vigour; (*kraft*) power; force; (*intensitet*) intensity; *den råa* ~*n* brute force; *med hela sin* ~ with all one's strength; *har aldrig varit min* ~ has never been my strong point; *pröva sin* ~ *på* try one's strength on; *vinna* ~ gain strength, (*om sak*) gain [in] force **2** (*krigs-, arbetar-*) force; (*numerär*) number[s *pl*]; *väpnad* ~ armed force **II** *v3* **1** (*stärka*) strengthen, confirm; (*ge* ~) fortify; -*t av mat och dryck* fortified with food and drink **2** (*bevisa*) prove, give proof of; (*med vittne*) attest, verify; (*bekräfta*) confirm; -*t avskrift* attested copy
styrke|demonstration display of [military] power **-förhållande** *ett ojämnt* ~ uneven odds **-grad** [degree of] strength **-tår** bracer, pick-me-up
styr|man ['sty:r-] mate; *förste* ~ first mate (officer) **-medel** instrument[s] of control **-ning** [-y:-] steering; (*manövrering*) operation control; (*ledning*) management **-organ** *flyg.* controls (*pl*); *data.* control unit **-sel** ['styrr-] *s9* (*stadga*) firmness; *bildl.* stability **-skena** guide rail **-snäcka** steering box **-spak** steering lever; *flyg.* control column **-spindel** steering knuckle **-stång** (*på cykel*) handlebar **-teori** control theory **-växel** steering gear **-åra** steering oar
styv *al* **1** (*stel*) stiff (*i lederna* in the joints); (*spänd*) tight, rigid (*fjäder* spring); ~ *bris* stiff

S

breeze; *visa sig på ~a linan* (*bildl.*) show off; *~ i korken* (*vard.*) cocky, snooty **2** *en ~ timme* a good hour; *ett ~t arbete* (*tungt*) a stiff (tough, hard) job **3** (*skicklig*) clever (*i* in, at), good (*i* at); capital (*simmare* swimmer); *~ i engelska* good at English

styv|barn stepchild **-bror** stepbrother **-dotter** stepdaughter

styver ['sty:-] *s9, s2* stiver; farthing; *hålla på ~n* stick to one's cash, be tightfisted

styv|far stepfather **-förälder** step-parent

styv|hala *sjö.* haul taut **-het** [-y:-] stiffness *etc.*

styv|moderlig stepmotherly; (*friare*) grudging, unfair (*behandling* treatment) **-mor** stepmother **-morsviol** wild pansy, heartsease, *AE.* Johnny-jump-up

styv|na [-y:-] stiffen, become (get, grow) stiff **-nackad** *a5, bildl.* obstinate **-sint** *a1* obstinate, headstrong, stubborn **-sinthet** obstinacy, stubbornness

styv|son stepson **-syskon** stepbrothers and stepsisters **-syster** stepsister

styvt [-y:-] *adv* **1** stiffly *etc.*; *hålla ~ på a*) (*ngt*) insist [up]on, *b*) (*ngn*) se great store by, think a lot of **2** (*duktigt*) *det var ~ gjort!* well done!

stå *stod stått* **I 1** *eg.* stand [up]; *han har redan lärt sig ~* he has already learnt to stand; *han stod hela tiden* he stood (was standing [up]) the whole time; *det ~r en stol där* there is a chair [standing] there; *få ~* (*inte sitta*) have to stand; *låta ngn ~* (*inte sitta*) let s.b. stand [up]; *~ ostadigt* wobble, (*om sak äv.*) be shaky (rickety); *~ stilla* keep still, not move; *tornet ~r ännu* the tower is still standing; *kom som du går och ~!* come just as you are! *~ och vänta* stand (be) waiting; *~ inte där och se dum ut!* don't stand there looking foolish! **2** (*vara*) be, stand; (*vara placerad*) be placed; (*ha sin plats*) be kept; (*äga bestånd*) remain, last, exist; (*vara skrivet*) be written; *grinden ~r öppen* the gate is open; *maten ~r och kallnar* the food is getting cold; *hans liv stod inte att rädda* his life couldn't be saved; *låta ngt ~* (*inte flytta*) leave, (*inte röra*) leave alone, (*om ord e.d.*) keep; *han ~r som ägare till* he is the owner of; *~ ensam i livet* be alone in the world; *det ~r dig fritt att* you are free (at liberty) to; *~ som objekt till* function (act) as the object of; *det kommer att ~ dig dyrt* you'll pay for this; *nu ~r vi där vackert!* now we are in a fix!; *~ som ett levande frågetecken* look the picture of bewilderment; *hur ~r det?* (*sport.*) what is the score?; *det ~r 6—4* the score (it) is six four; *var skall tallrikarna ~?* where do the plates go?; *så länge världen ~r* as long as the world remains (lasts); *det ~r i Bibeln* it says in the Bible, the Bible says; *vad ~r det i tidningen?* what's in the paper?; *det ~r Brown på dörren* there is Brown on the door; *orten ~r inte på kartan* the place is not marked on the map; *läsa vad som ~r om* read what is written about; *var ~r den dikten?* where is that poem to be found? **3** (*inte vara i gång*) *klocka ~r* the clock has stopped; *klockan har ~tt sedan i morse* the clock has not been going since this morning; *maskinerna ~r stilla* the engines are (stand) idle; *hur länge ~r tåget här?* how

long will the train stop (wait) here?; *affärerna* (*fabriken*) *~r stilla* business (the factory) is at a standstill; *mitt förstånd ~r stilla* I just can't think [any more] **4** (*äga rum*) take place; (*om slag*) be fought; *när skall bröllopet ~?* when is the wedding to be?; *bröllopet stod i dagarna tre* the wedding went on for three days; *slaget vid Brännkyrka stod år 1518* the battle of Brännkyrka was fought in 1518 **5** *~ sitt kast* take the consequences; *~ risken* run the risk, chance it **II** *rfl* **1** (*hålla sig*) keep; *mjölken ~r sig inte till i morgon* the milk won't keep until tomorrow; *målningen har ~tt sig bra* the paint has worn well; *det vackra vädret ~r sig* the fine weather will last **2** (*klara sig*) manage; *~ sig bra i konkurrensen* hold one's own in competition; *vi ~r oss på några smörgåsar a few sandwiches will keep us going; *vi ~r oss till middagen* we can do (manage) until dinner **III** (*med obetonad prep*) **1** *det är ingenting att ~ efter* (*eftertrakta*) that is not worth while; *~ efter ngns liv* seek a p.'s life **2** *~ för a*) (*ansvara för*) be responsible (answer) for, *b*) (*sköta*) be in charge of, *c*) (*innebära*) represent, stand for; *~ för betalningen* pay; *~ för dörren* (*bildl.*) be approaching (imminent); *~ för följderna* take the consequences; *~ för vad man säger* stand by what one has said; *det yttrandet får ~ för honom* if he has said so, he'll have to stand by it **3** *~ i affär* work in a shop; *~ i blom* be in bloom; *~ i förbindelse med* be in touch with; *~ i genitiv* be in the genitive; *~ i ljuset för ngn* stand in a p.'s light; *~ i tur* be next; *~ i vatten till fotknölarna* be up to one's ankles in water; *~ i vägen för ngn* be in a p.'s way; *aktierna ~r i 100 kronor* the shares are quoted at 100 kronor; *ha mycket att ~ i* have many things to attend to **4** *företaget ~r och faller med honom* the venture (business) stands or falls with him **5** *valet ~r mellan* the choice lies between **6** *klänningen ~r vackert mot hennes hår* the dress goes well with her hair; *uppgift ~r mot uppgift* one statement contradicts the other **7** *~ på benen* stand on one's legs, (*~ upp*) stand [up]; *~ på egna ben* stand on one's own feet; *det får ~ på framtiden* we must let the matter rest for the time being; *~ på näsan* fall on one's face; *~ på sin rätt* stand on one's rights; *barometern ~r på regn* the barometer is pointing to rain; *termometern ~r på noll* the thermometer is at zero **8** *hoppet ~r till* my (*etc.*) hope is in; *~ till förfogande* be available (at disposal); *~ till svars för* be held responsible for; *vattnet ~r mig till knäna* the water comes up to my knees **9** *~ under förmyndare* be under guardianship, have a guardian **10** *det ~r mig upp i halsen* I'm fed up to the teeth with it **11** *~ vid sitt ord* stand by (stick to) one's word **IV** (*med betonad partikel*) **1** *~ bakom* (*stödja*) be behind, support, (*ekonomiskt*) sponsor **2** *~ bi a*) (*räcka till*) last, hold out, *b*) (*stödja*) support **3** *~ efter a*) (*komma efter*) come after, follow, *b*) (*bli förbigången*) be passed over (*för ngn* by s.b.); *låta ngt ~ efter för ngt annat* let s.th. be neglected in favour of s.th. else **4** *~ emot, se motstå* **5** *~ fast* be firm; *~ fast vid* stand by **6** *~ framme* *(framtagen e.d.)* be out (ready), *(t. påseende)* be displayed, *(skräpa)* be [left] about **7** ~ *för (skymma)* stand in front of; *det ~r för mig att* I have an idea that **8** ~ *i (knoga)* work hard, keep at it; *arbeta och* ~ *i* be busy working **9** *jag lät pengarna* ~ *inne på banken* I left the money on deposit **10** ~ *kvar (förbli stående)* remain standing, *(stanna)* remain, stay **11** ~ *på (vara påkopplad)* be on; *det stod inte länge på förrän* it was not long before; *vinden stod på hela dagen* the wind blew all day; *fartyget ~r hårt på* the ship is fast aground; ~ *på sig (hävda sig)* hold one's own, *(inte ge vika)* be firm; ~ *på dig!* don't give in!; *vad ~r på?* what's going on? **12** *hur ~r det till?* how are you?; *hur ~r det till hemma?* how is your family?; *det ~r illa till med henne* she is in a bad way; *så ~r det till [med den saken]* that is how matters stand; *det här ~r inte rätt till* there is something the matter with this; *de åt så det stod härliga till* they were eating like anything **13** *han fick alltid* ~ *tillbaka för sin bror* he was always pushed into the background by his brother **14** ~ *upp, se uppstå* **15** ~ *ut a) (skjuta ut)* stand out, project, protrude, *b) (härda ut)* stand (put up with) it; ~ *ut med* stand, bear, put up with **16** ~ *över a) (i rang)* be above [in rank], *(vara överlägsen)* be superior *(ngn* to s.b.), *b) (hålla efter)* stand above, *c) (vänta)* wait *(till till), d) (i spel)* pass [one's turn], miss a turn

stående I *a4* standing; *(stilla-)* stationary *(bil* car); *bli* ~ *a) (bli kvar)* remain standing, *b) (stanna)* stop, come to a standstill; ~ *armé (skämt)* standing (army) joke; *en* ~ *rätt på matsedeln* a standing dish on the menu; *ett* ~ *uttryck* a stock phrase; *de närmast* ~ those immediately around him *(etc.)*; *på* ~ *fot* offhand **II** *s6* standing position; *~t blev tröttsamt* having to stand was tiring

ståhej [-'hejj] *s7* hullabaloo, fuss

stål *s7* steel **-band** steel strip (tape) **-blank** [as] bright as steel **-borste** wire brush **-fjäder** steel spring **-grå** steel[y] grey **-hjälm** steel helmet **-kant** steel edge **-klädd** steel clad **-konstruktion** steel structure **-lina** steel rope (wire, cable) **-penna** [pen] nib **-plåt** steel plate, sheet steel **-rör** steel tube **-sätta** *bildl.* steel, brace; ~ *sig* brace (harden) o.s. **-tråd** [steel] wire **-trådsnät** wire netting **-ull** steel wool (shavings *pl)* **-verk** steelworks *(sg o. pl)*

stånd *s7, i bet. 6 -et ständer* **1** *(skick)* state, condition; *(gott ~)* repair, keeping; *få till* ~ bring about; *komma till* ~ come (be brought) about, be realized; *sätta i* ~ *a) (ngt)* put in order, *b) (ngn)* put in a position, enable; *sätta ngn ur* ~ make s.b. incapable *(att tala* of speaking), make s.b. unfit *(att arbeta* for work); *sätta ngt ur* ~ damage s.th., put s.th. out of order; *vara i* ~ *till* be able *(att arbeta* to work), be capable *(att arbeta* of working); *vara ur* ~ *att* be unable to **2** *(ställning)* stand; *hålla* ~ hold one's ground, hold out; *hålla* ~ *mot* resist **3** *(salubod)* stall, booth **4** *(planta)* stand **5** *(levnadsställning)* station, status; *ogift* ~ unmarried state; *äkta ~et* the married state; *inträda i det äkta ~et* enter into matrimony **6**

(samhällsklass) rank, class; *(andligt* spiritual) estate; *gifta sig under sitt* ~ marry beneath one['s station]; *de fyra ~en* the four Estates **7** *vard. (erektion)* hard-on; *få* ~ *(äv.)*

stånd|a *se stå* **-aktig** *a1* steadfast, stable; *vara* ~ *(äv.)* stand firm, persevere **-aktighet** steadfastness, stability; perseverance

ståndar|e 1 *(stöd)* standard, upright **2** *bot.* stamen *(pl äv.* stamina) **-knapp** anther **-mjöl** pollen

stånd|punkt standpoint, position; *bildl.* point of view; *välja* ~ take up a position (an attitude); *ändra* ~ take up another position (attitude), revise one's opinion; *stå på en hög* ~ be at a very high level; *på sakernas nuvarande* ~ in the present state of things, as matters stand now **-rätt** *mil.* martial law

stånds|cirkulation movement of persons from one social class to another **-mässig** *a1* consistent with one's station [in life] **-person** person of rank **-riksdag** Diet of the Four Estates **-samhälle** *ung.* class society

stång *-en stänger* **1** *(tjock)* pole, staff; *(tunnare)* bar, rod; *(stift)* stick; *hålla ngn ~en (bildl.)* hold one's own against s.b.; *flagga på halv* ~ fly the flag [at] half-mast **2** *sjö.* pole, spar **3** *(i betsel)* bar **stånga** butt; *(spetsa på hornen)* toss [on the horns] **stångas** *dep* butt; *(stånga varandra)* butt each other

stångjärn bar (rod) iron

stångjärns|hammare tilt [hammer] **-smedja** ironworks forge **-smide** hammered iron

stång|korv sausage of barley and meat **-krok** *(fiskeredskap)* ledger tackle **-piska** queue **-störtning** *sport.* tossing the

1 stånka *s1* tankard

2 stånka *v1* puff and blow; *(stöna)* groan

stånkande *a4* puffing and blowing; groaning

ståplats standing room **-läktare** stand with standing accommodation

ståt *s3* splendour, grandeur; *med stor* ~ with great pomp, in great style **ståta** parade; ~ *med* make a great display of, show off

ståthållare governor

ståtlig [-å:-] *a1 (praktfull)* magnificent, grand; *(imponerande)* impressive *(byggnad* edifice); stately *(hållning* bearing); *en* ~ *karl* a fine--looking fellow

stått *sup. av stå*

stå'uppkomiker stand-up comedian

stäcka *v3* clip; *bildl.* foil, thwart, *(ngns planer* a p.'s plans)

städ *s7* anvil *(äv. anat.)*

städ|a *(göra rent)* clean, AE. *vard.* fix up *(en våning* a flat); *(ställa i ordning)* put things straight *(på skrivbordet* on the desk); *(ha storstädning i)* clean out; ~ *efter* tidy up after; ~ *efter sig* leave things tidy; ~ *undan* put away (out of the way); ~ *åt ngn* clean for s.b. **städad** *a5* tidy; *(proper)* decent, proper; *(om pers. äv.)* well-behaved

städ|are cleaner **-bolag** cleaning company (agency) **-dille** cleaning mania **-erska** charwoman, cleaning-woman; *(kontors-)* cleaner **-hjälp** charwoman, daily help

städja [-ä:-] *stadde statt* engage, hire

städ|ning [-ä:-] cleaning; tidying [up] *etc.*; char-

ring **-rock** overall; *AE.* smock
städse [-ä:-] always; constantly
städ|skrubb, -skåp broom cupboard
städsla [-ä:-] *se städja*
ställ *s7* **1** (*stöd*) rack, stand **2** (*omgång*) set
ställ|a I *v2* **1** (*placera*) put; place; set; (~ *upprätt*) place (set) upright, stand **2** (*sätta på visst sätt*) set right; (*inställa*) adjust, regulate (*instrument* instruments), set (*klockan på två* the clock at two) **3** (*rikta*) direct (*sina steg* one's steps); (*adressera*) address; ~ *anspråk på* make demands on; ~ *en fråga till* put a question to; ~ *problem under debatt* bring problems up for discussion; ~ *ngt på framtiden* let s.th. rest for the time being **4** (*lämna*) give (*borgen security*) **5** (*med prep uttryck*) ~ *i ordning* put in order (to rights); ~ *i skuggan* put in the shade, *bildl. äv.* obscure, overshadow; ~ *ngn inför rätta* commit s.b. for trail; ~*s inför frågan om* be faced with the question whether; ~ *ngn mot väggen* (*bildl.*) drive s.b. into a corner; ~ *stora förväntningar på* have great expectations of; ~ *ngn till ansvar för* hold s.b. responsible for; ~ *ngt till rätta* put (set) s.th. right **II** (*med betonad partikel*) **1** ~ *bort* put aside (down) **2** ~ *fram* put forward (*äv. klocka*); ~ *fram stolar åt* place chairs for **3** ~ *ifrån sig, se* ~ *bort* **4** ~ *in radion* tune in (*på en annan station* another station; *på program 3* to the third program); ~ *in i ett skåp* put into a cupboard; ~ *in sig på att* make up one's mind to **5** ~ *om a)* [re]adjust (*sin klocka* one's watch), *b)* (*ordna*) see about (to), arrange **6** ~ *till* arrange (*kalas* a party); ~ *till en scen* make a scene; *vad har han nu -t till?* what has he been up to now?; *så ni har -t till!* what a mess you have made [of it (things)]! **7** ~ *tillbaka* put back, replace (*i skåpet* in the cupboard) **8** ~ *undan* put away **9** ~ *upp a)* (*ställa högre*) put up, (*resa*) raise (*en stege mot väggen* a ladder against the wall), *b)* (*ordna*) arrange (*i en lång rad* in a long file), *mil.* draw up, *c)* (*deltaga*) take part, join in, (*låta deltaga*) put up; ~ *upp sig* form up, get into position; ~ *upp på linje* line up **10** ~ *upp för ngn* stand by s.o.; ~ *upp på ngn* back s.o. **11** ~ *ut* put out; ~ *ut på en mässa* exhibit goods at a fair; ~ *ut en växel på* make out (draw) a draft (bill) on **III** *rfl* **1** (*placera sig*) place (station) o.s. (*i vägen för ngn* in a p.'s way); stand (*framför* in front of; *på tå* on tiptoe; *på en stol* on a chair); ~ *sig i rad* line up; ~ *sig in hos ngn* curry favour with s.b.; ~ *sig på ngns sida* side (take sides) with s.b. **2** (*bete sig*) behave (conduct) o.s.; (*låtsas*) feign (*sjuk* illness); ~ *sig avvaktande* take up a wait-and-see attitude; *inte veta hur man skall* ~ *sig* not know what attitude to take; *det -er sig dyrt* it is (will be) expensive; *hur -er du dig till ...?* what is your attitude towards ...?
ställbar *a1* adjustable
ställ|d *a5* **1** placed *etc.*; *ha det gott -t* be well off; *en växel* ~ *på* a bill (draft) payable to **2** (*svarslös*) nonplussed; at a loss
ställ|e *s6* (*plats, rum*) place; ('*fläck*') spot; (*i skrift*) passage; *på* ~*t a*) eg. in (at) the place, *b*) (*genast*) on the spot, there and then; *på* ~*t marsch!* mark time!; *på* ~*t vila!* stand at ease!;

på annat ~ in (at) another place, somewhere else; *på ngt* ~ somewhere; *på ort och* ~ on the spot; *på rätt* ~ in the right place; *lägga ngt på rätt* ~ put s.th. in its proper place; *på vissa* (*sina*) ~*n* in some places, here and there **2** *i* ~*t* instead [of it], (*i dess* ~) in place of it (that); *i* ~*t för* instead of (*att komma* coming); *sätta ngt i* ~*t för* substitute s.th. for, replace s.th. with; *om jag vore i ditt* ~ if I were you; *upptaga ngn i barns* ~ adopt s.b.; *vara ngn i mors ställe* be a mother to s.b.
ställföreträd|ande *a4* acting, deputy, assistant; ~ *lidande* vicarious suffering **-are** deputy, proxy, substitute; *vara* ~ *för* deputize
ställning 1 (*sätt att stå etc.*) position (*äv. mil.*); (*läge*) situation; (*inställning*) attitude; (*social position*) status, standing; (*samlags-*) position; *sport.* core; *ekonomisk* ~ financial position; *liggande* ~ lying (recumbent) position; *statsrättslig* ~ [constitutional] status; *tillbakalutad* ~ recumbence, recumbency; *underordnad* ~ subordinate position; *i ledande* ~ in a key (leading) position; *ta* ~ *till* decide on, consider, make a decision on **2** *konkr.* stand; (*byggnads-*) scaffold[ing]; (*stomme*) frame
ställnings|krig positional war[fare] **-steg** *göra* ~ stand at attention **-tagande** *s6* attitude (*till* to); decision; *vårt* ~ our standpoint
ställverk *järnv.* signal box (cabin); *elektr.* bridge signal cabin
stäm|band [˟stämm-] vocal cord
stäm|d *a5* (*vänligt* favourably) disposed (inclined) (*mot* towards); *avogt* ~ *mot* prejudiced against **-gaffel** tuning fork
stämjärn [˟stämm-] [wood] chisel
1 stämm|a I *s1* **1** (*röst*) voice; *mus.* part; *första* ~*n* the first (leading, principal) part **2** (*röstträtt*) vote; *ha säte och* ~ *i* have a seat and a vote in **II** *v2* **1** *mus.* tune; pitch (*högre* higher); ~ *högre* (*äv.*) *lägre* (*äv.*) deepen; ~ *upp en sång* strike up a song **2** *bildl., det -er* [*sinnet*] *till eftertanke* it gives you s.th. to think about; *jfr äv. stämd* **3** (*passa ihop, överens-*) agree, accord, tally; *AE. äv.* check; ~ *med originalet* be in accordance with the original; *kassan -er* the cash account balances; *räkenskaperna -er inte* there are discrepancies in the accounts; *räkningen -er* the account is correct; *det -er!* quite right!, that's it!; ~ *av* (*bokför.*) tick off, balance; ~ *överens* agree, accord
2 stämma *v2* (*hejda*) stem, check; ~ *blod* sta[u]nch blood; *det är bättre att* ~ *i bäcken än i ån* it is better to nip it in the bud
3 stämma I *s1* (*sammankomst*) meeting, assembly **II** *v2* **1** *jur.* bring an action against, sue; ~ *ngn som vittne* summon s.b. as a witness **2** ~ *möte med ngn* arrange to meet s.b.
1 stämning 1 *mus.* pitch, key, tune; *hålla* ~*en* keep in tune **2** (*sinnestillstånd*) mood, temper; *en festlig* ~ a festive atmosphere; ~*en var hög* (*tryckt*) spirits (*pl*) ran high (were depressed); ~*en bland folket* (*äv.*) public sentiment; *upprörd* ~ agitation, excitement; *komma* (*vara*) *i* ~ get (be) in the right mood
2 stämning *jur.* writ, [writ of] summons; *delge ngn en* ~ serve a writ (summons) on s.b.; *ta ut* ~ *mot* cause a summons to be issued against,

sue
stämningsansökan application for a summons, plaint
stämnings|bild lyrical (sentimental) picture **-full** full of feeling; moving; solemn **-människa** spontaneous person
stämpel *s2* **1** (*verktyg*) stamp, punch; (*mynt-*) die **2** (*avtryck*) stamp (*äv. bildl.*); (*på frimärke*) postmark, cancel; (*guld-, silver-*) hallmark (*äv. bildl.*); (*på varor e.d.*) brand, mark **-avgift** stamp duty (tax) **-dyna** stamp pad **-färg** stamp[ing] (marking) ink **-klocka** time clock **-skatt** stamp duty (tax)
1 stämpla (*med stämpel*) stamp; mark, impress (*äv. bildl.*); (*guld, silver*) hallmark; (*post-*) postmark, cancel; (*skog*) blaze; (*med brännjärn*) brand (*äv. bildl.*)
2 stämpla (*konspirera*) plot, conspire
1 stämpling (*t. 1 stämpla*) stamping *etc.*
2 stämpling (*t. 2 stämpla*) ~*ar* conspiracy, plotting (*sg*), machinations
stäm|skruv [ˣstämm-] peg **-ton** concert pitch
ständer ['stänn-] *pl, se stånd 6*
ständig *a1* permanent (*sekreterare* secretary); constant (*oro* worry); perpetual; ~ *ledamot* life-member; ~*t utskott* standing committee
stäng|a *v2* shut (*dörren* the door); close; (*med lås*) lock; (*med regel*) bolt; (*med bom*) bar; (*hindra*) bar, obstruct (*utsikten* the view); *vi -er kl. 5* we close at five; ~ *butiken* shut up shop; ~ *dörren efter sig* shut the door behind one; ~ *sin dörr för* close one's door to; *dörren -er sig själv* the door shuts by (of) itself; ~ *en fabrik* shut down (close) a factory; ~ *av, se avstänga*; ~ *igen om sig* shut (lock) o.s. in; ~ *in sig* shut o.s. up; ~ *sig inne på sitt rum* keep (lock o.s. up in) one's room; ~ *till* close, shut [up], lock [up]; ~ *ute* keep (shut) out (*ljuset* the light); ~ *ngn ute* shut s.b. out
stängel *s2* stalk, stem; (*bladlös*) scape
stäng|ning shutting, closing *etc.* **-ningsdags, -ningstid** closing time
stängsel ['stäng-] *s7* fence; (*räcke*) rail[ing]; enclosure; *bildl.* bar, barrier **-tråd** fencing wire
stänk *s7* (*vatten-*) sprinkle, sprinkling, drop; (*smuts-*) splash; (*av vattenskum o.d.*) spray; *bildl.* touch, tinge (*av saknad* of regret); *få några grå ~ i håret* get a powdering of grey in one's hair
stänk|a *v3* sprinkle (*vatten på* water on; *tvätt* clothes); splash, sp[l]atter; (*småregna*) spit, sprinkle; (*dugga*) drizzle; ~ *ner* splash all over (*med* with); *regnet började* ~ it began to spit **-bord** *sjö.* washboard **-flaska** sprinkler bottle **-ning** sprinkle, sprinkling, splash[ing] **-skydd** (*på bil*) mudflap, splash guard **-skärm** (*på fordon*) mudguard, wing; *AE.* fender
stäpp *s3* steppe **-höns** Pallas's sandgrouse
stärbhus estate [of a deceased person] **-delägare** heir, beneficiary
stärk|a *v3* **1** (*göra stark[are]*) strengthen (*karaktären* the character); fortify (*ngn i hans tro* s.b. in his belief); (*i sht fysiskt*) invigorate; (*bekräfta*) confirm (*misstanken* the suspicion); ~ *sig med mat och dryck* take some refreshment[s] **2** (*styv-*) starch **-ande** *a4* strengthening *etc.*; ~ *medel* tonic, restorative **-else**

starch **-krage** starched collar **-ning** starching **-skjorta** starched shirt; (*frack-*) dress shirt
stätta *s1* stile
stäv *s2* stem
1 stäva *s1* (*mjölk-*) milk pail
2 stäva *v1, sjö.* head (*norrut* [to the] north)
stävja [-ä:-] check, put a stop to; (*tygla*) restrain; ~ *ngns iver* damp a p.'s ardour
stöd *s7, tekn.* support (*för ryggen* for one's back); prop, stay, foot; *bildl.* support; aid (*för minnet* for the memory); (*om pers.*) support[er]; *ekonomiskt* ~ economic aid (assistance); ~ *för ett påstående* support of a statement; *få* ~ *av* (*i tvist*) be backed up by; *ge* [*sitt*] ~ *åt* support; *med* ~ *av* with the support of; *som* ~ *för* (*bildl.*) in confirmation (as a proof) of; *ta* ~, *se stödja* [*sig*]
stöd|a *v2, se stödja* **-aktion** [action to] support **-de** *imperf. av stödja*
stöddig *a1* heavily built; substantial; *vard.* stuck-up
stödförband [emergency] splint
stödja [-ö:-] *stödde stött* support; (*stötta*) prop [up]; (*friare o. bildl.*) sustain; (*luta*) rest (*huvudet i handen* one's head in one's hand); (*grunda*) found, base (*sina uttalanden på* one's statements on); *inte kunna* ~ *på foten* not be able to stand on one's foot; ~ *sig* support o.s., (*luta sig*) lean, rest (*mot* against; *på* on); ~ *sig på* (*bildl.*) base one's opinion upon
stöd|jevävnad *anat.* connective tissue **-köp** supporting purchase **-lån** stand-by (emergency) loan **-mur** retaining wall **-område** development area **-punkt** point of support; *tekn.* fulcrum; *mil.* base **-trupper** *pl* supporting troops, reserves **-undervisning** remedial instruction **-åtgärder** support
stök *s7* (*städning*) cleaning; (*före helg o.d.*) preparation **stöka** clean up; potter; *gå ut och* ~ potter about; ~ *till* make a mess **stökig** *a1* untidy, messy
stöld *s3* stealing; (*en* ~) theft; *jur.* larceny; *föröva en* ~ steal; *grov* ~ grand larceny **-försäkra** insure against theft **-försäkring** theft insurance; (*inbrotts-*) burglary insurance **-gods** stolen goods (*pl*) **-kupp** raid **-säker** thief-proof
stön *s7* groan **stöna** groan; (*svagare*) moan **stönande** *s6, se stön*
stöp *s7, gå i* ~*et* come to nothing **stöpa** *v3* cast, mould; ~ *bly* (*äv.*) melt lead; ~ *ljus* dip candles; *stöpt i samma form* (*bildl.*) cast in the same mould **stöpning** [-ö:-] casting *etc.* **stöpslev** *vara i* ~*en* (*bildl.*) be in the melting pot
1 stör *s2, zool.* sturgeon
2 stör *s2* pole, stake
1 störa *v1* pole (*bönor* beans); stick (*ärtor* peas)
2 störa *v2* disturb (*ngn i hans arbete* s.b. at his work); (*göra intrång på*) interfere with (*ngn i hans arbete* a p.'s work); (*oroa*) trouble; harass (*fienden* the enemy); (*avbryta*) interrupt; *förlåt att jag stör* excuse me for disturbing you; *jag hoppas att jag inte stör* I hope I am not disturbing you; *inte så det stör* (*vard.*) not so that you'd notice; ~ *en radioutsändning* jam a broadcast
stör|ande *a4* disturbing; ~ *uppträdande* disorderly conduct **-ning** [-ö:-] disturbance; *ra-*

S

dio. äv. jamming, interference; (*-ande buller*) noise; (*själslig*) mental disorder; *atmosfäriska ~ar* atmospherics

störnings|skydd suppressor, interference eliminator **-sändare** *radio.* jamming station, jammer

större ['större] *komp. t. stor* larger, bigger *etc.*, *jfr stor*; major; (*ganska stor*) large, considerable, fair-sized; *bli ~* (*öka*) increase, (*växa*) grow, (*om barn*) grow up; *~ delen* the greater part, the majority; *desto ~ anledning att* all the more reason for (+ *ing- form*); *närmast ~ storlek* one size larger; *vara ~ än* (*i antal*) greater in number; *en ~ order* a large order

störst *superl. t. stor* largest, biggest *etc.*, *jfr stor*; (*ytterst stor*) utmost, maximum; *~a bredd* (*på fartyg*) overall width; *~a delen* the greatest part, (*huvuddelen*) the main (major) part, (*flertalet*) the greater number, most (*av dem* of them); *med ~a möjliga aktsamhet* with the greatest care, with all possible care; *till ~a delen* for the most part, mostly, (*huvudsakligen*) principally, mainly

stört absolutely, downright (*omöjligt* impossible)

störta 1 (*bringa att falla, äv. bildl.*) precipitate, throw (*ngn nedför trappan* s.b. down the stairs); (*stjälpa*) tip; (*avsätta*) overthrow (*en diktator* a dictator); *~ ngn i fördärvet* bring about (cause) a p.'s ruin, ruin s.b. **2** (*falla*) fall (tumble) [down] (*ner i* into); (*med flygplan*) crash; (*om häst*) fall; *~ omkull* fall (tumble) down; *~ samman* collapse, (*om byggnad*) fall in, *bildl.* break down; *~ till marken* drop to the ground **3** (*rusa*) rush, dash, dart (*fram* forward); *~ upp* spring to one's feet **4** *rfl* precipitate (throw) o.s. (*i* into); rush, dash; *~ sig på huvudet i vattnet* plunge headlong into the water; *~ sig över* fall upon (*ngn* s.b.) pitch into (*maten* the food)

stört|bombare dive bomber **-dyka** *flyg.* nose-dive **-dykning** *flyg.* nose dive **-flod** torrent (*äv. bildl.*) **-hjälm** crash helmet **-lopp** (*på skidor*) downhill race **-ning** *flyg.* crash **-regn** downpour, torrential rain **-regna** pour down; *vard.* rain cats and dogs **-sjö** heavy sea; *få en ~ över sig* ship a heavy sea; *en ~ av ovett* a torrent of abuse **-skur** heavy shower; *vard.* drencher; *bildl. se -sjö*

stöt *s2* thrust (*äv. bildl.*); *fäktn. äv.* pass; (*slag*) hit; blow; (*knuff*) push, shove; (*dunk*) knock, bump (*i huvudet* on the head); (*av vapen; biljard-*) stroke; (*sammanstötning*) shock (*äv. elektr.*); *aktas för ~ar* (*på kolli*) handle with care, fragile; *ta emot första ~en* take the first impact

stöt|a *v3* **I 1** ('*köra*') thrust; hit, blow *etc.*; *~ foten mot en sten* hit one's foot against a stone; *~ huvudet i taket* bang one's head on the ceiling; *~ kniven i bröstet på ngn* stab s.b. in the chest; *~ käppen i golvet* strike one's stick on the floor **2** (*krossa*) pound; (*i mortel äv.*) pestle **3** (*förarga*) offend, give offence to, (*starkare*) shock; (*såra*) hurt; *det -er ögat* it is an eyesore; *det -er örat* it jars upon my ear; *~ och blöta en fråga* thrash over a problem **4** (*om*

åkdon) bump, jolt; (*om skjutvapen*) kick; *fäktn.* thrust, make a pass **5** (*gränsa*) border (*till* [up]on); (*blåsa*) blow (*i trumpet* the trumpet; *~ i blått* incline to blue, have a tinge of blue in it; *~ på motstånd* meet with resistance; *det -er på bedrägeri* it verges (borders) on fraud **6** (*med betonad partikel*) *~ bort* push away, *bildl.* repel; *~ emot* knock (bump) against; *~ fram* (*ljud*) emit, jerk out, utter; *~ ifrån sig* push back (away), (*ngn*) repel; *~ ihop a*) knock (bump) together, (*med en skräll*) clash [together], (*kollidera*) collide, *b*) (*råkas*) run into; *~ ihop med a*) (*kollidera*) collide with, run into, *b*) (*träffa*) run across each other; *~ omkull* upset, knock over; *~ på a*) *sjö.* strike, *b*) (*råka*) come across *c*) (*påminna*) jog a p.'s memory (*om ngt* about s.th.); *~ till a*) (*knuffa till*) push, bump, *b*) (*ansluta sig till*) join, *c*) (*tillkomma*) come on; *~ ut a*) (*en båt från land*) push (shove) off, *b*) (*utesluta*) expel **II** *rfl*, *~ sig på knäet* hurt (bruise) one's knee; *~ sig med ngn* fall out with s.b., offend s.b.

stöt|ande *a4* (*anstötlig*) offensive, shocking; (*obehaglig*) objectionable **-dämpare** shock absorber

stöt|esten *bildl.* stumbling block **-fångare** bumper, fender; *AE.* (*på lokomotiv*) cowcatcher **-ig** *a1* shaky; jolting **-säker** shockproof

1 stött *sup. av stödja*

2 stött *a4* **1** (*skadad*) hurt, damaged; (*om frukt*) bruised **2** (*förolämpad*) offended (*på ngn* with s.b.; *över* at, about); *bli ~* take offence

stötta I *s1* prop, support, stay; (*gruv-*) pit prop; *sjö.* stanchion, pillar **II** *v1* prop [up]; *bildl.* support, bear up **stöttepelare** *eg.* prop, support; *bildl.* mainstay; *samhällets ~* the pillars of society

stöt|trupp shock troops (*pl*) **-vapen** thrusting weapon **-vis** by jerks; (*om vind*) in gusts; (*sporadiskt*) intermittently **-våg** shock wave

stövare harrier

stövel ['stövv-, 'stö:-] *s2* high boot **-knekt** bootjack **-krage, -skaft** bootleg

stövl|a [*stövv-, *stö:-] stalk, stride; trudge -'ett *s3* bootee

subaltern [-'tä:rn] *s3*, **-officer** subaltern [officer]

subba *s1*, *vard., neds.* cow, good-for-nothing

sub'jekt *s7* subject **-iv** ['subb-, -'ti:v] *a1* subjective **-ivism** subjectivism **-ivitet** subjectivity, subjectiveness

subjektskasus nominative case

sub|kultur subculture **-ku'tan** *a1* subcutaneous (*injektion* injection)

su'blim *a1* sublime

subli'mat *s4*, *s3* mercuric chloride, [corrosive] sublimate

sublim|era *kem. o. psyk.* sublimate, sublime **-ering** sublimation **-itet** sublimity

subma'rin *a1* submarine

subordin|ationsbrott breach of discipline, case of insubordination **-era** (*underordna*) subordinate; (*vara underordnad*) be subordinate (*under* to)

sub'rett *s3, teat.* soubrette

subsidi|er [-'si:-] *pl* subsidies **-era** subsidize

subskribent subscriber **subskribera** subscribe

(*på* for); *~d middag* a subscription dinner **sub-skription** [-p'ʃɷ:n] subscription

sub|'stans *s3* substance; (*ämne*) agent; *ytaktiv ~* surfactant **-stantiell** [-tsi'ell] *a1* substantial **-stantiv** *s7* noun, substantive **-stantivera** convert into a noun **-stantivisk** *a5* substantival (*användning* use); substantive (*sats* clause) **-stituera** substitute **-sti'tut** *s7* substitute **-strat** *s7* substratum (*pl* substrata), substrate **-'til** *a1* subtle; fine-drawn **-tilitet** *s3* subtlety **-tra'hend** *s3* subtrahend **-trahera** subtract (*från* from) **-traktion** [-k'ʃɷ:n] subtraction **-traktionstecken** minus sign **-tropisk** [-'trå:-] *a5* subtropical **-vention** [-n'ʃɷ:n] subvention **-ventionera** subsidize **-ver'siv** *a1* subversive

succé [suk'se:, syk-] *s3* success; *göra ~* be (score) a success, *teat. äv.* bring down the house **-författare** successful writer, best seller **-roman** best seller

succession [sukse'ʃɷ:n] [right of] succession

successionsordning order of succession

successiv [-'si:v, 'suks-] *a1* successive; gradual **successivt** [-i:-] *adv* gradually, by gradual stages

suck *s2* sigh (*av lättnad* of relief); *~arnas bro* the Bridge of Sighs; *dra en djup ~* heave a deep sigh; *utandas sin sista ~* breathe one's last **sucka** sigh (*av* with; *efter* for; *över* for, at)

suckat *s3, s4* candied peel

Su'dan *n* the Sudan **sudanesisk** [-'ne:-] *a5* Sudanese

sudd 1 *s7* (*klotter*) scribbling; (*med bläck o.d.*) smudge **2** *s2* (*tuss*) pad, wad **sudda 1** (*plumpa*) blot; (*smutsa*) soil, smear **2** *~ bort* (*ut*) erase, efface, rub out, (*från svarta tavlan*) wipe off; *~ ner* blur, smudge, blot; *~ över* blot out **3** (*festa*) go on the spree **suddgummi** eraser, rubber **suddig** *a1* blurred, blotched; (*otydlig*) fuzzy; (*om skrift*) indistinct; *foto.* fogged

suf'fix *s7* suffix

sufflé *s3* soufflé

suffler|a prompt **-ing** prompting

suff'lett *s3* hood; *hopfällbar ~* (*på bil*) folding top

sufflör *teat.* prompter **-lucka** prompt box

sufflös prompter

suffra'gett *s3* suffragette

suf|ism Sufism **-ist** Sufi

sug 1 *s7* (*-ning*) suck, draw **2** *s2* (*-anordning*) suction apparatus **3** *i uttr.: tappa ~en* (*ge upp*) lose heart, give up **suga** *sög sugit* suck (*honung* honey; *på tummen* one's thumb); (*om pump*) draw, fetch; *bildl.* drink in, imbibe; *~ musten ur ngn* take the life out of s.b.; *det suger i magen på mig* my stomach is crying out for food; *sjön suger* the sea air takes it out of one; *~ på ramarna* live on one's hump; *~ i sig* suck up, absorb; *~ ut* suck out, *bildl.* bleed, fleece; *~ ut jorden* impoverish the soil; *~ sig fast* adhere (*vid* to)

sug|ande *a4, en ~ känsla i magen* a sinking feeling; *en ~ uppförsbacke* a gruelling climb; *~ blickar* come-hither looks **-anordning** suction apparatus **-en** *a3* peckish; *vara ~ på* be longing for **-fisk** remora, suckerfish **-fot** sucker

foot

sugga *s1* sow

suggerera suggest **suggestibel** [-'ti:-] *a2* suggestible **suggestion** [-'ʃɷ:n] suggestion **sugges'tiv** *a1* suggestive

sug|hävert siphon **-it** *sup. av suga* **-kopp** suction cup **-kraft** suction power **-mun** suctorial mouth **-ning** [-u:-] sucking *etc.*, suction **-pump** suction pump **-rör** (*för dryck*) straw; *tekn.* suction pipe; *zool.* sucker **-skål** suction cup (disc) **-ventil** suction valve **-vårta** *zool.* sucker

sujett [sy'ʃett, su-] *s3* actor, *fem.* actress

sukta *~ efter ngt* sigh in vain for s.th.

1 sula I *s1* sole (*äv. tekn.*) **II** *v1* sole

2 sula *s1, zool.* booby

sulfa *s1* sulpha; *AE. äv.* sulfa **-preparat** sulpha drug

sulfat *s7, s4* sulphate; *AE.* sulfate **-fabrik** sulphate mill

sul'fid *s3* sulphide; *AE.* sulfide **sul'fit** *s7, s3* sulphite; *AE.* sulfite **sulfonamid** [-ˣfå:-] *s3* sulphonamide; *AE.* sulfonamide

sulky ['sulky] *s3* sulky; (*barnvagn*) pushchair, stroller

sul|läder sole leather **-ning** [-u:-] soling

sul'tan *s3* sultan **-'at** *s7* sultanate

summa *s1* sum; (*belopp äv.*) amount; (*slut-*) [sum] total; *en stor ~* a large sum [of money]; *rund ~* round (lump) sum; *~ summarum* all told, altogether, in all; *~ tillgångar* total assets; *en nätt ~* a tidy sum, a pretty penny

summarisk ['ma:-] *a5* summary; (*kortfattad*) succinct, brief; *~ översikt* summary

summer ['summ-] *s2* buzzer

summer|a sum (add) up **-ing** summation; *bildl.* summing-up, summary

summerton buzzer signal (tone)

summit *sup. av simma*

sump *s2* **1** (*kaffe-*) grounds (*pl*) **2** (*-mark*) fen, marsh **3** (*fisk-*) corf, fish chest; (*i båt*) well

sumpa *vard.* (*missa*) muff, miss

sump|bäver coypu, nutria **-feber** malaria, marsh fever **-gas** marsh gas **-höna** crake **-ig** *a1* (*sank*) swampy, marshy **-mark** *s3* fen, fenland, marsh, marshland, swamp

1 sund *s7* sound, strait[s *pl*]; *ett smalt ~* (*äv.*) a narrow passage (channel)

2 sund *a1* sound (*äv. bildl.*); (*hälsosam*) healthy; *en ~ själ i en ~ kropp* a sound mind in a sound body; *sunt förnuft* common sense

sund|het soundness; health **-hetsintyg** [clean] bill of health, health certificate

sunnan I *adv* from the south **II** *r* south wind **-vind** south wind

sun'nit *s3* Sunnite

sup *s2* dram; (*brännvin*) schnap[p]s

sup|a *söp -it* drink; (*starkare*) booze; *han -er* he is a heavy drinker, he is heavy on the booze; *~ ngn full* make s.b. drunk (tipsy); *~ sig full* get drunk (tipsy); *~ in* (*bildl.*) inhale, imbibe; *~ upp sina pengar* drink away one's money; *~ ur* drink up **-ande** *s6* drinking; boozing **-broder** drinking companion

sup|é *s3* supper **-era** have supper

su'perb *a1* superb

super|fosfat superphosphate **-intendent** superintendent **-lativ I** *s3* superlative **II** *a1* superlative **-makt** superpower **-ox'id** peroxide **-sonisk** [-'sɷ-] supersonic **-stjärna** superstar **-tanker** supertanker

sup|gille drinking bout, *vard.* booze, spree **-ig** *a1* addicted to drink[ing]

supinum [-ˣpi:-] *s4, best. form äv. supinum* [the] supine, (*motsv. i eng.*) past (perfect) participle

supit *sup. av supa*

supple|ant [-'ant, -'aŋ] deputy, substitute; (*i styrelse äv.*) deputy member

supple'ment *s7* supplement **-band** supplementary volume **-vinkel** supplementary angle **-'är** *a5* supplementary

supplera supplement, fill up

supp'lik *s3* supplication, petition **-ant** suppliant, petitioner

supponera suppose (*att* that)

supra|den'tal *språkv.* I *s5* supradental **II** *a5* supradental **-ledare** [ˣsu:-] superconductor **-ledning** [ˣsu:-] superconductivity

suprema'ti *s3* supremacy

sup'ut *s3, s2* tippler, boozer

sur *a1* **1** sour; (*syrlig*) acid, sharp; *kem.* acid, acetous; *bildl.* sour, surly; *se ~ ut* look sour (surly); *göra livet ~t för ngn* lead s.b. a dog's life; *det kommer ~t efter* one will have to pay for it afterwards; *bita i det ~a äpplet* swallow the bitter pill; *~t sa räven om rönnbären* "sour grapes", said the fox **2** (*fuktig*) wet, damp; *~ pipa* foul pipe; *~ ved* green wood; *~a ögon* bleary eyes

1 sura *sitta och ~* sulk

2 sura *s1, relig.* sura[h]

surdeg leaven

surfa [ˣsurfa, sörfa] surf, go surfing

surfing ['surr-, 'sörr-] surf-riding **-bräda** surfboard

sur|het [ˣsu:r-] sourness *etc.*; acidity **-kart** green fruit; *bildl.* sourpuss **-kål** *kokk.* sauerkraut **-mjölk** sour milk **-mulen** *a3* sullen, surly **-mulenhet** sullenness, surliness

sur|na [-u:-] sour, turn (get) sour **-puppa** *s1* sourpuss; grouch

surr *s7* hum[ming]; (*av röster äv.*) buzz[ing]; (*av maskin*) whir[ring]

1 surra hum; buzz; whir

2 surra *sjö., ~* [*fast*] frap, lash, make fast

surrealis|m surrealism **-tisk** *a5* surrealist[ic]

surro'gat *s7* substitute; makeshift

sur|stek *kokk. ung.* marinated roast beef **-strömming** fermented Baltic herring **-söt** bittersweet

surt [-u:-] *adv* sourly; *smaka ~* taste sour, have a sour taste; *~ förvärvade pengar* hard-earned money (*sg*)

surven ['surr-] *best. form., i uttr.: hela ~* (*vard.*) the whole lot

surögd *a1* bleary-eyed

sus *s7* **1** (*vindens etc.*) sough[ing]; sigh[ing]; (*friare*) murmur[ing]; *det gick ett ~ genom publiken* a murmur went through the audience **2** *leva i ~ och dus* lead a wild life, go the pace

susa 1 (*vina*) sough; sigh; *litt.* susurrate; *det ~r i öronen på mig* my ears are buzzing **2** (*ila*) whizz, swish; *~ förbi* sweep (*om bil:* flash)

past

susen ['su:-] *best. form vard., i uttr.: göra ~ do* the trick

susning [ˣsu:s-] *se sus 1*

sus'pekt *a1* suspect

suspen|dera suspend **-sion** suspension **-'siv** *a1* suspensive; **~t** *veto* delaying veto

suspenso'ar *s3* jockstrap, athletic supporter, suspensory [bandage]

sutare tench

sutenör pimp, ponce

suterrängvåning [-ˣräŋ-] basement

suttit *sup. av sitta*

sutur suture **-tråd** suture [thread]

suve'nir *se souvenir*

suve'rän I *s3* sovereign **II** *a1* sovereign (*stat* state); (*överlägsen*) supreme; superb (*tennisspelare* tennis player); *med ~t förakt* with supreme contempt **-itet** sovereignty; supremacy

svabb *s2* swab **svabba** swab

svacka *s1* depression, hollow

svada *s1* volubility, torrent of words; *ha en förfärlig ~* have the gift of the gab

svag *a1, allm.* weak (*förstånd* intellect; *kaffe* coffee; *skäl* argument; *syn* sight; *verb* verb); feeble (*försök* attempt; (*kraftlös*) powerless; (*klen*) delicate (*till hälsan* in health); (*om ljud, färg*) faint; (*om ljus*) weak, poor; (*lätt*) light (*cigarr* cigar); (*skral*) poor (*hälsa* health; *ursäkt* excuse); (*sakta*) soft (*bris* breeze); *ha en ~ aning om* have a faint idea of; *ett ~t hopp* a slight (faint) hope; *det ~a könet* the weaker sex; *köttet är ~t* the flesh is weak; *den ~a punkten* the weak point; *i ett ~t ögonblick* in a moment of weakness; *bli ~* weaken; *vara ~ för* have a weakness for, be fond of, (*ngn äv.*) have a soft spot for **-dricka** small beer **-het** weakness *etc.*; (*ålderdoms-*) infirmity; (*svag sida*) foible; (*böjelse*) weakness **-hetstecken** sign of weakness **-hetstillstånd** weak condition, general debility **-presterande** low-achieving; *de ~* the low achievers **-sint** *a1* feeble-minded **-ström** light (low-power) current **-strömsledning** communication (low-voltage) line **-synt** [-y:-] *a1* weak-sighted

svagt [-a:-] *adv* weakly *etc.*; (*klent*) poorly (*upplyst* illuminated)

svaj [svajj] *s7* **1** *ligga på ~* (*sjö.*) swing at anchor; *med mössan på ~* with one's cap at a jaunty angle **2** *radio.* wobbling, fading; (*om skivspelare*) wow and flutter **svaja 1** *sjö.* swing **2** (*vaja*) float **svajig** *a1* **1** swinging (*gång* gait) **2** (*flott*) stylish

sval *a1* cool (*äv. bildl.*)

sval|a *s1* swallow; *en ~ gör ingen sommar* one swallow does not make a summer **-bo** swallow's nest

svalde [-a:-] *imperf. av svälja*

svalg [svalj] *s7* **1** *anat.* throat; *fack.* pharynx **2** (*avgrund*) abyss, gulf

svalgång gallery

svalk|a I *s1* coolness, freshness **II** *v1* cool; (*uppfriska*) refresh; *~ sig* cool [o.s.] off, cool down, refresh o.s. **-ande** *a4* cooling, refreshing

svall *s7* surge; (*våg- äv.*) surging of [the] waves; (*dyning*) swell; *bildl.* flush, flow **svalla** surge;

swell; (*sjuda*) seethe; *diskussionens vågor ~de* the discussion became heated; *känslorna ~de* feelings ran high; ~ *över* overflow **svallning** surging; swelling; *hans blod råkade i ~* his blood began to boil **svallvåg** surge; (*efter fartyg*) wash

svaln|a [-a:l-] ~ [*av*] get cool, cool down (*äv. bildl.*) **-ing** cooling down

1 svalt [-a:-] *sup. av svälja*

2 svalt [svalt] *imperf. av svälta*

svalört lesser celandine, pilewort

svam|la ramble [on]; (*utbreda sig*) discourse (*om* upon) **-lig** *a1* rambling;(*oredig*) vaporous (*artikel* article) **-mel** ['svamm-] *s7* rant, verbiage; (*nonsens*) drivel

svamp *s2* **1** *bot.* fungus (*pl* fungi); (*ätbar*) mushroom; (*ej ätbar*) toadstool; *med.* fungoid growth; *plocka ~* go mushrooming **2** (*tvätt-*) sponge; *tvätta med ~* (*äv.*) sponge; *dricka som en ~* drink like a fish **-aktig** *a1* **1** *bot., med.* fungous; mushroom[-like] **2** spongy **-bildning** fungus [growth], fungosity **-dödande** ~ *medel* fungicide **-förgiftning** fungus poisoning **-ig** *a1* **1** *med.* fungoid **2** spongy **-infektion** fungus infection **-karta** mushroom (fungi) chart **-kännare** mycologist, expert on fungi **-kännedom** mycology **-odling** mushroom cultivation (growing) **-plockning** mushroom gathering

svan *s2, s1* swan **-damm** swannery **-dun** swan's-down **-esång** swan song (*äv. bildl.*)

svang *s, i uttr.: vara* (*komma*) *i ~* be (get) abroad

svanhopp *sport.* swallow dive, *AE.* swan dive

svank *s2, s7* hollow **svanka** be sway-backed

svankrygg sway-back **-ig** *a1* sway-backed

svann *imperf. av svinna*

svans *s2* tail; *astr.* trail (*äv. bildl.*); *bildl.* following, train

svans|a ~ *för* (*bildl.*) cringe to, fawn on **-kota** caudal vertebra **-lös** tailless **-motor** rear engine **-spets** tip of a tail

svanunge cygnet

svar *s7* answer (*på* to); reply; (*motåtgärd*) reply, counter; (*reaktion*) response; *jur.* rejoinder; ~ *betalt* reply paid (*förk.* R.P.); *jakande ~* (*äv.*) acceptance; *nekande ~* (*äv.*) refusal; ~ *med löneanspråk* replies stating salary expected; *bli ~et skyldig* not answer (reply); *inte bli ~et skyldig* have a reply ready; *få ~ på en fråga* get an answer to a question; *ge ngn ~ på tal* answer back, give s.b. tit for tat; *om ~ anhålles* an answer is requested, (*på bjudningskort*) R.S.V.P.; *som ~ på Ert brev* in reply to your letter; *stå till ~s för* be held responsible for

svar|a answer; reply (*på* to); (*skriftligen äv.*) write back; (*reagera*) respond; *rätt ~t!* that's right!; ~ *näsvist* give an impudent reply; *han ~de ingenting* he made no reply (*på* to); ~ *för* (*ansvara för*) answer (be responsible) for, account for; *jag ~r för att* I'll see to it that; ~ *i telefonen* answer the telephone; ~ *mot* correspond (answer) to, meet, match; *vad ~de du på det?* what did you reply (say) to that?; ~ *på en fråga* (*ett brev*) answer a question (letter); *jag ~de ja på hans fråga* I answered yes to his question

svarande *s9, jur.* defendant **-sidan** the

defending party, the defence

svaromål *s7, jur.* [defendant's] plea, defence; *ingå i ~* reply to a charge

svars|kupong reply coupon **-lös** at a loss for a reply; *bli ~* be nonplussed; *göra ~* reduce to silence; *inte vara ~* have an answer ready **-not** [note in] reply **-porto** return postage **-signal** *tel.* reply signal **-skrift** [written] reply

svart I *a1* black (*äv. bildl.*); (*dyster*) dark; *S~a havet* the Black Sea; *~e Petter* (*kortsp.*) old maid; *~a börsen* the black market; *familjens ~a får* the black sheep of the family; ~ *hål* black hole; *~a Maja* black Maria; *~a tavlan* the blackboard; *bli ~* get (grow) black, blacken; *stå på ~a listan* be on the black list **II** *s, best. form det svarta* black (*äv. schack.*); *de ~a* the blacks; *få ~ på vitt på ngt* get s.th. in black and white; *klä sig i ~* dress in black; *måla i ~* paint in black colours; *se allting i ~* look on the dark side of things

svartabörs|affär black market transaction **-haj** black-marketer, spiv

svart|betsa ebonize **-blå** blue-black **-broder** Black Friar, Dominican **-bygge** *ung.* house built without planning permission **-fläckig** blackspotted **-fot** (*indian*) Blackfoot; (*strejkbrytare*) blackleg, scab **-hårig** black-haired **-ing** darky **-jord** black earth **-klädd** [dressed] in black **-konst** (*magi*) black magic (art), necromancy **-krut** black powder **-kråka** carrion crow **-lista** blacklist **-mes** coal tit **-muskig** *a1* swarthy **-måla** paint in black colours **-målning** *bildl.* blackening **-na** blacken, get (grow, turn, go) black; *det ~de för ögonen på mig* everything went black for me -- **och-vitrandig** *a1* zebra striped, black-and-white striped **-peppar** black pepper **-prickig** black-dotted **-rock** (*präst*) black-coat **-rost** (*på säd*) black rust **-sjuk** jealous (*på* of) **-sjuka** jealousy **-skjorta** blackshirt, fascist **-soppa** goose-giblet soup **-syn** pessimism **-vit** black and white, monochrome (*film* film) **-ögd** *a1* black-eyed, dark-eyed

svarv *s2* [turning] lathe **svarva** turn [in a lathe] **svarvad** *a5* turned; *bildl.* well-turned, elaborate[d] **svarvare** turner, lathe operator **svarveri** turning-mill **svarvstol** [turning] lathe

svass|a ~ [*omkring*] strut about **-ande** *a4* (*om gång*) strutting; grandiloquent, highfalutin[g], hifalutin

svastika ['svass-] *s1* swastika

svavel ['sva:-] *s7* sulphur; *AE.* sulfur **-aktig** *a1* sulphur[e]ous **-bad** sulphur bath **-blomma** [-ˣblɷmma, ˣsva:-] flowers (*pl*) of sulphur **-haltig** *a1* sulphurous, sulphuric **-kis** sulphur pyrite, iron pyrites **-lukt** sulphurous smell **-predikant** fire-and-brimstone preacher **-sticka** sulphur match **-syra** sulphuric acid **-syrad** *a5, -syrat natron* sodium sulphate **-syrlighet** sulphurous acid **-väte** hydrogen sulphide

svavla [-a:-] *v1* sulphurate, sulphurize

Svea rike the land of Sweden **svear** *pl* Swedes

svecism *s3* Swedishism

sved *imperf. av svida*

1 sveda *s1* smart[ing pain]; ~ *och värk* physical suffering

2 sved|a *v2* singe; (*om frost*) nip; (*om solen*)

parch; *lukta -d* smell burnt
svedja [-e:-] burn woodland
svedje|bruk burn-beating **-land** burn-beaten
land
1 svek *imperf. av svika*
2 svek *s7* treachery, perfidy; (*bakslughet*) deceit,
guile; *jur.* fraud
svek|full treacherous, perfidious; deceitful,
guileful; fraudulent **-fullhet** treacherousness
etc.; guile **-lös** guileless, single-hearted
sven [svenn] *s3* swain, page; *riddare och ~ner*
knights and squires **-dom** *s2* chastity **-sexa**
stag party
svensk I *a1* Swedish; *~a kronor* Swedish kronor (*förk.* SEK); *en ~ mil* a Swedish mile, 10
kilometres **II** *s2* Swede **svenska** *s1* **1** (*språk*)
Swedish **2** (*kvinna*) Swedish woman
svensk|amerikan Swedish-American **-ameri-
kansk** Swedish-American **--engelsk** Anglo-
-Swedish; Swedish-English (*ordbok* dictionary) **-finne** Finn living in Sweden **--fransk**
Swedish-French, Franco-Swedish **-född** Swedish born, Swedish by birth **-het** Swedishness
-lärare Swedish teacher, teacher of Swedish
-språkig *a1* (*-talande*) Swedish-speaking **2**
(*avfattad på -a*) in Swedish, Swedish **-talande**
Swedish-speaking
svep *s7* sweep; *i ett ~* at one go **svepa** *v3* **1**
(*vira*) (*äv. ~ in*) wrap [up] (*i in*); (*lik*) shroud,
lay out; *~ om[kring] sig* wrap around one,
wrap o.s. up in **2** *sjömil.* sweep for (*minor
mines*) **3** (*hastigt dricka el. äta*) knock back **4**
(*blåsa hårt*) sweep (*fram* along) **svepande** *a4*
sweeping (*argument* argument)
svep|e *s6, bot.* involucre **-ning** [-e:-] **1** (*min-*)
sweeping **2** (*av lik*) shrouding; *konkr.* shroud
-skäl pretext, subterfuge; prevarication;
komma med ~ make excuses
Sverige ['svärje] *n* Sweden
svets *s2, abstr.* welding; *konkr.* weld
svets|a weld **-aggregat** welding set **-are** weld-
er **-loppa** welding spark **-låga** welding flame
-ning welding
svett *s3* perspiration; *vard.* sweat; *arbeta så ~en
lackar* work till one is dripping with perspiration; *i sitt anletes ~* in the sweat of one's brow
svettas *dep* perspire; *vard.* sweat (*äv. bildl.*);
jag ~ om fötterna my feet are sweaty
svett|bad (*stark -ning*) bath of perspiration;
(*bad*) sweat[ing bath] **-drivande** *a4* [*medel*]
sudorific, sudatory **-droppe** drop of perspiration **-drypande** all in a sweat, dripping with
perspiration **-ig** *a1* perspiring; *vard.* sweaty;
bli ~ perspire **-körtel** sweat gland **-ning**
sweat[ing], perspiration; *komma i ~* start
sweating **-pärla** bead of perspiration **-rem**
sweatband
svib|el ['svi:-] *s2, boktr.* pie[d type] **-la** [-i:-] pie
svicka *s1* spigot, plug
svid *s2, vard.* suit, outfit
svid|a *sved -it* smart; (*friare*) ache; *såret -er* (*äv.*)
the wound is very painful; *det -er i ögonen* [*på
mig*] my eyes smart; *röken -er i ögonen* the
smoke makes my eyes smart; *det -er i halsen*
[*på mig*] my throat feels sore, I have a sore
throat; *det -er i själen på mig att se* it breaks
my heart to see; *det -er men det -er gott* it

hurts but you feel better for it **-ande** *a4*
smarting; *med ~ hjärta* with an aching heart
-it *sup. av svida*
svik|a *svek -it* **1** (*överge*) fail, desert; (*i kärlek*)
jilt, *vard.* chuck; *~ en vän i nödens stund* leave
a friend in the lurch; *~ sitt löfte* break one's
promise, go back on one's word; *~ sin plikt*
fail in one's duty **2** (*svikta, tryta*) fail, fall
short; *krafterna svek mig* my strength gave out;
minnet (*modet*) *-er mig* my memory (courage)
fails me; *rösten svek honom* his voice failed
him **-it** *sup. av svika* **-lig** [-i:k-] *a1* fraudulent
(*förfarande* proceeding[s *pl*]), breach of trust
svikt *s2* **1** (*spänst*) spring[iness], elasticity; (*böj-
lighet*) flexibility; *ha ~* (*äv.*) be springy (flexible) **2** (*trampolin*) springboard; diving board
svikta 1 (*ge svikt*) be resilient; (*gunga*) shake,
rock **2** (*böja sig*) bend (*under* beneath); (*ge
efter*) give way, sag **3** *bildl.* flinch, give way,
waver
svikt|ande *a4, med aldrig ~* with never-failing
(unflinching) **-hopp** (*i simning*) springboard
diving; *gymn.* jumping on the spot
svim|färdig ready to drop **-ma** ~ [*av*] faint
[away], swoon, fall into a swoon, *vard.* pass
out; *~ av trötthet* faint with fatigue **-ning**
fainting, swoon; (*medvetslöshet*) unconsciousness **-ningsanfall** fainting-fit
svin *s7* pig; *koll. o. bildl.* swine; *bildl. äv.* hog
svin|a ~ *ner* make a dirty mess (*sig* of o.s.)
-aktig *a1* piggish, swinish; *bildl. äv.* mean;
(*oanständig*) indecent, filthy (*historia* story);
beastly (*tur* luck) **-aktighet** piggishness *etc.*;
meanness; *~er* (*i ord*) foul (filthy) things **-avel**
pig breeding **-borst** pig's (hog's) bristle
svindel *s9* **1** (*yrsel*) giddiness, dizziness; *med.*
vertigo; *få ~* turn giddy (dizzy) **2** (*svindleri*)
swindle, humbug, trickery
svindl|a 1 *det ~r för ögonen* my head is swim-
ming; *tanken ~r* the mind reels **2** (*bedriva -eri*)
swindle, cheat **-ande** *a4* giddying, dizzying;
giddy, dizzy (*höjd* height); *i ~ fart* at a
breakneck pace; *~ summor* prodigious sums
[of money] **-are** swindler, crook, cheat, humbug **-eri** *se svindel 2*; *~er* swindles
svineri filth, dirty habits
sving *s2, sport.* swing **svinga** swing; brandish
(*svärdet* the sword); *~ sig* swing o.s.; *~ sig ner*
swing down; *~ sig upp a*) (*i sadeln*) vault
(swing o.s. up) [into the saddle], *b*) (*om fågel*) take wing, soar, *c*) *bildl.* rise [in the world]
svin|gård piggery, pig farm **-hugg** *~ går igen*
tit for tat, the biter bit **-hus** piggery **-kall**
beastly cold **-koppor** *pl* impetigo (*sg*) **-kött**
pork **-läder** pigskin **-mat** pig (hog) feed; (*av
avfall*) pigwash, swill **-målla** *s1* fat hen, AE.
pigweed
svinn *s7* waste, wastage; loss **svanna** *svann
svunnit* (*om tid*) pass; *svunna tider* days gone
by
svin|pest swine fever, AE. hog cholera **-päls**
bildl. swine, dirty beggar **-skötare** pigman,
swineherd **-skötsel** pig-breeding **-stia** pigsty,
pigpen; *bildl.* sty
svira be on the spree
svirvel *s2* swivel
svischa swish

sviskon [-ån] *s7* prune
svit *s3* **1** *(följe)* suite **2** *(rad)* succession, series; *(av rum)* suite; *kortsp.* sequence; *i ~ (boktr.)* run-on **3** *(påföljd)* aftereffect; *med.* sequela *(pl sequelae)*
svor *imperf. av svära* **-dom** *s2* oath; *(förbannelse)* curse; *~ar* swearing, bad language *(sg)*
svull|en *a3* swollen *(kind cheek)*; puffed **-na ~** *[upp]* become swollen, swell **-nad** *s3* swelling
svulst *s3* **1** *(tumör)* tumour, tumefaction **2** *bildl.* bombast, pomposity, turgidity **-ig** *a1* bombastic; inflated, turgid **-ighet** *se svulst 2*
svult|en *a5* famished **-it** *sup. av svälta*
svunn|en *a5* bygone, past *(tid* time) **-it** *sup. av svinna*
svur|en *a5* sworn **-it** *sup. av svära*
svåger ['svå:-] *s2* brother-in-law
svål *s2 (svin-)* rind; *se äv. huvudsvål*
svångrem belt; *dra åt ~men (bildl.)* tighten one's belt
svår *a1* **1** *(besvärlig)* difficult *(för* for); *(mödosam)* hard *(uppgift* task; *för* for; *mot* on); *(invecklad)* complicated *(problem* problem); *~ examen* stiff examination; *ett ~t slag* a hard blow; *en ~ tid* hard times *(pl)*; *~ uppgift (äv.)* difficult problem, arduous task; *~ överresa* rough crossing; *ha ~t för att* find it difficult to; *ha ~t för ngt* find s.th. difficult; *ha ~t för att fatta* be slow on the uptake; *ha mycket ~t för att* have great difficulty in (+ ing-form); *ha det ~t a)* suffer greatly, *b) (ekonomiskt)* be badly off, *c) (slita ont)* have a rough time of it; *jag har ~t för att tro att* I find it hard to believe that; *det är ~t att* it is hard (difficult) to **2** *(allvarlig)* grave, serious, severe *(sjukdom* illness); *ett ~t fall a) eg.* a serious fall, *b) bildl.* a grave (difficult) case; *i ~are fall in* [more] serious cases; *~t fel a) (hos sak)* serious drawback, *b) (hos pers.)* serious fault, *c) (misstag)* grave error; *~ frestelse* sore (heavy) temptation; *~ förbrytelse* serious offence *(jur.* crime); *han har ~t hjärtfel* he has a serious heart condition; *~ hosta* bad cough; *~ kyla* severe cold; *~a lidanden* severe (great) suffering *(sg)*; *~ olycka* great misfortune, *(enstaka olyckshändelse)* serious accident; *ha ~a plågor* be in great pain; *~ sjö[gång]* rough sea **3** *vara ~ på ngt* be overfond of s.th.; *du är för ~!* you are too bad!, you are too bad!
svår|anträffbar hard to contact, elusive **-artad** [-a:r-] *a5* malignant *(sjukdom* illness) **-bedömd** *a5* difficult to appraise (assess, *vard.* size up) **-begriplig** hard (difficult) to understand; *(dunkel)* abstruse **-definierbar** difficult to define **-fattlig** *a1, se -begriplig* **-flirtad, -flörtad** *a5, eg.* unapproachable; *bildl.* hrd to convince **-framkomlig** *~ väg* difficult (rough) road **-förklarlig** difficult to explain **-gripbar** hard to get hold of; *bildl.* elusive **-hanterlig** difficult to manage (handle); *(friare, om pers.)* intractable, *(om sak)* awkward
svår|ighet difficulty; *(möda)* hardship; *(besvär)* trouble; *(olägenhet)* inconvenience; *(hinder)* obstacle; *göra ~er* make difficulties; *det möter inga ~er* that's not difficult, *vard.* that's all plain sailing; *däri ligger ~en* that's the trouble; *i ~er* in trouble; *utan ~* without any diffi-

culty **-ighetsgrad** degree of difficulty, factor **-ligen** [-å:-] hardly, scarcely **-läslig** *a1*, **-läst** [-ä:-] *a1* difficult to read; *(om handstil)* hardly legible **-löslig** *kem.* sparingly soluble **-löst** [-ö:-] *a4* difficult to solve; *(om gåta)* hard, intricate **-mod** melancholy; *(nedslagehet)* low spirits *(pl)*; *(dysterhet)* gloom, spleen **-modig** melancholy, sad; gloomy **-såld** difficult to sell; hard-selling
svår|t [-å:-] *adv* seriously *(sjuk* ill); badly *(sårad* wounded) **-tillgänglig** difficult of access (to get at); *(om pers. äv.)* distant, reserved **-tillgänglighet** difficulty of access; reserve **-uppnåelig** *a1* difficult (hard) to achieve **-åtkomlig** *se -tillgänglig* **-överskådlig** difficult to survey
svägerska sister-in-law
svälja *v2, el. svalde svalt* swallow *(äv. bildl.)*; *bildl. äv.* pocket; *~ förtreten* swallow one's annoyance; *~ ner* swallow; *~ orden* swallow one's words
sväll|a *v2* swell; *(höja sig)* rise; *(utvidga sig)* expand *(äv. bildl.)*; *seglen -er* the sails are swelling (filling); *~ upp* swell up (out), become swollen; *~ ut* swell [out], *(bukta ut)* bulge out **-ande** *a4* swelling; *(uppsvälld)* turgescent; *~ barm* ample bosom
svält *s3* starvation; *(hungersnöd)* famine; *dö av ~* die of starvation
svält|a 1 *svalt svultit* starve; *(starkare)* famish; *~ ihjäl* starve to death **2** *v3 (imperf. äv. svalt) (låta hungra)* starve; *~ sig* starve o.s.; *~ ut* starve out **-född** [half] starving, underfed **-gräns** *leva på ~en* live on the hunger line **-konstnär** person who needs very little food **-kost** starvation diet **-lön** starvation wages *(pl)*
svämma ~ över [rise and] overflow [its banks]
sväng *s2 (rörelse)* round; *(krök)* bend, turn; *(av flod, väg e.d.)* curve, wind[ing]; *ta ut ~en* take the corner wide; *ta sig en ~ (dansa)* shake a leg; *vägen gör en ~* the road bends (turns); *vara med i ~en* be in the swing **-ig** *a1* swinging
sväng|a *v2* **1** *(sätta i rörelse)* swing *(armarna* one's arms); *(vifta med)* wave; *(vapen)* brandish; *(vända)* turn *(bilen* the car) **2** *(hastigt röra sig)* swing *(fram o. tillbaka* to and fro); *(pendla)* oscillate *(äv. bildl.)*; *(svaja)* sway; *(om sträng)* vibrate; *(kring en tapp)* swing, pivot; *(rotera)* turn, rotate; *(göra en sväng)* turn; *~ av* turn off; *~ in på* turn into; *~ med armarna* swing one's arms; *~ om a)* turn round, *(om vind)* veer round, *bildl.* shift, change, *b) (i dans)* have a dance; *~ om på klacken* turn on one's heels; *~ om hörnet* turn the corner; *~ till (hastigt laga till)* knock up; *bilen -de upp på gården* the car swung up into the courtyard **3** *rfl (kretsa)* circle, rotate; *(göra undanflykter)* prevaricate; *~ sig med* flaunt *(latin* Latin) **-bar** *a1* revolving, pivoting **-borr** breast drill **-bro** swing (pivot, swivel) bridge
sväng|d *a5 (böjd)* bent, curved **-dörr** swing[ing] door; revolving door **-hjul** flywheel; *(i ur)* balance wheel **-ning** *(gungning)* swing; *(fram o. tillbaka)* oscillation, vibration; *(rotation)* wheeling, rotation
svängnings|radie turning radius **-rörelse** oscillatory motion, oscillation **-tal** frequency, num-

S

ber of oscillations
sväng|rum space to move, elbowroom (*äv. bildl.*) **-tapp** pivot, swivel
svära *svor svurit* **1** (*använda svordomar*) swear (*över* at); (*förbanna*) curse **2** (*gå ed*) swear (*på, att* that; *vid* by); (*avge löfte äv.*) vow; ~ *dyrt och heligt* make a solemn vow; ~ *falskt* perjure o.s., commit perjury; *jag kan* ~ *på att* I'll swear to it that; *det kan jag inte* ~ *på* (*vard.*) I won't swear to it that; ~ *sig fri* swear one's way out **3** ~ *mot* clash with (*äv. om färg*)
svärd [-ä:-] *s7* sword **-fisk** swordfish **-formig** [-å-] *a1, bot.* ensiform
svärdotter daughter-in-law
svärds|dans sword dance **-egg** sword edge **-fäste** sword hilt **-hugg** sword cut **-lilja** iris **-sidan** *i uttr.*: *på* ~ on the male (spear) side **-slukare** sword swallower
svär|far father-in-law **-förälder** parent-in-law
svärm *s2* swarm (*av* of); (*flock*) flock **svärma 1** (*om bin*) swarm, cluster; (*om mygg e.d.*) flutter about **2** ~ *i månskenet* spoon in the moonlight; ~ *för* fancy, (*starkare*) be mad about, (*för pers. äv.*) be crazy about **svärmare 1** (*drömmare*) dreamer; fantast **2** (*fjäril*) sphinx (hawk) moth **svärmeri 1** enthusiasm (*för* for); *religiöst* ~ fanaticism, religiosity **2** (*föräskelse*) infatuation; (*om pers.*) sweetheart **svärmisk** ['svärr-] *a5* dreamy; romantic, fanciful **svärmning** swarming [of bees]; flutter
svär|mor mother-in-law **-son** son-in-law
svärta I *s1* (*färg*) blacking; (*ämne*) blacking **2** *zool.* scoter **II** *v1* blacken; ~ *ner* blacken, *bildl. äv.* defame; *handskarna* ~*r av sig* the colour comes off the gloves
sväva 1 (*glida*) float, be suspended; (*om fågel*) soar; (*kretsa*) hover (*äv. bildl.*); (*hänga fritt*) hang; (*dansa fram*) flit (glide) along; ~ *genom luften* sail through the air; ~ *omkring* soar **2** ~ *i fara* be in danger; ~ *i okunnighet om* be in [a state of] ignorance about; ~ *mellan liv och död* hover between life and death; ~ *på målet* falter in one's speech **svävande** *a4* floating *etc.*; *bildl.* vague, uncertain **svävare, svävfarkost** hovercraft
sy *v4* sew (*för hand* by hand; *på maskin* on the machine); (*tillverka*) make; *absol.* do needlework; *kir.* sew up, suture; *låta* ~ *ngt* have s.th. made; ~ *fast* (*i*) sew on; ~ *ihop a*) sew up, stitch together, *b*) *bildl. ung.* implement, finalize; ~ *in* (*minska*) take in; ~ *om* remake **-ask** workbox **-ateljé** dressmaker's [workshop]
syba'rit *s3* sybarite
sy|behör *s7* sewing materials (*pl*), haberdashery; *AE. äv.* notions (*pl*) **-behörsaffär** haberdasher's [shop], haberdashery **-bord** worktable, sewing table **-båge** tambour
syd *s9, adv o. oböjligt a* south
Sydafrika *n* South Africa **sydafrikansk** South African **Sydamerika** *n* South America **sydamerikansk** South American **Sydeuropa** *n* Southern Europe **sydeuropeisk** South European
syd|frukt ~*er* citrus and tropical fruits **-gående** *a4* southbound **-kust** south[ern] coast **-lig** [-y:-] *a1* southern (*länder* countries); south, southerly (*vind* wind); ~*are* further south; ~

bredd south latitude **-ländsk** *a5* southern, of the South **-länning** southerner -'**ost** I *s2* (~*lig vind*) southeast wind; southeaster; (*väderstreck*) southeast (*förk.* SE) **II** *adv* southeast
Syd'ostasien Southeast Asia
syd|ostlig [-'ωsst-] *a1* southeast[ern] **-ostpassaden** *best. form* southeast trade wind **-pol** ~*en* the South Pole **-polsexpedition** Antarctic expedition **-sluttning** southfacing slope **-staterna** the Southern States; the South (*sg*) **-svensk** Southern Swedish **-sydost** south-southeast (*förk.* SSE) **-vart** southwards -'**väst** I *s2* (~*lig vind*) southwest wind; southwester; (*hatt*) sou'wester **II** *adv* southwest **-västlig** [-'väst-] *a1* southwest[ern] **-östlig** *se sydostlig*
syfili|s ['sy:-] *s2* syphilis **-tisk** [-'li:-] *a5* syphilitic
syfta aim (*på* at); (*häntyda*) allude (*på* to), hint (*på* at); ~ *högt* aim high; ~ *på* (*avse*) have in view (mind); ~ *till* (*eftersträva*) aim at; ~ *tillbaka på* refer [back] to
syft|e *s6* aim, purpose, end, object [in view]; *vad är* ~*t med* ...? what is the object (purpose) of ...?; *i* ~ *att lära känna* with a view to getting to know; *i detta* ~ to this (that) end (purpose); *i vilket* ~? to what end?; *med* ~ *på* with regard to **-emål** *se syfte* **-linje** sight line **-ning** aiming *etc.*; *tekn.* alignment
sy|förening sewing circle; *i Storbritannien äv.* Dorcas society **-junta** sewing guild
sykomor [-'må:r] *s3* sycamore
sy|korg work basket **-kunnig** able to sew
syl *s2* awl; *inte få en* ~ *i vädret* (*vard.*) not get a word in edgeways
syl'fid *s3* sylph **-isk** *a5* sylphlike
syll *s2, järnv.* sleeper, *AE.* crosstie, tie; *byggn.* [ground] sill
syllo'gism *s3* syllogism
sylt *s3* jam, preserve **sylta I** *s1* **1** *kokk.* brawn **2** (*krog*) third-rate eating house **II** *v1* preserve, make jam [of]; ~ *in sig* (*vard.*) get [o.s.] into a mess; ~ *in sig i* (*med*) (*vard.*) get mixed up in (with)
sylt|burk jam pot (jar); (*med sylt*) pot (jar) of jam **-gryta** preserving pan (kettle) **-lök** pearl onion; (*-ad lök*) pickled onions (*pl*) **-ning** preserving **-socker** preserving sugar
sylvass [as] sharp as an awl; ~*a blickar* piercing looks
sy|lön dressmaker's (tailor's) charges (*pl*) **-maskin** sewing machine
symbios [-'å:s] *s3* symbiosis
symbol [-'bå:l] *s3* symbol; (*om pers. äv.*) figurehead **-ik** *s3* symbolism **-isera** [-'se:-] symbolize **-isk** *a5* symbolic[al]; (*bildlig*) figurative; ~ *betalning* token payment **-ism** symbolism
symfo'n|i *s3* symphony **-iker** [-'få:-] **1** (*kompositör*) symphonist **2** (*orkestermedlem*) member of a symphony orchestra
symfoni|orkester symphony orchestra **-sk** [-'få:-] *a5* symphonic
symme'tr|i *s3* symmetry; *brist på* ~ lack of symmetry, asymmetry **-isk** [-'me:-] *a5* symmetric[al]
sym|patetisk [-'te:-] *a5* sympathetic; ~*t bläck*

(*äv.*) invisible ink **-pa'ti** *s3* sympathy (*för* for; *med* with); *gripas av ~ för ngn* take a liking to s.b.; *hysa ~ för* sympathize with; *~er och antipatier* likes and dislikes; *~erna var på hennes sida* she got all the sympathy **-patisera** sympathize (*med* with) **-patisk** [-'pa:-] *a5* nice, likeable; *äv.* sympathetic; attractive (*utseende* looks *pl*); *~a nervsystemet* the sympathetic nervous system **-patistrejk** sympathy (sympathetic) strike **-patisör** sympathizer

symposium [-'på:-] *s4* symposium

sym[p]tom [-'tå:m] *s7* symptom (*på* of) **-atisk** [-'ma:-] *a5* symptomatic

syn *s3* **1** (*-sinne*) [eye]sight; (*-förmåga*) vision; *~ och hörsel* sight and hearing; *få ~ på* catch sight of; *förlora ~en* lose one's [eye]sight; *förvända ~en på ngn* throw dust in a p.'s eyes; *ha god* (*dålig*) *~* have good (poor, weak) eyesight; *komma till ~es* appear **2** (*åsikt*) view, opinion; outlook; *hans ~ på* his view of; *ha en ljus ~ på* take a bright view of **3** *bära ~ för sägen* look like it; *för ~s skull* for the look of the thing; *till ~es* apparently, seemingly, to all appearances **4** (*ansikte*) face; *bli lång i ~en* pull a long face; *ljuga ngn mitt i ~en* lie in a p.'s face **5** (*anblick*) sight; *en härlig ~* a grand spectacle; *en ~ för gudar* a sight for the gods **6** (*dröm-*) vision; *ha ~er* have visions; *se i ~e* (*se orätt*) be mistaken **7** (*besiktning*) inspection, survey

syna inspect, survey; examine; *~ ngt i sömmarna* (*bildl.*) look thoroughly into s.th.

synagoga *s1* synagogue

sy'naps *s3* synapsis, synapse

syn|as *v3, dep* **1** (*ses*) be seen; (*vara -lig*) be visible (*för* to); (*visa sig*) appear (*för* to); *-s inte härifrån* cannot be seen from here; *det -s inte* it doesn't show; *fläcken -tes tydligt på* the spot could be seen clearly on; *det -tes på honom att* you could tell by looking at him that; *som -es* (*äv. bildl.*) as is evident, as you can see; *vilja ~* want to make a show; *vilja ~ vara förmer än* want to appear superior to; *~ till* appear, be seen; *ingen människa -tes till* not a soul was to be seen **2** (*tyckas*) appear, seem (*för ngn* to s.b.); *det -tes mig som om* it looked to me as if; *vägen -tes henne lång* it seemed a long way to her **-bar** *a1* visible; (*märkbar*) apparent; (*uppenbar*) obvious, evident **-barligen** [-a:-] apparently; (*tydligen*) evidently, obviously **-bild** visual picture **-centrum** visual centre

synd *s3* **1** sin; *~en straffar sig själv* sin carries its own punishment; *förlåt oss våra ~er* (*bibl.*) forgive us our trespasses; *begå en ~* commit a sin; *bekänna sin ~* confess one's guilt; *för mina ~ers skull* (*vard.*) for my sins; *hata ngn som ~en* hate s.b. like poison; *det är ingen ~ att dansa* there is no harm (sin) in dancing **2** (*skada*) pity; *så ~!* what a pity (shame)!; *det är ~ och skam att* it is really too bad that; *det är ~ att du inte kan komma* what a pity you can't come; *det är ~ om honom* one can't help feeling sorry for him; *det är ~ på så rara arter* (*vard.*) what a waste!; *det vore ~ att påstå att* you can't really say that; *tycka ~ om* pity,

feel sorry for

synda sin, commit a sin (*mot* against); (*bryta mot*) trespass (*mot* against)

synda|bekännelse confession of sin[s] **-bock** scapegoat; *vard.* whipping boy **-fall** *~et* the Fall [of man] **-flod** flood, deluge; *~en* the Flood; *före* (*efter*) *~en* antediluvian (postdiluvian) **-förlåtelse** remission of sins; *kyrkl.* absolution; *ge ngn ~* absolve s.b. of his (*etc.*) sin[s] **-pengar** (*orätt vunna*) ill-gotten gains; (*om pris*) exorbitant price (*sg*)

synda|re sinner **-register** *bildl.* list (register) of one's sins **-straff** punishment for [one's] sin[s]

synderska sinner, sinful woman

syndetikon [-'de:-, -ån] *s7* [fish] glue

synd|fri free from sin, sinless **-full** full of sin; sinful (*liv* life) **-ig** *a1* sinful; *det vore ~t att* it would be a sin to **-igt** *adv* **1** sinfully **2** *vard.* awfully

syndikal|ism syndicalism **-ist** *s3* syndicalist **-istisk** *a5* syndicalist[ic]

syndikat *s7* syndicate; combine; trust

syndrom [-'å:m] *s7* syndrome

syn|eförrättning inspection, survey **-fel** visual defect **-fält** field (range) of vision (sight) **-förmåga** [faculty of] vision, [eye]sight **-håll** *inom* (*utom*) *~* within (out of) sight (view) **-intryck** visual impression

synka (*vard. för synkronisera*) sync

synkop [-'kå:p] *s3* syncope

synkop|e ['synn-] *s3, språkv. o. med.* syncope **-era** syncopate **-ering** syncopation

synkrets *se synfält*; *bildl.* [mental] horizon, range of vision

synkron [-'krå:n] *a1* synchronous **-isera** synchronize; *~d växellåda* synchromesh gearbox **-isering** synchronization **-isk** *a1* synchronic **-motor** synchronous motor **-ur** synchronous clock

syn|lig [ˣsy:n-] *a1* visible (*för* to); (*iögonfallande*) conspicuous; (*märkbar*) discernible; *bli ~* become visible, (*komma i sikte*) come in sight, *sjö.* heave in sight; *~t bevis* physical evidence **-lighet** visibility **-minne** visual memory

synner|het *r, i ~* [more] particularly (especially); *i all ~ in particular; i ~ som* (*äv.*) all the more [so] as **-lig** *a1* particular; (*påfallande*) pronounced, marked **-ligen** particular; extraordinarily; *~ lämpad för* eminently suited for; *~ tacksam* extremely grateful; *samt och ~* (*allesamman*) all and sundry

synnerv optic (visual) nerve

synod [-'nå:d, -'nɷ:d] *s3* synod

syno'nym I *a1* synonymous **II** *s3, s7* synonym **-ordbok** dictionary of synonyms

sy'nop|s [-å-] *s3, -sis** [-'nåpp-] *s3* synopsis **-tisk** [-'nåpp-] *a5* synoptic (*karta* chart)

synorgan organ of sight

syn|punkt *bildl.* point of view, viewpoint; *från medicinsk ~* from a medical point of view; *från en annan ~* from a different angle **-rand** horizon **-sinne** [faculty of] vision, [eye]sight; *med ~t* (*äv.*) visually

syn|sk [-y:-] *a5* clairvoyant **-skadad** with defective vision **-skärpa** visual acuity **-sätt** out-

S

look, approach
synt *s2* synthesizer
syn|taktisk [-'tack-] *a5* syntactic[al] -'**tax** *s3* syntax -'**tes** *s3* synthesis
syntet|fiber synthetic (man-made) fibre -**isera** synthesize, synthetize -**tisk** [-'te:-] *a5* synthetic[al]
syn|vidd range of vision (sight) -**villa** optical illusion -**vinkel** visual (optic) angle; *bildl.* angle of approach
sy|nål [sewing] needle -**nålsbrev** packet of needles
syokonsulent [ˣsy:ɷ-] *ung.* careers master (mistress, adviser)
sypåse workbag
syra I *s1* **1** *kem.* acid; *frätande* ~ corrosive acid **2** (*syrlig smak*) acidity, sourness; *äpplenas friska* ~ the fresh tang of the apples **3** *bot.* dock, sorrel **II** *v1* acidify, sour -**angrepp** corrosion -**bad** acid bath -**fast** acid-proof, acid-resisting -**överskott** excess of acid, hyperacidity
syre *s6* oxygen -**brist** lack of oxygen -**fattig** deficient in oxygen -**förening** oxygen compound -**haltig** *a1* containing oxygen, oxygenous
sy'ren *s3* lilac, syringa -**buske** lilac [bush]
syretillförsel oxygen supply (feed)
syrgas oxygen -**apparat** oxygen apparatus -**behållare** oxygen cylinder (container)
Syrien ['sy:-] *n* Syria
syr|ier ['sy:-] *s9* Syrian -**isk** ['sy:-] *a5* Syrian
syrlig [ˣsy:r-] *a1* acid (*äv. bildl.*), sourish, somewhat sour; *göra* ~ acidify -**het** [sub]acidity, sourness; *bildl.* acidity
syrsa *s1* cricket
syrsätt|a oxygenate, oxygenize -**ning** oxygenation
syr'tut *s3* surtout; frock coat
sy|saker *pl, se sybehör* -**silke** sewing silk
syskon [-ån] *s7* brother[s] and sister[s]; *fack.* sibling[s] -**barn 1** (*kusin*) *vi är* ~ we are [first] cousins **2** (*pojke*) nephew, (*flicka*) niece -**bädd** *sova i* ~ bundle -**skara** family [of brothers and sisters]
syskrin workbox
sysselsatt *a4* occupied (*med* with; *med att* in + *ing-form*); (*upptagen*) engaged (*med* in, with; *med att* in + *ing-form*); (*strängt upptagen*) busy (*med* with; *med att* + *ing-form*); (*anställd*) employed (*vid* on; *med* in)
sysselsätt|a occupy; engage; keep busy; *hur många arbetare -er fabriken?* how many workers does the factory employ?; ~ *sig med* occupy (busy) o.s. with; *vad skall vi* ~ *barnen med?* what shall we occupy the children with? -**ning** (-*ande*) occupying; (*göromål*) occupation, employment; *konkr. äv.* work, something to do; *full* ~ full employment; *utan* ~ idle, with nothing to do, (*arbetslös*) out of work, unemployed -**ningsproblem** employment problem -**terapi** occupational therapy
syssl|a I *s1* **1** (*sysselsättning*) occupation *etc.*; (*göromål äv.*) work, business, task; *husliga -or* household (domestic) duties, *AE. äv.* chore; *sköta sina -or* do one's work; *tillfälliga -or* odd jobs **2** (*tjänst*) office, employment; *sköta sin*

~ discharge one's duties **II** *v1* busy o.s., be busy (*med* with); (*göra*) do; (*plocka*) potter (*med* over); (*yrkesmässigt ägna sig åt*) do [for a living]
syssling second cousin
sysslo|lös idle; (*arbetslös*) unemployed, out of work; (*overksam*) inactive; *gå* ~ go idle, do nothing -**löshet** idleness, inactivity; unemployment -**man** (*vid sjukhus*) manager, superintendent; (*i konkurs*) receiver; (*domkyrko-*) deacon
sys'tem *s7* system; (*friare*) method, plan; *periodiska* ~*et* the periodic table; *enligt ett* ~ on (according to) a system; *sätta i* ~, *se systematisera*
systematik *s3, ej pl* systematics (*pl, behandlas som sg*), systematism; (*klassificering*) classification -**er** [-'ma:-] systematist
systematiser|a systematize, reduce to a system -**ing** systematizing; (*med pl*) systematization
system|atisk [-'ma:-] *a5* systematic[al]; methodical -**bolag** [state-controlled] company for the sale of wines and spirits -**butik** [state-controlled] liquor shop
system|erare [-ˣme:-], -**man** computer programmer -**skifte** change of system -**teori** systems theory -**vetenskap** systems analysis
syster *s2* sister; (*sjuk-*) nurse -**dotter** niece -**fartyg** twin ship -**företag** sister company, affiliated firm -**lig** *a1* sisterly -**skap** sisterhood -**son** nephew
sytråd sewing cotton (thread)
syvende *till* ~ *och sist* in the final analysis
1 så *s2* tub, bucket
2 så I *adv* **1** (*på* ~ *sätt*) so, (*starkare*) thus; (*i* ~ *hög grad*) so, such; (*vid jämförelse*) as, (*nekande*) so; (*hur*) how; *den* ~ *kallade* the so-called; ~ *att säga* so to speak; *si och* ~ [rather] so-so; *än si än* ~ now this way now that; *han säger än si än* ~ he says one thing now and s.th. else later; *hur* ~? how then?, how do you mean?; *det förhåller sig* ~ *att* the fact is that; ~ *går det när* that is what happens when; ~ *får man inte göra* you must not do that; ~ *skall man inte göra* that is not the way to do it; ~ *sade han* those were his words; *det ser inte* ~ *ut* it doesn't look like it; *skrik inte* ~! don't shout like that!; ~ *slutade hans liv* that's how his life ended; *han var listigare än* ~ he was more cunning than that; *även om* ~ *skulle vara* even if that was so; ~ *är det* that's how it is; *är det inte* ~? isn't that right?; *det är* ~ *att* the thing is that; *det är nu en gång* ~ *att* it so happens that; *tack* ~ *mycket!* thank you so much!; ~ *dum är han inte* he is not that stupid; *det var* ~ *dåligt väder att* it was such bad weather that; *med* ~ *hög röst* in such a loud voice; *det är inte* ~ *lätt* it is not so easy; *hon blev* ~ *rädd att* she was so frightened that; *du skrämde mig* ~ you frightened me so; *inte* ~ *stor som* not so big as; *han skakade* ~ *stor han var* he was shaking all over; ~ *snällt av dig!* how nice of you!; ~ *stor du har blivit!* how tall you have grown!; ~ *du säger!* whatever are you saying? **2** (*i vissa uttryck*) ~ *radar* like this (that); ~ *där en 25 år* round about 25 years, (*om pers.*) somewhere about 25; ~ *där*

en tio pund a matter of ten pounds; ~ *här kan det inte fortsätta* it (things) can't go on like this; *rätt* ~ quite; *för* ~ *vitt* provided *(han kommer that he comes)* **3** ~*?* *(verkligen)* really?; ~ *[där] ja!* *(lugnande)* there you are!; *se* ~, *upp med hakan!* come now, cheer up! **4** *(sedan)* then; *först hon* ~ *han* first she then he **5** *(konjunktionellt)* then, and; *kom* ~ *får du se* come here and you will see; *om du säger det* ~ *är det* ~ if you say so, then it is so; *vill du* ~ *kommer jag* if you wish I shall come; *vänta* ~ *kommer jag* wait there and I shall come; *men* ~ *är jag också* but then I am **II** *pron, i* ~ *fall* in that (such a) case, if so; *i* ~ *måtto* to that (such an) extent *(att* that); *på* ~ *sätt* in that way **3 så** *v4* sow *(äv. bildl.)*; *(beså äv.)* seed
sådan [ˣså:-, *vard.* sånn] such; like this (that); *en* ~ *a)* *(fören.)* such a[n], *b)* *(självst.)* one of those; *en* ~ *som han* a man like him; ~ *där (här)* like that (this); ~ *är han* that is how he is; ~*t (självst.)* such a thing; *allt* ~*t* everything of the kind; *ngt* ~*t* such a thing, s.th. of the kind; ~*t händer* these things will happen; *det är* ~*t som händer varje dag* these are things that (such things as) happen every day; ~*t är livet* such is life; *en* ~ *vacker hatt!* what a beautiful hat!; ~*a påhitt!* what ideas!
sådd *s3* sowing; *(utsådd säd)* seed
såd|ig *a1* branny **-or** *pl* bran *(sg)*
så|'där *se 2 så I 2* **-'framt** *se såvida*
1 såg *imperf. av se*
2 såg *s2* saw; *(sågverk)* sawmill
såg|a saw *(av* off); ~ *till* saw; ~ *sönder* saw up **-blad** sawblade **-bock** sawhorse **-fisk** sawfish **-klinga** *(cirkel-)* circular sawblade **-ning** [-å:-] sawing **-spån** sawdust **-tandad** *a5* saw-toothed; *fack.* serrate[d] **-verk** sawmill; *AE.* lumber mill **-verksindustri** sawmill *(AE.* lumber) industry
så|'här *se 2 så I 2* **-ja** [ˣså:-] *se 2 så I 3*
såld *a5* sold; *gör du det är du* ~ *(vard.)* if you do that you are done for **sålde** *imperf. av sälja*
således 1 *(följaktligen)* consequently, accordingly **2** *(på det sättet)* thus
såll *s7* sieve, sifter, strainer; *(grovt)* riddle **sålla** sift, sieve; riddle; *bildl.* sift, screen
sålt *sup. av sälja*
sålunda thus; in this way (manner)
sång *s3* song; *(sjungande)* singing *(äv. som skolämne)*; *(kyrko-)* hymn; *(munkars)* chant, chanting; *(dikt)* poem; *(avdelning av dikt)* canto
sång|are 1 *pers.* singer; *(i kör äv.)* chorister; *(t. yrket)* professional singer; *(jazz- o.d.)* vocalist **2** *zool.* warbler **-bar** *a1* singable, melodious **-bok** song book **-erska** [female] singer *etc.*, *jfr sångare* **-fågel** songster, singing bird, songbird **-förening** singing club; choral society, glee club **-gudinna** muse **-kör** choir **-lektion** singing lesson **-lärare** singing master **-lärarinna** singing mistress **-mö** muse **-röst** singing voice **-spel** musical; ballad opera **-stämma** vocal part **-svan** whooper [swan] **-trast** song thrush **-övning** singing exercise
sånings|man sower **-maskin** sowing machine; *(rad-)* [sowing] drill
så'när almost
såp|a I *s1* soft soap **II** *v1*, ~ *[in]* soap **-bubbla**

soap bubble; *blåsa -bubblor* blow bubbles **-hal** slippery; *vägen var* ~ the road was like a skating rink **-lödder** soapsuds *(pl)*, lather **-vatten** suds *(pl)*, soapy water
sår *s7* wound *(äv. bildl.)*; *(bränn-)* burn; *(skär-)* cut; *(var-)* sore *(äv. bildl.)*; *ett gapande* ~ a gash, a deep cut
såra wound *(äv. bildl.)*; *bildl. äv.* hurt **sårad** *a5* wounded *(äv. bildl.)*; *(skadad)* injured; *djupt* ~ deeply hurt; ~ *fåfänga* pique; *känna sig* ~ feel hurt (offended) **sårande** *a4* *(kränkande)* insulting, offensive
sår|bar [-å:-] *a1* vulnerable; *bildl. äv.* susceptible; *vard.* touchy **-barhet** vulnerability *etc.*; touchiness **-feber** surgical fever **-förband** bandage **-ig a1** covered with sores; *(inflammerad)* ulcered **-salva** ointment [for wounds] **-skorpa** scab, crust
sås *s3* sauce; *(kött-)* gravy, juice **såsa 1** *(tobak)* sauce **2** *(söla)* dawdle, loiter **såskopp 1** *se såsskål* **2** *pers.* dawdler, slowcoach, *AE.* slowpoke
såsom ['så:såm] **1** *(liksom; i egenskap av)* as; ~ *den äldste i sällskapet* as the eldest present [at the gathering] **2** *(t. exempel)* for instance; such as
sås|sked sauce ladle, gravy spoon **-skål** gravy dish, sauce boat **-snipa** sauce boat
såt *a1, ej gärna i enstavig form,* ~*a vänner* intimate friends, great chums (pals)
så|tillvida [-ˣvi:-] ~ *som* [in] so far as, inasmuch as **-vida** [-ˣvi:-] provided *(inget oförutsett inträffar* [that] nothing unforeseen happens); ~ *annat ej överenskommits mellan parterna* unless the parties have agreed otherwise **-'vitt** as (so) far as *(jag vet* I know) **-'väl** ~ *stora som små* big as well as small, both big and small
säck *s2* sack; *(mindre)* bag; *en* ~ *potatis* a sack of potatoes; *köpa grisen i* ~*en* buy a pig in a poke; *i* ~ *och aska* in sackcloth and ashes; *svart som i en* ~ [as] black as ink; *det har varit i* ~ *innan det kom i påse* he *(etc.)* has picked that up from somewhere (someone) else; *bädda* ~ make an apple-pie bed **säcka** *(hänga som en säck)* be baggy; ~ *ihop (bildl.)* collapse
säck|hållare sack holder **-ig** *a1* baggy **-löpning** sack race **-pipa** bagpipe[s *pl*] **-pip[s]blåsare** piper, bagpiper **-väv** sacking, sackcloth
säd *s3* **1** *([frön av] sädesslag)* corn; *i sht AE.* grain; *(utsäde)* seed; *(gröda)* crop[s *pl*] **2** *(sperma)* sperm, semen; seed *(äv. bildl.)*
sädes|avgång ejaculation **-ax** ear of corn **-cell** sperm [cell] **-fält** cornfield **-korn** grain of corn **-kärve** [corn]sheaf *(pl* sheaves) **-slag** [kind (variety) of] corn (grain), cereal **-ärla** wagtail **-vätska** seminal fluid
säg|a [*vard.* ˣsäjja] *sade (vard. sa) sagt* **I** say *(ett ord* a word; *nej* no); *(berätta;* ~ *till, åt)* tell; ~ *ja [till ...] (äv.)* answer [...] in the affirmative, *(förslag)* agree to ...; ~ *nej [till ...] (äv.)* answer [...] in the negative; *gör som jag -er* do as I say (tell you); *vem har sagt det?* who said so?, who told you?; *-er du det?* you don't say?, really?; *det -er du bara!* you're only saying that!; *som man -er (brukar* ~) as the saying goes; *så att* ~ so to speak; *om jag*

S

så får ~ if I may say so; *om låt oss* ~ *en vecka* in [let us] say a week; ~ *vad man vill men* say what you will, but; *inte låta* ~ *sig ngt två gånger* not need to be told twice; *sagt och gjort* no sooner said than done; *ha mycket att* ~ *(bildl.)* have a great deal to say; *det vill* ~ that is [to say]; *förstå vad det vill* ~ *att* know what it is [like] to; *vad vill detta* ~*?* what is the meaning of this?; *han slog näven i bordet så det sa pang* he banged his fist down on the table; *det må jag [då]* ~*!, jag -er då det!* I must say!, well, I never!; *vad -er du!* you don't say [so]!, well, I never!; *vad var det jag sa!* well, I told you so!, what did I tell you?; *det -s att han är rik, han -s vara rik* he is said to be rich; *jag har hört* ~*s* I have heard [it said], I have been told **II** *(med betonad partikel)* **1** ~ *efter* repeat **2** ~ *emot* contradict **3** ~ *ifrån* speak one's mind; *säg ifrån när du är trött* let me *(etc.)* know when you are tired; ~ *ifrån på skarpen* put one's foot down **4** ~ *om* say over again, repeat; *det -er jag ingenting om* I am not surprised [to hear that], *(det har jag inget emot)* I have nothing against (no objection to) that **5** ~ *till ngn* tell s.b.; *gå utan att* ~ *till* go without leaving word; *säg till när du är färdig* let me *(etc.)* know when you are ready; ~ *till om ngt* order s.th. **6** ~ *upp en hyresgäst* give a tenant notice [to quit]; ~ *upp sin lägenhet* give notice [of removal]; ~ *upp ngn* give s.b. notice, *vard.* sack s.b.; ~ *upp sig (sin plats)* give notice; ~ *upp ett kontrakt* revoke (cancel) an agreement; ~ *upp bekantskapen med* break off relations with **7** ~ *åt ngn* tell s.b. *(att han skall komma* to come) **III** *rfl,* ~ *sig vara* pretend to be *(glad* happy); *han -er sig vara sjuk* he says he is ill; *det -er sig [av sig] själv[t]* it goes without saying

sägandes *i uttr.: skam till* ~ to my *(etc.)* shame I *(etc.)* must admit

sägen ['sä:-] *sägnen* [-ŋn-] *sägner* [-ŋn-] legend **-omspunnen** legendary

säk|er ['sä:-] *a2 (viss)* sure *(om, på* of, about), certain *(på* of); positive *(på* about); *(som ej medför fara)* safe *(förvar* custody), secure; *(pålitlig)* safe, trustworthy, reliable; *(garanterad)* assured *(ställning* position); ~ *blick* [a] sure eye; *-ra bevis* positive proofs; *gå en* ~ *död till mötes* [go to] meet certain death; *är det alldeles* ~*t?* is it really true?; *så mycket är* ~*t att* this much is certain that; *vara* ~ *på sin sak (vara viss)* be certain [that] one is right, be quite sure; *kan jag vara* ~ *på det?* can I be sure of that?; *är du* ~ *på det?* are you sure (certain) [about] that?; *jag är nästan* ~ *på att vinna* I am almost certain to win; *du kan vara* ~ *på att* you may rest assured that; *lova* ~*t att du gör det* be sure to do it; *det blir* ~*t regn* it is sure to rain; *vara* ~ *på handen* have a steady (sure) hand; *vara* ~ *i engelska* be good at English; *det är -rast att du* to make quite sure you had better; *-ra papper* good securities; *gå* ~ *för* be safe from, be above; *ingen går* ~ no one is safe (immune); *sitta* ~*t i sadeln, se sadel;* *ta det -ra före det osäkra* better be safe than sorry; *vara på den -ra sidan* be on the safe side; *från* ~ *källa* from a reliable source (a

trustworthy informant); ~ *smak* infallible taste; *ett* ~*t uppträdande* assured manners *(pl)*

säkerhet 1 certainty; safety, security; *(själv-)* confidence, assurance; reliability; *för* ~*s skull* for safety's sake; *den allmänna* ~*en* public safety; *i* ~ in safety, safe; *sätta sig i* ~ get out of harm's way; *med [all]* ~ certainly; *med* ~ *komma att* be sure (certain) to; *veta med* ~ *(äv.)* know for certain **2** *(borgen; garanti)* security; *ställa* ~ give (provide, furnish) security; ~ *i fast egendom* real security

säkerhets|anordning safety device (appliance) **-avstånd** safe distance **-bestämmelser** *pl* security (safety) regulations **-bälte** safety (seat) belt; *ta på sig* ~*t, vard.* belt up **-kedja** door (safety) chain **-lina** safety harness **-lås** safety lock **-marginal** safety margin, clearance **-nål** safety pin **-polis** security police **-risk** security risk **-rådet** the Security Council **-skäl** reasons of security **-synpunkt** security (safety) point of view **-tjänst** *(mot spionage etc.)* counterintelligence, security service **-tändsticka** safety match **-ventil** safety valve **-åtgärd** precautionary measure, precaution; *vidtaga* ~*er* take precautions

säker|ligen certainly, no doubt, undoubtedly **-ställa** ensure, guarantee; *(ekonomiskt äv.)* provide with sufficient funds; ~ *sig* protect (cover) o.s. *(för* against)

säkert ['sä:-] *adv (med visshet)* certainly, to be sure, no doubt; *AE. äv.* sure; *(stadigt)* securely, firmly; *(pålitligt)* steadily; *du känner dem* ~ I am sure you know them; *det vet jag [alldeles]* ~ I know that for certain (sure); *jag vet inte* ~ *om* I am not quite sure (certain) whether

säkr|a [-ä:-] **1** *(skydda)* safeguard, secure; *(ekonomiskt)* secure, guarantee **2** *(vapen)* put (set) at safety (half-cock); *(göra fast)* fasten, secure **-ing** *elektr.* fuse; *(trög)* delayed-action fuse; *(på vapen)* safety catch; *en* ~ *har gått* a fuse has blown

säl *s2* seal **-bisam** muskrat **-fångst** sealing

sälg [-j] *s2* sallow **-pipa** willow pipe

sälj|a *sålde sålt* sell; *(marknadsföra)* market; *(handla med)* trade in; ~ *ngt för 5 pund* sell s.th. for 5 pounds; ~ *i parti* sell wholesale; ~ *i minut* retail; ~ *ngt i fast räkning* receive a firm order for s.th.; ~ *slut* clear; ~ *ut* sell out **-are** seller; *jur. äv.* vendor; ~*ns marknad* seller's market **-bar** *a1* saleable, marketable; *inte* ~ unsaleable **-främjande** *a4,* ~ *åtgärder* sales promotion *(sg)* **-förmåga** ability to sell **-ingenjör** sales engineer **-kurs** selling rate (price); *sälj- och köpkurs* ask and bid price **-ledare** sales executive (manager)

säll *a1* blissful; *(salig)* blessed; *de* ~*a jaktmarkerna* the happy hunting grounds

sälla ~ *sig till* join, associate [o.s.] with

sällan seldom, rarely; ~ *eller aldrig* hardly ever; ~ *förekommande* [of] rare [occurrence]; *högst* ~ very seldom, *vard.* once in a blue moon; *inte så* ~ pretty frequently, quite often

sälle *s2* fellow; *en oförvägen* ~ a daredevil; *en rå* ~ a brute

sällhet felicity, bliss

sällsam *a1* strange; singular

sällskap *s7* **1** *(samling pers.)* party; company;

slutet (*blandat*) ~ private (mixed) party (company) **2** (*samfund*) society; (*församling*) assembly; (*förening äv.*) association, club **3** (*följeslagare; samvaro*) company; *får vi ~?* (*på vägen*) are you going my way?; *för ~s skull* for company; *göra ~ med ngn* go with s.b.; *gör du ~ med oss?* are you coming with us?; *hålla ngn ~* keep s.b. company; *råka i dåligt ~* get into bad company; *resa i ~ med ngn* travel together with s.b.

sällskap|**a** ~ *med* associate with **-lig** [-a:-] *a1* social; (*som trivs i sällskap*) sociable (*läggning* disposition)

sällskaps|**dam** [lady's] companion (*hos* to) **-dans** ballroom dance (dancing) **-hund** pet dog **-lek** party game **-liv** social life, society; *deltaga i ~et* move in society; *debutera i ~et* come out **-människa** sociable person **-resa** conducted tour **-rum** drawing room; (*på hotell e.d.*) lounge, assembly room **-sjuk** longing for company **-spel** party (parlour) game **-talang** social talent

Sällskapsöarna *pl* the Society Islands

sällspord [-ɷ:-] *a5, se -synt*

sällsynt [-y:-] *a1* rare, uncommon; unusual; *en ~ gäst* an infrequent (a rare) visitor; *en ~ varm dag* an exceptionally hot day **-het** rarity; *det hör till ~erna* it is a rare thing (is unusual); *det är ingen ~* it is by no means a rare thing **II** *adv, komp. t. illa* worse; badly, poorly

sämsk|**garva** chamois **-skinn** chamois [leather]; wash-leather

sämst *a o. adv, superl. t. dålig, illa* worst; *han är ~ i klassen* he is the worst in (at the bottom of) the class; *tycka ~ om* dislike most

sända *v2* **1** send; *hand. äv.* dispatch, transmit; (*pengar*) remit; ~ *med posten* post, mail; ~ *vidare* forward, send (pass) on **2** *radio.* transmit, broadcast; *TV* televise, telecast

sändar|**amatör** radio amateur **-anläggning** transmitting equipment

sändare *radio.* transmitter **sändebud 1** envoy; (*minister*) minister; (*ambassadör*) ambassador **2** messenger, emissary

sänder ['sänn-] *i uttr.: i ~* at a time; *en i ~* (*äv.*) one by one; *litet i ~* little by little; *en sak i ~* one thing at a time

sänd|**lista** mailing list **-ning 1** sending; (*varu-*) consignment; (*med fartyg*) shipment **2** *radio.* transmission, broadcast

sändningstid *radio.* air (transmission) time; *på bästa ~* (*i TV*) during peak viewing hours

säng *s2* **1** bed; (*själva möbeln äv.*) bedstead; *i ~en* in bed; *hålla sig i ~en* stay in bed; *skicka i ~* send to bed; *stiga ur ~en* get out of bed; *ta*

ngn på ~en catch s.b. in bed, *bildl.* catch s.b. napping; *dricka kaffe på ~en* have coffee in bed; *ligga till ~s* be in bed; *lägga till ~s* put to bed **2** (*trädgårds-*) bed **-botten** bottom of a (the) bed[stead] **-dags** *det är ~* it is time to go to bed; *vid ~* at bedtime **-försare** nightcap **-gavel** end of a (the) bed (bedstead) **-gående** *só, vid ~t* at bedtime, on retiring **-halm** bedstraw **-himmel** canopy **-kammare** bedroom **-kant** edge of a (the) bed; *vid ~en* at the bedside **-kläder** bedclothes; bedding (*sg*) **-lampa** bedside lamp **-liggande** [lying] in bed; (*sjuk*) confined to [one's] bed; (*sedan länge*) bedridden; *bli ~* (*lägga sig sjuk*) take to one's bed **-linne** bed-linen **-matta** bedside rug **-omhänge** bed-curtains, bed-hangings (*pl*) **-plats** sleeping accommodation; bed **-skåp** box bed, wardrobe bed **-stolpe** bedpost **-täcke** quilt **-värmare** warming pan; hot--water bottle **-vätare** bed-wetter **-vätning** bed-wetting **-överkast** bedspread, counterpane

sänk|**a I** *s1* **1** (*fördjupning*) hollow, depression [in the ground]; (*dal*) valley **2** *med., se sänkningsreaktion* **II** *v3* **1** (*få att sjunka*) sink; (*borra fartyg i sank*) scuttle; (*i vätska*) submerge **2** (*göra lägre, dämpa*) lower (*priset the price; sina anspråk* one's pretentions; *rösten* one's voice); ~ *blicken* drop one's eyes; ~ *fanan* dip the flag; ~ *priserna* (*äv.*) reduce the prices; ~ *vattennivån i en sjö* lower (sink) the level of a lake; ~ *skatterna* cut (lower, reduce) taxes **3** *rfl descend;* (*om sak*) sink, droop; (*om mark*) incline, slope; (*om pers.*) lower (demean) o.s.; ~ *sig till att* condescend to; *skymningen -er sig* twilight is falling; *solen -er sig i havet* the sun is sinking into the sea **-bar** *a1* folding down; *höj- och ~* vertically adjustable

sänk|**e** *só* (*på metrev*) sinker, lead; (*smides-*) die, swage **-håv** scap (scoop) net **-lod** plumb [bob], plummet **-ning 1** sinking *etc.*; (*av pris*) reduction, lowering **2** (*fördjupning*) declivity, downward slope **-ningsreaktion** sedimentation rate (reaction)

Säpo (*förk. för säkerhetspolisen*) the [Swedish] security police

sär|**a** ~ [*på*] separate, part **-art** specific nature (type) **-behandla** (*missgynna*) discriminate against, disfavour; (*gynna*) favour **-beskattning** individual (separate) taxation

särbo [ˣsä:r-] *ung.* LAT (*förk. för living apart together*)

sär|**deles** extraordinarily, exceedingly **-drag** characteristic; (*egenhet*) peculiarity **-egen** *a3* peculiar, singular **-fall** special case

särk *s2, åld.* shift; *vard.* (*nattsärk*) nightshirt

sär|**klass** *i* ~ a class of its own **-ling** individualist; eccentric, character **-märke, -prägel** *se särdrag* **-präglad** [-ä:g-] *a5* striking, peculiar, individual, distinctive **-skild** *a5* (*bestämd, viss*) special, particular; (*avskild*) separate; (*egen*) individual, peculiar; *vid ~a tillfällen* on special (*olika:* several) occasions; *ingenting -skilt* nothing special (in particular); *i detta ~a fall* in this specific case; *måste anges -skilt* must be specified separately **-skilja** separate, keep separate; (*åt-*) distinguish; (*ur-*) discern **-skilj-**

ande [-ʃ-] *s6* separation; distinction **-skilt** [-ʃ-] *adv* [e]specially *etc.*; *(för sig)* apart; *var och en* ~ each one separately; ~ *som* [e]specially as (since) **-skola 1** school for handicapped children **2** *(motsats samskola)* school for boys (girls) only **-skriva** write in two words **-ställning** *intaga en* ~ hold a unique (an exceptional) position **-tryck** offprint, separate impression; ~ *ur* reprinted from

säsong [-'såŋ] *s3* season; *mitt i* ~*en* in mid--season **-arbetare** seasonal worker **-arbetslöshet** seasonal unemployment **-betonad** seasonal **-biljett** season ticket

säte *s6 (sits)* seat; *(huvudkvarter)* headquarters *(pl)*; *(residens)* residence; *(bakdel)* seat, *vard.* behind; *ha sitt* ~ reside; *skillnad till säng och* ~ *(jur.)* separation from bed and board, judicial separation; *ha* ~ *och stämma* have a seat and vote

säter ['sä:-] *s2, se fäbod*

säteri *ung.* manor

sätes|bjudning *med.* breech presentation (birth) **-förlossning** breech delivery

1 sätt *s7* way, manner; fashion; *(tillvägagångs-)* method; *(umgänges-)* manners *(pl)*; *ha ett vinnande* ~ have winning manners; *vad är det för ett* ~? don't you know any better?, what do you think you are doing?; *på* ~ *och vis* in a way, in certain respects; *på allt* ~ in every way; *på annat* ~ in another (a different) way; *på bästa* ~ in the best [possible] way; *på det* ~*et* in this way (manner); *på ett eller annat* ~ somehow [or other], in some way; *på mer än ett* ~ in more ways than one; *inte på minsta* ~ not by any means, in no way; *det är på samma* ~ *med* it is the same [thing] with; *på sitt* ~ in his *(etc.)* way; *på så* ~ in that way, *(som svar)* I see

2 sätt *s7 (uppsättning)* set

sätt|a *satte satt* I **1** *(placera)* place, put; *(i sittande ställning)* seat *(ett barn på en stol a child on a chair)*; ~ *barn till världen* bring children into the world; ~ *en fläck på* make a mark (stain) on; ~ *frukt* form fruit; *inte* ~ *sin fot på en plats vidare* not set foot in a place any more; ~ *färg på* colour, bildl. *äv.* lend (give) colour to; ~ *händerna för öronen* put one's hands over one's ears; ~ *klockan på sex* set one's watch at six; ~ *komma (punkt)* put a comma (full stop); ~ *ngn främst* put s.b. first; ~ *ngn högt* esteem s.b. highly, think highly of s.b.; ~ *värde på* value **2** *(plantera)* plant, set **3** *boktr.* compose, set [up] **4** *komma* ~*ndes* come dashing (running) **II** *(med betonad partikel)* **1** ~ *av a)* ~ *av ngn någonstans* put s.b. down somewhere, *b)* *(rusa iväg)* dash off (away), *c)* *(pengar)* set apart, earmark **2** ~ *bort* put aside **3** ~ *efter (förfölja)* set off after; run after **4** ~ *fast a)* *(fästa)* fix *(på* to), *b)* *(ange)* report **5** ~ *fram* put (set) out, *(stolar)* draw up; ~ *fram en stol åt* bring [up] a chair for **6** ~ *för* put up *(fönsterluckor* shutters) **7** ~ *i a)* put in, *b)* *(införa)* install, *c)* *(installera)* install; ~ *i ngn ngt (inbilla)* put s.th. into a p.'s head; ~ *i sig mat (vard.)* stow away food **8** ~ *ihop* put together, bildl. *(utarbeta)* draw up, compose *(ett telegram* a telegram), *(ljuga)* invent, make up **9** ~

in a) put ... in, put in ..., *(brev e.d.)* file, *b)* *(börja)* set in, begin; ~ *in pengar i (bank)* deposit money in, put (place) money into, *(företag)* invest money in; ~ *ngn in i ngt* initiate s.b. into s.th. **10** ~ *ner* put down, *(plantera)* plant, set; reduce, depress **11** ~ *om* reset, replace, *(omplantera)* replant, boktr. reset, *(växel)* renew, prolong **12** ~ *på sig* put on *(kläder* clothes), take on *(en viktig min* consequential airs) **13** ~ *till alla klutar* clap on all sail; ~ *till livet* lose (sacrifice) one's life **14** ~ *undan* put by (aside) **15** ~ *upp a)* put up *(ett staket* a fence), put ... up *(på en hylla* on a shelf), *b)* *(grunda)* found, set up *(en affär* a business), *c)* *(skriftligt avfatta)* draw up *(ett kontrakt* a contract); ~ *upp ett anslag* stick up a bill; ~ *upp en armé* raise an army; ~ *upp gardiner* hang curtains; ~ *upp håret* put up one's hair; ~ *upp ngn mot ngn* prejudice s.b. against s.b.; ~ *upp en teaterpjäs* stage a play; *sätt upp det på mig* put it down to my account **16** ~ *ut a)* put out, *(ett barn)* expose, *b)* *(skriva ut)* put down *(datum* the date) **17** ~ *åt ngn (bildl.)* clamp down on s.b. **18** ~ *över (forsla över)* put across; ~ *över ett hinder* leap (jump) over a fence **III** *rfl* **1** *eg.* seat o.s.; ~ *sig [ner]* sit down *(i soffan* on the sofa); ~ *sig bekvämt (äv.)* find a comfortable seat; *han gick och satte sig vid* he went and sat down by; *gå och sätt er!* go and sit down! **2** *(placera sig)* place o.s.; put o.s. *(i spetsen för* at the head of); *det onda har satt sig i ryggen* the pain has settled in my *(etc.)* back; ~ *sig fast* stick; ~ *sig emot* oppose, rise (rebel) against; ~ *sig i respekt* make o.s. respected, ~ *sig in i* familiarize o.s. with, get aquainted with, get into *(ett ämne* a subject); ~ *sig upp i sängen* sit up in bed; ~ *sig över (bildl.)* disregard, ignore, not mind **3** *(sjunka [ihop])* settle; *huset har satt sig* the house has settled **4** *(om vätska)* settle; *(om grums e.d.)* settle to the bottom

sättar|e compositor, typesetter **-lärling** compositor's apprentice

sätteri composing room **-faktor** composing-room foreman

sätt|lök *(blomlök)* bulb **-maskin** boktr. composing (typesetting) machine, composer, typesetter **-ning 1** setting; *(plantering)* planting **2** boktr. composing, [type]setting **3** *(hopsjunkning)* sinking, settling **4** mus. setting, arrangement **-potatis** seed potatoe

säv *s3* rush

sävlig [ˣsä:v-] *a1* slow, leisurely; *vara* ~ *(äv.)* be a slowcoach, *AE.* slowpoke **-het** slowness

sävsångare sedge warbler

söcken ['söck-] *s, i uttr.: i helg och* ~ [on] weekdays and Sundays **-dag** weekday, workday

söder ['sö:-] **I** *s9* south; ~*n* the South **II** *adv* south; ~ *ifrån* from the south; ~ *ut* to the south **Söder|havet** the South Pacific **-havsöarna** *pl* the South Sea Islands

söder|sol *med* ~ facing south **-vägg** south-facing wall **-över** ['sö:-] in the south, southwards

södra [ˣsö:d-] *a, best. form* southern; ~ *halvklotet* the southern hemisphere; *S*~ *ishavet* the Antarctic Ocean

sög *imperf. av suga*
sök|a *v3* **1** seek (*lyckan* one's fortune); (*forska, spana*) search (*efter* for); (*leta efter*) look for (*nyckeln* the key), be on the lookout for (*arbete* work); (*försöka träffa*) call on, want ([have] come) to see; ~ *ngns blick* (*äv.*) try to catch a p.'s eye; ~ *bot för* seek a remedy (cure) for; ~ *efter* search (look) for; *han -te efter ord* he was at a loss for words; ~ *i fickorna* search (rummage) in one's pockets; ~ *kontakt med* try to [establish] contact [with]; ~ *lugn och ro* try to find (be in search of) peace and quiet; ~ *läkare* go to (consult) a doctor; ~ *sanningen* seek [the] truth; *kärleken -er icke sitt* (*bibl.*) love seeketh not its own; *vem -er ni?* whom do you want to see?; *en dam har -t er* a lady has called on (*per telefon*: rung, called) you **2** (*för-*) try; ~ *vinna ngt* try (seek) to win s.th. **3** (*an- om*) apply for (*plats* a post); try (compete) for (*ett stipendium* a scholarship) **4** (*lag-*) sue for (*skilsmässa* a divorce) **5** (*trötta*) try; *luften -er* the air is very relaxing **6** *rfl*, ~ *sig bort* try to get away; ~ *sig till* seek; ~ *sig till storstäderna* move to the cities; ~ *sig en annan plats* try to find another post **7** (*med betonad partikel*) ~ *fram* hunt out; ~ *igenom* search (look) through; ~ *upp a*) seek out, *b*) (*be-*) go to see; ~ *ut* (*välja*) choose, pick out
sökande I 1 *s6* search; pursuit **2** *s9, pers.* applicant, candidate (*t. en plats* for a post); (*rätts-*) claimant, plaintiff; *anmäla sig som* ~ send (give) in one's name as a candidate **II** *a4* searching (*blick* look); *en* ~ *själ* a seeker, an enquirer
sökaranläggning paging equipment **sökare 1** *foto.* [view]finder **2** (*-ljus*) [adjustable] spotlight **sökarljus** *se sökare 2*
sökt [-ö:-] *a4* (*lång-*) far-fetched; (*tillgjord*) affected
söl *s7* (*senfärdig*) tardiness; (*dröjsmål*) delay
1 söla (*vara långsam*) loiter, lag [behind]; (*dröja*) delay, tarry; ~ *på vägen hem* loiter on the way home
2 söla (*smutsa*) soil (*äv.* ~ *ner*)
sölig *a1* (*långsam*) loitering, tardy, laggard
sölja *s1* buckle, clasp
sölkorv *vard.* slowcoach, dawdler; loiterer; *AE.* slowpoke
1 söm [sömm] *s7, koll. äv. s9* (*hästsko-*) horse nail
2 söm [sömm] *s2* seam; *med., anat.* suture; *gå upp i ~men* come apart at the seam; *syna ngt i ~marna* scrutinize s.th.
sömlös seamless **sömma** sew, stitch
sömmersk|a seamstress; (*kläd-*) dressmaker **-etips** (*ung.*) pools coupon filled in by a greenhorn (*eg.* seamstress)
sömn *s3* sleep; *falla i* ~ go to sleep, fall asleep; *gnugga ~en ur ögonen* rub the sleep out of one's eyes; *gå* (*tala*) *i ~en* walk (talk) in one's sleep; *ha god* ~ sleep well, be a sound sleeper; *i ~en* in one's sleep; *gråta sig till ~s* cry o.s. to sleep
sömnad *s3* sewing, needlework
sömn|drucken heavy with sleep **-givande** soporific **-gångaraktig** *a1* somnambulistic **-gångare** sleepwalker, somnambulist

sömn|ig *a1* sleepy; (*dåsig*) drowsy; *~t väder* lethargic weather **-ighet** sleepiness *etc.* **-lös** sleepless; *ha en* ~ *natt* have a sleepless night **-löshet** sleeplessness; *med.* insomnia; *lida av* ~ be unable to sleep, suffer from insomnia **-medel** sleeping drug, soporific; hypnotic **-sjuka** (*afrikansk*) sleeping sickness **-tablett** sleeping tablet **-tuta** *s1* great sleeper; sleepyhead
sömsmån seam allowance
söndag ['sönn-] *s2* Sunday; *sön- och helgdagar* Sundays and public holidays
söndags|barn Sunday child; *han är ett* ~ (*äv.*) he was born under a lucky star **-bilaga** Sunday supplement **-bilist** Sunday driver **-bokstav** dominical letter **-fin** *göra sig* ~ put on one's Sunday best **-frid** sabbath calm **-kläder** *pl* Sunday clothes; *vard.* Sunday best **-promenad** Sunday walk **-seglare** Sunday sailor **-skola** Sunday school
sönder ['sönn-] **I** *pred. a* broken; (*-riven*) torn; (*i bitar*) [all] in pieces **II** *adv* (*isär*) asunder; (*i flera delar*) to pieces, (*mera planmässigt*) into pieces; (*itu*) in two; *gå* ~ get broken, break, smash [in two]; *krama* ~ squeeze to bits; *slå* ~ break, (*krossa äv.*) smash (*ett fönster* a window); *slå ngn* ~ *och samman* beat s.b. up **-bruten** broken [in two] **-bränd** *a5* burnt up (through); badly burnt **-dela** break up; (*stycka*) disjoint, dismember; *kem.* decompose **-delning** breaking up; disjointing *etc.*; *kem.* decomposition **-fall** disintegration, decomposition **-falla** fall to pieces; *bildl. o. fys.* disintegrate; (*kunna indelas*) be divisible (*i* into); *kem.* decompose (*i* into) **-fallshastighet** *kärnfys.* decay (disintegration) rate **-frusen** frozen to pieces **-kokt** [-⍟:-] *a4* boiled to bits **-körd** (*om väg*) rutted **-läst** tattered **-riven** *a5* torn to pieces **-skjuten** [-ʃ-] *a4* riddled with bullets **-skuren** *a5* cut to pieces **-slagen** broken; *han var* ~ *i ansiktet* his face was badly knocked about **-slitande** *a4* tearing apart; *bildl.* shattering (*sorg* sorrow); excruciating (*smärta* pain) **-smula** crumble, crush **-trasad** *a5* tattered [and torn], in rags
söndr|a (*dela*) divide; (*avskilja*) sever, separate; (*göra oense*) disunite; ~ *och härska* divide and rule; ~ *sig i två grupper* divide (split up) into two groups **-ig** *a1, se trasig* **-ing** (*splittring*) division; (*oenighet*) discord, dissension, disagreement; (*schism*) schism
söp *imperf. av supa*
1 sörja *s1* sludge; (*smuts*) mud
2 sörj|a *v2* **1** (*i sitt sinne*) grieve (*över* at, for, over), feel grief (*över* at); *det är ingenting att* ~ *över* that is nothing to worry about **2** (*en avliden*) mourn; (*bära sorgdräkt efter*) be in mourning for; ~ *förlusten av ngn* (*äv.*) grieve for (feel grief at) the loss of s.b. **3** ~ *för* (*ombesörja*) attend to, see to (about); (*ha omsorg om*) provide (make provisions) for (*sina barns framtid* the future of one's children); *det är väl -t för henne* she is well provided for
sörjig *a1* sludgy, slushy
sörpla drink noisily; ~ *i sig* lap up
söt *a1* **1** (*i smaken*) sweet (*äv. bildl.*); (*om vatten, mjölk*) fresh; ~ *doft* sweet scent **2** (*vacker*)

pretty, lovely; (*intagande*) charming, attractive; *AE. äv.* cute; *~a du!* my dear!

söt|a sweeten **-aktig** *a1* sweetish, sickly sweet **-ebrödsdagar** *pl* halcyon days

söt|ma ["sött-] *s1* sweetness **-mandel** sweet almond **-mjölk** fresh milk; (*oskummad*) whole (full-cream) milk **-ning** [-ö:-] sweetening; sugaring **-ningsmedel** sweetening [agent], sweetener **-nos** *s2* darling, poppet; *AE.* honey, cutie; *AE., vard.* tootsy **-potatis** batata; *koll.* batatas, sweet potatoes (*pl*) **-saker** *pl* sweets, sweetmeats; *AE.* candy; *vara förtjust i ~ (äv.)* have a sweet tooth **-sliskig** sickly sweet, mawkish **-sur** sour-sweet (*äv. bildl.*)

sött *adv* sweetly, in a sweet manner; *smaka ~* have a sweet taste; *sova ~* sleep peacefully

sötvatten freshwater

sötvattens|biologi limnology **-fisk** freshwater fish

söv|a *v2* **1** (*få att sova*) put to sleep; (*vagga t. sömns*) lull [to sleep]; (*göra sömnig*) make sleepy (drowsy); *bildl.* silence (*samvetet* one's conscience) **2** (*vid operation* an[a]esthetize; (*med kloroform äv.*) chloroform **-ande** *a4* soporific (*medel* drug); *~ mummel* drowsy murmur **-ning** [-ö:-] administration of an[a]esthetics **-ningsmedel** an[a]esthetic

T

ta *tog tagit* **I** take; (*~ fast*) catch, capture, seize; (*tillägna sig*) appropriate; (*~ med sig hit*) bring; (*~ sig*) have (*lektioner* lessons; *en cigarr* a cigar); (*göra*) make, do; *~ hand om* take charge of; *~ ngn i armen* take (seize) s.b. by the arm; *han vet hur han skall ~ henne* he knows just how to take her; *~ ledigt* take time off; *~ ngt för givet (på allvar)* take s.th. for granted (in earnest); *han tog det som ett skämt* he took it as a joke; *~ tid* take time; *~ fast tjuven* catch the thief; *han tog varenda boll* he caught every ball; *~ betalt* be paid; *~ bra betalt* know how to charge (make people pay); *vad ~r ni för ... ?* how much do you charge for ...?; *det tog honom hårt* it affected him deeply (hit him hard); *man ~r honom intе där man sätter honom* he has a will of his own; *vem ~r du mig för?* who do you think I am?; *~ fasta på* bear in mind, keep hold of; *skall vi ~ och öppna fönstret?* shall we open the window?; *kniven ~r inte* the knife does not bite; *var tog skottet?* where did it hit (go)?; *~ galoscher* put on rubbers; *var skall vi ~ pengarna ifrån?* where are we to find the money (get the money from)?; *~ det inte så noga* don't be too particular (fussy) about it; *~ pris* win a prize; *han ~r priset (bildl.)* he takes the cake; *~ tåget* take the train; *det ~r på krafterna* it tells on the (one's) strength; *han tog åt mössan* he touched his cap **II** (*med betonad partikel*) **1** *~ av a*) take off (... off), *b*) (*vika av*) turn off; *~ av [sig] kappan* take off one's coat **2** *~ bort* take away (... away), remove **3** *~ efter* imitate; copy **4** *~ emot a*) (*mot-*) receive, (*folk äv.*) see (*gäster* guests), (*an-*) accept (*erbjudandet* the offer), take in (*tvätt* laundry), take up (*avgifter* fees), *b*) (*avvärja*) parry (*stöten* the blow), *c*) (*vara i vägen*) be in the way, offer resistance, *d*) (*vara motbjudande*) be repugnant; *~ emot sig med händerna* put out one's hands to break one's fall; *~r doktorn emot?* can I see the doctor? **5** *~ fram* take out (... out) (*ur* of), produce (*biljetten* one's ticket) **6** *~ för sig av* help o.s. to **7** *~ hem a*) *kortsp.* take, get (*ett stick* a trick), *b*) *sjö.* reef (*seglen* the sails); *~ hem på* shorten (*skotet* the sheet) **8** *~ i* (*med händerna*) pull away, (*hjälpa till*) lend a hand, (*anstränga sig*) go at it [vigorously]; *det tog i att blåsa* the wind got up; *vad du ~r i!* you do go the whole hog, don't you? **9** *~ ifrån* take away [from], (*ngn ngt äv.*) deprive s.b. of s.th. **10** *~ igen* take back; (*förlorad tid äv.*) make up for; *~ igen sig* (*vila sig*) take a rest, (*repa sig*) recover, come round **11** *~ in a*) take in, (*bära in*) carry (bring) in, (*importera*) import, (*radiostation*) tune in to, *c*) (*förtjäna*) profit by, *d*) (*beställa*) order, *e*) (*läcka, bli överspolad*) ship (*vatten* water), *f*) (*ngn i en förening*) admit, *g*) (*slå sig ner*) put up (*hos ngn* at a p.'s house; *på hotell* at a hotel) **12** ~ *itu med* (*ngt*) set about [working at], set to work at, (*ngn*) take in hand **13** ~ *med* (*föra med sig*) bring; ~ *med ngt i räkningen* take s.th. into account **14** ~ *ner* take (fetch, bring) down, (*segel*) take in **15** ~ *om* take (read, sing, go through) again, *mus., teat., film äv.* repeat **16** ~ *på* [*sig*] *a*) (*klädesplagg o.d.*) put on, *b*) (*ansvar*) take upon o.s., (*för mycket arbete e.d.*) undertake, *c*) (*viktig min*) assume **17** ~ *till a*) take to (*vintermössan* one's winter cap), *b*) (*beräkna*) set up, charge (*för högt pris* a too high price), *c*) (*börja*) start, set about (*att* + *inf. el. ing-form*), *d*) (*överdriva*) overdo it, exaggerate; ~ *mod till sig* pluck up courage **18** ~ *tillbaka* take (carry, bring) back, (*ansökan, yttrande*) withdraw, (*löfte*) retract **19** ~ *undan* take away, (*för att gömma*) put out of the way **20** ~ *upp* (*jfr upp-*) *a*) take (carry, bring) up, (*från marken; passagerare*) pick up, *b*) (*öppna*) open, (*en knut*) undo, *c*) (*lån e.d.*) take up, *d*) (*order, skatter*) collect, *e*) *bildl.* bring up (*ett problem* a problem), (*en sång äv.*) strike up; ~ *upp sig, se repa sig, förkovra sig* **21** ~ *ur* take out [of], (*tömma äv.*) empty, (*fågel*) draw, (*fisk*) gut, (*fläck*) remove **22** ~ *ut a*) take (carry, bring) out, *b*) (*från bank*) withdraw, draw, *c*) (*lösa*) make out (*en rebus* a rebus), solve (*ett problem* a problem); ~ *ut en melodi på piano* pick out a tune on the piano; ~ *ut satsdelar* analyse [a sentence]; ~ *ut stegen* stride out **23** ~ *vid* (*börja, fortsätta*) step in, follow on, (*om sak*) begin, start; ~ [*illa*] *vid sig* be upset (put out) (*för* about) **24** ~ *åt sig a*) (*smuts e.d.*) attract, *b*) (*tillskriva sig*) take (*äran för* the credit for), *c*) (*känna sig träffad*) feel guilty; *vad ~r det åt dig?* what is the matter with you? **25** ~ *över take over* **III** *rfl* **1** take, have (*ett bad* a bath), (*servera sig äv.*) help o.s. to (*en kopp te* a cup of tea); ~ *sig för pannan* put one's hand to one's forehead **2** (*växa till*) grow (come) on, (*om eld*) begin to burn; (*bli bättre*) improve **3** (*med betonad partikel*) ~ *sig an* take up; ~ *sig fram a*) (*bana sig väg*) [manage to] get, (*hitta*) find one's way, *b*) (*ekonomiskt*) make one's way, get on; ~ *sig för ngt* (*att* + *inf.*) set about s.th. (+ *ing- form*); *inte veta vad man skall* ~ *sig till* not know what to do; *vad ~r du dig till?* what are you up to?; ~ *sig ut* (*eg. bet.*) find (make) one's way out (*ur* of); ~ *sig bra ut* look well, show to great advantage

tabbe *s2* blunder, bloomer; *AE.* boner

ta'bell *s3* table (*över* of) **-form** *i* ~ in tabular form; *uppställning i* ~ tabular statement; *ordna i* ~ tabulate **-huvud** table heading

tabernakel [-'na:-] *s7* tabernacle

tab'lett *s3* **1** (*läkemedel*) tablet; (*hals- etc.*) lozenge **2** (*tallriksunderlägg*) table mat **-förgiftning** poisoning from overdose of tablets, tablet poisoning

tab'lå *s3* tableau (*pl* tableaux), schedule; *teat.* tableau

tabu [-'bu:, 'ta:-] **I** *s6* taboo; *belägga med* ~ taboo **II** *oböjligt a* taboo **-föreställning** taboo

tabul|ator *s3* tabulator [key] **-era** tabulate

tabu'rett *s3* **1** tabo[u]ret; stool **2** (*statsråds-*

ämbete) ministerial office, seat in the Cabinet

tack *s7, s9* thanks (*pl*); *ja ~!* yes, please!; *nej ~!* no, thank you (thanks)!; ~ *så mycket!* many thanks!, thank you very much!; ~ *ska du ha!* thanks awfully!; ~ *för att du kom* thank you for coming; ~ *för lånet!* thank you [for the loan]!; ~ *för senast!* thank you for a lovely (nice) evening (party *etc.*)!; *hjärtligt ~ för ...!* most hearty thanks for ...!; *det är ~en för ...!* that's all the thanks you get for ...!; ~ *och lov!* thank heavens!; *vara ngn ~ skyldig* owe s.b. thanks; ~ *vare* thanks (owing) to

1 tacka *v1* thank (*ngn för* s.b. for); ~ *ja* (*och ta emot*) accept with many thanks; ~ *nej* [*till* ...] decline ... with thanks; *jo jag ~r* [*jag*]! well, I say!, well, well!; ~ *för det!* of course!; *det är ingenting att ~ för!* don't mention it!; ~ *vet jag* ... give me ... any day; *ha ngn att ~ för ngt* owe s.th. to s.b.

2 tacka *s1* (*fårhona*) ewe

3 tacka *s1* (*järn-, bly-*) pig; (*guld-, silver-, stål-*) ingot

tackbrev letter of thanks

tackel ['tack-] *s7* tackle [block]; ~ *och tåg* the rigging

tackjärn pig iron

tackkort thank-you card

tackl|a 1 *sjö.* rig **2** *sport.* tackle **3** ~ *av* (*magra*) grow (get) thin, fall away **-ing 1** *sjö.* rig[ging] **2** *sport.* tackle

tacknämlig [-ä:-] *a1* (*värd tack*) praiseworthy; (*gagnelig*) worthwhile, profitable, rewarding

tack- och avskedsföreställning farewell performance

tackoffer thank-offering

tacksam *a1* grateful (*för* for; *mot* to); (*mot försynen o.d.*) thankful (*för, över* for); (*uppskattande*) appreciative (*för* of); (*förbunden*) obliged; (*givande*) rewarding, worthwhile (*uppgift* task); *jag vore er mycket* ~ *om* I should be very much obliged to you if **-het** gratitude; thankfulness

tacksamhets|bevis token (mark) of gratitude **-skuld** debt of gratitude; *stå i* ~ *till* be indebted to (*ngn för* s.b. for)

tacksamt *adv* gratefully *etc.*; *vi emotser* ~ *Ert snara svar* we should appreciate your early reply; *vi erkänner* ~ *mottagandet av* we acknowledge, with thanks, [the] receipt of; ~ *avböja* regretfully decline

tacksägelse *framföra sina ~r till ngn* proffer one's thanks to s.b. **-gudstjänst** thanksgiving service

tacktal speech of thanks

tadel ['ta:-] *s7* blame, censure; *utan fruktan och* ~ without fear and without reproach **tadellös** [*x*ta:-] blameless **tadla** [-a:-] *se klandra*

1 ta'fatt *s3* (*lek*) tag

2 tafatt [*x*ta:-] *a1* awkward; clumsy

taffel ['taff-] *s2* **1** *hålla öppen* ~ keep open house **2** *mus.* square piano **-musik** mealtime music **-täckare** footman laying the [Royal] table

tafflig *a1, vard.* awkward, clumsy

tafs *s2* **1** (*på metrev*) trace, leader, *AE.* snell **2** *få på ~en* get it hot; *ge ngn på ~en* give s.b. it hot **tafsa** fiddle, tamper; ~ *på ngn* paw s.b.

taft *s3, s4* taffeta
tag *s7* **1** (*grepp*) grip, grasp (*omkring* round); hold (*i, om* of); *sport.* tackle; *fatta* (*gripa, hugga*) ~ *i* grasp (seize, catch) [hold of]; *få ~ i* (*på*) get hold of, (*komma över*) come across, pick up; *släppa ~et* leave hold of, let go, (*ge upp*) give in (up); *ta ett stadigt ~ i* take firm hold of **2** (*sim-, år-*) stroke; *simma med långa ~* swim with long strokes; *ta ett ~ med sopborsten* have a go with the broom; *ha ~en inne* have the knack [of the thing]; *komma* (*vara*) *i ~en* get started, be at it **3** (*gång, liten stund*) little while; *kom hit ett ~!* come here a second[, will you]!; *en i ~et* one at a time; *i första ~et* at the first try (*vard.* go); *jag ger mig inte i första ~et* I don't give up at the first try
taga *se ta* **tagas** *se tas*
tagel ['ta:-] *s7* horsehair **-madrass** horsehair mattress **-orm** hairworm **-skjorta** hair shirt
tag|en *a5* taken *etc.*; *bli* [*djupt*] ~ *av* be deeply affected by; *han såg mycket ~ ut* he looked deeply moved (*trött:* very tired); *strängt -et* strictly speaking; *över huvud -et* on the whole
tagg *s2* prickle; (*törn-*) thorn; *naturv.* spine; (*på -tråd*) barb **-ig** *a1* prickly; thorny; spiny **-svamp** hedgehog mushroom **-tråd** barbed wire, barbwire **-trådshinder** barbed-wire entanglement **-trådsstängsel** barbed-wire fence
tagit *sup. av ta*[*ga*]
tagla [ˈta:-] *sjö.* serve
tagning [-a:-] *film.* take
taiwa'nes *s3* Taiwanese **-isk** *a5* Taiwanese
tajma *vard.* time
tajt *a1, vard.* tight
tak *s7* (*ytter-*) roof; (*inner-*) ceiling (*äv. bildl.*); (*på bil etc.*) top; *bildl.* roof, shelter, cover, (*övre gräns*) ceiling; *brutet ~* mansard (curb) roof; *här är det högt* (*lågt*) *i ~* this room has a lofty (low) ceiling; *i ~et* on the ceiling; *grödan är under ~* the harvest is housed; *ha ~ över huvudet* have a roof over one's head; *vara utan ~ över huvudet* (*äv.*) have no shelter; *ingen fara på ~et* no harm done, all's well
taka *oböjligt a, pl, ~ händer* [legal] trust; *sätta ngt i ~ händer* deposit s.th. with a trustee (on trust)
tak|belysning ceiling lighting; ceiling fitting **-bjälke** beam [of the roof] **-bjälklag** tie beams (*pl*) **-dropp** (*från yttertak*) eaves drop; (*från innertak*) dropping from the ceiling **-fönster** skylight, fanlight **-krona** chandelier **-lagsfest** [-a:gs-] party for workmen when roof framework is completed **-lampa** ceiling lamp **-list** cornice **-lucka** roof hatch **-lök** *bot.* houseleek **-målning** ceiling painting; *~ar* (*äv.*) painted ceilings **-nock** roof ridge **-panna** roofing tile **-papp** roofing-felt **-räcke** (*på bil*) roof rack **-ränna** gutter **-skägg** eaves (*pl*) **-stol** roof truss
takt *s3* **1** (*finkänslighet*) tact, delicacy; (*urskillning*) discretion **2** (*av musikstycke*) bar; (*versfot*) foot **3** (*tempo*) time; *mus. äv.* measure; (*friare*) pace, rate; (*vid rodd*) stroke; *ange ~en* set the time (*vid rodd:* the pace); *gå i ~* keep in step; *hålla ~en* keep time; *hålla ~en med* keep pace with; *i ~ med musiken* in time to the music; *komma ur ~en* get out of time (step, the pace); *slå ~en* beat time; *stampa ~en* beat time with one's foot; *öka ~en* increase the speed (pace); *nu skall ni få se på andra ~er* this is where we get a move on **4** (*motors*) stroke **-art** time **-beteckning** time signature **-del** beat
tak|tegel roofing tile **-terrass** roof terrace, terrace roof
takt|fast (*om steg e.d.*) measured; *marschera ~* march in perfect time **-full** tactful; discreet **-fullhet** tactfulness; discretion
takt|ik *s3* tactics (*pl, behandlas som sg*) **-iker** ['tack-] tactician
tak'til *a1* tactile
taktisk ['tack-] *a4* tactical
takt|känsla 1 *mus.* sense of rhythm **2** (*-fullhet*) sense of tact, tactfulness **-lös** tactless, indiscreet **-löshet** want of tact; tactlessness **-mässig** *a1* rhythmical **-pinne** baton **-streck** bar, barline
tak|täckare roofer; (*med -tegel*) tiler; (*med halm*) thatcher **-täckning** roofing; tiling; thatching **-ås** roof ridge, ridgepole, rooftree
1 tal *s7, mat.* number; (*räkne-*) sum; *hela ~* integers, whole numbers; *ensiffriga ~* digits; *fyrsiffriga ~* numbers of four digits, four-figure numbers; *i runt ~* in round figures (numbers)
2 tal *s7* (*förmåga* (*sätt*) *att tala, språk*) speech; (*prat*) talk[ing]; (*sam-*) conversation; (*anförande*) speech, address; *~ets gåva* the gift of speech; *hålla ~* make a speech; *i ~ och skrift* verbally and in writing; *falla ngn i ~et* interrupt s.b., cut s.b. short; *det blev aldrig ~ om* there was never any question of; *det kan inte bli ~ om* there can be no talk (question) of; *föra på ~* bring up [for discussion]; *komma på ~* come (crop) up; *det är på ~ att* there is a talk of (+ *ing-form*); *på ~ om* speaking of
tala speak (*med* to; *om* about, of; *på* in); (*prata, konversera*) talk (*i telefon* on the telephone; *i sömnen* in one's sleep; *i näsan* through one's nose); *~ är silver, tiga är guld* speech is silver, silence is golden; *~ förstånd med* talk sense to; *får jag ~ ett par ord med dig?* can I have a word with you?; *~ rent* (*om barn*) speak properly; *allvarligt ~t* seriously speaking; *~ för* (*t. förmån för*) speak for (in favour of), (*tyda på*) indicate, point towards; *~ för sig själv* (*utan åhörare*) talk to o.s., (*i egen sak*) speak for o.s.; *de ~de i munnen på varandra* they were all talking at the same time; *~ om* speak (talk) about (of); *~ illa om* speak disparagingly about; *det är ingenting att ~ om!* (*avböjande*) don't mention it!; *för att inte ~ om* to say nothing of, not to mention; *låta ~ om sig* give rise to a lot of talk; *~ om* (*berätta*) tell; *~ inte om det för ngn!* don't tell anybody!; *~ sig hes* talk o.s. hoarse; *~ sig varm för* warm up to one's subject; *~ till ngn* speak to (address) s.b.; *~ ur skägget* speak up; *~ ut a*) (*så det hörs*) speak up (out), *b*) (*~ rent ut*) speak one's mind; *vi har ~t ut med varandra* we have had it out [with one another]; *~ vid ngn att han* tell (ask, arrange with) s.b. to (+ *inf.*)
talan *r* suit; (*kärandes*) claim; (*svarandes*) plea; *föra ngns ~* plead a p.'s cause, (*friare*) be a p.'s spokesman; *nedlägga sin ~* withdraw one's suit; *han har ingen ~* (*bildl.*) he has no

voice in the matter **talande** *a4* speaking *etc.*;
(uttrycksfull) expressive; *(menande)* significant
(blickar looks); *(om siffror)* telling; *den* ~ the
speaker

talang talent, gift, aptitude; *pers.* talented
(gifted) person **-full** talented, gifted **-fullt** *adv*
with great talent **-lös** untalented **-scout** talent
scout, star spotter

talar|e speaker; *(väl-)* orator; *föregående* ~ the
previous speaker; *han är ingen* ~ he's not
much of a speaker **-konst** art of [public]
speaking; rhetoric **-stol** platform, rostrum

tal|as *dep, höra* ~ *om* hear of; *jag har hört* ~
om honom I have heard of him; *vi får* ~ *vid
om saken* we must have a talk about it (talk
the matter over) **-man** speaker; *parl.* spokesman
(för of); *göra sig till* ~ *för* voice
the feelings of **-esätt** *(stående* current) phrase,
mode of expression, saying **-fel** speech defect
-film sound (talking) film; *vard.* talkie **-för** *a5*
talkative, loquacious **-förmåga** faculty (power)
of speech; *mista* ~*n* lose one's speech

talg [-j] *s3* tallow; *(njur-)* suet **-dank** tallow dip;
rush candle (light) **-ig** *a1* tallowy, greasy **-körtel**
sebaceous gland **-ljus** tallow candle **-oxe**
great tit

talhytt call (telephone) box

talis'man *s3* talisman

talj|a *s1*, **-block** tackle [blocks *pl*]

talk *s3* talc[um] **talka** talc **talkpuder** talcum
powder, talc

talkör chorus; choral speech

tall *s2 (träd)* [common] pine, pine tree, Scots
(Scotch) pine (fir); *(trä)* pinewoodm, redwood
-barr pine needle[s *pl*] **-barrsolja** pine-needle
oil

tallektion elocution lesson

tallium ['tall-] *s8* thallium

tallkott|e pine cone **-körtel** pineal gland
(body); *fack.* epiphysis

tallrik *s2* plate; *djup* ~ soup plate; *flat* ~
ordinary [dinner] plate; *en* ~ *gröt* a plate of
porridge **tallriksis** pancake ice

tall|ris pine twigs *(pl)* **-skog** pine forest **-tita**
s1 willow tit

tallös innumerable, countless

talman speaker; *parl.* Speaker of Parliament *(i
Sverige äv.* the Riksdag)

talmud [-'ta:l-] Talmud

talong [-'låŋ] *s3* counterfoil; *AE.* stub; *kortsp.*
talon

tal|organ organ of speech; *(röst)* voice **-pedagog**
speech therapist **-pjäs** *teat.* straight play
-registreringsapparat recording machine,
recorder

talrik numerous; ~*a (äv.)* numbers of **talrikt**
[-i:-] *adv* numerously, in large numbers; ~ *besökt*
well-attended

tal|roll *teat.* spoken part **-rubbning** impairment
of speech **-rör** speaking tube

tal|s [-a:-] *i uttr.: komma till* ~ *med* get to speak
to, talk to **-scen** dramatic theatre **-språk** spoken
(colloquial) language; *engelskt* ~ spoken
(etc.) English

talsystem number system, system of figures

talteknik elocution, speech training

talteori theory of numbers

tal|trast song thrush **-tratt** *tel.* mouthpiece
-trängd *a1* eager to speak; *(som vana)* loquacious,
garrulous **-övning** conversation exercise
(practice); *(uttals-)* speech training

tam *a1* tame; *(om djur)* domestic[ated] **-boskap**
domestic cattle *(pl)*

tambur hall; *(kapprum)* cloakroom

tambu'rin *s3* tambourin

tambur|major drum major; *vard. se följande*
-vaktmästare cloakroom attendant

tam|djur tame *(etc.)* animal **-fågel** poultry **-får**
domestic[ated] sheep **-het** tameness

tamp *s2* [rope's] end

tampas *dep* tussle

tamponer|a tampon **-ing** tamponage

tampong [-'påŋ] *s3* tampon

tamsvin pig

tamtam [ˣtamtam] *(gonggong)* gong, tam-tam;
(trumma) tom-tom

tand *-en tänder* tooth *(pl* teeth); *(vilddjurs)*
fang; *tekn.* tooth, cog; ~ *för* ~ a tooth for a
tooth; *tidens* ~ the ravages *(pl)* of time; *få tänder*
be teething, cut one's teeth; *försedd med
tänder* toothed; *ha ont i tänderna* have toothache;
hålla ~ *för tunga (bildl.)* keep one's own
councel; *visa tänderna* show one's *(om hund:*
bare its) teeth *(mot* at) **tanda** tooth; indent

tand|agnisslan *i uttr: gråt och* ~ weeping and
gnashing of teeth **-ben** toothbone **-borste**
toothbrush **-borstglas** tooth glass **-borstning**
[-å-] brushing of teeth **-brygga** dental bridge

tandem ['tann-] *(hästspann) s7, (cykel) s2* tandem
-cykel tandem cycle **-sadel** pillion; *AE.*
buddy seat

tand|garnityr set of teeth, denture **-hals** neck
of a tooth **-hygien** dental hygiene **-hygienist**
dental hygienist **-kirurgi** dental surgery **-klinik**
dental clinic **-krona** crown of a tooth
-kräm toothpaste **-kött** gum; *fack.* gingiva;
~*et* the gums *(pl)* **-läkarborr** dentist's drill
-läkare dentist, dental surgeon **-läkarexamen**
dental degree **-läkarstol** dentist's (dental)
chair **-lös** toothless **-ning** *konkr.* toothing;
(såg-) serration; *(kuggar)* teeth cogs *(pl)* **-pasta**
toothpaste, dentifrice **-petare** toothpick
-rad row of teeth **-reglering** prevention and
correction of irregular dentition; orthodontics
(pl) **-röta** [dental] caries **-skydd** *(i boxning)*
gumshield; mouthpiece; *sport.* chin protector
-sköterska dental nurse **-sprickning** teething,
cutting of the teeth **-sten** tartar; scale
-ställning brace[s *pl*] **-tekniker** dental
technician (mechanic) **-tråd** dental floss **-utdragning**
tooth extraction **-val** toothed whale
-vall alveolar ridge **-vård** dental care (service)
-värk toothache **-ömsning** second dentition

tangent [-nj-, *i sht tekn. o. geom.* -ŋg-] **1** *mus.,
tekn.* key **2** *geom.* tangent **-bord** *(i skrivmaskin)*
keyboard **-ial** [-ŋgen[t]si'a:l] *a1*, **-iell**
[-ŋgen[t]si'ell] tangential

Tanger [taŋ'ʃe:] *n* Tangier

tanger|a [-ŋg-, -nj-] **1** *(gränsa t.)* touch upon,
border on **2** *geom.* be a tangent to, touch **3**
sport. equal **-ingspunkt** tangential point; *bildl.*
point of contact

tango ['taŋgɷ] *s5* tango

tanig *a1* thin **-het** thinness

tank 1 *s2* (*behållare*) tank, container **2** *s2* (*stridsvagn*) tank **tanka** fill up, refuel **tanker** ['tann-] *s2* tanker **tankbil** petrol (*AE.* gas, gasoline) truck; *Storbritannien äv.* tank (tanker) lorry

tank|e *s2* thought (*på* of); (*idé*) idea (*om, på* of); (*åsikt*) opinion (*om* about); (*avsikt*) intention; (*plan*) plan (*på* for); *blotta ~ en på* the mere thought of; *var har du dina -ar?* what are you thinking about?; *ha -arna med sig* have one's wits about one; *ha en låg ~ om* have a poor opinion of; *ha ~ på att göra ngt* have got the idea of doing s.th.; *jag har aldrig haft en ~ ditåt* such a thought has never occurred to me; *i ~ att* with the idea (intention) of (+ ing-*form*); *försänkt i -ar* lost in thought; *jag hade ngt annat i -arna* I was thinking of s.th. else; *det leder* [*osökt*] *~n till* it makes one think of; *med ~ på* bearing ... in mind; *få ngn på andra -ar* make s.b. change his mind; *komma på bättre -ar* think better of it; *utbyta -ar om* exchange ideas about

tanke|ansträngning mental exertion (effort) **-arbete** brain work **-bana** line of thought **-diger** profound **-experiment** intellectual experiment **-frihet** freedom of thought **-förmåga** capacity for thinking **-gång** *s2* train of thought **-läsare** thought-reader, mind-reader **-möda** *se -ansträngning* **-skärpa** mental acumen **-ställare** warning, food for thought; *få sig en ~* get s.th. to think about **-utbyte** exchange of thoughts (ideas, opinions) **-verksamhet** mental activity **-väckande** *a4* thought-provoking **-värld** world of ideas **-överföring** telepathy, thought transference

tankfartyg tanker

tank|full thoughtful, contemplative **-lös** thoughtless, unreflecting; (*om pers. äv.*) scatterbrained **-löshet** thoughtlessness *etc.*; *en ~* a thoughtless act

tank|muff shroud **-ning** refuelling, filling up

tank|spridd *a5* absent-minded **-spriddhet** preoccupation (absence) of mind **-streck** dash

tankvagn tank wagon; *i sht AE.* [rail] tank car

tan'nin *s4, s3* tannin, tannic acid

tant *s3* aunt; (*smeksamt*) auntie; *~ Andersson* Mrs. Andersson

tan'tal *s3, s4, kem.* tantalum; (*malm*) tantalite

tantaluskval *pl* torments of Tantalus

tantiem [taŋt-, tant-, -i'e:m, -i'ä:m] *s7* commission on profit[s *pl*], bonus

tantig *a1* old-maidish; frumpy

tanzan|ier [-'(t)sa:-] *s9*, **-isk** *a5* Tanzanian

ta'pet *s3* wallpaper; (*vävd*) tapestry; *sätta upp ~er* hang (put up) wallpaper; *vara på ~en* (*bildl.*) be on the tapis **-klister** paperhanger's paste **-rulle** roll of wallpaper

tapetser|a [hang] paper, decorate; *~ om* repapper **-are** [-ˣse:-] upholsterer **-arverkstad** upholstery [work]shop, upholstery **-ing** paperhanging, wallpapering

tapioka [-i'åk:a, -iˣå:ka] *s1, bot.* tapioca

ta'pir *s3, zool.* tapir; (*schabrak-*) Malayan tapir

tapisseri tapestry **-affär** fancywork shop **-arbete** fancywork, tapestry work

tapp *s2* **1** (*i tunna e.d.*) tap, faucet; (*i badkar,* *båt e.d.*) plug **2** (*t. hopfästning*) peg; (*trä-*) tenon; (*axel*) journal; (*sväng-*) pivot, trunnion **3** (*syncell*) cone **4** (*hö-*) wisp; (*ull-*) flock; (*moln-*) wisp

1 tappa (*vätska*) tap (*äv. med.*); (*av-, ~ upp*) draw [off]; *~ på buteljer* draw [... off]; pour (tap) into bottles; *~ blod av* bleed, draw blood from; *~ i vatten i badkaret* run water into the bath; *~ ur vattnet ur* let the water out of

2 tappa (*släppa*) drop, let fall; (*förlora*) lose (*äv. ~ bort*); *~ i golvet* drop (*etc.*) on (to) the floor; *~ huvudet* (*bildl.*) lose one's head; *~ bort sig* get lost, lose o.s.; *~ bort varandra* lose (get separated from) each other

tapper ['tapp-] *a2* brave; courageous; (*ridderligt ~*) gallant **-het** bravery, valour; courage **-hetsmedalj** medal for valour; distinguished service medal

tapp|hål taphole, pouring hole **-kran** drain cock **-ning** (*av vätska*) drawing, tapping; *vin av en god ~* a vintage wine; *i annan ~* (*bildl.*) formulated differently, in a different form

tappt *i uttr: ge ~* give in

tapto ['tapp-] *s6* tattoo; *blåsa ~* beat (sound) the tattoo; *AE.* taps (*pl*)

tara *s1* tare

taran|tel [-'rann-] *s2* tarantula **-tella** [-ˣtella] *s1* tarantella

tarer|a tare **-ing** taring

ta'riff *s3* tariff; schedule (list) [of rates]

tarm *s2* intestine; *~arna* (*äv.*) the bowels (entrails, *vard.* guts) **-flora** intestinal flora **-kanal** intestinal canal **-katarr** intestinal catarrh **-käx** [-ç-] *s7* mesentery **-ludd** intestinal villi (*pl*) **-vred** *s7* ileus, intestinal obstruction **-vägg** intestinal wall

taro *s5* taro, elephant's ear, dasheen

tars *s3* tarsus (*pl* tarsi) **-led** tarsal joint

tar'tar *s3* Tartar **-biff** *se* råbiff **-sås** tartar sauce

tarte'lett *s3* tartlet

tarv *s7, förrätta sitt ~* ease nature **tarva** require, demand, call for **tarvas** *dep, se* behövas **tarvlig** *a1* (*enkel*) frugal (*måltid* meal); (*smaklös*) cheap (*klänning* dress); (*om pers. o. smak*) vulgar, common; (*lumpen*) shabby (*uppförande* behaviour) **tarvligt** *adv* frugally *etc.*; *bära sig ~ åt* behave shabbily (*mot* to) **tarvlighet** frugality; cheapness; vulgarity *etc.*; *~er* vulgarities

tas *togs tagits, dep, vard., hon är inte god att ~ med* she is a difficult person (child)

taskig *vard.* (*elak*) mean; (*orättvis*) unfair; (*dålig*) poor, lousy

taskspelar|e juggler, conjurer **-konst** *~er* juggling (conjuring) tricks

tass *s2* paw; *bort med ~arna!* hands off!; *räcka vacker ~* put out a paw nicely; *skaka ~ med* shake hands with **tassa** patter, pad

tassel ['tass-] *s7, tissel och ~* tittle-tattle **tassla** tittle-tattle

ta'tar *s3* Ta[r]tar

tattar|e *ung.* gypsy **-unge** gypsy kid

tatuer|a tattoo **-ing** tattooing

tautologi tautology

tavel|förfalskare forger of paintings **-galleri** picture gallery **-ram** picture frame **-samling** collection of pictures **-utställning** exhibition

of paintings
taverna [-ˣvärr-] *s1* tavern
tavla [ˣta:v-] *s1* **1** *konst.* picture (*äv. bildl.*) **2** (*platta*) table; (*anslags-*) board; *svarta ~n* the blackboard **3** *vard., vilken ~!* what a slip-up (*AE. boner*)!
tax *s2* dachshund
1 taxa *v1, flyg.* taxi
2 taxa *s1* (*pris*) rate, charge; (*för personbefordran e.d.*) fare; (*telefon-*) fee; (*förteckning*) list of rates, tariff; *enhetlig ~* standard (flat) rate; *full ~* full rate **-meter** [-ˈme:-] *s2* taximeter, fare meter **-meterbil** *se taxi*
taxe|bestämmelser tariff (fare) regulations **-höjning** increase of charges (*etc.*); (*av biljettpris*) increase in fares
taxer|a assess [... for taxes] (*till* at), tax; (*uppskatta*) rate; (*värdera*) estimate, value; *~d inkomst* assessed income; *han ~r för 5 000 pund om året* he is assessed at 5,000 pounds a year **-ing** [tax] assessment; *för hög ~* over-valuation; *~ till kommunal* (*statlig*) *inkomstskatt* assessment for local (national) income tax
taxerings|belopp sum charged, amount of assessment **-distrikt** assessment district **-kalender** taxpayers' (ratepayers') directory **-man** [tax] assessor **-myndighet** assessment authority **-nämnd** assessment board (committee) **-värde** rat[e]able value; *AE.* tax assessment [value] **-år** year of assessment
taxi [ˈtaksi] *s9* taxi [cab], cab **-båt** taxi boat **-chaufför** taxi driver, cab driver, cabman **-flyg** air taxi; taxiplane service **-station** taxi (cab) rank; *AE.* taxi (cab) stand
taˈzett [-s-] *s3* French daffodil
tbc [tebeˈse:] *best. form tbc-n* T.B., t.b. **-sjuk** *subst.* TB-sufferer
T-benstek T-bone steak
Tchad *n* Chad **tchad|ier** [ˈtʃa:-] *s9*, **-isk** [ˈtʃa:-] *a5* Chadian
TCO [teseˈʍ:] (*förk. för Tjänstemännens Centralorganisation*) *se under tjänsteman*
1 te *s4* tea; *koka* (*dricka*) *~* make (have) tea
2 te *v4, rfl* appear
teak [ti:k] *s3* teak
teater [-eˈa:-] *s2* theatre; *absurd ~* theatre of the absurd; *spela ~* act, *bildl.* play-act; *gå* (*vara*) *på ~n* go to (be at) the theatre; *gå in vid ~n* go on the stage **-affisch** playbill **-besök** visit to the theatre **-besökare** theatre-goer **-biljett** theatre ticket **-chef, -direktör** theatre manager **-folk** stage people **-föreställning** theatrical performance **-historia** stage history **-kikare** opera glasses (*pl*) **-kritiker** dramatic critic **-pjäs** [stage] play **-publik** theatre-goers (*pl*); audience **-recension** theatrical review **-sällskap** theatrical company **-viskning** stage whisper
teatralisk [-ˈtra:-] *a5* theatrical
te|bjudning tea party **-blad** tea leaf **-blask** *vard.* dishwater **-burk** tea caddy **-buske** tea plant
tecken [ˈteck-] *s7* sign (*på, till* of); (*känne-*) mark (*på* of); (*symbolisk figur*) symbol (*äv. kem.*); *mat.* sign; (*skriv-*) character, sign; (*signal*) signal (*till* for); *det är ett gott ~* it is a good sign; *göra ~ åt ngn* make signs (a sign)

to s.b.; *i enighetens ~* in a spirit of unity; *på givet ~* at a given sign (signal); *till ~ på* as a token (mark) of; *visa alla ~ till att* show every sign of (+ *ing-form*); *inte ett ~ till rädsla* not a vestige (trace) of fear **-förklaring** key to the (table of) signs **-ruta** (*t.ex. på miniräknare*) display **-språk** sign language **-tydare** auger
teckna 1 (*ge tecken*) sign (make signs, a sign) (*till, åt* to); (*med gester e.d.*) make a sign (*åt* to) **2** (*skriva*) sign; (*genom namnteckning utlova*) put one's name down for; *~ aktier* subscribe for (to) shares; *~ firman* sign for a company; *~ kontrakt* make (enter) into a contract **3** (*rita*) draw (*efter* from; *för* for); (*skildra äv.*) delineate, depict; *~ av* sketch [off]; *~d film* [animated] cartoon; *~d serie* comic strip; *djuret är vackert ~t* the animal is beautifully marked **4** *rfl* (*an- sig*) put one's name down (*för* for); (*av- sig*) be depicted (*i ngns ansikte* on a p.'s face); *~ sig för en försäkring* take out an insurance; *~ sig till minnes* commit to memory
teckn|are 1 drawer, artist; (*illustratör*) illustrator **2** (*aktie-*) [share] subscriber **-ing 1** drawing; *konkr. äv.* sketch; (*i ord*) description **2** *zool.* markings, lines (*pl*) **3** *hand.* subscription (*av aktier* to shares)
tecknings|bevis subscription certificate (*Storbritannien* warrant) **-lektion** drawing lesson **-lista** subscription list **-lärare** drawing master, art teacher **-rätt** *hand.* subscription right **-rättsbevis** *hand.* participation certificate **-undervisning** teaching of drawing
tedags *vid ~* at tea time
teddy|björn teddy bear **-kappa** artificial fur coat
tedeum [-ˣde:-] *s7, best. form äv. tedeum* Te Deum
tefat saucer; *flygande ~* flying saucer
1 teg *s2* strip (piece) of tilled land
2 teg *imperf. av tiga*
tegat *sup. av tiga*
tegel [ˈte:-] *s7* [building] brick; *koll.* bricks (*pl*); (*tak-*) tile, *koll.* tiles (*pl*); *eldfast ~* firebrick **-bruk** brickworks, brickyard; brick kiln **-bränning** brick-burning, tile-burning **-mur** brick wall **-panna** [roofing] tile; pantile **-röd** brick-red **-rör** tile (earthenware) pipe **-sten** brick **-stensroman** great thick novel, tome **-tak** tile[d] roof **-täckt** *a4* tiled
te|hus teahouse **-huv** tea cosy **-'in** *s4* theine
teis|m theism **-tisk** [-ˈiss-] *a5* theistic[al]
tejp *s3* tape **tejpa** tape
tek|a *sport.* face off **-ning** *sport.* face-off
tek|aka teacake **-kanna** teapot **-kittel** kettle
tekn|ik *s3* **1** (*ingenjörsvetenskap*) technics (*pl*); engineering, technology; *~ens framsteg* technological advances **2** (*tillvägagångssätt*) technique **-ikalitet** *s3* technicality **-iker** [ˈteck-] technician, engineer **-isk** [ˈteck-] *a5* technical; technological; *~ högskola* institute of technology; *~t missöde* technical hitch; *~t museum* museum of science and technology
tekno|krat technocrat **-log** technologist, technological student **-logi** *s3* technology **-logisk** *a5* technological
tekoindustri textile and clothing industry

T

te|kopp teacup; (som mått) teacupful [of] -kök tea urn
tele'fax s7 telefax
telefon [-'få:n] s3 telephone; vard. phone; det ringer i ~en the telephone is ringing; det är ~ till dig you are wanted on the telephone; svara i ~ answer the telephone; tala i ~ talk (speak) on the telephone; per ~ by (on the, over the) telephone -abonnent telephone subscriber -apparat telephone [apparatus] -automat slot telephone; AE. pay [tele]phone -avgift telephone rental (charge) -avlyssning wire-tapping -central telephone exchange -era telephone (efter for; till to); vard. phone, AE. call (till ngn s.b.) -förbindelse telephone connection -hytt call (telephone) box, phone booth; AE. telephone booth
telefo'n|i s3 telephony -ist telephone operator -katalog telephone directory (AE. book) -kiosk se telefonhytt -kontakt stå i ~ med keep in touch by telephone with -kort phone card -kö telephone queue [service] -ledning telephone circuit (wire) -lur receiver -nummer telephone number; hemligt ~ unlisted telephone number -påringning telephone call -reparatör telephone mechanic -räkning telephone bill -samtal telephone conversation; (påringning) telephone call; åberopande vårt ~ referring to our telephone conversation -station telephone exchange (call office; AE. office) -stolpe telephone pole -svarare telephone answering machine; pers. answering-service operator -terror threatening phone calls -tid telephone hours (pl) -tråd telephone wire -vakt telephone answering service -väckning alarm call -väkteri phone-in [radio programme] -växel telephone exchange
telefoto wirephoto, telephoto
telegraf s3 telegraph -arbetare telegraph-service worker -era wire, telegraph; (utom Europa äv.) cable -ering telegraphy; cabling
telegra'f|i s3 telegraphy -isk [-'gra:-] a5 telegraphic -iskt [-'gra:-] adv telegraphically; svara ~ wire (cable) back -ist telegraph operator; sjö. radio officer -station telegraph office -stolpe telegraph pole -verk telegraph service
telegram [-'gramm] s7 telegram; vard. wire; (utom Europa) cable[gram]; ~ med betalt svar reply-paid telegram -adress telegraphic (cable) address -avgift telegram (etc.) charge -bild telephoto -blankett telegram form (AE. blank) -byrå news (press) agency; Tidningarnas ~ [the] Swedish central news agency -pojke telegraph boy -remissa telegraphic remittance (money order, transfer) -stil telegraphic style
tele|kinesi telekinesis -kommunikation telecommunication[s pl] -objektiv telephoto lens -ologi teleology -pati s3 telepathy -patisk [-'pa:-] a5 telepathic -printer [-'prinn-] s2 teleprinter, AE. teletypewriter -printerremsa ticker tape
teleskop s7 telescope -antenn telescopic aerial (antenna) -isk [-'skå:-] a5 telescopic
tele|station telephone and telegraph office -teknik telecommunication [engineering] -tekniker telecommunication engineer -tek-

nisk telecommunication -verket [the Swedish] telecommunications administration -visera televise, telecast -vision television (förk. TV); vard. telly (Storbritannien), video (AE.); intern ~ closed-circuit television; komma i ~ appear on television, be on TV; se på ~ watch television (the TV); sända per ~, se -visera
televisions|apparat television (TV) [set] -kamera television camera -ruta viewing screen -sändare television transmitter -sändning television transmission (broadcast)
telex ['te:-] s2 telex; AE. teletype (varumärke)
telexa [ˣte:-] telex, teletype
telfer ['tell-] s2 [electric] hoist (telpher)
tel'lur s3, s4 tellurium
teln [-e:-] s2 net-rope
telning [ˣte:l-] (skott) sapling; (avkomma) offspring; (unge) kid
tema [ˣte:-, 'te:-] s6 1 (ämne) theme (äv. mus.) 2 (skolstil) composition; (översättning) translation 3 språkv., säga ~ på ett verb give the principle parts of a verb -tisk [-'ma:-] a5 thematic
temp s2, vard., ta ~en take one's temperature
tempel ['temm-] s7 temple -dans temple dance -herreorden the Order of Knights Templar[s] -skändare [-ʃ-] desecrator of a temple -tjänare temple servant; bibl. Levite
1 tempera ['temm-] s9 tempera, distemper
2 tem'pera v1 time, set a fuse
temperament s7 temperament
temperaments|full temperamental -sak en ~ a matter of temperament
temperatur temperature; absolut ~ thermodynamic (absolute) temperature -fall fall of (in the) temperature -förändring change of (in the) temperature
temperer|a 1 (värma) temper, warm, take the chill off 2 mus. temper -ad a5 (om vin e.d.) tempered; (om klimat e.d.) temperate -ing warming; tempering
tempo ['temm-] s6 1 (hastighet) pace, speed; mus. tempo (pl tempi); forcera ~t force the pace, speed up 2 (handgrepp) operation -arbetare semiskilled worker -arbete serial production -beteckning mus. expression mark -'ral a1 temporal -'rär a1 temporary
tempus ['temm-] n tense -följd sequence of tenses
ten s2 [metal] rod
ten'dens s3 tendency; (utvecklingsriktning) trend -fri nontendentious -roman novel with a purpose
tendentiös [-n(t)si'ö:s] a1 tendentious; (friare) bias[s]ed
tender ['tenn-] s2 tender
tendera tend (mot towards; [till] att to)
Teneriffa [-ˣriffa] n Tenerife
tenn s4 tin; engelskt ~ pewter -bägare pewter tankard -folie tinfoil -gjutare pewterer -gjuteri pewter foundry
tennis ['tenn-] s2 tennis -arm tennis elbow (arm) -bana tennis court -boll tennis ball -hall covered tennis court, tennis hall -racket tennis racket -sko tennis shoe -spelare tennis player -tävling tennis tournament
tenn|kanna pewter jug -lödning tin (soft)

soldering **-plåt** (*material*) sheet tin; *konkr.* tin sheet, tinplate **-soldat** tin soldier **-stop** pewter mug

te'nor *s3* tenor **-klav** tenor clef **-saxofon** tenor saxophone **-stämma** tenor voice

tensid *s3* surfactant, surface-active agent

tenta *vard., se* tentamen *o.* tentera

tentakel [-'tack-] *s3* tentacle, feeler

tent|amen *r,* -amen -amina examination; *muntlig* ~ oral examination, viva [voce]

tentamens|läsa revise, read (study) for an examination **-period** examination period **-skräck** horror of exams

ten'tand *s3* examinee, candidate

tentativ [-'ti:v, 'tenn-] *a1* tentative

tent|ator *s3* examiner **-era 1** (*prövas*) be examined (*för* by; *i* in) **2** (*pröva*) examine; *absol.* conduct an examination

teodl|are tea planter **-ing** tea growing; *konkr.* tea plantation

teodo'lit *s3* theodolite, *AE.* transit

teo|log theologian **-logi** *s3* theology; (*som studieämne äv.*) divinity; ~*e doktor* doctor of theology (divinity); ~*e studerande* theology student, student of theology (divinity) **-logisk** [-'lå:-] *a5* theological; ~ *fakultet* (*äv.*) faculty of theology

teo're|m *s7* theorem **-tiker** [-'re:-] theoretician, theorist **-tisera** theorize (*om, över* about) **-tisk** [-'re:-] *a5* theoretic[al]

teo'ri *s3* theory

teo|sof [-'så:f] *s3* theosophist **-sofi** [-så'fi:] *s3* theosophy **-sofisk** [-'så:-] *a5* theosophic[al]

tepåse tea bag

terapeut [-'pevt] *s3* therapist **-isk** [-'pevv-] *a5* therapeutic[al]

tera'pi *s3* therapy

term [tärm] *s3* term

termer ['tärr-] *pl* (*bad*) thermae

ter'mik [-'mi:k] *s3* thermal[s *pl*]

termin [-'mi:n] *s3* **1** (*del av läsår*) term; *AE.* semester **2** (*tidpunkt*) stated (fixed) time, term; (*förfallotid*) time of maturity, due date; (*betalnings-*) day (time) of payment; *betalning i* ~*er* payment by instalment

terminal [-'na:l] **I** *s3* terminal **II** *a1* terminal

terminologi *s3* terminology

termins|affär forward deal (transaction), time bargain **-avgift** term fee **-betyg** term report **-vis** by (in) instalments

termisk ['tärr-] *a5* thermal, thermic

termistor [-ˣmistår] *s3* thermistor

termit [-'mi:t] *s3* termite, white ant

termo|dynamik [ˣtärr-, -'i:k] thermodynamics (*pl, behandlas som sg*) **-dynamisk** [ˣtärm-, -'na:-] thermodynamic[al] **-elektrisk** [ˣtärr-, -'leck-] thermoelectric[al] **-element** [ˣtärr-] [bimetallic] thermocouple **-graf** *s3* thermograph **-meter** [-'me:-] *s2* thermometer; ~*n visar 5 grader* the thermometer stands at 5 degrees; ~*n faller* the temperature is falling **-meterskala** thermometric (thermometer) scale **-nukleär** [ˣtärr-, -'ä:r] thermonuclear **-plast** [ˣtärr-] thermoplastic

termos ['tärr-] *s2,* **-flaska** thermos [flask] (*varumärke*) **-kanna** vacuum jug

termostat *s3* thermostat **-reglerad** thermostat-

controlled

teros *bot.* tea rose

terpen *s3, kem.* terpene

terpen'tin *s3, s4* turpentine

terracotta [-ˣkåtta] *s9* terra cotta

terrarium [-'ra:-] *s4* vivarium; terrarium

ter'rass *s3,* **-era** *v1* terrace **-formig** [-å-] *a1* terraced

terrester [-'ress-] *a2* terrestrial

terrier ['tärr-] terrier

ter'rin *s3* tureen

territorial|gräns [-ˣa:l-] limit of territorial waters **-vatten** territorial waters (*pl*)

territor|i'ell *a1* territorial **-ium** [-'tø:-] *s4* territory

terror ['tärrår] *s9* terror **-balans** balance of terror **-dåd** terrorist act

terror|isera terrorize **-ism** terrorism **-ist** terrorist

terror|verksamhet terrorist activity **-vapen** *pl* terror weapons

ter'räng *s3* terrain; ground, country; land; *kuperad* ~ hilly country; *förlora* ~ lose ground **-bil** cross-country vehicle, *AE.* all-terrain vehicle (*förk.* ATV), jeep **-cykel** mountain bike **-förhållanden** *pl* nature (condition) (*sg*) of the ground **-gående** *a4* cross-country (*fordon* vehicle) **-löpning** cross-country running (run; *vid tävling*: racing, race) **-ritt** cross-country riding (ride)

ters [-ä-] *s3* tierce; *mus. äv.* third

tertiär [-tsi'ä:r] *a1* tertiary **-lån** loan secured by a third mortgage, third mortgage loan **-tiden** the Tertiary [Age]

terylen [-'le:n] *s3, s4* terylene (*urspr. varumärke*); *AE. äv.* dacron (*varumärke*)

terzin [-t'si:n] *s3* terza rima (*pl* terze rime)

tes *s3* thesis (*pl* theses)

te|servis tea service (set) **-sil** tea strainer **-sked** teaspoon; (*som mått*) teaspoonful [of] **-sort** type (blend) of tea; ~*er* (*äv.*) teas

1 test *s2* (*hår-*) wisp

2 test *s7, s9* (*prov*) test; *data.* check

testa test

testa|mentarisk [-'ta:-] *a5* testamentary **-mente** [-'menn-] *s6* **1** *jur.* [last] will [and testament]; *upprätta sitt* ~ make (draw up) one's will; *inbördes* ~ [con]joint will **2** *bibl., Gamla* (*Nya*) ~*et* the Old (New) Testament **-mentera** ~ *ngt till ngn* bequeath s.th. to s.b., leave s.b. s.th. **-mentsexekutor** executor [of a will] **-tor** *s3* testator; *fem.* testatrix

test|bild test pattern, test card; *AE. äv.* resolution chart **-cykel** ergometer bicycle **-flygare** test pilot

testikel [-'tick-] *s2* testicle, testis (*pl* testes)

testning testing

testosteron [-'rå:n] *s4* testosterone

testpilot test pilot

tetanus ['te:-] *r* tetanus

tetraeder [-'e:d-] *s2* tetrahedron

te|vagn tea trolley **-vatten** water for the tea; *sätta på* ~ put the kettle on; *-vattnet kokar* the kettle is boiling

teve *s2, se* TV *o.* television

te|veronika *s1,* **-ärenpris** *s3, bot.* germander speedwell

t.ex. e.g., for example; say

text *s3* text; (*bibelställe äv.*) passage; (*motsats musik*) words (*pl*); (*sammanhang*) context; ~ *i svit* (*boktr.*) run-on; *sätta ~ till musik* put the words to music; *gå vidare i ~en* (*bildl.*) go on; *lägga ut ~en* (*bildl.*) embroider things

text|a 1 (*skriva*) use (write in) block letters **2** (*uttala tydligt*) articulate **-analys** textual analysis **-are** calligrapher **-författare** author of a text; (*t. film*) scriptwriter; (*t. opera*) librettist; (*reklam-*) copywriter **-förklaring** textual commentary **-häfte** book of accompanying text

tex'til *al* textile **-fabrik** textile mill (factory) **-fiber** textile fibre **-ier** *pl* textiles, textile goods **-industri** textile industry **-konstnär, -konstnärinna** textile stylist, pattern designer **-lärare** teacher of textile craft **-varor** *pl, se textilier*

text|kritik textual criticism **-kritisk** critical **-ning** block writing, lettering **-reklam** editorial advertising **-sida** page of text **-ställe** passage, paragraph **--TV** teletext

textur texture

t.f. [*teeff] (*förk. för tillförordnad*) acting (*rektor* headmaster)

t.h. (*förk. för till höger*) to the right

thai|ländare *s9*, **-ländsk** *a5* Thai **-ländska** (*kvinna*) Thai woman **-siden** Thai silk **-språk** Thai

Themsen ['temm-] *r* the [River] Thames **-mynningen** the Thames Estuary

thinner ['tinn-] *s9* thinner **-sniffning** thinner sniffing

thoraxkirurgi [*tɷ:-, *tå:-] thoracic surgery

thriller ['trill-, *äv. eng. uttal*] *s9* thriller

thymus ['ty:-] *r* thymus (*pl äv.* thymi)

tia [*ti:a] *s1* ten; (*sedel*) ten-kronor note

tiar[a] [-*a:r(a)] *s3* [*s1*] tiara

Ti'bet *n* Tibet

tibe't|an *s3* Tibetan **-'ansk** [-a:-] *a5* Tibetan **-anska** [-'ta:n-] **I** (*språk*) Tibetan **II** (*kvinna*) Tibetan woman

1 ticka *s1* polypore

2 ticka *v1* tick

ticktack (*om mindre klocka*) ticktick; (*om större klocka*) ticktock; (*om hjärta*) ticktack

tid *s3* **1** time (*och rum* and space); (*-punkt äv.*) hour, moment; (*period*) period, space; (*tidsålder*) day[s *pl*], time[s *pl*]; *beställa* ~ make an appointment (*hos* with); *bestämma* [*en*] ~ set a day (date) (*för* for); *en* ~ *brukade jag* at one time I used to; *en ~s vila* a period of rest; *när jag får* ~ when I get time (an opportunity) (*med, till* for; *att* to); *har du* ~ *ett ögonblick?* can you spare a moment?; *allt har sin* ~ there's a time for everything; *kommer* ~ *kommer råd* don't cross your bridges until you get to them; *medan* ~ *är* while there is yet time; *ta* ~ (*sport.*) time; *ta god* ~ *på sig* take one's time; *det är god* ~ there is plenty of time (*med* (*till*) *det* for that); *det är hög* ~ *att* it is high time to; *~en är knapp* time is short; *den ~en den sorgen* worry about that when the time comes; *~en för avresan* the time (hour, date) for departure; *~en går* time passes; *~ens gång* the course of time; *~ens tand* the ravages of time; *ha ~en för sig* have the future before one; *hela* *~en* all the time; *nya ~en* the new age; *se ~en an* bide one's time, wait and see; *öppet alla ~er på dygnet* open day and night; *alla ~ers största målare* the greatest painter ever; *alla ~ers chans* the chance of a lifetime; *det var alla ~ers!* that was simply marvellous!; *andra ~er andra seder* manners change with the times; *det var andra ~er då* times were different then; *gamla ~er* ancient times, the old days; *långa ~er kunde han* for long periods he could **2** (*med föregående prep.*) *efter en* (*ngn*) ~ after a time (while), (*om särskilt fall*) some time afterwards; *efter en månads* ~ after [the lapse of] a (one) month, in a month's time; ~ *efter annan* from time to time; *vara efter sin* ~ be behind the times; *enligt den ~ens sed* in accordance with the custom of those times; *från vår* ~ from (of) our times; *för en* ~ for some time; *för en* ~ *av sex månader* for a period of six months; *nu för ~en* nowadays; *före sin* ~ ahead of one's time; *i* ~ in time (*för, till* for; *för att* for + ing-form); *i* ~ *och evighet* for all time; *i* ~ *och otid* at any time (all times); *i god* ~ in good time; *i rätt* (*rättan*) ~ at the right (in [due]) time; *i sinom* ~ in due course; *i två års* ~ for [a period of] two years; *i vår* ~ in our times (age); *förr i ~en* in former times, formerly; *i alla ~er* (*hittills*) from time immemorial; *med ~en* in [course of] time, as time goes on; *på Cromwells* ~ in Cromwell's day[s *pl*]; *springa på* ~ (*sport.*) run against time; *på bestämd* ~ at the appointed time; *på min* ~ in my time (day); *på senare* ~ in recent times; *på senaste* (*sista*) *~en* latterly, recently; *fara bort på en* ~ go away for a time; *det är på ~en att vi* it is about time we; *under ~en* in the meantime, meanwhile; *under ~en 1–0 maj* during the period 1–10 May; *under den närmaste ~en* during the next few days (weeks); *under en längre* ~ for a long (any great length of) time; *gå ur ~en* be removed; *vid ~en för* at the time of; *vid den ~en* at (by) that time; *vid den här ~en* by now (this time); *vid den här ~en på dagen* at (by) this time of the day; *vid en* ~ *som denna* at a time like this; *vid sjutiden* at about seven [o'clock]; *över ~en* beyond (past) the proper time **3** *~s nog* early enough

tidelag *s7* bestiality, sexual intercourse with animals

tide|räkning chronology; *gregorianska ~en* the Gregorian calendar **-varv** period, age, epoch

tidgivning [-ji:v-] time signalling; (*i radio*) time announcement

tidig *al* early **tidigare I** *a, komp. t. tidig* earlier; (*föregående äv.*) previous, former, prior **II** *adv* earlier; at an earlier hour, sooner; (*förut*) previously, formerly **tidigarelägga** advance; ~ *ett sammanträde* hold a meeting earlier **tidigast** *a, superl. t. tidig o. adv* earliest; *allra* ~ at the very earliest

tidigt *adv* early; *för* ~ too early (*för* for; *för att* to), (*i förtid*) prematurely (*född* born); *det blev* ~ *höst* autumn was early; ~ *på dagen* (*morgonen*) early in the day (morning); ~ *på våren* (*äv.*) in early spring; *vara* ~ *uppe* be up early; *vara för* ~ *ute* (*bildl.*) be premature

tid|kort timecard, clock card **-lön** time rate (wages); (*daglön*) day[work] rate; *ha ~ be paid by the hour* **-lös** timeless **-lösa** *s1, bot.* autumn crocus, meadow saffron **-mätare** time meter **-mätning** measurement of time, chronometry

tidning [-i:d-] newspaper; paper; *daglig ~* daily [paper]; *det står i ~en* it's in the paper

tidnings|anka hoax, canard **-artikel** newspaper article **-bilaga** newspaper supplement **-bud** person who delivers newspapers **-försäljare** newsagent, newsvendor; *AE.* newsdealer **-kiosk** newsstand, bookstall **-man** newspaperman, *fem.* newspaperwoman **-papper** hand. newsprint, news stock; *en bit ~* a piece of newspaper **-press** (*samtliga ~ar*) press **-redaktion** newspaper office **-redaktör** newspaper editor **-stöd** state newspaper subsidy **-urklipp** press cutting; *AE.* clipping; *bok för ~* scrapbook, press-cutting book **-utgivare** newspaper publisher

tid|punkt point [of time]; time; *vid ~en för* at the time of **-rymd** period, space of time

tids [-i:-] *se tid 3*

tids|adverb adverb of time **-anda** *~n* the spirit of the age **-befrakta**, **-befraktning** time charter **-begrepp** idea of time **-begränsad** limited in time **-begränsning** time limit **-besparande** *a4* timesaving **-besparing** time saved **-beställning** appointment **-bestämma** date; *-bestämt straff* fixed term [of imprisonment] **-brist** lack of time **-bunden** dated, of its period **-enhet** unit of time **-enlig** [-e:-] *a1* in keeping with the times; up-to-date **-faktor** time factor **-frist** time limit, deadline; (*anstånd*) respite **-fråga** *en ~* a matter of time **-följd** *i ~* in chronological order **-fördriv** *s7, till ~* as a pastime **-förlust** loss of time **-gräns** time limit **-inställd** timed; *~ bomb* time bomb **-inställning** *foto.* shutter setting

tidskrift periodical [publication], publication; journal, review; (*lättare*) magazine

tidskrifts|artikel article in a periodical (*etc.*) **-nummer** issue of a periodical (*etc.*) **-stöd** state magazine subsidy

tidskrivare time recorder

tids|läge situation at the time; *nuvarande ~* the present juncture **-nöd** lack of time **-period** period, space, time **-plan** timetable, time schedule **-signal** time signal **-skede** epoch **-skildring** picture of the time **-skillnad** difference in time **-spillan** *r* waste of time **-studie** time [and motion] study **-studieman** time-study man, timer **-trogen** true to the period; faithful **-typisk** characteristic of the time **-vinst** time-saving; *med stor ~* with a great gain of time **-ålder** age **-ödande** *a4* time-consuming, time-wasting

tid|tabell timetable; *AE. äv.* schedule **-tabellsenlig** [-e:n-] *a1* scheduled **-tagare** *sport.* timekeeper **-tagarur** stopwatch; timer **-tagning** timekeeping **-tals** [-a:-] (*stundtals*) at times; (*långa tider*) for periods together **-vatten** tide; tidal water **-vattenkraftverk** tidal power station **-vis** (*då o. då*) at times; (*med mellanrum*) intermittently, periodically

tig|a *teg tegat* (*äv. -it*) be (remain) silent (*med* about); *~ med ngt* (*äv.*) keep s.th. to o.s.; *~ som*

muren keep silent; *~ ihjäl* hush up; *tig!* shut up!; *han fick så han teg* it silenced him; *den som -er samtycker* silence gives consent

tiger ['ti:-] *s2* tiger **-haj** tiger shark **-hane** male tiger **-hjärta** *tröst för ett ~* a poor consolation **-hona** female tiger **-lilja** tiger lily **-skinn** (*på tiger*) tiger's coat; (*avdraget*) tiger skin **-språng** tiger's leap (*äv. bildl.*) **-unge** tiger cub

tigga *v2* beg (*av* of; *om* for); *AE. sl.* panhandle; *gå omkring och ~* go begging; *~ och be* beg and beg; *~ ihop* collect by begging; *~ sig fram* beg one's way along; *~ sig till ngt av ngn* coax s.th. out of s.b.; *~ stryk* (*vard.*) ask for a thrashing

tiggarbrev begging letter

tiggar|e beggar; *AE. sl.* panhandler; (*yrkesmässig äv.*) mendicant **-munk** mendicant friar **-påse** beggar's wallet **-ranunkel** crowfoot **-stav** beggar's staff; *bringa ngn till ~en* reduce s.b. to beggary

tigger|i begging **-ska** beggar-woman

tigit *sup. av tiga*

tigr|erad [-'re:-] *a5* tigrine **-inna** tigress

tik *s2* bitch

tilj|a *s1* (*planka*) board; *beträda ~n* go on the stage; *gå över ~n* (*om skådespel*) be performed

till I *prep* **1** rumsbet. (*äv. friare*) *a*) allm. to; (*in ~*) into; (*mot*) towards; *vägen ~ handelsboden* the road to the shop; *~ vänster* to the left; *ända ~ stationen* as far as the station; *ha gäster ~ middagen* have guests to dinner; *ha fisk ~ middag* have fish for dinner; *dricka öl ~ maten* have beer with one's food, *b*) (*ankomst*) at (*vid orter*), in (*vid länder, stora städer*); *ankomsten ~ Arlanda* (*Stockholm*) the arrival at Arlanda (in Stockholm); *han anlände ~ stationen* (*Sicilien*) he arrived at the station (in Sicily); *vid deras ankomst ~ staden* on their arrival in the city (at the town); *komma ~ ett resultat* arrive at a result, *c*) (*avresa*) for; *bussen* (*tåget*) *~ A.* the bus (train) for A.; *vid vår avresa ~ London* on our departure for London; *lösa biljett ~ A.* buy a ticket for A. **2** tidsbet. (*som svar på 'hur länge'*) till, until; (*ända ~*) [up] to; (*vid tidpunkt*) at; (*ej senare än*) by; (*avsett för viss tid*) for; *jag väntade ~ klockan sex* I waited till six o'clock; *jag väntade från klockan fem ~ klockan sex* I waited from five o'clock to (till) six o'clock; *~ långt in på natten* till far on into the night; *vi träffas ~ påsk* we will meet at Easter; *~ dess* by then; *ända ~ dess* up to that time; *du måste vara hemma ~ klockan sex* you must be home by six; *natten ~ lördagen* Friday night; *vi har ingen mat ~ i morgon* we have no food for tomorrow; *jag reser hem ~ jul* I am going home for Christmas; *köpa en ny hatt ~ våren* buy a new hat for the spring; *sammanträdet är bestämt ~ i morgon* the meeting is fixed for tomorrow; *jag har tre läxor ~ i morgon* I have three lessons for tomorrow **3** (*dativförhållande*) to; (*avsedd för*) for; *jag sade det ~ dig* I said it to you; *skriva ~ ngn* write to s.b.; *sjunga ~ gitarr* sing to [the accompaniment of] the guitar; *det finns post ~ dig* there are some letters for you; *fyra* *biljetter* ~ *söndag* four tickets for Sunday; *hans kärlek* ~ *pengar* his love of money; *av kärlek* ~ *nästan* out of love for one's neighbour; *vår tillit* ~ *honom* our confidence (trust) in him **4** (*genitivförhållande*) of; to; *hon är dotter till en general* she is a (the) daughter of a general; *dörren* ~ *huset* the door of the house; *författaren* ~ *pjäsen* the author of the play; *en källa* ~ (*bildl.*) a source of; *mor* ~ *två barn* the mother of two children; *nyckeln* ~ *garaget* the key to the garage; *en vän till mig* (*min syster's*) a friend of mine (my sister's); *ägaren* ~ *bilen* the owner of the car **5** (*efter verb*) *se verbet* **6** (*uttr. ändamålet*) for; (*såsom*) as, by way of; *köpa gardiner* ~ *köket* buy curtains for the kitchen; *sakna pengar* ~ lack money for; ~ *metspö använde han* he used ... as a fishing rod; *ge ngn ngt* ~ *julklapp* give s.b. s.th. as a Christmas present; *ha ngn* ~ *vän* have s.b. as a friend **7** (*uttr. verkan, resultat*) to; ~ *min fasa* to my horror; *vara* ~ *hinder för* be a hindrance to; ~ *skada för* to the detriment of **8** (*uttr. förändring*) into; *omvandlingen* ~ the transformation (change) into; *översättning* ~ *svenska* translation into Swedish; *en förändring* ~ *det bättre* a change for the better **9** (*vid pris o.d.*) at; (*vid måttsuppgift*) of; *jordgubbar* ~ *15 kronor litern* strawberries at 15 kronor per litre; ~ *en längd av sex meter* of a length of 6 metres **10** (*i fråga om*) in; (*genom*) by; ~ *antalet* (*utseendet*) in number (looks); ~ *det yttre* in external appearance; *läkare* ~ *yrket* doctor by profession **11** (*i egenskap av*) of; *det var en baddare* ~ *gädda!* that pike is a real whopper!; *ett nöt* ~ *karl* a fool of a man; *ett ruckel* ~ *hus* a ramshackle old house; *en slyngel* ~ *son* a rascal of a son **12** (*före inf.*) ~ *att börja med* to begin with; *ett gevär* ~ *att skjuta med* a gun for shooting (to shoot with); *han är inte karl* ~ *att* he's not the man to **13** ~ *och med* up to [and including], *AE.* through; ~ *och med söndag* (*äv.*) inclusive of Sunday, *AE.* through Sunday; *jfr II 4* **14** *svag* ~ *måttlig vind* light to moderate winds; *det var 20* ~ *30 personer där* there were 20 or (to) 30 persons there; *1* ~ *2 tabletter* one to two tablets **II** *adv* **1** (*ytterligare*) more; *en gång* ~ once more; *det kommer tre* ~ three more are coming; *ta en kaka* ~*!* have another biscuit!; *lika mycket* ~ as much again; *det gör varken* ~ *eller från* it makes no difference **2** (*på instrumenttavla o.d.*) on **3** (*tillhörande*) to it; *ett paraply med fodral* ~ an umbrella with a case to it; *en radio med batteri* ~ a radio and battery [to it] **4** ~ *och med* even (*jfr I 13*); ~ *och från* (*då o. då*) off and on; *hon går* ~ *och från* (*om städhjälp*) she comes in; *åt skolan* ~ towards the school; *vi skulle just* ~ *att börja* we were just about to start (on the point of starting) **III** *konj,* ~ *dess* [*att*] till, until

tillaga|a (*särskr. till-laga*) make (*soppa* soup; *te* tea); (*steka*) cook; (*göra i ordning*) get ready, prepare; (*tillblanda*) mix **-ning** (*särskr. till--lagning*) making *etc.*; preparation; ~ *av mat* cooking

tillbaka [-'ba:-] back; (*bakåt*) backwards; *sedan fem år* ~ for the last (past) five years; *sedan*

ngn tid ~ for some time [past] **-bildad** *a5, biol.* vestigial **-blick** retrospect; (*i film, bok*) flashback **-böjd** bent backwards **-dragen** *bildl.* retiring, unobtrusive, reserved **-draget** *adv, leva* ~ live in retirement **-gående** *a4* retrograde; retrogressive; *bildl. äv.* declining **-gång** (*nedgång*) retrogression, decline, setback (*i of*) **-lutad** *a5* leaning backwards; (*om pers. äv.*) leaning back, reclining; ~ *ställning* recumbence, recumbency **-satt** *a4, känna sig* ~ feel slighted (neglected) **-syftande** *a4* referring [back] to **-visa** (*förslag*) reject, refuse; (*påstående*) refute; (*beskyllning*) repudiate

till|be[dja] worship; (*friare*) adore **-bedjan** [-e:-] *best. form -bedjan, r* worship; adoration **-bedjansvärd** *a1* adorable **-bedjare** [-e:-] adorer; *hennes* ~ her admirer **-behör** *s7, pl* accessories, fittings, appliances; (*reservdelar*) spare parts **-blivelse** coming into being; (*begynnelse*) origin, birth **-bommad** *a5* barred and bolted **-bringa** spend, pass (*med att* in + ing-form) **-bringare** jug; *AE.* pitcher **-buck-lad** *a5* dented **-bud** (*olycks-*) narrow escape **-'buds** [-u:-] *se bud 5* **-byggnad** extension, addition **-börlig** [-ö:-] *a1* due; proper (*aktning* respect); (*lämplig*) fitting, appropriate **-bör-ligen** [-ö:-] duly *etc.* **-dela** allot (assign, give) [to]; award (*ngn ett pris* s.b. a prize, a prize to s.b.); confer, bestow (*ngn en utmärkelse* a distinction [up]on s.b.); (*vid ransonering*) allocate; ~ *ngn ett slag* deal s.b. a blow **-delning** allotment, assignment, allocation; award; conferment, bestowal; *konkr.* allowance, ration **-'dels** [-e:-] partly **-'dess** *konj.* ~ [*att*] till, until **till|dra[ga]** *rfl* **1** (*draga åt sig*) attract (*uppmärksamhet* attention) **2** (*hända*) happen, occur **-dragande** *a4* attractive **-dragelse** occurrence; (*viktig*) event **-döma** ~ *ngn ngt* adjudge s.th. to s.b., award s.b. s.th.; *-dömd ersättning* award **-erkänna** ~ *ngn ngt* award (grant) s.b. s.th.; *modern -erkändes vårdnaden om barnet* the mother was granted the custody of the child; ~ *ngt en viss vikt* ascribe (attach) a certain importance to s.th. **-falla** go (fall) to; accrue to **-fart** [-a:-] *s3* means of access **-fartsväg** approach, access road **-flykt** refuge (*mot, undan* from); *ta sin* ~ *till a*) (*en pers.*) take refuge with, go to for refuge, *b*) (*stad, land etc.*) take refuge in, *c*) *bildl.* resort (have recourse) to, take refuge in **-flyktsort** place of refuge (*undan* from) **-flöde** (*flods etc.*) feeder stream, affluent; *bildl.* inflow, influx **-foga 1** (*-lägga*) add (affix, append) (*till to*) **2** (*förorsaka*) inflict (*ngn skada* harm on s.b.), cause (*ngn en förlust* s.b. a loss); ~ *ngn ett nederlag* (*äv.*) defeat s.b. **-'freds** [-e:-] *oböjligt a* satisfied, content; ~ *med livet* at one with the world **tillfreds|ställ|a** [ˣtill-] satisfy, give satisfaction to, content; (*giva t. lags äv.*) please; (*begäran*) gratify; (*hunger e.d.*) appease; ~ *ngns anspråk* fulfil a p.'s expectations **-ställande** *a4* satisfactory (*för* to); (*glädjande*) gratifying (*för* to) **-ställd** *a5* satisfied, content (*med* with) **-ställelse** satisfaction (*över, med* at) **till|friskna** recover **-**(*efter, från* from); *absol. äv.* get well (*vard.* get better) again **-frisknande**

s6 recovery **-frusen** frozen (iced) over; (*om farvatten*) icebound **-fråga** ask; (*rådfråga*) consult (*om* as to, about); *han ~des om sina åsikter* he was asked his opinion **-frågan** *i uttr.: på* ~ when asked (*om* about) **-fullo** [-ˣfullo] *se full 3* **-fyllest** [-'fyll-] *se fyllest* **-fånga** [-ˣfåŋa] *se 1 fånga* **-fångataga** [-ˣfåŋa-] capture; *bli -fångatagen* be taken prisoner **-fångatagande** [-ˣfåŋa-] *s6* capturing, capture

tillfäll|e *s6* (*tidpunkt*) occasion; (*lägligt*) opportunity; (*möjlighet*) chance, possibility; *~t gör tjuven* opportunity makes the thief; *begagna ~t* take the opportunity; *bereda ngn ~ att* provide s.b. with an opportunity to (of + *ing-form*); *det finns ~n då* there are times when; *få* (*ha*) *~ att* find (get) an opportunity of (+ *ing- form*) (to); *så snart ~ ges* when an opportunity occurs (arises); *för ~t* (*för närvarande*) at present, just now, (*för ögonblicket*) for the time being; *inte vara i ~ att* be unable (in no position) to, not be in a position to; *vid ~* when opportunity occurs, when convenient; *vi ber Er meddela oss det vid ~* please let us know it at your convenience; *vid detta ~* on this occasion; *vid första* [*bästa*] *~* at the first opportunity, at your earliest convenience; *vid lämpligt ~* at a suitable (convenient) opportunity; *låta ~t gå sig ur händerna* let the opportunity slip, miss the opportunity

tillfällig *a1* (*då o. då förekommande*) occasional; (*av en händelse*) accidental, casual, incidental; (*kortvarig, provisorisk*) temporary; *~t arbete* casual work; *~a arbeten* odd jobs; *inkomst av ~ förvärvsverksamhet* income from incidental sources; *~t utskott* select committee **-het** accidental occurrence (circumstance); (*slump äv.*) chance; (*sammanträffande*) coincidence; *av en* [*ren*] *~* by pure chance **-hetsdikt** occasional poem

tillfälligt *adv* temporarily, for the time being **-vis** accidentally, by accident; (*oförutsett*) incidentally; (*av en slump*) by chance; (*helt apropå*) casually

tillför|a bring (*ngn ngt* s.th. to s.b.), supply, furnish (*ngn ngt* s.b. with s.th.; *-d effekt* (*fys.*) [power] input

tillförlitlig [-i:t-] *a1* reliable, trustworthy; authentic; *ur ~ källa* (*äv.*) on good authority **-het** reliability, trustworthiness; authenticity

till|förordna appoint temporarily; *~d* acting (*professor* professor), [appointed] pro tempore **-försel** *s9* supply, delivery, provision (*av* of); *~ av nytt kapital* provision of fresh capital **-förselväg** supply route, approach **-försikt** *s3* confidence (*till* in) **-försäkra** secure, ensure (*ngn ngt* s.b. s.th); *~ sig ngt* secure (make sure of) s.th. **-gift** [-j-] *s3* forgiveness; *be om ~* ask for forgiveness **-given** [-j-] *a3* attached; affectionate; (*om make, hund*) devoted; *vara ngn mycket ~* be very devoted (attached) to s.b.; *Din -givne* (*i brev*) Yours sincerely (*t. nära vän:* affectionately) **-givenhet** [-j-] attachment, devotion, attachment (*för* to); (*kärlek*) affection (*för* for) **-gjord** [-j-] affected; (*konstlad*) artificial **-gjordhet** [-j-] affectation; affected manners (*pl*)

tillgodo [-ˣgɷ:-] *se under godo* **-göra** *rfl* utilize; avail o.s. of; *bildl.* profit by (*undervisningen* the education) **-havande** *s6* balance in one's favour, balance due to one; (*i bank*) [credit] balance (*hos* with), holdings, assets (*pl*); *ha ett ~ hos* have a balance in one's favour with; *vårt ~ hos er* the amount you owe us, our account against you **-kvitto** credit note (*AE.* slip) **-räkna** *rfl*, *~ sig ngt* (*kreditera sig*) put s.th. to one's credit, (*rabatt*) allow o.s. s.th., *bildl.* take the credit for s.th. **-se** pay due attention to; satisfy, meet (*krav* demands); supply, provide for (*ngns behov* a p.'s needs)

till|grepp (*ur kassa e.d.*) misappropriation (*ur* from); (*stöld*) theft **-gripa 1** take unlawfully, seize upon; (*stjäla*) thieve; (*försnilla*) misappropriate **2** *bildl.* resort (have recourse) to **-gå 1** (*försiggå*) *det brukar ~ så att* what usually happens is that, the normal procedure is that; *spelet ~r så att* the rules of the game are that **2** *finnas att ~* be obtainable, be to be had (*hos from*); *ha ngn* (*ngt*) *att ~* have s.b. (s.th.) at hand **-gång** *s2* **1** (*förfogande*) access (*t. telefon* to telephone); *jag har ~ till bil i dag* I have the use of a car today **2** (*värdefull ~*) asset; (*bildl. om pers.*) asset; *~ar* means, assets, resources; *~ar och skulder* assets and liabilities; *leva över sina ~ar* live beyond one's means; *fasta* (*rörliga*) *~ar* fixed (current) assets; *han är en stor ~ för företaget* he is a great asset to the company **3** (*förråd*) supply (*på* of); *~ och efterfrågan* supply and demand; *~ på arbetskraft* supply of labour, labour supply **-gänglig** [-jäŋ-] *a1* **1** (*som man kan nå*) accessible (*för* to); (*som finns att -gå*) available (*för* to, for), obtainable; (*öppen*) open (*för* to); *med alla ~a medel* by every available means; *parken är ~ för besökare* the park is open to visitors **2** (*om pers.*) easy to approach, approachable; (*vänlig*) affable **-gänglighet** [-jäŋ-] **1** accessibility **2** affability

tillhanda [-ˣhann-] *se hand 3* **-hålla** (*saluföra*) sell; *~ ngn ngt* supply (furnish, provide) s.b. with s.th.; *~s* (*äv.*) be on sale

till|handla *rfl* buy o.s. (*av ngn* off, from s.b.) **-'hands** *se hand 4* **-hjälp** *med ~ av* with the aid (assistance) of; *med din ~* by your aid (help) **-hopa** [-'hɷ:-] [al]together, in all **-hygge** weapon **-håll** haunt (*för* of); *ha sitt ~ hos ngn* have one's quarters with s.b. **-hålla** *~ ngn att* urge s.b. to; *~ ngn att inte* tell s.b. not to

tillhör|a 1 belong to; (*vara medlem av äv.*) be a member of; (*räknas t.*) be among (one of); *jag tillhör inte dem som* I am not one of those who; *~ en förnäm släkt* (*äv.*) come of a distinguished family **2** *se tillkomma* **-ande** *a4* belonging to; appurtenant; *en maskin med ~ delar* a machine complete with fittings **-ig** *a1*, *en mig ~* a[n] ... belonging to me **-ighet** possession; [private] property; *mina ~er* (*äv.*) my belongings; *politisk ~* political affiliation

tillika [-ˣli:-, -'li:-] also, as well, ... too; (*dessutom*) besides, moreover; *~ med* together with

tillintet|gjord [-ˣinn-] (*nedbruten*) crushed (*av sorg* with sorrow) **-göra** (*nedgöra*) annihilate; (*besegra*) defeat completely; (*krossa*) crush (*äv. bildl.*); (*förhoppningar*) shatter; (*planer*) frustrate; *~nde blickar* withering looks **-görelse** [-j-] annihilation; demolition; ruin; shattering; frustration

tillit confidence, trust, faith (*till* in); reliance (*till* on); *sätta sin ~ till* put one's confidence in

tillitsfull confident; confiding, trustful

till|kalla summon, call; *~ hjälp* summon assistance; *~ läkare* send for a doctor **-klippning** cutting **-klippt** *a4* cut out **-knyckla** (*skrynkla*) crumple [up]; (*hatt e.d.*) batter [about] **-knäppt** *a4* buttoned-up; (*om pers.*) reserved **-komma 1** (*komma som tillägg*) *se komma* [*till*]; *dessutom -kommer* (*äv.*) in addition there is **2** (*uppstå*) *se komma* [*till*] **3** (*vara ngns rättighet*) be (a p.'s) due; (*åligga*) be incumbent [up]on; *det -kommer inte mig att* it is not for me to **4** *-komme ditt rike!* Thy Kingdom come! **-kommande** *a4* (*framtida*) future, coming, ... to come; *hennes ~* (*som subst.*) her husband-to-be (future husband) **-komst** [-å-] *s3* coming into being (existence); (*uppkomst*) origin, rise **-koppla** attach, hook on; *järnv.* couple [up]; (*motor*) put in[to] gear **-krånglad** *a5* (*-trasslad*) entangled; (*invecklad*) complicated **-kämpa** *rfl* obtain (gain) after a struggle; *~d* hard-won

tillkännagiv|a [-ˣçänn-] notify, announce, make known (*för* to); (*röja*) disclose; *härmed -es att* notice is hereby given that **-ande** *s6* notification, announcement, declaration; (*anslag äv.*) notice

till|mäle *s6* word of abuse, epithet; *grova ~n* (*äv.*) invectives **-mäta 1** (*uppmäta*) measure out to, allot **2** (*tillräkna*) attach to; *~ ngt betydelse* attach importance to s.th.; *~ sig äran* take the credit **-mätt** *a4* measured out; apportioned

tillmötes [-ˣmö:-] *se möte 1* **-gå** (*ngn*) oblige, meet; (*begäran, önskan*) comply with **-gående I** *a4* obliging (*sätt* manners), courteous; (*om pers.*) accommodating (*mot* to[wards]) **II** *s6* obligingness, courtesy, compliance; *tack för Ert ~* thank you for your kind assistance

till|namn surname, family name **-närmelsevis** [-ˣnärr-] approximately; *icke ~* nothing like

tillopp (*särskr. till-lopp*) (*tillflöde*) influx, inflow; (*av ånga*) induction, inlet; (*av människor*) rush, run

tillopps|kanal feeder; (*t. motor*) lead **-rör** delivery (feed) tube

till|'pass *se 5 pass* **-platta** flatten, compress; *känna sig ~d* (*bildl.*) feel crushed (sat on)

till|ra roll; trickle **-reda** prepare, get ready **-'reds** [-e:-] *vara* (*stå*) *~* be ready (*för, till* for; *för* (*till*) *att* to) **-rop** call, shout; *glada ~* joyous acclamations **-ropa** hail; (*om vakt*) *o.d.* challenge **-ryggalägga** [-ˣrygg-] cover

tillråd|a advise, recommend, suggest **-an** *r, på ngns ~* on the (by) advice of s.b. **-lig** *a1* advisable **-lighet** advisability

tillräck|lig *a1* sufficient, enough (*för, åt* for); *vi har ~t med* we have ... enough; *mer än ~t* more than enough, enough and to spare **-ligt** *adv* sufficiently, enough; *~ många* a sufficient number of; *~ ofta* often enough, sufficiently often

tillräkna *~ ngn ngt* put s.th. down to s.b.; *~ ngn förtjänsten av ngt* give s.b. the credit of s.th.; *~ sig* take (ascribe) to o.s.; *~ sig själv hela äran* take all the credit o.s.

tillräknelig [-ä:-] *a5* accountable (responsible) [for one's actions] **-het** accountability

tillrätta [-ˣrätta] *se rätta I 2* **-lagd** *a5, ~* [*för*] arranged (adjusted) to suit **-lägga** correct, make clear **-visa** reprove, censure; (*starkare*) reprimand, rebuke **-visning** reproof, censure; reprimand, rebuke

tills I *konj* (*t. dess att*) till, until **II** *prep* (*t. ngn tidpunkt*) up to; *~ för två år sedan* until two years ago; *~ vidare* until further notice; *~ på lördag* till (until) Saturday

till|sagd *a5* told; *han är ~* he has been told; *är det -sagt?* (*i butik*) are you being attended to [, Sir (Madam)]? **-sammans** together (*med* with); (*sammanlagt*) in all, altogether; (*gemensamt*) jointly; *alla ~* all together; *äta middag ~ med* dine with; *det blir 50 pund ~* it will be 50 pounds in all; *~ har vi 50 pund* we have 50 pounds between (*om fler än två:* amongst) us **-sats 1** (*-sättning*) adding, addition **2** (*ngt -satt*) added ingredient; (*liten ~*) dash; *bildl.* admixture, addition **-satsmedel** additive **-se** (*ha -syn över*) look after, superintend; (*sörja för*) see [to it] (*att ngt blir gjort* that s.th. is done) **-sinnes** [-ˣsinnes] in mind; *munter ~* in high spirits **-'sist** finally; at last **-skansa** *rfl* appropriate for o.s.; *~ sig makten* usurp power **-skjuta** contribute, pay in (*kapital* capital) **-skott** *s7* contribution; (*utökning*) addition, increase **-skottsvärme** incidental heat gain **-skriva 1** (*skriva t.*) write to **2** (*-räkna*) *~ ngn ngt* ascribe (attribute) s.th. to s.b., (*erkänna* *äv.*) credit s.b. with s.th.; *~ sig, se tillräkna* [*sig*] **-skrynkla** crease (crumple) up

tillskynd|a (*tillfoga*) cause (*ngn en förlust* s.b. a loss) **-an** *r, på ngns ~* at the instigation (instance) of s.b. **-are** initiator

tillskär|a cut out **-are** cutter **-ning** cutting out

till|slag (*tennis etc.*) hit; (*fotboll*) kick **-sluta** close, shut (*för* to) (*äv. bildl.*) **-slutning** [-u:-] **1** (*-slutande*) closing [up] *etc.* **2** (*an-*) *mötet hölls under stor ~* the meeting was very well attended **-spetsa** *eg.* sharpen, point; *bildl.* bring to a head; *läget har ~ts* the situation has become critical **-spillo** [-ˣspillo] *se spillo* **-spillogiva** (*låta gå förlorat*) allow to run to waste; *en -spillogiven dag* a wasted day **-stampa** (*jord o.d.*) stamp **-stoppa** stop (shut) [up] **-strömning** streaming in; (*om vätska*) inflow; (*-skott utifrån*) influx; (*publik-*) stream, rush **-stymmelse** *inte en ~ till* not a trace of; *utan varje ~ till* without any semblance of **-styrka** recommend, support, be in favour of **-styrkan** *r* recommendation **-stå** (*medge*) admit; (*bekänna*) confess (*för* to; *att* that)

1 tillstånd *s7* (*tillåtelse*) permission, leave; (*av myndighet äv.*) sanction; (*-sbevis*) permit, licence; *få ~ att* receive (be granted) permission to; *ha ~ att* (*äv.*) have been authorized (licenced) to; *med benäget ~ av* by kind permission of

2 tillstånd *s7* (*beskaffenhet; skick*) state, condition; (*sinnes-*) state [of mind]; *fast* (*flytande*

~ solid (liquid) form; *i dåligt* ~ in bad condition (repair); *i naturligt* ~ in the natural state; *miner.* native; *i berusat* ~ in a state of intoxication; *i medtaget* ~ in an exhausted condition
till|ståndsbevis permit, licence; *AE.* license, certificate **-städes** [-ˣstä:-] *vara* ~ be on the spot, (*närvarande*) be present; *komma* ~ arrive to the place **-städesvarande** *a4, de* ~ those present **-ställa** (*-sända*) send (forward) to; (*överlämna*) hand [over] to **-ställning 1** entertainment, (*fest*) party (*för* for, in honour of); *en lyckad* ~ a successful party **2** *det var just en skön* ~ (*iron.*) that's a nice business **-stöta** (*inträffa, tillkomma*) occur, happen; (*om sjukdom*) set in
tillsvidare [-ˈvi:-] *se vidare II 6* **-anställning** nontenured appointment
till|syn *s3, ha* ~ *över* supervise, superintend, be in charge of; *utan* ~ (*äv.*) unattended **-synes** [-ˣsy:-] *se syn 3* **-syningsman** supervisor (*över* of)
tillsyns|lärare deputy head teacher **-myndighet** supervising authority
till|säga *se säga [till]* **-sägelse** (*befallning*) order (*om* for); (*uppmaning*) summons; (*begäran*) demand (*om* for); (*tillrättavisning*) admonition, reprimand; *få* ~ [*om*] *att* receive orders (be told) to; *utan* ~ without being told *-sätta 1* (*utnämna*) appoint, nominate; ~ *en tjänst* nominate (appoint) s.b. to a post, fill a vacancy; ~ *en kommitté* set up a committee **2** (*-lägga*) add on (*till* to) **3** (*blanda i*) add (*till* to) **-sättande** *s6* **1** ~*t av tjänsten* the appointment to a post **2** addition **3** adding
tillta *se tilltaga*
till|tag (*företag*) venture; (*försök*) attempt; (*påhitt*) trick; *ett sådant* ~*!* (*äv.*) what a thing to do! **-taga** increase, grow **-tagande I** *a4* increasing *etc.* **II** *s6* increase, growth; *vara i* ~ be on the increase **-tagen** *a5, knappt* ~ on the small side, (*om mat e.d.*) scanty in quantity, (*om lön*) meagre; *väl* ~ a good (fair) size **-tagsen** [-taks-] *a3* enterprising, go-ahead; (*djärv*) bold, daring
till|tal address; *används i* ~ is used as a form of address; *svara på* ~ answer when [one is] spoken to **-tala 1** (*tala t.*) address, speak to; (*ngn på gatan*) accost; *den* ~*de* the person addressed (spoken to) **2** (*behaga*) attract, please; (*i sht om sak*) appeal to; *det* ~*r mig mycket* (*äv.*) I like it very much **-talande** *a4* attractive, pleasing (*för* to); acceptable (*förslag* proposal)
tilltals|form vocative form **-namn** Christian name normally used; ~*et understruket* (*på formulär e.d.*) underline the name used **-ord** word (form) of address
till|trasslad *a4* entangled; ~*e affärer* muddled finances **-tro I** *s9* credit, credence; confidence (*till* in); *sätta* ~ *till a*) (*ngn*) place confidence in, *b*) (*ngt*) give credit (credence) to; *vinna* ~ gain credence (*hos* with) **II** *v4,* ~ *ngn ngt* believe s.b. capable of s.th., give s.b. credit for s.th. **-träda** (*befattning*) enter upon [the duties of]; (*ta i besittning*) take over (*en egendom* a property); ~ *arv* come into [possession of] an

inheritance; ~ *sin tjänst* take up one's duties (an appointment) **-träde** *s6* **1** (*-trädande*) entry (*av* into possession of); entrance (*av ämbete* upon office) **2** (*inträde*) entrance, admission; (*tillstånd att inträda*) admittance; *luftens* ~ the access of the air; *bereda* ~ *för* give access to; *fritt* ~ admission (entrance) free; ~ *förbjudet* no admittance; *ha* ~ *till* have admission to; *barn äga ej* ~ children [are] not admitted; *obehöriga äga ej* ~ no admittance except on business **-trädesdag** day of taking possession; (*installationsdag*) inauguration day **-tugg** *s7* snack **-tvinga** *rfl* obtain (secure) by force **-tyga** *illa* ~ *ngt* (*ngn*) use (handle) s.th. (s.b.) roughly, *vard.* manhandle s.th. (s.b.); *han var illa* ~*d* he had been badly knocked about **-tänkt** *a4* (*påtänkt*) contemplated, proposed; (*planerad*) projected, intended **-valsämne** optional (*AE.* elective) subject **-vand** *a5* addicted (*vid* to)
tillvaratag|a [-ˣva:-] take charge of; (*bevaka*) look after; (*skydda*) protect, safeguard; (*utnyttja*) utilize (*tiden* time), take advantage of; ~ *sina intressen* look after (protect) one's interests **-ande** *s6,* ~*t av* the taking charge of (looking after)
tillvaro *s9* existence; life; *kampen för* ~*n* struggle for existence
tillverk|a manufacture, make, produce **-are** manufacturer *etc.* **-ning** (*-ande*) manufacture, make, production; (*det som -ats*) manufacture, make, product; (*-ningsmängd*) output, production; *ha ngt under* ~ have s.th. in production
tillverknings|kostnad cost of production **-pris** factory (cost) price **-process** manufacturing process
till|vinna *rfl* gain, obtain, secure; (*ngns respekt äv.*) win **-vita** ~ *ngn ngt* charge s.b. with s.th. **-vitelse** charge, imputation (*för* of; *för att* of + *ing-form*) **-väga** [-ˣvä:-] *se väg 2* **-vägagångssätt** course (line) of action, procedure **-välla** *rfl* usurp, arrogate to o.s. (*rätten att* the right of + *ing-form*) **-växa** grow; *bildl. äv.* increase (*i* in) **-växt** *s3* growth; (*ökning*) increase; *vara stadd i* ~ be increasing (growing, on the increase) **-växttakt** rate of growth **-yxa** rough-hew, rough-cut; (*friare*) roughly shape
tillåt|a (*särskr. till-låta*) **1** allow, permit; (*samtycka t.*) consent to; (*om sak*) admit (allow) of; (*finna sig i*) suffer; *tillåt mig fråga om ni* allow me to (let me) ask if you; *-er ni att jag röker?* do you mind my smoking?; *om ni -er* if you will allow me; *om vädret -er* weather permitting; *min ekonomi -er inte det* my finances won't allow it **2** *rfl* (*unna sig*) allow (permit) o.s.; (*ta sig friheten*) take the liberty to (of) + *ing-form* **-else** permission, leave; (*av myndighet e.d.*) licence, authorization; *be om* ~ *att* ask [for] permission to; *få* ~ *att* be allowed (permitted) to, get (be given) permission to; *med er* ~ with your permission **-en** *a5* allowed, permitted; (*laglig*) lawful; *är det -et att ...?* may I ...?; *det är inte -et att röka här* smoking is not allowed here; *högsta -na hastighet* the maximum speed allowed, the speed limit;

T

tillåtlig–tiotal

552

vara ~ (jakt.) be in season **-lig** [-å:-] *al* allowable, permissible

tillägg *(särskr. till-lägg) s7* addition; *(t. dokument äv.)* rider, additional paragraph; *(t. bok)* supplement, appendix; *(t. manuskript)* insertion; *(t. brev)* postscript; *(t. testamente)* codicil; *(löne-)* rise, bonus; *(anmärkning)* addendum *(pl addenda); rättelser och ~* corrections and additions, corrigenda and addenda; *procentuellt ~* [a] percentage addition; *dock med det ~et att* it being understood, however, that; *utan ~* without any addition **tilllägga** add *(till* to)

tilläggs|avgift extra (additional) fee, surcharge **-bestämmelse** additional (supplementary) regulation **-biljett** supplementary ticket **-pension** supplementary pension **-pensionering** *allmän ~ (förk. ATP)* national supplementary pensions scheme **-plats** *sjö.* berth, landing (mooring) place **-porto** surcharge, additional postage **-premie** *försäkr.* additional (extra) premium

till|ägna 1 *(dedicera)* dedicate *(ngn en bok* a book to s.b.) **2** *rfl (tillskansa sig)* appropriate, seize [upon], lay hands on; *(förvärva)* acquire *(kunskaper* knowledge); *(tillgodogöra sig)* assimilate, profit by; *orättmätigt ~ sig ngt* appropriate s.th. unlawfully **-ägnan** [-äŋn-] *r* dedication **-ämna** intend, have in view **-ämnad** *a5* intended; *(påtänkt)* premeditated

tillämp|a *(särskr. till-lämpa)* apply *(på* to); *(metod e.d.)* practise; *kunna ~s på (äv.)* be applicable to; *~ ngt i praktiken* put s.th. into practice; *~d forskning* applied research **-bar** *al* applicable **-lig** *al* applicable *(på* to); *stryk det ej ~a* strike out words not applicable; *i ~a delar* wherever applicable (relevant) **-ning** application *(på* to); *äga ~ på* be applicable to

tillända [-ˣänn-] *se 1 ända I 1* **-lupen** *a5* expired; *vara ~* be at (have come to) an end **till|öka** add to; *(göra större)* enlarge **-ökning** *(-ökande)* increasing, enlargement *(av, i* of); *konkr.* increase *(av* of); increment *(på lön* in one's salary); *vänta ~ [i familjen]* be expecting an addition to the family **-önska** wish **-önskan** wish; *med ~ om* best wishes for **-övers** [-'ö:-] *se* övers

tilta *s1, lantbr.* ridge
1 tima [ˣti:ma] *åld.* happen, occur
2 tima [ˣtajma] *vard.* time, coordinate
tim|antal number of hours **-arbete** work by the hour
tim'bal *s3* **1** *mus.* kettledrum; timbal **2** *kokk.* timbale
timbre ['täŋber] *s9* timbre
timer ['tajj-] *s9* time switch
tim|förtjänst hourly earnings *(pl)* **-glas** hourglass, sandglass
ti'mid *al, n sg obest. form undviks* timid
timing ['tajj-] timing, coordination
timjan *s9* thyme
tim|lig *al* temporal; *det ~a* things temporal; *lämna det ~a* depart this life **-lärare** *ung.* part-time teacher **-lön** hourly wage[s *pl*], payment by the hour; *få ~* be paid by the hour
timma *s2,* **timme** *s2* hour; *(lektion)* lesson; *en ~s resa* an hour's journey; *varannan ~* every

other hour; *åtta timmars arbetsdag* an eight-hour day; *efter en ~* an hour later; *i ~n* an hour; *i flera timmar* for [several] hours; *om en ~* in an hour; *per ~* per (by the) hour
timmer ['timm-] *s7* timber; *AE.* lumber **-avverkning** logging, timber cutting (felling) **-bil** timber lorry, *AE.* logging truck **-bröt** log jam (blockage) **-flottare** log driver **-flotte** log raft **-flottning** timber (log) driving **-huggare** woodcutter, logger; *AE.* lumberjack **-koja** log cabin **-lass** load of logs (timber) **-man** carpenter **-ränna** flume **-släp** log (timber) raft (transport) **-stock** log; *dra ~ar (snarka)* be driving one's hogs to market
timotej [-'tejj] *s3* timothy [grass], *AE.* herd's grass
tim|penning hourly wage **-plan** timetable
timra build with logs, construct out of timber; *absol.* do carpentry; *~d stuga* timbered cottage
timslag *på ~et* on the stroke of the hour
timslång of an hour's duration, lasting an hour
tim|tals [-a:-] for hours together, for hours and hours **-vis** by the hour **-visare** hour (small) hand
1 tina *s1* **1** *(laggkärl)* tub **2** *(fiskredskap)* creel
2 tina *v1, ~ [upp]* thaw *(äv. bildl.)*, melt; *(bildl. om pers.)* become less reserved (more sociable)
tindra twinkle; *(starkare)* sparkle, scintillate; *med ~nde ögon* starry-eyed
1 ting *s7 (sak)* thing; *(ärende äv.)* matter; *(föremål)* object; *saker och ~* [a lot of] things
2 ting *s7 (domstolssammanträde)* district-court sessions *(pl),* crown courts *(pl); Engl. förr* assizes, quarter sessions *(pl); hist.* thing; *sitta ~* be on duty at a district court
tinga *(beställa)* order [in advance], bespeak; *(ngn)* retain, engage; *(göra avtal om)* bargain for
tingeltangel [-'taŋ-, ˣtiŋ-] *s7* noisy funfair, cheap entertainment
tingest ['tiŋ-] *s2* thing, object; *vard.* contraption
tings|dag sessions day **-hus** courthouse, law courts *(pl)* **-meriterad** *a5, ~ jurist (ung.)* jurist with district-court practice **-meritering** *ung.* period of service in a district court **-notarie** clerk of a [district] court **-rätt** district (city) court; court of first instance **-sal** sessions hall **-tjänstgöring** court practice
tinktur tincture
tinn|e *s2* pinnacle; *bildl.* summit; *torn och ~ar* towers and pinnacles; *försedd med ~ar* pinnacled
tinning temple
tio [ˣti:ɷ, *vard.* ˣti:e] ten; *(för sms. jfr fem-);* *~-i-topp* top ten **-dubbel** tenfold **-dubbla** multiply by ten, increase tenfold **-falt** ten times, tenfold
tio|hörning [-ö:-] decagon **-kamp** *sport.* decathlon **-kampare** *sport.* decathlete **-kronesedel, -kronorssedel** ten-kronor note
tion|de [-å-] **I** *räkn.* tenth **II** *s9, s7* tithes *(pl); ge ~* pay [one's] tithes **-[de]del** tenth **-[de]dels** [-de:ls] *oböjligt a, en ~ sekund* one (a) tenth of a second
tio|pundssedel ten-pound note; *vard.* tenner **-tal** ten; *ett ~ (ung. tio)* about (some) ten; *i*

jämna ~ in multiples of ten; *under ett* ~ *år* for ten years [or so]; *på* ~*et* (*1910-talet*) in the nineteen-tens **-tiden** *vid* ~ [at] about ten [o'clock] **-tusental** *i* ~ in tens of thousands **-tusentals** [-'tu:-, *ˣ*ti:ʊ-, -a:-] *i* ~ *år* for tens of thousands of years **-årig** *a1* ten-year-old **-åring** ten-year-old boy (*etc.*), boy (*etc.*) of ten **-årsdag** tenth anniversary (*av* of) **-öring** ten--öre piece

1 tipp *s2* (*spets*) tip (*av* of)
2 tipp *s2* (*avstjälpningsplats*) tip, dump; (*på lastfordon*) tipping device; *lastbil med* ~ tipper truck (lorry), *AE.* dump (tip) truck
1 tippa (*stjälpa ur*) tip, dump
2 tippa (*förutsäga*) spot; *sport.* play the pools
1 tippning (*avstjälpning*) tipping, dumping; ~ *förbjuden!* no tipping allowed!
2 tippning *sport.* playing the pools
tippvagn 1 (*lastbil*) *se 2 tipp* **2** *järnv.* tipping truck; *AE.* dump car
tips *s7* **1** (*vink*) tip[-off], hint; *ge ngn ett* ~ give s.b. a tip **2** (*fotbolls-*) football pools; *vinna på* ~ win on the pools
tips|a tip **-kupong** [football-]pools coupon **-rad** line on a pools coupon **-vinst** [football-]pools win (dividend)
tiptop [-tåpp] *oböjligt a* tiptop, first-rate
ti'rad *s3* tirade
tisdag ['ti:s-] *s2* Tuesday; (*jfr fredag*)
tiss|el ['tiss-] *s7*, ~ *och tassel* tittle-tattle **-la** ~ *och tassla* tittle-tattle
tistel *s2*, *bot.* thistle
tistelstång shaft, pole
ti'tan 1 *s3*, *myt.* Titan **2** *s3*, *s4*, *kem.* titanium **-isk** *a5* (*jättelik*) titan[ic] **-vitt** titanium white
tit|el ['titt-] *s2* **1** (*bok- etc.*) title (*på* of); *med* ~*n* entitled **2** (*persons*) title; (*benämning*) designation, denomination; *lägga bort -larna* drop the Mr. (*etc.*)
titel|blad title page **-match** championship (title) match **-roll** *teat. e.d.* title role **-sida** title page **-sjuka** mania for titles **-vinjett** headpiece
titrer|a titrate **-ing** titration
1 titt *adv,* ~ *och tätt* frequently, repeatedly, over and over again
2 titt *s2* **1** (*blick*) look; (*hastig*) glance; (*i smyg*) peep; *ta sig en* ~ *på* have a look at **2** (*kort besök*) call (*hos* on; *på* at); *tack för* ~*en!* kind of you to look me up!
titta 1 look (*på* at); (*hastigt*) glance (*på* at); (*kika*) peep (*på* at); ~ *efter* gaze after, (*söka*) look for; ~ *i* have a look at (*in*); ~ *för djupt i glaset* be too fond of the bottle; ~ *sig i spegeln* look (have a look) at o.s. in the mirror; ~ *ngn djupt in i ögonen* look deep into a p.'s eyes; ~ *på* (*äv.*) have a look at; *vi skall ut och* ~ *på möbler* we are going to the shops to look at furniture; ~ *på TV* watch TV; *jag vill inte* ~ *åt honom* I can't bear the sight of him; *titt ut!* boo!, *AE.* peekaboo! **2** (*med betonad partikel*) ~ *efter* (*undersöka*) [look and] see; ~ *fram* peep out (forth); *vill du* ~ *hit ett ögonblick* will you come over here for a minute; ~ *in a)* look in (*genom fönstret* at the window), *b)* (*hälsa på* look (drop) in (*till* to see); ~ *in hos ngn* look s.b. up; ~ *in i* look into; ~ *ner* lower one's

eyes; ~ *på* look on, watch; ~ *upp* look up, raise one's eyes; ~ *ut genom fönstret* look out of the window; ~ *ut ngn* stare s.b. out of the room
tittar|e (*TV--*) **1** viewer **2** (*voyeur*) Peeping Tom, voyeur **-frekvens** television audience measurement (T.A.M.) rating **-siffror** *TV.* viewing figures **-storm** *TV-programmet utlöste en* ~ the TV switchboard was jammed with angry callers after the programme
titt|glugg spy hole **-hål** peephole **-hålsoperation** keyhole surgery **-skåp** peepshow -'ut *s2, leka* ~ play [at] bo-peep
titul|atur title[s *pl*] **-era** style, call; ~ *ngn* (*äv.*) address s.b. as -'**är** *a1* titular[y]
tivoli ['ti:-] *s6* amusement park; *AE. äv.* carnival
tixotrop [-'å:p-] *a1* thixotropic
tja [ça:] well!
tjafs [ç-] *s7* tommyrot **tjafsa** talk a lot of tommyrot
tjall|a [ç-] squeal **-are** informer, squealer
tjat [ç-] *s7* nagging **tjata** nag **tjatig** *a1* nagging; (*långtråkig*) tedious
tjatter ['çatt-] *s7*, **tjattra** [*ˣ*çatt-] *v1* jabber, chatter
tjeck [çeck] *s3* Czech **Tjeckien** ['çeck] *n* the Czech Republic **tjeckisk** ['çeck-] *a5* Czech; *T~a republiken* the Czech Republic
tjeckoslo'vak [çeck-] *s3* Czechoslovak **Tjeckoslovakien** [-'va:-] *n* Czechoslovakia
tjej [çejj] *s3* (*flicka*) girl, bird; (*kvinna*) woman
tjo [çɷ:] *s7*, ~ *och tjim* whoopee-making **tjoa** [*ˣ*çɷ:a] shout **tjo'hej** *interj* whoopee!
tjock [çåck] *a1* thick; (*om pers.*) stout, fat; (*tät*) dense, thick; ~ *grädde* thick cream; *det var* ~*t med folk på gatan* the street was packed with people
tjock|a [*ˣ*çåcka] *s1* fog **-bottnad** [-å-] *a5* thick-bottomed **-flytande** viscous, viscid, heavy, thick **-hudad** *a5* thick-skinned (*äv. bildl.*) **-huding** *zool.* pachyderm **-is** ['çåck-] *s2*, *vard.* fatty, fatso **-lek** *s2* thickness; (*dimension*) gauge; *med en* ~ *av 1 meter* 1 metre thick **-magad** *a5* big-bellied
tjock|na [*ˣ*çåck-] thicken; ~ *till* get (become) thicker **-olja** heavy fuel oil **-skalig** *a1* (*om nöt, ägg o.d.*) thick-shelled; (*om potatis, frukt o.d.*) thick-skinned, thick-peeled **-skalle** fathead, num[b]skull **-skallig** thickheaded (*äv. bildl.*) **-tarm** large intestine, *fack.* colon **-ända, -ände** thick-end, butt-end
tjog [çå:g] *s7* score; *ett* ~ *ägg* (*vanl.*) twenty eggs; *fem* ~ five score of **-tals** [-a:-] scores; ~ *med* scores of **-vis** by the score
tjuder ['çu:-] *s7* tether **tjudra** [*ˣ*çu:-] tether (*fast vid* up to)
tjuga [*ˣ*çu:-] *s1* hayfork
tjugo [*ˣ*çug:ɷ, *vard.* -ug. -ge] (*för sms . jfr. fem-*) twenty **-en** [-'enn, -'e:n] twenty-one -'**ett 1** *räkn* twenty-one **2** *kortsp.* blackjack, vingt-et-un, pontoon **-femårsjubileum** twenty-fifth anniversary **-femöring** twenty-five-öre piece **-första** twenty-first
tjugon|de [*ˣ*çu:gån-] twentieth **-[de]dag** ~*en* (~ *jul*) Hilarymas [Day] **-[de]del** twentieth
tjugo|tal *ett* ~ about (some) twenty; *på* ~*et* (*1920-talet*) in the [nineteen] twenties
tjur [çu:r] *s2* bull

T

tjura [ˣçu:-] sulk, be in a sulk
tjurfäkt|are bullfighter **-ning** bullfighting; *en* ~ a bullfight
tjurig [ˣçu:-] *a1* sulky **-het** sulkiness
tjur|kalv bull calf **-skalle** stubborn (pig-headed) person **-skallig** *a1* stubborn, pig-headed **-skallighet** stubbornness, pig-headedness
tjus|a [ˣçu:-] enchant, charm; *(friare)* fascinate **-arlock** kiss *(AE.* spit) curl **-ig** *a1* captivating, charming **-kraft** power to charm **-ning** [-u:-] charm, enchantment; fascination; *fartens* ~ the fascination of speed
tjut [çu:t] *s7* howling; *(ett* ~) howl **tjuta** *tjöt tjutit* howl; *(skrika)* shriek, yell; *(om mistlur)* hoot; *stormen tjuter kring knutarna* the storm is howling round the house **tjutit** *sup. av tjuta*
tjuv [çu:v] *s2* thief; *ta fast* ~*en!* stop thief!; *som en* ~ *om natten* like a thief in the night **-aktig** *a1* thievish **-eri** theft; *jur.* larceny **-fiska** poach fish **-fiskare** fish poacher **-fiske** fish poaching **-gods** stolen property (goods *pl*) **-godsgömma** cache **-godsgömmare** [-j-] receiver of stolen property *(etc.)*; *sl.* fence **-gubbe** old rascal **-hålla** keep back [for later] **-knep** *bildl.* sharp practice; dirty trick **-koppla** *(bil)* bypass the ignition switch **-larm** burglar alarm **-liga** gang of thieves (burglars) **-lyssna** eavesdrop **-lyssnare** eavesdropper; *radio.* wireless pirate **-läsa** read on the sly
tjuv|nad [ˣçu:-] *s3* stealing, theft; *jur.* larceny **-nadsbrott** larceny **-nyp** *ge ngn ett* ~ pinch s.b. on the sly, *bildl.* give s.b. a sly dig **-- och-rackarspel** *vard.* underhand dealings, skulduggery **-pojke** young rascal **-pojksaktig** *a1* roguish **-pojksstreck** dirty trick **-skytt** poacher **-skytte** poaching **-språk** argot, thieves' slang **-stanna** *(om motor)* stall **-start** *sport.* false start; *vard.* jumping (beating) the gun **-starta** *sport.* jump (beat) the gun **-streck** dirty trick **-titta** ~ *i* take a look into on the sly **-tjockt** *jag mår* ~ I feel lousy **-tryck** pirate edition **-åka** steal a ride **-åkare** fare dodger
tjäder ['çä:-] *s2* capercaillie; *koll. äv.* woodgrouse **-höna** hen-capercaillie **-lek** capercaillie courtship **-tupp** cock-capercaillie
tjäle [ˣçä:-] *s2* ground (soil) frost; *när* ~*n går ur jorden* when the frost in the ground breaks up
tjäll [ç-] *s7* humble abode
tjäl|lossning thawing of frozen soil, break of the frost **-skada** frost damage **-skott** frost heave; *(hål)* pothole
tjän|a [ˣçä:-] **1** *(förtjäna)* earn *(pengar* money); gain *(på affären* by the bargain); ~ *ihop* save up; ~ *in sin pension* earn one's pension **2** *(vara anställd)* serve *(hos* in a p.'s house; *som* as a[n]); ~ *staten* serve the State; ~ *hos ngn (äv.)* be in a p.'s service (employ); ~ *upp sig* work one's way up; ~ *ut (om soldat)* serve one's time; *den har* ~*t ut* it has seen its best days **3** *(användas)* serve, do duty *(som* as); ~ *ngn till efterrättelse* serve as an example to s.b.; *det* ~*r ingenting till att* there is no use (point) in (+ *ing-form*); *vad* ~*r det till?* what is the use (good) of that?
tjän|ande [ˣçä:-] *a4* serving *(till* as); ~ *andar*

ministering spirits **-are** servant; *(betjänt)* manservant; *en kyrkans* ~ a minister of the Church; *en statens* ~ a public servant; ~*!* hello!, *(vid avsked)* bye-bye! **-arinna** [maid]servant, domestic [servant] **-lig** [-ä:-] *a1* serviceable *(till* for); *(passande)* suitable *(till* for); *(ändamålsenlig)* expedient *(till* for); *vid* ~ *väderlek* when the weather is suitable
tjänst [ç-] *s3* **1** *(anställning)* service; *(befattning)* appointment, place, situation; *(högre)* office, post; *(prästerlig)* charge, ministry; *i* ~ on duty, in service; *i* ~*en* on official business, *(å ämbetets vägnar)* ex officio, officially; *i statens* ~ in the service of the State; *vara i ngns* ~ be employed by s.b., be in a p.'s service; *lämna sin* ~ resign one's appointment; *söka* ~ apply for a situation (job); *ta* ~ *(om tjänare)* go into service *(hos ngn* in a p.'s house), *(allmännare)* take a job (situation) *(som* as); *utom* ~*en* off duty **2** *(hjälp)* service *(mot* to); *be ngn om en* ~ ask a favour of s.b.; *göra ngn en* ~ do s.b. a service (good turn); *gör mig den* ~*en att* oblige me by (+ *ing-form*); *göra ngn den sista* ~*en* pay one's last respects to s.b.; *varmed kan jag stå till* ~? what can I do for you?; *till er* ~*!* at your service (command)! **3** *(nytta)* service; *göra* ~ do service (duty), serve, *(fungera)* work **-aktig** *a1* ready to render service, obliging **-duglig** fit for service; *(om sak)* serviceable
tjänste|ande servant; *vard.* slavey **-angelägenhet** official matter **-avtal** employment contract **-betyg** certificate of service **-bil** official (company) car **-bostad** housing accommodation supplied by a company; official residence **-brev** official letter; *skicka som* ~ send as official matter **-bruk** official use **-ed** oath of office **-fel** breach of duty **-flicka** servant [girl], maid **-folk** [domestic] servants *(pl)* **-förmåner** fringe benefits **-förrättande** *a4* acting; in charge **-grad** rank **-läkare** staff medical officer **-man** employee, clerk; *(högre)* official, officer; *(stats-)* civil servant; *vard.* white-collar worker; *Tjänstemännens centralorganisation (förk. TCO)* [the Swedish] central organization of salaried employees **-mannabana** white-collar career **-mannakår** staff of officers and employees **-meddelande** official communication **-pension** occupational pension **-plikt** **1** official duty **2** compulsory service **-resa** official journey, journey on official business; *(i privat tjänst)* business trip (journey) **-rum** office **-ställning** *mil.* official standing **-tid 1** *(anställningstid)* period of service **2** *(kontorstid)* office hours **-utövning** *under* ~ when discharging one's duties **-vikt** *(bils)* kerb weight plus driver's weight **-ålder** *gå efter* ~ go by seniority **-år** year[s *pl*] of service (in office) **-ärende** official matter
tjänstgör|a serve *(som* as; *på, vid* at); *(om pers. äv.)* act *(som* as); *(vara i tjänst)* be on duty, *(vid hovet o.d.)* be in attendance (waiting) *(hos* on) **-ande** *a4* on duty, in charge, *(vid hovet)* in attendance **-ing** service; duty; work; attendance; *ha* ~ be on duty
tjänstgörings|betyg testimonial, certificate of service **-reglemente** service regulations *(pl)*

-tid 1 (*daglig*) [office] hours (*pl*), hours (*pl*) of service (duty) **2** (*tid i samma tjänst*) [period of] service

tjänst|ledig *vara* ~ be on leave (off duty); ~ *för sjukdom* on sick leave; *ta* ~*t* take leave of absence **-ledighet** leave [of absence]; (*för sjukdom*) sick leave **-villig** obliging, helpful, eager to help

tjär|a [ˣçä:-] **l** *s1* tar **ll** *v1* tar; ~*t tak* tarred roof **-blomster** red German catchfly **-bloss** pitch torch, link **-fläck** tar stain **-ig** *a1* tarry **-kokare** tar-boiler

tjärn [çä:rn] *s2, s7* tarn

tjär|ning [ˣçä:r-] tarring **-papp** tarred [roofing] felt

tjöt [çö:t] *imperf. av tjuta*

toa [ˣto:a] *s9, vard., BE.* loo, *AE.* john

toa'lett *s3* **1** (*WC*) toilet, lavatory; (*offentlig*) public convenience, *AE.* washroom, rest room; (*på restaurang o.d.*) cloakroom, men's (ladies') room; *gå på* ~*en* go to the toilet **2** (*klädsel*) toilet, dress; *stor* ~ full dress; *göra* ~ make one's toilet; *göra* ~ *till middagen* dress for dinner **-artiklar** toilet requisites **-bord** dressing (toilet) table; *AE. äv.* dresser **-borste** lavatory brush **-papper** toilet paper (tissue) **-rum** toilet [room], lavatory; *se äv. toalett 1* **-saker** *pl* toiletries **-tvål** (*hopskr. toalettvål*) *en* ~ a bar (piece) of toilet soap

tobak [ˈtɒbb-, ˈtɒ:b-] *s3* tobacco; *ta sig en pipa* ~ have a pipe **-ist** tobacconist

tobaks|affär tobacconist's [shop], tobacco shop **-blandning** blend of tobacco **-burk** tobacco jar, humidor **-buss** quid **-handlare** tobacconist **-märke** brand of tobacco **-planta** tobacco plant **-pung** tobacco pouch **-rök** tobacco smoke **-rökning** tobacco smoking; ~ *förbjuden* no smoking **-varor** *pl* tobacco [products]

toddy [ˈtåddy, -i] *s2, pl äv. toddar* toddy

toffel [ˈtåff-] *s1* slipper; *stå under* ~*n* be henpecked, be tied to s.b.'s apron strings **-djur** slipper animalcule **-hjälte** henpecked husband **-regemente** petticoat government

tofs [-å-] *s2* tuft, bunch; (*på fågel äv.*) crest; (*på möbler, mössa*) tassel **-lärka** crested lark **-mes** crested tit **-vipa** lapwing, peewit

toft [-å-] *s3* thwart

tog *imperf. av ta*

toga [ˣtå:-] *s1* toga

togo'les *s3,* **-isk** *a5* Togolese

tok 1 *s2, pers.* fool; (*obetänksam pers.*) duffer **2** *oböjligt i uttr.: gå* (*vara*) *på* ~ go (be) wrong; *jag har fått på* ~ *för mycket* I have been given far too much **toka** *s1* fool of a woman (girl); *en liten* ~ a silly little thing

tokajer [-ˈkajj-] Tokay

tok|er [ˈto:-] **-ern** *-ar, se tok 1* **-eri** folly, nonsense; ~*er* (*upptåg*) foolish pranks **-ig** [ˣto:-] *a1* mad (*av* with; *efter* after; *i, på* on); (*oförståndig*) silly, foolish; (*löjlig*) ridiculous; (*-rolig*) comic, droll; (*mycket förtjust*) crazy (*i* about); *det låter inte så* ~*t* that doesn't sound too bad; *det är så man kan bli* ~ it's enough to drive one round the bend **-igt** [ˣto:-] *adv* madly *etc.*; *bära sig* ~ *åt* act foolishly (like a fool) **-rolig** [extremely] funny (comic, droll) **-stolle** madcap; crazy guy

toler|abel *a2* tolerable **-ans** [-ˈrans, -ˈraŋs] *s3* tolerance (*mot* towards) **-ant** [-ˈrant, -ˈraŋt] *a1* tolerant, forbearing (*mot* towards); (*friare*) broadminded **-era** tolerate, put up with

tolft [-å-] *s3* dozen

tolfte [-å-] twelfth **-del** twelfth

1 tolk [-å-] *s2* (*verktyg*) gauge; *AE.* gage

2 tolk [-å-] *s2* (*översättare o.d.*) interpreter; *göra sig till* ~ *för* (*bildl.*) voice, (*åsikt*) advocate

1 tolka [ˣtåll-] *sport.* go skijoring

2 tolka [ˣtåll-] (*översätta muntligt*) interpret; (*dikt*) translate, interpret; (*handskrift*) decipher; (*återge*) render; (*uttrycka känslor*) express, give expression to; ~ *på engelska* interpret into English; *hur skall jag* ~ *detta?* what am I to understand by this?

tolk|are (*av musik, roll o.d.*) interpreter, renderer **-ning** interpretation (*av* of); (*av handskrift*) decipherment; (*av dikt*) translation; (*muntlig*) interpretation; *felaktig* ~ misinterpretation; *fri* ~ free rendering **-ningsfråga** question of interpretation, matter of opinion

tolv [-å-] twelve; (*för sms. jfr fem-*); *klockan* ~ *på dagen* (*natten*) at noon (midnight)

tolv|a [-å-] *s1* twelve **-fingertarm** duodenum (*pl* duodena[s]) **-hundratalet** *på* ~ in the thirteenth century **-tiden** *vid* ~ at about twelve **-tonsmusik** twelve-tone music

Tolvöarna *pl* the Dodecanese [Islands]

t.o.m. *förk. för till och med, se till I 13 o. II 4*

tom [tɒmm] *a1* empty, void (*på* of) (*äv. bildl.*); (*ej upptagen*) vacant; (*naken*) bare; (*oskriven*) blank; (*öde o.* ~) deserted; ~*t prat* empty words; ~*t skryt* vain boasting; *känna sig* ~ *i huvudet* feel void of all thought (unable to think); *känna sig* ~ *i magen* feel empty inside; *det känns* ~*t efter dig* it feels so empty without you

tomat tomato **-juice** tomato juice **-ketchup** tomato ketchup **-puré** tomato purée **-soppa** tomato soup

tombola [ˈtåmm-] *s1* tombola

tom|butelj empty bottle **-fat** empty cask **-glas** *koll.* empty bottles (*pl*) **-gång** idling, idle running; *gå på* ~ idle, tick over **-het** emptiness, bareness (*etc.*); vacancy; *bildl.* void **-hänt** *a1* empty-handed

tomografi *s3* tomography

tom|rum empty space; (*lucka*) gap; (*på blankett o.d.*) blank; *fys.* vacuum; *bildl.* void, blank; *han har lämnat ett stort* ~ *efter sig* he has left a void (great blank) behind him

tomt [-å-] *s3* (*obebyggd*) [building] site, lot; (*kring villa e.d.*) garden, grounds (*pl*); *lediga* ~*er* vacant sites

tomte [-å-] *s2* brownie; goblin **-bloss** sparkler **-bolycka** married bliss **-nisse** little brownie

tomt|gräns boundary of a building site **-hyra** ground rent **-jobbare** land speculator **-karta** land register map **-mark** land for building on **-rätt** site-leasehold right **-rättsavgäld** [-j-] *s3* rent for a leasehold site

1 ton [tånn] *s7* (*viktenhet = 1 000 kg*) metric ton; (*Storbritannien, ca 1 016 kg*) long ton; (*AE., ca 907 kg*) short ton

2 ton [tɒ:n] *s3* (*mus.; färg-; bildl.*) tone; (*röst*

äv.) tone of voice; (*på -skala*) note; (*-höjd*) pitch; (*mus. o. friare*) key[note], tune; (*umgänges-*) tone, manners (*pl*); *~ernas rike* the realm of music; *ange ~en a) mus.* give (strike) the note, *b) bildl.* give (set) the tone; *i befallande ~* in a tone of command; *hålla ~* keep in tune; *hålla ut ~en* hold the note; *stämma ner ~en* (*bildl.*) temper one's tone; tone down; *ta sig ~* put on (assume) a lofty air (*mot ngn towards s.b.*); *träffa den rätta ~en* strike the right note; *takt och ~* good manners; *det hör till god ~* it is good form

ton|a (*ljuda*) sound; (*ge färgton åt*) tone (*äv. foto.*); *~ bort a*) (*förtona*) die away, *b*) (*få att upphöra, avlägsna*) fade out *-'al a1* tonal *-alitet* tonality *-ande a4* sounding; *fonet.* voiced (*ljud* sound) *-art mus.* key; *berömma ngn i alla ~er* sing a p.'s praises in every possible way *-band* recording tape *-dikt* symphonic (tone) poem *-diktare* composer

toner *s9* (*för kopiator, laserskrivare o.d.*) toner

tonfall intonation; accent

tonfisk tunny [fish], tuna

ton|givande *i ~ kretsar* in leading quarters *-gång ~ar a) mus.* progressions, successions of notes, *b) bildl.* strains *-höjd* pitch *-ing* toning, tinting *-konst* [art of] music *-kontroll* tone control *-läge mus.* pitch; (*rösts omfång*) range, compass *-lös* (*om röst*) toneless; (*om ljud*) flat, dull *-målning* tone picture

tonnage [tå'na:ʃ] *s4* tonnage

tonomfång range, compass

tonsill [tån'sill] *s3* tonsil

ton|skala musical scale *-steg* interval *-styrka* intensity of sound

tonsur [tån'su:r] tonsure

ton|sätta set to music *-sättare* composer *-sättning* [musical] composition *-vikt språkv.* stress; accent; *bildl.* emphasis; *lägga ~ på a) eg.* stress, put stress on, *b) bildl.* emphasize, lay stress on

tonår|en [ˣtånn-] *pl, i ~* in one's teens *-ing* teenager

tonåtergivning tone reproduction

to'pas *s3* topaz

topogra'f|i *s3* topography *-isk* [-'gra:-] *a5* topographic[al]

1 topp [-å-] *interj* done!, agreed!, a bargain!

2 topp [-å-] **I** *s2* top; (*bergs- äv.*) summit; (*väg-*) crest; (*friare*) peak, pinnacle; *från ~ till tå* from top to toe; *i ~en* at the top (*av* of); *med flaggan i ~* with the flag flying; *hissa flaggan i ~* run up the flag; *vara på ~en av sin förmåga* be at the height of one's powers **II** *adv, bli ~ tunnor rasande* boil over with rage, blow one's top

topp|a 1 (*-hugga*) pollard; (*växt*) top **2** (*stå överst på*) top, head *-befattning* top-level position (post) *-belastning* peak (maximum) load *-dressa trädg.* top-dress *-dressing trädg.* top dressing *-form vara i ~* be in top form *-formig* [-å-] *a1* conical *-hastighet* maximum (top) speed *-hemlig* top-secret *-ig a1* conical *-klass* top class *-konferens* summit conference (meeting) *-kraft* first-rate capacity *-kurs hand.* top (peak) rate *-lanterna* masthead light, top light *-lock* cylinder head *-luva*

[pointed] knitted cap *-modern* ultramodern *-murkla* [edible] morel *-märke* topmark *-mössa* pointed (conical) cap *-möte* summit meeting *-prestation* (*hopskr. topprestation*) top performance *-punkt* (*hopskr. toppunkt*) highest point, summit *-rida* bully *-segel* topsail *-siffra* peak (record) figure *-socker* loaf sugar *-styrd a5* top-down managed *-ventil* overhead valve

Tor *myt.* Thor

tordas [ˣtɷ:r-] *vard., se töras* **tordats** *vard., sup. av töras* **torde 1** (*i uppmaning*) will, (*artigare*) will please; *ni ~ observera* you will please (*anmodas:* are requested to) observe; *ni ~ erinra er* you will remember **2** (*uttr. förmodan*) probably; *det ~ dröja innan* it will probably be a long time before; *man ~ kunna påstå att* it may (can; might, could) probably be asserted that; *ni ~ ha rätt* I dare say you are right **tordes** *imperf. av töras*

tordmule [ˣtɷ:rd-] *s2* razorbill, razor-billed auk

tordyvel [ˣtɷ:rd-] *s2* dor [beetle]

tordön [ˣtɷ:r-] *s7* thunder **tordönsstämma** voice of thunder, thunderous voice

torft|ig [-å-] *a1* (*fattig*) poor; (*enkel*) plain; (*knapp*) scanty, meagre; *~a kunskaper* scanty knowledge (*sg*) *-ighet* poorness *etc. -igt adv* poorly *etc.*

torg [tårj] *s7* (*öppen plats*) square; (*salu-*) market, marketplace; *Röda ~et* the Red Square; *gå på ~et* go to the market, (*för att handla*) go marketing *-dag* market day *-föra* take (bring) to market, market, *bildl.* bring forward *-gumma* market woman *-handel* market trade, marketing *-kasse* market bag *-skräck* agoraphobia *-stånd* market stall

torium [ˈtɷ:-] *s8, kem.* thorium

tork [-å-] **1** *s2* drier, dryer **2** *oböjligt i uttr.: hänga på ~* hang [out] to dry; *hänga ut tvätten till ~* hang the washing out to dry

tork|a [-å-] **I** *s1* drought, dry weather; *svår ~* severe drought **II** *v1* **1** (*göra torr*) dry, get dry; *~ tvätt* dry the washing, rough-dry **2** (*~ av*) wipe [dry], dry; *~ disken* dry the dishes; *~ fötterna* wipe one's feet; *~ sina tårar* wipe away (dry) one's tears **3** (*bli torr*) dry, get dry; (*vissna äv.*) dry up **4** (*med betonad partikel*) *~ bort a*) (*av-*) wipe off (up), *b*) (*~ ut*) get dried up, (*om vätska*) dry up; *~ fast* dry and get stuck; *~ ihop* dry up; *~ in* dry in, *bildl. äv.* come to nothing; *~ upp a*) (*av-*) wipe (mop) up, *b*) (*bli torr*) dry up, get dry; *~ ut* dry up, run dry **5** *rfl* dry (wipe) o.s. (*med, på* with, on); *~ sig om händerna* dry one's hands; *~ dig om munnen!* wipe your mouth! *-arblad* (*på bil*) [windscreen] wiper blade *-huv* hood hairdryer (hairdrier) *-medel* siccative *-ning* drying; (*av-*) wiping [off], mopping [up] *-skåp* drying cabinet (cupboard) *-streck* clothesline *-ställ[ning]* drying rack; (*för disk*) plate rack *-tumlare* tumbler [drier], tumble drier *-ugn* drying kiln (oven, furnace)

1 torn [-ɷ:-] *s2, bot.* spine, thorn

2 torn [-ɷ:-] *s7* **1** tower; (*litet ~*) turret; (*spetsigt*) steeple; (*klock-*) belfry **2** (*schackpjäs*) rook, castle

torna ~ *upp sig* pile itself (themselves) up, *bildl.* tower aloft

tornad|o [-'na:-] *s5, s3* tornado

torner|a tourney, joust **-ing, -spel** tournament, tourney, joust

tornfalk kestrel

tornister [-'niss-] *s2* **1** (*proviantvätska*) canvas field bag **2** (*foderpåse*) nosebag

torn|seglare [common] swift **-spira** spire; steeple **-svala** *se tornseglare* **-uggla** barn owl **-ur** tower clock

torp [-å-] *s7* crofter's holding; (*sommarstuga*) cottage **-are** crofter

tor'ped [-å-] *s3* torpedo; *målsökande* ~ homing torpedo; *skjuta av en* ~ launch a torpedo **-båt** torpedo boat **-era** torpedo (*äv. bildl.*) **-ering** torpedoing

torr [-å-] *a1* dry; (*torkad*) dried; (*uttorkad*) parched, arid (*jord* ground); (*om klimat*) torrid; *bildl.* bald (*siffror* figures), (*tråkig*) dry, dull; *jag känner mig* ~ *i halsen* my throat feels dry; *han är inte* ~ *bakom öronen* he is [still] wet behind the ears; *på* ~*a land* on dry land; *ha sitt på det* ~*a* be comfortably off **-batteri** dry[-cell] battery **-boll** *vard.* stick-in-the-mud, sobersides **-dass** dry privy **-destillation** destructive (dry) distillation **-destillera** carbonize, burn without flame **-docka** *sjö.* dry dock **-het** dryness; parchedness; aridity **-hosta I** *s1* dry cough **II** *v1* have a dry cough **-jäst** dry (dried) yeast **-klosett** earth closet **-lägga 1** drain; (*mosse, sjö*) reclaim **2** (*införa spritförbud*) make dry **-läggning 1** drainage; reclamation **2** making (turning) dry **-mjölk** powdered (dried) milk **-nål, -nålsgravyr** *konst.* dry point **-rolig** (*hopskr. torrolig*) droll; (*om historia e.d.*) drily amusing **-rolighet** (*hopskr. torrolighet*) dry wit; drily witty remark **-schamponering** dry shampoo **-sim** swimming practice on land **-skaffning** cold food; *mil.* haversack ration **-skodd** *a5* dryshod **-spricka** sun shake **-substans** dry (solid) matter **-ögd** *a1* dry-eyed

torsdag ['to:rs-] *s2* Thursday; (*jfr fredag*)

torsion [tår'ʃɷ:n] torsion

torsionsfjäder torsion spring

1 torsk [-å-] *s2, med.* thrush

2 torsk [-å-] *s2, zool.* cod[fish]

torsk|fiske cod-fishing **-lever** cod liver **-leverolja** cod-liver oil **-rom** cod roe

torso ['tårr-] *-n torser, s3* torso

tortera torture

torts [-ɷ:-] *sup. av töras*

tor'tyr *s3* torture; *utsättas för* ~ be tortured (put to the torture) **-bänk** rack **-kammare** torture chamber **-redskap** instrument of torture

torv [-å-] *s3* peat; *ta upp* ~ dig [out] peat[s]

torv|a [-å-] *s1* (*gräs-*) [piece of] turf; (*jordbit*) plot [of ground]; *kärleken till den egna* ~*n* love of one's own little acre **-brikett** peat briquette **-mosse** peat bog (moor) **-mull** peat mould **-strö** peat litter **-tak** sod roof **-täcka** sod, turf

tosig *a1, se tokig*

tota ~ *ihop* (*till*) put together [some sort of] (*ett brev* a letter), get together (*en middag* a dinner)

to'tal *a1* total; entire, complete; ~*t krig* total war (warfare) **-bild** general (overall) view (picture) **-förbud** total prohibition **-förlust** total loss **-förstöra** totally destroy (demolish) **-försvar** total (military, economic, psychological and civil) defence **-haverera** become a total loss; ~*d bil* a completely smashed up car **-haveri** total loss; total wreck

totalisator *s3* totalizator; *vard.* tote; *spela på* ~ bet with the totalizator **-spel** tote-betting

total|itet totality **-i'tär** *a1* totalitarian **-kvadda** *vard.* wreck, smash up, *AE. sl.* total **-vägrare** conscientious objector who also refuses to do community service **-värde** aggregate (total) value

totem ['tå:-] *s9, s7* **-påle** totem [pole]

1 toto *s9, vard., se totalisator*

2 toto *barnspr.* (*häst*) gee-gee

tott [-å-] *s2* (*hår-, garn- etc.*) tuft [of ...]

tov|a I *s1* twisted (tangled) knot (bunch) **II** *v1,* ~ [*ihop*] *sig* become tangled **-ig** *a1* tangled, matted

tox|icitet [-å-] toxicity **-ikologi** *s3* toxicology **-'in** *s4, s3* toxin **-isk** ['tåks-] *a5* toxic

trad *s3* [shipping, (sea)] route

tradera hand down, transmit orally [from one generation to another]

tradig *a1* (*långtråkig*) tedious

tradition tradition **-'ell** *a1* traditional

traditions|bunden tradition bound; *vara* ~ be bound by (rooted in) tradition **-rik** rich in tradition

tra'fik *s3* **1** traffic; (*drift*) service; *genomgående* ~ through traffic; *gå i* [*regelbunden*] ~ *mellan* ply between; *visa hänsyn i* ~*en* show courtesy on the road; *sätta in en buss i* ~ put a bus into service; *vårdslöshet i* ~ careless driving; *ej i* ~ (*på skylt*) depot only **2** (*hantering*) traffic, trade; ~*en med narkotika* the traffic in narcotics **-abel** *a2* trafficable **-anhopning** traffic jam **-ant** user, customer; (*landsvägs-*) road-user; (*fotgängare*) pedestrian **-belastning** traffic load **-bil** (*last-*) lorry; (*taxi*) taxi[cab] **-buller** noise from traffic **-delare** traffic pillar (island) **-döden** the traffic toll

trafiker|a (*färdas på*) use, frequent, travel by; (*ombesörja trafik på*) operate, work, ply on; *livligt* ~*d* heavily trafficked, busy; ~ *en linje* operate a route **-bar** [-ˣke:r-] *a1* trafficable

trafik|flyg air service; civil aviation **-flygare** airline (commercial) pilot **-flygplan** passenger plane **-fyr** traffic light (signal) **-fälla** road trap **-förordning** traffic regulation **-förseelse** traffic offence **-försäkring** traffic insurance **-hinder** traffic obstacle; hold-up in [the] traffic **-knut** traffic centre (junction) **-konstapel** policeman on point duty; *AE., vard.* traffic cop **-kort** heavy vehicle licence **-led** traffic route **-ledare** *flyg.* control officer **-ljus** traffic light[s] **-märke** traffic sign **-olycka** traffic (road, street) accident **-polis** (*polisman*) policeman on point duty, traffic policeman; *koll.* traffic police **-signal** traffic signal (light) **-skylt** traffic sign, signpost **-stockning** traffic jam, congestion of the traffic **-stopp** traffic hold-up **-säkerhet** road safety **-säkerhetsverk** ~*et* [the Swedish] national road safety office **-teknik** transport engineering **-utskott**

~*et* [the Swedish parliamentary] standing committee on transport and communications **-vakt** traffic warden **-vett** good traffic sense **-väsen** traffic services (*pl*) **-övervakning** traffic supervision

tragedi [-ʃe'di:] *s3* tragedy -'**enn** *s3* tragedienne

traggla (*käxa*) go on (*om* about); (*knoga*) plod on (*med* with)

tra'g|ik *s3* tragedy; ~*en i* the tragedy of **-iker** ['tra:-] tragedian **-ikomisk** [-'kɔ:-] *a5* tragicomic[al] **-isk** ['tra:-] *a5* tragic[al] -'**öd** *s3* tragedian

trailer ['trej-] *s2*, (*släpvagn o. film.*) trailer

trakass|era pester, badger; persecute **-eri** pestering, badgering; persecution; ~*er* harassment

trakom [-'å:m] *s7* trachoma

trakt *s3* (*område*) district, parts (*pl*); region; *här i* ~*en* in this neighbourhood, hereabout[s], round about here

trakta ~ *efter* aspire to, aim at; ~ *efter ngns liv* seek a p.'s life

traktamente [-'menn-] *s6* allowance [for expenses], subsistence allowance

traktan *r, se diktan*

traktat 1 (*fördrag*) treaty; *ingå en* ~ make a treaty **2** (*småskrift*) tract

trakter|a 1 (*bjuda*) treat (*ngn med* s.b. to); (*underhålla*) regale (*ngn med* s.b. with); *inte vara vidare* ~*d av* not be flattered (particularly pleased) by **2** (*spela*) play; (*blåsa*) blow **-ing** (*förplägnad*) entertainment [provided]; *riklig* ~ sumptuous banquet, *vard.* plenty of food

traktor [-år] *s3* tractor; (*band-*) caterpillar [tractor]

traktör innkeeper; restaurateur, caterer

trala'la *interj* tra-la-la!

1 trall *s2, s7* (*golv-*) duckboard; *sjö.* grating

2 trall *s2* (*låt*) melody, tune; *den gamla* ~*en* (*bildl.*) the same old routine

1 tralla *v1*, ~ [*på*] warble, troll

2 tralla *s1* (*transport-*) truck; (*dressin*) trolley

tramp *s7* tramping, tramp **trampa I** *s1* (*på cykel o.d.*) pedal; (*på maskin*) treadle **II** *v1* tramp, tread; (*cykel, symaskin etc.*) treadle, pedal; (*tungt*) trample; (*orgel*) blow the bellows of; ~ *i klaveret* drop a brick, put one's foot in it; ~ *ngt i smutsen* (*bildl.*) trample s.th. in the dirt; ~ *ihjäl* trample to death; ~ *ner a*) (*jord*) tread down, *b*) (*gräs*) trample down, *c*) (*skor*) tread down at the heels; ~ *ngn på tårna* tread on a p.'s toes; ~ *sönder* tread (trample) to pieces; ~ *ur* (*koppling*) declutch; ~ *ut barnskorna* grow up; ~ *vatten* tread water

tramp|bil (*för barn*) pedal car **-båt 1** (*nöjesfarkost*) pedalo **2** (*fraktfartyg*) *se trampfartyg* **-cykel** pedal cycle **-dyna** pad, matrix

tramp|fart tramping, tramp trade; *gå i* ~ run in the tramp trade **-fartyg** tramp [vessel], tramp steamer

tramp|kvarn treadmill (*äv. bildl.*) **-mina** *mil.* antipersonnel mine

trampo'lin *s3* [high-diving] springboard; (*vid simhopp äv.*) diving board, high-board **-hopp** high-board diving

trams *s7, vard.* nonsense, drivel, rubbish **tramsa** act (play) the fool, fool around **tramsig**

a1 daft; *nu är du* ~ you are being silly

tran *s3, s4* train (whale) oil

tran|a *s1* crane **-bär** cranberry

trancher|a [-aŋ'ʃe:-, -an-] carve **-kniv** carving knife

trandans dancing of cranes

trankil [-aŋ'ki:l] *a1* cool, calm

tran|kokeri tryworks (*sg o. pl*), train-oil factory **-lampa** train-oil lamp

trans *s3* trance; *vara i* ~ be in a trance

trans|aktion transaction **-al'pin[sk]** [-i:-] transalpine **-atlantisk** [-'lann-] transatlantic

transcendent [-nsen'dent, -nʃen-] *a4*, -'**al** *a1* transcendent[al]

transfer ['trans-] *s9* transfer **-era** transfer **-summa** transfer fee

transform|ation transformation **-ator** *s3* transformer **-era** transform

transfusion [blood] transfusion

transistor [-ˣsistår] *s3* transistor **-isera** transistorize **-radio** transistor radio **-teknik** transistor technology

tran'sit ['trans-, -'si:t] *s3* transit **-era** pass (convey) in transit, transit **-ering** [forwarding in] transit **-hall** transit lounge (hall)

transitiv ['trann-] *a1* transitive

transito ['trann-] *s9* transit **-hall** *se transithall* **-handel** [-ˣsi:t-] transit trade (business)

Transjordanien [-'da:-] *n* Trans-Jordan

tran|skribera transcribe **-skription** [-p'ʃɔ:n] transcription

translator *s3* translator; *auktoriserad* ~ authorized (registered) translator

trans|mission transmission; *tekn. äv.* countershaft transmission **-missionsväxel** transmission gear **-mittera** transmit **-mutation** transmutation **-oce'an[sk]** [-a:-] *a5* transoceanic, overseas **-parang** transparency **-parent** [*äv.* -'raŋt] *a1* transparent **-piration** (*svettning*) perspiration; *bot.* transpiration **-pirationsmedel** deodorant **-pirera** (*svettas*) perspire; *bot.* transpire **-plan'tat** *s7* transplant, organ (tissue) transplanted **-plantation** transplantation, [skin] grafting **-plantera** transplant, graft **-ponera** transpose **-ponering** transposition

tran'sport [-å-] *s3* **1** (*forsling*) transport[ation], conveyance; (*fraktavgift*) cost of transport; *under* ~*en* in transit; *fördyra* ~*en* increase the cost of transport **2** (*överlåtelse av check etc.*) transfer; *bokför.* carried forward (*utgående saldo*), brought forward (*ingående saldo*) **3** (*förflyttning*) transfer, removal; *söka* ~ apply for transfer (*etc.*) **-abel** *a2* transportable **-apparat** conveyor **-arbetare** transport worker **-band** conveyor belt **-behållare** [transport] container **-chef** *mil.* transportation officer **-era** (*jfr transport*) **1** transport, carry, convey **2** (*överlåta*) transfer (*på* to); *bokför.* carry (bring) forward **3** (*förflytta*) transfer, remove **-fartyg** *mil.* transport vessel, troopship **-företag** [road] haulage (transport) business; *AE.* trucking business **-försäkring** transport (transportation) insurance **-kostnad** transport[ation] (carrying, shipping) cost **-medel** means of transport (conveyance) **-väsen** transport [service] **-ör** *tekn.* conveyor

trans|position *mus.* transposition **-sibirisk**

[-'bi:-] trans-Siberian **-substantiation** [-(t)sia-] transubstantiation

tran|sumera copy in extract **-sumt** [-'sumt] *s7* extract

transu'ran *s4, s3, kem.* transuranic element

transver's|al I *s1* transversal [line] II *a1* transverse, transversal **-'ell** *a1, se transversal II*

transves'tit *s3* transvestite **-ism** transvestism

tra'pets 1 *s7, s4, mat.* trapezium; *AE.* trapezoid **2** *s3, gymn.* trapeze **-konstnär** trapeze artiste

trapp|a I *s1 (utomhus)* stairs *(pl),* flight of stairs; *(farstu-)* doorstep[s *pl*]; *(inomhus)* stairs *(pl),* staircase, stairway, flight [of stairs]; *en ~ upp* on the first *(AE.* second) floor, *(i tvåvåningshus)* upstairs; *~ upp och ~ ner* up and down stairs; *i ~n* on the stairs; *nedför (uppför) ~n* down (up) the stairs, downstairs (upstairs) II *v1, ~ av* reduce; *~ ned* reduce; *~ upp* escalate, step up **-avsats** *(inomhus)* landing; *(utomhus)* platform **-gavel** stepped gable **-hus** stairwell **-ljus** staircase light **-räcke** [staircase] banisters *(pl)* **-steg** step, stair; *bildl. äv.* stage **-stege** stepladder **-uppgång** staircase; stairs *(pl)*

tras|a I *s1* **1** [piece of] rag; shred; *falla (slita) i -or* go to (tear [in]to) rags; *utan en ~ på kroppen* without a rag of clothing on one's body; *våt som en ~* wringing wet; *känna sig som en ~* feel washed out **2** *se damm-, skur-* II *v1, ~ sönder* tear [in]to rags (shreds, *äv. bildl.*) **-docka** rag doll **-grann** *(om pers.)* tawdry, shoddy; *(om sak)* gaudy **-hank** ragamuffin, tatterdemalion **-ig** *a1* ragged, tattered; *(om kläder äv.)* torn; *(i kanten)* frayed; *(sönderbruten)* broken; *(i olag)* out of order; *~a nerver* frayed nerves

traska trudge; trot *(i väg* off; *omkring* [a]round)

tras|matta rag (rug) [mat] **-proletariat** lumpenproletariat

trassat *hand.* drawee

trassel ['trass-] *s7* **1** *(oreda)* tangle; *bildl. äv.* muddle, confusion; *(besvärligheter)* trouble; bother *(sg),* complications *(pl);* *ställa till ~* make trouble *(för ngn* for s.b.), *vard.* kick up a fuss **2** *(textilavfall)* cotton waste, waste wool **-sudd** piece of cotton waste

trass|ent *hand.* drawer **-era** *hand.* draw

trassl|a *(krångla)* make a fuss, be troublesome; *~ ihop* get into a tangle, entangle; *~ in sig a)* get itself (o.s.) entangled *(i* in), *b) (bildl. om pers.)* entangle o.s., *get* o.s. involved *(i* in); *~ med betalningen* be irregular about paying; *~ till a) se ~ ihop, b) bildl.* muddle; *~ till sina affärer* get one's finances into a muddle; *~ [till] sig* get entangled; *~ sig fram a)* make one's way along with difficulty, *b) bildl.* muddle along; *~ sig ifrån* wriggle out of **-ig** *a1* tangled, entangled; *(friare)* muddled; *~a affärer* shaky finances

trast *s2* thrush

tratt *s2* funnel; *(matar- etc.; stormvarningssignal)* hopper

1 tratt *s1, hand.* draft, bill [of exchange]

2 tratt|a *v1, ~ i ngn ngt (äv. bildl.)* stuff s.b. with s.th.; *~ ngt i öronen på ngn* din s.th. into a p.'s ears; *~ ngn full med lögner* stuff s.b. with

a lot of lies

trattformig [-å-] *a1* funnel-shaped, funnelled

trauma ['trau-] *s6* trauma **-tisk** [-'ma:-] *a5* traumatic

trav *s4, s3* trot; *rida i ~* ride at a trot; *sätta av i ~* start trotting; *hjälpa ngn på ~en (bildl.)* put s.b. on the right track, give s.b. a start **1 trava** *(lägga i trave)* pile, stack *(virke* wood) **2 trava** trot; *~ på* trot along **trav|are** *se travhäst* **-bana** trotting course (track)

trave *s2* pile, stack *(böcker* of books; *ved* of wood)

travers [-'värs] *s3* **1** *(lyftkransanordning)* overhead [travelling] crane; *(tvärbalk)* cross member **2** *mil.* traverse

travestera *v1,* **traves'ti** *s3* travesty, spoof **trav|häst** trotter, trotting horse **-kusk** sulky driver **-sport** trotting **-tävling** trotting race **tre** three; *(för sms. jfr fem-);* *~ och ~ (~ i taget)* three at a time; *ett par ~ stycken* two or three; *alla ~ böckerna* all three books; *vi gjorde det alla ~* all [the] three of us did it; *i ~ exemplar* in triplicate, in three copies; *alla goda ting är ~* all good things are three in number

tre|a *s1* three; *(lägenhet)* three-room flat, flat with two bedrooms; *~n[s växel]* [the] third [gear]; *han kom ~* he came in third (as number three); *han blev ~* he was number three **-bent** [-e:-] *a4* three-legged **-dela** divide into three; *geom.* trisect **-dimensionell** *a1* three-dimensional, three-D

tredje [ˣtre:d-] third; *~ graden (jur.)* third degree; *~ klass* third class; *~ man a) (jur.)* third party, *b)* kortsp. [the] third hand; *~ riket* the Third Reich; *~ världen* the Third World; *~ statsmakten* the Press **-dag** *~ jul* the day after Boxing Day **-del** third; *en ~s* a third of; *två ~ar* two thirds **-klassbiljett** third-class ticket

tredsk [-e:-, *vard.* tresk] *a1* refractory, defiant **tredska** *s1* refractoriness, defiance; *jur.* obstinacy, contumacy **tredskas** *dep* be refractory **tredsko|dom** judgement by default **-domsförfarande** undefended proceedings *(pl)*

tredubb|el treble, threefold, triple; *det -la priset* treble (three times) the price **-la** treble, triple

treenig triune **-het** triunity, trinity; *~en* the Trinity

trefaldig *a1* threefold, treble, triple **-het** [ˣtre:-, -'fall-] *kyrkl.* [the] Trinity **-hetssöndag** *~en* Trinity Sunday

tre|falt threefold, trebly; thrice *(lycklig* blessed) **-fas** three-phase **-fasström** three-phase current **-fjärdedelstakt** [-ˣfjä:-r-] three-four [time], *AE.* three-four time **-fot** tripod **-glasfönster** triple glazing *(koll.)* **-hjulig** [-j-] *a1* three-wheeled **-hjuling** [-j-] three-wheeler; *(cykel)* tricycle; *(bil)* tricar **-hundratalet** the fourth century **-hundraårsjubileum** tercentenary, tercentennial **-hörning** [-ö:-] triangle **-kant** triangle **-kantig** triangular; *~ hatt* cocked (three-cornered) hat **-klang** *mus.* triad **-klöver** *bot.* three-leaf clover; *bildl.* trio **-kropparsproblemet** the three body problem **-'kvart** *på ~* at an angle

tre'kvarts *i ~ timme* for three quarters of an

hour **-lång** three-quarter length **-strumpa** knee hose (sock)
treledare three-wire, triple wire
trema s6 di[a]eresis (pl di[a]ereses)
tremakts|avtal tripartite agreement **-förbund** triple alliance **-fördrag** tripartite treaty
tre|mannadelegation three-man delegation **-mastare** three-master, three-masted schooner **-milsgräns** three-mile limit **-motorig** al three-engine[d]
tremul|ant mus. tremulant **-era** quaver, sing (play) with a tremolo **-ering** tremolo
tre|månadersväxel three-month bill **-männing** second cousin
trenchcoat ['tren(t)ʃkåt] s2 trench coat
trend s3 trend, fashion **-ig** al trendy
trenne three
trepaner|a trepan, trephine **-ing** trepanation, trephining
tre|procentig al three-percent **-radig** al three-rowed **-rumslägenhet** three-room[ed] flat; two-bedroom flat **-sidig** al trilateral **-siffrig** al three-figure; three-digit **-sitsig** al three-seated **-skift** three-shift **-snibb** triangular cloth **-spann** team of three horses, troika; köra ~ drive three in hand **-språkig** al trilingual **-stavig** al trisyllabic[al] **-steg** sport. triple jump, hop, step and jump **-stegsraket** three-stage rocket **-stjärnig** [-ʃä:-] al three-star (konjak brandy) **-stämmig** al for three voices, in three parts **-takt** mus. three-four time, AE. three-quarter time **-taktsmotor** three-stroke engine **-tal** (antal av tre) triad; kortsp., ~ i ess three aces; ~et [the number] three **-tiden** vid ~ [at] about three [o'clock]
tretti|o [ˣtretti(o), 'tretti(o)] thirty; klockan tre och ~ at three thirty **-onde** [-å-] thirtieth **-on-[de]del** thirtieth [part]
trettio|tal ett ~ some (about) thirty; på ~et (1930-talet) in the thirties **-årig** al thirty-year[-old]; ~a kriget the Thirty Years' War
tretton [-ån] thirteen **-dagen** Twelfth Day, Epiphany **-dagsafton** Twelfth Night **-de** thirteenth **-hundratalet** på ~ in the fourteenth century **-årig** al thirteen-year-old
tre|tumsspik three-inch nail **-tungad** a5 three-tongued; three-tailed (flagga flag) **-udd** trident **-uddig** al with three prongs
trev|a grope [about] (efter for); ~ efter ord fumble for words; ~ i mörkret go groping about (bildl. be groping) in the dark; ~ sig fram grope one's way along **-ande** a4 groping, fumbling; bildl. äv. tentative **-are** feeler
trev|lig [ˣtre:v-] al pleasant, agreeable; (mera vard.) nice; AE. äv. cute; (rolig) enjoyable; (om lägenhet o.d.) comfortable; (sällskaplig) sociable; ~ resa! a pleasant journey!, bon voyage!; vi hade mycket ~t we had a very nice time, we enjoyed ourselves very much; vi har haft mycket ~t we have had a wonderful time; det var ~t att [få] höra I am glad to hear that; det var just ~t! (iron.) what a pretty kettle of fish! **-ligt** adv pleasantly etc. **-nad** s3 comfort, comfortable feeling; sprida ~ omkring sig create a cheerful atmosphere
tre|våningshus three-storeyed house **-värd** kem. trivalent **-årig** al three-year[s'] **(om barn**

o. djur) three-year-old **-åring** child of three [years of age]; (om häst) three-year-old
tri s9, vard. trichlor[o]ethylene
triangel [-'aŋ-] s2 triangle **-drama** eternal-triangle drama **-formig** [-å-] al triangular **-mätning** triangulation **-punkt** triangulation point
triangul|ering [-ŋgu'le:-] triangulation **-'är** al triangular
trias ['tri:-] r Trias **-perioden** the Triassic period
tri'bad s3 tribade
1 tribun s3 (plattform) platform, tribune
2 tribun s3 (rom. ämbetsman) tribune
tribu'n|al s3, s4 tribunal **-'at** s7 tribunate, tribuneship
tri'but s3 tribute
1 trick s7, s2, kortsp. trick [over book]
2 trick s7 (knep) trick, dodge; (reklam- etc.) gimmick
trickfilmning trick filming **tricks** s7, se 2 trick **tricksa** use tricks; ~ med bollen dribble
triftong [-'tåŋ] s3, språkv. triphthong
trigonome'tr|i s3 trigonometry **-isk** [-'me:-] a5 trigonometric[al]
tri'kin s3 trichina (pl trichinae)
trikloretylen [-ˣklå:r-] trichlor[o]ethylene
trikolor [-'lå:r] s3, ~en the Tricolour
tri'kå s3 1 (tyg) tricot, stockinet[te] **2** ~er tights, pantyhose (behandlas som pl); hudfärgade ~er fleshings **-affär** knitwear shop **-fabrik** knitwear factory **-underkläder** pl machine-knitted (cotton) underwear **-varor** pl knitwear (sg), knitted (hosiery) goods
tril'jon s3 trillion; AE. quintillion
trilla 1 s1 (vagn) surrey **II** v1 **1** (rulla) roll; ~ piller make pills **2** (ramla) drop, fall, tumble; (om tårar) trickle; ~ omkull tumble over; ~ av pinn (vard.) kick the bucket
trilling triplet
tri|lo'bit s3 trilobite **-logi** s3 trilogy
trilsk al (motsträvig) contrary; (egensinnig) wilful; (omedgörlig) intractable; (tjurig) mulish, pig-headed **trilska** s1 contrariness etc. **trilskas** dep be contrary (etc.)
trim [trimm] s9, s7 trim; vara i ~ (sport. o. vard.) be in good trim
trima'ran s3 trimaran
trim|ma sjö. trim (äv. pälsen på hund); (justera motor o.d.) trim, adapt **-ning** trimming, trim
trind al (rund) round[-shaped], roundish; (fyllig) plump, vard. tubby, chubby **-het** roundness; rotundity
trio ['tri:o] s5 trio **triod** [-'å:d] s3 triode **triol** [-'o:l, -'å:l] s3 triplet
1 tripp s3, s2 (resa) [short] trip (äv. narkotika-rus); göra (ta sig) en ~ go for (take) a trip
2 tripp i uttr.: ~ trapp trull a) (spel) noughts and crosses, tick-tack-toe, b) bildl. one, two, three [going down in height]
tripp|a (gå på tå) trip along; (knarka) trip **-ande** a4 tripping; ~ steg mincing steps
trippel|allians ~en the Triple Alliance **-vaccinering** three-way D.P.T. (diphtheria, pertussis and tetanus) inoculation
trippmätare trip meter

trip'tyk *s3* triptych

triss *s3, kortsp., se* tretal

triss|a I *s1* [small] wheel, trundle, disc; (*i block e.d.*) pulley; (*sporr-*) rowel; *dra på -or!* (*vard.*) go to blazes! **II** *v1,* ~ *upp priserna* push up the prices

trist *a1* (*långtråkig*) tiresome, tedious; (*dyster*) gloomy, dismal; (*sorgsen*) sad, melancholy; (*föga uppbygglig*) depressing, dreary **-ess** tiresomeness *etc.*; melancholy

triton [-'tå:n, -'tω:n] *s3* triton

tri'umf *s3* triumph **-ator** *s3* triumphator **-båge** triumphal arch **-era** triumph; (*jubla*) exult **-erande** [-'fe:-] *a4* triumphant, exultant; ~ *leende* triumphant smile **-tåg** triumphal procession (*bildl.* march, progress) **-vagn** triumphator's chariot; car of triumph

trium'vir *s3* triumvir **-'at** *s7* triumvirate

triv|as *v2, dep* get on well, be happy; (*frodas*) thrive; (*blomstra*) flourish, prosper; *han -s i England* he likes being (likes it) in England; ~ *med* like, (*ngn äv.*) get on [well] with

trivi'al *a1* trivial; commonplace **-itet** *s3* triviality

trivsam [-i:-] *a1* pleasant, comfortable, cosy, snug; (*om pers.*) easy to get on with, congenial **-het** cosiness, hominess; congeniality

trivsel ['tri:v-] *s9* (*välbefinnande*) wellbeing, comfort[ableness]; (*trevnad*) ease, cosiness

tro I *s9* **1** belief (*på* in); (*tillit, tilltro*) faith, trust (*till, på* in); ~, *hopp och kärlek* faith, hope, love; *den kristna ~n* the Christian faith; *i den ~n att* believing (thinking) that; *leva i den ~n att* believe that; *i den fasta ~n att* convinced that; *i god* ~ in good faith, bona fide; *sätta ~ till* trust, believe, (*ngn äv.*) put confidence in **2** *svära ngn* ~ *och lydnad* swear allegiance to s.b.; *uppsäga ngn* ~ *och lydnad* withdraw one's allegiance from s.b.; *på* ~ *och loven* on one's honour; *skänka ngn sin* ~ give s.b. one's plighted word **II** *v4* **1** believe, trust; (*förmoda*) think, suppose, *AE. o. vard.* guess, reckon; (*föreställa sig*) imagine, fancy; *ja, jag ~r det* yes, I believe so; *jag skulle ~ det* I should think so; ~ *det den som vill!* believe that if you like!; *du kan aldrig* ~ *hur* you can't possibly imagine how; ~ *mig,* ... take my word for it, ...; believe me, ...; ..., *må du ~!* ..., I can tell you!; *det ~r du bara!* that's only your imagination (an idea of yours)!; *det var det jag ~dde!* [that's] just what I thought!; *det ~r jag det!* I should jolly well think so!; ~ *ngn om gott* expect well of s.b.; ~ *ngt om ngn* believe s.th. of s.b.; ~ *ngn på hans ord* take a p.'s word for it; ~ *ngn vara* believe s.b. to be; ~ *på* believe in (*äv. relig.*), (*hålla för sann*) think (believe) **2** *rfl* think (believe) o.s. (*säker* safe); ~ *sig vara* think that one is, consider (believe) o.s. to be; ~ *sig kunna* believe o.s. (that one is) capable of (+ *ing-form*) (able to)

tro|ende *a4* believing; *en* ~ a believer; *de* ~ (*äv.*) the faithful **-fast** true, constant (*vän* friend); loyal (*vänskap* friendship); faithful (*kärlek* love); (~ *av sig*) true-hearted, trusty **-fasthet** constancy; loyalty; faithfulness

trofé *s3* trophy

trogen *a3* faithful (*intill döden* unto death; *mot*

to); true (*sina ideal* to one's ideals); *sin vana* ~ true to habit

trohet faithfulness; fidelity; loyalty

trohets|brott breach of faith **-ed** (*avlägga* take the) oath of allegiance **-löfte** vow of fidelity **-plikt** allegiance

trohjärtad [-j-] *a5* true-hearted; (*ärlig*) frank; (*förtroendefull*) confiding

Troja ['tråjja] *n* Troy

tro'j|an [-å-] *s3,* **-'ansk** [-a:-] *a3* Trojan

trojka ['tråjj-] *s1* troika

troké *s3* trochee **trokeisk** [-'ke:isk] *a5* trochaic

trolig *a1* probable, likely; *AE. äv.* apt; (*trovärdig*) credible, plausible; *det är ~t att han* he will probably (is likely to); *det är föga ~t* it is hardly likely; *hålla* [*det*] *för ~t att* think it likely that; *söka göra ngt ~t* try to make s.th. plausible **-en, -tvis** very (most) likely, probably; *han kommer* ~ *inte* he is not likely to come

troll [-å-] *s7* troll; (*elakt*) hobgoblin; *när man talar om ~en står de i farstun* talk of the devil and he'll appear; *ditt lilla ~!* you little witch

troll|a (*utöva -dom*) conjure; (*om -konstnär*) perform conjuring tricks; ~ *bort* spirit (conjure) away; ~ *fram* conjure forth (up) **-bunden** spellbound **-dom** [-dωmm] *s2* witchcraft, sorcery; (*magi*) magic; *bruka* ~ use magic, practise witchcraft **-domskonst** ~*en* [the art of] witchcraft **-dryck** magic potion **-eri** magic, enchantment **-erikonstnär** *se* -konstnär **-formel** magic formula; charm, spell; (*besvärjelse*) incantation **-karl** magician, wizard; sorcerer **-konst** ~*er* (*häxas*) magic (*sg*); (*-konstnärs*) conjuring (jugglery) trick; *göra ~er* perform conjuring tricks **-konstnär** conjurer **-kraft** magic power **-krets** *bildl.* magic sphere **-kunnig** skilled in magic **-kvinna** *se -packa* **-makt** spell **-packa** *s1* witch, sorceress **-slag** *som genom ett* ~ as if by [a stroke of] magic **-slända** dragonfly **-spö, -stav** magic wand **-trumma** troll drum **-tyg** *s7* witchery, sorcery

trolov|ad *a5,* hans (hennes) ~*e* his (her) betrothed **-ning** betrothal **-ningsbarn** betrothal child

trolsk [-å-] *a1* magic[al]; (*tjusande*) bewitching; (*hemsk*) weird

trolös faithless, unfaithful, disloyal (*mot* to); (*förrädisk*) treacherous, perfidious (*mot* to, towards) **-het** faithlessness; breach of faith; ~ *mot huvudman* breach of trust committed by an agent on his principal

1 tromb [-å-] *s3* (*skydrag*) tornado

2 tromb [-å-] *s3* (*blodpropp*) thrombus (*pl* thrombi)

trombon [tråm'bå:n] *s3* trombone **-ist** trombonist

trombos [tråm'bå:s] *s3* thrombosis

tron *s3* throne; *avsäga sig ~en* abdicate; *bestiga ~en* ascend (accede to) the throne; *störta ngn från ~en* dethrone s.b.

tron|a be enthroned (*på* on) **-arvinge** heir to the throne **-avsägelse** abdication **-bestigning** accession to the throne **-följare** successor to the throne **-följd** succession [to the throne] **-följdsordning** act of succession; *Storbritannien* act of settlement **-himmel** canopy **-pre-**

T

tendent pretender (claimant) to the throne **-sal** throne room, room of state **-skifte** accession of a new monarch **-tal** speech from the throne

trop [-å:-] *s3, språkv.* trope

trop|ik *s3* tropic; *~erna* the Tropics, the torrid (tropic) zone (*sg*) **-ikhjälm** pith helmet, topee, topi **-isk** ['trå:-] *a5* tropic[al]

tropo'sfär *s3* troposphere

tropp [-å-] *s2* troop; (*infanteri-*) section; *gymn.* squad

tropp|a [-å-] **1** *mil.* troop (*fanan* the colour) **2** *~ av* move off **-chef** troop (section, squad) commander

tros|artikel article of faith; (*friare*) doctrine **-bekännare** *främmande ~* adherent of an alien creed **-bekännelse** confession (declaration) of [one's] faith; (*lära*) creed; *augsburgska ~n* the Augsburg Confession **-frihet** religious liberty **-frände** fellow believer **-gemenskap** communion in the faith **-iver** religious zeal **-ivrare** religious zealot

troskyldig true-hearted; frank (*blick* look)

troslära doctrine of faith, dogma

trosor *pl* briefs, panties

1 tross [-å-] *s2, sjö.* hawser; rope

2 tross [-å-] *s2, mil.* baggage [train]; supply vans (*pl*)

tros|sak matter of faith **-samfund** religious community **-sats** dogma

trossbotten *byggn.* double floor[ing]; *sjömil.* lower deck; (*manskapslogement*) crew's quarter

trosskydd panty liner (shield)

trosviss full of implicit faith **-het** certainty of belief; assured faith

trotjänar|e, -inna [*gammal*] ~ faithful old servant

trots [-å-] **I** *s7* defiance (*mot* of); (*motsträvighet*) obstinacy (*mot* to[wards]), scorn (*mot* of); *visa ~ mot ngn* bid defiance to (defy) s.b.; *i ~ av* in spite of; *på ~* in (out of) defiance; *alla ansträngningar till ~* in spite of all efforts **II** *prep* in spite of; notwithstanding, despite

trots|a defy; (*bjuda ... trots*) bid defiance to; (*utmana*) brave, scorn, stand up to; *det ~r all beskrivning* it is beyond description **-ig** *a1* defiant (*mot* to, towards); (*uppstudsig*) refractory (*mot* towards); (*hånfull*) scornful, insolent **-ighet** refractoriness *etc.*; defiance **-ålder** *~n* the obstinate age

trotto'ar *s3* pavement; *AE.* sidewalk **-kant** kerb; *AE.* curb **-servering** pavement restaurant (café)

tro'tyl *s3* trinitrotoluene, trotyl

trovärdig credible; (*tillförlitlig*) reliable, trustworthy; *från ~t håll* from a reliable quarter **-het** credibility; reliability, trustworthiness

trubadur troubadour

trubba ~ [*av, till*] blunt, make blunt

trubbel ['trubb-] *s7, vard.* trouble

trubb|ig *a1* blunt; (*avtrubbad*) blunted; (*ej spetsig*) pointless; (*om vinkel*) obtuse **-näsa** snub nose **-vinklig** *a1* obtuse-angled

truck *s2* truck; (*med lyftanordning*) lift truck **-förare** truck driver

trude'lutt *s3, vard.* ditty, little song

truga ~ *ngn att* press s.b. to, urge (importune, solicit) s.b. to; ~ *i* (*på*) *ngn ngt* press s.th. [up]on s.b.; ~ *sig på ngn* force o.s. [up]on s.b.; ~ *i sig maten* force o.s. to eat

truism *s3* truism

trum|broms drum (expanding) brake **-eld** drumfire

trumf *s7, s2* trump; *spader är ~* spades are trumps; *sitta med alla ~ på hand* have all the trumps; *spela ut sin sista ~* play one's last trump (*bildl.* card)

trumf|a trump, play trumps; ~ *i ngn ngt* drum (pound) s.th. into a p.'s head; ~ *igenom* force through, *AE. vard.* railroad; ~ *över ngn* out trump s.b. **-färg** trump suit **-kort** trump [card] **-spel** trump game **-äss** ace of trumps

trum|hinna eardrum, tympanic membrane **-ma I** *s1* **1** *mus.* drum; *slå på ~* beat the drum (*för* for) **2** *tekn.* drum, cylinder, barrel **II** *v1* drum; (*om regn äv.*) beat; ~ *ihop* (*bildl.*) drum (beat) up; ~ *på piano* strum on the piano **-minne** *data.* drum store

trumpen *a3* sulky, sullen; morose

trum'pet *s3* trumpet; *blåsa* [*i*] ~ play (sound) the trumpet

trumpet|a trumpet (*ut* forth) **-are** [-ˣpe:-] trumpeter; *mil. äv.* bugler **-fanfar** fanfare of trumpets **-signal** trumpet signal (call) **-stek** *s7, sjö.* sheepshank **-stöt** trumpet blast

trum|pinne drumstick **-skinn** drumhead **-slagare** drummer **-slagarpojke** drummer boy **-virvel** drum roll

trupi'al *s3, zool.* oriole

trupp *s3* troop; (*-styrka*) contingent; (*-enhet*) unit, detachment; (*idrotts-*) team; (*teater-*) troupe, company; *~er* (*mil.*) troops, forces **-förband** [military] unit **-revy** review [of troops] **-rörelse** military movement **-sammandragning[ar]** concentration of troops **-slag** branch of service, arm **-styrka** military force **-transport** transport[ation] of troops **-transportfartyg** troopship, troop carrier (transport) **-transportplan** transport plane, troop carrier [plane]

trust *s3* trust **-bildning** establishment of trusts **-väsen** trust system

1 trut *s2, zool.* gull

2 trut *s2, vard.* (*mun*) kisser; *hålla ~en* shut up; *vara stor i ~en* blow one's own trumpet

truta ~ *med munnen* pout [one's lips]

trutit *sup. av* tryta

tryck *s7* **1** (*fys. o. friare*) pressure (*på* on); weight (*över bröstet* on one's chest); *bildl.* constraint, strain; *språkv.* stress; *utöva ~* exert pressure, (*friare*) put pressure (*på* on); *det ekonomiska ~et* the financial strain **2** (*av bok e.d.*) print; (*av-*) impression; *komma ut i ~* appear (come out) in print; *ge ut i ~* print, publish

tryck|a *v3* **1** (*fys. o. friare*) press (*mot* against, to); (*klämma*) squeeze; (*tynga* [*på*]) lie heavy on, oppress; *tryck!* (*på dörr*) push!; *tryck på knappen!* press the button!; ~ *ngns hand* shake a p.'s hand; ~ *ngn till sitt bröst* press (clasp) s.b. to one's breast; ~ *en kyss på* imprint a kiss on **2** (*med betonad partikel*) ~ *av* a) (*ta av-tryck av*) impress, b) (*kopiera*) copy [off], c) (*avskjuta*) fire, *absol.* pull the trigger; ~ *fast*

press on; ~ *ihop* press (squeeze) together; ~ *in* (*ut*) press (force) in (out); ~ *sig intill* press up against; ~ *ner* press down, (*friare o. bildl.*) depress; ~ *upp* press up, force open **3** (*om villebråd*) squat; *ligga o.* ~ (*om pers.*) lie low **4** *boktr. o.d.* print; (*med stämpel*) stamp; ~ *en bok i 2 000 exemplar* print 2,000 copies of a book; ~ *om* reprint; *-es* (*på korrektur*) ready for press **-alster** publication; printed matter **-ande** *a4* pressing *etc.*; (*friare o. bildl.*) oppressive; (*om väder*) sultry, close; (*tung*) heavy; *värmen känns* ~ the heat is oppressive **-are** printer; (*dans*) *BE. sl.* smooch **-ark** printed sheet **-belastning** [compressive] load **-bokstav** (*textad*) block letter **-dräkt** pressure suit **-eri** printing works (house); (*motsats sätteri*) press room; *skicka till ~et* send to the printer[s] **-erifaktor** press-room (printer's) foreman **-fel** printer's error, misprint **-felsnisse** *s2* printer's gremlin **-frihet** freedom (liberty) of the press
tryckfrihets|brott breach of the press law **-förordning** press law **-mål** press-law suit
tryck|färdig ready for the press (for printing) **-färg** printing (printer's) ink **-godkännande** permission to print, imprimatur **-impregnera** impregnate under pressure **-kabin** *flyg.* pressure cabin **-kammare** pressure chamber **-knapp 1** (*strömbrytare*) push button **2** (*för knäppning*) press stud; *AE.* snap fastener **-kokare** pressure cooker **-kontakt** push-button switch **-luft** compressed air **-luftsborr** pneumatic drill **-luftsdriven** *a5* pneumatic, air--operated
tryck|ning 1 (*av böcker o.d.*) printing; *godkännes till* ~ ready for press; *lämna till* ~ hand in to be printed; *under* ~ in the press; *boken är under* ~ (*äv.*) the book is being printed **2** pressing *etc.*; pressure; (*med fingret*) press **-nings-kostnader** printing costs **-ort** place of publication, [printer's] imprint **-penna** automatic pencil **-press** printing press **-pump** pressure pump **-punkt 1** *fysiol.* pressure spot **2** *elektr.* pressure (feeding) point **-sak** *~er* printed matter (paper) **-sida** *boktr.* printed page **-stark** *språkv.* stressed, accented **-stil** [printing] type **-svag** *språkv.* unstressed, unaccented **-svärta** *se tryckfärg*
tryck|t 1 pressed *etc.* **2** *boktr.* printed (*hos* by); *~a kretsar* (*radio.*) printed circuits **3** (*nedstämd*) oppressed, dejected **-våg** blast wave **-år** year of publication
tryff|el ['tryff-] *s2* truffle **-era** garnish with truffles; *~d* (*äv.*) truffled
trygg *a1* safe, secure (*för* from); (*om pers.*) confident; (*orädd*) dauntless, assured
trygg|a make safe, secure (*för, emot* from); safeguard; ~ *framtiden* provide for the future; ~ *freden* guarantee the peace; *~d ålderdom* a carefree (secure) old age **-het** safety, security **-hetsavtal** job security agreement **-hetskänsla** feeling (sense) of security
tryggt *adv* safely *etc.*, with safety; ~ *påstå* confidently declare
try'må *s3* pier glass
tryne *s6* snout; *ett fult* ~ (*vard.*) an ugly mug
tryt|a *tröt trutit* (*fattas*) be lacking; (*ta slut*) run

short, be deficient; *förråden börjar* ~ supplies are getting low (running short); *krafterna börjar* ~ *his* (*etc.*) strength is beginning to ebb; *tålamodet tröt mig* my patience gave out
tråckel|stygn tacking-stitch **-tråd** tacking--thread
tråckl|a tack; ~ *fast ngt* tack s.th. on (*på, vid* to) **-ing** tacking
tråd *s2* thread; (*bomulls-*) cotton; (*metall-*) wire; (*glöd-*) filament; (*fiber*) fibre; *den röda ~en* (*i berättelse o.d.*) the main theme; *går som en röd* ~ *genom* runs all through, is the governing idea of; *få ngn på ~en* (*tel.*) get s.b. on the line; *hålla i ~arna* (*bildl.*) hold the reins; *hans liv hängde på en* ~ his life hung by a thread; *tappa ~en* (*bildl.*) lose the thread
tråda *v2*, ~ *dansen* dance
tråd|buss trolley bus **-drageri** [wire] drawing mill, wire mill **-fin** threadlike, finespun **-gardin** net (lace) curtain **-ig** *a1* fibrous, filamentous; (*om kött e.d.*) stringy **-kors** *fys.* cross wires (hairs) (*pl*) **-liknande** threadlike; filamentous **-lös** wireless (*telegrafi* telegraphy) **-radio** wire[d] broadcasting **-rakt** *adv* the way of the thread[s *pl*] **-rulle** (*med tråd*) reel of cotton, *AE.* spool of thread; (*för tråd*) cotton reel, *AE.* spool **-sliten** threadbare **-smal** [as] thin as a thread **-spik** wire nail **-ända** end of cotton (thread)
tråg *s7* trough; (*mindre djupt*) tray
tråk|a (*driva med*) tease, (*starkare*) pester; ~ *ihjäl* (*ut*) bore to death **-ig** *a1* (*lång-*) boring, tedious; (*om pers. äv.*) dull; (*ointressant*) uninteresting; (*besvärlig*) tiresome; (*oangenäm*) unpleasant, disagreable; *en* ~ *historia* a nasty affair; *en* ~ *människa* (*äv.*) a bore; *så ~t!* (*så synd*) what a pity!, (*det gör mig ont*) oh, I'm sorry!; *det var verkligen ~t!* that was too bad!; *det var ~t för dig!* how tiresome for you!; *det vore ~t om* I (we) should be [very] sorry if **-ighet** (*utan pl*) tediousness *etc.*; (*med pl*) trouble, annoyance **-igt** *adv* tediously *etc.*; ~ *nog* unfortunately, I am sorry to say; *ha ~t* be bored, have a tedious time of it **-måns** *s2* bore
tråla *s2*, **tråla** *v1* trawl **trålare** trawler **trålfiske** trawling
tråna pine, languish (*efter* for) **-ad** *s3* pining, languishing (*efter* for)
trång *-t trängre trängst* narrow (*i halsen* in (at) the neck); *över ryggen* across the back); (*åtsittande*) tight; (*om bostad e.d.*) cramped; *det är ~t i* there is very little space in, (*det är fullt med folk*) ... is very crowded; *det är ~t om saligheten* there's not much room to move **-bodd** *a1* overcrowded; *vara* ~ be cramped for space, live in overcrowded conditions **-boddhet** overcrowding, cramped housing accommodation **-bröstad** *a5* (*intolerant*) narrow--minded; (*pryd*) strait-laced **-mål** distress; (*penningknipa*) embarrassment, straits (*pl*); *råka i* ~ get into straits (*vard.* a tight corner) **-sinne** narrow-mindedness **-synt** [-y:-] *a1* narrow; *vara* ~ have a narrow outlook **-synthet** [-y:-] narrowness; narrow outlook
trångt *adv, bo* ~ live in [over]crowded conditions; *sitta* ~ *a*) sit close together, *bildl.* be hard up, be in a tight corner, *b*) (*om plagg*) fit

T

too tight
trånsjuka pining, languishing (*efter* for)
1 trä *v4, se 2 träda*
2 trä *s6* wood; *av ~ (äv.)* wooden; *ta i ~!* touch wood!
trä|aktig *a1* woodlike; *bildl.* woody, wooden **-ben** wooden leg **-bit** piece (bit) of wood **-blåsare** wood[wind] player; *-blåsarna* the woodwind (*sg*) **-blåsinstrument** woodwind instrument **-bjälke** timber beam **-bock 1** (*bock av trä*) wooden trestle **2** *pers.* dry stick **-bro** wooden bridge **-byggnad** wooden building
träck *s3* excrement[s *pl*]; (*djur-*) dung
träd *s7* tree; *växer inte på ~ (bildl.)* don't grow on trees; *inte se skogen för bara ~* not see the wood for the trees
1 träda *v2* (*gå, komma*) step, tread; *~ i förbindelse med* enter into a relationship with; *~ i kraft* come into force, take effect; *~ i likvidation* go into liquidation; *~ emellan* step between, *absol. äv.* intervene; *~ fram* come (step) forward; *~ tillbaka* retire, withdraw (*för* in favour of); *~ ut* step (walk) out
2 träda *v2* (*~ på*) thread (*på* on to); (*halsband äv.*) string; (*friare*) pass, slip; *~ en handske på handen* draw a glove on to the hand; *~ på en nål* thread a needle; *~ en nål (ett band)* igenom ngt run a needle (ribbon) through s.th.; *~ pärlor på ett band* thread pearls on [to] a string, string pearls; *~ upp* thread (*på* on [to])
3 träd|a *s1* (*trädesåker*) fallow [field], lay-land; *ligga i ~* lie fallow
träd|bevuxen wooded, timbered **-dunge** clump of trees **-fattig** with few trees **-fällning** wood cutting (felling) **-gren** branch [of a tree] **-gräns** timber (tree) line **-gård** ['träggå:rd, ˈträgg-] *s2* garden; *AE. äv.* yard; *anlägga en ~* lay out a garden; *botanisk (zoologisk) ~* botanical (zoological) gardens (*pl*)
trädgårds|anläggning (*-anläggande*) landscape gardening; *konkr.* garden[s *pl*], grounds **-arbetare** gardener, garden hand **-arbete** gardening, garden work **-arkitekt** landscape gardener (architect) **-fest** garden party **-förening** horticultural society **-gunga** lawn swing **-gång** garden path **-land** garden plot **-mästare** gardener **-möbel** [piece of] garden furniture **-odling** *abstr.* horticulture **-produkt** garden product; *-er (äv.)* garden produce (*sg*) **-redskap** garden[ing] tool **-skötsel** horticulture, gardening **-slang** garden hose **-sångare** *zool.* garden warbler **-täppa** garden plot **-utställning** horticultural show (exhibition), flower show
träd|krona crown of a (the) tree, tree top **-krypare** *zool.* tree creeper **-lös** treeless **-plantering** plantation of trees **-slag** variety of tree, tree species **-stam** tree trunk **-topp** tree top
träexport timber export[s *pl*]
träff *s2* **1** (*skott som -ar*) hit; *få in en ~* score a hit **2** (*möte*) rendezvous; *AE.* date; (*för fler än två*) meeting, get-together
träff|a 1 (*vid kast, skott e.d.*) hit; strike; *~ målet* (*sitt mål*) hit the target; *när ljudet ~r örat* when the sound strikes the ear; *inte ~ målet* (*äv.*) miss the mark **2** (*möta*) meet; see; *jag skall ~ dem i morgon* I shall see them to-

morrow; *~ ngn hemma* find s.b. at home; *~s herr A.?* is Mr. A. in (at home)?, (*i telefon*) can I speak to Mr. A.?, is Mr. A. available?; *doktorn ~s mellan 8 och 9* the doctor is at home to callers between 8 and 9; *~ på* [happen to] come across (come [up]on, meet with) **3** (*drabba*) hit, strike; *~s av solsting* get sunstroke **4** (*riktigt återge*) hit off; catch; *~* (*gissa*) rätt hit on the right answer; *~ den rätta tonen (äv. bildl.)* strike the right note **5** (*vidtaga*) make (*anstalter* arrangements); *~ ett val* make a choice **-ad** *a5* hit; *känna sig ~ (bildl.)* feel guilty **-ande** *a4* to the point; pertinent (*anmärkning* remark); (*välfunnen*) apposite, appropriate **-as** *dep* meet; *vi skall ~ i morgon* we shall meet (be seeing each other) tomorrow
träff|punkt point of impact **-säker** sure in aim; *bildl.* sure (*omdöme* judgment); apposite (*yttrande* remark); *en ~ skytt* a good marksman, a dead shot **-säkerhet** precision (accuracy) of aim; (*i omdöme*) rightness (sureness) of judgment
trä|fiber wood fibre **-fiberplatta** fibreboard, wallboard **-fri** wood-free **-förädling** woodworking, wood processing
trägen *a3* assiduous, persevering; *~ vinner* persevere and never fear **-het** assiduity, perseverance
trä|haltig *a1* woody; *-t papper* paper containing wood fibres **-hus** wooden (timber) house; *AE. äv.* frame house **-häst** wooden horse **-ig** *a1* woody; (*om grönsak o.d.*) tough, stringy; *bildl.* wooden **-industri** timber industry **-karl** *kortsp.* dummy **-karlsbridge** dummy bridge **-kol** charcoal **-kolsframställning** charcoal-burning **-konservering** wood preservation **-konstruktion** timber (wood[en]) structure (construction) **-kärl** wooden vessel
träl *s2* thrall; serf; *bildl.* slave, bondsman **träla** toil [like a slave], slave (*med* at)
trälast timber (*AE.* lumber) cargo
träl|bunden enslaved **-dom** *s2* bondage, thralldom; *bildl.* slavery, servitude **-domsok** yoke of bondage **-göra** *s6* drudgery
trä|mask woodworm **-massa** wood pulp **-massefabrik** pulp mill **-mjöl** wood meal (flour, dust)
trän|a train (*i* in; *till* for); (*öva sig*) practise; *börja ~* go into training **-ad** *a5* trained; (*erfaren*) experienced, practised **-are** trainer; coach
träng *s3* train; *Storbritannien* army service corps; *AE.* maintenance and supply troops (*pl*)
träng|a *v2* **I 1** (*vara trång*) be (feel) tight **2** (*driva, pressa*) drive, force, push, press; *fienden -er oss från alla håll* the enemy presses in upon us on every side; *han -de mig efter omkörningen* he cut me up after he overtook me **3** (*bana sig väg*) force one's (its) way (*österut* east[wards]); *inte ett ljud -de över hans läppar* not a sound escaped his lips **II** (*med betonad partikel*) **1** *~ av* force off **2** *~ fram* penetrate, force one's (its) way (*till* to) **3** *~ igenom* penetrate, (*om vatten*) come through; *uttrycket har -t igenom i skriftspråket* the expression has found its way into the written language **4** *~ ihop* (*ngt*) compress, (*människor*) crowd (pack) together; *~ ihop sig* crowd

together **5** ~ *in* ... [*i*] press (force) ... in[to]; ~ *in i* (*bildl.*) penetrate into; *kulan -de djupt in i* the bullet penetrated deep into **6** ~ *ner* force one's (its) way down (*i* into), (*i sht bildl.*) penetrate (*i* into; *till* to) **7** ~ *på* push (press) on **8** ~ *undan* force (push) out of its (his *etc.*) place (out of the way) **9** ~ *ut a*) (*ngn*) force (push) out, (*ngt*) displace, *b*) (*strömma ut*) force one's (its) way out, (*om rök, vätska o.d.*) issue [forth]; *ögonen -de ut ur sina hålor* his (*etc.*) eyes were starting out of their sockets **III** *rfl*, ~ *sig fram a*) eg. push one's way forward, *b*) *bildl.* push o.s. forward; ~ *sig in* intrude (*i* upon); ~ *sig på* force (thrust) o.s. upon (*ngn* s.b.), *absol.* intrude, obtrude ; *minnena -er sig på mig* memories come thronging in upon my mind
träng|ande *a4* (*tvingande*) pressing; (*angelägen*) urgent; *vid* ~ *behov* in an (a case of) emergency **-as** *v2, dep* push, jostle one another; (*skockas*) crowd [together]; *man behövde inte* ~ there was no crowding
träng|re ['träŋre] **I** *a, komp. t. trång* narrower; more limited; (*om plagg äv.*) tighter; *i den* ~ *familjekretsen* in the immediate family; *inom en* ~ *krets* [with]in a [strictly] limited circle **II** *adv* more narrowly; (*tätare*) closer [together] **-sel** ['träŋ-] *s9* crowding; (*folk-*) crush (throng) [of people]; *salen var fylld till* ~ the hall was thronged (packed, overcrowded) (*av* with); *det råder* ~ *på lärarbanan* the teaching profession is overcrowded **-st** (*jfr trängre*) **I** *a, superl. t. trång* narrowest *etc.* **II** *adv* most narrowly; closest
trängta yearn, pine (*efter* for; *efter att* to) **trängtan** *r* yearning
träning training; (*av ngn äv.*) coaching; (*övning*) practice; *ligga* (*lägga sig*) *i* ~ be in (go into) training (*för* for)
tränings|overall tracksuit **-skola** school for severely mentally retarded children **-värk** *ha* ~ be stiff [after training]
träns *s2* **1** (*snodd*) braid, cord **2** (*betsel*) snaffle [bit] **tränsa** (*förse med träns*) cord, braid
trä|panel wood panel[ling], wainscoting **-pinne** [round] piece of wood **-plugg** wooden plug (pin) **-ribba** wooden lath
träsk *s7* marsh, swamp, fen; *bildl.* sink
träskalle *bildl.* blockhead, num[b]skull
träskartad [-a:r-] *a5* marshy, fenny
träsked wooden spoon
träskmark marshy (fenny) ground
trä|sko wooden shoe; (*med -botten*) clog **-skodans** (*~ande*) clog dancing; (*en* ~) clog dance **-skruv** (*av trä*) wooden screw; (*av metall*) wood screw **-skyddsmedel** rot-proofing agent **-skål** wooden bowl **-slag** sort (kind) of wood **-slev** wooden ladle **-sliperi** mechanical pulp (wood-pulp) mill **-slöjd** woodwork, carpentry, joinery, sloyd *vard., jag har* ~ I've got a sore bottom **-snidare** woodcarver, wood engraver **-snideri** woodcarving, wood engraving **-snitt** woodcut **-sprit** wood alcohol (spirit) **-sticka** [wood] splinter **-svarv** wood lathe
trät|a I *s1* quarrel; *häftig* ~ fierce row **II** *v3* quarrel; (*svagare*) bicker (*om* about) **-girig** quarrelsome **-obroder** sparring partner, adversary

trä|tjära wood tar **-toffel** clog **-ull** wood wool, excelsior **-varor** *pl* timber (*sg*), wood products; (*bearbetade*) wooden goods **-varuhandel** timber (*AE.* lumber) trade (business) **-varuhandlare** timber merchant; *AE.* lumber dealer **-virke** timber, wood, (*i byggnad*) woodwork; *AE.* lumber **-vit** *en* ~ *bokhylla* a whitewood bookcase
trög *a1* slow (*i* at; *i att* at + *ing-form*); (*om pers. äv.*) inactive, inert, languid; (*senfärdig*) tardy (*i att* in + *ing-form*); (*slö*) dull (*äv. om affärer*); *fys.* inert; (*i rörelse*) sluggish; *låset är* ~*t* the lock is stiff; *ha* ~ *mage* be constipated **-djur** sloth; *bildl.* sluggard **-flytande** viscous, viscid; (*om vattendrag*) slow-flowing, sluggish **-het** slowness *etc.*; inactivity, inertia **-hetsmoment** moment of inertia **-läst** [-ä:-] *a4* heavy (dull) [to read] **-måns** *s2* sluggard, slacker
trög|t [-ö:-] *adv* slowly *etc.*; *affärerna går* ~ business is dull; *motorn går* ~ the engine is sluggish; *det går* ~ (*om arbete o.d.*) it's hard-going **-tänkt** *a1* slow-witted, slow-thinking, slow on the uptake
tröja [ˣtröjja] *s1* sweater, jersey; (*under-*) vest, singlet, *AE.* undershirt
tröska I *v1* thresh; ~ *igenom* (*bildl.*) plough through **II** *s1* **1** *se tröskverk* **2** (*skörde-*) combine [harvester]
tröskel *s2* threshold (*till* of); (*dörr- äv.*) doorstep **-värde** *fys.* threshold value
trösk|ning threshing **-verk** thresher, threshing machine
tröst *s3* consolation; solace; (*svagare*) comfort; *en klen* ~ a poor consolation; *det är en* ~ *i olyckan* that is some consolation; *hennes ålders* ~ a comfort in her old age; *skänka* ~ afford consolation; *söka* [*sin*] ~ *i* seek solace in
tröst|a console; solace; comfort; *Gud -e mig!* God have mercy upon me!; ~ *sig* console o.s. (*över* for); *hon ville inte låta* ~ *sig* she was inconsolable **-erik** full of consolation, consoling **-lös** (*som inte låter -a sig*) disconsolate; (*hopplös*) hopeless, desperate **-napp** dummy, comforter; *AE.* pacifier **-pris** consolation prize
tröt *imperf. av tryta*
trött *a1* tired (*av* with; *efter* after, as a result of; *på* of); (*uttröttad*) weary, fatigued; *jag är* ~ *på* (*äv.*) I am sick of; *jag är* ~ *i benen* my legs are tired (*av att* with, from + *ing-form*); *dansa sig* ~ dance till one is tired [out]
tröt|ta tire; weary, fatigue; *det* ~*r att stå* standing makes you tired (is tiring); ~ *ut ngn* tire s.b. out **-ande** *a4* tiring **-as** *dep* get tired (*etc.*) (*av* by) **-het** tiredness; weariness, fatigue **-hetskänsla** sense of fatigue **-köra** overdrive; overwork (*äv. bildl.*) **-na** tire, get tired, weary, get weary (*på* of; *på att* of + *ing-form*) **-sam** *a1* tiring, fatiguing
tsar [(t)sa:r] *s3* tsar, czar **-döme** *s6* (*-rike*) tsar's realm; (*-välde*) tsardom, czardom **-inna** tsarina, czarina
tsetsefluga tsetse (tzetze) fly
T-tröja T-shirt, tee-shirt
tu two; *ett* ~ *tre* all of a sudden; *de unga* ~ the

young couple; *det är inte ~ tal om den saken* there is no question about that; *på ~ man hand* in private
tub *s3* **1** tube **2** (*kikare*) telescope
tuba *s1* tuba **-blåsare** tuba player
tubba *~ ngn till* induce s.b. to
tuberkel [-'bärr-] *s3* tubercle **-bacill** tubercle bacillus
tuberku'lin *s4* tuberculin **-prov** tuberculin test
tuberkulos [-'lå:s] *s3* tuberculosis (*i* of) (*förk.* T.B.) **-sjuk** suffering from tuberculosis **-undersökning** examination for tuberculosis
tuberku'lös *a1* tuberculous, tubercular
tubformig [-å-] *a1* tubular
tudel|a divide into two [parts]; *geom.* bisect **-ning** dividing into two [parts]; *geom.* bisection
1 tuff *s3* (*bergart*) tuff; (*kalk-*) tufa
2 tuff *a1 vard.* (*hård*) tough (*kille* guy); (*snygg*) smart (*jacka* jacket)
tuffa (*om tåg*) puff
tuffing tough guy
tuff-tufftåg *barnspr.* puff-puff, *AE.* choo-choo
tugg|a I *s1* bite; chew **II** *v1* chew; (*mat äv.*) masticate; *hästen ~r på betslet* the horse is champing at the bit; *~ om* chew [over] again, *bildl.* repeat, keep harping on (*samma sak* the same string) **-buss** quid [of tobacco] **-gummi** (*hopskr. tuggummi*) chewing gum **-ning** chewing; mastication **-tobak** chewing tobacco
tuja [ˣtujja] *s1* arbor vitae
tukt *s3* discipline; *i Herrans ~ och förmaning* in good order **tukta 1** (*aga, äv. friare*) chastise, (*bestraffa*) punish **2** (*forma*) [hammer] dress (*sten* stone); prune (*träd* trees) **tuktan** *r* chastisement, castigation; correction **-hus** house of correction, penitentiary
1 tull *se årtull*
2 tull *s2* **1** (*avgift*) [customs] duty (*på* on); *hög ~* heavy duty; *belägga med ~* impose a duty on; *hur hög är ~en på ...?* what is the duty on ...?; *betala 2 pund i ~* pay two pounds [in] duty **2** (*-verk, -hus*) customs, Customs (*pl*); *~en* (*-personalen*) the customs officers (*pl*); *gå genom ~en* go through customs **3** (*stads-*) tollgate; (*infart t. stad*) entrance to a town
tull|a 1 (*betala tull*) pay [customs] duty (*för* on) **2** (*snatta*) *~ på* (*av*) pinch some of **-behandla** clear through the Customs, clear [in]; *-de varor* goods examined and cleared **-belägga** levy duty on; *-belagda varor* dutiable goods **-bestämmelser** customs regulations **-bevakning** customs supervision; *konkr.* preventive service **-deklaration** customs declaration **-deklarera** declare at Customs **-fri** duty-free, free of duty **-frihet** exemption from duty; *åtnjuta ~* be exempt from duty **-hus** custom-house, customs house **-kryssare** revenue cutter **-mur** tariff wall (barrier) **-myndighet[er]** customs authorities **-personal** customs officers (*pl*) **-pliktig** dutiable, liable to duty **-sats** tariff rate, [rate of] duty **-skydd** tariff protection **-station** customs station **-sänkning** tariff reduction **-taxa** customs tariff **-tjänsteman** customs officer (*högre:* official) **-union** customs union **-uppsyningsman** preventive officer **-verk** customs [and excise] department

-visitation customs examination **-visitera** examine **-väsen** customs administration
tulpan *s3* tulip
tulta I *v1* toddle **II** *s1* little girl, toddler girl
tum [tumm] *s9* inch; *en kung i varje ~* every inch a king; *jag viker inte en ~* I won't budge (give an inch)
tuml|a 1 (*falla*) tumble, fall (*över ända* over); *~ om* romp around; *~ om med varandra* have a tussle [together] **2** *~ en häst* caracole a horse **-are 1** (*delfin*) [common] porpoise **2** (*bägare*) tumbler
tumma 1 *~* [*på*] finger; *det ~r vi på!* let's shake upon it! **2** *~ på* (*jämka på*) compromise with (*hederskänslan* one's sense of honour), stretch (*en regel* stretch a point) **3** (*uppmäta i tum*) gauge
tumm|e *s2* thumb; *bita sig i ~n* (*bildl.*) get the wrong sow by the ear; *ha ~ med ngn* be chummy with s.b.; *hålla ~n på ögat på ngn* keep a tight hand on s.b.; *hålla -arna för ngn* keep one's fingers crossed for s.b.; *rulla -arna* twiddle one's thumbs; *-en upp!* thumbs up!
tummeliten [-ˣli:-] *r* Tom Thumb
tummelplats battlefield, battleground (*för* for)
tum|metott [-'tått, ˣtumme-] *s2* thumb **-nagel** thumbnail **-regel** rule of thumb
tums|bred an inch broad (wide) **-bredd** *en ~* the breadth (width) of an inch
tum|skruv thumbscrew; *sätta ~ar på ngn* (*bildl.*) put the thumbscrews on s.b., squeeze s.b. **-stock** folding rule **-sugning** thumbsucking
tu'mult *s7* tumult; commotion; (*oväsen*) uproar; (*upplopp*) disturbance, riot **-uarisk** [-'a:risk] *a5* tumultuous
tumvante [woollen] mitten
tumör tumour
tundra *s1* tundra
tung *-t* tyngre tyngst heavy; weighty; (*betungande*) cumbersome, burdensome; (*svår*) hard, grievous; *bildl.* ponderous, cumbrous (*stil* style); *~ industri* (*luft*) heavy industry (air); *med ~t hjärta* with a heavy heart; *jag känner mig ~ i huvudet* my head is heavy; *göra livet ~t för ngn* make life a burden to s.b.; *det känns ~t att* it feels hard to
tunga *s1* **1** tongue; (*på våg äv.*) needle, pointer; (*i musikinstrument*) reed; (*på flagga*) tail; *en elak* (*rapp*) *~* a malicious (ready) tongue; *vara ~n på vågen* tip the scale; *ha ett ord på ~n* have a word on the tip of one's tongue; *hålla tand för ~* keep one's own counsel; *hålla ~n rätt i mun* mind one's p's and q's; mind one's step; *räcka ut ~n åt* poke one's tongue out at **2** (*fisk*) sole
tungarbeta|d *a5* that is heavy to work; *ett -t kök* an inconvenient kitchen
tung|band *anat.* ligament of the tongue **-ben** *anat.* tongue bone
tungfotad *a5* heavy-footed
tunghäfta tongue-tie; *hon lider inte av ~* (*vard.*) her tongue is well oiled
tungmetall heavy metal
tungomål tongue
tungomålstalande *s6* gift of tongues, speaking in tongues

tungrodd *a5, eg.* that is heavy to row; *bildl.* heavy, unwieldy; (*om arbete*) [heavy and] time-consuming

tung|rot root of the tongue **-rygg** back of the tongue

tung|sinne melancholy **-sint** *a1* melancholy, gloomy **-spat** *s3* barytes, barite, heavy spar

tung|spene *anat.* uvula (*pl äv.* uvulae) **-spets** tip of the tongue

tungsövd [-ö:-] *a5, vara* ~ be a heavy sleeper

tungt *adv* heavily; *gå* ~ *a*) (*om pers.*) have a heavy tread, *b*) (*om maskin e.d.*) run heavily (heavy); ~ *vatten* heavy water; ~ *väte* heavy hydrogen, deuterium; ~ *vägande skäl* weighty reasons; *hans åsikt väger* ~ his opinion carries a lot of weight

tungus [-ŋ'gu:s] *s3* Tungus; ~*erna* the Tungus[ians]

tungvikt heavyweight **-are** heavyweight [boxer, wrestler]

tunik [-'ni:k, -'nick] *s3* tunic **tunika** ['tu:-] *s1* tunic

Tunisien [-'ni:-] *n* Tunisia

tunis|ier [-'ni:-] *s9* Tunisian **-isk** *a5* Tunisian

tunn *a1* thin; (*om tyg äv.*) flimsy; (*om rock o.d. äv.*) light; (*om tråd*) fine; (*om dryck*) weak, watery

1 tunna *v1*, ~ *av* (*smalna*) get (grow) thin (thinner), (*glesna*) thin

2 tunna *s1* barrel; cask; *hoppa i galen* ~ (*bildl.*) jump in the wrong box

tunn|band barrel hoop; (*leksak*) hoop **-bindare** cooper, hooper **-binderi** *abstr.* coopering; *konkr.* cooperage

tunnbröd *ung.* thin unleavened bread

tunnel *s2* tunnel; (*gång- äv.*) subway, *AE.* underpass **-bana** underground railway; *Storbritannien äv.* tube, underground; *AE. äv.* subway **-banestation** underground (tube; *AE.* subway) station

tunn|flytande *a4* thin (*vätska* liquid) **-het** thinness *etc.* **-hudad** *a5* that has a thin skin; *bildl.* thin-skinned **-hårig** thin on [the] top **-klädd** lightly clad

tunnland *n, ung.* acre

tunn|skalig *a1* thin-shelled (*etc., jfr skal*) **-sliten** threadbare **-sådd** *a1* thinly sown; *bildl.* few and far between **-tarm** small intestine

tunt *adv* thinly; (*glest*) sparsely

tupé *s3* toupee **tupera** backcomb, tease

tupp *s2* cock; rooster; *en* ~ *i halsen* a frog in one's throat

tupp|a *vard.*, ~ *av* pass out, black out **-fjät 1** *eg.* cock's stride **2** *bildl., bara ett* [*par*] ~ only a hand['s-]breadth; *inte ett* ~ not an iota **-fäktning** cockfighting **-kam** crest, cockscomb **-kyckling** cockerel; *bildl.* coxcomb, cocky young devil **-lur** catnap; *ta sig en* ~ (*äv.*) have forty winks

1 tur *s3* (*lycka; lyckträff*) luck; *ha* ~ have luck, be lucky; *ha* ~ *med sig* (*medföra* ~) bring luck; *ha* ~ *hos damerna* have a way with the ladies; *ha* ~*en att* have the [good] luck (be lucky enough) to; ~ *i oturen* (*ung.*) a blessing in disguise; *mer* ~ *än skicklighet* more good luck than good management; *det var* ~ *att* it was (is) lucky that, how fortunate that

2 tur *s3* **1** (*resa*) tour; (*kortare äv.*) round; trip; (*bil- äv.*) drive; (*cykel- äv.*) ride; (*promenad äv.*) walk, stroll; ~ *och retur*[-*resa*] return journey, *AE.* round trip; *reguljära* ~*er* regular service (*sg*) (*flyg.* flights; *sjö.* sailings); *göra en* ~ take (go for) a trip **2** (*i dans*) figure **3** (*följd, ordning*) turn; *i* ~ *och ordning* in turn, by turns; *nu är det min* ~ now it's my turn; *stå närmast i* ~ be next (on the list)

tur|a *v1*, **-as** *v1 dep*, ~ *om att* take [it in] turns to; ~ *om med ngn* take turns with s.b.

tur'ban *s3* turban **-klädd** turbaned

tur'bin *s3* turbine **-driven** turbine-powered, turbine-driven **-hjul** turbine wheel **-motor** turbine [engine], turbomotor

turbo|jetplan turbojet [aircraft] **-motor** turbo motor **-propplan** turboprop [aircraft]

turbu'l|ens *s3* turbulence **-'ent** *a1* turbulent

turism tourism **turist** tourist; sightseer **turista** [-'riss-] *vard.* travel as a tourist

turist|attraktion tourist attraction, sight **-broschyr** travel folder **-buss** touring (sightseeing) coach **-byrå** travel (tourist) agency (bureau) **-hotell** tourist hotel **-industri** tourist industry **-information** tourist information **-karta** touring map **-klass** tourist class **-land** tourist country **-ort** tourist resort **-säng** folding bed **-valuta** tourist (travel) allowance **-väsen** tourism; tourist services (*pl*)

turk *s2* **1** Turk **2** *vard.* Turkish bath **-cypriot** Turkish Cypriot

Turkiet [-'ki:-] *n* Turkey

turk|isk ['turr-] *a5* Turkish; Turkey (*matta* carpet) **-iska** *s1* **1** (*språk*) Turkish **2** (*kvinna*) Turkish woman

turkos [-'kå:s, -'kω:s] *s3* turquoise **-blå** turquoise blue

turlista timetable

turma'lin *s3* tourmaline

turn|é *s3* tour; *göra en* ~ tour, make a tour **-era 1** (*vara på turné*) tour **2** (*formulera*) turn, put; *väl* ~*d* well-turned **-ering** tournament

tur'nyr *s3* bustle

tur- och returbiljett return (*AE.* round-trip) ticket

tursam [ˣtu:r-] *a1* lucky, fortunate

turturduva [ˣturr-] turtledove

turvis [ˣtu:r-] by (in) turns, in turn

tusan *r, för* ~! hang it!; *det var* ~! well, I'll be blowed!; *av bara* ~ like blazes (the very deuce); *en* ~ *till karl* a devil of a fellow

1 tusch *s2, mus.* (*anslag*), *konst., fäkt., bildl.* touch; (*fanfar*) flourish

2 tusch *s3, s4* (*färg*) Indian ink

tuschteckning pen and ink drawing

tusen ['tu:-] thousand; *T*~ *och en natt* The Arabian Nights; ~ *sinom* ~ thousands and (upon) thousands; ~ *tack!* a thousand thanks!, *vard.* thanks awfully; *inte en på* ~ not one in a thousand; *flera* ~ several thousand[s of]; *jag ber* ~ *gånger om ursäkt!* [I beg] a thousand pardons! **-bladstårta** puff-pastry layer cake **-de I** *s6* thousand **II** (*ordningstal*) thousandth **-[de]del** thousandth [part] **-faldig** *a1* thousandfold **-foting** myriapod; centipede, millepede **-hövdad** *a5* many-headed **-konstnär** jack of all trades, handyman **-kronorssedel,**

T

-lapp thousand-kronor note **-sköna** [-ʃ-] *s1, bot.* [common] daisy **-tal 1** *ett* ~ some (about a) thousand **2** *på* ~*et* in the eleventh century **-tals** [-a:] thousands [of]; in thousands **-årig** *a1* a thousand years old; *det* ~*a riket* the millennium **-årsjubileum** millennial celebration
tuskaft *väv.* two-leaved twill
tuss *s2* wad
tussa ~ *hunden på ngn* set the dog on to s.b.; ~ *ihop* set at each other, *(friare)* set by the ears
tussilago [-'la:-] *s5, s9, bot.* coltsfoot
tut I *s7* toot[ing] **II** *interj* toot!
1 tuta *s1 (finger-)* fingerstall
2 tuta *v1* toot[le] *(i en lur* [on] a horn); *(med signalhorn)* hoot; ~ *ngt i öronen på ngn (bildl.)* din s.th. into a p.'s ears
tutning [-u:-] tooting; hooting
1 tutta *s1 (liten flicka)* little girl
2 tutta *v1,* ~ *[eld] på* set fire to, set on fire
tuva *s1* tussock, tuft; *(gräs- äv.)* tuft [of grass]; *liten* ~ *välter ofta stort lass* little strokes fell great oaks **tuvig** *a1* tufty
t.v. *förk. f. a) till vänster* to the left, *b) tills vidare, se vidare II 6*
TV [ˈteːveː] *s2 (jfr television)* TV; *Engl. vard.* telly; *AE. vard.* video
tvagning [-a:-] *åld.* washing; *(relig. el. skämts.)* ablutions
tvang *imperf. av tvinga*
TV-apparat TV [set]
tvedräkt *s3* dissension, discord
tweed [tviːd] *s3* tweed **-dräkt** tweed suit
tve|eggad *a5* two-edged; *bildl. äv.* double--edged **-gifte** bigamy **-hågsen** *a5* in two minds
tveka hesitate *(om* about, as to); be uncertain (doubtful) *(om hur man skall* [about] how to)
tvekamp duel; *(envig)* single combat
tvek|an *r* hesitation; uncertainty, indecision; *med (utan)* ~ with some (without [any]) hesitation **-ande** *a4* hesitating *etc.*; hesitant
tvekluven forked; *bot.* bipartite
tvek|lös unhesitating **-löst** [-öː-] *adv* without hesitation **-sam** [-eː-] *a1* uncertain, doubtful *(om* about, as to; *om huruvida* whether); *(obeslutsam)* irresolute; *känna sig* ~ *(äv.)* feel dubious **-samhet** hesitation, hesitance; doubt, doubtfulness
tvekönad [-çöː-] *a5* bisexual, hermaphrodite
tve|nne two **-stjärt** [common European] earwig **-talan** *beslå ngn med* ~ convict s.b. of self--contradiction **-tydig** *a1* ambiguous; double--barrelled; equivocal; *(oanständig)* indecent; *(tvivelaktig)* dubious **-tydighet** ambiguousness; ambiguity; indecency
tvi *interj* ugh!; pshaw!
tvilling twin **-bror** twin brother **-par** pair of twins **-stjärna** twin (double) star **-syskon** *de är* ~ they are twins **-syster** twin sister
tvills *s3* twill
tvina languish; ~ *bort, se förtvina*
tving *s2, tekn.* clamp, cramp
tvinga *tvang tvungit* **1** *v1* force *(ngn till ngt* s.b. to do s.th.); compel *(till att* to); *(friare äv.)* constrain; *(svagare)* oblige; ~ *fram* extort *(en bekännelse* a confession); ~ *i ngn ngt* force s.th. to eat (drink) s.th.; ~ *i sig ngt* force down s.th.;

~ *på ngn ngt* force s.th. on s.b.; ~ *till sig ngt* obtain s.th. by force **2** *rfl* force o.s. *(till att* to); constrain o.s.; ~ *sig fram* force one's way forward; ~ *sig på ngn* force o.s. on s.b. **tvingande** *a4* imperative *(skäl* reasons); *(trängande)* urgent; *(oemotståndlig)* irresistible; ~ *omständigheter* circumstances over which I *(etc.)* have no control; *utan* ~ *skäl* without urgent (very good) reasons
tvinna twine; twist; *(silke)* throw
tvinsot consumption
tvist *s3* strife, quarrel; *(ordstrid)* dispute, controversy; *ligga i* ~ *med* be at strife (controversy) with; *slita* ~*en* decide the dispute **tvista** dispute, quarrel *(om* about)
tviste|fråga question (point) at issue, matter (point) in dispute **-frö** seed of dissension, bone of contention **-mål** civil case **-ämne** subject of contention, controversial issue
tvivel [ˈtviː-] *s7* doubt; *(betänkligheter)* misgivings *(pl); det är (råder) intet* ~ *om* there is no doubt about; *utan* ~ without any doubt, no doubt, doubtless; *utan allt* ~ beyond all doubt, beyond [all] question **-aktig** *a1* doubtful; dubious, questionable *(ära* honour); *det är* ~*t om* it is doubtful whether
tvivelsmål doubt[s *pl*]; *draga ngt i* ~ call s.th. in question; *sväva i* ~ *om* have doubts [in one's mind] about
tvivl|a [-iː-] ~ *på* doubt, be doubtful about, *(misstro)* mistrust, have no faith in, *(ifrågasätta)* call in question **-ande** *a4* incredulous; sceptical; *ställa sig* ~ *till* doubt, feel dubious about **-are** doubter; sceptic
TV-|kamera TV camera **-mottagare** TV set **-pjäs** television play, teleplay **-program** TV programme **-ruta** TV screen **-studio** TV studio **-sändare** TV transmitter **-sändning** TV transmission (broadcast) **-tittande** viewing **-tittare** viewer
tvungen *a3* **1** *(tvingad)* forced; enforced; *vara* ~ *att* be forced (compelled) to, have to, *(i sht av inre tvång)* be obliged to; *vara så illa* ~ have no other choice, jolly well have to; *vara nödd och* ~ be compelled to **2** *det är en* ~ *sak* it (that) is a matter of necessity **3** *(tillgjord)* forced, constrained *(leende* smile) **tvungit** *sup. av tvinga*
1 två *v4* wash; *jag* ~*r mina händer (bildl.)* I wash my hands of it
2 två *räkn* two; ~ *och* ~ two and two; *en* ~ *tre stycken* two or three [of them]; *det skall vi bli* ~ *om!* I can put the lid on that!; *kl. halv* ~ at half past one; *jag tar båda* ~ I'll take both [of them]
två|a *s1* two; *(i spel)* äv. deuce; *(lägenhet)* two-room flat, one-bedroom flat; *hon kom* ~ she came [in] second; ~*n a) skol.* the second class, *b) (bilväxel)* [the] second [gear] **-basisk** *kem.* dibasic **-bent** [-eː-] *a4* two-legged **-bladig** *a1 (om växt)* two-leaved; *(om propeller, kniv e.d.)* two-bladed **-byggare** *bot.* di-[o]ecious plant **-cylindrig** *a1* twin-cylinder, two-cylinder *(motor* engine) **-dela** halve, split; ~*d* two-piece *(baddräkt* bathing suit), in two parts **-dimensionell** *a1* two-dimensional **-faldig** *a1* twofold; double **-familjshus** two-fami-

ly house; *AE.* duplex house **-fas** two-phase **-färgad** two-colour[ed] **-hjulig** [-j-] *a1* two--wheel[ed] **-hjuling** [-j-] two-wheeler **-hjärtbladig** *a1, bot.* dicotyledonous; ~ *växt* dicotyledon **-hundratalet** *på* ~ in the third century **-kammarsystem** bicameral (two-chamber) [parliamentary] system **-krona** two-kronor piece

tvål *s2* soap; *en* ~ a bar (cake) of soap **tvål|a** ~ *in* soap; lather; ~ *till ngn* crush s.b., deal s.b. a heavy blow **-ask** soap case **-bit** piece of soap **tvåledare** two-wire **tvål|fager** sleek **-flingor** *pl* soap-flakes **-ig** *a1* soapy **-kopp** soap dish **-lödder** soap lather **-lösning** soap solution **-opera** *AE.* soap opera **-vatten** soapy water; soapsuds (*pl*) **två|läppig** *a1, bot.* bilabiate **-mans** for two [men, persons], two-person **-manssäng** double bed **-mastare** two-master **-motorig** *a1* twin-engine[d]

tvång *s7* compulsion, coercion, constraint; (*våld*) force; *jur.* duress; *psykol.* compulsion; *det är inte ngt* ~ it is not absolutely necessary; *handla under* ~ act under compulsion (constraint); *rättsstridigt* ~ duress **tvångs|arbete** forced (compulsory) labour **-föreställning** obsession **-förflyttning** compulsory transfer **-försäljning** forced (compulsory) sale **-läge** *vara i* ~ be in an emergency situation **-mata** force-feed **-medel** means of coercion **-mässig** *a1* compulsive **-neuros** compulsion neurosis **-permittera** lay off **-sparande** compulsory saving **-tanke** obsession **-tröja** straitjacket (*äv. bildl.*) **-uppfostran** reformatory upbringing **-uppfostringsanstalt** reformatory, approved school **-uttagning** *mil.* conscription **-åtgärd** *vidtaga ~er* use coercive measures **två|partiregering** two-party government **-procentig** *a1* two-percent **-radig 1** two-line[d]; two-row[ed] (*korn* barley); double-breasted (*rock* coat) **-rumslägenhet** two-room[ed] flat, one-bedroom flat **-siffrig** *a1* two-figure **-sitsig** *a1* two-seat[ed]; *~t flygplan* two-seater **-språkig** *a1* bilingual **-stavig** *a1* two-syllable[d], dis[s]yllabic **-stegsraket** two-stage rocket **-struken** *mus.* two-line, twice-marked, twice--accented **-stämmig** *a1* for two voices, in two parts **-taktsmotor** two-stroke (*AE.* two-cycle) engine **-tiden** *vid* ~ at [about] two [o'clock] **-vingar** *pl, zool.* dipterans **-våningshus** two-storey[ed] house **-våningssäng** bunk bed **-vägskommunikation** two-way communication **-värd** *kem.* divalent **-årig** *a1* two-year--old; (*om växt*) biennial **-åring** child of two **-årsåldern** the age of two **-äggstvilling** fraternal twin **-öring** two-öre piece

tvär I *s, i uttr.: på ~en* across, crosswise; *sätta sig på ~en* a) (*om sak*) get stuck crossways, b) (*bildl. om pers.*) turn obstinate (awkward) **II** *a1* (*plötslig*) sudden; (*abrupt*) abrupt; (*brant*) steep; (*motsträvig*) refractory; (*vresig*) sullen, blunt, brusque; *göra en* ~ *krök* make a sharp turn; *ett ~t avbrott a*) *eg.* a sudden break (interruption), b) (*skarp kontrast*) a sharp contrast (*mot* to); *ta ett ~t slut* come to a sudden

end **tvär|a** cross, go across **-balk** crossbeam, stretcher **-brant** precipitous **-bromsa** slam on the brakes, brake suddenly **-gata** cross-street; *ta nästa* ~ *till höger!* take the next turning to the right! **-gående** *a4* transverse **-hand** handbreadth, hand's-breadth **-huggen** *a5* squared; *bildl.* abrupt **-linje** transverse line, cross-line **-mätt** *bli* ~ suddenly feel full **-randig** cross--striped, banded

tvärs across; ~ [*för*] (*sjö.*) abeam of; *akter* (*för*) *om* ~ abaft (before) the beam; *härs och* ~, *se härs;* ~ *igenom* right (straight) through; ~ *över* straight (right) across; *bo* ~ *över gatan* live just across the street; *gå* ~ *över gatan* cross the street **tvär|skepp** *byggn.* transept **-skepps** *adv* athwartships **-slå** crossbar, crosspiece **-snitt** cross section **-stanna** stop dead, come to a dead stop **-stopp** dead stop (halt) **-streck** cross-line; cross stroke (*äv. mus.*) **-säker** absolutely sure, positive; cocksure **-säkerhet** (*självsäkerhet*) cocksureness

tvärt *adv* squarely (*avskuren* cut); (*plötsligt*) abruptly; (*genast*) at once, directly; *svara* ~ reply straight off; *käppen gick* ~ *av* the stick broke right in two; *bryta ngt* ~ *av* break s.th. right off; *svara* ~ *nej* refuse flatly **-e'mot** quite contrary to; *göra* ~ do exactly the opposite of **-'om** on the contrary; (*svagare*) on the other hand; *och* (*eller*) ~ and (or) contrariwise (vice versa); *alldeles* ~ just the reverse; *det förhåller sig alldeles* ~ it is just the other way round; *snarare* ~ rather the reverse **tvär|tystna** become suddenly silent **-vetenskaplig** interdisciplinary, multidisciplinary **-vigg** *s2* contrary person; *vard.* crosspatch **-vägg** transverse wall

tvätt *s2* wash[ing]; (*kläder t.* ~) laundry; *kemisk* ~ dry-cleaning, (*-inrättning*) dry-cleaners; ~ *och strykning* washing and ironing; *är på* ~ is in the wash (*-inrättningen:* at the laundry); *gå bort i ~en* wash out; *skicka bort ~en* send the washing to the laundry **tvätt|a** wash; (*rengöra*) clean (*fönsterna* the windows); ~ *kemiskt* dry-clean; ~ *åt ngn* do a p.'s washing; ~ *bort* wash away; *jag måste* ~ *upp litet kläder* I must wash out a few clothes; ~ *sig* wash [o.s.], have a wash, *AE.* wash up; ~ *sig om händerna* wash one's hands **-anvisningar** *pl* washing intstructions **-balja** washtub **-bar** *a1* washable **-björn** [North American] rac[c]oon **-bräde** washboard **-eri** laundry **-erska** laundress; (*förr*) washerwoman **-fat** washbasin; *AE. äv.* washbowl **-gryta** washboiler, copper **-inrättning** laundry; *kemisk* ~ dry-cleaning establishment **-kläder** *pl* laundry, washing (*sg*), dirty linen **-korg** clothes basket **-lapp** [face] flannel (cloth); *AE.* washcloth, washrag **-maskin** washing machine **-medel** washing detergent (agent, powder), detergent **-ning** washing **-nota** laundry list **-omat** Launderette, *AE.* Laundromat (*varumärken*) **-pulver** washing powder **-rum** washroom, lavatory **-siden** washing silk **-skinnshandske** wash-leather glove **-stuga** (*rum*) laundry **-ställ**

washstand, (*väggfast*) washbasin **-svamp** [bath] sponge **-säck** laundry bag **-vante** washing glove **-vatten** washing water; (*använt*) dirty water, slops (*pl*) **-äkta** washable, washproof; (*om färg*) fast; *bildl.* authentic; (*inbiten*) out-and-out

TV-övervakning [closed-circuit] TV monitoring

1 ty *konj* for; because

2 ty *v4*, *rfl*, ~ *sig till* turn to

tyck|a *v3* **1** think (*om* about; *att* that); (*anse äv.*) be of the opinion (*att* that); *det -er jag* (*äv.*) that's what I think; *säg vad du -er!* tell us your opinion!; *han säger vad han -er* (*sin mening*) he says what he thinks; *jag -er nog att* I really (do) think; *vad -er du om ...?* what do you think of ...?; *han -er att han är någonting* he thinks a great deal of himself; *som du -er!* as you please!; *du -er väl inte illa vara att jag* I hope you don't mind my (+ *ing-form*); ~ *sig höra* think (imagine, fancy) that one hears; ~ *sig vara* think that one is, imagine o.s. to be **2** ~ *om* like (*starkare:* be fond of) (*att läsa* reading); *jag -er rätt bra om* I quite like; *jag -er mycket om* I like very much; *jag -er illa om* (*äv.*) I dislike; *jag -er mer om ... än ...* I like ... better than ..., I prefer ... to ...

tyck|as *v3*, *dep* seem; *det kan ~ så* it may seem so; *det -s mig som om* it seems to me as if; *vad -s?* what do you think (say)?

tyck|e *s6* **1** (*åsikt*) opinion; *i mitt ~* to my way of thinking, in my opinion **2** (*böjelse*) inclination, fancy (*för* for); (*smak*) liking; *fatta ~ för* take a liking (fancy) to; *om ~ och smak skall man inte tvista* (*ung.*) that's a matter of taste; *efter mitt ~* according to my taste **3** (*likhet*) likeness, resemblance; *han har ~ av sin far* he bears a resemblance to his father **-mycken** *a3* fastidious; touchy

tyd|a *v2* **1** (*tolka*) interpret; (*ut-*) decipher, solve; (*förklara*) explain; ~ *allt till det bästa* put the best construction on everything; *hur skall man ~* (*uppfatta*) *detta?* how should one take this? **2** ~ *på* indicate (*att* that; *gott omdöme* good judgement), point to, suggest; *allt -er på att han* everything points to his (+ *ing-form*)

tydbar [-y:-] *a1* interpretable **tydlig** [-y:-] *a1* (*lätt att se*) plain, clear, sharp; (*markerad*) marked, pronounced; (*distinkt*) distinct; (*påtaglig*) obvious, apparent, evident; *~a bevis på* distinct proofs of; ~ *bild* sharp picture; ~ *handstil* legible (fair) hand; *i ~a ordalag* in plain terms; *det är ~t att* it is obvious (evident) that; *ha ett ~t minne av* have a distinct remembrance of; *talar sitt ~a språk* speaks for itself; *undergå en ~ förbättring* improve noticeably **tydligen** [-y:-] evidently, obviously, apparently, patently **tydlighet** [-y:-] plainness *etc.*; *med all önskvärd ~* leaving no room for doubt **tydligt** [-y:-] *adv* (*skriva, tala etc.*) plainly, distinctly; (*uttrycka sig*) clearly; *vilket ~ framgår av* as is plain from **tydligtvis** [-y:-] *se* tydligen **tydning** [-y:-] interpretation; decipherment, solution **tydningsförsök** attempt at interpretation

tyfoidfeber [-ʼi:d-] typhoid fever

tyfon [-ʼfå:n] *s3* typhoon

tyfus [ʼty:-] *s2* (*fläckfeber*) typhus [fever]

1 tyg *s7*, *s4* (*vävnad*) material (*till* for); cloth, stuff; *i sht hand.* fabric; *~er* textiles

2 tyg 1 *i uttr.*: *allt vad ~en håller* (*med all kraft*) for all one is worth, (*i full fart*) at top speed **2** *s7*, *mil.* ordnance

tyg|blomma cloth flower **-bredd** width of cloth

tyg|el *s2* rein; bridle; *bildl. äv.* check; *ge hästen lösa -lar* give the horse a free rein; *ge sin fantasi fria* (*lösa*) *-lar* give [a free] rein to one's imagination; *med lösa -lar* with slack reins

tygellös *bildl.* (*otyglad*) unbridled; (*om liv, pers.*) dissolute, licentious; (*om levnadssätt äv.*) loose, wild **-het** unbridled behaviour; licentiousness *etc.*

tyg|förråd ordnance depot **-förvaltare** *ung.* ordnance officer **-hus** arsenal, armoury

tygknapp covered button

tygla [ʼty:g-] rein [in]; *bildl.* bridle; (*betvinga*) restrain, check; ~ *sig* restrain o.s.

tyg|packe bale of cloth **-sko** cloth shoe **-stycke** piece of cloth; (*rulle äv.*) roll of cloth

tykobrahedag [-ˣbra:-] *ung.* black-letter day

tyll *s3*, *s4* tulle; net

tymus *se* thymus

tyna languish, pine, fade (*bort* away)

tyng|a *v2* **1** (*vara tung*) weigh (*på* [up]on); (*kännas tung*) be (feel) heavy (*på* to); (*trycka*) press (*på* [up]on **2** (*plåga*) weigh down; *det -er mitt sinne* it preys on me (on my mind) **3** (*belasta*) weight (*med* with); burden, load (*minnet med* one's memory with) **-ande** *a4* heavy; weighty; *bildl. äv.* burdensome

tyngd I *a5* weighed down (*av sorg* by grief) **II** *s3* weight (*äv. konkr.*); load; *fys.* gravity; *en ~ har fallit från mitt bröst* a weight (load) has dropped off my mind; *ge ~ åt ett argument* give weight to an argument **-kraft** *~en* [the force of] gravity (gravitation) **-lagen** the law of gravitation **-lyftare** weightlifter **-lyftning** weightlifting **-lös** weightless **-löshet** weightlessness **-punkt** centre of gravity; *bildl.* main (crucial, central) point (*i* in)

tyngre [ʼtyŋ-] **I** *a*, *komp. t. tung.* heavier *etc.* (*jfr tung*); ~ *fordon* (*pl*) heavy-duty vehicles **II** *adv* more heavily **tyngst I** *a*, *superl. t. tung* heaviest *etc.* (*jfr tung*) **II** *adv* most heavily

typ *s3* **1** *boktr.* type; *fet* (*halvfet*) ~ boldface[d] (semibold) type **2** (*sort*) type; model; *han är ~en för en lärare* he's a typical teacher; *han är inte min ~* he's not my type **typa** (*fastställa typen av*) type

typ|arm typebar **-exempel** typical example, case in point **-fall** typical case **-huvud** face, typeface **-isk** [ʼty:-] *a5* typical, representative (*för* of)

typo|graf *s3* typographer **-grafi** *s3* typography **-grafisk** [-ʼgra:-] *a5* typographical **-logi** *s3* typology

typsnitt [type]face

tyʼrann *s3* tyrant **-ʼi** *s4* tyranny **-isera** tyrannize over; (*friare*) domineer over **-isk** *a5* tyrannical; (*friare äv.*) domineering

tyristor [-ˣriss-] thyristor

tyrolare [-ˣrå:-] Tyrolese, Tyrolean **Tyrolen** [-ʼrå:-] the Tyrol (Tirol) **tyrolerhatt** [-ˣrå:-]

Tyrolese hat **ty'rolsk** [-å:-] *a5* Tyrolese, Tyrolean

tysk I *a1* German; *T~a Riket* the German Empire, *(1918–45)* the Reich **II** *s2* German **tysk|a** *s1* **1** *(språk)* German **2** *(kvinna)* German woman **-fientlig** anti-German **Tyskland** ['tysk-] *n* Germany **tyskvänlig** pro-German

tyst I *a1* silent; still; *(lugn)* quiet; *(ljudlös)* noiseless; *(outtalad)* tacit, mute; *~ förbehåll* mental reservation; *hålla sig ~* keep quiet (silent); *han är inte ~ ett ögonblick* he can't keep silent (quiet) for a moment; *var ~!* be quiet!, silence!; *i det ~a* on the quiet, in a quiet way **II** *adv* silently; quietly, in silence; *håll ~!* keep quiet!; *hålla ~ med ngt* keep s.th. quiet; *det skall vi tala ~ om (vard.)* the less said about that, the better **tysta** silence; *~ munnen på ngn* stop a p.'s mouth, make s.b. hold his tongue; *~ ner a) (ngn)* [reduce ... to] silence, *b) (ngt, bildl.)* suppress, hush up; *låt maten ~ mun (munnen)* don't talk while you're eating **tyst|gående** *a4* noiseless, silent[-running] **-het** silence; quietness; *(hemlighet)* secrecy; *i [all] ~* in secrecy, secretly, privately; *i största ~* in the utmost secrecy **-hetslöfte** pledge (promise) of secrecy **-låten** *a3* aciturn; silent; *(förtegen)* reticent; *(hemlighetsfull)* secretive **-låtenhet** taciturnity; silence; reticency; secretiveness **tystna** become silent; *(om ljud äv.)* cease, stop **tystnad** *s3* silence; *djup (obrottslig) ~* profound (strict) silence; *bringa ngn till ~* reduce s.b. to silence, silence s.b.; *förbigå ngt med ~* pass s.th. over in silence; *under ~* in silence; *ålägga ngn ~* enjoin silence [up]on s.b. **tystnadsplikt** obligation to observe silence; *(läkares äv.)* professional secrecy; *bryta sin ~* commit a breach of professional secrecy

ty'värr unfortunately; *(som interj äv.)* alas!; *jag kan ~ inte komma* I am sorry [to say] I can't come; *~ måste vi meddela att* we regret to inform you that; *~ inte* I am afraid not

tå *s5* toe; *gå på ~* walk on one's toes (on tiptoe); *skorna är trånga i ~rna* my *(etc.)* shoes pinch at the toes; *stå på ~ för ngn (bildl.)* be at a p.'s beck and call; *trampa ngn på ~rna (äv. bildl.)* tread on a p.'s toes **-flört** *vard.* footsie **-flörta** *vard.* play footsie

1 tåg *s7 (rep)* rope
2 tåg *s7* **1** *(marsch)* march[ing]; *mil. äv.* expedition; *(fest- o.d.)* procession **2** *(järnvägs-)* train; *~et går kl. 2* the train leaves at two o'clock; *byta ~* change trains; *när kommer ~et?* when will the train be in (is the train due)?; *med ~[et]* by train; *på ~et* on the train; *~ till London* train[s *pl*] for London; *ta ~et till* take the (go by) train to

1 tåga *s1 (fiber)* filament, thread; *bildl.* nerve, sinew; *det är ~ i honom* he is tough
2 tåga *v1* march; walk in procession; *~ mot fienden* march against the enemy; *~ fram* march along

tåg|attentat train outrage **-biljett** railway ticket **-färja** train ferry **-förbindelse** train service (connection); *ha bra ~r med* have an excellent train service to and from **-klarerare**

[train] dispatcher **-konduktör** [train] guard; *AE.* conductor **-kupé** compartment **-ledes** by train **-luffa** travel on an interrail card **-luffare** traveller with an interrail card **-olycka** railway accident **-ombyte** change of trains **-ordning** marching order; *bildl.* slow bureaucratic procedure, red tape **-personal** train staff **-resa** train journey **-sätt** *ett ~ av 10 vagnar* a train of ten carriages (coaches) **-tid** *~er* train times **-tidtabell** railway timetable *(AE.* schedule) **-trafik** train service, railway traffic **-urspåring** derailment [of a train]

tågvirke cordage; ropes *(pl)*
tå|gångare *zool., ~ (pl)* digitigrades **-hätta** toecap **-hävning** [-ä:-] heel-raising **-järn** *(på tå)* toe plate

tål|a *v2* bear, endure; *(stå ut med)* stand; *(lida)* suffer, put up with; *han tål inte att ngn avbryter honom* he can't stand anyone['s] interrupting him; *jag tål henne inte* I can't stand (bear) her; *han tål inte skämt* he can't take a joke; *jag tål inte jordgubbar* strawberries upset (don't agree with) me; *han har fått vad han tål a) (av sprit e.d.)* he has had as much as he can stand, *b) (av stryk e.d.)* he has had all he can bear; *det tål att tänka på* it is worth consideration; *illa -d av* in bad favour with; *bör inte ~s* should not be tolerated

tålamod *s7* patience; *ha ~* have patience, be patient; *ha ~ med* be patient with, bear with; *förlora ~et* lose [one's] patience; *mitt ~ är slut* my patience is exhausted; *sätta ngns ~ på [hårt] prov* try a p.'s patience [severely] **tålamods|prov** *ett riktigt ~* a real trial to one's patience **-prövande** *a4* trying [to one's patience]

tålig *a1* patient **-het** patience
tålmodig patient; *(långmodig)* long-suffering **-het** patience; long-suffering
tåls [-å:-] *i uttr.: ge sig till ~* have patience, be patient

tånagel toenail
1 tång *s3 (växt)* seaweed; *(blås-)* rockweed
2 tång *-en tänger (verktyg)* tongs *(pl)*; pliers, pincers, nippers *(pl)*; *kir.* forceps; *en ~ (två tänger)* a pair (two pairs) of tongs *(etc.)*; *den vill jag inte ta i med ~* I wouldn't touch it with a bargepole

tångförlossning forceps delivery
tår *s2* **1** tear; *brista i (fälla) ~ar* burst into (shed) tears; *jag fick ~ar i ögonen* tears came into my eyes **2** *(skvätt)* drop; *ta sig en ~ på tand* have a drop [of brandy *(etc.)*] **-ad** *a5* filled with tears **-as** *dep* fill with tears; *(av blåst o.d.)* water

tår|drypande *a4* maudlin, sentimental **-dränkt** *a4* tearful **-eflod** stream of tears **-flöde** flood (torrent) of tears **-fylld** filled with tears; *(om blick, röst)* tearful **-gas** tear gas **-kanal** lacrimal (tear) duct **-körtel** lacrimal (tear) gland **-pil** *bot.* weeping willow

tårt|a [`tå:r-] *s1* cake, gâteau; *(mördegs-, smördegs- äv.)* tart; *~ på ~* the same thing twice over **-bit** piece of cake **-kartong** cake carton **-papper** cake doily **-spade** cake slice

tårögd *a1* with tears in one's eyes, with eyes filled with tears

T

tåspets tip of a (the, one's) toe **-dans** toe dance **-dansös** toe dancer

tåt *s2* piece (bit) of string (*grövre*: cord)

täck *a1* pretty; *det ~a könet* the fair sex

täck|a *v3* cover (*med* with); *eg. bet. äv.* coat; *trädg. äv.* cover over (up); (*skydda*) protect (*äv. växel*); *~ sina behov* supply (cover) one's needs; *~ en förlust* meet (cover) a loss; *-t bil* closed car **-ande** *s6* covering *etc.*; *till ~ av kostnaderna* to cover (defray) costs

täck|as *v3, dep* (*behaga*) *ni -[t]es erinra er* please be good enough to remember

täck|blad (*på cigarr*) wrapper **-dika** drain **-dike** covered drain **-dikning** underdrainage, pipe draining

täck|e *s6* cover[ing], coating; (*säng-*) [bed] quilt, *AE. äv.* comforter; (*skynke*) cloth; *spela under ~t med* (*bildl.*) be in collusion with **-else** cover[ing]; *dra ett ~ över* draw a veil over; *låta ~t falla* unveil, *bildl.* reveal, disclose **-färg** finishing (top) coat

täckhet prettiness

täck|jacka quilted jacket **-mantel** *under vänskapens ~* under the cloak (guise, veil) of friendship, under cover of friendship **-namn** assumed name **-ning** covering *etc.*; *hand.* cover (*för en check* for a cheque); (*skydd*) protection; *check utan ~* uncovered cheque; *till ~ av* in cover of, covering; *till ~ av vår faktura* in payment of our invoice **-vinge** wing sheath, shard **-vitt** lithopone

tälja *v2* ([*till*]*skära*) carve, whittle, cut

täljare *mat.* numerator

tälj|kniv (*slid-*) sheath knife; (*fäll-*) jackknife **-sten** soapstone, soaprock

tält *s7* tent **tälta 1** (*slå upp tält*) pitch one's tent **2** (*bo i tält*) tent; camp (be camping) [out] **tält|duk** canvas **-lina** guy line **-läger** camp **-makare** tentmaker **-pinne** tent peg **-stol** camp stool **-säng** camp bed

täm|ja *v2, -de -t -d* tame; domesticate; *bildl.* curb, harness

tämligen tolerably; fairly; (*vanl. gillande*) pretty; (*vanl. ogillande*) rather; *~ bra* pretty well, [fairly] tolerable, well enough; *det är ~ likgiltigt* it makes little difference; *det blev ~ sent* it was rather (pretty) late

tänd|a *v2* **1** (*få att brinna*) light (*äv. bildl.*); (*elektr. ljus*) turn (switch) on; *tekn.* ignite, fire; *bildl. äv.* kindle; *~* [*belysningen*] light up; *~* [*eld*] *på* set fire to, set ... on fire; *~ i spisen* make a fire; *stå som -a ljus* stand like statues; *hoppet -es på nytt* the spark of hope revived **2** (*fatta eld*) ignite, catch fire; light (*lätt* readily); (*om motor*) spark, fire; *bildl., vard., ~ på ngn* (*ngt*) get turned on by s.b. (s.th.); *hon -e på honom* he turned her on

tänd|ande *a4* lighting *etc.*; *den ~ gnistan* the igniting spark **-apparat** igniter, firing device; (*vid sprängning*) blasting machine **-are** (*cigarett- o.d.*) lighter **-gnista** ignition spark **-hatt** detonator, percussion (blasting) cap **-kulemotor** compression-ignition (ignition bulb) engine **-ning** lighting *etc.*; *tekn.* ignition; *hög ~* advanced spark; *justera ~en* adjust the ignition timing **-ningslås** ignition lock **-[nings]nyckel** ignition key **-ordning** (*i mo-*

tor) firing order **-sats** (*i tändmedel*) detonating composition, fuse body; (*på tändsticka*) head **-sticka** match; *tända en ~* strike a match **-sticksask** (*tom*) matchbox; (*med tändstickor i*) box of matches **-sticksfabrik** match factory **-stift** (*i motor*) sparking (*AE.* spark) plug; (*i vapen*) firing pin **-stiftskabel** ignition wire

tänj|a *v2* stretch; *~ ut* stretch, *bildl.* draw out, prolong; *~ ut sig* stretch; *~ på en princip* stretch a principle **-bar** *a1* stretchable; *tekn.* tensile, tensible; (*elastisk*) elastic

tänk|a *v3* **1** think (*högt* aloud; *på* of, about; *väl om ngn* well of s.b.); (*fundera äv.*) meditate; (*förmoda*) suppose; (*föreställa sig*) imagine; *~ olika om* hold divergent opinions about; *~ själv* think for o.s.; *~ för sig själv* think to o.s.; *säga vad man -er* (*äv.*) speak one's mind; *tänk först och tala sedan!* look before you leap!; *tänk om jag skulle ...!* supposing (what if) I should ...!; *tänk ...! a*) (*som utrop*) to think (*att jag är färdig* [that] I am ready), *b*) (*betänk*) think ...!, *c*) (*tänk efter*) reflect ...!; *ja* (*nej*) *tänk!* [oh], I say!; *det var det jag -te!* just as I thought!; *den är dyr kan jag ~* it is expensive, I shouldn't wonder; *~ på att* think of, reflect upon (+ ing-form); *ha mycket att ~ på* have a great deal to think about; *jag kom att ~ på att* the thought occurred to me that; *det vore ngt att ~ på* that's [a thing] quite worth considering; *när jag -er rätt på saken* when I come to think of it; *det är inte att ~ på* there's no thinking of that, that is out of the question; *jag skall ~ på saken* I will think it (the matter) over **2** (*med betonad partikel*) *~ efter* think, reflect, consider; *tänk noga efter!* think [it over] carefully!; *när man -er efter* (*äv.*) when one comes to think of it; *~ igenom* think ... out; *~ ut* think out, (*plan e.d.*) devise; *~ över* think over, consider **3** (*ämna*) intend (mean, be going; *AE. äv.* aim) to; (*anse*) consider; *vad -er du om det?* what do you think (is your opinion) of that? **4** *rfl* (*föreställa sig*) imagine, fancy; (*ämna* [*begiva*] *sig*) think of going [to]; *jag har -t mig att* my idea is that, I have thought that; *kan du ~ dig vad som ...?* can you imagine what ...?; *det kunde jag just ~ mig!* I might have known that (as much)!; *kan man ~ sig!* well, I never!; *det låter ~ sig* that's very possible; *~ sig för* think a (the) matter over; *du bör ~ dig för två gånger* you should think twice; *~ sig in i* imagine ... to o.s.; *vart har du -t dig?* where have you thought of going [to]?

tänk|ande *s6* thinking *etc.*; (*begrundan*) meditation, reflection **II** *a4* thinking, reflective; *en ~ människa* a thoughtful (reflecting) person **-are** thinker; *filos.* speculator **-bar** *a1* conceivable, thinkable; (*friare*) imaginable; *bästa ~a* the best possible; *i högsta ~a grad* to the highest degree imaginable; *den enda ~a* the only conceivable

tänke|språk adage, proverb **-sätt** way of thinking; (*friare*) turn of mind, way of looking at things

tänk|t *a4* thought *etc.*; (*ej verklig*) imagined (*situation* situation); imaginary (*linje* line); *det var inte så dumt ~* [*av dig*]*!* that was not such a bad idea [of yours]! **-värd** *a1* worth considering (taking into consideration); (*minnesvärd*) memorable

täpp|a I *s1* (*land*) garden plot (patch); *vara herre på ~n* rule (be cock of the) roost **II** *v3* ~ [*för, igen, till*] stop up, obstruct; *jag är -t i näsan* my nose feels stopped (stuffed) up; ~ *munnen på ngn* (*bildl.*) shut a p.'s mouth; *-t* stopped-up, choked-up

tära *v2* consume; ~ *på* waste [... away], reduce [... in bulk], (*förbruka*) use up; ~ *på reserverna* draw on the reserves; *sorgen tär på henne* sorrow is preying [up]on her **tärande** *a4* consuming; wasting (*sjukdom* illness); wearing (*bekymmer* anxiety) **tärd** [-ä:-] *a1* worn, wasted (*av* by); *se ~ ut* (*äv.*) look haggard; ~ *av bekymmer* (*äv.*) careworn

1 tärna [ˣtä:r-] *s1* (*brud-*) bridesmaid; *poet.* maid[en]

2 tärna [ˣtä:r-] *s1* (*fågel*) tern, sea swallow

tärning [ˣtä:r-] **1** die (*pl* dice); *falska ~ar* loaded (weighted) dice; *~en är kastad* (*bildl.*) the die is cast **2** *geom.* cube

tärnings|kast throw of a die (the dice) **-spel** game of dice; dice-playing

1 tät *s3* head; *gå i ~en för* walk (*friare*: place o.s.) at the head of

2 tät *a1* **1** (*motsats gles*) close; (*svårgenomtränglig o.d.*) thick, dense; (*kompakt*) compact, massive; (*utan springor e.d.*) tight **2** (*som ofta förekommer*) frequent (*besök* visits), repeated **3** (*rik*) well-to-do

täta *v1* tighten, make tight; (*stoppa till*) stop [up] (*en läcka* a leak); (*hermetiskt*) seal; *sjö.* caulk; *tekn.* pack

täta'tät *s3* tête-à-tête

tät|bebyggd *a5* densely built-up **-befolkad** [-å-] *a5* densely populated **-het** [-ä:-] **1** (*vävs e.d.*) closeness; (*skogs e.d.*) density, denseness; (*ogenomtränglighet*) impenetrability; *fys.* density **2** frequency

tät|na [-ä:-] become (get, grow) dense (compact); (*om rök e.d.*) thicken **-ning** [-ä:-] tightening; (*packning*) packing

tätnings|bricka grommet **-list** (*för fönster e.d.*) weather strip, strip seal; (*mot drag äv.*) draught-excluder

tät|ort [densely] built-up area, densely populated area **-ortsbebyggelse** city (town) buildings (*pl*)

tätt *adv* **1** closely; densely; *hålla ~* be watertight, *bildl.* keep quiet (close); *locket sluter ~* the lid fits tight; *husen ligger ~* the houses stand close together; ~ *åtsittande* tight, tight-fitting, skintight; ~ *efter* close behind; ~ *intill a*) *adv* close to, *b*) *prep* close up to **2** frequently, repeatedly; *breven duggade ~* the letters came thick and fast

tätting passerine

tätt|skriven *a3* closely written **-slutande** *a4* tight[-fitting]

tätört butterwort

tävla [ˣtä:v-] compete (*med* with; *om* for); *han har slutat ~* he doesn't enter competitions any more; *de ~de med varandra om priset* they competed for the prize; *skall vi ~ om vem som kommer först?* shall we race to see who comes first?; *de ~de om att säga henne artigheter*

they vied with each other in paying her compliments; *det här märket kan ~ med* this brand can stand comparison with; ~ *om makten* strive (struggle) for [the] power **tävlan** *r*, *som pl används* tävlingar competition (*i* in; *om* for); rivalry, emulation; *ädel ~* honourable rivalry; *delta utom ~* take part without competing for a prize **tävlande I** *s6* competing *etc.* **II** *a4* competing *etc.*; (*en ~*) competitor, (*löpare*) runner, (*i bridge e.d.*) tournament player **tävling** competition; contest; *AE. äv.* bee; *sport. äv.* (*löpning*) race, (*match*) match

tävlings|bana tournament ground; (*löpar-*) racetrack; (*kapplöpnings-*) racecourse **-bil** racing car, racer **-bidrag** entry; answer, solution **-domare** adjudicator, judge **-förare** racing driver **-regler** *pl* rules of (for) the competition (game) **-uppgift** problem (subject) for a prize competition

tö *s6* thaw **töa** thaw; ~ *bort* thaw [away]; ~ *upp* thaw (*äv. bildl.*)

töcken ['töck-] *s7* haze, mist; *höljd i ~* shrouded (veiled) in mist, misty, hazy **-gestalt** vague figure

töcknig *a1* hazy, misty

töff puff **töffa** puff

töj|a [ˣtöjja] *v2* stretch; ~ *ut* stretch out, extend; ~ *sig* stretch **-bar** *a1* stretchable; extensible **-ning** stretching; extension

tölp *s2* boor; (*drummel*) lout **-aktig** *a1*, **-ig** *a1* boorish, loutish

töm [tömm] *s2* rein

töm|ma *v2* **1** (*göra tom*) empty [out] (*i* into; *på* on [to]); (*dricka ur äv.*) drain; (*brevlåda*) clear; ~ *lidandets kalk* drain the cup of suffering; *salen -des hastigt* the hall emptied (was cleared [of people]) quickly **2** (*hälla*) pour [out] (*på flaskor* into bottles) **-ning** emptying [out] *etc.*; (*av brevlåda*) collection; (*tarmens*) evacuation; (*tappning*) pouring [out] **-ningstid** *post.* time of collection

tönt *s2*, *sl.* jerk, dope **-ig** *a1* awkward, clumsy

tör *det ~ dröja innan* it will probably be some time before

tör|as *tordes* torts (*vard. äv. inf.*: *tordas, sup.*: *tordats*) *dep* dare; *hon -s inte för sin mor* she doesn't dare because of her mother; *jag -s inte säga* I'm afraid to say; (*friare*) I can't tell exactly; *om jag -s fråga* if I may ask; *jag -s lova mitt liv på det* I'd stake my life on it

törhända [-ˣhänn-] *se måhända*

törn [-ö:-] *s2* **1** (*stöt*) blow, bump; *bildl.* shock; *ta ~* (*sjö.*) bear off **2** *sjö.* (*arbetsskift*) watch; *ha ~* have the watch **törna** ~ *emot* strike, bump into, *absol.* strike, make a bump; ~ *emot ngn* come into collision with s.b.; ~ *in* (*sjö.*) turn in

törn|beströdd *a5*, *bildl.* thorny **-bevuxen** overgrown with thorns **-buske** *se törne 1*

törne *s6* **1** (*buske*) thorn bush; (*vildros*) wild rose **2** (*tagg*) thorn; *ingen ros utan ~n* no rose without a thorn **-krona** crown of thorns **-krönt** [-ö:-] *a4* crowned with thorns **-stig** *bildl.* thorny path

törn|ig *a1* thorny (*äv. bildl.*) **-ros** rose (*jfr törne 1*)

Törnrosa [-ˣrω:-] the Sleeping Beauty

törn|rosasömn *bildl.* slumber, trance; sleep of the ages **-rosbuske** *se törne 1* **-skata** [red--backed] shrike; *koll.* butcherbird **-snår** thorn--brake, briery thicket **-tagg** thorn, prickle
törst *s3* thirst; *(längtan)* longing *(efter* for); *dö av ~* die of thirst **törsta** thirst *(efter* for); *~ efter hämnd* thirst for vengeance; *~ ihjäl* die of thirst **törstig** *a1* thirsty
tös *s3* girl, lass[ie]
töva *se dröja*
töväder thaw; *det är ~* a thaw has set in

U

U-balk channel [iron], U-iron
ubåt submarine; *(tysk)* U-boat
ubåts|bas *s3* submarine base **-fara** submarine menace **-fälla** decoy ship **-jagare** submarine chaser **-krig** submarine war[fare]
U.D. [ˣu:de:] *förk. för utrikesdepartementet*
udd *s2 (skarp spets)* [sharp] point; *(på gaffel o.d.)* prong; *(flik av tyg e.d.)* point, jag, *(rundad)* scallop; *bildl.* point, pungency; *satirens ~* the sting of satire; *bryta ~en av (bildl.)* turn the edge of; *med ~ mot (bildl.)* directed against
udda *oböjligt a* **1** *(om tal)* odd, uneven; *låta ~ vara jämnt* let s.th. pass **2** *(omaka)* odd; *~ varor (äv.)* oddments
udde *s2* cape; point; *(hög)* promontory
udd|ig *a1* pointed; *(rundad)* scalloped **-ljud** *språkv.* initial sound **-lös** pointless *(äv. bildl.)*
ufo ['u:fɷ] *s6* UFO *(förk. för unidentified flying object)* **-log** ufologist **-logi** ufology
ugand|ier [-'gann-] *s9*, **-isk** *a5* Ugandan
uggl|a *s1* owl; *det är -or i mossen* there is mischief brewing, something is up
uggle|skri owl's hoot; tu-whit tu-whoo **-unge** owlet, young owl
ugn [uŋn] *s2* furnace; *(bak-)* oven; *(bränn-, tork-)* kiln
ugns|bakad *a5* baked, roasted **-eldfast** oven-proof, heat-resisting **-lackera** stove enamel **-lucka** furnace *(etc.)* door **-pannkaka** batter pudding **-raka** oven rake **-steka** roast; *(potatis o.d.)* bake; *-stekt* roast[ed], baked **-svärta** stove polish (black) **-torka** oven (kiln) dry; bake *(tegel* bricks)
u-hjälp aid to developing countries
u'kas *s3* ukase
Ukraina [-ˣkrajj-] *n* [the] Ukraine **ukrain|are** [uˣkrajj-] *s9*, **-sk** *a5* Ukrainian
ukulele [-ˣle:-] *s5* ukulele
u-land developing country
ulk *s2* bullhead
ull *s3* wool; *(kamel-, get- äv.)* hair; *av ~* of wool, woollen; *ny ~* virgin wool; *han är inte av den ~en* he is not that sort (kind of man) **-fett** wool fat (grease) **-garn** wool[en yarn]; *(kamgarn)* worsted yarn **-ig** *a1* woolly, fleecy; *~a moln* fleecy clouds **-karda** wool card **-marknad** wool market **-strumpa** *se yllesstrumpa; gå på i -strumporna* go straight ahead **-tapp, -tott** tuft (flock) of wool
ulster ['uls-] *s2* ulster
ultim|ativ [-'ti:v, 'ult-] *a1* imperative; indispensable **-atum** [-ˣma:-] *s8* ultimatum; *ställa ~* present an ultimatum
ultimo ['ull-] *s6* the last day of the month
ultra ultra **-konservativ** ultraconservative **-kortvåg** ultrashort wave **-ljud** ultrasonic (supersonic) sound **-ma'rin I** *a1* ultramarine **II** *s3* ultramarine **-modern** ultramodern **-radikal** ultraradical, extreme radical **-rapid** *a1,*

n sg obest. form undviks slow-motion; *i* ~ in slow-motion **-röd** infrared, ultrared **-violett** ultraviolet

ulv *s2* wolf; *en* ~ *i fårakläder* a wolf in sheep's clothing; *man måste tjuta med ~arna* one must cry with the pack

umbra *s9* umber

umbär|a *nästan endast i inf.* do (go) without **-ande** *s6* privation, hardship; deprivation **-lig** [-ä:-] *a1* dispensable

umgicks [-j-] *imperf. av umgås* **umgås** *umgicks umgåtts, dep* **1** (*vara tillsammans*) associate, keep company; (*besöka*) be a frequent (regular) visitor (*hos* at a p.'s house); *de ~ mycket med varandra* they see a great deal of each other; ~ *i de högre kretsarna* move in exalted circles; *ha lätt att ~ med folk* (*äv.*) be a good mixer; *de ~ inte* they have nothing to do with one another **2** ~ *med planer på att* have plans to (+ *inf*), contemplate (+ *ing-form*) **3** (*handskas*) ~ *med* handle **umgåtts** *sup. av umgås*

um|gälla [-j-] *v2* pay for; *få* ~ suffer (smart) for **-gänge** [-jäŋe] *s6* (*samvaro*) intercourse; (*pers. man umgås med*) company, society; *ha stort* ~ have a large circle of friends; *sexuellt* ~ sexual intercourse

umgänges|former forms of [social] intercourse **-krets** [circle of] friends and acquaintances **-liv** social life **-rätt** right of parental access **-sätt** manners (*pl*) [in company]

undan I *adv* **1** (*bort*) away; (*ur vägen*) out of the way (*för* of); (*åt sidan*) aside (*för ngn* for s.b.); *komma* ~ get off, escape; *lägga* ~ put away **2** (*fort*) fast, rapidly; *det gick* ~ *i backen* we (*etc.*) whizzed down the hill; *det går* ~ *med arbetet* work is getting on fine **3** ~ *för* ~ little by little, one by one **II** *prep* (*bort från*) from; *fly* ~ *förföljarna* run away from the persecutors; *söka skydd* ~ *regnet* take shelter from the rain

undan|bad *imperf. av undanbe*[*dja*] **-be**[**dja**] [-e:-] *-bad - bett, rfl* decline, not seek (*återval* re-election); *jag -ber mig* kindly spare me **-bedjas** [-e:-] *-bads -betts, dep, rökning -bedes* please refrain from smoking; *blommor -bedes* no flowers by request **-bett** *sup. av undanbedja* **-dra**[**ga**] withdraw (*ngn ngt s.th.* from s.b.); (*beröva*) deprive (*ngn ngt s.b.* of s.th.); ~ *sig* shirk, elude, evade (*ansvar* responsibility); *straff* punishment); *det -drar sig mitt bedömande* it is beyond my power to judge **-dragande** *s6* evasion, withdrawal **-dräkt** *s3, jur.* petty embezzlement **-flykt** evasion; subterfuge; prevarication, excuse; *komma med ~er* make excuses, prevaricate excuses **-gjord** *a5* done, ready; over [and done with] **-glidande** *a4, bildl.* evasive **-gömd** [-j-] *a5* concealed, hidden away; (*om plats*) secluded, out-of-the-way **-hålla** withhold (*ngn ngt s.th.* from s.b.), keep back; ~ *sanningen* conceal the truth **-manöver** evasion action **-röja** remove; (*upphäva*) set aside **-röjning** clearance, removal **-skaffa** remove, get out of the way **-skymd** [-ʃ-] *a5* hidden, concealed; remote (*vrå* corner) **-stuvad** *a5* stowed away **-stökad** *a5* finished and done with

undan|ta *se undantaga* **-tag** *s7* exception (*från*

from, to); *~et bekräftar regeln* the exception proves the rule; *ingen regel utan* ~ [there is] no rule without an exception; *med* ~ *av* (*för*) with the exception of, except for, ... excepted; *utan* ~ without [an, any] exception; *sätta på undantag* set aside **-taga** exempt from, except; (*göra -tag*) make an exception for; *ingen -tagen* none excepted, exclusive of none **-tagandes** except [for], excepting, save

undantags|bestämmelse special stipulation (provision) **-fall** exception[al case]; *i ~, se -vis* **-lös** without exception **-tillstånd** (*proklamera* proclaim) a state of emergency **-vis** in exceptional cases, by way of (as an) exception

undantränga force out of its (his *etc.*) place; force (push, brush) aside (*äv. bildl.*); (*om idéer o.d.*) supersede, take the place of

1 under ['unn-] *s7* wonder, marvel; (*friare*) miracle; ~ *över alla ~!* wonder of wonders!; *naturens* ~ the wonders of Nature; *teknikens* ~ the marvels of science (technology); *göra* ~ work (do) wonders; *som genom ett* ~ as if by a miracle

2 under ['unn-] **I** *prep* **1** (*om rum*) under; underneath; (*på lägre nivå*) below, beneath; *långt* ~ far below; *sätta sitt namn* ~ *ngt* put one's name to (sign) s.th.; ~ *ytan* below the surface **2** (*om tid*) during (*natten* the night); in the course of (*samtalets gång* the conversation); (*om, på*) in (*våren* the spring); (*som svar på 'hur länge'*) for (*tre veckor* three weeks); ~ *hans regering* during (in) his reign; ~ *hela veckan* throughout the week, all the week **3** *bildl.* under (*drottning Viktoria* Queen Victoria; *befäl av* command of); below (*inköpspris* cost price); beneath (*min värdighet* me) **4** ~ *det* [*att*] while (*han talade* he was talking) **II** *adv* underneath; beneath; (*nedanför*) under; *skriva* ~ sign

under|arm forearm **-art** *biol.* subspecies (*pl lika*) **-avdelning** subdivision (*äv. mil.*), subsection, branch; *naturv.* subgroup

underbalanser|a *~d budget* budget [closing] with a deficit **-ing** ~ *av budget* deficit financing

under|bar *a1* wonderful, marvellous; (*övernaturlig*) miraculous **-barn** infant prodigy

underbefolkad *a5* underpopulated

underbefäl *s7* noncommissioned officer (*koll. officers pl*); *AE.* enlisted man **-havare** second--in-command

under|bemannad *a5* undermanned, short--handed **-ben** shank, lower part of the leg **-betala** underpay **-bett** underbite, protruding lower jaw **-betyg** *få* ~ fail (*i* in), be marked below standard **-binda** *kir.* ligate, ligature **-bjuda** underbid, undercut **-blåsa** *bildl.* fan, add fuel to **-bygga** support, substantiate **-byggnad 1** *eg.* foundation, substructure **2** *bildl.* grounding, schooling **-byxor** *pl* pants; *AE.* underpants; (*korta*) trunks, (*dam-*) knickers, (*trosor*) panties **-bädd** (*i sovkupé, hytt*) lower berth **-del** lower (under) part, bottom **-dimensionera** give too small dimensions, make too small; underestimate the size of **-domstol** *se underrätt* **-drift** understatement

underdånig *a1* humble, (*krypande*) obsequious;

U

~*st* Your Majesty's most obedient servant (subject) **-het** humility; (*inställsamhet*) servility, obsequiousness
under|exponer|a *foto.* underexpose **-ing** *foto.* underexposure
under'fund *komma ~ med* find out, get hold of, (*inse*) realize, (*upptäcka*) discover, get to know
underfundig *a1* cunning, artful; subtle
underförstå understand tacitly; ~*dd* implied, implicit; *det var ~tt dem emellan* it was understood (a tacit understanding) between them; ~*tt* (*nämligen*) that is to say
undergiven submissive; resigned (*sitt öde* to one's fate) **-het** [-j-] submissiveness, submission, resignation (*under, för* to)
under|gräva undermine (*äv. bildl.*) **-gå** undergo, go through; ~ *förändringar* change; ~ *examen* be examined **-gång** *s2* **1** (*ruin*) ruin, destruction; (*skeppsbrott*) wreck, loss; *gå sin ~ till mötes* be heading for disaster; *dömd till ~* doomed [to destruction] **2** (*passage*) subway; *AE.* underpass
undergör|ande [-j-] *a4* miraculous; wonder-working **-are** miracle worker, wonder-worker
underhaltig *a1* below (not up to) standard; [of] inferior [quality] **-het** inferiority, inferior (poor) quality
under'hand privately
underhandl|a negotiate (*med* with; *om* for, about); confer (*om* on); ~ *om* (*äv.*) discuss, negotiate **-are** negotiator **-ing** negotiation; *mil. äv.* parley; *ligga i ~ar med* be negotiating with
under'hands|besked confidential communication **-löfte** confidential (informal) promise
under|havande *s9* dependant, dependent; (*på gods*) tenant, *koll.* tenantry (*sg*) **-hud** corium **-huggare** underling; sidekick **-huset** the House of Commons (*AE.* Representatives)
underhåll *s7* **1** (*vidmakthållande*) maintenance, upkeep (*av* of) **2** (*understöd*) allowance; support; (*t. frånskild hustru*) alimony
underhåll|a 1 maintain, support; (*byggnad e.d.*) keep in repair; (*kunskaper*) keep up; *väl -en* well-kept, in good repair **2** (*roa*) entertain, amuse; divert; ~ *sig med* talk (converse) with **-ande** *a4* entertaining *etc.* **-are** entertainer **-ning** entertainment, amusement; diversion
underhållnings|litteratur light literature **-musik** light music **-program** entertainment program[me]
underhålls|bidrag alimony **-fri** requiring no maintenance **-kostnad** [cost of] maintenance (upkeep) **-skyldighet** maintenance obligation[s *pl*], duty to support **-tjänst** *mil.* maintenance [service]
under|ifrån from below (underneath) **-jorden** the lower (nether) regions (*pl*); Hades **-jordisk** subterranean; underground (*äv. bildl.*); *myt.* infernal; ~ *järnväg* underground, *AE.* subway; ~*a atomprov* underground nuclear tests **-kant** lower edge (side); *i ~* (*bildl.*) [rather] on the small (low) side
underkast|a 1 (*låta -gå*) subject (submit) to; ~ *ngn ett förhör* put s.b. through an interrogation; *bli ~d kritik* be subjected to criticism; *det är tvivel ~t* it is open to doubt **2** *rfl* (*kapitulera*) surrender; (*finna sig i*) submit [to], resign [o.s.

to] **-else** (*kapitulation*) surrender; (*lydnad*) submission (*under* to)
under|kjol underskirt **-klass** lower class; ~*en* the lower classes (*pl*) **-klassig** lower-class **-kläder** *pl* underwear, underclothing (*sg*); underclothes, undergarments; *vard.* undies **-klänning** slip, petticoat **-kropp** lower part of the body **-kunnig** *a1* aware (*om* of); *göra sig ~ om* acquaint o.s. with **-kurs** *hand., till ~ at* a discount, below par **-kuva** subdue, subjugate; (*besegra*) conquer **-kyla** supercool, undercool; *-kylt regn* freezing (supercooled) rain **-käke** lower jaw **-känna** disallow, not approve; *skol.* fail, reject; *bli -känd* (*skol.*) fail, *vard.* plough, *AE.* flunk **-kännande** [-ç-] *s6* disallowance; *skol.* rejection, failure
under|lag *s7* (*grundval*) foundation, basis (*äv. tekn.*); (*stöd*) support; *byggn.* bed[ding] **-lakan** bottom sheet **-leverantör** subcontractor
underlig *a1* strange, curious; odd, queer (*kurre* chap); ~ *till mods* queer; *det är inte ~t om* it is not to be wondered at if; *det ~a var* the funny thing about it was **-het** strangeness *etc.*; oddity; *hans ~er* his peculiarities
underligt *adv* strangely *etc.*; ~ *nog* strangely (oddly) enough
under|liv lower abdomen; (*kvinnliga könsorgan*) female organs of reproduction **-livssjukdomar** disorders of the female reproductive organs **-lydande I** *a4* dependent, subject **II** *s9* subordinate
underlåt|a (*låta bli*) omit; (*försumma*) neglect, fail; *han -lät att* he failed to; *jag kan inte ~ att säga* I cannot help saying **-enhet** omission; negligence **-enhetssynd** sin of omission
under|läge weak position; *vara i ~* be at a disadvantage; (*friare*) fall short, get the worst of it **-lägg** *s7* underlay, pad, mat **-lägsen** *a3* inferior (*ngn* to s.b.); *jag är ~ henne* (*äv.*) I am her inferior **-lägsenhet** inferiority **-läkare** assistant (house) physician (surgeon) **-läpp** lower lip **-lätta** facilitate, make easy (easier); *det kommer att ~ saken* it will simplify matters
under|medvetande subconsciousness **-medveten** subconscious; *det -medvetna* the subconscious [mind] **-mening** hidden meaning **-minera** undermine; sap **-målig** *a1* (*otillräcklig*) deficient; (*dålig*) inferior, poor **-närd** [-ä:-] *a5* underfed, undernourished **-näring** undernourishment, malnutrition **-officer** noncommissioned officer **-ordna** subordinate (*under* to) **-ordnad** *a5* subordinate; inferior, minor; (*en ~*) subordinate; *av ~ betydelse* of minor importance, incidental; ~ *sats* subordinate clause **-ordnande** [-å:-] *a4* subordinating (*konjunktion* conjunction) **-ordning** suborder **-pant 1** *jur.* collateral [security] **2** *bildl.* token **-presterande** underachieving **-pris** losing price; *sälja till ~* sell at a loss **-privilegierad** *a5* underprivileged **-rede** [base] frame; (*på bil*) chassis (*pl* chassis) **-redsbehandla** underseal, undercoat **-redsbehandling** underseal, undersealing, undercoat[ing] **-representerad** underrepresented **-rubrik** subheading **-rätt** lower (inferior) court, court of first instance
underrätta inform, notify, tell (*ngn om* s.b. of);

hand. advise, give notice; *göra sig ~d om* inquire (make inquiries) about; *hålla sig ~d om* keep o.s. informed about (as to); ~ *mig* let me know; *väl ~d* well informed
underrättelse information; intelligence; *(nyhet)* news; *(på förhand)* notice; *en ~* a piece of information *(etc.)*; *närmare ~r* further information *(sg)*, particulars; *inhämta ~r hos ngn om ngt* procure information from s.b. about s.th. **-tjänst** secret service, intelligence [service] **-verksamhet** *olovlig ~, se olovlig*
under|sida underside, bottom (underneath) side **-skatta** underrate, underestimate **-skott** deficit *(på* of*); (förlust)* loss **-skrida** be below, fall short of; ~ *ett pris* sell below a price **-skrift** signature; *(-skrivande)* signing; *förse med sin* ~ put one's signature to, sign; *utan ~ (äv.)* unsigned **-skriva** sign, put one's signature to; *(godkänna)* endorse, subscribe to **-skåp** hutch
underskön exquisitely beautiful
under|sköterska staff nurse **-slev** *s7* embezzlement; fraud; *begå ~* embezzle
underst ['unn-] *adv* at the [very] bottom *(i* of*)*
understa ['unn-] *superl. a* undermost; lowermost, lowest; ~ *lådan* the bottom drawer
under|stiga be (fall) below (short of); *(om pris)* not come up to **-streckare** feature article **-stryka** underline; *(betona)* emphasize **-ström** undercurrent **-stundom** [-ˣstundåm] at times **-stå** *rfl* presume, dare, make so bold as **-ställa** submit to; refer to; *-ställd* subordinate[d] to, placed under
under|stöd support; aid, assistance; *(penning-)* benefit; *periodiskt ~* periodical allowance **-stödja** support, assist, aid; *(ekonomiskt äv.)* subsidize, sponsor; *(förslag)* second **-stödjare** [-ö:-] supporter; sponsor
understöds|fond relief fund **-tagare** person receiving public assistance *(etc.)* **-verksamhet** public assistance
under|såte *s2* subject **-såtlig** [-å:-] *a1* as a subject; civic **-säng** lower bed **-sätsig** *a1* stocky, thickset **-sätsighet** stockiness
undersök|a examine; *(sakförhållande e.d.)* investigate, look (inquire) into **-ning** examination; investigation, inquiry; *vid närmare ~* on closer examination (investigation)
undersöknings|domare examining magistrate; *(vid dödsfall)* coroner **-kommission** commission of inquiry **-ledare** officer in charge of an investigation, investigator
underteckn|a sign, put one's name to; *~d (om brevskrivare)* I, the undersigned; *mellan ~de* between the undersigned **-ande** *s6* signing, signature; *vid ~t* on signature, on signing **-are** signer; signatory
under|titel subtitle **-ton** undertone **-trycka** suppress; *(kuva)* oppress, subjugate; *(hålla tillbaka)* repress, restrain **-tråd** *(på symaskin)* underthread **-tröja** vest; *AE.* undershirt; *AE. sl. (herr-)* skivvy **-utvecklad** *a5* underdeveloped; *~e länder, se utvecklingsland*
undervattens|båt submarine; *(tysk)* U-boat **-kabel** submarine cable **-klippa** sunken rock **-läge** submerged position; *intaga ~* submerge **-mina** submarine mine **-sten** sunken rock
undervegetation underbrush, undergrowth

underverk miracle; *världens sju ~* the seven wonders of the world; *uträtta ~* do (work) wonders
underviktig *a1* underweight
undervis|a teach, instruct **-ning** teaching, instruction; training, education; *högre ~* higher education, advanced instruction; *privat ~* private tuition; *programmerad ~* programmed instruction
undervisnings|anstalt educational institution **-börda** teaching load **-maskin** teaching machine **-material** teaching materials *(pl)* **-metod** teaching method **-plan** curriculum **-råd** head of division of the Swedish national board of education **-sal** instruction room **-sjukhus** teaching (training) hospital **-skyldighet** *med ~ i* with the obligation to teach **-språk** language of instruction **-vana** teaching experience **-väsen** educational system, education
under|värdera underrate, underestimate **-värdering** underestimation, underrating **-värme** heat from below **-årig** *a1* underage, minor
undfall|a escape; *uttrycket undföll mig* the expression slipped out; *låta sig ~ ngt* let s.th. slip out **-ande** *a4* compliant; submissive **-enhet** compliancy, complaisance; submissiveness
und|fly flee from; escape *(faran* danger*)* **-få** receive **-fägna** treat *(ngn med s.b.to)* **-fägnad** entertainment **-gå** escape; *ingen ~r sitt öde* there is no escaping one's fate; *jag kunde inte ~ att höra* I couldn't help hearing; *den kan inte ~ att göra intryck* it is bound to make an impression **-komma** escape; get away; ~ *sina förföljare* escape from one's pursuers
undra wonder *(över* at*); det ~r jag inte på* I don't wonder (am not surprised) [at that]; ~ *på att...!* no wonder ...!
undran *r* wonder
undre ['unn-] *a, komp. t. 2 under* [the] lower; bottom; ~ *världen* the underworld
und|seende *s6* deference; *ha ~ med* have forbearance with **-slippa** *se undgå, undkomma*; *låta ~ sig* let slip, allow to escape one **-sätta** relieve *(äv. mil.); (friare)* succour **-sättning** relief; succour; *komma till ngns ~* come to a p.'s rescue (succour) **-sättningsexpedition** relief expedition
undulat budgerigar; *vard.* budgie
und|vara *sup -varit, övriga former saknas* do without, dispense with; *inte kunna ~ (äv.)* not be able to spare **-vika** avoid *(att:* -ing-form*)*; keep away from, shun; *(med list)* evade, dodge; *som inte kan ~s* unavoidable **-vikande I** *s6* avoidance; *till ~ av* in order to avoid **II** *a4* evasive *(svar* reply*)* **III** *adv, svara ~* give an evasive answer
ung *-t yngre yngst* young *(för sina år* for one's years*); de ~a* the young, young people; *vid ~a år* early in life, at an early age; *som ~ var han* as a young man he was; *bli ~ på nytt* regain one's youth; *ha ett ~t sinne* be young at heart **-djur** *koll.* young stock *(sg)* **-dom** *s2* **1** *abstr.* youth; *i ~en, i sin ~* in one's youth **2** *(ung människa)* young person (man, girl), adolescent; *~ar* young people; *nationens ~* the youth of the nation **-domlig** *a1* youthful; juvenile
ungdoms|avdelning youth department; *(på*

bibliotek) juvenile department **-bjudning** party for young people **-brottslighet** juvenile delinquency **-brottsling** juvenile offender (delinquent) **-böcker** *pl* juvenile books **-fängelse** reformatory [school] **-förbund** youth association (club, *polit.* league) **-gård** youth centre **-kultur** youth culture **-kärlek** youthful passion **-ledare** youth leader **-litteratur** literature for the young **-minne** memory of one's youth **-tid** youth **-vårdsskola** *BE.* community home, borstal, *AE.* reformatory **-vän** *en* ~ a friend of one's youth **-år** *pl* children's

ung|e *s2* (*av djur*) *se fågel-, katt- etc.*; young; (*barn-*) kid, baby; *-ar* young [ones]; *få -ar* bring forth young; *som föder levande -ar* viviparous; *våra barn och andras -ar* our children and others' brats; *din otäcka* ~ you awful child

unge'fär [unj-, uŋ-] about; something like; approximately; ~ *detsamma* pretty much the same; ~ *100* (*äv.*) 100 or so, say 100; ~ *här* somewhere about here; *för* ~ *fem år sedan* some five years ago; *på ett* ~ approximately, roughly **-lig** *a1* approximate, rough (*beräkning* estimate) **-ligen** approximately; roughly

Ungern ['uŋ-] *n* Hungary

ung|ersk ['uŋ-] *a5* Hungarian **-erska** *s1* **1** (*språk*) Hungarian **2** (*kvinna*) Hungarian woman

ung|ersven [young] swain, lad **-flicksaktig** *a1* girlish **-herre** young gentleman **-häst** colt **-höns** pullet; *kokk.* spring chicken **-karl** bachelor

ungkarls|hotell hostel for single men **-tid** bachelor days **-våning** bachelor's apartment

ungmö maid[en]; *gammal* ~ old maid, spinster

ungrare [ˣuŋ-] Hungarian

ung|tjur stirk **-tupp** cockerel (*äv. bildl.*)

uni'form [-å-] *s3* uniform; full dress; *mil. äv.* regimentals (*pl*); *i* ~ (*äv.*) uniformed **-era 1** (*göra likformig*) make uniform **2** (*förse med uniform*) uniform **-itet** uniformity

uniforms|kappa regulation greatcoat **-klädd** in uniform, uniformed **-mössa** uniform cap **-rock** tunic

u'nik *a1* unique **unikum** ['uːni-] *s8* unique [specimen]

unilate'ral *a1* unilateral

uni'on *s3* union

unions|flagga union flag; *~n* (*Storbritannien*) Union Jack **-vänlig** pro-union

uni'sex *s7* unisex **-mode** unisex fashion

uni'son *a1* unison; ~ *sång* (*äv.*) community singing **uni'sont** [-ɷ-] *adv* in unison

univer'sal *a1* universal **-arvinge** residuary (sole) heir **-geni** all-round genius **-itet** universality **-medel** panacea, cure-all

univer'sell *a1* universal

universitet *s7* university; *ligga vid* ~ be at a university

universitets|adjunkt *ung* junior lecturer **-bibliotek** university library **-bildad** university trained **-examen** university degree **-filial** affiliated university, branch campus **-kanslern** the chancellor of the Swedish universities and colleges **-lektor** senior [university] lecturer, reader; *AE. äv.* assistant professor **-lärare**

university teacher **-rektor** rector; *Storbritannien ung.* vice chancellor; *AE. ung.* president **-studerande** university student, undergraduate **-studier** *pl* university (*Storbritannien* undergraduate) studies **-styrelse** *BE.* senate, *AE.* board of regents (directors) **-utbildning** university education

universum [-ˣvärr-] *s8* universe

unken *a3* musty; (*om lukt, smak äv.*) stale **unket** *adv, lukta* ~ smell musty (stale)

unna ~ *ngn ngt* not [be]grudge s.b. s.th.; *det är honom väl unt* he is very welcome to it; ~ *sig ngt* allow o.s. s.th.; *han ~r sig ingen ro* (*äv.*) he gives himself no rest

uns *s7* ounce (*förk. oz.*); *inte ett* ~ (*friare*) not a scrap

u.p.a. [uːpeːˈaː] (*förk. för utan personligt ansvar*) Ltd., Limited; without personal liability

upp up; (*-åt äv.*) upward[s]; (*ut*) out; *knyta* (*låsa*) ~ untie (unlock); *gata* ~ *och gata ner* up one street and down another; *hit* ~ up here; *denna sida ~!* this side up!; *det är* ~ *till dig* (*vard.*) it's up to you; ~ *med huvudet!* (*bildl.*) keep your chin up; ~ *med händerna!* hands up!, stick'em up!; ~ *ur* out of; *gå* ~ (*ur vattnet*) get out of the water; *hälla* ~ pour out; *vända* ~ *och ner på* turn upside down; *äta* ~ eat up **-amma** nurse, foster **-arbeta** (*jord*) cultivate; (*firma e.d.*) work up, develop

uppass|are waiter; *mil.* officer's [bat]man **-erska** waitress; (*på båt*) stewardess **-ning** waiting; attendance

upp|backa back up, support **-backning** backing up, backup, support **-bjuda** muster, summon (*alla sina krafter* all one's strength); exert (*energi* energy) **-bjudande** *s6, med* ~ *av alla sina krafter* exerting all one's strength **-bjudning** invitation (*till dans* to dance) **-blanda** mix [up], intermix; (*vätska*) dilute **-blomstrande** flourishing, prospering; developing (*industri* industry) **-blomstring** prosperity, rise, development **-blossande** *a4* blazing (flaring) up; ~ *vrede* (*äv.*) flash of anger **-blåsbar** [-å-] *a1* inflatable; pneumatic **-blåst** [-å-] *a1* inflated; puffed up; *bildl. vard.* stuck-up **-blött** *a4, marken var alldeles* ~ the ground was sopping wet **-bragt** *a4* indignant, irritated; (*starkare*) exasperated **-bringa 1** (*fartyg*) capture, seize **2** (*skaffa*) procure, obtain, raise **-bromsning** braking; *bildl.* slowing down **-brott** breaking-up; (*avresa*) departure, departing; *mil.* decampment; *göra* ~ *a*) (*från bjudning*) break up [the party], take leave, *b*) *mil.* break [up the] camp **-brottsorder** order[s *pl*] to march **-brottsstämning** breaking-up mood **-brusande** *a4, bildl.* hot-tempered, irascible, impetuous **-brusning** [-uː-] burst of passion **-bränd** *a5* burnt [up] **-buren** *a5, vara mycket* ~ be thought highly (*firad:* made much) of

uppbygg|a 1 *eg. bet., se bygga upp* **2** *bildl.* edify **-else** edification **-elselitteratur** edifying literature **-lig** *a1* edifying **-nad** building [up], construction; (*organisering*) build-up **-nadsarbete** reconstruction

upp|båd *s7, mil.* summons to arms, calling out; (*friare*) levy; *AE.* (*under sheriffs befäl*) posse; *ett stort* ~ a large force **-båda** summon to arms, call out; (*trupper äv.*) levy; (*friare*) mobilize (*hjälp* help) **-bära 1** (*erhålla*) receive, collect; ~ *skatt* collect taxes **2** (*vara föremål för*) suffer; come in for (*klander* criticism) **3** (*stödja*) support

uppbörd [-ö:-] *s3* collection [of taxes]; *förrätta* ~ collect taxes, take up the collection

uppbörds|distrikt revenue district **-kontor** [tax] collector's (revenue) office **-man** tax collector **-termin** collection period **-verk** inland revenue office; *AE.* internal revenue service

upp|daga discover; reveal **-datera** update **-dela** divide [up] **-delning** division, dividing [up] **-diktad** *a5* invented; trumped up

uppdra *se* dra [*upp*]

uppdrag commission; mission; (*uppgift*) task, *AE.* assignment; *hand.* order; *enligt* ~ by order (direction); *med* ~ *att* with orders (instructions) to; *på* ~ *av* at the request of, as instructed by, (*mer officiellt*) by order of; *få i* ~ *att göra ngt* be instructed (commissioned) to do s.th., be charged with doing s.th.; *ge ngn i* ~ *att* commission (instruct) s.b. to; *skiljas från ett* ~ be removed from office; *utföra ett* ~ *åt ngn* execute a commission for s.b.

uppdrag|a 1 *se* dra [*upp*]; (*uppfostra*) bring up; (*växter*) grow, rear **2** (*rita upp*) draw, trace; ~ *en jämförelse* draw a comparison (*mellan* between); ~ *gränserna för* delimit, *bildl. äv.* lay down the scope of **3** ~ *åt ngn att* instruct (order, commission) s.b. to **-en** *a5, klockan är* ~ the clock is wound up **-ning** (*av klocka*) winding up

upp|dragsgivare principal; (*arbetsgivare*) employer; (*kund*) customer, client **-driva** (*öka*) raise, increase; (*skaffa*) procure, obtain; *högt -drivna förväntningar* high expectations **-dykande** *s6* emersion; *bildl.* appearance **-dämma** dam up

uppe 1 (*mots. nere*) up (*äv. uppstigen*); (*i övre våningen*) upstairs; *vara tidigt* ~ be up early, (*som vana*) be an early riser (*vard.* bird); ~ *i landet* up country; *högt* ~ *på himlen* high in the sky **2** *vard.* (*öppen*) open **3** *vara* ~ *i tentamen* take (have) an [oral] exam

uppegga incite, egg on

uppehåll *s7* **1** (*avbrott*) interruption, break; (*paus*) pause, interval; (*tågs*) stop; *göra ett* ~ (*i tal o.d.*) make a pause, break off, (*allm. o. om tåg*) stop; *utan* ~ without stopping (a stop), incessantly **2** (*vistelse*) sojourn; (*kortare*) stay, stop; *göra* ~ *i* (*under resa*) stop over at

uppehålla 1 (*hindra*) detain, delay, keep [... back] **2** (*vidmakthålla*) keep up (*skenet* appearances); support (*livet* life); maintain (*en stor familj* a large family) **3** (*tjänst*) discharge the duties of **4** *rfl* (*vistas*) stay, live, reside; (*livnära sig*) support o.s. (*med musiklektioner* by giving music lessons); *bildl.* dwell (*vid småsaker* [up]on details)

uppehålls|ort [place of] residence; (*tillfällig*) place of sojourn, whereabouts; *jur.* domicile **-tillstånd** residence permit **-väder** dry (fair) weather

uppehälle *s6* subsistence, sustenance; *fritt* ~ free board and lodging; *förtjäna sitt* ~ earn

one's living; *sörja för ngns* ~ support s.b.

uppemot ['upp-, -'mɔ:t] nearly, almost

uppenbar *a1* obvious, evident; distinct, apparent; *när förseelsen blir* ~ when the offence comes to light **uppenbara 1** (*avslöja*) reveal, disclose **2** *rfl* reveal o.s. (*för* to) (*äv. relig.*); (*visa sig*) appear

uppenbarelse revelation (*om* of); *konkr.* apparation, vision **Uppenbarelseboken** the Revelation of St. John the Divine, [the Book of] Revelation[s], Apocalypse

uppenbarligen [-a:-] obviously *etc.*, patently

upp|fart ascent; (*väg*) approach, ramp; *under ~en* while driving up, on the way up **-fatta** apprehend; grasp; (*förstå*) comprehend, understand; (*tolka*) interpret; *jag kunde inte* ~ *vad han sa* I couldn't catch what he said; ~ *ngt såsom* take s.th. as **-fattning** apprehension; comprehension, understanding; (*föreställning*) idea, conception; *bilda sig en* ~ *om* form an opinion (idea) of

uppfinn|a invent; devise, contrive **-are** inventor **-ing** invention; (*nyhet äv.*) innovation

uppfinnings|förmåga [power of] invention, inventiveness **-rik** inventive; (*fyndig äv.*) ingenious **-rikedom** inventiveness; ingenuity

upp|flugen *a5* perched **-flytta** (*i lönegrad*) advance, promote; *bli ~d* (*skol.*) get one's remove **-flyttning** moving up; *skol.* remove; (*i lönegrad*) advance, rise

1 uppfordra (*uppmana*) call upon, request; (*t. strid*) challenge, summon

2 uppfordra (*forsla upp*) haul, raise [... to the surface], draw up

uppfordringsverk drawing engine; *gruv.* elevator (hoist) frame

uppfostr|a bring up; *AE. äv.* raise; (*bilda*) educate; (*uppöva äv.*) train; *illa ~d* badly brought up **-an** upbringing; education; training **-are** educator; tutor

uppfostrings|anstalt reformatory [school]; *Engl.* approved school; *AE.* institution for juveniles, workhouse **-bidrag** *jur.* alimony **-syfte** *i* ~ for educational purposes

upp|friska freshen up; refresh **-friskande** *a4* refreshing **-fräta** eat away; corrode completely **-fylla 1** (*fullgöra*) fulfil; (*plikt äv.*) perform, carry out; (*ngns önskningar äv.*) meet, comply with; *få sin önskan -fylld* have one's wish **2** (*fylla*) *bildl.* fill; ~ *jorden* (*bibl.*) replenish the earth; *-fylld av* filled with, full of **-fyllelse** accomplishment; (*av profetia*) fulfilment; *gå i* ~ be fulfilled (accomplished), come true **-fånga** catch; (*signaler*) pick up; (*hindrande*) intercept **-föda** bring up; nourish; (*djur*) breed, rear; *AE. äv.* raise **-födare** breeder **-födning** [-ö:-] breeding **-följa** follow up **-följning** follow-up, following-up **-följningsbrev** follow-up letter

uppför ['upp-] **I** *adv* uphill; *vägen bär* ~ it is uphill **II** *prep* up (*backen* the hill); *gå* ~ *trappan* (*äv.*) go upstairs

uppför|a 1 (*bygga*) build; raise, erect (*ett monument* a monument) **2** (*anteckna*) put down, enter **3** (*teaterstycke*) give, perform, present; (*musikstycke*) perform **4** *rfl* behave [o.s.], conduct o.s., carry o.s.; ~ *sig väl* (*illa*) behave

U

[well] (badly), (*som vana*) have good (bad) manners
uppförande *s6* **1** (*byggande*) building *etc.*; erection, construction; *är under* ~ is being built, is under construction **2** (*av teater-* o. *musikstycke*) performance **3** (*beteende*) behaviour, conduct; *dåligt* ~ (*äv.*) misbehaviour **-betyg** conduct marks **-rätt** performing rights (*pl*)
uppförs|backe ascent, rise **-väg** uphill road
upp|ge 1 (*meddela*) state; give (*namn o. adress* name and address); (*säga*) say; (*rapportera*) report; ~ *sig vara* state (say) that one is; ~ *namnet på* name, give the name of; ~ *ett pris* quote a price; *enligt vad han själv -gav* (*äv.*) on his own statement **2** (*överge, avstå från*) give up, abandon; ~ *andan* expire, breathe one's last **3** (*utstöta*) give (*ett skrik* a cry)
upp|gift [-j-] *s3* **1** (*meddelande*) statement (*om* of); (*upplysning*) information (*om* on); (*lista*) list, specification (*om* of); (*officiell*) report (*på* on); *närmare ~er* (*äv.*) further particulars; *enligt* ~ from information received, according to reports; *kompletterande ~er* supplementary data (details) (*om* on); *med* ~ *om* stating; *statiska ~er* returns, statistics **2** (*åliggande*) task, charge; (*kall*) mission, object (*i livet* in life); *förelägga ngn en* ~ set s.b. a task; *det är hans* ~ *att* it is his duty (business) to **3** (*i examen o.d.*) [examination *etc.*] question; *matematisk* ~ [mathematical] problem; *skriftlig* ~ [written] exercise **-giftslämnare** informant; respondent
upp|giva *se uppge* **-given** (*tillintetgjord*) overcome (*av trötthet* with fatigue); exhausted (*av sorg* with grief) **-gjord** settled, arranged; ~ *på förhand* prearranged **-gå 1** (*belöpa sig*) amount (*till* to); *i genomsnitt* ~ *till* average **2** (*sammansmälta*) ~ *i* be merged (*om firma e.d. äv.* incorporated) in **-gående I** *s6,* ~ *i* absorption by (*arbete* work) **II** *a4* rising; (*om himlakropp äv.*) ascending **-gång** *s2* **1** (*väg*) way up; (*trapp-*) stairs (*pl*), staircase **2** (*himlakropps*) rise **3** (*ökning*) rise, increase; upswing, upturn **-görelse** [-j-] **1** (*avtal*) agreement; (*överenskommelse äv.*) arrangement, settlement; (*affär*) transaction; ~ *i godo* amicable settlement, settlement out of court; *träffa en* ~ make an agreement, come to terms **2** (*dispyt*) dispute, showdown **-handla** purchase, buy (in, up) **-handling** purchase, purchasing, buying **-haussa** force up, boost
upphets|a excite; inflame; *bli ~d* get excited **-ande** *a4* exciting; inflammatory (*tal* speech) **-ning** excitement
upp|hetta heat, make hot; ~ *för mycket* overheat **-hettning** heating **-hinna** catch up, overtake **-hitta** find **-hittare** finder **-hjälpa** (*förbättra*) improve **-hostning** expectoration
upphov *s7* origin; source; (*orsak*) cause; (*början äv.*) beginning, origination; *ge* ~ *till* give rise (birth) to; *ha sitt* ~ *i* (*äv.*) originate in; *vara* ~ *till* be the cause of
upphovs|man author, originator (*till* of) **-rätt** copyright **-rättslig** ~ *lagstiftning* copyright legislation
upp|hällning 1 pouring out **2** *vara på ~en* be on the decline (wane), (*om förråd*) be running short **-hänga** suspend, hang [up] **-hängning**

suspension; mounting **-häva 1** (*återkalla*) revoke, withdraw; (*förklara ogiltig*) annul, declare invalid (void); (*kontrakt*) cancel; (*neutralisera*) neutralize **2** (*avbryta*) raise (*belägringen* the siege) **3** (*utstöta*) raise (*ett skri a* cry); ~ *sin röst* lift one's voice, begin to speak
upp|höja raise (*äv. mat.*); elevate; (*berömma*) extol; ~ *i kvadrat* square, raise to second power **-höjd** *a5* **1** *bildl.* elevated, exalted; *med -höjt lugn* with supreme composure **2** (*om arbete, bokstäver*) raised **-höjdhet** elevation; loftiness **-höjelse** elevation, exaltation; promotion **-höjning** *konkr.* elevation (*i marken* of the ground), rise; (*kulle*) eminence
upphör|a cease, stop (*med att göra ngt* doing s.th.); (*sluta*) end, come to an end; ~ *med* (*äv.*) discontinue, (*en vana*) give up; *firman har -t* the firm has closed down **-ande** *s6* ceasing *etc.*; cessation; (*avbrott äv.*) interruption; (*tillfälligt*) suspension
uppifrån I *adv* from above; ~ *och ner* from top to bottom **II** *prep* [down] from
uppiggande (*särskr. upp-piggande*) **I** *a4* stimulating, bracing (*verkan* effect); *något* ~ a pick-me-up **II** *adv, verka* ~ have a reviving (bracing) effect
upp|jagad *a5* [over]excited; heated (*fantasi* imagination); overstrained (*nerver* nerves) **-kalla 1** (*benämna*) call, name; *~d efter* called (named) after **2** (*be* [*ngn*] *att komma upp*) call up **3** (*mana*) call [up]on **-kastning** vomiting; *med.* emesis; *få* ~ *av* vomit **-klarna** clear up **-knäppt** *a4* unbuttoned (*äv. bildl.*) **-kok** boiling, warming up; *bildl.* rehash (*på* of); *ge ngt ett* ~ boil s.th. up
upp|komling [-å-] upstart, parvenu (*fem.* parvenue) **-komma** (*uppstå*) arise (*av* from), originate (*ur* in); (*börja*) begin; (*plötsligt*) start up; *de -komna skadorna* the damage (*sg*) incurred **-kommande** *a4* possible, arising; *vid* ~ *skada* in case of damage **-komst** [-å-] *s3* (*tillblivelse*) origin, beginning; appearance; *fack.* genesis; *ha sin* ~ *i* have its origin in, originate in **-konstruera** (*uppfinna*) invent; (*hitta på*) make up, create **-krupen** *a5, sitta* ~ be curled up (*i soffan* on the sofa) **-käftig** [-ç-] *a1* cheeky, saucy **-käftighet** [-ç-] cheek, sauce **-köp** (*-köpande*) buying [in], purchasing; (*ett* ~) purchase; *göra* ~ do one's purchasing (*vard.* shopping). **-köpa** buy [in, up], purchase **-köpare** buyer, purchaser **-körd** [-çö:-] *a5* **1** (*däst*) bloated **2** (*lurad*) fleeced
upp|laddning charge, charging (*äv. bildl.*); *bildl. äv.* build-up; *eg. äv.* electrification **-lag** *s7* store, stock, supply **-laga** *s1* edition; (*tidnings- äv.*) circulation; *bildl.* version; *förkortad* ~ abbreviated (abridged) edition; *~ns storlek* number of copies printed, print **-lagd** *a5* **1** (*om vara, fartyg*) laid up; *stort -lagt projekt* large-scale project **2** (*hågad*) inclined, disposed; (*känna sig* ~ *för att* be in a mood for, feel like (+ *ing-form*) **-lagesiffra** circulation figures (*pl*) **-lagring** storing, storage **-lagsnäring** reserve nutrition **-lagsplats** depot, storing place, storage yard **-land** *s7* surrounding area; (*innanför kusten*) hinterland **-lappning** *boktr.* making ready **-leta** find, hunt up

upp|leva (*erfara*) experience, meet with (*besvikelser* disappointments); (*leva tills ngt inträffar*) live to (*år 2000* the year 2000), [live to] see; (*bevittna*) witness; *han har -levt mycket* he has been through a lot (had an eventful life) **-levelse** (*erfarenhet*) experience; (*händelse*) event; *detta blev en ~ för mig* it was quite an experience for me **-linjera** rule [lines in] **-liva** (*förnya*) renew (*bekantskapen med* the acquaintance with); (*pigga upp*) cheer [up], exhilarate; *~ minnet* refresh (brush up) one's memory; *~ gamla minnen* revive old memories **-livande** *a4* cheering, stimulating **-livningsförsök** [-li:v-] *pl* attempts at resuscitation **upp|lopp 1** (*tumult*) riot, tumult **2** *sport.* finish **-luckra** loosen, break up; *bildl. äv.* relax (*bestämmelserna* the regulations, *moralen* morals) **-lupen** *a5, ~ ränta* accrued interest, interest due **-lyfta** lift up; *högt.* elevate; *med -lyft huvud* head high **-lyftande** *a4* elevating; sublime **upplys|a 1** (*göra ljus*) light [up], illuminate **2** (*underrätta*) inform (*ngn om s.b.* of), tell (*ngn om s.b.*); enlighten (*ngn i en fråga s.b.* on a point) **-ande** *a4* informative, illustrative (*exempel* example); (*förklarande*) explanatory (*anmärkningar* remarks); (*lärorik*) instructive **-ning 1** (*belysning*) lighting, illumination **2** (*underrättelse*) information (*om* about, of, on); (*förklaring*) explanation; (*kredit-*) credit[worthiness] report; *en ~* a piece of information; *~ar* information (*sg*); *närmare ~ar* further particulars (details) **3** ([*bibringande av*] *kunskaper*) enlightenment, elucidation; (*kultur*) civilization, culture; *~en* (*hist.*) the [Age of] Enlightenment

upplysnings|byrå information office (bureau) **-tiden** the Age of Enlightenment **-verksamhet** information service (activities *pl*) **-vis** by way of information; for your information **upp|lyst** [-y:-] *a1* **1** *eg.* illuminated, lighted (lit) up **2** *bildl.* enlightened **-låna** borrow, raise **-låning** borrowing [transaction[s *pl*]] **-låta** open (*för trafik* to traffic), make available (*för* to); *~ ett rum åt ngn* put a room at a p.'s disposal, grant s.b. the use of a room **-låtelse** grant, giving up; *~ nyttjanderätt* grant of enjoyment **-läggning 1** *sömn.* shortening, taking up **2** (*planering*) planning, arrangement; (*disposition*) disposition; (*av konto o.d.*) drawing up; (*av håret*) coiffure **3** (*magasinering*) storage, storing; (*av fartyg*) laying up **4** (*på fat etc.*) arrangement **-läsare** reader, reciter **-läsning** reading; recital **-läxning** sermon; *vard.* telling-off

upplös|a 1 (*knyta upp*) *se* lösa [*upp*] **2** (*komma* [*ngt*] *att upphöra*) dissolve, wind up (*ett företag* a company); (*skingra*) dissolve, dismiss; (*möte*) break up; (*trupper*) disband **3** (*sönderdela*) dissolve, disintegrate; *mat.* solve **4** (*bringa oreda i*) disorganize; *-löst i tårar* dissolved in tears **5** *rfl* dissolve, be dissolved (*i* into); (*sönderfalla*) decompose **-ande** *a4* dissolving *etc.* **-as** *v3, dep, se* upplösa **-bar** *a1* dissoluble **-ning** dissolution, winding up (*etc.*); (*samhälls-*) disintegration; (*dramas*) unravelling, denouement **-ningstillstånd** state of dissolution (decomposition); *vara i ~* (*bildl.*) be

on the point of collapse

upp|mana exhort; (*hövligt*) request, invite, (*enträget*) urge, incite; *besökare ~s att* visitors are recommended (requested) to **-maning** exhortation; request; summons, call; *på ~ av* at the request of, on the recommendation of **-marsch** marching-up; *mil.* deployment, drawing-up **-maskning** mending [of a ladder] **-mjuka** make soft, soften; (*göra smidig*) limber up; (*moderera*) modify, moderate **-mjukning** [-u:-] *sport.* limbering-up **uppmuntr|a** (*jfr muntra* [*upp*]); (*inge förhoppningar e.d.*) encourage; (*gynna*) favour, promote; (*uppmana*) exhort **-an** *best. form -an, pl -ingar* encouragement; favouring, patronage **-ande** *a4* encouraging; *föga ~* anything but encouraging, discouraging **uppmärk|sam** *a1* attentive (*äv. förekommande*) (*på, mot* to); (*aktgivande*) watchful, observant (*på* of); *göra ngn ~ på* draw (call) a p.'s attention to **-samhet** attention; (*som egenskap*) attentiveness; (*aktgivande*) watchfulness, observation; *rikta ngns ~ på* call a p.'s attention to; *undgå ngns ~* escape a p.'s attention; *visa ngn ~* pay attention to s.b.; *väcka ~* attract attention; *ägna ~ åt* give (pay) attention to **-samma** notice, observe; pay attention to; *bli ~d* attract attention; *en mycket ~d bok* a book that has created a stir **-samt** *adv* attentively; (*starkare*) intently

upp|mäta measure [out] **-mätning** measuring [up] **-nosig** *a1* impertinent, saucy, pert **-nå** reach, attain; arrive at; (*ernå*) obtain; (*vinna*) gain; *vid ~dd pensionsålder* at pensionable age **-näsa** snub (turned-up) nose **-näst** [-ä:-] *a4* snub-nosed

uppochnedvänd [-ˣne:d-] [turned] upside down; inverted, reversed; *bildl.* topsy-turvy

upp|odla cultivate **-odling** (*-odlande*) cultivation; *konkr.* cleared plot [of land] **-offra** sacrifice (*allt* everything; *sig o.s.*) **-offrande** [-å-] *a4* self-sacrificing **-offring** [-å-] sacrifice; *det har kostat henne stora ~ar* she has sacrificed a great deal **-packning** (*hopskr. uppackning*) unpacking **-passare** *se* uppassare **-piggande** *a4, se* uppiggande **-reklamera** boost, puff **-rensa** clean (clear) out; *mil.* mop up **-rensning** cleaning out; *mil.* mopping-up **upprep|a** repeat (*säga om o. om igen*) reiterate; (*förnya*) renew; *~de gånger* repeatedly, again and again **-repning** [-e:-] repetition; reiteration; renewal; recurrence

1 uppresa *s1* journey up; *på ~n* on my (*etc.*) journey up

2 upp|resa *v3* **1** (*uppföra*) raise; put up **2** *rfl* rise, revolt

uppretad *a5* irritated; exasperated (*folkhop* mob); enraged (*tjur* bull)

upprik|tig *a1* sincere; (*ärlig*) honest; (*öppen*) frank, candid; *~ vän* true friend; *säga ngn sin ~a mening* tell (give) s.b. one's honest opinion **-tighet** sincerity; frankness, candour; honesty **-tigt** *adv* sincerely *etc.*; *~ sagt* candidly [speaking]; *säg mig ~ ...!* tell me honestly ...!

upp|ringning [telephone] call **-rinnelse** origin, source **-rivande** *a4* harrowing, shocking **-riven** *a5, bildl.* (*nervös*) worked up; *~ av sorg*

U

broken by sorrow **-rop** (*av namn*) roll call, call-over; (*vädjan*) appeal; (*på auktion*) announcement **uppror** *s7* insurrection, rebellion; *mil.* mutiny; (*mindre*) revolt, uprising; (*oro*) agitation; *göra* ~ rise in rebellion, revolt; *hans känslor råkade i* ~ he flared up **-isk** *a5* rebellious; seditious, insubordinate **upprors|anda** rebellious spirit, spirit of revolt **-fana** *höja* ~*n* raise the standard of rebellion **-försök** attempted (attempt at) rebellion **-makare** instigator of rebellion; (*vid myteri*) ringleader; (*svagare*) troublemaker **upp|rusta** rearm **-rustning** *mil.* rearmament; (*renovering*) restoration, reparation **-rutten** rotten to the core **-ryckning** *bildl.* rousing, shaking-up; *ge ngn en* ~ give s.b. a shaking-up **-rymd** *a1* exhilarated, elated **-rymdhet** exhilaration, elation **-räcka** *ta emot ngt med* *-räckta händer* receive s.th. with open arms **-räkna** enumerate **-räkning** enumeration; (*höjning*) adjustment upwards **upprätt** *a4 o. adv* upright, erect; (*helt* ~ *äv.*) perpendicular **upprätt|a 1** (*grunda*) found, establish, set up (*en skola* a school); create (*en befattning* a post); ~ *förbindelser med* establish relations with **2** (*avfatta*) make, draw up (*ett testamente* a will) **3** (*rehabilitera*) rehabilitate; restore (*ngns rykte* a p.'s reputation); retrieve (*sin ära* one's honour) **-ande** *s6* raising, foundation; establishment; drawing-up **-else** reparation, redress; rehabilitation; *få* ~ obtain redress; *ge ngn* ~ make amends to s.b. (*för ngt* for s.th.) **-hålla** (*vidmakthålla*) maintain, keep up, uphold (*disciplin* discipline; *sköta*) hold (*en tjänst* a post); (*hålla i gång*) keep going **-hållande** *s6* maintenance, upholding *etc.* **-hållare** upholder *etc.*; *ordningens* ~ the upholders of law and order **-stående** *a4* upright, erect **upp|röjning** clearance, clearing **-röjningsarbete** clearance work **-röra** *bildl.* stir [up], irritate, disturb, upset **-rörande** *a4* agitating *etc.*; (*starkare*) shocking **-rörd** [-ö:-] *a1* indignant, excited; upset; *bli* ~ *över* be upset about **-rördhet** indignation, irritation; excitement **upp|sagd** *a5* (*om hyresgäst, personal*) under notice; (*om fördrag e.d.*) denounced; *bli* ~ get notice; *vara* ~ be under notice of dismissal **-samla** gather [up], collect **-samling** gathering, collection **uppsamlings|område** (*för evakuerade*) reception area **-plats** collecting centre; assembly point (*äv. mil.*) **uppsats** *s3* **1** (*i bok e.d.*) essay, paper (*om* on); (*i tidning*) article (*om* on); (*skol-*) composition **2** (*uppsättning, sats*) set **-skrivning** composition-writing, essay-writing **upp|satt** *a4* **1** (*om pers.*) exalted, distinguished; *en högt* ~ *person* a person of high station **2** *boktr.* in type **uppseende** attention; (*starkare*) sensation; scandal; *väcka* ~ attract attention (*genom* by) **-väckande** *a4* sensational; startling **upp|segling** *vara under* ~ (*bildl.*) be brewing **-sikt** control, superintendence, supervision; *ha*

~ *över* have charge of, supervise, superintend; *stå under* ~ be under supervision (superintendence) **-sjö** *en* ~ *på* (*bildl.*) an abundance (a wealth) of **-skakad** *a5* upset, shaken, shocked **-skakande** *a4* upsetting, shocking **-skatta** (*värdera*) estimate (*efter* by; *till* at), value; (*sätta värde på äv.*) appreciate (*dugligthet* ability); ~*d till 1 000 pund* valued at 1,000 pounds; ~*t pris* estimated price; *kan inte* ~*s nog högt* cannot be too highly prized **-skattning** estimation, valuation; appreciation **-skattningsvis** approximately, roughly, about **-skjuta 1** (*i tiden*) put off, postpone; (*sammanträde*) adjourn; *parl.* prorogue **2** (*raket*) launch **-skjutning** launch **upp|skov** *s7* postponement (*med* of), delay; (*anstånd*) respite (*med* for); *begära* ~ apply for a term of respite; *bevilja* ~ grant a respite (prolongation); *utan* ~ without delay, immediately, promptly **-skrivning** (*av valuta*) revaluation **-skruvad** *a5* **1** ~*e priser* exorbitant prices **2** wrought-up, worked-up **-skrämd** *a5* startled, frightened **-skuren** *a5* (*om bok*) with the pages cut; ~ *korv* sliced sausage; *-skuret* slices of cold meat **-skärrad** [-ʃ-] *a5* overexcited **-skörta** [-ʃ-] *bli* ~*d* be overcharged (fleeced) **-skörtning** [-ʃ-] swindle, cheating **upp|slag** *s7* **1** (*idé*) idea, project, impulse; *nya* ~ fresh suggestions, new ideas; *ge* ~ *till* give rise to, start, begin **2** (*på kläder*) facing; (*rock-*) lapel; (*ärm-*) cuff; (*på byxor*) turn-up, *AE.* cuff **3** (*i bok*) opening; (*i tidning*) [double-page] spread **-slagen** *a5* (*jfr slå* [*upp*]) **1** opened *etc.*; *som en* ~ *bok* (*bildl.*) like an open book; *med* ~ *rockkrage* with one's collar turned up **2** (*om förlovning*) broken [off] **uppslags|bok** encyclopaedia; reference book **-ord** [main] entry, headword **-rik** full of suggestions, ingenious **-verk** work of reference, reference work **-ända** *bildl.* clue **upp|slamma** silt [up]; *kem. äv.* dredge; ~*d* suspended, muddy **-slitande** *a4, bildl.* heart-rending **-slitsa** split open **-sluka** devour; *bildl.* engulf, absorb; *ett allt* ~*nde intresse* an all-absorbing interest **-sluppen** *a3* **1** (*i söm*) [ripped] open **2** *bildl.* exhilarated, in high spirits, jolly **-sluppenhet** exhilaration, high spirits (*pl*) **-slutning** [-u:-] *mil.* forming (*t. höger* to the right); (*tillströmning*) rallying, assembly **-snabba** speed up **-snappa** snatch (pick) up; ~ *ett ord* catch a word; ~ *ett brev* intercept a letter **-snyggad** *a5* tidied up **-spelning** audition **upp|spelt** [-e:-] *a1* exhilarated, jolly, gay **-spetad** *a5, sitta* ~ be perched (*på on*) **-sprucken** *a5* ripped (split) [up, open] **-spåra** *se spåra* [*upp*] **-spärrad** *a5* wide open; (*om näsborrar*) distended **-stapla** stack **-stekt** [-e:-] *a4* fried-up **-stigande** *s6*, **-stigning** (*jfr stiga* [*upp*]) rise, rising; (*på berg*) ascent; (*på tron*) ascension (*på* to); *flyg.* takeoff, ascent **-stoppad** [-å-] *a5* (*om djur*) stuffed **-stoppare** [-å-] taxidermist **-stoppning** stuffing; taxidermy **-sträckning** *bildl.* rating, telling-off, reprimand; *AE. vard.* calling down **-sträckt** *a4* (*finklädd*) dressed up **-ströms** upstream **-studsig** *a1* refractory, insubordinate **-stud-**

sighet refractoriness, insubordination **-styltad** *a5* stilted, affected; (*svulstig*) bombastic
upp|stå 1 (*-komma*) arise; come up; (*börja*) start **2** (*resa sig*) rise (*från de döda* from the dead) **-stående** *a4* stand-up (*krage* collar) **-ståndelse 1** *bildl.* commotion, excitement **2** (*från de döda*) resurrection **-stånden** *a5* risen **-ställa** (*jfr* ställa [*upp*]); ~ *fordringar* make stipulations; ~ *regler* lay down (establish) rules; ~ *som villkor* state as a condition, make it a condition (*att* that) **-ställning** arrangement; *mil.* formation (*på linje* in line), parade; (*i rad*) alignment; (*lista* o.d.) list, specification; ~*!* fall in!, attention!; ~ *i tabellform* tabular statement **-ställningsplats** *mil.* parade ground **-stötning** [-ö:-] belch; *med.* eructation **-suga** absorb, draw up **-sugningsförmåga** absorbency **-sving** *s7* upswing, rise, upsurge; *hand. äv.* boom **-svullen** *a5*, **-svälld** *a5* swollen; turgescent **-svällning** swelling **-syn 1** (*min*) look[s *pl*], countenance **2** *se uppsikt* **-syningsman** overseer, supervisor; inspector
uppsåt *s7* intent, intention; *i* ~ *att* with the intention of (*skada* damaging); *med ont* ~ with malicious intent; *utan* ~ unintentionally, *jur.* without premeditation; *utan ont* ~ without malice **-lig** [-å:-] *a1* intentional; (*överlagd*) wilful (*mord* murder) **-ligen** [-å:-] purposely, intentionally; ~ *eller av vårdslöshet* (*jur.*) prepensely or negligently
uppsäg|a *se säga* [*upp*]; ~ *ngn tro och lydnad* withdraw one's allegiance from s.b. **-bar** [-ä:-] *a1* subject to notice; (*om kontrakt*) terminable; (*om lån*) redeemable **-else, -ning** [-ä:-] notice; (*av kontrakt*) notice of termination, cancellation; (*av lån*) recalling; (*av fördrag e.d.*) withdrawal; (*av personal*) notice of dismissal (to quit), warning; *med 6 månaders* ~ at 6 months' notice **-ningstid** [period of] notice
upp|sända (*rikta*) offer up (*böner* prayers) **-sätta** *se sätta* [*upp*] **-sättning 1** (*-sättande*) putting up (*etc.*, *jfr* sätta [*upp*]) **2** *konkr.* set, collection; *tekn.* equipment, installation; *teat. o. film.* production, *konkr.* [stage-]setting; *full* ~ *av* full set of **-söka** (*leta reda på*) seek (hunt) out; (*besöka*) go to see, call on
upp|ta[ga] 1 *se ta* [*upp*] **2** (*antaga*) take up; take (*ngn som delägare* s.b. into partnership; *som ett skämt* as a joke); (*mottaga*) receive; (*i förening*) admit; ~*s till behandling* come (be brought) up for discussion; *målet skall* ~*s på nytt* (jur.) the case is to be resumed (to come on again) **3** (*ta i anspråk*) take up (*tid* time; *utrymme* room); engage (*alla ens tanker* all one's thoughts) **-tagen** *a5* **1** *eg.* taken up (*etc.*) **2** (*sysselsatt*) occupied, busy; (*om pers.*) engaged, busy; *jag är* ~ *i morgon eftermiddag* I am (shall be) engaged tomorrow afternoon **3** (*om sittplats*) occupied, taken, reserved; (*om telefonnummer*) engaged, AE. busy; *platsen* (*befattningen*) *är redan* ~ the post has already been filled (is no longer vacant) **4** (*på räkning e.d.*) listed **-tagetsignal** engaged tone, AE. busy signal **-tagning** (*grammofon-, radio-*) recording; (*film-*) filming, taking, shooting **upp|takt** *mus.* anacrusis; *bildl.* beginning, prelude, preamble **-taxera** (*höja taxering*)

raise a tax assessment **-teckna** take down, make a note of; (*folkvisor e.d.*) record, chronicle **-teckning** noting down (*etc.*); *konkr.* record, chronicle **-till** at the top **-tina** thaw **-trampa** tread, beat [out]; ~*d stig* beaten track **-trappa** escalate **-trappning** escalation **-träda 1** (*framträda*) appear (*offentligt* in public); (*om skådespelare äv.*) perform, give performances (a performance); ~ *som talare* speak; ~ *som vittne* give evidence **2** (*-föra sig*) behave [o.s.]; (*ingripa*) act (*med bestämdhet* resolutely); ~ *med fasthet* display firmness; ~ *oärligt* palter **-trädande I** *s6* (*framträdande*) appearance; (*beteende*) behaviour, conduct **II** *a4, de* ~ (*artisterna*) the performers (actors) **-träde** *s6* scene, scandal; *ställa till ett* ~ make a scene **-tuktelse** *ta ngn i* ~ give s.b. a good talking-to, take s.b. to task **-tåg** prank; practical joke; *ha dumma* ~ *för sig* be up to some silly lark **-tågsmakare** practical joker, wag
upp|täcka discover; (*avslöja*) detect, find out; (*uppspåra*) track down; *då* -*tes det att* (*äv.*) it then turned out that **-täckare** discoverer, finder; detector **-täckt** *s3* discovery; (*avslöjande*) revelation; *undgå* ~ (*äv.*) elude detection
upptäcks|färd expedition **-resande** explorer
upp|tända light; *bildl.* kindle, inflame, excite; *-tänd av iver* glowing with zeal; ~ *av raseri* enraged **-tänklig** *a1* conceivable, imaginable; *på alla* ~*a sätt* (*äv.*) in every possible way **-vaknande** [-va:k-] *s6* awakening
uppvakt|a (*hylla*) congratulate, honour; (*göra* [*ngn*] *sin kur*) court, AE. vard. äv. date; (*besöka*) call on; (*tjänstgöra hos kunglig pers.*) attend **-ande** *a4* attentive (*kavaljer* admirer); *de* ~ (*gratulanterna*) the congratulators; ~ *kammarherre* chamberlain-in-waiting **-ning 1** (*-ande*) attendance; waiting upon; (*hövlighetsvisit*) [complimentary, congratulatory] call; *göra ngn sin* ~ pay one's respects to s.b. **2** (*följe*) attendants (*pl*), gentlemen-in-waiting, ladies-in-waiting (*pl*); *tillhöra ngns* ~ belong to a p.'s suite, be in attendance on
uppvigl|a [-i:-] stir up [to rebellion (revolt)] **-are** [-i:-] agitator, instigator of rebellion (*etc.*) **-ing** [-i:-] agitation; instigation **-ingsförsök** attempt to instigate rebellion; attempted mutiny
upp|vilad *a5* rested **-vind** *flyg.* upwind **-visa** (*framvisa*) show, exhibit, display; (*förete*) present, produce (*en biljett* a ticket); (*blotta*) show up (*felaktigheter* errors) **-visande** *s6* showing etc.; *vid* ~ *on* presentation (*av* of); *mot* ~ *av* upon production of **-visning** show; *mil.* exhibition, review **-vuxen** grown up; *han är* ~ *i* he has grown up in **-väcka** raise (*från de döda* from the dead); rouse (*lidelser* passions) **-väga** *bildl.* [counter]balance, weigh against; compensate for, neutralize **-värdera** upgrade **-värma** warm (heat) [up]; *-värmd mat* warmed-up food **-värmning** heating; *sport.* warm-up **-växande** *a4* growing [up]; *det* ~ *släktet* the rising (coming) generation **-växt** growth; *jfr äv. följ.* **-växtmiljö** environment s.b. grew (grows) up in **-växttid** adolescence, youth; *under* ~*en* while growing up
uppåt ['upp-] **I** *adv* upward[s]; *stiga* ~ (*äv.*)

ascend **II** *prep* up to[wards]; ~ *landet (floden)* up country (the river) **III** *oböjligt a* (glad) in high spirits **-böjd** bent upwards **-gående** I *a4* ascending; rising; upward *(tendens* tendency) **II** *s6* ascension; *hand.* rise, hausse; *vara i* ~ be on the upgrade, *(om pris e.d.)* be rising **-riktad** *a5* directed upwards **-strävande** *a4* aspiring; struggling to rise [in the world]; *bildl. äv.* ambitious *(planer* plans) **-vänd** *a5* turned up[wards]
upp|äten *a5* eaten; *vara* ~ *av mygg* be stung all over by gnats **-öva** train, exercise **-över** ['upp-, -'ö:ver] *prep* over; ~ *öronen* head over heels *(förälskad* in love)
1 ur *i uttr.: i ~ och skur* in all weathers, *(friare)* through thick and thin
2 ur I *prep* out of, from *(minnet* memory); *(inifrån)* from within; ~ *funktion* unserviceable **II** *adv* out
3 ur *s7* watch; *(större)* clock; *fröken Ur* speaking clock, *(i Storbritannien äv.)* TIM
uraffär watchmaker's [shop]
uraktlåt|a neglect, omit, fail **-enhet** omission, failure
Uralbergen [u^{x}ra:l-] *pl* the Urals, the Ural Mountains
uralstring spontaneous generation
u'ran *s4, s3* uranium **-bränsle** uranium fuel **-fyndighet** uranium deposit **-haltig** *a1* uranous **-'id** *s3* uranide
ur|arta degenerate; *(friare)* turn *(till* into); ~*d* degenerate[d], depraved **-artning** [-a:-] degeneration **-arva** *oböjligt a, göra sig* ~ renounce all claim[s] on the estate
ur'ban *a1* **1** *(belevad)* urbane, affable **2** ([*stor*]*stads*) urban
urbaniser|ing [-'se:-] urbanization **-ingsprocess** urbanization process
ur|befolkning original population; ~*en (äv.)* the aborigines *(pl)* **-berg** primary (primitive) rock[s *pl*] **-bild** prototype, archetype, original *(för* of)
ur|blekt [-e:-] *a4* faded, *(-tvättad äv.)* washed out; *bli* ~ fade, discolour **-blåst** *a4* gutted *(hus* house) **-bota** *oböjligt a* **1** *jur., ~ brott* felony, capital offence **2** *(oförbätterlig)* hopeless, incorrigible
ur|cell, -djur primeval cell, protozoan
ure'mi *s3* uraemia
urfader first father, progenitor
ur|fånig idiotic **-gammal** extremely old; *(forn)* ancient; *en ~ rättighet* a time-honoured privilege **-germansk** Primitive Germanic
ur|gröpa hollow out; *(-gröpt äv.)* concave **-gröpning** hollow **-holka** hollow [out]; *(gräva ut)* excavate, dig out; *tekn.* scoop [out]; ~*d (äv.)* hollow, concave **-holkning** [-å-] *(-ande)* hollowing out, excavation; *konkr.* hollow, cavity
u'rin *s3* urine **-blåsa** [urinary] bladder **-drivande** *a4,* ~ *[medel]* diuretic **-era** urinate **-förgiftning** uraemia **-glas** urinal **-ledare** ureter
urin[ne]vånare original inhabitant, aboriginal; *pl äv.* aborigines
urin|o'ar *s3* urinal **-prov** specimen of urine **-rör** urethra **-syra** uric acid **-vägsinfektion**

inflammation of the urinary tract
ur|klipp [press] cutting; *AE.* clipping **-klippsbok** scrapbook, press-cutting book **-kokt** *a4* with all the flavour boiled out [of it]; *(friare)* overboiled
urkomisk irresistibly (screamingly) funny
urkoppling *(av maskin)* decoupling, declutching; *elektr.* disconnection, interruption
ur|kraft primitive force; *bildl.* immense power **-kristendom** primitive Christianity
ur|kund *s3* [original] document; record **-kundsförfalskning** forging (forgery) of documents **-källa** *bildl.* fountainhead *(äv. bildl.)*
ur|ladda discharge; *(kamera)* unload; ~*d (om batteri)* dead; ~ *sig (bildl.)* explode, burst **-laddning** discharge; *bildl.* explosion, outburst **-laka** soak; ~*d (kraftlös)* jaded, exhausted **-lasta** unload **-lastning** unloading
urmak|are watchmaker; clockmaker **-eri** *abstr.* watchmaking, clockmaking; *(verkstad)* watchmaker's [shop]
ur|minnes *oböjligt a* immemorial *(hävd* usage); *från ~ tider* from times immemorial (time out of mind) **-moder** first mother, progenitor **-modig** *a1* out-of-date, antiquated, outmoded **-människa** primitive man
urn|a [^{x}u:r-] urn **-lund** *ung.* garden of rest, outdoor columbarium
urnordisk Primitive Scandinavian
urnyckel watch (clock, winding) key
uro|grafi *s3* urography **-log** urologist **-logi** *s3* urology
ur|oxe aurochs **-plock** selection; assortment **-premiär** first performance *(för Sverige* in Sweden)
urring|a *v1* cut out; *(i halsen)* cut low; ~*d (om plagg)* low-necked, *(om pers.)* wearing a low-necked dress **-ning** *abstr.* cutting out; *konkr.* decolletage, neckline, low neck
ursinn|e fury, frenzy; rage **-ig** *a1* furious *(på* with; *över* at); *bli* ~ *(äv.)* fly into a rage (passion)
ur|skilja discern, make out **-skiljbar** *a1* discernible **-skillning** discernment; discrimination; judgement, discretion; *med* ~ *(äv.)* discriminately; *utan* ~ *(äv.)* indiscriminately
urskillnings|förmåga judgement **-lös** indiscriminate
urskog primeval (virgin) forest; *AE.* backwoods *(pl)*; jungle
urskuld|a exculpate; excuse *(sig* o.s.) **-ande** I *a4* apologetic *(min* air) **II** *s6* excuse, exculpation
ursprung *s7* origin; *(friare)* source, root; *(härkomst)* extraction; *leda sitt ~ från* derive one's (its) origin from, be derived from; *till sitt ~* in (by) origin; *av engelskt ~* of English extraction **-lig** *a1* original; primitive; *(okonstlad)* natural, simple **-ligen** originally; primarily **-lighet** originality, primitiveness
ursprungs|beteckning mark (indication) of origin **-bevis** certificate of origin **-land** country of origin
urspår|a run off the rails, derail; *bildl.* go wrong **-[n]ing** derailment
urståndsatt [-^{x}stånd-] *a4* incapacitated, incapable

ursäkt *s3* excuse (*för* for); apology; (*förevändning*) pretext; *anföra som* ~ plead ..., give ... as a pretext; *be om* ~ apologize, make apologies; *be ngn om* ~ beg a p.'s pardon, apologize to s.b.; *framföra sina* ~*er* make one's excuses (apologies) **ursäkt|a** excuse, pardon; ~*!* excuse me!, I beg your pardon!, [I'm] sorry!; ~ *att jag* excuse my (+ *ing-form*); ~ *sig* excuse o.s. (*med att* on the grounds that) **-lig** *a1* excusable, pardonable **urtag** recess, notch; *elektr.* socket, *AE.* outlet **urtavla** dial; clock face **ur|tida** *oböjligt a* primeval, prehistoric; *geol.* pal[a]eontological **-tiden** prehistoric times (*pl*) **-tima** *oböjligt a* extraordinary (*möte* session); ~ *riksdag* (*Storbritannien ung.*) autumn session **-tråkig** extremely dull **-typ** prototype; archetype **uru|guayare** [-ˣgajj-] *s9*, **-guaysk** [-'gajsk] *a5* Uruguayan **ur|uppförande** first (original) performance **-usel** extremely bad; *vard.* abysmal **ur|val** *s7* choice; selection; *hand. äv.* assortment; (*stickprov*) sample; *naturligt* ~ natural selection; *representativt* (*slumpmässigt*) ~ representative (probability) sample; *rikt* ~ large (rich) assortment (selection); ... *i* ~ (*som boktitel*) selections from ... **-valsmetod** selection method **-vattna** soak; ~*d* (*bildl.*) watered down, insipid **urverk** works (*pl*) of a clock (watch); *som ett* ~ (*äv. bildl.*) like clockwork **urvuxen** outgrown **uråldrig** extremely old, ancient **USA** [ˣu:essa:, -'a:] the U.S.[A.] (*sg*) **usans** [u-, y'saŋs] *s3* trade (commercial) custom; *enligt* ~ according to custom **usch** ugh!; *Irl., Sk.* och! **usel** ['u:-] *a2* wretched, miserable; *vard.* abysmal; (*om pers. äv.*) worthless; (*avskyvärd*) execrable; (*moraliskt*) vile, base; (*dålig*) poor, bad (*hälsa* health; *föda* food) **uselhet** wretchedness *etc.*; misery; (*moralisk*) meanness **uselt** *adv* wretchedly *etc.*; *ha det* ~ (*ekonomiskt*) be very badly off **usling** [ˣu:s-] wretch; (*starkare*) villain; (*stackare*) wretch **usurp|ator** *s3* usurper **-era** usurp **U-sväng** (*i trafik*) U-turn **ut** out; *år* ~ *och år in* year in year out; *nyheten kom* ~ (*äv.*) the news got abroad; *stanna månaden* ~ stay the month out; ~*!* get out!, out with you!; ~ *och in* in and out; *vända* ~ *och in på* turn inside out; *inte veta varken* ~ *eller in* not know which way to turn, be at one's wits end; *det kommer på ett* ~ it makes no difference, it is all one; *gå* ~ *i* go out into (*skogen* the woods); *han ville inte* ~ *med det* he wouldn't come out with it; *jag måste* ~ *med mycket pengar* I must pay out a lot of money; ~ *på* out into (*gatan* the street), out on (*isen* the ice); ~ *ur* out of **ut|ackordera** board out, *vard.* farm out **-agerad** *a5*, *saken är* ~ the matter is settled **utan I** *prep* without, with no (*pengar* money); ~ *arbete* out of work; *bli* ~ (*absol.*) have to go (do) without, get nothing; *inte bli* ~ have one's share; ~ *vidare* without further notice (ado),

vard. just like that; *prov* ~ *värde* sample of no value; *det är inte* ~ (*vard.*) it is not out of the question; *det är inte* ~ *att han har* it cannot be denied that he has; ~ *dem hade jag* but (were it not) for them I would have; ~ *att* without (*kunna* being able to); ~ *att ngn märker ngt* without anybody's noticing anything **II** *konj* but; *icke blott* ~ *även* not only ... but [also]; ~ *därför* [and] so **III** *adv* outside; *känna ngt* ~ *och innan* know s.th. inside out **utand|as** *dep* breathe out; exhale, expire; ~ *sin sista suck* breathe one's last [breath] **-ning** expiration, exhalation; *in- och* ~ inhalation and expiration **utanför I** *adv* outside **II** *prep* outside; in front of, before; *sjö.* off (*Godahoppsudden* the Cape of Good Hope); *en som står* ~ an outsider **utan|läsning** recitation by heart **-läxa** lesson [to be] learnt by heart **utannonsera** advertise **utanordn|a** ~ *ett belopp* order a sum of money to be paid [out] **-ing** directions for payment of a sum of money; *konkr.* voucher **utanpå I** *prep* outside, on the outside of; *gå* ~ (*vard.*) beat, surpass **II** *adv* outside **-skjorta** tunic [shirt] **utan|skrift** address [on the cover]; *det syns på* ~*en att han är lärare* you can see by his appearance that he is a teacher **-till** by heart **-tilläxa** (*särskr. utantill-läxa*) *se utanläxa* **-verk** *mil.* outwork, outer work; *bildl.* façade **ut|arbeta** work out; (*förslag e.d. äv.*) draw (make) up; (*sammanställa*) compile; (*omsorgsfullt*) elaborate; (*karta, katalog e.d.*) prepare **-arbetad** *a5* **1** worked out (*etc.*) **2** (*-sliten*) overworked, worn-out **-arbetande** *s6* working out (*etc.*); preparation; *är under* ~ is being prepared, is in course of preparation **-arma** impoverish, reduce to poverty; (*starkare*) pauperize; ~ *jorden* impoverish the soil; ~*d* (*äv.*) destitute **-armning** impoverishment **-arrendera** lease (let) [out] **-arrendering** leasing **ut'av** *se av* **ut|basunera** trumpet forth, blazon abroad **-bedja** *rfl* solicit, ask for, request **-bekomma** obtain (*sin lön* one's salary); obtain access to (*handlingar* documents) **-betala** pay [out, down], disburse **-betalning** payment, disbursement; *göra en* ~ make (effect) a payment **utbild|a** train; (*undervisa*) instruct; (*uppfostra*) educate; *mil. äv.* drill; (*utveckla*) develop; ~ *sig till läkare* study to become a doctor; ~ *sig till sångare* train o.s. to become a singer **-ad** *a5* trained *etc.*; skilled (*arbetare* worker); (*utvecklad*) developed **-ning** training *etc.*; (*undervisning*) instruction; (*uppfostran*) education; *få sin* ~ *vid* (*äv.*) be educated (trained) at; *språklig* ~ linguistic schooling **utbildnings|anstalt** educational (training) institution **-bevis** university course matriculation certificate **-bidrag** study grant; (*för doktorander*) postgraduate grant **-departement** ministry of education; (*i Sverige*) ministry of education and cultural affairs **-linje** study programme **-minister** minister of education; (*i Sverige*) minister of education and cultural affairs **-tid** period of training; apprenticeship **-utskott** ~*et* [the Swedish parliamentary] standing committee on education **ut|bjuda** offer [for sale], put up for sale **-blick** view; perspective **-blommad** *a5* faded **-blottad** destitute (*på* of); *i* *-blottat tillstånd* in a state of destitution **-blåsningsventil** exhaust valve; (*på ångmaskin*) blow-off [valve] **-bombad** *a5* bombed out **-bordare** [-ɔ:-] outboard motor **-breda** spread [out]; expand; (*ngt hopvikt*) unfold; ~ *sig* spread (itself), extend; ~ *sig över ett ämne* expiate upon a subject **-bredd** *a5* [widely] spread, widespread; prevalent (*åsikt* opinion); *med* ~*a armar* with open arms **-bredning** [-e:-] **1** (*-ande*) spreading *etc.* **2** spread, extension, distribution; (*av sjukdom, bruk*) prevalence **-bringa** propose (*en skål* a toast); ~ *ett leve för* cheer for **-brista 1** (*-ropa*) exclaim **2** *se brista 1* **-brodera** *bildl.* deck out **ut|brott** (*-brytande*) breaking out; (*av sinnesrörelse*) outburst (*av vrede* of rage), fit (*av dåligt humör* of temper); (*vulkan-*) eruption; (*krigs-*) outbreak; *komma till* ~ break out **-brunnen** *a5* burnt out; (*om vulkan*) extinct **-bryta 1** (*ta bort*) break out; *mat.* remove; ~ *ur sammanhanget* detach from the context **2** (*om krig, farsot e.d.*) break out **-brytarkung** escapologist, escape artist **-brytning** breaking out; breakout; (*från fängelse*) escape **-bränd** *a5* burnt out **-buad** (*från scenen*) booed off the stage; *hon blev* ~ she was booed, she got the bird **-bud** offer [for sale]; (*tillgång*) supply **-buktad** *a5* bent outwards **-buktning** bulge; protuberance **-byggd** *a5* built out; (*om fönster äv.*) projecting; *-byggt fönster* (*äv.*) bow window **-byggnad** *abstr.* extension, enlargement; *konkr.* annexe, addition **ut|byta** [ex]change (*mot* for); (*ömsesidigt*) interchange; ~ *erfarenheter* (*äv.*) compare notes; ~ *meddelanden* communicate [with each other] **-bytbar** [-y:-] **a1** replaceable; (*ömsesidigt*) interchangeable **-byte** exchange; (*ömsesidigt*) interchange; (*behållning*) gain, profit; *i* ~ in exchange (*mot* for); *få ngt i* ~ *mot* (*äv.*) get s.th. instead of; *lämna ngt i* ~ (*vid köp*) trade in s.th. (*mot* for); *ha* ~ *av ngt* derive benefit from s.th., profit by s.th. **-bär[n]ing** distribution; (*av post äv.*) delivery **-böling** outsider, stranger **-checka** [-çe-] check out **ut|data** *data.* output [data] **-debitera** impose (*skatt* taxes) **-debitering** imposition **-dela** distribute; deal (portion, hand) out; deliver (*post* mail); ~ *order om* give orders for; ~ *slag* deal out (administer) blows **-delning** distribution; dealing out *etc.*; (*av post*) delivery; (*på aktie*) dividend; *extra* ~ bonus, extra dividend; *ge 10% i* ~ yield a dividend of 10%; ~*en fastställdes till* a dividend of ... was declared **-dikning** drainage [by ditches] **-drag** extract, excerpt (*ur* from) **-dragbar** [-a:-] *a1* extensible **-dragen** *a5* drawn out; (*i tid*) lengthy, long [drawn-out] **utdrags|bord** extension table **-skiva** sliding leaf; (*på bord*) [pull-out] slide **-soffa** sofa bed **ut|driva** drive out (*ur* from); (*fack. o. friare*) expel; (*onda andar*) exorcise **-dunsta 1** (*avgå i gasform*) evaporate **2** (*avsöndra*) transpire,

perspire; (*om sak*) exhale (*fuktighet* moisture) **-dunstning** transpiration, perspiration; evaporation **-död** extinct; (*-rotad*) exterminated; (*friare*) deserted (*stad* town) **-döende I** *a4* dying, expiring **II** *s6* dying out; extinction; *är stadd i* ~ is dying out **-döma 1** (*genom dom*) impose (*ett straff* a penalty); adjudge (*ett belopp* an amount) **2** (*kassera*) reject; condemn (*ett fartyg* a vessel); *-dömda bostäder* condemned houses, houses declared unfit for habitation **ute 1** *rumsbet.* out; (*i det fria äv.*) outdoors, out-of-doors; (*utanför*) outside; *där* ~ out there; *vara* ~ *och* be out (+ *ing-form*); *fåren går* ~ *hela året* the sheep are in the open pasture the whole year round; *äta* ~ (*på restaurang*) dine out, (*i det fria*) dine out-of-doors **2** (*slut*) up; *allt hopp är* ~ all hope is gone, there is no hope; *tiden är* ~ [the] time is up; *det är* ~ *med honom* it is all up with him, he is quite done for **3** (*utsatt*) *de har varit* ~ *för en olycka* they met with an accident; *jag har aldrig varit* ~ *för ngt sådant* I have never experienced anything like that; *vara illa* ~ be in a spot **4** (*omodern*) out **ute|bli[va]** (*ej inträffa*) not (fail to) come off, not occur (happen); (*ej infinna sig*) stay away, not turn up (appear, come); ~ *inför rätta* fail to appear in court **-blivande** *s6* absence, failure to attend; *jur.* default **-bliven** *a5* that has failed to appear (*etc.*); (*frånvarande*) absent; ~ *betalning* nonpayment **-bruk** *för* ~ for outdoor use **-dass** *vard.* outside privy, *AE.* outhouse **utefter** ['u:t-, -'eff-] [all] along **ute|grill** outdoor grill **-gångsfår** sheep in open pasture **-gångsförbud** curfew [order] **-lek** outdoor game **-liggare** vagrant, homeless person **-liv 1** (*på restauranger e.d.*) idka ~ go out a lot **2** (*friluftsliv*) outdoor life **-lämna** leave out, omit; (*hoppa över*) pass over **-lämnande** *s6* omission **-löpande** *a4,* ~ *sedelmängd* volume of notes in circulation; ~ *växlar* outstanding bills **utensilier** [-'si:-] *pl* (*tillbehör*) accessories; (*redskap o.d.*) utensils, appliances **uterus** ['u:-] *r* uterus (*pl* uteri) **ute|servering** open-air restaurant (cafeteria *etc.*) **-sluta** *-slöt -slutit* exclude (*ur* from); (*ur förening*) expel; *fack.* eliminate; *det -sluter inte att jag* this does not prevent my (+ *ing- form*); *det är absolut -slutet* it is absolutely out of the question **-slutande I** *a4* exclusive, sole **II** *adv* exclusively, solely **III** *s6* exclusion; expulsion (*ur* from); elimination; *med* ~ *av* with the exclusion (exception) of **-slutit** *sup. av utesluta* **-slutning** [-u:-] *se -slutande III* **-slöt** *imperf. av utesluta* **-spelare** (*anfallsspelare*) forward, (*försvarsspelare*) defender; *alla -spelarna* all the players except the goalkeeper **-stående** *a4* **1** ~ *gröda* standing (growing) crops (*pl*) **2** (*som ej inbetalats*) outstanding; ~ *fordringar* accounts receivable, outstanding claims **-stänga** shut (lock) out; keep out; (*hindra*) debar; (*-sluta*) exclude; *bli -stängd* be shut (locked) out **-stängning** shutting out *etc.*; exclusion; debarment **ut|examinera** examine for the final degree; *AE.*

äv. graduate; *~d* certified, graduate; *bli ~d* pass one's final examination; *~d sjuksköterska* trained (registered, *AE.* graduate) nurse; *han är ~d från* he is a graduate of **-experimentera** discover (find out) by means of experiment
ut|fall 1 *fäkt.* lunge; *mil.* sally, sortie; *bildl.* (*attack*) attack; *göra ett ~* (*mil.*) make a sally, *fäkt.* make a lunge, *bildl.* launch an attack (*mot* against) **2** (*resultat*) result, outturn **3** (*bortfall*) disappearance, dropping out (*av en vokal* of a vowel) **4** (*radioaktivt*) fallout **-falla 1** *se falla ut* **2** (*om lott*) give (*med 100 pund* £100); *~ med vinst* (*om lott*) be a winning ticket; *~ till belåtenhet* give satisfaction; *skörden har -fallit bra* the harvest has been good; *utslaget -föll gynnsamt för oss* the verdict went in our favour
ut|fart 1 (*färd ut*) departure (*ur* from) **2** (*väg ut*) way out, exit; (*från stan*) main road [out of the town] **-fattig** miserably poor; (*utblottad*) destitute; (*utan pengar*) penniless **-fiska** overfish **-flaggning** registration of ships under a flag of convenience **-flugen** *a5, är ~* is (has) flown; *barnen är -flugna* the children have all left home **-flykt** excursion, outing, trip; (*i det gröna*) picnic; *göra en ~* make an excursion, take a trip (*till* to) **-flyktsmål** destination of an excursion; *vårt ~ var Bristol* (*äv.*) we made for Bristol **-flyttning** moving out, removal **-flöde** outflow, discharge, escape; *bildl.* emanation **-fodra** keep, feed (*med* on) **-fodring** [-ɷ:-] feed[ing], keep **-fordra** demand; challenge
ut|forma (*gestalta*) give final shape to, model; (*-arbeta*) work out; (*text e.d.*) draw up, formulate; *~ en annons* design (lay out) an advertisement **-formning** [-å-] shaping *etc.*; working out *etc.* **-forska** find out, investigate, search into; *geogr.* explore **-forskning** investigation; exploration **-frusen** *han är ~* he has been frozen out, he has been sent to Coventry **-frysa** freeze out, send to Coventry **-fråga** question, interrogate; (*korsförhöra*) cross--examine **-frågning** [-å:-] questioning, interrogation; cross-examination; (*av expert inför utskott o.d., äv.*) hearing **-fundera** think (work, find) out **-fyllnad** (*-fyllande*) filling up (in); *konkr.* filling; *bildl.* padding **-fälla** *kem.* precipitate **-fällbar** folding out, collapsible **-fällning 1** (*-fällande*) folding out **2** *kem.* precipitation, deposit **-färd** excursion (*jfr utflykt*)
ut|färda (*-ställa*) make out, draw up; issue (*fullmakt* power of attorney); (*påbjuda*) order, impose; *~ lagar* enact legislation; *stormvarning har ~ts för* a gale warning has been issued for; *~ en kommuniké* issue (publish) a communiqué **-fästa** offer (*en belöning* a reward); promise; *~ sig* promise, engage (*att* to) **-fästelse** promise, pledge **-för** ['u:t-] **I** *prep* down **II** *adv* down[wards]; *det bär* (*sluttar*) *~ it* slopes downhill; *gå ~* descend; *det går ~ med dem* (*bildl.*) they are going downhill
utför|a 1 *se föra* [*ut*] *o.* exportera **2** (*uträtta*) carry out, perform, effect, execute; (*göra*) do; *~ en plan* realize (carry out) a plan; *ett väl -t arbete* a good piece of work **3** *hand.* carry out (*en post* an item); *~ en summa* place (put) a

sum to account **-ande** *s6* **1** *eg.* taking out *etc.*; (*export*) exportation **2** (*uträttande*) carrying out, performance, execution; (*utformning*) design, model **3** (*framföringssätt*) style; (*talares*) delivery **4** *hand.* carrying out **-bar** *a1* practicable, feasible; realizable, executable
utför|lig [-ö:-] *a1* detailed; (*uttömmande*) exhaustive **-lighet** fullness (completeness) [of detail] **-ligt** *adv* in detail, fully; exhaustively
utförsbacke downhill
utförsel *s9* export[ation] **-förbud** export ban **-tillstånd** export licence (permit)
ut|försgåvor *pl* eloquence (*sg*); *han har goda ~* he is very eloquent **-försåkning** (*på skidor*) downhill [skiing]
utförsälj|a sell out (off) **-ning** clearance (closing-down) sale **-ningspris** (*detaljhandelspris*) retail price; (*realisationspris*) bargain (clearance) price
ut|gallring sorting out; (*av skog*) thinning [out]; *bildl.* elimination **-ge 1** *se ge* [*ut*] **2** *rfl, ~ sig för att vara* give o.s. out (pretend) to be **-gift** *s3* expense; *~er* (*äv.*) expenditure (*sg*); *inkomster och ~er* income and expenditure; *stora ~er* heavy expenses (expenditure); *få inkomster och ~er att gå ihop* make [both] ends meet
utgifts|konto expense account **-post** item of expenditure **-sida** debit side; *på ~n* on the debit side **-stat** estimate of expenditure
utgiva *se utge*
utgivar|e 1 (*av skrift*) publisher **2** (*utfärdare*) drawer (*av en växel* of a bill) **-korsband** (*angivelse på försändelse*) Printed Matter Rate
utgiv|en published **-ning** (*av bok*) publication; *under ~* in course of publication **-ningsår** year of publication
ut|gjuta pour out (*äv. bildl.*); shed (*tårar* tears); *~ sig* pour out one's feelings, (*i tal*) dilate (*över* on); *~ sig över* (*äv.*) pour o.s. out about; *~ sin vrede över* vent one's anger upon **-gjutelse** [-j-] pouring out; shedding; *bildl.* effusion **-gjutning** *med.* extravasation, suffusion **-grena** *rfl* branch out **-gräva** *se gräva* [*ut*] **-grävning** excavation
ut|gå 1 *se gå* [*ut*] **2** (*komma*) come, issue, proceed, (*från* from); *bildl.* start (*från* from); *förslaget -gick från honom* the proposal came from him **3** *~ från* (*förutsätta*) suppose, assume, take it, (*ta som ämne för utläggning*) start out from **4** (*betalas*) be paid (payable); *arvode ~r med* the fee payable (to be paid) is **5** (*utelämnas*) *denna post ~r* this item is to be deleted (left out, expunged) (*ur* from) **6** (*gå t. ända*) come to an end, expire **7** *~ som segrare* come off a victor (victorious) **-gående I** *a4* outgoing; *sjö. äv.* outward-bound; *~ balans* balance carried forward **II** *s6* going out; (*utgång*) departure; *på ~* (*sjö.*) outward bound **-gång 1** (*väg ut*) exit; way out **2** (*slut*) end, termination; (*av tidsfrist*) expiration; *vid ~en av 1968* by the end of 1968 **3** (*resultat*) result, outcome, issue; *få dödlig ~* prove fatal **4** *kortsp.* game; *få* (*göra*) *~* score game **-gången** *a5, han är ~* he has gone out; (*slutsåld*) sold out, no longer in stock; (*om bok*) out of print
utgångs|hastighet initial velocity **-läge** initial position, starting point **-material** source (ba-

sic, original) material **-psalm** concluding hymn, postlude **-punkt** starting point, point of departure; *(friare äv.)* basis *(för* of)

ut|gård outlying farm **-gåva** edition **-göra** *(bilda)* constitute, form, make; *(tillsammans ~)* compose, make up; *(belöpa sig t.)* amount to, be, total; *hyran -gör 900 kronor i månaden* the rent is 900 kronor a month; *~s av (vanl.)* consist (be composed) of **-hamn** outport, outer harbour **-huggning** *(skogsbruk)* clearing **-hungra** starve into surrender; *~d* famished, starving **-hus** outhouse **-hyrning** [-y:-] letting [out], renting, hiring [out]; *till ~* for hire; *se äv. hyra* **-hyrningsbyrå** estate agency, house-agent's office

uthållig *al* with staying power; persevering, persistent; tough **-het** *(fysisk)* staying power, stamina, perseverance, persistence; *som ger ~* staminal **-hetsprov** endurance test

uthärd|a endure, stand, bear **-lig** *al* endurable, bearable

ut|i *se i* **-ifrån I** *prep* from [out in] *(gatan* the street); from [out of] *(skogen* the woods) **II** *adv* from outside; *(från utlandet)* from abroad

util|ism utilitarianism **-ist** *s3*, **-istisk** [-'liss-] *a5* utilitarian **-itarism** *se utilism*

ut|jämna level *(äv. bildl.)*, even; *(-släta)* smooth [out]; *(göra lika)* equalize; *hand.* [counter]balance; *~ ett konto* settle an account **-jämning** levelling *etc.*; equalization; *fys. o. bildl.* compensation; *till ~ av (hand.)* in settlement of; *~ av motsättningar* the straightening out of differences **-kant** *(av skog e.d.)* border; *i stadens ~er* in the outskirts of the town **-kast 1** *bildl.* draft *(till* of); sketch; *(t. tavla e.d.)* design; *göra ett ~ till (äv.)* trace [... in outline], design **2** *(i bollspel)* throw-out **-kastare 1** *tekn.* ejector **2** *(ordningsvakt)* chucker-out; *AE.* bouncer

ut|kik [-çi:k] *s2* **1** lookout station, watch tower; *hålla ~* be on the lookout *(efter* for), watch **2** *(-kiksplats på fartyg)* lookout, crow's nest; *pers.* lookout [man] **-kikstorn** lookout [tower] **-klarera** enter (clear) outwards **-klarering** clearance outwards, outward clearance **-klassa** outclass **-klädd** dressed up *(till as a)* **-klädning** [-ä:-] dressing up **-komma** *se komma* [*ut*]; *en nyligen -kommen bok* a recently published book **-kommendera** order out **-komst** [-å-] *s3* living, livelihood **-komstmöjlighet** means of subsistence **-konkurrera** oust, outstrip; *bli ~d* be outclassed (crowded out)

ut|kora elect; *den ~de* the chosen one **-kristallisera** crystallize *(sig* o.s.) **-kräva** claim, require; *~ hämnd* take vengeance *(på* on); *~ skadestånd* demand damages **-kvittera** receipt [and receive]; *(pengar)* cash; *~ en försändelse* give a receipt for a consignment **-kyld** [-çy:-] *a5* chilled down; *rummet är -kylt (äv.)* the room has got quite cold **-kämpa** fight [out]; *strider ~des* battles were fought **-körare** delivery man **-körd** [-çö:-] *a5* **1** *(-jagad)* turned out [of doors] **2** *(-tröttad)* worn out **-körning** [-çö:-] *(av varor)* delivery **-körsport** [-çö:-]

utlandet *best. form, från (i, till) ~et* abroad; *i ~et (äv.)* in foreign countries

utlands|affärer *pl* foreign business *(sg)*

-svensk overseas (expatriate) Swede **-vistelse** sojourn (stay) abroad

ut|led[sen] thoroughly (utterly) tired; *vard.* bored to death *(på* of), fed up *(på* with) **-levad** *a5* decrepit; *(genom utsvävningar)* debauched **-ljud** *språkv.* final sound **-lokalisera** relocate [outside capital] **-lokalisering** relocation [outside capital] **-lopp** outflow; outlet *(äv. bildl.)*; *ge ~ åt* give vent to **-lotsning** piloting out **-lotta** dispose of by lottery; *(obligation e.d.)* draw **-lova** promise

ut|lysa give notice of, publish; *~ ett möte* convene (call) a meeting; *~ nyval* appeal to the country; *~ stejk* call a strike; *~ en tävlan* announce a competition **-låna** lend; *AE.* loan; *~ mot ränta* lend at interest; *boken är ~d* the book is out on loan **-låning** lending; *affärsbankernas ~* the advances of the commercial banks **-låningsränta** lending rate, interest rate for advances (loans) **-låta** *rfl* express o.s. *(om, över* [up]on); *(yttra äv.)* state, say **-låtande** *s6* [stated] opinion, report, statement [of opinion]; verdict; *(från högre myndighet)* rescript; *avge ett ~* deliver (give) an opinion *(om* on, about), present a report (verdict) *(om* on) **-lägg** *s7* outlay; expense[s *pl*], disbursement; *kontanta ~* out-of-pocket expenses **-lägga** *se lägga* [*ut*]; *(förklara)* interpret, comment **-läggning** laying [out]; *(förklaring)* interpretation, comments *(pl)*; *~ av kablar* cable-laying **-lämna** give (hand) out; issue *(biljetter* tickets); *(överlämna)* give up, surrender; *(brottsling t. främmande land)* extradite; *känna sig ~d (bildl.)* feel deserted **-lämning** giving out, distribution, issue; *(av post)* delivery; *(av brottsling)* extradition

ut|ländsk *a5* foreign **-ländska** *s1* foreign woman (lady) **-länning** foreigner **-länningskommission** aliens commission **-lärd** *vara ~* have served one's apprenticeship **-läsa** *(sluta sig t.)* gather, understand *(av* from) **-löpa 1** *(om fartyg)* put to sea, leave port **2** *(gå t. ända)* come to an end, expire; *kontraktet -löper den* the contract expires on **-löpare 1** *bot.* runner **2** *(från bergskedja)* spur; *bildl.* offshoot **-lösa 1** redeem; *(delägare)* buy out; *(pant)* get out of pawn **2** *(frigöra)* release; *(igångsätta)* start, trigger [off] **3** *(framkalla)* bring about, produce, create **-lösning 1** redeeming *etc.*; redemption **2** release; starting *etc.* **3** orgasm **-lösningsmekanism** release

utman|a challenge; *(trotsa)* defy; *~ ngn på duell (äv.)* call s.b. out **-ande** *a4* challenging; defying, defiant; *(om uppträdande)* provocative, *(i sht kvinnas)* enticing **-are** challenger **-ing** challenge *(äv. bildl.)*

ut|manövrera outmanoeuvre **-mark** outlying land

utmatt|ad *a5* exhausted; *vard.* knocked up **-ning** exhaustion

utmattnings|krig war of attrition **-tillstånd** state of exhaustion

ut|med ['ut-, -'me:d] [all] along; *~ varandra* alongside each other, side by side **-mejsla** chisel [out] **-minutera** sell by retail, retail **-minutering** retail sale [of liquors], retailing [of spirits] **-mynna** *(om vattendrag)* discharge (*i* into); (*om gata o.d.*) open out (*i* into); ~ *i* (*bildl.*) end [up] with, result in **-måla** *bildl.* paint, depict **-märglad** [-j-] *a5* emaciate[d], haggard **-märgling** [-j-] emaciation **utmärk|a** (*sätta märke vid*) mark [out]; (*beteckna*) denote; (*angiva*) indicate; (*karakterisera*) characterize, distinguish; (*hedra*) honour; ~ *med rött* indicate (mark) in red; ~ *sig* distinguish o.s. (*äv. iron.*) (*genom* by) **-ande** *a4* characteristic (*för* of); ~ *egenskap* characteristic, distinguishing quality; *det mest* ~ *draget i* (*äv.*) the outstanding feature of **utmärkelse** distinction; honour **-tecken** [mark of] distinction **utmärkt I** *a4* excellent, superb; *vard.* capital, splendid, first-rate, fine **II** *adv* excellently *etc.*; ~ *god* (*äv.*) excellent, delicious, exquisite; *må* ~ feel fine (first-rate) **utmät|a** *jur.* levy a distress (execution); *absol.* distrain **-ning** distraint, distress; *göra* ~ *hos ngn* distrain upon s.b., levy execution on a p.'s property **utmätnings|förfarande** attachment proceedings (*pl*) **-man** [court] bailiff, distrainer **utmönstr|a** (*kassera*) reject, discard **-ing** rejection, discarding **utnyttj|a** utilize, exploit, use; (*t. egen fördel*) take advantage of; ~ *situationen* make the most of the situation; *väl ~d tid* time well spent **-ande** *s6* utilization, exploitation **ut|nämna** appoint (*ngn t. överste* s.b. [a] colonel), nominate, make **-nämning** appointment, nomination **-nötning** wearing out **-nötningskrig** war of attrition **-nötningstaktik** wearing-down tactics (*pl*) **-nött** worn out; *bildl.* hackneyed, well-worn **utochinvänd** inside out **utom** [ˣu:tåm] **1** (*med undantag av*) except, save; with the exception of; *alla* ~ *jag* all except me; *ingen* ~ *jag* no one but me; *vara allt* ~ be anything but, be far from; ~ *att* except that, besides that; ~ *att det är för dyrt är det också* besides being too expensive it is also; ~ *när* except when **2** (*utanför*) outside (*dörren* the door); out of (*fara* danger); beyond (*allt tvivel* all doubt); *inom och* ~ *landet* at home and abroad **3** *vara* ~ *sig* be beside o.s. (*av* with), (*starkare*) go frantic, be transported (*av* with) **-bordsmotor** outboard motor **-europeisk** non-European **utomhus** outdoors, out-of-doors **-antenn** outdoor (open-air) aerial (*AE.* antenna) **-bruk** outdoor use **-grill** barbecue **-sport** outdoor sports (*pl*) **utom|lands** abroad **-ordentlig** extraordinary; (*förträfflig*) excellent; *av* ~ *betydelse* of extreme importance **-ordentligt** *adv* extraordinarily *etc.* **-skärs** [-ʃä:rs] beyond (off) the skerries; in open waters **-stående** *a4, en* ~ an outsider, the uninitiated **-äktenskaplig** extramarital; ~*a barn* illegitimate children **uto'p|i** *s3* utopia; utopian scheme **-isk** [-'tå:-] *a5* utopian **ut|organ** *data.* output device **-peka** point out; ~ *ngn som* indicate (designate) s.b. as **-pinad** *a5* harrowed, harassed; (*starkare*) excruciated **-placera** set out **-plantera** plant out

-plundra fleece, strip **-plåna** obliterate, efface, wipe out (*minnet av* the memory of); (*förinta*) annihilate **-plåning** obliteration; effacing *etc.*; annihilation **-portionera** portion out, distribute **-post** outpost, advanced post **-postera** station, post **utpress|a 1** *eg.* press (squeeze) out **2** ~ *pengar av* extort money from, blackmail **-are** blackmailer; *AE. äv.* racketeer **-ning** blackmail; extortion; *AE. äv.* racket **-ningsförsök** attempted blackmail **-ningspolitik** policy of extortion **ut|pricka** mark out; ~*d farled* buoyed-off fairway **-prickning** marking; *sjö.* beaconage, [system of] buoyage **-prova** test [out], try out; (*kläder*) try on **-provning** test; (*av kläder*) trying on **-prångla** hawk; ~ *falska mynt* utter (pass) base coin **-präglad** [-ä:-] *a5* pronounced, marked, decided **-pumpad** *a5, bildl.* done up, fagged out **-rangera** discard, scrap **-rannsaka** search out, fathom **utred|a 1** (*bringa ordning i*) disentangle; clear up; (*lösa*) solve; (*undersöka*) investigate, inquire into; (*grundligt*) analyse **2** *jur.* (*avveckla*) wind up; (*konkurs*) liquidate **-ning 1** disentanglement; (*undersökning*) investigation, inquest; analysis; *vara under* ~ be under consideration; *för vidare* ~ for further consideration; *offentliga* ~*ar* official reports **2** *jur.* winding up; liquidation **utrednings|arbete** investigation work **-man** investigator, examiner; (*i bo*) executor, administrator; (*i konkurs*) liquidator **ut|rensning** *bildl.* purge, cleanup **-resa** outward voyage (journey) **-resetillstånd** exit permit **-riggad** *a5* outrigged **-riggare** outrigger **utrikes I** *oböjligt a* foreign; *på* ~ *ort* abroad; ~ *resa* journey abroad **II** *adv* abroad; *resa* ~ go abroad **-departement** ~*et* [the] ministry for foreign affairs, *Storbritannien* Foreign Office, *AE.* the State Department **-handel** foreign trade **-handelsminister** minister for foreign trade **-korrespondent** foreign correspondent **-minister** minister for foreign affairs, foreign minister (*Storbritannien* secretary), *AE.* secretary of state **-ministerkonferens** foreign minister's conference **-nämnd** ~*en* the advisory council on foreign affairs, *AE.* the foreign relations committee **-politik** foreign politics (*pl*) (policy) **-politisk** relating to foreign politics (*etc.*); *det* ~*a läget* the political situation abroad **-representation** (*ett lands*) foreign service; (*en firmas*) foreign representation **-råd** head of department [of the ministry for foreign affairs] **-utskott** ~*et* [the Swedish parliamentry] standing committee on foreign affairs **utrikisk** [-'ri:-] *a5* foreign; *tala* ~*a* (*vard.*) speak a foreign lingo **ut|rop 1** exclamation; *ge till ett* ~ *av förvåning* give a cry of (cry out with) surprise **2** (*på auktion*) cry **-ropa 1** (*ropa högt*) exclaim; ejaculate **2** (*offentligt förkunna*) proclaim (*ngn t. kung* s.b. king) **3** (*på auktion*) cry; (*på gatan*) hawk **-ropare** (*på auktion*) crier; (*härold*) herald **-ropstecken** exclamation mark **-rota** eradicate, kill off, root out; (*fullständigt*) extirpate; (*ett folk*) exterminate **-rotning** [-ǝ:-] eradication, killing off *etc.*; extirpation; extermination; (*av folkgrupp*) genocide **-rotnings-hotad** under threat of extermination **-rotningskrig** war of extermination **-rotningsmedel** means of extermination; killer **-rusande** *a4*, *komma* ~ come out with a rush **ut|rusta** equip; (*med vapen äv.*) arm; (*fartyg o.d.*) fit out; (*förse*) furnish, supply, provide; *rikt ~d* (*bildl.*) richly endowed; *vara klent ~d å huvudets vägnar* be weak in the head **-rustning** equipment, outfit; *mil. äv.* kit; *maskinell* ~ machinery, mechanical equipment **-ryckning 1** tearing (pulling) out (*jfr rycka ut*) **2** (*uttåg*) march[ing] out; (*brandkårs etc.*) turnout; *mil.* decampment, departure; (*hemförlovning*) discharge from active service **-ryckningsfordon** rescue vehicle **-rymma** (*bostad e.d.*) vacate, clear out of; *mil.* evacuate; (*överge*) abandon; ~ *rättssalen* clear the court **-rymme** *s6* space, room (*äv. bildl.*); *bildl. äv.* scope; *ge* ~ *för* provide [space, room] for; *kräva mycket* ~ take up room, (*om sak äv.*) be bulky; *ett hus med många ~n* a house with plenty of storage space **utrymmes|besparande** *a4* space-saving **-krävande** requiring much space; bulky **-skäl** *i uttr.: av* ~ from considerations of space **ut|rymning** (*bortflyttning*) removal; (*av lägenhet*) quitting; *mil.* evacuation, abandonment **-räkna** (*beräkna*) calculate; work out (*kostnaden* the cost) **-räkning** calculation, working out; *det är ingen* ~ [*med det*] it is no good (not worth while) **-rätta** do (*en hel del* a great deal); ~ *ett uppdrag* carry out (perform) a commission; ~ *ett ärende* go on (do) an errand; *få ngt ~t* get s.th. done **-rättning** (*ärende*) job, errand, commission **-röna** ascertain, find out; (*konstatera*) establish **utsag|a** *s1* statement; saying; (*vittnesbörd*) evidence, testimony; *enligt hans -o* according to him (what he says) **ut|satt** *a4* **1** *se sätta* [*ut*] *o. utsätta* **2** (*fastställd*) appointed, fixed; *på* ~ *tid* at the appointed time, at the time fixed **3** (*blottställd*) exposed (*läge* position; *för* to); ~ *för kritik* subject[ed] to criticism; ~ *för fara* in danger; ~ *för förkylningar* liable to catch colds **-schasad** *se utsjasad* **-se** choose, select; ~ *ngn till ordförande* appoint s.b. chairman **1 utseende** *s6* (*val*) selecting *etc.*; appointment **2 utseende** *s6* (*yttre*) appearance, look; (*persons*) looks (*pl*); *av* ~*t att döma* to judge by appearances, from the look of him (*etc.*); *ha ett underligt* ~ have an odd look; *känna ngn till* ~*t* know s.b. by sight **ut|sida** outside; exterior; (*fasad*) front **-sikt** *s3* **1** *eg.* view; outlook; *ha* ~ *över* look (open) on to, overlook; *med* ~ *åt norr* facing north **2** *bildl.* prospect; chance, outlook; *ha alla* ~*er att* have every chance of; *ställa ngt i* ~ hold out the prospect of s.th. **utsikts|berg** hill with a [fine] view **-lös** hopeless **-plats** outlook **-torn** outlook tower **ut|sira** decorate, deck out; (*smycka*) adorn **-sirad** *a5* ornamented; ornamental (*bokstav* letter) **-sirning** [-i:r-] ornament[ation]; embel-

lishment **-sjasad** [-ʃ-] fagged out, dog-tired **-skeppa** ship [out]; export **-skeppningshamn** port of shipment **-skjutande** *a4* projecting; (*fram~*) protruding; salient (*hörn* angle) **-skjutning** discharge, firing, shooting; launching **-skjutningsramp** launching pad **1 utskott** [-å-] *s7* (*dålig vara*) rejections, throw-outs (*pl*) **2 utskott** [-å-] *s7* **1** (*kommitté*) committee **2** (*utväxt*) outgrowth **utskotts|behandling** debate in committee **-betänkande** committee report **utskotts|bräder** *pl* rejected deals, waste boards **-porslin** defective china **-varor** *pl* defective (damaged) goods; rejects **-virke** defective [sawn] goods (*pl*); *AE.* defective lumber **ut|skrattad** *a5* laughed to scorn **-skrift** clean (fair) copy; transcription **-skriva** *se skriva* [*ut*] **-skrivning 1** writing out [in full]; (*ren~*) transcription, copying; (*av kontrakt e.d.*) drawing up, making out **2** (*av skatter*) levy, imposition **3** *mil.* conscription, enlistment **4** (*från sjukhus*) discharge **-skuren** *a5* cut out **-skyld** [-ʃ-] *s3* tax; (*kommunal*) rate **-skällning** rating; *vard.* blowing up; *AE. vard. äv.* calling down **-skämd** disgraced **-skänka** serve on the premises **-skänkning** [-ʃ-] serving on the premises **-skänkningslokal** licensed house (premises *pl*), public house **-skärning** [-ʃ-] cutting [out] **ut|slag 1** (*beslut*) decision; *jur.* (*i civilmål*) judgement; (*skiljedom*) award; (*i brottmål*) sentence; (*jurys*) verdict; *fälla* ~ pronounce (give a) verdict; *hans ord fällde ~et* his words decided the matter **2** *med.* rash, eruption; *få* ~ break out into a rash **3** (*på våg e.d.*) turn of the scales, deviation; *mätaren gör* ~ the meter is registering **4** (*resultat*) result, decision; (*uttryck*) manifestation; (*yttring*) outcrop; *ett* ~ *av dåligt humör* a manifestation of bad temper **-slagen** *a5* (*om blomma*) in blossom; (*om träd*) in leaf; (*om hår*) brushed out; (*utspilld*) spilt; *sport.* eliminated **-slagning** [-a:-] *sport.* elimination; (*i boxning*) knockout **utslags|fråga** decisive issue; (*i tävling*) elimination question **-givande** *a4* decisive; *det blev* ~ *för mig* that decided me **-röst** casting vote **-tävlan** elimination (*sport.* knockout) competition (match) **ut|sliten** worn-out; *vard.* jaded, worn-out; (*om uttryck o.d.*) hackneyed, stale; ~ *fras* (*äv.*) cliché **-slockna** go out; (*om ätt*) die out; ~*d* (*äv.*) extinct **-slunga** hurl (fling) out; throw out; ~ *hotelser* threaten **-släpad** *a5*, *bildl.* worn-out; *vard.* dog-tired **-släpp** *s7* discharge (*av olja* of oil) **-släppa** (*sätta i omlopp*) issue, put on the market; (*jfr släppa* [*ut*]) **-smycka** adorn, decorate; deck out; (*försköna*) embellish (*en berättelse* a story) **-smyckning** adornment, ornamentation; embellishment; *konkr. äv.* ornament **-socknes** oböjligt *a* of another parish **-spark** *sport.* goal kick **-spekulerad** *a5* studied; artful, cunning **ut|spel** *kortsp.* lead; *bildl.* move, initiative **-spela** *a5*, *-spelat kort* card played [out] **-spelas** *dep* take place; *scenen* ~ *i* the scene is laid in **-spinna** *rfl* (*om samtal*) be carried on **-spionera** spy out **-spisa** cater; feed **-spisning** catering; feeding **-sprida** spread out; *(friare)* spread *(ett rykte* a rumour); *(utströ äv.)* scatter about **-språng** projection; protrusion; *(klipp-)* jut; *(bergs-)* shoulder **-spy** vomit, belch forth **-späda** dilute, thin [out] **-spädning** [-ä:-] dilution, thinning out **-spänd** spread [out], stretched; *(av luft)* inflated **-spärra 1** spread out, stretch open **2** *(från utbildning)* deny admission, exclude **-spökad** *a5* rigged out, guyed-up

ut|**staka** stake (set, mark, peg) out; *bildl.* lay down; *(föreskriva)* determine, prescribe **-stakad** *a5* marked out; fixed **-stakning** [-a:-] staking out *etc.* **-stansa** stamp (punch) [out] **-stoffera** dress up, garnish; *(berättelse e.d.)* pad out **-stråla** *(utgå som strålar)* [ir]radiate, emit, send forth *(ljus* light); ~ *värme* radiate (emit) heat; ~ *godhet* radiate goodness **-strålning 1** [ir]radiation, emission, emanation **2** *(persons)* charisma

ut|**sträcka** stretch [out], extend; ~ *sig* extend **-sträckning 1** *(-ande)* extension; *(i tid)* prolongation **2** *(vidd)* extent; extensiveness; wideness; *(dimension)* dimensions *(pl)*; *i stor* ~ to a great (large) extent; *i största möjliga* ~ to the fullest possible extent; *i viss* ~ to a certain degree (extent); *använda i stor* ~ make extensive use of, use extensively **-sträckt** *a4* outstretched; extended; *ligga* ~ lie full length *(framstupa* prostrate) **-studerad** *a5* *(raffinerad)* studied, artful; *(inpiskad)* thoroughpaced **-styra** fit out; *(pynta)* dress up, array; *så -styrd du är!* what a fright you look! **-styrsel** *s2* *(utrustning)* outfit; *(bruds)* trousseau; *(t.ex. boks)* get-up; *(förpackning)* package; *(tillbehör)* fittings *(pl)* **-styrselpjäs** spectacular play **-stå** suffer, endure; *(genomlida)* go through **-stående** *a4* protruding, projecting; salient *(hörn* angle); ~ *öron* protruding ears; ~ *kindknotor (äv.)* high (prominent) cheekbones

utställ|**a 1** *se ställa [ut]* **2** *(t. beskådande)* show; *(på -ning)* exhibit, expose, display **3** *(utfärda)* draw, make out; issue *(en växel* a bill) **-are 1** *(av varor)* exhibitor **2** *(av värdehandling)* drawer, issuer **-ning** exhibition, show; display; *(av tavlor äv.)* gallery

utställnings|**föremål** exhibit **-kommissarie** exhibition commissioner **-lokal** showrooms *(pl)*; *(med försäljning)* salesroom

ut|**stöta** *(utesluta)* expel, eject *(ur* from); *(ljud)* utter, emit; *(rökmoln)* puff out; *(om vulkan)* belch out *(lava* lava); *(ur kyrkan)* excommunicate; *vara -stött ur samhället* be a social outcast **-stötning** [-ö:-] ejection; expulsion **-suga** *(jord)* impoverish **-sugare** *pers.* extortioner, bloodsucker **-sugning** sucking out; *(evakuering)* evacuation; *(av jord)* impoverishment; *bildl.* extortion

utsugnings|**anordning** extractor **-ventil** evacuation valve

ut|**svulten** starved, famished **-svängd** *a5* curved (bent) outwards **-svängning** curve **-svävande** *a4* dissipated, dissolute, disorderly **-svävningar** [-ä:-] *pl* dissipation (sg), excesses; extravagances **-syning** rejection, discarding; *(av träd)* marking [out] **-så** sow [out] *(äv. bildl.)* **-såld** sold out; *-sålt (teat.)* all

tickets sold, house full, *AE.* full house **-säde** *s6* [planting] seed, grain **-sända 1** send out; *(utgiva)* publish, issue; *vår -sände medarbetare* our special correspondent **2** *(alstra)* send out, emit *(värme* heat) **3** *(i radio)* transmit, broadcast **-sändning 1** sending out; publication, issue **2** emission **3** transmission, broadcasting

ut|**sätta 1** *(blottställa)* expose, subject *(för* to) **2** *(fastställa)* appoint, fix *(dagen för* the day for) **3** *rfl* expose o.s., lay o.s. open *(för* to); *det vill jag inte* ~ *mig för (äv.)* I don't want to run that risk **-sökning** [-ö:-] *jur.* recovery of a debt by enforcement order **-sökt I** *al* exquisite, choice, select **II** *adv* exquisitely; ~ *fin (äv.)* very choice **-söndra** secrete, excrete **-söndrings-organ** secretory (excretive) organ **-sövd** [-ö:-] *a5* thoroughly rested

uttag 1 *elektr.* socket; *AE.* outlet **2** *(av pengar)* withdrawal; *varorna skall levereras för* ~ *efter köparens behov* the goods are to be delivered at (on) call **utta[ga]** *(jfr ta [ut])* take out; ~ *i förskott* draw in advance

uttag|**are** *(av pengar)* drawer **-bar** [-a:g-] *al* detachable **-ning** *(av pengar)* withdrawal; *sport.* selection **-ningstävling** trial [game]; trials *(pl)*

ut|**tal** pronunciation; *(artikulering)* articulation; *ha ett bra engelskt* ~ have a good English accent **-tala 1** *(frambringa)* pronounce; *(tydligt)* articulate **2** *(uttrycka)* express *(en önskan* a wish) **3** *rfl* speak *(om* of, about); pronounce *(för* for; *mot* against); ~ *sig om (äv.)* comment (express an opinion) on **-talande** *s6* pronouncement, statement; *göra ett* ~ make a statement

uttals|**beteckning** phonetic notation **-lära** phonetics *(pl, behandlas som sg)* **-ordbok** pronouncing dictionary

uttaxer|**a** levy **-ing** levy; *konkr.* taxes *(pl)*

utter ['utt-] *s2* otter **-skinn** otter's skin, otter

ut|**tittad** *a5* stared at **-tjatad** [-ç-] *a5* *(om ämne)* hackneyed; *vara* ~ be fed up **-tjänad** [-ç-] *a5* who (which) has served his *(etc.)* time; *en* ~ *soldat* a veteran **-tolka** *se 2 tolka* **-torkad** [-å-] *a5* dried up (out) **-torkning** drying up; *fack.* desiccation

uttryck expression; *(talesätt äv.)* phrase; *(tecken)* mark, token *(för* of); *stående* ~ set (stock) phrase; *tekniskt* ~ technical term; *ålderdomligt* ~ *(äv.)* archaism; *ge* ~ *åt* give expression (vent) to; *ta sig* ~ *i* find expression in, show itself in; *välja sina* ~ choose (pick) one's expressions

uttryck|**a** express *(en förhoppning* a hope; *en önskan* a wish); *som han -te det* as he put it; ~ *sig* express o.s.; *om jag så får* ~ *mig* if I may be permitted to say so **-lig** *al* express, explicit, definite; ~ *befallning* express (strict) order **-ligen** expressly, explicitly; strictly

uttrycks|**full** expressive; *(om blick, ord)* significant, eloquent **-fullhet** expressiveness **-fullt** *adv* expressively; with expression **-lös** expressionless; vacant, blank *(min* look) **-löshet** expressionlessness, inexpressiveness **-medel** means of expression **-sätt** way of expres-

sing o.s., manner of speaking; style
ut|tråkad *a5* bored [to death] **-träda** *se träda*
[*ut*]; *bildl.* retire, withdraw (*ur* from); ~ *ur* (*äv.*)
leave, resign one's membership of (in) **-träde**
s6 retirement, withdrawal; *anmäla sitt* ~ *ur*
(*förening*) announce one's resignation from
-tränga force aside; *bildl.* supersede, displace
-tröttad *a5* tired out, weary; (*utmattad*)
exhausted **-tröttning** (*uttröttande*) tiring out;
(*trötthet*) weariness, exhaustion **-tyda** interpret; (*dechiffrera*) decipher
ut|tåg march (marching) out, departure; *i sht*
bibl. exodus; *israeliternas* ~ *ur Egypten* the
Exodus **-tåga** march out, depart from **-tänja**
stretch, extend **-tänka** think out; (*hitta på*)
devise **-tömma** empty; *bildl.* exhaust (*sina*
tillgångar one's resources); *hans krafter är*
-tömda he is exhausted, he has no strength left;
han har -tömt ämnet he has exhausted the
subject **-tömmande** *a4* exhaustive,
comprehensive; *behandla* ~ treat exhaustively,
exhaust **-tömning** emptying; exhaustion,
draining; *med.* excretion, evacuation; ~ *av va-*
lutareserven exhaustion of (drain on) the foreign exchange reserves
ut|ur ['u:t-, -'u:r] out of **-vakad** *a5* tired out
through lack of sleep **-vald** chosen; selected
(*verk* works); select (*grupp* group); picked
(*trupper* troops); (*utsökt*) choice **-valsning** rolling out; sheeting **-vandra** emigrate **-vand-**
rare emigrant **-vandring** emigration; (*friare*)
migration
utveckla 1 *se veckla* [*ut*] **2** (*utbilda; klargöra*)
develop (*sina anlag* one's talents; *två hästkraf-*
ter two horsepower; *en plan* a plan); (*lägga i*
dagen) show, display (*energi* energy); *fys.*
generate (*värme* heat); ~ *sina synpunkter* (*äv.*)
expound one's views; *det är ~nde att resa*
travelling broadens the mind; *tidigt ~d* (*om*
barn) advanced for his (her) age **3** *rfl* develop
(*till into; från* out of); (*om blomma, fallskärm*
o. bildl.) unfold ; ~ *sig till* (*äv.*) grow into,
become **utveckling** development; progress;
growth; (*i sht fack.*) evolution; *vara stadd i* ~
be developing; *~en går i riktning mot* the trend
is towards
utvecklings|arbete development work **-bar** *al*
capable of development (progress) **-land**
developing country **-linje** trend **-lära** doctrine
(theory) of evolution; evolutionism **-möjlig-**
het possibility of development **-stadium**
stage of development **-störd** [-ö:-] *a5*
[mentally] retarded **-störning** retardation
utverka obtain, bring about, procure, secure
utvidg|a 1 (*utsträcka*) expand (*ett välde* an empire); (*göra bredare*) widen, broaden; (*göra*
längre) extend; (*förstora*) enlarge; *fys.* expand,
dilate **2** *rfl* widen, broaden; *fys.* expand, dilate;
(*friare*) extend, expand **-ning** expansion; extension; dilation
utvidgnings|förmåga expansive power,
extensibility; (*metalls*) ductility **-koefficient**
coefficient of expansion
utvikning [-i:-] *bildl.* deviation; digression (*från*
ämnet from the subject)
utviknings|blad gatefold, foldout **-brud**
centerfold girl

ut|vilad *a5* thoroughly rested **-vinna** extract,
win **-visa 1** (*visa bort*) send out; (*förvisa*)
banish; (*ur landet*) expel, deport; *sport.* order
off **2** (*visa*) indicate, show; (*bevisa*) prove; *det*
får framtiden ~ time will show **-visning** sending out; banishment; expulsion, deportation;
(*ishockey.*) penalty; (*fotboll.*) ordering off
utvisnings|beslut deportation (expulsion) order
-bås penalty box
ut|vissla *se vissla* [*ut*] **-vissling** hiss, whistle
-väg **1** *bildl.* expedient, resource, way out;
means; *finna en* ~ find some expedient; *jag ser*
ingen annan ~ I see no other way out
(alternative) **-välja** choose [out], select **-väl-**
jande *s6* choice, selection **-vändig** *al*
outward, external **-vändigt** *adv* outwardly; [on
the] outside **-värdera** evaluate **-värdshus**
out-of-town restaurant **-värtes I** *oböjligt a*
external, outward; *för* ~ *bruk* for external use
II *adv* *se* *-vändigt* **-växla** exchange;
interchange **-växling 1** (*utbyte*) exchange;
interchange **2** *tekn.* gear[ing]; *ha liten* (*stor*)
~ be low-geared (high-geared) **-växlings-**
anordning transmitter, gear mechanism **-växt**
outgrowth; protuberance; *bildl.* excrescence,
growth
utåt ['u:t-] **I** *prep* out into (towards); *fönstret*
vetter ~ *gatan* the window looks out onto the
street **II** *adv* outward[s]; *gå* ~ *med fötterna*
walk with one's toes turned out **-böjd** bent
outwards **-riktad** *a5* turned outwards,
out-turned; *bildl.* extrovert, outgoing
ut|ägor *pl* outlying fields **-öka** increase; extend,
expand; enlarge; *~d upplaga* enlarged edition
-ösa *bildl.* shower [a torrent of] (*ovett över*
abuse upon); ~ *sin vrede över* vent one's anger
upon
utöva (*bedriva*) carry on (*ett hantverk* a trade);
practise (*ett yrke* a profession); (*verkställa*)
exercise (*kontroll* control; *rättvisa* justice);
exert (*tryck* pressure); ~ *befäl* hold (exercise)
command; ~ *hämnd* take vengeance (*mot*
upon); ~ *inflytande på* exercise (exert)
influence on, influence; ~ *kritik* criticize; ~
värdskapet act as host **utövande I** *s6* exercise,
performance, execution **II** *a4* executive; ~
konstnär creative artist **utövare** practiser,
practician
utöver [-'ö:-, 'u:t-] *prep* [over and] above,
beyond; *gå* ~ exceed
utövning *se utövande I*
uv *s2* [great] horned owl
uver'tyr *se ouvertyr*
uvu'lar I *al* uvular **II** *s3* uvular

V

va *vard.* what?
vaccin [vak'si:n] *s4, s9* vaccine **-ation** vaccination **-ationstvång** compulsory vaccination **-era** vaccinate; inoculate **-ering** vaccination
vacker ['vack-] *a2* **1** beautiful; (*i sht om man*) handsome; (*förtjusande*) lovely; (*söt*) pretty; (*storslagen*) fine; (*tilltalande*) nice; (*fager*) fair; ~ *som en dag* [as] fair as a day in June; ~t *väder* beautiful (lovely) weather; *vackra lovord* high praise (*sg*); *en* ~ *dag* (*bildl.*) one fine day **2** (*ansenlig*) handsome (*summa* sum); *det är* ~t *så!* [it is] pretty good at that!, fair enough! **3** *iron.* fine, pretty
vackert *adv* **1** beautifully *etc.*; *huset ligger* ~ the house is beautifully situated; *det var* ~ *gjort av dig* it was a fine thing of you to do; *det där låter* ~ that sounds well; ~*!* (*vard.*) well done!, marvellous! **2** *iron.* nicely, prettily; *jo* ~*!* I should think so!, not likely!; *som det så* ~ *heter* as they so prettily put it **3** *det låter du* ~ *bli!* you will just not do so!; *du stannar* ~ *hemma!* you just stop at home!; *sitt* ~*!* (*t. hund*) beg!
vackl|a totter; (*ragla*) stagger; *bildl.* falter, waver, vacillate; *bruket* ~*r* the usage varies; *han* ~*de fram* he staggered along; ~ *hit och dit* (*äv.*) sway to and fro **-an** *r* wavering, vacillation; (*obeslutsamhet*) irresolution, indecision **-ande** *a4* tottering *etc.*; (*om hälsa*) uncertain, failing; *hans hälsa börjar bli* ~ his health is beginning to give way
1 vad *s3, s1* (*på ben*) calf (*pl* calves) [of the leg]
2 vad *s2* (*fisknot*) seine [net]; *fiska med* ~ seine
3 vad *s7, jur.* [notice of] appeal; *anmäla* ~ give notice of (lodge an) appeal
4 vad *s7* (*avtal*) bet (*om en summa* of a sum; *om resultatet* on the result); *slå* ~ bet, make a bet; *det kan jag slå* ~ *om* I['ll] bet you; *jag slår* ~ *om ett pund* I['ll] bet you one pound
5 vad *s7, se* vadställe
6 vad I *pron* **1** *interr.* what; ~*?* [I beg your] pardon?, *vard.* what?; *vet du* ~*!* I'll tell you what!; *nej,* ~ *säger du!* really!, well, I never!; ~ *nytt?* any news?; ~ *för en* what; ~ *för* [*en*] *bok* what book; ~ *för slag?* what?; ~ *är det för slags bok?* what kind of a book is that?; ~ *gråter du för?* why are you crying?, what are you crying for?; ~ *har du för anledning att* what reason have you for (+ *ing*-form); *jag vet inte* ~ *jag skall göra* I don't know what to do; ~ *är det?* what is the matter?; ~ *är det för dag i dag?* what day is it today? **2** *rel.* (*det som*) what; ~ *mig beträffar* as far as I am concerned; ~ *som är viktigt är att* the important thing is that; ~ *som helst* anything [whatever]; ~ *som än händer* whatever happens; ~ *värre är* what is [even] worse; *inte* ~ *jag vet* (*vard.*) not as far as I know **II** *adv* how (*du är snäll!* kind you are!)

vada wade (*över* across); ~ *över en flod* (*äv.*) ford a river; *han* ~*r i pengar* he's wallowing in money
vadan *åld., se* varifrån, varför
vadar|e, -fågel shore bird, wader
vadben splint bone, fibula
vadd *s2* wad[ding]; (*bomulls-*) cotton wool; *AE.* absorbent cotton; (*fönster-*) padding **-era** wad, pad; (*täcke, morgonrock etc.*) quilt **-ering** wadding, padding; (*med stickningar*) quilting **-täcke** quilt
vadeinlaga [document (notice) of] appeal
vadhelst [-'helst, 'va:d-] whatever
vadhåll|are better, backer **-ning** betting, wagering
vadmal [ˣvadd-, ˣva:d-] *s3, s4* rough homespun; frieze; russet
vadslagning [-a:g-] betting
vadställe ford[able place]
va'falls [I beg your] pardon?
vag *a1* vague; indistinct, undefined, hazy
vagabond [-'bånd, -'båŋd] *s3* vagabond, tramp; *AE. äv.* hobo; *jur.* vagrant **-era** vagabondize; *be* (go) *on the tramp* **-liv** vagabond life
1 vagel ['va:-] *s2* (*i ögat*) sty[e] (*pl äv.* sties)
2 vagel ['va:-] *s2* (*sittpinne*) perch, roost
vagg|a I *s1* cradle; *från -an till graven* from the cradle to the grave **II** *v1* rock (*i sömn* to sleep); (*svänga, vicka*) swing; (*gå* ~*nde*) waddle; ~*nde gång* rocking (waddling) gait **-visa** lullaby
vagn [vaŋn] *s2* **1** carriage; *AE.* car (*äv. järnv. person-*); (*större, gala-*) coach; (*last-, gods-*) wag[g]on, *AE.* car; (*kärra*) cart; *häst och* ~ a horse and carriage; (*direkt*) *genomgående* ~ (*järnv.*) through carriage **2** *fackl.* (*på kran*) trolley **-makare** coach-maker, coach-builder; cartwright **-makeri** (*tillverkning*) carriage-making, coach-building; (*verkstad*) carriage works (*sg o. pl*) **-park** *järnv.* rolling stock; (*bil-, buss-*) fleet [of cars (buses)]
vagns|axel axletree **-hjul** carriage (car) wheel
vagnskadeförsäkring insurance against material damage to a motor vehicle
vagns|korg carriage (wag[g]on) body **-last** cartload, carriage load; *järnv.* wag[g]onload, truckload **-lider** coach house
vagn|sätt *järnv.* train [of coaches]
vaja [ˣvajja] *v1* float, fly; (*fladdra*) flutter, stream
vajer ['vajj-] *s2* cable, wire
vak *s2* (*is-*) hole in the ice, ice hole
vaka I *s1* vigil, watch; (*lik-*) wake **II** *v1* **1** (*hålla vakt*) watch (*hos ngn* by a p.'s bedside); keep watch; (*hålla sig vaken*) stay up; ~ *över ngn* watch (keep watch) over s.b. **2** *sjö.* (*om båt*) ride
vak|ans [-'kans, -'kaŋs] *s3* vacancy **-ant** *a4* vacant, unoccupied
vakare *sjö.* buoy
vaken *a3* (*ej sovande*) *predik.* awake; *attr.* waking; (*uppmärksam*) observing, noticing (*barn* child); (*pigg*) wide-awake, brisk; (*mottaglig*) open (*blick* eye), alert (*sinne* mind); *i vaket tillstånd* when awake **-het** wakefulness; *bildl.* alertness
vak|na [ˣva:k-] wake [up], awake; *bildl. äv.* awaken; ~ *till besinning* come to one's sen-

ses; ~ *till medvetande* become conscious (*om of*); regain consciousness; ~ *på fel sida* get out of bed on the wrong side **-natt** wakeful night **vaksam** [ˣva:k-] *a1* watchful (*blick* eye); vigilant; on the alert **-het** watchfulness; vigilance **vakt** *s3* **1** (*-hållning*) watch (*äv. sjö.*); *mil.* guard, duty; *gå på* ~ mount guard, go on duty; *ha ~en* be on duty; *hålla* ~ keep watch, be on guard (duty); *slå* ~ *om* (*bildl.*) stand up for (*friheten* liberty), keep an eye on; *vara på sin* ~ be on one's guard (on the alert); *inte vara på sin* ~ be off one's guard **2** *pers.* guard, watchman; (*patrullerande*) *BE. äv.* roundsman; *mil.* sentry; (*-manskap*) [men (*pl*) on] guard, *sjö.* watch; *avlösa ~en* relieve the guard **vakt|a 1** (*bevaka*) guard; watch over, look after (*barn* children); ~ *får* tend (herd) sheep; ~ *på* watch **2** (*hålla vakt*) keep guard (watch) **3** *rfl, se akta 2* **-are** watcher, guardian; (*bro-, djur-e.d.*) keeper **-arrest** close arrest **-avlösning** changing of the guard **vaktel** *s2* quail **vakt|havande** *a4* on duty; *sjö. äv.* of the watch **-hund** watchdog **-hållning** patrol, patrolling; guard[ing] **-kur** sentry box **-man** *BE.* (*patrullerande*) roundsman **-manskap** [men (*pl*) on] guard **-mästare 1** (*vid ämbetsverk*) messenger; (*på museum*) attendant; (*skol-*) porter; *univ.* beadle; (*dörr-*) doorkeeper; (*platsanvisare*) usher; (*uppsyningsman*) caretaker **2** (*kypare*) waiter **-ombyte** changing of (relieving) the guard; ~[*t*] *sker kl.* the guard is relieved at **-parad** changing of the guard **-post** *se vakt 2* **-tjänst** guard (*sjö.* watch) duty **-torn** watchtower **vakuum** ['va:kum] *s8* vacuum **-förpackad** *a5* vacuum-packed **-förpackning** vacuum pack **-torkad** [-å-] *a5* vacuum-dried (*potatis* potatoes) **1 val** *s2, zool.* whale; ~*ar* (*koll.*) cetaceans **2 val** *s7* **1** (*väljande*) choice; (*ur-*) selection; *efter eget* ~ at one's own option, according to choice; *fritt* ~ option, free choice; *göra ett bra* ~ (*äv.*) choose well; *göra sitt* ~ make one's choice; *jag hade inget annat* ~ I had no alternative; *vara i ~et och kvalet* be in two minds (*om man skall gå el. inte* whether to go or not) **2** (*offentlig förrättning*) election; *allmänna* ~ general election (*sg*); *förrätta* ~ hold an election; *gå till* ~ go to the polls; *tillsatt genom* ~ elected, elective **valack** [-'lack, 'vall-] *s3* gelding **val|affisch** election poster **-agitation** electioneering; canvassing **-arbetare** electioneer **valbar** [ˣva:l-] *a1* eligible (*till* for); *ej* ~ ineligible **-het** eligibility **valberättigad** entitled to vote; *en* ~ an elector; *de ~e* the electorate (*sg*) **valborgsmässo|afton** [-bårjs-] Walpurgis night **-eld** bonfire on Walpurgis night **valbyrå** election office **val|d** [-a:-] *a5* chosen, selected; *några väl ~a ord* a few well-chosen words; ~*a skrifter* selected works **-dag** polling (election) day **-de** [-a:-] *imperf. av* välja **-deltagande** poll[ing], participation in the election; *stort* (*litet*) ~ heavy (low) polling **-distrikt** electoral (voting)

district (*AE.* precinct) **va'lens** *s3* valency; *AE.* valence **valeriana** [-ˣa:na] *s1* valerian **wales|are** [ˣœejls-] Welshman **-isk** ['œejls-] Welsh **-iska** ['œejl-] *s1* **1** (*språk*) Welsh **2** (*kvinna*) Welshwoman **valfisk** *åld.* whale **val|fiske** *vard.* fishing for votes, electioneering **-fläsk** election promise[s *pl*], bid for votes **-fri** optional; discretionary; ~*tt ämne* (*skol.*) optional subject, *AE.* elective **-frihet** [right of] option, freedom of choice **-fusk** electoral rigging **val|fångare** whaler; (*fartyg äv.*) whaling ship **-fångst** whaling **val|förrättare** election supervisor **-hemlighet** secrecy of the polls **valhänt** [-a:-] *a4* numb[ed]; *bildl.* awkward, clumsy (*försök* attempt), lame (*ursäkt* excuse); *vara* ~ (*eg.*) have numb hands **-het** numbness in the (one's) hands; *bildl.* clumsiness *etc.* **validitet** validity **valk** *s2* **1** (*förhårdnad*) callus, callosity **2** (*hår-*) pad; (*fett-*) roll of fat **valka** mill, full **valkampanj** election campaign **valkig** *a1* callous; horny **valkokeri** [whale] factory ship **val|konung** elective king **-krets** constituency **valkyria** [-ˈky:-] *s1* Valkyr[ie], Walkyrie **1 vall** *s2* (*upphöjning*) bank, embankment; (*strand-*) dike, dyke; *mil.* rampart **2 vall** *s2* (*slåtter-*) ley, temporary pasture; (*betes-*) pasture [ground (land)]; *driva i* ~ turn out to grass; *gå i* ~ be grazing **1 valla** *v1* tend (*boskap* cattle); (*vakta*) watch, guard; (*brottsling*) take to the scene of the crime **2 valla I** *s1* (*skid-*) ski wax **II** *v1* wax **vallag** electoral (election) law; *Storbritannien* Reform (Representation of the People) Act **vallar|e** herdsman, tender **-låt** *se vallvisa* **wallboard** ['vå:lbå:rd, 'œå:l-] *s3* fibreboard; (*hård*) hardboard; (*porös*) insulation fibreboard **vall|fart** pilgrimage **-fartsort** resort of pilgrims, shrine; *bildl.* Mecca **vallflicka** herdsmaid, shepherdess **vallfärda** go on a pilgrimage **vallgrav** moat, foss[e] **vall|horn** herdsman's horn **-hund** shepherd's dog; (*ras*) sheepdog, collie **vallmo** *s5* poppy **-frö** poppy seed **vallokal** polling station (place); poll[s *pl*] **val'lon** *s3*, **-sk** [-œ:-] *a5* Walloon **vall|pojke** shepherd boy **-visa** herdsman's song **vallväxter** *pl* pasture (ley) plants **vall|längd** electoral register **-löfte** electoral promise **vallört** comfrey **val|man** elector; voter **-manskår** electorate **-metod** voting method **-möte** election meeting **-nederlag** defeat [at the polls (elections)] **-nämnd** election (electoral) committee; ~*ens ordförande* (*ung.*) the returning officer **valnöt** walnut **valp** *s2* pup[py]; (*pojk-*) cub **valp|a** whelp **-aktig** *a1* puppyish

valplats field [of battle]
val|program election program[me]; platform **-propaganda** election propaganda
valpsjuka canine distemper
valrav [ˣvaːl-] *s3* spermaceti
valresultat election result[s *pl*] (returns *pl*)
valross [ˣvaːlråss] *s2* walrus; morse
valrörelse electioneering, election campaign
1 vals *s2* (*cylinder*) roll[er]; cylinder (*äv. skrivmaskins-*)
2 vals *s3* (*dans*) waltz
1 valsa *v1* (*dansa*) waltz
2 valsa *v1* (*låta passera genom valsar*) roll; (*plåt äv.*) laminate, sheet; *~t järn* rolled (sheet) iron; *~t stål* rolled (laminated) steel
val|sedel ballot [paper], voting paper **-seger** election victory
vals|formig [-å-] *a1* cylindrical **-järn** rolled iron
valskolkare [-å-] abstainer
vals|kvarn roller mill **-ning** rolling; lamination
valspråk motto, device
valstakt *i ~* in waltz-time
valsverk rolling mill
val|sätt electoral system; *proportionellt ~* proportional representation
valt [-aː-] *sup. av välja*
valtal election address (speech) **-are** election speaker
valthorn French horn **-blåsare** French-horn player
valurna ballot box
valuta [-ˣluː-] *s1* (*myntslag*) currency; *inhemsk ~* domestic currency; *utländsk ~* foreign exchange (currency); *~ bekommen* value received; *få ~ för* get good value for; *få ~ för sina pengar* (*äv.*) get one's money's worth **-bestämmelser** currency (*för utländsk valuta:* foreign exchange) regulations; *brott mot ~na* exchange control offences **-fond** monetary fund **-handel** exchange dealings (*pl*), foreign exchange **-kontor** [foreign] exchange control office **-kontroll** [foreign] exchange control **-kurs** rate of exchange **-marknad** foreign exchange market **-reserv** foreign exchange reserve[s *pl*] **-restriktioner** currency (*för utländsk valuta:* [foreign] exchange) restrictions **-tilldelning** [foreign] exchange allocation **-tillgångar** foreign exchange holdings
valv *s7* vault (*äv. bank-*); arch; *skeppsb.* counter **-båge** arch **-gång** archway **-konstruktion** arch vault[ing]
valör value; (*på sedlar o.d.*) denomination
vamp *s2, s3*, **vampa** vamp **vam'pyr** *s3* vampire
van *a5* (*övad*) practised, experienced; (*skicklig*) skilled; *han är gammal och ~* he's an old hand [at]; *vara* (*bli*) *~ vid* be (get) used (accustomed) to (*att* + *ing-form*); *bara man blir litet ~* (*äv.*) once you get into the knack of it; *med ~ hand* with a deft (skilled) hand
van|a *s1* (*sed, bruk*) custom; (*persons*) habit; (*erfarenhet*) experience (*vid* of); (*övning*) practice; *~ns makt* the force of habit; *ha dyrbara -or* have expensive habits; *av gammal ~* by force of habit, from [mere] habit; *sin ~ trogen* as is one's wont; *bli en ~* become a habit (*hos ngn* with s.b.); *ha ~n inne att* be used to;

ha för ~ att be in the habit of (+ *ing-form*)
vana'din *s4, s3* vanadium
vanart [ˣvaːn-] bad disposition; (*starkare*) depravation
vanartig *a1* depraved, demoralized; vicious **-het** depravity, depravation
van'dal *s3* vandal **-isera** vandalize **-ism** vandalism
vande [ˣvaːn-] *imperf. av vänja*
vandel [ˈvann-] *s9* conduct, behaviour, mode of life; *föra en hederlig ~* lead an honourable life
vandr|a walk (*äv. bildl.*); ramble, hike; (*ströva*) wander, stroll, rove, roam (*omkring* about); (*om djur, folk*) migrate **-ande** *a4* wandering; (*kring-*) itinerant, ambulatory; travelling (*gesäll* journeyman); (*flyttande*) migratory; *den ~ juden* the Wandering Jew; *~ blad* (*zool.*) leaf insect; *~ njure* floating kidney; *~ pinne* (*zool.*) stick insect, *AE.* walking stick
vandrar|e wanderer **-folk** nomadic (migratory) people **-hem** youth hostel
vandring wandering; (*kortare*) walk[ing tour]; (*genom livet*) way; (*folk-, djur-*) migration
vandrings|bibliotek travelling library **-lust** longing to travel, wanderlust **-man** *se vandrare* **-pokal** challenge cup **-pris** challenge prize **-utställning** travelling (touring) exhibition
vane|bildande *a4* habit-forming; addictive **-djur** creature of habit **-drinkare** habitual drinker **-förbrytare** habitual criminal; *vard.* jailbird **-människa** *se -djur* **-mässig** *a1* habitual, routine **-rökare** habitual smoker **-sak** matter of habit **-tänkande** *s6* thinking in grooves
van|fejd *s3* dishonour; infamy **-för** *a5* disabled, crippled, lame; (*en ~*) cripple, disabled person **-föreställning** misconception, wrong idea, false notion **-heder** dishonour, disgrace **-hedra** dishonour, disgrace; be a disgrace to **-hedrande** disgraceful, ignominious, dishonouring **-helga** profane, desecrate **-helgande a4** profaning, desecrating **-helgd** profanation, desecration; (*av kyrka e.d. äv.*) sacrilege **-hävd** neglect; *komma i ~* go (run) to waste; *ligga i ~* lie waste
va'nilj *s3* vanilla **-glass** vanilla ice **-sås** vanilla sauce; (*tjock äv.*) custard
vanillinsocker [-ˣliːn-] vanillin sugar
vank *r, utan ~* flawless; *utan ~ och lyte* without defect or blemish
vanka [*gå och*] *~* saunter (wander) (*omkring* about)
vanka|s *dep, det -des kakor* we (*etc.*) were treated to biscuits; *det ~ stryk* he (*etc.*) is in for a thrashing
vankelmod irresolution, indecision; hesitation; (*ombytlighet*) inconstancy **-ig** irresolute, inconstant; vacillating
vanlig [ˣvaːn-] *a1* **1** (*som sker efter vanan*) usual (*hos* with); habitual (*sysselsättning* occupation); (*bruklig*) customary; *det är det ~a* that's the usual thing; *på ~ tid* at the usual v–time; *på sin ~a plats* in its (*etc.*) usual place; *som ~t* as usual; *bättre än ~t* better than usual **2** (*ofta förekommande*) common (*blomma* flower; *fel* mistake; *namn* name); frequent

V

(*missuppfattning* misconception); (*allmän*) general (*uppfattning* belief); (*alldaglig, vardags-*) ordinary (*mat* food; *folk* people), *dial.* ornery; *mindre* ~ less (not very) common; *~t bråk* simple (vulgar, common) fraction; *vi ~a dödliga* we ordinary mortals; *den gamla ~a historien* the same old story; *~a människor* (*äv.*) the common run of people; *den ~a åsikten bland* the opinion generally held by; *i ~a fall* as a rule, ordinarily, in ordinary cases; *i ordets ~a bemärkelse* in the ordinary sense of the word; *på ~t sätt* in the ordinary (usual) manner (way) **vanligen** usually, generally; as a rule **vanlighet** usualness, frequency; *efter ~en* as usual; *mot ~en* contrary to the (his *etc.*) usual practice; *det hör inte till ~erna att* it is not very common that

vanligt *adv* usually *etc.* **-vis** *se vanligen*

van|lottad [-å-] *a5* badly off (*i fråga om* as regards) **-makt 1** (*medvetslöshet*) unconsciousness; *falla i ~* have a fainting-fit, faint, swoon **2** *bildl.* impotence; powerlessness **-mäktig 1** unconscious, fainting **2** impotent; powerless, vain

vann *imperf. av vinna*

vanna I *s1* **1** (*sädes-*) fan **2** (*glastillv.*) tank furnace **II** *v1* (*säd*) fan, winnow

van|pryda disfigure, spoil the look of **-prydnad** disfigurement **-ryktad** *a5* notorious, ill-famed **-rykte** disrepute, bad repute; discredit **van|sinne** insanity; mental disease; (*galenskap*) madness; *driva ngn till ~* drive s.b. mad (crazy); *det vore rena ~t* it would be insane (sheer madness) **-sinnig** *a1* insane; (*tokig*) crazy; (*galen*) mad; *bli ~* go mad; *det är så man kan bli ~* it is enough to drive one mad **-sinnigt** *adv* insanely; crazily; madly; (*förstärkande*) awfully, terribly; *~ roligt* awfully funny; *~ förälskad* madly in love **-skapt** [-a:-] *a4* deformed, misshapen

vansklig *a1* (*osäker*) hazardous, risky (*företag* enterprise); (*tvivelaktig*) doubtful; (*brydsam*) delicate (*uppgift* task); (*svår*) awkward

van|sköta mismanage, neglect; *trädgården är -skött* the garden is not looked after properly; *~ sig* be neglectful; *~ sin hälsa* neglect one's health **-skötsel** mismanagement; negligence; *av ~* for (from) want of proper care **-släktad** *a5* degenerate[d] **-släktas** *dep* degenerate **-styre** misrule **-ställa** disfigure, deform; (*friare*) spoil [the look[s] of], (*förvrida*) distort

1 vant *s7, s4, sjö.* shroud

2 vant [-a:-] *sup. av vänja*

vant|e *s2* (*finger-*) woollen (cotton) glove; (*tum-*) mitt[en]; *lägga -arna på* (*bildl.*) lay hands [up]on; *slå -arna i bordet* (*bildl.*) put the shutters up

van|tolka misinterpret; misconstrue **-trivas** *dep* feel ill at ease (uncomfortable); not feel at home; get on [very] badly (*med ngn* with s.b.); (*om djur, växter*) not thrive; *jag -trivs med mitt arbete* I am not at all happy in my work **-trivsel** discomfort, unhappiness; (*djurs, växters*) inability to thrive **-tro** false belief; disbelief **-vett** insanity; mania; *det vore rena ~et att* it would be sheer madness to **-vettig** *a1* mad; absurd, wild **-vård** neglect, negligence,

mismanagement **-vårda** *se vansköta* **-vördig** disrespectful (*mot* to); (*mot ngt heligt*) irreverent (*mot* to) **-vördnad** disrespect; irreverence **-ära I** *s1* dishonour, disgrace; (*skam*) shame, ignominy; *dra ~ över* bring shame (disgrace) upon **II** *v1* dishonour, disgrace

vapen ['va:-] *s7* **1** weapon; *koll.* arms (*pl*); *bära* (*föra*) ~ carry arms; *gripa till ~* take up arms; *med ~ i hand* weapon in hand; *nedlägga vapnen* lay down [one's] arms, surrender; *slå ngn med hans egna ~* beat s.b. at his own game **2** *her.* (*-märke*) arms (*pl*), coat of arms **-bragd** feat of arms; (*friare*) military achievement **-broder** brother-in-arms **-brödraskap** brotherhood of arms **-bärare** weapon carrier **-dragare** *hist.* armour-bearer; *bildl.* supporter **-fabrik** armament factory **-fri** ~ *tjänst* unarmed national (military) service **-för** *a5* fit for military service **-föring** handling (wielding) of a weapon **-förråd** armoury, arsenal **-gny** clash of arms, din of battle **-gren** fighting service, branch of the armed forces **-gömma** concealed store of arms (weapons)

vapen|handel trading in arms; armaments trade **-handlare** arms dealer **-hjälp** arms assistance **-hus** [church] porch **-licens** licence for carrying arms, firearms (*AE.* gun) licence **-lös** unarmed **-makt** (*med* by) force of arms **-rock** tunic **-samling** collection of arms **-skrammel** *bildl.* show of arms **-sköld** coat of arms, escutcheon, blazon **-slag** service branch, arm **-smed** armourer; gunsmith **-smedja** armourer's workshop **-smuggling** gunrunning **-stillestånd** armistice; truce **-stilleståndsvillkor** armistice terms **-tillverkning** manufacture of arms **-tjänst** military service **-vila** *se -stillestånd* **-vägran** refusal to bear arms **-vägrare** [-ä:-] conscientious objector; *vard.* conchie; draft resister (*AE.* dodger) **-övning** training in the use of arms

1 var *s7* (*kudd-*) case, slip

2 var *s7* (*i sår*) pus; *få ~ i ögonen* get infected eyes

3 var (*~t*) *pron a*) (*som adj.*) (*varenda*) every, (*varje särskild*) each; *b*) (*som subst.*) *se envar*; *~ dag* every day; *~ gång* every (each) time; *~ fjärde* every fourth (*timme* hour), every four (*timme* hours); *~ och en a*) (*som subst.*) every man (person), everybody, everyone, (*~ och en särskilt*) each [one] (*av* of), *b*) (*som adj.*) each, every; *de gick ~ och en till sig* each [of them] went home, they went each to his (*etc.*) own house; *~s och ens ensak* everybody's own business; *det tycker vi nog litet ~* pretty well every one of us thinks so; *~ för sig* each individually, separately; *de har ~ sin bok* each [of them] has his book, they have a book each; *göra ngt ~ sin gång* do s.th. by (in) turns; *på ~ sin sida om* on either side of; *de gick åt ~ sitt håll* they went their separate ways, they all went off in different directions

4 var *adv* where; (*-än, -helst äv.*) wherever; *här och ~* here and there; *~ som helst* anywhere; *~ någonstans* where[abouts]; *~ i all världen* wherever, where on earth

5 var *imperf. av 5 vara*

1 vara *vI, rfl, med.* suppurate, fester
2 vara *oböjligt s, ta ~ på* (*ta reda på*) take care of, (*använda väl*) make good use of (*tiden one's time*); *ta väl ~ på dig!* take good care of yourself!; *ta sig till ~* be careful, mind what one is doing; *ta sig till ~ för* be on one's guard against
3 var|a *sl* (*artikel*) article, product; *-or* (*äv.*) goods, merchandise, (*i sms. vanl.*) ware (*sg*); *-or och tjänster* goods and services; *explosiva -or* explosives; *korta -or* haberdashery; *tala för en ~* (*äv. bildl.*) speak (argue) in favour of s.th.
4 vara *vl* (*räcka*) last (*två timmar* [for] two hours); (*fortfara*) go on, continue; *så länge det ~r* as long as it lasts
5 vara *var varit, pres. är* **I** *huvudv* **1** *allm.* be; (*existera äv.*) exist; (*äga rum äv.*) take place; (*utgöra äv.*) make; *att ~ eller icke ~* to be or not to be; *~ från Sverige* (*om pers.*) be from Sweden, (*om sak*) come from Sweden; *~ vid posten* be working at the Post Office; *~ av den åsikten at*t be of the opinion that; *vad anser du ~ bäst?* what do you think is best?; *för att ~ så liten är han* considering he is so small he is; *såsom ~nde den äldste* being the oldest; *vi är fyra* there are four of us; *jag är för lång, är jag inte?* I'm too tall, aren't I (am I not)?; *om så är* if that be the case, if so; *det lilla som så mycket* (*the*) little there is; *snäll som jag är skall jag* as I am nice I will; *vad är att göra?* what is to be done?; *vad är den här knappen till?* what is this button [meant] for?; *hon är och handlar* she is out shopping; *när är premiären?* when is the opening night?; *båten är av plast* the boat is [made] of plastic; *tre och tre är sex* three and three are (is, make[s]) six; *det är att frukta att* it is to be feared that; *det är farliga saker* these are dangerous things; *det är ingenting för mig* that is not at all in my line; *det är inte mycket med den längre* it is not up to much any longer; *det är och förblir en gåta* it remains a mystery; *det är som det är* things are as they are; *det här är mina handskar* these gloves are mine; *hur är det att bo i London?* what's it like (how do you like) living in London?; *som det nu är* as things are (matters stand) now; *goddag, det är Lily* (*i telefon*) hello, [this is] Lily speaking, hello, Lily here; *är det herr A.?* (*vid tilltal*) are you Mr. A.?, (*i telefon*) is that Mr. A. speaking?; *vad är det nu då?* what is it (what is the matter) now?; *vad är det med TV:n?* what has happened to the TV; *de var två* there were two of them (*om lotten* to share the lottery ticket; *om arbetet* on the job); *jag var där en kvart* I stayed there for a quarter of an hour; *jag var och hälsade på dem* I went to see them; *de var och mötte honom* they were there to meet him; *om jag var* (*vore*) *rik* if I was (were) rich; *det var bra att du kunde komma* it's a good thing you could come; *det var det som var felet* that's what was wrong; *det var snällt av dig att komma* it's (it was) very kind of you to come; *var inte pjoskig!* don't make [such] a fuss!; *hur trevligt det än hade varit* however nice it would have been; *har du varit på teatern* (*Macbeth*)? have you

been to the theatre (to see "Macbeth")?; *jag vore tacksam om ni* I should be grateful if you; *det vore roligt* that would be fun **2** (*annan konstr.*) *deras sätt att ~* their manners; *hur därmed än må ~* be that as it may; *vi kan ~ sju i båten* there is room for seven of us (we can sit seven) in the boat; *vad får det lov att ~?* (*i butik*) what can I do for you?, (*t. gäst*) what can I offer you; *för att ~ utlänning är han* for a foreigner he is; *får det ~ en kopp kaffe?* would you like a cup of coffee; *det får ~ för mig* I would rather not, (*jag orkar inte*) I can't be bothered; *det får ~ som det är* we'll leave it at that (as it is); *det får ~ till en annan gång* it will have to wait until another time; *den dag som i dag är* this very day; *det är bara att komma* just come; *hur vore det om vi skulle gå och bada?* what about going swimming?; *under veckan som varit* during the last week* **II** *hjälpv* **1** *allm.* be; *jag är född 1931* I was born in 1931; *boken är tryckt i New York* the book was printed in New York **2** *de är bortresta* they are (have gone) away; *jag är ditbjuden i morgon* I have been invited there tomorrow; *han är utgången* he has gone out, he is out **III** (*med betonad partikel*) **1** *~ av* (*avbruten*) be [broken] off; *~ av med ngt* (*ha förlorat*) have lost, (*ha sluppit ifrån*) have got (be) rid of **2** *~ borta a*) *eg.* be away, *b*) (*försvunnen*) be missing, *c*) (*död*) be gone, *d*) *bildl.* be lost **3** *~ efter a*) (*förfölja*) be after, *b*) (*ej ha hunnit med*) be behind (*i skolan* at school); *han var långt efter oss* he was far behind us; *~ efter sin tid* be behind the times, *AE.* be a back number; *~ efter med betalningen* be in arrears with payment **4** *~ emot* be against **5** *~ för* (*gilla*) be in favour of; *fönsterluckorna var för* the shutters were closed (to) **6** *~ före a*) (*ha hunnit före*) be ahead (*sin tid* of the times), *b*) *jur.* be on, be before the court, *c*) (*dryftas*) be up [for discussion], (*behandlas*) be dealt with **7** *~ ifrån sig* be beside o.s. **8** *~ kvar a*) (*inte ha gått*) remain, stay [on], *b*) (*återstå*) remain, be left [over] **9** *~ med a*) (*deltaga*) take part, (*närvara*) be present (*på, vid* at), *b*) (*vara medräknad*) be included; *är osten med?* (*har vi med*) have we got the cheese?; *får jag ~ med?* may I join you (join in)?; *han var inte med planet* he wasn't on the plane; *är du med?* (*förstår du*) do you follow me?; *~ med sin tid* keep up with the times, be up to date; *hur är det med henne?* how is she?; *vad är det med henne?* what is the matter with her?; *~ med i* (*på*) (*deltaga i*) take part in, (*bevista*) attend; *~ med om* (*bevittna*) see, witness, (*uppleva*) experience, (*genomgå*) go through, (*råka ut för*) meet with, (*deltaga i*) take part in; *~ med om att* (*medverka*) do one's share towards (+ ing-form), (*hjälpa till*) help to (+ inf.); *hon är med på allt som är tokigt* she is in on anything crazy (mad) **10** *~ om sig* look after one's own interests, be on the make **11** *~ på a*) (*~ påsatt*) be on, *b*) (*röra vid*) be at; *~ på ngn* (*ligga efter*) be on at s.b., (*slå ner på*) be down on s.b. **12** *~ till* exist; *den är till för det* that's what it is there for; *~ till sig* be beside o.s. **13** *~ ur, knappen är ur* the button has come off;

nyckeln är ur the key is not in the lock **14** ~ *över a) (förbi)* be over (past), *b) (kvar)* left, [left] over; *snart är fienden över oss* the enemy will be over us any minute

varaktig *a1* lasting *(lycka* happiness); *(hållbar)* durable; *(beständig)* permanent *(adress* address); *~a konsumtionsvaror* consumer durables **-het** *(i tid)* duration; *(hållbarhet)* durability; *(beständighet)* permanency; *av kort ~ (äv.)* short-lived, brief

varande I *a4* being; *(existerande)* existing; *den i bruk ~* the ... in use **II** *s6* being; *(tillvaro)* existence

var|andra [-'and-, *vard.* -'rann] *(om två vanl.)* each other; *(om flera vanl.)* one another; *bredvid ~ (äv.)* side by side; *efter ~* one after the other (another); *två dagar efter ~* two days running, two days in succession; *tätt efter ~* close upon each other; *byta frimärken med ~* exchange stamps; *de rusade om ~* they rushed round one another; *två på ~ följande* two successive **-annan** [-ˣannan] **1** every other (second); *~ dag (äv.)* every two days; *~ vecka (äv.)* every two weeks, fortnightly; *~ gång (äv.)* alternately **2** *om vartannat* indiscriminately

varav ['vaːr-] *(av vilken)* from which (what); *~ följer att* and hence (so) it follows that; *~ 100 pund är* £100 of which is

var|bildning suppuration; *konkr.* abscess **-böld** boil

varda [ˣvaːr-] *vart, perf. part. vorden, se bliva; i ~nde* in the making

vardag ['vaːr-] *s2* weekday; *(arbetsdag äv.)* working day, *i sht AE.* workday; *om (på) ~arna, till ~s* on weekdays **-lig** [ˣvaːr-] *a1* everyday; *(alldaglig)* commonplace **-lighet** [ˣvaːr-] triviality

vardags|bestyr *pl* daily duties **-bruk** *till ~* for everyday use *(om kläder:* wear) **-klädd** dressed in everyday clothes **-kläder** *pl* everyday clothes **-kväll** weekday evening **-lag** *i uttr.: i ~* in everyday life, on weekdays **-liv** everyday life **-mat** everyday (ordinary) food (fare) **-middag** everyday dinner; *kom och ät ~ med oss* come and take potluck with us **-människa** ordinary (commonplace) person **-rum** living (sitting) room, lounge, parlour **-språk** colloquial language **-uttryck** everyday expression, colloquialism

vardera ['vaːr-] each; *på ~ sidan* on either side; *i vartdera fallet* in both cases, in each case

vare *konjunktiv av 5 vara* be; *ära ~ Gud* glory be to God; *~ därmed hur som helst* however that may be, be that as it may

varefter [-'eff-] after which; *(om tid äv.)* whereupon

varelse being; creature

varemot ['vaːr-] **I** *adv* against which; *(i jämförelse med vilken)* compared to which **II** *konj* while, whereas

varenda [-ˣenn-] every; *~ en* every [single] one

vare sig *~ ... eller inte* whether ... or not; *~ du vill eller inte* whether you want to or not; *han kom inte ~ i går eller i dag* he did not come either yesterday or today

varest ['vaːr-] where; and there

vareviga [-ˣeː-] every single *(dag* day)

varflytning flow[ing] of pus; pyorrhoea

varfågel [ˣvaːr-] great grey shrike

varför ['varr-, 'vaːr-] **1** *(av vilket skäl)* why; for what reason, on what account; *vard.* what for; *~ det?* why?; *~ inte?* why not? **2** *(och därför)* so, and therefore; wherefore **3** *(för vilken)* for which; *orsaken ~ jag slutade* the reason [why] I left

varg [-j] *s2* wolf; *hungrig som en ~* ravenous; *äta som en ~* eat voraciously; *~ i veum* outlaw **-avinter** bitter winter **-flock** pack of wolves **-grop** wolf pit **-hane** [he]wolf **-hona, -inna** she-wolf **-lik** *a5* wolfish **-skinnspäls** wolfskin fur[coat] **-tjut** howling of wolves (a wolf) **-unge** wolf cub; *(scout)* Cub [Scout], *(förr)* Wolf Cub

var'helst wherever

varhärd focus of suppuration

vari ['vaːri, -'iː] in which (what), wherein

varia ['vaː-] *pl* various things; *(som boktitel)* miscellanies **-bel** [-'aːbel] **I** *a2* variable, changeable **II** *s3* variable

vari|ans [-'ans, -'aŋs] *s3, stat.* variance **-'ant** variant; *(i textutgåva e.d.)* variant reading; *biol.* variety **-ation** variation

variations|bredd variation range; *stat.* range **-rikedom** abundance of variation

varibland ['vaːr-] among which; and among them *(etc.)*, including

varier|a 1 *(skifta)* vary; *(inom vissa gränser)* range *(mellan ... och* from ... to); *(vara ostadig)* fluctuate **2** *(förändra)* vary **-ande** *a4* varying, fluctuating

varieté *s3* **1** *(-föreställning)* variety [show], music-hall performance; *AE. äv.* vaudeville [show], burlesque **2** *(lokal)* variety theatre, music hall **-artist** variety (music-hall) artist **-föreställning** *se varieté 1*

varietet *s3, biol.* variety

varifrån ['vaːr-] *adv* **1** *interr.* where ... from, from where; *~ kommer han?* where does he come from? **2** *rel.* from which; *(från vilken plats)* from where; *vi kom till A., ~ vi fortsatte till* we arrived at A., from where we continued to

varig *a1* purulent; festering

varigenom ['vaːr-] *adv (jfr genom)* **1** *interr.* in what way; *(genom vilka medel)* by what means **2** *rel.* through which, by means of which; *(betecknande orsak)* whereby

varit *sup. av 5 vara*

varje *(jfr 3 var)* every; *(~ särskild)* each; *(vilken ... som helst)* any; *litet av ~* a little of everything; *i ~ fall* in any case, at any rate; *i ~ särskilt fall* in each [specific] case; *till ~ pris* at all costs, at any price **-handa** *oböjligt a* diverse, various, all sorts of [things]; *(som rubrik)* miscellanies

var'jämte besides (in addition to) which, and besides [that]

varken neither *(... eller ... nor)*; *han ~ ville eller kunde* he neither could nor would; *~ bättre eller sämre än* no better nor worse than; *~ det ena eller det andra (fågel eller fisk)* neither fish, flesh nor fowl

varl|ig [ˣvaːr-] *a1* gentle, soft; *jfr varsam* **-igt** *adv* gently

varm *a1* warm (*rock* coat; *färg* colour; *deltagande* sympathy); (*het*) hot (*bad* bath; *mat* food; *vatten* water); *bildl. äv.* hearty, cordial (*mottagande* reception), ardent (*beundrare* admirer); fervent; ~*t hjärta* warm heart; ~ *korv* hot dog; ~*a källor* hot springs; *fem grader* ~*t* five degrees above zero (freezing point); *bli* ~ get warm (hot), (*om maskin*) warm up; *jag blev* ~ *om hjärtat* my heart warmed; *bli* ~ *i kläderna* (*bildl.*) [begin to] find one's feet; *ge ngt med* ~ *hand* give s.th. gladly (readily, of one's own free will); *gå* ~ (*om maskin*) run hot, get overheated; *tala sig* ~ (*om maskin*) warm up to a subject; *vara* ~ *om händerna* have warm hands **-bad** hot bath **-blod** (*häst*) blood horse **-blodig** (*om djur*) warm-blooded; (*om pers.*) hot-blooded

varmed ['va:r-] *adv* **1** *interr.* with (by) what; ~ *kan jag stå till tjänst?* what can I do for you? **2** *rel.* with (by) which

varm|front *meteor.* warm front **-garage** heated garage **-gång** *tekn.* overheating, running hot **-hjärtad** [-j-] *a5* warm-hearted **-köra** (*motor*) warm up, run hot **-luft** hot air **-luftsridå** hot-air curtain **-rätt** hot dish

varmvatten hot water **-beredare** [electric] water heater; boiler, geyser **-flaska** hot-water bottle **-kran** hot[-water] tap

varn|a [ˣva:r-] warn (*för ngt* of s.th.; *för ngn* against s.b.; *för att* not to); (*mana t. försiktighet äv.*) caution (*för att* against + *ing*-form); *ett* ~*nde exempel* a warning (lesson)

varnagel [ˣva:r-] *r* example; *honom till straff och andra till* ~ as a punishment to himself and a warning to others

varning warning; (*varningsord äv.*) caution; (*vink*) hint; (*förmaning*) premonition; ~ *för* beware of; *ett* ~*ens ord* a word of warning (caution)

varnings|lampa warning light **-ljus** hazard warning light (flasher) **-märke** warning sign: (*trafik-*) danger sign **-signal** warning signal **-skott** warning shot **-triangel** warning triangle

varno'len *s3* white spirit; petroleum spirits (*pl*)

varom ['va:råm] **I** *adv, rel.* about (of) which; *interr.* about (of) what; ~ *mera nedan* about which more is said (written) below **II** *konj,* ~ *icke* and if not

1 varp *s2* (*i väv*) warp [wires *pl*]; (*handgjord*) chain; *sätta up en* ~ build up a warp; ~ *och inslag* warp and weft (*AE.* filling)

2 varp *s7* **1** *se notvarp* **2** *sjö.* warp, kedge

1 varpa *väv.* **I** *s1* warping machine **II** *v1* warp

2 varpa *s1* (*sten*) stone disc

varptråd warp thread

varpå ['va:r-] *adv, rel.* on which; *interr.* on what; (*om tid äv.*) whereupon, and so, after which; ~ *beror misstaget?* what is the reason for the mistake?, what is the mistake due to?

1 vars (*rel. pron, genitiv av vilken*) whose, of whom (which); *för* ~ *skull* for whose sake, for the sake of whom (which)

2 vars *interj, ja* (*jo*) ~ (*någorlunda*) not too bad; *nej,* ~ not really

var|sam [ˣva:r-] *a1* wary, cautious; (*aktsam*) careful **-samhet** care; caution **-samt** *adv*

warily *etc.*, gently; *behandlas* ~ handle with care

varse *oböjligt a, bli* ~ perceive, (*upptäcka*) discover, (*märka*) notice

varsebliv|a *se* [*bli*] *varse* **-ning** perception

varsel ['varr-] *s7* **1** (*förvarning*) premonitory sign, presage, foreboding **2** (*vid arbetstvist o.d.*) notice, warning; *utfärda* ~ *om strejk* give notice of a strike; *med kort* ~ at short notice

varsko [ˣva:r-] *v4* warn (*ngn om* s.b. of); give notice (*om flyttning* to quit); *polisen är* ~*dd* the police have been notified

varsla 1 (*vara förebud*) forebode, augur, portend; ~ *om* (*äv.*) be ominous of; *det* ~*r illa* that is no good omen, that augurs no good **2** (*varsko*) give notice (*om* of); ~ *om strejk, se varsel 2*

varsna *se* [*bli*] *varse*

varstans ['va:r-] *lite* ~ here, there and everywhere

Warszawa [var ˣsa:va] *n* Warsaw

1 vart *r, inte komma ngn* ~ get nowhere, make no progress; *jag kommer ingen* ~ *med honom* I can do nothing with him

2 vart *adv* where; *vard.* where to; ~ *som helst* anywhere; *jag vet inte* ~ *jag skall ta vägen* I don't know where to go; ~ *vill du komma* (*bildl.*) what are you driving at?

3 vart *imperf. av varda*

vartannat [-ˣann-] *se varannan 2*

vart|efter [-'eft-, 'vart-] (*efter hand som*) [according] as; (*så småningom*) little by little **-'hän** where

vartill ['va:r-] *adv, rel.* to (for) which; *interr.* for what [purpose]; ~ *nyttar det?* what is the good (use) of that?

vartåt [-'å:t, 'vart-] where; in what direction; *nu ser jag* ~ *det lutar* (*bildl.*) now I see which way things are going

varu|belåning loan on goods; *konkr.* pawnbroking business **-beteckning** description of goods **-bil** delivery van, *AE.* panel truck **-bud** delivery boy (messenger), *BE äv.* roundsman **-deklaration** merchandise description; informative label **-distribution** distribution of goods **-fordringar** *pl* commercial (trade) claims **-försändelse** consignment (*med fartyg:* shipment) [of goods] **-handel** trade, commerce **-hiss** goods (freight) lift, hoist; *AE.* freight elevator **-hus** department store **-huskedja** multiple retail organization; *AE.* chain store organization **-konto** trading (trade) account **-kännedom** knowledge of merchandise **-lager** stock [of goods], goods in stock; (*magasin*) warehouse; *inneliggande* ~ stock in trade

varulv werewolf

varu|magasin warehouse, storehouse **-märke** trademark **-märkesansökan** trademark application **-märkesskydd** trademark protection **-mässa** trade fair (exhibition)

varunder [-'unn-] under (*om tid:* during) which

varuprov sample

varur ['va:r-] *adv* out of which, from which

varu|rabatt trade discount **-skatt** purchase (*AE.* sales) tax; *allmän* ~ general purchase (*etc.*) tax **-slag** line (kind) of goods **-trans-**

V

port carriage (conveyance) of goods
varutöver [-'ö:-] over and above (besides, in addition to) which
varu|utbyte exchange of goods, trade **-växel** trade (commercial) bill
1 varv s7 (skepps-) shipyard, shipbuilding yard; (flottans) [naval] dockyard; på ~et in the shipyard
2 varv s7 **1** (omgång) turn; (hjul-) revolution; sport. round, lap, (vid stickning o.d.) row; linda ngt tre ~ runt wind s.th. three times round **2** (lager) layer; gå ner i ~ (bildl.) unwind
varva 1 (lägga i varv) put in layers **2** sport. lap
varvid ['va:r-] at which; (om tid äv.) when; ~ han (äv.) in doing which he
varv|ig a1 (skiktad) varved (lera clay) **-räknare** revolution counter, tachometer
varvs|arbetare shipyard worker **-chef** shipyard manager **-industri** shipbuilding industry
varvtal number of revolutions
varöver [-'ö:-] adv, rel. over (at) which; interr. over (at) what
vas s3 vase
va'sall s3 vassal **-stat** vassal state; satellite state
vasa|loppet the Vasa ski race, the Vasa run **-riddare** Knight of the Order of Vasa
vase'lin s4, s3 petrolatum, mineral jelly; vaseline (varumärke)
vask s2 (avlopp) sink
vask|a wash; (guld äv.) pan; (bergsvetenskap äv.) buddle **-malm** wash ore **-ning** panning; (guld-) placer-mining; **-tråg** washing trough; (guld-) cradle, rocker
vasomotorisk [-'tɔ:-] a5 vasomotor (nerv nerve)
1 vass s2 [common] reed; koll. reeds (pl); i ~en among (on) the reeds
2 vass a1 sharp (kniv knife); keen (egg edge) (äv. bildl.); sharp-edged (verktyg tool); (stickande) piercing; (sarkastisk) caustic (ton tone); ~a blickar keen (piercing) looks; ~ penna pointed (bildl. äv. caustic) pen; en ~ tunga a sharp (biting) tongue; ett strå ~are [än] (vard.) a cut above
vass|buk zool. sprat
vasskant i ~en at the edge of the reeds
vassla I s1 whey **II** v1, rfl turn (go, get) wheyey
vassleaktig a1 wheyey, wheyish
vassnäst [-ä:-] a4 sharp-nosed, with a pointed (sharp) nose
vass|rugge clump of reeds **-strå** (hopskr. vasstrå) reed
vassögd a1 sharp-eyed, with piercing eyes
Vatikanen [-'ka:-] r, best. form the Vatican
watt [v-] s9 watt
wattal (särskr. watt-tal) wattage
vatten ['vatt-] s7 **1** water; hårt (mjukt) ~ hard (soft) water; forsande ~ white water; rinnande ~ running water; per första öppet ~ per first open water (förk. f.o.w.); leda in ~ lay on water: lägga (sätta) i ~ put in water; ta in ~ (om båt) make (take in) water, water; på (i) svenska ~ on Swedish waters; under ~ under water, submerged; simma under vattnet swim below the surface; sätta under ~ flood, submerge **2** fiska i grumligt ~ fish in troubled

waters; få ~ på sin kvarn get grist to one's mill; det är som att hälla ~ på en gås it's like pouring water on a duck's back; kunna ngt som ett rinnande ~ know s.th. off pat; känna sig som fisken i vattnet feel thoroughly at home; ta sig ~ över huvudet (bildl.) take on more than one can manage, bite off more than one can chew; i de lugnaste vattnen går de största fiskarna still waters run deep **3** med. water (i knäet on the knee); ~ i lungsäcken wet pleurisy **4** kasta ~ (urinera) make (pass) water
vatten|avrinning drainage **-avvisande** water-repellent **-bad** water-bath **-behållare** water tank **-blandad** mixed with water **-brist** water shortage **-bryn** i ~et at the surface of the water, (vid stranden) at the water's edge **-buren** a5 waterborne **-cykel** water cycle, pedalo **-delare** watershed, divide **-djup** depth of water **-djur** aquatic animal **-domstol** water rights court, riparian court **-drag** watercourse **-droppe** drop of water **-fall** waterfall; falls, rapids (pl), cataract; bygga ut ett ~ harness a waterfall **-fallsverk** statens v~ [the Swedish] state power board **-fast** waterproof; water-resistant **-fattig** scantily supplied with water; (ofruktbar) arid **-fri** free from water; kem. anhydrous, dehydrated **-fågel** waterfowl (äv. koll.); aquatic bird **-färg** watercolour **-förande** a4 water-bearing **-förbrukning** water consumption **-förorening** water pollution **-förråd** supply of water **-försörjning** water supply **-glas 1** drinking-glass; en storm i ett ~ a storm in a teacup **2** kem. water glass **-grav** (sport.) water jump; (vallgrav) moat **-halt** water content **-haltig** a1 watery, containing water; kem. hydrous; med. serous **-kamma** wet comb **-kanna** (för vattning) watering can; (för tvättvatten) water jug **-kanon** water cannon **-karaff** carafe, water bottle **-kastare** hydrant **-klosett** water closet (förk. W.C.); AE. äv. bathroom **-konst** [artificial] fountain **-koppor** se vattkoppor **-kraft** water power **-kraftverk** hydroelectric power station (plant) **-kran** water tap; AE. faucet **-krasse** watercress **-kvarn** water mill **-kyld** [-çy:ld] a5 water-cooled (motor engine)
vatten|ledning water main, [water] conduit; (-ledningssystem) system of water mains; det finns ~ there is water laid on (i huset to the house) **-ledningsrör** water pipe; (huvudledning) water main[s pl] **-ledningsvatten** tap water **-linje** water line **-lås** waterseal, clean-out trap, drain trap **-löslig** soluble in water **-massa** volume (body) of water **-melon** watermelon **-märke** watermark **-mätare** (för flöde) water meter; (för innehåll) water gauge **-möja** s1, bot. water crowfoot **-odling** aquaculture **-pass** spirit (bubble) level **-pelare** column of water **-pistol** water pistol (AE. gun), squirt **-planing** aquaplaning **-polo** water polo **-post** [fire] hydrant **-prov 1** water sample; water test **2** hist. ordeal by water **-pump** water pump **-pöl** pool of water, puddle **-reglering** water regulation (control) **-reningsverk** water-purifying plant, sewage disposal plant **-reservoar** water reservoir (tank) **-ridå** water seal **-rik** abounding in water; ~ trakt well-wa-

tered country **-rätt** *jur.* water laws (rights) (*pl*) **-rättsdomare** judge of a water rights court **-rör** water pipe **-samling** pool of water; (*pöl*) puddle **-show** aquashow, *AE.* aquacade **-sjuk** boggy, waterlogged **-skada** water damage **-skadeförsäkring** water damage insurance **-skalle** *med.* hydrocephalus; *vard.* water on the brain **-skida** water-ski; *åka -skidor* water-ski **-skidåkning** water-skiing **-skott** *bot.* water shoot (sprout) **-slang** hose **-slipning** water sanding **-snok** grass snake **-spegel** mirror (surface) of the water **-sport** aquatic sports, aquatics (*pl*) **-spridare** water sprinkler **-stråle** jet of water **-stånd** water (sea) level; *högsta ~* high-water level **-stämpel** watermark **-stänk** splash of water **-torn** water tower; standpipe **-trampning** treading water **-tunna** water cask; (*för regnvatten*) water butt **-turbin** water (hydraulic) turbine **-täkt** *s3* water supply (resources *pl*) **-tät** (*om tyg e.d.*) waterproof; (*om fartyg, kärl*) watertight **-uppfordringsverk** water- raising plant **-uppsugande** *a4* water-absorbent, hygroscopic **-verk** waterworks (*sg o. pl*); water service **-vård** water conservation (protection) **-väg** waterway **-växt** aquatic plant, hydrophyte **-yta** surface of water **-åder** vein of water **-ånga** steam; water vapour **-ödla** newt

vattgröt porridge [made with water]

wattimme (*särskr. watt-timme*) watt-hour

vatt|koppor *pl* chickenpox (*sg*), *med.* varicella **-lägga** soak, put in water

vattna water (*äv. djur*); (*be-*) sprinkle, irrigate; *~ ur* soak (*sill* herring) **vattnas** *dep, det ~ i munnen på mig* it makes my mouth water (*när jag tänker på* to think of) **vattnig** *a1* watery; *bildl.* insipid; *med.* serous **vattning** watering; sprinkling, irrigation **vattra** water, wave; *~t tyg* moire, watered silk

vattu|mannen *V~* Aquarius **-siktig** *a1* dropsical **-skräck** rabies; (*hos människa äv.*) hydrophobia **-sot** dropsy

vattvälling water gruel; *var och en rosar sin ~* everyone swears by his own remedy

vax *s4* wax **vaxa** wax

vax|artad [-a:r-] *a5* waxy **-böna** wax (butter) bean **-docka** wax doll **-duk** oilcloth, American cloth **-figur** wax figure, waxwork **-gul** wax-coloured, waxen **-kabinett** waxworks (*sg o. pl*) **-kaka** honeycomb **-ljus** wax candle **-papper** wax paper **-plugg** plug of earwax

WC [*˟ve:se:] *s6* W.C., toilet, lavatory **--borste** lavatory brush

VD [*˟ve:de:] *förk. för verkställande direktör, se under verkställande*

ve I *oböjligt* s woe; *ditt väl och ~* your welfare (wellbeing); *svära ~ och förbannelse över* call down curses on II *interj, ~ dig!* woe betide ([be] to) you!; *~ mig!* woe is me!; *o, ~!* alas!; *~ och fasa!* alackaday!

veck *s7* fold; (*sytt äv.*) pleat, plait; (*invikning*) tuck; (*skrynkla; press-*) crease; (*i ansiktet*) wrinkle; *bilda ~* fold; *lägga ~* put in pleats (*på* on); *lägga sig i ~* form pleats; *lägga pannan i ~* pucker (knit) one's brow

1 vecka *v1* pleat, put pleats in; shirr *~ sig* fold, crease, (*om papper*) crumple

2 vecka *s1* week; [*i*] *förra ~n* last week; *~ för ~* week by week; *en gång i ~n* once a week, (*utkommande etc.*) weekly; *om en ~* in a week['s time]; *i dag om en ~* a week today, this day week; *på fredag i nästa ~* on the Friday of next week

veckig *a1* creased; (*skrynklig*) crumpled, crinkled

veckla wrap (*in i* up in); *~ ihop* fold up; *~ upp* (*ut*) unfold, (*flagga*) unfurl (*äv. ~ ut sig*)

vecko|avlönad weekly paid (*arbetare* worker); paid by the week **-avlöning** weekly wage[s *pl*] (pay, salary) **-dag** day of the week **-helg** weekend **-kort** weekly season (*AE.* commuter) ticket **-lön** se *-avlöning* **-pengar** *pl* [weekly] pocket money (allowance) (*sg*) **-press** weekly press; *~en* the weeklies (*pl*) **-slut** weekend **-tal** *i ~* for weeks together (on end) **-tidning** weekly [paper, magazine] **-tvätt** weekly wash **-vis** se *-tals*

veckända weekend

ved *s3* wood; (*bränsle äv.*) firewood **-artad** [-a:r-] *a5* woody, ligneous **-bod** woodshed

vederbör *i uttr.: den det ~* whom it may concern, the party concerned **-ande** I *a4* the proper, the ... in question; *~ myndighet* the proper (competent) authority, the authority concerned II *s9* the party concerned (in question); *pl* the parties concerned, those concerned; *höga ~* the authorities (*pl*), the person (people) in authority **-lig** [-ö:-] *a1* due, proper; appropriate; *i ~ ordning* in due course; *med ~t tillstånd* with the necessary authorization, (*friare*) with due permission; *på ~t avstånd* (*äv.*) at a discreet distance; *ta ~ hänsyn till* pay due regard (attention) to **-ligen** [-ö:-] duly, properly; in due course

veder|döpare anabaptist **-faras** *-fors -farits, dep* (*komma t. del*) fall to (*ngn* a p.'s lot); befall (happen to) (*ngn* s.b.) **-farits** *sup. av vederfaras* **-fors** [-ɔ:-] *imperf. av vederfaras* **-gälla** [-j-] *v2* repay; return (*ont med gott* good for evil) **-gällning** [-j-] retribution (*äv. relig.*); reprisal; (*lön*) requital, recompense; (*hämnd*) retaliation; *~ens stund* day of retribution; *torde mot ~ återlämnas* reward offered for the return of **-gällningsaktion** retaliatory action **-häftig 1** (*pålitlig*) reliable, trustworthy (*person* person); authentic, sure (*uppgift* statement) **2** *hand.* solvent; *icke ~* insolvent **-häftighet 1** reliability, trustworthiness; authenticity **2** solvency **-kvicka** *v3* (*uppfriska*) refresh; (*stärka*) invigorate; (*ge nya krafter*) restore **-kvickande** *a4* refreshing; recreative; restorative **-kvickelse** refreshment; recreation; comfort

veder|lag *s7* compensation; remuneration, recompense **-lägga** confute; refute (*ngn* s.b.); contradict, deny (*ett påstående* a statement); *som inte kan ~s* (*äv.*) irrefutable **-mäle** *s6* token, mark **-möda** hardship; travail **-sakare** adversary **-stygglig** *a1* abominable; (*ful*) hideous **-stygglighet** abomination; horror **-tagen** *a5* established (*bruk* custom); conventional (*uppfattning* idea); accepted **-vilja** antipathy (*mot* towards); loathing (*mot* of) **-värdig** repulsive, repugnant; (*avskyvärd*) dis-

V

gusting **-värdighet** repulsiveness; (*motgång*) vexation, contrariety; ~*er* (*äv.*) horrors
ve'dettbåt picket boat
ved|handlare firewood dealer **-huggning** woodcutting, woodchopping **-kap** circular saw **-kubbe** chopping block **-lår** firewood bin **-pinne** stick of wood **-skjul** woodshed **-spis** wood stove **-såg** wood saw **-trave** woodpile, wood stack **-trä** log, piece of wood, [split] billet
vegetabil|ier [-'bi:-] *pl* vegetables; crops **-isk** *a5* vegetable (*föda* food)
vegetar|i'an *s3* vegetarian **-isk** [-'ta:-] *a4* vegetarian (*kost* food)
veget|ation vegetation **-a'tiv** *a1* vegetative; ~*a nervsystemet* the autonomic nervous system **-era** vegetate (*äv. bildl.*); *bildl. äv.* lead an inactive life
Weichsel ['vajksel] *r* the Vistula
1 vek *imperf. av vika*
2 vek *a1* (*som lätt böjs*) pliant, pliable; (*svag*) weak; (*mjuk*) soft; (*känslig*) gentle, tender; ~*a livet* the waist; *ett* ~*t hjärta* a soft (tender) heart; *bli* ~ soften, grow soft; *bli* ~ *om hjärtat* feel one's heart soften
veke *s2* wick **-garn** wick yarn
vek|het [ˣve:k-] pliancy; weakness; softness; tenderness **-hjärtad** [-j-] *a5* tenderhearted, softhearted
veklagan lamentation, wailing
veklig [ˣve:k-] *a1* soft; effeminate; (*svag*) weak[ly]; *föra ett* ~*t liv* lead a very easy life **-het** softness *etc.*; effeminacy
vek|ling weakling; *vard.* milksop **-na** grow soft (tender), soften; (*ge vika*) relent
vektor [ˣvektår] *s3* vector **-algebra** vector algebra **-analys** vector analysis
vela *vard.* dither
ve'lar *a1 o. s3*, *språkv.* velar
velat *sup. av vilja*
velig *a1* irresolute, in two minds
wellpapp [ˣvell-] corrugated cardboard
veloci'ped *s3* bicycle
velour[s] [-'lɔ:r] *s3* velour[s]
weltervikt [ˣvell-], **-are** welterweight
velur *se velour[s]*
ve'läng *s3* vellum [paper]
vem [vemm] *pron* **1** *interr.* who (*som obj.* who[m]; *efter prep* whom); (*vilkendera*) which [of them]; ~ *av dem ...?* which of them ...?; *där?* who is there?; ~ *som* who; ~*s är felet?* whose fault is it?; ~ *får jag lov att hälsa ifrån?* what name shall I say? **2** *rel.*, ~ *som helst* anybody, anyone; *det kan* ~ *som helst se* anybody can see that; ~ *det vara må* whoever it may be
vemod *s7* [pensive] melancholy, [tender] sadness **-ig** *a1* melancholy, sad [at heart]; blue
vemodsfylld full of sadness (melancholy)
1 ven *imperf. av vina*
2 ven *s3, anat.* vein
vend *s3*, **-er** ['venn-] *s9* Wend **-isk** ['venn-] *a5* Wendish
Venedig [-'ne:-] *n* Venice
venerisk [-'ne:-] *a5* venereal (*sjukdom* disease)
veneti|an [-etsi'a:n] *s3*, **-anare** [-ˣa:na-] *s9,**-ansk** [-a:-] *a5* Venetian

ven'til *s3* **1** (*i rörledning e.d.*) valve **2** (*för luftväxling*) ventilator, vent[hole], air regulator **3** (*i fartygssida e.d.*) porthole; *AE.* air port **4** *mus.* valve **-ation** ventilation
ventilations|ruta quarterlight, *AE.* wing **-system** ventilation system
ventil|ator *s3* ventilator **-basun** valve trombone **-era 1** ventilate; air **2** (*dryfta*) discuss, debate, ventilate **-gummi** valve rubber **-hatt** valve (dust) cap **-slipning** valve grinding
ventrikel [-'trick-] *s2* (*magsäck*) stomach; (*hjärn-, hjärt-*) ventricle
venusberg *anat.* mons pubis (veneris)
ve'nös *a1* venous (*blod* blood)
veranda [-ˣrann-] *s1* veranda[h]; *AE. äv.* porch
verb *s7* verb
ver'bal *a1* verbal **-isera** verbalize **-substantiv** verbal noun
verbform verbal form
verifi|era verify **-kation** (*-ering*) verification; (*intyg, kvitto äv.*) voucher **-kationsnummer** voucher number
veritabel *a2* veritable, true
verk *s7* **1** (*arbete*) work; (*litt. o. konst. äv.*) production; (*gärning äv.*) deed; *samlade* ~ collected works; *ett ögonblicks* ~ the work of an instant; *gripa sig* ~*et an, gå* (*skrida*) *till* ~*et* set (go) to work; *sätta kronan på* ~*et* crown (put the seal on) the work; *sätta i* ~*et* carry out, put ... into practice, (*förverkliga*) realize; *i själva* ~*et* as a matter of fact, actually **2** (*ämbets-*) office, [civil service] department; *stadens* ~ municipal authorities; *statens* ~ government (civil service) departments **3** (*fabrik*) works **4** (*fästnings-, ur-*) works (*pl*); (*mekanism*) mechanism, apparatus
verka (*ha* ~*n*) work; act; *medicinen* ~*de inte* the medicin had no effect (did not work); *vi får se hur det* ~*r* we shall see how it works (what effect it has); ~ *lugnande* have a soothing effect **2** (*arbeta*) work; ~ *för* work for (in behalf of), devote o.s. to, interest o.s. in **3** (*förefalla*) seem, appear; *han* ~*r sympatisk* he makes an agreeable impression [upon one]; *hon* ~*r äldre än hon är* she strikes one as being older than she is
verkan *r, som pl används* verkningar (*resultat*) effect, result; (*in- äv.*) action; (*verkningskraft*) effectiveness; (*medicins*) efficacy; *orsak och* ~ cause and effect; *fördröjd* ~ retarded action; *förtaga* ~ *av* take away the effect[s] of, neutralize; *göra* ~ take effect, be effective; *inte göra* ~ be of no effect; *ha åsyftad* ~ have the desired effect; *till den* ~ *det hava kan* in the hope it may work **verkande** *a4* active; (*arbetande*) working; *kraftigt* ~ powerful, very effective; *långsamt* ~ slow[-acting]
verklig *a1* real; (*sann*) true (*vän* friend); (*äkta*) genuine, veritable; (*faktisk*) actual (*inkomst* income); *det* ~*a förhållandet* the actual situation, the [real] facts (*pl*), the truth of the matter; *i* ~*a livet* in real life **-en** really; actually, indeed; ~? indeed?, really?, you don't say [so]?; *jag hoppas* ~ *att* I do hope that; *jag vet* ~ *inte* I really don't know **-het** reality (*äv.* ~*en*); fact; (*sanning*) truth; *bli* ~ materialize, come true; *i* ~*en* in reality, in real life, (*i själva*

verket) as a matter of fact; *se ngn i ~en* see s.b. in the flesh

verklighets|flykt escapism **-främmande** out of touch with realities (real life) **-sinne** sense of reality **-skildring** realistic (true) description **-trogen** realistic, true to [real] life; (*om porträtt*) lifelike **-underlag** factual basis

verkmästare [industrial] supervisor, [factory] overseer, foreman

verkning *se verkan*

verknings|full effective **-grad** [degree of] efficiency, effectiveness; *ha hög ~* be highly efficient **-kraft** efficiency **-krets** incidence **-lös** ineffective **-område** sphere of influence **-radie** radius of action, range **-sätt** [mode of] action (operation)

verksam *a1* **1** (*effektiv*) effective (*medicin* medicine) **2** (*arbetsam*) industrious, busy; (*aktiv*) active; (*driftig*) energetic; *ta ~ del i* take an active part in; *vara ~ som* work as **-het** activity; (*rörelse, handling*) action; (*arbete*) work; (*handels- e.d.*) business, operations (*pl*); *oamerikansk ~* un-American activities (*pl*); *inställa ~en* cease one's activities, stop work; *sätta i ~* set working; *träda i ~* come into action (operation), start work; *vara i ~* be at work, (*om sak*) be in operation (action)

verksamhets|berättelse annual report **-form** form of activity **-fält** field of action; (*persons*) sphere of activity; *hand.* line [of business] **-lust** energy, craving for action **-år** *hand.* financial year

verkskydd industrial civil defence [unit]

verksläkare staff medical officer

verkstad ['värk-] *-en verkstäder* workshop; [repair, machine] shop; (*bil-*) garage; *mekanisk ~* engineering plant (workshop); *skyddad ~* sheltered workshop

verkstads|arbetare engineering worker, mechanic **-chef** works (*AE.* plant) manager **-golv** shop floor **-industri** engineering industry **-klubb** trade union branch, works committee

verkställ|a carry out (into effect), perform; (*t.ex. dom*) execute; *~ betalningar* make (effect) payments **-ande** *a4* executive (*makt* power); *~ direktör* managing director, general manager, *AE.* president; *vice ~ direktör* deputy managing director (general manager), *AE.* [executive] vice president; *~ utskott* executive committee **-are** executor **-ighet** execution; effect; *gå i ~* be put into effect, be carried out

verk|tum [Swedish] inch **-tyg** tool, instrument (*äv. bildl.*); *eg. äv.* implement

verktygs|låda tool box **-skåp** tool cupboard (locker) **-utrustning** tool kit (outfit) **-väska** tool bag

vermiceller [-'sell-] *pl, kokk.* vermicelli

verm[o]ut ['värmut] *s2* vermouth

vernissage [-'sa:ʃ] *s5* opening of an exhibition; private view

vero'nal *s4, s3* veronal (*varumärke*)

veronika [-'rå:-] *s1, bot.* speedwell

vers *s3, s2* verse (*äv. i Bibeln*); (*strof*) stanza, strophe; (*dikt*) poem; *sjunga på sista ~en* be on one's (its) last legs; *skriva ~* write poetry (poems)

ver'sal *s3, boktr.* capital [letter]; cap

vers|byggnad metrical structure **-drama** verse (metrical) drama

verserad [-'se:-] *a5* well-mannered

vers|form metrical form **-fot** metrical foot

versifier|a versify **-ing** versification

version [-'ʃɔ:n] version

vers|konst metrical art **-krönika** verse drama **-lära** prosody; metrics (*pl, behandlas som sg*) **-makare** versifier **-mått** metre **-rad** line of poetry

vertebrat vertebrate

verti'kal vertical **-plan** vertical plane

verv *s3* verve, animation

ve'sir *s3* vizier

vespa *s1* Vespa scooter

vesper ['vess-] *s2* vesper

vessla *s1* **1** weasel; ferret **2** (*fordon*) snow cat[erpillar]

ves'tal *s3* vestal [virgin]

Westfalen [ˣvest-] *n* Westphalia **westfalisk** [ˣvest-] *a5* Westphalian; *~a freden* the Peace of Westphalia

vesti'bul *s3* vestibule; entrance hall, lobby

vet|a *visste -at* **1** know; be aware of; *det är inte gott att ~* one never knows (can tell); *du vet väl att* I suppose you know (are aware of the fact) that; *inte ~ vad man vill* not know one's own mind; *vad vet jag?* how should I know?; *vet du vad, ...!* tell you what, ...!; *~ sin plats* know one's place; *vet skäms!* be ashamed of yourself!; *det -e fåglarna!* goodness knows!; *så mycket du vet det!* and now you know!; *så vitt jag vet* as far as (for all) I know; *inte så vitt jag vet* not that I know of; *~ att* know how to (*uppföra sig* behave); *få ~* get to know, hear, learn (*av* from), be told (*av* by); *jag fick ~ det av honom själv* I had it from his own lips; *hur fick du ~ det?* how did you get to know that (of it)?; *man kan aldrig ~* you never know (can tell); *låta ngn [få] ~* let s.b. know; *det måtte väl jag ~!* I ought to know! **2** (*med betonad partikel*) *~ av* know of; *han vill inte ~ av* a) (*ngn*) he won't have anything to do with, b) (*ngt*) he won't hear of; *innan man vet ordet av* before you can say Jack Robinson; *~ med sig* be conscious (aware) (*att man är* of being, that one is); *~ om* know [of, about]; *inte ~ om* (*äv.*) be ignorant of; *inte ~ till sig* not know what to do; *~ varken ut eller in* not know which way to turn **3** *rfl, inte ~ sig ha sett* not know that one has seen; *hon visste sig ingen levande[s] råd* she was at her wits' end

vetande I *a4, mindre ~* not quite right in the head, feeble-minded **II** *s6* knowledge; (*kunskaper äv.*) learning; *mot bättre ~* against one's better judgement; *tro och ~* faith and knowledge

vetat *sup. av veta*

vete *s6* wheat; *rostat ~* puffed wheat **-ax** ear of wheat **-bröd** white bread **-bulle** bun **-grodd** wheat germ **-kli** bran **-korn** grain of wheat **-mjöl** wheat flour

vetenskap *s3* science; (*-sgren*) branch of science (scholarship); *de humanistiska ~erna* the humanities (arts); *det är en hel ~* (*mycket invecklat*) it's an art in itself **-lig** [-a:-] *a1* scientific; (*lärd*) scholarly **-lighet** [-a:-]

scholarliness; scientific character **-ligt** [-a:-]
adv scientifically; *bevisa* ~ prove scientifically
vetenskaps|akademi academy of science[s]
-gren branch of science (scholarship) **-histo-
ria** history of science **-man** scientist; (*huma-
nist*) scholar **-teori** epistemology, theory of
science and research
vete'ran *s3* veteran **-bil** veteran car
veteri'när *s3* veterinary surgeon, *AE.* veteri-
narian; *vard.* vet **-besiktning** veterinary inspection **-högskola** veterinary college
veter|lig *a1* known; *göra ~t, se kungöra* **-ligen,
-ligt** as far as is known; *mig* ~ as far as I know,
to my knowledge
vetgirig eager to learn (know), craving for
knowledge, inquiring, inquisitive **-het** thirst
for knowledge; inquiring mind; inquisitiveness
veto *s6* veto; *inlägga sitt* ~ interpose one's veto;
inlägga sitt ~ *mot* veto, put one's veto on **-rätt**
[right of] veto
vetskap [ˣve:t-] *s3* knowledge; *få* ~ *om* get to
know, learn about; *utan min* ~ (*äv.*) unknown
to me
vett *s7* [good] sense; wit; *med* ~ *och vilja*
knowingly, wittingly; *ha* ~ *att* have the good
sense to; *vara från ~et* be out of one's senses
vett|a *-e -at,* ~ *mot* (*åt*) face (*norr* the north)
vette *s2* stool pidgeon, decoy
vett|lig *a1* sensible; (*omdömesgill*) judicious **-lös**
senseless **-skrämd** *a5* frightened (scared) out
of one's senses (wits) **-villing** madman
vev *s2* crank, handle
vev|a I *s1, i samma* ~ just at that (the same)
moment **II** *v1,* ~ [*på*] turn [the crank (handle)
[of]]; grind (*på ett positiv* an organ); ~ *på*
grind away **-axel** crankshaft **-hus** crankcase
-stake connecting rod **-tapp** crankpin
v.g.v. *förk. för var god vänd, se vända 1*
whisky ['viss-] *s3* whisky; (*skotsk*) Scotch
[whisky]; (*AE.*) rye, bourbon **-grogg** *en* ~ a
whisky and soda, *AE.* a highball
vi we; ~ *andra* (*äv.*) the rest of us; ~ *själva* we
ourselves; ~ *bröder* my brother[s] and I, we
brothers
via via, by way of; through
via'dukt *s3* viaduct
vi'al *s3, bot.* vetchling
vibr|afon [-'få:n] *s3* vibraphone **-ation** vibra-
tion **-ationsfri** vibrationless, vibration-free
-ator *s3* vibrator **-era** vibrate
vice *oböjligt a* **1** vice[-]; deputy (*talman* speaker) **2** ~ *versa* vice versa, the other way round
-amiral vice admiral **-konsul** vice consul **-ko-
nung** viceroy **-korpral** (*vid armén*) lance
corporal, *AE.* private 1st class; (*vid flyget*) aircraftman 1st class, *AE.* airman 2nd class **-pre-
sident** vice president **-värd** proprietor's (landlord's) agent, caretaker; *AE.* superintendent
vichyvatten soda water
1 vicka rock, sway; *bordet ~r* the table wobbles;
~ *på foten* wag one's foot; *sitta och* ~ *på stolen* sit and swing on (sit balancing) one's
chair; ~ *omkull* tip (tilt) over, upset; ~ *till* tip
up, (*om båt äv.*) give a lurch
2 vicka *vard. för vikariera* sub[stitute] (*för* for)
vicker ['vick-] *s2* vetch; *koll.* vetches (*pl*)
1 vid *prep* **1** *rumsbet., allm.* at; (*bredvid, invid;*

med hjälp av) by; (*geogr. läge*) on; (*i närheten av*) near; (*vid gata, torg; anställd vid*) in;
(*i prep. attr.*) of; (*efter fästa, binda e.d.*) to;
sitta ~ *ett bord* sit at (*bredvid* by) a table; *röka
~ bordet* smoke at table; *sitta och prata* ~ *en
kopp te* have a chat over a cup of tea; *bilen
stannade* ~ *grinden* the car stopped at the gate;
klimatet ~ *kusten* the climate at the coast; *sätta
ett kryss* ~ *ett namn* put a cross against a name;
sitta ~ *ratten* be at the wheel; *tåget stannar
inte* ~ *den stationen* the train does not stop at
that station; *studera* ~ *universitetet* study (be)
at the university; *sitta* ~ *brasan* sit by the fire;
steka ~ *sakta eld* fry over a slow fire; *leda ngn
~ handen* lead s.b. by the hand; *vi bor* ~ *kusten* we live by (near) the coast; *sida* ~ *sida* side
by side; ~ *min sida* by (at) my side; *skuldra* ~
skuldra shoulder to shoulder; *stolen står* ~
väggen the chair stands by (*intill* against) the
wall; ~ *gränsen* on the border; *staden ligger
~ havet* the town is [situated] on the sea; ~ *ho-
risonten* on the horizon; *en gata* ~ *torget* a
street near (off) the square; *huset ligger* ~ *torget* the house is in the square; *anställd* ~
employed in (at); *tjänstgöra* ~ *flottan* serve in
the Navy; *vara* (*gå in*) ~ *teatern* be (go) on
the stage; *slaget* ~ *Waterloo* the battle of
Waterloo; *binda* [*fast*] *ngt* ~ tie s.th. [on] to;
fäst ~ (*äv. bildl.*) attached to **2** *tidsbet., allm.*
at; (*omedelbart efter*) on; (*omkring*) about; ~
den här tiden på året at this time of the year;
~ *den här tiden i morgon* at this time
tomorrow; ~ *jultiden* at Christmas; ~ *tiden för*
at the time of; ~ *midnatt* at (*omkring* about)
midnight; ~ *nymåne* at new moon; ~ *sin död
var han* at the time of his death (when he died)
he was; ~ *fyrtio års ålder* at the age of forty;
~ *första ögonkastet* at first sight; ~ *min ankomst till* on my arrival in; ~ *ett tillfälle* on
one occasion; ~ *sextiden* about six o'clock; ~
användningen av when using; ~ *halka* when it
is slippery; ~ *kaffet talade vi om* when we were
having coffee we talked about; ~ *sjukdom* in
case of illness **3** *oegentl. bet.*; ~ *behov* when
necessary, if required; ~ *fara* in case of danger; ~ *Gud!* by God!; ~ *allt vad heligt är* by
everything that is sacred; ~ *gott mod* in good
heart; ~ *namn Z.* called (named) Z., by the
name of Z.; *hålla* ~ *makt* maintain, keep up;
hålla fast ~ stick to; *stå* ~ *vad man sagt* stand
by (keep to) what one has said; *van* ~ used
(accustomed) to; *vara* ~ *liv* be alive **II** *adv* **1**
sitta ~ [*sitt arbete*] stick to one's work **2** ~
pass 15 personer about 15 people, 15 persons
or so
2 vid *a1* wide; (*-sträckt*) vast, extensive; broad
(*dal* valley); (*om klädesplagg*) loose[ly fitting];
i ~a kretsar (*äv.*) widely; *det öppnar ~a per-
spektiv* it opens up wide vistas; *på ~a havet*
on the open sea; *i ~a världen* in the wide world
vida *adv* **1** (*långt*) ~ [*omkring*] [far and] wide;
~ *berömd* renowned **2** (*mycket*) far (*bättre* better)
vidare *a, komp. t.* **2** *vid* **1** (*med större vidd*)
wider *etc.* (*jfr 2 vid*); *bli* (*göra*) ~ widen
2 (*ytterligare*) further (*underrättelser* particulars); more; *ni får* ~ *besked* (*äv.*) you will hear

more **II** adv **1** (komp. t. vida 1, 2 vitt) wider, more widely; (längre) farther, further (t.ex. gå, föra, läsa ~) on; (i tid) longer, more; ~! go on!; den behövs inte ~ it is no longer needed; innan vi går ~ before we go any further; läsa ~ read on, continue to read; och så ~ and so on (forth) **2** (ytterligare) further, more; ~ meddelas att it is further stated that; jag har inget ~ att tillägga I have nothing to add; jag kommer inte ~ att ... I won't ... any more; vi talar inte ~ om det! don't let us talk any more about that! **3** (dessutom) further[more], also; se ~ sidan 5 see also page 5 **4** (igen) again; låt det inte hända ~ don't let it happen again **5** (särskilt) inte ~ not particularly (very); det är inget ~ att bo här it's not very pleasant living here; vi hade inte (inget) ~ roligt it wasn't much fun, we did not enjoy ourselves very much **6** tills ~ until further notice, for the present; utan ~ without further notice (any more ado), vard. just like that

vidare|befordra forward, send on; (upplysningar o.d. äv.) pass on **-befordran** forwarding; för ~ till to be forwarded to **-utbildning** further (advanced) training (education) **-utveckling** further development

vid|bränd a5, är ~ has got burnt **-bränt** adv, smaka ~ have a burnt taste; det luktar ~ there is a smell of [something] burning

vidbrättad a5 wide-brimmed

vidd s3 **1** (omfång) width; wideness fack. amplitude; (kläders etc.) fullness, looseness **2** bildl. (utsträckning) extent; (omfattning) scope; i hela sin ~ to (in) its whole extent; ~en av hans kunskaper the scope of his knowledge **3** (-sträckt yta) expanse; plain

vide s6 willow; (korg-) osier **-korg** wicker basket

video ['vi:-] s5 **1** tekn. video **2** se -bandspelare **-band** video tape **-bandspelare** video [cassette] recorder **-förstärkare** video amplifier **-våld** video violence

vidertryck backing [up]

videsnår osiery

vidfilm wide-screen film; i ~ on wide screen

vid|foga append, affix **-fästa** attach, fix on

vidg|a (äv. rfl) widen (äv. bildl.); expand, enlarge; (spänna ut) dilate; ~ sina vyer broaden one's mind **-as** dep, se vidga **-ning** widening; expansion, enlargement; dilation

vid|gå own (att man är being), confess **-gående** s6 owning, confession **-hålla** maintain; keep (adhere, vard. stick) to; insist on **-häfta 1** (häfta fast vid) adhere, stick **2** se vidlåda **-häftning** adherence, adhesion **-häftningsförmåga** adhesiveness, adhesive capacity (power) **-hängande** a4 attached, fastened (tied) on; ~ adresslapp tag, tie-on label

vidimer|a attest, ~s signed in the presence of, witnessed **-ing** attestation

vidja ['vi:d-] s1 osier switch, wicker

vid|kommande s6, för mitt ~ as far as I am concerned **-kännas** v2, dep **1** (erkänna) own, admit, acknowledge **2** (lida) suffer, bear, endure (en förlust a loss); ~ kostnaderna bear the costs

vidlyftig a1 **1** (omfattande) extensive; (omständ-

lig) wordy (berättelse narrative); ~a resor extensive travels **2** (tvivelaktig) questionable (affär transaction); (utsvävande) fast (herre liver); ett ~t fruntimmer a woman of easy virtue **-het 1** extensiveness etc. **2** (i seder) dissipation; (-a äventyr) escapades (pl)

vid|låda be inherent in; de fel som -låder (äv.) the [inherent] faults of **-makthålla** maintain, keep up, preserve **-makthållande** s6 maintenance, upholding, preservation

vidrig [ˣvi:d-] a1 **1** (motbjudande) repulsive, disgusting; (förhatlig) odious; (otäck) horrid **2** (ogynnsam) contrary; adverse (omständigheter circumstances) **-het 1** repulsiveness etc. **2** contrariness; adversity

vidrigt adv repulsively etc.; lukta ~ have a terrible smell; smaka ~ taste abominable

vidräkning settlement of accounts; vard. showdown; en skarp ~ med a sharp attack on

vidskepelse [-ʃ-] superstition

vidskeplig [-ʃe:-] a1 superstitious **-het** superstitiousness, superstition

vidsträckt a1 extensive, wide; vast (område area); expansive (utsikt view); ~a befogenheter extensive powers; göra ~a resor (äv.) travel extensively; i ~ bemärkelse in a wide (broad) sense

vidstående a4 adjoining (sida page)

vid|syn broad outlook (views pl) **-synt** [-y:-] a1 broad-minded **-synthet** broad- mindedness

vid|ta[ga] **1** (företaga) take (åtgärder steps); make (anstalter arrangements) **2** (fortsätta) come; (börja) begin; efter lunchen -tog after the lunch followed **-tala** arrange with; jag har ~t honom om saken I have spoken to him about it

vidunder monster; (enastående företeelse) prodigy **-lig** [ˣvi:d-, -'unn-] monstrous; (orimlig) preposterous **-lighet** monstrosity

vid|vinkelobjektiv foto. wide-angle lens **-öppen** wide-open

Wien [vi:n] n Vienna

wien|are [ˣvi:nare] Viennese (pl lika) **-erbröd** Danish pastry **-erschnitzel** [-ʃnitsel] s2 Wiener schnitzel **-sk** [-i:-] a5 Viennese

Vierwaldstättersjön [fi:rvalt ˣʃtätter-] the Lake of Lucerne

vietna'mes s3 Vietnamese (pl lika) **-isk** [-'me:-] a5 Vietnamese

vift s3, ute på ~ out on the spree

vift|a I s1 whisk **II** v1 wave (farväl åt ngn s.b. farewell); ~ bort whisk away (flugor flies); ~ med wave; brandish; ~ på svansen wag its tail **-ning** waving, wave; wag

vig a1 agile, supple, lithe

vig|a v2 **1** (helga, in-) consecrate; (präst) ordain; (ägna) dedicate, devote (sitt liv åt one's life to); ~ ngn till biskop consecrate s.b. bishop; ~ ngn till den sista vilan commit s.b. to his (etc.) last resting place; -d jord consecrated ground **2** (förena genom vigsel) marry; ~s get married (vid to)

1 vigg s2 (fågel) tufted duck

2 vigg s2, vard. touch; slå en ~ hos ngn touch s.b. for money

vigga vard. touch

vighet [ˣvi:g-] agility, suppleness, litheness

vigil|lans [-'lans, -'laŋs] *s3, se 2 vigg* **-era** *se vigga*

vigsel ['vi:g-, 'vick-] *s2* marriage [ceremony], wedding; *borgerlig ~* civil marriage; *kyrklig ~* church (religious) marriage; *förrätta ~* officiate at a marriage **-akt** marriage ceremony, spousal (*ofta pl*) **-attest, -bevis** marriage certificate (lines *pl*) **-formulär** marriage formula **-förrättare** person officiating at a wedding **-ring** wedding ring

vig|vatten holy water **-vattenskål** holy water stoup

vigör vigour; fettle; *vid full ~* in full vigour (capital form)

vik *s2* bay; (*mindre*) creek; (*havs-*) gulf; *ha en vän i ~en* (*vard.*) have a friend at court

vik|a *vek -it el. -t* **1** fold; (*~ dubbel äv.*) double; (*fåll*) turn in; *får ej ~s* do not bend **2** (*gå undan*) yield, give in (*för* to); (*flytta sig*) budge; *mil.* retreat; *bildl.* waver, flinch; *~ för övermakten* yield to [superior] numbers; *inte ~ en tum* not move an inch; *han vek inte från hennes sida* he did not budge from her side; *~ om hörnet* turn [round] the corner; *~ åt sidan* turn aside; *vik hädan!* get thee behind me! **3** *ge ~* give way (in) (*för* to), (*böja sig*) yield (*för* to), (*falla ihop*) collapse; *inte ge ~* (*äv.*) hold one's own, keep firm **4** *vard.* (*reservera*) set aside; *platsen är -t för honom* the post is earmarked for him **5** *rfl* double up; (*böja sig*) bend; *benen vek sig under mig* my legs gave way under me; *gå och ~ sig* (*vard.*) turn in **6** (*med betonad partikel*) *~ av* turn off; *~ ihop* fold up; *~ in* fold in, *sömn.* turn in; *~ in på* turn into (*en gata* a street); *~ ner* turn down; *~ tillbaka a*) fold back, *b*) (*dra sig undan*) fall back, (*om pers.*) retire; *~ undan a*) fold back, *b*) (*gå åt sidan*) give way, stand aside, (*för slag e.d.*) dodge; *~ upp a*) turn up, (*ärmar äv.*) tuck up, *b*) (*veckla upp*) unfold; *~ ut* unfold **vikande** *a4, aldrig ~* never yielding, (*ständig*) incessant

vikare *zool.* ringed seal

vikari'at *s7* deputyship; temporary post

vikarie [-'ka:-] *s5* deputy; (*för lärare*) substitute; (*för läkare, präst*) locum [tenens]

vikarier|a *~ för ngn* deputize for s.b., act as a p.'s substitute **-ande** *a4* deputy; acting (*professor* professor)

vik|bar [ˣvi:k-] *a1* foldable **-dörr** folding door

viking Viking

vikinga|balk law of the Vikings **-färd** Viking expedition **-skepp** Viking ship **-tiden** the Viking Age **-tåg** Viking raid

vikit *sup. av vika*

1 vikt [-i:-] *sup. o. perf. part. av vika*

2 vikt [vikt] *s3* **1** weight (*äv. konkr.*); *fys.* gravity; *efter ~* by weight; *i lös ~* in bulk; *specifik ~* specific gravity; *förlora i ~* lose weight; *hålla ~en* be full weight; watch one's weight (diet); *inte hålla ~en* be (fall) short in weight **2** (*betydelse*) importance; weight; *lägga ~ vid* lay stress on; *av största ~* of the utmost importance; [*inte*] *vara av ~* be of [no] consequence (importance)

vikta *stat.* weight

vikt|enhet unit of weight **-förlust** loss of weight

viktig *a1* **I** (*betydelsefull*) important, of importance; (*allvarlig*) serious (*problem* problem); (*angelägen*) urgent (*sak* matter); *ytterst ~* vital[ly important], of utmost importance; *det ~aste* the main (most important) thing, the essential point **2** (*högfärdig*) self-important, stuck-up; *göra sig ~* put on airs **-petter** *s2* stuck-up fellow

vikt|klass *sport.* class, weight **-lös** weightless **-löshet** weightlessness **-minskning** reduction in weight **-mängd** weight

viktori'ansk [-a:-] *a5* Victorian

vikt|sats set of weights **-system** system of weights

viktualiehandlare [-ˣa:li-] provision merchant

viktualier [-'a:li-] *pl* provisions, victuals

viktökning increase in (of) weight

vila I *s1* rest (*äv. om maskin e.d.*), recumbence, recumbency; (*ro äv.*) repose; *en stunds ~* a little rest; *i ~* at rest; *söka ~* seek repose; *den sista (eviga) ~n* the final rest **II** *v1* rest (*mot* against, on); repose; *absol. äv.* be at rest; (*vara stödd äv.*) lean (*mot* on); *arbetet ~r* work is at a standstill; *här ~r* here lies; *~ i frid!* sleep in peace!; *saken får ~ tills vidare* the matter must rest there [for the present]; *avgörandet ~r hos honom* the decision rests with him; *~ sig* rest [o.s.], take a rest; *~ på* rest on, (*vara grundad på*) be based (founded) on; *~ på hanen* have one's finger on the trigger; *~ på årorna* rest on one's oars; *det ~r en förbannelse över a*) (*ngn*) a curse has fallen on, *b*) (*ngt*) there is a curse upon; *~ ut* have a good rest

vild *a1* **1** wild; (*ociviliserad, otämjd*) savage (*stammar* tribes) (*ouppodlad, ödslig*) uncultivated; (*förvildad*) feral; *~a djur* wild (savage) animals; *V~a Västern* the Wild West **2** *bildl.* wild; (*otyglad äv.*) unruly (*pojke* boy); (*rasande*) furious (*fart* pace); *~a fantasier* wild ideas; *~ flykt* headlong flight; *~ förtvivlan* wild despair; *föra ett vilt liv* lead a wild (dissipated) life; *vilt raseri* frenzied rage; *bli ~* go mad (frantic) (*av glädje* with joy); *vara ~* (*utom sig*) be beside o.s., be mad (*av* with); *vara ~ i* (*på, efter*) be mad for; *vara ~ på att* be wild to **-and** wild duck **-apel** crab apple [tree] **-basare** scapegrace **-djur** wild beast; *bildl. äv.* brute

vild|e *s2* savage; *AE. polit.* maverick **-fågel** wildfowl **-gås** wild goose **-havre** wild oats (*pl*); *så sin ~* sow one's wild oats **-het** wildness; savagery; (*sinnelag äv.*) wild character; (*-sinthet*) ferocity **-hjärna** madcap **-honung** wild honey **-inna** female savage, wild woman **-katt** wildcat **-mark** wilderness; wilds (*pl*) **-marksliv** life in the wilds **-ros** wild rose **-sint** *a1* fierce, savage, ferocious **-svin** [wild] boar **-svinshona** wild sow **-vin** Virginia creeper, *AE.* American ivy, woodbine **-vuxen** that runs wild, wild

vilja I *s1* will; (*önskan*) wish, desire; (*avsikt*) intention; *med bästa ~ i världen* with the best will in the world; *av egen fri ~* of one's own accord (free will); *med litet god ~* with a little good will; *ngns sista ~* a p.'s last will [and testament]; *driva sin ~ igenom* work one's will; *få sin ~ igenom* get (have) one's own way, have one's will; *med eller mot sin ~* whether one will (likes it) or not; *göra ngt med ~ do* s.th. on purpose (deliberately, purposely) **II** *ville velat* **1** will; (*vara villig* [*att*] *äv.*) be willing [to]; (*åstunda, önska*) want, wish, desire; (*ha lust* [*till*]) like, please; (*ämna*) intend, mean; (*stå i begrepp att*) be about (going) to; *~ ngns bästa* desire a p.'s good; *~ ngn väl* wish s.b. well; *~ är ett och kunna ett annat* to be willing is one thing, to be able another; *det ena du vill, det andra du skall* what I would I cannot and what I would not I must; *det är det jag vill* that is what I want; *du kan om du vill* you can if you want to; *jag både vill och inte vill* (*äv.*) I am in two minds; *som du vill!* [just] as you like!; *låta ngn göra som han vill* let s.b. have his own way (mind); *det vill jag verkligen hoppas* I should hope so; *det vill tyckas som om* it would seem as though; *slumpen ville att vi* [as] chance would have it, we; *vad vill du ha?* what do you want?, (*om mat e.d.*) what will you have?; *vad vill du att jag skall göra?* what do you want me to do?; *vad vill du mig?* what do you want of me?; *jag vill gärna* I should like to (*gå dit* go there), I shall be glad to (*komma* come; *hjälpa dig* help you); *motorn vill gärna stanna* the engine is apt to stop; *jag skulle ~* I should like to; *jag skulle ~ ha* I should like [to have]; *nej, det vill jag inte* no, I won't; *han vill inte att hon skall a*) (*tillåter inte*) he won't have her (+ *ing-form*), *b*) (*tycker inte om*) he does not like her (+ *ing-form*), *c*) (*önskar inte*) he does not want her to (+ *inf.*); *jag vill inte gärna* I would rather not, I prefer not to; *härmed vill jag inte ha sagt* by this I don't mean; *du vill väl inte säga att ...?* you surely don't mean to say that ...?; *jag ville inte* I did not want to, (*vägrade*) I would not **2** (*med betonad partikel*) *inte ~ fram med a*) (*pengar*) not want to fork out, *b*) (*sanningen etc.*) not want to come out with; *~ hem* want to go home; *det vill till mycket pengar* it takes (requires) a lot of money; *det vill till att kunna arbeta om* it takes a lot of work if; *~ åt* (*ngn*) want to get at s.b., (*ngt*) want to get hold of s.th. **3** *rfl, om det vill sig väl* (*illa*) if all goes well (if things go wrong); *det vill sig inte för mig* nothing is going right for me; *det ville sig så väl att vi* (*äv.*) as [good] luck would have it, we

vilje|akt [act of] volition **-ansträngning** effort of will **-fast** firm of purpose **-kraft** willpower **-liv** volitional life **-lös** without a will of one's own, weak-minded; (*apatisk*) apathetic

vilje|s *i uttr.: göra ngn till ~* do as s.b. wants, humour s.b. **-stark** strong-willed; (*beslutsam*) resolute, determined **-styrka** *se viljekraft* **-svag** weak-willed **-yttring** manifestation of the (one's) will

vilk|en 1 *rel. a*) *självst.* (*om pers.*) who, (*om sak*) which, (*i inskränkande satser äv.*) that, *b*) *fören.* which; *-a alla* all of whom, (*om saker*) all of which; *de -as namn* those whose names; *den stad i ~ jag bor* (*äv.*) the town where I live; *gör -et du vill* do as (what) you like; *om hon kommer, -et är föga troligt* if she comes, which is not very likely **2** *interr. a*) (*vid*

urval) which, *b*) (*i obegränsad bet.*) (*fören. om pers. o. saker, självst. om saker*) what, (*självst. om pers.*) who, (*vid urval*) which of them; *~ bok skall jag köpa?* (*~ av dessa*) which (*~ av alla:* what) book shall I buy?; *-a är dina skäl?* what are your reasons?; *åt -et håll skall vi gå?* which way shall we go?; *~ härlig dag!* what a lovely day!; *-a vackra blommor!* what beautiful flowers! **3** *indef.*, *~ som helst* anyone, anybody; *får jag ta ~ som helst* [*av de här två*]? may I take either [of these two]?; *~ som helst som* whoever, whichever; *~ ... än* whichever, whatever, (*om pers.*) whoever

vilkendera which [of them (the two)]

vill *pres. av vilja*

1 villa *s1* **I** (*villfarelse*) illusion, delusion; (*förvirring*) confusion; *optisk ~* optical illusion; *då blir den sista ~n värre än den första* (*bibl.*) so the last error shall be worse than the first **II** *v1*, *~ bort* confuse; *~ bort sig* lose one's way, *bildl.* go astray; *på ~nde hav* on the boundless sea

2 villa *s1* house; (*större*) villa; (*enplans-*) bungalow; (*stuga*) cottage

villa|bebyggelse *området är avsett för ~* the area is reserved for the building of one-family houses **-kvarter** *se -område* **-olja** light fuel oil **-område** residential district (neighbourhood) **-stad** residential (garden) suburb **-ägare** houseowner

ville *imperf. av vilja*

villebråd *s7* game; (*jagat el. dödat*) quarry

villervalla *s1* (*förvirring*) confusion; (*oreda*) muddle, jumble; *allmän ~* general confusion

villfara grant, comply with (*ngns önskan* a p.'s wish)

villfarelse delusion; mistake; *sväva i den ~n att* be under the delusion that; *ta ngn ur hans ~r* enlighten s.b., open a p.'s eyes

villig *a1* willing; ready; prepared; *vara ~* (*äv.*) agree (*att komma* to come) **-het** willingness; readiness

villkor [-å:r] *s7* **1** condition; *pl* (*i kontrakt, fördrag e.d.*) terms; (*bestämmelser*) stipulation, (*förbehåll*) provision, reserve; *på goda ~* on favourable (fair) terms; *på inga ~* on no condition; *på ~ att* on [the] condition that, provided [that]; *på överenskomna ~* on the terms agreed upon; *ställa som ~* make ... a condition; *ställa som ~ att* make it a condition that; *uppställa som ~* state as a condition; *våra ~ är följande* our terms are as follows **2** (*levnads-*) *pl* condition (*sg*), circumstances; *leva i* (*under*) *svåra ~* be badly off, live in reduced circumstances **-lig** [-å:-] *a1* conditional; *~ dom* suspended (qualified, conditional) sentence; *få ~ dom* (*äv.*) be put on probation; *~ frigivning* conditional release **-ligt** [-å:-] *adv* conditionally; *~ dömd* (*person*) probationer; *~ frigiven* on parole, released conditionally

villkors|bisats conditional clause **-lös** unconditional (*kapitulation* surrender)

villo|lära false doctrine; (*kätteri*) heresy **-spår** *komma* (*vara*) *på ~* get (be) on the wrong track; *föra ngn på ~* (*äv.*) throw s.b. off the scent **-väg** false path, wrong way; *föra ngn på ~ar* lead s.b. astray

V

villrådig irresolute (*om* as to); *vara* ~ (*äv.*) be in two minds (*om huruvida* as to whether) **-het** irresolution; hesitation

villsam *a1*, *bildl.* confusing, puzzling; *~ma vägar* devious paths

vilo|dag day of rest **-hem** nursing (convalescent) home **-läge** rest[ing] position, *i* ~ at rest **-läger** place of repose **-paus** break, pause **-rum** (*grav*) last resting place **-stund** hour of rest, leisure hour **-tid** time of rest

vilsam [ˣviːl-] *a1* restful

vilse *adv o. oböjligt a* astray; *gå* ~ go astray, lose one's way (o.s.), (*i skogen*) get lost [in the woods]; *föra ngn* ~ lead s.b. astray, *bildl. äv.* mislead s.b. **-förd** [-öː-] *a5* led astray, misguided, misled **-gången** *a5*, **-kommen** [-å-] *a5* gone astray; stray; *känna sig -kommen* feel lost **-leda** lead astray, mislead; (*leda på fel spår*) throw off the scent, lead by the nose **-ledande** *a4* misleading, deceptive; ~ *framställning* (*äv.*) misrepresentation

vilsen lost; confused

vil|soffa couch **-stol** (*fåtölj*) easy chair, armchair; (*fällstol*) folding (reclining) chair

vilt I *adv* wildly *etc., jfr vild*; *växa* ~ grow wild; ~ *främmande* perfectly (quite) strange; *en* ~ *främmande människa* an absolute (perfect, complete) stranger **II** *s7* game **-bestånd** stock of game **-handel** poulterer's [shop] **-reservat** wildlife refuge **-vård** wildlife conservation, game protection **-vårdare** game warden

vimla swarm, be crowded, teem (*av* with); abound (*av* in); *det ~r av folk på stranden* the beach is swarming with people; *det ~r av fisk i sjön* the lake is teeming with fish

vimmel ['vimm-] *s7* crowd, throng **-kantig** *a1* giddy, dizzy; (*förvirrad*) bewildered; *den gjorde mig* ~ (*äv.*) it made my head swim

vimpel *s2* streamer; *sjö. o. mil.* pennant

vimsig *a1* scatterbrained, featherbrained

1 vin *s4* (*-ranka*) vine; (*dryck*) wine; ~ *av årets skörd* this year's vintage; *där ~et går in går vettet ut* when the wine is in the wit is out; *skörda ~et* gather in the vintage

2 vin *s7* (*-ande*) whine, whiz[z]; whistle; *stormens* ~ the howl of the storm

vin|a *ven -it* whine, whistle; sough; *kulorna ven* the bullets whistled (whizzed); *vinden -er* the wind is howling; *i ~nde fart* at a headlong (rattling) pace

vin|beredning wine-making **-berg** hill planted with vines **-bergssnäcka** edible snail **-bär** (*svart*) blackcurrant; (*rött*) redcurrant **-bärsbuske** currant bush **-bärssaft** *svart* ~ blackcurrant juice

1 vind *s2* (*blåst*) wind; *väder och* ~ wind and weather; *god* (*nordlig*) ~ fair (north[erly]) wind; *svag* ~ light breeze; *växlande ~ar* variable (*sjö.* baffling) winds; *vad blåser det för* ~ *i dag?* what is the wind today?, *bildl.* (*eftersom du kommer*) what wind has blown you in here?; *med ~ens hastighet* with lightning speed, like the wind; *borta med ~en* gone with the wind; *~en har vänt sig* the wind has shifted (veered); *få* ~ *i seglen* catch the wind, *bildl.* get a good start; *gå upp i* ~ sail near the wind; *driva* ~ *för våg* be adrift, be drifting [at the mercy of the winds]; *låta ngt gå* ~ *för våg* let s.th. take care of itself; *lämna sina barn* ~ *för våg* leave one's children to fend for themselves; *skingras för alla ~ar* be scattered to the winds

2 vind *s2* (*i byggnad*) attic, garret; loft; *på ~en* in the attic (*etc.*)

3 vind *a1* (*skev*) warped; askew; (*sned o.* ~) twisted

1 vinda I *s1* (*nyst-*) winder, reel **II** *v1*, ~ [*upp*] wind [up]; (*ankare*) hoist, heave [up]

2 vinda *v1* (*skela*) squint, have a squint, be cross-eyed

3 vinda *s1*, *bot.* bindweed

vindbrygga drawbridge

vind|böjtel *s2*, *pers.* weathercock **-driven 1** weather-driven; *bildl.* rootless **2** (*om väderkvarn*) wind-driven

vindel *s2* whorl; spiral **-trappa** winding (spiral) staircase

vind|energi wind energy **-fläkt** breath of wind **-flöjel** weathercock, [weather] vane **-fång 1** (*förstuga*) [small] entry, porch **2** (*yta*) surface exposed to the wind; *ha stort* ~ catch a great deal of wind **-fälle** *s6* windfall[en tree] **- hastighet** velocity of wind, wind velocity

vindi|cera reclaim, vindicate **-kation** claim for restitution of property

vindil gust [of wind]

vindistrikt winegrowing district

vind|kantring change of wind **-kast** sudden shift of wind

vindkraft wind power **-anläggning**, **-verk** wind power station (plant)

vindkåre breeze

vindla wind, meander

vindling whorl; *fack. äv.* convolution (*i hjärnan* of the brain); *~ar* (*i flod, väg e.d.*) windings

vind|motor wind wheel **-mätare** anemometer, wind gauge **-pinad** *a5* windswept; (*om träd o.d.*) windblown **-pust** whiff (puff) of wind **-riktning** direction of the wind **-ros** *meteor.* wind rose; (*kompass-*) compass card **-ruta** windscreen; *AE.* windshield **-rutespolare** windscreen washer **-rutetorkare** windscreen (*AE.* windshield) wiper

vindruva grape

vindruvsklase bunch of grapes

vinds|fönster attic (garret) window **-glugg** skylight

vind|sidan the windward side; *åt* ~ windward **-skala** scale of wind force

vinds|kammare attic (garret) [room] **-kontor** boxroom [in the attic (garret)] **-kupa** attic

vindskydd windshield, windbreak

vindslucka ceiling hatch

vindspel winch, windlass

vindsrum [room in the] attic, garret [room]

vindstilla I *oböjligt a* calm, becalmed **II** *s1* calm

vindstrappa staircase up to the attic

vind|strut windsock, air sock, wind cone (sleeve) **-styrka** wind force **-stöt** gust [of wind], squall

vindsvåning attic [storey]

vind|tunnel wind tunnel (channel) **-turbin** wind turbine **-tyg** windproof cloth **-tygsjacka** windcheater, windjammer, *AE.* windbreaker

(varumärke) **-tät** windproof **- vridning** shift (change) of wind
vindögd *a1* squint-eyed **-het** squint
vinerbröd *se* **wienerbröd**
vinflaska bottle of wine; *(tom)* wine bottle
ving|ad *s6* winged **-ben** wing bone **-bredd** wingspread; *flyg.* [wing]span **-bruten** broken--winged *(äv. bildl.)*
ving|e *s2* wing *(äv. bot.)*; *(på fläkt)* blade; *flaxa med -arna* flap (flutter) the wings; *flyga högre än -arna bär* fly too high; *få luft under -arna (bildl.)* get started, get going; *pröva -arna (bildl.)* try paddling one's own canoe; *ta ngn under sina -ars skugga (bildl.)* take s.b. under one's wing **-frukt** key, key-fruit **-klaff** *flyg.* wing flap **-klippa** clip ...'s wings; pinion
vingla *(gå ostadigt)* stagger; *(stå ostadigt)* wobble, sway [to and fro]
vinglas wineglass
vinglig *a1 (som rör sig ostadigt)* staggering *(gång gait); (som står ostadigt)* wobbly *(stol* chair) **-het** unsteadiness
vinglögg mulled wine
ving|lös wingless **-mutter** wing (butterfly) nut **-par** pair of wings **-penna** wing quill, pinion **-skjuten** *a5* winged **-slag** wing-beat **-snäcka** pteropod, sea butterfly **-spegel** *zool.* speculum **-spets** wing tip, tip of the wing; *avstånd mellan -arna* span **-sus** swish of wings **-tippa** *flyg.* dip wings
vin|gud god of wine **-gård** vineyard **-gårds-man** vinedresser **-handlare** wine merchant, vintner
vinit *sup. av* **vina**
vin'jett *s3* vignette, [printer's] flower; *(slut-)* tailpiece
vinjäst wine yeast
vink *s2* **1** wave; *(med handen)* beck; *lyda ngns minsta ~* obey a p.'s every sign, be at a p.'s beck and call; *vid minsta ~ från* at a nod from **2** *(antydan)* hint; *en tydlig ~* a broad hint; *en fin ~ (äv.)* a gentle reminder; *ge ngn en ~* give (drop) s.b. a hint; *förstå ~en* take the hint
vinka **1** *(med handen)* wave *(åt at; farväl* farewell); *(göra tecken)* beckon *(åt to; ngn till sig* s.b. to come up [to one]); *~ avvärjande* make a deprecating gesture; *~ åt ngn att (äv.)* sign to s.b. to **2** *vi har inte mycket tid att ~ på* we have not much time to spare
vinkel *s2* **1** *mat.* angle; *(på rör)* knee, elbow; *(verktyg)* try square; *död ~* dead angle; *spetsig (trubbig) ~* acute (obtuse) angle; *i ~ at an* angle; *i rät ~ mot* at right angles to; *i 60° ~* at an angle of 60 degrees; *bilda ~ mot* form an angle with **2** *(vrå)* nook; *(hörn)* corner; *i alla vinklar och vrår* in every nook and corner **-ben** side (leg) of an angle **-formig** [-å-] *a1* angular **-hake** set square, triangle; *boktr.* composing stick **-järn** angle iron (bar) **-linjal** T-square **-mått** square rule, joint hook **-rät** perpendicular, at right angles *(mot* to); *gå ~t mot varandra* be at right angles to each other **-spets** vertex [of an angle]
vinkl|a angle, slant; weight; bias **-ing** angle, slant; weighting; bias
vinkning waving *etc., se* **vinka**
vin|krus wine jar, tankard **-kylare** wine cooler

-källare wine cellar **-kännare** connoisseur of wine **-lista** wine list **-löv** vine leaf **-lövsranka** vine leaves *(pl)*
vinn *oböjligt s, lägga sig ~ om, se* **vinnlägga** *[sig]*
vinn|a *vann vunnit* **1** *(segra* [i]; *erhålla vinst)* win *(ett krig* a war; *pris* a prize; *en process* a suit; *på lotteri* in a lottery); *~ i bridge (på tips)* win at bridge (the pools); *~ i ärlig strid* win a fair fight; *~ på poäng* win by points; *~ över ngn (äv.)* beat s.b. **2** *(skaffa sig)* gain; *(förvärva)* acquire; *(uppnå)* attain, obtain; *~ avsättning för* find a [ready] market for; *~ [ngns] bifall* meet with [a p.'s] approval; *~ erkännande* gain (receive) recognition; *~ gehör* obtain a hearing; *~ ngns hjärta* win a p.'s heart; *~ insteg* gain (obtain) a footing; *~ inträde* obtain admission; *~ laga kraft* gain legal force, become legal[ly binding]; *~ ngn för sin sak* get s.b. on one's side, win s.b. for one's cause; *~ spridning* become popular; *~ sitt syfte* gain (attain) one's end; *~ terräng (tid)* gain ground (time) **3** *(förändras t. sin fördel)* gain *(vid jämförelse* by comparison); *([för]tjäna)* profit *(på affären* by the transaction); *du -er ingenting på att* you'll gain nothing by *(+ ing-form)*; *hon -er i längden (vid närmare bekantskap)* she improves on closer acquaintance, she grows on you; *~ på bytet* profit by (win on) the bargain (change); *rummet kommer att ~ på ommöbleringen* the room will improve with refurnishing **4** *~ på ngn (knappa in)* gain [ground] on s.b., *trägen -er* perseverance carries the day
vinn|ande *a4* winning; *(tilltalande äv.)* attractive **-are** winner **-ing** gain; profit; *snöd ~* sordid gain, filthy lucre
vinnings|lysten covetous, mercenary, greedy **-lystnad** greed, covetousness **-syfte** *i ~ with* the intention of gain
vinnlägga *rfl, ~ sig om* take pains *(att skriva fint* to write well; *ett gott uppförande* to behave well); strive after
vin|odlare wine-grower; viticulturer, viticulturist **-odling** wine-growing; viticulture **-press** winepress **-provare** wine-taster **-provning** wine-tasting **-ranka** [grape]vine **-rättighet** licence to serve wine **-röd** wine-red
vinsch *s2, s3* winch; hoist **vinscha** hoist
vin|skörd vintage, wine harvest **-sort** sort of wine
vinst *s3* gain; *i sht hand.* profit[s *pl*]; *(behållning)* proceeds *(pl)*, return; *(i lotteri)* prize; *(på spel)* winnings *(pl)*; *~ och förlust* profit and loss; *på ~ och förlust (bildl.)* at random (a venture), on speculation; *del i ~* share in profits; *högsta ~en* the first prize; *ren ~* net (clear) profit; *ta in 10 pund i ren ~* make a clear profit of £10; *ge ~* yield a profit, turn out well; *gå med ~ (om företag)* be a paying concern; *sälja med ~* sell at a profit; *utfalla med ~ (om lott)* be a winning ticket **-andel** share of (in) [the] profits **-begär** greed, cupidity **-delning** profit--sharing
vinsten [ˣviːn-] tartar; *kem.* potassium bitartrate, potassium hydrogen tartrate; *renad ~* cream of tartar

vinst|givande profitable, remunerative, lucrative **-kupong** dividend warrant **-lista** [lottery] prize list, lottery list **-lott** winning ticket **-marginal** profit margin **-medel** *pl* profits
vinst- och förlust|konto, -räkning profit and loss account
vinstock [grape]vine
vinstsida *på ~n* on the credit side
vin|stuga tavern, bodega **-syra** tartaric acid **-säck** wineskin
vint|er ['vinn-] *s2* winter; *i ~* this winter; *mitt i ~n* in the middle of [the] winter, in midwinter; *i -ras* last winter; *om (på) ~n (-rarna)* in winter
vinter|badare winter bather **-bona** make fit for winter habitation **-bostad** winter residence **-dag** winter['s] day **-dvala** winter (hibernal) sleep; *ligga i ~* hibernate **-däck** snow tyre **-frukt** winter fruit **-fälttåg** winter campaign **-förråd** winter stock (supply) **-gatan** the Milky Way, the Galaxy **-grön** evergreen **-gröna** *s1 (Pyrola)* wintergreen; *(trädgårds-)* [lesser] periwinkle **-gäck** [-j-] *s2, bot.* winter aconite **-halvår** winter half (term) **-härdig** hardy **-idrott** winter sports *(pl)* **-kappa** winter coat **-klädd** winter-clad **-kläder** *pl* winter clothes (clothing *sg*) **-kvarter** *s7 (lägga sig i* go into) winter quarters *(pl)* **-kyla** cold of winter, winter cold **-körning** *(bil-)* winter motoring
vinter|lig *a1* wintry; brumous **-olympiad** Olympic Winter Games **-rock** winter coat, greatcoat **-solstånd** winter solstice **-sport** *s3* winter sports *(pl)* **-sportort** winter sports resort **-sömn** *se vinterdvala* **-tid I** *s3* wintertime, winter season **II** *adv* in [the] winter **-trädgård** winter garden **-väg** winter road
vintrig *a1* wint[e]ry, winterly, winter-like
vinthund greyhound
vintunna wine cask (barrel)
vi'nyl *s3* vinyl **-plast** vinyl plastic **-platta** vinyl tile
vinår *(gott* good) vintage [year]
vin|jäger [-'nä:-] *s2*, **-ättika** wine vinegar
vi'ol *s3* violet
viola ['vi:-, -'å:la] *s1* viola, tenor violin
viol|blå violet-blue **-'ett** *a1* violet; *(rödaktig äv.)* purple; *(blålila äv.)* mauve
vio'lin *s3* violin **-ist** violinist; *förste ~* first violin[ist] **-klav** treble (G) clef
violoncell [-lån'sell, -låŋ'sell] *s3* [violon]cello
viol|doft fragrance of violets **-rot** orrisroot
VIP [vipp] *s2* VIP *(initialord för very important person)*
vipa *s1, zool.* lapwing, peewit
vipp *s2, vard., vara på ~en att* be on the point of (+ ing-form); *det var på ~en att han föll* he was within an ace of falling; *kola ~en (sl.)* kick the bucket
1 vippa *s1* **1** puff; *jfr damm-, puder-* **2** *bot.* panicle
2 vipp|a *v1* tilt (tip) [up]; *(röra sig upp o. ner)* rock, bob up and down; *~ på stjärten* wag[gle] one's tail
vipp|arm rocker [arm], lever arm **-kärra** tilt cart **-port** *(hopskr. vipport) (garagedörr)* overhead door
vips *~ var han borta* hey presto, he was gone!
1 vira *s9 (kortspel)* vira

2 vira *v1* wind *(med* [round] with; *om[kring]* round); *(veckla)* wrap; *(krans)* weave; *~ in* wrap up *(i* in); *~ av* unwind
vi'ril *a1* virile
virka crochet
virke *s6* wood, timber; *AE.* lumber; *färskt ~* green wood; *hyvlat ~* planed wood; *ohyvlat ~* rough sawn timber; *kvistfritt ~* clean timber; *han är av hårdare ~ än sin bror* he's of a tougher fibre than his brother
virkes|avfall wood waste **-mätning** timber scaling **-upplag** stock of timber (wood)
virk|garn crochet yarn **-ning** crocheting; *konkr.* [piece of] crochet [work] **-nål** crochet hook
viro|log virologist **-logi** virology **-logisk** *a5* virological
virrig *a1 (om pers.)* muddleheaded, scatterbrained; *(om sak)* muddled, confused *(svar* reply); *(osammanhängande)* disconnected *(tal* speech) **-het** confused state of mind, muddleheadedness *etc.*
virrvarr *s7* confusion, muddle; *vard.* mess; *ett ~ av* a confused (tangled) heap of
virtu'ell *a5* virtual; *~t minne (data.)* virtual memory; *~ verklighet* virtual reality
virtu'os I *s3* virtuoso; master **II** *a1* masterly **-itet** virtuosity
viru'l|en|s *s3* virulence **-'ent** *a1* virulent
virus ['vi:-] *s7, best. form äv. virus* virus **-sjukdom** virus disease
virvel *s2* **1** whirl *(äv. bildl.)*; turbulence; *(ström-)* whirlpool, *(mindre)* eddy; *fack. o. bildl.* vortex *(pl* vortexes, vortices); *(hår-)* vertex *(pl* vertexes, vertices); *en ~ av nöjen* a whirl of pleasures; *dansens virvlar* the whirls of the dance **2** *(trum-)* roll; *slå en ~* beat a roll **-rörelse** whirling motion, gyration, turbulence **-storm** cyclone **-vind** whirlwind
virvla whirl; *(om vatten)* eddy; *~ runt* whirl round; *~ upp* whirl up
1 vis *s7 (sätt)* manner, way; *på det ~et* in that way, *(i utrop)* oh, that's how it is!, I see!; *på sätt och ~* in a way; *på intet ~* in no way; *på sitt ~ är hon snäll* she is quite nice in her own way
2 vis *a1* wise; *en ~ [man] (äv.)* a sage; *Greklands sju ~e* the seven sages; *de ~es sten* the philosophers' stone; *de tre ~e männen* the three wise men, the three Magi; *av skadan bli man ~* experience is the father of wisdom; once bit, twice shy
1 vis|a *s1* song; ballad; *Höga ~n* the Song of Songs (Solomon); *ord och inga -or* plain words (speaking); *hon är en ~ i hela stan* she is the talk of the town; *alltid samma ~* always the same old story; *slutet på ~n blev att* the end of the story was that
2 visa *v1* **1** show *(vänlighet* kindness; *hur man skall* how to); *(peka)* point *(på* out, to); *(ut-)* indicate, show *(tiden* the time); *(förete)* present, show *(ett glatt ansikte* a happy face), produce *(biljetten* one's ticket); *(ådagalägga)* exhibit, display *(skicklighet* skill); *(be-)* prove, show; *erfarenheten ~r att* experience proves (tells us) that; *utställningen ~s kl.* the exhibition may be seen (visited) at; *~ ngn en artighet* show courtesy to s.b.; *~ med exempel*

demonstrate by example; ~ *ngn på dörren* show s.b. the door, turn s.b. out; ~ *tänderna* (*bildl.*) show fight; *gå före och* ~ *vägen* lead the way; ~ *ngn vägen till* show s.b. the way to, direct s.b. to; *klockan ~r på 8* the clock says 8; *termometern ~r på 20* the thermometer says 20 **2** (*med betonad partikel*) ~ *bort* dismiss (*äv. bildl.*), send away; ~ *fram* show, (*ta fram*) produce (*biljetten* one's ticket); ~ *tillbaka* turn back, *bildl.* reject; ~ *upp* show [up], *bildl.* exhibit, produce; ~ *ut* send out **3** *rfl* show o.s. (itself); (*framträda*) appear (*av* from; *för* to; *offentligt* in public); (*bli sedd*) be seen; (*dyka upp*) turn up; *det kommer snart att* ~ *sig* (*bli uppenbart*) it will soon be seen; *åter* ~ *sig* reappear; ~ *sig från sin bästa sida* show one's best side; ~ *sig för pengar* go round in a show; ~ *sig vara* turn out (prove) [to be]; ~ *sig vänlig* be kind, show kindness (*mot* to)

visar|e (*på ur*) hand; (*på instrument*) pointer, indicator, needle **-tavla** dial

visa'vi I *adv o. prep* vis-à-vis, opposite **II** *s3* vis--à-vis, lady (*etc.*) opposite

visbok song book, book of ballads

vischan *s, best. form, vard.* the back of beyond; *AE.* the sticks (*pl*); *på* ~ at the back of beyond, *AE.* out in the sticks

visdiktare song (ballad) writer

visdom *s2* wisdom; (*klokhet äv.*) prudence

visdoms|ord word of wisdom, maxim **-tand** wisdom tooth

vise *s2* queen [bee]

visent European bison, wisent

viser|a visa (*ett pass* a passport) **-ing** visa[ing]

vishet [ˣviːs-] wisdom

vishets|lära philosophy **-regel** maxim

vision vision **-'är** *al o. s3* visionary

1 vi'sir *s3* (*titel*) vizier

2 vi'sir *s7* (*på hjälm*) visor; *fälla upp ~et* raise the visor; *med öppet* ~ (*bildl.*) straightforwardly

visirskiva *foto.* focussing screen

vi'sit *s3* call; visit; *avlägga* ~ *hos ngn* pay s.b. a visit, call on s.b.; *fransysk* ~ flying call **-ation** inspection, examination; (*kropps-*) search; *jur.* revision **-ationsresa** tour of visitation **-dräkt** afternoon dress **-era** inspect; (*tull-*) examine; (*jur. o. friare*) search **-ering** examination; search **-kort** [visiting] card

1 viska I *s1* whisk; (*borste äv.*) wisp **II** *v1* sponge (*ett eldvapen* a firearm)

2 viska *v1* whisper (*ngt t. ngn* s.th. to s.b.); *litt.* susurrate; ~ *ngt i ngns öra* whisper s.th. in a p.'s ear

visk|ning whisper **-ningskampanj** whispering campaign

viskos [-ˈkåːs] *s3* viscose **-itet** viscosity

visky [ˈviss-] *se* whisky

vis'kös *al* viscous

visligen [ˣviːs-] wisely

vismut [ˈviss-] *s3* bismuth

visning [ˣviːs-] show[ing]; demonstration; (*före-äv.*) exhibition; ~ *varje timme* hourly tours

visp *s2* whisk; (*grädd-, ägg-*) beater

visp|a whip (*grädde* cream); (*ägg e.d.*) beat [up] **-grädde** double cream; whipping cream; whipped cream **-ning** whipping *etc.*

---

viss *al* **1** (*säker*) sure, certain (*om, på* about, of); (*tvärsäker*) positive (*på* of); *det är sant och ~t* it is true [enough]; *döden är* ~ death is certain **2** (*odefinierbar*) certain (*skäl* reasons); (*bestämd äv.*) given, fixed (*tid* time); *en* ~ some (*tvekan* hesitation), a certain degree of (*skicklighet* skill); *en* ~ *herr A.* a certain Mr. A.; *hon har ngt ~t* she has a certain s.th.; *på ~a håll* in certain (some) quarters; *till* ~ *grad* to (in) a certain degree (extent); *ställd till* ~ *person* made out to a certain name, personal

vissel|konsert hissing consert **-pipa** whistle

vissen *a3* faded, wilted (*äv. bildl.*); dry, dead; *vard.* (*dålig*) off colour, rotten, (*krasslig*) under the weather

viss|erligen it is true (*är den dyr* that it is expensive), certainly; ~ *... men* it is true [that] (certainly) ... but **-het** certainty; (*tillförsikt*) assurance; *med* ~ (*äv.*) for certain; *få* ~ *om* find out [for certain]; *skaffa sig* ~ *om* ascertain, make sure about

viss|la I *s1* whistle **II** *v1* whistle; ~ *på* whistle for, (*hund*) whistle to; ~ *ut ngn* hiss s.b. [off the stage], *vard.* give s.b. the bird **-ing** (*-ande*) whistling; (*en* ~) whistle; (*kulas*) whizz, whistle

vissna fade; wither, wilt; die down; ~ *bort* (*om pers.*) fade away

visso *s, i uttr.: till yttermera* ~ to make doubly sure, what is more

visst *adv* **1** (*säkerligen*) certainly; to be sure; (*naturligtvis*) by all means; *det kan jag* ~ of course I can; ~ *skall du göra det* [you should do so] by all means; *det tror jag* ~ *det* I most certainly think so; *helt* ~ [most] certainly; ~ *inte* not at all, by no means; *ja* ~! [yes] certainly!, of course!, yes, indeed!, *AE. äv.* sure!; *ja* ~ *ja!* yes, of course, that's true! **2** (*nog*) probably, no doubt; *han har* ~ *rest* he has left, I think; *du tror* ~ you seem to believe (think); *vi har* ~ *träffats förr* I'm sure we must have met be fore

visste *imperf. av veta*

vis|stump scrap of a song **-sångare** ballad singer

vist *s2* (*kortspel*) whist

vist|as *dep* stay; be; (*bo*) live; *hur länge har ni -ats här?* how long have you been [staying] here? **-else** stay; (*boende*) residence **-elseort** [place of] residence, dwelling place, abode; *jur.* domicile

visthus[bod] storehouse; (*matbod*) pantry

visu|alisera visualize **-aliserare** (*i reklambranschen*) visualizer **-'ell** *al* visual

visum *s8* visa (*pl* visas) **-ansökan** application for visa **-tvång** compulsory visa system

vit *al* white; *de ~a* white people, the whites; *~a frun* the White Lady; ~ *slavhandel* white--slave traffic; *~a varor* white goods, linen drapery (*sg*); *sjön går* ~ the sea is white with foam

vit|a *s1* white [of an egg] **-aktig** *al* whitish

vi'tal *al* vital, of vital importance; (*livskraftig*) vigorous; (*mycket viktig äv.*) momentous **-isera** vitalize **-isering** vitalizing **-itet** vitality; vigour

vita'min *s4* vitamin; *fettlösliga* (*vattenlösliga*)

~*er* fat-soluble (watersoluble) vitamins **-behov** vitamin requirement[s *pl*] **-berikad** *a5* vitamin enriched **-brist** vitamin deficiency; avitaminosis **-fattig** deficient in vitamins **-halt** vitamin content **-isera** vitaminize **-isering** vitaminization **-källa** source of vitamins **-piller** vitamin pill **-preparat** vitamin preparation **-rik** rich in vitamins
vit|beta *bot.* white beet **-bok 1** *s2, bot.* hornbeam **2** ~*en -böcker, dipl.* white book
vite *s6* penalty, fine; *vid* ~ under penalty of a fine; *vid ~ av 10 pund* under [a] penalty of a £10 fine; *tillträde vid ~ förbjudet* trespassers will be prosecuted
vitesföreläggande order to pay a fine
vit|fläckig white-spotted **-glödande** incandescent, white-hot **-glödga** bring to a white heat **-gran** white spruce **-grå** whitish grey; hoary **-gul** pale yellow, flaxen **-het** whiteness **-hårig** white-haired; hoary **-kalka** whitewash **-klädd** dressed in white **-klöver** white clover **-kål** white cabbage **-kålshuvud** white cabbage **-limma** whitewash
vitling [ˣvitt-] *zool.* whiting
vit|lök garlic **-löksklyfta** clove of garlic **-mena** *v1* whitewash **-mening** whitewashing; *konkr.* whitewash **-metall** white metal **-mossa** sphagnum, peat moss **-måla** paint white; ~*d* painted white
vit|na [-i:-] whiten, grow (*hastigt:* turn) white **-peppar** white pepper **-prickig** dotted with (spotted) white **-randig** striped [with] white **-rappa** roughcast with white plaster
vi'trin *s3 (skåp)* display cabinet, vitrine; *(låda)* display case
vitri'ol *s3* vitriol
vit|rysk *a1,* **-ryss** *s3* Byelorussian, White Russian
Vitryssland Byelorussia, White Russia
vits *s2 (ordlek)* pun; *(kvickhet)* joke, jest, witticism; *inte förstå* ~*en med ngt* not see the point of s.th.
vits|a pun, crack jokes, joke **-are** punster, joker **-ig** *a1* full of puns (*etc.*); witty
vit|sippa wood anemone, windflower **-skäggig** with a white beard, white-bearded
vits|ord *(vittnesbörd)* testimonial; *(omdöme)* verdict; *(i betyg)* grade, mark; *få goda ~* be highly recommended; *äga ~* be considered lawful evidence **-orda** testify (bear testimony) to; ~ *ngn* give s.b. a good character; ~ *ngns duglighet* recommend s.b., testify to a p.'s ability
1 vitt *best. form det vita* white; *klädd i ~* [dressed] in white; *göra svart till ~* swear black is white
2 vitt *adv* **1** *(vida)* widely *(skild* separated); wide, far *(åtskilda* apart); ~ *och brett,* ~ *omkring* far and wide; *orda ~ och brett om* talk at great length on; ~ *utbredd* widespread; *vara ~ skild från (bildl. äv.)* differ greatly from **2** *så ~ jag vet* as far as I know; *så ~ möjligt* as far as possible; *för så ~ (ifall)* provided, if
vitt|bekant widely known, famous; *(ökänd)* notorious **-berest** *vara* ~ have travelled a great deal, be a travelled person **-berömd** renowned, farfamed, illustrious **-berömdhet** wide renown
vitten ['vitt-] *r el. n, inte vara värd en (ett)* ~ not be worth a damn
vitter ['vitt-] *a2* literary; *en ~ man (äv.)* a man of letters **-het** literature, belles-lettres *(pl, behandlas som sg)* **-hetsakademi** academy of literature *(etc.)*
vitt|förgrenad *a5* with many ramifications, widely ramified **-gående** *a4* far-reaching *(följder* consequences); extensive *(reformer* reforms)
vittja examine [and empty] *(nät* nets); ~ *ngns fickor (vard.)* pick a p.'s pockets
vittn|a *(inför domstol)* witness; give evidence *(om* of); *(intyga)* testify *(om* to), *(skriftligt)* certify; ~ *om (bära -esbörd om)* bear witness to, *(visa äv.)* show
vittne *s6* witness *(till* of); *ha* ~*n på* have witnesses to; *i* ~*ns närvaro* before witnesses; *inkalla ngn som* ~ call s.b. as a witness; *vara* ~ *till* be [a] witness to, witness
vittnes|berättelse deposition [of a witness], evidence **-bås** witness box; *AE.* witness stand **-börd** [-ö:-] *s7* testimony; *jur.* evidence; *bära* ~ *testify; bära falskt* ~ bear false witness **-ed** oath [of a witness] **-ersättning** compensation to witnesses, witness's fee **-förhör** hearing of witnesses; *anställa* ~ examine a witness **-gill** competent to witness; ~ *person* competent witness **-mål** evidence; *(skriftligt)* deposition; *avlägga* ~ give evidence
vitt|omfattande far-reaching, extensive; comprehensive *(studier* studies)
vittr|a weather, decompose
1 vittring *geol.* weathering, decomposition
2 vittring *jakt.* scent; *få upp* ~ pick up the scent; *känna* ~ *efter (äv. bildl.)* catch the scent
vittsvävande high-aspiring, ambitious
vit|tvätt white washing **-varuaffär** linen-draper's business (shop) **-vin** white wine **-öga** white of the eye; *se döden i* ~*t* face death [bravely]
viv *s7, poet.* spouse
vivel *s2* weevil, snout beetle
vivisektion vivisection
vivre ['vi:ver, -re] *s7* board and lodging; *fritt* ~ free board and lodging, all found
vivör snout beetle, *(bildl.)* man about town, rake, roué
Vlissingen [ˣfliss-] *n* Flushing
vo'all *s3* voile
vodka [-å-] *s1* vodka
voffla [-å-] *s1, se våffla*
Vogeserna [få'ge:-] *pl* the Vosges
wok *s2* wok **woka** stirfry
vokabel *s3* vocable, word **-samling** *s2* vocabulary
vokabu'lär *s3* vocabulary
vo'kal I *s3* vowel **II** *a1* vocal **-isation** vocalization **-isera** vocalize **-ist** vocalist; *som* ~ on the vocals **-musik** vocal music **-möte** hiatus
vokativ ['våck-] *s3* vocative
vo'lang *s3* flounce, frill
volauvent [vållå'vaŋ] *s3* vol-au-vent
volfram ['vålf-] *s3, s4* tungsten, wolfram
volleyboll ['vålli-] volleyball
volm, volma *se vålm, vålma*
volontär [vållån'tä:r] *s3 (på kontor)* voluntary

worker, unsalaried clerk; *mil.* volunteer

1 volt [-å-] *s3* **1** (*luftsprång*) somersault; *slå en* ~ turn a somersault **2** (*på ridbana*) volt

2 volt [-å-] *s9, elektr.* volt

volt|astapel voltaic (galvanic) pile **-meter** coulometer, voltameter

volumi'nös *a1* voluminous; (*skrymmande*) bulky

vo'lym *s3* volume **-kontroll** volume control **-procent** percentage by volume

vom [våmm] *se* **våm**

vomera vomit

vorden [ˣvoːr-] *perf. part. av varda, se bliva*

vore (*imperf. konj. av 5 vara*) were; (*skulle vara*) should be (*1 pers.*), would be (*2 o. 3 pers.*); *det ~ trevligt* it would be nice

workout [*ung.* 'wöːkaot] *s3* workout

voter|a vote **-ing** voting, vote; *begära ~* demand a division (*om* on); *vid ~* on a vote

votivtavla [-ˣtiːv-] votive tablet

votum *s8* vote

vov|ve *s2 vard. o. barnspr.* doggy, doggie **--vov** *interj* bow-wow

vrak *s7* wreck (*äv. bildl.*); *bli ~* get wrecked

vraka reject

vrak|gods wreckage, stranded goods; (*flytande*) flotsam; (*kastat över bord*) jetsam **-plundrare** wrecker **-plundring** plundering of wrecks, wrecking

vrakpris bargain price, cut rate; *för ~* dirt-cheap

vrakspillror *pl* wreckage (*sg*), pieces of wreckage

1 vred *imperf. av vrida*

2 vred *s7* handle; (*runt äv.*) knob

3 vred *a1, n sg obest. form undviks* wrathful, irate; very angry; (*starkare*) furious (*på ngn* with s.b.)

vrede *s9* wrath; (*ursinne*) fury, rage; (*ilska*) anger; *koka av ~* foam with rage; *låta sin ~ gå ut över* vent one's anger on; *snar till ~* quick to anger

vredes|mod *i uttr.: i ~* in anger **-utbrott** outburst of anger, fit of rage

vredg|ad *a5, se vred; äv.* incensed, angered **-as** *dep* get angry, become incensed

vrenskas *dep* be difficult to manage; (*om häst*) be restive (balky)

vresig *a1* cross, sullen, surly

vrick|a 1 (*vrida fram o. åter*) wriggle **2** (*båt*) scull **3** (*stuka*) sprain; *~ foten* sprain one's ankle **-ad** *a5, vard.* (*tokig*) nuts, cracked **-borr** gimlet; (*större*) auger **-ning 1** wriggling; (*en ~*) wriggle **2** sculling **3** spraining; (*en ~*) sprain; (*ur led*) dislocation **-åra** scull[ing oar]

vrid|a *vred -it* **1** (*vända*) turn (*på huvudet* one's head); (*hårt*) wring (*nacken av en tupp* a cock's neck; *sina händer* one's hands) (*sno*) twist, wind; (*häftigt*) wrench; (*slita*) wrest; *~ och vända på ett problem* turn a problem over; *~ tvätt* wring [out] washing; *~ ur led* put out of joint, dislocate **2** (*med betonad partikel*) *av* twist (wrench) off, (*kontakt*) switch off; *~ fram klockan* put the clock (one's watch) forward; *~ loss* wrench (wrest) loose; *~ om* turn (*nyckeln* the key); *~ på* (*gasen*) turn on, (*strömmen*) switch on; *~ runt* turn round, revolve; *~ sönder* break [by twisting]; *~ till*

(*kran e.d.*) turn off; *~ tillbaka klockan* put the clock (one's watch) back; *~ upp* (*klocka*) wind up; *~ ur* (*tvätt*) wring out **3** *rfl* turn, revolve (*runt en axel* round an axle); (*sno sig*) twist, wind; writhe (*av smärta* with pain); wriggle (*som en mask* like a worm)

vrid|bar [-iː-] *a1* revolving, rotating, turnable **-en** *a5* twisted; (*för-*) distorted, warped; *bildl.* (*rubbad*) cracked, unhinged **-hållfasthet** torsional (twisting) strength **-it** *sup. av vrida* **-kondensator** adjustable disc condenser **-maskin** (*för tvätt*) wringer, mangle **-moment** torque, torsional moment **-motstånd** rheostat **-ning** [-iːd-] turning *etc.*; (*en ~*) turn *etc.* **-ningsrörelse** rotary movement **-scen** revolving stage

vrist *s3* instep; (*ankel*) ankle; *anat.* tarsus; *smäckra ~er* slim ankles **-rem** shoe-strap

vrå *s5* (*hörn*) corner, nook; (*undangömt ställe*) recess, cranny; *i en undangömd ~ av världen* in an out-of-the-way spot

vråk *s2, zool.* buzzard

vrål *s7* roar[ing], howl[ing], bellow[ing]

vrål|a roar, howl, bellow **-apa** howler [monkey] **-åk** *vard.* flashy high-powered car

vrång *a1* **1** (*ogin*) disobliging, perverse, contrary; *vara ~ mot ngn* (*vard.*) make things difficult for s.b. **2** (*orätt*) wrong; *~ dom* miscarriage of justice, wrong verdict **-bild** distorted picture, caricature **-het** contrariness **-strupe** *få ngt i ~n* have s.th. go down the wrong way

vräk|a *v3* **1** heave; (*kasta*) toss; (*huller om buller*) tumble; *~ bort* toss (throw) away; *~ i sig maten* gobble down the food; *~ omkull* throw over; *~ ur sig* (*bildl.*) spit out (*skällsord* invectives); *~ ut* heave (*etc.*) out, (*pengar*) throw to the winds **2** *rfl* (*kasta sig*) throw (fling) o.s. down (*i* in); *bildl. vard.* play the swell; *~ sig i en fåtölj* lounge about in an armchair; *~ sig i lyx* roll in luxury

vräkig *a1* ostentatious, extravagant; *vard.* flashy **-het** ostentation, extravagance

vräk|ning [- äː-] (*avhysning*) eviction, ejection **-ningsbeslut** eviction order

vränga *v2* **1** (*vända ut o. in på*) turn inside out **2** (*för-*) twist (*lag* the law)

vulgari|sera vulgarize **-tet** vulgarity

vul'gär *a1* vulgar, common **-latin** popular Latin

vul'kan *s3* volcano

vulkaniser|a vulcanize **-ing** vulcanization

vulkan|isk [-ˈkaː-] *a5* volcanic **-kägla** volcanic cone **-utbrott** volcanic eruption **-ö** volcanic island

vulst *s3* **1** *byggn.* torus, round **2** (*plåtslageri.*) upset **3** (*på däck*) bead, heel

vunn|en *a5* gained *etc., se vinna*; *därmed är föga* there is little [to be] gained by that; *därmed är ändå ngt -et* that's something anyway **-it** *sup. av vinna*

vurm *s2* mania, craze, passion (*för* for) **vurma** have a craze (passion) (*för* for)

vurpa I *s1* (*kullkörning*) fall; (*kullerbytta*) somersault **II** *v1* overturn, make a somersault

vuxen *a3* **1** (*full-*) grown-up (*barn* children), adult; *barn och vuxna* children and grown-ups (adults) **2** *vara situationen* ~ be equal to the occasion; *vara* ~ *sin uppgift* be equal (up) to one's task **-gymnasium** upper secondary school for adults **-studerande** adult student **-undervisning, -utbildning** adult education

vy *s3* view; (*utsikt äv.*) sight **-kort** picture postcard

vyss hushaby! **vyss[j]a** [ˣvyssa, ˣvyʃa] lull (*i sömn, till sömns* to sleep)

våd *s3* (*kjol-*) gore; (*tapet-*) length

våda *s1* **1** *jur., av* ~ by misadventure (accident) **2** (*fara*) risk, danger **-dråp** unintentional homicide; *jur.* chance-medley **-skott** accidental shot

våd|eld accidental fire **-lig** [-å:-] *a1* **1** *se farlig* **2** *vard.* (*förfärlig*) awful **-ligt** *adv, vard.* awfully

våffel|järn waffle iron **-vävnad** honeycomb (towelling) fabric

våffla *s1* waffle

1 våg *s2* (*för vägning*) balance; (*butiks-, hushålls- e.d.*) scales (*pl*); *V~en* (*astr.*) Libra, the Scales

2 våg *s1* (*bölja, ljud-, ljus- etc.*) wave (*äv. bildl.*); (*dyning*) roller; (*störtsjö*) breaker; *poet.* billow; *gå i ~or* surge; (*friare äv.*) go in waves, undulate; *~orna går höga* the sea is running high; *diskussionens ~or gick höga* it was a very heated discussion

1 våga (*göra vågig*) ~ *håret* have one's hair waved

2 våga 1 (*tordas*) dare [to]; venture; (*djärvas*) make so bold as to; ~ *försöket* try the experiment; ~ *en gissning* hazard a guess; *friskt ~t är hälften vunnet* boldly ventured is half won; *du skulle bara ~!* you dare!; *~r jag besvära er att ...?* may (might) I trouble you to ...?; *jag ~r påstå att* I venture to say that **2** (*äventyra*) risk, jeopardize (*sitt liv* one's life); (*sätta på spel*) stake (*sitt huvud på* one's life on); *jag ~r hundra mot ett att* I'll stake a hundred to one that **3** *rfl* venture; ~ *sig dit* (*fram*) venture [to go] there (to appear); ~ *sig på a*) (*ngt*) dare to tackle, *b*) (*ngn*) venture to approach (attack); ~ *sig ut i kylan* brave (venture out in) the cold; ~ *sig ut på djupet* dare to go into deep water

vågad *a5* (*djärv*) daring, bold; (*riskfylld*) risky, hazardous; (*frivol*) risqué, *vard.* near the bone; *det är litet vågat att* it's a bit risky to

våg|berg ridge of a wave **-brytare** breakwater, pier, jetty **-dal** trough between two waves; *en* ~ (*bildl.*) the doldrums (*pl*)

våghals daredevil, madcap **-ig** *a1* foolhardy, reckless, rash

våg|ig *a1* wavy; waving, undulating **-kam** crest of a wave **-linje** wave-line; wavy (sinuous) line **-längd** wavelength

våg|mästarroll *polit., spela en* ~ hold the balance of power **-rät** horizontal, level; *~a ord* (*i korsord*) clues across **-rätt** *adv* horizontally; ~ *5* (*i korsord*) 5 across

vågrörelse undulatory (wave) motion, undulation

vågsam [-å:-] *a1* risky, hazardous

vågskvalp lapping [of waves]

vågskål scale (pan) [of a balance]; *lägga i ~en* put in (on) the scale; *väga tungt i ~en* (*bildl.*) be weighty, carry weight

våg|spel, -stycke bold venture, daring (risky) enterprise

våg|svall surging sea, surge **-topp** crest of a wave

våld *s7* **1** (*makt, välde*) power; (*besittning*) posession; *få* (*ha*) *i sitt* ~ get (have) in one's power; *råka i ngns* ~ fall into a p.'s power; *ge sig i ngns* ~ deliver o.s. into a p.'s hands; *dra för fan i ~!* go to hell (the devil)! **2** (*maktmedel, tvång*) force; (*över-*) violence; (*våldsdåd*) outrage, assault (*mot* upon); *bildl.* violation (*mot den personliga friheten* of personal liberty); *med* ~ by force, forcibly; *med milt* ~ with gentle compulsion; *yttre* ~ violence; *begå* ~ resort to violence; *begå nesligt* ~ *mot, se våldtaga; bruka* ~ *mot* use force (violence) against; *bruka större* ~ *än nöden kräver* employ more force than the situation demands; *göra* ~ *på* violate; *göra* ~ *på sig* restrain o.s.; *öppna med* ~ force open **-föra** [*sig på*] violate **-gästa** ~ [*hos*] abuse a p.'s hospitality, descend on s.b. [for a meal] **-sam** *a1* violent; (*om pers. äv.*) vehement; (*ursinnig*) furious; (*larmande*) tumultuous (*oväsen* noise); ~ *död* violent death; *göra ~t motstånd mot* violently resist **-samhet** violence; vehemence; fury; *~er* (*äv.*) excesses **-samt** *adv* violently; ~ *rolig* terrifically (terribly) funny

vålds|brott crime (act) of violence **-dåd** act of violence; outrage **-härskare** tyrant **-man** *se -verkare* **-politik** policy of violence **-verkare** perpetrator of an outrage, assailant **-åtgärder** forcible means

våld|taga violate, rape; *jur.* assault **-täkt** *s3* rape; *jur.* indecent assault **-täktsförsök** attempted rape **-täktsman** person guilty of rape, rapist

våll|a (*förorsaka*) cause, be the cause of; bring about; (*åsamka*) give (*ngn besvär* s.b. trouble); ~ *ngn smärta* (*äv.*) make s.b. suffer **-ande I** *s6, för* ~ *av annans död* for causing another person's death, for manslaughter **II** *a4, vara* ~ *till* be the cause of

vålm *s2* haycock **vålma** cock

vålnad [ˣvå:l-] *s3* ghost, phantom, apparition; *Skottl.* wraith

våm [våmm] *s2* rumen, paunch, first stomach

vånda *s1* agony; throes (*pl*) **våndas** *dep* suffer (be in) agony; ~ *inför ngt* dread s.th.; ~ *över ngt* go through agonies over s.th.

våning 1 (*lägenhet*) flat; *AE.* apartment; *en* ~ *på tre rum och kök* a three-room[ed] flat with a kitchen **2** (*etage*) stor[e]y; floor; *övre ~en* the upper (top) floor; *ett tre ~ar högt hus* a three-storey[ed] house; *på första ~en* (*botten-*) on the ground (*AE.* first) floor; *på andra ~en* (*en trappa upp*) on the first (*AE.* second) floor **vånings|byte** exchange of flats **-hotell** apartment hotel **-plan** floor **-säng** bunk bed

våp *s7* goose, simpleton, silly **-ig** *a1* soft

1 vår *pron; fören.* our; *självst.* ours; *de ~a* our people, (*a trupper*) our men; *allas* ~ *vän* the friend of all of us, our mutual friend; *vi skall göra ~t* (*~t bästa*) we shall do our part (our utmost)

2 vår *s2* spring; *poet.* springtime; *i livets ~* in the prime of life; *i ~ this spring; i ~as* last spring; *om (på) ~en (~arna)* in spring

vår|as *dep, det ~* spring is on its way **-blomma** spring flower **-bruk** spring farming **-brytning** *i ~en* as winter gives way to spring

1 vård [-å:-] *s2 (minnesmärke)* monument, memorial

2 vård [-å:-] *s2 (omvårdnad)* care (*om* of); (*tillsyn äv.*) charge, custody; (*sjuk- äv.*) nursing; *få god ~* be well cared for (looked after); *ha ~ om* have charge (the care) of; *den som har ~ om* the man (*etc.*) in (who takes) charge of; *lämna ngt i ngns ~* leave s.th. in a p.'s charge

vård|a **1** take care of, look after; (*sjuka*) nurse; (*ansa*) tend; (*bevara*) preserve (*minnet av* the memory of); *han ~s på sjukhus* he is [being treated] in hospital **2** *rfl,* ~ *sig om* take care of, cherish, cultivate **-ad** *a5* careful; (*om klädsel, hår*) well-groomed; (*väl-*) well-kept; (*prydlig*) neat (*handstil* handwriting); *-at språk* correct language; *använd ett -at språk!* mind how you speak!; *ett -at yttre* well-groomed appearance

vårdag spring day **-jämning** vernal equinox

vård|anstalt nursing home (institution) **-are** caretaker; (*sjuk-*) male nurse, attendant; (*djur-*) keeper; (*bevarare*) preserver **-arinna** nurse; *jfr vård*are **-fall** *vara ett ~* be in need of professional care **-hem** nursing home **-kas[e]** *s2* beacon **-nad** *s3* guardianship; *ha ~en om* have the custody of **-nadsbidrag** child maintenance allowance **-nadshavare** guardian, custodian; *jur.* next friend **-personal** medical (nursing) staff

vårdslös [ˣvå:rds-, ˣvårs-] careless (*i* in; *med* with); negligent (*i* in; *med* of); (*försumlig äv.*) neglectful (*med sitt utseende* of one's appearance); (*slarvig*) slovenly (*klädsel* dress) **vårdslösa** neglect, be careless about, be neglectful of **vårdslöshet** carelessness, negligence, neglect; *grov ~* gross negligence; ~ *i trafiken* careless driving

vård|tecken token **-yrke** occupation in medical or social services

vårflod spring flood

vårfrudagen Lady (Annunciation) Day

vår|hatt spring hat **-himmel** spring sky **-känsla** *ha -känslor* have the spring feeling **-lig** [-å:-] *a1* vernal, of spring, spring **-lik** springlike **-luft** spring air **-lök** *bot.* gagea **-mode** spring fashion **-regn** spring rain **-sidan** *på ~* when spring comes (came) **-sol** spring (vernal) sun **-städa** spring-clean **-städning** spring-cleaning **-sådd** spring sowing **-säd** spring (summer) corn (grain)

vårt|a [ˣvå:r-] *s1* wart **-bitare** *zool.* long-horned grasshopper **-björk** silver birch

vår|tecken sign of spring **-termin** spring term

vårtlik wartlike, warty

vårtrötthet spring fever

vårtsvin wart hog

vår|vind spring (vernal) breeze **-vinter** late winter

våt *a1* wet (*av* with); (*fuktig*) moist, damp; (*flytande*) liquid, fluid; *bli (vara) ~ om fötterna*

get (have) wet feet; *hålla ihop i ~ och torrt* stick together through thick and thin **-docka** *sjö.* wet dock **-dräkt** wet suit **-mark** wetland **-stark** *~t papper* wet-strength paper **-varm** warm and wet **-varor** *pl* liquids; (*sprit-*) alcoholic beverages **-värmande** *a4,* ~ *omslag* fomentation **-äng** marsh meadow

väbel [ˈväː-] *s2, mil.* regimental sergeant major

väck [*puts*] ~ gone, lost, vanished

väck|a *v3* **1** (*göra vaken*) wake [up]; rouse [from sleep]; (*på beställning*) call; *bildl.* awaken (*äv. relig.*), [a]rouse (*till to; ur* from, out of); ~ *ngn till besinning* call s.b. to his (her) senses; ~ *till liv* bring back to life, *bildl. äv.* arouse, revive **2** (*framkalla*) awaken (*medlidande* compassion), cause (*förvåning* astonishment); arouse (*nyfikenhet* curiosity; *misstankar* suspicion (*sg*); *sympati* sympathy); (*upp- äv.*) raise (*förhoppningar* hopes); excite (*avund* envy; *beundran* admiration), call up (*gamla minnen* old memories), call forth (*gillande* approbation), provoke (*vrede* anger); (*ge upphov t.*) create, cause (*oro* alarm); ~ *intresse* awaken (arouse) an interest; ~ *tanken på ngt* evoke the idea of s.th., suggest s.th.; ~ *uppmärksamhet* attract attention **3** (*framställa*) bring up, raise (*en fråga* a question); ~ *förslag om* propose, suggest

väckande *s6,* ~ *av åtal* [the] bringing [of] an action

väckarklocka alarm clock

väckelse [religious] revival **-möte** revivalist meeting **-predikant** revivalist **-rörelse** revivalist movement, revival

väckning awakening; (*per telefon*) alarm call; *får jag be om ~ kl. 6* I should like to be called at 6 *väckt* *a4* woken, awakened *etc.*; *relig.* saved

vädd *s2, bot.* scabious

väd|er [ˈväː-] *s7* **1** weather; *-rets makter* the clerk (*sg*) of the weather; *ett sådant ~!* what weather!; *i alla ~* in all weathers, *bildl. äv.* in rain and shine; *det är fult (vackert) ~* it is dirty (nice) weather; *det ser ut att bli vackert ~* the weather looks promising; *det vackra -ret fortsätter* it is keeping fine; *vad är det för ~?* what is the weather like?; *om -ret tillåter* weather permitting **2** (*luft, vind*) air, wind; ~ *och vind* wind and weather; *hårt ~* stormy weather; *prata i -ret* talk rubbish through one's hat; *släppa ~* break wind; *gå till ~s* rise [in the air], *sjö.* go [up] aloft

väder|beständig weatherproof, weather-resistant **-biten** *a5* weather-beaten **-karta** weather map (chart) **-korn** scent; *gott ~ [a]* keen scent, [a] sharp nose; *hunden har fått ~ på* the dog has picked up the scent of (has scented) **-kvarn** windmill **- lek** weather

väderleks|förhållanden *pl* weather conditions **-förändring** change in the weather **-karta** weather map (chart) **-prognos** weather forecast **-rapport** weather report (forecast) **-station** meteorological (weather) station **-tjänst** weather service (bureau); meteorological office **-utsikter** *pl* weather forecast (*sg*)

väder|rapport weather forecast **-spåman** weather prophet **-spänd** flatulent **- spänning** flatulence **-streck** quarter; point of the com-

V

pass; *i vilket ~?* in what quarter?; *de fyra ~en* the four cardinal points
vädja [ˣväː d-] ~ *till* appeal to (*äv. jur.*) **vädjan** *r* appeal **vädjande** *a4* appealing (*blick* look) **vädjobana** lists (*pl*); (*livets* life's) arena
vädr|a [ˣväː d-] **1** (*lufta*) air; ~ *kläder* (*äv.*) give the clothes an airing **2** (*få vittring av*) scent (*äv. bildl.*); sniff **-ing** airing *etc.*
vädur *s2* ram; V~*en* (*astr.*) Ram, Aries
väft *s3* weft
väg *s2* **1** *konkr.* road; (*mer abstr. o. bildl.*) way; (*bana*) path, course; (*färd-*) journey, drive, ride, walk; (*sträcka*) distance; (*rutt*) route; (*levnadsbana*) career; ~*en till* the road to; *allmän* (*enskild*) ~ public (private) road; *den breda* (*smala*) ~*en* (*bildl.*) the broad (narrow) path; *förbjuden ~!* no thoroughfare!; *halva ~en* halfway; *raka ~en* the straight course; *gå raka ~en hem* go straight home; *fyra timmars ~* four hours' journey (drive, walk); *bryta nya ~ar* (*bildl.*) break new ground; *det är lång ~ till* it is a long way to; *vilken ~ gick de?* which way did they go (road did they take)?; *gå ~en fram* [be] walk[ing] along the road; *gå all världens ~* go the way of all flesh; *gå sin ~* go away, *vard.* be off; *gå din ~!* go away!, make yourself scarce!; *gå sin egen ~* go one's own way; *gå skilda ~ar* split;*om du har ~arna hitåt* if you happen to be [coming] this way; *resa sin ~* go away, leave; *ta ~en* take the road (*genom* through; *över, förbi* by); *vart skall du ta ~en?* where are you going (off to)?; *inte veta vart man skall ta ~en* not know where to go; *vart har min hatt tagit ~en?* what has become of my hat?; *gå före och visa ~en* lead the way **2** (*föregånget av prep*) *i* ~ off; *gå* (*komma*) *i ~en för ngn* be (get) in a p.'s way; *ge sig i ~* be off (*till* for); *ngt i den ~en* s.th. like that (of that sort); *lägga hinder i ~en för ngn* put obstacles in a p.'s way; *längs ~en* along the road[side]; *på ~en* on the way (*dit* there); *på diplomatisk ~* through diplomatic channels, diplomatically; *på laglig ~* by legal means, legally; *inte på långa ~ar* (*bildl.*) not by a long way (chalk); *ett gott stycke på ~* well on the way; *följa ngn ett stycke på ~* accompany s.b. part of the way; *vara på ~ till* be on one's way to; *vara på ~ att* be on the point of (+ *ing-form*); *vara på god ~ att* be well on the way to; *gå till ~a* proceed, go about it; *under ~en* on the (one's) road (way), en route; *ur ~en* out of the way; *ur ~en!* get out of the way!, stand aside!; *gå ur ~en för ngn* get out of a p.'s way; *det vore inte ur ~en om* (*att*) it wouldn't be a bad idea to; *vid ~en* near (by the side of) the road, by the roadside
väg|a *v2* weigh (*äv. bildl.*); *hur mycket -er du?* how much do you weigh?; *hon -er hälften så mycket som jag* she is half my weight; *det -er jämnt* the scales are even; *det står och -er mellan* (*bildl.*) the decision lies (*vard.* it is a toss--up) between; ~ *skälen för och emot* weigh the pros and cons; *sitta och* ~ *på stolen* sit balancing [on] one's chair; *det är väl -t* it is good weight; *hans ord -er tungt* his words carry great weight; ~ *upp a*) eg. weigh out, *b*) (~ *mer än*) poise up, *c*) (*upp-, bildl.*) [counter]balance

-ande *a4* weighty; [*tungt*] ~ *skäl* weighty reasons
väg|arbetare roadworker **-arbete** roadwork; (*på skylt*) Road Up!, Men at Work!, Road under Repair! **-bana** roadway; *slirig* ~ slippery roadway (road surface) **-bank** road embankment
vägbar [-äː-] *a1* ponderable
väg|beläggning road surface (metalling) **-bom** [road] barrier **-byggare** road builder (maker) **-bygge** road construction (work, building, making) **-farande I** *a4* travelling; *poet.* wayfaring **II** *s9* traveller; (*trafikant*) road user **-förbindelse** road communication; *det finns ~ till* there is a road going to **-förvaltning** road maintenance authority
vägg *s2* wall; (*tunn skilje-*) partition; *bo ~ i ~ med* live next door to; *~arna har öron* walls have ears; *köra huvudet i ~en* (*bildl.*) run one's head against a wall; *ställa ngn mot ~en* (*bildl.*) drive s.b. into a corner, press s.b. hard; *uppåt ~arna* (*bildl.*) all wrong, wide of the mark; *det är som att tala till en ~-* it's like talking to a brick wall **-almanack[a]** wall calendar **-block** *byggn.* wall panel **-bonad** wall hanging, tapestry **-fast** fixed to the wall; *~a inredningar* fixtures; ~ *skåp* wall cabinet (cupboard) **-klocka** wall clock **-kontakt** wall socket (plug) **-lus** bedbug **-målning** mural (wall) painting **-pelare** pilaster **-uttag** point, wall socket **-yta** wall space (surface)
väg|hyvel road grader (drag) **-hållning** [road making and] road maintenance; (*bils*) roadholding **-kant** roadside **-karta** road map **-korsning** [road] crossing, crossroads **-krök** curve (bend) in the road **-lag** *s7* state of the road; *halt* ~ slippery road **-leda** guide; direct; *några ~nde ord* a few [introductory] directions **-ledare** guide; councellor **-ledning** guidance; *till ~ för* for the guidance of; *tjäna som* ~ serve as a guide **-märke** road sign **-mätare** mileometer; *AE.* odometer **-mätarställning** mileage
vägnar [ˣväːgnar] *pl*, [*p*]*å ngns* ~ on behalf of s.b.; *å tjänstens* (*ämbetets*) ~ by (in) virtue of one's office, ex officio; *rikt utrustad å huvudets* ~ well equipped with brains, very clever, brainy
vägning [ˣväːg-] weighing
väg|nät road network **-- och vattenbyggare** civil engineer **-- och vattenbyggnad[s-konst]** civil engineering, road construction and hydraulic engineering **-port** [road] underpass, road arch
vägr|a [ˣväːg-] refuse; (*om häst äv.*) balk, jib; ~ *att mottaga* refuse [to accept], decline **-an** *r* refusal; declining
väg|ren verge, shoulder **-rätt** right of way **-skatt** road tax **-skrapa** road grader (scraper) **-skylt** road (traffic) sign **-skäl** fork [in a road]; *vid ~et* at the crossroads **-spärr** road block; *mil.* barricade **-sträcka** stretch [of a road], road section; (*avstånd*) distance **-styrelse** highway (road) board **-trafikförordning** highway code, road (*AE.* highway) traffic act; *överträdelse av ~en* (*vanl.*) motoring offence **-underhåll** road maintenance **-verk** ~*et* [the

Swedish] national road administrtion **-vett** road sense **-visare 1** *pers.* guide **2** (*bok*) guide, guidebook, directory **3** (*skylt*) direction post (sign), signpost **-vält** [road]roller **-övergång** viaduct, flyover, overpass

väj‖a [*väjja] *v2* make way (*för* for); give way, yield (*för* to); *sjö.* veer, give way; ~ *för* (*undvika*) avoid; *inte* ~ *för ngt* (*bildl.*) not mind anything, stick at nothing **-ningsplikt** *sjö.* obligation to veer (give way)

väktare custodian, watchman, guard[ian]; *ordningens* ~ the guardians of law and order

väl I *n* welfare, wellbeing; *det allmännas* ~ the common weal; *vårt* ~ *och we beror på* our happiness is dependent upon **II** *bättre bäst, adv* **1** *beton.* [vä:l] **a)** (*bra, gott*) well; ~ *förfaren* experienced; *allt ~!* all's well!; *så ~!* what a good thing!; *befinna sig* ~ be well; *det går aldrig ~!* it can't turn out well!; *om allt går* ~ if nothing goes wrong; *hålla sig* ~ *med ngn* keep in with s.b.; *ligga* ~ *till* be in a favourable position; *låta sig* ~ *smaka* enjoy one's food; *stå* ~ *hos ngn* be on the right side of s.b.; *ta* ~ *upp* receive favourably; *tala* ~ *om* speak well of; *veta mycket* ~ *att* be perfectly (fully) aware that; *det var för* ~ *att* it was a blessing that, **b)** (*alltför*) rather [too], over; (*över*) over, rather over [...] than; ~ *mycket* rather too much; ~ *stor* rather (almost too) big; *gott och* ~ well over (*1 timme* one hour); *länge och* ~ for ages, no end of a time, **c)** (*omsider, en gång*) once; *det hade inte* ~ *börjat förrän* no sooner had it begun than; *när hon* ~ *hade somnat var hon* once asleep she was, **d)** *inte henne men* ~ *hennes syster* not her but her sister **2** *obetonat* [väll] **a)** (*uttryckande förmodan el. förhoppning*) surely; (*förmodar jag*) I suppose; (*hoppas jag*) I hope; *du kommer* ~ *?* I hope you will come!; *du är* ~ *inte sjuk* you are surely not ill?, you are not ill, are you?; *han får* ~ *vänta* he will have to wait; *jag gör* ~ *det då* I suppose I had better do that then; *det kan* ~ *hända* that's possible; *det kan mycket* ~ *tänkas att hon* there is every possibility of her (+ *ing- form*); *det var* ~ *det jag trodde* that's just what I thought; *de är* ~ *framme nu* they must be there by now; *det är* ~ *inte möjligt* it can't be possible; *det hade* ~ *varit bättre att ...* wouldn't it have been better to ...?; *du vet* ~ *att* I suppose you know; you must know, **b)** (*som fyllnadsord i frågor*) *vem kunde* ~ *ha trott det?* who would have believed such a thing?; *vad är* ~ *lycka?* what is happiness [after all]? **3** *så* ~ *som* as well as **II** *interj, ja ~!* of course!; *nå ~!* well then!

väl‖'an well [then]! **-artad** [-a:r-] *a5* well-behaved **-avlönad** well-paid **-befinnande** wellbeing **-behag** pleasure; complacency **-behållen** safe [and sound]; (*om sak*) in good condition; *komma fram* ~ arrive safely **-behövlig** badly (much) needed **-bekant** well-known **-beställd** well-to-do, well-off **-betänkt** well-advised, judicious; *mindre* ~ ill-advised, injudicious **-boren** honourable **-borenhet** [-å:-] *Ers* ~ your Excellency **-bärgad** well-to-do; wealthy

väld‖e *s6* **1** (*rike*) state, empire **2** (*makt*) domi-

nation, power; *bringa ett folk under sitt* ~ bring a people under one's domination (sway), subject a people **-ig** *a1* **1** (*stor*) huge; enormous; (*vidsträckt*) immense, vast **2** (*mäktig*) mighty **-igt** *adv, vard.* awfully, tremendously, terrifically

väl‖doftande fragrant **-etablerad** well-established **-funnen** *a5* apt (*uttryck* phrase) **-fylld** well-filled **-fägnad** food and drink; good cheer **-färd** [-ä:-] *s3* welfare; wellbeing **-färdssamhället** welfare state **-född** well-fed; plump **-förrättad** *s5, efter -förrättat värv gick han* having completed his job he went **-försedd** *a5* well-stocked, well-supplied **-förtjänt** well-earned; well-deserved; *få sitt ~a straff* get the punishment one deserves; *det var ~!* that served you (*etc.*) right! **-gjord** well-made **-grundad** well-founded; good (*anledning* reason) **-gräddad** *a5* well-baked **-gång** prosperity, success; *lycka och ~!* all good wishes for the future! **-gångsskål** toast; *dricka en ~ för ngn* drink [to] a p.'s health **-gångsönskningar** *pl* good wishes **-gärning** kind (charitable) deed; (*om sak*) blessing, boon; *det var då en ~ att* it was a real blessing (boon) that **-gödd** [-j-] *a5* well-fattened

välgör‖ande [-j-] *a4* (*nyttig*) beneficial (*solsken* sunshine); (*hälsosam*) salutary (*sömn* sleep); refreshing; ~ *ändamål* charitable purposes; *vara ~ för ngn* (*äv.*) be good for s.b., do s.b. [a lot of] good **-are** benefactor **-enhet** charity **-enhetsinrättning** charitable institution **-enhetsmärke** charity seal (*frimärke*: stamp) **-erska** benefactress

väl‖hållen well-kept **-hängd** (*mör*) tender **-informerad** [-å-] *a5* well-informed (*kretsar* circles)

välja *valde valt* **1** (*ut-*) choose (*bland* from, out of; *mellan* between; *till* as); (*noga*) select, pick (*sina ord* one's words), pick out (*äv.* ~ *ut*); *få* ~ be allowed to choose, have one's choice; *låta ngn* ~ give s.b. the choice; *inte ha mycket att* ~ *på* not have much choice; ~ *bort* (*skolämne*) drop **2** (*genom röstning*) elect (*ngn t. president* s.b. president); (*t. eng. parl.*) return; ~ *in ngn* elect s.b. [as] a member (*i* of); ~ *in ngn i styrelse* elect s.b. to a board; ~ *om* relect **-väljare** voter, elector **-kår** electorate

välklädd well-dressed **-het** being well dressed

välkom‖men [-å-] *a5* welcome; ~*!* I am (*etc.*) glad to see you!; *hälsa ngn* ~ welcome s.b. **-na** welcome

välkomst‖bägare [-å-] *tömma en* ~ drink a toast of welcome **-hälsning** [address of] welcome **-ord** *pl* word of welcome

välkänd well-known

välla *v2* **1** gush (well, spring) (*fram* forth, up; *fram ur* from); ~ *upp* ooze **2** *tekn.* weld

vällevnad good (luxurious) living, [life of] luxury

välling gruel **-klocka** farm[yard] bell

väl‖ljud euphony; *mus.* harmony, melody **-ljudande** [-j-] *a4* euphonious; harmonious, melodious; (*om instrument*) with a beautiful tone; (*om toner*) sweet **-lovlig** *i ~a ärenden* on lawful occasions **-lukt** sweet smell (scent); perfume, fragrance; *sprida* ~ fill with fra-

grance, smell sweet **-luktande** *a4* sweet- -smelling, sweet-scented; aromatic; fragrant **-lust** voluptuousness; sensual pleasure **-lustig** *a1* voluptuous; sensual; *(liderlig)* libidinous **-lusting** voluptuary; sensualist; *(liderlig pers.)* libertine, debauchee **-läsning** elocution **-makt** prosperity **-menande** *a4* well-meaning, well- -intentioned **-mening** good intention; *i bästa* ~ with the best of intentions **-ment** [-e:-] *a4* well-meant **-meriterad** *a5* highly qualified, meritorious **-motiverad** *a5* well-founded, well-justified **-måenде** *a4* thriving; *(blomstrande)* flourishing, prosperous; *(-bärgad)* well-to-do; *se ~ ut* look prosperous (thriving) **-måga** *s1* wellbeing, good health; *i högönsklig* ~ in the best of health **-ordnad** well-arranged, well-organized; well-managed *(affärer* affairs) **-orienterad** well-informed **-pressad** *a5* well-pressed **-rakad** *a5* clean-shaved **-renommerad** [-å-] *a5* well-reputed, well-established **-riktad** *a5* well-aimed, well-directed **-sedd** *a5* acceptable; welcome *(gäst* guest) **väl|signa** [-iŋna] bless **-signad** *a5* blessed; *(besvärlig, vard. äv.)* confounded; *i -at tillstånd* in the family way **välsignelse** blessing; *(bön)* benediction; *ha ~ med sig* bring a blessing [in its *(etc.)* train]; *det är ingen ~ med* no good will come of **-bringande** *a4* blessed, beneficial **-rik** full of blessings **väl|sinnad** *a5* well-disposed **-sittande** *a4* well- -fitting **-situerad** *a5* well-situated, in good circumstances **-skapad** *a5* well-shaped; *(-formad äv.)* shapely; *ett -skapt gossebarn* a bonny boy **-skriven** *a5* well-written *(bok* book) **-skrivning** *skol.* writing **-skött** [-ʃ-] *a4* well- -managed *(affär* business); well-kept *(trädgård* garden); well-tended *(händer* hands); well looked after *(baby* baby) **-smakande** *a4* appetizing; *(läcker)* delicious; *(svagare)* palatable **-sorterad** *(med god sortering)* well-stocked, well-assorted; *vara ~* have a wide range (large assortment) of goods **-stånd** prosperity; wealth **-sydd** *a5* well-tailored, well-cut **vält** *s2* roller; *jordbr. äv.* packer
1 välta I *s1 (timmer-)* log pile **II** *v1* roll
2 välta *v3* **1** *(stjälpa)* upset *(äv. ~ omkull)* **2** *(ramla omkull)* fall over; *(köra omkull)* turn over, *(om bil)* overturn
vältalare orator
vältalig *a1* eloquent **-het** eloquence
vältra 1 *(flytta)* roll [... over], trundle; *~ skulden på ngn* throw the blame on s.b.; *~ bort (åt sidan)* roll away **2** *rfl, ~ sig i gräset* roll over in the grass; *~ sig i smutsen* wallow in the mud; *~ sig i pengar* roll in money
väl|tränad *a5* fit **-underrättad** *a5, se välin- formerad* **-uppfostrad** *a5* well-bred, well- -mannered; *deras barn är ~e* their children are well brought up **-utrustad** well-equipped, well-appointed
välva *v2* **1** *(förse med valv)* vault, arch **2** *rfl* form a vault (an arch), vault **3** *~ stora planer* revolve great plans
välvil|ja benevolence; good will, kindness; *hysa ~ mot* be well-disposed towards; *visa ngn ~* show s.b. kindness; *mottogs med ~* was favour-

ably received **-lig** benevolent; kind[ly] **-ligt** *adv* benevolently; kindly; *~ inställd mot* favourably disposed towards
välvning vaulting, arching; *konkr.* vault, arch
väl|vårdad well-kept; *(om pers.)* groomed **-växt** *a4* shapely, well-formed
vämj|as *v2 el. vämdes vämts, dep, ~ vid* be disgusted (nauseated) at (by) **-elig** *a1* nauseous, disgusting; loathsome **-else** loathing, disgust; *(starkare)* nausea; *känna ~ vid* be revolted by
1 vän [vä:n] *a1* fair; lovely, graceful
2 vän [vänn] *s3* friend; *vard.* pal, chum; *min lilla ~ (i tilltal)* my dear [child]; *en ~ till mig* a friend of mine, one of my friends; *~ av ordning* a lover of law and order; *släkt och ~ner* friends and relations; *goda ~ner* close friends; *ha en ~ i ngn (ngn till ~)* have a friend in s.b., have a p.'s friendship; *bli (vara) ~ med* make (be) friends with; *jag är mycket god ~ med honom* he is one of my greatest friends; *inte vara ngn ~ av (äv.)* not be fond of, dislike
vänd|a *v2* **1** *(ge (intaga) annat läge)* turn; *(rikta äv.)* direct; *sjö.* go about; *~ en bil* turn a car [round]; *~ hö* turn over hay; *~ ngn ryggen* turn one's back upon s.b.; *~ stegen hemåt* direct one's steps homewards; *var god vänd!* please turn over (p.t.o.), *AE. äv.* over; *vänd mot öster* facing the east; *med ansiktet vänt mot* facing; *~ allt till det bästa* make the best of it; *~ ngt till sin fördel* turn s.th. to one's advantage; *~ om (tillbaka)* turn [back]; *~ på* turn [over]; *~ på huvudet* turn one's head; *~ på sig* turn round; *~ på slanten* look twice at one's money; *vrida och ~ på* turn and twist; *~ upp och ner (ut och in) på* turn upside down (inside out); *~ åter* return **2** *rfl* turn *(omkring* about, round); *(om vind)* shift, veer; *(förändras)* change; *~ sig kring en axel (äv.)* revolve on an axle; *~ sig i sängen (äv.)* turn over in bed; *bladet har vänt sig* the tables are turned; *inte veta vart man skall ~ sig* not know which way to turn; *hans lycka -e sig* his luck changed; *~ sig ifrån* turn away from; *~ sig mot* turn towards *(fientligt:* against, upon); *~ sig om* turn round; *~ sig till ngn a) eg. bet.* turn to[wards] s.b., *b) (med fråga e.d.)* address s.b., *c) (för att få ngt)* apply (appeal) to s.b. *(för att få* for), see s.b. *(för att få* about)
vändbar *a1* turnable; *(omkastbar)* reversible *(kappa* coat)
vände[l]rot *bot.* valerian
vänd|kors turnstile **-krets** tropic[al circle]; *Kräftans (Stenbockens) ~* the tropic of Cancer (Capricorn) **-ning 1** *(-ande)* turning *etc.* **2** *([in]riktning)* turn; *(förändring)* change *(t. det bättre* for the better); *(uttryckssätt)* turn [of phrase], term; *ta en annan ~* take a new turn; *ta en allvarlig ~* take a serious turn; *vara kvick i ~arna* be alert (nimble); *vara långsam i ~arna* be slow on one's feet, *vard.* be a slow-coach *(AE.* slowpoke) **-punkt** turning point *(äv. bildl.)*; *bildl. äv.* crisis; *utgöra en ~* mark a turning point **-radie** turning radius **-skiva 1** *järnv.* turntable **2** *(på plog)* mouldboard **-tapp** trunnion
vän|fast constant in friendship, [loyally] attached to one's friends **-gåva** gift from a

friend **-inna** girlfriend, ladyfriend
vänja *vande vant* **1** accustom (*vid* to), familiarize (*vid* with); (*härda*) inure, harden (*vid* to); ~*s vid att* be trained to the habit of (+ *ing--form*); ~ *ngn av med att* get s.b. out of [the habit of] (+ *ing-form*); ~ *ngn av med en ovana* cure s.b. of a bad habit **2** *rfl* accustom o.s. (*vid* to); (*bli van*) get accustomed (used) (*vid* to); ~ *sig av med att* get out (rid o.s.) of the habit of (+ *ing-form*)
vänkrets circle of friends
vän|lig *a1* kind (*mot* to); (*välvillig äv.*) kindly; (*-skaplig*) friendly; ~*t ansikte* (*leende, råd*) friendly face (smile, piece of advice); *så ~t av er!* how kind of you!; *ett ~t mottagande* a kind reception, a friendly welcome **-ligen** kindly **-lighet** kindness; kindliness; friendliness; *i all* ~ in a friendly way, as a friend **-ligt** *adv* kindly *etc.*; ~ *sinnad* friendly
vän|ort sister community; adopted town (city) **-pris** *till* ~ at a price as between friends
vänskap *s3* friendship (*för, till* for); *fatta* ~ *för* get friendly with; *hysa* ~ *för* have a friendly feeling towards (for); *för gammal* ~*s skull* for old times' (friendship's) sake **-lig** [-a:-] *a1* friendly; *leva på* ~ *fot med* be on friendly terms with **-lighet** [-a:-] friendliness, amicability; *i all* ~, *se under vänlighet* **-ligt** [-a:-] *adv* in a friendly way; amicably; ~ *sinnad* friendly
vänskaps|band tie (bond) of friendship; *knyta* ~ *med* form a friendship with **-bevis** token of friendship **-full** kind, friendly **-match** friendly [match] **-pakt** treaty of friendship, friendship pact
Vänskapsöarna *pl* the Friendly Islands, Tonga
vänslas *dep* bill and coo, spoon; (*om hund*) fawn
vänster ['vänn-] **I** *a, best. form vänstra* left (*jfr höger*) **II** **1** *oböjligt s, till* ~ to the left (*om* of) **2** *s9, polit.,* ~*n* the Left **-extremist, -extremistisk** left-wing extremist **-flygel** *polit.* left wing; *tillhöra* ~*n* be a leftist **-gänga** left--hand[ed] thread **-hänt** *a4* left-handed **-inner** *sport.* inside left **-parti** left- wing party; ~*et kommunisterna* (*vpk*) left party communists **-prassel** *vard.* extramarital relations, (sl.) a little bit on the side **-radikal** leftist **-sida** (*i bok*) left-hand page **-styrning** (*av bil*) left--hand drive **-sväng** left turn **-trafik** left-hand traffic **-vriden** ~ *kommentar* pro-leftist commentary **-vridning** *polit.* veering (swing) to the left; leftism **-ytter** *sport.* outside left
vänsäll popular; *vara* ~ have many friends
vänt|a **1** (*motse, förvänta* [*sig*]) expect (*besked* an answer; *att ngn skall komma* s.b. to come; *av* from); (*förstå*) await, be in store for; *det är att* ~ it is to be expected; *det var inte annat att* ~ what else could you expect?; *som man kunde ha* ~*t sig* as might have been expected; *han* ~*s hit i dag* he is expected to arrive here today; *döden* ~*r oss alla* death awaits us all; *du vet inte vad som* ~*r dig* you don't know what is in store for you; ~ *ut ngn* wait for s.b. to go (come) **2** (*avvakta, bida*) wait (*på* for; *på att ngn skall* for s.b. to; *och se* and see); ~ *lite!* wait a bit!; ~ *länge* wait a long time; *få* ~ have to wait; *gå och* ~ wait

[and wait]; *låta ngn* ~ keep s.b. waiting; *låta* ~ *på sig* a) (*om pers.*) keep people (*etc.*) waiting, be late, b) (*om svar.e.d.*) be long in coming; ~ *med* (*uppskjuta*) put off, (*sitt omdöme e.d.*) postpone, reserve; ~ *inte med middagen* don't wait dinner **3** *rfl* expect (*mycket av* a lot from; *ett kyligt mottagande* a cool reception); *det hade jag inte* ~*t mig av dig* I didn't expect that from you
väntan *r* wait, waiting; (*för-*) expectation; (*spänd* ~) suspense; *i* ~ *på* while waiting for, awaiting, pending
vänte|lista waiting list **-tid** time of waiting, wait, waiting period; *under* ~*en kan vi* while we are waiting we can
vänthall waiting room
väntjänst *göra ngn en* ~ do s.b. a good turn
vänt|rum, -sal waiting room
väpna [ˣväː p-] arm **väpnare** *hist.* [e]squire
väppling trefoil, clover
1 värd [-äː-] *s2* host; *se äv. hyres-, värdshus-; fungera som* ~ act as host, do the honours
2 vär|d [-äː-] *a5* **1** worth (*besväret* the trouble; *att läsa[s]* reading); (*värdig, förtjänt av*) worthy (*all uppmuntran* of every encouragement; *beröm* of praise); *inte vara mycket* ~ (*bildl.*) be good for nothing; *arbetaren är* ~ *sin lön* the labourer is worthy of his hire; ~ *priset* worth the price, good value; *det är* ~*t att lägga märke till* it is worth noting; *det är inte mödan* ~*t* it is not worth while; *det är fara* ~*t att* it is to be feared that; *det är inte* ~*t att du gör det* you had better not do it **2** (*aktningsvärd*) esteemed; *Er* ~*a skrivelse* your esteemed letter
värddjur host
värde [ˣväːr-] *s6* value; (*inre* ~) worth; *det bokförda* ~*t* the book value; *stora* ~*n* (*summor*) large sums, (*föremål*) valuable property; *pengar eller pengars* ~ money or its equivalent; *av noll och intet* ~ null and void, of no value whatsoever; *av ringa* ~ of small value; *till ett* ~ *av* to a (the) value of; *prov utan* ~ sample of no value; *ha stort* ~ be of great value; *sjunka* (*stiga*) *i* ~ fall (rise) in value; *sätta på* attach value to, lay (put, set) store by, (*uppskatta*) appreciate; *uppskatta ngt till sitt fulla* ~ appreciate s.th. fully
värdebeständig of stable value; ~ *pension* with constant purchasing power; ~*a tillgångar* real-value assets **-het** stability of value
värde|full valuable (*för* to); *det skulle vara mycket* ~*t om* it would be very useful (helpful) if **-föremål** article (object) of value, valuable [thing] **-försändelse** registered (insured) postal matter (*brev*: letter; *paket*: parcel) **-gemenskap** community of values **-laddad** loaded with subjective judgements **-lös** worthless; of no value, valueless **-minskning** depreciation, decrease (fall) in value **-minskningskonto** depreciation account **-mässig** *a1* in terms of value; *den* ~*a stegringen* the rise in value **-mätare** standard of value **-papper** valuable document; security; bond; *koll.* (*aktier*) stock (*sg*); *belåning av* ~ loans on (pledging of) securities, hypothecation **-post** registered (insured) mail
värder|a **1** (*bestämma värdet av*) value, esti-

V

mate (till at); (på uppdrag) appraise; (om myndighet) assess; ~ för högt (äv.) overestimate 2 (uppskatta) value, appreciate; (högakta) esteem, estimate; vår ~de medarbetare our esteemed colleague -ing valuation; estimation, estimate; appraisement; assessment; ~ar (allm.) set of values

värderings|grund basis of valuation -man valuer; (för skada) claims assessor

värde|sak article (object) of value; ~er valuables -stegring rise in value, appreciation -säker se värdebeständig -sätta se värdera o. [sätta] värde [på]

värdfolk vårt ~ our host and hostess

värdig [ˣväː r-] a1 worthy (efterträdare successor); (aktningsvärd) dignified; (passande för) fitting, seemly (ngn for s.b); på ett ~t sätt in a dignified manner, with dignity -as dep deign (condescend) to -het dignity; (som egenskap) worthiness; (ämbetsställning) position; (rang) rank; hålla på sin ~ stand on one's dignity; anse det under sin ~ att consider it beneath one (one's dignity) to

värdinna hostess; lady of the house

värdinneplikter pl duties of a hostesss

värdshus [ˣväː rds-, ˣvärs-] inn; tavern; (restaurang) restaurant -värd innkeeper, landlord

värdskap [ˣväː rd-] s7 duties (pl) of [a] host (etc.); utöva ~et do the honours, act as host

värdväxt host

1 värja v2 defend (sitt liv one's life; sig o.s.); man kan inte ~ sig från misstanken att one cannot help suspecting that

2 värja s1 sword; (stick-) rapier

värj|fäktning sword fight -fäste sword hilt -stöt sword thrust

värk s2 ache, pain[s pl]; ~ar labour pains; reumatisk ~ rheumatic pains

värk|a v3 ache; det -er i armen my arm aches; det -er i hela kroppen (äv.) I ache all over; ~ ut work out -bruten crippled with rheumatism

värld [väː rd] s2 world; (jord) earth; gamla (nya) ~en the Old (New) World; en man av ~ a man of the world; undre ~en the underworld; hur i all ~en? how on earth?; hela ~en the whole world, (alla människor) all the world, everybody; från hela ~en from all over the world; det är väl inte hela ~en! it doesn't matter all that much!; hur lever ~en med dig? (vard.) how's the world treating you?; inte se mycket ut för ~en not look much; slå sig fram i ~en make one's way in the world; för allt i ~en! for goodness' sake!; inte för allt i ~en not for [all] the world; förr i ~en formerly, in former days; så går det till här i ~en that's the way of the world; se sig om i ~en see the world; komma till ~en come into the world; bringa ur ~en settle [once and for all]

världs|alltet the universe; fack. cosmos -artikel article with a worldwide market -artist international (world-famous) performer -banken the World Bank -bekant universally known -berömd world-famous -bild idea (conception) of the world -brand world conflagration -dam woman of the world, lady of fashion -del part of the world, continent -fred world (universal) peace -frånvarande

who is living in a world of his own -frånvänd a5 detached -främmande ignorant of the world; unrealistic -förakt contempt of the world -föraktare cynic -förbättrare reformer -handel world (international) trade -hav ocean -herravälde universal (world) supremacy (dominion) -historia world history; -historien the history of the world -historisk of the history of the world -hushållning world economy; universal economics (pl) -händelse event of worldwide importance, historic event -karta map of the world, world map -klass i ~ of international caliber -klok worldly-wise -klokhet worldly wisdom -kongress world congress -krig world war; första (andra) ~et (äv.) World War I (II); utlösa ett ~ unleash a world war

världslig [ˣväː rds-] a1 worldly (ting matter); (av denna värld) mundane, of the world; (motsats helig) profane; (motsats kyrklig) secular; ~ makt temporal power; ~a ting (äv.) temporal affairs; ~a nöjen worldly pleasures

världsligt adv worldly; ~ sinnad (äv.) worldly-minded

världs|litteratur world literature -läge ~t the world situation -makt world power -man man of the world -marknad world market -medborgare citizen of the world; cosmopolitan -medborgarskap world citizenship -mästare world champion -mästerskap world championship -omfattande worldwide; global -omsegling circumnavigation of the earth; sailing round the world -opinion world opinion -ordning world order; den nuvarande ~en (äv.) the present order of things in the world -organisation world organization -politik world politics (pl) -politisk of world politics; en ~ händelse a political event of world importance -press world press -problem world problem -rekord world record -rykte world[wide] fame (renown) -rymden best. form outer space -språk world language -stad metropolis -stat world state -trött weary of the world -utställning world fair -van experienced in the ways of the world -välde world empire -åskådning ideology; [general] view of life

värma v2 warm; (hetta) heat; ~ upp warm (heat) up

värme s9, fackl. s7 warmth; (hetta) heat (äv. fys.); bildl. äv. fervour, ardour; hålla ~n keep warm; stark ~ great (intense) heat; i 60° ~ at 60° above zero -alstring heat production -anläggning heating plant, [central] heating -apparat heater -behandla treat with heat -behandling med. thermotherapy; tekn. heattreatment -beständig heat-resistant -bölja heat wave -central district heating plant -dyna [electric] heating pad -element (radiator) radiator; (elektriskt) electric heater -energi thermal energy -enhet thermal (heat) unit -filt electric blanket -flaska hot-water bottle -förlust heat loss, loss of heat -isolera insulate against heat -isolering thermal insulation -kraftverk thermal power station -källa source of heat -känslig sensitive to heat -lampa infrared lamp -ledare heat conductor;

dålig ~ bad (poor) conductor of heat **-ledning** central heating; *fys.* heat (thermal) conduction **-ledningselement** radiator **-lära** thermology **-motor** heat engine **-mätare** heat meter, calorimeter **-panel** heating panel **-panna** heating boiler, central heater **-platta** hotplate **-pump** heat pump **- skåp** (*i kök*) warming cupboard; (*i laboratorium*) incubator **-sköld** heat shield **- slag** *med.* heatstroke **-slinga** heating coil **-strålning** thermal (heat) radiation **-ugn** [re]heating furnace **-utvidgning** heat (thermal) expansion **-verk** heating plant **-värde** calorific value **-växlare** heat exchanger

värmning heating

värn [-ä:-] 7 defence, safeguard; protection; (*skytte-*) fire trench **värna** ~ [*om*] defend, safeguard; protect **värnlös** defenceless; ~*a barn* (*vanl.*) orphans

värnplikt *allmän* ~ compulsory military service, Storbritannien [compulsory] national service; *AE.* universal military training; *fullgöra sin* ~ do one's military service **-ig** liable for (to) military service; *en* ~ a conscript (*AE.* draftee); ~ *officer* conscript officer

värnplikts|tjänstgöring national service training **-vägran** refusal to do military service **-ålder** call-up (*AE.* draft) age **-skatt** national defence levy

värp|a *v3* lay [eggs] **-höna** laying hen

värre ['värre] **I** *a, komp. t.* ond worse (*jfr illa o. ond*); *bli* ~ *och* ~ get worse and worse, go from bad to worse; *det var* ~ *det!* that's too bad!; *och vad* ~ *är* and what's worse **II** *adv, komp. t. illa* worse; (*allvarligare*) more seriously (*sjuk* ill); *dess* ~ unfortunately; *så mycket* ~ so much the worse; *vi hade roligt* ~ we had no end of fun; *hon var fin* ~ she was dressed [up] to the nines

värst I *a, superl. t.* ond worst (*jfr illa o. ond*); *släkten är* ~ preserve me (us) from relatives!; *frukta det* ~*a* fear the worst; *det* ~*a återstår* the worst is yet to come; *det* ~*a är att* the worst of it is that; *det var* ~ (*det* ~*a*)*!* well, I never!; *det var det* ~*a jag har hört!* I never heard the like!; *du skall då alltid vara* ~ you always have to go one better; *i* ~*a fall* at worst, if the worst comes to the worst; *mitt under* ~*a* in the midst of [the], at the height of; *när ... var som* ~ when ... was at its worst (height) **II** *adv, superl. t. illa* [the] most; *när jag var som* ~ *sjuk* when I was at my worst; *inte så* ~ not very (*bra* good); *jag är inte så* ~ glad åt det it doesn't make me any too happy

värsting teenage hoodlum, tearaway

värv *s7* (*sysselsättning*) work; (*uppgift*) task; (*åliggande*) function, duty; *fullgöra sitt* ~ (*äv.*) do one's part; *fredliga* (*krigiska*) ~ (*äv.*) the arts of peace (war)

värv|a secure (*kunder* customers; *röster* votes); *mil.* enlist; ~ *röster* canvass [for votes], electioneer; *låta* ~ *sig* (*mil.*) enlist; ~ *trupper* raise (levy) troops **-ning** enlistment; *ta* ~ enlist [in the army]

väsa *v3* hiss; ~ *fram* hiss [out]

väsen ['vä:-] **1** *-det -den el. väsen* (*äv. väsende* ['ʰvä:-] *s6*) (*varelse*) being; *det högsta* ~*det* the Supreme Being; *inte ett levande* ~ not a living soul **2** *böjs enl. 1* (*sätt att vara*) being, nature, person, character; (*innersta natur*) essence; *till sitt* ~ of disposition **3** *-det, pl väsen* (*buller*) noise; (*ståhej*) fuss, ado; *mycket* ~ *för ingenting* much ado about nothing; *göra mycket* ~ make a great fuss (*av ngn* of s.b.; *av ngt* about s.th.); *göra* ~ *av sig* make o.s. felt [in the world]; *hon gör inte mycket* ~ *av sig* (*äv.*) she is not very pushing **-de** *se väsen 1*

väsens|besläktad kindred **-främmande** alien (*för* to) **-skild** essentially different **-skillnad** essential difference

väsentlig [-'senn-] *a1* essential; principle, main; (*betydelsefull*) important; (*avsevärd*) considerable; *det* ~*a* the essentials (*pl*); *det* ~*a i* the essential part of; *en högst* ~ *skillnad* a very important difference; *mindre* ~ (*äv.*) not so important; *i* ~ *grad* essentially, to a considerable extent; *i allt* ~*t* in [all] essentials, essentially **-en** essentially; principally, mainly; (*i väsentlig grad*) substantially **-het** essential thing; ~*er* vital points, essentials

väsk|a *s1* bag; (*hand-*) handbag; (*res-*) suitcase, valise **-ryckare** bag-snatcher

västljud [ʰvä:s-] *språkv.* fricative

väsnas [ʰvä:s-] *dep* be noisy, make a noise

väsning [ʰvä:s-] hissing; *en* ~ a hiss

vässa sharpen; whet

1 väst *s2* (*plagg*) waistcoat; (*AE. o. dam-*) vest

2 väst *s9 o. adv* (*väderstreck*) west, West

Västafrika West Africa

västan **I** *adv,* ~ [*ifrån*] from the west **II** *r, se följ.* **-vind** west wind; ~*en* (*poet.*) Zephyrus

Väst|asien Western Asia **-australien** Western Australia

västblocket the Western bloc

väster ['väss-] **I** *s9* **1** (*väderstreck*) the west; (*jfr norr*) **2** ~*n* the West (Occident); *Vilda V~n* the Wild West **II** *adv* west **-landet** the West (Occident) **-ländsk** *a5* western, occidental **-länning** westerner, occidental **-ut** westward[s]

Västeuropa Western Europe

västeuropeisk West European

västficka waistcoat pocket

västficksformat vest-pocket size

väst|front ~*en* the Western front **-got** Visigoth **-gotisk** Visigothic **-götaklimax** [ʰvästjö:-, ʰväfö:-] anticlimax

Västindien the West Indies (*pl*)

västindisk West Indian

västklänning jumper (*AE.*)

väst|kust west coast **-lig** *a1* west[erly] (*vind* wind); western (*landskap* provinces); *den* ~*a världen* the Western World, the West; *vinden är* ~ the wind is [from the] west; ~*ast* westernmost, most westerly (western) **-makterna** the Western Powers **-maktspolitik** Western policy **-nordväst** west-north-west **-orienterad** *bildl.* Western[at]ed

väst|ra *a, best. form* [the] western; *i* ~ *Sverige* (*äv.*) in the west of Sweden **-romersk** Western Roman; ~*a riket* the Western [Roman] Empire **-sida** *på* ~*n* to the **-sydväst** west-southwest **-tysk** *s2 o. a5* West German

Västtyskland West Germany; (*officiellt*) the Federal Republic of Germany

väst|vart ['väst-] westward[s] -världen the Western world
väta I *s1* wet; moisture, damp[ness]; *aktas för* ~ to be kept dry, keep dry II *v3*, ~ [*ner*] wet; ~ *ner sig* get [o.s.] wet; ~ *i sängen* wet the bed
väte *s6* hydrogen -atom hydrogen atom -bomb hydrogen bomb, H-bomb -bombskrig thermonuclear war -cyanid hydrogen cyanide, hydrocyanic acid -kraft hydrogen power -peroxid hydrogen peroxide -superoxid *se -peroxid*
vätgas hydrogen gas
vätmedel wetting agent
vätsk|a I *s1* liquid, fluid; *vid sunda -or* in good form II *v1*, ~ [*sig*] run, discharge fluid
vätske|balans fluid balance -form liquid state -kylning liquid-cooling -pelare liquid column
vätteros *bot.* toothwort
väv *s2* (*tyg*) fabric; (*varp*) web; *sätta upp en* ~ loom a web
väv|a *v2* weave -are weaver -arfågel weaver, weaverbird -bom beam
väv|d [-ä:-] *a5* woven -eri weaving mill -erska woman weaver -nad [-ä:-] *s3* [woven] fabric; *biol. o. bildl.* tissue; ~*er* (*äv.*) textiles; *en ~ av lögner* a tissue of lies -nadsindustri weaving industry -ning [-ä:-] weaving -plast coated (plastic-coated) fabric -sked [weaving] reed -stol loom; (*hand-*) hand loom; (*maskin-*) power loom
väx|a *v3* **1** grow (*t. ngt* into s.th.); (*öka*) increase (*i antal* in numbers); ~ *i styrka* increase in strength; ~ *sig* grow (*stark* strong); *låta skägget* ~ grow a beard; ~ *ngn över huvudet a*) eg. *bet.* outgrow s.b., *b*) *bildl.* get beyond a p.'s control **2** (*med betonad partikel*) ~ *bort* disappear with time; ~ *fast vid* grow [on] to; ~ *fram* grow (come) up (*ur* out of), (*utvecklas*) develop; ~ *ifatt ngn* catch s.b. up in height (size); ~ *ifrån* outgrow (*ngn* s.b.), grow out of (*en vana* a habit); ~ *igen* (*om stig e.d.*) become grassed, (*om dike e.d.*) fill up [with grass]; ~ *ihop* grow together; ~ *in i a*) eg. *bet.* grow into, *b*) *bildl.* grow familiar with; ~ *om* outgrow; ~ *till sig* improve in looks; ~ *upp* grow up; ~ *upp till kvinna* grow into womanhood; ~ *ur* grow out of, outgrow; ~ *ut* grow out, (*bli utvuxen*) attain its (*etc.*) full growth; ~ *över* overgrow
växande *a4* growing, increasing; ~ *gröda* (*äv.*) standing crops (*pl*); ~ *skog* standing forest
1 väx|el ['väks-] *s2, bank.* bill [of exchange] (*förk.* B/E); (*tratta*) draft; *egen* (*främmande*) ~ bill payable (receivable); *förfallen* ~ bill due; *prima* (*sekunda*) ~ first (second) of exchange; *acceptera en* ~ accept a bill; *dra en* ~ *för ett belopp på ngn på sex månader* draw [for] an amount on s.b. at six months; *dra -lar på framtiden* (*bildl.*) count too much on the future; *inlösa en* ~ discharge (honour) a bill; *omsätta* (*utställa*) *en* ~ renew (draw) a bill
2 väx|el ['väks-] *s2* **1** (*-pengar*) [small] change; *inte ha ngn* ~ *på sig* have no change [about one] **2** *tekn.* gear; *järnv.* points (*pl*), AE. switch[es *pl*]; *fyra -lar framåt* (*på bil*) four forward gears; *lägga om* ~*n* (*järnv.*) reverse the points; *passera en* ~ (*om tåg*) take a point **3**

(*telefon-*) [telephone] exchange; (*-bord*) switchboard; *sitta i* ~*n* be a switchboard operator
växel|acceptant acceptor [of a bill] -affär **1** (*enskild*) bill transaction **2** *göra* ~*er* do exchange business -belopp amount of a bill -blankett bill[-of-exchange] form
växel|bord switchboard -bruk rotation of crops, crop rotation; *bedriva* ~ practise rotation farming
växel|diskontering discounting of bills -fordringar *pl, bokför.* bills receivable -förfalskning forging (forgery) of bills
växel|kassa small-change cash -kontor exchange office -kurs rate [of exchange], exchange rate
växellag bills of exchange (negotiable instruments) act
växel|lok[omotiv] shunting engine; AE. switch engine -låda gearbox; AE. transmission [case] -pengar *pl* [small] change (*sg*)
växel|protest protest of a bill -rytteri kite--flying, bill-jobbing
växel|spak (*i bil*) gear lever, AE. gearshift -spel interplay, interaction -spår *järnv.* siding (AE. switch) track -spänning *elektr.* alternating voltage -station *tel.* subexchange -ström alternating current (*förk.* A.C.) -strömsmotor alternating-current motor -sång alternating song; *kyrklig* ~ antiphon
växeltagare payee [of a bill]
växeltelefonist switchboard operator
växel|utställare drawer [of a bill]
växel|varm ~*a djur* cold-blooded animals -verkan reciprocal action, interaction -vis alternately; in (by) turns
väx|la **1** (*pengar*) change; (*utbyta*) exchange (*ringar* rings); *kan du* ~ *5 kronor åt mig?* (*äv.*) can you give me change for 5 kronor?; ~ *en sedel* break a note (*i* into); ~ *ett par ord med* have a word with; *vi har aldrig* ~*t ett ont ord* we have never had words; ~ *fel* give the wrong change; ~ *in* (*pengar*) change, cash **2** (*tåg e.d.*) shunt, switch; (*i bil*) change (shift) gear, AE. shift the gears **3** (*skifta*) vary, change; (~ *om*) alternate; (*om priser*) fluctuate
växlande *a4* varying, changing; variable (*vindar* winds); ~ *framgång* varying success; ~ *öden* (*äv.*) vicissitudes
väx|ling **1** (*-ande*) changing *etc.* **2** (*skiftning*) change; variation, fluctuation; (*inbördes*) alternation; (*regelbunden*) rotation; *årstidernas* ~*ar* the rotations of the seasons; *ödets* ~*ar* the vicissitudes of fortune **3** (*av tåg*) shunting, switching; (*av bil*) gear changing (shifting) -ingsrik full of changes (*etc.*)
växt I *a4* (*väl* well) grown II *s3* **1** (*tillväxt*) growth; *hämma i* ~*en* check the growth of; *stanna i* ~*en* stop growing **2** (*kroppsbyggnad*) shape, figure, build; *av ståtlig* ~ of a fine stature; *liten* (*stor*) *till* ~*en* short (tall) of stature **3** (*planta*) plant; (*ört*) herb; (*utväxt*) growth, tumour; *samla* ~*er* collect wild flowers -art plant species -biologi plant biology -cell plant cell -del part of a plant -familj plant family -fett vegetable fat -fiber plant (vegetable) fibre -färg vegetable dye -följd rotation (suc-

cession) of crops **-förädling** plant breeding (improvement) **-geografi** plant geography, phytogeography **-gift** vegetable poison; (*bekämpningsmedel*) herbicide, weedkiller **-hus** greenhouse; (*uppvärmt*) hothouse **-huseffekt** greenhouse effect **-kraft** growing power **-lighet** vegetation **-liv** plant life; vegetation, flora **-lära** botany **-namn** plant name **-period** period of growth **-press** botanical (plant) press **-riket** the plant (vegetable) kingdom **-saft** [plant] sap **-sjukdom** plant disease **-skyddsmedel** plant protectant **-släkte** plant family **-sätt** growth habit (form) **-värk** growing pains (*pl*) **-värld** flora; *jfr äv. -riket* **-ätande** *a4* herbivorous

vörda [ˣvö:r-] revere, venerate; (*högakta*) respect **vördig** *a1, se vördnadsbjudande*; (*i titel*) reverend **vördnad** *s3* reverence, veneration; *sonlig ~* filial piety; *betyga ngn sin ~* pay one's respects to s.b.; *hysa ~ för* revere, venerate, respect; *inviga ~* (*äv.*) command respect **vördnads|betygelse** mark (token) of respect (reverence) **-bjudande** venerable; (*friare äv.*) imposing, grand **-full** reverent[ial], respectful (*mot* of) **-värd** venerable

vörd|sam *a1* respectful **-samt** *adv* respectfully; deferentially; (*i brevslut*) Yours respectfully **vört** *s3* wort **-bröd** bread flavoured with wort

x-a [ˣeksa] ~ [*över*] 'x' out
Xantippa [ksanˣtippa] Xant[h]ippe
xantippa *s1* shrew
x-axel [ˣeks-] x-axis
Xenofon [ˈksenåfån] Xenophon
xenon [kseˈnå:n] *s4, kem.* xenon
xerograˈfi [kse:-] *s3* xerography
X-krok [ˣeks-] picture hook
x-kromosom X-chromosome
xylofon [ksylɷˈfå:n] *s3* xylophone
xyloˈgraf *s3* xylographer **-graˈfi** *s3* xylography
xylol [ksyˈlå:l] *s3, kem.* xylene, xylol
xylos [ksyˈlå:s] *s3, kem.* xylose

X

yacht [jått] *s3* yacht **-klubb** yacht[ing] club
yankee ['jänki] *s5* [*pl* -kier] Yankee; *vard.* Yank
y-axel y-axis
yeme'nit *se jemenit*
Y-kromosom Y-chromosome
yla howl **ylande** *s6* howling
ylle *s6* wool; *av* ~ [made] of wool, woollen **-filt**
woollen blanket; (*material*) wool felt **-foder**
woollen lining **-fodrad** [-ɷ:-] *a5* wool-lined,
flannel-lined **-halsduk** woollen scarf **-kläder**
pl woollen clothing (*sg*) **-muslin** delaine
-skjorta flannel shirt **-strumpa** woollen
stocking (*kort:* sock) **-tröja** jersey, sweater;
(*undertröja*) woollen vest **-tyg** woollen material (cloth); paisley (*ett slags tunt mönstrat*
~) **-varor** woollen goods, woollens **-väveri**
woollen mill (factory)
ymnig *a1* abundant, plentiful; heavy (*regn* rain)
-het abundance, profusion **-hetshorn** horn of
plenty, cornucopia **ymnigt** *adv* abundantly
etc.; (*blöda* bleed) profusely; *förekomma* ~
abound, be plentiful **ymp** *s2* graft; bud **ymp|a**
1 *med.* inoculate **2** *trädg.* graft **-kniv** grafting
knife **-kvist** graft, scion - **ning 1** *med.*
inoculation **2** *trädg.* grafting **-vax** grafting wax
yngel ['yŋel] *s7, koll.* brood; (*fisk-, grod-*) fry;
(*i romkorn*) spawn (*äv. bildl.* neds.); *ett* ~ one
of the brood (*etc.*)
yngla [ˣyŋla] breed; spawn; ~ *av sig* (*eg. o. friare*) multiply
yngling youth, young man; (*skol-*) [school]boy
-aålder [years (*pl*) of] adolescence
yngre ['yŋ-] *a, komp. t. ung* **1** younger (*än*
than); (*i tjänsten*) junior; (*senare*) later, more
recent; *han är 3 år* ~ *än jag* (*äv.*) he is my
junior by 3 years; *se* ~ *ut än man är* (*äv.*) not
look one's years; *den* ~ *herr A.* Mr. A. Junior;
Dumas den ~ Dumas the younger; *Pitt den* ~
the younger Pitt; *de* ~ the juniors, the younger
people **2** (*ganska ung*) young[ish], fairly young
(*herre* gentleman)
yngst *a, superl. t. ung* (*jfr yngre*) youngest; latest, most recent; *den* ~*e i* the youngest
[member] of; *den* ~*e i tjänsten* the most recently appointed member of the staff
ynka *se ömka* **ynkedom** [-dɷmm] *s2, det var
rena* ~*en* it was a poor show (pitiable affair,
pitiable performance) **ynklig** *a1* pitiable, miserable **ynkrygg** funk; milksop
ynnest ['ynn-] *s2* (*visa ngn en* do s.b. a) favour
-bevis [mark (token) of] favour
yppa 1 reveal, disclose (*för* to); ~ *en hemlighet
för ngn* (*äv.*) let s.b. into a secret **2** *rfl* (*uppstå*) arise, crop up; (*erbjuda sig*) offer, present
itself, turn up
ypperlig *a1* excellent, splendid; superb; (*av hög
kvalitet*) superior, first-class **ypperst** *superl.
a* best, finest, most outstanding; choicest (*kva-

litet quality); noblest, greatest (*man* man)
yppig *a1* **1** (*om växtlighet e.d.*) luxuriant; lush
(*gräs* grass); (*om figur*) full, buxom; ~ *barm*
ample bosom **2** (*luxuös*) luxurious, sumptuous
-het 1 luxuriance; lushness *etc.* **2** luxurious-
ness, sumptuousness
yr *a1* (*i huvudet*) dizzy, giddy; (*ostyrig*) giddy,
harum-scarum; *bli* ~ turn (go) dizzy (*etc.*); ~
av glädje giddy with joy; ~ *i mössan* flustered,
flurried, all in a fluster (flurry); *som* ~*a höns*
like giddy geese **yra I** *s1* **1** *se snöyra* **2** (*under sjukdom*) delirium; (*vild* ~) frenzy; *i stridens* ~ in the frenzy of the fray **II** *v1* **1** (*tala i
yrsel*) be delirious; ~ *om ngt* rave about s.th.
2 (*virvla*) whirl; *snön yr* the snow is whirling
(driving) about, *skummet yr om stäven* the
spray is swirling round the stem; *dammet yr i
luften* there are clouds of dust in the air; ~ *igen*
(*om väg*) get blocked with snow; ~ *omkring*
go whirling about **yrhätta** madcap, tomboy
yrka (*begära*) demand; ~ *ansvar på ngn* demand
a p.'s conviction, prefer a charge against s.b.;
~ *bifall* (*parl.*) move that the motion be agreed
to; ~ *bifall till* support; ~ *på* demand, claim
(*ersättning* compensation); apply for (*uppskov*
a postponement); (*ihärdigt*) insist [up]on (*att
ngn gör ngt* a p.'s doing s.th.) **yrkande** *s6* **1**
(*utan pl*) demanding *etc.* **2** (*med pl*) demand;
claim (*på ersättning* for compensation); *parl.*
motion; *på* ~ *av* at the instance of
yrke *s6* profession; (*sysselsättning*) occupation;
(*hantering*) trade; (*kall*) vocation; *lärare till* ~*t*
a teacher by profession; *fria* ~*n* [liberal]
professions; *han har till* ~ *att undervisa*
teaching is his profession
yrkes|arbetande *a4* working in a profession
(*etc.*); *de* ~ the working population **-arbetare**
skilled worker **-arbete** profession, skilled
work **-erfarenhet** professional experience
-fiskare fisherman by trade **-gren** occupational branch **-grupp** occupational group
-hemlighet trade (business) secret **-inspek-
tion** ~*en* the [Swedish] labour inspectorate
-kunnig skilled, trained **-kvinna** professional
woman **-liv** working (professional) life **-lärare**
vocational teacher **-man** craftsman, skilled
worker **-medicin** occupational medicine **-mu-
siker** professional musician **-mässig** *a1*
professional **-område** vocational (occupational) field (sphere) **-orientering** vocational
guidance **-register** trade register, (*i tel.kata-
log*) classified telephone directory, *AE.* yellow
pages **-rådgivning** *se - orientering* **-sjukdom**
occupational disease **-skada** industrial injury
- skadeförsäkring industrial injury insurance
-skicklig skilled **-skicklighet** professional
(occupational) skill, skill in one's work **-skola**
vocational (trade) school **-stolthet** professional pride **-titel** professional title **-trafik**
commercial traffic **-undervisning** vocational
training **-utbildad** *a5* skilled, trained **-utbild-
ning** vocational training **-val** choice of career
(vocation, occupation, profession) **-verksam-
het** economic activity, trade **-vägledning** *se
-orientering*
yrsel ['yrr-] *s2* dizziness, giddiness; (*omtöck-
ning*) delirium; *ligga i* ~ be delirious; *jag greps*

av ~ (*äv.*) my head began to swim **-anfall** *få ett* ~ have an attack of giddiness
yr|snö whirling (driving) snow **-vaken** drowsy [with sleep], startled out of [one's] sleep **-väder** snowstorm, blizzard
ysta (*en ost*) make; (*mjölk*) make into cheese; ~ *sig* curdle, coagulate
yster ['yss-] *a2* frisky, lively, boisterous; *en* ~ *häst* a frisky (spirited) horse; *en* ~ *lek* a romping game
ystning cheese-making; (*löpning*) curdling [process]
yt|a *s1* **1** surface; *geom. äv.* face; *på* ~*n* on the (its *etc.*) surface; *endast se till* ~*n* take a superficial view of things, take s.th. at its face value **2** (*areal*) area **-aktiv** surface-active **-behandla** finish **-behandling** finish[ing], surface treatment **-beklädnad** facing **-beläggning** surface coating, surfacing, coating **-beräkning** area calculation **-bildning** *geogr.* configuration **-enhet** unit [of] area **-innehåll** area **-lager** surface layer (coating)
ytlig ['*y:t-] *a1* superficial (*äv. bildl.*); skin-deep (*sår* wound); (*grund*) shallow; (*flyktig*) cursory; *en* ~ *kännedom om* (*äv.*) a smattering of **-het** superficiality
yt|läge *sjö.* surface position **-mått** square measure **-spänning** surface tension
ytter ['ytt-] *s2*, *sport.* outside forward **-bana** *sport.* outside track **-dörr** outer (front) door **-fil** ouside lane **-kant** outer edge, fringe, verge **-kläder** *pl* outdoor clothes **-kurva** outer curve
ytterlig *a1* extreme; (*fullständig*) utter; (*överdriven*) excessive **-are I** *komp. a* further; additional; (*mera*) more **II** *adv* (*vidare*) further; (*ännu mera*) still more; ~ *ett exemplar* another (one more) copy; ~ *några dagar* a few days more; *har förbättrats* ~ has been further improved **-het** extreme; (*-hetsåtgärd*) extremity; ~*erna berör varandra* extremes meet; *gå till* ~*er* go to extremes; *till* ~ *oartig* extremely (exceedingly) impolite
ytterlighets|fall extreme case **-man** extremist **-parti** extremist party **-åtgärd** extreme measure
ytterligt *adv* extremely; exceedingly, excessively
ytter|mera *oböjligt a, till* ~ *visso* what is more **-mått** outer dimension; external measurements (*pl*) **-plagg** outdoor garment **-ring** tyre, tire **-rock** overcoat, greatcoat **-sida** outer side, exterior, outside **-skor** outdoor shoes **-skär** *åka* ~ skate on the outside edge **-skärgård** outer isles
ytterst ['ytt-] *superl. adv* **1** (*längst ut*) farthest out (off), outermost **2** (*synnerligen*) extremely, exceedingly, most **3** (*i sista hand*) ultimately, finally
yttersta *best. superl. a* **1** (*längst ut belägen*) outermost, remotest; (*friare*) utmost; *bildl.* extreme; *den* ~ *gränsen* the utmost limit; ~ *vänstern* the extreme left **2** (*störst, högst*) utmost; extreme; *göra sitt* ~ do one's utmost, make every effort; *i* ~ *nöd* in direst necessity; *i* ~ *okunnighet* in utter ignorance; *till det* ~ to the utmost (limit), (*kämpa* fight) to the bitter end, (*pressa* press) to the last ounce, (*i* (*till*)

högsta grad) to an extreme pitch **3** (*sist*) last; ~ *domen* the last judgment; *på* ~ *dagen* on the last day; *göra ett* ~ *försök* make one last (a final) attempt; *ligga på sitt* ~ be in extremis (at the point of death)
ytter|tak roof **-trappa** *s1* steps (*pl*), flight of steps **-vägg** outer (outside) wall **-världen** the outer (outside) world **-öra** external ear
yttra I (*uttala*) utter, say; (*ge uttryck åt*) express; ~ *några ord* utter (speak) a few words **II** *rfl* **1** (*ta t. orda*) speak (*vid ett sammanträde* at a meeting); (*uttala sig*) express an (one's) opinion (*om* about, on) **2** (*visa sig*) manifest itself; *sjukdomen* ~*r sig i* the symptoms of the disease are
yttrande *s6* **1** (*utan pl*) uttering **2** (*med pl*) utterance; (*anmärkning*) remark, observation, statement [of opinion]; *avge sitt* ~ submit one's comments **-frihet** freedom of speech (expression)
yttre ['ytt-] **I** *komp. a* (*längre ut belägen*) outer (*hamn* harbour; *skärgård* archipelago); (*utvändig*) external, exterior (*diameter* diameter), outside (*mått* measurement); *bildl.* external (*fiender* enemies; *förbindelser* relations), outward (*skönhet* beauty); extrinsic (*företräden* advantages); (*utrikes*) foreign (*mission* missions); *Y*~ *Mongoliet* Outer Mongolia; ~ *orsak* external cause; ~ *rymden* outer space; ~ *skada* external (outer) damage; *i* ~ *måtto* (*vanl.*) outwardly, externally **II** *n* exterior, outside; [external] appearance; *till det* ~ externally, outwardly
yttring manifestation, mark (*av* of)
yt|vatten surface water **-verkan** *elektr.* skin effect **-vidd** area
yuppie ~*n* ~*s* yuppie
yvas *v2, dep,* ~ *över* be proud of, glory in
yverboren ['*y:-, -å:-] *a5, bildl.* ultrapatriotic
yvig *a1* bushy (*svans* tail; *skägg* beard); thick (*hår* hair); ~*a fraser* high-flown phrases
yx|a I *s1* axe; *kasta* ~*n i sjön* (*bildl.*) throw up (in) the sponge **II** *v1,* ~ *till* rough-hew **-hammare** axe-head **-hugg** cut (blow) with (of) an (the) axe **-skaft** axe handle (helve); *goddag* ~*!* neither rhyme nor reason!

Y

Z

zair|ier [sa'i:-] Zaïrese **-isk** *a5* Zaïrese
zamb|ier ['samm-] Zambian **-isk** *a5* Zambian
zenit ['se:-] *oböjligt s* [the] zenith **-avstånd** zenith distance
zeppelinare [s-, -ˣli:-] zeppelin; *vard.* zep[p]
zigenarblod [siˣje:-] gypsy blood
zigenar|e gypsy, gipsy **-flicka** gypsy girl **-läger** gypsy camp (encampment) **-musik** gypsy music **-språk** gypsy language, Rom[m]any
zigenerska [siˣje:-] gypsy woman (girl) **zigensk** [si'je:nsk] *a5* gypsy
zimbabw|ier [sim'babb-] Zimbabwean **-isk** *a5* Zimbabwean
zink [s-] *s3* zinc **-haltig** *a1* zinc-bearing, zinciferous **-legering** zinc alloy **- plåt** zinc plate (sheet) **-salva** zinc ointment **-spat** zinc spar **-vitt** *s9* zinc (Chinese) white
zinnia ['sinnia] *s1* (*växt*) zinnia
zirkonium [sir'kɔ:-] *s8* zirconium
zodia'k|alljus [s-] zodiacal light **-en** [-'a:-] *s, best. form* the zodiac
zon [sɔ:n] *s3* zone **-gräns** zonal boundary **-indelning** zone division **-tariff** zone tariff, zonal rate
zoofysiologi [ˣsåå:-] zoophysiology, zoophysics
zoo|log [såå-] zoologist **-logi** *s3* zoology **-logisk** *a5* zoological; ~ trädgård zoological gardens (*pl*), *vard.* zoo
zooma [ˣso:-] *foto.* zoom
zoo|tomi [sååtåˣmi:] *s3* zootomy **-tomisk** [-'tå:-] *a5* zootomic[al]
zucchini [so'ki:ni] *s5, bot.* zucchini, squash
zulu ['su:lu] *s3* Zulu **-kaffer** Zulu-Kaffir **-språket** Zulu
zygot [sy'gå:t] *s3, naturv.* zygote
Zürich ['sy:riç] *n* Zürich, Zurich

Å

1 å *s2* [small] river; stream; *AE. äv.* creek; *gå över ~n efter vatten* give o.s. unnecessary trouble, put o.s. to unnecessary inconvenience
2 å *prep., se på*
3 å *interj* oh!, *Irl., Sk.* och!
åberopa 1 (*anföra*) adduce (*som exempel* as an example); (*hänvisa t.*) refer to, quote, cite; (*t. försvar*) plead; ~ *som ursäkt* allege as an excuse; *~nde vårt brev* referring to our letter **2** *rfl, se 1*
åberopande *s6, under ~ av a*) on the plea (*att* that), *b*) hand. referring to (*vårt brev* our letter)
åbo *s5* farm tenant with fixity of tenure, copyholder **-rätt** copyhold right, hereditary lease
åbrodd [ˣå:-, -å-] *s2* (*växt*) southernwood, lad's love
åbäka *rfl* make ridiculous gestures; (*göra sig till*) show off **åbäke** *s6* huge and clumsy creature (*om sak:* thing); monster, monstrosity; *ett ~ till karl* a great lump of a fellow **åbäkig** *a1* unwieldy, hulky, shapeless
ådagalägg|a [ˣå:-, -ˣda:-] (*visa*) show [o.s. to possess], manifest, display, exhibit; (*bevisa*) prove **-ande** *s6* manifestation *etc.*
åder ['å:-] *s1* vein (*äv. bildl.*); (*puls-*) artery; *geol.* vein, lode; (*i trä*) vein, grain; (*käll-*) spring **-brock, -bråck** varicose veins (*pl*), *fack.* varix (*pl* varices) **-förkalkad** *a5* suffering from arteriosclerosis; *hon börjar bli ~* (*äv.*) she is getting senile **-förkalkning** arteriosclerosis, *vard.* hardening of the arteries **-låta** bleed (*äv. bildl.*); *bildl. äv.* drain **-låtning** [-å:-] bleeding, blood-letting; *bildl.* drain, depletion
ådra [ˣå:-] **I** *s1, se åder* **II** *v1* vein; (*sten, trä e.d. äv.*) grain, streak
ådraga 1 (*förorsaka*) cause (*ngn obehag* s.b. inconvenience); bring down upon **2** *rfl* bring down upon o.s.; contract (*sjukdom* an illness); catch (*förkylning* a cold); (*utsätta sig för*) incur (*kritik* criticism); ~ *sig uppmärksamhet* attract attention
ådr|ig [ˣå:-] *a1* veined, veiny; (*om trä, sten e.d.*) grained, streaked; *bot.* venous **-ing** veining; *konkr. äv.* veinage, grain, streak; *bot.* venation
ådöma sentence (*ngn ngt* s.b. to s.th.); inflict (*ngn straff* a penalty upon s.b.); ~ *ngn böter* impose a fine on (fine) s.b.
åh *se 3 å*
å|'hej heave-ho! **-hoj** [å'håjj] *skepp ~!* ship ahoy **-'hå** aha!, oh!
åhöra listen to, hear
åhörar|e hearer, listener; *koll.* audience **-dag** *skol.* parents' day **-läktare** [public] gallery
å|ja ['å:-] (*tämligen*) fairly **-jo** ['å:-] (*jo då*) oh yes; (*tämligen*) fairly
åk *s7* **1** *vard.* (*bil*) car **2** *sport.* run
åk|a *v3* **1** *eg. bet.* ride (*baklänges* backwards; *karusell* on the merry-go-round); (*färdas*) go ([*med*] *tåg etc.* by train *etc.*); (*köra*) drive ([*i*

en] *bil* a car); *absol.* go by car (*etc.*); ~ *cykel* ride a bicycle (*vard.* bike); ~ *framlänges* sit facing the engine; ~ *första klass* travel (go) first class; ~ *gratis* travel free; ~ *hiss* take the lift; ~ *efter häst* drive behind a horse; ~ *kana* slide; ~ *kälke* toboggan; ~ *skidor* ski; ~ *skridskor* skate; *får jag* ~ *med dig?* can you give me a lift? **2** (*glida*) slide, glide, slip; *skjortan -er jämt upp* my (*etc.*) shirt keeps riding up; *vasen -te i golvet* the vase fell on the floor **3** (*med betonad partikel*) ~ *av* slip off; ~ *bort* go away; ~ *efter* (*hämta*) fetch [by car *etc.*].; ~ *fast* get (be) caught by the police; ~ *förbi* pass, drive past; ~ *in a*) eg. drive in, *b*) *vard.* (*i fängelse*) land in jail; [*få*] ~ *med* get a lift; ~ *om* overtake, pass; ~ *omkull a*) fall (*på cykel* from one's bicycle; *på vägen* on the road), *b*) (*ngn, ngt*) run down; ~ *ut a*) eg. go for a drive, *b*) *vard.* (*kastas ut*) be turned (kicked) out

åkall|a invoke, call upon **-an** *r* invocation

åkar|brasa *ta sig* (*slå*) *en* ~ slap o.s. to keep warm **-dräng** carter

åkar|e haulage contractor, carrier **-häst** carthorse **-kamp** *vard.* [old] hack **-taxa** (*för gods*) cartage

åkdon vehicle

åker ['å:-] *s2* (*-fält*) [tilled] field; (*-jord*) arable [land]; ~ *och äng* arable and pasture land; *ute på* ~ *n* out in the field[s *pl*] **-areal** area under cultivation, arable acreage **-bruk** *se jordbruk* **-bär** arctic raspberry (bramble)

åkeri haulage contractor[s], haul[i]er; *AE.* trucker

åker|jord arable (tilled) land, cultivated field **-lapp** patch of cultivated ground **-mark** *se -jord* **-ren** headland **-senap** charlock, wild mustard **-sork** field vole **-spöke** *vard.* scarecrow **-stubb** stubble **-tistel** creeping thistle, *AE.* Canada thistle **-vicker** vetch **-vinda** bindweed **-ärt** field pea

åklaga ['å:-] prosecute

åklagar|e prosecutor; *Skottl.* procurator fiscal; *allmän* ~ public prosecutor, *AE.* district attorney **-myndighet** public prosecution authority **-sidan** the prosecution **-vittne** witness for the prosecution

åkomma ['ª:kå-] *s1* complaint; affection

åk|sjuka travel sickness **-tur** ride, drive; *göra* (*ta*) *en* ~ go for a ride (drive)

ål *s2* (*fisk*) eel; *hal som en* ~ [as] slippery as an eel **åla** crawl

ålder ['åll-] *s2* age; *av* ~ traditionally, of old; *böjd av* ~ bent with age; *personer av alla åldrar* persons of all ages; *efter* ~ according to age (*i tjänsten*: seniority); *liten för sin* ~ small for one's age; *ha* ~*n inne* be old enough (*för* for; *för att* to); *hon är i min* ~ she is [about] my age; *i sin bästa* ~ in the prime of life; *vid 35 års* ~ at the age of thirty-five; *vid hög* ~ at an advanced (a great) age; *mogen* ~ maturity

ålderdom [-dåmm] *s2* old age **-lig** *a1* ancient (*sed* custom); (*gammaldags*) old-fashioned; (*föråldrad*) archaic; ~*t uttryck* archaic expression **-ligt** *adv,* ~ *klädd* dressed in old-fashioned clothes

ålderdoms|hem home for the aged, old

people's home **-krämpor** infirmities of old age **-svag** decrepit, senile **-svaghet** decrepitude, senility

ålderman alderman; (*i skrå*) [guild]master

ålders|betyg birth certificate **-fördelning** age structure **-grupp** age group **-gräns** age limit **-klass** age class **-pension** retirement pension; (*folkpension*) old age pension **-president** president by seniority; (*i underhuset*) Father of the House [of Commons] **-sjukdomar** *läran om* ~*na* geriatrics (*pl, behandlas som sg*) **-skillnad** difference of (in) age **-streck** *falla för* ~*et* reach retiral age **-tecken** sign of age

ålderstigen *a5* old, aged; advanced in years

ålderstillägg seniority increment

åldfru royal housekeeper

åldr|ad *a5* aged **-ande** *a4 o. s6* ag[e]ing **-as** *dep* grow old[er], age **-ig** *a1* old; aged **-ing** old man (woman *etc.*); ~*ar* old people **-ingsvård** care of the aged

åligg|a be incumbent [up]on, rest [up]on (with); *det -er honom att* (*äv.*) it is his duty to; *det -er köparen att* the buyer shall **-ande** *s6* duty; obligation; (*uppgift*) task; *sköta sina* ~*n* discharge one's duties

ål|kista eel hatch (trap) **-ning** [ˣå:l-] *mil.* crawling **-skinn** eel skin

ålägga enjoin (*ngn att göra ngt* s.b. to do s.th.; *ngn ngt* s.th. on s.b.); order, command; (*tilldela*) impose (*ngn en uppgift* a task on s.b.); ~ *sig ngt* impose s.th. on o.s.

åma *rfl, se åbäka*

åminnelse commemoration; *till* ~ *av* in commemoration of **-gudstjänst** memorial service

ånej ['å:-] (*nej då*) oh no!; (*inte vidare*) not very

ång|a I *s1* (*vatten-*) steam; (*dunst*) vapour (*äv. fys.*); *bilda* ~ make steam; *få upp* ~ *i* (*äv. bildl.*) get up steam; *hålla* ~*n uppe* (*äv. bildl.*) keep up steam; *släppa ut* ~ let off steam **II** *v1* steam (*av* with); *det* ~*r från lokomotivet* the engine is steaming; ~ *bort* steam off; *tåget* ~*de in på* the train steamed into **-are** steamer, steamship (*förk.* S/S, S.S.); *med* ~*n X* by the X, by S.S. X **-bad** vapour bath **-bildning** steam generation; vaporization **-båt** *se -are*

ångbåts|bolag steamship company **-brygga** landing stage, jetty, pier **-förbindelse** steamship service **-resa** steamer voyage **-trafik** steamship service (traffic) **-turer** *pl* sailings of steamers; (*förteckning*) list of sailings

ång|central steam power station **-driven** *a5* (*om maskin*) steam-operated, steam-driven; (*om båt*) steam-propelled

ånger ['åŋer] *s9* repentance (*över* for, of); remorse, compunction; (*ledsnad*) regret (*över* at, for) **-full** repentant (*över* of); remorseful (*över* at); regretful **-köpt** [-çö:pt] *a4, se -full*; *vara* ~ *över ngt* regret it (what one has done) **-vecka** cooling-off week

ångest ['åŋ-] *s2* agony; anguish; *i dödlig* ~ in deadly (mortal) fear (*för* of) **-full** filled with agony; anguished **-känsla** [feeling of] alarm (anguish) **-skrik** cry of agony, anguished cry

ång|fartyg *se ångare* **-koka** steam **-kraft** steam power **-kraftverk** steam power station (plant) **-kvarn** steam mill **-lok, -maskin** steam-engine **-panna** [steam-]boiler **-preparerad** *a5*

Å

evaporated; ~e havregryn rolled oats
ångra regret; feel sorry for (att man gjort doing); repent [of] (sina synder one's sins); ~ sig regret, be sorry, repent; det skall du inte behöva ~ you will not have cause to regret it
ång|slup steam cutter (launch) **-spruta** steam fire engine **-strykjärn** steam iron **-stråle** jet of steam **-ström** r, fys. angstrom [unit], (förk. Å., A.U.) **-tryck** boiler (steam, vapour) pressure **-turbin** steam turbine **-vissla** steam whistle **-vält** steamroller
ånyo [å⁺ny:ɷ] anew, afresh, [once] again
år s7 year; ~ 1960 a) adv in [the year] 1960, b) s the year 1960; nådens ~ 1960 the year of grace 1960; 1960 ~s modell the 1960 model; 1808 ~s krig the war of 1808; ~ för ~ year by year; ~ ut och ~ in year in and year out; Gott Nytt År! [A] Happy New Year!; ~ts skörd this year's harvest; två ~s fängelse two years' imprisonment; ett halvt ~ six months; ett och ett halvt ~ eighteen months; hela ~et the whole year, all the year round; under hela ~et throughout the year, all through the year; bära sina ~ med heder carry one's years well, wear well; när fyller du ~? when is your birthday?; ha ~en inne be of the age; med ~en with time; om ett ~ in a year['s time]; per ~ a year, yearly, annually, per annum; på ~ och dag for years [and years]; vi är vänner sedan många ~ tillbaka we have been friends for many years; till ~en [kommen] advanced in years; under senare ~ in recent years; under de senaste ~en during the last few years
åra s1 oar; (mindre) scull; (paddel-) paddle
åratal i uttr.: i (under) ~ for years [and years]
årblad oar blade
årder ['å:r-] s4, s3 wooden plough
år|gång s2 **1** (av tidskrifter e.d.) [annual] volume; en ~ (äv.) a year's issue; gamla ~ar back-volumes, old files **2** (av vin) vintage **3** (åldersklass) de yngre ~arna the younger age groups; min ~ people of my year **-hundrade** century
årklyka rowlock; AE. oarlock
årlig ['⁺å:r-] a1 annual, yearly **-en** annually, yearly; ~ återkommande annual; det inträffar ~ it happens every year
års [å:rs] adv, så här ~ at this time of [the] year **-avgift** annual charge (fee); (i förening e.d.) annual subscription (AE. dues pl) **-avslutning** breaking-up; AE. commencement **-barn** vi är ~ we were born in the same year **-berättelse** annual report **-bok** yearbook, annual **-bokstav** year hallmark **-dag** anniversary **-fest** annual festival (celebration) **-gammal** one-year-old; ett ~t barn a one-year-old child; ett ~t djur (äv.) a yearling **-hyra** annual rent **-inkomst** annual (yearly) income **-klass** age class (group); stat. generation **-kontingent** mil. annual contingent (quota) **-kontrakt** contract by the year **-kort** season ticket [for a year] **-kull** age group; (av elever) batch; efterkrigstidens stora ~ar the large number of children born after the war, äv. the high birth rate of the postwar period **-kurs** form; AE. grade; (läroplan) curriculum **-lång** yearlong; lasting one year (many years) **-lön** annual salary; ha

30 000 i ~ have an annual income of 30,000 **-modell** (av senaste of the latest) model **-möte** annual meeting **-omsättning** annual turnover (sales) **-redogörelse** annual report **-ring** annual ring **-ränta** annual interest **-skifte** turn of the year **-skrift** yearbook **-tid** season, time of the year **-vinst** annual profit **-växt** year's crop[s pl]
årtag stroke of the oar[s pl]
år|tal date, year **-tionde** decade
årtull rowlock; AE. oarlock
årtusende millennium (pl äv. millennia); ett ~ (vanl.) a thousand years; i ~n for thousands of years
ås s2 ridge
å|samka se ådraga **-se** (se på) watch; (bevittna) witness
åsido [å⁺si:dɷ] aside, on one side; lämna ngt ~ (äv.) leave s.th. out of consideration; skämt ~ joking apart **-sätta** (ej bry sig om) disregard, set aside; (försumma) neglect, ignore; känna sig -satt feel slighted **-sättande** s6 disregard, setting aside; neglect; med ~ av alla hänsyn having no consideration
åsikt s3 opinion, view (om of, on, about); ~erna är delade opinions differ (are divided); egna ~er views of one's own; enligt min ~ in my opinion; ha (hysa) en ~ have (hold) an opinion; vara av den ~en att be of the opinion that, hold the view that; vad är din ~ i saken? what is your view of (on) the matter?, what do you think about it
åsikts|brytning difference of opinion **-frihet** freedom of opinion **-förtryck** suppression of free opinion **-utbyte** exchange of views
åsk|a I s1 thunder; (-väder) thunderstorm; ~n går it is thundering, there is thunder; ~n slog ner i X. X. was struck by lightning; det är ~ i luften there is thunder in the air; vara rädd för ~n be afraid of thunder **II** v1, det ~r it is thundering **-by** thundershower **-front** thundery front **-knall** thunderclap **-ledare** lightning conductor (rod) **-lik** thundery **-moln** thundercloud **-nedslag** stroke of lightning **-regn** thundery rain **-skräll** thunderclap, peal of thunder **-skur** thundershower **-vigg** thunderbolt **-väder** thunderstorm
åskåda [⁺å:-] se åse
åskådar|e spectator; onlooker, looker-on; (mera tillfällig) bystander; -na (på teater e.d.) the audience, (vid idrottstävling) the crowd; bli ~ till ngt witness s.th. **-läktare** [grand]stand; (utan tak) bleachers (pl) **-platser** pl places [for spectators]
åskådlig [-å:d-] a1 (klar) clear, lucid; (tydlig) perspicuous; ett ~t exempel an object lesson; en ~ skildring (äv.) a graphic description **-göra** make clear, visualize; illustrate (med by) **-het** clearness, clarity; perspicuity
åskådning [-å:d-] (uppfattning) opinions, views (pl); outlook; vilken är hans politiska ~? what is his political position?, where does he stand politically?
åskådnings|materiel audiovisual materials in education: som ~ (friare) as an illustration **-undervisning** audiovisual education
åsna [⁺å:s-] s1 donkey; bildl. o. bibl. ass; envis

som en ~ [as] stubborn as a mule
åsne|aktig *a1* asslike, asinine **-brygga** *bildl.* crib **-drivare** donkey driver **-föl** ass's (donkey's) foal **-hingst** he-ass, jackass **-skri** bray (braying) of donkeys (a donkey)
åsninna she-ass
å'stad off; *bege sig* ~ go away (off), set out; *gå* ~ *och* go [off] and
åstadkomm|a [ˣå:-] *(få t. stånd)* bring about, effect *(en förändring* a change); *(förorsaka)* cause, make *(stor skada* great damage); *(frambringa)* produce; *(göra)* do; *(prestera)* achieve; ~ *ett gott arbete* do it well, *(friare)* do a good job of work; ~ *förvirring* cause confusion; ~ *underverk* work wonders **-ande** *s6, för* ~ *av* [in order] to bring about *(etc.)*
åstund|a desire, long for; *(åtrå)* covet **-an** *r* desire, longing
åsyfta *(ha t. mål)* aim at, have in view; *(avse, mena)* intend, mean *(med* by); *ha ~d verkan* have the desired effect
åsyn sight; *blotta ~en av honom* the mere (very) sight of him; *i allas* ~ in public, in full view of everybody; *i broderns* ~ before his (her) brother, under the very eyes of his (her) brother; *försvinna ur ngns* ~ be lost to (pass out of) a p.'s sight (view); *vid ~en av* at the sight of **åsyna** *oböjligt a,* ~ *vittne* eyewitness *(till* of)
åsätta ~ *en prislapp på ngt* put (fix) a price ticket on [to] s.th.; ~ *ett pris på en vara* put a price on an article; *det åsatta priset* the price marked
1 åt *imperf. av äta*
2 åt I *prep (se äv. under resp. verb)* **1** *rumsbet.* to; *([i riktning] mot)* towards, in the direction of; ~ *vänster (norr)* to the left (north); *gå* ~ *sidan* step aside; *jag har ngt* ~ *magen* there is s.th. the matter with my stomach; *han tog sig* ~ *hjärtat* he put his hand to his heart **2** *glad* ~ happy about; *nicka (skratta)* ~ nod (laugh) at; *vad går det* ~ *dig?* what is the matter with you?; *göra ngt* ~ *saken* do s.th. about it; *hon tog* ~ *sig* she took it personally **3** *(uttr. dativförh.)* to; *(för ngn[s räkning])* for; *ge ngt* ~ *ngn* give s.th. to s.b., give s.b. s.th.; *köpa ngt* ~ *ngn* buy s.th. for s.b., buy s.b. s.th.; *jag skall laga rocken* ~ *dig* I'll mend your coat [for you]; *säga ngt* ~ *ngn* say s.th. to s.b., tell s.b. s.th. **4** *fyra* ~ *gången* four at a time **II** *adv (se äv. under resp. verb)* tight; *sitta* ~ be (fit) tight
åtag|a *rfl* undertake, take upon o.s.; ~ *sig ansvaret för* assume (take the responsibility) for; ~ *sig ngt* take s.th. on, take a matter in hand **-ande** *s6* undertaking; *(förpliktelse äv.)* obligation, commitment, engagement
åtal *s7 (av allm. åklagare)* prosecution; *(av enskild)* [legal] action; *allmänt* ~ public prosecution; *enskilt* ~ private action; *väcka* ~ *mot ngn för ngt* take proceedings against s.b. for s.th., *(mot målsägare äv.)* bring an action against (sue) s.b. for s.th. **åtala** *(om allm. åklagare)* prosecute; *(om enskild)* bring an action against; *bli ~d för* be prosecuted for; *den ~de (vanl.)* the defendant; *frikänna en ~d* acquit an accused **åtalbar** *a1* actionable, indictable
åtals|eftergift nolle prosequi; *bevilja* ~ refuse

to prosecute a case, withdraw a charge; *han beviljades* ~ the charge brought against him was withdrawn, his case was dropped **-punkt** count [of an indictment]
åtanke remembrance; *ha i* ~ remember, bear in mind; *komma i* ~ be remembered (thought of)
åtbörd [-ö:-] *s3* gesture, motion; *göra ~er* gesticulate
åtel *s2* carrion
åtdraga tighten *(en bult* a bolt)
åter [ˈå:-] **1** *(ånyo)* again, once more; *nej och* ~ *nej!* no, a thousand times no!, no, and no again!; *tusen och* ~ *tusen* thousands upon thousands; *affären öppnas* ~ the shop reopens (will be reopened) **2** *(tillbaka)* back [again]; *fram och* ~ there and back, *(av o. an)* to and fro **3** *(däremot)* again, on the other hand **-anpassa** readjust **-anpassning** readjustment **-anskaffa** replace **-anskaffning** replacement **-anskaffningsvärde** replacement value (cost) **-anställa** re-engage, re-employ; *AE.* rehire **-använda** recycle **-användning** recycling **-berätta** *(i ord -ge)* relate; *(berätta i andra hand)* retell **-besätta** *mil.* reoccupy; *(tjänst e.d.)* refill **-besök** *(hos läkare e.d.)* next visit (appointment); *göra ett* ~ make another visit **-betala** pay back, repay; *(lån e.d. äv.)* refund **-betalning** repayment, reimbursement, refund **-betalningsskyldighet** obligation to repay (refund) **-blick** retrospect *(på* of); *(i film e.d.)* flashback *(på* to); *göra (kasta) en* ~ *på* look back upon
åter|bud *(t. inbjudan)* excuse; *(avbeställning)* cancellation, annulment; *ge (skicka)* ~ a) *(att man inte kommer)* send word [to say] that one cannot come, send an excuse, *(t. tävling)* drop out, b) *(att ngt inställs)* cancel a party (dinner etc.), *(att ngt återkallas)* send a cancellation; *ge* ~ *till doktorn* cancel one's appointment with the doctor; *vi har fått några* ~ a few people [sent word that they] could not come **-bäring** refund; bonus; *(i detaljhandel o. försäkr.)* dividend **-börda** [-ö:-] *v1* restore; ~ *ngn t. hemlandet* repatriate s.b. **-erövra** recapture, win back **-erövring** recapture, reconquest
åter|fall relapse *(i* into) **-falla 1** *(i brott etc.)* relapse *(i, till* into) **2** *(falla tillbaka)* recoil *(på* upon) **-fallsförbrytare** recidivist, backslider **-finna** find again; *(-få)* recover; *adresser -finns på s. 50* for addresses see p. 50; *citatet -finns på s. 50* the quotation is to be found on p. 50 **-finnande** *s6, han var vid ~t* when he was found again, he was **-fordra** demand back, reclaim; *(lån)* call in **-få** get back; recover, regain *(medvetandet* consciousness) **-färd** *se återresa* **-föra** bring back; *(bildl.)* trace s.th. back to **-förena** reunite, bring together again; ~ *sig med* rejoin **-förening** reunion; *Tysklands* ~ the reunification of Germany **-försäkra** reinsure; ~ *sig (bildl.)* take measures *(mot* against) **-försäkring** reinsurance **-försälja** resell; *(i minut)* retail **-försäljare** retail dealer, retailer; *pris för* ~ trade price; *sälja till* ~ sell to the trade **-försäljning** resale, reselling **-förvisa** *jur.* refer back, *AE.* remand **-förvärv** recovery, retrieval
åter|ge 1 *(ge tillbaka)* give back, return; ~ *ngn*

friheten give s.b. his freedom **2** (*tolka*) render; (*framställa äv.*) reproduce, represent; ~ *i ord* express in words; ~ *i tryck* reproduce in print; ~ *på engelska* render in[to] English **-givande** [-j-] *s6*, **-givning** [-ji:v-] *s2* rendering; reproduction, representation; (*ljud-*) reproduction **-glans** reflection **-gå 1** (*gå tillbaka*) go back, return; ~ *till arbetet* go back to work **2** (*om köp*) be cancelled; *låta ett köp* ~ cancel a purchase **-gång 1** (*-vändande*) return (*t. arbetet* to work) **2** *jur.* (*av egendom*) reversion; (*av köp*) cancellation, annulment; ~ *av äktenskap* annulment (nullity) of marriage **3** *bildl.* retrogression **-gälda** (*-betala*) repay; (*vedergälla äv.*) return, reciprocate; ~ *ont med gott* return good for evil

återhåll|a restrain, keep back (*ett leende* a smile), suppress; (*hejda*) check; *verka ~nde* have a curbing effect; *med -en andedräkt* with bated breath **-sam** *a1* (*måttfull*) moderate, temperate; (*behärskad*) restrained **-samhet** moderation, temperance; restraint

åter|hämta fetch back; *bildl.* recover, regain (*sina krafter* one's strength); ~ *sig* recover **-hämtning** recovery **-igen** ['å:-] again; (*däremot*) on the other hand **-införa** reintroduce **-insätta** reinstate, reinstall **-inträda** re-enter; ~ *i tjänst* resume one's duties **-inträde** re-entry, re-entrance (*i* into); resumption (*i* of)

åter|kalla 1 (*ropa tillbaka*) call back; recall **2** (*ta tillbaka*) cancel (*en beställning* an order); revoke (*en befallning* an order); withdraw (*en ansökan* an application) **3** *bildl.*, ~ *ngn till livet* (*verkligheten*) bring s.b. back to life (reality); ~ *ngt i minnet* recall s.th., call s.th. to mind **-kallelse 1** recall **2** cancellation; revocation; withdrawal **-kasta** (*ljus*) reflect; (*ljud*) reverberate, re-echo; *ljudet ~des av bergväggen* the sound was thrown back from the cliff **-klang** reverberation; echo (*äv. bildl.*) **-klinga** echo, resound, reverberate (*av with*) **-knyta** (*på nytt uppta*) re-establish (*förbindelser* connections), renew (*vänskap* friendship); ~ *till vad man tidigare sagt* refer (go back) to what one said earlier **-komma** come back, return; *bildl.* return, revert, recur; *ett sådant tillfälle -kommer aldrig* an opportunity like this will never turn up (come) again; *vi ber att få* ~ *längre fram* you will be hearing from us (we will write to you) again later on **-kommande** *a4* recurrent; *ofta* ~ frequent; ~ *till vårt brev av* further (with reference) to our letter of **-komst** [-å-] *s3* return **-koppling** *radio.* feedback [coupling] **-kräva** reclaim **-köp** repurchase **-köpa** repurchase, buy back **-köpsrätt** right of repurchase (redemption); *försäljning med* ~ sale with option of repurchase

åter|lämna return, give (hand) back **-lämnande** *s6* return **-lösa** redeem **-lösning** redemption **-marsch** march back; (*-tåg*) retreat **-remiss** recommitment, return for reconsideration; *yrka* ~ move [that a (the) bill be sent back] for reconsideration; *vi har fått ... på* ~ ... has been referred back to us **-remittera** refer back, return for reconsideration, recommit **-resa** journey back; *på ~n* on one's (the) way back **-se** see (*träffa:* meet) again; ~

varandra (*äv.*) meet again **-seende** meeting [again]; *på ~!* see you again (later)!, *vard.* be seeing you!; *~ts glädje* the joy of reunion **-skaffa** recover **-skapa** re-create **-skall** echo, reverberation **-sken** reflection **-skänka** give back; ~ *ngn livet* restore s.b. to life **-spegla** reflect, mirror **-spegling** reflection **-stod** rest, remainder; *ekon.* balance; (*lämning*) remnant, remains (*pl*) **-studsa** rebound; (*om ljud*) be reflected; (*om kula*) ricochet **-studsning** rebound[ing] **-stå** remain; (*vara kvar*) be left [over]; *det ~r ännu fem lådor* there are still five cases left; *det ~r att se* it remains to be seen; *det värsta ~r ännu* the worst is yet to come, (*att göra*) the worst still remains to be done; *det ~r mig inget annat än att* I have no choice but to **-stående** *a4* remaining; ~ *delen av året* the rest (remaining part) of the year; *hans* ~ *liv* the rest of his life **-ställa 1** (*försätta i sitt förra tillstånd*) restore; ~ *ngt i dess forna skick* restore s.th. to its former state; ~ *jämvikten* restore equilibrium; ~ *ordningen* restore order **2** (*-lämna*) return, restore, give back **-ställande** *s6* restoration, repair; return **-ställare** *en* ~ a hair of the dog [that bit one last night], a pick-me-up **-ställd** *a5, han är fullt* ~ *efter sin sjukdom* he has quite recovered from his illness **-ställningstecken** *mus.* natural, *AE.* cancel **-sända** send back, return **-ta[ga] 1** take back; (*-erövra*) recapture; (*-vinna*) recover **2** (*-gå t.*) resume **3** (*åter ta t. orda*) resume **4** (*-kalla*) withdraw, cancel (*en beställning* an order); retract (*ett löfte* a promise) **-tåg** retreat; *anträda ~et* start retreating; *befinna sig på* ~ be in (on the) retreat

återuppbygg|a rebuild, reconstruct **-ande, -nad** rebuilding, reconstruction **-nadsarbete** reconstruction work

återupp|föra *se återuppbygga* **-liva** revive; (*drunknad*) resuscitate; (*bekantskap*) renew; ~ *gamla minnen* revive old memories **-livningsförsök** [-li:v-] attempt (effort) at resuscitation **-repa** repeat, reiterate **-repning** [-e:-] repetition, reiteration **-rustning** rearmament **-rätta** (*på nytt upprätta*) re-establish, restore; (*ge -rättelse åt*) rehabilitate **-rättelse** rehabilitation **-stå** rise again, arise anew; (*friare*) be revived **-ståndelse** resurrection **-ta[ga]** resume, take up again; ~ *arbetet* resume [one's] work; ~ *ngt till behandling* reconsider s.th. **-täcka** rediscover **-täckt** rediscovery **-väcka** reawaken; revive; ~ *ngn från de döda* raise s.b. from the dead

åter|utsända *radio.* retransmit; (*program*) rebroadcast **-utsändning** *radio.* retransmission; rebroadcast **-val** re-election; *undanbe sig* ~ decline re-election **-verka** react, retroact, have repercussions (*på* on) **-verkan, -verkning** reaction, retroaction, repercussion **-vinna** win back; (*-få*) regain, recover (*fattningen* one's composure); (*-använda*) recycle **-vinning** recycling **-visit** return visit **-väg** way back; *på ~en kom vi* on our way back we came **-välja** re-elect **-vända** return, turn (go, come) back; revert (*till ett ämne* to a subject) **-vändo** *i uttr.: det finns ingen* ~ there is no turning back; *utan* ~ (*oåterkallelig*) irrevocable **-vändsgata,**

-vändsgränd blind alley, cul-de-sac; *bildl. äv.* impasse, dead end **-växt** regrowth, fresh growth; *bildl.* rising (coming) generation; *sörja för ~en* (*bildl.*) ensure the continuance (continued growth)

åt|följa accompany; (*som uppvaktning*) attend; (*följa efter*) follow **-följande** *a4* accompanying etc.; (*bifogad*) enclosed; *med ty ~* with the ensuing **-gång** (*förbrukning*) consumption; (*avsättning*) sale; *ha stor ~* sell well; *ha strykande ~* have a rapid sale **-gången** *a5, illa ~* roughly treated (handled), badly knocked about **-gärd** [-jä:-] *s3* measure; (*mått o. steg*) step, move; *föranledde ingen ~* could not be considered; *lämna utan ~* not be able to consider; *vidtaga ~er* take measures (action) **-gärda** [-jä:r-] *vi måste ~* we must do s.th. about **-görande** [-j-] *s6* action; *det skedde utan A:s ~* A. had nothing to do with it, it was none of A.'s doing **-hutning** [-u:-] reprimand, rating **-hävor** *pl* manners; behaviour (*sg*); *utan ~* without a lot of fuss **-komlig** [-å-] *a1* within reach (*för* of); *lätt ~* easily accessible, within easy reach

åtkomst [-å-] *s3* possession, acquisition **-handling** title deed (document) **-tid** *data.* access time

åt|lyda obey; (*föreskrift e.d.*) observe; *bli -lydd* be obeyed **-lydnad** obedience **-löje** ridicule; (*föremål för löje*) laughing stock; *göra sig till ett ~* make a laughing stock (fool) of o.s., make o.s. ridiculous; *göra ngn till ett ~* make s.b. a laughing stock, hold s.b. up to ridicule

åtminstone [-ˣminstå-] at least; (*minst äv.*) at the least; (*i varje fall*) at any rate

åtnjut|a enjoy (*aktning* esteem); *~ aktning* (*äv.*) be held in esteem **-ande** *s6* enjoyment; *komma i ~ av* come into possession of, get the benefit of

åtra [ˣå:-] *rfl* change one's mind; (*återta sitt ord*) go back on one's word

åtrå [ˣå:-] **I** *s9* desire (*efter* for); (*sinnlig äv.*) lust (*efter* for) **II** *v4* desire; (*trakta efter*) covet **-värd** *a1* desirable

åt|sida (*hitre sida*) near side; (*på mynt*) obverse **-sittande** *a4* tight[-fitting], snug[-fitting] **-skild** separate[d]; *bildl. äv.* distinct; *ligga ~a* lie apart **-skilja** separate; part; (*skilja från varandra*) distinguish [between] **-skillig** [-ʃ-] *a1, fören.* a great (good) deal of; *självst.* a great (good) deal; *~a* (*flera*) several, (*många*) quite a number of, a great (good) many, (*olika*) various; *det finns ~a som tror det* there are many who think so **-skilligt** [-ʃ-] *adv* a good deal, considerably, not a little; *~ mer än 100 personer* well over a hundred people **-skillnad** *göra ~* make a distinction (*mellan* between); *utan ~* without distinction, indifferently **-skils** [-ʃ-] apart, asunder **-smitande** *a4* tight[-fitting] **-stramning** [-a:-] *eg.* contraction; (*ekonomisk*) tightening[-up]; (*kredit- etc.*) squeeze, restraint; (*på börsen*) stiffening

åtta I *räkn* eight; *~ dagar* (*vanl.*) a week; *~ dagar i dag* this day week **II** *s1* eight **-dubbel** eightfold; octuple **-hundratalet** the ninth century **-hörnig** [-ö:-] *a1* octagonal, eight-cornered **-hörning** [-ö:-] octagon **-sidig** *a1*

eight-sided, octahedral **-timmarsdag** eight-hour [working] day

åttio [ˣåtti(ɷ), ˈåtti(ɷ)] eighty **-nde** [-å-] eightieth **-n[de]del** eightieth [part] **-tal** *ett ~* some eighty (*personer* persons); *på ~et* in the eighties

ått|kantig *a1* octagonal **-onde** [-å-] eighth; *var ~ dag* every (once a) week **-on[de]del** eighth [part]; *fem ~ar* five eighths **-ondelsnot** *mus.* quaver; *AE.* eighth note

åverkan damage, injury; *göra ~ på* do damage to, damage; *utsätta för ~* tamper with

åvila rest with ([up]on), lie upon

åvägabringa [åˣvä:-] bring about, effect

äckel ['äkk-] *s7* **1** nausea, sick feeling; *bildl.* disgust; *känna ~ inför ngt* feel sick at s.th.; *jag känner ~ vid blotta tanken* the mere thought [of it] makes me feel sick **2** (*-lig person*) repulsive chap **äckla** nauseate, sicken; *bildl.* disgust; *det ~r mig* it sickens me **äcklas** *dep* be disgusted (*vid* by, at) **äcklig** *a1* nauseating; (*friare*) sickening; (*motbjudande*) repulsive

ädel ['ä:-] *a2* noble; (*om metall, stenar*) precious; (*av ~ ras*) thoroughbred; (*högsint*) noble-minded, magnanimous; *av ~ börd* of noble birth; *kroppens ädlare delar* the vital parts [of the body]; *~t vilt* big game; *~t vin* fine vintage **-boren** noble-born **-gas** inert (rare) gas **-het** nobility, nobleness **-metall** precious metal **-mod** noble-mindedness, generosity; magnanimity **-modig** noble-minded, generous; magnanimous **-ost** blue cheese **-sten** precious stone; (*arbetad*) gem, jewel **-trä** (*lövträ*) hardwood

ädling ['ä:d-] nobleman, noble [man]

äg|a I *s1* **1** *i sg end. i uttr.: ha i sin -o* possess; *komma i ngns -o* come into a p.'s hands; *vara i ngns -o* be in a p.'s possession; *vara i privat -o* be private property; *övergå i privat -o* pass into private ownership **2** *pl -or* grounds; property (*sg*) **II** *v2* **1** (*rå om*) own, be the owner of; (*besitta*) possess; (*ha*) have; *allt vad jag -er och har* all I possess, all my worldly possessions; *han -er en förmögenhet* he is worth a fortune; *~ giltighet* be valid; *det -er sin riktighet* it is true (a fact); *~ rum* take place; *~ rätt att* have a (the) right to **2** *~ att a*) (*ha rättighet*) have a (the) right to, be entitled to, *b*) (*vara skyldig att*) have (be required) to **ägande|rätt** right of possession; ownership, proprietorship (*till* of); (*upphovsrätt*) copyright; *jur.* title (*till* to); *~en har övergått till* the right of possession has passed to **-rättsbevis** document of title

ägar|e owner, proprietor; *övergå till ny ~* come under new ownership **-inna** owner, proprietress

ägg *s7* egg; *biol.* ovum (*pl* ova); *det är som Columbi ~* (*ung.*) it's as plain as a pikestaff; *där har vi ~et* (*bildl.*) there is the crux of the matter **-bildning** ovulation **-cell** ovum (*pl* ova) **-formig** [-å-] *a1* egg-shaped; *fack.* oviform **-gula** (*hopskr. äggula*) yolk; *en ~* (*vanl.*) the yolk of an egg **-kläckning** hatching, incubation **-kläckningsmaskin** [chicken, poultry] incubator **-kopp** egg cup **-ledare** *anat.* Fallopian tube; *zool.* oviduct **-lossning** ovulation **-läggning** egg-laying **-läggningsrör** ovipositor **-pulver** egg powder **-rund** oval **-röra** scrambled eggs (*pl*) **-sjuk** *gå omkring som en ~ höna* be wanting to get s.th. off one's chest **-skal** eggshell **-sked** egg spoon **-stanning**

baked egg **-stock** ovary **-stocksinflammation** ovaritis **-toddy** eggnog **-vita 1** (*vitan i ägg*) egg white, white of [an] egg; *en ~* (*vanl.*) the white of an egg **2** (*ämne*) albumin; (*i ägg*) albumen, white of egg **3** (*sjukdom*) albuminuria, Bright's disease **-viteämne** protein; (*enkelt*) albumin

ägna ['äŋna] **I** devote; *högt.* dedicate (*sitt liv åt* one's life to); (*skänka*) bestow (*omsorg åt* care on); *~ intresse åt* take an interest in; *~ en tanke åt ... give ... a thought; ~ sin tid åt* devote one's time to; *~ ngt sin uppmärksamhet* give one's attention to s.th. **II** *opers., som det ~r och anstår* as befits (becomes) **III** *rfl* **1** *~ sig åt* devote o.s. to (*att göra ngt* doing s.th.), *högt.* dedicate o.s. to, (*utöva*) follow (*ett yrke* a trade), pursue (*ett kall* a calling), (*slå sig på*) go in for, take up (*affärer* business) **2** (*lämpa sig*) *~ sig för* be suited (adapted) for (to), (*om sak äv.*) lend itself to

ägnad ['äŋnad] *a5* suited, fitted; *inte ~ att inge förtroende* not calculated (likely) to inspire confidence; *~ att väcka farhågor* likely to cause alarm

ägo *se äga I 1* **-delar** *pl* property (*sg*), belongings, possessions; *jordiska ~* worldly goods

ägor *pl, se äga I 2*

äh oh!, ah!; (*avvisande äv.*) pooh!

äkta I *a1* (*oböjligt a*) **1** genuine, real; (*autentisk*) authentic; (*om konstverk*) original; (*om färg*) fast; (*uppriktig*) sincere; (*sann*) true (*konstnär* artist); *~ pärlor* real (genuine) pearls; *~ silver* sterling (pure, real) silver **2** *~ barn* legitimate child; *~ hälft* (*vard.*) better half; *~ maka* (*make*) [wedded (lawful)] wife (husband); *~ par* married couple, husband and wife **II** *s, i uttr.: ta ngn till ~, se följ.* **III** *v1* wed, espouse

äktenskap *s7* marriage; *jur. äv.* wedlock, matrimony; *efter fem års ~* after five years of married life; *barn i* (*utom*) *~et* child born in (out of) wedlock; *ingå ~ med* marry; *ingå nytt ~* marry again, remarry; *leva i ett lyckligt ~* have a happy married life; *till ~ ledig* unmarried, on the marriage market **-lig** *a1* matrimonial; conjugal, marital; married (*samliv* life); *~ börd* legitimate birth; *~a rättigheter* marital rights

äktenskaps|anbud proposal (offer) of marriage **-annons** matrimonial advertisement **-betyg** certificate of marital (matrimonial) capacity **-brott** adultery **-brytare** adulterer **-bryterska** adulteress **-byrå** matrimonial agency **-förord** marriage settlement (articles *pl*) **-hinder** impediment to marriage **-löfte** promise of marriage; *brutet ~* breach of promise **-mäklare** matrimonial agent, *vard.* matchmaker **-rådgivning** marriage guidance **-skillnad** divorce, dissolution of marriage **-tycke** *de har ~* they are so well matched **-ålder** marrying age

äkt|het (*jfr äkta I 1*) genuineness, reality; authenticity; originality; sincerity; (*färg-*) fastness; *bevisa ~en av* authenticate **-hetsbevis** proof of authenticity **-svensk** genuinely Swedish

äld|re ['äll-] *a, komp. t. gammal* older (*än* than); (*om släktskapsförh.*) elder; (*i tjänst*) senior (*än* to); *(tidigare)* earlier; *(ganska gammal)* elderly; ~ *järnåldern* the early Iron Age; ~ *människor* old (elderly) people; ~ *årgång (av tidskrift e.d.)* old (back) volume; *av* ~ *datum* of an earlier date; *i* ~ *tider* in older (more ancient) times; *de som är* ~ *än jag* my elders (seniors), those older than myself; *herr A. den* ~ Mr. A. Senior; *Dumas den* ~ Dumas the elder; *Pitt den* ~ the elder Pitt **-omsorg** old-age care

äldst *[vard.* älst*] a, superl. t. gammal* oldest; *(om släktskapsförh.)* eldest; *(av två äv.)* older (elder); *(i tjänst)* senior; *(tidigast)* earliest; *de* ~*a (i församling e.d.)* the Elders; *den* ~*e (i kår e.d.)* the doyen

älg [älj] *s2* elk; *AE.* moose **-antilop** eland **-gräs** *bot.* meadowsweet **-jakt** *(jagande)* elk-hunting; *(jaktparti)* elk-hunt; *vara på* ~ be out elk--hunting **-kalv** elk calf **-ko** cow (female) elk **-stek** roast elk **-tjur** bull (male) elk **-ört** *se -gräs*

älsk|a love; *(tycka mycket om)* like, be [very] fond of **-ad** *a5* beloved; *(predik. äv.)* loved; ~*e Tom!* Tom darling!, *(i brev)* my dear Tom; *min* ~*e* my beloved (darling) **-ande** *a4* loving *(par* couple); *de* ~ the lovers

älskar|e lover; *förste* ~ *(teat.)* juvenile lead; *inte vara ngn* ~ *av* not be fond of **-inna** mistress **-roll** *teat.* [part of the] juvenile lead

älsklig *a1* charming, sweet, lovable **-het** charm, sweetness, lovable character

älskling darling; *(i tilltal äv.)* love; *AE.* honey; *(käresta)* sweetheart

älsklings|barn favourite child **-elev** favourite (pet) pupil **-rätt** favourite dish

älsk|og *s2* love **-ogskrank** *a1* lovesick

älskvärd amiable, kind **-het** amiability, kindness

älta knead *(deg* dough); work *(smör* butter); *bildl.* go over again and again; ~ *samma sak* go harping on the same string

ältranunkel *bot.* lesser spearwort

älv *s2* river

älv|a *s1* fairy, elf *(pl* elves); *poet.* fay **-[a]-drottning** fairy queen; ~*en (äv.)* Queen Mab **-[a]kung** fairy king **-dans** fairy dance **-lik** fairy-like

älvmynning mouth of a (the) river, river mouth

ämabel [-'ma:-] *a2, se älskvärd*

ämbar *s7* pail, bucket

ämbete *s6* office; *bekläda (inneha) ett* ~ hold an office; *i kraft av sitt* ~, *[p]å* ~*ts vägnar* by (in) virtue of one's office, in one's official capacity, ex officio

ämbets|ansvar official responsibility **-broder** colleague **-brott** malpractice, misconduct [in office] **-byggnad** government office [building] **-dräkt** official dress, uniform **-ed** oath of office; *avlägga* ~*en* be sworn in **-examen** *filosofisk* ~ Master of Arts *(förk.* M.A.), Bachelor of Education *(förk.* B.Ed.); *avlägga filosofisk* ~ pass (take) one's Master's degree **-förrättning** official function **-man** official, public (Government) officer; *(i statens tjänst äv.)* civil servant

ämbetsmanna|bana official (civil service) career **-delegation** delegation of officials **-kår** body of civil servants; officials *(pl)*, official

class **-välde** bureaucracy

ämbets|plikt official duty **-rum** office **-tid** period of office; *under sin* ~ while in office **-verk** government office, civil service department

ämna intend (mean, plan, *AE.* aim) to; *jag* ~*de just* I was just going to; ~ *sig hem (ut)* intend to go home (out); *vart* ~*r du dig?* where are you going (you off to)?

ämne *s6* **1** *(material)* material; *(för bearbetning)* blank; *(arbetsstycke)* workpiece; *han har* ~ *i sig till en stor konstnär* he has the makings of a great artist **2** *(materia)* matter, substance, stuff; *fasta* ~*n* solids; *flytande* ~*n* liquids; *enkla* ~*n* elements; *sammansatta* ~*n* compounds; *organiskt* ~ organic matter **3** *(tema, samtals-, skol-* etc.) subject; matter; theme; *(samtalsäv.)* topic; *frivilligt* ~ *(skol.)* optional *(AE.* elective) subject; *obligatoriskt* ~ *(skol.)* compulsory subject; ~*t för romanen* the subject for the novel; *litteraturen i* ~*t* the literature on this subject; *byta* ~ change the subject; *hålla sig till* ~*t* keep to the subject (point); *komma till* ~*t* come to the point; ~ *till betraktelse* food for thought

ämnes|grupp group of subjects, subject group **-kombination** combination of subjects **-konferens** *skol.* staff meeting of teachers of the same subject **-lärare** teacher of a special subject **-namn** material noun **-område** subject field **-omsättning** metabolism; *fel på* ~*en* metabolic disturbance **-val** choice of subject

än [änn] **I** *adv* **1** *se* **ännu 2** *hur gärna jag* ~ *ville* however much I should like to; *när (var) jag* ~ whenever (wherever) I, no matter when (where) I; *om* ~ *aldrig så litet* however small [it may be], no matter how small; *vad som* ~ *må hända* whatever happens; *vem han* ~ *må vara* whoever he may be **3** ~ ... ~ now ..., now, sometimes ..., sometimes; ~ *si* ~ *så* now this way, now that; ~ *huttra,* ~ *svettas* shiver and sweat by turns **4** ~ *sen då?* well, what of it?, *vard.* so what? **II** *konj* **1** *(i jämförelser)* than; *mindre* ~ smaller than; *inte mindre* ~ no less than; *ingen mindre* ~ no less a person than **2** *ingen annan* ~ no other than *(kungen* the king), no one but; *inget annat* ~ nothing else but; *han är allt annat* ~ *dum* he is anything but stupid

1 ända I *s5* **1** *(äv. ände)* end; *(yttersta del äv.)* extremity; *(spetsig)* tip; *nedre (övre)* ~*n av* the bottom (top) of; *världens* ~ the ends *(pl)* of the world; *allting har en* ~ there is an end to everything; *det är ingen* ~ *på* there is no end to; *ta en* ~ *med förskräckelse* come to a sad end; *börja i galen* ~ start at the wrong end; *stå på* ~ stand on end, *(om hår äv.)* bristle; *gå till* ~ come to an end, expire; *falla över* ~ tumble (topple) over **2** *vard. (stuss)* behind, bottom, posterior, rear; *en spark i* ~*n* a kick on the behind (in the pants); *sätta sig på* ~*n (ramla)* fall on one's behind **3** *(stump)* bit, piece; *sjö.* [bit of] rope **4** *dagen i* ~ all day long **5** *(syfte) till den* ~*n* to that end **II** *v1* end **2 ända** *adv* right *(till* to; *hit* here); *(hela vägen)* all the way *(hem* home); ~ *fram till* right up to; ~ *från början* right from the beginning; ~ *från 1500-talet* ever since the sixteenth

century; ~ *från Indien* all the way from India; ~ *in i minsta detalj* down to the very last detail; ~ *in i det sista* down (up) to the very end; ~ *till slutet* to the very end; ~ *till påsk* right up to Easter; ~ *till midnatt* [all the time] till (until) midnight; ~ *till kyrkan* as far as (all the way to) the church; ~ *till nu* until (till, [right] up to) now, (*t. våra dagar*) down to the present time
ändalykt *s3* **1** (*slut*) *en sorglig* ~ a tragic end **2** (*stuss*) posterior
ändamål *s7* purpose; end; (*syfte äv.*) object; (*avsikt*) aim; ~*et med* the purpose of; ~*et helgar medlen* the end justifies the means; *för detta* ~ for this purpose, to this end; *det fyller sitt* ~ it is suited to (serves) its purpose; *ha ngt till* ~ have s.th. as an end; *välgörande* ~ charitable (charity, welfare) purposes
ändamåls|enlig [-e:-] *a1* [well] adapted (suited) to its purpose, suitable; (*lämplig*) appropriate; (*praktisk*) practical; *vara mycket* ~ be very much to the purpose **-enlighet** [-e:n-] fitness, practicality, expediency **-lös** purposeless; aimless; (*gagnlös*) useless
ändas *dep* end, terminate (*på* in, with)
ände *s2, se I* **ända** *I 1*
änd|else ending **-hållplats** bus (tram) terminus **-lig** *a1* finite **-lös** endless; (*som aldrig tar slut äv.*) interminable; *mat.* infinite **-morän** end (terminal) moraine
ändock yet, still, nevertheless, for all that
ändpunkt terminal point, end
ändr|a **1** alter; (*byta*) change, shift; (*rätta*) correct; (*förbättra*) amend; (*modifiera*) modify; (*revidera*) revise; ~ *en klänning* alter a dress; ~ *mening* change one's opinion (mind) (*om* about); *inte* ~ *en min* (*vanl.*) not move a muscle; *det* ~*r inte mitt beslut* it does not alter my decision; *det* ~*r ingenting i sak* it makes no difference in substance; *domen* ~*des till böter* the sentence was commuted into a fine; *paragraf 6 skall* ~*s* paragraph 6 shall be amended; *obs* ~*d tid!* note the alteration of time!; ~ *om* alter; ~ *om ngt till* change (transform) s.th. into; ~ *på* alter, change **2** *rfl* alter, change; (*rätta sig*) correct o.s.; (*fatta annat beslut*) change one's mind; (*byta åsikt äv.*) change one's opinion **-ing** alteration (*äv. av klädesplagg*); change; correction; amendment; *tekn. e.d.* modification; *en* ~ *till det bättre* a change for the better; *en obetydlig* ~ a slight modification **-ingsförslag** proposed alteration (amendment)
änd|station terminus (*pl äv.* termini), terminal [station] **-tarm** rectum **-tarmsöppning** anus, anal orifice
ändå ["änn-, -'då:] **1** (*likväl*) yet, still; (*icke desto mindre*) nevertheless; (*i alla fall*) all the same; *det är* ~ *något* it's something, anyway; *om han* ~ *kunde komma!* if only (I do wish) he could come! **2** (*ännu*) still, even (*mer* more)
äng *s2* meadow; *poet.* mead
ängd *s3, se* trakt
ängel *s2* angel; *det gick en* ~ *genom rummet* there was a sudden hush in the room; *han kom som en räddande* ~ he came like an angel to the rescue

ängla|lik angelic[al]; *hon har ett* ~*t tålamod* she has the patience of an angel (of Job) **-makerska** baby-farmer **-skara** angelic host **-vakt** guardian angel **-vinge** wing of an angel
ängs|blomma meadow flower **-kavle** [-a:-] *s2, bot.* foxtail
ängsl|a alarm, cause alarm, make anxious **-an** *r* anxiety; (*oro*) alarm, uneasiness; (*starkare*) apprehension, fright **-as** *dep* be (feel) anxious (*för, över* about); (*oroa sig*) worry (*för* about) **-ig** *a1* (*rädd*) anxious, uneasy (*för* about); ~ *av sig* timid, timorous; *var inte* ~*!* don't worry (be afraid)!; *jag är* ~ *för att ngt kan ha hänt* I am afraid (fear) s.th. may have happened **2** (*ytterst noggrann*) scrupulous; *med* ~ *noggrannhet* with [over]scrupulousness
ängs|mark meadow land **-syra** sorrel **-ull** [common] cotton grass
änka *s1* widow; (*änkenåd*) dowager; *vara* ~ *efter* be [the] widow of; *hon blev tidigt* ~ she was early left a widow
änke|drottning queen dowager; (*regerande monarks mor*) queen mother **-fru** widow; ~ *A.* Mrs. A.[, widow of the late Mr. A.] **-man** widower **-nåd** *s3* dowager -- **och pupillkassa** widows' and orphans' fund **-pension** widow's pension **-stånd** widowhood **-stöt** knock on the funny (*AE.* crazy) bone **-säte** dowager's residence
änkling widower
ännu [¨ännu, -'nu:] **1** (*fortfarande*) still; (*om ngt som ej inträffat*) yet; (*hittills*) as yet, so far; *har de kommit* ~? have they come yet?; *inte* ~ not yet; *medan det* ~ *är tid* while there is still time, while the going is good; *det har* ~ *aldrig hänt* it has never happened so far; *det dröjer* ~ *länge innan* it will be a long time before; ~ *så länge* so far, up to now, (*för närvarande*) for the present; ~ *när han var 80* even at the age of eighty; ~ *så sent som i går* only (as recently as, as late as) yesterday **2** (*ytterligare*) more; ~ *en* one more, yet (still) another; ~ *en gång* once more, (*återigen*) again; *det tar* ~ *en stund* it will take a while yet **3** (*vid komp.*) still, even (*bättre* better)
änterhake *sjö.* grapnel, grappling iron (hook)
äntligen at last; (*omsider äv.*) at length
äntr|a board (*ett fartyg* a ship); (*klättra*) climb (*uppför en lina* up a rope) **-ing** boarding; climbing
äppel|blom *koll.* apple-blossom[s *pl*] **-blomma** apple-blossom **-brännvin** apple brandy; *AE.* applejack **-kaka** apple cake **-kart** green apple[s *pl*] **-klyfta** slice of [an] apple **-kompott** stewed apples **-kärna** apple pip **-mos** mashed apples (*pl*), apple sauce **-must** apple juice **-paj** apple-pie **-skal** apple-peel **-skrott** [-å-] *s2* apple-core **-sort** brand of apple **-träd** apple tree **-vecklare** *zool.* codling moth **-vin** cider **-år** *ett gott* ~ a good year for apples
äpple *s6* apple; ~*t faller inte långt från trädet* he (she) is a chip of the old block; like father, like son
är *pres. av* vara
ära I *s1* honour; (*heder*) credit; (*berömmelse*) glory, reknown; ~ *vare Gud!* Glory be to God!; ~*ns fält* military exploits (*pl*), field of glory;

en ~ns knöl a downright swine; *det är en stor ~ för oss att* it is a great honour for us to; *få ~n för* get the credit for; *får jag den ~n att* may I have the honour of (+ *ing- form*); *ge ngn ~n för* give s.b. the credit for, credit s.b. with; *det gick hans ~ för när* that wounded (piqued) his pride; *göra ngn den ~n att* do s.b. the honour (favour) of (+ *ing-form*); *ha ~n att* have the honour of (+ *ing-form*); *har den ~n [att gratulera!]* congratulations!, *(på födelsedag)* many happy returns [of the day]!, happy birthday!; *sätta en (sin) ~ i att* make a point of (+ *ing-form*); *vinna ~* gain honour (credit); *bortom all ~ och redlighet* miles from anywhere (civilization); *... i all ~* with all deference (respect) to ...; *göra ngt med den ~n* do s.th. with credit; *på min ~!* upon my honour!; *dagen till ~* in honour of the day; *till ngns ~* in a p.'s honour; *till Guds ~* for the glory of God **II** *vl* (*vörda*) respect, revere, venerate; *~s den som ~s bör* honour where (to whom) honour is due

ärad *a5* honoured; *(om kund e.d.)* esteemed; *Ert ~e [brev]* your letter, åld. your favour (esteemed letter)

ärbar [ˣäːr-] *a1* decent, modest **-het** decency, modesty; *i all ~* in all decency

äre|betygelse *se hedersbetygelse* **-girig** ambitious; aspiring **-girighet** ambition[s *pl*]; aspiration[s *pl*] **-kränka** defame **-kränkande** *a4* defamatory; *(i skrift)* libellous **-kränkning** defamation; *(skriftlig)* libel **-lysten** *se -girig* **-lystnad** *se -girighet* **-lös** infamous **-minne** memorial *(över* to, in honour of)

ärende *s6* **1** *(uträttning)* errand; *(uppdrag)* commission; *(besked)* message; *framföra sitt ~* state one's errand, give one's message; *får jag fråga vad ert ~ är?* what brings you here, if I may ask?; *gå ~n* go [on] errands, be an errand boy (girl) *(åt* for); *gå ngns ~n* (*bildl.*) run a p.'s errands; *göra sig ett ~ till* find an excuse for going to; *boken har ett ~* the book has a message; *ha ett ~ i (till) stan* have business in town; *ha ett ~ till ngn* have to see s.b. about; *i lovliga ~n* on lawful business (errands); *med oförrättat ~* without having achieved one's object **2** *(angelägenhet)* matter; *löpande ~n* [the] usual routine, current matters; *utrikes ~n* foreign affairs; *handlägga ett ~* deal with (handle) a matter

ärenpris *s3, bot.* [common] speedwell

äre|port triumphal arch **-rörig** *a1* slanderous, defamatory, calumnious **-varv** *sport.* lap of honour **-vördig** venerable

ärftlig *a1* hereditary *(anlag* disposition); *(om titel e.d.)* inheritable; *det är ~t (vanl.)* it runs in the family **-het** heredity; *(sjukdoms e.d.)* hereditariness

ärftlighets|forskare geneticist **-forskning** genetics *(pl, behandlas som sg)*, genetic research **-lära** genetics *(pl, behandlas som sg)*, science of heredity

ärftligt *adv* hereditarily; by inheritance; *vara ~ belastad* have a hereditary taint

ärg [-j] *s3* verdigris; patina **ärga** [-j-] *(bli -ig, ~ sig)* become coated with verdigris; *~ av sig* give off verdigris **ärggrön** verdigris green **är-**

gig *a1* verdigrised; *konst.* patinated

ärke|biskop archbishop **-biskopinna** archbishop's wife **-biskoplig** archiepiscopal **-biskopsdöme** *s6* archdiocese, archbishopric, archbishop's diocese **-bov** archvillain, unmitigated scoundrel **-fiende** archenemy **-hertig** archduke **-hertigdöme** archduchy **-nöt** nitwit, utter fool **-reaktionär** archreactionary; *en ~ (äv.)* a die-hard **-skälm** archrogue **-stift** *se -biskopsdöme* **-säte** archiepiscopal see **-ängel** archangel

ärla [ˣäːr-] *s1* wagtail

ärlig [ˣäːr-] *a1* honest; *(hederlig)* honourable *(avsikt* intention); *(rättfram)* straightforward; *(uppriktig)* sincere; *vard.* straight, on the level; *~t spel* fair play; *om jag skall vara helt ~* to be quite honest, honestly; *säga sin ~a mening* give one's honest opinion **-en** honestly *etc.*; *det har du ~ förtjänat* you have fairly earned it, that is no more than your due; *~ förtjäna sitt uppehälle* make an honest living **-het** honesty, straightforwardness; *~ varar längst* honesty is the best policy; *i ~ens namn måste jag* to be quite honest I must

ärligt *adv, se -en; ~ talat* to be quite honest with you

ärm *s2* sleeve **-bräda** sleeve board **-hål** armhole **-hållare** armband; *AE.* arm (sleeve) garter **-linning** wristband **-lös** sleeveless

ärna [ˣäːr-] *se ämna*

äro|full glorious; honourable *(återtåg* retreat) **-rik** *(-full)* glorious; *(som förvärvat stor ära)* illustrious *(krigare* warrior)

ärr *s7* scar; *fack.* cicatrice **ärra** *rfl,* **ärras** *dep* scar; *fack.* cicatrize

ärr|bildning scar formation; *fack.* cicatrization **-ig** *a1* scarred; *(kopp-)* pockmarked

ärt *s3,* **ärta** *s1* pea

ärt|balja, -skida pea pod; *(tom)* pea shell **-soppa** pea soup **-törne** *bot.* gorse **-växt** leguminous plant

ärva *v2 [få] ~* inherit *(av, efter* from); *~ ngn* be a p.'s heir; *~ en tron* succeed to a throne; *jag har fått ~* I have come into money **ärvd** *a5* inherited; *(medfödd)* hereditary **ärvdabalk** laws *(pl)* of inheritance, inheritance code

äsch ah!, oh!; *(besviket)* dash it!; *~, det gör ingenting!* oh, never mind!, oh, it doesn't matter!

äsk|a demand, ask for; *~ tystnad* call for silence **-ande** *s6* demand, claim, request

äsping *(orm)* [young female] viper

äss *s7* ace

ässja [ˣäʃa] *s1* forge

ät|a *åt -it* **1** eat; *(frukost etc.)* have; *har du -it ännu?* have you had [your] dinner *(etc.)* yet?; *vi sitter och -er* we are at (are having [our]) dinner *(etc.)*; *~ frukost* have breakfast; *~ middag* have dinner, dine; *~ gott* get good food; *tycka om att ~ gott* be fond of good food; *~ litet (mycket)* be a poor (big) eater; *~ på ngt* eat (munch) s.th.; *~ ngn ur huset* eat s.b. out of house and home **2** *rfl,* *~ sig mätt* have enough to eat; *~ sig sjuk* eat o.s. sick; *~ (nöta) sig igenom* wear its way through; *~ sig in i (om djur)* eat into **3** *(med betonad partikel)* ~ *upp* eat [up], consume; *jag har -it upp* I have finished [my food]; *det skall du få ~ upp!*

Ä

(*bildl.*) you'll have that back [with interest]!; ~ *upp sig* put on weight, fatten [up]; ~ *ut ngn* (*bildl.*) cut s.b. out
ät|bar [ˣä:t-] *a1* eatable (*mat* food) **-it** *sup. av äta* **-lig** [ˣä:t-] *a1* edible (*svamp* mushroom)
ätt *s3* family; (*furstlig*) dynasty; *den siste av sin* ~ the last of his (*etc.*) line; ~*en utslocknade år* the family died out in **ättartavla** genealogy, genealogical table
ätte|fader [first] ancestor **-hög** barrow **-lägg** *s2* scion
ättestupa *s1, ung.* [suicidal] precipice
ättika *s1* vinegar; *kem.* acetum; *lägga in i* ~ pickle
ättiksgurka pickled cucumber, gherkin
ättik|sprit vinegar essence **-sur** [as] sour as vinegar; *bildl.* vinegary **-syra** acetic acid
ättling descendant, offspring
även also, ... too; (*likaledes*) ... as well; (*till och med*) even (*om* if, though); *icke blott* ... *utan* ~ not only ... but also **-ledes** also, likewise **-som** as well as **-så** also, likewise
äventyr *s7* **1** adventure; (*missöde*) misadventure **2** (*vågstycke*) hazardous venture (enterprise) **3** *jur., vid* ~ *att* at the risk of; *vid* ~ *av böter* on pain (under penalty) of fines (a fine) **4** *till* ~*s* perchance, peradventure
äventyr|a risk, hazard, jeopardize; imperil, endanger ~*ar* adventurer **-erska** adventuress **-lig** [-y:-] *a1* adventurous; (*riskabel*) venturesome, risky, hazardous **-lighet** [-y:-] adventurousness *etc.*
äventyrs|lust love of adventure **-lysten** adventure-loving, fond of adventure **-roman** adventure story, story of adventure; romance
ävlan [ˣä:v-] *r* striving[s *pl*] **ävlas** *dep* strive (*efter* for, after)

Ö

ö *s2* island; (*i vissa geogr. namn*) isle; *bo på en* ~ live on (*om stor ö:* in) an island
ÖB [ˣö:be:] *förk. för överbefälhavaren*
öbo *s5* islander
öda *v2,* ~ [*bort*] waste
1 öde *s6* fate; (*bestämmelse*) destiny; ~*t* Fate; Destiny; ~*n* destinies, (*levnads-*) fortunes; *skiftande* ~*n* changing fortunes, vicissitudes [of fortune]; *ett sorgligt* ~ a tragic fate; ~*ts skickelse* the decree of fate, Fate; *efter många* ~*n och äventyr* after many adventures; *hans* ~ *är beseglat* his fate is sealed; *dela ngns* ~ share a p.'s fate (lot); *finna sig i sitt* ~ submit (resign o.s.) to one's fate; *förena sina* ~*n med ngn* cast in one's lot with s.b.
2 öde *oböjligt a* desert, waste; (*övergiven*) deserted; (*enslig*) lonely; (*ödslig*) desolate; (*obebodd*) uninhabited; *ligga* ~ *a*) (*folktom*) be deserted, *b*) (*om åkerjord*) lie waste
öde|bygd depopulated (deserted) area **-gård** deserted (derelict) farm **-kyrka** abandoned church **-lägga** lay waste; (*skövla*) ravage, devastate; (*förstöra*) ruin, destroy **-läggelse** (*-läggning*) laying waste; (*om resultatet*) devastation, ruin, destruction
ö'dem *s7, med.* oedema (*pl* oedemata)
ödemark waste, desert; (*vildmark*) wilderness; (*obygd*) wilds (*pl*), AE. backwoods (*pl*)
ödes|bestämd fated **-diger** (*skickelsediger*) fateful; (*avgörande äv.*) decisive; (*olycksbringande*) fatal, disastrous, ill-fated **-gudinnor** *pl* Fates **-mättad** fateful, fatal **-timma** fateful (fatal) hour, hour of destiny
ödla [ˣö:d-] *s1* lizard; (*vatten-*) newt, eft
öd|mjuk [ˣö:d-] *a1* humble; (*undergiven*) submissive **-mjuka** *rfl* humble o.s. (*inför* before) **-mjukhet** humility, humbleness; submission; *i all* ~ in all humility
ödsla [ˣö:d-, ˣödd-] ~ [*med*] be wasteful with (of); ~ *bort* waste, squander
ödslig [ˣö:d-, ˣödd-] *a1* desolate, deserted; (*dyster*) dreary **-het** desolateness *etc.*; desolation
ödsligt *adv, ligga* ~ be lonely; *en* ~ *belägen* a desolate
öfolk (*öbor*) islanders (*pl*); (*nation*) insular nation
ög|a *-at -on* **1** eye; ~ *för* ~ an eye for an eye; *stå* ~ *mot* ~ stand face to face with; *anstränga -onen* strain one's eyes; *falla i -onen* catch (strike) the eye; *få ett blått* ~ get a black eye; *få upp -onen för* have one's eyes opened to; *göra stora -on* open one's eyes wide, stare; *ha -onen med sig* keep one's eyes open, be observant; *inte ha -on för ngn annan än* have eyes for nobody but; *ha ett gott* ~ *till* have one's eyes on; *jag har ljuset i -onen* the light is in my eyes; *ha ngt för -onen* keep s.th. before one['s sight]; *ha svaga -on* have a poor eyesight; *hålla ett* ~ *på* keep an eye on; *i mina*

(folks) -*on* in my (people's) eyes (opinion); *inför allas* -*on* in sight (before the eyes) of everybody; *finna nåd inför ngns* -*on* find favour with s.b.; *kasta ett* ~ *på* have a look at, glance at; *med blotta* ~*t* with the naked eye; *mellan fyra* -*on* in private, privately; *samtal mellan fyra* -*on* private talk, tête-à-tête; *mitt för* -*onen på* before the very eyes of, in full view of; *det var nära* ~*t* that was a narrow escape (close shave); *jag ser dåligt på vänstra (högra)* ~*t* the sight is poor in my left (right) eye; *se ngn rakt i* -*onen* look s.b. straight in the face; *skämmas* -*onen ur sig* be thoroughly ashamed of o.s.; *slå ner* -*onen* cast down one's eyes; *så långt* ~*t når* as far as the eye can reach **2** *(på tärning)* pip **3** *(på potatis)* eye

ögla [ˣö:g-, ˣögg-] *s1* loop, eye; *göra en* ~ *på loop*

ögna [ˣöŋna] ~ *i* have a glance (look) at, glance at; ~ *igenom* glance through, scan

ögon|blick *s7* moment; instant; *ett* ~*!* one moment, please!, just a moment (minute)!; *ett* ~*s verk* the work of a moment (an instant); *ett obevakat* ~ an unguarded moment; *har du tid ett* ~*?* can you spare [me] a moment?; *det tror jag inte ett* ~ I don't believe that for a moment; *för* ~*et* at the moment, at present, just now; *i nästa* ~ [the] next moment; *i samma* ~ *jag såg det* the moment I saw it; *om ett* ~ in a moment (an instant); *på ett* ~ in a moment (an instant), in the twinkling of an eye **-blicklig** *a1* instantaneous; immediate, instant **-blickligen** instantly, immediately; *(genast)* at once **-blicksbild** snapshot

ögon|bryn eyebrow; *höja (rynka)* ~*en* raise (knit) one's eyebrows **-droppar** *pl* eye drops (lotion *sg*) **-frans** eyelash **-fröjd, -fägnad** feast for the eye, delightful sight **-färg** colour of the (one's) eyes **-glob** eyeball **-håla** eye socket, *fack.* orbit **-hår** eyelash **-inflammation** ophthalmia **-kast** glance; *vid första* ~*et* at first sight, at the first glance **-klinik** eye hospital (clinic) **-lock** eyelid **-läkare** eye specialist; ophthalmologist, oculist *ha gott* ~ have a sure eye; *efter* ~ by [the] eye **-märke** sighting (aiming) point **-sikte** *förlora ur* ~ lose sight of **-sjukdom** eye (ophthalmic) disease **-skenlig** [-ʃe:n-] *a1* apparent; *(påtaglig)* evident, self-evident; *(tydlig)* obvious **-skugga** eye shadow **-specialist** *se* -*läkare* **-sten** *bildl., ngns* ~ the apple of a p.'s eye **-tjänare** timeserver, fawner **-tröst** *bot.* eyebright **-vita** the white of the eye **-vittne** eyewitness **-vrå** corner of the (one's) eye

ögrupp group (cluster) of islands

ök *s7 (lastdjur)* beast of burden; *(dragdjur)* beast of draught; *(häst)* jade

öka 1 *(göra större)* increase *(med* by); *(ut-, till-)* add to; *(utvidga)* enlarge; *(förhöja)* enhance *(värdet av* the value of); ~ *farten (äv.)* speed up, accelerate; ~ *kapitalet med 1 miljon* add 1 million to the capital; ~ *kraftigt* increase rapidly, undergo a rapid growth; ~ *priset på* raise (increase, put up) the price of; ~ *till det dubbla (tredubbla)* double (treble); ~ *på* increase; ~ *ut a) (dryga ut)* eke out, *b) (utvidga)* enlarge *(lokalerna* the premises), increase *(sitt vetande*

one's knowledge) **2** *(tilltaga)* increase; *(om vind äv.)* rise; ~ *i vikt* put on weight **ökad** *a5* increased *etc.*; *(ytterligare)* added; additional *(utgifter* expenditure *sg)*; *ge* ~ *glans åt* lend additional lustre to **ökas** *dep se öka 2*

öken ['ö:-, 'ökk-] *s2* desert; *bibl.* wilderness; *öknens skepp (kamelen)* the ship of the desert **-artad** [-a:r-] *a5* desertlike **-folk** desert people **-kängor** desert boots **-område** desert region **-råtta** *mil. vard.* desert rat **-räv** fennec **-vandring** wandering[s *pl*] in the wilderness **-vind** desert wind; *(samum)* simoom, simoon

öklimat insular climate

öknamn nickname; *ge [ett]* ~ nickname

ökning [ˣö:k-] increase *(i* of); addition; enlargement; enhancement; ~ *av farten* acceleration of [the] speed

ökänd [ˣö:çänd] notorious

öl *s7* beer; *ljust* ~ light beer, pale ale; *mörkt* ~ dark beer, stout

ölandstok shrubby cinquefoil

öl|back case of beer; *(tom)* beer case **-bryggeri** brewery **-burk** beer can **-butelj, -flaska** bottle of beer; *(tom)* beer bottle **-glas** beer glass; *(glas öl)* glass of beer **-kafé** beerhouse, public house, pub **-mage** brewer's drop **-sejdel** beer mug; *(med lock)* tankard **-sinne** *ha gott (dåligt)* ~ carry one's liquor well (badly) **-stuga** *åld.* alehouse; *AE. äv.* beer parlor **-utkörare** [brewer's] drayman **-öppnare** bottle (beer-can) opener

öm [ömm] *a1* **1** *(ömtålig)* tender, sore *(fötter* feet); *en* ~ *punkt (bildl.)* a tender spot, a sore point; *vara* ~ *i hela kroppen* be (feel) sore (aching) all over **2** *(kärleksfull)* tender, loving, fond; ~ *omtanke* solicitude; *hysa* ~*ma känslor för ngn* have tender feelings for s.b. **-fotad** *a5*, *vara* ~ have tender (sore) feet, be footsore **-het 1** *(smärta)* tenderness, soreness **2** *(kärleksfullhet)* tenderness, [tender] affection, love **-hetsbehov** need for affection **-hetsbetygelse** proof (token) of affection, endearment **-hjärtad** [-j-] *a5* tenderhearted

ömk|a commiserate, pity; ~ *sig över ngt* complain about s.th.; ~ *sig över ngn* feel sorry for (pity) s.b. **-an** *r* compassion, pity **-ansvärd** [-ä:-] *a1* pitiable; *(stackars)* poor, wretched **-lig** *a1* pitiful, miserable; deplorable, lamentable; *en* ~ *min* a piteous air; *en* ~ *syn* a pitiful (sad) sight; *ett* ~*t tillstånd* a piteous state

ömm|a 1 *(vara öm)* be tender (sore); ~ *för tryck* ache at pressure **2** *(hysa medkänsla)* feel [compassion] *(för* for), sympathize *(för* with) **-ande** *a4* **1** *se öm* **2** *(ömkansvärd)* distressing *(omständigheter* circumstances); *i* ~ *fall* in deserving cases

ömsa change; ~ *skinn (om orm äv.)* cast (slough) its skin

ömse *oböjligt a, på* ~ *håll (sidor)* on both sides (each side) **-sidig** *a1* mutual, reciprocal; ~*a anklagelser* cross accusations; ~*t beroende* interdependence; ~*t försäkringsbolag* mutual insurance company; *kontraktet gäller med 6 månaders* ~ *uppsägning* the contract is subject to 6 months' notice by either party; *till* ~ *belåtenhet* to our mutual satisfaction **-sidighet** reciprocity, mutuality **-vis** alternately; *(i tur o.*

ordning) by turns
ömsint *a4* tender[hearted] **-het** tenderness of heart
ömsom [ˣömmsåm] ~ ... ~ ... sometimes ..., sometimes ..., ... and ... alternately
ömtålig *al* **1** (*som lätt skadas*) damageable, easily damaged; (*om matvara*) perishable; (*om tyg*) flimsy; (*bräcklig*) frail, fragile **2** (*om hälsa*) delicate; (*känslig*) sensitive; (*mottaglig*) susceptible (*för* to) **3** (*lättsårad*) touchy; (*grannlaga*) delicate (*fråga* question) **-het** liability to damage; perishableness *etc.*; fragility; delicacy; sensitiveness; susceptibility; touchiness
önskļa 1 wish; (*åstunda*) desire; (*vilja ha*) want; *jag ~r att han ville komma* I [do] wish he would come; *vad ~s?* (*i butik*) what can I do for you[, Madam (Sir)]?; *om så ~s* if desired, if you wish; *stryk det som ej ~s* delete as required; *lämna mycket övrigt att ~* leave a great deal to be desired; *~de upplysningar* information desired; *icke ~d* unwanted, undesirable **2** *rfl* wish for, desire; *~ sig ngt i julklapp* want (wish for) s.th. for Christmas; *~ sig bort* wish o.s. (wish one were) far away; *~ sig tillbaka till* wish one were back in **-an** *r, som pl används pl av* önskning wish, desire; *enligt ~* as desired, according to your (his *etc.*) wishes; *uttrycka en ~ att* express a wish to; *med ~ om* with best wishes for
önskeļdröm [cherished] dream; pipe dream **-lista** want list; (*t. jul e.d.*) list of presents one would like **-mål** wish, desire; object desired, desideratum (*pl* desiderata); *ett länge närt ~* a long-felt want **-program** request programme **-tänkande** *s6* wishful thinking **-väder** ideal weather
önskļning *se* önskan **-värd** [-ä:-] *al* desirable, to be desired; *icke ~* undesirable **-värdhet** [-ä:-] desirability, desirableness
öppļen *a3* open; aboveboard; (*uppriktig*) frank, candid; (*mottaglig*) susceptible (*för* to); *~ båt* (*äv.*) undecked boat; *~ eld* open fire; *-et förvar* (*i bank*) safe custody; *-et köp* purchase on approval; *på -et köp* on a sale-or-return basis; *~ spis* fireplace; *frågan får stå ~* the matter must be left open; *platsen står ~ för hans räkning* the post is reserved for him; *vara ~, hålla -et* keep open; *för ~ ridå* with the curtain up, *bildl.* in public; *i ~ räkning* in open account; *i ~ sjö* on the open sea; *på -na fältet* in the open field; *vid* (*per*) *första* (*sista*) *-et vatten* at (per) first (last) open water (*förk.* f.o.w. *resp.* l.o.w.)
öppenļhet openness; frankness, candour; sincerity; susceptibility **-hjärtig** [-j-] *al* open-hearted, frank, unreserved **-hjärtighet** [-j-] open-heartedness
öppet *adv* openly *etc.*; *~ och ärligt* squarely and fairly; *förklara ~* declare freely; *ligga ~* have an exposed situation **-hållande** *s6* business (service, opening and closing) hours (*pl*)
öppnļa 1 open; (*låsa upp*) unlock; *~ för ngn* open the door for s.b., let s.b. in; *~ affär* open (start) a shop (business); *affären ~r* (*~s*) *kl. 9* the shop opens at nine [o'clock]; *~ kredit* open a credit; *~ vägen för* (*bildl.*) pave the way for; *~ ngns ögon för* open a p.'s eyes to; *vi såg*

dörren ~s we saw the door open[ing]; *~!* open up!; *~s här* open here; *~s för trafik i mars* will be open to traffic in March; *dörren ~s utåt* the door opens outwards **2** *rfl* open; (*vidga sig*) open out **-ing 1** opening (*äv. i schack*); (*hål*) aperture, hole; (*mynning*) orifice; (*springa*) chink; (*för mynt*) slot; (*i mur e.d.*) gap, break; (*glänta*) glade, clearing **2** (*avföring*) motion, defecation
öppningsļanförande opening (introductory) address **-bud** opening bid **-ceremoni** opening ceremony, inauguration (ceremony)
örļa *-at* *-on* **1** ear (*äv. bildl.*); *dra -onen åt sig* become wary, take alarm; *gå in genom ena -t och ut genom det andra* go in at one ear and out at the other; *ha ~ för musik* have an ear for music; *få det hett om -onen* be in for it, get into hot water; *höra dåligt* (*vara döv*) *på ena -t* hear badly with (be deaf in) one ear; *mycket skall man höra innan -onen faller av!* I've never heard such a thing!, well, I never!, what next!; *han ville inte höra på det -t* (*bildl.*) he wouldn't listen at all; *vara idel ~* be all ears; *klia sig bakom -t* scratch one's head; *det har kommit till mina -on* it has come to my ears; *som ett slag för -t* like a [shattering] blow; *det susar* (*ringer*) *i -onen* my ears are buzzing (singing); *tala för döva -on* talk to deaf ears; *inte vara torr bakom -onen* be very green; *små grytor har också -on* little pitchers have long ears; *upp över -onen förälskad* head over heels in love **2** (*handtag*) handle; (*på tillbringare*) ear **-clips** *pl* ear clips
öre *s6* öre; *inte ha ett ~* not have [got] a penny, be penniless; *inte ett rött ~* not a bean; *inte värd ett rött* (*ruttet*) *~* not worth a brass farthing; *inte för fem ~* not a bit; *räkna ut priset på -t* work out the price to the last penny; *jag kan inte säga på -t vad det kostar* I cannot tell you the exact price; *till sista -t* to the last farthing
Öre'sund *n* the Sound
örļfil [ˣö:r-] *s2* box on the ear **-fila** *~* [*upp*] *ngn* box a p.'s ears, cuff s.b. **-hänge** (*smycke*) earring; (*långt*) eardrop; (*schlager*) hit
örike island state (country)
öring salmon trout
örlig [ˣö:r-] *r*, **örlog** [-å-] *s* [naval] war
örlogsļfartyg warship, man-of-war (*pl* men-of-war) **-flagg[a]** naval (man-of-war) flag **-flotta** navy, naval force **-hamn** naval port **-kapten** lieutenant commander **-man** man-of-war **-varv** naval dockyard (*AE.* shipyard)
örn [ö:rn] *s2* eagle **-blick** eagle eye **-bo** eyrie, aerie, eagle's nest **-bräken** *s2* bracken, brake
örngott [-å-] *s7* pillowcase, pillowslip
örnļnäbb eagle's beak **-näsa** aquiline nose **-näste** *se* örnbo **-unge** eaglet, young eagle
öronļbedövande *a4* deafening **-clips** *se* örclips **-inflammation** inflammation of (in) the ear[s]; *med.* otitis **-lappsfåtölj** wing chair **-klinik** ear clinic **-läkare** ear specialist, aurist, otologist **-lös** *en ~ kopp* a cup without a handle **-mussla** [ear] concha; (*hörpropp*) earphone **-märkning** earmarking **-näsahalsläkare** ear, nose and throat specialist, oto[rhino]laryngologist, *vard.* E.N.T. specialist **-propp** (*vaxpropp*)

plug of wax; (*mot ljud*) earplugg **-sjukdom** disease of the ear, aural disease **-skydd** earflap; earmuff **-susning** singing (buzzing) in one's ears **-trumpet** auditory (Eustachian) tube

ör|snibb ear lobe, lobe of the ear **-språng** earache; *med.* otalgia

ört *s3* herb, plant; ~*er* (*äv.*) herbaceous plants **örtagård** garden **örtte** herbal tea

örvax earwax; *fack.* cerumen

ös|a *v3* **1** scoop; (*sleva*) ladle (*upp* out); (*hälla*) pour; ~ *en båt* bale (bail) a boat; ~ *en stek* baste a joint; ~ *presenter över ngn* shower s.b. with gifts; ~ *på ngn arbete* overburden s.b. with work; ~ *ur sig otidigheter över* shower abuse on; ~ *ut pengar* throw one's money around, waste (squander) one's money **2** *det (regnet)* -*er ner* it is pouring down, *vard.* it is raining cats and dogs **-kar** bailer, dipper **-regn** pouring rain, downpour **-regna** pour

öst *r* east; *jfr nord*

Östafrika East Africa

östan *r*, **-vind** *s2* east[erly] wind

östasiatisk East Asiatic **Östasien** Eastern Asia **Östberlin** East Berlin

östblocket the Eastern bloc

öster ['öss-] **I** *oböjligt s o. s9* the east; *Ö~n* the East (Orient) **II** *adv* [to the] east (*om* of) **-ifrån** from the east

Österlandet *n* the East (Orient) **öster|ländsk** *a5* oriental, eastern **-länning** Oriental

österrikare Austrian **Österrike** *n* Austria **österrikisk** *a5* Austrian

Östersjön the Baltic [Sea]

Östeuropa Eastern Europe **östeuropeisk** East European

öst|front ~*en* the Eastern front **-got** Ostrogoth **-gotisk** Ostrogothic **-kust** east coast

östlig *a1* easterly; east[ern]; *jfr nordlig* **östra** *best. a* the east; the eastern; *jfr norra*

östrogen [-'je:n] *s7, med.* [o]estrogen

östromersk *Ö~a riket* the Eastern Roman Empire; the Byzantine Empire

östron [-'å:n] *s7, med.* [o]estrone

öst|stat eastern state, East European state **-tysk** East German

Östtyskland East Germany; (*officiellt*) the German Democratic Republic, the GDR

öva 1 (*träna*) train (*ngn i ngt* s.b. in s.th.; *ngn i att* s.b. to); *mil.* drill, exercise; ~ *in* practise, (*roll e.d.*) rehearse; ~ *upp* train, exercise, (*utveckla*) develop; ~ *upp sig i engelska* brush up one's English **2** (*ut-*) exercise (*inflytande* influence); ~ *kritik* [*mot*] criticize; ~ *rättvisa* do justice; ~ *våld* use (make use of) violence **3** *rfl* practise; ~ *sig i att* practise (+ *ing-form*); ~ *sig i pianospelning* (*skjutning*) practise on the piano (with the rifle); ~ *sig i tålamod* learn to be patient **övad** *a5* practised; trained; (*erfaren*) experienced; (*skicklig*) skilled

över ['ö:-] **I** *prep* **1** over; (*högre än, ovanför*) above; (*tvärs-*) across; (*i tidsangivelse*) past, *AE. äv.* after; *bron ~ floden* the bridge across the river; *gå ~ gatan* walk across the street, *vanl.* cross the street; *bo ~ gården* live across the [court]yard; *500 meter ~ havet* 500 metres above sea level; ~ *hela kroppen* all over the body; ~ *hela landet* throughout (all over) the country; ~ *hela linjen* all along the line; ~ *hela vintern* throughout (all through) the winter; *tak ~ huvudet* a roof over one's head; *högt ~ våra huvuden* high above our heads; *bred ~ höfterna* broad across the hips; *höjd ~ alla misstankar* above (beyond) suspicion; *plötsligt var stormen ~ oss* suddenly the storm came upon us; *leva ~ sina tillgångar* live beyond one's means; *klockan är* [*fem*] ~ *sex* it is [five] past (*AE. äv.* after) six; ~ *veckoslutet* over the weekend; *det är inte så ~ sig* (*inget vidare*) it's not all that good **2** (*via*) via, by [way of] **3** (*mer än*) over, more than, above; ~ *hälften* over (more than) half; *dra* [*tio minuter*] ~ *tiden* run over the time [by ten minutes] **4** (*uttr. makt, -höghet o.d.*) over; (*i fråga om rang*) above; *löjtnant är ~ sergeant* a lieutenant ranks (is) above a sergeant; *makt ~* power over; *överlägsenhet ~* supremacy to **5** (*uttr. genitivförh.*) of; (*om, angående*) [up]on; *essä ~* essay on; *karta ~* map of; *föreläsa ~* lecture on **6** (*med anledning av*) at; of; *glad* (*förvånad*) ~ glad (surprised) at; *lycklig ~* happy about; *rörd ~* touched by; *undra ~* wonder at **II** *adv* **1** over; above; across; *jfr över I; resa ~ till Finland* go over to Finland; *gå ~ till grannen* walk round (pop over) to the neighbour's; *arbeta ~* work overtime; *50 pund och ~ på det* 50 pounds and more **2** (*kvar*) left, [left] over; *det som blir ~* what is left, the remainder; *det blev pengar ~* I have (he has *etc.*) some money left **3** (*slut*) over, at an end; (*förbi äv.*) past; *nu är sommaren ~* summer is over now; *smärtan har gått ~* the pain has passed

överaktiv ['ö:-] hyperactive

överallt ['ö:-, -'allt] everywhere; *AE. vard.* every place; ~ *där* wherever; *han är smutsig ~* he is dirty all over

över|ambitiös overambitious **-anstränga 1** overstrain, overexert (*hjärtat* one's heart); ~ *ekonomin* overstrain the economy **2** *rfl* overstrain o.s.; (*arbeta för mycket*) overwork o.s., work too hard **-ansträngd** overworked; (*rent fysiskt*) overstrained **-ansträngning** overwork; overstrain, overexertion (*av hjärtat* of the (one's) heart) **-antvarda** [-a:r-] deliver up, entrust (*åt* to); ~ *ngn i rättvisans händer* deliver s.b. into the hands of justice **-arbeta 1** (*bearbeta för mycket*) overelaborate **2** (*omarbeta*) revise **-arm** upper arm; *anat.* brachium (*pl* brachia) **-armsben** humerus

över|balans *ta* ~*en* lose one's balance, overbalance, topple over **-balansera** ~*d budget* budget that shows a surplus **-befolkad** [-å-] *a5* overpopulated **-befolkning** overpopulation **-befäl** *abstr.* supreme command (*över* of); *konkr. koll.* [commissioned] officers (*pl*) **-befälhavare** commander in chief, supreme commander; ~*n* [the] supreme commander of the armed forces **-begåvad** hyperintelligent **-belasta** overload (*äv. elektr.*); *bildl.* overstrain, overtax **-belastning** overloading; *bildl.* overtaxing **-beskydda** overprotect **-beskyddande** overprotective **-betala** overpay **-betona** overemphasize, lay too much stress on **-bett** overbite **-betyg** honours (*pl*), mark above the pass standard **-bevisa** convict (*ngn om* s.b. of); (*-tyga*) convince (*ngn om* s.b. of) **-bevisning** conviction **-bibliotekarie** chief (head) librarian **-bjuda** outbid, overbid; *bildl.* [try to] outdo, rival; *de -bjöd varandra i artighet* they tried to outdo one another in courtesy **över|blick** survey, general view (*över* of); *ta en* ~ *över* (*äv.*) survey **-blicka** survey; *bildl.* take in (*situationen* the situation); *följder som inte kan ~s* consequences that cannot be foreseen **-bliven** *a5* remaining, left over; *komma på -blivna kartan* remain on the shelf **-boka** overbook **-'bord** [-ɔ:-] *falla* (*spolas*) ~ fall (be washed) overboard; *man ~!* man overboard!; *kasta ~* (*äv.*) jettison **- bringa** deliver, convey; hand in **-bringare** bearer (*av ett budskap* of a message) **- brygga** *vl* bridge [over]; ~ *motsättningar* reconcile differences **-bud** higher bid, overbid **-byggnad** superstructure (*äv. bildl.*) **-bädd** upper bed (*i hytt e.d.* berth) **över|del** top (*äv. av plagg*), upper part **-dimensionera** oversize, overdimension; *~d* (*äv.*) oversize[d] **-direktör** (*i statligt verk*) deputy director-general **-domare** (*i tennis*) referee **-dos, -dosera** overdose **-drag** cover[ing]; (*på möbel*) cover; (*på kudde*) [pillow]case; (*av fernissa e.d.*) coat[ing]; (*tids-*) running over the time **-dragning** (*av konto*) overdraft **-dragskläder** *pl* overalls, coveralls **-dramatisera** exaggerate; *sl.* pile on the agony **överdrift** exaggeration; (*i tal äv.*) overstatement; (*ytterlighet*) excess; *gå till* ~ go too far, go to extremes, (*om pers. äv.*) carry things too far; *man kan utan* ~ *säga att* it is no exaggeration to say that **över|driva** exaggerate, overstate; overact, overdo (*en roll* a part); (*gå för långt*) overdo it; *-driver du inte nu?* aren't you piling it on a bit? **-driven** *a5* exaggerated; excessive, exorbitant; *-drivet bruk av* excessive use of; *-drivet nit* overzealousness; *hon är så -driven* she overdoes it **-drivet** *adv* exaggeratedly *etc.*; ~ *noga* too careful, overcareful, overscrupulous; ~ *känslig* (*äv*) hypersensitive; ~ *sparsam* overeconomical, (*i småsaker*) cheeseparing, (*gnidig*) stingy, niggardly **över|dåd** (*slösaktighet*) extravagance; (*lyx*) luxury; (*dumdristighet*) foolhardiness, rashness **-dådig** *a1* **1** (*slösaktig*) extravagant; (*lyxig*) luxurious, sumptuous **2** (*utmärkt*) excellent, superb, first-rate **3** (*dumdristig*) foolhardy, rash **-dängare** past master (*i* in, at); *vara en ~ i* (*äv.*) be terrifically good at; *han är en ~ i skjutning* he is a crack shot **över'ens** *vara* ~ be agreed (*om* on; *om att* that); *komma ~ om* agree (come to an agreement, *AE. äv.* get together) on (about); *komma ~ om att träffas* agree to meet, arrange a meeting; *komma bra ~ med ngn* get on well with s.b.; *de kommer bra* (*dåligt*) ~ they get on (don't get on) well [together] **-komma** [ˣö:-, -ˣens-] agree (*om* on, about); (*göra upp*) arrange, settle; *den -komna tiden* the time agreed [up]on (fixed); *som -kommet* as agreed **-kommelse** [-å-] agreement; arrangement; *enligt* ~ by (according to) agreement, as agreed [upon]; *gällande ~r* existing (current) agreements;

träffa en ~ make (come to) an agreement, come to terms; *tyst* ~ tacit understanding, gentlemen's agreement **-stämma** [ˣö:ver-, -ˣens-] agree, be in accordance, accord; (*passa ihop äv.*) correspond, tally; *inte* ~ (*äv.*) disagree **-stämmelse** agreement; accord[ance]; conformity; (*motsvarighet*) correspondence; *bristande* ~ incongruity, discrepancy; *i* ~ *med* (*enligt*) in accordance (conformity) with, according to; *bringa* (*stå*) *i* ~ *med* bring into (be in) agreement (line) with **över|exekutor** chief executory authority (officer) **-exponera** overexpose **-exponering** overexposure **-fall, -falla** assault, attack; (*från bakhåll*) ambush **-fart** crossing; (*-resa äv.*) voyage, passage **-fett** *a5* superfatted **-flyga** fly over **-flygla** [-y:-] *mil.* outflank; (*-träffa*) surpass, exceed; (*-lista*) outmanoeuvre, outdo **-flygning** flight over, overflight; (*vid flygparad*) fly-past **-flytta** move over (across); (*friare*) transfer **-flyttning** moving [over] *etc.*; transport; (*friare*) transfer **över|flöd** *s7* (*ymnighet*) abundance, profusion, plenty (*av, på* of); (*materiellt*) affluence; (*övermått*) superfluity, superabundance; (*på arbetskraft, information*) redundance; (*lyx*) luxury; *ha ~ på, ha ... i* ~ have an abundance of, have ... in plenty, have plenty of; *finnas i* ~ be abundant **-flöda** abound (*av, på* in, with); *~nde* abundant, profuse **-flödig** *a1* superfluous; (*onödig äv.*) unnecessary; *känna sig* ~ feel unwanted (in the way) **-flödighet** superfluousness **-flödssamhälle** affluent society **över|full** overfull, too full; (*om lokal e.d.*) overcrowded, crammed; ~ *sysselsättning* overfull employment, overemployment **-furir** (*vid armén*) sergeant, *AE.* staff sergeant; (*vid marinen*) petty officer, *AE.* petty oficer 1. class; (*vid flyget*) sergeant, *AE.* technical sergeant **-fyllnad** repletion; (*på marknaden*) glut **-färd** *se -fart* **-föra 1** *se föra* [*över*] **2** (*-flytta*) transfer, transmit; *bokför.* carry over (forward); ~ *blod* transfuse blood; ~ *smitta* transmit infection (contagion); *i -förd bemärkelse* in a figurative (transferred) sense **3** (*-sätta*) translate, turn (*till* into) **-förenkla** oversimplify **-förfinad** *a5* overrefined **-förfriskad** *a5* tipsy, intoxicated **-föring** transfer[ence] (*äv. tekn.*); conveyance, transport[ation] (*av trupper* of troops); (*av blod*) transfusion; (*av smitta*) transmission (*äv. radio.*); ~ *av pengar* transfer of money **-förmyndare** chief guardian **-förtjust** overjoyed, delighted **över|ge, -giva** abandon; desert; (*lämna äv.*) leave; (*ge upp äv.*) give up; ~ *ett fartyg* abandon a ship; ~ *en plan* abandon (give up) a plan **-given** [-j-] *a5* abandoned *etc.*; *ensam och* ~ forlorn **-givenhet** [-j-] abandonment; forlornness **-glänsa** outshine, eclipse **-grepp** (*inkräktande*) encroachment (*mot* on); (*-våld*) outrage; ~ (*pl*) excesses (*mot* against) **-gripande** *a4* overarching **över|gå 1** *eg.*, *se gå* [*över*] **2** (*-träffa*) [sur]pass (*ngns förväntningar* a p.'s expectations) **3** (*-stiga*) exceed, be beyond (above); *det ~r mitt förstånd* it is above my comprehension (beyond me) **4** (*drabba*) overtake, befall **5** (*-flyt-*

tas) change hands, be transferred; *färger som ~r i varandra* colours that merge (melt) into each other; *sommaren -gick i höst* summer turned into autumn; *~ till annat parti* go over to another party; *~ till dagordningen* proceed (pass) to the business of the day; *~ till katolicismen* embrace (be converted to) Catholicism, become a Catholic; *~ till professionalism* turn professional; *~ till annan verksamhet* pass on to other activities; *äganderätten har -gått till* the title has been transferred to **-gående** *a4* passing; *(kortvarig äv.)* transient, transitory, of short duration; *av ~ natur* of a temporary (transitory) nature **-gång** *s2* **1** *abstr.* crossing *(över* of); *(omställning)* changeover; *(utveckling)* transition; *(mellantillstånd)* intermediate stage; *(omvändelse)* conversion; *~ förbjuden!* do not cross! **2** *(-gångsställe) (vid järnväg e.d.)* crossing; *(fotgängar-, se övergångsställe)* **3** *se övergångsbiljett; ta ~ till tunnelbana* change to the underground

övergångs|bestämmelse provisional (transitional, temporary) regulation **-biljett** transfer [ticket] **-form** transitional (intermediate) form **-stadium** transitory (transition[al]) stage **-ställe** *(för fotgängare)* [pedestrian, zebra] crossing, *AE.* crosswalk **-summa** transfer fee **-tid** transition[al] period, period (time) of transition **-tillstånd** transition[al] state, state of transition **-ålder (***klimakterium)* change of life, climacteric [age, period]; *(pubertet)* [years *(pl)* of] puberty

över|göda overfeed, surfeit **-gödsling** top dressing **-halning** [-a:-] **1** *(fartygs slingring)* lurch; *göra en ~* *(äv. bildl.)* lurch **2** *(utskällning) ge ngn en ~* give s.b. a good rating **-hand** *(ta) ~* get the upper hand *(över* of), prevail *(över* over), *(om tankar, växter e.d.)* be[come] rampant; *hungern tog ~en* hunger got the better of them (us *etc.*) **-handsknop** *~ i åtta* figure eight knot **-het** *~en* the authorities, the powers that be *(pl)* **-hetsperson** person in authority; *(ämbetsman)* public officer **-hetta** overheat, superheat **-hettning** overheating, superheating

över|hopa *~ ngn med ngt* heap (shower) s.th. upon s.b., heap (shower) s.b. with; *~d med arbete* overburdened with work; *~d med skulder* loaded with debts, *vard.* up to one's neck in debt **-hoppad** [-å -] *a5, bli ~ (om text e.d.)* be omitted (left out), *(om pers.)* be passed over **-hovmästarinna** mistress of the robes **-hud** scarfskin, epidermis **-hus** *parl.* upper house (chamber); *~et* the House of Lords *(Storbritannien)*, the Senate *(AE.)*

överhuvud [ˈöː-] *s7, s6* head; *(ledare)* chief **över huvud** [-ˈhu:-] *adv (i jakande sats)* on the whole; *(i nekande, frågande, villkorlig sats)* at all; *det är ~ [taget]* svårt att on the whole it is difficult to; *han vet ~ taget ingenting* he knows nothing at all

över|hängande *a4 (nära förestående, hotande)* impending; *(om fara äv.)* imminent; *(brådskande)* urgent; *det är ingen ~ fara* there is no immediate danger **-höghet** supremacy, sovereignty **-hölja** *bildl., ~ ngn med ngt* heap s.th. upon s.b., heap s.b. with s.th. **-höljan** [-ˈhö:-]

se [över] hövan

över|ila *rfl* be rash (hasty), act rashly; *(förgå sig)* lose one's head **-ilad** *a5* rash, hasty; *gör ingenting -ilat!* don't do anything rash! **-ilning** rashness, precipitation; *handla i ~* act rashly **-ingenjör** chief engineer **-inseende** supervision **-isad** *a5* covered with ice, iced up **-jaget** *psykol.* the superego **-jordisk** *(himmelsk)* unearthly, celestial; *(eterisk)* ethereal, divine *(skönhet* beauty*)* **-jägmästare** chief forest officer

över|kant upper edge (side); *i ~ (bildl.)* rather on the large (big, long *etc.*) side, too large *(etc.)* if anything **-kapacitet** surplus capacity **-kast** *(säng-)* bedspread, counterpane **-klaga** appeal against, lodge (enter) an appeal against; *beslutet kan ej ~s* the decision is final **-klagande** *s6* appeal *(av* against*)* **-klass** upper class; *~en* the upper classes *(pl)* **-klasskvinna** upper-class woman **-klädd** covered; *(om möbel)* upholstered **-komlig** [-å-] *a1* surmountable *(hinder* obstacle*); till ~t pris* at a reasonable (moderate) price **-kommando** supreme (high) command **-kompensation** overcompensation **-konstapel** *(polis-)* [police] sergeant; *(kriminal-)* detective sergeant **-korsad** [-å-] *a5* crossed-out

över|kropp upper part of the body; *med naken ~* stripped to the waist **-kucku** *s2, vard.* top dog **-kultiverad** overrefined **-kurs** *hand.* premium [rate]; *till ~* at a premium **-kvalificerad** overqualified , too highly qualified **-käke** upper jaw; *anat.* maxilla **-käksben** *anat.* maxillary [bone] upper jawbone **-känslig** hypersensitive, oversensitive; *(allergisk)* allergic *(för* to*)* **-känslighet** hypersensitiveness *etc.*; allergy *(för* to*)* **-körd** [-çö:rd] *a5, bli ~* be (get) run over (knocked down)

över'lag *adv* generally **över|lagd** *a5 (noga* well*)* considered; *(uppsåtlig)* premeditated; *-lagt mord* premeditated (wilful) murder, criminal homicide **-lakan** top sheet **-lappa** overlap **-lappning** overlapping **-lasta** overload, overburden; *(fartyg)* overfreight; *~ minnet* overburden (encumber) one's memory; *~ (berusa) sig* get intoxicated, intoxicate o.s. **-lastad** *a5* **1** *(berusad)* intoxicated, the worse for liquor **2** *(alltför utsmyckad)* overburdened with ornaments **-leva** survive; *~ ngn (äv.)* outlive s.b.; *~ sig själv (om sak)* outlive its day, become out of date; *det kommer han aldrig att ~* he will never get over it, it will be the death of him **-levande** *a4* surviving; *de ~* the survivors *(från* of*)* **-leverans** excess delivery **-levnad** survival **-liggare** *univ.* "perpetual student" **-lista** outwit; *han -de mig (äv.)* he was too sharp for me **-ljudsbang** supersonic bang **-ljudshastighet** supersonic speed **-ljudsplan** supersonic aircraft (aeroplane)

över|lopps [-å-] *i uttr.: till ~* to spare **-energi** surplus energy **-gärning** *teol.* work of supererogation; *det vore en ~ att* it would be quite superfluous to

över|lupen *a5* **1** *(-vuxen)* overgrown *(med, av* with*)* **2** *(-hopad)* overburdened *(med arbete* with work*); (hemsökt)* overrun *(av besökare* with visitors*)*; deluged *(av förfrågningar* with inquiries) **-lycklig** overjoyed **-låta 1** (*avhända sig*) transfer, make over (*ngt t. ngn* s.th. to s.b.); *jur. äv.* convey, assign, remise; *biljetten får ej ~s* the ticket is not transferable **2** (*hänskjuta*) leave (*ngt i ngns hand* s.th. in a p.'s hands); *jag -låter åt dig att* I leave it to you to **-låtelse** transfer; *jur. äv.* conveyance, assignment **-låtelsehandling** deed (instrument) of conveyance (transfer, assignment) **-läge** *bildl.* advantage, superior position **över|lägga** confer, deliberate (*om* on, about); *~ om* (*äv.*) discuss **-läggning** deliberation; (*övervägande äv.*) consideration; (*diskussion äv.*) discussion **-lägsen** *a3* superior (*ngn* to s.b.); (*storartad*) excellent; (*högdragen*) supercilious; *han är mig ~* (*äv.*) he is my superior; *~ seger* signal (easy) victory **-lägsenhet** superiority (*över* to); (*högdragenhet*) superciliousness **-lägset** *adv* in a superior manner; excellently; superciliously **-läkare** consultant; chief (senior, head) physician (*kirurg* surgeon) **överlämn|a 1** deliver [up, over]; (*framlämna*) hand over; (*skänka*) present, give; (*anförtro*) entrust, leave; (*uppge*) surrender (*ett fort* a fort); *~ ett meddelande* deliver a message; *~ blommor till ngn* present flowers to s.b., present s.b. with flowers; *~ i ngns vård* leave in a p.'s care, entrust to s.b.; *jag ~r åt dig att* I leave it to you to; *~d åt sig själv* left to o.s. **2** *rfl* surrender (*åt fienden* to the enemy); *~ sig åt sorgen* surrender [o.s.] (give way) to grief **-ande** *s6* delivery, handing over; presentation; surrender **över|läpp** upper lip **-lärare** headmaster **-löpare** deserter; *polit.* defector, renegade **över|maga** oböjligt *a* (*-modig*) presumptuous, overweening **-makt** (*i styrka*) superior force; (*i antal*) superior numbers (*pl*); *ha ~en* be superior in numbers (*över* over); *kämpa mot ~en* fight against odds; *vika för ~en* yield to superior force (numbers) **-man** superior; *finna sin ~* meet (find) one's match; *ej ha sin ~* have no superior; *vara ngns ~* (*äv.*) be more than a match for s.b. **-manna** overpower **-mod** (*förmätenhet*) presumption, overweening confidence (pride); (*våghalsighet*) recklessness; *ungdomligt ~* youthful recklessness **-modig** (*förmäten*) presumptuous, overweening; (*våghalsig*) reckless **-mogen** overripe **-mognad** overripeness **-morgon** *i ~* the day after tomorrow **-mått** *bildl.* excess; (*-flöd äv.*) exuberance; *ett ~ av* an excess of; *till ~* to excess **-måttan** [-ˣmått-] *adv* extremely, beyond measure; *roa sig ~* have no end of fun **-mäktig** superior (*fiende* enemy); *sorgen blev mig ~* I was overcome by grief; *smärtan blev honom ~* the pain became too much for him **-människa** superman **-mänsklig** superhuman **-mätt** surfeited, satiated (*på* with) **-mätta** surfeit, satiate; *kem.* supersaturate **-mättnad** surfeit; (*leda*) satiety **-mättning** *kem.* supersaturation **över|nationell** supranational **-natta** stay the night, stay overnight; (*på hotell e.d. äv.*) spend the night **-nattning** *i ~ i Hamburg* stop overnight in Hamburg **-naturlig** supernatural **-nervös** very nervous, highly strung **-nog** more

than enough; *nog och ~* enough and to spare **-ord** *pl* (*skryt*) boasting (*sg*); (*överdrift*) exaggeration (*sg*); *det är inga ~* that is no exaggeration **-ordna** *~ ngn över* place s.b. above **-ordnad** [-å:-] *a5* superior; *~ sats* principle clause; *~ ställning* responsible position; *han är min ~e* he is above me, he is my chief; *mina närmaste ~e* my immediate superiors **över|plats** (*i hytt e.d.*) upper berth **-prestation** overachievement **-presterande** overachieving **-pris** excessive price; *betala ~ för ngt* be overcharged for s.th.; *sälja ngt till ~* overcharge for s.th.; sell s.th. at too high a price **-produktion** overproduction **överrask|a** surprise; (*överrumpla äv.*) take by surprise; (*obehagligt*) startle; *~ ngn med att stjäla* catch (surprise) s.b. in the act of stealing; *~ ngn med en present* surprise s.b. with a gift, give s.b. a gift as a surprise; *glatt ~d* pleasantly surprised; *~d över* surprised at; *~d av regnet* caught in the rain **-ning** surprise; *glad ~* pleasant surprise; *det kom som en ~ för mig* (*äv.*) it took me by surprise; *till min stora ~* (*äv.*) much to my surprise **över|rede** (*av vagn e.d.*) body **-reklamerad** *a5* overrated **-resa** crossing, passage; voyage **-retad** *a5* overexcited; *i -retat tillstånd* (*äv.*) in a state of overexcitement **-retning** overexcitation **-rock** overcoat; (*vinter-*) greatcoat **-rumpla** surprise, take unawares; *låta sig ~s* let o.s. be caught napping, be off one's guard **-rumpling** surprise **-rumplingstaktik** surprise tactics (*pl, behandlas som sg*) **-räcka** hand [over]; (*skänka*) present **-rösta 1** (*ropa högre än*) shout (cry) louder than; *larmet ~de dem* the din drowned their voices; *han ~de* ... he made himself (his voice was) heard above ... **2** (*i omröstning*) outvote **övers** ['ö:-] *i uttr.: ha tid till ~* have spare time; *har du en tia till ~?* have you [got] ten kronor to spare?; *inte ha mycket* (*ngt*) *till ~ för* have no time for, not think much of **över|se** *~ med ngt* overlook s.th.; *~ med ngn* excuse a p.'s behaviour **-seende I** *a4* indulgent (*mot* towards) **II** *s6* indulgence; *ha ~ med* be indulgent towards, make allowance[s] for; *jag ber om ~ med* I hope you will overlook **-sida** top [side], upper side **-siggiven** [-ˣji:-] in despair (*över, för* about, at) **-sikt** *s3* survey (*över, av* of); (*sammanfattning*) summary, synopsis (*över, av* of) **-siktlig** *a1, se överskådlig* **-siktskarta** key map **-sinnlig** supersensual; (*andlig*) spiritual **-sittare** bully; *spela ~* play the bully; *spela ~ mot ngn* bully (browbeat) s.b. **-sittaraktig** *a1* bullying **-sittarfasoner, -sitteri** bullying [manner] **över|skatta** overrate, overestimate **-skattning** overrating, overestimation **-skeppa** ship across **-skjutande** [-ʃ-] *a4* **1** additional (*dag* day); surplus, excess (*belopp* amount); *~ skatt* surplus tax **2** (*framskjutande*) projecting (*klippa* rock) **-skott** surplus; excess; (*nettoförtjänst äv.*) profit **-skottslager** surplus stock **-skrida** cross (*gränsen* the frontier); *bildl.* exceed, overstep (*sina befogenheter* one's authority); *~ sitt konto* overdraw one's account; *~ sina till-*

gångar exceed one's means **-skrift** heading; title **-skugga** overshadow (*äv. bildl.*); *det allt ~nde problemet* the all-pervading problem **-skyla** cover [up]; (*dölja*) disguise; (*släta över*) gloss over, palliate **-skådlig** [-å:-] *a1* (*klar, redig*) clear, lucid; (*-siktlig*) perspicuous; *inom en ~ framtid* in the foreseeable future **-skådlighet** [-å:-] clearness, lucidity; perspicuity **-sköljning** wash, washing **-sköterska** head nurse, sister

över|slag 1 (*förhandsberäkning*) [rough] estimate (calculation) (*över of*); *göra ett ~ över* (*äv.*) estimate, calculate ... [roughly] **2** (*volt*) somersault **3** *elektr.* flashover **-slagsberäkning** rough estimate **-snöad** *a5* covered with snow **-spel 1** *kortsp.* extra trick **2** *teat.* overacting **-spela** overact **-spelad** *det är -spelat nu* it's not relevant any longer, it's a thing of the past now **-spelning** [-e:l-] practising [on the piano *etc.*] **-spänd** (*hypernervös*) overstrung, highly strung, *AE.* high-strung; (*svärmisk*) romantic **-spändhet** overstrung state; romanticism **- spänning** *elektr.* overvoltage

överst ['ö:-] *adv* uppermost, on top; *~ på sidan* at the top of the page; *stå ~ på listan* head the list **översta** *best. superl. a,* [*den*] ~ the top (*lådan* drawer); (*av två*) the upper; *den allra ~* the topmost (*grenen* branch)

överstatlig supranational

överste ['ö:-] *s2* (*vid armén*) colonel; (*vid flyget*) group captain, *AE.* colonel; *~ av 1.graden* (*vid armén*) brigadier, *AE.* brigadier general; (*vid flyget*) air commodore, *AE.* brigadier general **-löjtnant** [-*löjt-] (*vid armén*) lieutenant colonel; (*vid flyget*) wing commander, *AE.* lieutenant colonel **-'präst** high priest

överstig|a *bildl.* exceed, be beyond (above); *ett pris ej ~nde* a price not exceeding; *det -er mina krafter* it is beyond my powers, it is too much for me

överstimulera overstimulate

överstinna colonel's wife; *~n A.* Mrs. A.

över|strykning crossing-out, deletion **-strö** sprinkle, powder, dust **-stycke** top [piece, part]; (*dörr-*) lintel **-'styr** *i uttr.: gå ~* (*om företag o.d.*) fail, go to rack and ruin, (*om plan e.d.*) come to nothing, (*välta*) topple over **-styrd** [-y:-] *a5, tekn.* oversteered; *radio.* overmodulated **-styrelse** central (national) board **-styrning** *tekn.* oversteering; *radio.* overload, overmodulation **-stånden** *a5, vara ~ be* over (surmounted); *nu är det värsta -ståndet* the worst is over now; *ett -ståndet stadium* a thing of the past; *en ~ operation* a completed operation; *-ståndna faror* surmounted dangers **-ståthållare** governor [general] **-ståthållarämbetet** (*i Stockholm*) the office of the governor of Stockholm **-stämma** *mus.* upper part **-stämpla** overprint (*ett frimärke* a stamp) **-stökad** *a5* over [and done with] **-svallande** *a4* overflowing (*vänlighet* kindness); (*om pers.*) effusive, gushing; *~ glädje* exuberant joy, rapture, excess of joy

över|svämma (*strömma ut över*) flood, inundate (*äv. bildl.*); *stora områden är ~de* large areas are flooded; *~ marknaden* flood (glut) the market **-svämning** flood; (*-svämmande*)

flooding, inundation **-syn** inspection, overhaul; *ge motorn en ~* give the engine an overhaul, overhaul the engine **-synt** [-y:-] *a4* long-sighted; *fack.* hypermetropic **-synthet** [-y:-] long--sightedness; *fack.* hypermetropia **-sålla** strew, cover; *~d med blommor* (*äv.*) starred with flowers **-sända** send; forward; (*penga*) remit **-säng** upper bed **-sätta** translate (*från* from; *till* into); (*återge*) render; *~ till engelska* (*äv.*) turn into English **-sättare** translator **-sättning** translation (*till* into); (*version*) version; (*återgivning*) rendering; *trogen ~* true (faithful) translation; *i ~ av* translated by **-sättningsfel** mistranslation, translation error **-sättningsrätt** right of translation; translation rights (*pl*)

över|ta *se* **övertaga -tag** *bildl.* advantage (*över* over); *få ~et över* get the better of; *ha ~et* (*äv.*) have the best of it **-taga** take over; *~ ansvaret* take [over] the responsibility; *~ ledningen av* take charge of, assume the management of; *~ makten* come into power, take over (control) **-tagande** *s6* taking over **-tala** persuade; *vard.* get round; (*förmå äv.*) induce; *~ ngn att* persuade s.b. to (*komma* come), coax s.b. into (*komma* coming); *låta ~ sig att* [let o.s.] be talked into, be persuaded into (*komma* coming) **-talig** *a1* supernumerary **-talning** [-a:-] persuasion; *efter många ~ar* after much persuasion **-talningsförmåga** persuasive powers (*pl*), powers (*pl*) of persuasion **-talningsförsök** attempt at persuasion **-teckna** oversubscribe (*ett lån* a loan) **-teckning** oversubscription

över|tid overtime; *arbeta på ~* work overtime **-tidsarbete** overtime [work] **-tidsblockad** overtime ban **-tidsersättning** overtime pay (payment, compensation) **-tolka** overinterprete **-ton** overtone (*äv. bildl.*) **-tramp** *sport.* failure; *göra ~* overstep the mark (*äv. bildl.*) **-trassera** overdraw **-trassering** overdraft **-tro** (*vidskepelse*) superstition; (*blind tro*) blind faith (*på* in) **-trumfa** *bildl.* go one better than, outdo **-tryck 1** *fys.* overpressure; (*över atmosfärtrycket*) pressure exceeding atmospheric pressure **2** (*påtryck*) overprint **-trycksventil** pressure relief valve **-träda** transgress; (*förbud*) infringe, break; (*kränka*) violate **-trädelse** transgression; infringement, breach; violation; trespass; *~ beivras* trespassers will be prosecuted **-träffa** surpass, exceed; (*besegra*) outdo, *vard.* beat; *~ ngn i ngt* be better than s.b. in (at) s.th.; *~ sig själv* surpass (excel) o.s. **-tydlig** overexplicit

över|tyga convince (*om* of; *om att* that); *du kan vara ~d om att* you may rest assured that; *~ sig om ngt* make sure of (ascertain) s.th. **-tygande** *a4* convincing; (*i ord äv.*) persuasive; (*bindande äv.*) cogent, conclusive **-tygelse** conviction; (*tro*) belief; *i den fasta ~n att* in the firm conviction that, being firmly convinced that; *handla mot sin ~* act against one's convictions **-täcka** cover **-tänd** *a5, byggnaden var helt ~* the building was all in flames **-tänkt** *a4, ett väl ~ svar* a well-considered answer

över|upplaga *boktr.* [over]plus; over copies (*pl*) **-uppseende, -uppsikt** superintendence,

Ö

supervision **-uppsyningsman** [chief] supervisor (overseer, inspector) **-utbilda** overeducate
över|vaka superintend, supervise; ~ *(tillse) att* see [to it] that **-vakare** supervisor; *(av villkorligt dömd)* probation officer **-vakning** [-a:-] supervision, superintendence; *(av villkorligt dömd)* probation; *stå under* ~ be on probation **-vara** *-var -varit (pres. saknas)* attend, be present at; *festen -vars av Mr. S.* Mr. S. was present at the party **-vattensläge** surface position **-vikt 1** *eg.* overweight, excess (surplus) weight; *(bagage- äv.)* excess luggage *(AE.* baggage); *betala* ~ pay [an] excess luggage charge **2** *bildl.* predominance, preponderance, advantage; *få (ha) ~en (äv.)* predominate, preponderate **-viktig** *a1* overweight, too heavy **-vinna** overcome; *(besegra äv.)* vanquish, conquer, defeat; ~ *en fiende* overcome an enemy; ~ *sina betänkligheter* overcome one's scruples; ~ *sig själv* get the better of o.s. **-vintra** pass the winter, winter; *(ligga i ide)* hibernate **-vintring** wintering; *(i ide)* hibernation **-vunnen** *a5, det är ett -vunnet stadium* that is a thing of the past, I have got over that stage **-vuxen** overgrown; ~ *med ogräs (äv.)* overrun with weeds **-våld** outrage; *jur.* assault **-våning** upper floor (storey)
1 överväg|a *(noga genomtänka)* reflect [up]on, ponder over; *(betänka)* consider; *(överlägga med sig själv)* deliberate; *(planera)* contemplate, plan; *i väl -da ordalag* in well-considered words; *när man -er vad* considering what; *jag skall* ~ *saken* I will consider the matter (think the matter over); *ett väl -t beslut* a well-considered decision
2 överväg|a *(väga mer än)* outweigh; *(överstiga i antal)* be in majority; *fördelarna -er olägenheterna* the advantages outweigh the disadvantages
1 övervägande *s6* consideration; deliberation; *ta ngt i (under)* ~ take s.th. into consideration; *efter moget* ~ after careful consideration; *vid närmare* ~ on [further] consideration, on second thoughts
2 övervägande I *a4* predominant, preponderating; *den* ~ *delen* the greater part, the majority; *frågan är med* ~ *ja besvarad* the great majority is in favour, the ayes have it; *till* ~ *del* mainly, chiefly **II** *adv (t. största delen)* mainly, chiefly; ~ *vackert väder* mainly fair
över|väldiga overpower, overwhelm *(äv. bildl.)*; ~*d av trötthet* overcome by fatigue **-väldigande** *a4* overpowering, overwhelming; *en* ~ *majoritet* an overwhelming (a crushing) majority **-vältra** ~ *ansvaret på* shift the responsibility on **-värdera** overestimate, overrate, overvalue **-värme** *(t.ex. i ugn)* heat from above, top heat **-växel** *(i bil)* overdrive **-årig** *a1 (över viss ålder)* overage, above the prescribed age; *(över pensionsålder)* superannuated **-ösa** ~ *ngn med ngt* shower (heap) s.th. upon s.b.
övlig [ˣö:v-] **1** usual, customary; *på ~t sätt* in the usual manner
övning [ˣö:v-] **1** *(övande)* practice; *(träning)* training; ~ *ger färdighet* practice makes perfect; *sakna* ~ *i* have no (be out of) practice in

(att teckna drawing) **2** *(utövning)* exercise; *~ar (äv.)* practice *(sg); andliga (gymnastiska) ~ar* religious (physical) exercises
övnings|bil driving-school car; learner's car **-exempel** exercise; *mat. o.d.* problem **-flygning** training (practice) flight **-fält** *mil.* training (drill) ground **-häfte** exercise book, notebook **-köra** learn how to drive; get driving practice **-körning** practice driving **-lärare** teacher in a practical subject **-område** *mil.* military training (manoeuvres) area **-uppgift** exercise **-ämne** *skol.* practical subject
övre [ˈö:v-] *komp. a* upper; *(översta äv.)* top
övrig [ˣö:v-] *a1 (återstående)* remaining; *(annan)* other; *det ~a* the rest (remainder); *de ~a* the others, the rest *(sg); lämna mycket ~t att önska* leave a great deal to be desired; *det ~a Sverige* the rest of Sweden; *för ~t a) (annars)* otherwise, in other respects, for (as to) the rest, b) *(dessutom)* besides, moreover, c) *(i förbigående sagt)* by the way, incidentally
övärld archipelago *(pl* archipelagos)
ÖÄ *förk. för överståthållarämbetet*